McGraw-Hill's Homework Manager, the most powerful Homework Manager system available.

- **Textbook specific exercises and problems**
- **Automatically-graded assignments and analysis**
- **Immediate grading and feedback for students**
- **Algorithmic exercises and problems**
- **Instructor course management tools**

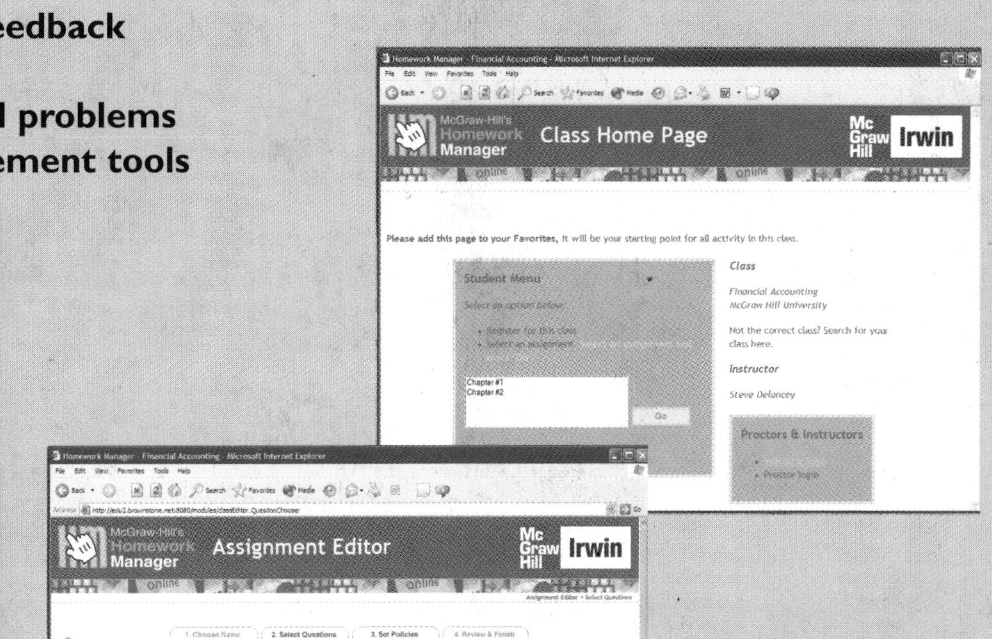

Wherever you find this Icon within this book, you know that the problem or exercise is available in McGraw-Hill's Homework Manager.

Please visit www.mhhe.com/hm, for a guided tour of Homework Manager and to experience Homework Manager content.

17 edition

Fundamental Accounting Principles

Kermit D. Larson
University of Texas at Austin

John J. Wild
University of Wisconsin at Madison

Barbara Chiappetta
Nassau Community College

Boston Burr Ridge, IL Dubuque, IA Madison, WI New York
San Francisco St. Louis Bangkok Bogotá Caracas Kuala Lumpur
Lisbon London Madrid Mexico City Milan Montreal New Delhi
Santiago Seoul Singapore Sydney Taipei Toronto

To my wife **Nancy.**
To my wife **Gail** and children, **Kimberly, Jonathan, Stephanie,** and **Trevor.**
To my husband **Bob,** my sons **Michael** and **David,** and my **mother.**

FUNDAMENTAL ACCOUNTING PRINCIPLES
Published by McGraw-Hill/Irwin, a business unit of The McGraw-Hill Companies, Inc., 1221 Avenue of the Americas, New York, NY, 10020.

This book is printed on acid-free paper.

2 3 4 5 6 7 8 9 0 DOW/DOW 0 9 8 7 6 5 4

ISBN 0-07-251243-1 (combined edition)
ISBN 0-07-287003-6 (volume 1, chapters 1–12)
ISBN 0-07-287002-8 (volume 2, chapters 12–25)
ISBN 0-07-286993-3 (volume 1 with working papers, chapters 1–12)
ISBN 0-07-287016-8 (volume 2 with working papers, chapters 12–25)
ISBN 0-07-286999-2 (Principles of Financial Accounting, chapters 1–17)

Editorial director: *Brent Gordon*
Publisher: *Stewart Mattson*
Sponsoring editor: *Steve Schuetz*
Developmental editor I: *Kelly Odom*
Marketing manager: *Richard Kolasa*
Senior producer, Media technology: *Ed Przyzycki*
Senior project manager: *Lori Koetters*
Senior production supervisor: *Michael R. McCormick*
Lead designer: *Matthew Baldwin*
Photo research coordinator: *Judy Kausal*
Photo researcher: *Sarah Evertson*
Lead supplement producer: *Becky Szura*
Senior digital content specialist: *Brian Nacik*
Cover designer: *Matthew Baldwin*
Cover image: © *Corbis Images*
Typeface: *10.5/12 Times Roman*
Compositor: *The GTS Companies/York, PA Campus*
Printer: *R.R. Donnelley*

Library of Congress Cataloging-in-Publication Data

Larson, Kermit D.
Fundamental accounting principles / Kermit D. Larson, John J. Wild, Barbara Chiappetta.—17th ed.
p. cm.
A variety of multi-media instructional aids are available to support the text.
Includes index.
ISBN 0-07-251243-1 (alk. paper)
1. Accounting. I. Wild, John J. II. Chiappetta, Barbara. III. Title.
HF5635.P975 2005 2003061454
657—dc22

www.mhhe.com

The first edition of Fundamental Accounting Principles was published fifty years ago, into a world very different from the one we live in today.

Technological tools that have reshaped the accounting profession—handheld computers, telecommunications, the Internet—could scarcely have been imagined by the men and women filling in ledgers or punching figures into adding machines. What they had were principles: tried-and-true rules and practices for collecting and interpreting information comprehensively, accurately, and responsibly.

Technology makes certain accounting functions easier, but students require a firm grounding in principles to become good business people—in any era. Teaching these principles in a way that is engaging to students while providing instructors with the support they need has been the goal of Fundamental Accounting Principles since the first copy rolled off the press.

Over the years instructors have turned to Fundamental Accounting Principles confident that they have selected the most accurate, best organized, and best written book on the market. Feedback on the book's pedagogy, real world examples, and assignment materials has always been outstanding. We've long believed in doing whatever it takes to keep students engaged, from creating interesting chapter opening vignettes to integrating leading-edge technology tools.

With fifty years of success and the expertise of our talented author team, **Fundamental Accounting Principles achieves new heights in student motivation, creative pedagogy, technology integration, and end-of-chapter material.**

Thank you for choosing Fundamental Accounting Principles. Here's to the next fifty years!

Fundamental Accounting Principles Rates #1

As with the past fifty years, we actively solicited your feedback when planning the 17th edition of Fundamental Accounting Principles (FAP). Independent research* confirmed what we already knew: **Instructors find FAP more satisfying to use than *any* other principles textbook.**

Top Five Textbooks	Rated as Very Satisfied or Satisfied by Instructors	Mean Rating*
FAP, Larson/Wild/Chiappetta	**100%**	**4.46**
Competitor #1	75%	3.83
Competitor #2	64%	3.83
Competitor #3	60%	3.76
Competitor #4	47%	3.79

**Instructors ranked books from very dissatisfied (1) to very satisfied (5).*

"It (FAP) is the best text I have ever used (in 15 years of teaching). It is the best resource text available for my students to keep and include in their professional library after the course."
— L. Hass, Glen Oaks Community College

The choice is clear: of the five best-selling principles books, FAP scores consistently highest in user satisfaction.

Fundamental Accounting Principles also rates #1 with instructors surveyed† in each of the following key areas:

#1 in Accuracy
#1 in Clarity
#1 in Pedagogy
#1 in Organization
#1 in Real-World Examples
#1 in Problems and Exercises
#1 in Supplements

And remember, a book that satisfies your needs is that much more likely to satisfy your students' needs as well.

"With the help of the book, my instructor, and especially the FAP CD-ROM, I am excelling in the class and like it so much I am considering becoming an Accounting major myself! Thanks and keep up the good work!"

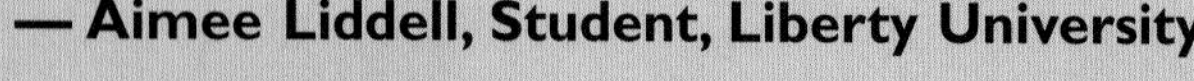

— Aimee Liddell, Student, Liberty University

†Independent study conducted by Professional Research Group, February 2003.

Kermit D. Larson is the Arthur Andersen & Co. Alumni Professor of Accounting Emeritus at the University of Texas at Austin. He served as chairman of the University of Texas, Department of Accounting and was visiting professor at Tulane University. His scholarly articles have been published in a variety of journals, including The Accounting Review, Journal of Accountancy, and Abacus. He is the author of several books, including Financial Accounting and Fundamentals of Financial and Managerial Accounting, both published by McGraw-Hill/Irwin.

Professor Larson is a member of the American Accounting Association, the Texas Society of CPAs, and the American Institute of CPAs. His positions with the AAA have included vice president, southwest regional vice president, and chairperson of several committees, including the Committee of Concepts and Standards. He was a member of the committee that planned the first AAA doctoral consortium and served as its director.

Professor Larson served as president of the Richard D. Irwin Foundation. He also served on the Accounting Accreditation Committee and on the Accounting Standards Committee of the AACSB. He was a member of the Constitutional Drafting Committee of the Federation of Schools of Accountancy and a member of the Commission on Professional Accounting Education. He has been an expert witness on cases involving mergers, antitrust litigation, consolidation criteria, franchise taxes, and expropriation of assets by foreign governments. Professor Larson served on the Board of Directors and Executive Committee of Tekcon, Inc., and on the National Accountants Advisory Board of Safe-Guard Business Systems. In his leisure time, he enjoys skiing and is an avid sailor and golfer.

John J. Wild is a professor of accounting and the Robert and Monica Beyer Distinguished Professor at the University of Wisconsin at Madison. He previously held appointments at Michigan State University and the University of Manchester in England. He received his BBA, MS, and PhD from the University of Wisconsin.

Professor Wild teaches accounting courses at both the undergraduate and graduate levels. He has received the Mabel W. Chipman Excellence-in-Teaching Award, the departmental Excellence-in-Teaching Award, and the Teaching Excellence Award from the 2003 graduation class at the University of Wisconsin. He also received the Beta Alpha Psi and Roland F. Salmonson Excellence-in Teaching Award from Michigan State University. Professor Wild is a past KPMG Peat Marwick National Fellow and is a recipient of fellowships from the American Accounting Association and the Ernst and Young Foundation.

Professor Wild is an active member of the American Accounting Association and its sections. He has served on several committees of these organizations, including the Outstanding Accounting Educator Award, Wildman Award, National Program Advisory, Publications, and Research Committees. Professor Wild is author of Financial Accounting and Financial Statement Analysis, both published by McGraw-Hill/Irwin. His research appears in The Accounting Review, Journal of Accounting Research, Journal of Accounting and Economics, Contemporary Accounting Research, Journal of Accounting, Auditing and Finance, Journal of Accounting and Public Policy, and other business periodicals. He is past associate editor of Contemporary Accounting Research and has served on several editorial boards including The Accounting Review.

Professor Wild, his wife, and four children enjoy travel, music, sports, and community activities.

Barbara Chiappetta received her BBA in Accountancy and MS in Education from Hofstra University and is a tenured full professor at Nassau Community College. For the past 17 years, she has been an active executive board member of the Teachers of Accounting at Two-Year Colleges (TACTYC), serving 10 years as vice president and as president from 1993 through 1999. As an active member of the American Accounting Association, she has served on the Northeast Regional Steering Committee, chaired the Curriculum Revision Committee of the Two-Year Section, and participated in numerous national committees.

In 1998, Professor Chiappetta was inducted into the American Accounting Association Hall of Fame for the Northeast Region. She received the Nassau Community College dean of instruction's Faculty Distinguished Achievement Award in 1995. Professor Chiappetta was honored with the State University of New York Chancellor's Award for Teaching Excellence in 1997. As a confirmed believer in the benefits of active learning pedagogy, Professor Chiappetta has authored Student Learning Tools, an active learning workbook for a first-year accounting course, published by McGraw-Hill/Irwin.

In her leisure time, Professor Chiappetta enjoys tennis and participates on a U.S.T.A. team. She also enjoys the challenge of bridge. Her husband, Robert, is an entrepreneur in the leisure sport industry. She has two sons—Michael, a lawyer, specializing in intellectual property law in New York, and David, a composer, pursuing a career in music for film in Los Angeles.

Achieve New Heights

Fundamental Accounting Principles, 17e

The principles course is crucial for accounting majors and non-majors alike. It is a student's first step into the world of accounting, one which quickly immerses them in unfamiliar and challenging new concepts.

Much of your students' future success in both accounting and business is determined in the time spent in the principles course. Will your students struggle with this new material? Or will they understand that accounting is a vital discipline relevant to any career, and use that knowledge to **achieve new heights of success** in business and throughout their lives?

Fundamental Accounting Principles has always been dedicated to presenting accounting concepts as vital tools that anyone can learn to successfully use. The 17th edition expands on this traditional strength by especially focusing on three areas: **student engagement, technology, and end-of-chapter material**.

FAP 17e portrays accounting as it truly is—a language of business communication that is vital to student success.

"FAP has good coverage for [the Principles course] and excellent exercises, problems, and end-of-chapter materials."
— S. McClure, Tri-County Tech

New heights in student engagement

Instructors repeatedly raise a common concern: the biggest hurdle they face is getting students interested and motivated in the materials. FAP provides solutions. It is more engaging and student-friendly than any competing book, from the book's eye-catching design to its comprehensive and stimulating end-of-chapter material. Each new book includes the actual shareholders' report from Krispy Kreme Doughnuts, which gets real financial data in students' hands. Moreover, engaging chapter-opening vignettes focus on small businesses and entrepreneurs to show how accounting knowledge is a springboard to success.

Krispy Kreme DOUGHNUTS

> "I think FAP does a better job motivating and sustaining student interest in accounting."
> **— L. Kolar, Bucks County Community College**

New heights in technology

Match our technology assets against those of any other book, and we're confident you'll agree: FAP's technology is, hands-down, the best in the market.

- **Carol Yachts General Ledger and Peachtree Complete Accounting 2004**
- **ALEKS for Financial Accounting and ALEKS for the Accounting Cycle**
- **Mcgraw-Hill's Homework Manager**
- **Topic Tackler**
- **Online Learning Center**

To learn more about these and other technology enhancements, see page xi.

New heights of end-of-chapter material

FAP's end-of-chapter content is tightly coordinated with the main body of the chapter. Icons for C.A.P. learning objectives make it easy for students to flip back in the chapter to a particular discussion, or to pick up the solution strategy for a specific assignment. In addition, FAP takes technology integration to a new level with two powerful and popular study aids, Homework Manager and Topic Tackler, both specifically written to coordinate with FAP. We also revised and expanded the two problem sets for every chapter of FAP, with a third set available on the text's Online Learning Center.

By addressing students in language that speaks to them, by providing your class with market-leading technology support, and by ensuring the textbook package is strong in the areas you rely on most, FAP helps you ***achieve new heights of success*** in the classroom—and beyond.

Decision Center

Whether we prepare, analyze, or apply accounting information, one skill remains essential: decision making. To help develop good decision-making habits *and* to illustrate the relevance of accounting, FAP uses a unique pedagogical framework called the Decision Center. This framework is comprised of a variety of approaches and subject areas, giving students insight into every aspect of business decision making. Answers to Decision Maker and Ethics boxes are at the end of each chapter.

A decision icon calls out all relevant material within chapters, whether it's a boxed item or end-of-chapter item.

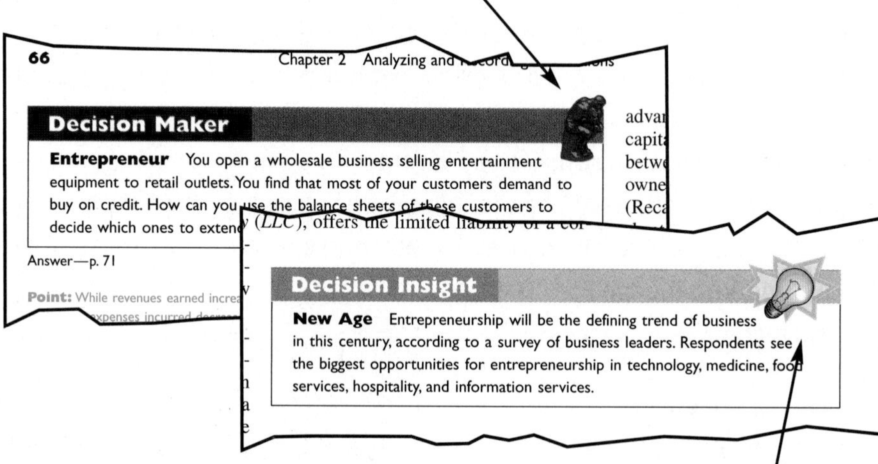

An entrepreneurial icon calls out all relevant material within chapters, whether it's an opening vignette, box, or end-of-chapter assignment.

"The Decision sidebars are one of the particular strengths of the text. They help the student stop and think about what he or she has read or can be used by the professor to stimulate discussion when introducing a topic. They are excellent tools!"

— M. Conway, Kingsborough Community College

CAP Model

The Conceptual/Analytical/Procedural (CAP) Model allows courses to be specially designed to meet your teaching needs or those of a diverse faculty. This model identifies learning objectives, textual materials, assignments, and test items by C, A, or P, allowing different instructors to teach from the same materials, yet easily customize their courses toward a conceptual, analytical, or procedural approach (or a combination thereof) based on personal preferences.

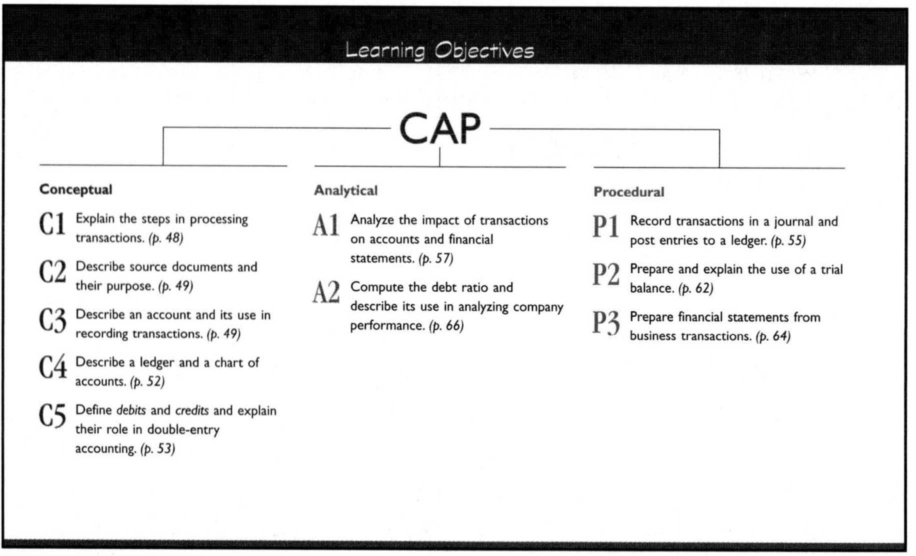

Chapter Preview Flow Chart

New to the 17th edition, this feature provides a handy textual/visual guide at the start of every chapter. Students can now begin their reading with a clear understanding of what they will learn and when, allowing them to stay more focused and organized along the way.

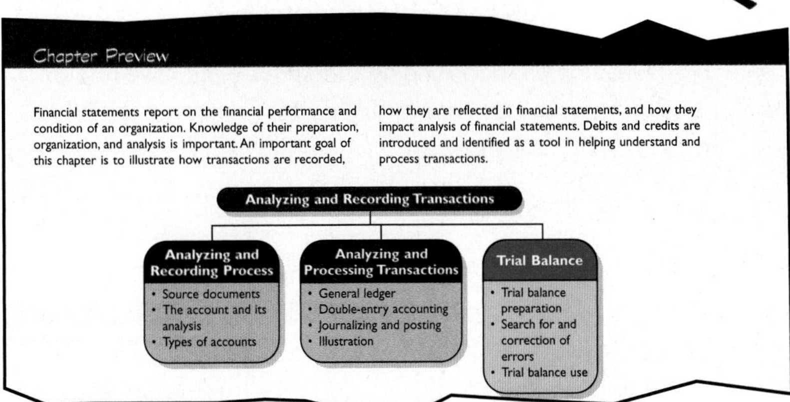
Chapter Preview

Financial statements report on the financial performance and condition of an organization. Knowledge of their preparation, organization, and analysis is important. An important goal of this chapter is to illustrate how transactions are recorded, how they are reflected in financial statements, and how they impact analysis of financial statements. Debits and credits are introduced and identified as a tool in helping understand and process transactions.

Quick Check

These short question/answer features reinforce the material immediately preceding them. They allow the reader to pause and reflect on the topics described, then receive immediate feedback before going on to new topics. Answers are provided at the end of each chapter.

Quick Check

8. What types of transactions increase equity? What types decrease equity?
9. Why are accounting systems called *double entry?*
10. For each transaction, double-entry accounting requires which of the following: (*a*) Debits to asset accounts must create credits to liability or equity accounts, (*b*) a debit to a liability account must create a credit to an asset account, or (*c*) total debits must equal total credits.
11. An owner invests $15,000 cash along with equipment having a market value of $23,000 in a proprietorship. Prepare the necessary journal entry.
12. Explain what a compound journal entry is.
13. Why are posting reference numbers entered in the journal when entries are posted to ledger accounts?

Answers—p. 73

"I think FAP does a better job with learning objectives than my book because of the CAP learning objectives organization."

— S. McClure, Tri-County Tech

FastForward

FastForward is a case that takes students through the Accounting Cycle, chapters 1-4. The FastForward icon is placed in the margin at key points when this case is discussed.

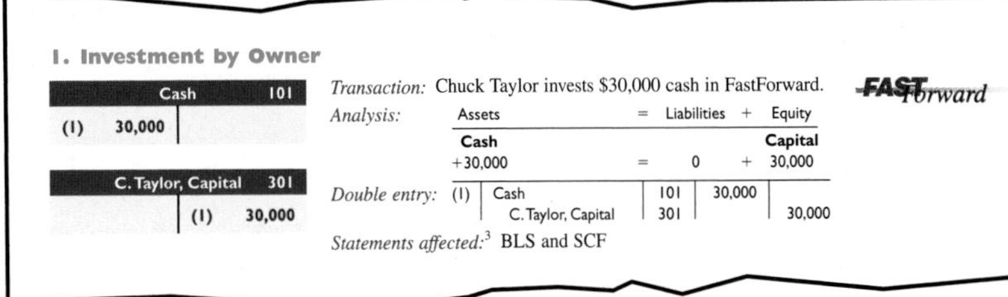
1. Investment by Owner

Cash	101
(1) 30,000	

C. Taylor, Capital	301
	(1) 30,000

Transaction: Chuck Taylor invests $30,000 cash in FastForward.

Analysis:

Assets	=	Liabilities	+	Equity
Cash				Capital
+30,000	=	0	+	30,000

Double entry:

			Debit	Credit
(1)	Cash	101	30,000	
	C. Taylor, Capital	301		30,000

Statements affected:[3] BLS and SCF

Marginal Student Annotations

These annotations provide students with additional hints, tips, and examples to help them more fully understand the concepts and retain what they have learned. They also include notes on global implications of accounting and further examples.

cord for each customer, but for now, we
s and decreases in receivables in a sin-

itten promise of another entity to pay a
the holder of the note. A company hold-
s an asset that is recorded in a Note (or

are assets that represent prepayments of
expenses are later incurred, the amounts
ccounts. Common examples of prepaid

Point: A college parking fee is a prepaid account from the student's standpoint. At the beginning of the term, it represents an asset that entitles a student to park on or near campus. The benefits of the parking fee expire as the term progresses. At term-end, prepaid parking (asset) equals zero as it has been entirely recorded as parking expense.

Once a student has finished reading the chapter, how well he or she retains the material can depend greatly on the questions, exercises, and problems that reinforce it. FAP has consistently led the way in comprehensive, accurate end-of-chapter exercises. Independent survey research reports that instructors are more satisfied with FAP's end-of-chapter materials than any other textbook—and the 17th edition is no exception.

Demonstration Problems present both a problem and a complete solution, allowing students to review the entire problem-solving process and achieve success in the principles course.

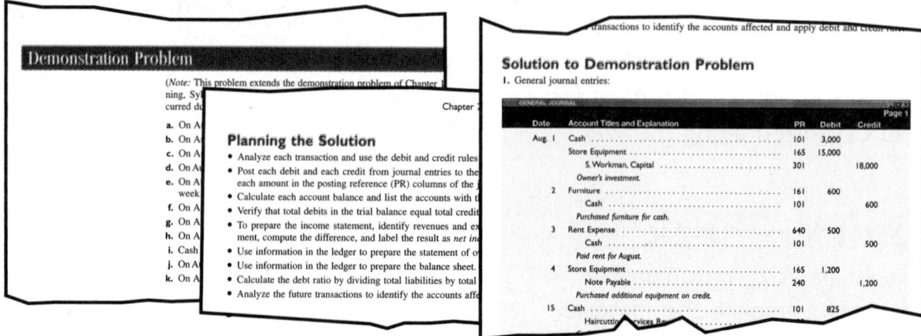
Demonstration Problem

(*Note:* This problem extends the demonstration problem of Chapter ...

Planning the Solution

- Analyze each transaction and use the debit and credit rules ...
- Post each debit and each credit from journal entries to the ... each amount in the posting reference (PR) columns of the ...
- Calculate each account balance and list the accounts with ...
- Verify that total debits in the trial balance equal total credit...
- To prepare the income statement, identify revenues and ex... ment, compute the difference, and label the result as *net in...*
- Use information in the ledger to prepare the statement of o...
- Use information in the ledger to prepare the balance sheet.
- Calculate the debt ratio by dividing total liabilities by total ...
- Analyze the future transactions to identify the accounts aff...

Solution to Demonstration Problem

1. General journal entries:

Date	Account Titles and Explanation	PR	Debit	Credit
Aug. 1	Cash	101	3,000	
	Store Equipment	165	15,000	
	S. Workman, Capital	301		18,000
	Owner's investment.			
2	Furniture	161	600	
	Cash	101		600
	Purchased furniture for cash.			
3	Rent Expense	640	500	
	Cash	101		500
	Paid rent for August.			
4	Store Equipment	165	1,200	
	Note Payable	240		1,200
	Purchased additional equipment on credit.			
15	Cash	101	825	

Chapter Summaries provide students with a review organized by learning objectives. Chapter Summaries are a component of the CAP model (see page viii), which recaps each conceptual, analytical, and procedural objective.

Key Terms are bolded in the text and repeated at the end of the chapter with page numbers indicating their location. The 17th edition now includes a Glossary of key terms at the back of the book. Key Terms are also available as online flash cards at the book's Website.

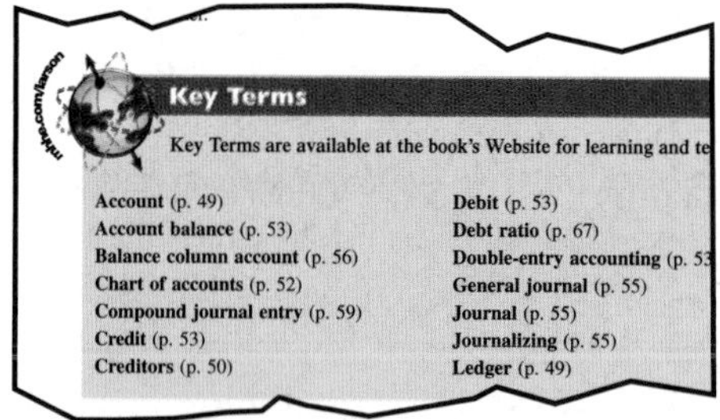
Key Terms

Key Terms are available at the book's Website for learning and te...

Account (p. 49)
Account balance (p. 53)
Balance column account (p. 56)
Chart of accounts (p. 52)
Compound journal entry (p. 59)
Credit (p. 53)
Creditors (p. 50)
Debit (p. 53)
Debt ratio (p. 67)
Double-entry accounting (p. 5...
General journal (p. 55)
Journal (p. 55)
Journalizing (p. 55)
Ledger (p. 49)

Quick Study are short exercises that often focus on one learning objective. The numerical ones are included in Homework Manager. There are usually 8-10 Quick Study assignments per chapter.

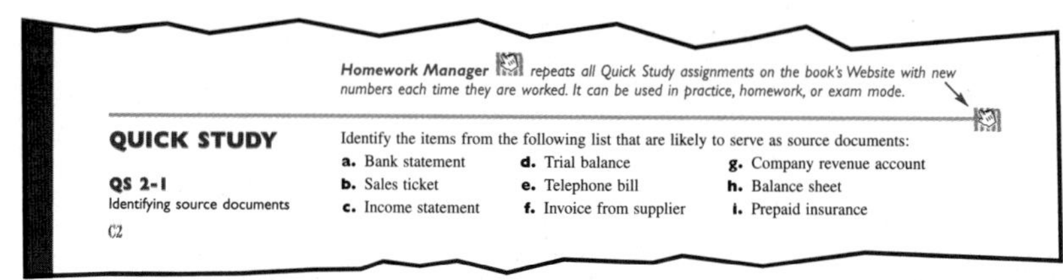
Homework Manager repeats all Quick Study assignments on the book's Website with new numbers each time they are worked. It can be used in practice, homework, or exam mode.

QUICK STUDY

QS 2-1
Identifying source documents
C2

Identify the items from the following list that are likely to serve as source documents:

a. Bank statement **b.** Sales ticket **c.** Income statement **d.** Trial balance **e.** Telephone bill **f.** Invoice from supplier **g.** Company revenue account **h.** Balance sheet **i.** Prepaid insurance

Exercises are one of FAP's ongoing strengths, and the 17th edition again shows its competitive advantage. There are about 10-15 per chapter and most are included in Homework Manager.

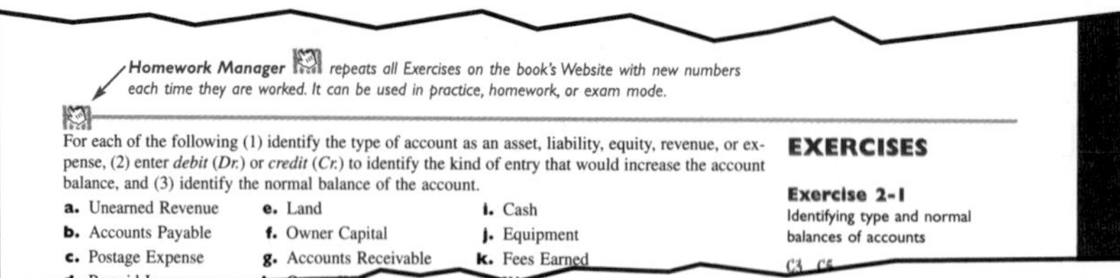
Homework Manager repeats all Exercises on the book's Website with new numbers each time they are worked. It can be used in practice, homework, or exam mode.

For each of the following (1) identify the type of account as an asset, liability, equity, revenue, or expense, (2) enter *debit (Dr.)* or *credit (Cr.)* to identify the kind of entry that would increase the account balance, and (3) identify the normal balance of the account.

a. Unearned Revenue **b.** Accounts Payable **c.** Postage Expense **e.** Land **f.** Owner Capital **g.** Accounts Receivable **i.** Cash **j.** Equipment **k.** Fees Earned

EXERCISES

Exercise 2-1
Identifying type and normal balances of accounts

Problem Sets A & B are proven problems that can be assigned as homework or for in-class projects. Problem Set C is available on the book's Website. All problems are coded according to the CAP model (see page viii), and many are included in Homework Manager.

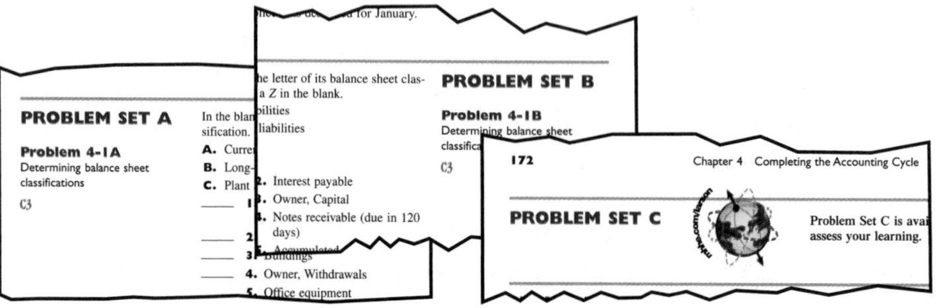
PROBLEM SET A

Problem 4-1A
Determining balance sheet classifications
C3

In the blan... sification. ...

A. Curre... **B.** Long-... **C.** Plant ...

...he letter of its balance sheet clas... a Z in the blank.

...bilities
...liabilities

2. Interest payable
3. Owner, Capital
4. Notes receivable (due in 120 days)
4. Owner, Withdrawals
5. Office equipment

PROBLEM SET B

Problem 4-1B
Determining balance sheet classifica...
C3

172 Chapter 4 Completing the Accounting Cycle

PROBLEM SET C

Problem Set C is avai... assess your learning.

End-of-Chapter Materials

Beyond the Numbers exercises encourage your students to use the figures and understand their meaning, learning how accounting data applies to a variety of business situations. These creative and fun exercises are all new or updated, and are divided into 10 sections:

- Reporting in Action
- Comparative Analysis
- Ethics Challenge
- Communicating in Practice
- Taking It to the Net
- Teamwork in Action
- Hitting the Road—NEW
- Business Week Activity
- Entrepreneurial Decision
- Global Decision—NEW

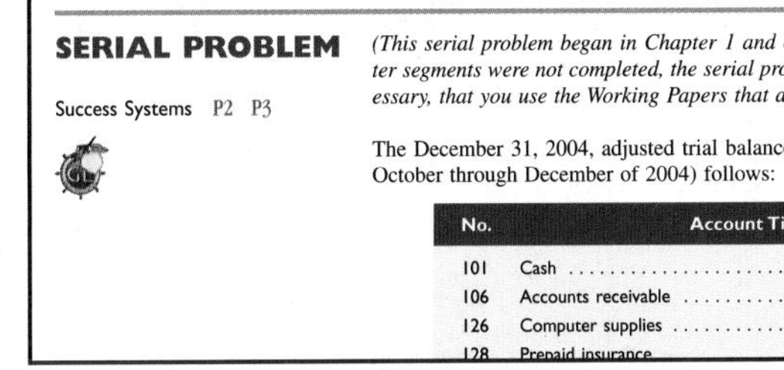

Serial Problems use a continuous running case study to illustrate chapter concepts in a familiar context. Serial Problems can be followed continuously from the first chapter or picked up at any later point in the book; enough information is provided to ensure students can get right to work.

SERIAL PROBLEM

Success Systems P2 P3

(This serial problem began in Chapter 1 and ... ter segments were not completed, the serial pro... essary, that you use the Working Papers that a...

The December 31, 2004, adjusted trial balanc... October through December of 2004) follows:

No.	Account Ti...
101	Cash ....
106	Accounts receivable ....
126	Computer supplies ....
128	Prepaid insurance

> "Some of the overall strengths of FAP include clearly stated learning objectives. Each chapter is written in a clear, concise language supported by a lot of exhibits and appropriate end-of-chapter materials to reinforce the learning process."
>
> **— M. Bentil, Pierce College**

The End of the Chapter Is Only the Beginning

FAP's valuable and proven assignments aren't just confined to the book. From problems that require technological solutions to materials found exclusively online, FAP's end-of-chapter material is fully integrated with its technology package.

- Quick Studies, Exercises, and Problems available on Homework Manager (see page xii) are marked with an icon.

- Problems supported by the all-new General Ledger Application Software or Peachtree are marked with an icon.

- The Online Learning Center (OLC) includes more *Taking It To The Net* exercises, Personal Interactive Quizzes, more Excel template assignments, and Problem Set C.

- Problems supported with Microsoft Excel templates are marked with an icon.

- Material that receives additional coverage (slide shows, videos, audio, etc.) in Topic Tackler is marked with an icon.

Put Away Your Red Pen

We've always prided ourselves on the accuracy of FAP's assignment materials, and the market confirms this. Independent research reports that instructors pointed to the accuracy of FAP's assignment materials as a key factor in their satisfaction with the book, much more than did instructors using competing books. The 17th edition continues that tradition of accuracy.

The authors extend special thanks to accuracy checkers **Marc Giullian**, Montana State University-Bozeman; **Suzanne King**, University of Charleston; **Barbara Schnathorst**, The Write Solution, Inc.; and **Jo Lynne Koehn**, Central Missouri State University.

In teaching and learning from FAP, the book itself is only the beginning. Our comprehensive technology package provides ample opportunity for both assessment and reinforcement, while offering valuable practice in learning and using the digital tools that are integral to the modern accounting and business workplace.

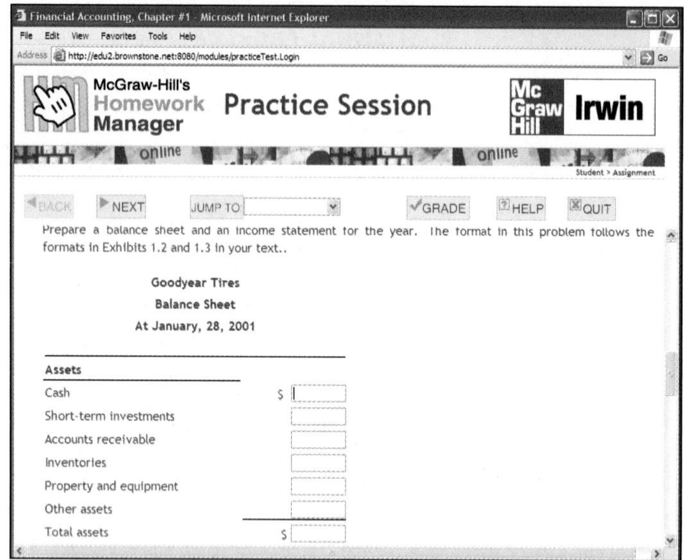

McGraw-Hill's Homework Manager

This Web-based study and review aid uses a sophisticated algorithm to generate "lookalike" versions of FAP's assignment materials. These new exercises and problems contain different values but are structured identically to those in FAP, allowing students to practice and refine their skills. The algorithm can generate infinite variations of any selected assignments, which also discourages sharing of answers.

Instructors can use Homework Manager to build custom homework assignments, tests, or quizzes that can be completed either online or with pencil and paper. Online assignments are graded automatically and the results stored in a secure online gradebook. Tests and quizzes prepared from Homework Manager overcome any inconsistencies between "test bank drawn" problems and the language and approach in the book—now there is complete consistency!

Homework Manager gives you:

- Textbook-specific quick studies, exercises, and problems
- Automatically-graded assignments and analysis for instructors
- Immediate grading and feedback for students
- Algorithmic-generated quick studies, exercises, and problems
- Instructor course management tools
- 100% consistency between test problems and the textbook

Quick Studies, Exercises, and Problems appearing in FAP that are reproduced in Homework Manager are marked with an icon.

"On the whole, in my opinion, FAP's activites are better and there are more of them."

— J. Miller, Mercer County Community College

Technology for Assessment and Learning

ALEKS®

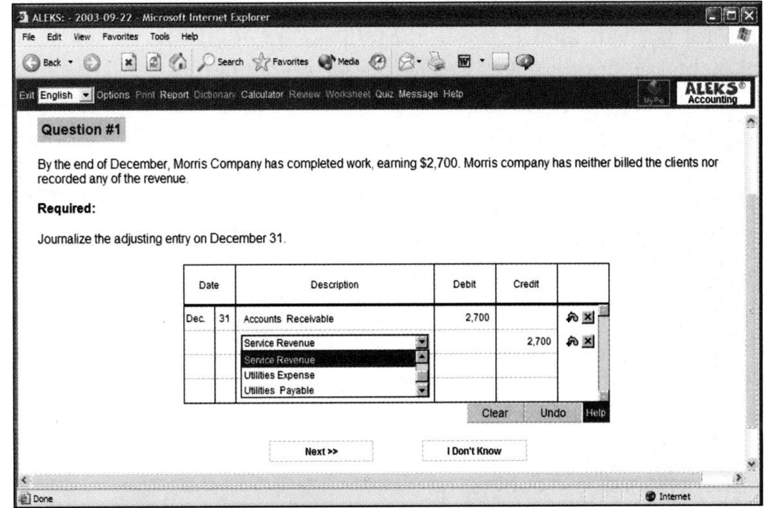

ALEKS® for the Accounting Cycle and ALEKS® for Financial Accounting

Available from McGraw-Hill over the World Wide Web, ALEKS (Assessment and LEarning in Knowledge Spaces) provides precise assessment and individualized instruction in the fundamental skills your students need to succeed in accounting.

ALEKS motivates your students because ALEKS can tell what a student knows, doesn't know, and is most ready to learn next. ALEKS does this using the ALEKS Assessment and Knowledge Space Theory as an artificial intelligence engine to exactly identify a student's knowledge of accounting. When students focus on precisely what they are ready to learn, they build the confidence and learning momentum that fuel success.

To learn more about adding ALEKS to your principles course, visit www.business.aleks.com.

GradeSummit

The online resource GradeSummit tells your students everything they need to know in order to study effectively. GradeSummit provides a series of practice tests written to coincide with FAP's coverage. Once a student has taken a particular test, GradeSummit returns a detailed results page showing exactly where the student did well and where he or she needs to improve. They can compare their results with those of their other classmates, or even with those of every other student using the text nationwide.

With that information, students can plan their studying to focus exclusively on their weak areas, without wasting effort on material they've already mastered. And they can come back to take a retest on those subjects later, comparing their new score with their previous efforts.

Carol Yacht's General Ledger and Peachtree Complete 2004 CD-ROM

Carol Yacht's General Ledger Software is McGraw-Hill/Irwin's custom-built general ledger package for FAP. Carol Yacht's General Ledger can help your students master every aspect of the general ledger, from inputting sales and cash receipts to calculating ratios for analysis or inventory valuations.

Carol Yacht's General Ledger allows students to review an entire report, and then double-click on any single transaction to review or edit it. All reports are immediately updated to reflect the revised figures. When it comes to learning how an individual transaction effects the outcome of financial reports, no other approach matches that of Carol Yacht's General Ledger.

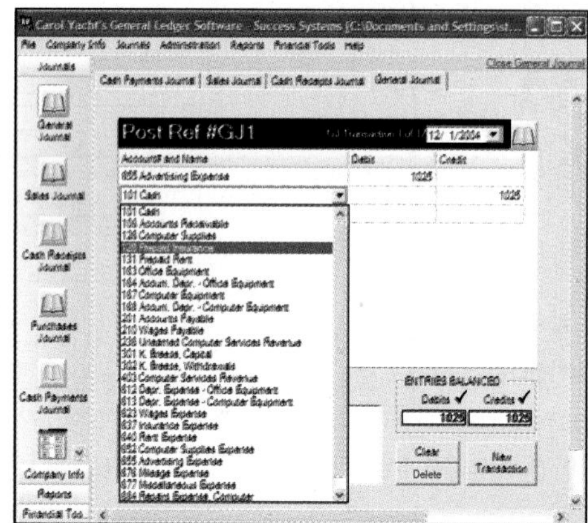

Also on Carol Yacht's General Ledger CD, students receive the educational version of Peachtree Complete 2004, along with templates containing data for many of FAP's exercises and problems. Familiarity with Peachtree Complete is essential for many students entering the job market, and Carol Yacht's Peachtree templates that accompany FAP 17e makes sure they get plenty of practice.

Students can use Carol Yacht's General Ledger to solve numerous problems from FAP; the data for these problems are already included on the Carol Yacht's General Ledger CD-ROM. You can even populate Carol Yacht's General Ledger with your own custom data.

Online Learning Center (OLC) with PowerWeb

www.mhhe.com/larson

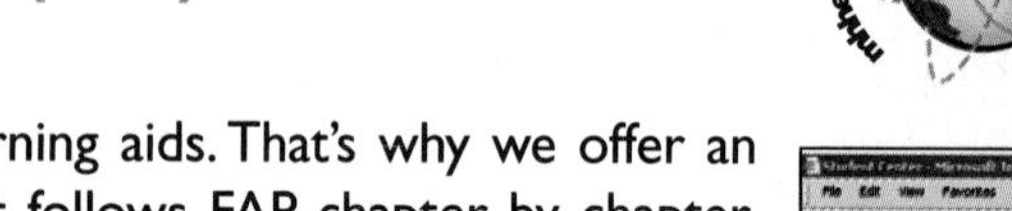

More students are using online learning aids. That's why we offer an Online Learning Center (OLC) that follows FAP chapter by chapter. It doesn't require any building or maintenance on your part; it's ready to go the moment your students type in the address.

As your students study and learn from FAP, they can visit the OLC Website and work with a multitude of helpful tools:

- Tutorial
- Glossary
- NetTutor
- PowerWeb
- Chapter Objectives
- Chapter Overview
- Text Company Links
- Interactive Quizzes A & B
- Key Term Flashcards
- PowerPoint Presentation
- Additional appendices
- Cogg Hill Practice Set
- Updates
- Mobile Resources
- Audio Narrated PowerPoint
- Excel Template Assignments
- More *Taking It To The Net*
- Problem Set C
- Business Week Articles

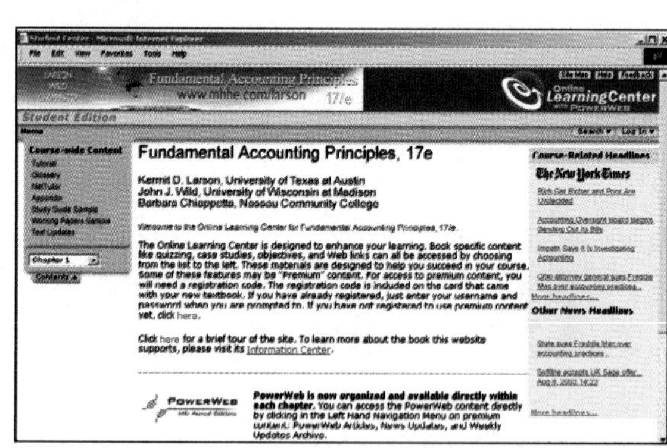

A secured Instructor Resource Center stores your essential course materials to save you prep time before class. Everything you need to run a lively classroom and an efficient course is included:

- Sample Syllabi
- Additional chapter materials
- Transition Notes
- Instructors Manual
- Solutions to Excel Template Assignments
- Cogg Hill Solutions Manual
- Updates
- Solutions Manual
- PowerPoint Presentations
- Textbook Company Links
- More *Taking It To The Net* Solutions
- Business Week Articles
- Problem Set C Solutions

PowerWeb provides high quality, peer-reviewed content including up-to-date articles from leading periodicals and journals, current news, weekly updates with assessment, interactive exercises, Web research guide, study tips, and much more. PowerWeb is free with your FAP adoption.

Topic Tackler—FREE with new book

This software is a complete tutorial focusing on those areas in the principles of accounting course that give students the most trouble. Providing help on at least 2 key topics per chapter, this program delves into the material using the following learning aids:

- Video clips
- PowerPoint slide-shows (many include animations and/or audio)
- Drag-and-drop, fill-in-the-blank exercises
- Self-test quizzes

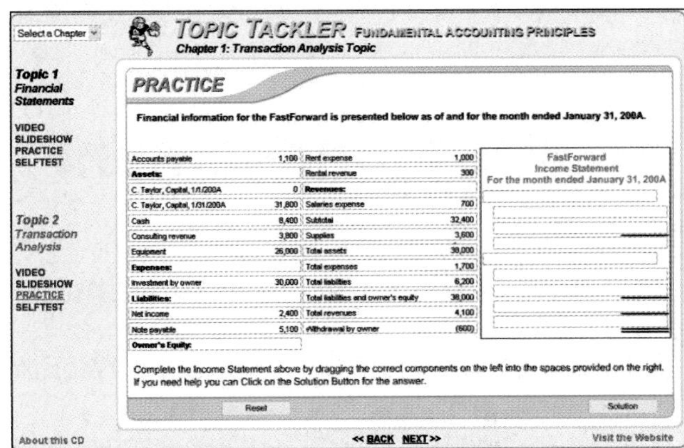

This highly engaging presentation will put your students in control of the most fundamental aspects of principles of accounting.

Concepts appearing in FAP that receive additional treatment in Topic Tackler are marked with an icon at the appropriate location in the margin of the page.

NetTutor™

NetTutor

NetTutor allows tutors and students to communicate with each other in a variety of ways:

- The Live Tutor Center via NetTutor's WWWhiteboard enables a tutor to hold an interactive on-line tutorial with several students, whose questions are placed in a queue and answered sequentially.
- The Q&A Center allows students to submit questions at any time and retrieve answers within 24 hours.
- The Archive Center allows students to browse for answers to previously asked questions. They can also search for questions pertinent to a particular topic. If they encounter an answer they do not understand, they can ask a follow-up question.

NetTutor™ v5.1

Welcome to the: MH: Accounting. We are currently offering the following services. The Live Tutor is available 9am to 12pm Monday-Thursday and 9am to 9pm on Fridays. All times Eastern Daylight Time (EDT). Holiday Hours. The Archive Center, Bulletin and Q & A Center are open 24 hours a day.

Site Notes --

Welcome to NetTutor™, version 5.1. Click here to see the New Features. If you have any problems, please send email to info@nettutor.com.

If you need help or have questions, please email info@nettutor.com.

Students are issued 5 hours of free NetTutor time when they purchase a new copy of FAP. Additional time can be purchased in 5-hour increments.

In today's learning environment, a computer is as indispensible a tool as a blackboard or an overhead projector. McGraw-Hill/Irwin continues to lead in innovative classroom technology, and FAP's teaching tools put it far ahead of any other book.

Course Management

PageOut
McGraw-Hill's Course Management System

PageOut is the easiest way to create a Website for your accounting course.

There's no need for HTML coding, graphic design, or a thick how-to book. Just fill in a series of boxes with plain English and click on one of our professional designs. In no time, your course is online with a Website that contains your syllabus!

Should you need assistance in preparing your Website, we can help you. Our team of specialists is ready to take your course materials and build a custom Website to your specifications. Simply call a McGraw-Hill/Irwin PageOut specialist to start the process. (For information on how to do this, see "Superior Service" on page xvii.) Best of all, PageOut is **free** when you adopt FAP! To learn more, please visit www.pageout.net.

Third-Party Course Management Systems

For the ambitious instructor, we offer FAP content for complete online courses. To make this possible, we have joined forces with the most popular delivery platforms currently available. These platforms are designed for instructors who want complete control over course content and how it is presented to students. You can customize the FAP Online Learning Center content and author your own course materials. It's entirely up to you.

Products like WebCT, Blackboard, and eCollege all expand the reach of your course. Online discussion and message boards will now complement your office hours. Thanks to a sophisticated tracking system, you will know which students need more attention – even if they don't ask for help. That's because online testing scores are recorded and automatically placed in your grade book, and if a student is struggling with coursework, a special alert message lets you know.

Remember, FAP's content is flexible enough to use with any platform currently available. If your department or school is already using a platform, we can help. For information on McGraw-Hill/Irwin's course management supplements, including Instructor Advantage and Knowledge Gateway, see "Superior Service" on the next page.

Superior Service

No matter which online course solution you choose, you can count on the highest level of service. That's what sets McGraw-Hill apart. Once you choose FAP, our specialists offer free training and answer any question you have through the life of your adoption.

Instructor Advantage and Instructor Advantage Plus

Instructor Advantage is a special level of service McGraw-Hill offers in conjunction with WebCT and Blackboard. A team of platform specialists is always available, either by toll-free phone or e-mail, to ensure everything runs smoothly through the life of your adoption. Instructor Advantage is available <u>free</u> to all McGraw-Hill customers.

Instructor Advantage Plus is available to qualifying McGraw-Hill adopters (see your representative for details). **IA Plus** guarantees you a full day of on-site training by a Blackboard or WebCT specialist, for yourself and up to nine colleagues. Thereafter, you will enjoy the benefits of unlimited telephone and e-mail support throughout the life of your adoption. **IA Plus** users also have the opportunity to access the **McGraw-Hill Knowledge Gateway**.

Knowledge Gateway

Developed with the help of our partner Eduprise, the McGraw-Hill Knowledge Gateway is an all-purpose service and resource center for instructors teaching FAP online.

The First Level of **Knowledge Gateway** is available to all professors browsing the McGraw-Hill Higher Education Website, and consists of an introduction to OLC content, access to the first level of the Resource Library, technical support, and information on Instructional Design Services available through Eduprise.

The Second Level is password-protected and provides access to the expanded Resource Library, technical and pedagogical support for WebCT, Blackboard, and TopClass, the online Instructional Design helpdesk and an online discussion forum for users. The **Knowledge Gateway** provides a considerable advantage for teaching online—and it's only available through McGraw-Hill.

To see how these platforms can assist your online FAP course, visit www.mhhe.com/solutions.

Content Changes for

FAP's revisions are in response to feedback from both instructors and students. Many of these revisions are summarized below. Feedback suggests that FAP is the book instructors want to teach from and students want to learn from. Some overall revisions include:

- New chapter-opening flowchart
- Revised assignments throughout
- Updated ratio analyses
- New and revised entrepreneurial elements
- New assignments using chapter openers
- Serial problem running through nearly all chapters
- New Krispy Kreme annual report and comparisons to Tastykake, Grupo Bimbo (Mexican), and the industry
- New Harley-Davidson financial statements

Chapter 1

The Chocolate Farm NEW opener

New, early introduction to transaction analysis

Transaction analysis uses expanded accounting equation to aid student learning

Revised, early introduction to financial statements

New, early introduction to key accounting principles

Revised section on accounting and related careers

Revised table on compensation

Moved return-risk analysis and business activities to appendixes for instructor flexibility

Chapter 2

York Entertainment NEW opener

Streamlined and revised introduction to accounts

Revised discussion on analyzing and processing transactions

Revised section on preparing financial statements

Chapter 3

Mellies NEW opener

Streamlined discussion on adjusting accounts

New visual linkages from adjusting entries to the accounts

New presentation on preparing financial statements from trial balance

Chapter 4

Premier Snowskate NEW opener

Streamlined discussion of accounting work sheet

Revised Excel screen captures with acetates for work sheet

Shortened section on closing process

Reduced presentation on operating cycles

Chapter 5

Damani Dada NEW opener

New table summarizing merchandising entries

Revised description of credit terms and discounts

Revised and simplified presentation of income statement formats

Simplified descriptions of debit and credit memoranda

Chapter 6

FunKo NEW opener

New discussion on internal controls and inventory

New introduction to inventory cost flow assumptions

Added simplified journal entries to inventory computations

Revised discussion of "lower of cost or market"

Moved gross profit and retail inventory methods to appendix for instructor flexibility

Chapter 7

Rap-Up NEW opener

Revised visuals for special journals

Streamlined coverage of posting

Revised discussion of technology in accounting including ERP

Added new exercises on special journals without postings

Chapter 8

Dylan's Candy Bar NEW opener

Enhanced discussion on internal controls

New material on Internet fraud

Simplified presentation of voucher system of control

Streamlined discussion of bank reconciliation

Moved control of purchase discounts to appendix for instructor flexibility

Chapter 9

Manzi Metals NEW opener

New material on credit vs debit cards

Simplified discussion on disposing of receivables

Streamlined discussion on estimating bad debts

Deleted section on discounting notes receivable

Moved short-term investments to Chapter 15

Chapter 10

Queston Construction NEW opener

Simplified discussion of partial-year depreciation and changes in estimates

Shortened and simplified section on "Additional Expenditures"

Simplified section on exchange of similar assets

Revised discussion of intangible assets per new standards

Shortened section on goodwill and moved goodwill estimation to an appendix

Chapter 11

EEC NEW opener

Revised payroll liabilities for current tax rates

Shortened section on contingent liabilities

Removed noninterest-bearing notes from this chapter

Revised appendix on payroll records

Moved "income tax liabilities" to appendix for instructor flexibility

Chapter 12

Koch Entertainment NEW opener

Increased discussion of limited liability companies

Revised section for partner return on equity

Streamlined partnership liquidation

Chapter 13

Get Real Girl, Inc. NEW opener

Shortened introductory materials on corporations

Streamlined section on preferred stock

Shortened section on stock dividends

Streamlined reporting of discontinued operations

Simplified section on "changes in accounting principles"

Shortened sections on book value per share and dividend yield

Chapter 14

Noodles & Company NEW opener

New visual linkages from bond interest computations to amortization entries

Moved effective interest amortization to chapter appendix for instructor flexibility

Streamlined presentation on notes payable

Removed materials on noninterest-bearing notes

Chapter 15

TradeStation Group NEW opener

New, simplified organization for investments

New presentation of both short-term and long-term investments

New illustrations on adjustments for unrealized gains and losses on securities

Moved investments in international operations to appendix for instructor flexibility

Chapter 16

Atomic Toys NEW opener

Simplified preparation of statement of cash flows

New 3-stage process of analyzing investing and financing cash flows

Moved investments in international operations to appendix for instructor flexibility

Chapter 17

The Motley Fool NEW opener

Krispy Kreme vs Tastykake NEW comparative analysis

Streamlined section on common-size analysis

Chapter 18

Rap Snacks NEW opener

Streamlined flow of costs discussion with revised visuals

Expanded discussion of cost controls with service businesses

Revised presentation of manufacturing statement

Chapter 19

A. D. Morgan NEW opener

Streamlined discussion of overapplied and underapplied overhead

Expanded section on costing and pricing for service businesses

Chapter 20

All American Meats NEW opener

Simplified presentation of equivalent units of production

Streamlined discussion on costing for multiple departments

Chapter 21

Life Is Good NEW opener

Simplified discussion of activity-based costing

Streamlined section on joint costs

Chapter 22

Vosges Haut Chocolat NEW opener

Streamlined break-even point analysis

Chapter 23

Aquent NEW opener

Streamlined section on budget administration

Moved production and manufacturing budgets to appendix for instructor flexibility

Chapter 24

Technology Enabled Clothing NEW opener

Expanded discussion of service applications

Streamlined overhead cost variance analysis

Chapter 25

AnthroTronix NEW opener

Further emphasis on applied applications of managerial accounting

Expanded applications to service businesses

Instructor Supplements

Instructor's Resource CD-ROM

Volume 1: 0072869844

Volume 2: 0072870192

This is your all-in-one resource. It allows you to create custom presentations from your own materials or from FAP's text-specific materials provided in the CD's asset library:

- Solutions Manual
- Test Bank, Computerized Test Bank
- Instructor's Resource Manual
- PowerPoint® Presentations *Prepared by Jon A. Booker, Charles W. Caldwell, and Susan C. Galbreath.* Presentations illustrate crucial chapter concepts and procedures, and allow for custom-revision of lecture slides by instructors.
- Excel Templates and solutions
- Link to PageOut
- Video Clips

Solutions Manual

Volume 1: 0072869828 (Solutions Transparencies 0072869801)

Volume 2: 0072869909 (Solutions Transparencies 0072869887)

Written by John J. Wild and Jo Lynne Koehn.

Test Bank

Volume 1: 0072869798

Volume 2: 0072869895

Written by Marilyn Sagrillo and John J. Wild.

Brownstone Diploma 6.2 Computerized Test Bank

Available for Windows only, located on the Instructor's Resource CD-ROM.

Instructor's Resource Manual

Volume 1: 0072869836

Volume 2: 0072869917

Written by Barbara Chiappetta and Janice Klimek.

This manual contains (for each chapter) a Lecture Outline, a chart linking all assignment materials to Learning Objectives, a list of relevant active learning activities, and additional visuals with transparency masters. An electronic version is available on the Website and on the Instructor's Resource CD-ROM.

Financial and Managerial Accounting Video Library

Financial Videos: 0072376163

Managerial Videos: 0072376171

These short, action-oriented videos, developed by Dallas County Community College for the Accounting in Action distance-learning course, provide an impetus for lively classroom discussion. Tied closely to FAP's pedagogical framework, these videos avoid dry talking-head footage in favor of dynamic, documentary-style explorations of how businesses use accounting information.

Contributing Authors

The FAP Team wishes to thank the following contributors for their excellent work.

Jo Lynne Koehn is a professor at Central Missouri State University. She received her PhD and Master's of Accountancy from the University of Wisconsin—Madison. Her scholarly articles are published in a variety of journals including *Issues in Accounting Education, The CPA Journal, The Tax Advisor,* and *Accounting Enquiries.* Professor Koehn is a member of the American Accounting Association and the American Institute of CPAs. She also holds a Certified Financial Planning license. In her leisure time, Professor Koehn indulges her passion for golf and participates in the Executive Women's Golf Association of Kansas City. Professor Koehn also enjoys reading, traveling, and visiting bookstores.

Marilyn Sagrillo is an associate professor at the University of Wisconsin—Green Bay. She received her BA and MS from Northern Illinois University and her PhD from the University of Wisconsin—Madison. Her scholarly articles are published in *Accounting Enquiries, Journal of Accounting Case Research,* and the *Missouri Society of CPAs Casebook.* She is a member of the American Accounting Association and the Institute of Management Accountants. In 1989 she received the UWGB Founder's Association Faculty Award for Excellence in Teaching. Professor Sagrillo is an active volunteer for the Midwest Renewable Energy Association. She also enjoys reading, traveling, and hiking.

Student Supplements

Topic Tackler (free with new books)

Revised by Joan Cook and Laura Ruff.

See page xv for complete description.

Carol Yacht's General Ledger & Peachtree Complete 2004 CD-ROM

ISBN 0072870079

GL Software developed by Jack E. Terry, ComSource Associates, Inc.

Peachtree templates prepared by Carol Yacht.

The CD-ROM includes fully functioning versions of McGraw-Hill's own General Ledger Application software as well as Peachtree Complete 2004. Problem templates are included that allow you to assign FAP problems for working in either Yacht's General Ledger or Peachtree Complete 2004.

Study Guide

Volume 1: ISBN 007286981X

Volume 2: ISBN 0072869860

Chapters 1-17: ISBN 0072869968

Prepared by Barbara Chiappetta.

Covers each chapter and appendix with reviews of the learning objectives, outlines of the chapters, summaries of chapter materials, and additional problems with solutions.

Special thanks to **Joan Cook** and **Laura Ruff**, *Milwaukee Area Technical College,* for their efforts in revising the Topic Tackler CD-ROM, and to **Janice Klimek**, *Central Missouri State University,* for accuracy checking Topic Tackler.

Working Papers

Volume 1: 0072869852

Volume 2: 0072869925

Chapters 1-17: 007286995X

Written by John J. Wild.

Working Papers are available to help direct students in solving all assignments. Each chapter also contains one set of papers that can be used for either the A or B series of problems.

Excel Working Papers

Volume 1: 0072870109

Volume 2: 0072870117

Chapters 1-17: 0072870125

Written by John J. Wild.

Working Papers delivered in Excel spreadsheets. Excel Working Papers are available on CD-ROM and can be bundled with the printed Working Papers; see your representative for information.

Telecourse Guide

Volume 1: 0072869941

Volume 2: 0072869879

Prepared by the Dallas County Community College District.

Student Learning Tools

ISBN 0256255776

Prepared by Barbara Chiappetta.

This workbook helps students develop and use critical thinking and learning-to-learn skills in a collaborative team environment. It contains class activities, writing assignments, and team presentation assignments.

Achieving New Heights in

Publishing a textbook is a serious undertaking, and in creating the 17th edition of FAP we had a 50-year tradition of quality and innovation to live up to.

The process began more than two years before publication, when our editorial staff commissioned a survey of the principles market. This independent research confirmed that FAP users were more satisfied by far with their chosen textbook than users of any other book. However, that wasn't enough for us.

Early in 2003, we and our research partners surveyed 156 non-users for suggestions on how to improve FAP; at the same time we asked 35 current users what they liked about the book, and what they would change if they could. This information proved invaluable as we began the development process.

The next step was to meet face-to-face with principles instructors at 5 focus groups throughout the country. A mix of users and non-users came to meet with us in Orlando, Dallas, Chicago, Phoenix, and Los Angeles, where they were able to speak to the authors in person and talk at length about what they needed in a principles book. When the authors sat down to write, they did so having firsthand feedback and suggestions from instructors.

The book you hold in your hands is the most market-driven book available. It is the result of a lengthy dialogue between user, author, and instructor. FAP is what principles instructors all over the country are looking for: a book with solid content, engaging explanations and examples, unmatched assignment materials, and first-class technology.

We would like to acknowledge the assistance of the following colleagues for their help in making FAP the best book of its kind.

Cynthia Ash, Davenport University-South Bend
Sister Virginia Assumpta McNabb, Immaculata College
Harold Averkamp, University of Wisconsin-Whitewater
Courtney Baillie, Nebraska Wesleyan University
William Barnhart, El Centro College
Mary Barnum, Grand Rapids Community College
Sandy Barz, Rocky Mountain College
Abdul Baten, NOVA Community College-Manassas
Jim Bates, Mountain Empire Community College
Robert Bauman, Allan Hancock CommunityCollege
James Q. Beisel, Longview Community College
Irene Bembenista, Davenport University-Merrillville
Dr. Michael Bentil, Peirce College
Joseph Bentley, Bunker Hill Community College
JulieAnne Adamich, St. Petersburg College
Rayla Black, Faulkner University
Phoebe Blackburn, Bristol Community College
Linda Bolduc, Mount Wachusett Community College
Deborah Boyce-Panella, Mohawk Valley Community College
Sanithia Boyd, Arkansas State University
James Bryant, Community College of Baltimore County-Catonsville
Ronald Burnette, Macomb Community College South
Leon Button, Scottsdale Community College
Carolyn Byrd, St. Petersburg College-Clearwater
Eric Carlsen, Kean University
Robert Carpenter, Eastfield College
Lloyd Carroll, Borough of Manhattan Community College
Trudy Chiaravalli, Lansing Community College
Tom Chilcote, Messiah College
Steven Christian, Jackson Community College
Dan Chrzan, Springfield College
Anthony Cioffi, Lorain County Community College
Ron Collyer, Santa Fe Community College
Elizabeth Conner, U. of Colorado - Denver
Margaret Conway, Kingsborough Community College
James Cosby, John Tyler Community College
Ralph Cotham, University of Arkansas-Little Rock
Ken Couvillion, San Joaquin Delta College
David G. Coy, Adrian College
Louann Cummings, University of Findlay
Stanley Dabrowski, Hudson County Community College
Walter DeAguero, Saddleback College
Stanley Deal, Azusa Pacific College
David Dearman, Arkansas State University
Mary Kathryn Demarest, Carroll Community College
Louis DePaul, Ivy Tech State College
Michael Deschamps, Chaffey College
William Dillion, Carson-Newman College
Vicky Dominguez, Community College of Southern Nevada
Kevin Dooley, Kapiolani Community College
David Doyon, Southern New Hampshire University
Phyllis N. Driver, Carson-Newman College
Sam Duah, Bowie State University
Ken Duffie, Brookdale Community College
Richard Dugger, Kilgore College
Helen Edwards, College of the Redwoods
Randalei Ellis, Black Hills State University
Lori Epping, University of South Dakota
Larry Farmer, Middle Tenn. State University
Jim Ficek, Iowa Western Community College
Carolyn Fitzmorris, Hutchinson Community College
Steve Flynn, Thomas More College
James Forcier, Las Positas Community College
Kelly Ford, Dowling College
Richard Frederics, Lasell College
Benjamin Gardiner, Franklin Pierce College
Daniel Gibbons, Waubonsee Community College
Thomas J. Gilday, Thomas More College
Mike Glasscock, Amarillo College
Ellen Goldberg, Northern Virginia Community College
Jack Goodwin, Tidewater Community College - Portsmouth
Barbara Gregorio, Nassau Community College
Jennifer Gregorski, Assumption College
Steve Grice, Troy State University
Debbie Griest, Lake Tahoe Community College
Joyce Griffin, Kansas City Kansas Community College
Dennis Gutting, Orange County Community College
Amy Haas, Kingsborough Community College
Gene Hale, Iowa Wesleyan College
Mary Halford, Prince George's Community College
Patricia Halliday, Santa Monica College
Sara Harris, Arapahoe Community College
William Harvey, Henry Ford Community College
Larry Hass, Glen Oaks Community College
Robert D. Hayes, Tennessee State University
William Herd, Springfield Tech Community College
Leonard Heritage, Tacoma Community College
Jim Hoffman, Ancilla College
Merrily Hoffman, San Jacinto College
Jay Holmen, U. of Wisconsin - Eau Claire
Patricia Holmes, Des Moines Area Community College
Paul Holt, Texas A&M-Kingsville
John Horgan, Iowa Western
Kathy Horton, College of DuPage
Larry Huus, University of Minnesota
Verne Ingram, Red Rocks Community College
Tim Ireland, Columbia College of Missouri

Christine Iruno, Westfield State College

Lynn Isvik, Upper Iowa University

Mary Jackson-Heard, Norfolk State University

Lori Jacobson, North Idaho College

Catherine Jeppson, Calif.St.U.-Northridge

Peg Johnson, Omaha Metro Community College

Sharon Johnson, Kansas City Kansas Community College

Thomas Kam, Hawaii Pacific University

John Karayan, Calif. State Polytech University-Pomona

John Kim, SUNY-Hunter College

Deanna King, Ivy Tech College-Terre Haute

Deb Kiss, Davenport University

Shirly Kleiner, Johnson County Community College

Mary Kline, Black Hawk College

Dave Knight, Borough of Manhattan Community College

Sherrie Koechling-Andraes, Lincoln University

Elizabeth M. Kolar, Bucks County Community College

Leon Korte, U. of South Dakota

Terry Kubican, Old Dominion University

Phillip Landers, Pennsylvania College of Technology

Sandra Lang, McKendree College

David Lanning, SUNY-Tompkins Cortland Community College

Tom Largay, Thomas College

Brian Lazarus, Baltimore City Community College

Mike Leahy, North County C.C.

Martin Lecker, SUNY Rockland Community College

Edward LeMay, Massasoit Community College

Louieco Lewis, Stillman College

Daniel Litt, UCLA

James Lock, NOVA-Alexandria

Ronald Loesel, Davenport Univ.-Saginaw

Angelo Luciano, Columbia College-Chicago

Stephen Ludwig, NW Missouri State

Kathy Lukcso, Germanna Community College

Terri Lukshaitis, Davenport University-Gaylord

John Lynch, Ivy Tech State College

Linda Mallory, Central Virginia Community College

Jeff Mankin, Lipscomb University

Frank Marino, Assumption College

Ken Mark, Kansas City Kansas Community College

Barbara Marotta, NOVA-Woodbridge

Dr. Otto Martinson, Old Dominion University

Carol McCain, Reedley College

Cynthia McCall, Des Moines Area Community College

Susan McClure, Tri-County Technical College

Clarice McCoy, Brookhaven College

Florence McGovern, Bergen C.C.

James McKinnie, NE State Technical Community College

Shea Mears, Des Moines Area Community College

David Medved, Davenport University - Dearborn

Kenneth Meisinger, U. of Colorado-Colorado Springs

Trini Melcher, Calif. State University - San Marcos

Mary Ann Merryman, St. Mary's College

John Miller, Metropolitan Community College

Josephine Miller-Mathias, Mercer County Community College

Scott E. Miller, Gannon University

Norma R. Montague, Central Carolina Community College

Henry Moore, Florida Community College-Jacksonville

Louella Moore, Arkansas State University

Joe Moran, College of DuPage

Andrea Murowski, Brookdale Community College

Charles Murphy, Bunker Hill Community College

Dr. Ali Naggar, West Chester University

V.R. Nemani, Trinity College

Dave Nichols, University of Mississippi

Jason Nielsen, Harrisburg Area C.C.

Connie Nieser, Oklahoma City Community College

Patricia Novak, Southeast Community College

Franklin Olive, Jr., Manchester College

Liz Ott, Casper College

George Otto, Truman College

Bill Padley, Madison Area Tech College

Ronald Palma, Cape Cod Community College

Judy Parker, North Idaho College

Jeff Phillips, Clark Atlanta University

Anthony Piltz, Rocky Mountain College

Von Plessner, Northwest State Community College

Barbara Powers, Wytheville C.C.

Michael Prockton, Finger Lakes Community College

Debbie Rankin, Lincoln University

Paulette Ratliff, Arkansas State University

Clara Richardson, McMurry University

Thomas Rim, National University

Frank Rodjius, Northwestern Univ.

Donald Rogoff, Cal. State University-Northridge

Dan Roland, Hilbert College

Laura Rose, Dalton State College

Gary Ross, Harding College

David Schultz, Central Nebraska Community College

Jerry Scott, Ivy Tech State College-Sellersburg

William Shaver, J. Sargeant Reynolds Community College

Jim Shelton, Freed-Hardeman University

Leon Singleton, Santa Monica College

Brenda Skornogoski, Montana State University-Northern

Daniel Small, J. Sargeant Reynolds Community College

Warren Smock, Ivy Tech State College

Richard Snapp, Olympic College

Tom Snavely, Yavapai College

Laura Solano, Pueblo Community College

John Stancil, Florida Southern University

Undine Stinnette, Roosevelt University

Gary Stout, Cal State University-Northridge

Gina Sturgill, Concord College

Kan Sugandh, DeVry Institute of Technology-Pomona

William Sullivan, Assumption College

Ron Summers, Oklahoma City Community College

Rahmat Tavallali, Walsh University

Steve Teeter, Utah Valley State College

James Thomas, Cosumnes River College

Leslie Thysell, Richard Bland College

Christine Todd, William Woods University

Tom Turner, Des Moines Area Community College

Karen Ulbrich, Parkland College

Frank Urbancic, University of South Alabama - Mobile

Robert Urell, Irvine Valley College

John VanSantvoord, Southern New Hampshire University

Jay Wahlund, Minot State University

Pat Walczak, Lansing Community College

Scott Wallace, Blue Mountain Community College

Debra Warren, Chadron State College

Jeffrey Waybright, Spokane Community College

Christian Widmer, Tidewater Community College-VA Beach

Jack Wiehler, San Joaquin Delta College

Jo Winegar, Scott Community College

Rahnl Wood, NW Missouri State University

Joe Woods, University of Arkansas-Little Rock

Ray Wurzburger, New River Community College

Lori Zulauf, Slippery Rock University

Brief Contents

Contents

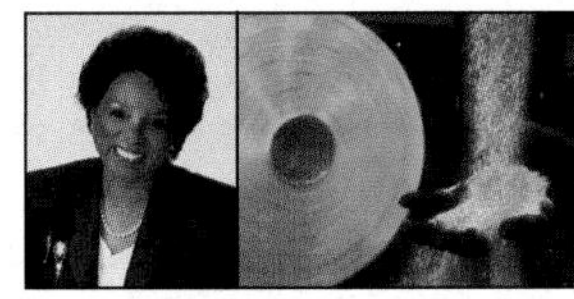

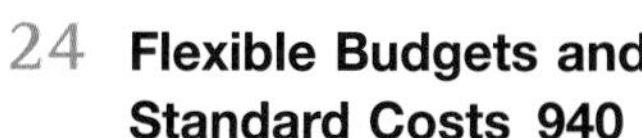

Fundamental Accounting Principles

"I love chocolate, and so I'm having fun making money"—Elise Macmillan (Evan Macmillan on right)

1 Accounting in Business

A Look at This Chapter

Accounting plays a crucial role in the information age. In this chapter, we discuss the importance of accounting to different types of organizations and describe its many users and uses. We explain that ethics are crucial to accounting. We also describe business transactions and how they are reflected in financial statements.

A Look Ahead

Chapter 2 further describes and analyzes business transactions. We explain the analysis and recording of transactions, the ledger and trial balance, and the double-entry system. More generally, Chapters 2 through 4 focus on accounting and analysis, and they illustrate (via the accounting cycle) how financial statements reflect business activities.

Learning Objectives

***Learning Objectives** are organized by conceptual, analytical, and procedural.*

CAP

Conceptual

C1 Explain the purpose and importance of accounting in the information age. *(p. 4)*

C2 Identify users and uses of accounting. *(p. 5)*

C3 Identify opportunities in accounting and related fields. *(p. 6)*

C4 Explain why ethics are crucial to accounting. *(p. 8)*

C5 Explain the meaning of generally accepted accounting principles, and define and apply several key principles of accounting. *(p. 9)*

Analytical

A1 Define and interpret the accounting equation and each of its components. *(p. 12)*

A2 Analyze business transactions using the accounting equation. *(p. 13)*

A3 Compute and interpret return on assets. *(p. 20)*

Procedural

P1 Identify and prepare basic financial statements and explain how they interrelate. *(p. 17)*

Decision Feature

Sweet Taste of Success

DENVER—Elise and Evan Macmillan—sister and brother entrepreneurs—aim to satisfy. "Our whole business is about customers," says Elise. These teenagers head **The Chocolate Farm** **(TheChocolateFarm.com)**, which specializes in making chocolates and in helping their customers make them.

"We thought our business was going to be a one-day thing," says Elise, "but it turned into a real business." This meant Elise and Evan had to deal with issues such as organization form, accounting and information systems, transaction analysis, and financial reports. Adds Elise, "I'm kept busy with the company's future plans and new product ideas and everything else that there is to a company."

Special attention is directed at accounting information; because without income, The Chocolate Farm would be knee-deep in cocoa. Elise and Evan were able to set up a transaction-based accounting system to profitably handle customer sales and orders. They also used accounting information to make good business decisions. Relying on sales and expense information, Elise and Evan focused efforts on their best-sellers such as *Brown Cows, Mint Sheep Munch, Pecan Turtles,* and *Pigs in Mud.* Moreover, after an analysis of the accounting information, they decided to expand and now employ more than a dozen people.

Evan admits that even with the best accounting information, one must accept some risk. We "accept the fact that it's a risk," says Evan, but that's the reality of money making. Elise concurs, "I love chocolate, and so I'm having fun making money." The Farm now produces more than $1 million per year in revenues. We could all become chocolate-lovers with results like that!

[Sources: *Ernst & Young Website,* January 2004; *The Chocolate Farm Website,* January 2004; *Entrepreneur Magazine,* May 2002; *Denver Business Journal,* January 2002; *The Wall Street Journal,* March 2003.]

*A **Decision Feature** launches each chapter showing the relevance of accounting for a real entrepreneur. An **Entrepreneurial Decision** problem at the end of the assignments returns to this feature with a mini-case.*

*A **Preview** opens each chapter with a summary of topics covered.*

Today's world is one of information—its preparation, communication, analysis, and use. Accounting is at the heart of this information age. Knowledge of accounting gives us career opportunities and the insight to take advantage of them. By studying this book, you will learn about concepts, procedures, and analyses that will help you make better decisions throughout your life. In this chapter we describe accounting, the users and uses of accounting information, the forms and activities of organizations, and several accounting principles. We also introduce transaction analysis and financial statements.

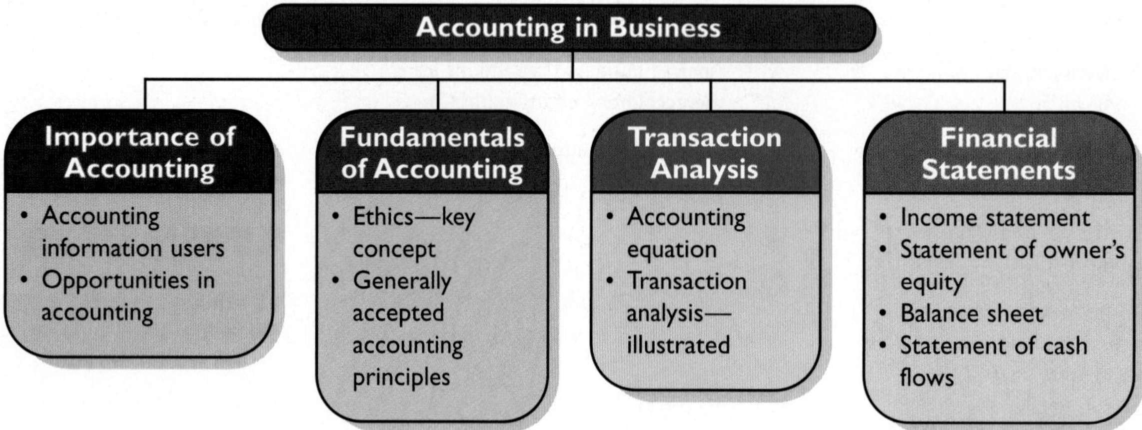

Importance of Accounting

C1 Explain the purpose and importance of accounting in the information age.

We live in an information age—a time of communication and immediate access to data, news, facts, and commentary. Information affects how we live, whom we associate with, and the opportunities we have. To fully benefit from the available information, we need knowledge of the information system. An information system involves the collecting, processing, and reporting of information to decision makers.

Providing information about what businesses own, what they owe, and how they perform is an important aim of accounting. **Accounting** is an information and measurement system that identifies, records, and communicates relevant, reliable, and comparable information about an organization's business activities. *Identifying* business activities requires selecting transactions and events relevant to an organization. Examples are the sale of vehicles by **Ford** and the receipt of ticket money by **TicketMaster**. *Recording* business activities requires keeping a chronological log of transactions and events measured in dollars and classified and summarized in a useful format. *Communicating* business activities requires preparing accounting reports such as financial statements. It also requires analyzing and interpreting such reports. (The financial statements and notes of **Krispy Kreme** are shown in Appendix A of this book. This appendix also shows the financial statements of **Tastykake** and **Harley-Davidson**.) Exhibit 1.1 summarizes accounting activities.

We must guard against a narrow view of accounting. The most common contact with accounting is through credit approvals, checking accounts, tax forms, and payroll. These

Exhibit 1.1

Accounting Activities

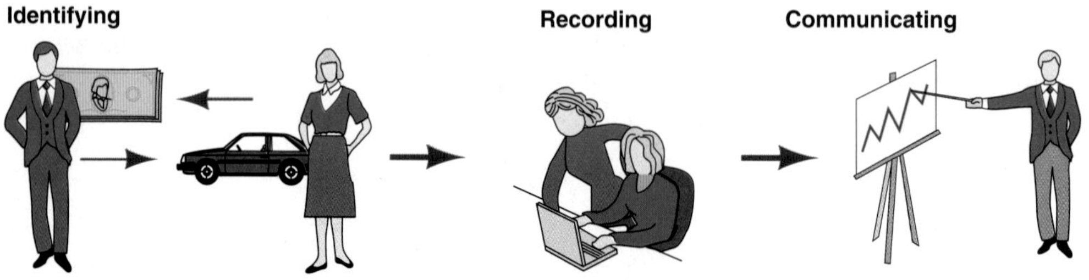

experiences are limited and tend to focus on the recordkeeping parts of accounting. **Recordkeeping,** or **bookkeeping,** is the recording of transactions and events, either manually or electronically. This is just one part of accounting. Accounting also identifies and communicates information on transactions and events, and it includes the crucial processes of analysis and interpretation.

Margin notes further enhance the textual material.

Point: Technology is only as useful as the accounting data available, and users' decisions are only as good as their understanding of accounting. The best software and recordkeeping cannot make up for lack of accounting knowledge.

Technology is a key part of modern business and plays a major role in accounting. Technology reduces the time, effort, and cost of recordkeeping while improving clerical accuracy. Some small organizations continue to perform various accounting tasks manually, but even they are impacted by information technology. As technology has changed the way we store, process, and summarize masses of data, accounting has been freed to expand. Consulting, planning, and other financial services are now closely linked to accounting. These services require sorting through data, interpreting their meaning, identifying key factors, and analyzing their implications.

Users of Accounting Information

Accounting is often called the *language of business* because all organizations set up an accounting information system to communicate data to help people make better decisions. Exhibit 1.2 shows that the accounting information system serves many kinds of users who can be divided into two groups: external users and internal users.

Exhibit 1.2
Users of Accounting Information

Infographics reinforce key concepts through visual learning.

C2 Identify users and uses of accounting.

External Information Users **External users** of accounting information are *not* directly involved in running the organization. They include shareholders (investors), lenders, directors, customers, suppliers, regulators, lawyers, brokers, and the press. External users have limited access to an organization's information. Yet many of their important decisions depend on information that is reliable, relevant, and comparable.

Financial accounting is the area of accounting aimed at serving external users by providing them with financial statements. These statements are known as *general-purpose financial statements*. The term *general-purpose* refers to the broad range of purposes for which external users rely on these statements.

Each external user has special information needs depending on the types of decisions to be made. *Lenders* (creditors) loan money or other resources to an organization. Banks, savings and loans, co-ops, and mortgage and finance companies often are lenders. Lenders look for information to help them assess whether an organization is likely to repay its loans with interest. *Shareholders* (investors) are the owners of a corporation. They use accounting reports in deciding whether to buy, hold, or sell stock. Shareholders typically elect a *board of directors* to oversee their interests in an organization. Since directors are responsible to shareholders, their information needs are similar. *External* (independent) *auditors* examine financial statements to verify that they are prepared according to generally accepted accounting principles. *Employees* and *labor unions* use financial statements to judge the fairness of

Point: World Wrestling Entertainment has more than 70 mil. shares of stock outstanding.

wages, assess future job prospects, and bargain for better wages. *Regulators* often have legal authority over certain activities of organizations. For example, the Internal Revenue Service (IRS) and other tax authorities require organizations to file accounting reports in computing taxes. Other regulators include utility boards that use accounting information to set utility rates and securities regulators that require reports for companies that sell their stock to the public.

Point: Microsoft's high income levels encouraged antitrust actions against it.

Accounting serves the needs of many other external users. *Voters, legislators,* and *government officials* use accounting information to monitor and evaluate a government's receipts and expenses. *Contributors* to nonprofit organizations use accounting information to evaluate the use and impact of their donations. *Suppliers* use accounting information to judge the soundness of a customer before making sales on credit, and *customers* use financial reports to assess the staying power of potential suppliers.

Internal Information Users **Internal users** of accounting information are those directly involved in managing and operating an organization. They use the information to help improve the efficiency and effectiveness of an organization. **Managerial accounting** is the area of accounting that serves the decision-making needs of internal users. Internal reports are not subject to the same rules as external reports and are designed with the special needs of internal users in mind.

Decision Insight *boxes highlight relevant items from practice.*

There are several types of internal users, and many are managers of key operating activities. *Research and development managers* need information about projected costs and revenues of proposed changes in products and services. *Purchasing managers* need to know what, when, and how much to purchase. *Human resource managers* need information about employees' payroll, benefits, performance, and compensation. *Production managers* depend on information to monitor costs and ensure quality. *Distribution managers* need reports for timely, accurate, and efficient delivery of products and services. *Marketing managers* use reports about sales and costs to target consumers, set prices, and monitor consumer needs, tastes, and price concerns. *Service managers* require information on both the costs and benefits of looking after products and services.

Decision Insight

Know-Nothing CEO The know-nothing defense of CEOs such as **Global Crossing**'s Gary Winnick and **Enron**'s Jeffrey Skilling and Kenneth Lay could soon be shattered. Through novel legal moves, prosecutors are achieving convictions provided they prove that the CEO knew the company's internal picture was different than the picture shown to outsiders.

Both internal and external users rely on internal controls to monitor and control company activities. *Internal controls* are procedures set up to protect company property and equipment, ensure reliable accounting reports, promote efficiency, and encourage adherence to company policies. Examples are good records, physical controls (locks, passwords, guards), and independent reviews.

Opportunities in Accounting

C3 Identify opportunities in accounting and related fields.

Accounting information affects many aspects of our lives. When we earn money, pay taxes, invest savings, budget earnings, and plan for the future, we are influenced by accounting. Accounting has four broad areas of opportunities: financial, managerial, taxation, and accounting-related. Exhibit 1.3 lists selected opportunities in each area.

The majority of accounting opportunities are in *private accounting,* as shown in Exhibit 1.4. *Public accounting* offers the next largest number of opportunities. Still other opportunities exist in government (and not-for-profit) agencies, including business regulation and investigation of law violations.

Point: The "top 5" greatest investors of the 20th century, as compiled in a recent survey:
1. Warren Buffett, Berkshire Hathaway
2. Peter Lynch, Fidelity Funds
3. John Templeton, Templeton Group
4. Benjamin Graham & David Dodd, professors
5. George Soros, Soros Fund

Accounting specialists are highly regarded. Their professional standing often is denoted by a certificate. Certified public accountants (CPAs) must meet education and experience requirements, pass an examination, and exhibit ethical character. Many accounting specialists hold certificates in addition to or instead of the CPA. Two of the most common are the

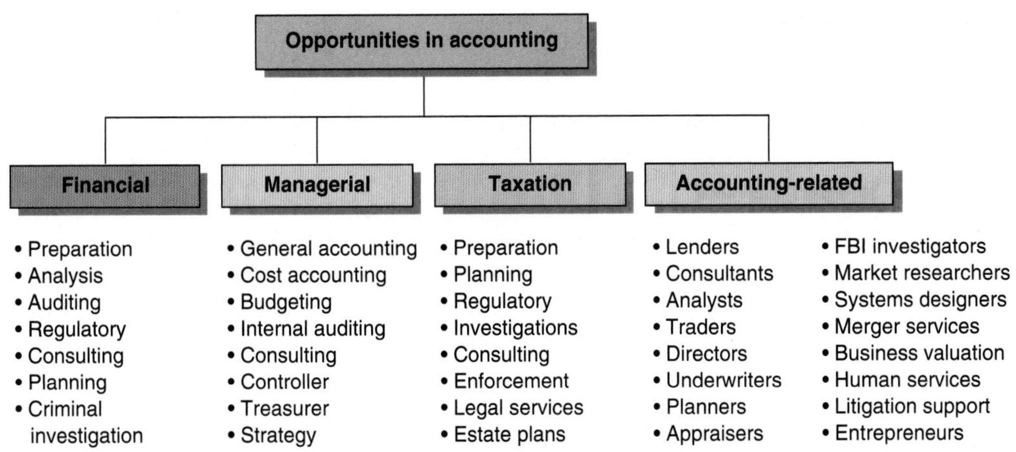

Exhibit 1.3
Accounting Opportunities

certificate in management accounting (CMA) and the certified internal auditor (CIA). Employers also look for specialists with designations such as certified bookkeeper (CB), certified payroll professional (CPP), and personal financial specialist (PFS).

Exhibit 1.4
Accounting Jobs by Area

Individuals with accounting knowledge are always in demand as they can help with financial analysis, strategic planning, e-commerce, product feasibility analysis, information technology, and financial management. Benefit packages can include flexible work schedules, telecommuting options, career path alternatives, casual work environments, extended vacation time, and child and elder care.

Demand for accounting specialists is boosting salaries. Exhibit 1.5 reports average annual salaries for several accounting positions. Salary variation depends on location, company size, professional designation, experience, and other factors. For example, salaries for chief financial officers (CFO) range from under $75,000 to more than $1 million per year. Likewise, salaries for bookkeepers range from under $30,000 to more than $80,000.

Point: The firm of Ernst & Young gave its interns a vacation at Disney World.

Point: The CFOs of Cisco Systems and Qualcom received an annual salary of more than $20 mil.

Exhibit 1.5
Accounting Salaries for Selected Fields

Field	Title (experience)	2003 Salary	2008 Estimate*
Public Accounting:	Partner	$181,000	$231,000
	Manager (6–8 years)	89,500	114,000
	Senior (3–5 years)	68,500	87,500
	Junior (0–2 years)	49,000	62,500
Private Accounting:	CFO	221,000	282,000
	Controller/Treasurer	140,000	179,000
	Manager (6–8 years)	83,000	106,000
	Senior (3–5 years)	69,000	88,000
	Junior (0–2 years)	47,000	60,000
Recordkeeping:	Full-charge bookkeeper	55,000	70,000
	Accounts manager	48,500	62,000
	Payroll manager	52,000	66,000
	Accounting clerk (0–1 years)	30,500	39,000

* Estimates assume a 5% compounded annual increase over current levels.

Point: For updated salary information:
www.AICPA.org
Abbott-Langer.com
Kforce.com

Quick Check is a chance to stop and reflect on key points.

Quick Check

1. What is the purpose of accounting?
2. What is the relation between accounting and recordkeeping?
3. Identify some advantages of technology for accounting.
4. Who are the internal and external users of accounting information?
5. Identify at least five types of managers who are internal users of accounting information.
6. What are internal controls and why are they important?

Answers—p. 26

Fundamentals of Accounting

Accounting is guided by principles, standards, concepts, and assumptions. This section describes several of these key fundamentals of accounting.

Ethics—A Key Concept

C4 Explain why ethics are crucial to accounting.

The goal of accounting is to provide useful information for decisions. For information to be useful, it must be trusted. This demands ethics in accounting. **Ethics** are beliefs that distinguish right from wrong. They are accepted standards of good and bad behavior.

Identifying the ethical path is sometimes difficult. The preferred path is a course of action that avoids casting doubt on one's decisions. For example, accounting users are less likely to trust an auditor's report if the auditor's pay depends on the success of the client. To avoid such concerns, ethics rules are often set. For example, auditors are banned from direct investment in their client and cannot accept pay that depends on figures in the client's reports. Exhibit 1.6 gives guidelines for making ethical decisions.

Point: Sarbanes-Oxley Act requires each issuer of securities to disclose whether it has adopted a code of ethics for its senior financial officers and the contents of that code.

Exhibit 1.6

Guidelines for Ethical Decision Making

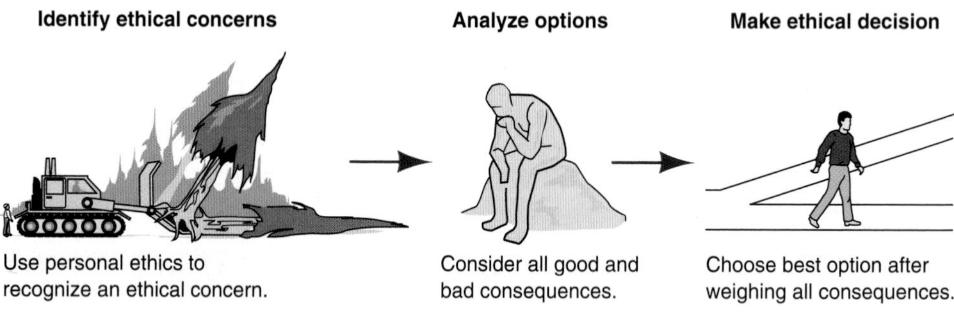

Providers of accounting information often face ethical choices as they prepare financial reports. These choices can affect the price a buyer pays and the wages paid to workers. They can even affect the success of products and services. Misleading information can lead to a wrongful closing of a division that harms workers, customers, and suppliers. There is an old saying worth remembering: *Good ethics are good business.*

Some extend ethics to *social responsibility,* which refers to a concern for the impact of actions on society. An organization's social responsibility can include donations to hospitals, colleges, community programs, and law enforcement. It also can include programs to reduce pollution, increase product safety, improve worker conditions, and support continuing education. These programs are not limited to large companies. For example, many independently owned theaters and small businesses offer discounts to students and senior citizens. Still others help sponsor events such as the Special Olympics and summer reading programs.

Global: Business ethics differ across countries. This is due to cultural, political, legal, economic, and other important factors.

Point: A survey of executives, educators, and legislators showed that 9 of 10 participants believe organizations are troubled by ethical problems.

Point: The American Institute of Certified Public Accountants' *Code of Professional Conduct* is available at www.AICPA.org.

Graphical displays are often used to illustrate key points.

Generally Accepted Accounting Principles

Financial accounting practice is governed by concepts and rules known as **generally accepted accounting principles (GAAP).** To use and interpret financial statements effectively, we need to understand these principles. A main purpose of GAAP is to make information in financial statements relevant, reliable, and comparable. *Relevant information* affects the decisions of its users. *Reliable information* is trusted by users. *Comparable information* is helpful in contrasting organizations.

Decision Insight

Virtuous Returns Virtue is not always its own reward. Compare the S&P 500 with the Domini Social Index (DSI), which covers 400 companies that have especially good records of social responsibility. Notice that returns for companies with socially responsible behavior are at least as high as those of the S&P 500.

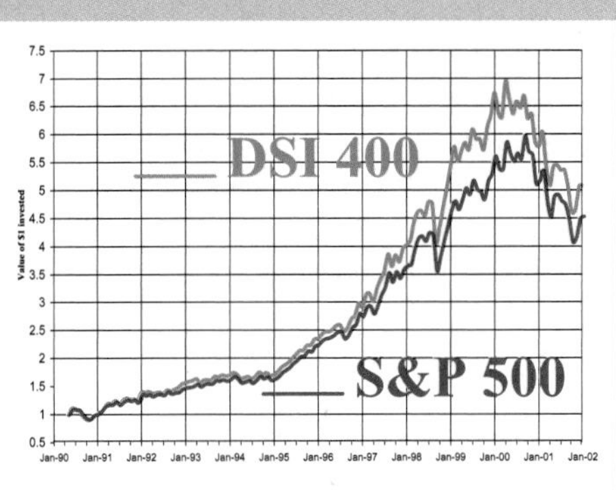

Setting Accounting Principles Two main groups establish generally accepted accounting principles in the United States. The **Financial Accounting Standards Board (FASB)** is the private group that sets both broad and specific principles. The **Securities and Exchange Commission (SEC)** is the government group that establishes reporting requirements for companies that issue stock to the public.

C5 Explain the meaning of generally accepted accounting principles, and define and apply several key principles of accounting.

In today's global economy, there is increased demand by external users for comparability in accounting reports. This often arises when companies wish to raise money from lenders and investors in different countries. To that end, the **International Accounting Standards Board (IASB)** issues *International Financial Reporting Standards* (*IFRS*) that identify preferred accounting practices. The IASB hopes to create more harmony among accounting practices of different countries. If standards are harmonized, one company can use a single set of financial statements in all financial markets. Many countries' standard setters support the IASB, and interest in moving U.S. GAAP toward the IASB's practices is growing, yet the IASB does not have the authority to impose its standards on companies.

Point: State ethics codes require CPAs who audit financial statements to disclose areas where those statements fail to comply with GAAP. If CPAs fail to report noncompliance, they can lose their licenses and be subject to criminal action and fines.

Principles of Accounting Accounting principles are of two types. *General principles* are the basic assumptions, concepts, and guidelines for preparing financial statements. *Specific principles* are detailed rules used in reporting business transactions and events. General principles stem from long-used accounting practices. Specific principles arise more often from the rulings of authoritative groups.

We need to understand both general and specific principles to effectively use accounting information. Several general principles are described in this section and several others are described in later chapters. General principles are portrayed as building blocks of GAAP in Exhibit 1.7. The specific principles are described as we encounter them.

Point: An audit examines whether financial statements are prepared using GAAP. It does *not* attest to the absolute accuracy of the statements.

Point: The largest accounting firms are Deloitte & Touche, Ernst & Young, PricewaterhouseCoopers, and KPMG.

The **objectivity principle** means that accounting information is supported by independent, unbiased evidence. It demands more than a person's opinion. Information is not reliable if it is based only on what a preparer thinks might be true. A preparer can be too optimistic or pessimistic. The objectivity principle is intended to make financial statements useful by ensuring they report reliable and verifiable information.

Exhibit 1.7

Building Blocks for GAAP

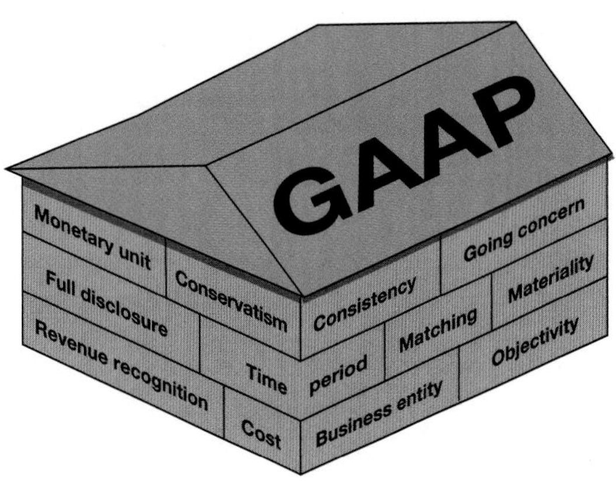

The **cost principle** means that accounting information is based on actual cost. Cost is measured on a cash or equal-to-cash basis. This means if cash is given for a service, its cost is measured as the amount of cash paid. If something besides cash is exchanged (such as

Decision Insight

Name that Value Abuse of the objectivity and cost principles brought down executives at **Itex Corp** who bartered assets of little or no value and then reported them at grossly inflated values—recognizing fictitious gains and assets. The deals involved difficult-to-value assets such as artwork and stamps.

a car traded for a truck), cost is measured as the cash value of what is given up or received. The cost principle emphasizes reliability, and information based on cost is considered objective. To illustrate, suppose a company pays $5,000 for equipment. The cost principle requires that this purchase be recorded at a cost of $5,000. It makes no difference if the owner thinks this equipment is worth $7,000.

The **going-concern principle** means that accounting information reflects an assumption that the business will continue operating instead of being closed or sold. This implies, for example, that property is reported at cost instead of, say, liquidation values that assume closure.

Point: The cost principle is also called the *historical cost principle.*

Point: For currency conversion: cnnfn.com/markets/currencies

The **monetary unit principle** means that we can express transactions and events in monetary, or money, units. Money is the common denominator in business. Examples of monetary units are the dollar in the United States, Canada, Australia, and Singapore; the pound sterling in the United Kingdom; and the peso in Mexico, the Philippines, and Chile. The monetary unit a company uses in its accounting reports usually depends on the country where it operates, but many companies today are expressing reports in more than one monetary unit.

Example: Cadbury Schweppes, a leading beverage and confectionery producer, recently reported sales of £5,500 million. What is the U.S.$ equivalent of these sales if the exchange rate is £1 = $1.50? *Answer:* $8,250 million (£5,500 × $1.50).

Revenue (sales) is the amount received from selling products and services. The **revenue recognition principle** provides guidance on when a company must recognize revenue. To *recognize* means to record it. If revenue is recognized too early, a company would look more profitable than it is. If revenue is recognized too late, a company would look less profitable than it is. The following three concepts are important to revenue recognition. (1) *Revenue is recognized when earned.* The earnings process is normally complete when services are rendered or a seller transfers ownership of products to the buyer. (2) *Proceeds from selling products and services need not be in cash.* A common noncash proceed received by a seller is a customer's promise to pay at a future date, called *credit sales.* (3) *Revenue is measured by the cash received plus the cash value of any other items received.*

Example: When a bookstore sells a textbook on credit is its earnings process complete? *Answer:* The bookstore can record sales for these books minus an amount expected for returns.

The **business entity principle** means that a business is accounted for separately from other business entities, including its owner. The reason for this principle is that separate information about each business is necessary for good decisions. A business entity can take one of three legal forms: *sole proprietorship, partnership,* or *corporation.*

Point: Abuse of the entity principle was a main culprit in the collapse of Enron.

1. A **sole proprietorship,** or simply **proprietorship,** is a business owned by one person. No special legal requirements must be met to start a proprietorship. It is a separate entity for accounting purposes, but it is *not* a separate legal entity from its owner. This means, for example, that a court can order an owner to sell personal belongings to pay a proprietorship's debt. This *unlimited liability* of a proprietorship is a disadvantage. However, an advantage is that a proprietorship's income is not subject to a business income tax but is instead reported and taxed on the owner's personal income tax return. Proprietorship characteristics are summarized in Exhibit 1.8.
2. A **partnership** is a business owned by two or more people, called *partners.* Like a proprietorship, no special legal requirements must be met in starting a partnership. The only requirement is an agreement between partners to run a business together. The agreement can be either oral or

Decision Insight

Revenues for the New York Yankees baseball team include ticket sales, television and cable broadcasts, radio rights, concessions, and advertising. Revenues from ticket sales are earned when the Yankees play each game. Advance ticket sales are not revenues; instead, they represent a liability until the Yankees play the game for which the ticket was sold.

Characteristic	Proprietorship	Partnership	Corporation
Business entity	yes	yes	yes
Legal entity	no	no	yes
Limited liability	no*	no*	yes
Unlimited life	no	no	yes
Business taxed	no	no	yes
One owner allowed	yes	no	yes

* Proprietorships and partnerships that are set up as LLCs provide limited liability.

Exhibit 1.8

Characteristics of Businesses

written and usually indicates how income and losses are to be shared. A partnership, like a proprietorship, is *not* legally separate from its owners. This means that each partner's share of profits is reported and taxed on that partner's tax return. It also means *unlimited liability* for its partners. However, at least three types of partnerships limit liability. A *limited partnership* (*LP*) includes a general partner(s) with unlimited liability and a limited partner(s) with liability restricted to the amount invested. A *limited liability partnership* (*LLP*) restricts partners' liabilities to their own acts and the acts of individuals under their control. This protects an innocent partner from the negligence of another partner, yet all partners remain responsible for partnership debts. A *limited liability company* (*LLC*), offers the limited liability of a corporation and the tax treatment of a partnership (or proprietorship). Most proprietorships and partnerships are now organized as an LLC.

Decision Insight

Web Info Most organizations maintain Websites that include accounting information—see **Krispy Kreme's (KrispyKreme.com)** Website as one example. The SEC keeps an online database called EDGAR **(www.sec.gov/edgar.shtml),** which has accounting information for thousands of companies that sell their stock to the public.

Lightbulb icon highlights entrepreneurial-related info.

Decision Insight

New Age Entrepreneurship will be the defining trend of business in this century, according to a survey of business leaders. Respondents see the biggest opportunities for entrepreneurship in technology, medicine, food services, hospitality, and information services.

3. A **corporation** is a business legally separate from its owners, meaning it is responsible for its own acts and its own debts. Separate legal status means that a corporation can conduct business with the rights, duties, and responsibilities of a person. A corporation acts through its managers, who are its legal agents. Separate legal status also means that its owners, who are called **shareholders** (or **stockholders**), are not personally liable for corporate acts and debts. This limited liability is its main advantage. A main disadvantage is what's called *double taxation*—meaning that (1) the corporation income is taxed and (2) any distribution of income to its owners through dividends is taxed as part of the owners' personal income (usually at the 15% rate). An exception to this is an *S corporation,* a corporation with certain characteristics that give it a tax status that removes its corporate income tax. Owners of S corporations report their share of corporate income with their personal income. (*Note:* For lower income taxpayers, the dividend tax is less than 15%, and in some cases zero.) Ownership of corporations is divided into units called **shares** or **stock.** When a corporation issues only one class of stock, we call it **common stock** (or *capital stock*).

***Decision Ethics** boxes are role-playing exercises that stress ethics in accounting and business.*

Decision Ethics

Entrepreneur You and a friend develop a new design for in-line skates that improves speed and performance by 25% to 40%. You plan to form a business to manufacture and market these skates. You and your friend want to minimize taxes, but your prime concern is potential lawsuits from individuals who might be injured on these skates. What form of organization do you set up?

Answer—p. 26

Point: Sole proprietorships and partnerships are usually managed on a regular basis by their owners. In a corporation, the owners (shareholders) elect a board of directors who appoint managers to run the business.

Quick Check

7. What three-step guidelines can help people make ethical decisions?
8. Why are ethics and social responsibility valuable to organizations?
9. Why are ethics crucial in accounting?
10. Who sets U.S. accounting rules?
11. How are U.S. companies affected by international accounting standards?
12. How are the objectivity and cost principles related?
13. Why is the business entity principle important?
14. Why is the revenue recognition principle important?
15. What are the three basic forms of business organization?
16. Identify the owners of corporations and the terminology for ownership units.

Answers—p. 26

Transaction Analysis and the Accounting Equation

A1 Define and interpret the accounting equation and each of its components.

To understand accounting information, we need to know how an accounting system captures relevant data about transactions, and classifies, records, and reports data.

Accounting Equation

The accounting system reflects two basic aspects of a company: what it owns and what it owes. **Assets** are resources with future benefits that are owned or controlled by a company. Examples are cash, supplies, equipment, and land. The claims on a company's assets—what it owes—are separated into owner and nonowner claims. **Liabilities** are what a company owes its nonowners (creditors) in future products or services. **Equity** (also called owner's equity or capital) refers to the claims of its owner(s). Together, liabilities and equity are the source of funds to acquire assets. The relation of assets, liabilities, and equity is reflected in the following **accounting equation:**

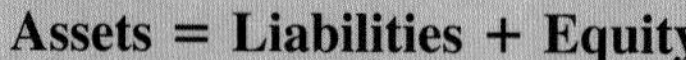

Assets = Liabilities + Equity

Liabilities are usually shown before equity in this equation because creditors' claims must be paid before the claims of owners. (The terms in this equation can be rearranged; for example, Assets − Liabilities = Equity.) The accounting equation applies to all transactions and events, to all companies and forms of organization, and to all points in time. To illustrate, **Krispy Kreme**'s assets equal $410,487, its liabilities equal $137,135, and its equity equals $273,352 ($ in thousands). Let's now look at the accounting equation in more detail.

***Real company names** are printed in bold magenta.*

Assets **Assets** are resources owned or controlled by a company. These resources are expected to yield future benefits. Examples are Web servers for an online services company, musical instruments for a rock band, and land for a vegetable grower. The term *receivable* is used to refer to an asset that promises a future inflow of resources. A company that provides a service or product on credit is said to have an account receivable from that customer.

Point: The phrase "on credit" implies that the cash payment will occur at a future date.

Liabilities **Liabilities** are creditors' claims on assets. These claims reflect obligations to provide assets, products, or services to others. The term *payable* refers to a liability that promises a future outflow of resources. Examples are wages payable to employees, accounts payable to suppliers, notes payable to banks, and taxes payable to the government.

Equity **Equity** is the owner's claim on assets. Equity is equal to assets minus liabilities. This is the reason equity is also called *net assets* or *residual equity (interest)*.

For a proprietorship, owner investments and revenues increase equity, and owner withdrawals and expenses decrease it. **Owner investments** are the assets an owner puts into the company—included under the title **Owner, Capital. Revenues** are the gross increase in equity from a company's earnings activities. Examples are consulting services provided, sales of products, facilities rented to others, and commissions from services. **Owner withdrawals** are the assets an owner takes from the company for personal use. **Expenses** decrease equity and are the cost of assets or services used to earn revenues. Examples are costs of employee time, use of supplies, and the advertising, utilities, and insurance services from others. This breakdown of equity yields the following **expanded accounting equation:**

*Key **terms** are printed in bold and defined again in the end-of-book **glossary.***

Point: Revenues and owner investments increase equity. Expenses and owner withdrawals decrease equity.

$$\text{Assets} = \text{Liabilities} + \overbrace{\text{Owner Capital} - \text{Owner Withdrawals} + \text{Revenues} - \text{Expenses}}^{\text{Equity}}$$

Net income occurs when revenues exceed expenses. Net income increases equity. A **net loss** occurs when expenses exceed revenues, which decreases equity. The accounting equation can be used to track changes in a company's assets, liabilities, and equity, which is the focus of the next section.

Transaction Analysis

A2 Analyze business transactions using the accounting equation.

Business activities can be described in terms of transactions and events. **External transactions** are exchanges of value between two entities, which yield changes in the accounting equation. **Internal transactions** are exchanges within an entity; they can also affect the accounting equation. An example is a company's use of its supplies, which are reported as expenses when used. **Events** refer to those happenings that affect an entity's accounting equation *and* can be reliably measured. They include business events such as changes in the market value of certain assets and liabilities, and natural events such as floods and fires that destroy assets and create losses. They do not include, for example, the signing of service or product contracts, which by themselves do not impact the accounting equation.

This section uses the accounting equation to analyze 11 selected transactions and events of FastForward, a start-up consulting business, in its first month of operations. Remember that each transaction and event leaves the equation in balance and that assets *always* equal the sum of liabilities and equity.

*Topic Tackler **icon** references additional help on the CD.*

Topic Tackler 1-1

Transaction 1: Investment by Owner On December 1, Chuck Taylor forms an athletic shoe consulting business, which he names FastForward. He sets it up as a proprietorship. Taylor owns and manages the business. The marketing plan for the business is to focus primarily on consulting with sports clubs, amateur athletes, and others who place orders for athletic shoes with manufacturers. Taylor personally invests $30,000 cash in the new company and deposits the cash in a bank account opened under the name of FastForward. After this transaction, the cash (an asset) and the owner's equity each equal $30,000. The source of increase in equity is the owner's investment, which is included in the column titled C. Taylor, Capital. (*Note:* Owner investments are always included under the title *"Owner name," Capital.*) The effect of this transaction on FastForward is reflected in the accounting equation as follows:

Point: There are 3 basic types of company operations: (1) **Services**—providing services for profit, (2) **Merchandisers**—buying products and selling them for profit, and (3) **Manufacturers**—creating products and selling them for profit.

	Assets	=	Liabilities	+	Equity
	Cash	=			**C. Taylor, Capital**
(1)	+$30,000	=			+$30,000

Transaction 2: Purchase Supplies for Cash FastForward uses $2,500 of its cash to buy supplies of brand name athletic shoes for testing over the next few months. This transaction is an exchange of cash, an asset, for another kind of asset, supplies. It merely changes

the form of assets from cash to supplies. The decrease in cash is exactly equal to the increase in supplies. The supplies of athletic shoes are assets because of the expected future benefits from the test results of their performance. This transaction is reflected in the accounting equation as follows:

	Assets			=	Liabilities	+	Equity
	Cash	+	Supplies	=			C. Taylor, Capital
Old Bal.	$30,000			=			$30,000
(2)	−2,500	+	$2,500				
New Bal.	$27,500	+	$ 2,500	=			$30,000
	$30,000				$30,000		

Transaction 3: Purchase Equipment for Cash FastForward spends $26,000 to acquire equipment for testing athletic shoes. Like transaction 2, transaction 3 is an exchange of one asset, cash, for another asset, equipment. The equipment is an asset because of its expected future benefits from testing athletic shoes. This purchase changes the makeup of assets but does not change the asset total. The accounting equation remains in balance.

	Assets					=	Liabilities	+	Equity
	Cash	+	Supplies	+	Equipment	=			C. Taylor, Capital
Old Bal.	$27,500	+	$2,500			=			$30,000
(3)	−26,000			+	$26,000				
New Bal.	$1,500	+	$2,500	+	$ 26,000	=			$30,000
	$30,000						$30,000		

Example: If FastForward pays $500 cash in transaction 4, how does this partial payment affect the liability to CalTech? What would be FastForward's cash balance? *Answers:* The liability to CalTech would be reduced to $6,600 and the cash balance would be reduced to $1,000.

Transaction 4: Purchase Supplies on Credit Taylor decides he needs more supplies of athletic shoes. These additional supplies total $7,100, but as we see from the accounting equation in transaction 3, FastForward has only $1,500 in cash. Taylor arranges to purchase them on credit from CalTech Supply Company. Thus, FastForward acquires supplies in exchange for a promise to pay for them later. This purchase increases assets by $7,100 in supplies, and liabilities (called *accounts payable* to CalTech Supply) increase by the same amount. The effects of this purchase on the accounting equation follow:

	Assets					=	Liabilities	+	Equity
	Cash	+	Supplies	+	Equipment	=	Accounts Payable	+	C. Taylor, Capital
Old Bal.	$1,500	+	$2,500	+	$26,000	=			$30,000
(4)		+	7,100				+$7,100		
New Bal.	$1,500	+	$9,600	+	$26,000	=	$ 7,100	+	$30,000
	$37,100						$37,100		

Transaction 5: Provide Services for Cash FastForward earns revenues by consulting with clients about test results on athletic shoes. It earns net income only if its revenues are greater than its expenses incurred in earning them. In one of its first jobs, FastForward provides consulting services to an athletic club and immediately collects $4,200 cash. The accounting equation reflects this increase in cash of $4,200 and in equity of $4,200. This increase in equity is identified in the far right column under Revenues because the cash is earned by providing consulting services.

	Assets					=	Liabilities	+	Equity		
	Cash	+	Supplies	+	Equipment	=	Accounts Payable	+	C. Taylor, Capital	+	Revenues
Old Bal.	$1,500	+	$9,600	+	$26,000	=	$7,100	+	$30,000		
(5)	+4,200									+	$4,200
New Bal.	$5,700	+	$9,600	+	$26,000	=	$7,100	+	$30,000	+	$ 4,200
			$41,300						$41,300		

Transactions 6 and 7: Payment of Expenses in Cash FastForward pays $1,000 rent to the landlord of the building where its store is located. Paying this amount allows FastForward to occupy the space for the month of December. The rental payment is reflected in the following accounting equation as transaction 6. FastForward also pays the biweekly $700 salary of the company's only employee. This is reflected in the accounting equation as transaction 7. Both transactions 6 and 7 are December expenses for FastForward. The costs of both rent and salary are expenses, as opposed to assets, because their benefits are used in December (they have no future benefits after December). These transactions also use up an asset (cash) in carrying out FastForward's operations. The accounting equation shows that both transactions reduce cash and equity. The far right column identifies these decreases as Expenses.

	Assets					=	Liabilities	+	Equity				
	Cash	+	Supplies	+	Equipment	=	Accounts Payable	+	C. Taylor, Capital	+	Revenues	−	Expenses
Old Bal.	$5,700	+	$9,600	+	$26,000	=	$7,100	+	$30,000	+	$4,200		
(6)	−1,000											−	$1,000
Bal.	4,700	+	9,600	+	26,000	=	7,100	+	30,000	+	4,200	−	1,000
(7)	− 700											−	700
New Bal.	$4,000	+	$9,600	+	$26,000	=	$7,100	+	$30,000	+	$4,200	−	$ 1,700
			$39,600						$39,600				

Transaction 8: Provide Services and Facilities for Credit FastForward provides consulting services of $1,600 and rents its test facilities for $300 to an amateur sports club. The rental involves allowing club members to try recommended shoes at FastForward's testing grounds. The sports club is billed for the $1,900 total. This transaction results in a new asset, called *accounts receivable,* from this client. It also yields an increase in equity from the two revenue components reflected in the Revenues column of the accounting equation:

	Assets							=	Liabilities	+	Equity				
	Cash	+	Accounts Receivable	+	Supplies	+	Equipment	=	Accounts Payable	+	C. Taylor, Capital	+	Revenues	−	Expenses
Old Bal.	$4,000	+		+	$9,600	+	$26,000	=	$7,100	+	$30,000	+	$4,200	−	$1,700
(8)		+	$1,900									+	1,600		
												+	300		
New Bal.	$4,000	+	$ 1,900	+	$9,600	+	$26,000	=	$7,100	+	$30,000	+	$6,100	−	$1,700
				$41,500							$41,500				

Transaction 9: Receipt of Cash from Accounts Receivable The client in transaction 8 (the amateur sports club) pays $1,900 to FastForward 10 days after it is billed for consulting services. This transaction 9 does not change the total amount of assets and

Point: Receipt of cash is not always a revenue.

does not affect liabilities or equity. It converts the receivable (an asset) to cash (another asset). It does not create new revenue. Revenue was recognized when FastForward rendered the services in transaction 8, not when the cash is now collected. This emphasis on the earnings process instead of cash flows is a goal of the revenue recognition principle and yields useful information to users. The new balances follow:

	Assets							=	Liabilities	+	Equity				
	Cash	+	Accounts Receivable	+	Supplies	+	Equipment	=	Accounts Payable	+	C. Taylor, Capital	+	Revenues	−	Expenses
Old Bal.	$4,000	+	$1,900	+	$9,600	+	$26,000	=	$7,100	+	$30,000	+	$6,100	−	$1,700
(9)	+1,900	−	1,900												
New Bal.	$5,900	+	$ 0	+	$9,600	+	$26,000	=	$7,100	+	$30,000	+	$6,100	−	$1,700
	$41,500								$41,500						

Transaction 10: Payment of Accounts Payable FastForward pays CalTech Supply $900 cash as partial payment for its earlier $7,100 purchase of supplies (transaction 4), leaving $6,200 unpaid. The accounting equation shows that this transaction decreases FastForward's cash by $900 and decreases its liability to CalTech Supply by $900. Equity does not change. This event does not create an expense even though cash flows out of FastForward (instead the expense is recorded when FastForward derives the benefits from these supplies).

	Assets							=	Liabilities	+	Equity				
	Cash	+	Accounts Receivable	+	Supplies	+	Equipment	=	Accounts Payable	+	C. Taylor, Capital	+	Revenues	−	Expenses
Old Bal.	$5,900	+	$ 0	+	$9,600	+	$26,000	=	$7,100	+	$30,000	+	$6,100	−	$1,700
(10)	− 900								− 900						
New Bal.	$5,000	+	$ 0	+	$9,600	+	$26,000	=	$6,200	+	$30,000	+	$6,100	−	$1,700
	$40,600								$40,600						

Transaction 11: Withdrawal of Cash by Owner The owner of FastForward withdraws $600 cash for personal use. Withdrawals (decreases in equity) are not reported as expenses because they are not part of the company's earnings process. Since withdrawals are not company expenses, they are not used in computing net income.

	Assets							=	Liabilities	+	Equity						
	Cash	+	Accounts Receivable	+	Supplies	+	Equipment	=	Accounts Payable	+	C. Taylor, Capital	−	C. Taylor, Withdrawals	+	Revenues	−	Expenses
Old Bal.	$5,000	+	$ 0	+	$9,600	+	$26,000	=	$6,200	+	$30,000			+	$6,100	−	$1,700
(11)	− 600											−	$600				
New Bal.	$4,400	+	$ 0	+	$9,600	+	$26,000	=	$6,200	+	$30,000	−	$600	+	$6,100	−	$1,700
	$40,000								$40,000								

Summary of Transactions

Point: Knowing how financial statements are prepared improves our analysis of them. We develop the skills for analysis of financial statements throughout the book. Chapter 17 focuses on financial statement analysis.

We summarize in Exhibit 1.9 the effects of these 11 transactions of FastForward using the accounting equation. Two points should be noted. First, the accounting equation remains in balance after each transaction. Second, transactions can be analyzed by their effects on components of the accounting equation. For example, in transactions 2, 3, and 9, one asset increased while another decreased by equal amounts.

Exhibit 1.9

Summary of Transactions Using the Accounting Equation

	Assets								= Liabilities +			Equity					
	Cash	+	Accounts Receivable	+	Supplies	+	Equipment	=	Accounts Payable	+	C.Taylor, Capital	−	C.Taylor, Withdrawals	+	Revenues	−	Expenses
(1)	**$30,000**							=			**$30,000**						
(2)	**− 2,500**			+	**$2,500**												
Bal.	27,500			+	2,500			=			30,000						
(3)	**−26,000**					+	**$26,000**										
Bal.	1,500			+	2,500	+	26,000	=			30,000						
(4)				+	**7,100**				**+$7,100**								
Bal.	1,500			+	9,600	+	26,000	=	7,100	+	30,000						
(5)	**+ 4,200**													+	**$4,200**		
Bal.	5,700			+	9,600	+	26,000	=	7,100	+	30,000			+	4,200		
(6)	**− 1,000**															−	**$1,000**
Bal.	4,700			+	9,600	+	26,000	=	7,100	+	30,000			+	4,200	−	1,000
(7)	**− 700**															−	**700**
Bal.	4,000			+	9,600	+	26,000	=	7,100	+	30,000			+	4,200	−	1,700
(8)		+	**$1,900**											+	**1,600**		
														+	**300**		
Bal.	4,000	+	1,900	+	9,600	+	26,000	=	7,100	+	30,000			+	6,100	−	1,700
(9)	**+ 1,900**	−	**1,900**														
Bal.	5,900	+	0	+	9,600	+	26,000	=	7,100	+	30,000			+	6,100	−	1,700
(10)	**− 900**								**− 900**								
Bal.	5,000	+	0	+	9,600	+	26,000	=	6,200	+	30,000			+	6,100	−	1,700
(11)	**− 600**											−	**$600**				
Bal.	$ 4,400	+	$ 0	+	$ 9,600	+	$ 26,000	=	$ 6,200	+	$ 30,000	−	$ 600	+	$6,100	−	$1,700

Quick Check

17. When is the accounting equation in balance, and what does that mean?

18. How can a transaction not affect any liability and equity accounts?

19. Describe a transaction increasing equity and one decreasing it.

20. Identify a transaction that decreases both assets and liabilities.

Answers—p. 26

Financial Statements

P1 Identify and prepare basic financial statements and explain how they interrelate.

This section shows how financial statements are prepared from the analysis of business transactions. The four financial statements and their purposes are:

1. ***Income statement***—describes a company's revenues and expenses along with the resulting net income or loss over a period of time due to earnings activities.
2. ***Statement of owner's equity***—explains changes in equity from net income (or loss) and from the owner investments and withdrawals over a period of time.
3. ***Balance sheet***—describes a company's financial position (types and amounts of assets, liabilities, and equity) at a point in time.
4. ***Statement of cash flows***—identifies cash inflows (receipts) and cash outflows (payments) over a period of time.

Topic Tackler 1-2

We prepare these financial statements using the 11 selected transactions of FastForward. (These statements are technically called *unadjusted*—we explain this in Chapters 2 and 3.)

Income Statement

Point: Net income is sometimes called earnings or profit.

Point: Decision makers often compare income to the operating cash flows from the statement of cash flows to help assess how much income is in the form of cash.

FastForward's income statement for December is shown at the top of Exhibit 1.10. Information about revenues and expenses is conveniently taken from the Equity columns of Exhibit 1.9. Revenues are reported first on the income statement. They include consulting revenues of $5,800 from transactions 5 and 8 and rental revenue of $300 from transaction 8. Expenses are reported after revenues. (For convenience in this chapter, we list larger amounts first, but we can sort expenses in different ways.) Rent and salary expenses are from transactions 6 and 7. Expenses reflect the costs to generate the revenues reported. Net income (or loss) is reported at the bottom of the statement and is the amount earned in December. Owner's investments and withdrawals are *not* part of income.

Statement of Owner's Equity

Point: The statement of owner's equity is also called the *statement of changes in owner's equity.* Note: Beg. Capital + Owner Investments + Net Income − Withdrawals = End. Capital

The statement of owner's equity reports information about how equity changes over the reporting period. This statement shows beginning capital, events that increase it (owner investments and net income), and events that decrease it (withdrawals and net loss). Ending capital is computed in this statement and is carried over and reported on the balance sheet. FastForward's statement of owner's equity is the second report in Exhibit 1.10. The beginning capital balance is measured as of the start of business on December 1. It is zero because FastForward did not exist before then. An existing business reports the beginning balance as of the end of the prior reporting period (such as from November 30). FastForward's statement shows that Taylor's initial investment created $30,000 of equity. It also shows the $4,400 of net income earned during the period. This links the income statement to the statement of owner's equity (see line ①). The statement also reports Taylor's $600 withdrawal and FastForward's $33,800 end-of-period capital balance.

Balance Sheet

Decision Maker boxes are role-playing exercises that stress the relevance of accounting.

FastForward's balance sheet is the third report in Exhibit 1.10. This statement refers to FastForward's financial condition at the close of business on December 31. The left side of the balance sheet lists FastForward's assets: cash, supplies, and equipment. The upper right side of the balance sheet shows that FastForward owes $6,200 to creditors. Any other liabilities (such as a bank loan) would be listed here. The equity (capital) balance is $33,800. Note the link between the ending balance of the statement of owner's equity and the equity balance here—see line ②. (This presentation of the balance sheet is called the *account form:* assets on the left and liabilities and equity on the right. Another presentation is the *report form:* assets on top, followed by liabilities and then equity at the bottom. Either presentation is acceptable.)

Decision Maker

Retailer You open a wholesale business selling entertainment equipment to retail outlets. You find that most of your customers demand to buy on credit. How can you use the balance sheets of these customers to help you decide which ones to extend credit to?

Answer—p. 26

Statement of Cash Flows

Point: Statement of cash flows has three main sections: operating, investing, and financing.

Point: Payment for supplies is an operating activity because supplies are expected to be used up in short-term operations (typically less than one year).

FastForward's statement of cash flows is the final report in Exhibit 1.10. The first section reports cash flows from *operating activities*. It shows the $6,100 cash received from clients and the cash paid for supplies, rent, and employee salaries. Outflows are in parentheses to denote subtraction. Net cash provided by operating activities for December is $1,000. If cash paid exceeded cash received, we would call it "cash used by operating activities." The second section reports *investing activities,* which involve buying and selling assets such as land and equipment that are held for *long-term use* (typically more than one-year). The only investing activity is the $26,000 purchase of equipment. The third section shows cash flows from *financing activities,* which include the *long-term* borrowing and repaying of cash from lenders and the owner's cash investments and withdrawals. FastForward reports $30,000

Exhibit 1.10

Financial Statements and Their Links

FASTFORWARD
Income Statement
For Month Ended December 31, 2004

Revenues:		
Consulting revenue ($4,200 + $1,600)	$ 5,800	
Rental revenue	300	
Total revenues		$ 6,100
Expenses:		
Rent expense	1,000	
Salaries expense	700	
Total expenses		1,700
Net income		$ 4,400

FASTFORWARD
Statement of Owner's Equity
For Month Ended December 31, 2004

C. Taylor, Capital, December 1, 2004		$ 0
Plus: Investments by owner	$30,000	
Net income	4,400	34,400
		34,400
Less: Withdrawals by owner		600
C. Taylor, Capital, December 31, 2004		$33,800

FASTFORWARD
Balance Sheet
December 31, 2004

Assets		Liabilities	
Cash	$ 4,400	Accounts payable	$ 6,200
Supplies	9,600	Total liabilities	6,200
Equipment	26,000		
		Equity	
		C. Taylor, Capital	33,800
Total assets	$40,000	Total liabilities and equity	$ 40,000

FASTFORWARD
Statement of Cash Flows
For Month Ended December 31, 2004

Cash flows from operating activities:		
Cash received from clients ($4,200 + $1,900)	$ 6,100	
Cash paid for supplies ($2,500 + $900)	(3,400)	
Cash paid for rent	(1,000)	
Cash paid to employee	(700)	
Net cash provided by operating activities		$ 1,000
Cash flows from investing activities:		
Purchase of equipment	(26,000)	
Net cash used by investing activities		(26,000)
Cash flows from financing activities:		
Investments by owner	30,000	
Withdrawals by owner	(600)	
Net cash provided by financing activities		29,400
Net increase in cash		$ 4,400
Cash balance, December 1, 2004		0
Cash balance, December 31, 2004		$ 4,400

Point: A statement's heading identifies the company, the statement title, and the date or time period.

Point: Arrow lines show how the statements are linked. ① Net income is used to compute equity. ② Equity is used to prepare the balance sheet. ③ Cash from the balance sheet is used to reconcile the statement of cash flows.

Point: The income statement, the statement of owner's equity, and the statement of cash flows are prepared for a *period* of time. The balance sheet is prepared as of a *point* in time.

Point: A single ruled line denotes an addition or subtraction. Final totals are double underlined. Negative amounts are often in parentheses.

Point: Investing activities refer to long-term asset investments by the company, *not* to owner investments.

from the owner's initial investment and the $600 owner withdrawal. The net cash effect of all transactions is a $29,400 cash inflow. The final part of the statement shows FastForward increased its cash balance by $4,400 in December. Since it started with no cash, the ending balance is also $4,400—see line ③.

Quick Check

21. Explain the link between the income statement and the statement of owner's equity.
22. Describe the link between the balance sheet and the statement of owner's equity.
23. Discuss the three major sections of the statement of cash flows.

Answers—p. 27

Decision Analysis (a section at the end of each chapter) introduces and explains ratios helpful in decision making using real company data. Instructors can skip this section and cover all ratios in Chapter 17.

Decision Analysis — Return on Assets

A3 Compute and interpret return on assets.

A *Decision Analysis* section at the end of each chapter is devoted to financial statement analysis. We organize financial statement analysis into four areas: (1) liquidity and efficiency, (2) solvency, (3) profitability, and (4) market prospects—the back inside cover has a ratio listing with definitions and grouping by area. When analyzing ratios, we need benchmarks to identify good, bad, or average levels. Common benchmarks include the company's prior levels and those of its competitors.

This chapter presents a profitability measure, that of return on assets. Return on assets is useful in evaluating management, analyzing and forecasting profits, and planning activities. **Dell Computer** has its marketing department compute return on assets for *every* mailing. *Return on assets* (*ROA*), also called *return on investment* (*ROI*), is defined in Exhibit 1.11.

Exhibit 1.11
Return on Assets

$$\textbf{Return on assets} = \frac{\textbf{Net income}}{\textbf{Average total assets}}$$

Net income is from the annual income statement, and average total assets is computed by adding the beginning and ending amounts for that same period and dividing by 2. To illustrate, **Nike** reports net income of $663.3 million in 2002. At the beginning of fiscal 2002, its total assets are $5,819.6 million and at the end of fiscal 2002, they total $6,443.0 million. Nike's return on assets for 2002 is:

$$\text{Return on assets} = \frac{\$663.3 \text{ mil.}}{(\$5{,}819.6 \text{ mil.} + \$6{,}443.0 \text{ mil.})/2} = 10.8\%$$

*Each **Decision Analysis** section ends with a role-playing scenario to show the usefulness of ratios.*

Is a 10.8% return on assets good or bad for Nike? To help answer this question, we compare (benchmark) Nike's return with its prior performance, the returns of competitors (such as **Reebok**, **Converse**, **Skechers**, and **Vans**), and the returns from alternative investments. Nike's return for each of the prior five years is in the second column of Exhibit 1.12, which ranges from 7.4% to 10.8%. These returns show an increase in its productive use of assets in recent years. We also compute Reebok's returns in the third column of Exhibit 1.12. In four of the five years, Nike's return exceeds Reebok's, and its average return is higher for this period. We also compare Nike's return to the normal return for manufacturers of athletic footwear and apparel (fourth column). Industry averages are available from services such as **Dun & Bradstreet**'s *Industry Norms and Key Ratios* and **Robert Morris Associates**' *Annual Statement Studies.* When compared to the industry, Nike performs well.

Decision Maker

Business Owner You own a small winter ski resort that earns a 21% return on its assets. An opportunity to purchase a winter ski equipment manufacturer is offered to you. This manufacturer earns a 19% return on its assets. The industry return for this manufacturer is 14%. Do you purchase this manufacturer?

Answer—p. 26

Nike Fiscal Year	Return on Assets		
	Nike	Reebok	Industry
2002	10.8%	6.8%	3.6%
2001	10.1	5.3	6.4
2000	10.4	0.7	5.1
1999	8.5	1.4	6.4
1998	7.4	7.7	6.1

Exhibit 1.12

Nike, Reebok, and Industry Returns

*The **Demonstration Problem** is a review of key chapter content. The Planning the Solution offers strategies in solving the problem.*

Demonstration Problem

After several months of planning, Sylvia Workman started a haircutting business called Expressions. The following events occurred during its first month:

a. On August 1, Workman invested $3,000 cash and $15,000 of equipment in Expressions.
b. On August 2, Expressions paid $600 cash for furniture for the shop.
c. On August 3, Expressions paid $500 cash to rent space in a strip mall for August.
d. On August 4, it purchased $1,200 of equipment on credit for the shop (using a long-term note payable).
e. On August 5, Expressions opened for business. Cash received from services provided in the first week and a half of business (ended August 15) is $825.
f. On August 15, it provided $100 of haircutting services on account.
g. On August 17, it received a $100 check for services previously rendered on account.
h. On August 17, it paid $125 cash to an assistant for working during the grand opening.
i. Cash received from services provided during the second half of August is $930.
j. On August 31, it paid a $400 installment toward principal on the note payable entered into on August 4.
k. On August 31, Workman made a $900 cash withdrawal for personal use.

Required

1. Arrange the following asset, liability, and equity titles in a table similar to the one in Exhibit 1.9: Cash; Accounts Receivable; Furniture; Store Equipment; Note Payable; S. Workman, Capital; S. Workman, Withdrawals; Revenues; and Expenses. Show the effects of each transaction using the accounting equation.
2. Prepare an income statement for August.
3. Prepare a statement of owner's equity for August.
4. Prepare a balance sheet as of August 31.
5. Prepare a statement of cash flows for August.
6. Determine the return on assets ratio for August.

Planning the Solution

- Set up a table like Exhibit 1.9 with the appropriate columns for accounts.
- Analyze each transaction and show its effects as increases or decreases in the appropriate columns. Be sure the accounting equation remains in balance after each transaction.
- Prepare the income statement, and identify revenues and expenses. List those items on the statement, compute the difference, and label the result as *net income* or *net loss*.
- Use information in the Equity columns to prepare the statement of owner's equity.
- Use information in the last row of the transactions table to prepare the balance sheet.
- Prepare the statement of cash flows; include all events listed in the Cash column of the transactions table. Classify each cash flow as operating, investing, or financing.
- Calculate return on assets by dividing net income by average assets.

Solution to Demonstration Problem

1.

	Assets							=	Liabilities +		Equity						
	Cash	**+**	**Accounts Receivable**	**+**	**Furniture**	**+**	**Store Equipment**	**=**	**Note Payable**	**+**	**S. Workman, Capital**	**−**	**S. Workman Withdrawals**	**+**	**Revenues**	**−**	**Expenses**
a.	**$3,000**						**$15,000**				**$18,000**						
b.	**− 600**			+	**$600**												
Bal.	2,400	+		+	600	+	15,000	=			18,000						
c.	**− 500**															−	**$500**
Bal.	1,900	+		+	600	+	15,000	=			18,000					−	500
d.						+	**1,200**		**+$1,200**								
Bal.	1,900	+		+	600	+	16,200	=	1,200	+	18,000					−	500
e.	**+ 825**													+	**$825**		
Bal.	2,725	+		+	600	+	16,200	=	1,200	+	18,000			+	825	−	500
f.		+	**$100**											+	**100**		
Bal.	2,725	+	100	+	600	+	16,200	=	1,200	+	18,000			+	925	−	500
g.	**+ 100**	−	**100**														
Bal.	2,825	+	0	+	600	+	16,200	=	1,200	+	18,000			+	925	−	500
h.	**− 125**															−	**125**
Bal.	2,700	+	0	+	600	+	16,200	=	1,200	+	18,000			+	925	−	625
i.	**+ 930**													+	**930**		
Bal.	3,630	+	0	+	600	+	16,200	=	1,200	+	18,000			+	1,855	−	625
j.	**− 400**								**− 400**								
Bal.	3,230	+	0	+	600	+	16,200	=	800	+	18,000			+	1,855	−	625
k.	**− 900**											−	**$900**				
Bal.	$2,330	+	0	+	$600	+	$ 16,200	=	$ 800	+	$ 18,000	−	$900	+	$1,855	−	$625

2.

EXPRESSIONS
Income Statement
For Month Ended August 31

Revenues:		
Haircutting services revenue		$1,855
Expenses:		
Rent expense	$500	
Wages expense	125	
Total expenses		625
Net Income		$1,230

3.

EXPRESSIONS
Statement of Owner's Equity
For Month Ended August 31

S. Workman, Capital, August 1*		$ 0
Plus: Investments by owner	$18,000	
Net income	1,230	19,230
		19,230
Less: Withdrawals by owner		900
S. Workman, Capital, August 31		$18,330

* If Expressions had been an existing business from a prior period, the beginning capital balance would equal the Capital account balance from the end of the prior period.

4.

EXPRESSIONS Balance Sheet August 31			
Assets		**Liabilities**	
Cash	$ 2,330	Note payable	$ 800
Furniture	600	**Equity**	
Store equipment	16,200	S. Workman, Capital	18,330
Total assets	$19,130	Total liabilities and equity	$19,130

5.

EXPRESSIONS Statement of Cash Flows For Month Ended August 31		
Cash flows from operating activities:		
Cash received from customers	$1,855	
Cash paid for rent	(500)	
Cash paid for wages	(125)	
Net cash provided by operating activities		$1,230
Cash flows from investing activities:		
Cash paid for furniture		(600)
Cash flows from financing activities:		
Cash received from owner	3,000	
Cash paid for owner withdrawal	(900)	
Partial repayment of (long-term) note payable	(400)	
Net cash provided by financing activities		1,700
Net increase in cash		$2,330
Cash balance, August 1		0
Cash balance, August 31		$2,330

6. Return on assets $= \frac{\text{Net income}}{\text{Average assets}} = \frac{\$1,230}{(\$18,000^* + \$19,130)/2} = \frac{\$1,230}{\$18,565} = \underline{\underline{6.63\%}}$

* Uses the initial $18,000 investment as the begining balance for the startup period only.

APPENDIX

1A Return and Risk Analysis

A4 Explain the relation between return and risk.

This appendix explains return and risk analysis and its role in business and accounting.

Net income is often linked to **return.** Return on assets (ROA) is stated in ratio form as income divided by assets invested. For example, banks report return from a savings account in the form of an interest return such as 4%. If we invest in a savings account or in U.S. Treasury bills, we expect a return of around 2% to 7%. We could also invest in a company's stock, or even start our own business. How do we decide among these investment options? The answer depends on our trade-off between return and risk.

Decision Insight

Celebrity Investing How do fame and fortune translate into return and risk? A poll asked people which celebrity is the best investment. Similar to business investments, many people named performers with years of earning power ahead—see results to the right.

Oprah Winfrey	27%
Steven Spielberg	19
Tiger Woods	15
Michael Jordan	14
Tom Cruise	8
Jerry Seinfeld	4
Madonna	2

Risk is the uncertainty about the return we will earn. All business investments involve risk, but some investments involve more risk than others. The lower the risk of an investment, the lower is our expected return. The reason that savings accounts pay such a low return is the low risk of not being repaid with interest (the government guarantees most savings accounts from default). If we buy a share of Nike or any other company, we might obtain a large return. However, we have no guarantee of any return; there is even the risk of loss.

The bar graph in Exhibit 1A.1 shows recent returns for bonds with different risks. *Bonds* are written promises by organizations to repay amounts loaned with interest. U.S. Treasury bonds provide a low expected return, but they also offer low risk since they are backed by the U.S. government. High-risk corporate bonds offer a much larger potential return but with much higher risk.

The trade-off between return and risk is a normal part of business. Higher risk implies higher, but riskier, expected returns. To help us make better decisions, we use accounting information to assess both return and risk.

Exhibit 1A.1

Average Returns for Bonds with Different Risks

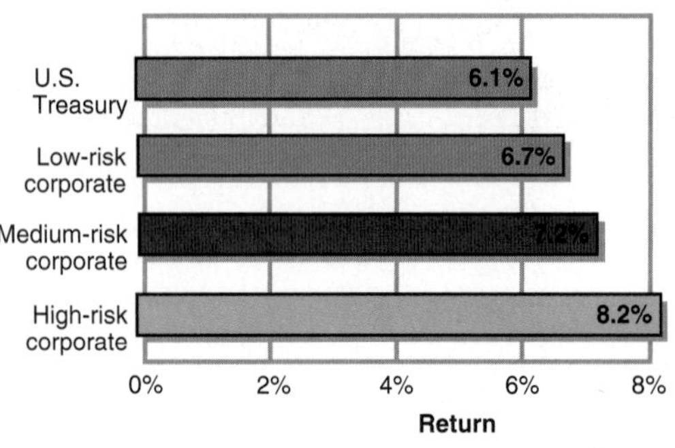

APPENDIX

1B Business Activities and the Accounting Equation

C6 Identify and describe the three major activities in organizations.

This appendix explains how the accounting equation is derived from business activities.

There are three major types of business activities: financing, investing, and operating. Each of these requires planning. *Planning* involves defining an organization's ideas, goals, and actions. Most public corporations use the *Management Discussion and Analysis* section in their annual reports to communicate plans. However, planning is not cast in stone. This adds *risk* to both setting plans and analyzing them.

Point: Management must understand accounting data to set financial goals, make financing and investing decisions, and evaluate operating performance.

Point: Investing (assets) and financing (liabilities plus equity) totals are *always* equal.

Financing *Financing activities* provide the means organizations use to pay for resources such as land, buildings, and equipment to carry out plans. Organizations are careful in acquiring and managing financing activities because they can determine success or failure. The two sources of financing are owner and nonowner. *Owner financing* refers to resources contributed by the owner along with any income the owner leaves in the organization. *Nonowner* (or *creditor*) *financing* refers to resources contributed by creditors (lenders). *Financial management* is the task of planning how to obtain these resources and to set the right mix between owner and creditor financing.

Investing *Investing activities* are the acquiring and disposing of resources (assets) that an organization uses to acquire and sell its products or services. Assets are funded by an organization's financing. Organizations differ on the amount and makeup of assets. Some require land and factories to operate. Others need only an office. Determining the amount and type of assets for operations is called *asset management*.

Invested amounts are referred to as *assets.* Financing is made up of creditor and owner financing, which hold claims on assets. Creditors' claims are called *liabilities,* and the owner's claim is called *equity.* This basic equality is called the *accounting equation* and can be written as: Assets = Liabilities + Equity.

Operating *Operating activities* involve using resources to research, develop, purchase, produce, distribute, and market products and services. Sales and revenues are the inflow of assets from selling products and services. Costs and expenses are the outflow of assets to support operating activities. *Strategic management* is the process of determining the right mix of operating activities for the type of organization, its plans, and its market.

Exhibit 1B.1 summarizes business activities. Planning is part of each activity and gives them meaning and focus. Investing (assets) and financing (liabilities and equity) are set opposite each other to stress their balance. Operating activities are below investing and financing activities to show that operating activities are the result of investing and financing.

Exhibit 1B.1

Activities in Organizations

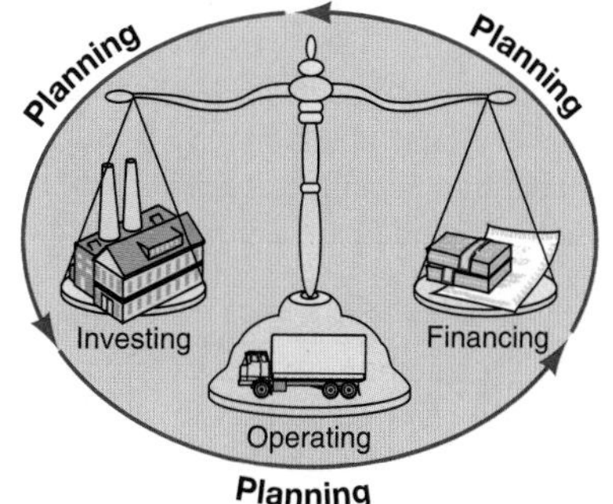

A ***Summary*** *organized by learning objectives concludes each chapter.*

Summary

C1 Explain the purpose and importance of accounting in the information age. Accounting is an information and measurement system that aims to identify, record, and communicate relevant, reliable, and comparable information about business activities. It helps assess opportunities, products, investments, and social and community responsibilities.

C2 Identify users and uses of accounting. Users of accounting are both internal and external. Some users and uses of accounting include (a) managers in controlling, monitoring, and planning; (b) lenders for measuring the risk and return of loans; (c) shareholders for assessing the return and risk of stock; (d) directors for overseeing management; and (e) employees for judging employment opportunities.

C3 Identify opportunities in accounting and related fields. Opportunities in accounting include financial, managerial, and tax accounting. They also include accounting-related fields such as lending, consulting, managing, and planning.

C4 Explain why ethics are crucial to accounting. The goal of accounting is to provide useful information for decision making. For information to be useful, it must be trusted. This demands ethical behavior in accounting.

C5 Explain the meaning of generally accepted accounting principles, and define and apply several key principles of accounting. Generally accepted accounting principles are a common set of standards applied by accountants. Accounting principles aid in producing relevant, reliable, and comparable information. The business entity principle means that a business is accounted for separately from its owner(s). The objectivity principle means independent, objective evidence supports the information. The cost principle means financial statements are based on actual costs incurred. The monetary unit principle assumes transactions can be reflected in money terms. The going-concern principle means financial statements assume the business will continue. The revenue recognition principle means revenue is recognized when earned.

C6[B] Identify and describe the three major activities in organizations. Organizations carry out three major activities: financing, investing, and operating. Financing is the means used to pay for resources such as land, buildings, and machines. Investing refers to the buying and selling of resources used in acquiring and selling products and services. Operating activities are those necessary for carrying out the organization's plans.

A1 Define and interpret the accounting equation and each of its components. The accounting equation is: Assets = Liabilities + Equity. Assets are resources owned by a company. Liabilities are creditors' claims on assets. Equity is the owner's claim on assets (*the residual*). The expanded accounting equation is: Assets = Liabilities + [Owner Capital − Owner Withdrawals + Revenues − Expenses].

A2 Analyze business transactions using the accounting equation. A *transaction* is an exchange of economic consideration between two parties. Examples include exchanges of products, services, money, and rights to collect money. Transactions always have at least two effects on one or more components of the accounting equation. This equation is always in balance.

A3 Compute and interpret return on assets. Return on assets is computed as net income divided by average assets. For example, if we have an average balance of $100 in a savings account and it earns $5 interest for the year, the return on assets is $5/$100, or 5%.

A4[A] Explain the relation between return and risk. *Return* refers to income, and *risk* is the uncertainty about the return we hope to make. All investments involve risk. The lower the risk of an investment, the lower is its expected return. Higher risk implies higher, but riskier, expected return.

P1 Identify and prepare basic financial statements and explain how they interrelate. Four financial statements report on an organization's activities: balance sheet, income statement, statement of owner's equity, and statement of cash flows.

Guidance Answers to **Decision Maker** and **Decision Ethics**

Entrepreneur (p. 11) You should probably form the business as a corporation if potential lawsuits are of prime concern. The corporate form of organization protects your personal property from lawsuits directed at the business and places only the corporation's resources at risk. A downside of the corporate form is double taxation: The corporation must pay taxes on its income, and you normally must pay taxes on any money distributed to you from the business (even though the corporation already paid taxes on this money). You should also examine the ethical and socially responsible aspects of starting a business in which you anticipate injuries to others. Formation as an LLC or S corp. should also be explored.

Retailer (p. 18) You can use the accounting equation (Assets = Liabilities + Equity) to help identify risky customers to whom you would likely not want to extend credit. A balance sheet provides amounts for each of these key components. The lower a customer's equity is relative to liabilities, the less likely you would extend credit. A low equity means the business has little value that does not already have creditor claims to it.

Business Owner (p. 20) The 19% return on assets for the manufacturer exceeds the 14% industry return (and many others). This is a positive factor for a potential purchase. Also, the purchase of this manufacturer is an opportunity to spread your risk over two businesses as opposed to one. Still, you should hesitate to purchase a business whose return of 19% is lower than your current resort's return of 21%. You are probably better off directing efforts to increase investment in your resort, assuming you can continue to earn a 21% return.

Guidance Answers to **Quick Checks**

1. Accounting is an information and measurement system that identifies, records, and communicates relevant information to help people make better decisions.
2. Recordkeeping, also called *bookkeeping,* is the recording of financial transactions and events, either manually or electronically. Recordkeeping is essential to data reliability; but accounting is this and much more. Accounting includes identifying, measuring, recording, reporting, and analyzing business events and transactions.
3. Technology offers increased accuracy, speed, efficiency, and convenience in accounting.
4. External users of accounting include lenders, shareholders, directors, customers, suppliers, regulators, lawyers, brokers, and the press. Internal users of accounting include managers, officers, and other internal decision makers involved with strategic and operating decisions.
5. Internal users (managers) include those from research and development, purchasing, human resources, production, distribution, marketing, and servicing.
6. Internal controls are procedures set up to protect assets, ensure reliable accounting reports, promote efficiency, and encourage adherence to company policies. Internal controls are crucial for relevant and reliable information.
7. Ethical guidelines are threefold: (1) identify ethical concerns using personal ethics, (2) analyze options considering all good and bad consequences, and (3) make ethical decisions after weighing all consequences.
8. Ethics and social responsibility yield good behavior, and they often result in higher income and a better working environment.
9. For accounting to provide useful information for decisions, it must be trusted. Trust requires ethics in accounting.
10. Two major participants in setting rules include the SEC and the FASB. (*Note:* Accounting rules reflect society's needs, not those of accountants or any other single constituency).
11. Most U.S. companies are not directly affected by international accounting standards. International standards are put forth as preferred accounting practices. However, stock exchanges and other parties are increasing the pressure to narrow differences in worldwide accounting practices. International accounting standards are playing an important role in that process.
12. The objectivity and cost principles are related in that most users consider information based on cost as objective. Information prepared using both principles is considered highly reliable and often relevant.
13. Users desire information about the performance of a specific entity. If information is mixed between two or more entities, its usefulness decreases.
14. The revenue recognition principle gives preparers guidelines on when to recognize (record) revenue. This is important; for example, if revenue is recognized too early, the statements report revenue sooner than it should and the business looks more profitable than it is. The reverse is also true.
15. The three basic forms of business organization are sole proprietorships, partnerships, and corporations.
16. Owners of corporations are called *shareholders* (or *stockholders*). Corporate ownership is divided into units called *shares* (or *stock*). The most basic of corporate shares is common stock (or capital stock).
17. The accounting equation is: Assets = Liabilities + Equity. This equation is always in balance, both before and after each transaction.
18. A transaction that changes the makeup of assets would not affect liability and equity accounts. FastForward's transactions 2 and 3 are examples. Each exchanges one asset for another.
19. Earning revenue by performing services, as in FastForward's transaction 5, increases equity (and assets). Incurring expenses while servicing clients, such as in transactions 6 and 7, decreases equity (and assets). Other examples include owner investments that increase equity and withdrawals that decrease equity.
20. Paying a liability with an asset reduces both asset and liability totals. One example is FastForward's transaction 10 that reduces a payable by paying cash.

21. An income statement reports a company's revenues and expenses along with the resulting net income or loss. A statement of owner's equity shows changes in equity, including that from net income or loss. Both statements report transactions occurring over a period of time.

22. The balance sheet describes a company's financial position (assets, liabilities, and equity) at a point in time. The equity account in the balance sheet is obtained from the statement of owner's equity.

23. Cash flows from operating activities report cash receipts and payments from the primary business the company engages in. Cash flows from investing activities involve cash transactions from buying and selling long-term assets. Cash flows from financing activities include long-term cash borrowings and repayments to lenders and the cash investments and withdrawals of the owner.

A list of key terms with page references concludes each chapter (a complete glossary is at the end of the book and also on the book's Website).

Key Terms

Key Terms are available at the book's Website for learning and testing in an online Flashcard Format.

Accounting (p. 4)
Accounting equation (p. 12)
Assets (p. 12)
Audit (p. 9)
Balance sheet (p. 17)
Bookkeeping (p. 5)
Business entity principle (p. 10)
Common stock (p. 11)
Corporation (p. 11)
Cost principle (p. 9)
Equity (p. 12)
Ethics (p. 8)
Events (p. 13)
Expanded accounting equation (p. 13)
Expenses (p. 13)
External transactions (p. 13)
External users (p. 5)
Financial accounting (p. 5)
Financial Accounting Standards Board (FASB) (p. 9)
Generally Accepted Accounting Principles (GAAP) (p. 9)
Going-concern principle (p. 10)
Income statement (p. 17)
Internal transactions (p. 13)
Internal users (p. 6)
International Accounting Standards Board (IASB) (p. 9)
Liabilities (p. 12)
Managerial accounting (p. 6)
Monetary unit principle (p. 10)
Net assets (p. 12)
Net income (p. 13)
Net loss (p. 13)
Objectivity principle (p. 9)
Owner investment (p. 13)
Owner withdrawals (p. 13)
Partnership (p. 10)
Proprietorship (p. 10)
Recordkeeping (p. 5)
Return (p. 23)
Return on assets (p. 20)
Revenues (p. 13)
Revenue recognition principle (p. 10)
Risk (p. 24)
Securities and Exchange Commission (SEC) (p. 9)
Shareholders (p. 11)
Shares (p. 11)
Sole proprietorship (p. 10)
Statement of cash flows (p. 17)
Statement of owner's equity (p. 17)
Stock (p. 11)
Stockholders (p. 11)
Withdrawals (p. 13)

Personal Interactive Quiz

Personal Interactive Quizzes A and B are available at the book's Website to reinforce and assess your learning.

Superscript letter A (B) denotes assignments based on Appendix 1A (1B).

Discussion Questions

1. What is the purpose of accounting in society?

2. Identify three actual businesses that offer services and three actual businesses that offer products.

3. Why do organizations license and monitor accounting and accounting-related professionals?

4. Technology is increasingly used to process accounting data. Why then must we study and understand accounting?

5. Identify four kinds of external users and describe their uses of accounting information.

6. What are at least three questions business owners might be able to answer by looking at accounting information?
7. Describe the internal role of accounting for organizations.
8. What type of accounting information might be useful to those who carry out the marketing activities of a business?
9. Identify three types of services typically offered by accounting professionals.
10. Why is accounting described as a service activity?
11. Identify at least three tasks you would expect to be performed by government accounting professionals.
12. What work do tax accounting professionals perform in addition to preparing tax returns?
13. What ethical issues might accounting professionals face in dealing with confidential information?
14. Identify the two main categories of accounting principles.
15. What does the objectivity principle prescribe for information reported in financial statements? Why?
16. A business reports its own office stationery on the balance sheet at its $430 cost, although it cannot be sold for more than $10 as scrap paper. Which accounting principle(s) justifies this treatment?
17. Why is the revenue recognition principle needed? What does it prescribe?
18. Describe the three basic forms of business organization and their key characteristics.
19. Identify three types of organizations that can be formed as either profit-oriented entities or government (or non-profit) entities.
20. Define (*a*) *assets,* (*b*) *liabilities,* (*c*) *equity,* and (*d*) *net assets.*
21. What events or transactions change equity?
22. What do accountants mean by the term *revenue?*
23. Define *net income* and explain its computation.
24. Identify the four basic financial statements of a business.
25. What information is reported in an income statement?
26. Give two examples of expenses a business might incur.
27. What information is reported in a balance sheet?
28. The statement of cash flows reports on what major activities?
29. Define and explain return on assets.
30.[A] Explain return and risk. Discuss the trade-off between them.
31.[B] Describe the three major activities in organizations.
32.[B] Explain why investing (assets) and financing (liabilities and equity) totals are always equal.
33. Refer to the financial statements of **Krispy Kreme** in Appendix A. To what level of significance are dollar amounts rounded? What time period does its income statement cover?
34. Identify the dollar amounts of **Tastykake**'s 2002 assets, liabilities, and equity shown in its statements in Appendix A near the end of the book.
35. Access the SEC EDGAR database (www.SEC.gov) and retrieve **Harley-Davidson**'s 2002 10-K (filed 2003-03-28). Identify its auditor. What responsibility does its independent auditor claim regarding its financial statements?

Red numbers denote Discussion Questions that involve decision-making.

***Quick Study** exercises give readers a brief test of key elements.*

***Homework Manager** repeats all numerical Quick Study assignments on the book's Website with new numbers each time it is worked. It can be used in practice, homework, or exam mode.*

QUICK STUDY

QS 1-1
Identifying accounting users
C2

Identify the following users as either external users (E) or internal users (I).

a. Managers	**d.** FBI and CIA	**g.** Consumer group	**j.** Shareholders
b. Controllers	**e.** Sales staff	**h.** Customers	**k.** Congress
c. Business press	**f.** Brokers	**i.** Lenders	**l.** District attorney

QS 1-2
Identifying accounting terms
C1

(*a*) Identify the meaning of these accounting-related acronyms: GAAP, SEC, and FASB, and then briefly explain the importance of each to accounting. (*b*) Identify the international accounting standards setting organization, and then briefly explain its purpose.

QS 1-3
Accounting opportunities
C3

Identify at least three main areas of opportunities for accounting professionals. For each area, identify at least three job possibilities linked to accounting.

QS 1-4
Identifying ethical concerns
C4

Accounting professionals must sometimes choose between two or more acceptable methods of accounting for business transactions and events. Explain why these situations can involve difficult matters of ethical concern.

Thinker icon highlights assignments that use decision-making skills.

QS 1-5
Identifying transactions and events
A2

Accounting provides information about an organization's business transactions and events that both affect the accounting equation and can be reliably measured. Identify at least two examples of both (*a*) business transactions and (*b*) business events that meet these requirements.

QS 1-6
Explaining internal control
C1

An important responsibility of many accounting professionals is to design and implement internal control procedures for organizations. Explain the purpose of internal control procedures.

QS 1-7
Identifying accounting principles
C5 

Identify which general accounting principle best describes each of the following practices:

a. Marilyn Choi owns both Sailing Passions and Dockside Supplies. In preparing financial statements for Dockside Supplies, Choi makes sure that the expense transactions of Sailing Passions are kept separate from Dockside's statements.

b. In December 2004, A-Plus Floors received a customer's order and cash prepayment to install carpet in a new house that would not be ready for installation until March 2005. A-Plus Floors should record the revenue from the customer order in March 2005, not in December 2004.

c. If $30,000 cash is paid to buy land, the land is reported on the buyer's balance sheet at $30,000.

QS 1-8
Applying the accounting equation
A1  

a. Total assets of HLC Financial Co. equal $40,000 and its equity is $10,000. What is the amount of its liabilities?

b. Total assets of Deep Valley Co. equal $55,000 and its liabilities and equity amounts are equal. What is the amount of its liabilities? What is the amount of its equity?

QS 1-9
Applying the accounting equation
A1

Use the accounting equation to compute the missing financial statement amounts (*a*), (*b*), and (*c*).

Company	Assets	=	Liabilities	+	Equity
1	$30,000		$ (*a*)		$20,000
2	$ (*b*)		$50,000		$30,000
3	$90,000		$10,000		$ (*c*)

QS 1-10
Identifying and computing assets, liabilities, and equity
A2  **Harley-Davidson**

Use **Harley-Davidson**'s December 31, 2002, financial statements, in Appendix A near the end of the book, to answer the following:

a. Identify the dollar amounts of Harley's 2002 (1) assets, (2) liabilities, and (3) equity.

b. Using Harley's amounts from part *a*, verify that Assets = Liabilities + Equity.

QS 1-11
Classifying items by financial statements
P1

Indicate in which financial statement each item would most likely appear: income statement (I), balance sheet (B), statement of owner's equity (E), or statement of cash flows (CF).

a. Assets
b. Revenues
c. Liabilities
d. Equipment
e. Withdrawals
f. Expenses
g. Total liabilities and equity
h. Cash from operating activities
i. Net decrease (or increase) in cash

QS 1-12
Computing and interpreting return on assets
A3  

In a recent year's financial statements, **Boeing Company**, which is the largest aerospace company in the United States, reported the following. Compute and interpret Boeing's return on assets (assume competitors average a 6% return on assets).

Sales	$21,924 million
Net income	856 million
Average total assets	21,463 million

Homework Manager repeats all numerical Exercises on the book's Website with new numbers each time they are worked. It can be used in practice, homework, or exam mode.

EXERCISES

Exercise 1-1
Distinguishing business organizations
C5

The following describe several different business organizations. Determine whether the description refers to a sole proprietorship, partnership, or corporation.

a. Ownership of Spirit Company is divided into 1,000 shares of stock.
b. Delta is owned by Sarah Gomez, who is personally liable for the debts of the business.
c. Jo Chen and Al Fitch own Financial Services, a financial services provider. Neither Chen nor Fitch has personal responsibility for the debts of Financial Services.
d. Sung Kwon and Frank Heflin own Get-It-There, a courier service. Both are personally liable for the debts of the business.
e. XLT Services does not have separate legal existence apart from the one person who owns it.
f. BioProducts does not pay income taxes and has one owner.
g. Tampa Biz pays its own income taxes and has two owners.

Exercise 1-2
Identifying accounting principles
C5

Match each of the numbered descriptions with the principle it best reflects. Indicate your answer by writing the letter for the appropriate principle in the blank space next to each description.

A. General accounting principle
B. Cost principle
C. Business entity principle
D. Revenue recognition principle
E. Specific accounting principle
F. Objectivity principle
G. Going-concern principle

_______ **1.** Usually created by a pronouncement from an authoritative body.
_______ **2.** Financial statements reflect the assumption that the business continues operating.
_______ **3.** Derived from long-used and generally accepted accounting practices.
_______ **4.** Financial statement information is supported by evidence other than someone's opinion or belief.
_______ **5.** Every business is accounted for separately from its owner or owners.
_______ **6.** Revenue is recorded only when the earnings process is complete.
_______ **7.** Information is based on actual costs incurred in transactions.

Exercise 1-3
Describing accounting responsibilities
C2 C3

Many accounting professionals work in one of the following three areas:

A. Financial accounting **B.** Managerial accounting **C.** Tax accounting

Identify the area of accounting that is most involved in each of the following responsibilities:

_______ **1.** External auditing.
_______ **2.** Cost accounting.
_______ **3.** Budgeting.
_______ **4.** Internal auditing.
_______ **5.** Planning transactions to minimize taxes.
_______ **6.** Preparing external financial statements.
_______ **7.** Reviewing reports for SEC compliance.
_______ **8.** Investigating violations of tax laws.

Exercise 1-4
Identifying accounting users and uses
 C2 

Much of accounting is directed at servicing the information needs of those users that are external to an organization. Identify at least three external users of accounting information and indicate two questions they might seek to answer through their use of accounting information.

Exercise 1-5
Identifying ethical concerns
C4 

Assume the following role and describe a situation in which ethical considerations play an important part in guiding your decisions and actions:

a. You are a student in an introductory accounting course.
b. You are a manager with responsibility for several employees.
c. You are an accounting professional preparing tax returns for clients.
d. You are an accounting professional with audit clients that are competitors in business.

Exercise 1-6
Learning the language of business
C1–C4

Match each of the numbered descriptions with the term or phrase it best reflects. Indicate your answer by writing the letter for the term or phrase in the blank provided.

A. Audit **C.** Ethics **E.** SEC **G.** Net income
B. GAAP **D.** Tax accounting **F.** Public accountants **H.** IASB

_____ **1.** Amount a business earns after paying all expenses and costs associated with its sales and revenues.

_____ **2.** An examination of an organization's accounting system and records that adds credibility to financial statements.

_____ **3.** Principles that determine whether an action is right or wrong.

_____ **4.** Accounting professionals who provide services to many clients.

_____ **5.** An accounting area that includes planning future transactions to minimize taxes paid.

Exercise 1-7
Using the accounting equation
A1 A2 

Answer the following questions. (*Hint:* Use the accounting equation.)

a. Fong's Medical Supplies has assets equal to $123,000 and liabilities equal to $53,000 at year-end. What is the total equity for Fong's business at year-end?

b. At the beginning of the year, Beyonce Company's assets are $200,000 and its equity is $150,000. During the year, assets increase $70,000 and liabilities increase $30,000. What is the equity at the end of the year?

c. At the beginning of the year, New Wave Company's liabilities equal $60,000. During the year, assets increase by $80,000, and at year-end assets equal $180,000. Liabilities decrease $10,000 during the year. What are the beginning and ending amounts of equity?

Check (c) Beg. equity, $40,000

Exercise 1-8
Using the accounting equation
A1

Determine the missing amount from each of the separate situations a, b, and c below.

Assets	=	Liabilities	+	Equity
a. ?	=	$30,000	+	$65,000
b. $ 89,000	=	$22,000	+	?
c. $132,000	=	?	+	$20,000

Exercise 1-9
Identifying effects of transactions on the accounting equation
A1 A2 

Provide an example of a transaction that creates the described effects for the separate cases *a* through *g*.

a. Decreases an asset and decreases equity.
b. Increases an asset and increases a liability.
c. Decreases a liability and increases a liability.
d. Decreases an asset and decreases a liability.
e. Increases an asset and decreases an asset.
f. Increases a liability and decreases equity.
g. Increases an asset and increases equity.

Exercise 1-10
Analysis using the accounting equation
A1 A2 

Mulan began a new consulting firm on January 5. The accounting equation showed the following balances after each of the company's first five transactions. Analyze the accounting equation for each transaction and describe each of the five transactions with their amounts.

	Assets								=	Liabilities	+	Equity		
Transaction	Cash	+	Accounts Receivable	+	Office Supplies	+	Office Furniture		=	Accounts Payable	+	Mulan, Capital	+	Revenues
a.	$20,000	+	$ 0	+	$ 0	+	$ 0		=	$ 0	+	$20,000	+	$ 0
b.	19,000	+	0	+	1,500	+	0		=	500	+	20,000	+	0
c.	11,000	+	0	+	1,500	+	8,000		=	500	+	20,000	+	0
d.	11,000	+	3,000	+	1,500	+	8,000		=	500	+	20,000	+	3,000
e.	11,500	+	3,000	+	1,500	+	8,000		=	500	+	20,000	+	3,500

Exercise 1-11
Identifying effects of transactions on accounting equation
A1 A2 

The following table shows the effects of five transactions (*a* through *e*) on the assets, liabilities, and equity of Bonita Boutique. Write short descriptions of the probable nature of each transaction.

	Assets				= Liabilities	+ Equity	
	Cash	+ Accounts Receivable	+ Office Supplies	+ Land	= Accounts Payable	+ Bonita, Capital	+ Revenues
	$ 10,500	+ $ 0	+ $1,500	+ $ 9,500	= $ 0	+ $21,500	+ $ 0
a.	− 2,000			+ 2,000			
b.			+ 500		+500		
c.		+ 950					+ 950
d.	− 500				−500		
e.	+ 950	− 950					
	$ 8,950	+ $ 0	+ $2,000	+ $ 11,500	= $ 0	+ $21,500	+ $950

Exercise 1-12
Identifying effects of transactions on the accounting equation and computing return on assets
A1 A2 

Pamela Maben began a professional practice on June 1 and plans to prepare financial statements at the end of each month. During June, Maben (the owner) completed these transactions:

a. Owner invested $50,000 cash along with equipment that had a $10,000 market value.
b. Paid $1,600 cash for rent of office space for the month.
c. Purchased $12,000 of additional equipment on credit (due within 30 days).
d. Completed work for a client and immediately collected the $2,000 cash earned.
e. Completed work for a client and sent a bill for $7,000 to be paid within 30 days.
f. Purchased additional equipment for $8,000 cash.
g. Paid an assistant $2,400 cash as wages for the month.
h. Collected $5,000 cash on the amount owed by the client described in transaction *e*.
i. Paid $12,000 cash to settle the liability created in transaction *c*.
j. Owner withdrew $500 cash for personal use.

Required

Create a table like the one in Exhibit 1.9, using the following headings for columns: Cash; Accounts Receivable; Equipment; Accounts Payable; Maben, Capital; Maben, Withdrawals; Revenues; and Expenses. Then use additions and subtractions to show the effects of the transactions on individual items of the accounting equation. Show new balances after each transaction.

Check Net income, $5,000

Exercise 1-13
Preparing an income statement
P1

On October 1, Sasha Shandi organized Best Answers a new consulting firm. On October 31, the company's records show the following items and amounts. Use this information to prepare an October income statement for the business.

Cash	$ 2,000	Cash withdrawals by owner	$ 3,360
Accounts receivable	13,000	Consulting fees earned	15,000
Office supplies	4,250	Rent expense	2,550
Land	36,000	Salaries expense	6,000
Office equipment	28,000	Telephone expense	660
Accounts payable	7,500	Miscellaneous expenses	680
Owner investments	74,000		

Check Net income, $5,110

Exercise 1-14
Preparing a statement of owner's equity P1

Use the information in Exercise 1-13 to prepare an October statement of owner's equity for Best Answers.

Exercise 1-15
Preparing a balance sheet P1

Use the information in Exercise 1-13 (if completed, you can also use your solution to Exercise 1-14) to prepare an October 31 balance sheet for Best Answers.

Exercise 1-16
Preparing a statement of cash flows
P1

Use the information in Exercise 1-13 to prepare an October 31 statement of cash flows for Best Answers. Also assume the following:

a. The owner's initial investment consists of $38,000 cash and $36,000 in land.

b. The $28,000 equipment purchase is paid in cash.

c. The accounts payable balance of $7,500 consists of the $4,250 office supplies purchase and $3,250 in employee salaries yet to be paid.

d. The rent, telephone, and miscellaneous expenses are paid in cash.

e. Only $2,000 cash has been collected for the $15,000 consulting services provided.

Check Net increase in cash, $2,000

Exercise 1-17
Identifying sections of the statement of cash flows
P1

Indicate the section where each of the following would appear on the statement of cash flows.

A. Cash flows from operating activity
B. Cash flows from investing activity
C. Cash flows from financing activity

______ **1.** Cash paid for wages
______ **2.** Cash withdrawal by owner
______ **3.** Cash purchase of equipment
______ **4.** Cash paid for advertising
______ **5.** Cash paid on an account payable
______ **6.** Cash invested by owner
______ **7.** Cash received from clients
______ **8.** Cash paid for rent

Exercise 1-18
Analysis of return on assets
A3

Geneva Group reports net income of $20,000 for 2005. At the beginning of 2005, Geneva Group had $100,000 in assets. By the end of 2005, assets had grown to $150,000. What is Geneva Group's 2005 return on assets? How would you assess its performance if competitors average a 10% return on assets?

Exercise 1-19[B]
Identifying business activities
C6

Match each transaction or event to one of the following activities of an organization: financing activities (F), investing activities (I), or operating activities (O).

a. ______ An owner contributes resources to the business.
b. ______ An organization purchases equipment.
c. ______ An organization advertises a new product.
d. ______ The organization borrows money from a bank.
e. ______ An organization sells some of its land.

Problem Set B *located at the end of* ***Problem Set A*** *is provided for each problem to reinforce the learning process.* ***Problem Set C*** *(with solutions for instructors) is provided on this book's Website.*

PROBLEM SET A

Problem 1-1A
Computing missing information using accounting knowledge
A1 A2

The following financial statement information is from five separate companies:

	Company A	Company B	Company C	Company D	Company E
December 31, 2004:					
Assets	$45,000	$35,000	$29,000	$80,000	$123,000
Liabilities	23,500	22,500	14,000	38,000	?
December 31, 2005:					
Assets	48,000	41,000	?	125,000	112,500
Liabilities	?	27,500	19,000	64,000	75,000
During year 2005:					
Owner investments	5,000	1,500	7,750	?	4,500
Net income	7,500	?	9,000	12,000	18,000
Owner cash withdrawals	2,500	3,000	3,875	0	9,000

Required

1. Answer the following questions about Company A:

  a. What is the equity amount on December 31, 2004?

  b. What is the equity amount on December 31, 2005?

  c. What is the amount of liabilities on December 31, 2005?

2. Answer the following questions about Company B:

  a. What is the equity amount on December 31, 2004?

  b. What is the equity amount on December 31, 2005?

  c. What is net income for year 2005?

3. Calculate the amount of assets for Company C on December 31, 2005.

4. Calculate the amount of owner investments for Company D during year 2005.

5. Calculate the amount of liabilities for Company E on December 31, 2004.

Check (1*b*) $31,500

(2*c*) $2,500

(3) $46,875

Problem 1-2A
Identifying effects of transactions on financial statements

A1 A2 

Identify how each of the following separate transactions affects financial statements. For the balance sheet, identify how each transaction affects total assets, total liabilities, and total equity. For the income statement, identify how each transaction affects net income. For the statement of cash flows, identify how each transaction affects cash flows from operating activities, cash flows from financing activities, and cash flows from investing activities. For increases, place a "+" in the column or columns. For decreases, place a "−" in the column or columns. If both an increase and a decrease occur, place a "+/−" in the column or columns. The first transaction is completed as an example.

		Balance Sheet			Income Statement	Statement of Cash Flows		
	Transaction	Total Assets	Total Liab.	Total Equity	Net Income	Operating Activities	Financing Activities	Investing Activities
1	Owner invests cash in business	+		+			+	
2	Receives cash for services provided							
3	Pays cash for employee wages							
4	Incurs legal costs on credit							
5	Borrows cash by signing long-term note payable							
6	Owner withdraws cash							
7	Buys land by signing note payable							
8	Provides services on credit							
9	Buys office equipment for cash							
10	Collects cash on receivable from (8)							

Problem 1-3A
Preparing an income statement

P1 

The following is selected financial information for Valdez Energy Company for the year ended December 31, 2005: revenues, $65,000; expenses, $50,000; net income, $15,000.

Required

Prepare the 2005 calendar-year income statement for Valdez Energy Company.

Problem 1-4A
Preparing a balance sheet

P1

The following is selected financial information for Amico as of December 31, 2005: liabilities, $34,000; equity, $56,000; assets, $90,000.

Required

Prepare the balance sheet for Amico as of December 31, 2005.

The following is selected financial information of Trimark for the year ended December 31, 2005:

Problem 1-5A
Preparing a statement of cash flows

P1 

Cash used by investing activities	$(3,000)
Net increase in cash	200
Cash used by financing activities	(3,800)
Cash from operating activities	7,000
Cash, December 31, 2004	3,300

Required

Prepare the 2005 calendar-year statement of cash flows for Trimark.

The following is selected financial information for Boardwalk for the year ended December 31, 2005:

Problem 1-6A
Preparing a statement of owner's equity

P1

B. Walk, Capital, Dec. 31, 2005	$15,000	B. Walk, Withdrawals	$2,000
Net income	9,000	B. Walk, Capital, Dec. 31, 2004	8,000

Required

Prepare the 2005 calendar-year statement of owner's equity for Boardwalk.

J. D. Simpson started The Simpson Co., a new business that began operations on May 1. Simpson Co. completed the following transactions during that first month:

Problem 1-7A
Analyzing transactions and preparing financial statements

C5 A2 P1

mhhe.com/larson

May 1 J. D. Simpson, the owner, invested $60,000 cash in the business.
1 Rented a furnished office and paid $3,200 cash for May's rent.
3 Purchased $1,680 of office equipment on credit.
5 Paid $800 cash for this month's cleaning services.
8 Provided consulting services for a client and immediately collected $4,600 cash.
12 Provided $3,000 of consulting services for a client on credit.
15 Paid $850 cash for an assistant's salary for the first half of this month.
20 Received $3,000 cash payment for the services provided on May 12.
22 Provided $2,800 of consulting services on credit.
25 Received $2,800 cash payment for the services provided on May 22.
26 Paid $1,680 cash for the office equipment purchased on May 3.
27 Purchased $60 of advertising in this month's (May) local paper on credit; cash payment is due June 1.
28 Paid $850 cash for an assistant's salary for the second half of this month.
30 Paid $200 cash for this month's telephone bill.
30 Paid $480 cash for this month's utilities.
31 J. D. Simpson withdrew $1,200 cash for personal use.

Required

1. Arrange the following asset, liability, and equity titles in a table like Exhibit 1.9: Cash; Accounts Receivable; Office Equipment; Accounts Payable; J. D. Simpson, Capital; J. D. Simpson, Withdrawals; Revenues; and Expenses.
2. Show effects of the transactions on the accounts of the accounting equation by recording increases and decreases in the appropriate columns. Do not determine new account balances after each transaction. Determine the final total for each account and verify that the equation is in balance.
3. Prepare an income statement for May, a statement of owner's equity for May, a May 31 balance sheet, and a statement of cash flows for May.

Check (2) Ending balances: Cash, $61,140; Expenses, $6,440

(3) Net income, $3,960; Total assets, $62,820

Problem 1-8A

Analyzing transactions and preparing financial statements

C5 A2 P1 

mhhe.com/larson

Curtis Hamilton started a new business and completed these transactions during December:

Dec. 1 Curtis Hamilton transferred $56,000 cash from a personal savings account to a checking account in the name of Hamilton Electric as its initial capital.
2 Rented office space and paid $800 cash for the December rent.
3 Purchased $14,000 of electrical equipment by paying $3,200 cash and agreeing to pay the $10,800 balance in 30 days.
5 Purchased office supplies by paying $900 cash.
6 Completed electrical work and immediately collected $1,000 cash for the work.
8 Purchased $3,800 of office equipment on credit.
15 Completed electrical work on credit in the amount of $4,000.
18 Purchased $500 of office supplies on credit.
20 Paid $3,800 cash for the office equipment purchased on December 8.
24 Billed a client $600 for electrical work completed; the balance is due in 30 days.
28 Received $4,000 cash for the work completed on December 15.
29 Paid the assistant's salary of $1,200 cash for this month.
30 Paid $440 cash for this month's utility bill.
31 C. Hamilton withdrew $700 cash for personal use.

Required

1. Arrange the following asset, liability, and equity titles in a table like Exhibit 1.9: Cash; Accounts Receivable; Office Supplies; Office Equipment; Electrical Equipment; Accounts Payable; C. Hamilton, Capital; C. Hamilton, Withdrawals; Revenues; and Expenses.

Check (2) Ending balances: Cash, $49,960, Accounts Payable, $11,300

(3) Net income, $3,160: Total assets, $69,760

2. Use additions and subtractions to show the effects of each transaction on the accounts in the accounting equation. Show new balances after each transaction.

3. Use the increases and decreases in the columns of the table from part 2 to prepare an income statement, a statement of owner's equity, and a statement of cash flows for the month. Also prepare a balance sheet as of the end of the month.

Analysis Component

4. Assume that the owner investment transaction on December 1 was $40,000 cash instead of $56,000 and that Hamilton Electric obtained the $16,000 difference by borrowing it from a bank. Explain the effect of this change on total assets, total liabilities, and total equity.

Problem 1-9A

Analyzing effects of transactions

C5 P1 A1 A2

Miranda Right started Right Consulting, a new business, and completed the following transactions during its first year of operations:

a. M. Right invests $60,000 cash and office equipment valued at $30,000 in the business.
b. Purchased a $300,000 building to use as an office. Right paid $50,000 in cash and signed a note payable promising to pay the $250,000 balance over the next ten years.
c. Purchased office equipment for $6,000 cash.
d. Purchased $4,000 of office supplies and $1,000 of office equipment on credit.
e. Paid a local newspaper $1,000 cash for printing an announcement of the office's opening.
f. Completed a financial plan for a client and billed that client $4,000 for the service.
g. Designed a financial plan for another client and immediately collected an $8,000 cash fee.
h. M. Right withdrew $1,800 cash from the company bank account for personal use.
i. Received a $3,000 partial cash payment from the client described in transaction *f*.
j. Made a $500 cash payment on the equipment purchased in transaction *d*.
k. Paid $2,500 cash for the office secretary's wages.

Required

1. Create a table like the one in Exhibit 1.9, using the following headings for the columns: Cash; Accounts Receivable; Office Supplies; Office Equipment; Building; Accounts Payable; Notes Payable; M. Right, Capital; M. Right, Withdrawals; Revenues; and Expenses.

Check (2) Ending balances: Cash, $9,200; Expenses, $3,500

(3) Net income, $8,500

2. Use additions and subtractions to show the effects of these transactions on individual items of the accounting equation. Show new balances after each transaction.

3. Once you have completed the table, determine the company's net income.

Problem 1-10A
Computing and interpreting return on assets
A3 

Coca-Cola and **PepsiCo** both produce and market beverages that are direct competitors. Key financial figures (in $ millions) for these businesses over the past year follow:

Key Figures	Coca-Cola	PepsiCo
Sales	$400	$250.0
Net income	50	37.5
Average invested (assets)	625	312.5

Required

1. Compute return on assets for (*a*) Coca-Cola and (*b*) PepsiCo.
2. Which company is more successful in its total amount of sales to consumers?
3. Which company is more successful in returning net income from its amount invested?

Check (1*a*) 8%; (1*b*) 12%

Analysis Component

4. Write a one-paragraph memorandum explaining which company you would invest your money in and why. (Limit your explanation to the information provided.)

Problem 1-11A
Determining expenses, liabilities, equity and return on assets
A1 A3 

Zia manufactures, markets, and sells cellular telephones. The average total assets for Zia is $250,000. In its most recent year, Zia reported net income of $55,000 on revenues of $455,000.

Required

1. What is Zia's return on assets?
2. Does return on assets seem satisfactory for Zia given that its competitors average a 12% return on assets?
3. What are total expenses for Zia in its most recent year?
4. What is the average total amount of liabilities plus equity for Zia?

Check (3) $400,000
(4) $250,000

Problem 1-12A[A]
Identifying risk and return
A4 

All business decisions involve aspects of risk and return.

Required

Identify both the risk and the return in each of the following activities:

1. Investing $1,000 in a 4% savings account.
2. Placing a $1,000 bet on your favorite sports team.
3. Investing $10,000 in Yahoo! stock.
4. Taking out a $10,000 college loan to earn an accounting degree.

Problem 1-13A[B]
Describing organizational activities
C6

A startup company often engages in the following transactions in its first year of operations. Classify these transactions in one of the three major categories of an organization's business activities.

A. Financing **B.** Investing **C.** Operating

______ **1.** Owner investing land in business.
______ **2.** Purchasing a building.
______ **3.** Purchasing land.
______ **4.** Borrowing cash from a bank.
______ **5.** Purchasing equipment.
______ **6.** Selling and distributing products.
______ **7.** Paying for advertising.
______ **8.** Paying employee wages.

Problem 1-14A[B]
Describing organizational activities C6

An organization undertakes various activities in pursuit of business success. Identify an organization's three major business activities, and describe each activity.

PROBLEM SET B

Problem 1-1B
Computing missing information using accounting knowledge

A1 A2 

The following financial statement information is from five separate companies:

	Company V	Company W	Company X	Company Y	Company Z
December 31, 2004:					
Assets	$45,000	$70,000	$121,500	$82,500	$124,000
Liabilities	30,000	50,000	58,500	61,500	?
December 31, 2005:					
Assets	49,000	90,000	136,500	?	160,000
Liabilities	26,000	?	55,500	72,000	52,000
During year 2005:					
Owner investments	6,000	10,000	?	38,100	40,000
Net income	?	30,000	16,500	24,000	32,000
Owner cash withdrawals	4,500	2,000	0	18,000	6,000

Required

1. Answer the following questions about Company V:
   a. What is the amount of equity on December 31, 2004?
   b. What is the amount of equity on December 31, 2005?
   c. What is net income for year 2005?
2. Answer the following questions about Company W:
   a. What is the amount of equity on December 31, 2004?
   b. What is the amount of equity on December 31, 2005?
   c. What is the amount of liabilities on December 31, 2005?
3. Calculate the amount of owner investments for Company X during 2005.
4. Calculate the amount of assets for Company Y on December 31, 2005.
5. Calculate the amount of liabilities for Company Z on December 31, 2004.

Check (1*b*) $23,000

(2c) $32,000

(4) $137,100

Problem 1-2B
Identifying effects of transactions on financial statements

A1 A2 

Identify how each of the following separate transactions affects financial statements. For the balance sheet, identify how each transaction affects total assets, total liabilities, and total equity. For the income statement, identify how each transaction affects net income. For the statement of cash flows, identify how each transaction affects cash flows from operating activities, cash flows from financing activities, and cash flows from investing activities. For increases, place a "+" in the column or columns. For decreases, place a "−" in the column or columns. If both an increase and a decrease occur, place "+/−" in the column or columns. The first transaction is completed as an example.

		Balance Sheet			Income Statement	Statement of Cash Flows		
	Transaction	Total Assets	Total Liab.	Total Equity	Net Income	Operating Activities	Financing Activities	Investing Activities
1	Owner invests cash in business	+		+			+	
2	Buys building by signing note payable							
3	Pays cash for salaries incurred							
4	Provides services for cash							
5	Pays cash for rent incurred							
6	Incurs utilities costs on credit							
7	Buys store equipment for cash							
8	Owner withdraws cash							
9	Provides services on credit							
10	Collects cash on receivable from (9)							

Problem 1-3B
Preparing an income statement
P1

Selected financial information for Online Co. for the year ended December 31, 2005, follows:

Revenues	$58,000	Expenses	$30,000	Net income	$28,000

Required

Use the information provided to prepare the 2005 calendar-year income statement for Online Co.

Problem 1-4B
Preparing a balance sheet
P1

The following is selected financial information for RWB Company as of December 31, 2005:

Liabilities	$74,000	Equity	$40,000	Assets	$114,000

Required

Use the information provided to prepare the balance sheet for RWB as of December 31, 2005.

Problem 1-5B
Preparing a statement of cash flows
P1

Selected financial information of BuyRight Co. for the year ended December 31, 2005, follows:

Cash from investing activities	$2,600
Net increase in cash	1,400
Cash from financing activities	2,800
Cash used by operating activities	(4,000)
Cash, December 31, 2004	1,300

Required

Use this information to prepare the 2005 calendar-year statement of cash flows for BuyRight.

Problem 1-6B
Preparing a statement of owner's equity
P1

The following is selected financial information of ComEx for the year ended December 31, 2005:

C. Tex, Capital, Dec. 31, 2005	$47,000	C. Tex, Withdrawals	$ 8,000
Net income	6,000	C. Tex, Capital, Dec. 31, 2004	49,000

Required

Prepare the 2005 calendar-year statement of owner's equity for ComEx.

Problem 1-7B
Analyzing transactions and preparing financial statements
C5 A2 P1

Ken Stone launched a new business, Ken's Maintenance Co., that began operations on June 1. The following transactions were completed by the company during that first month:

June 1 K. Stone invested $120,000 cash in the business.
2 Rented a furnished office and paid $4,500 cash for June's rent.
4 Purchased $2,400 of equipment on credit.
6 Paid $1,125 cash for the next week's advertising of the opening of the business.
8 Completed maintenance services for a customer and immediately collected $750 cash.
14 Completed $6,300 of maintenance services for First Union Center on credit.
16 Paid $900 cash for an assistant's salary for the first half of the month.
20 Received $6,300 cash payment for services completed for First Union Center on June 14.
21 Completed $3,500 of maintenance services for Skyway Co. on credit.
24 Completed $825 of maintenance services for Comfort Motel on credit.
25 Received $3,500 cash payment from Skyway Co. for the work completed on June 21.
26 Made payment of $2,400 cash for the equipment purchased on June 4.
28 Paid $900 cash for an assistant's salary for the second half of this month.
29 K. Stone withdrew $2,000 cash for personal use.
30 Paid $120 cash for this month's telephone bill.
30 Paid $525 cash for this month's utilities.

Required

1. Arrange the following asset, liability, and equity titles in a table like Exhibit 1.9: Cash; Accounts Receivable; Equipment; Accounts Payable; K. Stone, Capital; K. Stone, Withdrawals; Revenues; and Expenses.

Check (2) Ending balances: Cash, $118,080; Expenses, $8,070

2. Show the effects of the transactions on the accounts of the accounting equation by recording increases and decreases in the appropriate columns. Do not determine new account balances after each transaction. Determine the final total for each account and verify that the equation is in balance.

(3) Net income, $3,305; Total assets, $121,305

3. Prepare a June income statement, a June statement of owner's equity, a June 30 balance sheet, and a June statement of cash flows.

Problem 1-8B
Analyzing transactions and preparing financial statements
C5 A2 P1

Swender Excavating Co., owned by Patrick Swender, began operations in July and completed these transactions during that first month:

July	1	P. Swender invested $60,000 cash in the business as its initial capital.
	2	Rented office space and paid $500 cash for the July rent.
	3	Purchased excavating equipment for $4,000 by paying $800 cash and agreeing to pay the $3,200 balance in 30 days.
	6	Purchased office supplies for $500 cash.
	8	Completed work for a customer and immediately collected $2,200 cash for the work.
	10	Purchased $3,800 of office equipment on credit.
	15	Completed work for a customer on credit in the amount of $2,400.
	17	Purchased $1,920 of office supplies on credit.
	23	Paid $3,800 cash for the office equipment purchased on July 10.
	25	Billed a customer $5,000 for work completed; the balance is due in 30 days.
	28	Received $2,400 cash for the work completed on July 15.
	30	Paid an assistant's salary of $1,260 cash for this month.
	31	Paid $260 cash for this month's utility bill.
	31	P. Swender withdrew $1,200 cash for personal use.

Required

1. Arrange the following asset, liability, and equity titles in a table like Exhibit 1.9: Cash; Accounts Receivable; Office Supplies; Office Equipment; Excavating Equipment; Accounts Payable; P. Swender, Capital; P. Swender, Withdrawals; Revenues; and Expenses.

Check (2) Ending balances: Cash, $56,280; Accounts Payable, $5,120

2. Use additions and subtractions to show the effects of each transaction on the accounts in the accounting equation. Show new balances after each transaction.

(3) Net income, $7,580: Total assets, $71,500

3. Use the increases and decreases in the columns of the table from part 2 to prepare an income statement, a statement of owner's equity, and a statement of cash flows for the month. Also prepare a balance sheet as of the end of the month.

Analysis Component

4. Assume that Swender's $4,000 purchase of excavating equipment on July 3 was financed from an additional personal investment of another $4,000 cash in the business (instead of the purchase conditions described in the transaction). Explain the effect of this change on total assets, total liabilities, and equity.

Problem 1-9B
Analyzing effects of transactions
C5 P1 A1 A2

Tiana Moore started a new business, Tiana's Solutions, that completed the following transactions during its first year of operations:

a. T. Moore invests $95,000 cash and office equipment valued at $20,000 in the business.
b. Purchased a $120,000 building to use as an office. Moore paid $20,000 in cash and signed a note payable promising to pay the $100,000 balance over the next ten years.
c. Purchased office equipment for $20,000 cash.
d. Purchased $1,400 of office supplies and $3,000 of office equipment on credit.
e. Paid a local newspaper $400 cash for printing an announcement of the office's opening.
f. Completed a financial plan for a client and billed that client $1,800 for the service.
g. Designed a financial plan for another client and immediately collected a $2,000 cash fee.
h. T. Moore withdrew $5,000 cash from the company bank account for personal use.
i. Received $1,800 cash from the client described in transaction *f*.
j. Made a $2,000 cash payment on the equipment purchased in transaction *d*.
k. Paid $2,000 cash for the office secretary's wages.

Required

1. Create a table like the one in Exhibit 1.9, using the following headings for the columns: Cash; Accounts Receivable; Office Supplies; Office Equipment; Building; Accounts Payable; Notes Payable; T. Moore, Capital; T. Moore, Withdrawals; Revenues; and Expenses.

2. Use additions and subtractions to show the effects of these transactions on individual items of the accounting equation. Show new balances after each transaction.

3. Once you have completed the table, determine the company's net income.

Check (2) Ending balances: Cash, $49,400; Expenses, $2,400

(3) Net income, $1,400

Problem 1-10B
Computing and interpreting return on assets

A3

AT&T and GTE produce and market telecommunications products and are competitors. Key financial figures (in $ millions) for these businesses over the past year follow:

Key Figures	AT&T	GTE
Sales	$79,609	$19,957
Net income	139	2,538
Average invested (assets)	87,261	37,019

Required

1. Compute return on assets for (*a*) AT&T and (*b*) GTE.

2. Which company is more successful in the total amount of sales to consumers?

3. Which company is more successful in returning net income from its amount invested?

Check (1*a*) 0.16%; (1*b*) 6.9%

Analysis Component

4. Write a one-paragraph memorandum explaining which company you would invest your money in and why. (Limit your explanation to the information provided.)

Problem 1-11B
Determining expenses, liabilities, equity, and return on assets

A1 A3

Aspen Company manufactures, markets, and sells snowmobile equipment. The average total assets for Aspen Company is $2,000,000. In its most recent year, Aspen reported net income of $100,000 on revenues of $1,200,000.

Required

1. What is Aspen Company's return on assets?

2. Does return on assets seem satisfactory for Aspen given that its competitors average a 9.5% return on assets?

3. What are the total expenses for Aspen Company in its most recent year?

4. What is the average total amount of liabilities plus equity for Aspen Company?

Check (3) $1,100,000

(4) $2,000,000

Problem 1-12B[A]
Identifying risk and return

A4

All business decisions involve aspects of risk and return.

Required

Identify both the risk and the return in each of the following activities:

1. Stashing $1,000 under your mattress.

2. Placing a $500 bet on a horse running in the Kentucky Derby.

3. Investing $10,000 in Nike stock.

4. Investing $10,000 in U.S. Savings Bonds.

Problem 1-13B[B]
Describing organizational activities

C6

A startup company often engages in the following activities during its first year of operations. Classify each of the following activities into one of the three major activities of an organization:

A. Financing **B.** Investing **C.** Operating

_____ **1.** Providing client services.

_____ **2.** Obtaining a bank loan.

_____ **3.** Purchasing machinery.

_____ **4.** Researching products.

_____ **5.** Supervising workers.

_____ **6.** Owner investing money in business.

_____ **7.** Renting office space.

_____ **8.** Paying utilities expenses.

Problem 1-14B[B]
Describing organizational activities C6

Identify in outline format the three major business activities of an organization. For each of these activities, identify at least two specific transactions or events normally undertaken by the business's owners or managers.

PROBLEM SET C

Problem Set C is available at the book's Website to further reinforce and assess your learning.

This serial problem starts in this chapter and continues throughout most chapters of the book. It is most readily solved if you use the Working Papers that accompany this book.

SERIAL PROBLEM

Success Systems

On October 1, 2004, Kay Breeze launched a computer services company, **Success Systems,** that is organized as a sole proprietorship and provides consulting services, computer system installations, and custom program development. Breeze adopts the calendar year for reporting purposes and expects to prepare the company's first set of financial statements on December 31, 2004.

Required

Create a table like the one in Exhibit 1.9 using the following headings for columns: Cash; Accounts Receivable; Computer Supplies; Office Equipment; Accounts Payable; K. Breeze, Capital; K. Breeze, Withdrawals; Revenues; and Expenses. Then use additions and subtractions to show the effects of the October transactions for Success Systems on the individual items of the accounting equation. Show new balances after each transaction.

Oct. 1 Kay Breeze invested $55,000 cash, a $20,000 computer system, and $8,000 of office equipment in the business.
3 Purchased $1,420 of computer supplies on credit from Cain Office Products.
6 Billed Easy Leasing $4,800 for services performed in installing a new Web server.
8 Paid $1,420 cash for the computer supplies purchased from Cain Office Products on October 3.
10 Hired Sherry Adams as a part-time assistant for $125 per day, as needed.
12 Billed Easy Leasing another $1,400 for services performed.
15 Received $4,800 cash from Easy Leasing on its account.
17 Paid $805 cash to repair computer equipment damaged when moving it.
20 Paid $1,940 cash for an advertisement in the local newspaper.
22 Received $1,400 cash from Easy Leasing on its account.
28 Billed Clark Company $5,208 for services performed.
31 Paid $875 cash for Sherry Adams's wages for seven days of work.
31 Breeze withdrew $3,600 cash for personal use.

Check Ending balances: Cash, $52,560; Revenues, $11,408; Expenses, $3,620

Beyond the Numbers (BTN) *is a special problem section aimed to refine communication, conceptual, analysis, and research skills. It includes many activities helpful in developing an active learning environment.*

BEYOND THE NUMBERS

REPORTING IN ACTION

A1 A3 A4

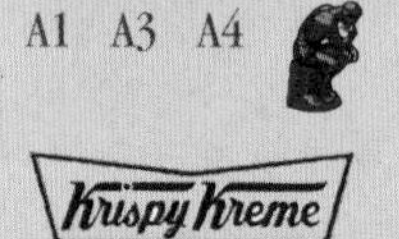

BTN 1-1 Key financial figures for **Krispy Kreme**'s fiscal year ended February 2, 2003, follow:

Key Figure	In Thousands
Liabilities + Equity	$410,487
Net income	33,478
Revenues	491,549

Required

1. What is the total amount of assets invested in Krispy Kreme?
2. What is Krispy Kreme's return on assets? Its assets at February 3, 2002, equal $255,376 (in thousands).
3. How much are total expenses for Krispy Kreme?
4. Does Krispy Kreme's return on assets seem satisfactory if competitors average a 3% return?

Check (2) 10.1%

Roll On

5. Access Krispy Kreme's financial statements (Form 10-K) for fiscal years ending after February 2, 2003, from its Website (KrispyKreme.com) or from the SEC Website (www.SEC.gov). Compute its return on assets for those fiscal years. Compare the February 2, 2003, fiscal year-end return on assets to any subsequent years' returns you are able to compute, and interpret the results.

COMPARATIVE ANALYSIS

A1 A3 A4 

BTN 1-2 Key comparative figures ($ thousands) for both **Krispy Kreme** and **Tastykake** follow:

Key Figure	Krispy Kreme	Tastykake
Liabilities + Equity	$410,487	$116,560
Net income	33,478	2,000*
Revenues (sales)	491,549	162,263

* Restructuring charges are removed from income.

Required

1. What is the total amount of assets invested in (*a*) Krispy Kreme and (*b*) Tastykake?
2. What is the return on assets for (*a*) Krispy Kreme and (*b*) Tastykake? Krispy Kreme's beginning-year assets equal $255,376 (in thousands) and Tastykake's beginning-year assets equal $116,137 (in thousands).
3. How much are expenses for (*a*) Krispy Kreme and (*b*) Tastykake?
4. Is return on assets satisfactory for (*a*) Krispy Kreme and (*b*) Tastykake? (Assume competitors average a 3% return.)
5. What can you conclude about Krispy Kreme and Tastykake from these computations?

Check (2b) 1.7%

ETHICS CHALLENGE

C4 C5 

BTN 1-3 Juanita Cruz works in a public accounting firm and hopes to eventually be a partner. The management of Allnet Company invites Cruz to prepare a bid to audit Allnet's financial statements. In discussing the audit fee, Allnet's management suggests a fee range in which the amount depends on the reported profit of Allnet. The higher its profit, the higher will be the audit fee paid to Cruz's firm.

Required

1. Identify the parties potentially affected by this audit and the fee plan proposed.
2. What are the ethical factors in this situation? Explain.
3. Would you recommend that Cruz accept this audit fee arrangement? Why or why not?
4. Describe some ethical considerations guiding your recommendation.

COMMUNICATING IN PRACTICE

A1 C2  

BTN 1-4 Refer to this chapter's opening feature about **The Chocolate Farm**. Assume that the Macmillans wish to expand The Chocolate Farm to include a store devoted to selling food decorations related to the main business. They meet with a loan officer of a Denver bank to discuss a loan.

Required

1. Prepare a half-page report outlining the information you would request from the Macmillans if you were the loan officer.
2. Indicate whether the information you request and your loan decision are affected by the form of business organization for the proposed Chocolate Farm store.

TAKING IT TO THE NET

A3

mhhe.com/larson

BTN 1-5 Visit the EDGAR database at (www.SEC.gov). Access the Form 10-K report of World Wrestling Entertainment (ticker WWE) filed on July 26, 2002.

Required

1. On page 16 of the 10-K report you will find comparative income statements of WWE for the years 1998–2002. How would you describe the revenue trend for WWE over this five-year period?
2. Has the WWE been profitable (see net income) over this five-year period?

TEAMWORK IN ACTION

C1

BTN 1-6 Teamwork is important in today's business world. Successful teams schedule convenient meetings, maintain regular communications, and cooperate with and support their members. This assignment aims to establish support/learning teams, initiate discussions, and set meeting times.

Required

1. Form teams and open a team discussion to determine a regular time and place for your team to meet between each scheduled class meeting. Notify your instructor via a memorandum or e-mail message as to when and where your team will hold regularly scheduled meetings.
2. Develop a list of telephone numbers and/or e-mail addresses of your teammates.

Book's Website provides free and easy access to all articles for every Business Week *Activity.*

BUSINESS WEEK ACTIVITY

C1

mhhe.com/larson

BTN 1-7 *Business Week* publishes a ranking of the top 1,000 companies based on several performance measures. This issue is called the *Business Week Global 1000.* Obtain the July 14, 2003, publication of this issue—this book's Website maintains free access to this article.

Required

1. What are the top 10 companies on the basis of market value?
2. Are any of the top 10 companies in the same industry?
3. How many of the top 10 based on market capitalization are not U.S. companies?

ENTREPRENEURIAL DECISION

A1 A2  

BTN 1-8 Refer to this chapter's opening feature about **The Chocolate Farm**. Assume the Macmillans decide to open a small retail store to supplement their chocolate operations.

Required

1. The Macmillans obtain a $50,000 bank loan and contribute $30,000 of their own assets to support the opening of the new store.
   a. What is the new store's total amount of liabilities plus equity?
   b. What is the new store's total amount of assets?
2. If the Macmillans earn $20,000 of income in the first year the retail store operates, compute the store's return on assets (assume average assets equal $80,000). Assess its performance if competitors average a 10% return.

Check (2) 25%

HITTING THE ROAD

C2   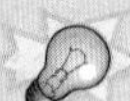

BTN 1-9 You are to interview a local business owner. (This can be a friend or relative.) Opening lines of communication with members of the business community can provide personal benefits of business networking. If you do not know the owner, you should call ahead to introduce yourself and explain your position as a student and your assignment requirements. You should request a thirty minute appointment for a face-to-face or phone interview to discuss the form of organization and operations of the business. Be prepared to make a good impression.

Required

1. Identify and describe the main operating activities and the form of organization for this business.
2. Determine and explain why the owner(s) chose this particular form of organization.
3. Identify any special advantages and/or disadvantages the owner(s) experiences in operating with this form of business organization.

BTN 1-10 Grupo Bimbo (GrupoBimbo.com) is a leader in the baking industry and also competes with both **Krispy Kreme** and **Tastykake**. Key financial figures for Grupo Bimbo follow:

GLOBAL DECISION

A1 A3 A4

Key Figure*	Pesos in Millions
Average assets	27,750
Net income	1,003
Revenues	41,373
Return on assets	3.6%

* Figures prepared in accordance with Generally Accepted Accounting Principles in Mexico.

Required

1. Identify any concerns you have in comparing Grupo Bimbo's income, revenue, liabilities, and equity figures to those of Krispy Kreme and Tastykake (in BTN 1-2) for purposes of making business decisions.
2. Identify any concerns you have in comparing Grupo Bimbo's return on assets ratio to those of Krispy Kreme and Tastykake (in BTN 1-2) for purposes of making business decisions.

"I want everything done . . . like, yesterday"—Tanya York

Analyzing and Recording Transactions

A Look Back

Chapter 1 considered the role of accounting in the information age and introduced financial statements. We described different forms of organizations and identified users and uses of accounting. We explained the accounting equation and applied it to transaction analysis.

A Look at This Chapter

This chapter focuses on the accounting process. We describe transactions and source documents as inputs for analysis. We explain the analysis and recording of transactions. The accounting equation, T-account, general ledger, trial balance, and debits and credits are shown as useful tools in the accounting process.

A Look Ahead

Chapter 3 extends our focus on processing information. We explain the importance of adjusting accounts and the procedures in preparing financial statements.

CAP

Conceptual

C1 Explain the steps in processing transactions. *(p. 48)*

C2 Describe source documents and their purpose. *(p. 49)*

C3 Describe an account and its use in recording transactions. *(p. 49)*

C4 Describe a ledger and a chart of accounts. *(p. 52)*

C5 Define *debits* and *credits* and explain their role in double-entry accounting. *(p. 53)*

Analytical

A1 Analyze the impact of transactions on accounts and financial statements. *(p. 57)*

A2 Compute the debt ratio and describe its use in analyzing company performance. *(p. 67)*

Procedural

P1 Record transactions in a journal and post entries to a ledger. *(p. 55)*

P2 Prepare and explain the use of a trial balance. *(p. 64)*

P3 Prepare financial statements from business transactions. *(p. 65)*

Decision Feature

Against Long Odds

LOS ANGELES—Tanya York produced her first film at 19. Since then she has produced hundreds of films with her company **York Entertainment (YorkEntertainment.com)**. York's company has become an urban powerhouse and distributes its titles under the York Urban, York Latino, and York En Espanol labels. Says York, "I'm Jamaican myself, so I can kind of relate to being a minority in a world where so much is aimed at the majority, so, in that way I'm happy to be able to offer films with an urban appeal."

York insists that the business and accounting side of production is as important as the artistic side. "With producing you're involved in all aspects of the entertainment industry," she says, "the creative side as well as the business side." York knows that attention to financial statements and know-how of the accounting system of debits and credits is crucial to success. An understanding of the accounting details enabled York to assess and enhance her company's profitability and financial position.

York relies on the financial numbers in devising strategies to enhance income. At the same time, she does not lose sight of giving the public what they want. Adds York, "I don't see my job as changing the public [demands]." Instead she fulfills them. This includes filling her movies with stars like Ice T, Kurupt, Destiny's Child, Kool Mo Dee, and Mac 10.

York continues to grow her company. With revenues near $20 million, she shows a keen understanding of accounting information in making good business decisions. Still, she insists anyone can use such information in a business to achieve similar success. "I came to America and through hard work built a company."

Without a doubt, Tanya York has not only tasted success but is living it. Adds York, "I like to always have new challenges in front of me."

[Sources: *York Entertainment Website,* January 2004; *Cinescape,* 2002; *Rolling Out Urban Style,* January 2002; *Entrepreneur,* November 2002; *Los Angeles Daily News,* February 2003.]

Financial statements report on the financial performance and condition of an organization. Knowledge of their preparation, organization, and analysis is important. A main goal of this chapter is to illustrate how transactions are recorded, how they are reflected in financial statements, and how they impact analysis of financial statements. Debits and credits are introduced and identified as a tool in helping understand and process transactions.

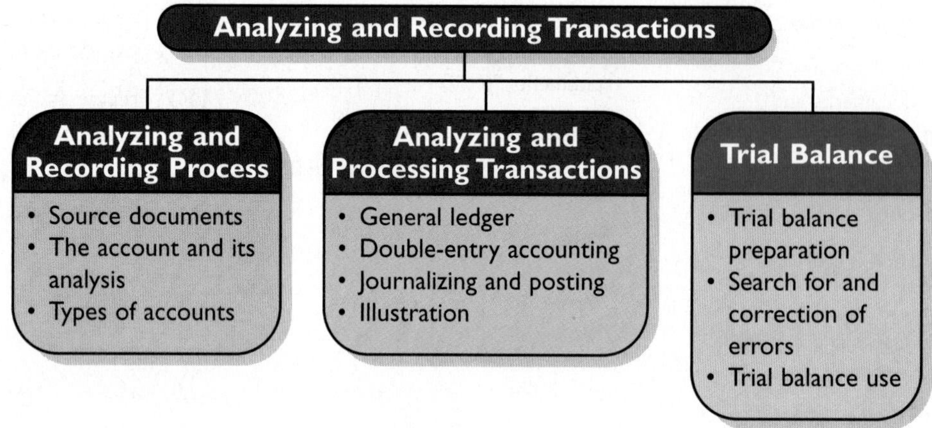

Analyzing and Recording Process

The accounting process identifies business transactions and events, analyzes and records their effects, and summarizes and presents information in reports and financial statements. These reports and statements are used for making investing, lending, and other business decisions. The steps in the accounting process that focus on *analyzing and recording* transactions and events are shown in Exhibit 2.1.

Exhibit 2.1

The Analyzing and Recording Process

C1 Explain the steps in processing transactions.

Business transactions and events are the starting points. Relying on source documents, transactions and events are analyzed using the accounting equation to understand how they affect company performance and financial position. These effects are recorded in accounting records, informally referred to as the *accounting books,* or simply the *books*. Additional steps such as posting and then preparing a trial balance help summarize and classify the effects of transactions and events. Ultimately, the accounting process provides information in useful reports or financial statements to decision makers.

Source Documents

C2 Describe source documents and their purpose.

Source documents identify and describe transactions and events entering the accounting process. They are the sources of accounting information and can be in either hard copy or electronic form. Examples are sales tickets, checks, purchase orders, bills from suppliers, employee earnings records, and bank statements. To illustrate, when an item is purchased on credit, the seller usually prepares at least two copies of a sales invoice. One copy is given to the buyer. Another copy, often sent electronically, results in an entry in the seller's information system to record the sale. Sellers use invoices for recording sales and for control; buyers use them for recording purchases and for monitoring purchasing activity. Note that many cash registers record information for each sale on a tape or electronic file locked inside the register. This record can be used as a source document for recording sales in the accounting records. Source documents, especially if obtained from outside the organization, provide objective and reliable evidence about transactions and events and their amounts.

Point: To ensure that all sales are rung up on the register, most sellers require customers to have their receipts to exchange or return purchased items.

Decision Ethics

Cashier Your manager requires that you, as cashier, immediately enter each sale. Recently, lunch hour traffic has increased and the assistant manager asks you to avoid delays by taking customers' cash and making change without entering sales. The assistant manager says she will add up cash and enter sales after lunch. She says that, in this way, the register will always match the cash amount when the manager arrives at three o'clock. What do you do?

Answer—p. 72

The Account and Its Analysis

C3 Describe an account and its use in recording transactions.

An **account** is a record of increases and decreases in a specific asset, liability, equity, revenue, or expense item. Information from an account is analyzed, summarized, and presented in reports and financial statements. The **general ledger,** or simply **ledger,** is a record containing all accounts used by a company. The ledger is often in electronic form. While most companies' ledgers contain similar accounts, a company may use one or more unique accounts because of its type of operations. Accounts are arranged into three general categories (based on the accounting equation), as shown in Exhibit 2.2.

Exhibit 2.2

Accounts Organized by the Accounting Equation

Asset Accounts Assets are resources owned or controlled by a company and that have expected future benefits. Most accounting systems include (at a minimum) separate accounts for the assets described here.

A *Cash* account reflects a company's cash balance. All increases and decreases in cash are recorded in the Cash account. It includes money and any medium of exchange that a bank accepts for deposit (coins, checks, money orders, and checking account balances).

Accounts receivable are held by a seller and refer to promises of payment from customers to sellers. These transactions are often called *credit sales* or *sales on account* (or *on credit*). Accounts receivable are increased by credit sales and are decreased by customer payments. A company needs a separate record for each customer, but for now, we use the simpler practice of recording all increases and decreases in receivables in a single account called Accounts Receivable.

Point: Customers and others who owe a company are called its **debtors.**

A *note receivable,* or promissory note, is a written promise of another entity to pay a definite sum of money on a specified future date to the holder of the note. A company holding a promissory note signed by another entity has an asset that is recorded in a Note (or Notes) Receivable account.

Point: A college parking fee is a prepaid account from the student's standpoint. At the beginning of the term, it represents an asset that entitles a student to park on or near campus. The benefits of the parking fee expire as the term progresses. At term-end, prepaid parking (asset) equals zero as it has been entirely recorded as parking expense.

Prepaid accounts (also called *prepaid expenses*) are assets that represent prepayments of future expenses (*not* current expenses). When the expenses are later incurred, the amounts in prepaid accounts are transferred to expense accounts. Common examples of prepaid

Point: Prepaid accounts that apply to current *and* future periods are assets. These assets are adjusted at the end of each period to reflect only those amounts that have not yet expired and to record as expenses those amounts that have expired.

accounts include prepaid insurance, prepaid rent, and prepaid services (such as club memberships). Prepaid accounts expire with the passage of time (such as with rent) or through use (such as with prepaid meal tickets). When financial statements are prepared, prepaid accounts are adjusted so that (1) all expired and used prepaid accounts are recorded as regular expenses and (2) all unexpired and unused prepaid accounts are recorded as assets (reflecting future use in future periods). To illustrate, when an insurance fee, called a *premium,* is paid in advance, the cost is typically recorded in the asset account Prepaid Insurance. Over time, the expiring portion of the insurance cost is removed from this asset account and reported in expenses on the income statement. Any unexpired portion remains in Prepaid Insurance and is reported on the balance sheet as an asset. (An exception exists for prepaid accounts that will expire or be used before the end of the current accounting period when financial statements are prepared. In this case, the prepayments *can* be recorded immediately as expenses.)

Supplies are assets until they are used. When they are used up, their costs are reported as expenses. The costs of unused supplies are recorded in a Supplies asset account. Supplies are often grouped by purpose—for example office supplies and store supplies. *Office supplies* include stationery, paper, toner, and pens. *Store supplies* include packaging materials, plastic and paper bags, gift boxes and cartons, and cleaning materials. The costs of these unused supplies can be recorded in an Office Supplies or a Store Supplies asset account. When supplies are used, their costs are transferred from the asset accounts to expense accounts.

Point: Some assets are described as *intangible* because they do not have physical existence or their benefits are highly uncertain. A recent balance sheet for Coca-Cola Company shows nearly $3.5 billion in intangible assets.

Equipment is an asset. When equipment is used and gets worn down its cost is gradually reported as an expense (called depreciation). Equipment is often grouped by its purpose—for example, office equipment and store equipment. *Office equipment* includes computers, printers, desks, chairs, shelves, and other office equipment. Costs incurred for these items are recorded in an Office Equipment asset account. The Store Equipment account includes the costs of assets used in a store such as counters, showcases, ladders, hoists, and cash registers.

Buildings such as stores, offices, warehouses, and factories are assets because they provide expected future benefits to those who control or own them. Their costs are recorded in a Buildings asset account. When several buildings are owned, separate accounts are sometimes kept for each of them.

The cost of *land* owned by a business is recorded in a Land account. The cost of buildings located on the land is separately recorded in one or more building accounts.

Decision Insight

Boss-Aid Entrepreneurs were asked whom they would want—if they could have anyone—to help run their businesses for a week. Bill Gates led, with 24%, followed by Donald Trump and Warren Buffet—see selected survey results.

Bill Gates	24%
Donald Trump	6.8
Warren Buffet	5.8
Lee Iacocca	5.2
Ross Perot	3.1
Hillary Clinton	1.4

Liability Accounts Liabilities are claims (by creditors) against assets, which means they are obligations to transfer assets or provide products or services to other entities. **Creditors** are individuals and organizations that own the right to receive payments from a company. If a company fails to pay its obligations, the law gives creditors a right to force the sale of that company's assets to obtain the money to meet creditors' claims. When assets are sold under these conditions, creditors are paid first, but only up to the amount of their claims. Any remaining money, the residual, goes to the owners of the company. Creditors often use a balance sheet to help decide whether to loan money to a company. A loan is less risky if the borrower's liabilities are small in comparison to assets because there are more resources than claims on resources. The more common liability accounts are described here.

Point: Accounts Payable are also called *Trade Payables.*

Accounts payable refer to oral or implied promises to pay later, which commonly arise from purchases of merchandise. Payables can also arise from purchases of supplies, equipment, and services. Accounting systems keep separate records about each creditor. We describe these individual records in Chapter 4.

A *note payable* refers to a formal promise, usually denoted by the signing of a promissory note, to pay a future amount. It is recorded in either a Short-Term Note Payable account or a Long-Term Note Payable account, depending on when it must be repaid. We explain details of short- and long-term classification in Chapter 4.

Unearned Revenue refers to a liability that is settled in the future when a company delivers its products or services. When customers pay in advance for products or services (before revenue is earned), the revenue recognition principle requires that the seller consider this payment as unearned revenue. Examples of unearned revenue include magazine subscriptions collected in advance by a publisher, sales of gift certificates by stores, and season ticket sales by sports teams. The seller would record these in liability accounts such as Unearned Subscriptions, Unearned Store Sales, and Unearned Ticket Revenue. When products and services are later delivered, the earned portion of the unearned revenue is transferred to revenue accounts such as Subscription Fees, Store Sales, and Ticket Sales.[1]

Decision Insight

Cash Spread The **Green Bay Packers** have *Unearned Revenues* of nearly $40 million in advance ticket sales. When the team plays its regular season home games, it settles this liability to its ticket holders and transfers the amount earned to *Ticket Revenues.*

Point: If a subscription is cancelled the publisher should refund the unused portion to the subscriber.

Accrued liabilities are amounts owed that are not yet paid. Examples are wages payable, taxes payable, and interest payable. These are often recorded in separate liability accounts by the same title. If they are not large in amount, one or more ledger accounts can be added and reported as a single amount on the balance sheet. (Financial statements often have amounts reported that are a summation of several ledger accounts.)

Equity Accounts The owner's claim on a company's assets is called *equity* or *owner's equity.* Equity is the owners' *residual interest* in the assets of a business after deducting liabilities. There are four subcategories of equity: owner's capital, owner's withdrawals, revenues, and expenses. We show this visually in Exhibit 2.3 by expanding the accounting equation.

Point: Equity is also called *net assets.*

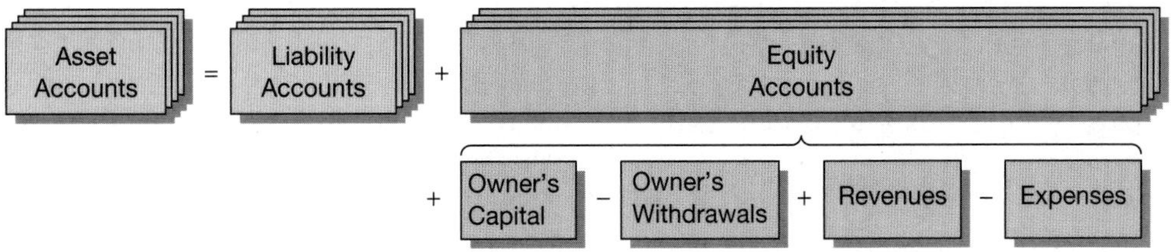

Exhibit 2.3
Expanded Accounting Equation

When an owner invests in a company, the invested amount is recorded in an account titled **Owner, Capital** (where the owner's name is inserted in place of "owner"). An account called *C. Taylor, Capital* is used for FastForward. Any further investments are recorded in this account. When the owner withdraws assets for personal use the withdrawal decreases both the company's assets and its total equity. (Owners of proprietorships cannot receive salaries because they are not legally separate from their companies and cannot enter into salary, or any other, contracts with themselves.) Withdrawals are

Point: The Owner's Withdrawals account (also called *Drawing* or *Personal* account) is sometimes referred to as a *contra equity* account because it reduces the normal balance of equity.

[1] In practice, account titles vary. As one example, Subscription Fees is sometimes called Subscription Fees Revenue, Subscription Fees Earned, or Earned Subscription Fees. As another example, Rent Earned is sometimes called Rent Revenue, Rental Revenue, or Earned Rent Revenue. We must use good judgment when reading financial statements because titles can differ even within the same industry. For example, product sales are called *revenues* at **Krispy Kreme,** but *net sales* at **Tastykake.** Generally, the term *revenues* or *fees* is more commonly used with service businesses, and *net sales* or *sales* with product businesses.

Point: The withdrawal of assets by the owners of a corporation is called a *dividend.*

not expenses of the business. They are simply the opposite of owner investments. An Owner, Withdrawals account is used in recording withdrawals by the owner. An account called *C. Taylor, Withdrawals,* is used to record Taylor's withdrawals from FastForward.

Revenues and expenses are the final two categories of equity. Examples of revenue accounts are Sales, Commissions Earned, Professional Fees Earned, Rent Earned, and Interest Revenue. *Revenues increase equity* and result from products or services provided to customers. Examples of expense accounts are Advertising Expense, Store Supplies Expense, Office Salaries Expense, Office Supplies Expense, Rent Expense, Utilities Expense, and Insurance Expense. *Expenses decrease equity* and result from assets or services used in a company's operations. The variety of revenues and expenses can be seen by looking at the *chart of accounts* that follows the index at the back of this book. (Different companies sometimes use different account titles than those in this book's chart of accounts. For example, some might use Interest Revenue instead of Interest Earned, or Rental Expense instead of Rent Expense. It is important only that an account title describe the item it represents.)

Decision Insight

Sports Accounts The **Boston Celtics** report the following major revenue and expense accounts:

Revenues	Expenses
Basketball ticket sales	Team salaries
TV & radio broadcast fees	Game costs
Advertising revenues	NBA franchise costs
Basketball playoff receipts	Promotional costs

Analyzing and Processing Transactions

This section explains several crucial tools and processes that comprise an accounting system. These include a ledger, T-accounts, debits and credits, double-entry accounting, journalizing, and posting.

Ledger and Chart of Accounts

C4 Describe a ledger and a chart of accounts.

The collection of all accounts for an information system is called a *ledger* (or *general ledger*). If accounts are in files on a hard drive, the sum of those files is the ledger. If the accounts are pages in a file, that file is the ledger. A company's size and diversity of operations affect the number of accounts needed. A small company can get by with as few as 20 or 30 accounts; a large company can require several thousand. The **chart of accounts** is a list of all accounts a company uses and includes an identification number assigned to each account. A small business might use the following numbering system for its accounts:

Decision Insight

Accoun-tech Using technology, **Sears** shrank its annual financial plan from 100 flowcharts with more than 300 steps to just *one* sheet of paper with 25 steps! Technology also allows Sears execs to analyze budgets and financial plans on their PCs. Sears says it slashed $100 million in recordkeeping costs.

101–199	Asset accounts
201–299	Liability accounts
301–399	Equity accounts
401–499	Revenue accounts
501–699	Expense accounts

These numbers provide a three-digit code that is useful in recordkeeping. In this case, the first digit assigned to asset accounts is a 1, the first digit assigned to liability accounts is a 2, and so on. The second and third digits relate to the accounts' subcategories. Exhibit 2.4 shows a partial chart of accounts for FastForward.

Account Number	Account Name	Account Number	Account Name
101	Cash	301	C. Taylor, Capital
106	Accounts receivable	302	C. Taylor, Withdrawals
126	Supplies	403	Consulting revenue
128	Prepaid insurance	406	Rental revenue
167	Equipment	622	Salaries expense
201	Accounts payable	637	Insurance expense
236	Unearned consulting revenue	640	Rent expense
		652	Supplies expense
		690	Utilities expense

Exhibit 2.4

Partial Chart of Accounts for FastForward

Debits and Credits

C5 Define *debits* and *credits* and explain their role in double-entry accounting.

A **T-account** represents a ledger account and is a tool used to understand the effects of one or more transactions. Its name comes from its shape like the letter *T*. The layout of a T-account (shown in Exhibit 2.5) is (1) the account title on top, (2) a left, or debit side, and (3) a right, or credit, side.

The left side of an account is called the **debit** side, often abbreviated *Dr.* The right side is called the **credit** side, abbreviated *Cr.*[2] To enter amounts on the left side of an account is to *debit* the account. To enter amounts on the right side is to *credit* the account. Do not make the error of thinking that the terms *debit* and *credit* mean increase or decrease. Whether a debit or a credit is an increase or decrease depends on the account. In an account where a debit is an increase, the credit is a decrease; in an account where a debit is a decrease, the credit is an increase. The difference between total debits and total credits for an account, including any beginning balance, is the **account balance.** When the sum of debits exceeds the sum of credits, the account has a *debit balance*. It has a *credit balance* when the sum of credits exceeds the sum of debits. When the sum of debits equals the sum of credits, the account has a *zero balance*.

Point: Think of *debit* and *credit* as accounting directions for left and right.

Account Title	
(Left side) **Debit**	(Right side) **Credit**

Exhibit 2.5

The T-Account

Double-Entry Accounting

Double-entry accounting requires that each transaction affect, and be recorded in, at least two accounts. It also means the *total amount debited must equal the total amount credited* for each transaction. Thus, the sum of the debits for all entries must equal the sum of the credits for all entries, and the sum of debit account balances in the ledger must equal the sum of credit account balances.

The system for recording debits and credits follows from the usual accounting equation—see Exhibit 2.6. Two points are important here. First, like any simple mathematical relation, net increases or decreases on one side have equal net effects on the other side. For example, a net increase in assets must be accompanied by an identical net increase on the liabilities

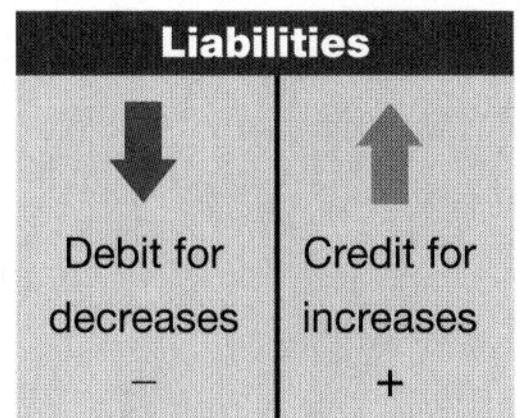

Exhibit 2.6

Debits and Credits in the Accounting Equation

[2] These abbreviations are remnants of 18th-century English recordkeeping practices where the terms *debitor* and *creditor* were used instead of *debit* and *credit*. The abbreviations use the first and last letters of these terms, just as we still do for Saint (St.) and Doctor (Dr.).

Point: Debits and credits do not mean favorable or unfavorable. A debit to an asset increases it, as does a debit to an expense. A credit to a liability increases it, as does a credit to a revenue.

and equity side. Recall that some transactions affect only one side of the equation, meaning that two or more accounts on one side are affected, but their net effect on this one side is zero. Second, the left side is the *normal balance* side for assets, and the right side is the *normal balance* side for liabilities and equity. This matches their layout in the accounting equation where assets are on the left side of this equation, and liabilities and equity are on the right.

Equity increases from revenues and owner investments and it decreases from expenses and owner withdrawals. These important equity relations are conveyed by expanding the accounting equation to include debits and credits in double-entry form as shown in Exhibit 2.7.

Exhibit 2.7

Debit and Credit Effects for Component Accounts

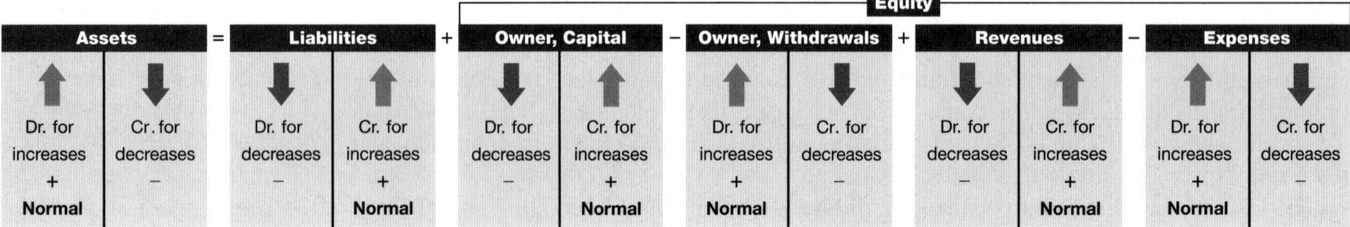

Increases (credits) to capital and revenues *increase* equity; increases (debits) to withdrawals and expenses *decrease* equity. The normal balance of each account (asset, liability, capital, withdrawals, revenue, or expense) refers to the left or right (debit or credit) side where *increases* are recorded. Understanding these diagrams and rules is required to prepare, analyze, and interpret financial statements.

The T-account for FastForward's Cash account, reflecting its first 11 transactions (from Exhibit 1.9), is shown in Exhibit 2.8. The total increases in its Cash account are $36,100, the total decreases are $31,700, and the account's debit balance is $4,400.

Exhibit 2.8

Computing the Balance for a T-Account

Cash			
Investment by owner	30,000	Purchase of supplies	2,500
Consulting services revenue earned	4,200	Purchase of equipment	26,000
Collection of account receivable	1,900	Payment of rent	1,000
		Payment of salary	700
		Payment of account payable	900
		Withdrawal by owner	600
Balance	**4,400**		

Point: The ending balance is on the side with the largest dollar amount.

Quick Check

1. Identify examples of accounting source documents.
2. Explain the importance of source documents.
3. Identify each of the following as either an asset, a liability, or equity: (*a*) Prepaid Rent, (*b*) Unearned Fees, (*c*) Building, (*d*) Wages Payable, and (*e*) Office Supplies.
4. What is an account? What is a ledger?
5. What determines the number and types of accounts a company uses?
6. Does *debit* always mean increase and *credit* always mean decrease?
7. Describe a chart of accounts.

Answers—pp. 72–73

Journalizing and Posting Transactions

P1 Record transactions in a journal and post entries to a ledger.

Processing transactions is a crucial part of accounting. The four usual steps of this process are depicted in Exhibit 2.9. Steps 1 and 2—involving transaction analysis and double-entry accounting—were introduced in prior sections. This section extends that discussion and focuses on steps 3 and 4 of the accounting process. Step 3 is to record each transaction in a journal. A **journal** gives a complete record of each transaction in one place. It also shows debits and credits for each transaction. The process of recording transactions in a journal is called **journalizing.** Step 4 is to transfer (or *post*) entries from the journal to the ledger. The process of transferring journal entry information to the ledger is called **posting.**

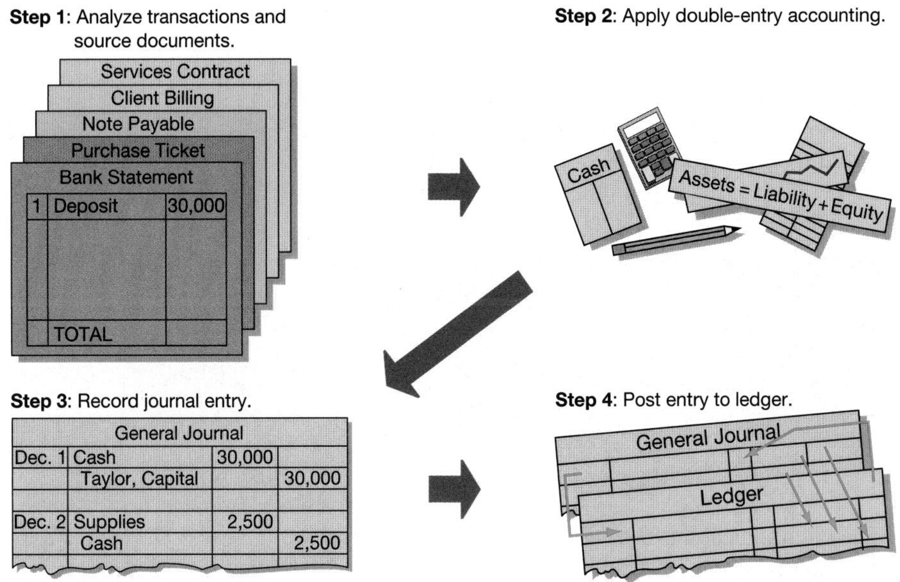

Exhibit 2.9

Steps in Processing Transactions

Journalizing Transactions The process of journalizing transactions requires an understanding of a journal. While companies can use various journals, every company uses a **general journal.** It can be used to record any transaction and includes the following information about each transaction: (1) date of transaction, (2) titles of affected accounts, (3) dollar amount of each debit and credit, and (4) explanation of the transaction. Exhibit 2.10 shows how the first two transactions of FastForward are recorded in a general journal. This process is similar for manual and computerized systems. Computerized journals are often designed to look like a manual journal page, and also include error-checking routines that ensure debits equal credits for each entry. Shortcuts allow recordkeepers to select account names and numbers from pull-down menus.

To record entries in a general journal, apply these steps; refer to the entries in Exhibit 2.10 when reviewing these steps. ① Date the transaction: Enter the year at the top of the first column and the month and day on the first line of each journal entry. ② Enter titles

GENERAL JOURNAL

Date	Account Titles and Explanation	PR	Debit	Page 1 Credit
2004 Dec. 1	Cash		30,000	
	C. Taylor, Capital			30,000
	Investment by owner.			
Dec. 2	Supplies		2,500	
	Cash			2,500
	Purchased supplies for cash.			

Exhibit 2.10

Partial General Journal for FastForward

of accounts debited and then enter amounts in the Debit column on the same line. Account titles are taken from the chart of accounts and are aligned with the left margin of the Account Titles and Explanation column. ③ Enter titles of accounts credited and then enter amounts in the Credit column on the same line. Account titles are from the chart of accounts and are indented from the left margin of the Account Titles and Explanation column to distinguish them from debited accounts. ④ Enter a brief explanation of the transaction on the line below the entry (it often references a source document). This explanation is indented about half as far as the credited account titles to avoid confusing it with accounts, and it is italicized.

A blank line is left between each journal entry for clarity. When a transaction is first recorded, the **posting reference (PR) column** blank is left blank (in a manual system). Later, when posting entries to the ledger, the identification numbers of the individual ledger accounts are entered in the PR column.

Balance Column Account T-accounts are simple and direct means to show how the accounting process works. However, actual accounting systems need more structure and therefore use **balance column accounts,** as in Exhibit 2.11.

Exhibit 2.11

Cash Account in Balance Column Format

Cash				Account No. 101	
Date	**Explanation**	**PR**	**Debit**	**Credit**	**Balance**
2004					
Dec. 1		G1	30,000		30,000
Dec. 2		G1		2,500	27,500
Dec. 3		G1		26,000	1,500
Dec. 10		G1	4,200		5,700

The balance column account format is similar to a T-account in having columns for debits and credits. It is different in including transaction date and explanation columns. It also has a column with the balance of the account after each entry is recorded. To illustrate, FastForward's Cash account in Exhibit 2.11 is debited on December 1 for the $30,000 owner investment, yielding a $30,000 debit balance. The account is credited on December 2 for $2,500, yielding a $27,500 debit balance. On December 3, it is credited again, this time for $26,000, and its debit balance is reduced to $1,500. The Cash account is debited for $4,200 on December 10, and its debit balance increases to $5,700; and so on.

The heading of the Balance column does not show whether it is a debit or credit balance. Instead, an account is assumed to have a *normal balance*. Unusual events can sometimes temporarily give an account an abnormal balance. An *abnormal balance* refers to a balance on the side where decreases are recorded. For example, a customer might mistakenly overpay a bill. This gives that customer's account receivable an abnormal (credit) balance. An abnormal balance is often identified by circling it or by entering it in red or some other unusual color. A zero balance for an account is usually shown by writing zeros or a dash in the Balance column to avoid confusion between a zero balance and one omitted in error.

Point: There are no exact rules for writing journal entry explanations. An explanation should be short yet describe why an entry is made.

Posting Journal Entries Step 4 of processing transactions is to post journal entries to ledger accounts (see Exhibit 2.9). To ensure that the ledger is up-to-date, entries are posted as soon as possible. This might be daily, weekly, or when time permits. All entries must be posted to the ledger before financial statements are prepared to ensure that account balances are up-to-date. When entries are posted to the ledger, the debits in journal entries are transferred into ledger accounts as debits, and credits are transferred into ledger accounts as credits. Exhibit 2.12 shows the four steps to post a journal entry. First, identify the ledger account that is debited in the entry; then, in the ledger, enter the entry date, the journal and page in its PR column, the debit amount, and the new balance of the ledger account. (The letter *G* shows it came from the General Journal. Other journals are discussed in Chapter 7.) Second, enter the ledger account number in the PR column of the journal. Steps three and four repeat the first two steps for credit entries and amounts. The posting process creates a link

Point: Computerized systems often provide a code beside a balance such as *dr.* or *cr.* to identify its balance.

Point: A journal is often referred to as the *book of original entry.* The ledger is referred to as the *book of final entry* because financial statements are prepared from it.

Point: Posting is automatic and immediate with accounting software.

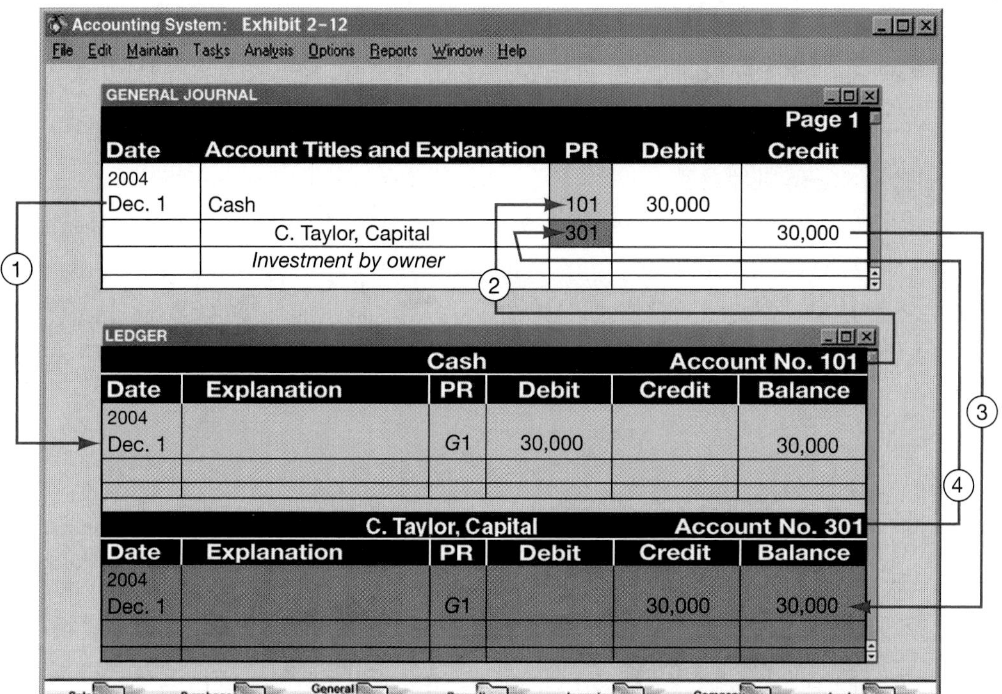
Accounting System: Exhibit 2-12

GENERAL JOURNAL — Page 1

Date	Account Titles and Explanation	PR	Debit	Credit
2004				
Dec. 1	Cash	101	30,000	
	C. Taylor, Capital	301		30,000
	Investment by owner			

LEDGER

Cash — Account No. 101

Date	Explanation	PR	Debit	Credit	Balance
2004					
Dec. 1		G1	30,000		30,000

C. Taylor, Capital — Account No. 301

Date	Explanation	PR	Debit	Credit	Balance
2004					
Dec. 1		G1		30,000	30,000

Key:
1. Identify debit account in Ledger: enter date, journal page, amount, and balance.
2. Enter the debit account number from the Ledger in the PR column of the journal.
3. Identify credit account in Ledger: enter date, journal page, amount, and balance.
4. Enter the credit account number from the Ledger in the PR column of the journal.

Exhibit 2.12

Posting an Entry to the Ledger

Point: The fundamental concepts of a manual (pencil-and-paper) system are identical to those of a computerized information system.

between the ledger and the journal entry. This link is a useful cross-reference for tracing an amount from one record to another.

Point: Explanations are typically included in ledger accounts only for unusual transactions or events.

Analyzing Transactions—An Illustration

We return to the activities of FastForward to show how double-entry accounting is useful in analyzing and processing transactions. Analysis of each transaction follows the four steps of Exhibit 2.9. First, we review the transaction and any source documents. Second, we analyze the transaction using the accounting equation. Third, we use double-entry accounting to record the transaction in journal entry form. Fourth, the entry is posted (for simplicity, we use T-accounts to represent ledger accounts). We also identify the financial statements affected by each transaction. Study each transaction thoroughly before proceeding to the next transaction. The first 11 transactions are from Chapter 1, and we analyze five additional December transactions of FastForward (numbered 12 through 16) that were omitted earlier.

A1 Analyze the impact of transactions on accounts and financial statements.

Topic Tackler 2-1

1. Investment by Owner

Cash	101
(1) 30,000	

C. Taylor, Capital	301
	(1) 30,000

Transaction: Chuck Taylor invests $30,000 cash in FastForward.

Analysis:

Assets	=	Liabilities	+	Equity
Cash				Capital
+30,000	=	0	+	30,000

Double entry:

(1)	Cash	101	30,000	
	C. Taylor, Capital	301		30,000

Statements affected:[3] BLS and SCF

FAST Forward

[3] We use abbreviations for the statements: income statement (IS), balance sheet (BLS), statement of cash flows (SCF), and statement of owner's equity (SOE).

2. Purchase Supplies for Cash

Supplies			126
(2)	2,500		

Cash			101
(1)	30,000	(2)	2,500

Transaction: FastForward pays $2,500 cash for supplies.

Analysis:

Assets		=	Liabilities	+	Equity
Cash	**Supplies**				
−2,500	+2,500	=	0	+	0

Changes the composition of assets but not the total.

Double entry:

(2)	Supplies	126	2,500	
	Cash	101		2,500

Statements affected: BLS and SCF

3. Purchase Equipment for Cash

Equipment			167
(3)	26,000		

Cash			101
(1)	30,000	(2)	2,500
		(3)	26,000

Transaction: FastForward pays $26,000 cash for equipment.

Analysis:

Assets		=	Liabilities	+	Equity
Cash	**Equipment**				
−26,000	+26,000	=	0	+	0

Changes the composition of assets but not the total.

Double entry:

(3)	Equipment	167	26,000	
	Cash	101		26,000

Statements affected: BLS and SCF

4. Purchase Supplies on Credit

Supplies			126
(2)	2,500		
(4)	7,100		

Accounts Payable			201
		(4)	7,100

Transaction: FastForward purchases $7,100 of supplies on credit from a supplier.

Analysis:

Assets	=	Liabilities	+	Equity
Supplies		**Accounts Payable**		
+7,100	=	+7,100	+	0

Double entry:

(4)	Supplies	126	7,100	
	Accounts Payable	201		7,100

Statements affected: BLS

5. Provide Services for Cash

Cash			101
(1)	30,000	(2)	2,500
(5)	4,200	(3)	26,000

Consulting Revenue			403
		(5)	4,200

Transaction: FastForward provides consulting services and immediately collects $4,200 cash.

Analysis:

Assets	=	Liabilities	+	Equity
Cash				**Consulting Revenue**
+4,200	=	0		+4,200

Double entry:

(5)	Cash	101	4,200	
	Consulting Revenue	403		4,200

Statements affected: BLS, IS, SCF, and SOE

6. Payment of Expense in Cash

Rent Expense			640
(6)	1,000		

Cash			101
(1)	30,000	(2)	2,500
(5)	4,200	(3)	26,000
		(6)	1,000

Transaction: FastForward pays $1,000 cash for December rent.

Analysis:

Assets	=	Liabilities	+	Equity
Cash				Rent Expense
−1,000	=	0		−1,000

Double entry:

(6)	Rent Expense	640	1,000	
	Cash	101		1,000

Statements affected: BLS, IS, SCF, and SOE

7. Payment of Expense in Cash

Salaries Expense			622
(7)	700		

Cash			101
(1)	30,000	(2)	2,500
(5)	4,200	(3)	26,000
		(6)	1,000
		(7)	700

Transaction: FastForward pays $700 cash for employee salary.

Analysis:

Assets	=	Liabilities	+	Equity
Cash				Salaries Expense
−700	=	0		−700

Double entry:

(7)	Salaries Expense	622	700	
	Cash	101		700

Statements affected: BLS, IS, SCF, and SOE

Point: *Salary* usually refers to compensation for an employee who receives a fixed amount for a given time period, whereas *wages* usually refers to compensation based on time worked.

8. Provide Consulting and Rental Services on Credit

Accounts Receivable			106
(8)	1,900		

Consulting Revenue			403
		(5)	4,200
		(8)	1,600

Rental Revenue			406
		(8)	300

Transaction: FastForward provides consulting services of $1,600 and rents its test facilities for $300. The customer is billed $1,900 for these services.

Analysis:

Assets	=	Liabilities	+	Equity	
Accounts Receivable				Consulting Revenue	Rental Revenue
+1,900	=	0		+1,600	+300

Double entry:

(8)	Accounts Receivable	106	1,900	
	Consulting Revenue	403		1,600
	Rental Revenue	406		300

Statements affected: BLS, IS, and SOE

Point: Transaction 8 is a **compound journal entry,** which affects three or more accounts.

9. Receipt of Cash on Account

Cash			101
(1)	30,000	(2)	2,500
(5)	4,200	(3)	26,000
(9)	1,900	(6)	1,000
		(7)	700

Accounts Receivable			106
(8)	1,900	(9)	1,900

Transaction: FastForward receives $1,900 cash from the client billed in transaction 8.

Analysis:

Assets		=	Liabilities	+	Equity
Cash	Accounts Receivable				
+1,900	−1,900	=	0	+	0

Double entry:

(9)	Cash	101	1,900	
	Accounts Receivable	106		1,900

Statements affected: BLS and SCF

Point: The *revenue recognition principle* requires revenue to be recognized when earned, which is when the company provides products or services to a customer. This is not necessarily the same time that the customer pays. A customer can pay before or after products or services are provided.

10. Partial Payment of Accounts Payable

Accounts Payable			201
(10)	**900**	(4)	7,100

Cash			101
(1)	30,000	(2)	2,500
(5)	4,200	(3)	26,000
(9)	1,900	(6)	1,000
		(7)	700
		(10)	**900**

Transaction: FastForward pays CalTech Supply $900 cash toward the payable of transaction 4.

Analysis:

Assets	=	Liabilities	+	Equity
Cash		**Accounts Payable**		
−900	=	−900	+	0

Double entry:

(10)	Accounts Payable	201	900	
	Cash	101		900

Statements affected: BLS and SCF

11. Withdrawal of Cash by Owner

C. Taylor, Withdrawals 302			
(11)	**600**		

Cash			101
(1)	30,000	(2)	2,500
(5)	4,200	(3)	26,000
(9)	1,900	(6)	1,000
		(7)	700
		(10)	900
		(11)	**600**

Transaction: Chuck Taylor withdraws $600 cash from FastForward for personal use.

Analysis:

Assets	=	Liabilities	+	Equity
Cash				**Withdrawals**
−600	=	0		−600

Double entry:

(11)	C. Taylor, Withdrawals	302	600	
	Cash	101		600

Statements affected: BLS, SCF, and SOE

12. Receipt of Cash for Future Services

Cash			101
(1)	30,000	(2)	2,500
(5)	4,200	(3)	26,000
(9)	1,900	(6)	1,000
(12)	**3,000**	(7)	700
		(10)	900
		(11)	600

Unearned Consulting Revenue			236
		(12)	**3,000**

Transaction: FastForward receives $3,000 cash in advance of providing consulting services to a customer.

Analysis:

Assets	=	Liabilities	+	Equity
Cash		**Unearned Consulting Revenue**		
+3,000	=	+3,000	+	0

Accepting $3,000 cash obligates FastForward to perform future services and is a liability. No revenue is earned until services are provided.

Double entry:

(12)	Cash	101	3,000	
	Unearned Consulting Revenue	236		3,000

Statements affected: BLS and SCF

Point: Luca Pacioli is considered a pioneer in accounting and the first to devise double-entry accounting.

13. Pay Cash for Future Insurance Coverage

Prepaid Insurance			128
(13)	2,400		

Cash			101
(1)	30,000	(2)	2,500
(5)	4,200	(3)	26,000
(9)	1,900	(6)	1,000
(12)	3,000	(7)	700
		(10)	900
		(11)	600
		(13)	**2,400**

Transaction: FastForward pays $2,400 cash (insurance premium) for a 24-month insurance policy. Coverage begins on December 1.

Analysis:

Assets		=	Liabilities	+	Equity
Cash	**Prepaid Insurance**				
−2,400	+2,400	=	0	+	0

Changes the composition of assets from cash to prepaid insurance. Expense is incurred as insurance coverage expires.

Double entry:

(13)	Prepaid Insurance	128	2,400	
	Cash	101		2,400

Statements affected: BLS and SCF

14. Purchase Supplies for Cash

Supplies			126
(2)	2,500		
(4)	7,100		
(14)	**120**		

Cash			101
(1)	30,000	(2)	2,500
(5)	4,200	(3)	26,000
(9)	1,900	(6)	1,000
(12)	3,000	(7)	700
		(10)	900
		(11)	600
		(13)	2,400
		(14)	**120**

Transaction: FastForward pays $120 cash for supplies.

Analysis:

Assets		=	Liabilities	+	Equity
Cash	**Supplies**				
−120	+120	=	0	+	0

Double entry:

(14)	Supplies	126	120	
	Cash	101		120

Statements affected: BLS and SCF

15. Payment of Expense in Cash

Utilities Expense			690
(15)	**230**		

Cash			101
(1)	30,000	(2)	2,500
(5)	4,200	(3)	26,000
(9)	1,900	(6)	1,000
(12)	3,000	(7)	700
		(10)	900
		(11)	600
		(13)	2,400
		(14)	120
		(15)	**230**

Transaction: FastForward pays $230 cash for December utilities expense.

Analysis:

Assets	=	Liabilities	+	Equity
Cash				**Utilities Expense**
−230	=	0		−230

Double entry:

(15)	Utilities Expense	690	230	
	Cash	101		230

Statements affected: BLS, IS, SCF, and SOE

16. Payment of Expense in Cash

Salaries Expense			622
(7)	700		
(16)	**700**		

Cash			101
(1)	30,000	(2)	2,500
(5)	4,200	(3)	26,000
(9)	1,900	(6)	1,000
(12)	3,000	(7)	700
		(10)	900
		(11)	600
		(13)	2,400
		(14)	120
		(15)	230
		(16)	**700**

Transaction: FastForward pays $700 cash in employee salary for work performed in the latter part of December.

Analysis:

Assets	=	Liabilities	+	Equity
Cash				**Salaries Expense**
−700	=	0		−700

Double entry:

(16)	Salaries Expense	622	700	
	Cash	101		700

Statements affected: BLS, IS, SCF, and SOE

Point: We could merge transactions 15 and 16 into one *compound entry.*

Accounting Equation Analysis

Summary of debit and credit rules:

Accounts	Increase (normal bal.)	Decrease
Asset	Debit	Credit
Liability	Credit	Debit
Capital	Credit	Debit
Withdrawals	Debit	Credit
Revenue	Credit	Debit
Expense	Debit	Credit

Point: Technology does not provide the judgment required to analyze most business transactions. Analysis requires the expertise of skilled and ethical professionals.

Exhibit 2.13 shows the accounts (in T-account form) of FastForward after all 16 transactions are recorded, posted and the balances computed. The accounts are grouped into three major columns corresponding to the accounting equation: assets, liabilities, and equity. Note several important points. First, as with each transaction, the totals for the three columns must obey the accounting equation. Specifically, assets equal $42,070 ($3,950 + $0 + $9,720 + $2,400 + $26,000); liabilities equal $9,200 ($6,200 + $3,000); and equity equals $32,870 ($30,000 − $600 + $5,800 + $300 − $1,400 − $1,000 − $230). These numbers prove the accounting equation: Assets of $42,070 = Liabilities of $9,200 + Equity of $32,870. Second, the capital, withdrawals, revenue, and expense accounts reflect the transactions that change equity. Their balances underlie the statement of owner's equity. Third, the revenue and expense account balances will be summarized and reported in the income statement. Fourth, increases and decreases in the cash account make up the elements reported in the statement of cash flows.

Exhibit 2.13

Ledger for FastForward (in T-Account Form)

Assets = Liabilities + Equity

Assets

Cash 101

(1)	30,000	(2)	2,500
(5)	4,200	(3)	26,000
(9)	1,900	(6)	1,000
(12)	3,000	(7)	700
		(10)	900
		(11)	600
		(13)	2,400
		(14)	120
		(15)	230
		(16)	700
Balance	**3,950**		

Accounts Receivable 106

(8)	1,900	(9)	1,900
Balance	**0**		

Supplies 126

(2)	2,500		
(4)	7,100		
(14)	120		
Balance	**9,720**		

Prepaid Insurance 128

(13)	**2,400**		

Equipment 167

(3)	**26,000**		

Liabilities

Accounts Payable 201

(10)	900	(4)	7,100
		Balance	**6,200**

Unearned Consulting Revenue 236

		(12)	**3,000**

Equity

C. Taylor, Capital 301

		(1)	**30,000**

C. Taylor, Withdrawals 302

(11)	**600**		

Consulting Revenue 403

		(5)	4,200
		(8)	1,600
		Balance	**5,800**

Rental Revenue 406

		(8)	**300**

Salaries Expense 622

(7)	700		
(16)	700		
Balance	**1,400**		

Rent Expense 640

(6)	**1,000**		

Utilities Expense 690

(15)	**230**		

Accounts in this white area reflect those reported on the income statement.

$42,070 = $9,200 + $32,870

Quick Check

8. What types of transactions increase equity? What types decrease equity?
9. Why are accounting systems called *double entry?*
10. For each transaction, double-entry accounting requires which of the following: (*a*) Debits to asset accounts must create credits to liability or equity accounts, (*b*) a debit to a liability account must create a credit to an asset account, or (c) total debits must equal total credits.
11. An owner invests $15,000 cash along with equipment having a market value of $23,000 in a proprietorship. Prepare the necessary journal entry.
12. Explain what a compound journal entry is.
13. Why are posting reference numbers entered in the journal when entries are posted to ledger accounts?

Answers—p. 73

Trial Balance

Double-entry accounting requires the sum of debit account balances to equal the sum of credit account balances. A trial balance is used to verify this. A **trial balance** is a list of accounts and their balances at a point in time. Account balances are reported in the appropriate debit or credit column of a trial balance. Exhibit 2.14 shows the trial balance for FastForward after its 16 entries have been posted to the ledger. (This is an *unadjusted* trial balance—Chapter 3 will explain the necessary adjustments.)

Point: Knowing how financial statements are prepared improves our analysis of them.

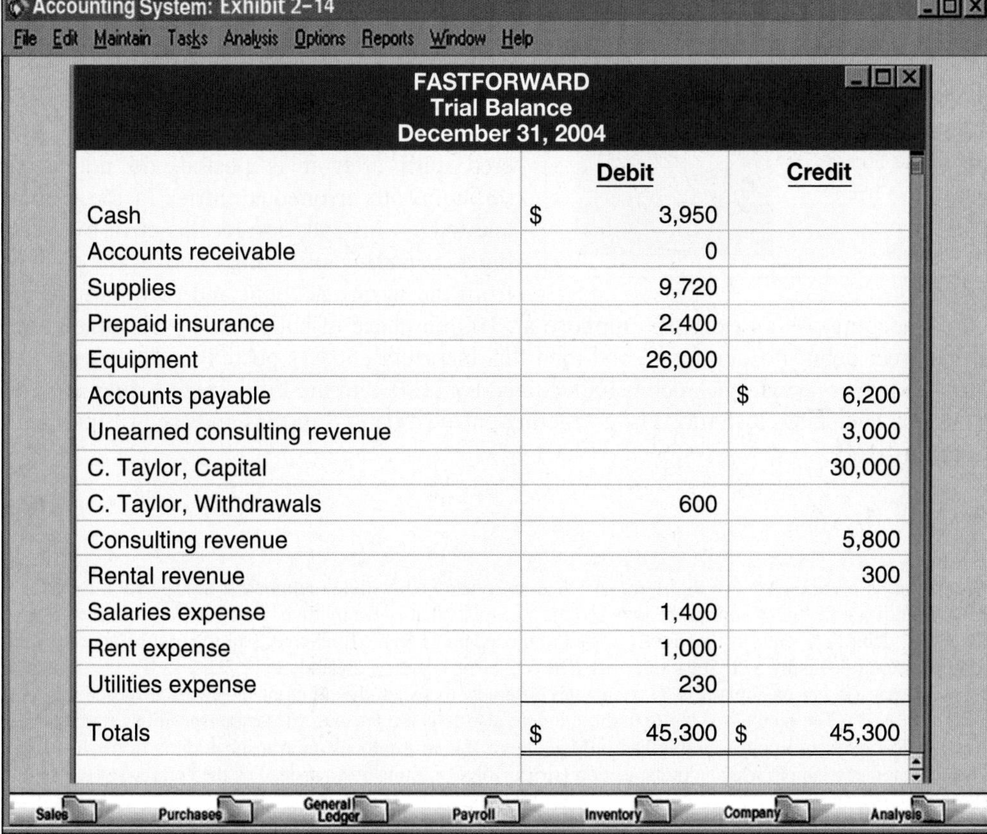

Accounting System: Exhibit 2-14

File Edit Maintain Tasks Analysis Options Reports Window Help

FASTFORWARD
Trial Balance
December 31, 2004

	Debit	Credit
Cash	$ 3,950	
Accounts receivable	0	
Supplies	9,720	
Prepaid insurance	2,400	
Equipment	26,000	
Accounts payable		$ 6,200
Unearned consulting revenue		3,000
C. Taylor, Capital		30,000
C. Taylor, Withdrawals	600	
Consulting revenue		5,800
Rental revenue		300
Salaries expense	1,400	
Rent expense	1,000	
Utilities expense	230	
Totals	$ 45,300	$ 45,300

Exhibit 2.14

Trial Balance (unadjusted)

Preparing a Trial Balance

P2 Prepare and explain the use of a trial balance.

Preparing a trial balance involves three steps:

1. List each account title and its amount (from ledger) in the trial balance. If an account has a zero balance, list it with a zero in its normal balance column (or omit it entirely).
2. Compute the total of debit balances and the total of credit balances.
3. Verify (*prove*) total debit balances equal total credit balances.

Point: The ordering of accounts in a trial balance typically follows their identification number from the chart of accounts.

Point: A trial balance is *not* a financial statement but a mechanism for checking equality of debits and credits in the ledger. Financial statements do not have debit and credit columns.

The total of debit balances equals the total of credit balances for the trial balance in Exhibit 2.14. Note that equality of these two totals does not guarantee that no errors were made. For example, the column totals still will be equal when a debit or credit of a correct amount is made to a wrong account. Another error that does not cause unequal column totals is when equal debits and credits of an incorrect amount are entered.

Searching for and Correcting Errors If the trial balance does not balance (when its columns are not equal), the error (or errors) must be found and corrected. An efficient way to search for an error is to check the journalizing, posting, and trial balance preparation in *reverse order.* Step 1 is to verify that the trial balance columns are correctly added. If step 1 fails to find the error, step 2 is to verify that account balances are accurately entered from the ledger. Step 3 is to see whether a debit (or credit) balance is mistakenly listed in the trial balance as a credit (or debit). A clue to this error is when the difference between total debits and total credits equals twice the amount of the incorrect account balance. If the error is still undiscovered, Step 4 is to recompute each account balance in the ledger. Step 5 is to verify that each journal entry is properly posted. Step 6 is to verify that the original journal entry has equal debits and credits. At this point, any errors should be uncovered.[4]

Example: If a credit to Unearned Revenue were incorrectly posted from the journal as a credit to the Revenue ledger account, would the ledger still balance? Would the financial statements be correct? *Answers:* The ledger would balance, but liabilities would be understated, equity would be overstated, and income would be overstated (all because of overstated revenues).

If an error in a journal entry is discovered before the error is posted, it can be corrected in a manual system by drawing a line through the incorrect information. The correct information is written above it to create a record of change for the auditor. Many computerized systems allow the operator to replace the incorrect information directly.

Decision Insight

Gorge'em *Disgorgement* is one of the government's strongest weapons for going after shady executives. When the SEC wins a court order or settles a case against executives, it can require them to give back their salaries, including stock gains.

If an error in a journal entry is not discovered until after it is posted, do not strike through both erroneous entries in the journal and ledger. Instead, correct this error by creating a *correcting entry* that removes the amount from the wrong account and records it to the correct account. As an example, suppose a $100 purchase of supplies is journalized with an incorrect debit to Equipment, and then this incorrect entry is posted to the ledger. The Supplies ledger account balance is understated by $100, and the Equipment ledger account balance is overstated by $100. The correcting entry is: debit Supplies and credit Equipment (both for $100).

Point: The IRS requires companies to keep records that can be audited.

[4] *Transposition* occurs when two digits are switched, or transposed, within a number. If transposition is the only error, it yields a difference between the two trial balance totals that is evenly divisible by 9. For example, assume that a $691 debit in an entry is incorrectly posted to the ledger as $619. Total credits in the trial balance are then larger than total debits by $72 ($691 − $619). The $72 error is *evenly* divisible by 9 (72/9 = 8). The first digit of the quotient (in our example it is 8) equals the difference between the digits of the two transposed numbers (the 9 and the 1). The number of digits in the quotient also tells the location of the transposition, starting from the right. The quotient in our example had only one digit (8), so it tells us the transposition is in the first digit. Consider another example where a transposition error involves posting $961 instead of the correct $691. The difference in these numbers is $270, and its quotient is 30 (270/9). The quotient has two digits, so it tells us to check the second digit from the right for a transposition of two numbers that have a difference of 3.

Using a Trial Balance to Prepare Financial Statements

This section shows how to prepare *financial statements* from the trial balance in Exhibit 2.14 and information on the December transactions of FastForward. The statements differ from those in Chapter 1 because of several additional transactions. These statements are also more precisely called *unadjusted statements* because we need to make some further accounting adjustments (described in Chapter 3).

P3 Prepare financial statements from business transactions.

How financial statements are linked in time is illustrated in Exhibit 2.15. A balance sheet reports on an organization's financial position at a *point in time*. The income statement, statement of owner's equity, and statement of cash flows report on financial performance over a *period of time*. The three statements in the middle column of Exhibit 2.15 link balance sheets from the beginning to the end of a reporting period. They explain how financial position changes from one point to another.

Exhibit 2.15

Links between Financial Statements Across Time

Income statement
Beginning balance sheet
Statement of owner's equity
Ending balance sheet
Statement of cash flows
Point in time
Period of time
Point in time

Preparers and users (including regulatory agencies) determine the length of the reporting period. A one-year, or annual, reporting period is common, as are semiannual, quarterly, and monthly periods. The one-year reporting period is known as the *accounting,* or *fiscal, year*. Businesses whose accounting year begins on January 1 and ends on December 31 are known as *calendar-year* companies. Many companies choose a fiscal year ending on a date other than December 31. **Krispy Kreme** is a *noncalendar-year* company as reflected in the headings of its February 2 year-end financial statements in Appendix A near the end of the book.

Topic Tackler 2-2

Point: A statement's heading lists the 3 W's: **Who**—name of organization, **What**—name of statement, **When**—statement's point in time or period of time.

Income Statement An income statement reports the revenues earned less the expenses incurred by a business over a period of time. FastForward's income statement for December is shown at the top of Exhibit 2.16. Information about revenues and expenses is conveniently taken from the trial balance in Exhibit 2.14. Net income of $3,470 is reported at the bottom of the statement. Owner investments and withdrawals are *not* part of income.

"I'LL TELL YOU, HARRIS, THEY DON'T MAKE ACCOUNTANTS LIKE THEY USED TO. THOSE I HAD IN THE '90'S, NEVER BROUGHT ME FIGURES LIKE THESE."

Statement of Owner's Equity The statement of owner's equity reports information about how equity changes over the reporting period. FastForward's statement of owner's equity is the second report in Exhibit 2.16. It shows the $30,000 owner investment plus the $3,470 of net income earned during the month. It also reports the $600 withdrawal and the $32,870 end-of-month equity (capital) balance. (The beginning capital balance in the statement of owner's equity is rarely zero. An exception is for the first period of a company's operations. The beginning capital balance in January 2005 is $32,870, which is December's ending balance.)

Balance Sheet The balance sheet reports the financial position of a company at a point in time, usually at the end of a month, quarter, or year. FastForward's balance sheet is the third report in Exhibit 2.16. This statement refers to FastForward's financial condition at the close of business on December 31. The left side of the balance sheet lists its assets: cash, supplies, prepaid insurance, and equipment. The upper right side of the balance sheet shows that it owes $6,200 to creditors and $3,000 in services to customers who paid in advance.

Point: An income statement is also called an *earnings statement, a statement of operations,* or a *P&L* (profit and loss) *statement*. A balance sheet is also called a *statement of financial position.*

Decision Maker

Entrepreneur You open a wholesale business selling entertainment equipment to retail outlets. You find that most of your customers demand to buy on credit. How can you use the balance sheets of these customers to decide which ones to extend credit to?

Answer—p. 72

The equity section shows an ending capital balance of $32,870. Note the link between the ending balance of the statement of owner's equity and the capital balance here. (Recall that this presentation of the balance sheet is called the *account form:* assets on the left and liabilities and equity on the right. Another presentation is the *report form:* assets on top, followed by liabilities and then equity. Either presentation is acceptable.)

Point: While revenues increase equity and expenses decrease equity, the amounts are not reported in detail in the statement of owner's equity. Instead, their effects are reflected through net income.

Presentation Issues Dollar signs are not used in journals and ledgers. They do appear in financial statements and other reports such as trial balances. The usual practice is to put dollar signs beside only the first and last numbers in a column. **Krispy Kreme**'s

Exhibit 2.16

Financial Statements and Their Links

FASTFORWARD
Income Statement
For Month Ended December 31, 2004

Revenues		
Consulting revenue ($4,200 + $1,600)	$ 5,800	
Rental revenue	300	
Total revenues		$ 6,100
Expenses		
Rent expense	1,000	
Salaries expense	1,400	
Utilities expense	230	
Total expenses		2,630
Net income		$ 3,470

Point: Arrow lines show how the statements are linked.

FASTFORWARD
Statement of Owner's Equity
For Month Ended December 31, 2004

C. Taylor, Capital, December 1, 2004		$ 0
Plus: Investments by owner	$30,000	
Net income	3,470	33,470
		33,470
Less: Withdrawals by owner		600
C. Taylor, Capital, December 31, 2004		$32,870

FASTFORWARD
Balance Sheet
December 31, 2004

Assets		Liabilities	
Cash	$ 3,950	Accounts payable	$ 6,200
Supplies	9,720	Unearned revenue	3,000
Prepaid insurance	2,400	Total liabilities	9,200
Equipment	26,000		
		Equity	
		C. Taylor, Capital	32,870
Total assets	$42,070	Total liabilities and equity	$ 42,070

Point: To *foot* a column of numbers is to add them.

financial statements in Appendix A show this. When amounts are entered in a journal, ledger, or trial balance, commas are optional to indicate thousands, millions, and so forth. However, commas are always used in financial statements. Companies also commonly round amounts in reports to the nearest dollar, or even to a higher level. Krispy Kreme is typical of many companies in that it rounds its financial statement amounts to the nearest thousand. This decision is based on the perceived impact of rounding for users' business decisions.

Example: How would the balance sheet in Exhibit 2.16 change if FastForward pays $2,000 of its payable on December 31 using its Cash account? What would be the new amount of total assets? Would the balance sheet still balance? *Answers:* Cash would be $1,950, accounts payable would be $4,200, total assets (and liabilities plus equity) would be $40,070, and the balance sheet would still balance.

Quick Check

14. Where are dollar signs typically entered in financial statements?

15. If a $4,000 debit to Equipment in a journal entry is incorrectly posted to the ledger as a $4,000 credit, and the ledger account has a resulting debit balance of $20,000, what is the effect of this error on the Trial Balance column totals?

16. Describe the link between the income statement and the statement of owner's equity.

17. Explain the link between the balance sheet and the statement of owner's equity.

18. Define and describe revenues and expenses.

19. Define and describe assets, liabilities, and equity.

Answers—p. 73

Debt Ratio

Decision Analysis

A2 Compute the debt ratio and describe its use in analyzing company performance.

An important business objective is gathering information to help assess a company's risk of failing to pay its debts. Companies finance their assets with either liabilities or equity. A company that finances a relatively large portion of its assets with liabilities is said to have a high degree of *financial leverage*. Higher financial leverage involves greater risk because liabilities must be repaid and often require regular interest payments (equity financing does not). The risk that a company might not be able to meet such required payments is higher if it has more liabilities (is more highly leveraged). One way to assess the risk associated with a company's use of liabilities is to compute the **debt ratio** as in Exhibit 2.17.

$$\textbf{Debt ratio} = \frac{\textbf{Total liabilities}}{\textbf{Total assets}}$$

Exhibit 2.17

Debt Ratio

To see how to apply the debt ratio, let's look at **Stride Rite**'s liabilities and assets. Stride Rite makes Keds, Pro-Keds, and other footwear. Exhibit 2.18 computes and reports its debt ratio at the end of each year from 1998 to 2002.

Stride Rite's debt ratio ranges from a low of 0.24 to a high of 0.31. Its ratio is low compared with the industry ratio. Stride Rite reports that it carries no long-term debt, which is unusual. This analysis implies a low risk from its financial leverage. Is this good or bad? To answer that question we

Point: Compare the equity amount to the liability amount to assess the extent of owner versus nonowner financing.

	2002	2001	2000	1999	1998
Total liabilities (in mil.)	$ 82	$100	$110	$101	$102
Total assets (in mil.)	$335	$362	$359	$351	$347
Debt ratio	**0.24**	**0.28**	**0.31**	**0.29**	**0.29**
Industry debt ratio	0.45	0.49	0.48	0.46	0.52

Exhibit 2.18

Computation and Analysis of Debt Ratio

Decision Maker

Investor You consider buying stock in **Converse.** As part of your analysis, you compute its debt ratio for 2001, 2002, and 2003 as: 0.35, 0.74, and 0.94, respectively. Based on the debt ratio, is Converse a low-risk investment? Has the risk of buying Converse stock changed over this period? (*Note:* The industry ratio averages 0.40.)

Answer—p. 72

need to compare the company's return on the borrowed money to the rate it is paying creditors. If the company's return is higher, it is successfully borrowing money to make more money. Be aware that a company's success with making money from borrowed money can quickly turn unprofitable if its own return drops below the rate it is paying creditors.

Demonstration Problem

(*Note:* This problem extends the demonstration problem of Chapter 1.) After several months of planning, Sylvia Workman started a haircutting business called Expressions. The following events occurred during its first month:

a. On August 1, Workman invested $3,000 cash and $15,000 of equipment in Expressions.
b. On August 2, Expressions paid $600 cash for furniture for the shop.
c. On August 3, Expressions paid $500 cash to rent space in a strip mall for August.
d. On August 4, it purchased $1,200 of equipment on credit for the shop (using a long-term note payable).
e. On August 5, Expressions opened for business. Cash received from services provided in the first week and a half of business (ended August 15) is $825.
f. On August 15, it provided $100 of haircutting services on account.
g. On August 17, it received a $100 check for services previously rendered on account.
h. On August 17, it paid $125 to an assistant for working during the grand opening.
i. Cash received from services provided during the second half of August is $930.
j. On August 31, it paid a $400 installment toward principal on the note payable entered into on August 4.
k. On August 31, Workman made a $900 cash withdrawal for personal use.

Required

1. Open the following ledger accounts in balance column format (account numbers are in parentheses): Cash (101); Accounts Receivable (102); Furniture (161); Store Equipment (165); Note Payable (240); S. Workman, Capital (301); S. Workman, Withdrawals (302); Haircutting Services Revenue (403); Wages Expense (623); and Rent Expense (640). Prepare general journal entries for the transactions.
2. Post the journal entries from (1) to the ledger accounts.
3. Prepare a trial balance as of August 31.
4. Prepare an income statement for August.
5. Prepare a statement of owner's equity for August.
6. Prepare a balance sheet as of August 31.
7. Determine the debt ratio as of August 31.

Extended Analysis

8. In the coming months, Expressions will experience a greater variety of business transactions. Identify which accounts are debited and which are credited for the following transactions. (*Hint:* You need to use some accounts not opened in part 1.)
   a. Purchase supplies with cash.
   b. Pay cash for future insurance coverage.
   c. Receive cash for services to be provided in the future.
   d. Purchase supplies on account.

Planning the Solution

- Analyze each transaction and use the debit and credit rules to prepare a journal entry for each.
- Post each debit and each credit from journal entries to their ledger accounts and cross-reference each amount in the posting reference (PR) columns of the journal and ledger.
- Calculate each account balance and list the accounts with their balances on a trial balance.
- Verify that total debits in the trial balance equal total credits.
- To prepare the income statement, identify revenues and expenses. List those items on the statement, compute the difference, and label the result as *net income* or *net loss*.
- Use information in the ledger to prepare the statement of owner's equity.
- Use information in the ledger to prepare the balance sheet.
- Calculate the debt ratio by dividing total liabilities by total assets.
- Analyze the future transactions to identify the accounts affected and apply debit and credit rules.

Solution to Demonstration Problem

1. General journal entries:

GENERAL JOURNAL — Page 1

Date	Account Titles and Explanation	PR	Debit	Credit
Aug. 1	Cash	101	3,000	
	Store Equipment	165	15,000	
	S. Workman, Capital	301		18,000
	Owner's investment.			
2	Furniture	161	600	
	Cash	101		600
	Purchased furniture for cash.			
3	Rent Expense	640	500	
	Cash	101		500
	Paid rent for August.			
4	Store Equipment	165	1,200	
	Note Payable	240		1,200
	Purchased additional equipment on credit.			
15	Cash	101	825	
	Haircutting Services Revenue	403		825
	Cash receipts from 10 days of operations.			
15	Accounts Receivable	102	100	
	Haircutting Services Revenue	403		100
	To record revenue for services provided on account.			
17	Cash	101	100	
	Accounts Receivable	102		100
	To record cash received as payment on account.			
17	Wages Expense	623	125	
	Cash	101		125
	Paid wages to assistant.			
31	Cash	101	930	
	Haircutting Services Revenue	403		930
	Cash receipts from second half of August.			
31	Note Payable	240	400	
	Cash	101		400
	Paid an installment on the note payable.			
31	S. Workman, Withdrawals	302	900	
	Cash	101		900
	Cash withdrawal by owner.			

2. Post journal entries from (part 1) to the ledger accounts:

General Ledger

Cash — Account No. 101

Date	PR	Debit	Credit	Balance
Aug. 1	G1	3,000		3,000
2	G1		600	2,400
3	G1		500	1,900
15	G1	825		2,725
17	G1	100		2,825
17	G1		125	2,700
31	G1	930		3,630
31	G1		400	3,230
31	G1		900	2,330

Accounts Receivable — Account No. 102

Date	PR	Debit	Credit	Balance
Aug. 15	G1	100		100
17	G1		100	0

Furniture — Account No. 161

Date	PR	Debit	Credit	Balance
Aug. 2	G1	600		600

Store Equipment — Account No. 165

Date	PR	Debit	Credit	Balance
Aug. 1	G1	15,000		15,000
4	G1	1,200		16,200

Note Payable — Account No. 240

Date	PR	Debit	Credit	Balance
Aug. 4	G1		1,200	1,200
31	G1	400		800

S. Workman, Capital — Account No. 301

Date	PR	Debit	Credit	Balance
Aug. 1	G1		18,000	18,000

S. Workman, Withdrawals — Account No. 302

Date	PR	Debit	Credit	Balance
Aug. 31	G1	900		900

Haircutting Services Revenue — Account No. 403

Date	PR	Debit	Credit	Balance
Aug. 15	G1		825	825
15	G1		100	925
31	G1		930	1,855

Wages Expense — Account No. 623

Date	PR	Debit	Credit	Balance
Aug. 17	G1	125		125

Rent Expense — Account No. 640

Date	PR	Debit	Credit	Balance
Aug. 3	G1	500		500

3. Prepare a trial balance from the ledger:

EXPRESSIONS
Trial Balance
August 31

	Debit	Credit
Cash	$ 2,330	
Accounts receivable	0	
Furniture	600	
Store equipment	16,200	
Note payable		$ 800
S. Workman, Capital		18,000
S. Workman, Withdrawals	900	
Haircutting services revenue		1,855
Wages expense	125	
Rent expense	500	
Totals	$20,655	$20,655

4.

EXPRESSIONS
Income Statement
For Month Ended August 31

Revenues		
Haircutting services revenue		$1,855
Operating expenses		
Rent expense	$500	
Wages expense	125	
Total operating expenses		625
Net Income		$1,230

5.

EXPRESSIONS
Statement of Owner's Equity
For Month Ended August 31

S. Workman, Capital, August 1		$ 0
Plus: Investments by owner	$18,000	
Net income	1,230	19,230
		19,230
Less: Withdrawals by owner		900
S. Workman, Capital, August 31		$18,330

6.

EXPRESSIONS
Balance Sheet
August 31

Assets		**Liabilities**	
Cash	$ 2,330	Note payable	$ 800
Furniture	600	**Equity**	
Store equipment	16,200	S. Workman, Capital	18,330
Total assets	$19,130	Total liabilities and equity	$19,130

7. Debt ratio $= \dfrac{\text{Total liabilities}}{\text{Total assets}} = \dfrac{\$800}{\$19{,}130} = \mathbf{4.18\%}$

8a. Supplies *debited*
Cash *credited*

8b. Prepaid Insurance *debited*
Cash *credited*

8c. Cash *debited*
Unearned Services Revenue *credited*

8d. Supplies *debited*
Accounts Payable *credited*

Summary

C1 **Explain the steps in processing transactions.** The accounting process identifies business transactions and events, analyzes and records their effects, and summarizes and prepares information useful in making decisions. Transactions and events are the starting points in the accounting process. Source documents help in their analysis. The effects of transactions and events are recorded in journals. Posting along with a trial balance helps summarize and classify these effects.

C2 Describe source documents and their purpose. Source documents identify and describe transactions and events. Examples are sales tickets, checks, purchase orders, bills, and bank statements. Source documents provide objective and reliable evidence, making information more useful.

C3 Describe an account and its use in recording transactions. An account is a detailed record of increases and decreases in a specific asset, liability, equity, revenue, or expense. Information from accounts is analyzed, summarized, and presented in reports and financial statements for decision makers.

C4 Describe a ledger and a chart of accounts. The ledger (or general ledger) is a record containing all accounts used by a company and their balances. It is referred to as the *books*. The chart of accounts is a list of all accounts and usually includes an identification number assigned to each account.

C5 Define *debits* and *credits* and explain their role in double-entry accounting. *Debit* refers to left, and *credit* refers to right. Debits increase assets, expenses, and withdrawals while credits decrease them. Credits increase liabilities, owner capital, and revenues; debits decrease them. Double-entry accounting means each transaction affects at least two accounts and has at least one debit and one credit. The system for recording debits and credits follows from the accounting equation. The left side of an account is the normal balance for assets, withdrawals, and expenses, and the right side is the normal balance for liabilities, capital, and revenues.

A1 Analyze the impact of transactions on accounts and financial statements. We analyze transactions using concepts of double-entry accounting. This analysis is performed by determining a transaction's effects on accounts. These effects are recorded in journals and posted to ledgers.

A2 Compute the debt ratio and describe its use in analyzing company performance. A company's debt ratio is computed as total liabilities divided by total assets. It reveals how much of the assets are financed by creditor (nonowner) financing. The higher this ratio, the more risk a company faces because liabilities must be repaid at specific dates.

P1 Record transactions in a journal and post entries to a ledger. Transactions are recorded in a journal. Each entry in a journal is posted to the accounts in the ledger. This provides information that is used to produce financial statements. Balance column accounts are widely used and include columns for debits, credits, and the account balance.

P2 Prepare and explain the use of a trial balance. A trial balance is a list of accounts from the ledger showing their debit or credit balances in separate columns. The trial balance is a summary of the ledger's contents and is useful in preparing financial statements and in revealing recordkeeping errors.

P3 Prepare financial statements from business transactions. The balance sheet, the statement of owner's equity, the income statement, and the statement of cash flows use data from the trial balance (and other financial statements) for their preparation.

Guidance Answers to **Decision Maker** and **Decision Ethics**

Cashier The advantages to the process proposed by the assistant manager include improved customer service, fewer delays, and less work for you. However, you should have serious concerns about internal control and the potential for fraud. In particular, the assistant manager could steal cash and simply enter fewer sales to match the remaining cash. You should reject her suggestion without the manager's approval. Moreover, you should have an ethical concern about the assistant manager's suggestion to ignore store policy.

Entrepreneur We can use the accounting equation (Assets = Liabilities + Equity) to help us identify risky customers to whom we would likely not want to extend credit. A balance sheet provides amounts for each of these key components. The lower a customer's equity is relative to liabilities, the less likely you would extend credit. A low equity means the business has little value that does not already have creditor claims to it.

Investor The debt ratio suggests the stock of Converse is of higher risk than normal and that this risk is rising. The average industry ratio of 0.40 further supports this conclusion. The 2003 debt ratio for Converse is twice the industry norm. Also, a debt ratio approaching 1.0 indicates little to no equity.

Guidance Answers to **Quick Checks**

1. Examples of source documents are sales tickets, checks, purchase orders, charges to customers, bills from suppliers, employee earnings records, and bank statements.
2. Source documents serve many purposes, including recordkeeping and internal control. Source documents, especially if obtained from outside the organization, provide objective and reliable evidence about transactions and their amounts.
3.

Assets	Liabilities	Equity
a,c,e	b,d	—

4. An account is a record in an accounting system that records and stores the increases and decreases in a specific asset, liability, equity, revenue, or expense. The ledger is a collection of all the accounts of a company.

5. A company's size and diversity affect the number of accounts in its accounting system. The types of accounts depend on information the company needs to both effectively operate and report its activities in financial statements.

6. No. Debit and credit both can mean increase or decrease. The particular meaning in a circumstance depends on the *type of account*. For example, a debit increases the balance of asset, withdrawals, and expense accounts, but it decreases the balance of liability, capital, and revenue accounts.

7. A chart of accounts is a list of all of a company's accounts and their identification numbers.

8. Equity is increased by revenues and by owner investments. Equity is decreased by expenses and owner withdrawals.

9. The name *double entry* is used because all transactions affect at least two accounts. There must be at least one debit in one account and at least one credit in another account.

10. Answer is (*c*).

11.

Cash	15,000	
Equipment	23,000	
Owner, Capital		38,000
Investment by owner of cash and equipment.		

12. A compound journal entry affects three or more accounts.

13. Posting reference numbers are entered in the journal when posting to the ledger as a cross-reference that allows the record-keeper or auditor to trace debits and credits from one record to another.

14. At a minimum, dollar signs are placed beside the first and last numbers in a column. It is also common to place dollar signs beside any amount that appears after a ruled line to indicate that an addition or subtraction has occurred.

15. The Equipment account balance is incorrectly reported at $20,000—it should be $28,000. The effect of this error understates the trial balance's Debit column total by $8,000. This results in an $8,000 difference between the column totals.

16. An income statement reports a company's revenues and expenses along with the resulting net income or loss. A statement of owner's equity reports changes in equity, including that from net income or loss. Both statements report transactions occurring over a period of time.

17. The balance sheet describes a company's financial position (assets, liabilities, and equity) at a point in time. The capital account in the balance sheet is obtained from the statement of owner's equity.

18. Revenues are inflows of assets in exchange for products or services provided to customers as part of the main operations of a business. Expenses are outflows or the using up of assets that result from providing products or services to customers.

19. Assets are the resources a business owns or controls that carry expected future benefits. Liabilities are the obligations of a business, representing the claims of others against the assets of a business. Equity reflects the owner's claims on the assets of the business after deducting liabilities.

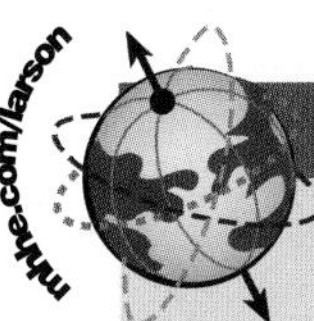

Key Terms

Key Terms are available at the book's Website for learning and testing in an online Flashcard Format.

Account (p. 49)
Account balance (p. 53)
Balance column account (p. 56)
Chart of accounts (p. 52)
Compound journal entry (p. 59)
Credit (p. 53)
Creditors (p. 50)
Debit (p. 53)
Debt ratio (p. 67)
Double-entry accounting (p. 53)
General journal (p. 55)
Journal (p. 55)
Journalizing (p. 55)
Ledger (p. 49)
Owner, capital (p. 51)
Posting (p. 55)
Posting reference (PR) column (p. 56)
Source documents (p. 49)
T-account (p. 53)
Trial balance (p. 63)
Unearned revenue (p. 51)

Personal Interactive Quiz

Personal Interactive Quizzes A and B are available at the book's Website to reinforce and assess your learning.

Discussion Questions

1. Provide the names of two (*a*) asset accounts, (*b*) liability accounts, and (*c*) equity accounts.
2. What is the difference between a note payable and an account payable?
3. Discuss the steps in processing business transactions.
4. What kinds of transactions can be recorded in a general journal?
5. Are debits or credits typically listed first in general journal entries? Are the debits or the credits indented?

6. If assets are valuable resources and asset accounts have debit balances, why do expense accounts have debit balances?

7. Should a transaction be recorded first in a journal or the ledger? Why?

8. Why does the recordkeeper prepare a trial balance?

9. If a wrong amount is journalized and posted to the accounts, how should the error be corrected?

10. Identify the four financial statements of a business.

11. What information is reported in an income statement?

12. Why does the user of an income statement need to know the time period that it covers?

13. What information is reported in a balance sheet?

14. Define (*a*) *assets,* (*b*) *liabilities,* (*c*) *equity,* and (*d*) *net assets.*

15. Which financial statement is sometimes called the *statement of financial position?*

16. Review the **Krispy Kreme** balance sheet in Appendix A. Identify three accounts on its balance sheet that carry debit balances and three accounts on its balance sheet that carry credit balances.

17. Review the **Tastykake** balance sheet in Appendix A. Identify two different liability accounts that include the word *payable* in the account title.

18. Locate **Harley-Davidson**'s income statement in Appendix A. What is the title of its revenue account?

Red numbers denote Discussion Questions that involve decision-making.

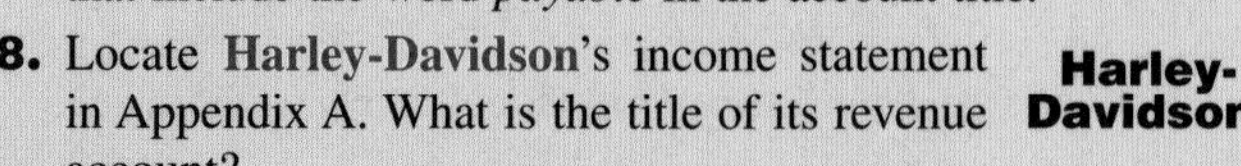

Homework Manager *repeats all Quick Study assignments on the book's Website with new numbers each time they are worked. It can be used in practice, homework, or exam mode.*

QUICK STUDY

QS 2-1
Identifying source documents
C2

Identify the items from the following list that are likely to serve as source documents:

a. Bank statement
b. Sales ticket
c. Income statement
d. Trial balance
e. Telephone bill
f. Invoice from supplier
g. Company revenue account
h. Balance sheet
i. Prepaid insurance

QS 2-2
Identifying financial statement items
C3 P3

Identify the financial statement(s) where each of the following items appears. Use I for income statement, E for statement of owner's equity, and B for balance sheet:

a. Service fees earned
b. Owner cash withdrawal
c. Office equipment
d. Accounts payable
e. Cash
f. Utilities expenses
g. Office supplies
h. Prepaid rent
i. Unearned fees

QS 2-3
Linking debit or credit with normal balance
C5

Indicate whether a debit or credit *decreases* the normal balance of each of the following accounts:

a. Office Supplies
b. Repair Services Revenue
c. Interest Payable
d. Accounts Receivable
e. Salaries Expense
f. Owner Capital
g. Prepaid Insurance
h. Buildings
i. Interest Revenue
j. Owner Withdrawals
k. Unearned Revenue
l. Accounts Payable

QS 2-4
Analyzing debit or credit by account
C5 A1

Identify whether a debit or credit yields the indicated change for each of the following accounts:

a. To increase Store Equipment
b. To increase Owner Withdrawals
c. To decrease Cash
d. To increase Utilities Expense
e. To increase Fees Earned
f. To decrease Unearned Revenue
g. To decrease Prepaid Insurance
h. To increase Notes Payable
i. To decrease Accounts Receivable
j. To increase Owner Capital

QS 2-5
Identifying normal balance
C5

Identify whether the normal balances (in parentheses) assigned to the following accounts are correct or incorrect.

a. Office supplies (Debit)
b. Owner Withdrawals (Credit)
c. Fees Earned (Debit)
d. Wages Expense (Credit)
e. Cash (Debit)
f. Prepaid Insurance (Credit)
g. Wages Payable (Credit)
h. Building (Debit)

QS 2-6
Preparing journal entries
P1

Prepare journal entries for each of the following selected transactions:

a. On January 13, Chico Chavez opens a landscaping business called Showcase Yards by investing $70,000 cash along with equipment having a $30,000 value.

b. On January 21, Showcase Yards purchases office supplies on credit for $280.

c. On January 29, Showcase Yards receives $7,800 cash for performing landscaping services.

d. On January 30, Showcase Yards receives $1,000 cash in advance of providing landscaping services to a customer.

QS 2-7
Identifying a posting error
P2 

A trial balance has total debits of $20,000 and total credits of $24,500. Which one of the following errors would create this imbalance? Explain.

a. A $2,250 debit to Rent Expense in a journal entry is incorrectly posted to the ledger as a $2,250 credit, leaving the Rent Expense account with a $3,000 debit balance.

b. A $4,500 debit to Salaries Expense in a journal entry is incorrectly posted to the ledger as a $4,500 credit, leaving the Salaries Expense account with a $750 debit balance.

c. A $2,250 credit to Consulting Fees Earned in a journal entry is incorrectly posted to the ledger as a $2,250 debit, leaving the Consulting Fees Earned account with a $6,300 credit balance.

QS 2-8
Classifying accounts in financial statements
P3

Indicate the financial statement on which each of the following items appears. Use I for income statement, E for statement of owner's equity, and B for balance sheet:

a. Office Supplies
b. Services Revenue
c. Interest Payable
d. Accounts Receivable
e. Salaries Expense
f. Equipment
g. Prepaid Insurance
h. Buildings
i. Interest Revenue
j. Withdrawals

Homework Manager *repeats all Exercises on the book's Website with new numbers each time they are worked. It can be used in practice, homework, or exam mode.*

EXERCISES

Exercise 2-1
Identifying type and normal balances of accounts
C3 C5

For each of the following (1) identify the type of account as an asset, liability, equity, revenue, or expense, (2) enter *debit* (*Dr.*) or *credit* (*Cr.*) to identify the kind of entry that would increase the account balance, and (3) identify the normal balance of the account.

a. Unearned Revenue
b. Accounts Payable
c. Postage Expense
d. Prepaid Insurance
e. Land
f. Owner Capital
g. Accounts Receivable
h. Owner Withdrawals
i. Cash
j. Equipment
k. Fees Earned
l. Wages Expense

Exercise 2-2
Analyzing effects of transactions on accounts
A1 

Tavon Co. recently notified a client that it must pay a $48,000 fee for services provided. Tavon agreed to accept the following three items in full payment: (1) $7,500 cash, (2) computer equipment worth $75,000, and (3) assume responsibility for a $34,500 note payable related to the computer equipment. The entry Tavon makes to record this transaction includes which one or more of the following?

a. $34,500 increase in a liability account
b. $7,500 increase in the Cash account
c. $7,500 increase in a revenue account
d. $48,000 increase in an asset account
e. $48,000 increase in a revenue account

Exercise 2-3
Analyzing account entries and balances
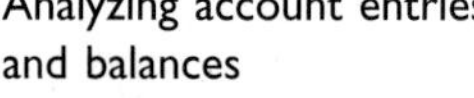
A1 

Use the information in each of the following separate cases to calculate the unknown amount:

a. During October, Shandra Company had $97,500 of cash receipts and $101,250 of cash disbursements. The October 31 Cash balance was $16,800. Determine how much cash the company had at the close of business on September 30.

b. On September 30, Li Ming Co. had a $97,500 balance in Accounts Receivable. During October, the company collected $88,950 from its credit customers. The October 31 balance in Accounts Receivable was $100,500. Determine the amount of sales on account that occurred in October.

c. Nasser Co. had $147,000 of accounts payable on September 30 and $136,500 on October 31. Total purchases on account during October were $270,000. Determine how much cash was paid on accounts payable during October.

Exercise 2-4
Preparing general journal entries
A1 P1

Prepare general journal entries for the following transactions of a new business called Pose for Pics.

Aug.	1	Hashim Paris, the owner, invested $7,500 cash and $32,500 of photography equipment in the business.
	1	Paid $3,000 cash for an insurance policy covering the next 24 months.
	5	Purchased office supplies for $1,400 cash.
	20	Received $2,650 cash in photography fees earned.
	31	Paid $875 cash for August utilities.

Exercise 2-5
Preparing T-accounts and a trial balance
C3 P2

Use the information in Exercise 2-4 to prepare an August 31 trial balance for Pose-for-Pics. Open these T-accounts: Cash; Office Supplies; Prepaid Insurance; Photography Equipment; H. Paris, Capital; Photography Fees Earned; and Utilities Expense. Post the general journal entries to these T-accounts (which will serve as the ledger), and prepare a trial balance.

Exercise 2-6
Recording effects of transactions in T-accounts
C5 A1

Record the transactions below for Dejonge Company by recording the debit and credit entries directly in the following T-accounts: Cash; Accounts Receivable; Office Supplies; Office Equipment; Accounts Payable; Dejonge, Capital; Dejonge, Withdrawals; Fees Earned; and Rent Expense. Use the letters beside each transaction to identify entries. Determine the ending balance of each T-account.

a. Robert Dejonge invested $12,750 cash in the business.

b. Purchased office supplies for $375 cash.

c. Purchased $7,050 of office equipment on credit.

d. Received $1,500 cash as fees for services provided to a customer.

e. Paid $7,050 cash to settle the payable for the office equipment purchased in transaction *c*.

f. Billed a customer $2,700 as fees for services provided.

g. Paid the monthly rent with $525 cash.

h. Collected $1,125 cash toward the account receivable created in transaction *f*.

i. Dejonge withdrew $1,000 cash for personal use.

Check Cash ending balance, $6,425

Exercise 2-7
Preparing a trial balance P2

After recording the transactions of Exercise 2-6 in T-accounts and calculating the balance of each account, prepare a trial balance. Use May 31, 2005, as its report date.

Exercise 2-8
Analyzing and journalizing revenue transactions
A1 P1 

Examine the following transactions and identify those that create revenues for Jade Services, a company owned by Mia Jade. Prepare general journal entries to record those transactions and explain why the other transactions did not create revenues.

a. Mia Jade invests $38,250 cash in the business.
b. Provided $1,350 of services on credit.
c. Provided services to a client and received $1,575 cash.
d. Received $9,150 cash from a client in payment for services to be provided next year.
e. Received $4,500 cash from a client in partial payment of an account receivable.
f. Borrowed $150,000 cash from the bank by signing a promissory note.

Exercise 2-9
Analyzing and journalizing expense transactions
A1 P1 

Examine the following transactions and identify those that create expenses for Jade Services. Prepare general journal entries to record those transactions and explain why the other transactions did not create expenses.

a. Paid $14,100 cash for office supplies that were purchased more than 1 year ago.
b. Paid $1,125 cash for the two-week salary of the receptionist.
c. Paid $45,000 cash for equipment.
d. Paid $930 cash for monthly utilities.
e. Owner withdrew $5,000 cash for personal use.

Exercise 2-10
Preparing an income statement
C4 P3

On October 1, Ming Lue organized a new consulting firm called Tech Today. On October 31, the company's records show the following items and amounts. Use this information to prepare an October income statement for the business.

Cash	$ 8,360	M. Lue, Withdrawals	$ 3,000
Accounts receivable	17,000	Consulting fees earned	17,000
Office supplies	3,250	Rent expense	4,550
Patents	46,000	Salaries expense	8,000
Office equipment	18,000	Telephone expense	560
Accounts payable	8,000	Miscellaneous expenses	280
M. Lue, Capital	84,000		

Check Net income, $3,610

Exercise 2-11
Preparing a statement of owner's equity P3

Use the information in Exercise 2-10 to prepare an October statement of owner's equity for Tech Today.

Exercise 2-12
Preparing a balance sheet P3

Use the information in Exercise 2-10 (if completed, you can also use your solution to Exercise 2-11) to prepare an October 31 balance sheet for Tech Today.

Exercise 2-13
Computing net income
A1 P3 

A sole proprietorship had the following assets and liabilities at the beginning and end of a recent year:

	Assets	Liabilities
Beginning of the year	$ 70,000	$30,000
End of the year	115,000	46,000

Determine the net income earned or net loss incurred by the business during the year for each of the following *separate* cases:

a. Owner made no investments in the business and withdrew no assets during the year.

b. Owner made no investments in the business but withdrew $1,250 per month for personal use.

c. Owner withdrew no assets during the year but invested an additional $45,000 cash.

d. Owner withdrew $1,250 per month for personal use and invested an additional $25,000 cash.

Exercise 2-14
Analyzing changes in a company's equity
C5 P3

Compute the missing amount in each of the following separate companies *a* through *d*:

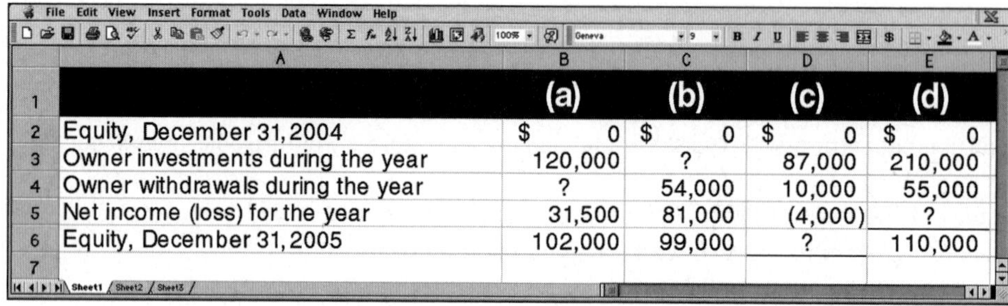

	A	B	C	D	E
1		(a)	(b)	(c)	(d)
2	Equity, December 31, 2004	$ 0	$ 0	$ 0	$ 0
3	Owner investments during the year	120,000	?	87,000	210,000
4	Owner withdrawals during the year	?	54,000	10,000	55,000
5	Net income (loss) for the year	31,500	81,000	(4,000)	?
6	Equity, December 31, 2005	102,000	99,000	?	110,000
7					

Exercise 2-15
Interpreting and describing transactions from T-accounts
C1 A1

Assume the following T-accounts reflect Joy Co.'s general ledger and that seven transactions *a* through *g* are posted to them. Provide a short description of each transaction. Include the amounts in your descriptions.

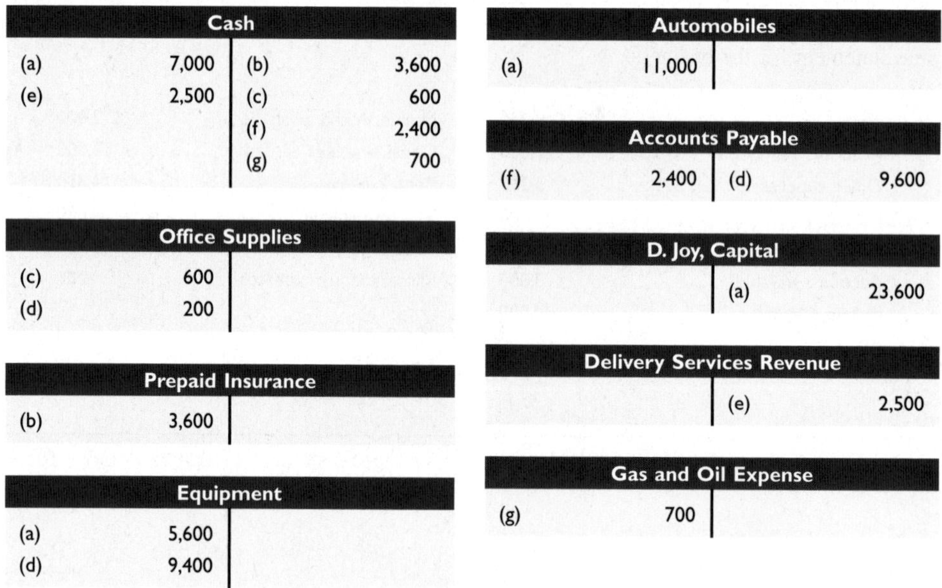

Cash

	Debit		Credit
(a)	7,000	(b)	3,600
(e)	2,500	(c)	600
		(f)	2,400
		(g)	700

Office Supplies

	Debit		Credit
(c)	600		
(d)	200		

Prepaid Insurance

	Debit		Credit
(b)	3,600		

Equipment

	Debit		Credit
(a)	5,600		
(d)	9,400		

Automobiles

	Debit		Credit
(a)	11,000		

Accounts Payable

	Debit		Credit
(f)	2,400	(d)	9,600

D. Joy, Capital

	Debit		Credit
		(a)	23,600

Delivery Services Revenue

	Debit		Credit
		(e)	2,500

Gas and Oil Expense

	Debit		Credit
(g)	700		

Exercise 2-16
Preparing general journal entries A1 P1

Use information from the T-accounts in Exercise 2-15 to prepare general journal entries for each of the seven transaction *a* through *g*.

Exercise 2-17
Identifying effects of posting errors on the trial balance A1 P2

Posting errors are identified in the following table. In column (1), enter the amount of the difference between the two (debit and credit) trial balance columns due to the error. In column (2), identify the trial balance column (debit or credit) with the larger amount if they are not equal. In column (3), identify the account(s) affected by the error. In column (4), indicate the amount by which the account(s) in column (3) is (are) under- or overstated. Answers for the first error are given.

	Description of Posting Error	(1) Difference between Debit and Credit Columns	(2) Column with the Larger Total	(3) Identify Account(s) Incorrectly Stated	(4) Amount that Account(s) is Over- or Understated
a.	$2,400 debit to Rent Expense is posted as a $1,590 debit.	$810	Credit	Rent Expense	Rent Expense understated $810
b.	$4,050 credit to Cash is posted twice as two credits to Cash.				
c.	$9,900 debit to the owner's withdrawals account is debited to owner's capital.				
d.	$2,250 debit to Prepaid Insurance is posted as a debit to Insurance Expense.				
e.	$42,000 debit to Machinery is posted as a debit to Accounts Payable.				
f.	$4,950 credit to Services Revenue is posted as a $495 credit.				
g.	$1,440 debit to Store Supplies is not posted.				

Exercise 2-18
Analyzing a trial balance error
A1 P2

You are told the column totals in a trial balance are not equal. After careful analysis, you discover only one error. Specifically, a correctly journalized credit purchase of a computer for $16,950 is posted from the journal to the ledger with a $16,950 debit to Office Equipment and another $16,950 debit to Accounts Payable. The balance of the Office Equipment account has a debit balance of $40,100 on the trial balance. Answer each of the following questions and compute the dollar amount of any misstatement:

a. Is the debit column total of the trial balance overstated, understated, or correctly stated?

b. Is the credit column total of the trial balance overstated, understated, or correctly stated?

c. Is the balance of the Office Equipment account overstated, understated, or correctly stated in the trial balance?

d. Is the balance of the Accounts Payable account overstated, understated, or correctly stated in the trial balance?

e. If the debit column total of the trial balance is $360,000 before correcting the error, what is the total of the credit column before correction?

Exercise 2-19
Interpreting the debt ratio and return on assets
A2 

a. Calculate the debt ratio and the return on assets using the year-end information for each of the following six separate companies ($ in thousands):

Case	Assets	Liabilities	Average Assets	Net Income
Company 1	$ 90,500	$ 12,000	$ 100,000	$ 20,000
Company 2	64,000	47,000	40,000	3,800
Company 3	32,500	26,500	50,000	660
Company 4	147,000	56,000	200,000	21,000
Company 5	92,000	31,000	40,000	7,500
Company 6	104,500	51,500	70,000	12,000

b. Of the six companies, which business relies most heavily on creditor financing?

c. Of the six companies, which business relies most heavily on equity financing?

d. Which two companies indicate the greatest risk?

e. Which two companies earn the highest return on assets?

f. Which one company would investors likely prefer based on the risk-return relation?

PROBLEM SET A

Problem 2-1A

Preparing and posting general journal entries; preparing a trial balance

C4 C5 A1 P1 P2

Roberto Ricci opens a computer consulting business called Viva Consultants and completes the following transactions in its first month of operations:

April 1 Ricci invests $100,000 cash along with office equipment valued at $24,000 in the business.
2 Prepaid $7,200 cash for twelve months' rent for office space. (*Hint:* Debit Prepaid Rent for $7,200.)
3 Made credit purchases for $12,000 in office equipment and $2,400 in office supplies. Payment is due within 10 days.
6 Completed services for a client and immediately received $2,000 cash.
9 Completed an $8,000 project for a client, who must pay within 30 days.
13 Paid $14,400 cash to settle the account payable created on April 3.
19 Paid $6,000 cash for the premium on a 12-month insurance policy. (*Hint:* Debit Prepaid Insurance for $6,000.)
22 Received $6,400 cash as partial payment for the work completed on April 9.
25 Completed work for another client for $2,640 on credit.
28 Ricci withdrew $6,200 cash for personal use.
29 Purchased $800 of additional office supplies on credit.
30 Paid $700 cash for this month's utility bill.

Required

1. Prepare general journal entries to record these transactions (use account titles listed in part 2).

2. Open the following ledger accounts—their account numbers are in parentheses (use the balance column format): Cash (101); Accounts Receivable (106); Office Supplies (124); Prepaid Insurance (128); Prepaid Rent (131); Office Equipment (163); Accounts Payable (201); R. Ricci, Capital (301); R. Ricci, Withdrawals (302); Services Revenue (403); and Utilities Expense (690). Post journal entries from part 1 to the ledger accounts and enter the balance after each posting.

3. Prepare a trial balance as of the end of this month's operations.

Check (2) Ending balances: Cash, $73,900; Accounts Receivable, $4,240; Accounts Payable, $800

(3) Total debits, $137,440

Problem 2-2A

Preparing and posting journal entries; preparing a trial balance

C4 C5 A1 P1 P2

Shelton Engineering completed the following transactions in the month of June.

a. Shania Shelton, the owner, invested $105,000 cash, office equipment with a value of $6,000, and $45,000 of drafting equipment to launch the business.

b. Purchased land worth $54,000 for an office by paying $5,400 cash and signing a long-term note payable for $48,600.

c. Purchased a portable building with $75,000 cash and moved it onto the land acquired in *b*.

d. Paid $6,000 cash for the premium on an 18-month insurance policy.

e. Completed and delivered a set of plans for a client and collected $5,700 cash.

f. Purchased $22,500 of additional drafting equipment by paying $10,500 cash and signing a long-term note payable for $12,000.

g. Completed $12,000 of engineering services for a client. This amount is to be received in 30 days.

h. Purchased $2,250 of additional office equipment on credit.

i. Completed engineering services for $18,000 on credit.

j. Received a bill for rent of equipment that was used on a recently completed job. The $1,200 rent must be paid within 30 days.

k. Collected $7,200 cash in partial payment from the client described in transaction *g*.

l. Paid $1,500 cash for wages to a drafting assistant.

m. Paid $2,250 cash to settle the account payable created in transaction *h*.

n. Paid $675 cash for minor repairs to the drafting equipment.

o. Shelton withdrew $9,360 cash for personal use.

p. Paid $1,500 cash for wages to a drafting assistant.

q. Paid $3,000 cash for advertisements in the local newspaper during June.

Required

1. Prepare general journal entries to record these transactions (use the account titles listed in part 2).

2. Open the following accounts—their account numbers are in parentheses (use the balance column format): Cash (101); Accounts Receivable (106); Prepaid Insurance (108); Office Equipment (163); Drafting Equipment (164); Building (170); Land (172); Accounts Payable (201); Notes Payable (250); S. Shelton, Capital (301); S. Shelton, Withdrawals (302); Engineering Fees Earned (402); Wages Expense (601); Equipment Rental Expense (602); Advertising Expense (603); and Repairs Expense (604). Post the journal entries from part 1 to the accounts and enter the balance after each posting.

3. Prepare a trial balance as of the end of this month's operations.

Check (2) Ending balances: Cash, $2,715; Accounts Receivable, $22,800; Accounts Payable, $1,200

(3) Trial balance totals, $253,500

Problem 2-3A
Preparing and posting general journal entries; preparing a trial balance

C4 C5 A1 P1 P2

mhhe.com/larson

Santo Birch opens a Web consulting business called Show-Me-the-Money Consultants and completes the following transactions in March:

March 1 Birch invested $150,000 cash along with $22,000 of office equipment in the business.
2 Prepaid $6,000 cash for six months' rent for an office. (*Hint:* Debit Prepaid Rent for $6,000.)
3 Made credit purchases of office equipment for $3,000 and office supplies for $1,200. Payment is due within 10 days.
6 Completed services for a client and immediately received $4,000 cash.
9 Completed a $7,500 project for a client, who must pay within 30 days.
10 Paid $4,200 cash to settle the account payable created on March 3.
19 Paid $5,000 cash for the premium on a 12-month insurance policy.
22 Received $3,500 cash as partial payment for the work completed on March 9.
25 Completed work for another client for $3,820 on credit.
29 Birch withdrew $5,100 cash for personal use.
30 Purchased $600 of additional office supplies on credit.
31 Paid $200 cash for this month's utility bill.

Required

1. Prepare general journal entries to record these transactions (use the account titles listed in part 2).

2. Open the following accounts—their account numbers are in parentheses (use the balance column format): Cash (101); Accounts Receivable (106); Office Supplies (124); Prepaid Insurance (128); Prepaid Rent (131); Office Equipment (163); Accounts Payable (201); S. Birch, Capital (301); S. Birch, Withdrawals (302); Services Revenue (403); and Utilities Expense (690). Post the journal entries from part 1 to the accounts and enter the balance after each posting.

3. Prepare a trial balance as of the end of this month's operations.

Check (2) Ending balances: Cash, $137,000; Accounts Receivable, $7,820; Accounts Payable, $600

(3) Total debits, $187,920

Problem 2-4A
Computing net income from equity analysis, preparing a balance sheet, and calculating the debt ratio

C3 A1 A2 P3

mhhe.com/larson

The accounting records of Crist Crate Services show the following assets and liabilities as of December 31, 2004, and 2005:

	December 31	
	2004	2005
Cash	$ 52,500	$ 18,750
Accounts receivable	28,500	22,350
Office supplies	4,500	3,300
Office equipment	138,000	147,000
Trucks	54,000	54,000
Building	0	180,000
Land	0	45,000
Accounts payable	7,500	37,500
Note payable	0	105,000

Late in December 2005, the business purchased a small office building and land for $225,000. The business paid $120,000 cash toward the purchase and a $105,000 note payable was signed for the balance. Crist had to invest $35,000 cash in the business to enable it to pay the $120,000 cash. Crist also withdraws $3,000 cash per month from the business for personal use.

Required

1. Prepare balance sheets for the business as of December 31, 2004, and 2005. (Remember that total equity equals the difference between assets and liabilities.)
2. By comparing equity amounts from the balance sheets and using the additional information presented in this problem, prepare a calculation to show how much net income was earned by the business during 2005.
3. Compute the 2005 year-end debt ratio for the business.

Check (2) Net income, $58,900

(3) Debt ratio, 30.29%

Problem 2-5A
Analyzing account balances and reconstructing transactions

C1 C4 A1 P2 

Carlos Beltran started an engineering firm called Beltran Engineering. He began operations and completed seven transactions in May, which included his initial investment of $17,000 cash. After these transactions, the ledger included the following accounts with normal balances:

Cash	$26,660
Office supplies	660
Prepaid insurance	3,200
Office equipment	16,500
Accounts payable	16,500
C. Beltran, Capital	17,000
C. Beltran, Withdrawals	3,740
Engineering fees earned	24,000
Rent expense	6,740

Required

1. Prepare a trial balance for this business at the end of May.

Check (1) Trial balance totals, $57,500

Analysis Components

2. Analyze the accounts and their balances and prepare a list that describes each of the seven most likely transactions and their amounts.
3. Prepare a report of cash received and cash paid showing how the seven transactions in part 2 yield the $26,660 ending Cash balance.

(3) Cash paid, $14,340

Problem 2-6A
Recording transactions; posting to ledger; preparing a trial balance

C4 A1 P1 P2

Business transactions completed by Eric Piburn during the month of September are as follows:

a. Piburn invested $23,000 cash along with office equipment valued at $12,000 in a new sole proprietorship named EP Consulting.
b. Purchased land valued at $8,000 and a building valued at $33,000. The purchase is paid with $15,000 cash and a long-term note payable for $26,000.
c. Purchased $600 of office supplies on credit.
d. Piburn invested his personal automobile in the business. The automobile has a value of $7,000 and is to be used exclusively in the business.
e. Purchased $1,100 of additional office equipment on credit.
f. Paid $800 cash salary to an assistant.
g. Provided services to a client and collected $2,700 cash.
h. Paid $430 cash for this month's utilities.
i. Paid $600 cash to settle the account payable created in transaction *c*.
j. Purchased $4,000 of new office equipment by paying $2,400 cash and trading in old equipment with a recorded net cost and value of $1,600. (*Hint:* Credit Office Equipment (old) for $1,600.)

k. Completed $2,400 of services for a client, who must pay within 30 days.
l. Paid $800 cash salary to an assistant.
m. Received $1,000 cash on the receivable created in transaction *k*.
n. Piburn withdrew $1,050 cash from the business for personal use.

Required

1. Prepare general journal entries to record these transactions (use the account titles listed in part 2).
2. Open the following accounts—their account numbers are in parentheses (use the balance column format): Cash (101); Accounts Receivable (106); Office Supplies (108); Office Equipment (163); Automobiles (164); Building (170); Land (172); Accounts Payable (201); Notes Payable (250); E. Piburn, Capital (301); E. Piburn, Withdrawals (302); Fees Earned (402); Salaries Expense (601); and Utilities Expense (602). Post the journal entries from part 1 to the accounts and enter the balance after each posting.
3. Prepare a trial balance as of the end of this month's operations.

Check (2) Ending balances: Cash, $5,620; Office Equipment, $15,500

(3) Trial balance totals, $74,200

PROBLEM SET B

Problem 2-1B
Preparing and posting general journal entries; preparing a trial balance
C4 C5 A1 P1 P2

Lummus Management Services opens for business and completes these transactions in September:

Sept. 1 Rhonda Lummus, the owner, invests $28,000 cash along with office equipment valued at $25,000 in the business.
2 Prepaid $10,500 cash for twelve months' rent for office space. (*Hint:* Debit Prepaid Rent for $10,500.)
4 Made credit purchases for $9,000 in office equipment and $1,200 in office supplies. Payment is due within 10 days.
8 Completed work for a client and immediately received $2,600 cash.
12 Completed a $13,400 project for a client, who must pay within 20 days.
13 Paid $10,200 cash to settle the account payable created on September 4.
19 Paid $5,200 cash for the premium on an 18-month insurance policy. (*Hint:* Debit Prepaid Insurance for $5,200.)
22 Received $7,800 cash as partial payment for the work completed on September 12.
24 Completed work for another client for $1,900 on credit.
28 Lummus withdrew $5,300 cash for personal use.
29 Purchased $1,700 of additional office supplies on credit.
30 Paid $460 cash for this month's utility bill.

Required

1. Prepare general journal entries to record these transactions (use account titles listed in part 2).
2. Open the following ledger accounts—their account numbers are in parentheses (use the balance column format): Cash (101); Accounts Receivable (106); Office Supplies (124); Prepaid Insurance (128); Prepaid Rent (131); Office Equipment (163); Accounts Payable (201); R. Lummus, Capital (301); R. Lummus, Withdrawals (302); Service Fees Earned (401); and Utilities Expense (690). Post journal entries from part 1 to the ledger accounts and enter the balance after each posting.
3. Prepare a trial balance as of the end of this month's operations.

Check (2) Ending balances: Cash, $6,740; Accounts Receivable, $7,500; Accounts Payable, $1,700

(3) Total debits, $72,600

Problem 2-2B
Preparing and posting journal entries; preparing a trial balance
C4 C5 A1 P1 P2 

At the beginning of April, Brooke Grechus launched a custom computer programming company called Softways. The company had the following transactions during April:

a. Brooke Grechus invested $45,000 cash, office equipment with a value of $4,500, and $28,000 of computer equipment in the company.
b. Purchased land worth $24,000 for an office by paying $4,800 cash and signing a long-term note payable for $19,200.
c. Purchased a portable building with $21,000 cash and moved it onto the land acquired in *b*.

d. Paid $6,600 cash for the premium on a two-year insurance policy.
e. Provided services to a client and collected $3,200 cash.
f. Purchased $3,500 of additional computer equipment by paying $700 cash and signing a long-term note payable for $2,800.
g. Completed $3,750 of services for a client. This amount is to be received within 30 days.
h. Purchased $750 of additional office equipment on credit.
i. Completed client services for $9,200 on credit.
j. Received a bill for rent of a computer testing device that was used on a recently completed job. The $320 rent must be paid within 30 days.
k. Collected $4,600 cash from the client described in transaction *i*.
l. Paid $1,600 cash for wages to an assistant.
m. Paid $750 cash to settle the account payable created in transaction *h*.
n. Paid $425 cash for minor repairs to the computer equipment.
o. Grechus withdrew $3,875 cash for personal use.
p. Paid $1,600 cash for wages to an assistant.
q. Paid $800 cash for advertisements in the local newspaper during April.

Required

1. Prepare general journal entries to record these transactions (use the account titles listed in part 2).

Check (2) Ending balances: Cash, $10,650; Accounts Receivable, $8,350; Accounts Payable, $320

2. Open the following accounts—their account numbers are in parentheses (use the balance column format): Cash (101); Accounts Receivable (106); Prepaid Insurance (108); Office Equipment (163); Computer Equipment (164); Building (170); Land (172); Accounts Payable (201); Notes Payable (250); B. Grechus, Capital (301); B. Grechus, Withdrawals (302); Fees Earned (402); Wages Expense (601); Computer Rental Expense (602); Advertising Expense (603); and Repairs Expense (604). Post the journal entries from part 1 to the accounts and enter the balance after each posting.

(3) Trial balance totals, $115,970

3. Prepare a trial balance as of the end of this month's operations.

Problem 2-3B
Preparing and posting general journal entries; preparing a trial balance
C4 C5 A1 P1 P2

Shaw Management Services opens for business and completes these transactions in November:

Nov.	1	Kita Shaw, the owner, invested $30,000 cash along with $15,000 of office equipment in the business.
	2	Prepaid $4,500 cash for six months' rent for an office. (*Hint:* Debit Prepaid Rent for $4,500.)
	4	Made credit purchases of office equipment for $2,500 and of office supplies for $600. Payment is due within 10 days.
	8	Completed work for a client and immediately received $3,400 cash.
	12	Completed a $10,200 project for a client, who must pay within 30 days.
	13	Paid $3,100 cash to settle the account payable created on November 4.
	19	Paid $1,800 cash for the premium on a 24-month insurance policy.
	22	Received $5,200 cash as partial payment for the work completed on November 12.
	24	Completed work for another client for $1,750 on credit.
	28	Shaw withdrew $5,300 cash for personal use.
	29	Purchased $249 of additional office supplies on credit.
	30	Paid $531 cash for this month's utility bill.

Required

1. Prepare general journal entries to record these transactions (use account titles listed in part 2).

Check (2) Ending balances: Cash, $23,369; Accounts Receivable, $6,750; Accounts Payable, $249

2. Open the following accounts—their account numbers are in parentheses (use the balance column format): Cash (101); Accounts Receivable (106); Office Supplies (124); Prepaid Insurance (128); Prepaid Rent (131); Office Equipment (163); Accounts Payable (201); K. Shaw, Capital (301); K. Shaw, Withdrawals (302); Services Revenue (403); and Utilities Expense (690). Post the journal entries from part 1 to the accounts and enter the balance after each posting.

(3) Total debits, $60,599

3. Prepare a trial balance as of the end of this month's operations.

Problem 2-4B
Computing net income from equity analysis, preparing a balance sheet, and computing the debt ratio

C3 A1 A2 P3 

The accounting records of Schmit Co. show the following assets and liabilities as of December 31, 2004, and 2005:

	December 31	
	2004	2005
Cash	$14,000	$ 10,000
Accounts receivable	25,000	30,000
Office supplies	10,000	12,500
Office equipment	60,000	60,000
Machinery	30,500	30,500
Building	0	260,000
Land	0	65,000
Accounts payable	5,000	15,000
Note payable	0	260,000

Late in December 2005, the business purchased a small office building and land for $325,000. The business paid $65,000 cash toward the purchase and a $260,000 note payable was signed for the balance. Schmit had to invest an additional $25,000 cash to enable it to pay the $65,000 cash. Schmit also withdraws $1,000 cash per month from the business for personal use.

Required

1. Prepare balance sheets for the business as of December 31, 2004, and 2005. (Remember that total equity equals the difference between assets and liabilities.)
2. By comparing equity amounts from the balance sheets and using the additional information presented in the problem, prepare a calculation to show how much net income was earned by the business during 2005.
3. Calculate the December 31, 2005, debt ratio for the business.

Check (2) Net income, $45,500

(3) Debt ratio, 58.76%

Problem 2-5B
Analyzing account balances and reconstructing transactions

C1 C4 A1 P2 

Miguel Gould started a Web consulting firm called Gould Solutions. He began operations and completed seven transactions in April that resulted in the following accounts, which all have normal balances:

Cash	$12,485
Office supplies	560
Prepaid rent	1,500
Office equipment	11,450
Accounts payable	11,450
M. Gould, Capital	10,000
M. Gould, Withdrawals	6,200
Consulting fees earned	16,400
Operating expenses	5,655

Required

1. Prepare a trial balance for this business at the end of April.

Check (1) Trial balance total, $37,850

Analysis Component

2. Analyze the accounts and their balances and prepare a list that describes each of the seven most likely transactions and their amounts.
3. Present a report that shows how the seven transactions in part 2 yield the $12,485 Cash balance.

(3) Cash paid, $13,915

Problem 2-6B
Recording transactions; posting to ledger; preparing a trial balance

C4 A1 P1 P2

Czekai Consulting completed the following transactions during June:

a. Chris Czekai, the sole proprietor, invested $80,000 cash along with office equipment valued at $30,000 in the new business.
b. Purchased land valued at $30,000 and a building valued at $170,000. The purchase is paid with $40,000 cash and a long-term note payable for $160,000.

c. Purchased $2,400 of office supplies on credit.

d. Czekai invested her personal automobile in the business. The automobile has a value of $18,000 and is to be used exclusively in the business.

e. Purchased $6,000 of additional office equipment on credit.

f. Paid $1,500 cash salary to an assistant.

g. Provided services to a client and collected $6,000 cash.

h. Paid $800 cash for this month's utilities.

i. Paid $2,400 cash to settle the account payable created in transaction *c*.

j. Purchased $20,000 of new office equipment by paying $18,600 cash and trading in old equipment with a recorded net cost and value of $1,400. (*Hint:* Credit Office Equipment (old) for $1,400.)

k. Completed $5,200 of services for a client, who must pay within 30 days.

l. Paid $1,500 cash salary to an assistant.

m. Received $3,800 cash on the receivable created in transaction *k*.

n. Czekai withdrew $6,400 cash from the business for personal use.

Required

1. Prepare general journal entries to record these transactions (use the account titles listed in part 2).

Check (2) Ending balances: Cash, $18,600; Office Equipment, $54,600

2. Open the following accounts—their account numbers are in parentheses (use the balance column format): Cash (101); Accounts Receivable (106); Office Supplies (108); Office Equipment (163); Automobiles (164); Building (170); Land (172); Accounts Payable (201); Notes Payable (250); C. Czekai, Capital (301); C. Czekai, Withdrawals (302); Fees Earned (402); Salaries Expense (601); and Utilities Expense (602). Post the journal entries from part 1 to the accounts and enter the balance after each posting.

(3) Trial balance totals, $305,200

3. Prepare a trial balance as of the end of this month's operations.

PROBLEM SET C

Problem Set C is available at the book's Website to further reinforce and assess your learning.

SERIAL PROBLEM

Success Systems

(This serial problem started in Chapter 1 and continues through most of the book. If the Chapter 1 segment was not completed, the problem can begin at this point. It is helpful, but not necessary, to use the Working Papers that accompany this book.)

On October 1, 2004, Kay Breeze launched a computer services company called Success Systems, which is organized as a sole proprietorship and provides consulting services, computer system installations, and custom program development. Breeze adopts the calendar year for reporting purposes and expects to prepare the company's first set of financial statements on December 31, 2004. The company's initial chart of accounts follows:

Account	No.	Account	No.
Cash	101	K. Breeze, Capital	301
Accounts Receivable	106	K. Breeze, Withdrawals	302
Computer Supplies	126	Computer Services Revenue	403
Prepaid Insurance	128	Wages Expense	623
Prepaid Rent	131	Advertising Expense	655
Office Equipment	163	Mileage Expense	676
Computer Equipment	167	Miscellaneous Expenses	677
Accounts Payable	201	Repairs Expense—Computer	684

Required

1. Prepare journal entries to record each of the following transactions for Success Systems.

Oct.	1	Breeze invested $55,000 cash, a $20,000 computer system, and $8,000 of office equipment in the business.
	2	Paid $3,300 cash for four months' rent. (*Hint:* Debit Prepaid Rent for $3,300.)
	3	Purchased $1,420 of computer supplies on credit from Cain Office Products.
	5	Paid $2,220 cash for one year's premium on a property and liability insurance policy. (*Hint:* Debit Prepaid Insurance for $2,220.)
	6	Billed Easy Leasing $4,800 for services performed in installing a new Web server.
	8	Paid $1,420 cash for the computer supplies purchased from Cain Office Products on October 3.
	10	Hired Sherry Adams as a part-time assistant for $125 per day, as needed.
	12	Billed Easy Leasing another $1,400 for services performed.
	15	Received $4,800 cash from Easy Leasing on its account.
	17	Paid $805 cash to repair computer equipment damaged when moving it.
	20	Paid $1,940 cash for an advertisement in the local newspaper.
	22	Received $1,400 cash from Easy Leasing on its account.
	28	Billed Clark Company $5,208 for services performed.
	31	Paid $875 cash for Sherry Adams's wages for seven days' work.
	31	Breeze withdrew $3,600 cash for personal use.
Nov.	1	Reimbursed Breeze in cash for business automobile mileage allowance (Breeze logged 1,000 miles at $0.32 per mile).
	2	Received $4,633 cash from Chang Corporation for computer services performed.
	5	Purchased computer supplies for $1,125 cash from Cain Office Products.
	8	Billed Gomez Co. $5,668 for services performed.
	13	Received notification from Alex's Engineering Co. that Success Systems' bid of $3,950 for an upcoming project is accepted.
	18	Received $2,208 cash from Clark Company as partial payment of the October 28 bill.
	22	Donated $250 cash to the United Way in the company's name.
	24	Completed work for Alex's Engineering Co. and sent it a bill for $3,950.
	25	Sent another bill to Clark Company for the past-due amount of $3,000.
	28	Reimbursed Breeze in cash for business automobile mileage (1,200 miles at $0.32 per mile).
	30	Paid $1,750 cash for Sherry Adams's wages for 14 days' work.
	30	Breeze withdrew $2,000 cash for personal use.

2. Open ledger accounts (in balance column format) and post the journal entries from part 1 to them.

3. Prepare a trial balance as of the end of November.

BEYOND THE NUMBERS

REPORTING IN ACTION

A1 A2

BTN 2-1 Refer to **Krispy Kreme**'s financial statements in Appendix A for the following questions.

Required

1. What amount of total liabilities does it report for each of the fiscal years ended 2002 and 2003?

2. What amount of total assets does it report for each of the fiscal years ended 2002 and 2003?

3. Calculate its debt ratio for each of the fiscal years ended 2002 and 2003.

4. In which fiscal year did it employ more financial leverage (2002 or 2003)? Explain.

Roll On

5. Access its financial statements (10-K report) for a fiscal year ending after February 2, 2003, from its Website (KrispyKreme.com) or the SEC's EDGAR database (www.SEC.gov). Recompute its debt ratio for any subsequent year's data and compare it with the February 2, 2003, debt ratio.

COMPARATIVE ANALYSIS

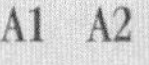

BTN 2-2 Key comparative figures ($ thousands) for both **Krispy Kreme** and **Tastykake** follow:

Key Figures	Krispy Kreme Current Year	Krispy Kreme Prior Year	Tastykake Current Year	Tastykake Prior Year
Total liabilities	$131,942	$ 65,218	$ 69,035	$ 61,072
Total assets	410,487	255,376	116,560	116,137

1. What is the debt ratio for Krispy Kreme in the current year and the prior year?

2. What is the debt ratio for Tastykake in the current year and the prior year?

3. Which of the two companies has a higher degree of financial leverage? What does this imply?

ETHICS CHALLENGE

C1 C2 

BTN 2-3 Review the *Decision Ethics* case from the first part of this chapter involving the cashier. The guidance answer suggests that you should not comply with the assistant manager's request.

Required

Propose and evaluate two other courses of action you might consider, and explain why.

COMMUNICATING IN PRACTICE

C1 C3 A1 P3 

BTN 2-4 Amy Renkmeyer is an aspiring entrepreneur and your friend. She is having difficulty understanding the purposes of financial statements and how they fit together across time.

Required

Write a one-page memorandum to Renkmeyer explaining the purposes of the four financial statements and how they are linked across time.

TAKING IT TO THE NET

A1 

mhhe.com/larson

BTN 2-5 Access EDGAR online (www.SEC.gov) and locate the 10-K report of **Amazon.com** (ticker AMZN) filed on January 24, 2002. Review its financial statements reported for fiscal years ended 1999, 2000, and 2001 to answer the following questions:

Required

1. What are the amounts of its net losses reported for each of these three years?

2. Does Amazon's operations provide cash or use cash for each of these three years?

3. If Amazon has a 2000 net loss and a net use of cash in operations in 2000, how is it possible that its cash balance at December 31, 2000, shows an increase relative to its balance at January 1, 2000?

TEAMWORK IN ACTION

C1 C3 C5 A1

BTN 2-6 The expanded accounting equation consists of assets, liabilities, capital, withdrawals, revenues, and expenses. It can be used to reveal insights into changes in a company's financial position.

Required

1. Form *learning teams* of six (or more) members. Each team member must select one of the six components and each team must have at least one expert on each component: (*a*) assets, (*b*) liabilities, (*c*) capital, (*d*) withdrawals, (*e*) revenues, and (*f*) expenses.

2. Form *expert teams* of individuals who selected the same component in part 1. Expert teams are to draft a report that each expert will present to his or her learning team addressing the following:

   a. Identify for its component the (i) increase and decrease side of the account and (ii) normal balance side of the account.

   b. Describe a transaction, with amounts, that increases its component.

c. Using the transaction and amounts in (*b*), verify the equality of the accounting equation and then explain any effects on the income statement and statement of cash flows.
d. Describe a transaction, with amounts, that decreases its component.
e. Using the transaction and amounts in (*d*), verify the equality of the accounting equation and then explain any effects on the income statement and statement of cash flows.

3. Each expert should return to his/her learning team. In rotation, each member presents his/her expert team's report to the learning team. Team discussion is encouraged.

BUSINESS WEEK ACTIVITY

A2

mhhe.com/larson

BTN 2-7 Read the article "Leveraged for Success" in the April 18, 2002, issue of ***Business Week***.

Required

1. Explain why debt financing can be a less expensive alternative than equity financing.
2. What can happen if a company takes on too much debt?
3. Name five companies cited by the article that are using a high degree of leverage but still maintaining top credit ratings.

ENTREPRENEURIAL DECISION

A1 A2 P3

BTN 2-8 Liang Lu is a young entrepreneur who operates Lu Music Services, offering singing lessons and instruction on musical instruments. Lu wishes to expand but needs a loan. The bank requests Lu to prepare a balance sheet and key financial ratios. Lu has not kept formal records but is able to provide the following accounts and their amounts as of December 31, 2005:

Cash	$ 1,800	Accounts Receivable	$4,800	Prepaid Insurance . .	$ 750
Prepaid Rent	4,700	Store Supplies	3,300	Equipment	25,000
Accounts Payable . . .	1,100	Unearned Lesson Fees	7,800	Total Equity*	31,450
Annual net income . .	20,000				

* The total equity amount reflects all owner investments, owner withdrawals, revenues, and expenses as of December 31, 2005.

Required

1. Prepare a balance sheet as of December 31, 2005, for Lu Music Services.
2. Compute Lu's debt ratio and its return on assets (from Chapter 1). Assume average assets equal its ending balance.
3. Do you think the prospects of a $15,000 bank loan are good? Why or why not?

A1 A2 P3

BTN 2-9 Assume that Tanya York of **York Entertainment** wants to grow company revenues by 10% each year for the next five years. York has determined that achieving that revenue growth will require additional financing. Accordingly, the company has sought and been offered a $5 million line of credit by a Los Angeles bank to help fund current operations and new movie projects. York is not required to use the line of credit, but it does have preapproval to use the line of credit as needed. If the line of credit is used, an annual interest rate of 8% will be charged on the money borrowed.

Required

1. What will York's annual revenues be in five years if the revenue growth target rate is achieved?
2. If York decides to borrow against the line of credit, what must it do to successfully employ financial leverage?

HITTING THE ROAD

C1

BTN 2-10 Obtain a recent copy of the most prominent newspaper distributed in your area. Research the classified section and prepare a report answering the following questions (attach relevant classified clippings to your report). Alternatively, you may want to search the Web for the required information. One suitable Website is **America's Job Bank** (**www.AJB.org**). For documentation, you should print copies of Websites accessed.

1. Identify the number of listings for accounting positions and the various accounting job titles.
2. Identify the number of listings for other job titles, with examples, that require or prefer accounting knowledge/experience but are not specifically accounting positions.
3. Specify the salary range for the accounting and accounting-related positions if provided.
4. Indicate the job that appeals to you, the reason for its appeal, and its requirements.

GLOBAL DECISION

A2

BTN 2-11 Grupo Bimbo (GrupoBimbo.com) competes with several companies, including Krispy Kreme and Tastykake. Key financial ratios for the current fiscal year follow:

Key Figure	Grupo Bimbo	Krispy Kreme	Tastykake
Return on assets	3.6%	10.1%	1.7%
Debt ratio	56.0%	32.1%	59.2%

Required

1. Which company is most profitable according to return on assets?
2. Which company is most risky according to the debt ratio?
3. Which company deserves increased investment based on a joint analysis of return on assets and the debt ratio?

"Stay focused and keep doing what you believe in"—Melody Kulp (second from left; David Reinstein is on the far left)

Adjusting Accounts and Preparing Financial Statements

A Look Back

Chapter 2 explained the analysis and recording of transactions. We showed how to apply and interpret company accounts, T-accounts, double-entry accounting, ledgers, postings, and trial balances.

A Look at This Chapter

This chapter explains the timing of reports and the need to adjust accounts. Adjusting accounts is important for recognizing revenues and expenses in the proper period. We describe the adjusted trial balance and how it is used to prepare financial statements.

A Look Ahead

Chapter 4 highlights the completion of the accounting cycle. We explain the important final steps in the accounting process. These include closing procedures, the post-closing trial balance, and reversing entries.

CAP

Conceptual

C1 Explain the importance of periodic reporting and the time period principle. *(p. 94)*

C2 Explain accrual accounting and how it makes financial statements more useful. *(p. 95)*

C3 Identify the types of adjustments and their purpose. *(p. 97)*

Analytical

A1 Explain how accounting adjustments link to financial statements. *(p. 104)*

A2 Compute profit margin and describe its use in analyzing company performance. *(p. 108)*

Procedural

P1 Prepare and explain adjusting entries. *(p. 97)*

P2 Explain and prepare an adjusted trial balance. *(p. 105)*

P3 Prepare financial statements from an adjusted trial balance. *(p. 106)*

Decision Feature

Sparkling Financials

EL SEGUNDO, CA—One afternoon 23-year-old Melody Kulp was playing outside with the young cousin of a friend when she placed yard-picked flowers in the girl's hair and thought how much prettier they looked than headbands or hair clips. The next day, with some silk flowers and Velcro she purchased, Kulp made similar hair accessories, called them *Sparkles,* and began wearing them.

When a friend wore one to work at Fred Segal's, the shop's buyer asked to meet with Kulp about putting together a product line. Kulp quickly organized a business—dubbed **Mellies (Mellies.com)**—and then converted a 10′ × 10′ room in her house into a minifactory. The rest is the stuff of Hollywood movies.

After only three years, Mellies is a $40 million accessories company. With her 25-year-old partner David Reinstein, Melody Kulp now manages 15 employees and plans to launch a cosmetics line. The young entrepreneurs learned a lot in a hurry. She had to meet creditors and bankers, set up a reliable accounting system, draw up financial statements, and analyze and interpret financial data. It was at times overwhelming, says Kulp, but "the key is to stay focused and keep doing what you believe in."

Kulp knows how important a timely and reliable accounting system is for Mellies' continued success. Historical and projected financial statements have enabled her company to obtain the necessary financing to propel it to new heights.

This chapter focuses on the accounting system underlying financial statements. Says Kulp, "We've got the system set up where we can look ahead, rather than live day to day." That look ahead reveals sparkling financials.

[Sources: Mellies Website, January 2004; *Success Publishing,* 2000; *Entrepreneur,* November 2000.]

Financial statements reflect revenues when earned and expenses when incurred. This is known as *accrual accounting*. Accrual accounting requires several steps. We described many of these steps in Chapter 2. We showed how companies use accounting systems to collect information about *external* transactions and events. We also explained how journals, ledgers, and other tools are useful in preparing financial statements. This chapter describes the accounting process for producing useful information involving *internal* transactions and events. An important part of this process is adjusting the account balances so that financial statements at the end of a reporting period reflect the effects of all transactions. We then explain the important steps in preparing financial statements.

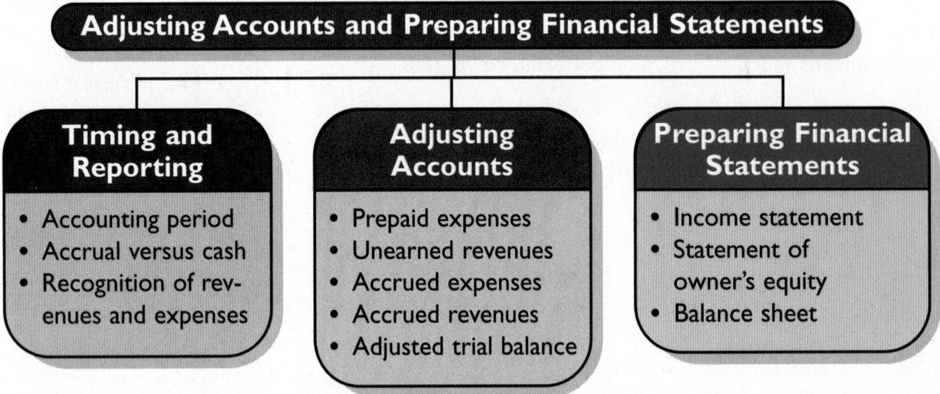

Timing and Reporting

Regular, or periodic, reporting is an important part of the accounting process. This section describes the impact on the accounting process of the point in time or the period of time that a report refers to.

The Accounting Period

C1 Explain the importance of periodic reporting and the time period principle.

"Krispy Kreme announces earnings per share of . . ."

The value of information is often linked to its timeliness. Useful information must reach decision makers frequently and promptly. To provide timely information, accounting systems prepare reports at regular intervals. This results in an accounting process impacted by the time period (or periodicity) principle. The **time period principle** assumes that an organization's activities can be divided into specific time periods such as a month, a three-month quarter, a six-month interval, or a year. Exhibit 3.1 shows various **accounting,** or *reporting,*

Exhibit 3.1

Accounting Periods

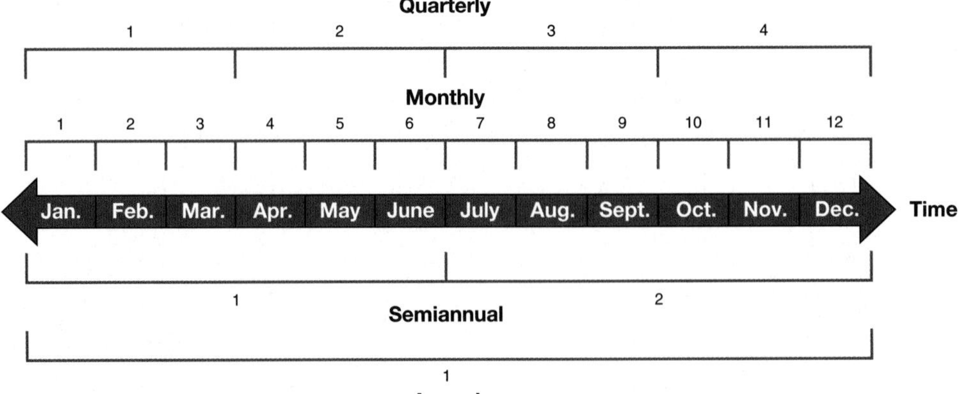

periods. Most organizations use a year as their primary accounting period. Reports covering a one-year period are known as **annual financial statements.** Many organizations also prepare **interim financial statements** covering one, three, or six months of activity.

The annual reporting period is not always a calendar year ending on December 31. An organization can adopt a **fiscal year** consisting of any 12 consecutive months. It is also acceptable to adopt an annual reporting period of 52 weeks. For example, **Gap**'s fiscal year consistently ends the final week of January or the first week of February each year.

Companies with little seasonal variation in sales often choose the calendar year as their fiscal year. For example, the financial statements of **Marvel Enterprises** reflect a fiscal year that ends on December 31. Companies experiencing seasonal variations in sales often choose a **natural business year** end, which is when sales activities are at their lowest level for the year. The natural business year for retailers such as **Wal-Mart**, **Dell**, and **FUBU** usually ends around January 31, after the holiday season.

Accrual Basis versus Cash Basis

After external transactions and events are recorded for an accounting period, several accounts still need adjustments before their balances appear in financial statements. This need arises because internal transactions and events remain unrecorded. **Accrual basis accounting** uses the adjusting process to recognize revenues when earned and to match expenses with revenues.

C2 Explain accrual accounting and how it makes financial statements more useful.

Cash basis accounting recognizes revenues when cash is received and records expenses when cash is paid. This means that cash basis net income for a period is the difference between cash receipts and cash payments. Cash basis accounting is not consistent with generally accepted accounting principles.

It is commonly held that accrual accounting better reflects business performance than information about cash receipts and payments. Accrual accounting also increases the *comparability* of financial statements from one period to another. Yet cash basis accounting is useful for several business decisions—which is the reason companies must report a statement of cash flows.

Topic Tackler 3-1

To see the difference between these two accounting systems, let's consider FastForward's Prepaid Insurance account. FastForward paid $2,400 for 24 months of insurance coverage beginning on December 1, 2004. Accrual accounting requires that $100 of insurance expense be reported on December's income statement. Another $1,200 of expense is reported in year 2005, and the remaining $1,100 is reported as expense in the first 11 months of 2006. Exhibit 3.2 illustrates this allocation of insurance cost across these three years. The accrual basis balance sheet reports any unexpired premium as a Prepaid Insurance asset.

Point: IBM's revenues from services to customers are recorded when services are performed. Its revenues from product sales are recorded when products are shipped.

A cash basis income statement for December 2004 reports insurance expense of $2,400, as shown in Exhibit 3.3. The cash basis income statements for years 2005 and 2006 report

Exhibit 3.2

Accrual Basis Accounting for Allocating Prepaid Insurance to Expense

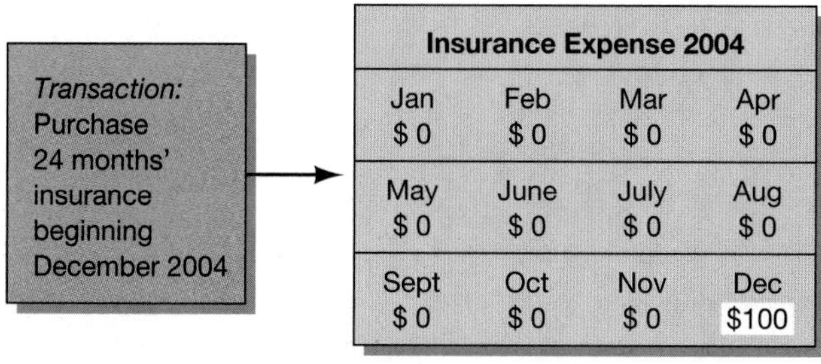

Insurance Expense 2004			
Jan $0	Feb $0	Mar $0	Apr $0
May $0	June $0	July $0	Aug $0
Sept $0	Oct $0	Nov $0	Dec $100

Insurance Expense 2005			
Jan $100	Feb $100	Mar $100	Apr $100
May $100	June $100	July $100	Aug $100
Sept $100	Oct $100	Nov $100	Dec $100

Insurance Expense 2006			
Jan $100	Feb $100	Mar $100	Apr $100
May $100	June $100	July $100	Aug $100
Sept $100	Oct $100	Nov $100	Dec $0

Exhibit 3.3

Cash Basis Accounting for Allocating Prepaid Insurance to Expense

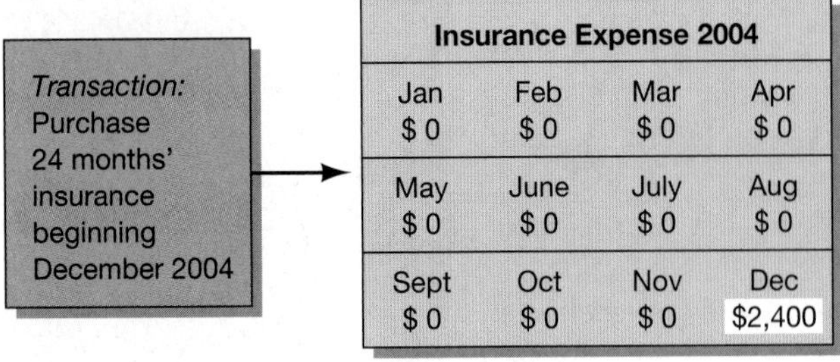

Insurance Expense 2004			
Jan $ 0	Feb $ 0	Mar $ 0	Apr $ 0
May $ 0	June $ 0	July $ 0	Aug $ 0
Sept $ 0	Oct $ 0	Nov $ 0	Dec $2,400

Insurance Expense 2005			
Jan $0	Feb $0	Mar $0	Apr $0
May $0	June $0	July $0	Aug $0
Sept $0	Oct $0	Nov $0	Dec $0

Insurance Expense 2006			
Jan $0	Feb $0	Mar $0	Apr $0
May $0	June $0	July $0	Aug $0
Sept $0	Oct $0	Nov $0	Dec $0

Point: Recording revenue early overstates current-period revenue and income; recording it late understates current-period revenue and income.

no insurance expense. The cash basis balance sheet never reports an insurance asset because it is immediately expensed. Note that reported income for 2004–2006 fails to match the cost of insurance with the insurance benefits received for those years and months.

Recognizing Revenues and Expenses

Decision Insight

Numbers Game **Ascential Software**, a software provider, recorded revenue when products were passed to distributors. It admits now that there were "errors in the way revenues had been recorded," and its CEO is in jail. **Centennial Technologies**, a computers manufacturer, recognized revenue when it shipped products. What is not common is that Centennial's CEO shipped products to the warehouses of friends and reported it as revenue. Risky or improper revenue recognition practices are often revealed by a large increase in the *Accounts Receivable to Sales* ratio.

We use the time period principle to divide a company's activities into specific time periods, but not all activities are complete when financial statements are prepared. Thus, adjustments often are required to get correct account balances.

We rely on two principles in the adjusting process: revenue recognition and matching. Chapter 1 explained that the *revenue recognition principle* requires that revenue be recorded when earned, not before and not after. Most companies earn revenue when they provide services and products to customers. A major goal of the adjusting process is to have revenue recognized (reported) in the time period when it is earned.

The **matching principle** aims to record expenses in the same accounting period as the revenues that are earned as a result of these expenses. This matching of expenses with the revenue benefits is a major part of the adjusting process.

Matching expenses with revenues often requires us to predict certain events. When we use financial statements, we must understand that they require estimates and therefore include measures that are not precise. **Walt Disney**'s annual report explains that its production costs from movies are matched to revenues based on a ratio of current revenues from the movie divided by its predicted total revenues.

Point: Recording expense early overstates current-period expense and understates current-period income; recording it late understates current-period expense and overstates current-period income.

Quick Check

1. Describe a company's annual reporting period.
2. Why do companies prepare interim financial statements?
3. What two accounting principles most directly drive the adjusting process?
4. Is cash basis accounting consistent with the matching principle? Why or why not?
5. If your company pays a $4,800 premium on April 1, 2004, for two years' insurance coverage, how much insurance expense is reported in 2005 using cash basis accounting?

Answers—p. 115

Adjusting Accounts

The process of adjusting accounts involves analyzing each account balance and the transactions and events that affect it to determine any needed adjustments. An **adjusting entry** is recorded to bring an asset or liability account balance to its proper amount. This entry also updates a related expense or revenue account.

C3 Identify the types of adjustments and their purpose.

Framework for Adjustments

Adjustments are necessary for transactions and events that extend over more than one period. It is helpful to group adjustments by the timing of cash receipt or cash payment in relation to the recognition of the related revenues or expenses. Exhibit 3.4 identifies four types of adjustments.

Topic Tackler 3-2

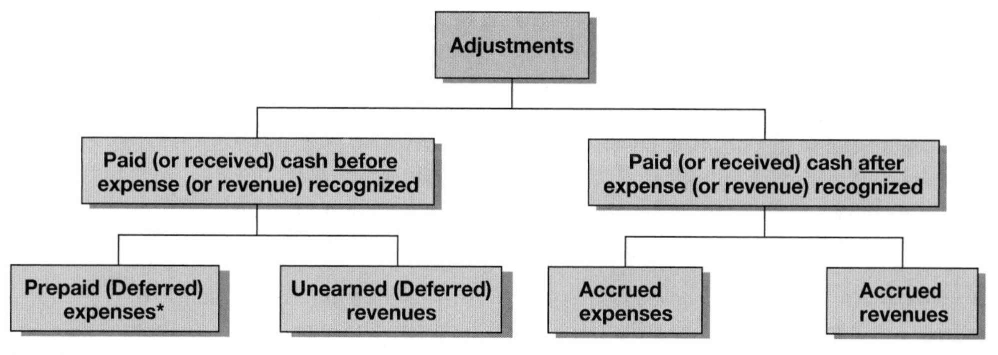

*Includes depreciation.

Exhibit 3.4

Types of Adjustments

The left side of this exhibit shows prepaid expenses (including depreciation) and unearned revenues, which reflect transactions when cash is paid or received *before* a related expense or revenue is recognized. They are also called *deferrals* because the recognition of an expense (or revenue) is *deferred* until after the related cash is paid (or received). The right side of this exhibit shows accrued expenses and accrued revenues, which reflect transactions when cash is paid or received *after* a related expense or revenue is recognized. Adjusting entries are necessary for each of these so that revenues, expenses, assets, and liabilities are correctly reported. It is helpful to remember that each adjusting entry affects one or more income statement accounts *and* one or more balance sheet accounts (but not the Cash account).

Point: Adjusting is a 3-step process: (1) Compute current account balance, (2) Compute what current account balance should be, and (3) Record entry to get from step *1* to step 2.

Prepaid (Deferred) Expenses

P1 Prepare and explain adjusting entries.

Prepaid expenses refer to items *paid for* in advance of receiving their benefits. Prepaid expenses are assets. When these assets are used, their costs become expenses. Adjusting entries for prepaids increase expenses and decrease assets as shown in the T-accounts of Exhibit 3.5. Such adjustments reflect transactions and events that use up prepaid expenses (including passage of time). To illustrate the accounting for prepaid expenses, this section focuses on prepaid insurance, supplies, and depreciation.

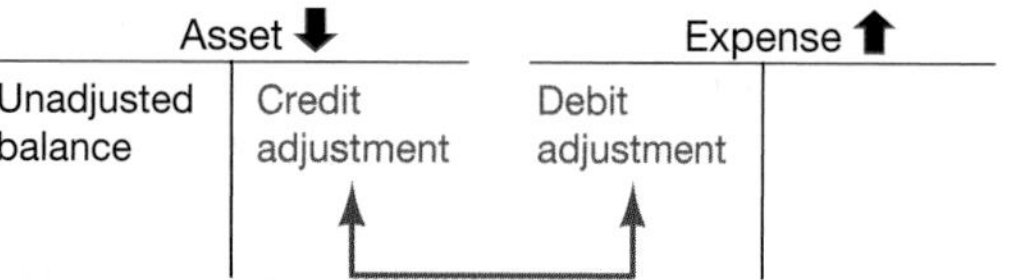

Exhibit 3.5

Adjusting for Prepaid Expenses

Prepaid Insurance We illustrate prepaid insurance using FastForward's payment of $2,400 for 24 months of insurance benefits beginning on December 1, 2004. With the passage of time, the benefits of the insurance gradually expire and a portion of the Prepaid

Insurance asset becomes expense. For instance, one month's insurance coverage expires by December 31, 2004. This expense is $100, or 1/24 of $2,400. The adjusting entry to record this expense and reduce the asset, along with T-account postings, follows:

Assets = Liabilities + Equity
−100 −100

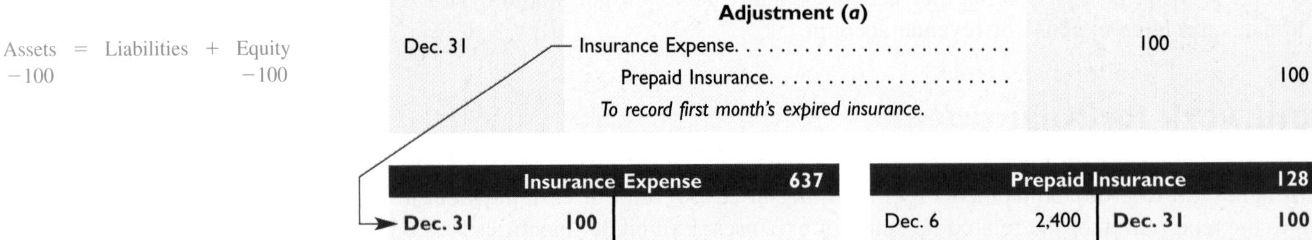

Point: Many companies record adjusting entries only at the end of each year because of the time and cost necessary.

Point: Source documents provide information for most daily transactions, and in many businesses the recordkeepers record them. Adjustments require more knowledge and are usually handled by senior accounting professionals.

After adjusting and posting, the $100 balance in Insurance Expense and the $2,300 balance in Prepaid Insurance are ready for reporting in financial statements. *Not* making the adjustment on or before December 31 would (1) understate expenses by $100 and overstate net income by $100 for the December income statement and (2) overstate both prepaid insurance (assets) and equity (because of net income) by $100 in the December 31 balance sheet. It is also evident from Exhibit 3.2 that 2005's adjustments must transfer a total of $1,200 from Prepaid Insurance to Insurance Expense, and 2006's adjustments must transfer the remaining $1,100 to Insurance Expense.

Supplies Supplies are a prepaid expense often requiring adjustment. To illustrate, FastForward purchased $9,720 of supplies in December and used some of them. When financial statements are prepared at December 31, the cost of supplies used during December must be recognized. When FastForward computes (takes inventory of) its remaining unused supplies at December 31, it finds $8,670 of supplies remaining of the $9,720 total supplies. The $1,050 difference between these two amounts is December's supplies expense. The adjusting entry to record this expense and reduce the Supplies asset account, along with T-account postings, follows:

Assets = Liabilities + Equity
−1,050 −1,050

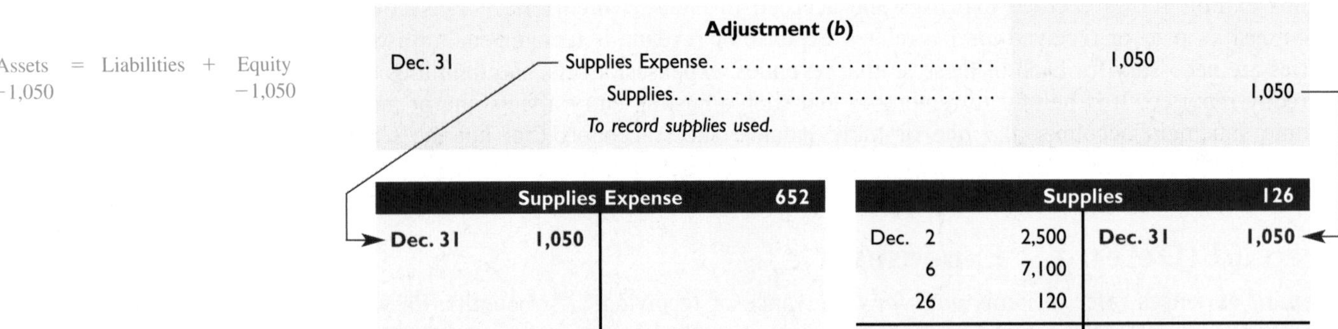

The balance of the Supplies account is $8,670 after posting—equaling the cost of the remaining supplies. *Not* making the adjustment on or before December 31 would (1) understate expenses by $1,050 and overstate net income by $1,050 for the December income statement and (2) overstate both supplies and equity (because of net income) by $1,050 in the December 31 balance sheet.

Point: An alternative method to record prepaids is to initially debit expense for the total amount. Appendix 3A discusses this alternative. The adjusted financial statement information is identical under either method.

Other Prepaid Expenses Other prepaid expenses, such as Prepaid Rent, are accounted for exactly as Insurance and Supplies are. We should also note that some prepaid expenses are both paid for and fully used up within a single accounting period. One example is when a company pays monthly rent on the first day of each month. This payment creates a prepaid expense on the first day of each month that fully expires by the end of the month. In these special cases, we can record the cash paid with a debit to an expense account instead of an asset account. This practice is described more completely later in the chapter.

Decision Maker

Investor A small publishing company signs a well-known athlete to write a book. The company pays the athlete $500,000 to sign plus future book royalties. A note to the company's financial statements says that "prepaid expenses include $500,000 in author signing fees to be matched against future expected sales." Is this accounting for the signing bonus acceptable? How does it affect your analysis?

Answer—p. 114

Depreciation A special category of prepaid expenses is **plant assets,** which refers to long-term tangible assets used to produce and sell products and services. Plant assets are expected to provide benefits for more than one period. Examples of plant assets are buildings, machines, vehicles, and fixtures. All plant assets, with a general exception for land, eventually wear out or decline in usefulness. The costs of these assets are deferred but are gradually reported as expenses in the income statement over the assets' useful lives (benefit periods). **Depreciation** is the process of allocating the costs of these assets over their expected useful lives. Depreciation expense is recorded with an adjusting entry similar to that for other prepaid expenses.

Point: Depreciation does not necessarily measure the decline in market value.

To illustrate, recall that FastForward purchased equipment for $26,000 in early December to use in earning revenue. This equipment's cost must be depreciated. The equipment is expected to have a useful life (benefit period) of four years and to be worth about $8,000 at the end of four years. This means the *net* cost of this equipment over its useful life is $18,000 ($26,000 − $8,000). We can use any of several methods to allocate this $18,000 net cost to expense. FastForward uses a method called **straight-line depreciation,** which allocates equal amounts of an asset's net cost to depreciation during its useful life. Dividing the $18,000 net cost by the 48 months in the asset's useful life gives a monthly cost of $375 ($18,000/48). The adjusting entry to record monthly depreciation expense, along with T-account postings, follows:

Point: An asset's expected value at the end of its useful life is called *salvage value.*

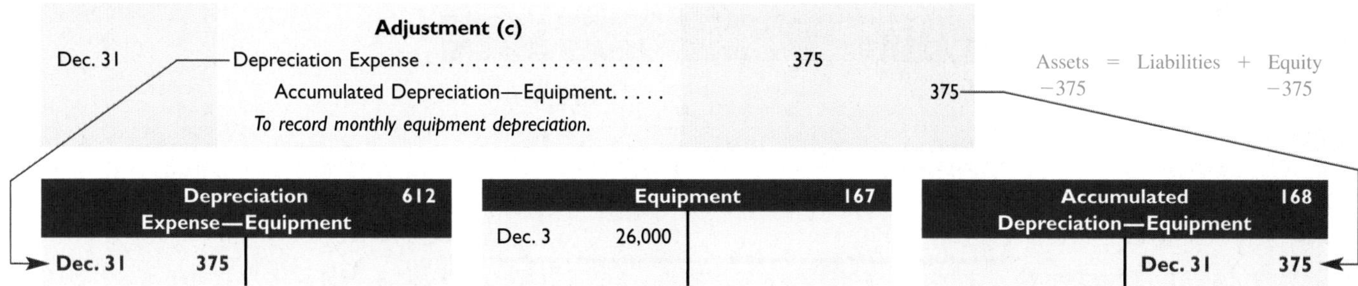

After posting the adjustment, the Equipment account ($26,000) less its Accumulated Depreciation ($375) account equals the $25,625 net cost of the 47 remaining months in the benefit period. The $375 balance in the Depreciation Expense account is reported in the December income statement. *Not* making the adjustment at December 31 would (1) understate expenses by $375 and overstate net income by $375 for the December income statement and (2) overstate both assets and equity (because of income) by $375 in the December 31 balance sheet.

The accumulated depreciation is kept in a separate contra account. A **contra account** is an account linked with another account, it has an opposite normal balance, and it is reported as a subtraction from that other account's balance. For instance, FastForward's contra account of Accumulated Depreciation—Equipment is subtracted from the Equipment account in the balance sheet (see Exhibit 3.7).

Point: The cost principle requires an asset to be initially recorded at acquisition cost. Depreciation causes the asset's book value (cost less accumulated depreciation) to decline over time.

Decision Maker

Entrepreneur You are preparing an offer to purchase a family-run restaurant. The depreciation schedule for the restaurant's building and equipment shows costs of $175,000 and accumulated depreciation of $155,000. This leaves a net for building and equipment of $20,000. Is this information useful in helping you decide on a purchase offer?

Answer—p. 115

A contra account allows balance sheet readers to know both the full costs of assets and the total amount of depreciation. By knowing both these amounts, decision makers can better assess a company's capacity and its need to replace assets. For example, FastForward's balance sheet shows both the $26,000 original cost of equipment and the $375 balance in the accumulated depreciation contra account. This information reveals that the equipment is close to new. If FastForward reports equipment only at its net amount of $25,625, users cannot assess the equipment's age or its need for replacement. The title of the contra account, *Accumulated Depreciation,* indicates that this account includes total depreciation expense for all prior periods for which the asset was used. To illustrate, the Equipment and the Accumulated Depreciation accounts appear as in Exhibit 3.6 on February 28, 2005, after three months of adjusting entries.

Exhibit 3.6

Accounts after Three Months of Depreciation Adjustments

Equipment	167		
Dec. 3	26,000		

Accumulated Depreciation—Equipment			168
		Dec. 31	375
		Jan. 31	375
		Feb. 28	375
		Balance	1,125

The $1,125 balance in the accumulated depreciation account is subtracted from its related $26,000 asset cost. The difference ($24,875) between these two balances is the cost of the asset that has not yet been depreciated. This difference is called the **book value,** or *net amount,* which equals the asset's costs less its accumulated depreciation. These account balances are reported in the assets section of the February 28 balance sheet in Exhibit 3.7.

Point: The net cost of equipment is also called the *depreciable basis.*

Exhibit 3.7

Equipment and Accumulated Depreciation on February 28 Balance Sheet

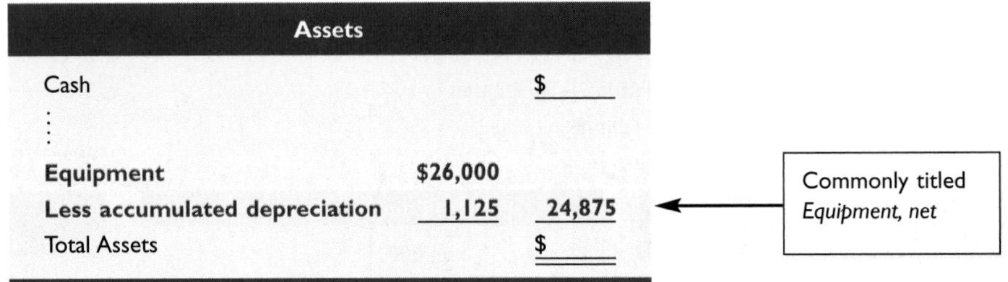

Assets		
Cash		$
⋮		
Equipment	$26,000	
Less accumulated depreciation	1,125	24,875
Total Assets		$

Unearned (Deferred) Revenues

The term **unearned revenues** refers to cash received in advance of providing products and services. Unearned revenues, also called *deferred revenues,* are liabilities. When cash is accepted, an obligation to provide products or services is accepted. As products or services are provided, the unearned revenues become *earned* revenues. Adjusting entries for unearned revenues involve increasing revenues and decreasing unearned revenues, as shown in Exhibit 3.8.

Exhibit 3.8

Adjusting for Unearned Revenues

An example of unearned revenues is from **The New York Times Company**, which reports unexpired (unearned) subscriptions of more than $60 million: "Proceeds from . . . subscriptions are deferred at the time of sale and are recognized in earnings on a pro rata basis over the terms of the subscriptions."

Point: To *defer* is to postpone. We postpone reporting amounts received as revenues until they are earned.

Unearned revenues are more than 10% of the current liabilities for the Times. Another example comes from the **Boston Celtics**. When the Celtics receive cash from advance ticket sales and broadcast fees, they record it in an unearned revenue account called *Deferred Game Revenues.* The Celtics recognize this unearned revenue with adjusting entries on a game-by-game basis. Since the NBA regular season begins in October and ends in April, revenue recognition is mainly limited to this period. For a recent season, the Celtics' quarterly revenues were $0 million for July–September; $34 million for October–December; $48 million for January–March; and $17 million for April–June.

FastForward has unearned revenues. It agreed on December 26 to provide consulting services to a client for a fixed fee of $3,000 for 60 days. On that same day, this client paid the 60-day fee in advance, covering the period December 27 to February 24. The entry to record the cash received in advance is

Dec. 26	Cash	3,000	
	Unearned Consulting Revenue		3,000
	Received advance payment for services over the next 60 days.		

Assets = Liabilities + Equity
+3,000 +3,000

This advance payment increases cash and creates an obligation to do consulting work over the next 60 days. As time passes, FastForward will earn this payment through consulting. By December 31, it has provided five days' service and earned 5/60 of the $3,000 unearned revenue. This amounts to $250 ($3,000 × 5/60). The *revenue recognition principle* implies that $250 of unearned revenue must be reported as revenue on the December income statement. The adjusting entry to reduce the liability account and recognize earned revenue, along with T-account postings, follows:

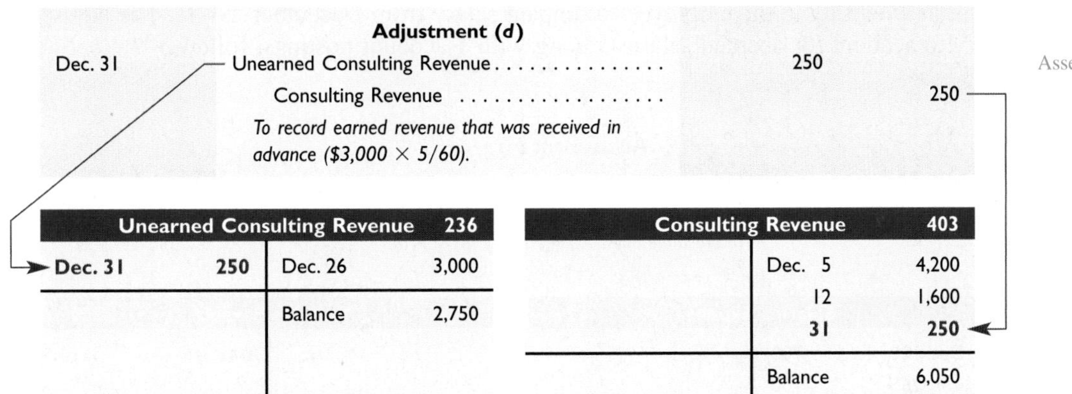

Assets = Liabilities + Equity
−250 +250

The adjusting entry transfers $250 from unearned revenue (a liability account) to a revenue account. *Not* making the adjustment (1) understates revenue and net income by $250 in the December income statement and (2) overstates unearned revenue and understates equity by $250 on the December 31 balance sheet.

Accrued Expenses

Accrued expenses refer to costs that are incurred in a period but are both unpaid and unrecorded. Accrued expenses must be reported on the income statement of the period when incurred. Adjusting entries for recording accrued expenses involves increasing expenses and increasing liabilities as shown in Exhibit 3.9. This adjustment

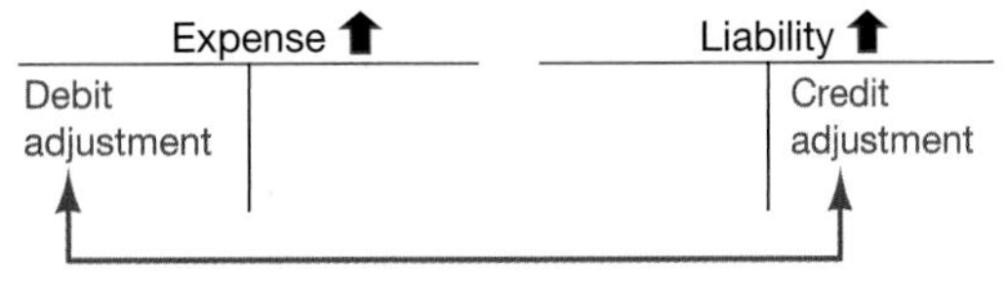

Exhibit 3.9
Adjusting for Accrued Expenses

Point: Accrued expenses are also called *accrued liabilities.*

recognizes expenses incurred in a period but not yet paid. Common examples of accrued expenses are salaries, interest, rent, and taxes. We use salaries and interest to show how to adjust accounts for accrued expenses.

Accrued Salaries Expense FastForward's employee earns $70 per day, or $350 for a five-day workweek beginning on Monday and ending on Friday. This employee is paid every two weeks on Friday. On December 12 and 26, the wages are paid, recorded in the journal, and posted to the ledger. The calendar in Exhibit 3.10 shows three working days after the December 26 payday (29, 30, and 31). This means the employee has earned three days' salary by the close of business on Wednesday, December 31, yet this salary cost is not paid or recorded.

Exhibit 3.10

Salary Accrual and Paydays

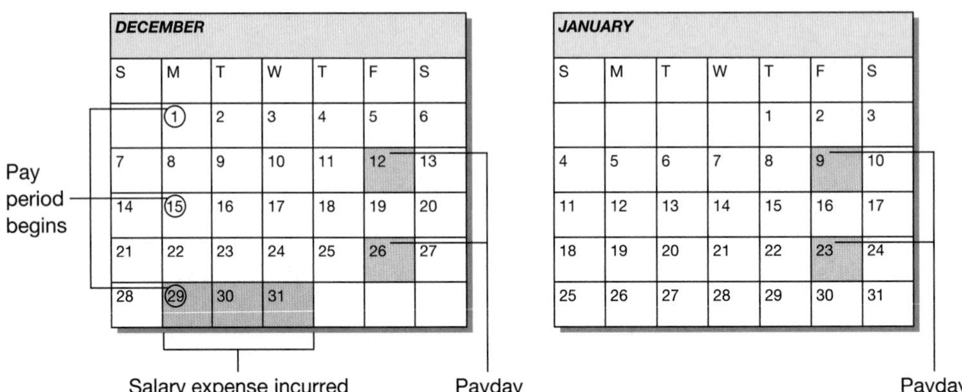

Point: Assume: (1) the last payday for the year is December 19, (2) the next payday is January 2, and (3) December 25 is a paid holiday. Record the December 31 adjusting entry. *Answer:* We must accrue pay for eight working days (8 × $70):
Salaries Expense . . . 560
Salaries Payable 560

The financial statements would be incomplete if FastForward fails to report the added expense and liability to the employee for unpaid salary from December 29–31. The adjusting entry to account for accrued salaries, along with T-account postings, follows:

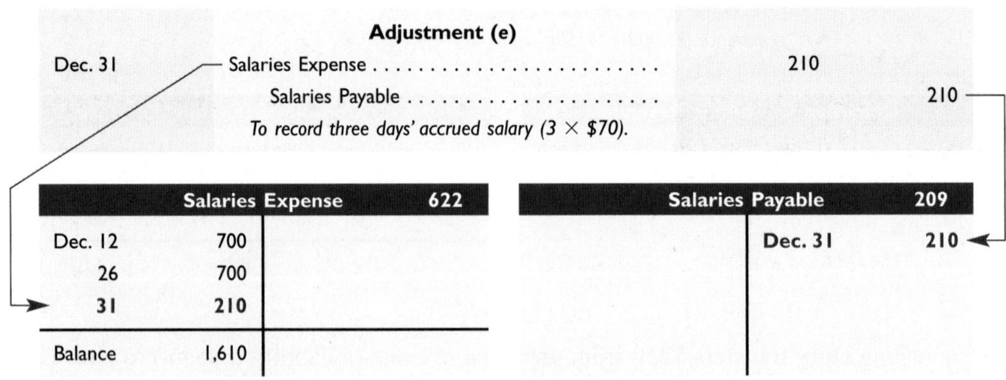

Point: An employer records salaries expense and a vacation pay liability when employees earn vacation pay.

Salaries expense of $1,610 is reported on the December income statement and $210 of salaries payable (liability) is reported in the balance sheet. *Not* making the adjustment (1) understates salaries expense and overstates net income by $210 in the December income statement and (2) understates salaries payable (liabilities) and overstates equity by $210 on the December 31 balance sheet.

Accrued Interest Expense Companies commonly have accrued interest expense on notes payable and other long-term liabilities at the end of a period. Interest expense is incurred with the passage of time. Unless interest is paid on the last day of an accounting period, we need to adjust for interest expense incurred but not yet paid. This means we must accrue interest cost from the most recent payment date up to the end of the period. The formula for computing accrued interest is:

Principal amount owed × Annual interest rate × Fraction of year since last payment date.

To illustrate, if a company has a $6,000 loan from a bank at 6% annual interest, then 30 days' accrued interest expense is $30—computed as $6,000 × 0.06 × 30/360. The adjusting entry would be to debit Interest Expense for $30 and credit Interest Payable for $30.

Point: Interest computations assume a 360-day year.

Future Payment of Accrued Expenses Adjusting entries for accrued expenses foretell cash transactions in future periods. Specifically, accrued expenses at the end of one accounting period result in *cash payments* in a *future* period(s). To illustrate, recall that FastForward recorded accrued salaries of $210. On January 9, the first payday of the next period, the following entry settles the accrued liability (salaries payable) and records salaries expense for seven days of work in January:

Jan. 9	Salaries Payable (3 days at $70 per day)	210	
	Salaries Expense (7 days at $70 per day)	490	
	Cash...............................		700
	Paid two weeks' salary including three days accrued in December.		

Assets	=	Liabilities	+	Equity
−700		−210		−490

The $210 debit reflects the payment of the liability for the three days' salary accrued on December 31. The $490 debit records the salary for January's first seven working days (including the New Year's Day holiday) as an expense of the new accounting period. The $700 credit records the total amount of cash paid to the employee.

Accrued Revenues

The term **accrued revenues** refers to revenues earned in a period that are both unrecorded and not yet received in cash (or other assets). An example is a technician who bills customers only when the job is done. If one-third of a job is complete by the end of a period, then the technician must record one-third of the expected billing as revenue in that period—even though there is no billing or collection. The adjusting entries for accrued revenues increase assets and increase revenues as shown in Exhibit 3.11. Accrued revenues commonly arise from services, products, interest, and rent. We use service fees and interest to show how to adjust for accrued revenues.

Point: Accrued revenues are also called *accrued assets.*

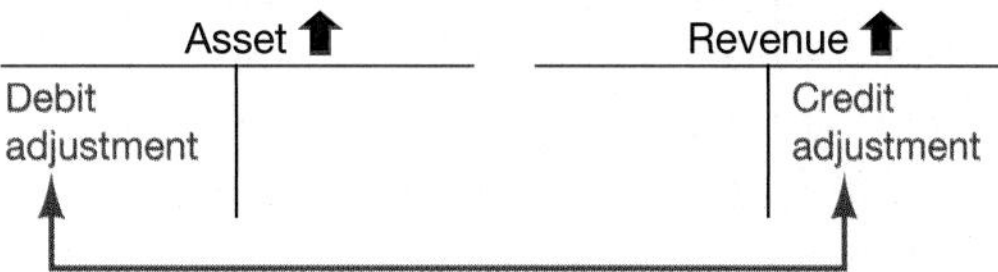

Exhibit 3.11

Adjusting for Accrued Revenues

Accrued Services Revenue Accrued revenues are not recorded until adjusting entries are made at the end of the accounting period. These accrued revenues are earned but unrecorded because either the buyer has not yet paid for them or the seller has not yet billed the buyer. FastForward provides an example. In the second week of December, it agreed to provide 30 days of consulting services to a local sports club for a fixed fee of $2,700. The terms of the initial agreement call for FastForward to provide services from December 12, 2004, through January 10, 2005, or 30 days of service. The club agrees to pay FastForward $2,700 on January 10, 2005, when the service period is complete. At December 31, 2004, 20 days of services have already been provided. Since the contracted services are not yet entirely provided, FastForward has neither billed the club nor recorded the services already provided. Still, FastForward has earned two-thirds of the 30-day fee, or $1,800 ($2,700 × 20/30). The *revenue recognition principle* implies that it must report the $1,800 on the December income statement. The balance sheet also must report that the club owes FastForward $1,800.

The year-end adjusting entry to account for accrued services revenue is

Assets	=	Liabilities	+	Equity
+1,800				+1,800

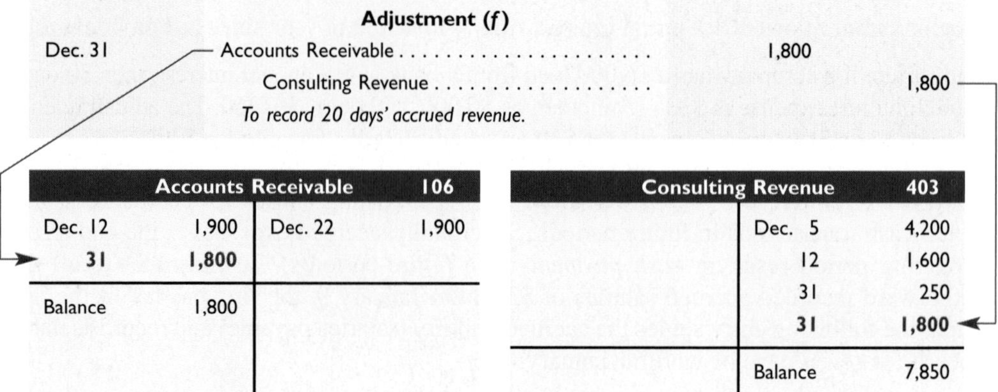

Adjustment (*f*)

Dec. 31	Accounts Receivable	1,800	
	Consulting Revenue		1,800
	To record 20 days' accrued revenue.		

Accounts Receivable			106
Dec. 12	1,900	Dec. 22	1,900
31	**1,800**		
Balance	1,800		

Consulting Revenue			403
		Dec. 5	4,200
		12	1,600
		31	250
		31	**1,800**
		Balance	7,850

Example: What is the adjusting entry if the 30-day consulting period began on December 22? *Answer:* One-third of the fee is earned:
Accounts Receivable . . . 900
Consulting Revenue . . . 900

Accounts receivable are reported on the balance sheet at $1,800, and the $7,850 of consulting revenue is reported on the income statement. *Not* making the adjustment would understate (1) both consulting revenue and net income by $1,800 in the December income statement and (2) both accounts receivable (assets) and equity by $1,800 on the December 31 balance sheet.

Decision Maker

Loan Officer The owner of an electronics store applies for a business loan. The store's financial statements reveal large increases in current-year revenues and income. Analysis shows that these increases are due to a promotion that let consumers buy now and pay nothing until January 1 of next year. The store recorded these sales as accrued revenue. Does your analysis raise any concerns?

Answer—p. 115

Accrued Interest Revenue In addition to the accrued interest expense we described earlier, interest can yield an accrued revenue when a debtor owes money (or other assets) to a company. If a company is holding notes or accounts receivable that produce interest revenue, we must adjust the accounts to record any earned and yet uncollected interest revenue. The adjusting entry is similar to the one for accruing services revenue. Specifically, we debit Interest Receivable (asset) and credit Interest Revenue.

Future Receipt of Accrued Revenues Accrued revenues at the end of one accounting period result in *cash receipts* in a *future* period(s). To illustrate, recall that FastForward made an adjusting entry for $1,800 to record 20 days' accrued revenue earned from its consulting contract. When FastForward receives $2,700 cash on January 10 for the entire contract amount, it makes the following entry to remove the accrued asset (accounts receivable) and recognize the revenue earned in January. The $2,700 debit reflects the cash received. The $1,800 credit reflects the removal of the receivable, and the $900 credit records the revenue earned in January.

Assets	=	Liabilities	+	Equity
+2,700				+900
−1,800				

Jan. 10	Cash	2,700	
	Accounts Receivable (20 days at $90 per day)		1,800
	Consulting Revenue (10 days at $90 per day)		900
	Received cash for the accrued asset and recorded earned consulting revenue.		

Links to Financial Statements

A1 Explain how accounting adjustments link to financial statements.

The process of adjusting accounts is intended to bring an asset or liability account balance to its correct amount. It also updates a related expense or revenue account. These adjustments are necessary for transactions and events that extend over more than one period. (Adjusting entries are posted like any other entry.)

Exhibit 3.12 summarizes the four types of transactions requiring adjustment. Understanding this exhibit is important to understanding the adjusting process and its

Category	Before Adjusting: Balance Sheet	Before Adjusting: Income Statement	Adjusting Entry
Prepaid expenses†	Asset overstated Equity overstated	Expense understated	Dr. Expense Cr. Asset*
Unearned revenues†	Liability overstated Equity understated	Revenue understated	Dr. Liability Cr. Revenue
Accrued expenses	Liability understated Equity overstated	Expense understated	Dr. Expense Cr. Liability
Accrued revenues	Asset understated Equity understated	Revenue understated	Dr. Asset Cr. Revenue

* For depreciation, the credit is to Accumulated Depreciation (contra asset).

† Exhibit assumes that Prepaid Expenses are initially recorded as assets and that Unearned Revenues are initially recorded as liabilities.

Exhibit 3.12

Summary of Adjustments and Financial Statement Links

importance to financial statements. Remember that each adjusting entry affects one or more income statement accounts *and* one or more balance sheet accounts (but not cash).

Information about some adjustments is not always available until several days or even weeks after the period-end. This means that some adjusting and closing entries are recorded later than, but dated as of, the last day of the period. One example is a company that receives a utility bill on January 10 for costs incurred for the month of December. When it receives the bill, the company records the expense and the payable as of December 31. Other examples include long-distance phone usage and costs of many Web billings. The December income statement reflects these additional expenses incurred, and the December 31 balance sheet includes these payables, although the amounts were not actually known on December 31.

Decision Ethics

Financial Officer At year-end, the president instructs you, the financial officer, not to record accrued expenses until next year because they will not be paid until then. The president also directs you to record in current-year sales a recent purchase order from a customer that requires merchandise to be delivered two weeks after the year-end. Your company would report a net income instead of a net loss if you carry out these instructions. What do you do?

Answer—p. 115

Quick Check

6. If an adjusting entry for accrued revenues of $200 at year-end is omitted, what is this error's effect on the year-end income statement and balance sheet?
7. What is a contra account? Explain its purpose.
8. What is an accrued expense? Give an example.
9. Describe how an unearned revenue arises. Give an example.

Answers—p. 115

Adjusted Trial Balance

P2 Explain and prepare an adjusted trial balance.

An **unadjusted trial balance** is a list of accounts and balances prepared *before* adjustments are recorded. An **adjusted trial balance** is a list of accounts and balances prepared *after* adjusting entries have been recorded and posted to the ledger.

Exhibit 3.13 shows both the unadjusted and the adjusted trial balances for FastForward at December 31, 2004. The order of accounts in the trial balance is usually set up to match the order in the chart of accounts. Notice that several new accounts arise from the adjusting entries. Each adjustment is identified by a letter in parentheses that links it to an adjusting entry explained earlier. Each amount in the Adjusted Trial Balance columns is computed by taking that account's amount from the Unadjusted Trial Balance columns and adding or subtracting any adjustment(s). To illustrate, Supplies has a $9,720 Dr. balance in the unadjusted columns. Subtracting the $1,050 Cr. amount shown in the adjustments

Exhibit 3.13

Unadjusted and Adjusted Trial Balances

FASTFORWARD
Trial Balances
December 31, 2004

Acct. No.	Account Title	Unadjusted Trial Balance Dr.	Unadjusted Trial Balance Cr.	Adjustments Dr.	Adjustments Cr.	Adjusted Trial Balance Dr.	Adjusted Trial Balance Cr.
101	Cash	$ 3,950				$ 3,950	
106	Accounts receivable	0		*(f)* $1,800		1,800	
126	Supplies	9,720			*(b)* $1,050	8,670	
128	Prepaid insurance	2,400			*(a)* 100	2,300	
167	Equipment	26,000				26,000	
168	Accumulated depreciation—Equip.		$ 0		*(c)* 375		$ 375
201	Accounts payable		6,200				6,200
209	Salaries payable		0		*(e)* 210		210
236	Unearned consulting revenue		3,000	*(d)* 250			2,750
301	C. Taylor, Capital		30,000				30,000
302	C. Taylor, Withdrawals	600				600	
403	Consulting revenue		5,800		*(d)* 250		7,850
					(f) 1,800		
406	Rental revenue		300				300
612	Depreciation expense—Equip.	0		*(c)* 375		375	
622	Salaries expense	1,400		*(e)* 210		1,610	
637	Insurance expense	0		*(a)* 100		100	
640	Rent expense	1,000				1,000	
652	Supplies expense	0		*(b)* 1,050		1,050	
690	Utilities expense	230				230	
	Totals	$45,300	$45,300	$3,785	$3,785	$47,685	$47,685

columns yields an adjusted $8,670 Dr. balance for Supplies. An account can have more than one adjustment, such as for Consulting Revenue. Also, some accounts might not require adjustment for this period, such as Accounts Payable.

Preparing Financial Statements

P3 Prepare financial statements from an adjusted trial balance.

We can prepare financial statements directly from information in the *adjusted* trial balance. An adjusted trial balance (see the right-most columns in Exhibit 3.13) includes all accounts and balances appearing in financial statements, and is easier to work from than the entire ledger when preparing financial statements.

Exhibit 3.14 shows how revenue and expense balances are transferred from the adjusted trial balance to the income statement (red lines). The net income and the withdrawals amount is then used to prepare the statement of owner's equity (black lines). Asset and liability balances on the adjusted trial balance are then transferred to the balance sheet (blue lines). The ending capital is determined on the statement of owner's equity and transferred to the balance sheet (green lines).

We usually prepare financial statements in the following order: income statement, statement of owner's equity, and balance sheet. This order makes sense since the balance sheet uses information from the statement of owner's equity, which in turn uses information from the income statement. The statement of cash flows is usually the final statement prepared.

Point: Sarbanes-Oxley Act requires that financial statements filed with the SEC be certified by the CEO and CFO, including a declaration that the statements fairly present the issuer's operations and financial condition. Violators can receive a $5,000,000 fine and/or 20 years imprisonment.

Exhibit 3.14

Preparing the Financial Statements (Adjusted Trial Balance from Exhibit 3.13)

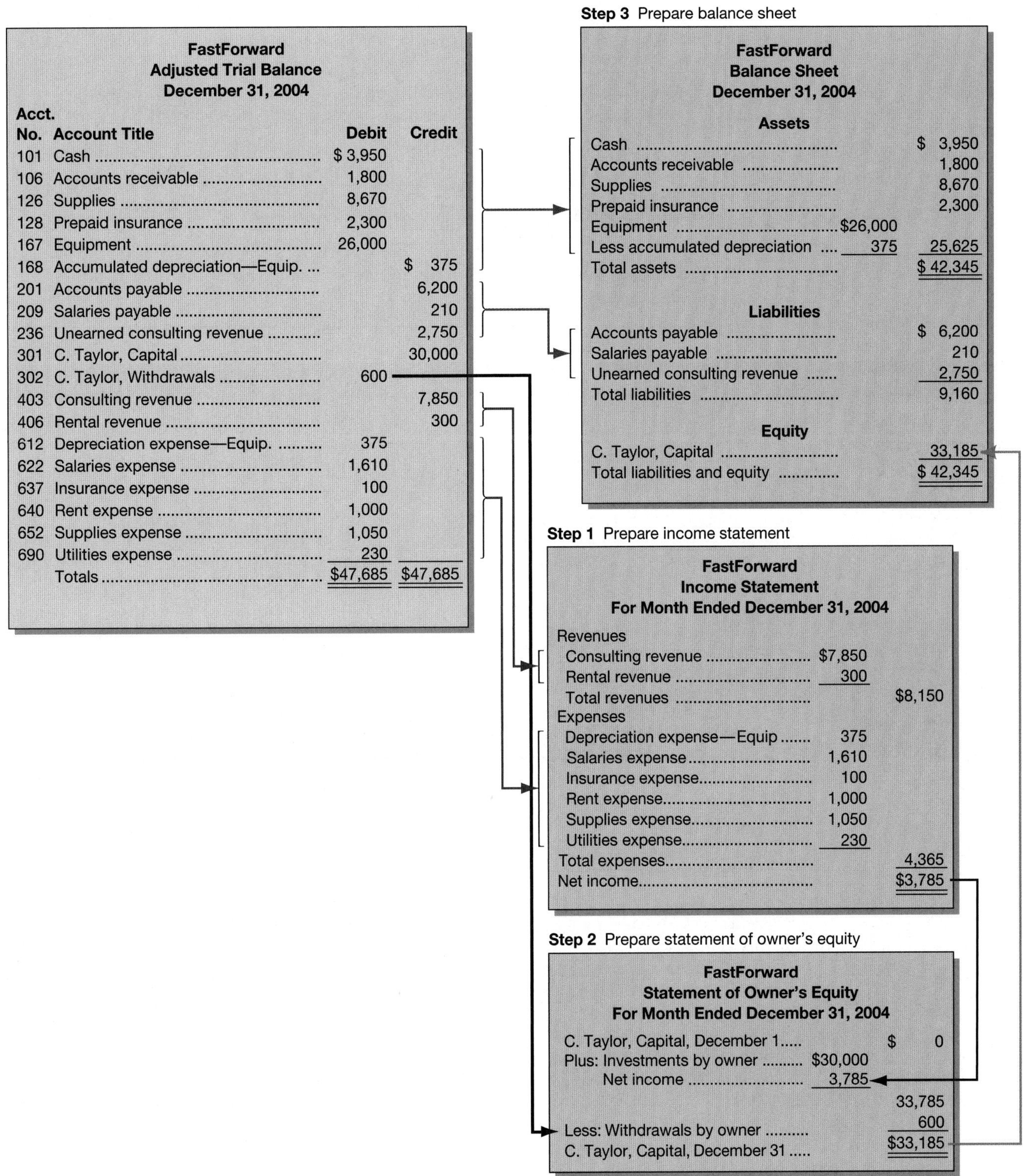

FastForward
Adjusted Trial Balance
December 31, 2004

Acct. No.	Account Title	Debit	Credit
101	Cash	$ 3,950	
106	Accounts receivable	1,800	
126	Supplies	8,670	
128	Prepaid insurance	2,300	
167	Equipment	26,000	
168	Accumulated depreciation—Equip.		$ 375
201	Accounts payable		6,200
209	Salaries payable		210
236	Unearned consulting revenue		2,750
301	C. Taylor, Capital		30,000
302	C. Taylor, Withdrawals	600	
403	Consulting revenue		7,850
406	Rental revenue		300
612	Depreciation expense—Equip.	375	
622	Salaries expense	1,610	
637	Insurance expense	100	
640	Rent expense	1,000	
652	Supplies expense	1,050	
690	Utilities expense	230	
	Totals	$47,685	$47,685

Step 3 Prepare balance sheet

FastForward
Balance Sheet
December 31, 2004

Assets		
Cash		$ 3,950
Accounts receivable		1,800
Supplies		8,670
Prepaid insurance		2,300
Equipment	$26,000	
Less accumulated depreciation	375	25,625
Total assets		$ 42,345
Liabilities		
Accounts payable		$ 6,200
Salaries payable		210
Unearned consulting revenue		2,750
Total liabilities		9,160
Equity		
C. Taylor, Capital		33,185
Total liabilities and equity		$ 42,345

Step 1 Prepare income statement

FastForward
Income Statement
For Month Ended December 31, 2004

Revenues		
Consulting revenue	$7,850	
Rental revenue	300	
Total revenues		$8,150
Expenses		
Depreciation expense—Equip	375	
Salaries expense	1,610	
Insurance expense	100	
Rent expense	1,000	
Supplies expense	1,050	
Utilities expense	230	
Total expenses		4,365
Net income		$3,785

Step 2 Prepare statement of owner's equity

FastForward
Statement of Owner's Equity
For Month Ended December 31, 2004

C. Taylor, Capital, December 1		$ 0
Plus: Investments by owner	$30,000	
Net income	3,785	
		33,785
Less: Withdrawals by owner		600
C. Taylor, Capital, December 31		$33,185

Quick Check

10. Music-Mart records $1,000 of accrued salaries on December 31. Five days later, on January 5 (the next payday), salaries of $7,000 are paid. What is the January 5 entry?

11. Jordan Air has the following information in its unadjusted and adjusted trial balances:

	Unadjusted		Adjusted	
	Debit	Credit	Debit	Credit
Prepaid insurance	$6,200		$5,900	
Salaries payable		$ 0		$1,400

What are the adjusting entries that Jordan Air likely recorded?

12. What accounts are taken from the adjusted trial balance to prepare an income statement?

13. In preparing financial statements from an adjusted trial balance, what statement is usually prepared second?

Answers—p. 115

Decision Analysis — Profit Margin

A2 Compute profit margin and describe its use in analyzing company performance.

A useful measure of a company's operating results is the ratio of its net income to net sales. This ratio is called **profit margin,** or *return on sales,* and is computed as in Exhibit 3.15.

Exhibit 3.15

Profit Margin

$$\textbf{Profit margin} = \frac{\textbf{Net income}}{\textbf{Net sales}}$$

This ratio is interpreted as reflecting the percent of profit in each dollar of sales. To illustrate how we compute and use profit margin, let's look at the results of **Limited Brands, Inc.,** in Exhibit 3.16 for the period 2000–2003.

Exhibit 3.16

Limited Brands's Profit Margin

	2003	2002	2001	2000
Net income (in mil.)	$ 502	$ 519	$ 428	$ 461
Net sales (in mil.)	$8,445	$8,423	$9,080	$8,765
Profit margin	**5.9%**	**6.2%**	**4.7%**	**5.3%**
Industry profit margin	**1.8%**	**1.5%**	**2.5%**	**2.9%**

The Limited's average profit margin is 5.5% during this period. This favorably compares to the average industry profit margin of 2.2%. Moreover, Limited's most recent two years' profit margins are markedly better than earlier years.

Thus, while 2001 was a difficult year for Limited in generating profits on its sales, Limited's performance has slightly improved in 2002–2003. Future success, of course, depends on Limited maintaining and preferably increasing its profit margin.

Demonstration Problem 1

The following information relates to Fanning's Electronics on December 31, 2005. The company, which uses the calendar year as its annual reporting period, initially records prepaid and unearned items in balance sheet accounts (assets and liabilities, respectively).

a. The company's weekly payroll is $8,750, paid each Friday for a five-day workweek. December 31, 2005, falls on a Monday, but the employees will not be paid their wages until Friday, January 4, 2006.

b. Eighteen months earlier, on July 1, 2004, the company purchased equipment that cost $20,000. Its useful life is predicted to be five years, at which time the equipment is expected to be worthless (zero salvage value).

c. On October 1, 2005, the company agreed to work on a new housing development. The company is paid $120,000 on October 1 in advance of future installation of similar alarm systems in 24 new homes. That amount was credited to the Unearned Services Revenue account. Between October 1 and December 31, work on 20 homes was completed.

d. On September 1, 2005, the company purchased a 12-month insurance policy for $1,800. The transaction was recorded with an $1,800 debit to Prepaid Insurance.

e. On December 29, 2005, the company performed a $7,000 service that has not been billed and not recorded as of December 31, 2005.

Required

1. Prepare any necessary adjusting entries on December 31, 2005, in relation to transactions and events *a* through *e*.
2. Prepare T-accounts for the accounts affected by adjusting entries, and post the adjusting entries. Determine the adjusted balances for the Unearned Revenue and the Prepaid Insurance accounts.
3. Complete the following table and determine the amounts and effects of your adjusting entries on the year 2005 income statement and the December 31, 2005, balance sheet. Use up (down) arrows to indicate an increase (decrease) in the Effect columns.

Entry	Amount in the Entry	Effect on Net Income	Effect on Total Assets	Effect on Total Liabilities	Effect on Total Equity

Planning the Solution

- Analyze each situation to determine which accounts need to be updated with an adjustment.
- Calculate the amount of each adjustment and prepare the necessary journal entries.
- Show the amount of each adjustment in the designated accounts, determine the adjusted balance, and identify the balance sheet classification of the account.
- Determine each entry's effect on net income for the year and on total assets, total liabilities, and total equity at the end of the year.

Solution to Demonstration Problem 1

1. Adjusting journal entries.

(*a*) Dec. 31	Wages Expense.	1,750	
	Wages Payable.		1,750
	To accrue wages for the last day of the year ($8,750 × 1/5).		
(*b*) Dec. 31	Depreciation Expense—Equipment	4,000	
	Accumulated Depreciation—Equipment.		4,000
	To record depreciation expense for the year ($20,000/5 years = $4,000 per year).		
(*c*) Dec. 31	Unearned Services Revenue.	100,000	
	Services Revenue.		100,000
	To recognize services revenue earned ($120,000 × 20/24).		

[continued on next page]

[continued from previous page]

(*d*) Dec. 31	Insurance Expense.	600	
	Prepaid Insurance.		600
	To adjust for expired portion of insurance ($1,800 × 4/12).		
(e) Dec. 31	Accounts Receivable	7,000	
	Services Revenue.		7,000
	To record services revenue earned.		

2. T-accounts for adjusting journal entries *a* through *e*.

Wages Expense			
(*a*)	1,750		

Wages Payable			
		(*a*)	1,750

Depreciation Expense—Equipment			
(*b*)	4,000		

Accumulated Depreciation—Equipment			
		(*b*)	4,000

Unearned Revenue			
		Unadj. Bal.	120,000
(*c*)	100,000		
		Adj. Bal.	20,000

Services Revenue			
		(*c*)	100,000
		(*e*)	7,000
		Adj. Bal.	107,000

Insurance Expense			
(*d*)	600		

Prepaid Insurance			
Unadj. Bal.	1,800		
		(*d*)	600
Adj. Bal.	1,200		

Accounts Receivable			
(*e*)	7,000		

3. Financial statement effects of adjusting journal entries.

Entry	Amount in the Entry	Effect on Net Income	Effect on Total Assets	Effect on Total Liabilities	Effect on Total Equity
a	$ 1,750	$ 1,750 ↓	No effect	$ 1,750 ↑	$ 1,750 ↓
b	4,000	4,000 ↓	$4,000 ↓	No effect	4,000 ↓
c	100,000	100,000 ↑	No effect	$100,000 ↓	100,000 ↑
d	600	600 ↓	$ 600 ↓	No effect	600 ↓
e	7,000	7,000 ↑	$7,000 ↑	No effect	7,000 ↑

Demonstration Problem 2

Use the following adjusted trial balance to answer questions 1–3.

CHOI COMPANY
Adjusted Trial Balance
December 31

	Debit	Credit
Cash	$ 3,050	
Accounts receivable	400	
Prepaid insurance	830	
Supplies	80	
Equipment	217,200	

[continued on next page]

[continued from previous page]

Accumulated depreciation—Equipment		$ 29,100
Wages payable		880
Interest payable		3,600
Unearned rent		460
Long-term notes payable		150,000
M. Choi, Capital		40,340
M. Choi, Withdrawals	21,000	
Rent earned		57,500
Wages expense	25,000	
Utilities expense	1,900	
Insurance expense	3,200	
Supplies expense	250	
Depreciation expense—Equipment	5,970	
Interest expense	3,000	
Totals	$281,880	$281,880

1. Prepare the annual income statement from the adjusted trial balance of Choi Company.

Answer:

CHOI COMPANY
Income Statement
For Year Ended December 31

Revenues		
Rent earned		$57,500
Expenses		
Wages expense	$25,000	
Utilities expense	1,900	
Insurance expense	3,200	
Supplies expense	250	
Depreciation expense—Equipment	5,970	
Interest expense	3,000	
Total expenses		39,320
Net income		$18,180

2. Prepare a statement of owner's equity from the adjusted trial balance of Choi Company. Choi's capital account balance of $40,340 consists of a $30,340 beginning-year balance, plus a $10,000 owner investment during the current year.

Answer:

CHOI COMPANY
Statement of Owner's Equity
For Year Ended December 31

M. Choi, Beginning-year Capital, December 31		$30,340
Plus: Owner investments	$10,000	
Net income	18,180	28,180
		58,520
Less: Withdrawals by owner		21,000
M. Choi, Year-end Capital, December 31		$37,520

3. Prepare a balance sheet from the adjusted trial balance of Choi Company.

Answer:

CHOI COMPANY Balance Sheet December 31		
Assets		
Cash		$ 3,050
Accounts receivable		400
Prepaid insurance		830
Supplies		80
Equipment	$217,200	
Less accumulated depreciation	29,100	188,100
Total assets		$192,460
Liabilities		
Wages payable		$ 880
Interest payable		3,600
Unearned rent		460
Long-term note payable		150,000
Total liabilities		154,940
Equity		
M. Choi, Capital		37,520
Total liabilities and equity		$192,460

APPENDIX

3A Alternative Accounting for Prepayments

This appendix explains an alternative in accounting for prepaid expenses and unearned revenues.

Recording the Prepayment of Expenses in Expense Accounts

P4 Identify and explain alternatives in accounting for prepaids.

An alternative method is to record *all* prepaid expenses with debits to expense accounts. If any prepaids remain unused or unexpired at the end of an accounting period, then adjusting entries must transfer the cost of the unused portions from expense accounts to prepaid expense (asset) accounts. This alternative method is acceptable. The financial statements are identical under either method, but the adjusting entries are different. To illustrate the differences between these two methods, let's look at FastForward's cash payment of December 6 for 24 months of insurance coverage beginning on December 1. FastForward recorded that payment with a debit to an asset account, but it could have recorded a debit to an expense account. These alternatives are shown in Exhibit 3A.1.

Exhibit 3A.1

Alternative Initial Entries for Prepaid Expenses

		Payment Recorded as Asset		Payment Recorded as Expense	
Dec. 6	Prepaid Insurance	2,400			
	Cash		2,400		
Dec. 6	Insurance Expense			2,400	
	Cash				2,400

At the end of its accounting period on December 31, insurance protection for one month has expired. This means $100 ($2,400/24) of insurance coverage expired and is an expense for December. The adjusting entry depends on how the original payment was recorded. This is shown in Exhibit 3A.2.

Exhibit 3A.2

Adjusting Entry for Prepaid Expenses for the Two Alternatives

		Payment Recorded as Asset		Payment Recorded as Expense	
Dec. 31	Insurance Expense	100			
	Prepaid Insurance		100		
Dec. 31	Prepaid Insurance			2,300	
	Insurance Expense				2,300

When these entries are posted to the accounts in the ledger, we can see that these two methods give identical results. The December 31 adjusted account balances in Exhibit 3A.3 show Prepaid Insurance of $2,300 and Insurance Expense of $100 for both methods.

Exhibit 3A.3

Account Balances under Two Alternatives for Recording Prepaid Expenses

Payment Recorded as Asset

Prepaid Insurance			128
Dec. 6	2,400	Dec. 31	100
Balance	**2,300**		

Insurance Expense			637
Dec. 31	**100**		

Payment Recorded as Expense

Prepaid Insurance			128
Dec. 31	**2,300**		

Insurance Expense			637
Dec. 6	2,400	Dec. 31	2,300
Balance	**100**		

Recording the Prepayment of Revenues in Revenue Accounts

As with prepaid expenses, an alternative method is to record *all* unearned revenues with credits to revenue accounts. If any revenues are unearned at the end of an accounting period, then adjusting entries must transfer the unearned portions from revenue accounts to unearned revenue (liability) accounts. This alternative method is acceptable. The adjusting entries are different for these two alternatives, but the financial statements are identical. To illustrate the accounting differences between these two methods, let's look at FastForward's December 26 receipt of $3,000 for consulting services covering the period December 27 to February 24. FastForward recorded this transaction with a credit to a liability account. The alternative is to record it with a credit to a revenue account, as shown in Exhibit 3A.4.

Exhibit 3A.4

Alternative Initial Entries for Unearned Revenues

		Receipt Recorded as Liability		Receipt Recorded as Revenue	
Dec. 26	Cash	3,000			
	Unearned Consulting Revenue		3,000		
Dec. 26	Cash			3,000	
	Consulting Revenue				3,000

By the end of its accounting period on December 31, FastForward has earned $250 of this revenue. This means $250 of the liability has been satisfied. Depending on how the initial receipt is recorded, the adjusting entry is as shown in Exhibit 3A.5.

Exhibit 3A.5

Adjusting Entry for Unearned Revenues for the Two Alternatives

		Receipt Recorded as Liability		Receipt Recorded as Revenue	
Dec. 31	Unearned Consulting Revenue	250			
	Consulting Revenue		250		
Dec. 31	Consulting Revenue			2,750	
	Unearned Consulting Revenue				2,750

After adjusting entries are posted, the two alternatives give identical results. The December 31 adjusted account balances in Exhibit 3A.6 show unearned consulting revenue of $2,750 and consulting revenue of $250 for both methods.

Exhibit 3A.6

Account Balances under Two Alternatives for Recording Unearned Revenues

Receipt Recorded as Liability

Unearned Consulting Revenue			236
Dec. 31	250	Dec. 26	3,000
		Balance	**2,750**

Consulting Revenue			403
		Dec. 31	**250**

Receipt Recorded as Revenue

Unearned Consulting Revenue			236
		Dec. 31	**2,750**

Consulting Revenue			403
Dec. 31	2,750	Dec. 26	3,000
		Balance	**250**

Summary

C1 Explain the importance of periodic reporting and the time period principle. The value of information is often linked to its timeliness. To provide timely information, accounting systems prepare periodic reports at regular intervals. The time period principle assumes that an organization's activities can be divided into specific time periods for periodic reporting.

C2 Explain accrual accounting and how it makes financial statements more useful. Accrual accounting recognizes revenue when earned and expenses when incurred—not necessarily when cash inflows and outflows occur. This information is valuable in assessing a company's financial position and performance.

C3 Identify the types of adjustments and their purpose. Adjustments can be grouped according to the timing of cash receipts and cash payments relative to when they are recognized as revenues or expenses as follows: prepaid expenses, unearned revenues, accrued expenses, and accrued revenues. Adjusting entries are necessary so that revenues, expenses, assets, and liabilities are correctly reported.

A1 Explain how accounting adjustments link to financial statements. Accounting adjustments bring an asset or liability account balance to its correct amount. They also update related expense or revenue accounts. Every adjusting entry affects one or more income statement accounts *and* one or more balance sheet accounts. An adjusting entry never affects cash.

A2 Compute profit margin and describe its use in analyzing company performance. *Profit margin* is defined as the reporting period's net income divided by its net sales. Profit margin reflects on a company's earnings activities by showing how much income is in each dollar of sales.

P1 Prepare and explain adjusting entries. *Prepaid expenses* refer to items paid for in advance of receiving their benefits. Prepaid expenses are assets. Adjusting entries for prepaids involve increasing (debiting) expenses and decreasing (crediting) assets. *Unearned* (or *prepaid*) *revenues* refer to cash received in advance of providing products and services. Unearned revenues are liabilities. Adjusting entries for unearned revenues involves increasing (crediting) revenues and decreasing (debiting) unearned revenues. *Accrued expenses* refer to costs incurred in a period that are both unpaid and unrecorded. Adjusting entries for recording accrued expenses involve increasing (debiting) expenses and increasing (crediting) liabilities. *Accrued revenues* refer to revenues earned in a period that are both unrecorded and not yet received in cash. Adjusting entries for recording accrued revenues involve increasing (debiting) assets and increasing (crediting) revenues.

P2 Explain and prepare an adjusted trial balance. An adjusted trial balance is a list of accounts and balances prepared after recording and posting adjusting entries. Financial statements are often prepared from the adjusted trial balance.

P3 Prepare financial statements from an adjusted trial balance. Revenue and expense balances are reported on the income statement. Asset, liability, and equity balances are reported on the balance sheet. We usually prepare statements in the following order: income statement, statement of owner's equity, balance sheet, and statement of cash flows.

P4[A] Identify and explain alternatives in accounting for prepaids. Charging all prepaid expenses to expense accounts when they are purchased is acceptable. When this is done, adjusting entries must transfer any unexpired amounts from expense accounts to asset accounts. Crediting all unearned revenues to revenue accounts when cash is received is also acceptable. In this case, the adjusting entries must transfer any unearned amounts from revenue accounts to unearned revenue accounts.

Guidance Answers to **Decision Maker** and **Decision Ethics**

Investor Prepaid expenses are items paid for in advance of receiving their benefits. They are assets and are expensed as they are used up. The publishing company's treatment of the signing bonus is acceptable provided future book sales can at least match the $500,000 expense. As an investor, you are concerned about the risk of future book sales. The riskier the likelihood of future book sales is, the more likely your analysis is to treat the $500,000, or a portion of it, as an expense, not a prepaid expense (asset).

Entrepreneur Depreciation is a process of cost allocation, not asset valuation. Knowing the depreciation schedule is not especially useful in your estimation of what the building and equipment are currently worth. Your own assessment of the age, quality, and usefulness of the building and equipment is more important.

Loan Officer Your concern in lending to this store arises from analysis of current-year sales. While increased revenues and income are fine, your concern is with collectibility of these promotional sales. If the owner sold products to customers with poor records of paying bills, then collectibility of these sales is low. Your analysis must assess this possibility and recognize any expected losses.

Financial Officer Omitting accrued expenses and recognizing revenue early can mislead financial statement users. One action is to request a second meeting with the president so you can explain that accruing expenses when incurred and recognizing revenue when earned are required practices. If the president persists, you might discuss the situation with legal counsel and any auditors involved. Your ethical action might cost you this job, but the potential pitfalls for falsification of statements, reputation loss, personal integrity, and other costs are too great.

Guidance Answers to **Quick Checks**

1. An annual reporting (or accounting) period covers one year and refers to the preparation of annual financial statements. The annual reporting period is not always a calendar year that ends on December 31. An organization can adopt a fiscal year consisting of any consecutive 12 months or 52 weeks.
2. Interim financial statements (covering less than one year) are prepared to provide timely information to decision makers.
3. The revenue recognition principle and the matching principle lead most directly to the adjusting process.
4. No. Cash basis accounting is not consistent with the matching principle because it reports expenses when paid, not in the period when revenue is earned as a result of those expenses.
5. No expense is reported in 2005. Under cash basis accounting, the entire $4,800 is reported as an expense in April 2004 when the premium is paid.
6. If the accrued revenues adjustment of $200 is not made, then both revenues and net income are understated by $200 on the current year's income statement, and both assets and equity are understated by $200 on the balance sheet.
7. A contra account is an account that is subtracted from the balance of a related account. Use of a contra account provides more information than simply reporting a net amount.
8. An accrued expense is a cost incurred in a period that is both unpaid and unrecorded prior to adjusting entries. One example is salaries earned but not yet paid at period-end.
9. An unearned revenue arises when a firm receives cash (or other assets) from a customer before providing the services or products to the customer. A magazine subscription paid in advance is one example; season ticket sales is another.
10.

Salaries Payable	1,000	
Salaries Expense	6,000	
Cash		7,000
Paid salary including accrual from December.		

11. The probable adjusting entries of Jordan Air are:

Insurance Expense	300	
Prepaid Insurance		300
To record insurance expired.		
Salaries Expense	1,400	
Salaries Payable		1,400
To record accrued salaries.		

12. Revenue accounts and expense accounts.
13. Statement of owner's equity.

Key Terms

Key Terms are available at the book's Website for learning and testing in an online Flashcard Format.

Accounting period (p. 94)
Accrual basis accounting (p. 95)
Accrued expenses (p. 101)
Accrued revenues (p. 103)
Adjusted trial balance (p. 105)
Adjusting entry (p. 97)
Annual financial statements (p. 95)
Book value (p. 100)
Cash basis accounting (p. 95)
Contra account (p. 99)
Depreciation (p. 99)
Fiscal year (p. 95)
Interim financial statements (p. 95)
Matching principle (p. 96)
Natural business year (p. 95)
Plant assets (p. 99)
Prepaid expenses (p. 97)
Profit margin (p. 108)
Straight-line depreciation method (p. 99)
Time period principle (p. 94)
Unadjusted trial balance (p. 105)
Unearned revenues (p. 100)

Personal Interactive Quiz

Personal Interactive Quizzes A and B are available at the book's Website to reinforce and assess your learning.

Superscript letter A denotes assignments based on Appendix 3A.

Discussion Questions

1. What is the difference between the cash basis and the accrual basis of accounting?
2. Why is the accrual basis of accounting generally preferred over the cash basis?
3. What type of business is most likely to select a fiscal year that corresponds to its natural business year instead of the calendar year?
4. Where is a prepaid expense reported in the financial statements?
5. What type of asset(s) requires adjusting entries to record depreciation?
6. What contra account is used when recording and reporting the effects of depreciation? Why is it used?
7. Where is unearned revenue reported in financial statements?
8. What is an accrued revenue? Give an example.
9. [A] If a company initially records prepaid expenses with debits to expense accounts, what type of account is debited in the adjusting entries for those prepaid expenses?
10. Review the balance sheet of **Krispy Kreme** in Appendix A. Identify two asset accounts that require adjustment before annual financial statements can be prepared. What would be the effect on the income statement if these two asset accounts were not adjusted?
11. Review the balance sheet of **Tastykake** in Appendix A. In addition to Prepayments, identify two accounts (either assets or liabilities) requiring adjusting entries.
12. Refer to **Harley-Davidson**'s balance sheet in Appendix A. If it made an adjustment for unpaid wages at year-end, where would the Accrued Wages Expense be reported on its balance sheet?

Red numbers denote Discussion Questions that involve decision-making.

***Homework Manager** repeats all numerical Quick Study assignments on the book's Website with new numbers each time they are worked. It can be used in practice, homework, or exam mode.*

QUICK STUDY

QS 3-1
Identifying accounting adjustments
C3

Classify the following adjusting entries as involving prepaid expenses (PE), unearned revenues (UR), accrued expenses (AE), or accrued revenues (AR).

a. ______ To record revenue earned that was previously received as cash in advance.
b. ______ To record annual depreciation expense.
c. ______ To record wages expense incurred but not yet paid (nor recorded).
d. ______ To record revenue earned but not yet billed (nor recorded).
e. ______ To record expiration of prepaid insurance.

QS 3-2
Adjusting prepaid expenses
P1

a. On July 1, 2005, Beyonce Company paid $1,800 for six months of insurance coverage. No adjustments have been made to the Prepaid Insurance account, and it is now December 31, 2005. Prepare the journal entry to reflect expiration of the insurance as of December 31, 2005.

b. Tyrell Company has a Supplies account balance of $1,000 on January 1, 2005. During 2005, it purchased $3,000 of supplies. As of December 31, 2005, a supplies inventory shows $1,300 of supplies available. Prepare the adjusting journal entry to correctly report the balance of the Supplies account and the Supplies Expense account as of December 31, 2005.

QS 3-3
Adjusting for depreciation
P1

a. Carlos Company purchases $30,000 of equipment on January 1, 2005. The equipment is expected to last five years and be worth $5,000 at the end of that time. Prepare the entry to record one year's depreciation expense for the equipment as of December 31, 2005.

b. Chavez Company purchases $40,000 of land on January 1, 2005. The land is expected to last indefinitely. What depreciation adjustment, if any, should be made with respect to the Land account as of December 31, 2005?

QS 3-4
Adjusting for unearned revenues
A1 P1

a. Eager receives $20,000 cash in advance for 4 months of legal services on October 1, 2005, and records it by debiting Cash and crediting Unearned Revenue both for $20,000. It is now December 31, 2005, and Eager has provided legal services as planned. What adjusting entry should Eager make to account for the work performed from October 1 through December 31, 2005?

b. S. Morford started a new publication called *Contest News*. Her subscribers pay $48 to receive 12 issues. With every new subscriber, Morford debits Cash and credits Unearned Subscription Revenue for the amounts received. Morford has 100 new subscribers as of July 1, 2005. She sends *Contest News* to each of these subscribers every month from July through December. Assuming no changes in subscribers, prepare the journal entry that Morford must make as of December 31, 2005, to adjust the Subscription Revenue account and the Unearned Subscription Revenue account.

QS 3-5
Accruing salaries
A1 P1

Matia Mouder employs one college student every summer in her coffee shop. The student works the five weekdays and is paid on the following Monday. (For example, a student who works Monday through Friday, June 1 through June 5, is paid for that work on Monday, June 8.) Mouder adjusts her books monthly, if needed, to show salaries earned but unpaid at month-end. The student works the last week of July—Friday is August 1. If the student earns $100 per day, what adjusting entry must Mouder make on July 31 to correctly record accrued salaries expense for July?

QS 3-6
Recording and analyzing adjusting entries
A1

Adjusting entries affect at least one balance sheet account and at least one income statement account. For the following entries, identify the account to be debited and the account to be credited. Indicate which of the accounts is the income statement account and which is the balance sheet account.

a. Entry to record revenue earned that was previously received as cash in advance.
b. Entry to record annual depreciation expense.
c. Entry to record wage expenses incurred but not yet paid (nor recorded).
d. Entry to record revenue earned but not yet billed (nor recorded).
e. Entry to record expiration of prepaid insurance.

QS 3-7
Preparing adjusting entries
C3 P1

During the year, Lola Co. recorded prepayments of expenses in asset accounts, and cash receipts of unearned revenues in liability accounts. At the end of its annual accounting period, the company must make three adjusting entries: (1) accrue salaries expense, (2) adjust the Unearned Services Revenue account to recognize earned revenue, and (3) record services revenue earned for which cash will be received the following period. For each of these adjusting entries (1), (2), and (3), indicate the account from *a* through *g* to be debited and the account to be credited.

a. Accounts Receivable
b. Prepaid Salaries
c. Cash
d. Salaries Payable
e. Unearned Services Revenue
f. Salaries Expense
g. Services Revenue

QS 3-8
Interpreting adjusting entries
C2 P2

The following information is taken from Cruz Company's unadjusted and adjusted trial balances:

	Unadjusted		Adjusted	
	Debit	Credit	Debit	Credit
Prepaid insurance	$4,100		$3,700	
Interest payable		$ 0		$800

Given this information, which of the following is likely included among its adjusting entries?

a. A $400 credit to Prepaid Insurance and an $800 debit to Interest Payable.
b. A $400 debit to Insurance Expense and an $800 debit to Interest Payable.
c. A $400 debit to Insurance Expense and an $800 debit to Interest Expense.

QS 3-9
Computing accrual and cash income
C1 C2

In its first year of operations, Harden Co. earned $39,000 in revenues and received $33,000 cash from these customers. The company incurred expenses of $22,500 but had not paid $2,250 of them at year-end. Harden also prepaid $3,750 cash for expenses that would be incurred the next year. Calculate the first year's net income under both the cash basis and the accrual basis of accounting.

QS 3-10
Determining effects of adjusting entries
C3 A1 

In making adjusting entries at the end of its accounting period, Gomez Consulting failed to record $1,600 of insurance coverage that had expired. This $1,600 cost had been initially debited to the Prepaid Insurance account. The company also failed to record accrued salaries expense of $1,000. As a result of these two oversights, the financial statements for the reporting period will [choose one] (1) understate assets by $1,600; (2) understate expenses by $2,600; (3) understate net income by $1,000; or (4) overstate liabilities by $1,000.

QS 3-11
Analyzing profit margin
A2

Yang Company reported net income of $37,925 and net sales of $390,000 for the current year. Calculate Yang's profit margin and interpret the result. Assume that Yang's competitors' average profit margin is 15%.

QS 3-12A
Preparing adjusting entries
C3 P4

Diego Consulting initially records prepaid and unearned items in income statement accounts. Given Diego Consulting's accounting practices, which of the following applies to the preparation of adjusting entries at the end of its first accounting period?

a. Earned but unbilled (and unrecorded) consulting fees are recorded with a debit to Unearned Consulting Fees and a credit to Consulting Fees Earned.

b. Unpaid salaries are recorded with a debit to Prepaid Salaries and a credit to Salaries Expense.

c. The cost of unused office supplies is recorded with a debit to Supplies Expense and a credit to Office Supplies.

d. Unearned fees (on which cash was received in advance earlier in the period) are recorded with a debit to Consulting Fees Earned and a credit to Unearned Consulting Fees.

Homework Manager *repeats all numerical Exercises on the book's Website with new numbers each time they are worked. It can be used in practice, homework, or exam mode.*

EXERCISES

Exercise 3-1
Classifying adjusting entries
C3

In the blank space beside each adjusting entry, enter the letter of the explanation *A* through *F* that most closely describes the entry:

A. To record this period's depreciation expense.
B. To record accrued salaries expense.
C. To record this period's use of a prepaid expense.
D. To record accrued interest revenue.
E. To record accrued interest expense.
F. To record the earning of previously unearned income.

		Account	Debit	Credit
____	1.	Salaries Expense	13,280	
		Salaries Payable		13,280
____	2.	Interest Expense	2,208	
		Interest Payable		2,208
____	3.	Insurance Expense	3,180	
		Prepaid Insurance		3,180
____	4.	Unearned Professional Fees	19,250	
		Professional Fees Earned		19,250
____	5.	Interest Receivable	3,300	
		Interest Revenue		3,300
____	6.	Depreciation Expense	38,217	
		Accumulated Depreciation		38,217

Exercise 3-2
Preparing adjusting entries
P1

For each of the following separate cases, prepare adjusting entries required for financial statements for the year ended (or date of) December 31, 2005. (Assume that prepaid expenses are initially recorded in asset accounts and that fees collected in advance of work are initially recorded as liabilities.)

a. One-third of the work related to $30,000 cash received in advance is performed this period.

b. Wages of $9,000 are earned by workers but not paid as of December 31, 2005.

c. Depreciation on the company's equipment for 2005 is $19,127.

d. The Office Supplies account had a $480 debit balance on December 31, 2004. During 2005, $5,349 of office supplies is purchased. A physical count of supplies at December 31, 2005, shows $587 of supplies available.

e. The Prepaid Insurance account had a $5,000 balance on December 31, 2004. An analysis of insurance policies shows that $2,200 of unexpired insurance benefits remain at December 31, 2005.

f. The company has earned (but not recorded) $750 of interest from investments in CDs for the year ended December 31, 2005. The interest revenue will be received on January 10, 2006.

g. The company has a bank loan and has incurred (but not recorded) interest expenses of $3,500 for the year ended December 31, 2005. The company must pay the interest on January 2, 2006.

Check (e) Dr. Insurance Expense, $2,800; (*f*) Cr. Interest Revenue, $750

Exercise 3-3
Preparing adjusting entries
P1

Prepare adjusting journal entries for the year ended (or date of) December 31, 2005, for each of these separate situations. Assume that prepaid expenses are initially recorded in asset accounts. Also assume that fees collected in advance of work are initially recorded as liabilities.

a. Depreciation on the company's equipment for 2005 is computed to be $16,000.

b. The Prepaid Insurance account had a $7,000 debit balance at December 31, 2005, before adjusting for the costs of any expired coverage. An analysis of the company's insurance policies showed that $1,040 of unexpired insurance coverage remains.

c. The Office Supplies account had a $300 debit balance on December 31, 2004; and $2,680 of office supplies was purchased during the year. The December 31, 2005, physical count showed $354 of supplies available.

d. One-half of the work related to $10,000 cash received in advance was performed this period.

e. The Prepaid Insurance account had a $5,600 debit balance at December 31, 2005, before adjusting for the costs of any expired coverage. An analysis of insurance policies showed that $4,600 of coverage had expired.

f. Wage expenses of $4,000 have been incurred but are not paid as of December 31, 2005.

Check (c) Dr. Office Supplies Expense, $2,626; (e) Dr. Insurance Expense, $4,600

Exercise 3-4
Adjusting and paying accrued wages
C1 P1

Pablo Management has five part-time employees, each of whom earns $100 per day. They are normally paid on Fridays for work completed Monday through Friday of the same week. They were paid in full on Friday, December 28, 2005. The next week, the five employees worked only four days because New Year's Day was an unpaid holiday. Show (*a*) the adjusting entry that would be recorded on Monday, December 31, 2005, and (*b*) the journal entry that would be made to record payment of the employees' wages on Friday, January 4, 2006.

Exercise 3-5
Determining cost flows through accounts
C1 A1 P1

Determine the missing amounts in each of these four separate situations *a* through *d*:

	a	b	c	d
Supplies available—prior year-end	$ 300	$1,600	$1,360	?
Supplies purchased during the current year	2,100	5,400	?	$6,000
Supplies available—current year-end	750	?	1,840	800
Supplies expense for the current year	?	1,300	9,600	6,575

Exercise 3-6
Adjusting and paying accrued expenses
A1 P1

The following three separate situations require adjusting journal entries to prepare financial statements as of April 30. For each situation, present both the April 30 adjusting entry and the subsequent entry during May to record the payment of the accrued expenses.

a. On April 1, the company retained an attorney at a flat monthly fee of $2,500. This amount is payable on the 12th of the following month.

b. A $780,000 note payable requires 9.6% annual interest, or $6,240 to be paid at the end of each 30 days. The interest was last paid on April 20 and the next payment is due on May 20. As of April 30, $2,080 of interest has accrued.

c. Total weekly salaries expense for all employees is $9,000. This amount is paid at the end of the day on Friday of each five-day workweek. April 30 falls on Tuesday of this year, which means that the employees had worked two days since the last payday. The next payday is May 3.

Check (*b*) May 20 Dr. Interest Expense, $4,160

Exercise 3-7
Determining assets and expenses for accrual and cash accounting
C2

On March 1, 2003, a company paid a $16,200 premium on a 36-month insurance policy for coverage beginning on that date. Refer to that policy and fill in the blanks in the following table:

Balance Sheet Insurance Asset Using			Insurance Expense Using		
	Accrual Basis	Cash Basis		Accrual Basis	Cash Basis
Dec. 31, 2003	$_____	$_____	2003	$_____	$_____
Dec. 31, 2004	_____	_____	2004	_____	_____
Dec. 31, 2005	_____	_____	2005	_____	_____
Dec. 31, 2006	_____	_____	2006	_____	_____
			Total	$_____	$_____

Check 2005 insurance expense: Accrual, $5,400; Cash, $0. Dec. 31, 2005, asset: Accrual, $900; Cash, $0.

Exercise 3-8
Analyzing and preparing adjusting entries
A1 P1 P3

Following are two income statements for Kendis Co. for the year ended December 31. The left column is prepared before any adjusting entries are recorded, and the right column includes the effects of adjusting entries. The company records cash receipts and payments related to unearned and prepaid items in balance sheet accounts. Analyze the statements and prepare the eight adjusting entries that likely were recorded. (*Note:* 30% of the $6,000 adjustment for Fees Earned has been earned but not billed, and the other 70% has been earned by performing services that were paid for in advance.)

KENDIS CO.
Income Statements
For Year Ended December 31

	Unadjusted	Adjusted
Revenues		
Fees earned	$24,000	$30,000
Commissions earned	42,500	42,500
Total revenues	66,500	72,500
Expenses		
Depreciation expense—Computers	0	1,500
Depreciation expense—Office furniture	0	1,750
Salaries expense	12,500	14,950
Insurance expense	0	1,300
Rent expense	4,500	4,500
Office supplies expense	0	480
Advertising expense	3,000	3,000
Utilities expense	1,250	1,320
Total expenses	21,250	28,800
Net income	$45,250	$43,700

Exercise 3-9
Computing and interpreting profit margin
A2

Use the following information to compute profit margin for each separate company *a* through *e:*

	Net Income	Net Sales		Net Income	Net Sales
a.	$ 5,390	$ 44,830	**d.**	$55,234	$1,458,999
b.	87,644	398,954	**e.**	70,158	435,925
c.	93,385	257,082			

Which of the five companies is the most profitable according to the profit margin ratio? Interpret that company's profit margin ratio.

Exercise 3-10^A
Adjusting for prepaids recorded as expenses and unearned revenues recorded as revenues
P4

On-The-Mark Construction began operations on December 1. In setting up its accounting procedures, the company decided to debit expense accounts when it prepays its expenses and to credit revenue accounts when customers pay for services in advance. Prepare journal entries for items *a* through *d* and the adjusting entries as of its December 31 period-end for items *e* through *g*.

a. Supplies are purchased on December 1 for $3,000 cash.

b. The company prepaid its insurance premiums for $1,440 cash on December 2.

c. On December 15, the company receives an advance payment of $12,000 cash from a customer for remodeling work.

d. On December 28, the company receives $3,600 cash from another customer for remodeling work to be performed in January.

e. A physical count on December 31 indicates that On-The-Mark has $1,920 of supplies available.

f. An analysis of the insurance policies in effect on December 31 shows that $240 of insurance coverage had expired.

g. As of December 31, only one remodeling project has been worked on and completed. The $6,300 fee for this project had been received in advance.

Check (*f*) Cr. Insurance Expense, $1,200; (*g*) Dr. Remodeling Fees Earned, $9,300

Exercise 3-11[A]

Recording and reporting revenues received in advance

P4

Cosmo Company experienced the following events and transactions during July:

July	1	Received $2,000 cash in advance of performing work for Jill Dwyer.
	6	Received $8,400 cash in advance of performing work for Lisa Poe.
	12	Completed the job for Dwyer.
	18	Received $7,500 cash in advance of performing work for Vern Hillsman.
	27	Completed the job for Poe.
	31	None of the work for Hillsman has been performed.

a. Prepare journal entries (including any adjusting entries as of the end of the month) to record these events using the procedure of initially crediting the Unearned Fees account when payment is received from a customer in advance of performing services.

b. Prepare journal entries (including any adjusting entries as of the end of the month) to record these events using the procedure of initially crediting the Fees Earned account when payment is received from a customer in advance of performing services.

c. Under each method, determine the amount of earned fees reported on the income statement for July and the amount of unearned fees reported on the balance sheet as of July 31.

Check (c) Fees Earned, $10,400

PROBLEM SET A

Problem 3-1A

Identifying adjusting entries with explanations

C3 P1

For each of the following entries, enter the letter of the explanation that most closely describes it in the space beside each entry. (You can use letters more than once.)

A. To record receipt of unearned revenue.

B. To record this period's earning of prior unearned revenue.

C. To record payment of an accrued expense.

D. To record receipt of an accrued revenue.

E. To record an accrued expense.

F. To record an accrued revenue.

G. To record this period's use of a prepaid expense.

H. To record payment of a prepaid expense.

I. To record this period's depreciation expense.

		Account	Debit	Credit
_____	1.	Rent Expense	2,000	
		Prepaid Rent		2,000
_____	2.	Interest Expense	1,000	
		Interest Payable		1,000
_____	3.	Depreciation Expense	4,000	
		Accumulated Depreciation		4,000
_____	4.	Unearned Professional Fees	3,000	
		Professional Fees Earned		3,000
_____	5.	Insurance Expense	4,200	
		Prepaid Insurance		4,200
_____	6.	Salaries Payable	1,400	
		Cash		1,400
_____	7.	Prepaid Rent	4,500	
		Cash		4,500
_____	8.	Salaries Expense	6,000	
		Salaries Payable		6,000
_____	9.	Interest Receivable	5,000	
		Interest Revenue		5,000
_____	10.	Cash	9,000	
		Accounts Receivable (from consulting)		9,000
_____	11.	Cash	7,500	
		Unearned Professional Fees		7,500
_____	12.	Cash	2,000	
		Interest Receivable		2,000

Problem 3-2A
Preparing adjusting and subsequent journal entries

C1 A1 P1

Maja Co. follows the practice of recording prepaid expenses and unearned revenues in balance sheet accounts. Maja's annual accounting period ends on December 31, 2005. The following information concerns the adjusting entries to be recorded as of that date:

a. The Office Supplies account started the year with a $3,000 balance. During 2005, the company purchased supplies for $12,400, which was added to the Office Supplies account. The inventory of supplies available at December 31, 2005, totaled $2,640.

b. An analysis of the company's insurance policies provided these facts:

Policy	Date of Purchase	Months of Coverage	Cost
A	April 1, 2004	24	$15,840
B	April 1, 2005	36	13,068
C	August 1, 2005	12	2,700

The total premium for each policy was paid in full (for all months) at the purchase date, and the Prepaid Insurance account was debited for the full cost. (Note that year-end adjusting entries for Prepaid Insurance were properly recorded in all prior years.)

c. The company has 15 employees, who earn a total of $2,100 in salaries each working day. They are paid each Monday for their work in the five-day workweek ending on the previous Friday. Assume that December 31, 2005, is a Tuesday, and all 15 employees worked the first two days of that week. Because New Year's Day is a paid holiday, they will be paid salaries for five full days on Monday, January 6, 2006.

d. The company purchased a building on January 1, 2005. It cost $855,000 and is expected to have a $45,000 salvage value at the end of its predicted 30-year life.

e. Since the company is not large enough to occupy the entire building it owns, it rented space to a tenant at $2,400 per month, starting on November 1, 2005. The rent was paid on time on November 1, and the amount received was credited to the Rent Earned account. However, the tenant has not paid the December rent. The company has worked out an agreement with the tenant, who has promised to pay both December and January rent in full on January 15. The tenant has agreed not to fall behind again.

f. On November 1, the company rented space to another tenant for $2,175 per month. The tenant paid five months' rent in advance on that date. The payment was recorded with a credit to the Unearned Rent account.

Required

1. Use the information to prepare adjusting entries as of December 31, 2005.

2. Prepare journal entries to record the first subsequent cash transaction in 2006 for parts *c* and *e*.

Check (1*b*) Dr. Insurance Expense, $12,312 (1*d*) Dr. Depreciation Expense, $27,000

Problem 3-3A
Preparing adjusting entries, adjusted trial balance, and financial statements

A1 P1 P2 P3

mhhe.com/larson

Watson Technical Institute (WTI), a school owned by Tom Watson, provides training to individuals who pay tuition directly to the school. WTI also offers training to groups in off-site locations. Its unadjusted trial balance as of December 31, 2005, follows. WTI initially records prepaid expenses and unearned revenues in balance sheet accounts. Descriptions of items *a* through *h* that require adjusting entries on December 31, 2005, follow.

Additional Information Items

a. An analysis of the school's insurance policies shows that $3,000 of coverage has expired.

b. An inventory count shows that teaching supplies costing $2,600 are available at year-end 2005.

c. Annual depreciation on the equipment is $12,000.

d. Annual depreciation on the professional library is $6,000.

e. On November 1, the school agreed to do a special six-month course (starting immediately) for a client. The contract calls for a monthly fee of $2,200, and the client paid the first five months' fees in advance. When the cash was received, the Unearned Training Fees account was credited. The fee for the sixth month will be recorded when it is collected in 2006.

f. On October 15, the school agreed to teach a four-month class (beginning immediately) for an individual for $3,000 tuition per month payable at the end of the class. The services are being provided as agreed, and no payment has yet been received.

g. The school's two employees are paid weekly. As of the end of the year, two days' wages have accrued at the rate of $100 per day for each employee.

h. The balance in the Prepaid Rent account represents rent for December.

WATSON TECHNICAL INSTITUTE Unadjusted Trial Balance December 31, 2005		
	Debit	**Credit**
Cash	$ 26,000	
Accounts receivable	0	
Teaching supplies	10,000	
Prepaid insurance	15,000	
Prepaid rent	2,000	
Professional library	30,000	
Accumulated depreciation—Professional library		$ 9,000
Equipment	70,000	
Accumulated depreciation—Equipment		16,000
Accounts payable		36,000
Salaries payable		0
Unearned training fees		11,000
T. Watson, Capital		63,600
T. Watson, Withdrawals	40,000	
Tuition fees earned		102,000
Training fees earned		38,000
Depreciation expense—Professional library	0	
Depreciation expense—Equipment	0	
Salaries expense	48,000	
Insurance expense	0	
Rent expense	22,000	
Teaching supplies expense	0	
Advertising expense	7,000	
Utilities expense	5,600	
Totals	$ 275,600	$ 275,600

Required

1. Prepare T-accounts (representing the ledger) with balances from the unadjusted trial balance.

2. Prepare the necessary adjusting journal entries for items *a* through *h* and post them to the T-accounts. Assume that adjusting entries are made only at year-end.

3. Update balances in the T-accounts for the adjusting entries and prepare an adjusted trial balance.

4. Prepare Watson Technical Institute's income statement and statement of owner's equity for the year 2005 and prepare its balance sheet as of December 31, 2005.

Check (2e) Cr. Training Fees Earned, $4,400; (2*f*) Cr. Tuition Fees Earned, $7,500; (3) Adj. Trial balance totals, $301,500; (4) Net income, $38,500; Ending T. Watson, Capital $62,100

Problem 3-4A
Interpreting unadjusted and adjusted trial balances, and preparing financial statements

C3 A1 P1 P2 P3

mhhe.com/larson

A six-column table for JJW Company follows. The first two columns contain the unadjusted trial balance for the company as of July 31, 2005. The last two columns contain the adjusted trial balance as of the same date.

Required

Analysis Component

1. Analyze the differences between the unadjusted and adjusted trial balances to determine the eight adjustments that likely were made. Show the results of your analysis by inserting these adjustment amounts in the table's two middle columns. Label each adjustment with a letter *a* through *h* and provide a short description of it at the bottom of the table.

Preparation Component

Check (2) Net income, $37,020; J. J. Winner, Capital (7/31/2005), $55,440; Total assets, $131,340

2. Use the information in the adjusted trial balance to prepare the company's (*a*) income statement and its statement of owner's equity for the year ended July 31, 2005 (*note:* J. Winner, Capital at July 31, 2004, was $28,420, and the current-year withdrawals were $10,000), and (*b*) the balance sheet as of July 31, 2005.

	Unadjusted Trial Balance		Adjustments		Adjusted Trial Balance	
Cash	$ 27,000				$ 27,000	
Accounts receivable	12,000				22,460	
Office supplies	18,000				3,000	
Prepaid insurance	7,320				4,880	
Office equipment	92,000				92,000	
Accum. depreciation—Office equip.		$ 12,000				$ 18,000
Accounts payable		9,300				10,200
Interest payable		0				800
Salaries payable		0				6,600
Unearned consulting fees		16,000				14,300
Long-term notes payable		44,000				44,000
J. Winner, Capital		28,420				28,420
J. Winner, Withdrawals	10,000				10,000	
Consulting fees earned		156,000				168,160
Depreciation expense—Office equip.	0				6,000	
Salaries expense	71,000				77,600	
Interest expense	1,400				2,200	
Insurance expense	0				2,440	
Rent expense	13,200				13,200	
Office supplies expense	0				15,000	
Advertising expense	13,800				14,700	
Totals	$265,720	$265,720			$290,480	$290,480

Problem 3-5A
Preparing financial statements from the adjusted trial balance and calculating profit margin
P3 A1 A2

The adjusted trial balance for Callahay Company as of December 31, 2005, follows:

	Debit	Credit
Cash	$ 22,000	
Accounts receivable	44,000	
Interest receivable	10,000	
Notes receivable (due in 90 days)	160,000	
Office supplies	8,000	
Automobiles	160,000	
Accumulated depreciation—Automobiles		$ 42,000
Equipment	130,000	
Accumulated depreciation—Equipment		10,000
Land	70,000	
Accounts payable		88,000
Interest payable		12,000
Salaries payable		11,000
Unearned fees		22,000
Long-term notes payable		130,000
J. Callahay, Capital		247,800
J. Callahay, Withdrawals	38,000	

[continued on next page]

[continued from previous page]

Fees earned		420,000
Interest earned		16,000
Depreciation expense—Automobiles	18,000	
Depreciation expense—Equipment	10,000	
Salaries expense	180,000	
Wages expense	32,000	
Interest expense	24,000	
Office supplies expense	26,000	
Advertising expense	50,000	
Repairs expense—Automobiles	16,800	
Totals	$998,800	$998,800

Required

1. Use the information in the adjusted trial balance to prepare (*a*) the income statement for the year ended December 31, 2005; (*b*) the statement of owner's equity for the year ended December 31, 2005; and (*c*) the balance sheet as of December 31, 2005.

2. Calculate the profit margin for year 2005.

Check (1) Total assets, $552,000

Problem 3-6A[A]
Recording prepaid expenses and unearned revenues

P1 P4

Quisp Co. had the following transactions in the last two months of its year ended December 31:

Nov.	1	Paid $1,500 cash for future newspaper advertising.
	1	Paid $2,160 cash for 12 months of insurance through October 31 of the next year.
	30	Received $3,300 cash for future services to be provided to a customer.
Dec.	1	Paid $2,700 cash for a consultant's services to be received over the next three months.
	15	Received $7,650 cash for future services to be provided to a customer.
	31	Of the advertising paid for on November 1, $900 worth is not yet used.
	31	A portion of the insurance paid for on November 1 has expired. No adjustment was made in November to Prepaid Insurance.
	31	Services worth $1,200 are not yet provided to the customer who paid on November 30.
	31	One-third of the consulting services paid for on December 1 have been received.
	31	The company has performed $3,000 of services that the customer paid for on December 15.

Required

1. Prepare entries for these transactions under the method that records prepaid expenses as assets and records unearned revenues as liabilities. Also prepare adjusting entries at the end of the year.

2. Prepare entries for these transactions under the method that records prepaid expenses as expenses and records unearned revenues as revenues. Also prepare adjusting entries at the end of the year.

Analysis Component

3. Explain why the alternative sets of entries in requirements 1 and 2 do not result in different financial statement amounts.

PROBLEM SET B

Problem 3-1B
Identifying adjusting entries with explanations

C3 P1

For each of the following entries, enter the letter of the explanation that most closely describes it in the space beside each entry. (You can use letters more than once.)

A. To record payment of a prepaid expense.
B. To record this period's use of a prepaid expense.
C. To record this period's depreciation expense.
D. To record receipt of unearned revenue.
E. To record this period's earning of prior unearned revenue.
F. To record an accrued expense.
G. To record payment of an accrued expense.
H. To record an accrued revenue.
I. To record receipt of accrued revenue.

			Debit	Credit
____	1.	Unearned Professional Fees	6,000	
		Professional Fees Earned		6,000
____	2.	Interest Receivable	3,500	
		Interest Revenue		3,500
____	3.	Salaries Payable	9,000	
		Cash		9,000
____	4.	Depreciation Expense	8,000	
		Accumulated Depreciation		8,000
____	5.	Cash	9,000	
		Unearned Professional Fees		9,000
____	6.	Insurance Expense	4,000	
		Prepaid Insurance		4,000
____	7.	Interest Expense	5,000	
		Interest Payable		5,000
____	8.	Cash	1,500	
		Accounts Receivable (from services)		1,500
____	9.	Salaries Expense	7,000	
		Salaries Payable		7,000
____	10.	Cash	1,000	
		Interest Receivable		1,000
____	11.	Prepaid Rent	3,000	
		Cash		3,000
____	12.	Rent Expense	7,500	
		Prepaid Rent		7,500

Problem 3-2B
Preparing adjusting and subsequent journal entries

C1 A1 P1

Nomo Co. follows the practice of recording prepaid expenses and unearned revenues in balance sheet accounts. Nomo's annual accounting period ends on October 31, 2005. The following information concerns the adjusting entries that need to be recorded as of that date:

a. The Office Supplies account started the fiscal year with a $500 balance. During the fiscal year, the company purchased supplies for $3,650, which was added to the Office Supplies account. The supplies available at October 31, 2005, totaled $700.

b. An analysis of the company's insurance policies provided these facts:

Policy	Date of Purchase	Months of Coverage	Cost
A	April 1, 2004	24	$3,000
B	April 1, 2005	36	3,600
C	August 1, 2005	12	660

The total premium for each policy was paid in full (for all months) at the purchase date, and the Prepaid Insurance account was debited for the full cost. (Note that year-end adjusting entries for Prepaid Insurance were properly recorded in all prior fiscal years.)

c. The company has four employees, who earn a total of $800 for each workday. They are paid each Monday for their work in the five-day workweek ending on the previous Friday. Assume that October 31, 2005, is a Monday, and all five employees worked the first day of that week. They will be paid salaries for five full days on Monday, November 7, 2005.

d. The company purchased a building on November 1, 2004, that cost $155,000 and is expected to have a $20,000 salvage value at the end of its predicted 25-year life.

e. Since the company does not occupy the entire building it owns, it rented space to a tenant at $600 per month, starting on September 1, 2005. The rent was paid on time on September 1, and the amount received was credited to the Rent Earned account. However, the October rent has not been paid. The company has worked out an agreement with the tenant, who has promised to pay both October and November rent in full on November 15. The tenant has agreed not to fall behind again.

f. On September 1, the company rented space to another tenant for $525 per month. The tenant paid five months' rent in advance on that date. The payment was recorded with a credit to the Unearned Rent account.

Required

1. Use the information to prepare adjusting entries as of October 31, 2005.
2. Prepare journal entries to record the first subsequent cash transaction in 2006 for parts *c* and *e*.

Check (1*b*) Dr. Insurance Expense, $2,365; (1*d*) Dr. Depreciation Expense, $5,400.

Problem 3-3B

Preparing adjusting entries, adjusted trial balance, and financial statements

A1 P1 P2 P3

Following is the unadjusted trial balance for Alcorn Institute as of December 31, 2005, which initially records prepaid expenses and unearned revenues in balance sheet accounts. The Institute provides one-on-one training to individuals who pay tuition directly to the business and offers extension training to groups in off-site locations. Shown after the trial balance are items *a* through *h* that require adjusting entries as of December 31, 2005.

	A	B	C
1	**ALCORN INSTITUTE** **Unadjusted Trial Balance** **December 31, 2005**		
2		**Debit**	**Credit**
3	Cash	$ 50,000	
4	Accounts receivable	0	
5	Teaching supplies	60,000	
6	Prepaid insurance	18,000	
7	Prepaid rent	2,600	
8	Professional library	10,000	
9	Accumulated depreciation—Professional library		$ 1,500
10	Equipment	30,000	
11	Accumulated depreciation—Equipment		16,000
12	Accounts payable		12,200
13	Salaries payable		0
14	Unearned training fees		27,600
15	M. Alcorn, Capital		68,500
16	M. Alcorn, Withdrawals	20,000	
17	Tuition fees earned		105,000
18	Training fees earned		62,000
19	Depreciation expense—Professional library	0	
20	Depreciation expense—Equipment	0	
21	Salaries expense	43,200	
22	Insurance expense	0	
23	Rent expense	28,600	
24	Teaching supplies expense	0	
25	Advertising expense	18,000	
26	Utilities expense	12,400	
27	Totals	$ 292,800	$292,800
28			

Additional Information Items

a. An analysis of the Institute's insurance policies shows that $6,400 of coverage has expired.

b. An inventory count shows that teaching supplies costing $2,500 are available at year-end 2005.

c. Annual depreciation on the equipment is $4,000.

d. Annual depreciation on the professional library is $2,000.

e. On November 1, the Institute agreed to do a special four-month course (starting immediately) for a client. The contract calls for a $4,600 monthly fee, and the client paid the first two months' fees in advance. When the cash was received, the Unearned Training Fees account was credited. The last two months' fees will be recorded when collected in 2006.

f. On October 15, the Institute agreed to teach a four-month class (beginning immediately) to an individual for $2,200 tuition per month payable at the end of the class. The class started on October 15, but no payment has yet been received.

g. The Institute's only employee is paid weekly. As of the end of the year, three days' wages have accrued at the rate of $180 per day.

h. The balance in the Prepaid Rent account represents rent for December.

Check (2e) Cr. Training Fees Earned, $9,200; (2*f*) Cr. Tuition Fees Earned, $5,500; (3) Adj. trial balance totals, $304,840; (4) Net income, $6,460; Ending M. Alcorn, Capital, $54,960

Required

1. Prepare T-accounts (representing the ledger) with balances from the unadjusted trial balance.
2. Prepare the necessary adjusting journal entries for items *a* through *h*, and post them to the T-accounts. Assume that adjusting entries are made only at year-end.
3. Update balances in the T-accounts for the adjusting entries and prepare an adjusted trial balance.
4. Prepare Alcorn Institute's income statement and statement of owner's equity for the year 2005, and prepare its balance sheet as of December 31, 2005.

Problem 3-4B

Interpreting unadjusted and adjusted trial balances, and preparing financial statements

C3 A1 P1 P2 P3 

A six-column table for Daxu Consulting Company follows. The first two columns contain the unadjusted trial balance for the company as of December 31, 2005, and the last two columns contain the adjusted trial balance as of the same date.

	Unadjusted Trial Balance		Adjustments		Adjusted Trial Balance	
Cash	$ 48,000				$ 48,000	
Accounts receivable	70,000				76,660	
Office supplies	30,000				7,000	
Prepaid insurance	13,200				8,600	
Office equipment	150,000				150,000	
Accumulated depreciation—Office equip.		$ 30,000				$ 40,000
Accounts payable		36,000				42,000
Interest payable		0				1,600
Salaries payable		0				11,200
Unearned consulting fees		30,000				17,800
Long-term notes payable		80,000				80,000
D. Chen, Capital		70,200				70,200
D. Chen, Withdrawals	10,000				10,000	
Consulting fees earned		264,000				282,860
Depreciation expense—Office equip.	0				10,000	
Salaries expense	115,600				126,800	
Interest expense	6,400				8,000	
Insurance expense	0				4,600	
Rent expense	24,000				24,000	
Office supplies expense	0				23,000	
Advertising expense	43,000				49,000	
Totals	$510,200	$510,200			$545,660	$545,660

Required

Analysis Component

1. Analyze the differences between the unadjusted and adjusted trial balances to determine the eight adjustments that likely were made. Show the results of your analysis by inserting these adjustment amounts in the table's two middle columns. Label each adjustment with a letter *a* through *h* and provide a short description of it at the bottom of the table.

Preparation Component

Check (2) Net income, $37,460; D. Chen, Capital (12/31/05), $97,660; Total assets, $250,260

2. Use the information in the adjusted trial balance to prepare this company's (*a*) income statement and its statement of owner's equity for the year ended December 31, 2005 (*note:* D. Chen, Capital at December 31, 2004, was $70,200, and the current-year withdrawals were $10,000), and (*b*) the balance sheet as of December 31, 2005.

Problem 3-5B
Preparing financial statements from the adjusted trial balance and calculating profit margin
P3 A1 A2

The adjusted trial balance for Lightning Courier as of December 31, 2005, follows:

	Debit	Credit
Cash	$ 48,000	
Accounts receivable	110,000	
Interest receivable	6,000	
Notes receivable (due in 90 days)	200,000	
Office supplies	12,000	
Trucks	124,000	
Accumulated depreciation—Trucks		$ 48,000
Equipment	260,000	
Accumulated depreciation—Equipment		190,000
Land	90,000	
Accounts payable		124,000
Interest payable		22,000
Salaries payable		30,000
Unearned delivery fees		110,000
Long-term notes payable		190,000
J. Hallam, Capital		115,000
J. Hallam, Withdrawals	40,000	
Delivery fees earned		580,000
Interest earned		24,000
Depreciation expense—Trucks	24,000	
Depreciation expense—Equipment	46,000	
Salaries expense	64,000	
Wages expense	290,000	
Interest expense	25,000	
Office supplies expense	33,000	
Advertising expense	26,400	
Repairs expense—Trucks	34,600	
Totals	$1,433,000	$1,433,000

Required

1. Use the information in the adjusted trial balance to prepare (a) the income statement for the year ended December 31, 2005, (b) the statement of owner's equity for the year ended December 31, 2005, and (c) the balance sheet as of December 31, 2005.

2. Calculate the profit margin for year 2005.

Check (1) Total assets, $612,000

Problem 3-6B^A
Recording prepaid expenses and unearned revenues
P1 P4

Quake Co. had the following transactions in the last two months of its fiscal year ended May 31:

Apr.	1	Paid $3,450 cash for future consulting services.
	1	Paid $2,700 cash for 12 months of insurance through March 31 of the next year.
	30	Received $7,500 cash for future services to be provided to a customer.
May	1	Paid $3,450 cash for future newspaper advertising.
	23	Received $9,450 cash for future services to be provided to a customer.
	31	Of the consulting services paid for on April 1, $1,500 worth has been received.
	31	A portion of the insurance paid for on April 1 has expired. No adjustment was made in April to Prepaid Insurance.
	31	Services worth $3,600 are not yet provided to the customer who paid on April 30.
	31	Of the advertising paid for on May 1, $1,050 worth is not yet used.
	31	The company has performed $4,500 of services that the customer paid for on May 23.

Required

1. Prepare entries for these transactions under the method that records prepaid expenses and unearned revenues in balance sheet accounts. Also prepare adjusting entries at the end of the year.
2. Prepare entries for these transactions under the method that records prepaid expenses and unearned revenues in income statement accounts. Also prepare adjusting entries at the end of the year.

Analysis Component

3. Explain why the alternative sets of entries in parts 1 and 2 do not result in different financial statement amounts.

PROBLEM SET C

Problem Set C is available at the book's Website to further reinforce and assess your learning.

SERIAL PROBLEM

Success Systems

This serial problem began in Chapter 1 and continues through most of the book. If previous chapter segments were not completed, the serial problem can still begin at this point. It is helpful, but not necessary, that you use the Working Papers that accompany the book.

After the success of the company's first two months, Kay Breeze continues to operate Success Systems. (Transactions for the first two months are described in the serial problem of Chapter 2.) The November 30, 2004, unadjusted trial balance of Success Systems (reflecting its transactions for October and November of 2004) follows:

No.	Account Title	Debit	Credit
101	Cash	$ 48,052	
106	Accounts receivable	12,618	
126	Computer supplies	2,545	
128	Prepaid insurance	2,220	
131	Prepaid rent	3,300	
163	Office equipment	8,000	
164	Accumulated depreciation—Office equipment		$ 0
167	Computer equipment	20,000	
168	Accumulated depreciation—Computer equipment		0
201	Accounts payable		0
210	Wages payable		0
236	Unearned computer services revenue		0
301	K. Breeze, Capital		83,000
302	K. Breeze, Withdrawals	5,600	
403	Computer services revenue		25,659
612	Depreciation expense—Office equipment	0	
613	Depreciation expense—Computer equipment	0	
623	Wages expense	2,625	
637	Insurance expense	0	
640	Rent expense	0	
652	Computer supplies expense	0	
655	Advertising expense	1,940	
676	Mileage expense	704	
677	Miscellaneous expenses	250	
684	Repairs expense—Computer	805	
	Totals	$108,659	$108,659

Success Systems had the following transactions and events in December 2004:

Dec. 2 Paid $1,025 cash to Hilldale Mall for Success Systems' share of mall advertising costs.
3 Paid $500 cash for minor repairs to the company's computer.
4 Received $3,950 cash from Alex's Engineering Co. for the receivable from November.
10 Paid cash to Sherry Adams for six days of work at the rate of $125 per day.

14 Notified by Alex's Engineering Co. that Success's bid of $7,000 on a proposed project has been accepted. Alex's paid a $1,500 cash advance to Success Systems.
15 Purchased $1,100 of computer supplies on credit from Cain Office Products.
16 Sent a reminder to Gomez Co. to pay the fee for services recorded on November 8.
20 Completed a project for Chang Corporation and received $5,625 cash.
22–26 Took the week off for the holidays.
28 Received $3,000 cash from Gomez Co. on its receivable.
29 Reimbursed Breeze's business automobile mileage (600 miles at $0.32 per mile).
31 Breeze withdrew $1,500 cash for personal use.

The following additional facts are collected for use in making adjusting entries prior to preparing financial statements for the company's first three months:

a. The December 31 inventory count of computer supplies shows $580 still available.
b. Three months have expired since the 12-month insurance premium was paid in advance.
c. As of December 31, Sherry Adams has not been paid for four days of work at $125 per day.
d. The company's computer is expected to have a four-year life with no salvage value.
e. The office equipment is expected to have a five-year life with no salvage value.
f. Prepaid rent for three of the four months has expired.

Required

1. Prepare journal entries to record each of the December transactions and events for Success Systems. Post these entries to the accounts in the ledger.
2. Prepare adjusting entries to reflect *a* through *f*. Post these entries to the accounts in the ledger.
3. Prepare an adjusted trial balance as of December 31, 2004.
4. Prepare an income statement for the three months ended December 31, 2004.
5. Prepare a statement of owner's equity for the three months ended December 31, 2004.
6. Prepare a balance sheet as of December 31, 2004.

Check (3) Adjusted trial balance totals, $119,034

(6) Total assets, $93,248

BEYOND THE NUMBERS

REPORTING IN ACTION

C1 C2 A1 A2

BTN 3-1 Refer to **Krispy Kreme**'s financial statements in Appendix A to answer the following:

1. Identify and write down the revenue recognition principle as explained in the chapter.
2. Research Krispy Kreme's footnotes to discover how it applies the revenue recognition principle. Report what you discover.
3. What is Krispy Kreme's profit margin for 2003 and for 2002?

Roll On

4. Access Krispy Kreme's financial statements (10-K) for fiscal years ending after February 2, 2003, at its Website (KrispyKreme.com) or the SEC's EDGAR database (www.SEC.gov). Compare the February 2, 2003, fiscal year profit margin to any subsequent year's profit margin that you are able to calculate.

COMPARATIVE ANALYSIS

A2

BTN 3-2 Key figures for the recent two years of both **Krispy Kreme** and **Tastykake** follow:

Key Figures	Krispy Kreme		Tastykake	
($ thousands)	Current Year	Prior Year	Current Year	Prior Year
Net income	$ 33,478	$ 26,378	$ 2,000*	$ 8,048*
Net sales	491,549	394,354	162,263	166,245

* Net income without restructuring charges.

Required

1. Compute profit margins for (*a*) Krispy Kreme and (*b*) Tastykake for the two years of data shown.
2. Which company is more successful on the basis of profit margin? Explain.

ETHICS CHALLENGE

C1 C2 A1 

BTN 3-3 Jackie Bergez works for Sea Biscuit Co. She and Bob Welch, her manager, are preparing adjusting entries for annual financial statements. Bergez computes depreciation and records it as

Depreciation Expense—Equipment	123,000	
Accumulated Depreciation—Equipment		123,000

Welch agrees with her computation but says the credit entry should be directly to the Equipment account. He argues that while accumulated depreciation is technically correct, "it is less hassle not to use a contra account and just credit the Equipment account directly. And besides, the balance sheet shows the same amount for total assets under either method."

Required

1. How should depreciation be recorded? Do you support Bergez or Welch?
2. Evaluate the strengths and weaknesses of Welch's reasons for preferring his method.
3. Indicate whether the situation Bergez faces is an ethical problem.

COMMUNICATING IN PRACTICE

C1 A2 

BTN 3-4 The class should be divided into teams. Teams are to select an industry (such as automobile manufacturing, airlines, defense contractors), and each team member is to select a different company in that industry. Each team member is to acquire the annual report of the company selected. Annual reports can be downloaded from company Websites or from the SEC's EDGAR database at (www.SEC.gov).

Required

1. Use the annual report to compute the return on assets, debt ratio, and profit margin.
2. Communicate with team members via a meeting, e-mail, or telephone to discuss the meaning of the ratios, how different companies compare to each other, and the industry norm. The team must prepare a single memo reporting the ratios for each company and identifying the conclusions or consensus of opinion reached during the team's discussion. The memo is to be copied and distributed to the instructor and all classmates.

TAKING IT TO THE NET

C1 A2 

mhhe.com/larson

BTN 3-5 Access the **Cannondale** promotional Website (Cannondale.com).

1. What is the primary product that Cannondale sells?
2. Review its form 10-K. You can access this from the EDGAR system (www.SEC.gov). You must scroll down the form to find the financial statements.
3. What is Cannondale's fiscal year-end?
4. What are Cannondale's net sales for the annual period ended June 29, 2002?
5. What is Cannondale's net income for the annual period ended June 29, 2002?
6. Compute Cannondale's profit margin ratio for the annual period ended June 29, 2002.
7. Do you think its decision to use a year-end of late June or early July relates to its natural business year?

TEAMWORK IN ACTION

C3 A1 P1 

BTN 3-6 Four types of adjustments are described in the chapter: (1) prepaid expenses, (2) unearned revenues, (3) accrued expenses, and (4) accrued revenues.

Required

1. Form *learning teams* of four (or more) members. Each team member must select one of the four adjustments as an area of expertise (each team must have at least one expert in each area).
2. Form *expert teams* from the individuals who have selected the same area of expertise. Expert teams are to discuss and write a report that each expert will present to his or her learning team addressing the following:
   a. Description of the adjustment and why it's necessary.
   b. Example of a transaction or event, with dates and amounts, that requires adjustment.

c. Adjusting entry(ies) for the example in requirement *b*.
d. Status of the affected account(s) before and after the adjustment in requirement *c*.
e. Effects on financial statements of not making the adjustment.

3. Each expert should return to his or her learning team. In rotation, each member should present his or her expert team's report to the learning team. Team discussion is encouraged.

BUSINESS WEEK ACTIVITY

C2 

mhhe.com/larson

BTN 3-7 Read the article "It's Like When Someone Robs a Bank," in the August 19, 2002, issue of ***Business Week***. (Access the book's Website for a free link.)

Required

1. Describe the type of overall accounting reform that FASB Chairman Herz favors.
2. What does Herz assert as being at the core of most recent scandals in corporate America?
3. What is meant by "principles-based accounting"?
4. Why is "principles-based accounting" controversial?

ENTREPRENEURIAL DECISION

A2  

BTN 3-8 Melody Kulp of **Mellies** (see chapter's opening feature) is aware of Robin Drucker, who operates a collection agency. For a 50% commission, Drucker collects on accounts receivables for her clients' customers who are delinquent in their payments. For example, assume that a company turns over a $100 accounts receivable to Drucker. If she can collect the $100 from the customer, Drucker keeps $50 and remits the other $50 to her client. Kulp is negotiating with Drucker to offer her a discount from the normal 50% commission that Drucker charges. Kulp has proposed a fee of 40% on amounts collected by Drucker, and leaving 60% of the receivable for Mellies. Currently, Mellies uses a different collection agency that charges a 50% commission.

Required

1. Why would a company hire a collection agency to pursue its accounts receivable?
2. Assume that Mellies' profit margin is 8%. What is Mellies' net income on sales of $40 million?
3. Assume that Mellies currently pays 2% of its $40 million sales to collection agencies. What is the current amount of commission expense Mellies pays to collect delinquent accounts?
4. If Mellies is able to successfully negotiate with the Drucker agency for the reduced collection fee, how will its commission expense for collecting accounts change?
5. How would Mellies' profit margin change if it hires the Drucker collection agency at a 40% commission?

HITTING THE ROAD

C1

BTN 3-9 Visit the Website of a major company that interests you. Use the Investor Relations link at the Website to obtain the toll-free telephone number of the Investor Relations Department. Call the company, ask to speak to Investor Relations, and request a copy of the company's most recent annual report. You should receive the requested report within one to two weeks. Once you have received your report, consult it throughout the term to see the principles that you are learning in class are being applied in practice.

GLOBAL DECISION

A2 C1 C2 

BTN 3-10 **Grupo Bimbo** is a major producer and distributor of bakery products. Access its 2002 annual financial report at the company's Website (GrupoBimbo.com) to answer the following questions.

Required

1. Identify and report the revenue recognition policy applied by Grupo Bimbo?
2. What are the five types of assets depreciated by Grupo Bimbo? Which two assets classified as property, plant, and equipment are not depreciated?
3. What is Grupo Bimbo's profit margin for both fiscal years ended 2002 and 2001?

"Snowskates let you live out your skateboarding fantasies on the snow"—Andy Wolf

4 Completing the Accounting Cycle

A Look Back

Chapter 3 explained the timing of reports. We described why adjusting accounts is important for recognizing revenues and expenses in the proper period. We explained how to prepare an adjusted trial balance and use it in preparing financial statements.

A Look at This Chapter

This chapter emphasizes the final steps in the accounting process and reviews the entire accounting cycle. We explain the closing process, including accounting procedures and the use of a post-closing trial balance. We show how a work sheet aids in preparing financial statements. A classified balance sheet and its use in analyzing information are explained.

A Look Ahead

Chapter 5 looks at accounting for merchandising activities. We describe the sale and purchase of merchandise and their implications for preparing and analyzing financial statements.

CAP

Conceptual

C1 Explain why temporary accounts are closed each period. *(p. 140)*

C2 Identify steps in the accounting cycle. *(p. 143)*

C3 Explain and prepare a classified balance sheet. *(p. 146)*

Analytical

A1 Compute the current ratio and describe what it reveals about a company's financial condition. *(p. 148)*

Procedural

P1 Prepare a work sheet and explain its usefulness. *(p. 136)*

P2 Describe and prepare closing entries. *(p. 141)*

P3 Explain and prepare a post-closing trial balance. *(p. 143)*

Decision Feature

Snowskate on Upstart

PORTLAND—Andy Wolf was a frustrated skateboarder when he moved to Portland a few years ago because of its snow-covered surroundings for much of the year. Wolf toyed with the idea of making a skateboard for snow. His answer was the "snowskate"—similar in size and shape to a skateboard but ridden without bindings to allow *shove-its* and *flip tricks* that aren't possible with snowboards. He now heads the upstart **Premier Snowskate (PremierSnowsk8.com),** the maker of snowskates.

Wolf says his early business experiences were tough as people reacted to him as if "all he knows how to do is ride a snowboard and play Nintendo." People were wrong. One of Wolf's first goals was to control costs. "I wanted to keep the price under $100 retail," says Wolf; "that's how I sourced my materials." He also monitored revenues and kept track of financial performance. Closing procedures were important in helping identify the proper costs and revenues for specific periods. He also relied on classified balance sheets so that he would know what was due and when.

Still, it was tough. "It was still a job," says Wolf. "I had to handle my business, do my own deals, set up my traveling, and work with reps." Accounting work sheets helped Wolf identify temporary and permanent accounts, make crucial adjustments, and prepare and analyze financial reports. Yet the final business decisions were his to make.

Today, his decisions look good as forward-thinking resorts are building snowskate parks. "We're finding that resorts are totally into it," says Wolf. "Either embrace it or have it run them over."

Now for Wolf: How is he dealing with success? "I kind of hate to admit it," says Wolf, "but snowskates are going mainstream." From skateboarder to entrepreneur who uses accounting data—that must hurt. However, with annual sales projected to top $3 million this year, the hurt is tolerable. Admits Wolf, "I'm pretty damn lucky."

[Sources: *Premier Snowskates Website,* January 2004; *Entrepreneur Magazine,* May 2002; *Snowskates Underground,* May 2001; *USA Today,* January 2003; *Sports Guide,* December 2002; *Transworld Snowboarding,* February 2003.]

Many of the important steps leading to financial statements were explained in earlier chapters. We described how transactions and events are analyzed, journalized, and posted. This chapter describes important adjustments that are often necessary to properly reflect revenues when earned and expenses when incurred. This chapter also describes financial statement preparation. It explains the closing process that readies revenue, expense, and withdrawal accounts for the next reporting period and updates the capital account. A work sheet is shown to be a useful tool for these final steps and in preparing financial statements. It also explains how accounts are classified on a balance sheet to increase their usefulness to decision makers.

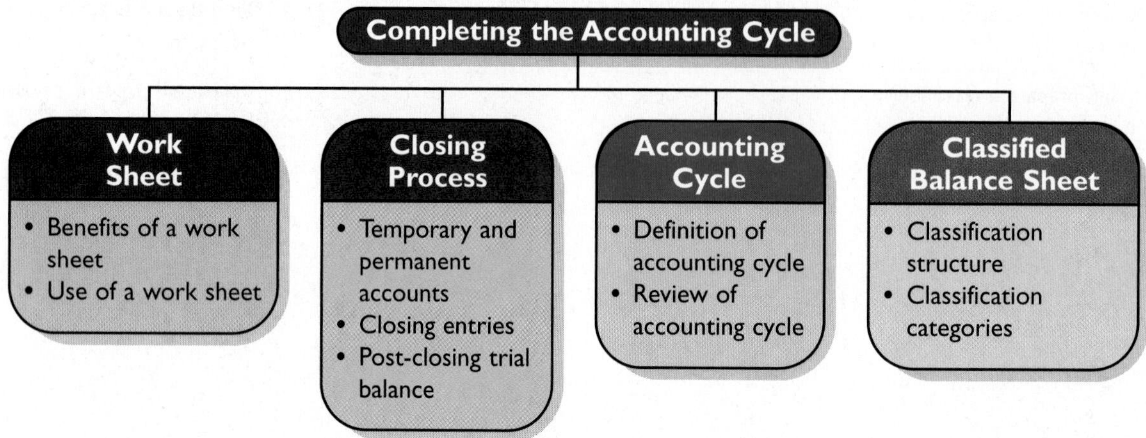

Work Sheet as a Tool

Information preparers use various analyses and internal documents when organizing information for internal and external decision makers. Internal documents are often called **working papers.** One widely used working paper is the **work sheet,** which is a useful tool for preparers in working with accounting information. It is usually not available to external decision makers.

Benefits of a Work Sheet

P1 Prepare a work sheet and explain its usefulness.

A work sheet is *not* a required report, yet using a manual or electronic work sheet has several potential benefits. Specifically, a work sheet:

- Aids the preparation of financial statements.
- Reduces the possibility of errors when working with many accounts and adjustments.
- Links accounts and adjustments to their impacts in financial statements.
- Assists in planning and organizing an audit of financial statements—as it can be used to reflect any adjustments necessary.
- Helps in preparing interim (monthly and quarterly) financial statements when the journalizing and posting of adjusting entries are postponed until the year-end.
- Shows the effects of proposed or "what if" transactions.

Point: Since a work sheet is *not* a required report or an accounting record, its format is flexible and can be modified by its user to fit his/her preferences.

Decision Insight

Accoun-tech An electronic work sheet using spreadsheet software such as Excel allows us to easily change numbers, assess the impact of alternative strategies, and quickly prepare financial statements at less cost. It can also increase the available time for analysis and interpretation.

Use of a Work Sheet

When a work sheet is used to prepare financial statements, it is constructed at the end of a period before the adjusting process. The complete work sheet includes a list of the accounts, their balances and adjustments, and their sorting into financial statement columns. It provides two columns each for the unadjusted trial balance, the adjustments, the adjusted trial balance, the income statement, and the balance sheet (including the statement of owner's equity). To describe and interpret the work sheet, we use the information from FastForward. Preparing the work sheet has five important steps. Each step, 1 through 5, is color-coded and explained with reference to Exhibits 4.1 and 4.2.

1 Step 1. Enter Unadjusted Trial Balance

Refer to Exhibit 4.1. The first step in preparing a work sheet is to list the title of every account and its account number that is expected to appear on its financial statements. This includes all accounts in the ledger plus any new ones from adjusting entries. Most adjusting entries—including expenses from salaries, supplies, depreciation, and insurance—are predictable and recurring. The unadjusted balance for each account is then entered in the appropriate Debit or Credit column of the unadjusted trial balance columns. The totals of these two columns must be equal. Exhibit 4.1 shows FastForward's work sheet after completing this first step. Sometimes blank lines are left on the work sheet based on past experience to indicate where lines will be needed for adjustments to certain accounts. Exhibit 4.1 shows Consulting Revenue as one example. An alternative is to squeeze adjustments on one line or to combine the effects of two or more adjustments in one amount. In the unusual case when an account is not predicted, we can add a new line for such an account following the *Totals* line.

2 Step 2. Enter Adjustments

Refer to Exhibit 4.1a (turn over first transparency). The second step in preparing a work sheet is to enter adjustments in the Adjustments columns. The adjustments shown are the same ones shown in Exhibit 3.13. An identifying letter links the debit and credit of each adjusting entry. This is called *keying* the adjustments. After preparing a work sheet, adjusting entries must still be entered in the journal and posted to the ledger. The Adjustments columns provide the information for those entries.

Point: A recordkeeper often can complete the procedural task of journalizing and posting adjusting entries by using a work sheet and the guidance that *keying* provides.

3 Step 3. Prepare Adjusted Trial Balance

Refer to Exhibit 4.1b (turn over second transparency). The adjusted trial balance is prepared by combining the adjustments with the unadjusted balances for each account. As an example, the Prepaid Insurance account has a $2,400 debit balance in the Unadjusted Trial Balance columns. This $2,400 debit is combined with the $100 credit in the Adjustments columns to give Prepaid Insurance a $2,300 debit in the Adjusted Trial Balance columns. The totals of the Adjusted Trial Balance columns confirm the equality of debits and credits.

Point: To avoid omitting the transfer of an account balance, start with the first line (cash) and continue in account order.

4 Step 4. Sort Adjusted Trial Balance Amounts to Financial Statements

Refer to Exhibit 4.1c (turn over third transparency). This step involves sorting account balances from the adjusted trial balance to their proper financial statement columns. Expenses go to the Income Statement Debit column and revenues to the Income Statement Credit column. Assets and withdrawals go to the Balance Sheet & Statement of Owner's Equity Debit column. Liabilities and owner's capital go to the Balance Sheet & Statement of Owner's Equity Credit column.

5 Step 5. Total Statement Columns, Compute Income or Loss, and Balance Columns

Refer to Exhibit 4.1d (turn over fourth transparency). Each financial statement column (from Step 4) is totaled. The difference between the totals of the Income Statement columns is net income or net loss. This occurs because revenues are entered in the Credit column and expenses in the Debit column. If the Credit total exceeds the Debit total, there is net income. If the Debit total exceeds the Credit total, there is a net loss. For FastForward, the Credit total exceeds the Debit total, giving a $3,785 net income.

[continued on p. 140]

Exhibit 4.1

Work Sheet with Unadjusted Trial Balance

FastForward
Work Sheet
For Month Ended December 31, 2004

(1)

No.	Account	Unadjusted Trial Balance Dr.	Unadjusted Trial Balance Cr.	Adjustments Dr.	Adjustments Cr.	Adjusted Trial Balance Dr.	Adjusted Trial Balance Cr.	Income Statement Dr.	Income Statement Cr.	Balance Sheet & Statement of Owner's Equity Dr.	Balance Sheet & Statement of Owner's Equity Cr.
101	Cash	3,950									
106	Accounts receivable	0									
126	Supplies	9,720									
128	Prepaid insurance	2,400									
167	Equipment	26,000									
168	Accumulated depreciation—Equip.		0								
201	Accounts payable		6,200								
209	Salaries payable		0								
236	Unearned consulting revenue		3,000								
301	C. Taylor, Capital		30,000								
302	C. Taylor, Withdrawals	600									
403	Consulting revenue		5,800								
406	Rental revenue		300								
612	Depreciation expense—Equip.	0									
622	Salaries expense	1,400									
637	Insurance expense	0									
640	Rent expense	1,000									
652	Supplies expense	0									
690	Utilities expense	230									
	Totals	45,300	45,300								

List all accounts from the ledger and those expected to arise from adjusting entries.

Enter all amounts available from ledger accounts. Column totals must be equal.

A work sheet collects and summarizes information used to prepare adjusting entries, financial statements, and closing entries.

Exhibit 4.2

Financial Statements Prepared from the Work Sheet

FASTFORWARD
Income Statement
For Month Ended December 31, 2004

Revenues		
Consulting revenue	$ 7,850	
Rental revenue	300	
Total revenues		$ 8,150
Expenses		
Depreciation expense—Equipment	375	
Salaries expense	1,610	
Insurance expense	100	
Rent expense	1,000	
Supplies expense	1,050	
Utilities expense	230	
Total expenses		4,365
Net income		$ 3,785

FASTFORWARD
Statement of Owner's Equity
For Month Ended December 31, 2004

C. Taylor, Capital, December 1		$ 0
Add: Investment by owner	$30,000	
Net income	3,785	33,785
		33,785
Less: Withdrawals by owner		600
C. Taylor, Capital, December 31		$33,185

FASTFORWARD
Balance Sheet
December 31, 2004

Assets		
Cash		$ 3,950
Accounts receivable		1,800
Supplies		8,670
Prepaid insurance		2,300
Equipment	$26,000	
Accumulated depreciation—Equipment	(375)	25,625
Total assets		$42,345
Liabilities		
Accounts payable		$ 6,200
Salaries payable		210
Unearned consulting revenue		2,750
Total liabilities		9,160
Equity		
C. Taylor, Capital		33,185
Total liabilities and equity		$42,345

Decision Maker

Entrepreneur You make a printout of the electronic work sheet used to prepare financial statements. There is no depreciation adjustment, yet you own a large amount of equipment. Does the absence of depreciation adjustment concern you?

Answer—p. 154

The net income from the Income Statement columns is then entered in the Balance Sheet & Statement of Owner's Equity Credit column. Adding net income to the last Credit column implies that it is to be added to owner's capital. If a loss occurs, it is added to the Debit column. This implies that it is to be subtracted from owner's capital. The ending balance of owner's capital does not appear in the last two columns as a single amount, but it is computed in the statement of owner's equity using these account balances. When net income or net loss is added to the proper Balance Sheet & Statement of Owner's Equity column, the totals of the last two columns must balance. If they do not, one or more errors have been made. The error can either be mathematical or involve sorting one or more amounts to incorrect columns.

Work Sheet Applications and Analysis

A work sheet does not substitute for financial statements. It is a tool we can use at the end of an accounting period to help organize data and prepare financial statements. FastForward's financial statements are shown in Exhibit 4.2. Its income statement amounts are taken from the Income Statement columns of the work sheet. Similarly, amounts for its balance sheet and its statement of owner's equity are taken from the Balance Sheet & Statement of Owner's Equity columns of the work sheet.

A work sheet is also useful to journalize adjusting entries as the information is in the Adjustments columns. It is important to remember that a work sheet is not a journal. This means that even when a work sheet is prepared, it is necessary to both journalize adjustments and post them to the ledger.

Work sheets are also useful in analyzing the effects of proposed, or what-if, transactions. This is done by entering financial statement amounts in the Unadjusted (what-if) columns. Proposed transactions are then entered in the Adjustments columns. We then compute "adjusted" amounts from these proposed transactions. The extended amounts in the financial statement columns show the effects of these proposed transactions. These financial statement columns yield **pro forma financial statements** because they show the statements *as if* the proposed transactions occurred.

Quick Check

1. Where do we get the amounts to enter in the Unadjusted Trial Balance columns of a work sheet?
2. What are the advantages of using a work sheet to help prepare adjusting entries?
3. What are the overall benefits of a work sheet?

Answers—p. 155

Closing Process

C1 Explain why temporary accounts are closed each period.

The **closing process** is an important step at the end of an accounting period *after* financial statements have been completed. It prepares accounts for recording the transactions and the events of the *next* period. In the closing process we must (1) identify accounts for closing, (2) record and post the closing entries, and (3) prepare a post-closing trial balance. The purpose of the closing process is twofold. First, it resets revenue, expense, and withdrawals account balances to zero at the end of each period. This is done so that these accounts can properly measure income and withdrawals for the next period. Second, it helps in summarizing a period's revenues and expenses. This section explains the closing process.

Temporary and Permanent Accounts

Temporary (or *nominal*) **accounts** accumulate data related to one accounting period. They include all income statement accounts, the withdrawals account, and the Income Summary account. They are temporary because the accounts are opened at the beginning of a period, used to record transactions and events for that period, and then closed at the end of the period. *The closing process applies only to temporary accounts.* **Permanent** (or *real*) **accounts** report on activities related to one or more future accounting periods. They carry their ending balances into the next period and generally consist of all balance sheet accounts. These asset, liability, and equity accounts are not closed.

Temporary Accounts

Revenues
Expenses
Owner Withdrawals
Income Summary

Permanent Accounts

Assets
Liabilities
Owner Capital

Recording Closing Entries

To record and post **closing entries** is to transfer the end-of-period balances in revenue, expense, and withdrawals accounts to the permanent capital account. Closing entries are necessary at the end of each period after financial statements are prepared because

- Revenue, expense, and withdrawals accounts must begin each period with zero balances.
- Owner's capital must reflect revenues, expenses, and withdrawals.

Topic Tackler 4-1

An income statement aims to report revenues and expenses for a *specific accounting period.* The statement of owner's equity reports similar information, including withdrawals. Since revenue, expense, and withdrawals accounts must accumulate information separately for each period, they must start each period with zero balances. To close these accounts, we transfer their balances first to an account called *Income Summary.* **Income Summary** is a temporary account (only used for the closing process) that contains a credit for the sum of all revenues (and gains) and a debit for the sum of all expenses (and losses). Its balance equals net income or net loss and it is transferred to the capital account. Next, the withdrawals account balance is transferred to the capital account. After these closing entries are posted, the revenue, expense, withdrawals, and Income Summary accounts have zero balances. These accounts are then said to be *closed* or *cleared.*

Point: To understand the closing process, focus on its *outcomes—updating* the capital account balance to its proper ending balance, and getting *temporary accounts* to show *zero balances* for purposes of accumulating data for the next period.

Exhibit 4.3 uses the adjusted account balances of FastForward (from the Adjusted Trial Balance columns of Exhibit 4.1 or from the left side of Exhibit 4.4) to show the four steps necessary to close its temporary accounts. We explain each step.

Step 1: Close Credit Balances in Revenue Accounts to Income Summary The first closing entry transfers credit balances in revenue (and gain) accounts to the Income Summary account. We bring accounts with credit balances to zero by debiting them. For FastForward, this journal entry is step 1 in Exhibit 4.4. This entry closes revenue accounts and leaves them with zero balances. The accounts are now ready to record revenues when they occur in the next period. The $8,150 credit entry to Income Summary equals total revenues for the period.

P2 Describe and prepare closing entries.

Step 2: Close Debit Balances in Expense Accounts to Income Summary The second closing entry transfers debit balances in expense (and loss) accounts to the Income Summary account. We bring expense accounts' debit balances to zero by crediting them. With a balance of zero, these accounts are ready to accumulate a record of expenses for the next period. This second closing entry for FastForward is step 2 in Exhibit 4.4. Exhibit 4.3 shows that posting this entry gives each expense account a zero balance.

Point: It is possible to close revenue and expense accounts directly to owner's capital. Computerized accounting systems do this.

Step 3: Close Income Summary to Owner's Capital After steps 1 and 2, the balance of Income Summary is equal to December's net income of $3,785. The third closing entry transfers the balance of the Income Summary account to the capital account. This entry closes the Income Summary account and is step 3 in Exhibit 4.4. The Income Summary account has a zero balance after posting this entry. It continues to have a zero balance until the closing process again occurs at the end of the next period. (If a net loss occurred because

Point: The Income Summary is used only for closing entries.

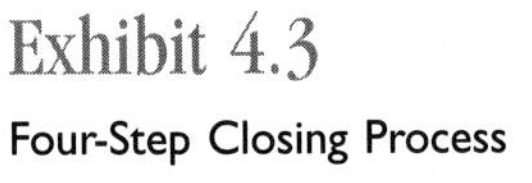

Exhibit 4.3

Four-Step Closing Process

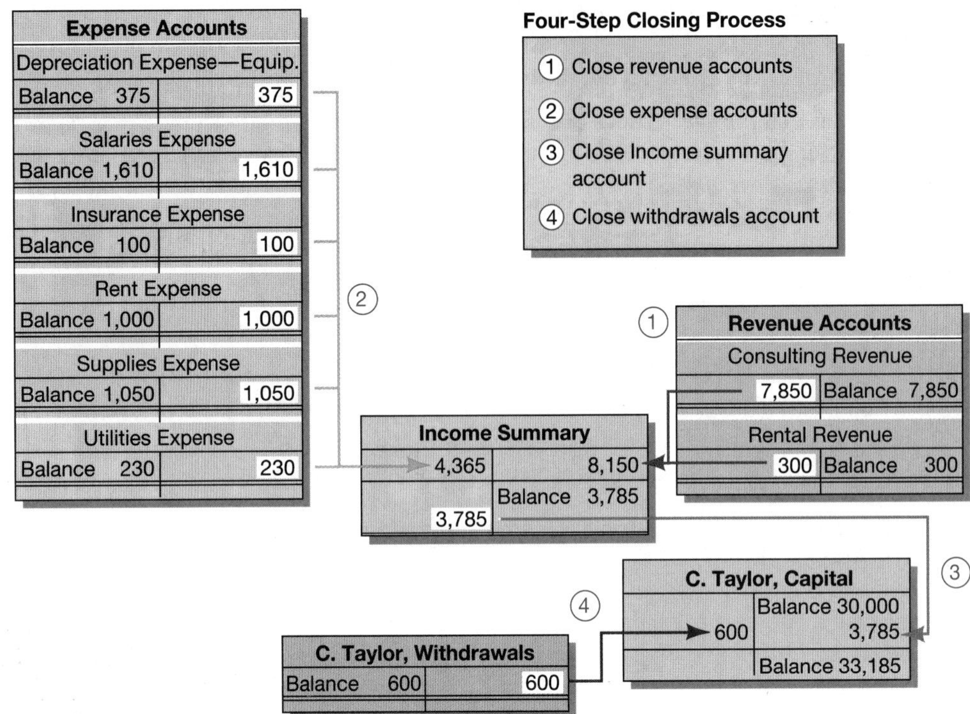

Exhibit 4.4

Preparing Closing Entries

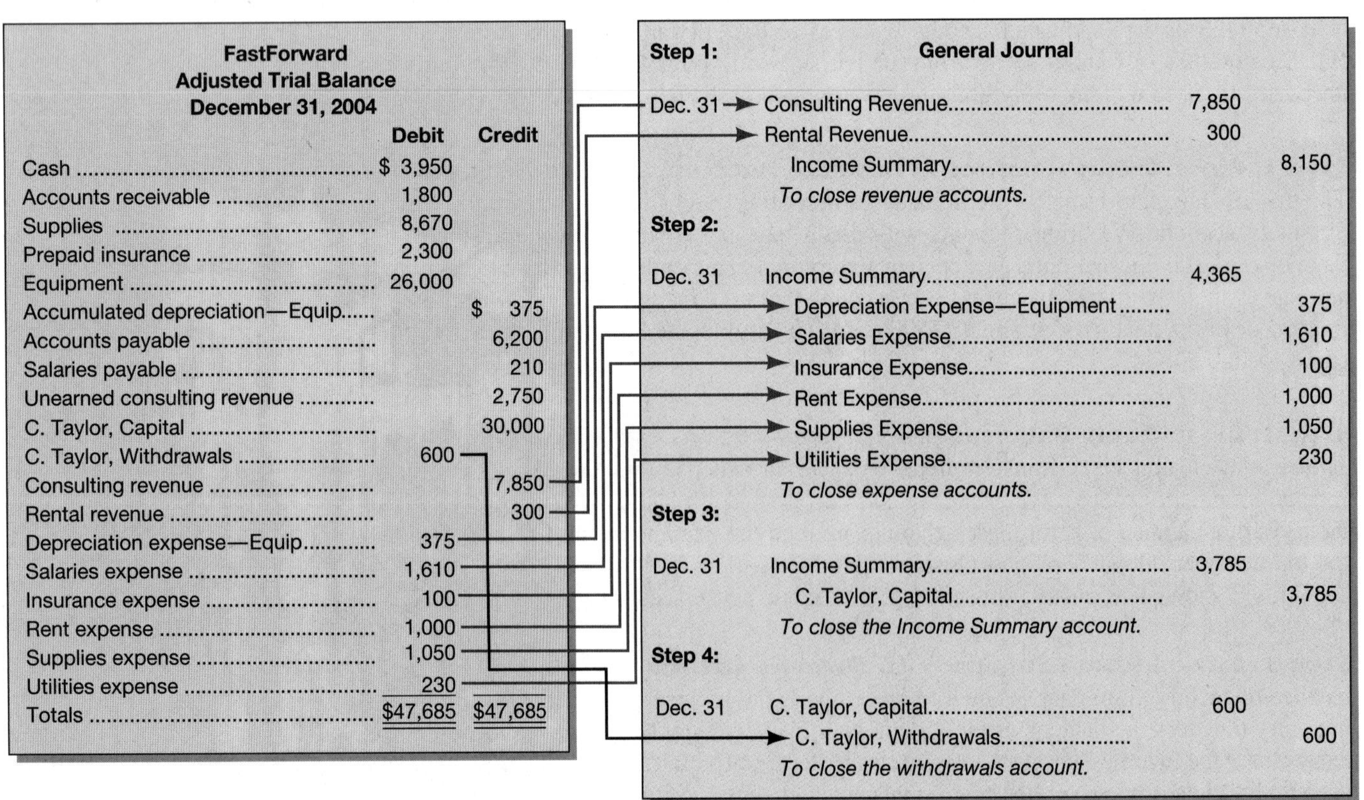

FastForward
Adjusted Trial Balance
December 31, 2004

	Debit	Credit
Cash	$ 3,950	
Accounts receivable	1,800	
Supplies	8,670	
Prepaid insurance	2,300	
Equipment	26,000	
Accumulated depreciation—Equip.		$ 375
Accounts payable		6,200
Salaries payable		210
Unearned consulting revenue		2,750
C. Taylor, Capital		30,000
C. Taylor, Withdrawals	600	
Consulting revenue		7,850
Rental revenue		300
Depreciation expense—Equip.	375	
Salaries expense	1,610	
Insurance expense	100	
Rent expense	1,000	
Supplies expense	1,050	
Utilities expense	230	
Totals	$47,685	$47,685

General Journal

Step 1:			
Dec. 31	Consulting Revenue	7,850	
	Rental Revenue	300	
	Income Summary		8,150
	To close revenue accounts.		
Step 2:			
Dec. 31	Income Summary	4,365	
	Depreciation Expense—Equipment		375
	Salaries Expense		1,610
	Insurance Expense		100
	Rent Expense		1,000
	Supplies Expense		1,050
	Utilities Expense		230
	To close expense accounts.		
Step 3:			
Dec. 31	Income Summary	3,785	
	C. Taylor, Capital		3,785
	To close the Income Summary account.		
Step 4:			
Dec. 31	C. Taylor, Capital	600	
	C. Taylor, Withdrawals		600
	To close the withdrawals account.		

expenses exceeded revenues, the third entry is reversed: debit Owner Capital and credit Income Summary.)

Step 4: Close Withdrawals Account to Owner's Capital The fourth closing entry transfers any debit balance in the withdrawals account to the owner's capital account—see step 4 in Exhibit 4.4. This entry gives the withdrawals account a zero balance, and the account is now ready to accumulate next period's withdrawals. This entry also reduces the capital account balance to the $33,185 amount reported on the balance sheet.

Notice that we can select the accounts and amounts needing to be closed by identifying individual revenue, expense, and withdrawals accounts in the ledger. This is illustrated in Exhibit 4.4 where we prepare closing entries using the adjusted trial balance.[1] (Information for closing entries is also in the financial statement columns of the work sheet.)

Decision Insight

Instant Numbers Quantum leaps in technology are increasing the importance of accounting analysis and interpretation. We are moving toward what some call the "virtual financial statement"—up-to-date financials with the click of a mouse. This reality increases the value of those individuals with the skills to use accounting data.

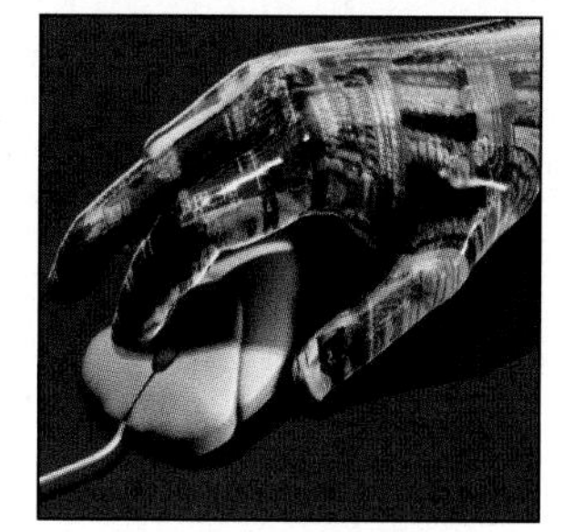

Post-Closing Trial Balance

Exhibit 4.5 shows the entire ledger of FastForward as of December 31 after adjusting and closing entries are posted. (The transaction and adjusting entries are in Chapters 2 and 3.) Note that the temporary accounts (revenues, expenses, and withdrawals) have balances equal to zero.

P3 Explain and prepare a post-closing trial balance.

A **post-closing trial balance** is a list of permanent accounts and their balances from the ledger after all closing entries have been journalized and posted. It lists the balances for all accounts not closed. These accounts comprise a company's assets, liabilities, and equity, which are identical to those in the balance sheet. The aim of a post-closing trial balance is to verify that (1) total debits equal total credits for permanent accounts and (2) all temporary accounts have zero balances. FastForward's post-closing trial balance is shown in Exhibit 4.6. The post-closing trial balance usually is the last step in the accounting process.

Accounting Cycle

The term **accounting cycle** refers to the steps in preparing financial statements. It is called a *cycle* because the steps are repeated each reporting period. Exhibit 4.7 shows the 10 steps in the cycle, beginning with analyzing transactions and ending with a post-closing trial balance or reversing entries. Steps 1 through 3 usually occur regularly as a company enters into transactions. Steps 4 through 9 are done at the end of a period. Reversing entries in step 10 are optional and are explained in Appendix 4A.

C2 Identify steps in the accounting cycle.

Decision Insight

Data Dash A few years ago **Sun Microsystems** took a month to prepare statements after its year-end. Today, it takes less than 24 hours to deliver preliminary figures to key decision makers. What is Sun's secret? Transactions are entered into a network of computerized systems.

[1] The closing process has focused on proprietorships. It is identical for partnerships with the exception that each owner has separate capital and withdrawals accounts (for steps 3 and 4). The closing process for a corporation is similar with the exception that it uses a Retained Earnings account instead of a Capital account, and a Dividend account instead of a Withdrawals account.

Exhibit 4.5

General Ledger after the Closing Process for FastForward

Asset Accounts

Cash Acct. No. 101

Date	Explan.	PR	Debit	Credit	Balance
2004					
Dec. 1		G1	30,000		30,000
2		G1		2,500	27,500
3		G1		26,000	1,500
5		G1	4,200		5,700
6		G1		2,400	3,300
12		G1		1,000	2,300
12		G1		700	1,600
22		G1	1,900		3,500
24		G1		900	2,600
24		G1		600	2,000
26		G1	3,000		5,000
26		G1		120	4,880
26		G1		230	4,650
26		G1		700	**3,950**

Accounts Receivable Acct. No. 106

Date	Explan.	PR	Debit	Credit	Balance
2004					
Dec. 12		G1	1,900		1,900
22		G1		1,900	0
31	Adj.	G1	1,800		**1,800**

Supplies Acct. No. 126

Date	Explan.	PR	Debit	Credit	Balance
2004					
Dec. 2		G1	2,500		2,500
6		G1	7,100		9,600
26		G1	120		9,720
31	Adj.	G1		1,050	**8,670**

Prepaid Insurance Acct. No. 128

Date	Explan.	PR	Debit	Credit	Balance
2004					
Dec. 6		G1	2,400		2,400
31	Adj.	G1		100	**2,300**

Equipment Acct. No. 167

Date	Explan.	PR	Debit	Credit	Balance
2004					
Dec. 3		G1	26,000		**26,000**

Accumulated Depreciation—Equipment Acct. No. 168

Date	Explan.	PR	Debit	Credit	Balance
2004					
Dec. 31	Adj.	G1		375	**375**

Liability and Equity Accounts

Accounts Payable Acct. No. 201

Date	Explan.	PR	Debit	Credit	Balance
2004					
Dec. 6		G1		7,100	7,100
24		G1	900		**6,200**

Salaries Payable Acct. No. 209

Date	Explan.	PR	Debit	Credit	Balance
2004					
Dec. 31	Adj	G1		210	**210**

Unearned Consulting Revenue Acct. No. 236

Date	Explan.	PR	Debit	Credit	Balance
2004					
Dec. 26		G1		3,000	3,000
31	Adj.	G1	250		**2,750**

C. Taylor, Capital Acct. No. 301

Date	Explan.	PR	Debit	Credit	Balance
2004					
Dec. 1		G1		30,000	30,000
31	**Closing**	**G1**		**3,785**	**33,785**
31	**Closing**	**G1**	**600**		**33,185**

C. Taylor, Withdrawals Acct. No. 302

Date	Explan.	PR	Debit	Credit	Balance
2004					
Dec. 24		G1	600		600
31	**Closing**	**G1**		**600**	**0**

Revenue and Expense Accounts (including Income Summary)

Consulting Revenue Acct. No. 403

Date	Explan.	PR	Debit	Credit	Balance
2004					
Dec. 5		G1		4,200	4,200
12		G1		1,600	5,800
31	Adj.	G1		250	6,050
31	Adj.	G1		1,800	7,850
31	**Closing**	**G1**	**7,850**		**0**

Rental Revenue Acct. No. 406

Date	Explan.	PR	Debit	Credit	Balance
2004					
Dec. 12		G1		300	300
31	**Closing**	**G1**	**300**		**0**

Depreciation Expense—Equipment Acct. No. 612

Date	Explan.	PR	Debit	Credit	Balance
2004					
Dec. 31	Adj.	G1	375		375
31	**Closing**	**G1**		**375**	**0**

Salaries Expense Acct. No. 622

Date	Explan.	PR	Debit	Credit	Balance
2004					
Dec. 12		G1	700		700
26		G1	700		1,400
31	Adj.	G1	210		1,610
31	**Closing**	**G1**		**1,610**	**0**

Insurance Expense Acct. No. 637

Date	Explan.	PR	Debit	Credit	Balance
2004					
Dec. 31	Adj.	G1	100		100
31	**Closing**	**G1**		**100**	**0**

Rent Expense Acct. No. 640

Date	Explan.	PR	Debit	Credit	Balance
2004					
Dec. 12		G1	1,000		1,000
31	**Closing**	**G1**		**1,000**	**0**

Supplies Expense Acct. No. 652

Date	Explan.	PR	Debit	Credit	Balance
2004					
Dec. 31	Adj.	G1	1,050		1,050
31	**Closing**	**G1**		**1,050**	**0**

Utilities Expense Acct. No. 690

Date	Explan.	PR	Debit	Credit	Balance
2004					
Dec. 26		G1	230		230
31	**Closing**	**G1**		**230**	**0**

Income Summary Acct. No. 901

Date	Explan.	PR	Debit	Credit	Balance
2004					
Dec. 31	**Closing**	**G1**		**8,150**	**8,150**
31	**Closing**	**G1**	**4,365**		**3,785**
31	**Closing**	**G1**	**3,785**		**0**

FASTFORWARD
Post-Closing Trial Balance
December 31, 2004

	Debit	Credit
Cash	$ 3,950	
Accounts receivable	1,800	
Supplies	8,670	
Prepaid insurance	2,300	
Equipment	26,000	
Accumulated depreciation—Equipment		$ 375
Accounts payable		6,200
Salaries payable		210
Unearned consulting revenue		2,750
C. Taylor, Capital		33,185
Totals	$42,720	$42,720

Exhibit 4.6

Post-Closing Trial Balance

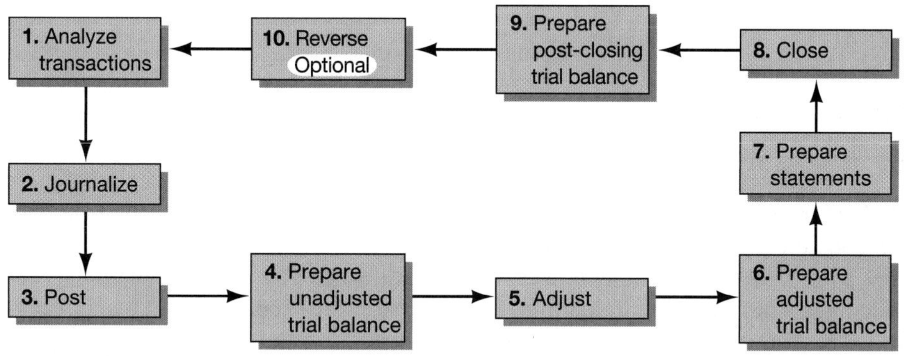

Exhibit 4.7

Steps in the Accounting Cycle*

Explanations

1. Analyze transactions	Analyze transactions to prepare for journalizing.
2. Journalize	Record accounts, including debits and credits, in a journal.
3. Post	Transfer debits and credits from the journal to the ledger.
4. Prepare unadjusted trial balance	Summarize unadjusted ledger accounts and amounts.
5. Adjust	Record adjustments to bring account balances up to date; journalize and post adjusting entries.
6. Prepare adjusted trial balance	Summarize adjusted ledger accounts and amounts.
7. Prepare statements	Use adjusted trial balance to prepare financial statements.
8. Close	Journalize and post entries to close temporary accounts.
9. Prepare post-closing trial balance	Test clerical accuracy of the closing procedures.
10. Reverse (optional)	Reverse certain adjustments in the next period—optional step; see Appendix 4A.

*Steps 4, 6, and 9 can be done on a work sheet. A work sheet is useful in planning adjustments, but adjustments (step 5) must always be journalized and posted. Steps 3, 4, 6, and 9 are automatic with a computerized system.

Quick Check

4. What are the major steps in preparing closing entries?
5. Why are revenue and expense accounts called *temporary?* Can you identify and list any other temporary accounts?
6. What accounts are listed on the post-closing trial balance?

Answers—p. 155

Classified Balance Sheet

C3 Explain and prepare a classified balance sheet.

Our discussion to this point has been limited to unclassified financial statements. This section describes a classified balance sheet. Chapter 5 describes a classified income statement. An **unclassified balance sheet** is one whose items are broadly grouped into assets, liabilities, and equity. One example is FastForward's balance sheet in Exhibit 4.2. A **classified balance sheet** organizes assets and liabilities into important subgroups that provide more information to decision makers.

Classification Structure

Topic Tackler 4-2

A classified balance sheet has no required layout, but it usually contains the categories in Exhibit 4.8. One of the more important classifications is the separation between current and noncurrent items for both assets and liabilities. Current items are those expected to come due (either collected or owed) within one year or the company's operating cycle, whichever is longer. The **operating cycle** is the time span from when *cash is used* to acquire goods and services until *cash is received* from the sale of those goods and services. "Operating" refers to company operations and "cycle" refers to the circular flow of cash used for company inputs and then cash received from its outputs. The length of a company's operating cycle depends on its activities. For a service company, the operating cycle is the time span between (1) paying employees who perform the services and (2) receiving cash from customers. For a merchandiser selling products, the operating cycle is the time span between (1) paying suppliers for merchandise and (2) receiving cash from customers.

Exhibit 4.8

Typical Categories in a Classified Balance Sheet

Assets	Liabilities and Equity
Current assets	Current liabilities
Noncurrent assets	Noncurrent liabilities
Long-term investments	Equity
Plant assets	
Intangible assets	

Point: Current is also called *short term*, and noncurrent is also called *long term*.

Most operating cycles are less than one year. This means most companies use a one-year period in deciding which assets and liabilities are current. A few companies have an operating cycle longer than one year. For instance, producers of certain beverages (wine) and products (ginseng) that require aging for several years have operating cycles longer than one year. A balance sheet lists current assets before noncurrent assets and current liabilities before noncurrent liabilities. This consistency in presentation allows users to quickly identify current assets that are most easily converted to cash and current liabilities that are shortly coming due. Items in current assets and current liabilities are listed in the order of how quickly they will be converted to, or paid in, cash.

Classification Categories

This section describes the most common categories in a classified balance sheet. The balance sheet for Snowboarding Components in Exhibit 4.9 shows these typical categories. Its assets are classified as either current or noncurrent. Its noncurrent assets include three main categories: long-term investments, plant assets, and intangible assets. Its liabilities are classified as either current or long term. Not all companies use the same categories of assets and liabilities for their balance sheets. **K2**'s balance sheet lists only three asset classes: current assets; property, plant and equipment; and other assets.

Point: Short-term investments maturing within three months are combined with cash on both the balance sheet and cash flow statement. This combination is called *cash and cash equivalents*.

Current Assets **Current assets** are cash and other resources that are expected to be sold, collected, or used within one year or the company's operating cycle, whichever is longer. Examples are cash, short-term investments, accounts receivable, short-term notes receivable, goods for sale (called *merchandise* or *inventory*), and prepaid expenses. The individual prepaid expenses of a company are usually small in amount compared to many other assets and are often combined and shown as a single item. The prepaid expenses in Exhibit 4.9 likely include items such as prepaid insurance, prepaid rent, office supplies,

SNOWBOARDING COMPONENTS
Balance Sheet
January 31, 2005

Assets			
Current assets			
Cash		$ 6,500	
Short-term investments		2,100	
Accounts receivable		4,400	
Merchandise inventory		27,500	
Prepaid expenses		2,400	
Total current assets			$ 42,900
Long-term investments			
Notes receivable		1,500	
Investments in stocks and bonds		18,000	
Land held for future expansion		48,000	
Total long-term investments			67,500
Plant assets			
Store equipment	$ 33,200		
Less accumulated depreciation	8,000	25,200	
Buildings	170,000		
Less accumulated depreciation	45,000	125,000	
Land		73,200	
Total plant assets			223,400
Intangible assets			10,000
Total assets			$343,800
Liabilities			
Current liabilities			
Accounts payable		$15,300	
Wages payable		3,200	
Notes payable		3,000	
Current portion of long-term liabilities		7,500	
Total current liabilities			$ 29,000
Long-term liabilities (net of current portion)			150,000
Total liabilities			179,000
Equity			
T. Hawk, Capital			164,800
Total liabilities and equity			$343,800

Exhibit 4.9

Example of a Classified Balance Sheet

and store supplies. Prepaid expenses are usually listed last because they will not be converted to cash (instead, they are used).

Long-Term Investments A second major balance sheet classification is **long-term** (or *noncurrent*) **investments.** Notes receivable and investments in stocks and bonds are long-term assets when they are expected to be held for more than the longer of one year or the operating cycle. Land held for future expansion is a long-term investment because it is *not* used in operations.

Global: In the U.K. and many countries influenced by U.K. reporting, noncurrent assets are listed first and current assets are listed second.

Plant Assets Plant assets are tangible assets that are both *long lived* and *used to produce* or *sell products and services*. Examples are equipment, machinery, buildings, and land that are used to produce or sell products and services. The order listing for plant assets is usually from most liquid to least liquid such as equipment and machinery to buildings and land.

Point: Plant assets are also called **fixed assets; property, plant and equipment;** or **long-lived assets.**

Intangible Assets **Intangible assets** are long-term resources that benefit business operations. They usually lack physical form and have uncertain benefits. Examples are patents, trademarks, copyrights, franchises, and goodwill. Their value comes from the privileges or rights granted to or held by the owner. **Huffy Corporation** reports intangible assets of $48.1 million, which is more than 15 percent of its total assets. Its intangibles include trademarks, patents, and licensing agreements.

Current Liabilities **Current liabilities** are obligations due to be paid or settled within one year or the operating cycle, whichever is longer. They are usually settled by paying out current assets such as cash. Current liabilities often include accounts payable, notes payable, wages payable, taxes payable, interest payable, and unearned revenues. Also, any portion of a long-term liability due to be paid within one year or the operating cycle, whichever is longer, is a current liability. Unearned revenues are current liabilities when they will be settled by delivering products or services within one year or the operating cycle, whichever is longer. Current liabilities are reported in the order of those to be settled first.

Point: Many financial ratios are distorted if accounts are not classified correctly. We must be especially careful when analyzing accounts whose balances are separated into short and long term.

Long-Term Liabilities **Long-term liabilities** are obligations *not* due within one year or the operating cycle, whichever is longer. Notes payable, mortgages payable, bonds payable, and lease obligations are common long-term liabilities. If a company has both short- and long-term items in each of these categories, they are commonly separated into two accounts in the ledger.

Point: Many companies report two or more subgroups for long-term liabilities. See the balance sheets in Appendix A for examples.

Equity Equity is the owner's claim on assets. For a proprietorship, this claim is reported in the equity section with an owner's capital account. (For a partnership, the equity section reports a capital account for each partner. For a corporation, the equity section is divided into two main subsections, common stock and retained earnings.)

Quick Check

7. Identify which of the following assets are classified as (1) current assets or (2) plant assets: (*a*) land used in operations, (*b*) office supplies, (*c*) receivables from customers due in 10 months, (*d*) insurance protection for the next nine months, (*e*) trucks used to provide services to customers, (*f*) trademarks.
8. Cite two examples of assets classified as investments on the balance sheet.
9. Explain the operating cycle for a service company.

Answers—p. 155

Decision Analysis — Current Ratio

A1 Compute the current ratio and describe what it reveals about a company's financial condition.

An important use of financial statements is to help assess a company's ability to pay its debts in the near future. Such analysis affects decisions by suppliers when allowing a company to buy on credit. It also affects decisions by creditors when lending money to a company, including loan terms such as interest rate, due date, and collateral requirements. It can also affect a manager's decisions about using cash to pay existing debts when they come due. The **current ratio** is an important measure of a company's ability to pay its short-term obligations. It is defined in Exhibit 4.10 as current assets divided by current liabilities:

Exhibit 4.10
Current Ratio

$$\textbf{Current ratio} = \frac{\textbf{Current assets}}{\textbf{Current liabilities}}$$

Using financial information from **Limited Brands, Inc.**, we compute its current ratio for the recent four-year period. The results are in Exhibit 4.11.

Fiscal Year ($ Millions)	2003	2002	2001	2000
Current assets	$3,606	$2,784	$2,068	$2,285
Current liabilities	$1,259	$1,454	$1,000	$1,236
Current ratio	**2.9**	**1.9**	**2.1**	**1.8**
Industry current ratio	2.8	2.9	3.3	3.4

Exhibit 4.11

Limited Brands's Current Ratio

Limited Brands's current ratio rose to 2.9 in 2003 compared to lower ratios for prior years. Still, the current ratio for each of these years suggests that the company's short-term obligations can be covered with its short-term assets. However, if its ratio would approach 1.0, Limited would expect to face challenges in covering liabilities. If the ratio were *less* than 1.0, current liabilities would exceed current assets, and the company's ability to pay short-term obligations would be in doubt.

Decision Maker

Analyst You are analyzing the financial condition of a fitness club to assess its ability to meet upcoming loan payments. You compute its current ratio as 1.2. You also find that a major portion of accounts receivable is due from one client who has not made any payments in the past 12 months. Removing this receivable from current assets drops the current ratio to 0.7. What do you conclude?

Answer—p. 154

Demonstration Problem

The partial work sheet of Midtown Repair Company at December 31, 2005, follows:

	Adjusted Trial Balance		Income Statement		Balance Sheet and Statement of Owner's Equity	
	Debit	**Credit**	**Debit**	**Credit**	**Debit**	**Credit**
Cash	95,600					
Notes receivable (current)	50,000					
Prepaid insurance	16,000					
Prepaid rent	4,000					
Equipment	170,000					
Accumulated depreciation—Equipment		57,000				
Accounts payable		52,000				
Long-term notes payable		63,000				
C. Trout, Capital		178,500				
C. Trout, Withdrawals	30,000					
Repair services revenue		180,800				
Interest revenue		7,500				
Depreciation expense—Equipment	28,500					
Wages expense	85,000					
Rent expense	48,000					
Insurance expense	6,000					
Interest expense	5,700					
Totals	538,800	538,800				

Required

1. Complete the work sheet by extending the adjusted trial balance totals to the appropriate financial statement columns.
2. Prepare closing entries for Midtown Repair Company.

3. Set up the Income Summary and the C. Trout, Capital account in the general ledger (in balance column format) and post the closing entries to these accounts.
4. Determine the balance of the C. Trout, Capital account to be reported on the December 31, 2005, balance sheet.
5. Prepare an income statement, statement of owner's equity, and classified balance sheet (in report form) as of December 31, 2005.

Planning the Solution

- Extend the adjusted trial balance account balances to the appropriate financial statement columns.
- Prepare entries to close the revenue accounts to Income Summary, to close the expense accounts to Income Summary, to close Income Summary to the capital account, and to close the withdrawals account to the capital account.
- Post the first and second closing entries to the Income Summary account. Examine the balance of income summary and verify that it agrees with the net income shown on the work sheet.
- Post the third and fourth closing entries to the capital account.
- Use the work sheet's two right-most columns and your answer in part 4 to prepare the classified balance sheet.

Solution to Demonstration Problem

1. Completing the work sheet:

	Adjusted Trial Balance		Income Statement		Balance Sheet and Statement of Owner's Equity	
	Debit	Credit	Debit	Credit	Debit	Credit
Cash	95,600				95,600	
Notes receivable (current)	50,000				50,000	
Prepaid insurance	16,000				16,000	
Prepaid rent	4,000				4,000	
Equipment	170,000				170,000	
Accumulated depreciation—Equipment		57,000				57,000
Accounts payable		52,000				52,000
Long-term notes payable		63,000				63,000
C. Trout, Capital		178,500				178,500
C. Trout, Withdrawals	30,000				30,000	
Repair services revenue		180,800		180,800		
Interest revenue		7,500		7,500		
Depreciation expense—Equipment	28,500		28,500			
Wages expense	85,000		85,000			
Rent expense	48,000		48,000			
Insurance expense	6,000		6,000			
Interest expense	5,700		5,700			
Totals	538,800	538,800	173,200	188,300	365,600	350,500
Net Income			15,100			15,100
Totals			188,300	188,300	365,600	365,600

2. Closing entries:

Dec. 31	Repair Services Revenue	180,800	
	Interest Revenue	7,500	
	Income Summary		188,300
	To close revenue accounts.		

[continued on next page]

[continued from previous page]

Dec. 31	Income Summary	173,200	
	Depreciation Expense—Equipment		28,500
	Wages Expense		85,000
	Rent Expense		48,000
	Insurance Expense		6,000
	Interest Expense		5,700
	To close expense accounts.		
Dec. 31	Income Summary	15,100	
	C. Trout, Capital		15,100
	To close the Income Summary account.		
Dec. 31	C. Trout, Capital	30,000	
	C. Trout, Withdrawals		30,000
	To close the withdrawals account.		

3. Set up the Income Summary and the capital ledger accounts and post the closing entries.

Income Summary — Account No. 901

Date	Explanation	PR	Debit	Credit	Balance
2005					
Jan. 1	Beginning balance				0
Dec. 31	Close revenue accounts			188,300	188,300
31	Close expense accounts		173,200		15,100
31	Close income summary		15,100		0

C. Trout, Capital — Account No. 301

Date	Explanation	PR	Debit	Credit	Balance
2005					
Jan. 1	Beginning balance				178,500
Dec. 31	Close Income Summary			15,100	193,600
31	Close C. Trout, Withdrawals		30,000		163,600

4. The final capital balance of $163,600 (from part 3) will be reported on the December 31, 2005 balance sheet. The final capital balance reflects the increase due to the net income earned during the year and the decrease for the owner's withdrawals during the year.

5.

MIDTOWN REPAIR COMPANY
Income Statement
For Year Ended December 31, 2005

Revenues		
Repair services revenue	$180,800	
Interest revenue	7,500	
Total revenues		$188,300
Expenses		
Depreciation expense—Equipment	28,500	
Wages expense	85,000	
Rent expense	48,000	
Insurance expense	6,000	
Interest expense	5,700	
Total expenses		173,200
Net income		$ 15,100

MIDTOWN REPAIR COMPANY Statement of Owner's Equity For Year Ended December 31, 2005		
C. Trout, Capital, December 31, 2004		$178,500
Add: Investment by owner	$ 0	
Net income	15,100	15,100
		193,600
Less: Withdrawals by owner		30,000
C. Trout, Capital, December 31, 2005		$163,600

MIDTOWN REPAIR COMPANY Balance Sheet December 31, 2005		
Assets		
Current assets		
Cash		$ 95,600
Notes receivable		50,000
Prepaid insurance		16,000
Prepaid rent		4,000
Total current assets		165,600
Plant assets		
Equipment	$170,000	
Less: Accumulated depreciation—Equipment	(57,000)	
Total plant assets		113,000
Total assets		$278,600
Liabilities		
Current liabilities		
Accounts payable		$ 52,000
Long-term liabilities		
Long-term notes payable		63,000
Total liabilities		115,000
Equity		
C. Trout, Capital		163,600
Total liabilities and equity		$278,600

APPENDIX

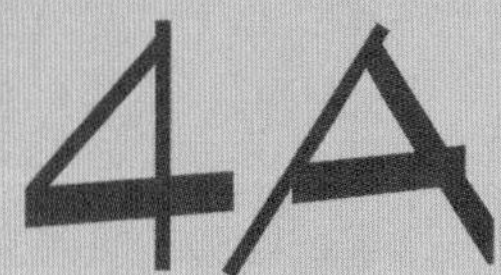

4A Reversing Entries

Point: As a general rule, adjusting entries that create new asset or liability accounts are likely candidates for reversing.

Reversing entries are optional. They are recorded in response to accrued assets and accrued liabilities that were created by adjusting entries at the end of a reporting period. The purpose of reversing entries is to simplify a company's recordkeeping. Exhibit 4A.1 shows an example of FastForward's reversing entries. The top of the exhibit shows the adjusting entry FastForward recorded on December 31 for its employee's earned but unpaid salary. The entry recorded three days' salary of $210, which increased December's total salary expense to $1,610. The entry also recognized a liability of $210. The expense is reported on December's income statement. The expense account is then closed. The

Exhibit 4A.1

Reversing Entries for an Accrued Expense

Accrue salaries expense on December 31, 2004

Salaries Expense 210
Salaries Payable 210

Salaries Expense

Date	Expl.	Debit	Credit	Balance
2004				
Dec. 12	(7)	700		700
26	(16)	700		1,400
31	*(e)*	210		1,610

Salaries Payable

Date	Expl.	Debit	Credit	Balance
2004				
Dec. 31	*(e)*		210	210

— OR —

No reversing entry recorded on January 1, 2005

NO ENTRY

Salaries Expense

Date	Expl.	Debit	Credit	Balance
2005				

Salaries Payable

Date	Expl.	Debit	Credit	Balance
2004				
Dec. 31	*(e)*		210	210
2005				

Reversing entry recorded on January 1, 2005

Salaries Payable 210
Salaries Expense 210

Salaries Expense*

Date	Expl.	Debit	Credit	Balance
2005				
Jan. 1			210	(210)

Salaries Payable

Date	Expl.	Debit	Credit	Balance
2004				
Dec. 31	*(e)*		210	210
2004				
Jan. 1		210		0

Pay the accrued and current salaries on January 9, the first payday in 2005

Salaries Expense 490
Salaries Payable 210
Cash 700

Salaries Expense

Date	Expl.	Debit	Credit	Balance
2005				
Jan. 9		490		490

Salaries Payable

Date	Expl.	Debit	Credit	Balance
2004				
Dec. 31	*(e)*		210	210
2005				
Jan. 9		210		0

Salaries Expense 700
Cash 700

Salaries Expense*

Date	Expl.	Debit	Credit	Balance
2005				
Jan. 1			210	(210)
Jan. 9		700		490

Salaries Payable

Date	Expl.	Debit	Credit	Balance
2004				
Dec. 31	*(e)*		210	210
2005				
Jan. 1		210		0

Under both approaches, the expense and liability accounts have identical balances after the cash payment on January 9.

Salaries Expense $490
Salaries Payable .... $ 0

*Circled numbers in the *Balance* column indicate abnormal balances.

ledger on January 1, 2005, shows a $210 liability and a zero balance in the Salaries Expense account. At this point, the choice is made between using or not using reversing entries.

Accounting *without* Reversing Entries

The path down the left side of Exhibit 4A.1 is described in the chapter. To summarize here, when the next payday occurs on January 9, we record payment with a compound entry that debits both the expense and liability accounts and credits Cash. Posting that entry creates a $490 balance in the expense account and reduces the liability account balance to zero because the debt has been settled. The disadvantage of this approach is the slightly more complex entry required on January 9. Paying the accrued liability means that this entry differs from the routine entries made on all other paydays. To construct the proper entry on January 9, we must recall the effect of the December 31 adjusting entry. Reversing entries overcome this disadvantage.

Accounting *with* Reversing Entries

P4 Prepare reversing entries and explain their purpose.

The right side of Exhibit 4A.1 shows how a reversing entry on January 1 overcomes the disadvantage of the January 9 entry when not using reversing entries. A reversing entry is the exact opposite of an adjusting entry. For FastForward, the Salaries Payable liability account is debited for $210, meaning that this account now has a zero balance after the entry is posted. The Salaries Payable account temporarily understates the liability, but this is not a problem since financial statements are not prepared before the liability is settled on January 9. The credit to the Salaries Expense account is unusual because it gives the account an *abnormal credit balance*. We highlight an abnormal balance by circling it. Because of the reversing entry, the January 9 entry to record payment is straightforward. This entry debits the Salaries Expense account and credits Cash for the full $700 paid. It is the same as all other entries made to record 10 days' salary for the employee. Notice that after the payment entry is posted, the Salaries Expense account has a $490 balance that reflects seven days' salary of $70 per day (see the lower right side of Exhibit 4A.1). The zero balance in the Salaries Payable account is now correct. The lower section of Exhibit 4A.1 shows that the expense and liability accounts have exactly the same balances whether reversing entries are used or not. This means that both approaches yield identical results.

Summary

C1 Explain why temporary accounts are closed each period. Temporary accounts are closed at the end of each accounting period for two main reasons. First, the closing process updates the capital account to include the effects of all transactions and events recorded for the period. Second, it prepares revenue, expense, and withdrawals accounts for the next reporting period by giving them zero balances.

C2 Identify steps in the accounting cycle. The accounting cycle consists of 10 steps: (1) analyze transactions, (2) journalize, (3) post, (4) prepare an unadjusted trial balance, (5) adjust accounts, (6) prepare an adjusted trial balance, (7) prepare statements, (8) close, (9) prepare a post-closing trial balance, and (10) prepare (optional) reversing entries.

C3 Explain and prepare a classified balance sheet. Classified balance sheets report assets and liabilities in two categories: current and noncurrent. Noncurrent assets often include long-term investments, plant assets, and intangible assets. Owner's equity for proprietorships (and partnerships) report the capital account balance. A corporation separates equity into common stock and retained earnings.

A1 Compute the current ratio and describe what it reveals about a company's financial condition. A company's current ratio is defined as current assets divided by current liabilities. We use it to evaluate a company's ability to pay its current liabilities out of current assets.

P1 Prepare a work sheet and explain its usefulness. A work sheet can be a useful tool in preparing and analyzing financial statements. It is helpful at the end of a period in preparing adjusting entries, an adjusted trial balance, and financial statements. A work sheet usually contains five pairs of columns: Unadjusted Trial Balance, Adjustments, Adjusted Trial Balance, Income Statement, and Balance Sheet & Statement of Owner's Equity.

P2 Describe and prepare closing entries. Closing entries involve four steps: (1) close credit balances in revenue (and gain) accounts to Income Summary, (2) close debit balances in expense (and loss) accounts to Income Summary, (3) close Income Summary to the capital account, and (4) close withdrawals account to owner's capital.

P3 Explain and prepare a post-closing trial balance. A post-closing trial balance is a list of permanent accounts and their balances after all closing entries have been journalized and posted. Its purpose is to verify that (1) total debits equal total credits for permanent accounts and (2) all temporary accounts have zero balances.

P4[A] Prepare reversing entries and explain their purpose. Reversing entries are an optional step. They are applied to accrued expenses and revenues. The purpose of reversing entries is to simplify subsequent journal entries. Financial statements are unaffected by the choice to use or not use reversing entries.

Guidance Answers to **Decision Maker** and **Decision Ethics**

Entrepreneur Yes, you are concerned about the absence of a depreciation adjustment. Equipment does depreciate, and financial statements must recognize this occurrence. Its absence suggests an error or a misrepresentation.

Analyst A current ratio of 1.2 suggests that current assets are sufficient to cover current liabilities, but it implies a minimal buffer in case of errors in measuring current assets or current liabilities. Removing tardy receivables reduces the current ratio to 0.7. Your assessment is that the club will have some difficulty meeting its loan payments.

Guidance Answers to **Quick Checks**

1. Amounts in the Unadjusted Trial Balance columns are taken from current account balances in the ledger. The balances for new accounts expected to arise from adjusted entries can be left blank or set at zero.
2. A work sheet offers the advantage of listing on one page all necessary information to make adjusting entries.
3. A work sheet can help in (a) accounting efficiency and avoiding errors, (b) linking transactions and events to their effects in financial statements, (c) showing adjustments for audit purposes, (d) preparing interim financial statements, and (e) showing effects from proposed, or what-if, transactions.
4. The major steps in preparing closing entries are to close (1) credit balances in revenue accounts to Income Summary, (2) debit balances in expense accounts to Income Summary, (3) Income Summary to owner's capital, and (4) any withdrawals account to owner's capital.
5. Revenue (and gain) and expense (and loss) accounts are called *temporary* because they are opened and closed each period. The Income Summary and owner's withdrawals accounts are also temporary.
6. Permanent accounts make up the post-closing trial balance. These accounts are asset, liability, and equity accounts.
7. Current assets: (*b*), (*c*), (*d*). Plant assets: (*a*), (*e*). Item (*f*) is an intangible asset.
8. Investment in common stock, investment in bonds, and land held for future expansion.
9. For a service company, the operating cycle is the usual time between (1) paying employees who do the services and (2) receiving cash from customers for services provided.

Key Terms

Key Terms are available at the book's Website for learning and testing in an online Flashcard Format.

Accounting cycle (p. 143)
Classified balance sheet (p. 146)
Closing entries (p. 141)
Closing process (p. 140)
Current assets (p. 146)
Current liabilities (p. 148)
Current ratio (p. 148)
Income Summary (p. 141)
Intangible assets (p. 148)
Long-term investments (p. 147)
Long-term liabilities (p. 148)
Operating cycle (p. 146)
Permanent accounts (p. 141)
Post-closing trial balance (p. 143)
Pro forma financial statements (p. 140)
Reversing entries (p. 152)
Temporary accounts (p. 141)
Unclassified balance sheet (p. 146)
Working papers (p. 136)
Work sheet (p. 136)

Personal Interactive Quiz

Personal Interactive Quizzes A and B are available at the book's Website to reinforce and assess your learning.

Superscript letter A denotes assignments based on Appendix 4A.

Discussion Questions

1. What accounts are affected by closing entries? What accounts are not affected?
2. What two purposes are accomplished by recording closing entries?
3. What are the steps in recording closing entries?
4. What is the purpose of the Income Summary account?
5. Explain whether an error has occurred if a post-closing trial balance includes a Depreciation Expense account.
6. What tasks are aided by a work sheet?
7. Why are the debit and credit entries in the Adjustments columns of the work sheet identified with letters?
8. What is a company's operating cycle?
9. What classes of assets and liabilities are shown on a typical classified balance sheet?
10. How is unearned revenue classified on the balance sheet?
11. What are the characteristics of plant assets?
12. [A] How do reversing entries simplify recordkeeping?
13. [A] If a company recorded accrued salaries expense of $500 at the end of its fiscal year, what reversing entry could be made? When would it be made?

14. Refer to the balance sheet for **Krispy Kreme** in Appendix A. What five noncurrent asset categories are used on its classified balance sheet?

15. Refer to **Tastykake**'s balance sheet in Appendix A. Identify the accounts listed as current liabilities.

16. Refer to **Harley-Davidson**'s financial statements in Appendix A. What journal entry was likely recorded as of December 31, 2002, to close its Income Summary account?

Harley-Davidson

Red numbers denote Discussion Questions that involve decision-making.

Homework Manager  *repeats all numerical Quick Study assignments on the book's Website with new numbers.*

QUICK STUDY

QS 4-1
Determining effects of closing entries
C1 P2 

Argosy Company began the current period with a $14,000 credit balance in the D. Argosy, Capital account. At the end of the period, the company's adjusted account balances include the following temporary accounts with normal balances:

Service fees earned	$35,000	Interest revenue	$3,500
Salaries expense	19,000	D. Argosy, Withdrawals	6,000
Depreciation expense	4,000	Utilities expense	2,300

After closing the revenue and expense accounts, what will be the balance of the Income Summary account? After all closing entries are journalized and posted, what will be the balance of the D. Argosy, Capital account?

QS 4-2
Identifying the accounting cycle
C2

List the following steps of the accounting cycle in their proper order:

a. Preparing the post-closing trial balance.
b. Posting the journal entries.
c. Journalizing and posting adjusting entries.
d. Preparing the adjusted trial balance.
e. Journalizing and posting closing entries.
f. Analyzing transactions and events.
g. Preparing the financial statements.
h. Preparing the unadjusted trial balance.
i. Journalizing transactions and events.

QS 4-3
Classifying balance sheet items
C3

The following are common categories on a classified balance sheet:

A. Current assets
B. Long-term investments
C. Plant assets
D. Intangible assets
E. Current liabilities
F. Long-term liabilities

For each of the following items, select the letter that identifies the balance sheet category where the item typically would appear.

_____ **1.** Trademarks
_____ **2.** Accounts receivable
_____ **3.** Land not currently used in operations
_____ **4.** Notes payable (due in three years)
_____ **5.** Cash
_____ **6.** Wages payable
_____ **7.** Store equipment
_____ **8.** Accounts payable

QS 4-4
Identifying current accounts and computing the current ratio
C3 A1

Compute Jamar Company's current ratio using the following information:

Accounts receivable	$15,000	Long-term notes payable	$20,000
Accounts payable	10,000	Office supplies	1,800
Buildings	42,000	Prepaid insurance	2,500
Cash	6,000	Unearned services revenue	4,000

QS 4-5
Interpreting a work sheet
P1 

The following information is taken from the work sheet for Wayman Company as of December 31, 2005. Using this information, determine the amount for K. Wayman, Capital, that should be reported on its December 31, 2005, balance sheet.

	Income Statement		Balance Sheet and Statement of Owner's Equity	
	Dr.	Cr.	Dr.	Cr.
K. Wayman, Capital				65,000
K. Wayman, Withdrawals			32,000	
Totals	115,000	174,000		

QS 4-6
Applying a work sheet
P1

In preparing a work sheet, indicate the financial statement Debit column to which a normal balance in the following accounts should be extended. Use IS for the Income Statement Debit column and BS for the Balance Sheet and Statement of Owner's Equity Debit column.

_____ **a.** Insurance expense
_____ **b.** Equipment
_____ **c.** Owner, Withdrawals
_____ **d.** Depreciation expense—Equipment
_____ **e.** Prepaid rent
_____ **f.** Accounts receivable

QS 4-7
Ordering work sheet steps
P1

List the following steps in preparing a work sheet in their proper order by writing numbers 1–5 in the blank spaces provided.

a. _____ Prepare an adjusted trial balance on the work sheet.
b. _____ Prepare an unadjusted trial balance on the work sheet.
c. _____ Enter adjustments data on the work sheet.
d. _____ Extend adjusted balances to appropriate financial statement columns.
e. _____ Total the statement columns, compute net income (loss), and complete work sheet.

QS 4-8
Preparing a partial work sheet
P1

The ledger of Terrel Company includes the following unadjusted normal balances: Prepaid Rent $800, Services Revenue $11,600, and Wages Expense $5,000. Adjusting entries are required for **(a)** accrued rent expense $240; **(b)** accrued services revenue $180; and **(c)** accrued wages expense $160. Enter these unadjusted balances and the necessary adjustments on a work sheet and complete the work sheet for these accounts. *Note:* You must include the following accounts: Accounts Receivable, Wages Payable, and Rent Expense.

QS 4-9
Prepare closing entries from the ledger P2

The ledger of Avril Company includes the following accounts with normal balances: L. Avril, Capital $6,000; L. Avril, Withdrawals $400; Services Revenue $10,000; Wages Expense $5,200; and Rent Expense $800. Prepare the necessary closing entries at December 31.

QS 4-10
Identify post-closing accounts P3

Identify the accounts listed in QS 4-9 that would be included in a post-closing trial balance.

QS 4-11[A]
Reversing entries
P4

On December 31, 2004, Yates Co. prepared an adjusting entry for $6,700 of earned but unrecorded management fees. On January 16, 2005, Yates received $15,500 cash in management fees, which included the accrued fees earned in 2004. Assuming the company uses reversing entries, prepare the January 1, 2005, reversing entry and the January 16, 2005, cash receipt entry.

Homework Manager *repeats all numerical Exercises on the book's Website with new numbers.*

EXERCISES

Exercise 4-1
Preparing and posting closing entries
P2

Use the March 31 fiscal year-end information from the following ledger accounts (assume that all accounts have normal balances) to prepare closing journal entries and then post those entries to the appropriate ledger accounts.

General Ledger

M. Mallon, Capital — Acct. No. 301

Date	PR	Debit	Credit	Balance
Mar. 31	G2			42,000

Salaries Expense — Acct. No. 622

Date	PR	Debit	Credit	Balance
Mar. 31	G2			21,000

[continued on next page]

[continued from previous page]

M. Mallon, Withdrawals Acct. No. 302

Date	PR	Debit	Credit	Balance
Mar. 31	G2			25,000

Insurance Expense Acct. No. 637

Date	PR	Debit	Credit	Balance
Mar. 31	G2			4,500

Check M. Mallon, Capital (ending balance), $38,900

Services Revenue Acct. No. 401

Date	PR	Debit	Credit	Balance
Mar. 31	G2			74,000

Rent Expense Acct. No. 640

Date	PR	Debit	Credit	Balance
Mar. 31	G2			9,600

Depreciation Expense Acct. No. 603

Date	PR	Debit	Credit	Balance
Mar. 31	G2			17,000

Income Summary Acct. No. 901

Date	PR	Debit	Credit	Balance

Exercise 4-2

Preparing closing entries and a post-closing trial balance

P2 P3

The adjusted trial balance for Schwepker Marketing Co. follows. Complete the four right-most columns of the table by first entering information for the four closing entries (keyed *1* through *4*) and second by completing the post-closing trial balance.

No.	Account Title	Adjusted Trial Balance		Closing Entry Information		Post-Closing Trial Balance	
		Dr.	Cr.	Dr.	Cr.	Dr.	Cr.
101	Cash	$ 8,200					
106	Accounts receivable	24,000					
153	Equipment	41,000					
154	Accumulated depreciation—Equipment		$ 16,500				
193	Franchise	30,000					
201	Accounts payable		14,000				
209	Salaries payable		3,200				
233	Unearned fees		2,600				
301	C. Schwepker, Capital		64,500				
302	C. Schwepker, Withdrawals	14,400					
401	Marketing fees earned		79,000				
611	Depreciation expense—Equipment	11,000					
622	Salaries expense	31,500					
640	Rent expense	12,000					
677	Miscellaneous expenses	7,700					
901	Income summary						
	Totals	$179,800	$179,800				

Exercise 4-3

Preparing closing entries and a post-closing trial balance

C1 P2 P3

The following adjusted trial balance contains the accounts and balances of Showers Company as of December 31, 2005, the end of its fiscal year. (1) Prepare the December 31, 2005, closing entries for Showers Company. (2) Prepare the December 31, 2005, post-closing trial balance for Showers Company.

No.	Account Title	Debit	Credit
101	Cash	$18,000	
126	Supplies	12,000	
128	Prepaid insurance	2,000	
167	Equipment	23,000	
168	Accumulated depreciation—Equipment		$ 6,500
301	R. Showers, Capital		46,600

[continued on next page]

[continued from previous page]

302	R. Showers, Withdrawals	6,000	
404	Services revenue		36,000
612	Depreciation expense—Equipment	2,000	
622	Salaries expense	21,000	
637	Insurance expense	1,500	
640	Rent expense	2,400	
652	Supplies expense	1,200	
	Totals	$89,100	$89,100

Check (2) R. Showers, Capital (ending), $48,500; Total debits, $55,000

Exercise 4-4
Preparing a classified balance sheet
C3

Use the following adjusted trial balance of Webb Trucking Company to prepare a classified balance sheet as of December 31, 2005.

Account Title	Debit	Credit
Cash	$ 7,000	
Accounts receivable	16,500	
Office supplies	2,000	
Trucks	170,000	
Accumulated depreciation—Trucks		$ 35,000
Land	75,000	
Accounts payable		11,000
Interest payable		3,000
Long-term notes payable		52,000
K. Webb, Capital		161,000
K. Webb, Withdrawals	19,000	
Trucking fees earned		128,000
Depreciation expense—Trucks	22,500	
Salaries expense	60,000	
Office supplies expense	7,000	
Repairs expense—Trucks	11,000	
Totals	$390,000	$390,000

Check Total assets, $235,500; K. Webb, Capital, $169,500

Exercise 4-5
Preparing the financial statements
C2

Use the information in the adjusted trial balance reported in Exercise 4-4 to prepare Webb Trucking Company's (1) income statement, and (2) statement of owner's equity. The K. Webb, Capital account balance is $161,000 at December 31, 2004.

Exercise 4-6
Computing the current ratio
A1

Use the information in the adjusted trial balance reported in Exercise 4-4 to compute the current ratio as of the balance sheet date. Interpret the current ratio for this company. (Assume that the industry norm for the current ratio is 1.5.)

Exercise 4-7
Computing and analyzing the current ratio

Calculate the current ratio in each of the following separate cases. Identify the company case with the strongest liquidity position. (These cases represent competing companies in the same industry.)

	Current Assets	Current Liabilities
Case 1	$ 78,000	$31,000
Case 2	104,000	75,000
Case 3	44,000	48,000
Case 4	84,500	80,600
Case 5	60,000	99,000

Exercise 4-8
Preparing adjusting entries from a work sheet
P1

Use the following information from the Adjustments columns of a 10-column work sheet to prepare the necessary adjusting journal entries (*a*) through (*e*):

No.	Account Title	Adjustments Debit	Adjustments Credit
109	Interest receivable	(*d*) $ 580	
124	Office supplies		(*b*) $1,650
128	Prepaid insurance		(*a*) 900
164	Accumulated depreciation—Office equipment		(*c*) 3,300
209	Salaries payable		(*e*) 660
409	Interest revenue		(*d*) 580
612	Depreciation expense—Office equipment	(*c*) 3,300	
620	Office salaries expense	(*e*) 660	
636	Insurance expense—Office equipment	(*a*) 432	
637	Insurance expense—Store equipment	(*a*) 468	
650	Office supplies expense	(*b*) 1,650	
	Totals	$7,090	$7,090

Exercise 4-9
Extending adjusted account balances on a work sheet
P1

These 16 accounts are from the Adjusted Trial Balance columns of a company's 10-column work sheet. In the blank space beside each account, write the letter of the appropriate financial statement column (A, B, C, or D) to which a normal account balance is extended.

A. Debit column for the Income Statement columns.
B. Credit column for the Income Statement columns.
C. Debit column for the Balance Sheet and Statement of Owner's Equity columns.
D. Credit column for the Balance Sheet and Statement of Owner's Equity columns.

_____	**1.** Office Supplies	_____	**9.** Service Fees Revenue
_____	**2.** Accounts Payable	_____	**10.** Insurance Expense
_____	**3.** Owner, Capital	_____	**11.** Accumulated Depreciation
_____	**4.** Wages Payable	_____	**12.** Interest Revenue
_____	**5.** Machinery	_____	**13.** Accounts Receivable
_____	**6.** Interest Receivable	_____	**14.** Rent Expense
_____	**7.** Interest Expense	_____	**15.** Depreciation Expense
_____	**8.** Owner, Withdrawals	_____	**16.** Cash

Exercise 4-10
Extending accounts in a work sheet
P1

The Adjusted Trial Balance columns of a 10-column work sheet for Poppe Company follow. Complete the work sheet by extending the account balances into the appropriate financial statement columns and by entering the amount of net income for the reporting period.

No.	Account Title	Debit	Credit
101	Cash	$ 6,000	
106	Accounts receivable	26,200	
153	Trucks	41,000	
154	Accumulated depreciation—Trucks		$ 16,500
183	Land	30,000	
201	Accounts payable		14,000
209	Salaries payable		3,200
233	Unearned fees		2,600
301	J. Poppe, Capital		64,500
302	J. Poppe, Withdrawals	14,400	
401	Plumbing fees earned		79,000
611	Depreciation expense—Trucks	5,500	
622	Salaries expense	37,000	
640	Rent expense	12,000	
677	Miscellaneous expenses	7,700	
	Totals	$179,800	$179,800

Check Net income, $16,800

Exercise 4-11
Completing the income statement columns and preparing closing entries

P1 P2

These partially completed Income Statement columns from a 10-column work sheet are for Red Sail Rental Co. (1) Use the information to determine the amount that should be entered on the net income line of the work sheet. (2) Prepare Red Sail's closing entries. The owner, L. Welch, did not make any withdrawals this period.

Account Title	Debit	Credit
Rent earned		102,000
Salaries expense	45,300	
Insurance expense	6,400	
Dock rental expense	15,000	
Boat supplies expense	3,200	
Depreciation expense—Boats	19,500	
Totals		
Net income		
Totals		

Check Net income, $12,600

Exercise 4-12
Preparing a work sheet and recording closing entries

P1 P2

The following unadjusted trial balance contains the accounts and balances of Dalton Delivery Company as of December 31, 2005, its first year of operations. (1) Use the following information about the company's adjustments to complete a 10-column work sheet for Dalton.

a. Unrecorded depreciation on the trucks at the end of the year is $35,000.

b. The total amount of accrued interest expense at year-end is $8,000.

c. The cost of unused office supplies still available at year-end is $1,000.

(2) Prepare the year-end closing entries for Dalton, and determine the capital amount to be reported on the year-end balance sheet.

	A	B	C
1	Account Title	Debit	Credit
2	Cash	$ 14,000	
3	Accounts receivable	33,000	
4	Office supplies	4,000	
5	Trucks	340,000	
6	Accumulated depreciation—Trucks		$ 70,000
7	Land	150,000	
8	Accounts payable		22,000
9	Interest payable		6,000
10	Long-term notes payable		104,000
11	V. Dalton, Capital		322,000
12	V. Dalton, Withdrawals	38,000	
13	Delivery fees earned		256,000
14	Depreciation expense—Truck	45,000	
15	Salaries expense	120,000	
16	Office supplies expense	14,000	
17	Interest expense	6,000	
18	Repairs expense—trucks	16,000	
19	Totals	$780,000	$780,000
20			

Check Adj. trial balance totals, $817,000; Net income, $15,000

Exercise 4-13[A]
Preparing reversing entries

P4

The following two events occurred for Totten Co. on October 31, 2005, the end of its fiscal year:

a. Totten rents a building from its owner for $3,200 per month. By a prearrangement, the company delayed paying October's rent until November 5. On this date, the company paid the rent for both October and November.

b. Totten rents space in a building it owns to a tenant for $750 per month. By prearrangement, the tenant delayed paying the October rent until November 8. On this date, the tenant paid the rent for both October and November.

Required

1. Prepare adjusting entries that Totten must record for these events as of October 31.

2. Assuming Totten does *not* use reversing entries, prepare journal entries to record Totten's payment of rent on November 5 and the collection of rent on November 8 from Totten's tenant.

3. Assuming that Totten uses reversing entries, prepare reversing entries on November 1 and the journal entries to record Totten's payment of rent on November 5 and the collection of rent on November 8 from Totten's tenant.

Exercise 4-14[A]
Preparing reversing entries
P4

Hinson Company records prepaid assets and unearned revenues in balance sheet accounts. The following information was used to prepare adjusting entries for Hinson Company as of August 31, the end of the company's fiscal year:

a. The company has earned $5,000 in unrecorded service fees.
b. The expired portion of prepaid insurance is $2,700.
c. The company has earned $1,900 of its Unearned Service Fees account balance.
d. Depreciation expense for office equipment is $2,300.
e. Employees have earned but have not been paid salaries of $2,400.

Prepare any necessary reversing entries for the accounting adjustments *a* through *e* assuming that Hinson uses reversing entries in its accounting system.

PROBLEM SET A

Problem 4-1A
Determining balance sheet classifications
C3

In the blank space beside each numbered balance sheet item, enter the letter of its balance sheet classification. If the item should not appear on the balance sheet, enter a *Z* in the blank.

A. Current assets
B. Long-term investments
C. Plant assets
D. Intangible assets
E. Current liabilities
F. Long-term liabilities
G. Equity

_____ **1.** Accumulated depreciation—Trucks
_____ **2.** Cash
_____ **3.** Buildings
_____ **4.** Store supplies
_____ **5.** Office equipment
_____ **6.** Land (used in operations)
_____ **7.** Repairs expense
_____ **8.** Office supplies
_____ **9.** Current portion of long-term note payable
_____ **10.** Long-term investment in stock
_____ **11.** Depreciation expense—Building
_____ **12.** Prepaid rent
_____ **13.** Interest receivable
_____ **14.** Taxes payable
_____ **15.** Automobiles
_____ **16.** Notes payable (due in 3 years)
_____ **17.** Accounts payable
_____ **18.** Prepaid insurance
_____ **19.** Owner, Capital
_____ **20.** Unearned services revenue

Problem 4-2A
Applying the accounting cycle
C1 C2 P2 P3

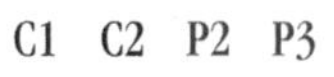

mhhe.com/larson

On April 1, 2005, Jennifer Stafford created a new travel agency, See-It-Now Travel. The following transactions occurred during the company's first month:

April	1	Stafford invested $20,000 cash and computer equipment worth $40,000 in the business.
	2	Rented furnished office space by paying $1,700 cash for the first month's (April) rent.
	3	Purchased $1,100 of office supplies for cash.
	10	Paid $3,600 cash for the premium on a 12-month insurance policy. Coverage begins on April 11.
	14	Paid $1,800 cash for two weeks' salaries earned by employees.
	24	Collected $7,900 cash on commissions from airlines on tickets obtained for customers.
	28	Paid another $1,800 cash for two weeks' salaries earned by employees.
	29	Paid $250 cash for minor repairs to the company's computer.
	30	Paid $650 cash for this month's telephone bill.
	30	Stafford withdrew $1,500 cash for personal use.

The company's chart of accounts follows:

101	Cash	405	Commissions Earned
106	Accounts Receivable	612	Depreciation Expense—Computer Equip.
124	Office Supplies	622	Salaries Expense
128	Prepaid Insurance	637	Insurance Expense
167	Computer Equipment	640	Rent Expense
168	Accumulated Depreciation—Computer Equip.	650	Office Supplies Expense
209	Salaries Payable	684	Repairs Expense
301	J. Stafford, Capital	688	Telephone Expense
302	J. Stafford, Withdrawals	901	Income Summary

Required

1. Use the balance column format to set up each ledger account listed in its chart of accounts.

2. Prepare journal entries to record the transactions for April and post them to the ledger accounts. The company records prepaid and unearned items in balance sheet accounts.

3. Prepare an unadjusted trial balance as of April 30.

4. Use the following information to journalize and post adjusting entries for the month:

   a. Two-thirds of one month's insurance coverage has expired.

   b. At the end of the month, $700 of office supplies are still available.

   c. This month's depreciation on the computer equipment is $600.

   d. Employees earned $320 of unpaid and unrecorded salaries as of month-end.

   e. The company earned $1,650 of commissions that are not yet billed at month-end.

5. Prepare the income statement and the statement of owner's equity for the month of April and the balance sheet at April 30, 2005.

6. Prepare journal entries to close the temporary accounts and post these entries to the ledger.

7. Prepare a post-closing trial balance.

Check (3) Unadj. trial balance totals, $67,900

(4*a*) Dr. Insurance Expense, $200

(5) Net income, $1,830; Capital (4/30/2005), $60,330; Total assets, $60,650

(7) P-C trial balance totals, $61,250

Problem 4-3A

Preparing trial balances, closing entries, and financial statements

C3 P2 P3 

mhhe.com/larson

The adjusted trial balance of Kobe Repairs on December 31, 2005, follows:

KOBE REPAIRS
Adjusted Trial Balance
December 31, 2005

No.	Account Title	Debit	Credit
101	Cash	$ 13,000	
124	Office supplies	1,200	
128	Prepaid insurance	1,950	
167	Equipment	48,000	
168	Accumulated depreciation—Equipment		$ 4,000
201	Accounts payable		12,000
210	Wages payable		500
301	S. Kobe, Capital		40,000
302	S. Kobe, Withdrawals	15,000	
401	Repair fees earned		77,750
612	Depreciation expense—Equipment	4,000	
623	Wages expense	36,500	
637	Insurance expense	700	
640	Rent expense	9,600	
650	Office supplies expense	2,600	
690	Utilities expense	1,700	
	Totals	$134,250	$134,250

Check (1) Ending capital balance, $47,650

(2) P-C trial balance totals, $64,150

Required

1. Prepare an income statement and a statement of owner's equity for the year 2005, and a classified balance sheet at December 31, 2005. There are no owner investments in 2005.

2. Enter the adjusted trial balance in the first two columns of a six-column table. Use columns three and four for closing entry information and the last two columns for a post-closing trial balance. Insert an Income Summary account as the last item in the trial balance.

3. Enter closing entry information in the six-column table and prepare journal entries for them.

Analysis Component

4. Assume for this part only that:

a. None of the $700 insurance expense had expired during the year. Instead, assume it is a prepayment of the next period's insurance protection.

b. There are no earned and unpaid wages at the end of the year. (*Hint:* Reverse the $500 wages payable accrual.)

Describe the financial statement changes that would result from these two assumptions.

Problem 4-4A
Preparing closing entries, financial statements, and ratios

C3 A1 P2

The adjusted trial balance for Sharp Construction as of December 31, 2005, follows:

SHARP CONSTRUCTION
Adjusted Trial Balance
December 31, 2005

No.	Account Title	Debit	Credit
101	Cash	$ 4,000	
104	Short-term investments	22,000	
126	Supplies	7,100	
128	Prepaid insurance	6,000	
167	Equipment	39,000	
168	Accumulated depreciation—Equipment		$ 20,000
173	Building	130,000	
174	Accumulated depreciation—Building		55,000
183	Land	45,000	
201	Accounts payable		15,500
203	Interest payable		1,500
208	Rent payable		2,500
210	Wages payable		1,500
213	Property taxes payable		800
233	Unearned professional fees		6,500
251	Long-term notes payable		66,000
301	J. Sharp, Capital		82,700
302	J. Sharp, Withdrawals	12,000	
401	Professional fees earned		96,000
406	Rent earned		13,000
407	Dividends earned		1,900
409	Interest earned		1,000
606	Depreciation expense—Building	10,000	
612	Depreciation expense—Equipment	5,000	
623	Wages expense	31,000	
633	Interest expense	4,100	
637	Insurance expense	9,000	
640	Rent expense	12,400	
652	Supplies expense	6,400	
682	Postage expense	3,200	
683	Property taxes expense	4,000	
684	Repairs expense	7,900	
688	Telephone expense	2,200	
690	Utilities expense	3,600	
	Totals	$363,900	$363,900

J. Sharp invested $50,000 cash in the business during year 2005 (the December 31, 2004, credit balance of the J. Sharp, Capital account was $32,700). Sharp Construction is required to make a $6,600 payment on its long-term notes payable during 2006.

Required

1. Prepare the income statement and the statement of owner's equity for the calendar-year 2005, and the classified balance sheet at December 31, 2005.
2. Prepare the necessary closing entries at December 31, 2005.
3. Use the information in the financial statements to compute these ratios: (a) return on assets (total assets at December 31, 2004, was $200,000), (b) debt ratio, (c) profit margin ratio (use total revenues as the denominator), and (d) current ratio.

Check (1) Total assets (12/31/2005), $178,100; Net income, $13,100

Problem 4-5A
Preparing a work sheet, adjusting and closing entries, and financial statements

C3 P1 P2 

The following unadjusted trial balance is for Adams Construction Co. as of the end of its 2005 fiscal year. The June 30, 2004, credit balance of the owner's capital account was $52,660, and the owner invested $25,000 cash in the company during the 2005 fiscal year.

ADAMS CONSTRUCTION CO.
Unadjusted Trial Balance
June 30, 2005

No.	Account Title	Debit	Credit
101	Cash	$ 17,500	
126	Supplies	8,900	
128	Prepaid insurance	6,200	
167	Equipment	131,000	
168	Accumulated depreciation—Equipment		$ 25,250
201	Accounts payable		5,800
203	Interest payable		0
208	Rent payable		0
210	Wages payable		0
213	Property taxes payable		0
251	Long-term notes payable		24,000
301	S. Adams, Capital		77,660
302	S. Adams, Withdrawals	30,000	
401	Construction fees earned		134,000
612	Depreciation expense—Equipment	0	
623	Wages expense	45,860	
633	Interest expense	2,640	
637	Insurance expense	0	
640	Rent expense	13,200	
652	Supplies expense	0	
683	Property taxes expense	4,600	
684	Repairs expense	2,810	
690	Utilities expense	4,000	
	Totals	$ 266,710	$ 266,710

Required

1. Prepare a 10-column work sheet for fiscal year 2005, starting with the unadjusted trial balance and including adjustments based on these additional facts:
   - **a.** The supplies available at the end of fiscal year 2005 had a cost of $3,200.
   - **b.** The cost of expired insurance for the fiscal year is $3,900.
   - **c.** Annual depreciation on equipment is $8,500.
   - **d.** The June utilities expense of $550 is not included in the unadjusted trial balance because the bill arrived after the trial balance was prepared. The $550 amount owed needs to be recorded.
   - **e.** The company's employees have earned $1,600 of accrued wages at fiscal year-end.
   - **f.** The rent expense incurred and not yet paid or recorded at fiscal year-end is $200.
   - **g.** Additional property taxes of $900 have been assessed for this fiscal year but have not been paid or recorded in the accounts.
   - **h.** The long-term note payable bears interest at 1% per month. The unadjusted Interest Expense account equals the amount paid for the first 11 months of the 2005 fiscal year. The $240 accrued interest for June has not yet been paid or recorded. (Note that the company is required to make a $5,000 payment toward the note payable during the 2006 fiscal year.)

Check (3) Total assets, $120,250; current liabilities, $14,290; Net income, $39,300

2. Use the work sheet to enter the adjusting and closing entries; then journalize them.
3. Prepare the income statement and the statement of owner's equity for the year ended June 30 and the classified balance sheet at June 30, 2005.

Analysis Component

4. Analyze the following separate errors and describe how each would affect the 10-column work sheet. Explain whether the error is likely to be discovered in completing the work sheet and, if not, the effect of the error on the financial statements.
   a. Assume that the adjustment for supplies used consisted of a credit to Supplies for $3,200 and a debit for $3,200 to Supplies Expense.
   b. When the adjusted trial balance in the work sheet is completed, the $17,500 Cash balance is incorrectly entered in the Credit column.

Problem 4-6A[A]
Preparing adjusting, reversing, and next period entries

P4

The following six-column table for Bullseye Ranges includes the unadjusted trial balance as of December 31, 2005.

BULLSEYE RANGES
December 31, 2005

Account Title	Unadjusted Trial Balance		Adjustments		Adjusted Trial Balance	
	Dr.	Cr.	Dr.	Cr.	Dr.	Cr.
Cash	$ 13,000					
Accounts receivable	0					
Supplies	5,500					
Equipment	130,000					
Accumulated depreciation—Equipment		$ 25,000				
Interest payable		0				
Salaries payable		0				
Unearned member fees		14,000				
Notes payable		50,000				
T. Allen, Capital		58,250				
T. Allen, Withdrawals	20,000					
Member fees earned		53,000				
Depreciation expense—Equipment	0					
Salaries expense	28,000					
Interest expense	3,750					
Supplies expense	0					
Totals	$200,250	$200,250				

Required

1. Complete the six-column table by entering adjustments that reflect the following information:
   a. As of December 31, 2005, employees had earned $900 of unpaid and unrecorded salaries. The next payday is January 4, at which time $1,600 of salaries will be paid.
   b. The cost of supplies still available at December 31, 2005, is $2,700.
   c. The notes payable requires an interest payment to be made every three months. The amount of unrecorded accrued interest at December 31, 2005, is $1,250. The next interest payment, at an amount of $1,500, is due on January 15, 2006.
   d. Analysis of the unearned member fees account shows $5,600 remaining unearned at December 31, 2005.
   e. In addition to the member fees included in the revenue account balance, the company has earned another $9,100 in unrecorded fees that will be collected on January 31, 2006. The company is also expected to collect $8,000 on that same day for new fees earned in January 2006.
   f. Depreciation expense for the year is $12,500.

Check (1) Adjusted trial balance totals, $224,000

2. Prepare journal entries for the adjustments entered in the six-column table for part 1.
3. Prepare journal entries to reverse the effects of the adjusting entries that involve accruals.
4. Prepare journal entries to record the cash payments and cash collections described for January.

PROBLEM SET B

Problem 4-1B
Determining balance sheet classifications

C3

In the blank space beside each numbered balance sheet item, enter the letter of its balance sheet classification. If the item should not appear on the balance sheet, enter a *Z* in the blank.

A. Current assets
B. Long-term investments
C. Plant assets
D. Intangible assets
E. Current liabilities
F. Long-term liabilities
G. Equity

_____ **1.** Machinery
_____ **2.** Prepaid insurance
_____ **3.** Current portion of long-term note payable
_____ **4.** Interest receivable
_____ **5.** Rent receivable
_____ **6.** Land (used in operations)
_____ **7.** Copyrights
_____ **8.** Rent revenue
_____ **9.** Depreciation expense—Trucks
_____ **10.** Long-term investment in stock
_____ **11.** Office supplies
_____ **12.** Interest payable
_____ **13.** Owner, Capital
_____ **14.** Notes receivable (due in 120 days)
_____ **15.** Accumulated depreciation—Trucks
_____ **16.** Salaries payable
_____ **17.** Commissions earned
_____ **18.** Interest payable
_____ **19.** Office equipment
_____ **20.** Notes payable (due in 5 years)

Problem 4-2B
Applying the accounting cycle

C1 C2 P2 P3

On July 1, 2005, Lucinda Fogle created a new self-storage business, KeepSafe Co. The following transactions occurred during the company's first month:

July 1 Fogle invested $20,000 cash and buildings worth $120,000 in the business.
2 Rented equipment by paying $1,800 cash for the first month's (July) rent.
5 Purchased $2,300 of office supplies for cash.
10 Paid $5,400 cash for the premium on a 12-month insurance policy. Coverage begins on July 11.
14 Paid an employee $900 cash for two weeks' salary earned.
24 Collected $8,800 cash for storage fees from customers.
28 Paid another $900 cash for two weeks' salary earned by an employee.
29 Paid $850 cash for minor repairs to a leaking roof.
30 Paid $300 cash for this month's telephone bill.
31 Fogle withdrew $1,600 cash for personal use.

The company's chart of accounts follows:

101	Cash	401	Storage Fees Earned
106	Accounts Receivable	606	Depreciation Expense—Buildings
124	Office Supplies	622	Salaries Expense
128	Prepaid Insurance	637	Insurance Expense
173	Buildings	640	Rent Expense
174	Accumulated Depreciation—Buildings	650	Office Supplies Expense
209	Salaries Payable	684	Repairs Expense
301	L. Fogle, Capital	688	Telephone Expense
302	L. Fogle, Withdrawals	901	Income Summary

Required

1. Use the balance column format to set up each ledger account listed in its chart of accounts.
2. Prepare journal entries to record the transactions for July and post them to the ledger accounts. Record prepaid and unearned items in balance sheet accounts.

Check (3) Unadj. trial balance totals, $148,800

(4*a*) Dr. Insurance Expense, $300

(5) Net income, $2,570; Capital (7/31/2005), $140,970; Total assets, $141,150

(7) P-C trial balance totals, $142,350

3. Prepare an unadjusted trial balance as of July 31.
4. Use the following information to journalize and post adjusting entries for the month:
   a. Two-thirds of one month's insurance coverage has expired.
   b. At the end of the month, $1,550 of office supplies are still available.
   c. This month's depreciation on the buildings is $1,200.
   d. An employee earned $180 of unpaid and unrecorded salary as of month-end.
   e. The company earned $950 of storage fees that are not yet billed at month-end.
5. Prepare the income statement and the statement of owner's equity for the month of July and the balance sheet at July 31, 2005.
6. Prepare journal entries to close the temporary accounts and post these entries to the ledger.
7. Prepare a post-closing trial balance.

Problem 4-3B

Preparing trial balances, closing entries, and financial statements

C3 P2 P3 

Heel-To-Toe-Shoes' adjusted trial balance on December 31, 2005, follows:

HEEL-TO-TOE SHOES
Adjusted Trial Balance
December 31, 2005

No.	Account Title	Debit	Credit
101	Cash	$ 13,450	
125	Store supplies	4,140	
128	Prepaid insurance	2,200	
167	Equipment	33,000	
168	Accumulated depreciation—Equipment		$ 9,000
201	Accounts payable		1,000
210	Wages payable		3,200
301	P. Holt, Capital		31,650
302	P. Holt, Withdrawals	16,000	
401	Repair fees earned		62,000
612	Depreciation expense—Equipment	3,000	
623	Wages expense	28,400	
637	Insurance expense	1,100	
640	Rent expense	2,400	
651	Store supplies expense	1,300	
690	Utilities expense	1,860	
	Totals	$106,850	$106,850

Required

Check (1) Ending capital balance, $39,590

(2) P-C trial balance totals, $52,790

1. Prepare an income statement and a statement of owner's equity for the year 2005, and a classified balance sheet at December 31, 2005. There are no owner investments in 2005.
2. Enter the adjusted trial balance in the first two columns of a six-column table. Use the middle two columns for closing entry information and the last two columns for a post-closing trial balance. Insert an Income Summary account as the last item in the trial balance.
3. Enter closing entry information in the six-column table and prepare journal entries for them.

Analysis Component

4. Assume for this part only that:
   a. None of the $1,100 insurance expense had expired during the year. Instead, assume it is a prepayment of the next period's insurance protection.
   b. There are no earned and unpaid wages at the end of the year. (*Hint:* Reverse the $3,200 wages payable accrual.)

   Describe the financial statement changes that would result from these two assumptions.

The adjusted trial balance for Giovanni Co. as of December 31, 2005, follows:

Problem 4-4B
Preparing closing entries, financial statements, and ratios
C3 A1 P2

GIOVANNI CO. Adjusted Trial Balance December 31, 2005			
No.	Account Title	Debit	Credit
101	Cash	$ 6,400	
104	Short-term investments	10,200	
126	Supplies	3,600	
128	Prepaid insurance	800	
167	Equipment	18,000	
168	Accumulated depreciation—Equipment		$ 3,000
173	Building	90,000	
174	Accumulated depreciation—Building		9,000
183	Land	28,500	
201	Accounts payable		2,500
203	Interest payable		1,400
208	Rent payable		200
210	Wages payable		1,180
213	Property taxes payable		2,330
233	Unearned professional fees		650
251	Long-term notes payable		32,000
301	J. Giovanni, Capital		91,800
302	J. Giovanni, Withdrawals	6,000	
401	Professional fees earned		47,000
406	Rent earned		3,600
407	Dividends earned		500
409	Interest earned		1,120
606	Depreciation expense—Building	2,000	
612	Depreciation expense—Equipment	1,000	
623	Wages expense	17,500	
633	Interest expense	1,200	
637	Insurance expense	1,425	
640	Rent expense	1,800	
652	Supplies expense	900	
682	Postage expense	310	
683	Property taxes expense	3,825	
684	Repairs expense	579	
688	Telephone expense	421	
690	Utilities expense	1,820	
	Totals	$196,280	$196,280

J. Giovanni invested $30,000 cash in the business during year 2005 (the December 31, 2004, credit balance of the J. Giovanni, Capital account was $61,800). Giovanni Company is required to make a $6,400 payment on its long-term notes payable during 2006.

Required

1. Prepare the income statement and the statement of owner's equity for the calendar year 2005 and the classified balance sheet at December 31, 2005.

2. Prepare the necessary closing entries at December 31, 2005.

3. Use the information in the financial statements to calculate these ratios: (a) return on assets (total assets at December 31, 2004, was $150,000), (b) debt ratio, (c) profit margin ratio (use total revenues as the denominator), and (d) current ratio.

Check (1) Total assets (12/31/2005), $145,500; Net income, $19,440

Problem 4-5B
Preparing a work sheet, adjusting and closing entries, and financial statements

C3 P1 P2

The following unadjusted trial balance is for Crush Demolition Company as of the end of its April 30, 2005, fiscal year. The April 30, 2004, credit balance of the owner's capital account was $36,900, and the owner invested $30,000 cash in the company during the 2005 fiscal year.

	CRUSH DEMOLITION COMPANY Unadjusted Trial Balance April 30, 2005		
No.	**Account Title**	**Debit**	**Credit**
101	Cash	$ 9,000	
126	Supplies	18,000	
128	Prepaid insurance	14,600	
167	Equipment	140,000	
168	Accumulated depreciation—Equipment		$ 10,000
201	Accounts payable		16,000
203	Interest payable		0
208	Rent payable		0
210	Wages payable		0
213	Property taxes payable		0
251	Long-term notes payable		20,000
301	J. Bonair, Capital		66,900
302	J. Bonair, Withdrawals	24,000	
401	Demolition fees earned		177,000
612	Depreciation expense—Equipment	0	
623	Wages expense	51,400	
633	Interest expense	2,200	
637	Insurance expense	0	
640	Rent expense	8,800	
652	Supplies expense	0	
683	Property taxes expense	8,400	
684	Repairs expense	6,700	
690	Utilities expense	6,800	
	Totals	$ 289,900	$ 289,900

Required

1. Prepare a 10-column work sheet for fiscal year 2005, starting with the unadjusted trial balance and including adjustments based on these additional facts:

- **a.** The supplies available at the end of fiscal year 2005 had a cost of $8,100.
- **b.** The cost of expired insurance for the fiscal year is $11,500.
- **c.** Annual depreciation on equipment is $18,000.
- **d.** The April utilities expense of $700 is not included in the unadjusted trial balance because the bill arrived after the trial balance was prepared. The $700 amount owed needs to be recorded.
- **e.** The company's employees have earned $2,200 of accrued wages at fiscal year-end.
- **f.** The rent expense incurred and not yet paid or recorded at fiscal year-end is $5,360.
- **g.** Additional property taxes of $450 have been assessed for this fiscal year but have not been paid or recorded in the accounts.
- **h.** The long-term note payable bears interest at 1% per month. The unadjusted Interest Expense account equals the amount paid for the first 11 months of the 2005 fiscal year. The $200 accrued interest for April has not yet been paid or recorded. (Note that the company is required to make a $4,000 payment toward the note payable during the 2006 fiscal year.)

2. Use the work sheet to enter the adjusting and closing entries; then journalize them.

3. Prepare the income statement and the statement of owner's equity for the year ended April 30, and the classified balance sheet at April 30, 2005.

Check (3) Total assets, $132,200; current liabilities, $28,910; Net income, $44,390

Analysis Component

4. Analyze the following separate errors and describe how each would affect the 10-column work sheet. Explain whether the error is likely to be discovered in completing the work sheet and, if not, the effect of the error on the financial statements.

a. Assume the adjustment for expiration of the insurance coverage consisted of a credit to Prepaid Insurance for $3,100 and a debit for $3,100 to Insurance Expense.

b. When the adjusted trial balance in the work sheet is completed, the $6,700 Repairs Expense account balance is extended to the Debit column of the balance sheet columns.

Problem 4-6B[A]

Preparing adjusting, reversing, and next period entries

P4

The following six-column table for Solutions Co. includes the unadjusted trial balance as of December 31, 2005:

SOLUTIONS CO. December 31, 2005						
Account Title	**Unadjusted Trial Balance**		**Adjustments**		**Adjusted Trial Balance**	
	Dr.	**Cr.**	**Dr.**	**Cr.**	**Dr.**	**Cr.**
Cash	$ 9,000					
Accounts receivable	0					
Supplies	6,600					
Machinery	40,100					
Accumulated depreciation—Machinery		$15,800				
Interest payable		0				
Salaries payable		0				
Unearned rental fees		5,200				
Notes payable		20,000				
G. Clay, Capital		13,200				
G. Clay, Withdrawals	10,500					
Rental fees earned		37,000				
Depreciation expense—Machinery	0					
Salaries expense	23,500					
Interest expense	1,500					
Supplies expense	0					
Totals	$91,200	$91,200				

Required

1. Complete the six-column table by entering adjustments that reflect the following information:

a. As of December 31, 2005, employees had earned $420 of unpaid and unrecorded wages. The next payday is January 4, at which time $1,250 in wages will be paid.

b. The cost of supplies still available at December 31, 2005, is $2,450.

c. The notes payable requires an interest payment to be made every three months. The amount of unrecorded accrued interest at December 31, 2005, is $500. The next interest payment, at an amount of $600, is due on January 15, 2006.

d. Analysis of the unearned rental fees shows that $3,100 remains unearned at December 31, 2005.

e. In addition to the machinery rental fees included in the revenue account balance, the company has earned another $2,350 in unrecorded fees that will be collected on January 31, 2006. The company is also expected to collect $4,400 on that same day for new fees earned in January 2006.

f. Depreciation expense for the year is $3,800.

2. Prepare journal entries for the adjustments entered in the six-column table for part 1.

3. Prepare journal entries to reverse the effects of the adjusting entries that involve accruals.

4. Prepare journal entries to record the cash payments and cash collections described for January.

Check (1) Adjusted trial balance totals, $98,270

PROBLEM SET C

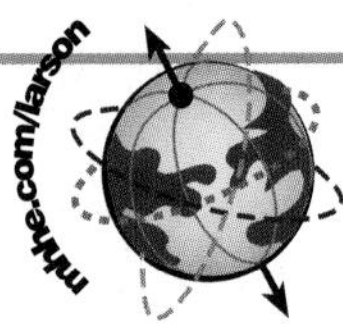

Problem Set C is available at the book's Website to further reinforce and assess your learning.

SERIAL PROBLEM

Success Systems P2 P3

(This serial problem began in Chapter 1 and continues through most of the book. If previous chapter segments were not completed, the serial problem can begin at this point. It is helpful, but not necessary, that you use the Working Papers that accompany the book.)

The December 31, 2004, adjusted trial balance of Success Systems (reflecting its transactions from October through December of 2004) follows:

No.	Account Title	Debit	Credit
101	Cash	$ 58,160	
106	Accounts receivable	5,668	
126	Computer supplies	580	
128	Prepaid insurance	1,665	
131	Prepaid rent	825	
163	Office equipment	8,000	
164	Accumulated depreciation—Office equipment		$ 400
167	Computer equipment	20,000	
168	Accumulated depreciation—Computer equipment		1,250
201	Accounts payable		1,100
210	Wages payable		500
236	Unearned computer services revenue		1,500
301	K. Breeze, Capital		83,000
302	K. Breeze, Withdrawals	7,100	
403	Computer services revenue		31,284
612	Depreciation expense—Office equipment	400	
613	Depreciation expense—Computer equipment	1,250	
623	Wages expense	3,875	
637	Insurance expense	555	
640	Rent expense	2,475	
652	Computer supplies expense	3,065	
655	Advertising expense	2,965	
676	Mileage expense	896	
677	Miscellaneous expenses	250	
684	Repairs expense—Computer	1,305	
901	Income summary		0
	Totals	$119,034	$119,034

Required

Check Post-closing trial balance totals, $94,898

1. Record and post the necessary closing entries for Success Systems.
2. Prepare a post-closing trial balance as of December 31, 2004.

BEYOND THE NUMBERS

REPORTING IN ACTION

C1 P2

BTN 4-1 Refer to **Krispy Kreme**'s financial statements in Appendix A to answer the following:

Required

1. For the fiscal year ended February 2, 2003, what amount will be credited to Income Summary to summarize its revenues earned?
2. For the fiscal year ended February 2, 2003, what amount will be debited to Income Summary to summarize its expenses incurred?

3. For the fiscal year ended February 2, 2003, what will be the balance of its Income Summary account before it is closed?

4. In its statement of cash flows for the year ended February 2, 2003, what amount of cash is paid in dividends to common stockholders?

Roll On

5. Access Krispy Kreme's annual report for fiscal years ending after February 2, 2003, at its Website (KrispyKreme.com) or the SEC's EDGAR database (www.SEC.gov). How has the amount of net income closed to Income Summary changed in the fiscal years ending after February 2, 2003? How has the amount of cash paid as dividends changed in the fiscal years ending after February 2, 2003?

COMPARATIVE ANALYSIS

A1 

BTN 4-2 Key figures ($ thousands) for the recent two years of both **Krispy Kreme** and **Tastykake** follow:

Key Figures	Krispy Kreme		Tastykake	
	Current Year	Prior Year	Current Year	Prior Year
Current assets	$141,128	$101,769	$36,095	$35,169
Current liabilities	59,687	52,533	19,307	16,885

Required

1. Compute the current ratio for both years and both companies.

2. Which has the better ability to pay short-term obligations according to the current ratio?

3. Analyze and comment on each company's current ratios for the past two years.

4. How do Krispy Kreme's and Tastykake's current ratios compare to their industry average ratio of about 1.0 to 1.2?

ETHICS CHALLENGE

C2

BTN 4-3 On January 20, 2005, Jennifer Nelson, the accountant for Travon Enterprises, is feeling pressure to complete the annual financial statements. The company president has said he needs up-to-date financial statements to share with the bank on January 21 at a dinner meeting that has been called to discuss Travon's obtaining loan financing for a special building project. Jennifer knows that she will not be able to gather all the needed information in the next 24 hours to prepare the entire set of adjusting entries that must be posted before the financial statements accurately portray the company's performance and financial position for the fiscal period ended December 31, 2004. Jennifer ultimately decides to estimate several expense accruals at the last minute. When deciding on estimates for the expenses, she uses low estimates because she does not want to make the financial statements look worse than they are. Jennifer finishes the financial statements before the deadline and gives them to the president without mentioning that several accounts use estimated balances.

Required

1. Identify several courses of action that Jennifer could have taken instead of the one she took.

2. If you were in Jennifer's situation, what would you have done? Briefly justify your response.

COMMUNICATING IN PRACTICE

C1 P2

BTN 4-4 Assume that one of your classmates states that a company's books should be ongoing and therefore not closed until that business is terminated. Write a one-half page memo to this classmate explaining the concept of the closing process by drawing analogies between (1) a scoreboard for an athletic event and the revenue and expense accounts of a business or (2) a sports team's record book and the capital account. (*Hint:* Think about what would happen if the scoreboard is not cleared before the start of a new game.)

TAKING IT TO THE NET

A1

mhhe.com/larson

BTN 4-5 Access Motley Fool's discussion of the current ratio at Fool.com/School/Valuation/CurrentAndQuickRatio.htm. (Note that if the page changed, search the site for the *current ratio*.)

Required

1. What level for the current ratio is generally regarded as sufficient to meet near-term operating needs?
2. Once you have calculated the current ratio for a company, what should you compare it against?
3. What are the implications for a company that has a current ratio that is too high?

TEAMWORK IN ACTION

P1 P2 P3

BTN 4-6 The unadjusted trial balance and information for the accounting adjustments of Noseworthy Investigators follow. Each team member involved in this project is to assume one of the four responsibilities listed. After completing each of these responsibilities, the team should work together to prove the accounting equation utilizing information from teammates (1 and 4). If your equation does not balance, you are to work as a team to resolve the error. The team's goal is to complete the task as quickly and accurately as possible.

Unadjusted Trial Balance		
Account Title	Debit	Credit
Cash	$15,000	
Supplies	11,000	
Prepaid insurance	2,000	
Equipment	24,000	
Accumulated depreciation—Equipment		$ 6,000
Accounts payable		2,000
D. Noseworthy, Capital		31,000
D. Noseworthy, Withdrawals	5,000	
Investigation fees earned		32,000
Rent expense	14,000	
Totals	$71,000	$71,000

Additional Year-End Information

a. Insurance that expired in the current period amounts to $1,200.
b. Equipment depreciation for the period is $3,000.
c. Unused supplies total $4,000 at period-end.
d. Services in the amount of $500 have been provided but have not been billed or collected.

Responsibilities for Individual Team Members

1. Determine the accounts and adjusted balances to be extended to the balance sheet columns of the work sheet for Noseworthy. Also determine total assets and total liabilities.
2. Determine the adjusted revenue account balance and prepare the entry to close this account.
3. Determine the adjusted account balances for expenses and prepare the entry to close these accounts.
4. Prepare T-accounts for both D. Noseworthy, Capital (reflecting the unadjusted trial balance amount) and Income Summary. Prepare the third and fourth closing entries. Ask teammates assigned to parts 2 and 3 for the postings for Income Summary. Obtain amounts to complete the third closing entry and post both the third and fourth closing entries. Provide the team with the ending capital account balance.
5. The entire team should prove the accounting equation using post-closing balances.

HITTING THE ROAD

C2

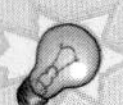

BTN 4-7 Select a company that you can visit in person or interview on the telephone. Call ahead to the company to arrange a time when you can interview an employee (preferably an accountant) who helps prepare the annual financial statements. Inquire about the following aspects of its *accounting cycle:*

1. Does it prepare interim financial statements? What time period(s) is used for interim statements?
2. Does the company use the cash or accrual basis of accounting?

3. Does the company use a work sheet in preparing financial statements? Why or why not?
4. Does the company use a spreadsheet program? If so, which software program is used?
5. How long does it take after the end of its reporting period to complete annual statements?

BTN 4-8 Read the article "Weighing the Balance Sheet" in the April 1, 2002, issue of *Business Week*.

BUSINESS WEEK ACTIVITY

A1 C3

mhhe.com/larson

Required

1. This article explains how to evaluate whether a company has a financially strong balance sheet. What does the author of this article look for when evaluating the debt level carried by companies?
2. The article reports a table showing 12 companies that passed the test for strong balance sheets. Identify the range of the current ratio for these 12 companies and name the company with the highest and the company with the lowest current ratios.
3. What is the range of the return on assets ratio for the 12 companies with attractive numbers according to the article? Identify the company with the highest and the company with the lowest return on assets.
4. Some investors will not buy tobacco or asbestos-related companies even if they have a very strong balance sheet. What risk factor are these investors concerned with so that it is more important for these companies than the level of debt on their balance sheets?

BTN 4-9 Review this chapter's opening feature involving Andy Wolf and his startup company, Premier Snowskates.

ENTREPRENEURIAL DECISION

A1 C3 P2 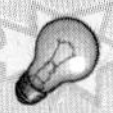 

Required

1. What is a conservative estimate for the units of snowskates that will be sold if annual sales are $3 million and Andy Wolf meets his targeted retail price?
2. What ratios studied in Chapters 1 through 4 do you recommend that Andy use to monitor the financial performance of his company?
3. What portions of the classified balance sheet do you believe are most relevant in assisting Andy in discovering what obligations are due and when?
4. What objectives are met when Andy applies closing procedures each fiscal year?

BTN 4-10 Grupo Bimbo (GrupoBimbo.com) is a leader in the baking and foods industry. Key financial information (millions of pesos) for Grupo Bimbo for its recent fiscal years follows:

GLOBAL DECISION

A1 

Key Figures*	Current Year	Prior Year
Current assets	$7,155	$4,867
Current liabilities	5,409	4,026

*Key figures prepared in accordance with accounting principles generally accepted in Mexico.

Required

1. Compute the current ratio for Grupo Bimbo for both the current and prior years.
2. Comment on the level and the change in the current ratios computed in part 1.

"I felt we should go into something that we had some connection to"—Dwayne Lewis (standing; Michael Cherry sitting)

Accounting for Merchandising Operations

A Look Back

Chapter 4 focused on the final steps of the accounting process. We explained the importance of proper revenue and expense recognition and described the closing process. We also showed how to prepare financial statements from a work sheet.

A Look at This Chapter

This chapter emphasizes merchandising activities. We explain how reporting merchandising activities differs from reporting service activities. We also analyze and record merchandise purchases and sales transactions and explain the adjustments and closing process for merchandisers.

A Look Ahead

Chapter 6 extends our analysis of merchandising activities and focuses on the valuation of inventory. Topics include the items in inventory, costs assigned, costing methods used, and inventory estimation techniques.

CAP

Conceptual

C1 Describe merchandising activities and identify income components for a merchandising company. *(p. 178)*

C2 Identify and explain the inventory asset of a merchandising company. *(p. 179)*

C3 Describe both perpetual and periodic inventory systems. *(p. 179)*

C4 Analyze and interpret cost flows and operating activities of a merchandising company. *(p. 187)*

Analytical

A1 Compute the acid-test ratio and explain its use to assess liquidity. *(p. 193)*

A2 Compute the gross margin ratio and explain its use to assess profitability. *(p. 193)*

Procedural

P1 Analyze and record transactions for merchandise purchases using a perpetual system. *(p. 180)*

P2 Analyze and record transactions for merchandise sales using a perpetual system. *(p. 185)*

P3 Prepare adjustments and close accounts for a merchandising company. *(p. 188)*

P4 Define and prepare multiple-step and single-step income statements. *(p. 190)*

Decision Feature

Dada, Dada, Dada . . .

EL SEGUNDO, CA—Dwayne Lewis and Michael Cherry had a dream—a dream to own and run a company. With one lone product (a five-panel polo hat) and $1,000 in pooled paychecks, they launched **Damani Dada (DamaniDada.com).** The two dreamed that Damani Dada would bring an ultra-hip style to the urban fashion scene. A mere seven years after its launch, Dada projects annual sales of more than $50 million.

The early days, however, were far from easy as Lewis and Cherry struggled alone against long odds. "It was very tricky to try and learn the business without a mentor," recalls Lewis. "We always struggled with the task of maintaining a strong financial backing, and we had to learn a lot by making mistakes." Among those struggles was implementing and learning a merchandising system—one that could capture and communicate the costs and sales information so desperately needed by the young entrepreneurs.

A crucial part of their success was tracking merchandising activities. This was necessary for setting prices and making policies for everything from discounts and allowances to returns on both sales and purchases. Also, use of a perpetual inventory system enabled them to stock the right type and amount of merchandise and to avoid the costs of out-of-stock and excess inventory. This chapter describes how the accounting system captures merchandising information for these and other business decisions. It also introduces analysis tools for assessing the financial condition and performance of merchandisers.

Damani Dada successfully weathered the storm and now offers a full line of both men's and women's apparel and footwear. NBA star Chris Webber's chrome Dada shoes were the talk of the 2003 All-Star Game. But it's still a battle. "Business is war," says Lewis. "You have to be mentally strong, willing to sacrifice, and willing to accept delayed gratification."

[Sources: *Damani Dada Website,* January 2004; *Entrepreneur,* November 2000; *ESPN Sports Business,* February 2003.]

Merchandising activities are a major part of modern business. Consumers expect a wealth of products, discount prices, inventory on demand, and high quality. This chapter introduces the business and accounting practices used by companies engaged in merchandising activities. We show how financial statements reflect these merchandising activities and explain the new financial statement items created by merchandising activities. We also analyze and record merchandise purchases and sales, and explain the adjustments and the closing process for merchandising companies.

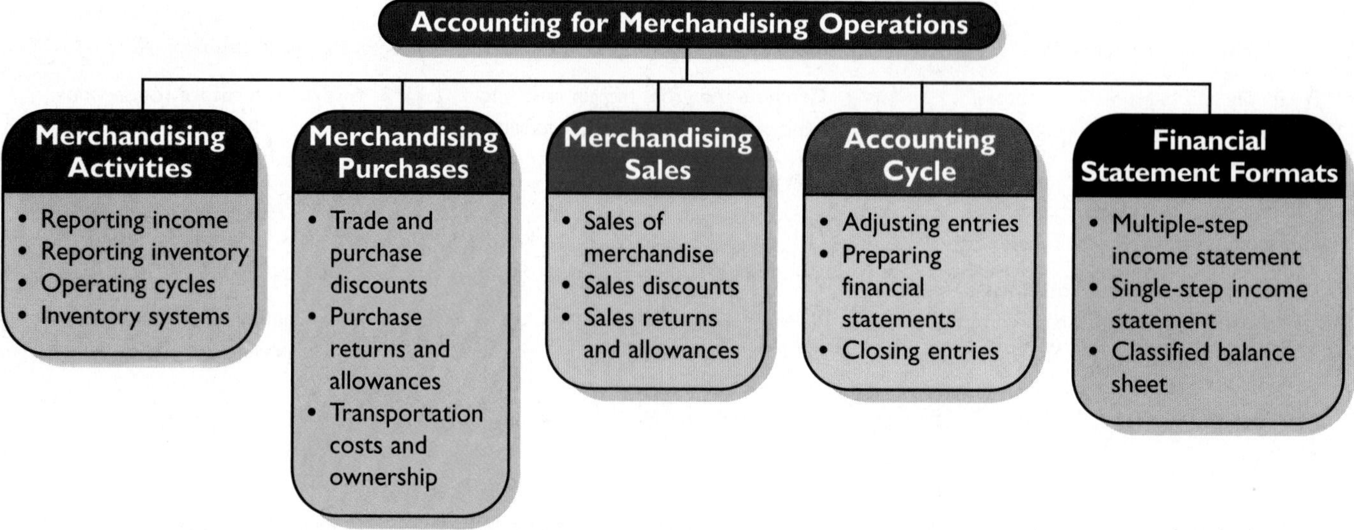

Merchandising Activities

C1 Describe merchandising activities and identify income components for a merchandising company.

Point: **Fleming, SuperValu,** and **SYSCO** are wholesalers. **Gap, Oakley,** and **Wal-Mart** are retailers.

Previous chapters emphasized the accounting and reporting activities of service companies. A merchandising company's activities differ from those of a service company. **Merchandise** consists of products, also called *goods,* that a company acquires to resell to customers. A **merchandiser** earns net income by buying and selling merchandise. Merchandisers are often identified as either wholesalers or retailers. A **wholesaler** is an *intermediary* that buys products from manufacturers or other wholesalers and sells them to retailers or other wholesalers. A **retailer** is an intermediary that buys products from manufacturers or wholesalers and sells them to consumers. Many retailers sell both products and services.

Reporting Income for a Merchandiser

Net income to a merchandiser equals revenues from selling merchandise minus both the cost of merchandise sold to customers and the cost of other expenses for the period (see Exhibit 5.1). The usual accounting term for revenues from selling merchandise is *sales,* and

Exhibit 5.1

Computing Income for a Merchandising Company versus a Service Company

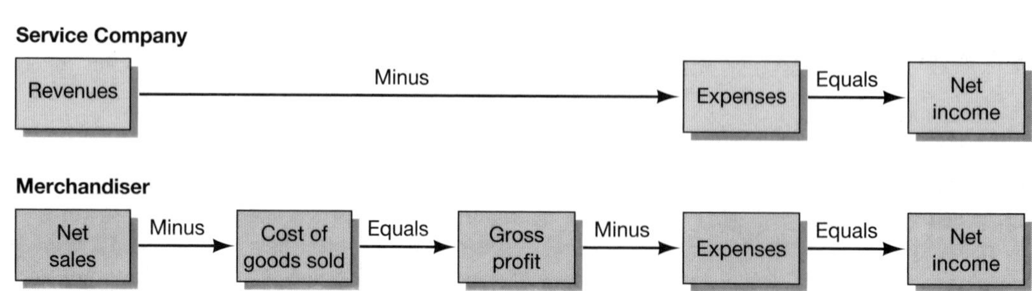

the term used for the expense of buying and preparing the merchandise is **cost of goods sold.** (Note that many service companies use the term *sales* instead of revenues, and cost of goods sold is also called *cost of sales.*)

The income statement for Z-Mart in Exhibit 5.2 illustrates these key components of a merchandiser's net income. The first two lines show that products are acquired at a cost of $230,400 and sold for $314,700. The third line shows an $84,300 **gross profit,** also called **gross margin,** which equals net sales less cost of goods sold. Finally, $71,400 of other expenses are reported, which leaves $12,900 in net income.

Z-MART
Income Statement
For Year Ended December 31, 2005

Net sales	$314,700
Cost of goods sold	**230,400**
Gross profit	**84,300**
Expenses	71,400
Net income	$ 12,900

Exhibit 5.2

Merchandiser's Income Statement

Point: Analysis of gross profit is important to effective business decisions, and is described later in the chapter.

Reporting Inventory for a Merchandiser

A merchandiser's balance sheet includes a current asset called *merchandise inventory,* an item not on a service company's balance sheet. **Merchandise inventory,** or simply *inventory,* refers to products that a company owns and intends to sell. The cost of this asset includes the cost incurred to buy the goods, ship them to the store, and make them ready for sale.

C2 Identify and explain the inventory asset of a merchandising company.

Operating Cycle for a Merchandiser

A merchandising company's operating cycle begins by purchasing merchandise and ends by collecting cash from selling the merchandise. The length of an operating cycle differs across the types of businesses. Department stores often have operating cycles of two to five months. Operating cycles for grocery merchants usually range from two to eight weeks.

Exhibit 5.3 illustrates an operating cycle for a merchandiser with credit sales. The cycle moves from (*a*) cash purchases of merchandise to (*b*) inventory for sale to (*c*) credit sales to (*d*) accounts receivable to (*e*) cash. Companies try to keep their operating cycles short because assets tied up in inventory and receivables are not productive.

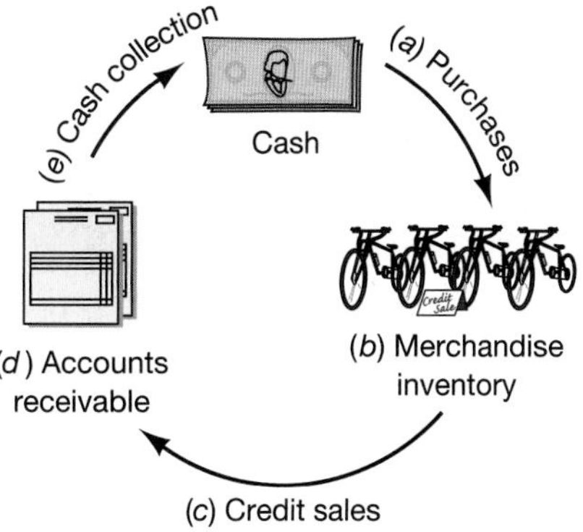

Exhibit 5.3

Merchandiser's Operating Cycle

Point: Cash sales shorten operating cycles. Credit purchases lengthen operating cycles.

Inventory Systems

Cost of goods sold is the cost of merchandise sold to customers during a period. It is often the largest single expense on a merchandiser's income statement. **Inventory** refers to products a company owns and expects to sell in its normal operations. Exhibit 5.4 shows that a company's merchandise available for sale consists of what it begins with (beginning inventory) and what it purchases (net cost of purchases). The merchandise available is either sold (cost of goods sold) or kept for future sales (ending inventory).

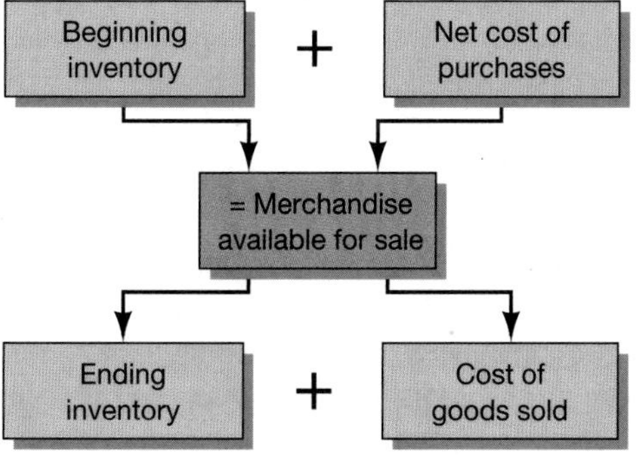

Exhibit 5.4

Merchandiser's Cost Flow for a Single Time Period

Two alternative inventory accounting systems can be used to collect information about cost of goods sold and cost of inventory: *perpetual system* or *periodic system*. The **perpetual**

C3 Describe both perpetual and periodic inventory systems.

Decision Insight

Technology and perpetual inventory systems are helping with purchasing activities, slashing inventory cycles, keeping popular items in stock, and cutting return rates. Technology has "totally changed the industry," says the chairman of **Western Merchandisers**, a supplier to more than 1,000 **Wal-Marts**.

inventory system continually updates accounting records for merchandising transactions—specifically, for those records of inventory available for sale and inventory sold. The **periodic inventory system** updates the accounting records for merchandise transactions only at the *end of a period*. Technological advances and competitive pressures have dramatically increased the use of the perpetual system.

Quick Check

1. Describe a merchandiser's cost of goods sold.
2. What is gross profit for a merchandising company?
3. Explain why use of the perpetual inventory system has dramatically increased.

Answers—p. 204

The following sections on purchasing, selling, and adjusting merchandise use the perpetual system. Appendix 5A uses the periodic system (with the perpetual results on the side). An instructor can choose to cover either one or both inventory systems.

Accounting for Merchandise Purchases

The cost of merchandise purchased for resale is recorded in the Merchandise Inventory asset account. To illustrate, Z-Mart records a $1,200 cash purchase of merchandise on November 2 as follows:

Assets = Liabilities + Equity
+1,200
−1,200

Nov. 2	Merchandise Inventory	1,200	
	Cash		1,200
	Purchased merchandise for cash.		

P1 Analyze and record transactions for merchandise purchases using a perpetual system.

The invoice for this merchandise is shown in Exhibit 5.5. The buyer usually receives the original invoice, and the seller keeps a copy. This *source document* serves as the purchase invoice of Z-Mart (buyer) and the sales invoice for Trex (seller). The amount recorded for merchandise inventory includes its purchase cost, shipping fees, taxes, and any other costs necessary to make it ready for sale. This section explains how we compute the recorded cost of merchandise purchases.

Trade Discounts

Topic Tackler 5-1

When a manufacturer or wholesaler prepares a catalog of items it has for sale, it usually gives each item a **list price,** also called a *catalog price.* However, an item's intended *selling price* equals list price minus a given percent called a **trade discount.** The amount of trade discount usually depends on whether a buyer is a wholesaler, retailer, or final consumer. A wholesaler buying in large quantities is often granted a larger discount than a retailer buying in smaller quantities. Note that a buyer records the net amount of list price minus trade discount. For example, in the November 2 purchase of merchandise by Z-Mart, the merchandise was listed in the seller's catalog at $2,000 and Z-Mart received a 40% trade discount. This meant that Z-Mart's purchase price was $1,200, computed as $2,000 − (40% × $2,000).

Point: The Merchandise Inventory account reflects the cost of goods available for resale.

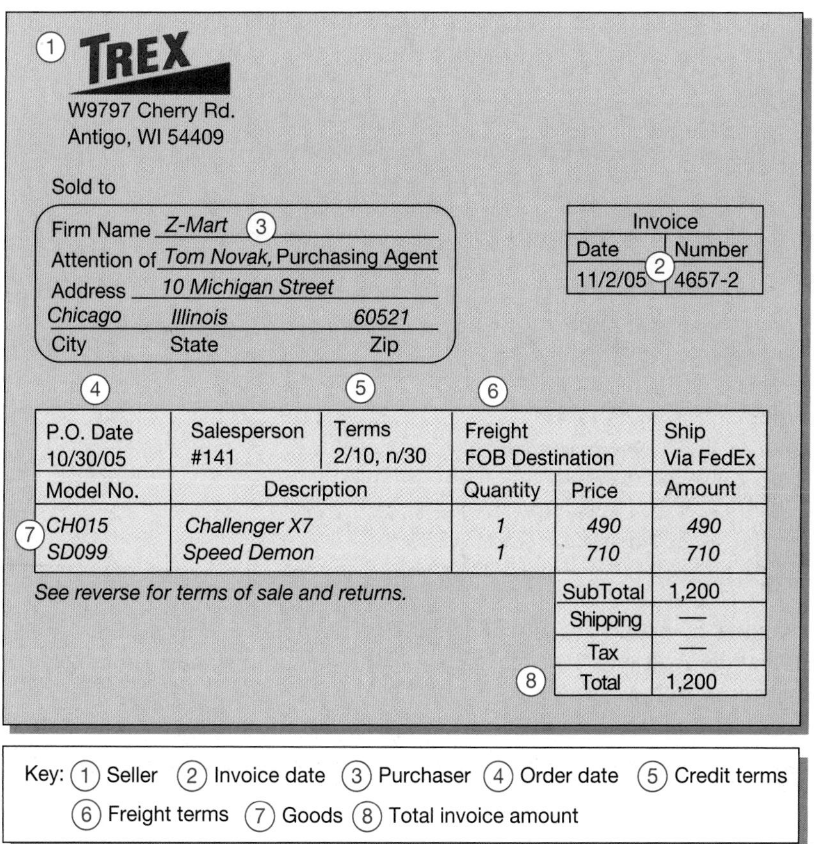

① TREX
W9797 Cherry Rd.
Antigo, WI 54409

Sold to
Firm Name *Z-Mart* ③
Attention of *Tom Novak,* Purchasing Agent
Address *10 Michigan Street*
Chicago *Illinois* *60521*
City State Zip

Invoice	
Date	Number
11/2/05 ②	4657-2

P.O. Date ④	Salesperson	Terms ⑤	Freight ⑥		Ship
10/30/05	#141	2/10, n/30	FOB Destination		Via FedEx
Model No.	Description		Quantity	Price	Amount
⑦ *CH015*	*Challenger X7*		*1*	*490*	*490*
SD099	*Speed Demon*		*1*	*710*	*710*
				SubTotal	1,200
				Shipping	—
				Tax	—
			⑧	Total	1,200

See reverse for terms of sale and returns.

Key: ① Seller ② Invoice date ③ Purchaser ④ Order date ⑤ Credit terms ⑥ Freight terms ⑦ Goods ⑧ Total invoice amount

Exhibit 5.5

Invoice

Purchase Discounts

The purchase of goods on credit requires a clear statement of expected future payments and dates to avoid misunderstandings. **Credit terms** for a purchase include the amounts and timing of payments from a buyer to a seller. Credit terms usually reflect an industry's practices. To illustrate, when sellers require payment within 10 days after the end of the month of the invoice date, the invoice will show credit terms as "n/10 EOM," which stands for net 10 days after end of month (**EOM**). When sellers require payment within 30 days after the invoice date, the invoice shows credit terms of "n/30," which stands for *net 30 days.*

Exhibit 5.6 portrays credit terms. The amount of time allowed before full payment is due is called the **credit period.** Sellers can grant a **cash discount** to encourage buyers to pay earlier. A buyer views a cash discount as a **purchase discount.** A seller views a cash discount as a **sales discount.** Any cash discounts are described in the credit terms on the invoice. For example, credit terms of "2/10, n/60" mean that full payment is due within a 60-day credit period, but the buyer can deduct 2% of the invoice amount if payment is made within 10 days of the invoice date. This reduced payment applies only for the **discount period.**

Point: Since both the buyer and seller know the invoice date, this date is used in determining the discount and credit periods.

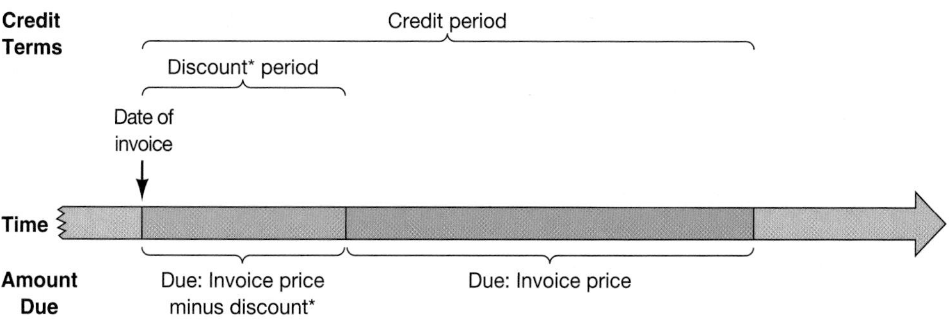

*Discount refers to a purchase discount for a buyer and a sales discount for a seller.

Exhibit 5.6

Credit Terms

Point: Appendix 5A repeats journal entries *a* through *f* using a periodic inventory system.

To illustrate how a buyer accounts for a purchase discount, assume that Z-Mart's $1,200 purchase of merchandise is on credit with terms of 2/10, n/30. Its entry is

Assets = Liabilities + Equity
+1,200 +1,200

(a) Nov. 2	Merchandise Inventory	1,200	
	Accounts Payable		1,200
	Purchased merchandise on credit, invoice dated Nov. 2, terms 2/10, n/30.		

If Z-Mart pays the amount due on (or before) November 12, the entry is

Assets = Liabilities + Equity
−24 −1,200
−1,176

(b) Nov. 12	Accounts Payable	1,200	
	Merchandise Inventory		24
	Cash		1,176
	Paid for the $1,200 purchase of Nov. 2 less the discount of $24 (2% × $1,200).		

Point: These entries illustrate what is called the *gross method* of accounting for purchases with discount terms.

The Merchandise Inventory account after these entries reflects the net cost of merchandise purchased, and the Accounts Payable account shows a zero balance. Both ledger accounts, in T-account form, follow:

Merchandise Inventory			
Nov. 2	1,200	Nov. 12	24
Balance	1,176		

Accounts Payable			
Nov. 12	1,200	Nov. 2	1,200
		Balance	0

Decision Maker

Entrepreneur You purchase a batch of products on terms of 3/10, n/90, but your company has limited cash and you must borrow funds at an 11% annual rate if you are to pay within the discount period. Do you take advantage of the purchase discount?

Answer—p. 203

A buyer's failure to pay within a discount period can be expensive. To illustrate, if Z-Mart does not pay within the 10-day 2% discount period, it can delay payment by 20 more days. This delay costs Z-Mart $24, computed as 2% × $1,200. Most buyers take advantage of a purchase discount because of the usually high interest rate implied from not taking it.[1] Also, good cash management means that no invoice is paid until the last day of the discount or credit period.

Purchase Returns and Allowances

Purchase returns refer to merchandise a buyer acquires but then returns to the seller. A *purchase allowance* is a reduction in the cost of defective or unacceptable merchandise that a buyer acquires. Buyers often keep defective but still marketable merchandise if the seller grants an acceptable allowance.

Point: The sender (maker) of a *debit memorandum* will debit the account of the memo's receiver. The memo's receiver will credit the account of the sender.

When a buyer returns or takes an allowance on merchandise, the buyer issues a **debit memorandum** to inform the seller of a debit made to the seller's account in the buyer's records. To illustrate, on November 15 Z-Mart (buyer) issues a $300 debit memorandum for

[1] The *implied annual interest rate* formula is:

(365 days ÷ [Credit period − Discount period]) × Cash discount rate.

For terms of 2/10, n/30, missing the 2% discount for an additional 20 days is equal to an annual interest rate of 36.5%, computed as (365 days/[30 days − 10 days]) × 2% discount rate. *Favorable purchase discounts* are those with implied annual interest rates that exceed the purchaser's annual rate for borrowing money.

an allowance from Trex for defective merchandise. Z-Mart's November 15 entry to update its Merchandise Inventory account to reflect the purchase allowance is

(c) Nov. 15	Accounts Payable	300	
	Merchandise Inventory		300
	Allowance for defective merchandise.		

Assets = Liabilities + Equity
−300 −300

If this had been a return, then the total *recorded cost* (all costs less any discounts) of the defective merchandise would be entered. The buyer's cost of returned and defective merchandise is usually offset against the buyer's current account payable balance to the seller. When cash is refunded, the Cash account is debited instead of Accounts Payable.

When goods are returned, a buyer can take a purchase discount on only the remaining balance of the invoice. For example, suppose Z-Mart purchases $1,000 of merchandise offered with a 2% cash discount. Two days later, Z-Mart returns $100 of goods before paying the invoice. When Z-Mart later pays within the discount period, it takes the 2% discount only on the $900 remaining balance. The discount is $18 (2% × $900) and the cash payment is $882 ($900 − $18).

Decision Ethics

Credit Manager As the new credit manager, you are being trained by the outgoing manager. She explains that the system prepares checks for amounts net of favorable cash discounts, and the checks are dated the last day of the discount period. She also tells you that checks are not mailed until five days later, adding that "the company gets free use of cash for an extra five days, and our department looks better. When a supplier complains, we blame the computer system and the mailroom." Do you continue this payment policy?

Answer—p. 203

Example: Z-Mart pays $980 cash for $1,000 of merchandise purchased within its 2% discount period. Later, Z-Mart returns $100 of the original $1,000 merchandise. The return entry is

Cash	98	
Merchandise Inventory . . .		98

Transportation Costs and Ownership Transfer

The buyer and seller must agree on who is responsible for paying any freight costs and who bears the risk of loss during transit for merchandising transactions. This is essentially the same as asking at what point ownership transfers from the seller to the buyer. The point of transfer is called the **FOB** (*free on board*) point, which determines who pays transportation costs (and often other incidental costs of transit such as insurance).

Exhibit 5.7 identifies two alternative points of transfer. (1) *FOB shipping point,* also called *FOB factory,* means the buyer accepts ownership when the goods depart the seller's place of business. The buyer is then responsible for paying shipping costs and bearing the risk of damage or loss when goods are in transit. The goods are part of the buyer's inventory when they are in transit since ownership has transferred to the buyer. **Cannondale**, a major bike manufacturer, uses FOB shipping point. (2) *FOB destination* means ownership of goods transfers to the buyer when the goods arrive at the buyer's place of business. The seller is responsible for paying shipping charges and bears the risk of damage or loss in transit. The

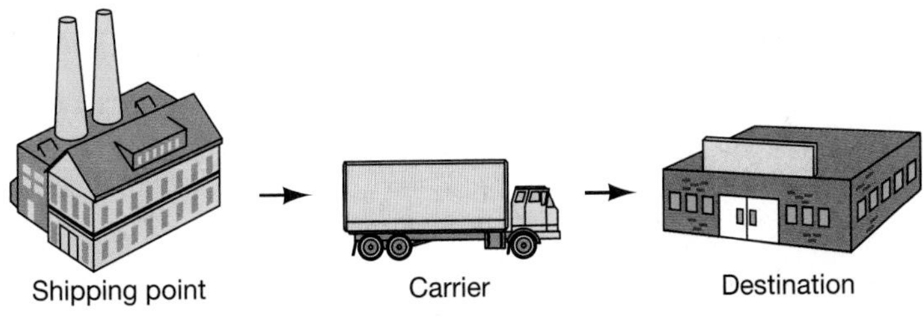

	Ownership Transfers when Goods Passed to	Transportation Costs Paid by
FOB shipping point	Carrier	Buyer
FOB destination	Buyer	Seller

Exhibit 5.7

Ownership Transfer and Transportation Costs

Point: **Compaq Computer** at one time shipped its products FOB shipping point, but it found delivery companies unreliable. Compaq then changed its agreements to FOB destination, took control of shipping, and eliminated its problems.

Point: The party not responsible for shipping costs sometimes pays the carrier. In these cases, the party paying these costs either bills the party responsible or, more commonly, adjusts its account payable or account receivable with the other party. For example, a buyer paying a carrier when terms are FOB destination can decrease its account payable to the seller by the amount of shipping cost.

seller does not record revenue from this sale until the goods arrive at the destination because this transaction is not complete before that point.

Z-Mart's $1,200 purchase on November 2 is on terms of FOB destination. This means Z-Mart is not responsible for paying transportation costs. When a buyer is responsible for paying transportation costs, the payment is made to a carrier or directly to the seller depending on the agreement. The cost principle requires that any necessary transportation costs of a buyer (often called *transportation-in* or *freight-in*) be included as part of the cost of purchased merchandise. To illustrate, Z-Mart's entry to record a $75 freight charge from an independent carrier for merchandise purchased FOB shipping point is

Assets = Liabilities + Equity
+75
−75

(*d*) Nov. 24	Merchandise Inventory	75	
	Cash		75
	Paid freight costs on purchased merchandise.		

A seller records the costs of shipping goods to customers in a Delivery Expense account when the seller is responsible for these costs. Delivery Expense, also called *transportation-out* or *freight-out,* is reported as a selling expense in the seller's income statement.

In summary, purchases are recorded as debits to Merchandise Inventory. Any later purchase discounts, returns, and allowances are credited (decreases) to Merchandise Inventory. Transportation-in is debited (added) to Merchandise Inventory. Z-Mart's itemized costs of merchandise purchases for year 2005 are in Exhibit 5.8.

Exhibit 5.8

Itemized Costs of Merchandise Purchases

Z-MART
Itemized Costs of Merchandise Purchases
For Year Ended December 31, 2005

Invoice cost of merchandise purchases	$235,800
Less: Purchase discounts received	(4,200)
Purchase returns and allowances	(1,500)
Add: Costs of transportation-in	2,300
Total cost of merchandise purchases	**$232,400**

Point: Some companies have separate accounts for purchase discounts, returns and allowances, and transportation-in. These accounts are then transferred to Merchandise Inventory at period-end. This is a *hybrid system* of perpetual and periodic. That is, Merchandise Inventory is updated on a perpetual basis but only for purchases and cost of goods sold.

The accounting system described here does not provide separate records (accounts) for total purchases, total purchase discounts, total purchase returns and allowances, and total transportation-in. Yet nearly all companies collect this information in supplementary records because managers need this information to evaluate and control each of these cost elements. **Supplementary records,** also called *supplemental records,* refer to information outside the usual general ledger accounts.

Quick Check

4. How long are the credit and discount periods when credit terms are 2/10, n/60?
5. Identify which items are subtracted from the *list* amount and not recorded when computing purchase price: (*a*) freight-in; (*b*) trade discount; (*c*) purchase discount; (*d*) purchase return.
6. What does *FOB* mean? What does *FOB destination* mean?

Answers—p. 204

Accounting for Merchandise Sales

Merchandising companies also must account for sales, sales discounts, sales returns and allowances, and cost of goods sold. A merchandising company such as Z-Mart reflects these items in its gross profit computation, as shown in Exhibit 5.9. This section explains how this information is derived from transactions.

Z-MART
Computation of Gross Profit
For Year Ended December 31, 2005

Sales		$321,000
Less: Sales discounts	$4,300	
Sales returns and allowances	2,000	6,300
Net sales		314,700
Cost of goods sold		230,400
Gross profit		**$ 84,300**

Exhibit 5.9
Gross Profit Computation

Sales of Merchandise

P2 Analyze and record transactions for merchandise sales using a perpetual system.

Each sales transaction for a seller of merchandise involves two parts. One part is the revenue received in the form of an asset from a customer. The second part is the recognition of the cost of merchandise sold to a customer. Accounting for a sales transaction under the perpetual system requires recording information about both parts. This means that each sales transaction for merchandisers, whether for cash or on credit, requires two entries: one for revenue and one for cost. To illustrate, Z-Mart sold $2,400 of merchandise on credit on November 3. The revenue part of this transaction is recorded as

Point: Growth of superstores such as **Price Club** and **Costco** is fed by the efficient use of perpetual inventory.

(e) Nov. 3	Accounts Receivable	2,400	
	Sales		2,400
	Sold merchandise on credit.		

Assets = Liabilities + Equity
+2,400 +2,400

This entry reflects an increase in Z-Mart's assets in the form of an accounts receivable. It also shows the increase in revenue (Sales). If the sale is for cash, the debit is to Cash instead of Accounts Receivable.

The cost part of each sales transaction ensures that the Merchandise Inventory account under a perpetual inventory system reflects the updated cost of the merchandise available for sale. For example, the cost of the merchandise Z-Mart sold on November 3 is $1,600, and the entry to record the cost part of this sales transaction is

Topic Tackler 5-2

(e) Nov. 3	Cost of Goods Sold	1,600	
	Merchandise Inventory		1,600
	To record the cost of Nov. 3 sale.		

Assets = Liabilities + Equity
−1,600 −1,600

Point: The Cost of Goods Sold account is only used in a perpetual system.

Sales Discounts

Sales discounts on credit sales can benefit a seller by decreasing the delay in receiving cash and reducing future collection efforts.

At the time of a credit sale, a seller does not know whether a customer will pay within the discount period and take advantage of a purchases discount. This means the seller usually does not record a sales discount until a customer actually pays within the discount period. To illustrate, Z-Mart completes a credit sale for $1,000 on November 12 with terms of 2/10, n/60. The entry to record the revenue part of this sale is

Decision Insight

Suppliers and Demands Merchandising companies often bombard suppliers with demands. These include special discounts for new stores, payment of fines for shipping errors, and free samples. Merchandisers' goals are to reduce inventories, shorten lead times, and eliminate errors.

Nov. 12	Accounts Receivable	1,000	
	Sales		1,000
	Sold merchandise under terms of 2/10, n/60.		

Assets = Liabilities + Equity
+1,000 +1,000

This entry records the receivable and the revenue as if the customer will pay the full amount. The customer has two options, however. One option is to wait 60 days until January 11 and pay the full $1,000. In this case, Z-Mart records that payment as

Assets = Liabilities + Equity
+1,000
−1,000

Jan. 11	Cash	1,000	
	Accounts Receivable		1,000
	Received payment for Nov. 12 sale.		

Point: Sales discounts is seldom reported on income statements distributed to external users.

The customer's second option is to pay $980 within a 10-day period ending November 22. If the customer pays on (or before) November 22, Z-Mart records the payment as

Assets = Liabilities + Equity
+980 −20
−1,000

Nov. 22	Cash	980	
	Sales Discounts	20	
	Accounts Receivable		1,000
	Received payment for Nov. 12 sale less discount.		

Decision Insight

Catalina Supermarkets uses bar codes, software, and the Web to help execs keep tabs on who buys what foods, how often, and at what price. Its high-profit customer rate is up because most discounts and services, such as coupons and free delivery, are given almost exclusively to its best customers.

Sales Discounts is a contra revenue account, meaning the Sales Discounts account is deducted from the Sales account when computing a company's net sales (see Exhibit 5.9). Management monitors Sales Discounts to assess the effectiveness and cost of its discount policy.

Sales Returns and Allowances

Sales returns refer to merchandise that customers return to the seller after a sale. Many companies allow customers to return merchandise for a full refund. *Sales allowances* refer to reductions in the selling price of merchandise sold to customers. This can occur with damaged or defective merchandise that a customer is willing to purchase with a decrease in selling price. Sales returns and allowances usually involve dissatisfied customers and the possibility of lost future sales, and managers need information about returns and allowances to monitor these problems.

Point: Published income statements rarely disclose Sales Returns and Allowances.

Decision Insight

Return to Sender Book merchandisers such as **Barnes & Noble** and **Borders Books** can return unsold books to publishers at purchase price. Publishers say returns of new hardcover books run between 35% and 50%.

To illustrate, recall Z-Mart's sale of merchandise on November 3 for $2,400 that had cost $1,600. Assume that the customer returns part of the merchandise on November 6, and the returned items sell for $800 and cost $600. The revenue part of this transaction must reflect the decrease in sales from the customer's return of merchandise as follows:

Assets = Liabilities + Equity
−800 −800

(f) Nov. 6	Sales Returns and Allowances	800	
	Accounts Receivable		800
	Customer returns merchandise of Nov. 3 sale.		

If the merchandise returned to Z-Mart is not defective and can be resold to another customer, Z-Mart returns these goods to its inventory. The entry to restore the cost of such goods to the Merchandise Inventory account is

Assets = Liabilities + Equity
+600 +600

Nov. 6	Merchandise Inventory	600	
	Cost of Goods Sold		600
	Returned goods added to inventory.[2]		

[2] This entry changes if the goods returned are defective—that is, the returned inventory is recorded at its estimated value, not its cost. To illustrate, if the goods (costing $600) returned to Z-Mart are defective and estimated to be worth $150, the following entry is made: Dr. Merchandise Inventory for $150, Dr. Loss from Defective Merchandise for $450, and Cr. Cost of Goods Sold for $600.

To illustrate sales allowances, assume that $800 of the merchandise Z-Mart sold on November 3 is defective but the buyer decides to keep it because Z-Mart offers a $100 price reduction. Z-Mart records the allowance and decreases expected assets as follows:

Nov. 6	Sales Returns and Allowances	100	
	Accounts Receivable		100
	To record sales allowance on Nov. 3 sale.		

Assets = Liabilities + Equity
−100 −100

The seller usually prepares a credit memorandum to confirm a buyer's return or allowance. A seller's **credit memorandum** informs a buyer of the seller's credit to the buyer's Account Receivable (on the seller's books).

Point: The sender (maker) of a credit memorandum will *credit* the account of the receiver. The receiver of a credit memorandum will *debit* the account of the sender.

Quick Check

7. Why are sales discounts and sales returns and allowances recorded in contra revenue accounts instead of directly in the Sales account?
8. Under what conditions are two entries necessary to record a sales return?
9. When merchandise is sold on credit and the seller notifies the buyer of a price allowance, does the seller create and send a credit memorandum or a debit memorandum?

Answers—p. 204

Completing the Accounting Cycle

C4 Analyze and interpret cost flows and operating activities of a merchandising company.

Exhibit 5.10 shows the flow of merchandising costs during a period and where these costs are reported at period-end. This chapter already discussed how a merchandiser's purchases and sales transactions during a period are analyzed, recorded, and reported. Specifically, beginning inventory plus the net cost of purchases is the merchandise available for sale. As inventory is sold, its cost is recorded in cost of goods sold on the income statement; what remains is ending inventory on the balance sheet. Note that a period's ending inventory is the next period's beginning inventory.

Each of the steps in the accounting cycle described in Chapter 4 for a service company applies to a merchandiser. This section extends that discussion to three remaining steps of the accounting cycle for a merchandiser—adjustments, statement preparation, and closing.

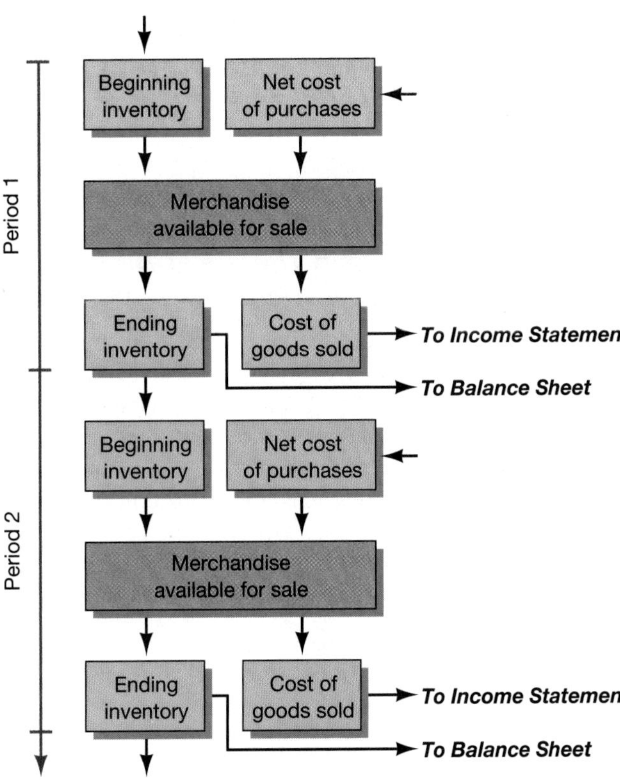

Exhibit 5.10

Merchandising Cost Flow in the Accounting Cycle

Adjusting Entries for Merchandisers

P3 Prepare adjustments and close accounts for a merchandising company.

Adjusting entries are generally the same for merchandising companies and service companies, including those for prepaid expenses (including depreciation), accrued expenses, unearned revenues, and accrued revenues. However, a merchandiser using a perpetual inventory system is usually required to make another adjustment to update the Merchandise Inventory account to reflect any loss of merchandise, including theft and deterioration. **Shrinkage** is the term used to refer to the loss of inventory and it is computed by comparing a physical count of inventory with recorded amounts. A physical count is usually performed at least once annually.

Decision Insight

Who Shrunk Inventory Shrinkage can be a sizable cost for many merchandisers. Recent annual losses due to shrinkage are

Musicland	$22 million
Sports Authority	9 million

Companies often invest considerable resources to reduce shrinkage.

To illustrate, Z-Mart's Merchandise Inventory account at the end of year 2005 has a balance of $21,250, but a physical count reveals that only $21,000 of inventory exists. The adjusting entry to record this $250 shrinkage is

Point: About two-thirds of shoplifting losses are thefts by employees.

Assets = Liabilities + Equity
−250 −250

Dec. 31	Cost of Goods Sold	250	
	Merchandise Inventory		250
	To adjust for $250 shrinkage revealed by a physical count of inventory.		

Preparing Financial Statements

The financial statements of a merchandiser, and their preparation, are similar to those for a service company described in Chapters 3 and 4. The income statement mainly differs by the inclusion of *cost of goods sold* and *gross profit.* Also, net sales is affected by discounts, returns, and allowances, and some additional expenses are possible such as delivery expense and loss from defective merchandise. The balance sheet mainly differs by the inclusion of *merchandise inventory* as part of current assets. The statement of owner's equity is unchanged. A work sheet can be used to help prepare these statements, and one is illustrated in Appendix 5B for Z-Mart.

Point: CompUSA's costs of shipping merchandise to its stores is included in the costs of its inventories as required by the cost principle.

Closing Entries for Merchandisers

Closing entries are similar for service companies and merchandising companies using a perpetual system. The difference is that we must close some new temporary accounts that arise from merchandising activities. Z-Mart has several temporary accounts unique to merchandisers: Sales (of goods), Sales Discounts, Sales Returns and Allowances, and Cost of Goods Sold. Their existence in the ledger means that the first two closing entries for a merchandiser are slightly different from the ones described in Chapter 4 for a service company. These differences are set in boldface in the closing entries of Exhibit 5.11.

Point: The Inventory account is not affected by the closing process under a perpetual system.

Summary of Merchandising Entries

Exhibit 5.12 summarizes the key adjusting and closing entries of a merchandiser (using a perpetual inventory system) that are different from those of a service company described in prior chapters (the Demonstration Problem 2 illustrates these merchandising entries).

Exhibit 5.11

Closing Entries for a Merchandiser

Step 1: Close Credit Balances in Temporary Accounts to Income Summary.

Z-Mart has one temporary account with a credit balance; it is closed with this entry:

Dec. 31	**Sales**	**321,000**	
	Income Summary		321,000
	To close credit balances in temporary accounts.		

Step 2: Close Debit Balances in Temporary Accounts to Income Summary.

The second entry closes temporary accounts having debit balances such as Cost of Goods Sold, Sales Discounts, and Sales Returns and Allowances and is shown here:

Dec. 31	Income Summary	308,100	
	Sales Discounts		**4,300**
	Sales Returns and Allowances		**2,000**
	Cost of Goods Sold		**230,400**
	Depreciation Expense—Store Equipment		3,000
	Depreciation Expense—Office Equipment		700
	Office Salaries Expense		25,300
	Sales Salaries Expense		18,500
	Insurance Expense		600
	Rent Expense—Office Space		900
	Rent Expense—Selling Space		8,100
	Office Supplies Expense		1,800
	Store Supplies Expense		1,200
	Advertising Expense		11,300
	To close debit balances in temporary accounts.		

Step 3: Close Income Summary to Owner's Capital.

The third closing entry is exactly the same for a merchandising company and a service company. It updates the owner's capital account for the net income or loss and is shown here:

Dec. 31	Income Summary	12,900	
	K. Marty, Capital		12,900
	To close the Income Summary account.		

The $12,900 amount in the entry is net income reported on the income statement in Exhibit 5.2.

Step 4: Close Withdrawals Account to Owner's Capital.

The fourth closing entry is exactly the same for a merchandising company and a service company. It closes the withdrawals account and adjusts the owner's capital account balance to the amount shown on the balance sheet. This entry for Z-Mart is

Dec. 31	K. Marty, Capital	4,000	
	K. Marty, Withdrawals		4,000
	To close the withdrawals accounts.		

When these entries are posted, all temporary accounts are set to zero and are ready to record events for the next period. The capital account is now updated to reflect all current and prior period transactions.

Exhibit 5.12

Summary of Merchandising Entries

	Merchandising Transactions	Merchandising Entries	Dr.	Cr.
Purchases	Purchasing merchandise for resale.	Merchandise Inventory	#	
		Cash or Accounts Payable		#
	Paying freight costs on purchases; FOB shipping point.	Merchandise Inventory	#	
		Cash		#
	Paying within discount period.	Accounts Payable	#	
		Merchandise Inventory		#
		Cash		#
	Recording purchase returns or allowances.	Cash or Accounts Payable	#	
		Merchandise Inventory		#
Sales	Selling merchandise.	Cash or Accounts Receivable	#	
		Sales		#
		Cost of Goods Sold	#	
		Merchandise Inventory		#
	Receiving payment within discount period.	Cash	#	
		Sales Discounts	#	
		Accounts Receivable		#
	Granting sales returns or allowances.	Sales Returns and Allowances	#	
		Cash or Accounts Receivable		#
		Merchandise Inventory	#	
		Cost of Goods Sold		#
	Paying freight costs on sales; FOB destination.	Delivery Expense	#	
		Cash		#

	Merchandising Events	Adjusting and Closing Entries	Dr.	Cr.
Adjusting	Adjusting due to shrinkage (recorded amount larger than physical inventory).	Cost of Goods Sold	#	
		Merchandise Inventory		#
Closing	Closing temporary accounts with credit balances.	Sales	#	
		Income Summary		#
	Closing temporary accounts with debit balances.	Income Summary	#	
		Sales Returns and Allowances		#
		Sales Discounts		#
		Cost of Goods Sold		#
		Delivery Expense		#
		"Other Expenses"		#

Quick Check

10. When a merchandiser uses a perpetual inventory system, why is it sometimes necessary to adjust the Merchandise Inventory balance with an adjusting entry?

11. What temporary accounts do you expect to find in a merchandising business but not in a service business?

12. Describe the closing entries normally made by a merchandising company.

Answers—p. 204

Financial Statement Formats

Generally accepted accounting principles do not require companies to use any one presentation format for financial statements so we see many different formats in practice. This section describes two common income statement formats: multiple-step and single-step. The classified balance sheet of a merchandiser is also explained.

P4 Define and prepare multiple-step and single-step income statements.

Multiple-Step Income Statement

A **multiple-step income statement** format shows detailed computations of net sales and other costs and expenses, and reports subtotals for various classes of items. Exhibit 5.13

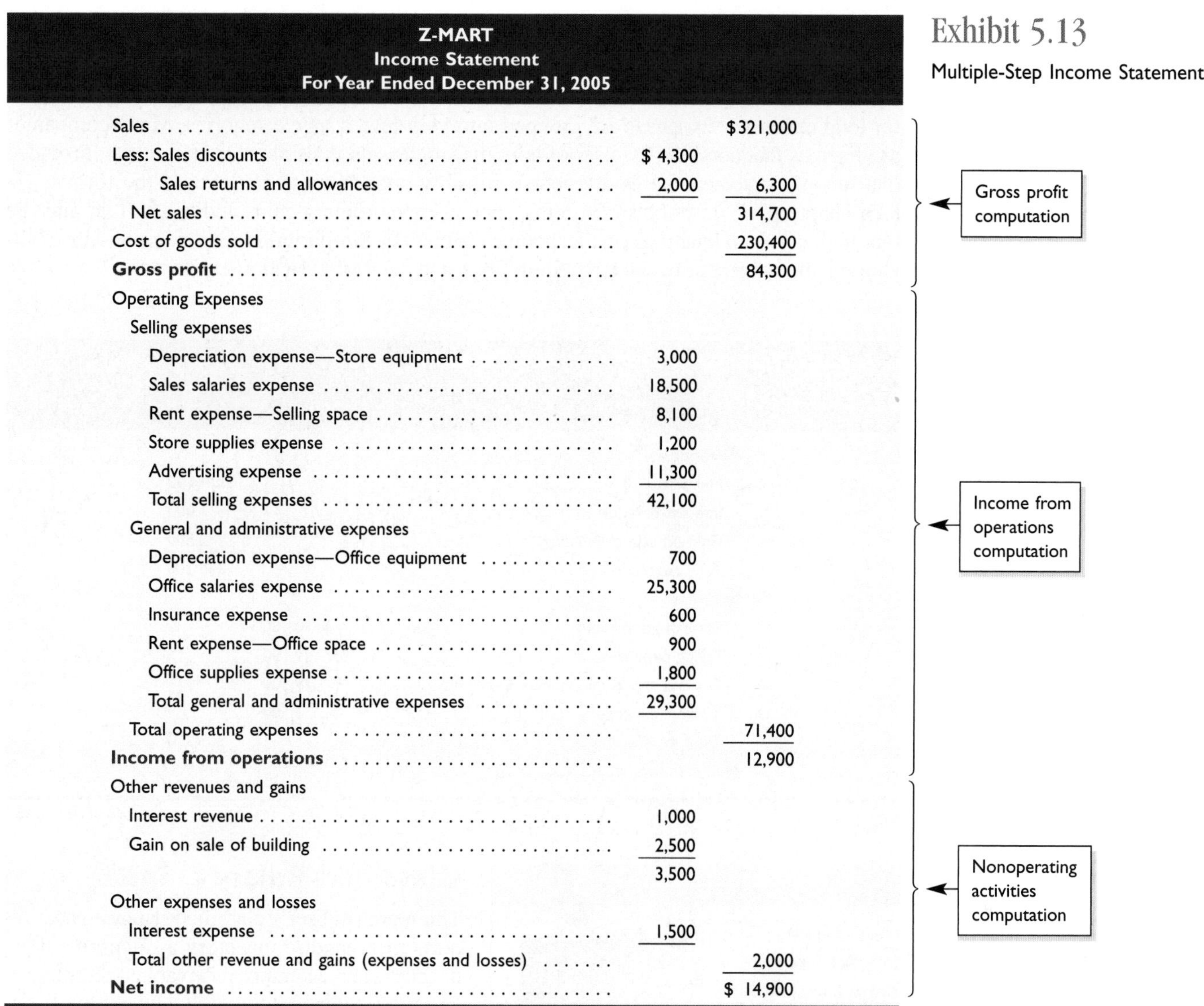

Z-MART
Income Statement
For Year Ended December 31, 2005

Sales		$321,000
Less: Sales discounts	$ 4,300	
Sales returns and allowances	2,000	6,300
Net sales		314,700
Cost of goods sold		230,400
Gross profit		84,300
Operating Expenses		
Selling expenses		
Depreciation expense—Store equipment	3,000	
Sales salaries expense	18,500	
Rent expense—Selling space	8,100	
Store supplies expense	1,200	
Advertising expense	11,300	
Total selling expenses	42,100	
General and administrative expenses		
Depreciation expense—Office equipment	700	
Office salaries expense	25,300	
Insurance expense	600	
Rent expense—Office space	900	
Office supplies expense	1,800	
Total general and administrative expenses	29,300	
Total operating expenses		71,400
Income from operations		12,900
Other revenues and gains		
Interest revenue	1,000	
Gain on sale of building	2,500	
	3,500	
Other expenses and losses		
Interest expense	1,500	
Total other revenue and gains (expenses and losses)		2,000
Net income		$ 14,900

Exhibit 5.13

Multiple-Step Income Statement

shows a multiple-step income statement for Z-Mart. The statement has three main parts: (1) *gross profit,* determined by net sales less cost of goods sold, (2) *income from operations,* determined by gross profit less operating expenses, and (3) *net income,* determined by income from operations adjusted for nonoperating items.

Operating expenses are classified into two sections. **Selling expenses** include the expenses of promoting sales by displaying and advertising merchandise, making sales, and delivering goods to customers. **General and administrative expenses** support a company's overall operations and include expenses related to accounting, human resource management, and financial management. Note that expenses are allocated between sections when they contribute to more than one. Z-Mart allocates rent expense of $9,000 from its store building between two sections: $8,100 to selling expense and $900 to general and administrative expense.

Nonoperating activities consist of other expenses, revenues, losses, and gains that are unrelated to a company's operations. They are reported in two sections. (1) *Other revenues and gains,* which often include interest revenue, dividend revenue, rent revenue, and gains from asset disposals. (2) *Other expenses and losses,* which often include interest expense, losses from asset disposals, and casualty losses. When a company has no reportable nonoperating activities, its income from operations is simply labeled net income.

Point: Z-Mart did not have any nonoperating activities, however, Exhibit 5.13 includes some for illustrative purposes.

Single-Step Income Statement

A **single-step income statement** is another widely used format, and is shown in Exhibit 5.14 for Z-Mart. It lists cost of goods sold as another expense and shows only one subtotal for total expenses. Expenses are grouped into very few, if any, categories. Many companies use formats that combine features of both the single- and multiple-step statements. Provided that income statement items are shown sensibly, management can choose the format. (In later chapters, we describe some items, such as extraordinary gains and losses, that must be reported in certain locations on the income statement.) Similar presentation options are available for the statement of owner's equity and statement of cash flows.

Point: Many companies report interest expense and interest income in separate categories after income from operations and before subtracting income taxes expense. As one example, see Krispy Kreme's income statement in Appendix A.

Exhibit 5.14

Single-Step Income Statement

Z-MART
Income Statement
For Year Ended December 31, 2005

Revenues		
Net sales		$314,700
Interest revenue		1,000
Gain on sale of building		2,500
Total revenues		318,200
Expenses		
Cost of goods sold	$230,400	
Selling expenses	42,100	
General and administrative expenses	29,300	
Interest expense	1,500	
Total expenses		303,300
Net income		$ 14,900

Decision Insight

Head Start Incubators offer start-ups a space plus services such as management advice, office support, and financial, legal, and technical help. Studies show that nearly 90% of entrepreneurs that "hatch" from incubators (usually after two to three years) are still in business six years later—which is more than double the usual success rate.

Classified Balance Sheet

The merchandiser's classified balance sheet reports merchandise inventory as a current asset, usually after accounts receivable according to an asset's nearness to liquidity. Inventory is usually less liquid than accounts receivable because receivables must first be sold before cash is received, but more liquid than supplies and prepaid expenses. Exhibit 5.15 shows the current asset section of Z-Mart's classified balance sheet (other sections are as shown in Chapter 4).

Exhibit 5.15

Classified Balance Sheet (partial) of a Merchandiser

Z-MART
Balance Sheet (partial)
December 31, 2005

Assets	
Current assets	
Cash	$ 8,200
Accounts receivable	11,200
Merchandise inventory	**21,000**
Office supplies	550
Store supplies	250
Prepaid insurance	300
Total current assets	$ 41,500

Acid-Test and Gross Margin Ratios

Decision Analysis

Acid-Test Ratio

A1 Compute the acid-test ratio and explain its use to assess liquidity.

For many merchandisers, inventory makes up a large portion of current assets. Inventory must be sold and any resulting accounts receivable must be collected before cash is available. Chapter 4 explained that the current ratio, defined as current assets divided by current liabilities, is useful in assessing a company's ability to pay current liabilities. Since it is sometimes unreasonable to assume that inventories are a source of payment for current liabilities, we look to other measures.

One measure of a merchandiser's ability to pay its current liabilities (its *liquidity*) is the acid-test ratio. It differs from the current ratio by excluding less liquid current assets such as inventory and prepaid expenses that take longer to be converted to cash. The **acid-test ratio,** also called *quick ratio,* is defined as *quick assets* (cash, short-term investments, and current receivables) divided by current liabilities—see Exhibit 5.16.

$$\text{Acid-test ratio} = \frac{\text{Cash and equivalents} + \text{Short-term investments} + \text{Current receivables}}{\text{Current liabilities}}$$

Exhibit 5.16

Acid-Test (Quick) Ratio

Exhibit 5.17 shows both the acid-test and current ratios of retailer **JCPenney** for fiscal years 1999 through 2003. JCPenney's acid-test ratio reveals a decline in 2000–2001 that exceeds the decline in the retailing industry. Still, JCPenney's current ratio (never less than 1.7) suggests that its short-term obligations can be covered with short-term assets.

An acid-test ratio less than 1.0 means that current liabilities exceed quick assets. A rule of thumb is that the acid-test ratio should have a value of, or higher than, 1.0 to conclude that a company is unlikely to face near-term liquidity problems. A value less than 1.0 raises liquidity concerns unless a company can generate enough cash from inventory sales or if much of its liabilities are not due until late in the next period. Similarly, a value greater than 1.0 can hide a liquidity problem if payables are due shortly and receivables are not collected until late in the next period. Analysis of JCPenney reveals a slight concern with its liquidity in 2000–2001, especially when benchmarked against the industry ratio. However, in 2002–2003 JCPenney raised its acid-test ratio to a reasonable level (and its inventory is fairly liquid).

Point: Successful use of a just-in-time inventory system can narrow the gap between the acid-test ratio and the current ratio.

Decision Maker

Supplier A retailer requests to purchase supplies on credit from your company. You have no prior experience with this retailer. The retailer's current ratio is 2.1, its acid-test ratio is 0.5, and inventory makes up most of its current assets. Do you extend credit?

Answer—p. 203

($ in millions)	2003	2002	2001	2000	1999
Total quick assets	$3,179	$3,538	$1,837	$2,076	$ 4,779
Total current assets	$8,353	$8,677	$7,257	$8,174	$11,007
Total current liabilities	$4,159	$4,499	$4,235	$4,272	$ 5,912
Acid-test ratio	**0.76**	**0.79**	**0.43**	**0.49**	**0.81**
Current ratio	**2.01**	**1.93**	**1.71**	**1.91**	**1.86**
Industry acid-test ratio	0.5	0.5	0.8	0.8	0.9
Industry current ratio	2.5	2.6	3.0	2.8	3.1

Exhibit 5.17

JCPenney's Acid-Test and Current Ratios

Gross Margin Ratio

A2 Compute the gross margin ratio and explain its use to assess profitability.

The cost of goods sold makes up much of expenses for merchandisers. Without sufficient gross profit, a merchandiser will likely fail. Users often compute the gross margin ratio to help understand this relation. It differs from the profit margin ratio in that it excludes all costs except cost of goods sold. The **gross margin ratio** is defined as *gross margin* (net sales minus cost of goods sold) divided by net sales—see Exhibit 5.18.

$$\text{Gross margin ratio} = \frac{\text{Net sales} - \text{Cost of goods sold}}{\text{Net sales}}$$

Exhibit 5.18

Gross Margin Ratio

Decision Maker

Financial Officer Your company has a 36% gross margin ratio and a 17% net profit margin ratio. Industry averages are 44% for gross margin and 16% for net profit margin. Do these comparative results concern you?

Answer—p. 204

Point: The power of a ratio is often its ability to identify areas for more detailed analysis.

Exhibit 5.19 shows the gross margin ratio of **JCPenney** for fiscal years 1999–2003. For JCPenney, each $1 of sales in 2003 yielded about 30¢ in gross margin to cover all other expenses and still produce a profit. This 30¢ margin is up from 29¢ in 2002 and from 28¢ in 2001. This rebound is an important (and positive) development. Success for merchandisers such as JCPenney depends on adequate gross margin. Overall, both the acid-test ratio and the gross margin ratio suggest that the financial condition and performance of JCPenney has markedly improved over the past two years.

Exhibit 5.19

JCPenney's Gross Margin Ratio

($ in millions)	2003	2002	2001	2000	1999
Gross margin	$ 9,774	$ 9,215	$ 8,815	$ 9,457	$ 9,140
Net sales	$32,347	$32,004	$31,846	$31,743	$29,761
Gross margin ratio	30.2%	28.8%	27.7%	29.8%	30.7%

Demonstration Problem 1

Use the following adjusted trial balance and additional information to complete the requirements:

KC ANTIQUES
Adjusted Trial Balance
December 31, 2005

	Debit	Credit
Cash	$ 20,000	
Merchandise inventory	60,000	
Store supplies	1,500	
Equipment	45,600	
Accumulated depreciation—Equipment		$ 16,600
Accounts payable		9,000
Salaries payable		2,000
K. Carter, Capital		79,000
K. Carter, Withdrawals	10,000	
Sales		343,250
Sales discounts	5,000	
Sales returns and allowances	6,000	
Cost of goods sold	159,900	
Depreciation expense—Store equipment	4,100	
Depreciation expense—Office equipment	1,600	
Sales salaries expense	30,000	
Office salaries expense	34,000	
Insurance expense	11,000	
Rent expense (70% is store, 30% is office)	24,000	
Store supplies expense	5,750	
Advertising expense	31,400	
Totals	$449,850	$449,850

KC Antiques' *supplementary records* for 2005 reveal the following itemized costs for merchandising activities:

Invoice cost of merchandise purchases	$150,000
Purchase discounts received	2,500
Purchase returns and allowances	2,700
Cost of transportation-in	5,000

Required

1. Use the supplementary records to compute the total cost of merchandise purchases for 2005.
2. Prepare a 2005 multiple-step income statement. (Inventory at December 31, 2004, is $70,100.)
3. Prepare a single-step income statement for 2005.
4. Prepare closing entries for KC Antiques at December 31, 2005.
5. Compute the acid-test ratio and the gross margin ratio. Explain the meaning of each ratio and interpret them for KC Antiques.

Planning the Solution

- Compute the total cost of merchandise purchases for 2005.
- To prepare the multiple-step statement, first compute net sales. Then, to compute cost of goods sold, add the net cost of merchandise purchases for the year to beginning inventory and subtract the cost of ending inventory. Subtract cost of goods sold from net sales to get gross profit. Then classify expenses as selling expenses or general and administrative expenses.
- To prepare the single-step income statement, begin with net sales. Then list and subtract the expenses.
- The first closing entry debits all temporary accounts with credit balances and opens the Income Summary account. The second closing entry credits all temporary accounts with debit balances. The third entry closes the Income Summary account to the owner's capital account, and the fourth entry closes the withdrawals account to the capital account.
- Identify the quick assets on the adjusted trial balance. Compute the acid-test ratio by dividing quick assets by current liabilities. Compute the gross margin ratio by dividing gross profit by net sales.

Solution to Demonstration Problem 1

1.

Invoice cost of merchandise purchases	$150,000
Less: Purchases discounts received	2,500
Purchase returns and allowances	2,700
Add: Cost of transportation-in	5,000
Total cost of merchandise purchases	$149,800

2. Multiple-step income statement

KC ANTIQUES Income Statement For Year Ended December 31, 2005		
Sales		$343,250
Less: Sales discounts	$ 5,000	
Sales returns and allowances	6,000	11,000
Net sales		332,250
Cost of goods sold*		159,900
Gross profit		172,350
Expenses		
Selling expenses		
Depreciation expense—Store equipment	4,100	
Sales salaries expense	30,000	
Rent expense—Selling space	16,800	
Store supplies expense	5,750	
Advertising expense	31,400	
Total selling expenses	88,050	

[continued on next page]

[continued from previous page]

General and administrative expenses		
Depreciation expense—Office equipment	1,600	
Office salaries expense	34,000	
Insurance expense	11,000	
Rent expense—Office space	7,200	
Total general and administrative expenses	53,800	
Total operating expenses		141,850
Net income		$ 30,500

* Cost of goods sold can also be directly computed (applying concepts from Exhibit 5.4):

Merchandise inventory, December 31, 2004	$ 70,100
Total cost of merchandise purchases (from part 1)	149,800
Goods available for sale	219,900
Merchandise inventory, December 31, 2005	60,000
Cost of goods sold	$159,900

3. Single-step income statement

KC ANTIQUES
Income Statement
For Year Ended December 31, 2005

Net sales		$332,250
Expenses		
Cost of goods sold	$159,900	
Selling expenses	88,050	
General and administrative expenses	53,800	
Total expenses		301,750
Net income		$ 30,500

4.

Dec. 31	Sales	343,250	
	Income Summary		343,250
	To close credit balances in temporary accounts.		
Dec. 31	Income Summary	312,750	
	Sales Discounts		5,000
	Sales Returns and Allowances		6,000
	Cost of Goods Sold		159,900
	Depreciation Expense—Store Equipment		4,100
	Depreciation Expense—Office Equipment		1,600
	Sales Salaries Expense		30,000
	Office Salaries Expense		34,000
	Insurance Expense		11,000
	Rent Expense		24,000
	Store Supplies Expense		5,750
	Advertising Expense		31,400
	To close debit balances in temporary accounts.		
Dec. 31	Income Summary	30,500	
	K. Carter, Capital		30,500
	To close the Income Summary account.		
Dec. 31	K. Carter, Capital	10,000	
	K. Carter, Withdrawals		10,000
	To close the withdrawals account.		

5. Acid-test ratio = (Cash and equivalents + Short-term investments + Current receivables)/Current liabilities
= Cash/(Accounts payable + Salaries payable)
= $20,000/($9,000 + $2,000) = $20,000/$11,000 = 1.82

Gross margin ratio = Gross profit/Net sales = $172,350/$332,250 = 0.52 (or 52%)

KC Antiques has a healthy acid-test ratio of 1.82. This means it has more than $1.80 in liquid assets to satisfy each $1.00 in current liabilities. The gross margin of 0.52 shows that KC Antiques spends 48¢ ($1.00 − $0.52) of every dollar of net sales on the costs of acquiring the merchandise it sells. This leaves 52¢ of every dollar of net sales to cover other expenses incurred in the business and to provide a profit.

Demonstration Problem 2

Prepare journal entries to record the following merchandising transactions for both the seller (BMX) and buyer (Sanuk).

May 4 BMX sold $1,500 of merchandise on account to Sanuk, terms FOB shipping point, n/45, invoice dated May 4. The cost of the merchandise was $900.

May 6 Sanuk paid transportation charges of $30 on the May 4 purchase from BMX.

May 8 BMX sold $1,000 of merchandise on account to Sanuk, terms FOB destination, n/30, invoice dated May 8. The cost of the merchandise was $700.

May 10 BMX paid transportation costs of $50 for delivery of merchandise sold to Sanuk on May 8.

May 16 BMX issued Sanuk a $200 credit memorandum for merchandise returned. The merchandise was purchased by Sanuk on account on May 8. The cost of the merchandise returned was $140.

May 18 BMX received payment from Sanuk for purchase of May 8.

May 21 BMX sold $2,400 of merchandise on account to Sanuk, terms FOB shipping point, 2/10, n/EOM. BMX prepaid transportation costs of $100, which were added to the invoice. The cost of the merchandise was $1,440.

May 31 BMX received payment from Sanuk for purchase of May 21, less discount (2% × $2,400).

Solution to Demonstration Problem 2

	BMX (Seller)			Sanuk (Buyer)		
May 4	Accounts Receivable—Sanuk	1,500		Merchandise Inventory	1,500	
	Sales		1,500	Accounts Payable—BMX		1,500
	Cost of Goods Sold	900				
	Merchandise Inventory		900			
6	No entry.			Merchandise Inventory	30	
				Cash		30
8	Accounts Receivable—Sanuk	1,000		Merchandise Inventory	1,000	
	Sales		1,000	Accounts Payable—BMX		1,000
	Cost of Goods Sold	700				
	Merchandise Inventory		700			
10	Delivery Expense	50		No entry.		
	Cash		50			
16	Sales Returns & Allowances	200		Accounts Payable—BMX	200	
	Accounts Receivable—Sanuk		200	Merchandise Inventory		200
	Merchandise Inventory	140				
	Cost of Goods Sold		140			
18	Cash	800		Accounts Payable—BMX	800	
	Accounts Receivable—Sanuk		800	Cash		800
21	Accounts Receivable—Sanuk	2,400		Merchandise Inventory	2,500	
	Sales		2,400	Accounts Payable—BMX		2,500
	Accounts Receivable—Sanuk	100				
	Cash		100			
	Cost of Goods Sold	1,440				
	Merchandise Inventory		1,440			
31	Cash	2,452		Accounts Payable—BMX	2,500	
	Sales Discounts	48		Merchandise Inventory		48
	Accounts Receivable—Sanuk		2,500	Cash		2,452

APPENDIX

Periodic (and Perpetual) Inventory System

A **periodic inventory system** requires updating the inventory account only at the *end of a period* to reflect the quantity and cost of both the goods available and the goods sold. Thus, during the period, the Merchandise Inventory balance remains unchanged. It reflects the beginning inventory balance until it is updated at the end of the period. During the period the cost of merchandise is recorded in a temporary *Purchases* account. When a company sells merchandise, it records revenue but not the cost of the goods sold. At the end of the period when a company prepares financial statements, it takes a *physical count of inventory* by counting the quantities and costs of merchandise available. The cost of goods sold is then computed by subtracting the ending inventory amount from the cost of merchandise available for sale.

Recording Merchandise Transactions

P5 Record and compare merchandising transactions using both periodic and perpetual inventory systems.

Under a periodic system, each purchase, purchase return and allowance, purchase discount, and transportation-in transaction is recorded in a separate temporary account. At period-end, each of these temporary accounts is closed and the Merchandise Inventory account is updated. To illustrate, journal entries under the periodic inventory system are shown for the most common transactions (codes ***a*** through ***f*** link these transactions to those in the chapter, and we drop explanations for simplicity). For comparison, perpetual system journal entries are shown to the right of each periodic entry.

Purchases The periodic system uses a temporary *Purchases* account that accumulates the cost of all purchase transactions during each period. Z-Mart's November 2 entry to record the purchase of merchandise for $1,200 on credit with terms of 2/10, n/30 is

(a) Periodic			Perpetual		
Purchases	1,200		Merchandise Inventory	1,200	
Accounts Payable		1,200	Accounts Payable		1,200

Purchase Discounts The periodic system uses a temporary *Purchase Discounts* account that accumulates discounts taken on purchase transactions during the period. If payment in (*a*) is delayed until after the discount period expires, the entry is to debit Accounts Payable and credit Cash for $1,200 each. However, if Z-Mart pays the supplier for the previous purchase in (*a*) within the discount period, the required payment is $1,176 ($1,200 × 98%) and is recorded as

(b) Periodic			Perpetual		
Accounts Payable	1,200		Accounts Payable	1,200	
Purchase Discounts . . .		24	Merchandise Inventory . . .		24
Cash		1,176	Cash		1,176

Purchase Returns and Allowances Z-Mart returned merchandise purchased on November 2 because of defects. In the periodic system, the temporary *Purchase Returns and Allowances* account accumulates the cost of all returns and allowances during a period. The recorded cost (including discounts) of the defective merchandise is $300, and Z-Mart records the November 15 return with this entry:

(c) Periodic			Perpetual		
Accounts Payable	300		Accounts Payable	300	
Purchase Returns and Allowances		300	Merchandise Inventory . . .		300

Transportation-In Z-Mart paid a $75 freight charge to transport merchandise to its store. In the periodic system, this cost is charged to a temporary *Transportation-In* account.

(d)

Periodic			Perpetual		
Transportation-In	75		Merchandise Inventory	75	
Cash		75	Cash		75

Sales Under the periodic system, the cost of goods sold is *not* recorded at the time of each sale. (We later show how to compute total cost of goods sold at the end of a period.) Z-Mart's November 3 entry to record sales of $2,400 in merchandise on credit (when its cost is $1,600) is:

(e)

Periodic			Perpetual		
Accounts Receivable	2,400		Accounts Receivable	2,400	
Sales		2,400	Sales		2,400
			Cost of Goods Sold	1,600	
			Merchandise Inventory ...		1,600

Sales Returns A customer returned part of the merchandise from the transaction in (*e*), where the returned items sell for $800 and cost $600. (*Recall:* The periodic system records only the revenue effect, not the cost effect, for sales transactions.) Z-Mart restores the merchandise to inventory and records the November 6 return as

(f)

Periodic			Perpetual		
Sales Returns and Allowances	800		Sales Returns and Allowances	800	
Accounts Receivable .		800	Accounts Receivable		800
			Merchandise Inventory	600	
			Cost of Goods Sold		600

Adjusting and Closing Entries

The periodic and perpetual inventory systems have slight differences in adjusting and closing entries. The period-end Merchandise Inventory balance (unadjusted) is $19,000 under the periodic system and $21,250 under the perpetual system. Since the periodic system does not update the Merchandise Inventory balance during the period, the $19,000 amount is the beginning inventory. However, the $21,250 balance under the perpetual system is the recorded ending inventory before adjusting for any inventory shrinkage.

A physical count of inventory taken at the end of the period reveals $21,000 of merchandise available. The adjusting and closing entries for the two systems are shown in Exhibit 5A.1. The periodic

Exhibit 5A.1

Comparison of Adjusting and Closing Entries—Periodic and Perpetual

Periodic			Perpetual		
Adjusting Entry—Shrinkage			**Adjusting Entry—Shrinkage**		
None			Cost of Goods Sold	250	
			Merchandise Inventory		250
Closing Entries			**Closing Entries**		
(1) Sales	321,000		(1) Sales	321,000	
Merchandise Inventory	**21,000**		Income Summary		321,000
Purchase Discounts	**4,200**				
Purchase Returns and Allowances	**1,500**				
Income Summary		347,700			

[continued on next page]

[continued from previous page]

	Dr.	Cr.		Dr.	Cr.
(2) Income Summary	334,800		(2) Income Summary	308,100	
Sales Discounts		4,300	Sales Discounts		4,300
Sales Returns and Allowances		2,000	Sales Returns and Allowances		2,000
Merchandise Inventory		**19,000**			
Purchases		**235,800**	**Cost of Goods Sold**		**230,400**
Transportation-In		**2,300**			
Depreciation Expense—Store eq.		3,000	Depreciation Expense—Store eq.		3,000
Depreciation Expense—Office eq.		700	Depreciation Expense—Office eq.		700
Office Salaries Expense		25,300	Office Salaries Expense		25,300
Sales Salaries Expense		18,500	Sales Salaries Expense		18,500
Insurance Expense		600	Insurance Expense		600
Rent Expense—Office space		900	Rent Expense—Office space		900
Rent Expense—Selling space		8,100	Rent Expense—Selling space		8,100
Office Supplies Expense		1,800	Office Supplies Expense		1,800
Store Supplies Expense		1,200	Store Supplies Expense		1,200
Advertising Expense		11,300	Advertising Expense		11,300
(3) Income Summary	12,900		(3) Income Summary	12,900	
K. Marty, Capital		12,900	K. Marty, Capital		12,900
(4) K. Marty, Capital	4,000		(4) K. Marty, Capital	4,000	
K. Marty, Withdrawals		4,000	K. Marty, Withdrawals		4,000

system records the ending inventory of $21,000 in the Merchandise Inventory account (which includes shrinkage) in the first closing entry and removes the $19,000 beginning inventory balance from the account in the second closing entry.*

By updating Merchandise Inventory and closing Purchases, Purchase Discounts, Purchase Returns and Allowances, and Transportation-In, the periodic system transfers the cost of goods sold amount to Income Summary. Review the periodic side of Exhibit 5A.1 and notice that the boldface items affect Income Summary as follows:

Credit to Income Summary in the first closing entry includes amounts from:	
Merchandise inventory (ending)	$ 21,000
Purchase discounts	4,200
Purchase returns and allowances	1,500
Debit to Income Summary in the second closing entry includes amounts from:	
Merchandise inventory (beginning)	(19,000)
Purchases	(235,800)
Transportation-in	(2,300)
Net effect on Income Summary	**$(230,400)**

This $230,400 effect on Income Summary is the cost of goods sold amount. The periodic system transfers cost of goods sold to the Income Summary account but without using a Cost of Goods Sold account. Also, the periodic system does not separately measure shrinkage. Instead, it computes cost of goods available for sale, subtracts the cost of ending inventory, and defines the difference as cost of goods sold, which includes shrinkage.

* (This approach is called the *closing entry method.* An alternative approach, referred to as the *adjusting entry method,* would not make any entries to Merchandise Inventory in the closing entries of Exhibit 5A.1, but instead would make two adjusting entries. Using Z-Mart data, the two adjusting entries would be: (1) Dr. Income Summary and Cr. Merchandise Inventory for $19,000 each, and (2) Dr. Merchandise Inventory and Cr. Income Summary for $21,000 each. The first entry removes the beginning balance of Merchandise Inventory, and the second entry records the actual ending balance.)

Preparing Financial Statements

The financial statements of a merchandiser using the periodic system are similar to those for a service company described in prior chapters. The income statement mainly differs by the inclusion of *cost of goods sold* and *gross profit*—of course, net sales is affected by discounts, returns, and allowances. The cost of goods sold section under the periodic system follows

Calculation of Cost of Goods Sold
For Year Ended December 31, 2005

Beginning inventory	$ 19,000
Cost of goods purchased	232,400
Cost of goods available for sale	251,400
Less ending inventory	21,000
Cost of goods sold	$230,400

The balance sheet mainly differs by the inclusion of *merchandise inventory* in current assets—see Exhibit 5.15. The statement of owner's equity is unchanged. Finally, a work sheet can be used to help prepare these statements. The only differences under the periodic system from the work sheet illustrated in Appendix 5B using the perpetual system follow:

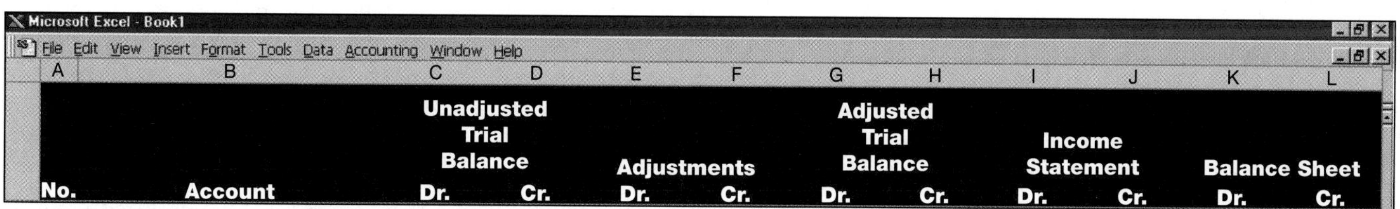

	No.	Account	Unadjusted Trial Balance Dr.	Unadjusted Trial Balance Cr.	Adjustments Dr.	Adjustments Cr.	Adjusted Trial Balance Dr.	Adjusted Trial Balance Cr.	Income Statement Dr.	Income Statement Cr.	Balance Sheet Dr.	Balance Sheet Cr.

(1) Delete the following row for Merchandise Inventory

5	119	Merchandise Inventory	21,250			(g) 250	21,000				21,000	

and substitute the following row:

5	119	Merchandise Inventory	19,000				19,000		19,000	21,000	21,000	

(2) Delete the following cost of goods sold row

20	502	Cost of goods sold	230,150		(g) 250		230,400		230,400			

and substitute the following 4 rows:

20a	505	Purchases	235,800				235,800		235,800			
20b	506	Purchases returns & allow.		1,500				1,500		1,500		
20c	507	Purchases discounts		4,200				4,200		4,200		
20d	508	Transportation-In	2,300				2,300		2,300			

Of course, the worksheet column totals will slightly differ, but not the net income amount.

Quick Check

13. What account is used in a perpetual inventory system but not in a periodic system?

14. Which of the following accounts are temporary accounts under a periodic system? (*a*) Merchandise Inventory; (*b*) Purchases; (*c*) Transportation-In.

15. How is cost of goods sold computed under a periodic inventory system?

16. Do reported amounts of ending inventory and net income differ if the adjusting entry method of recording the change in inventory is used instead of the closing entry method?

Answer—p. 204

APPENDIX

5B Work Sheet—Perpetual System

Exhibit 5B.1 shows the work sheet for preparing financial statements of a merchandiser. It differs slightly from the work sheet layout in Chapter 4—the differences are in bold. Also, the adjustments in the work sheet reflect the following: (*a*) Expiration of \$600 of prepaid insurance. (*b*) Use of \$1,200 of store supplies. (*c*) Use of \$1,800 of office supplies. (*d*) Depreciation of \$3,000 for store equipment. (*e*) Depreciation of \$700 for office equipment. (*f*) Accrual of \$300 of unpaid office salaries and \$500 of unpaid store salaries. (*g*) Inventory shrinkage of \$250. Once the adjusted amounts are extended into the financial statement columns, the information is used to develop financial statements.

Exhibit 5B.1

Work Sheet for Merchandiser (using a perpetual system)

	A	B	C	D	E	F	G	H	I	J	K	L
1			Unadjusted Trial Balance		Adjustments		Adjusted Trial Balance		Income Statement		Balance Sheet and Statement of Owner's Equity	
2	**No.**	**Account**	**Dr.**	**Cr.**	**Dr.**	**Cr.**	**Dr.**	**Cr.**	**Dr.**	**Cr.**	**Dr.**	**Cr.**
3	101	Cash	8,200				8,200				8,200	
4	106	Accounts receivable	11,200				11,200				11,200	
5	**119**	**Merchandise Inventory**	**21,250**			*(g)* 250	**21,000**				**21,000**	
6	124	Office supplies	2,350			*(c)* 1,800	550				550	
7	125	Store supplies	1,450			*(b)* 1,200	250				250	
8	128	Prepaid insurance	900			*(a)* 600	300				300	
9	163	Office equipment	4,200				4,200				4,200	
10	164	Accum. depr.—Office equip.		700		*(e)* 700		1,400				1,400
11	165	Store equipment	30,000				30,000				30,000	
12	166	Accum. depr.—Store equip.		3,000		*(d)* 3,000		6,000				6,000
13	201	Accounts payable		16,000				16,000				16,000
14	209	Salaries payable				*(f)* 800		800				800
15	301	K. Marty, Capital		42,600				42,600				42,600
16	302	K. Marty, Withdrawals	4,000				4,000				4,000	
17	**413**	**Sales**		**321,000**				**321,000**		321,000		
18	**414**	**Sales returns and allowances**	**2,000**				**2,000**		2,000			
19	**415**	**Sales discounts**	**4,300**				**4,300**		4,300			
20	**502**	**Cost of goods sold**	**230,150**		*(g)* 250		**230,400**		230,400			
21	612	Depr. expense—Store equip.			*(d)* 3,000		3,000		3,000			
22	613	Depr. expense—Office equip.			*(e)* 700		700		700			
23	620	Office salaries expense	25,000		*(f)* 300		25,300		25,300			
24	621	Sales salaries expense	18,000		*(f)* 500		18,500		18,500			
25	637	Insurance expense			*(a)* 600		600		600			
26	641	Rent expense—Office space	900				900		900			
27	642	Rent expense—Selling space	8,100				8,100		8,100			
28	650	Office supplies expense			*(c)* 1,800		1,800		1,800			
29	651	Store supplies expense			*(b)* 1,200		1,200		1,200			
30	655	Advertising expense	11,300				11,300		11,300			
31		Totals	383,300	383,300	8,350	8,350	387,800	387,800	308,100	321,000	79,700	66,800
32		Net income							12,900			12,900
33		Totals							321,000	321,000	79,700	79,700
34												

Summary

C1 Describe merchandising activities and identify income components for a merchandising company. Merchandisers buy products and resell them. Examples of merchandisers include Wal-Mart, Home Depot, The Limited, and Barnes & Noble. A merchandiser's costs on the income statement include an amount for cost of goods sold. Gross profit, or gross margin, equals sales minus cost of goods sold.

C2 Identify and explain the inventory asset of a merchandising company. The current asset section of a merchandising company's balance sheet includes *merchandise inventory,* which refers to the products a merchandiser sells and are available for sale at the balance sheet date.

C3 Describe both perpetual and periodic inventory systems. A perpetual inventory system continuously tracks the cost of goods available for sale and the cost of goods sold. A periodic system accumulates the cost of goods purchased during the period and does not compute the amount of inventory or the cost of goods sold until the end of a period.

C4 Analyze and interpret cost flows and operating activities of a merchandising company. Cost of merchandise purchases flows into Merchandise Inventory and from there to Cost of Goods Sold on the income statement. Any remaining inventory is reported as a current asset on the balance sheet.

A1 Compute the acid-test ratio and explain its use to assess liquidity. The acid-test ratio is computed as quick assets (cash, short-term investments, and current receivables) divided by current liabilities. It indicates a company's ability to pay its current liabilities with its existing quick assets. An acid-test ratio equal to or greater than 1.0 is often adequate.

A2 Compute the gross margin ratio and explain its use to assess profitability. The gross margin ratio is computed as gross margin (net sales minus cost of goods sold) divided by net sales. It indicates a company's profitability before considering other expenses.

P1 Analyze and record transactions for merchandise purchases using a perpetual system. For a perpetual inventory system, purchases of inventory (net of trade discounts) are added to the Merchandise Inventory account. Purchase discounts and purchase returns and allowances are subtracted from Merchandise Inventory, and transportation-in costs are added to Merchandise Inventory.

P2 Analyze and record transactions for merchandise sales using a perpetual system. A merchandiser records sales at list price less any trade discounts. The cost of items sold is transferred from Merchandise Inventory to Cost of Goods Sold. Refunds or credits given to customers for unsatisfactory merchandise are recorded in Sales Returns and Allowances, a contra account to Sales. If merchandise is returned and restored to inventory, the cost of this merchandise is removed from Cost of Goods Sold and transferred back to Merchandise Inventory. When cash discounts from the sales price are offered and customers pay within the discount period, the seller records Sales Discounts, a contra account to Sales.

P3 Prepare adjustments and close accounts for a merchandising company. With a perpetual system, it is often necessary to make an adjustment for inventory shrinkage. This is computed by comparing a physical count of inventory with the Merchandise Inventory balance. Shrinkage is normally charged to Cost of Goods Sold. Temporary accounts closed to Income Summary for a merchandiser include Sales, Sales Discounts, Sales Returns and Allowances, and Cost of Goods Sold.

P4 Define and prepare multiple-step and single-step income statements. Multiple-step income statements include greater detail for sales and expenses than do single-step income statements. They also show details of net sales and report expenses in categories reflecting different activities.

P5[A] Record and compare merchandising transactions using both periodic and perpetual inventory systems. Transactions involving the sale and purchase of merchandise are recorded and analyzed under both the periodic and perpetual inventory systems. Adjusting and closing entries for both inventory systems are illustrated and explained.

Guidance Answers to **Decision Maker** and **Decision Ethics**

Entrepreneur For terms of 3/10, n/90, missing the 3% discount for an additional 80 days equals an implied annual interest rate of 13.69% computed as (365 days ÷ 80 days) × 3%. Since you can borrow funds at 11% (assuming no other processing costs), it is better to borrow and pay within the discount period. You save 2.69% (13.69% − 11%) in interest costs by paying early.

Credit Manager Your decision is whether to comply with prior policy or to create a new policy and not abuse discounts offered by suppliers. Your first step should be to meet with your superior to find out if the late payment policy is the actual policy and, if so, its rationale. If it is the policy to pay late, you must apply your own sense of ethics. One point of view is that the late payment policy is unethical. A deliberate plan to make late payments means the company lies when it pretends to make payment within the discount period. Another view is that the late payment policy is acceptable. In some markets, attempts to take discounts through late payments are accepted as a continued phase of "price negotiation." Also, your company's suppliers can respond by billing your company for the discounts not accepted because of late payments. However, this is a dubious viewpoint, especially since the prior manager proposes that you explain late payments as computer or mail problems and since some suppliers have complained.

Supplier A current ratio of 2.1 suggests sufficient current assets to cover current liabilities. An acid-test ratio of 0.5 suggests, however, that quick assets can cover only about one-half of current liabilities. This implies that the retailer depends on money from sales of inventory to pay current liabilities. If sales of inventory decline or profit margins decrease, the likelihood that this retailer will default on its payments increases. Your decision is probably not to extend credit. If you do extend credit, you are likely to closely monitor the retailer's financial condition. (It is better to hold unsold inventory than uncollectible receivables.)

Financial Officer Your company's net profit margin is about equal to the industry average and suggests typical industry performance. However, gross margin reveals that your company is paying far more in cost of goods sold or receiving far less in sales price than competitors. Your attention must be directed to finding the problem with cost of goods sold, sales, or both. One positive note is that your company's expenses make up 19% of sales (36% − 17%). This favorably compares with competitors' expenses that make up 28% of sales (44% − 16%).

Guidance Answers to **Quick Checks**

1. Cost of goods sold is the cost of merchandise purchased from a supplier that is sold to customers during a specific period.
2. Gross profit (or gross margin) is the difference between net sales and cost of goods sold.
3. Widespread use of computing and related technology has dramatically increased the use of the perpetual inventory system.
4. Under credit terms of 2/10, n/60, the credit period is 60 days and the discount period is 10 days.
5. (*b*) trade discount.
6. *FOB* means "free on board." It is used in identifying the point when ownership transfers from seller to buyer. *FOB destination* means that the seller transfers ownership of goods to the buyer when they arrive at the buyer's place of business. It also means that the seller is responsible for paying shipping charges and bears the risk of damage or loss during shipment.
7. Recording sales discounts and sales returns and allowances separately from sales gives useful information to managers for internal monitoring and decision making.
8. When a customer returns merchandise *and* the seller restores the merchandise to inventory, two entries are necessary. One entry records the decrease in revenue and credits the customer's account. The second entry debits inventory and reduces cost of goods sold.
9. Credit memorandum—seller credits accounts receivable from buyer.
10. Merchandise Inventory may need adjusting to reflect shrinkage.
11. Sales (of goods), Sales Discounts, Sales Returns and Allowances, and Cost of Goods Sold (and maybe Delivery Expense).
12. Four closing entries: (1) close credit balances in temporary accounts to Income Summary, (2) close debit balances in temporary accounts to Income Summary, (3) close Income Summary to owner's capital, and (4) close withdrawals account to owner's capital.
13. Cost of Goods Sold.
14. (*b*) Purchases and (*c*) Transportation-In.
15. Under a periodic inventory system, the cost of goods sold is determined at the end of an accounting period by adding the net cost of goods purchased to the beginning inventory and subtracting the ending inventory.
16. Both methods report the same ending inventory and income.

Key Terms

Key Terms are available at the book's Website for learning and testing in an online Flashcard Format.

Acid-test ratio (p. 193)
Cash discount (p. 181)
Cost of goods sold (p. 179)
Credit memorandum (p. 187)
Credit period (p. 181)
Credit terms (p. 181)
Debit memorandum (p. 182)
Discount period (p. 181)
EOM (p. 181)
FOB (p. 183)
General and administrative expenses (p. 191)
Gross margin (p. 179)
Gross margin ratio (p. 193)
Gross profit (p. 179)
Inventory (p. 179)
List price (p. 180)
Merchandise (p. 178)
Merchandise inventory (p. 179)
Merchandiser (p. 178)
Multiple-step income statement (p. 190)
Periodic inventory system (p. 180)
Perpetual inventory system (p. 179)
Purchase discount (p. 181)
Retailer (p. 178)
Sales discount (p. 181)
Selling expenses (p. 191)
Shrinkage (p. 188)
Single-step income statement (p. 192)
Supplementary records (p. 184)
Trade discount (p. 180)
Wholesaler (p. 178)

Personal Interactive Quiz

Personal Interactive Quizzes A and B are available at the book's Website to reinforce and assess your learning.

Superscript letter A (B) denotes assignments based on Appendix 5A (5B).

Discussion Questions

1. In comparing the accounts of a merchandising company with those of a service company, what additional accounts would the merchandising company likely use, assuming it employs a perpetual inventory system?
2. What items appear in financial statements of merchandising companies but not in the statements of service companies?
3. Explain how a business can earn a positive gross profit on its sales and still have a net loss.
4. Why do companies offer a cash discount?
5. How does a company that uses a perpetual inventory system determine the amount of inventory shrinkage?
6. Distinguish between cash discounts and trade discounts. Is the amount of a trade discount on purchased merchandise recorded in the accounts?
7. What is the difference between a sales discount and a purchase discount?
8. Why would a company's manager be concerned about the quantity of its purchase returns if its suppliers allow unlimited returns?
9. Does the sender (maker) of a debit memorandum record a debit or a credit in the recipient's account? What entry (debit or credit) does the recipient record?
10. What is the difference between the single-step and multiple-step income statement formats?
11. Refer to the income statement for **Krispy Kreme** in Appendix A. What term is used instead of cost of goods sold? Does the company present a detailed calculation of its cost of goods sold?
12. Refer to the balance sheet for **Tastykake** in Appendix A. What does Tastykake call its inventory account? What alternate name could it use?
13. Refer to the income statement of **Harley-Davidson** in Appendix A. Does its income statement report a gross profit figure? If yes, what is the amount?
14. Buyers negotiate purchase contracts with suppliers. What type of shipping terms should a buyer attempt to negotiate to minimize freight-in costs?

Red numbers denote Discussion Questions that involve decision-making.

***Homework Manager** repeats all numerical Quick Study assignments on the book's Website with new numbers.*

QUICK STUDY

QS 5-1
Recording purchases—perpetual system
P1

Prepare journal entries to record each of the following purchases transactions of a merchandising company. Show supporting calculations and assume a perpetual inventory system.

Mar. 5 Purchased 500 units of product with a list price of $5 per unit. The purchaser is granted a trade discount of 20%; terms of the sale are 2/10, n/60; invoice is dated March 5.
Mar. 7 Returned 50 defective units from the March 5 purchase and received full credit.
Mar. 15 Paid the amount due from the March 5 purchase, less the return on March 7.

QS 5-2
Recording sales—perpetual system
P2

Prepare journal entries to record each of the following sales transactions of a merchandising company. Show supporting calculations and assume a perpetual inventory system.

Apr. 1 Sold merchandise for $2,000, granting the customer terms of 2/10, EOM; invoice dated April 1. The cost of the merchandise is $1,400.
Apr. 4 The customer in the April 1 sale returned merchandise and received credit for $500. The merchandise, which had cost $350, is returned to inventory.
Apr. 11 Received payment for the amount due from the April 1 sale less the return on April 4.

QS 5-3
Computing and analyzing gross margin
C1 A2 

Compute net sales, gross profit, and the gross margin ratio for each separate case *a* through *d*. Interpret the gross margin ratio for case *a*.

	a	b	c	d
Sales	$130,000	$512,000	$35,700	$245,700
Sales discounts	4,200	16,500	400	3,500
Sales returns and allowances	17,000	5,000	5,000	700
Cost of goods sold	76,600	326,700	21,300	125,900

QS 5-4
Accounting for shrinkage—perpetual system
P3

Nix'It Company's ledger on July 31, its fiscal year-end, includes the following accounts that have normal balances (Nix'It uses the perpetual inventory system):

Merchandise inventory	$ 34,800	Sales returns and allowances	$ 3,500
T. Nix, Capital	115,300	Cost of goods sold	102,000
T. Nix, Withdrawals	7,000	Depreciation expense	7,300
Sales	157,200	Salaries expense	29,500
Sales discounts	1,700	Miscellaneous expenses	2,000

A physical count of its July 31 year-end inventory discloses that the cost of the merchandise inventory still available is $32,900. Prepare the entry to record any inventory shrinkage.

QS 5-5
Closing entries P3

Refer to QS 5-4 and prepare journal entries to close the balances in temporary revenue and expense accounts. Remember to consider the entry for shrinkage that is made to solve QS 5-4.

QS 5-6
Computing and interpreting acid-test ratio
A1 

Use the following information on current assets and current liabilities to compute and interpret the acid-test ratio. Explain what the acid-test ratio of a company measures.

Cash	$1,200	Prepaid expenses	$ 600
Accounts receivable	2,700	Accounts payable	4,750
Inventory	5,000	Other current liabilities	950

QS 5-7
Contrasting liquidity ratios A1

Identify similarities and differences between the acid-test ratio and the current ratio. Compare and describe how the two ratios reflect a company's ability to meet its current obligations.

QS 5-8^A
Contrasting periodic and perpetual systems
C3

Identify whether each description best applies to a periodic or a perpetual inventory system.

a. Provides more timely information to managers.
b. Requires an adjusting entry to record inventory shrinkage.
c. Markedly increased in frequency and popularity in business within the past decade.
d. Records cost of goods sold each time a sales transaction occurs.

QS 5-9^A
Recording purchases—periodic system P5

Refer to QS 5-1 and prepare journal entries to record each of the merchandising transactions assuming that the periodic inventory system is used.

QS 5-10^A
Recording purchases—periodic system P5

Refer to QS 5-2 and prepare journal entries to record each of the merchandising transactions assuming that the periodic inventory system is used.

Homework Manager repeats all numerical Exercises on the book's Website with new numbers.

EXERCISES

Exercise 5-1
Recording entries for merchandise purchases

P1

Prepare journal entries to record the following transactions for a retail store. Assume a perpetual inventory system.

Apr. 2 Purchased merchandise from Blue Company under the following terms: $3,600 price, invoice dated April 2, credit terms of 2/15, n/60, and FOB shipping point.

3 Paid $200 for shipping charges on the April 2 purchase.

4 Returned to Blue Company unacceptable merchandise that had an invoice price of $600.

17 Sent a check to Blue Company for the April 2 purchase, net of the discount and the returned merchandise.

18 Purchased merchandise from Fox Corp. under the following terms: $7,500 price, invoice dated April 18, credit terms of 2/10, n/30, and FOB destination.

21 After negotiations, received from Fox a $2,100 allowance on the April 18 purchase.

28 Sent a check to Fox paying for the April 18 purchase, net of the discount and allowance.

Check April 28, Cr. Cash $5,292

Exercise 5-2
Analyzing and recording merchandise transactions—both buyer and seller

P1 P2

Taos Company purchased merchandise for resale from Tucson Company with an invoice price of $22,000 and credit terms of 3/10, n/60. The merchandise had cost Tucson $15,000. Taos paid within the discount period. Assume that both buyer and seller use a perpetual inventory system.

1. Prepare entries that the buyer should record for the purchase and the cash payment.

2. Prepare entries that the seller should record for the sale and the cash collection.

3. Assume that the buyer borrowed enough cash to pay the balance on the last day of the discount period at an annual interest rate of 8% and paid it back on the last day of the credit period. Compute how much the buyer saved by following this strategy. (Assume a 365-day year and round dollar amounts to the nearest cent.)

Check (3) $426 savings

Exercise 5-3
Applying merchandising terms

C1

Insert the letter for each term in the blank space beside the definition that it most closely matches:

A. Cash discount
B. Credit period
C. Discount period
D. FOB destination
E. FOB shipping point
F. Gross profit
G. Merchandise inventory
H. Purchase discount
I. Sales discount
J. Trade discount

_____ **1.** Ownership of goods is transferred when delivered to the buyer's place of business.
_____ **2.** Time period in which a cash discount is available.
_____ **3.** Difference between net sales and the cost of goods sold.
_____ **4.** Reduction in a receivable or payable if it is paid within the discount period.
_____ **5.** Purchaser's description of a cash discount received from a supplier of goods.
_____ **6.** Ownership of goods is transferred when the seller delivers goods to the carrier.
_____ **7.** Reduction below list or catalog price that is negotiated in setting the price of goods.
_____ **8.** Seller's description of a cash discount granted to buyers in return for early payment.
_____ **9.** Time period that can pass before a customer's payment is due.
_____ **10.** Goods a company owns and expects to sell to its customers.

Exercise 5-4
Recording sales returns and allowances

P2

Spare Parts was organized on May 1, 2005, and made its first purchase of merchandise on May 3. The purchase was for 1,000 units at a price of $10 per unit. On May 5, Spare Parts sold 600 of the units for $14 per unit to DeSoto Co. Terms of the sale were 2/10, n/60. Prepare entries for Spare Parts to record the May 5 sale and each of the following separate transactions *a* through *c* using a perpetual inventory system.

a. On May 7, DeSoto returns 200 units because they did not fit the customer's needs. Spare Parts restores the units to its inventory.

b. On May 8, DeSoto discovers that 50 units are damaged but of some use and, therefore, keeps the units. Spare Parts sends DeSoto a credit memorandum for $300 to compensate for the damage.

c. On May 15, DeSoto returns 100 defective units and Spare Parts concludes that these units cannot be resold. As a result, Spare Parts discards them—it removes these units' cost from cost of good sold and records a loss from defective merchandise.

Check (c) Cr. Cost of Good Sold $1,000

Exercise 5-5
Recording purchase returns and allowances P1

Refer to Exercise 5-4 and prepare the appropriate journal entries for DeSoto Co. to record the May 5 purchase and each of the three separate transactions *a* through *c*. DeSoto is a retailer that uses a perpetual inventory system and purchases these units for resale.

Exercise 5-6
Analyzing and recording merchandise transactions—both buyer and seller
P1 P2

On May 11, Smythe Co. accepts delivery of $30,000 of merchandise it purchases for resale from Hope Corporation. With the merchandise is an invoice dated May 11, with terms of 3/10, n/90, FOB shipping point. The cost of the goods for Hope is $20,000. When the goods are delivered, Smythe pays $335 to Express Shipping for delivery charges on the merchandise. On May 12, Smythe returns $1,200 of goods to Hope, who receives them one day later and restores them to inventory. The returned goods had cost Hope $800. On May 20, Smythe mails a check to Hope Corporation for the amount owed. Hope receives it the following day. (Both Smythe and Hope use a perpetual inventory system)

Check (1) May 20, Cr. Cash $27,936

1. Prepare journal entries that Smythe Co. records for these transactions.
2. Prepare journal entries that Hope Corporation records for these transactions.

Exercise 5-7
Sales returns and allowances
C1 P2

Explain why a company's manager wants the accounting system to record customers' returns of unsatisfactory goods in the Sales Returns and Allowances account instead of the Sales account. In addition, explain whether this information would be useful for external decision makers.

Exercise 5-8
Recording effects of merchandising activities
C4

The following supplementary records summarize Titus Company's merchandising activities for year 2005. Set up T-accounts for Merchandise Inventory and Cost of Goods Sold. Then record the summarized activities in those T-accounts and compute account balances.

Cost of merchandise sold to customers in sales transactions	$186,000
Merchandise inventory, December 31, 2004	27,000
Invoice cost of merchandise purchases	190,500
Shrinkage determined on December 31, 2005	700
Cost of transportation-in	1,900
Cost of merchandise returned by customers and restored to inventory	2,200
Purchase discounts received	1,600
Purchase returns and allowances	4,100

Check Merchandise Inventory (12/31/2005), $29,200

Exercise 5-9
Calculating revenues, expenses, and income
C1 C4

Fill in the blanks in the following separate income statements *a* through *e*. Identify any negative amount by putting it in parentheses.

	a	b	c	d	e
Sales	$60,000	$42,500	$36,000	$?	$23,600
Cost of goods sold					
Merchandise inventory (beginning)	6,000	17,050	7,500	7,000	2,560
Total cost of merchandise purchases	36,000	?	?	32,000	5,600
Merchandise inventory (ending)	?	(2,700)	(9,000)	(6,600)	?
Cost of goods sold	34,050	15,900	?	?	5,600
Gross profit	?	?	3,750	45,600	?
Expenses	9,000	10,650	12,150	2,600	6,000
Net income (loss)	$?	$15,950	$ (8,400)	$43,000	$?

Exercise 5-10
Preparing adjusting and closing entries for a merchandiser
P3

The following list includes some permanent accounts and all of the temporary accounts from the December 31, 2005, unadjusted trial balance of Deacon Co., a business owned by Julie Deacon. Use these account balances along with the additional information to journalize (*a*) adjusting entries and (*b*) closing entries. Deacon Co. uses a perpetual inventory system.

	Debit	Credit
Merchandise inventory	$ 28,000	
Prepaid selling expenses	5,000	
J. Deacon, Withdrawals	2,200	
Sales		$429,000
Sales returns and allowances	16,500	
Sales discounts	4,000	
Cost of goods sold	211,000	
Sales salaries expense	47,000	
Utilities expense	14,000	
Selling expenses	35,000	
Administrative expenses	95,000	

Additional Information

Accrued sales salaries amount to $1,600. Prepaid selling expenses of $2,000 have expired. A physical count of year-end merchandise inventory shows $27,450 of goods still available.

Check Entry to close Income Summary: Cr. J. Deacon, Capital $2,350

Exercise 5-11
Interpreting a physical count error as inventory shrinkage
A1 A2 P3

A retail company recently completed a physical count of ending merchandise inventory to use in preparing adjusting entries. In determining the cost of the counted inventory, company employees failed to consider that $2,000 of incoming goods had been shipped by a supplier on December 31 under an FOB shipping point agreement. These goods had been recorded in Merchandise Inventory as a purchase, but they were not included in the physical count because they were in transit. Explain how this overlooked fact affects the company's financial statements and the following ratios: return on assets, debt ratio, current ratio, profit margin ratio, and acid-test ratio.

Exercise 5-12
Computing and analyzing acid-test and current ratios
A1

Compute the current ratio and acid-test ratio for each of the following separate cases. Which company case is in the best position to meet short-term obligations? Explain.

	Case X	Case Y	Case Z
Cash	$ 800	$ 910	$1,100
Short-term investments	0	0	500
Current receivables	0	990	800
Inventory	2,000	1,000	4,000
Prepaid expenses	1,200	600	900
Total current assets	$4,000	$3,500	$7,300
Current liabilities	$2,200	$1,100	$3,650

Exercise 5-13[A]
Preparing journal entries for both the periodic and perpetual systems
P1 P2 P5

Journalize the following merchandising transactions for CSI Systems assuming it uses (*a*) a periodic inventory system and (*b*) a perpetual inventory system.

1. On November 1, CSI Systems purchases merchandise for $1,400 on credit with terms of 2/5, n/30, FOB shipping point; invoice dated November 1.
2. On November 5, CSI Systems pays cash for the November 1 purchase.
3. On November 7, CSI Systems discovers and returns $100 of defective merchandise purchased on November 1 for a cash refund.
4. On November 10, CSI Systems pays $80 cash for transportation costs with the November 1 purchase.
5. On November 13, CSI Systems sells merchandise for $1,500 on credit. The cost of the merchandise is $750.
6. On November 16, the customer returns merchandise from the November 13 transaction. The returned items sell for $200 and cost $100.

Exercise 5-14^A
Recording purchases—periodic system P5

Refer to Exercise 5-1 and prepare journal entries to record each of the merchandising transactions assuming that the periodic inventory system is used.

Exercise 5-15^A
Recording purchases and sales—periodic system P5

Refer to Exercise 5-2 and prepare journal entries to record each of the merchandising transactions assuming that the periodic inventory system is used by both the buyer and the seller. (Skip the part 3 requirement.)

Exercise 5-16^A
Buyer and seller transactions—periodic system P5

Refer to Exercise 5-6 and prepare journal entries to record each of the merchandising transactions assuming that the periodic inventory system is used by both the buyer and the seller.

PROBLEM SET A

Problem 5-1A
Preparing journal entries for merchandising activities—perpetual system

P1 P2

Check Aug. 9, Dr. Delivery Expense, $120

Aug. 18, Cr. Cash $4,695

Aug. 29, Dr. Cash $2,970

Prepare journal entries to record the following merchandising transactions of Stone Company, which applies the perpetual inventory system. (*Hint:* It will help to identify each receivable and payable; for example, record the purchase on August 1 in Accounts Payable—Abilene.)

Aug. 1 Purchased merchandise from Abilene Company for $6,000 under credit terms of 1/10, n/30, FOB destination, invoice dated August 1.
4 At Abilene's request, Stone paid $100 cash for freight charges on the August 1 purchase, reducing the amount owed to Abilene.
5 Sold merchandise to Lux Corp. for $4,200 under credit terms of 2/10, n/60, FOB destination, invoice dated August 5. The merchandise had cost $3,000.
8 Purchased merchandise from Welch Corporation for $5,300 under credit terms of 1/10, n/45, FOB shipping point, invoice dated August 8. The invoice showed that at Stone's request, Welch paid the $240 shipping charges and added that amount to the bill.
9 Paid $120 cash for shipping charges related to the August 5 sale to Lux Corp.
10 Lux returned merchandise from the August 5 sale that had cost Stone $500 and been sold for $700. The merchandise was restored to inventory.
12 After negotiations with Welch Corporation concerning problems with the merchandise purchased on August 8, Stone received a credit memorandum from Welch granting a price reduction of $800.
15 Received balance due from Lux Corp. for the August 5 sale less the return on August 10.
18 Paid the amount due Welch Corporation for the August 8 purchase less the price reduction granted.
19 Sold merchandise to Trax for $3,600 under credit terms of 1/10, n/30, FOB shipping point, invoice dated August 19. The merchandise had cost $2,500.
22 Trax requested a price reduction on the August 19 sale because the merchandise did not meet specifications. Stone sent Trax a $600 credit memorandum to resolve the issue.
29 Received Trax's cash payment for the amount due from the August 19 purchase.
30 Paid Abilene Company the amount due from the August 1 purchase.

Problem 5-2A
Preparing journal entries for merchandising activities—perpetual system

P1 P2

Prepare journal entries to record the following merchandising transactions of Bask Company, which applies the perpetual inventory system. (*Hint:* It will help to identify each receivable and payable; for example, record the purchase on July 1 in Accounts Payable—Black.)

July 1 Purchased merchandise from Black Company for $6,000 under credit terms of 1/15, n/30, FOB shipping point, invoice dated July 1.
2 Sold merchandise to Coke Co. for $800 under credit terms of 2/10, n/60, FOB shipping point, invoice dated July 2. The merchandise had cost $500.
3 Paid $100 cash for freight charges on the purchase of July 1.
8 Sold merchandise that had cost $1,200 for $1,600 cash.
9 Purchased merchandise from Lane Co. for $2,300 under credit terms of 2/15, n/60, FOB destination, invoice dated July 9.
11 Received a $200 credit memorandum from Lane Co. for the return of part of the merchandise purchased on July 9.

12 Received the balance due from Coke Co. for the invoice dated July 2, net of the discount.
16 Paid the balance due to Black Company within the discount period.
19 Sold merchandise that cost $900 to AKP Co. for $1,250 under credit terms of 2/15, n/60, FOB shipping point, invoice dated July 19.
21 Issued a $150 credit memorandum to AKP Co. for an allowance on goods sold on July 19.
24 Paid Lane Co. the balance due after deducting the discount.
30 Received the balance due from AKP Co. for the invoice dated July 19, net of discount.
31 Sold merchandise that cost $3,200 to Coke Co. for $5,000 under credit terms of 2/10, n/60, FOB shipping point, invoice dated July 31.

Check July 12, Dr. Cash $784
July 16, Cr. Cash $5,940
July 24, Cr. Cash $2,058
July 30, Dr. Cash $1,078

Problem 5-3A
Preparing adjusting entries and income statements; and computing gross margin, acid-test, and current ratios

A1 A2 P3 P4

mhhe.com/larson

The following unadjusted trial balance is prepared at fiscal year-end for Rex Company:

	REX COMPANY Unadjusted Trial Balance January 31, 2005		
1		Debit	Credit
2	Cash	$ 2,200	
3	Merchandise inventory	11,500	
4	Store supplies	4,800	
5	Prepaid insurance	2,300	
6	Store equipment	41,900	
7	Accumulated depreciation—Store equipment		$ 15,000
8	Accounts payable		9,000
9	T. Rex, Capital		32,000
10	T. Rex, Withdrawals	2,000	
11	Sales		104,000
12	Sales discounts	1,000	
13	Sales returns and allowances	2,000	
14	Cost of goods sold	37,400	
15	Depreciation expense—Store equipment	0	
16	Salaries expense	31,000	
17	Insurance expense	0	
18	Rent expense	14,000	
19	Store supplies expense	0	
20	Advertising expense	9,900	
21	Totals	$160,000	$160,000
22			

Rent expense and salaries expense are equally divided between selling activities and the general and administrative activities. Rex Company uses a perpetual inventory system.

Required

1. Prepare adjusting journal entries to reflect each of the following:
   a. Store supplies still available at fiscal year-end amount to $1,650.
   b. Expired insurance, an administrative expense, for the fiscal year is $1,500.
   c. Depreciation expense on store equipment, a selling expense, is $1,400 for the fiscal year.
   d. To estimate shrinkage, a physical count of ending merchandise inventory is taken. It shows $11,100 of inventory is still available at fiscal year-end.

2. Prepare a multiple-step income statement for fiscal year 2005.

3. Prepare a single-step income statement for fiscal year 2005.

4. Compute the current ratio, acid-test ratio, and gross margin ratio as of January 31, 2005.

Check (2) Gross profit, $63,200; (3) Total expenses, $98,750; Net income, $2,250

Problem 5-4A
Computing merchandising amounts and formatting income statements
C4 P4

BizKid Company's adjusted trial balance on August 31, 2005, its fiscal year-end, follows:

	Debit	Credit
Merchandise inventory	$ 31,000	
Other (noninventory) assets	120,400	
Total liabilities		$ 35,000
N. Kidman, Capital		101,650
N. Kidman, Withdrawals	8,000	
Sales		212,000
Sales discounts	3,250	
Sales returns and allowances	14,000	
Cost of goods sold	82,600	
Sales salaries expense	29,000	
Rent expense—Selling space	10,000	
Store supplies expense	2,500	
Advertising expense	18,000	
Office salaries expense	26,500	
Rent expense—Office space	2,600	
Office supplies expense	800	
Totals	$348,650	$348,650

On August 31, 2004, merchandise inventory was $25,000. Supplementary records of merchandising activities for the year ended August 31, 2005, reveal the following itemized costs:

Invoice cost of merchandise purchases	$91,000
Purchase discounts received	1,900
Purchase returns and allowances	4,400
Costs of transportation-in	3,900

Required

1. Compute the company's net sales for the year.

2. Compute the company's total cost of merchandise purchased for the year.

3. Prepare a multiple-step income statement that includes separate categories for selling expenses and for general and administrative expenses.

4. Prepare a single-step income statement that includes these expense categories: cost of goods sold, selling expenses, and general and administrative expenses.

Check (2) $88,600; (3) Gross profit, $112,150; Net income, $22,750; (4) Total expenses, $172,000

Problem 5-5A
Preparing closing entries and interpreting information about discounts and returns
C4 P3

Use the data for BizKid Company in Problem 5-4A to complete the following requirements:

Required

1. Prepare closing entries as of August 31, 2005 (the perpetual inventory system is used).

Check (1) $22,750 Dr. to close Income Summary

Analysis Component

2. The company makes all purchases on credit, and its suppliers uniformly offer a 3% sales discount. Does it appear that the company's cash management system is accomplishing the goal of taking all available discounts? Explain.

3. In prior years, the company experienced a 5% returns and allowance rate on its sales, which means approximately 5% of its gross sales were eventually returned outright or caused the company to grant allowances to customers. How do this year's results compare to prior years' results?

(3) Current-year rate, 6.6%

Problem 5-6A[B]
Preparing a work sheet for a merchandiser

Refer to the data and information in Problem 5-3A.

Required

Prepare and complete the entire 10-column work sheet for Rex Company. Follow the structure of Exhibit 5B.1 in Appendix 5B.

PROBLEM SET B

Problem 5-1B
Preparing journal entries for merchandising activities—perpetual system

P1 P2

Prepare journal entries to record the following merchandising transactions of Wave Company, which applies the perpetual inventory system. (*Hint:* It will help to identify each receivable and payable; for example, record the purchase on July 3 in Accounts Payable—CAP.)

July 3 Purchased merchandise from CAP Corp. for $15,000 under credit terms of 1/10, n/30, FOB destination, invoice dated July 3.

4 At CAP's request, Wave paid $250 cash for freight charges on the July 3 purchase, reducing the amount owed to CAP.

7 Sold merchandise to Morris Co. for $10,500 under credit terms of 2/10, n/60, FOB destination, invoice dated July 7. The merchandise had cost $7,500.

10 Purchased merchandise from Murdock Corporation for $14,200 under credit terms of 1/10, n/45, FOB shipping point, invoice dated July 10. The invoice showed that at Wave's request, Murdock paid the $600 shipping charges and added that amount to the bill.

11 Paid $300 cash for shipping charges related to the July 7 sale to Morris Co.

12 Morris returned merchandise from the July 7 sale that had cost Wave $1,250 and been sold for $1,750. The merchandise was restored to inventory.

14 After negotiations with Murdock Corporation concerning problems with the merchandise purchased on July 10, Wave received a credit memorandum from Murdock granting a price reduction of $2,000.

17 Received balance due from Morris Co. for the July 7 sale less the return on July 12.

20 Paid the amount due Murdock Corporation for the July 10 purchase less the price reduction granted.

21 Sold merchandise to Ulsh for $9,000 under credit terms of 1/10, n/30, FOB shipping point, invoice dated July 21. The merchandise had cost $6,250.

24 Ulsh requested a price reduction on the July 21 sale because the merchandise did not meet specifications. Wave sent Ulsh a credit memorandum for $1,500 to resolve the issue.

30 Received Ulsh's cash payment for the amount due from the July 21 purchase.

31 Paid CAP Corp. the amount due from the July 3 purchase.

Check July 17, Dr. Cash $8,575
July 20, Cr. Cash $12,678
July 30, Dr. Cash $7,425

Problem 5-2B
Preparing journal entries for merchandising activities—perpetual system

P1 P2

Prepare journal entries to record the following merchandising transactions of Yang Company, which applies the perpetual inventory system. (*Hint:* It will help to identify each receivable and payable; for example, record the purchase on May 2 in Accounts Payable—Bots.)

May 2 Purchased merchandise from Bots Co. for $9,000 under credit terms of 1/15, n/30, FOB shipping point, invoice dated May 2.

4 Sold merchandise to Chase Co. for $1,200 under credit terms of 2/10, n/60, FOB shipping point, invoice dated May 4. The merchandise had cost $750.

5 Paid $150 cash for freight charges on the purchase of May 2.

9 Sold merchandise that had cost $1,800 for $2,400 cash.

10 Purchased merchandise from Snyder Co. for $3,450 under credit terms of 2/15, n/60, FOB destination, invoice dated May 10.

12 Received a $300 credit memorandum from Snyder Co. for the return of part of the merchandise purchased on May 10.

14 Received the balance due from Chase Co. for the invoice dated May 4, net of the discount.

17 Paid the balance due to Bots Co. within the discount period.

20 Sold merchandise that cost $1,450 to Tex Co. for $2,800 under credit terms of 2/15, n/60, FOB shipping point, invoice dated May 20.

22 Issued a $400 credit memorandum to Tex Co. for an allowance on goods sold from May 20.

25 Paid Snyder Co. the balance due after deducting the discount.

30 Received the balance due from Tex Co. for the invoice dated May 20, net of discount and allowance.

31 Sold merchandise that cost $4,800 to Chase Co. for $7,500 under credit terms of 2/10, n/60, FOB shipping point, invoice dated May 31.

Check May 14, Dr. Cash $1,176
May 17, Cr. Cash $8,910
May 30, Dr. Cash $2,352

Problem 5-3B
Preparing adjusting entries and income statements; and computing gross margin, acid-test, and current ratios
A1 A2 P3 P4

The following unadjusted trial balance is prepared at fiscal year-end for FAB Products Company:

	FAB PRODUCTS COMPANY Unadjusted Trial Balance October 31, 2005	Debit	Credit
2	Cash	$ 4,400	
3	Merchandise inventory	23,000	
4	Store supplies	9,600	
5	Prepaid insurance	4,600	
6	Store equipment	83,800	
7	Accumulated depreciation—Store equipment		$ 30,000
8	Accounts payable		16,000
9	A. Fab, Capital		64,000
10	A. Fab, Withdrawals	2,000	
11	Sales		208,000
12	Sales discounts	2,000	
13	Sales returns and allowances	4,000	
14	Cost of goods sold	74,800	
15	Depreciation expense—Store equipment	0	
16	Salaries expense	62,000	
17	Insurance expense	0	
18	Rent expense	28,000	
19	Store supplies expense	0	
20	Advertising expense	19,800	
21	Totals	$318,000	$318,000

Rent expense and salaries expense are equally divided between selling activities and the general and administrative activities. FAB Products Company uses a perpetual inventory system.

Required

1. Prepare adjusting journal entries to reflect each of the following:
   a. Store supplies still available at fiscal year-end amount to $3,300.
   b. Expired insurance, an administrative expense, for the fiscal year is $3,000.
   c. Depreciation expense on store equipment, a selling expense, is $2,800 for the fiscal year.
   d. To estimate shrinkage, a physical count of ending merchandise inventory is taken. It shows $22,200 of inventory is still available at fiscal year-end.
2. Prepare a multiple-step income statement for fiscal year 2005.
3. Prepare a single-step income statement for fiscal year 2005.
4. Compute the current ratio, acid-test ratio, and gross margin ratio as of October 31, 2005.

Check (2) Gross profit, $126,400; (3) Total expenses, $197,500; Net income, $4,500

Problem 5-4B
Computing merchandising amounts and formatting income statements
C1 C4 P4

Albin Company's adjusted trial balance on March 31, 2005, its fiscal year-end, follows:

	Debit	Credit
Merchandise inventory	$ 46,500	
Other (noninventory) assets	190,600	
Total liabilities		$ 52,500
R. Albin, Capital		152,475
R. Albin, Withdrawals	2,000	
Sales		318,000
Sales discounts	4,875	
Sales returns and allowances	21,000	
Cost of goods sold	123,900	
Sales salaries expense	43,500	
Rent expense—Selling space	15,000	

[continued on next page]

[continued from previous page]

Store supplies expense	3,750	
Advertising expense	27,000	
Office salaries expense	39,750	
Rent expense—Office space	3,900	
Office supplies expense	1,200	
Totals	$522,975	$522,975

On March 31, 2004, merchandise inventory was $37,500. Supplementary records of merchandising activities for the year ended March 31, 2005, reveal the following itemized costs:

Invoice cost of merchandise purchases	$136,500
Purchase discounts received	2,850
Purchase returns and allowances	6,600
Costs of transportation-in	5,850

Required

1. Calculate the company's net sales for the year.

2. Calculate the company's total cost of merchandise purchased for the year.

3. Prepare a multiple-step income statement that includes separate categories for selling expenses and for general and administrative expenses.

4. Prepare a single-step income statement that includes these expense categories: cost of goods sold, selling expenses, and general and administrative expenses.

Check (2) $132,900; (3) Gross profit, $168,225; Net income, $34,125; (4) Total expenses, $258,000

Problem 5-5B
Preparing closing entries and interpreting information about discounts and returns
C4 P3

Use the data for Albin Company in Problem 5-4B to complete the following requirements:

Required

1. Prepare closing entries as of March 31, 2005 (the perpetual inventory system is used).

Analysis Component

2. The company makes all purchases on credit, and its suppliers uniformly offer a 3% sales discount. Does it appear that the company's cash management system is accomplishing the goal of taking all available discounts? Explain.

3. In prior years, the company experienced a 5% returns and allowance rate on its sales, which means approximately 5% of its gross sales were eventually returned outright or caused the company to grant allowances to customers. How do this year's results compare to prior years' results?

Check (1) $34,125 Dr. to close Income Summary

(3) Current-year rate, 6.6%

Problem 5-6B[B]
Preparing a work sheet for a merchandiser

Refer to the data and information in Problem 5-3B.

Required

Prepare and complete the entire 10-column work sheet for FAB Products Company. Follow the structure of Exhibit 5B.1 in Appendix 5B.

PROBLEM SET C

Problem Set C is available at the book's Website to further reinforce and assess your learning.

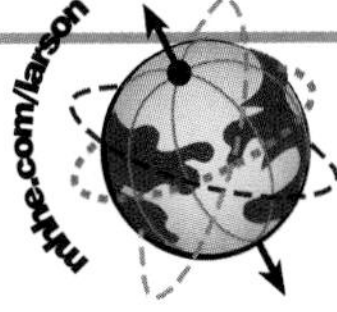

SERIAL PROBLEM

Success Systems

(This serial problem began in Chapter 1 and continues through most of the book. If previous chapter segments were not completed, the serial problem can begin at this point. It is helpful, but not necessary, that you use the Working Papers that accompany the book.)

Kay Breeze created Success Systems on October 1, 2004. The company has been successful, and its list of customers has grown. To accommodate the growth, the accounting system is modified to set up separate accounts for each customer. The following chart of accounts includes the account number used for each account and any balance as of December 31, 2004. Breeze decided to add a fourth digit with a decimal point to the 106 account number that had been used for the single Accounts Receivable account. This modification allows the company to continue using the existing chart of accounts.

No.	Account Title	Dr.	Cr.
101	Cash	58,160	
106.1	Alex's Engineering Co.	0	
106.2	Wildcat Services	0	
106.3	Easy Leasing	0	
106.4	Clark Co.	3,000	
106.5	Chang Corp.	0	
106.6	Gomez Co.	2,668	
106.7	Delta Co.	0	
106.8	KC, Inc.	0	
106.9	Dream, Inc.	0	
119	Merchandise inventory	0	
126	Computer supplies	580	
128	Prepaid insurance	1,665	
131	Prepaid rent	825	
163	Office equipment	8,000	
164	Accumulated depreciation—Office equipment		400
167	Computer equipment	20,000	
168	Accumulated depreciation—Computer equipment		1,250
201	Accounts payable		1,100

No.	Account Title	Dr.	Cr.
210	Wages payable		500
236	Unearned computer services revenue		1,500
301	K. Breeze, Capital		90,148
302	K. Breeze, Withdrawals	0	
403	Computer services revenue		0
413	Sales		0
414	Sales returns and allowances	0	
415	Sales discounts	0	
502	Cost of goods sold	0	
612	Depreciation expense—Office equipment	0	
613	Depreciation expense—Computer equipment	0	
623	Wages expense	0	
637	Insurance expense	0	
640	Rent expense	0	
652	Computer supplies expense	0	
655	Advertising expense	0	
676	Mileage expense	0	
677	Miscellaneous expenses	0	
684	Repairs expense—Computer	0	

In response to requests from customers, Breeze will begin selling computer software. The company will extend credit terms of 1/10, n/30, FOB shipping point, to all customers who purchase this merchandise. However, no cash discount is available on consulting fees. Note that additional accounts (Nos. 119, 413, 414, 415, and 502) are added to its general ledger to accommodate the company's new merchandising activities. Also, Success Systems does not use reversing entries and, therefore, all revenue and expense accounts have zero balances as of January 1, 2005. Its transactions for January through March follow:

Jan. 4 Paid cash to Sherry Adams for five days' work at the rate of $125 per day. Four of the five days relate to wages payable that were accrued in the prior year.

5 Kay Breeze invested an additional $25,000 cash in the business.

7 Purchased $5,800 of merchandise from Kansas Corp. with terms of 1/10, n/30, FOB shipping point, invoice dated January 7.

9 Received $2,668 cash from Gomez Co. as full payment on its account.

Check Jan. 11, Dr. Unearned Computer Services Revenue $1,500

11 Completed a five-day project for Alex's Engineering Co. and billed it $5,500, which is the total price of $7,000 less the advance payment of $1,500.

13 Sold merchandise with a retail value of $5,200 and a cost of $3,560 to Chang Corp., invoice dated January 13.

15 Paid $600 cash for freight charges on the merchandise purchased on January 7.

16 Received $4,000 cash from Delta Co. for computer services provided.

17 Paid Kansas Corp. for the invoice dated January 7, net of the discount.

Check Jan. 20, No entry to Cost of Goods Sold

20 Chang Corp. returned $500 of defective merchandise from its invoice dated January 13. The returned merchandise, which had a $320 cost, is discarded. (The policy of Success Systems is to leave the cost of defective products in cost of goods sold.)

22 Received the balance due from Chang Corp., net of both the discount and the credit for the returned merchandise.

24 Returned defective merchandise to Kansas Corp. and accepted a credit against future purchases. The defective merchandise invoice cost, net of the discount, was $496.

26 Purchased $9,000 of merchandise from Kansas Corp. with terms of 1/10, n/30, FOB destination, invoice dated January 26.

26 Sold merchandise with a $4,640 cost for $5,800 on credit to KC, Inc., invoice dated January 26.

29 Received a $496 credit memorandum from Kansas Corp. concerning the merchandise returned on January 24.

31 Paid cash to Sherry Adams for 10 days' work at $125 per day.

Feb. 1 Paid $2,475 cash to Summit Mall for another three months' rent in advance.

3 Paid Kansas Corp. for the balance due, net of the cash discount, less the $496 amount in the credit memorandum.

5 Paid $600 cash to the local newspaper for an advertising insert in today's paper.

11 Received the balance due from Alex's Engineering Co. for fees billed on January 11.

15 Kay Breeze withdrew $4,800 cash for personal use.

23 Sold merchandise with a $2,660 cost for $3,220 on credit to Delta Co., invoice dated February 23.
26 Paid cash to Sherry Adams for eight days' work at $125 per day.
27 Reimbursed Kay Breeze for business automobile mileage (600 miles at $0.32 per mile).
Mar. 8 Purchased $2,730 of computer supplies from Cain Office Products on credit, invoice dated March 8.
9 Received the balance due from Delta Co. for merchandise sold on February 23.
11 Paid $960 cash for minor repairs to the company's computer.
16 Received $5,260 cash from Dream, Inc., for computing services provided.
19 Paid the full amount due to Cain Office Products, including amounts created on December 15 and March 8.
24 Billed Easy Leasing for $8,900 of computing services provided.
25 Sold merchandise with a $2,002 cost for $2,800 on credit to Wildcat Services, invoice dated March 25.
30 Sold merchandise with a $1,100 cost for $2,220 on credit to Clark Company, invoice dated March 30.
31 Reimbursed Kay Breeze for business automobile mileage (400 miles at $0.32 per mile).

The following additional facts are available for preparing adjustments on March 31 prior to financial statement preparation:

a. The March 31 amount of computer supplies still available totals $2,005.
b. Three more months have expired since the company purchased its annual insurance policy at a $2,220 cost for 12 months of coverage.
c. Sherry Adams has not been paid for seven days of work at the rate of $125 per day.
d. Three months have passed since any prepaid rent has been transferred to expense. The monthly rent expense is $825.
e. Depreciation on the computer equipment for January 1 through March 31 is $1,250.
f. Depreciation on the office equipment for January 1 through March 31 is $400.
g. The March 31 amount of merchandise inventory still available totals $704.

Required

1. Prepare journal entries to record each of the January through March transactions.
2. Post the journal entries in part 1 to the accounts in the company's general ledger. (*Note:* Begin with the ledger's post-closing adjusted balances as of December 31, 2004.)
3. Prepare a partial work sheet consisting of the first six columns (similar to the one shown in Exhibit 5B.1) that includes the unadjusted trial balance, the March 31 adjustments (*a*) through (*g*), and the adjusted trial balance. Do not prepare closing entries and do not journalize the adjustments or post them to the ledger.
4. Prepare an income statement (from the adjusted trial balance in part 3) for the three months ended March 31, 2005. Use a single-step format. List all expenses without differentiating between selling expenses and general and administrative expenses.
5. Prepare a statement of owner's equity (from the adjusted trial balance in part 3) for the three months ended March 31, 2005.
6. Prepare a classified balance sheet (from the adjusted trial balance) as of March 31, 2005.

Check (2) Ending balances: Cash, $77,845; Sales, $19,240;

(3) Unadj. totals, $161,198; Adj. totals, $163,723;

(4) Net income, $18,686;

(5) K. Breeze, Capital (3/31/05), $129,034;

(6) Total assets, $129,909

BEYOND THE NUMBERS

REPORTING IN ACTION

C4 A1

BTN 5-1 Refer to **Krispy Kreme**'s financial statements in Appendix A to answer the following.

Required

1. Assume that the amounts reported for inventories and cost of sales reflect items purchased in a form ready for resale. Compute the net cost of goods purchased for the fiscal year ended February 2, 2003.
2. Compute the current ratio and acid-test ratio as of February 2, 2003, and February 3, 2002. Interpret and comment on the ratio results.

Roll On

3. Access Krispy Kreme's financial statements (form 10-K) for fiscal years ending after February 2, 2003, from its Website (KrispyKreme.com) or the SEC's EDGAR database (www.SEC.gov). Recompute and interpret the current ratio and acid-test ratio for these current fiscal years.

COMPARATIVE ANALYSIS

A2

BTN 5-2 Key comparative figures ($ thousands) for both **Krispy Kreme** and **Tastykake** follow:

	Krispy Kreme		Tastykake	
Key Figures	**Current Year**	**Prior Year**	**Current Year**	**Prior Year**
Revenues (net sales)	$491,549	$394,354	$162,263	$166,245
Cost of sales	381,489	316,946	111,187	103,297

Required

1. Compute the dollar amount of gross margin and the gross margin ratio for the two years shown for both companies.
2. Which company earns more in gross margin for each dollar of net sales?
3. Did the gross margin ratio improve or decline for these companies?

ETHICS CHALLENGE

C1 P2

BTN 5-3 Amy Martinez is a student who plans to attend approximately four professional events a year at her college. Each event necessitates a financial outlay of $100–$200 for a new suit and accessories. After incurring a major hit to her savings for the first event, Amy developed a different approach. She buys the suit on credit the week before the event, wears it to the event, and returns it the next week to the store for a full refund on her charge card.

Required

1. Comment on the ethics exhibited by Amy and possible consequences of her actions.
2. How does the merchandising company account for the suits that Amy returns?

COMMUNICATING IN PRACTICE

C3 C4 P3

BTN 5-4 You are the financial officer for Music Plus, a retailer that sells goods for home entertainment needs. The business owner, Vic Velakturi, recently reviewed the annual financial statements you prepared and sent you an e-mail stating that he thinks you overstated net income. He explains that although he has invested a great deal in security, he is sure shoplifting and other forms of inventory shrinkage have occurred, but he does not see any deduction for shrinkage on the income statement. The store uses a perpetual inventory system.

Required

Prepare a brief memorandum that responds to the owner's concerns.

TAKING IT TO THE NET

A2 C1

mhhe.com/larson

BTN 5-5 Access the SEC's EDGAR database (www.sec.gov) and obtain the April 22, 2003, filing of its fiscal 2003 10-K report (for the year ended February 1, 2003) for **J. Crew Group, Inc.**

Required

Prepare a table that reports the gross margin ratios for J. Crew using the revenues and cost of goods sold data from J. Crew's income statement for each of its most recent four years. Analyze and comment on the trend in its gross margin ratio.

TEAMWORK IN ACTION

C1 C4

BTN 5-6 Best Brands' general ledger and supplementary records at the end of its current period reveal the following:

Sales	$430,000	Merchandise inventory (beginning of period)	$ 49,000
Sales returns	18,000	Invoice cost of merchandise purchases	180,000
Sales discounts	6,600	Purchase discounts received	4,500
Cost of transportation-in	11,000	Purchase returns and allowances	5,500
Operating expenses	20,000	Merchandise inventory (end of period)	42,000

Required

1. *Each* member of the team is to assume responsibility for computing *one* of the following items. You are not to duplicate your teammates' work. Get any necessary amounts to compute your item from the appropriate teammate. Each member is to explain his or her computation to the team in preparation for reporting to the class.
   a. Net sales
   b. Total cost of merchandise purchases
   c. Cost of goods sold
   d. Gross profit
   e. Net income

Point: In teams of four, assign the same student *a* and e. Rotate teams for reporting on a different computation and the analysis in step 3.

2. Check your net income with the instructor. If correct, proceed to step 3.
3. Assume that a physical inventory count finds that actual ending inventory is $38,000. Discuss how this affects previously computed amounts in step 1.

BUSINESS WEEK ACTIVITY

C1 C4

mhhe.com/larson

BTN 5-7 Read the article, "The End of Fuzzy Math?" in the December 11, 2000, issue of *Business Week*. The book's Website provides free access to the article.

Required

1. How does the article define *fulfillment costs?*
2. Where does **Amazon.com** account for fulfillment costs on its income statement?
3. Where do similar companies, such as catalog companies and direct marketers, account for fulfillment costs on their income statements?
4. Does the FASB specify how to account for fulfillment costs? Explain.
5. Why is the issue of accounting for fulfillment costs important to investors?

ENTREPRENEURIAL DECISION

C1 C4 P4

BTN 5-8 Dwayne Lewis and Michael Cherry have earned well beyond the $1,000 they used to launch **Damani Dada** (see chapter's opening feature). Good entrepreneurs continually rethink and refine business strategies. Assume that Damani Dada's most recent income statement follows:

DAMANI DADA
Income Statement ($ thousands)
For Year Ended April 30, 2005

Net sales	$50,000
Cost of sales	35,000
Expenses	4,000
Net income	$11,000

To increase income, Lewis and Cherry are proposing to offer sales discounts of 3/10, n/30, and to ship merchandise FOB shipping point. Assume that Damani Dada presently offers no discounts and ships merchandise FOB destination. The sales discounts are predicted to increase net sales by 14%, and the ratio of cost of sales divided by net sales is expected to remain unchanged. Since delivery expenses are zero under this proposal, the expenses are predicted to increase by only 10%.

Required

1. Prepare a forecasted income statement for the year ended April 30, 2006, based on this proposal.
2. Do you recommend that it implement the proposal given your analysis in part 1? Explain.
3. Identify any concerns you might express to Lewis and Cherry regarding their proposal.

HITTING THE ROAD

C1

Point: This activity complements the Ethics Challenge assignment.

BTN 5-9 Arrange an interview (in person or by phone) with the manager of a retail shop in a mall or in the downtown area of your community. Explain to the manager that you are a student studying merchandising activities and the accounting for sales returns and sales allowances. Ask the manager what the store policy is regarding returns. Also find out if the sales allowances are ever negotiated with customers. Inquire whether management perceives that customers are abusing return policies and what actions management takes to counter potential abuses. Be prepared to discuss your findings in class.

GLOBAL DECISION

A2 P4

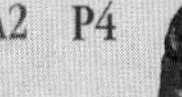

BTN 5-10 **Grupo Bimbo (GrupoBimbo.com), Krispy Kreme,** and **Tastykake** are all competitors in the global marketplace. Key comparative figures for each company follow:

	Net Sales	Cost of Sales
Grupo Bimbo*	41,373,269	19,155,865
Krispy Kreme**	$ 491,549	$ 381,489
Tastykake**	$ 162,263	$ 111,187

*Thousands of pesos (Grupo Bimbo).
**Thousands of dollars (Krispy Kreme and Tastykake).

Required

1. Rank the three companies (highest to lowest) based on the gross margin ratio.
2. Which of the companies uses a multiple-step income statement format? (Access their annual reports.)
3. Which company's income statement would likely be most easily interpreted by potential investors? Provide a brief justification for your choice.

"I am the COF—Chairman of Fun!"—Mike Becker

Inventories and Cost of Sales

A Look Back

Chapter 5 focused on merchandising activities and how they are reported and analyzed. We also analyzed and recorded merchandise purchases and sales and explained accounting adjustments and the closing process for merchandising companies.

A Look at This Chapter

This chapter emphasizes accounting for inventory. We describe the methods available for assigning costs to inventory and explain the items and costs making up merchandise inventory. We also analyze the effects of inventory on both financial and tax reporting, and we discuss other methods of estimating and measuring inventory.

A Look Ahead

Chapter 7 emphasizes accounting information systems. We describe fundamental system principles, the system's components, use of special journals and subsidiary ledgers, and technology-based systems. We also discuss segment data.

CAP

Conceptual

C1 Identify the items making up merchandise inventory. *(p. 222)*

C2 Identify the costs of merchandise inventory. *(p. 223)*

Analytical

A1 Analyze the effects of inventory methods for both financial and tax reporting. *(p. 229)*

A2 Analyze the effects of inventory errors on current and future financial statements. *(p. 232)*

A3 Assess inventory management using both inventory turnover and days' sales in inventory. *(p. 233)*

Procedural

P1 Compute inventory in a perpetual system using the methods of specific identification, FIFO, LIFO, and weighted average. *(p. 224)*

P2 Compute the lower of cost or market amount of inventory. *(p. 231)*

Decision Feature

Wacky Inventor of Wobblers

SNOHOMISH, WA—Mike Becker long collected nostalgia-based toys from his childhood. Becker imagined that "there's got to be people like me out there [who love such toys], where I could have a cool little business based on that love."

Drawing on his life savings of $35,000, Becker started **FunKo** **(Funko.com)** making Wacky Wobblers (bobbleheads) out of his garage. His Wobblers are based on characters and personalities from his youth. "It's about invoking a feeling," says Becker. "We want people to say, 'Oh, I remember that!'" Becker has now sold more than 600,000 of 50 different Wobblers (selling for about $15 each) in the past 5 years. He projects sales this year of more than $2 million.

Still, the road to the top was shaky. Becker struggled with purchases and sales and had to confront discounts, returns, and allowances. One of his biggest obstacles, and continuing challenges, is maintaining the right inventories and controlling costs of sales. "It was kind of by trial and error," says Becker. "I didn't understand what the heck I was doing. I didn't have any distribution networks, sales reps, employees, or even a place of business." Success is more than good products, says Becker; it depends on assigning and monitoring costs of inventory and applying sound inventory management procedures.

With business booming, he continues to keep watch over inventory turnover and days' sales in inventory. This chapter focuses on these issues, including measuring, monitoring and managing such inventories. Yet Becker keeps all in perspective. "I guess we totally underestimated the possibility that there were so many other weirdos like us out there."

[Sources: *FunKo Website,* January 2004; *Entrepreneur,* November 2002; *Puget Sound Business Journal,* June 8, 2001; *Tri-City Herald,* January 2002; *Seattle Times,* April 13, 2002.]

Merchandisers' activities include the purchasing and reselling of merchandise. We explained accounting for merchandisers in Chapter 5, including that for purchases and sales. In this chapter, we extend the study and analysis of inventory by explaining the methods used to assign costs to merchandise inventory *and* to cost of goods sold. Retailers, wholesalers, and other merchandising companies that purchase products for resale use the principles and methods described. Understanding inventory accounting helps in the analysis and interpretation of financial statements, and in helping people run their own businesses.

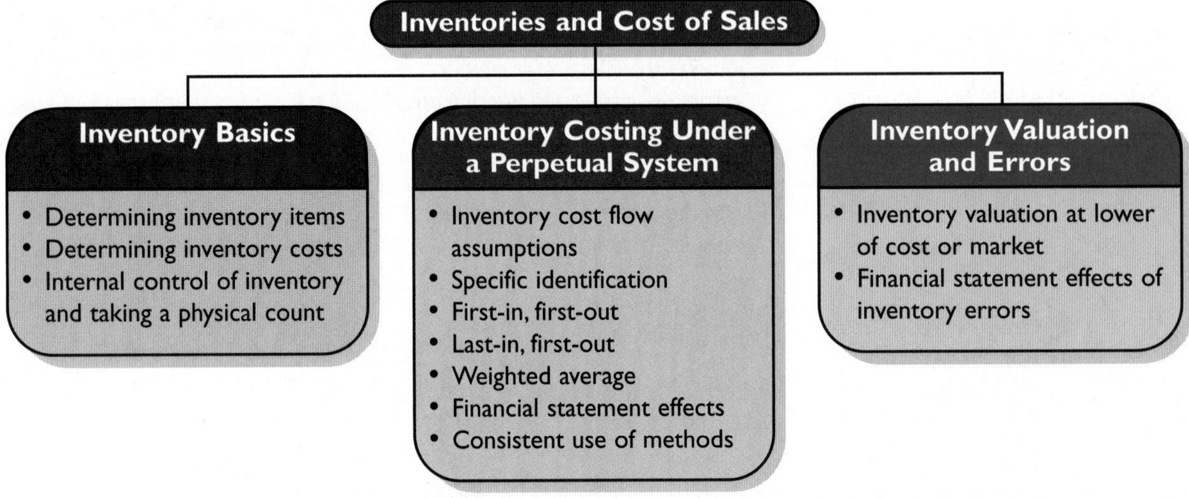

Inventory Basics

This section identifies the items and costs making up merchandise inventory. It also describes the importance of internal controls in taking a physical count of inventory.

Determining Inventory Items

C1 Identify the items making up merchandise inventory.

Merchandise inventory includes all goods that a company owns and holds for sale. This rule holds regardless of where the goods are located when inventory is counted. Certain inventory items require special attention, including goods in transit, goods on consignment, and goods that are damaged or obsolete.

Goods in Transit Does a purchaser's inventory include goods in transit from a supplier? The answer is that if ownership has passed to the purchaser, the goods are included in the purchaser's inventory. We determine this by reviewing the shipping terms: *FOB destination* or *FOB shipping point.* If the purchaser is responsible for paying freight, ownership passes when goods are loaded on the transport vehicle. If the seller is responsible for paying freight, ownership passes when goods arrive at their destination.

Goods on Consignment Goods on consignment are goods shipped by the owner, called the **consignor,** to another party, the **consignee.** A consignee sells goods for the owner. The consignor continues to own the consigned goods and reports them in its inventory. **Upper Deck**, for instance, pays sports celebrities such as Tiger Woods to sign memorabilia, which are offered to shopping networks on consignment. Upper Deck, the consignor, must report these items in its inventory until sold.

Goods Damaged or Obsolete Damaged and obsolete (and deteriorated) goods are not counted in inventory if they cannot be sold. If these goods can be sold at a reduced price, they are included in inventory at a conservative estimate of their **net realizable value.** Net realizable value is sales price minus the cost of making the sale. The period when damage or obsolescence (or deterioration) occurs is the period when the loss in value is reported.

Decision Insight

A wireless portable computer with a two-way radio allows clerks to quickly record inventory by scanning bar codes and to instantly send and receive data. It gives managers access to up-to-date information on inventory and its location.

Determining Inventory Costs

C2 Identify the costs of merchandise inventory.

Merchandise inventory includes costs of expenditures necessary, directly or indirectly, to bring an item to a salable condition and location. This means that the cost of an inventory item includes its invoice cost minus any discount, and plus any added or incidental costs necessary to put it in a place and condition for sale. Added or incidental costs can include import duties, freight, storage, insurance, and costs incurred in an aging process (for example, aging wine or cheese).

Accounting principles prescribe that incidental costs be assigned to inventory. Also, the *matching principle* states that inventory costs should be recorded against revenue in the period when inventory is sold. However, some companies use the *materiality principle* (*cost-to-benefit constraint*) to avoid assigning incidental costs of acquiring merchandise to inventory. These companies argue either that incidental costs are immaterial or that the effort in assigning these costs to inventory outweighs the benefit.

Decision Insight

Some retailers are adding bar code readers on shopping carts for customers to swipe products over the reader, charging it to a credit card. There is no need to stand in a checkout line. Customers simply pass through a gate to verify that everything in the cart is scanned.

Internal Controls and Taking a Physical Count

The Inventory account under a perpetual system is updated for each purchase and sale, but events can cause the account balance to be different from the actual inventory available. Such events include theft, loss, damage, and errors. Thus, nearly all companies take a *physical count of inventory* at least once each year—informally called *taking an inventory.* This often occurs at the end of a fiscal year or when inventory amounts are low. This physical count is used to adjust the Inventory account balance to the actual inventory available.

A business must apply internal controls when taking a physical count of inventory that would usually include the following:

- *Prenumbered inventory tickets* are prepared and distributed to *counters*—each ticket must be accounted for.
- Counters of inventory are assigned that do not include those responsible for the inventory.
- Counters confirm the validity of inventory, including its existence, amounts, quality, and so forth.
- A second count should occur by a different counter.
- A manager confirms that all inventories are ticketed once, and only once.

Point: The Inventory account is a controlling account for the inventory subsidiary ledger. This *subsidiary ledger* contains a separate record (units and costs) for each separate product, and it can be in electronic or paper form. Subsidiary records assist managers in planning and monitoring inventory.

Quick Check

1. What accounting principle most guides the allocation of cost of goods available for sale between ending inventory and cost of goods sold?
2. If **Skechers** sells goods to **Target** with terms FOB shipping point, which company reports these goods in its inventory while they are in transit?
3. An art gallery purchases a painting for $11,400 on terms FOB shipping point. Additional costs in obtaining and offering the artwork for sale include $130 for transportation-in, $150 for import duties, $100 for insurance during shipment, $180 for advertising, $400 for framing, and $800 for office salaries. For computing inventory, what cost is assigned to the painting?

Answers—p. 245

Inventory Costing Under a Perpetual System

Accounting for inventory affects both the balance sheet and the income statement. A major goal in accounting for inventory is to properly match costs with sales. We use the *matching principle* to decide how much of the cost of the goods available for sale is deducted from sales and how much is carried forward as inventory and matched against future sales.

Management decisions in accounting for inventory involve the following

- Costing method (specific identification, FIFO, LIFO, or weighted average).
- Inventory system (perpetual or periodic).
- Items included in inventory and their costs.
- Use of market values or other estimates.

Decisions on these points affect the reported amounts for inventory, cost of goods sold, gross profit, income, current assets, and other accounts.

One of the most important issues in accounting for inventory is determining the per unit costs assigned to inventory items. When all units are purchased at the same unit cost, this process is simple. When identical items are purchased at different costs, however, a question arises as to which amounts to record in cost of goods sold and which amounts remain in inventory.

Four methods are commonly used to assign costs to inventory and to cost of goods sold: (1) specific identification; (2) first-in, first-out; (3) last-in, first-out; and (4) weighted average. Exhibit 6.1 shows the frequency in the use of these methods.

Exhibit 6.1

Frequency in Use of Inventory Methods

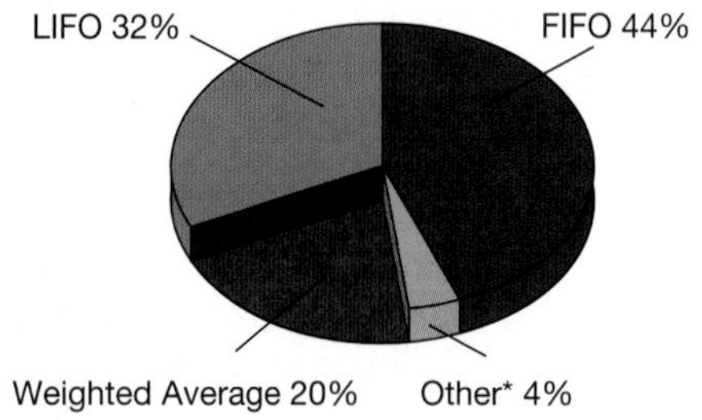

*Includes specific identification.

Each method assumes a particular pattern for how costs flow through inventory. Each of these four methods is acceptable whether or not the actual physical flow of goods follows the cost flow assumption. Physical flow of goods depends on the type of product and the way it is stored. (Perishable goods such as fresh fruit demand that a business attempt to sell them in a first-in, first-out physical flow. Other products such as crude oil and minerals such as coal, gold, decorative stone can be sold in a last-in, first-out physical flow.) **Physical flow and cost flow need not be the same.**

Inventory Cost Flow Assumptions

P1 Compute inventory in a perpetual system using the methods of specific identification, FIFO, LIFO, and weighted average.

This section introduces inventory cost flow assumptions. Assume that three identical units are purchased at the following three dates and costs: May 1 at $45, May 3 at $65, and May 6 at $70. One unit is then sold on May 7 for $100. Exhibit 6.2 gives a visual layout of the flow of costs to either the gross profit section of the income statement or the inventory reported on the balance sheet for FIFO, LIFO, and weighted average.

(1) *FIFO assumes costs flow in the order incurred.* The unit purchased on May 1 for $45 is the earliest cost incurred—it is sent to cost of goods sold on the income statement. The remaining two units ($65 and $70) are reported in inventory on the balance sheet.

(2) *LIFO assumes costs flow in the reverse order incurred.* The unit purchased on May 6 for $70 is the most recent cost incurred—it is sent to cost of goods sold on the income statement. The remaining two units ($45 and $65) are reported in inventory on the balance sheet.

(3) *Weighted average assumes costs flow at an average of the costs available.* The units available at the May 7 sale average $60 in cost, computed as ($45 + $65 + $70)/3. One unit's $60 average cost is sent to cost of goods sold on the income statement. The remaining two units' average costs are reported in inventory at $120 on the balance sheet.

Cost flow assumptions can markedly impact gross profit and inventory. Exhibit 6.2 shows that gross profit as a percent of net sales ranges from 30% to 55% due to nothing else but the cost flow assumption.

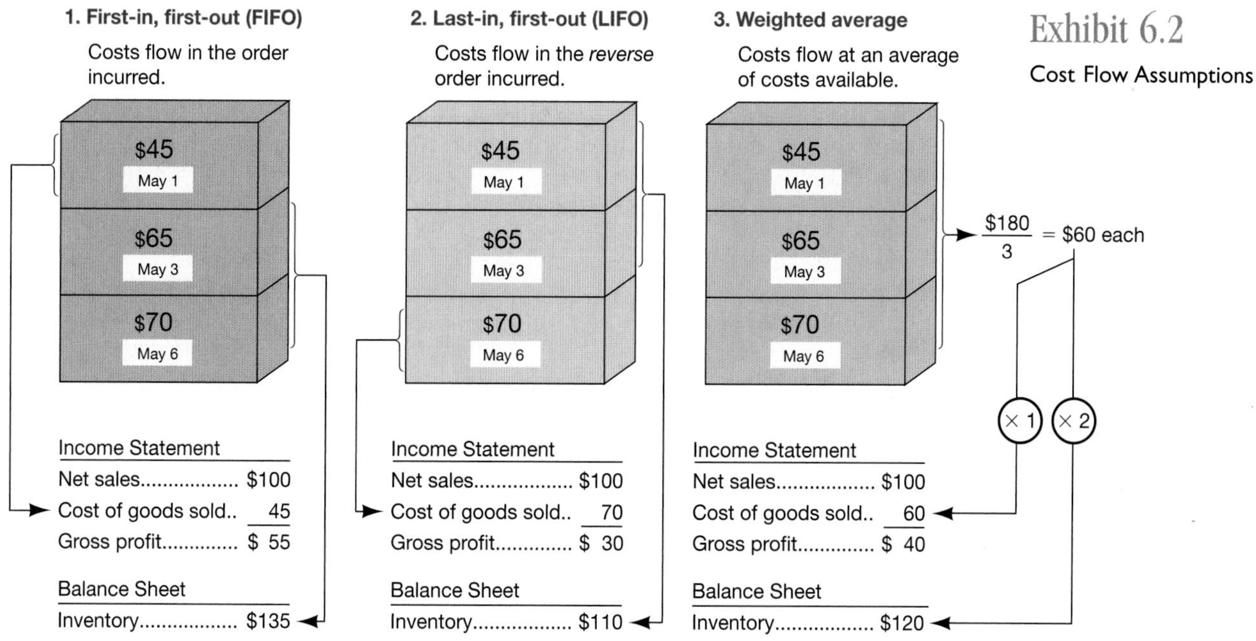

Exhibit 6.2

Cost Flow Assumptions

The following sections on inventory costing methods use the perpetual system. Appendix 6A uses the periodic system. An instructor can choose to cover either one or both inventory systems.

Inventory Costing Illustration

This section provides a comprehensive illustration of inventory costing methods. We use information from Trekking, a sporting goods store. Among its many products, Trekking carries one type of mountain bike whose sales are directed at resorts that provide inexpensive mountain bikes for complimentary guest use. Its customers usually purchase in amounts of 10 or more bikes. We use Trekking's data from August 2005. Its mountain bike (unit) inventory at the beginning of August and its purchases and sales during August are shown in Exhibit 6.3. It ends August with 12 bikes remaining in inventory.

Point: Inventories are a large portion of current assets for most wholesalers, retailers, and manufacturers. Accounting for inventories is key to determining cost of goods sold and gross profit.

Exhibit 6.3

Purchases and Sales of Goods

Date	Activity	Units Acquired at Cost	Units Sold at Retail	Unit Inventory
Aug. 1	Beginning inventory	10 units @ $ 91 = $ 910		10 units
Aug. 3	Purchases	15 units @ $106 = $ 1,590		25 units
Aug. 14	Sales		20 units @ $130	5 units
Aug. 17	Purchases	20 units @ $115 = $ 2,300		25 units
Aug. 28	Purchases	10 units @ $119 = $ 1,190		35 units
Aug. 31	Sales		23 units @ $150	12 units
	Totals	55 units $5,990	43 units	

Trekking uses the perpetual inventory system, which means that its merchandise inventory account is continually updated to reflect purchases and sales. (**Appendix 6A describes the assignment of costs to inventory using a periodic system.**) Regardless of what inventory method or system is used, cost of goods available for sale must be allocated between cost of goods sold and ending inventory.

Point: The perpetual inventory system is now the most dominant system across U.S. businesses.

Point: Cost of goods sold plus ending inventory equals cost of goods available for sale.

Specific Identification

When each item in inventory can be identified with a specific purchase and invoice, we can use **specific identification** (also called *specific invoice inventory pricing*) to assign costs.

Point: Three key variables determine the dollar value of ending inventory: (1) inventory quantity, (2) costs of inventory, and (3) cost flow assumption.

We also need sales records that identify exactly which items were sold and when. Trekking's internal documents reveal that 7 of the 12 unsold units in ending inventory were from the August 28 purchase and 5 were from the August 17 purchase. We use this information and the specific identification method to assign costs to the 12 units in ending inventory and to the 43 units sold as shown in Exhibit 6.4. Carefully study this exhibit to see the flow of costs both in and out of inventory. Notice that each unit, whether sold or remaining in inventory, has its own specific cost attached to it.

Exhibit 6.4

Specific Identification Computations

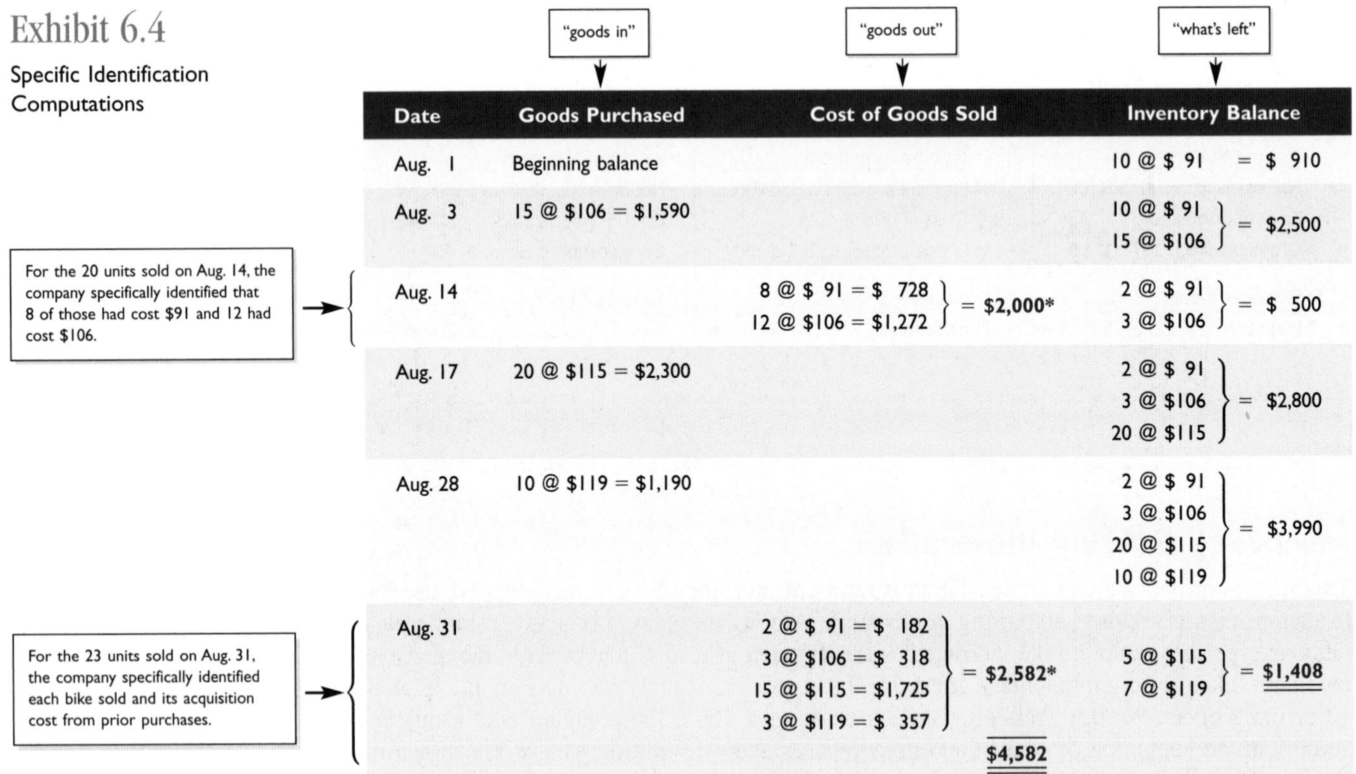

Date	Goods Purchased ("goods in")	Cost of Goods Sold ("goods out")		Inventory Balance ("what's left")	
Aug. 1	Beginning balance			10 @ $ 91	= $ 910
Aug. 3	15 @ $106 = $1,590			10 @ $ 91 15 @ $106	= $2,500
Aug. 14		8 @ $ 91 = $ 728 12 @ $106 = $1,272	= $2,000*	2 @ $ 91 3 @ $106	= $ 500
Aug. 17	20 @ $115 = $2,300			2 @ $ 91 3 @ $106 20 @ $115	= $2,800
Aug. 28	10 @ $119 = $1,190			2 @ $ 91 3 @ $106 20 @ $115 10 @ $119	= $3,990
Aug. 31		2 @ $ 91 = $ 182 3 @ $106 = $ 318 15 @ $115 = $1,725 3 @ $119 = $ 357	= $2,582*	5 @ $115 7 @ $119	= $1,408
			$4,582		

For the 20 units sold on Aug. 14, the company specifically identified that 8 of those had cost $91 and 12 had cost $106.

For the 23 units sold on Aug. 31, the company specifically identified each bike sold and its acquisition cost from prior purchases.

* Identification of items sold (and their costs) is obtained from internal documents that track each unit from its purchase to its sale.

Point: Specific identification is usually only practical for companies with expensive, custom-made inventory.

When using specific identification, Trekking's cost of goods sold reported on the income statement totals **$4,582**, the sum of $2,000 and $2,582 from the third column of Exhibit 6.4. Trekking's ending inventory reported on the balance sheet is **$1,408**, which is the final inventory balance from the fourth column of Exhibit 6.4.

The purchases and sales entries for Exhibit 6.4 follow (the boldface numbers are those determined by the cost flow assumption):

Purchases

Date	Account	Debit	Credit
Aug. 3	Merchandise Inventory	1,590	
	Accounts Payable		1,590
17	Merchandise Inventory	2,300	
	Accounts Payable		2,300
28	Merchandise Inventory	1,190	
	Accounts Payable		1,190

Sales

Date	Account	Debit	Credit
Aug. 14	Accounts Receivable	2,600	
	Sales		2,600
14	Cost of Goods Sold	**2,000**	
	Merchandise Inventory		**2,000**
31	Accounts Receivable	3,450	
	Sales		3,450
31	Cost of Goods Sold	**2,582**	
	Merchandise Inventory		**2,582**

First-In, First-Out

The **first-in, first-out (FIFO)** method of assigning costs to both inventory and cost of goods sold assumes that inventory items are sold in the order acquired. When sales occur, the costs of the earliest units acquired are charged to cost of goods sold. This leaves the costs from the most recent purchases in ending inventory. Use of FIFO for computing the cost of inventory and cost of goods sold is shown in Exhibit 6.5.

Point: The "Goods Purchased" column is identical for all methods. Data are taken from Exhibit 6.3.

Exhibit 6.5

FIFO Computations—Perpetual System

Date	Goods Purchased	Cost of Goods Sold	Inventory Balance
Aug. 1	Beginning balance		10 @ $ 91 = $ 910
Aug. 3	15 @ $106 = $1,590		10 @ $ 91 15 @ $106 } = $2,500
Aug. 14		10 @ $ 91 = $ 910 10 @ $106 = $1,060 } = $1,970	5 @ $106 = $ 530
Aug. 17	20 @ $115 = $2,300		5 @ $106 20 @ $115 } = $2,830
Aug. 28	10 @ $119 = $1,190		5 @ $106 20 @ $115 10 @ $119 } = $4,020
Aug. 31		5 @ $106 = $ 530 18 @ $115 = $2,070 } = $2,600 $4,570	2 @ $115 10 @ $119 } = $1,420

For the 20 units sold on Aug. 14, the first 10 sold are assigned the earliest cost of $91 (from beg. bal.). The next 10 sold are assigned the next earliest cost of $106.

For the 23 units sold on Aug. 31, the first 5 sold are assigned the earliest available cost of $106 (from Aug. 3 purchase). The next 18 sold are assigned the next earliest cost of $115 (from Aug. 17 purchase).

Trekking's FIFO cost of goods sold reported on its income statement (reflecting the 43 units sold) is **$4,570** ($1,970 + $2,600), and its ending inventory reported on the balance sheet (reflecting the 12 units unsold) is **$1,420**.

The purchases and sales entries for Exhibit 6.5 follow (the boldface numbers are those affected by the cost flow assumption):

Point: Under FIFO, a unit sold is assigned the earliest (oldest) cost from inventory. This leaves the most recent costs in ending inventory.

Purchases

Aug. 3	Merchandise Inventory.	1,590	
	Accounts Payable		1,590
17	Merchandise Inventory.	2,300	
	Accounts Payable		2,300
28	Merchandise Inventory.	1,190	
	Accounts Payable		1,190

Sales

Aug. 14	Accounts Receivable	2,600	
	Sales		2,600
14	Cost of Goods Sold.	**1,970**	
	Merchandise Inventory. . .		**1,970**
31	Accounts Receivable	3,450	
	Sales		3,450
31	Cost of Goods Sold.	**2,600**	
	Merchandise Inventory. . .		**2,600**

Last-In, First-Out

The **last-in, first-out (LIFO)** method of assigning costs assumes that the most recent purchases are sold first. These more recent costs are charged to the goods sold, and the costs of the earliest purchases are assigned to inventory. As with other methods, LIFO is acceptable even when the physical flow of goods does not follow a last-in, first-out pattern. One appeal of LIFO is that by assigning costs from the most recent purchases to cost of goods sold, LIFO comes closest to matching current costs of goods sold with revenues (compared to FIFO or weighted average). Exhibit 6.6 shows how LIFO assigns the costs of mountain bikes to the 12 units in ending inventory and to the 43 units sold.

Topic Tackler 6-1

Point: Under LIFO, a unit sold is assigned the most recent (latest) cost from inventory. This leaves the oldest costs in inventory.

Exhibit 6.6

LIFO Computations—Perpetual System

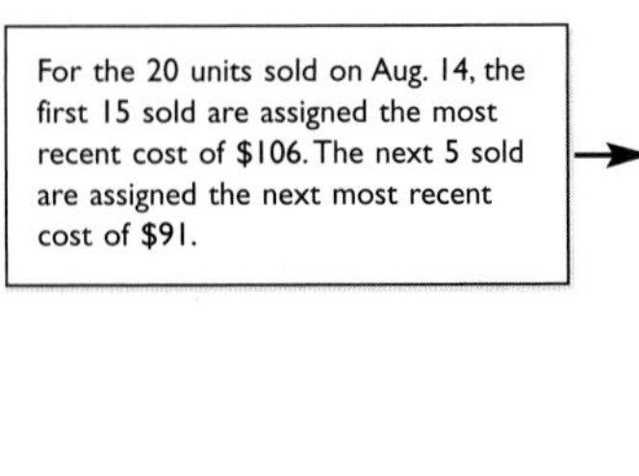

For the 23 units sold on Aug. 31, the first 10 sold are assigned the most recent cost of $119. The next 13 sold are assigned the next most recent cost of $115.

Date	Goods Purchased	Cost of Goods Sold		Inventory Balance	
Aug. 1	Beginning balance			10 @ $ 91	= $ 910
Aug. 3	15 @ $106 = $1,590			10 @ $ 91 15 @ $106	= $ 2,500
Aug. 14		15 @ $106 = $1,590 5 @ $ 91 = $ 455	= **$2,045**	5 @ $ 91	= $ 455
Aug. 17	20 @ $115 = $2,300			5 @ $ 91 20 @ $115	= $ 2,755
Aug. 28	10 @ $119 = $1,190			5 @ $ 91 20 @ $115 10 @ $119	= $ 3,945
Aug. 31		10 @ $119 = $1,190 13 @ $115 = $1,495	= **$2,685**	5 @ $ 91 7 @ $115	= **$1,260**
			$4,730		

Trekking's LIFO cost of goods sold reported on the income statement is **$4,730** ($2,045 + $2,685), and its ending inventory reported on the balance sheet is **$1,260**.

The purchases and sales entries for Exhibit 6.6 follow (the boldface numbers are those affected by the cost flow assumption):

Purchases

Date	Account	Debit	Credit
Aug. 3	Merchandise Inventory	1,590	
	Accounts Payable		1,590
17	Merchandise Inventory	2,300	
	Accounts Payable		2,300
28	Merchandise Inventory	1,190	
	Accounts Payable		1,190

Sales

Date	Account	Debit	Credit
Aug. 14	Accounts Receivable	2,600	
	Sales		2,600
14	Cost of Goods Sold	**2,045**	
	Merchandise Inventory		**2,045**
31	Accounts Receivable	3,450	
	Sales		3,450
31	Cost of Goods Sold	**2,685**	
	Merchandise Inventory		**2,685**

Weighted Average

The **weighted average** (also called **average cost**) method of assigning cost requires that we compute the weighted average cost per unit of inventory at the time of each sale. Weighted average cost per unit at the time of each sale equals the cost of goods available for sale divided by the units available. The results using weighted average for Trekking are shown in Exhibit 6.7.

Point: Under weighted average, a unit sold is assigned the average cost of all items currently available for sale at the date of each sale.

Trekking's cost of goods sold reported on the income statement (reflecting the 43 units sold) is **$4,622** ($2,000 + $2,622), and its ending inventory reported on the balance sheet (reflecting the 12 units unsold) is **$1,368**.

The purchases and sales entries for Exhibit 6.7 follow (the boldface numbers are those affected by the cost flow assumption):

Purchases

Date	Account	Debit	Credit
Aug. 3	Merchandise Inventory	1,590	
	Accounts Payable		1,590
17	Merchandise Inventory	2,300	
	Accounts Payable		2,300
28	Merchandise Inventory	1,190	
	Accounts Payable		1,190

Sales

Date	Account	Debit	Credit
Aug. 14	Accounts Receivable	2,600	
	Sales		2,600
14	Cost of Goods Sold	**2,000**	
	Merchandise Inventory		**2,000**
31	Accounts Receivable	3,450	
	Sales		3,450
31	Cost of Goods Sold	**2,622**	
	Merchandise Inventory		**2,622**

Date	Goods Purchased	Cost of Goods Sold	Inventory Balance	
Aug. 1	Beginning balance		10 @ $ 91	= $ 910
Aug. 3	15 @ $106 = $1,590		10 @ $ 91 15 @ $106	= $2,500 (or $100 per unit)[a]
Aug. 14		20 @ $100 = $2,000	5 @ $100	= $ 500 (or $100 per unit)[b]
Aug. 17	20 @ $115 = $2,300		5 @ $100 20 @ $115	= $2,800 (or $112 per unit)[c]
Aug. 28	10 @ $119 = $1,190		5 @ $100 20 @ $115 10 @ $119	= $3,990 (or $114 per unit)[d]
Aug. 31		23 @ $114 = $2,622	12 @ $114	= $1,368 (or $114 per unit)[e]
		$4,622		

[a] $100 per unit = ($2,500 inventory balance ÷ 25 units in inventory).

[b] $100 per unit = ($500 inventory balance ÷ 5 units in inventory).

[c] $112 per unit = ($2,800 inventory balance ÷ 25 units in inventory).

[d] $114 per unit = ($3,990 inventory balance ÷ 35 units in inventory).

[e] $114 per unit = ($1,368 inventory balance ÷ 12 units in inventory).

Exhibit 6.7

Weighted Average Computations—Perpetual System

For the 20 units sold on Aug. 14, the cost assigned is the $100 *average cost* per unit from the inventory balance column at the time of sale.

For the 23 units sold on Aug. 31, the cost assigned is the $114 *average cost* per unit from the inventory balance column at the time of sale.

Advances in technology have greatly reduced the cost of a perpetual inventory system. Many companies are now asking whether they can afford *not* to have a perpetual inventory system because timely access to inventory information is a competitive advantage and it can help reduce the level of inventory, which reduces costs.

Decision Insight

Inventory War The Pentagon applies accounting tools to shrink inventories and speed deliveries. Use of bar codes, laser cards, radio tags, and perpetual accounting systems speeds delivery from factory to foxhole.

Financial Statement Effects of Costing Methods

A1 Analyze the effects of inventory methods for both financial and tax reporting.

When purchase prices do not change, each inventory costing method assigns the same cost amounts to inventory and to cost of goods sold. When purchase prices are different, however, the methods nearly always assign different cost amounts. We show these differences in Exhibit 6.8 using Trekking's data.

Exhibit 6.8

Financial Statement Effects of Inventory Costing Methods

TREKKING COMPANY
For Month Ended August 31

	Specific Identification	FIFO	LIFO	Weighted Average
Income Statement				
Sales	$6,050	$6,050	$6,050	$6,050
Cost of goods sold	4,582	4,570	4,730	4,622
Gross profit	1,468	1,480	1,320	1,428
Expenses	450	450	450	450
Income before taxes	1,018	1,030	870	978
Income tax expense (30%)	305	309	261	293
Net income	$ 713	$ 721	$ 609	$ 685
Balance Sheet				
Inventory	$1,408	$1,420	$1,260	$1,368

When purchase costs *regularly rise,* as in Trekking's case, note the following:

Point: FIFO is preferred when costs are rising and managers have incentives to report higher income for reasons such as bonus plans, job security, and reputation.

- FIFO assigns the lowest amount to cost of goods sold—yielding the highest gross profit and net income.
- LIFO assigns the highest amount to cost of goods sold—yielding the lowest gross profit and net income, which also yields a temporary tax advantage by postponing payment of some income tax.
- Weighted average yields results between FIFO and LIFO.
- Specific identification always yields results that depend on which units are sold.

Point: LIFO inventory is often less than the inventory's replacement cost because LIFO inventory is valued using the oldest inventory purchase costs.

When costs *regularly decline,* the reverse occurs for FIFO and LIFO.

All four inventory costing methods are acceptable. However, a company must disclose the inventory method it uses in its financial statements or notes. Each method offers certain advantages as follows:

- FIFO assigns an amount to inventory on the balance sheet that approximates its current cost; it also mimics the actual flow of goods for most businesses.
- LIFO assigns an amount to cost of goods sold on the income statement that approximates its current cost; it also better matches current costs with revenues in computing gross profit.
- Weighted average tends to smooth out erratic changes in costs.
- Specific identification exactly matches the costs of items with the revenues they generate.

Decision Maker

Financial Planner One of your clients asks if the inventory account of a company using FIFO needs any "adjustments" for analysis purposes in light of recent inflation. What is your advice? Does your advice depend on changes in the costs of these inventories?

Answer—p. 245

Decision Insight

Giving for Growth A recent survey found 76% of consumers saying they'd switch from their current product to one with a "good cause" if price and quality are equal. Many entrepreneurs combine their business ventures with their social passions for a win-win situation.

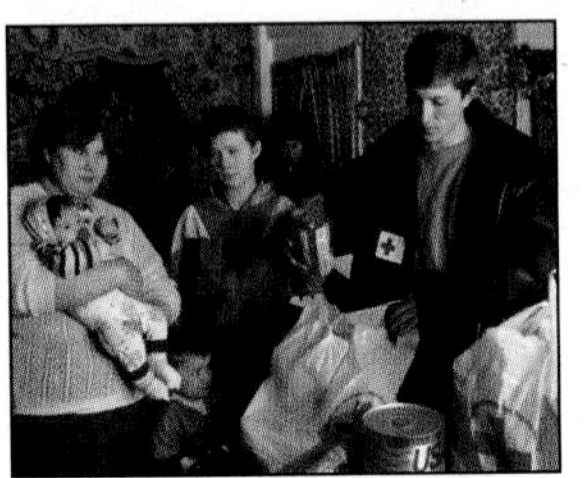

Tax Effects of Costing Methods Trekking's segment income statement in Exhibit 6.8 includes income tax expense (at a rate of 30%) because it was formed as a corporation. Since inventory costs affect net income, they have potential tax effects. Trekking gains a temporary tax advantage by using LIFO. Many companies use LIFO for this reason.

Companies can and often do use different costing methods for financial reporting and tax reporting. *The only exception is when LIFO is used for tax reporting; in this case, the IRS requires that it also be used in financial statements.*

Consistency in Using Costing Methods

Global: LIFO is acceptable under international accounting standards.

The **consistency principle** prescribes that a company use the same accounting methods period after period so that financial statements are comparable across periods—the only exception is when a change from one method to another will improve its financial reporting. The *full-disclosure principle* prescribes that the notes to the statements report this type of change, its justification, and its effect on net income.

The consistency principle does *not* require a company to use one method exclusively. For example, it can use different methods to value different categories of inventory.

Decision Ethics

Inventory Manager Your compensation as inventory manager includes a bonus plan based on gross profit. Your superior asks your opinion on changing the inventory costing method from FIFO to LIFO. Since costs are expected to continue to rise, your superior predicts that LIFO would match higher current costs against sales, thereby lowering taxable income (and gross profit). What do you recommend?

Answer—p. 245

Quick Check

4. Describe one advantage for each of the inventory costing methods: specific identification, FIFO, LIFO, and weighted average.
5. When costs are rising, which method reports higher net income—LIFO or FIFO?
6. When costs are rising, what effect does LIFO have on a balance sheet compared to FIFO?
7. A company takes a physical count of inventory at the end of 2005 and finds that ending inventory is understated by $10,000. Would this error cause cost of goods sold to be overstated or understated in 2005? In year 2006? If so, by how much?

Answers—p. 245

Valuing Inventory at LCM and the Effects of Inventory Errors

This section examines the role of market costs in determining inventory on the balance sheet and also the financial statement effects of inventory errors.

Lower of Cost or Market

P2 Compute the lower of cost or market amount of inventory.

We explained how to assign costs to ending inventory and cost of goods sold using one of four costing methods (FIFO, LIFO, weighted average, or specific identification). However, *accounting principles require that inventory be reported at the market value (cost) of replacing inventory when market value is lower than cost.* Merchandise inventory is then said to be reported on the balance sheet at the **lower of cost or market (LCM).**

Computing the Lower of Cost or Market *Market* in the term *LCM* is defined as the current replacement cost of purchasing the same inventory items in the usual manner. A decline in replacement cost reflects a loss of value in inventory. When the recorded cost of inventory is higher than the replacement cost, a loss is recognized. When the recorded cost is lower, no adjustment is made.

LCM is applied in one of three ways: (1) to each individual item separately, (2) to major categories of items, or (3) to the entire inventory. The less similar the items that make up inventory, the more likely companies are to apply LCM to individual items. To illustrate, we apply LCM to the ending inventory of a motorsports retailer in Exhibit 6.9.

Point: Advances in technology encourage the individual-item approach for LCM.

Exhibit 6.9

Lower of Cost or Market Computations

Inventory Items	Units	Per Unit Cost	Per Unit Market	Total Cost	Total Market	LCM Applied to Items	LCM Applied to Categories	LCM Applied to Whole
Cycles								
Roadster	20	$8,000	$7,000	$160,000	$140,000	$ 140,000		
Sprint	10	5,000	6,000	50,000	60,000	50,000		
Category subtotal				210,000	200,000		$ 200,000	
Off-Road								
Trax-4	8	5,000	6,500	40,000	52,000	40,000		
Blazer	5	9,000	7,000	45,000	35,000	35,000		
Category subtotal				85,000	87,000		85,000	
Totals				$295,000	$287,000	$265,000	$285,000	$287,000

When LCM is applied to the *entire* inventory, the market amount is $287,000. Since this market amount is $8,000 lower than the $295,000 recorded cost, the $287,000 amount is reported for inventory on the balance sheet. When LCM is applied to the major *categories* of inventory, the market is $285,000. When LCM is applied to individual *items* of inventory, the market is $265,000. Since market amounts for these cases are less than the $295,000 recorded cost, the market amount is reported for inventory. Any one of these three applications of LCM is acceptable. The retailer **Best Buy** applies LCM and reports that its "merchandise inventories are recorded at the lower of average cost or market."

Global: In Canada, the Netherlands, and the United Kingdom, the *market* in LCM is defined as "net realizable value" (selling price less costs to complete and sell).

Recording the Lower of Cost or Market Inventory must be adjusted downward when market is less than cost. To illustrate, if LCM is applied to the individual items of inventory in Exhibit 6.9, the Merchandise Inventory account must be adjusted from the $295,000 recorded cost down to the $265,000 market amount as follows

Cost of Goods Sold	30,000	
Merchandise Inventory		30,000
To adjust inventory cost to market.		

Accounting rules require that inventory be adjusted to market when market is less than cost, but inventory usually cannot be written up to market when market exceeds cost. If recording inventory down to market is acceptable, why are companies not allowed to record inventory up to market? One view is that a gain from a market increase should not be realized until a sales transaction verifies the gain. However, this problem also applies when market is less than cost. A second and primary reason is the **conservatism principle,** which prescribes the use of the less optimistic amount when more than one estimate of the amount to be received or paid exists and these estimates are about equally likely.

Financial Statement Effects of Inventory Errors

A2 Analyze the effects of inventory errors on current and future financial statements.

Topic Tackler 6-2

Companies must take care in both taking a physical count of inventory and in assigning a cost to it. An inventory error causes misstatements in cost of goods sold, gross profit, net income, current assets, and equity. It also causes misstatements in the next period's statements because ending inventory of one period is the beginning inventory of the next.

Income Statement Effects Exhibit 6.10 shows the effects of inventory errors on key amounts in the current period's income statement. Notice that inventory errors yield opposite effects in cost of goods sold and net income. Inventory errors also carry over to the next period, yielding reverse effects.

Exhibit 6.10

Effects of Inventory Errors on the Current Period's Income Statement

Inventory Error	Cost of Goods Sold	Net Income
Understate ending inventory	Overstated	Understated
Understate beginning inventory	Understated	Overstated
Overstate ending inventory*	Understated	Overstated
Overstate beginning inventory*	Overstated	Understated

* These errors are less likely under a perpetual system because they imply more inventory than is recorded (or less shrinkage than expected). Thus, management will normally follow up and discover and correct these errors before they impact any accounts.

To illustrate, consider an inventory error for a company with $100,000 in sales for each of the years 2004, 2005, and 2006. If this company maintains a steady $20,000 inventory level during this period and makes $60,000 in purchases in each of these years, its cost of goods sold is $60,000 and its gross profit is $40,000 each year. What if this company errs in computing its 2004 ending inventory and reports $16,000 instead of the correct amount of $20,000? The effects of this error are shown in Exhibit 6.11. The $4,000 understatement of the year 2004 ending inventory causes a $4,000 overstatement in year 2004 cost of goods sold and a $4,000 understatement in both gross profit and net income for year 2004. Since year 2004 ending inventory becomes year 2005 beginning inventory, this error causes an understatement in 2005 cost of goods sold and a $4,000 overstatement in both gross profit and net income for year 2005. Notice that an inventory error in period 1 (2004) does not affect the period 3, year 2006. An inventory error is said to be *self-correcting* because it always yields an offsetting error in the next period. This, however, does not make inventory errors less serious. Managers, lenders, owners, and other users make important decisions from analysis of changes in net income and cost of goods sold.

Point: A former internal auditor at Coca-Cola alleges that just before midnight at the 2002 period-end, fully loaded Coke trucks were ordered to drive about 2 feet away from the loading dock so that Coke could record millions of dollars in extra sales.

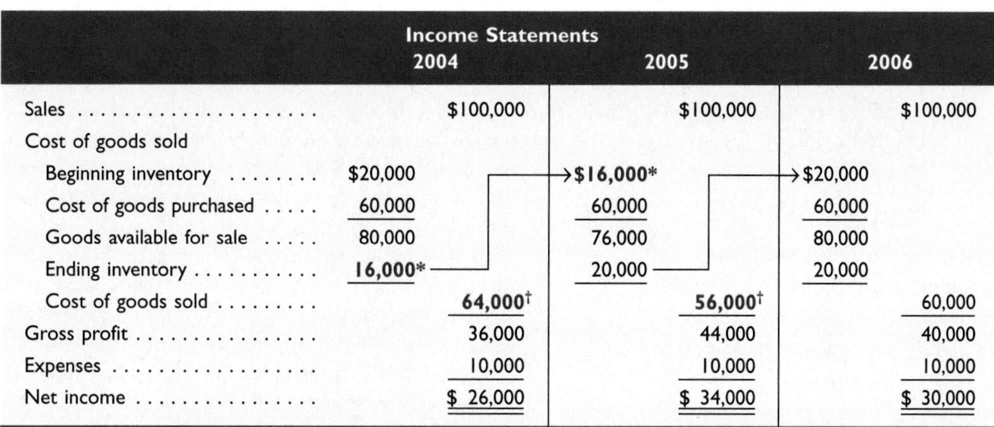

Income Statements	2004		2005		2006	
Sales		$100,000		$100,000		$100,000
Cost of goods sold						
Beginning inventory	$20,000		→$16,000*		→$20,000	
Cost of goods purchased	60,000		60,000		60,000	
Goods available for sale	80,000		76,000		80,000	
Ending inventory	16,000*		20,000		20,000	
Cost of goods sold		64,000†		56,000†		60,000
Gross profit		36,000		44,000		40,000
Expenses		10,000		10,000		10,000
Net income		$ 26,000		$ 34,000		$ 30,000

* Correct amount is $20,000. † Correct amount is $60,000.

Exhibit 6.11

Effects of Inventory Errors on Three Periods' Income Statements

Example: If year 2004 ending inventory in Exhibit 6.11 is overstated by $3,000, what is the effect on cost of goods sold, gross profit, assets, and equity? *Answer:* Cost of goods sold is understated by $3,000 in 2004 and overstated by $3,000 in 2005. Gross profit and net income are overstated in 2004 and understated in 2005. Assets and equity are overstated in 2004.

Balance Sheet Effects Balance sheet effects of an inventory error can be seen by considering the components of the accounting equation: Assets = Liabilities + Equity. For example, understating ending inventory understates both current and total assets. An understatement in ending inventory also yields an understatement in equity because of the understatement in net income. Exhibit 6.12 shows the effects of inventory errors on the current period's balance sheet amounts. Errors in *beginning* inventory do not yield misstatements in the end-of-period balance sheet, but they do affect that current period's income statement.

Inventory Error	Assets	Equity
Understate ending inventory	Understated	Understated
Overstate ending inventory	Overstated	Overstated

Exhibit 6.12

Effects of Inventory Errors on Current Period's Balance Sheet

Quick Check

8. Use LCM applied separately to individual items to compute ending inventory if the data are as follows:

Product	Units	Unit Recorded Cost	Unit Market Cost
A	20	$ 6	$ 5
B	40	9	8
C	10	12	15

Answer—p. 246

Inventory Turnover and Days' Sales in Inventory

Decision Analysis

Inventory Turnover

A3 Assess inventory management using both inventory turnover and days' sales in inventory.

Earlier chapters described two important ratios useful in evaluating a company's short-term liquidity: current ratio and acid-test ratio. A merchandiser's ability to pay its short-term obligations also depends on how quickly it sells its merchandise inventory. **Inventory turnover,** also called *merchandise inventory turnover,* is one ratio used to assess this and is defined in Exhibit 6.13.

$$\textbf{Inventory turnover} = \frac{\textbf{Cost of goods sold}}{\textbf{Average inventory}}$$

Exhibit 6.13

Inventory Turnover

Point: We must take care when comparing turnover ratios across companies that use different costing methods (such as FIFO and LIFO).

This ratio reveals how many *times* a company turns over (sells) its inventory during a period. If a company's inventory greatly varies within a year, average inventory amounts can be computed from interim periods such as quarters or months.

Users apply inventory turnover to help analyze short-term liquidity and to assess whether management is doing a good job controlling the amount of inventory available. A low ratio compared to that of competitors suggests inefficient use of assets. The company may be holding more inventory than it needs to support its sales volume. Similarly, a very high ratio compared to that of competitors suggests inventory might be too low. This can cause lost sales if customers must back order merchandise. Inventory turnover has no simple rule except to say *a high ratio is preferable provided inventory is adequate to meet demand.*

Decision Insight

Dell-ocity From its roots in a college dorm room, **Dell** now sells 50 million dollars' worth of computers each day from its Website. The speed of Web technology has allowed Dell to slash inventories. Dell's operating cycle is less than 15 hours and its days' sales in inventory is 3 days. Michael Dell asserts, "Speed is everything in this business."

Days' Sales in Inventory

Point: Inventory turnover is higher and days' sales in inventory is lower for industries such as foods and other perishable products. The reverse holds for nonperishable product industries.

To better interpret inventory turnover, many users measure the adequacy of inventory to meet sales demand. **Days' sales in inventory,** also called *days' stock on hand,* is a ratio that reveals how much inventory is available in terms of the number of days' sales. It can be interpreted as the number of days one can sell from inventory if no new items are purchased. This ratio is often viewed as a measure of the buffer against out-of-stock inventory and is useful in evaluating liquidity of inventory. It is defined in Exhibit 6.14.

Exhibit 6.14

Days' Sales in Inventory

$$\textbf{Days' sales in inventory} = \frac{\textbf{Ending inventory}}{\textbf{Cost of goods sold}} \times 365$$

Days' sales in inventory focuses on ending inventory and it estimates how many days it will take to convert inventory at the end of a period into accounts receivable or cash. Notice that days' sales in inventory focuses on *ending* inventory whereas inventory turnover focuses on *average* inventory.

Analysis of Inventory Management

Inventory management is a major emphasis for merchandisers. They must both plan and control inventory purchases and sales. Toys "R" Us is one of those merchandisers. Its inventory in fiscal year 2003 was $2,190 million. This inventory constituted 62% of its current assets and 23% of its total assets. We apply the analysis tools in this section to Toys "R" Us, as shown in Exhibit 6.15.

Its 2003 inventory turnover of 3.7 times means that Toys "R" Us turns over its inventory 3.7 times per year, or once every 99 days (365 days ÷ 3.7). We prefer inventory turnover to be high provided inventory is not out of stock and the company is not losing customers. The 2003 days' sales in inventory of 102 days reveals that it is carrying 102 days of sales in inventory. This inventory buffer seems more than adequate. Toys "R" Us would benefit from further management efforts to increase inventory turnover and reduce inventory levels.

Decision Maker

Entrepreneur Analysis of your retail store yields an inventory turnover of 5.0 and a days' sales in inventory of 73 days. The industry norm for inventory turnover is 4.4 and for days' sales in inventory is 74 days. What is your assessment of inventory management?

Answer—p. 245

Exhibit 6.15

Inventory Turnover and Days' Sales in Inventory for Toys "R" Us

($ in millions)	2003	2002	2001
Cost of goods sold	$7,799	$7,604	$7,815
Ending inventory	$2,190	$2,041	$2,307
Inventory turnover	**3.7** times	**3.5** times	**3.6** times
Industry inventory turnover	2.6 times	2.5 times	2.8 times
Days' sales in inventory	**102** days	**98** days	**108** days
Industry days' sales in inventory	139 days	146 days	130 days

Demonstration Problem

Craig Company uses a perpetual inventory system for its one product. Its beginning inventory, purchases, and sales during year 2005 follow:

Date	Activity	Units Acquired at Cost		Units Sold at Retail	Unit Inventory
Jan. 1	Beg. Inventory . .	400 units @ $14 =	$5,600		400 units
Jan. 15	Sale			200 units @ $30	200 units
March 10	Purchase	200 units @ $15 =	$3,000		400 units
April 1	Sale			200 units @ $30	200 units
May 9	Purchase	300 units @ $16 =	$4,800		500 units
Sept. 22	Purchase	250 units @ $20 =	$5,000		750 units
Nov. 1	Sale			300 units @ $35	450 units
Nov. 28	Purchase	100 units @ $21 =	$2,100		550 units
	Totals	1,250 units	$20,500	700 units	

Additional tracking data for applying specific identification: (1) January 15 sale—200 units @ $14, (2) April 1 sale—200 units @ $15, and (3) November 1 sale—200 units @ $14 and 100 units @ $20.

Required

1. Calculate the cost of goods available for sale.
2. Apply the four different methods of inventory costing (FIFO, LIFO, weighted average, and specific identification) to calculate ending inventory and cost of goods sold under each method.
3. In preparing financial statements for year 2005, the financial officer was instructed to use FIFO but failed to do so and instead computed cost of goods sold according to LIFO. Determine the impact on year 2005's income from the error. Also determine the effect of this error on year 2006's income. Assume no income taxes.
4. Management wants a report that shows how changing from FIFO to another method would change net income. Prepare a table showing (1) the cost of goods sold amount under each of the four methods, (2) the amount by which each cost of goods sold total is different from the FIFO cost of goods sold, and (3) the effect on net income if another method is used instead of FIFO.

Planning the Solution

- Compute cost of goods available for sale by multiplying the units of beginning inventory and each purchase by their unit costs to determine the total cost of goods available for sale.
- Prepare a perpetual FIFO table starting with beginning inventory and showing how inventory changes after each purchase and after each sale (see Exhibit 6.5).
- Prepare a perpetual LIFO table starting with beginning inventory and showing how inventory changes after each purchase and after each sale (see Exhibit 6.6).
- Make a table of purchases and sales recalculating the average cost of inventory prior to each sale to arrive at the weighted average cost of ending inventory. Total the average costs associated with each sale to determine cost of goods sold (see Exhibit 6.7).
- Prepare a table showing the computation of cost of goods sold and ending inventory using the specific identification method (see Exhibit 6.4).
- Compare the year-end 2005 inventory amounts under FIFO and LIFO to determine the misstatement of year 2005 income that results from using LIFO. The errors for year 2005 and 2006 are equal in amount but opposite in effect.
- Create a table showing cost of goods sold under each method and how net income would differ from FIFO net income if an alternate method is adopted.

Solution to Demonstration Problem

1. Cost of goods available for sale (this amount is the same for all methods):

Date		Units	Unit Cost	Total Cost
Jan. 1	Beg. Inventory	400	$14	$ 5,600
March 10	Purchase	200	15	3,000
May 9	Purchase	300	16	4,800
Sept. 22	Purchase	250	20	5,000
Nov. 28	Purchase	100	21	2,100
Total cost of goods available for sale				$20,500

2a. FIFO perpetual method:

Date	Goods Purchased	Cost of Goods Sold	Inventory Balance	
Jan. 1	Beginning balance		400 @ $14	= $ 5,600
Jan. 15		200 @ $14 = $2,800	200 @ $14	= $ 2,800
Mar. 10	200 @ $15 = $3,000		200 @ $14 200 @ $15	= $ 5,800
April 1		200 @ $14 = $2,800	200 @ $15	= $ 3,000
May 9	300 @ $16 = $4,800		200 @ $15 300 @ $16	= $ 7,800
Sept. 22	250 @ $20 = $5,000		200 @ $15 300 @ $16 250 @ $20	= $12,800
Nov. 1		200 @ $15 = $3,000 100 @ $16 = $1,600	200 @ $16 250 @ $20	= $ 8,200
Nov. 28	100 @ $21 = $2,100		200 @ $16 250 @ $20 100 @ $21	= **$10,300**
Total cost of goods sold		**$10,200**		

Note to students: **In a classroom situation,** once we compute cost of goods available for sale, we can compute the amount for either cost of goods sold or ending inventory—it is a matter of preference. **In practice,** the costs of items sold are identified as sales are made and immediately transferred from the inventory account to the cost of goods sold account. The previous solution showing the line-by-line approach illustrates actual application in practice. The following alternate solutions illustrate that, once the concepts are understood, other solution approaches are available—although this is only shown for FIFO, it could be shown for all methods.

Alternate Methods to Compute FIFO Perpetual Numbers

[FIFO Alternate No. 1: Computing cost of goods sold first]

Cost of goods available for sale (from part 1)			$ 20,500
Cost of goods sold			
Jan. 15	Sold (200 @ $14)	$2,800	
April 1	Sold (200 @ $14)	2,800	
Nov. 1	Sold (200 @ $15 and 100 @ $16)	4,600	10,200
Ending inventory			**$10,300**

[FIFO Alternate No. 2: Computing ending inventory first]

Cost of goods available for sale (from part 1)			$ 20,500
Ending inventory*			
Nov. 28	Purchase (100 @ $21)	$2,100	
Sept. 22	Purchase (250 @ $20)	5,000	
May 9	Purchase (200 @ $16)	3,200	
Ending inventory			**10,300**
Cost of goods sold			**$10,200**

* Since FIFO assumes that the earlier costs are the first to flow out, we determine ending inventory by assigning the most recent costs to the remaining items.

2b. LIFO perpetual method:

Date	Goods Purchased	Cost of Goods Sold	Inventory Balance	
Jan. 1	Beginning balance		400 @ $14	= $ 5,600
Jan. 15		200 @ $14 = $2,800	200 @ $14	= $ 2,800
Mar. 10	200 @ $15 = $3,000		200 @ $14 200 @ $15	= $ 5,800
April 1		200 @ $15 = $3,000	200 @ $14	= $ 2,800
May 9	300 @ $16 = $4,800		200 @ $14 300 @ $16	= $ 7,600
Sept. 22	250 @ $20 = $5,000		200 @ $14 300 @ $16 250 @ $20	= $12,600
Nov. 1		250 @ $20 = $5,000 50 @ $16 = $ 800	200 @ $14 250 @ $16	= $ 6,800
Nov. 28	100 @ $21 = $2,100		200 @ $14 250 @ $16 100 @ $21	= **$ 8,900**
Total cost of goods sold		**$11,600**		

2c. Weighted average perpetual method:

Date	Goods Purchased	Cost of Goods Sold	Inventory Balance	
Jan. 1	Beginning balance		400 @ $14	= $ 5,600
Jan. 15		200 @ $14 = $2,800	200 @ $14	= $ 2,800
Mar. 10	200 @ $15 = $3,000		200 @ $14 200 @ $15 (avg. cost is $14.5)	= $ 5,800
April 1		200 @ $14.5 = $2,900	200 @ $14.5	= $ 2,900
May 9	300 @ $16 = $4,800		200 @ $14.5 300 @ $16 (avg. cost is $15.4)	= $ 7,700

[continued on next page]

[continued from previous page]

Sept. 22	250 @ $20 = $5,000		200 @ $14.5 300 @ $16 250 @ $20 } = $ 12,700 (avg. cost is $16.93)
Nov. 1		300 @ $16.93 = $5,079	450 @ $16.93 = $ 7,618.5
Nov. 28	100 @ $21 = $2,100		450 @ $16.93 100 @ $21 } = $9,718.5
Total cost of goods sold*		$10,779	

* The cost of goods sold ($10,779) plus ending inventory ($9,718.5) is $2.5 less than the cost of goods available for sale ($20,500) due to rounding.

2d. Specific identification method:

Date	Goods Purchased	Cost of Goods Sold	Inventory Balance
Jan. 1	Beginning balance		400 @ $14 = $ 5,600
Jan. 15		200 @ $14 = $2,800	200 @ $14 = $ 2,800
Mar. 10	200 @ $15 = $3,000		200 @ $14 200 @ $15 } = $ 5,800
April 1		200 @ $15 = $3,000	200 @ $14 = $ 2,800
May 9	300 @ $16 = $4,800		200 @ $14 300 @ $16 } = $ 7,600
Sept. 22	250 @ $20 = $5,000		200 @ $14 300 @ $16 250 @ $20 } = $12,600
Nov. 1		200 @ $14 = $2,800 100 @ $20 = $2,000	300 @ $16 150 @ $20 } = $ 7,800
Nov. 28	100 @ $21 = $2,100		300 @ $16 150 @ $20 100 @ $21 } = $ 9,900
Total cost of goods sold		$10,600	

3. Mistakenly using LIFO when FIFO should have been used overstates cost of goods sold in year 2005 by $1,400, which is the difference between the FIFO and LIFO amounts of ending inventory. It understates income in 2005 by $1,400. In year 2006, income is overstated by $1,400 because of the understatement in beginning inventory.

4. Analysis of the effects of alternative inventory methods:

	Cost of Goods Sold	Difference from FIFO Cost of Goods Sold	Effect on Net Income if Adopted Instead of FIFO
FIFO	$10,200	—	—
LIFO	11,600	+$1,400	$1,400 lower
Weighted average	10,779	+ 579	579 lower
Specific identification	10,600	+ 400	400 lower

APPENDIX

Inventory Costing Under a Periodic System 6A

The basic aim of the periodic system and the perpetual system is the same: to assign costs to inventory and cost of goods sold. The same four methods are used to assign costs under both systems: specific identification; first-in, first-out; last-in, first-out; and weighted average. We use information from Trekking to show how to assign costs using these four methods with a periodic system. Data for sales and purchases are reported in the chapter (see Exhibit 6.3). Recall that we explained the accounting under a periodic system in Appendix 5A.

P3 Compute inventory in a periodic system using the methods of specific identification, FIFO, LIFO, and weighted average.

Specific Identification

We use the information in Exhibit 6.3 and the specific identification method to assign costs to the 12 units in ending inventory and to the 43 units sold as shown in Exhibit 6A.1. Carefully study Exhibit 6A.1 to see the flow of costs both in and out of inventory. Notice that each unit, whether sold or remaining in inventory, has its own specific cost attached to it.

Exhibit 6A.1

Specific Identification Computations

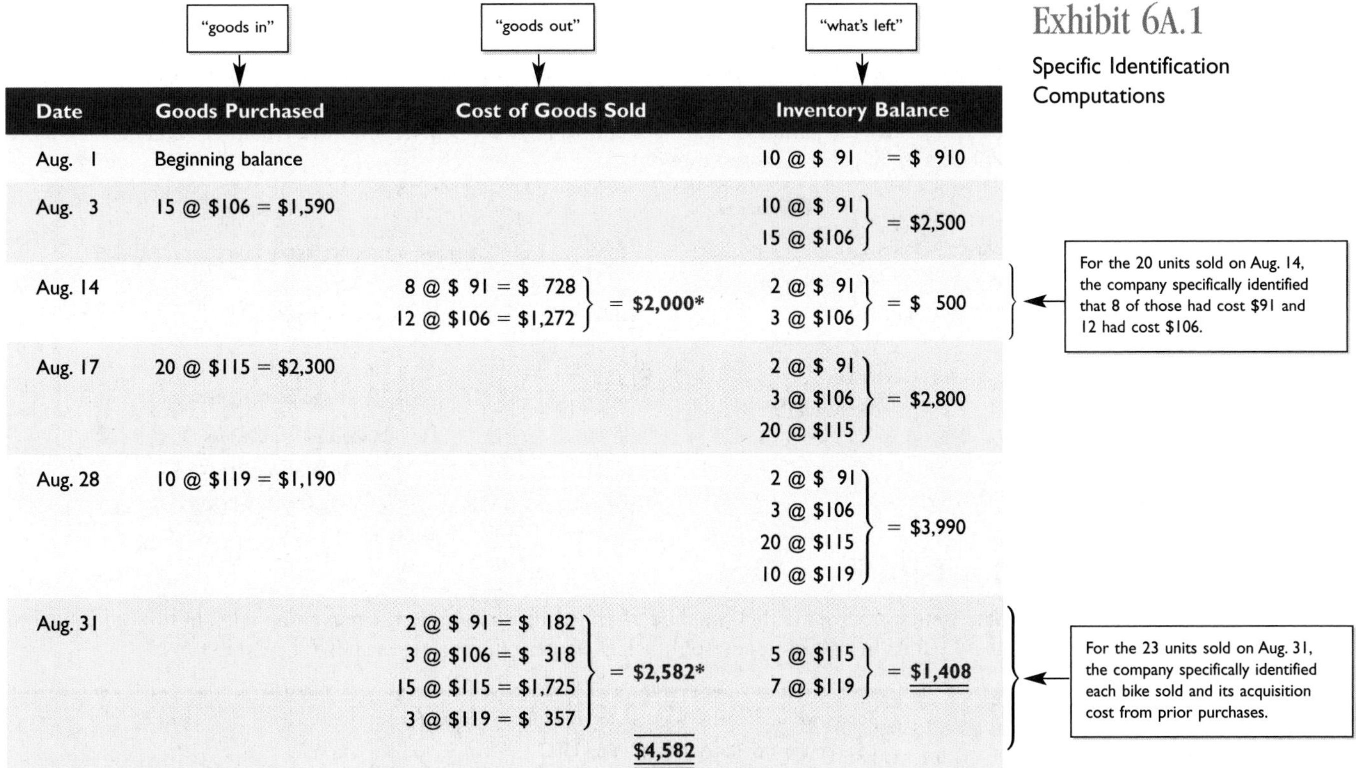

Date	Goods Purchased ("goods in")	Cost of Goods Sold ("goods out")		Inventory Balance ("what's left")	
Aug. 1	Beginning balance			10 @ $ 91	= $ 910
Aug. 3	15 @ $106 = $1,590			10 @ $ 91 15 @ $106	= $2,500
Aug. 14		8 @ $ 91 = $ 728 12 @ $106 = $1,272	= $2,000*	2 @ $ 91 3 @ $106	= $ 500
Aug. 17	20 @ $115 = $2,300			2 @ $ 91 3 @ $106 20 @ $115	= $2,800
Aug. 28	10 @ $119 = $1,190			2 @ $ 91 3 @ $106 20 @ $115 10 @ $119	= $3,990
Aug. 31		2 @ $ 91 = $ 182 3 @ $106 = $ 318 15 @ $115 = $1,725 3 @ $119 = $ 357	= $2,582*	5 @ $115 7 @ $119	= $1,408
			$4,582		

For the 20 units sold on Aug. 14, the company specifically identified that 8 of those had cost $91 and 12 had cost $106.

For the 23 units sold on Aug. 31, the company specifically identified each bike sold and its acquisition cost from prior purchases.

* Identification of items sold (and their costs) is obtained from internal documents that track each unit from its purchase to its sale.

When using specific identification, Trekking's cost of goods sold reported on the income statement totals **$4,582**, the sum of $2,000 and $2,582 from the third column of Exhibit 6A.1. Trekking's ending inventory reported on the balance sheet is **$1,408**, which is the final inventory balance from the fourth column of Exhibit 6A.1. The purchases and sales entries for Exhibit 6A.1 follow (the

Point: The assignment of costs to the goods sold and to inventory using specific identification is the same for both the perpetual and periodic systems.

boldface numbers are those affected by the cost flow assumption):

Purchases				Sales			
Aug. 3	Purchases	1,590		Aug. 14	Accounts Receivable	2,600	
	Accounts Payable		1,590		Sales................		2,600
17	Purchases	2,300		31	Accounts Receivable	3,450	
	Accounts Payable		2,300		Sales................		3,450
28	Purchases	1,190			**Adjusting Entry**		
	Accounts Payable		1,190	31	Merchandise Inventory.......	**1,408**	
					Income Summary		498
					Merchandise Inventory...		**910**

First-In, First-Out

The first-in, first-out (FIFO) method of assigning cost to both inventory and cost of goods sold using the periodic system is shown in Exhibit 6A.2.

Exhibit 6A.2

FIFO Computations—Periodic System

Exhibit 6.3 shows that the 12 units in ending inventory consist of 10 units from the latest purchase on Aug. 28 and 2 units from the next latest purchase on Aug. 17.

Total cost of 55 units available for sale (from Exhibit 6.3)		$5,990
Less ending inventory priced using FIFO		
10 units from August 28 purchase at $119 each	$1,190	
2 units from August 17 purchase at $115 each	230	
Ending inventory		**1,420**
Cost of goods sold		**$4,570**

Point: The assignment of costs to the goods sold and to inventory using FIFO is the same for both the perpetual and periodic systems.

Trekking's ending inventory reported on the balance sheet is **$1,420**, and its cost of goods sold reported on the income statement is **$4,570**. These amounts are the same as those computed using the perpetual system. This always occurs because the most recent purchases are in ending inventory under both systems. The purchases and sales entries for Exhibit 6A.2 follow (the boldface numbers are those affected by the cost flow assumption):

Purchases				Sales			
Aug. 3	Purchases................	1,590		Aug. 14	Accounts Receivable	2,600	
	Accounts Payable.......		1,590		Sales		2,600
17	Purchases................	2,300		31	Accounts Receivable	3,450	
	Accounts Payable.......		2,300		Sales		3,450
28	Purchases................	1,190			**Adjusting Entry**		
	Accounts Payable.......		1,190	31	Merchandise Inventory......	**1,420**	
					Income Summary		510
					Merchandise Inventory ..		**910**

Last-In, First-Out

The last-in, first-out (LIFO) method of assigning costs to the 12 remaining units in inventory (and to the 43 units in cost of goods sold) using the periodic system is shown in Exhibit 6A.3.

Exhibit 6A.3

LIFO Computations—Periodic System

Exhibit 6.3 shows that the 12 units in ending inventory consist of 10 units from the earliest purchase (beg. inv.) and 2 units from the next earliest purchase on Aug. 3.

Total cost of 55 units available for sale (from Exhibit 6.3)		$5,990
Less ending inventory priced using LIFO		
10 units in beginning inventory at $91 each	$910	
2 units from August 3 purchase at $106 each	212	
Ending inventory		**1,122**
Cost of goods sold		**$4,868**

Trekking's ending inventory reported on the balance sheet is **$1,122**, and its cost of goods sold reported on the income statement is **$4,868**. When LIFO is used with the periodic system, cost of goods sold is assigned costs from the most recent purchases for the period. With a perpetual system, cost of goods sold is assigned costs from the most recent purchases at the point of *each sale*. The purchases and sales entries for Exhibit 6A.3 follow (the boldface numbers are those affected by the cost flow assumption):

Purchases

Aug. 3	Purchases	1,590	
	Accounts Payable		1,590
17	Purchases	2,300	
	Accounts Payable		2,300
28	Purchases	1,190	
	Accounts Payable		1,190

Sales

Aug. 14	Accounts Receivable	2,600	
	Sales		2,600
31	Accounts Receivable	3,450	
	Sales		3,450
	Adjusting Entry		
31	Merchandise Inventory	**1,122**	
	Income Summary		212
	Merchandise Inventory		**910**

Weighted Average

The weighted average method of assigning cost involves three important steps. The first two steps are shown in Exhibit 6A.4. First, multiply the per unit cost for beginning inventory and each particular purchase by the corresponding number of units (from Exhibit 6.3). Second, add these amounts and divide by the total number of units available for sale to find the weighted average cost per unit.

Exhibit 6A.4

Weighted Average Cost per Unit

Step 1:	10 units @ $ 91 = $ 910
	15 units @ $106 = 1,590
	20 units @ $115 = 2,300
	10 units @ $119 = 1,190
	55 $5,990
Step 2:	$5,990/55 units = **$108.91** weighted average cost per unit

Example: In Exhibit 6A.4, if 5 more units had been purchased at $120 each, what would be the weighted average cost per unit?
Answer: $109.83 ($6,590/60)

The third step is to use the weighted average cost per unit to assign costs to inventory and to the units sold as shown in Exhibit 6A.5.

Exhibit 6A.5

Weighted Average Computations—Periodic

Step 3:	Total cost of 55 units available for sale (from Exhibit 6.3)	$5,990
	Less **ending inventory** priced on a weighted average cost basis: 12 units at $108.91 each (from Exhibit 6A.4)	1,307
	Cost of goods sold	**$4,683**

Trekking's ending inventory reported on the balance sheet is **$1,307**, and its cost of goods sold reported on the income statement is **$4,683** when using the weighted average (periodic) method. The purchases and sales entries for Exhibit 6A.5 follow (the boldface numbers are those affected by the cost flow assumption):

Point: Weighted average usually yields different results for the perpetual and the periodic systems because under a perpetual system it recomputes the per unit cost prior to each sale, whereas under a periodic system, the per unit cost is computed only at the end of a period.

Purchases

Aug. 3	Purchases	1,590	
	Accounts Payable		1,590
17	Purchases	2,300	
	Accounts Payable		2,300
28	Purchases	1,190	
	Accounts Payable		1,190

Sales

Aug. 14	Accounts Receivable	2,600	
	Sales		2,600
31	Accounts Receivable	3,450	
	Sales		3,450
	Adjusting Entry		
31	Merchandise Inventory	**1,307**	
	Income Summary		397
	Merchandise Inventory . . .		**910**

Financial Statement Effects

When purchase prices do not change, each inventory costing method assigns the same cost amounts to inventory and to cost of goods sold. When purchase prices are different, however, the methods nearly always assign different cost amounts. We show these differences in Exhibit 6A.6 using Trekking's data. When purchase costs *regularly rise,* as in Trekking's case, note the following:

Point: LIFO inventory is often less than the inventory's replacement cost because LIFO inventory is valued using the oldest inventory purchase costs.

Exhibit 6A.6

Financial Statement Effects of Inventory Costing Methods

TREKKING COMPANY For Month Ended August 31	Specific Identification	FIFO	LIFO	Weighted Average
Income Statement				
Sales	$ 6,050	$ 6,050	$ 6,050	$ 6,050
Cost of goods sold	**4,582**	**4,570**	**4,868**	**4,683**
Gross profit	1,468	1,480	1,182	1,367
Expenses	450	450	450	450
Income before taxes	1,018	1,030	732	917
Income tax expense (30%)	305	309	220	275
Net income	**$ 713**	**$ 721**	**$ 512**	**$ 642**
Balance Sheet				
Inventory	**$1,408**	**$1,420**	**$1,122**	**$1,307**

- FIFO assigns the lowest amount to cost of goods sold—yielding the highest gross profit and net income.
- LIFO assigns the highest amount to cost of goods sold—yielding the lowest gross profit and net income, which also yields a temporary tax advantage by postponing payment of some income tax.
- Weighted average yields results between FIFO and LIFO.
- Specific identification always yields results that depend on which units are sold.

When costs *regularly decline,* the reverse occurs for FIFO and LIFO.

All four inventory costing methods are acceptable in practice. A company must disclose the inventory method it uses. Each method offers certain advantages as follows:

- FIFO assigns an amount to inventory on the balance sheet that approximates its current cost; it also mimics the actual flow of goods for most businesses.
- LIFO assigns an amount to cost of goods sold on the income statement that approximates its current cost; it also better matches current costs with revenues in computing gross profit.
- Weighted average tends to smooth out erratic changes in costs.
- Specific identification exactly matches the costs of items with the revenues they generate.

While Dilbert's suggestion may be easier said than done, it does reinforce the importance of inventory management. This includes attention to inventory turnover, days' sales in inventory, and other measures.

Quick Check

9. A company reports the following beginning inventory and purchases, and it ends the period with 30 units in inventory.

Beginning Inventory	100 units at $10 cost per unit
Purchase 1	40 units at $12 cost per unit
Purchase 2	20 units at $14 cost per unit

a. Compute ending inventory using the FIFO periodic system.

b. Compute cost of goods sold using the LIFO periodic system.

Answers—p. 246

APPENDIX

Inventory Estimation Methods 6B

P4 Apply both the retail inventory and gross profit methods to estimate inventory.

Inventory sometimes requires estimation for two reasons. First, companies may require **interim statements** (financial statements prepared for periods of less than one year), but they only annually take a physical count of inventory. Second, companies may require an inventory estimate if some casualty such as fire or flood makes taking a physical count impossible. Note that estimates are usually only required for companies that use the periodic system. Companies using a perpetual system would presumably have updated inventory data.

This appendix describes two methods to estimate inventory.

Retail Inventory Method

Point: When a retailer takes a physical inventory, it can restate the retail value of inventory to a cost basis by applying the cost-to-retail ratio. It can also estimate the amount of shrinkage by comparing the inventory computed with the amount from a physical inventory.

To avoid the time-consuming and expensive process of taking a physical inventory each month or quarter, some companies use the **retail inventory method** to estimate cost of goods sold and ending inventory. Some companies even use the retail inventory method to prepare the annual statements. **Home Depot**, for instance, says in its recent annual report: "Inventories are stated at the lower of cost (first-in, first-out) or market, as determined by the retail inventory method." A company may also estimate inventory for audit purposes or when inventory is damaged or destroyed.

The retail inventory method uses a three-step process to estimate ending inventory. We need to know the amount of inventory a company had at the beginning of the period in both *cost* and *retail* amounts. We already explained how to compute the cost of inventory. The *retail amount of inventory* refers to its dollar amount measured using selling prices of inventory items. We also need to know the net amount of goods purchased (minus returns, allowances, and discounts) in the period, both at cost and at retail. The amount of net sales at retail is also needed. The process is shown in Exhibit 6B.1.

The reasoning behind the retail inventory method is that if we can get a good estimate of the cost-to-retail ratio, we can multiply ending inventory at retail by this ratio to estimate ending inventory at cost. We show in Exhibit 6B.2 how these steps are applied to estimate ending inventory for

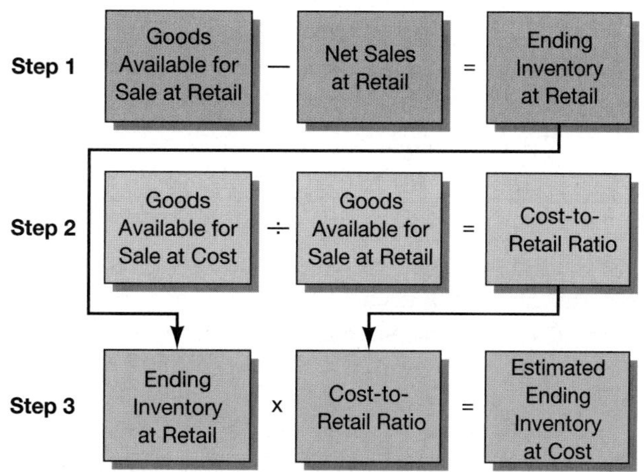

Exhibit 6B.1

Retail Inventory Method of Inventory Estimation

Exhibit 6B.2

Estimated Inventory Using the Retail Inventory Method

		At Cost	At Retail
	Goods available for sale		
	Beginning inventory	$ 20,500	$ 34,500
	Cost of goods purchased	39,500	65,500
Step 1:	Goods available for sale	60,000	100,000
	Deduct net sales at retail		**70,000**
	Ending inventory at retail		**$ 30,000**
Step 2:	**Cost-to-retail ratio: ($60,000 ÷ $100,000) = 60%**		
Step 3:	**Estimated ending inventory at cost ($30,000 × 60%)**	**$18,000**	

Example: What is the cost of ending inventory in Exhibit 6B.2 if the cost of beginning inventory is $22,500 and its retail value is $34,500? *Answer:* $30,000 × 62% = $18,600

a typical company. First, we find that $100,000 of goods (at retail selling prices) was available for sale. We see that $70,000 of these goods were sold, leaving $30,000 (retail value) of merchandise in ending inventory. Second, the cost of these goods is 60% of the $100,000 retail value. Third, since cost for these goods is 60% of retail, the estimated cost of ending inventory is $18,000.

Gross Profit Method

The **gross profit method** estimates the cost of ending inventory by applying the gross profit ratio to net sales (at retail). This type of estimate often is needed when inventory is destroyed, lost, or stolen. These cases require an inventory estimate so that a company can file a claim with its insurer. Users also apply this method to see whether inventory amounts from a physical count are reasonable. This method uses the historical relation between cost of goods sold and net sales to estimate the proportion of cost of goods sold making up current sales. This cost of goods sold estimate is then subtracted from cost of goods available for sale to estimate the ending inventory at cost. These two steps are shown in Exhibit 6B.3.

Exhibit 6B.3

Gross Profit Method of Inventory Estimation

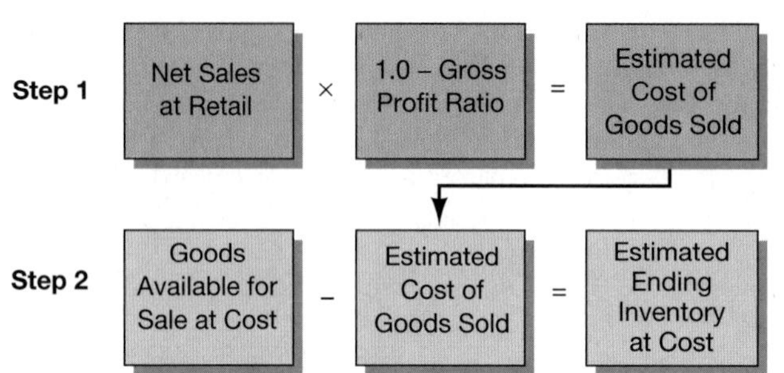

Point: A fire or other catastrophe can result in an insurance claim for lost inventory or income. Backup and off-site storage of data help ensure coverage for such losses.

Point: Reliability of the gross profit method depends on a good estimate of the gross profit ratio.

To illustrate, assume that a company's inventory is destroyed by fire in March 2005. When the fire occurs, the company's accounts show the following balances for January through March: sales, $31,500; sales returns, $1,500; inventory (January 1, 2005), $12,000; and cost of goods purchased, $20,500. If this company's gross profit ratio is 30%, then 30% of each net sales dollar is gross profit and 70% is cost of goods sold. We show in Exhibit 6B.4 how this 70% is used to estimate lost inventory of $11,500. To understand this exhibit, think of subtracting cost of goods sold from the goods available for sale to get ending inventory.

Exhibit 6B.4

Estimated Inventory Using the Gross Profit Method

	Goods available for sale		
	Inventory, January 1, 2005	$12,000	
	Cost of goods purchased	20,500	
	Goods available for sale (at cost)	32,500	
	Net sales at retail ($31,500 − $1,500)		$30,000
Step 1:	**Estimated cost of goods sold ($30,000 × 70%)**	**(21,000)** ←	× 0.70
Step 2:	**Estimated March inventory at cost**	**$11,500**	

Quick Check

10. Using the retail method and the following data, estimate the cost of ending inventory.

	Cost	Retail
Beginning inventory	$324,000	$530,000
Cost of goods purchased	195,000	335,000
Net sales		320,000

Answer—p. 246

Summary

C1 Identify the items making up merchandise inventory. Merchandise inventory refers to goods owned by a company and held for resale. Three special cases merit our attention. Goods in transit are reported in inventory of the company that holds ownership rights. Goods on consignment are reported in the consignor's inventory. Goods damaged or obsolete are reported in inventory at their net realizable value.

C2 Identify the costs of merchandise inventory. Costs of merchandise inventory include expenditures necessary to bring an item to a salable condition and location. This includes its invoice cost minus any discount plus any added or incidental costs necessary to put it in a place and condition for sale.

A1 Analyze the effects of inventory methods for both financial and tax reporting. When purchase costs are rising or falling, the inventory costing methods are likely to assign different costs to inventory. Specific identification exactly matches costs and revenues. Weighted average smooths out cost changes. FIFO assigns an amount to inventory closely approximating current replacement cost. LIFO assigns the most recent costs incurred to cost of goods sold and likely better matches current costs with revenues.

A2 **Analyze the effects of inventory errors on current and future financial statements.** An error in the amount of ending inventory affects assets (inventory), net income (cost of goods sold), and equity for that period. Since ending inventory is next period's beginning inventory, an error in ending inventory affects next period's cost of goods sold and net income. Inventory errors in one period are offset in the next period.

A3 **Assess inventory management using both inventory turnover and days' sales in inventory.** We prefer a high inventory turnover, provided that goods are not out of stock and customers are not turned away. We use days' sales in inventory to assess the likelihood of goods being out of stock. We prefer a small number of days' sales in inventory if we can serve customer needs and provide a buffer for uncertainties.

P1 **Compute inventory in a perpetual system using the methods of specific identification, FIFO, LIFO, and weighted average.** Costs are assigned to the cost of goods sold account *each time* a sale occurs in a perpetual system. Specific identification assigns a cost to each item sold by referring to its actual cost (for example, its net invoice cost). Weighted average assigns a cost to items sold by dividing the current balance in the inventory account by the total items available for sale to determine cost per unit. We then multiply the number of units sold by this cost per unit to get the cost of each sale. FIFO assigns cost to items sold assuming that the earliest units purchased are the first units sold. LIFO assigns cost to items sold assuming that the most recent units purchased are the first units sold.

P2 **Compute the lower of cost or market amount of inventory.** Inventory is reported at market cost when market is *lower* than recorded cost, called the *lower of cost or market (LCM) inventory.* Market is typically measured as replacement cost. Lower of cost or market can be applied separately to each item, to major categories of items, or to the entire inventory.

P3[A] **Compute inventory in a periodic system using the methods of specific identification, FIFO, LIFO, and weighted average.** Periodic inventory systems allocate the cost of goods available for sale between cost of goods sold and ending inventory *at the end of a period.* Specific identification and FIFO give identical results whether the periodic or perpetual system is used. LIFO assigns costs to cost of goods sold assuming the last units purchased for the period are the first units sold. The weighted average cost per unit is computed by dividing the total cost of beginning inventory and net purchases for the period by the total number of units available. Then, it multiplies cost per unit by the number of units sold to give cost of goods sold.

P4[B] **Apply both the retail inventory and gross profit methods to estimate inventory.** The retail inventory method involves three steps: (1) goods available at retail minus net sales at retail equals ending inventory at retail, (2) goods available at cost divided by goods available at retail equals the cost-to-retail ratio, and (3) ending inventory at retail multiplied by the cost-to-retail ratio equals estimated ending inventory at cost. The gross profit method involves two steps: (1) net sales at retail multiplied by 1 minus the gross profit ratio equals estimated cost of goods sold, and (2) goods available at cost minus estimated cost of goods sold equals estimated ending inventory at cost.

Guidance Answers to **Decision Maker** and **Decision Ethics**

Financial Planner The FIFO method implies that the oldest costs are the first ones assigned to cost of goods sold. This leaves the most recent costs in ending inventory. You report this to your client and note that in most cases, the ending inventory of a company using FIFO is reported at or near its replacement cost. This means that your client need not in most cases adjust the reported value of inventory. Your answer changes only if there are major increases in replacement cost compared to the cost of recent purchases reported in inventory. When major increases in costs occur, your client might wish to adjust inventory (for internal reports) for the difference between the reported cost of inventory and its replacement cost. (*Note:* Decreases in costs of purchases are recognized under the lower of cost or market adjustment.)

Inventory Manager It seems your company can save (or at least postpone) taxes by switching to LIFO, but the switch is likely to reduce bonus money that you think you have earned and deserve. Since the U.S. tax code requires companies that use LIFO for tax reporting also to use it for financial reporting, your options are further constrained. Your best decision is to tell your superior about the tax savings with LIFO. You also should discuss your bonus plan and how this is likely to hurt you unfairly. You might propose to compute inventory under the LIFO method for reporting purposes but use the FIFO method for your bonus calculations. Another solution is to revise the bonus plan to reflect the company's use of the LIFO method.

Entrepreneur Your inventory turnover is markedly higher than the norm, whereas days' sales in inventory approximates the norm. Since your turnover is already 14% better than average, you are probably best served by directing attention to days' sales in inventory. You should see whether you can reduce the level of inventory while maintaining service to customers. Given your higher turnover, you should be able to hold less inventory.

Guidance Answers to **Quick Checks**

1. The matching principle.
2. **Target** reports these goods in its inventory.
3. Total cost assigned to the painting is $12,180, computed as $11,400 + $130 + $150 + $100 + $400.
4. Specific identification exactly matches costs and revenues. Weighted average tends to smooth out cost changes. FIFO assigns an amount to inventory that closely approximates current replacement cost. LIFO assigns the most recent costs incurred

to cost of goods sold and likely better matches current costs with revenues.

5. FIFO—it gives a lower cost of goods sold, a higher gross profit, and a higher net income when costs are rising.

6. When costs are rising, LIFO gives a lower inventory figure on the balance sheet as compared to FIFO. FIFO's inventory amount approximates current replacement costs.

7. Cost of goods sold would be overstated by $10,000 in 2005 and understated by $10,000 in year 2006.

8. The reported LCM inventory amount (using items) is $540, computed as [(20 × $5) + (40 × $8) + (10 × $12)].

9.[A] a. FIFO periodic inventory = (20 × $14) + (10 × $12) = $400

b. LIFO periodic cost of goods sold = (20 × $14) + (40 × $12) + (70 × $10) = $1,460

10.[B] Estimated ending inventory (at cost) is $327,000. It is computed as follows:

Step 1: ($530,000 + $335,000) − $320,000 = $545,000

Step 2: $\frac{\$324{,}000 + \$195{,}000}{\$530{,}000 + \$335{,}000} = 60\%$

Step 3: $545,000 × 60% = $327,000

Key Terms

Key Terms are available at the book's Website for learning and testing in an online Flashcard Format.

Average cost (p. 228)
Conservatism principle (p. 232)
Consignee (p. 222)
Consignor (p. 222)
Consistency principle (p. 230)
Days' sales in inventory (p. 234)
First-in, first-out (FIFO) (p. 227)
Gross profit method (p. 244)
Interim statements (p. 243)
Inventory turnover (p. 233)
Last-in, first-out (LIFO) (p. 227)
Lower of cost or market (LCM) (p. 231)
Net realizable value (p. 223)
Retail inventory method (p. 243)
Specific identification (p. 225)
Weighted average (p. 228)

Personal Interactive Quiz

Personal Interactive Quizzes A and B are available at the book's Website to reinforce and assess your learning.

Superscript letter [A] ([B]) denotes assignments based on Appendix 6A (6B).

Discussion Questions

1. Describe the flow of costs from inventory to cost of goods sold for the following methods: (*a*) FIFO and (*b*) LIFO.

2. Where is the amount of merchandise inventory disclosed in the financial statements?

3. Why are incidental costs sometimes ignored in inventory costing? Under what principle is this permitted?

4. If costs are declining, will the LIFO or FIFO method of inventory valuation result in the lower cost of goods sold?

5. What does the full-disclosure principle prescribe if a company changes from one acceptable accounting method to another?

6. Can a company change its inventory method each accounting period? Explain.

7. Does the accounting principle of consistency preclude any changes from one accounting method to another?

8. If inventory errors are said to correct themselves, why are accounting users concerned when such errors are made?

9. Explain the following statement: "Inventory errors correct themselves."

10. What is the meaning of *market* as it is used in determining the lower of cost or market for inventory?

11. What guidance does the principle of conservatism offer?

12. What factors contribute to (or cause) inventory shrinkage?

13.[A] What accounts are used in a periodic inventory system but not in a perpetual inventory system?

14.[B] When preparing interim financial statements, what two methods can companies utilize to estimate cost of goods sold and ending inventory?

15. Refer to Krispy Kreme's financial statements in Appendix A. On February 2, 2003, what percent of current assets are represented by inventory? Krispy Kreme

16. Refer to Tastykake's financial statements in Appendix A. Compute its cost of goods available for sale for the year ended December 28, 2002. Tastykake

17. What percent of Harley-Davidson's current assets are inventory as of December 31, 2002, and as of December 31, 2001? Harley-Davidson

Red numbers denote Discussion Questions that involve decision-making.

Homework Manager repeats all numerical Quick Study assignments on the book's Website with new numbers.

QUICK STUDY

QS 6-1
Assigning costs to inventory—perpetual systems
P1

Tevin Trader starts a merchandising business on December 1 and enters into three inventory purchases:

December 7	10 units @ $ 6 cost
December 14	20 units @ $12 cost
December 21	15 units @ $14 cost

Trader sells 15 units for $25 each on December 15. Eight of the sold units are from the December 7 purchase and seven are from the December 14 purchase. Trader uses a perpetual inventory system. Determine the costs assigned to the December 31 ending inventory when costs are assigned based on (*a*) FIFO, (*b*) LIFO, (*c*) weighted average, and (*d*) specific identification.

Check (c) $360

QS 6-2
Computing goods available for sale
P1

Senona Company reports beginning inventory of 10 units at $50 each. Every week for four weeks it purchases an additional 10 units at respective costs of $51, $52, $55, and $60 per unit for weeks 1 through 4. Calculate the cost of goods available for sale and the units available for sale for this four-week period.

QS 6-3
Inventory costing methods
P1

A company reports the following beginning inventory and purchases for January. On January 26, 345 units were sold. What is the cost of the 140 units that remain in ending inventory, assuming costs are assigned based on (*a*) FIFO, (*b*) LIFO, and (*c*) weighted average? (Round unit costs to the nearest cent.)

	Units	Unit Cost
Beginning inventory on January 1	310	$3.00
Purchase on January 9	75	3.20
Purchase on January 25	100	3.35

QS 6-4
Contrasting inventory costing methods
A1 

Identify the inventory costing method best described by each of the following separate statements. Assume a period of increasing costs.

1. The preferred method when each unit of product has unique features that markedly affect cost.
2. Matches recent costs against net sales.
3. Provides a tax advantage (deferral) to a corporation.
4. Yields a balance sheet inventory amount often markedly less than its replacement cost.
5. Results in a balance sheet inventory amount approximating replacement cost.

QS 6-5
Inventory ownership
C1

1. At year-end, Jolie Co. had shipped $850 of merchandise FOB destination to China Co. Which company should include the $850 of merchandise in transit as part of its year-end inventory?
2. Jolie Company has shipped $500 of goods to China Co., and China Co. has arranged to sell the goods for Jolie. Identify the consignor and the consignee. Which company should include any unsold goods as part of its inventory?

QS 6-6
Inventory ownership
C1

Crafts Galore, a distributor of handmade gifts, operates out of owner Jenny Finn's house. At the end of the current period, Jenny reports she has 1,500 units (products) in her basement, 30 of which were damaged by water and cannot be sold. She also has another 250 units in her van, ready to deliver per a customer order, terms FOB destination, and another 70 units out on consignment to a friend who owns a retail store. How many units should Jenny include in her company's period-end inventory?

QS 6-7
Inventory costs
C2

A car dealer acquires a used car for $3,000, terms FOB shipping point. Additional costs in obtaining and offering the car for sale include $150 for transportation-in, $200 for import duties, $50 for insurance during shipment, $25 for advertising, and $250 for sales staff salaries. For computing inventory, what cost is assigned to the used car?

QS 6-8
Inventory costs
C2

Duke & Son, antique dealers, purchased the contents of an estate for $37,500. Terms of the purchase were FOB shipping point, and the cost of transporting the goods to Duke & Son's warehouse was $1,200. Duke & Son insured the shipment at a cost of $150. Prior to putting the goods up for sale, they cleaned and refurbished them at a cost of $490. Determine the cost of the inventory acquired from the estate.

QS 6-9
Applying LCM to inventories
P2

Talisman Trading Co. has the following products in its ending inventory. Compute lower of cost or market for inventory (*a*) as a whole and (*b*) applied separately to each product.

Product	Quantity	Cost per Unit	Market per Unit
Mountain bikes	9	$360	$330
Skateboards	12	210	270
Gliders	25	480	420

QS 6-10
Inventory errors
A2 

In taking a physical inventory at the end of year 2005, Nadir Company erroneously forgot to count certain units. Explain how this error affects the following: (*a*) 2005 cost of goods sold, (*b*) 2005 gross profit, (*c*) 2005 net income, (*d*) 2006 net income, (*e*) the combined two-year income, and (*f*) income for years after 2006.

QS 6-11
Analyzing inventory A3

Market Company begins the year with $200,000 of goods in inventory. At year-end, the amount in inventory has increased to $230,000. Cost of goods sold for the year is $1,600,000. Compute Market's inventory turnover and days' sales in inventory. Assume that there are 365 days in the year.

QS 6-12[A]
Costing methods—periodic system P3

Refer to QS 6-1 and assume the periodic inventory system is used. Determine the costs assigned to the December 31 ending inventory when costs are assigned based on (*a*) FIFO, (*b*) LIFO, (*c*) weighted average, and (*d*) specific identification.

QS 6-13[A]
Costing methods—periodic system P3

Refer to QS 6-3 and assume the periodic inventory system is used. Determine the costs assigned to the ending inventory when costs are assigned based on (*a*) FIFO, (*b*) LIFO, and (*c*) weighted average. (Round unit costs to the nearest cent.)

QS 6-14[B]
Estimating inventories—gross profit method
P4

Dooling Store's inventory is destroyed by a fire on September 5, 2005. The following data for year 2005 are available from the accounting records. Estimate the cost of the inventory destroyed.

Jan. 1 inventory	$180,000
Jan. 1 through Sept. 5 purchases (net)	$342,000
Jan. 1 through Sept. 5 sales (net)	$675,000
Year 2005 estimated gross profit rate	42%

***Homework Manager** repeats all numerical Exercises on the book's Website with new numbers.*

EXERCISES

Exercise 6-1
Inventory costing methods—perpetual
P1

Lakia Corporation reported the following current-year purchases and sales data for its only product:

Date	Activities	Units Acquired at Cost		Units Sold at Retail
Jan. 1	Beginning inventory	120 units @ $6.00 =	$ 720	
Jan. 10	Sales			70 units @ $15
Mar. 7	Purchase	200 units @ $5.50 =	1,100	
Mar. 15	Sales			125 units @ $15
July 28	Purchase	500 units @ $5.00 =	2,500	
Oct. 3	Purchase	375 units @ $4.40 =	1,650	
Oct. 5	Sales			600 units @ $15
Dec. 19	Purchase	100 units @ $4.10 =	410	
	Totals	1,295 units	$6,380	795 units

Lakia uses a perpetual inventory system. Ending inventory consists of 500 units, 400 from the July 28 purchase and 100 from the December 19 purchase. Determine the cost assigned to ending inventory and to cost of goods sold using (*a*) specific identification, (*b*) weighted average, (*c*) FIFO, and (*d*) LIFO.

Check Ending inventory: LIFO, $2,498; WA, $2,350

Exercise 6-2
Income effects of inventory methods
A1

Use the data in Exercise 6-1 to prepare comparative income statements for Lakia Corporation (calendar year-end 2005) similar to those shown in Exhibit 6.8 for the four inventory methods. Assume expenses are $1,250. The applicable income tax rate is 30%.

1. Which method yields the highest net income?

2. Does net income using weighted average fall between that using FIFO and LIFO?

3. If costs are rising instead of declining, which method would yield the highest net income?

Exercise 6-3
Inventory costing methods (perpetual)—FIFO and LIFO
P1

Henin Co. reported the following current-year purchases and sales data for its only product:

Date	Activities	Units Acquired at Cost		Units Sold at Retail
Jan. 1	Beginning inventory	100 units @ $10 =	$ 1,000	
Jan. 10	Sales			90 units @ $40
Mar. 14	Purchase	250 units @ $15 =	3,750	
Mar. 15	Sales			140 units @ $40
July 30	Purchase	400 units @ $20 =	8,000	
Oct. 5	Sales			300 units @ $40
Oct. 26	Purchase	600 units @ $25 =	15,000	
	Totals	1,350 units	$27,750	530 units

Henin uses a perpetual inventory system. Determine the costs assigned to ending inventory and to cost of goods sold using (*a*) FIFO and (*b*) LIFO. Compute the gross margin for each method.

Check Ending inventory: LIFO, $18,750

Exercise 6-4
Specific Identification P1

Refer to the data in Exercise 6-3. Assume that ending inventory is made up of 200 units from the March 14 purchase, 20 units from the July 30 purchase, and all the units of the October 26 purchase. Using the specific identification method, calculate (*a*) the cost of goods sold and (*b*) the gross margin.

Exercise 6-5
Lower of cost or market
P2

Tanzy Company's ending inventory includes the following items. Compute the lower of cost or market for ending inventory (*a*) as a whole and (*b*) applied separately to each product.

		Per Unit	
Product	Units	Cost	Market
Helmets	22	$50	$54
Bats	15	78	72
Shoes	36	95	91
Uniforms	40	36	36

Check (*b*) $6,896

Exercise 6-6
Analysis of inventory errors
A2

Ringo Company had $900,000 of sales in each of three consecutive years 2004–2006, and it purchased merchandise costing $500,000 in each of those years. It also maintained a $200,000 inventory from the beginning to the end of the three-year period. In accounting for inventory, it made an error at the end of year 2004 that caused its year-end 2004 inventory to appear on its statements as $180,000 rather than the correct $200,000.

1. Determine the correct amount of the company's gross profit in each of the years 2004–2006.

Check 2004 gross profit, $380,000

2. Prepare comparative income statements as in Exhibit 6.11 to show the effect of this error on the company's cost of goods sold and gross profit for each of the years 2004–2006.

Exercise 6-7
Inventory turnover and days' sales in inventory
A3

Use the following information for Ryder Co. to compute inventory turnover for 2005 and 2004, and its days' sales in inventory at December 31, 2005 and 2004. (Round answers to the tenths place.) Comment on Ryder's efficiency in using its assets to increase sales from 2004 to 2005.

	2005	2004	2003
Cost of goods sold	$643,825	$426,650	$391,300
Inventory (Dec. 31)	96,400	86,750	91,500

Exercise 6-8
Comparing LIFO numbers to FIFO numbers; ratio analysis
A1 A3

Checkers Company uses LIFO for inventory costing and reports the following financial data. It also recomputed inventory and cost of goods sold using FIFO for comparison purposes.

	2005	2004
LIFO inventory	$150	$100
LIFO cost of goods sold	730	670
FIFO inventory	220	125
FIFO cost of goods sold	685	—
Current assets (using LIFO)	210	180
Current liabilities	190	170

Check (1) FIFO: Current ratio, 1.5; Inventory turnover, 4.0 times

1. Compute its current ratio, inventory turnover, and days' sales in inventory for 2005 using (*a*) LIFO numbers and (*b*) FIFO numbers.

2. Comment on and interpret the results of part 1.

Exercise 6-9^A
Inventory costing—periodic system P3

Refer to Exercise 6-1 and assume the periodic inventory system is used. Determine the costs assigned to ending inventory and to cost of goods sold using (*a*) specific identification, (*b*) weighted average, (*c*) FIFO, and (*d*) LIFO.

Exercise 6-10^A
Inventory costing—periodic system P3

Refer to Exercise 6-3 and assume the periodic inventory system is used. Determine the costs assigned to ending inventory and to cost of goods sold using (*a*) FIFO, and (*b*) LIFO. Compute the gross margin for each method.

Exercise 6-11^A
Alternative cost flow assumptions—periodic
P3

Rod & Roy Co. reported the following current-year data for its only product. The company uses a periodic inventory system, and its ending inventory consists of 300 units, 100 from each of the last three purchases. Determine the cost assigned to ending inventory and to cost of goods sold using (*a*) specific identification, (*b*) weighted average, (*c*) FIFO, and (*d*) LIFO. Which method yields the highest net income?

Jan. 1	Beginning inventory	200 units @ $2.00 =	$ 400
Mar. 7	Purchase	440 units @ $2.25 =	990
July 28	Purchase	1080 units @ $2.50 =	2,700
Oct. 3	Purchase	960 units @ $2.80 =	2,688
Dec. 19	Purchase	320 units @ $2.90 =	928
	Totals	3,000 units	$7,706

Check Inventory: LIFO, $625; FIFO, $870

Exercise 6-12^A
Alternative cost flow assumptions—periodic
P3

Nyhus Gifts reported the following current-year data for its only product. The company uses a periodic inventory system, and its ending inventory consists of 300 units, 100 from each of the last three purchases. Determine the cost assigned to ending inventory and to cost of goods sold using (*a*) specific identification, (*b*) weighted average, (*c*) FIFO, and (*d*) LIFO. Which method yields the lowest net income?

Jan. 1	Beginning inventory	280 units @ $3.00 =	$ 840
Mar. 7	Purchase	600 units @ $2.80 =	1,680
July 28	Purchase	800 units @ $2.50 =	2,000
Oct. 3	Purchase	1,100 units @ $2.30 =	2,530
Dec. 19	Purchase	250 units @ $2.00 =	500
	Totals	3,030 units	$7,550

Check Inventory: LIFO, $896; FIFO, $615

Exercise 6-13B
Estimating ending inventory—retail method
P4

In 2005, Wichita Company had retail sales (net) of $130,000. The following additional information is available from its records at the end of 2005. Use the retail inventory method to estimate Wichita's 2005 ending inventory at cost.

	At Cost	At Retail
Beginning inventory	$31,900	$64,200
Cost of goods purchased	57,810	98,400

Check End. Inventory, $17,930

Exercise 6-14B
Estimating ending inventory—gross profit method
P4

On January 1, KB Store had $450,000 of inventory at cost. In the first quarter of the year, it purchased $1,590,000 of merchandise, returned $23,100, and paid freight charges of $37,600 on purchased merchandise, terms FOB shipping point. The store's gross profit averages 30%. The store had $2,000,000 of retail sales (net) in the first quarter of the year. Use the gross profit method to estimate its cost of inventory at the end of the first quarter.

PROBLEM SET A

Problem 6-1A
Alternative cost flows—perpetual
P1

Parker Company uses a perpetual inventory system. It entered into the following calendar-year 2005 purchases and sales transactions:

Date	Activities	Units Acquired at Cost	Units Sold at Retail
Jan. 1	Beginning inventory	600 units @ $44/unit	
Feb. 10	Purchase	200 units @ $40/unit	
Mar. 13	Purchase	100 units @ $20/unit	
Mar. 15	Sales		400 units @ $75/unit
Aug. 21	Purchase	160 units @ $60/unit	
Sept. 5	Purchase	280 units @ $48/unit	
Sept. 10	Sales		200 units @ $75/unit
	Totals	1,340 units	600 units

Required

1. Compute cost of goods available for sale and the number of units available for sale.
2. Compute the number of units in ending inventory.
3. Compute the cost assigned to ending inventory using (*a*) FIFO, (*b*) LIFO, (*c*) specific identification (*Note:* The units sold consist of 500 units from beginning inventory and 100 units from the March 13 purchase), and (*d*) weighted average.
4. Compute the gross profit earned by the company for each of the four costing methods in part 3.

Check (3) Ending inventory: FIFO, $33,040; LIFO, $35,440; WA, $34,055;

(4) LIFO gross profit, $21,000

Analysis Component

5. If the company's manager earns a bonus based on a percent of gross profit, which method of inventory costing will the manager likely prefer?

Problem 6-2A
Analysis of inventory errors
A2 

mhhe.com/larson

Stover Company's financial statements report the following. Stover recently discovered that in making physical counts of inventory, it had made the following errors: Inventory on December 31, 2004, is understated by $66,000, and inventory on December 31, 2005, is overstated by $30,000.

Key Figures	For Year Ended December 31		
	2004	2005	2006
(a) Cost of goods sold	$ 715,000	$ 847,000	$ 770,000
(b) Net income	220,000	275,000	231,000
(c) Total current assets	1,155,000	1,265,000	1,100,000
(d) Total equity	1,287,000	1,430,000	1,232,000

Required

1. For each key financial statement figure—(*a*), (*b*), (*c*), and (*d*) above—prepare a table similar to the following to show the adjustments necessary to correct the reported amounts.

Figure: ________	2004	2005	2006
Reported amount	________	________	________
Adjustments for: 12/31/2004 error	________	________	________
12/31/2005 error	________	________	________
Corrected amount	________	________	________

Check (1) Corrected net income: 2004, $286,000; 2005, $179,000; 2006, $261,000

Analysis Component

2. What is the error in total net income for the combined three-year period resulting from the inventory errors? Explain.

3. Explain why the understatement of inventory by $66,000 at the end of 2004 results in an understatement of equity by the same amount in that year.

Problem 6-3A
Lower of cost or market
P2

A physical inventory of Ireland Unlimited taken at December 31 reveals the following:

Item	Units	Per Unit Cost	Per Unit Market
Audio equipment			
Receivers	335	$ 90	$ 98
CD players	250	111	100
DVD players	316	86	95
Speakers	194	52	41
Video equipment			
Televisions	470	150	125
VCRs	281	93	84
Video cameras	202	310	322
Car audio equipment			
DVD radios	175	70	84
CD radios	160	97	105

Required

Calculate the lower of cost or market for the inventory (*a*) as a whole, (*b*) by major category, and (*c*) applied separately to each item.

Check (b) $270,332; (c) $263,024

Problem 6-4A[A]
Alternative cost flows—periodic
P3

Viper Company began year 2005 with 20,000 units of product in its January 1 inventory costing $15 each. It made successive purchases of its product in year 2005 as follows:

Mar. 7	28,000 units @ $18 each
May 25	30,000 units @ $22 each
Aug. 1	20,000 units @ $24 each
Nov. 10	33,000 units @ $27 each

The company uses a periodic inventory system. On December 31, 2005, a physical count reveals that 35,000 units of its product remain in inventory.

Required

1. Compute the number and total cost of the units available for sale in year 2005.

2. Compute the amounts assigned to the 2005 ending inventory and the cost of goods sold using (*a*) FIFO, (*b*) LIFO, and (*c*) weighted average.

Check (2) Cost of goods sold: FIFO, $1,896,000; LIFO, $2,265,000; WA, $2,077,557

Problem 6-5A[A]
Income comparisons and cost flows—periodic
A1 P3

True Blue Corp. sold 5,500 units of its product at $45 per unit in year 2005 and incurred operating expenses of $6 per unit in selling the units. It began the year with 600 units in inventory and made successive purchases of its product as follows:

Jan. 1	Beginning inventory	600 units @ $18 per unit
Feb. 20	Purchase	1,500 units @ $19 per unit
May 16	Purchase	700 units @ $20 per unit
Oct. 3	Purchase	400 units @ $21 per unit
Dec. 11	Purchase	3,300 units @ $22 per unit
	Total	6,500 units

Required

1. Prepare comparative income statements similar to Exhibit 6.8 for the three inventory costing methods of FIFO, LIFO, and weighted average. Include a detailed cost of goods sold section as part of each statement. The company uses a periodic inventory system, and its income tax rate is 30%.

2. How would the financial results from using the three alternative inventory costing methods change if True Blue had been experiencing declining costs in its purchases of inventory?

3. What advantages and disadvantages are offered by using (*a*) LIFO and (*b*) FIFO? Assume the continuing trend of increasing costs.

Check (1) Net income: LIFO, $69,020; FIFO, $71,540; WA, $70,603

Problem 6-6A[B]
Retail inventory method
P4

mhhe.com/larson

The records of Nilson Company provide the following information for the year ended December 31:

	At Cost	At Retail
January 1 beginning inventory	$ 471,350	$ 927,150
Cost of goods purchased	3,276,030	6,279,350
Sales		5,495,700
Sales returns		44,600

Required

1. Use the retail inventory method to estimate the company's year-end inventory.

2. A year-end physical inventory at retail prices yields a total inventory of $1,675,800. Prepare a calculation showing the company's loss from shrinkage at cost and at retail.

Check (1) Inventory, $912,808 cost; (2) Inventory shortage at cost, $41,392

Problem 6-7A^B
Gross profit method
P4

Wayman Company wants to prepare interim financial statements for the first quarter. The company wishes to avoid making a physical count of inventory. Wayman's gross profit rate averages 35%. The following information for the first quarter is available from its records:

January 1 beginning inventory	$ 300,260
Cost of goods purchased	939,050
Sales	1,191,150
Sales returns	9,450

Check Estimated ending inventory, $471,205

Required

Use the gross profit method to estimate the company's first-quarter ending inventory.

PROBLEM SET B

Problem 6-1B
Alternative cost flows—perpetual
P1

Venus Company uses a perpetual inventory system. It entered into the following calendar-year 2005 purchases and sales transactions:

Date	Activities	Units Acquired at Cost	Units Sold at Retail
Jan. 1	Beginning inventory	600 units @ $55/unit	
Jan. 10	Purchase	450 units @ $56/unit	
Feb. 13	Purchase	200 units @ $57/unit	
Feb. 15	Sales		430 units @ $90/unit
July 21	Purchase	230 units @ $58/unit	
Aug. 5	Purchase	345 units @ $59/unit	
Aug. 10	Sales		335 units @ $90/unit
	Total	1,825 units	765 units

Required

1. Compute cost of goods available for sale and the number of units available for sale.

2. Compute the number of units in ending inventory.

Check (3) Ending inventory: FIFO, $61,055; LIFO, $59,250; WA, $60,293;

3. Compute the cost assigned to ending inventory using (*a*) FIFO, (*b*) LIFO, (*c*) specific identification (*Note:* The units sold consist of 600 units from beginning inventory and 165 units from the February 13 purchase), and (*d*) weighted average.

(4) LIFO gross profit, $24,805

4. Compute gross profit earned by the company for each of the four costing methods in part 3.

Analysis Component

5. If the company's manager earns a bonus based on a percent of gross profit, which method of inventory costing will the manager likely prefer?

Problem 6-2B
Analysis of inventory errors
A2

Hector Company's financial statements report the following. Hector recently discovered that in making physical counts of inventory, it had made the following errors: Inventory on December 31, 2004, is overstated by $17,000, and inventory on December 31, 2005, is understated by $25,000.

	For Year Ended December 31		
Key Figures	**2004**	**2005**	**2006**
(*a*) Cost of goods sold	$205,200	$212,800	$196,030
(*b*) Net income	174,800	211,270	183,910
(*c*) Total current assets	266,000	276,500	262,950
(*d*) Total equity	304,000	316,000	336,000

Required

1. For each key financial statement figure—(*a*), (*b*), (*c*), and (*d*) above—prepare a table similar to the following to show the adjustments necessary to correct the reported amounts.

Figure: ________	2004	2005	2006
Reported amount	________	________	________
Adjustments for: 12/31/2004 error	________	________	________
12/31/2005 error	________	________	________
Corrected amount	________	________	________

Check (1) Corrected net income: 2004, $157,800; 2005, $253,270; 2006, $158,910

Analysis Component

2. What is the error in total net income for the combined three-year period resulting from the inventory errors? Explain.
3. Explain why the overstatement of inventory by $17,000 at the end of 2004 results in an overstatement of equity by the same amount in that year.

Problem 6-3B
Lower of cost or market
P2

A physical inventory of Office Deals taken at December 31 reveals the following:

Item	Units	Per Unit Cost	Per Unit Market
Office furniture			
Desks	436	$261	$305
Credenzas	295	227	256
Chairs	587	49	43
Bookshelves	321	93	82
Filing cabinets			
Two-drawer	214	81	70
Four-drawer	398	135	122
Lateral	175	104	118
Office equipment			
Fax machines	430	168	200
Copiers	545	317	288
Telephones	352	125	117

Required

Calculate the lower of cost or market for the inventory (*a*) as a whole, (*b*) by major category, and (*c*) applied separately to each item.

Check (*b*) $607,707; (*c*) $584,444

Problem 6-4B[A]
Alternative cost flows—periodic
P3

Elfrink Co. began year 2005 with 6,300 units of product in its January 1 inventory costing $35 each. It made successive purchases of its product in year 2005 as follows:

Jan. 4	10,500 units @ $33 each
May 18	13,000 units @ $32 each
July 9	12,000 units @ $29 each
Nov. 21	15,500 units @ $26 each

The company uses a periodic inventory system. On December 31, 2005, a physical count reveals that 16,500 units of its product remain in inventory.

Required

1. Compute the number and total cost of the units available for sale in year 2005.
2. Compute the amounts assigned to the 2005 ending inventory and the cost of goods sold using (*a*) FIFO, (*b*) LIFO, and (*c*) weighted average.

Check (2) Cost of goods sold: FIFO, $1,302,000; LIFO, $1,176,900; WA, $1,234,681

Problem 6-5B[A]
Income comparisons and cost flows—periodic
A1 P3

Rikkers Corp. sold 2,500 units of its product at $98 per unit in year 2005 and incurred operating expenses of $14 per unit in selling the units. It began the year with 740 units in inventory and made successive purchases of its product as follows:

Jan. 1	Beginning inventory	740 units @ $58 per unit
April 2	Purchase	700 units @ $59 per unit
June 14	Purchase	600 units @ $61 per unit
Aug. 29	Purchase	500 units @ $64 per unit
Nov. 18	Purchase	800 units @ $65 per unit
	Total	3,340 units

Check (1) Net income: LIFO, $40,500; FIFO, $44,805; WA, $42,519

Required

1. Prepare comparative income statements similar to Exhibit 6.8 for the three inventory costing methods of FIFO, LIFO, and weighted average. Include a detailed cost of goods sold section as part of each statement. The company uses a periodic inventory system, and its income tax rate is 25%.
2. How would the financial results from using the three alternative inventory costing methods change if Rikkers had been experiencing decreasing prices in its purchases of inventory?
3. What advantages and disadvantages are offered by using (*a*) LIFO and (*b*) FIFO? Assume the continuing trend of increasing costs.

Problem 6-6B[B]
Retail inventory method
P4

The records of Alaina Co. provide the following information for the year ended December 31:

	At Cost	At Retail
January 1 beginning inventory	$ 81,670	$114,610
Cost of goods purchased	492,250	751,730
Sales		786,120
Sales returns		4,480

Check (1) Inventory, $55,902 cost; (2) Inventory shortage at cost, $4,059

Required

1. Use the retail inventory method to estimate the company's year-end inventory.
2. A year-end physical inventory at retail prices yields a total inventory of $78,550. Prepare a calculation showing the company's loss from shrinkage at cost and at retail.

Problem 6-7B[B]
Gross profit method
P4

Ernst Equipment Co. wants to prepare interim financial statements for the first quarter. The company wishes to avoid making a physical count of inventory. Ernst's gross profit rate averages 30%. The following information for the first quarter is available from its records:

January 1 beginning inventory	$ 752,880
Cost of goods purchased	2,159,630
Sales	3,710,250
Sales returns	74,200

Check Estim. ending inventory, $367,275

Required

Use the gross profit method to estimate the company's first quarter ending inventory.

PROBLEM SET C

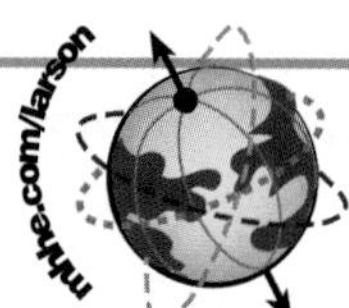

Problem Set C is available at the book's Website to further reinforce and assess your learning.

SERIAL PROBLEM

Success Systems 

(This serial problem began in Chapter 1 and continues through most of the book. If previous chapter segments were not completed, the serial problem can begin at this point.)

Selected accounts and balances for the three months ended March 31, 2005, for Success Systems follows:

January 1 beginning inventory	$ 0
Cost of goods sold	14,052
March 31 ending inventory	704

Required

1. Compute inventory turnover and days' sales in inventory for the three months ended March 31, 2005.
2. Assess its performance if competitors average 10 times for inventory turnover and 29 days for days' sales in inventory.

BEYOND THE NUMBERS

REPORTING IN ACTION

C2 A3 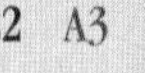

BTN 6-1 Refer to **Krispy Kreme**'s financial statements in Appendix A to answer the following:

Required

1. What amount of inventories did Krispy Kreme hold as a current asset on February 2, 2003? On February 3, 2002?
2. Inventories represent what percent of total assets on February 2, 2003? On February 3, 2002?
3. Comment on the relative size of Krispy Kreme's inventories compared to its other types of assets.
4. What accounting method did Krispy Kreme use to compute inventory amounts on its balance sheet?
5. Compute inventory turnover for fiscal year ended February 2, 2003, and days' sales in inventory as of February 2, 2003. (*Note:* Cost of goods sold is titled operating expenses for Krispy Kreme.)

Roll On

6. Access Krispy Kreme's financial statements for fiscal years ended after February 2, 2003, from its Website (KrispyKreme.com) or the SEC's EDGAR database (www.SEC.gov). Answer questions 1 through 5 using the current Krispy Kreme information and compare results to those prior years.

COMPARATIVE ANALYSIS

A3 

BTN 6-2 Key comparative figures ($ thousands) for both **Krispy Kreme** and **Tastykake** follow:

	Krispy Kreme			Tastykake		
Key Figures	Current Year	One Year Prior	Two Years Prior	Current Year	One Year Prior	Two Years Prior
Inventory	$ 24,365	$ 16,159	$ 12,031	$ 6,777	$ 8,412	$ 5,930
Cost of sales	381,489	316,946	250,690	111,187	103,297	105,036

Required

1. Calculate inventory turnover for both companies for the most recent two years shown.
2. Calculate days' sales in inventory for both companies for the three years shown.
3. Comment on and interpret your findings from parts 1 and 2.

ETHICS CHALLENGE

A1   

BTN 6-3 Golf Away Corp. is a retail sports store carrying golf apparel and equipment. The store is at the end of its second year of operation and is struggling. A major problem is that its cost of inventory has continually increased in the past two years. In the first year of operations, the store assigned inventory costs using LIFO. A loan agreement the store has with its bank, its prime source of financing, requires the store to maintain a certain profit margin and current ratio. The store's owner is currently looking over Golf Away's preliminary financial statements for its second year. The numbers are not favorable. The only way the store can meet the required financial ratios agreed on with the bank is to change from LIFO to FIFO. The store originally decided on LIFO because of its tax advantages. The owner recalculates ending inventory using FIFO and submits those numbers and statements to the loan officer at the bank for the required bank review. The owner thankfully reflects on the available latitude in choosing the inventory costing method.

Required

1. How does Golf Away's use of FIFO improve its net profit margin and current ratio?
2. Is the action by Golf Away's owner ethical? Explain.

COMMUNICATING IN PRACTICE

A1   

BTN 6-4 You are a financial adviser with a client in the wholesale produce business that just completed its first year of operations. Due to weather conditions, the cost of acquiring produce to resell has escalated during the later part of this period. Your client, Jariah Gish, mentions that because the business sells perishable goods, she has striven to maintain a FIFO flow of goods. Although sales are good, the increasing cost of inventory has put the business in a tight cash position. Gish has expressed concern regarding the ability of the business to meet income tax obligations.

Required

Prepare a memorandum that identifies, explains, and justifies the inventory method you recommend your client, Ms. Gish, adopt.

TAKING IT TO THE NET

A3

mhhe.com/larson

BTN 6-5 Access the 2002 annual 10-K report for Oakley, Inc. (Ticker OO), filed on March 31, 2003, from the EDGAR filings at www.SEC.gov.

Required

1. What product does Oakley sell that is especially popular with college students?
2. What inventory method does Oakley use? (*Hint:* See the notes to its financial statements.)
3. Compute Oakley's gross margin and gross margin ratio for the current year.
4. Compute Oakley's inventory turnover and days' sales in inventory for the current year.

TEAMWORK IN ACTION

A1 P1

Point: Step 1 allows four choices or areas for expertise. Larger teams will have some duplication of choice, but the specific identification method should not be duplicated.

BTN 6-6 Each team member has the responsibility to become an expert on an inventory method. This expertise will be used to facilitate teammates' understanding of the concepts relevant to that method.

1. Each learning team member should select an area for expertise by choosing one of the following inventory methods: specific identification, LIFO, FIFO, or weighted average.
2. Form expert teams made up of students who have selected the same area of expertise. The instructor will identify where each expert team will meet.
3. Using the following data, each expert team must collaborate to develop a presentation that illustrates the relevant concepts and procedures for its inventory method. Each team member must write the presentation in a format that can be shown to the learning team.

Data

Wiseman Corp. uses a perpetual inventory system. It had the following beginning inventory and current year purchases of its product:

Jan. 1	Beginning inventory	50 units @ $10 =	$ 500
Jan. 14	Purchase	150 units @ $12 =	1,800
Apr. 30	Purchase	200 units @ $15 =	3,000
Sept. 26	Purchase	300 units @ $20 =	6,000

Wiseman Corp. transacted sales on the following dates at a $35 per unit sales price:

Jan. 10	30 units	(specific cost: 30 @ $10)
Feb. 15	100 units	(specific cost: 100 @ $12)
Oct. 5	350 units	(specific cost: 100 @ $15 and 250 @ $20)

Concepts and Procedures to Illustrate in Expert Presentation

a. Identify and compute the costs to assign to the units sold.
b. Identify and compute the costs to assign to the units in ending inventory.
c. How likely is it that this inventory costing method will reflect the actual physical flow of goods? How relevant is that factor in determining whether this is an acceptable method to use?
d. What is the impact of this method versus others in determining net income and income taxes?
e. How closely does the ending inventory amount reflect replacement cost?

4. Re-form learning teams. In rotation, each expert is to present to the team the presentation developed in part 3. Experts are to encourage and respond to questions.

BUSINESS WEEK ACTIVITY

A3

mhhe.com/larson

BTN 6-7 Read the article "iPod: A Seed for Growth?" from the August 27, 2002, issue of *Business Week*. (The book's Website provides a free link.)

Required

1. What percent of the U.S. market for digital music players does Apple have?
2. What firms are emerging with products to compete with the Apple iPod?
3. Why might the Toshiba product hold an inventory cost edge over the Apple iPod?
4. How does Apple expect its unit sales of the iPod to grow from 2002 to 2006?

ENTREPRENEURIAL DECISION

A3

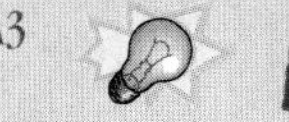

BTN 6-8 Review the chapter's opening feature highlighting Mike Becker and his company, FunKo. Assume that FunKo consistently maintains an inventory level of $500,000, meaning that its average and ending inventory levels are the same. Also assume its annual cost of sales is $1,050,000. To cut costs, Becker proposes to slash inventory to a constant level of $125,000 with no impact on cost of sales.

Required

1. Compute the company's inventory turnover and its days' sales in inventory under (*a*) current conditions and (*b*) proposed conditions.
2. Evaluate and comment on the merits of Becker's proposal given your analysis in part 1. Identify any concerns you would express about the proposal.

HITTING THE ROAD

C1 C2

BTN 6-9 Visit four retail stores with another classmate. In each store, identify whether the store uses a bar-coding system to help manage its inventory. Try to find at least one store that does not use bar-coding. If a store does not use bar-coding, ask the store's manager or clerk whether he or she knows which type of inventory method the store employs. Create a table that shows columns for the name of store visited, type of merchandise sold, use or nonuse of bar-coding, and the inventory method used if bar-coding is not employed. You might also inquire as to what the store's inventory turnover is and how often physical inventory is taken.

GLOBAL DECISION

A3

BTN 6-10 Key figures (pesos millions) for Grupo Bimbo (GrupoBimbo.com) follow:

Key Figures	Current Year	One Year Prior	Two Years Prior
Inventory	905	767	725
Cost of sales	19,156	15,708	13,939

Required

1. Use these data and those from BTN 6-2 to compute (*a*) inventory turnover and (*b*) days' sales in inventory for the most recent two years shown for Grupo Bimbo, Krispy Kreme, and Tastykake.
2. Comment on and interpret your findings from part 1.

"I still want to achieve something greater"—Devin Lazerine

Accounting Information Systems

A Look Back

Chapters 5 and 6 focused on merchandising activities and accounting for inventory. We explained both the perpetual and periodic inventory systems, accounting for inventory transactions, and methods for assigning costs to inventory.

A Look at This Chapter

This chapter emphasizes accounting information systems. We describe fundamental system principles, the system's components, use of special journals and subsidiary ledgers, and technology-based systems. We also briefly discuss segment reporting.

A Look Ahead

Chapter 8 focuses on internal controls and accounting for cash and cash equivalents. We explain good internal control procedures and their importance for accounting.

CAP

Conceptual

C1 Identify fundamental principles of accounting information systems. *(p. 262)*

C2 Identify components of accounting information systems. *(p. 263)*

C3 Explain the goals and uses of special journals. *(p. 265)*

C4 Describe the use of controlling accounts and subsidiary ledgers. *(p. 266)*

C5 Explain how technology-based information systems impact accounting. *(p. 276)*

Analytical

A1 Compute segment return on assets and use it to evaluate segment performance. *(p. 278)*

Procedural

P1 Journalize and post transactions using special journals. *(p. 267)*

P2 Prepare and prove the accuracy of subsidiary ledgers. *(p. 269)*

Decision Feature

Wrapping Up Rap Deals

CALABASAS, CA—Devin Lazerine's not your typical rap mogul, but then again, he is only 20. Devin is the founder of ***Rap-Up*** **(Rap-Up.com),** a nationwide hip-hop and R&B magazine that he launched four years ago.

Lazerine admits he has had to overcome many hurdles, including those of publishers. "They [publishers] don't know too much about hip-hop music. They think it's vulgar and something they don't want to touch at all." But overcome he has—today, *Rap-Up* has a circulation of more than 200,000. Lazerine did not reveal revenues, but his per monthly issues costs are about $120,000.

Lazerine says his path to success was rocky and with constant challenges. One of those challenges was implementing an accounting system. Controls had to be implemented, technology had to be purchased, and information had to be collected.

Interestingly, Lazerine's age was a barrier in the rap industry. He learned to avoid phone contact, afraid his youthful voice would hurt his credibility. "I was at school once when they [record publicists] called," admits Lazerine. "My mom picked up and said where I was, and they were like, 'What? I thought he was the editor-in-chief of a magazine?' "

Another hurdle for Lazerine was to address the need to track business transactions. He eventually set up several special journals for this purpose, including subsidiary ledgers to track subscribers and their balances owed.

What does the future hold for this rap mogul? When asked about his role models, Lazerine doesn't rattle off Ludacris or Ja Rule; instead, he mentions J Records head Clive Davis and Def Jam founder Russell Simmons. Thus, his interest in the business side of rap is natural. Lazerine adds that understanding and using accounting information systems help him direct and plan *Rap-Up* operations. "My ultimate goal," reveals Lazerine, "is to become a music mogul/entrepreneur." With his current record, he may well become hip-hop's business star.

[Sources: *Rap-Up Website,* January 2004; *Entrepreneur,* November 2002; *Folio Magazine,* May 1, 2002; *Entertainment,* July 19, 2001; *USA Weekend,* March 9, 2003.]

With increases in the number and complexity of business activities, the demands placed on accounting information systems increase. Accounting information systems must meet this challenge in an efficient and effective manner. In this chapter, we learn about fundamental principles guiding information systems, and we study components making up these systems. We also explain procedures that use special journals and subsidiary ledgers to make accounting information systems more efficient. An understanding of the details of accounting reports makes us better decision makers when using financial information, and it improves our ability to analyze and interpret financial statements.

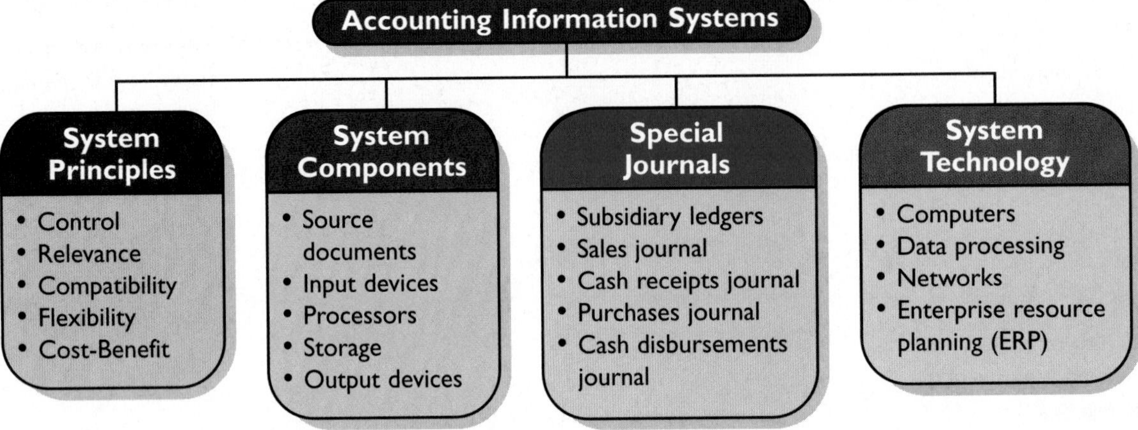

Fundamental System Principles

C1 Identify fundamental principles of accounting information systems.

Accounting information systems collect and process data from transactions and events, organize them in useful reports, and communicate results to decision makers. With the increasing complexity of business and the growing need for information, accounting information systems are more important than ever. All decision makers need to have a basic knowledge of how accounting information systems work. This knowledge gives decision makers a competitive edge as they gain a better understanding of information constraints, measurement limitations, and potential applications. It allows them to make more informed decisions and to better balance the risks and returns of different strategies. This section explains five basic principles of accounting information systems, shown in Exhibit 7.1.

Exhibit 7.1

System Principles

Control
Relevance
Compatibility
Flexibility
Cost-Benefit Principle
System Principles

Control Principle

Managers need to control and monitor business activities. The **control principle** prescribes that an accounting information system have internal controls. **Internal controls** are methods and procedures allowing managers to control and monitor business activities. They include policies to direct operations toward common goals, procedures to ensure reliable financial reports, safeguards to protect company assets, and methods to achieve compliance with laws and regulations. Chapter 8 describes detailed control procedures.

Point: A hacker stole 300,000 credit card numbers from online music retailer **CDUniverse** due to internal control failure.

Relevance Principle

Decision makers need relevant information to make informed decisions. The **relevance principle** prescribes that an accounting information system report useful, understandable, timely, and pertinent information for effective decision making. The system must be designed to capture data that make a difference in decisions. To ensure this, we must consider all decision makers when identifying relevant information for disclosure.

Compatibility Principle

Accounting information systems must be consistent with the aims of a company. The **compatibility principle** prescribes that an accounting information system conform with a company's activities, personnel, and structure. It also must adapt to a company's unique characteristics. The system must not be intrusive but must work in harmony with and be driven by company goals. Most start-up entrepreneurs require only a simple information system. **Harley-Davidson**, on the other hand, demands both a merchandising and a manufacturing information system able to assemble data from its global operations.

Flexibility Principle

Accounting information systems must be able to adjust to changes. The **flexibility principle** prescribes that an accounting information system be able to adapt to changes in the company, business environment, and needs of decisions makers. Technological advances, competitive pressures, consumer tastes, regulations, and company activities constantly evolve. A system must be designed to adapt to these changes.

Cost-Benefit Principle

The **cost-benefit principle** prescribes that the benefits from an activity in an accounting information system outweigh the costs of that activity. The costs and benefits of an activity such as producing a specific report will impact the decisions of both external and internal users. Decisions regarding other systems principles (control, relevance, compatibility, and flexibility) are also affected by the cost-benefit principle.

Components of Accounting Systems

Accounting information systems consist of people, records, methods, and equipment. The systems are designed to capture information about a company's transactions and to provide output including financial, managerial, and tax reports. All accounting information systems have these same goals, and thus share some basic components. These components apply whether or not a system is heavily computerized, yet the components of computerized systems usually provide more accuracy, speed, efficiency, and convenience than those of manual systems.

The five basic **components of accounting systems** are source documents, input devices, information processors, information storage, and output devices. Exhibit 7.2 shows these components as a series of steps, yet we know that much two-way communication occurs between many of these components. We briefly describe each of these key components in this section.

C2 Identify components of accounting information systems.

Exhibit 7.2

Accounting System Components

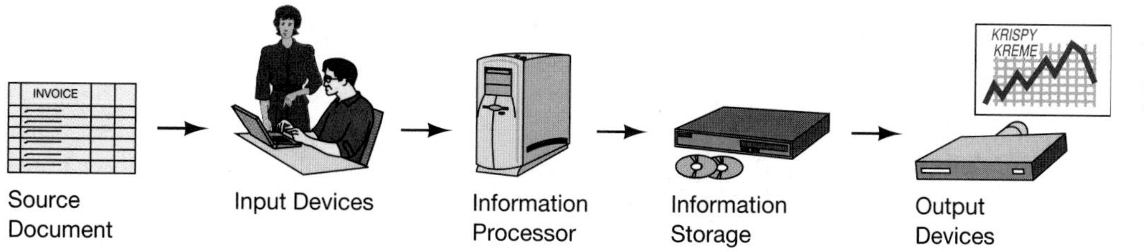

Source Documents

We introduced source documents in Chapters 1 and 2 and explained their importance for both business transactions and information collection. Source documents provide the basic information processed by an accounting system. Examples of source documents include bank statements and checks, invoices from suppliers, billings to customers, cash register files, and employee earnings records. Source documents can be paper, although they increasingly are taking the form of electronic files and Web communications. A growing number of companies are sending documents directly from their systems to their customers' and suppliers' systems. The Web is playing a major role in this transformation from paper-based to *paperless* systems.

Accurate source documents are crucial to accounting information systems. Input of faulty or incomplete information seriously impairs the reliability and relevance of the information system. We commonly refer to this as "garbage in, garbage out." Information systems are set up with attention on control procedures to limit the possibility of entering faulty data in the system.

Decision Insight

Remote Input Scanners are increasingly embedded in cell phones and other handheld devices to gain access to Websites equipped with bar code readers. The phones can scan the bar codes in and then the user gains access to sites that market products and services.

Input Devices

Input devices capture information from source documents and enable its transfer to the system's information processing component. These devices often involve converting data on source documents from written or electronic form to a form usable for the system. Journal entries, both electronic and paper based, are a type of input device. Keyboards, scanners, and modems are some of the most common input devices in practice today. For example, bar code readers capture code numbers and transfer them to the organization's computer for processing. Moreover, a scanner can capture writing samples and other input directly from source documents.

Point: Understanding a manual accounting system is useful in understanding an electronic system.

Controls are used to ensure that only authorized individuals input data to the system. Controls increase the system's reliability and allow information to be traced back to its source.

Information Processors

Information processors are systems that interpret, transform, and summarize information for use in analysis and reporting. An important part of an information processor in accounting systems is professional judgment. Accounting principles are never so structured that they limit the need for professional judgment. Other parts of an information processor include journals, ledgers, working papers, and posting procedures. Each assists in transforming raw data to useful information.

Increasingly, computer technology (both computing hardware and software) is assisting manual information processors. This assistance is freeing accounting professionals to take on increased analysis, interpretive, and managerial roles. Web-based application service providers (ASPs) offer another type of information processor.

Information Storage

Point: A financial accounting database can be designed to support a wide range of internal reports for management.

Information storage is the accounting system component that keeps data in a form accessible to information processors. After being input and processed, data are stored for use in future analyses and reports. The database must be accessible to preparers of periodic financial reports. Auditors rely on this database when they audit both financial statements and a company's controls. Companies also maintain files of source documents.

Older systems consisted almost exclusively of paper documents, but most modern systems depend on electronic storage devices. Advances in information storage enable accounting systems to increasingly store more detailed data. This means managers have more

Decision Insight

Geek Chic Cyberfashion pioneers are creating geek chic, a kind of wearable computer. Cyberfashion draws on digital cellular phones, lithium batteries, and miniature monitors. Special thread is woven into clothing to carry low-voltage signals from one part of the system to another, and fabric keyboards are sewn into clothes. These creations give new meaning to the term *software*.

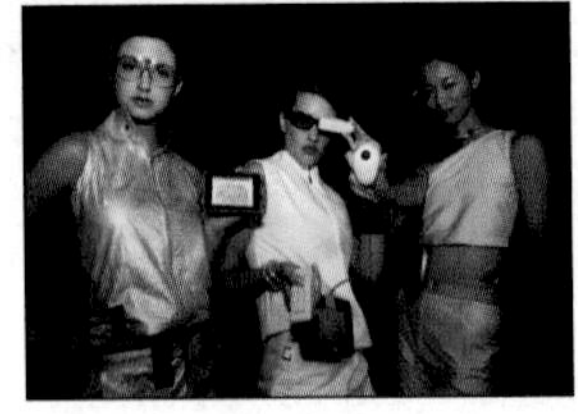

data to access and work with in planning and controlling business activities. Note that information storage can be online, meaning that data can be accessed whenever, and from wherever, it is needed. Off-line storage means access often requires assistance and authorization. Information storage is increasingly augmented by Web sources such as SEC databases, benchmarking services, and financial and product markets.

Decision Insight

Direct Output A screenless computer display, called *virtual retinal display* (VRD), scans rows of pixels directly onto the user's retina by means of a laser. VRDs can simulate three-dimensional virtual worlds, including 3D financial graphics.

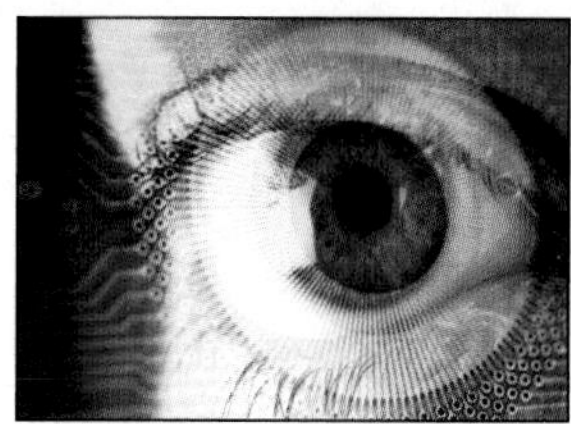

Output Devices

Output devices are the means to take information out of an accounting system and make it available to users. Common output devices are printers, monitors, LCD projectors, and Web communications. Output devices provide users a variety of items including graphics, analysis reports, bills to customers, checks to suppliers, employee paychecks, financial statements, and internal reports. When requests for output occur, an information processor takes the needed data from a database and prepares the necessary report, which is then sent to an output device. A special type of output is an electronic funds transfer (EFT). One example is the transfer of payroll from the company's bank account to its employees' bank accounts. This requires an interface to allow a company's accounting system to send payroll data directly to the bank's accounting system. This interface can involve a company recording its payroll data on CD and forwarding it to the bank. The bank then uses this output to transfer wages earned to employees' accounts.

Decision Ethics

Accountant Your client requests advice in purchasing software for its accounting system. You have been offered a 10% commission by a software company for each purchase of its system by one of your clients. Does this commission arrangement affect your evaluation of software? Do you tell your client about the commission arrangement?

Answer—p. 287

Quick Check

1. Identify the five primary components of an accounting information system.
2. What is the aim of information processors in an accounting system?
3. How are data in the information storage component of an accounting system used?

Answers—p. 288

Special Journals in Accounting

This section describes the underlying records of accounting information systems. Designed correctly, these records support efficiency in processing transactions and events. They are part of all systems in various forms and are increasingly electronic. Even in technologically advanced systems, a basic understanding of the records we describe in this section aids in using, interpreting, and applying accounting information. It also improves our knowledge of computer-based systems. Remember that all accounting systems have common purposes and internal workings whether or not they depend on technology.

C3 Explain the goals and uses of special journals.

This section focuses on special journals and subsidiary ledgers that are an important part of accounting systems. We describe how special journals are used to capture transactions, and we explain how subsidiary ledgers are set up to capture details of accounts. This section uses a *perpetual* inventory system, and the special journals are set up using this system. Appendix 7A describes the change in special journals required for a *periodic* system. We also include a note at the bottom of each of the special journals explaining the change required if a company uses a periodic system.

Basics of Special Journals

Point: Companies can use as many special journals as necessary given their unique business activities.

A **general journal** is an all-purpose journal in which we can record any transaction. Use of a general journal for all transactions is usually more costly for a business *and* is a less effective control procedure. Moreover, for less technologically advanced systems, use of a general journal requires that each debit and each credit entered be individually posted to its respective ledger account. To enhance internal control and reduce costs, transactions are organized into common groups. A **special journal** is used to record and post transactions of similar type. Most transactions of a merchandiser, for instance, can be categorized into the journals shown in Exhibit 7.3. This section assumes the use of these four special journals along with the general journal. The general journal continues to be used for transactions not covered by special journals and for adjusting, closing, and correcting entries. We show in the following discussion that special journals are *efficient tools in helping journalize and post transactions.* This is done, for instance, by accumulating debits and credits of similar transactions, which allows posting of amounts as column *totals* rather than as individual amounts. The advantage of this system increases as the number of transactions increases. Special journals allow an *efficient division of labor,* which is also an effective control procedure.

Point: A specific transaction is recorded in only *one* journal.

Exhibit 7.3

Using Special Journals with a General Journal

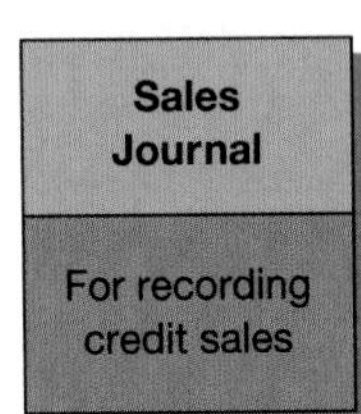

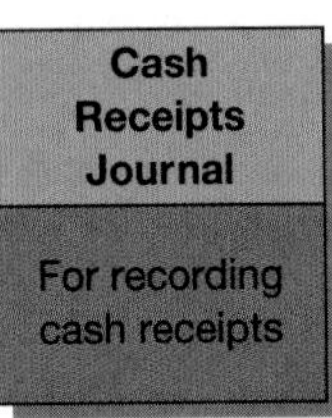

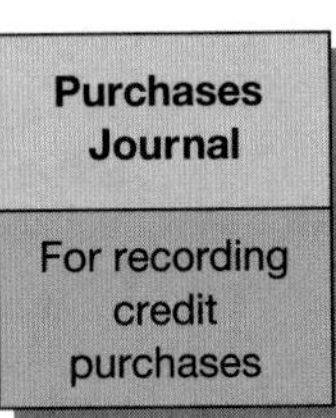

Cash Disbursement Journal
For recording cash payments

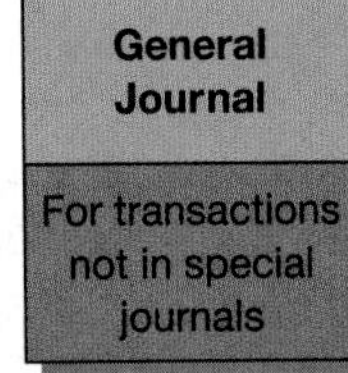

It is important to note that special journals and subsidiary ledgers *are designed in a manner that is best suited for each business.* The most likely candidates for special journal status are recurring transactions—for many businesses those are sales, cash receipts, purchases, and cash disbursements. However, good systems design for a business could involve collapsing sales and cash receipts in one journal, or purchases and cash disbursement in another. It could also involve adding more special journals or additional subsidiary ledgers for other recurring transactions. This design decision extends to journal and ledger format. That is, the selection on number of columns, column headings, and so forth is based on what is best suited for each business. Thus, you should read the following sections as one example of a common systems design, but not the only design.

Subsidiary Ledgers

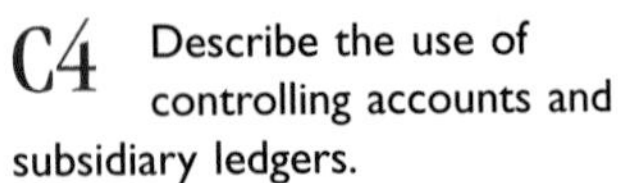
C4 Describe the use of controlling accounts and subsidiary ledgers.

To understand special journals, it is necessary to understand the workings of a **subsidiary ledger,** which is a list of individual accounts with a common characteristic. A subsidiary ledger contains detailed information on specific accounts in the general ledger. Information systems often include several subsidiary ledgers. Two of the most important are:

- *Accounts receivable ledger*—stores transaction data of individual customers.
- *Accounts payable ledger*—stores transaction data of individual suppliers.

Individual accounts in subsidiary ledgers are often arranged alphabetically, which is the approach taken here. We describe accounts receivable and accounts payable ledgers in this section. Our discussion of special journals uses these ledgers.

Topic Tackler 7-1

Accounts Receivable Ledger When we recorded credit sales in prior chapters, we debited (increased) Accounts Receivable. When a company has more than one credit customer, the accounts receivable records must show how much *each* customer purchased, paid, and has yet to pay. This information is collected by keeping a separate account receivable for each credit customer. A separate account for each customer *could* be kept in the general ledger with the other financial statement accounts, but this is uncommon. Instead, the general ledger usually has a single Accounts Receivable account, and a *subsidiary ledger* is set up to keep a separate account for each customer. This subsidiary ledger is called the **accounts receivable ledger** (also called *accounts receivable subsidiary ledger* or *customers ledger*), and it can exist in electronic or paper form.

Exhibit 7.4 shows the relation between the Accounts Receivable account and its individual accounts in the subsidiary ledger. After all items are posted, the balance in the Accounts Receivable account must equal the sum of all balances of its customers' accounts. The Accounts Receivable account is said to control the accounts receivable ledger and is called a **controlling account.** Since the accounts receivable ledger is a supplementary record controlled by an account in the general ledger, it is called a *subsidiary* ledger.

Point: When a general ledger account has a subsidiary ledger, any transaction that impacts one of them also impacts the other—some refer to this as *general and subsidiaries ledgers kept in tandem.*

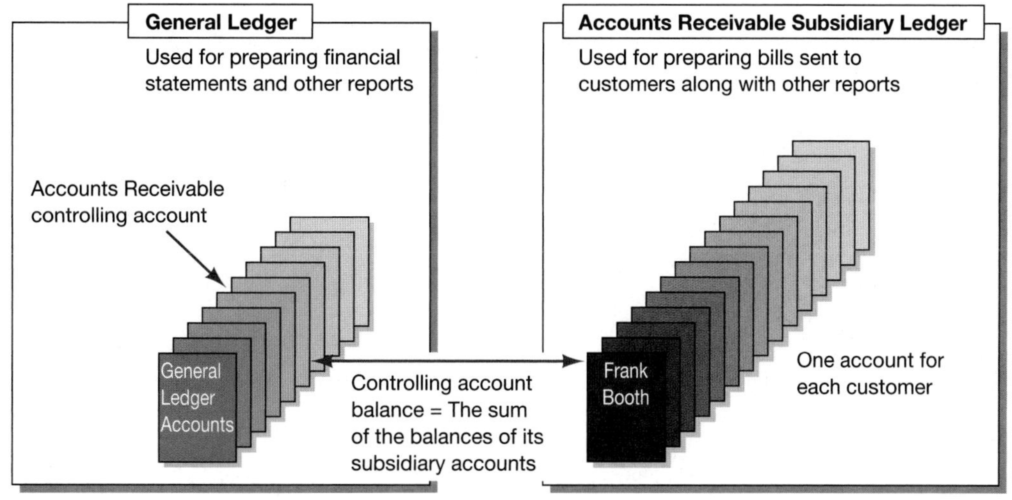

Exhibit 7.4

Accounts Receivable Controlling Account and Its Subsidiary Ledger

Accounts Payable Ledger There are other controlling accounts and subsidiary ledgers. We know, for example, that many companies buy on credit from several suppliers. This means that companies must keep a separate account for each supplier by keeping an Accounts Payable controlling account in the general ledger and a separate account for each supplier (creditor) in an **accounts payable ledger** (also called *accounts payable subsidiary ledger* or *creditors ledger*).

Point: Subsidiary ledgers: (1) remove excessive details from general ledger, (2) provide up-to-date info on customer or other specific account balances, (3) aid in error identification for individual accounts, and (4) help with division of labor (recordkeeping tasks).

Other Subsidiary Ledgers Subsidiary ledgers are common for several other accounts. A company with many classes of equipment, for example, might keep only one Equipment account in its general ledger, but its Equipment account would control a subsidiary ledger in which each class of equipment is recorded in a separate account. Similar treatment is common for investments, inventory, and any accounts needing separate detailed records. **Arctic Cat** reports sales information by product line in its annual report. Yet its accounting system keeps much more detailed sales records. Arctic Cat, for instance, sells hundreds of different products and must be able to analyze the sales performance of each. This detail can be captured by many different general ledger sales accounts but is instead captured by using supplementary records that function like subsidiary ledgers. Overall, subsidiary ledgers are applied in many different ways to ensure that the accounting system captures sufficient details to support analyses that decision makers need.

Sales Journal

A typical **sales journal** is used to record sales of inventory *on credit.* Sales of inventory for cash are not recorded in a sales journal but in a cash receipts journal. Sales of noninventory assets on credit are recorded in the general journal.

P1 Journalize and post transactions using special journals.

Topic Tackler 7-2

Journalizing Credit sale transactions are recorded with information about each sale entered separately in a sales journal. This information is often taken from a copy of the sales ticket or invoice prepared at the time of sale. The top portion of Exhibit 7.5 shows a typical sales journal from a merchandiser. It has columns for recording the date, customer's name, invoice number, posting reference, and the retail and cost amounts of each credit sale. The sales journal in this exhibit is called a **columnar journal,** which is any journal with more than one column.

Point: Each transaction in the sales journal includes a debit to accounts receivable and a credit to sales.

Each transaction recorded in the sales journal yields an entry in the "Accounts Receivable Dr., Sales Cr." column. We usually need only one column for these two accounts. (An exception is when managers need more information about taxes, returns, and other sales details.) Each transaction in the sales journal also yields an entry in the "Cost of Goods Sold Dr., Inventory Cr." column. This entry reflects the perpetual inventory system of tracking costs with each sale. To illustrate, on February 2, this company sold merchandise on account to Jason Henry for $450. The invoice number is 307, and the cost of this merchandise is

Exhibit 7.5

Sales Journal with Posting*

Accounting System: Exhibit 7–5

File Edit Maintain Tasks Analysis Options Reports Window Help

Sales Journal Page 3

Date	Account Debited	Invoice Number	PR	Accounts Receivable Dr. Sales Cr.	Cost of Goods Sold Dr. Inventory Cr.
Feb. 2	Jason Henry	307	✓	450	315
7	Albert Co.	308	✓	500	355
13	Kam Moore	309	✓	350	260
15	Paul Roth	310	✓	200	150
22	Jason Henry	311	✓	225	155
25	Frank Booth	312	✓	175	95
28	Albert Co.	313	✓	250	170
28	Totals			2,150	1,500
				(106/413)	(502/119)

Individual amounts are posted immediately to the subsidiary ledger.

Totals are posted at the end of the period to General Ledger accounts.

Accounts Receivable Ledger

Albert Co.

Date	PR	Debit	Credit	Balance
Feb. 7	S3	500		500
28	S3	250		750

Frank Booth

Date	PR	Debit	Credit	Balance
Feb. 25	S3	175		175

Jason Henry

Date	PR	Debit	Credit	Balance
Feb. 2	S3	450		450
22	S3	225		675

Kam Moore

Date	PR	Debit	Credit	Balance
Feb. 13	S3	350		350

Paul Roth

Date	PR	Debit	Credit	Balance
Feb. 15	S3	200		200

General Ledger

Accounts Receivable No. 106

Date	PR	Debit	Credit	Balance
Feb. 28	S3	2,150		2,150

Inventory No. 119

Date	PR	Debit	Credit	Balance
Feb. 1	bal.			15,700
28	S3		1,500	14,200

Sales No. 413

Date	PR	Debit	Credit	Balance
Feb. 28	S3		2,150	2,150

Cost of Goods Sold No. 502

Date	PR	Debit	Credit	Balance
Feb. 28	S3	1,500		1,500

Customer accounts are in a subsidiary ledger and the financial statement accounts are in the General Ledger.

Sales Purchases General Ledger Payroll Inventory Company Analysis

*The Sales Journal in a *periodic* system would exclude the column on the far right titled "Cost of Goods Sold Dr., Inventory Cr." (see Exhibit 7A.1).

$315. This information is captured on one line in the sales journal. No further explanations or entries are necessary, saving time and effort. Moreover, this sales journal is consistent with most inventory systems that use bar codes to record both sales and costs with each sale transaction. Note that the Posting Reference (PR) column is not used when entering transactions but instead is used when posting.

Point: Continuously updated customer accounts provide timely information for customer inquiries on those accounts. Keeping creditor accounts updated provides timely information on current amounts owed.

Posting A sales journal is posted as reflected in the arrow lines of Exhibit 7.5. Two types of posting can be identified: (1) posting to the subsidiary ledger(s) and (2) posting to the general ledger.

Posting to subsidiary ledger. Individual transactions in the sales journal are posted regularly (typically concurrently) to customer accounts in the accounts receivable ledger. These postings keep customer accounts up-to-date, which is important for the person granting credit to customers. When sales recorded in the sales journal are individually posted to customer accounts in the accounts receivable ledger, check marks are entered in the sales journal's PR column. Check marks are used rather than account numbers because customer accounts usually are arranged alphabetically in the accounts receivable ledger. Note that posting debits to Accounts Receivable twice—once to Accounts Receivable and once to the customer's subsidiary account—does not violate the accounting equation of debits equal credits. The equality of debits and credits is always maintained in the general ledger.

Point: PR column is only checked *after* the amount(s) is posted.

Posting to general ledger. The sales journal's account columns are totaled at the end of each period (the month of February in this case). For the "sales" column, the $2,150 total is debited to Accounts Receivable and credited to Sales in the general ledger (see Exhibit 7.5). For the "cost" column, the $1,500 total is debited to Cost of Goods Sold and credited to Inventory in the general ledger. When totals are posted to accounts in the general ledger, the account numbers are entered below the column total in the sales journal for tracking. For example, we enter (106/413) below the total in the sales column after this amount is posted to account number 106 (Accounts Receivable) and account number 413 (Sales).

Point: Postings are automatic in a computerized system.

A company identifies in the PR column of its subsidiary ledgers the journal and page number from which an amount is taken. We identify a journal by using an initial. Items posted from the sales journal carry the initial ***S*** before their journal page numbers in a PR column. Likewise, items from the cash receipts journal carry the initial ***R***; items from the cash disbursements journal carry the initial ***D***; items from the purchases journal carry the initial ***P***; and items from the general journal carry the initial ***G***.

Proving the Ledgers Account balances in the general ledger and subsidiary ledgers are periodically proved (or reviewed) for accuracy after posting. To do this we first prepare a trial balance of the general ledger to confirm that debits equal credits. Second, we test a subsidiary ledger by preparing a *schedule* of individual accounts and amounts. A **schedule of accounts receivable** lists each customer and the balance owed. If this total equals the balance of the Accounts Receivable controlling account, the accounts in the accounts receivable ledger are assumed correct. Exhibit 7.6 shows a schedule of accounts receivable drawn from the accounts receivable ledger of Exhibit 7.5.

P2 Prepare and prove the accuracy of subsidiary ledgers.

Exhibit 7.6

Schedule of Accounts Receivable

Schedule of Accounts Receivable February 28	
Albert Co.	$ 750
Frank Booth	175
Jason Henry	675
Kam Moore	350
Paul Roth	200
Total accounts receivable	$2,150

Additional Issues We consider three additional issues with the sales journal: (1) recording sales taxes, (2) recording sales returns and allowances, and (3) using actual sales invoices as a journal.

Point: In accounting, the word *schedule* generally means a list.

Sales taxes. Governmental agencies such as cities and states often require sellers to collect sales taxes from customers and to periodically send these taxes to the appropriate agency.

When using a columnar sales journal, we can keep a record of taxes collected by adding a Sales Taxes Payable column as follows:

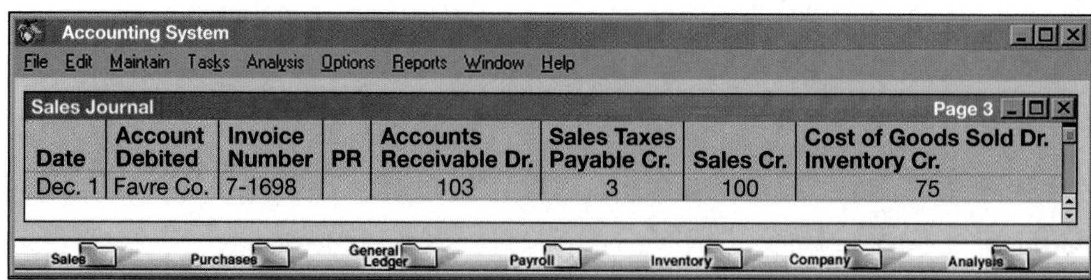

Date	Account Debited	Invoice Number	PR	Accounts Receivable Dr.	Sales Taxes Payable Cr.	Sales Cr.	Cost of Goods Sold Dr. Inventory Cr.
Dec. 1	Favre Co.	7-1698		103	3	100	75

Individual amounts in the Accounts Receivable column would continue to be posted immediately to customer accounts in the accounts receivable ledger. Individual amounts in the Sales Taxes Payable and Sales columns are not posted. Column totals would continue to be posted as usual. (A company that collects sales taxes on its cash sales can also use a Sales Taxes Payable column in its cash receipts journal.)

Sales returns and allowances. A company with only a few sales returns and allowances can record them in a general journal with an entry such as this:

Assets = Liabilities + Equity
−175 −175

May 17	Sales Returns and Allowances	414	175	
	Accounts Receivable—Ray Ball	106/✓		175
	Customer returned merchandise.			

The debit in this entry is posted to the Sales Returns and Allowances account (no. 414). The credit is posted to both the Accounts Receivable controlling account (no. 106) and to the customer's account. When we enter the account number and the check mark, 106/✓, in the PR column on the credit line, this means both the Accounts Receivable controlling account in the general ledger and the Ray Ball account in the accounts receivable ledger are credited for $175. [*Note:* If the returned goods can be resold to another customer, the company would debit (increase) the Inventory account and credit (decrease) the Cost of Goods Sold account. If the returned goods are defective (worthless), the company could simply leave their costs in the Cost of Goods Sold account (see Chapter 5).] A company with a large number of sales returns and allowances can save time by recording them in a separate sales returns and allowances journal.

Sales invoices as a sales journal. To save costs, some small companies avoid using a sales journal for credit sales and instead post each sales invoice amount directly to the customer's account in the accounts receivable ledger. They then put copies of invoices in a file. At the end of the period, they total all invoices for that period and make a general journal entry to debit Accounts Receivable and credit Sales for the total amount. The file of invoice copies act as a sales journal. This is called *direct posting of sales invoices.*

Quick Check

4. When special journals are used, where are cash payments by check recorded?
5. How does a columnar journal save posting time and effort?
6. How do debits and credits remain equal when credit sales are posted twice (once to Accounts Receivable and once to the customer's subsidiary account)?
7. How do we identify the journal from which an amount in a ledger account was posted?
8. How are sales taxes recorded in the context of special journals?
9. What is direct posting of sales invoices?

Answers—p. 288

Cash Receipts Journal

A **cash receipts journal** is typically used to record all receipts of cash. Exhibit 7.7 shows one common form of the cash receipts journal.

Exhibit 7.7

Cash Receipts Journal with Posting*

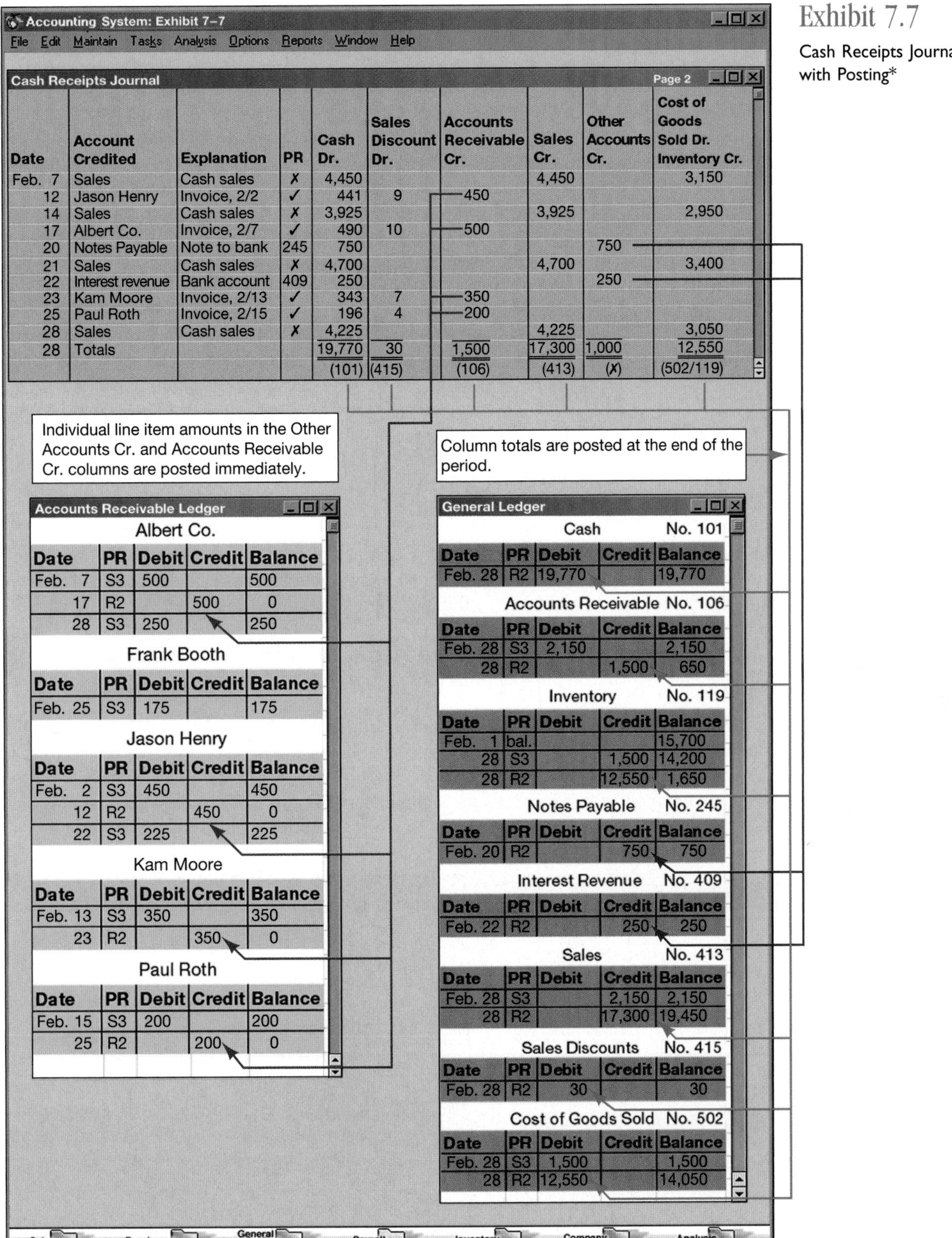

Date	Account Credited	Explanation	PR	Cash Dr.	Sales Discount Dr.	Accounts Receivable Cr.	Sales Cr.	Other Accounts Cr.	Cost of Goods Sold Dr. Inventory Cr.
Feb. 7	Sales	Cash sales	✗	4,450			4,450		3,150
12	Jason Henry	Invoice, 2/2	✓	441	9	450			
14	Sales	Cash sales	✗	3,925			3,925		2,950
17	Albert Co.	Invoice, 2/7	✓	490	10	500			
20	Notes Payable	Note to bank	245	750				750	
21	Sales	Cash sales	✗	4,700			4,700		3,400
22	Interest revenue	Bank account	409	250				250	
23	Kam Moore	Invoice, 2/13	✓	343	7	350			
25	Paul Roth	Invoice, 2/15	✓	196	4	200			
28	Sales	Cash sales	✗	4,225			4,225		3,050
28	Totals			19,770	30	1,500	17,300	1,000	12,550
				(101)	(415)	(106)	(413)	(✗)	(502/119)

Accounts Receivable Ledger

Albert Co.

Date	PR	Debit	Credit	Balance
Feb. 7	S3	500		500
17	R2		500	0
28	S3	250		250

Frank Booth

Date	PR	Debit	Credit	Balance
Feb. 25	S3	175		175

Jason Henry

Date	PR	Debit	Credit	Balance
Feb. 2	S3	450		450
12	R2		450	0
22	S3	225		225

Kam Moore

Date	PR	Debit	Credit	Balance
Feb. 13	S3	350		350
23	R2		350	0

Paul Roth

Date	PR	Debit	Credit	Balance
Feb. 15	S3	200		200
25	R2		200	0

General Ledger

Cash No. 101

Date	PR	Debit	Credit	Balance
Feb. 28	R2	19,770		19,770

Accounts Receivable No. 106

Date	PR	Debit	Credit	Balance
Feb. 28	S3	2,150		2,150
28	R2		1,500	650

Inventory No. 119

Date	PR	Debit	Credit	Balance
Feb. 1	bal.			15,700
28	S3		1,500	14,200
28	R2		12,550	1,650

Notes Payable No. 245

Date	PR	Debit	Credit	Balance
Feb. 20	R2		750	750

Interest Revenue No. 409

Date	PR	Debit	Credit	Balance
Feb. 22	R2		250	250

Sales No. 413

Date	PR	Debit	Credit	Balance
Feb. 28	S3		2,150	2,150
28	R2		17,300	19,450

Sales Discounts No. 415

Date	PR	Debit	Credit	Balance
Feb. 28	R2	30		30

Cost of Goods Sold No. 502

Date	PR	Debit	Credit	Balance
Feb. 28	S3	1,500		1,500
28	R2	12,550		14,050

*The Cash Receipts Journal in a *periodic* system would exclude the column on the far right titled "Cost of Goods Sold Dr., Inventory Cr." (see Exhibit 7A.2).

Point: Each transaction in the cash receipts journal involves a debit to Cash. Credit accounts will vary.

Journalizing and Posting Cash receipts can be separated into one of three types: (1) cash from credit customers in payment of their accounts, (2) cash from cash sales, and (3) cash from other sources. The cash receipts journal in Exhibit 7.7 has a separate credit column for each of these three sources. We describe how to journalize transactions from each of these three sources. (An Explanation column is included in the cash receipts journal to identify the source.)

Cash from credit customers. *Journalizing.* To record cash received in payment of a customer's account, the customer's name is first entered in the Account Credited column—see transactions dated February 12, 17, 23, and 25. Then the amounts debited to both Cash and the Sales Discount (if any) are entered in their respective columns, and the amount credited to the customer's account is entered in the Accounts Receivable Cr. column.

Posting. Individual amounts in the Accounts Receivable Cr. column are posted immediately to customer accounts in the subsidiary accounts receivable ledger. The $1,500 column total is posted at the end of the period (month in this case) as a credit to the Accounts Receivable controlling account in the general ledger.

Cash sales. *Journalizing.* The amount for each cash sale is entered in the Cash Dr. column and the Sales Cr. column. The February 7, 14, 21, and 28 transactions are examples. (Cash sales are usually journalized daily or at point of sale, but are journalized weekly in Exhibit 7.7 for brevity.) Each cash sale also yields an entry to Cost of Goods Sold Dr. and Inventory Cr. for the cost of merchandise—see the far right column.

Point: Some software packages put cash sales in the sales journal.

Posting. For cash sales, we place an *x* in the PR column to indicate that its amount is not individually posted. We do post the $17,300 Sales Cr. total and the $12,550 total from the "cost" column.

Example: Record in the cash receipts journal a $700 cash sale of land when the land carries a $700 original cost. *Answer:* Debit the Cash column for $700, and credit the Other Accounts column for $700 (the account credited is Land).

Cash from other sources. *Journalizing.* Examples of cash from other sources are money borrowed from a bank, cash interest received on account, and cash sale of noninventory assets. The transactions of February 20 and 22 are illustrative. The Other Accounts Cr. column is used for these transactions.

Posting. Amounts from these transactions are immediately posted to their general ledger accounts and the PR column identifies those accounts.

Footing, Crossfooting, and Posting To be sure that total debits and credits in a columnar journal are equal, we often crossfoot column totals before posting them. To *foot* a column of numbers is to add it. To *crossfoot* in this case is to add the Debit column totals, then add the Credit column totals, and compare the two sums for equality. Footing and crossfooting of the numbers in Exhibit 7.7 results in the report in Exhibit 7.8.

Point: Subsidiary ledgers and their controlling accounts are *in balance* only after all posting is complete.

Exhibit 7.8

Footing and Crossfooting Journal Totals

Debit Columns		Credit Columns	
Cash Dr.	$19,770	Accounts Receivable Cr.	$ 1,500
Sales Discounts Dr.	30	Sales Cr.	17,300
Cost of Goods Sold Dr.	12,550	Other Accounts Cr.	1,000
		Inventory Cr.	12,550
Total	$32,350	Total	$32,350

Decision Maker

Entrepreneur You want to know how promptly customers are paying their bills. This information can help you decide whether to extend credit and to plan your cash payments. Where do you find this information?

Answer—p. 287

At the end of the period, after crossfooting the journal to confirm that debits equal credits, the total amounts from the columns of the cash receipts journal are posted to their general ledger accounts. The Other Accounts Cr. column total is not posted because the individual amounts are directly posted to their general ledger accounts. We place an *x* below the Other

Accounts Cr. column to indicate that this column total is not posted. The account numbers for the column totals that are posted are entered in parentheses below each column. (*Note:* Posting items immediately from the Other Accounts Cr. column with a delayed posting of their offsetting items in the Cash column total causes the general ledger to be out of balance during the period. Posting the Cash Dr. column total at the end of the period corrects this imbalance in the general ledger before the trial balance and financial statements are prepared.)

Purchases Journal

A **purchases journal** is typically used to record all credit purchases, including those for inventory. Purchases for cash are recorded in the Cash Disbursements Journal.

Journalizing Entries in the purchases journal in Exhibit 7.9 reflect purchase invoices or other source documents. We use the invoice date and terms to compute the date when payment

Point: The number of special journals and the design of each are based on a company's specific needs.

Exhibit 7.9

Purchases Journal with Posting*

Accounting System: Exhibit 7–9

File Edit Maintain Tasks Analysis Options Reports Window Help

Purchases Journal — Page 1

Date	Account	Date of Invoice	Terms	PR	Accounts Payable Cr.	Inventory Dr.	Office Supplies Dr.	Other Accounts Dr.
Feb. 3	Horning Supply Co.	2/2	n/30	✓	350	275	75	
5	Ace Mfg. Co.	2/5	2/10, n/30	✓	200	200		
13	Wynet & Co.	2/10	2/10, n/30	✓	150	150		
20	Smite Co.	2/18	2/10, n/30	✓	300	300		
25	Ace Mfg. Co.	2/24	2/10, n/30	✓	100	100		
28	Store Supplies/ITT Co.	2/28	n/30	125/✓	225	125	25	75
28	Totals				1,325	1,150	100	75
					(201)	(119)	(124)	(X)

Individual amounts in the Other Accounts Dr. and the Accounts Payable Cr. columns are posted immediately.

Column totals, except for Other Accounts Dr. column, are posted at the end of the period.

Accounts Payable Ledger

Ace Mfg. Company

Date	PR	Debit	Credit	Balance
Feb. 5	P1		200	200
25	P1		100	300

Horning Supply Company

Date	PR	Debit	Credit	Balance
Feb. 3	P1		350	350

ITT Company

Date	PR	Debit	Credit	Balance
Feb. 28	P1		225	225

Smite Company

Date	PR	Debit	Credit	Balance
Feb. 20	P1		300	300

Wynet and Company

Date	PR	Debit	Credit	Balance
Feb. 13	P1		150	150

General Ledger

Inventory No. 119

Date	PR	Debit	Credit	Balance
Feb. 1	bal.			15,700
28	S3		1,500	14,200
28	R2		12,550	1,650
28	P1	1,150		2,800

Office Supplies No. 124

Date	PR	Debit	Credit	Balance
Feb. 28	P1	100		100

Store Supplies No. 125

Date	PR	Debit	Credit	Balance
Feb. 28	P1	75		75

Accounts Payable No. 201

Date	PR	Debit	Credit	Balance
Feb. 28	P1		1,325	1,325

Sales Purchases General Ledger Payroll Inventory Company Analysis

*The Purchases Journal in a *periodic* system replaces "Inventory Dr." with "Purchases Dr." (see Exhibit 7A.3).

for each purchase is due. The Accounts Payable Cr. column is used to record the amounts owed to each creditor. Inventory purchases are recorded in the Inventory Dr. column.

To illustrate, inventory costing $200 is purchased from Ace Manufacturing on February 5. The creditor's name (Ace) is entered in the Account column, the invoice date is entered in the Date of Invoice column, the purchase terms are entered in the Terms column, and the $200 amount is entered in the Accounts Payable Cr. and the Inventory Dr. columns. When a purchase involves an amount recorded in the Other Accounts Dr. column, we use the Account column to identify the general ledger account debited. For example, the February 28 transaction involves purchases of inventory, office supplies, and store supplies from ITT. The journal has no column for store supplies, so the Other Accounts Dr. column is used. In this case, Store Supplies is entered in the Account column along with the creditor's name (ITT). This purchases journal also includes a separate column for credit purchases of office supplies. A separate column such as this is useful when several transactions involve debits to the same account. Each company uses its own judgment in deciding on the number of separate columns necessary.

Point: Each transaction in the purchases journal involves a credit to Accounts Payable. Debit accounts will vary.

Point: The Other Accounts Dr. column allows the purchases journal to be used for any purchase transaction on credit.

Posting The amounts in the Accounts Payable Cr. column are immediately posted to individual creditor accounts in the accounts payable subsidiary ledger. Individual amounts in the Other Accounts Dr. column are immediately posted to their general ledger accounts. At the end of the period, all column totals except the Other Accounts Dr. column are posted to their general ledger accounts.

Exhibit 7.10

Schedule of Accounts Payable

Schedule of Accounts Payable February 28	
Ace Mfg. Company	$ 300
Horning Supply Company	350
ITT Company	225
Smite Company	300
Wynet & Company	150
Total accounts payable	$1,325

Proving the Ledger Accounts payable balances in the subsidiary ledger are proved after posting the purchases journal. We prove the subsidiary ledger by preparing a **schedule of accounts payable,** which is a list of accounts from the accounts payable ledger with their balances and the total. If this total equals the balance of the Accounts Payable controlling account, the accounts in the accounts payable ledger are assumed correct. Exhibit 7.10 shows a schedule of accounts payable drawn from the accounts payable ledger of Exhibit 7.9.

Point: The balance in the Accounts Payable controlling account must equal the sum of the individual account balances in the accounts payable subsidiary ledger after posting.

Cash Disbursements Journal

A **cash disbursements journal,** also called a *cash payments journal,* is typically used to record all cash payments.

Journalizing The cash disbursements journal shown in Exhibit 7.11 illustrates repetitive entries to the Cash Cr. column of this journal (reflecting cash payments). Also note the frequent credits to Inventory (which reflect purchase discounts) and the debits to Accounts Payable. For example, on February 15, the company pays Ace on account (credit terms of 2/10, n/30—see February 5 transaction in Exhibit 7.9). Since payment occurs in the discount period, the company pays $196 ($200 invoice less $4 discount). The $4 discount is credited to Inventory. Note that when this company purchases inventory for cash, it is recorded using the Other Accounts Dr. column and the Cash Cr. column as illustrated in the February 3 and 12 transactions. Generally, the Other Accounts column is used to record cash payments on items for which no column exists. For example, on February 15, the company pays salaries expense of $250. The title of the account debited (Salaries Expense) is entered in the Account Debited column.

The cash disbursements journal has a column titled Ck. No. (check number). For control over cash disbursements, all payments except for those of small amounts are made by check.

Point: Each transaction in the cash disbursements journal involves a credit to Cash. Debit accounts will vary.

Decision Maker

Controller You wish to analyze your company's cash payments to suppliers and its purchases discounts. Where do you find this information?

Answer—p. 287

Exhibit 7.11

Cash Disbursements Journal with Posting*

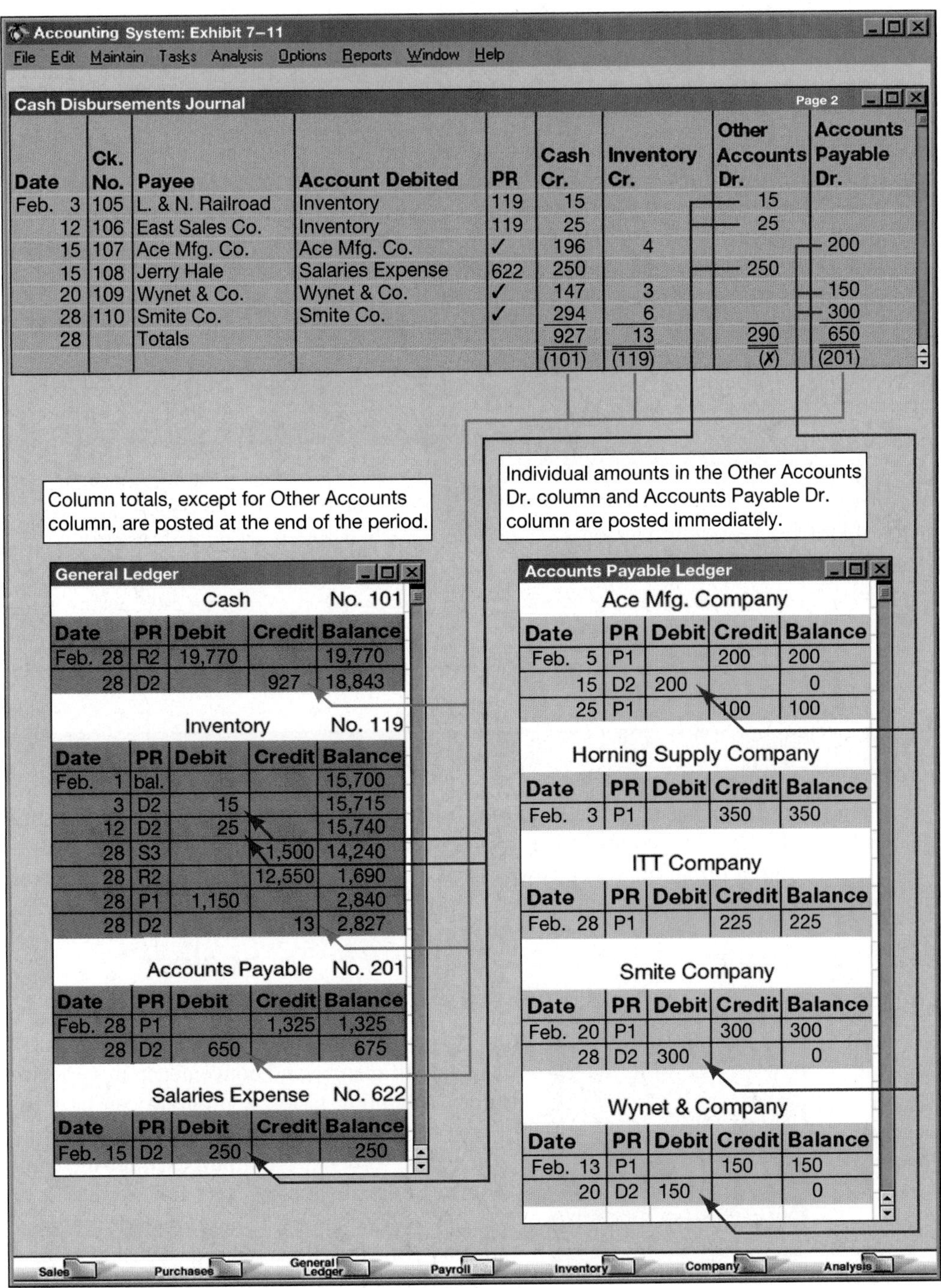

Accounting System: Exhibit 7–11

File Edit Maintain Tasks Analysis Options Reports Window Help

Cash Disbursements Journal — Page 2

Date	Ck. No.	Payee	Account Debited	PR	Cash Cr.	Inventory Cr.	Other Accounts Dr.	Accounts Payable Dr.
Feb. 3	105	L. & N. Railroad	Inventory	119	15		15	
12	106	East Sales Co.	Inventory	119	25		25	
15	107	Ace Mfg. Co.	Ace Mfg. Co.	✓	196	4		200
15	108	Jerry Hale	Salaries Expense	622	250		250	
20	109	Wynet & Co.	Wynet & Co.	✓	147	3		150
28	110	Smite Co.	Smite Co.	✓	294	6		300
28		Totals			927	13	290	650
					(101)	(119)	(✗)	(201)

Column totals, except for Other Accounts column, are posted at the end of the period.

Individual amounts in the Other Accounts Dr. column and Accounts Payable Dr. column are posted immediately.

General Ledger

Cash — No. 101

Date	PR	Debit	Credit	Balance
Feb. 28	R2	19,770		19,770
28	D2		927	18,843

Inventory — No. 119

Date	PR	Debit	Credit	Balance
Feb. 1	bal.			15,700
3	D2	15		15,715
12	D2	25		15,740
28	S3		1,500	14,240
28	R2		12,550	1,690
28	P1	1,150		2,840
28	D2		13	2,827

Accounts Payable — No. 201

Date	PR	Debit	Credit	Balance
Feb. 28	P1		1,325	1,325
28	D2	650		675

Salaries Expense — No. 622

Date	PR	Debit	Credit	Balance
Feb. 15	D2	250		250

Accounts Payable Ledger

Ace Mfg. Company

Date	PR	Debit	Credit	Balance
Feb. 5	P1		200	200
15	D2	200		0
25	P1		100	100

Horning Supply Company

Date	PR	Debit	Credit	Balance
Feb. 3	P1		350	350

ITT Company

Date	PR	Debit	Credit	Balance
Feb. 28	P1		225	225

Smite Company

Date	PR	Debit	Credit	Balance
Feb. 20	P1		300	300
28	D2	300		0

Wynet & Company

Date	PR	Debit	Credit	Balance
Feb. 13	P1		150	150
20	D2	150		0

*The Cash Disbursements Journal in a *periodic* system replaces "Inventory Cr." with "Purchases Discounts Cr." (see Exhibit 7A.4).

Checks should be prenumbered and each check's number entered in the journal in numerical order in the column headed Ck. No. This makes it possible to scan the numbers in the column for omitted checks. When a cash disbursements journal has a column for check numbers, it is sometimes called a **check register.**

Posting Individual amounts in the Other Accounts Dr. column of a cash disbursements journal are immediately posted to their general ledger accounts. Individual amounts in the Accounts Payable Dr. column are also immediately posted to creditors' accounts in the subsidiary Accounts Payable ledger. At the end of the period, we crossfoot column totals and post the Accounts Payable Dr. column total to the Accounts Payable controlling account.

Also, the Inventory Cr. column total is posted to the Inventory account, and the Cash Cr. column total is posted to the Cash account.

General Journal Transactions

When special journals are used, we still need a general journal for adjusting, closing, and any other transactions for which no special journal has been set up. Examples of these other transactions might include purchases returns and allowances, purchases of plant assets by issuing a note payable, sales returns if a sales returns and allowances journal is not used, and receipt of a note receivable from a customer. We described the recording of transactions in a general journal in Chapters 2 and 3.

Quick Check

10. What are the normal recording and posting procedures when using special journals and controlling accounts with subsidiary ledgers?
11. What is the process for posting to a subsidiary ledger and its controlling account?
12. How do we prove the accuracy of account balances in the general ledger and subsidiary ledgers after posting?
13. Why does a company need a general journal when using special journals for sales, purchases, cash receipts, and cash disbursements?

Answers—p. 288

Technology-Based Accounting Systems

C5 Explain how technology-based information systems impact accounting.

Accounting information systems are supported with technology, which can range from simple calculators to advanced computerized systems. Since technology is increasingly important in accounting information systems, we discuss the impact of computer technology, how data processing works with accounting data, and the role of computer networks.

Decision Insight

Middleware is software allowing different computer programs in a company or across companies to work together. It allows transfer of purchase orders, invoices, and other electronic documents between accounting systems. For example, suppliers can monitor inventory levels of their buyers for production and shipping purposes.

Computer Technology in Accounting

Computer technology provides accuracy, speed, efficiency, and convenience in performing accounting tasks. A program can be written, for instance, to process customers' merchandise orders. Multipurpose off-the-shelf software applications exist for a variety of business operations. These include familiar accounting programs such as Peachtree® and QuickBooks®. Off-the-shelf programs are designed to be user friendly and menu driven, and many operate more efficiently as *integrated* systems. In an integrated system, actions taken in one part of the system automatically affect related parts. When a credit sale is recorded in an integrated system, for instance, several parts of the system are automatically updated, such as posting.

Computer technology can dramatically reduce the time and effort devoted to recordkeeping. Less effort spent on recordkeeping means more time for accounting professionals to concentrate on analysis and managerial decision making. These advances have created a greater demand for accounting professionals who understand financial reports and can draw

Decision Insight

A new generation of Windows- and Web-based accounting support is available. With the touch of a key, users can create real-time inventory reports showing all payments, charges, and credit limits at any point in the accounting cycle. Many services also include "alert signals" notifying the company when, for example, a large order exceeds a customer's credit limit or when purchases need to be made.

insights and information from mountains of processed data. Accounting professionals have expertise in determining relevant and reliable information for decision making. They also can assess the effects of transactions and events on a company and its financial statements.

Data Processing in Accounting

Accounting systems differ with regard to how input is entered and processed. **Online processing** enters and processes data as soon as source documents are available. This means that databases are immediately updated. **Batch processing** accumulates source documents for a period of time and then processes them all at once such as daily, weekly, or monthly. The advantage of online processing is timeliness. This often requires additional costs related to both software and hardware requirements. Companies such as **NetLedger** (NetLedger.com) are making online processing of accounting data a reality for many businesses. The advantage of batch processing is that it requires only periodic updating of databases. Records used to send bills to customers, for instance, might require updating only once a month. The disadvantage of batch processing is the lack of updated databases for management to use when making business decisions.

Computer Networks in Accounting

Networking, or linking computers with each other, can create information advantages (and cost efficiencies). **Computer networks** are links among computers giving different users and different computers access to common databases, programs, and hardware. Many college computer labs, for instance, are networked. A small computer network is called a *local area network (LAN);* it links machines with *hard-wire* hookups. Large computer networks extending over long distances often rely on *modem* or *wireless* communication.

Demand for information sometimes requires advanced networks such as the systems **Federal Express** and **UPS** use to track packages and bill customers and the system **Wal-Mart** uses to monitor inventory levels in its stores. These networks include many computers and satellite communications to gather information and to provide ready access to its databases from all locations.

Enterprise Resource Planning Software

Enterprise resource planning (ERP) software includes the programs that manage a company's vital operations. They extend from order taking to manufacturing to accounting. When working properly, these integrated programs can speed decision making, identify costs for reduction, and give managers control over operations with the click of a mouse. For many managers, ERP software allows them to scrutinize business, identify where inventories are piling up, and see what plants are most efficient. The software is designed to link every part of a company's operations. This software allowed **Monsanto** to slash production planning from six weeks to three, trim its inventories, and increase its bargaining power with suppliers. Monsanto estimates that this software saves the company $200 million per year.

Total ERP Market: About $13 Billion

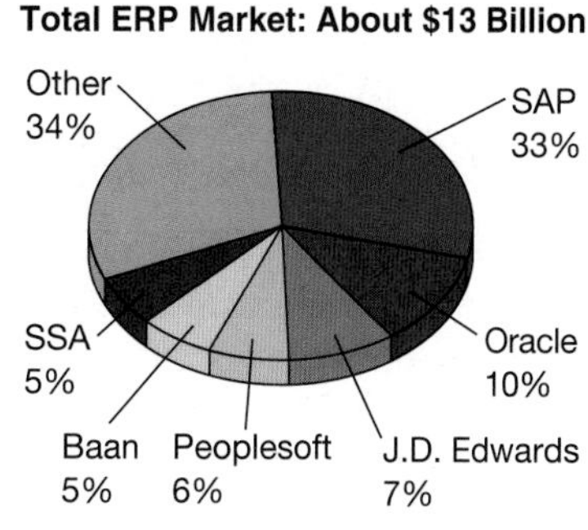

ERP has six major suppliers. **SAP** leads the market, with **Oracle** a distant second. SAP software is used by roughly half of the world's 500 largest companies. It links ordering, inventory, production, purchasing, planning, tracking, and human resources. A transaction or event triggers an immediate chain reaction of events throughout the enterprise. It is making companies more efficient and profitable.

ERP is pushing into cyberspace. Now companies can share data with customers and suppliers. Applesauce maker **Mott's** is using SAP so that distributors can check the status of orders and place them over the Net, and the **Coca-Cola Company** uses it to ship soda on time. ERP is also increasingly used by small business. For example, **NetLedger**'s accounting services to small and medium businesses are powered by Oracle's system.

Quick Check

14. Identify an advantage of an integrated computer-based accounting system.
15. What advantages do computer systems offer over manual systems?
16. Identify an advantage of computer networks.
17. Describe ERP software and its potential advantages to businesses.

Answers—p. 288

Decision Analysis — Segment Return on Assets

Good accounting information systems collect financial data for a company's various segments. A *segment* refers to a part of a company that is separately identified by its products or services, or by the geographic market it serves. **Harley-Davidson** reports that it operates in two business segments: (1) motorcycles and related and (2) financial services. Users of financial statements are especially interested in segment information to better understand a company's activities because segments often vary on profitability, risk, and growth.

Full disclosure by segments is rare because managers are reluctant to release information that can harm its competitive position. Exhibit 7.12 shows survey results on the number of companies with different (reported) segments.

One measure of success for business segments is the **segment return on assets** ratio defined as follows:

Exhibit 7.12

Companies Reporting Operations by These Segments*

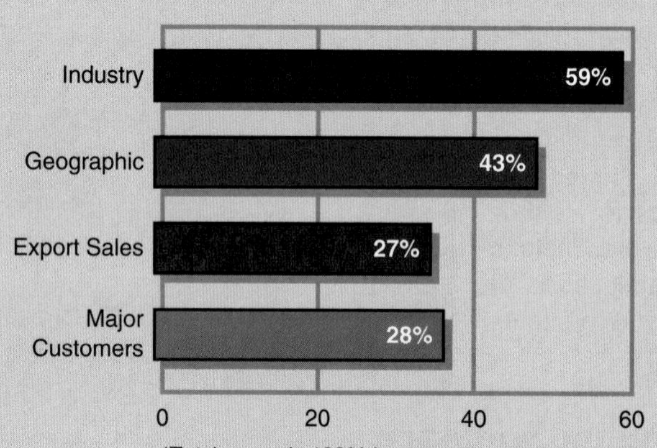

*Total exceeds 100% because companies can report more than one type of segment.

Point: Publicly traded companies must report segment information, including their sales, operating income, identifiable assets, capital expenditures, depreciation, depletion, and amortization.

A1 Compute segment return on assets and use it to evaluate segment performance.

$$\text{Segment return on assets} = \frac{\text{Segment operating income}}{\text{Segment average assets}}$$

This ratio reflects on the profitability of a segment. Exhibit 7.13 shows the segment return on assets for Harley-Davidson from 2000 through 2002.

Exhibit 7.13

Harley-Davidson's Segment Return on Assets ($ millions)

	2002			2001			2000
Segment	Operating Income*	Average Assets	Return on Assets	Operating Income	Average Assets	Return on Assets	Return on Assets
Motorcycles and related	$791	$1,464	54%	$613	$1,272	48%	44%
Financial services	104	1,310	8	61	977	6	4

* A segment's operating income is usually measured as income before taxes, and assets is usually measured as identifiable assets.

The trend in Harley's segment return on assets is increasing for both segments, but its motorcycles segment is much more profitable (54%) than its financial services (8%) segment. Harley should consider further investment in its motorcycles segment if such returns can be sustained. Analysis can also be extended to geographical segments and any other segments that are reported.

Decision Maker

Banker A bicycle merchandiser requests a loan from you to expand operations. Its net income is $220,000, reflecting a 10% increase over the prior year. You ask about segment results. The owner reports that $160,000 of net income is from Cuban operations, reflecting a 60% increase over the prior year. The remaining $60,000 of net income is from U.S. operations, reflecting a 40% decrease. Does this segment information impact your loan decision?

Answer—p. 287

Demonstration Problem—Perpetual System

Pepper Company completed the following selected transactions and events during March of this year. (Terms of all credit sales for the company are 2/10, n/30.)

Mar. 4 Sold merchandise on credit to Jennifer Nelson, Invoice No. 954, for $16,800 (cost is $12,200).

6 Purchased $1,220 of office supplies on credit from Mack Company. Invoice dated March 3, terms n/30.

6 Sold merchandise on credit to Dennie Hoskins, Invoice No. 955, for $10,200 (cost is $8,100).

11 Purchased $52,600 of merchandise, invoice dated March 6, terms 2/10, n/30, from Defore Industries.

12 Borrowed $26,000 cash by giving Commerce Bank a long-term promissory note payable.

14 Received cash payment from Jennifer Nelson for the March 4 sale less the discount.

16 Received a $200 credit memorandum from Defore Industries for unsatisfactory merchandise Pepper purchased on March 11 and later returned.

16 Received cash payment from Dennie Hoskins for the March 6 sale less the discount.

18 Purchased $22,850 of store equipment on credit from Schmidt Supply, invoice dated March 15, terms n/30.

20 Sold merchandise on credit to Marjorie Allen, Invoice No. 956, for $5,600 (cost is $3,800).

21 Sent Defore Industries Check No. 516 in payment of its March 6 dated invoice less the return and the discount.

22 Purchased $41,625 of merchandise, invoice dated March 18, terms 2/10, n/30, from Welch Company.

26 Issued a $600 credit memorandum to Marjorie Allen for defective merchandise Pepper sold on March 20 and Allen later returned.

31 Issued Check No. 517, payable to Payroll, in payment of $15,900 sales salaries for the month. Cashed the check and paid the employees.

31 Cash sales for the month are $134,680 (cost is $67,340). (Cash sales are recorded daily but are recorded only once here to reduce repetitive entries.)

Required

1. Open the following selected general ledger accounts: Cash (101), Accounts Receivable (106) Inventory (119), Office Supplies (124), Store Equipment (165), Accounts Payable (201), Long-Term Notes Payable (251), Sales (413), Sales Returns and Allowances (414), Sales Discounts (415), Cost of Goods Sold (502), and Sales Salaries Expense (621). Open the following accounts receivable ledger accounts: Marjorie Allen, Dennie Hoskins, and Jennifer Nelson. Open the following accounts payable ledger accounts: Defore Industries, Mack Company, Schmidt Supply, and Welch Company.
2. Enter the transactions using a sales journal, a purchases journal, a cash receipts journal, a cash disbursements journal, and a general journal similar to the ones illustrated in the chapter. Regularly post to the individual customer and creditor accounts. Also, post any amounts that should be posted as individual amounts to general ledger accounts. Foot and crossfoot the journals and make the month-end postings. *Pepper Co. uses the perpetual inventory system.*
3. Prepare a trial balance for the selected general ledger accounts in part 1 and prove the accuracy of subsidiary ledgers by preparing schedules of accounts receivable and accounts payable.

Planning the Solution

- Set up the required general ledger, the subsidiary ledger accounts, and the five required journals as illustrated in the chapter.

- Read and analyze each transaction and decide in which special journal (or general journal) the transaction is recorded.
- Record each transaction in the proper journal (and post the appropriate individual amounts).
- Once you have recorded all transactions, total the journal columns. Post from each journal to the appropriate ledger accounts.
- Prepare a trial balance to prove the equality of the debit and credit balances in your general ledger.
- Prepare schedules of accounts receivable and accounts payable. Compare the totals of these schedules to the Accounts Receivable and Accounts Payable controlling account balances, making sure that they agree.

Solution to Demonstration Problem—Perpetual System

Sales Journal — Page 2

Date	Account Debited	Invoice Number	PR	Accounts Receivable Dr. Sales Cr.	Cost of Goods Sold Dr. Inventory Cr.
Mar. 4	Jennifer Nelson	954	✓	16,800	12,200
6	Dennie Hoskins	955	✓	10,200	8,100
20	Marjorie Allen	956	✓	5,600	3,800
31	Totals			32,600	24,100
				(106/413)	(502/119)

Cash Receipts Journal — Page 3

Date	Account Credited	Explanation	PR	Cash Dr.	Sales Discount Dr.	Accounts Receivable Cr.	Sales Cr.	Other Accounts Cr.	Cost of Goods Sold Dr. Inventory Cr.
Mar. 12	L.T. Notes Payable	Note to bank	251	26,000				26,000	
14	Jennifer Nelson	Invoice, 3/4	✓	16,464	336	16,800			
16	Dennie Hoskins	Invoice, 3/6	✓	9,996	204	10,200			
31	Sales	Cash sales	x	134,680			134,680		67,340
31	Totals			187,140	540	27,000	134,680	26,000	67,340
				(101)	(415)	(106)	(413)	(x)	(502/119)

Purchases Journal — Page 3

Date	Account	Date of Invoice	Terms	PR	Accounts Payable Cr.	Inventory Dr.	Office Supplies Dr.	Other Accounts Dr.
Mar. 6	Office Supplies/Mack Co	3/3	n/30	✓	1,220		1,220	
11	Defore Industries	3/6	2/10, n/30	✓	52,600	52,600		
18	Store Equipment/Schmidt Supp	3/15	n/30	165/✓	22,850			22,850
22	Welch Company	3/18	2/10, n/30	✓	41,625	41,625		
31	Totals				118,295	94,225	1,220	22,850
					(201)	(119)	(124)	(x)

Cash Disbursements Journal — Page 3

Date	Ck. No.	Payee	Account Debited	PR	Cash Cr.	Inventory Cr.	Other Accounts Dr.	Accounts Payable Dr.
Mar. 21	516	Defore Industries	Defore Industries	✓	51,352	1,048		52,400
31	517	Payroll	Sales Salaries Expense	621	15,900		15,900	
31		Totals			67,252	1,048	15,900	52,400
					(101)	(119)	(x)	(201)

General Journal — Page 2

Date	Account	PR	Debit	Credit
Mar. 16	Accounts Payable—Defore Industries	201/✓	200	
	Inventory	119		200
	To record credit memorandum received.			
26	Sales Returns and Allowances	414	600	
	Accounts Receivable—Marjorie Allen	106/✓		600
	To record credit memorandum issued.			

Accounts Receivable Ledger

Marjorie Allen

Date	PR	Debit	Credit	Balance
Mar. 20	S2	5,600		5,600
26	G2		600	5,000

Dennie Hoskins

Date	PR	Debit	Credit	Balance
Mar. 6	S2	10,200		10,200
16	R3		10,200	0

Jennifer Nelson

Date	PR	Debit	Credit	Balance
Mar. 4	S2	16,800		16,800
14	R3		16,800	0

Accounts Payable Ledger

Defore Industries

Date	PR	Debit	Credit	Balance
Mar. 11	P3		52,600	52,600
16	G2	200		52,400
21	D3	52,400		0

Mack Company

Date	PR	Debit	Credit	Balance
Mar. 6	P3		1,220	1,220

Schmidt Supply

Date	PR	Debit	Credit	Balance
Mar. 18	P3		22,850	22,850

Welch Company

Date	PR	Debit	Credit	Balance
Mar. 22	P3		41,625	41,625

General Ledger (Partial Listing)

Cash Acct. No. 101

Date	PR	Debit	Credit	Balance
Mar. 31	R3	187,140		187,140
31	D3		67,252	119,888

Accounts Receivable Acct. No. 106

Date	PR	Debit	Credit	Balance
Mar. 26	G2		600	(600)
31	S2	32,600		32,000
31	R3		27,000	5,000

Inventory Acct. No. 119

Date	PR	Debit	Credit	Balance
Mar. 16	G2		200	(200)
21	D3		1,048	(1,248)
31	P3	94,225		92,977
31	S2		24,100	68,877
31	R3		67,340	1,537

Office Supplies Acct. No. 124

Date	PR	Debit	Credit	Balance
Mar. 31	P3	1,220		1,220

Store Equipment Acct. No. 165

Date	PR	Debit	Credit	Balance
Mar. 18	P3	22,850		22,850

Accounts Payable Acct. No. 201

Date	PR	Debit	Credit	Balance
Mar. 16	G2	200		(200)
31	P3		118,295	118,095
31	D3	52,400		65,695

Long-Term Notes Payable Acct. No. 251

Date	PR	Debit	Credit	Balance
Mar. 12	R3		26,000	26,000

Sales Acct. No. 413

Date	PR	Debit	Credit	Balance
Mar. 31	S2		32,600	32,600
31	R3		134,680	167,280

Sales Returns and Allowances Acct. No. 414

Date	PR	Debit	Credit	Balance
Mar. 26	G2	600		600

Sales Discounts Acct. No. 415

Date	PR	Debit	Credit	Balance
Mar. 31	R3	540		540

Cost of Goods Sold Acct. No. 502

Date	PR	Debit	Credit	Balance
Mar. 31	R3	67,340		67,340
31	S2	24,100		91,440

Sales Salaries Expense Acct. No. 621

Date	PR	Debit	Credit	Balance
Mar. 31	D3	15,900		15,900

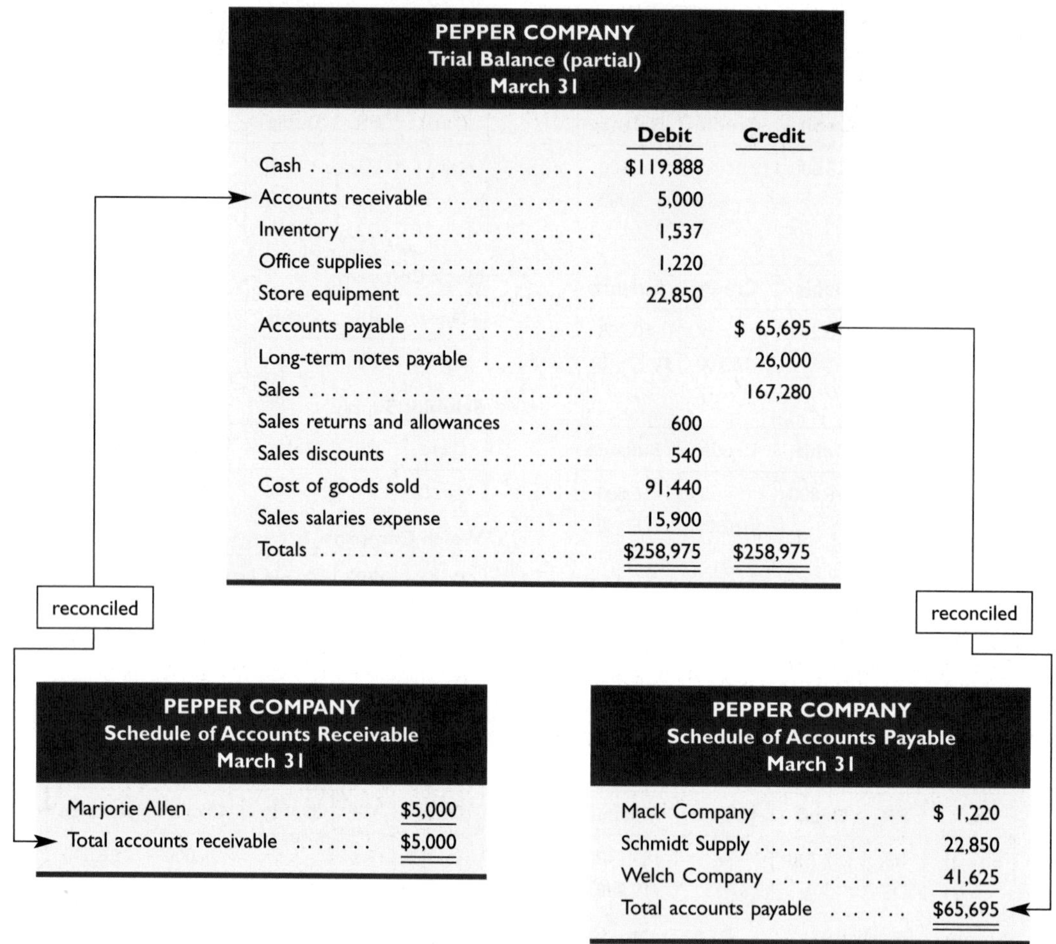

PEPPER COMPANY
Trial Balance (partial)
March 31

	Debit	Credit
Cash	$119,888	
Accounts receivable	5,000	
Inventory	1,537	
Office supplies	1,220	
Store equipment	22,850	
Accounts payable		$ 65,695
Long-term notes payable		26,000
Sales		167,280
Sales returns and allowances	600	
Sales discounts	540	
Cost of goods sold	91,440	
Sales salaries expense	15,900	
Totals	$258,975	$258,975

PEPPER COMPANY
Schedule of Accounts Receivable
March 31

Marjorie Allen	$5,000
Total accounts receivable	$5,000

PEPPER COMPANY
Schedule of Accounts Payable
March 31

Mack Company	$ 1,220
Schmidt Supply	22,850
Welch Company	41,625
Total accounts payable	$65,695

APPENDIX

7A Special Journals under a Periodic System

P3 Journalize and post transactions using special journals in a periodic inventory system.

This appendix describes special journals under a periodic inventory system. Each journal is slightly impacted. The sales journal and the cash receipts journal both require one less column (namely that of Cost of Goods Sold Dr., Inventory Cr.). The Purchases Journal replaces the Inventory Dr. column with a Purchases Dr. column in a periodic system. The cash disbursements journal replaces the Inventory Cr. column with a Purchases Discounts Cr. column in a periodic system. These changes are illustrated.

Sales Journal

The sales journal using the periodic inventory system is shown in Exhibit 7A.1. The difference in the sales journal between the perpetual and periodic system is the exclusion of the column to record cost of goods sold and inventory amounts for each sale. The periodic system does *not* record the increase in cost of goods sold and the decrease in inventory at the time of each sale.

Exhibit 7A.1

Sales Journal—Periodic System

Sales Journal — Page 3

Date	Account Debited	Invoice Number	PR	Accounts Receivable Dr. Sales Cr.
Feb. 2	Jason Henry	307	✓	450
7	Albert Co.	308	✓	500
13	Kam Moore	309	✓	350
15	Paul Roth	310	✓	200
22	Jason Henry	311	✓	225
25	Frank Booth	312	✓	175
28	Albert Co.	313	✓	250
28	Total			2,150
				(106/413)

Cash Receipts Journal

The cash receipts journal using the periodic system is shown in Exhibit 7A.2. Note the absence of the column on the far right side to record debits to Cost of Goods Sold and credits to Inventory for the cost of merchandise sold (seen under the perpetual system). Consistent with the cash receipts journal shown in Exhibit 7.7, we show only the weekly (summary) cash sale entries.

Exhibit 7A.2

Cash Receipts Journal—Periodic System

Cash Receipts Journal — Page 2

Date	Account Credited	Explanation	PR	Cash Dr.	Sales Discount Dr.	Accounts Receivable Cr.	Sales Cr.	Other Accounts Cr.
Feb. 7	Sales	Cash sales	x	4,450			4,450	
12	Jason Henry	Invoice, 2/2	✓	441	9	450		
14	Sales	Cash sales	x	3,925			3,925	
17	Albert Co.	Invoice, 2/7	✓	490	10	500		
20	Notes Payable	Note to bank	245	750				750
21	Sales	Cash sales	x	4,700			4,700	
22	Interest revenue	Bank account	409	250				250
23	Kam Moore	Invoice, 2/13	✓	343	7	350		
25	Paul Roth	Invoice, 2/15	✓	196	4	200		
28	Sales	Cash sales	x	4,225			4,225	
28	Totals			19,770	30	1,500	17,300	1,000
				(101)	(415)	(106)	(413)	(x)

Purchases Journal

The purchases journal using the periodic system is shown in Exhibit 7A.3. This journal under a perpetual system included an Inventory column where the periodic system now has a Purchases column.

Exhibit 7A.3

Purchases Journal—Periodic System

Purchases Journal — Page 1

Date	Account	Date of Invoice	Terms	PR	Accounts Payable Cr.	Purchases Dr.	Office Supplies Dr.	Other Accounts Dr.
Feb. 3	Horning Supply Co.	2/2	n/30	✓	350	275	75	
5	Ace Mfg. Co.	2/5	2/10, n/30	✓	200	200		
13	Wynet and Co.	2/10	2/10, n/30	✓	150	150		
20	Smite Co.	2/18	2/10, n/30	✓	300	300		
25	Ace Mfg. Co.	2/24	2/10, n/30	✓	100	100		
28	Store Supplies/ITT Co.	2/28	n/30	125/✓	225	125	25	75
28	Totals				1,325	1,150	100	75
					(201)	(505)	(124)	(x)

Cash Disbursements Journal

The cash disbursements journal using a periodic system is shown in Exhibit 7A.4. This journal under the perpetual system included an Inventory column where the periodic system now has the Purchases Discounts column.

Exhibit 7A.4

Cash Disbursements Journal—Periodic System

Cash Disbursements Journal — Page 2

Date	Ck. No.	Payee	Account Debited	PR	Cash Cr.	Purchases Discounts Cr.	Other Accounts Dr.	Accounts Payable Dr.
Feb. 3	105	L. and N. Railroad	Purchases	505	15		15	
12	106	East Sales Co.	Purchases	505	25		25	
15	107	Ace Mfg. Co.	Ace Mfg. Co.	✓	196	4		200
15	108	Jerry Hale	Salaries Expense	622	250		250	
20	109	Wynet and Co.	Wynet and Co.	✓	147	3		150
28	110	Smite Co.	Smite Co.	✓	294	6		300
28		Totals			927	13	290	650
					(101)	(507)	(x)	(201)

Demonstration Problem—Periodic System

Refer to Pepper Company's selected transactions described under the Demonstration Problem—Perpetual System to fulfill the following requirements.

Required

1. Open the following selected general ledger accounts: Cash (101), Accounts Receivable (106), Office Supplies (124), Store Equipment (165), Accounts Payable (201), Long-Term Notes Payable (251), Sales (413), Sales Returns and Allowances (414), Sales Discounts (415), Purchases (505), Purchases Returns and Allowances (506), Purchases Discounts (507), and Sales Salaries Expense (621). Open the following accounts receivable ledger accounts: Marjorie Allen, Dennie Hoskins, and Jennifer Nelson. Open the following accounts payable ledger accounts: Defore Industries, Mack Company, Schmidt Supply, and Welch Company.
2. Enter the transactions using a sales journal, a purchases journal, a cash receipts journal, a cash disbursements journal, and a general journal similar to the ones illustrated in Appendix 7A. Regularly post to the individual customer and creditor accounts. Also, post any amounts that should be posted as individual amounts to general ledger accounts. Foot and crossfoot the journals and make the month-end postings. *Pepper Co. uses the periodic inventory system in this problem.*
3. Prepare a trial balance for the selected general ledger accounts in part 1 and prove the accuracy of subsidiary ledgers by preparing schedules of accounts receivable and accounts payable.

Solution to Demonstration Problem—Periodic System

Sales Journal — Page 2

Date	Account Debited	Invoice Number	PR	Accounts Receivable Dr. Sales Cr.
Mar. 4	Jennifer Nelson	954	✓	16,800
6	Dennie Hoskins	955	✓	10,200
20	Marjorie Allen	956	✓	5,600
31	Totals			32,600
				(106/413)

Cash Receipts Journal — Page 3

Date	Account Credited	Explanation	PR	Cash Dr.	Sales Discount Dr.	Accounts Receivable Cr.	Sales Cr.	Other Accounts Cr.
Mar. 12	L.T. Notes Payable	Note to bank	251	26,000				26,000
14	Jennifer Nelson	Invoice, 3/4	✓	16,464	336	16,800		
16	Dennie Hoskins	Invoice, 3/6	✓	9,996	204	10,200		
31	Sales	Cash sales	x	134,680			134,680	
31	Totals			187,140	540	27,000	134,680	26,000
				(101)	(415)	(106)	(413)	(x)

Purchases Journal — Page 3

Date	Account	Date of Invoice	Terms	PR	Accounts Payable Cr.	Purchases Dr.	Office Supplies Dr.	Other Accounts Dr.
Mar. 6	Office Supplies/Mack Co	3/3	n/30	✓	1,220		1,220	
11	Defore Industries	3/6	2/10, n/30	✓	52,600	52,600		
18	Store Equipment/Schmidt Supp	3/15	n/30	165/✓	22,850			22,850
22	Welch Company	3/18	2/10, n/30	✓	41,625	41,625		
31	Totals				118,295	94,225	1,220	22,850
					(201)	(505)	(124)	(x)

Cash Disbursements Journal — Page 3

Date	Ck. No.	Payee	Account Debited	PR	Cash Cr.	Purch. Discount Cr.	Other Accounts Dr.	Accounts Payable Dr.
Mar. 21	516	Defore Industries	Defore Industries	✓	51,352	1,048		52,400
31	517	Payroll	Sales Salaries Expense	621	15,900		15,900	
31		Totals			67,252	1,048	15,900	52,400
					(101)	(507)	(x)	(201)

General Journal — Page 2

Date	Account	PR	Debit	Credit
Mar. 16	Accounts Payable—Defore Industries	201/✓	200	
	Purchases Returns and Allowances	506		200
	To record credit memorandum received.			
26	Sales Returns and Allowances	414	600	
	Accounts Receivable—Marjorie Allen	106/✓		600
	To record credit memorandum issued.			

Accounts Receivable Ledger

Marjorie Allen

Date	PR	Debit	Credit	Balance
Mar. 20	S2	5,600		5,600
26	G2		600	5,000

Dennie Hoskins

Date	PR	Debit	Credit	Balance
Mar. 6	S2	10,200		10,200
16	R3		10,200	0

Jennifer Nelson

Date	PR	Debit	Credit	Balance
Mar. 4	S2	16,800		16,800
14	R3		16,800	0

Accounts Payable Ledger

Defore Industries

Date	PR	Debit	Credit	Balance
Mar. 11	P3		52,600	52,600
16	G2	200		52,400
21	D3	52,400		0

Mack Company

Date	PR	Debit	Credit	Balance
Mar. 6	P3		1,220	1,220

Schmidt Supply

Date	PR	Debit	Credit	Balance
Mar. 18	P3		22,850	22,850

Welch Company

Date	PR	Debit	Credit	Balance
Mar. 22	P3		41,625	41,625

General Ledger (Partial Listing)

Cash Acct. No. 101

Date	PR	Debit	Credit	Balance
Mar. 31	R3	187,140		187,140
31	D3		67,252	119,888

Accounts Receivable Acct. No. 106

Date	PR	Debit	Credit	Balance
Mar. 26	G2		600	(600)
31	S2	32,600		32,000
31	R3		27,000	5,000

Office Supplies Acct. No. 124

Date	PR	Debit	Credit	Balance
Mar. 31	P3	1,220		1,220

Store Equipment Acct. No. 165

Date	PR	Debit	Credit	Balance
Mar. 18	P3	22,850		22,850

Accounts Payable Acct. No. 201

Date	PR	Debit	Credit	Balance
Mar. 16	G2	200		(200)
31	P3		118,295	118,095
31	D3	52,400		65,695

Long-Term Notes Payable Acct. No. 251

Date	PR	Debit	Credit	Balance
Mar. 12	R3		26,000	26,000

Sales Acct. No. 413

Date	PR	Debit	Credit	Balance
Mar. 31	S2		32,600	32,600
31	R3		134,680	167,280

Sales Returns and Allowances Acct. No. 414

Date	PR	Debit	Credit	Balance
Mar. 26	G2	600		600

Sales Discounts Acct. No. 415

Date	PR	Debit	Credit	Balance
Mar. 31	R3	540		540

Purchases Acct. No. 505

Date	PR	Debit	Credit	Balance
Mar. 31	P3	94,225		94,225

Purchases Returns and Allowances Acct. No. 506

Date	PR	Debit	Credit	Balance
Mar. 16	G2		200	200

Purchases Discounts Acct. No. 507

Date	PR	Debit	Credit	Balance
Mar. 31	D3		1,048	1,048

Sales Salaries Expense Acct. No. 621

Date	PR	Debit	Credit	Balance
Mar. 31	D3	15,900		15,900

PEPPER COMPANY
Trial Balance (partial)
March 31

	Debit	Credit
Cash	$119,888	
Accounts receivable	5,000	
Office supplies	1,220	
Store equipment	22,850	
Accounts payable		$ 65,695
Long-term notes payable		26,000
Sales		167,280
Sales returns and allowances	600	
Sales discounts	540	
Purchases	94,225	
Purchases returns and allowances		200
Purchases discounts		1,048
Sales salaries expense	15,900	
Totals	$260,223	$260,223

PEPPER COMPANY
Schedule of Accounts Receivable
March 31

Marjorie Allen	$5,000
Total accounts receivable	$5,000

PEPPER COMPANY
Schedule of Accounts Payable
March 31

Mack Company	$ 1,220
Schmidt Supply	22,850
Welch Company	41,625
Total accounts payable	$65,695

Summary

C1 Identify fundamental principles of accounting information systems. Accounting information systems are governed by five fundamental principles: control, relevance, compatibility, flexibility, and cost-benefit.

C2 Identify components of accounting information systems. The five basic components of an accounting information system are source documents, input devices, information processors, information storage, and output devices.

C3 Explain the goals and uses of special journals. Special journals are used for recording transactions of similar type, each meant to cover one kind of transaction. Four of the most common special journals are the sales journal, cash receipts journal, purchases journal, and cash disbursements journal. Special journals are efficient and cost-effective tools in the journalizing and posting processes.

C4 Describe the use of controlling accounts and subsidiary ledgers. A general ledger keeps controlling accounts such as Accounts Receivable and Accounts Payable, but details on individual accounts making up the controlling account are kept in subsidiary ledgers (such as an accounts receivable ledger). The balance in a controlling account must equal the sum of its subsidiary account balances after posting is complete.

C5 Explain how technology-based information systems impact accounting. Technology-based information systems aim to increase the accuracy, speed, efficiency, and convenience of accounting procedures.

A1 Compute segment return on assets and use it to evaluate segment performance. A business segment is a part of a company that is separately identified by its products or services or by the geographic market it serves. Analysis of a company's segments is aided by the segment return on assets (segment operating income divided by segment average assets).

P1 Journalize and post transactions using special journals. Each special journal is devoted to similar kinds of transactions. Transactions are journalized on one line of a special journal, with columns devoted to specific accounts, dates, names, posting references, explanations, and other necessary information. Posting is threefold: (1) individual amounts in the Other Accounts column are posted to their general ledger accounts on a regular (daily) basis, (2) individual amounts in a column whose total is *not* posted to a controlling account at the end of a period (month) are posted regularly (daily) to their general ledger accounts, and (3) total amounts for all columns except the Other Accounts column are posted at the end of a period (month) to their column's account title in the general ledger. Most companies also maintain subsidiary ledgers for special accounts such as accounts receivable and accounts payable. Transactions that impact subsidiary ledgers are posted on a regular (daily) basis.

P2 Prepare and prove the accuracy of subsidiary ledgers. Account balances in the general ledger and its subsidiary ledgers are tested for accuracy after posting is complete. This procedure is twofold: (1) prepare a trial balance of the general ledger to confirm that debits equal credits and (2) prepare a schedule to confirm that the controlling account's balance equals the subsidiary ledger's balance.

P3[A] Journalize and post transactions using special journals in a periodic inventory system. Transactions are journalized and posted using special journals in a periodic system. The methods are similar to those in a perpetual system; the primary difference is that both cost of goods sold and inventory are not adjusted at the time of each sale. This usually results in the deletion (or renaming) of one or more columns devoted to these accounts in each special journal.

Guidance Answers to Decision Maker and Decision Ethics

Accountant The main issue is whether commissions have an actual or perceived impact on the integrity and objectivity of your advice. You probably should not accept a commission arrangement (the AICPA Code of Ethics prohibits it when you perform the audit or a review). In any event, you should tell the client of your commission arrangement. Also, you need to seriously examine the merits of agreeing to a commission arrangement when you are in a position to exploit it.

Entrepreneur The accounts receivable ledger has much of the information you need. It lists detailed information for each customer's account, including the amounts, dates for transactions, and dates of payments. It can be reorganized into an "aging schedule" to show how long customers wait before paying their bills.

Controller Much of the information you need is in the accounts payable ledger. It contains information for each supplier, the amounts due, and when payments are made. This subsidiary ledger along with information on credit terms should enable you to conduct your analyses.

Banker This merchandiser's segment information is likely to greatly impact your loan decision. The risks associated with the company's two sources of net income are quite different. While net income is up by 10%, U.S. operations are performing poorly and Cuban operations are subject to many uncertainties. These uncertainties depend on political events, legal issues, business relationships, Cuban economic conditions, and a host of other risks. Overall, net income results suggested a low-risk loan opportunity, but the segment information reveals a high-risk situation.

Guidance Answers to Quick Checks

1. The five components are source documents, input devices, information processors, information storage, and output devices.
2. Information processors interpret, transform, and summarize the recorded accounting information so that it can be used in analysis, interpretation, and decision making.

3. Data saved in information storage are used to prepare periodic financial reports and special-purpose internal reports as well as source documentation for auditors.
4. All cash payments by check are recorded in the cash disbursements journal.
5. Columnar journals allow us to accumulate repetitive debits and credits and post them as column totals rather than as individual amounts from each entry.
6. The equality of debits and credits is kept within the general ledger. The subsidiary ledger keeps the customer's individual account and is used only for supplementary information.
7. An initial and the page number of the journal from which the amount was posted are entered in the PR column next to the amount.
8. A separate column for Sales Taxes Payable can be included in both the cash receipts journal and the sales journal.
9. This refers to a procedure of using copies of sales invoices as a sales journal. Each invoice amount is posted directly to the customer's account. All invoices are totaled at period-end for posting to the general ledger accounts.
10. The normal recording and posting procedures are threefold. First, transactions are entered in a special journal if applicable. Second, individual amounts are posted to any subsidiary ledger accounts. Third, column totals are posted to general ledger accounts if not already individually posted.
11. Controlling accounts are debited periodically for an amount or amounts equal to the sum of their respective debits in the subsidiary ledgers (equals journal column totals), and they are credited periodically for an amount or amounts equal to the sum of their respective credits in the subsidiary ledgers (from journal column totals).
12. Tests for accuracy of account balances in the general ledger and subsidiary ledgers are twofold. First, we prepare a trial balance of the general ledger to confirm that debits equal credits. Second, we prove the subsidiary ledgers by preparing schedules of accounts receivable and accounts payable.
13. The general journal is still needed for adjusting, closing, and correcting entries and for special transactions such as sales returns, purchases returns, and certain asset purchases.
14. Integrated systems can save time and minimize errors. This is so because actions taken in one part of the system automatically affect and update related parts.
15. Computer systems offer increased accuracy, speed, efficiency, and convenience.
16. Computer networks can create advantages by linking computers, and giving different users and different computers access to common databases, programs, and hardware.
17. ERP software involves integrated programs, from order taking to manufacturing to accounting. It can speed decision-making, help identify costs for reduction, and aid managers in controlling operations.

Key Terms

Key Terms are available at the book's Website for learning and testing in an online Flashcard Format.

Accounting information systems (p. 262)
Accounts payable ledger (p. 267)
Accounts receivable ledger (p. 267)
Batch processing (p. 277)
Cash disbursements journal (p. 274)
Cash receipts journal (p. 271)
Check register (p. 275)
Columnar journal (p. 268)
Compatibility principle (p. 263)
Components of accounting systems (p. 263)
Computer networks (p. 277)
Controlling account (p. 267)
Control principle (p. 262)
Cost-benefit principle (p. 263)
Enterprise resource planning (ERP) software (p. 277)
Flexibility principle (p. 263)
General journal (p. 266)
Information processors (p. 264)
Information storage (p. 264)
Input devices (p. 264)
Internal controls (p. 262)
Online processing (p. 277)
Output devices (p. 265)
Purchases journal (p. 273)
Relevance principle (p. 262)
Sales journal (p. 267)
Schedule of accounts payable (p. 274)
Schedule of accounts receivable (p. 269)
Segment return on assets (p. 278)
Special journal (p. 266)
Subsidiary ledger (p. 266)

Personal Interactive Quiz

Personal Interactive Quizzes A and B are available at the book's Website to reinforce and assess your learning.

Superscript ^{A} denotes assignments based on Appendix 7A.

Discussion Questions

1. What are the five fundamental principles of accounting information systems?
2. What are five basic components of an accounting system?
3. What are source documents? Give two examples.

4. What is the purpose of an input device? Give examples of input devices for computer systems.
5. What is the difference between data that are stored off-line and data that are stored online?
6. What purpose is served by the output devices of an accounting system?
7. When special journals are used, they are usually used to record each of four different types of transactions. What are these four types of transactions?
8. What notations are entered into the Posting Reference column of a ledger account?
9. When a general journal entry is used to record sales returns, the credit of the entry must be posted twice. Does this cause the trial balance to be out of balance? Explain.
10. Describe the procedures involving the use of copies of a company's sales invoices as a sales journal.
11. Credits to customer accounts and credits to Other Accounts are individually posted from a cash receipts journal such as the one in Exhibit 7.7. Why not put both types of credits in the same column and save journal space?
12. Why should sales to and receipts of cash from credit customers be recorded and posted immediately?
13. Locate the note that discusses **Krispy Kreme's** operations by segments in Appendix A. In what segment does it predominantly operate?

14. Does the income statement of **Tastykake** in Appendix A indicate the net income earned by its business segments? If so, list them.

15. Does the balance sheet of **Harley-Davidson** in Appendix A indicate the identifiable assets owned by its business segments? If so, list them.

Harley-Davidson

Red numbers denote Discussion Questions that involve decision-making.

***Homework Manager** repeats all numerical Quick Studies on the book's Website with new numbers.*

QUICK STUDY

QS 7-1
Accounting information system principles
C1

Place the letter of each system principle in the blank next to its best description.

A. Control principle
B. Relevance principle
C. Compatibility principle
D. Flexibility principle
E. Cost-benefit principle

1. ______ The principle prescribes the accounting information system to change in response to technological advances and competitive pressures.
2. ______ The principle prescribes the accounting information system to help monitor activities.
3. ______ The principle prescribes the accounting information system to provide timely information for effective decision making.
4. ______ The principle prescribes the accounting information system to adapt to the unique characteristics of the company.
5. ______ The principle that affects all other accounting information system principles.

QS 7-2
Accounting information system
C2

Fill in the blanks to complete the following descriptions:

1. With ______ processing, source documents are accumulated for a period and then processed all at the same time, such as once a day, week, or month.
2. A computer ______ allows different computer users to share access to data and programs.
3. A ______ is an input device that captures writing and other input directly from source documents.
4. ______ ______ ______ software comprises programs that help manage a company's vital operations, from manufacturing to accounting.

QS 7-3
Accounting information system components
C2

Identify the most likely role in an accounting system played by each of the numbered items 1 through 12 by assigning a letter from the list A through E on the left:

A. Source documents
B. Input devices
C. Information processors
D. Information storage
E. Output devices

______ 1. Bar code reader
______ 2. Filing cabinet
______ 3. Bank statement
______ 4. Computer scanner
______ 5. Computer keyboard
______ 6. Zip drive
______ 7. Computer monitor
______ 8. Invoice from a supplier
______ 9. Computer software
______ 10. Computer printer
______ 11. Digital camera
______ 12. MP3 player

QS 7-4
Identifying the special journal of entry
C3

Damron Electronics uses a sales journal, a purchases journal, a cash receipts journal, a cash disbursements journal, and a general journal as illustrated in this chapter. Damron recently completed the following transactions *a* through *h*. Identify the journal in which each transaction should be recorded.

a. Paid cash to a creditor.
b. Sold merchandise on credit.
c. Purchased shop supplies on credit.
d. Paid an employee's salary in cash.
e. Borrowed cash from the bank.
f. Sold merchandise for cash.
g. Purchased merchandise on credit.
h. Purchased inventory for cash.

QS 7-5
Entries in the general journal
C3

Lue Gifts uses a sales journal, a purchases journal, a cash receipts journal, a cash disbursements journal, and a general journal as illustrated in this chapter. Journalize its November transactions that should be recorded in the general journal. For those not recorded in the general journal, identify the special journal where each should be recorded.

Nov. 2 Purchased $2,900 of merchandise on credit from the Elko Co., terms 2/10, n/30.
12 The owner, T. Lue, contributed an automobile worth $15,000 to the business.
16 Sold $1,100 of merchandise (cost is $700) on credit to K. Gould, terms n/30.
19 K. Gould returned $150 of (worthless) merchandise originally purchased on November 16 (assume the cost of this merchandise is left in cost of goods sold).

QS 7-6
Required segment reporting
A1

Debray is a company with publicly traded securities and it operates in more than one industry. Which of the following items of information about each industry segment must the company report?

a. Operating income
b. Depreciation
c. Inventory
d. Sales
e. Cash flows
f. Capital expenditures
g. Identifiable assets
h. Amortization

***Homework Manager** repeats all numerical Exercises on the book's Website with new numbers.*

EXERCISES

Exercise 7-1
Sales journal—perpetual
P1

Hutton Company uses a sales journal, a purchases journal, a cash receipts journal, a cash disbursement journal, and a general journal. The following transactions occur in the month of March:

Mar. 2 Sold merchandise costing $300 to B. Fager for $450 cash, invoice no. 5703.
5 Purchased $2,300 of merchandise on credit from Marsh Corp.
7 Sold merchandise costing $800 to J. Dryer for $1,150, terms 2/10, n/30, invoice no. 5704.
8 Borrowed $8,000 cash by signing a note payable to the bank.
12 Sold merchandise costing $200 to R. Land for $320, terms n/30, invoice no. 5705.
16 Received $1,127 cash from J. Dryer to pay for the purchase of March 7.
19 Sold used store equipment for $900 cash to Malone, Inc.
25 Sold merchandise costing $350 to T. Burton for $550, terms n/30, invoice no. 5706.

Prepare headings for a sales journal like the one in Exhibit 7.5. Journalize the March transactions that should be recorded in this sales journal.

Exercise 7-2
Identifying journal of entry C3

Refer to Exercise 7-1 and for each of the March transactions identify the journal in which it would be recorded. Assume the company uses a sales journal, purchases journal, cash receipts journal, cash disbursements journal, and general journal as illustrated in this chapter.

Exercise 7-3[A]
Sales journal—periodic P3

Prepare headings for a sales journal like the one in Exhibit 7A.1. Journalize the March transactions shown in Exercise 7-1 that should be recorded in the sales journal assuming that the periodic inventory system is used.

Exercise 7-4
Cash receipts journal—perpetual
P1

Moeder Co. uses a sales journal, a purchases journal, a cash receipts journal, a cash disbursements journal, and a general journal. The following transactions occur in the month of November.

Nov. 3 Purchased $3,100 of merchandise on credit from Hargrave Co., terms n/20.
7 Sold merchandise costing $840 on credit to J. York for $900, subject to a $18 sales discount if paid by the end of the month.
9 Borrowed $2,750 cash by signing a note payable to the bank.
13 J. Emling, the owner, contributed $4,000 cash to the company.
18 Sold merchandise costing $130 to B. Box for $230 cash.
22 Paid Hargrave Co. $3,100 cash for the merchandise purchased on November 3.

27 Received $882 cash from J. York in payment of the November 7 purchase.
30 Paid salaries of $1,600 in cash.

Prepare headings for a cash receipts journal like the one in Exhibit 7.7. Journalize the November transactions that should be recorded in the cash receipts journal.

Exercise 7-5
Identifying journal of entry C3

Refer to Exercise 7-4 and for each of the November transactions identify the journal in which it would be recorded. Assume the company uses a sales journal, purchases journal, cash receipts journal, cash disbursements journal, and general journal as illustrated in this chapter.

Exercise 7-6[A]
Cash receipts journal—periodic P3

Prepare headings for a cash receipts journal like the one in Exhibit 7A.2. Journalize the November transactions shown in Exercise 7-4 that should be recorded in the cash receipts journal assuming that the periodic inventory system is used.

Exercise 7-7
Purchases journal—perpetual P1

Redmon Company uses a sales journal, a purchases journal, a cash receipts journal, a cash disbursements journal, and a general journal. The following transactions occur in the month of June.

June 1 Purchased $8,100 of merchandise on credit from Vick, Inc., terms n/30.
8 Sold merchandise costing $900 on credit to R. Panke for $1,500 subject to a $30 sales discount if paid by the end of the month.
14 Purchased $240 of store supplies from Poe Company on credit, terms n/30.
17 Purchased $260 of office supplies on credit from Rehmer Company, terms n/30.
24 Sold merchandise costing $400 to L. Barnett for $630 cash.
28 Purchased store supplies from Piburn's for $90 cash.
29 Paid Vick, Inc., $8,100 cash for the merchandise purchased on June 1.

Prepare headings for a purchases journal like the one in Exhibit 7.9. Journalize the June transactions that should be recorded in the purchases journal.

Exercise 7-8
Identifying journal of entry C3

Refer to Exercise 7-7 and for each of the June transactions identify the journal in which it would be recorded. Assume the company uses a sales journal, purchases journal, cash receipts journal, cash disbursements journal, and general journal as illustrated in this chapter.

Exercise 7-9[A]
Purchases journal—periodic P3

Prepare headings for a purchases journal like the one in Exhibit 7A.3. Journalize the June transactions from Exercise 7-7 that should be recorded in the purchases journal assuming the periodic inventory system is used.

Exercise 7-10
Cash disbursements journal—perpetual P1

Politte Supply uses a sales journal, a purchases journal, a cash receipts journal, a cash disbursements journal, and a general journal. The following transactions occur in the month of April.

Apr. 3 Purchased merchandise for $2,750 on credit from Scott, Inc., terms 2/10, n/30.
9 Issued check no. 210 to Kidman Corp. to buy store supplies for $450.
12 Sold merchandise costing $400 on credit to C. Myers for $670, terms n/30.
17 Issued check no. 211 for $1,500 to pay off a note payable to City Bank.
20 Purchased merchandise for $3,500 on credit from LeBron, terms 2/10, n/30.
29 Issued check no. 212 to LeBron to pay the amount due for the purchase of April 20, less the discount.
30 Paid salary of $1,700 to B. Decker by issuing check no. 213.
31 Issued check no. 214 to Scott, Inc., to pay the amount due for the purchase of April 3.

Prepare headings for a cash disbursements journal like the one in Exhibit 7.11. Journalize the April transactions that should be recorded in the cash disbursements journal.

Exercise 7-11
Identifying journal of entry C3

Refer to Exercise 7-10 and for each of the April transactions identify the journal in which it would be recorded. Assume the company uses a sales journal, purchases journal, cash receipts journal, cash disbursements journal, and general journal as illustrated in this chapter.

Exercise 7-12[A]
Cash disbursements journal—periodic P3

Prepare headings for a cash disbursements journal like the one in Exhibit 7A.4. Journalize the April transactions from Exercise 7-10 that should be recorded in the cash disbursements journal assuming that the periodic inventory system is used.

Exercise 7-13
Special journal transactions and error discovery
P1 

Porter Pharmacy uses the following journals: sales journal, purchases journal, cash receipts journal, cash disbursements journal, and general journal. On June 5, Porter purchased merchandise priced at $12,000, subject to credit terms of 2/10, n/30. On June 14, the pharmacy paid the net amount due for the merchandise. In journalizing the payment, the pharmacy debited Accounts Payable for $12,000 but failed to record the cash discount on the purchases. Cash was properly credited for the actual $11,760 paid. (*a*) In what journals would the June 5 and the June 14 transactions be recorded? (*b*) What procedure is likely to discover the error in journalizing the June 14 transaction?

Exercise 7-14
Posting to subsidiary ledger accounts; preparing a schedule of accounts receivable
P1 P2

At the end of May, the sales journal of Clear View appears as follows:

Sales Journal

Date	Account Debited	Invoice Number	PR	Accounts Receivable Dr. Sales Cr.	Cost of Goods Sold Dr. Inventory Cr.
May 6	Aaron Reckers	190		2,880	2,200
10	Sara Reed	191		1,940	1,600
17	Anna Page	192		850	500
25	Sara Reed	193		340	200
31	Totals			6,010	4,500

Clear View also recorded the return of defective merchandise with the following entry:

May 20	Sales Returns and Allowances	250	
	Accounts Receivable—Anna Page		250
	Customer returned (worthless) merchandise.		

Required

1. Open an accounts receivable subsidiary ledger that has a T-account for each customer listed in the sales journal. Post to the customer accounts the entries in the sales journal and any portion of the general journal entry that affects a customer's account.
2. Open a general ledger that has T-accounts for Accounts Receivable, Inventory, Sales, Sales Returns and Allowances, and Cost of Goods Sold. Post the sales journal and any portion of the general journal entry that affects these accounts.
3. Prepare a schedule of accounts receivable and prove that its total equals the balance in the Accounts Receivable controlling account.

Check (3) Accounts Receivable, $5,760

Exercise 7-15
Accounts receivable ledger; posting from sales journal
P1 P2

Winslow Company posts its sales invoices directly and then binds them into a Sales Journal. Winslow had the following credit sales to these customers during June:

June 2	Joe Mack	$ 3,600
8	Eric Horner	6,100
10	Tess Cox	13,400
14	Hong Jiang	20,500
20	Tess Cox	11,200
29	Joe Mack	7,300
	Total credit sales	$62,100

Required

1. Open an accounts receivable subsidiary ledger having a T-account for each customer. Post the invoices to the subsidiary ledger.
2. Open an Accounts Receivable controlling T-account and a Sales T-account to reflect general ledger accounts. Post the end-of-month total from the sales journal to these accounts.
3. Prepare a schedule of accounts receivable and prove that its total equals the Accounts Receivable controlling account balance.

Exercise 7-16
Purchases journal and error identification
P1 

A company that records credit purchases in a purchases journal and records purchases returns in a general journal made the following errors. Indicate when each error should be discovered.

1. Posted a purchases return to the Accounts Payable account and to the creditor's subsidiary account but did not post the purchases return to the Inventory account.
2. Posted a purchases return to the Inventory account and to the Accounts Payable account but did not post to the creditor's subsidiary account.
3. Correctly recorded a $4,000 purchase in the purchases journal but posted it to the creditor's subsidiary account as a $400 purchase.
4. Made an addition error in determining the balance of a creditor's subsidiary account.
5. Made an addition error in totaling the Office Supplies column of the purchases journal.

Exercise 7-17
Computing and analyzing segment return on assets
A1 

Refer to Exhibit 7.13 and complete the segment return on assets table for Wolfe Company. Analyze your findings and identify the segment with the highest, and that with the lowest, segment return on assets.

	Segment Operating Income (in $ mil.)		Segment Assets (in $ mil.)		Segment Return on Assets
Segment	2004	2003	2004	2003	2004
Specialty					
Skiing Group	$ 62	$ 58	$ 581	$440	
Skating Group	9	6	53	42	
Specialty Footwear	22	19	155	136	
Other Specialty	11	4	37	24	
Subtotal	104	87	826	642	
General Merchandise					
South America	32	36	305	274	
United States	7	8	52	35	
Europe	5	3	14	12	
Subtotal	44	47	371	321	
Total	$148	$134	$1197	$963	

Check Europe segment return, 38.5%

PROBLEM SET A

Problem 7-1A
Special journals, subsidiary ledgers, and schedule of accounts receivable—perpetual
C4 P1 P2 

Wise Company completes these transactions during April of the current year (the terms of all its credit sales are 2/10, n/30):

Apr. 2 Purchased $13,300 of merchandise on credit from Negi Company, invoice dated April 2, terms 2/10, n/60.
3 Sold merchandise on credit to Brooke Sledd, Invoice No. 760, for $3,000 (cost is $2,000).
3 Purchased $1,380 of office supplies on credit from Madison, Inc. Invoice dated April 2, terms n/10 EOM.
4 Issued Check No. 587 to *U.S. View* for advertising expense, $999.
5 Sold merchandise on credit to Paul Kohr, Invoice No. 761, for $8,000 (cost is $6,500).
6 Received an $85 credit memorandum from Madison, Inc., for the return of some of the office supplies received on April 3.
9 Purchased $11,125 of store equipment on credit from Ned's Supply, invoice dated April 9, terms n/10 EOM.
11 Sold merchandise on credit to Amy Nilson, Invoice No. 762, for $9,500 (cost is $7,000).
12 Issued Check No. 588 to Negi Company in payment of its April 2 invoice, less the discount.
13 Received payment from Brooke Sledd for the April 3 sale, less the discount.
13 Sold $4,100 of merchandise on credit to Brooke Sledd (cost is $2,600), Invoice No. 763.
14 Received payment from Paul Kohr for the April 5 sale, less the discount.
16 Issued Check No. 589, payable to Payroll, in payment of sales salaries expense for the first half of the month, $9,750. Cashed the check and paid employees.

16 Cash sales for the first half of the month are $50,840 (cost is $33,880). (Cash sales are recorded daily from cash register data but are recorded only twice in this problem to reduce repetitive entries.)
17 Purchased $12,750 of merchandise on credit from Price Company, invoice dated April 17, terms 2/10, n/30.
18 Borrowed $50,000 cash from First State Bank by signing a long-term note payable.
20 Received payment from Amy Nilson for the April 11 sale, less the discount.
20 Purchased $730 of store supplies on credit from Ned's Supply, invoice dated April 19, terms n/10 EOM.
23 Received a $400 credit memorandum from Price Company for the return of defective merchandise received on April 17.
23 Received payment from Brooke Sledd for the April 13 sale, less the discount.
25 Purchased $10,375 of merchandise on credit from Negi Company, invoice dated April 24, terms 2/10, n/60.
26 Issued Check No. 590 to Price Company in payment of its April 17 invoice, less the return and the discount.
27 Sold $3,070 of merchandise on credit to Paul Kohr, Invoice No. 764 (cost is $2,420).
27 Sold $5,700 of merchandise on credit to Amy Nilson, Invoice No. 765 (cost is $3,305).
30 Issued Check No. 591, payable to Payroll, in payment of the sales salaries expense for the last half of the month, $9,750.
30 Cash sales for the last half of the month are $70,975 (cost is $55,900).

Required

1. Prepare a sales journal like that in Exhibit 7.5 and a cash receipts journal like that in Exhibit 7.7. Number both journal pages as page 3. Then review the transactions of Wise Company and enter those that should be journalized in the sales journal and those that should be journalized in the cash receipts journal. Ignore any transactions that should be journalized in a purchases journal, a cash disbursements journal, or a general journal.

2. Open the following general ledger accounts: Cash, Accounts Receivable, Inventory, Long-Term Notes Payable, Cost of Goods Sold, Sales, and Sales Discounts. Enter the March 31 balances for Cash ($85,000), Inventory ($125,000), and Long-Term Notes Payable ($210,000). Also open accounts receivable subsidiary ledger accounts for Paul Kohr, Brooke Sledd, and Amy Nilson.

3. Verify that amounts that should be posted as individual amounts from the journals have been posted. (Such items are immediately posted.) Foot and crossfoot the journals and make the month-end postings.

Check Trial balance totals, $415,185

4. Prepare a trial balance of the general ledger and prove the accuracy of the subsidiary ledger by preparing a schedule of accounts receivable.

Analysis Component

5. Assume that the total for the schedule of Accounts Receivable does not equal the balance of the controlling account in the general ledger. Describe steps you would take to discover the error(s).

Problem 7-2A[A]

Special journals, subsidiary ledgers, and schedule of accounts receivable—periodic

C4 P2 P3

Check Trial balance totals, $415,185

Assume that Wise Co. in Problem 7-1A uses the periodic inventory system.

Required

1. Prepare headings for a sales journal like the one in Exhibit 7A.1. Prepare headings for a cash receipts journal like the one in Exhibit 7A.2. Journalize the April transactions shown in Problem 7-1A that should be recorded in the sales journal and the cash receipts journal assuming the *periodic* inventory system is used.

2. Open the general ledger accounts with balances as shown in Problem 7-1A (do not open a Cost of Goods Sold ledger account). Under the periodic system, an Inventory account exists but is inactive until its balance is updated to the correct inventory balance at year-end. In this problem, the Inventory account remains inactive but must be included to correctly complete the trial balance.

3. Complete parts 3, 4, and 5 of Problem 7-1A using the results of parts 1 and 2 of this problem.

Problem 7-3A

Special journals, subsidiary ledgers, and schedule of accounts payable—perpetual

C4 P1 P2

The April transactions of Wise Company are described in Problem 7-1A.

Required

1. Prepare a general journal, a purchases journal like that in Exhibit 7.9, and a cash disbursements journal like that in Exhibit 7.11. Number all journal pages as page 3. Review the April transactions of Wise Company and enter those transactions that should be journalized in the general journal, the purchases journal, or the cash disbursements journal. Ignore any transactions that should be journalized in a sales journal or cash receipts journal.

2. Open the following general ledger accounts: Cash, Inventory, Office Supplies, Store Supplies, Store Equipment, Accounts Payable, Long-Term Notes Payable, Sales Salaries Expense, and Advertising Expense. Enter the March 31 balances of Cash ($85,000), Inventory ($125,000), and Long-Term Notes Payable ($210,000). Also open accounts payable subsidiary ledger accounts for Ned's Supply, Negi Company, Price Company, and Madison, Inc.

3. Verify that amounts that should be posted as individual amounts from the journals have been posted. (Such items are immediately posted.) Foot and crossfoot the journals and make the month-end postings.

4. Prepare a trial balance of the general ledger and a schedule of accounts payable.

Check Trial balance totals, $233,525

Problem 7-4A[A]

Special journals, subsidiary ledgers, and schedule of accounts payable—periodic

C4 P2 P3

Refer to Problem 7-1A and assume that Wise Co. uses the periodic inventory system.

Required

1. Prepare a general journal, a purchases journal like that in Exhibit 7A.3, and a cash disbursements journal like that in Exhibit 7A.4. Number all journal pages as page 3. Review the April transactions of Wise Company (Problem 7-1A) and enter those transactions that should be journalized in the general journal, the purchases journal, or the cash disbursements journal. Ignore any transaction that should be journalized in a sales journal or cash receipts journal.

2. Open the following general ledger accounts: Cash, Inventory, Office Supplies, Store Supplies, Store Equipment, Accounts Payable, Long-Term Notes Payable, Purchases, Purchases Returns and Allowances, Purchases Discounts, Sales Salaries Expense, and Advertising Expense. Enter the March 31 balances of Cash ($85,000), Inventory ($125,000), and Long-Term Notes Payable ($210,000). Also open accounts payable subsidiary ledger accounts for Ned's Supply, Negi Company, Price Company, and Madison, Inc.

3. Complete parts 3 and 4 of Problem 7-3A using the results of parts 1 and 2 of this problem.

Check Trial balance totals, $234,438

Problem 7-5A

Special journals, subsidiary ledgers, trial balance—perpetual

C4 P1 P2

mhhe.com/larson

(If the Working Papers that accompany this textbook are not being used, omit this problem.)
You have just taken over the accounting for Choi Enterprises, whose annual accounting period ends December 31. The company's previous accountant journalized its transactions through December 15 and posted all items that required posting as individual amounts (see the journals and ledgers in the Working Papers). The company's transactions beginning on December 16 follow (terms for all its credit sales are 2/10, n/30):

Dec. 16 Sold merchandise on credit to Hanna Seppa, Invoice No. 916, for $7,700 (cost is $4,600).
17 Received a $1,040 credit memorandum from Funk Company for the return of merchandise received on December 15.
17 Purchased $615 of office supplies on credit from KK's Supply Company, invoice dated December 16, terms n/10 EOM.
18 Received a $40 credit memorandum from KK's Supply Company for the return of office supplies received on December 17.
20 Issued a $500 credit memorandum to Bo Brown for defective (worthless) merchandise sold on December 15 and returned for credit.
21 Purchased $6,700 of store equipment on credit from KK's Supply Company, invoice dated December 21, terms n/10 EOM.
22 Received payment from Hanna Seppa for the December 12 sale less the discount.
23 Issued Check No. 623 to Crossland Company in payment of its December 15 invoice less the discount.
24 Sold merchandise on credit to Shilo Jones, Invoice No. 917, for $1,200 (cost is $600).
24 Issued Check No. 624 to Funk Company in payment of its December 15 invoice less the return and the discount.
25 Received payment from Bo Brown for the December 15 sale less the return and the discount.

26 Purchased $8,100 of merchandise from Crossland Company, invoice dated December 25, terms 2/10, n/60.
29 Sold a neighboring merchant five boxes of file folders (office supplies) at their cost of $50 cash.
30 Ken Choi, the sole owner of Choi Enterprises, used Check No. 625 to withdraw $2,500 in cash from the business for personal use.
31 Issued Check No. 626 to Jamie Inman, the company's only sales employee, in payment of her $2,020 salary for the last half of December.
31 Issued Check No. 627 to Access Electric Company in payment of its $710 December electric bill.
31 Cash sales for the last half of the month are $29,600 (cost is $11,200). (Cash sales are recorded daily but are recorded only twice in this problem to reduce repetitive entries.)

Required

1. Record these transactions in the journals provided in the working papers.
2. Verify that amounts that should be posted as individual amounts to the general ledger accounts have been posted, including posting to the customer and creditor accounts. (Such items are immediately posted.) Foot and crossfoot the journals and make the month-end postings.
3. Prepare a December 31 trial balance and prove the accuracy of the subsidiary ledgers by preparing schedules of both accounts receivable and accounts payable.

Check Trial balance totals, $219,408

Problem 7-6A
Special journals, subsidiary ledgers, trial balance—perpetual
C4 P1 P2

mhhe.com/larson

Bishop Company completes these transactions and events during March of the current year (terms for all its credit sales are 2/10, n/30):

Mar. 1 Purchased $42,600 of merchandise from Soy Industries, invoice dated March 1, terms 2/15, n/30.
2 Sold merchandise on credit to Min Cho, Invoice No. 854, for $15,800 (cost is $7,900).
3 Purchased $1,120 of office supplies on credit from Stacy Company, invoice dated March 3, terms n/10 EOM.
3 Sold merchandise on credit to Lance Snow, Invoice No. 855, for $9,200 (cost is $4,600).
6 Borrowed $72,000 cash from Federal Bank by signing a long-term note payable.
9 Purchased $20,850 of office equipment on credit from Tells Supply, invoice dated March 9, terms n/10 EOM.
10 Sold merchandise on credit to Taylor Few, Invoice No. 856, for $4,600 (cost is $2,300).
12 Received payment from Min Cho for the March 2 sale less the discount.
13 Sent Soy Industries Check No. 416 in payment of the March 1 invoice less the discount.
13 Received payment from Lance Snow for the March 3 sale less the discount.
14 Purchased $31,625 of merchandise from the JW Company, invoice dated March 13, terms 2/10, n/30.
15 Issued Check No. 417, payable to Payroll, in payment of sales salaries expense for the first half of the month, $15,900. Cashed the check and paid the employees.
15 Cash sales for the first half of the month are $164,680 (cost is $138,000). (Cash sales are recorded daily, but are recorded only twice here to reduce repetitive entries.)
16 Purchased $1,670 of store supplies on credit from Stacy Company, invoice dated March 16, terms n/10 EOM.
17 Received a $2,425 credit memorandum from JW Company for the return of unsatisfactory merchandise purchased on March 14.
19 Received a $630 credit memorandum from Tells Supply for office equipment received on March 9 and returned for credit.
20 Received payment from Taylor Few for the sale of March 10 less the discount.
23 Issued Check No. 418 to JW Company in payment of the invoice of March 13 less the return and the discount.
27 Sold merchandise on credit to Taylor Few, Invoice No. 857, for $13,910 (cost is $6,220).
28 Sold merchandise on credit to Lance Snow, Invoice No. 858, for $5,315 (cost is $2,280).
31 Issued Check No. 419, payable to Payroll, in payment of sales salaries expense for the last half of the month, $15,900. Cashed the check and paid the employees.
31 Cash sales for the last half of the month are $174,590 (cost is $143,000).
31 Verify that amounts impacting customer and creditor accounts were posted and that any amounts that should have been posted as individual amounts to the general ledger accounts were posted. Foot and crossfoot the journals and make the month-end postings.

Required

1. Open the following general ledger accounts: Cash; Accounts Receivable; Inventory (March 1 beg. bal. is $300,000); Office Supplies; Store Supplies; Office Equipment; Accounts Payable; Long-Term Notes Payable; M. Bishop, Capital (March 1 beg. bal. is $300,000); Sales; Sales Discounts; Cost of Goods Sold; and Sales Salaries Expense. Open the following accounts receivable subsidiary ledger accounts: Taylor Few, Min Cho, and Lance Snow. Open the following accounts payable subsidiary ledger accounts: Stacy Company, Soy Industries, Tells Supply, and JW Company.
2. Enter these transactions in a sales journal like Exhibit 7.5, a purchases journal like Exhibit 7.9, a cash receipts journal like Exhibit 7.7, a cash disbursements journal like Exhibit 7.11, or a general journal. Number all journal pages as page 2.
3. Prepare a trial balance of the general ledger and prove the accuracy of the subsidiary ledgers by preparing schedules of both accounts receivable and accounts payable.

Check Trial balance totals, $783,105

Problem 7-7A[A]
Special journals, subsidiary ledgers, trial balance—periodic
C4 P2 P3

Assume that Bishop Co. in Problem 7-6A uses the periodic inventory system.

Required

1. Open the following general ledger accounts: Cash; Accounts Receivable; Inventory (March 1 beg. bal. is $300,000); Office Supplies; Store Supplies; Office Equipment; Accounts Payable; Long-Term Notes Payable; M. Bishop, Capital (March 1 beg. bal. is $300,000); Sales; Sales Discounts; Purchases; Purchases Returns and Allowances; Purchases Discounts; and Sales Salaries Expense. Open the following accounts receivable subsidiary ledger accounts: Taylor Few, Min Cho, and Lance Snow. Open the following Accounts Payable subsidiary ledger accounts: Stacy Company, Soy Industries, Tells Supply, and JW Company.
2. Enter the transactions from Problem 7-6A in a sales journal like that in Exhibit 7A.1, a purchases journal like that in Exhibit 7A.3, a cash receipts journal like that in Exhibit 7A.2, a cash disbursements journal like that in Exhibit 7A.4, or a general journal. Number journal pages as page 2.
3. Prepare a trial balance of the general ledger and prove the accuracy of the subsidiary ledgers by preparing schedules of both accounts receivable and accounts payable.

Check Trial balance totals, $786,966

PROBLEM SET B

Problem 7-1B
Special journals, subsidiary ledgers, schedule of accounts receivable—perpetual
C4 P1 P2

Alcorn Industries completes these transactions during July of the current year (the terms of all its credit sales are 2/10, n/30):

July 1 Purchased $6,300 of merchandise on credit from Tahoe Company, invoice dated June 30, terms 2/10, n/30.
3 Issued Check No. 300 to *The Weekly* for advertising expense, $575.
5 Sold merchandise on credit to Kim Newsom, Invoice No. 918, for $18,400 (cost is $9,700).
6 Sold merchandise on credit to Ruth Baker, Invoice No. 919, for $7,500 (cost is $4,300).
7 Purchased $1,050 of store supplies on credit from Pryor, Inc., invoice dated July 7, terms n/10 EOM.
8 Received a $150 credit memorandum from Pryor, Inc., for the return of store supplies received on July 7.
9 Purchased $37,710 of store equipment on credit from Caro's Supply, invoice dated July 8, terms n/10 EOM.
10 Issued Check No. 301 to Tahoe Company in payment of its June 30 invoice, less the discount.
13 Sold merchandise on credit to Stephanie Meyer, Invoice No. 920, for $8,350 (cost is $5,030).
14 Sold merchandise on credit to Kim Newsom, Invoice No. 921, for $4,100 (cost is $2,800).
15 Received payment from Kim Newsom for the July 5 sale, less the discount.
15 Issued Check No. 302, payable to Payroll, in payment of sales salaries expense for the first half of the month, $30,620. Cashed the check and paid employees.
15 Cash sales for the first half of the month are $121,370 (cost is $66,330). (Cash sales are recorded daily using data from the cash registers but are recorded only twice in this problem to reduce repetitive entries.)
16 Received payment from Ruth Baker for the July 6 sale, less the discount.
17 Purchased $8,200 of merchandise on credit from Dixon Company, invoice dated July 17, terms 2/10, n/30.
20 Purchased $750 of office supplies on credit from Caro's Supply, invoice dated July 19, terms n/10 EOM.
21 Borrowed $20,000 cash from College Bank by signing a long-term note payable.

23 Received payment from Stephanie Meyer for the July 13 sale, less the discount.
24 Received payment from Kim Newsom for the July 14 sale, less the discount.
24 Received a $2,400 credit memorandum from Dixon Company for the return of defective merchandise received on July 17.
26 Purchased $9,770 of merchandise on credit from Tahoe Company, invoice dated July 26, terms 2/10, n/30.
27 Issued Check No. 303 to Dixon Company in payment of its July 17 invoice, less the return and the discount.
29 Sold merchandise on credit to Ruth Baker, Invoice No. 922, for $28,090 (cost is $22,850).
30 Sold merchandise on credit to Stephanie Meyer, Invoice No. 923, for $15,750 (cost is $9,840).
31 Issued Check No. 304, payable to Payroll, in payment of the sales salaries expense for the last half of the month, $30,620.
31 Cash sales for the last half of the month are $79,020 (cost is $51,855).

Required

1. Prepare a sales journal like that in Exhibit 7.5 and a cash receipts journal like that in Exhibit 7.7. Number both journals as page 3. Then review the transactions of Alcorn Industries and enter those transactions that should be journalized in the sales journal and those that should be journalized in the cash receipts journal. Ignore any transactions that should be journalized in a purchases journal, a cash disbursements journal, or a general journal.
2. Open the following general ledger accounts: Cash, Accounts Receivable, Inventory, Long-Term Notes Payable, Cost of Goods Sold, Sales, and Sales Discounts. Enter the June 30 balances for Cash ($100,000), Inventory ($200,000), and Long-Term Notes Payable ($300,000). Also open accounts receivable subsidiary ledger accounts for Kim Newsom, Stephanie Meyer, and Ruth Baker.
3. Verify that amounts that should be posted as individual amounts from the journals have been posted. (Such items are immediately posted.) Foot and crossfoot the journals and make the month-end postings.
4. Prepare a trial balance of the general ledger and prove the accuracy of the subsidiary ledger by preparing a schedule of accounts receivable.

Check Trial balance totals, $602,580

Analysis Component

5. Assume that the total for the schedule of Accounts Receivable does not equal the balance of the controlling account in the general ledger. Describe steps you would take to discover the error(s).

Problem 7-2B[A]
Special journals, subsidiary ledgers, and schedule of accounts receivable—periodic
C4 P2 P3

Assume that Alcorn Industries in Problem 7-1B uses the periodic inventory system.

Required

1. Prepare headings for a sales journal like the one in Exhibit 7A.1. Prepare headings for a cash receipts journal like the one in Exhibit 7A.2. Journalize the July transactions shown in Problem 7-1B that should be recorded in the sales journal and the cash receipts journal assuming the periodic inventory system is used.
2. Open the general ledger accounts with balances as shown in Problem 7-1B (do not open a Cost of Goods Sold ledger account). Under the periodic system, an Inventory account exists but is inactive until its balance is updated to the correct inventory balance at year-end. In this problem, the Inventory account remains inactive but must be included to correctly complete the trial balance.
3. Complete parts 3, 4, and 5 of Problem 7-1B using the results of parts 1 and 2 of this problem.

Check Trial balance totals, $602,580

Problem 7-3B
Special journals, subsidiary ledgers, and schedule of accounts payable—perpetual
C4 P1 P2

The July transactions of Alcorn Industries are described in Problem 7-1B.

Required

1. Prepare a general journal, a purchases journal like that in Exhibit 7.9, and a cash disbursements journal like that in Exhibit 7.11. Number all journal pages as page 3. Review the July transactions of Alcorn Industries and enter those transactions that should be journalized in the general journal, the purchases journal, or the cash disbursements journal. Ignore any transactions that should be journalized in a sales journal or cash receipts journal.

2. Open the following general ledger accounts: Cash, Inventory, Office Supplies, Store Supplies, Store Equipment, Accounts Payable, Long-Term Notes Payable, Sales Salaries Expense, and Advertising Expense. Enter the June 30 balances of Cash ($100,000), Inventory ($200,000), and Long-Term Notes Payable ($300,000). Also open accounts payable subsidiary ledger accounts for Caro's Supply, Tahoe Company, Dixon Company, and Pryor, Inc.
3. Verify that amounts that should be posted as individual amounts from the journals have been posted. (Such items are immediately posted.) Foot and crossfoot the journals and make the month-end postings.
4. Prepare a trial balance of the general ledger and a schedule of accounts payable.

Check Trial balance totals, $349,130

Problem 7-4B^A
Special journals, subsidiary ledgers, and schedule of accounts payable—periodic
C4 P2 P3

Refer to Problem 7-1B and assume that Alcorn uses the periodic inventory system.

Required

1. Prepare a general journal, a purchases journal like that in Exhibit 7A.3, and a cash disbursements journal like that in Exhibit 7A.4. Number all journal pages as page 3. Review the July transactions of Alcorn Company (Problem 7-1B) and enter those transactions that should be journalized in the general journal, the purchases journal, or the cash disbursements journal. Ignore any transaction that should be journalized in a sales journal or cash receipts journal.
2. Open the following general ledger accounts: Cash, Inventory, Office Supplies, Store Supplies, Store Equipment, Accounts Payable, Long-Term Notes Payable, Purchases, Purchases Returns and Allowances, Purchases Discounts, Sales Salaries Expense, and Advertising Expense. Enter the June 30 balances of Cash ($100,000), Inventory ($200,000), and Long-Term Notes Payable ($300,000). Also open accounts payable subsidiary ledger accounts for Tahoe Company, Pryor, Inc., Caro's Supply, and Dixon Company.
3. Complete parts 3 and 4 of Problem 7-3B using the results of parts 1 and 2 of this problem.

Check Trial balance totals, $351,772

Problem 7-5B
Special journals, subsidiary ledgers, trial balance—perpetual
C4 P1 P2

(If the Working Papers that accompany this textbook are not being used, omit this problem.)
You have just taken over the accounting for YES Products, whose annual accounting period ends December 31. The company's previous accountant journalized its transactions through December 15 and posted all items that required posting as individual amounts (see the journals and ledgers in the working papers). The company's transactions beginning on December 16 follow (terms for all its credit sales are 2/10, n/30):

Dec. 16 Purchased $765 of office supplies on credit from Black Supply Company, invoice dated December 16, terms n/10 EOM.
16 Sold merchandise on credit to Brad Sills, Invoice No. 916, for $4,290 (cost is $2,821).
18 Issued a $200 credit memorandum to Leslie Wilson for defective (worthless) merchandise sold on December 15 and returned for credit.
19 Received a $640 credit memorandum from Chiefs Company for the return of merchandise received on December 15.
20 Received a $143 credit memorandum from Black Supply Company for the return of office supplies received on December 16.
20 Purchased $7,475 of store equipment on credit from Black Supply Company, invoice dated December 19, terms n/10 EOM.
21 Sold merchandise on credit to Mo Carp, Invoice No. 917, for $5,520 (cost is $3,210).
22 Received payment from Brad Sills for the December 12 sale less the discount.
25 Received payment from Leslie Wilson for the December 15 sale less the return and the discount.
25 Issued Check No. 623 to Chiefs Company in payment of its December 15 invoice less the return and the discount.
25 Issued Check No. 624 to Blue Company in payment of its December 15 invoice less a 2% discount.
28 Purchased $6,030 of merchandise from Blue Company, invoice dated December 28, terms 2/10, n/60.
28 Sold a neighboring merchant a carton of tape (store supplies) at its cost of $58 cash.
29 Sarah Morris, the sole owner of YES Products, used Check No. 625 to withdraw $4,000 in cash from the business for personal use.
30 Issued Check No. 626 to Bush Electric Company in payment of the $990 December electric bill.
30 Issued Check No. 627 to Sue Hart, the company's only sales employee, in payment of her $2,620 salary for the last half of December.
31 Cash sales for the last half of the month are $66,128 (cost is $33,850). (Cash sales are recorded daily but are recorded only twice here to reduce repetitive entries.)

Required

1. Record these transactions in the journals provided in the working papers.

2. Verify that amounts that should be posted as individual amounts to the general ledger accounts have been posted, including posting to the customer and creditor accounts. (These amounts are immediately posted.) Foot and crossfoot the journals and make the month-end postings.

Check Trial balance totals, $255,598

3. Prepare a December 31 trial balance and prove the accuracy of the subsidiary ledgers by preparing schedules of both accounts receivable and accounts payable.

Problem 7-6B
Special journals, subsidiary ledgers, trial balance—perpetual
C4 P1 P2

Suppan Company completes these transactions during November of the current year (terms for all its credit sales are 2/10, n/30):

Nov. 1 Purchased $5,062 of office equipment on credit from Blix Supply, invoice dated November 1, terms n/10 EOM.
2 Borrowed $86,250 cash from Kansas Bank by signing a long-term note payable.
4 Purchased $11,400 of merchandise from ATM Industries, invoice dated November 3, terms 2/10, n/30.
5 Purchased $1,020 of store supplies on credit from Globe Company, invoice dated November 5, terms n/10 EOM.
8 Sold merchandise on credit to Sid Ragan, Invoice No. 439, for $6,350 (cost is $3,710).
10 Sold merchandise on credit to Carlos Mane, Invoice No. 440, for $12,500 (cost is $7,500).
11 Purchased $2,887 of merchandise from Xu Company, invoice dated November 10, terms 2/10, n/30.
12 Sent ATM Industries Check No. 633 in payment of its November 3 invoice less the discount.
15 Issued Check No. 634, payable to Payroll, in payment of sales salaries expense for the first half of the month, $8,435. Cashed the check and paid the employees.
15 Cash sales for the first half of the month are $27,170 (cost is $17,000). (Cash sales are recorded daily but are recorded only twice in this problem to reduce repetitive entries.)
15 Sold merchandise on credit to Tony Timmons, Invoice No. 441, for $4,250 (cost is $1,450).
16 Purchased $559 of office supplies on credit from Globe Company, invoice dated November 16, terms n/10 EOM.
17 Received a $487 credit memorandum from Xu Company for the return of unsatisfactory merchandise purchased on November 11.
18 Received payment from Sid Ragan for the November 8 sale less the discount.
19 Received payment from Carlos Mane for the November 10 sale less the discount.
19 Issued Check No. 635 to Xu Company in payment of its invoice of November 10 less the return and the discount.
22 Sold merchandise on credit to Carlos Mane, Invoice No. 442, for $2,595 (cost is $1,060).
24 Sold merchandise on credit to Tony Timmons, Invoice No. 443, for $3,240 (cost is $1,090).
25 Received payment from Tony Timmons for the sale of November 15 less the discount.
26 Received a $922 credit memorandum from Blix Supply for the return of office equipment purchased on November 1.
30 Issued Check No. 636, payable to Payroll, in payment of sales salaries expense for the last half of the month, $8,435. Cashed the check and paid the employees.
30 Cash sales for the last half of the month are $35,703 (cost is $20,400).
30 Verify that amounts impacting customer and creditor accounts were posted and that any amounts that should have been posted as individual amounts to the general ledger accounts were posted. Foot and crossfoot the journals and make the month-end postings.

Required

1. Open the following general ledger accounts: Cash; Accounts Receivable; Inventory (November 1 beg. bal. is $40,000); Office Supplies; Store Supplies; Office Equipment; Accounts Payable; Long-Term Notes Payable; J. Suppan, Capital (November 1 beg. bal. is $40,000); Sales; Sales Discounts; Cost of Goods Sold; and Sales Salaries Expense. Open the following accounts receivable subsidiary ledger accounts: Carlos Mane, Tony Timmons, and Sid Ragan. Open the following accounts payable subsidiary ledger accounts: Globe Company, ATM Industries, Blix Supply, and Xu Company.

2. Enter these transactions in a sales journal like that in Exhibit 7.5, a purchases journal like that in Exhibit 7.9, a cash receipts journal like that in Exhibit 7.7, a cash disbursements journal like that in Exhibit 7.11, or a general journal. Number all journal pages as page 2.

Check Trial balance totals, $223,777

3. Prepare a trial balance of the general ledger and prove the accuracy of the subsidiary ledgers by preparing schedules of both accounts receivable and accounts payable.

Problem 7-7B^A
Special journals, subsidiary ledgers, trial balance—periodic
C4 P2 P3

Assume that Suppan Company in Problem 7-6B uses the periodic inventory system.

Required

1. Open the following general ledger accounts: Cash; Accounts Receivable; Inventory (November 1 beg. bal. is $40,000); Office Supplies; Store Supplies; Office Equipment; Accounts Payable; Long-Term Notes Payable; J. Suppan, Capital (November 1 beg. bal. is $40,000); Sales; Sales Discounts; Purchases; Purchases Returns and Allowances; Purchases Discounts; and Sales Salaries Expense. Open the following accounts receivable subsidiary ledger accounts: Carlos Mane, Tony Timmons, and Sid Ragan. Open the following accounts payable subsidiary ledger accounts: Globe Company, ATM Industries, Blix Supply, and Xu Company.

2. Enter the transactions from Problem 7-6B in a sales journal like that in Exhibit 7A.1, a purchases journal like that in Exhibit 7A.3, a cash receipts journal like that in Exhibit 7A.2, a cash disbursements journal like that in Exhibit 7A.4, or a general journal. Number journal pages as page 2.

3. Prepare a trial balance of the general ledger and prove the accuracy of the subsidiary ledgers by preparing schedules of both accounts receivable and accounts payable.

Check Trial balance totals, $224,540

PROBLEM SET C

Problem Set C is available at the book's Website to further reinforce and assess your learning.

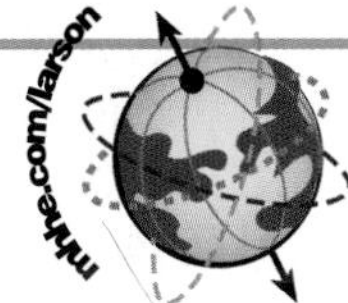

SERIAL PROBLEM

Success Systems

(This serial problem began in Chapter 1 and continues through most of the book. If previous chapter segments were not completed, the serial problem can begin at this point. It is helpful, but not necessary, that you use the Working Papers that accompany the book.)

Assume that Kay Breeze expands Success Systems' accounting system to include special journals.

Required

1. Locate the transactions related to January through March 2005 for Success Systems in Chapter 5.

2. Enter the Success Systems transactions for January through March in a sales journal like that in Exhibit 7.5 (insert "n/a" in the Invoice column), a cash receipts journal like that in Exhibit 7.7, a purchases journal like that in Exhibit 7.9 (use Computer Supplies heading instead of Office Supplies), and a cash disbursements journal like that in Exhibit 7.11 (insert "n/a" in the Check Number column), or a general journal. Number journal pages as page 2. If the transaction does not specify the name of the payee, state "not specified" in the Payee column of the cash disbursements journal.

3. The transactions on the following dates should be journalized in the general journal: January 5, 11, 20, 24, and 29 (no entry required) and March 24. Do not record and post the adjusting entries for the end of March.

COMPREHENSIVE PROBLEM—PERPETUAL

Colo Company

mhhe.com/larson

(If the Working Papers that accompany this book are not available, omit this comprehensive problem.) Assume it is Monday, May 1, the first business day of the month, and you have just been hired as the accountant for Colo Company, which operates with monthly accounting periods. All of the company's accounting work is completed through the end of April and its ledgers show April 30 balances. During your first month on the job, the company experiences the following transactions and events (terms for all its credit sales are 2/10, n/30 unless stated differently):

May 1 Issued Check No. 3410 to S&P Management Co. in payment of the May rent, $3,710. (Use two lines to record the transaction. Charge 80% of the rent to Rent Expense—Selling Space and the balance to Rent Expense—Office Space.)

2 Sold merchandise on credit to Hensel Company, Invoice No. 8785, for $6,100 (cost is $4,100).

2 Issued a $175 credit memorandum to Knox, Inc., for defective (worthless) merchandise sold on April 28 and returned for credit. The total selling price (gross) was $4,725.

3 Received a $798 credit memorandum from Peyton Products for the return of merchandise purchased on April 29.

4 Purchased the following on credit from Gear Supply Co.: merchandise, $37,072; store supplies, $574; and office supplies, $83. Invoice dated May 4, terms n/10 EOM.

5 Received payment from Knox, Inc., for the balance from the April 28 sale less the May 2 return and the discount.
8 Issued Check No. 3411 to Peyton Products to pay for the $7,098 of merchandise purchased on April 29 less the May 3 return and a 2% discount.
9 Sold store supplies to the merchant next door at their cost of $350 cash.
10 Purchased $4,074 of office equipment on credit from Gear Supply Co., invoice dated May 10, terms n/10 EOM.
11 Received payment from Hensel Company for the May 2 sale less the discount.
11 Purchased $8,800 of merchandise from Garcia, Inc., invoice dated May 10, terms 2/10, n/30.
12 Received an $854 credit memorandum from Gear Supply Co. for the return of defective office equipment received on May 10.
15 Issued Check No. 3412, payable to Payroll, in payment of sales salaries, $5,320, and office salaries, $3,150. Cashed the check and paid the employees.
15 Cash sales for the first half of the month are $59,220 (cost is $38,200). (Cash sales are recorded daily but are recorded only twice here to reduce repetitive entries.)
15 Post to the customer and creditor accounts. Also post individual items that are not included in column totals at the end of the month to the general ledger accounts. (Such items are posted daily but are posted only twice each month because they are few in number.)
16 Sold merchandise on credit to Hensel Company, Invoice No. 8786, for $3,990 (cost is $1,890).
17 Purchased $13,650 of merchandise from Fink Corp., invoice dated May 14, terms 2/10, n/60.
19 Issued Check No. 3413 to Garcia, Inc., in payment of its May 10 invoice less the discount.
22 Sold merchandise to Lee Services, Invoice No. 8787, for $6,850 (cost is $4,990), terms 2/10, n/60.
23 Issued Check No. 3414 to Fink Corp. in payment of its May 14 invoice less the discount.
24 Purchased the following on credit from Gear Supply Co.: merchandise, $8,120; store supplies, $630; and office supplies, $280. Invoice dated May 24, terms n/10 EOM.
25 Purchased $3,080 of merchandise from Peyton Products, invoice dated May 23, terms 2/10, n/30.
26 Sold merchandise on credit to Crane Corp., Invoice No. 8788, for $14,210 (cost is $8,230).
26 Issued Check No. 3415 to Perennial Power in payment of the May electric bill, $1,283.
29 The owner of Colo Company, Jenny Colo, used Check No. 3416 to withdraw $7,000 cash from the business for personal use.
30 Received payment from Lee Services for the May 22 sale less the discount.
30 Issued Check No. 3417, payable to Payroll, in payment of sales salaries, $5,320, and office salaries, $3,150. Cashed the check and paid the employees.
31 Cash sales for the last half of the month are $66,052 (cost is $42,500).
31 Post to the customer and creditor accounts. Also post individual items that are not included in column totals at the end of the month to the general ledger accounts. Foot and crossfoot the journals and make the month-end postings.

Required

1. Enter these transactions in a sales journal, a purchases journal, a cash receipts journal, a cash disbursements journal, or a general journal as illustrated in this chapter. Post when instructed to do so. Assume a perpetual inventory system.

Check (2) Unadjusted trial balance totals, $545,020; Adjustments' column totals, $2,407

2. Prepare a trial balance in the Trial Balance columns of the work sheet form provided with the working papers. Complete the work sheet using the following information for accounting adjustments:

a. Expired insurance, $553.

b. Ending store supplies inventory, $2,632.

c. Ending office supplies inventory, $504.

d. Depreciation of store equipment, $567.

e. Depreciation of office equipment, $329.

Prepare and post adjusting and closing entries.

(3) Net income, $31,647; Total assets, $385,791

3. Prepare a May 2005 multiple-step income statement, a May 2005 statement of owner's equity, and a May 31, 2005, classified balance sheet.

4. Prepare a post-closing trial balance. Also prove the accuracy of subsidiary ledgers by preparing schedules of both accounts receivable and accounts payable.

BEYOND THE NUMBERS

REPORTING IN ACTION

A1

BTN 7-1 Refer to **Krispy Kreme**'s financial statements in Appendix A to answer the following:

1. Identify the note disclosing Krispy Kreme's business segments.

2. Describe the nature and activities of each of Krispy Kreme's business segments.

Roll On

3. Access Krispy Kreme's annual report for fiscal years ending after February 2, 2003, from its Website (KrispyKreme.com) or the SEC's EDGAR database (www.SEC.gov). Has Krispy Kreme changed its reporting policy regarding segment information?

COMPARATIVE ANALYSIS

A1

BTN 7-2 Key figures for **Krispy Kreme** follow ($ millions):

	Krispy Kreme		
Revenue by Segment	**Current Year**	**One Year Prior**	**Two Years Prior**
Company Store	$320	$266	$214
Franchise	19	14	9
KKM&D	348	269	201

Required

1. Compute the percent change in revenue (rounded to whole numbers) for each segment and for each of the most recent two years shown. Interpret and comment on your findings.

2. Identify the segment experiencing the largest growth in revenue for Krispy Kreme.

ETHICS CHALLENGE

C5

BTN 7-3 Erica Gray, CPA, is a sole practitioner. She has been practicing as an auditor for 10 years. Recently a long-standing audit client asked Gray to design and implement an integrated computer-based accounting information system. The fees associated with this additional engagement with the client are very attractive. However, Gray wonders if she can remain objective on subsequent audits in her evaluation of the client's accounting system and its records if she was responsible for its design and implementation. Gray knows that professional auditing standards require her to remain independent in fact and appearance from her auditing clients.

Required

1. What do you believe auditing standards are mainly concerned with when they require independence in fact? In appearance?

2. Why is it important that auditors remain independent of their clients?

3. Do you think Gray can accept this engagement and remain independent? Justify your response.

COMMUNICATING IN PRACTICE

C3 C4

BTN 7-4 Your friend, Wendy Geiger, owns a small retail store that sells candies and nuts. Geiger acquires her goods from a few select vendors. She generally makes purchase orders by phone and on credit. Sales are primarily for cash. Geiger keeps her own manual accounting system using a general journal and a general ledger. At the end of each business day, she records one summary entry for cash sales. Geiger recently began offering items in creative gift packages. This has increased sales substantially, and she is now receiving orders from corporate and other clients who order large quantities and prefer to buy on credit. As a result of increased credit transactions in both purchases and sales, keeping the accounting records has become extremely time consuming. Geiger wants to continue to maintain her own manual system and calls you for advice. Write a memo to her advising how she might modify her current manual accounting system to accommodate the expanded business activities. Geiger is accustomed to checking her ledger by using a trial balance. Your memo should explain the advantages of what you propose and of any other verification techniques you recommend.

TAKING IT TO THE NET

A1 

mhhe.com/larson

BTN 7-5 Access the May 1, 2002, filing of the fiscal 2002 10-K report for **Dell Computer** (ticker DELL) at **www.sec.gov**. Read the footnote that details Dell's segment information and answer the following:

1. Dell's operations are divided among which three geographic segments?
2. In fiscal year 2002, which geographic area had the largest dollar amount of operating income? Which had the largest amount of identifiable assets?
3. Compute the return on assets for each segment for fiscal year 2002. Use operating income and average total assets by segment for your calculation. Which segment has the highest return on assets?
4. For what product groups does Dell provide segment data? What percent of Dell's net revenue is earned by each product group?

TEAMWORK IN ACTION

C4 P1 P2

BTN 7-6 Each member of the team is to assume responsibility for one of the following tasks:

a. Journalizing in the purchases journal.
b. Journalizing in the cash disbursements journal.
c. Maintaining and verifying the Accounts Payable ledger.
d. Journalizing in the sales journal and the general journal.
e. Journalizing in the cash receipts journal.
f. Maintaining and verifying the Accounts Receivable ledger.

The team should abide by the following procedures in carrying out responsibilities.

Required

1. After tasks *a–f* are assigned, each team member is to quickly read the list of transactions in Problem 7-6A, identifying with initials the journal in which each transaction is to be recorded. Upon completion, the team leader is to read transaction dates, and the appropriate team member is to vocalize responsibility. Any disagreement between teammates must be resolved.
2. Journalize and continually update subsidiary ledgers. Journal recorders should alert teammates assigned to subsidiary ledgers when an entry must be posted to their subsidiary.
3. Team members responsible for tasks *a*, *b*, *d*, and *e* are to summarize and prove journals; members responsible for tasks *c* and *f* are to prepare both payables and receivables schedules.
4. The team leader is to take charge of the general ledger, rotating team members to obtain amounts to be posted. The person responsible for a journal must complete posting references in that journal. Other team members should verify the accuracy of account balance computations. To avoid any abnormal account balances, post in the following order: P, S, G, R, D. (*Note:* Posting any necessary individual general ledger amounts are also done at this time.)
5. The team leader is to read out general ledger account balances while another team member fills in the trial balance form. Concurrently, one member should keep a running balance of debit account balance totals and another credit account balance totals. Verify the final total of the trial balance and the schedules. If necessary, the team must resolve any errors. Turn in the trial balance and schedules to the instructor.

BUSINESS WEEK ACTIVITY

C1 C2

mhhe.com/larson

BTN 7-7 Read the article, "The Battle to Streamline Business Software" in the December 4, 2002, edition of ***Business Week***. (This book's Website provides a free link.)

Required

1. What functions are integrated by enterprise resource planning, or ERP, software?
2. How long does **Oregon Health and Sciences University** in Portland think it will take for it to earn a return on its $25 million dollar investment in **Oracle** software?
3. Which companies are identified in the article as the large (likely long-standing) names in the business software market?
4. In dollar terms, what is the current size of the ERP software market? What annual growth rate is predicted for this market through 2006?

ENTREPRENEURIAL DECISION

P1 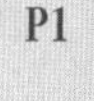 

BTN 7-8 Refer to the chapter's opening feature about Devin Lazerine and his ***Rap-Up*** magazine.

Required

1. What is the current circulation (to the nearest one hundred thousand) of *Rap-Up* magazine?
2. Assume that Devin charges $2.40 per issue for subscribers and $3.60 per issue to newsstands that purchase copies of *Rap-Up*. Also assume that *Rap-Up*'s circulation (refer to your answer in part 1) is equally divided between newsstand and subscription sales.
   - **a.** If Devin uses one mass mailing to ship magazines to newsstands each month, what journal entry would Devin make to record the sale upon shipment of the magazines? (You may ignore cost of goods sold and show only the revenue side of the transaction.)
   - **b.** Assume that *Rap-Up* is a monthly publication. With the current level of subscribers, how much annual revenue will be earned from subscription sales?
   - **c.** What journal entry does Devin record when an individual subscription order with payment is received? (*Note:* Subscribers pay $28.80 per year.)
   - **d.** What journal entry does Devin record when an individual subscriber's magazine is mailed out each month?
   - **e.** Construct a table to show annual revenue, cost of goods sold ($0.60 per issue), gross margin and gross margin percentage by each business segment (newsstand and subscription).
3. Devin is thinking of adding a sales subsidiary ledger to his accounting system. What information might the sales subsidiary ledger be designed to account for beyond each customer and the amount owed?

GLOBAL DECISION

A1 

BTN 7-9 Access and refer to the 2002 annual report for **Grupo Bimbo** at GrupoBimbo.com.

Required

1. Skim the management and discussion section until you find information relating to Grupo Bimbo's geographic segments. Identify those segments.
2. What three financial figures does it disclose for each geographic segment?
3. Does Grupo Bimbo have a dominant segment? Explain.
4. Does the total of sales by region match with the total amount of sales reported on Grupo Bimbo's consolidated statement of income?

"*They [customers] love that it's very childhood, nostalgic*"—Dylan Lauren (on right, Jeff Rubin on left)

Cash and Internal Controls

A Look Back

Chapter 7 focused on accounting information systems. We explained the fundamental principles and components of information systems, the use of special journals and subsidiary ledgers, and technology-based systems. We also discussed the analysis of segment data.

A Look at This Chapter

This chapter extends our study of accounting to the area of internal control and the analysis of cash. We describe procedures that are good for internal control. We also explain the control of and the accounting for cash, including control features of banking activities.

A Look Ahead

Chapter 9 focuses on receivables, which are some of the most liquid assets other than cash. We explain how to account and report on receivables and their related accounts. This includes estimating uncollectible receivables and computing interest earned.

CAP

Conceptual

C1 Define internal control and identify its purpose and principles. *(p. 308)*

C2 Define cash and cash equivalents and explain how to report them. *(p. 312)*

C3 Identify control features of banking activities. *(p. 319)*

Analytical

A1 Compute the days' sales uncollected ratio and use it to assess liquidity. *(p. 325)*

Procedural

P1 Apply internal control to cash receipts and disbursements. *(p. 313)*

P2 Explain and record petty cash fund transactions. *(p. 316)*

P3 Prepare a bank reconciliation. *(p. 322)*

Decision Feature

Sweet Success

NEW YORK—A 10-foot chocolate bunny named Jeffrey greets you as you enter the store—that should be warning enough! This elite designer candy store, christened **Dylan's Candy Bar (DylansCandyBar.com),** is the brainchild of co-founders Dylan Lauren and Jeff Rubin (the bunny is named for him). This sweet-lovers heaven offers more than 5,000 different choices of sweets from all over the world. In just under two years of operation, it has become a hip hangout for locals and tourists—and it has made candy cool. Says Lauren, "Park Avenue women come in, and the first thing they ask for is Gummi bears. They love that it's very childhood, nostalgic."

The New York store projects more than $5 million in sales this year. While marketing is an important part of its success, Lauren and Rubin's management of internal controls and cash is equally impressive. Several control procedures monitor its business activities and safeguard its assets. An example is the biometric time and attendance control system using fingerprint characteristics. Says Rubin, "There's no fooling the system! It is going to help us remotely manage our employees while eliminating human error and dishonesty. [It] is a cost effective and important business management tool." Similar controls are applied throughout the store. Rubin notes that such controls raise productivity and cut expenses.

The store's cash management practices are equally impressive, including controls over cash receipts, disbursements, and petty cash. The use of bank reconciliations further helps with the store's control and management of cash.

Internal controls are crucial when on a busy day its store brings in more than 8,000 customers, and their cash. Moreover, expansion is already underway in Orlando, Houston, Chicago, Toronto, and Las Vegas. Through it all, Lauren says it is "totally fun." And how is it that Lauren maintains her slim figure. "I work out a lot!" she exclaims.

[Sources: *Dylan's Candy Bar Website,* January 2004; *Entrepreneur,* December 2002; *USA Today,* October 26, 2001; *PR Newswire,* November 2001; ECommerce-Guide.com, June 2003.]

We all are aware of reports and experiences involving theft and fraud. These occurrences affect us in several ways: We lock doors, chain bikes, review sales receipts, and acquire alarm systems. A company also takes actions to safeguard, control, and manage what it owns. Experience tells us that small companies are most vulnerable, usually due to weak internal controls. It is management's responsibility to set up policies and procedures to safeguard a company's assets, especially cash. To do so, management *and* employees must understand and apply principles of internal control. This chapter describes these principles and how to apply them. It focuses special attention on cash because it is easily transferable and often at high risk of loss. An understanding of these controls and procedures makes us more secure in carrying out business activities and in assessing the activities of other companies.

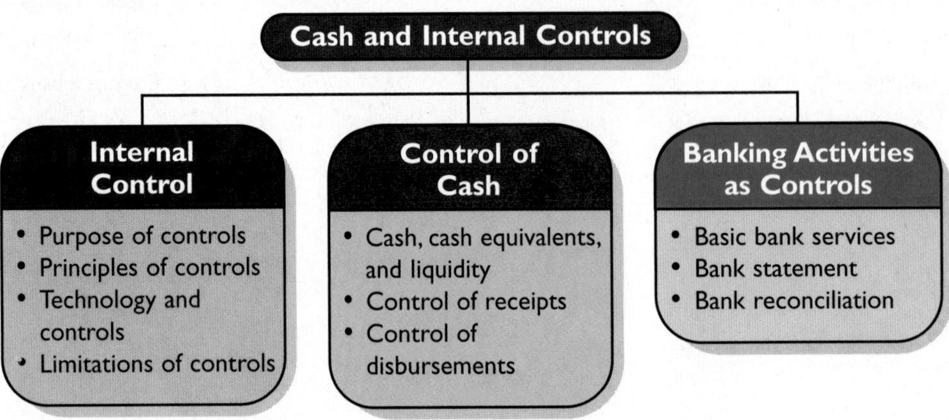

Internal Control

This section describes internal control and its fundamental principles. We also discuss the impact of technology on internal control and the limitations of control procedures.

Purpose of Internal Control

C1 Define internal control and identify its purpose and principles.

Managers (or owners) of small businesses often control the entire operation. These managers usually purchase all assets, hire and manage employees, negotiate all contracts, and sign all checks. They know from personal contact and observation whether the business is actually receiving the assets and services paid for. Most companies, however, cannot maintain this close personal supervision. They must delegate responsibilities and rely on formal procedures rather than personal contact in controlling business activities.

Point: With company growth comes increased reporting and controls to safeguard assets and manage operations.

Managers use an internal control system to monitor and control business activities. An **internal control system** consists of the policies and procedures managers use to

- Protect assets.
- Ensure reliable accounting.
- Promote efficient operations.
- Urge adherence to company policies.

A properly designed internal control system is a key part of systems design, analysis, and performance. Managers place a high priority on internal control systems because they can prevent avoidable losses, help managers plan operations, and monitor company and employee performance. Internal controls do not provide guarantees, but they lower the company's risk of loss.

Decision Insight

What's the Password? Good internal control prevents unauthorized access to assets and accounting records by requiring passwords. It takes a password, for instance, to boot up most office PCs, log onto a network, and access voice mail, e-mail, and online services—not to mention personal ID numbers on credit and cash cards.

Principles of Internal Control

Topic Tackler 8-1

Internal control policies and procedures vary from company to company according to such factors as the nature of the business and its size. Certain fundamental internal control principles apply to all companies. The **principles of internal control** are to

1. Establish responsibilities.
2. Maintain adequate records.
3. Insure assets and bond key employees.
4. Separate recordkeeping from custody of assets.
5. Divide responsibility for related transactions.
6. Apply technological controls.
7. Perform regular and independent reviews.

Point: **Sarbanes-Oxley Act** requires that each annual report contain an *internal control report,* which must: (1) state managers' responsibility for establishing and maintaining adequate internal controls for financial reporting; and (2) assess the effectiveness of those controls.

This section explains these seven principles and describes how internal control procedures minimize the risk of fraud and theft. These procedures also increase the reliability and accuracy of accounting records.

Establish Responsibilities Proper internal control means that responsibility for a task is clearly established and assigned to one person. When a problem occurs in a company where responsibility is not identified, determining who is at fault is difficult. For instance, if two salesclerks share the same cash register and there is a cash shortage, neither clerk can be held accountable. To prevent this problem, one clerk might be given responsibility for handling all cash sales. Alternately, a company can use a register with separate cash drawers for each clerk. Most of us have waited at a retail counter during a shift change while employees swap cash drawers.

Point: Many companies have a mandatory vacation policy for employees who handle cash. When another employee must cover for the one on vacation, it is more difficult to hide cash frauds.

Maintain Adequate Records Good recordkeeping is part of an internal control system. It helps protect assets and ensures that employees use prescribed procedures. Reliable records are also a source of information that managers use to monitor company activities. When detailed records of equipment are kept, for instance, items are unlikely to be lost or stolen without detection. Similarly, transactions are less likely to be entered in wrong accounts if a chart of accounts is set up and carefully used. Many preprinted forms and internal documents are also designed for use in a good internal control system. When sales slips are properly designed, for instance, sales personnel can record needed information efficiently with less chance of errors or delays to customers. When sales slips are prenumbered and controlled, each one issued is the responsibility of one salesperson, preventing the salesperson from pocketing cash by making a sale and destroying the sales slip. Computerized point-of-sale systems achieve the same control results.

Point: The Association of Certified Fraud Examiners **(cfenet.com)** estimates that employee fraud costs small companies an average of about $130,000 per incident.

Insure Assets and Bond Key Employees Good internal control means that assets are adequately insured against casualty and that employees handling large amounts of cash and easily transferable assets are bonded. An employee is *bonded* when a company purchases an insurance policy, or a bond, against losses from theft by that employee. Bonding reduces the risk of loss. It also discourages theft because bonded employees know an independent bonding company will be involved when theft is uncovered and is unlikely to be sympathetic with an employee involved in theft.

Decision Insight

Check It Out What lurks behind that spiffy résumé you just reviewed? The Association of Certified Fraud Examiners **(cfenet.com)** provides links to search engines to verify Social Security numbers, addresses, and phone numbers. Also, **KnowX.com** lets you check lawsuits and bankruptcies, and **EmployeeScreen.com** offers background searches, including employment verification.

Separate Recordkeeping from Custody of Assets A person who controls or has access to an asset must not keep that asset's accounting records. This principle reduces the risk of theft or waste of an asset because the person with control over it knows that another person keeps its records. Also, a recordkeeper who does not have access to the asset

Decision Insight

Tag Time A new technique exists for marking all physical assets. It involves embedding a less than one-inch-square tag of nylon fibers that creates a unique optical signature recordable by scanners. The manufacturer hopes to embed tags in everything from compact discs and credit cards to designer clothes.

has no reason to falsify records. This means that to steal an asset and hide the theft from the records, two or more people must *collude*—or agree in secret to commit the fraud.

Divide Responsibility for Related Transactions Good internal control divides responsibility for a transaction or a series of related transactions between two or more individuals or departments. This is to ensure that the work of one individual acts as a check on the other. This principle, often called *separation of duties,* is not a call for duplication of work. Each employee or department should perform unduplicated effort. Examples of transactions with divided responsibility are placing purchase orders, receiving merchandise, and paying vendors. These tasks should not be given to one individual or department. Assigning responsibility for two or more of these tasks to one party increases mistakes and perhaps fraud. Having an independent person, for example, check incoming goods for quality and quantity encourages more care and attention to detail than having the person who placed the order do the checking. Added protection can result from identifying a third person to approve payment of the invoice. A company can even designate a fourth person with authority to write checks as another protective measure.

Point: There's a new security device—a person's ECG (electrocardiogram) reading, which is as unique as a fingerprint and a lot harder to lose or steal than a PIN. An ECG also shows that a living person is actually there, whereas fingerprint and facial recognition software can be fooled. ECGs can be read through fingertip touches.

Apply Technological Controls Cash registers, check protectors, time clocks, and personal identification scanners are examples of devices that can improve internal control. Technology often improves the effectiveness of controls. A cash register with a locked-in tape or electronic file makes a record of each cash sale. A check protector perforates the amount of a check into its face and makes it difficult to alter the amount. A time clock registers the exact time an employee both arrives at and departs from the job. Mechanical change and currency counters quickly and accurately count amounts, and personal scanners limit access to only authorized individuals. Each of these and other technological controls are an effective part of many internal control systems.

Point: Evidence of any internal control failure for a company reduces user reliance on its financial statements.

Decision Insight

About Face Face-recognition software snaps a digital picture of the face and converts key facial features—say, the distance between the eyes—into a series of numerical values. These can be stored on an ID or ATM card as a simple bar code to prohibit unauthorized access.

Perform Regular and Independent Reviews Changes in personnel, stress of time pressures, and technological advances present opportunities for shortcuts and lapses. To counter these factors, regular reviews of internal control systems are needed to ensure that procedures are followed. These reviews are preferably done by internal auditors not directly involved in the activities. Their impartial perspective encourages an evaluation of the efficiency as well as the effectiveness of the internal control system. Many companies also pay for audits by independent, external auditors. These external auditors test the company's financial records to give an opinion as to whether its financial statements are presented fairly. Before external auditors decide on how much testing is needed, they evaluate the effectiveness of the internal control system. This evaluation is often helpful to a client.

Decision Maker

Entrepreneur As owner of a start-up information services company, you hire a systems analyst. One of her first recommendations is to require all employees to take at least one week of vacation per year. Why would she recommend a "forced vacation" policy?

Answer—p. 333

Technology and Internal Control

Point: Information on Internet fraud can be found at these Websites: ftc.gov/ftc/consumer.htm sec.gov/investor/pubs/cyberfraud.htm www.fraud.org

The fundamental principles of internal control are relevant no matter what the technological state of the accounting system, from purely manual to fully automated systems. Technology impacts an internal control system in several important ways. Perhaps the most obvious is that technology allows us quicker access to databases and information. Used effectively, technology greatly improves managers' abilities to monitor and control business activities. This section describes some technological impacts we must be alert to.

> **Decision Insight**
>
> **Undo Shredding?** A Website that specializes in high-tech spy tools sold several $5,000 paper shredders fitted with scanners and wireless transmitters. When unsuspecting companies fed in confidential documents, the illegally obtained information was sent to the spy's e-mail address.
>
> 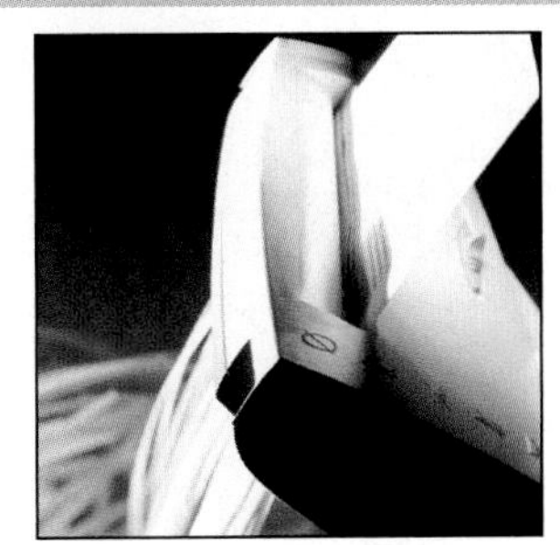

Reduced Processing Errors Technologically advanced systems reduce the number of errors in processing information. Provided the software and data entry are correct, the risk of mechanical and mathematical errors is nearly eliminated. However, we must remember that erroneous software or data entry does exist. Also, less human involvement in data processing can cause data entry errors to go undiscovered. Moreover, errors in software can produce consistent but erroneous processing of transactions. Continually checking and monitoring all types of systems are important.

More Extensive Testing of Records A company's review and audit of electronic records can include more extensive testing when information is easily and rapidly accessed. When accounting records are kept manually, auditors and others likely select only small samples of data to test. When data are accessible with computer technology, however, auditors can quickly analyze large samples or even the entire database.

Limited Evidence of Processing Many data processing steps are increasingly done by computer. Accordingly, fewer hard-copy items of documentary evidence are available for review. Yet technologically advanced systems can provide new evidence. They can, for instance, record who made the entries, the date and time, the source of the entry, and so on. Technology can also be designed to require the use of passwords or other identification before access to the system is granted. This means that internal control depends more on the design and operation of the information system and less on the analysis of its resulting documents.

Point: External decision makers look to several sources when assessing a company's internal controls. Sources include the auditor's report, management report on controls (if available), management discussion and analysis, and financial press.

Crucial Separation of Duties Technological advances in accounting information systems often yield some job eliminations or consolidations. While those who remain have the special skills necessary to operate advanced programs and equipment, a company with a reduced workforce risks losing its crucial separation of duties. The company must establish ways to control and monitor employees to minimize risk of error and fraud. For instance, the person who designs and programs the information system must not be the one who operates it. The company must also separate control over programs and files from the activities related to cash receipts and disbursements. For instance, a computer operator should not control check-writing activities. Achieving acceptable separation of duties can be especially difficult and costly in small companies with few employees.

> **Decision Insight**
>
> **Hot Prospects** A recent survey cites the shortage of accounting techies as one barrier to company growth. The most prized recruits are those adept at enterprise software, the Web, intranets, and accounting.

Limitations of Internal Control

All internal control policies and procedures have limitations which usually arise from either (1) the human element, or (2) the cost-benefit principle.

Internal control policies and procedures are applied by people. This human element creates several potential limitations that we can categorize as either (1) human error or (2) human fraud. *Human error* can occur from negligence, fatigue, misjudgment, or confusion. *Human fraud* involves intent by people to defeat internal controls, such as *management override,* for personal gain. Fraud also includes collusion to thwart the separation of duties. The human element highlights the importance of establishing an *internal control environment* to convey management's commitment to internal control policies and procedures.

Point: When the electronic manufacturer Casio (Casio.com) started an e-commerce site, it found 13% of its first-year customer purchases were fraudulent.

Point: Cybercrime.gov pursues computer and intellectual property crimes, including that of e-commerce.

The second major limitation on internal control is the *cost-benefit principle,* which dictates that the costs of internal controls must not exceed their benefits. Analysis of costs and benefits must consider all factors, including the impact on morale. Most companies, for instance, have a legal right to read employees' e-mails, yet companies seldom exercise that right unless they are confronted with evidence of potential harm to the company. The same holds for drug testing, phone tapping, and hidden cameras. The bottom line is that managers must establish internal control policies and procedures with a net benefit to the company.

Quick Check

1. Principles of internal control suggest that (choose one): (*a*) Responsibility for a series of related transactions (such as placing orders, receiving and paying for merchandise) should be assigned to one employee; (*b*) Responsibility for individual tasks should be shared by more than one employee so that one serves as a check on the other; or (*c*) Employees who handle considerable cash and easily transferable assets should be bonded.
2. What are some impacts of computing technology on internal control?

Answers—p. 333

Control of Cash

Cash is a necessary asset of every company. Most companies also own *cash equivalents* (defined below), which are assets similar to cash. Cash and cash equivalents are the most liquid of all assets and are easily hidden and moved. An effective system of internal controls protects these assets and it should meet three basic guidelines:

1. Handling cash is separate from recordkeeping of cash.
2. Cash receipts are promptly deposited in a bank.
3. Cash disbursements are made by check.

The first guideline applies separation of duties to minimize errors and fraud. When duties are separated, two or more people must collude to steal cash and conceal this action in the accounting records. The second guideline uses immediate (say, daily) deposits of all cash receipts to produce a timely independent record of the cash received. It also reduces the likelihood of cash theft (or loss) and the risk that an employee could personally use the money before depositing it. The third guideline uses payments by check to develop an independent bank record of cash disbursements. This guideline also reduces the risk of cash theft (or loss).

This section begins with definitions of cash and cash equivalents. Discussion then focuses on controls and accounting for both cash receipts and disbursements. The exact procedures used to achieve control over cash vary across companies. They depend on factors such as company size, number of employees, volume of cash transactions, and sources of cash.

Cash, Cash Equivalents, and Liquidity

C2 Define cash and cash equivalents and explain how to report them.

Good accounting systems help in managing the amount of cash and controlling who has access to it. Cash is the usual means of payment when paying for assets, services, or liabilities. **Liquidity** refers to a company's ability to pay for its near-term obligations. Cash and similar assets are called **liquid assets** because they can be readily used to settle such obligations. A company needs liquid assets to effectively operate.

Point: The most liquid assets are usually reported first on a balance sheet; the least liquid assets are reported last.

Cash includes currency and coins along with the amounts on deposit in bank accounts, checking accounts (called *demand deposits*), and many savings accounts (called *time deposits*). Cash also includes items that are acceptable for deposit in these accounts such as customer checks, cashier checks, certified checks, and money orders. **Cash equivalents** are short-term, highly liquid investment assets meeting two criteria: (1) readily convertible to a known cash amount and (2) sufficiently close to their due date so that their market value is not sensitive to interest rate changes. Only investments purchased within three months of their due date usually satisfy these criteria. Examples of cash equivalents are short-term investments in assets such as U.S. Treasury bills and money market funds. To increase their return, many companies invest idle cash in cash equivalents. Most companies combine cash equivalents with cash as a single item on the balance sheet.

Decision Insight

Days' Cash Expense Coverage The ratio of *cash (and cash equivalents) to average daily cash expenses* indicates the number of days a company can operate without additional cash inflows. It reflects on company liquidity.

Point: The e-commerce company i2 Technologies reports cash and cash equivalents of $538 million in its recent balance sheet. This amount makes up nearly one-third of its total assets.

Control of Cash Receipts

P1 Apply internal control to cash receipts and disbursements.

Internal control of cash receipts ensures that cash received is properly recorded and deposited. Cash receipts can arise from transactions such as cash sales, collections of customer accounts, receipts of interest earned, bank loans, sales of assets, and owner investments. This section explains internal control over two important types of cash receipts: over-the-counter and by mail.

Over-the-Counter Cash Receipts For purposes of internal control, over-the-counter cash receipts from sales should be recorded on a cash register at the time of each sale. To help ensure that correct amounts are entered, each register should be located so customers can read the amounts entered. Clerks also should be required to enter each sale before wrapping merchandise and to give the customer a receipt for each sale. The design of each cash register should provide a permanent, locked-in record of each transaction. In many systems, the register is directly linked with computing and accounting services. Less advanced registers simply print a record of each transaction on a paper tape or electronic file locked inside the register.

Decision Insight

Money Talk Projected cash receipts and cash disbursements are often summarized in a *cash budget.* Provided that sufficient cash exists for effective operations, managers wish to minimize the cash they hold because of its low return versus other investment opportunities.

Proper internal control prescribes that custody over cash should be separate from its recordkeeping. For over-the-counter cash receipts, this separation begins with the cash sale. The clerk who has access to cash in the register should not have access to its locked-in record. At the end of the clerk's work period, the clerk should count the cash in the register, record the amount, and turn over the cash and a record of its amount to the company cashier. The cashier, like the clerk, has access to the cash but should not have access to accounting records (or the register tape or file). A third employee compares the record of total register transactions (or the register tape or file) with the cash receipts reported by the cashier. This record is the basis for a journal entry recording over-the-counter cash receipts. The third employee has access to the records for cash but not to the actual cash. The clerk and the cashier have access to cash but not to the accounting records. None of them can make a mistake or divert cash without the difference being revealed.

Decision Insight

Link Time **Wal-Mart** uses a network of information links with its point-of-sale cash registers to coordinate sales, purchases, and distribution. Its supercenters, for instance, ring up to 15,000 separate sales on heavy days. By using cash register information, the company can fix pricing mistakes quickly and capitalize on sales trends.

Cash over and short. Sometimes errors in making change are discovered from differences between the cash in a cash register and the record of the amount of cash receipts. Although a clerk is careful, one or more customers can be given too much or too little change. This means that at the end of a work period, the cash in a cash register might not equal the record of cash receipts. This difference is reported in the **Cash Over and Short**

Point: Retailers often require cashiers to restrictively endorse checks immediately on receipt by stamping them "For deposit only."

account, also called *Cash Short and Over,* which is an income statement account recording the income effects of cash overages and cash shortages. To illustrate, if a cash register's record shows $550 but the count of cash in the register is $555, the entry to record cash sales and its overage is

Assets = Liabilities + Equity
+555 + 5
+550

Cash	555	
Cash Over and Short		**5**
Sales		550
To record cash sales and a cash overage.		

On the other hand, if a cash register's record shows $625 but the count of cash in the register is $621, the entry to record cash sales and its shortage is:

Assets = Liabilities + Equity
+621 − 4
+625

Cash	621	
Cash Over and Short	**4**	
Sales		625
To record cash sales and a cash shortage.		

Since customers are more likely to dispute being shortchanged than being given too much change, the Cash Over and Short account usually has a debit balance at the end of an accounting period. A debit balance reflects an expense. It can be shown on the income statement as part of general and administrative expenses. (Note that since the amount is usually small, it is often combined with other small expenses and reported as part of *miscellaneous expenses;* or as part of *miscellaneous revenues* if it has a credit balance.)

Point: Collusion implies that two or more individuals are knowledgeable or involved with the activities of the other(s).

Point: A complete set of financial statements includes a statement of cash flows, which provides useful information about a company's sources and uses of cash and cash equivalents during a period of time.

Cash Receipts by Mail Control of cash receipts that arrive through the mail starts with the person who opens the mail. Preferably, two people are assigned the task of, and are present for, opening the mail. In this case, theft of cash receipts by mail requires collusion between these two employees. Specifically, the person(s) opening the mail enters a list (in triplicate) of money received. This list should contain a record of each sender's name, the amount, and an explanation of why the money is sent. The first copy is sent with the money to the cashier. A second copy is sent to the recordkeeper in the accounting area. A third copy is kept by the clerks who opened the mail. The cashier deposits the money in a bank, and the recordkeeper records the amounts received in the accounting records.

This process reflects good internal control. That is, when the bank balance is reconciled by another person (explained later in the chapter), errors or acts of fraud by the mail clerks, the cashier, or the recordkeeper are revealed. They are revealed because the bank's record of cash deposited must agree with the records from each of the three. Moreover, if the mail clerks do not report all receipts correctly, customers will question their account balances. If the cashier does not deposit all receipts, the bank balance does not agree with the recordkeeper's cash balance. The recordkeeper and the person who reconciles the bank balance do not have access to cash and therefore have no opportunity to divert cash to themselves. This system makes errors and fraud highly unlikely. The exception is employee collusion.

Decision Insight

Look West In the annual Small Business Survival Index (**SBSC.org**), the first 4 of the top 5 states ranked as most entrepreneur friendly are west of the Mississippi: (1) South Dakota, (2) Nevada, (3) Wyoming, (4) Texas, and (5) Florida. Factors considered included taxes, regulations, costs, and crime.

Control of Cash Disbursements

Control of cash disbursements is especially important as most large thefts occur from payment of fictitious invoices. One key to controlling cash disbursements is to require all expenditures to be made by check. The only exception is small payments made from petty cash.

Another key is to deny access to the accounting records to anyone other than the owner who has the authority to sign checks. A small business owner often signs checks and knows from personal contact that the items being paid for are actually received. This arrangement is impossible in large businesses. Instead, internal control procedures must be substituted for personal contact. Such procedures are designed to assure the check signer that the obligations recorded are properly incurred and should be paid. This section describes these and other internal control procedures, including the voucher system and petty cash system. The management of cash disbursements for purchases is described in Appendix 8B.

> **Decision Insight**
>
> **Hidden Risks** The basic purposes of paper and electronic documents are similar. However, the internal control system must change to reflect different risks, including confidential and competitive-sensitive information that is at greater risk in electronic systems.

Voucher System of Control A **voucher system** is a set of procedures and approvals designed to control cash disbursements and the acceptance of obligations. The voucher system of control establishes procedures for

- Verifying, approving, and recording obligations for eventual cash disbursement.
- Issuing checks for payment of verified, approved, and recorded obligations.

A reliable voucher system follows standard procedures for every transaction. This applies even when multiple purchases are made from the same supplier.

A voucher system's control over cash disbursements begins when a company incurs an obligation that will result in payment of cash. A key factor in this system is that only approved departments and individuals are authorized to incur such obligations. The system often limits the type of obligations that a department or individual can incur. In a large retail store, for instance, only a purchasing department should be authorized to incur obligations for merchandise inventory. Another key factor is that procedures for purchasing, receiving, and paying for merchandise are divided among several departments (or individuals). These departments include the one requesting the purchase, the purchasing department, the receiving department, and the accounting department. To coordinate and control responsibilities of these departments, a company uses several different business documents. Exhibit 8.1 shows how documents are accumulated in a **voucher,** which is an internal document (or file) used to accumulate information to control cash

> **Decision Insight**
>
> **Cyber Setup** The FTC is on the cutting edge of cybersleuthing. Opportunists in search of easy money are lured to **WeMarket4U.net/netops.** Take the bait and you get warned—and possibly targeted. (The top 4 fraud complaints as compiled by the Internet Fraud Complaint Center are shown to the right.)
>
> 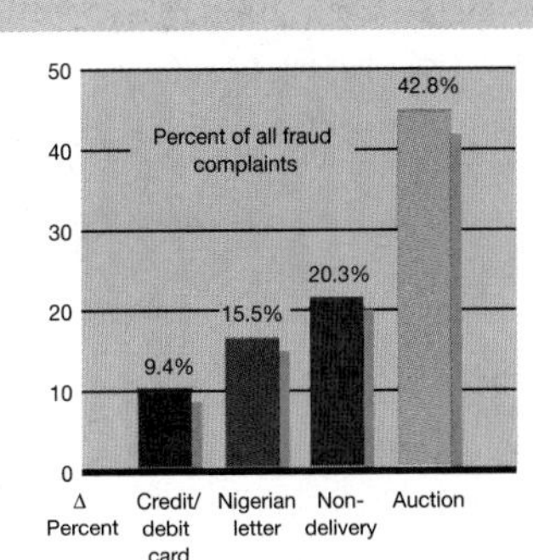
>

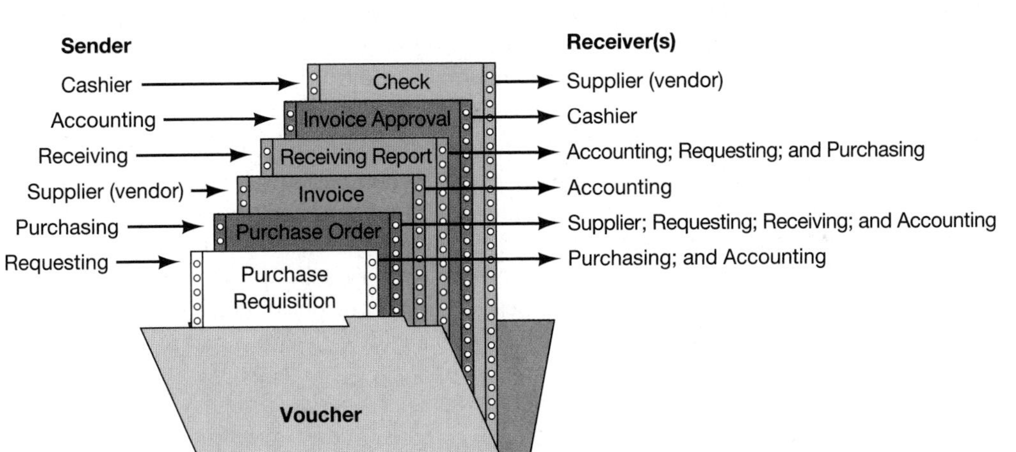

Exhibit 8.1

Document Flow in a Voucher System

Point: **MCI,** formerly WorldCom, paid a whopping $500 million in SEC fines for accounting fraud. Among the charges were that it inflated earnings by as much as $10 billion.

disbursements and to ensure that a transaction is properly recorded. This specific example begins with a *purchase requisition* and concludes with a *check* drawn against cash. Appendix 8A describes each document entering and leaving a voucher system. It also describes the internal control objective served by each document.

A voucher system should be applied not only to purchases of inventory but to all expenditures. To illustrate, when a company receives a monthly telephone bill, it should review and verify the charges, prepare a voucher (file), and insert the bill. This transaction is then recorded with a journal entry. If the amount is currently due, a check is issued. If not, the voucher is filed for payment on its due date. If no voucher is prepared, verifying the invoice and its amount after several days or weeks can be difficult. Also, without records, a dishonest employee could collude with a dishonest supplier to get more than one payment for an obligation, payment for excessive amounts, or payment for goods and services not received. An effective voucher system helps prevent such frauds.

Decision Insight

Hoodwinked Fictitious sales receipts and altered inventory tags deceived auditors, investors, and creditors of **Centennial Technologies.** Its CEO was eventually indicted on five counts of fraud. Many of these shenanigans could have been avoided with internal controls.

Point: A *voucher* is an internal document (or file).

Quick Check

3. Why must a company hold liquid assets?
4. Why does a company hold cash equivalent assets in addition to cash?
5. Identify at least two assets that are classified as cash equivalents.
6. Good internal control procedures for cash include which of the following? (*a*) All cash disbursements, other than those for very small amounts, are made by check; (*b*) One employee should count cash received from sales and promptly deposit cash receipts; or (*c*) Cash receipts by mail should be opened by one employee who is then responsible for recording and depositing receipts.
7. Should all companies require a voucher system? At what point in a company's growth would you recommend a voucher system?

Answers—p. 333

P2 Explain and record petty cash fund transactions.

Petty Cash System of Control A basic principle for controlling cash disbursements is that all payments must be made by check. An exception to this rule is made for *petty cash disbursements,* which are the small payments required for items such as postage, courier fees, minor repairs, and low-cost supplies. To avoid the time and cost of writing checks for small amounts, a company sets up a petty cash fund to make small payments. (**Petty cash** activities are part of an *imprest system,* which designates advance money to establish the fund, to withdraw from the fund, and to reimburse the fund.)

Operating a petty cash fund. Establishing a petty cash fund requires estimating the total amount of small payments likely to be made during a short period such as a week or month. A check is then drawn by the company cashier for an amount slightly in excess of this estimate. This check is recorded with a debit to the Petty Cash account (an asset) and a credit to Cash. The check is cashed, and the currency is given to an employee designated as the *petty cashier* or *petty cash custodian.* The petty cashier is responsible for keeping this cash safe, making payments from the fund, and keeping records of it in a secure place referred to as the *petty cashbox.*

For example, when each cash disbursement is made, the person receiving payment should sign a prenumbered *petty cash receipt,* also called *petty cash ticket*—see Exhibit 8.2. The petty cash receipt is then placed in the petty cashbox with the remaining money. Under this system, the sum of all receipts plus the remaining cash equals the total fund amount. A $100 petty cash fund, for instance, contains any combination of cash and petty cash receipts that totals

Point: A petty cash fund is used only for business expenses.

Petty Cash Receipt Z-Mart			No. 9
For	Freight charges	Date	11/5/05
Charge to	Merchandise Inventory	Amount	$6.75
Approved by	Jim Gibbs	Received by	Dick Fitch

Exhibit 8.2

Petty Cash Receipt

$100 (examples are $80 cash plus $20 in receipts, or $10 cash plus $90 in receipts). Each disbursement reduces cash and increases the amount of receipts in the petty cashbox.

The petty cash fund should be reimbursed when it is nearing zero and at the end of an accounting period when financial statements are prepared. For this purpose, the petty cashier sorts the paid receipts by the type of expense or account and then totals the receipts. The petty cashier presents all paid receipts to the company cashier, who stamps all receipts *paid* so they cannot be reused, files them for recordkeeping, and gives the petty cashier a check for their sum. When this check is cashed and the money placed in the cashbox, the total money in the cashbox is restored to its original amount. The fund is now ready for a new cycle of petty cash payments.

Point: Petty cash receipts with either no signature or a forged signature usually indicate misuse of petty cash. Companies respond with surprise petty cash counts for verification.

Illustrating a petty cash fund. To illustrate, assume Z-Mart establishes a petty cash fund on November 1 and designates one of its office employees as the petty cashier. A $75 check is drawn, cashed, and the proceeds given to the petty cashier. The entry to record the setup of this petty cash fund is

Nov. 1	Petty Cash	75	
	Cash		75
	To establish a petty cash fund.		

Assets = Liabilities + Equity
+75
−75

After the petty cash fund is established, the *Petty Cash account is not debited or credited again unless the amount of the fund is changed.* (A fund probably should be increased if it requires reimbursement too frequently. On the other hand, if the fund is too large, some of its money should be redeposited in the Cash account.)

Next, assume that Z-Mart's petty cashier makes several November payments from petty cash. Each person who received payment is required to sign a receipt. On November 27, after making a $26.50 cash payment for tile cleaning, only $3.70 cash remains in the fund. The petty cashier then summarizes and totals the petty cash receipts as shown in Exhibit 8.3.

Point: Reducing or eliminating a petty cash fund would require a credit to Petty Cash.

Point: Although *individual* petty cash disbursements are not evidenced by a check, the initial petty cash fund is evidenced by a check, and later petty cash expenditures are evidenced by a check to replenish them *in total.*

Z-MART Petty Cash Payments Report			
Miscellaneous Expenses			
Nov. 2	Washing windows	$20.00	
Nov. 27	Tile cleaning	26.50	$ 46.50
Merchandise Inventory (transportation-in)			
Nov. 5	Transport of merchandise purchased	6.75	
Nov. 20	Transport of merchandise purchased	8.30	15.05
Delivery Expense			
Nov. 18	Customer's package delivered		5.00
Office Supplies Expense			
Nov. 15	Purchase of office supplies immediately used		4.75
Total			**$71.30**

Exhibit 8.3

Petty Cash Payments Report

Point: This report can also include receipt number and names of those who approved and received cash payment (see Demo Problem 2).

The petty cash payments report and all receipts are given to the company cashier in exchange for a $71.30 check to reimburse the fund. The petty cashier cashes the check and puts the $71.30 cash in the petty cashbox. The company records this reimbursement as follows:

Assets	=	Liabilities	+	Equity
−71.30				−46.50
				−15.05
				− 5.00
				− 4.75

Nov. 27	Miscellaneous Expenses	46.50	
	Merchandise Inventory	15.05	
	Delivery Expense	5.00	
	Office Supplies Expense	4.75	
	Cash		71.30
	To reimburse petty cash.		

Point: To avoid errors in recording petty cash reimbursement, follow these steps: (1) prepare payments report, (2) compute cash needed by subtracting cash remaining from total fund amount, (3) record entry, and (4) check "Dr. = Cr." in entry—any difference is Cash Over and Short.

A petty cash fund is usually reimbursed at the end of an accounting period so that expenses are recorded in the proper period, even if the fund is not low on money. If the fund is not reimbursed at the end of a period, the financial statements would show both an overstated cash asset and understated expenses (or assets) that were paid out of petty cash. Some companies do not reimburse the petty cash fund at the end of each period under the principle that this amount is immaterial to users of financial statements.

Increasing or decreasing a petty cash fund. A decision to increase or decrease a petty cash fund is often made when reimbursing it. To illustrate, assume Z-Mart decides to *increase* its petty cash fund from $75 to $100 on November 27 when it reimburses the fund. The entries required are to (1) reimburse the fund as usual (see the preceding November 27 entry, and (2) increase the fund amount as follows:

Nov. 27	Petty Cash	25	
	Cash		25
	To increase the petty cash fund amount.		

Decision Ethics

Internal Auditor You make a surprise count of a $300 petty cash fund. You arrive at the petty cashier when she is on the telephone. She politely asks that you return after lunch so that she can finish her business on the telephone. You agree and return after lunch. In the petty cashbox, you find 14 new $20 bills with consecutive serial numbers plus receipts totaling $20. What is your evaluation?

Answer—p. 333

Alternatively, if Z-Mart *decreases* the petty cash fund from $75 to $55 on November 27, the entry is to (1) credit Petty Cash for $20 (decreasing the fund from $75 to $55) and (2) debit Cash for $20 (reflecting the $20 transfer from Petty Cash to Cash).

Cash over and short. Sometimes a petty cashier fails to get a receipt for payment or overpays for the amount due. When this occurs and the fund is later reimbursed, the petty cash payments report plus the cash remaining will not total to the fund balance. This mistake causes the fund to be *short*. This shortage is recorded as an expense in the reimbursing entry with a debit to the Cash Over and Short account. (An overage in the petty cash fund is recorded with a credit to Cash Over and Short in the reimbursing entry.) To illustrate, prepare the entry to reimburse a $200 petty cash fund when its payments report shows $178 in miscellaneous expenses and $15 cash remains.

Event	Petty Cash	Cash	Expenses
Set up fund	Dr.	Cr.	—
Reimburse fund	—	Cr.	Dr.
Increase fund	Dr.	Cr.	—
Decrease fund	Cr.	Dr.	—

Miscellaneous Expenses	178	
Cash Over and Short	7	
Cash		185
To reimburse petty cash.		

Quick Check

8. Why are some cash payments made from a petty cash fund, and not by check?

9. Why should a petty cash fund be reimbursed at the end of an accounting period?

10. Identify at least two results of reimbursing a petty cash fund.

Answers—p. 333

Banking Activities as Controls

Banks (and other financial institutions) provide many services, including helping companies control cash. Banks safeguard cash, provide detailed and independent records of cash transactions, and are a source of cash financing. This section describes these services and the documents provided by banking activities that increase managers' control over cash.

Basic Bank Services

C3 Identify control features of banking activities.

This section explains basic bank services—such as the bank account, the bank deposit, and checking—that contribute to the control of cash.

Bank Account, Deposit, and Check A *bank account* is a record set up by a bank for a customer. It permits a customer to deposit money for safekeeping and helps control withdrawals. To limit access to a bank account, all persons authorized to write checks on the account must sign a **signature card,** which bank employees use to verify signatures on checks. Many companies have more than one bank account to serve different needs and to handle special transactions such as payroll.

Each bank deposit is supported by a **deposit ticket,** which lists items such as currency, coins, and checks deposited along with their corresponding dollar amounts. The bank gives the customer a copy of the deposit ticket or a deposit receipt as proof of the deposit. Exhibit 8.4 shows one type of deposit ticket.

Exhibit 8.4

Deposit Ticket

Front

Deposit Ticket

VideoBuster Company
901 Main Street
Hillcrest, NY 11749

Date October 2 20 05
Memo Deposit checks

99-DT/101

CASH	CURRENCY	36	50
	COIN		
LIST CHECKS SINGLY			
TOTAL FROM OTHER SIDE		203	50
TOTAL		240	00
NET DEPOSIT		240	00

USE OTHER SIDE FOR ADDITIONAL LISTINGS
BE SURE EACH ITEM IS PROPERLY ENDORSED

FN First National
Hillcrest, New York 11750

I:012410497 I: 457923 • 02 75

CHECKS AND OTHER ITEMS ARE RECEIVED FOR DEPOSIT SUBJECT TO THE PROVISIONS OF THE UNIFORM COMMERCIAL CODE OR ANY APPLICABLE COLLECTION AGREEMENT

Back

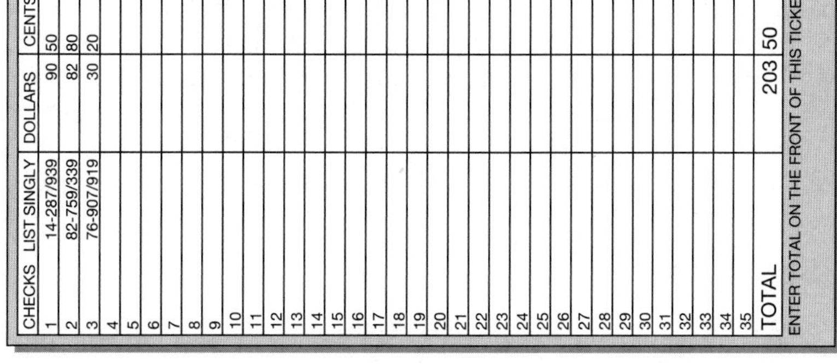

CHECKS LIST SINGLY		DOLLARS	CENTS
1	14-287/939	90	50
2	82-759/339	82	80
3	76-907/919	30	20
4			
5			
6			
7			
8			
9			
10			
11			
12			
13			
14			
15			
16			
17			
18			
19			
20			
21			
22			
23			
24			
25			
26			
27			
28			
29			
30			
31			
32			
33			
34			
35			
TOTAL		203	50

ENTER TOTAL ON THE FRONT OF THIS TICKET

To withdraw money from an account, the depositor can use a **check,** which is a document signed by the depositor instructing the bank to pay a specified amount of money to a designated recipient. A check involves three parties: a *maker* who signs the check, a *payee* who is the recipient, and a *bank* (or *payer*) on which the check is drawn. The bank provides a depositor the checks

Decision Insight

Web-bank Many companies balance checkbooks and pay bills via the Web. Customers value the convenience and low cost of banking services anytime, anywhere. Services include the ability to stop payment on a check, move money between accounts, get up-to-date balances, and identify cleared checks and deposits.

that are serially numbered and imprinted with the name and address of both the depositor and bank. Both checks and deposit tickets are imprinted with identification codes in magnetic ink for computer processing. Exhibit 8.5 shows one type of check. It is accompanied with an optional *remittance advice* explaining the payment. When a remittance advice is unavailable, the *memo* line is often used for a brief explanation.

Exhibit 8.5

Check with Remittance Advice

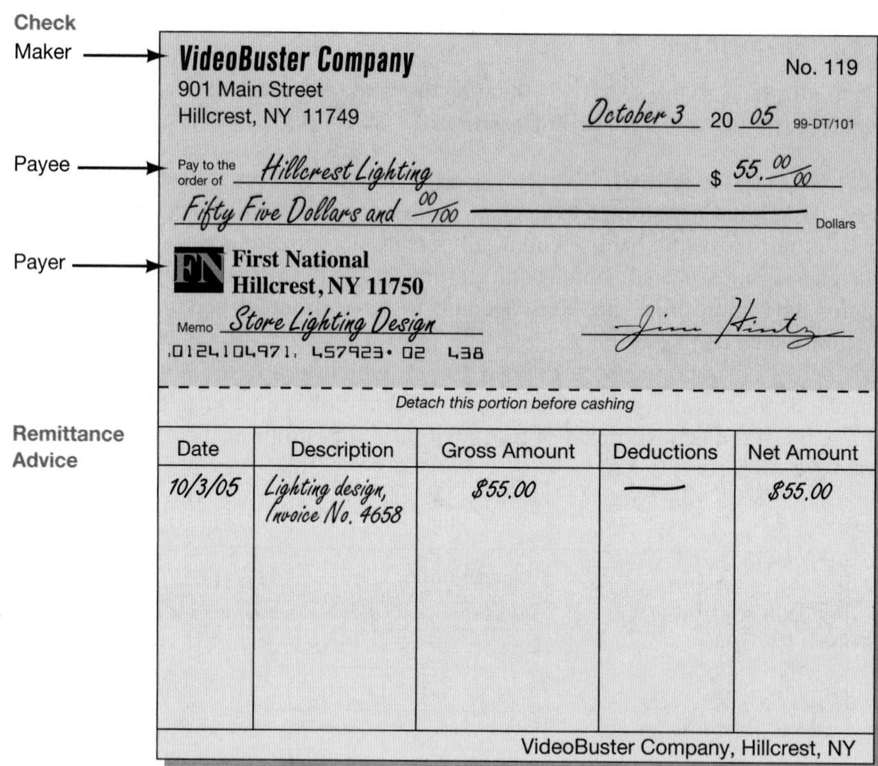

Check Maker → VideoBuster Company
901 Main Street
Hillcrest, NY 11749

No. 119

October 3 20 05 99-DT/101

Payee → Pay to the order of Hillcrest Lighting $ 55.00/00

Fifty Five Dollars and 00/100 Dollars

Payer → FN First National
Hillcrest, NY 11750

Memo Store Lighting Design

Jim Hintz

:012410497 1: 457923• 02 438

Detach this portion before cashing

Remittance Advice

Date	Description	Gross Amount	Deductions	Net Amount
10/3/05	Lighting design, Invoice No. 4658	$55.00	—	$55.00

VideoBuster Company, Hillcrest, NY

Electronic Funds Transfer **Electronic funds transfer (EFT)** is the electronic communication transfer of cash from one party to another. No paper documents are necessary. Banks simply transfer cash from one account to another with a journal entry. Companies are increasingly using EFT because of its convenience and low cost. For instance, it can cost up to 50 cents to process a check through the banking system, whereas EFT cost is near zero. We now commonly see items such as payroll, rent, utilities, insurance, and interest payments being handled by EFT. The bank statement lists cash withdrawals by EFT with the checks and other deductions. Cash receipts by EFT are listed with deposits and other additions. A bank statement is sometimes a depositor's only notice of an EFT.

Bank Statement

Point: Good internal control is to deposit all cash receipts daily and make all payments for goods and services by check. This controls access to cash and creates an independent record of all cash activities.

Usually once a month, the bank sends each depositor a **bank statement** showing the activity in the account. Different banks use different formats for their bank statements, but all of them include the following items of information:

1. Beginning-of-period balance of the depositor's account.
2. Checks and other debits decreasing the account during the period.
3. Deposits and other credits increasing the account during the period.
4. End-of-period balance of the depositor's account.

This information reflects the bank's records. Exhibit 8.6 shows one type of bank statement. Identify each of these four items in that statement. Part Ⓐ of Exhibit 8.6 summarizes changes

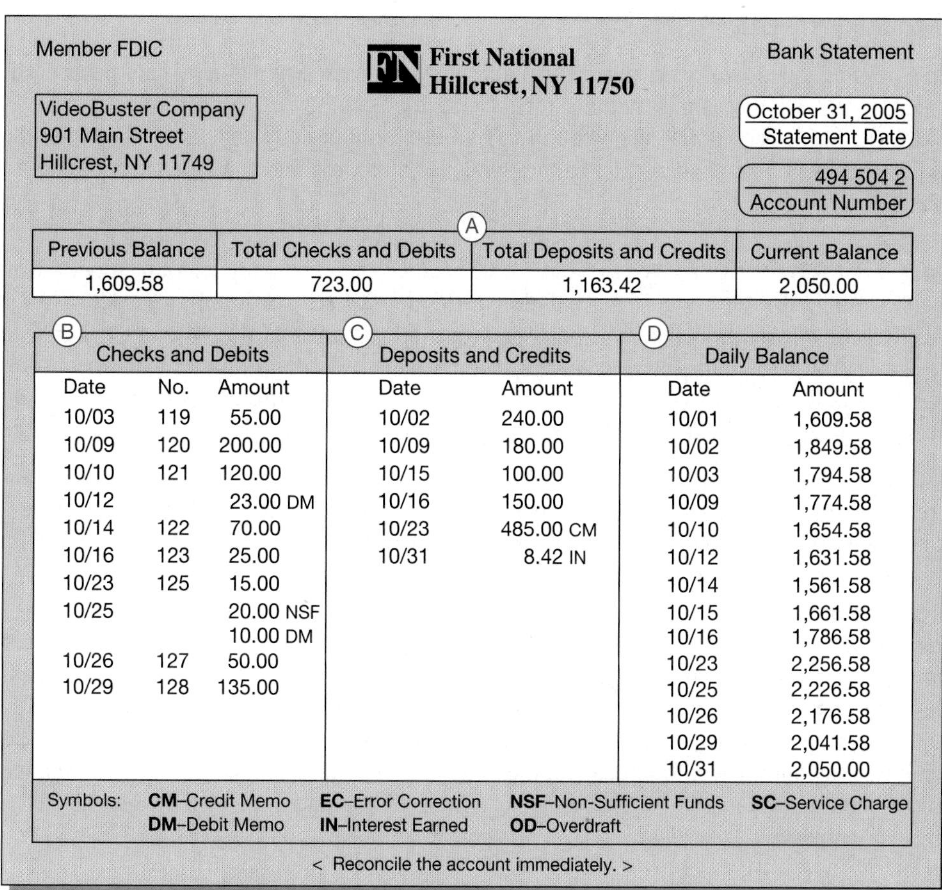

Member FDIC

First National
Hillcrest, NY 11750

Bank Statement

VideoBuster Company
901 Main Street
Hillcrest, NY 11749

October 31, 2005
Statement Date

494 504 2
Account Number

(A)

Previous Balance	Total Checks and Debits	Total Deposits and Credits	Current Balance
1,609.58	723.00	1,163.42	2,050.00

(B) Checks and Debits

Date	No.	Amount
10/03	119	55.00
10/09	120	200.00
10/10	121	120.00
10/12		23.00 DM
10/14	122	70.00
10/16	123	25.00
10/23	125	15.00
10/25		20.00 NSF
		10.00 DM
10/26	127	50.00
10/29	128	135.00

(C) Deposits and Credits

Date	Amount
10/02	240.00
10/09	180.00
10/15	100.00
10/16	150.00
10/23	485.00 CM
10/31	8.42 IN

(D) Daily Balance

Date	Amount
10/01	1,609.58
10/02	1,849.58
10/03	1,794.58
10/09	1,774.58
10/10	1,654.58
10/12	1,631.58
10/14	1,561.58
10/15	1,661.58
10/16	1,786.58
10/23	2,256.58
10/25	2,226.58
10/26	2,176.58
10/29	2,041.58
10/31	2,050.00

Symbols: **CM**–Credit Memo **DM**–Debit Memo **EC**–Error Correction **IN**–Interest Earned **NSF**–Non-Sufficient Funds **OD**–Overdraft **SC**–Service Charge

< Reconcile the account immediately. >

Exhibit 8.6

Bank Statement

in the account. Part (B) lists paid checks along with other debits. Part (C) lists deposits and credits to the account, and part (D) shows the daily account balances.

In reading a bank statement note that a depositor's account is a liability on the bank's records. This is so because the money belongs to the depositor, not the bank. When a depositor increases the account balance, the bank records it with a *credit* to that liability account. This means that debit memos from the bank produce *credits* on the depositor's books, and credit memos from the bank produce *debits* on the depositor's books.

Enclosed with a bank statement is a list of the depositor's canceled checks (or the actual canceled checks) along with any debit or credit memoranda affecting the account. **Canceled checks** are checks the bank has paid and deducted from the customer's account during the period. Other deductions that can appear on a bank statement include (1) service charges and fees assessed by the bank, (2) checks deposited that are uncollectible, (3) corrections of previous errors, (4) withdrawals through automated teller machines (ATMs), and (5) periodic payments arranged in advance by a depositor. (Most company checking accounts do not allow ATM withdrawals because of the company's desire to make all disbursements by check.) Except for service charges, the bank notifies the depositor of each deduction with a debit memorandum when the bank reduces the balance. A copy of each debit memorandum is usually sent with the statement.

Global: If cash is in more than one currency, a company usually translates these amounts into U.S. dollars using the exchange rate as of the balance sheet date.

Transactions that increase the depositor's account include amounts the bank collects on behalf of the depositor and the corrections of previous errors. Credit memoranda notify the depositor of all increases when they are recorded. A copy of each credit memorandum is often sent with the bank statement. Banks that pay interest on checking accounts often compute the amount of interest earned on the average cash balance and would credit it to the depositor's account each period. In Exhibit 8.6, the bank credits $8.42 of interest to the account.

Global: A company must disclose any restrictions on cash accounts located outside the United States.

Bank Reconciliation

P3 Prepare a bank reconciliation.

When a company deposits all cash receipts and makes all cash payments (except petty cash) by check, it can use the bank statement for proving the accuracy of its cash records. This is done using a **bank reconciliation,** which is a report explaining any differences between the checking account balance according to the depositor's records and the balance reported on the bank statement.

Topic Tackler 8-2

Purpose of Bank Reconciliation The balance of a checking account reported on the bank statement rarely equals the balance in the depositor's accounting records. This is usually due to information that one party has that the other does not. We must therefore prove the accuracy of both the depositor's records and those of the bank. This means we must *reconcile* the two balances and explain or account for any differences in them. Among the factors causing the bank statement balance to differ from the depositor's book balance are these:

- **Outstanding checks. Outstanding checks** are checks written (or drawn) by the depositor, deducted on the depositor's records, and sent to the payees but not yet received by the bank for payment at the bank statement date.
- **Deposits in transit** (also called **outstanding deposits**). **Deposits in transit** are deposits made and recorded by the depositor but not yet recorded on the bank statement. For example, companies can make deposits (in the night depository) at the end of a business day after the bank is closed. If such a deposit occurred on a bank statement date, it would not appear on this period's statement. The bank would record such a deposit on the next business day, and it would appear on the next period's bank statement. Deposits mailed to the bank near the end of a period also can be in transit and unrecorded when the statement is prepared.
- **Deductions for uncollectible items and for services.** A company sometimes deposits another party's check that is uncollectible (usually meaning the balance in such an account is not large enough to cover the check). This check is called a *non-sufficient funds (NSF)* check. The bank would have initially credited the depositor's account for the amount of the check. When the bank learns the check is uncollectible, it debits (reduces) the depositor's account for the amount of that check. The bank may also charge the depositor a fee for processing an uncollectible check and notify the depositor of the deduction by sending a debit memorandum. The depositor should record each deduction when a debit memorandum is received, but an entry is sometimes not made until the bank reconciliation is prepared. Other possible bank charges to a depositor's account that are first reported on a bank statement include printing new checks and service fees.
- **Additions for collections and for interest.** Banks sometimes act as collection agents for their depositors by collecting notes and other items. Banks can also receive electronic funds transfers to the depositor's account. When a bank collects an item, it is added to the depositor's account, less any service fee. The bank also sends a credit memorandum to notify the depositor of the transaction. When the memorandum is received, the depositor should record it; yet it sometimes remains unrecorded until the bank reconciliation is prepared. The bank statement also includes a credit for any interest earned.
- **Errors.** Both banks and depositors can make errors. Bank errors might not be discovered until the depositor prepares the bank reconciliation. Also, depositor errors are sometimes discovered when the bank balance is reconciled. Error testing includes: (a) comparing deposits on the bank statement with deposits in the accounting records and (b) comparing canceled checks on the bank statement with checks recorded in the accounting records.

Point: Small businesses with few employees often allow recordkeepers to both write checks and keep the general ledger. If this is done, it is essential that the owner do the bank reconciliation.

Point: The person preparing the bank reconciliation should not be responsible for processing cash receipts, managing checks, or maintaining cash records.

Illustration of a Bank Reconciliation We follow nine steps in preparing the bank reconciliation. It is helpful to refer to the bank reconciliation in Exhibit 8.7 when studying steps 1 through 9.

1 Identify the bank statement balance of the cash account (*balance per bank*). VideoBuster's bank balance is $2,050.

2 Identify and list any unrecorded deposits and any bank errors understating the bank balance. Add them to the bank balance. VideoBuster's $145 deposit placed in the bank's night depository on October 31 is not recorded on its bank statement.

3 Identify and list any outstanding checks and any bank errors overstating the bank balance. Deduct them from the bank balance. VideoBuster's comparison of canceled checks with its books shows two checks outstanding: No. 124 for $150 and No. 126 for $200.

4 Compute the *adjusted bank balance,* also called the *corrected* or *reconciled balance.*

5 Identify the company's book balance of the cash account (*balance per book*). VideoBuster's book balance is $1,404.58.

6 Identify and list any unrecorded credit memoranda from the bank, any interest earned, and errors understating the book balance. Add them to the book balance. Enclosed with VideoBuster's bank statement is a credit memorandum showing the bank collected a note receivable for the company on October 23. The note's proceeds of $500 (minus a $15 collection fee) are credited to the company's account. VideoBuster's bank statement also shows a credit of $8.42 for interest earned on the average cash balance. There was no prior notification of this item, and it is not yet recorded.

7 Identify and list any unrecorded debit memoranda from the bank, any service charges, and errors overstating the book balance. Deduct them from the book balance. Debits on VideoBuster's bank statement that are not yet recorded include (a) a $23 charge for check printing and (b) an NSF check for $20 plus a related $10 processing fee. (The NSF check is dated October 16 and was included in the book balance.)

8 Compute the *adjusted book balance,* also called *corrected* or *reconciled balance.*

9 Verify that the two adjusted balances from steps 4 and 8 are equal. If so, they are reconciled. If not, check for accuracy and missing data to achieve reconciliation.

Point: Outstanding checks are identified by comparing canceled checks on the bank statement with checks recorded. This includes identifying any outstanding checks listed on the *previous* period's bank reconciliation that are not included in the canceled checks on this period's bank statement.

Adjusting Entries from a Bank Reconciliation A bank reconciliation often identifies unrecorded items that need recording by the company. In VideoBuster's reconciliation, the adjusted balance of $1,845 is the correct balance as of October 31. But the company's accounting records show a $1,404.58 balance. We must prepare journal entries to adjust the book balance to the correct balance. *It is important to remember that only the items reconciling the book balance require adjustment.* A review of Exhibit 8.7 indicates that four entries are required for VideoBuster.

Point: The adjusting entries could be combined into one compound entry.

Exhibit 8.7

Bank Reconciliation

VIDEOBUSTER
Bank Reconciliation
October 31, 2005

①	Bank statement balance		$ 2,050.00	⑤	Book balance		$ 1,404.58
②	Add			⑥	Add		
	Deposit of Oct. 31 in transit		145.00		Collect $500 note less $15 fee	$485.00	
			2,195.00		Interest earned	8.42	493.42
③	Deduct						1,898.00
	Outstanding checks			⑦	Deduct		
	No. 124	$150.00			Check printing charge	23.00	
	No. 126	200.00	350.00		NSF check plus service fee	30.00	53.00
④	**Adjusted bank balance**		**$1,845.00**	⑧	**Adjusted book balance**		**$1,845.00**

⑨ Balances are equal (reconciled)

Collection of note. The first entry is to record the proceeds of its note receivable collected by the bank less the expense of having the bank perform that service.

Assets = Liabilities + Equity
+485 −15
−500

Oct. 31	Cash	485	
	Collection Expense	15	
	Notes Receivable		500
	To record the collection fee and proceeds for a note collected by the bank.		

Interest earned. The second entry records interest credited to its account by the bank.

Assets = Liabilities + Equity
+8.42 +8.42

Oct. 31	Cash	8.42	
	Interest Revenue		8.42
	To record interest earned on the cash balance in the checking account.		

Check printing. The third entry records expenses for the check printing charge.

Assets = Liabilities + Equity
−23 −23

Oct. 31	Miscellaneous Expenses	23	
	Cash		23
	Check printing charge.		

NSF check. The fourth entry records the NSF check that is returned as uncollectible. The $20 check was originally received from F. Heflin in payment of his account and then deposited. The bank charged $10 for handling the NSF check and deducted $30 total from VideoBuster's account. This means the entry must reverse the effects of the original entry made when the check was received and must record (add) the $10 bank fee.

Point: The company will try to collect the entire NSF amount of $30.

Assets = Liabilities + Equity
+30
−30

Oct. 31	Accounts Receivable—F. Heflin	30	
	Cash		30
	To charge Heflin's account for $20 NSF check and $10 bank fee.		

After these four entries are recorded, the book balance of cash is adjusted to the correct amount of $1,845 (computed as $1,404.58 + $485 + $8.42 − $23 − $30).

Point: The Demo Problem 1 shows an adjusting entry for an error correction.

Quick Check

11. What is a bank statement?
12. What is the meaning of the phrase *to reconcile a bank balance?*
13. Why do we reconcile the bank statement balance of cash and the depositor's book balance of cash?
14. List at least two items affecting the bank balance side of a bank reconciliation and indicate whether the items are added or subtracted.
15. List at least three items affecting the book balance side of a bank reconciliation and indicate whether the items are added or subtracted.

Answers—p. 333

Days' Sales Uncollected

Decision Analysis

A1 Compute the days' sales uncollected ratio and use it to assess liquidity.

Many companies attract customers by selling to them on credit. This means that cash receipts from customers are delayed until accounts receivable are collected. Users of accounting information often want to know how quickly a company can convert its accounts receivable into cash. This is important for evaluating a company's liquidity. One measure of the receivables' nearness to cash is the **days' sales uncollected,** also called *days' sales in receivables*. This measure is computed by dividing the current balance of receivables by net credit sales over the year just completed and then multiplying by 365 (number of days in a year). Since net credit sales usually are not reported to external users, the net sales (or revenues) figure is commonly used in the computation as in Exhibit 8.8.

Exhibit 8.8

Days' Sales Uncollected

$$\textbf{Days' sales uncollected} = \frac{\textbf{Accounts receivable}}{\textbf{Net sales}} \times 365$$

We use days' sales uncollected to estimate how much time is likely to pass before the current amount of accounts receivable is received in cash. For evaluation purposes, we need to compare this estimate to that for other companies in the same industry. We also make comparisons between current and prior periods.

To illustrate, we select data from the annual reports of two toy manufacturers, **Hasbro** and **Mattel**. Their days' sales uncollected figures are shown in Exhibit 8.9.

Exhibit 8.9

Analysis using Days' Sales Uncollected

Company	Figure ($ millions)	2002	2001	2000
Hasbro	Accounts receivable	$555	$572	$686
	Net sales	$2,816	$2,856	$3,787
	Days' sales uncollected	**72 days**	**73 days**	**66 days**
Mattel	Accounts receivable	$491	$666	$840
	Net sales	$4,885	$4,688	$4,565
	Days' sales uncollected	**37 days**	**52 days**	**67 days**

Days' sales uncollected for Hasbro in 2002 is computed as ($555/$2,816) × 365 days = 72 days. This means that it will take about 72 days to collect cash from ending accounts receivable. This number reflects one or more of the following factors: a company's ability to collect receivables, customer financial health, customer payment strategies, and discount terms. To further assess days' sales uncollected for Hasbro, we compare it to two prior years and to those of Mattel. We see that Hasbro's days' sales uncollected has slightly increased from 66 days in 2000 to 72 days in 2002, which is not good for its liquidity. In comparison, Mattel has improved on this factor. Specifically, Mattel's days' sales uncollected has declined from 67 days in 2000 to 37 days in 2002. The less time that money is tied up in receivables often translates into increased profitability.

Decision Maker

Sales Representative The sales staff is told to take action to help reduce days' sales uncollected. What can you, a salesperson, do to reduce days' sales uncollected?

Answer—p. 333

Demonstration Problem 1

Prepare a bank reconciliation for Jamboree Enterprises for the month ended November 30, 2005. The following information is available to reconcile Jamboree Enterprises' book balance of cash with its bank statement balance as of November 30, 2005:

a. After all posting is complete on November 30, the company's book balance of Cash has a $16,380 debit balance, but its bank statement shows a $38,520 balance.

b. Checks No. 2024 for $4,810 and No. 2036 for $5,000 are outstanding.

c. In comparing the canceled checks on the bank statement with the entries in the accounting records, it is found that Check No. 2025 in payment of rent is correctly drawn for $1,000 but is erroneously entered in the accounting records as $880.

d. The November 30 deposit of $17,150 was placed in the night depository after banking hours on that date, and this amount does not appear on the bank statement.

e. In reviewing the bank statement, a check written by Jumbo Enterprises in the amount of $160 was erroneously drawn against Jamboree's account.

f. A credit memorandum enclosed with the bank statement indicates that the bank collected a $30,000 note and $900 of related interest on Jamboree's behalf. This transaction was not recorded by Jamboree prior to receiving the statement.

g. A debit memorandum for $1,100 lists a $1,100 NSF check received from a customer, Marilyn Welch. Jamboree had not recorded the return of this check before receiving the statement.

h. Bank service charges for November total $40. These charges were not recorded by Jamboree before receiving the statement.

Planning the Solution

- Set up a bank reconciliation with a bank side and a book side (as in Exhibit 8.7). Leave room to both add and deduct items. Each column will result in a reconciled, equal balance.
- Examine each item *a* through *h* to determine whether it affects the book or the bank balance and whether it should be added or deducted from the bank or book balance.
- After all items are analyzed, complete the reconciliation and arrive at a reconciled balance between the bank side and the book side.
- For each reconciling item on the book side, prepare an adjusting entry. Additions to the book side require an adjusting entry that debits Cash. Deductions on the book side require an adjusting entry that credits Cash.

Solution to Demonstration Problem 1

JAMBOREE ENTERPRISES
Bank Reconciliation
November 30, 2005

Bank statement balance		$ 38,520	Book balance		$ 16,380
Add			Add		
Deposit of Nov. 30	$17,150		Collection of note	$30,000	
Bank error	160	17,310	Interest earned	900	30,900
		55,830			47,280
Deduct			Deduct		
Outstanding checks		9,810	NSF check	1,100	
			Recording error	120	
			Service charge	40	1,260
Adjusted bank balance		**$46,020**	**Adjusted book balance**		**$46,020**

Required Adjusting Entries for Jamboree

Nov. 30	Cash	30,900	
	Notes Receivable		30,000
	Interest Earned		900
	To record collection of note with interest.		
Nov. 30	Accounts Receivable—M. Welch	1,100	
	Cash		1,100
	To reinstate account due from an NSF check.		

[continued on next page]

[continued from previous page]

Nov. 30	Rent Expense	120	
	Cash		120
	To correct recording error on check no. 2025.		
Nov. 30	Bank Service Charges	40	
	Cash		40
	To record bank service charges.		

Demonstration Problem 2

Bacardi Company established a $150 petty cash fund with Dean Martin as the petty cashier. When the fund balance reached $19 cash, Martin prepared a petty cash payment report, which follows:

Petty Cash Payments Report

Receipt No.	Account Charged		Approved by	Received by
12	Delivery Expense	$ 29	Martin	A. Smirnoff
13	Merchandise Inventory	18	Martin	J. Daniels
15	(Omitted)	32	Martin	C. Carlsberg
16	Miscellaneous Expense	41	(Omitted)	J. Walker
	Total	$120		

Required

1. Identify four internal control weaknesses from the payment report.

2. Prepare general journal entries to record:

a. Establishment of the petty cash fund.

b. Reimbursement of the fund. (Assume for this part only that petty cash receipt no. 15 was issued for miscellaneous expenses.)

3. What is the Petty Cash account balance immediately before reimbursement? Immediately after reimbursement?

Solution to Demonstration Problem 2

1. Four internal control weaknesses are

a. Petty cash ticket no. 14 is missing. Its omission raises questions about the petty cashier's management of the fund.

b. The $19 cash balance means that $131 has been withdrawn ($150 − $19 = $131). However, the total amount of the petty cash receipts is only $120 ($29 + $18 + $32 + $41). The fund is $11 short of cash ($131 − $120 = $11). Was petty cash receipt no. 14 issued for $11? Management should investigate.

c. The petty cashier (Martin) did not sign petty cash receipt no. 16. This omission could have been an oversight on his part or he might not have authorized the payment. Management should investigate.

d. Petty cash receipt no. 15 does not indicate which account to charge. This omission could have been an oversight on the petty cashier's part. Management could check with C. Carlsberg and the petty cashier (Martin) about the transaction. Without further information, debit Miscellaneous Expense.

2. Petty cash general journal entries:

a. Entry to establish the petty cash fund:

Petty Cash	150	
Cash		150

b. Entry to reimburse the fund:

Delivery Expense	29	
Merchandise Inventory	18	
Miscellaneous Expense ($41 + $32)	73	
Cash Over and Short	11	
Cash		131

3. The Petty Cash account balance *always* equals its fund balance, in this case $150. This account balance does not change unless the fund is increased or decreased.

APPENDIX

Documents in a Voucher System

P4 Describe the voucher system to control cash disbursements.

This appendix describes the important business documents of a voucher system of control.

Purchase Requisition Department managers are usually not allowed to place orders directly with suppliers for control purposes. Instead, a department manager must inform the purchasing department of its needs by preparing and signing a **purchase requisition,** which lists the merchandise needed and requests that it be purchased—see Exhibit 8A.1. Two copies of the purchase requisition are sent to the purchasing department, which then sends one copy to the accounting department. When the accounting department receives a purchase requisition, it creates and maintains a voucher for this transaction. The requesting department keeps the third copy.

Exhibit 8A.1

Purchase Requisition

Purchase Requisition
Z-Mart
No. 917

From Sporting Goods Department
To Purchasing Department
Date October 28, 2005
Preferred Vendor Trex

Request purchase of the following item(s):

Model No.	Description	Quantity
CH 015	Challenger X7	1
SD 099	SpeedDemon	1

Reason for Request Replenish inventory
Approval for Request J.Z.

For Purchasing Department use only: Order Date 10/30/05 P.O. No. P98

Point: It is important to note that a voucher system is designed to uniquely meet the needs of a specific business. Thus, you should read this appendix as one example of a common voucher system design, but *not* the only design.

Purchase Order A **purchase order** is a document the purchasing department uses to place an order with a **vendor** (seller or supplier). A purchase order authorizes a vendor to ship ordered merchandise at the stated price and terms—see Exhibit 8A.2. When the purchasing department receives a purchase requisition, it prepares at least five copies of a purchase order. The copies are distributed as follows: *copy 1* to the vendor as a purchase request and as authority to ship merchandise; *copy 2,* along with a copy of the purchase requisition, to the accounting department, where it is entered in the voucher and used in approving payment of the invoice; *copy 3* to the requesting department to inform its manager that action is being taken; *copy 4* to the receiving department without order quantity so it can compare with goods received and provide independent count of goods received; and *copy 5* retained on file by the purchasing department.

Invoice An **invoice** is an itemized statement of goods prepared by the vendor listing the customer's name, items sold, sales prices, and terms of sale. An invoice is also a bill sent to the buyer from the supplier. From the vendor's point of view, it is a *sales invoice*. The buyer, or **vendee,** treats it as a *purchase invoice*. When receiving a purchase order, the vendor ships the ordered merchandise to the buyer and includes or mails a copy of the invoice covering the shipment to the buyer. The invoice is sent to the buyer's accounting department where it is placed in the voucher. (Refer back to Exhibit 5.5, which shows Z-Mart's purchase invoice.)

Purchase Order

Z-Mart
10 Michigan Street
Chicago, Illinois 60521

No. P98

To: Trex
W9797 Cherry Road
Antigo, Wisconsin 54409

Date 10/30/05
FOB Destination
Ship by As soon as possible
Terms 2/15, n/30

Request shipment of the following item(s):

Model No.	Description	Quantity	Price	Amount
CH 015	Challenger X7	1	490	490
SD 099	SpeedDemon	1	710	710

All shipments and invoices must include purchase order number

Ordered by J.W.

Exhibit 8A.2

Purchase Order

Receiving Report Many companies maintain a separate department to receive all merchandise and purchased assets. When each shipment arrives, this receiving department counts the goods and checks them for damage and agreement with the purchase order. It then prepares four or more copies of a **receiving report,** which is used within the company to notify the appropriate persons that ordered goods have been received and to describe the quantities and condition of the goods. One copy is sent to accounting and placed in the voucher. Copies are also sent to the requesting department and the purchasing department to notify them that the goods have arrived. The receiving department retains a copy in its files.

Invoice Approval When a receiving report arrives, the accounting department should have copies of the following documents in the voucher: purchase requisition, purchase order, and invoice. With the information in these documents, the accounting department can record the purchase and approve its payment. In approving an invoice for payment, it checks and compares information across all documents. To facilitate this checking and to ensure that no step is omitted, it often uses an **invoice approval,** also called *check authorization*—see Exhibit 8A.3. An invoice approval is a checklist of steps necessary for approving an invoice for recording and payment. It is a separate document either filed in the voucher or preprinted (or stamped) on the voucher.

Invoice Approval

Document		By	Date
Purchase requisition	917	TZ	10/28/05
Purchase order	P98	JW	10/30/05
Receiving report	R85	SK	11/3/05
Invoice:	4657		11/12/05
Price		JK	11/12/05
Calculations		JK	11/12/05
Terms		JK	11/12/05
Approved for payment		BC	

Exhibit 8A.3

Invoice Approval

As each step in the checklist is approved, the person initials the invoice approval and records the current date. Final approval implies the following steps have occurred:

1. **Requisition check:** Items on invoice are requested per purchase requisition.
2. **Purchase order check:** Items on invoice are ordered per purchase order.
3. **Receiving report check:** Items on invoice are received, per receiving report.
4. **Invoice check: Price:** Invoice prices are as agreed with the vendor.
   Calculations: Invoice has no mathematical errors.
   Terms: Terms are as agreed with the vendor.

Point: Recording a purchase is initiated by an invoice approval, not an invoice. An invoice approval verifies that the amount is consistent with that requested, ordered, and received. This controls and verifies purchases and related liabilities.

Voucher Once an invoice has been checked and approved, the voucher is complete. A complete voucher is a record summarizing a transaction. Once the voucher certifies a transaction, it authorizes recording an obligation. A voucher also contains approval for paying the obligation on an appropriate date. The physical form of a voucher varies across companies. Many are designed so that the invoice and other related source documents are placed inside the voucher, which can be a folder.

Completion of a voucher usually requires a person to enter certain information on both the inside and outside of the voucher. Typical information required on the inside of a voucher is shown in Exhibit 8A.4, and that for the outside is shown in Exhibit 8A.5. This information is taken from the invoice and the supporting documents filed in the voucher. A complete voucher is sent to an authorized individual (often called an *auditor*). This person performs a final review, approves the accounts and amounts for debiting (called the *accounting distribution*), and authorizes recording of the voucher.

Exhibit 8A.4
Inside of a Voucher

Z-Mart
Chicago, Illinois

Voucher No. 4657

Date Oct. 28, 2005
Pay to Trex
City Antigo State Wisconsin

For the following: (attach all invoices and supporting documents)

Date of Invoice	Terms	Invoice Number and Other Details	Terms
Nov. 2, 2005	2/15, n/30	Invoice No. 4657	1,200
		Less discount	24
		Net amount payable	1,176

Payment approved
N.O. Neal
Auditor

After a voucher is approved and recorded (in a journal called a **voucher register**), it is filed by its due date. A check is then sent on the payment date from the cashier, the voucher is marked "paid", and the voucher is sent to the accounting department and recorded (in a journal called the **check register**). The person issuing checks relies on the approved voucher and its signed supporting documents as proof that an obligation has been incurred and must be paid. The purchase requisition and purchase order confirm the purchase was authorized. The receiving report shows that items have been received, and the invoice approval form verifies that the invoice has been checked for errors. There is little chance for error and even less chance for fraud without collusion unless all the documents and signatures are forged.

Exhibit 8A.5
Outside of a Voucher

Voucher No. 4657

Accounting Distribution

Account Debited	Amount
Merch. Inventory	1,200
Store Supplies	
Office Supplies	
Sales Salaries	
Other	
Total Vouch. Pay. Cr.	1,200

Due Date November 12, 2005
Pay to Trex
City Antigo
State Wisconsin

Summary of charges:
Total charges 1,200
Discount 24
Net payment 1,176

Record of payment:
Paid
Check No.

APPENDIX

Control of Purchase Discounts

This appendix explains how a company can better control its cash *disbursements* to take advantage of favorable purchases discounts. Chapter 5 described the entries to record the receipt and payment of an invoice for a merchandise purchase with and without discount terms. Those entries were prepared under what is called the **gross method** of recording purchases, which initially records the invoice at its *gross* amount ignoring any cash discount.

P5 Apply the net method to control purchase discounts.

The **net method** is another means of recording purchases, which initially records the invoice at its *net* amount of any cash discount. The net method gives management an advantage in controlling and monitoring cash payments involving purchase discounts.

To explain, when invoices are recorded at *gross* amounts, the amount of any discounts taken is deducted from the balance of the Merchandise Inventory account when cash payment is made. This means that the amount of any discounts lost is not reported in any account or on the income statement. Lost discounts recorded in this way are unlikely to come to the attention of management. When purchases are recorded at *net* amounts, a **Discounts Lost** expense account is recorded and brought to management's attention. Management can then seek to identify the reason for discounts lost such as oversight, carelessness, or unfavorable terms. (Chapter 5 explains how managers assess whether a discount is favorable or not.)

Perpetual Inventory System To illustrate, assume that a company purchases merchandise on November 2 at a $1,200 invoice price with terms of 2/10, n/30. Its November 2 entries under the gross and net methods are

Gross Method			Net Method		
Merchandise Inventory	1,200		Merchandise Inventory	1,176	
Accounts Payable		1,200	Accounts Payable		1,176

If the invoice is paid on November 12 within the discount period, it records the following

Gross Method			Net Method		
Accounts Payable	1,200		Accounts Payable	1,176	
Merchandise Inventory		24	Cash		1,176
Cash		1,176			

If the invoice is *not* paid within the discount period, it records the following November 12 entry (which is the date corresponding to the end of the discount period)

Gross Method			Net Method		
No entry			**Discounts Lost**	24	
			Accounts Payable		24

Then, when the invoice is later paid on December 2, outside the discount period, it records the following

Gross Method			Net Method		
Accounts Payable	1,200		Accounts Payable	1,200	
Cash		1,200	Cash		1,200

(Note that the discount lost can be recorded when the cash payment is made with a single entry. However, in this case, when financial statements are prepared after a discount is lost and before the cash payment is made, an adjusting entry is required to recognize any unrecorded discount lost in the period when incurred.)

Periodic Inventory System The preceding entries assume a perpetual inventory system. If a company is using a *periodic system*, its November 2 entries under the gross and net methods are

Gross Method—Periodic		
Purchases	1,200	
Accounts Payable		1,200

Net Method—Periodic		
Purchases	1,176	
Accounts Payable		1,176

If the invoice is paid on November 12 within the discount period, it records the following

Gross Method—Periodic		
Accounts Payable	1,200	
Purchases Discounts		24
Cash		1,176

Net Method—Periodic		
Accounts Payable	1,176	
Cash		1,176

If the invoice is *not* paid within the discount period, it records the following November 12 entry

Gross Method—Periodic		
No entry		

Net Method—Periodic		
Discounts Lost	24	
Accounts Payable		24

Then, when the invoice is later paid on December 2, outside the discount period, it records the following

Gross Method—Periodic		
Accounts Payable	1,200	
Cash		1,200

Net Method—Periodic		
Accounts Payable	1,200	
Cash		1,200

Summary

C1 Define internal control and identify its purpose and principles. An internal control system consists of the policies and procedures managers use to protect assets, ensure reliable accounting, promote efficient operations, and urge adherence to company policies. It can prevent avoidable losses and help managers both plan operations and monitor company and human performance. Principles of good internal control include establishing responsibilities, maintaining adequate records, insuring assets and bonding employees, separating recordkeeping from custody of assets, dividing responsibilities for related transactions, applying technological controls, and performing regular independent reviews.

C2 Define cash and cash equivalents and explain how to report them. Cash includes currency, coins, and amounts on (or acceptable for) deposit in checking and savings accounts. Cash equivalents are short-term, highly liquid investment assets readily convertible to a known cash amount and sufficiently close to their maturity date so that market value is not sensitive to interest rate changes. Cash and cash equivalents are liquid assets because they are readily converted into other assets or can be used to pay for goods, services, or liabilities.

C3 Identify control features of banking activities. Banks offer several services that promote the control and safeguarding of cash. A bank account is a record set up by a bank permitting a customer to deposit money for safekeeping and to draw checks on it. A bank deposit is money contributed to the account with a deposit ticket as proof. A check is a document signed by the depositor instructing the bank to pay a specified amount of money to a designated recipient.

A1 Compute the days' sales uncollected ratio and use it to assess liquidity. Many companies attract customers by selling to them on credit. This means that cash receipts from customers are delayed until accounts receivable are collected. Users want to know how quickly a company can convert its accounts receivable into cash. The days' sales uncollected ratio, one measure reflecting company liquidity, is computed by dividing the ending balance of receivables by annual net sales, and then multiplying by 365.

P1 Apply internal control to cash receipts and disbursements. Internal control of cash receipts ensures that all cash received is properly recorded and deposited. Attention focuses on two important types of cash receipts: over-the-counter and by mail. Good internal control for over-the-counter cash receipts includes use of a cash register, customer review, use of receipts, a permanent transaction record, and separation of the custody of cash from its recordkeeping. Good internal control for cash receipts by mail includes at least two people assigned to open mail and a listing of each sender's name, amount, and explanation.

P2 Explain and record petty cash fund transactions. Petty cash disbursements are payments of small amounts for items such as postage, courier fees, minor repairs, and supplies. A company usually sets up one or more petty cash funds. A petty fund cashier is responsible for safekeeping the cash, making payments from this fund, and keeping receipts and records. A Petty Cash account is debited only when the fund is established or increased in amount. When the fund is replenished, petty cash disbursements are recorded with debits to expense (or asset) accounts and a credit to cash.

P3 Prepare a bank reconciliation. A bank reconciliation proves the accuracy of the depositor's and the bank's records. The bank statement balance is adjusted for items such as outstanding checks and unrecorded deposits made on or before the bank statement date but not reflected on the statement. The book balance is adjusted for items such as service charges, bank collections for the depositor, and interest earned on the account.

P4A Describe the voucher system to control cash disbursements. A voucher system is a set of procedures and approvals designed to control cash disbursements and acceptance of obligations. The voucher system of control relies on several important documents, including the voucher and its supporting files. A key factor in this system is that only approved departments and individuals are authorized to incur certain obligations.

P5B Apply the net method to control purchase discounts. The net method aids management in monitoring and controlling purchase discounts. When invoices are recorded at gross amounts, the amount of discounts taken is deducted from the balance of the Inventory account. This means that the amount of any discounts lost is not reported in any account and is unlikely to come to the attention of management. When purchases are recorded at net amounts, a Discounts Lost account is brought to management's attention as an operating expense. Management can then seek to identify the reason for discounts lost, such as oversight, carelessness, or unfavorable terms.

Guidance Answers to **Decision Maker** and **Decision Ethics**

Entrepreneur A forced vacation policy is part of a good system of internal controls. When employees are forced to take vacations, their ability to hide any fraudulent behavior decreases because others must perform the vacationers' duties. A replacement employee potentially can uncover fraudulent behavior or falsified records. A forced vacation policy is especially important for employees in sensitive positions of handling money or in control of easily transferable assets.

Internal Auditor Since you were asked to postpone your count, along with the fact the fund consists of 14 new $20 bills, you have legitimate concerns about whether money is being used for personal use. It is possible the most recent reimbursement of the fund was for $280 (14 × $20) or more. In that case, this reimbursement can leave the fund with sequentially numbered $20 bills. But if the most recent reimbursement was for less than $280, the presence of 14 sequentially numbered $20 bills suggests that the new bills were obtained from a bank as replacement for bills that had been removed. Neither situation shows that the cashier is stealing money, but the second case indicates that the cashier "borrowed" the cash and later replaced it after the auditor showed up. In writing your report, you must not conclude that the cashier is unethical unless other evidence supports it. You should consider additional surprise counts of this petty cashier over the next few weeks.

Sales Representative A salesperson can take several steps to reduce days' sales uncollected. These include (1) decreasing the ratio of sales on account to total sales by encouraging more cash sales, (2) identifying customers most delayed in their payments and encouraging earlier payments or cash sales, and (3) applying stricter credit policies to eliminate credit sales to customers that never pay.

Guidance Answers to **Quick Checks**

1. (*c*)
2. Technology reduces processing errors. It also allows more extensive testing of records, limits the amount of hard evidence, and highlights the importance of separation of duties.
3. A company holds liquid assets so that it can purchase other assets, buy services, and pay obligations.
4. It owns cash equivalents because they yield a return greater than what cash earns (and are readily exchanged for cash).
5. Examples of cash equivalents are 90-day U.S. Treasury bills, money market funds, and commercial paper (notes).
6. (*a*)
7. A voucher system is used when an owner/manager can no longer control purchasing procedures through personal supervision and direct participation.
8. If all cash payments are made by check, numerous checks for small amounts must be written. Since this practice is expensive and time-consuming, a petty cash fund is often established for making small (immaterial) cash payments.
9. If the petty cash fund is not reimbursed at the end of an accounting period, the transactions involving petty cash are not yet recorded and the petty cash asset is overstated.
10. First, petty cash transactions are recorded when the petty cash fund is reimbursed. Second, reimbursement provides cash to allow the fund to continue being used. Third, reimbursement identifies any cash shortage or overage in the fund.
11. A bank statement is a report prepared by the bank describing the activities in a depositor's account.

12. To reconcile a bank balance means to explain the difference between the cash balance in the depositor's accounting records and the cash balance on the bank statement.

13. The purpose of the bank reconciliation is to determine whether the bank or the depositor has made any errors and whether the bank has entered any transactions affecting the account that the depositor has not recorded.

14. Outstanding checks—subtracted
Unrecorded deposits—added

15. Debit memos—subtracted
NSF checks—subtracted
Bank service charges—subtracted
Interest earned—added
Credit memos—added

Key Terms

Key Terms are available at the book's Website for learning and testing in an online Flashcard Format.

Bank reconciliation (p. 322)
Bank statement (p. 320)
Canceled checks (p. 321)
Cash (p. 312)
Cash equivalents (p. 312)
Cash Over and Short (p. 313)
Check (p. 319)
Check register (p. 330)
Days' sales uncollected (p. 325)
Deposits in transit (p. 322)
Deposit ticket (p. 319)
Discounts Lost (p. 331)
Electronic funds transfer (EFT) (p. 320)
Gross method (p. 331)
Internal control system (p. 308)
Invoice (p. 328)
Invoice approval (p. 329)
Liquid assets (p. 312)
Liquidity (p. 312)
Net method (p. 331)
Outstanding checks (p. 322)
Petty cash fund (p. 316)
Principles of internal control (p. 309)
Purchase order (p. 328)
Purchase requisition (p. 328)
Receiving report (p. 329)
Signature card (p. 319)
Vendee (p. 328)
Vendor (p. 328)
Voucher (p. 315)
Voucher register (p. 330)
Voucher system (p. 315)

Personal Interactive Quiz

Personal Interactive Quizzes A and B are available at the book's Website to reinforce and assess your learning.

Superscript letter A (B) denotes assignments based on Appendix 8A (8B).

Discussion Questions

1. List the seven broad principles of internal control.

2. Why should responsibility for related transactions be divided among different departments or individuals?

3. Internal control procedures are important in every business, but at what stage in the development of a business do they become especially critical?

4. Which of the following assets is most liquid? Which is least liquid? Inventory, building, accounts receivable, or cash.

5. Why should the person who keeps the records of an asset not be the person responsible for its custody?

6. When a store purchases merchandise, why are individual departments not allowed to directly deal with suppliers?

7. What is a petty cash receipt? Who should sign it?

8. Why should cash receipts be deposited on the day of receipt?

9. **Krispy Kreme**'s statement of cash flows in Appendix A describes changes in cash and cash equivalents for the year ended February 2, 2003. What amount is provided (used) by investing activities? What amount is provided (used) by financing activities?

10. Refer to **Tastykake**'s balance sheet in Appendix A. Compare and discuss the amount of its cash with its other current assets (both in amount and percent) as of December 28, 2002. Compare and assess the cash amount at December 28, 2002, with its amount at December 29, 2001.

11. **Harley-Davidson**'s balance sheet in Appendix A reports that cash and equivalents decreased during the fiscal year ended December 31, 2002. Identify at least three major causes of this change in cash and equivalents.

Red numbers denote Discussion Questions that involve decision-making.

Homework Manager *repeats all numerical Quick Studies on the book's Website with new numbers.*

QUICK STUDY

QS 8-1
Internal control objectives
C1

An internal control system consists of all policies and procedures used to protect assets, ensure reliable accounting, promote efficient operations, and urge adherence to company policies.

1. What is the main objective of internal control procedures, and how is it achieved?

2. Why should recordkeeping for assets be separated from custody over the assets?

3. Why should the responsibility for a transaction be divided between two or more individuals or departments?

QS 8-2
Internal control for cash
P1

A good system of internal control for cash provides adequate procedures for protecting both cash receipts and cash disbursements.

1. What are three basic guidelines that help achieve this protection?

2. Identify two control systems or procedures for cash disbursements.

QS 8-3
Cash, liquidity, and return
C1 C2

Good accounting systems help with the management and control of cash and cash equivalents.

1. Define and contrast the terms *liquid asset* and *cash equivalent.*

2. Why would companies invest their idle cash in cash equivalents?

QS 8-4
Cash and equivalents
C2

Good accounting systems help in managing cash and controlling who has access to it.

1. What items are included in the category of cash?

2. What items are included in the category of cash equivalents?

3. What does the term *liquidity* refer to?

QS 8-5
Petty cash accounting
P2

1. The petty cash fund of the Rio Agency is established at $75. At the end of the current period, the fund contained $14 and had the following receipts: film rentals, $19, and refreshments for meetings, $23 (both expenditures to be classified as Entertainment Expense); postage, $6; and printing, $13. Prepare journal entries to record (*a*) establishment of the fund and (*b*) reimbursement of the fund at the end of the current period.

2. Identify the two events that cause a Petty Cash account to be credited in a journal entry.

QS 8-6
Bank reconciliation
P3

1. For each of the following items, indicate whether its amount (i) affects the bank or book side of a bank reconciliation and (ii) represents an addition or a subtraction in a bank reconciliation:

a. Outstanding checks
b. Debit memos
c. NSF checks
d. Unrecorded deposits
e. Interest on cash balance
f. Credit memos
g. Bank service charges

2. Which of the items in part 1 require an adjusting journal entry?

QS 8-7
Days' sales uncollected
A1

The following annual account balances are taken from Next Level Sports at December 31:

	2005	2004
Accounts receivable	$ 75,692	$ 70,484
Net sales	2,591,933	2,296,673

What is the change in the number of days' sales uncollected between years 2005 and 2004? According to this analysis, is the company's collection of receivables improving? Explain your answer.

QS 8-8[B]
Purchase discounts
P5

An important part of cash management is knowing when, and if, to take purchase discounts. (*a*) Which accounting method uses a Discounts Lost account? (*b*) What is the advantage of this method for management?

Homework Manager repeats all numerical Exercises on the book's Website with new numbers.

EXERCISES

Exercise 8-1
Internal control recommendations
C1  

What internal control procedures would you recommend in each of the following situations?

1. A concession company has one employee who sells T-shirts and sunglasses at the beach. Each day, the employee is given enough shirts and sunglasses to last through the day and enough cash to make change. The money is kept in a box at the stand.
2. An antique store has one employee who is given cash and sent to garage sales each weekend. The employee pays cash for this merchandise that the antique store resells.

Exercise 8-2
Control of cash receipts by mail
P1 

Some of Castel Co.'s cash receipts from customers are sent to the company with the regular mail. Castel's recordkeeper opens these letters and deposits the cash received each day. (*a*) Identify any internal control problem(s) in this arrangement. (*b*) What changes do you recommend?

Exercise 8-3
Analyzing internal control
C1 

Bemis Company is a rapidly growing start-up business. Its recordkeeper, who was hired one year ago, left town after the company's manager discovered that a large sum of money had disappeared over the past six months. An audit disclosed that the recordkeeper had written and signed several checks made payable to her fiancé and then recorded the checks as salaries expense. The fiancé, who cashed the checks but never worked for the company, left town with the recordkeeper. As a result, the company incurred an uninsured loss of $84,000. Evaluate Bemis's internal control system and indicate which principles of internal control appear to have been ignored.

Exercise 8-4
Petty cash fund with a shortage
P2

Check (2) Cr. Cash $234 and Dr. Cash $100

Gannon Company establishes a $400 petty cash fund on September 9. On September 30, the fund shows $166 in cash along with receipts for the following expenditures: transportation-in, $32; postage expenses, $113; and miscellaneous expenses, $87. The petty cashier could not account for a $2 shortage in the fund. Gannon uses the perpetual system in accounting for merchandise inventory. Prepare (1) the September 9 entry to establish the fund and (2) the September 30 entry to both reimburse the fund and reduce it to $300.

Exercise 8-5
Petty cash fund accounting
P2

Check (3) Cr. Cash $472 (total)

Dane Co. establishes a $200 petty cash fund on January 1. One week later, the fund shows $28 in cash along with receipts for the following expenditures: postage, $64; transportation-in, $19; delivery expenses, $36; and miscellaneous expenses, $53. Dane uses the perpetual system in accounting for merchandise inventory. Prepare journal entries to (1) establish the fund on January 1, (2) reimburse it on January 8, and (3) both reimburse the fund and increase it to $500 on January 8, assuming no entry in part 2.

Exercise 8-6
Bank reconciliation and adjusting entries
P3

Prepare a table with the following headings for a monthly bank reconciliation dated September 30:

Bank Balance		Book Balance			Not Shown on the Reconciliation
Add	Deduct	Add	Deduct	Adjust	

For each item 1 through 12, place an *x* in the appropriate column to indicate whether the item should be added to or deducted from the book or bank balance, or whether it should not appear on the reconciliation. If the book balance is to be adjusted, place a *Dr.* or *Cr.* in the Adjust column to indicate whether the Cash balance should be debited or credited. At the left side of your table, number the items to correspond to the following list.

1. Bank service charge.
2. Checks written and mailed to payees on October 2.
3. Checks written by another depositor but charged against this company's account.
4. Principal and interest on a note collected by the bank but not yet recorded by the company.
5. Special bank charge for collection of note in part 4 on this company's behalf.
6. Check written against the company's account and cleared by the bank; erroneously not recorded by the company's recordkeeper.
7. Interest earned on the cash balance in the bank.
8. Night deposit made on September 30 after the bank closed.
9. Checks outstanding on August 31 that cleared the bank in September.
10. NSF check from customer returned on September 25 but not yet recorded by this company.
11. Checks written by the company and mailed to payees on September 30.
12. Deposit made on September 5 and processed by the bank on September 6.

Exercise 8-7
Voucher system
P1

The voucher system of control is designed to control cash disbursements and the acceptance of obligations.
1. The voucher system of control establishes procedures for what two processes?
2. What types of expenditures should be overseen by a voucher system of control?
3. When is the voucher initially prepared? Explain.

Exercise 8-8
Bank reconciliation
P3

Cruz Clinic deposits all cash receipts on the day when they are received and makes all cash payments by check. At the close of business on June 30, 2004, its Cash account shows an $11,352 debit balance. Cruz Clinic's June 30 bank statement shows $10,332 on deposit in the bank on that day. Prepare a bank reconciliation for Cruz Clinic using the following information:

a. Outstanding checks as of June 30 total $1,713.
b. The June 30 bank statement included an $18 debit memorandum for bank services.
c. Check No. 919, listed with the canceled checks, was correctly drawn for $489 in payment of a utility bill on June 15. Cruz Clinic mistakenly recorded it with a debit to Utilities Expense and a credit to Cash in the amount of $498.
d. The June 30 cash receipts of $2,724 were placed in the bank's night depository after banking hours and were not recorded on the June 30 bank statement.

Check Reconciled bal., $11,343

Exercise 8-9
Adjusting entries from bank reconciliation P3

Prepare the adjusting journal entries that Cruz Clinic must record as a result of preparing the bank reconciliation in Exercise 8-8.

Exercise 8-10
Liquid assets and accounts receivable
A1 

Deacon Co. reported annual net sales for 2004 and 2005 of $565,000 and $647,000, respectively. Its year-end balances of accounts receivable follow: December 31, 2004, $51,000; and December 31, 2005, $83,000. (*a*) Calculate its days' sales uncollected at the end of each year. (*b*) Evaluate and comment on any changes in the amount of liquid assets tied up in receivables.

Exercise 8-11[A]
Documents in a voucher system
P4

Management uses a voucher system to help control and monitor cash disbursements. Identify at least four key documents that are part of a voucher system of control. Explain each document's purpose, where it originates, and how it flows through the voucher system (including its copies).

Exercise 8-12B
Record invoices at gross or net amounts
P5

Trade Imports uses the perpetual system in accounting for merchandise inventory and had the following transactions during the month of October. Prepare entries to record these transactions assuming that Trade Imports records invoices (*a*) at gross amounts and (*b*) at net amounts.

Oct. 2 Purchased merchandise at a $4,000 price, invoice dated October 2, terms 2/10, n/30.
10 Received a $400 credit memorandum (at full invoice price) for the return of merchandise that it purchased on October 2.
17 Purchased merchandise at a $4,400 price, invoice dated October 16, terms 2/10, n/30.
26 Paid for the merchandise purchased on October 17, less the discount.
31 Paid for the merchandise purchased on October 2. Payment was delayed because the invoice was mistakenly filed for payment today. This error caused the discount to be lost.

PROBLEM SET A

Problem 8-1A
Analyzing internal control
C1 

For each of these five separate cases, identify the principle of internal control that is violated. Recommend what the business should do to ensure adherence to principles of internal control.

1. Heather Flatt records all incoming customer cash receipts for her employer and posts the customer payments to their respective accounts.
2. At Netco Company, Jeff and Jose alternate lunch hours. Jeff is the petty cash custodian, but if someone needs petty cash when he is at lunch, Jose fills in as custodian.
3. Nadine Cox posts all patient charges and payments at the P-Town Medical Clinic. Each night Nadine backs up the computerized accounting system to a tape and stores the tape in a locked file at her desk.
4. Barto Sayles prides himself on hiring quality workers who require little supervision. As office manager, Barto gives his employees full discretion over their tasks and for years has seen no reason to perform independent reviews of their work.
5. Desi West's manager has told her to reduce costs. Desi decides to raise the deductible on the plant's property insurance from $5,000 to $10,000. This cuts the property insurance premium in half. In a related move, she decides that bonding the plant's employees is a waste of money since the company has not experienced any losses due to employee theft. Desi saves the entire amount of the bonding insurance premium by dropping the bonding insurance.

Problem 8-2A
Establish, reimburse, and adjust petty cash
P2

Shawnee Co. set up a petty cash fund for payments of small amounts. The following transactions involving the petty cash fund occurred in May (the last month of the company's fiscal year):

May 1 Prepared a company check for $250 to establish the petty cash fund.
15 Prepared a company check both to replenish the fund for the following expenditures made since May 1 and to increase the fund to $450.
a. Paid $78 for janitorial services.
b. Paid $63.68 for miscellaneous expenses.
c. Paid postage expenses of $43.50.
d. Paid $57.15 to *The County Gazette* (the local newspaper) for an advertisement.
e. Counted $11.15 remaining in the petty cash box.
31 The petty cashier reports that $293.39 cash remains in the fund and decides that the May 15 increase in the fund was too large. A company check is drawn both to replenish the fund for the following expenditures made since May 15 and to reduce the fund to $400.
f. Paid postage expenses of $48.36.
g. Reimbursed the office manager for business mileage, $38.50.
h. Paid $39.75 to deliver merchandise to a customer, terms FOB destination.

Required

1. Prepare journal entries to establish the fund on May 1, to replenish it on May 15 and on May 31, and to reflect any increase or decrease in the fund balance on those dates.

Check (1) Total Cr. to Cash: May 15, $438.85; May 31, $106.61

Analysis Component

2. Explain how the company's financial statements are affected if the petty cash fund is not replenished and no entry is made on May 31.

Problem 8-3A

Establish, reimburse, and increase petty cash

P2

Inoke Gallery had the following petty cash transactions in February of the current year:

Feb. 2 Wrote a $300 check, cashed it, and gave the proceeds and the petty cashbox to Bo Brown, the petty cashier.
5 Purchased bond paper for the copier for $10.13 that is immediately used.
9 Paid $22.50 COD shipping charges on merchandise purchased for resale, terms FOB shipping point. Metro uses the perpetual system to account for merchandise inventory.
12 Paid $9.95 postage to express mail a contract to a client.
14 Reimbursed Alli Buck, the manager, $58 for business mileage on her car.
20 Purchased stationery for $77.76 that is immediately used.
23 Paid a courier $18 to deliver merchandise sold to a customer, terms FOB destination.
25 Paid $15.10 COD shipping charges on merchandise purchased for resale, terms FOB shipping point.
27 Paid $64 for postage expenses.
28 The fund had $21.23 remaining in the petty cash box. Sorted the petty cash receipts by accounts affected and exchanged them for a check to reimburse the fund for expenditures. The fund amount is also increased to $400.

Required

1. Prepare the journal entry to establish the petty cash fund.
2. Prepare a petty cash payments report for February with these categories: delivery expense, mileage expense, postage expense, merchandise inventory (for transportation-in), and office supplies expense. Sort the payments into the appropriate categories and total the expenditures in each category.
3. Prepare the journal entries for part 2 to both (*a*) reimburse and (*b*) increase the fund amount.

Check (3a & 3b) Cr. Cash $378.77

Problem 8-4A

Prepare a bank reconciliation and record adjustments

P3

mhhe.com/larson

The following information is available to reconcile Clark Company's book balance of cash with its bank statement cash balance as of July 31, 2005:

a. After all posting is complete on July 31, the company's Cash account has a $26,193 debit balance, but its July bank statement shows a $28,020 cash balance.

b. Check No. 3031 for $1,380 and Check No. 3040 for $552 were outstanding on the June 30 bank reconciliation. Check No. 3040 is listed with the July canceled checks, but Check No. 3031 is not. Also, Check No. 3065 for $336 and Check No. 3069 for $2,148, both written in July, are not among the canceled checks on the July 31 statement.

c. In comparing the canceled checks on the bank statement with the entries in the accounting records, it is found that Check No. 3056 for July rent was correctly written and drawn for $1,250 but was erroneously entered in the accounting records as $1,230.

d. A credit memorandum enclosed with the July bank statement indicates the bank collected $9,000 cash on a noninterest-bearing note for Clark, deducted a $45 collection fee, and credited the remainder to its account. Clark had not recorded this event before receiving the statement.

e. A debit memorandum for $805 lists a $795 NSF check plus a $10 NSF charge. The check had been received from a customer, Jim Shaw. Clark has not yet recorded this check as NSF.

f. Enclosed with the July statement is a $15 debit memorandum for bank services. It has not yet been recorded because no previous notification had been received.

g. Clark's July 31 daily cash receipts of $10,152 were placed in the bank's night depository on that date, but do not appear on the July 31 bank statement.

Required

1. Prepare the bank reconciliation for this company as of July 31, 2005.
2. Prepare the journal entries necessary to bring the company's book balance of cash into conformity with the reconciled cash balance as of July 31, 2005.

Check (1) Reconciled balance, $34,308; (2) Cr. Note Receivable $9,000

Analysis Component

3. Assume that the July 31, 2005, bank reconciliation for this company is prepared and some items are treated incorrectly. For each of the following errors, explain the effect of the error on (i) the adjusted bank statement cash balance and (ii) the adjusted cash account book balance.
   a. The company's unadjusted cash account balance of $26,193 is listed on the reconciliation as $26,139.
   b. The bank's collection of the $9,000 note less the $45 collection fee is added to the bank statement cash balance on the reconciliation.

Problem 8-5A
Prepare a bank reconciliation and record adjustments

P3

mhhe.com/larson

Els Company most recently reconciled its bank statement and book balances of cash on August 31 and it reported two checks outstanding, No. 5888 for $1,038.05 and No. 5893 for $484.25. The following information is available for its September 30, 2005, reconciliation:

From the September 30 Bank Statement

Previous Balance	Total Checks and Debits	Total Deposits and Credits	Current Balance
16,800.45	9,620.05	11,182.85	18,363.25

Checks and Debits

Date	No.	Amount
09/03	5888	1,038.05
09/04	5902	731.90
09/07	5901	1,824.25
09/17		588.25 NSF
09/20	5905	937.00
09/22	5903	399.10
09/22	5904	2,080.00
09/28	5907	213.85
09/29	5909	1,807.65

Deposits and Credits

Date	Amount
09/05	1,103.75
09/12	2,226.90
09/21	4,093.00
09/25	2,351.70
09/30	22.50 IN
09/30	1,385.00 CM

Daily Balance

Date	Amount
08/31	16,800.45
09/03	15,762.40
09/04	15,030.50
09/05	16,134.25
09/07	14,310.00
09/12	16,536.90
09/17	15,948.65
09/20	15,011.65
09/21	19,104.65
09/22	16,625.55
09/25	18,977.25
09/28	18,763.40
09/29	16,955.75
09/30	18,363.25

From Els Company's Accounting Records

Cash Receipts Deposited

Date			Cash Debit
Sept.	5		1,103.75
	12		2,226.90
	21		4,093.00
	25		2,351.70
	30		1,582.75
			11,358.10

Cash Disbursements

Check No.		Cash Credit
5901		1,824.25
5902		731.90
5903		399.10
5904		2,050.00
5905		937.00
5906		859.30
5907		213.85
5908		276.00
5909		1,807.65
		9,099.05

Cash — Acct. No. 101

Date		Explanation	PR	Debit	Credit	Balance
Aug.	31	Balance				15,278.15
Sept.	30	Total receipts	R12	11,358.10		26,636.25
	30	Total disbursements	D23		9,099.05	17,537.20

Additional Information

Check No. 5904 is correctly drawn for $2,080 to pay for computer equipment; however, the recordkeeper misread the amount and entered it in the accounting records with a debit to Computer Equipment and a credit to Cash of $2,050. The NSF check shown in the statement was originally received from a customer, S. Nilson, in payment of her account. Its return has not yet been recorded by the company. The credit memorandum is from the collection of a $1,400 note for Els Company by the bank. The bank deducted a $15 collection fee. The collection and fee are not yet recorded.

Required

1. Prepare the September 30, 2005, bank reconciliation for this company.
2. Prepare the journal entries to adjust the book balance of cash to the reconciled balance.

Check (1) Reconciled balance, $18,326.45 (2) Cr. Note Receivable $1,400

Analysis Component

3. The bank statement reveals that some of the prenumbered checks in the sequence are missing. Describe three situations that could explain this.

PROBLEM SET B

Problem 8-1B
Analyzing internal control
C1

For each of these five separate cases, identify the principle of internal control that is violated. Recommend what the business should do to ensure adherence to principles of internal control.

1. Latoya Tally is the company's computer specialist and oversees its computerized payroll system. Her boss recently asked her to put password protection on all office computers. Latoya has put a password in place that allows only the boss access to the file where pay rates are changed and personnel are added or deleted from the payroll.
2. Lake Theater has a computerized order-taking system for its tickets. The system is active all week and backed up every Friday night.
3. X2U Company has two employees handling acquisitions of inventory. One employee places purchase orders and pays vendors. The second employee receives the merchandise.
4. The owner of Super-Aid uses a check protector to perforate checks, making it difficult for anyone to alter the amount of the check. The check protector sits on the owner's desk in an office that contains company checks and is often unlocked.
5. LeAnn Company is a small business that has separated the duties of cash receipts and cash disbursements. The employee responsible for cash disbursements reconciles the bank account monthly.

Problem 8-2B
Establishing, reimbursing, and adjusting petty cash
P2

Pepco Co. establishes a petty cash fund for payments of small amounts. The following transactions involving the petty cash fund occurred in January (the last month of the company's fiscal year).

Jan. 3 A company check for $150 is written and made payable to the petty cashier to establish the petty cash fund.

14 A company check is written both to replenish the fund for the following expenditures made since January 3 and to increase the fund to $175.

a. Purchased office supplies for $16.29 that are immediately used up.
b. Paid $17.60 COD shipping charges on merchandise purchased for resale, terms FOB shipping point. Pepco uses the perpetual system to account for inventory.
c. Paid $36.57 to All-Tech for minor repairs to a computer.
d. Paid $14.82 for items classified as miscellaneous expenses.
e. Counted $62.28 remaining in the petty cash box.

31 The petty cashier reports that $17.35 remains in the fund and decides that the February 14 increase in the fund was not large enough. A company check is written both to replenish the fund for the following expenditures made since January 14 and to increase it to $250.

f. Paid $40 to *The Smart Shopper* for an advertisement in January's newsletter.
g. Paid $38.19 for postage expenses.
h. Paid $58 to Take-You-There for delivery of merchandise, terms FOB destination.

Required

Check (1) Total Cr. to Cash: Jan. 14, $112.72; Jan. 31, $232.65

1. Prepare journal entries to establish the fund on January 3, to replenish it on January 14 and January 31, and to reflect any increase or decrease in the fund balance on those dates.

Analysis Component

2. Explain how the company's financial statements are affected if the petty cash fund is not replenished and no entry is made on January 31.

Problem 8-3B
Establish, reimburse, and increase petty cash
P2

RPM Music Center had the following petty cash transactions in March of the current year:

March 5 Wrote a $200 check, cashed it, and gave the proceeds and the petty cashbox to Liz Buck, the petty cashier.
6 Paid $14.50 COD shipping charges on merchandise purchased for resale, terms FOB shipping point. RPM uses the perpetual system to account for merchandise inventory.
11 Paid $8.75 delivery charges on merchandise sold to a customer, terms FOB destination.
12 Purchased file folders for $12.13 that are immediately used.
14 Reimbursed Will Nelson, the manager, $9.65 for office supplies purchased and used.
18 Purchased printer paper for $22.54 that is immediately used.
27 Paid $47.10 COD shipping charges on merchandise purchased for resale, terms FOB shipping point.
28 Paid postage expenses of $16.
30 Reimbursed Nelson $58.80 for business car mileage.
31 Cash of $11.53 remained in the fund. Sorted the petty cash receipts by accounts affected and exchanged them for a check to reimburse the fund for expenditures. The fund amount is also increased to $250.

Required

1. Prepare the journal entry to establish the petty cash fund.

Check (2) Total expenses $189.47

2. Prepare a petty cash payments report for March with these categories: delivery expense, mileage expense, postage expense, merchandise inventory (for transportation-in), and office supplies expense. Sort the payments into the appropriate categories and total the expenses in each category.

(3a & 3b) Cr. Cash $238.47

3. Prepare the journal entries for part 2 to both (*a*) reimburse and (*b*) increase the fund amount.

Problem 8-4B
Prepare a bank reconciliation and record adjustments
P3 

The following information is available to reconcile Style Co.'s book balance of cash with its bank statement cash balance as of December 31, 2005:

a. After posting is complete, the December 31 cash balance according to the accounting records is $31,743.70, and the bank statement cash balance for that date is $45,091.80.
b. Check No. 1273 for $1,084.20 and Check No. 1282 for $390.00, both written and entered in the accounting records in December, are not among the canceled checks. Two checks, No. 1231 for $2,289.00 and No. 1242 for $370.50, were outstanding on the most recent November 30 reconciliation. Check No. 1231 is listed with the December canceled checks, but Check No. 1242 is not.
c. When the December checks are compared with entries in the accounting records, it is found that Check No. 1267 had been correctly drawn for $2,435 to pay for office supplies but was erroneously entered in the accounting records as $2,453.
d. Two debit memoranda are enclosed with the statement and are unrecorded at the time of the reconciliation. One debit memorandum is for $749.50 and dealt with an NSF check for $732 received from a customer, Titus Industries, in payment of its account. The bank assessed a $17.50 fee for processing it. The second debit memorandum is a $79.00 charge for check printing. Style did not record these transactions before receiving the statement.
e. A credit memorandum indicates that the bank collected $20,000 cash on a note receivable for the company, deducted a $20 collection fee, and credited the balance to the company's Cash account. Style did not record this transaction before receiving the statement.
f. Style's December 31 daily cash receipts of $7,666.10 were placed in the bank's night depository on that date, but do not appear on the December 31 bank statement.

Required

1. Prepare the bank reconciliation for this company as of December 31, 2005.

2. Prepare the journal entries necessary to bring the company's book balance of cash into conformity with the reconciled cash balance as of December 31, 2005.

Check (1) Reconciled balance, $50,913.20; (2) Cr. Note Receivable $20,000

Analysis Component

3. Explain the nature of the communications conveyed by a bank when the bank sends the depositor (*a*) a debit memorandum and (*b*) a credit memorandum.

Problem 8-5B
Prepare a bank reconciliation and record adjustments
P3

Safe Systems Co. most recently reconciled its bank balance on April 30 and reported two checks outstanding at that time, No. 1771 for $781.00 and No. 1780 for $1,325.90. The following information is available for its May 31, 2005, reconciliation:

From the May 31 Bank Statement

Previous Balance	Total Checks and Debits	Total Deposits and Credits	Current Balance
18,290.70	12,898.90	16,416.80	21,808.60

Checks and Debits			Deposits and Credits		Daily Balance	
Date	No.	Amount	Date	Amount	Date	Amount
05/01	1771	781.00	05/04	2,438.00	04/30	18,290.70
05/02	1783	195.30	05/14	2,898.00	05/01	17,509.70
05/04	1782	1,285.50	05/22	1,801.80	05/02	17,314.40
05/11	1784	1,449.60	05/25	7,200.00 CM	05/04	18,466.90
05/18		431.80 NSF	05/26	2,079.00	05/11	17,017.30
05/25	1787	8,032.50			05/14	19,915.30
05/26	1785	157.20			05/18	19,483.50
05/29	1788	554.00			05/22	21,285.30
05/31		12.00 SC			05/25	20,452.80
					05/26	22,374.60
					05/29	21,820.60
					05/31	21,808.60

From Safe Systems' Accounting Records

Cash Receipts Deposited

Date			Cash Debit
May	4		2,438.00
	14		2,898.00
	22		1,801.80
	26		2,079.00
	31		2,526.30
			11,743.10

Cash Disbursements

Check No.		Cash Credit
1782		1,285.50
1783		195.30
1784		1,449.60
1785		157.20
1786		353.10
1787		8,032.50
1788		544.00
1789		639.50
		12,656.70

Cash — Acct. No. 101

Date		Explanation	PR	Debit	Credit	Balance
Apr.	30	Balance				16,183.80
May	31	Total receipts	R7	11,743.10		27,926.90
	31	Total disbursements	D8		12,656.70	15,270.20

Additional Information

Check No. 1788 is correctly drawn for $554 to pay for May utilities; however, the recordkeeper misread the amount and entered it in the accounting records with a debit to Utilities Expense and a credit to Cash for $544. The bank paid and deducted the correct amount. The NSF check shown in the statement was originally received from a customer, S. Bax, in payment of her account. The company has not yet recorded its return. The credit memorandum is from a $7,300 note that the bank collected for the company. The bank deducted a $100 collection fee and deposited the remainder in the company's account. The collection and fee have not yet been recorded.

Required

Check (1) Reconciled balance, $22,016.40; (2) Cr. Note Receivable $7,300

1. Prepare the May 31, 2005, bank reconciliation for Safe Systems.
2. Prepare the journal entries to adjust the book balance of cash to the reconciled balance.

Analysis Component

3. The bank statement reveals that some of the prenumbered checks in the sequence are missing. Describe three possible situations to explain this.

PROBLEM SET C

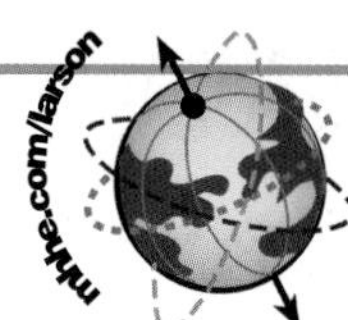

Problem Set C is available at the book's Website to further reinforce and assess your learning.

SERIAL PROBLEM

Success Systems

P3

(This serial problem began in Chapter 1 and continues through most of the book. If previous chapter segments were not completed, the serial problem can begin at this point. It is helpful, but not necessary, that you use the Working Papers that accompany the book.)

Kay Breeze receives the March bank statement for Success Systems on April 11, 2005. The March 31 bank statement shows an ending cash balance of $77,354. A comparison of the bank statement with the general ledger Cash account, No. 101, reveals the following:

a. Breeze notices that the bank erroneously cleared a $500 check against her account that she did not issue. The check documentation included with the bank statement shows that this check was actually issued by a company named Sierra Systems.
b. On March 25, the bank issues a $50 debit memorandum for the safety deposit box that Success Systems agreed to rent from the bank beginning March 25.
c. On March 26, the bank issues a $102 debit memorandum for printed checks that Success Systems ordered from the bank.
d. On March 31, the bank issues a credit memorandum for $33 interest earned on Success Systems' checking account for the month of March.
e. Breeze notices that the check she issued for $128 on March 31, 2005, has not yet cleared the bank.
f. Breeze verifies that all deposits made in March do appear on the March bank statement.
g. The general ledger Cash account, No. 101, shows an ending cash balance per books as $77,845 (prior to any reconciliation).

Required

1. Prepare a bank reconciliation in good form (refer to Exhibit 8.7) for Success Systems for the month ended March 31, 2005.
2. Prepare any necessary adjusting entries. Use Miscellaneous Expenses, No. 677, for any bank charges. Use Interest Revenue, No. 404, for any interest earned on the checking account for the month of March.

BEYOND THE NUMBERS

REPORTING IN ACTION

C2 A1

BTN 8-1 Refer to **Krispy Kreme**'s financial statements in Appendix A to answer the following:

1. For both fiscal year-end 2003 and 2002, identify the total amount of cash and cash equivalents. Determine the percent this amount represents of total current assets, total current liabilities, total shareholders' equity, and total assets for both years. Comment on any trends.
2. For both fiscal 2003 and 2002, use the information in the statement of cash flows to determine the percent change between the beginning and ending year amounts of cash and cash equivalents.
3. Compute the days' sales uncollected as of February 2, 2003, and February 3, 2002. Has the collection of receivables improved?

Roll On

4. Access Krispy Kreme's financial statements for fiscal years ending after February 2, 2003, from its Website (KrispyKreme.com) or the SEC's EDGAR database (www.SEC.gov). Recompute its days' sales uncollected for fiscal years ending after February 2, 2003. Compare this to the days' sales uncollected for 2003 and 2002.

COMPARATIVE ANALYSIS

A1

BTN 8-2 Key comparative figures ($ thousands) for both **Krispy Kreme** and **Tastykake** follow:

Key Figures	Krispy Kreme Current Year	Krispy Kreme Prior Year	Tastykake Current Year	Tastykake Prior Year
Accounts receivable	$ 34,373	$ 26,894	$ 20,882	$ 22,233
Net sales	491,549	394,354	162,263	166,244

Required

Compute days' sales uncollected for both companies for each of the two years shown. Comment on any trends for both companies. Which company has the larger percent change in days' sales uncollected?

ETHICS CHALLENGE

C1

BTN 8-3 Carol Benton, Sue Knox, and Marcia Diamond work for a family physician, Dr. Gwen Conrad, who is in private practice. Dr. Conrad is knowledgeable about office management practices and has segregated the cash receipt duties as follows. Benton opens the mail and prepares a triplicate list of money received. She sends one copy of the list to Knox, the cashier, who deposits the receipts daily in the bank. Diamond, the recordkeeper, receives a copy of the list and posts payments to patients' accounts. About once a month the office clerks have an expensive lunch they pay for as follows. First, Knox endorses a patient's check in Dr. Conrad's name and cashes it at the bank. Benton then destroys the remittance advice accompanying the check. Finally, Diamond posts payment to the customer's account as a miscellaneous credit. The three justify their actions by their relatively low pay and knowledge that Dr. Conrad will likely never miss the money.

Required

1. Who is the best person in Dr. Conrad's office to reconcile the bank statement?
2. Would a bank reconciliation uncover this office fraud?
3. What are some ways to detect this type of fraud?
4. Suggest additional internal controls that Dr. Conrad could implement.

COMMUNICATING IN PRACTICE

P5

BTN 8-4[B] Assume you are a business consultant. The owner of a company sends you an e-mail expressing concern that the company is not taking advantage of its discounts offered by vendors. The company currently uses the gross method of recording purchases. The owner is considering a review of all invoices and payments from the previous period. Due to the volume of purchases, however, the owner recognizes this is time-consuming and costly. The owner seeks your advice about monitoring purchase discounts in the future. Provide a response in memorandum form.

TAKING IT TO THE NET

C1 P1

mhhe.com/larson

BTN 8-5 Visit the Association of Certified Fraud Examiners Website at **cfenet.com**. Research the fraud facts (see media center—fraud statistics) presented at this site and fill in the blanks in the following statements.

1. It is estimated that ____% of revenues will be lost in 2002 as a result of occupational fraud and abuse. Applied to the U.S. gross domestic product, this translates to losses of approximately $____ billion, or about $____ per employee.
2. Organizations with fraud hotlines cut their fraud losses by approximately ____% per scheme. Internal audits, external audits, and background checks also significantly reduce fraud losses.
3. Small businesses are the most vulnerable to occupational fraud and abuse. The average scheme in a small business causes $____ in losses. The average scheme in the largest companies costs $____.
4. The most common method for detecting occupational fraud is through tips from ____, customers, vendors, and anonymous sources. The second most common method of discovery is ____.
5. The typical occupational fraud perpetrator is a first-time offender. Only ____% of occupational fraudsters in this study were known to have prior convictions for fraud-related offenses.
6. All occupational frauds fall into one of three categories: ____, corruption, or ____statements.
7. Over ____% of occupational frauds involve asset misappropriations. Cash is the targeted asset ____% of the time.
8. Corruption schemes account for ____% of all occupational frauds, and they cause over $____ in losses, on average.
9. Fraudulent statements are the most costly form of occupational fraud with median losses of $____ million per scheme.
10. Frauds committed by employees cause median losses of $____, while frauds committed by managers and executives cause median losses of $____. When managers and employees conspire in a fraud scheme, the median loss rises to $____.
11. Losses caused by perpetrators older than 60 are ____times higher than losses caused by employees 25 and younger.
12. The average fraud scheme lasted ____ months before it was detected.

TEAMWORK IN ACTION

C1

BTN 8-6 Organize the class into teams. Each team must prepare a list of 10 internal controls a consumer could observe in a typical retail department store. When called upon, the team's spokesperson must be prepared to share controls identified by the team that have not been shared by another team's spokesperson.

BUSINESS WEEK ACTIVITY

C1 P1

mhhe.com/larson

BTN 8-7 Read the article "To Cure Fraud, Start at the Top" in the October 18, 2002, issue of *Business Week*. (The book's Website provides a free link.)

Required:

1. Which fraud case does Pergola (the interviewee) state was the most significant?
2. What are the character traits of individuals who might be more likely to commit fraud?
3. Which corporate structures make it easier for fraud to thrive?
4. How do corporate recruiters keep potential fraudsters from joining the company?
5. What role can co-workers play in stopping fraud?

ENTREPRENEURIAL DECISION

C1 P1

BTN 8-8 Refer to the chapter's opening feature, "Sweet Success," describing the entrepreneurial efforts of Dylan Lauren and Jeff Rubin with **Dylan's Candy Bar**.

Required

List the seven principles of internal control. For each principle, identify how Lauren and Rubin could implement it in their candy store.

HITTING THE ROAD

C1 

BTN 8-9 Visit a part of your college that serves the student community with either products or services. Some examples are food services, libraries, and book stores. Identify and describe between four and eight internal controls being implemented.

GLOBAL DECISION

C2 

BTN 8-10 Review the consolidated statement of changes in financial position for Grupo Bimbo for the year ended December 31, 2002, at GrupoBimbo.com.

Required

1. What item caused the largest change (excluding net income) in the Operations section of the statement?
2. What item caused the largest change in the Financing section of the statement?
3. What item caused the largest change in the Investing section of the statement?
4. Did the cash and marketable securities as of December 31, 2002, increase or decrease relative to December 31, 2001?
5. Calculate the percentage change in both the cash and the marketable securities balances between December 31, 2001 and December 31, 2002.
6. At December 31, 2002, what percentage of current assets is comprised of cash and marketable securities?

"My goal is to become the Oprah of raw materials"—Barbara Manzi

Accounting for Receivables

A Look Back

Chapter 8 focused on internal control and reporting for cash. We described procedures that are good for internal control, and we explained the accounting for and management of cash.

A Look at This Chapter

This chapter emphasizes receivables. We explain that they are liquid assets and describe how companies account for and report them. We also discuss the importance of estimating uncollectibles.

A Look Ahead

Chapter 10 focuses on plant assets, natural resources, and intangible assets. We explain how to account for, report, and analyze these long-term assets.

CAP

Conceptual

C1 Describe accounts receivable and how they occur and are recorded. *(p. 350)*

C2 Describe a note receivable and the computation of its maturity date and interest. *(p. 359)*

C3 Explain how receivables can be converted to cash before maturity. *(p. 363)*

Analytical

A1 Compute accounts receivable turnover and use it to help assess financial condition. *(p. 364)*

Procedural

P1 Apply the direct write-off and allowance methods to account for accounts receivable. *(p. 354)*

P2 Estimate uncollectibles using methods based on sales and accounts receivable. *(p. 356)*

P3 Record the receipt of a note receivable. *(p. 361)*

P4 Record the honoring and dishonoring of a note and adjustments for interest. *(p. 361)*

Decision Feature

Heavy into Metals

BROOKSVILLE, FL—"When you're an African-American entrepreneur, and a woman in a male-dominated industry, you learn some lessons very quickly, " says Barbara Manzi. Manzi launched **Manzi Metals** (**ManziMetals.com**) from her home eight years ago. Her lessons learned have translated into an annual $3 million in revenues as a distributor of aluminum, steel, titanium, brass, and other alloys.

Manzi, who runs Manzi Metals along with her son Louis, had to overcome long odds in achieving success. "There were 12 children in our family," she says. "But if I had listened to [those]... who told me I'd never do anything except get married, I would have gone astray." Instead, Manzi pursued her dreams.

Today, Manzi Metals is a major distributor of all types of metals in any shapes or sizes. Manzi strives for the highest quality service but maintains competitive prices. This includes special attention to customers and keeping control over receivables. Decisions such as selling on credit or not, and setting policies and criteria for extending credit, can make or break a startup.

Manzi, who has "a passion for people," never loses sight of the personal touch when making these business decisions. Recognizing economic downturns and adjusting past due accounts when appropriate are as much people decisions as accounting applications. Still, keeping an eye on accounts receivable turnover and uncollectible accounts is part of good business operations. This chapter focuses on these and related issues. Such factors, says Manzi, must be studied and carefully interpreted. "You have to get it right the first time," she says. "There's no room for mistakes!"

[Sources: *Manzi Metals Website,* January 2004; *Business Week,* January 2003; *Entre World,* February 2003.]

This chapter focuses on accounts receivable and short-term notes receivable. We describe each of these assets, their uses, and how they are accounted for and reported in financial statements. This knowledge helps us use accounting information to make better business decisions. It can also help in predicting future company performance and financial condition as well as in managing one's own business.

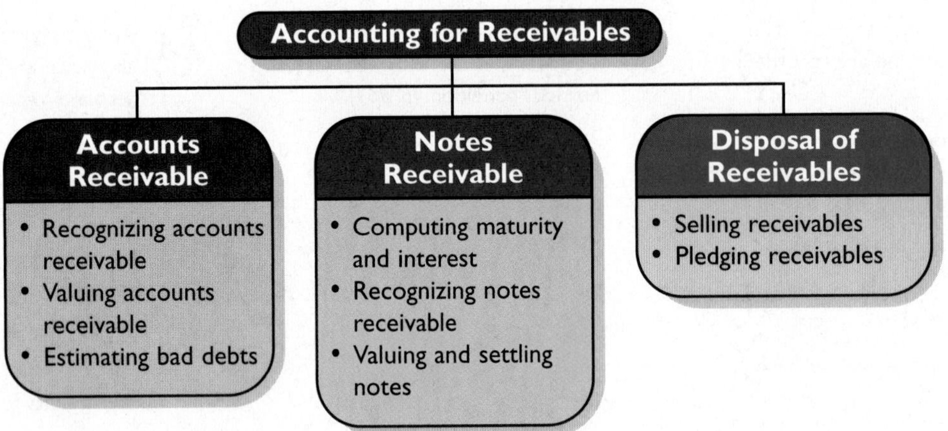

Accounts Receivable

A *receivable* is an amount due from another party. The two most common receivables are accounts receivable and notes receivable. Other receivables include interest receivable, rent receivable, tax refund receivable, and receivables from employees. **Accounts receivable** are amounts due from customers for credit sales. This section begins by describing how accounts receivable occur. It includes receivables that occur when customers use credit cards issued by third parties and when a company gives credit directly to customers. When a company does extend credit directly to customers, it must (1) maintain a separate account receivable for each customer and (2) account for bad debts from credit sales.

Recognizing Accounts Receivable

C1 Describe accounts receivable and how they occur and are recorded.

Accounts receivable occur from credit sales to customers. The amount of credit sales has increased in recent years, reflecting several factors including an efficient financial system. Retailers such as **Limited Brands** and **Best Buy** hold millions of dollars in accounts receivable. Similar amounts are held by wholesalers such as **SUPERVALU** and **SYSCO**. Exhibit 9.1 shows recent dollar amounts of accounts receivable and their percent of total assets for four well-known companies.

Sales on Credit Credit sales are recorded by increasing (debiting) Accounts Receivable. A company must also maintain a separate account for each customer that tracks how much that customer purchases, has already paid, and still owes. This information provides the basis for sending bills to customers and for other business analyses. To maintain this information, companies that extend credit directly to their customers keep a separate account receivable for each one of them. The general ledger continues to have a single Accounts Receivable account along with the other financial

Exhibit 9.1

Accounts Receivable for Selected Companies

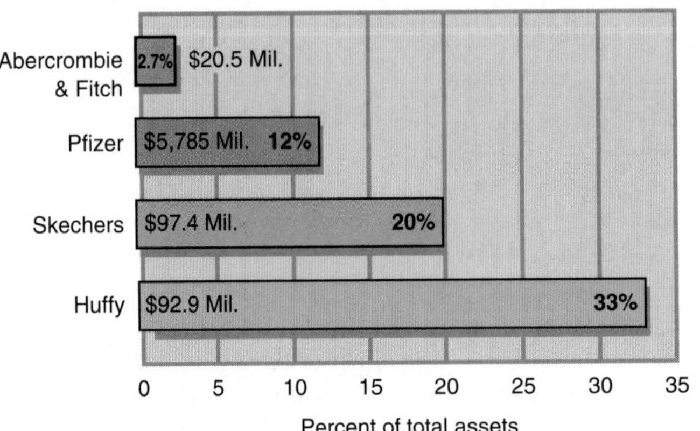

statement accounts, but a supplementary record is created to maintain a separate account for each customer. This supplementary record is called the *accounts receivable ledger*.

Exhibit 9.2 shows the relation between the Accounts Receivable account in the general ledger and its individual customer accounts in the accounts receivable ledger for TechCom, a small electronics wholesaler. This exhibit reports a $3,000 ending balance of TechCom's accounts receivable for June 30. TechCom's transactions are mainly in cash, but it has two major credit customers: CompStore and RDA Electronics. Its *schedule of accounts receivable* shows that the $3,000 balance of the Accounts Receivable account in the general ledger equals the total of its two customers' balances in the accounts receivable ledger.

Point: Receivables, cash, cash equivalents, and short-term investments make up the most liquid assets of a company.

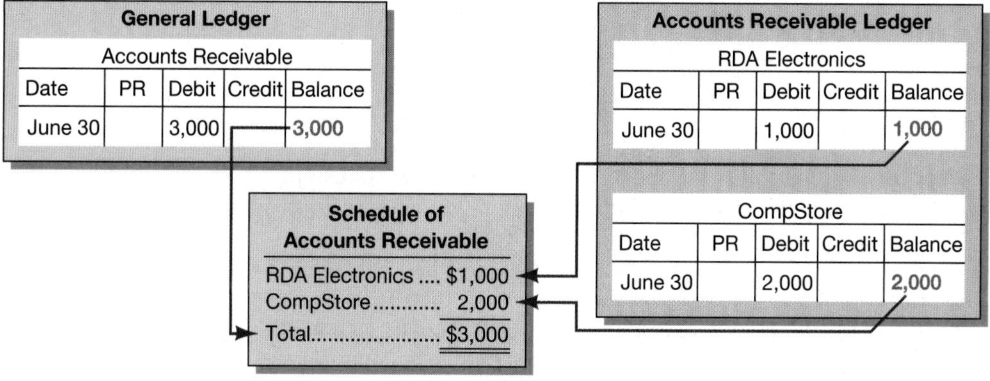

Exhibit 9.2

General Ledger and the Accounts Receivable Ledger (before July 1 transactions)

To see how accounts receivable from credit sales are recognized in the accounting records, we look at two transactions on July 1 between TechCom and its credit customers—see Exhibit 9.3. The first is a credit sale of $950 to CompStore. A credit sale is posted with both a debit to the Accounts Receivable account in the general ledger and a debit to the customer account in the accounts receivable ledger. The second transaction is a collection of $720 from RDA Electronics from a prior credit sale. Cash receipts from a credit customer are posted with a credit to both the Accounts Receivable account in the general ledger and to the customer account in the accounts receivable ledger. (Posting debits or credits to Accounts Receivable in two separate ledgers does not violate the requirement that debits equal credits. The equality of debits and credits is maintained in the general ledger. The accounts receivable ledger is a supplementary record providing information on each customer.)

July 1	Accounts Receivable—CompStore	950	
	Sales		950
	*To record credit sales**		
July 1	Cash	720	
	Accounts Receivable—RDA Electronics		720
	To record collection of credit sales.		

* We omit the entry to Dr. Cost of Sales and Cr. Merchandise Inventory to focus on sales and receivables.

Exhibit 9.3

Accounts Receivable Transactions

Assets = Liabilities + Equity
+950 +950

Assets = Liabilities + Equity
+720
−720

Exhibit 9.4 shows the general ledger and the accounts receivable ledger after recording the two July 1 transactions. The general ledger shows the effects of the sale, the collection, and the resulting balance of $3,230. These events are also reflected in the individual customer accounts: RDA Electronics has an ending balance of $280, and CompStore's ending balance is $2,950. The $3,230 sum of the individual accounts equals the debit balance of the Accounts Receivable account in the general ledger.

Point: Software helps merchants build Web storefronts quickly and easily. Merchants simply enter product details such as names and prices, and out comes a respectable-looking Website complete with order forms. They also offer security with credit card orders and can track sales and site visits.

Like TechCom, many large retailers such as **Sears** and **JCPenney** sell on credit. Many also maintain their own credit cards to grant credit to approved customers and to earn interest on any balance not paid within a specified period of time. This allows them to avoid the fee charged by credit card companies. The entries in this case are the same as those for TechCom

Exhibit 9.4

General Ledger and the Accounts Receivable Ledger (after July 1 transactions)

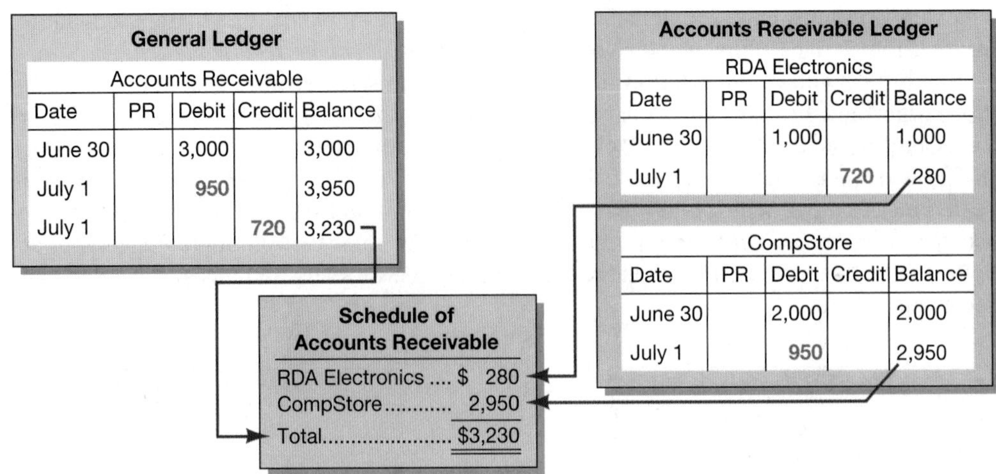

General Ledger

Accounts Receivable

Date	PR	Debit	Credit	Balance
June 30		3,000		3,000
July 1		950		3,950
July 1			720	3,230

Accounts Receivable Ledger

RDA Electronics

Date	PR	Debit	Credit	Balance
June 30		1,000		1,000
July 1			720	280

CompStore

Date	PR	Debit	Credit	Balance
June 30		2,000		2,000
July 1		950		2,950

Schedule of Accounts Receivable

RDA Electronics	$ 280
CompStore	2,950
Total	$3,230

except for the possibility of added interest revenue. If a customer owes interest on a bill, we debit Interest Receivable and credit Interest Revenue for that amount.

Credit Card Sales Many companies allow their customers to pay for products and services using third-party credit cards such as **Visa**, **MasterCard**, or **American Express**, and debit cards (also called bankcards). This practice gives customers the ability to make purchases without cash or checks. Once credit is established with a credit card company or bank, the customer does not have to open an account with each store. Customers using these cards can make single monthly payments instead of several payments to different creditors and can defer their payments.

Sellers allow customers to use third-party credit cards and debit cards instead of granting credit directly for several reasons. First, the seller does not have to evaluate each customer's credit standing or make decisions about who gets credit and how much. Second, the seller avoids the risk of extending credit to customers who cannot or do not pay. This risk is transferred to the card company. Third, the seller typically receives cash from the card company sooner than had it granted credit directly to customers. Fourth, a variety of credit options for customers offers a potential increase in sales volume. **Sears** historically offered credit only to customers using a Sears card but later changed its policy to permit customers to charge purchases to third-party credit card companies in a desire to increase sales. It reported: "SearsCharge increased its share of Sears retail sales even as the company expanded the payment options available to its customers with the acceptance . . . of [Visa,] MasterCard, and American Express in addition to the Discover Card."

Decision Insight

Debit Card vs. Credit Card A buyer's debit card purchase reduces the buyer's cash account balance at the card company, which is often a bank. Since the buyer's cash account balance is a liability (with a credit balance) for the card company to the buyer, the card company would debit that account for a buyer's purchase—hence, the term *debit card.* A credit card reflects authorization by the card company of a line of credit for the buyer with predetermined interest rates and payment terms—hence, the term *credit card.* Most credit card companies waive interest charges on the line of credit if the buyer pays its balance in full each month.

Point: Visa USA transacted more than $1 trillion in 2003 from its credit, debit and prepaid cards.

There are guidelines in how companies account for credit card and debit card sales. Some credit cards, but mostly debit cards, credit a seller's Cash account immediately upon deposit. In this case the seller deposits a copy of each card sales receipt in its bank account just as it deposits a customer's check. Some other cards require the seller to remit a copy (often electronically) of each receipt to the card company. Until payment is received, the seller has an account receivable from the card company. In both cases, the seller pays a fee for services provided by the card company, often ranging

Decision Maker

Entrepreneur As a small retailer, you are considering allowing customers to purchase merchandise using credit cards. Until now, your store accepted only cash and checks. What form of analysis do you use to make this decision?

Answer—p. 367

from 1% to 5% of card sales. This charge is deducted from the credit to the seller's account or the cash payment to the seller.

The procedures used in accounting for credit card sales depend on whether cash is received immediately on deposit or cash receipt is delayed until the credit card company makes the payment. To illustrate, if TechCom has $100 of credit card sales with a 4% fee, and its $96 cash is received immediately on deposit, the entry is

Point: Web merchants pay twice as much in credit card association fees as other retailers because they suffer 10 times as much fraud.

July 15	Cash.	96	
	Credit Card Expense	4	
	Sales		100
	*To record credit card sales less a 4% credit card expense.**		

* We omit the entry to Dr. Cost of Sales and Cr. Merchandise Inventory to focus on credit card expense.

Assets	=	Liabilities	+	Equity
+96				+100
				−4

However, if instead TechCom must remit the credit card sales receipts to the credit card company and wait for the $96 cash payment, the entry on the date of sale is

July 15	**Accounts Receivable—Credit Card Co.**	96	
	Credit Card Expense	4	
	Sales		100
	*To record credit card sales less 4% credit card expense.**		

* We omit the entry to Dr. Cost of Sales and Cr. Merchandise Inventory to focus on credit card expense.

Assets	=	Liabilities	+	Equity
+96				+100
				−4

When cash is later received from the credit card company, the entry is

July 25	Cash.	96	
	Accounts Receivable—Credit Card Co..		96
	To record cash receipt.		

Assets	=	Liabilities	+	Equity
+96				
−96				

Point: Third-party credit card costs can be large. JCPenney recently reported sales exceeding $30,000 million along with third-party credit card costs of nearly $100 million.

Some firms report credit card expense in the income statement as a type of discount deducted from sales to get net sales. Other companies classify it as a selling expense or even as an administrative expense. Arguments can be made for each alternative.

Installment Sales and Receivables Many companies allow their credit customers to make periodic payments over several months. For example, **Harley-Davidson** holds more than $400 million in installment receivables. The seller refers to such assets as *installment accounts receivable,* which are amounts owed by customers from credit sales for which payment is required in periodic amounts over an extended time period. Source documents for installment accounts receivable include sales slips or invoices describing the sales transactions. The customer is usually charged interest. Although installment accounts receivable may have credit periods of more than one year, they are classified as current assets if the seller regularly offers customers such terms.

Quick Check

1. In recording credit card sales, when do you debit Accounts Receivable and when do you debit Cash?
2. A company accumulates sales receipts and remits them to the credit card company for payment. When are the credit card expenses recorded? When are these expenses incurred?

Answers—p. 368

Valuing Accounts Receivable

When a company directly grants credit to its customers, it expects that some customers will not pay what they promised. The accounts of these customers are *uncollectible accounts,* commonly called **bad debts.** The total amount of uncollectible accounts is an expense of selling on credit. Why do companies sell on credit if they expect some accounts

Decision Insight

Bad Debts Costs are rising for credit card issuers owing to default rates. Much of this is the fault of issuers who offer credit cards with low "teaser" rates. In response, credit card users have increased their debts, and many are unable to pay them.

Credit Card Default Rates	
Banc One	6.8%
First Chicago	6.7
Discover	6.1
Citicorp	5.5
Chase	5.1
Capital One	5.1
Advanta	5.1

to be uncollectible? The answer is that companies believe that granting credit will increase total sales and net income enough to offset bad debts. Companies use two methods to account for uncollectible accounts: (1) direct write-off method and (2) allowance method. We describe both.

Direct Write-Off Method The **direct write-off method** of accounting for bad debts records the loss from an uncollectible account receivable when it is determined to be uncollectible. No attempt is made to predict bad debts expense. To illustrate, if TechCom determines on January 23 that it cannot collect $520 owed to it by its customer J. Kent, it recognizes the loss using the direct write-off method as follows:

P1 Apply the direct write-off and allowance methods to account for accounts receivable.

Assets = Liabilities + Equity
−520 −520

Jan. 23	Bad Debts Expense	520	
	Accounts Receivable—J. Kent		520
	To write off an uncollectible account.		

The debit in this entry charges the uncollectible amount directly to the current period's Bad Debts Expense account. The credit removes its balance from the Accounts Receivable account in the general ledger (and its subsidiary ledger).

Sometimes an account written off is later collected. This can be due to factors such as continual collection efforts or a customer's good fortune. If the account of J. Kent that was written off directly to Bad Debts Expense is later collected in full, the following two entries record this recovery:

Point: Managers realize that some portion of credit sales will be uncollectible, but which credit sales are uncollectible is unknown.

Assets = Liabilities + Equity
+520 +520

Assets = Liabilities + Equity
+520
−520

Mar. 11	Accounts Receivable—J. Kent	520	
	Bad Debts Expense		520
	To reinstate account previously written off.		
Mar. 11	Cash	520	
	Accounts Receivable—J. Kent		520
	To record full payment of account.		

Companies must weigh at least two accounting principles when considering the use of the direct write-off method: the (1) matching principle and (2) materiality principle.

Point: If a customer fails to pay within the credit period, most companies send out repeated billings and make other efforts to collect.

Matching principle applied to bad debts. The **matching principle** requires expenses to be reported in the same accounting period as the sales they helped produce. This means that if extending credit to customers helped produce sales, the bad debts expense linked to those sales is matched and reported in the same period. The direct write-off method usually does not best match sales and expenses because bad debts expense is not recorded until an account becomes uncollectible, which often occurs in a period after that of the credit sale. To match bad debts expense with the sales it produces therefore requires a company to estimate future uncollectibles.

Point: Pier 1 Imports reports $7 million of bad debts expense matched against $413 million of credit sales in a recent fiscal year.

Materiality principle applied to bad debts. The **materiality principle** states that an amount can be ignored if its effect on the financial statements is unimportant to users' business decisions. The materiality principle permits the use of the direct write-off method when bad debts expenses are very small in relation to a company's other financial statement items such as sales and net income.

Point: Under the direct write-off method, expense is recorded each time an account is written off. Under the allowance method, expense is recorded with an adjusting entry equal to the total estimated uncollectibles for that period's sales.

Allowance Method The **allowance method** of accounting for bad debts matches the *estimated* loss from uncollectible accounts receivable against the sales they helped produce. We must use estimated losses because when sales occur, management does not know which customers will not pay their bills. This means that at the end of each period, the allowance method requires an estimate of the total bad debts expected to result from that period's sales. This method has two advantages over the direct write-off method: (1) it records estimated bad debts expense in the period when the related sales are recorded and (2) it reports accounts receivable on the balance sheet at the estimated amount of cash to be collected.

Topic Tackler 9-1

Point: The Office of the Comptroller of the Currency reported that losses from bad debts are a major factor when banks fail.

Recording bad debts expense. The allowance method estimates bad debts expense at the end of each accounting period and records it with an adjusting entry. TechCom, for instance, had credit sales of $300,000 during its first year of operations. At the end of the first year, $20,000 of credit sales remained uncollected. Based on the experience of similar businesses, TechCom estimated that $1,500 of its accounts receivable would be uncollectible. This estimated expense is recorded with the following adjusting entry:

Dec. 31	Bad Debts Expense	1,500	
	Allowance for Doubtful Accounts		1,500
	To record estimated bad debts.		

Assets = Liabilities + Equity
−1,500 −1,500

The estimated Bad Debts Expense of $1,500 is reported on the income statement (as either a selling expense or an administrative expense) and offsets the $300,000 credit sales it helped produce. The **Allowance for Doubtful Accounts** is a contra asset account. A contra account is used instead of reducing accounts receivable directly because at the time of the adjusting entry, the company does not know which customers will not pay. After the bad debts adjusting entry is posted, TechCom's account balances for Accounts Receivable and its Allowance for Doubtful Accounts are as shown in Exhibit 9.5.

Point: Credit approval is usually not assigned to the selling department because its main goal is to increase sales, and it may approve customers at the expense of increased bad debts. Instead, approval is assigned to a separate credit-granting or administrative department.

Accounts Receivable				Allowance for Doubtful Accounts			
Dec. 31	20,000					Dec. 31	1,500

Exhibit 9.5

General Ledger Balances after Bad Debts Adjusting Entry

The Allowance for Doubtful Accounts credit balance of $1,500 has the effect of reducing accounts receivable to its estimated realizable value. **Realizable value** refers to the expected proceeds from converting an asset into cash. Although credit customers owe $20,000 to TechCom, only $18,500 is expected to be realized in cash collections from these customers. In the balance sheet, the Allowance for Doubtful Accounts is subtracted from Accounts Receivable and is often reported as shown in Exhibit 9.6.

Point: Bad Debts Expense is also called *Uncollectible Accounts Expense*. The Allowance for Doubtful Accounts is also called *Allowance for Uncollectible Accounts*.

Current assets		
Accounts receivable	**$20,000**	
Less allowance for doubtful accounts	**1,500**	**$18,500**

Exhibit 9.6

Balance Sheet Presentation of the Allowance for Doubtful Accounts

Sometimes the Allowance for Doubtful Accounts is not reported separately. This alternative presentation is shown in Exhibit 9.7 (also see Appendix A).

Current assets	
Accounts receivable (net of $1,500 doubtful accounts)	**$18,500**

Exhibit 9.7

Alternative Presentation of the Allowance for Doubtful Accounts

Writing off a bad debt. When specific accounts are identified as uncollectible, they are written off against the Allowance for Doubtful Accounts. To illustrate, TechCom decides that J. Kent's $520 account is uncollectible and makes the following entry to write it off:

Jan. 23	Allowance for Doubtful Accounts	520	
	Accounts Receivable—J. Kent............		520
	To write off an uncollectible account.		

Assets = Liabilities + Equity
+520
−520

Point: The Bad Debts Expense account is not debited in the write-off entry because it was recorded in the period when sales occurred.

Posting this write-off entry to the Accounts Receivable account removes the amount of the bad debt from the general ledger (it is also posted to the accounts receivable subsidiary ledger). The general ledger accounts now appear as in Exhibit 9.8 (assuming no other transactions affecting these accounts).

Exhibit 9.8

General Ledger Balances after Write-Off

Accounts Receivable			
Dec. 31	20,000		
		Jan. 23	520

Allowance for Doubtful Accounts			
		Dec. 31	1,500
Jan. 23	520		

Point: In posting a write-off, the ledger's Explanation column indicates the reason for this credit so it is not misinterpreted as payment in full.

The write-off does not affect the realizable value of accounts receivable as shown in Exhibit 9.9. Neither total assets nor net income is affected by the write-off of a specific account. Instead, both assets and net income are affected in the period when bad debts expense is predicted and then recorded with an adjusting entry.

Exhibit 9.9

Realizable Value before and after Write-Off of a Bad Debt

	Before Write-Off	After Write-Off
Accounts receivable	$ 20,000	$ 19,480
Less allowance for doubtful accounts	1,500	980
Estimated realizable accounts receivable	**$18,500**	**$18,500**

Recovering a bad debt. When a customer fails to pay and the account is written off as uncollectible, his or her credit standing is jeopardized. To help restore credit standing, a customer sometimes volunteers to pay all or part of the amount owed. A company makes two entries when collecting an account previously written off by the allowance method. The first is to reverse the write-off and reinstate the customer's account. The second entry records the collection of the reinstated account. To illustrate, if on March 11 Kent pays in full his account previously written off, the entries are

Assets = Liabilities + Equity
+520
−520

Assets = Liabilities + Equity
+520
−520

Mar. 11	Accounts Receivable—J. Kent	520	
	Allowance for Doubtful Accounts		520
	To reinstate account previously written off.		
Mar. 11	Cash	520	
	Accounts Receivable—J. Kent		520
	To record full payment of account.		

Example: If TechCom used a collection agency and paid a 35% commission on $520 collected from Kent, how is this recorded? *Answer:*

Cash	338	
Collection Expense	182	
Accts. Recble.—J. Kent		520

In this illustration, Kent paid the entire amount previously written off, but sometimes a customer pays only a portion of the amount owed. A question then arises as to whether the entire balance of the account or just the amount paid is returned to accounts receivable. This is a matter of judgment. If we believe this customer will later pay in full, we return the entire amount owed to accounts receivable, but if we expect no further collection, we return only the amount paid.

Estimating Bad Debts Expense

P2 Estimate uncollectibles using methods based on sales and accounts receivable.

Companies with direct credit sales must attempt to estimate bad debts expense to both manage their receivables and set credit policies. The allowance method also requires an estimate of bad debts expense to prepare an adjusting entry at the end of each accounting period. There are two common methods. One is based on the income statement relation between bad debts expense and sales. The second is based on the balance sheet relation between accounts receivable and the allowance for doubtful accounts.

Point: The focus is on *credit* sales because cash sales do not produce bad debts. If cash sales are a small or stable percent of credit sales, total sales can be used.

Percent of Sales Method The *percent of sales method* uses income statement relations to estimate bad debts. It is based on the idea that a given percent of a company's credit sales for the period are uncollectible. To illustrate, assume that Musicland has credit sales of $400,000 in year 2005. Based on past experience, Musicland estimates 0.6% of credit sales to be uncollectible. This implies that Musicland expects $2,400 of bad debts expense from its sales (computed as $400,000 × 0.006 = $2,400). The adjusting entry to record this estimated expense is

Dec. 31	Bad Debts Expense	2,400	
	Allowance for Doubtful Accounts		2,400
	To record estimated bad debts.		

Assets = Liabilities + Equity
−2,400 −2,400

The allowance account ending balance on the balance sheet for this method would rarely equal the bad debts expense on the income statement. This is so because unless a company is in its first period of operations, its allowance account has a zero balance only if the prior amounts written off as uncollectible *exactly* equal the prior estimated bad debts expenses. (When computing bad debts expense as a percent of sales, managers monitor and adjust the percent so it is not too high or too low.)

Point: When using the *percent of sales method* for estimating uncollectibles, the estimate of bad debts is the number used in the adjusting entry.

Accounts Receivable Methods The *accounts receivable methods* use balance sheet relations to estimate bad debts—mainly the relation between accounts receivable and the allowance amount. The goal of the bad debts adjusting entry for these methods is to make the Allowance for Doubtful Accounts balance equal to the portion of accounts receivable that is estimated to be uncollectible. The estimated balance for the allowance account is obtained in one of two ways: (1) computing the percent uncollectible from the total accounts receivable or (2) aging accounts receivable.

Decision Insight

Bum Loans Want to pick up some cheap debt? **Sprint** recently put $145 million of its unpaid telephone bills up for sale on the Net, and **Bank One** listed $211 million of unpaid credit card receivables on **E-Debt.com.** Insiders say Sprint's $145 million portfolio fetched $2 million—better low margins than none.

Bum Loan Sources
E-Debt.com
DebtMarketplace.com
AssetExchange.com

Point: When using an accounts receivable method for estimating uncollectibles, the allowance account balance is adjusted to equal the estimate of uncollectibles.

Percent of accounts receivable method. The *percent of accounts receivable method* assumes that a given percent of a company's receivables is uncollectible. This percent is based on past experience and is impacted by current conditions such as economic trends and customer difficulties. The total dollar amount of all receivables is multiplied by this percent to get the estimated dollar amount of uncollectible accounts—reported in the balance sheet as the Allowance for Doubtful Accounts.

To illustrate, assume that Musicland has $50,000 of accounts receivable on December 31, 2005. Experience suggests 5% of its receivables are uncollectible. This means that after the adjusting entry is posted, we want the Allowance for Doubtful Accounts to show a $2,500 credit balance (5% of $50,000). (*Note:* Its beginning balance is $2,200, which is 5% of the $44,000 accounts receivable on December 31, 2004—see Exhibit 9.10.) Also, during 2005, accounts of customers are written off on February 6, July 10, and November 20. Thus, the account has a $200 credit balance prior to the December 31, 2005, adjustment. The adjusting entry to give the allowance account the estimated $2,500 balance is

Global: In China, government regulation constrains the *percents* used to estimate bad debts.

Dec. 31	Bad Debts Expense	2,300	
	Allowance for Doubtful Accounts		2,300
	To record estimated bad debts.		

Assets = Liabilities + Equity
−2,300 −2,300

Exhibit 9.10 shows the effects of these transactions and adjustments on the allowance account.

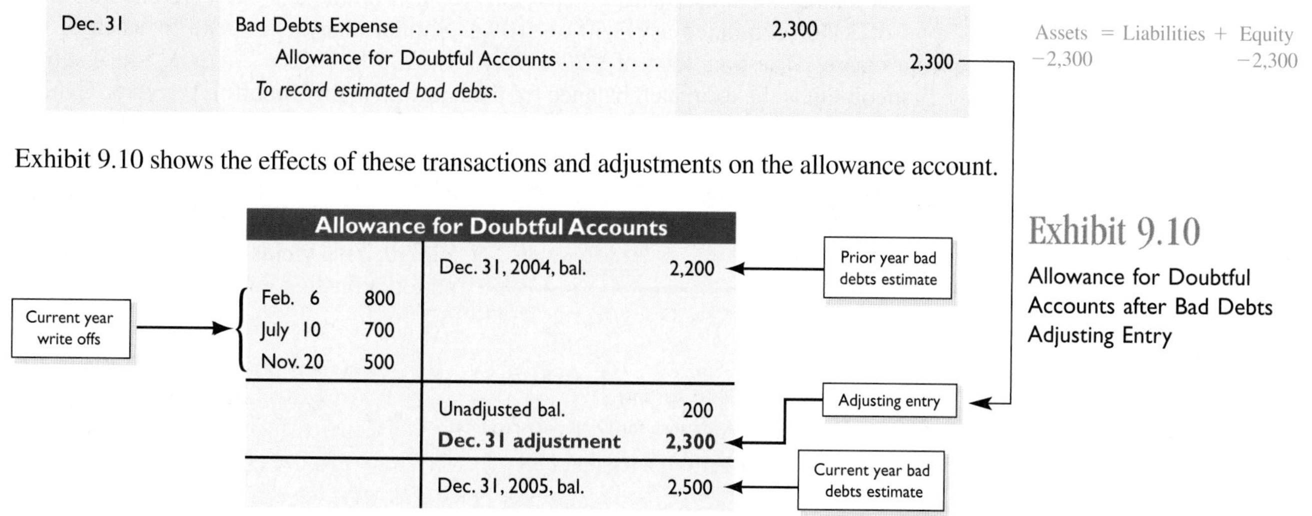

Exhibit 9.10

Allowance for Doubtful Accounts after Bad Debts Adjusting Entry

Aging of accounts receivable method. The **aging of accounts receivable** method uses both past and current receivables information to estimate the allowance amount. Specifically, each receivable is classified by how long it is past its due date. Then estimates of uncollectible amounts are made assuming that the longer an amount is past due, the more likely it is to be uncollectible. Classifications are often based on 30-day periods. After the amounts are classified (or aged), experience is used to estimate the percent of each uncollectible class. These percents are applied to the amounts in each class and then totaled to get the estimated balance of the Allowance for Doubtful Accounts. This computation is performed by setting up a schedule such as Exhibit 9.11.

Decision Insight

When you buy online with a credit card, you put your account number at risk. If, however, you slide a smart card into a reader on your PC and enter your password, the merchant never gets your account number but only a code authorizing the sale.

Exhibit 9.11

Aging of Accounts Receivable

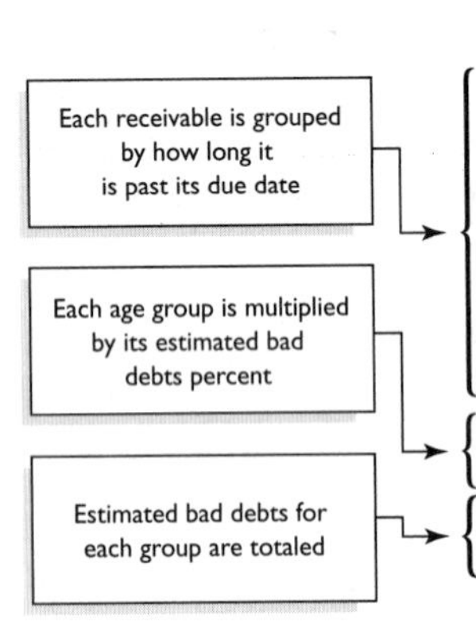

MUSICLAND
Schedule of Accounts Receivable by Age

Customer	Totals	Not Yet Due	1 to 30 Days Past Due	31 to 60 Days Past Due	61 to 90 Days Past Due	Over 90 Days Past Due
Carlos Abbot	$ 450	$ 450				
Jaime Allen	710			$ 710		
Chavez Andres	500	300	$ 200			
Belicia Co.	740				$ 100	$ 640
Zamora Services	1,000	810	190			
Totals	$ 49,900	$ 37,000	$ 6,500	$ 3,500	$ 1,900	$ 1,000
Percent uncollectible		x 2%	x 5%	x 10%	x 25%	x 40%
Estimated uncollectible	$ 2,290	$ 740	$ 325	$ 350	$ 475	$ 400

Point: Experience shows the longer a receivable is past due, the lower is the likelihood of collection. An aging schedule exploits this relation.

Point: Spreadsheet software is especially useful for estimating bad debts. Using both current and past data, estimates of bad debts are obtained under different assumptions.

Exhibit 9.11 lists each customer's individual balances assigned to one of five classes based on its days past due. The amounts in each class are totaled and multiplied by the estimated percent of uncollectible accounts for each class. The percents used are regularly reviewed to reflect changes in the company and economy.

To explain, notice that Musicland has $3,500 in accounts receivable that are 31 to 60 days past due. Its management estimates 10% of the amounts in this age class are uncollectible, or a total of $350 (computed as $3,500 × 10%). Similar analysis is done for each of the other four classes. The final total of $2,290($740 + $325 + $350 + $475 + $400) shown in the first column is the estimated balance for the Allowance for Doubtful Accounts. Exhibit 9.12 shows that since the allowance account has an unadjusted credit balance of $200, the required adjustment to the Allowance for Doubtful Accounts is $2,090. This yields the following end-of-period adjusting entry:

Exhibit 9.12

Computation of the Required Adjustment for an Accounts Receivable Method

Unadjusted balance	$ 200 credit
Estimated balance	2,290 credit
Required adjustment	**$2,090 credit**

Assets = Liabilities + Equity
−2,090 −2,090

Dec. 31	Bad Debts Expense	2,090	
	Allowance for Doubtful Accounts		2,090
	To record estimated bad debts.		

Alternatively, if the allowance account had an unadjusted *debit* balance of $500 (instead of the $200 credit balance), its required adjustment would be computed as follows:

Global: International practices vary as to when receivables are written off. Some do not write off an account until it is 1 to 2 years past due.

Unadjusted balance	$ 500 debit	
Estimated balance	2,290 credit	← Current year bad debts estimate
Adjusting entry → **Required adjustment ....**	**$ 2,790 credit**	

The entry to record the end-of-period adjustment for this alternative case is

Dec. 31	Bad Debts Expense	2,790	
	Allowance for Doubtful Accounts		2,790
	To record estimated bad debts.		

Assets = Liabilities + Equity
−2,790 −2,790

The aging of accounts receivable method is a more detailed examination of specific accounts and is usually the most reliable of the estimation methods.

Exhibit 9.13 summarizes the principles guiding all three estimation methods and their focus of analysis.

Decision Maker

Labor Union Chief One week prior to labor contract negotiations, financial statements are released showing no income growth. A 10% growth was predicted. Your analysis finds that the company increased its allowance for uncollectibles from 1.5% to 4.5% of receivables. Without this change, income would show a 9% growth. Does this analysis impact negotiations?

Answer—p. 368

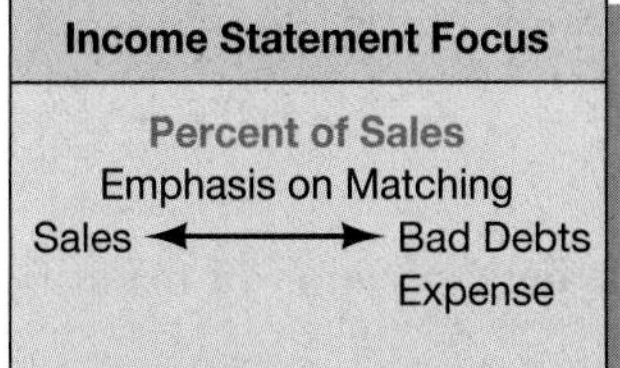

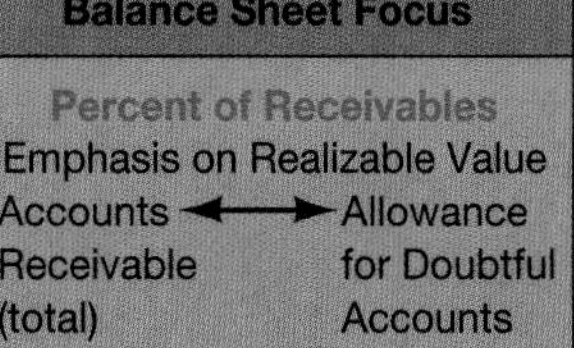

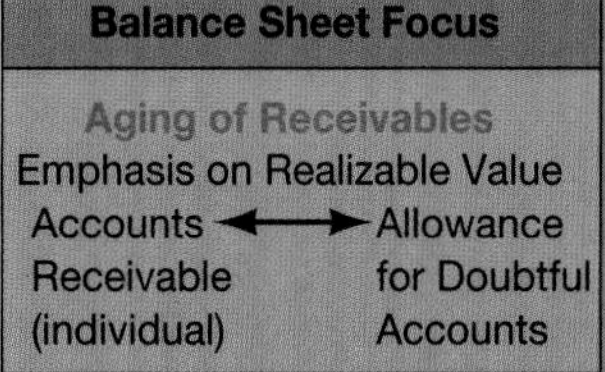

Exhibit 9.13
Methods to Estimate Bad Debts

Quick Check

3. Why must bad debts expense be estimated if such an estimate is possible?
4. What term describes the balance sheet valuation of Accounts Receivable less the Allowance for Doubtful Accounts?
5. Why is estimated bad debts expense credited to a contra account (Allowance for Doubtful Accounts) rather than to the Accounts Receivable account?
6. SnoBoard Company's year-end balance in its Allowance for Doubtful Accounts is a credit of $440. By aging accounts receivable, it estimates that $6,142 is uncollectible. Prepare SnoBoard's year-end adjusting entry for bad debts.
7. Record entries for these transactions assuming the allowance method is used:

   Jan. 10 The $300 account of customer Cool Jam is determined uncollectible.

   April 12 Cool Jam unexpectedly pays in full the account that was deemed uncollectible on January 10.

Answers—p. 368

Notes Receivable

C2 Describe a note receivable and the computation of its maturity date and interest.

A **promissory note** is a written promise to pay a specified amount of money, usually with interest, either on demand or at a definite future date. Promissory notes are used in many transactions, including paying for products and services, and lending and borrowing money. Sellers sometimes ask for a note to replace an account receivable when a customer requests additional time to pay a past-due account. For legal reasons, sellers generally prefer to receive notes when the credit period is long and when the receivable is for a large amount. If a lawsuit is needed to collect from a customer, a note is the buyer's written acknowledgment of the debt, its amount, and its terms.

Topic Tackler 9-2

Exhibit 9.14 shows a simple promissory note dated July 10, 2005. For this note, Julia Browne promises to pay TechCom or to its order (according to TechCom's instructions) a specified amount of money ($1,000), called the **principal of a note,** at a definite future date (October 8, 2005). As the one who signed the note and promised to pay it at maturity, Browne is the **maker of the note.** As the person to whom the note is payable, TechCom is the **payee of the note.** To Browne, the note is a liability called a *note payable*. To TechCom, the same note is an asset called a *note receivable*. This note bears interest at 12%, as written on the note. **Interest** is the charge for using (not paying) the money until a later date. To a borrower, interest is an expense. To a lender, it is revenue.

Exhibit 9.14

Promissory Note

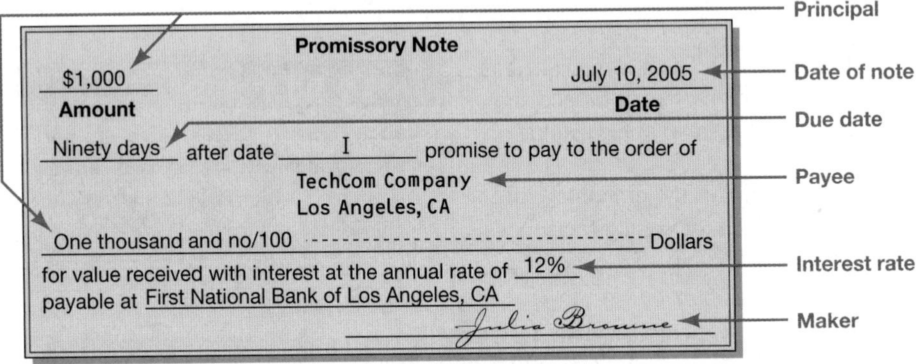

Computing Maturity and Interest

This section describes key computations for notes including the determination of maturity date, period covered, and interest computation.

Maturity Date and Period The **maturity date of a note** is the day the note (principal and interest) must be repaid. The *period* of a note is the time from the note's (contract) date to its maturity date. Many notes mature in less than a full year, and the period they cover is often expressed in days. When the time of a note is expressed in days, its maturity date is the specified number of days after the note's date. As an example, a five-day note dated June 15 matures and is due on June 20. A 90-day note dated July 10 matures on October 8. This October 8 due date is computed as shown in Exhibit 9.15. The period of a note is sometimes expressed in months or years. When months are used, the note matures and is payable in the month of its maturity on the *same day of the month* as its original date. A nine-month note dated July 10, for instance, is payable on April 10. The same analysis applies when years are used.

Exhibit 9.15

Maturity Date Computation

Days in July	31	
Minus the date of the note	10	
Days remaining in July		21
Add days in August		31
Add days in September		30
Days to equal 90 days, or **maturity date of October 8**		8
Period of the note in days		90

Interest Computation *Interest* is the cost of borrowing money for the borrower or, alternatively, the profit from lending money for the lender. Unless otherwise stated, the rate of interest on a note is the rate charged for the use of the principal for one year. The formula for computing interest on a note is shown in Exhibit 9.16.

Principal of the note × **Annual interest rate** × **Time expressed in years** = **Interest**

Exhibit 9.16

Computation of Interest Formula

To simplify interest computations, a year is commonly treated as having 360 days (called the *banker's rule*). **We treat a year as having 360 days for interest computations in the examples and assignments.** Using the promissory note in Exhibit 9.14 where we have a 90-day, 12%, $1,000 note, the total interest is computed as follows:

$$\$1{,}000 \times 12\% \times \frac{90}{360} = \$1{,}000 \times 0.12 \times 0.25 = \$30$$

Recognizing Notes Receivable

P3 Record the receipt of a note receivable.

Notes receivable are usually recorded in a single Notes Receivable account to simplify recordkeeping. The original notes are kept on file, including information on the maker, rate of interest, and due date. (When a company holds a large number of notes, it sometimes sets up a controlling account and a subsidiary ledger for notes. This is similar to the handling of accounts receivable.) To illustrate the recording for the receipt of a note, we use the $1,000, 90-day, 12% promissory note in Exhibit 9.14. TechCom received this note at the time of a product sale to Julia Browne. This transaction is recorded as follows:

July 10*	Notes Receivable	1,000	
	Sales		1,000
	Sold goods in exchange for a 90-day, 12% note.		

* We omit the entry to Dr. Cost of Sales and Cr. Merchandise Inventory to focus on sales and receivables.

Assets	= Liabilities	+ Equity
+1,000		+1,000

When a seller accepts a note from an overdue customer as a way to grant a time extension on a past-due account receivable, it will often collect part of the past-due balance in cash. This partial payment forces a concession from the customer, reduces the customer's debt (and the seller's risk), and produces a note for a smaller amount. To illustrate, assume that TechCom agreed to accept $232 in cash along with a $600, 60-day, 15% note from Jo Cook to settle her $832 past-due account. TechCom made the following entry to record receipt of this cash and note:

Point: Notes receivable often are a major part of a company's assets. Likewise, notes payable often are a large part of a company's liabilities.

Oct. 5	Cash	232	
	Notes Receivable	600	
	Accounts Receivable—J. Cook		832
	Received cash and note to settle account.		

Assets	= Liabilities	+ Equity
+232		
+600		
−832		

Valuing and Settling Notes

P4 Record the honoring and dishonoring of a note and adjustments for interest.

Recording an Honored Note The principal and interest of a note are due on its maturity date. The maker of the note usually *honors* the note and pays it in full. To illustrate, when J. Cook pays the note above on its due date, TechCom records it as follows:

Dec. 4	Cash	615	
	Notes Receivable		600
	Interest Revenue		15
	Collect note with interest of $600 × 15% × 60/360.		

Assets	= Liabilities	+ Equity
+615		+15
−600		

Interest Revenue, also called *Interest Earned,* is reported on the income statement.

Recording a Dishonored Note When a note's maker is unable or refuses to pay at maturity, the note is *dishonored.* The act of dishonoring a note does not relieve the maker of the obligation to pay. The payee should use every legitimate means to collect. How do companies report this event? The balance of the Notes Receivable account should include only those notes that have not matured. Thus, when a note is dishonored, we remove the amount of this note from the Notes Receivable account and charge it back to an account receivable from its maker. To illustrate, TechCom holds an $800, 12%, 60-day note of Greg Hart. At maturity, Hart dishonors the note. TechCom records this dishonoring of the note as follows:

Point: When posting a dishonored note to a customer's account, an explanation is included so as not to misinterpret the debit as a sale on account.

Assets = Liabilities + Equity
+816 +16
−800

Oct. 14	Accounts Receivable—G. Hart	816	
	Interest Revenue		16
	Notes Receivable		800
	To charge account of G. Hart for a dishonored note and interest of $800 × 12% × 60/360.		

Charging a dishonored note back to the account of its maker serves two purposes. First, it removes the amount of the note from the Notes Receivable account and records the dishonored note in the maker's account. Second, and more important, if the maker of the dishonored note applies for credit in the future, his or her account will reveal all past dealings, including the dishonored note. Restoring the account also reminds the company to continue collection efforts from Hart for both principal and interest. The entry records the full amount, including interest, to ensure that it is included in collection efforts.

Point: Reporting the details of notes is consistent with the **full disclosure principle,** which requires financial statements (including footnotes) to report all relevant information.

Recording End-of-Period Interest Adjustment When notes receivable are outstanding at the end of a period, any accrued interest earned is computed and recorded. To illustrate, on December 16, TechCom accepts a $3,000, 60-day, 12% note from a customer in granting an extension on a past-due account. When TechCom's accounting period ends on December 31, $15 of interest has accrued on this note ($3,000 × 12% × 15/360). The following adjusting entry records this revenue:

Assets = Liabilities + Equity
+15 +15

Dec. 31	Interest Receivable	15	
	Interest Revenue		15
	To record accrued interest earned.		

Interest Revenue appears on the income statement, and Interest Receivable appears on the balance sheet as a current asset. When the December 16 note is collected on February 14, TechCom's entry to record the cash receipt is

Assets = Liabilities + Equity
+3,060 +45
−15
−3,000

Feb. 14	Cash	3,060	
	Interest Revenue		45
	Interest Receivable		15
	Notes Receivable		3,000
	Received payment of note and its interest.		

Total interest earned on the 60-day note is $60. The $15 credit to Interest Receivable on February 14 reflects the collection of the interest accrued from the December 31 adjusting entry. The $45 interest earned reflects TechCom's revenue from holding the note from January 1 to February 14 of the current period.

Quick Check

8. Irwin purchases $7,000 of merchandise from Stamford on December 16, 2005. Stamford accepts Irwin's $7,000, 90-day, 12% note as payment. Stamford's accounting period ends on December 31, and it does not make reversing entries. Prepare entries for Stamford on December 16, 2005, and December 31, 2005.
9. Using the information in Quick Check 8, prepare Stamford's March 16, 2006, entry if Irwin dishonors the note.

Answers—p. 368

Disposing of Receivables

Companies can convert receivables to cash before they are due. Reasons for this include the need for cash or the desire not to be involved in collection activities. Converting receivables is usually done either by (1) selling them or (2) using them as security for a loan. A recent survey shows that about 20% of companies obtain cash from either selling receivables or pledging them as security. In some industries such as textiles, apparel and furniture, this is common practice.

Selling Receivables

C3 Explain how receivables can be converted to cash before maturity.

A company can sell all or a portion of its receivables to a finance company or bank. The buyer, called a *factor,* charges the seller a *factoring fee* and then the buyer takes ownership of the receivables and receives cash when they come due. By incurring a factoring fee, the seller receives cash earlier and can pass the risk of bad debts to the factor. The seller can also choose to avoid costs of billing and accounting for the receivables. To illustrate, if TechCom sells $20,000 of its accounts receivable and is charged a 4% factoring fee, it records this sale as follows:

Global: Firms in export sales increasingly sell their receivables to factors.

Aug. 15	Cash	19,200	
	Factoring Fee Expense	800	
	Accounts Receivable		20,000
	Sold accounts receivable for cash, less 4% fee.		

Assets	= Liabilities	+ Equity
+19,200		−800
−20,000		

The accounting for sales of notes receivable is similar to that for accounts receivable. The detailed entries are covered in advanced courses.

Pledging Receivables

A company can raise cash by borrowing money and *pledging* its receivables as security for the loan. Pledging receivables does not transfer the risk of bad debts to the lender because the borrower retains ownership of the receivables. If the borrower defaults on the loan, the lender has a right to be paid from the cash receipts of the receivable when collected. To illustrate, when TechCom borrows $35,000 and pledges its receivables as security, it records this transaction as follows:

Point: When accounts receivable are sold, each subsidiary ledger account is credited along with the controlling account for the total.

Point: Chock Full O'Nuts reports, "Outstanding borrowings . . . are collateralized by, among other things, the trade accounts receivable."

Aug. 20	Cash	35,000	
	Notes Payable		35,000
	Borrowed money with a note secured by pledging receivables.		

Assets	= Liabilities	+ Equity
+35,000	+35,000	

Decision Insight

Money Source **Zenith** obtained a three-year, $60 million loan by pledging accounts receivable as collateral, and **Intel** converted accounts receivable to a note receivable for a major customer.

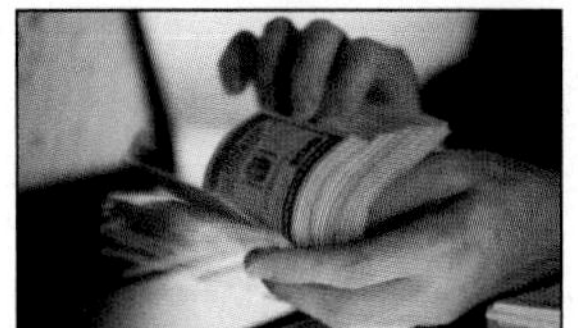

Since pledged receivables are committed as security for a specific loan, the borrower's financial statements disclose the pledging of them. TechCom, for instance, includes the following note with its statements: *Accounts receivable of $40,000 are pledged as security for a $35,000 note payable.*

Decision Analysis — Accounts Receivable Turnover

A1 Compute accounts receivable turnover and use it to help assess financial condition.

For a company selling on credit, we want to assess both the quality and liquidity of its accounts receivable. *Quality* of receivables refers to the likelihood of collection without loss. Experience shows that the longer receivables are outstanding beyond their due date, the lower the likelihood of collection. *Liquidity* of receivables refers to the speed of collection. **Accounts receivable turnover** is a measure of both the quality and liquidity of accounts receivable. It indicates how often, on average, receivables are received and collected during the period. The formula for this ratio is shown in Exhibit 9.17.

Exhibit 9.17

Accounts Receivable Turnover

$$\textbf{Accounts receivable turnover} = \frac{\textbf{Net sales}}{\textbf{Average accounts receivable}}$$

We prefer to use net *credit* sales in the numerator because cash sales do not create receivables. However, since financial statements rarely report net credit sales, our analysis uses net sales. The denominator is the *average* accounts receivable balance, computed as (Beginning balance + Ending balance) ÷ 2. TechCom has an accounts receivable turnover of 5.1. This indicates its average accounts receivable balance is converted into cash 5.1 times during the period. Exhibit 9.18 shows graphically this turnover activity for TechCom.

Exhibit 9.18

Rate of Accounts Receivable Turnover for TechCom

Accounts receivable turnover also reflects how well management is doing in granting credit to customers in a desire to increase sales. A high turnover in comparison with competitors suggests that management should consider using more liberal credit terms to increase sales. A low turnover suggests management should consider stricter credit terms and more aggressive collection efforts to avoid having its resources tied up in accounts receivable.

Point: **Credit risk ratio** is computed by dividing the Allowance for Doubtful Accounts by Accounts Receivable. The higher this ratio, the higher is credit risk.

To illustrate, we take data from two competitors: **Dell Computer** and **Apple Computer**. Exhibit 9.19 shows accounts receivable turnover for both companies.

Exhibit 9.19

Analysis Using Accounts Receivable Turnover

Company	Figure ($ millions)	2002	2001	2000
Dell	Net sales	$35,404	$31,168	$31,888
	Average accounts receivable	$ 2,428	$ 2,347	$ 2,752
	Accounts receivable turnover	**14.6**	**13.3**	**11.6**
Apple	Net sales	$ 5,742	$ 5,363	$ 7,983
	Average accounts receivable	$ 516	$ 710	$ 817
	Accounts receivable turnover	**11.1**	**7.6**	**9.8**

Dell's 2002 turnover is computed ($ millions) as $35,404/$2,428 = 14.6. This means that Dell's average accounts receivable balance was converted into cash 14.6 times in 2002. Also, its turnover improved in 2002 (versus its prior two years), and it is superior to that of Apple. Is Dell's turnover too high? Since sales are markedly growing over this time period, Dell's turnover does not appear to be too high. Instead, it seems to be doing well in managing receivables. Similarly, Apple has improved its management of receivables during this period. Turnover for competitors is generally in the range of 7 to 11 for this same period.[1]

Decision Maker

Family Physician Your practice is less profitable, so you hire a health care analyst. The analyst highlights several points including the following: *"Accounts receivable turnover is too low. Tighter credit policies are recommended along with discontinuing service to those most delayed in payments."* How do you interpret these recommendations? What actions do you take?

Answer—p. 368

Demonstration Problem

Clayco Company completes the following selected transactions during year 2005:

July 14	Writes off a $750 account receivable arising from a sale to Briggs Company that dates to 10 months ago. (Clayco Company uses the allowance method.)
30	Clayco Company receives a $1,000, 90-day, 10% note in exchange for merchandise sold to Sumrell Company (the merchandise cost $600).
Aug. 15	Receives $2,000 cash plus a $10,000 note from JT Co. in exchange for merchandise that sells for $12,000 (its cost is $8,000). The note is dated August 15, bears 12% interest, and matures in 120 days.
Nov. 1	Completed a $200 credit card sale with a 4% fee (the cost of sales is $150). The cash is received immediately from the credit card company.
3	Sumrell Company refuses to pay the note that was due to Clayco Company on October 28. Prepare the journal entry to charge the dishonored note plus accrued interest to Sumrell Company's accounts receivable.
5	Completed a $500 credit card sale with a 5% fee (the cost of sales is $300). The payment from the credit card company is received on Nov. 9.
15	Received the full amount of $750 from Briggs Company that was previously written off on July 14. Record the bad debts recovery.
Dec. 13	Received payment of principal plus interest from JT for the August 15 note.

Required

1. Prepare journal entries to record these transactions on Clayco Company's books.
2. Prepare an adjusting journal entry as of December 31, 2005, assuming the following:
   a. Bad debts expense is estimated to be $20,400 by aging accounts receivable. The unadjusted balance of the Allowance for Doubtful Accounts is $1,000 debit.
   b. Alternatively, assume that bad debts expense is estimated using the percent of sales method. The Allowance for Doubtful Accounts had a $1,000 debit balance before adjustment, and the company estimates bad debts to be 1% of its credit sales of $2,000,000.

Planning the Solution

- Examine each transaction to determine the accounts affected, and then record the entries.
- For the year-end adjustment, record the bad debts expense for the two approaches.

[1] As an estimate of *average days' sales uncollected,* we compute how many days (*on average*) it takes to collect receivables as follows: 365 days ÷ accounts receivable turnover. An increase in this *average collection period* can signal a decline in its customers' financial condition.

Solution to Demonstration Problem

1.

Date	Account	Debit	Credit
July 14	Allowance for Doubtful Accounts	750	
	Accounts Receivable—Briggs Co.		750
	Wrote off an uncollectible account.		
July 30	Notes Receivable—Sumrell Co.	1,000	
	Sales		1,000
	Sold merchandise for a 90-day, 10% note.		
July 30	Cost of Goods Sold	600	
	Merchandise Inventory		600
	To record the cost of July 30 sale.		
Aug. 15	Cash	2,000	
	Notes Receivable—JT Co.	10,000	
	Sales		12,000
	Sold merchandise to customer for $2,000 cash and $10,000 note.		
Aug. 15	Cost of Goods Sold	8,000	
	Merchandise Inventory		8,000
	To record the cost of Aug. 15 sale.		
Nov. 1	Cash	192	
	Credit Card Expense	8	
	Sales		200
	To record credit card sale less a 4% credit card expense.		
Nov. 1	Cost of Goods Sold	150	
	Merchandise Inventory		150
	To record the cost of Nov. 1 sale.		
Nov. 3	Accounts Receivable—Sumrell Co.	1,025	
	Interest Revenue		25
	Notes Receivable—Sumrell Co.		1,000
	To charge account of Sumrell Company for a $1,000 dishonored note and interest of $1,000 × 10% × 90/360.		
Nov. 5	Accounts Receivable—Credit Card Co.	475	
	Credit Card Expense	25	
	Sales		500
	To record credit card sale less a 5% credit card expense.		
Nov. 5	Cost of Goods Sold	300	
	Merchandise Inventory		300
	To record the cost of Nov. 5 sale.		
Nov. 9	Cash	475	
	Accounts Receivable—Credit Card Co.		475
	To record cash receipt from Nov. 5 sale.		
Nov. 15	Accounts Receivable—Briggs Co.	750	
	Allowance for Doubtful Accounts		750
	To reinstate the account of Briggs Company previously written off.		
Nov. 15	Cash	750	
	Accounts Receivable—Briggs Co.		750
	Cash received in full payment of account.		
Dec. 13	Cash	10,400	
	Interest Revenue		400
	Note Receivable—JT Co.		10,000
	Collect note with interest of $10,000 × 12% × 120/360.		

2a. Aging of accounts receivable method:

Dec. 31	Bad Debts Expense	21,400	
	Allowance for Doubtful Accounts		21,400
	To adjust allowance account from a $1,000 debit balance to a $20,400 credit balance.		

2b. Percent of sales method:*

Dec. 31	Bad Debts Expense	20,000	
	Allowance for Doubtful Accounts		20,000
	To provide for bad debts as 1% × $2,000,000 in credit sales.		

---

* For the income statement approach, which requires estimating bad debts as a percent of sales or credit sales, the Allowance account balance is *not* considered when making the adjusting entry.

Summary

C1 Describe accounts receivable and how they occur and are recorded. Accounts receivable are amounts due from customers for credit sales. A subsidiary ledger lists amounts owed by each customer. Credit sales arise from at least two sources: (1) sales on credit and (2) credit card sales. *Sales on credit* refers to a company's granting credit directly to customers. Credit card sales involve customers' use of third-party credit cards.

C2 Describe a note receivable and the computation of its maturity date and interest. A note receivable is a written promise to pay a specified amount of money at a definite future date. The maturity date is the day the note (principal and interest) must be repaid. Interest rates are normally stated in annual terms. The amount of interest on the note is computed by expressing time as a fraction of one year and multiplying the note's principal by this fraction and the annual interest rate.

C3 Explain how receivables can be converted to cash before maturity. Receivables can be converted to cash before maturity in three ways. First, a company can sell accounts receivable to a factor, who charges a factoring fee. Second, a company can borrow money by signing a note payable that is secured by pledging the accounts receivable. Third, notes receivable can be discounted at (sold to) a financial institution.

A1 Compute accounts receivable turnover and use it to help assess financial condition. Accounts receivable turnover is a measure of both the quality and liquidity of accounts receivable. The accounts receivable turnover measure indicates how often, on average, receivables are received and collected during the period. Accounts receivable turnover is computed as net sales divided by average accounts receivable.

P1 Apply the direct write-off and allowance methods to account for accounts receivable. The direct write-off method charges Bad Debts Expense when accounts are written off as uncollectible. This method is acceptable only when the amount of bad debts expense is immaterial. Under the allowance method, bad debts expense is recorded with an adjustment at the end of each accounting period that debits the Bad Debts Expense account and credits the Allowance for Doubtful Accounts. The uncollectible accounts are later written off with a debit to the Allowance for Doubtful Accounts.

P2 Estimate uncollectibles using methods based on sales and accounts receivable. Uncollectibles are estimated by focusing on either (1) the income statement relation between bad debts expense and credit sales or (2) the balance sheet relation between accounts receivable and the allowance for doubtful accounts. The first approach emphasizes the matching principle using the income statement. The second approach emphasizes realizable value of accounts receivable using the balance sheet.

P3 Record the receipt of a note receivable. A note received is recorded at its principal amount by debiting the Notes Receivable account. The credit amount is to the asset, product, or service provided in return for the note.

P4 Record the honoring and dishonoring of a note and adjustments for interest. When a note is honored, the payee debits the money received and credits both Notes Receivable and Interest Revenue. Dishonored notes are credited to Notes Receivable and debited to Accounts Receivable (to the account of the maker in an attempt to collect), and Interest Revenue is recorded for interest earned for the time the note is held.

Guidance Answers to **Decision Maker** and **Decision Ethics**

Entrepreneur Analysis of credit card sales should weigh the benefits against the costs. The primary benefit is the potential to increase sales by attracting customers who prefer the convenience of credit cards. The primary cost is the fee charged by the credit card company for providing this service. Analysis should therefore estimate the expected increase in dollar sales from allowing credit card sales and then subtract (1) the normal costs and expenses and (2) the credit card fees associated with this expected increase in dollar sales. If your analysis shows an increase in profit from allowing credit card sales, your store should probably accept them.

Labor Union Chief Yes, this information is likely to impact your negotiations. The obvious question is why the company markedly increased this allowance. The large increase in this allowance means a substantial increase in bad debts expense *and* a decrease in earnings. This change (coming immediately prior to labor contract discussions) also raises concerns since it reduces the union's bargaining power for increased compensation. You want to ask management for supporting documentation justifying this increase. You also want data for two or three prior years and similar data from competitors. These data should give you some sense of whether the change in the allowance for uncollectibles is justified.

Family Physician The recommendations are twofold. First, the analyst suggests more stringent screening of patients' credit standing. Second, the analyst suggests dropping patients who are most overdue in payments. You are likely bothered by both suggestions. They are probably financially wise recommendations, but you are troubled by eliminating services to those less able to pay. One alternative is to follow the recommendations while implementing a care program directed at patients less able to pay for services. This allows you to continue services to patients less able to pay and lets you discontinue services to patients able but unwilling to pay.

Guidance Answers to **Quick Checks**

1. If cash is immediately received when credit card sales receipts are deposited, the company debits Cash at the time of sale. If the company does not receive payment until after it submits receipts to the credit card company, it debits Accounts Receivable at the time of sale. (Cash is later debited when payment is received from the credit card company.)

2. Credit card expenses are usually *recorded* and *incurred* at the time of their related sales, not when cash is received from the credit card company.

3. If possible, bad debts expense must be matched with the sales that gave rise to the accounts receivable. This requires that companies estimate future bad debts at the end of each period before they learn which accounts are uncollectible.

4. Realizable value (also called *net realizable value*).

5. The estimated amount of bad debts expense cannot be credited to the Accounts Receivable account because the specific customer accounts that will prove uncollectible cannot yet be identified and removed from the accounts receivable subsidiary ledger. Moreover, if only the Accounts Receivable account is credited, its balance would not equal the sum of its subsidiary account balances.

6.

Dec. 31	Bad Debts Expense	5,702	
	Allowance for Doubtful Accounts		5,702

7.

Jan. 10	Allowance for Doubtful Accounts	300	
	Accounts Receivable—Cool Jam		300
Apr. 12	Accounts Receivable—Cool Jam	300	
	Allowance for Doubtful Accounts		300
Apr. 12	Cash	300	
	Accounts Receivable—Cool Jam		300

8.

Dec. 16	Note Receivable—Irwin	7,000	
	Sales		7,000
Dec. 31	Interest Receivable	35	
	Interest Revenue		35
	($7,000 × 12% × 15/360)		

9.

Mar. 16	Accounts Receivable—Irwin	7,210	
	Interest Revenue		175
	Interest Receivable		35
	Notes Receivable—Irwin		7,000

Key Terms

Key Terms are available at the book's Website for learning and testing in an online Flashcard Format.

Accounts receivable (p. 350)
Accounts receivable turnover (p. 364)
Aging of accounts receivable (p. 358)
Allowance for Doubtful Accounts (p. 355)
Allowance method (p. 354)
Bad debts (p. 353)
Direct write-off method (p. 354)
Interest (p. 360)
Maker of the note (p. 360)
Matching principle (p. 354)
Materiality principle (p. 354)
Maturity date of a note (p. 360)
Payee of the note (p. 360)
Principal of a note (p. 360)
Promissory note (or note) (p. 359)
Realizable value (p. 355)

Personal Interactive Quiz

Personal Interactive Quizzes A and B are available at the book's Website to reinforce and assess your learning.

Discussion Questions

1. How do sellers benefit from allowing their customers to use credit cards?
2. Why does the direct write-off method of accounting for bad debts usually fail to match revenues and expenses?
3. Explain the accounting principle of materiality.
4. Explain why writing off a bad debt against the Allowance for Doubtful Accounts does not reduce the estimated realizable value of a company's accounts receivable.
5. Why does the Bad Debts Expense account usually not have the same adjusted balance as the Allowance for Doubtful Accounts?
6. Why might a business prefer a note receivable to an account receivable?
7. Refer to **Krispy Kreme**'s balance sheet in Appendix A. What percent of accounts receivable at February 2, 2003, has been set aside as an allowance for doubtful accounts? How does this percent compare to the prior year?
8. Refer to the balance sheet of **Tastykake** in Appendix A. Does it use the direct write-off method or allowance method to account for doubtful accounts? What is the realizable value of its accounts receivable as of December 28, 2002? What is another name for the Allowance for Doubtful Accounts?
9. Refer to the balance sheet of **Harley-Davidson** in Appendix A. What two types of receivables does Harley show in its current asset section of the balance sheet?

Red numbers denote Discussion Questions that involve decision-making.

***Homework Manager** repeats all numerical Quick Studies on the book's Website with new numbers.*

QUICK STUDY

QS 9-1
Credit card sales
C1

Prepare journal entries for the following credit card sales transactions (the company uses the perpetual inventory system):

1. Sold $10,000 of merchandise, that cost $7,500, on MasterCard credit cards. The net cash receipts from sales are immediately deposited in the seller's bank account. MasterCard charges a 5% fee.
2. Sold $3,000 of merchandise, that cost $1,500, on an assortment of credit cards. Net cash receipts are received 7 days later, and a 4% fee is charged.

QS 9-2
Allowance method for bad debts
P1

Milner Corp. uses the allowance method to account for uncollectibles. On October 31, it wrote off a $1,000 account of a customer, C. Schaub. On December 9, it receives a $200 payment from Schaub.

1. Prepare the journal entry or entries for October 31.
2. Prepare the journal entry or entries for December 9; assume no additional money is expected from Schaub.

QS 9-3
Percent of accounts receivable and percent of sales methods
P1 P2

Wecker Company's year-end unadjusted trial balance shows accounts receivable of $89,000, allowance for doubtful accounts of $500 (credit), and sales of $270,000. Uncollectibles are estimated to be 1.5% of accounts receivable.

1. Prepare the December 31 year-end adjusting entry for uncollectibles.
2. What amount would have been used in the year-end adjusting entry if the allowance account had a year-end unadjusted debit balance of $200?
3. Assume the same facts as in part 1, except that Wecker estimates uncollectibles as 1.0% of sales. Prepare the December 31 year-end adjusting entry for uncollectibles.

QS 9-4
Note receivable
P3 P4

On August 2, 2005, JLK Co. receives a $5,500, 90-day, 12% note from customer Tom Menke as payment on his $5,500 account. Prepare JLK's journal entries for August 2 and for the note's maturity date assuming the note is honored by Menke.

QS 9-5
Note receivable
C2 P4

Dekon Company's December 31 year-end unadjusted trial balance shows an $8,000 balance in Notes Receivable. This balance is from one 6% note dated December 1, with a period of 45 days. Prepare journal entries for December 31 and for the note's maturity date assuming it is honored.

QS 9-6
Accounts receivable turnover
A1 

The following data are taken from the comparative balance sheets of Fulton Company. Compute and interpret its accounts receivable turnover for year 2005 (competitors average a turnover of 7.5).

	2005	2004
Accounts receivable	$152,900	$133,700
Net sales	754,200	810,600

***Homework Manager** repeats all numerical Exercises on the book's Website with new numbers.*

EXERCISES

Exercise 9-1
Accounting for credit card sales
C1 

Petri Company allows customers to use two credit cards in charging purchases. With the Omni Card, Petri receives an immediate credit to its account when it deposits sales receipts. Omni Card assesses a 4% service charge for credit card sales. The second credit card that Petri accepts is the Continental Bank Card. Petri sends its accumulated receipts to Continental Bank on a weekly basis and is paid by Continental about a week later. Continental Bank assesses a 2.5% charge on sales for using its card. Prepare journal entries to record the following selected credit card transactions of Petri Company:

Apr. 8 Sold merchandise for $9,200 (that had cost $6,800) and accepted the customer's Omni Card. The Omni receipts are immediately deposited in Petri's bank account.
12 Sold merchandise for $5,400 (that had cost $3,500) and accepted the customer's Continental Bank Card. Transferred $5,400 of credit card receipts to Continental Bank, requesting payment.
20 Received Continental Bank's check for the April 12 billing, less the service charge.

Exercise 9-2
Accounts receivable subsidiary ledger; schedule of accounts receivable
C1

Sami Company recorded the following selected transactions during November 2005:

Nov. 5	Accounts Receivable—Surf Shop	4,417	
	Sales		4,417
10	Accounts Receivable—Yum Enterprises	1,250	
	Sales		1,250
13	Accounts Receivable—Matt Albin............	733	
	Sales		733
21	Sales Returns and Allowances	189	
	Accounts Receivable—Matt Albin		189
30	Accounts Receivable—Surf Shop	2,606	
	Sales		2,606

1. Open a general ledger having T-accounts for Accounts Receivable, Sales, and Sales Returns and Allowances. Also open an accounts receivable subsidiary ledger having a T-account for each customer. Post these entries to both the general ledger and the accounts receivable ledger.

2. Prepare a schedule of accounts receivable (see Exhibit 9.4) and compare its total with the balance of the Accounts Receivable controlling account as of November 30.

Check Accounts Receivable ending balance, $8,817

Exercise 9-3
Percent of sales method; write-off
P1 P2

At year-end (December 31), Alvare Company estimates its bad debts as 0.5% of its annual credit sales of $875,000. Alvare records its Bad Debts Expense for that estimate. On the following February 1, Alvare decides that the $420 account of P. Coble is uncollectible and writes it off as a bad debt. On June 5, Coble unexpectedly pays the amount previously written off. Prepare the journal entries of Alvare to record these transactions and events of December 31, February 1, and June 5.

Exercise 9-4
Percent of accounts receivable method
P1 P2

At each calendar year-end, Cabool Supply Co. uses the percent of accounts receivable method to estimate bad debts. On December 31, 2005, it has outstanding accounts receivable of $53,000, and it estimates that 4% will be uncollectible. Prepare the adjusting entry to record bad debts expense for year 2005 under the assumption that the Allowance for Doubtful Accounts has (*a*) a $915 credit balance before the adjustment and (*b*) a $1,332 debit balance before the adjustment.

Exercise 9-5
Selling and pledging accounts receivable
C3

On June 30, Peña Co. has $125,900 of accounts receivable. Prepare journal entries to record the following selected July transactions. Also prepare any footnotes to the July 31 financial statements that result from these transactions. (The company uses the perpetual inventory system.)

July 4 Sold $6,295 of merchandise (that had cost $4,000) to customers on credit.
9 Sold $18,000 of accounts receivable to Center Bank. Center charges a 4% factoring fee.
17 Received $3,436 cash from customers in payment on their accounts.
27 Borrowed $10,000 cash from Center Bank, pledging $13,000 of accounts receivable as security for the loan.

Exercise 9-6
Honoring a note
P4

Prepare journal entries to record these selected transactions for Eduardo Company:

Nov. 1 Accepted a $5,000, 180-day, 6% note dated November 1 from Melosa Allen in granting a time extension on her past-due account receivable.
Dec. 31 Adjusted the year-end accounts for the accrued interest earned on the Allen note.
Apr. 30 Allen honors her note when presented for payment.

Exercise 9-7
Dishonoring a note
P4

Prepare journal entries to record the following selected transactions of Paloma Company:

Mar. 21 Accepted a $3,100, 180-day, 10% note dated March 21 from Salma Hernandez in granting a time extension on her past-due account receivable.
Sept. 17 Hernandez dishonors her note when it is presented for payment.
Dec. 31 After exhausting all legal means of collection, Paloma Company writes off Hernandez's account against the Allowance for Doubtful Accounts.

Exercise 9-8
Notes receivable transactions and entries
C2 P3 P4

Prepare journal entries for the following selected transactions of Deshawn Company:

2004

Dec. 13 Accepted a $10,000, 60-day, 8% note dated December 13 in granting Latisha Clark a time extension on her past-due account receivable.
31 Prepared an adjusting entry to record the accrued interest on the Clark note.

Check Dec. 31, Cr. Interest Revenue $40

2005

Feb. 11 Received Clark's payment for principal and interest on the note dated December 13.

Check Feb. 11, Dr. Cash $10,133

Mar. 3 Accepted a $4,000, 10%, 90-day note dated March 3 in granting a time extension on the past-due account receivable of Shandi Company.
17 Accepted a $2,000, 30-day, 9% note dated March 17 in granting Juan Torres a time extension on his past-due account receivable.
Apr. 16 Torres dishonors his note when presented for payment.
May 1 Wrote off the Torres account against the Allowance for Doubtful Accounts.
June 1 Received the Shandi payment for principal and interest on the note dated March 3.

Check June 1, Dr. Cash $4,100

Exercise 9-9
Accounts receivable turnover
A1 

The following information is from the annual financial statements of Waseem Company. Compute its accounts receivable turnover for 2004 and 2005. Compare the two years results and give a possible explanation for any change (competitors average a turnover of 11).

	2005	2004	2003
Net sales	$305,000	$236,000	$288,000
Accounts receivable (December 31)	22,900	20,700	17,400

PROBLEM SET A

Problem 9-1A
Sales on account and credit card sales
C1

Atlas Co. allows select customers to make purchases on credit. Its other customers can use either of two credit cards: Zisa or Access. Zisa deducts a 3% service charge for sales on its credit card and credits the bank account of Atlas immediately when credit card receipts are deposited. Atlas deposits the Zisa credit card receipts each business day. When customers use Access credit cards, Atlas accumulates the receipts for several days before submitting them to Access for payment. Access deducts a 2% service charge and usually pays within one week of being billed. Atlas completes the following transactions in June. (The terms of all credit sales are 2/15, n/30, and all sales are recorded at the gross price.)

June 4 Sold $750 of merchandise (that had cost $500) on credit to Anne Cianci.
5 Sold merchandise for $5,900 (that had cost $3,200) to customers who used their Zisa credit cards.
6 Sold merchandise for $4,800 (that had cost $2,800) to customers who used their Access credit cards.
8 Sold merchandise for $3,200 (that had cost $1,900) to customers who used their Access credit cards.
10 Submitted Access card receipts accumulated since June 6 to the credit card company for payment.
13 Wrote off the account of Nakia Wells against the Allowance for Doubtful Accounts. The $329 balance in Wells' account stemmed from a credit sale in October of last year.
17 Received the amount due from Access.
18 Received Cianci's check paying for the purchase of June 4.

Check June 17, Dr. Cash $7,840

Required

Prepare journal entries to record the preceding transactions and events. (The company uses the perpetual inventory system.)

Problem 9-2A
Accounts receivable transactions and bad debts adjustments
C1 P1 P2

Lopez Company began operations on January 1, 2004. During its first two years, the company completed a number of transactions involving sales on credit, accounts receivable collections, and bad debts. These transactions are summarized as follows:

2004

a. Sold $1,803,750 of merchandise (that had cost $1,475,000) on credit, terms n/30.
b. Wrote off $20,300 of uncollectible accounts receivable.
c. Received $789,200 cash in payment of accounts receivable.
d. In adjusting the accounts on December 31, the company estimated that 1.5% of accounts receivable will be uncollectible.

Check (*d*) Dr. Bad Debts Expense $35,214

2005

e. Sold $1,825,700 of merchandise (that had cost $1,450,000) on credit, terms n/30.
f. Wrote off $28,800 of uncollectible accounts receivable.
g. Received $1,304,800 cash in payment of accounts receivable.
h. In adjusting the accounts on December 31, the company estimated that 1.5% of accounts receivable will be uncollectible.

Check (*h*) Dr. Bad Debts Expense $36,181

Required

Prepare journal entries to record Lopez's 2004 and 2005 summarized transactions and its year-end adjustments to record bad debts expense. (The company uses the perpetual inventory system.)

Problem 9-3A
Estimating and reporting bad debts
P1 P2

On December 31, 2005, Ethan Co. records show the following results for the calendar-year:

Cash sales	$1,803,750
Credit sales	3,534,000

In addition, its unadjusted trial balance includes the following items:

Accounts receivable	$1,070,100 debit
Allowance for doubtful accounts	15,750 debit

Required

1. Prepare the adjusting entry for Ethan Co. to recognize bad debts under each of the following independent assumptions:
a. Bad debts are estimated to be 2% of credit sales.
b. Bad debts are estimated to be 1% of total sales.
c. An aging analysis estimates that 5% of year-end accounts receivable are uncollectible.

Check Bad Debts Expense: (1*a*) $70,680, (1*c*) $69,255

2. Show how Accounts Receivable and the Allowance for Doubtful Accounts appear on the December 31, 2005, balance sheet given the facts in part 1*a*.

3. Show how Accounts Receivable and the Allowance for Doubtful Accounts appear on the December 31, 2005, balance sheet given the facts in part 1*c*.

Problem 9-4A
Aging accounts receivable and accounting for bad debts

P1 P2 

Carmack Company has credit sales of $2.6 million for year 2005. On December 31, 2005, the company's Allowance for Doubtful Accounts has an unadjusted credit balance of $13,400. Carmack prepares a schedule of its December 31, 2005, accounts receivable by age. On the basis of past experience, it estimates the percent of receivables in each age category that will become uncollectible. This information is summarized here:

December 31, 2005 Accounts Receivable	Age of Accounts Receivable	Expected Percent Uncollectible
$730,000	Not yet due	1.25%
354,000	1 to 30 days past due	2.00
76,000	31 to 60 days past due	6.50
48,000	61 to 90 days past due	32.75
12,000	Over 90 days past due	68.00

Required

1. Estimate the required balance of the Allowance for Doubtful Accounts at December 31, 2005, using the aging of accounts receivable method.

2. Prepare the adjusting entry to record bad debts expense at December 31, 2005.

Check (2) Dr. Bad Debts Expense $31,625

Analysis Component

3. On June 30, 2006, Carmack Company concludes that a customer's $3,750 receivable (created in 2005) is uncollectible and that the account should be written off. What effect will this action have on Carmack's 2006 net income? Explain.

Problem 9-5A
Analyzing and journalizing notes receivable transactions

C2 C3 P3 P4 

The following selected transactions are from Ohlde Company:

2004

Dec. 16 Accepted a $9,600, 60-day, 9% note dated this day in granting Todd Duke a time extension on his past-due account receivable.

31 Made an adjusting entry to record the accrued interest on the Duke note.

2005

Feb. 14 Received Duke's payment of principal and interest on the note dated December 16.

Check Feb. 14, Cr. Interest Revenue $108

Mar. 2 Accepted a $4,120, 8%, 90-day note dated this day in granting a time extension on the past-due account receivable from Mare Co.

17 Accepted a $2,400, 30-day, 7% note dated this day in granting Jolene Halaam a time extension on her past-due account receivable.

Apr. 16 Halaam dishonored her note when presented for payment.

June 2 Mare Co. refuses to pay the note that was due to Ohlde Co. on May 31. Prepare the journal entry to charge the dishonored note plus accrued interest to Mare Co.'s accounts receivable.

Check June 2, Cr. Interest Revenue $82

July 17 Received payment from Mare Co. for the maturity value of its dishonored note plus interest for 46 days beyond maturity at 8%.

Aug. 7 Accepted a $5,440, 90-day, 10% note dated this day in granting a time extension on the past-due account receivable of Birch and Byer Co.

Sept. 3 Accepted a $2,080, 60-day, 10% note dated this day in granting Kevin York a time extension on his past-due account receivable.

Check Nov. 2, Cr. Interest Revenue $35

Nov. 2 Received payment of principal plus interest from York for the September 3 note.
Nov. 5 Received payment of principal plus interest from Birch and Byer for the August 7 note.
Dec. 1 Wrote off the Jolene Halaam account against Allowance for Doubtful Accounts.

Required

1. Prepare journal entries to record these transactions and events.

Analysis Component

2. What reporting is necessary when a business pledges receivables as security for a loan and the loan is still outstanding at the end of the period? Explain the reason for this requirement and the accounting principle being satisfied.

PROBLEM SET B

Problem 9-1B

Sales on account and credit card sales

C1

Able Co. allows select customers to make purchases on credit. Its other customers can use either of two credit cards: Commerce Bank or Aztec. Commerce Bank deducts a 3% service charge for sales on its credit card and immediately credits the bank account of Able when credit card receipts are deposited. Able deposits the Commerce Bank credit card receipts each business day. When customers use the Aztec card, Able accumulates the receipts for several days and then submits them to Aztec for payment. Aztec deducts a 2% service charge and usually pays within one week of being billed. Able completed the following transactions in August (terms of all credit sales are 2/10, n/30; and all sales are recorded at the gross price).

Aug. 4 Sold $2,780 of merchandise (that had cost $1,750) on credit to Stacy Dalton.
10 Sold merchandise for $3,248 (that had cost $2,456) to customers who used their Commerce Bank credit cards.
11 Sold merchandise for $1,575 (that had cost $1,150) to customers who used their Aztec cards.
14 Received Dalton's check paying for the purchase of August 4.
15 Sold merchandise for $2,960 (that had cost $1,758) to customers who used their Aztec cards.
18 Submitted Aztec card receipts accumulated since August 11 to the credit card company for payment.
22 Wrote off the account of Ness City against the Allowance for Doubtful Accounts. The $398 balance in Ness City's account stemmed from a credit sale in November of last year.
25 Received the amount due from Aztec.

Check Aug. 25, Dr. Cash $4,444

Required

Prepare journal entries to record the preceding transactions and events. (The company uses the perpetual inventory system.)

Problem 9-2B

Accounts receivable transactions and bad debts adjustments

C1 P1 P2

Crist Co. began operations on January 1, 2004, and completed several transactions during 2004 and 2005 that involved sales on credit, accounts receivable collections, and bad debts. These transactions are summarized as follows:

2004

a. Sold $673,490 of merchandise (that had cost $500,000) on credit, terms n/30.
b. Received $437,250 cash in payment of accounts receivable.
c. Wrote off $8,330 of uncollectible accounts receivable.
d. In adjusting the accounts on December 31, the company estimated that 1% of accounts receivable will be uncollectible.

Check (*d*) Dr. Bad Debts Expense $10,609

2005

e. Sold $930,100 of merchandise (that had cost $650,000) on credit, terms n/30.
f. Received $890,220 cash in payment of accounts receivable.
g. Wrote off $10,090 of uncollectible accounts receivable.
h. In adjusting the accounts on December 31, the company estimated that 1% of accounts receivable will be uncollectible.

Check (*h*) Dr. Bad Debts Expense $10,388

Required

Prepare journal entries to record Crist's 2004 and 2005 summarized transactions and its year-end adjusting entry to record bad debts expense. (The company uses the perpetual inventory system.)

Problem 9-3B
Estimating and reporting bad debts

P1 P2

On December 31, 2005, Klimek Co.'s records show the following results for the year:

Cash sales	$1,015,000
Credit sales	1,241,000

In addition, its unadjusted trial balance includes the following items:

Accounts receivable	$475,000 debit
Allowance for doubtful accounts	5,200 credit

Required

1. Prepare the adjusting entry for Klimek Co. to recognize bad debts under each of the following independent assumptions:

   a. Bad debts are estimated to be 2.5% of credit sales.

   b. Bad debts are estimated to be 1.5% of total sales.

   c. An aging analysis estimates that 6% of year-end accounts receivable are uncollectible.

2. Show how Accounts Receivable and the Allowance for Doubtful Accounts appear on the December 31, 2005, balance sheet given the facts in part 1*a*.

3. Show how Accounts Receivable and the Allowance for Doubtful Accounts appear on the December 31, 2005, balance sheet given the facts in part 1*c*.

Check Bad debts expense: (1*b*) $33,840, (1*c*) $23,300

Problem 9-4B
Aging accounts receivable and accounting for bad debts

P1 P2

Quisp Company has credit sales of $3.5 million for year 2005. On December 31, 2005, the company's Allowance for Doubtful Accounts has an unadjusted debit balance of $4,100. Quisp prepares a schedule of its December 31, 2005, accounts receivable by age. On the basis of past experience, it estimates the percent of receivables in each age category that will become uncollectible. This information is summarized here:

December 31, 2005 Accounts Receivable	Age of Accounts Receivable	Expected Percent Uncollectible
$296,400	Not yet due	2.0%
177,800	1 to 30 days past due	4.0
58,000	31 to 60 days past due	8.5
7,600	61 to 90 days past due	39.0
3,700	Over 90 days past due	82.0

Required

1. Compute the required balance of the Allowance for Doubtful Accounts at December 31, 2005, using the aging of accounts receivable method.

2. Prepare the adjusting entry to record bad debts expense at December 31, 2005.

Check (2) Dr. Bad Debts Expense $28,068

Analysis Component

3. On July 31, 2006, Quisp concludes that a customer's $2,345 receivable (created in 2005) is uncollectible and that the account should be written off. What effect will this action have on Quisp's 2006 net income? Explain.

Problem 9-5B
Analyzing and journalizing notes receivable transactions
C2 C3 P3 P4 

The following selected transactions are from Seeker Company:

2004

Nov. 1 Accepted a $4,800, 90-day, 8% note dated this day in granting Julie Stephens a time extension on her past-due account receivable.

Dec. 31 Made an adjusting entry to record the accrued interest on the Stephens note.

2005

Jan. 30 Received Stephens's payment for principal and interest on the note dated November 1.

Check Jan. 30, Cr. Interest Revenue $32

Feb. 28 Accepted a $12,600, 6%, 30-day note dated this day in granting a time extension on the past-due account receivable from Kramer Co.

Mar. 1 Accepted a $6,200, 60-day, 8% note dated this day in granting Shelly Myers a time extension on her past-due account receivable.

30 The Kramer Co. dishonored its note when presented for payment.

April 30 Received payment of principal plus interest from Myers for the March 1 note.

Check April 30, Cr. Interest Revenue $83

June 15 Accepted a $2,000, 60-day, 10% note dated this day in granting a time extension on the past-due account receivable of Rhonda Rye.

21 Accepted a $9,500, 90-day, 12% note dated this day in granting Jack Striker a time extension on his past-due account receivable.

Aug. 14 Received payment of principal plus interest from R. Rye for the note of June 15.

Sep. 19 Received payment of principal plus interest from J. Striker for the June 21 note.

Check Sep. 19, Cr. Interest Revenue $285

Nov. 30 Wrote off Kramer Co.'s account against Allowance for Doubtful Accounts.

Required

1. Prepare journal entries to record these transactions and events.

Analysis Component

2. What reporting is necessary when a business pledges receivables as security for a loan and the loan is still outstanding at the end of the period? Explain the reason for this requirement and the accounting principle being satisfied.

PROBLEM SET C

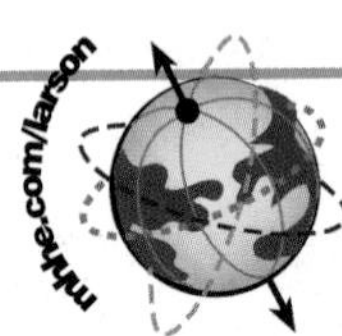

Problem Set C is available at the book's Website to further reinforce and assess your learning.

SERIAL PROBLEM

Success Systems

(This serial problem began in Chapter 1 and continues through most of the book. If previous chapter segments were not completed, the serial problem can begin at this point. It is helpful, but not necessary, that you use the Working Papers that accompany the book.)

Kay Breeze, owner of Success Systems, realizes that she needs to begin accounting for bad debts expense. Assume that Success Systems has total revenues of $43,853 during the first three months of 2005. The Accounts Receivable balance on March 31, 2005, is $22,720.

Required

1. Prepare the adjusting entry needed for Success Systems to recognize bad debts expense on March 31, 2005, under each of the following independent assumptions (assume a zero balance in the Allowance for Doubtful Accounts at March 31).

a. Bad debts are estimated to be 1% of total revenues.

b. Bad debts are estimated to be 2% of accounts receivable.

2. Assume that Success Systems' Accounts Receivable balance at June 30, 2005, is $20,250 and that one account of $100 has been written off against the Allowance for Doubtful Accounts since March 31, 2005. If Breeze uses the method prescribed in Part 1*b*, what adjusting journal entry must be made to recognize bad debts expense on June 30, 2005?

3. Should Breeze consider adopting the direct write-off method of accounting for bad debts expense rather than one of the allowance methods considered in part 1?

BEYOND THE NUMBERS

REPORTING IN ACTION

A1 

BTN 9-1 Refer to **Krispy Kreme**'s financial statements in Appendix A to answer the following:

1. What is the amount of its accounts receivable (net) on February 2, 2003?
2. Krispy Kreme's most liquid assets include (a) Cash and Cash Equivalents, (b) Short-Term Investments, (c) Accounts Receivable, (d) Accounts Receivable, Affiliates, and (e) Other Receivables. Compute the percent that liquid assets are of current liabilities as of February 2, 2003. Do the same for February 3, 2002. Comment on the company's ability to satisfy current liabilities at the end of the fiscal year 2003 as compared to the end of fiscal year 2002.
3. What criteria did Krispy Kreme's use to classify items as cash equivalents?
4. Compute Krispy Kreme's accounts receivable turnover as of February 2, 2003.

Roll On

5. Access Krispy Kreme's financial statements for fiscal years ending after February 2, 2003, at its Website (KrispyKreme.com) or the SEC's EDGAR database (www.sec.gov). Recompute parts 2 and 4 and comment on any changes since February 2, 2003.

COMPARATIVE ANALYSIS

A1 P2 

BTN 9-2 Key comparative figures ($ thousands) for both **Krispy Kreme** and **Tastykake** follow:

	Krispy Kreme			Tastykake		
Key Figures	Current Year	One-Year Prior	Two-Years Prior	Current Year	One-Year Prior	Two-Years Prior
Allowance for doubtful accounts	$ 1,453	$ 1,182	$ 1,302	$ 3,606	$ 3,752	$ 3,329
Accounts receivable, net	34,373	26,894	19,855	20,882	22,233	20,772
Net sales	491,549	394,354	300,715	162,263	166,245	162,877

Required

1. Compute the accounts receivable turnover for both Krispy Kreme and Tastykake for each of the two most recent years using the data shown.
2. Using results from part 1, compute how many days it takes each company, *on average,* to collect receivables.
3. Which company is more efficient in collecting its accounts receivable?
4. Which company estimates a higher percent of uncollectible accounts receivable?

Hint: Average collection period equals 365 divided by the accounts receivable turnover.

ETHICS CHALLENGE

P1 P2 

BTN 9-3 Kelly Steinman is the manager of a medium-size company. A few years ago, Steinman persuaded the owner to base a part of her compensation on the net income the company earns each year. Each December she estimates year-end financial figures in anticipation of the bonus she will receive. If the bonus is not as high as she would like, she offers several recommendations to the accountant for year-end adjustments. One of her favorite recommendations is for the controller to reduce the estimate of doubtful accounts.

Required

1. What effect does lowering the estimate for doubtful accounts have on the income statement and balance sheet?
2. Do you think Steinman's recommendation to adjust the allowance for doubtful accounts is within her right as manager, or do you think this action is an ethics violation? Justify your response.
3. What type of internal control(s) might be useful for this company in overseeing the manager's recommendations for accounting changes?

COMMUNICATING IN PRACTICE

P1 P2 

BTN 9-4 As the accountant for Pure-Air Distributing, you attend a sales managers' meeting devoted to a discussion of credit policies. At the meeting, you report that bad debts expense is estimated to be \$59,000 and accounts receivable at year-end amount to \$1,750,000 less a \$43,000 allowance for doubtful accounts. Sid Omar, a sales manager, expresses confusion over why bad debts expense and the allowance for doubtful accounts are different amounts. Write a one-page memorandum to him explaining why a difference in bad debts expense and the allowance for doubtful accounts is not unusual. The company estimates bad debts expense as 2% of sales.

TAKING IT TO THE NET

C1

mhhe.com/larson

BTN 9-5 Access Surg II, Inc.'s, February 7, 2003, filing of its 10-KSB (small business 10-K) for the fiscal year-end of December 31, 2002 at www.SEC.gov.

Required

1. How does its accounts receivable balance for the fiscal year-end 2002 compare with its fiscal year-end 2001 balance?
2. What event accounts for its 2002 accounts receivable balance being zero?

TEAMWORK IN ACTION

P2

BTN 9-6 Each member of a team is to participate in estimating uncollectibles using the aging schedule and percents shown in Problem 9-4A. The division of labor is up to the team. Your goal is to accurately complete this task as soon as possible. After estimating uncollectibles, check your estimate with the instructor. If the estimate is correct, the team then should prepare the adjusting entry and the presentation of accounts receivable (net) for the December 31, 2005, balance sheet.

BUSINESS WEEK ACTIVITY

C1 P1

mhhe.com/larson

BTN 9-7 Read the article, "How Plastic Put Sears in a Pickle" in the October 30, 2002, issue of *Business Week*. (The book's Website provides a free link.)

Required

1. What two types of credit cards does Sears issue to its customers?
2. What is Sears' overall bad-debt charge-off rate as a percent of its receivables?
3. How many years does it usually take before a retailer's charge-off rates on new charge card programs peak?
4. What are the average balances carried by customers on the Sears MasterCard and on the Sears card? How do these balances compare to balances carried by consumers on general-purchase cards?

ENTREPRENEURIAL DECISION

C1 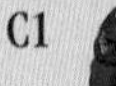 

BTN 9-8 The chapter's opening feature introduces Barbara Manzi and her business, Manzi Metals, a distributor of aluminum, steel, titanium, brass, and other alloys. Manzi Metals generates \$3 million in annual sales. Assume that all sales are cash sales and that Manzi's net profit margin is 30%. Manzi's buyers would like to either use credit cards with their purchases or buy on credit. Therefore, Manzi has decided to pursue one of two plans (neither plan will impact cash sales nor alter current costs as a percent of sales):

Plan A. *Manzi accepts credit cards.* This plan is expected to yield new credit sales equal to 20% of current cash sales. Cost estimates of this plan as a percent of net credit sales are: credit card fee, 4.8%; recordkeeping, 1.2%.

Plan B. *Manzi grants credit directly to qualified buyers.* This plan is expected to yield new credit sales equal to 24% of current cash sales. Cost estimates of this plan as a percent of net credit sales are: uncollectibles, 6.7%; collection expenses, 1.3%; recordkeeping, 2.0%.

Required

Check (1b) Net income, \$12,000

1. Compute the *added* monthly net income (loss) expected under (*a*) Plan A and (*b*) Plan B.
2. Should Manzi pursue either plan? Discuss the financial and nonfinancial factors relevant to this decision.

HITTING THE ROAD

C1 

BTN 9-9 Many commercials include comments similar to the following: "Bring your **VISA**" or "We do not accept **American Express**." Conduct your own research by contacting at least 5 companies via interviews, phone calls, or the Internet to determine the reason(s) companies discriminate in their use of credit cards. (The instructor may assign this as a team activity.)

GLOBAL DECISION

C1 P1

BTN 9-10 **Grupo Bimbo**, **Krispy Kreme**, and **Tastykake** are all competitors in the global marketplace. Review the Consolidated Balance Sheet for Grupo Bimbo for the year ended December 31, 2002, at GrupoBimbo.com.

Required

1. Contrast the presentation of the accounts receivable balance on the Grupo Bimbo balance sheet with that of both Krispy Kreme and Tastykake on their balance sheets in Appendix A.
2. As a potential investor in these companies, which presentation do you prefer: Grupo Bimbo's or that of Krispy Kreme and Tastykake? Explain.

"There are well over 2 million Hispanic owned businesses in the U.S. today"—Tina Cordova

Plant Assets, Natural Resources, and Intangibles

A Look Back

Chapters 8 and 9 focused on short-term assets: cash, cash equivalents, and receivables. We explained why they are known as liquid assets and described how companies account and report for them.

A Look at This Chapter

This chapter introduces us to long-term assets, including plant assets, natural resource assets, and intangible assets. We explain how to account for a long-term asset's cost, the allocation of an asset's cost to periods benefiting from it, the recording of additional costs after an asset is purchased, and the disposal of an asset.

A Look Ahead

Chapter 11 focuses on current liabilities. We explain how they are computed, recorded, and reported in financial statements. We also explain the accounting for payroll and contingencies.

CAP

Conceptual

C1 Describe plant assets and issues in accounting for them. *(p. 382)*

C2 Explain depreciation and the factors affecting its computation. *(p. 385)*

C3 Explain depreciation for partial years and changes in estimates. *(p. 390)*

Analytical

A1 Compare and analyze alternative depreciation methods. *(p. 389)*

A2 Compute total asset turnover and apply it to analyze a company's use of assets. *(p. 401)*

Procedural

P1 Apply the cost principle to compute the cost of plant assets. *(p. 383)*

P2 Compute and record depreciation using the straight-line, units-of-production, and declining-balance methods. *(p. 386)*

P3 Distinguish between revenue and capital expenditures, and account for them. *(p. 392)*

P4 Account for asset disposal through discarding, selling, and exchanging an asset. *(p. 394)*

P5 Account for natural resource assets and their depletion. *(p. 397)*

P6 Account for intangible assets. *(p. 398)*

Decision Feature

Climbing the Ladder

ALBUQUERQUE—Tina Cordova attended medical school and dreamed of being a doctor, but life had other plans. She found herself divorced with a child to support. Life became about survival. Cordova waited tables but something inside told her life had more to offer.

With her life savings of $5,000, she launched **Queston Construction**, a company devoted to roofing and commercial construction. When Cordova sat for the contractor's license exam, she was the only woman among more than 100 men. "Not one of them was particularly glad to see me," she laughs. Cordova soon found herself working with a crew of two men while removing old roofing, laying new roofing, and driving the dump truck. "I figured that the worst thing that could happen was that I'd have to go back to working for someone else," says Cordova. Her first-year sales of $50,000 was meager but enough to continue.

Today, Cordova oversees a crew of 28—swelling to 40 during high season—and reports annual sales of more than $3 million. One of her greatest challenges is maintaining the right kind, size, and amount of plant assets necessary to maintain her business. Cordova says that maintaining a strong sales to assets ratio is crucial. This includes monitoring and controlling asset costs ranging from expensive construction equipment and trucks to building and land costs. To be successful, Cordova's sales must cover these plant asset costs as well as yield a return adequate to pay other expenses and meet income goals. This chapter focuses on these and other crucial issues related to long-term assets. Cordova says that effective acquisition, use, and disposal of long-term assets are keys to business success.

Cordova doesn't look back at her dreams and what might have been. "Never in a million years," insists Cordova. "I have found my place." That place is at the top of the ladder.

[Sources: *Hispanic Magazine*, April 2003; *Small Business Association Website*, October 2002; *House of Representatives Committee on Small Business*, August 2001.]

This chapter focuses on long-term assets used to operate a company. These assets can be grouped into plant assets, natural resource assets, and intangible assets. Plant assets are a major investment for most companies. They make up a large part of assets on most balance sheets, and they yield depreciation, often one of the largest expenses on income statements. The acquisition or building of a plant asset is often referred to as a *capital expenditure.* Capital expenditures are important events because they impact both the short- and long-term success of a company. Natural resource assets and intangible assets have similar impacts. This chapter describes the purchase and use of these assets. We also explain what distinguishes these assets from other types of assets, how to determine their cost, how to allocate their costs to periods benefiting from their use, and how to dispose of them.

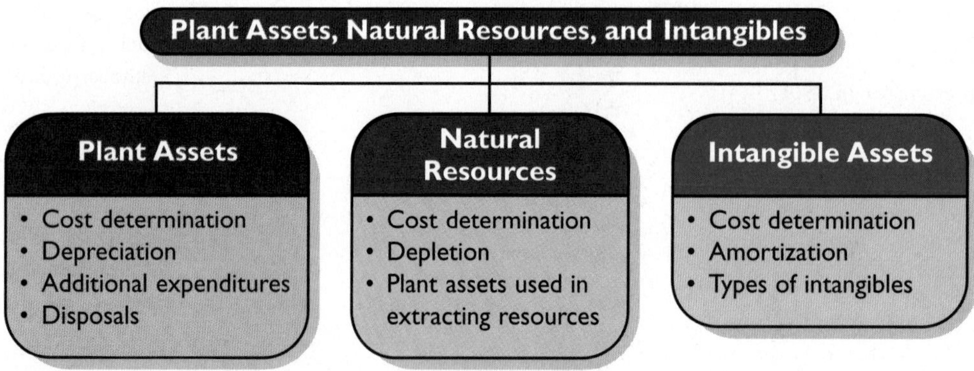

Section 1—Plant Assets

Plant assets are tangible assets used in a company's operations that have a useful life of more than one accounting period. Plant assets are also called *plant and equipment; property, plant, and equipment;* or *fixed assets.* For many companies, plant assets make up the single largest class of assets they own. Exhibit 10.1 shows plant assets as a percent of total assets for several companies. Not only do they make up a large percent of these companies' assets but also their dollar values are large. **McDonald's** plant assets, for instance, are reported at more than $18 billion, and **Wal-Mart** reports plant assets of more than $48 billion.

Exhibit 10.1

Plant Assets of Selected Companies

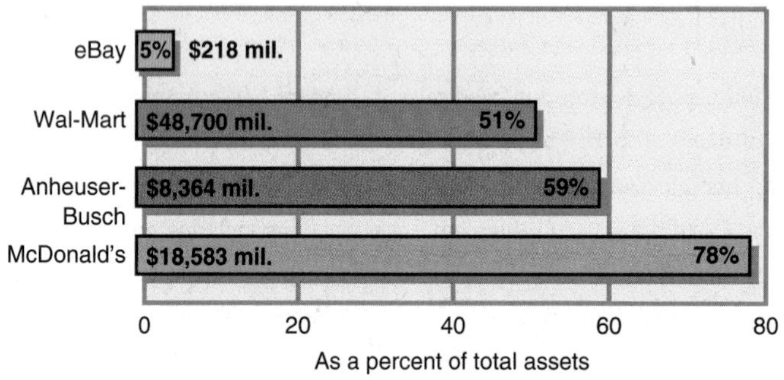

C1 Describe plant assets and issues in accounting for them.

Plant assets are set apart from other assets by two important features. First, *plant assets are used in operations.* This makes them different from, for instance, inventory that is held for sale and not used in operations. The distinctive feature here is use, not type of asset. A company that purchases a computer to resell it, reports it on the balance sheet as inventory. If the same company purchases this computer to use in operations, however, it is a plant asset. Another example is land held for future expansion, which is reported as a long-term investment. However, if this land holds a factory used in operations, the land is part of plant assets. Another example is equipment held for use in the event of a breakdown or for peak periods of production, which is reported in plant assets. If this same equipment is removed from use and held for sale, however, it is not reported in plant assets.

Point: Amazon.com's plant assets of $239 million make up 12% of its total assets.

The second important feature is that *plant assets have useful lives extending over more than one accounting period.* This makes plant assets different from current assets such as supplies that are normally consumed in a short time period after they are placed in use.

The accounting for plant assets reflects these two features. Since plant assets are used in operations, we try to match their costs against the revenues they generate. Also, since their useful lives extend over more than one period, our matching of costs and revenues must extend over several periods. Specifically, we value plant assets (balance sheet effect) and then allocate their costs to periods benefiting from their use (income statement effect).

Point: It can help to view plant assets as prepaid expenses that benefit several future accounting periods.

Exhibit 10.2 shows four main issues in accounting for plant assets: (1) computing the costs of plant assets, (2) allocating the costs of plant assets (less any salvage amounts) against revenues for the periods they benefit, (3) accounting for expenditures such as repairs and improvements to plant assets, and (4) recording the disposal of plant assets. The following sections discuss these issues.

Topic Tackler 10-1

Exhibit 10.2

Issues in Accounting for Plant Assets

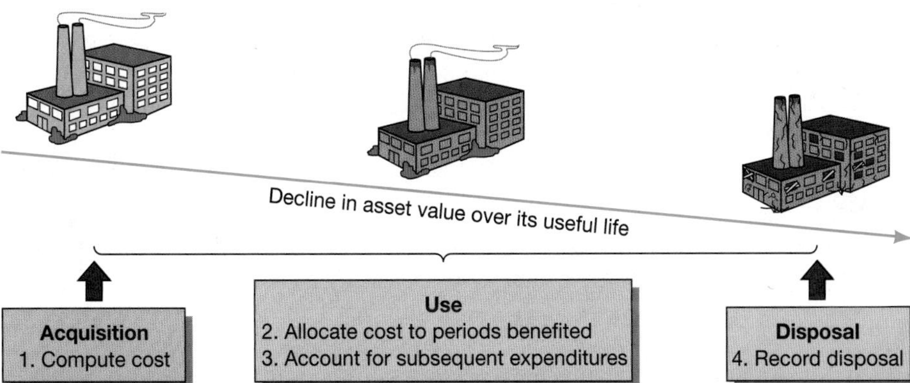

Cost Determination

Plant assets are recorded at cost when acquired. This is consistent with the *cost principle.* **Cost** includes all normal and reasonable expenditures necessary to get the asset in place and ready for its intended use. The cost of a factory machine, for instance, includes its invoice cost less any cash discount for early payment, plus any necessary freight, unpacking, assembling, installing, and testing costs. Examples are the costs of building a base or foundation for a machine, providing electrical hook-ups, and testing the asset before using it in operations.

To be recorded as part of the cost of a plant asset, an expenditure must be normal, reasonable, and necessary in preparing it for its intended use. If an asset is damaged during unpacking, the repairs are not added to its cost. Instead, they are charged to an expense account. Nor is a paid traffic fine for moving heavy machinery on city streets without a proper permit part of the machinery's cost; but payment for a proper permit is included in the cost of machinery. Charges are sometimes incurred to modify or customize a new plant asset. These charges are added to the asset's cost. We explain in this section how to determine the cost of plant assets for each of its four major classes.

Global: International accounting standards encourage use of the cost principle for plant assets. Plant asset revaluation is permitted if it is consistently applied across periods.

Land

P1 Apply the cost principle to compute the cost of plant assets.

When land is purchased for a building site, its cost includes the total amount paid for the land, including any real estate commissions, title insurance fees, legal fees, and any accrued property taxes paid by the purchaser. Payments for surveying, clearing, grading, and draining also are included in the cost of land. Other costs include government assessments, whether incurred at the time of purchase or later, for items such as public roadways, sewers, and sidewalks. These assessments are included because they permanently add to the land's value. Land purchased as a building site sometimes includes structures that must be removed. In such cases, the total purchase price is charged to the Land account as is the cost of removing the structures, less any amounts recovered through sale of salvaged materials. To illustrate, assume the **Hockey Co.** paid $167,000 cash to acquire land for a retail

Exhibit 10.3

Computing Cost of Land

Cash price of land	$ 167,000
Net cost of garage removal	13,000
Closing costs	10,000
Cost of land	**$190,000**

store. This land had an old service garage that was removed at a net cost of $13,000 ($15,000 in costs less $2,000 proceeds from salvaged materials). Additional closing costs total $10,000, consisting of brokerage fees ($8,000), legal fees ($1,500), and title costs ($500). The cost of this land to Hockey Co. is $190,000 and is computed as shown in Exhibit 10.3.

Land Improvements

Land has an unlimited life and is not usually used up over time. **Land improvements** such as parking lot surfaces, driveways, fences, shrubs, and lighting systems, however, have limited useful lives and are used up. While the costs of these improvements increase the usefulness of the land, they are charged to a separate Land Improvement account so that their costs can be allocated to the periods they benefit.

Buildings

A Building account is charged for the costs of purchasing or constructing a building that is used in operations. When purchased, a building's costs usually include its purchase price, brokerage fees, taxes, title fees, and attorney fees. Its costs also include all expenditures to ready it for its intended use, including any necessary repairs or renovations such as wiring, lighting, flooring, and wall coverings. When a company constructs a building or any plant asset for its own use, its costs include materials and labor plus a reasonable amount of indirect overhead cost. Overhead includes the costs of items such as heat, lighting, power, and depreciation on machinery used to construct the asset. Costs of construction also include design fees, building permits, and insurance during construction. However, costs such as insurance to cover the asset *after* it is placed in use are operating expenses.

Machinery and Equipment

The costs of machinery and equipment consist of all costs normal and necessary to purchase them and prepare them for their intended use. These include the purchase price, taxes, transportation charges, insurance while in transit, and the installing, assembling, and testing of the machinery and equipment.

Lump-Sum Purchase

Example: If appraised values in Exhibit 10.4 are land, $24,000; land improvements, $12,000; and building, $84,000, what cost is assigned to the building? *Answer:* (1) $24,000 + $12,000 + $84,000 = $120,000 (total appraisal) (2) $84,000/$120,000 = 70% (building's percent of total) (3) 70% × $90,000 = $63,000 (building's apportioned cost)

Plant assets sometimes are purchased as a group in a single transaction for a lump-sum price. This transaction is called a *lump-sum purchase,* or *group, bulk,* or *basket purchase.* When this occurs, we allocate the cost of the purchase among the different types of assets acquired based on their *relative market values,* which can be estimated by appraisal or by using the tax-assessed valuations of the assets. To illustrate, Oakley paid $90,000 cash to acquire a group of items consisting of land appraised at $30,000, land improvements appraised at $10,000, and a building appraised at $60,000. The $90,000 cost is allocated on the basis of these appraised values as shown in Exhibit 10.4.

Exhibit 10.4

Computing Costs in a Lump-Sum Purchase

	Appraised Value	Percent of Total	Apportioned Cost
Land	$ 30,000	30% ($30,000/$100,000)	**$27,000** ($90,000 × 30%)
Land improvements	10,000	10 ($10,000/$100,000)	**9,000** ($90,000 × 10%)
Building	60,000	60 ($60,000/$100,000)	**54,000** ($90,000 × 60%)
Totals	$100,000	100%	$ 90,000

Quick Check

1. Identify the asset class for each of the following: (*a*) supplies, (*b*) office equipment, (*c*) inventory, (*d*) land for future expansion, and (*e*) trucks used in operations.
2. Identify the account charged for each of the following: (*a*) purchase price of a vacant lot to be used in operations and (*b*) cost of paving that same vacant lot.
3. Calculate the amount recorded as the cost of a new machine given the following payments related to its purchase: gross purchase price, $700,000; sales tax, $49,000; purchase discount taken, $21,000; freight cost—terms FOB shipping point, $3,500; normal assembly costs, $3,000; cost of necessary foundation for machine, $2,500; cost of parts used in maintaining the machine, $4,200.

Answers—p. 406

Depreciation

Depreciation is the process of allocating the cost of a plant asset to expense in the accounting periods benefiting from its use. Depreciation does not measure the decline in the asset's market value each period, nor does it measure the asset's physical deterioration. Since depreciation reflects the cost of using a plant asset, depreciation charges are only recorded when the asset is actually in service. This section describes the factors we must consider in computing depreciation, the depreciation methods used, revisions in depreciation, and depreciation for partial periods.

Topic Tackler 10-2

Factors in Computing Depreciation

Factors that determine depreciation are (1) cost, (2) salvage value, and (3) useful life.

C2 Explain depreciation and the factors affecting its computation.

Cost The **cost** of a plant asset consists of all necessary and reasonable expenditures to acquire it and to prepare it for its intended use.

Salvage Value The total amount of depreciation to be charged off over an asset's benefit period equals the asset's cost minus its salvage value. **Salvage value,** also called *residual value* or *scrap value,* is an estimate of the asset's value at the end of its benefit period. This is the amount the owner expects to receive from disposing the asset at the end of its benefit period. If the asset is expected to be traded in on a new asset, its salvage value is the expected trade-in value.

Point: If we expect additional costs in preparing a plant asset for disposal, the salvage value equals the expected amount from disposal less any disposal costs.

Useful Life The **useful life** of a plant asset is the length of time it is productively used in a company's operations. Useful life, also called *service life,* might not be as long as the asset's total productive life. For example, the productive life of a computer can be eight years or more. Some companies, however, trade in old computers for new ones every two years. In this case, these computers have a two-year useful life, meaning the cost of these computers (less their expected trade-in values) is charged to depreciation expense over a two-year period.

Point: Useful life and salvage value are estimates. Estimates require judgment based on consideration of all available information.

Several variables often make the useful life of a plant asset difficult to predict. A major variable is the wear and tear from use in operations. Two other variables, inadequacy and obsolescence, also demand consideration. **Inadequacy** refers to the insufficient capacity of a company's plant assets to meet its growing productive demands. **Obsolescence** refers to a plant asset that is no longer useful in producing goods or services with a competitive advantage because of new inventions and improvements. Both inadequacy and obsolescence

Decision Insight

Life Line Life expectancy of plant assets is often in the eye of the beholder. For instance, **Converse** and **Stride Rite** are competitors, yet their buildings' life expectancies are quite different. Converse depreciates buildings over 5 to 10 years, but Stride Rite depreciates them over 10 to 40 years. Such differences markedly impact financial statements.

Global: While U.S. accounting must consider inadequacy and obsolescence in estimating useful life, the accounting in many other countries does not.

are difficult to predict because of demand changes, new inventions, and improvements. A company usually disposes of an inadequate or obsolete asset before it wears out.

A company is often able to better predict a new asset's useful life when it has past experience with a similar asset. When it has no such experience, a company relies on the experience of others or on engineering studies and judgment. In note 1 of its annual report, **Brunswick**, a manufacturer of boats and motors, reports the following useful lives:

Estimated useful lives of buildings and equipment;	
Buildings	5–40 years
Equipment	2–20 years

Depreciation Methods

Depreciation methods are used to allocate a plant asset's cost over the accounting periods in its useful life. The most frequently used method of depreciation is the straight-line method. Another common depreciation method is the units-of-production method. We explain both of these methods in this section. This section also describes accelerated depreciation methods, with a focus on the declining-balance method.

The computations in this section use information about a machine that inspects athletic shoes before packaging. Manufacturers such as **Converse**, **Reebok**, **Adidas**, and **Fila** use this machine. Data for this machine are in Exhibit 10.5.

Exhibit 10.5

Data for Athletic Shoe-Inspecting Machine

Cost	$10,000
Salvage value	1,000
Depreciable cost	$ 9,000
Useful life	
Accounting periods	5 years
Units inspected	36,000 shoes

P2 Compute and record depreciation using the straight-line, units-of-production, and declining-balance methods.

Straight-Line Method **Straight-line depreciation** charges the same amount of expense to each period of the asset's useful life. A two-step process is used. We first compute the *depreciable cost* of the asset; this amount is also called the *cost to be depreciated.* It is computed by subtracting the asset's salvage value from its total cost. Second, depreciable cost is divided by the number of accounting periods in the asset's useful life. The formula for straight-line depreciation, along with its computation for the inspection machine described above, is shown in Exhibit 10.6.

Exhibit 10.6

Straight-Line Depreciation Formula and Example

$$\frac{\textbf{Cost} - \textbf{Salvage value}}{\textbf{Useful life in periods}} = \frac{\$10{,}000 - \$1{,}000}{5 \text{ years}} = \$1{,}800 \text{ per year}$$

If this machine is purchased on December 31, 2003, and used throughout its predicted useful life of five years, the straight-line method allocates an equal amount of depreciation to each of the years 2004 through 2008. We make the following adjusting entry at the end of each of the five years to record straight-line depreciation of this machine:

Dec. 31	Depreciation Expense	1,800	
	Accumulated Depreciation—Machinery.....		1,800
	To record annual depreciation.		

Assets = Liabilities + Equity
−1,800 −1,800

Example: If salvage value of the machine is estimated to be $2,500, what is the annual depreciation expense? *Answer:* ($10,000 − $2,500)/5 years = $1,500

The $1,800 Depreciation Expense is reported on the income statement among operating expenses. The $1,800 Accumulated Depreciation is a contra asset account to the Machinery account in the balance sheet. The graph on the left in Exhibit 10.7 shows the $1,800 per year expenses reported in each of the five years. The graph on the right shows the amounts reported on each of the six December 31 balance sheets while the company owns the asset.

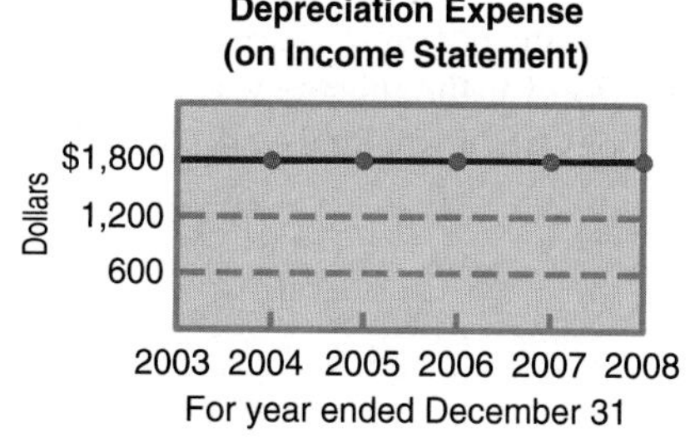

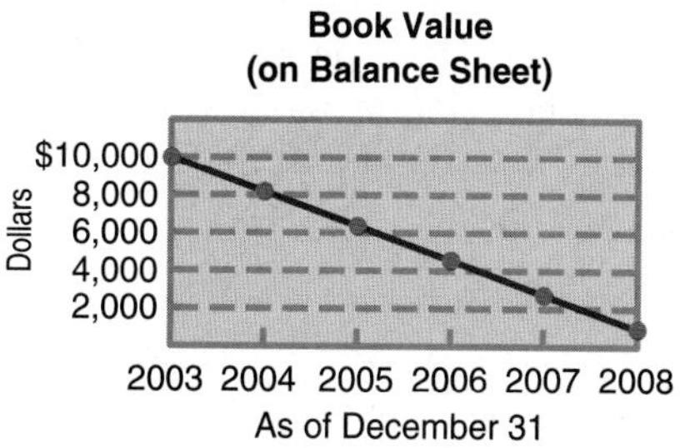

Exhibit 10.7

Financial Statement Effects of Straight-Line Depreciation

The net balance sheet amount is the asset's **book value** and is computed as the asset's total cost less its accumulated depreciation. For example, at the end of year 2 (December 31, 2005), its book value is $6,400 and is reported in the balance sheet as follows:

Machinery	$10,000	
Less accumulated depreciation	3,600	$6,400

The book value of this machine declines by $1,800 each year due to depreciation. From the graphs in Exhibit 10.7 we can see why this method is called straight line.

We also can compute the *straight-line depreciation rate,* defined as 100% divided by the number of periods in the asset's useful life. For the inspection machine, this rate is 20% (100% ÷ 5 years). We use this rate, along with other information, to compute the machine's *straight-line depreciation schedule* shown in Exhibit 10.8. Note three points in Exhibit 10.8. First, depreciation expense is the same each period. Second, accumulated depreciation is the sum of current and prior periods' depreciation expense. Third, book value declines each period until it equals salvage value at the end of the machine's useful life.

Point: Depreciation requires estimates for salvage value and useful life. Decision ethics are relevant when managers might be tempted to choose estimates to achieve desired results on financial statements.

Exhibit 10.8

Straight-Line Depreciation Schedule

	Depreciation for the Period			End of Period	
Annual Period	Depreciable Cost*	Depreciation Rate	Depreciation Expense	Accumulated Depreciation	Book Value†
2003	—	—	—	—	$10,000
2004	$9,000	20%	$1,800	$1,800	8,200
2005	9,000	20	1,800	3,600	6,400
2006	9,000	20	1,800	5,400	4,600
2007	9,000	20	1,800	7,200	2,800
2008	9,000	20	1,800	9,000	**1,000**

* $10,000 − $1,000. † Book value is total cost minus accumulated depreciation.

Units-of-Production Method The straight-line method charges an equal share of an asset's cost to each period. If plant assets are used up in about equal amounts each accounting period, this method produces a reasonable matching of expenses with revenues. However, the use of some plant assets varies greatly from one period to the next. A builder, for instance, might use a piece of construction equipment for a month and then not use it again for several months. When equipment use varies from period to period, the units-of-production depreciation method can better match expenses with revenues. **Units-of-production depreciation** charges a varying amount to expense for each period of an asset's useful life depending on its usage.

A two-step process is used to compute units-of-production depreciation. We first compute *depreciation per unit* by subtracting the asset's salvage value from its total cost and then dividing by the total number of units expected to be produced during its useful life. Units of production can be expressed in product or other units such as hours used or miles driven. The second step is to compute depreciation expense for the period by multiplying the units produced in the period by the depreciation per unit. The formula for units-of-production depreciation, along with its computation for the machine described in Exhibit 10.5, is shown in Exhibit 10.9. (*Note:* 7,000 shoes are inspected and sold in its first year.)

Exhibit 10.9

Units-of-Production Depreciation Formula and Example

Step 1

$$\textbf{Depreciation per unit} = \frac{\textbf{Cost} - \textbf{Salvage value}}{\textbf{Total units of production}} = \frac{\$10{,}000 - \$1{,}000}{36{,}000 \text{ shoes}} = \$0.25 \text{ per shoe}$$

Step 2

Depreciation expense = Depreciation per unit × Units produced in period

$\$0.25$ per shoe $\times$ 7,000 shoes $= \$1{,}750$

Using data on the number of shoes inspected by the machine, we can compute the *units-of-production depreciation schedule* shown in Exhibit 10.10. For example, depreciation for the first year is $1,750 (7,000 shoes at $0.25 per shoe). Depreciation for the second year is $2,000 (8,000 shoes at $0.25 per shoe). Other years are similarly computed. Notice in Exhibit 10.10 that (1) depreciation expense depends on unit output, (2) accumulated depreciation is the sum of current and prior periods' depreciation expense, and (3) book value declines each period until it equals salvage value at the end of the asset's useful life. **Boise Cascade** is one of many companies using the units-of-production depreciation method. It reports that most of its "paper and wood products manufacturing facilities determine depreciation by a units-of-production method."

Example: Refer to Exhibit 10.10. If the number of shoes inspected in 2008 is 5,500, what is depreciation expense for that year?
Answer: $1,250 (never depreciate below salvage value)

Exhibit 10.10

Units-of-Production Depreciation Schedule

	Depreciation for the Period			End of Period	
Annual Period	Number of Units	Depreciation per Unit	Depreciation Expense	Accumulated Depreciation	Book Value
2003	—	—	—	—	$10,000
2004	7,000	$0.25	**$1,750**	$1,750	8,250
2005	8,000	0.25	**2,000**	3,750	6,250
2006	9,000	0.25	**2,250**	6,000	4,000
2007	7,000	0.25	**1,750**	7,750	2,250
2008	5,000	0.25	**1,250**	9,000	**1,000**

Declining-Balance Method An **accelerated depreciation method** yields larger depreciation expenses in the early years of an asset's life and less depreciation in later years. Of several accelerated methods, the most common is the **declining-balance method** of depreciation, which uses a depreciation rate that is a multiple of the straight-line rate and applies it to the asset's beginning-of-period book value. The amount of depreciation declines each period because book value declines each period.

A common depreciation rate for the declining-balance method is double the straight-line rate. This is called the *double-declining-balance* (*DDB*) method. This method is applied in three steps: (1) compute the asset's straight-line depreciation rate, (2) double the straight-line rate, and (3) compute depreciation expense by multiplying this rate by the asset's beginning-of-period book value. To illustrate, let's return to the machine in Exhibit 10.5 and

Global: German firms commonly apply accelerated depreciation of up to three times the straight-line rate.

Point: In the DDB method, *double* refers to the rate and *declining balance* refers to book value. The rate is applied to beginning book value each period.

apply the double-declining-balance method to compute depreciation expense. Exhibit 10.11 shows the first-year depreciation computation for the machine. The three-step process is to (1) divide 100% by five years to determine the straight-line rate of 20% per year, (2) double this 20% rate to get the declining-balance rate of 40% per year, and (3) compute depreciation expense as 40% multiplied by the beginning-of-period book value.

Exhibit 10.11

Double-Declining-Balance Depreciation Formula

Step 1

Straight-line rate = 100% ÷ Useful life = 100% ÷ 5 years = 20%

Step 2

Double-declining-balance rate = 2 × Straight-line rate = 2 × 20% = 40%

Step 3

Depreciation expense = Double-declining-balance rate × Beginning-period book value

40% × $10,000 = $4,000 (for 2004)

The *double-declining-balance depreciation schedule* is shown in Exhibit 10.12. The schedule follows the formula except for year 2008, when depreciation expense is $296. This $296 is not equal to 40% × $1,296, or $518.40. If we had used the $518.40 for depreciation expense in 2008, ending book value would equal $777.60, which is less than the $1,000 salvage value. Instead, the $296 is computed by subtracting the $1,000 salvage value from the $1,296 book value at the beginning of the fifth year (the year when DDB depreciation cuts into salvage value).

Example: What is DDB depreciation expense in year 2007 if the salvage value is $2,000? *Answer:* $2,160 − $2,000 = $160

Exhibit 10.12

Double-Declining-Balance Depreciation Schedule

	Depreciation for the Period			End of Period	
Annual Period	Beginning of Period Book Value	Depreciation Rate	Depreciation Expense	Accumulated Depreciation	Book Value
2003	—	—	—	—	$10,000
2004	$10,000	40%	$4,000	$4,000	6,000
2005	6,000	40	2,400	6,400	3,600
2006	3,600	40	1,440	7,840	2,160
2007	2,160	40	864	8,704	1,296
2008	1,296	40	296*	9,000	**1,000**

* Year 2008 depreciation is $1,296 − $1,000 = $296 (never depreciate book value below salvage value).

Comparing Depreciation Methods Exhibit 10.13 shows depreciation expense for each year of the machine's useful life under each of the three depreciation methods.

A1 Compare and analyze alternative depreciation methods.

Exhibit 10.13

Depreciation Expense for the Different Methods

	A	B	C	D
1	**Period**	**Straight-Line**	**Units-of-Production**	**Double-Declining-Balance**
2	2004	$1,800	$1,750	$4,000
3	2005	1,800	2,000	2,400
4	2006	1,800	2,250	1,440
5	2007	1,800	1,750	864
6	2008	1,800	1,250	296
7	Totals	$9,000	$9,000	$9,000
8				

While the amount of depreciation expense per period differs for different methods, total depreciation expense is the same over the machine's useful life. Each method starts with a total cost of $10,000 and ends with a salvage value of $1,000. The difference is the pattern

Global: Some Canadian companies use an "increasing charge" depreciation (the opposite of accelerated).

Decision Insight

Vogue About 83% of companies use straight-line depreciation for plant assets, 5% use units-of-production, and 4% use declining-balance. Another 8% use an unspecified accelerated method—most likely declining-balance.

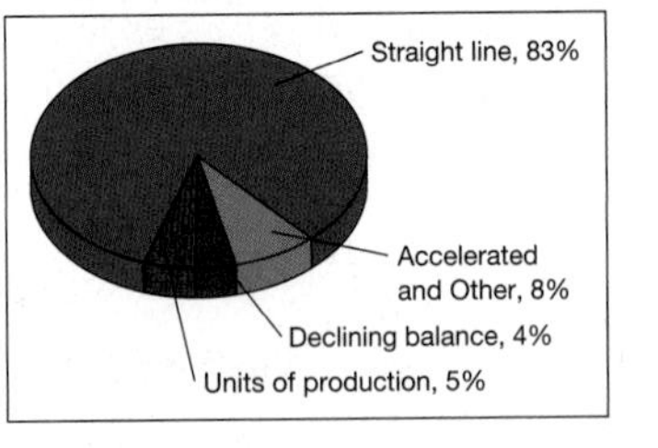

in depreciation expense over the useful life. The book value of the asset when using straight-line is always greater than the book value from using double-declining-balance, except at the beginning and end of the asset's useful life, when it is the same. Also, the straight-line method yields a steady pattern of depreciation expense while the units-of-production depreciation depends on the number of units produced. Each of these methods is acceptable because it allocates cost in a systematic and rational manner.

Depreciation for Tax Reporting The records a company keeps for financial accounting purposes are usually separate from the records it keeps for tax accounting purposes. This is so because financial accounting aims to report useful information on financial performance and position, whereas tax accounting reflects government objectives in raising revenues. Differences between these two accounting systems are normal and expected. Depreciation is a common example of how the records differ. For example, many companies use accelerated depreciation in computing taxable income. Reporting higher depreciation expense in the early years of an asset's life reduces the company's taxable income in those years and increases it in later years, when the depreciation expense is lower. The company's goal here is to *postpone* its tax payments. This means the company can use these resources now to earn additional income before payment is due.

Point: Understanding depreciation for financial accounting will help in learning MACRS for tax accounting. Rules for MACRS are available from www.IRS.com.

Global: A few countries require the depreciation method chosen for financial reporting to match the method chosen for tax reporting.

The U.S. federal income tax law has rules for depreciating assets. These rules include the **Modified Accelerated Cost Recovery System (MACRS),** which allows straight-line depreciation for some assets, but it requires accelerated depreciation for most kinds of assets. MACRS separates depreciable assets into different classes and defines the depreciable life and rate for each class. MACRS is not acceptable for financial reporting because it often allocates costs over an arbitrary period that is less than the asset's useful life. Details of MACRS are covered in tax accounting courses.

Decision Insight

Instant Numbers Computer technology greatly simplifies depreciation computations and revisions. Many inexpensive, off-the-shelf software packages and business calculators allow a user to choose from a variety of depreciation methods and quickly produce depreciation schedules.

Partial-Year Depreciation

C3 Explain depreciation for partial years and changes in estimates.

Plant assets are purchased and disposed of at various times. When an asset is purchased (or disposed of) at a time other than the beginning or end of an accounting period, depreciation is recorded for part of a year. This is done so that the year of purchase or the year of disposal is charged with its share of the asset's depreciation.

To illustrate, assume that the machine in Exhibit 10.5 is purchased and placed in service on October 8, 2003, and the annual accounting period ends on December 31. Since this machine is purchased and used for nearly three months in 2003, the calendar-year income statement should report depreciation expense on the machine for that part of the year. Normally, depreciation assumes that the asset is purchased on the first day of the month nearest the actual date of purchase. In this case, since the purchase occurred on October 8, we assume an October 1 purchase date. This means that three months' depreciation is recorded in 2003. Using straight-line depreciation, we compute three months' depreciation of $450 as follows:

$$\frac{\$10{,}000 - \$1{,}000}{5 \text{ years}} \times \frac{3}{12} = \$450$$

Example: If the machine's salvage value is zero and purchase occurs on Oct. 8, 2003, how much depreciation is recorded at Dec. 31, 2003? *Answer:* $10,000/5 × 3/12 = $500

A similar computation is necessary when an asset disposal occurs during a period. To illustrate, assume that the machine is sold on June 24, 2008. Depreciation is recorded for the period January 1 through June 24 when it is disposed of. This partial year's depreciation, computed to the nearest whole month, is

$$\frac{\$10{,}000 - \$1{,}000}{5 \text{ years}} \times \frac{6}{12} = \$900$$

Change in Estimates for Depreciation

Depreciation is based on estimates of salvage value and useful life. During the useful life of an asset, new information may indicate that these estimates are inaccurate. If our estimate of an asset's useful life and/or salvage value changes, what should we do? The answer is to use the new estimate to compute depreciation for current and future periods. This means that we revise the depreciation expense computation by spreading the cost yet to be depreciated over the remaining useful life. This approach is used for all depreciation methods.

Point: Remaining depreciable cost equals book value less revised salvage value at the point of revision.

Let's return to the machine described in Exhibit 10.8 using straight-line depreciation. At the beginning of this asset's third year, its book value is \$6,400, computed as \$10,000 minus \$3,600. Assume that at the beginning of its third year, the estimated number of years remaining in its useful life changes from three to four years *and* its estimate of salvage value changes from \$1,000 to \$400. Straight-line depreciation for each of the four remaining years is computed as shown in Exhibit 10.14.

Point: Income is overstated (and depreciation understated) when useful life is too high; a useful life that is too low yields opposite results.

$$\frac{\textbf{Book value} - \textbf{Revised salvage value}}{\textbf{Revised remaining useful life}} = \frac{\$6{,}400 - \$400}{4 \text{ years}} = \$1{,}500 \text{ per year}$$

Exhibit 10.14

Computing Revised Straight-Line Depreciation

Thus, \$1,500 of depreciation expense is recorded for the machine at the end of the third through sixth years—each year of its remaining useful life. Since this asset was depreciated at \$1,800 per year for the first two years, it is tempting to conclude that depreciation expense was overstated in the first two years. However, these expenses reflected the best information available at that time. We do not go back and restate prior years' financial statements for this type of new information. Instead, we adjust the current and future periods' statements to reflect this new information. Revising an estimate of the useful life or salvage value of a plant asset is referred to as a **change in an accounting estimate** and is reflected in current and future financial statements, not in prior statements.

Example: If at the beginning of its second year the machine's remaining useful life changes from four to three years and salvage value from \$1,000 to \$400, how much straight-line depreciation is recorded in remaining years? *Answer:* Revised depreciation = (\$8,200 − \$400)/3 = \$2,600.

Reporting Depreciation

Both the cost and accumulated depreciation of plant assets are reported on the balance sheet or in its notes. **Titan Motorcycle**, for instance, reports the following:

Property and equipment:	
Land, building, and vehicles	\$ 689,748
Machinery and equipment	1,116,318
Displays and leasehold improvements	837,414
Gross property and equipment	2,643,480
Less accumulated depreciation	629,575
Net property and equipment	\$2,013,905

Many companies also show plant assets on one line with the net amount of cost less accumulated depreciation. When this is done, the amount of accumulated depreciation is disclosed in a note. **Krispy Kreme** reports only the net amount of its property and equipment in its balance sheet in Appendix A. To satisfy the full-disclosure principle, Krispy Kreme describes its depreciation methods in its Note 2 and the amounts comprising plant assets in its Note 5.

Point: A company usually keeps records for each asset showing its cost and depreciation to date. The combined records for individual assets are a type of *plant asset subsidiary ledger.*

Reporting both the cost and accumulated depreciation of plant assets helps users compare the assets of different companies. For example, a company holding assets costing \$50,000 and accumulated depreciation of \$40,000 is likely in a situation different from a company

Decision Ethics

Controller You are the controller for a struggling company. Its operations require regular investments in equipment, and depreciation is its largest expense. Its competitors frequently replace equipment—often depreciated over three years. The company president instructs you to revise useful lives of equipment from three to six years and to use a six-year life on all new equipment. What actions do you take?

Answer—p. 406

with new assets costing $10,000. While the net undepreciated cost of $10,000 is the same in both cases, the first company may have more productive capacity available but likely is facing the need to replace older assets. These insights are not provided if the two balance sheets report only the $10,000 book values.

Users must remember that plant assets are reported on a balance sheet at their undepreciated costs (book value), not at market values. This emphasis on costs rather than market values is based on the *going-concern principle* described in Chapter 1. This principle states that, unless there is evidence to the contrary, we assume that a company continues in business. This implies that plant assets are held and used long enough to recover their cost through the sale of products and services. Since plant assets are not for sale, their market values are not reported.

Point: Depreciation is higher and income lower in the short run when using accelerated versus straight-line methods.

Accumulated Depreciation is a contra asset account with a normal credit balance. It does *not* reflect funds accumulated to buy new assets when the assets currently owned are replaced. If a company has funds available to buy assets, the funds are shown on the balance sheet among liquid assets such as Cash or Investments.

Quick Check

4. On January 1, 2005, a company pays $77,000 to purchase office furniture with a zero salvage value. The furniture's useful life is somewhere between 7 and 10 years. What is the year 2005 straight-line depreciation on the furniture using (*a*) a 7-year useful life and (*b*) a 10-year useful life?
5. What does the term *depreciation* mean in accounting?
6. A company purchases a machine for $96,000 on January 1, 2005. Its useful life is five years or 100,000 units of product, and its salvage value is $8,000. During 2005, 10,000 units of product are produced. Compute the book value of this machine on December 31, 2005, assuming (*a*) straight-line depreciation and (*b*) units-of-production depreciation.
7. In early January 2005, a company acquires equipment for $3,800. The company estimates this equipment to have a useful life of three years and a salvage value of $200. Early in 2007, the company changes its estimates to a total four-year useful life and zero salvage value. Using the straight-line method, what is depreciation for the year ended 2007?

Answers—p. 406

Additional Expenditures

P3 Distinguish between revenue and capital expenditures, and account for them.

After a company acquires a plant asset and puts it into service, it often makes additional expenditures for that asset's operation, maintenance, repair, and improvement. In recording these expenditures, it must decide whether to capitalize or expense them (to capitalize an expenditure is to debit the asset account). The issue is whether more useful information is provided by reporting these expenditures as current period expenses or by adding them to the plant asset's cost and depreciating them over its remaining useful life.

Point: When an amount is said to be *capitalized* to an account, the amount is added to the account's normal balance.

Revenue expenditures, also called *income statement expenditures,* are additional costs of plant assets that do not materially increase the asset's life or productive capabilities. They are recorded as expenses and deducted from revenues in the current period's income statement. Examples of revenue expenditures are cleaning, repainting, adjustments, and lubricants. **Capital expenditures,** also called *balance sheet expenditures,* are additional costs of plant assets that provide benefits extending beyond the current period. They are debited to asset accounts and reported on the balance sheet. Capital expenditures increase or improve the type or amount of service an asset provides. Examples are roofing replacement, plant expansion, and major overhauls of machinery and equipment.

	Financial Statement Effect		
Cost Category	Accounting	Expense Timing	Current Income
Revenue expenditure	Income stmt. account debited	Expensed currently	Lower
Capital expenditure	Balance sheet account debited	Expensed in future	Higher

Financial statements are affected for several years by the accounting choice of recording costs as either revenue expenditures or capital expenditures. Managers must be careful in classifying them. This classification decision is based on whether these expenditures are identified as either ordinary repairs or as betterments and extraordinary repairs.

Ordinary Repairs

Ordinary repairs are expenditures to keep an asset in normal, good operating condition. They are necessary if an asset is to perform to expectations over its useful life. Ordinary repairs do not extend an asset's useful life beyond its original estimate or increase its productivity beyond original expectations. Examples are normal costs of cleaning, lubricating, adjusting, and replacing small parts of a machine. Ordinary repairs are treated as *revenue expenditures.* This means their costs are reported as expenses on the current period income statement. Following this rule, **Brunswick** reports that "maintenance and repair costs are expensed as incurred."

Point: Many companies apply the *materiality principle* to treat *low-cost plant assets* (say, less than $500) as revenue expenditures.

Betterments and Extraordinary Repairs

Accounting for betterments and extraordinary repairs is similar. **Betterments,** also called *improvements,* are expenditures that make a plant asset more efficient or productive. A betterment often involves adding a component to an asset or replacing one of its old components with a better one, and does not always increase an asset's useful life. An example is replacing manual controls on a machine with automatic controls. One special type of betterment is an *addition,* such as adding a new wing or dock to a warehouse. Since a betterment benefits future periods, it is debited to the asset account as a capital expenditure. The new book value (less salvage value) is then depreciated over the asset's remaining useful life. To illustrate, suppose a company pays $8,000 for a machine with an eight-year useful life and no salvage value. After three years and $3,000 of depreciation, it adds an automated control system to the machine at a cost of $1,800. This results in reduced labor costs in future periods. The cost of the betterment is added to the Machinery account with this entry:

Example: Assume a company owns a Web server. Identify each item as a revenue or capital expenditure: (1) purchase price, (2) necessary wiring, (3) platform for operation, (4) circuits to increase capacity, (5) cleaning after each three months of use, (6) repair of a faulty connection, and (7) replaced a worn cooling fan. *Answer:* Capital expenditures: 1, 2, 3, 4; Revenue expenditures: 5, 6, 7.

Jan. 2	Machinery	1,800	
	Cash		1,800
	To record installation of automated system.		

Assets	=	Liabilities	+	Equity
+1,800				
−1,800				

After the betterment, the remaining cost to be depreciated is $6,800, computed as $8,000 − $3,000 + $1,800. Depreciation expense for the remaining five years is $1,360 per year, computed as $6,800/5 years.

Point: Both extraordinary repairs and betterments demand revised depreciation schedules.

Extraordinary repairs are expenditures extending the asset's useful life beyond its original estimate. Extraordinary repairs are *capital expenditures* because they benefit future periods. Their costs are debited to the asset account. For example, **America West Airlines** reports: "the cost of major scheduled airframe, engine and certain component overhauls are capitalized (and expensed) . . . over the periods benefited."

Decision Maker

Entrepreneur Your start-up Internet services company needs cash, and you are preparing financial statements to apply for a short-term loan. A friend suggests that you treat as many expenses as possible as capital expenditures. What are the impacts on financial statements of this suggestion? What do you think is the aim of this suggestion?

Answer—p. 406

Disposals of Plant Assets

Plant assets are disposed of for several reasons. Some are discarded because they wear out or become obsolete. Others are sold because of changing business plans. Regardless of the reason, disposals of plant assets occur in one of three basic ways: discarding, sale, or exchange. The general steps in accounting for a disposal of plant assets is described in Exhibit 10.15.

Exhibit 10.15

Accounting for Disposals of Plant Assets

1. Record depreciation up to the date of disposal—this also updates Accumulated Depreciation.
2. Record the removal of the disposed asset's account balances—including its Accumulated Depreciation.
3. Record any cash (and/or other assets) received or paid in the disposal.
4. Record any gain or loss—computed by comparing the disposed asset's book value with the market value of any assets received.*

* One exception to step 4 is the case of a gain on a similar asset exchange—it is described later in this section.

Discarding Plant Assets

P4 Account for asset disposal through discarding, selling, and exchanging an asset.

A plant asset is *discarded* when it is no longer useful to the company and it has no market value. To illustrate, assume that a machine costing $9,000 with accumulated depreciation of $9,000 is discarded. When accumulated depreciation equals the asset's cost, it is said to be *fully depreciated* (zero book value). The entry to record the discarding of this asset is

Assets	= Liabilities	+ Equity
+9,000		
−9,000		

June 5	Accumulated Depreciation—Machinery	9,000	
	Machinery		9,000
	To discard fully depreciated machinery.		

This entry reflects all four steps of Exhibit 10.15. Step 1 is unnecessary since the machine is fully depreciated. Step 2 is reflected in the debit to Accumulated Depreciation and credit to Machinery. Since no other asset is involved, step 3 is irrelevant. Finally, since book value is zero and no other asset is involved, no gain or loss is recorded in step 4.

How do we account for discarding an asset that is not fully depreciated or one whose depreciation is not up-to-date? To answer this, consider equipment costing $8,000 with accumulated depreciation of $6,000 on December 31 of the prior fiscal year-end. This equipment is being depreciated using the straight-line method over eight years with zero salvage. On July 1 of the current year it is discarded. Step 1 is to bring depreciation up-to-date:

Point: Recording depreciation expense up-to-date gives an up-to-date book value for determining gain or loss.

Assets	= Liabilities	+ Equity
−500		−500

July 1	Depreciation Expense	500	
	Accumulated Depreciation—Equipment		500
	To record 6 months' depreciation ($1,000 × 6/12).		

Steps 2 through 4 of Exhibit 10.15 are reflected in the second (and final) entry:

Assets	= Liabilities	+ Equity
+6,500		−1,500
−8,000		

July 1	Accumulated Depreciation—Equipment	6,500	
	Loss on Disposal of Equipment	1,500	
	Equipment		8,000
	To discard equipment with a $1,500 book value.		

Point: Gain or loss is determined by comparing "value given" (book value) to "value received."

The loss is computed by comparing the equipment's $1,500 book value ($8,000 − $6,000 − $500) with the zero net cash proceeds. This loss is reported in the Other Expenses and Losses section of the income statement. Discarding an asset can sometimes require a cash payment that would increase the loss. The income statement reports any loss from discarding an asset, and the balance sheet reflects the changes in the asset and accumulated depreciation accounts.

Selling Plant Assets

Companies often sell plant assets when they restructure or downsize operations. To illustrate the accounting for selling plant assets, we consider BTO's March 31 sale of equipment that cost $16,000 and has accumulated depreciation of $12,000 at December 31 of the prior calendar year-end. Annual depreciation on this equipment is $4,000 computed using straight-line depreciation. Step 1 of this sale is to record depreciation expense and update accumulated depreciation to March 31 of the current year:

March 31	Depreciation Expense	1,000	
	Accumulated Depreciation—Equipment.		1,000
	To record 3 months' depreciation ($4,000 × 3/12).		

Assets = Liabilities + Equity
−1,000 −1,000

Steps 2 through 4 of Exhibit 10.15 can be reflected in one final entry that depends on the amount received from the asset's sale. We consider three different possibilities.

Sale at Book Value If BTO receives $3,000, an amount equal to the equipment's book value as of March 31, no gain or loss occurs on disposal. The entry is

March 31	Cash	3,000	
	Accumulated Depreciation—Equipment	13,000	
	Equipment		16,000
	To record sale of equipment for no gain or loss.		

Assets = Liabilities + Equity
+3,000
+13,000
−16,000

Sale above Book Value If BTO receives $7,000, an amount that is $4,000 above the equipment's book value as of March 31, a gain on disposal occurs. The entry is

March 31	Cash	7,000	
	Accumulated Depreciation—Equipment	13,000	
	Gain on Disposal of Equipment.		4,000
	Equipment		16,000
	To record sale of equipment for a $4,000 gain.		

Assets = Liabilities + Equity
+7,000 +4,000
+13,000
−16,000

Sale below Book Value If BTO receives $2,500, an amount that is $500 below the equipment's book value as of March 31, a loss on disposal occurs. The entry is

March 31	Cash	2,500	
	Loss on Disposal of Equipment	500	
	Accumulated Depreciation—Equipment	13,000	
	Equipment.		16,000
	To record sale of equipment for a $500 loss.		

Assets = Liabilities + Equity
+2,500 −500
+13,000
−16,000

Exchanging Plant Assets

Many plant assets such as machinery, automobiles, and office equipment are disposed of by exchanging them for newer assets. In a typical exchange of plant assets, a *trade-in allowance* is received on the old asset and the balance is paid in cash. Accounting for the exchange of assets depends on whether the old and the new assets are similar or dissimilar in the functions they perform. Trading an old truck for a new truck is an exchange of similar assets, whereas trading a truck for a machine is an exchange of dissimilar assets. This section describes the accounting for the exchange of similar assets. Similar asset exchanges are common, whereas dissimilar asset exchanges are not (the latter are discussed in advanced courses).

Accounting for exchanges of similar assets depends on whether the book value of the asset given up is less or more than the market value of the asset received. When the market value of the asset received is less than the book value of the asset given up, the difference is recognized as a loss. However, when the value of the asset received is more than the asset's book value given up, the gain is *not* recognized.

Receiving Less in Exchange: A Loss Let's assume that a company exchanges both old equipment and $33,000 in cash for new equipment. The old equipment originally cost

Point: Trade-in allowance minus book value equals the gain (or loss if negative) on exchange.

$36,000 and has accumulated depreciation of $20,000 at the time of exchange. The new equipment has a market value of $42,000. These details are reflected in the middle (Loss) columns of Exhibit 10.16.

Exhibit 10.16

Computing Gain or Loss on *Similar* Asset Exchange

Similar Plant Asset Exchange	Loss		Gain	
Market value of assets received		$42,000		$52,000
Book value of assets given up:				
Equipment ($36,000 − $20,000)	$16,000		$16,000	
Cash	33,000	49,000	33,000	49,000
Gain (loss) on exchange		**$(7,000)**		**$ 3,000**

The entry to record this similar asset exchange is

Assets	= Liabilities	+ Equity
+42,000		−7,000
+20,000		
−36,000		
−33,000		

Date	Account	Debit	Credit
Jan. 3	Equipment (**new**)	42,000	
	Loss on Exchange of Assets	7,000	
	Accumulated Depreciation—Equipment (**old**)	20,000	
	Equipment (**old**)		36,000
	Cash		33,000
	To record exchange of old equipment and cash for new equipment.		

Point: Parenthetical journal entry notes to "new" and "old" equipment are for illustration only. Both the debit and credit are to the same Equipment account in the general ledger.

The book value of the assets given up consists of the $33,000 cash and the $16,000 ($36,000 − $20,000) book value of the old equipment. The total $49,000 book value of assets given up is compared to the $42,000 market value of the new equipment received. This yields a loss of $7,000 ($42,000 − $49,000).

Receiving More in Exchange: A Gain Let's assume the same facts as in the preceding similar asset exchange *except* that the new equipment received has a market value of $52,000 instead of $42,000. The entry to record this similar asset exchange is

Assets	= Liabilities	+ Equity
+49,000		
+20,000		
−36,000		
−33,000		

Date	Account	Debit	Credit
Jan. 3	Equipment (**new**)	49,000	
	Accumulated Depreciation—Equipment (**old**)	20,000	
	Equipment (**old**)		36,000
	Cash		33,000
	To record exchange of old equipment and cash for new equipment.		

Point: No gain is recognized for similar asset exchanges.

Exhibit 10.16 shows that there is a "gain" from this exchange in the far right (Gain) columns. This gain is *not* recognized in the entry because of a rule prohibiting recognizing a gain on similar asset exchanges.[1] The $49,000 recorded for the new equipment equals its cash price ($52,000) less the unrecognized gain ($3,000) on the exchange. The $49,000 cost recorded is called the *cost basis* of the new machine. This cost basis is the amount we use to compute depreciation and its book value. The cost basis of the new asset also can be computed by summing the book values of the assets given up as shown in Exhibit 10.17.

Exhibit 10.17

Cost Basis of New Asset when Gain Not Recognized

Cost of old equipment	$ 36,000
Less accumulated depreciation	20,000
Book value of old equipment	16,000
Cash paid in the exchange	33,000
Cost recorded for new equipment	**$49,000**

[1] The reason a gain from a similar asset exchange is not recognized is that the earnings process is not considered complete for the exchanged asset. The decision to recognize a loss from a similar asset exchange is an application of *accounting conservatism* in measuring and recording asset values.

Quick Check

8. Early in the fifth year of a machine's six-year useful life, it is overhauled, and its useful life is extended to nine years. This machine originally cost $108,000 and the overhaul cost is $12,000. Prepare the entry to record the overhaul cost.
9. Explain the difference between revenue expenditures and capital expenditures and how both are recorded.
10. What is a betterment? How is a betterment recorded?
11. A company acquires equipment on January 10, 2005, at a cost of $42,000. Straight-line depreciation is used with a five-year life and $7,000 salvage value. On June 27, 2006, the company sells this equipment for $32,000. Prepare the entry(ies) for June 27, 2006.
12. A company trades an old Web server for a new one. The cost of the old server is $30,000, and its accumulated depreciation at the time of the trade is $23,400. The new server has a cash price of $45,000. Prepare entries to record the trade under two different assumptions where the company receives a trade-in allowance of (*a*) $3,000 and (*b*) $7,000.

Answers—p. 406

Example: Assume the old equipment in Exh. 10.17 is sold for $19,000 and, in a *separate* transaction, new equipment is bought for $52,000. Record both transactions. *Answer:*

Cash	19,000	
Accum. Depr — Eq.	20,000	
Equipment (old)		36,000
Gain on Sale of Eq.		3,000
Equipment (new)	52,000	
Cash		52,000

Section 2—Natural Resources

Natural resources are assets that are physically consumed when used. Examples are standing timber, mineral deposits, and oil and gas fields. Since they are consumed when used, they are often called *wasting assets*. These assets represent soon-to-be inventories of raw materials that will be converted into one or more products by cutting, mining, or pumping. Until that conversion takes place, they are noncurrent assets and are shown in a balance sheet using titles such as timberlands, mineral deposits, or oil reserves. Natural resources are reported under either plant assets or its own separate category. **Alcoa**, for instance, reports its natural resources under the balance sheet title *Properties, plants and equipment.* In a note to its financial statements, Alcoa reports a separate amount for *Land and land rights, including mines.* **Weyerhaeuser**, on the other hand, reports its timber holdings in a separate balance sheet category titled *Timber and timberlands.*

Cost Determination and Depletion

P5 Account for natural resource assets and their depletion.

Natural resources are recorded at cost, which includes all expenditures necessary to acquire the resource and prepare it for its intended use. **Depletion** is the process of allocating the cost of a natural resource to the period when it is consumed. Natural resources are reported on the balance sheet at cost less *accumulated depletion.* The depletion expense per period is usually based on units extracted from cutting, mining, or pumping. This is similar to units-of-production depreciation. **Exxon Mobil** uses this approach to amortize the costs of discovering and operating its oil wells.

To illustrate depletion of natural resources, let's consider a mineral deposit with an estimated 250,000 tons of available ore. It is purchased for $500,000, and we expect zero salvage value. The depletion charge per ton of ore mined is $2, computed as $500,000 ÷ 250,000 tons. If 85,000 tons are mined and sold in the first year, the depletion charge for that year is $170,000. These computations are detailed in Exhibit 10.18. Depletion expense for the first year is recorded as follows:

Dec. 31	Depletion Expense—Mineral Deposit	170,000	
	Accumulated Depletion—Mineral Deposit		170,000
	To record depletion of the mineral deposit.		

Assets = Liabilities + Equity
−170,000 −170,000

Exhibit 10.18

Depletion Formula and Example

Step 1

$$\textbf{Depletion per unit} = \frac{\textbf{Cost} - \textbf{Salvage value}}{\textbf{Total units of capacity}} = \frac{\$500{,}000 - \$0}{250{,}000 \text{ tons}} = \$2 \text{ per ton}$$

Step 2

$$\textbf{Depletion expense} = \textbf{Depletion per unit} \times \textbf{Units extracted and sold in period}$$
$$= \$2 \times 85{,}000 = \$170{,}000$$

The period-end balance sheet reports the mineral deposit as shown in Exhibit 10.19.

Exhibit 10.19

Balance Sheet Presentation of Natural Resources

Mineral deposit	$500,000	
Less accumulated depletion	170,000	$330,000

Since all 85,000 tons of the mined ore are sold during the year, the entire $170,000 of depletion is reported on the income statement. If some of the ore remains unsold at year-end, however, the depletion related to the unsold ore is carried forward on the balance sheet and reported as Ore Inventory, a current asset.

Plant Assets Used in Extracting Resources

The conversion of natural resources by mining, cutting, or pumping usually requires machinery, equipment, and buildings. When the usefulness of these plant assets is directly related to the depletion of a natural resource, their costs are depreciated using the units-of-production method in proportion to the depletion of the natural resource. For example, if a machine is permanently installed in a mine and 10% of the ore is mined and sold in the period, then 10% of the machine's cost (less any salvage value) is allocated to depreciation expense. The same procedure is used when a machine is abandoned once resources have been extracted. If, however, a machine will be moved to and used at another site when extraction is complete, the machine is depreciated over its own useful life.

Section 3—Intangible Assets

P6 Account for intangible assets.

Intangible assets are nonphysical assets (used in operations) that confer on their owners long-term rights, privileges, or competitive advantages. Examples are patents, copyrights, licenses, leaseholds, franchises, goodwill, and trademarks. Lack of physical substance does not necessarily make an asset intangible. Notes and accounts receivable, for instance, lack physical substance, but they are not intangibles. This section identifies the more common types of intangible assets and explains the accounting for them.

Cost Determination and Amortization

Point: Goodwill is not amortized; instead, it is annually tested for impairment.

Point: The cost to acquire a Website address is an intangible asset.

An intangible asset is recorded at cost when purchased. Its cost is systematically allocated to expense over its estimated useful life through the process of **amortization.** If an intangible asset has an **indefinite useful life**—meaning that no legal, regulatory, contractual, competitive, economic, or other factors limit its useful life—it should not be amortized. (If an intangible with an indefinite useful life is later judged to have a limited useful life, it is amortized over that limited useful life.) Amortization of intangible assets is similar to depreciation of plant assets and the depletion of natural resources in that it is a process of cost allocation. However, only the straight-line method is used for amortizing intangibles *unless* the company can show that another method is preferred. The effects of amortization are recorded in a contra account (Accumulated Amortization). The gross acquisition cost of intangible assets is disclosed in the balance sheet along with their accumulated amortization (these disclosures are new per *SFAS 142*). The eventual disposal of an intangible asset involves removing its book value, recording any other asset(s) received or given up, and recognizing any gain or loss for the difference.

Many intangibles have limited useful lives due to laws, contracts, or other asset characteristics. Examples are patents, copyrights, and leaseholds. Other intangibles such as goodwill, trademarks, and trade names have useful lives that cannot be easily determined. The cost of intangible assets is amortized over the periods expected to benefit by their use, but in no case can this period be longer than the asset's legal existence. The values of some intangible assets such as goodwill continue indefinitely into the future and are not amortized. (An intangible asset that is not amortized is tested annually for **impairment**—if necessary, an impairment loss is recorded. Details for this test are in advanced courses.)

Intangible assets are often shown in a separate section of the balance sheet immediately after plant assets. **Callaway Golf**, for instance, follows this approach in reporting more than $100 million of intangible assets in its recent balance sheet. Companies usually disclose their amortization periods for intangibles. The remainder of our discussion focuses on accounting for specific types of intangible assets.

Types of Intangibles

Patents The federal government grants patents to encourage the invention of new technology, mechanical devices, and production processes. A **patent** is an exclusive right granted to its owner to manufacture and sell a patented item or to use a process for 20 years. When patent rights are purchased, the cost to acquire the rights is debited to an account called Patents. If the owner engages in lawsuits to successfully defend a patent, the cost of lawsuits is debited to the Patents account. However, the costs of research and development leading to a new patent are expensed when incurred.

Mention "drug war" and most people think of fighting cocaine or heroin use. But another drug war is under way: Brand-name drugmakers are fighting to stop generic copies of their products from hitting the market once their patents expire. Successfully delaying a generic rival can mean hundreds of millions of dollars in extra sales.

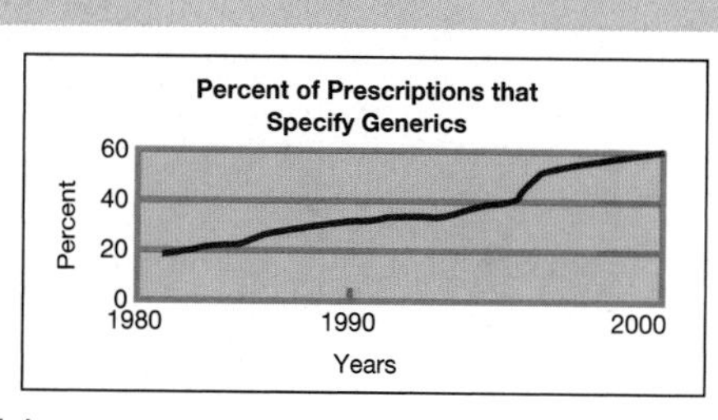

A patent's cost is amortized over its estimated useful life (not to exceed 20 years). If we purchase a patent costing $25,000 with a useful life of 10 years, we make the following adjusting entry at the end of each of the 10 years to amortize one-tenth of its cost:

Dec. 31	Amortization Expense—Patents	2,500	
	Accumulated Amortization—Patents		2,500
	To amortize patent costs over its useful life.		

Assets	=	Liabilities	+	Equity
−2,500				−2,500

The $2,500 debit to Amortization Expense appears on the income statement as a cost of the product or service provided under protection of the patent. The Accumulated Amortization—Patents account is a contra asset account to Patents.

Copyrights A **copyright** gives its owner the exclusive right to publish and sell a musical, literary, or artistic work during the life of the creator plus 70 years, although the useful life of most copyrights is much shorter. The costs of a copyright are amortized over its useful life. The only identifiable cost of many copyrights is the fee paid to the Copyright Office of the federal government or international agency granting the copyright. If this fee is immaterial, it is charged directly to an expense account, but if the identifiable costs of a copyright are material, they are capitalized (recorded in an asset account) and periodically amortized by debiting an account called Amortization Expense—Copyrights.

Leaseholds Property is rented under a contract called a **lease.** The property's owner, called the **lessor,** grants the lease. The one who secures the right to possess and use the property is called the **lessee.** A **leasehold** refers to the rights the lessor grants to the lessee under the terms of the lease. A leasehold is an intangible asset for the lessee.

Point: A leasehold account implies existence of future benefits that the lessee controls because of a prepayment. It also meets the definition of an asset.

Certain leases require no advance payment from the lessee but require monthly rent payments. In this case, we do not set up a Leasehold account. Instead, the monthly payments are debited to a Rent Expense account. If a long-term lease requires the lessee to pay the final period's rent in advance when the lease is signed, the lessee records this advance payment with a debit to the Leasehold account. Since the advance payment is not used until the final period, the Leasehold account balance remains intact until that final period when its balance is transferred to Rent Expense. (Some long-term leases give the lessee essentially the same rights as a purchaser. This results in a tangible asset and a liability reported by the lessee. Chapter 11 describes these so-called *capital leases.*)

A long-term lease can increase in value when current rental rates for similar property rise while the required payments under the lease remain constant. This increase in value of a lease is not reported on the lessee's balance sheet. However, if the property is subleased and the new tenant makes a cash payment to the original lessee for the rights under the old lease, the new tenant debits this payment to a Leasehold account, which is amortized to Rent Expense over the remaining life of the lease.

Leasehold Improvements A lessee sometimes pays for alterations or improvements to the leased property such as partitions, painting, and storefronts. These alterations and improvements are called **leasehold improvements,** and the lessee debits these costs to a Leasehold Improvements account. Since leasehold improvements become part of the property and revert to the lessor at the end of the lease, the lessee amortizes these costs over the life of the lease or the life of the improvements, whichever is shorter. The amortization entry debits Amortization Expense—Leasehold Improvements and credits Accumulated Amortization—Leasehold Improvements.

Franchises and Licenses **Franchises** and **licenses** are rights that a company or government grants an entity to deliver a product or service under specified conditions. Many organizations grant franchise and license rights—**McDonald's**, **Pizza Hut**, and **Major League Baseball** are just a few examples. The costs of franchises and licenses are debited to a Franchises and Licenses asset account and are amortized over the lives of the agreements.

Trademarks and Trade Names Companies often adopt unique symbols or select unique names and brands in marketing their products. A **trademark** or **trade (brand) name** is a symbol, name, phrase, or jingle identified with a company, product, or service. Examples are Nike swoosh, Marlboro Man, Big Mac, Coca-Cola, and Corvette. Ownership and exclusive right to use a trademark or trade name is often established by showing that one company used it before another. Ownership is best established by registering a trademark or trade name with the government's Patent Office. The cost of developing, maintaining, or enhancing the value of a trademark or trade name (such as advertising) is charged to expense when incurred. If a trademark or trade name is purchased, however, its cost is debited to an asset account and then amortized over its expected useful life.

Global: Some Australian and U.K. companies value brand names separately on their balance sheets.

Point: McDonald's "golden arches" is one of the world's most valuable trademarks, yet this asset is not shown on McDonald's balance sheet.

Goodwill **Goodwill** has a specific meaning in accounting. Goodwill is the amount by which a company's value exceeds the value of its individual assets and liabilities. This usually implies that the company as a whole has certain valuable attributes not measured among its individual assets and liabilities. These can include superior management, skilled workforce, good supplier or customer relations, quality products or services, good location, or other competitive advantages.

Point: IBM's balance sheet reports more than $4 billion of goodwill.

To keep accounting information from being too subjective, goodwill is not recorded unless an entire company or business segment is purchased. Purchased goodwill is measured by taking the purchase price of the company and subtracting the market value of its individual

Global: International accounting standards call for charging goodwill against income. The amortization period suggested is 20 or fewer years.

net assets (excluding goodwill). For instance, **Yahoo!** paid nearly $3.0 billion to acquire **GeoCities**; about $2.8 of the $3.0 billion was for goodwill and other intangibles.

Goodwill is measured as the excess of the cost of an acquired entity over the value of the acquired net assets. Goodwill is recorded as an asset, and it is *not* amortized. Instead, the FASB (*SFAS 142*) requires that goodwill be annually tested for impairment. If the book value of goodwill does not exceed its fair (market) value, goodwill is not impaired. However, if the book value of goodwill does exceed its fair value, an impairment loss is recorded equal to that excess. (Details of this test are in advanced courses.)

Point: Accounting for goodwill is different for financial accounting and tax accounting. The IRS requires the amortization of goodwill over a period not to exceed 15 years.

Quick Check

13. Give an example of a natural resource and of an intangible asset.
14. A company pays $650,000 for an ore deposit. The deposit is estimated to have 325,000 tons of ore that will be mined over the next 10 years. During the first year, it mined, processed, and sold 91,000 tons. What is that year's depletion expense?
15. On January 6, 2005, a company pays $120,000 for a patent with a remaining 17-year legal life to produce a toy expected to be marketable for three years. Prepare entries to record its acquisition and the December 31, 2005, amortization entry.

Answers—p. 407

Total Asset Turnover

Decision Analysis

A company's assets are important in determining its ability to generate sales and earn income. Managers devote much attention to deciding what assets a company acquires, how much it invests in assets, and how to use assets most efficiently and effectively. One important measure of a company's ability to use its assets is **total asset turnover,** defined in Exhibit 10.20.

A2 Compute total asset turnover and apply it to analyze a company's use of assets.

$$\textbf{Total asset turnover} = \frac{\textbf{Net sales}}{\textbf{Average total assets}}$$

Exhibit 10.20

Total Asset Turnover

The numerator reflects the net amounts earned from the sale of products and services. The denominator reflects the average total resources devoted to operating the company and generating sales.

To illustrate, let's look at total asset turnover in Exhibit 10.21 for two competing companies: **Coors** and **Anheuser-Busch**.

Company	Figure ($ in millions)	2002	2001	2000	1999
Coors	Net sales	$ 3,776	$ 2,429	$ 2,414	$ 2,236
	Average total assets	$ 3,019	$ 1,684	$ 1,588	$ 1,503
	Total asset turnover	**1.25**	**1.44**	**1.52**	**1.49**
Anheuser-Busch	Net sales	$13,566	$12,912	$12,499	$11,895
	Average total assets	$14,032	$13,547	$12,914	$12,593
	Total asset turnover	**0.97**	**0.95**	**0.97**	**0.94**

Exhibit 10.21

Analysis Using Total Asset Turnover

To show how we use total asset turnover, let's look at Coors. We express Coors's use of assets in generating net sales by saying "it turned its assets over 1.25 times during 2002." This means that each $1.00 of assets produced $1.25 of net sales. Is a total asset turnover of 1.25 good or bad? It is safe to say that all companies desire a high total asset turnover. Like many ratio analyses, however, a company's total asset turnover must be interpreted in comparison with that of prior years and of its competitors. Interpreting the total asset turnover also requires an understanding of the company's operations. Some operations are capital intensive, meaning that a relatively large amount is invested in assets to generate sales. This suggests a relatively lower total asset turnover. Other companies' operations are labor intensive, meaning that they generate sales more by the efforts of people than the use of assets. In that case, we expect a higher total asset turnover. Companies with low total

Point: A measure of **plant asset useful life** equals the plant asset cost divided by depreciation expense.

Point: A measure of **plant asset age** is estimated by dividing accumulated depreciation by depreciation expense. Older plant assets can signal needed asset replacements; it may also signal use of less efficient assets.

Decision Maker

Environmentalist A paper manufacturer claims it cannot afford more environmental controls. It points to its low total asset turnover of 1.9 and argues that it cannot compete with companies whose total asset turnover is much higher. Examples cited are food stores (5.5) and auto dealers (3.8). How do you respond?

Answer—p. 406

asset turnover require higher profit margins (examples are hotels and real estate); companies with high total asset turnover can succeed with lower profit margins; examples are food stores and toy merchandisers. Coors's turnover recently declined, but it is superior to that for Anheuser-Busch. Total asset turnover for Coors's competitors, available in industry publications such as Dun & Bradstreet, is generally in the range of 1.0 to 1.2 over this same period. Overall, Coors appears to be competitive and doing slightly better than its competitors on total asset turnover.

Demonstration Problem

On July 14, 2004, Tulsa Company pays $600,000 to acquire a fully equipped factory. The purchase involves the following assets:

Asset	Appraised Value	Salvage Value	Useful Life	Depreciation Method
Land	$160,000			Not depreciated
Land improvements	80,000	$ 0	10 years	Straight-line
Building	320,000	100,000	10 years	Double-declining-balance
Machinery	240,000	20,000	10,000 units	Units-of-production*
Total	$800,000			

* The machinery is used to produce 700 units in 2004 and 1,800 units in 2005.

Required

1. Allocate the total $600,000 purchase cost among the separate assets.
2. Compute the 2004 (six months) and 2005 depreciation expense for each asset and compute total depreciation expense for both years.
3. On the first day of 2006, Tulsa exchanged the machinery that was acquired on July 14, 2004, and $5,000 cash for similar machinery with a $210,000 market value. Journalize the exchange of these similar assets.
4. On the last day of calendar year 2006, Tulsa discarded machinery that had been on its books for five years. The machinery's original cost was $12,000 (estimated life of five years) and its salvage value was $2,000. No depreciation had been recorded for the fifth year when the disposal occurred. Journalize the fifth year of depreciation (straight-line method) and the asset's disposal.
5. At the beginning of year 2006, Tulsa purchased a patent for $100,000 cash. The company estimated the patent's useful life to be 10 years. Journalize the patent acquisition and its amortization for the year 2006.
6. Late in the year 2006, Tulsa acquired an ore deposit for $600,000 cash. It added roads and built mine shafts for an additional cost of $80,000. Salvage value of the mine is estimated to be $20,000. The company estimated 330,000 tons of available ore. In year 2006, Tulsa mined and sold 10,000 tons of ore. Journalize the mine's acquisition and its first year's depletion.

Planning the Solution

- Complete a three-column table showing the following amounts for each asset: appraised value, percent of total value, and apportioned cost.
- Using allocated costs, compute depreciation for 2004 (only one-half year) and 2005 (full year) for each asset. Summarize those computations in a table showing total depreciation for each year.
- Remember that gains on exchanges of similar assets are not recognized. Make a journal entry to add the acquired machinery to the books and to remove the old machinery, along with its accumulated depreciation, and to record the cash given in the exchange.
- Remember that depreciation must be recorded up-to-date before discarding an asset. Calculate and record depreciation expense for the fifth year using the straight-line method. Since salvage value

is not received at the end of a discarded asset's life, the amount of any salvage value becomes a loss on disposal. Record the loss on the disposal as well as the removal of the discarded asset and its related accumulated depreciation.

- Record the patent (an intangible asset) at its purchase price. Use straight-line amortization over its useful life to calculate amortization expense.
- Record the ore deposit (a natural resource asset) at its cost, including any added costs to ready the mine for use. Calculate depletion per ton using the depletion formula. Multiply the depletion per ton by the amount of tons mined and sold to calculate depletion expense for the year.

Solution to Demonstration Problem

1. Allocation of the total cost of $600,000 among the separate assets:

Asset	Appraised Value	Percent of Total Value	Apportioned Cost
Land	$160,000	20%	**$120,000** ($600,000 × 20%)
Land improvements	80,000	10	**60,000** ($600,000 × 10%)
Building	320,000	40	**240,000** ($600,000 × 40%)
Machinery	240,000	30	**180,000** ($600,000 × 30%)
Total	$800,000	100%	$ 600,000

2. Depreciation for each asset. (*Note:* Land is not depreciated.)

Land Improvements	
Cost	$ 60,000
Salvage value	0
Depreciable cost	$ 60,000
Useful life	10 years
Annual depreciation expense ($60,000/10 years)	$ 6,000
2004 depreciation ($6,000 × 6/12)	**$ 3,000**
2005 depreciation	**$ 6,000**
Building	
Straight-line rate = 100%/10 years = 10%	
Double-declining-balance rate = 10% × 2 = 20%	
2004 depreciation ($240,000 × 20% × 6/12)	**$ 24,000**
2005 depreciation [($240,000 − $24,000) × 20%]	**$ 43,200**
Machinery	
Cost	$180,000
Salvage value	20,000
Depreciable cost	$160,000
Total expected units of production	10,000 units
Depreciation per unit ($160,000/10,000 units)	$ 16
2004 depreciation ($16 × 700 units)	**$ 11,200**
2005 depreciation ($16 × 1,800 units)	**$ 28,800**

Total depreciation expense:

	2004	2005
Land improvements	$ 3,000	$ 6,000
Building	24,000	43,200
Machinery	11,200	28,800
Total	$38,200	$78,000

3. Record the exchange of similar assets (machinery) with a gain on the exchange: The book value on the exchange date is $180,000 (cost) − $40,000 (accumulated depreciation). The book value of the machinery given up in the exchange ($140,000) plus the $5,000 cash paid is less than the $210,000 value of the machine acquired. The entry to record this exchange of similar assets does not recognize the $65,000 gain on exchange:

Machinery (new)	145,000*	
Accumulated Depreciation—Machinery (old)	40,000	
Machinery (old)		180,000
Cash		5,000
To record exchange of similar assets.		

* Market value of the acquired asset of $210,000 minus $65,000 gain.

4. Record the depreciation up to date on the discarded asset:

Depreciation Expense—Machinery	2,000	
Accumulated Depreciation—Machinery		2,000
To record depreciation on date of disposal: ($12,000 − $2,000)/5		

Record the removal of the discarded asset and its loss on disposal:

Accumulated Depreciation—Machinery	10,000	
Loss on Disposal of Machinery	2,000	
Machinery		12,000
To record the discarding of machinery with a $2,000 book value.		

5.

Patent	100,000	
Cash		100,000
To record patent acquisition.		

Amortization Expense—Patent	10,000	
Accumulated Amortization—Patent		10,000
To record amortization expense: $100,000/10 years = $10,000.		

6.

Ore Deposit	680,000	
Cash		680,000
To record ore deposit acquisition and its related costs.		

Depletion Expense—Ore Deposit	20,000	
Accumulated Depletion—Ore Deposit		20,000
To record depletion expense: ($680,000 − $20,000)/330,000 tons = $2 per ton. 10,000 tons mined and sold × $2 = $20,000 depletion.		

APPENDIX

10A Goodwill Estimation

A company has goodwill when its expected future income is greater than the normal income for its industry (competitors). To illustrate, consider the information in Exhibit 10A.1 for two competing companies, Z2 and Burton, of roughly equal size in the snowboard industry.

	Z2	Burton
Net assets* (excluding goodwill)	$190,000	$190,000
Normal return on net assets in the industry	10%	10%
Normal net income	19,000	19,000
Expected net income	24,000	19,000
Expected net income above normal	**$ 5,000**	**$ 0**

* Net assets (also called *equity*) equal total assets minus total liabilities.

Exhibit 10A.1

Data for Goodwill Illustration

The expected net income for Z2 is $24,000. This is $5,000 higher than the $19,000 industry norm based on the 10% return on net assets (equity) for its competitors. This implies that Z2 has goodwill that yields above normal net income. In contrast, Burton's expected income of $19,000 equals the norm for this industry. This implies zero goodwill for Burton. This means that Z2 buyers are willing to pay more than just the value of its net assets—specifically, to acquire its goodwill asset.

In accounting, goodwill is recorded when an entire company or business segment is purchased. The buyer and seller can estimate goodwill in more than one way. For instance, how do we value Z2's $5,000 per year above normal net income? One method is to value goodwill at some *multiple* of above normal net income. If we choose a multiple of 6, our goodwill estimate for Z2 is 6 × $5,000, or $30,000. Another method is to assume the $5,000 above normal net income continues indefinitely (often called *capitalizing*). This is like an *annuity*. For example, if we assume a 16% discount (interest) rate, the goodwill estimate is $5,000/16%, or $31,250. Whatever method we choose, the value of goodwill is confirmed only by the price the seller is willing to accept and the buyer is willing to pay.

Summary

C1 Describe plant assets and issues in accounting for them. Plant assets are tangible assets used in the operations of a company and have a useful life of more than one accounting period. Plant assets are set apart from other tangible assets by two important features: use in operations and useful lives longer than one period. The four main accounting issues with plant assets are (1) computing their costs, (2) allocating their costs to the periods they benefit, (3) accounting for subsequent expenditures, and (4) recording their disposal.

C2 Explain depreciation and the factors affecting its computation. *Depreciation* is the process of allocating to expense the cost of a plant asset over the accounting periods that benefit from its use. Depreciation does not measure the decline in a plant asset's market value or its physical deterioration. Three factors determine depreciation: cost, salvage value, and useful life. Salvage value is an estimate of the asset's value at the end of its benefit period. Useful (service) life is the length of time an asset is productively used.

C3 Explain depreciation for partial years and changes in estimates. Partial-year depreciation is often required because assets are bought and sold throughout the year. Depreciation is revised when changes in estimates such as salvage value and useful life occur. If the useful life of a plant asset changes, for instance, the remaining cost to be depreciated is spread over the remaining (revised) useful life of the asset.

A1 Compare and analyze alternative depreciation methods. The amount of depreciation expense per period is usually different for different methods, yet total depreciation expense over an asset's life is the same for all methods. Each method starts with the same total cost and ends with the same salvage value. The difference is in the pattern of depreciation expense over the asset's life. Common methods are straight-line, double-declining-balance, and units-of-production.

A2 Compute total asset turnover and apply it to analyze a company's use of assets. Total asset turnover measures a company's ability to use its assets to generate sales. It is defined as net sales divided by average total assets. While all companies desire a high total asset turnover, it must be interpreted in comparison with that for prior years and its competitors.

P1 Apply the cost principle to compute the cost of plant assets. Plant assets are recorded at cost when purchased. Cost includes all normal and reasonable expenditures necessary to get the asset in place and ready for its intended use. The cost of a lump-sum purchase is allocated among its individual assets.

P2 Compute and record depreciation using the straight-line, units-of-production, and declining-balance methods. The straight-line method divides cost less salvage value by the asset's useful life to determine depreciation expense per period. The units-of-production method divides cost less salvage value by the estimated number of units the asset will produce over its life to determine depreciation per unit. The declining-balance method multiplies the asset's beginning-of-period book value by a factor that is often double the straight-line rate.

P3 Distinguish between revenue and capital expenditures, and account for them. Revenue expenditures expire in the current period and are debited to expense accounts and matched with current revenues. Ordinary repairs are an example of revenue expenditures. Capital expenditures benefit future periods and are debited to asset accounts. Examples of capital expenditures are extraordinary repairs and betterments.

P4 Account for asset disposal through discarding, selling, or exchanging an asset. When a plant asset is discarded, sold, or exchanged, its cost and accumulated depreciation are removed from the accounts. Any cash proceeds from discarding or selling an asset are recorded and compared to the asset's book value to determine gain or loss. When similar assets are exchanged, losses are recognized but gains are not. When gains are not recognized, the new asset account is debited for the book value of the old asset plus any cash (assets) paid.

P5 Account for natural resource assets and their depletion. The cost of a natural resource is recorded in a noncurrent asset account. Depletion of a natural resource is recorded by allocating its cost to depletion expense using the units-of-production method. Depletion is credited to an Accumulated Depletion account.

P6 Account for intangible assets. An intangible asset is recorded at the cost incurred to purchase it. The cost of an intangible asset with a definite useful life is allocated to expense using the straight-line method, which is called *amortization.* Goodwill and intangible assets with an indefinite useful life are not amortized—they are annually tested for impairment. Intangible assets include patents, copyrights, leaseholds, goodwill, and trademarks.

Guidance Answers to **Decision Maker** and **Decision Ethics**

Controller The president's instructions may reflect an honest and reasonable prediction of the future. Since the company is struggling financially, the president may have concluded that the normal pattern of replacing assets every three years cannot continue. Perhaps the strategy is to avoid costs of frequent replacements and stretch use of equipment a few years longer until financial conditions improve. However, if you believe the president's decision is unprincipled, you might confront the president with your opinion that it is unethical to change the estimate to increase income. Another possibility is to wait and see whether the auditor will prohibit this change in estimate. In either case, you should insist that the statements be based on reasonable estimates.

Entrepreneur Treating an expense as a capital expenditure means that reported expenses will be lower and income higher in the short run. This is so because a capital expenditure is not expensed immediately but is spread over the asset's useful life. Treating an expense as a capital expenditure also means that asset and equity totals are reported at larger amounts in the short run. This continues until the asset is fully depreciated. Your friend is probably trying to help, but the suggestion is misguided. Only an expenditure benefiting future periods is a capital expenditure.

Environmentalist The paper manufacturer's comparison of its total asset turnover with food stores and auto dealers is misdirected. These other industries' turnovers are higher because their profit margins are lower (about 2%). Profit margins for the paper industry are usually 3% to 3.5%. You need to collect data from competitors in the paper industry to show that a 1.9 total asset turnover is about the norm for this industry. You might also want to collect data on this company's revenues and expenses, along with compensation data for its high-ranking officers and employees.

Guidance Answers to **Quick Checks**

1. a. Supplies—current assets
   b. Office equipment—plant assets
   c. Inventory—current assets
   d. Land for future expansion—long-term investments
   e. Trucks used in operations—plant assets
2. a. Land b. Land Improvements
3. \$700,000 + \$49,000 − \$21,000 + \$3,500 + \$3,000 + \$2,500 = \$737,000
4. a. Straight-line with 7-year life: (\$77,000/7) = \$11,000
   b. Straight-line with 10-year life: (\$77,000/10) = \$7,700
5. Depreciation is a process of allocating the cost of plant assets to the accounting periods that benefit from the assets' use.
6. a. Book value using straight-line depreciation: \$96,000 − [(\$96,000 − \$8,000)/5] = \$78,400
   b. Book value using units of production: \$96,000 − [(\$96,000 − \$8,000) × (10,000/100,000)] = \$87,200
7. (\$3,800 − \$200)/3 = \$1,200 (original depreciation per year)
   \$1,200 × 2 = \$2,400 (accumulated depreciation)
   (\$3,800 − \$2,400)/2 = \$700 (revised depreciation)
8.

Machinery	12,000	
Cash		12,000

9. A revenue expenditure benefits only the current period and should be charged to expense in the current period. A capital expenditure yields benefits that extend beyond the end of the current period and should be charged to an asset.
10. A betterment involves modifying an existing plant asset to make it more efficient, usually by replacing part of the asset with an improved or superior part. The cost of a betterment is debited to the asset account.
11.

Depreciation Expense	3,500	
Accumulated Depreciation		3,500
Cash	32,000	
Accumulated Depreciation	10,500	
Gain on Sale of Equipment		500
Equipment		42,000

12.

(a)		
Equipment	45,000	
Loss on Exchange of Assets	3,600	
Accumulated Depreciation—Equipment	23,400	
Equipment		30,000
Cash ($45,000 − $3,000)		42,000

(b)		
Equipment*	44,600	
Accumulated Depreciation—Equipment	23,400	
Equipment		30,000
Cash ($45,000 − $7,000)		38,000

* Includes $400 unrecognized gain.

13. Examples of natural resources are timberlands, mineral deposits, and oil reserves. Examples of intangible assets are patents, copyrights, leaseholds, leasehold improvements, goodwill, trademarks, and licenses.

14. ($650,000/325,000 tons) × 91,000 tons = $182,000

15.

Date	Account	Debit	Credit
Jan. 6	Patents	120,000	
	Cash		120,000
Dec. 31	Amortization Expense	40,000*	
	Accumulated Amortization—Patents		40,000

* $120,000/3 years = $40,000.

Key Terms

Key Terms are available at the book's Website for learning and testing in an online Flashcard Format.

Accelerated depreciation method (p. 388)
Amortization (p. 398)
Betterments (p. 393)
Book value (p. 387)
Capital expenditures (p. 392)
Change in an accounting estimate (p. 391)
Copyright (p. 399)
Cost (p. 383)
Declining-balance method (p. 388)
Depletion (p. 397)
Depreciation (p. 385)
Extraordinary repairs (p. 393)
Franchises (p. 400)
Goodwill (p. 400)
Impairment (p. 399)
Inadequacy (p. 385)
Indefinite useful life (p. 398)
Intangible assets (p. 398)
Land improvements (p. 384)
Lease (p. 400)
Leasehold (p. 400)
Leasehold improvements (p. 400)
Lessee (p. 400)
Lessor (p. 400)
Licenses (p. 400)
Modified Accelerated Cost Recovery System (MACRS) (p. 390)
Natural resources (p. 397)
Obsolescence (p. 385)
Ordinary repairs (p. 393)
Patent (p. 399)
Plant assets (p. 382)
Revenue expenditures (p. 392)
Salvage value (p. 385)
Straight-line depreciation (p. 386)
Total asset turnover (p. 401)
Trademark or trade (brand) name (p. 400)
Units-of-production depreciation (p. 387)
Useful life (p. 385)

Personal Interactive Quiz

Personal Interactive Quizzes A and B are available at the book's Website to reinforce and assess your learning.

Superscript letter A denotes assignments based on Appendix 10A.

Discussion Questions

1. What is the general rule for costs included in a plant asset?
2. What characteristics of a plant asset make it different from other assets?
3. What is the balance sheet classification for land that is held for future expansion? Why is such land not classified as a plant asset?
4. What is different between land and land improvements?
5. Why is the Modified Accelerated Cost Recovery System not generally accepted for financial accounting purposes?
6. Does the balance in the Accumulated Depreciation—Machinery account represent funds to replace the machinery when it wears out? If not, what does it represent?
7. What accounting principle justifies charging low-cost plant asset purchases immediately to an expense account?

8. What is the difference between ordinary repairs and extraordinary repairs? How should each be recorded?

9. Identify events that might lead to disposal of a plant asset.

10. What is the process of allocating the cost of natural resources to expense as they are used?

11. What are the characteristics of an intangible asset?

12. Is the declining-balance method an acceptable way to compute depletion of natural resources? Explain.

13. What general procedures are applied in accounting for the acquisition and potential cost allocation of intangible assets?

14. When do we know that a company has goodwill? When can goodwill appear in a company's balance sheet?

15. Assume that a company buys another business and pays for its goodwill. If the company plans to incur costs each year to maintain the value of the goodwill, must it also amortize this goodwill?

16. How does accounting for long-term assets impact the statement of cash flows?

17. How is total asset turnover computed? Why would a financial statement user be interested in total asset turnover?

18. Refer to **Krispy Kreme**'s balance sheet in Appendix A. What title does Krispy Kreme use for its plant assets? What is its book value of plant assets as of February 2, 2003, and February 3, 2002?

19. Refer to **Tastykake**'s balance sheet in Appendix A. How are Tastykake's plant assets reported (with amounts) on its 2002 balance sheet?

20. Refer to the December 31, 2002, balance sheet of **Harley-Davidson** in Appendix A. What long-term assets discussed in this chapter are reported?

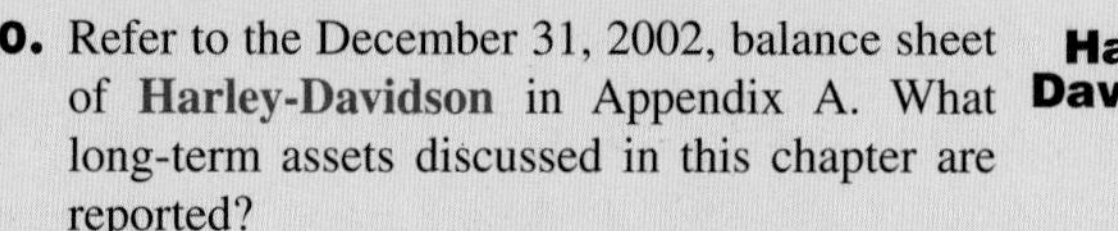

Harley-Davidson

Red numbers denote Discussion Questions that involve decision-making.

***Homework Manager** repeats all numerical Quick Studies on the book's Website with new numbers.*

QUICK STUDY

QS 10-1
Cost of plant assets
P1

Bowl-4-Fun installs automatic scorekeeping equipment with an invoice cost of $180,000. The electrical work required for the installation costs $18,000. Additional costs are $3,000 for delivery and $12,600 for sales tax. During the installation, a component of the equipment is carelessly left on a lane and hit by the automatic lane-cleaning machine. The cost of repairing the component is $2,250. What is the total recorded cost of the automatic scorekeeping equipment?

QS 10-2
Defining assets
C1

Identify the main difference between (1) plant assets and current assets, (2) plant assets and inventory, and (3) plant assets and long-term investments.

QS 10-3
Depreciation methods
P2

On January 2, 2005, the Crossover Band acquires sound equipment for concert performances at a cost of $55,900. The band estimates it will use this equipment for four years, during which time it anticipates performing about 120 concerts. It estimates that after four years it can sell the equipment for $1,900. During year 2005, the band performs 40 concerts. Compute the year 2005 depreciation using the (1) straight-line method and (2) units-of-production method.

QS 10-4
Computing revised depreciation
C3

Refer to the facts in QS 10-3. Assume that Crossover Band chose straight-line depreciation but realizes early in the second year that due to concert bookings beyond expectations, this equipment will last only a total of three years. The salvage value remains unchanged. Compute the revised depreciation for both the second and third years.

QS 10-5
Double-declining-balance method
P2

A fleet of refrigerated delivery trucks is acquired on January 5, 2005, at a cost of $930,000 with an estimated useful life of eight years and an estimated salvage value of $150,000. Compute the depreciation expense for the first three years using the double-declining-balance method.

QS 10-6
Revenue and capital expenditures
P3

1. Classify the following as either a revenue or a capital expenditure:
   a. Completed an addition to an office building for $250,000 cash.
   b. Paid $160 for the monthly cost of replacement filters on an air-conditioning system.
   c. Paid $300 cash per truck for the cost of their annual tune-ups.
   d. Paid $50,000 cash to replace a compressor on a refrigeration system that extends its useful life by four years.

2. Prepare the journal entries to record transactions *a* and *d* of part 1.

Esteban Co. owns a machine that costs $38,400 with accumulated depreciation of $20,400. Esteban exchanges the machine for a similar but newer model that has a market value of $48,000. Record the exchange assuming Esteban also paid cash of (1) $32,000 and (2) $24,000.

QS 10-7
Similar asset exchange
P4

Corazon Company acquires an ore mine at a cost of $1,300,000. It incurs additional costs of $200,000 to access the mine, which is estimated to hold 500,000 tons of ore. The estimated value of the land after the ore is removed is $150,000.

1. Prepare the entry(ies) to record the cost of the ore mine.
2. Prepare the year-end adjusting entry if 90,000 tons of ore are mined and sold the first year.

QS 10-8
Natural resources and depletion
P5

Which of the following assets are reported on the balance sheet as intangible assets? Which are reported as natural resources? *(a)* Oil well, *(b)* Trademark, *(c)* Leasehold, *(d)* Gold mine, *(e)* Building, *(f)* Copyright, *(g)* Franchise, *(h)* Timberland.

QS 10-9
Classify assets
P5 P6 

On January 4 of this year, Best Boutique incurs a $95,000 cost to modernize its store. Improvements include new floors, ceilings, wiring, and wall coverings. These improvements are estimated to yield benefits for 10 years. Best leases its store and has eight years remaining on the lease. Prepare the entry to record (1) the cost of modernization and (2) amortization at the end of this current year.

QS 10-10
Intangible assets and amortization
P6

Eastman Company reports the following ($ millions): net sales of $13,557 for 2005 and $12,670 for 2004; end-of-year total assets of $14,968 for 2005 and $18,810 for 2004. Compute its total asset turnover for 2005 and assess its level if competitors average a total asset turnover of 2.0 times.

QS 10-11
Computing total asset turnover
A2 

***Homework Manager** repeats all numerical Exercises on the book's Website with new numbers.*

EXERCISES

Farha Co. purchases a machine for $11,500, terms 2/10, n/60, FOB shipping point. The seller prepaid the $260 freight charges, adding the amount to the invoice and bringing its total to $11,760. The machine requires special steel mounting and power connections costing $795. Another $375 is paid to assemble the machine and get it into operation. In moving the machine to its steel mounting, $190 in damages occurred. Also, $30 of materials is used in adjusting the machine to produce a satisfactory product. The adjustments are normal for this machine and are not the result of the damages. Compute the cost recorded for this machine. (Farha pays for this machine within the cash discount period.)

Exercise 10-1
Cost of plant assets
P1 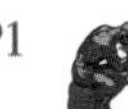

Cerner Manufacturing purchases a large lot on which an old building is located as part of its plans to build a new plant. The negotiated purchase price is $225,000 for the lot plus $120,000 for the old building. The company pays $34,500 to tear down the old building and $51,000 to landscape the lot. It also pays a total of $1,440,000 in construction costs—this amount consists of $1,354,500 for the new building and $85,500 for lighting and paving a parking area next to the building. Prepare a single journal entry to record these costs incurred by Cerner, all of which are paid in cash.

Exercise 10-2
Recording costs of assets
C1 P1

Ming Yue Company pays $368,250 for real estate plus $19,600 in closing costs. The real estate consists of land appraised at $166,320; land improvements appraised at $55,440; and a building appraised at $174,240. Allocate the total cost among the three purchased assets and prepare the journal entry to record the purchase.

Exercise 10-3
Lump-sum purchase of plant assets C1

In early January 2004, LabTech purchases computer equipment for $147,000 to use in operating activities for the next four years. It estimates the equipment's salvage value at $30,000. Prepare tables showing depreciation and book value for each of the four years assuming (1) straight-line and (2) double-declining-balance depreciation.

Exercise 10-4
Depreciation methods
P2

Exercise 10-5
Depreciation methods
P2

Check (3) $6,768

Feng Company installs a computerized manufacturing machine in its factory at the beginning of the year at a cost of $42,300. The machine's useful life is estimated at 10 years, or 363,000 units of product, with a $6,000 salvage value. During its second year, the machine produces 35,000 units of product. Determine the machine's second-year depreciation under the (1) straight-line, (2) units-of-production, and (3) double-declining-balance methods.

Exercise 10-6
Depreciation methods; partial year depreciation C3

On April 1, 2004, Stone's Backhoe Co. purchases a trencher for $250,000. The machine is expected to last five years and have a salvage value of $25,000. Compute depreciation expense for year 2005 using the (1) straight-line and (2) double-declining-balance methods.

Exercise 10-7
Revising depreciation
C3

Check (2) $3,400

Summit Fitness Club uses straight-line depreciation for a machine costing $21,750, with an estimated four-year life and a $2,250 salvage value. At the beginning of the third year, Summit determines that the machine has three more years of remaining useful life, after which it will have an estimated $1,800 salvage value. Compute (1) the machine's book value at the end of its second year and (2) the amount of depreciation for each of the final three years given the revised estimates.

Exercise 10-8
Income effects of depreciation methods
A1 

Check (2) Year 3 NI, $53,328

Mulan Enterprises pays $235,200 for equipment that will last five years and have a $52,500 salvage value. By using the machine in its operations for five years, the company expects to earn $85,500 annually, after deducting all expenses except depreciation. Prepare a table showing income before depreciation, depreciation expense, and net (pretax) income for each year and for the total five-year period, assuming (1) straight-line depreciation and (2) double-declining-balance depreciation.

Exercise 10-9
Extraordinary repairs; plant asset age
P3

Check (3) $207,450

Passat Company owns a building that appears on its prior year-end balance sheet at its original $561,000 cost less $420,750 accumulated depreciation. The building is depreciated on a straight-line basis assuming a 20-year life and no salvage value. During the first week in January of the current calendar year, major structural repairs are completed on the building at a $67,200 cost. The repairs extend its useful life for 7 years beyond the 20 years originally estimated.

1. Determine the building's age (plant asset age) as of the prior year-end balance sheet date.
2. Prepare the entry to record the cost of the structural repairs that are paid in cash.
3. Determine the book value of the building immediately after the repairs are recorded.
4. Prepare the entry to record the current calendar year's depreciation.

Exercise 10-10
Ordinary repairs, extraordinary repairs and betterments
P3

Patterson Company pays $262,500 for equipment expected to last four years and have a $30,000 salvage value. Prepare journal entries to record the following costs related to the equipment:

1. During the second year of the equipment's life, $21,000 cash is paid for a new component expected to increase the equipment's productivity by 10% a year.
2. During the third year, $5,250 cash is paid for normal repairs necessary to keep the equipment in good working order.
3. During the fourth year, $13,950 is paid for repairs expected to increase the useful life of the equipment from four to five years.

Exercise 10-11
Exchanging similar assets
P4 

Check (2) $14,500

Jericho Construction trades in an old tractor for a new tractor, receiving a $28,000 trade-in allowance and paying the remaining $82,000 in cash. The old tractor had cost $95,000, and straight-line accumulated depreciation of $52,500 had been recorded to date under the assumption that it would last eight years and have a $11,000 salvage value. Answer the following questions:

1. What is the book value of the old tractor at the time of exchange?
2. What is the loss on this similar asset exchange?
3. What amount should be recorded (debited) in the asset account for the new tractor?

Exercise 10-12
Recording plant asset disposals
P4

On January 2, 2005, Atlantic Co. disposes of a machine costing $42,000 with accumulated depreciation of $22,625. Prepare the entries to record the disposal under each of the following separate assumptions:

1. Machine is sold for $16,250 cash.
2. Machine is traded in on a similar but newer machine having a $58,500 cash price. A $20,000 trade-in allowance is received, and the balance is paid in cash.
3. Machine is traded in on a similar but newer machine having a $58,500 cash price. A $15,000 trade-in allowance is received, and the balance is paid in cash.

Check (2) Dr. Machinery, $57,875

Exercise 10-13
Partial year depreciation; disposal of plant asset
P4

Finesse Co. purchases and installs a machine on January 1, 2004, at a total cost of $92,750. Straight-line depreciation is taken each year for four years assuming a seven-year life and no salvage value. The machine is disposed of on July 1, 2008, during its fifth year of service. Prepare entries to record the partial year's depreciation on July 1, 2008, and to record the disposal under the following separate assumptions: (1) the machine is sold for $35,000 cash and (2) Finesse receives an insurance settlement of $30,000 resulting from the total destruction of the machine in a fire.

Exercise 10-14
Depletion of natural resources
P2 P5

On April 2, 2005, Idaho Mining Co. pays $3,633,750 for an ore deposit containing 1,425,000 tons. The company installs machinery in the mine costing $171,000, with an estimated seven-year life and no salvage value. The machinery will be abandoned when the ore is completely mined. Idaho began mining on May 1, 2005, and mined and sold 156,200 tons of ore during the remaining eight months of 2005. Prepare the December 31, 2005, entries to record both the ore deposit depletion and the mining machinery depreciation. Mining machinery depreciation should be in proportion to the mine's depletion.

Exercise 10-15
Amortization of intangible assets
P6

Busch Gallery purchases the copyright on an oil painting for $236,700 on January 1, 2005. The copyright legally protects its owner for 19 more years. However, the company plans to market and sell prints of the original for only 12 years. Prepare entries to record the purchase of the copyright on January 1, 2005, and its annual amortization on December 31, 2005.

Exercise 10-16[A]
Goodwill estimation
P6 

Corey Alt has devoted years to developing a profitable business that earns an attractive return. Alt is now considering selling the business and is attempting to estimate its goodwill. The value of the business's net assets (excluding goodwill) is $437,000, and in a typical year net income is about $85,000. Most businesses of this type are expected to earn a return of about 10% on their net assets. Estimate the value of this business's goodwill for the following separate cases assuming it is (1) equal to 10 times the amount that net income is above normal and (2) computed by capitalizing at a rate of 8% the amount that net income is above normal.

Check (2) $516,250

Exercise 10-17
Cash flows related to assets
C1
Harley-Davidson

Refer to the statement of cash flows for **Harley-Davidson** in Appendix A for the fiscal year ended December 31, 2002, to answer the following:

1. What amount of cash is used to purchase property and equipment?
2. How much depreciation and amortization are recorded?
3. What total amount of net cash is used in investing activities?

Exercise 10-18
Evaluating efficient use of assets
A2 

Joy Co. reports net sales of $4,862,000 for 2004 and $7,542,000 for 2005. End-of-year balances for total assets are 2003, $1,586,000; 2004, $1,700,000; and 2005, $1,882,000. (*a*) Compute Joy's total asset turnover for 2004 and 2005. (*b*) Comment on Joy's efficiency in using its assets if its competitors average a total asset turnover of 3.0.

PROBLEM SET A

Problem 10-1A
Plant asset costs; depreciation methods

C1 C2 A1 P1 P2

excel
mhhe.com/larson

Check (2) $23,490
(3) $15,750

Xavier Construction negotiates a lump-sum purchase of several assets from a company that is going out of business. The purchase is completed on January 1, 2005, at a total cash price of $787,500 for a building, land, land improvements, and six vehicles. The estimated market values of the assets are building, $408,000; land, $289,000; land improvements, $42,500; and four vehicles, $110,500. The company's fiscal year ends on December 31.

Required

1. Prepare a table to allocate the lump-sum purchase price to the separate assets purchased (round percents to the nearest 1%). Prepare the journal entry to record the purchase.
2. Compute the depreciation expense for year 2005 on the building using the straight-line method, assuming a 15-year life and a $25,650 salvage value.
3. Compute the depreciation expense for year 2005 on the land improvements assuming a five-year life and double-declining-balance depreciation.

Analysis Component

4. Defend or refute this statement: Accelerated depreciation results in payment of less taxes over the asset's life.

Problem 10-2A
Asset cost allocation; straight-line depreciation

C1 C2 P1 P2

mhhe.com/larson

Check (1) Land costs, $2,381,800; Building 2 costs, $616,000

(3) Depr.—Land Improv. 1 and 2, $28,000 and $7,900

In January 2005, Keona Co. pays $2,800,000 for a tract of land with two buildings on it. It plans to demolish Building 1 and build a new store in its place. Building 2 will be a company office; it is appraised at $641,300, with a useful life of 20 years and an $80,000 salvage value. A lighted parking lot near Building 1 has improvements (Land Improvements 1) valued at $408,100 that are expected to last another 14 years with no salvage value. Without the buildings and improvements, the tract of land is valued at $1,865,600. Keona also incurs the following additional costs:

Cost to demolish Building 1	$ 422,600
Cost of additional land grading	167,200
Cost to construct new building (Building 3), having a useful life of 25 years and a $390,100 salvage value	2,019,000
Cost of new land improvements (Land Improvements 2) near Building 2 having a 20-year useful life and no salvage value	158,000

Required

1. Prepare a table with the following column headings: Land, Building 2, Building 3, Land Improvements 1, and Land Improvements 2. Allocate the costs incurred by Keona to the appropriate columns and total each column (round percents to the nearest 1%).
2. Prepare a single journal entry to record all the incurred costs assuming they are paid in cash on January 1, 2005.
3. Using the straight-line method, prepare the December 31 adjusting entries to record depreciation for the 12 months of 2005 when these assets were in use.

Problem 10-3A
Computing and revising depreciation; revenue and capital expenditures

C3 P1 P3

Check Dec. 31, 2004, Dr. Depr. Expense—Equip., $60,238

Clarion Contractors completed the following transactions and events involving the purchase and operation of equipment in its business:

2004

Jan. 1 Paid $255,440 cash plus $15,200 in sales tax and $2,500 in transportation (FOB shipping point) for a new loader. The loader is estimated to have a four-year life and a $34,740 salvage value. Loader costs are recorded in the Equipment account.

Jan. 3 Paid $3,660 to enclose the cab and install air conditioning in the loader to enable operations under harsher conditions. This increased the estimated salvage value of the loader by another $1,110.

Dec. 31 Recorded annual straight-line depreciation on the loader.

2005

Jan. 1 Paid $4,500 to overhaul the loader's engine, which increased the loader's estimated useful life by two years.
Feb. 17 Paid $920 to repair the loader after the operator backs it into a tree.
Dec. 31 Recorded annual straight-line depreciation on the loader.

Check Dec. 31, 2005, Dr. Depr. Expense—Equip., $37,042

Required

Prepare journal entries to record these transactions and events.

Problem 10-4A
Computing and revising depreciation; selling plant assets
C3 P2 P4

Chen Company completed the following transactions and events involving its delivery trucks:

2004

Jan. 1 Paid $19,415 cash plus $1,165 in sales tax for a new delivery truck estimated to have a five-year life and a $3,000 salvage value. Delivery truck costs are recorded in the Trucks account.
Dec. 31 Recorded annual straight-line depreciation on the truck.

2005

Dec. 31 Due to new information obtained earlier in the year, the truck's estimated useful life was changed from five to four years, and the estimated salvage value was increased to $3,500. Recorded annual straight-line depreciation on the truck.

Check Dec. 31, 2005, Dr. Depr. Expense—Trucks, $4,521

2006

Dec. 31 Recorded annual straight-line depreciation on the truck.
Dec. 31 Sold the truck for $6,200 cash.

Dec. 31, 2006, Dr. Loss on Disposal of Trucks, $1,822

Required

Prepare journal entries to record these transactions and events.

Problem 10-5A
Depreciation methods; disposal of plant asset
C3 P1 P2 P4

Part 1. A machine costing $210,000 with a four-year life and an estimated $20,000 salvage value is installed in Calhoon Company's factory on January 1. The factory manager estimates the machine will produce 475,000 units of product during its life. It actually produces the following units: year 1, 121,400; year 2, 122,400; year 3, 119,600; and year 4, 118,200. The total number of units produced by the end of year 4 exceeds the original estimate—this difference was not predicted. (The machine must not be depreciated below its estimated salvage value.)

Required

Prepare a table with the following column headings and compute depreciation for each year (and total depreciation of all years combined) for the machine under each depreciation method.

Year	Straight-Line	Units-of-Production	Double-Declining-Balance

Check Year 4: Units-of-Production Depreciation, $44,640; DDB Depreciation, $6,250

Part 2. Calhoon purchases a used machine for $167,000 cash on January 2 and readies it for use the next day at a $3,420 cost. On January 3, it is installed on a required operating platform costing $1,080, and it is readied for operations. The company predicts the machine will be used for six years and have a $14,600 salvage value. Depreciation is to be charged on a straight-line basis. On December 31, at the end of its fifth year in operations, it is disposed of.

Required

a. Prepare journal entries to record the machine's purchase and the costs to ready and install it. Cash is paid for all costs incurred.

b. Prepare journal entries to record depreciation of the machine at December 31 of its first year in operations and at December 31 in the year of its disposal.

(*b*) Depr. Exp., $26,150

c. Prepare journal entries to record the machine's disposal under each of the following separate assumptions: (i) it is sold for $13,500 cash; (ii) it is sold for $45,000 cash; and (iii) it is destroyed in a fire and the insurance company pays $24,000 cash to settle the loss claim.

(iii) Dr. Loss from Fire, $16,750

Problem 10-6A
Intangible assets and natural resources
A1 P5 P6 

Part 1. On July 1, 2000, Sweetman Company signed a contract to lease space in a building for 15 years. The lease contract calls for annual (prepaid) rental payments of $70,000 on each July 1 throughout the life of the lease and for the lessee to pay for all additions and improvements to the leased property. On June 25, 2005, Sweetman decides to sublease the space to Kirk & Associates for the remaining 10 years of the lease—Kirk pays $185,000 to Sweetman for the right to sublease and it agrees to assume the obligation to pay the $70,000 annual rent to the building owner beginning July 1, 2005. After taking possession of the leased space, Kirk pays for improving the office portion of the leased space at a $129,840 cost. The improvements are paid for on July 5, 2005, and are estimated to have a useful life equal to the 16 years remaining in the life of the building.

Required

Prepare entries for Kirk to record (*a*) its payment to Sweetman for the right to sublease the building space, (*b*) its payment of the 2005 annual rent to the building owner, and (*c*) its payment for the office improvements. Prepare Kirk's year-end adjusting entries required at December 31, 2005, to (*d*) amortize the $185,000 cost of the sublease, (*e*) amortize the office improvements, and (*f*) record rent expense.

Check Dr. Rent Expense for: (*d*) $9,250, (*f*) $35,000

Part 2. On July 23 of the current year, Dakota Mining Co. pays $4,836,000 for land estimated to contain 7,800,000 tons of recoverable ore. It installs machinery costing $390,000 that has a 10-year life and no salvage value and is capable of mining the ore deposit in eight years. The machinery is paid for on July 25, seven days before mining operations begin. The company removes and sells 400,000 tons of ore during its first five months of operations. Depreciation of the machinery is in proportion to the mine's depletion as the machinery will be abandoned after the ore is mined.

Required

Preparation Component

Prepare entries to record (*a*) the purchase of the land, (*b*) the cost and installation of machinery, (*c*) the first five months' depletion assuming the land has a net salvage value of zero after the ore is mined, and (*d*) the first five months' depreciation on machinery.

(*c*) Depletion, $248,000; (*d*) Depreciation, $20,000

Analysis Component

Describe both the similarities and differences in amortization, depletion, and depreciation.

Problem 10-7A[A]
Goodwill estimation and analysis
P6 

mhhe.com/larson

Rent-Center, an equipment rental business, has the following balance sheet on December 31, 2005:

Assets		
Cash		$ 93,930
Equipment	$678,800	
Accumulated depreciation—Equipment	271,500	407,300
Buildings	340,000	
Accumulated depreciation—Buildings	182,400	157,600
Land		93,000
Total assets		$751,830
Liabilities and Equity		
Accounts payable		$ 18,650
Long-term note payable		337,250
Total equity		395,930
Total liabilities and equity		$751,830

Normal annual net income averages 20% of equity in this industry. Rent-Center regularly expects to earn $100,000 annually. The balance sheet amounts are reasonable estimates of market values for both assets (except goodwill) and liabilities. In negotiations to sell the business, Rent-Center proposes to measure goodwill by capitalizing at a rate of 15% the amount of above-normal net income. The potential buyer thinks that goodwill should be valued at five times the amount of above-normal net income.

Required

1. Compute the amount of goodwill as proposed by Rent-Center.
2. Compute the amount of goodwill as proposed by the potential buyer.

Check (1) $138,760
(2) $104,070

3. The buyer purchases the business for the net asset amount (assets less liabilities) reported on the December 31, 2005, balance sheet plus the amount proposed by Rent-Center for goodwill. What is the buyer's purchase price?

4. If the buyer earns $100,225 of net income in its first year after acquiring the business under the terms in part 3, what rate of return does the buyer earn on this investment for the first year? Explain how goodwill impacts the buyer's net income computation.

Check (4) 18.7%

PROBLEM SET B

Problem 10-1B
Plant asset costs; depreciation methods

C1 C2 A1 P1 P2

Niemeyer Company negotiates a lump-sum purchase of several assets from a contractor who is relocating. The purchase is completed on January 1, 2005, at a total cash price of $1,610,000 for a building, land, land improvements, and six trucks. The estimated market values of the assets are building, $784,800; land, $540,640; land improvements, $226,720; and three trucks, $191,840. The company's fiscal year ends on December 31.

Required

1. Prepare a table to allocate the lump-sum purchase price to the separate assets purchased (round percents to the nearest 1%). Prepare the journal entry to record the purchase.

2. Compute the depreciation expense for year 2005 on the building using the straight-line method, assuming a 12-year life and a $100,500 salvage value.

Check (2) $52,000

3. Compute the depreciation expense for year 2005 on the land improvements assuming a 10-year life and double-declining-balance depreciation.

(3) $41,860

Analysis Component

4. Defend or refute this statement: Accelerated depreciation results in payment of more taxes over the asset's life.

Problem 10-2B
Asset cost allocation; straight-line depreciation

C1 C2 P1 P2

In January 2005, InTech pays $1,350,000 for a tract of land with two buildings. It plans to demolish Building A and build a new shop in its place. Building B will be a company office; it is appraised at $472,770, with a useful life of 15 years and a $90,000 salvage value. A lighted parking lot near Building B has improvements (Land Improvements B) valued at $125,145 that are expected to last another six years with no salvage value. Without the buildings and improvements, the tract of land is valued at $792,585. InTech also incurs the following additional costs:

Cost to demolish Building A	$ 117,000
Cost of additional land grading	172,500
Cost to construct new building (Building C), having a useful life of 20 years and a $295,500 salvage value	1,356,000
Cost of new land improvements (Land Improvements C) near building C, having a 10-year useful life and no salvage value	101,250

Required

1. Prepare a table with the following column headings: Land, Building B, Building C, Land Improvements B, and Land Improvements C. Allocate the costs incurred by InTech to the appropriate columns and total each column (round percents to the nearest 1%).

Check (1) Land costs, $1,059,000; Building B costs, $459,000

2. Prepare a single journal entry to record all incurred costs assuming they are paid in cash on January 1, 2005.

3. Using the straight-line method, prepare the December 31 adjusting entries to record depreciation for the 12 months of 2005 when these assets were in use.

(3) Depr.—Land Improv. B and C, $20,250 and $10,125

Problem 10-3B
Computing and revising depreciation; revenue and capital expenditures

C3 P1 P3

Xpress Delivery Service completed the following transactions and events involving the purchase and operation of equipment for its business:

2004

Jan. 1 Paid $24,950 cash plus $1,950 in sales tax for a new delivery van that was estimated to have a five-year life and a $3,400 salvage value. Van costs are recorded in the Equipment account.

Jan. 3 Paid $1,550 to install sorting racks in the van for more accurate and quicker delivery of packages. This increases the estimated salvage value of the van by another $200.

Dec. 31 Recorded annual straight-line depreciation on the van.

Check Dec. 31, 2004, Dr. Depr. Expense—Equip., $4,970

2005

Jan. 1 Paid $1,970 to overhaul the van's engine, which increased the van's estimated useful life by two years.
May 10 Paid $600 to repair the van after the driver backed it into a loading dock.
Dec. 31 Record annual straight-line depreciation on the van.

Check Dec. 31, 2005, Dr. Depr. Expense—Equip., $3,642

Required

Prepare journal entries to record these transactions and events.

Problem 10-4B
Computing and revising depreciation; selling plant assets
C3 P2 P4

Field Instruments completed the following transactions and events involving its machinery:

2004

Jan. 1 Paid $106,600 cash plus $6,400 in sales tax for a new machine. The machine is estimated to have a six-year life and a $9,800 salvage value.
Dec. 31 Recorded annual straight-line depreciation on the machinery.

2005

Dec. 31 Due to new information obtained earlier in the year, the machine's estimated useful life was changed from six to four years, and the estimated salvage value was increased to $13,050. Recorded annual straight-line depreciation on the machinery.

Check Dec. 31, 2005, Dr. Depr. Expense—Machinery, $27,583

2006

Dec. 31 Recorded annual straight-line depreciation on the machinery.
Dec. 31 Sold the machine for $25,240 cash.

Dec. 31, 2006, Dr. Loss on Disposal of Machine, $15,394

Required

Prepare journal entries to record these transactions and events.

Problem 10-5B
Depreciation methods; disposal of plant assets
C3 P1 P2 P4

Part 1. On January 2, Gannon Co. purchases and installs a new machine costing $312,000 with a five-year life and an estimated $28,000 salvage value. Management estimates the machine will produce 1,136,000 units of product during its life. Actual production of units is as follows: year 1, 245,600; year 2, 230,400; year 3, 227,000; year 4, 232,600; and year 5, 211,200. The total number of units produced by the end of year 5 exceeds the original estimate—this difference was not predicted. (The machine must not be depreciated below its estimated salvage value.)

Required

Prepare a table with the following column headings and compute depreciation for each year (and total depreciation of all years combined) for the machine under each depreciation method.

Check DDB depreciation, Year 3, $44,928; U-of-P depreciation, Year 4, $58,150

Year	Straight-Line	Units-of-Production	Double-Declining-Balance

Part 2. On January 1, Gannon purchases a used machine for $130,000 and readies it for use the next day at a cost of $3,390. On January 4, it is mounted on a required operating platform costing $4,800, and it is readied for operations. Management estimates the machine will be used for seven years and have an $18,000 salvage value. Depreciation is to be charged on a straight-line basis. On December 31, at the end of its sixth year of use, the machine is disposed of.

Required

a. Prepare journal entries to record the machine's purchase and the costs to ready and install it. Cash is paid for all costs incurred.

b. Prepare journal entries to record depreciation of the machine at December 31 of its first year in operations and at December 31 in the year of its disposal.

(*b*) Depr. Exp., $17,170

c. Prepare journal entries to record the machine's disposal under each of the following separate assumptions: (i) it is sold for $30,000 cash; (ii) it is sold for $50,000 cash; and (iii) it is destroyed in a fire and the insurance company pays $20,000 cash to settle the loss claim.

(iii) Dr. Loss from Fire, $15,170

Problem 10-6B
Intangible assets and natural resources
A1 P5 P6

Part 1. On January 1, 2000, Liberty Co. entered into a 12-year lease on a building. The lease contract requires (1) annual (prepaid) rental payments of $26,400 each January 1 throughout the life of the lease and (2) for the lessee to pay for all additions and improvements to the leased property. On January 1, 2007, Liberty decides to sublease the space to Moberly Co. for the remaining five years of the lease—Moberly pays $30,000 to Liberty for the right to sublease and agrees to assume the obligation to pay the $26,400 annual rent to the building owner beginning January 1, 2007. After taking possession of the leased space, Moberly pays for improving the office portion of the leased space at an $18,000 cost. The improvements are paid for on January 3, 2007, and are estimated to have a useful life equal to the 13 years remaining in the life of the building.

Required

Prepare entries for Moberly to record (*a*) its payment to Liberty for the right to sublease the building space, (*b*) its payment of the 2007 annual rent to the building owner, and (*c*) its payment for the office improvements. Prepare Moberly's year-end adjusting entries required on December 31, 2007, to (*d*) amortize the $30,000 cost of the sublease, (*e*) amortize the office improvements, and (*f*) record rent expense.

Check Dr. Rent Expense: (*d*) $6,000, (*f*) $26,400

Part 2. On February 19 of the current year, Rock Chalk Co. pays $4,450,000 for land estimated to contain 5 million tons of recoverable ore. It installs machinery costing $200,000 that has a 16-year life and no salvage value and is capable of mining the ore deposit in 12 years. The machinery is paid for on March 21, eleven days before mining operations begin. The company removes and sells 352,000 tons of ore during its first nine months of operations. Depreciation of the machinery is in proportion to the mine's depletion as the machinery will be abandoned after the ore is mined.

Required

Preparation Component

Prepare entries to record (*a*) the purchase of the land, (*b*) the cost and installation of machinery, (*c*) the first nine months' depletion assuming the land has a net salvage value of zero after the ore is mined, and (*d*) the first nine months' depreciation on machinery.

(*c*) Depletion, $313,280; (*d*) Depreciation, $14,080

Analysis Component

Describe both the similarities and differences in amortization, depletion, and depreciation.

Problem 10-7B^A
Goodwill estimation and analysis
P6

Pack Casual Wear has the following balance sheet on December 31, 2005:

Assets		
Cash		$ 138,700
Merchandise inventory		607,950
Buildings	$451,500	
Accumulated depreciation—Buildings	210,800	240,700
Land		192,400
Total assets		$1,179,750
Liabilities and Equity		
Accounts payable		$ 98,325
Long-term note payable		414,050
Total equity		667,375
Total liabilities and equity		$1,179,750

Normal annual net income averages 32% of equity in this industry. Pack regularly expects to earn $230,000 annually. The balance sheet amounts are reasonable estimates of market values for both assets (except goodwill) and liabilities. In negotiations to sell the business, Pack proposes to measure goodwill by capitalizing at a rate of 10% the amount of above-normal net income. The potential buyer believes that goodwill should be valued at eight times the amount of above-normal net income.

Required

Check (1) $164,400
(2) $131,520

1. Compute the amount of goodwill as proposed by Pack.
2. Compute the amount of goodwill as proposed by the potential buyer.
3. The buyer purchases the business for the net asset amount (assets less liabilities) reported on the December 31, 2005, balance sheet plus the amount proposed by Pack for goodwill. What is the buyer's purchase price?

(4) 24.1%

4. If the buyer earns $200,175 of net income in its first year after acquiring the business under the terms in part 3, what rate of return does the buyer earn on this investment for the first year? Is the goodwill asset amortized or not? Explain.

PROBLEM SET C

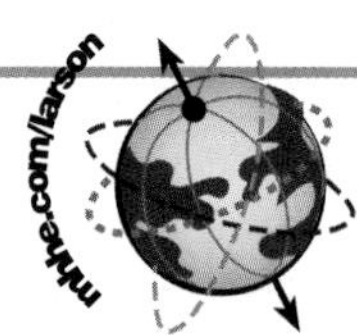

Problem Set C is available at the book's Website to further reinforce and assess your learning.

SERIAL PROBLEM

Success Systems

(This serial problem began in Chapter 1 and continues through most of the book. If previous chapter segments were not completed, the serial problem can begin at this point. It is helpful, but not necessary, for you to use the Working Papers that accompany the book.)

Selected ledger account balances for Success Systems follow.

	For the Three Months Ended December 31, 2004	For the Three Months Ended March 31, 2005
Office equipment	$ 8,000	$ 8,000
Accumulated depreciation—Office equipment	400	800
Computer equipment	20,000	20,000
Accumulated depreciation—Computer equipment	1,250	2,500
Total revenue	31,284	43,853
Total assets	93,248	129,909

Required

1. Assume that Success Systems does not acquire additional office equipment or computer equipment in 2005. Compute the amounts for the year ended December 31, 2005, for Depreciation Expense—Office Equipment and for Depreciation Expense—Computer Equipment (assume use of the straight-line method).
2. What is the book value of both the Office Equipment account and the Computer Equipment account as of December 31, 2005?
3. Compute the 3-month total asset turnover for Success Systems as of March 31, 2005. Use total revenue for the numerator and average the December 31, 2004, total assets and the March 31, 2005, total assets for the denominator. Interpret its total asset turnover if competitors average 2.5 for annual periods.

BEYOND THE NUMBERS

REPORTING IN ACTION

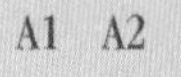

BTN 10-1 Refer to the financial statements of Krispy Kreme in Appendix A to answer the following:

1. What percent of the original cost of Krispy Kreme's property, plant, and equipment remains to be depreciated as of February 2, 2003, and February 3, 2002? Assume these assets have no salvage value.
2. Over what length(s) of time is Krispy Kreme amortizing its intangible assets?
3. What is the change in total property and equipment (before accumulated depreciation) for the year ended February 2, 2003? What is the amount of cash provided (used) by investing activities for property and equipment for the year ended February 2, 2003? What is one possible explanation for the difference between these two amounts?
4. Compute its total asset turnover for the year ended February 2, 2003.

Roll On

5. Access Krispy Kreme's financial statements for fiscal years ending after February 2, 2003, at its Website (KrispyKreme.com) or the SEC's EDGAR database (www.SEC.gov). Recompute Krispy's total asset turnover for the additional years' data you collect. Comment on any differences relative to the turnover computed in part 4.

COMPARATIVE ANALYSIS

A2

BTN 10-2 Key comparative figures ($ thousands) for **Krispy Kreme** and **Tastykake** follow:

	Krispy Kreme			Tastykake		
Key Figures	Current Year	One Year Prior	Two Years Prior	Current Year	One Year Prior	Two Years Prior
Total assets	$410,487	$255,376	$171,493	$116,560	$116,137	$112,192
Net sales	491,549	394,354	300,715	162,263	166,245	162,877

Required

1. Compute total asset turnover for the most recent two years for both Krispy Kreme and Tastykake using the data shown.

2. Which company is more efficient in generating net sales given the total assets it employs?

ETHICS CHALLENGE

C1 C2  

BTN 10-3 Flo Choi owns a small business and manages its accounting. Her company just finished a year in which a large amount of borrowed funds was invested in a new building addition as well as in equipment and fixture additions. Choi's banker requires her to submit semiannual financial statements so he can monitor the financial health of her business. He has warned her that if profit margins erode, he might raise the interest rate on the borrowed funds to reflect the increased loan risk from the bank's point of view. Choi knows profit margin is likely to decline this year. As she prepares year-end adjusting entries, she decides to apply the following depreciation rule: All asset additions are considered to be in use on the first day of the following month. (The previous rule assumed assets are in use on the first day of the month nearest to the purchase date.)

Required

1. Identify decisions that managers like Choi must make in applying depreciation methods.

2. Is Choi's rule an ethical violation, or is it a legitimate decision in computing depreciation?

3. How will Choi's depreciation rule affect the profit margin of her business?

COMMUNICATING IN PRACTICE

A2 

BTN 10-4 Teams are to select an industry, and each team member is to select a different company in that industry. Each team member is to acquire the financial statements (form 10-K) of the company selected—see the company's Website or the SEC's EDGAR database (www.SEC.gov). Use the financial statements to compute total asset turnover. Communicate with teammates via a meeting, e-mail, or telephone to discuss the meaning of this ratio, how different companies compare to each other, and the industry norm. The team must prepare a one-page report that describes the ratios for each company and identifies the conclusions reached during the team's discussion.

TAKING IT TO THE NET

C1 P6

mhhe.com/larson

BTN 10-5 Access **Adaptec**'s (ticker: ADPT) 10-K report for its fiscal year ended March 31, 2002, filed on June 24, 2002, at www.SEC.gov to answer the following.

Required

1. Read the overview of Adaptec's business and briefly describe the types of products it produces.

2. On page 12 of its 10-K, what information is provided regarding the company's patents?

3. Does Adaptec show any patent-related revenue or expense on its consolidated statement of operations (income statement)?

TEAMWORK IN ACTION

C2 A1 P2 

Point: This activity can follow an overview of each method. Step 1 allows for three areas of expertise. Larger teams will have some duplication of areas, but the straight-line choice should not be duplicated. Expert teams can use the book and consult with the instructor.

BTN 10-6 Each team member is to become an expert on one depreciation method to facilitate teammates' understanding of that method. Follow these procedures:

a. Each team member is to select an area for expertise from one of the following depreciation methods: straight-line, units-of-production, or double-declining-balance.

b. Expert teams are to be formed from those who have selected the same area of expertise. The instructor will identify the location where each expert team meets.

c. Using the following data, expert teams are to collaborate and develop a presentation answering the requirements. Expert team members must write the presentation in a format they can show to their learning teams.

Data and Requirements On January 8, 2004, Whitewater Riders purchases a van to transport rafters back to the point of departure at the conclusion of the rafting adventures they operate. The cost of the van is $44,000. It has an estimated salvage value of $2,000 and is expected to be used for four years and driven 60,000 miles. The van is expected to be driven 12,000 miles in 2004, 18,000 miles in 2005, 21,000 in 2006, and 10,000 in 2007.

1. Compute annual depreciation expense for each year of the van's estimated useful life.
2. Explain when and how annual depreciation is recorded.
3. Explain the impact on income of this depreciation method versus others over the van's life.
4. Identify the van's book value for each year of its life and illustrate the reporting of this amount for any one year.

d. Re-form original learning teams. In rotation, experts are to present to their teams the results from part *c*. Experts are to encourage and respond to questions.

BUSINESS WEEK ACTIVITY

C1 P6

mhhe.com/larson

BTN 10-7 Read the article "How Much Is the Goodwill Worth?" in the September 16, 2002, issue of ***Business Week***. (The book's Website provides a free link.)

Required

1. Explain how goodwill is calculated in accounting terms.
2. Before the accounting rules changed, how was goodwill accounted for?
3. How have the accounting rules governing goodwill recently changed?
4. Why is it a good idea to become familiar with accounting for goodwill?

ENTREPRENEURIAL DECISION

 A2  

BTN 10-8 Review the chapter's opening feature involving **Queston Construction**. Assume that it generates annual sales of $3 million on an average total asset base of $1,000,000. To increase sales, Cordova proposes to expand her construction company, which would increase average total assets by $500,000. This expansion is expected to increase net sales by $2,500,000.

Required

1. Compute the company's total asset turnover under (*a*) current conditions and (*b*) proposed conditions.
2. Evaluate and comment on the merits of Cordova's proposal given your analysis in part 1. Identify any concerns you would express about the proposal.

HITTING THE ROAD

C1 P5 P6

BTN 10-9 Team up with one or more classmates for this activity. Identify companies in your community or area that must account for at least one of the following assets: natural resource; patent; lease; leasehold improvement; copyright; trademark; or goodwill. You might find a company having more than one type of asset. Once you identify a company with a specific asset, describe the accounting this company uses to allocate the cost of that asset to the periods benefited from its use.

BTN 10-10 Grupo Bimbo, Krispy Kreme, and Tastykake are all competitors in the global marketplace. Key comparative figures (in millions) for these companies' recent annual accounting periods follow.

GLOBAL DECISION

A2

	Grupo Bimbo (millions of pesos)			Krispy Kreme		Tastykake	
Key Figures	Current Year	Prior Year	Two Years Prior	Current Year	Prior Year	Current Year	Prior Year
Total assets	31,719	23,781	25,035	$410	$255	$117	$116
Net sales	41,373	34,968	32,008	$492	$394	$162	$166
Total asset turnover	?	?	—	1.48	1.85	1.39	1.46

Required

1. Compute total asset turnover for the most recent two years for Grupo Bimbo using the data shown.
2. Which company of the three is most efficient in generating net sales given the total assets it employs?

"I like to be independent and to be able to control my own destiny"—André Downey

11 Current Liabilities and Payroll Accounting

A Look Back

Chapter 10 focused on long-term assets including plant assets, natural resources, and intangibles. We showed how to record their costs, allocate their costs to periods benefiting from their use, record their disposal, and assess their turnover.

A Look at This Chapter

This chapter emphasizes current liabilities. We explain how to identify, compute, record, and report current liabilities in financial statements. We also analyze and interpret these liabilities, including those related to employee payroll.

A Look Ahead

Chapter 12 explains the partnership form of organization. It also describes the accounting concepts and procedures for the basic transactions of partnerships.

CAP

Conceptual

C1 Describe current and long-term liabilities and their characteristics. *(p. 424)*

C2 Identify and describe known current liabilities. *(p. 426)*

C3 Explain how to account for contingent liabilities. *(p. 436)*

Analytical

A1 Compute the times interest earned ratio and use it to analyze liabilities. *(p. 437)*

Procedural

P1 Prepare entries to account for short-term notes payable. *(p. 427)*

P2 Compute and record *employee* payroll deductions and liabilities. *(p. 429)*

P3 Compute and record *employer* payroll expenses and liabilities. *(p. 431)*

P4 Account for estimated liabilities, including warranties and bonuses. *(p. 433)*

Decision Feature

Cleaning Up in Business

LANDOVER, MD—26-year-old André Downey saw opportunity in environmental cleanup. Downey, however, faced obstacles in funding his business because banks did not share his enthusiasm. Convinced of his eventual success, Downey obtained 10 credit cards that, in sum, provided him $100,000 for his start-up called **Environmental, Engineering & Construction, Inc. (EECinc.com).** That was 1993. Today, Downey's company projects annual revenues of more than $3 million.

"There is a lot of risk involved," admits Downey. "But if you're successful, the benefits definitely outweigh the risks." His company focuses on cleanup of environmental hazards such as black toxic mold, asbestos, and lead.

Downey's service-oriented business demands good employees and he is devoted to them. "Luckily, I have good people working for me," says Downey. "So I can go to the next level." This next level requires Downey to attend to many aspects of business, including the crucial task of managing liabilities for payroll, supplies, employee benefits, vacations, training, and taxes. Without his effective management of liabilities, especially payroll and employee benefits, his company would not be where it is today. Adds Downey, if you want your business to be successful, monitoring and controlling liabilities is a must.

This chapter focuses on measuring and analyzing current liabilities like those Downey insists must be dealt with by good business owners. To ignore them, especially those requiring payments to government agencies and to key employees, is too risky. "This way," says Downey, "if I fail, it's on me." Given his revenue projections, Downey is cleaning up with more than the environment.

[Sources: *Environmental, Engineering & Construction Website,* January 2004; *Black Enterprise,* November 2002; *Gazette Community News,* December 2002.]

Previous chapters introduced liabilities such as accounts payable, notes payable, wages payable, and unearned revenues. This chapter further explains these liabilities and additional ones such as warranties, taxes, payroll, vacation pay, and bonuses. It also describes contingent liabilities and introduces some basic long-term liabilities. The focus is on how to define, classify, measure, report, and analyze these liabilities so that this information is useful to business decision makers.

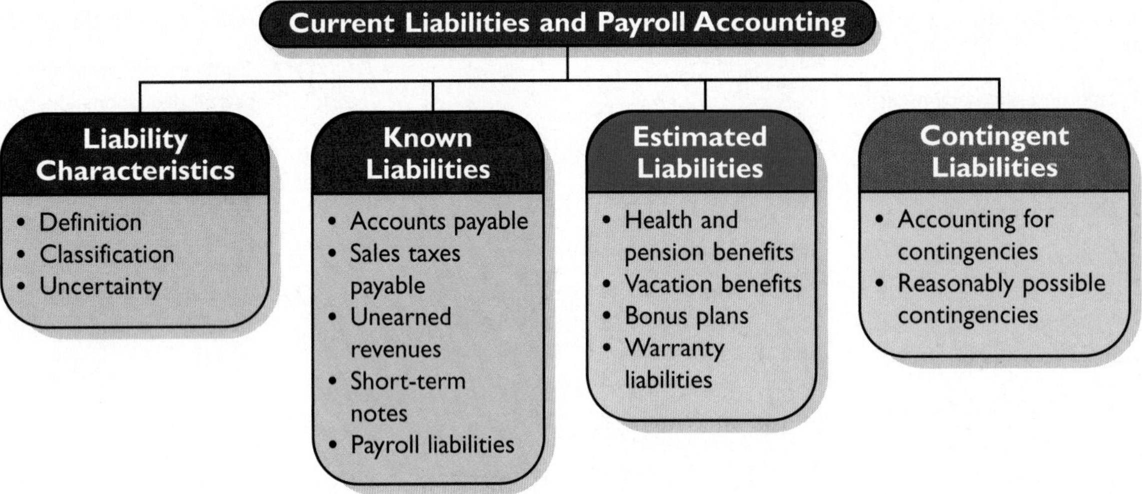

Characteristics of Liabilities

This section discusses important characteristics of liabilities and how liabilities are classified and reported.

Defining Liabilities

C1 Describe current and long-term liabilities and their characteristics.

A *liability* is a probable future payment of assets or services that a company is presently obligated to make as a result of past transactions or events. This definition includes three crucial factors:

- A past transaction or event.
- A present obligation.
- A future payment of assets or services.

Exhibit 11.1

Characteristics of a Liability

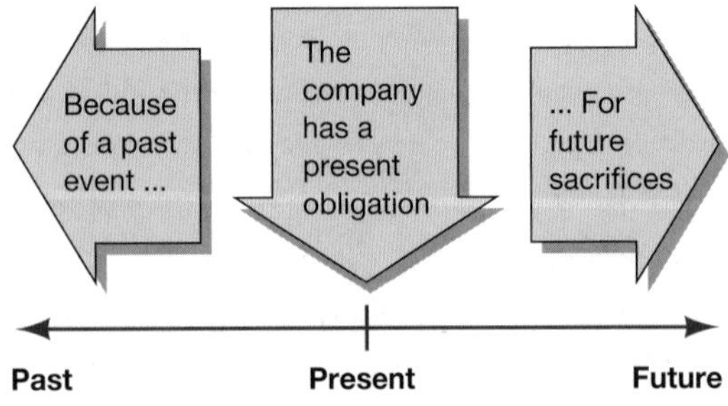

These three important elements are portrayed visually in Exhibit 11.1. Liabilities do not include all expected future payments. For example, most companies expect to pay wages to their employees in upcoming months and years, but these future payments are not liabilities because no past event such as employee work resulted in a present obligation. Instead, such liabilities arise when employees perform their work and earn the wages.

Classifying Liabilities

Information about liabilities is more useful when the balance sheet identifies them as either current or long term. Decision makers need to know when obligations are due so they can plan for them and take appropriate action.

Current Liabilities **Current liabilities,** also called *short-term liabilities,* are obligations due within one year or the company's operating cycle, whichever is longer. They are expected to be paid using current assets or by creating other current liabilities. Common examples of current liabilities are accounts payable, short-term notes payable, wages payable, warranty liabilities, lease liabilities, taxes payable, and unearned revenues.

Point: Improper classification of liabilities can distort key ratios used in financial statement analysis and decision making.

Current liabilities differ across companies because they depend on the type of company operations. **Univision Communications,** for instance, reported the following current liabilities related to its Spanish-language media operations ($000s):

Music copyright and artist royalties	$25,611
Deferred advertising revenues	4,250

Harley-Davidson reports a much different set of current liabilities. It discloses current liabilities made up of items such as warranty, recall, and dealer incentive liabilities.

Long-Term Liabilities A company's obligations not expected to be paid within the longer of one year or the company's operating cycle are reported as **long-term liabilities.** They can include long-term notes payable, warranty liabilities, lease liabilities, and bonds payable. They are sometimes reported on the balance sheet in a single long-term liabilities total or in multiple categories. **Domino's Pizza,** for instance, reports long-term liabilities of $641 million. They are reported after current liabilities. A single liability also can be divided between the current and noncurrent sections if a company expects to make payments toward it in both the short and long term. Domino's reports ($ millions) long-term debt, $599; and current portion of long-term debt, $3. The second item is reported in current liabilities. We sometimes see liabilities that do not have a fixed due date but instead are payable on the creditor's demand. These are reported as current liabilities because of the possibility of payment in the near term. Exhibit 11.2 shows amounts of current liabilities and as a percent of total liabilities for selected companies.

Global: In some countries such as France, the balance sheet does not separate current liabilities into their own category.

Point: The current ratio will be overstated if a company fails to classify any portion of long-term debt due next period as a current liability.

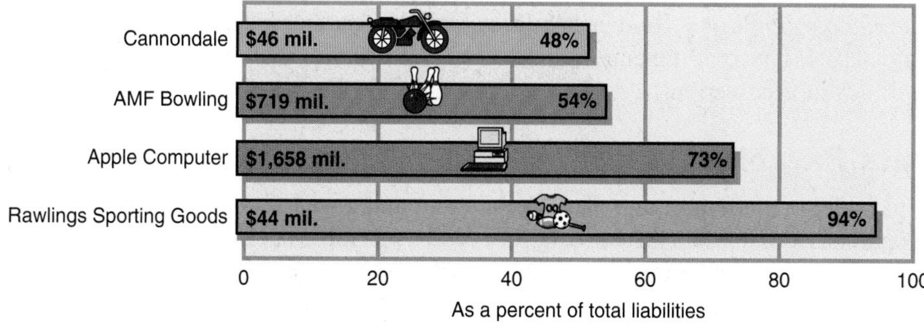

Exhibit 11.2

Current Liabilities of Selected Companies

Uncertainty in Liabilities

Accounting for liabilities involves addressing three important questions: Whom to pay? When to pay? How much to pay? Answers to these questions are often decided when a liability is incurred. For example, if a company has a $100 account payable to a specific individual, payable on March 15, the answers are clear. The company knows whom to pay, when to pay, and how much to pay. However, the answers to one or more of these questions are uncertain for some liabilities.

Uncertainty in Whom to Pay Liabilities can involve uncertainty in whom to pay. For instance, a company can create a liability with a known amount when issuing a note that is payable to its holder. In this case, a specific amount is payable to the note's holder at a specified date, but the company does not know who the holder is until that date. Despite this uncertainty, the company reports this liability on its balance sheet.

Point: An *accrued expense* is an unpaid expense that is also a liability. This is the reason accrued expenses are also called *accrued liabilities.*

Uncertainty in When to Pay A company can have an obligation of a known amount to a known creditor but not know when it must be paid. For example, a legal services firm can accept fees in advance from a client who plans to use the firm's services in the future. This means that the firm has a liability that it settles by providing services at an unknown future date. Although this uncertainty exists, the legal firm's balance sheet must report this liability. These types of obligations are reported as current liabilities because they are likely to be settled in the short term.

Uncertainty in How Much to Pay A company can be aware of an obligation but not know how much will be required to settle it. For example, a company using electrical power is billed only after the meter has been read. This cost is incurred and the liability created before a bill is received. A liability to the power company is reported as an estimated amount if the balance sheet is prepared before a bill arrives.

Quick Check

1. What is a liability? Identify its crucial characteristics.
2. Is every expected future payment a liability?
3. If a liability is payable in 15 months, is it classified as current or long term?

Answers—p. 448

Known (Determinable) Liabilities

Most liabilities arise from situations with little uncertainty. They are set by agreements, contracts, or laws and are measurable. These liabilities are **known liabilities,** also called *definitely determinable liabilities.* Known liabilities include accounts payable, notes payable, payroll, sales taxes, unearned revenues, and leases. We describe how to account for these known liabilities in this section.

Accounts Payable

C2 Identify and describe known current liabilities.

Accounts payable, or trade accounts payable, are amounts owed to suppliers for products or services purchased on credit. Accounting for accounts payable is primarily explained and illustrated in our discussion of merchandising activities in Chapters 5 and 6.

Sales Taxes Payable

Nearly all states and many cities levy taxes on retail sales. Sales taxes are stated as a percent of selling prices. The seller collects sales taxes from customers when sales occur and remits these collections (often monthly) to the proper government agency. Since sellers currently owe these collections to the government, this amount is a current liability. **Home Depot**, for instance, reports sales taxes payable of $307 million in its recent annual report. To illustrate, if Home Depot sells materials on August 31 for $6,000 cash that are subject to a 5% sales tax, the revenue portion of this transaction is recorded as follows:

Assets	= Liabilities	+ Equity
+6,300	+300	+6,000

Aug. 31	Cash	6,300	
	Sales		6,000
	Sales Taxes Payable ($6,000 × 0.05)		300
	To record cash sales and 5% sales tax.		

Sales Taxes Payable is debited and Cash credited when it remits these collections to the government. Sales Taxes Payable is not an expense. It arises because laws require sellers to collect this cash from customers for the government.[1]

Unearned Revenues

Unearned revenues (also called *deferred revenues, collections in advance,* and *prepayments*) are amounts received in advance from customers for future products or services. Advance ticket sales for sporting events or music concerts are examples. The **New York Jets**, for instance, report "deferred game revenues" from advance ticket sales in its balance sheet. To illustrate, assume the Jets sell $5 million of season tickets for 8 home games; its entry is

Point: To *defer* a revenue means to postpone recognition of a revenue collected in advance until it is earned. Sport teams must defer recognition of ticket sales until games are played.

June 30	Cash	5,000,000	
	Unearned Season Ticket Revenue		5,000,000
	To record sale of season tickets.		

Assets = Liabilities + Equity
+5,000,000 +5,000,000

When a home game is played, the Jets record revenue for that portion earned:

Oct. 31	Unearned Season Ticket Revenue	625,000	
	Season Ticket Revenue		625,000
	To record season ticket revenues earned.		

Assets = Liabilities + Equity
−625,000 +625,000

Unearned Season Ticket Revenue is an unearned revenue account and is reported as a current liability. Unearned revenues also arise with airline ticket sales, magazine subscriptions, construction projects, hotel reservations, and custom orders.

Short-Term Notes Payable

P1 Prepare entries to account for short-term notes payable.

A **short-term note payable** is a written promise to pay a specified amount on a definite future date within one year or the company's operating cycle, whichever is longer. These promissory notes are negotiable (as are checks), meaning they can be transferred from party to party by endorsement. The written documentation provided by notes is helpful in resolving disputes and for pursuing legal actions involving these liabilities. Most notes payable bear interest to compensate for use of the money until payment is made. Short-term notes payable can arise from many transactions. A company that purchases merchandise on credit can sometimes extend the credit period by signing a note to replace an account payable. Such notes also can arise when money is borrowed from a bank. We describe both of these cases.

Point: Required characteristics for negotiability of a note: (1) unconditional promise, (2) in writing, (3) specific amount, and (4) definite due date.

Note Given to Extend Credit Period A company can replace an account payable with a note payable. A common example is a creditor that requires the substitution of an interest-bearing note for an overdue account payable that does not bear interest. A less common situation occurs when a debtor's weak financial condition motivates the creditor to accept a note, sometimes for a lesser amount, and to close the account to ensure that this customer makes no additional credit purchases.

---

[1] Sales taxes can be computed from total sales receipts when sales taxes are not separately identified on the register. To illustrate, assume a 5% sales tax and $420 in total sales receipts (which includes sales taxes). Sales are computed as follows:

$$\text{Sales} = \text{Total sales receipts}/(1 + \text{Sales tax percentage}) = \$420/1.05 = \$400$$

Thus, the sales tax amount equals total sales receipts minus sales, or $420 − $400 = $20.

To illustrate, let's assume that on August 23, Irwin asks to extend its past-due $600 account payable to McGraw. After some negotiations, McGraw agrees to accept $100 cash and a 60-day, 12%, $500 note payable to replace the account payable. Irwin records the transaction with this entry:

Assets = Liabilities + Equity
−100 −600
+500

Aug. 23	Accounts Payable—McGraw	600	
	Cash		100
	Notes Payable—McGraw		500
	Gave $100 cash and a 60-day, 12% note for payment on account.		

Point: Accounts payable are detailed in a subsidiary ledger, but notes payable are sometimes not. A file with copies of notes often serves as a subsidiary ledger.

Signing the note does not resolve Irwin's debt. Instead, the form of debt is changed from an account payable to a note payable. McGraw prefers the note payable over the account payable because it earns interest and it is written documentation of the debt's existence, term, and amount. When the note comes due, Irwin pays the note and interest by giving McGraw a check for $510. Irwin records that payment with this entry:

Assets = Liabilities + Equity
−510 −500 −10

Oct. 22	Notes Payable—McGraw	500	
	Interest Expense	10	
	Cash		510
	Paid note with interest ($500 × 12% × 60/360).		

Point: Companies commonly compute interest using a 360-day year. This is known as the *banker's rule.*

Interest expense is computed by multiplying the principal of the note ($500) by the annual interest rate (12%) for the fraction of the year the note is outstanding (60 days/360 days).

Point: Cash received from long-term borrowing is reported on the statement of cash flows as a source of financing Cash from short-term borrowing is part of operating activities. Interest incurred on a note is reported on the income statement as an expense.

Point: When money is borrowed from a bank, the loan is reported as an asset (receivable) on the bank's balance sheet.

Note Given to Borrow from Bank A bank nearly always requires a borrower to sign a promissory note when making a loan. When the note matures, the borrower repays the note with an amount larger than the amount borrowed. The difference between the amount borrowed and the amount repaid is *interest.* This section considers a type of note whose signer promises to pay *principal* (the amount borrowed) plus interest. In this case, the *face value* of the note equals principal. Face value is the value shown on the face (front) of the note. To illustrate, assume that a company needs $2,000 for a project and borrows this money from a bank at 12% annual interest. The loan is made on September 30, 2005, and is due in 60 days. Specifically, the borrowing company signs a note with a face value equal to the amount borrowed. The note includes a statement similar to this: *"I promise to pay $2,000 plus interest at 12% within 60 days after September 30."* This simple note is shown in Exhibit 11.3.

Exhibit 11.3

Note with Face Value Equal to Amount Borrowed

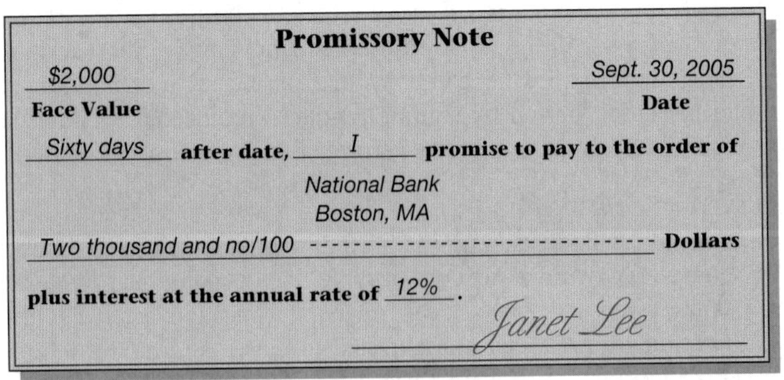
Promissory Note

$2,000 — Face Value — Sept. 30, 2005 — Date

Sixty days after date, I promise to pay to the order of

National Bank
Boston, MA

Two thousand and no/100 ---------- Dollars

plus interest at the annual rate of 12%.

Janet Lee

The borrower records its receipt of cash and the new liability with this entry:

Assets = Liabilities + Equity
+2,000 +2,000

Sept. 30	Cash	2,000	
	Notes Payable		2,000
	Borrowed $2,000 cash with a 60-day, 12%, $2,000 note.		

When principal and interest are paid, the borrower records payment with this entry:

Nov. 29	Notes Payable	2,000	
	Interest Expense	40	
	Cash		2,040
	Paid note with interest ($2,000 × 12% × 60/360).		

Assets	= Liabilities	+ Equity
−2,040	−2,000	−40

End-of-period interest adjustment. When the end of an accounting period occurs between the signing of a note payable and its maturity date, the *matching principle* requires us to record the accrued but unpaid interest on the note. To illustrate, let's return to the note in Exhibit 11.3, but assume that the company borrows $2,000 cash on December 16, 2005, instead of September 30. This 60-day note matures on February 14, 2006, and the company's fiscal year ends on December 31. Thus, we need to record interest expense for the final 15 days in December.

Decision Insight

Many franchisors such as **Curves for Women** use notes to help entrepreneurs acquire their franchises. Many allow the franchise fee and equipment to be paid with notes. Payments on these notes are collected monthly and are secured by the franchisees' assets.

Specifically, we know that 15 days of the 60-day loan period for the $2,000, 12% note have elapsed by December 31. This means that one-fourth (15 days/60 days) of the $40 total interest is an expense of year 2005. The borrower records this expense with the following adjusting entry:

2005			
Dec. 31	Interest Expense	10	
	Interest Payable		10
	To record accrued interest on note ($2,000 × 12% × 15/360).		

Assets	= Liabilities	+ Equity
	+10	−10

Example: If this note is dated December 1 instead of December 16, how much expense is recorded on December 31? *Answer:* $2,000 × 12% × 30/360 = $20

When this note matures on February 14, the borrower must recognize 45 days of interest expense for year 2006 and remove the balances of the two liability accounts:

2006			
Feb. 14	Interest Expense*	30	
	Interest Payable	10	
	Notes Payable	2,000	
	Cash		2,040
	*Paid note with interest. *($2,000 × 12% × 45/360)*		

Assets	= Liabilities	+ Equity
−2,040	−10	−30
	−2,000	

Payroll Liabilities

P2 Compute and record employee payroll deductions and liabilities.

An employer incurs several expenses and liabilities from having employees. These expenses and liabilities are often large and arise from salaries and wages earned, from employee benefits, and from payroll taxes levied on the employer. **Anheuser-Busch**, for instance, reports payroll-related current liabilities of more than $280 million from "accrued salaries, wages and benefits." We discuss payroll liabilities and related accounts in this section. The appendix to this chapter describes details about payroll reports, records, and procedures.

Point: Internal control is important for payroll accounting. Managers must monitor (1) employee hiring, (2) timekeeping, (3) payroll listings, and (4) payroll payments. Poor controls led the U.S. Army to pay nearly $10 million to deserters, fictitious soldiers, and other unauthorized entities.

Employee Payroll Deductions **Gross pay** is the total compensation an employee earns including wages, salaries, commissions, bonuses, and any compensation earned before deductions such as taxes. (*Wages* usually refer to payments to employees at an hourly rate. *Salaries* usually refer to payments to employees at a monthly or yearly rate.) **Net pay,** also called *take-home pay,* is gross pay less all deductions. **Payroll deductions,** commonly called *withholdings,* are amounts withheld from an employee's gross pay, either required or voluntary. Required deductions result from laws and include income taxes and Social Security taxes. Voluntary deductions, at an employee's option, include pension and health contributions, union dues, and charitable giving. Exhibit 11.4 shows the typical payroll deductions of an employee. The employer withholds payroll deductions from employees' pay and is obligated to transmit this money to the designated organization. The employer records payroll deductions as current liabilities until these amounts are transmitted. This section discusses the major payroll deductions.

Decision Insight

Delay or failure to pay withholding taxes to the government has severe consequences. For example, a 100% penalty can be levied, with interest, on the unpaid balance. The government can even close a company, take its assets, and pursue legal actions against those involved.

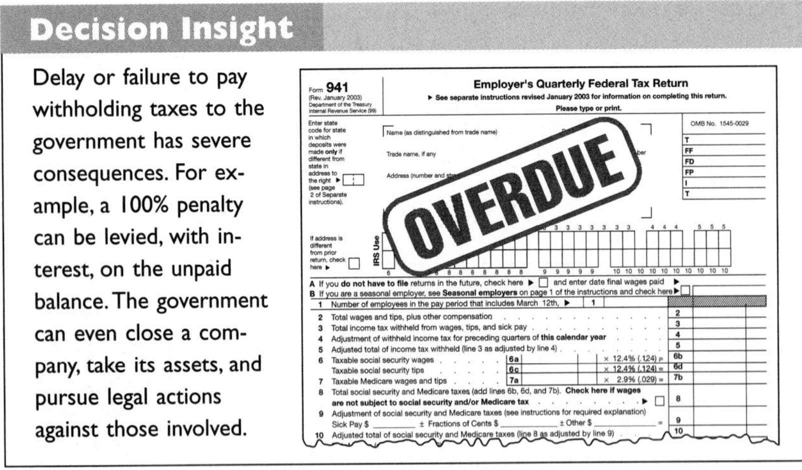

Form **941** (Rev. January 2003) Department of the Treasury Internal Revenue Service (99)

Employer's Quarterly Federal Tax Return

▶ **See separate instructions revised January 2003 for information on completing this return.**

Please type or print.

Enter state code for state in which deposits were made **only** if different from state in address to the right ▶ (see page 2 of Separate instructions).

Name (as distinguished from trade name)

Trade name, if any

Address (number and st

OMB No. 1545-0029

T / FF / FD / FP / I / T

If address is different from prior return, check here ▶

IRS Use

A If you **do not have to file** returns in the future, check here ▶ ☐ and enter date final wages paid ▶

B If you are a seasonal employer, see **Seasonal employers** on page 1 of the instructions and check here ▶ ☐

1 Number of employees in the pay period that includes March 12th, ▶ 1

2 Total wages and tips, plus other compensation . . . 2

3 Total income tax withheld from wages, tips, and sick pay . . . 3

4 Adjustment of withheld income tax for preceding quarters of **this calendar year** . . . 4

5 Adjusted total of income tax withheld (line 3 as adjusted by line 4) . . . 5

6 Taxable social security wages . . . 6a × 12.4% (.124) = 6b

Taxable social security tips . . . 6c × 12.4% (.124) = 6d

7 Taxable Medicare wages and tips . . . 7a × 2.9% (.029) = 7b

8 Total social security and Medicare taxes (add lines 6b, 6d, and 7b). **Check here if wages are not subject to social security and/or Medicare tax** . . . ▶ ☐ 8

9 Adjustment of social security and Medicare taxes (see instructions for required explanation) Sick Pay $ ____ ± Fractions of Cents $ ____ ± Other $ ____ = 9

10 Adjusted total of social security and Medicare taxes (line 8 as adjusted by line 9) 10

Exhibit 11.4

Payroll Deductions

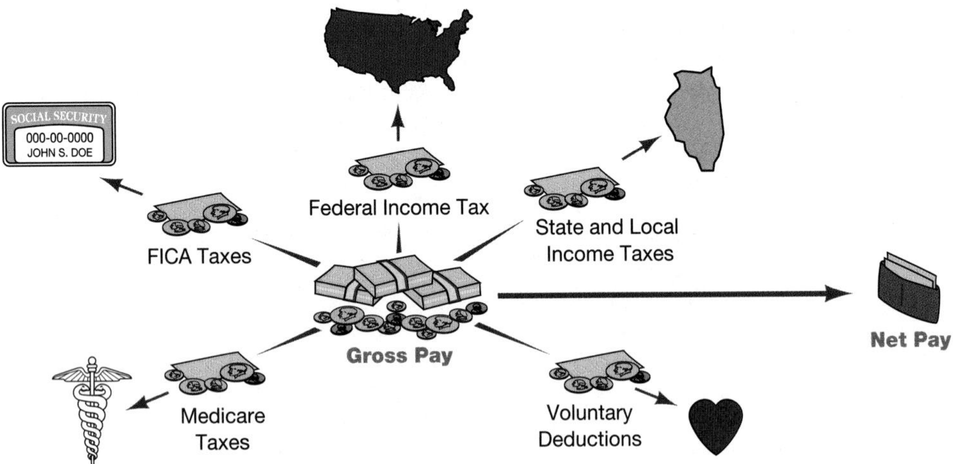

Employee FICA taxes. The federal Social Security system provides retirement, disability, survivorship, and medical benefits to qualified workers. Laws *require* employers to withhold **Federal Insurance Contributions Act (FICA) taxes** from employees' pay to cover costs of the system. Employers usually separate FICA taxes into two groups: (1) retirement, disability, and survivorship and (2) medical. For the first group, the Social Security system provides monthly cash payments to qualified retired workers for the rest of their lives. These payments are often called *Social Security benefits.* Taxes related to this group are often called *Social Security taxes.* For the second group, the system provides monthly payments to deceased workers' surviving families and to disabled workers who qualify for assistance. These payments are commonly called *Medicare benefits;* like those in the first group, they are paid with *Medicare taxes* (part of FICA taxes).

Topic Tackler 11-1

Law requires employers to withhold FICA taxes from each employee's salary or wages on each payday. The taxes for Social Security and Medicare are computed separately. For example, for the year 2003, the amount withheld from each employee's pay for Social Security tax was 6.2% of the first $87,000 the employee earns in the calendar year, or a maximum of $5,394. The Medicare tax was 1.45% of *all* amounts the employee earns; there is no maximum limit to Medicare tax.

Point: The sources of U.S. tax receipts are roughly as follows:

10%	Corporate income tax
50	Personal income tax
35	FICA and FUTA taxes
5	Other taxes

Employers must pay withheld taxes to the Internal Revenue Service (IRS) on specific filing dates during the year. Employers who fail to send the withheld taxes to the IRS on time can be assessed substantial penalties. Until all the taxes are sent to the IRS, they are included in employers' current liabilities. For any changes in rates or with the maximum earnings level, check the IRS Website at www.IRS.gov.

Employee income tax. Most employers are required to withhold federal income tax from each employee's paycheck. The amount withheld is computed using tables published by the IRS. The amount depends on the employee's annual earnings rate and the number of *withholding allowances* the employee claims. Allowances reduce the amount of taxes one owes the government. The more allowances one claims, the less tax the employer will withhold. Employees can claim allowances for themselves and their dependents. They also can claim additional allowances if they expect major declines in their taxable income for medical expenses. (An employee who claims more allowances than appropriate is subject to a fine.) Most states and many local governments require employers to withhold income taxes from employees' pay and to remit them promptly to the proper government agency. Until they are paid, withholdings are reported as a current liability on the employer's balance sheet.

Point: Part-time employees may claim "exempt from withholding" if they did not have any income tax liability in the prior year and do not expect any in the current year.

Point: IRS withholding tables are based on projecting weekly (or other period) pay into an annual figure.

Employee voluntary deductions. Beyond Social Security, Medicare, and income taxes, employers often withhold other amounts from employees' earnings. These withholdings arise from employee requests, contracts, unions, or other agreements. They can include amounts for charitable giving, medical insurance premiums, pension contributions, and union dues. Until they are paid, such withholdings are reported as part of employers' current liabilities.

Recording employee payroll deductions. Employers must accrue payroll expenses and liabilities at the end of each pay period. To illustrate, assume that an employee earns a salary of $2,000 per month. At the end of January, the employer's entry to accrue payroll expenses and liabilities for this employee is

Date	Account	Debit	Credit
Jan. 31	Salaries Expense	2,000	
	FICA—Social Security Taxes Payable (6.2%)		124
	FICA—Medicare Taxes Payable (1.45%)		29
	Employee Federal Income Taxes Payable*		213
	Employee Medical Insurance Payable*		85
	Employee Union Dues Payable*		25
	Accrued Payroll Payable		1,524
	To record accrued payroll for January.		

Assets	=	Liabilities	+	Equity
		+124		−2,000
		+29		
		+213		
		+85		
		+25		
		+1,524		

*Amounts taken from employer's accounting records.

Salaries Expense (debit) shows that the employee earns a gross salary of $2,000. The first five payables (credits) show the liabilities the employer owes on behalf of this employee to cover FICA taxes, income taxes, medical insurance, and union dues. The Accrued Payroll Payable account (credit) records the $1,524 net pay the employee receives from the $2,000 gross pay earned. When the employee is paid, another entry (or a series of entries) is required to record the check written and distributed (or funds transferred). The entry to record cash payment to this employee is to debit Accrued Payroll Payable and credit Cash for $1,524.

Decision Insight

Check List Millions are lost annually to check schemes. Companies are fighting back with an internal control method called *positive pay*. Here's how it works: A company regularly (daily) sends the bank a "positive file" listing all checks written. When a check reaches the bank for payment, the bank compares the check against the positive file. This flags any forged checks and altered authentic checks.

Employer Payroll Taxes

Employers must pay payroll taxes in addition to those required of employees. Employer taxes include FICA and unemployment taxes.

P3 Compute and record *employer* payroll expenses and liabilities.

Employer FICA tax. Employers must pay FICA taxes *equal in amount to* the FICA taxes withheld from their employees. An employer's tax is credited to the same FICA Taxes Payable accounts used to record the Social Security and Medicare taxes withheld from employees. (A self-employed person must pay both the employee and employer FICA taxes.)

Federal and state unemployment taxes. The federal government participates with states in a joint federal and state unemployment insurance program. Each state administers its program. These programs provide unemployment benefits to qualified workers. The federal government approves state programs and pays a portion of their administrative expenses.

Federal Unemployment Taxes (FUTA). Employers are subject to a federal unemployment tax on wages and salaries paid to their employees. For the year 2003, employers were required to pay FUTA taxes of as much as 6.2% of the first $7,000 earned by each employee. This federal tax can be reduced by a credit of up to 5.4% for taxes paid to a state program. As a result, the net federal unemployment tax is often only 0.8%.

Decision Insight

eTax Technology helps reduce errors and increase speed in computing taxes as compared with manual computation of taxes. Also, tax tables and forms can be downloaded off the Web (**www.IRS.gov**) and then used to accurately and quickly compute payroll taxes.

State Unemployment Taxes (SUTA). All states support their unemployment insurance programs by placing a payroll tax on employers. (A few states require employees to make a contribution. In the book's assignments, we assume that this tax is only on the employer.) In most states, the base rate for SUTA taxes is 5.4% of the first $7,000 paid each employee. This base rate is adjusted according to an employer's merit rating. The state assigns a **merit rating** that reflects a company's stability or instability in employing workers. A good rating reflects stability in employment and means an employer can pay less than the 5.4% base rate. A low rating reflects high turnover or seasonal hirings and layoffs. To illustrate, an employer with 50 employees each of whom earns $7,000 or more per year saves $15,400 annually if it has a merit rating of 1.0% versus 5.4%. This is computed by comparing taxes of $18,900 at the 5.4% rate to only $3,500 at the 1.0% rate.

Decision Ethics

Web Designer You take a summer job working for a family friend who runs a small IT service. On your first payday, the owner slaps you on the back, gives you full payment in cash, winks, and adds: "No need to pay those high taxes, eh." What action do you take?

Answer—p. 448

Recording employer payroll taxes. Employer payroll taxes are an added expense beyond the wages and salaries earned by employees. These taxes are often recorded in an entry separate from the one recording payroll expenses and deductions. To illustrate, assume that the $2,000 recorded salaries expense from the previous example is earned by an employee whose earnings have not yet reached $5,000 for the year. Also assume that the federal unemployment tax rate is 0.8% and the state unemployment tax rate is 5.4%. Consequently, the FICA portion of the employer's tax is $153, computed by multiplying both the 6.2% and 1.45% by the $2,000 gross pay. Moreover, state unemployment (SUTA) taxes are $108 (5.4% of the $2,000 gross pay), and federal unemployment (FUTA) taxes are $16 (0.8% of $2,000). The entry to record the employer's payroll tax expense and related liabilities is

Example: If the employer's merit rating in this example reduces its SUTA rate to 2.9%, what is its SUTA liability? *Answer:* SUTA payable = $2,000 × 2.9% = $58

Assets	=	Liabilities	+	Equity
		+124		−277
		+29		
		+108		
		+16		

Jan. 31	Payroll Taxes Expense	277	
	FICA—Social Security Taxes Payable (6.2%)		124
	FICA—Medicare Taxes Payable (1.45%)		29
	State Unemployment Taxes Payable		108
	Federal Unemployment Taxes Payable		16
	To record employer payroll taxes.		

Multi-Period Known Liabilities

Many known liabilities extend over multiple periods. These often include unearned revenues and notes payable. For example, if **Sports Illustrated** sells a four-year magazine subscription, it records amounts received for this subscription in an Unearned Subscription Revenues account. Amounts in this account are liabilities, but are they current or long term? They are *both.* The portion of the Unearned Subscription Revenues account that will be fulfilled in the next year is reported as a current liability. The remaining portion is reported as a long-term liability.

The same analysis applies to notes payable. For example, a borrower reports a three-year note payable as a long-term liability in the first two years it is outstanding. In the third year, the borrower reclassifies this note as a current liability since it is due within one year or the operating cycle, whichever is longer. The **current portion of long-term debt** refers to that part of long-term debt due within one year or the operating cycle, whichever is longer. Long-term debt is reported under long-term liabilities, but the *current portion due* is reported under current liabilities. To illustrate, assume that a $7,500 debt is paid in installments of $1,500 per year for five years. The $1,500 due within the year is reported as a current liability. No journal entry is necessary for this reclassification. Instead, we simply classify the amounts for debt as either current or long term when the balance sheet is prepared.

Some known liabilities are rarely reported in long-term liabilities. These include accounts payable, sales taxes, and wages and salaries.

Decision Insight

Small is Big The Small Business Administration (**SBA.gov**) publishes a yearly report of likely sources of small business loans. It shows that small businesses number more than 25 million, employ 53% of the private workforce, make 47% of all sales, create most new jobs, and produce 55% of innovations.

Quick Check

4. Why does a creditor prefer a note payable to a past-due account payable?
5. A company pays its one employee $3,000 per month. This company's FUTA rate is 0.8% on the first $7,000 earned; its SUTA rate is 4.0% on the first $7,000; its Social Security tax rate is 6.2% of the first $87,000; and its Medicare tax rate is 1.45% of all amounts earned. The entry to record this company's March payroll includes what amount for total payroll taxes expense?
6. Identify whether the employer or employee or both incurs each of the following: (*a*) FICA taxes, (*b*) FUTA taxes, (*c*) SUTA taxes, and (*d*) withheld income taxes.

Answers—p. 448

Estimated Liabilities

P4 Account for estimated liabilities, including warranties and bonuses.

An **estimated liability** is a known obligation that is of an uncertain amount but that can be reasonably estimated. Common examples are employee benefits such as pensions, health care and vacation pay, and warranties offered by a seller. We discuss each of these in this section. Other examples of estimated liabilities include property taxes and certain contracts to provide future services.

Health and Pension Benefits

Many companies provide **employee benefits** beyond salaries and wages. An employer often pays all or part of medical, dental, life, and disability insurance. Many employers also contribute to *pension plans,* which are agreements by employers to provide benefits (payments) to employees after retirement. Many companies also provide medical care and insurance benefits to their retirees. When payroll taxes and charges for employee benefits are totaled, payroll cost often exceeds employees' gross earnings by 25% or more.

Decision Insight

Postgame Gripes Several ex-players sued **Major League Baseball** over a pension system they say unfairly excludes them and fails to reward them for their contributions. Gripes include a failure to extend pensions to players whose careers ended years ago or were interrupted by war. A full pension exceeds $120,000 per year.

To illustrate, assume that an employer agrees to (1) pay an amount for medical insurance equal to $8,000 and (2) contribute an additional 10% of the employees' $120,000 gross salary to a retirement program. The entry to record these accrued benefits is

Assets = Liabilities + Equity
+8,000 −20,000
+12,000

Jan. 31	Employee Benefits Expense	20,000	
	Employee Medical Insurance Payable		8,000
	Employee Retirement Program Payable		12,000
	To record costs of employee benefits.		

Vacation Benefits

Many employers offer paid vacation benefits, also called *paid absences.* To illustrate, assume that salaried employees earn 2 weeks' vacation per year. This benefit increases employers' payroll expenses because employees are paid for 52 weeks but work for only 50 weeks. Total annual salary is the same, but the cost per week worked is greater than the amount paid per week. For example, if an employee is paid $20,800 for 52 weeks but works only 50 weeks, the total weekly expense to the employer is $416 ($20,800/50 weeks) instead of the $400 cash paid weekly to the employee ($20,800/52 weeks). The $16 difference between these two amounts is recorded weekly as follows:

Assets = Liabilities + Equity
+16 −16

	Vacation Benefits Expense	16	
	Vacation Benefits Payable		16
	To record vacation benefits accrued.		

Vacation Benefits Expense is an operating expense, and Vacation Benefits Payable is a current liability. When the employee takes a vacation, the employer reduces (debits) the Vacation Benefits Payable and credits Cash (no additional expense is recorded).

Global: Bonuses are considered part of salary expense in most countries. In Japan, bonuses to members of the board of directors and to external auditors are directly charged against equity rather than treated as an expense.

Bonus Plans

Many companies offer bonuses to employees, and many of the bonuses depend on net income. To illustrate, assume that an employer offers a bonus to its employees equal to 5% of the company's annual net income (to be equally shared by all). The company's expected annual net income is $210,000. The year-end adjusting entry to record this benefit is

Assets = Liabilities + Equity
+10,000 −10,000

Dec. 31	Employee Bonus Expense*.	10,000	
	Bonus Payable		10,000
	To record expected bonus costs.		

* Bonus Expense (B) equals 5% of the quantity $210,000 minus the bonus—computed as:

$B = 0.05\ (\$210{,}000 - B)$
$B = \$10{,}500 - 0.05B$
$1.05B = \$10{,}500$
$\mathbf{B = \$10{,}500/1.05 = \$10{,}000}$

When the bonus is paid, Bonus Payable is debited and Cash is credited for $10,000.

Warranty Liabilities

A **warranty** is a seller's obligation to replace or correct a product (or service) that fails to perform as expected within a specified period. Most new cars, for instance, are sold with a warranty covering parts for a specified period of time. **Ford Motor Company** reported more than $14 billion in "dealer and customer allowances and claims" in its recent annual report. To comply with the *full disclosure* and *matching principles,* the seller reports the expected warranty expense in the period when revenue from the sale of the product or service is reported. The seller reports this warranty obligation as a liability, although the existence,

Point: Zenith recently reported $32.1 million on its balance sheet for warranties.

amount, payee, and date of future sacrifices are uncertain. This is because such warranty costs are probable and the amount can be estimated using, for instance, past experience with warranties.

To illustrate, a dealer sells a used car for $16,000 on December 1, 2005, with a maximum one-year or 12,000-mile warranty covering parts. This dealer's experience shows that warranty expense averages about 4% of a car's selling price, or $640 in this case ($16,000 × 4%). The dealer records the estimated expense and liability related to this sale with this entry:

2005			
Dec. 1	Warranty Expense	640	
	Estimated Warranty Liability		640
	To record estimated warranty expense.		

Assets = Liabilities − Equity
+640 −640

This entry alternatively could be made as part of end-of-period adjustments. Either way, the estimated warranty expense is reported on the 2005 income statement and the warranty liability on the 2005 balance sheet. To further extend this example, suppose the customer returns the car for warranty repairs on January 9, 2006. The dealer performs this work by replacing parts costing $200. The entry to record partial settlement of the estimated warranty liability is

Point: Recognition of expected warranty liabilities is necessary to comply with the matching and full disclosure principles.

2006			
Jan. 9	Estimated Warranty Liability	200	
	Auto Parts Inventory		200
	To record costs of warranty repairs.		

Assets = Liabilities + Equity
−200 −200

This entry reduces the balance of the estimated warranty liability. Warranty expense was previously recorded in 2005, the year the car was sold with the warranty. Finally, what happens if total warranty expenses are more or less than the estimated 4%, or $640? The answer is that management should monitor actual warranty expenses to see whether the 4% rate is accurate. If experience reveals a large difference from the estimate, the rate for current and future sales should be changed. Differences are expected, but they should be small.

Multi-Period Estimated Liabilities

Estimated liabilities can be both current and long term. For example, pension liabilities to employees are long term to workers who will not retire within the next period. For employees who are retired or will retire within the next period, a portion of pension liabilities is current. Other examples include employee health benefits and warranties. Specifically, many warranties are for 30 or 60 days in length. Estimated costs under these warranties are properly reported in current liabilities. Many other automobile warranties are for three years or 36,000 miles. A portion of these warranties is reported as long term.

Quick Check

7. Estimated liabilities involve an obligation to pay which of these? (*a*) An uncertain but reasonably estimated amount owed on a known obligation or (*b*) A known amount to a specific entity on an uncertain due date.
8. A car is sold for $15,000 on June 1, 2005, with a one-year warranty on parts. Warranty expense is estimated at 1.5% of selling price at each calendar year-end. On March 1, 2006, the car is returned for warranty repairs costing $135. The amount recorded as warranty expense on March 1 is (*a*) $0; (*b*) $60; (*c*) $75; (*d*) $135; (*e*) $225.

Answers—p. 449

Contingent Liabilities

C3 Explain how to account for contingent liabilities.

A **contingent liability** is a potential obligation that depends on a future event arising from a past transaction or event. An example is a pending lawsuit. Here, a past transaction or event leads to a lawsuit whose result depends on the outcome of the suit. Future payment of a contingent liability depends on whether an uncertain future event occurs.

Accounting for Contingent Liabilities

Accounting for contingent liabilities depends on the likelihood that a future event will occur and the ability to estimate the future amount owed if this event occurs. Three categories are identified (see the table in the margin)

	Probable	Reasonably Possible	Remote
Amount estimable	Record contingent liability	Disclose liability in notes	No action
Amount not estimable	Disclose liability in notes	Disclose liability in notes	No action

(1) The future event is *probable* (likely) and the amount owed can be *reasonably estimated.* We record this amount as a liability. Examples are the estimated liabilities described earlier such as warranties, vacation pay, and income taxes.

(2) The future event is *remote* (unlikely). We do not record or disclose information on remote contingent liabilities.

(3) Likelihood of the future event is between these two extremes. That is, if the future event is *reasonably possible* (could occur), we disclose information about the contingent liability in notes to the financial statements.

This section identifies contingent liabilities that often fall in the third category—when the future event is reasonably possible. Disclosing information about contingencies in this third category is motivated by the *full-disclosure principle,* which requires information relevant to decision makers be reported.

Point: A contingency is an *if.* Namely, if a future event occurs, then financial consequences are likely for the entity.

Reasonably Possible Contingent Liabilities

This section discusses common examples of reasonably possible contingent liabilities.

Point: A sale of a note receivable is often a contingent liability. It becomes a liability if the original signer of the note fails to pay it at maturity.

Potential Legal Claims Many companies are sued or at risk of being sued. The accounting issue is whether the defendant should recognize a liability on its balance sheet or disclose a contingent liability in its notes while a lawsuit is outstanding and not yet settled. The answer is that a potential claim is recorded in the accounts *only* if payment for damages is probable and the amount can be reasonably estimated. If the potential claim cannot be reasonably estimated or is less than probable but reasonably possible, it is disclosed. **Ford Motor Company,** for example, includes the following note in its recent annual report: "Various legal actions, governmental investigations and proceedings and claims are pending . . . arising out of alleged defects in our products."

Decision Insight

Hot Claims Remember the infamous lawsuit against **McDonald's** that awarded an 81-year-old New Mexico woman $2.9 million—later reduced to $640,000—after she spilled hot coffee in her lap? Well, copycat litigation is booming. Companies from **Burger King** to **Starbucks** now print cautions on coffee cups, chili bowls, and so forth.

Debt Guarantees Sometimes a company guarantees the payment of debt owed by a supplier, customer, or another company. The guarantor usually discloses the guarantee in its financial statement notes as a contingent liability. If it is probable that the debtor will default, the guarantor needs to record and report the guarantee in its financial statements as a liability. The **Boston Celtics** report a unique guarantee when it comes to coaches and players: "Certain of the contracts provide for guaranteed payments which must be paid even if the employee [player] is injured or terminated."

Decision Insight

Pricing Priceless What's it worth to see from one side of the Grand Canyon to the other? What's the cost when beaches are closed due to pollution? One method to measure these environmental liabilities is **contingent valuation,** by which people are asked to answer such questions. Regulators use their answers to levy fines and assess punitive damages.

Other Contingencies Other examples of contingencies include environmental damages, possible tax assessments, insurance losses, and government investigations. **Sunoco**, for instance, reports that "federal, state and local laws . . . result in liabilities and loss contingencies. Sunoco accrues . . . cleanup costs [that] are probable and reasonably estimable. [Sunoco also] believes it is reasonably possible (i.e., less than probable but greater than remote) that additional . . . losses will be incurred." Many of Sunoco's contingencies are revealed only in notes.

Point: Auditors and managers often have different views about whether a contingency is recorded, disclosed, or omitted.

Uncertainties All organizations face uncertainties from future events such as natural disasters and the development of new competing products or services. These uncertainties are not contingent liabilities because they are future events *not* arising from past transactions. Accordingly, they are not disclosed.

Topic Tackler 11-2

Quick Check

9. A future payment is reported as a liability on the balance sheet if payment is contingent on a future event that (*a*) is reasonably possible but the payment cannot be reasonably estimated; (*b*) is probable and the payment can be reasonably estimated; or (*c*) is not probable but the payment is known.
10. Under what circumstances is a future payment reported in the notes to the financial statements as a contingent liability?

Global: Accounting for contingencies varies across countries. International accounting standards require disclosure only for contingent liabilities that are reasonably possible or probable.

Answers—p. 449

Times Interest Earned Ratio

Decision Analysis

A1 Compute the times interest earned ratio and use it to analyze liabilities.

A company incurs interest expense on many of its current and long-term liabilities. Examples extend from its short-term notes and the current portion of long-term liabilities to its long-term notes and bonds. Interest expense is often viewed as a *fixed expense* because the amount of these liabilities is likely to remain in one form or another for a substantial period of time. This means that the amount of interest is unlikely to vary due to changes in sales or other operating activities. While fixed expenses can be advantageous when a company is growing, they create risk. This risk stems from the possibility that a company might be unable to pay fixed expenses if sales decline. To illustrate, consider X-Caliber's results for year 2005 and two possible outcomes for year 2006 in Exhibit 11.5.

Exhibit 11.5

Actual and Projected Results

($ thousands)	Year 2005	Year 2006 Projections	
		Sales Increase	Sales Decrease
Sales	$600	$900	$300
Expenses (75% of sales)	450	675	225
Income before interest	150	225	75
Interest expense (fixed)	60	60	60
Net income	$ 90	$165	$ 15

Expenses excluding interest are at, and expected to remain at, 75% of sales. Expenses such as these that change with sales volume are called *variable expenses*. However, interest expense is at, and expected to remain at, $60,000 per year due to its fixed nature.

The middle numerical column of Exhibit 11.5 shows that X-Caliber's income nearly doubles to $165,000 if sales increase by 50% to $900,000. In contrast, the far right column shows that income falls sharply if sales decline by 50%. These results reveal that the amount of fixed interest expense affects a company's risk of its ability to pay interest, which is numerically reflected in the **times interest earned** ratio in Exhibit 11.6.

Exhibit 11.6

Times Interest Earned

$$\textbf{Times interest earned} = \frac{\textbf{Income before interest expense and income taxes}}{\textbf{Interest expense}}$$

For 2005, X-Caliber's times interest earned is computed as $150,000/$60,000, or 2.5 times. This ratio suggests that X-Caliber faces low to moderate risk because its sales must decline sharply before it would be unable to cover its interest expenses. (X-Caliber is an LLC and does not pay income taxes.)

Experience shows that when times interest earned falls below 1.5 to 2.0 and remains at that level or lower for several periods, the default rate on liabilities increases sharply. This reflects increased risk for companies and their creditors. We also must interpret the times interest earned ratio in light of information about the variability of a company's income before interest. If income is stable from year to year or if it is growing, the company can afford to take on added risk by borrowing. If its income greatly varies from year to year, fixed interest expense can increase the risk that it will not earn enough income to pay interest.

Decision Maker

Entrepreneur You wish to invest in a franchise for either one of two national chains. Each franchise has an expected annual net income *after* interest and taxes of $100,000. Net income for the first franchise includes a regular fixed interest charge of $200,000. The fixed interest charge for the second franchise is $40,000. Which franchise is riskier to you if sales forecasts are not met? Does your decision change if the first franchise has more variability in its income stream?

Answer—p. 448

Demonstration Problem

The following transactions and events took place at Kern Company during its recent calendar-year reporting period (Kern does not use reversing entries):

a. In September 2005, Kern sold $140,000 of merchandise covered by a 180-day warranty. Prior experience shows that costs of the warranty equal 5% of sales. Compute September's warranty expense and prepare the adjusting journal entry for the warranty liability as recorded at September 30. Also prepare the journal entry on October 8 to record a $300 cash expenditure to provide warranty service on an item sold in September.

b. On October 12, 2005, Kern arranged with a supplier to replace Kern's overdue $10,000 account payable by paying $2,500 cash and signing a note for the remainder. The note matures in 90 days and has a 12% interest rate. Prepare the entries recorded on October 12, December 31, and January 10, 2006, related to this transaction.

c. In late December, Kern learns it is facing a product liability suit filed by an unhappy customer. Kern's lawyer advises that although it will probably suffer a loss from the lawsuit, it is not possible to estimate the amount of damages at this time.

d. Sally Kline works for Kern. For the pay period ended November 30, her gross earnings are $3,000. Kline has $800 deducted for federal income taxes and $200 for state income taxes from each paycheck. Additionally, a $35 premium for her health care insurance and a $10 donation for the United Way are deducted. Kline pays FICA Social Security taxes at a rate of 6.2% and FICA Medicare taxes at a rate of 1.45%. She has not earned enough this year to be exempt from any FICA taxes. Journalize the payment of Kline's wages by Kern.

e. On November 1, Kern borrows $5,000 cash from a bank in return for a 60-day, 12%, $5,000 note. Record the note's issuance on November 1 and its repayment with interest on December 31.

f.[B] Kern has estimated and recorded its quarterly income tax payments. In reviewing its year-end tax adjustments, it identifies an additional $5,000 of income tax expense that should be recorded. A portion of this additional expense, $1,000, is deferrable to future years. Record this year-end income taxes expense adjusting entry.

g. For this calendar-year, Kern's net income is $1,000,000, its interest expense is $275,000, and its income taxes expense is $225,000. Calculate Kern's times interest earned ratio.

Planning the Solution

- For *a*, compute the warranty expense for September and record it with an estimated liability. Record the October expenditure as a decrease in the liability.
- For *b*, eliminate the liability for the account payable and create the liability for the note payable. Compute interest expense for the 80 days that the note is outstanding in 2005 and record it as an

additional liability. Record the payment of the note, being sure to include the interest for the 10 days in 2006.

- For *c,* decide whether the company's contingent liability needs to be disclosed or accrued (recorded) according to the two necessary criteria: probable loss and reasonably estimable.
- For *d,* set up payable accounts for all items in Kline's paycheck that require deductions. After deducting all necessary items, credit the remaining amount to Accrued Payroll Payable.
- For *e,* record the issuance of the note. Calculate 60 days' interest due using the 360-day convention in the interest formula.
- For *f,* determine how much of the income taxes expense is payable in the current year and how much needs to be deferred.
- For *g,* apply and compute times interest earned.

Solution to Demonstration Problem

a. Warranty expense = 5% × $140,000 = $7,000

Sept. 30	Warranty Expense	7,000	
	Estimated Warranty Liability		7,000
	To record warranty expense for the month.		
Oct. 8	Estimated Warranty Liability.	300	
	Cash		300
	To record the cost of the warranty service.		

b. Interest expense for 2005 = 12% × $7,500 × 80/360 = $200
Interest expense for 2006 = 12% × $7,500 × 10/360 = $25

Oct. 12	Accounts Payable	10,000	
	Notes Payable		7,500
	Cash.		2,500
	Paid $2,500 cash and gave a 90-day, 12% note to extend the due date on the account.		
Dec. 31	Interest Expense.	200	
	Interest Payable		200
	To accrue interest on note payable.		
Jan. 10	Interest Expense.	25	
	Interest Payable	200	
	Notes Payable.	7,500	
	Cash		7,725
	Paid note with interest, including the accrued interest payable.		

c. Disclose the pending lawsuit in the financial statement notes. Although the loss is probable, no liability can be accrued since the loss cannot be reasonably estimated.

d.

Nov. 30	Salaries Expense	3,000.00	
	FICA—Social Security Taxes Payable (6.2%) . .		186.00
	FICA—Medicare Taxes Payable (1.45%)		43.50
	Employee Federal Income Taxes Payable.		800.00
	Employee State Income Taxes Payable		200.00
	Employee Medical Insurance Payable		35.00
	Employee United Way Payable.		10.00
	Accrued Payroll Payable		1,725.50
	To record Kline's accrued payroll.		

e.

Nov. 1	Cash	5,000	
	Notes Payable		5,000
	Borrowed cash with a 60-day, 12% note.		

When the note and interest are paid 60 days later, Kern Company records this entry:

Dec. 31	Notes Payable	5,000	
	Interest Expense	100	
	Cash		5,100
	Paid note with interest ($5,000 × 12% × 60/360).		

f.

Dec. 31	Income Taxes Expense	5,000	
	Income Taxes Payable		4,000
	Deferred Income Tax Liability		1,000
	To record added income taxes expense and the deferred tax liability.		

g. $$\text{Times interest earned} = \frac{\$1{,}000{,}000 + \$275{,}000 + \$225{,}000}{\$275{,}000} = \underline{\underline{5.45 \text{ times}}}$$

APPENDIX

11A Payroll Reports, Records, and Procedures

Understanding payroll procedures and keeping adequate payroll reports and records are essential to a company's success. This appendix focuses on payroll accounting and its reports, records, and procedures.

Payroll Reports

Most employees and employers are required to pay local, state, and federal payroll taxes. Payroll expenses involve liabilities to individual employees, to federal and state governments, and to other organizations such as insurance companies. Beyond paying these liabilities, employers are required to prepare and submit reports explaining how they computed these payments.

C4 Identify and describe payroll reporting.

Reporting FICA Taxes and Income Taxes The Federal Insurance Contributions Act (FICA) requires each employer to file an Internal Revenue Service (IRS) **Form 941,** the *Employer's Quarterly Federal Tax Return,* within one month after the end of each calendar quarter. A sample Form 941 is shown in Exhibit 11A.1 for Phoenix Sales & Service, a landscape design company. Accounting information and software are helpful in tracking payroll transactions and reporting the accumulated information on Form 941. Specifically, the employer reports total wages subject to income

Exhibit 11A.1

Form 941

Form **941** (Rev. January 2003) Department of the Treasury Internal Revenue Service (99)

Employer's Quarterly Federal Tax Return

▶ See separate instructions revised January 2003 for information on completing this return.

Please type or print.

Enter state code for state in which deposits were made **only** if different from state in address to the right ▶ (see page 2 of Separate instructions).

OMB No. 1545-0029

Name (as distinguished from trade name): Phoenix Sales & Service

Date quarter ended: Dec. 31, 2005

Trade name, if any

Employer identification number: 86-3214587

Address (number and street): 1214 Mill Road, Phoenix, AZ 85621, USA

City, State, and ZIP code

T / FF / FD / FP / I / T

If address is different from prior return, check here ▶ ☐ — IRS Use

A If you **do not have to file** returns in the future, check here ▶ ☐ and enter date final wages paid ▶

B If you are a seasonal employer, see **Seasonal employers** on page 1 of the instructions and check here ▶ ☐

1	Number of employees in the pay period that includes March 12th, ▶ 1		
2	Total wages and tips, plus other compensation	2	36,599.00
3	Total income tax withheld from wages, tips, and sick pay	3	3,056.47
4	Adjustment of withheld income tax for preceding quarters of **this calendar year**	4	
5	Adjusted total of income tax withheld (line 3 as adjusted by line 4)	5	3,056.47
6	Taxable social security wages — 6a $ 36,599.00 × 12.4% (.124) =	6b	4,538.28
	Taxable social security tips — 6c $ × 12.4% (.124) =	6d	
7	Taxable Medicare wages and tips — 7a $ 36,599.00 × 2.9% (.029) =	7b	1,061.37
8	Total social security and Medicare taxes (add lines 6b, 6d, and 7b). **Check here if wages are not subject to social security and/or Medicare tax** ▶ ☐	8	5,599.65
9	Adjustment of social security and Medicare taxes (see instructions for required explanation) Sick Pay $ ____ ± Fractions of Cents $ ____ ± Other $ ____ =	9	
10	Adjusted total of social security and Medicare taxes (line 8 as adjusted by line 9)	10	5,599.65
11	**Total taxes** (add lines 5 and 10)	11	8,656.12
12	Advance earned income credit (EIC) payments made to employees (see instructions)	12	
13	Net taxes (subtract line 12 from line 11). **If $2,500 or more, this must equal line 17, column (d) below (or line D of Schedule B (Form 941))**	13	8,656.12
14	Total deposits for quarter, including overpayment applied from a prior quarter	14	8,656.12
15	**Balance due** (subtract line 14 from line 13). See instructions	15	
16	**Overpayment.** If line 14 is more than line 13, enter excess here ▶ $ 0.00 and check if to be: ☐ Applied to next return **or** ☐ Refunded.		

- **All filers:** If line 13 is less than $2,500, **do not** complete line 17 **or** Schedule B (Form 941). ▶ ☐
- **Semiweekly schedule depositors:** Complete Schedule B (Form 941) and check here ▶ ☐
- **Monthly schedule depositors:** Complete line 17, columns (a) through (d), and check here ▶ ☒

17 Monthly Summary of Federal Tax Liability. (Complete **Schedule B (Form 941)** instead, if you were a semiweekly schedule depositor.)

(a) First month liability	(b) Second month liability	(c) Third month liability	(d) Total liability for quarter
3,079.11	2,049.77	3,527.24	8,656.12

Third Party Designee — Do you want to allow another person to discuss this return with the IRS (see separate instructions)? ☐ **Yes.** Complete the following. ☒ **No.**

Designee's name ▶ Phone no. ▶ ( ) Personal identification number (PIN) ▶

Sign Here — Under penalties of perjury, I declare that I have examined this return, including accompanying schedules and statements, and to the best of my knowledge and belief, it is true, correct, and complete.

Signature ▶ Print your Name and Title ▶ Date ▶

For Privacy Act and Paperwork Reduction Act Notice, see back of Payment Voucher. Cat. No. 17001Z Form **941** (Rev. 1-2003)

tax withholding on line 2 of Form 941. (For simplicity, this appendix uses *wages* to refer to both wages and salaries.) The income tax withheld is reported on lines 3 and 5. The combined amount of employee and employer FICA (Social Security) taxes for Phoenix Sales & Service is reported on line 6a (taxable Social Security wages, $36,599 × 12.4% = $4,538.28). The 12.4% is the sum of the Social Security tax withheld, computed as 6.2% tax withheld from the employee wages for the quarter plus the 6.2% tax levied on the employer. The combined amount of employee Medicare wages is reported on line 7. The 2.9% is the sum of 1.45% withheld from employee wages for the quarter plus 1.45% tax levied on the employer. Total FICA taxes are reported on lines 8 and 10 and are added to the total income taxes withheld of $3,056.47 to yield a total of $8,656.12. For this

COPYRIGHT JOHN S. PRITCHETT WWW.PRITCHETTCARTOONS.COM

Although the IRS may not be at the end of the rainbow, this cartoon reinforces the importance of taxation in all business activities and management decisions.

year, assume that income up to $87,000 is subject to Social Security tax. There is no income limit on amounts subject to Medicare tax. Congress sets annual limits on the amount owed for Social Security tax.

Federal depository banks are authorized to accept deposits of amounts payable to the federal government. Deposit requirements depend on the amount of tax owed. For example, when the sum of FICA taxes plus the employee income taxes is less than $500 for a quarter, the taxes can be paid when Form 941 is filed. Companies with large payrolls are often required to pay monthly or even semiweekly. If taxes owed are $100,000 or more at the end of any day, they must be paid by the end of the next banking day.

Reporting FUTA Taxes and SUTA Taxes An employer's federal unemployment taxes (FUTA) are reported on an annual basis by filing an *Annual Federal Unemployment Tax Return,* IRS **Form 940.** It must be mailed on or before January 31 following the end of each tax year. Ten more days are allowed if all required tax deposits are filed on a timely basis and the full amount of tax is paid on or before January 31. FUTA payments are made quarterly to a federal depository bank if the total amount due exceeds $100. If $100 or less is due, the taxes are remitted annually. Requirements for paying and reporting state unemployment taxes (SUTA) vary depending on the laws of each state. Most states require quarterly payments and reports.

Reporting Wages and Salaries Employers are required to give each employee an annual report of his or her wages subject to FICA and federal income taxes along with the amounts of these taxes withheld. This report is called a *Wage and Tax Statement,* or **Form W-2.** It must be given to employees before January 31 following the year covered by the report. Exhibit 11A.2 shows Form W-2 for one of the employees at Phoenix Sales & Service. Copies of the W-2 Form must be sent to the Social Security Administration, where the amount of the employee's wages subject to FICA taxes and FICA taxes withheld are posted to each employee's Social Security account. These posted amounts become the basis for determining an employee's retirement and survivors' benefits. The Social Security Administration also transmits to the IRS the amount of each employee's wages subject to federal income taxes and the amount of taxes withheld.

Payroll Records

Employers must keep payroll records in addition to reporting and paying taxes. These records usually include a payroll register and an individual earnings report for each employee.

C5 Identify and describe payroll records.

Payroll Register A **payroll register** usually shows the pay period dates, hours worked, gross pay, deductions, and net pay of each employee for each pay period. Exhibit 11A.3 shows a payroll register for Phoenix Sales & Service. It is organized into nine columns:

Col. 1 Employee identification (ID); Employee name; Social Security number (SS No.); Reference (check number); and Date (date check issued)
Col. 2 Pay Type (regular and overtime)
Col. 3 Pay Hours (number of hours worked as regular and overtime)
Col. 4 Gross Pay (amount of gross pay)[2]
Col. 5 FIT (federal income taxes withheld); FUTA (federal unemployment taxes)
Col. 6 SIT (state income taxes withheld); SUTA (state unemployment taxes)
Col. 7 FICA-SS_EE (social security taxes withheld, employee); FICA-SS_ER (social security taxes, employer)
Col. 8 FICA-Med_EE (medicare tax withheld, employee); FICA-Med_ER (medicare tax, employer)
Col. 9 Net pay (Gross pay less amounts withheld from employees)

[2] The Gross Pay column shows regular hours worked on the first line multiplied by the regular pay rate—this equals regular pay. Overtime hours multiplied by the overtime premium rate equals overtime premium pay reported on the second line. If employers are engaged in interstate commerce, federal law sets a minimum overtime rate of pay to employees. For this company, workers earn 150% of their regular rate for hours in excess of 40 per week.

a Control number
AR101
OMB No. 1545-0008

b Employer identification number
86-3214587

c Employer's name, address, and ZIP code
Phoenix Sales & Service
1214 Mill Road
Phoenix, AZ 85621
USA

d Employee's social security number
333-22-9999

e Employee's first name and initial Last name
Robert Austin

18 Roosevelt Blvd., Apt C
Tempe, AZ 86322

f Employee's address and ZIP code

1 Wages, tips, other compensation	4910.00
2 Federal income tax withheld	333.37
3 Social security wages	4910.00
4 Social security tax withheld	304.42
5 Medicare wages and tips	4910.00
6 Medicare tax withheld	71.20
7 Social security tips	
8 Allocated tips	
9 Advance EIC payment	
10 Dependent care benefits	
11 Nonqualified plans	
12a	
13 Statutory employee / Retirement plan / Third-party sick pay	
12b	
14 Other	
12c	
12d	

15 State	Employer's state ID number	16 State wages, tips, etc.	17 State income tax	18 Local wages, tips, etc.	19 Local income tax	20 Locality name
AZ	13-902319	4910.00	26.68			

Form **W-2** Wage and Tax Statement **2003** Department of the Treasury—Internal Revenue Service
Copy 1 For State, City, or Local Tax Department

Exhibit 11A.2

Form W-2

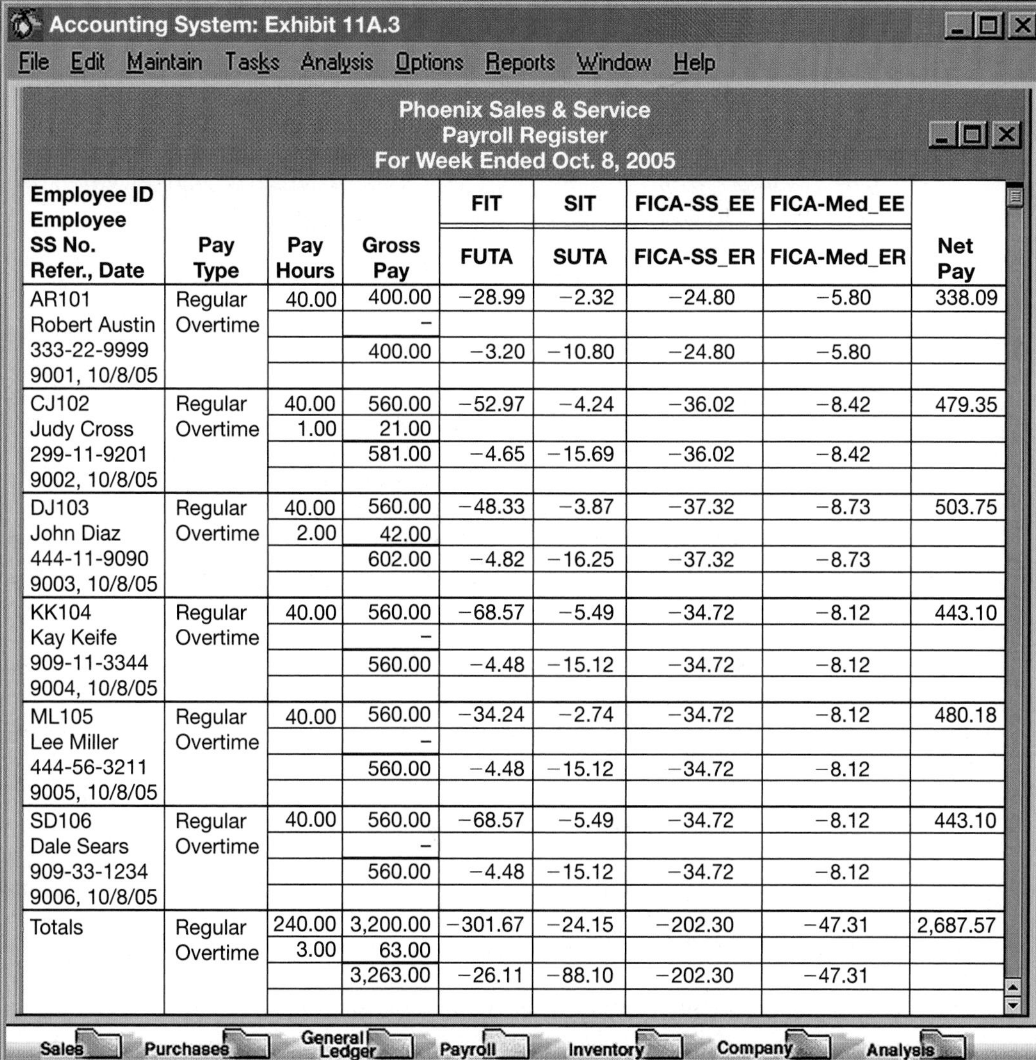

Accounting System: Exhibit 11A.3
File Edit Maintain Tasks Analysis Options Reports Window Help

Phoenix Sales & Service
Payroll Register
For Week Ended Oct. 8, 2005

Employee ID / Employee / SS No. / Refer., Date	Pay Type	Pay Hours	Gross Pay	FIT / FUTA	SIT / SUTA	FICA-SS_EE / FICA-SS_ER	FICA-Med_EE / FICA-Med_ER	Net Pay
AR101	Regular	40.00	400.00	−28.99	−2.32	−24.80	−5.80	338.09
Robert Austin	Overtime		–					
333-22-9999			400.00	−3.20	−10.80	−24.80	−5.80	
9001, 10/8/05								
CJ102	Regular	40.00	560.00	−52.97	−4.24	−36.02	−8.42	479.35
Judy Cross	Overtime	1.00	21.00					
299-11-9201			581.00	−4.65	−15.69	−36.02	−8.42	
9002, 10/8/05								
DJ103	Regular	40.00	560.00	−48.33	−3.87	−37.32	−8.73	503.75
John Diaz	Overtime	2.00	42.00					
444-11-9090			602.00	−4.82	−16.25	−37.32	−8.73	
9003, 10/8/05								
KK104	Regular	40.00	560.00	−68.57	−5.49	−34.72	−8.12	443.10
Kay Keife	Overtime		–					
909-11-3344			560.00	−4.48	−15.12	−34.72	−8.12	
9004, 10/8/05								
ML105	Regular	40.00	560.00	−34.24	−2.74	−34.72	−8.12	480.18
Lee Miller	Overtime		–					
444-56-3211			560.00	−4.48	−15.12	−34.72	−8.12	
9005, 10/8/05								
SD106	Regular	40.00	560.00	−68.57	−5.49	−34.72	−8.12	443.10
Dale Sears	Overtime		–					
909-33-1234			560.00	−4.48	−15.12	−34.72	−8.12	
9006, 10/8/05								
Totals	Regular	240.00	3,200.00	−301.67	−24.15	−202.30	−47.31	2,687.57
	Overtime	3.00	63.00					
			3,263.00	−26.11	−88.10	−202.30	−47.31	

Sales Purchases General Ledger Payroll Inventory Company Analysis

Exhibit 11A.3

Payroll Register

Net pay for each employee is computed as gross pay minus the items on the first line of columns 5–8. The employer's payroll tax for each employee is computed as the sum of items on the third line of columns 5–8. A payroll register includes all data necessary to record payroll. In some software programs the entries to record payroll are made in a special *payroll journal.*

Payroll Check Payment of payroll is usually done by check or electronic funds transfer. Exhibit 11A.4 shows a *payroll check* for a Phoenix employee. This check is accompanied with a detachable *statement of earnings* (at top) showing gross pay, deductions, and net pay.

Exhibit 11A.4

Check and Statement of Earnings

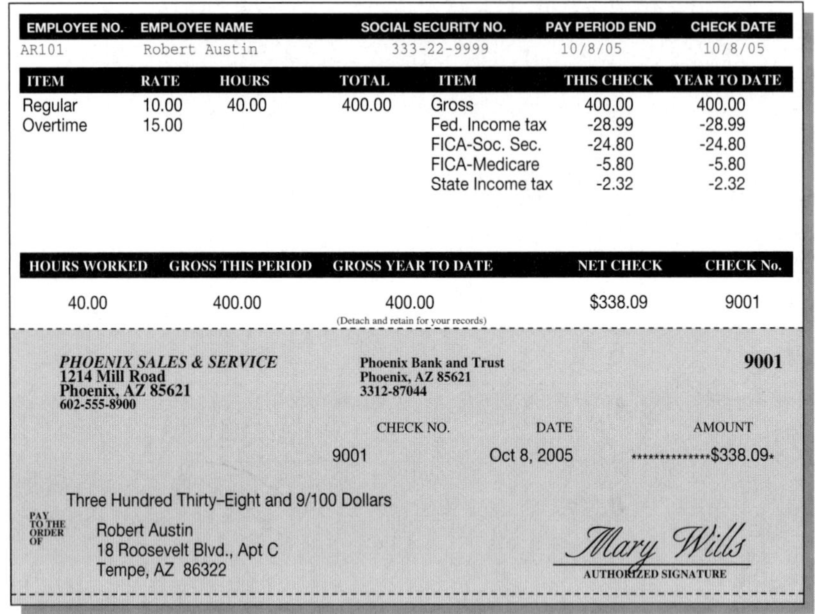

EMPLOYEE NO.	EMPLOYEE NAME	SOCIAL SECURITY NO.	PAY PERIOD END	CHECK DATE
AR101	Robert Austin	333-22-9999	10/8/05	10/8/05

ITEM	RATE	HOURS	TOTAL	ITEM	THIS CHECK	YEAR TO DATE
Regular	10.00	40.00	400.00	Gross	400.00	400.00
Overtime	15.00			Fed. Income tax	-28.99	-28.99
				FICA-Soc. Sec.	-24.80	-24.80
				FICA-Medicare	-5.80	-5.80
				State Income tax	-2.32	-2.32

HOURS WORKED	GROSS THIS PERIOD	GROSS YEAR TO DATE	NET CHECK	CHECK No.
40.00	400.00	400.00	$338.09	9001

(Detach and retain for your records)

PHOENIX SALES & SERVICE
1214 Mill Road
Phoenix, AZ 85621
602-555-8900

Phoenix Bank and Trust
Phoenix, AZ 85621
3312-87044

9001

CHECK NO.	DATE	AMOUNT
9001	Oct 8, 2005	**************$338.09*

Three Hundred Thirty-Eight and 9/100 Dollars

PAY TO THE ORDER OF Robert Austin
18 Roosevelt Blvd., Apt C
Tempe, AZ 86322

Mary Wills
AUTHORIZED SIGNATURE

Decision Insight

Virtual Reports Off-the-shelf and Web-based programs can produce payroll reports including the (1) payroll register, (2) payroll checks, and (3) employee earnings report.

Employee Earnings Report An **employee earnings report** is a cumulative record of an employee's hours worked, gross earnings, deductions, and net pay. Payroll information on this report is taken from the payroll register. The employee earnings report for R. Austin at Phoenix Sales & Service is shown in Exhibit 11A.5.

An employee earnings report accumulates information that can show when an employee's earnings reach the tax-exempt points for FICA, FUTA, and SUTA taxes. It also gives data an employer needs to prepare Form W-2.

Payroll Procedures

Employers must be able to compute federal income tax for payroll purposes. This section explains how we compute this tax and how to use a payroll bank account.

P5 Compute payroll taxes.

Computing Federal Income Taxes To compute the amount of taxes withheld from each employee's wages, we need to determine both the employee's wages earned and the employee's number of *withholding allowances.* Each employee records the number of withholding allowances claimed on a withholding allowance certificate, **Form W-4,** filed with the employer. When the number of withholding allowances increases, the amount of income taxes withheld decreases.

Employers often use a **wage bracket withholding table** similar to the one shown in Exhibit 11A.6 to compute the federal income taxes withheld from each employee's gross pay. The table in

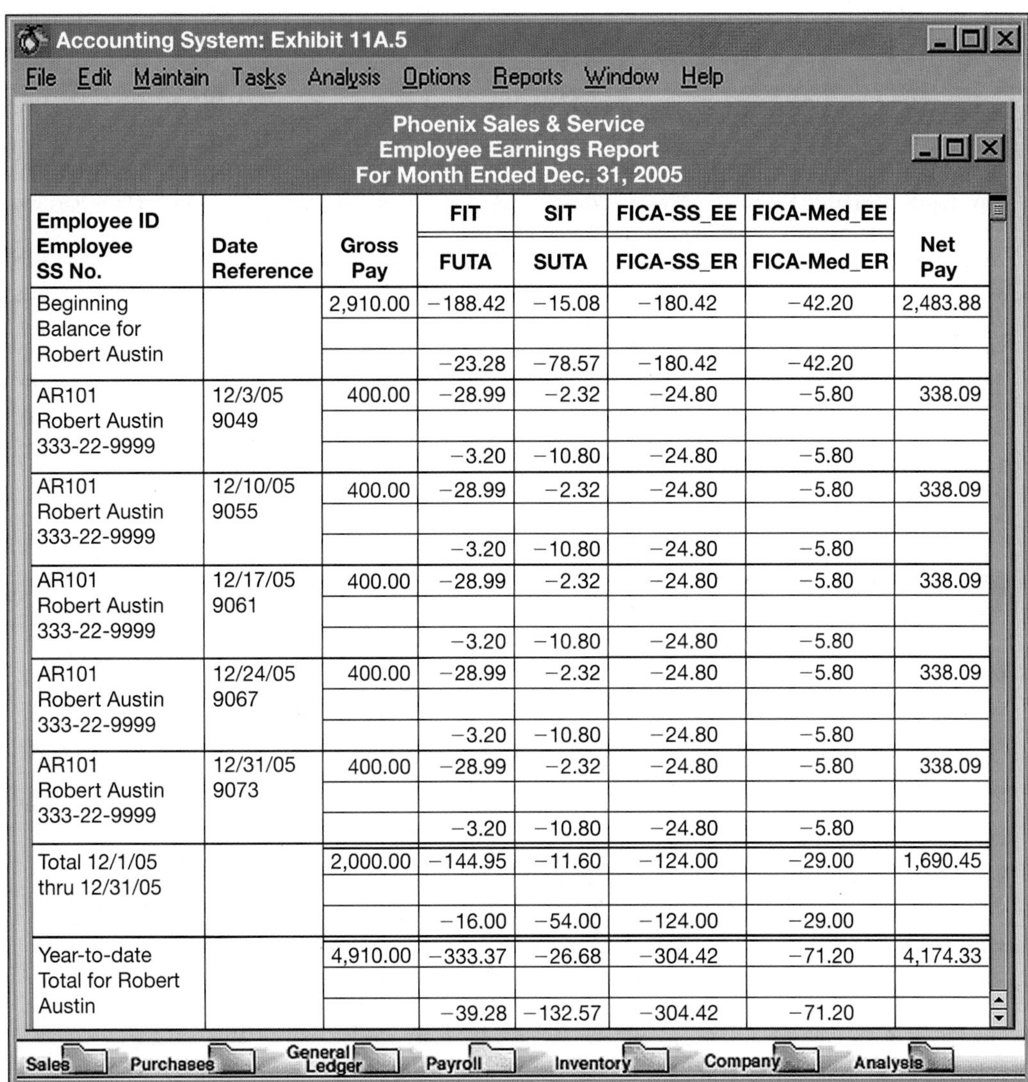

Accounting System: Exhibit 11A.5

File Edit Maintain Tasks Analysis Options Reports Window Help

Phoenix Sales & Service
Employee Earnings Report
For Month Ended Dec. 31, 2005

Employee ID Employee SS No.	Date Reference	Gross Pay	FIT / FUTA	SIT / SUTA	FICA-SS_EE / FICA-SS_ER	FICA-Med_EE / FICA-Med_ER	Net Pay
Beginning Balance for Robert Austin		2,910.00	−188.42	−15.08	−180.42	−42.20	2,483.88
			−23.28	−78.57	−180.42	−42.20	
AR101 Robert Austin 333-22-9999	12/3/05 9049	400.00	−28.99	−2.32	−24.80	−5.80	338.09
			−3.20	−10.80	−24.80	−5.80	
AR101 Robert Austin 333-22-9999	12/10/05 9055	400.00	−28.99	−2.32	−24.80	−5.80	338.09
			−3.20	−10.80	−24.80	−5.80	
AR101 Robert Austin 333-22-9999	12/17/05 9061	400.00	−28.99	−2.32	−24.80	−5.80	338.09
			−3.20	−10.80	−24.80	−5.80	
AR101 Robert Austin 333-22-9999	12/24/05 9067	400.00	−28.99	−2.32	−24.80	−5.80	338.09
			−3.20	−10.80	−24.80	−5.80	
AR101 Robert Austin 333-22-9999	12/31/05 9073	400.00	−28.99	−2.32	−24.80	−5.80	338.09
			−3.20	−10.80	−24.80	−5.80	
Total 12/1/05 thru 12/31/05		2,000.00	−144.95	−11.60	−124.00	−29.00	1,690.45
			−16.00	−54.00	−124.00	−29.00	
Year-to-date Total for Robert Austin		4,910.00	−333.37	−26.68	−304.42	−71.20	4,174.33
			−39.28	−132.57	−304.42	−71.20	

Sales Purchases General Ledger Payroll Inventory Company Analysis

Exhibit 11A.5
Employee Earnings Report

SINGLE Persons—WEEKLY Payroll Period
(For Wages Paid in 2003)

If the wages are –		And the number of withholding allowances claimed is —										
At least	But less than	0	1	2	3	4	5	6	7	8	9	10
		The amount of income tax to be withheld is —										
$600	$610	$81	$69	$60	$51	$42	$33	$25	$16	$8	$3	$0
610	620	83	70	61	53	44	35	26	17	9	4	0
620	630	86	72	63	54	45	36	28	19	10	5	0
630	640	89	73	64	55	47	38	29	20	12	6	0
640	650	91	76	65	57	48	39	31	22	13	7	1
650	660	94	78	67	59	60	41	32	23	15	8	2
660	670	97	81	69	60	61	42	34	25	16	9	3
670	680	99	84	70	62	63	44	35	26	18	10	4
680	690	102	85	72	63	64	45	37	28	19	11	5
690	700	103	89	73	65	65	47	38	29	21	12	6
700	710	108	92	70	66	67	48	40	31	22	13	7
710	720	110	94	79	69	69	60	41	32	24	15	8
720	730	113	97	81	69	60	61	43	34	25	16	9
730	740	116	100	84	71	62	63	44	35	27	18	10
740	750	118	103	87	72	63	64	45	37	28	19	11

Exhibit 11A.6
Wage Bracket Withholding Table

Exhibit 11A.6 is for a single employee paid weekly. Tables are also provided for married employees and for biweekly, semimonthly, and monthly pay periods (most payroll software includes these tables). When using a wage bracket withholding table to compute federal income tax withheld from an employee's gross wages, we need to locate an employee's wage bracket within the first two columns. We then find the amount withheld by looking in the withholding allowance column for that employee.

P6 Record payment of payroll.

Payroll Bank Account Companies with few employees often pay them with checks drawn on the company's regular bank account. Companies with many employees often use a special **payroll bank account** to pay employees. When this account is used, a company either (1) draws one check for total payroll on the regular bank account and deposits it in the payroll bank account or (2) executes an *electronic funds transfer* to the payroll bank account. Individual payroll checks are then drawn on this payroll bank account. Since only one check for the total payroll is drawn on the regular bank account each payday, use of a special payroll bank account helps with internal control. It also helps in reconciling the regular bank account. When companies use a payroll bank account, they usually include check numbers in the payroll register. The payroll register in Exhibit 11A.3 shows check numbers in column 1. For instance, Check No. 9001 is issued to Robert Austin. With this information, the payroll register serves as a supplementary record of wages earned by and paid to employees.

Quick Check

11. What two items determine the amount deducted from an employee's wages for federal income taxes?
12. What amount of income tax is withheld from the salary of an employee who is single with three withholding allowances and earnings of $675 in a week? (*Hint:* Use the wage bracket withholding table in Exhibit 11A.6.)
13. Which of the following steps are executed when a company draws one check for total payroll and deposits it in a special payroll bank account? (*a*) Write a check to the payroll bank account for the total payroll and record it with a debit to Accrued Payroll Payable and a credit to Cash. (*b*) Deposit a check (or transfer funds) for the total payroll in the payroll bank account. (*c*) Issue individual payroll checks drawn on the payroll bank account. (*d*) All of the above.

Answers—p. 449

APPENDIX 11B Income Taxes

This appendix explains current liabilities involving income taxes for corporations.

Income Tax Liabilities Corporations are subject to income taxes and must estimate their income tax liability when preparing financial statements. Since income tax expense is created by earning income, a liability is incurred when income is earned. This tax must be paid quarterly under federal regulations. To illustrate, consider a corporation that prepares monthly financial statements. Based on its income in January 2005, this corporation estimates that it owes income taxes of $12,100. The following adjusting entry records this estimate:

Assets	=	Liabilities	+	Equity
		+12,100		−12,100

Jan. 31	Income Taxes Expense	12,100	
	Income Taxes Payable		12,100
	To accrue January income taxes.		

The tax liability is recorded each month until the first quarterly payment is made. If the company's estimated taxes for this first quarter total $30,000, the entry to record its payment is

Apr. 10	Income Taxes Payable	30,000	
	Cash		30,000
	Paid estimated quarterly income taxes based on first quarter income.		

Assets	=	Liabilities	+	Equity
−30,000		−30,000		

This process of accruing and then paying estimated income taxes continues through the year. When annual financial statements are prepared at year-end, the corporation knows its actual total income and the actual amount of income taxes it must pay. This information allows it to properly record income taxes expense for the fourth quarter so that the total of the four quarters' expense amounts equals the actual taxes paid to the government.

Deferred Income Tax Liabilities An income tax liability for corporations can arise when the amount of income before taxes that the corporation reports on its income statement is not the same as the amount of income reported on its income tax return. This difference occurs because income tax laws and GAAP measure income differently. (Differences between tax laws and GAAP arise because Congress uses tax laws to generate receipts, stimulate the economy, and influence behavior, whereas GAAP are intended to provide financial information useful for decision making. Also, tax accounting often follows the cash basis, whereas GAAP follows the accrual basis.)

Some differences between tax laws and GAAP are temporary. *Temporary differences* arise when the tax return and the income statement report a revenue or expense in different years. As an example, companies are often able to deduct higher amounts of depreciation in the early years of an asset's life and smaller amounts in later years for tax reporting in comparison to GAAP. This means that in the early years, depreciation for tax reporting is often more than depreciation on the income statement. In later years, depreciation for tax reporting is often less than depreciation on the income statement. When temporary differences exist between taxable income on the tax return and the income before taxes on the income statement, corporations compute income taxes expense based on the income reported on the income statement. The result is that income taxes expense reported in the income statement is often different from the amount of income taxes payable to the government. This difference is the **deferred income tax liability.**

To illustrate, assume that in recording its usual quarterly income tax payments, a corporation computes $25,000 of income taxes expense. It also determines that only $21,000 is currently due and $4,000 is deferred to future years (a timing difference). The entry to record this end-of-period adjustment is

Dec. 31	Income Taxes Expense	25,000	
	Income Taxes Payable		21,000
	Deferred Income Tax Liability		4,000
	To record tax expense and deferred tax liability.		

Assets	=	Liabilities	+	Equity
		+21,000		−25,000
		+4,000		

The credit to Income Taxes Payable reflects the amount currently due to be paid. The credit to Deferred Income Tax Liability reflects tax payments deferred until future years when the temporary difference reverses.

Temporary differences also can cause a company to pay income taxes *before* they are reported on the income statement as expense. If so, the company reports a *Deferred Income Tax Asset* on its balance sheet.

Summary

C1 Describe current and long-term liabilities and their characteristics. Liabilities are probable future payments of assets or services that past transactions or events obligate an entity to make. Current liabilities are due within one year or the operating cycle, whichever is longer. All other liabilities are long term.

C2 Identify and describe known current liabilities. Known (determinable) current liabilities are set by agreements or laws and are measurable with little uncertainty. They include accounts payable, sales taxes payable, unearned revenues, notes payable, payroll liabilities, and the current portion of long-term debt.

C3 Explain how to account for contingent liabilities. If an uncertain future payment depends on a probable future event and the amount can be reasonably estimated, the payment is recorded as a liability. The uncertain future payment is reported as a contingent liability (in the notes) if (*a*) the future event is reasonably possible but not probable or (*b*) the event is probable but the payment amount cannot be reasonably estimated.

C4[A] Identify and describe payroll reporting. Employers report FICA taxes and federal income tax withholdings using Form 941. FUTA taxes are reported on Form 940. Earnings and deductions are reported to each employee and the federal government on Form W-2.

C5[A] Identify and describe payroll records. An employer's payroll records include a payroll register for each pay period, payroll checks and statements of earnings, and individual employee earnings reports.

A1 Compute the times interest earned ratio and use it to analyze liabilities. Times interest earned is computed by dividing a company's net income before interest expense and income taxes by the amount of interest expense. The times interest earned ratio reflects a company's ability to pay interest obligations.

P1 Prepare entries to account for short-term notes payable. Short-term notes payable are current liabilities; most bear interest. When a short-term note's face value equals the amount borrowed, it identifies a rate of interest to be paid at maturity.

P2 Compute and record *employee* payroll deductions and liabilities. Employee payroll deductions include FICA taxes, income taxes, and voluntary deductions such as for pensions and charities. They make up the difference between gross and net pay.

P3 Compute and record *employer* payroll expenses and liabilities. An employer's payroll expenses include employees' gross earnings, any employee benefits, and the payroll taxes levied on the employer. Payroll liabilities include employees' net pay amounts, withholdings from employee wages, any employer-promised benefits, and the employer's payroll taxes.

P4 Account for estimated liabilities, including warranties and bonuses. Liabilities for health and pension benefits, warranties, and bonuses are recorded with estimated amounts. These items are recognized as expenses when incurred and matched with revenues generated.

P5[A] Compute payroll taxes. Federal income tax deductions depend on the employee's earnings and the number of withholding allowances claimed. Wage bracket withholding tables are available for different pay periods and employee classes.

P6[A] Record payment of payroll. Employers with a large number of employees often use a separate payroll bank account. When this is done, the payment of employees is recorded with a transfer of cash from the regular bank account to the payroll bank account.

Guidance Answers to **Decision Maker** and **Decision Ethics**

Web Designer You need to be concerned about being an accomplice to unlawful payroll activities. Not paying federal and state taxes on wages earned is illegal and unethical. Such payments also will not provide the employee with Social Security and some Medicare credits. The best course of action is to request payment by check. If this fails to change the owner's payment practices, you must consider quitting this job.

Entrepreneur Risk is partly reflected by the times interest earned ratio. This ratio for the first franchise is 1.5 [($100,000 + $200,000)/$200,000], whereas the ratio for the second franchise is 3.5 [($100,000 + $40,000)/$40,000]. This analysis shows that the first franchise is more at risk of incurring a loss if its sales decline. The second question asks about variability of income. If income greatly varies, this increases the risk an owner will not earn sufficient income to cover interest. Since the first franchise has the greater variability, it is a riskier investment.

Guidance Answers to **Quick Checks**

1. A liability involves a probable future payment of assets or services that an entity is presently obligated to make as a result of past transactions or events.
2. No, an expected future payment is not a liability unless an existing obligation was created by a past event or transaction.
3. In most cases, a liability due in 15 months is classified as long term. It is classified as a current liability if the company's operating cycle is 15 months or longer.
4. A creditor prefers a note payable instead of a past-due account payable so as to (*a*) charge interest and/or (*b*) have evidence of the debt and its terms for potential litigation or disputes.
5. $1,000(.008) + $1,000(.04) + $3,000(.062) + $3,000(.0145) = $277.50
6. (*a*) FICA taxes are incurred by both employee and employer.
   (*b*) FUTA taxes are incurred by the employer.
   (*c*) SUTA taxes are incurred by the employer.
   (*d*) Withheld income taxes are incurred by the employee.

7. (*a*)
8. (*a*) Warranty expense was previously estimated and recorded.
9. (*b*)
10. A future payment is reported in the notes as a contingent liability if (*a*) the uncertain future event is probable but the amount of payment cannot be reasonably estimated or (*b*) the uncertain future event is not probable but has a reasonable possibility of occurring.
11. An employee's gross earnings and number of withholding allowances determine the deduction for federal income taxes.
12. $62
13. (*d*)

Key Terms

Key Terms are available at the book's Website for learning and testing in an online Flashcard Format.

Contingent liability (p. 436)
Current liabilities (p. 425)
Current portion of long-term debt (p. 433)
Deferred income tax liability (p. 447)
Employee benefits (p. 433)
Employee earnings report (p. 444)
Estimated liability (p. 433)
Federal depository bank (p. 442)
Federal Insurance Contributions Act (FICA) Taxes (p. 430)
Federal Unemployment Taxes (FUTA) (p. 432)
Form 940 (p. 442)
Form 941 (p. 440)
Form W-2 (p. 442)
Form W-4 (p. 444)
Gross pay (p. 429)
Known liabilities (p. 426)
Long-term liabilities (p. 425)
Merit rating (p. 432)
Net pay (p. 430)
Payroll bank account (p. 446)
Payroll deductions (p. 430)
Payroll register (p. 442)
Short-term note payable (p. 427)
State Unemployment Taxes (SUTA) (p. 432)
Times interest earned (p. 437)
Wage bracket withholding table (p. 444)
Warranty (p. 434)

Personal Interactive Quiz

Personal Interactive Quizzes A and B are available at the book's Website to reinforce and assess your learning.

Superscript letter A (B) denotes assignments based on Appendix 11A (11B).

Discussion Questions

1. What are the three important questions concerning the uncertainty of liabilities?
2. What is the difference between a current and a long-term liability?
3. What is an estimated liability?
4. If $894.40 is the total of a sale that includes its sales tax of 4%, what is the selling price of the item only?
5. What is the combined amount (in percent) of the employee and employer Social Security tax rate?
6. What is the current Medicare tax rate? This rate is applied to what maximum level of salary and wages?
7. What determines the amount deducted from an employee's wages for federal income taxes?
8. Which payroll taxes are the employee's responsibility and which are the employer's responsibility?
9. What is an employer's unemployment merit rating? How are these ratings assigned to employers?
10. Why are warranty liabilities usually recognized on the balance sheet as liabilities even when they are uncertain?
11. Suppose that a company has a facility located where disastrous weather conditions often occur. Should it report a probable loss from a future disaster as a liability on its balance sheet? Explain.
12.[A] What is a wage bracket withholding table?

13.[A] What amount of income tax is withheld from the salary of an employee who is single with two withholding allowances and earning $725 per week? What if the employee earned $625 and has no withholding allowances? (Use Exhibit 11A.6.)

14. Refer to **Krispy Kreme**'s financial statements in Appendix A. As an alternative to short-term notes, Krispy Kreme meets short-term borrowing needs through revolving lines of credit. Briefly explain how a line of credit differs from a short-term note payable.

15. Refer to **Tastykake**'s balance sheet in Appendix A. What accounts related to income taxes are on its balance sheet? Explain the meaning of each income tax account you identify.

16. Refer to **Harley-Davidson**'s balance sheet in Appendix A. Which current liability account reports its payroll-related liabilities (if any) as of December 31, 2002?

Red numbers denote Discussion Questions that involve decision-making.

***Homework Manager** repeats all numerical Quick Studies on the book's Website with new numbers.*

QUICK STUDY

QS 11-1
Classifying liabilities C1

Which of the following items are normally classified as a current liability for a company that has a 15-month operating cycle?

1. Salaries payable.
2. Note payable due in 18 months.
3. FICA taxes payable.
4. Note payable maturing in 2 years.
5. Note payable due in 11 months.
6. Portion of long-term note due in 15 months.

QS 11-2
Accounting for sales taxes
C2

Gomez Computing sells merchandise for $5,000 cash on September 30 (cost of merchandise is $2,900). The sales tax law requires Gomez to collect 4% sales tax on every dollar of merchandise sold. Record the entry for the $5,000 sale and its applicable sales tax. Also record the entry that shows the remittance of the 4% tax on this sale to the state government on October 15.

QS 11-3
Unearned revenue C2

Ticketmaster receives $4,000,000 in advance ticket sales for a four-date tour of the Rolling Stones. Record the advance ticket sales on October 31. Record the revenue earned for the first concert date of November 5, assuming it represents one-fourth of the advance ticket sales.

QS 11-4
Interest-bearing note transactions
P1

On November 7, 2005, Ortez Company borrows $150,000 cash by signing a 90-day, 8% note payable with a face value of $150,000. (1) Compute the accrued interest payable on December 31, 2005, (2) prepare the journal entry to record the accrued interest expense at December 31, 2005, and (3) prepare the journal entry to record payment of the note at maturity.

QS 11-5
Record employer payroll taxes
P2 P3

Meredith Co. has five employees, each of whom earns $2,600 per month and has been employed since January 1. FICA Social Security taxes are 6.2% of gross pay and FICA Medicare taxes are 1.45% of gross pay. FUTA taxes are 0.8% and SUTA taxes are 2.8% of the first $7,000 paid to each employee. Prepare the March 31 journal entry to record the March payroll taxes expense.

QS 11-6
Recording warranty repairs
P4

On September 11, 2004, Home Store sells a mower for $400 with a one-year warranty that covers parts. Warranty expense is estimated at 5% of sales. On July 24, 2005, the mower is brought in for repairs covered under the warranty requiring $35 in materials taken from the Repair Parts Inventory. Prepare the July 24, 2005, entry to record the warranty repairs.

QS 11-7
Accounting for bonuses P4

Paris Company offers an annual bonus to employees if the company meets certain net income goals. Prepare the journal entry to record a $10,000 bonus owed to its workers (to be shared equally) at calendar year-end.

QS 11-8
Accounting for contingent liabilities
C3

The following legal claims exist for Kalamazoo Co. Identify the accounting treatment for each claim as either (*a*) a liability that is recorded or (*b*) an item described in notes to its financial statements.

1. Kalamazoo (defendant) estimates that a pending lawsuit could result in damages of $1,000,000; it is reasonably possible that the plaintiff will win the case.

2. Kalamazoo faces a probable loss on a pending lawsuit; the amount is not reasonably estimable.

3. Kalamazoo estimates damages in a case at $2,500,000 with a high probability of losing the case.

QS 11-9
Times interest earned
A1

Compute the times interest earned for Dechow Company, which reports income before interest expense and income taxes of $1,575,000 and interest expense of $137,000. Interpret its times interest earned—assume that its competitors average a times interest earned of 4.0.

QS 11-10[B]
Record deferred income tax liability
P4

Cather Corporation has made and recorded its quarterly income tax payments. After a final review of taxes for the year, the company identifies an additional $30,000 of income tax expense that should be recorded. A portion of this additional expense, $8,000, is deferred for payment in future years. Record Cather's year-end adjusting entry for income tax expense.

***Homework Manager** repeats all numerical Exercises on the book's Website with new numbers.*

EXERCISES

Exercise 11-1
Classifying liabilities
C1

The following items appear on the balance sheet of a company with a two-month operating cycle. Identify the proper classification of each item as follows: *C* if it is a current liability, *L* if it is a long-term liability, or *N* if it is not a liability.

_____	**1.** Sales taxes payable.	_____	**6.** Notes payable (due in 6 to 12 months).
_____	**2.** FUTA taxes payable.	_____	**7.** Notes payable (due in 120 days).
_____	**3.** Accounts receivable.	_____	**8.** Current portion of long-term debt.
_____	**4.** Accrued payroll payable.	_____	**9.** Notes payable (mature in five years).
_____	**5.** Wages payable.	_____	**10.** Notes payable (due in 13 to 24 months).

Exercise 11-2
Adjusting entries for liabilities
C2 C3 P4

Prepare any necessary adjusting entries at December 31, 2005, for Yacht Company's year-end financial statements for each of the following separate transactions and events:

1. During December, Yacht Company sold 3,000 units of a product that carries a 60-day warranty. December sales for this product total $120,000. The company expects 8% of the units to need warranty repairs, and it estimates the average repair cost per unit will be $15.

2. A disgruntled employee is suing Yacht Company. Legal advisers believe that the company will probably need to pay damages, but the amount cannot be reasonably estimated.

3. Employees earn vacation pay at a rate of one day per month. During December, 20 employees qualify for one vacation day each. Their average daily wage is $120 per employee.

4. Yacht Company guarantees the $5,000 debt of a supplier. The supplier will probably not default on the debt.

5. Yacht Company records an adjusting entry for $2,000,000 of previously unrecorded cash sales (costing $1,000,000) and its sales taxes at a rate of 5%.

6. The company earned $40,000 of $100,000 previously received in advance for services.

Exercise 11-3
Computing and recording bonuses C2

Check (1) $29,126

For the year ended December 31, 2005, Winter Company has implemented an employee bonus program equal to 3% of Winter's net income, which employees will share equally. Winter's net income (prebonus) is expected to be $1,000,000, and bonus expense is deducted in computing net income.

1. Compute the amount of the bonus payable to the employees at year-end (use the method described in the chapter and round to the nearest dollar).

2. Prepare the journal entry at December 31, 2005, to record the bonus due the employees.

3. Prepare the journal entry at January 19, 2006, to record payment of the bonus to employees.

Exercise 11-4
Accounting for note payable
P1

Check (2b) Interest expense, $1,880

Perfect Systems borrows $94,000 cash on May 15, 2005, by signing a 60-day, 12% note.

1. On what date does this note mature?
2. Suppose the face value of the note equals $94,000, the principal of the loan. Prepare the journal entries to record (*a*) issuance of the note and (*b*) payment of the note at maturity.

Exercise 11-5
Interest-bearing notes payable with year-end adjustments
P1

Check (2) $2,250
(3) $1,125

Kwon Co. borrows $150,000 cash on November 1, 2005, by signing a 90-day, 9% note with a face value of $150,000.

1. On what date does this note mature?
2. How much interest expense results from this note in 2005? (Assume a 360-day year.)
3. How much interest expense results from this note in 2006? (Assume a 360-day year.)
4. Prepare journal entries to record (*a*) issuance of the note, (*b*) accrual of interest at the end of 2005, and (*c*) payment of the note at maturity.

Exercise 11-6
Computing payroll taxes
P2 P3

MRI Co. has one employee, and the company is subject to the following taxes:

Tax	Rate	Applied To
FICA—Social Security	6.20%	First $87,000
FICA—Medicare	1.45	All gross pay
FUTA	0.80	First $7,000
SUTA	2.90	First $7,000

Compute MRI's amounts for each of these four taxes as applied to the employee's gross earnings for September under each of three separate situations (*a*), (*b*), and (*c*):

Check (*a*) FUTA, $4.80; SUTA, $17.40

	Gross Pay through August	Gross Pay for September
a.	$ 6,400	$ 800
b.	18,200	2,100
c.	82,000	8,000

Exercise 11-7
Payroll-related journal entries
P2 P3

Using the data in situation *a* of Exercise 11-6, prepare the employer's September 30 journal entries to record (1) salary expense and its related payroll liabilities for this employee and (2) the employer's payroll taxes expense and its related liabilities. The employee's federal income taxes withheld by the employer are $135 for this pay period.

Exercise 11-8
Warranty expense and liability computations and entries
P4

Chang Co. sold a copier costing $3,800 with a two-year parts warranty to a customer on August 16, 2005, for $5,500 cash. Chang uses the perpetual inventory system. On November 22, 2006, the copier requires on-site repairs that are completed the same day. The repairs cost $199 for materials taken from the Repair Parts Inventory. These are the only repairs required in 2006 for this copier. Based on experience, Chang expects to incur warranty costs equal to 4% of dollar sales. It records warranty expense with an adjusting entry at the end of each year.

Check (1) $220

1. How much warranty expense does the company report in 2005 for this copier?
2. How much is the estimated warranty liability for this copier as of December 31, 2005?
3. How much warranty expense does the company report in 2006 for this copier?

(4) $21

4. How much is the estimated warranty liability for this copier as of December 31, 2006?
5. Prepare journal entries to record (*a*) the copier's sale; (*b*) the adjustment on December 31, 2005, to recognize the warranty expense; and (*c*) the repairs that occur in November 2006.

Exercise 11-9
Computing and interpreting times interest earned
A1

Use the following information from separate companies *a* through *f* to compute times interest earned. Which company indicates the strongest ability to pay interest expense as it comes due?

	Net Income (Loss)	Interest Expense	Income Taxes
a.	$140,000	$48,000	$ 35,000
b.	140,000	15,000	50,000
c.	140,000	8,000	70,000
d.	265,000	12,000	130,000
e.	79,000	12,000	30,000
f.	(4,000)	12,000	0

Check (b) 13.67

Exercise 11-10[A]
Net pay and tax computations
P5

The payroll records of Clix Software show the following information about Trish Farqua, an employee, for the weekly pay period ending September 30, 2005. Farqua is single and claims one allowance. Compute her Social Security tax (6.2%), Medicare tax (1.45%), federal income tax withholding, state income tax (0.5%), and net pay for the current pay period. The state income tax is 0.5 percent on the first $9,000 earned. (Use the withholding table in Exhibit 11A.6.)

Total (gross) earnings for current pay period	$ 735
Cumulative earnings of previous pay periods	9,700

Check Net pay, 578.77

Exercise 11-11[A]
Gross and net pay computation
P5 P6

LaShonda Blake, an unmarried employee, works 48 hours in the week ended January 12. Her pay rate is $12 per hour, and her wages are subject to no deductions other than FICA—Social Security, FICA— Medicare, and federal income taxes. She claims two withholding allowances. Compute her regular pay, overtime pay (overtime premium is 50% of the regular rate for hours in excess of 40 per week), and gross pay. Then compute her FICA tax deduction (use 6.2% for the Social Security portion and 1.45% for the Medicare portion), income tax deduction (use the wage bracket withholding table of Exhibit 11A.6), total deductions, and net pay.

Check Net pay, $513.26

Exercise 11-12[B]
Accounting for income taxes
P4

Ming Corporation prepares financial statements for each month-end. As part of its accounting process, estimated income taxes are accrued each month for 30% of the current month's net income. The income taxes are paid in the first month of each quarter for the amount accrued for the prior quarter. The following information is available for the fourth quarter of year 2005. When tax computations are completed on January 20, 2006, Ming determines that the quarter's Income Taxes Payable account balance should be $29,100 on December 31, 2005 (its unadjusted balance is $23,640).

October 2005 net income	$27,900
November 2005 net income	18,200
December 2005 net income	32,700

1. Determine the amount of the accounting adjustment (dated as of December 31, 2005) to produce the proper ending balance in the Income Taxes Payable account.

Check (1) $5,460

2. Prepare journal entries to record (*a*) the December 31, 2005, adjustment to the Income Taxes Payable account and (*b*) the January 20, 2006, payment of the fourth-quarter taxes.

PROBLEM SET A

Problem 11-1A
Short-term notes payable transactions and entries
P1

Tytus Co. entered into the following transactions involving short-term liabilities in 2004 and 2005.

2004

Apr. 20 Purchased $38,500 of merchandise on credit from Frier, terms are 1/10, n/30. Tytus uses the perpetual inventory system.

May 19 Replaced the April 20 account payable to Frier with a 90-day, $30,000 note bearing 9% annual interest along with paying $8,500 in cash.

mhhe.com/larson

July 8 Borrowed $60,000 cash from Community Bank by signing a 120-day, 10% interest-bearing note with a face value of $60,000.
? Paid the amount due on the note to Frier at the maturity date.
? Paid the amount due on the note to Community Bank at the maturity date.
Nov. 28 Borrowed $21,000 cash from UMB Bank by signing a 60-day, 8% interest-bearing note with a face value of $21,000.
Dec. 31 Recorded an adjusting entry for accrued interest on the note to UMB Bank.

2005

? Paid the amount due on the note to UMB Bank at the maturity date.

Required

1. Determine the maturity date for each of the three notes described.
2. Determine the interest due at maturity for each of the three notes. (Assume a 360-day year.)
3. Determine the interest expense to be recorded in the adjusting entry at the end of 2004.
4. Determine the interest expense to be recorded in 2005.
5. Prepare journal entries for all the preceding transactions and events for years 2004–2005.

Check (2) Frier, $675
(3) $154
(4) $126

Problem 11-2A
Warranty expense and liability estimation
P4

On October 29, 2004, Lue Co. began operations by purchasing razors for resale. Lue uses the perpetual inventory method. The razors have a 90-day warranty that requires the company to replace any nonworking razor. When a razor is returned, the company discards it and mails a new one from Merchandise Inventory to the customer. The company's cost per new razor is $18 and its retail selling price is $80 in both 2004 and 2005. The manufacturer has advised the company to expect warranty costs to equal 7% of dollar sales. The following transactions and events occurred:

2004

Nov. 11 Sold 75 razors for $6,000 cash.
30 Recognized warranty expense related to November sales with an adjusting entry.
Dec. 9 Replaced 15 razors that were returned under the warranty.
16 Sold 210 razors for $16,800 cash.
29 Replaced 30 razors that were returned under the warranty.
31 Recognized warranty expense related to December sales with an adjusting entry.

2005

Jan. 5 Sold 130 razors for $10,400 cash.
17 Replaced 50 razors that were returned under the warranty.
31 Recognized warranty expense related to January sales with an adjusting entry.

Required

1. Prepare journal entries to record these transactions and adjustments for 2004 and 2005.
2. How much warranty expense is reported for November 2004 and for December 2004?
3. How much warranty expense is reported for January 2005?
4. What is the balance of the Estimated Warranty Liability account as of December 31, 2004?
5. What is the balance of the Estimated Warranty Liability account as of January 31, 2005?

Check (3) $728
(4) $786 Cr.
(5) $614 Cr.

Problem 11-3A
Computing and analyzing times interest earned

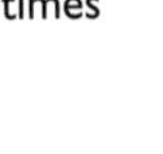

Shown here are condensed income statements for two different companies (both are organized as LLCs and pay no income taxes):

Ace Co.	
Sales	$500,000
Variable expenses (80%)	400,000
Income before interest	100,000
Interest expense (fixed)	30,000
Net income	$ 70,000

Deuce Co.	
Sales	$500,000
Variable expenses (60%)	300,000
Income before interest	200,000
Interest expense (fixed)	130,000
Net income	$ 70,000

Required

1. Compute times interest earned for Ace Co.
2. Compute times interest earned for Deuce Co.
3. What happens to each company's net income if sales increase by 30%?
4. What happens to each company's net income if sales increase by 50%?
5. What happens to each company's net income if sales increase by 80%?
6. What happens to each company's net income if sales decrease by 10%?
7. What happens to each company's net income if sales decrease by 20%?
8. What happens to each company's net income if sales decrease by 40%?

Check (3) Ace net income, $100,000 (43% increase)

(6) Deuce net income, $50,000 (29% decrease)

Analysis Component

9. Comment on the results from parts 3 through 8 in relation to the fixed-cost strategies of the two companies and the ratio values you computed in parts 1 and 2.

Problem 11-4A
Payroll expenses, withholdings, and taxes

P2 P3

mhhe.com/larson

Legal Stars pays its employees each week. Its employees' gross pay is subject to these taxes:

Tax	Rate	Applied To
FICA—Social Security	6.20%	First $87,000
FICA—Medicare	1.45	All gross pay
FUTA	0.80	First $7,000
SUTA	2.15	First $7,000

The company is preparing its payroll calculations for the week ended August 25. Payroll records show the following information for the company's four employees:

	A	B	C	D
1			Current Week	
2		Gross Pay		
3	Name	through 8/18	Gross Pay	Income Tax Withholding
4	Dale	$86,200	$2,000	$252
5	Ted	29,700	900	99
6	Kate	6,750	450	54
7	Chas	1,050	400	36
8				

In addition to gross pay, the company must pay one-half of the $32 per employee weekly health insurance; each employee pays the remaining one-half. The company also contributes an extra 8% of each employee's gross pay (at no cost to employees) to a pension fund.

Required

Compute the following for the week ended August 25 (round amounts to the nearest cent):

1. Each employee's FICA withholdings for Social Security.
2. Each employee's FICA withholdings for Medicare.
3. Employer's FICA taxes for Social Security.
4. Employer's FICA taxes for Medicare.
5. Employer's FUTA taxes.
6. Employer's SUTA taxes.
7. Each employee's net (take-home) pay.
8. Employer's total payroll-related expense for each employee.

Check (3) $158.10
(4) $54.38
(5) $5.20

(7) Total net pay, $3,032.52

Problem 11-5A
Entries for payroll transactions
P2 P3

On January 8, the end of the first weekly pay period of the year, Royal Company's payroll register showed that its employees earned $11,380 of office salaries and $32,920 of sales salaries. Withholdings from the employees' salaries include FICA Social Security taxes at the rate of 6.2%, FICA Medicare taxes at the rate of 1.45%, $6,340 of federal income taxes, $670 of medical insurance deductions, and $420 of union dues. No employee earned more than $7,000 in this first period.

Required

Check (1) Cr. Accrued Payroll Payable, $33,481.05

(2) Dr. Payroll Taxes Expense, $5,515.35

1. Calculate FICA Social Security taxes payable and FICA Medicare taxes payable. Prepare the journal entry to record Royal Company's January 8 (employee) payroll expenses and liabilities.
2. Prepare the journal entry to record Royal's (employer) payroll taxes resulting from the January 8 payroll. Royal's merit rating reduces its state unemployment tax rate to 4.0% of the first $7,000 paid each employee. The federal unemployment tax rate is 0.8%.

Problem 11-6A[A]
Entries for payroll transactions
P2 P3 P5 P6

Polo Company has 10 employees, each of whom earns $2,600 per month and is paid on the last day of each month. All 10 have been employed continuously at this amount since January 1. Polo uses a payroll bank account and special payroll checks to pay its employees. On March 1, the following accounts and balances exist in its general ledger:

a. FICA—Social Security Taxes Payable, $3,224; FICA—Medicare Taxes Payable, $754. (The balances of these accounts represent total liabilities for *both* the employer's and employees' FICA taxes for the February payroll only.)

b. Employees' Federal Income Taxes Payable, $3,900 (liability for February only).

c. Federal Unemployment Taxes Payable, $416 (liability for January and February together).

d. State Unemployment Taxes Payable, $2,080 (liability for January and February together).

During March and April, the company had the following payroll transactions:

Mar. 15 Issued check payable to Fleet Bank, a federal depository bank authorized to accept employers' payments of FICA taxes and employee income tax withholdings. The $7,878 check is in payment of the February FICA and employee income taxes.

Check March 31: Cr. Accrued Payroll Payable, $20,111

31 Recorded the March payroll and transferred funds from the regular bank account to the payroll bank account. Issued checks payable to each employee in payment of the March payroll. The payroll register shows the following summary totals for the March pay period:

Salaries and Wages				Federal	
Office Salaries	Shop Wages	Gross Pay	FICA Taxes*	Income Taxes	Net Pay
$10,400	$15,600	$26,000	$1,612 $ 377	$3,900	$20,111

* FICA taxes are Social Security and Medicare, respectively.

March 31: Dr. Payroll Taxes Expenses, $2,853

31 Recorded the employer's payroll taxes resulting from the March payroll. The company has a merit rating that reduces its state unemployment tax rate to 4.0% of the first $7,000 paid each employee. The federal rate is 0.8%.

April 15: Cr. Cash, $7,878 (Fleet)

Apr. 15 Issued check to Fleet Bank in payment of the March FICA and employee income taxes.

15 Issued check to the State Tax Commission for the January, February, and March state unemployment taxes. Mailed the check and the first quarter tax return to the Commission.

30 Issued check payable to Fleet Bank in payment of the employer's FUTA taxes for the first quarter of the year.

30 Mailed Form 941 to the IRS, reporting the FICA taxes and the employees' federal income tax withholdings for the first quarter.

Required

Prepare journal entries to record the transactions and events for both March and April.

PROBLEM SET B

Problem 11-1B
Short-term notes payable transactions and entries

P1

Bargen Co. entered into the following transactions involving short-term liabilities in 2004 and 2005.

2004

Apr. 22	Purchased $4,000 of merchandise on credit from Quinn Products, terms are 1/10, n/30. Bargen uses the perpetual inventory system.
May 23	Replaced the April 22 account payable to Quinn Products with a 60-day, $3,600 note bearing 15% annual interest along with paying $400 in cash.
July 15	Borrowed $9,000 cash from Blackhawk Bank by signing a 120-day, 10% interest-bearing note with a face value of $9,000.
?	Paid the amount due on the note to Quinn Products at maturity.
?	Paid the amount due on the note to Blackhawk Bank at maturity.
Dec. 6	Borrowed $16,000 cash from City Bank by signing a 45-day, 9% interest-bearing note with a face value of $16,000.
31	Recorded an adjusting entry for accrued interest on the note to City Bank.

2005

?	Paid the amount due on the note to City Bank at maturity.

Required

1. Determine the maturity date for each of the three notes described.

2. Determine the interest due at maturity for each of the three notes. (Assume a 360-day year.)

3. Determine the interest expense to be recorded in the adjusting entry at the end of 2004.

4. Determine the interest expense to be recorded in 2005.

5. Prepare journal entries for all the preceding transactions and events for years 2004–2005.

Check (2) Quinn, $90
(3) $100
(4) $80

Problem 11-2B
Warranty expense and liability estimation

P4

On November 10, 2004, Byung Co. began operations by purchasing coffee grinders for resale. Byung uses the perpetual inventory method. The grinders have a 60-day warranty that requires the company to replace any nonworking grinder. When a grinder is returned, the company discards it and mails a new one from Merchandise Inventory to the customer. The company's cost per new grinder is $14 and its retail selling price is $35 in both 2004 and 2005. The manufacturer has advised the company to expect warranty costs to equal 10% of dollar sales. The following transactions and events occurred.

2004

Nov. 16	Sold 50 grinders for $1,750 cash.
30	Recognized warranty expense related to November sales with an adjusting entry.
Dec. 12	Replaced six grinders that were returned under the warranty.
18	Sold 150 grinders for $5,250 cash.
28	Replaced 17 grinders that were returned under the warranty.
31	Recognized warranty expense related to December sales with an adjusting entry.

2005

Jan. 7	Sold 60 grinders for $2,100 cash.
21	Replaced 38 grinders that were returned under the warranty.
31	Recognized warranty expense related to January sales with an adjusting entry.

Required

1. Prepare journal entries to record these transactions and adjustments for 2004 and 2005.

2. How much warranty expense is reported for November 2004 and for December 2004?

3. How much warranty expense is reported for January 2005?

4. What is the balance of the Estimated Warranty Liability account as of December 31, 2004?

5. What is the balance of the Estimated Warranty Liability account as of January 31, 2005?

Check (3) $210
(4) $378 Cr.
(5) $56 Cr.

Problem 11-3B
Computing and analyzing times interest earned

A1 

Shown here are condensed income statements for two different companies (both are organized as LLCs and pay no income taxes):

Virgo Co.	
Sales	$120,000
Variable expenses (50%)	60,000
Income before interest	$ 60,000
Interest expense (fixed)	45,000
Net income	$ 15,000

Zodiac Co.	
Sales	$120,000
Variable expenses (75%)	90,000
Income before interest	$ 30,000
Interest expense (fixed)	15,000
Net income	$ 15,000

Required

1. Compute times interest earned for Virgo.
2. Compute times interest earned for Zodiac.
3. What happens to each company's net income if sales increase by 10%?
4. What happens to each company's net income if sales increase by 40%?
5. What happens to each company's net income if sales increase by 90%?
6. What happens to each company's net income if sales decrease by 20%?
7. What happens to each company's net income if sales decrease by 50%?
8. What happens to each company's net income if sales decrease by 80%?

Check (4) Virgo net income, $39,000 (160% increase)

(6) Zodiac net income, $9,000 (40% decrease)

Analysis Component

9. Comment on the results from parts 3 through 8 in relation to the fixed cost strategies of the two companies and the ratio values you computed in parts 1 and 2.

Problem 11-4B
Payroll expenses, withholdings, and taxes

P2 P3

Sea Biz Company pays its employees each week. Employees' gross pay is subject to these taxes:

Tax	Rate	Applied To
FICA—Social Security	6.20%	First $87,000
FICA—Medicare	1.45	All gross pay
FUTA	0.80	First $7,000
SUTA	1.75	First $7,000

The company is preparing its payroll calculations for the week ended September 30. Payroll records show the following information for the company's four employees:

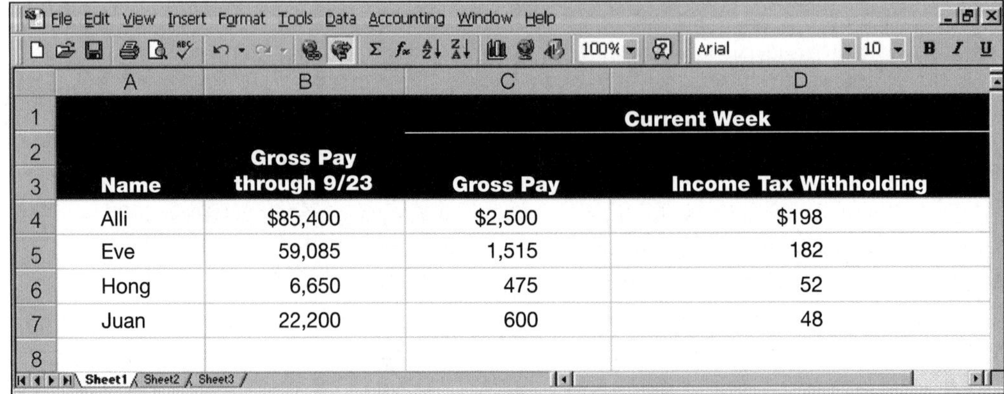

Name	Gross Pay through 9/23	Current Week Gross Pay	Current Week Income Tax Withholding
Alli	$85,400	$2,500	$198
Eve	59,085	1,515	182
Hong	6,650	475	52
Juan	22,200	600	48

In addition to gross pay, the company must pay one-half of the $44 per employee weekly health insurance; each employee pays the remaining one-half. The company also contributes an extra 5% of each employee's gross pay (at no cost to employees) to a pension fund.

Required

Compute the following for the week ended September 30 (round amounts to the nearest cent):

1. Each employee's FICA withholdings for Social Security.
2. Each employee's FICA withholdings for Medicare.
3. Employer's FICA taxes for Social Security.
4. Employer's FICA taxes for Medicare.
5. Employer's FUTA taxes.
6. Employer's SUTA taxes.
7. Each employee's net (take-home) pay.
8. Employer's total payroll-related expense for each employee.

Check (3) $259.78
(4) $73.81
(5) $2.80
(7) Total net pay, $4,188.41

Problem 11-5B
Entries for payroll transactions
P2 P3

Palmer Company's first weekly pay period of the year ends on January 8. On that date, the column totals in Palmer's payroll register indicate its sales employees earned $69,490, its office employees earned $42,450, and its delivery employees earned $2,060. The employees are to have withheld from their wages FICA Social Security taxes at the rate of 6.2%, FICA Medicare taxes at the rate of 1.45%, $17,250 of federal income taxes, $2,320 of medical insurance deductions, and $275 of union dues. No employee earned more than $7,000 in the first pay period.

Required

1. Calculate FICA Social Security taxes payable and FICA Medicare taxes payable. Prepare the journal entry to record Palmer Company's January 8 (employee) payroll expenses and liabilities.
2. Prepare the journal entry to record Palmer's (employer) payroll taxes resulting from the January 8 payroll. Palmer's merit rating reduces its state unemployment tax rate to 3.4% of the first $7,000 paid each employee. The federal unemployment tax rate is 0.8%.

Check (1) Cr. Accrued Payroll Payable, $85,434
(2) Dr. Payroll Taxes Expense, $13,509

Problem 11-6B[A]
Entries for payroll transactions
P2 P3 P5 P6

JLK Company has five employees, each of whom earns $1,200 per month and is paid on the last day of each month. All five have been employed continuously at this amount since January 1. JLK uses a payroll bank account and special payroll checks to pay its employees. On June 1, the following accounts and balances exist in its general ledger:

a. FICA—Social Security Taxes Payable, $744; FICA—Medicare Taxes Payable, $174. (The balances of these accounts represent total liabilities for *both* the employer's and employees' FICA taxes for the May payroll only.)
b. Employees' Federal Income Taxes Payable, $900 (liability for May only).
c. Federal Unemployment Taxes Payable, $96 (liability for April and May together).
d. State Unemployment Taxes Payable, $480 (liability for April and May together).

During June and July, the company had the following payroll transactions:

June 15 Issued check payable to Security Bank, a federal depository bank authorized to accept employers' payments of FICA taxes and employee income tax withholdings. The $1,818 check is in payment of the May FICA and employee income taxes.

30 Recorded the June payroll and transferred funds from the regular bank account to the payroll bank account. Issued checks payable to each employee in payment of the June payroll. The payroll register shows the following summary totals for the June pay period:

Check June 30: Cr. Accrued Payroll Payable, $4,641

Salaries and Wages					
Office Salaries	Shop Wages	Gross Pay	FICA Taxes*	Federal Income Taxes	Net Pay
$2,000	$4,000	$6,000	$372 $ 87	$900	$4,641

* FICA taxes are Social Security and Medicare, respectively.

Check June 30: Dr. Payroll Taxes Expenses, $699

July 15: Cr. Cash $1,818 (Security Bank)

30 Recorded the employer's payroll taxes resulting from the June payroll. The company has a merit rating that reduces its state unemployment tax rate to 4.0% of the first $7,000 paid each employee. The federal rate is 0.8%.

July 15 Issued check payable to Security Bank in payment of the June FICA and employee income taxes.

15 Issued check to the State Tax Commission for the April, May, and June state unemployment taxes. Mailed the check and the second quarter tax return to the State Tax Commission.

31 Issued check payable to Security Bank in payment of the employer's FUTA taxes for the second quarter of the year.

31 Mailed Form 941 to the IRS, reporting the FICA taxes and the employees' federal income tax withholdings for the second quarter.

Required

Prepare journal entries to record the transactions and events for both June and July.

PROBLEM SET C

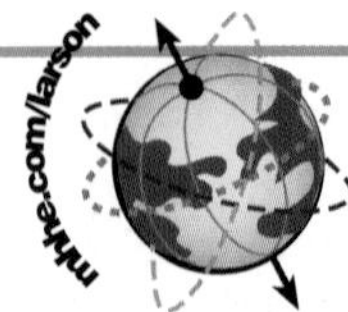

Problem Set C is available at the book's Website to further reinforce and assess your learning.

SERIAL PROBLEM

Success Systems

(This serial problem began in Chapter 1 and continues through most of the book. If previous chapter segments were not completed, the serial problem can begin at this point. It is helpful, but not necessary, for you to use the Working Papers that accompany the book.)

Review the February 26 and March 25 transactions for Success Systems found in Chapter 5.

Required

1.[A] Assume that Sherry Adams is an unmarried employee. Her wages are subject to no deductions other than FICA Social Security taxes, FICA Medicare taxes, and federal income taxes. Her federal income taxes for this pay period total $189. Compute her net pay for the eight days' work paid on February 26.

2. Make the required journal entry to record the payroll payment to Sherry Adams as calculated in part 1.

3. Make the required journal entry to record the (employer) payroll tax expenses for the February 26 payroll. Assume Sherry Adams has not met earnings limits for FUTA and SUTA—the FUTA rate is 0.8% and the SUTA rate is 4%.

4. Record the entry(ies) for the merchandise sold on March 25 if a 4% sales tax rate applies.

COMPREHENSIVE PROBLEM

Bug-Off Exterminators (Review of Chapters 1–11)

Bug-Off Exterminators provides pest control services and sells extermination products manufactured by other companies. The following six-column table contains the company's unadjusted trial balance as of December 31, 2005.

BUG-OFF EXTERMINATORS
December 31, 2005

	Unadjusted Trial Balance		Adjustments		Adjusted Trial Balance	
Cash	$ 17,000					
Accounts receivable	4,000					
Allowance for doubtful accounts		$ 828				
Merchandise inventory	11,700					
Trucks	32,000					
Accum. depreciation—Trucks		0				
Equipment	45,000					
Accum. depreciation—Equipment		12,200				
Accounts payable		5,000				

[continued on next page]

[continued from previous page]

Estimated warranty liability		1,400						
Unearned services revenue		0						
Long-term notes payable		15,000						
Interest payable		0						
T. Newman, Capital		59,700						
T. Newman, Withdrawals	10,000							
Extermination services revenue		60,000						
Interest revenue		872						
Sales (of merchandise)		71,026						
Cost of goods sold	46,300							
Depreciation expense—Trucks	0							
Depreciation expense—Equipment	0							
Wages expense	35,000							
Interest expense	0							
Rent expense	9,000							
Bad debts expense	0							
Miscellaneous expense	1,226							
Repairs expense	8,000							
Utilities expense	6,800							
Warranty expense	0							
Totals	$226,026	$226,026						

The following information applies to the company at the end of the current year:

a. The bank reconciliation as of December 31, 2005, includes these facts:

Balance per bank	$15,100
Balance per books	17,000
Outstanding checks	1,800
Deposit in transit	2,450
Interest earned (on bank account)	52
Bank service charges (miscellaneous expense)	15

Reported on the bank statement is a canceled check that the company failed to record. (Information from the bank reconciliation allows you to determine the amount of this check, which is a payment on an account payable.)

b. An examination of customers' accounts shows that accounts totaling $679 should be written off as uncollectible. Using an aging of receivables, the company determines that the ending balance of the Allowance for Doubtful Accounts should be $700.

c. A truck is purchased and placed in service on January 1, 2005. Its cost is being depreciated with the straight-line method using these facts and estimates:

Original cost	$32,000
Expected salvage value	8,000
Useful life (years)	4

d. Two items of equipment (a sprayer and an injector) were purchased and put into service in early January 2003. They are being depreciated with the straight-line method using these facts and estimates:

	Sprayer	Injector
Original cost	$27,000	$18,000
Expected salvage value	3,000	2,500
Useful life (years)	8	5

e. On August 1, 2005, the company is paid $3,840 in advance to provide monthly service for an apartment complex for one year. The company began providing the services in August. When the cash was received, the full amount was credited to the Extermination Services Revenue account.

f. The company offers a warranty for the services it sells. The expected cost of providing warranty service is 2.5% of the extermination services revenue of $57,760 for 2005. No warranty expense has been recorded for 2005. All costs of servicing warranties in 2005 were properly debited to the Estimated Warranty Liability account.

g. The $15,000 long-term note is a 8%, five-year, interest-bearing note with interest payable annually on December 31. The note was signed with First National Bank on December 31, 2005.

h. The ending inventory of merchandise is counted and determined to have a cost of $11,700. Bug-Off uses a perpetual inventory system.

Required

1. Use the preceding information to determine amounts for the following items:

Check (1*a*) Cash, $15,750
(1*b*) $551 credit

a. Correct (reconciled) ending balance of Cash, and the amount of the omitted check.

b. Adjustment needed to obtain the correct ending balance of the Allowance for Doubtful Accounts.

c. Depreciation expense for the truck used during year 2005.

d. Depreciation expense for the two items of equipment used during year 2005.

e. The adjusted 2005 ending balances of the Extermination Services Revenue and Unearned Services Revenue accounts.

(1*f*) Estim. warranty liability, $2,844 Cr.

f. The adjusted 2005 ending balances of the accounts for Warranty Expense and Estimated Warranty Liability.

g. The adjusted 2005 ending balances of the accounts for Interest Expense and Interest Payable. (Round amounts to nearest whole dollar.)

(2) Adjusted trial balance totals, $238,207

2. Use the results of part 1 to complete the six-column table by first entering the appropriate adjustments for items *a* through *g* and then completing the adjusted trial balance columns. (*Hint:* Item *b* requires two adjustments.)

3. Prepare journal entries to record the adjustments entered on the six-column table. Assume Bug-Off's adjusted balance for Merchandise Inventory matches the year-end physical count.

(4) Net income, $9,274; Total assets, $82,771

4. Prepare a single-step income statement, a statement of owner's equity (withdrawals during 2005 were $10,000), and a classified balance sheet.

BEYOND THE NUMBERS

REPORTING IN ACTION

A1 P4

BTN 11-1 Refer to the financial statements of **Krispy Kreme** in Appendix A to answer the following:

1. Compute times interest earned for the fiscal years ended 2003, 2002, and 2001. Comment on Krispy Kreme's ability to cover its interest expense for this period.

2. What evidence can you identify as an indication that Krispy Kreme has temporary differences between income reported on its income statement and income reported on its tax return?

Roll On

3. Access Krispy Kreme's financial statements for fiscal years ending after February 2, 2003, at its Website (**KrispyKreme.com**) or the SEC's EDGAR database (**www.SEC.gov**). Compute its times interest earned for years ending after February 2, 2003, and compare your results to those in part 1.

COMPARATIVE ANALYSIS

A1

BTN 11-2 Key comparative figures ($ thousands) for both **Krispy Kreme** and **Tastykake** follow:

	Krispy Kreme			Tastykake		
Key Figures	Current Year	One Year Prior	Two Years Prior	Current Year	One Year Prior	Two Years Prior
Net income	$33,478	$26,378	$14,725	$2,000*	$8,048*	$8,144
Income taxes	21,295	16,168	9,058	0	3,775	4,609
Interest expense	1,781	337	607	1,066	1,103	1,540

* Net income without restructuring charges.

Required

1. Compute times interest earned for the three years' data shown for each company.

2. Comment on which company appears stronger in its ability to pay interest obligations if income should decline.

ETHICS CHALLENGE

P4

BTN 11-3 Cannon Bly is a sales manager for an automobile dealership. He earns a bonus each year based on revenue from the number of autos sold in the year less related warranty expenses. Actual warranty expenses have varied over the prior 10 years from a low of 3% of an automobile's selling price to a high of 10%. In the past, Bly has tended to estimate warranty expenses on the high end to be conservative. He must work with the dealership's accountant at year-end to arrive at the warranty expense accrual for cars sold each year.

1. Does the warranty accrual decision create any ethical dilemma for Bly?

2. Since warranty expenses vary, what percent do you think Bly should choose for the current year? Justify your response.

COMMUNICATING IN PRACTICE

C3

BTN 11-4 Dustin Clemens is the accounting and finance manager for a manufacturer. At year-end, he must determine how to account for the company's contingencies. His manager, Tom Pretti, objects to Clemens's proposal to recognize an expense and a liability for warranty service on units of a new product introduced in the fourth quarter. Pretti comments, "There's no way we can estimate this warranty cost. We don't owe anyone anything until a product fails and it is returned. Let's report an expense if and when we do any warranty work."

Required

Prepare a one-page memorandum for Clemens to send to Pretti defending his proposal.

TAKING IT TO THE NET

C1 A1

BTN 11-5 Access the March 12, 2003, filing of the December 31, 2002, annual 10-K report of **McDonald's Corporation** (Ticker: MCD), which is available from www.SEC.gov.

Required

1. Identify the current liabilities on McDonald's balance sheet as of December 31, 2002.

2. What portion (in percent) of McDonald's long-term debt matures within the next 12 months?

3. Use the consolidated statement of income for the year ended December 31, 2002, to compute McDonald's times interest earned ratio. Comment on the result.

TEAMWORK IN ACTION

C2 P1

BTN 11-6 Assume that your team is in business and you must borrow $6,000 cash for short-term needs. You have been shopping banks for a loan, and you have the following two options:

A. Sign a $6,000, 90-day, 10% interest-bearing note dated June 1.

B. Sign a $6,000, 120-day, 8% interest-bearing note dated June 1.

Required

1. Discuss these two options and determine the best choice. Ensure that all teammates concur with the decision and understand the rationale.

2. Each member of the team is to prepare *one* of the following journal entries:

  a. Option A—at date of issuance.

  b. Option B—at date of issuance.

  c. Option A—at maturity date.

  d. Option B—at maturity date.

3. In rotation, each member is to explain the entry he or she prepared in part 2 to the team. Ensure that all team members concur with and understand the entries.

4. Assume that the funds are borrowed on December 1 (instead of June 1) and your business operates on a calendar-year reporting period. Each member of the team is to prepare *one* of the following entries:
   a. Option A—the year-end adjustment.
   b. Option B—the year-end adjustment.
   c. Option A—at maturity date.
   d. Option B—at maturity date.
5. In rotation, each member is to explain the entry he or she prepared in part 4 to the team. Ensure that all team members concur with and understand the entries.

BUSINESS WEEK ACTIVITY

P4

mhhe.com/larson

BTN 11-7 Read the article "Bed, Board—and Big Trouble" in the October 23, 2002, online issue of ***Business Week***. (This book's Website provides a free link.)

Required

1. What arrangement does the motel owner have with the long-term resident?
2. What risks is the motel operator exposed to by this arrangement?
3. How will the state of New York probably classify the tenant, and what should the motel owner do to respond to New York's probable action? Are there payroll tax implications?

ENTREPRENEURIAL DECISION

A1 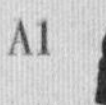 

BTN 11-8 Review the chapter's opening feature involving André Downey and **Environmental, Engineering & Construction**. EEC is considering a major technological investment in a plant asset to improve its environmental cleanup process. Assume that this investment would cut variable costs from 60% of sales to 45% of sales. However, fixed interest expense would increase from $540,000 per year to $1,140,000 per year to fund the $4,800,000 plant asset investment (with zero salvage, 50-year life, and depreciated using the straight-line method). Also assume that its recent income statement (absent this potential investment) appears as follows (assume zero income taxes):

EEC Income Statement For Year Ended January 31, 2005	
Sales	$3,000,000
Depreciation	60,000
Variable expenses (60%)	1,800,000
Income before interest	1,140,000
Interest expense (fixed)	540,000
Net income	$ 600,000

Required

1. Compute EEC's times interest earned ratio at January 31, 2005.
2. If EEC expects sales to remain at $3,000,000, what would net income and times interest earned equal if it makes the investment?
3. What would net income and times interest earned equal if sales increase to $3,600,000 and the investment is (*a*) not made and (*b*) made?
4. What would net income and times interest earned equal if sales increase to $4,639,998 and the investment is (*a*) not made and (*b*) made?
5. What would net income and times interest earned equal if sales increase to $5,400,000 and the investment is (*a*) not made and (*b*) made?
6. Comment on the results from parts 1 through 5 and their relation to the times interest earned ratio.

HITTING THE ROAD

P2

BTN 11-9 Check your phone book or the Social Security Administration Website (www.SSA.gov) to locate the Social Security office near you. Visit the office to request a personal earnings and estimate form. Fill out the form and mail according to the instructions. You will receive a statement from the Social Security Administration regarding your earnings history and future Social Security benefits you can receive. (*Note:* Formerly the request could be made online. The online service has been discontinued and is now under review by the Social Security Administration due to security concerns.) It is good to request an earnings and benefit statement every 5 to 10 years to make sure you have received credit for all wages earned and for which you and your employer have paid taxes into the system.

BTN 11-10 **Grupo Bimbo**, **Krispy Kreme**, and **Tastykake** are all competitors in the global marketplace. Key comparative figures for Grupo Bimbo **(GrupoBimbo.com)** for the year ended December 31, 2002 (along with selected figures from Krispy Kreme and Tastykake) follow:

GLOBAL DECISION

A1 

	Grupo Bimbo (millions of pesos)		Krispy Kreme		Tastykake	
Key Figures	Current Year	Prior Year	Current Year	Prior Year	Current Year	Prior Year
Net income	$1,003	$1,682	—	—	—	—
Income taxes	575	805	—	—	—	—
Interest expense	703	193	—	—	—	—
Times interest earned	?	?	31.8	127.2	2.9	10.2

Required

1. Compute the times interest earned ratio for the most recent two years for Grupo Bimbo using the data shown.
2. Which company of the three presented provides the best coverage of interest expense?

"*I started everything from nothing and figured it out along the way*"—Michael Koch

Accounting for Partnerships

A Look Back

Chapter 11 focused on current liabilities. We explained how liabilities are identified, computed, recorded, and reported in financial statements. Attention was directed at notes, payroll, sales taxes, warranties, employee benefits, and contingencies.

A Look at This Chapter

This chapter explains the partnership form of organization. Important characteristics of this form of organization are described along with the accounting concepts and procedures for its most fundamental transactions.

A Look Ahead

Chapter 13 extends our discussion to the corporate form of organization. We describe the accounting for stock issuances, dividends, and other equity transactions. We also explain how income, earnings per share, and retained earnings are reported.

CAP

Conceptual

C1 Identify characteristics of partnerships and similar organizations. *(p. 468)*

Analytical

A1 Compute partner return on equity and use it to evaluate partnership performance. *(p. 480)*

Procedural

P1 Prepare entries for partnership formation. *(p. 471)*

P2 Allocate and record income and loss among partners. *(p. 471)*

P3 Account for the admission and withdrawal of partners. *(p. 474)*

P4 Prepare entries for partnership liquidation. *(p. 478)*

Decision Feature

Sound of Success

PORT WASHINGTON, NY—Michael Koch knows the value of a good idea and a partnership. Koch was 24, having just moved to the United States from Innsbruck, and had a job pressing CDs. "I quickly realized I'd better get something else going, because pressing CDs . . . was kind of hard," says Koch. "So I had to look around for something else to do." Koch soon found his niche. He partnered with a friend, and says Koch, "We started importing classical CDs." Koch soon expanded from classical music to rap, jazz, rock, punk, country, and Broadway. He set up **Koch Entertainment LLC (www.KochEnt.com)** to focus those efforts.

Koch believes the knowledge of partnerships and their financial implications is important to successful operation. By partnering with others, Koch was able to make serious inroads in the music industry in a relatively short time. His partnering approach extends to the artists. "We don't dictate their creative process as much as larger labels," says Koch. "We focus more on the artist and the relationship."

That partnership philosophy pervades his company, which Koch chose to set up as an LLC (an organizational form with partnership characteristics). He emphasizes the importance of attending to partnership formation, agreements, and financial statements to stay afloat. He points to his own LLC's success as supportive evidence. "Obviously we're doing something right," say Koch.

Koch is not finished with partnerships. He recently signed an agreement to partner with the BBC to market its CDs. First on the list: *Bob the Builder*. If that isn't diversity, nothing is. Koch has also done well by partnering with WWF and Pokémon. He also has partnerships with Dwight Yoakam, Ani DeFranco, Jody Watley, Rancid, and Nick Cave. Koch points to this diversity in artists as a strength: "Let the music speak for itself," he says.

Knowledge of partnerships has set Koch on the road to success. Not bad for someone who started with nothing!

[Sources: *Koch Entertainment Website*, January 2004; *Entrepreneur*, May 2003; *Newsday*, April 2003; *Billboard*, June 2002.]

The three basic types of business organizations are proprietorships, partnerships, and corporations. Partnerships are similar to proprietorships, except they have more than one owner. This chapter explains partnerships and looks at several variations of them such as limited partnerships, limited liability partnerships, S corporations, and limited liability companies. Understanding the advantages and disadvantages of the partnership form of business organization is important for making informed business decisions.

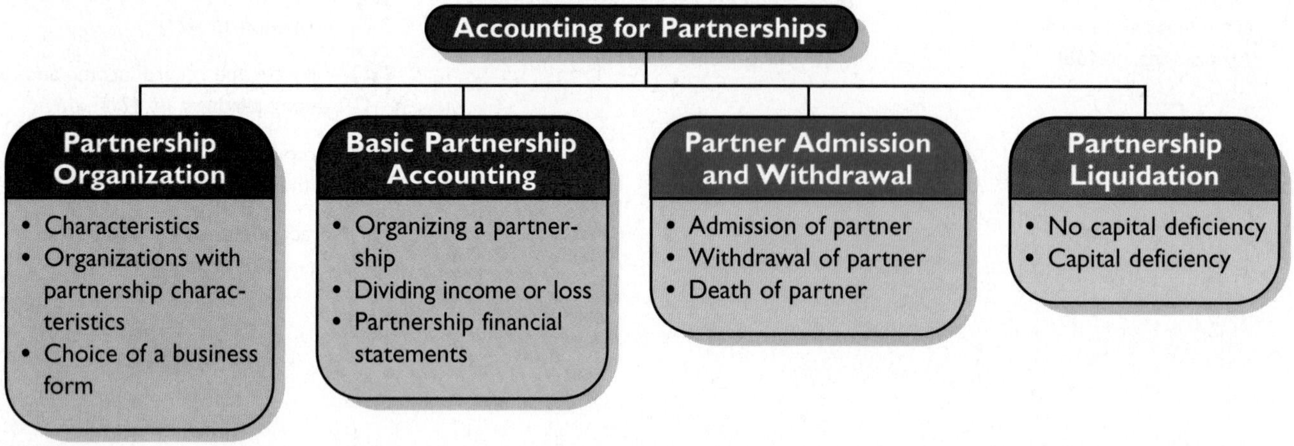

Accounting for Partnerships

Partnership Organization	Basic Partnership Accounting	Partner Admission and Withdrawal	Partnership Liquidation
• Characteristics • Organizations with partnership characteristics • Choice of a business form	• Organizing a partnership • Dividing income or loss • Partnership financial statements	• Admission of partner • Withdrawal of partner • Death of partner	• No capital deficiency • Capital deficiency

Partnership Form of Organization

C1 Identify characteristics of partnerships and similar organizations.

A **partnership** is an unincorporated association of two or more people to pursue a business for profit as co-owners. Many businesses are organized as partnerships. They are especially common in small retail and service businesses. Many professional practitioners, including physicians, lawyers, investors, and accountants, also organize their practices as partnerships.

Characteristics of Partnerships

Partnerships are an important type of organization because they offer certain advantages with their unique characteristics. We describe these characteristics in this section.

Voluntary Association A partnership is a voluntary association between partners. Joining a partnership increases the risk to one's personal financial position. Some courts have ruled that partnerships are created by the actions of individuals even when there is no expressed agreement to form one.

Partnership Agreement Forming a partnership requires that two or more legally competent people (who are of age and of sound mental capacity) agree to be partners. Their agreement becomes a **partnership contract,** also called *articles of copartnership.* Although it should be in writing, the contract is binding even if it is only expressed verbally. Partnership agreements normally include details of the partners' (1) names and contributions, (2) rights and duties, (3) sharing of income and losses, (4) withdrawal arrangement, (5) dispute procedures, (6) admission and withdrawal of partners, and (7) rights and duties in the event a partner dies.

Point: When a new partner is admitted, all parties usually must agree to the admission.

Limited Life The life of a partnership is limited. Death, bankruptcy, or any event taking away the ability of a partner to enter into or fulfill a contract ends a partnership. Any one of the partners can also terminate a partnership at will.

Point: The end of a partnership is referred to as its *dissolution.*

Taxation A partnership has the same tax status as a proprietorship and is not subject to taxes on its income. The income or loss of a partnership is allocated to the partners according to the partnership agreement, and it is included in determining the taxable income for each partner's tax return. Partnership income or loss is allocated each year whether or not cash is distributed to partners.

Point: Partners are taxed on their share of partnership income, not on their withdrawals.

Mutual Agency **Mutual agency** implies that each partner is a fully authorized agent of the partnership. As its agent, a partner can commit or bind the partnership to any contract within the scope of the partnership business. For instance, a partner in a merchandising business can sign contracts binding the partnership to buy merchandise, lease a store building, borrow money, or hire employees. These activities are all within the scope of a merchandising firm. A partner in a law firm, acting alone, however, cannot bind the other partners to a contract to buy snowboards for resale or rent an apartment for parties. These actions are outside the normal scope of a law firm's business. Partners also can agree to limit the power of any one or more of the partners to negotiate contracts for the partnership. This agreement is binding on the partners and on outsiders who know it exists. It is not binding on outsiders who do not know it exists. Outsiders unaware of the agreement have the right to assume each partner has normal agency powers for the partnership. Mutual agency exposes partners to the risk of unwise actions by any one partner.

Point: The majority of states adhere to the Uniform Partnership Act for the basic rules of partnership formation, operation, and dissolution.

Unlimited Liability **Unlimited liability** implies that each partner can be called on to pay a partnership's debts. When a partnership cannot pay its debts, creditors usually can apply their claims to partners' *personal* assets. If a partner does not have enough assets to meet his or her share of the partnership debt, the creditors can apply their claims to the assets of the other partners. A partnership in which all partners have *mutual agency* and *unlimited liability* is called a **general partnership.** Mutual agency and unlimited liability are two main reasons that most general partnerships have only a few members.

Point: Limited life, mutual agency, and unlimited liability are disadvantages of a partnership.

Co-Ownership of Property Partnership assets are owned jointly by all partners. Any investment by a partner becomes the joint property of all partners. Partners have a claim on partnership assets based on their capital account and the partnership contract.

Organizations with Partnership Characteristics

Organizations exist that combine certain characteristics of partnerships with other forms of organizations. We discuss several of these forms in this section.

Limited Partnerships Some individuals who want to invest in a partnership are unwilling to accept the risk of unlimited liability. Their needs can be met with a **limited partnership.** This type of organization is identified in its name with the words "Limited Partnership," or "Ltd.," or "LP." A limited partnership has two classes of partners, general and limited. At least one partner must be a **general partner,** who assumes management duties and unlimited liability for the debts of the partnership. The **limited partners** have no personal liability beyond the amounts they invest in the partnership. Limited partners have no active role except as specified in the partnership agreement. A limited partnership agreement often specifies unique procedures for allocating income and losses between general and limited partners. The accounting procedures are similar for both limited and general partnerships.

Decision Insight

Team Up The **Boston Celtics** is organized as a limited partnership. It owns and operates the Boston Celtics NBA team. The general partner of the Boston Celtics is Paul E. Gaston.

Limited Liability Partnerships Most states allow individuals to form a **limited liability partnership.** This is identified in its name with the words "Limited Liability Partnership" or by "LLP." This type of partnership is designed to protect innocent partners from malpractice or negligence claims resulting from the acts of another partner. When a partner provides service resulting in a malpractice claim, that partner has personal liability for the claim. The remaining partners who were not responsible for the actions resulting in the claim are not personally liable for it. However, most states hold all partners personally liable for other partnership debts. Accounting for a limited liability partnership is the same as for a general partnership.

Point: Many accounting services firms are set up as LLPs.

S Corporations Certain corporations with 75 or fewer stockholders can elect to be treated as a partnership for income tax purposes. These corporations are called *Sub-Chapter S* or simply **S corporations.** This distinguishes them from other corporations, called *Sub-Chapter C* or simply **C corporations.** S corporations provide stockholders the same limited liability feature that C corporations do. The advantage of an S corporation is that it does not pay income taxes. If stockholders work for an S corporation, their salaries are treated as expenses of the corporation. The remaining income or loss of the corporation is allocated to stockholders for inclusion on their personal tax returns. Except for C corporations having to account for income tax expenses and liabilities, the accounting procedures are the same for both S and C corporations.

Point: The majority of proprietorships and partnerships that are being organized today are being set up as an LLC.

Limited Liability Companies A relatively new form of business organization is the **limited liability company.** The names of these businesses usually include the words "Limited Liability Company" or an abbreviation such as "LLC" or "LC." This form of business has certain features similar to a corporation and others similar to a limited partnership. The owners, who are called *members,* are protected with the same limited liability feature as owners of corporations. While limited partners cannot actively participate in the management of a limited partnership, the members of a limited liability company can assume an active management role. A limited liability company usually has a limited life. For income tax purposes, a limited liability company is typically treated as a partnership. This treatment depends on factors such as whether the members' equity interests are freely transferable and whether the company has continuity of life. A limited liability company's accounting system is designed to help management comply with the dictates of the articles of organization and company regulations adopted by its members. The accounting system also must provide information to support the company's compliance with state and federal laws, including taxation.

Point: Accounting for LLCs is similar to that for partnerships (and proprietorships). One difference is that Owner (Partner), Capital is usually called *Members, Capital* for LLCs.

Choosing a Business Form

Choosing the proper business form is crucial. Many factors should be considered, including taxes, liability risk, tax and fiscal year-end, ownership structure, estate planning, business risks, and earnings and property distributions. The following table summarizes several important characteristics of business organizations:

	Proprietorship	Partnership	LLP	LLC	S Corp.	Corporation
Business entity	yes	yes	yes	yes	yes	yes
Legal entity	no	no	no	yes	yes	yes
Limited liability	no	no	limited*	yes	yes	yes
Business taxed	no	no	no	no	no	yes
One owner allowed ..	yes	no	no	yes	yes	yes

* A partner's personal liability for LLP debts is limited. Most LLPs carry insurance to protect against malpractice.

Point: Small Business Administration provides suggestions and information on setting up the proper form for your organization—see SBA.gov.

We must remember that this table is a summary, not a detailed list. Many details underlie each of these business forms, and several details differ across states. Also, state and federal laws change, and a body of law is still developing around LLCs. Business owners should look at these details and consider unique business arrangements such as organizing various parts of their businesses in different forms.

Quick Check

1. A partnership is terminated in the event (*a*) a partnership agreement is not in writing, (*b*) a partner dies, (*c*) a partner exercises mutual agency.
2. What does the term *unlimited liability* mean when applied to a general partnership?
3. Which of the following forms of organization do not provide limited liability to *all* of its owners: (*a*) S corporation, (*b*) limited liability company, (*c*) limited partnership?

Answers—p. 483

Basic Partnership Accounting

Since ownership rights in a partnership are divided among partners, partnership accounting

- Uses a capital account for each partner.
- Uses a withdrawals account for each partner.
- Allocates net income or loss to partners according to the partnership agreement.

This section describes partnership accounting for organizing a partnership, distributing income and loss, and preparing financial statements.

Organizing a Partnership

P1 Prepare entries for partnership formation.

When partners invest in a partnership, their capital accounts are credited for the invested amounts. Partners can invest both assets and liabilities. Each partner's investment is recorded at an agreed-on value, normally the market values of the contributed assets and liabilities at the date of contribution. To illustrate, Kayla Zayn and Hector Perez organize a partnership called BOARDS that offers year-round facilities for skateboarding and snowboarding. Zayn's initial net investment in BOARDS is $30,000, made up of cash ($7,000), boarding facilities ($33,000), and a note payable reflecting a bank loan for the new business ($10,000). Perez's initial investment is cash of $10,000. These amounts are the values agreed on by both partners. The entries to record these investments follow:

Zayn's Investment

Jan. 11	Cash	7,000	
	Boarding facilities	33,000	
	Note payable		10,000
	K. Zayn, Capital		30,000
	To record the investment of Zayn.		

Assets	= Liabilities +	Equity
+7,000	+10,000	+30,000
+33,000		

Perez's Investment

Jan. 11	Cash	10,000	
	H. Perez, Capital		10,000
	To record the investment of Perez.		

Assets	= Liabilities +	Equity
+10,000		+10,000

Note that in accounting for a partnership, the following additional relations hold true: (1) Partners' withdrawals are debited to their own separate withdrawals accounts. (2) Partners' capital accounts are credited (or debited) for their shares of net income (or net loss) when closing the accounts at the end of a period. (3) Each partner's withdrawals account is closed to that partner's capital account. Note, too, that separate capital and withdrawals accounts are kept for each partner.

Point: Both equity and cash are reduced when a partner withdraws cash from a partnership.

Decision Insight

Nutty Partners The Hawaii-based **ML Macadamia Orchards LP** is one of the world's largest growers of macadamia nuts. It reported the following partners' capital balances ($ thousands) in its recent balance sheet:

General Partner	$ 549
Limited Partners	$54,300

Dividing Income or Loss

P2 Allocate and record income and loss among partners.

Partners are not employees of the partnership but are its owners. If partners devote their time and services to their partnership, they are understood to do so for profit, not for salary. This means there are no salaries to partners that are reported as expenses on the partnership income statement. However, when net income or loss of a partnership is allocated among partners, the partners can agree to allocate "salary allowances" reflecting the relative value of services provided. Partners also can agree to allocate "interest allowances" based on the amount invested. For instance, since Zayn contributes three times the investment of Perez, it is only fair that this be considered when allocating income between them. Like salary allowances, these interest allowances are not expenses on the income statement.

Partners can agree to any method of dividing income or loss. In the absence of an agreement, the law says that the partners share income or loss of a partnership equally. If partners agree on how to share income but say nothing about losses, they share losses the same way they share income. Three common methods to divide income or loss use (1) a stated ratio basis, (2) the ratio of capital balances, or (3) salary and interest allowances and any remainder according to a fixed ratio. We explain each of these methods in this section.

Point: Partners can agree on one ratio to divide income and another ratio to divide a loss.

Allocation on Stated Ratios The *stated ratio* (also called the *income-and-loss-sharing ratio,* the *profit and loss ratio,* or the *P&L ratio*) method of allocating partnership income or loss gives each partner a fraction of the total. Partners must agree on the fractional share each receives. To illustrate, assume the partnership agreement of K. Zayn and H. Perez says Zayn receives two-thirds and Perez one-third of partnership income and loss. If their partnership's net income is $60,000, it is allocated to the partners when the Income Summary account is closed as follows:

Point: The fractional basis can be stated as a proportion, ratio, or percent. For example, a 3:2 basis is the same as ⅗ and ⅖, or 60% and 40%.

Dec. 31	Income Summary	60,000	
	K. Zayn, Capital		40,000
	H. Perez, Capital		20,000
	To allocate income and close Income Summary.		

Assets = Liabilities + Equity
−60,000
+40,000
+20,000

Allocation on Capital Balances The *capital balances* method of allocating partnership income or loss assigns an amount based on the ratio of each partner's relative capital balance. If Zayn and Perez agree to share income and loss on the ratio of their beginning capital balances—Zayn's $30,000 and Perez's $10,000—Zayn receives three-fourths of any income or loss ($30,000/$40,000) and Perez receives one-fourth ($10,000/$40,000). The journal entry follows the same format as that using stated ratios (see preceding entries).

Point: To determine the percent of income received by each partner, divide an individual partner's share by total net income.

Topic Tackler 12-1

Allocation on Services, Capital, and Stated Ratios The *services, capital, and stated ratio* method of allocating partnership income or loss recognizes that service and capital contributions of partners often are not equal. Salary allowances can make up for differences in service contributions. Interest allowances can make up for unequal capital contributions. Also, the allocation of income and loss can include *both* salary and interest allowances. To illustrate, assume that the partnership agreement of K. Zayn and H. Perez reflects differences in service and capital contributions as follows: (1) annual salary allowances of $36,000 to Zayn and $24,000 to Perez, (2) annual interest allowances of 10% of a partner's beginning-year capital balance, and (3) equal share of any remaining balance of income or loss. These salaries and interest allowances are *not* reported as expenses on the income statement. They are simply a means of dividing partnership income or loss. The remainder of this section provides two illustrations using this three-point allocation agreement.

Illustration when income exceeds allowance. If BOARDS has first-year net income of $70,000, and Zayn and Perez apply the three-point partnership agreement described in the prior paragraph, income is allocated as shown in Exhibit 12.1. Zayn gets $42,000 and Perez gets $28,000 of the $70,000 total.

Illustration when allowances exceed income. The sharing agreement between Zayn and Perez must be followed even if net income is less than the total of the allowances. For example, if BOARDS' first-year net income is $50,000 instead of $70,000, it is allocated to the partners as shown in Exhibit 12.2. Computations for salaries and interest are identical to those in Exhibit 12.1. However, when we apply the total allowances against income, the balance of income is negative. This $(14,000) negative balance is allocated equally to the partners per their sharing agreement. This means that a negative $(7,000) is allocated to each partner. In this case, Zayn ends up with $32,000 and Perez with $18,000. If BOARDS had experienced a net loss, Zayn and Perez would share it in the same manner as the $50,000 income. The only difference is that they would have begun with a negative amount because of the loss. Specifically, the partners would still have been allocated their salary and interest

Point: When allowances exceed income, the amount of this negative balance often is referred to as a *sharing agreement loss* or *deficit.*

Point: Check to make sure the sum of the dollar amounts allocated to each partner equals net income or loss.

Exhibit 12.1

Dividing Income When Income Exceeds Allowances

	Zayn	Perez	Total
Net income			$70,000
Salary allowances			
Zayn	$ 36,000		
Perez		$ 24,000	
Interest allowances			
Zayn (10% × $30,000)	3,000		
Perez (10% × $10,000)		1,000	
Total salaries and interest	39,000	25,000	64,000
Balance of income			6,000
Balance allocated equally			
Zayn	3,000 ←		
Perez		3,000 ←	
Total allocated			6,000
Balance of income			$ 0
Income of each partner	$42,000	$28,000	

Exhibit 12.2

Dividing Income When Allowances Exceed Income

	Zayn	Perez	Total
Net income			$50,000
Salary allowances			
Zayn	$ 36,000		
Perez		$ 24,000	
Interest allowances			
Zayn (10% × $30,000)	3,000		
Perez (10% × $10,000)		1,000	
Total salaries and interest	39,000	25,000	64,000
Balance of income			(14,000)
Balance allocated equally			
Zayn	(7,000) ←		
Perez		(7,000) ←	
Total allocated			(14,000)
Balance of income			$ 0
Income of each partner	$32,000	$18,000	

allowances, further adding to the negative balance of the loss. This *total* negative balance *after* salary and interest allowances would have been allocated equally between the partners. These allocations would have been applied against the positive numbers from any allowances to determine each partner's share of the loss.

Point: When a loss occurs, it is possible for a specific partner's capital to increase (when closing income summary) if that partner's allowance is in excess of his or her share of the negative balance. This implies that decreases to the capital balances of other partners exceed the partnership's loss amount.

Quick Check

4. Denzel and Shantell form a partnership by contributing $70,000 and $35,000, respectively. They agree to an interest allowance equal to 10% of each partner's capital balance at the beginning of the year, with the remaining income shared equally. Allocate first-year income of $40,000 to each partner.

Answers—p. 483

Partnership Financial Statements

Partnership financial statements are similar to those of other organizations. The **statement of partners' equity,** also called *statement of partners' capital,* is one exception. It shows *each* partner's beginning capital balance, additional investments, allocated income or loss, withdrawals, and ending capital balance. To illustrate, Exhibit 12.3 shows the statement of

Decision Insight

Beach Buddies The **Casa Munras Hotel Partners LP** operates the Casa Munras Garden Hotel and several leased retail stores in Monterey, California. Its recent statement of partners' equity reports that total partners' withdrawals equal $1,350 is distributed to the general partner and the remainder of $133,650 to limited partners.

partners' equity for BOARDS prepared using the sharing agreement of Exhibit 12.1. Recall that BOARDS' income was $70,000; also, assume that Zayn withdrew $20,000 and Perez $12,000 at year-end.

The equity section of the balance sheet of a partnership usually shows the separate capital account balance of each partner. In the case of BOARDS, both K. Zayn, Capital, and H. Perez, Capital, are listed in the equity section along with their balances of $52,000 and $26,000, respectively.

Exhibit 12.3

Statement of Partners' Equity

BOARDS
Statement of Partners' Equity
For Year Ended December 31, 2005

	Zayn		Perez		Total
Beginning capital balances		$ 0		$ 0	$ 0
Plus					
Investments by owners		30,000		10,000	40,000
Net income					
Salary allowances	$36,000		$24,000		
Interest allowances	3,000		1,000		
Balance allocated	3,000		3,000		
Total net income		42,000		28,000	70,000
		72,000		38,000	110,000
Less partners' withdrawals		(20,000)		(12,000)	(32,000)
Ending capital balances		**$52,000**		**$26,000**	**$78,000**

Admission and Withdrawal of Partners

P3 Account for the admission and withdrawal of partners.

A partnership is based on a contract between individuals. When a partner is admitted or withdraws, the present partnership ends. Still, the business can continue to operate as a new partnership consisting of the remaining partners. This section considers how to account for the admission and withdrawal of partners.

Admission of a Partner

A new partner is admitted in one of two ways: by purchasing an interest from one or more current partners or by investing cash or other assets in the partnership.

Topic Tackler 12-2

Purchase of Partnership Interest The purchase of partnership interest is a *personal transaction between one or more current partners and the new partner.* To become a partner, the current partners must accept the purchaser. Accounting for the purchase of partnership interest involves reallocating current partners' capital to reflect the transaction. To illustrate, at the end of BOARDS' first year, H. Perez sells one-half of his partnership interest to Tyrell Rasheed for $18,000. This means that Perez gives up a $13,000 recorded interest ($26,000 × 1/2) in the partnership (see the ending capital balance in Exhibit 12.3). The partnership records this as follows:

Assets = Liabilities + Equity
−13,000
+13,000

Jan. 4	H. Perez, Capital	13,000	
	T. Rasheed, Capital		13,000
	To record admission of Rasheed by purchase.		

After this entry is posted, BOARDS' equity shows K. Zayn, Capital; H. Perez, Capital; and T. Rasheed, Capital, and their respective balances of $52,000, $13,000, and $13,000.

Two aspects of this transaction are important. First, the partnership, does *not* record the $18,000 Rasheed paid Perez. The partnership's assets, liabilities, and *total equity* are unaffected by this transaction among partners. Second, Zayn and Perez must agree that Rasheed is to become a partner. If they agree to accept Rasheed, a new partnership is formed and a new contract with a new income-and-loss-sharing agreement is prepared. If Zayn or Perez refuses to accept Rasheed as a partner, then (under the Uniform Partnership Act) Rasheed gets Perez's sold share of partnership income and loss. If the partnership is liquidated, Rasheed gets Perez's sold share of partnership assets. Rasheed gets no voice in managing the company unless Rasheed is admitted as a partner.

Point: Partners' withdrawals are not constrained by the partnership's annual income or loss.

Investing Assets in a Partnership Admitting a partner by accepting assets is a *transaction between the new partner and the partnership.* The invested assets become partnership property. To illustrate, if Zayn (with a $52,000 interest) and Perez (with a $26,000 interest) agree to accept Rasheed as a partner in BOARDS after an investment of $22,000 cash, this is recorded as follows:

Jan. 4	Cash	22,000	
	T. Rasheed, Capital		22,000
	To record admission of Rasheed by investment.		

Assets	= Liabilities +	Equity
+22,000		+22,000

After this entry is posted, both assets (cash) and equity (T. Rasheed, Capital) increase by $22,000. Rasheed now has a 22% equity in the assets of the business, computed as $22,000 divided by the entire partnership equity ($52,000 + $26,000 + $22,000). Rasheed does not necessarily have a right to 22% of income. Dividing income and loss is a separate matter on which partners must agree.

Bonus to old partners. When the current value of a partnership is greater than the recorded amounts of equity, the partners usually require a new partner to pay a bonus for the privilege of joining. To illustrate, assume that Zayn and Perez agree to accept Rasheed as a partner with a 25% interest in BOARDS if Rasheed invests $42,000. Recall the partnership's accounting records show Zayn's recorded equity in the business is $52,000 and Perez's recorded equity is $26,000 (see Exhibit 12.3). Rasheed's equity is determined as follows:

Equities of existing partners ($52,000 + $26,000)	$ 78,000
Investment of new partner	42,000
Total partnership equity	$120,000
Equity of Rasheed (25% × $120,000)	$ 30,000

Although Rasheed invests $42,000, the equity attributed to Rasheed in the new partnership is only $30,000. The $12,000 difference is called a *bonus* and is allocated to existing partners (Zayn and Perez) according to their income-and-loss-sharing agreement. A bonus is shared in this way because it is viewed as reflecting a higher value of the partnership that is not yet reflected in income. The entry to record this transaction follows:

Jan. 4	Cash	42,000	
	T. Rasheed, Capital		30,000
	K. Zayn, Capital ($12,000 × ½)		6,000
	H. Perez, Capital ($12,000 × ½)		6,000
	To record admission of Rasheed and bonus.		

Assets	= Liabilities +	Equity
+42,000		+30,000
		+6,000
		+6,000

Bonus to new partner. Alternatively, existing partners can grant a bonus to a new partner. This usually occurs when they need additional cash or the new partner has exceptional talents. The bonus to the new partner is in the form of a larger share of equity than the amount invested. To illustrate, assume that Zayn and Perez agree to accept Rasheed as a partner with a 25% interest in the partnership, but they require Rasheed to invest only $18,000. Rasheed's equity is determined as follows:

Equities of existing partners ($52,000 + $26,000)	$78,000
Investment of new partner	18,000
Total partnership equity	$96,000
Equity of Rasheed (25% × $96,000)	$24,000

The old partners contribute the $6,000 bonus (computed as $24,000 minus $18,000) to Rasheed according to their income-and-loss-sharing ratio. Moreover, Rasheed's 25% equity does not necessarily entitle Rasheed to 25% of future income or loss. This is a separate matter for agreement by the partners. The entry to record the admission and investment of Rasheed is

Assets	= Liabilities	+ Equity
+18,000		−3,000
		−3,000
		+24,000

Jan. 4	Cash	18,000	
	K. Zayn, Capital ($6,000 × ½)	3,000	
	H. Perez, Capital ($6,000 × ½)..............	3,000	
	T. Rasheed, Capital.....................		24,000
	To record Rasheed's admission and bonus.		

Withdrawal of a Partner

A partner generally withdraws from a partnership in one of two ways. (1) First, the withdrawing partner can sell his or her interest to another person who pays for it in cash or other assets. For this, we need only debit the withdrawing partner's capital account and credit the new partner's capital account. (2) The second case is when cash or other assets of the partnership are distributed to the withdrawing partner in settlement of his or her interest. To illustrate these cases, assume that Perez withdraws from the partnership of BOARDS in some future period. The partnership shows the following capital balances at the date of Perez's withdrawal: K. Zayn, $84,000; H. Perez, $38,000; and T. Rasheed, $38,000. The partners (Zayn, Perez, and Rasheed) share income and loss equally. Accounting for Perez's withdrawal depends on whether a bonus is paid. We describe three possibilities.

No Bonus If Perez withdraws and takes cash equal to Perez's capital balance, the entry is

Assets	= Liabilities	+ Equity
−38,000		−38,000

Oct. 31	H. Perez, Capital..........................	38,000	
	Cash..............................		38,000
	To record withdrawal of Perez from partnership with no bonus.		

Perez can take any combination of assets to which the partners agree to settle Perez's equity. Perez's withdrawal creates a new partnership between the remaining partners. A new partnership contract and a new income-and-loss-sharing agreement are required.

Bonus to Remaining Partners A withdrawing partner is sometimes willing to take less than the recorded value of his or her equity to get out of the partnership or because the recorded value is overstated. Whatever the reason, when this occurs, the withdrawing partner in effect gives the remaining partners a bonus equal to the equity left behind. The remaining partners share this unwithdrawn equity according to their income-and-loss-sharing ratio. To illustrate, if Perez withdraws and agrees to take $34,000 cash in settlement of

Perez's capital balance, the entry is

Oct. 31	H. Perez, Capital	38,000	
	Cash		34,000
	K. Zayn, Capital		2,000
	T. Rasheed, Capital		2,000
	To record withdrawal of Perez and bonus to remaining partners.		

Assets	= Liabilities +	Equity
−34,000		−38,000
		+2,000
		+2,000

Perez withdrew $4,000 less than Perez's recorded equity of $38,000. This $4,000 is divided between Zayn and Rasheed according to their income-and-loss-sharing ratio.

Bonus to Withdrawing Partner A withdrawing partner may be able to receive more than his or her recorded equity for at least two reasons. First, the recorded equity may be understated. Second, the remaining partners may agree to remove this partner by giving assets of greater value than this partner's recorded equity. In either case, the withdrawing partner receives a bonus. The remaining partners reduce their equity by the amount of this bonus according to their income-and-loss-sharing ratio. To illustrate, if Perez withdraws and receives $40,000 cash in settlement of Perez's capital balance, the entry is

Oct. 31	H. Perez, Capital	38,000	
	K. Zayn, Capital	1,000	
	T. Rasheed, Capital	1,000	
	Cash		40,000
	To record Perez's withdrawal from partnership with a bonus to Perez.		

Assets	= Liabilities +	Equity
−40,000		−38,000
		−1,000
		−1,000

Falcon Cable Communications LLC has a partnership withdrawal agreement. Falcon owns and operates cable television systems and has two managing general partners. The partnership agreement states that either partner "can offer to sell to the other partner the offering partner's entire partnership interest . . . for a negotiated price. If the partner receiving such an offer rejects it, the offering partner may elect to cause [the partnership] . . . to be liquidated and dissolved."

Death of a Partner

A partner's death dissolves a partnership. A deceased partner's estate is entitled to receive his or her equity. The partnership contract should contain provisions for settlement in this case. These provisions usually require (1) closing the books to determine income or loss since the end of the previous period and (2) determining and recording current market values for both assets and liabilities. The remaining partners and the deceased partner's estate then must agree to a settlement of the deceased partner's equity. This can involve selling the equity to remaining partners or to an outsider, or it can involve withdrawing assets.

Decision Ethics

Financial Planner You are hired by the two remaining partners of a three-member partnership after the third partner's death. The partnership agreement states that a deceased partner's estate is entitled to a "share of partnership assets equal to the partner's relative equity balance" (partners' equity balances are equal). The estate argues it is entitled to one-third of the current value of partnership assets. The remaining partners say the distribution should use asset book values, which are 75% of current value. They also point to partnership liabilities, which equal 40% of total asset book value and 30% of current value. How would you resolve this situation?

Answer—p. 483

Liquidation of a Partnership

When a partnership is liquidated, its business ends and four concluding steps are required:

1. Record the sale of noncash assets for cash and any gain or loss from their liquidation.
2. Allocate any gain or loss from liquidation of the assets in step 1 to the partners using their income-and-loss-sharing ratio.

3. Pay or settle all partner liabilities.
4. Distribute any remaining cash to partners based on their capital balances.

Partnership liquidation usually falls into one of two cases, as described in this section.

No Capital Deficiency

P4 Prepare entries for partnership liquidation.

No capital deficiency means that all partners have a zero or credit balance in their capital accounts for final distribution of cash. To illustrate, assume that Zayn, Perez, and Rasheed operate their partnership in BOARDS for several years, sharing income and loss equally. The partners then decide to liquidate. On the liquidation date, the current period's income or loss is transferred to the partners' capital accounts according to the sharing agreement. After that transfer, assume the partners' recorded equity balances (immediately prior to liquidation) are Zayn, $70,000; Perez, $66,000; and Rasheed, $62,000.

Next, assume that BOARDS sells its noncash assets for a net gain of $6,000. In a liquidation, gains or losses usually result from the sale of noncash assets, which are called *losses and gains from liquidation.* Partners share losses and gains from liquidation according to their income-and-loss-sharing agreement (equal for these partners) yielding the partners' revised equity balances of Zayn, $72,000; Perez, $68,000; and Rasheed, $64,000.[1] Then, after partnership assets are sold and any gain or loss is allocated, the liabilities must be paid. After creditors are paid, any remaining cash is divided among the partners according to their capital account balances. BOARDS' only liability at liquidation is $20,000 in accounts payable. The entries to record the payment to creditors and the final distribution of cash to partners follow:

Assets	= Liabilities	+ Equity
−20,000	−20,000	

Date	Account	Debit	Credit
Jan. 15	Accounts Payable	20,000	
	Cash		20,000
	To pay claims of creditors.		
Jan. 15	K. Zayn, Capital	72,000	
	H. Perez, Capital	68,000	
	T. Rasheed, Capital	64,000	
	Cash		204,000
	To distribute remaining cash to partners.		

Assets	= Liabilities	+ Equity
−204,000		−72,000
		−68,000
		−64,000

It is important to remember that the final cash payment is distributed to partners according to their capital account balances, whereas gains and losses from liquidation are allocated according to the income-and-loss-sharing ratio.

[1] The concepts behind these entries are not new. For example, assume that BOARDS has two noncash assets recorded as boarding facilities, $15,000, and land, $25,000. The entry to sell these assets for $46,000 is

Date	Account	Debit	Credit
Jan. 15	Cash	46,000	
	Boarding facilities		15,000
	Land		25,000
	Gain from Liquidation		6,000
	Sold noncash assets at a gain.		

We then record the allocation of any loss or gain (a gain in this case) from liquidation according to the partners' income-and-loss-sharing agreement as follows:

Date	Account	Debit	Credit
Jan. 15	Gain from Liquidation	6,000	
	K. Zayn, Capital		2,000
	H. Perez, Capital		2,000
	T. Rasheed, Capital		2,000
	To allocate liquidation gain to partners.		

Capital Deficiency

Capital deficiency means that at least one partner has a debit balance in his or her capital account at the point of final cash distribution. This can arise from liquidation losses, excessive withdrawals before liquidation, or recurring losses in prior periods. A partner with a capital deficiency must, if possible, cover the deficit by paying cash into the partnership.

To illustrate, assume that Zayn, Perez, and Rasheed operate their partnership in BOARDS for several years, sharing income and losses equally. The partners then decide to liquidate. Immediately prior to the final distribution of cash, the partners' recorded capital balances are Zayn, $19,000; Perez, $8,000; and Rasheed, $(3,000). Rasheed's capital deficiency means that Rasheed owes the partnership $3,000. Both Zayn and Perez have a legal claim against Rasheed's personal assets. The final distribution of cash in this case depends on how this capital deficiency is handled. Two possibilities exist.

Partner Pays Deficiency Rasheed is obligated to pay $3,000 into the partnership to cover the deficiency. If Rasheed is willing and able to pay, the entry to record receipt of payment from Rasheed follows:

Jan. 15	Cash	3,000	
	T. Rasheed, Capital		3,000
	To record payment of deficiency by Rasheed.		

Assets	= Liabilities +	Equity
+3,000		+3,000

After the $3,000 payment, the partners' capital balances are Zayn, $19,000; Perez, $8,000; and Rasheed, $0. The entry to record the final cash distributions to partners is

Jan. 15	K. Zayn, Capital	19,000	
	H. Perez, Capital	8,000	
	Cash		27,000
	To distribute remaining cash to partners.		

Assets	= Liabilities +	Equity
−27,000		−19,000
		−8,000

Partner Cannot Pay Deficiency The remaining partners with credit balances absorb any partner's unpaid deficiency according to their income-and-loss-sharing ratio. To illustrate, if Rasheed is unable to pay the $3,000 deficiency, Zayn and Perez absorb it. Since they share income and loss equally, Zayn and Perez each absorb $1,500 of the deficiency. This is recorded as follows:

Jan. 15	K. Zayn, Capital	1,500	
	H. Perez, Capital	1,500	
	T. Rasheed, Capital		3,000
	To transfer Rasheed deficiency to Zayn and Perez.		

Assets	= Liabilities +	Equity
		−1,500
		−1,500
		+3,000

After Zayn and Perez absorb Rasheed's deficiency, the capital accounts of the partners are Zayn, $17,500; Perez, $6,500; and Rasheed, $0. The entry to record the final cash distribution to the partners is

Jan. 15	K. Zayn, Capital	17,500	
	H. Perez, Capital	6,500	
	Cash		24,000
	To distribute remaining cash to partners.		

Assets	= Liabilities +	Equity
−24,000		−17,500
		−6,500

Rasheed's inability to cover this deficiency does not relieve Rasheed of the liability. If Rasheed becomes able to pay at a future date, Zayn and Perez can each collect $1,500 from Rasheed.

Decision Analysis — Partner Return on Equity

A1 Compute partner return on equity and use it to evaluate partnership performance.

An important role of partnership financial statements is to aid current and potential partners in evaluating partnership success compared with other opportunities. One measure of this success is the **partner return on equity** ratio:

$$\textbf{Partner return on equity} = \frac{\textbf{Partner net income}}{\textbf{Average partner equity}}$$

This measure is separately computed for each partner. To illustrate, Exhibit 12.4 reports selected data from the **Boston Celtics LP**. The return on equity for the *total* partnership is computed as $216/[($84 + $252)/2] = 128.6%. However, return on equity is quite different across the partners. For example, the **Boston Celtics LP I** partner return on equity is computed as $44/[($122 + $166)/2] = 30.6%, whereas the **Celtics LP** partner return on equity is computed as $111/[($270 + $333)/2] = 36.8%. Partner return on equity provides *each* partner an assessment of its return on its equity invested in the partnership. A specific partner often uses this return to decide whether additional investment or withdrawal of resources is best for that partner. Exhibit 12.4 reveals that year 2002 produced good returns for all partners (the Boston Celtics LP II return is not computed because its average equity is negative due to an unusual and large distribution in the prior year).

Exhibit 12.4

Selected Data from Boston Celtics LP

($ thousands)	Total	Boston Celtics LP I	Boston Celtics LP II	Celtics LP
Balance at June 30, 2001	$ 84	$122	$(307)	$270
Net income (loss) for year	216	44	61	111
Cash distribution	(48)	—	—	(48)
Balance at June 30, 2002	$252	$166	$(246)	$333
Partner return on equity	**128.6%**	**30.6%**	**n.a.**	**36.8%**

Demonstration Problem

The following transactions and events affect the partners' capital accounts in several successive partnerships. Prepare a table with six columns, one for each of the five partners along with a total column to show the effects of the following events on the five partners' capital accounts.

Part 1

4/13/2004 Ries and Bax create R&B Company. Each invests $10,000, and they agree to share income and losses equally.

12/31/2004 R&B Co. earns $15,000 in income for its first year. Ries withdraws $4,000 from the partnership, and Bax withdraws $7,000.

1/1/2005 Royce is made a partner in RB&R Company after contributing $12,000 cash. The partners agree that a 10% interest allowance will be given on each partner's beginning-year capital balance. In addition, Bax and Royce are to receive $5,000 salary allowances. The remainder of the income or loss is to be divided evenly.

12/31/2005 The partnership's income for the year is $40,000, and withdrawals at year-end are Ries, $5,000; Bax, $12,500; and Royce, $11,000.

1/1/2006 Ries sells her interest for $20,000 to Murdock, whom Bax and Royce accept as a partner in the new BR&M Co. Income or loss is to be shared equally after Bax and Royce each receives $25,000 salary allowances.

12/31/2006 The partnership's income for the year is $35,000, and year-end withdrawals are Bax, $2,500, and Royce, $2,000.

1/1/2007 Elway is admitted as a partner after investing $60,000 cash in the new Elway & Associates partnership. He is given a 50% interest in capital after the other partners transfer $3,000 to his account from each of theirs. A 20% interest allowance (on the beginning-year capital balances) will be used in sharing any income or loss, there will be no salary allowances, and Elway will receive 40% of the remaining balance—the other three partners will each get 20%.

12/31/2007 Elway & Associates earns $127,600 in income for the year, and year-end withdrawals are Bax, $25,000; Royce, $27,000; Murdock, $15,000; and Elway, $40,000.

1/1/2008 Elway buys out Bax and Royce for the balances of their capital accounts after a revaluation of the partnership assets. The revaluation gain is $50,000, which is divided in using a 1:1:1:2 ratio (Bax:Royce:Murdock:Elway). Elway pays the others from personal funds. Murdock and Elway will share income on a 1:9 ratio.

2/29/2008 The partnership earns $10,000 of income since the beginning of the year. Murdock retires and receives partnership cash equal to her capital balance. Elway takes possession of the partnership assets in his own name, and the company is dissolved.

Part 2

Journalize the events affecting the partnership for the year ended December 31, 2005.

Planning the Solution

- Evaluate each transaction's effects on the capital accounts of the partners.
- Each time a new partner is admitted or a partner withdraws, allocate any bonus based on the income-or-loss-sharing agreement.
- Each time a new partner is admitted or a partner withdraws, allocate subsequent net income or loss in accordance with the new partnership agreement.
- Prepare entries to (1) record Royce's initial investment; (2) record the allocation of interest, salaries, and remainder; (3) show the cash withdrawals from the partnership; and (4) close the withdrawal accounts on December 31, 2005.

Solution to Demonstration Problem

Part 1

Event	Ries	Bax	Royce	Murdock	Elway	Total
4/13/2004						
Initial Investment	$10,000	$10,000				$ 20,000
12/31/2004						
Income (equal)	7,500	7,500				15,000
Withdrawals	(4,000)	(7,000)				(11,000)
Ending balance	$13,500	$10,500				$ 24,000
1/1/2005						
New investment			$12,000			$ 12,000
12/31/2005						
10% interest	1,350	1,050	1,200			3,600
Salaries		5,000	5,000			10,000
Remainder (equal)	8,800	8,800	8,800			26,400
Withdrawals	(5,000)	(12,500)	(11,000)			(28,500)
Ending balance	$18,650	$12,850	$16,000			$ 47,500
1/1/2006						
Transfer interest	(18,650)			$18,650		$ 0
12/31/2006						
Salaries		25,000	25,000			50,000
Remainder (equal)		(5,000)	(5,000)	(5,000)		(15,000)
Withdrawals		(2,500)	(2,000)			(4,500)
Ending balance	$ 0	$30,350	$34,000	$13,650		$ 78,000
1/1/2007						
New investment					$ 60,000	60,000
Bonuses to Elway		(3,000)	(3,000)	(3,000)	9,000	0
Adjusted balance		$27,350	$31,000	$10,650	$ 69,000	$138,000

[continued on next page]

[continued from previous page]

12/31/2007					
20% interest	5,470	6,200	2,130	13,800	27,600
Remainder (1:1:1:2)	20,000	20,000	20,000	40,000	100,000
Withdrawals	(25,000)	(27,000)	(15,000)	(40,000)	(107,000)
Ending Balance	$27,820	$30,200	$17,780	$ 82,800	$158,600
1/1/2008					
Gain (1:1:1:2)	10,000	10,000	10,000	20,000	50,000
Adjusted balance	$37,820	$40,200	$27,780	$102,800	$208,600
Transfer interests	(37,820)	(40,200)		78,020	0
Adjusted balance	$ 0	$ 0	$27,780	$180,820	$208,600
2/29/2008					
Income (1:9)			1,000	9,000	10,000
Adjusted balance			$28,780	$189,820	$218,600
Settlements			(28,780)	(189,820)	(218,600)
Final balance			$ 0	$ 0	$ 0

Part 2

2005			
Jan. 1	Cash	12,000	
	Royce, Capital		12,000
	To record investment of Royce.		
Dec. 31	Income Summary	40,000	
	Ries, Capital		10,150
	Bax, Capital		14,850
	Royce, Capital		15,000
	To allocate interest, salaries, and remainders.		
Dec. 31	Ries, Withdrawals	5,000	
	Bax, Withdrawals	12,500	
	Royce, Withdrawals	11,000	
	Cash		28,500
	To record cash withdrawals by partners.		
Dec. 31	Ries, Capital	5,000	
	Bax, Capital	12,500	
	Royce, Capital	11,000	
	Ries, Withdrawals		5,000
	Bax, Withdrawals		12,500
	Royce, Withdrawals		11,000
	To close withdrawal accounts.		

Summary

C1 Identify characteristics of partnerships and similar organizations. Partnerships are voluntary associations, involve partnership agreements, have limited life, are not subject to income tax, include mutual agency, and have unlimited liability. Organizations that combine selected characteristics of partnerships and corporations include limited partnerships, limited liability partnerships, S corporations, and limited liability companies.

A1 Compute partner return on equity and use it to evaluate partnership performance. Partner return on equity provides each partner an assessment of his or her return on equity invested in the partnership.

P1 Prepare entries for partnership formation. A partner's initial investment is recorded at the market value of the assets contributed to the partnership.

P2 Allocate and record income and loss among partners. A partnership agreement should specify how to allocate partnership income or loss among partners. Allocation can be based on a stated ratio, capital balances, or salary and interest allowances to compensate partners for differences in their service and capital contributions.

P3 Account for the admission and withdrawal of partners. When a new partner buys a partnership interest directly from one or more existing partners, the amount of cash paid from one partner to another does not affect the partnership total recorded equity. When a new partner purchases equity by investing additional assets in the partnership, the new partner's investment can yield a bonus either to existing partners or to the new partner. The entry to record a withdrawal can involve payment from either (1) the existing partners' personal assets or (2) partnership assets. The latter can yield a bonus to either the withdrawing or remaining partners.

P4 **Prepare entries for partnership liquidation.** When a partnership is liquidated, losses and gains from selling partnership assets are allocated to the partners according to their income-and-loss-sharing ratio. If a partner's capital account has a deficiency that the partner cannot pay, the other partners share the deficit according to their relative income-and-loss-sharing ratio.

Guidance Answer to **Decision Ethics**

Financial Planner The partnership agreement apparently fails to mention liabilities or use the term *net assets.* To give the estate one-third of total assets is not fair to the remaining partners because if the partner had lived and the partners had decided to liquidate, the liabilities would need to be paid out of assets before any liquidation. Also, a settlement based on the deceased partner's recorded equity would fail to recognize excess of current value over book value. This value increase would be realized if the partnership were liquidated. A fair settlement would seem to be a payment to the estate for the balance of the deceased partner's equity based on the *current value of net assets.*

Guidance Answers to **Quick Checks**

1. (*b*)
2. *Unlimited liability* means that the creditors of a partnership require each partner to be personally responsible for all partnership debts.
3. (*c*)
4.

	Denzel	Shantell	Total
Net Income			$40,000
Interest allowance (10%)	$ 7,000	$ 3,500	10,500
Balance of income	↓	↓	**$29,500**
Balance allocated equally	14,750	14,750	29,500
Balance of income			$ 0
Income of partners	**$21,750**	**$18,250**	

Key Terms

Key Terms are available at the book's Website for learning and testing in an online Flashcard Format.

C corporation (p. 470)
General partner (p. 469)
General partnership (p. 469)
Limited liability company (LLC) (p. 470)
Limited liability partnership (p. 469)
Limited partners (p. 469)
Limited partnership (p. 469)
Mutual agency (p. 469)
Partner return on equity (p. 480)
Partnership (p. 468)
Partnership contract (p. 468)
Partnership liquidation (p. 478)
S corporation (p. 470)
Statement of partners' equity (p. 473)
Unlimited liability (p. 469)

Personal Interactive Quiz

Personal Interactive Quizzes A and B are available at the book's Website to reinforce and assess your learning.

Discussion Questions

1. If a partnership contract does not state the period of time the partnership is to exist, when does the partnership end?
2. What does the term *mutual agency* mean when applied to a partnership?
3. Can partners limit the right of a partner to commit their partnership to contracts? Would such an agreement be binding (*a*) on the partners and (*b*) on outsiders?

4. Assume that Amey and Lacey are partners. Lacey dies, and her son claims the right to take his mother's place in the partnership. Does he have this right? Why or why not?
5. Assume that the Barnes and Ardmore partnership agreement provides for a two-third/one-third sharing of income but says nothing about losses. The first year of partnership operation resulted in a loss, and Barnes argues that the loss should be shared equally because the partnership agreement said nothing about sharing losses. Is Barnes correct? Explain.
6. Allocation of partnership income among the partners appears on what financial statement?
7. What does the term *unlimited liability* mean when it is applied to partnership members?
8. How does a general partnership differ from a limited partnership?
9. George, Burton, and Dillman have been partners for three years. The partnership is being dissolved. George is leaving the firm, but Burton and Dillman plan to carry on the business. In the final settlement, George places a $75,000 salary claim against the partnership. He contends that he has a claim for a salary of $25,000 for each year because he devoted all of his time for three years to the affairs of the partnership. Is his claim valid? Why or why not?
10. Kay, Kat, and Kim are partners. In a liquidation, Kay's share of partnership losses exceeds her capital account balance. Moreover, she is unable to meet the deficit from her personal assets, and her partners shared the excess losses. Does this relieve Kay of liability?
11. After all partnership assets have been converted to cash and all liabilities paid, the remaining cash should equal the sum of the balances of the partners' capital accounts. Why?
12. Assume a partner withdraws from a partnership and receives assets of greater value than the book value of his equity. Should the remaining partners share the resulting reduction in their equities in the ratio of their relative capital balances or according to their income-and-loss-sharing ratio?

Red numbers denote Discussion Questions that involve decision-making.

***Homework Manager** repeats all numerical Quick Studies on the book's Website with new numbers.*

QUICK STUDY

QS 12-1
Partnership liability
C1

Kent and Davis are partners in operating a store. Without consulting Kent, Davis enters into a contract to purchase merchandise for the store. Kent contends that he did not authorize the order and refuses to pay for it. The vendor sues the partners for the contract price of the merchandise. (*a*) Must the partnership pay for the merchandise? Why? (*b*) Does your answer differ if Kent and Davis are partners in a public accounting firm?

QS 12-2
Partnership income allocation
P2

Ann Keeley and Susie Norton are partners in a business they started two years ago. The partnership agreement states that Keeley should receive a salary allowance of $30,000 and that Norton should receive a $40,000 salary allowance. Any remaining income or loss is to be shared equally. Determine each partner's share of the current year's net income of $104,000.

QS 12-3
Partnership income allocation
P2

Jakes and Ness are partners who agree that Jakes will receive a $50,000 salary allowance and that any remaining income or loss will be shared equally. If Ness's capital account is credited for $1,000 as his share of the net income in a given period, how much net income did the partnership earn in that period?

QS 12-4
Liability in limited partnerships
P1

Lamb organized a limited partnership and is the only general partner. Maxi invested $20,000 in the partnership and was admitted as a limited partner with the understanding that he would receive 10% of the profits. After two unprofitable years, the partnership ceased doing business. At that point, partnership liabilities were $85,000 larger than partnership assets. How much money can the partnership's creditors obtain from Maxi's personal assets to satisfy the unpaid partnership debts?

QS 12-5
Partner admission through purchase of interest P3

Mintz agrees to pay Bogg and Meyer $10,000 each for a one-third (33⅓%) interest in the Bogg and Meyer partnership. Immediately prior to Mintz's admission, each partner had a $30,000 capital balance. Make the journal entry to record Mintz's purchase of the partners' interest.

QS 12-6
Admission of a partner P3

Jones and Jordan are partners, each with $30,000 in their partnership capital accounts. Holly is admitted to the partnership by investing $30,000 cash. Make the entry to show Holly's admission to the partnership.

QS 12-7
Partner return on equity
A1 

Gilson and Lott's company is organized as a partnership. At the prior year-end, partnership equity totaled $300,000 ($200,000 from Gilson and $100,000 from Lott). For the current year, partnership net income is $50,000 ($40,000 allocated to Gilson and $10,000 allocated to Lott), and year-end total partnership equity is $400,000 ($280,000 from Gilson and $120,000 from Lott). Compute the total partnership return on equity *and* the individual partner return on equity ratios.

***Homework Manager** repeats all numerical Exercises on the book's Website with new numbers.*

EXERCISES

Exercise 12-1
Characteristics of partnerships
C1

Next to the following list of eight characteristics of business organizations, write a brief description of how each characteristic applies to general partnerships.

Characteristic	Application to General Partnerships
1. Life	
2. Owners' liability	
3. Legal status	
4. Tax status of income	
5. Owners' authority	
6. Ease of formation	
7. Transferability of ownership	
8. Ability to raise large amounts of capital	

Exercise 12-2
Forms of organization
C1  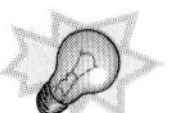

For each of the following separate cases, recommend a form of business organization. With each recommendation, explain how business income would be taxed if the owners adopt the form of organization recommended. Also list several advantages that the owners will enjoy from the form of business organization that you recommend.

a. Ross, Jenks, and Keim are recent college graduates in computer science. They want to start a Website development company. They all have college debts and currently do not own any substantial computer equipment needed to get the company started.

b. Dr. Langholz and Dr. Clark are recent graduates from medical residency programs. Both are family practice physicians and would like to open a clinic in an underserved rural area. Although neither has any funds to bring to the new venture, a banker has expressed interest in making a loan to provide start-up funds for their practice.

c. Milan has been out of school for about five years and has become quite knowledgeable about the commercial real estate market. He would like to organize a company that buys and sells real estate. Milan believes he has the expertise to manage the company but needs funds to invest in commercial property.

Exercise 12-3
Journalizing partnership transactions
P2 

On March 1, 2005, Abbey and Adams formed a partnership. Abbey contributed $88,000 cash and Adams contributed land valued at $70,000 and a building valued at $100,000. The partnership also assumed responsibility for Adams's $80,000 long-term note payable associated with the land and building. The partners agreed to share income as follows: Abbey is to receive an annual salary allowance of $30,000, both are to receive an annual interest allowance of 10% of their beginning-year capital investment, and any remaining income or loss is to be shared equally. On October 20, 2005, Abbey withdrew $32,000 cash and Adams withdrew $25,000 cash. After the adjusting and closing entries are made to the revenue and expense accounts at December 31, 2005, the Income Summary account had a credit balance of $79,000.

1. Prepare journal entries to record (*a*) the partners' initial capital investments, (*b*) their cash withdrawals, and (*c*) the December 31 closing of both the Withdrawals and Income Summary accounts.

2. Determine the balances of the partners' capital accounts as of December 31, 2005.

Check (2) Adams, $89,600

Exercise 12-4
Income allocation in a partnership
P2  

Cosmo and Ellis began a partnership by investing $50,000 and $75,000, respectively. During its first year, the partnership earned $165,000. Prepare calculations showing how the $165,000 income should be allocated to the partners under each of the following three separate plans for sharing income and loss: (1) the partners failed to agree on a method to share income; (2) the partners agreed to share income and loss in proportion to their initial investments (round proportions to the nearest hundredth);

and (3) the partners agreed to share income by granting a $55,000 per year salary allowance to Cosmo, a $45,000 per year salary allowance to Ellis, 10% interest on their initial capital investments, and the remaining balance shared equally.

Check Plan 3, Cosmo, $86,250

Exercise 12-5
Income allocation in a partnership
P2

Check (2) Cosmo, $(4,100)

Assume that the partners of Exercise 12-4 agreed to share net income and loss by granting annual salary allowances of $55,000 to Cosmo and $45,000 to Ellis, 10% interest allowances on their investments, and any remaining balance shared equally.

1. Determine the partners' shares of Cosmo and Ellis given a first-year net income of $94,400.

2. Determine the partners' shares of Cosmo and Ellis given a first-year net loss of $15,700.

Exercise 12-6
Sale of partnership interest P3

The partners in the Biz Partnership have agreed that partner Madonna may sell her $90,000 equity in the partnership to Streisand, for which Streisand will pay Madonna $75,000. Present the partnership's journal entry to record the sale of Madonna's interest to Streisand on September 30.

Exercise 12-7
Admission of new partner

P3

The Treed Partnership has total partners' equity of $510,000, which is made up of Elm, Capital, $400,000, and Oak, Capital, $110,000. The partners share net income and loss in a ratio of 80% to Elm and 20% to Oak. On November 1, Ash is admitted to the partnership and given a 15% interest in equity and a 15% share in any income and loss. Prepare the journal entry to record the admission of Ash under each of the following separate assumptions: Ash invests cash of (1) $90,000; (2) $125,000; and (3) $60,000.

Exercise 12-8
Retirement of partner
P3

Holland, Flowers, and Tulip have been partners while sharing net income and loss in a 5:3:2 ratio. On January 31, the date Tulip retires from the partnership, the equities of the partners are Holland, $350,000; Flowers, $240,000; and Tulip, $180,000. Present journal entries to record Tulip's retirement under each of the following separate assumptions: Tulip is paid for her equity using partnership cash of (1) $180,000; (2) $200,000; and (3) $150,000.

Exercise 12-9
Liquidation of partnership

P4

Check (1) Red, $(5,000)

The Red, White & Blue partnership was begun with investments by the partners as follows: Red, $175,000; White, $220,000; and Blue, $205,000. The operations did not go well, and the partners eventually decided to liquidate the partnership, sharing all losses equally. On August 31, after all assets were converted to cash and all creditors were paid, only $60,000 in partnership cash remained.

1. Compute the capital account balance of each partner after the liquidation of assets and the payment of creditors.

2. Assume that any partner with a deficit agrees to pay cash to the partnership to cover the deficit. Present the journal entries on August 31 to record (*a*) the cash receipt from the deficient partner(s) and (*b*) the final disbursement of cash to the partners.

3. Assume that any partner with a deficit is not able to reimburse the partnership. Present journal entries (*a*) to transfer the deficit of any deficient partners to the other partners and (*b*) to record the final disbursement of cash to the partners.

Exercise 12-10
Liquidation of partnership P4

Check (b) Lee, Capital after allocation, $(10,900)

Tuttle, Ritter, and Lee are partners who share income and loss in a 1:4:5 ratio. After lengthy disagreements among the partners and several unprofitable periods, the partners decided to liquidate the partnership. Immediately before liquidation, the partnership balance sheet shows: total assets, $116,000; total liabilities, $88,000; Tuttle, Capital, $1,200; Ritter, Capital, $11,700; and Lee, Capital, $15,100. The cash proceeds from selling the assets were sufficient to repay all but $24,000 to the creditors. (*a*) Calculate the loss from selling the assets. (*b*) Allocate the loss to the partners. (*c*) Determine how much of the remaining liability should be paid by each partner.

Exercise 12-11
Liquidation of limited partnership
P4

Assume that the Tuttle, Ritter, and Lee partnership of Exercise 12-10 is a limited partnership. Tuttle and Ritter are general partners and Lee is a limited partner. How much of the remaining $24,000 liability should be paid by each partner?

Exercise 12-12
Partner return on equity
A1

Hunt Sports Enterprises LP is organized as a limited partnership consisting of two individual partners: Soccer LP and Football LP. Both partners separately operate a minor league soccer team and a semipro football team. Compute partner return on equity for each limited partnership (and the total) for the year ended June 30, 2005, using the following selected data on partner capital balances from Hunt Sports Enterprises LP:

	Soccer LP	Football LP	Total
Balance at 6/30/04	$378,000	$1,516,000	$1,894,000
Annual net income	44,268	891,796	936,064
Cash distribution	—	(100,000)	(100,000)
Balance at 6/30/05	$422,268	$2,307,796	$2,730,064

PROBLEM SET A

Problem 12-1A
Allocating partnership income
P2

Kim Ries, Tere Bax, and Josh Thomas invested $40,000, $56,000, and $64,000, respectively, in a partnership. During its first calendar-year, the firm earned $124,500.

Required

Prepare the entry to close the firm's Income Summary account as of its December 31 year-end and to allocate the $124,500 net income to the partners under each of the following separate assumptions: The partners (1) have no agreement on the method of sharing income and loss; (2) agreed to share income and loss in the ratio of their beginning capital investments; and (3) agreed to share income and loss by providing annual salary allowances of $33,000 to Ries, $28,000 to Bax, and $40,000 to Thomas; granting 10% interest on the partners' beginning capital investments; and sharing the remainder equally.

Check (3) Thomas, Capital, $48,900

Problem 12-2A
Allocating partnership income and loss; sequential years
P2

Rex Baker and Ty Farney are forming a partnership to which Baker will devote one-half time and Farney will devote full time. They have discussed the following alternative plans for sharing income and loss: (*a*) in the ratio of their initial capital investments, which they have agreed will be $21,000 for Baker and $31,500 for Farney; (*b*) in proportion to the time devoted to the business; (*c*) a salary allowance of $3,000 per month to Farney and the balance in accordance with the ratio of their initial capital investments; or (*d*) a salary allowance of $3,000 per month to Farney, 10% interest on their initial capital investments, and the balance shared equally. The partners expect the business to perform as follows: Year 1, $18,000 net loss; Year 2, $45,000 net income; and Year 3, $75,000 net income.

Required

Prepare three tables with the following column headings:

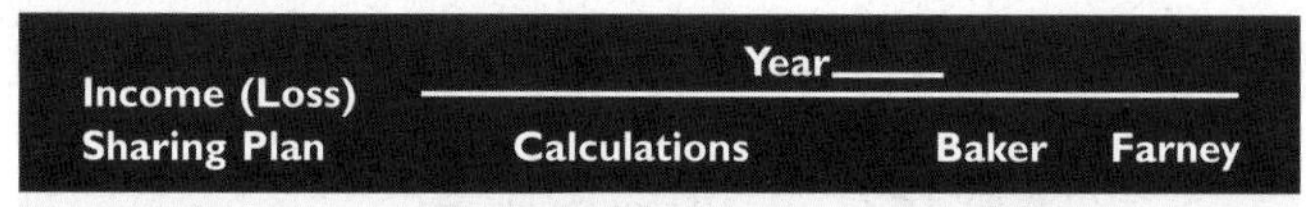

Income (Loss) Sharing Plan	Year____ Calculations	Baker	Farney

Complete the tables, one for each of the first three years, by showing how to allocate partnership income or loss to the partners under each of the four plans being considered. (Round answers to the nearest whole dollar.)

Check Plan d, Year 1, Farney's share, $9,525

Problem 12-3A
Partnership income allocation, statement of partners' equity, and closing entries
P2

Bill Beck, Ron Beck, and Barb Beck formed the BRB Partnership by making capital contributions of $183,750, $131,250, and $210,000, respectively. They predict annual partnership net income of $225,000 and are considering the following alternative plans of sharing income and loss: (*a*) equally; (*b*) in the ratio of their initial capital investments; or (*c*) salary allowances of $40,000 to Bill, $30,000 to Ron, and $45,000 to Barb; interest allowances of 10% on their initial capital investments; and the balance shared equally.

Required

1. Prepare a table with the following column headings:

Income (Loss) Sharing Plan	Calculations	Bill	Ron	Barb	Total

Use the table to show how to distribute net income of $225,000 for the calendar year under each of the alternative plans being considered. (Round answers to the nearest whole dollar.)

Check (2) Barb, Ending Capital, $223,000

2. Prepare a statement of partners' equity showing the allocation of income to the partners assuming they agree to use plan (*c*), that income earned is $104,500, and that Bill, Ron, and Barb withdraw $17,000, $24,000, and $32,000, respectively, at year-end.

3. Prepare the December 31 journal entry to close Income Summary assuming they agree to use plan (*c*) and that net income is $104,500. Also close the withdrawals accounts.

Problem 12-4A
Partner withdrawal and admission

P3

Part 1. Goering, Gore, and Schmit are partners and share income and loss in a 3:2:5 ratio. The partnership's capital balances are as follows: Goering, $84,000; Gore, $69,000; and Schmit, $147,000. Gore decides to withdraw from the partnership, and the partners agree to not have the assets revalued upon Gore's retirement. Prepare journal entries to record Gore's February 1 withdrawal from the partnership under each of the following separate assumptions: Gore (*a*) sells his interest to Getz for $80,000 after Goering and Schmit approve the entry of Getz as a partner; (*b*) gives his interest to a son-in-law, Swanson, and thereafter Goering and Schmit accept Swanson as a partner; (*c*) is paid $69,000 in partnership cash for his equity; (*d*) is paid $107,000 in partnership cash for his equity; and (*e*) is paid $15,000 in partnership cash plus equipment recorded on the partnership books at $35,000 less its accumulated depreciation of $11,600.

Check (1e) Cr. Schmit, Capital, $19,125

(2c) Cr. Gore, Capital, $4,650

Part 2. Assume that Gore does not retire from the partnership described in Part 1. Instead, Ford is admitted to the partnership on February 1 with a 25% equity. Prepare journal entries to record Ford's entry into the partnership under each of the following separate assumptions: Ford invests (*a*) $100,000; (*b*) $72,500; and (*c*) $131,000.

Problem 12-5A
Liquidation of a partnership

P4

Quick, Drake, and Sage share income and loss in a 3:2:1 ratio. The partners have decided to liquidate their partnership. On the day of liquidation their balance sheet appears as follows:

QUICK, DRAKE, AND SAGE
Balance Sheet
May 31

Assets		Liabilities and Equity	
Cash	$ 90,400	Accounts payable	$122,750
Inventory	268,600	Quick, Capital	46,500
		Drake, Capital	106,250
		Sage, Capital	83,500
Total assets	$359,000	Total liabilities and equity	$359,000

Required

Prepare journal entries for (*a*) the sale of inventory, (*b*) the allocation of its gain or loss, (*c*) the payment of liabilities at book value, and (*d*) the distribution of cash in each of the following four separate cases: Inventory is sold for (1) $300,000; (2) $250,000; (3) $160,000 and any partners with capital deficits pay in the amount of their deficits; and (4) $125,000 and the partners have no assets other than those invested in the partnership. (Round to the nearest dollar.)

Check (4) Cash distribution, Sage, $51,134

PROBLEM SET B

Problem 12-1B
Allocating partnership income

P2

Matt Albin, Ryan Peters, and Seth Ramsey invested $82,000, $49,200, and $32,800, respectively, in a partnership. During its first calendar-year, the firm earned $135,000.

Required

Prepare the entry to close the firm's Income Summary account as of its December 31 year-end and to allocate the $135,000 net income to the partners under each of the following separate assumptions. (Round answers to whole dollars.) The partners (1) have no agreement on the method of sharing income and loss; (2) agreed to share income and loss in the ratio of their beginning capital investments; and (3) agreed to share income and loss by providing annual salary allowances of $48,000 to Albin, $36,000 to Peters, and $25,000 to Ramsey; granting 10% interest on the partners' beginning capital investments; and sharing the remainder equally.

Check (3) Ramsey, Capital, $31,480

Problem 12-2B
Allocating partnership income and loss; sequential years

P2

Maria Barto and J. R. Black are forming a partnership to which Barto will devote one-third time and Black will devote full time. They have discussed the following alternative plans for sharing income and loss: (*a*) in the ratio of their initial capital investments, which they have agreed will be $52,000 for Barto and $78,000 for Black; (*b*) in proportion to the time devoted to the business; (*c*) a salary allowance of $2,000 per month to Black and the balance in accordance with the ratio of their initial capital investments; or (*d*) a salary allowance of $2,000 per month to Black, 10% interest on their initial capital investments, and the balance shared equally. The partners expect the business to perform as follows: Year 1, $18,000 net loss; Year 2, $38,000 net income; and Year 3, $94,000 net income.

Required

Prepare three tables with the following column headings:

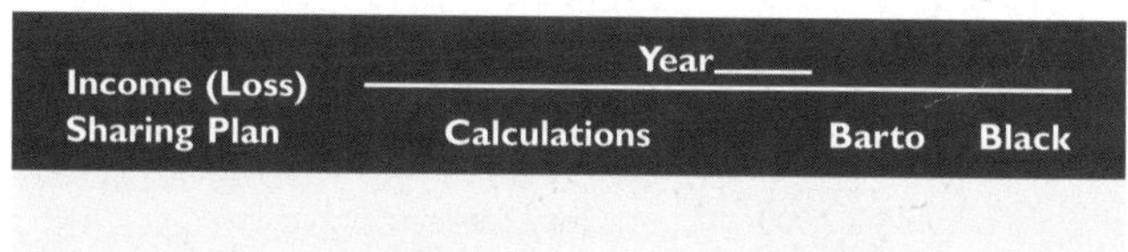

Income (Loss) Sharing Plan	Year____ Calculations	Barto	Black

Complete the tables, one for each of the first three years, by showing how to allocate partnership income or loss to the partners under each of the four plans being considered. (Round answers to the nearest whole dollar.)

Check Plan d, Year 1, Black's share, $4,300

Problem 12-3B
Partnership income allocation, statement of partners' equity, and closing entries

P2

Staci Cook, Lin Xi, and Kevin Schwartz formed the CXS Partnership by making capital contributions of $72,000, $108,000, and $60,000, respectively. They predict annual partnership net income of $120,000 and are considering the following alternative plans of sharing income and loss: (*a*) equally; (*b*) in the ratio of their initial capital investments; or (*c*) salary allowances of $20,000 to Cook, $15,000 to Xi, and $40,000 to Schwartz; interest allowances of 12% on their initial capital investments; and the balance shared equally.

Required

1. Prepare a table with the following column headings:

Income (Loss) Sharing Plan	Calculations	Cook	Xi	Schwartz	Total

   Use the table to show how to distribute net income of $120,000 for the calendar year under each of the alternative plans being considered. (Round answers to the nearest whole dollar.)
2. Prepare a statement of partners' equity showing the allocation of income to the partners assuming they agree to use plan (*c*), that income earned is $43,800, and that Cook, Xi, and Schwartz withdraw $9,000, $19,000, and $12,000, respectively, at year-end.
3. Prepare the December 31 journal entry to close Income Summary assuming they agree to use plan (*c*) and that net income is $43,800. Also close the withdrawals accounts.

Check (2) Schwartz, Ending Capital, $75,200

Problem 12-4B
Partner withdrawal and admission
P3

Part 1. Gibbs, Gier, and Gill are partners and share income and loss in a 5:1:4 ratio. The partnership's capital balances are as follows: Gibbs, $303,000; Gier, $74,000; and Gill, $223,000. Gibbs decides to withdraw from the partnership, and the partners agree not to have the assets revalued upon Gibbs's retirement. Prepare journal entries to record Gibbs's April 30 withdrawal from the partnership under each of the following separate assumptions: Gibbs (*a*) sells her interest to Grady for $250,000 after Gier and Gill approve the entry of Grady as a partner; (*b*) gives her interest to a daughter-in-law, Gannon, and thereafter Gier and Gill accept Gannon as a partner; (*c*) is paid $303,000 in partnership cash for her equity; (*d*) is paid $175,000 in partnership cash for her equity; and (*e*) is paid $100,000 in partnership cash plus manufacturing equipment recorded on the partnership books at $269,000 less its accumulated depreciation of $168,000.

Check (1e) Cr. Gill, Capital, $81,600

Part 2. Assume that Gibbs does not retire from the partnership described in Part 1. Instead, Grise is admitted to the partnership on April 30 with a 20% equity. Prepare journal entries to record the entry of Grise under each of the following separate assumptions: Grise invests (*a*) $150,000; (*b*) $98,000; and (*c*) $213,000.

(2c) Cr. Gier, Capital, $5,040

Problem 12-5B
Liquidation of a partnership
P4

Rasure, Ramirez, and Roney, who share income and loss in a 2:1:2 ratio, plan to liquidate their partnership. At liquidation, their balance sheet appears as follows:

RASURE, RAMIREZ, AND RONEY
Balance Sheet
January 18

Assets		Liabilities and Equity	
Cash	$174,300	Accounts payable	$171,300
Equipment	308,600	Rasure, Capital	150,200
		Ramirez, Capital	97,900
		Roney, Capital	63,500
Total assets	$482,900	Total liabilities and equity	$482,900

Required

Prepare journal entries for (*a*) the sale of equipment, (*b*) the allocation of its gain or loss, (*c*) the payment of liabilities at book value, and (*d*) the distribution of cash in each of the following four separate cases: Equipment is sold for (1) $325,000; (2) $265,000; (3) $100,000 and any partners with capital deficits pay in the amount of their deficits; and (4) $75,000 and the partners have no assets other than those invested in the partnership.

Check (4) Cash distribution, Rasure, $36,800

PROBLEM SET C

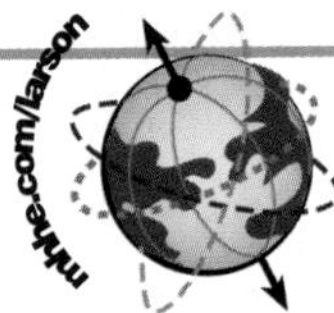

Problem Set C is available at the book's Website to further reinforce and assess your learning.

SERIAL PROBLEM

Success Systems

At the start of 2005, Kay Breeze is considering adding a partner to her business. She envisions the new partner taking the lead in generating sales of both services and merchandise for Success Systems. Kay Breeze's equity in Success Systems as of January 1, 2005, is reflected in the following capital balance:

K. Breeze, Capital	$90,148

Required

1. Breeze is evaluating whether the prospective partner should be an equal partner with respect to capital investment and profit sharing (1:1) or whether the agreement should be 3:1 with Breeze retaining three-fourths interest with rights to three-fourths of the profits. What factors should she consider in deciding which partnership agreement to offer?

2. Prepare the January 1, 2005, journal entry(ies) necessary to admit a new partner to Success Systems through the purchase of a partnership interest for each of the following two separate cases (*a*) 1:1 sharing agreement and (*b*) 3:1 sharing agreement.
3. Prepare the January 1, 2005, journal entry(ies) required to admit a new partner if the new partner invests cash of $30,050.
4. After posting the entry in part 3, what would be the new partner's equity percentage?

BEYOND THE NUMBERS

REPORTING IN ACTION

C1 

BTN 12-1 Take a step back in time and imagine **Krispy Kreme** in its infancy as a company. The year is 1937.

Required

1. Read the history of Krispy Kreme at KrispyKreme.com/history.html. Can you determine from its history whether it was originally organized as a sole proprietorship, partnership, or corporation?
2. Assume that Krispy Kreme was originally organized as a partnership. Krispy Kreme's income statement in Appendix A varies in several key ways from what it would look like for a partnership. Explain how a corporate income statement differs from a partnership income statement.
3. Compare the Krispy Kreme balance sheet in Appendix A to what a partnership balance sheet would have shown in 1937. Identify and explain any account differences you would anticipate.

COMPARATIVE ANALYSIS

C1  

BTN 12-2 Over the years **Krispy Kreme** and **Tastykake** have evolved into large corporations. Today it is difficult to imagine them as fledgling start-ups. Research each company's history online.

Required

1. Which company is older?
2. Which company was named by the founder's wife after tasting the first bakery samples?
3. Which company first sold its cakes for $0.10 each and had $28 in sales on the first day of business?
4. Which company has developed more of a global presence?
5. Which company had its first initial public offering of stock in April 2000?

ETHICS CHALLENGE

P2 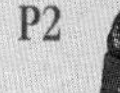 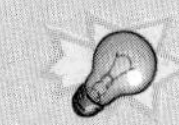

BTN 12-3 Doctors Maben, Orlando, and Clark have been in a group practice for several years. Maben and Orlando are family practice physicians, and Clark is a general surgeon. Clark receives many referrals for surgery from his family practice partners. Upon the partnership's original formation, the three doctors agreed to a two-part formula to share income. Every month each doctor receives a salary allowance of $3,000. Additional income is divided according to a percent of patient charges the doctors generate for the month. In the current month, Maben generated 10% of the billings, Orlando 30%, and Clark 60%. The group's income for this month is $50,000. Clark has expressed dissatisfaction with the income-sharing formula and asks that income be split entirely on patient charge percents.

Required

1. Compute the income allocation for the current month using the original agreement.
2. Compute the income allocation for the current month using Clark's proposed agreement.
3. Identify the ethical components of this partnership decision for the doctors.

COMMUNICATING IN PRACTICE

C1

BTN 12-4 Assume that you are studying for an upcoming accounting exam with a good friend. Your friend says that she has a solid understanding of general partnerships but is less sure that she understands organizations that combine certain characteristics of partnerships with other forms of business organization. You offer to make some study notes for your friend to help her learn about limited partnerships, limited liability partnerships, S Corporations, and limited liability companies. Prepare a one-page set of well-organized, complete study notes on these four forms of business organization.

TAKING IT TO THE NET

P1 P2

mhhe.com/larson

BTN 12-5 Access the September 27, 2002, filing of the June 30, 2002, 10-K report for **Henley Limited Partnership** (formerly the Boston Celtics Limited Partnership) at www.SEC.gov.

Required

1. Locate the June 30, 2002, balance sheet for the Boston Celtics Limited Partnership. List the account titles used in the equity section of this balance sheet.
2. How many units of limited partnership interest are authorized, issued, and outstanding as of June 30, 2002?
3. What are the equity balances of the general partners and limited partners as of June 30, 2002?
4. What is the partnership's largest asset and its amount as of June 30, 2002?

TEAMWORK IN ACTION

P2

BTN 12-6 This activity requires teamwork to reinforce understanding of accounting for partnerships.

Required

1. Assume that Baker, Warner, and Rice form the BWR Partnership by making capital contributions of \$200,000, \$300,000, and \$500,000, respectively. BWR predicts annual partnership net income of \$600,000. The partners are considering various plans for sharing income and loss. Assign a different team member to compute how the projected \$600,000 income would be shared under each of the following separate plans:
   a. Shared equally.
   b. In the ratio of the partners' initial capital investments.
   c. Salary allowances of \$50,000 to Baker, \$60,000 to Warner, and \$70,000 to Rice, with the remaining balance shared equally.
   d. Interest allowances of 10% on the partners' initial capital investments, with the remaining balance shared equally.
2. In sequence, each member is to present his or her income-sharing calculations with the team.
3. As a team, identify and discuss at least one other possible way that income could be shared.

BUSINESS WEEK ACTIVITY

C1

mhhe.com/larson

BTN 12-7 Read the article "Take Me Online to the Ball Game," in the April 9, 2001, issue of *Business Week*. (This book's Website provides a free link.)

Required

1. What is the business relation between **Major League Baseball** (MLB) and **MLB.com**?
2. Based on your reading of the article, who are the limited partners of MLB.com?
3. What does the media analyst quoted in the article think of MLB.com's self-sufficient strategy?
4. Why do MLB.com executives think they can be successful?
5. Does the article lend any insight into the profit-sharing formula for MLB.com? Explain.

ENTREPRENEURIAL DECISION

C1

BTN 12-8 Revisit the chapter's opening feature involving Michael Koch and his company **Koch Entertainment LLC**. Assume that Koch has decided to organize all future business endeavors with artists as general partnerships.

Required

1. What details should Koch and his future partners specify in their general partnership agreements?
2. What advantages should Koch and his future partners be aware of with respect to organizing as general partnerships?
3. What disadvantages should Koch and his future partners be aware of with respect to organizing as general partnerships?

BTN 12-9 Access **Grupo Bimbo**'s Website at GrupoBimbo.com. Research the history, philosophy, and commitments of the company using the "about Grupo Bimbo" link.

GLOBAL DECISION

C1

Required

1. Grupo Bimbo was founded when and where?
2. Can you determine its original form of business organization from reading its company history?
3. What commitment does Grupo Bimbo have toward social responsibility?
4. When was Grupo Bimbo first listed on the Mexican Stock Exchange (Bolsa Mexica Valores)? (*Hint:* See company FAQs under the "about Grupo Bimbo" link.)
5. Why doesn't Grupo Bimbo trade its stock abroad?

"Turning a profit to me is getting the dolls into the hands of kids"—Julz Chavez

13 Accounting for Corporations

A Look Back

Chapter 12 focused on the partnership form of organization. We described crucial characteristics of partnerships and the accounting and reporting of their important transactions.

A Look at This Chapter

This chapter emphasizes details of the corporate form of organization. The accounting concepts and procedures for equity transactions are explained. We also describe how to report and analyze income, earnings per share, and retained earnings.

A Look Ahead

Chapter 14 focuses on long-term liabilities. We explain how to value, record, amortize, and report these liabilities in financial statements.

CAP

Conceptual

C1 Identify characteristics of corporations and their organization. *(p. 496)*

C2 Describe the components of stockholders' equity. *(p. 499)*

C3 Explain characteristics of common and preferred stock. *(p. 503)*

C4 Explain the form and content of a complete income statement. *(p. 512)*

C5 Explain the items reported in retained earnings. *(p. 516)*

Analytical

A1 Compute earnings per share and describe this ratio's use. *(p. 514)*

A2 Compute book value and explain its use in analysis. *(p. 518)*

A3 Compute dividend yield and explain its use in analysis. *(p. 519)*

A4 Compute price-earnings ratio and describe its use in analysis. *(p. 519)*

Procedural

P1 Record the issuance of corporate stock. *(p. 500)*

P2 Distribute dividends between common stock and preferred stock. *(p. 503)*

P3 Record transactions involving cash dividends. *(p. 506)*

P4 Account for stock dividends and stock splits. *(p. 507)*

P5 Record purchases and sales of treasury stock and the retirement of stock. *(p. 510)*

Decision Feature

Real Girls Invade Corporate World

SAN FRANCISCO—The daughter of a migrant farmworker, Julz Chavez grew up with handmade toys. The oldest of 11 children, Chavez dreamed of making her own dolls—ones that looked like her. "If your skin is darker, your lips are fuller, and your body's fuller," says Chavez, "you look at the usual dolls and think 'I don't look like that.'" Three decades later, Chavez is an entrepreneur and founder of **Get Real Girl, Inc. (GetRealGirl.com),** a start-up corporation that produces ethnically diverse, active, and intelligent dolls. Skylar is Asian-American, Gabi is Brazilian, and Nakia is African-American; they travel the world with interesting stories to tell.

Chavez's road to the corporate world is a story in itself. She endured the usual moves of a migrant family working in southwestern United States. Still, she was able to graduate and land jobs as an idea person for several toy companies. The jobs frustrated Chavez. She faced the prevailing notion that girls wanted pink, "feminine" toys—like Barbie. So she took a job with Barbie's company, Mattel. "I thought, 'I'm going to change this—I'm going to go work for the biggest toy company in the world.'" Again she met resistance and finally quit to launch her own corporation.

With little money, Chavez struggled to get financial backing. Investors "wanted to see that you're successful, but without the money, you can't be successful," says Chavez. She also had to contend with corporate formation, organization form, capital stock, stock issuance, and various other accounting-related, corporate issues. Still, Chavez persisted. "I'm the outcome of that [worker] struggle to get out of the fields and into business," she says. She was determined "to make real change."

With the motto "Be your own role model," Get Real Girl produced its first dolls in 2000. "This is going to be real girls living in the real world," insists Chavez. Although she continues to confront the realities of a corporate world, such as stock distributions, dividends, and income and equity reporting, her business is making some inroads. Sales projections for next year exceed $5 million. From meager beginnings—where her parents could afford to buy her only one toy a year—Chavez is living her dream. She's also helping young children who, like the young Chavez, need dreams and role models.

[Sources: *Get Real Girl Website,* January 2004; *Entrepreneur,* April 2002; *Mercury News,* July 2002; *Sacramento Bee,* February 2002.]

This chapter focuses on corporations and accounting for them. The first part of the chapter describes the basics of the corporate form of organization and explains the accounting for common and preferred stock. We then focus on several special financing transactions, including cash and stock dividends, stock splits, and treasury stock. Next, we discuss the form and content of a complete income statement as well as earnings per share. The final section considers accounting for retained earnings, including prior period adjustments, retained earnings restrictions, and reporting guidelines.

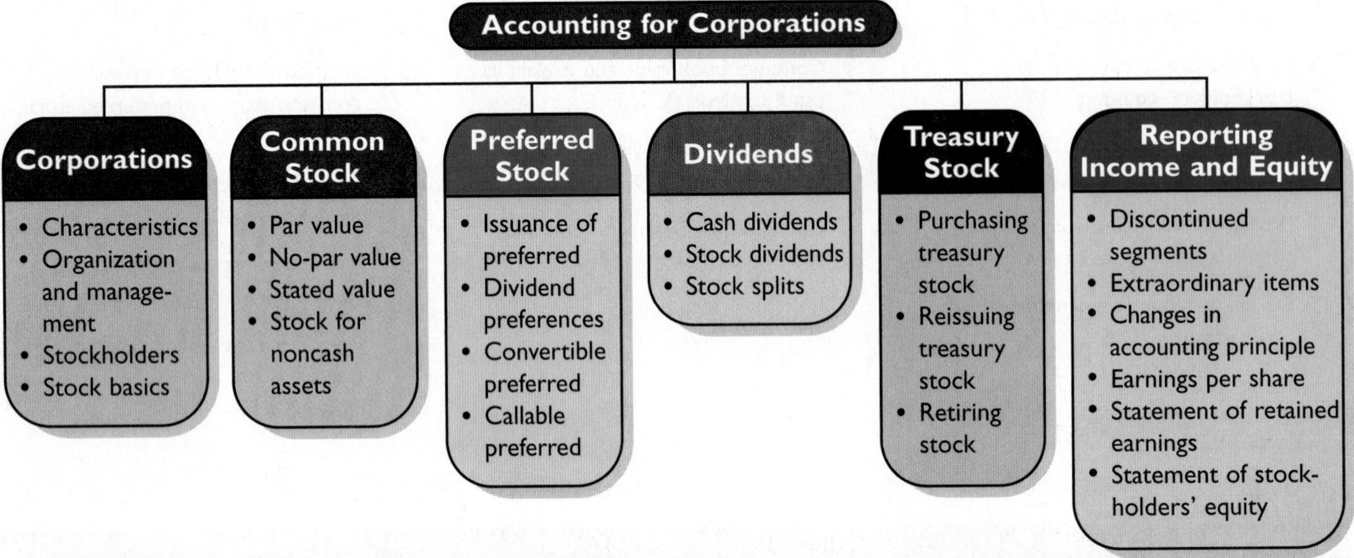

Corporate Form of Organization

A **corporation** is an entity created by law that is separate from its owners. It has most of the rights and privileges granted to individuals. Owners of corporations are called *stockholders* or *shareholders.* Corporations can be separated into two types. A *privately held* (or *closely held*) corporation does not offer its stock for public sale and usually has few stockholders. A *publicly held* corporation offers its stock for public sale and can have thousands of stockholders. *Public sale* usually refers to issuance and trading on an organized stock market.

Characteristics of Corporations

C1 Identify characteristics of corporations and their organization.

Corporations represent an important type of organization. Their unique characteristics offer advantages and disadvantages.

Advantages of Corporate Characteristics

- **Separate legal entity:** A corporation conducts its affairs with the same rights, duties, and responsibilities of a person. It takes actions through its agents, who are its officers and managers.
- **Limited liability of stockholders:** Stockholders are neither liable for corporate acts nor corporate debt.
- **Transferable ownership rights:** The transfer of shares from one stockholder to another usually has no effect on the corporation or its operations except when this causes a change in the directors who control or manage the corporation.
- **Continuous life:** A corporation's life continues indefinitely because it is not tied to the physical lives of its owners.
- **Lack of mutual agency for stockholders:** A corporation acts through its agents, who are its officers and managers. Stockholders, who are not its officers and managers, do not have the power to bind the corporation to contracts—referred to as *lack of mutual agency.*
- **Ease of capital accumulation:** Buying stock is attractive to investors because (1) stockholders are not liable for the corporation's acts and debts, (2) stocks usually are transferred

Point: The *business entity principle* requires a corporation to be accounted for separately from its owners (shareholders).

Global: U.S., U.K., and Canadian corporations finance much of their operations with stock issuances, but companies in countries such as France, Germany, and Japan finance mainly with note and bond issuances.

easily, (3) the life of the corporation is unlimited, and (4) stockholders are not corporate agents. These advantages enable corporations to accumulate large amounts of capital from the combined investments of many stockholders.

Decision Insight

Share Success Marc Andreessen cofounded **Netscape** at age 22, only four months after earning his degree. One year later, he and friends issued Netscape shares to the public. The stock soared, making Andreessen a multimillionaire.

Disadvantages of Corporate Characteristics

- **Government regulation:** A corporation must meet requirements of a state's incorporation laws, which subject the corporation to state regulation and control. Proprietorships and partnerships avoid many of these regulations and governmental reports.
- **Corporate taxation:** Corporations are subject to the same property and payroll taxes as proprietorships and partnerships plus *additional* taxes. The most burdensome of these are federal and state income taxes that together can take 40% or more of corporate pretax income. Moreover, corporate income is usually taxed a second time as part of stockholders' personal income when they receive cash distributed as dividends. This is called *double taxation.* (The usual dividend tax is 15%; however, it is less than 15% for lower income taxpayers, and in some cases zero.)

Point: Proprietorships and partnerships are not subject to income taxes. Their income is taxed as the personal income of their owners.

Point: Double taxation is less severe when a corporation's owner-manager collects a salary that is taxed only once as part of his or her personal income.

Corporate Organization and Management

This section describes the incorporation, costs, and management of corporate organizations.

Point: A corporation is not required to have an office in its state of incorporation. Thus, a majority of large corporations are incorporated in Delaware mainly because directors must exercise only "due care" in shareholder interests.

Incorporation A corporation is created by obtaining a charter from a state government. A charter application usually must be signed by the prospective stockholders called *incorporators* or *promoters* and then filed with the proper state official. When the application process is complete and fees paid, the charter is issued and the corporation is formed. Investors then purchase the corporation's stock, meet as stockholders, and elect a board of directors. Directors oversee a corporation's affairs.

Decision Insight

Seed Money Sources for start-up money include (1) "angel" investors such as parents, siblings, friends, or anyone else who believes in a company, (2) employees, investors, and even suppliers who can be paid with stock, (3) venture capitalists (investors) who have a record of success with entrepreneurs. See the National Venture Capital Association (NVCA.org) for other sources.

Organization Expenses **Organization expenses** (also called *organization costs*) are the costs to organize a corporation; they include legal fees, promoters' fees, and amounts paid to obtain a charter. The corporation records (debits) these costs to an expense account called *Organization Expenses*. Organization costs are expensed as incurred because it is difficult to determine the amount and timing of their future benefits.

Management of a Corporation The ultimate control of a corporation rests with stockholders who control a corporation by electing its *board of directors,* or simply, *directors*. Each stockholder usually has one vote for each share of stock owned. This control relation is shown in Exhibit 13.1. Directors are responsible for and have final authority for managing corporate activities. A board can act only as a collective body and usually limits its actions to setting general policy.

A corporation usually holds a stockholder meeting at least once a year to elect directors and transact business as its bylaws require. A group of stockholders

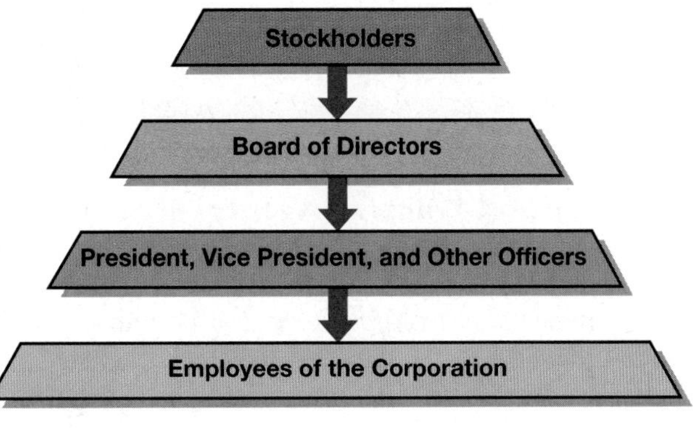

Exhibit 13.1
Corporate Structure

Point: *Bylaws* are guidelines that govern the behavior of individuals employed by and managing the corporation.

Global: Some corporate labels are:

Country	Label
United States	Inc.
France	SA
United Kingdom	
Public	PLC
Private	LTD
Germany	
Public	AG
Private	GmbH
Sweden	AB
Italy	SpA

owning or controlling votes of more than a 50% share of a corporation's stock can elect the board and control the corporation. Stockholders who do not attend stockholders' meetings must have an opportunity to delegate their voting rights to an agent by signing a **proxy,** a document that gives a designated agent the right to vote the stock.

Day-to-day direction of corporate business is delegated to executive officers appointed by the board. A corporation's chief executive officer (CEO) is often its president. Several vice presidents, who report to the president, are commonly assigned specific areas of management responsibility such as finance, production, and marketing. One person often has the dual role of chairperson of the board of directors and CEO. In this case, the president is usually designated the chief operating officer (COO).

Stockholders of Corporations

This section explains stockholder rights, stock purchases and sales, and the role of registrar and transfer agents.

Rights of Stockholders When investors buy stock, they acquire all *specific* rights the corporation's charter grants to stockholders. They also acquire *general* rights granted stockholders by the laws of the state in which the company is incorporated. When a corporation has only one class of stock, it is identified as **common stock.** State laws vary, but common stockholders usually have the general right to

1. Vote at stockholders' meetings.
2. Sell or otherwise dispose of their stock.
3. Purchase their proportional share of any common stock later issued by the corporation. This **preemptive right** protects stockholders' proportionate interest in the corporation. For example, a stockholder who owns 25% of a corporation's common stock has the first opportunity to buy 25% of any new common stock issued.
4. Receive the same dividend, if any, on each common share of the corporation.
5. Share in any assets remaining after creditors are paid when, and if, the corporation is liquidated. Each share receives the same amount of remaining liquidated assets.

Stockholders also have the right to receive timely financial reports.

Global: Stockholders' access to financial information varies across countries both in scope and by level of ownership. For instance, stockholders of Mexican companies holding small percent ownership often have difficulty obtaining quality financial information.

Stock Certificates and Transfer Investors who buy a corporation's stock, sometimes receive a *stock certificate* as proof of share ownership. Many corporations issue only one certificate for each block of stock purchased. A certificate can be for any number of shares. Exhibit 13.2 shows a stock certificate of the **Green Bay Packers.** A certificate shows the company name, stockholder name, number of shares, and other crucial information. Issuance of certificates is becoming less common. Instead, many stockholders maintain accounts with the corporation or their stockbrokers and never receive actual certificates.

Exhibit 13.2

Stock Certificate

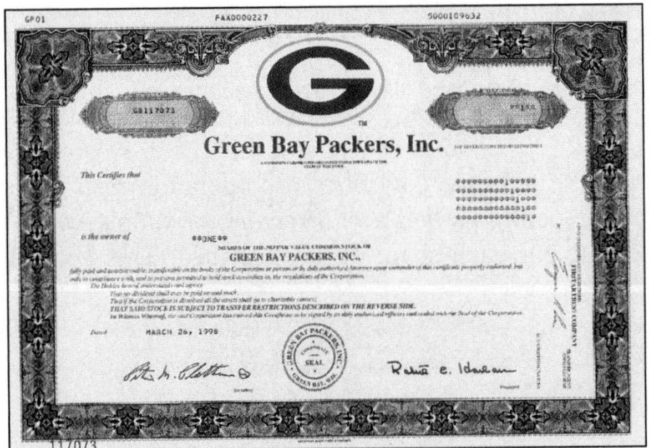

Registrar and Transfer Agents If a corporation's stock is traded on a major stock exchange, the corporation must have a registrar and a transfer agent. A *registrar* keeps stockholder records and prepares official lists of stockholders for stockholder meetings and dividend payments. A *transfer agent* assists with purchases and sales of shares by receiving and issuing certificates as necessary. Registrars and transfer agents are usually large banks or trust companies with computer facilities and staff to do this work.

Basics of Capital Stock

Capital stock is a general term that refers to any shares issued to obtain capital (owner financing). This section introduces terminology and accounting for capital stock.

Authorized Stock **Authorized stock** is the number of shares that a corporation's charter allows it to sell. The number of authorized shares usually exceeds the number of shares issued (and outstanding), often by a large amount. (*Outstanding stock* refers to issued stock held by stockholders.) No formal journal entry is required for stock authorization. A corporation must apply to the state for a change in its charter if it wishes to issue more shares than previously authorized. A corporation discloses the number of shares authorized in the equity section of its balance sheet or notes. **Krispy Kreme**'s balance sheet in Appendix A reports 300,000 shares authorized in 2003.

C2 Describe the components of stockholders' equity.

Decision Insight

Stock Trading Online brokerage service fees are as low as $5 to $10 per trade. Brokerage firms say technology has slashed their costs. Many also offer wireless or broker-assisted trading, stock research services, and real-time account balances.

Selling (Issuing) Stock A corporation can sell stock directly or indirectly. To *sell directly,* it advertises its stock issuance to potential buyers. This type of issuance is most common with privately held corporations. To *sell indirectly,* a corporation pays a brokerage house (investment banker) to issue its stock. Some brokerage houses *underwrite* an indirect issuance of stock; that is, they buy the stock from the corporation and take all gains or losses from its resale.

Decision Insight

Pricing Stock A prospectus accompanies a stock's initial public offering (IPO), giving financial information about the company issuing the stock. A prospectus should help answer these questions to price an IPO: (1) Is the underwriter reliable? (2) Is there growth in revenues, profits, and cash flows? (3) What is management's view of operations? (4) Are current owners selling? (5) What are the risks?

Market Value of Stock **Market value per share** is the price at which a stock is bought and sold. Expected future earnings, dividends, growth, and other company and economic factors influence market value. Traded stocks' market values are available daily in newspapers such as *The Wall Street Journal* and online. The current market value of previously issued shares (for example, the price of stock in trades between investors) does not impact the issuing corporation's stockholders' equity.

Classes of Stock When all authorized shares have the same rights and characteristics, the stock is called *common stock.* A corporation is sometimes authorized to issue more than one class of stock, including preferred stock and different classes of common stock. **American Greetings**, for instance, has two types of common stock: Class A stock has 1 vote per share and Class B stock has 10 votes per share.

Decision Insight

Stock Quote The **Krispy Kreme** stock quote is interpreted as (left to right): **Hi,** highest price in past 52 weeks; **Lo,** lowest price in past 52 weeks; **Sym,** company exchange symbol; **Div,** dividends paid per share in past year; **Yld %,** dividend divided by closing price; **PE,** stock price per share divided by earnings per share; **Vol 100s,** number (in 100s) of shares traded; **Hi,** highest price for the day; **Lo,** lowest price for the day; **Close,** closing price for the day; **Net Chg,** change in closing price from prior day.

52 Weeks				Yld		Vol				Net
Hi	Lo	Sym	Div	%	PE	100s	Hi	Lo	Close	Chg
41.55	26.42	KKD	0.0	0.0	55	4606	31.41	30.91	30.95	+0.20

Par Value Stock **Par value stock** is a class of stock assigned a **par value,** which is an amount assigned per share by the corporation in its charter. For example, **Novell**'s common stock has a par value of $0.10. Other commonly assigned par values are $10, $5, $1 and $0.01. There is no restriction on the assigned par value. In many states, the par value of a stock establishes **minimum legal capital,** which refers to the least amount that the buyers of stock must contribute to the corporation or be subject to paying at a future date. For example, if a corporation issues 1,000 shares of $10 par value stock, the corporation's minimum legal capital in these states would be $10,000. Minimum legal capital is intended to protect a corporation's creditors. Since creditors cannot demand payment from stockholders' personal assets, their claims are limited to the corporation's assets and any minimum legal capital. At liquidation, creditor claims are paid before any amounts are distributed to stockholders.

Point: Managers are motivated to set a low par value when minimum legal capital or state issuance taxes are based on par value.

Point: Minimum legal capital was intended to protect creditors by requiring a minimum amount of net assets in the corporation. However, such net assets can be lost by unprofitable operations.

Point: Par, no-par, and stated value do *not* set the stock's market value.

No-Par Value Stock **No-par value stock,** or simply *no-par stock,* is stock *not* assigned a value per share by the corporate charter. Its advantage is that it can be issued at any price without the possibility of a minimum legal capital deficiency.

Exhibit 13.3

Equity Composition

Proprietorship	Corporation
C. Taylor, Capital (Normal bal.)	Common Stock (Normal bal.) — Contributed Capital
	Contributed Capital in Excess of Par (Normal bal.) — Contributed Capital
	Retained Earnings (Normal bal.)

Stated Value Stock **Stated value stock** is no-par stock to which the directors assign a "stated" value per share. Stated value per share becomes the minimum legal capital per share in this case.

Stockholders' Equity A corporation's equity is known as **stockholders' equity,** also called *shareholders' equity* or *corporate capital.* Stockholders' equity consists of (1) contributed (or paid-in) capital and (2) retained earnings; see Exhibit 13.3. **Contributed capital** is the total amount of cash and other assets the corporation receives from its stockholders in exchange for common stock. **Retained earnings** is the cumulative net income (and loss) retained by a corporation.

Point: Contributed capital comes from stock-related transactions, whereas retained earnings comes from operations.

Quick Check

1. Which of the following is *not* a characteristic of the corporate form of business? (*a*) Ease of capital accumulation, (*b*) Stockholder responsibility for corporate debts, (*c*) Ease in transferability of ownership rights, or (*d*) Double taxation.
2. Why is a corporation's income said to be taxed twice?
3. What is a proxy?

Answers—p. 526

Common Stock

P1 Record the issuance of corporate stock.

Accounting for the issuance of common stock affects only contributed capital accounts; no retained earnings accounts are affected.

Topic Tackler 13-1

Issuing Par Value Stock

Par value stock can be issued at par, at a premium (above par), or at a discount (below par). In each case, stock can be exchanged for either cash or noncash assets.

Issuing Par Value Stock at Par When common stock is issued at par value, we record amounts for both the asset(s) received and the par value stock issued. To illustrate, the entry to record Dillon Snowboards' issuance of 30,000 shares of $10 par value stock for $300,000 cash on June 5, 2005, follows

Assets	= Liabilities +	Equity
+300,000		+300,000

June 5	Cash	300,000	
	Common Stock, $10 Par Value		300,000
	Issued 30,000 shares of $10 par value common stock at par.		

Exhibit 13.4 shows the stockholders' equity of Dillon Snowboards at year-end 2005 (its first year of operations) after income of $65,000 and no dividend payments.

Issuing Par Value Stock at a Premium A **premium on stock** occurs when a corporation sells its stock for more than par (or stated) value. To illustrate, if Dillon Snowboards issues its $10 par value common stock at $12 per share, its stock is sold at a $2 per share premium. The premium, known as **contributed capital in excess of par value,** is reported as part of equity; it is not revenue and is not listed on the income statement. The entry to

Point: The "Contributed Capital in Excess of Par Value, Common Stock" account is also called "Premium on Common Stock."

Stockholders' Equity	
Contributed capital	
Common Stock—$10 par value; 50,000 shares authorized; 30,000 shares issued and outstanding	$300,000
Retained earnings	65,000
Total stockholders' equity	$365,000

Exhibit 13.4

Stockholders' Equity for Stock Issued at Par

record Dillon Snowboards' issuance of 30,000 shares of $10 par value stock for $12 per share on June 5, 2005, follows

June 5	Cash	360,000	
	Common Stock, $10 Par Value		300,000
	Contributed Capital in Excess of Par Value, Common Stock		**60,000**
	Sold and issued 30,000 shares of $10 par value common stock at $12 per share.		

Assets	= Liabilities +	Equity
+360,000		+300,000
		+60,000

Point: The *Contributed Capital* terminology is interchangeable with *Paid-In Capital.*

The Contributed Capital in Excess of Par Value account is added to the par value of the stock in the equity section of the balance sheet as shown in Exhibit 13.5.

Stockholders' Equity		
Contributed capital		
Common Stock—$10 par value; 50,000 shares authorized; 30,000 shares issued and outstanding	$300,000	
Contributed capital in excess of par value, common stock	**60,000**	
Total contributed capital		$360,000
Retained earnings		65,000
Total stockholders' equity		$425,000

Exhibit 13.5

Stockholders' Equity for Stock Issued at a Premium

Issuing Par Value Stock at a Discount A **discount on stock** occurs when a corporation sells its stock for less than par (or stated) value. Most states prohibit the issuance of stock at a discount. In states that allow stock to be issued at a discount, its buyers usually become contingently liable to creditors for the discount. If stock is issued at a discount, the amount by which issue price is less than par is debited to a *Discount on Common Stock* account, a contra to the common stock account, and its balance is subtracted from the par value of stock in the equity section of the balance sheet. This discount is not an expense and does not appear on the income statement.

Point: Retained earnings can be negative, reflecting accumulated losses. Amazon.com had an accumulated deficit of $3 billion at the start of 2003.

Issuing No-Par Value Stock

When no-par stock is issued and is not assigned a stated value, the amount the corporation receives becomes legal capital and is recorded as Common Stock. This means that the entire proceeds are credited to a no-par stock account. To illustrate, a corporation records its issue of 1,000 shares of no-par stock for $40 cash per share as follows:

Oct. 20	Cash	40,000	
	Common Stock, No-Par Value		40,000
	Issued 1,000 shares of no-par value common stock at $40 per share.		

Assets	= Liabilities +	Equity
+40,000		+40,000

Frequency of Stock Types

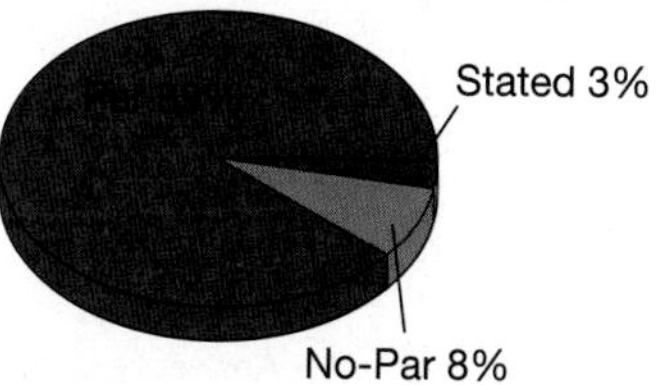

Issuing Stated Value Stock

When no-par stock is issued and assigned a stated value, its stated value becomes legal capital and is credited to a stated value stock account. Assuming that stated value stock is issued at an amount in excess of stated value (the usual case), the excess is credited to

Point: A *premium* is the amount by which issue price exceeds par (or stated) value. It is recorded in a separate equity account.

Contributed Capital in Excess of Stated Value, Common Stock, which is reported in the contributed capital part of the stockholders' equity section. To illustrate, a corporation that issues 1,000 shares of no-par common stock having a stated value of $40 per share in return for $50 cash per share records this as follows:

Assets	= Liabilities +	Equity
+50,000		+40,000
		+10,000

Oct. 20	Cash	50,000	
	Common Stock, $40 Stated Value		40,000
	Contributed Capital in Excess of Stated Value, Common Stock		10,000
	Issued 1,000 shares of $40 per share stated value stock at $50 per share.		

Issuing Stock for Noncash Assets

Point: Stock issued for noncash assets should be recorded at the market value of either the stock or the noncash asset, whichever is more clearly determinable.

A corporation can receive assets other than cash in exchange for its stock. (It can also assume liabilities on the assets received such as a mortgage on property received.) The corporation records the assets received at their market values as of the date of the transaction. The stock given in exchange is recorded at its par (or stated) value with any excess recorded in the Contributed Capital in Excess of Par (or Stated) Value account. (If no-par stock is issued, the stock is recorded at the assets' market value.) To illustrate, the entry to record receipt of land valued at $105,000 in return for issuance of 4,000 shares of $20 par value common stock is

Assets	= Liabilities +	Equity
+105,000		+80,000
		+25,000

June 10	Land	105,000	
	Common Stock, $20 Par Value		80,000
	Contributed Capital in Excess of Par Value, Common Stock		25,000
	Exchanged 4,000 shares of $20 par value common stock for land.		

Point: Any type of stock can be issued for noncash assets.

A corporation sometimes gives shares of its stock to promoters in exchange for their services in organizing the corporation, which the corporation records as **Organization Expenses.** The entry to record receipt of services valued at $12,000 in organizing the corporation in return for 600 shares of $15 par value common stock is

Assets	= Liabilities +	Equity
		−12,000
		+9,000
		+3,000

June 5	Organization Expenses	12,000	
	Common Stock, $15 Par Value		9,000
	Contributed Capital in Excess of Par Value, Common Stock		3,000
	Gave promoters 600 shares of $15 par value common stock in exchange for their services.		

Corporations sometimes issue stock through a **stock subscription,** which is the sale of stock to investors who agree to buy a certain number of shares at specified future dates and prices. The usual case occurs when a new corporation is formed and the organizers want commitments for both immediate and future financing needs.

Quick Check

4. A company issues 7,000 shares of its $10 par value common stock in exchange for equipment valued at $105,000. The entry to record this transaction includes a credit to (*a*) Contributed Capital in Excess of Par Value, Common Stock, for $35,000. (*b*) Retained Earnings for $35,000. (*c*) Common Stock, $10 Par Value, for $105,000.
5. What is a premium on stock?
6. Who is intended to be protected by minimum legal capital?

Answers—p. 526

Preferred Stock

A corporation can issue two basic kinds of stock, common and preferred. **Preferred stock** has special rights that give it priority (or senior status) over common stock in one or more areas. Special rights typically include a preference for receiving dividends and for the distribution of assets if the corporation is liquidated. Preferred stock carries all rights of common stock unless the corporate charter nullifies them. Most preferred stock, for instance, does not confer the right to vote. Exhibit 13.6 shows that preferred stock is issued by about one-fourth of large corporations. All corporations issue common stock.

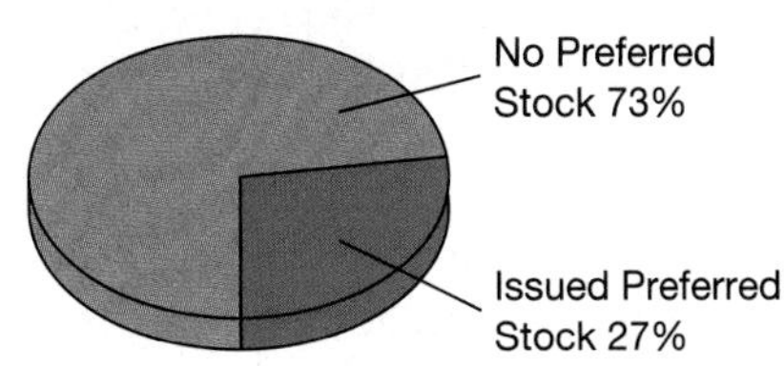

Exhibit 13.6

Corporations and Preferred Stock

Issuance of Preferred Stock

C3 Explain characteristics of common and preferred stock.

Preferred stock usually has a par value. Like common stock, it can be sold at a price different from par. Preferred stock is recorded in its own separate contributed capital accounts. To illustrate, if Dillon Snowboards issues 50 shares of $100 par value preferred stock for $6,000 cash on July 1, 2005, the entry is

July 1	Cash	6,000	
	Preferred Stock, $100 Par Value		5,000
	Contributed Capital in Excess of Par Value, Preferred Stock		1,000
	Issued preferred stock for cash.		

Assets	= Liabilities	+ Equity
+6,000		+5,000
		+1,000

The preferred stock accounts are included as part of contributed capital. The equity section of the year-end balance sheet for Dillon Snowboards, including preferred stock, is shown in Exhibit 13.7. (This exhibit assumes that common stock was issued at par.) Note that issuing no-par preferred stock is similar to issuing no-par common stock. Also, the entries for issuing preferred stock for noncash assets are similar to those for common stock.

Exhibit 13.7

Stockholders' Equity with Common and Preferred Stock

Stockholders' Equity		
Contributed capital		
Common stock—$10 par value; 50,000 shares authorized; 30,000 shares issued and outstanding	$300,000	
Preferred stock—$100 par value; 1,000 shares authorized; 50 shares issued and outstanding	**5,000**	
Contributed capital in excess of par value, preferred stock	**1,000**	
Total contributed capital		$306,000
Retained earnings		65,000
Total stockholders' equity		$371,000

Dividend Preference of Preferred Stock

P2 Distribute dividends between common stock and preferred stock.

Preferred stock usually carries a preference for dividends, meaning that preferred stockholders are allocated their dividends before any dividends are allocated to common stockholders. The dividends allocated to preferred stockholders are usually expressed as a dollar amount per share or a percent applied to par value. A preference for dividends does *not* ensure dividends. If the directors do not declare a dividend, neither the preferred nor the common stockholders receive one.

Cumulative or Noncumulative Dividend Most preferred stocks carry a cumulative dividend right. **Cumulative preferred stock** has a right to be paid both the current and all prior periods' unpaid dividends before any dividend is paid to common stockholders. When preferred stock is cumulative and the directors either do not declare a dividend to preferred stockholders or declare one that does not cover the total amount of cumulative

Point: Dividend preference does not imply that preferred stockholders receive more dividends than common stockholders, nor does it guarantee a dividend.

dividend, the unpaid dividend amount is called **dividend in arrears.** Accumulation of dividends in arrears on cumulative preferred stock does not guarantee they will be paid. **Noncumulative preferred stock** confers no right to prior periods' unpaid dividends if they were not declared in those prior periods.

Example: What dividends do cumulative preferred stockholders receive in 2005 if the corporation paid only $2,000 of dividends in 2004? How does this affect dividends to common stockholders in 2005? *Answers:* $16,000 ($7,000 dividends in arrears, plus $9,000 current preferred dividends). Dividends to common stockholders decrease to $26,000.

To illustrate the difference between cumulative and noncumulative preferred stock, assume that a corporation's outstanding stock includes (1) 1,000 shares of $100 par, 9% preferred stock—yielding $9,000 per year in potential dividends, and (2) 4,000 shares of $50 par value common stock. During 2004, the first year of operations, the directors declare cash dividends of $5,000. In year 2005, they declare cash dividends of $42,000. See Exhibit 13.8 for the allocation of dividends for these two years. Note that allocation of year 2005 dividends depends on whether the preferred stock is noncumulative or cumulative. With noncumulative preferred, the preferred stockholders never receive the $4,000 skipped in 2004. If the preferred stock is cumulative, the $4,000 in arrears is paid in 2005 before any other dividends are paid.

Exhibit 13.8

Allocation of Dividends (noncumulative vs. cumulative preferred stock)

	Preferred	Common
Preferred Stock Is Noncumulative		
Year 2004	$ 5,000	$ 0
Year 2005		
Step 1: Current year's preferred dividend	$ 9,000	
Step 2: Remainder to common		$33,000
Preferred Stock Is Cumulative		
Year 2004	$ 5,000	$ 0
Year 2005		
Step 1: Dividend in arrears	$ 4,000	
Step 2: Current year's preferred dividend	9,000	
Step 3: Remainder to common		$29,000
Totals for year 2005	$13,000	$29,000

A liability for a dividend does not exist until the directors declare a dividend. If a preferred dividend date passes and the corporation's board fails to declare the dividend on its cumulative preferred stock, the dividend in arrears is not a liability. The *full-disclosure principle* requires a corporation to report (usually in a note) the amount of preferred dividends in arrears as of the balance sheet date.

Participating or Nonparticipating Dividend **Nonparticipating preferred stock** has a feature that limits dividends to a maximum amount each year. This maximum is often stated as a percent of the stock's par value or as a specific dollar amount per share. Once preferred stockholders receive this amount, the common stockholders receive any and all additional dividends. **Participating preferred stock** has a feature allowing preferred stockholders to share with common stockholders in any dividends paid in excess of the percent or dollar amount stated on the preferred stock. This participation feature does not apply until common stockholders receive dividends equal to the preferred stock's dividend percent. Many corporations are authorized to issue participating preferred stock but rarely do, and most managers never expect to issue it.[1]

[1] Participating preferred stock is usually authorized as a defense against a possible corporate *takeover* by an "unfriendly" investor (or a group of investors) who intends to buy enough voting common stock to gain control. Taking a term from spy novels, the financial world refers to this type of plan as a *poison pill* that a company swallows if enemy investors threaten its capture. A poison pill usually works as follows: A corporation's common stockholders on a given date are granted the right to purchase a large amount of participating preferred stock at a very low price. This right to purchase preferred shares is *not* transferable. If an unfriendly investor buys a large block of common shares (whose right to purchase participating preferred shares does *not* transfer to this buyer), the board can issue preferred shares at a low price to the remaining common shareholders who retained the right to purchase. Future dividends are then divided between the newly issued participating preferred shares and the common shares. This usually transfers value from common shares to preferred shares, causing the unfriendly investor's common stock to lose much of its value and reduces the potential benefit of a hostile takeover.

Convertible Preferred Stock

Preferred stock is more attractive to investors if it carries a right to exchange preferred shares for a fixed number of common shares. **Convertible preferred stock** gives holders the option to exchange their preferred shares for common shares at a specified rate. When a company prospers and its common stock increases in value, convertible preferred stockholders can share in this success by converting their preferred stock into more valuable common stock.

Callable Preferred Stock

Callable preferred stock gives the issuing corporation the right to purchase (retire) this stock from its holders at specified future prices and dates. Many issues of preferred stock are callable. The amount paid to call and retire a preferred share is its **call price,** or *redemption value,* and is set when the stock is issued. The call price normally includes the stock's par value plus a premium giving holders additional return on their investment. When the issuing corporation calls and retires a preferred stock, the terms of the agreement often require it to pay the call price *and* any dividends in arrears.

Point: The issuing corporation has the right, or option, to retire its callable preferred stock.

Reasons for Issuing Preferred Stock

Corporations issue preferred stock for several reasons. One is to raise capital without sacrificing control. For example, suppose a company's organizers have $100,000 cash to invest and organize a corporation that needs $200,000 of capital to start. If they sell $200,000 worth of common stock (with $100,000 to the organizers), they would have only 50% control and would need to negotiate extensively with other stockholders in making policy. However, if they issue $100,000 worth of common stock to themselves and sell outsiders $100,000 of 8%, cumulative preferred stock with no voting rights, they retain control.

A second reason to issue preferred stock is to boost the return earned by common stockholders. To illustrate, suppose a corporation's organizers expect to earn an annual after-tax income of $24,000 on an investment of $200,000. If they sell and issue $200,000 worth of common stock, the $24,000 income produces a 12% return on the $200,000 of common stockholders' equity. However, if they issue $100,000 of 8% preferred stock to outsiders and $100,000 of common stock to themselves, their own return increases to 16% per year, as shown in Exhibit 13.9.

Net (after-tax) income	$24,000
Less preferred dividends at 8%	(8,000)
Balance to common stockholders	$16,000
Return to common stockholders ($16,000/$100,000)	16%

Exhibit 13.9

Return to Common Stockholders When Preferred Stock Is Issued

Common stockholders earn 16% instead of 12% because assets contributed by preferred stockholders are invested to earn $12,000 while the preferred dividend is only $8,000. Use of preferred stock to increase return to common stockholders is an example of **financial leverage** (also called *trading on the equity*). As a general rule, when the dividend rate on preferred stock is less than the rate the corporation earns on its assets, the effect of issuing preferred stock is to increase (or *lever*) the rate earned by common stockholders.

Other reasons for issuing preferred stock include its appeal to some investors who believe that the corporation's common stock is too risky or that the expected return on common stock is too low.

Point: Financial leverage also occurs when debt is issued and the interest rate paid on it is less than the rate earned from using the assets the creditors lend the company.

Decision Maker

Concert Organizer Assume that you alter your business strategy from organizing concerts targeted at under 1,000 people to those targeted at between 5,000 to 20,000 people. You also incorporate because of increased risk of lawsuits and a desire to issue stock for financing. It is important that you control the company for decisions on whom to schedule. What types of stock do you offer?

Answer—p. 525

Quick Check

7. In what ways does preferred stock often have priority over common stock?
8. Increasing the return to common stockholders by issuing preferred stock is an example of (*a*) Financial leverage. (*b*) Cumulative earnings. (*c*) Dividend in arrears.
9. A corporation has issued and outstanding (i) 9,000 shares of $50 par value, 10% cumulative, nonparticipating preferred stock and (ii) 27,000 shares of $10 par value common stock. No dividends have been declared for the two prior years. During the current year, the corporation declares $288,000 in dividends. The amount paid to common shareholders is (*a*) $243,000. (*b*) $153,000. (*c*) $135,000.

Answers—p. 526

Dividends

P3 Record transactions involving cash dividends.

This section describes both cash and stock dividend transactions.

Cash Dividends

The decision to pay cash dividends rests with the board of directors and involves more than evaluating the amounts of retained earnings and cash. The directors, for instance, may decide to keep the cash to invest in the corporation's growth, to meet emergencies, to take advantage of unexpected opportunities, or to pay off debt. Alternatively, many corporations pay cash dividends to their stockholders at regular dates. These cash flows provide a return to investors and almost always affect the stock's market value.

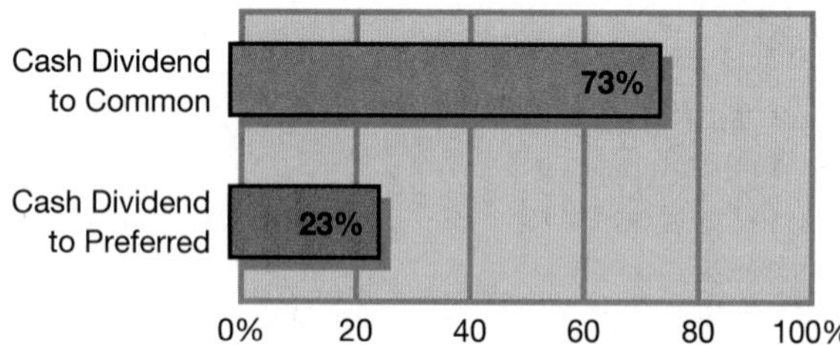

Accounting for Cash Dividends Dividend payment involves three important dates: declaration, record, and payment. **Date of declaration** is the date the directors vote to declare and pay a dividend. This creates a legal liability of the corporation to its stockholders. **Date of record** is the future date specified by the directors for identifying those stockholders listed in the corporation's records to receive dividends. The date of record usually follows the date of declaration by at least two weeks. Persons who own stock on the date of record receive dividends. **Date of payment** is the date when the corporation makes payment; it follows the date of record by enough time to allow the corporation to arrange checks, money transfers, or other means to pay dividends.

Point: A cash dividend reduces a company's assets (and its working capital).

To illustrate, the entry to record a January 9 declaration of a $1 per share cash dividend by the directors of Z-Tech, Inc., with 5,000 outstanding shares is

Assets = Liabilities + Equity
+5,000 −5,000

Date of Declaration

Jan. 9	Retained Earnings	5,000	
	Common Dividend Payable.		5,000
	Declared $1 per common share cash dividend.[2]		

Topic Tackler 13-2

Common Dividend Payable is a current liability. The date of record for the Z-Tech dividend is January 22. *No formal journal entry is needed on the date of record.* The February 1 date of payment requires an entry to record both the settlement of the liability and the reduction of the cash balance, as follows:

Assets = Liabilities + Equity
−5,000 −5,000

Date of Payment

Feb. 1	Common Dividend Payable	5,000	
	Cash.		5,000
	Paid $1 per common share cash dividend.		

[2] An alternative entry is to debit Dividends instead of Retained Earnings. The balance in Dividends is then closed to Retained Earnings at the end of the reporting period. The effect is the same: Retained Earnings is decreased and a Dividend Payable is increased. For simplicity, all assignments use the Retained Earnings account to record dividend declarations.

Deficits and Cash Dividends A corporation with a debit (abnormal) balance for retained earnings is said to have a **retained earnings deficit,** which arises when a company incurs cumulative losses and/or pays more dividends than total earnings from current and prior years. A deficit is reported as a deduction on the balance sheet, as shown in Exhibit 13.10. Most states prohibit a corporation with a deficit from paying a cash dividend to its stockholders. This legal restriction is designed to protect creditors by preventing distribution of assets to stockholders when the company may be in financial difficulty.

Point: It is often said a dividend is a distribution of retained earnings, but it is more precise to describe a dividend as a distribution of assets to satisfy stockholder claims.

Point: The Retained Earnings Deficit account is also called *Accumulated Deficit.*

Common stock—$10 par value, 5,000 shares authorized, issued, and outstanding	$50,000
Retained earnings deficit	**(6,000)**
Total stockholders' equity	$44,000

Exhibit 13.10

Stockholders' Equity with a Deficit

Some state laws allow cash dividends to be paid by returning a portion of the capital contributed by stockholders. This type of dividend is called a **liquidating cash dividend,** or simply *liquidating dividend,* because it returns a part of the original investment back to the stockholders. This requires a debit entry to one of the contributed capital accounts instead of Retained Earnings at the declaration date.

Decision Insight

Where's the Money Cash dividends have declined as a percent of stock prices. More companies are instead buying back shares, paying down debt, or expanding business when they have extra cash.

Quick Check

10. What type of an account is the Common Dividend Payable account?
11. What three crucial dates are involved in the process of paying a cash dividend?
12. When does a dividend become a company's legal obligation?

Answers—p. 526

Stock Dividends

P4 Account for stock dividends and stock splits.

A **stock dividend,** declared by a corporation's directors, is a distribution of additional shares of the corporation's own stock to its stockholders without the receipt of any payment in return. Stock dividends and cash dividends are different. A stock dividend does not reduce assets and equity but instead transfers a portion of equity from retained earnings to contributed capital.

Reasons for Stock Dividends Stock dividends exist for at least two reasons. First, directors are said to use stock dividends to keep the market price of the stock affordable. For example, if a corporation continues to earn income but does not issue cash dividends, the price of its common stock likely increases. The price of such a stock may become so high that it discourages some investors from buying the stock (especially in lots of 100 and 1,000). When a corporation has a stock dividend, it increases the number of outstanding shares and lowers the per share stock price. Another reason for a stock dividend is to provide evidence of management's confidence that the company is doing well and will continue to do well.

Point: Berkshire Hathaway has not declared a cash dividend since 1967. Its recent stock price was about $75,000 per share.

Accounting for Stock Dividends A stock dividend affects the components of equity by transferring part of retained earnings to contributed capital accounts, sometimes described as *capitalizing* retained earnings. Accounting for a stock dividend depends on whether it is a small or large stock dividend. A **small stock dividend** is a distribution of 25% or less of previously outstanding shares. It is recorded by capitalizing retained earnings for an amount equal to the market value of the shares to be distributed. A **large stock dividend** is a distribution of more than 25% of previously outstanding shares. A large stock dividend is recorded by capitalizing retained earnings for the minimum amount required by state law governing the corporation. Most states require capitalizing retained earnings equal to the par or stated value of the stock.

To illustrate stock dividends, we use the equity section of X-Quest's balance sheet shown in Exhibit 13.11 just *before* its declaration of a stock dividend on December 31.

Exhibit 13.11

Stockholders' Equity *before* Declaring a Stock Dividend

Stockholders' Equity (before dividend)	
Common stock—$10 par value, 15,000 shares authorized, 10,000 shares issued and outstanding	$100,000
Contributed capital in excess of par value, common stock	8,000
Total contributed capital	108,000
Retained earnings	35,000
Total stockholders' equity	$143,000

Recording a small stock dividend. Assume that X-Quest's directors declare a 10% stock dividend on December 31. This stock dividend of 1,000 shares, computed as 10% of its 10,000 issued and outstanding shares, is to be distributed on January 20 to the stockholders of record on January 15. Since the market price of X-Quest's stock on December 31 is $15 per share, this small stock dividend declaration is recorded as follows:

Point: Small stock dividends are recorded at market value.

Date of Declaration

Dec. 31	Retained Earnings	15,000	
	Common Stock Dividend Distributable		10,000
	Contributed Capital in Excess of Par Value, Common Stock		5,000
	Declared a 1,000-share (10%) stock dividend.		

Assets = Liabilities + Equity
−15,000
+10,000
+5,000

The $10,000 credit in the declaration entry equals the par value of the shares and is recorded in a contributed capital account, *Common Stock Dividend Distributable*. Its balance exists only until the shares are issued. The $5,000 credit equals the amount by which market value exceeds par value. This amount increases the Contributed Capital in Excess of Par Value account in anticipation of the issue of shares. In general, the balance sheet changes in three ways when a stock dividend is declared. First, the amount of equity attributed to common stock increases; for X-Quest, from $100,000 to $110,000 for 1,000 additional declared shares. Second, contributed capital in excess of par increases by the excess of market value over par value for the declared shares. Third, retained earnings decreases, reflecting the transfer of amounts to both common stock and contributed capital in excess of par. The stockholders' equity of X-Quest is shown in Exhibit 13.12 *after* its 10% stock dividend is declared on December 31.

Point: The term *Distributable* (not *Payable*) is used for stock dividends.

Point: The credit to Contributed Capital in Excess of Par Value is recorded when the stock dividend is declared. This account is not affected when stock is later distributed.

Point: A stock dividend is never a liability on a balance sheet because it never reduces assets.

Exhibit 13.12

Stockholders' Equity *after* Declaring a Stock Dividend

Stockholders' Equity (after dividend)	
Common stock—$10 par value, 15,000 shares authorized, 10,000 shares issued and outstanding	$100,000
Common stock dividend distributable—1,000 shares	**10,000**
Contributed capital in excess of par value, common stock	**13,000**
Total contributed capital	123,000
Retained earnings	**20,000**
Total stockholders' equity	$143,000

No entry is made on the date of record for a stock dividend. On January 20, the date of payment, X-Quest distributes the new shares to stockholders and records this entry:

Point: A stock dividend does not affect assets (or working capital).

Date of Payment

Jan. 20	Common Stock Dividend Distributable	10,000	
	Common Stock, $10 Par Value		10,000
	To record issuance of common stock dividend.		

Assets = Liabilities + Equity
−10,000
+10,000

The combined effect of these stock dividend entries is to transfer (or capitalize) $15,000 of retained earnings to contributed capital accounts. The amount of capitalized retained earnings equals the market value of the 1,000 issued shares ($15 × 1,000 shares). Note that a stock dividend has no effect on the ownership percent of individual stockholders.

Decision Maker

Entrepreneur A company you cofounded and own stock in announces a 50% stock dividend. Has the value of your stock investment increased, decreased, or remained the same?

Answer—p. 525

Recording a large stock dividend. A corporation capitalizes retained earnings equal to the minimum amount required by state law for a large stock dividend. For most states, this amount is the par or stated value of the newly issued shares. To illustrate, suppose X-Quest's board declares a stock dividend of 30% instead of 10% on December 31. Since this dividend is more than 25%, it is treated as a large stock dividend. Thus, the par value of the 3,000 dividend shares is capitalized at the date of declaration with this entry:

Point: Large stock dividends are recorded at par or stated value.

Date of Declaration

Dec. 31	Retained Earnings	30,000	
	Common Stock Dividend Distributable		30,000
	Declared a 3,000-share (30%) stock dividend.		

Assets = Liabilities + Equity
−30,000
+30,000

This transaction decreases retained earnings and increases contributed capital by $30,000. On the date of payment the company debits Common Stock Dividend Distributable and credits Common Stock for $30,000. Note that the effects from a large stock dividend on balance sheet accounts are similar to those for a small stock dividend except for the absence of any effect on contributed capital in excess of par.

Stock Splits

A **stock split** is the distribution of additional shares to stockholders according to their percent ownership. When a stock split occurs, the corporation "calls in" its outstanding shares and issues more than one new share in exchange for each old share. Splits can be done in any ratio, including 2-for-1, 3-for-1, or higher. Stock splits reduce the par or stated value per share.

To illustrate, CompTec has 100,000 outstanding shares of $20 par value common stock with a current market value of $88 per share. A 2-for-1 stock split cuts par value in half as it replaces 100,000 shares of $20 par value stock with 200,000 shares of $10 par value stock. Market value is reduced from $88 per share to about $44 per share. The split does not affect any equity amounts reported on the balance sheet or any individual stockholder's percent ownership. Both the Contributed Capital and Retained Earnings accounts are unchanged by a split, and *no journal entry is made*. The only effect on the accounts is a change in the stock account description. CompTec's 2-for-1 split on its $20 par value stock means that after the split, it changes its stock account title to Common Stock, $10 Par Value. This stock's description on the balance sheet also changes to reflect the additional authorized, issued, and outstanding shares and the new par value.

Point: A **reverse stock split** is the opposite of a stock split. It increases both the market value per share and the par or stated value per share by specifying the split ratio to be less than 1-for-1, such as 1-for-2. A reverse stock split results in fewer shares.

The difference between stock splits and large stock dividends is often blurred. Many companies report stock splits in their financial statements without calling in the original shares by simply changing their par value. This type of "split" is really a large stock dividend and results in additional shares issued to stockholders by capitalizing retained earnings or transferring other contributed capital to Common Stock. This approach avoids administrative costs of splitting the stock. **Harley-Davidson** recently declared a 2-for-1 stock split executed in the form of a 100% stock dividend.

Quick Check

13. How does a stock dividend impact assets and retained earnings?

14. What distinguishes a large stock dividend from a small stock dividend?

15. What amount of retained earnings is capitalized for a small stock dividend?

Answers—p. 526

Treasury Stock

P5 Record purchases and sales of treasury stock and the retirement of stock.

Corporations acquire shares of their own stock for several reasons: (1) to use their shares to acquire another corporation, (2) to purchase shares to avoid a hostile takeover of the company, (3) to reissue them to employees as compensation, and (4) to maintain a strong market for their stock or to show management confidence in the current price.

A corporation's reacquired shares are called **treasury stock,** which is similar to unissued stock in several ways: (1) neither treasury stock nor unissued stock is an asset, (2) neither receives cash dividends or to stock dividends, and (3) neither allows the exercise of voting rights. However, treasury stock does differ from unissued stock in one major way: The corporation can resell treasury stock at less than par without having the buyers incur a liability, provided it was originally issued at par value or higher. Treasury stock purchases also require management to exercise ethical sensitivity because funds are being paid to specific stockholders instead of all stockholders. Managers must be sure the purchase is in the best interest of all stockholders. These concerns cause companies to fully disclose treasury stock transactions.

Corporations and Treasury Stock

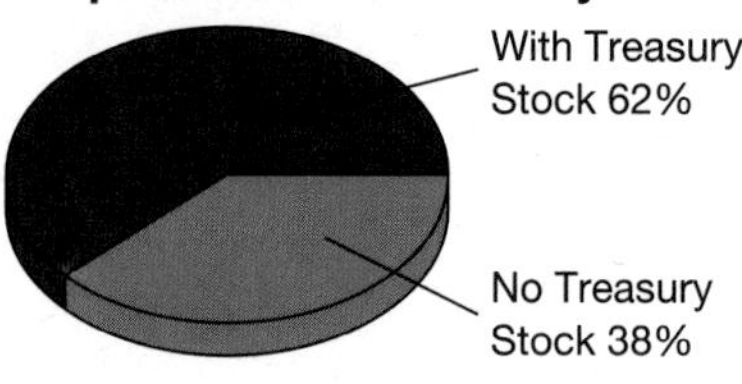

Purchasing Treasury Stock

Purchasing treasury stock reduces the corporation's assets and equity by equal amounts. (We describe the *cost method* of accounting for treasury stock, which is the most widely used method. The *par value* method is another method explained in advanced courses.) To illustrate, Exhibit 13.13 shows Cyber Corporation's account balances *before* any treasury stock purchase (Cyber has no liabilities).

Exhibit 13.13

Account Balances *before* Purchasing Treasury Stock

Assets		Stockholders' Equity	
Cash	$ 30,000	Common stock—$10 par; 10,000 shares authorized, issued, and outstanding	$100,000
Other assets	95,000	Retained earnings	25,000
Total assets	$125,000	Total stockholders' equity	$125,000

Global: Many countries, such as China, Japan, and Singapore, do not permit purchase of treasury stock.

Cyber then purchases 1,000 of its own shares for $11,500, which is recorded as follows:

Assets	= Liabilities +	Equity
−11,500		−11,500

May 1	Treasury Stock, Common	11,500	
	Cash		11,500
	Purchased 1,000 treasury shares at $11.50 per share.		

Point: Treasury stock does not carry voting or dividend rights.

This entry reduces equity through the debit to the Treasury Stock account, which is a contra equity account. Exhibit 13.14 shows account balances *after* this transaction.

Exhibit 13.14

Account Balances *after* Purchasing Treasury Stock

Assets		Stockholders' Equity	
Cash	$ 18,500	Common stock—$10 par; 10,000 shares authorized and issued; 1,000 shares in treasury	$100,000
Other assets	95,000	Retained earnings, $11,500 restricted by treasury stock purchase	25,000
		Less cost of treasury stock	**(11,500)**
Total assets	$113,500	Total stockholders' equity	$113,500

Point: The Treasury Stock account is *not* an asset. This contra equity account is a subtraction in the equity section.

The treasury stock purchase reduces Cyber's cash, total assets, and total equity by $11,500 but does not reduce the balance of either the Common Stock or the Retained Earnings account. The equity reduction is reported by deducting the cost of treasury stock in the equity section. Also, two disclosures are evident. First, the stock description reveals that 1,000 issued shares are in treasury, leaving only 9,000 shares still outstanding. Second, the description for retained earnings reveals that it is partly restricted.

Point: A treasury stock purchase is also called a *stock buyback*.

Reissuing Treasury Stock

Treasury stock can be reissued by selling it at cost, above cost, or below cost.

Selling Treasury Stock at Cost If treasury stock is reissued at cost, the entry is the reverse of the one made to record the purchase. For instance, if on May 21 Cyber reissues 100 of the treasury shares purchased on May 1 at the same $11.50 per share cost, the entry is

May 21	Cash	1,150	
	Treasury Stock, Common		1,150
	Received $11.50 per share for 100 treasury shares costing $11.50 per share.		

Assets = Liabilities + Equity
+1,150 +1,150

Selling Treasury Stock *above* Cost If treasury stock is sold for more than cost, the amount received in excess of cost is credited to the Contributed Capital, Treasury Stock account. This account is reported as a separate item in the contributed capital section of stockholders' equity. No gain is ever reported from the sale of treasury stock. To illustrate, if Cyber receives $12 cash per share for 400 treasury shares costing $11.50 per share, the entry is

Point: Treasury stock does not represent ownership. A company cannot own a part of itself.

June 3	Cash	4,800	
	Treasury Stock, Common		4,600
	Contributed Capital, Treasury Stock ...		**200**
	Received $12 per share for 400 treasury shares costing $11.50 per share.		

Assets = Liabilities + Equity
+4,800 +4,600
+200

Selling Treasury Stock *below* Cost When treasury stock is sold below cost, the entry to record the sale depends on whether the Contributed Capital, Treasury Stock account has a credit balance. If it has a zero balance, the excess of cost over the sales price is debited to Retained Earnings. If the Contributed Capital, Treasury Stock account has a credit balance, it is debited for the excess of the cost over the selling price but not to exceed the balance in this account. When the credit balance in this contributed capital account is eliminated, any remaining difference between the cost and selling price is debited to Retained Earnings. To illustrate, if Cyber sells its remaining 500 shares of treasury stock at $10 per share, equity is reduced by $750 (500 shares × $1.50 per share excess of cost over selling price), as shown in this entry:

Point: The term *treasury stock* is believed to arise from the fact that reacquired stock is held in a corporation's treasury.

Point: The Contributed Capital, Treasury Stock account can have a zero or credit balance but never a debit balance.

July 10	Cash	5,000	
	Contributed Capital, Treasury Stock	**200**	
	Retained Earnings	**550**	
	Treasury Stock, Common		5,750
	Received $10 per share for 500 treasury shares costing $11.50 per share.		

Assets = Liabilities + Equity
+5,000 −200
−550
+5,750

This entry eliminates the $200 credit balance in the contributed capital account created on June 3 and then reduces the Retained Earnings balance by the remaining $550 excess of cost over selling price. A company never reports a loss (or gain) from the sale of treasury stock.

Retiring Stock

A corporation can purchase its own stock and retire it. Retiring stock reduces the number of issued shares. Retired stock is the same as authorized and unissued shares. Purchases and retirements of stock are permissible under state law only if they do not jeopardize the interests of creditors and stockholders. When stock is purchased for retirement, we remove

Point: Wrigley Company recently reported that its "Directors adopted a resolution retiring the entire balance of shares of Common Stock held in the corporate treasury."

Point: Recording stock retirement results in canceling the equity from the original issuance of the shares.

all contributed capital amounts related to the retired shares. If the purchase price exceeds the net amount removed from contributed capital, this excess is debited to Retained Earnings. If the net amount removed from contributed capital exceeds the purchase price, this excess is credited to the Contributed Capital from Retirement of Stock account. A company's assets and equity are always reduced by the amount paid for the retiring stock.

Quick Check

16. Purchase of treasury stock (*a*) has no effect on assets; (*b*) reduces total assets and total equity by equal amounts; or (*c*) is recorded with a debit to Retained Earnings.

17. Southern Co. purchases shares of Northern Corp. Should either company classify these shares as treasury stock?

18. How does treasury stock affect the authorized, issued, and outstanding shares?

19. When a company purchases treasury stock, (*a*) retained earnings are restricted by the amount paid; (*b*) Retained Earnings is credited; or (*c*) it is retired.

Answers—p. 526

Reporting Income and Equity

When a company's revenue and expense transactions are from normal, continuing operations, a simple income statement is usually adequate. When a company's activities include income-related events not part of its normal, continuing operations, it must disclose information to help users understand these events and predict future performance. To meet these objectives, companies separate the income statement into continuing operations, discontinued segments, extraordinary items, changes in accounting principles, and earnings per share. For illustration, Exhibit 13.15 shows such an income statement for ComUS.

Continuing Operations

C4 Explain the form and content of a complete income statement.

The first major section (①) shows the revenues, expenses, and income from continuing operations. Users especially rely on this information to predict future operations. Many users view this section as the most important. Earlier chapters explained the items comprising income from continuing operations.

Discontinued Segments

A **business segment** is a part of a company's operations that serves a particular line of business or class of customers. A segment has assets, liabilities, and financial results of operations that can be distinguished from those of other parts of the company. A company's gain or loss from selling or closing down a segment is separately reported. Section ② of Exhibit 13.15 reports both (1) income from operating the discontinued segment for the current period prior to its disposal and (2) the loss from disposing of the segment's net assets. The income tax effects of each are reported separately from the income taxes expense in section ①.

Extraordinary Items

Section ③ reports **extraordinary gains and losses,** which are those that are *both unusual* and *infrequent*. An **unusual gain or loss** is abnormal or otherwise unrelated to the company's regular activities and environment. An **infrequent gain or loss** is not expected to recur given the company's operating environment. Reporting extraordinary items in a separate category helps users predict future performance, absent the effects of extraordinary items. Items usually considered extraordinary include (1) expropriation (taking away) of property by a foreign government, (2) condemning of property by a domestic government body, (3) prohibition against using an asset by a newly enacted law, and (4) losses and gains from an unusual and infrequent calamity ("act of God"). Items *not* considered extraordinary

Exhibit 13.15

Income Statement (all-inclusive) for a Corporation

ComUS
Income Statement
For Year Ended December 31, 2005

①	Net sales		$8,478,000
	Operating expenses		
	Cost of goods sold	$5,950,000	
	Depreciation expense	35,000	
	Other selling, general, and administrative expenses	515,000	
	Interest expense	20,000	
	Total operating expenses		(6,520,000)
	Other gains (losses)		
	Loss on plant relocation		(45,000)
	Gain on sale of surplus land		72,000
	Income from continuing operations before taxes		1,985,000
	Income taxes expense		(595,500)
	Income from continuing operations		1,389,500
②	**Discontinued segment**		
	Income from operating Division A (net of $180,000 taxes)	420,000	
	Loss on disposal of Division A (net of $66,000 tax benefit)	(154,000)	266,000
	Income before extraordinary items and cumulative effect of change in accounting principle		1,655,500
③	**Extraordinary items**		
	Gain on land expropriated by state (net of $61,200 taxes)	142,800	
	Loss from earthquake damage (net of $270,000 tax benefit)	(630,000)	(487,200)
④	**Cumulative effect of a change in accounting principle**		
	Effect on prior years' income (through Dec. 31, 2004) of changing depreciation methods (net of $24,000 taxes)		56,000
	Net income		$1,224,300
⑤	**Earnings per common share (200,000 outstanding shares)**		
	Income from continuing operations		$ 6.95
	Discontinued operations		1.33
	Income before extraordinary items and cumulative effect of change in accounting principle		8.28
	Extraordinary items		(2.44)
	Cumulative effect of a change in accounting principle		0.28
	Net income (basic earnings per share)		$ 6.12

include (1) write-downs of inventories and write-offs of receivables, (2) gains and losses from disposing of segments, and (3) financial effects of labor strikes.

Gains and losses that are neither unusual nor infrequent are reported as part of continuing operations. Gains and losses that are *either* unusual *or* infrequent, but *not* both, are reported as part of continuing operations *but* after the normal revenues and expenses.

Decision Maker

Small Business Owner You own an orange grove near Jacksonville, Florida. A bad frost destroys about one-half of your oranges. You are currently preparing an income statement for a bank loan. Can you claim the loss of oranges as extraordinary?

Answer—p. 525

Changes in Accounting Principles

The *consistency principle* directs a company to apply the same accounting principles across periods, yet a company can change from one acceptable accounting principle (such as FIFO, LIFO, or straight-line) to another as long as the change improves the usefulness of

Point: Changes in principles are sometimes required when new accounting standards are issued.

information in its financial statements. Changes in accounting principles usually affect income in more than one way. To illustrate, ComUS purchased its only depreciable asset early in 2002 for $320,000. This asset has an eight-year life, a $40,000 salvage value, and was depreciated using double-declining-balance for 2002, 2003, and 2004. Early in 2005, ComUS decides its income statement would be more useful if depreciation is computed using straight-line. Double-declining-balance had yielded $185,000 of depreciation from 2002 through 2004, whereas if the straight-line method had been used, depreciation would have been $105,000. The cumulative effect on prior year income statements (those for 2002–2004) is to reduce depreciation expense by $80,000 and increase pretax income by $80,000. Since ComUS is subject to a 30% income tax, the after-tax effect of this change is $56,000 ($80,000 × [1 − 0.30]).

The income statement in Exhibit 13.15 shows how to report the change in an accounting principle. First, section ① reports $35,000 of depreciation using the newly adopted straight-line method. Straight-line depreciation also will be used in 2006 through 2009. Second, the income statement reports the $56,000 catch-up adjustment in section ④. This item is the cumulative effect of the change in accounting principle. Finally, a note describes the accounting change, why it is an improvement, and what income would have been under the prior method.

Quick Check

20. Which of the following is an extraordinary item? (*a*) a settlement paid to a customer injured while using the company's product, (*b*) a loss to a plant from damages caused by a meteorite, or (*c*) a loss from selling old equipment.
21. Identify the five major sections of an income statement that are potentially reported.
22. A company using FIFO for the past 15 years decides to switch to LIFO. The effect of this event on prior years' net income is (*a*) reported as a prior period adjustment to retained earnings; (*b*) ignored because it is a change in an accounting estimate; or (*c*) reported on the current year income statement.

Answers—p. 526

Earnings per Share

A1 Compute earnings per share and describe this ratio's use.

The final section of the income statement in Exhibit 13.15 reports earnings per share for each of the four subcategories of income (continuing operations, discontinued segments, extraordinary items, and the effect of accounting principle changes) when they exist. **Earnings per share,** also called *net income per share,* is the amount of income earned per each share of a company's outstanding common stock. The **basic earnings per share** formula is in Exhibit 13.16. The weighted-average common shares outstanding is explained by first considering the simple case of no changes in shares outstanding and second when shares outstanding changes.

Point: Earnings per share is often referred to as *EPS*.

Exhibit 13.16

Basic Earnings per Share

$$\textbf{Basic earnings per share} = \frac{\textbf{Net income} - \textbf{Preferred dividends}}{\textbf{Weighted-average common shares outstanding}}$$

No Changes in Common Shares Outstanding Assume that Quantum Co. earns $40,000 net income in 2005 and declares dividends of $7,500 on its noncumulative preferred stock. (If preferred stock is *non*cumulative, the income available [numerator] is the current period net income less any preferred dividends *declared* in that same period. If preferred stock is cumulative, the income available [numerator] is the current period net income less the preferred dividends whether declared or not.) Quantum has 5,000 common shares outstanding during all of 2005. Its basic EPS is

$$\text{Basic earnings per share} = \frac{\$40{,}000 - \$7{,}500}{5{,}000 \text{ shares}} = \$6.50$$

Changes in Common Shares Outstanding (Stock Sales and Purchases) Assume that Quantum earns $40,000 in 2005 and declares preferred dividends of $7,500. Also assume that it begins the year with 5,000 common shares outstanding, sells 4,000 additional shares on July 1, and purchases 3,000 treasury shares on November 1. Thus, 5,000 shares were outstanding for the first six months, 9,000 were outstanding for July through October (four months), and 6,000 were outstanding for the final two months. Exhibit 13.17 shows how to compute Quantum's weighted-average number of shares outstanding for 2005.

Global: Some countries, such as Japan and Australia, use the number of shares outstanding at the end of the period when computing EPS.

Exhibit 13.17

Computing Weighted-Average Shares Outstanding

Time Period	Outstanding Shares		Fraction of Year		Weighted Average
January–June	5,000	×	6/12	=	2,500
July–October	9,000	×	4/12	=	3,000
November–December	6,000	×	2/12	=	1,000
Weighted-average shares outstanding					**6,500**

Quantum's basic EPS is

$$\text{Basic earnings per share} = \frac{\$40{,}000 - \$7{,}500}{6{,}500 \text{ shares}} = \$5$$

Changes in Common Shares Outstanding (Stock Splits and Dividends) We restate the number of shares outstanding during the period to reflect a stock split or dividend *as if it occurred at the beginning of the period.* To illustrate, use the preceding facts and assume that Quantum executed a 2-for-1 stock split on December 1, 2005. We include an additional column reflecting the effect of the split in Exhibit 13.18. The December shares already reflect the split and do not require adjustment.

Exhibit 13.18

Computing Weighted-Average Shares Outstanding when Stock Splits (or Dividends) Occur

Time Period	Outstanding Shares		Effect of Split		Fraction of Year		Weighted Average
January–June	5,000	×	2	×	6/12	=	5,000
July–October	9,000	×	2	×	4/12	=	6,000
November	6,000	×	2	×	1/12	=	1,000
December	12,000	×	1	×	1/12	=	1,000
Weighted-average shares outstanding							**13,000**

Quantum's basic EPS under the 2-for-1 stock split is

$$\text{Basic earnings per share} = \frac{\$40{,}000 - \$7{,}500}{13{,}000 \text{ shares}} = \$2.50$$

We use the same computations for stock dividends. For instance, if the 2-for-1 stock split had been a 10% stock dividend, the outstanding shares prior to the dividend are multiplied by 1.1 instead of 2.0 because 110% (or 1.1) of the original number of shares are now outstanding, computed as 100% + 10%.[3]

Decision Insight

Future Fortunes Some managers have fortunes to reap from unexercised stock options. Four of the larger treasure chests are:

Lawrence Ellison (Oracle)	$3,434 million
John Chambers (Cisco)	1,126 million
Scott McNealy (Sun)	849 million
Stephen Case (AOL)	524 million

Decision Ethics

Director The board of Intex is planning its stockholders' meeting agenda. The first item is whether to disclose a contract just signed that will increase future income. One officer argues, "The meeting should focus on actual results." After agreeing not to disclose the contract, the next item is a motion for stockholders to approve a two-year option to managers to buy shares at a price equal to the average stock price over the next 2 weeks. What action (if any) do you take?

Answer—p. 525

Stock Options

The majority of corporations whose shares are publicly traded issue **stock options,** which are rights to purchase common stock at a fixed price over a specified period. As the stock's price rises above the fixed price, the option's value increases. **Starbucks** and **Home Depot** offer stock options to both full- and part-time employees. Stock options are said to motivate managers and employees to (1) focus on company performance, (2) take a long-run perspective, and (3) remain with the company. A stock option is like having an investment with no risk ("a carrot with no stick").

To illustrate, Quantum grants each of its employees the option to purchase 100 shares of its $1 par value common stock at its current market price of $50 per share anytime within the next 10 years. If the stock price rises to $70 per share, an employee can exercise the option at a gain of $20 per share (acquire a $70 stock at the $50 option price). With 100 shares, a single employee would have a total gain of $2,000, computed as $20 × 100 shares.

Quick Check

23. FDI reports 2005 net income of $250,000 and pays preferred dividends of $70,000. On January 1, 2005, FDI had 25,000 outstanding common shares, and it purchased 5,000 treasury shares on July 1. Its 2005 basic EPS is *(a)* $8; *(b)* $9; or *(c)* $10.
24. How are stock splits and stock dividends treated in computing the weighted-average number of outstanding common shares?
25. What EPS figures are reported for a complex capital structure company?

Answers—p. 526

Statement of Retained Earnings

C5 Explain the items reported in retained earnings.

Retained earnings generally consist of a company's cumulative net income less any net losses and dividends declared since its inception. Retained earnings are part of stockholders' claims on the company's net assets, but this does *not* imply that a certain amount of cash or other assets is available to pay stockholders. For example, **Harley-Davidson** has $2.4 billion in

[3] A corporation can be classified as having either a simple or complex capital structure. The term **simple capital structure** refers to a company with only common stock and nonconvertible preferred stock outstanding. The term **complex capital structure** refers to companies with dilutive securities. **Dilutive securities** include options, rights to purchase common stock, and any bonds or preferred stock that are convertible into common stock. A company with a complex capital structure must often report two EPS figures: basic and diluted. **Diluted earnings per share** is computed by adding all dilutive securities to the denominator of the basic EPS computation. It reflects the decrease in basic EPS *assuming* that all dilutive securities are converted into common shares. Since ComUS had a simple capital structure, it reported only basic EPS.

retained earnings, but only $0.3 billion in cash. This section describes events and transactions affecting retained earnings and how retained earnings are reported.

Restrictions and Appropriations The term **restricted retained earnings** refers to both *statutory* and *contractual* restrictions. A common statutory (or legal) restriction is to limit treasury stock purchases to the amount of retained earnings. The balance sheet in Exhibit 13.14 provides an example. A common *contractual restriction* involves loan agreements that restrict paying dividends beyond a specified amount or percent of retained earnings. Restrictions are usually described in the notes. The term **appropriated retained earnings** refers to a voluntary transfer of amounts from the Retained Earnings account to the Appropriated Retained Earnings account to inform users of special activities that require funds.

Global: Some countries, such as Japan, require companies to set up reserves at specified rates for the protection of creditors.

Prior Period Adjustments **Prior period adjustments** are corrections of material errors in prior period financial statements. These errors include arithmetic mistakes, unacceptable accounting, and missed facts. Prior period adjustments are reported in the *statement of retained earnings* (or the statement of stockholders' equity), net of any income tax effects. Prior period adjustments result in changing the beginning balance of retained earnings for events occurring prior to the earliest period reported in the current set of financial statements. To illustrate, assume that ComUS makes an error in a 2003 journal entry for the purchase of land by incorrectly debiting an expense account. When this is discovered in 2005, the statement of retained earnings includes a prior period adjustment, as shown in Exhibit 13.19. This exhibit also shows the usual format of the statement of retained earnings.

Point: If a year 2003 error is discovered in 2004, the company records the adjustment in 2004. But if the financial statements include 2003 and 2004 figures, the adjustment is not reported as a correction of 2004's beginning retained earnings balance. Instead, the statements report the correct amounts for 2003, and a note describes the correction.

Exhibit 13.19

Statement of Retained Earnings with a Prior Period Adjustment

ComUS Statement of Retained Earnings For Year Ended December 31, 2005	
Retained earnings, Dec. 31, 2004, as previously reported	$4,745,000
Prior period adjustment	
Cost of land incorrectly expensed (net of $63,000 income taxes)	**147,000**
Retained earnings, Dec. 31, 2004, as adjusted	4,892,000
Plus net income	1,224,300
Less cash dividends declared	(301,800)
Retained earnings, Dec. 31, 2005	$5,814,500

Note that many items reported in financial statements are based on estimates. Future events are certain to reveal that some of these estimates were inaccurate even when based on the best data available at the time. These inaccuracies are *not* considered errors and are *not* reported as prior period adjustments. Instead, they are identified as **changes in accounting estimates** and are accounted for in current and future periods. To illustrate, we know that depreciation is based on estimated useful lives and salvage values. As time passes and new information becomes available, managers may need to change these estimates and the resulting depreciation expense for current and future periods.

Point: Accounting for changes in estimates is sometimes criticized as two wrongs to make a right. Consider a change in an asset's life. Depreciation neither before nor after the change is the amount computed if the revised estimate were originally selected. Regulators chose this approach to avoid restating prior period numbers.

This cartoon reinforces the trade-off of risk (dangerous) and return (thrilling ride) when buying stock.

Statement of Stockholders' Equity

Instead of a separate statement of retained earnings, companies commonly report a statement of stockholders' equity that includes changes in retained earnings. A **statement of stockholders' equity** lists the beginning and ending balances of each equity account and describes the changes that occur during the period. The companies in Appendix A report such a statement. The usual format is to provide a column for each component of equity and use the rows to describe events occurring in the period. Exhibit 13.20 shows a condensed statement for **Outback Steakhouse**.

Exhibit 13.20

Statement of Stockholders' Equity

OUTBACK STEAKHOUSE Statement of Stockholders' Equity					
($ thousands)	Common Stock Amount	Contributed Capital in Excess of Par	Retained Earnings	Treasury Stock	Total
Balance, Dec. 31, 2001	**$786**	**$220,648**	**$762,414**	**$(42,004)**	**$ 941,844**
Net income	—	—	156,364	—	156,364
Issuance of Common Stock	2	15,578	—	—	15,580
Purchase of Treasury Stock	—	—	—	(81,650)	(81,650)
Reissuance of Treasury Stock	—	—	(6,767)	36,706	29,939
Cash Dividends ($0.12 per share)	—	—	(9,101)	—	(9,101)
Balance, Dec. 31, 2002	**$788**	**$236,226**	**$902,910**	**$(86,948)**	**$1,052,976**

Decision Analysis — Book Value per Share, Dividend Yield, and Price-Earnings Ratio

Book Value per Share

A2 Compute book value and explain its use in analysis.

Point: Book value per share is also referred to as *stockholders' claim to assets on a per share basis.*

Case 1: Common Stock (Only) Outstanding. **Book value per common share,** defined in Exhibit 13.21, is the recorded amount of stockholders' equity applicable to *common* shares on a per share basis. To illustrate, we use Dillon Snowboards' data from Exhibit 13.4. Dillon has 30,000 outstanding common shares, and the stockholders' equity applicable to common shares is $365,000. Dillon's book value per common share is $12.17, computed as $365,000 divided by 30,000 shares.

Exhibit 13.21

Book Value per Common Share

$$\textbf{Book value per common share} = \frac{\textbf{Stockholders' equity applicable to common shares}}{\textbf{Number of common shares outstanding}}$$

Case 2: Common and Preferred Stock Outstanding. To compute book value when both common and preferred shares are outstanding, we allocate total stockholders' equity between the two types of shares. The **book value per preferred share** is computed first; its computation is shown in Exhibit 13.22.

Exhibit 13.22

Book Value per Preferred Share

$$\textbf{Book value per preferred share} = \frac{\textbf{Stockholders' equity applicable to preferred shares}}{\textbf{Number of preferred shares outstanding}}$$

The stockholders' equity applicable to preferred shares equals the preferred share's call price (or par value if the preferred is not callable) plus any cumulative dividends in arrears. The remaining stockholders' equity is the portion applicable to common shares. To illustrate, consider LTD's stockholders' equity in Exhibit 13.23. Its preferred stock is callable at $108 per share, and two years of cumulative preferred dividends are in arrears.

Exhibit 13.23

Stockholders' Equity with Preferred and Common Stock

Stockholders' Equity	
Preferred stock—$100 par value, 7% cumulative, 2,000 shares authorized, 1,000 shares issued and outstanding	$100,000
Common stock—$25 par value, 12,000 shares authorized, 10,000 shares issued and outstanding	250,000
Contributed capital in excess of par value, common stock	15,000
Retained earnings	82,000
Total stockholders' equity	$447,000

The book value computations are in Exhibit 13.24. Note that equity is first allocated to preferred shares before the book value of common shares is computed.

Total stockholders' equity		$447,000
Less equity applicable to preferred shares		
Call price (1,000 shares × $108)	$108,000	
Dividends in arrears ($100,000 × 7% × 2 years)	14,000	(122,000)
Equity applicable to common shares		$325,000
Book value per preferred share ($122,000/1,000 shares)		**$ 122.00**
Book value per common share ($325,000/10,000 shares)		**$ 32.50**

Exhibit 13.24

Computing Book Value per Preferred and Common Share

Book value per share reflects the value per share if a company is liquidated at balance sheet amounts. Book value is also the starting point in many stock valuation models, merger negotiations, price setting for public utilities, and loan contracts. The main limitation in using book value is the potential difference between recorded value and market value for assets and liabilities. Investors often adjust their analysis for estimates of these differences.

Decision Maker

Investor You are considering investing in **BMX**, whose book value per common share is $4 and price per common share on the stock exchange is $7. From this information, are BMX's net assets priced higher or lower than its recorded values?

Answer—p. 526

Dividend Yield

A3 Compute dividend yield and explain its use in analysis.

Investors buy shares of a company's stock in anticipation of receiving a return from either or both cash dividends and stock price increases. Stocks that pay large dividends on a regular basis, called *income stocks,* are attractive to investors who want recurring cash flows from their investments. In contrast, some stocks pay little or no dividends but are still attractive to investors because of their expected stock price increases. The stocks of companies that distribute little or no cash but use their cash to finance expansion are called *growth stocks.* One way to help identify whether a stock is an income stock or a growth stock is to analyze its dividend yield. **Dividend yield,** defined in Exhibit 13.25, shows the annual amount of cash dividends distributed to common shares relative to their market value.

$$\textbf{Dividend yield} = \frac{\textbf{Annual cash dividends per share}}{\textbf{Market value per share}}$$

Exhibit 13.25

Dividend Yield

Dividend yield can be computed for current and prior periods using actual dividends and stock prices and for future periods using expected values. Exhibit 13.26 shows recent dividend and stock price data for **Microsoft** and **Altria Group** to compute dividend yield.

Company	Cash Dividends per Share	Market Value per Share	Dividend Yield
Microsoft	$0.08	$25	0.3%
Altria Group	2.56	30	8.5

Exhibit 13.26

Dividend and Stock Price Information

Dividend yield is near zero for Microsoft, implying it is a growth stock. An investor in Microsoft would look for increases in stock prices (and eventual cash from the sale of stock). Altria has a dividend yield of 8.5%, implying it is an income stock for which dividends are important in assessing its value.

Point: The *payout ratio* equals cash dividends declared on common stock divided by net income. A low payout ratio suggests that a company is retaining earnings for future growth.

Price-Earnings Ratio

A4 Compute price-earnings ratio and describe its use in analysis.

A stock's market value is determined by its *expected* future cash flows. A comparison of a company's EPS and its market value per share reveals information about market expectations. This comparison is traditionally made using a **price-earnings (or PE) ratio,** expressed also as *price earnings, price to* *earnings,* or *PE.* Some analysts interpret this ratio as what price the market is willing to pay for a company's current earnings stream. Price-earnings ratios can differ across companies that have similar earnings because of either higher or lower expectations of future earnings. The price-earnings ratio is defined in Exhibit 13.27.

Point: The average PE ratio of stocks in the 1950–2003 period is about 14.

Exhibit 13.27

Price-Earnings Ratio

$$\textbf{Price-earnings ratio} = \frac{\textbf{Market value (price) per share}}{\textbf{Earnings per share}}$$

Point: Average PE ratios for U.S. stocks have increased over the past two decades. Some analysts interpret this as a signal the market is overpriced. But higher ratios can at least partly reflect accounting changes that have reduced reported earnings.

This ratio is often computed using EPS from the most recent period. However, many users compute this ratio using *expected* EPS for the next period.

Some analysts view stocks with high PE ratios (higher than 20 to 25) as more likely to be overpriced and stocks with low PE ratios (less than 5 to 8) as more likely to be underpriced. These investors prefer to sell or avoid buying stocks with high PE ratios and to buy or hold stocks with low PE ratios. However, investment decision making is rarely so simple as to rely on a single ratio. For instance, a stock with a high PE ratio can prove to be a good investment if its earnings continue to increase beyond current expectations. Similarly, a stock with a low PE ratio can prove to be a poor investment if its earnings decline below expectations.

Decision Maker

Manager You plan to invest in one of two companies identified as having identical future prospects. One has a PE of 19 and the other a PE of 25. Which do you invest in? Does it matter if your *estimate* of PE for these two companies is 29 as opposed to 22?

Answer—p. 526

Demonstration Problem 1

Barton Corporation began operations on January 1, 2005. The following transactions relating to stockholders' equity occurred in the first two years of the company's operations.

2005

Jan. 1 Authorized the issuance of 2 million shares of $5 par value common stock and 100,000 shares of $100 par value, 10% cumulative, preferred stock.
Jan. 2 Issued 200,000 shares of common stock for $12 cash per share.
Jan. 3 Issued 100,000 shares of common stock in exchange for a building valued at $820,000 and merchandise inventory valued at $380,000.
Jan. 4 Paid $10,000 cash to the company's founders for organization activities.
Jan. 5 Issued 12,000 shares of preferred stock for $110 cash per share.

2006

June 4 Issued 100,000 shares of common stock for $15 cash per share.

Required

1. Prepare journal entries to record these transactions.
2. Prepare the stockholders' equity section of the balance sheet as of December 31, 2005, and December 31, 2006, based on these transactions.
3. Prepare a table showing dividend allocations and dividends per share for 2005 and 2006 assuming Barton declares the following cash dividends: 2005, $50,000, and 2006, $300,000.
4. Prepare the January 2, 2005, journal entry for Barton's issuance of 200,000 shares of common stock for $12 cash per share assuming
   a. Common stock is no-par stock without a stated value.
   b. Common stock is no-par stock with a stated value of $10 per share.

Planning the Solution

- Record journal entries for the transactions for 2005 and 2006.
- Determine the balances for the 2005 and 2006 equity accounts for the balance sheet.
- Prepare the contributed capital portion of the 2005 and 2006 balance sheets.
- Prepare a table similar to Exhibit 13.8 showing dividend allocations for 2005 and 2006.
- Record the issuance of common stock under both specifications of no-par stock.

Solution to Demonstration Problem 1

1. Journal entries:

Date	Account	Debit	Credit
2005			
Jan. 2	Cash	2,400,000	
	Common Stock, $5 Par Value		1,000,000
	Contributed Capital in Excess of Par Value, Common Stock		1,400,000
	Issued 200,000 shares of common stock.		
Jan. 3	Building	820,000	
	Merchandise Inventory	380,000	
	Common Stock, $5 Par Value		500,000
	Contributed Capital in Excess of Par Value, Common Stock		700,000
	Issued 100,000 shares of common stock.		
Jan. 4	Organization Expenses	10,000	
	Cash		10,000
	Paid founders for organization costs.		
Jan. 5	Cash	1,320,000	
	Preferred Stock, $100 Par Value		1,200,000
	Contributed Capital in Excess of Par Value, Preferred Stock		120,000
	Issued 12,000 shares of preferred stock.		
2006			
June 4	Cash	1,500,000	
	Common Stock, $5 Par Value		500,000
	Contributed Capital in Excess of Par Value, Common Stock		1,000,000
	Issued 100,000 shares of common stock.		

2. Balance sheet presentations (at December 31 year-end):

	2005	2006
Stockholders' Equity		
Contributed capital		
Preferred stock—$100 par value, 10% cumulative, 100,000 shares authorized, 12,000 shares issued and outstanding	$1,200,000	$1,200,000
Contributed capital in excess of par value, preferred stock	120,000	120,000
Total capital contributed by preferred stockholders	1,320,000	1,320,000
Common stock—$5 par value, 2,000,000 shares authorized, 300,000 shares issued and outstanding in 2005, and 400,000 shares issued and outstanding in 2006	1,500,000	2,000,000
Contributed capital in excess of par value, common stock	2,100,000	3,100,000
Total capital contributed by common stockholders	3,600,000	5,100,000
Total contributed capital	$4,920,000	$6,420,000

3. Dividend allocation table:

	Common	Preferred
2005 ($50,000)		
Preferred—current year (12,000 shares × $10 = $120,000)	$ 0	$ 50,000
Common—remainder (300,000 shares outstanding)	0	0
Total for the year	$ 0	$ 50,000
2006 ($300,000)		
Preferred—dividend in arrears from 2005 ($120,000 − $50,000)	$ 0	$ 70,000
Preferred—current year	0	120,000
Common—remainder (400,000 shares outstanding)	110,000	0
Total for the year	$110,000	$190,000
Dividends per share		
2005	$ 0.00	$ 4.17
2006	$ 0.28	$ 15.83

4. Journal entries:

a. For 2005:

Jan. 2	Cash	2,400,000	
	Common Stock, No-Par Value		2,400,000
	Issued 200,000 shares of no-par common stock at $12 per share.		

b. For 2005:

Jan. 2	Cash	2,400,000	
	Common Stock, $10 Stated Value		2,000,000
	Contributed Capital in Excess of Stated Value, Common Stock		400,000
	Issued 200,000 shares of $10 stated value common stock at $12 per share.		

Demonstration Problem 2

Precision Company began year 2005 with the following balances in its stockholders' equity accounts:

Common stock—$10 par, 500,000 shares authorized, 200,000 shares issued and outstanding	$2,000,000
Contributed capital in excess of par, common stock	1,000,000
Retained earnings	5,000,000
Total	$8,000,000

All outstanding common stock was issued for $15 per share when the company was created.

Part 1

Prepare journal entries to account for the following transactions during year 2005:

Jan. 10 The board declared a $0.10 cash dividend per share to shareholders of record Jan. 28.
Feb. 15 Paid the cash dividend declared on January 10.
Mar. 31 Declared a 20% stock dividend. The market value of the stock is $18 per share.
May 1 Distributed the stock dividend declared on March 31.
July 1 Purchased 30,000 shares of treasury stock at $20 per share.
Sept. 1 Sold 20,000 treasury shares at $26 cash per share.
Dec. 1 Sold the remaining 10,000 shares of treasury stock at $7 cash per share.

Part 2

Use the following information to prepare a complete income statement of Precision Corp. (a technology consulting company) for year 2005, including EPS results for each category of income.

Cumulative effect of a change in depreciation method (net of tax benefit)	$ (136,500)
Operating expenses related to continuing operations	(2,072,500)
Extraordinary gain from insurance coverage of earthquake damage (net of tax)	182,000
Gain on disposal of discontinued segment assets (net of tax)	29,000
Gain on sale of long-term investments	400,000
Loss from operating discontinued segment (net of tax benefit)	(120,000)
Income taxes on income from continuing operations	(225,000)
Prior period adjustment for error (net of tax benefit)	(75,000)
Net sales	4,140,000
Loss on sale of equipment	(650,000)

Planning the Solution

- Calculate the total cash dividend to record by multiplying the cash dividend declared by the number of shares as of the date of record.
- Decide whether the stock dividend is a small or large dividend. Then analyze each event to determine the accounts affected and the appropriate amounts to be recorded.
- Based on shares of outstanding stock at the beginning of the year and the transactions during the year, compute the weighted-average number of outstanding shares for the year.
- Assign each listed item to an appropriate income statement category.
- Prepare an income statement similar to Exhibit 13.15, including EPS results.

Solution to Demonstration Problem 2

Part 1

Date	Account	Debit	Credit
Jan. 10	Retained Earnings	20,000	
	Common Dividend Payable		20,000
	Declared a $0.10 per share cash dividend.		
Feb. 15	Common Dividend Payable	20,000	
	Cash		20,000
	Paid $0.10 per share cash dividend.		
Mar. 31	Retained Earnings	720,000	
	Common Stock Dividend Distributable		400,000
	Contributed Capital in Excess of Par Value, Common Stock		320,000
	Declared a small stock dividend of 20% or 40,000 shares; market value is $18 per share.		
May 1	Common Stock Dividend Distributable	400,000	
	Common Stock		400,000
	Distributed 40,000 shares of common stock.		
July 1	Treasury Stock, Common	600,000	
	Cash		600,000
	Purchased 30,000 common shares at $20 per share.		
Sept. 1	Cash	520,000	
	Treasury Stock, Common		400,000
	Contributed Capital, Treasury Stock		120,000
	Sold 20,000 treasury shares at $26 per share.		
Dec. 1	Cash	70,000	
	Contributed Capital, Treasury Stock	120,000	
	Retained Earnings	10,000	
	Treasury Stock, Common		200,000
	Sold 10,000 treasury shares at $7 per share.		

Part 2

Compute the weighted-average number of outstanding common shares:

Time Period	Outstanding Shares		Effect of Dividend		Fraction of Year		Weighted Average
January–April	200,000	×	1.2	×	4/12	=	80,000
May–June	240,000*	×	1	×	2/12	=	40,000
July–August	210,000	×	1	×	2/12	=	35,000
September–November	230,000	×	1	×	3/12	=	57,500
December	240,000	×	1	×	1/12	=	20,000
Weighted-average shares outstanding							**232,500**

* 200,000 shares × 1.2 = 240,000 shares.

PRECISION CORPORATION Income Statement For Year Ended December 31, 2005		
Net sales		$4,140,000
Operating expenses		(2,072,500)
Other gains (losses)		
Gain on sale of long-term investments		400,000
Loss on sale of equipment		(650,000)
Income from continuing operations before taxes		1,817,500
Income taxes expense		225,000
Income from continuing operations		1,592,500
Discontinued segment		
Loss from operating discontinued segment (net of tax benefit)	$(120,000)	
Gain on disposal of discontinued segment (net of tax)	29,000	(91,000)
Income before extraordinary item and cumulative effect of a change in accounting principle		1,501,500
Extraordinary item		
Extraordinary gain from insurance coverage of earthquake damage (net of tax)		182,000
Cumulative effect of a change in accounting principle		
Cumulative effect of change in deprec. method (net of tax benefit)		(136,500)
Net income		$1,547,000
Earnings per share (232,500 weighted-average shares)		
Income from continuing operations		$ 6.85
Discontinued operations		(0.39)
Income before extraordinary item and cumulative effect of change in accounting principle		6.46
Extraordinary item		0.78
Cumulative effect of change in accounting principle		(0.59)
Net income (basic earnings per share)		$ 6.65

Summary

C1 Identify characteristics of corporations and their organization. Corporations are legal entities whose stockholders are not liable for its debts. Stock is easily transferred, and the life of a corporation does not end with the incapacity of a stock holder. A corporation acts through its agents, who are its officers and managers. Corporations are regulated and subject to income taxes.

C2 Describe the components of stockholders' equity. Authorized stock is the stock that a corporation's charter authorizes it to sell. Issued stock is the portion of authorized shares sold. Par value stock is a value per share assigned by the charter. No-par value stock is stock *not* assigned a value per share by the charter. Stated value stock is no-par stock to which the directors assign a value per share. Stockholders' equity is made up of (1) contributed capital and (2) retained earnings. Contributed capital consists of funds raised by stock issuances. Retained earnings consists of cumulative net income (losses) not distributed.

C3 **Explain characteristics of common and preferred stock.** Preferred stock has a priority (or senior status) relative to common stock in one or more areas, usually (1) dividends and (2) assets in case of liquidation. Preferred stock usually does not carry voting rights and can be convertible or callable. Convertibility permits the holder to convert preferred to common. Callability permits the issuer to buy back preferred stock under specified conditions.

C4 **Explain the form and content of a complete income statement.** An income statement has five *potential* sections: (1) continuing operations, (2) discontinued segments, (3) extraordinary items, (4) changes in accounting, and (5) earnings per share.

C5 **Explain the items reported in retained earnings.** Many companies face statutory and contractual restrictions on retained earnings. Corporations can voluntarily appropriate retained earnings to inform others about their disposition. Prior period adjustments are corrections of errors in prior financial statements.

A1 **Compute earnings per share and describe this ratio's use.** A company with a simple capital structure computes basic EPS by dividing net income less any preferred dividends by the weighted-average number of outstanding common shares. A company with a complex capital structure must usually report both basic and diluted EPS.

A2 **Compute book value and explain its use in analysis.** Book value per common share is equity applicable to common shares divided by the number of outstanding common shares. Book value per preferred share is equity applicable to preferred shares divided by the number of outstanding preferred shares.

A3 **Compute dividend yield and explain its use in analysis.** Dividend yield is the ratio of a stock's annual cash dividends per share to its market value (price) per share. Dividend yield can be compared with the yield of other companies to determine whether the stock is expected to be an income or growth stock.

A4 **Compute price-earnings ratio and describe its use in analysis.** A common stock's price-earnings (PE) ratio is computed by dividing the stock's market value (price) per share by its EPS. A stock's PE is based on expectations that can prove to be better or worse than eventual performance.

P1 **Record the issuance of corporate stock.** When stock is issued, its par or stated value is credited to the stock account and any excess is credited to a separate contributed capital account. If a stock has neither par nor stated value, the entire proceeds are credited to the stock account. Stockholders must contribute assets equal to minimum legal capital or be potentially liable for the deficiency.

P2 **Distribute dividends between common stock and preferred stock.** Preferred stockholders usually hold the right to dividend distributions before common stockholders. When preferred stock is cumulative and in arrears, the amount in arrears must be distributed to preferred before any dividends are distributed to common.

P3 **Record transactions involving cash dividends.** Cash dividends involve three events. On the date of declaration, the directors bind the company to pay the dividend. A dividend declaration reduces retained earnings and creates a current liability. On the date of record, recipients of the dividend are identified. On the date of payment, cash is paid to stockholders and the current liability is removed.

P4 **Account for stock dividends and stock splits.** Neither a stock dividend nor a stock split alters the value of the company. However, the value of each share is less due to the distribution of additional shares. The distribution of additional shares is according to individual stockholders' ownership percent. Small stock dividends (≤25%) are recorded by capitalizing retained earnings equal to the market value of distributed shares. Large stock dividends (>25%) are recorded by capitalizing retained earnings equal to the par or stated value of distributed shares. Stock splits do not yield journal entries but do yield changes in the description of stock.

P5 **Record purchases and sales of treasury stock and the retirement of stock.** When a corporation purchases its own previously issued stock, it debits the cost of these shares to Treasury Stock. Treasury stock is subtracted from equity in the balance sheet. If treasury stock is reissued, any proceeds in excess of cost are credited to Contributed Capital, Treasury Stock. If the proceeds are less than cost, they are debited to Contributed Capital, Treasury Stock to the extent a credit balance exists. Any remaining amount is debited to Retained Earnings. When stock is retired, all accounts related to the stock are removed.

Guidance Answers to **Decision Maker** and **Decision Ethics**

Concert Organizer You have two basic options: (1) different classes of common stock or (2) common and preferred stock. Your objective is to issue to yourself stock that has all or a majority of the voting power. The other class of stock would carry limited or no voting rights. In this way, you maintain control and are able to raise the necessary funds.

Entrepreneur The 50% stock dividend provides you no direct income. A stock dividend often reveals management's optimistic expectations about the future and can improve a stock's marketability by making it affordable to more investors. Accordingly, a stock dividend usually reveals "good news" and because of this, it likely increases (slightly) the market value for your stock.

Small Business Owner The frost loss is probably not extraordinary. Jacksonville experiences enough recurring frost damage to make it difficult to argue this event is both unusual and infrequent. Still, you want to highlight the frost loss and hope the bank views this uncommon event separately from continuing operations.

Director This case deals with insider trading in a company's stock. The ethical conflict is between your director responsibilities to stockholders (and the public) and your interest in increasing personal wealth from the options. If information about the new contract is kept private until after the option plan is approved and the options are priced, you are likely to make more money. (*Note:* Insider trading laws may make nondisclosure in this case a crime.)

You should raise ethical and legal concerns to the board. You might also consider whether staying on the board of this company is proper since it appears there was some intent to deceive outsiders.

Investor Book value reflects recorded values. BMX's book value is $4 per common share. Stock price reflects the market's expectation of net asset value (both tangible and intangible items). BMX's market value is $7 per common share. Comparing these figures suggests BMX's market value of net assets is higher than its recorded values (by an amount of $7 versus $4 per share).

Manager Since one company requires a payment of $19 for each $1 of earnings, and the other requires $25, you would prefer the stock with the PE of 19; it is a better deal given identical prospects. You should make sure these companies' earnings computations are roughly the same, for example, no extraordinary items, unusual events, and so forth. Also, your PE estimates for these companies do matter. If you are willing to pay $29 for each $1 of earnings for these companies, both are solid investments because you obviously expect both to exceed current market expectations.

Guidance Answers to **Quick Checks**

1. (*b*)
2. A corporation pays taxes on its income, and its stockholders normally pay personal income taxes (at the 15% rate or lower) on any cash dividends received from the corporation.
3. A proxy is a legal document used to transfer a stockholder's right to vote to another person.
4. (*a*)
5. A stock premium is an amount in excess of par (or stated) value paid by purchasers of newly issued stock.
6. Minimum legal capital intends to protect creditors of a corporation by obligating stockholders to some minimum level of equity financing and by constraining a corporation from excessive payments to stockholders.
7. Typically, preferred stock has a preference in receipt of dividends and in distribution of assets.
8. (*a*)
9. (*b*)

Total cash dividend	$288,000
To preferred shareholders	135,000*
Remainder to common shareholders	$153,000

* 9,000 × $50 × 10% × 3 years = $135,000.

10. Common Dividend Payable is a current liability account.
11. The date of declaration, date of record, and date of payment.
12. A dividend is a legal liability at the date of declaration, on which date it is recorded as a liability.
13. A stock dividend does not transfer assets to stockholders, but it does require an amount of retained earnings to be transferred to a contributed capital account(s).
14. A small stock dividend is 25% or less of the previous outstanding shares. A large stock dividend is more than 25%.
15. Retained earnings equal to the distributable shares' market value should be capitalized for a small stock dividend.
16. (*b*)
17. No. The shares are an investment for Southern Co. and are issued and outstanding shares for Northern Corp.
18. Treasury stock does not affect the number of authorized or issued shares, but it reduces the outstanding shares.
19. (*a*)
20. (*b*)
21. The five (potentially reportable) major sections are income from continuing operations, discontinued segments, extraordinary items, cumulative effects of changes in accounting principles, and earnings per share.
22. (*c*)
23. (*a*) Weighted-average shares: (25,000 × 6/12) + (20,000 × 6/12) = 22,500. Earnings per share: ($250,000 − $70,000)/22,500 = $8.
24. The number of shares previously outstanding is retroactively restated to reflect the stock split or stock dividend as if it occurred at the beginning of the period.
25. Basic EPS and diluted EPS.

Key Terms

Key Terms are available at the book's Website for learning and testing in an online Flashcard Format.

Appropriated retained earnings (p. 517)
Authorized stock (p. 499)
Basic earnings per share (p. 514)
Book value per common share (p. 518)
Book value per preferred share (p. 518)
Business segment (p. 512)
Callable preferred stock (p. 505)
Call price (p. 505)
Capital stock (p. 499)
Changes in accounting estimates (p. 517)
Common stock (p. 498)
Complex capital structure (p. 516)
Contributed capital (p. 500)
Contributed capital in excess of par value (p. 500)
Convertible preferred stock (p. 505)
Corporation (p. 496)
Cumulative preferred stock (p. 503)
Date of declaration (p. 506)
Date of payment (p. 506)
Date of record (p. 506)
Diluted earnings per share (p. 516)
Dilutive securities (p. 516)
Discount on stock (p. 501)
Dividend in arrears (p. 504)
Dividend yield (p. 519)
Earnings per share (EPS) (p. 514)

Extraordinary gains or losses (p. 512)
Financial leverage (p. 505)
Infrequent gain or loss (p. 512)
Large stock dividend (p. 507)
Liquidating cash dividend (p. 507)
Market value per share (p. 499)
Minimum legal capital (p. 499)
Noncumulative preferred stock (p. 504)
Nonparticipating preferred stock (p. 504)
No-par value stock (p. 500)
Organization expenses (p. 502)
Participating preferred stock (p. 504)
Par value (p. 499)
Par value stock (p. 499)
Preemptive right (p. 498)
Preferred stock (p. 503)
Premium on stock (p. 500)
Price-earnings (PE) ratio (p. 519)
Prior period adjustment (p. 517)
Proxy (p. 498)
Restricted retained earnings (p. 517)
Retained earnings (p. 500)
Retained earnings deficit (p. 507)
Reverse stock split (p. 509)
Simple capital structure (p. 516)
Small stock dividend (p. 507)
Stated value stock (p. 500)
Statement of stockholders' equity (p. 517)
Stock dividend (p. 507)
Stockholders' equity (p. 500)
Stock options (p. 516)
Stock split (p. 509)
Stock subscription (p. 502)
Treasury stock (p. 510)
Unusual gain or loss (p. 512)

Personal Interactive Quiz

Personal Interactive Quizzes A and B are available at the book's Website to reinforce and assess your learning.

Discussion Questions

1. What are organization expenses? Provide examples.
2. How are organization expenses reported?
3. Who is responsible for directing a corporation's affairs?
4. What is the preemptive right of common stockholders?
5. List the general rights of common stockholders.
6. Why would an investor find convertible preferred stock attractive?
7. What is the difference between the par value and the call price of a share of preferred stock?
8. Identify and explain the importance of the three dates relevant to corporate dividends.
9. Why is the term *liquidating dividend* used to describe cash dividends debited against contributed capital accounts?
10. How does declaring a stock dividend affect the corporation's assets, liabilities, and total equity? What effects does the eventual distribution of the stock have?
11. What is the difference between a stock dividend and a stock split?
12. Courts have ruled that a stock dividend is not taxable income to stockholders. What justifies this decision?
13. How does the purchase of treasury stock affect the purchaser's assets and total equity?
14. Why do laws place limits on treasury stock purchases?
15. Where on the income statement does a company report an unusual gain not expected to occur more often than once every two years?
16. After taking five years of straight-line depreciation expense for an asset that was expected to have an eight-year useful life, a company decides that the asset will last six more years. Is this decision a change in accounting principles? How do the financial statements describe this change?
17. How are EPS results computed for a corporation with a simple capital structure?
18. Review the balance sheet for Krispy Kreme in Appendix A and determine the classes of stock that it has issued.

19. Refer to the balance sheet for Tastykake in Appendix A. What is the par value of its common stock? Suggest a rationale for the amount of par value it assigned.
20. Refer to the financial statements for Tastykake in Appendix A. How many treasury stock shares does it report as of December 28, 2002? Compute the average cost per treasury share.
21. Refer to the financial statements for Harley-Davidson in Appendix A. Was it a net seller or net purchaser of treasury stock for the fiscal year ended December 31, 2002? Explain.

Harley-Davidson

Red numbers denote Discussion Questions that involve decision-making.

Homework Manager *repeats all numerical Quick Studies on the book's Website with new numbers.* 

QUICK STUDY

QS 13-1
Characteristics of corporations
C1

Of the following statements, which are true for the corporate form of organization?

1. It is a separate legal entity.
2. Ownership rights cannot be easily transferred.
3. Owners are not agents of the corporation.
4. Capital is more easily accumulated than with most other forms of organization.
5. It has a limited life.
6. Owners have unlimited liability for corporate debts.
7. Corporate income that is distributed to shareholders is usually taxed twice.

QS 13-2
Issuance of common stock
P1

Prepare the journal entry to record each separate transaction. (*a*) On March 1, DVD Co. issues 44,500 shares of $4 par value common stock for $255,000 cash. (*b*) On April 1, GT Co. issues no-par value common stock for $50,000 cash. (*c*) On April 6, MTV issues 2,000 shares of $20 par value common stock for $35,000 of inventory, $135,000 of machinery, and acceptance of a $84,000 note payable.

QS 13-3
Dividend allocation between classes of shareholders
P2 

Hilton Company's stockholders' equity includes 75,000 shares of $5 par value, 8% cumulative preferred stock and 200,000 shares of $1 par value common stock. Both classes of stock have been outstanding since the company's inception. Hilton did not declare any dividends in the prior year, but it now declares and pays a $108,000 cash dividend in the current year. Determine the amount distributed to each class of stockholders for this two-year-old company.

QS 13-4
Accounting for cash dividends
P3

Prepare journal entries to record the following transactions for Skylar Corporation:

May 15 Declared a $48,000 cash dividend payable to common stockholders.
July 31 Paid the dividend declared on May 15.

QS 13-5
Accounting for small stock dividend
C2 P4

The stockholders' equity section of Catalina Company's balance sheet as of April 1 follows. On April 2, Catalina declares and distributes a 10% stock dividend. The stock's per share market value on April 2 is $25. Prepare the stockholders' equity section immediately after the stock dividend.

Common stock—$5 par value, 375,000 shares authorized, 150,000 shares issued and outstanding	$ 750,000
Contributed capital in excess of par value, common stock	352,500
Total contributed capital	1,102,500
Retained earnings	633,000
Total stockholders' equity	$1,735,500

QS 13-6
Purchase and sale of treasury stock P5

On May 3, Lassman Corporation purchased 3,000 shares of its own stock for $27,000 cash. On November 4, Lassman reissued 750 shares of this treasury stock for $7,080. Prepare the May 3 and November 4 journal entries to record Lassman's purchase and reissuance of treasury stock.

QS 13-7
Accounting for changes in estimates; error adjustments
C4 C5 

Answer the following questions related to a company's activities for the current year:

1. A review of the notes payable files discovers that three years ago the company reported the entire amount of a payment (principal and interest) on an installment note payable as interest expense. This mistake had a material effect on the amount of income in that year. How should the correction be reported in the current year financial statements?
2. After using an expected useful life of seven years and no salvage value to depreciate its office equipment over the preceding three years, the company decided early this year that the equipment will last only two more years. How should the effects of this decision be reported in the current year financial statements?

QS 13-8
Basic earnings per share A1

Barnes Company earned a net income of $450,000 this year. The number of common shares outstanding during the entire year was 200,000, and preferred shareholders received a $10,000 cash dividend. Compute Barnes Company's basic earnings per share.

QS 13-9
Weighted-average shares outstanding A1

On January 1, Vendetta Company had 100,000 shares of common stock outstanding. On February 1, it issued 20,000 additional shares of common stock. On June 1, it issued another 40,000 shares of common stock. Compute Vendetta's weighted-average shares outstanding for the calendar year.

QS 13-10
Weighted-average shares outstanding A1 P4

On January 1, Brazil Company had 150,000 shares of common stock outstanding. On April 1, it purchased 12,000 treasury shares and on June 2, it declared a 10% stock dividend. Compute Brazil's weighted-average shares outstanding for the calendar-year.

QS 13-11
Book value per common share
A2

The stockholders' equity section of Axel Company's balance sheet follows. The preferred stock's call price is $30. Determine the book value per share of the common stock.

Preferred stock—5% cumulative, $10 par value, 10,000 shares authorized, issued and outstanding	$100,000
Common stock—$5 par value, 100,000 shares authorized, 75,000 shares issued and outstanding	375,000
Retained earnings	445,000
Total stockholders' equity	$920,000

QS 13-12
Dividend yield
A3 

Fiona Company expects to pay a $2.10 per share cash dividend this year on its common stock. The current market value of Fiona stock is $28.50 per share. Compute the expected dividend yield on the Fiona stock. Would you classify the Fiona stock as a growth or an income stock?

QS 13-13
Price-earnings ratio A4 

Compute Fox Company's price-earnings ratio if its common stock has a market value of $30.75 per share and its EPS is $4.10. Would an analyst likely consider this stock potentially over- or underpriced?

***Homework Manager** repeats all numerical Exercises on the book's Website with new numbers.*

EXERCISES

Exercise 13-1
Characteristics of corporations
C1

Describe how each of the following characteristics of organizations applies to corporations.

1. Owner authority and control	5. Duration of life
2. Ease of formation	6. Owner liability
3. Transferability of ownership	7. Legal status
4. Ability to raise large capital amounts	8. Tax status of income

Exercise 13-2
Accounting for par and no-par stock issuances
P1

Aloha Corporation issues 6,000 shares of its common stock for $144,000 cash on February 20. Prepare journal entries to record this event under each of the following separate situations:

1. The stock has neither par nor stated value.
2. The stock has a $20 par value.
3. The stock has a $8 stated value.

Exercise 13-3
Recording stock issuances
P1

Prepare journal entries to record the following four separate issuances of stock:

1. Two thousand shares of no-par common stock are issued to the corporation's promoters in exchange for their efforts, estimated to be worth $30,000. The stock has no stated value.
2. Two thousand shares of no-par common stock are issued to the corporation's promoters in exchange for their efforts, estimated to be worth $30,000. The stock has a $1 per share stated value.
3. Four thousand shares of $10 par value common stock are issued for $70,000 cash.
4. One thousand shares of $100 par value preferred stock are issued for $120,000 cash.

Exercise 13-4
Identifying characteristics of preferred stock
C2 C3

Match each description 1 through 6 with the characteristic of preferred stock that it best describes by writing the letter of the characteristic in the blank next to each description.

A. Callable	**B.** Convertible	**C.** Cumulative
D. Noncumulative	**E.** Nonparticipating	**F.** Participating

______ **1.** Holders of the stock are not entitled to receive dividends in excess of the stated rate.

______ **2.** Holders of the stock lose any dividends that are not declared in the current year.

______ **3.** Holders of the stock are entitled to receive current and all past dividends before common stockholders receive any dividends.

______ **4.** Holders of this stock can exchange it for shares of common stock.

______ **5.** The issuing corporation can retire the stock by paying a prespecified price.

______ **6.** Holders of the stock can receive dividends exceeding the stated rate under certain conditions.

Exercise 13-5
Dividends on common and noncumulative preferred stock
P2

Citicool's outstanding stock consists of (*a*) 40,000 shares of noncumulative 7.5% preferred stock with a $10 par value and (*b*) 100,000 shares of common stock with a $1 par value. During its first four years of operation, the corporation declared and paid the following cash dividends:

2003	$ 10,000
2004	24,000
2005	100,000
2006	196,000

Check Total paid to preferred, $94,000

Determine the amount of dividends paid each year to each of the two classes of stockholders. Also compute the total dividends paid to each class for the four years combined.

Exercise 13-6
Dividends on common and cumulative preferred stock P2

Use the data in Exercise 13-5 to determine the amount of dividends paid each year to each of the two classes of stockholders assuming that the preferred stock is cumulative. Also determine the total dividends paid to each class for the four years combined.

Exercise 13-7
Stock dividends and splits
P4 

On June 30, 2005, Scizzory Corporation's common stock is priced at $31 per share before any stock dividend or split, and the stockholders' equity section of its balance sheet appears as follows:

Common stock—$10 par value, 60,000 shares authorized, 25,000 shares issued and outstanding	$250,000
Contributed capital in excess of par value, common stock	100,000
Total contributed capital	350,000
Retained earnings	330,000
Total stockholders' equity	$680,000

1. Assume that the company declares and immediately distributes a 100% stock dividend. This event is recorded by capitalizing retained earnings equal to the stock's par value. Answer these questions about stockholders' equity as it exists *after* issuing the new shares:
  a. What is the retained earnings balance?
  b. What is the amount of total stockholders' equity?
  c. How many shares are outstanding?

Check (1*b*) $680,000

2. Assume that the company implements a 2-for-1 stock split instead of the stock dividend in part 1. Answer these questions about stockholders' equity as it exists *after* issuing the new shares:
  a. What is the retained earnings balance?
  b. What is the amount of total stockholders' equity?
  c. How many shares are outstanding?

(2*a*) $330,000

3. Explain the difference, if any, to a stockholder from receiving new shares distributed under a large stock dividend versus a stock split.

Exercise 13-8
Stock dividends and per share book values
P4 

The stockholders' equity of Whiz.com at the beginning of the day on February 5 follows:

Common stock—$25 par value, 150,000 shares authorized, 60,000 shares issued and outstanding	$1,500,000
Contributed capital in excess of par value, common stock	525,000
Total contributed capital	2,025,000
Retained earnings	675,000
Total stockholders' equity	$2,700,000

On February 5, the directors declare a 20% stock dividend distributable on February 28 to the February 15 stockholders of record. The stock's market value is $40 per share on February 5 before the stock dividend. The stock's market value is $34 per share on February 28.

1. Prepare entries to record both the dividend declaration and its distribution.
2. One stockholder owned 750 shares on February 5 before the dividend. Compute the book value per share and total book value of this stockholder's shares immediately before and after the stock dividend of February 5.
3. Compute the total market value of the investor's shares in part 2 as of February 5 and February 28.

Check (2) Book value per share: before, $45.00; after, $37.50

Exercise 13-9
Recording and reporting treasury stock transactions

P5 

On October 10, the stockholders' equity of Noble Systems appears as follows:

Common stock—$10 par value, 36,000 shares authorized, issued, and outstanding	$360,000
Contributed capital in excess of par value, common stock	108,000
Total contributed capital	468,000
Retained earnings	432,000
Total stockholders' equity	$900,000

1. Prepare journal entries to record the following transactions for Noble Systems:
   a. Purchased 4,500 shares of its own common stock at $30 per share on October 11.
   b. Sold 1,200 treasury shares on November 1 for $36 cash per share.
   c. Sold all remaining treasury shares on November 25 for $25 cash per share.
2. Explain how Noble's equity section changes after the October 11 treasury stock purchase, and prepare the revised equity section of its balance sheet at that time.

Check (1c) Dr. Retained Earnings, $9,300

Exercise 13-10
Income statement categories

C4

In 2005, Randa Merchandising, Inc., sold its interest in a chain of wholesale outlets, taking the company completely out of the wholesaling business. The company still operates its retail outlets. A listing of the major sections of an income statement follows:

A. Income (loss) from continuing operations
B. Income (loss) from operating, or gain (loss) from disposing, a discontinued segment
C. Extraordinary gain (loss)
D. Cumulative effect of a change in accounting principle

Indicate where each of the following income-related items for this company appears on its 2005 income statement by writing the letter of the appropriate section in the blank beside each item.

Section	Item	Debit	Credit
______	1. Net sales		$2,700,000
______	2. Gain on state's condemnation of company property (net of tax)		330,000
______	3. Cost of goods sold	$1,380,000	
______	4. Effect of change from FIFO to LIFO (net of tax)		135,000
______	5. Income taxes expense	207,000	
______	6. Depreciation expense	262,500	
______	7. Gain on sale of wholesale business segment (net of tax)		675,000
______	8. Loss from operating wholesale business segment (net of tax)	555,000	
______	9. Salaries expense	540,000	

Exercise 13-11
Income statement presentation
C4

Use the financial data for Randa Merchandising, Inc., in Exercise 13-10 to prepare its income statement for calendar year 2005. (Ignore the earnings per share section.)

Exercise 13-12
Reporting a change in accounting principle
C4 C5

Fast Tek put an asset costing $225,000 into service on January 1, 2004. Its predicted useful life is six years with an expected salvage value of $22,500. The company uses double-declining-balance depreciation and records $75,000 of depreciation in 2004 and $50,000 of depreciation in 2005. The scheduled depreciation expense for 2006 is $33,250. After consulting with the company's auditors, management decides to change to straight-line depreciation in 2006 without changing either the predicted useful life or salvage value. Under this new method, the annual depreciation expense for this asset is $33,750. The cumulative effect on prior year income statements (for 2004–2005) is to decrease depreciation expense by $57,500 and increase pretax income by $57,500. This company has a 35% income tax rate.

1. How much depreciation expense is reported on the company's income statement for this asset in 2006 and in each of the remaining years of its life?

Check (2) After-tax cumulative effect, $37,375

2. What amount is reported on the company's 2006 income statement as the after-tax cumulative effect of the change in accounting principle?

Exercise 13-13
Weighted-average shares and earnings per share
A1

Nexus Company reports $1,350,000 of net income for 2005 and declares $195,000 of cash dividends on its preferred stock for 2005. At the beginning of 2005, the company had 270,000 outstanding shares of common stock. Two events change the number of outstanding common shares during 2005:

May 1 Issued 180,000 common shares for cash.
Nov. 1 Purchased 108,000 shares of its own common stock.

1. What amount of net income is available to common stockholders for 2005?

Check (2) 372,000 shares

2. What is the weighted-average number of common shares outstanding for 2005?

3. What is the company's basic EPS for 2005?

Exercise 13-14
Weighted-average shares and earnings per share
A1

C4 Company reports $480,000 of net income for 2005 and declares $65,000 of cash dividends on its preferred stock for 2005. At the beginning of 2005, the company had 50,000 outstanding shares of common stock. Three events change the number of outstanding common shares during year 2005.

June 1 Issued 30,000 common shares for cash.
Sept. 1 Purchased 13,000 shares of its own common stock.
Oct. 1 Completed a 3-for-1 stock split.

1. What amount of net income is available to common stockholders for 2005?

Check (2) 189,500 shares

2. What is the weighted-average number of common shares outstanding for 2005?

3. What is the company's basic EPS for 2005?

Exercise 13-15
Book value per share
A2

The equity section of Anna Corporation's balance sheet shows the following:

Preferred stock—6% cumulative, $25 par value, $30 call price, 5,000 shares issued and outstanding	$125,000
Common stock—$10 par value, 40,000 shares issued and outstanding	400,000
Retained earnings	267,500
Total stockholders' equity	$792,500

Determine the book value per share of the preferred and common stock under two separate situations:

Check (1) Book value of common, $16.06

1. No preferred dividends are in arrears.

2. Three years of preferred dividends are in arrears.

Exercise 13-16
Dividend yield computation and interpretation

A3 

Compute the dividend yield for each of these four separate companies. Which company's stock would probably *not* be classified as an income stock?

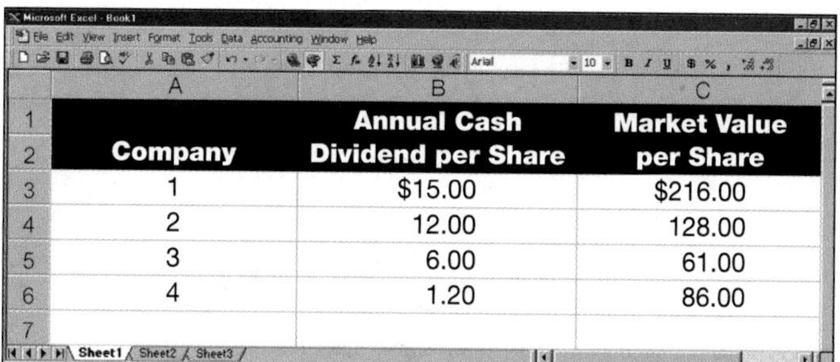

Company	Annual Cash Dividend per Share	Market Value per Share
1	$15.00	$216.00
2	12.00	128.00
3	6.00	61.00
4	1.20	86.00

Exercise 13-17
Price-earnings ratio computation and interpretation

A4 

Compute the price-earnings ratio for each of these four separate companies. Which stock might an analyst likely investigate as being potentially undervalued by the market?

Company	Earnings per Share	Market Value per Share
1	$10.00	$166.00
2	9.00	86.00
3	6.50	90.00
4	36.00	240.00

PROBLEM SET A

Problem 13-1A
Stockholders' equity transactions and analysis

C2 C3 P1 

Oxygen Co. is incorporated at the beginning of this year and engages in a number of transactions. The following journal entries impacted its stockholders' equity during its first year of operations:

a.	Cash	150,000	
	Common Stock, $25 Par Value		125,000
	Contributed Capital in Excess of Par Value, Common Stock		25,000
b.	Organization Expenses	75,000	
	Common Stock, $25 Par Value		62,500
	Contributed Capital in Excess of Par Value, Common Stock		12,500
c.	Cash	21,500	
	Accounts Receivable	7,500	
	Building	30,000	
	Notes Payable		19,000
	Common Stock, $25 Par Value		25,000
	Contributed Capital in Excess of Par Value, Common Stock		15,000
d.	Cash	60,000	
	Common Stock, $25 Par Value		37,500
	Contributed Capital in Excess of Par Value, Common Stock		22,500

Required

1. Explain each journal entry (*a*) through (*d*).

2. How many shares of common stock are outstanding at year-end?

3. What is the amount of minimum legal capital (based on par value) at year-end?

4. What is the total contributed capital at year-end?

5. What is the book value per share of the common stock at year-end if contributed capital plus retained earnings equals $347,500?

Check (2) 10,000 shares
(3) $250,000
(4) $325,000

Problem 13-2A
Cash dividends, treasury stock, and statement of retained earnings
C2 C5 P3 P5

Context Corporation reports the following components of stockholders' equity on December 31, 2005:

Common stock—$10 par value, 50,000 shares authorized, 20,000 shares issued and outstanding	$200,000
Contributed capital in excess of par value, common stock	30,000
Retained earnings	135,000
Total stockholders' equity	$365,000

In year 2006, the following transactions affected its stockholders' equity accounts:

Jan. 1	Purchased 2,000 shares of its own stock at $20 cash per share.
Jan. 5	Directors declared a $2 per share cash dividend payable on Feb. 28 to the Feb. 5 stockholders of record.
Feb. 28	Paid the dividend declared on January 5.
July 6	Sold 750 of its treasury shares at $24 cash per share.
Aug. 22	Sold 1,250 of its treasury shares at $17 cash per share.
Sept. 5	Directors declared a $2 per share cash dividend payable on October 28 to the September 25 stockholders of record.
Oct. 28	Paid the dividend declared on September 5.
Dec. 31	Closed the $194,000 credit balance (from net income) in the Income Summary account to Retained Earnings.

Required

1. Prepare journal entries to record these transactions for 2006.

2. Prepare a statement of retained earnings for the year ended December 31, 2006.

3. Prepare the stockholders' equity section of the company's balance sheet as of December 31, 2006.

Check (2) Retained earnings, Dec. 31, 2006, $252,250.

Problem 13-3A
Equity analysis—journal entries and account balances
P3 P4

At September 30, the end of Excel Company's third quarter, the following stockholders' equity accounts are reported:

Common stock, $12 par value	$720,000
Contributed capital in excess of par value, common stock	180,000
Retained earnings	640,000

In the fourth quarter, the following entries related to its equity accounts are recorded:

Date	Account	Debit	Credit
Oct. 2	Retained Earnings	120,000	
	Common Dividend Payable		120,000
Oct. 25	Common Dividend Payable	120,000	
	Cash		120,000
Oct. 31	Retained Earnings	150,000	
	Common Stock Dividend Distributable		72,000
	Contributed Capital in Excess of Par Value, Common Stock		78,000
Nov. 5	Common Stock Dividend Distributable	72,000	
	Common Stock, $12 Par Value		72,000

[continued on next page]

[continued from previous page]

Dec. 1	Memo—Change the title of the common stock account to reflect the new par value of $4.		
Dec. 31	Income Summary	420,000	
	Retained Earnings		420,000

Required

1. Explain each journal entry.

2. Complete the following table showing the equity account balances at each indicated date:

	Oct. 2	Oct. 25	Oct. 31	Nov. 5	Dec. 1	Dec. 31
Common stock	$____	$____	$____	$____	$____	$____
Common stock dividend distributable	____	____	____	____	____	____
Contributed capital in excess of par, common stock	____	____	____	____	____	____
Retained earnings	____	____	____	____	____	____
Total equity	$____	$____	$____	$____	$____	$____

Check Total equity: Oct. 2, $1,420,000; Dec. 31, $1,840,000

Problem 13-4A
Analysis of changes in stockholders' equity accounts

C5 P3 P4 P5 

The equity sections from Salazar Group's 2005 and 2006 year-end balance sheets follow:

Stockholders' Equity (December 31, 2005)

Common stock—$4 par value, 50,000 shares authorized, 20,000 shares issued and outstanding	$ 80,000
Contributed capital in excess of par value, common stock	60,000
Total contributed capital	140,000
Retained earnings	160,000
Total stockholders' equity	$300,000

Stockholders' Equity (December 31, 2006)

Common stock—$4 par value, 50,000 shares authorized, 23,700 shares issued, 1,500 shares in treasury	$ 94,800
Contributed capital in excess of par value, common stock	89,600
Total contributed capital	184,400
Retained earnings ($15,000 restricted by treasury stock)	200,000
	384,400
Less cost of treasury stock	(15,000)
Total stockholders' equity	$369,400

The following transactions and events affected its equity accounts during year 2006:

Jan. 5	Declared a $0.50 per share cash dividend, date of record January 10.
Mar. 20	Purchased treasury stock for cash.
Apr. 5	Declared a $0.50 per share cash dividend, date of record April 10.
July 5	Declared a $0.50 per share cash dividend, date of record July 10.
July 31	Declared a 20% stock dividend when the stock's market value is $12 per share.
Aug. 14	Issued stock dividend that was declared on July 31.
Oct. 5	Declared a $0.50 per share cash dividend, date of record October 10.

Required

1. How many common shares are outstanding on each cash dividend date?

2. What is the total dollar amount for each of the four cash dividends?

3. What is the amount of the capitalization of retained earnings for the stock dividend?

4. What is the per share cost of the treasury stock purchased?

5. How much net income did the company earn during year 2006?

Check (3) $44,400

(4) $10

(5) $124,000

Problem 13-5A
Income statement computations and format

C4

Selected account balances from the adjusted trial balance for Chex Corporation as of its calendar year-end December 31, 2005, follow:

	Debit	Credit
a. Interest revenue		$ 12,000
b. Depreciation expense—Equipment	$ 36,000	
c. Loss on sale of equipment	24,750	
d. Accounts payable		42,000
e. Other operating expenses	97,500	
f. Accumulated depreciation—Equipment		73,500
g. Gain from settlement of lawsuit		42,000
h. Cumulative effect of change in accounting principle (pretax)	63,000	
i. Accumulated depreciation—Buildings		163,500
j. Loss from operating a discontinued segment (pretax)	19,500	
k. Gain on insurance recovery of tornado damage (pretax and extraordinary)		28,500
l. Net sales		970,500
m. Depreciation expense—Buildings	54,000	
n. Correction of overstatement of prior year's sales (pretax)	15,000	
o. Gain on sale of discontinued segment's assets (pretax)		33,000
p. Loss from settlement of lawsuit	24,000	
q. Income taxes expense	?	
r. Cost of goods sold	487,500	

Required

Answer each of the following questions by providing supporting computations:

1. Assume that the company's income tax rate is 30% for all items. Identify the tax effects and after-tax amounts of the five items labeled pretax.

2. What is the amount of income from continuing operations before income taxes? What is the amount of the income taxes expense? What is the amount of income from continuing operations?

Check (3) $9,450

(4) $219,975

(5) $195,825

3. What is the total amount of after-tax income (loss) associated with the discontinued segment?

4. What is the amount of income (loss) before the extraordinary items and the cumulative effect of changes in accounting principle?

5. What is the amount of net income for the year?

Problem 13-6A
Change in accounting principle (depreciation) and its disclosure

C4  
mhhe.com/larson

On January 1, 2003, Virtuality, Inc., purchases equipment costing $600,000 with an expected salvage value of $30,000 at the end of its five-year useful life. Depreciation is allocated to 2003, 2004, and 2005 with the double-declining-balance method. Early in 2006, the company changes to the straight-line method to produce more useful financial statements and to be consistent with industry competitors.

Required

1. Do generally accepted accounting principles allow Virtuality to change depreciation methods in 2006?

Check (2) 2004, $144,000

(3) 2004, $114,000

(4) After-tax cumulative effect, $89,880

2. Prepare a table to show the annual amount of depreciation expense allocated to 2003 through 2005 using the double-declining-balance method.

3. Prepare a table to show the annual amount of depreciation expense that would have been allocated to 2003 through 2005 using the straight-line method.

4. The cumulative effect on prior year income statements (for 2003–2005) is to decrease depreciation expense by $128,400 and increase pretax income by $128,400. The company's income tax rate is 30%. What are the pretax and after-tax cumulative effects of the accounting change?

5. How should the cumulative effect of the change in accounting principle be reported? Does the cumulative effect increase or decrease net income?

6. How much depreciation expense is reported on the company's income statement for 2006?

Analysis Component

(7) 2006 retained earnings understated by $44,940

7. Assume that Virtuality mistakenly treats the change in depreciation methods as a change in accounting estimate. Using your answers from parts 2, 3, and 4, describe the effect of this error on the 2006 financial statements.

Problem 13-7A
Earnings per share calculation and presentation

C4 A1

mhhe.com/larson

The annual income statements for Cortez, Inc., as reported when they were initially published in 2003, 2004, and 2005 follow:

	2003	2004	2005
Net sales	$370,000	$425,000	$412,500
Operating expenses	232,500	260,000	245,500
Income from continuing operations	137,500	165,000	167,000
Loss on discontinued segment	(52,500)	—	—
Income before extraordinary items	85,000	165,000	167,000
Extraordinary gain (loss)	—	33,000	(70,000)
Net income	$ 85,000	$198,000	$ 97,000

The company also experienced changes in the number of outstanding shares from the following events:

Outstanding shares on December 31, 2002	40,000
2003	
Treasury stock purchase on April 1	− 4,000
Issuance of new shares on June 30	+ 12,000
10% stock dividend on October 1	+ 4,800
Outstanding shares on December 31, 2003	52,800
2004	
Issuance of new shares on July 1	+ 16,000
Treasury stock purchase on November 1	− 4,800
Outstanding shares on December 31, 2004	64,000
2005	
Issuance of new shares on August 1	+ 20,000
Treasury stock purchase on September 1	− 4,000
3-for-1 stock split on October 1	+160,000
Outstanding shares on December 31, 2005	240,000

Required

1. Compute the weighted average of the common shares outstanding for year 2003.

2. Compute the EPS component amounts to report with the year 2003 income statement for: income from continuing operations, the loss on discontinued segment, and net income.

3. Compute the weighted average of the common shares outstanding for year 2004.

4. Compute the EPS component amounts to report with the year 2004 income statement for: income from continuing operations, the extraordinary gain, and net income.

5. Compute the weighted average of the common shares outstanding for year 2005.

6. Compute the EPS component amounts to report with the year 2005 income statement for: income from continuing operations, the extraordinary loss, and net income.

Check (1) 47,300 shares

(2) EPS, $1.80

(3) 60,000 shares

(4) EPS, $3.30

Analysis Component

7. Explain how you would use the EPS data from part 6 to predict EPS for 2006.

Problem 13-8A
Computation of book values and dividend allocations

C3 A2 P2

Razz Corporation's common stock is currently selling on a stock exchange at $170 per share, and its current balance sheet shows the following stockholders' equity section:

Preferred stock—5% cumulative, $___ par value, 1,000 shares authorized, issued, and outstanding	$100,000
Common stock—$___ par value, 4,000 shares authorized, issued, and outstanding	160,000
Retained earnings	300,000
Total stockholders' equity	$560,000

Required

1. What is the current market value (price) of this corporation's common stock?

2. What are the par values of the corporation's preferred stock and its common stock?

3. If no dividends are in arrears, what are the book values per share of the preferred stock and the common stock?

Check (4) Book value of common, $112.50

4. If two years' preferred dividends are in arrears, what are the book values per share of the preferred stock and the common stock?

(5) Book value of common, $110

5. If two years' preferred dividends are in arrears and the preferred stock is callable at $110 per share, what are the book values per share of the preferred stock and the common stock?

(6) Dividends per common share, $1.25

6. If two years' preferred dividends are in arrears and the board of directors declares cash dividends of $20,000, what total amount will be paid to the preferred and to the common shareholders? What is the amount of dividends per share for the common stock?

Analysis Component

7. What are some factors that can contribute to a difference between the book value of common stock and its market value (price)?

PROBLEM SET B

Problem 13-1B
Stockholders' equity transactions and analysis

C2 C3 P1

Nilson Company is incorporated at the beginning of this year and engages in a number of transactions. The following journal entries impacted its stockholders' equity during its first year of operations:

		Debit	Credit
a.	Cash	60,000	
	Common Stock, $1 Par Value		1,500
	Contributed Capital in Excess of Par Value, Common Stock		58,500
b.	Organization Expenses	20,000	
	Common Stock, $1 Par Value		500
	Contributed Capital in Excess of Par Value, Common Stock		19,500
c.	Cash	6,650	
	Accounts Receivable	4,000	
	Building	12,500	
	Notes Payable		3,150
	Common Stock, $1 Par Value		400
	Contributed Capital in Excess of Par Value, Common Stock		19,600
d.	Cash	30,000	
	Common Stock, $1 Par Value		600
	Contributed Capital in Excess of Par Value, Common Stock		29,400

Required

1. Explain each journal entry (*a*) through (*d*).

Check (2) 3,000 shares

2. How many shares of common stock are outstanding at year-end?

(3) $3,000

3. What is the amount of minimum legal capital (based on par value) at year-end?

(4) $130,000

4. What is the total contributed capital at year-end?

5. What is the book value per share of the common stock at year-end if contributed capital plus retained earnings equals $141,500?

Problem 13-2B
Cash dividends, treasury stock, and statement of retained earnings

C2 C5 P3 P5

Baycore Corp. reports the following components of stockholders' equity on December 31, 2005:

Common stock—$1 par value, 160,000 shares authorized, 100,000 shares issued and outstanding	$ 100,000
Contributed capital in excess of par value, common stock	700,000
Retained earnings	1,080,000
Total stockholders' equity	$1,880,000

It completed the following transactions related to stockholders' equity in year 2006:

Jan. 10 Purchased 20,000 shares of its own stock at $12 cash per share.
Mar. 2 Directors declared a $1.50 per share cash dividend payable on March 31 to the March 15 stockholders of record.
Mar. 31 Paid the dividend declared on March 2.
Nov. 11 Sold 12,000 of its treasury shares at $13 cash per share.
Nov. 25 Sold 8,000 of its treasury shares at $9.50 cash per share.
Dec. 1 Directors declared a $2.50 per share cash dividend payable on January 2, 2003, to the December 10 stockholders of record.
Dec. 31 Closed the $536,000 credit balance (from net income) in the Income Summary account to Retained Earnings.

Required

1. Prepare journal entries to record these transactions for 2006.
2. Prepare a statement of retained earnings for the year ended December 31, 2006.
3. Prepare the stockholders' equity section of the company's balance sheet as of December 31, 2006.

Check (2) Retained earnings, Dec. 31, 2006, $1,238,000

Problem 13-3B
Equity analysis—journal entries and account balances
P3 P4

At December 31, the end of Intertec Communication's third quarter, the following stockholders' equity accounts are reported:

Common stock, $10 par value	$480,000
Contributed capital in excess of par value, common stock	192,000
Retained earnings	800,000

In the fourth quarter, the following entries related to its equity accounts are recorded:

Jan. 17	Retained Earnings	48,000	
	Common Dividend Payable		48,000
Feb. 5	Common Dividend Payable	48,000	
	Cash		48,000
Feb. 28	Retained Earnings	126,000	
	Common Stock Dividend Distributable		60,000
	Contributed Capital in Excess of Par Value, Common Stock		66,000
Mar. 14	Common Stock Dividend Distributable	60,000	
	Common Stock, $10 Par Value		60,000
Mar. 25	Memo—Change the title of the common stock account to reflect the new par value of $5.		
Mar. 31	Income Summary	360,000	
	Retained Earnings		360,000

Required

1. Explain each journal entry.
2. Complete the following table showing the equity account balances at each indicated date:

	Jan. 17	Feb. 5	Feb. 28	Mar. 14	Mar. 25	Mar. 31
Common stock	$____	$____	$____	$____	$____	$____
Common stock dividend distributable	____	____	____	____	____	____
Contributed capital in excess of par, common stock	____	____	____	____	____	____
Retained earnings	____	____	____	____	____	____
Total equity	$____	$____	$____	$____	$____	$____

Check Total equity: Jan. 17, $1,424,000; Mar. 31, $1,784,000

Problem 13-4B
Analysis of changes in stockholders' equity accounts
C5 P3 P4 P5 

The equity sections from Jetta Corporation's 2005 and 2006 balance sheets follow:

Stockholders' Equity (December 31, 2005)	
Common stock—$20 par value, 15,000 shares authorized, 8,500 shares issued and outstanding	$170,000
Contributed capital in excess of par value, common stock	30,000
Total contributed capital	200,000
Retained earnings	135,000
Total stockholders' equity	$335,000

Stockholders' Equity (December 31, 2006)	
Common stock—$20 par value, 15,000 shares authorized, 9,500 shares issued, 500 shares in treasury	$190,000
Contributed capital in excess of par value, common stock	52,000
Total contributed capital	242,000
Retained earnings ($20,000 restricted by treasury stock)	147,600
	389,600
Less cost of treasury stock	(20,000)
Total stockholders' equity	$369,600

The following transactions and events affected its equity accounts during year 2006:

Feb. 15 Declared a $0.40 per share cash dividend, date of record five days later.
Mar. 2 Purchased treasury stock for cash.
May 15 Declared a $0.40 per share cash dividend, date of record five days later.
Aug. 15 Declared a $0.40 per share cash dividend, date of record five days later.
Oct. 4 Declared a 12.5% stock dividend when the stock's market value is $42 per share.
Oct. 20 Issued stock dividend that was declared on October 4.
Nov. 15 Declared a $0.40 per share cash dividend, date of record five days later.

Required

1. How many common shares are outstanding on each cash dividend date?
2. What is the total dollar amount for each of the four cash dividends?
3. What is the amount of the capitalization of retained earnings for the stock dividend?
4. What is the per share cost of the treasury stock purchased?
5. How much net income did the company earn during year 2006?

Check (3) $42,000
(4) $40
(5) $68,000

Problem 13-5B
Income statement computations and format C4

Selected account balances from the adjusted trial balance for Bar Harbor Corp. as of its calendar year-end December 31, 2005, follow:

	Debit	Credit
a. Accumulated depreciation—Buildings		$ 200,000
b. Interest revenue		10,000
c. Cumulative effect of change in accounting principle (pretax)		46,000
d. Net sales		1,320,000
e. Income taxes expense	$?	
f. Loss on hurricane damage (pretax and extraordinary)	32,000	
g. Accumulated depreciation—Equipment		110,000
h. Other operating expenses	164,000	
i. Depreciation expense—Equipment	50,000	
j. Loss from settlement of lawsuit	18,000	
k. Gain from settlement of lawsuit		34,000

[continued on next page]

[continued from previous page]

l. Loss on sale of equipment	12,000	
m. Loss from operating a discontinued segment (pretax)	60,000	
n. Depreciation expense—Buildings	78,000	
o. Correction of overstatement of prior year's expense (pretax)		24,000
p. Cost of goods sold	520,000	
q. Loss on sale of discontinued segment's assets (pretax)	90,000	
r. Accounts payable		66,000

Required

Answer each of the following questions by providing supporting computations:

1. Assume that the company's income tax rate is 25% for all items. Identify the tax effects and after-tax amounts of the five items labeled pretax.

2. What is the amount of income from continuing operations before income taxes? What is the amount of income taxes expense? What is the amount of income from continuing operations?

3. What is the total amount of after-tax income (loss) associated with the discontinued segment?

4. What is the amount of income (loss) before the extraordinary items and the cumulative effect of changes in accounting principle?

5. What is the amount of net income for the year?

Check (3) $(112,500)

(4) $279,000

(5) $289,500

Problem 13-6B
Change in accounting principle (depreciation) and its disclosure
C4

On January 1, 2003, Belize Corp. purchases equipment costing $200,000 with an expected salvage value of zero at the end of its five-year useful life. Depreciation is allocated to 2003, 2004, and 2005 with the double-declining-balance method. Early in 2006, the company changes to the straight-line method to produce more useful financial statements and to be consistent with industry competitors.

Required

1. Do generally accepted accounting principles allow Belize to change depreciation methods in 2006?

2. Prepare a table to show the annual amount of depreciation expense allocated to 2003 through 2005 using the double-declining-balance method.

3. Prepare a table to show the annual amount of depreciation expense that would have been allocated to 2003 through 2005 using the straight-line method.

4. The cumulative effect on prior year income statements (for 2003–2005) is to decrease depreciation expense by $36,800 and increase pretax income by $36,800. The company's income tax rate is 25%. What are the pretax and after-tax cumulative effects of the change?

5. How should the cumulative effect of the change in accounting principle be reported? Does the cumulative effect increase or decrease net income?

6. How much depreciation expense is reported on the company's income statement for 2006?

Check (2) 2004, $48,000

(3) 2004, $40,000

(4) After-tax cumulative effect, $27,600

Analysis Component

7. Assume that Belize mistakenly treats the change in depreciation methods as a change in accounting estimate. Using your answers from parts 2, 3, and 4, describe the effect of this error on the 2006 financial statements.

(7) 2006 retained earnings understated by $13,800

Problem 13-7B
Earnings per share calculation and presentation
C4 A1

The annual income statements for Peña, Inc., as reported when they were initially published in 2003, 2004, and 2005 follow:

	2003	2004	2005
Net sales	$250,000	$300,000	$400,000
Operating expenses	160,000	215,000	270,000
Income from continuing operations	90,000	85,000	130,000
Loss on discontinued segment	(26,145)	—	—
Income before extraordinary items	63,855	85,000	130,000
Extraordinary gain (loss)	—	14,100	(37,125)
Net income	$ 63,855	$ 99,100	$ 92,875

The company also experienced changes in the number of outstanding shares from the following events:

Outstanding shares on December 31, 2002	10,000
2003	
Treasury stock purchase on July 1	− 1,000
Issuance of new shares on September 30	+ 3,500
20% stock dividend on December 1	+ 2,500
Outstanding shares on December 31, 2003	15,000
2004	
Issuance of new shares on March 31	+ 4,000
Treasury stock purchase on October 1	− 1,500
Outstanding shares on December 31, 2004	17,500
2005	
Issuance of new shares on July 1	+ 3,000
Treasury stock purchase on October 1	− 1,750
2-for-1 stock split on November 1	+18,750
Outstanding shares on December 31, 2005	37,500

Required

Check (1) 12,450 shares

(2) EPS, $5.13

(3) 17,625 shares

(4) EPS, $5.62

1. Compute the weighted average of the common shares outstanding for year 2003.
2. Compute the EPS component amounts to report with the year 2003 income statement for: income from continuing operations, the loss on discontinued segment, and net income.
3. Compute the weighted average of the common shares outstanding for year 2004.
4. Compute the EPS component amounts to report with the year 2004 income statement for: income from continuing operations, the extraordinary gain, and net income.
5. Compute the weighted average of the common shares outstanding for year 2005.
6. Compute the EPS component amounts to report with the year 2005 income statement for: income from continuing operations, the extraordinary loss, and net income.

Analysis Component

7. Explain how you would use the EPS data from part 6 to predict EPS for 2006.

Problem 13-8B
Computation of book values and dividend allocations

C3 A2 P2 

Scotch, Inc.'s common stock is currently selling on a stock exchange at $45 per share, and its current balance sheet shows the following stockholders' equity section:

Preferred stock—8% cumulative, $___ par value, 1,500 shares authorized, issued, and outstanding	$ 187,500
Common stock—$___ par value, 18,000 shares authorized, issued, and outstanding	450,000
Retained earnings	562,500
Total stockholders' equity	$1,200,000

Required

1. What is the current market value (price) of this corporation's common stock?
2. What are the par values of the corporation's preferred stock and its common stock?
3. If no dividends are in arrears, what are the book values per share of the preferred stock and the common stock?

Check (4) Book value of common, $54.58

(5) Book value of common, $53.33

4. If two years' preferred dividends are in arrears, what are the book values per share of the preferred stock and the common stock?
5. If two years' preferred dividends are in arrears and the preferred stock is callable at $140 per share, what are the book values per share of the preferred stock and the common stock?

6. If two years' preferred dividends are in arrears and the board of directors declares cash dividends of $50,000, what total amount will be paid to the preferred and to the common shareholders? What is the amount of dividends per share for the common stock?

(6) Dividends per common share, $0.28

Analysis Component

7. Discuss why the book value of common stock is not always a good estimate of its market value.

PROBLEM SET C

Problem Set C is available at the book's Website to further reinforce and assess your learning.

SERIAL PROBLEM

Success Systems

(This serial problem began in Chapter 1 and continues through most of the book. If previous chapter segments were not completed, the serial problem can begin at this point. It is helpful, but not necessary, for you to use the Working Papers that accompany the book.)

Success Systems was initially organized as a proprietorship. Assume that on April 1, 2005, Kay Breeze reorganizes her business from a proprietorship to a corporation of which Breeze is the sole owner. The Success Systems, Inc., corporate charter authorizes the issuance of 25,000 shares of $1 par value common stock. Kay Breeze's equity in Success Systems immediately prior to the reorganization is reflected in the following capital balance:

K. Breeze, Capital	$129,034

Required

1. Prepare the April 1, 2005, journal entry to reflect Kay Breeze's exchange of her capital for 10,000 shares of $1 par value common stock. Assume that any capital in excess of the par value of the stock issued should be assigned to contributed capital in excess of par.
2. Prepare an updated equity section of the balance sheet at the close of business on April 1, 2005, reflecting the corporate ownership of Success Systems, Inc.

BEYOND THE NUMBERS

REPORTING IN ACTION

C2 C3 C4 A1 A2

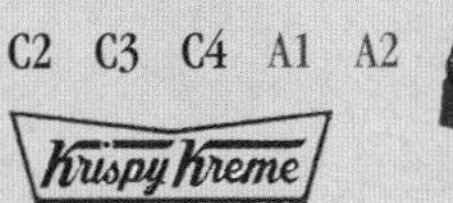

BTN 13-1 Refer to Krispy Kreme's financial statements in Appendix A to answer the following:

1. Has Krispy Kreme issued any preferred stock? If so, what are its features?
2. How many shares of common stock are issued and outstanding at the end of fiscal years 2003 and 2002? How do these numbers compare with the weighted-average common shares outstanding at the end of fiscal years 2003 and 2002?
3. What is the book value of its entire common stock at February 2, 2003?
4. What is the total amount of cash dividends paid to common stockholders for fiscal years 2003 and 2002?
5. Identify and compare basic EPS amounts across years 2003, 2002, and 2001. Identify and comment on any significant changes.
6. Does Krispy Kreme hold any treasury stock as of February 2, 2003? As of February 3, 2002?
7. Does Krispy Kreme report any changes in accounting principles or the occurrence of extraordinary items for fiscal years 2003 or 2002? Are there gains or losses on disposal of a business segment for fiscal years 2003 or 2002?

Roll On

8. Access Krispy Kreme's financial statements for fiscal years ending after February 2, 2003, from its Website (KrispyKreme.com) or the SEC's EDGAR database (www.SEC.gov). Has the number of common shares outstanding increased since February 2, 2003? Has Krispy Kreme increased the total amount of cash dividends paid compared to the total amount for fiscal year 2003?

COMPARATIVE ANALYSIS

A1 A2 A3 A4

BTN 13-2 Key comparative figures for both **Krispy Kreme** and **Tastykake** follow:

Key Figures	Krispy Kreme	Tastykake
Net income (in thousands)	$ 33,478	$ 2,000*
Cash dividends declared per common share	$ 0.00	$ 0.48
Common shares outstanding (in thousands)	55,093	8,075
Market value (price) per share	$ 30.41	$ 9.20
Equity applicable to common shares (in thousands)	$273,352	$47,525

* Restructuring charges are removed from income.

Required

1. Compute the book value per common share for each company using these data.
2. Compute the basic EPS for each company using these data.
3. Compute the dividend yield for each company using these data. Does the dividend yield of either company characterize it as an income or growth stock? Explain.
4. Compute, compare, and interpret the price-earnings ratio for each company using these data.

ETHICS CHALLENGE

C4

BTN 13-3 This chapter describes ComUS's change in accounting principle from the double-declining-balance depreciation method to the straight-line method. ComUS argues that its income statement computed using the straight-line method is more useful. This change in accounting principle adds $56,000 to net income for year 2005. As this company's auditor, you must review the decision to change the accounting principle. You review the equipment in question and learn that it is a piece of high-tech equipment whose risk of obsolescence in the near future is high. You also are aware that management receives year-end bonuses based on net income.

Required

As the auditor, would you support the change in depreciation method or ask management to continue using the double-declining-balance method? Justify your response.

COMMUNICATING IN PRACTICE

A1 A4

Hint: Make a transparency of each team's memo for a class discussion.

BTN 13-4 Teams are to select an industry, and each team member is to select a different company in that industry. Each team member then is to acquire the selected company's financial statements (or Form 10-K) from the SEC EDGAR site (www.SEC.gov). Use these data to identify basic EPS. Use the financial press (or finance.yahoo.com/quote) to determine the market price of this stock, and then compute the price-earnings ratio. Communicate with teammates via a meeting, e-mail, or telephone to discuss the meaning of this ratio, how companies compare, and the industry norm. The team must prepare a single memorandum reporting the ratio for each company and identifying the team conclusions or consensus of opinion. The memorandum is to be duplicated and distributed to the instructor and teammates.

TAKING IT TO THE NET

C2

mhhe.com/larson

BTN 13-5 Access the March 28, 2003, filing of the 2002 calendar-year 10-K report of **HCA, Inc.**, (ticker HCA) from www.SEC.gov.

Required

1. How many classes of stock has HCA issued?
2. What are the par values of the classes of stock you identified in part 1?
3. How much cash did HCA raise in 2002 from issuing stock?
4. What total amount of cash did HCA pay in 2002 to repurchase stock?
5. What amount did HCA pay out in cash dividends for 2002?

TEAMWORK IN ACTION

P5

BTN 13-6 This activity requires teamwork to reinforce understanding of accounting for treasury stock.

1. Write a brief team statement (*a*) generalizing what happens to a corporation's financial position when it engages in a stock "buyback" and (*b*) identifying reasons that a corporation would engage in this activity.

2. Assume that an entity acquires 100 shares of its $100 par value common stock at a cost of $134 cash per share. Discuss the entry to record this acquisition. Next, assign *each* team member to prepare *one* of the following entries (assume each entry applies to all shares):

a. Reissue treasury shares at cost.

b. Reissue treasury shares at $150 per share.

c. Reissue treasury shares at $120 per share; assume the contributed capital account from treasury shares has a $1,500 balance.

d. Reissue treasury shares at $120 per share; assume the contributed capital account from treasury shares has a $1,000 balance.

e. Reissue treasury shares at $120 per share; assume the contributed capital account from treasury shares has a zero balance.

3. In sequence, each member is to present his/her entry to the team and explain the *similarities* and *differences* between that entry and the previous entry.

Hint: Instructor should be sure each team accurately completes part 1 before proceeding.

BUSINESS WEEK ACTIVITY

C1 C2

mhhe.com/larson

BTN 13-7 Read the commentary "So Much Cash, So Few Dividends" from the January 20, 2003, issue of *Business Week*. (The book's Website provides a free link.)

Required

1. Why are start-up tech companies reluctant to pay dividends to shareholders?

2. Have large tech companies historically paid dividends?

3. Do most institutional investors want tech companies to pay dividends if the tax on dividends is eliminated?

4. How have tech companies used stockpiles of cash in the past?

5. How would tech company CEOs fare if these companies start to pay dividends?

ENTREPRENEURIAL DECISION

C2 C3 P3

BTN 13-8 Assume that Julz Chavez's launch of **Get Real Girl** requires $312,500 of start-up capital. Chavez contributes $250,000 of personal assets in return for 5,000 shares of common stock but needs to raise another $62,500 in cash. There are two alternative plans for raising the additional cash. Plan A is to sell 1,250 shares of common stock to one or more investors for $62,500 cash. Plan B is to sell 625 shares of cumulative preferred stock to one or more investors for $62,500 cash (this preferred stock would have a $100 par value, an annual 8% dividend rate, and be issued at par).

1. If the business is expected to earn $45,000 of after-tax net income in the first year, what rate of return on beginning equity will Chavez personally earn under each alternative? Which plan will provide the higher expected return to Chavez?

2. If the business is expected to earn $10,500 of after-tax net income in the first year, what rate of return on beginning equity will Chavez personally earn under each alternative? Which plan will provide the higher expected return to Chavez?

3. Analyze and interpret the differences between the results for parts 1 and 2.

HITTING THE ROAD

A1 A3 A4

BTN 13-9 Watch 30 to 60 minutes of financial news on the **CNBC** television channel. Take notes on companies that are catching analysts' attention. You might hear reference to over- and undervaluation of firm and to reports about PE ratios, dividend yields, and earnings per share. Be prepared to give a brief description to the class of your observations of CNBC.

GLOBAL DECISION

A1 C4 C5

BTN 13-10 Access the annual report of **Grupo Bimbo** (GrupoBimbo.com) for the year ended December 31, 2002. Review its statements of income and its statements of changes in financial position.

Required

1. What is Grupo Bimbo's trend in earnings per share for the three years 2000 to 2002?

2. Has Grupo Bimbo increased or decreased its weighted-average shares outstanding from 2001 to 2002?

3. Has Grupo Bimbo increased or decreased cash dividends declared to shareholders from 2001 to 2002?

"Being a first-time entrepreneur leading a fast-growth company is like running full speed through the dark over unfamiliar terrain"—Aaron Kennedy

14 Long-Term Liabilities

A Look Back

Chapter 13 focused on the corporate form of organization. We described stock issuances, dividends, and other equity transactions. We also explained how to report and analyze income, earnings per share, and retained earnings.

A Look at This Chapter

This chapter describes the accounting for and analysis of bonds and notes. We explain their characteristics, payment patterns, interest computations, retirement, and reporting requirements. An appendix to this chapter introduces leases and pensions.

A Look Ahead

Chapter 15 focuses on investments in securities. We explain how to identify, account for, and report investments in both debt and equity securities. We also describe accounting for transactions listed in a foreign currency.

CAP

Conceptual

C1 Describe the types of bonds and the procedures for issuing them. *(p. 549)*

C2 Explain the types and payment patterns of notes. *(p. 561)*

Analytical

A1 Compare bond financing with stock financing. *(p. 548)*

A2 Explain collateral agreements and their effects on loan risk. *(p. 565)*

A3 Compute the ratio of pledged assets to secured liabilities and explain its use. *(p. 565)*

Procedural

P1 Prepare entries to record bond issuance and bond interest expense. *(p. 551)*

P2 Compute and record amortization of bond discount. *(p. 552)*

P3 Compute and record amortization of bond premium. *(p. 555)*

P4 Record the retirement of bonds. *(p. 560)*

P5 Prepare entries to account for notes. *(p. 562)*

Decision Feature

Using His Noodle(s) for Business Financing

BOULDER, CO—Aaron Kennedy never planned to be an entrepreneur. An evening dinner at an Asian noodle shop in New York's Greenwich Village changed all that. "All of sudden this idea hit me," says Kennedy. "There are noodle dishes all over the world. I thought, 'What if they were all on one menu? Why not bring all of these influences together and make it affordable and fast.'"

Kennedy quickly developed his global noodle concept: "high-quality food made to order." He wanted his noodles "quick and convenient, very affordable and served in a very appealing dining environment." This led to his launch of **Noodles & Company (Noodles.com).** "We're not fast food—we're casual dining," notes Kennedy.

The global noodle concept required financing to become reality. Since Kennedy lacked collateral and had no entrepreneurial experience, he approached 25 friends and family members for the $250,000 start-up financing. It was challenging, says Kennedy. He had to confront the realities of debt, interest payments, collateral agreements, and pledged assets. Moreover, he had to achieve the accounting numbers necessary to stay afloat.

With grit and determination, Kennedy obtained his financing. Six months later, he launched his first noodle shop in Denver, followed by the second in Madison, Wisconsin. "The first two restaurants nearly killed us—physically and fiscally," recalls Kennedy. Yet Noodles not only achieved the income to pay the debt with interest but also produced revenue growth for expansion. Kennedy now has taken on additional financing, which he predicts "should culminate in accelerating growth." An important new factor, says Kennedy, is Noodles' "new franchised area operator program."

Kennedy admits he is both surprised and humbled by Noodles' success but realizes that simple concepts are often the best. "Noodles are staples," Kennedy says. His task: "bring the noodles to the people." By all accounts, Kennedy has applied his noodles well.

[Sources: *Noodles & Co. Website,* January 2004; *Rocky Mountain News,* February 2002; *Augustana Magazine,* Fall 2002; *Shopping Centers Today,* December 2002; *UW Update,* Summer 2002; *Forbes,* May 2003; *Catlin Group Website,* June 2003.]

Individuals, companies, and governments issue bonds to finance their activities. In return for financing, bonds promise to repay the lender with interest. This chapter explains the basics of bonds and the accounting for their issuance and retirement. The chapter also describes long-term notes as another financing source, including interest-bearing, noninterest-bearing, and installment notes. We explain how present value concepts impact both the accounting for and reporting of bonds and notes. Appendixes to this chapter discuss present value concepts applicable to liabilities, effective interest amortization, and the accounting for leases and pensions.

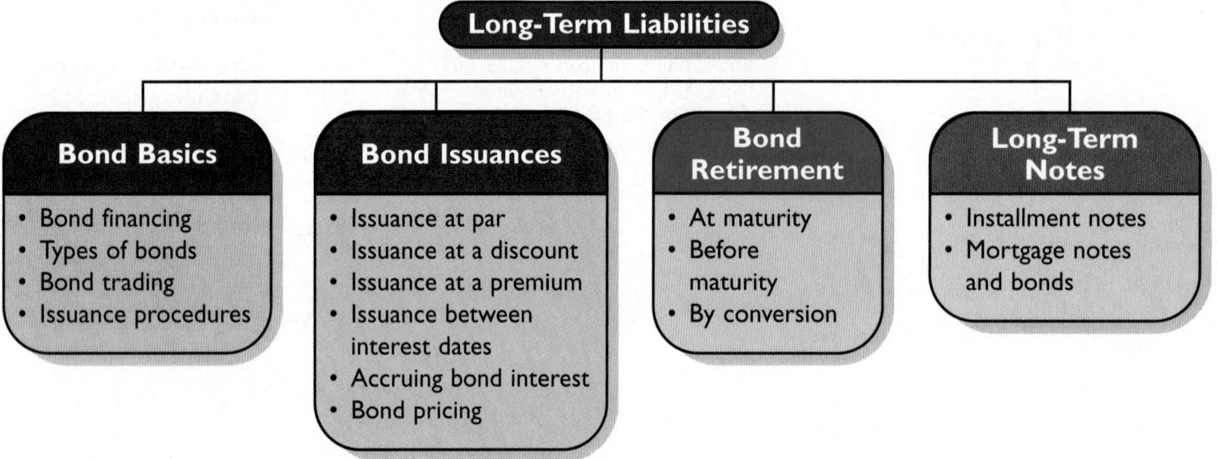

Basics of Bonds

This section explains the basics of bonds and a company's motivation for issuing them.

Bond Financing

Projects that demand large amounts of money often are funded from bond issuances. (Both for-profit and nonprofit companies, as well as governmental units, such as nations, states, cities, and school districts, issue bonds.) A **bond** is its issuer's written promise to pay an amount identified as the par value of the bond with interest. The **par value of a bond,** also called the *face amount* or *face value,* is paid at a specified future date known as the bond's *maturity date.* Most bonds also require the issuer to make semiannual interest payments. The amount of interest paid each period is determined by multiplying the par value of the bond by the bond's contract rate of interest. This section explains both advantages and disadvantages of bond financing.

A1 Compare bond financing with stock financing.

Advantages of Bonds There are three main advantages of bond financing:

1. *Bonds do not affect owner control.* Equity financing reflects ownership in a company, whereas bond financing does not. A person who contributes $1,000 of a company's $10,000 equity financing typically controls one-tenth of all owner decisions. A person who owns a $1,000, 11%, 20-year bond has no ownership right. This person, or bondholder, is to receive from the bond issuer 11% interest, or $110, each year the bond is outstanding and $1,000 when it matures in 20 years.

2. *Interest on bonds is tax deductible.* Bond interest payments are tax deductible for the issuer, but equity payments (distributions) to owners are not. To illustrate, assume that a corporation with no bond financing earns $15,000 in income *before* paying taxes at a 40% tax rate, which amounts to $6,000 ($15,000 × 40%) in taxes. If a portion of its financing is in bonds, however, the resulting bond interest is deducted in computing taxable income. That is, if bond interest expense is $10,000, the taxes owed would be $2,000 ([$15,000 − $10,000] × 40%), which is less than the $6,000 owed with no bond financing.

3. *Bonds can increase return on equity.* A company that earns a higher return with borrowed funds than it pays in interest on those funds increases its return on equity. This process is called *financial leverage* or *trading on the equity.*

To illustrate the third point, consider Magnum Co., which has $1 million in equity and is planning a $500,000 expansion to meet increasing demand for its product. Magnum predicts the $500,000 expansion will yield $125,000 in additional income before paying any interest. It currently earns $100,000 per year and has no interest expense. Magnum is considering three plans. Plan A is not to expand. Plan B is to expand and raise $500,000 from equity financing. Plan C is to expand and issue $500,000 of bonds that pay 10% annual interest ($50,000). Exhibit 14.1 shows how these three plans affect Magnum's net income, equity, and return on equity (net income/equity). Analysis shows that the owner(s) will earn a higher return on equity if expansion occurs. Moreover, the preferred expansion plan is to issue bonds. Projected net income under Plan C ($175,000) is smaller than under Plan B ($225,000), but the return on equity is larger because of less equity investment. Plan C has another advantage if income is taxable. This illustration reflects a general rule: *Return on equity increases when the expected rate of return from the new assets is higher than the rate of interest expense on the debt financing.*

Point: Financial leverage can be achieved by issuing either bonds, notes, or preferred stock.

Example: Compute return on equity for all three plans if Magnum currently earns $150,000 instead of $100,000.
Answer ($ in 000s):
Plan A = 15% ($150/$1,000)
Plan B = 18.3% ($275/$1,500)
Plan C = 22.5% ($225/$1,000)

Exhibit 14.1

Financing with Bonds versus Equity

	Plan A Do Not Expand	Plan B Equity Financing	Plan C Bond Financing
Income before interest expense	$ 100,000	$ 225,000	$ 225,000
Interest expense	—	—	(50,000)
Net income	**$ 100,000**	**$ 225,000**	**$ 175,000**
Equity	$1,000,000	$1,500,000	$1,000,000
Return on equity	**10.0%**	**15.0%**	**17.5%**

Disadvantages of Bonds The two main disadvantages of bond financing are:

1. *Bonds can decrease return on equity.* When a company earns a lower return with the borrowed funds than it pays in interest, it decreases its return on equity. This downside risk of financial leverage is more likely to arise when a company has periods of low income or net losses.
2. *Bonds require payment of both periodic interest and the par value at maturity.* Bond payments can be especially burdensome when income and cash flow are low. Equity financing, in contrast, does not require any payments because cash withdrawals (dividends) are paid at the discretion of the owner (or board).

Point: Debt financing is desirable when interest is tax deductible, when owner control is preferred, and when return on equity is higher than interest rate on debt.

A company must weigh the risks and returns of the disadvantages and advantages of bond financing when deciding whether to issue bonds to finance operations.

Types of Bonds

This section describes the more common types of bonds and their characteristics.

C1 Describe the types of bonds and the procedures for issuing them.

Secured and Unsecured Bonds **Secured bonds** have specific assets of the issuer pledged (or *mortgaged*) as collateral. This arrangement gives bondholders added protection against the issuer's default. If the issuer fails to pay interest or par value, the secured bondholders can demand that the collateral be sold and the proceeds used to pay the bond obligation. **Unsecured bonds,** also called *debentures,* are backed by the issuer's general credit standing. Unsecured bonds are riskier than secured bonds. An issuer generally must be financially strong to successfully issue debentures at a favorable interest rate. *Subordinated debentures* refer to creditors whose claims on the issuer's assets are second to those of other unsecured liabilities. In a liquidation, subordinated debentures are not repaid until the claims of the more senior, unsecured liabilities have been settled.

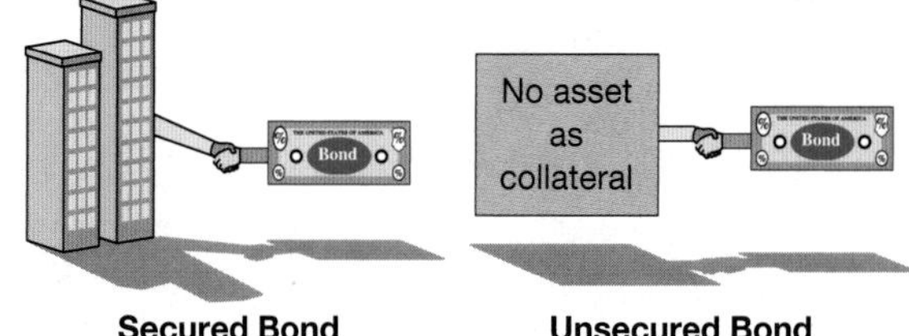

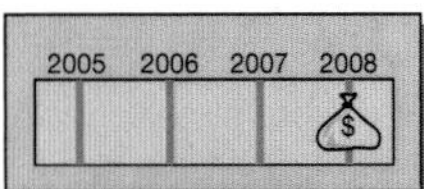

Term Bond

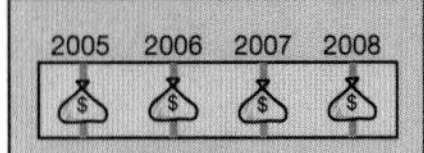

Serial Bond

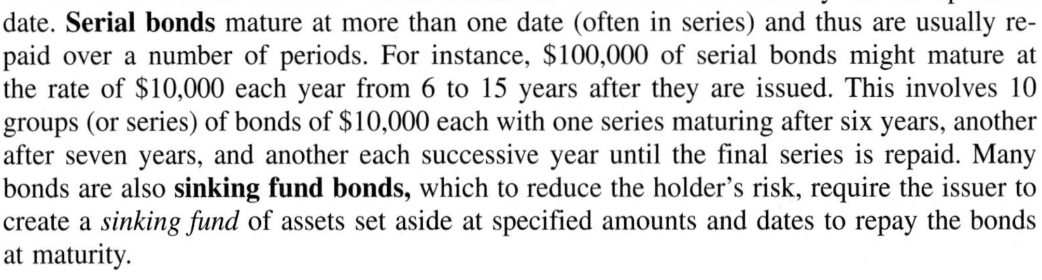

Term and Serial Bonds **Term bonds** are scheduled for maturity on one specified date. **Serial bonds** mature at more than one date (often in series) and thus are usually repaid over a number of periods. For instance, $100,000 of serial bonds might mature at the rate of $10,000 each year from 6 to 15 years after they are issued. This involves 10 groups (or series) of bonds of $10,000 each with one series maturing after six years, another after seven years, and another each successive year until the final series is repaid. Many bonds are also **sinking fund bonds,** which to reduce the holder's risk, require the issuer to create a *sinking fund* of assets set aside at specified amounts and dates to repay the bonds at maturity.

Registered Bond

Bearer Bond

Registered Bonds and Bearer Bonds Bonds issued in the names and addresses of their holders are **registered bonds.** The issuer makes bond payments by sending checks (or cash transfers) to these registered holders. When selling a bond to another holder, a registered holder must notify the issuer of the change. Registered bonds offer the issuer the practical advantage of not having to actually issue bond certificates, which protects holders against loss or theft of bonds.

Bonds payable to whoever holds them (the *bearer*) are called **bearer bonds** or *unregistered bonds*. Sales or exchanges might not be recorded, so the holder of a bearer bond is presumed to be its rightful owner. As a result, lost or stolen bearer bonds are difficult to replace. Many bearer bonds are also **coupon bonds.** This term reflects interest coupons that are attached to the bonds. Each coupon matures on a specific interest payment date. When each coupon matures, the holder presents it to a bank or broker for collection. At maturity, the holder follows the same process and presents the bond certificate for collection. Income tax law discourages companies from issuing coupon bonds because there is no readily available record of who actually receives the interest.

Decision Insight

Munis More than a million municipal bonds, or "munis," can be purchased, and many are tax exempt. Munis are issued by state, city, town, and county governments to pay for public projects including schools, libraries, roads, bridges, and stadiums.

Convertible Bond Callable Bond

Convertible and Callable Bonds **Convertible bonds** can be exchanged for a fixed number of shares of the issuing corporation's common stock. Convertible bonds offer bondholders the potential to participate in future increases in a stock's market value. Bondholders still receive periodic interest while the bonds are held and the par value if they hold the bond to maturity. In most cases, the bondholders decide whether and when to convert the bonds to stock. **Callable bonds** have an option exercisable by the issuer to retire them at a stated dollar amount prior to maturity.

Decision Insight

Quotes The bond quote here is interpreted (left to right) as **Bonds,** issuer name; **Rate,** contract interest rate (7%); **Mat,** matures in year 2025 when principal is paid; **Yld,** yield rate (5.9%) of bond at current price; **Vol,** daily dollar worth ($130,000) of trades (in 1,000s); **Close,** closing price (119.25) for the day as percent of par value; **Chg,** change (1.25) in closing price from prior day's close.

Bonds	Rate	Mat	Yld	Vol	Close	Chg
IBM	7	25	5.9	130	119¼	+1¼

Bond Trading

Bonds are securities that can be readily bought and sold. A large number of bonds trade on both the New York Exchange and the American Exchange. A bond *issue* consists of a number of bonds, usually in denominations of $1,000 or $5,000, and is sold to many different lenders. After bonds are issued, they often are bought and sold by investors, meaning that any particular bond probably has a number of owners before it matures. Since bonds are exchanged (bought and sold) in the market, they have a market value (price). For convenience, bond market values are expressed as a percent of their par (face) value. For example, a company's bonds might be trading at 103½, meaning they can be bought or sold for 103.5% of their par value. Bonds can also trade below par value. For instance, if a company's bonds are trading at 95, they can be bought or sold at 95% of their par value.

Point: Issuers of coupon bonds cannot deduct the related interest expense for taxable income. This is to prevent abuse by taxpayers who own coupon bonds but fail to report interest income on their tax returns.

Bond-Issuing Procedures

State and federal laws govern bond issuances. Bond issuers also want to ensure that they do not violate any of their existing contractual agreements when issuing bonds. Authorization of bond issuances includes the number of bonds authorized, their par value, and the contract interest rate. The legal document identifying the rights and obligations of both the bondholders and the issuer is called the **bond indenture,** which is the legal contract between the issuer and the bondholders. A bondholder may also receive a bond certificate as evidence of the company's debt. A **bond certificate,** such as that shown in Exhibit 14.2, includes specifics such as the issuer's name, the par value, the contract interest rate, and the maturity date. Many companies reduce costs by not issuing paper certificates to bondholders.

Point: *Indenture* refers to a bond's legal contract; *debenture* refers to an unsecured bond.

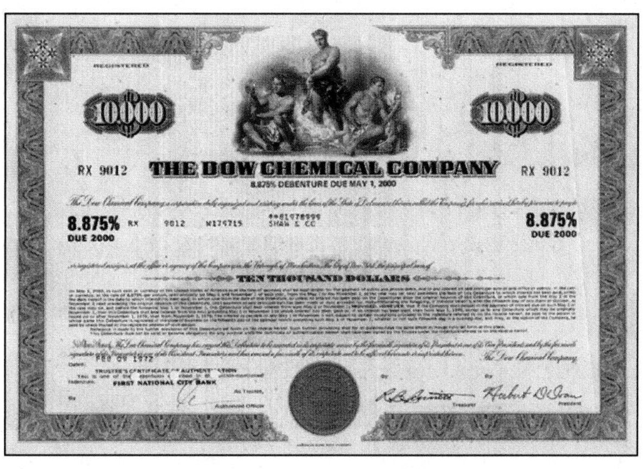

Exhibit 14.2

Bond Certificate

The issuing company normally sells its bonds to an investment firm called an *underwriter,* which resells them to the public. An issuing company can also sell bonds directly to investors. When an underwriter sells bonds to a large number of investors, a *trustee* represents and protects the bondholders' interests. The trustee monitors the issuer to ensure that it complies with the obligations in the bond indenture. Most trustees are large banks or trust companies. The trustee writes and accepts the terms of a bond indenture before it is issued. When bonds are offered to the public, called *floating an issue,* they must be registered with the Securities and Exchange Commission (SEC). SEC registration requires the issuer to file certain financial information. Most company bonds are issued in par value units of $1,000 or $5,000. A *baby bond* has a par value of less than $1,000, such as $100.

Point: The *spread* between the dealer's cost and what buyers pay can be huge. Dealers are said to earn more than $25 billion in annual spread revenue. A tight oligopoly of Wall Street brokers and dealers continues to control bond prices.

Global: In the United Kingdom, government bonds are called *gilts*—short for gilt-edged investments.

Bond Issuances

This section explains accounting for bond issuances at par, below par (discount), and above par (premium). It also describes how to amortize a discount or premium and record bonds issued between interest payment dates.

Topic Tackler 14-1

Issuing Bonds at Par

P1 Prepare entries to record bond issuance and bond interest expense.

To illustrate an issuance of bonds at par value, suppose a company receives authorization to issue $800,000 of 9%, 20-year bonds dated January 1, 2005, that mature on December 31, 2024, and pay interest semiannually on each June 30 and December 31. After accepting the bond indenture on behalf of the bondholders, the trustee can sell all or a portion of the bonds to an underwriter. If all bonds are sold at par value, the issuer records the sale as:

2005			
Jan. 1	Cash	800,000	
	Bonds Payable		800,000
	Sold bonds at par.		

Assets = Liabilities + Equity
+800,000 +800,000

This entry reflects increases in the issuer's cash *and* long-term liabilities.

The issuer records the first semiannual interest payment as follows:

2005			
June 30	Bond Interest Expense	36,000	
	Cash		36,000
	Paid semiannual interest (9% × $800,000 × ½ year).		

Assets = Liabilities + Equity
−36,000 −36,000

The issuer pays and records its semiannual interest obligation every six months until the bonds mature. When they mature, the issuer records its payment of principal as:

2024			
Dec. 31	Bonds Payable	800,000	
	Cash..............................		800,000
	Paid bond principal at maturity.		

Assets	= Liabilities	+ Equity
−800,000	−800,000	

Bond Discount or Premium

The bond issuer pays the interest rate specified in the indenture, the **contract rate,** also referred to as the *coupon rate, stated rate,* or *nominal rate*. The annual interest paid is determined by multiplying the bond par value by the contract rate. The contract rate is usually stated on an annual basis, even if interest is paid semiannually. For example, if a company issues a $1,000, 8% bond paying interest semiannually, it pays annual interest of $80 (8% × $1,000) in two semiannual payments of $40 each.

Decision Insight

Ratings Game Many bond buyers rely on rating services to assess bond risk. The best known are **Standard & Poor's** and **Moody's.** These services focus on the issuer's financial statements and other factors in setting ratings. Standard & Poor's ratings, from best quality to default, are AAA, AA, A, BBB, BB, B, CCC, CC, C, and D. Ratings can include a plus (+) or minus (−) to show relative standing within a category.

The contract rate sets the amount of interest the issuer pays in *cash,* which is not necessarily the *bond interest expense* actually incurred by the issuer. Bond interest expense depends on the bond's market value at issuance, which is determined by market expectations of the risk of lending to the issuer. The bond's **market rate** of interest is the rate that borrowers are willing to pay and lenders are willing to accept for a particular bond and its risk level. As the risk level increases, the rate increases to compensate purchasers for the bonds' increased risk. Also, the market rate is generally higher when the time period until the bond matures is longer due to the risk of adverse events occurring over a longer time period.

Point: Business acquisitions are sometimes financed by issuing "junk bonds" that carry high market rates of interest but offer little security. Bondholders can suffer huge losses if the bond issuers do not generate adequate cash flows to pay interest and principal.

Many bond issuers try to set a contract rate of interest equal to the market rate they expect as of the bond issuance date. When the contract rate and market rate are equal, a bond sells at par value, but when they are not equal, a bond does not sell at par value. Instead, it is sold at a *premium* above par value or at a *discount* below par value. Exhibit 14.3 shows the relation between the contract rate, market rate, and a bond's issue price.

Exhibit 14.3

Relation between Bond Issue Price, Contract Rate, and Market Rate

Contract Rate Is		Bond Sells
Above market rate	➡	At a premium
Equal to market rate	➡	At par value
Below market rate	➡	At a discount

Quick Check

1. Unsecured bonds backed only by the issuer's general credit standing are called (*a*) serial bonds, (*b*) debentures, (*c*) registered bonds, or (*d*) convertible bonds.
2. How do you compute the amount of interest a bond issuer pays in cash each year?
3. When the contract rate is above the market rate, do bonds sell at a premium or a discount? Do purchasers pay more or less than the par value of the bonds?

Answers—p. 576

Issuing Bonds at a Discount

P2 Compute and record amortization of bond discount.

A **discount on bonds payable** occurs when a company issues bonds with a contract rate less than the market rate. This means that the issue price is less than par value. To illustrate, assume that **Fila** announces an offer to issue bonds with a $100,000 par value, an 8% annual contract rate (paid semiannually), and a five-year life. Also assume that the market rate for Fila bonds is 10%. These bonds then will sell at a discount since the contract rate is less than the market rate. The exact issue price for these bonds is 92.277 (or 92.277% of par value); we show how to compute this issue price later in the chapter. These bonds obligate the issuer to pay two separate types of future cash flows:

1. Par value of $100,000 cash at the end of the bonds' five-year life.
2. Cash interest payments of $4,000 (4% × $100,000) at the end of each semiannual period during the bonds' five-year life.

The exact pattern of cash flows for the Fila bonds is shown in Exhibit 14.4.

Point: The difference between the contract rate and the market rate of interest on a new bond issue is usually a fraction of a percent. We use a difference of 2% to emphasize the effects.

Exhibit 14.4

Cash Flows for Fila Bonds

0	6 mo.	12 mo.	18 mo.	24 mo.	. . .	48 mo.	54 mo.	60 mo.
	$4,000	$4,000	$4,000	$4,000		$4,000	$4,000	$100,000 $4,000

When Fila accepts $92,277 cash for its bonds on the issue date of December 31, 2005, it records the sale as follows:

Dec. 31	Cash	92,277	
	Discount on Bonds Payable	7,723	
	Bonds Payable		100,000
	Sold bonds at a discount on their issue date.		

Assets = Liabilities + Equity
+92,277 +100,000
−7,723

These bonds are reported in the long-term liability section of the issuer's December 31, 2005, balance sheet as shown in Exhibit 14.5. A discount is deducted from the par value of bonds to yield the **carrying (book) value of bonds.** Discount on Bonds Payable is a contra liability account.

Point: Book value at issuance always equals the issuer's cash amount borrowed.

Exhibit 14.5

Balance Sheet Presentation of Bond Discount

Long-term liabilities		
Bonds payable, 8%, due December 31, 2010	$100,000	
Less discount on bonds payable	7,723	$92,277

Amortizing a Bond Discount Fila receives $92,277 for its bonds; in return it must pay bondholders $100,000 after five years (plus semiannual interest payments). The $7,723 discount is paid to bondholders at maturity and is part of the cost of using the $92,277 for five years. The upper portion of panel A in Exhibit 14.6 shows that total bond interest expense of $47,723 is the difference between the total amount repaid to bondholders ($140,000) and the amount borrowed from bondholders ($92,277). Alternatively, we can compute total bond interest expense as the sum of the 10 interest payments and the bond discount. This alternative computation is shown in the lower portion of panel A.

Decision Maker

Bond Rater You must assign a rating to a bond that reflects its risk to bondholders. Identify factors you consider in assessing bond risk. Indicate the likely levels (relative to the norm) for the factors you identify for a bond that sells at a discount.

Answer—p. 576

Point: *Zero-coupon bonds* do not pay periodic interest (contract rate is zero). These bonds always sell at a discount because their 0% contract rate is always below the market rate.

The total $47,723 bond interest expense must be allocated across the 10 semiannual periods in the bonds' life, and the bonds' carrying value must be updated at each balance sheet date. This is accomplished using the straight-line method (or the effective interest method in Appendix 14B). Both methods systematically reduce the bond discount to zero over the five-year life. This process is called *amortizing a bond discount.*

Decision Insight

Junk Bonds Junk bonds are company bonds with low credit ratings because of a higher than average likelihood of default on repayment. On the upside, the high risk of junk bonds can yield high returns if the issuer survives and repays its debt. Junk bond issuances are now running over $100 billion a year.

Straight-Line Method The **straight-line method** allocates an equal portion of the total bond interest expense to each interest period. To apply the straight-line method to Fila's

Exhibit 14.6

Interest Computation and Entry for Bonds Issued at a Discount

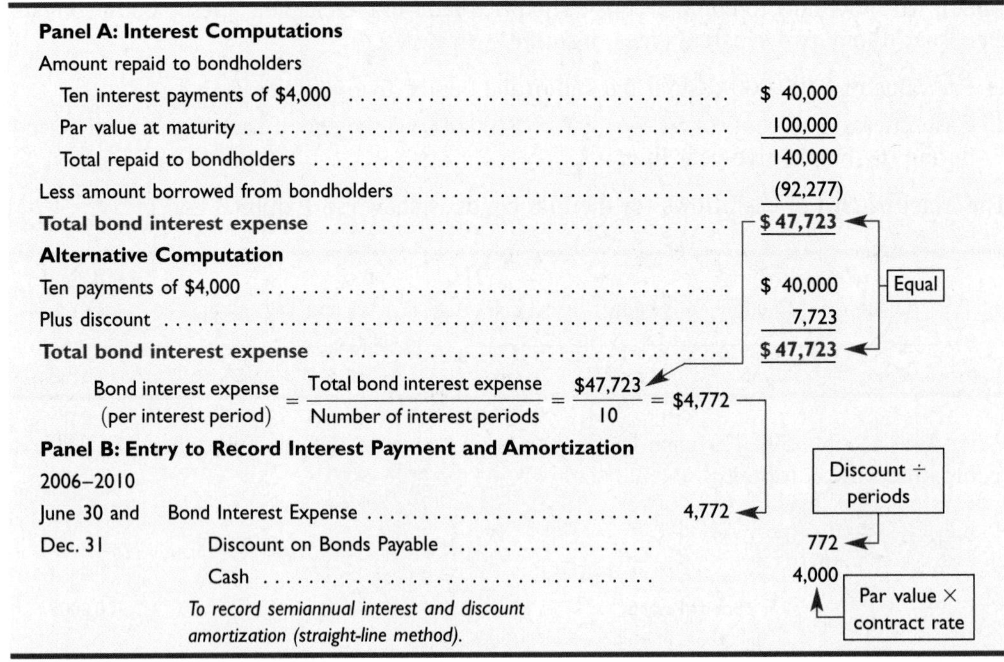

Panel A: Interest Computations

Amount repaid to bondholders	
Ten interest payments of $4,000	$ 40,000
Par value at maturity	100,000
Total repaid to bondholders	140,000
Less amount borrowed from bondholders	(92,277)
Total bond interest expense	**$ 47,723**
Alternative Computation	
Ten payments of $4,000	$ 40,000
Plus discount	7,723
Total bond interest expense	**$ 47,723**

$$\text{Bond interest expense (per interest period)} = \frac{\text{Total bond interest expense}}{\text{Number of interest periods}} = \frac{\$47,723}{10} = \$4,772$$

Panel B: Entry to Record Interest Payment and Amortization

2006–2010 June 30 and Dec. 31	Bond Interest Expense	4,772	
	Discount on Bonds Payable		772
	Cash		4,000
	To record semiannual interest and discount amortization (straight-line method).		

Topic Tackler 14-2

bonds, we divide the total bond interest expense of $47,723 by 10 (the number of semiannual periods in the bonds' life). This gives a bond interest expense of $4,772 per period (all computations, including those for assignments, are rounded to the nearest whole dollar). Alternatively, we can find this number by first dividing the $7,723 discount by 10, which yields the $772 amount of discount to be amortized each interest period. When the $772 is added to the $4,000 cash payment, the bond interest expense for each period is $4,772. Panel B of Exhibit 14.6 shows how the issuer records bond interest expense and updates the balance of the bond liability account at the end of *each* of the 10 semiannual interest periods (June 30, 2006, through December 31, 2010).

Exhibit 14.7 shows the pattern of decreases in the Discount on Bonds Payable account and the pattern of increases in the bonds' carrying value. The following points summarize the discount bonds' straight-line amortization:

Exhibit 14.7

Straight-Line Amortization of Bond Discount

Semiannual Period-End	Unamortized Discount*	Carrying Value†
(0) 12/31/2005	$7,723	$ 92,277
(1) 6/30/2006	6,951	93,049
(2) 12/31/2006	6,179	93,821
(3) 6/30/2007	5,407	94,593
(4) 12/31/2007	4,635	95,365
(5) 6/30/2008	3,863	96,137
(6) 12/31/2008	3,091	96,909
(7) 6/30/2009	2,319	97,681
(8) 12/31/2009	1,547	98,453
(9) 6/30/2010	775	99,225
(10) 12/31/2010	**0‡**	**100,000**

The two columns always sum to par value for a discount bond.

* Total bond discount ($7,723) less accumulated periodic amortization ($772 per semiannual interest period).

† Bond par value ($100,000) less unamortized discount.

‡ Adjusted for rounding.

1. At issuance, the $100,000 par value consists of the $92,277 cash received by the issuer plus the $7,723 discount.
2. During the bonds' life, the (unamortized) discount decreases each period by the $772 amortization ($7,723/10), and the carrying value (par value less unamortized discount) increases each period by $772.
3. At maturity, the unamortized discount equals zero, and the carrying value equals the $100,000 par value that the issuer pays the holder.

Notice that the issuer incurs a $4,772 bond interest expense each period but pays only $4,000 cash. The $772 unpaid portion of this expense is added to the bonds' carrying value. (The total $7,723 unamortized discount is "paid" when the bonds mature; $100,000 is paid at maturity but only $92,277 was received at issuance.)

Global: Some countries such as Italy report bonds and notes at their par (face) value, not at book (carrying) value.

Quick Check

Five-year, 6% bonds with a $100,000 par value are issued at a price of $91,893. Interest is paid semiannually, and the bonds' market rate is 8% on the issue date. Use this information to answer the following questions:

4. Are these bonds issued at a discount or a premium? Explain your answer.
5. What is the issuer's journal entry to record the issuance of these bonds?
6. What is the amount of bond interest expense recorded at the first semiannual period using the straight-line method?

Answers—p. 576

Issuing Bonds at a Premium

P3 Compute and record amortization of bond premium.

When the contract rate of bonds is higher than the market rate, the bonds sell at a price higher than par value. The amount by which the bond price exceeds par value is the **premium on bonds.** To illustrate, assume that **Adidas** issues bonds with a $100,000 par value, a 12% annual contract rate, semiannual interest payments, and a five-year life. Also assume that the market rate for Adidas bonds is 10% on the issue date. The Adidas bonds will sell at a premium because the contract rate is higher than the market rate. The exact issue price for these bonds is 107.72 (or 107.72% of par value); we show how to compute this issue price later in the chapter. These bonds obligate the issuer to pay out two separate future cash flows:

1. Par value of $100,000 cash at the end of the bonds' five-year life.
2. Cash interest payments of $6,000 (6% × $100,000) at the end of each semiannual period during the bonds' five-year life.

The exact pattern of cash flows for the Adidas bonds is shown in Exhibit 14.8.

Exhibit 14.8

Cash Flows for Adidas Bonds

								$100,000
	$6,000	$6,000	$6,000	$6,000	. . .	$6,000	$6,000	$6,000
0	6 mo.	12 mo.	18 mo.	24 mo.		48 mo.	54 mo.	60 mo.

When Adidas accepts $107,720 cash for its bonds on the issue date of December 31, 2005, it records this transaction as follows:

Dec. 31	Cash	107,720	
	Premium on Bonds Payable		7,720
	Bonds Payable		100,000
	Sold bonds at a premium on their issue date.		

Assets	=	Liabilities	+	Equity
+107,720		+100,000		
		+7,720		

These bonds are reported in the long-term liability section of the issuer's December 31, 2005, balance sheet as shown in Exhibit 14.9. A premium is added to par value to yield the carrying (book) value of bonds. Premium on Bonds Payable is an adjunct (also called *accretion*) liability account.

Exhibit 14.9

Balance Sheet Presentation of Bond Premium

Long-term liabilities		
Bonds payable, 12%, due December 31, 2010	$100,000	
Plus premium on bonds payable	7,720	$107,720

Amortizing a Bond Premium Adidas receives $107,720 for its bonds; in return, it pays bondholders $100,000 after five years (plus semiannual interest payments). The

$7,720 premium not repaid to bondholders at maturity goes to reduce the issuer's expense of using the $107,720 for five years. The upper portion of panel A of Exhibit 14.10 shows that total bond interest expense of $52,280 is the difference between the total amount repaid to bondholders ($160,000) and the amount borrowed from bondholders ($107,720). Alternatively, we can compute total bond interest expense as the sum of the 10 interest payments less the bond premium. The premium is subtracted because it will not be paid to bondholders when the bonds mature; see the lower portion of panel A. Total bond interest expense must be allocated over the 10 semiannual periods using the straight-line method (or the effective interest method in Appendix 14B).

Exhibit 14.10

Interest Computation and Entry for Bonds Issued at a Premium

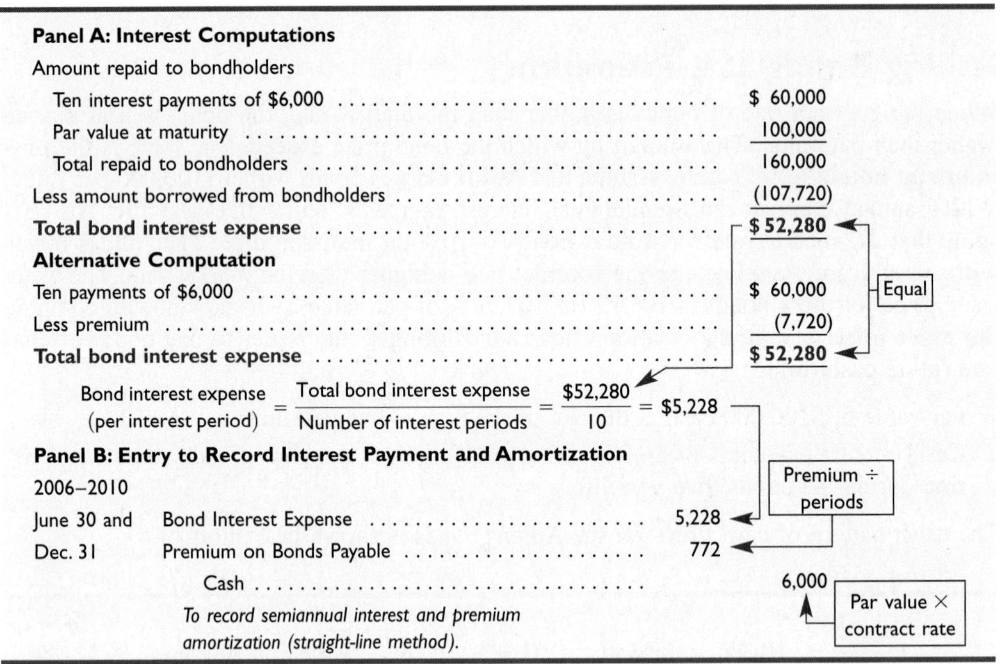

Panel A: Interest Computations

Amount repaid to bondholders	
Ten interest payments of $6,000	$ 60,000
Par value at maturity	100,000
Total repaid to bondholders	160,000
Less amount borrowed from bondholders	(107,720)
Total bond interest expense	**$ 52,280**
Alternative Computation	
Ten payments of $6,000	$ 60,000
Less premium	(7,720)
Total bond interest expense	**$ 52,280**

$$\text{Bond interest expense (per interest period)} = \frac{\text{Total bond interest expense}}{\text{Number of interest periods}} = \frac{\$52{,}280}{10} = \$5{,}228$$

Panel B: Entry to Record Interest Payment and Amortization

2006–2010			
June 30 and	Bond Interest Expense	5,228	
Dec. 31	Premium on Bonds Payable	772	
	Cash		6,000
	To record semiannual interest and premium amortization (straight-line method).		

Point: A premium decreases Bond Interest Expense while a discount increases it.

Straight-Line Method The straight-line method allocates an equal portion of total bond interest expense to each of the bonds' semiannual interest periods. To apply this method to Adidas bonds, we divide the five years' total bond interest expense of $52,280 by 10 (the number of semiannual periods in the bonds' life). This gives a total bond interest expense of $5,228 per period. Panel B of Exhibit 14.10 shows how the issuer records bond interest expense and updates the balance of the bond liability account for *each* semiannual period (June 30, 2006, through December 31, 2010).

Exhibit 14.11

Straight-Line Amortization of Bond Premium

Semiannual Period-End	Unamortized Premium*	Carrying Value†
(0) 12/31/2005	$7,720	$107,720
(1) 6/30/2006	6,948	106,948
(2) 12/31/2006	6,176	106,176
(3) 6/30/2007	5,404	105,404
(4) 12/31/2007	4,632	104,632
(5) 6/30/2008	3,860	103,860
(6) 12/31/2008	3,088	103,088
(7) 6/30/2009	2,316	102,316
(8) 12/31/2009	1,544	101,544
(9) 6/30/2010	772	100,772
(10) 12/31/2010	**0**	**100,000**

* Total bond premium ($7,720) less accumulated periodic amortization ($772 per semiannual interest period).

† Bond par value ($100,000) plus unamortized premium.

Carrying value is adjusted to par and the amortized premium to zero during the bond life.

Exhibit 14.11 shows the pattern of decreases in the unamortized Premium on Bonds Payable account and in the bonds' carrying value. The following points summarize straight-line amortization of the premium bonds:

1. At issuance, the $100,000 par value plus the $7,720 premium equals the $107,720 cash received by the issuer.

2. During the bonds' life, the (unamortized) premium decreases each period by the $772 amortization ($7,720/10), and the carrying value decreases each period by the same $772.
3. At maturity, the unamortized premium equals zero, and the carrying value equals the $100,000 par value that the issuer pays the holder.

Issuing Bonds between Interest Dates

An issuer can sell bonds at a date other than an interest payment date. When this occurs, the buyers normally pay the issuer the purchase price plus any interest accrued since the prior interest payment date. This accrued interest is then repaid to these buyers on the next interest payment date. To illustrate, suppose **Avia** sells $100,000 of its 9% bonds at par on March 1, 2005, sixty days after the stated issue date. The interest on Avia bonds is payable semiannually on each June 30 and December 31. Since 60 days have passed, the issuer collects accrued interest from the buyers at the time of issuance. This amount is $1,500 ($100,000 × 9% × 60/360 year). This case is reflected in Exhibit 14.12.

Decision Insight

Amor-tech Spreadsheet and accounting software such as **Excel** and **Peachtree** make amortization tables easier. Enter the bonds' par value, selling price, contract rate, and life and out comes a complete amortization table.

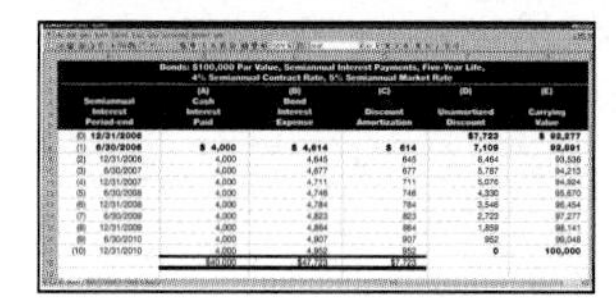

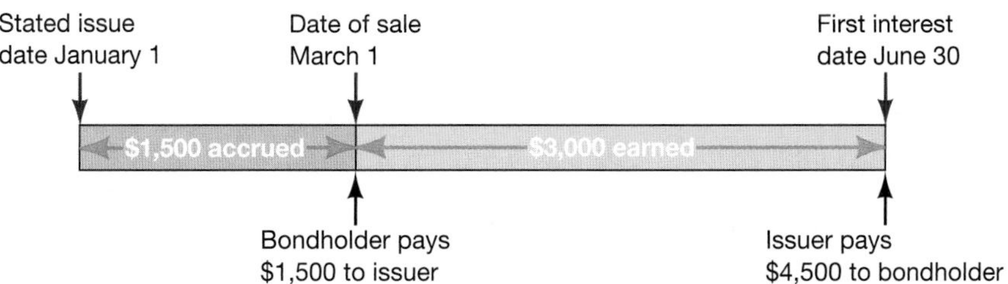

Exhibit 14.12

Accruing Interest between Interest Payment Dates

Avia records the issuance of these bonds on March 1, 2005, as follows:

Mar. 1	Cash	101,500	
	Interest Payable		1,500
	Bonds Payable		100,000
	Sold bonds at par with accrued interest.		

Assets = Liabilities + Equity
+101,500 +100,000
+1,500

Note that liabilities for interest payable and bonds payable are recorded in separate accounts. When the June 30, 2005, semiannual interest date arrives, Avia pays the full semiannual interest of $4,500 ($100,000 × 9% × ½ year) to the bondholders. This payment includes the four months' interest of $3,000 earned by the bondholders from March 1 to June 30 *plus* the repayment of the 60 days' accrued interest collected by Avia when the bonds were sold. Avia records this first semiannual interest payment as follows:

Example: How much interest is collected from a buyer of $50,000 of Avia bonds sold at par 150 days after the contract issue date? *Answer:* $1,875 (computed as $50,000 × 9% × 150/360 year)

June 30	Interest Payable	1,500	
	Bond Interest Expense	3,000	
	Cash		4,500
	Paid semiannual interest on the bonds.		

Assets = Liabilities + Equity
−4,500 −1,500 −3,000

The practice of collecting and then repaying accrued interest with the next interest payment is to simplify the issuer's administrative efforts. To explain, suppose an issuer sells bonds on 15 or 20 different dates between the stated issue date and the first interest payment date. If the issuer does not collect accrued interest from buyers, it needs to pay different amounts of cash to each of them according to the time that passed after purchasing the bonds. The issuer needs to keep detailed records of buyers and the dates they bought bonds. Issuers

Global: In some countries such as Kuwait, Saudi Arabia, and Iran, charging explicit interest for use of money is rare due to Islamic law.

avoid this recordkeeping by having each buyer pay accrued interest at purchase. Issuers then pay the full semiannual interest to all buyers, regardless of when they bought bonds.

Accruing Bond Interest Expense

If a bond's interest period does not coincide with the issuer's accounting period, an adjusting entry is needed to recognize bond interest expense accrued since the most recent interest payment. To illustrate, assume that the Adidas bonds described in Exhibit 14.11 are sold on the stated issue date of September 1, 2005, instead of December 31, 2005. As a result, four months' interest (and premium amortization) accrue before the end of the 2005 calendar year. Interest for this period equals $3,485, or 4/6 of the first six months' interest of $5,228. Also, the premium amortization is $515, or 4/6 of the first six months' amortization of $772. The sum of the bond interest expense and the amortization is $4,000 ($3,485 + $515), which equals 4/6 of the $6,000 cash payment due on February 28, 2006. Adidas records these effects with an adjusting entry at December 31, 2005:

Assets = Liabilities + Equity
−515 −3,485
+4,000

Dec. 31	Bond Interest Expense	3,485	
	Premium on Bonds Payable	515	
	Interest Payable		4,000
	To record four months' accrued interest and premium amortization.		

Similar entries are made on each December 31 throughout the bonds' five-year life. When the $6,000 cash payment occurs on each February 28 interest payment date, Adidas must recognize bond interest expense and amortization for January and February. It must also eliminate the interest payable liability created by the December 31 adjusting entry. For example, Adidas records its payment on February 28, 2006, as:

Assets = Liabilities + Equity
−6,000 −4,000 −1,743
−257

Feb. 28	Interest Payable	4,000	
	Bond Interest Expense ($5,228 × 2/6)	1,743	
	Premium on Bonds Payable ($772 × 2/6)........	257	
	Cash..............................		6,000
	To record 2 months' interest and amortization and eliminate accrued interest liability.		

The interest payments made each August 31 are recorded as usual because the entire six-month interest period is included within this company's calendar-year reporting period.

Bond Pricing

Point: InvestingInBonds.com is an excellent bond research and learning source.

Prices for bonds traded on an organized exchange are often published in newspapers and through online services. This information normally includes the bond price (called *quote*), its contract rate, and its current market (called *yield*) rate. However, only a fraction of bonds are traded on organized exchanges. To compute the price of a bond, we apply present value concepts. This section explains how to use *present value concepts* to price the Fila discount bond and the Adidas premium bond described earlier.

Point: A bond's market value (price) at issuance equals the present value of all its future cash payments (the interest [discount] rate used is the bond's market rate).

Point: Many calculators provide present value functions for computation of bond prices.

Present Value of a Discount Bond The issue price of bonds is found by computing the present value of the bonds' cash payments, discounted at the bonds' market rate. When computing the present value of the Fila bonds, we work with *semiannual* compounding periods because this is the time between interest payments; the annual market rate of 10% is considered a semiannual rate of 5%. Also, the five-year bond life is viewed as 10 semiannual periods. The price computation is twofold: (1) find the present value of the $100,000 par value paid at maturity and (2) find the present value of the series of 10 semiannual payments of $4,000 each; see Exhibit 14.4. These present values can be found by using *present value tables*. Appendix B at the end of this book shows present value tables and describes their use. Table B.1 at the end of Appendix B is used for the single $100,000 maturity payment, and Table B.3 in Appendix B is used for the $4,000 series of interest payments. Specifically, we go to Table B.1, row 10, and across to the 5% column to identify the present value factor of 0.6139 for the maturity payment. Next, we go to Table B.3, row 10, and across to the 5% column, where the present value factor is 7.7217 for the series of interest payments. We compute bond price by multiplying the cash flow payments by their corresponding present value factors and adding them together; see Exhibit 14.13.

Point: The general approach to bond pricing is identical for discount bonds and premium bonds.

Cash Flow	Table	Present Value Factor	Amount	Present Value
$100,000 par (maturity) value	B.1	0.6139	× $100,000 =	$ 61,390
$4,000 interest payments	B.3	7.7217	× 4,000 =	30,887
Price of bond				**$92,277**

Exhibit 14.13

Computing Issue Price for the Fila Discount Bonds

Present Value of a Premium Bond We find the issue price of the Adidas bonds by using the market rate to compute the present value of the bonds' future cash flows. When computing the present value of these bonds, we again work with *semiannual* compounding periods because this is the time between interest payments. The annual 10% market rate is applied as a semiannual rate of 5%, and the five-year bond life is viewed as 10 semiannual periods. The computation is twofold: (1) find the present value of the $100,000 par value paid at maturity and (2) find the present value of the series of 10 payments of $6,000 each; see Exhibit 14.8. These present values can be found by using present value tables. First, go to Table B.1, row 10, and across to the 5% column where the present value factor is 0.6139 for the maturity payment. Second, go to Table B.3, row 10, and across to the 5% column, where the present value factor is 7.7217 for the series of interest payments. The bonds' price is computed by multiplying the cash flow payments by their corresponding present value factors and adding them together; see Exhibit 14.14.

Point: There are nearly 5 million individual U.S. bond issues, ranging from huge treasuries to tiny municipalities. This compares to about 12,000 individual U.S. stocks that are traded.

Cash Flow	Table	Present Value Factor	Amount	Present Value
$100,000 par (maturity) value	B.1	0.6139	× $100,000 =	$ 61,390
$6,000 interest payments	B.3	7.7217	× 6,000 =	46,330
Price of bond				**$107,720**

Exhibit 14.14

Computing Issue Price for the Adidas Premium Bonds

Quick Check

On December 31, 2004, a company issues 16%, 10-year bonds with a par value of $100,000. Interest is paid on June 30 and December 31. The bonds are sold to yield a 14% annual market rate at an issue price of $110,592. Use this information to answer questions 7 through 9:

7. Are these bonds issued at a discount or a premium? Explain your answer.

8. Using the straight-line method to allocate bond interest expense, the issuer records the second interest payment (on December 31, 2005) with a debit to Premium on Bonds Payable in the amount of (*a*) $7,470, (*b*) $530, (*c*) $8,000, or (*d*) $400.

9. How are these bonds reported in the long-term liability section of the issuer's balance sheet as of December 31, 2005?

10. On May 1, a company sells 9% bonds with a $500,000 par value that pay semiannual interest on each January 1 and July 1. The bonds are sold at par plus interest accrued since January 1. The issuer records the first semiannual interest payment on July 1 with (*a*) a debit to Interest Payable for $15,000, (*b*) a debit to Bond Interest Expense for $22,500, or (*c*) a credit to Interest Payable for $7,500.

Answers—p. 576

Bond Retirement

This section describes the retirement of bonds (1) at maturity, (2) before maturity, and (3) by conversion to stock.

Bond Retirement at Maturity

P4 Record the retirement of bonds.

The carrying value of bonds at maturity always equals par value. For example, both Exhibits 14.7 (a discount) and 14.11 (a premium) show that the carrying value of bonds at the end of their lives equals par value ($100,000). The retirement of these bonds at maturity, assuming interest is already paid and entered, is recorded as follows:

Assets	=	Liabilities	+	Equity
−100,000		−100,000		

2010			
Dec. 31	Bonds Payable	100,000	
	Cash		100,000
	To record retirement of bonds at maturity.		

Bond Retirement before Maturity

Point: Bond retirement is also referred to as *bond redemption.*

Point: Gains and losses from retiring bonds were *previously* reported as extraordinary items. New standards require that they now be judged by the "unusual and infrequent" criteria for reporting purposes.

Issuers sometimes wish to retire some or all of their bonds prior to maturity. For instance, if interest rates decline significantly, an issuer may wish to replace high-interest-paying bonds with new low-interest bonds. Two common ways to retire bonds before maturity are to (1) exercise a call option or (2) purchase them on the open market. In the first instance, an issuer can reserve the right to retire bonds early by issuing callable bonds. The bond indenture can give the issuer an option to *call* the bonds before they mature by paying the par value plus a *call premium* to bondholders. In the second case, the issuer retires bonds by repurchasing them on the open market at their current price. Whether bonds are called or repurchased, the issuer is unlikely to pay a price that exactly equals their carrying value. When a difference exists between the bonds' carrying value and the amount paid, the issuer records a gain or loss equal to the difference.

Callable Bond

To illustrate the accounting for retiring callable bonds, assume that a company issued callable bonds with a par value of $100,000. The call option requires the issuer to pay a call premium of $3,000 to bondholders in addition to the par value. Next, assume that after the June 30, 2005, interest payment, the bonds have a carrying value of $104,500. Then on July 1, 2005, the issuer calls these bonds and pays $103,000 to bondholders. The issuer recognizes a $1,500 gain from the difference between the bonds' carrying value of $104,500 and the retirement price of $103,000. The issuer records this bond retirement as:

Assets	=	Liabilities	+	Equity
−103,000		−100,000		+1,500
		−4,500		

July 1	Bonds Payable	100,000	
	Premium on Bonds Payable	4,500	
	Gain on Bond Retirement		1,500
	Cash..............................		103,000
	To record retirement of bonds before maturity.		

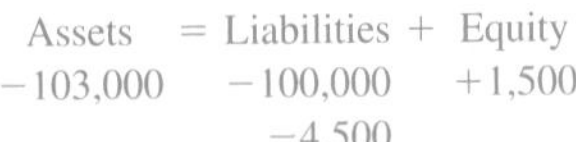

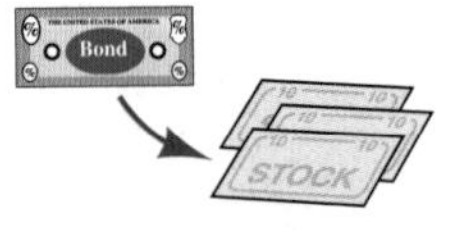

Convertible Bond

An issuer usually must call all bonds when it exercises a call option. However, to retire as many or as few bonds as it desires, an issuer can purchase them on the open market. If it retires less than the entire class of bonds, it recognizes a gain or loss for the difference between the carrying value of those bonds retired and the amount paid to acquire them.

Decision Insight

Convertible bonds have delivered about 80% of the returns of diversified stock funds but with only about 66% of the price volatility. Convertibles protect holders against stock price declines and give holders the chance to make more money if stock prices increase.

Bond Retirement by Conversion

We described convertible bonds earlier in the chapter and explained how these bondholders have the right to convert their bonds to stock. When conversion occurs, the bonds' carrying value is transferred to equity accounts and no gain or loss is recorded. (The market prices of the bonds and stock are *not* relevant to this entry; the material in Chapter 13 is helpful in understanding this transaction.) To illustrate, assume that on January 1 the $100,000 par value bonds of **Converse**, with a carrying value of $100,000, are converted to 15,000 shares of $2 par value common stock. The entry to record this conversion is:

Jan. 1	Bonds Payable	100,000	
	Common Stock		30,000
	Contributed Capital in Excess of Par Value . .		70,000
	To record retirement of bonds by conversion.		

Assets	=	Liabilities	+	Equity
		−100,000		+30,000
				+70,000

Quick Check

11. Six years ago, a company issued $500,000 of 6%, eight-year bonds at a price of 95. The current carrying value is $493,750. The company decides to retire 50% of these bonds by buying them on the open market at a price of 102½. What is the amount of gain or loss on retirement of these bonds?

Answer—p. 576

Long-Term Notes Payable

Like bonds, notes are issued to obtain assets such as cash. Unlike bonds, notes are typically transacted with a *single* lender such as a bank. An issuer initially records a note at its selling price; that is, the note's face value minus any discount or plus any premium. Over the note's life, the amount of interest expense allocated to each period is computed by multiplying the market rate (at issuance of the note) by the beginning-of-period note balance. The note's carrying (book) value at any time equals its face value minus any unamortized discount or plus any unamortized premium; carrying value is also computed as the present value of all remaining payments, discounted using the market rate at issuance.

Installment Notes

C2 Explain the types and payment patterns of notes.

An **installment note** is an obligation requiring a series of payments to the lender. Installment notes are common for franchises and other businesses when lenders and borrowers agree to spread payments over several periods. To illustrate, assume that Foghog borrows $60,000 from a bank to purchase equipment. It signs an 8% installment note requiring six annual payments of principal plus interest and it records the note's issuance as follows:

Dec. 31	Cash	60,000	
	Notes Payable		60,000
	Borrowed $60,000 by signing an 8%, six-year installment note.		

Assets	=	Liabilities	+	Equity
+60,000		+60,000		

Payments on an installment note normally include the accrued interest expense plus a portion of the amount borrowed (the *principal*). Two payment patterns are common: (1) accrued interest plus equal principal payments and (2) equal payments. This section describes these two patterns and how to account for them.

Accrued Interest plus Equal Principal Payments The payment pattern of accrued interest plus equal amounts of principal creates cash flows that decrease in size over the note's life. This decrease occurs because each principal payment reduces the note's principal balance, yielding less interest expense for the next period.

To illustrate, assume that Foghog's $60,000, six-year, 8% note requires it to make an annual year-end payment equal to *accrued interest plus $10,000 of principal*. Exhibit 14.15 shows these payments and changes in the note balance. Column A lists the note's annual beginning balance.

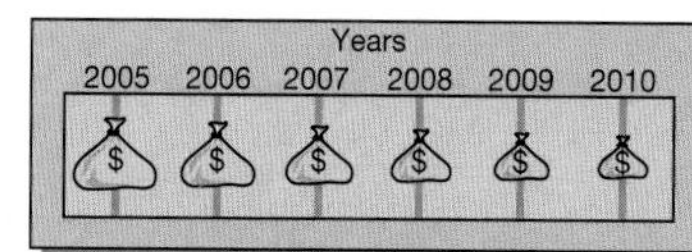

Exhibit 14.15

Installment Note: Accrued Interest plus Equal Principal Payments

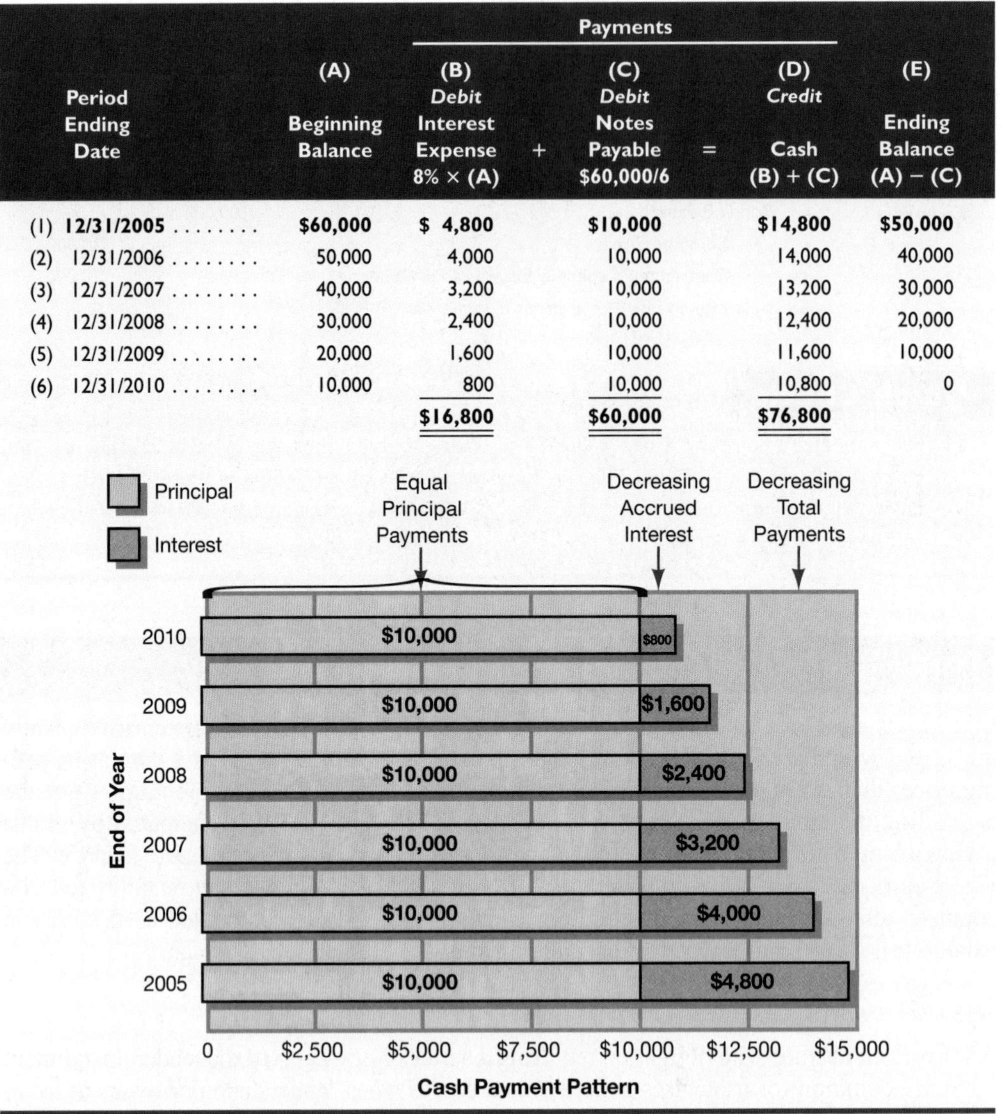

Period Ending Date	(A) Beginning Balance	Payments (B) *Debit* Interest Expense 8% × (A)	+	Payments (C) *Debit* Notes Payable $60,000/6	=	Payments (D) *Credit* Cash (B) + (C)	(E) Ending Balance (A) − (C)
(1) **12/31/2005**	**$60,000**	**$ 4,800**		**$10,000**		**$14,800**	**$50,000**
(2) 12/31/2006	50,000	4,000		10,000		14,000	40,000
(3) 12/31/2007	40,000	3,200		10,000		13,200	30,000
(4) 12/31/2008	30,000	2,400		10,000		12,400	20,000
(5) 12/31/2009	20,000	1,600		10,000		11,600	10,000
(6) 12/31/2010	10,000	800		10,000		10,800	0
		$16,800		**$60,000**		**$76,800**	

P5 Prepare entries to account for notes.

Columns B, C, and D list each annual cash payment and its breakdown into interest and principal. Specifically, column B shows interest expense for each year at 8% of the beginning balance. Column C shows that each principal payment reduces the Notes Payable account balance by $10,000. Column D is the total annual payment. Column E shows the note's ending balance, which equals the beginning balance in column A minus the principal payment in column C. We include *debit* or *credit* in column headings to show the accounting effects. Note that the sum of debits to both interest expense and notes payable equals the credit to Cash. Also notice that total interest expense is $16,800 and total principal is $60,000, meaning cash payments for the five years total $76,800. The graph in the lower portion of Exhibit 14.15 shows the decreasing pattern in total payments, made up of decreasing accrued interest and constant principal payments. After all six payments are recorded, the balance of the Notes Payable account is zero. Foghog records its first two payments (for years 2005 and 2006) as follows:

Assets	=	Liabilities	+	Equity
−14,800		−10,000		−4,800

2005			
Dec. 31	Interest Expense	4,800	
	Notes Payable	10,000	
	Cash		14,800
	To record first installment payment.		

2006			
Dec. 31	Interest Expense	4,000	
	Notes Payable	10,000	
	Cash		14,000
	To record second installment payment.		

Assets	=	Liabilities	+	Equity
−14,000		−10,000		−4,000

Equal Total Payments The equal total payments pattern consists of changing amounts of both interest and principal. To illustrate, assume that Foghog borrows $60,000 by signing a $60,000 note that requires six *equal payments* of $12,979 at the end of each year. (The present value of an annuity of six annual payments of $12,979, discounted at 8%, equals $60,000; we show this computation later in the section.) The $12,979 includes both interest and principal, the amounts of which change with each payment. Exhibit 14.16 shows the pattern of equal total payments and its two parts, interest and principal. Column A shows the note's beginning balance. Column B shows accrued interest for each year at 8% of the beginning note balance. Column C shows the impact on the note's principal, which equals the difference between the total payment in column D and the interest expense in column B. Column E shows the note's year-end balance.

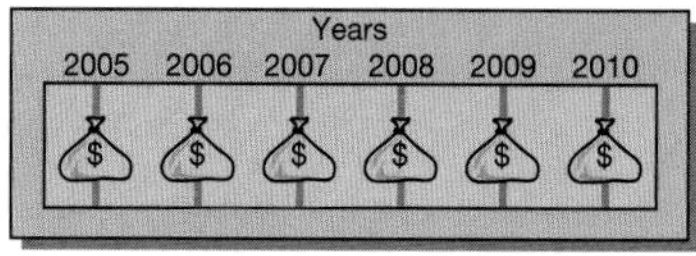

Point: Most consumer notes are installment notes that require equal total payments.

Exhibit 14.16

Installment Note: Equal Total Payments

Period Ending Date	(A) Beginning Balance	Payments: (B) *Debit* Interest Expense 8% × (A)	+	(C) *Debit* Notes Payable (D) − (B)	=	(D) *Credit* Cash (computed)	(E) Ending Balance (A) − (C)
(1) **12/31/2005**	**$60,000**	**$ 4,800**		**$ 8,179**		**$12,979**	**$51,821**
(2) 12/31/2006	51,821	4,146		8,833		12,979	42,988
(3) 12/31/2007	42,988	3,439		9,540		12,979	33,448
(4) 12/31/2008	33,448	2,676		10,303		12,979	23,145
(5) 12/31/2009	23,145	1,852		11,127		12,979	12,018
(6) 12/31/2010	12,018	961		12,018		12,979	0
		$17,874		**$60,000**		**$77,874**	

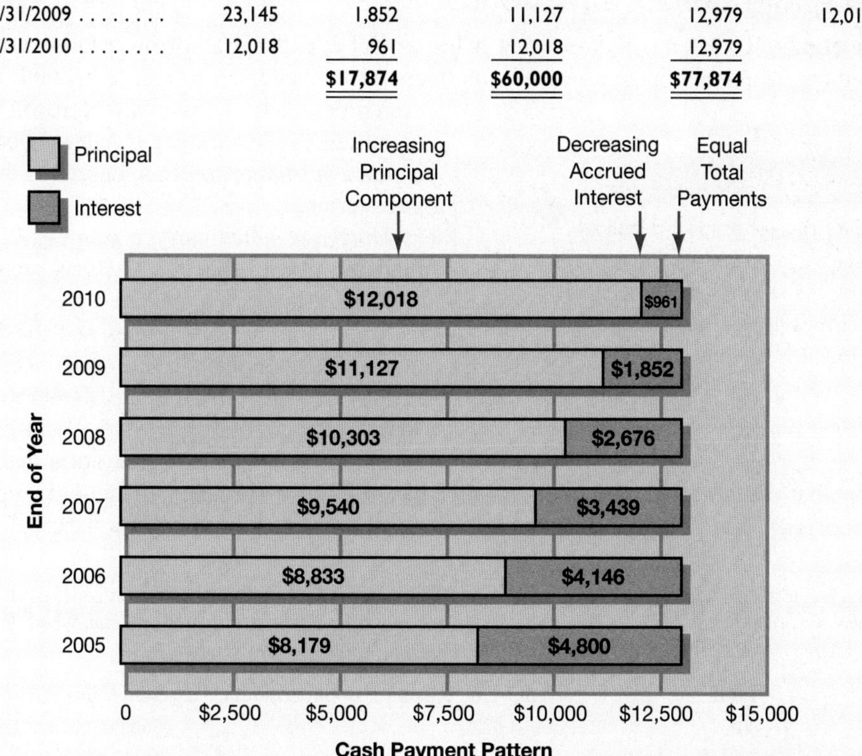

Point: The Truth-in-Lending Act requires lenders to provide information about loan costs including finance charges and interest rate.

Although the six cash payments are equal, accrued interest decreases each year because the principal balance of the note declines. As the amount of interest decreases each year, the portion of each payment applied to principal increases. This pattern is graphed in the lower part of Exhibit 14.16. Foghog uses the amounts in Exhibit 14.16 to record its first two payments (for years 2005 and 2006) as follows:

Assets	= Liabilities	+ Equity
−12,979	−8,179	−4,800

Date	Account	Debit	Credit
2005			
Dec. 31	Interest Expense	4,800	
	Notes Payable	8,179	
	Cash		12,979
	To record first installment payment.		

Assets	= Liabilities	+ Equity
−12,979	−8,833	−4,146

Date	Account	Debit	Credit
2006			
Dec. 31	Interest Expense	4,146	
	Notes Payable	8,833	
	Cash		12,979
	To record second installment payment.		

Decision Insight

Entrepreneur Aid Small Business Administration (SBA) provides loan programs, workshops, software, and other useful services for start-ups. It also operates an online library with facts and advice for entrepreneurs (**SBA.gov**). It reports that reliable accounting is crucial in securing financing at favorable terms.

Foghog records similar entries but with different amounts for each of the remaining four payments. After six years, the Notes Payable account balance is zero.

It is useful to compare the two payment patterns in Exhibits 14.15 and 14.16. The series of equal total payments yields more interest expense over the life of the note because the first three payments in Exhibit 14.16 are smaller and do not reduce the principal as quickly as the first three payments in Exhibit 14.15.[1]

Mortgage Notes and Bonds

A **mortgage** is a legal agreement that helps protect a lender if a borrower fails to make required payments on bonds or notes. A mortgage gives the lender a right to be paid from the cash proceeds of the sale of a borrower's assets identified in the mortgage. A legal document, called a *mortgage contract,* describes the mortgage terms.

Mortgage notes carry a mortgage contract pledging title to specific assets as security for the note. Mortgage notes are especially popular in the purchase of homes and the acquisition of plant assets. Less common *mortgage bonds* are backed by the issuer's assets. Accounting for mortgage notes and bonds is similar to that for unsecured notes and bonds, except that the mortgage agreement must be disclosed. For example, **Musicland** reports that its "mortgage note payable is collateralized by land, buildings and certain fixtures."

Decision Maker

Entrepreneur You are an electronics retailer planning a holiday sale on a custom stereo system that requires no payments for two years. At the end of two years, buyers must pay the full amount. The system's suggested retail price is $4,100, but you are willing to sell it today for $3,000 cash. What is your holiday sale price if payment will not occur for two years and the market interest rate is 10%?

Answer—p. 576

Example: Suppose the $60,000 installment loan has an 8% interest rate with eight equal annual payments. What is the annual payment? *Answer* (using Table B.3): $60,000/5.7466 = $10,441

[1] Table B.3 in Appendix B is used to compute the dollar amount of the six payments that equal the initial note balance of $60,000 at 8% interest. We go to Table B.3, row 6, and across to the 8% column, where the present value factor is 4.6229. The dollar amount is then computed by solving this relation:

Table	Present Value Factor		Dollar Amount		Present Value
B.3	4.6229	×	?	=	$60,000

The dollar amount is computed by dividing $60,000 by 4.6229, yielding $12,979.

Global: Countries vary in the preference given to debtholders vs. stockholders when a company is in financial distress. Some countries such as Germany, France, and Japan give preference to stockholders over debtholders.

Quick Check

12. Which of the following is true for an installment note requiring a series of equal total cash payments? (*a*) Payments consist of increasing interest and decreasing principal; (*b*) Payments consist of changing amounts of principal but constant interest; or (*c*) Payments consist of decreasing interest and increasing principal.

13. How is the interest portion of an installment note payment computed?

14. When a borrower records an interest payment on an installment note, how are the balance sheet and income statement affected?

Answers—p. 576

Pledged Assets to Secured Liabilities Ratio

Decision Analysis

A2 Explain collateral agreements and their effects on loan risk.

Collateral agreements can reduce the risk of loss for both bonds and notes. Unsecured bonds and notes are riskier because the issuer's obligation to pay interest and principal has the same priority as all other unsecured liabilities in the event of bankruptcy. If a company is unable to pay its debts in full, the unsecured creditors (including the holders of debentures) lose all or a portion of their balances.

A company's ability to borrow money with or without collateral agreements depends on its credit rating. In some cases, debt financing is unavailable unless the borrower can provide security to creditors with a collateral agreement. Even if unsecured loans are available, the creditors are likely to charge a higher rate of interest to compensate for the added risk. To borrow funds at a more favorable rate, many bonds and notes are secured by collateral agreements in the form of mortgages.

A3 Compute the ratio of pledged assets to secured liabilities and explain its use.

Notes to financial statements often describe the amounts of assets pledged as security against liabilities. Buyers (investors) of a company's secured debt obligations need to determine whether the debtor's pledged assets provide adequate security. One method to evaluate this is to compute the ratio of **pledged assets to secured liabilities** as in Exhibit 14.17.

$$\textbf{Pledged assets to secured liabilities} = \frac{\textbf{Book value of pledged assets}}{\textbf{Book value of secured liabilities}}$$

Exhibit 14.17

Ratio of Pledged Assets to Secured Liabilities

To illustrate, assume that a company owns assets with a book value of \$230,000 pledged against loans with a balance of \$100,000. The pledged assets to secured liabilities ratio is 2.3 (expressed as 2.3 to 1) and is computed as \$230,000/\$100,000. There are no exact guidelines for interpreting this ratio, but a 2.3 value is sufficiently high to provide secured creditors with some comfort that their loans are covered by the borrower's assets. As another example, a recent annual report of **Chock Full O'Nuts** reveals that "borrowings under the Loan Agreements . . . are collateralized by . . . accounts receivable and inventories, and substantially all of the machinery and equipment and real estate." We can use this information to compute its pledged assets to secured liabilities ratio of 20.6 (\$206 million/\$10 million). This ratio implies that more than \$20 of collateral exists for each \$1 of secured liabilities. This huge collateral commitment likely accounts for the low interest rate that Chock Full O'Nuts pays on these secured liabilities.

Pledging more assets for the benefit of secured creditors puts unsecured creditors at greater risk. Also, when using this ratio, be aware that book values of a company's net assets are unlikely to exactly reflect market values. The ratio is improved if reliable market values are used for the ratio instead of book values.

Decision Maker

Bond Investor You plan to purchase debenture bonds from one of two companies in the same industry that are similar in size and performance. The first company has \$350,000 of unsecured liabilities, \$575,000 of secured liabilities, and \$1,265,000 in book value of pledged assets. The second company has \$1,200,000 of unsecured liabilities, \$800,000 of secured liabilities, and \$2,000,000 in book value of pledged assets. Which company's debenture bonds are less risky based on the ratio of pledged assets to secured liabilities?

Answer—p. 576

Demonstration Problem

Water Sports Company (WSC) patented and successfully test-marketed a new product. To expand its ability to produce and market the new product, WSC needs to raise $800,000 of financing. On January 1, 2004, the company obtained the money in two ways:

a. WSC signed a $400,000, 10% installment note to be repaid with five equal annual installments to be made on December 31 of 2004 through 2008.

b. WSC issued five-year bonds with a par value of $400,000. The bonds have a 12% annual contract rate and pay interest on June 30 and December 31. The bonds' annual market rate is 10% as of January 1, 2004.

Required

1. For the installment note, (*a*) compute the size of each annual payment, (*b*) prepare an amortization table such as Exhibit 14.16, and (*c*) prepare the journal entry for the first payment.

2. For the bonds, (*a*) compute their issue price; (*b*) prepare the January 1, 2004, journal entry to record their issuance; (*c*) prepare an amortization table using the straight-line method; (*d*) prepare the June 30, 2004, journal entry to record the first interest payment; and (*e*) prepare a journal entry to record retiring the bonds at a $416,000 call price on January 1, 2006.

3.[B] Redo parts 2(*c*), 2(*d*), and 2(*e*) assuming the bonds are amortized using the effective interest method.

Planning the Solution

- For the installment note, divide the borrowed amount by the annuity factor (from Table B.3) using the 10% rate and five payments to compute the amount of each payment. Prepare a table similar to Exhibit 14.16 and use the numbers in the table's first line for the journal entry.
- Compute the bonds' issue price by using the market rate to find the present value of their cash flows (use tables found in Appendix B). Then use this result to record the bonds' issuance. Next, prepare an amortization table like Exhibit 14.11 (and Exhibit 14B.2) and use it to get the numbers needed for the journal entry. Also use the table to find the carrying value as of the date of the bonds' retirement that you need for the journal entry.

Solution to Demonstration Problem

Part 1: Installment Note

a. Annual payment = Note balance/Annuity factor = $400,000/3.7908 = $105,519 (Note: Annuity factor is for five payments and a rate of 10%.)

b. Amortization table follows:

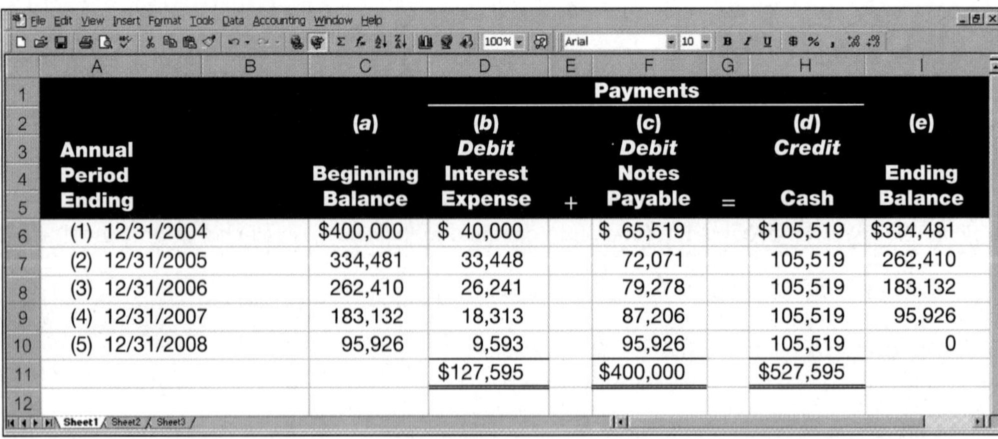

Annual Period Ending	(a) Beginning Balance	Payments: (b) Debit Interest Expense	+	Payments: (c) Debit Notes Payable	=	Payments: (d) Credit Cash	(e) Ending Balance
(1) 12/31/2004	$400,000	$ 40,000		$ 65,519		$105,519	$334,481
(2) 12/31/2005	334,481	33,448		72,071		105,519	262,410
(3) 12/31/2006	262,410	26,241		79,278		105,519	183,132
(4) 12/31/2007	183,132	18,313		87,206		105,519	95,926
(5) 12/31/2008	95,926	9,593		95,926		105,519	0
		$127,595		$400,000		$527,595	

c. Journal entry for December 31, 2004, payment:

Dec. 31	Interest Expense	40,000	
	Notes Payable	65,519	
	Cash		105,519
	To record first installment payment.		

Part 2: Bonds (straight-line amortization)

a. Compute the bonds' issue price:

Cash Flow	Table	Present Value Factor*	Amount	Present Value
Par (maturity) value	B.1 in App. B (PV of 1)	0.6139	× 400,000	= $245,560
Interest payments	B.3 in App. B (PV of annuity)	7.7217	× 24,000	= 185,321
Price of bond				$430,881

* Present value factors are for 10 payments using a semiannual market rate of 5%.

b. Journal entry for January 1, 2004, issuance:

Jan. 1	Cash	430,881	
	Premium on Bonds Payable		30,881
	Bonds Payable		400,000
	Sold bonds at a premium.		

c. Straight-line amortization table for premium bonds:

Semiannual Period-End	Unamortized Premium	Carrying Value
(0) 1/1/2004	$30,881	$430,881
(1) 6/30/2004	27,793	427,793
(2) 12/31/2004	24,705	424,705
(3) 6/30/2005	21,617	421,617
(4) 12/31/2005	18,529	418,529
(5) 6/30/2006	15,441	415,441
(6) 12/31/2006	12,353	412,353
(7) 6/30/2007	9,265	409,265
(8) 12/31/2007	6,177	406,177
(9) 6/30/2008	3,089	403,089
(10) 12/31/2008	0*	400,000

* Adjusted for rounding.

d. Journal entry for June 30, 2004, payment:

June 30	Bond Interest Expense	20,912	
	Premium on Bonds Payable	3,088	
	Cash		24,000
	Paid semiannual interest on bonds.		

e. Journal entry for January 1, 2006, bond retirement:

Jan. 1	Bonds Payable	400,000	
	Premium on Bonds Payable	18,529	
	Cash		416,000
	Gain on Retirement of Bonds		2,529
	To record bond retirement (carrying value as of Dec. 31, 2005).		

Part 3: Bonds (effective interest amortization)[B]

c. Effective interest amortization table for premium bonds:

Semiannual Interest Period	(A) Cash Interest Paid 6% × $400,000	(B) Interest Expense 5% × Prior (E)	(C) Premium Amortization (A) − (B)	(D) Unamortized Premium Prior (D) − (C)	(E) Carrying Value $400,000 + (D)
(0) 1/1/2004				$30,881	$430,881
(1) 6/30/2004	$ 24,000	$ 21,544	$ 2,456	28,425	428,425
(2) 12/31/2004	24,000	21,421	2,579	25,846	425,846
(3) 6/30/2005	24,000	21,292	2,708	23,138	423,138
(4) 12/31/2005	24,000	21,157	2,843	20,295	420,295
(5) 6/30/2006	24,000	21,015	2,985	17,310	417,310
(6) 12/31/2006	24,000	20,866	3,134	14,176	414,176
(7) 6/30/2007	24,000	20,709	3,291	10,885	410,885
(8) 12/31/2007	24,000	20,544	3,456	7,429	407,429
(9) 6/30/2008	24,000	20,371	3,629	3,800	403,800
(10) 12/31/2008	24,000	20,200*	3,800	0	400,000
	$240,000	$209,119	$30,881		

* Adjusted for rounding.

d. Journal entry for June 30, 2004, payment:

June 30	Bond Interest Expense	21,544	
	Premium on Bonds Payable	2,456	
	Cash		24,000
	Paid semiannual interest on bonds.		

e. Journal entry for January 1, 2006, bond retirement:

Jan. 1	Bonds Payable	400,000	
	Premium on Bonds Payable	20,295	
	Cash		416,000
	Gain on Retirement of Bonds		4,295
	To record bond retirement (carrying value as of December 31, 2005).		

APPENDIX

14A Present Values of Bonds and Notes

This appendix explains how to apply present value techniques to measure a long-term liability when it is created and to assign interest expense to the periods until it is settled. Appendix B at the end of the book provides additional discussion of present value concepts.

Present Value Concepts

C3 Explain and compute the present value of an amount to be paid at a future date.

The basic present value concept is that cash paid (or received) in the future has less value now than the same amount of cash paid (or received) today. To illustrate, if we must pay $1 one year from now, its present value is less than $1. To see this, assume that we borrow $0.9259 today that must be paid back in one year with 8% interest. Our interest expense for this loan is computed as $0.9259 × 8%, or $0.0741. When the $0.0741 interest is added to the $0.9259 borrowed, we get the $1 payment necessary to repay our loan with interest. This is formally computed in Exhibit 14A.1. The $0.9259 borrowed is the present value of the $1 future payment. More generally, an amount borrowed equals the present value of the future payment. (This same interpretation applies to an investment. If $0.9259 is invested at 8%, it yields $0.0741 in revenue after one year. This amounts to $1, made up of principal and interest.)

Exhibit 14A.1

Components of a One-Year Loan

Amount borrowed	**$0.9259**
Interest for one year at 8%	0.0741
Amount owed after 1 year	$1.0000

To extend this example, assume that we owe $1 two years from now instead of one year, and the 8% interest is compounded annually. *Compounded* means that interest during the second period is based on the total of the amount borrowed plus the interest accrued from the first period. The second period's interest is then computed as 8% multiplied by the sum of the amount borrowed plus interest earned in the first period. Exhibit 14A.2 shows how we compute the present value of $1 to be paid in two years. This amount is $0.8573. The first year's interest of $0.0686 is added to the principal so that the second year's interest is based on $0.9259. Total interest for this two-year period is $0.1427, computed as $0.0686 plus $0.0741.

Point: Benjamin Franklin is said to have described compounding as "the money, money makes, makes more money."

Exhibit 14A.2

Components of a Two-Year Loan

Amount borrowed	**$0.8573**
Interest for first year ($0.8573 × 8%)	0.0686
Amount owed after 1 year	$ 0.9259
Interest for second year ($0.9259 × 8%)	0.0741
Amount owed after 2 years	$ 1.0000

Present Value Tables

The present value of $1 that we must repay at some future date can be computed by using this formula: $1/(1 + i)^n$. The symbol i is the interest rate per period and n is the number of periods until the future payment must be made. Applying this formula to our two-year loan, we get $\$1/(1.08)^2$, or $0.8573. This is the same value shown in Exhibit 14A.2. We can use this formula to find any present value. However, a simpler method is to use a *present value table,* which lists present values computed with this formula for various interest rates and time periods. Many people find it helpful in learning present value concepts to first work with the table and then move to using a calculator.

Exhibit 14A.3

Present Value of 1

	Rate		
Periods	6%	8%	10%
1	0.9434	**0.9259**	0.9091
2	0.8900	**0.8573**	0.8264
3	0.8396	0.7938	0.7513
4	0.7921	0.7350	0.6830
5	0.7473	0.6806	0.6209
6	0.7050	0.6302	0.5645
7	0.6651	0.5835	0.5132
8	0.6274	0.5403	0.4665
9	0.5919	0.5002	0.4241
10	0.5584	0.4632	0.3855

Exhibit 14A.3 shows a present value table for a future payment of 1 for up to 10 periods at three different interest rates. Present values in this table are rounded to four decimal places. This table is drawn from the larger and more complete Table B.1 in Appendix B at the end of the book. Notice that the first value in the 8% column is 0.9259, the value we computed earlier for the present value of a $1 loan for one year at 8% (see Exhibit 14A.1). Go to the second row in the same 8% column and find the present value of 1 discounted at 8% for two years, or 0.8573. This $0.8573 is the present value of our obligation to repay $1 after two periods at 8% interest (see Exhibit 14A.2).

Example: Use Exhibit 14A.3 to find the present value of $1 discounted for 2 years at 6%. *Answer:* Present value = $0.8900

Applying a Present Value Table

To illustrate how to measure a liability using a present value table, assume that a company plans to borrow cash and repay it as follows: $2,000 after one year, $3,000 after two years, and $5,000 after three

Exhibit 14A.4

Present Value of a Series of Unequal Payments

Periods	Payments	Present Value of 1 at 10%	Present Value of Payments
1	$2,000	0.9091	$ 1,818
2	3,000	0.8264	2,479
3	5,000	0.7513	3,757
Present value of all payments			$8,054

years. How much does this company receive today if the interest rate on this loan is 10%? To answer, we need to compute the present value of the three future payments, discounted at 10%. This computation is shown in Exhibit 14A.4 using present values from Exhibit 14A.3. The company can borrow $8,054 today at 10% interest in exchange for its promise to make these three payments at the scheduled dates.

Present Value of an Annuity

C4 Explain and compute the present value of a series of equal amounts to be paid at future dates.

The $8,054 present value for the loan in Exhibit 14A.4 equals the sum of the present values of the three payments. When payments are not equal, their combined present value is best computed by adding the individual present values as shown in Exhibit 14A.4. Sometimes payments follow an **annuity,** which is a series of *equal* payments at equal time intervals. The present value of an annuity is readily computed.

To illustrate, assume that a company must repay a 6% loan with a $5,000 payment at each year-end for the next four years. This loan amount equals the present value of the four payments discounted at 6%. Exhibit 14A.5 shows how to compute this loan's present value of $17,326 by multiplying each payment by its matching present value factor taken from Exhibit 14A.3.

Exhibit 14A.5

Present Value of a Series of Equal Payments (Annuity) by Discounting Each Payment

Periods	Payments	Present Value of 1 at 6%	Present Value of Payments
1	$5,000	0.9434	$ 4,717
2	5,000	0.8900	4,450
3	5,000	0.8396	4,198
4	5,000	0.7921	3,961
Present value of all payments		**3.4651**	**$17,326**

However, the series of $5,000 payments is an annuity, so we can compute its present value with either of two shortcuts. First, the third column of Exhibit 14A.5 shows that the sum of the present values of 1 at 6% for periods 1 through 4 equals 3.4651. One shortcut is to multiply this total of 3.4651 by the $5,000 annual payment to get the combined present value of $17,326. It requires one multiplication instead of four.

The second shortcut uses an *annuity table* such as the one shown in Exhibit 14A.6, which is drawn from the more complete Table B.3 in Appendix B. We go directly to the annuity table to get the present value factor for a specific number of payments and interest rate. We then multiply this factor by the amount of the payment to find the present value of the annuity. Specifically, find the row for four periods and go across to the 6% column, where the factor is 3.4651. This factor equals the present value of an annuity with four payments of 1, discounted at 6%. We then multiply 3.4651 by $5,000 to get the $17,326 present value of the annuity.

Exhibit 14A.6

Present Value of an Annuity of 1

	Rate		
Periods	6%	8%	10%
1	0.9434	0.9259	0.9091
2	1.8334	1.7833	1.7355
3	2.6730	2.5771	2.4869
4	**3.4651**	3.3121	3.1699
5	4.2124	3.9927	3.7908
6	4.9173	4.6229	4.3553
7	5.5824	5.2064	4.8684
8	6.2098	5.7466	5.3349
9	6.8017	6.2469	5.7590
10	7.3601	6.7101	6.1446

Example: Use Exhibit 14A.6 to find the present value of an annuity of eight $15,000 payments with an 8% interest rate. *Answer:* Present value = $15,000 × 5.7466 = $86,199

Compounding Periods Shorter than a Year

The present value examples all involved periods of one year. In many situations, however, interest is compounded over shorter periods. For example, the interest rate on bonds is usually stated as an annual rate but interest is often paid every six months (semiannually). This means that the present value of interest payments from such bonds must be computed using interest periods of six months.

Assume that a borrower wants to know the present value of a series of 10 *semiannual payments* of $4,000 made over five years at an *annual interest rate* of 12%. The interest rate is stated as an annual rate of 12%, but it is actually a rate of 6% per semiannual interest period. To compute the present value of this series of $4,000 payments, go to row 10 of Exhibit 14A.6 and across to the 6% column to find the factor 7.3601. The present value of this annuity is $29,440 (7.3601 × $4,000).

Example: If this borrower makes five semiannual payments of $8,000, what is the present value of this annuity at a 12% annual rate? *Answer:* 4.2124 × $8,000 = $33,699

Appendix B further describes present value concepts and includes more complete present value tables and assignments.

Quick Check

15. A company enters into an agreement to make four annual year-end payments of $1,000 each, starting one year from now. The annual interest rate is 8%. The present value of these four payments is (*a*) $2,923, (*b*) $2,940, or (*c*) $3,312.
16. Suppose a company has an option to pay either (*a*) $10,000 after one year or (*b*) $5,000 after six months and another $5,000 after one year. Which choice has the lower present value?

Answers—p. 576

APPENDIX

Effective Interest Amortization 14B

Effective Interest Amortization of a Discount Bond

The straight-line method yields changes in the bonds' carrying value while the amount for bond interest expense remains constant. This gives the impression of a changing interest rate when users divide a constant bond interest expense over a changing carrying value. As a result, accounting standards allow use of the straight-line method only when its results do not differ materially from those obtained using the effective interest method. The **effective interest method,** or simply *interest method,* allocates total bond interest expense over the bonds' life in a way that yields a constant rate of interest. This constant rate of interest is the market rate at the issue date. Thus, bond interest expense for a period equals the carrying value of the bond at the beginning of that period multiplied by the market rate when issued.

Point: The effective interest method consistently computes bond interest expense using the market rate at issuance. This rate is applied to a changing carrying value.

Exhibit 14B.1 shows an effective interest amortization table for the Fila bonds (as described in Exhibit 14.4). The key difference between the effective interest and straight-line methods lies in

Exhibit 14B.1

Effective Interest Amortization of Bond Discount

Bonds: $100,000 Par Value, Semiannual Interest Payments, Five-Year Life, 4% Semiannual Contract Rate, 5% Semiannual Market Rate

Semiannual Interest Period-End	(A) Cash Interest Paid	(B) Bond Interest Expense	(C) Discount Amortization	(D) Unamortized Discount	(E) Carrying Value
(0) **12/31/2005**				**$7,723**	**$ 92,277**
(1) **6/30/2006**	**$4,000**	**$4,614**	**$ 614**	**7,109**	**92,891**
(2) 12/31/2006	4,000	4,645	645	6,464	93,536
(3) 6/30/2007	4,000	4,677	677	5,787	94,213
(4) 12/31/2007	4,000	4,711	711	5,076	94,924
(5) 6/30/2008	4,000	4,746	746	4,330	95,670
(6) 12/31/2008	4,000	4,784	784	3,546	96,454
(7) 6/30/2009	4,000	4,823	823	2,723	97,277
(8) 12/31/2009	4,000	4,864	864	1,859	98,141
(9) 6/30/2010	4,000	4,907	907	952	99,048
(10) 12/31/2010	4,000	4,952	952	**0**	**100,000**
	$40,000	$47,723	$7,723		

Column (**A**) is par value ($100,000) multiplied by the semiannual contract rate (4%).
Column (**B**) is prior period's carrying value multiplied by the semiannual market rate (5%).
Column (**C**) is the difference between interest paid and bond interest expense, or [(B) − (A)].
Column (**D**) is the prior period's unamortized discount less the current period's discount amortization.
Column (**E**) is par value less unamortized discount, or [$100,000 − (D)].

Global: The U.S. generally requires use of the effective interest method, but some countries prefer straight-line amortization, and Brazil requires it.

computing bond interest expense. Instead of assigning an equal amount of bond interest expense to each period, the effective interest method assigns a bond interest expense amount that increases over the life of a discount bond. **Both methods allocate the *same* $47,723 of total bond interest expense to the bonds' life, but in different patterns.** Specifically, the amortization table in Exhibit 14B.1 shows that the balance of the discount (column D) is amortized until it reaches zero. Also, the bonds' carrying value (column E) changes each period until it equals par value at maturity. Compare columns D and E to the corresponding columns in Exhibit 14.7 to see the amortization patterns. Total bond interest expense is $47,723, consisting of $40,000 of semiannual cash payments and $7,723 of the original bond discount, the same for both methods.

Except for differences in amounts, journal entries recording the expense and updating the liability balance are the same under the effective interest method and the straight-line method. We can use the numbers in Exhibit 14B.1 to record each semiannual entry during the bonds' five-year life (June 30, 2006, through December 31, 2010). For instance, we record the interest payment at the end of the first semiannual period as:

Assets	= Liabilities	+ Equity
−4,000	+614	−4,614

2006			
June 30	Bond Interest Expense	4,614	
	Discount on Bonds Payable		614
	Cash		4,000
	To record semiannual interest and discount amortization (effective interest method).		

Effective Interest Amortization of a Premium Bond

Exhibit 14B.2 shows the amortization table using the effective interest method for the Adidas bonds (as described in Exhibit 14.8). Column A lists the semiannual cash payments. Column B shows the amount of bond interest expense, computed as the 5% semiannual market rate at issuance multiplied by the beginning-of-period carrying value. The amount of cash paid in column A is larger than the bond interest expense because the cash payment is based on the higher 6% semiannual contract rate. The excess cash payment over the interest expense reduces the principal. These amounts are shown in column C. Column E shows the carrying value after deducting the amortized premium in column

Exhibit 14B.2

Effective Interest Amortization of Bond Premium

Bonds: $100,000 Par Value, Semiannual Interest Payments, Five-Year Life, 6% Semiannual Contract Rate, 5% Semiannual Market Rate

Semiannual Interest Period-End	(A) Cash Interest Paid	(B) Bond Interest Expense	(C) Premium Amortization	(D) Unamortized Premium	(E) Carrying Value
(0) **12/31/2005**				**$7,720**	**$107,720**
(1) **6/30/2006**	**$6,000**	**$5,386**	**$ 614**	**7,106**	**107,106**
(2) 12/31/2006	6,000	5,355	645	6,461	106,461
(3) 6/30/2007	6,000	5,323	677	5,784	105,784
(4) 12/31/2007	6,000	5,289	711	5,073	105,073
(5) 6/30/2008	6,000	5,254	746	4,327	104,327
(6) 12/31/2008	6,000	5,216	784	3,543	103,543
(7) 6/30/2009	6,000	5,177	823	2,720	102,720
(8) 12/31/2009	6,000	5,136	864	1,856	101,856
(9) 6/30/2010	6,000	5,093	907	949	100,949
(10) 12/31/2010	6,000	5,051*	949	**0**	**100,000**
	$60,000	$52,280	$7,720		

Column (**A**) is par value ($100,000) multiplied by the semiannual contract rate (6%).
Column (**B**) is prior period's carrying value multiplied by the semiannual market rate (5%).
Column (**C**) is the difference between interest paid and bond interest expense, or [(A) − (B)].
Column (**D**) is the prior period's unamortized premium less the current period's premium amortization.
Column (**E**) is par value plus unamortized premium, or [$100,000 + (D)].
* Adjusted for rounding.

C from the prior period's carrying value. Column D shows the premium's reduction by periodic amortization. When the issuer makes the first semiannual interest payment, the effect of premium amortization on bond interest expense and bond liability is recorded as follows:

2006			
June 30	Bond Interest Expense	5,386	
	Premium on Bonds Payable	614	
	Cash		6,000
	To record semiannual interest and premium amortization (effective interest method).		

Assets	=	Liabilities	+	Equity
−6,000		−614		−5,386

Similar entries with different amounts are recorded at each payment date until the bond matures at the end of 2010. The effective interest method yields decreasing amounts of bond interest expense and increasing amounts of premium amortization over the bonds' life.

APPENDIX 14C

Leases and Pensions

This appendix briefly explains the accounting and analysis for both leases and pensions.

Lease Liabilities

C5 Describe the accounting for leases and pensions.

A **lease** is a contractual agreement between a *lessor* (asset owner) and a *lessee* (asset renter or tenant) that grants the lessee the right to use the asset for a period of time in return for cash (rent) payments. Nearly one-fourth of all equipment purchases is financed with leases. The advantages of lease financing include the lack of an immediate large cash payment and the potential to deduct rental payments in computing taxable income. From an accounting perspective, leases can be classified as either operating or capital leases.

Operating Leases **Operating leases** are short-term (or cancelable) leases in which the lessor retains the risks and rewards of ownership. Examples include most car and apartment rental agreements. The lessee records such lease payments as expenses; the lessor records them as revenue. The lessee does not report the leased item as an asset or a liability (it is the lessor's asset). To illustrate, if an employee of Amazon leases a car for $300 at an airport while on company business, Amazon (lessee) records this cost as:

Point: Home Depot's recent annual report indicates that its rental expenses from operating leases total more than $500 million.

July 4	Rental Expense	300	
	Cash		300
	To record lease rental payment.		

Assets	=	Liabilities	+	Equity
−300				−300

Capital Leases **Capital leases** are long-term (or noncancelable) leases by which the lessor transfers substantially all risks and rewards of ownership to the lessee.[2] Examples include most leases of airplanes and department store buildings. The lessee records the leased item as its own

[2] A *capital lease* meets any one or more of four criteria: (1) transfers title of leased asset to lessee, (2) contains a bargain purchase option, (3) has a lease term that is 75% or more of the leased asset's useful life, or (4) has a present value of lease payments that is 90% or more of the leased asset's market value.

asset along with a lease liability at the start of the lease term; the amount recorded equals the present value of all lease payments. To illustrate, assume that K2 Co. enters into a six-year lease of a building in which it will sell sporting equipment. The lease transfers all building ownership risks and rewards to K2 (the present value of its $12,979 annual lease payments is $60,000). K2 records this transaction as follows:

Assets = Liabilities + Equity
+60,000 +60,000

2005			
Jan. 1	Leased Asset—Building	60,000	
	Lease Liability		60,000
	To record leased asset and lease liability.		

Point: Home Depot reports *"certain retail locations are leased under capital leases."* The net present value of its Lease Liability is about $270 million.

K2 reports the leased asset as a plant asset and the lease liability as a long-term liability. The portion of the lease liability expected to be paid in the next year is reported as a current liability.[3] At each year-end, K2 records depreciation on the leased asset (assume straight-line depreciation, six-year lease term, and no salvage value) as follows:

Assets = Liabilities + Equity
−10,000 −10,000

Dec. 31	Depreciation Expense—Building	10,000	
	Accumulated Depreciation—Building.		10,000
	To record depreciation on leased asset.		

K2 also accrues interest on the lease liability at each year-end. Interest expense is computed by multiplying the remaining lease liability by the interest rate on the lease. Specifically, K2 records its annual interest expense as part of its annual lease payment ($12,979) as follows (for its first year):

Assets = Liabilities + Equity
−12,979 −8,179 −4,800

2005			
Dec. 31	Interest Expense.	4,800	
	Lease Liability.	8,179	
	Cash.		12,979
	*To record first annual lease payment.**		

* These numbers are computed from a *lease payment schedule.* For simplicity, we use the same numbers from Exhibit 14.16 for this lease payment schedule—with different headings as follows:

		Payments			
	(A)	**(B)** *Debit*	**(C)** *Debit*	**(D)** *Credit*	**(E)**
Period Ending Date	**Beginning Balance of Lease Liability**	**Interest on Lease Liability 8% × (A)** +	**Lease Liability (D) − (B)** =	**Cash Lease Payment**	**Ending Balance of Lease Liability (A) − (C)**
12/31/2005	**$60,000**	**$ 4,800**	**$ 8,179**	**$12,979**	**$51,821**
12/31/2006	51,821	4,146	8,833	12,979	42,988
12/31/2007	42,988	3,439	9,540	12,979	33,448
12/31/2008	33,448	2,676	10,303	12,979	23,145
12/31/2009	23,145	1,852	11,127	12,979	12,018
12/31/2010	12,018	961	12,018	12,979	0
		$17,874	**$60,000**	**$77,874**	

[3] Most lessees try to keep leased assets and lease liabilities off their balance sheets by failing to meet any one of the four criteria of a capital lease. This is because a lease liability increases a company's total liabilities, making it more difficult to obtain additional financing. The acquisition of assets without reporting any related liabilities (or other asset outflows) on the balance sheet is called **off-balance-sheet financing.**

Pension Liabilities

A **pension plan** is a contractual agreement between an employer and its employees for the employer to provide benefits (payments) to employees after they retire. Most employers pay the full cost of the pension, but sometimes employees pay part of the cost. An employer records its payment into a pension plan with a debit to Pension Expense and a credit to Cash. A *plan administrator* receives payments from the employer, invests them in pension assets, and makes benefit payments to *pension recipients* (retired employees). Insurance and trust companies often serve as pension plan administrators.

Point: Fringe benefits are often 40% or more of salaries and wages, and pension benefits make up nearly 15% of fringe benefits.

Many pensions are known as *defined benefit plans* that define future benefits; the employer's contributions vary, depending on assumptions about future pension assets and liabilities. Several disclosures are necessary in this case. Specifically, a pension liability is reported when the accumulated benefit obligation is *more than* the plan assets, a so-called *underfunded plan*. The accumulated benefit obligation is the present value of promised future pension payments to retirees. *Plan assets* refer to the market value of assets the plan administrator holds. A pension asset is reported when the accumulated benefit obligation is *less than* the plan assets, a so-called *overfunded plan*. An employer reports pension expense when it receives the benefits from the employees' services, which is sometimes decades before it pays pension benefits to employees. (*Other Postretirement Benefits* refer to nonpension benefits such as health care and life insurance benefits. Similar to a pension, costs of these benefits are estimated and liabilities accrued when the employees earn them.)

Point: Two types of pension plans are (1) *defined benefit plan*—the retirement benefit is defined and the employer estimates the contribution necessary to pay these benefits and (2) *defined contribution plan*—the pension contribution is defined and the employer and/or employee contributes amounts specified in the pension agreement.

Summary

C1 Describe the types of bonds and the procedures for issuing them. Certain bonds are secured by the issuer's assets; other bonds, called *debentures,* are unsecured. Serial bonds mature at different points in time; term bonds mature at one time. Registered bonds have each bondholder's name recorded by the issuer; bearer bonds are payable to the holder. Convertible bonds are exchangeable for shares of the issuer's stock. Callable bonds can be retired by the issuer at a set price. Bonds are often issued by an underwriter and monitored by a trustee.

C2 Explain the types and payment patterns of notes. Notes repaid over a period of time are called *installment notes* and usually follow one of two payment patterns: (1) decreasing payments of interest plus equal amounts of principal or (2) equal total payments. Mortgage notes also are common.

C3[A] Explain and compute the present value of an amount to be paid at a future date. The basic concept of present value is that an amount of cash to be paid or received in the future is worth less than the same amount of cash to be paid or received today. Another important present value concept is that interest is compounded, meaning interest is added to the balance and used to determine interest for succeeding periods.

C4[A] Explain and compute the present value of a series of equal amounts to be paid at future dates. An annuity is a series of equal payments occurring at equal time intervals. An annuity's present value can be computed as the sum of individual present values for each payment. An alternative and preferred approach is to compute the present value of the series using the present value table for an annuity (or a calculator).

C5[C] Describe the accounting for leases and pensions. A lease is a rental agreement between the lessor and the lessee. When the lessor retains the risks and rewards of asset ownership (an *operating lease*), the lessee debits Rent Expense and credits Cash for its lease payments. When the lessor substantially transfers the risks and rewards of asset ownership to the lessee (a *capital lease*), the lessee capitalizes the leased asset and records a lease liability. Pension agreements can result in either pension assets or pension liabilities.

A1 Compare bond financing with stock financing. Bond financing is used to fund business activities. Advantages of bond financing versus stock include (1) no effect on owner control, (2) tax savings, and (3) increased earnings due to financial leverage. Disadvantages include (1) interest and principal payments and (2) amplification of poor performance.

A2 Explain collateral agreements and their effects on loan risk. Collateral agreements alter the risk of loss for creditors. Unsecured bonds and notes are riskier because the issuer's obligation to pay interest and principal has the same priority as all other unsecured liabilities in the event of bankruptcy. To borrow funds at a more favorable rate, many bonds and notes are secured by collateral agreements called *mortgages.*

A3 Compute the ratio of pledged assets to secured liabilities and explain its use. Both secured and unsecured creditors are concerned about the relation between the amount of assets the debtor owns and the amount of secured liabilities. Secured creditors are at less risk when the ratio of pledged assets to secured liabilities is larger, but the risks of unsecured creditors are often increased when this ratio is high because their claims to assets are secondary to secured creditors.

P1 Prepare entries to record bond issuance and bond interest expense. When bonds are issued at par, Cash is debited and Bonds Payable is credited for the bonds' par value. At bond interest payment dates (usually semiannual), Bond Interest Expense is debited and Cash credited; the latter for an amount equal to the bond par value multiplied by the bond contract rate.

P2 Compute and record amortization of bond discount. Bonds are issued at a discount when the contract rate is less than the market rate, making the issue (selling) price less than par. When this occurs, the issuer records a credit to Bonds Payable (at par) and debits both Discount on Bonds Payable and Cash. The amount of bond interest expense assigned to each period is computed using either the straight-line or effective interest method.

P3 Compute and record amortization of bond premium. Bonds are issued at a premium when the contract rate is higher than the market rate, making the issue (selling) price greater than par. When this occurs, the issuer records a debit to Cash and credits both Premium on Bonds Payable and Bonds Payable (at par). The amount of bond interest expense assigned to each period is computed using either the straight-line or effective interest method. The Premium on Bonds Payable is allocated to reduce bond interest expense over the life of the bonds.

P4 Record the retirement of bonds. Bonds are retired at maturity with a debit to Bonds Payable and a credit to Cash at par value. The issuer can retire the bonds early by exercising a call option or purchasing them in the market. Bondholders can also retire bonds early by exercising a conversion feature on convertible bonds. The issuer recognizes a gain or loss for the difference between the amount paid and the bond carrying value.

P5 Prepare entries to account for notes. Interest is allocated to each period in a note's life by multiplying its beginning-period carrying value by its market rate at issuance. If a note is repaid with equal payments, the payment amount is computed by dividing the borrowed amount by the present value of an annuity factor (taken from a present value table) using the market rate and the number of payments.

Guidance Answers to **Decision Maker** and **Decision Ethics**

Bond Rater Bonds with longer repayment periods (life) have higher risk. Also, bonds issued by companies in financial difficulties or facing higher than normal uncertainties have higher risk. Moreover, companies with higher than normal debt and large fluctuations in earnings are considered of higher risk. Discount bonds are more risky on one or more of these factors.

Entrepreneur This is a "present value" question. The market interest rate (10%) and present value ($3,000) are known, but the payment required two years later is unknown. This amount ($3,630) can be computed as $3,000 × 1.10 × 1.10. Thus, the sale price is $3,630 when no payments are received for two years. Note that the $3,630 received two years from today is equivalent to $3,000 cash today.

Bond Investor The ratio of pledged assets to secured liabilities for the first company is 2.2 ($1,265,000/$575,000) and for the second company is 2.5 ($2,000,000/$800,000), suggesting that secured creditors of the second company are at less risk than those of the first company. But *debenture bonds are unsecured.* Therefore, since the first company has fewer secured liabilities, it is of lower risk for unsecured debenture bonds. The first company also has fewer liabilities and, since the companies are of equal size, the first company's liabilities make up a smaller portion of total assets. Consequently, as a buyer of unsecured debenture bonds, you prefer the first company.

Guidance Answers to **Quick Checks**

1. (*b*)
2. Multiply the bond's par value by its contract rate of interest.
3. Bonds sell at a premium when the contract rate exceeds the market rate and the purchasers pay more than their par value.
4. The bonds are issued at a discount, meaning that issue price is less than par value. A discount occurs because the bond contract rate (6%) is less than the market rate (8%).
5.

Cash	91,893	
Discount on Bonds Payable	8,107	
Bonds Payable		100,000

6. $3,811 (Total bond interest expense of $38,107 divided by 10 periods; or the $3,000 semiannual cash payment plus the $8,107 discount divided by 10 periods.)
7. The bonds are issued at a premium, meaning issue price is higher than par value. A premium occurs because the bonds' contract rate (16%) is higher than the market rate (14%).
8. (*c*) For each semiannual period: $10,592/20 periods = $530 premium amortization.
9.

Bonds payable, 16%, due 12/31/2014	$100,000	
Plus premium on bonds payable	9,532*	$109,532

* Original premium balance of $10,592 less $530 and $530 amortized on 6/30/2005 and 12/31/2005, respectively.

10. (*a*) Reflects payment of accrued interest recorded back on May 1; $500,000 × 9% × 4/12 = $15,000.
11. $9,375 loss. Computed as the difference between the repurchase price of $256,250 [50% of ($500,000 × 102.5%)] and the carrying value of $246,875 (50% of $493,750).
12. (*c*)
13. The interest portion of an installment payment equals the period's beginning loan balance multiplied by the market interest rate at the time of the note's issuance.
14. On the balance sheet, the account balances of the related liability (note payable) and asset (cash) accounts are decreased. On the income statement, interest expense is recorded.
15. (*c*) Computed as 3.3121 × $1,000 = $3,312.
16. The option of paying $10,000 after one year has a lower present value. It postpones paying the first $5,000 by six months. More generally, the present value of a further delayed payment is always lower than a less delayed payment.

Key Terms

Key Terms are available at the book's Website for learning and testing in an online Flashcard Format.

Annuity (p. 570)
Bearer bonds (p. 550)
Bond (p. 548)
Bond certificate (p. 551)
Bond indenture (p. 551)
Callable bonds (p. 550)
Capital leases (p. 573)
Carrying value of bonds (p. 553)
Contract rate (p. 552)
Convertible bonds (p. 550)
Coupon bonds (p. 550)
Discount on bonds payable (p. 552)
Effective interest method (p. 571)
Installment note (p. 561)
Lease (p. 573)
Market rate (p. 552)
Mortgage (p. 564)
Off-balance-sheet financing (p. 574)
Operating leases (p. 573)
Par value of a bond (p. 548)
Pension plan (p. 575)
Pledged assets to secured liabilities (p. 565)
Premium on bonds (p. 555)
Registered bonds (p. 550)
Secured bonds (p. 549)
Serial bonds (p. 550)
Sinking fund bonds (p. 550)
Straight-line method (p. 553)
Term bonds (p. 550)
Unsecured bonds (p. 549)

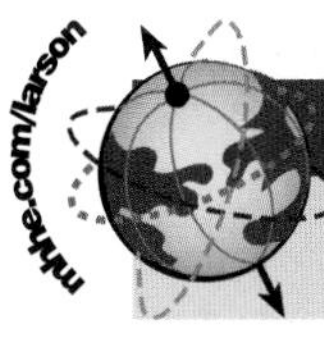

Personal Interactive Quiz

Personal Interactive Quizzes A and B are available at the book's Website to reinforce and assess your learning.

Superscript letter B (C) denotes assignments based on Appendix 14B (14C).

Discussion Questions

1. What is the main difference between a bond and a share of stock?
2. What is the main difference between notes payable and bonds payable?
3. What are the duties of a trustee for bondholders?
4. What is the advantage of issuing bonds instead of obtaining financing from the company's owners?
5. What is a bond indenture? What provisions are usually included in it?
6. What are the *contract* rate and the *market* rate for bonds?
7. What factors affect the market rates for bonds?
8. [B] Does the straight-line or effective interest method produce an interest expense allocation that yields a constant rate of interest over a bond's life? Explain.
9. Why does a company that issues bonds between interest dates collect accrued interest from the bonds' purchasers?
10. If you know the par value of bonds, the contract rate, and the market rate, how do you compute the bonds' price?
11. What is the issue price of a $2,000 bond sold at 98¼? What is the issue price of a $6,000 bond sold at 101½?
12. Describe two common payment patterns for installment notes.
13. Explain why unsecured creditors are concerned when the pledged assets to secured liabilities ratio for a borrower increases.
14. What obligation does an entrepreneur (owner) have to investors that purchase bonds to finance the business?
15. Refer to **Krispy Kreme**'s annual report in Appendix A. Is there any indication that Krispy Kreme has issued bonds?
16. Refer to the statement of cash flows for **Tastykake** in Appendix A. For the year ended December 28, 2002, what is its "Net borrowings (payments) of long-term debt"?

17. Refer to the annual report for **Harley-Davidson** in Appendix A. For the year ended December 31, 2002, did it raise more cash by issuing stock or debt?

Harley-Davidson

18. [C] When can a lease create both an asset and a liability for the lessee?
19. [C] Compare and contrast an operating lease with a capital lease.
20. [C] Describe the two basic types of pension plans.

Red numbers denote Discussion Questions that involve decision-making.

***Homework Manager** repeats all numerical Quick Studies on the book's Website with new numbers.*

QUICK STUDY

QS 14-1
Bond terminology
C1

Enter the letter of the description *A* through *H* that best fits each term 1 through 8.

A. Records and tracks the bondholders' names.
B. Is unsecured; backed only by the issuer's credit standing.
C. Has varying maturity dates for amounts owed.
D. Identifies rights and responsibilities of the issuer and the bondholders.
E. Can be exchanged for shares of the issuer's stock.
F. Is unregistered; interest is paid to whoever possesses them.
G. Maintains a separate asset account from which bondholders are paid at maturity.
H. Pledges specific assets of the issuer as collateral.

1. _______ Debenture
2. _______ Bond indenture
3. _______ Bearer bond
4. _______ Registered bond
5. _______ Sinking fund bond
6. _______ Convertible bond
7. _______ Secured bond
8. _______ Serial bond

QS 14-2
Bond computations—straight-line
P1 P2

Alberto Company issues 8%, 10-year bonds with a par value of $350,000 and semiannual interest payments. On the issue date, the annual market rate for these bonds is 10%, which implies a selling price of 87½. The straight-line method is used to allocate interest expense.

1. What are the issuer's cash proceeds from issuance of these bonds?
2. What total amount of bond interest expense will be recognized over the life of these bonds?
3. What is the amount of bond interest expense recorded on the first interest payment date?

QS 14-3[B]
Bond computations—effective interest
P1 P3

Sanchez issues 10%, 15-year bonds with a par value of $120,000 and semiannual interest payments. On the issue date, the annual market rate for these bonds is 8%, which implies a selling price of 117¼. The effective interest method is used to allocate interest expense.

1. What are the issuer's cash proceeds from issuance of these bonds?
2. What total amount of bond interest expense will be recognized over the life of these bonds?
3. What amount of bond interest expense is recorded on the first interest payment date?

QS 14-4
Journalize bond issuance P1

Prepare the journal entry for the issuance of the bonds in both QS 14-2 and QS 14-3. Assume that both bonds are issued for cash on January 1, 2005.

QS 14-5
Computing bond price
P2 P3

Using the bond details in both QS 14-2 and QS 14-3, confirm that the bonds' selling prices given in each problem are approximately correct. Use the present value tables B.1 and B.3 in Appendix B.

QS 14-6
Issuing bonds between interest dates
P1

Gooden Company plans to issue 8% bonds on January 1, 2005, with a par value of $2,000,000. The company sells $1,800,000 of the bonds on January 1, 2005. The remaining $200,000 sells at par on March 1, 2005. The bonds pay interest semiannually as of June 30 and December 31. Record the entry for the March 1 cash sale of bonds.

QS 14-7
Bond retirement by call option
P4

On July 1, 2005, Taurasi Company exercises a $5,000 call option (plus par value) on its outstanding bonds that have a carrying value of $208,000 and par value of $200,000. The company exercises the call option after the semiannual interest is paid on June 30, 2005. Record the entry to retire the bonds.

QS 14-8
Bond retirement by stock conversion P4

On January 1, 2005, the $1,000,000 par value bonds of Gruden Company with a carrying value of $1,000,000 are converted to 500,000 shares of $0.50 par value common stock. Record the entry for the conversion of the bonds.

QS 14-9
Computing payments for an installment note C2

Valdez Company borrows $170,000 cash from a bank and in return signs an installment note for five annual payments of equal amount, with the first payment due one year after the note is signed. Use Table B.3 in Appendix B to compute the amount of the annual payment for each of the following annual market rates: (*a*) 4%, (*b*) 8%, and (*c*) 12%.

QS 14-10
Interpretation of collateral agreement
A2 

Note 2 of **Collins Industries**' annual report states: "The credit facility [line] is collateralized by receivables, inventories, equipment and certain real property. Under the terms of the Agreement, the Company is required to maintain certain financial ratios and other financial conditions. The Agreement also prohibits the Company from incurring certain additional indebtedness, limits certain investments, advances or loans and restricts substantial asset sales, capital expenditures and cash dividends." What restrictions has the bank that granted the credit placed on Collins Industries?

QS 14-11
Ratio of pledged assets to secured liabilities
A3 

Compute the ratio of pledged assets to secured liabilities for the following two companies. Which company appears to have the riskier secured liabilities?

	Xiang Co.	Xu Co.
Pledged assets	$387,000	$172,000
Total assets	550,000	490,000
Secured liabilities	163,000	158,000
Unsecured liabilities . . .	266,000	390,000

QS 14-12[C]
Recording operating leases C5

Lauren Wright, an employee of ETrain.com, leases a car at O'Hare airport for a three-day business trip. The rental cost is $350. Prepare the entry by ETrain.com to record Lauren's short-term car lease cost.

QS 14-13[C]
Recording capital leases
C5

Juicyfruit, Inc., signs a five-year lease for office equipment with Office Solutions. The present value of the lease payments is $20,859. Prepare the journal entry that Juicyfruit records at the inception of this capital lease.

 ***Homework Manager*** *repeats all numerical Exercises on the book's Website with new numbers.*

EXERCISES

Round dollar amounts to the nearest whole dollar. Assume no reversing entries are used.

Exercise 14-1
Recording bond issuance and interest
P1

On January 1, 2005, Kidman Enterprises issues bonds that have a $1,700,000 par value, mature in 20 years, and pay 9% interest semiannually on June 30 and December 31. The bonds are sold at par.

1. How much interest will Kidman pay (in cash) to the bondholders every six months?
2. Prepare journal entries to record (*a*) the issuance of bonds on January 1, 2005; (*b*) the first interest payment on June 30, 2005; and (*c*) the second interest payment on December 31, 2005.
3. Prepare the journal entry for issuance assuming the bonds are issued at (*a*) 98 and (*b*) 102.

Exercise 14-2
Straight-line amortization of bond discount
P2

ACT issues bonds with a par value of $90,000 on January 1, 2005. The annual contract rate on them is 8%, and interest is paid semiannually on June 30 and December 31. The bonds mature in three years. The annual market rate at the date of issuance is 10%, and the bonds are sold for $85,431.

1. What is the amount of the discount on these bonds at issuance?
2. How much total bond interest expense will be recognized over the life of these bonds?
3. Prepare an amortization table like the one in Exhibit 14.7 for these bonds; use the straight-line method to amortize the discount.

Exercise 14-3[B]
Effective interest amortization of bond discount
P2

Welch Company issues bonds dated January 1, 2005, with a par value of $250,000. The annual contract rate on them is 9%, and interest is paid semiannually on June 30 and December 31. The bonds mature in three years. The annual market rate at the date of issuance is 12%, and the bonds are sold for $231,570.

1. What is the amount of the discount on these bonds at issuance?
2. How much total bond interest expense will be recognized over the life of these bonds?
3. Prepare an amortization table like the one in Exhibit 14B.1 for these bonds; use the effective interest method to amortize the discount.

Exercise 14-4
Straight-line amortization of bond premium
P3

Prairie Dunes Company issues bonds dated January 1, 2004, with a par value of $800,000. The annual contract rate is 13%, and interest is paid semiannually on June 30 and December 31. The bonds mature in three years. The annual market rate at the date of issuance is 12%, and the bonds are sold for $819,700.

1. What is the amount of the premium on these bonds at issuance?
2. How much total bond interest expense will be recognized over the life of these bonds?
3. Prepare an amortization table like the one in Exhibit 14.11 for these bonds; use the straight-line method to amortize the premium.

Exercise 14-5B
Effective interest amortization of bond premium P3

Refer to the bond details in Exercise 14-4 and prepare an amortization table like the one in Exhibit 14B.2 for these bonds using the effective interest method to amortize the premium.

Exercise 14-6
Computing bond interest and price, and recording bond issuance
P2 

Check (4) $518,465

Jester Company issues bonds with a par value of $600,000 on their stated issue date. The bonds mature in 10 years and pay 6% annual interest in semiannual payments. On the issue date, the annual market rate for the bonds is 8%.

1. What is the amount of each semiannual interest payment for these bonds?
2. How many semiannual interest payments will be made on these bonds over their life?
3. Use the interest rates given to determine whether the bonds are issued at par, at a discount, or at a premium.
4. Compute the price of the bonds as of their issue date.
5. Prepare the journal entry to record the bonds' issuance.

Exercise 14-7
Computing bond interest and price, and recording bond issuance
P3 

Check (4) $81,086

Metro, Inc., issues bonds with a par value of $75,000 on their stated issue date. The bonds mature in five years and pay 10% annual interest in semiannual payments. On the issue date, the annual market rate for the bonds is 8%.

1. What is the amount of each semiannual interest payment for these bonds?
2. How many semiannual interest payments will be made on these bonds over their life?
3. Use the interest rates given to determine whether the bonds are issued at par, at a discount, or at a premium.
4. Compute the price of the bonds as of their issue date.
5. Prepare the journal entry to record the bonds' issuance.

Exercise 14-8
Bond computations, straight-line amortization, and bond retirement
P2 P4

Check (6) $4,095 loss

On January 1, 2004, Steadman issues $350,000 of 10%, 15-year bonds at a price of 97¾. Six years later, on January 1, 2010, Steadman retires 20% of these bonds by buying them on the open market at 104½. All interest is accounted for and paid through December 31, 2009, the day before the purchase. The straight-line method is used to amortize any bond discount.

1. How much does the company receive when it issues the bonds on January 1, 2004?
2. What is the amount of the discount on the bonds at January 1, 2004?
3. How much amortization of the discount is recorded on the bonds for the entire period from January 1, 2004, through December 31, 2009?
4. What is the carrying (book) value of the bonds as of the close of business on December 31, 2009? What is the carrying value of the 20% soon-to-be-retired bonds on this same date?
5. How much did the company pay on January 1, 2010, to purchase the bonds that it retired?
6. What is the amount of the recorded gain or loss from retiring the bonds?
7. Prepare the journal entry to record the bond retirement at January 1, 2010.

Exercise 14-9
Recording bond issuance with accrued interest
P1

Check (1) $51,000

On May 1, 2005, Kidman Enterprises issues bonds dated January 1, 2005, that have a $1,700,000 par value, mature in 20 years, and pay 9% interest semiannually on June 30 and December 31. The bonds are sold at par plus four months' accrued interest.

1. How much accrued interest do the bond purchasers pay Kidman on May 1, 2005?
2. Prepare journal entries to record (*a*) the issuance of bonds on May 1, 2005; (*b*) the first interest payment on June 30, 2005; and (*c*) the second interest payment on December 31, 2005.

Exercise 14-10
Straight-line amortization and accrued bond interest expense
P1 P2

Simon issues four-year bonds with a $50,000 par value on June 1, 2004, at a price of $47,974. The annual contract rate is 7%, and interest is paid semiannually on November 30 and May 31.

1. Prepare an amortization table like the one in Exhibit 14.7 for these bonds. Use the straight-line method of interest amortization.
2. Prepare journal entries to record the first two interest payments and to accrue interest as of December 31, 2004.

Exercise 14-11
Installment note with equal principal payments C2 P5

Check (1) $6,250

On January 1, 2005, Perez borrows $25,000 cash by signing a four-year, 7% installment note that requires annual payments of accrued interest and equal amounts of principal on December 31 of each year from 2005 through 2008.

1. How much principal is included in each of the four annual payments?
2. Prepare an amortization table for this installment note like the one in Exhibit 14.15.

Exercise 14-12
Installment note entries P5

Use the information in Exercise 14-11 to prepare the journal entries for Perez to record the loan on January 1, 2005, and the four payments from December 31, 2005, through December 31, 2008.

Exercise 14-13
Installment note with equal total payments C2 P5
Check (1) $7,381

On January 1, 2005, Randa borrows $25,000 cash by signing a four-year, 7% installment note. The note requires four equal total payments of accrued interest and principal on December 31 of each year from 2005 through 2008.

1. Compute the amount of each of the four equal total payments.
2. Prepare an amortization table for this installment note like the one in Exhibit 14.16.

Exercise 14-14
Installment note entries P5

Use the information in Exercise 14-13 to prepare the journal entries for Randa to record the loan on January 1, 2005, and the four payments from December 31, 2005, through December 31, 2008.

Exercise 14-15
Pledged assets to secured liabilities
A3

An unsecured creditor of Telnet Co. is monitoring Telnet's financing activities. Two years ago, Telnet's ratio of pledged assets to secured liabilities was 1.7. One year ago, the ratio climbed to 2.3, and the most recent financial report shows the ratio is now 3.1. Describe what this trend likely indicates about the company's activities, specifically from the point of view of this unsecured creditor.

Exercise 14-16^C
Identifying capital and operating leases
C5

Indicate whether the company in each separate case 1 through 3 has entered into an operating lease or a capital lease.

1. The lessor retains title to the asset, and the lease term is three years on an asset that has a five-year useful life.
2. The title is transferred to the lessee, the lessee can purchase the asset for $1 at the end of the lease, and the lease term is five years. The leased asset has an expected useful life of six years.
3. The present value of the lease payments is 95% of the leased asset's market value, and the lease term is 70% of the leased asset's useful life.

Exercise 14-17^C
Accounting for capital lease
C5

Flyer (lessee) signs a five-year capital lease for office equipment with a $20,000 annual lease payment. The present value of the five annual lease payments is $82,000, based on a 7% interest rate.

1. Prepare the journal entry Flyer will record at inception of the lease.
2. If the leased asset has a 5-year useful life with no salvage value, prepare the journal entry Flyer will record each year to recognize depreciation expense related to the leased asset.

Exercise 14-18^C
Analyzing lease options
C3 C4 C5

General Motors advertised three alternatives for a 25-month lease on a new Blazer: (1) zero dollars down and a lease payment of $1,750 per month for 25 months, (2) $5,000 down and $1,500 per month for 25 months, or (3) $38,500 down and no payments for 25 months. Use the present value Table B.3 in Appendix B to determine which is the best alternative (assume you have enough cash to accept any alternative and the annual interest rate is 12% compounded monthly).

PROBLEM SET A

Round dollar amounts to the nearest whole dollar. Assume no reversing entries are used.

Problem 14-1A

Computing bond price and recording issuance

P1 P2 P3

Check (1) Premium, $2,718

(3) Discount, $2,294

Stowers Research issues bonds dated January 1, 2005, that pay interest semiannually on June 30 and December 31. The bonds have a $20,000 par value, an annual contract rate of 10%, and mature in 10 years.

Required

For each of the following three separate situations, (*a*) determine the bonds' issue price on January 1, 2005, and (*b*) prepare the journal entry to record their issuance.

1. Market rate at the date of issuance is 8%.
2. Market rate at the date of issuance is 10%.
3. Market rate at the date of issuance is 12%.

Problem 14-2A

Straight-line amortization of both bond discount and bond premium

P1 P2 P3

mhhe.com/larson

Check (3) $2,071,776

(4) 12/31/2005 carrying value, $1,764,460

Heathrow issues $2,000,000 of 6%, 15-year bonds dated January 1, 2004, that pay interest semiannually on June 30 and December 31. The bonds are issued at a price of $1,728,224.

Required

1. Prepare the January 1, 2004, journal entry to record the bonds' issuance.
2. For each semiannual period, compute (*a*) the cash payment, (*b*) the straight-line discount amortization, and (*c*) the bond interest expense.
3. Determine the total bond interest expense to be recognized over the bonds' life.
4. Prepare the first two years of an amortization table like Exhibit 14.7 using the straight-line method.
5. Prepare the journal entries to record the first two interest payments.
6. Assume that the bonds are issued at a price of $2,447,990. Repeat parts 1 through 5.

Problem 14-3A

Straight-line amortization of bond premium; computing bond price

P1 P3

mhhe.com/larson

Check (2) 6/30/2006 carrying value, $505,331

Saturn issues 6.5%, five-year bonds dated January 1, 2004, with a $500,000 par value. The bonds pay interest on June 30 and December 31 and are issued at a price of $510,666. The annual market rate is 6% on the issue date.

Required

1. Calculate the total bond interest expense over the bonds' life.
2. Prepare a straight-line amortization table like Exhibit 14.11 for the bonds' life.
3. Prepare the journal entries to record the first two interest payments.

Problem 14-4A[B]

Effective interest amortization of bond premium; computing bond price P1 P3

Check (2) 6/30/2006 carrying value, $505,728

(4) $504,653

Refer to the bond details in Problem 14-3A.

Required

1. Compute the total bond interest expense over the bonds' life.
2. Prepare an effective interest amortization table like the one in Exhibit 14B.2 for the bonds' life.
3. Prepare the journal entries to record the first two interest payments.
4. Use the market rate at issuance to compute the present value of the remaining cash flows for these bonds as of December 31, 2006. Compare your answer with the amount shown on the amortization table as the balance for that date (from part 2) and explain your findings.

Problem 14-5A

Straight-line amortization of bond discount

P1 P2

Check (2) $195,639

(3) 12/31/2005 carrying value, $617,181

Patton issues $650,000 of 5%, four-year bonds dated January 1, 2004, that pay interest semiannually on June 30 and December 31. They are issued at $584,361 and their market rate is 8% at the issue date.

Required

1. Prepare the January 1, 2004, journal entry to record the bonds' issuance.
2. Determine the total bond interest expense to be recognized over the bonds' life.
3. Prepare a straight-line amortization table like the one in Exhibit 14.7 for the bonds' first two years.
4. Prepare the journal entries to record the first two interest payments.

Analysis Component

5. Assume the market rate on January 1, 2004, is 4% instead of 8%. Without providing numbers, describe how this change affects the amounts reported on Patton's financial statements.

Problem 14-6A[B]
Effective interest amortization of bond discount P1 P2

Check (2) $195,639
(3) 12/31/2005 carrying value, $614,614

eXcel
mhhe.com/larson

Refer to the bond details in Problem 14-5A.

Required

1. Prepare the January 1, 2004, journal entry to record the bonds' issuance.
2. Determine the total bond interest expense to be recognized over the bonds' life.
3. Prepare an effective interest amortization table like the one in Exhibit 14B.1 for the bonds' first two years.
4. Prepare the journal entries to record the first two interest payments.

Problem 14-7A[B]
Effective interest amortization of bond premium; retiring bonds

P1 P3 P4  
mhhe.com/larson

Check (3) 6/30/2005 carrying value, $91,224
(5) $2,635 gain

McFad issues $90,000 of 11%, three-year bonds dated January 1, 2004, that pay interest semiannually on June 30 and December 31. They are issued at $92,283. Their market rate is 10% at the issue date.

Required

1. Prepare the January 1, 2004, journal entry to record the bonds' issuance.
2. Determine the total bond interest expense to be recognized over the bonds' life.
3. Prepare an effective interest amortization table like Exhibit 14B.2 for the bonds' first two years.
4. Prepare the journal entries to record the first two interest payments.
5. Prepare the journal entry to record the bonds' retirement on January 1, 2006, at 98.

Analysis Component

6. Assume that the market rate on January 1, 2004, is 12% instead of 10%. Without presenting numbers, describe how this change affects amounts reported on McFad's financial statements.

Problem 14-8A
Installment notes

C2 P5 

Check (2) 10/31/2008 ending balance, $92,759
(4) 10/31/2007 ending balance, $160,000

On November 1, 2004, Leetch Ltd. borrows $400,000 cash from a bank by signing a five-year installment note bearing 8% interest. The note requires equal total payments each year on October 31.

Required

1. Compute the total amount of each installment payment.
2. Complete an amortization table for this installment note similar to the one in Exhibit 14.16.
3. Prepare the journal entries in which Leetch records (*a*) accrued interest as of December 31, 2004 (the end of its annual reporting period), and (*b*) the first annual payment on the note.
4. Assume that the note does not require equal total payments but five payments of accrued interest and equal amounts of principal. Complete an amortization table for this note similar to the one in Exhibit 14.15. Prepare the journal entries to record (*a*) accrued interest as of December 31, 2004 (the end of its annual reporting period), and (*b*) the note's first annual payment.

Problem 14-9A
Ratio of pledged assets to secured liabilities

A2 A3 

On January 1, 2005, Wildcat Company issues at par its 11%, four-year bonds with a $135,000 par value. They are secured by a mortgage that specifies assets totaling $225,000 as collateral. Also on January 1, 2005, Athens Company issues at par its 11%, four-year bonds with a par value of $60,000. Athens secures its bonds with a mortgage that includes $150,000 of pledged assets. The December 31, 2004, balance sheet information for both companies follows:

	Wildcat Co.	Athens Co.
Total assets	$900,000*	$450,000†
Liabilities		
Secured	$210,000	$ 75,000
Unsecured	150,000	165,000
Equity	540,000	210,000
Total liabilities and equity	$900,000	$450,000

* 43% are pledged. †54% are pledged.

Required

Check Wildcat, 1.77 to 1

1. Compute the ratio of pledged assets to secured liabilities for each company at January 1, 2005.

Analysis Component

2. Which company's bonds appear less risky? What other information might help to evaluate the risks of these companies' bonds?

Problem 14-10A[C]
Capital lease accounting

C5

Montana Company signs a five-year capital lease with Elway Company for office equipment. The annual lease payment is $20,000, and the interest rate is 8%.

Required

Check (1) $79,854

(3) Year 3 ending balance, $35,664

1. Compute the present value of Montana's five-year lease payments.

2. Prepare the journal entry to record Montana's capital lease at its inception.

3. Complete a lease payment schedule for the five years of the lease with the following headings. Assume that the beginning balance of the lease liability (present value of lease payments) is $79,854. (*Hint:* To find the amount allocated to interest in year 1, multiply the interest rate by the beginning-of-year lease liability. The amount of the annual lease payment not allocated to interest is allocated to principal. Reduce the lease liability by the amount allocated to principal to update the lease liability at each year-end.)

Period Ending Date	Beginning Balance of Lease Liability	Interest on Lease Liability	Reduction of Lease Liability	Cash Lease Payment	Ending Balance of Lease Liability

4. Use straight-line depreciation and prepare the journal entry to depreciate the leased asset at the end of year 1. Assume zero salvage value and a five-year life for the office equipment.

PROBLEM SET B

Problem 14-1B
Computing bond price and recording issuance

P1 P2 P3

Sedona Systems issues bonds dated January 1, 2005, that pay interest semiannually on June 30 and December 31. The bonds have a $45,000 par value, an annual contract rate of 12%, and mature in five years.

Required

For each of the following three separate situations, (*a*) determine the bonds' issue price on January 1, 2005, and (*b*) prepare the journal entry to record their issuance.

Check (1) Premium, $3,475

(3) Discount, $3,162

1. Market rate at the date of issuance is 10%.

2. Market rate at the date of issuance is 12%.

3. Market rate at the date of issuance is 14%.

Problem 14-2B
Straight-line amortization of both bond discount and bond premium

P1 P2 P3

ParFour issues $1,700,000 of 10%, 10-year bonds dated January 1, 2004, that pay interest semiannually on June 30 and December 31. The bonds are issued at a price of $1,505,001.

Required

Check (3) $1,894,999

(4) 6/30/2005 carrying value, $1,534,251

1. Prepare the January 1, 2004, journal entry to record the bonds' issuance.

2. For each semiannual period, compute (*a*) the cash payment, (*b*) the straight-line discount amortization, and (*c*) the bond interest expense.

3. Determine the total bond interest expense to be recognized over the bonds' life.

4. Prepare the first two years of an amortization table like Exhibit 14.7 using the straight-line method.

5. Prepare the journal entries to record the first two interest payments.

6. Assume that the bonds are issued at a price of $2,096,466. Repeat parts 1 through 5.

Problem 14-3B
Straight-line amortization of bond premium; computing bond price

P1 P3

Zooba Company issues 9%, five-year bonds dated January 1, 2004, with a $160,000 par value. The bonds pay interest on June 30 and December 31 and are issued at a price of $166,494. Their annual market rate is 8% on the issue date.

Required

1. Calculate the total bond interest expense over the bonds' life.
2. Prepare a straight-line amortization table like Exhibit 14.11 for the bonds' life.
3. Prepare the journal entries to record the first two interest payments.

Check (2) 6/30/2006 carrying value, $163,249

Problem 14-4B[B]
Effective interest amortization of bond premium; computing bond price P1 P3

Refer to the bond details in Problem 14-3B.

Required

1. Compute the total bond interest expense over the bonds' life.
2. Prepare an effective interest amortization table like the one in Exhibit 14B.2 for the bonds' life.
3. Prepare the journal entries to record the first two interest payments.
4. Use the market rate at issuance to compute the present value of the remaining cash flows for these bonds as of December 31, 2006. Compare your answer with the amount shown on the amortization table as the balance for that date (from part 2) and explain your findings.

Check (2) 6/30/2006 carrying value, $163,568

(4) $162,903

Problem 14-5B
Straight-line amortization of bond discount

P1 P2

Roney issues $120,000 of 6%, 15-year bonds dated January 1, 2004, that pay interest semiannually on June 30 and December 31. They are issued at $99,247, and their market rate is 8% at the issue date.

Required

1. Prepare the January 1, 2004, journal entry to record the bonds' issuance.
2. Determine the total bond interest expense to be recognized over the life of the bonds.
3. Prepare a straight-line amortization table like the one in Exhibit 14.7 for the bonds' first two years.
4. Prepare the journal entries to record the first two interest payments.

Check (2) $128,753

(3) 6/30/2005 carrying value, $101,323

Problem 14-6B[B]
Effective interest amortization of bond discount

P1 P2

Refer to the bond details in Problem 14-5B.

Required

1. Prepare the January 1, 2004, journal entry to record the bonds' issuance.
2. Determine the total bond interest expense to be recognized over the bonds' life.
3. Prepare an effective interest amortization table like the one in Exhibit 14B.1 for the bonds' first two years.
4. Prepare the journal entries to record the first two interest payments.

Check (2) $128,753;
(3) 6/30/2005 carrying value, $100,402

Problem 14-7B[B]
Effective interest amortization of bond premium; retiring bonds

P1 P3 P4

Hutton issues $900,000 of 13%, four-year bonds dated January 1, 2004, that pay interest semiannually on June 30 and December 31. They are issued at $987,217, and their market rate is 10% at the issue date.

Required

1. Prepare the January 1, 2004, journal entry to record the bonds' issuance.
2. Determine the total bond interest expense to be recognized over the bonds' life.
3. Prepare an effective interest amortization table like the one in Exhibit 14B.2 for the bonds' first two years.
4. Prepare the journal entries to record the first two interest payments.
5. Prepare the journal entry to record the bonds' retirement on January 1, 2006, at 106.

Check (3) 6/30/2005 carrying value, $958,406

(5) $6,174 loss

Analysis Component

6. Assume that the market rate on January 1, 2004, is 14% instead of 10%. Without presenting numbers, describe how this change affects amounts reported on Hutton's financial statements.

Problem 14-8B
Installment notes
C2 P5

On October 1, 2004, Milan Enterprises borrows $300,000 cash from a bank by signing a three-year installment note bearing 10% interest. The note requires equal total payments each year on September 30.

Required

1. Compute the total amount of each installment payment.
2. Complete an amortization table for this installment note similar to the one in Exhibit 14.16.
3. Prepare the journal entries in which Milan records (*a*) accrued interest as of December 31, 2004 (the end of its annual reporting period) and (*b*) the first annual payment on the note.
4. Assume that the note does not require equal total payments but three payments of accrued interest and equal amounts of principal. Complete an amortization table for this note similar to the one in Exhibit 14.15. Prepare the journal entries to record (*a*) accrued interest as of December 31, 2004 (the end of its annual reporting period) and (*b*) the note's first annual payment.

Check (2) 9/30/2006 ending balance, $109,673

(4) 9/30/2006 ending balance, $100,000

Problem 14-9B
Ratio of pledged assets to secured liabilities
A2 A3

On January 1, 2005, Hunt Company issues $45,000 of its 12%, 10-year bonds at par that are secured by a mortgage that specifies assets totaling $120,000 as collateral. Also on January 1, 2005, Hound Company issues its 12%, 10-year bonds at their par value of $150,000. Hound secures its bonds by a mortgage that includes $225,000 of pledged assets. The December 31, 2004, balance sheet information for both companies follows:

	Hunt Co.	Hound Co.
Total assets	$180,000*	$750,000†
Liabilities		
Secured	$ 39,000	$ 57,000
Unsecured	42,000	505,500
Equity	99,000	187,500
Total liabilities and equity	$180,000	$750,000

* 32% are pledged. † 10% are pledged.

Required

1. Compute the ratio of pledged assets to secured liabilities for each company at January 1, 2005.

Check Hunt, 2.11 to 1

Analysis Component

2. Which company's bonds appear less risky? What other information might help to evaluate the risks of these companies' bonds?

Problem 14-10B[C]
Capital lease accounting
C5

Preston Company signs a five-year capital lease with Starbuck Company for office equipment. The annual lease payment is $10,000, and the interest rate is 10%.

Required

1. Compute the present value of Preston's lease payments.
2. Prepare the journal entry to record Preston's capital lease at its inception.
3. Complete a lease payment schedule for the five years of the lease with the following headings. Assume that the beginning balance of the lease liability (present value of lease payments) is $37,908. (*Hint:* To find the amount allocated to interest in year 1, multiply the interest rate by the beginning-of-year lease liability. The amount of the annual lease payment not allocated to interest is allocated to principal. Reduce the lease liability by the amount allocated to principal to update the lease liability at each year-end.)

Check (1) $37,908

(3) Year 3 ending balance, $17,356

Period Ending Date	Beginning Balance of Lease Liability	Interest on Lease Liability	Reduction of Lease Liability	Cash Lease Payment	Ending Balance of Lease Liability

4. Use straight-line depreciation and prepare the journal entry to depreciate the leased asset at the end of year 1. Assume zero salvage value and a five-year life for the office equipment.

Problem Set C is available at the book's Website to further reinforce and assess your learning.

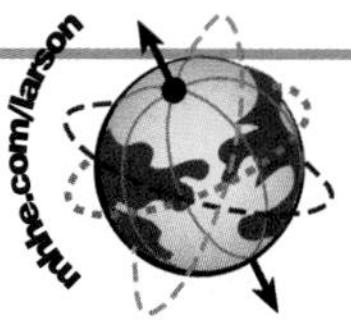

PROBLEM SET C

SERIAL PROBLEM

Success Systems

(This serial problem began in Chapter 1 and continues through most of the book. If previous chapter segments were not completed, the serial problem can begin at this point. It is helpful, but not necessary, for you to use the Working Papers that accompany the book.)

Kay Breeze has consulted with her local banker and is considering financing an expansion of her business by obtaining a long-term bank loan. Selected account balances at March 31, 2005, for Success Systems, Inc., follow:

Accounts receivable	$22,720	Total assets	$129,909
Merchandise inventory	704	Total liabilities	875
Plant assets, net	24,700	Total equity	129,034

Required

1. The bank has offered a long-term secured note to Success Systems. This bank's loan procedures require that selected pledged assets (accounts receivable, inventory, and net plant assets) to its secured loan ratio be at least 6. As of March 31, 2005, what is the maximum amount that Success Systems could borrow from this bank?
2. If Success Systems borrows the maximum amount allowed from the bank, what percentage of assets would be financed (*a*) by debt, and (*b*) by equity?

BEYOND THE NUMBERS

REPORTING IN ACTION

C1 A1

BTN 14-1 Refer to **Krispy Kreme**'s financial statements in Appendix A to answer the following:

1. Does Krispy Kreme have any issued and outstanding bonds or long-term notes payable?
2. How much cash is paid to reduce long-term debt for the year ended February 2, 2003?
3. Did it have any additions to long-term debt that provided cash for year-end February 2, 2003?

Roll On

4. Access Krispy Kreme's financial statements for a year ending after February 2, 2003, from its Website (KrispyKreme.com) or the SEC's EDGAR database (www.sec.gov). Has it issued additional long-term debt since the year-end February 2, 2003? If yes, identify the amount(s).

COMPARATIVE ANALYSIS

A3

BTN 14-2 Key comparative figures ($ thousands) for both **Krispy Kreme** and **Tastykake** follow:

Key Figures	Krispy Kreme Current Year	Krispy Kreme Prior Year	Tastykake Current Year	Tastykake Prior Year
Current receivables, net	$ 46,319	$ 38,682	$20,882	$22,233
Inventory	24,365	16,159	6,777	8,412
Property and equipment, net	202,558	112,577	58,391	59,702
Long-term debt (includes current portion)	53,201	4,643	13,500	14,900

Required

1. Assume that both Krispy Kreme and Tastykake have pledged substantially all of their current receivables, inventory, and property and equipment to collateralize their long-term debt. Compute the ratio of pledged assets to secured liabilities for both companies.
2. Use the ratio you computed in part 1 to determine which company's long-term debt is less risky.

ETHICS CHALLENGE

C5 A1

BTN 14-3 Brevard County needs a new county government building that would cost $24 million. The politicians feel that voters will not approve a municipal bond issue to fund the building since it would increase taxes. They opt to have a state bank issue $24 million of tax-exempt securities to pay for the building construction. The county then will make yearly lease payments (of principal and interest) to repay the obligation. Unlike conventional municipal bonds, the lease payments are not binding obligations on the county and, therefore, require no voter approval.

Required

1. Do you think the actions of the politicians and the bankers in this situation are ethical?
2. How do the tax-exempt securities used to pay for the building compare in risk to a conventional municipal bond issued by Brevard County?

COMMUNICATING IN PRACTICE

P3

BTN 14-4 Your business associate mentions that she is considering investing in corporate bonds currently selling at a premium. She says that since the bonds are selling at a premium, they are highly valued and her investment will yield more than the going rate of return for the risk involved. Reply with a memorandum to confirm or correct your associate's interpretation of premium bonds.

TAKING IT TO THE NET

C1

mhhe.com/larson

BTN 14-5 Access the March 26, 2003, filing of the 2002 calendar-year 10-K report of **Coca-Cola Co.** (Ticker KO) from www.SEC.gov. Refer to Coca-Cola's statement of cash flows for the year ended December 31, 2002, to answer the following questions.

Required

1. Did the company issue any new debt in 2002? If yes, identify the amount.
2. Did the company repay any of its debt in 2002? If yes, identify the amount.
3. Did it obtain more new financing in 2002 from issuing debt or from issuing stock? List amounts.
4. The company's 10-K report shows three years of cash flow data. Does it reveal a trend of issuing more or less debt over this three-year period? Explain.

TEAMWORK IN ACTION

P2 P3

BTN 14-6[B] Break into teams and complete the following requirements related to effective interest amortization for a premium bond.

1. Each team member is to independently prepare a blank table with proper headings for amortization of a bond premium. When all have finished, compare tables and ensure all are in agreement.

Parts 2 and 3 require use of these facts: On January 1, 2005, BC issues $100,000, 9%, five-year bonds at 104.1. The market rate at issuance is 8%. BC pays interest semiannually on June 30 and December 31.

2. In rotation, *each* team member must explain how to complete *one* line of the bond amortization table, including all computations for his or her line. (Round amounts to the nearest dollar.) All members are to fill in their tables during this process. You need not finish the table; stop after all members have explained a line.
3. In rotation, *each* team member is to identify a separate column of the table and indicate what the final number in that column will be and explain the reasoning.
4. Reach a team consensus as to what the total bond interest expense on this bond issue will be if the bond is not retired before maturity.
5. As a team, prepare a list of similarities and differences between the amortization table just prepared and the amortization table if the bond had been issued at a discount.

Hint: Rotate teams to report on parts 4 and 5. Consider requiring entries for issuance and interest payments.

BUSINESS WEEK ACTIVITY

C1

mhhe.com/larson

BTN 14-7 Read the article "Going Solo" from the November 6, 2000, issue of ***Business Week***. (The book's Website provides a free link.)

Required

1. Summarize this article's main topic.
2. Why do you think the article refers to foreign investment as "hot money"?
3. What interest rate would you have earned if you had purchased Polish treasury bills in 2000?
4. What do emerging countries offer to lure foreigners to invest in their countries?
5. Why do foreign countries sometimes have trouble retaining foreign investment?

ENTREPRENEURIAL DECISION

A1  

BTN 14-8 Aaron Kennedy is the entrepreneur and owner of **Noodles & Company**. Assume that Kennedy's franchise program currently has $250,000 in equity; he is considering a $100,000 expansion to meet increased demand. The $100,000 expansion will yield $16,000 in additional annual income before interest expense. Assume that Kennedy's franchise program currently earns $40,000 annual income before interest expense of $10,000, yielding a return on equity of 12% ($30,000/$250,000). To fund the expansion, Kennedy is considering the issuance of a 10-year, $100,000 note with annual interest payments (the principal due at the end of 10 years).

Required

1. Using return on equity as the decision criterion, show computations to support or reject Kennedy's expansion if interest on the $100,000 note is (*a*) 10%, (*b*) 15%, (*c*) 16%, (*d*) 17%, and (*e*) 20%.
2. What general rule do the results in part 1 illustrate?

HITTING THE ROAD

A1 

BTN 14-9 Visit your city or county library. Ask the librarian to help you locate the recent financial records of your city or county government. Examine the records.

Required

1. Determine the amount of long-term bonds and notes currently outstanding.
2. Read the supporting information to your municipality's financial statements and record:
   a. Market interest rate(s) when the bonds and/or notes were issued.
   b. Date(s) when the bonds and/or notes will mature.
   c. Any rating(s) on the bonds and/or notes received from **Moody's**, **Standard & Poor's**, or another rating agency.

GLOBAL DECISION

A3 

BTN 14-10 **Grupo Bimbo (GrupoBimbo.com)**, **Krispy Kreme**, and **Tastykake** are competitors in the global marketplace. Selected results from these companies follow:

	Grupo Bimbo (millions of pesos)		Krispy Kreme ($ thousands)		Tastykake ($ thousands)	
Key Figures	**Current Year**	**Prior Year**	**Current Year**	**Prior Year**	**Current Year**	**Prior Year**
Current receivables, net	3,794	3,207	$ 46,319	$ 38,682	$20,882	$22,233
Inventory	905	767	24,365	16,159	6,777	8,412
Property and equipment, net	15,444	14,683	202,558	112,577	58,391	59,702
Long-term debt (includes current portion)	11,466	5,004	53,201	4,643	13,500	14,900
Pledged assets to secured liabilities	?	?	5.14	36.06	6.37	6.06

Required

1. Compute Grupo Bimbo's ratio of pledged assets to secured liabilities for the current and prior year. (Assume each company has pledged its current receivables, inventory, and net property and equipment to collateralize its long-term debt.)
2. Use the data provided and the ratios you computed in part 1 to determine which company's long-term debt is least risky.
3. Was Grupo Bimbo a net borrower or net repayer of debt in 2002?

"To build a great company you have to build a great team of people—people that are completely focused, who see this as their opportunity to achieve their lifelong financial goals"—Ralph Cruz (on right; Bill Cruz on left)

Investments and International Operations

A Look Back

Chapter 14 focused on long-term liabilities. We explained how these liabilities are valued, recorded, amortized, and reported in financial statements. We also described the accounting for leases and pensions.

A Look at This Chapter

This chapter focuses on investments in securities. We explain how to identify, account for, and report investments in both debt and equity securities. We also introduce foreign exchange rates and describe accounting for transactions listed in a foreign currency.

A Look Ahead

Chapter 16 focuses on reporting and analyzing a company's cash flows. Special emphasis is directed at the statement of cash flows—reported under the indirect method.

CAP

Conceptual

C1 Distinguish between debt and equity securities and between short-term and long-term investments. *(p. 592)*

C2 Identify and describe the different classes of investments in securities. *(p. 593)*

C3 Describe how to report equity securities with controlling influence. *(p. 599)*

Analytical

A1 Compute and analyze the components of return on total assets. *(p. 600)*

Procedural

P1 Account for trading securities. *(p. 595)*

P2 Account for held-to-maturity securities. *(p. 596)*

P3 Account for available-for-sale securities. *(p. 596)*

P4 Account for equity securities with significant influence. *(p. 597)*

Decision Feature

Sound of Success

PLANTATION, FL—Bill and Ralph Cruz remember it as if it were yesterday. The Cruz brothers, then teenagers, combined their life savings of $2,400 and invested in securities. By week's end, they had amassed a $400 profit. "At the time we were poor, starving musicians," said Bill; "$400 seemed like we were set for life." However, success in trading securities can be short lived, and by the next week they had lost their profit and much of their original investment.

Although that first experience was unprofitable, the young musicians were hooked. The Cruz brothers had dreamed of becoming violinists but their attention turned to trading securities. "A lot of what we learned then [in music] we transferred to our business," says Bill. That business, now called the **TradeStation Group [TradeStation.com],** is based on an award-winning trading platform which enables very active individual and professional traders to design custom trading strategies, and then test, refine and automate the execution of those strategies. "The TradeStation trading platform monitors all the markets for you and the minute it spots buy or sell opportunities based on your criteria, it generates a real time buy or sell order that is usually executed instantaneously through our direct-access order execution technology," says Ralph.

The Cruz brothers also recognize the importance of knowing the accounting and reporting requirements for investments. The Cruzes point out that accounting rules for recognizing gains and losses for different portfolios can affect the trading strategies and successes of traders. It is important for investors to understand these rules to not inadvertently hurt their trading profits or accelerate gains recognition. This knowledge extends to investments in both equity and debt securities.

Bill Cruz says a future goal is to further their international brokerage base. "There's really no reason that a good portion of our revenue shouldn't come from active traders outside the U.S. who trade futures and NYSE and Nasdaq securities," says Bill. He also highlights unique accounting and reporting requirements that international traders in securities must consider. The one-time musicians have set lofty plans. "Our goal," says Bill, "is to be one of the largest online brokerages." Smart money says don't bet against them.

[Sources: *TradeStation Website,* January 2004, *Hispanic Magazine,* April 2003; *South Florida Business Journal Website Archive,* June 2003.]

This chapter's main focus is investments in securities. Many companies have investments, and many of these are in the form of debt and equity securities issued by other companies. We describe investments in these securities and how to account for them. An increasing number of companies also invest in international operations. We explain in the appendix how to account for and report international transactions listed in foreign currencies.

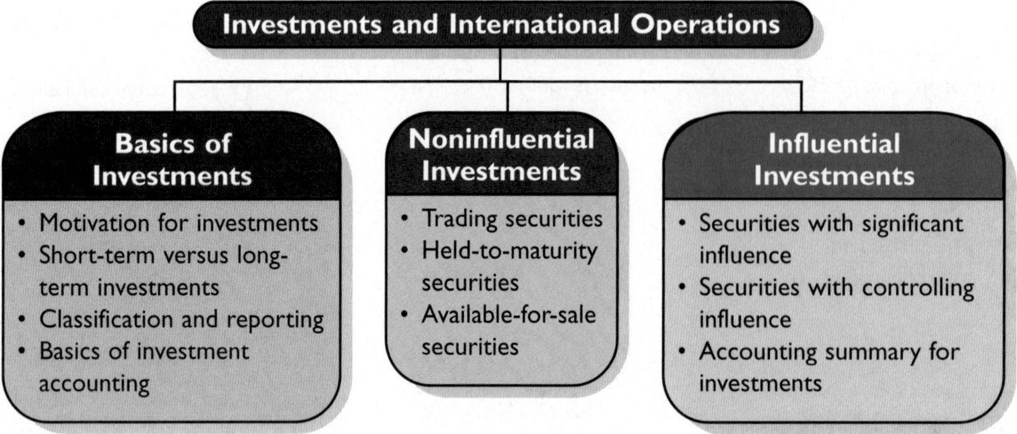

Basics of Investments

C1 Distinguish between debt and equity securities and between short-term and long-term investments.

This section describes the motivation for investments, the distinction between short- and long-term investments, and the different classes of investments.

Motivation for Investments

Point: Reporting securities at market value is referred to as *mark-to-market* accounting.

Companies make investments for at least three reasons. First, companies transfer *excess cash* into investments to produce higher income. Second, some entities, such as mutual funds and pension funds, are set up to produce income from investments. Third, companies make investments for strategic reasons. Examples are investments in competitors, suppliers, and even customers. Exhibit 15.1 shows short-term (S-T) and long-term (L-T) investments as a percent of total assets for several companies.

Exhibit 15.1

Investments of Selected Companies

Krispy Kreme S-T 6% L-T 1%
Dell Computer S-T 3% L-T 34%
Starbucks S-T 10% L-T 5%
Merrill Lynch S-T 7% L-T 22%
0% 20% 40%
Percent of total assets

Short-Term versus Long-Term Investments

Cash equivalents are investments that are both readily converted to known amounts of cash and mature within three months. Many investments, however, mature between 3 and 12 months. These investments are **short-term investments,** also called *temporary investments* and *marketable securities*. Specifically, short-term investments are securities that (1) management intends to convert to cash within one year or the operating cycle, whichever is longer, and (2) are readily convertible to cash. Short-term investments are reported under current assets and serve a purpose similar to cash equivalents.

Long-term investments in securities are defined as those securities that are not readily convertible to cash or are not intended to be converted into cash in the short term. Long-term investments can also include funds earmarked for a special purpose, such as bond sinking funds and investments in land or other assets not used in the company's operations. Long-term investments are reported in the noncurrent section of the balance sheet, often in its own separate line titled *Long-Term Investments.*

Topic Tackler 15-1

Investments in securities can include both debt and equity securities. *Debt securities* reflect a creditor relationship such as investments in notes, bonds, and certificates of deposit;

they are issued by governments, companies, and individuals. *Equity securities* reflect an owner relationship such as shares of stock issued by companies.

Classes of and Reporting for Investments

Accounting for investments in securities depends on three factors: (1) security type, either debt or equity, (2) the company's intent to hold the security either short term or long term, and (3) the company's (investor's) percent ownership in the other company's (investee's) equity securities. Exhibit 15.2 identifies five classes of securities using these three factors. It describes each of these five classes of securities and the reporting required under each class.

C2 Identify and describe the different classes of investments in securities.

Exhibit 15.2

Investments in Securities

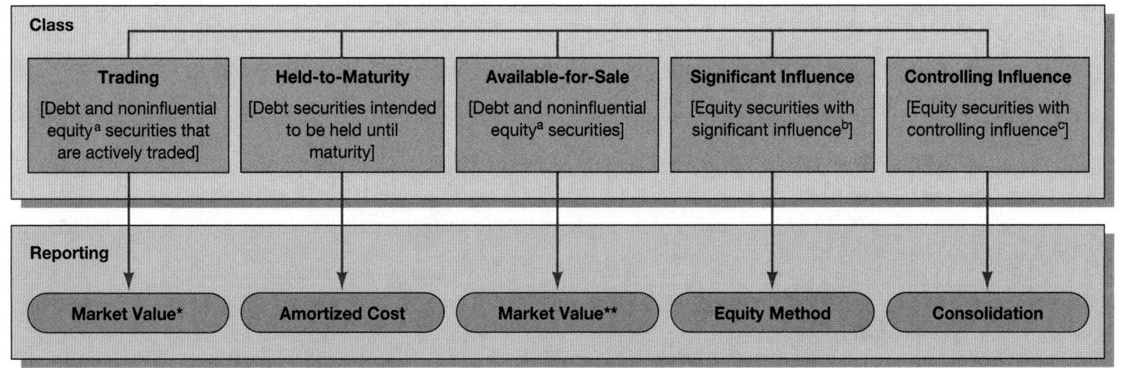

[a] Holding less than 20% of voting stock (equity securities only). [b] Holding 20% or more, but not more than 50%, of voting stock.
[c] Holding more than 50% of voting stock.
* Unrealized gains and losses reported on the income statement.
** Unrealized gains and losses reported in the equity section of the balance sheet and in comprehensive income.

Basics of Accounting for Investments

This section introduces the accounting basics for investments, including that for acquisition, disposition, and any interest or dividends.

Accounting Basics for Debt Securities Debt securities are recorded at cost when purchased. Interest revenue for investments in debt securities is recorded when earned.

Acquisition. Assume that Music City paid $29,500 plus a $500 brokerage fee on September 1, 2005, to buy Dell's 7%, two-year bonds payable with a $30,000 par value. The bonds pay interest semiannually on August 31 and February 28. Music City intends to hold the bonds until they mature on August 31, 2007, called held-to-maturity (HTM) securities. The entry to record this purchase is

Example: What is cost per share? *Answer:* Cost per share is the total cost of acquisition, including broker fees, divided by number of shares acquired.

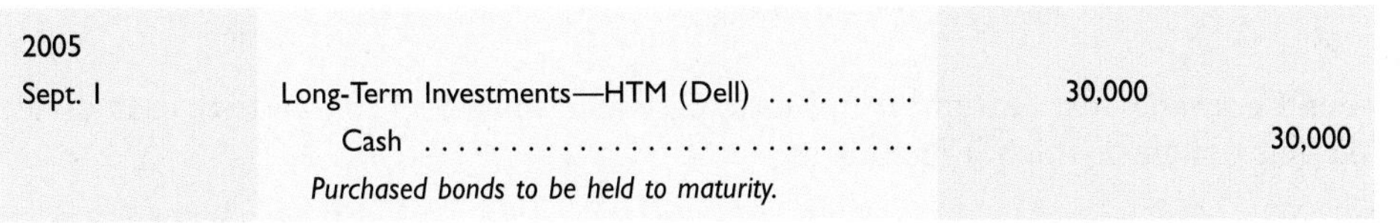

2005			
Sept. 1	Long-Term Investments—HTM (Dell)	30,000	
	Cash		30,000
	Purchased bonds to be held to maturity.		

Assets = Liabilities + Equity
+30,000
−30,000

Interest earned. On December 31, 2005, at the end of its accounting period, Music City accrues interest receivable as follows:

Dec. 31	Interest Receivable	700	
	Interest Revenue		700
	Accrued interest earned ($30,000 × 7% × 4/12).		

Assets = Liabilities + Equity
+700 +700

The $700 reflects 4/6 of the semiannual cash receipt of interest—the portion Music City earned as of December 31. Relevant sections of Music City's financial statements at December 31, 2005, are shown in Exhibit 15.3.

Exhibit 15.3

Financial Statement Presentation of Debt Securities

On the income statement for year 2005:	
Interest revenue	**$ 700**
On the December 31, 2005, balance sheet:	
Long-term investments—Held-to-maturity securities (at amortized cost)	**$30,000**

On February 28, 2006, Music City records receipt of semiannual interest:

Assets	= Liabilities	+ Equity
+1,050		+350
−700		

Feb. 28	Cash	1,050	
	Interest Receivable		700
	Interest Revenue		350
	Received six months' interest on Dell bonds.		

Disposition. When the bonds mature, the proceeds (not including the interest entry) are recorded as:

Assets	= Liabilities	+ Equity
+30,000		
−30,000		

2007			
Aug. 31	Cash	30,000	
	Long-Term Investments—HTM (Dell)		30,000
	Received cash from matured bonds.		

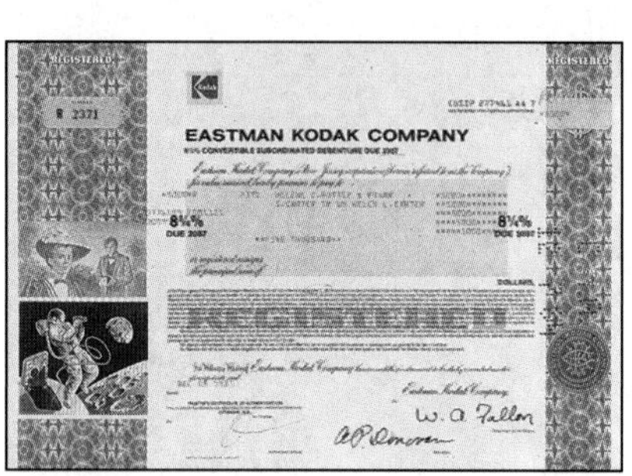

The cost of a debt security can be either higher or lower than its maturity value. When the investment is long term, the difference between cost and maturity value is amortized over the remaining life of the security. We assume for ease of computations that the cost of a long-term debt security equals its maturity value.

Accounting Basics for Equity Securities

Equity securities are recorded at cost when acquired, including commissions or brokerage fees paid. Any cash dividends received are credited to Dividend Revenue and reported in the income statement. When the securities are sold, sale proceeds are compared with the cost, and any gain or loss is recorded.

Acquisition. Assume that Music City purchases 1,000 shares of Intex common stock at par value for $86,000 on October 10, 2005. It records this purchase of available-for-sale (AFS) securities as follows:

Assets	= Liabilities	+ Equity
+86,000		
−86,000		

Oct. 10	Long-Term Investments—AFS (Intex)..........	86,000	
	Cash		86,000
	Purchased 1,000 shares of Intex.		

Dividend earned. On November 2, Music City receives a $1,720 quarterly cash dividend on the Intex shares, which it records as:

Assets	= Liabilities	+ Equity
+1,720		+1,720

Nov. 2	Cash	1,720	
	Dividend Revenue		1,720
	Received dividend of $1.72 per share.		

Disposition. On December 20, Music City sells 500 of the Intex shares for $45,000 cash and records this sale as:

Assets	= Liabilities	+ Equity
+45,000		+2,000
−43,000		

Dec. 20	Cash	45,000	
	Long-Term Investments—AFS (Intex)		43,000
	Gain on Sale of Long-Term Investments.....		2,000
	Sold 500 Intex shares ($86,000 × 500/1,000).		

Accounting for *Non*influential Investments

Companies must value and report most noninfluential investments at *fair market value,* or simply *market value.* The exact reporting requirements depend on whether the investments are classified as (1) trading, (2) held-to-maturity, or (3) available-for-sale.

P1 Account for trading securities.

Trading Securities **Trading securities** are *debt and equity securities* that the company intends to actively manage and trade for profit. Frequent purchases and sales are expected and are made to earn profits on short-term price changes.

Point: Trading securities are *always* reported under current assets.

Valuing and reporting trading securities. The entire portfolio of trading securities is reported at its market value; this requires a "market adjustment" from the cost of the portfolio. The term *portfolio* refers to a group of securities. Any **unrealized gain (or loss)** from a change in the market value of the portfolio of trading securities is reported on the income statement. Most users believe accounting reports are more useful when changes in market value for trading securities are reported in income.

To illustrate, TechCom's portfolio of trading securities had a total cost of $11,500 and a market value of $13,000 on December 31, 2005, the first year it held trading securities. The difference between the $11,500 cost and the $13,000 market value reflects a $1,500 gain. It is an unrealized gain because it is not yet confirmed by actual sales. The market adjustment for trading securities is recorded with an adjusting entry at the end of each period to equal the difference between the portfolio's cost and its market value. TechCom records this gain as:

Point: The phrase *unrealized gain (or loss)* refers to a change in market value that is not yet realized through an actual sale.

Point: Market Adjustment—Trading is a *permanent account,* shown as a deduction or addition to Short-Term Investments—Trading.

Dec. 31	Market Adjustment—Trading	1,500	
	Unrealized Gain—Income		1,500
	To reflect an unrealized gain in market values of trading securities.		

Assets	=	Liabilities	+	Equity
+1,500				+1,500

The Unrealized Gain (or Loss) is reported in the Other Revenues and Gains (or Expenses and Losses) section on the income statement. The total cost of the trading securities portfolio is maintained in one account, and the market adjustment is recorded in a separate account. For example, TechCom's investment in trading securities is reported in the current assets section of its balance sheet as follows:

Point: Unrealized Gain (or Loss)—Income is a *temporary account* that is closed to Income Summary at the end of each period.

Example: If TechCom's trading securities have a cost of $14,800 and a market of $16,100 at Dec. 31, 2006, its adjusting entry is
Unrealized Loss—Income 200
Market Adj.—Trading 200
This is computed as: $1,500 Beg. Dr. + $200 Cr. = $1,300 End. Dr.

Current Assets		
Short-term investments—Trading (at cost)	$11,500	
Market adjustment—Trading	1,500	
Short-term investments—Trading (at market)		$13,000
or simply		
Short-term investments—Trading (at market; cost is $11,500)		$13,000

Selling trading securities. When individual trading securities are sold, the difference between the net proceeds (sale price less fees) and the cost of the individual trading securities that are sold is recognized as a gain or a loss. Any prior period market adjustment is *not* used to compute the gain or loss from sale. A gain is reported in the Other Revenues and Gains section on the income statement, whereas a loss is shown in Other Expenses and Losses. When the period-end market adjustment for trading securities is computed, it excludes the cost and market value of securities sold.

Point: Security prices are sometimes listed in fraction form. For example, a debt security with a price of $22\frac{1}{4}$, is the same as $22.25.

Decision Insight

Flip-Flop About 70 years ago banks switched from reporting market values for short-term investments to reporting them at cost. We now see a return to market value reporting driven by S&L and banking failures that many allege could have been mitigated through the disclosure of market value changes.

P2 Account for held-to-maturity securities.

Held-to-Maturity Securities **Held-to-maturity (HTM) securities** are *debt* securities a company intends and is able to hold until maturity. They are reported in current assets if their maturity dates are within one year or the operating cycle, whichever is longer. HTM securities are reported in long-term assets when the maturity dates extend beyond one year or the operating cycle, whichever is longer. All HTM securities are recorded at cost when purchased, and interest revenue is recorded when earned.

The portfolio of HTM securities is reported at (amortized) cost, which is explained in advanced courses. There is no market adjustment to the portfolio of HTM securities—neither to the short-term nor long-term portfolios. The basics of accounting for HTM securities were described earlier in this chapter.

Decision Maker

Money Manager You expect interest rates to sharply fall within a few weeks and remain at this lower rate. What is your strategy for holding investments in fixed-rate bonds and notes?

Answer—p. 608

Point: Only debt securities can be classified as *held-to-maturity;* equity securities have no maturity date.

P3 Account for available-for-sale securities.

Available-for-Sale Securities **Available-for-sale (AFS) securities** are *debt and equity securities* not classified as trading or held-to-maturity securities. AFS securities are purchased to yield interest, dividends, or increases in market value. They are not actively managed like trading securities. If the intent is to sell AFS securities within the longer of one year or operating cycle, they are classified as short-term investments. Otherwise, they are classified as long-term.

Decision Insight

Trading Secrets Trading records for mutual fund companies are kept secret for many reasons, including regulatory requirements and potential lawsuits.

Point: Many users believe that since AFS securities are not actively traded, reporting market value changes in income would unnecessarily increase income variability and decrease usefulness.

Valuing and reporting available-for-sale securities. As with trading securities, companies adjust the cost of the portfolio of AFS securities to reflect changes in market value. This is done with a market adjustment to its total portfolio cost. However, any unrealized gain or loss for the portfolio of AFS securities is *not* reported on the income statement. Instead, it is reported in the equity section of the balance sheet (and is part of *comprehensive income,* explained later). To illustrate, assume that Music City had no prior period investments in available-for-sale securities other than those purchased in the current period. Exhibit 15.4 shows both the cost and market value of those investments on December 31, 2005, the end of its reporting period.

Exhibit 15.4

Cost and Market Value of Available-for-Sale Securities

	Cost	Market Value	Unrealized Gain (Loss)
Improv bonds	$30,000	$29,050	$ (950)
Intex common stock, 500 shares	43,000	45,500	2,500
Total	$73,000	$74,550	**$1,550**

Example: If market value in Exhibit 15.4 is $70,000 (instead of $74,550), what entry is made? *Answer:*
Unreal. Loss—Equity ... 3,000
Market Adj.—AFS 3,000

The year-end adjusting entry to record the market value of these investments follows:

Dec. 31	Market Adjustment—Available-for-Sale (LT)	1,550	
	Unrealized Gain—Equity		1,550
	To record adjustment to market value of available-for-sale securities.		

Assets = Liabilities + Equity
+1,550 +1,550

Point: Unrealized Loss—Equity and Unrealized Gain—Equity are *permanent* (balance sheet) *accounts* reported in the equity section.

Exhibit 15.5 shows the December 31, 2005, balance sheet presentation—it assumes these investments are long term, but they can also be short term. It is also common to combine the cost of investments with the balance in the Market Adjustment account and report the net as a single amount.

Exhibit 15.5

Balance Sheet Presentation of Available-for-Sale Securities

Long-term investments—Available-for-sale (at cost)	$73,000	
Market adjustment— Available-for-sale	1,550	
Long-term investments—Available-for-sale (at market)		$74,550
or simply		
Long-term investments—Available-for-sale (at market; cost is $73,000)		$74,550
Equity		
. . . usual equity accounts . . .		
Add unrealized gain on available-for-sale securities*		$ 1,550

* Often included under the caption Accumulated Other Comprehensive Income.

Let's extend this illustration and assume that at the end of its next calendar year (December 31, 2006), Music City's portfolio of long-term AFS securities has an $81,000 cost and an $82,000 market value. It records the adjustment to market value as follows:

Dec. 31	Unrealized Gain—Equity	550	
	Market Adjustment—Available-for-Sale (LT)		550
	To record adjustment to market value of available-for-sale securities.		

Point: Income can be window-dressed upward by selling AFS securities with unrealized gains; income is reduced by selling those with unrealized losses.

Assets = Liabilities + Equity
−550 −550

The effects of the 2005 and 2006 securities transactions are reflected in the following T-accounts:

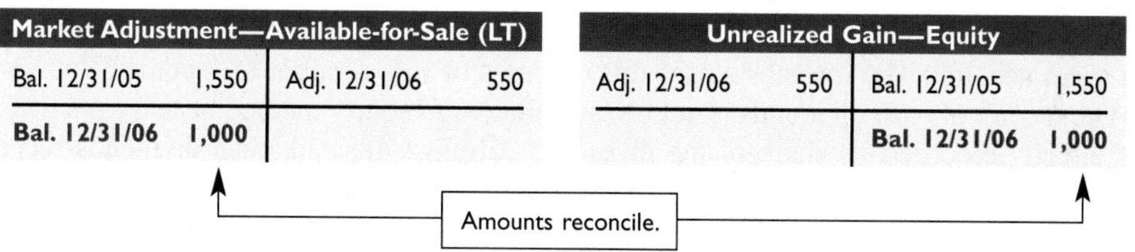

Example: If cost is $83,000 and market is $82,000 at Dec. 31, 2006, it records the following adjustment:

Unreal. Gain—Equity	1,550	
Unreal. Loss—Equity	1,000	
Mkt. Adj.—AFS		2,550

Selling available-for-sale securities. Accounting for the sale of individual AFS securities is identical to that described for the sale of trading securities. When individual AFS securities are sold, the difference between the cost of the individual securities sold and the net proceeds (sale price less fees) is recognized as a gain or loss.

Point: Market Adjustment—Available-for-Sale is a permanent account, shown as a deduction or addition to the Investment account.

Quick Check

1. How are short-term held-to-maturity securities reported (valued) on the balance sheet?
2. How are trading securities reported (valued) on the balance sheet?
3. Where are unrealized gains and losses on available-for-sale securities reported?
4. Where are unrealized gains and losses on trading securities reported?

Answers—p. 608

Accounting for Influential Investments

Investment in Equity Securities with Significant Influence

P4 Account for equity securities with significant influence.

A long-term investment classified as **equity securities with significant influence** implies that the investor can exert significant influence over the investee. An investor that owns 20% or more (but not more than 50%) of a company's voting stock is usually presumed to have a significant influence over the investee. In some cases, however, the 20% test of significant influence is overruled by other, more persuasive, evidence. This evidence can either lower the 20% requirement or increase it. The **equity method** of accounting and reporting is used for long-term investments in equity securities with significant influence, which is explained in this section.

Long-term investments in equity securities with significant influence are recorded at cost when acquired. To illustrate, Micron Co. records the purchase of 3,000 shares (30%) of Star Co. common stock at a total cost of $70,650 on January 1, 2005, as follows:

Assets	= Liabilities	+ Equity
+70,650		
−70,650		

Jan. 1	Long-Term Investments—Star	70,650	
	Cash		70,650
	To record purchase of 3,000 Star shares.		

The investee's (Star) earnings increase both its net assets and the claim of the investor (Micron) on the investee's net assets. Thus, when the investee reports its earnings, the investor records its share of those earnings in its investment account. To illustrate, assume that Star reports net income of $20,000 for 2005. Micron then records its 30% share of those earnings as follows:

Assets	= Liabilities	+ Equity
+6,000		+6,000

Dec. 31	Long-Term Investments—Star	6,000	
	Earnings from Long-Term Investment		6,000
	To record 30% equity in investee earnings.		

The debit reflects the increase in Micron's equity in Star. The credit reflects 30% of Star's net income that appears on Micron's income statement. If the investee incurs a net loss instead of a net income, the investor records its share of the loss and reduces (credits) its investment account. The investor closes this earnings or loss account to Income Summary.

Point: *Insider trading* usually refers to officers and employees who buy or sell shares in their firm based on information unavailable to the public. Generally, insider trading is illegal in the U.S., but some countries permit it.

The receipt of cash dividends is not revenue under the equity method because the investor has already recorded its share of the investee's earnings. Instead, cash dividends received by an investor from an investee are viewed as a conversion of one asset to another; that is, dividends reduce the balance of the investment account. To illustrate, Star declares and pays $10,000 in cash dividends on its common stock. Micron records its 30% share of these dividends received on January 9, 2006 as:

Assets	= Liabilities	+ Equity
+3,000		
−3,000		

Jan. 9	Cash	3,000	
	Long-Term Investments—Star		3,000
	To record share of dividend paid by Star.		

The book value of an investment under the equity method equals the cost of the investment plus (minus) the investor's equity in the *undistributed* (*distributed*) earnings of the investee. Once Micron records these transactions, its Long-Term Investments account appears as in Exhibit 15.6.

Exhibit 15.6

Investment in Star Common Stock (Ledger Account)

Date	Explanation	Debit	Credit	Balance
2005				
Jan. 1	Investment acquisition	70,650		70,650
Dec. 31	Share of earnings	6,000		76,650
2006				
Jan. 9	Share of dividend		3,000	73,650

Micron's account balance on January 9, 2006, for its investment in Star is $73,650. This is the investment's cost *plus* Micron's equity in Star's earnings since its purchase *less* Micron's equity in Star's cash dividends since its purchase. When an investment in equity securities is sold, the gain or loss is computed by comparing proceeds from the sale with the book value of the investment on the date of sale. If Micron sells its Star stock for $80,000 on January 10, 2006, it records the sale as:

Jan. 10	Cash	80,000	
	Long-Term Investments—Star.		73,650
	Gain on Sale of Investment.		6,350
	Sold 3,000 shares of stock for $80,000.		

Assets = Liabilities + Equity
+80,000 +6,350
−73,650

Investment in Equity Securities with Controlling Influence

C3 Describe how to report equity securities with controlling influence.

A long-term investment classified as **equity securities with controlling influence** implies that the investor can exert a controlling influence over the investee. An investor who owns more than 50% of a company's voting stock has control over the investee. This investor can dominate all other shareholders in electing the corporation's board of directors and has control over the investee's management. In some cases, controlling influence can extend to situations of less than 50% ownership. Exhibit 15.7 summarizes the accounting for investments in equity securities based on an investor's ownership in the stock.

Equity Method with Consolidation (50%+)
Equity Method (20%–50%)
Market Value Method (Under 20%)

Exhibit 15.7

Accounting for Equity Investments by Percent of Ownership

The *equity method with consolidation* is used to account for long-term investments in equity securities with controlling influence. The investor reports *consolidated financial statements* when owning such securities. The controlling investor is called the **parent,** and the investee is called the **subsidiary.** Many companies are parents with subsidiaries. Examples are (1) **McGraw-Hill**, the parent of *Business Week,* Standard & Poor's, and Compustat; (2) **Gap, Inc.**, the parent of Gap, Old Navy, and Banana Republic; and (3) **Brunswick**, the parent of Mercury Marine, Sea Ray, and U.S. Marine. A company owning all the outstanding stock of a subsidiary can, if it desires, take over the subsidiary's assets, retire the subsidiary's stock, and merge the subsidiary into the parent. However, there often are financial, legal, and tax advantages if a business operates as a parent controlling one or more subsidiaries. When a company operates as a parent with subsidiaries, each entity maintains separate accounting records. From a legal viewpoint, the parent and each subsidiary are separate entities with all rights, duties, and responsibilities of individual companies.

Consolidated financial statements show the financial position, results of operations, and cash flows of all entities under the parent's control, including all subsidiaries. These statements are prepared as if the business were organized as one entity. The parent uses the equity method in its accounts, but the investment account is *not* reported on the parent's financial statements. Instead, the individual assets and liabilities of the parent and its subsidiaries are combined on one balance sheet. Their revenues and expenses also are combined on one income statement, and their cash flows are combined on one statement of cash flows. The procedures for preparing consolidated financial statements are in advanced courses.

Accounting Summary for Investments in Securities

Exhibit 15.8 summarizes the accounting for investments in securities. Recall that many investment securities are classified as either short term or long term depending on management's

Exhibit 15.8
Accounting for Investments in Securities

Class of Investment Securities	Accounting Method
Short-Term Investment in Securities	
Held-to-maturity (debt) securities	Cost (without any discount or premium amortization)
Trading (debt and equity) securities	Market value (with market adjustment to income)
Available-for-sale (debt and equity) securities	Market value (with market adjustment to equity)
Long-Term Investment in Securities	
Held-to-maturity (debt) securities	Cost (with any discount or premium amortization)
Available-for-sale (debt and equity) securities	Market value (with market adjustment to equity)
Equity securities with significant influence	Equity method
Equity securities with controlling influence	Equity method (with consolidation)

intent and ability to convert them in the future. Understanding the accounting for these investments enables us to draw better conclusions from financial statements in making business decisions.

Comprehensive Income The term **comprehensive income** refers to all changes in equity for a period except those due to investments and distributions to owners. This means that it includes (1) the revenues, gains, expenses, and losses reported in net income *and* (2) the gains and losses that bypass net income but affect equity. An example of an item that bypasses net income is unrealized gains and losses on available-for-sale securities. These items make up *other comprehensive income* and are usually reported as a part of the statement of stockholders' equity. (Two other options are as a second separate income statement or as a combined income statement of comprehensive income; these less common options are described in advanced courses.) Most often this simply requires one additional column for Other Comprehensive Income in the usual columnar form of the statement of stockholders' equity (the details of this are left for advanced courses). The FASB encourages, but does *not* require, other comprehensive income items to be grouped under the caption *Accumulated Other Comprehensive Income* in the equity section of the balance sheet, which would include unrealized gains and losses on available-for-sale securities. For instructional benefits, we use actual account titles for these items in the equity section instead of this general, less precise caption.

Quick Check

5. Give at least two examples of assets classified as long-term investments.
6. What are the requirements for an equity security to be listed as a long-term investment?
7. Identify similarities and differences in accounting for long-term investments in debt securities that are held-to-maturity versus those available-for-sale.
8. What are the three possible classifications of long-term equity investments? Describe the criteria for each class and the method used to account for each.

Answers—p. 608

Decision Analysis — Components of Return on Total Assets

A1 Compute and analyze the components of return on total assets.

A company's **return on total assets** (or simply *return on assets*) is important in assessing financial performance. The return on total assets can be separated into two components, profit margin and total asset turnover, for additional analyses. Exhibit 15.9 shows how these two components determine return on total assets.

Exhibit 15.9
Components of Return on Total Assets

Return on total assets = Profit margin × Total asset turnover

$$\frac{\text{Net income}}{\text{Average total assets}} = \frac{\text{Net income}}{\text{Net sales}} \times \frac{\text{Net sales}}{\text{Average total assets}}$$

Profit margin reflects the percent of net income in each dollar of net sales. Total asset turnover reflects a company's ability to produce net sales from total assets. All companies desire a high return on total assets. By considering these two components, we can often discover strengths and weaknesses not revealed by return on total assets alone. This improves our ability to assess future performance and company strategy.

To illustrate, consider return on total assets and its components for **Reebok** in Exhibit 15.10.

Year	Return on Total Assets	=	Profit Margin	×	Total Asset Turnover
2002	7.4%	=	4.0%	×	1.84
2001	6.8%	=	3.4%	×	1.99
2000	5.3%	=	2.8%	×	1.89
1999	0.7%	=	0.4%	×	1.78

Exhibit 15.10

Reebok's Components of Return on Total Assets

At least three findings emerge. First, Reebok's return on total assets steadily improved from 1999 through 2002. Second, total asset turnover might have slightly improved but nothing noteworthy. Third, Reebok's profit margin sharply rose between 1999 and 2002. These components reveal the dual role of profit margin and total asset turnover in determining return on total assets. They also reveal that the driver of Reebok's rebound is not total asset turnover but profit margin.

Generally, if a company is to maintain or improve its return on total assets, it must meet any decline in either profit margin or total asset turnover with an increase in the other. If not, return on assets will decline. Companies consider these components in planning strategies. A component analysis can also reveal where a company is weak and where changes are needed, especially in a competitor analysis. If asset turnover is lower than the industry norm, for instance, a company should focus on raising asset turnover at least to the norm. The same applies to profit margin.

Decision Maker

Retailer You are an entrepreneur and owner of a retail sporting goods store. The store's recent annual performance reveals (industry norms in parentheses): return on total assets = 11% (11.2%); profit margin = 4.4% (3.5%); and total asset turnover = 2.5 (3.2). What does your analysis of these figures reveal?

Answer—p. 608

Demonstration Problem—1

Garden Company completes the following selected transactions related to its short-term investments during 2005:

May 8 Purchased 300 shares of FedEx stock as a short-term investment in available-for-sale securities at $40 per share plus $975 in broker fees.

Sept. 2 Sold 100 shares of its investment in FedEx stock at $47 per share and held the remaining 200 shares; broker's commission was $225.

Oct. 2 Purchased 400 shares of Ajay stock for $60 per share plus $1,600 in commissions. The stock is held as a short-term investment in available-for-sale securities.

Required

1. Prepare journal entries for the above transactions of Garden Co. for 2005.
2. Prepare an adjusting journal entry as of December 31, 2005, if the market prices of the equity securities held by Garden Company are $48 per share for FedEx and $55 per share for Ajay. (Year 2005 is the first year Garden Co. acquired short-term investments.)

Solution to Demonstration Problem—1

1.

Date	Account	Debit	Credit
May 8	Short-Term Investments—AFS (FedEx).	12,975	
	Cash.		12,975
	Purchased 300 shares of FedEx stock (300 × $40) + $975.		

[continued on next page]

[continued from previous page]

Sept. 2	Cash	4,475	
	Gain on Sale of Short-Term Investment		150
	Short-Term Investments—AFS (FedEx)		4,325
	Sold 100 shares of FedEx for $47 per share less a $225 commission. The original cost is ($12,975 × 100/300).		
Oct. 2	Short-Term Investments—AFS (Ajay)	25,600	
	Cash		25,600
	Purchased 400 shares of Ajay for $60 per share plus $1,600 in commissions.		

2. Computation of unrealized gain or loss:

Short-Term Investments in Available-for-Sale Securities	Shares	Cost per Share	Total Cost	Market Value per Share	Total Market Value	Unrealized Gain (Loss)
FedEx	200	$43.25	$ 8,650	$48.00	$ 9,600	
Ajay	400	64.00	25,600	55.00	22,000	
Total			$34,250		$31,600	$(2,650)

Adjusting entry:

Dec. 31	Unrealized Loss—Equity	2,650	
	Market Adjustment—Available-for-Sale (ST)		2,650
	To reflect an unrealized loss in market values of available-for-sale securities.		

Demonstration Problem—2

The following transactions relate to Brown Company's long-term investments during 2005 and 2006. Brown did not own any long-term investments prior to 2005. Show (1) the appropriate journal entries and (2) the relevant portions of each year's balance sheet and income statement that reflect these transactions for both 2005 and 2006.

2005

Sept. 9 Purchased 1,000 shares of Packard, Inc., common stock for $80,000 cash. These shares represent 30% of Packard's outstanding shares.

Oct. 2 Purchased 2,000 shares of AT&T common stock for $60,000 cash. These shares represent less than a 1% ownership in AT&T.

17 Purchased as a long-term investment 1,000 shares of Apple Computer common stock for $40,000 cash. These shares are less than 1% of Apple's outstanding shares.

Nov. 1 Received $5,000 cash dividend from Packard.

30 Received $3,000 cash dividend from AT&T.

Dec. 15 Received $1,400 cash dividend from Apple.

31 Packard's 2002 net income is $70,000.

31 Market values for the investments in equity securities are Packard, $84,000; AT&T, $48,000; and Apple Computer, $45,000.

31 For preparing financial statements, note the following post-closing account balances: Common Stock, $500,000, and Retained Earnings, $350,000.

2006

Jan. 1 Sold Packard, Inc., shares for $108,000 cash.

May 30 Received $3,100 cash dividend from AT&T.

June 15 Received $1,600 cash dividend from Apple.

Aug. 17 Sold the AT&T stock for $52,000 cash.
19 Purchased 2,000 shares of Coca-Cola common stock for $50,000 cash as a long-term investment. The stock represents less than a 5% ownership in Coca-Cola.
Dec. 15 Received $1,800 cash dividend from Apple.
31 Market values of the investments in equity securities are Apple, $39,000, and Coca-Cola, $48,000.
31 For preparing financial statements, note the following post-closing account balances: Common Stock, $500,000, and Retained Earnings, $410,000.

Planning the Solution

- Account for the investment in Packard under the equity method.
- Account for the investments in AT&T, Apple, and Coca-Cola as long-term investments in available-for-sale securities.
- Prepare the information for the two years' balance sheets by including the appropriate asset and equity accounts.

Solution to Demonstration Problem—2

1. Journal entries for 2005

Date	Account	Debit	Credit
Sept. 9	Long-Term Investments—Packard	80,000	
	Cash		80,000
	Acquired 1,000 shares, representing a 30% equity in Packard.		
Oct. 2	Long-Term Investments—AFS (AT&T)	60,000	
	Cash		60,000
	Acquired 2,000 shares as a long-term investment in available-for-sale securities.		
Oct. 17	Long-Term Investments—AFS (Apple)	40,000	
	Cash		40,000
	Acquired 1,000 shares as a long-term investment in available-for-sale securities.		
Nov. 1	Cash	5,000	
	Long-Term Investments—Packard		5,000
	Received dividend from Packard.		
Nov. 30	Cash	3,000	
	Dividend Revenue		3,000
	Received dividend from AT&T.		
Dec. 15	Cash	1,400	
	Dividend Revenue		1,400
	Received dividend from Apple.		
Dec. 31	Long-Term Investments—Packard	21,000	
	Earnings from Investment (Packard).		21,000
	To record 30% share of Packard's annual earnings of $70,000.		
Dec. 31	Unrealized Loss—Equity	7,000	
	Market Adjustment—Available-for-Sale (LT)* .		7,000
	To record change in market value of long-term available-for-sale securities.		

* Market adjustment computations:

	Cost	Market Value	Unrealized Gain (Loss)
AT&T	$ 60,000	$48,000	$(12,000)
Apple	40,000	45,000	5,000
Total	$100,000	$93,000	$ (7,000)

Required balance of the Market Adjustment—Available-for-Sale (LT) account	$(7,000)
Existing balance	0
Necessary adjustment (credit)	$(7,000)

2. The December 31, 2005, selected balance sheet items appear as follows:

Assets	
Long-term investments	
Available-for-sale securities (at market; cost is $100,000)	$93,000
Investment in equity securities	96,000
Total long-term investments	$189,000
Stockholders' Equity	
Common stock	500,000
Retained earnings	350,000
Unrealized loss—Equity	(7,000)

The relevant income statement items for the year ended December 31, 2005, follow:

Dividend revenue	$ 4,400
Earnings from investment	21,000

1. Journal entries for 2006

Date	Account	Debit	Credit
Jan. 1	Cash	108,000	
	Long-Term Investments—Packard		96,000
	Gain on Sale of Long-Term Investments		12,000
	Sold 1,000 shares for cash.		
May 30	Cash	3,100	
	Dividend Revenue		3,100
	Received dividend from AT&T.		
June 15	Cash	1,600	
	Dividend Revenue		1,600
	Received dividend from Apple.		
Aug. 17	Cash	52,000	
	Loss on Sale of Long-Term Investments	8,000	
	Long-Term Investments—AFS (AT&T)		60,000
	Sold 2,000 shares for cash.		
Aug. 19	Long-Term Investments—AFS (Coca-Cola)	50,000	
	Cash		50,000
	Acquired 2,000 shares as a long-term investment in available-for-sale securities.		
Dec. 15	Cash	1,800	
	Dividend Revenue		1,800
	Received dividend from Apple.		
Dec. 31	Market Adjustment—Available-for-Sale (LT)*	4,000	
	Unrealized Loss—Equity		4,000
	To record change in market value of long-term available-for-sale securities.		

* Market adjustment computations:

	Cost	Market Value	Unrealized Gain (Loss)
Apple	$40,000	$39,000	$(1,000)
Coca-Cola	50,000	48,000	(2,000)
Total	$90,000	$87,000	$(3,000)

Required balance of the Market Adjustment—Available-for-Sale (LT) account	$(3,000)
Existing balance (credit)	(7,000)
Necessary adjustment (debit)	$ 4,000

2. The December 31, 2006, balance sheet items appear as follows:

Assets	
Long-term investments	
Available-for-sale securities (at market; cost is $90,000)	$ 87,000
Stockholders' Equity	
Common stock	500,000
Retained earnings	410,000
Unrealized loss—Equity	(3,000)

The relevant income statement items for the year ended December 31, 2006, follow:

Dividend revenue	$ 6,500
Gain on sale of long-term investments	12,000
Loss on sale of long-term investments	(8,000)

APPENDIX

Investments in International Operations 15A

Many entities from small entrepreneurs to large corporations conduct business internationally. Some entities' operations occur in so many different countries that the companies are called **multinationals.** Many of us think of **Coca-Cola** and **McDonald's**, for example, as primarily U.S. companies, but most of their sales occur outside the United States. Exhibit 15A.1 shows the percent of international sales and income for selected U.S. companies. Managing and accounting for multinationals presents challenges. This section describes some of these challenges and how to account for and report these activities.

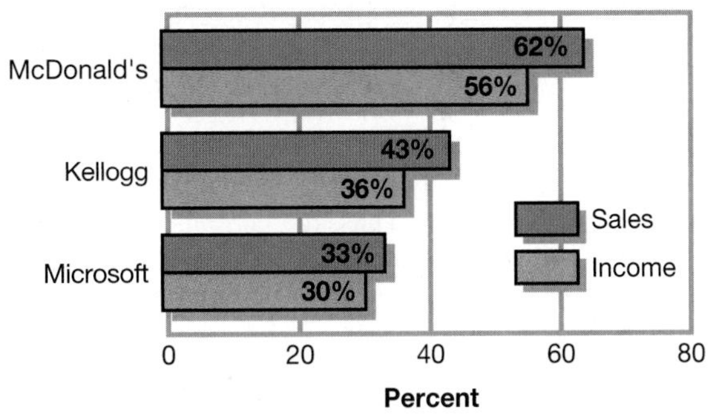

Exhibit 15A.1

International Sales and Income as a Percent of Their Totals

Topic Tackler 15-2

Two major accounting challenges that arise when companies have international operations relate to transactions that involve more than one currency. The first is to account for sales and purchases listed in a foreign currency. The second is to prepare consolidated financial statements with international subsidiaries. For ease in this discussion, we use companies with a U.S. base of operations and assume the need to prepare financial statements in U.S. dollars. This means the *reporting currency* of these companies is the U.S. dollar.

Point: Transactions *listed* or *stated* in a foreign currency are said to be *denominated* in that currency.

Exchange Rates between Currencies

C4 Explain foreign exchange rates between currencies.

Markets for the purchase and sale of foreign currencies exist all over the world. In these markets, U.S. dollars can be exchanged for Canadian dollars, British pounds, Japanese yen, Euros, or any other legal currencies. The price of one currency stated in terms of another currency is called a **foreign exchange rate.** Exhibit 15A.2 lists recent exchange rates for selected currencies. The exchange rate for British pounds and U.S. dollars is $1.6152, meaning 1 British pound could be purchased for $1.6152. On that same day, the exchange rate between Mexican pesos and U.S. dollars is $0.1063, or 1 Mexican peso can be purchased for $0.1063. Exchange rates

Decision Insight

Rush to Russia Investors are still eager to buy Russian equities even in the face of rampant crime, corruption, and slow economic growth. Why? Many argue Russia remains a bargain-priced, if risky, bet on future growth. Some analysts argue that natural-resource-rich Russia is one of the least expensive emerging markets.

Exhibit 15A.2

Foreign Exchange Rates for Selected Currencies*

Source (unit)	Price in $U.S.	Source (unit)	Price in $U.S.
Britain (pound)	$1.6152	Canada (dollar)	$0.7400
Mexico (peso)	0.1063	Japan (yen)	0.0085
Taiwan (dollar)	0.0305	Europe (Euro)	1.1703

* Rates will vary over time based on economic, political, and other changes.

Point: For currency conversion, see XE.com

fluctuate due to changing economic and political conditions, including the supply and demand for currencies and expectations about future events.

Sales and Purchases Listed in a Foreign Currency

P5 Record transactions listed in a foreign currency.

When a U.S. company makes a credit sale to an international customer, accounting for the sale and the account receivable is straightforward if sales terms require the international customer's payment in U.S. dollars. If sale terms require (or allow) payment in a foreign currency, however, the U.S. company must account for the sale and the account receivable in a different manner.

Decision Insight

Global Greenback What do changes in foreign exchange rates mean? A decline in the price of the U.S. dollar against other currencies usually yields increased international sales for U.S. companies, without hiking prices or cutting costs, and puts them on a stronger competitive footing abroad. At home, they can raise prices without fear that foreign rivals will undercut them.

To illustrate, consider the case of the U.S.-based manufacturer Boston Company, which makes credit sales to London Outfitters, a British retail company. A sale occurs on December 12, 2005, for a price of £10,000 with payment due on February 10, 2006. Boston Company keeps its accounting records in U.S. dollars. To record the sale, Boston Company must translate the sales price from pounds to dollars. This is done using the exchange rate on the date of the sale. Assuming the exchange rate on December 12, 2005, is $1.80, Boston records this sale as follows:

Assets = Liabilities + Equity
+18,000 +18,000

Dec. 12	Accounts Receivable—London Outfitters.......	18,000	
	Sales*		18,000
	To record a sale at £10,000, when the exchange rate equals $1.80. * (£10,000 × $1.80)		

When Boston Company prepares its annual financial statements on December 31, 2005, the current exchange rate is $1.84. Thus, the current dollar value of Boston Company's receivable is $18,400 (10,000 × $1.84). This amount is $400 higher than the amount recorded on December 12. Accounting principles require a receivable to be reported in the balance sheet at its current dollar value. Thus, Boston Company must make the following entry to record the increase in the dollar value of this receivable at year-end:

Assets = Liabilities + Equity
+400 +400

Dec. 31	Accounts Receivable—London Outfitters.......	400	
	Foreign Exchange Gain.................		400
	To record the increased value of the British pound for the receivable.		

Point: Foreign exchange gains are credits, and foreign exchange losses are debits.

On February 10, 2006, Boston Company receives London Outfitters' payment of £10,000. It immediately exchanges the pounds for U.S. dollars. On this date, the exchange rate for pounds is $1.78. Thus, Boston Company receives only $17,800 (£10,000 × $1.78). It records the cash receipt and the loss associated with the decline in the exchange rate as follows:

Assets = Liabilities + Equity
+17,800 −600
−18,400

Feb. 10	Cash	17,800	
	Foreign Exchange Loss	600	
	Accounts Receivable—London Outfitters ...		18,400
	Received foreign currency payment of an account and converted it into dollars.		

Gains and losses from foreign exchange transactions are accumulated in the Foreign Exchange Gain (or Loss) account. After year-end adjustments, the balance in the Foreign Exchange Gain (or Loss) account is reported on the income statement and closed to the Income Summary account.

Accounting for credit purchases from an international seller is similar to the case of a credit sale to an international customer. In particular, if the U.S. company is required to make payment in a foreign currency, the account payable must be translated into dollars before the U.S. company can record it. If the exchange rate is different when preparing financial statements and when paying for the purchase, the U.S. company must recognize a foreign exchange gain or loss at those dates.

Example: Assume that a U.S. company makes a credit purchase from a British company for £10,000 when the exchange rate is $1.62. At the balance sheet date, this rate is $1.72. Does this imply a gain or loss for the U.S. company? *Answer:* A loss.

Consolidated Statements with International Subsidiaries

A second challenge in accounting for international operations involves preparing consolidated financial statements when the parent company has one or more international subsidiaries. Consider a U.S.-based company that owns a controlling interest in a French subsidiary. The reporting currency of the U.S. parent is the dollar. The French subsidiary maintains its financial records in euros. Before preparing consolidated statements, the parent must translate financial statements of the French company into U.S. dollars. After this translation is complete (including that for accounting differences), it prepares consolidated statements the same as for domestic subsidiaries. Procedures for translating an international subsidiary's account balances depend on the nature of the subsidiary's operations. The process requires the parent company to select appropriate foreign exchange rates and to apply those rates to the foreign subsidiary's account balances. This is described in advanced courses.

Decision Maker

Entrepreneur You are a U.S. home builder that purchases lumber from mills in both the U.S. and Canada. The price of the Canadian dollar in terms of the U.S. dollar jumps from US$0.70 to US$0.80. Are you now more or less likely to buy lumber from Canadian or U.S. mills?

Answer—p. 608

Global: A weaker U.S. dollar often increases global sales for U.S. companies.

Summary

C1 Distinguish between debt and equity securities and between short-term and long-term investments. *Debt securities* reflect a creditor relationship and include investments in notes, bonds, and certificates of deposit. *Equity securities* reflect an owner relationship and include shares of stock issued by other companies. Short-term investments in securities are current assets that meet two criteria: (1) They are expected to be converted into cash within one year or the current operating cycle of the business, whichever is longer and (2) they are readily convertible to cash, or *marketable*. All other investments in securities are long-term. Long-term investments also include assets not used in operations and those held for special purposes, such as land for expansion.

C2 Identify and describe the different classes of investments in securities. Investments in securities are classified into one of five groups: (1) trading securities, which are always short-term, (2) debt securities held-to-maturity, (3) debt and equity securities available-for-sale, (4) equity securities in which an investor has a significant influence over the investee, and (5) equity securities in which an investor has a controlling influence over the investee.

C3 Describe how to report equity securities with controlling influence. If an investor owns more than 50% of another company's voting stock and controls the investee, the investor's financial reports are prepared on a consolidated basis. These reports are prepared as if the company were organized as one entity.

C4[A] Explain foreign exchange rates between currencies. A foreign exchange rate is the price of one currency stated in terms of another. An entity with transactions in a foreign currency when the exchange rate changes between the transaction dates and their settlement will experience exchange gains or losses.

A1 Compute and analyze the components of return on total assets. Return on total assets has two components: profit margin and total asset turnover. A decline in one component must be met with an increase in another if return on assets is to be maintained. Component analysis is helpful in assessing company performance compared to that of competitors and its own past.

P1 Account for trading securities. Investments are initially recorded at cost, and any dividend or interest from these investments is recorded in the income statement. Investments classified as trading securities are reported at market value. Unrealized gains and losses on trading securities are reported in income. When investments are sold, the difference between the net proceeds from the sale and the cost of the securities is recognized as a gain or loss.

P2 Account for held-to-maturity securities. Debt securities held-to-maturity are reported at cost when purchased. Interest revenue is recorded as it accrues. The cost of long-term held-to-maturity securities is adjusted for the amortization of any difference between cost and maturity value.

P3 Account for available-for-sale securities. Debt and equity securities available-for-sale are recorded at cost when purchased. Available-for-sale securities are reported at their market values on the balance sheet with unrealized gains or losses shown in the equity section. Gains and losses realized on the sale of these investments are reported in the income statement.

P4 Account for equity securities with significant influence. The equity method is used when an investor has a significant influence over an investee. This usually exists when an investor owns 20% or more of the investee's voting stock but not more than 50%. The equity method means an investor records its share of investee earnings with a debit to the investment account and a credit to a revenue account. Dividends received reduce the investment account balance.

P5[A] **Record transactions listed in a foreign currency.** When a company makes a credit sale to a foreign customer and sales terms call for payment in a foreign currency, the company must translate the foreign currency into dollars to record the receivable. If the exchange rate changes before payment is received, exchange gains or losses are recognized in the year they occur. The same treatment is used when a company makes a credit purchase from a foreign supplier and is required to make payment in a foreign currency.

Guidance Answers to **Decision Maker** and **Decision Ethics**

Money Manager If you have investments in fixed-rate bonds and notes when interest rates fall, the value of your investments increases. This is so because the bonds and notes you hold continue to pay the same (high) rate while the market is demanding a new lower interest rate. Your strategy is to continue holding your investments in bonds and notes, and, potentially, to increase these holdings through additional purchases.

Retailer Your store's return on assets is 11%, which is similar to the industry norm of 11.2%. However, disaggregation of return on assets reveals that your store's profit margin of 4.4% is much higher than the norm of 3.5%, but your total asset turnover of 2.5 is much lower than the norm of 3.2. These results suggest that, as compared with competitors, you are less efficient in using assets. You need to focus on increasing sales or reducing assets. You might consider reducing prices to increase sales, provided such a strategy does not reduce your return on assets. For instance, you could reduce your profit margin to 4% to increase sales. If total asset turnover increases to more than 2.75 when profit margin is lowered to 4%, your overall return on assets is improved.

Entrepreneur You are now less likely to buy Canadian lumber because it takes more U.S. money to buy a Canadian dollar (and lumber). For instance, the purchase of lumber from a Canadian mill with a $1,000 (Canadian dollars) price would have cost the U.S. builder $700 (U.S. dollars, computed as C$1,000 × US$0.70) before the rate change, and $800 (US dollars, computed as C$1,000 × US$0.80) after the rate change.

Guidance Answers to **Quick Checks**

1. Short-term held-to-maturity securities are reported at cost.
2. Trading securities are reported at market value.
3. The equity section of the balance sheet (and in comprehensive income).
4. The income statement.
5. Long-term investments include (1) long-term funds earmarked for a special purpose, (2) debt and equity securities that do not meet current asset requirements, and (3) long-term assets not used in the regular operations of the business.
6. An equity investment is classified as long term if it is not marketable or, if marketable, it is not held as an available source of cash to meet the needs of current operations.
7. Debt securities held-to-maturity and debt securities available-for-sale are both recorded at cost. Also, interest on both is accrued as earned. However, only long-term securities held-to-maturity require amortization of the difference between cost and maturity value. In addition, only securities available-for-sale require a period-end adjustment to market value.
8. Long-term equity investments are placed in one of three categories and accounted for as follows: (a) **available-for-sale** (noninfluential, less than 20% of outstanding stock)—market value; (b) **significant influence** (20% to 50% of outstanding stock)—equity method; and (c) **controlling influence** (holding more than 50% of outstanding stock)—equity method with consolidation.

Key Terms

Key Terms are available at the book's Website for learning and testing in an online Flashcard Format.

Available-for-sale (AFS) securities (p. 596)
Comprehensive income (p. 600)
Consolidated financial statements (p. 599)
Equity method (p. 598)
Equity securities with controlling influence (p. 599)
Equity securities with significant influence (p. 597)
Foreign exchange rate (p. 605)
Held-to-maturity (HTM) securities (p. 596)
Long-term investments (p. 592)
Multinational (p. 605)
Parent (p. 599)
Return on total assets (p. 600)
Short-term investments (p. 592)
Subsidiary (p. 599)
Trading securities (p. 595)
Unrealized gain (loss) (p. 595)

Personal Interactive Quiz

Personal Interactive Quizzes A and B are available at the book's Website to reinforce and assess your learning.

Superscript A denotes assignments based on Appendix 15A.

Discussion Questions

1. Under what two conditions should investments be classified as current assets?
2. On a balance sheet, what valuation must be reported for short-term investments in trading securities?
3. If a short-term investment in available-for-sale securities costs $6,780 and is sold for $7,500, how should the difference between these two amounts be recorded?
4. Identify the three classes of noninfluential and two classes of influential investments in securities.
5. Under what conditions should investments be classified as current assets? As long-term assets?
6. If a company purchases its only long-term investments in available-for-sale debt securities this period and their market value is below cost at the balance sheet date, what entry is required to recognize this unrealized loss?
7. On a balance sheet, what valuation must be reported for debt securities classified as available-for-sale?
8. Under what circumstances are long-term investments in debt securities reported at cost and adjusted for amortization of any difference between cost and maturity value?
9. For investments in available-for-sale securities, how are unrealized (holding) gains and losses reported?
10. In accounting for investments in equity securities, when should the equity method be used?
11. Under what circumstances does a company prepare consolidated financial statements?
12.^A What are two major challenges in accounting for international operations?
13.^A Assume a U.S. company makes a credit sale to a foreign customer that is required to make payment in its foreign currency. In the current period, the exchange rate is $1.40 on the date of the sale and is $1.30 on the date the customer pays the receivable. Will the U.S. company record an exchange gain or loss?
14.^A If a U.S. company makes a credit sale to a foreign customer required to make payment in U.S. dollars, can the U.S. company have an exchange gain or loss on this sale?
15. What amount does **Krispy Kreme** report as Accumulated Other Comprehensive Income on its balance sheet as of February 2, 2003, and February 3, 2002?

16. Refer to the balance sheet of **Tastykake** in Appendix A. How can you tell that Tastykake uses the consolidated method of accounting?
17. Refer to the financial statements of **Harley-Davidson** in Appendix A. Compute its return on total assets for the year ended December 31, 2002.

Harley-Davidson

Red numbers denote Discussion Questions that involve decision-making.

***Homework Manager** repeats all numerical Quick Studies on the book's Website with new numbers.*

QUICK STUDY

QS 15-1
Short-term equity investments C2 P1

On April 18, Dice Co. made a short-term investment in 500 common shares of XLT Co. The purchase price is $45 per share and the broker's fee is $150. The intent is to actively manage these shares for profit. On May 30, Dice Co. receives $1 per share from XLT in dividends. Prepare the April 18 and May 30 journal entries.

QS 15-2
Available-for-sale securities C2 P3

Fender Co. purchased short-term investments in available-for-sale securities at a cost of $100,000 on November 25, 2005. At December 31, 2005, these securities had a market value of $94,000. This is the first and only time the company has purchased such securities.

1. Prepare the December 31, 2005, year-end adjusting entry for the securities' portfolio.
2. For each account in the entry for part 1, explain how it is reported in financial statements.
3. Prepare the April 6, 2006, entry when Fender sells one-half of these securities for $52,000.

QS 15-3
Available-for-sale securities C2 P3

Prepare Hoffman Company's journal entries to reflect the following transactions for the current year:

May 7 Purchases 100 shares of Lov stock as a short-term investment in available-for-sale securities at a cost of $25 per share plus $200 in broker fees.

June 6 Sells 100 shares of its investment in Lov stock at $28 per share. The broker's commission on this sale is $75.

QS 15-4
Available-for-sale securities
C2 P3

Galaxy Company completes the following transactions during the current year:

May 9 Purchases 400 shares of X&O stock as a short-term investment in available-for-sale securities at a cost of $50 per share plus $400 in broker fees.

June 2 Sells 200 shares of its investment in X&O stock at $56 per share. The broker's commission on this sale is $180.

Dec. 31 The closing market price of the X&O stock is $46 per share.

Prepare the May 9 and June 2 journal entries and the December 31 adjusting entry. This is the first and only time the company purchased such securities.

QS 15-5
Identifying long-term investments
C1

Which of the following statements are true of long-term investments?

a. They can include investments in trading securities.
b. They are always easily sold and therefore qualify as being marketable.
c. They can include debt and equity securities available-for-sale.
d. They are held as an investment of cash available for current operations.
e. They can include debt securities held-to-maturity.
f. They can include bonds and stocks not intended to serve as a ready source of cash.
g. They can include funds earmarked for a special purpose, such as bond sinking funds.

QS 15-6
Describing investments in securities
C1 C2 C3

Complete the following descriptions by filling in the blanks.

1. Accrual of interest on bonds held as long-term investments requires a credit to ____ ____.
2. The controlling investor (more than 50% ownership) is called the ____, and the investee company is called the ____.
3. Trading securities are classified as ____ assets.
4. Equity securities giving an investor significant influence are accounted for using the ____ ____.
5. Available-for-sale debt securities are reported on the balance sheet at ____ ____.

QS 15-7
Debt securities transactions
C2 P2

On February 1, 2005, Charo Mendez purchased 6% bonds issued by CR Utilities at a cost of $30,000, which is their par value. The bonds pay interest semiannually on July 31 and January 31. For 2005, prepare entries to record the July 31 receipt of interest and the December 31 year-end interest accrual.

QS 15-8
Recording equity securities
C2 P3

On May 20, 2005, Allegra Co. paid $750,000 to acquire 25,000 common shares (10%) of TKR Corp. as a long-term investment. On August 5, 2006, Allegra sold one-half of these shares for $475,000. What valuation method should be used to account for this stock investment? Prepare entries to record both the acquisition and the sale of these shares.

QS 15-9
Equity method transactions
C2 P4

Assume the same facts as in QS 15-8 except that the stock acquired represents 40% of TKR Corp.'s outstanding stock. Also assume that TKR Corp. paid a $125,000 dividend on November 1, 2005, and reported a net income of $550,000 for 2005. Prepare the entries to record the receipt of the dividend and the December 31, 2005, year-end adjustment required for the investment account.

QS 15-10
Recording market adjustment for securities
P3

During the current year, Patton Consulting Group acquired long-term available-for-sale securities at a $35,000 cost. At its December 31 year-end, these securities had a market value of $29,000. This is the first and only time the company purchased such securities.

1. Prepare the necessary year-end adjusting entry related to these securities.
2. Explain how each account used in part 1 is reported in the financial statements.

QS 15-11
Return on total assets A1

How is return on total assets computed? What does this ratio reflect?

QS 15-12
Component return on total assets A1

Write the formula to separate the return on total assets into its components. Explain how components of the return on total assets are helpful to financial statement users.

QS 15-13[A]
Foreign currency transactions
P5

A U.S. company sells a British company a product with the transaction listed in British pounds. On the date of the sale, the transaction of $16,000 is billed as £10,000, reflecting an exchange rate of 1.60 (that is, $1.60 per pound). Prepare the entry to record (1) the sale and (2) the receipt of payment in pounds when the exchange rate is 1.50.

QS 15-14[A]
Foreign currency transactions
P5

On March 1, 2005, a U.S. company made a credit sale requiring payment in 30 days from a Malaysian company, Hamac Sdn. Bhd., in 20,000 Malaysian ringgits. Assuming the exchange rate between Malaysian ringgits and U.S. dollars is $0.6811 on March 1 and $0.6985 on March 31, prepare the entries to record the sale on March 1 and the cash receipt on March 31.

***Homework Manager** repeats all numerical Exercises on the book's Website with new numbers.*

EXERCISES

Exercise 15-1
Accounting for transactions in short-term securities
C2 P1 P2 P3

Prepare journal entries to record the following transactions involving the short-term securities investments of Smart Co., all of which occurred during year 2005:

a. On February 15, paid $100,000 cash to purchase FTR's 90-day short-term debt securities ($100,000 principal), dated February 15, that pay 8% interest (categorized as held-to-maturity securities).

b. On March 22, purchased 700 shares of FIX Company stock at $30 per share plus a $150 brokerage fee. These shares are categorized as trading securities.

c. On May 16, received a check from FTR in payment of the principal and 90 days' interest on the debt securities purchased in transaction *a*.

Check (c) Dr. Cash $102,000

d. On August 1, paid $60,000 cash to purchase Better Buy's 10% debt securities ($60,000 principal), dated July 30, 2005, and maturing January 30, 2006 (categorized as available-for-sale securities).

e. On September 1, received a $1.00 per share cash dividend on the FIX Company stock purchased in transaction *b*.

f. On October 8, sold 350 shares of FIX Co. stock for $40 per share, less a $140 brokerage fee.

(*f*) Dr. Cash $13,860

g. On October 30, received a check from Better Buy for 90 days' interest on the debt securities purchased in transaction *d*.

Exercise 15-2
Accounting for trading securities
C1 P1

Forex Co. purchases investments in trading securities at a cost of $56,000 on December 27, 2005. (This is its first and only purchase of such securities.) At December 31, 2005, these securities had a market value of $66,000.

1. Prepare the December 31, 2005, year-end adjusting entry for the trading securities' portfolio.

2. Explain how each account in the entry of part 1 is reported in financial statements.

3. Prepare the January 3, 2006, entry when Forex sells one-half of these securities for $30,000.

Check (3) Gain, $2,000

Exercise 15-3
Adjusting available-for-sale securities to market
C2 P3

On December 31, 2005, Rollo Company held the following short-term investments in its portfolio of available-for-sale securities. Rollo had no short-term investments in its prior accounting periods. Prepare the December 31, 2005, adjusting entry to report these investments at market value.

	Cost	Market Value
Vicks Corporation bonds payable	$79,600	$90,600
Pace Corporation notes payable	60,600	52,900
Lake Lugano Company common stock	85,500	82,100

Check Unrealized loss, $100

Exercise 15-4
Transactions in short- and long-term investments
C1 C2

Prepare journal entries to record the following transactions involving both the short- and long-term investments of Sophia Corp., all of which occurred during calendar year 2005. Use the account Short-Term Investments for any transactions that you determine are short term.

a. On February 15, paid $150,000 cash to purchase American General's 120-day short-term notes at par, which are dated February 15 and pay 10% interest (classified as held-to-maturity).

b. On March 22, bought 700 shares of Fran Industries common stock at $25 cash per share plus a $250 brokerage fee (classified as long-term available-for-sale securities).

c. On June 15, received a check from American General in payment of the principal and 120 days' interest on the notes purchased in transaction *a*.

d. On July 30, paid $50,000 cash to purchase MP3 Electronics' 8% notes at par, dated July 30, 2005, and maturing on January 30, 2006 (classified as trading securities).

e. On September 1, received a $0.50 per share cash dividend on the Fran Industries common stock purchased in transaction *b*.

f. On October 8, sold 350 shares of Fran Industries common stock for $32 cash per share, less a $175 brokerage fee.

g. On October 30, received a check from MP3 Electronics for three months' interest on the notes purchased in transaction *d*.

Exercise 15-5
Market adjustment to available-for-sale securities
P3

On December 31, 2005, Manhattan Co. held the following short-term available-for-sale securities:

	Cost	Market Value
Nintendo Co. common stock	$68,900	$75,300
Atlantic Richfield Co. bonds payable	24,500	22,800
Kellogg Co. notes payable	50,000	47,200
McDonald's Corp. common stock	91,400	86,600

Manhattan had no short-term investments prior to the current period. Prepare the December 31, 2005, year-end adjusting entry to record the market adjustment for these securities.

Exercise 15-6
Market adjustment to available-for-sale securities
P3

Berroa Co. began operations in 2004. The cost and market values for its long-term investments portfolio in available-for-sale securities are shown below. Prepare Berroa's December 31, 2005, adjusting entry to reflect any necessary market adjustment for these investments.

	Cost	Market Value
December 31, 2004	$79,483	$72,556
December 31, 2005	85,120	90,271

Exercise 15-7
Multi-year market adjustments to available-for-sale securities
P3 

Ticker Services began operations in 2003 and maintains long-term investments in available-for-sale securities. The year-end cost and market values for its portfolio of these investments follow. Prepare journal entries to record each year-end market adjustment for these securities.

	Cost	Market Value
December 31, 2003	$374,000	$362,560
December 31, 2004	426,900	453,200
December 31, 2005	580,700	686,450
December 31, 2006	875,500	778,800

Exercise 15-8
Classifying investments in securities; recording market values
C1 C2 P2 P3 P4 

Information regarding Central Company's individual investments in securities during its calendar-year 2005, with the December 31, 2005, market values, follows:

a. Investment in Beeman Company bonds: $418,500 cost, $455,000 market value. Central intends to hold these bonds until they mature in 2008.

b. Investment in Baybridge common stock: 29,500 shares; $332,450 cost; $361,375 market value. Central owns 32% of Baybridge's voting stock and has a significant influence over Baybridge.

c. Investment in Carrollton common stock: 12,000 shares; $169,750 cost; $183,000 market value. This investment amounts to 3% of Carrollton's outstanding shares, and Central's goal with this investment is to earn dividends over the next few years.

d. Investment in Newtech common stock: 3,500 shares; $95,300 cost; $93,625 market value. Central's goal with this investment is to reap an increase in market value of the stock over the next three to five years. Newtech has 30,000 common shares outstanding.

e. Investment in Flockhart common stock: 16,300 shares; $102,860 cost; $109,210 market value. This stock is marketable and is held as an investment of cash available for operations.

Identify whether each investment should be classified as a short-term or long-term investment. For each long-term investment, indicate in which of the long-term investment classifications it should be placed. Prepare a journal entry dated December 31, 2005, to record the market value adjustment of the long-term investments in available-for-sale securities. Central had no long-term investments prior to year 2005.

Check Unrealized gain, $11,575

Exercise 15-9
Securities transactions; equity method
P4 C2

Prepare journal entries to record the following transactions and events of Kash Company.

2005

Jan. 2	Purchased 30,000 shares of Bushtex Co. common stock for $204,000 cash plus a broker's fee of $3,480 cash. Bushtex has 90,000 shares of common stock outstanding and its policies will be significantly influenced by Kash.
Sept. 1	Bushtex declared and paid a cash dividend of $3.10 per share.
Dec. 31	Bushtex announced that net income for the year is $624,900.

2006

June 1	Bushtex declared and paid a cash dividend of $3.60 per share.
Dec. 31	Bushtex announced that net income for the year is $699,750.
Dec. 31	Kash sold 10,000 shares of Bushtex for $162,500 cash.

Exercise 15-10
Return on total assets
A1

The following information is available from the financial statements of Wright Industries. Compute Wright's return on total assets for 2005 and 2006. (Round percentages to one decimal place.) Comment on the company's efficiency in using its assets in 2005 and 2006.

	2004	2005	2006
Total assets, December 31	$190,000	$320,000	$750,000
Net income	28,200	36,400	58,300

Exercise 15-11[A]
Foreign currency transactions
P5

Desi of New York sells its products to customers in the United States and the United Kingdom. On December 16, 2005, Desi sold merchandise on credit to Bronson Ltd. of London at a price of 17,000 pounds. The exchange rate on that day for £1 was $1.5238. On December 31, 2005, when Desi prepared its financial statements, the rate was £1 for $1.4990. Bronson paid its bill in full on January 15, 2006, at which time the exchange rate was £1 for $1.5156. Desi immediately exchanged the 17,000 pounds for U.S. dollars. Prepare Desi's journal entries on December 16, December 31, and January 15 (round to the nearest dollar).

Exercise 15-12[A]
Computing foreign exchange gains and losses on receivables
C4 P5

On May 8, 2005, Jett Company (a U.S. company) made a credit sale to Lopez (a Mexican company). The terms of the sale required Lopez to pay 800,000 pesos on February 10, 2006. Jett prepares quarterly financial statements on March 31, June 30, September 30, and December 31. The exchange rates for pesos during the time the receivable is outstanding follow:

May 8, 2005	$0.1984
June 30, 2005	0.2013
September 30, 2005	0.2029
December 31, 2005	0.1996
February 10, 2006	0.2047

Compute the foreign exchange gain or loss that Jett should report on each of its quarterly income statements for the last three quarters of 2005 and the first quarter of 2006. Also compute the amount reported on Jett's balance sheets at the end of each of its last three quarters of 2005.

PROBLEM SET A

Problem 15-1A
Recording transactions and market adjustments for trading securities

C2 P1

Ryder Company, which began operations in 2005, invests its idle cash in trading securities. The following transactions are from its short-term investments in its trading securities:

2005

Jan. 20	Purchased 900 shares of Ford Motor Co. at $36 per share plus a $125 commission.
Feb. 9	Purchased 4,400 shares of Lucent at $10 per share plus a $200 commission.
Oct. 12	Purchased 500 shares of Z-Seven at $8 per share plus a $100 commission.

2006

Apr. 15	Sold 900 shares of Ford Motor Co. at $39 per share less a $185 commission.
July 5	Sold 500 shares of Z-Seven at $10.25 per share less a $100 commission.
22	Purchased 800 shares of Hunt Corp. at $30 per share plus a $225 commission.
Aug. 19	Purchased 1,000 shares of Donna Karan at $12 per share plus a $100 commission.

2007

Feb. 27	Purchased 3,400 shares of HCA at $22 per share plus a $220 commission.
Mar. 3	Sold 800 shares of Hunt at $25 per share less a $125 commission.
June 21	Sold 4,400 shares of Lucent at $8 per share less a $180 commission.
30	Purchased 1,000 shares of Black & Decker at $47.50 per share plus a $195 commission.
Nov. 1	Sold 1,000 shares of Donna Karan at $22 per share less a $208 commission.

Required

1. Prepare journal entries to record these short-term investment activities for the years shown. (Ignore any year-end adjusting entries.)

Check (2) Dr. Market Adjustment—Trading $2,385

2. On December 31, 2007, prepare the adjusting entry to record any necessary market adjustment for the portfolio of trading securities when HCA's share price is $24 and Black & Decker's share price is $43.50. (The Market Adjustment—Trading account had an unadjusted balance of zero.)

Problem 15-2A
Recording, adjusting, and reporting short-term available-for-sale securities

C2 P3

Perry Company had no short-term investments prior to year 2005. It had the following transactions involving short-term investments in available-for-sale securities during 2005:

Apr. 16	Purchased 8,000 shares of Gem Co. stock at $24.25 per share plus a $360 brokerage fee.
May 1	Paid $200,000 to buy 90-day U.S. Treasury bills (debt securities): $200,000 principal amount, 6% interest, securities dated May 1.
July 7	Purchased 4,000 shares of PepsiCo stock at $49.25 per share plus a $350 brokerage fee.
20	Purchased 2,000 shares of Xerox stock at $16.75 per share plus a $410 brokerage fee.
Aug. 3	Received a check for principal and accrued interest on the U.S. Treasury bills that matured on July 29.
15	Received an $0.85 per share cash dividend on the Gem Co. stock.
28	Sold 4,000 shares of Gem Co. stock at $30 per share less a $450 brokerage fee.
Oct. 1	Received a $1.90 per share cash dividend on the PepsiCo shares.
Dec. 15	Received a $1.05 per share cash dividend on the remaining Gem Co. shares.
31	Received a $1.30 per share cash dividend on the PepsiCo shares.

Required

1. Prepare journal entries to record the preceding transactions and events.

Check (2) Cost = $328,440

2. Prepare a table to compare the cost and market values of Perry's short-term investments in available-for-sale securities. The year-end market values per share are Gem Co., $26.50; PepsiCo, $46.50; and Xerox, $13.75.

(3) Dr. Unrealized Loss—Equity $8,940

3. Prepare an adjusting entry, if necessary, to record the market adjustment for the portfolio of short-term investments in available-for-sale securities.

Analysis Component

4. Explain the balance sheet presentation of a market adjustment for these short-term investments.

5. How do these short-term investments affect Perry's (*a*) income statement for year 2005 and (*b*) the equity section of its balance sheet at year-end 2005?

Problem 15-3A
Recording, adjusting, and reporting long-term available-for-sale securities
C2 P3

Shaq Security, which began operations in 2005, invests in long-term available-for-sale securities. Following is a series of transactions and events determining its long-term investment activity:

2005

Jan. 20 Purchased 900 shares of Johnson & Johnson at $18.75 per share plus a $590 commission.
Feb. 9 Purchased 2,200 shares of Sony at $46.88 per share plus a $2,578 commission.
June 12 Purchased 500 shares of Mattel at $55.50 per share plus a $832 commission.
Dec. 31 Per share market values for stocks in the portfolio are Johnson & Johnson, $20.38; Mattel, $57.25; Sony, $39.00.

2006

Apr. 15 Sold 900 shares of Johnson & Johnson at $21.75 per share less a $685 commission.
July 5 Sold 500 shares of Mattel at $49.13 per share less a $491 commission.
July 22 Purchased 1,600 shares of Sara Lee at $36.25 per share plus a $1,740 commission.
Aug. 19 Purchased 1,800 shares of Eastman Kodak at $28.00 per share plus a $1,260 commission.
Dec. 31 Per share market values for stocks in the portfolio are Kodak, $31.75; Sara Lee, $30.00; Sony, $36.50.

2007

Feb. 27 Purchased 3,400 shares of Microsoft at $23.63 per share plus a $1,606 commission.
June 21 Sold 2,200 shares of Sony at $40.00 per share less an $2,640 commission.
June 30 Purchased 1,200 shares of Black & Decker at $47.50 per share plus a $1,995 commission.
Aug. 3 Sold 1,600 shares of Sara Lee at $31.25 per share less a $1,750 commission.
Nov. 1 Sold 1,800 shares of Eastman Kodak at $42.75 per share less a $2,309 commission.
Dec. 31 Per share market values for stocks in the portfolio are Black & Decker, $56.50; Microsoft, $28.00.

Required

1. Prepare journal entries to record these transactions and events and any year-end market adjustments to the portfolio of long-term available-for-sale securities.

2. Prepare a table that summarizes the (*a*) total cost, (*b*) total market adjustment, and (*c*) total market value of the portfolio of long-term available-for-sale securities at each year-end.

3. Prepare a table that summarizes (*a*) the realized gains and losses and (*b*) the unrealized gains or losses for the portfolio of long-term available-for-sale securities at each year-end.

Check (2b) Market adjustment: 12/31/05, $(18,994); 12/31/06; $(31,664)

(3b) Unrealized Gain for 2007, $22,057

Problem 15-4A
Long-term investment transactions; unrealized and realized gains and losses
C2 C3 P3 P4

Park Co.'s long-term available-for-sale portfolio at December 31, 2004, consists of the following:

Available-for-Sale Securities	Cost	Market Value
80,000 shares of Company A common stock	$1,070,600	$ 980,000
14,000 shares of Company B common stock	318,750	308,000
35,000 shares of Company C common stock	1,325,500	1,281,875

Park enters into the following long-term investment transactions during year 2005.

Jan. 29 Sold 7,000 shares of Company B common stock for $158,375 less a brokerage fee of $3,100.
Apr. 17 Purchased 20,000 shares of Company W common stock for $395,000 plus a brokerage fee of $6,800. The shares represent a 30% ownership in Company W.
July 6 Purchased 9,000 shares of Company X common stock for $253,125 plus a brokerage fee of $3,500. The shares represent a 10% ownership in Company X.
Aug. 22 Purchased 100,000 shares of Company Y common stock for $750,000 plus a brokerage fee of $8,200. The shares represent a 51% ownership in Company Y.
Nov. 13 Purchased 17,000 shares of Company Z common stock for $533,800 plus a brokerage fee of $6,900. The shares represent a 5% ownership in Company Z.
Dec. 9 Sold 80,000 shares of Company A common stock for $1,030,000 less a brokerage fee of $4,100.

The market values of its investments at December 31, 2005, are B, $162,750; C, $1,220,625; W, $382,500; X, $236,250; Y, $1,062,500; Z, $557,600.

Required

1. Determine the amount Park should report on its December 31, 2005, balance sheet for its long-term investments in available-for-sale securities.

Check (2) Cr. Unrealized Gain—Equity, $40,000

2. Prepare any necessary December 31, 2005, adjusting entry to record the market value adjustment for the long-term investments in available-for-sale securities.
3. What amount of gains or losses on transactions relating to long-term investments in available-for-sale securities should Park report on its December 31, 2005, income statement?

Problem 15-5A
Accounting for long-term investments in securities; with and without significant influence

C2 P3 P4

Pillar Steel Co., which began operations on January 4, 2005, had the following subsequent transactions and events in its long-term investments:

2005

Jan. 5 Pillar purchased 30,000 shares (20%) of Kildaire's common stock for $780,000.
Oct. 23 Kildaire declared and paid a cash dividend of $1.60 per share.
Dec. 31 Kildaire's net income for 2005 is $582,000, and the market value of its stock at December 31 is $27.75 per share.

2006

Oct. 15 Kildaire declared and paid a cash dividend of $1.30 per share.
Dec. 31 Kildaire's net income for 2006 is $738,000, and the market value of its stock at December 31 is $30.45 per share.

2007

Jan. 2 Pillar sold all of its investment in Kildaire for $947,000 cash.

Part 1

Assume that Pillar has a significant influence over Kildaire with its 20% share of stock.

Required

1. Prepare journal entries to record these transactions and events for Pillar.

Check (2) Carrying value per share, $31.90

2. Compute the carrying (book) value per share of Pillar's investment in Kildaire common stock as reflected in the investment account on January 1, 2007.
3. Compute the net increase or decrease in Pillar's equity from January 5, 2005, through January 2, 2007, resulting from its investment in Kildaire.

Part 2

Assume that although Pillar owns 20% of Kildaire's outstanding stock, circumstances indicate that it does not have a significant influence over the investee and that it is classified as an available-for-sale security investment.

Required

(1) 1/2/07 Dr. Unrealized Gain—Equity $133,500

1. Prepare journal entries to record the preceding transactions and events for Pillar. Also prepare an entry dated January 2, 2007, to remove any balance related to the market adjustment.
2. Compute the cost per share of Pillar's investment in Kildaire common stock as reflected in the investment account on January 1, 2007.

(3) Net increase, $254,000

3. Compute the net increase or decrease in Pillar's equity from January 5, 2005, through January 2, 2007, resulting from its investment in Kildaire.

Problem 15-6A[A]
Foreign currency transactions

C4 P5

Roundtree Co., a U.S. corporation with customers in several foreign countries, had these selected transactions for 2005 and 2006:

2005

Apr. 8 Sold merchandise to Salinas & Sons of Mexico for $7,938 cash. The exchange rate for pesos is $0.1323 on this day.
July 21 Sold merchandise on credit to Sumito Corp. in Japan. The price of 1.5 million yen is to be paid 120 days from the date of sale. The exchange rate for yen is $0.0096 on this day.

Oct. 14 Sold merchandise for 19,000 pounds to Smithers Ltd. of Great Britain, payment in full to be received in 90 days. The exchange rate for pounds is $1.5181 on this day.

Nov. 18 Received Sumito's payment in yen for its July 21 purchase and immediately exchanged the yen for dollars. The exchange rate for yen is $0.0091 on this day.

Dec. 20 Sold merchandise for 17,000 ringgits to Hamid Albar of Malaysia, payment in full to be received in 30 days. On this day, the exchange rate for ringgits is $0.6852.

Dec. 31 Recorded adjusting entries to recognize exchange gains or losses on Roundtree's annual financial statements. Rates for exchanging foreign currencies on this day follow:

Pesos (Mexico)	$0.1335
Yen (Japan)	0.0095
Pounds (Britain)	1.5235
Ringgits (Malaysia)	0.6807

2006

Jan. 12 Received full payment in pounds from Smithers for the October 14 sale and immediately exchanged the pounds for dollars. The exchange rate for pounds is $1.5314 on this day.

Jan. 19 Received Hamid Albar's full payment in ringgits for the December 20 sale and immediately exchanged the ringgits for dollars. The exchange rate for ringgits is $0.6771 on this day.

Required

1. Prepare journal entries for the Roundtree transactions and adjusting entries (round amounts to the dollar).
2. Compute the foreign exchange gain or loss to be reported on Roundtree's 2005 income statement.

Check (2) 2005 total foreign exchange loss, $723

Analysis Component

3. What actions might Roundtree consider to reduce its risk of foreign exchange gains or losses?

PROBLEM SET B

Problem 15-1B
Recording transactions and market adjustments for trading securities
C2 P1

Deal Co., which began operations in 2005, invests its idle cash in trading securities. The following transactions relate to its short-term investments in its trading securities.

2005

Mar. 10 Purchased 1,200 shares of AOL at $59.15 per share plus a $773 commission.
May 7 Purchased 2,500 shares of MTV at $36.25 per share plus a $1,428 commission.
Sept. 1 Purchased 600 shares of UPS at $57.25 per share plus a $625 commission.

2006

Apr. 26 Sold 2,500 shares of MTV at $34.50 per share less a $1,025 commission.
27 Sold 600 shares of UPS at $60.50 per share less a $894 commission.
June 2 Purchased 1,800 shares of SPW at $172 per share plus a $1,625 commission.
14 Purchased 450 shares of Wal-Mart at $50.25 per share plus a $541.50 commission.

2007

Jan. 28 Purchased 1,000 shares of PepsiCo at $43 per share plus a $1,445 commission.
31 Sold 1,800 shares of SPW at $168 per share less a $1,020 commission.
Aug. 22 Sold 1,200 shares of AOL at $56.75 per share less a $1,240 commission.
Sept. 3 Purchased 750 shares of Vodaphone at $40.50 per share plus a $840 commission.
Oct. 9 Sold 450 shares of Wal-Mart at $53.75 per share less a $610.50 commission.

Required

1. Prepare journal entries to record these short-term investment activities for the years shown. (Ignore any year-end adjusting entries.)
2. On December 31, 2007, prepare the adjusting entry to record any necessary market adjustment for the portfolio of trading securities when PepsiCo's share price is $41 and Vodaphone's share price is $37. (The Market Adjustment—Trading account had an unadjusted balance of zero.)

Check (2) Cr. Market Adjustment—Trading $6,910

Problem 15-2B
Recording, adjusting, and reporting short-term available-for-sale securities

Day Systems had no short-term investments prior to 2005. It had the following transactions involving short-term investments in available-for-sale securities during 2005.

Feb. 6 Purchased 1,700 shares of Nokia stock at $41.25 per share plus a $1,500 brokerage fee.
15 Paid $10,000 to buy six-month U.S. Treasury bills (debt securities): $10,000 principal amount, 6% interest, securities dated February 15.
Apr. 7 Purchased 600 shares of Dell Co. stock at $39.50 per share plus a $627 brokerage fee.
June 2 Purchased 1,250 shares of Merck stock at $72.50 per share plus a $1,945 brokerage fee.
30 Received a $0.19 per share cash dividend on the Nokia shares.
Aug. 11 Sold 425 shares of Nokia stock at $46 per share less a $525 brokerage fee.
16 Received a check for principal and accrued interest on the U.S. Treasury bills purchased February 15.
24 Received a $0.10 per share cash dividend on the Dell shares.
Nov. 9 Received a $0.20 per share cash dividend on the remaining Nokia shares.
Dec. 18 Received a $0.15 per share cash dividend on the Dell shares.

Required

1. Prepare journal entries to record the preceding transactions and events.

Check (2) Cost = $170,616

2. Prepare a table to compare the cost and market values of the short-term investments in available-for-sale securities. The year-end market values per share are Nokia, $40.25; Dell, $41; and Merck, $59.

(3) Dr. Unrealized Loss—Equity, $20,947

3. Prepare an adjusting entry, if necessary, to record the market adjustment for the portfolio of short-term investments in available-for-sale securities.

Analysis Component

4. Explain the balance sheet presentation of a market adjustment to these short-term investments.

5. How do these short-term investments affect (*a*) its income statement for year 2005 and (*b*) the equity section of its balance sheet at the 2005 year-end?

Problem 15-3B
Recording, adjusting, and reporting long-term available-for-sale securities

C2 P3

Venice Enterprises, which began operations in 2005, invests in long-term available-for-sale securities. Following is a series of transactions and events involving its long-term investment activity:

2005

Mar. 10 Purchased 2,400 shares of Apple Computer at $33.25 per share plus $1,995 commission.
Apr. 7 Purchased 5,000 shares of Ford at $17.50 per share plus $2,625 commission.
Sept. 1 Purchased 1,200 shares of Polaroid at $49.00 per share plus $1,176 commission.
Dec. 31 Per share market values for stocks in the portfolio are Apple, $35.50; Ford, $17.00; Polaroid, $51.75.

2006

Apr. 26 Sold 5,000 shares of Ford at $16.38 per share less a $2,237 commission.
June 2 Purchased 3,600 shares of Duracell at $18.88 per share plus a $2,312 commission.
June 14 Purchased 900 shares of Sears at $24.50 per share plus a $541 commission.
Nov. 27 Sold 1,200 shares of Polaroid at $52 per share less a $1,672 commission.
Dec. 31 Per share market values for stocks in the portfolio are Apple, $35.50; Duracell, $18.00; Sears, $26.00.

2007

Jan. 28 Purchased 2,000 shares of Coca-Cola Co. at $41 per share plus a $3,280 commission.
Aug. 22 Sold 2,400 shares of Apple at $29.75 per share less a $2,339 commission.
Sept. 3 Purchased 1,500 shares of Motorola at $29.00 per share plus an $870 commission.
Oct. 9 Sold 900 shares of Sears at $27.50 per share less a $619 commission.
Oct. 31 Sold 3,600 shares of Duracell at $16.00 per share less a $1,496 commission.
Dec. 31 Per share market values for stocks in the portfolio are Coca-Cola, $46.00; Motorola, $22.00.

Required

1. Prepare journal entries to record these transactions and events and any year-end market adjustments to the portfolio of long-term available-for-sale securities.

2. Prepare a table that summarizes the (*a*) total cost, (*b*) total market adjustment, and (*c*) total market value for the portfolio of long-term available-for-sale securities at each year-end.

3. Prepare a table that summarizes (*a*) the realized gains and losses and (*b*) the unrealized gains or losses for the portfolio of long-term available-for-sale securities at each year-end.

Check (2b) Market adjustment: 12/31/05, $404; 12/31/06, $(1,266)

(3b) Unrealized loss for 2007, $4,650

Problem 15-4B
Long-term investment transactions; unrealized and realized gains and losses
C2 C3 P3 P4

Capollo's long-term available-for-sale portfolio at December 31, 2004, consists of the following:

Available-for-Sale Securities	Cost	Market Value
45,000 shares of Company R common stock	$1,118,250	$1,198,125
17,000 shares of Company S common stock	616,760	586,500
22,000 shares of Company T common stock	294,470	303,600

Capollo enters into the following long-term investment transactions during year 2005:

Jan. 13 Sold 4,250 shares of Company S common stock for $144,500 less a brokerage fee of $2,390.

Mar. 24 Purchased 31,000 shares of Company U common stock for $565,750 plus a brokerage fee of $9,900. The shares represent a 62% ownership in Company U.

Apr. 5 Purchased 85,000 shares of Company V common stock for $267,750 plus a brokerage fee of $4,500. The shares represent a 10% ownership in Company V.

Sept. 2 Sold 22,000 shares of Company T common stock for $313,500 less a brokerage fee of $5,400.

Sept. 27 Purchased 5,000 shares of Company W common stock for $101,000 plus a brokerage fee of $2,100. The shares represent a 25% ownership in Company W.

Oct. 30 Purchased 10,000 shares of Company X common stock for $97,500 plus a brokerage fee of $2,340. The shares represent a 13% ownership in Company X.

The market values of its investments at December 31, 2005, are R, $1,136,250; S, $420,750; U, $545,600; V, $269,875; W, $109,375; X, $91,250.

Required

1. Determine the amount Capollo should report on its December 31, 2005, balance sheet for its long-term investments in available-for-sale securities.

2. Prepare any necessary December 31, 2005, adjusting entry to record the market value adjustment of the long-term investments in available-for-sale securities.

3. What amount of gains or losses on transactions relating to long-term investments in available-for-sale securities should Capollo report on its December 31, 2005, income statement?

Check (2) Dr. Unrealized Loss—Equity, $34,785; Cr. Market Adjustment, $93,530

Problem 15-5B
Accounting for long-term investments in securities; with and without significant influence
C2 P3 P4

Bengal Company, which began operations on January 3, 2005, had the following subsequent transactions and events in its long-term investments.

2005

Jan. 5 Bengal purchased 15,000 shares (25%) of Bloch's common stock for $187,500.
Aug. 1 Bloch declared and paid a cash dividend of $0.95 per share.
Dec. 31 Bloch's net income for 2005 is $92,000, and the market value of its stock is $12.90 per share.

2006

Aug. 1 Bloch declared and paid a cash dividend of $1.25 per share.
Dec. 31 Bloch's net income for 2006 is $76,000, and the market value of its stock is $13.55 per share.

2007

Jan. 8 Bengal sold all of its investment in Bloch for $204,750 cash.

Part 1

Assume that Bengal has a significant influence over Bloch with its 25% share.

Required

1. Prepare journal entries to record these transactions and events for Bengal.

Check (2) Carrying value per share, $13.10

2. Compute the carrying (book) value per share of Bengal's investment in Bloch common stock as reflected in the investment account on January 7, 2007.

3. Compute the net increase or decrease in Bengal's equity from January 5, 2005, through January 8, 2007, resulting from its investment in Bloch.

Part 2

Assume that although Bengal owns 25% of Bloch's outstanding stock, circumstances indicate that it does not have a significant influence over the investee and that it is classified as an available-for-sale security investment.

Required

(1) 1/8/07 Dr. Unrealized Gain—Equity $15,750

1. Prepare journal entries to record these transactions and events for Bengal. Also prepare an entry dated January 8, 2007, to remove any balance related to the market adjustment.

2. Compute the cost per share of Bengal's investment in Bloch common stock as reflected in the investment account on January 7, 2007.

(3) Net increase, $50,250

3. Compute the net increase or decrease in Bengal's equity from January 5, 2005, through January 8, 2007, resulting from its investment in Bloch.

Problem 15-6B[A]
Foreign currency transactions
C4 P5

Datamix, a U.S. corporation with customers in several foreign countries, had these selected transactions for 2005 and 2006:

2005

May 26 Sold merchandise for 6.5 million yen to Fuji Company of Japan, payment in full to be received in 60 days. On this day, the exchange rate for yen is $0.0094.

June 1 Sold merchandise to Fordham Ltd. of Great Britain for $72,613 cash. The exchange rate for pounds is $1.5277 on this day.

July 25 Received Fuji's payment in yen for its May 26 purchase and immediately exchanged the yen for dollars. The exchange rate for yen is $0.0090 on this day.

Oct. 15 Sold merchandise on credit to Martinez Brothers of Mexico. The price of 373,000 pesos is to be paid 90 days from the date of sale. On this day, the exchange rate for pesos is $0.1340.

Dec. 6 Sold merchandise for 242,000 yuans to Chi-Ying Company of China, payment in full to be received in 30 days. The exchange rate for yuans is $0.1975 on this day.

Dec. 31 Recorded adjusting entries to recognize exchange gains or losses on Datamix's annual financial statements. Rates of exchanging foreign currencies on this day follow:

Yen (Japan)	$0.0094
Pounds (Britain)	1.5318
Pesos (Mexico)	0.1560
Yuans (China)	0.2000

2006

Jan. 5 Received Chi-Ying's full payment in yuans for the December 6 sale and immediately exchanged the yuans for dollars. The exchange rate for yuans is $0.2060 on this day.

Jan. 13 Received full payment in pesos from Martinez for the October 15 sale and immediately exchanged the pesos for dollars. The exchange rate for pesos is $0.1420 on this day.

Required

1. Prepare journal entries for the Datamix transactions and adjusting entries.

Check 2005 total foreign exchange gain, $6,211

2. Compute the foreign exchange gain or loss to be reported on Datamix's 2005 income statement.

Analysis Component

3. What actions might Datamix consider to reduce its risk of foreign exchange gains or losses?

PROBLEM SET C

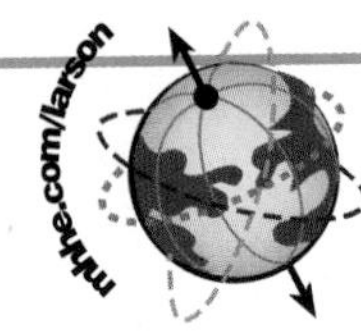

Problem Set C is available at the book's Website to reinforce and assess your learning.

SERIAL PROBLEM

Success Systems

(This serial problem began in Chapter 1 and continues through most of the book. If previous chapter segments were not completed, the serial problem can begin at this point. It is helpful, but not necessary, for you to use the Working Papers that accompany the book.)

While reviewing the March 31, 2005, balance sheet of Success Systems, Kay Breeze notes that the business has built a large cash balance of $77,845. Its most recent bank money market statement shows that the funds are earning an annualized return of 0.75%. Breeze decides to make several investments with the desire to earn a higher return on the idle cash balance. Accordingly, in April 2005, Success Systems makes the following investments in trading securities:

April 16 Purchases 200 shares of Johnson & Johnson stock at $55 per share plus $240 commission.
April 30 Purchases 100 shares of Starbucks Corporation at $24 per share plus $120 commission.

On June 30, 2005, the per share market price of the Johnson & Johnson shares is $60 and the Starbucks shares is $21.

Required

1. Prepare journal entries to record the April purchases of trading securities.
2. On June 30, 2005, prepare the adjusting entry to record any necessary market adjustment to its portfolio of trading securities.

BEYOND THE NUMBERS

REPORTING IN ACTION

C3 C4 A1 

BTN 15-1 Refer to **Krispy Kreme**'s financial statements in Appendix A to answer the following:

1. Are Krispy Kreme's financial statements consolidated? How can you tell?
2. What is Krispy Kreme's *comprehensive income* for the year ended February 2, 2003?
3. Does Krispy Kreme have any foreign operations? How can you tell?
4. Compute Krispy Kreme's return on total assets for the year ended February 2, 2003.

Roll On

5. Access Krispy Kreme's annual report for a fiscal year ending after February 2, 2003, from either its Website (**KrispyKreme.Com**) or the SEC's EDGAR database (**www.SEC.gov**). Recompute Krispy Kreme's return on total assets for the years subsequent to February 2, 2003.

COMPARATIVE ANALYSIS

A1 

BTN 15-2 Key comparative figures ($ millions) for **Krispy Kreme** and **Tastykake** follow:

	Krispy Kreme			Tastykake		
Key Figures	Current Year	1 Year Prior	2 Years Prior	Current Year	1 Year Prior	2 Years Prior
Net income	$ 33,478	$ 26,378	$ 14,725	$ 2,000*	$ 8,048*	$ 8,144
Net sales	491,549	394,354	300,715	162,263	166,245	162,877
Total assets	410,487	255,376	171,493	116,560	116,137	112,192

* Restructuring charges are removed from income.

Required

1. Compute return on total assets for Krispy Kreme and Tastykake for the two most recent years.
2. Separate the return on total assets computed in part 1 into its components for both companies and both years according to the formula in Exhibit 15.9.
3. Which company has the higher total return on assets? The higher profit margin? The higher total asset turnover? What does this comparative analysis reveal?

ETHICS CHALLENGE

C2 P2 P3

BTN 15-3 Kendra Wecker is the controller for Wildcat Company, which has numerous long-term investments in debt securities. Wildcat's investments are mainly in 10-year bonds. Wecker is preparing its year-end financial statements. In accounting for long-term debt securities, she knows that each long-term investment must be designated as a held-to-maturity or an available-for-sale security.

Interest rates rose sharply this past year causing the portfolio's market value to substantially decline. The company does not intend to hold the bonds for the entire 10 years. Wecker also earns a bonus each year, which is computed as a percent of net income.

Required

1. Will Wecker's bonus depend in any way on the classification of the debt securities?
2. What criteria must Wecker use to classify the securities as held-to-maturity or available-for-sale?
3. Is there likely any company oversight of Wecker's classification of the securities?

COMMUNICATING IN PRACTICE

C2 P4

BTN 15-4 Assume that you are Jackson Company's accountant. Company owner Abel Terrio has reviewed the 2006 financial statements you prepared and questions the $6,000 loss reported on the sale of its investment in Blackhawk Co. common stock. Jackson acquired 50,000 shares of Blackhawk's common stock on December 31, 2004, at a cost of $500,000. This stock purchase represented a 40% interest in Blackhawk. The 2005 income statement reported that earnings from all investments were $126,000. On January 3, 2006, Jackson Company sold the Blackhawk stock for $575,000. Blackhawk did not pay any dividends during 2005 but reported a net income of $202,500 for that year. Terrio believes that because the Blackhawk stock purchase price was $500,000 and was sold for $575,000, the 2006 income statement should report a $75,000 gain on the sale.

Required

Draft a one-half page memorandum to Terrio explaining why the $6,000 loss on sale of Blackhawk stock is correctly reported.

TAKING IT TO THE NET

C1 C2

mhhe.com/larson

BTN 15-5 Access the September 6, 2002, 10-K filing (for year-end June 30, 2002) of **Microsoft** (MSFT) at www.SEC.gov. Review footnote 4, "Cash and Short-term Investments."

Required

1. How does the total for cash and short-term investments held as of June 30, 2002, compare to the prior year-end amount?
2. Identify the five types of short-term investments held by Microsoft as of June 30, 2002.
3. What were Microsoft's gains and losses from cash and short-term investments sold in 2002?
4. Was the cost or market of the short-term investments higher as of June 30, 2002?

TEAMWORK IN ACTION

C1 C2 C3 P1 P2 P3 P4

BTN 15-6 Each team member is to become an expert on a specific classification of long-term investments. This expertise will be used to facilitate other teammates' understanding of the concepts and procedures relevent to the classification chosen.

1. Each team member must select an area for expertise by choosing one of the following classifications of long-term investments.
   a. Held-to-maturity debt securities
   b. Available-for-sale debt and equity securities
   c. Equity securities with significant influence
   d. Equity securities with controlling influence
2. Learning teams are to disburse and expert teams are to be formed. Expert teams are made up of those who select the same area of expertise. The instructor will identify the location where each expert team will meet.
3. Expert teams will collaborate to develop a presentation based on the following requirements. Students must write the presentation in a format they can show to their learning teams in part (4).

Requirements for Expert Presentation

a. Write a transaction for the acquisition of this type of investment security. The transaction description is to include all necessary data to reflect the chosen classification.

b. Prepare the journal entry to record the acquisition.

   [*Note:* The expert team on equity securities with controlling influence will substitute requirements (*d*) and (*e*) with a discussion of the reporting of these investments.]

c. Identify information necessary to complete the end-of-period adjustment for this investment.

d. Assuming that this is the only investment owned, prepare any necessary year-end entries.

e. Present the relevant balance sheet section(s).

4. Re-form learning teams. In rotation, experts are to present to their teams the presentations they developed in part 3. Experts are to encourage and respond to questions.

BUSINESS WEEK ACTIVITY

C2

mhhe.com/larson

BTN 15-7 Read the article "Accounting: Bringing the Future into Play" in the March 11, 2002, issue of *Business Week*. (This book's Website provides a free link.)

Required

1. On what types of data do accountants focus? How does this compare with the data desired by investors?

2. Explain the phrase "marking to market."

3. What ideas have been proposed to allow marking to market that will also limit fraud by insiders?

4. How do accountants respond to the economists' argument that mark-to-market accounting will result in "asymmetrical" information for investors?

5. What is the best argument for mark-to-market accounting?

ENTREPRENEURIAL DECISION

C1 C2 P3  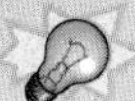

BTN 15-8 Bill and Ralph Cruz, of **TradeStation Group**, know it is important for their clients to understand the accounting rules for recognizing gains and losses on investments in securities. Several clients, with little experience in investing, recently expressed confusion in the difference between unrealized and realized gains and losses. They also expressed concern about the low yields on their certificate of deposit (CD) investments and inquired about investment alternatives.

Required

1. Assume that you are an assistant to Ralph Cruz. He asks you to prepare a brief email to his business client Andy Iglesias of Iglesias Company, explaining the difference between unrealized and realized gains and losses on securities. Prepare this email.

2. If the client, Iglesias Company, purchases available-for-sale securities, will any unrealized gains or losses on those securities affect its income statement? Explain.

3. Cruz asks you to email another client, Gloria Perez, explaining the benefits of long-term investments in stocks rather than CDs. Prepare this brief email.

HITTING THE ROAD C4

BTN 15-9^A Assume that you are planning a spring break trip to Europe. Identify three locations where you can find exchange rates for the dollar relative to the Euro or other currencies.

GLOBAL DECISION

A1 

BTN 15-10 **Grupo Bimbo**, **Krispy Kreme**, and **Tastykake** are competitors in the global marketplace.

	Grupo Bimbo (millions of pesos)			Krispy Kreme		Tastykake	
Key Figure	Current Year	One Year Prior	Two Years Prior	Current Year	Prior Year	Current Year	Prior Year
Net income	1,002.7	1,682.0	2,004.9	—	—	—	—
Total assets	31,718.6	23,781.3	25,035.1	—	—	—	—
Net sales	41,373.3	34,968.1	32,007.8	—	—	—	—
Profit margin	?	?	—	6.80%	6.70%	1.20%	4.80%
Total asset turnover	?	?	—	1.48	1.85	1.39	1.46

Required

1. Compute Grupo Bimbo's return on total assets for the most recent two years using the data shown.

2. Which of these three companies has the highest return on total assets? Profit margin? Total asset turnover?

"The most important thing I've learned is to wait out the [cash] storm"—Chance Roth

16 Reporting the Statement of Cash Flows

A Look Back

Chapter 15 focused on investments in securities. We explained how to identify, account for, and report investments in both debt and equity securities. We also introduced foreign exchange rates and described accounting for transactions listed in a foreign currency.

A Look at This Chapter

This chapter focuses on reporting and analyzing cash inflows and cash outflows. We emphasize how to prepare and interpret the statement of cash flows.

A Look Ahead

Chapter 17 focuses on tools to help us analyze financial statements. We also describe comparative analysis and the application of ratios for financial analysis.

CAP

Conceptual

C1 Explain the purpose and importance of cash flow information. *(p. 626)*

C2 Distinguish among operating, investing, and financing activities. *(p. 627)*

C3 Identify and disclose noncash investing and financing activities. *(p. 628)*

C4 Describe the format of the statement of cash flows. *(p. 629)*

Analytical

A1 Analyze the statement of cash flows. *(p. 643)*

A2 Compute and apply the cash flow on total assets ratio. *(p. 644)*

Procedural

P1 Prepare a statement of cash flows. *(p. 630)*

P2 Compute cash flows from operating activities using the indirect method. *(p. 634)*

P3 Determine cash flows from both investing and financing activities. *(p. 639)*

Decision Feature

Cashing In with the Toy Biz

SAN DIEGO—Cash may not be king, but it is crucial to the king's survival. Just ask Chance Roth, the young owner of **Atomic Toys (AtomicToys.com)**, an upstart toy designer, manufacturer, and distributor. He opened Atomic Toys's doors in 1999, and its revenues are projected to reach $4 million this year. Yet all was not easy; cash flow was a constant battle, especially in the beginning. While the toy biz can be wild and crazy, Roth says he had to change "from the wild-eyed, creative entrepreneur into a street-smart businessman." This meant keeping a watchful eye on cash flows, especially those from operating activities. Adds Roth, "There comes a time when you realize it's not Monopoly money anymore."

Roth learned that a start-up could produce sales at the same time its cash is running short—a common and constant struggle. "We couldn't physically manufacture enough product to satisfy the demand," says Roth. "Our product was flying off the shelf." Exploding sales meant increasing cash outflows for manufacturing and distribution. Roth says he had to carefully monitor the cash flows associated with each of the operating, investing, and financing activities. With cash under control, says Roth, "now we're poised to capitalize on that [sales] success."

Roth continues to closely scrutinize and personally oversee cash flows. "For me to take the company where it needs to go," he says, "I've got to continually step up to the plate and make it happen." Cash flow responsibility is one of those steps. This chapter focuses on cash flow: its measurement, presentation, analysis, and interpretation. It describes the importance of separately analyzing cash flows according to operating, investing, and financing activities.

Roth knows first-hand the importance of cash flow information, especially for start-ups. "It's going to be very, very difficult for at least the first two or three years," he adds. "But by just sticking it out and letting the waves crash and pound while steadily making progress," the company will win the battle of cash flows. Cash analysis demands serious attention and work. However, says Roth, "We all have to grow up sometime—even in toys!"

[Sources: *Atomic Toys Website,* January 2004; *Entrepreneur,* May 2003; *Playthings,* February, 2002 and 2003.]

Profitability is a main goal of most managers, but not the only goal. A company cannot achieve or maintain profits without carefully managing cash. Managers and other users of information pay close attention to a company's cash position and the events and transactions affecting cash. Information about cash events and transactions is reported in the statement of cash flows. This chapter explains how we prepare, analyze, and interpret a statement of cash flows. It also discusses the importance of cash flow information for predicting future performance and making managerial decisions. More generally, effectively using the statement of cash flows is crucial for managing and analyzing the operating, investing, and financing activities of businesses.

Reporting the Statement of Cash Flows

Basics of Cash Flow Reporting
- Purpose
- Importance
- Measurement
- Classification
- Noncash activities
- Format
- Preparation

Cash Flows from Operating
- Indirect and direct methods of reporting
- Application of indirect method of reporting
- Summary of indirect method adjustments

Cash Flows from Investing
- Three-stage process of analysis
- Analysis of noncurrent assets
- Analysis of other assets

Cash Flows from Financing
- Three-stage process of analysis
- Analysis of noncurrent liabilities
- Analysis of equity

Basics of Cash Flow Reporting

This section describes the basics of cash flow reporting, including its purpose, measurement, classification, format, and preparation.

Purpose of the Statement of Cash Flows

C1 Explain the purpose and importance of cash flow information.

The purpose of the **statement of cash flows** is to report all major cash receipts (inflows) and cash payments (outflows) during a period. This includes separately identifying the cash flows related to operating, investing, and financing activities. The statement of cash flows does more than simply report changes in cash. It is the detailed disclosure of individual cash flows that makes this statement useful to users. Information in this statement helps users answer questions such as these:

- How does a company obtain its cash?
- Where does a company spend its cash?
- What explains the change in the cash balance?

Point: Internal users rely on the statement of cash flows to make investing and financing decisions. External users rely on this statement to assess the amount and timing of a company's cash flows.

The statement of cash flows addresses important questions such as these by summarizing, classifying, and reporting a company's cash inflows and cash outflows for each period.

Importance of Cash Flows

Topic Tackler 16-1

Information about cash flows can influence decision makers in important ways. For instance, we look more favorably at a company that is financing its expenditures with cash from operations than one that does it by selling its assets. Information about cash flows helps users decide whether a company has enough cash to pay its existing debts as they mature. It is also relied upon to evaluate a company's ability to meet unexpected obligations and pursue unexpected opportunities. External information users especially want to assess a company's ability to take advantage of new business opportunities. Internal users such as managers use cash flow information to plan day-to-day operating activities and make long-term investment decisions.

Macy's striking turnaround is an example of how analysis and management of cash flows can lead to improved financial stability. Several years ago Macy's obtained temporary protection from bankruptcy, at which time it desperately needed to improve its cash flows. It did so by engaging in aggressive cost-cutting measures. As a result, Macy's annual cash flow rose to $210 million, up from a negative cash flow of $38.9 million in the prior year. Macy's eventually met its financial obligations and then successfully merged with **Federated Department Stores**.

The case of **W. T. Grant Co.** is a classic example of the importance of cash flow information in predicting a company's future performance and financial strength. Grant reported net income of more than $40 million per year for three consecutive years. At that same time, it was experiencing an alarming decrease in cash provided by operations. For instance, net cash outflow was more than $90 million by the end of that three-year period. Grant soon went bankrupt. Users who relied solely on Grant's income numbers were unpleasantly surprised. This reminds us that cash flows as well as income statement and balance sheet information are crucial in making business decisions.

Decision Insight

Valuation Some experts who value private companies do so on the basis of a multiple of operating cash flow. Medium-sized private companies usually sell for five to seven times their operating cash flows. Larger companies often can command somewhat higher multiples.

Measurement of Cash Flows

Cash flows are defined to include both *cash* and *cash equivalents*. The statement of cash flows explains the difference between the beginning and ending balances of cash and cash equivalents. We continue to use the phrases *cash flows* and the *statement of cash flows,* but we must remember that both phrases refer to cash and cash equivalents. Recall that a cash equivalent must satisfy two criteria: (1) be readily convertible to a known amount of cash and (2) be sufficiently close to its maturity so its market value is unaffected by interest rate changes. In most cases, a debt security must be within three months of its maturity to satisfy these criteria. Companies must disclose and follow a clear policy for determining cash and cash equivalents and apply it consistently from period to period. **American Express**, for example, defines its cash equivalents as "time deposits with original maturities of 90 days or less, excluding those that are restricted by law or regulation."

Decision Insight

Know Cash "A lender must have a complete understanding of a borrower's cash flows to assess both the borrowing needs and repayment sources. This requires information about the major types of cash inflows and outflows. I have seen many companies, whose financial statements indicate good profitability, experience severe financial problems because the owners or managers lacked a good understanding of cash flows."—Mary E. Garza, **NationsBank**.

Classification of Cash Flows

C2 Distinguish among operating, investing, and financing activities.

Since cash and cash equivalents are combined, the statement of cash flows does not report transactions between cash and cash equivalents such as cash paid to purchase cash equivalents and cash received from selling cash equivalents. However, all other cash receipts and cash payments are classified and reported on the statement as operating, investing, or financing activities. Individual cash receipts and payments for each of these three categories are labeled to identify their originating transactions or events. A net cash inflow (source) occurs when the receipts in a category exceed the payments. A net cash outflow (use) occurs when the payments in a category exceed the receipts.

Operating Activities **Operating activities** include those transactions and events that determine net income. Examples are the production and purchase of merchandise, the sale of goods and services to customers, and the expenditures to administer the business. Not all

Global: Some countries such as Saudi Arabia and Italy do not require the statement of cash flows.

items in income, such as unusual gains and losses, are operating activities (we discuss these exceptions later in the chapter). Exhibit 16.1 lists the more common cash inflows and outflows from operating activities.

Exhibit 16.1

Cash Flows from Operating Activities

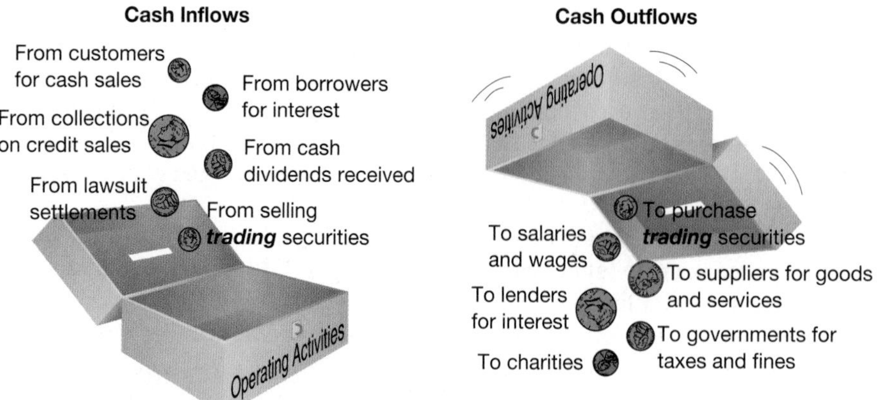

Investing Activities **Investing activities** generally include those transactions and events that affect long-term assets, namely, the purchase and sale of long-term assets. They also include the (1) purchase and sale of short-term investments other than cash equivalents and trading securities and (2) lending and collecting money for notes receivable. Exhibit 16.2 lists examples of cash flows from investing activities. Proceeds from collecting the principal amounts of notes deserve special mention. If the note results from sales to customers, its cash receipts are classed as operating activities whether short term or long term. If the note results from a loan to another party apart from sales, however, the cash receipts from collecting the note principal are classed as an investing activity. The FASB requires the collection of interest on loans be reported as an operating activity.

Point: Investing activities exclude transactions in trading securities.

Point: Common errors include misclassification of *cash dividends received* and *cash interest received* as investing activities and *cash interest paid* as financing. The FASB requires these cash flows be reported as operating activities.

Exhibit 16.2

Cash Flows from Investing Activities

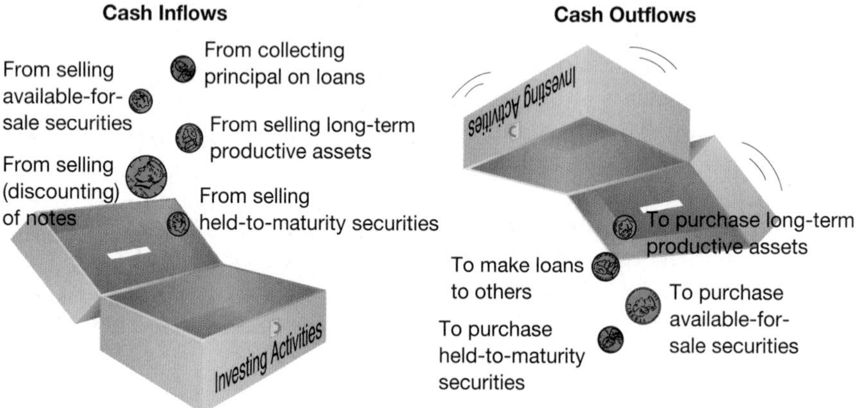

Financing Activities **Financing activities** include those transactions and events that affect long-term liabilities and equity. Examples are (1) obtaining cash from issuing debt and repaying the amounts borrowed and (2) receiving cash from or distributing cash to owners. These activities involve transactions with a company's owners and creditors. They also often involve borrowing and repaying principal amounts relating to both short- and long-term debt. Notice that payments of interest expense are classified as operating activities. Also, cash payments to settle credit purchases of merchandise, whether on account or by note, are operating activities. Exhibit 16.3 lists examples of cash flows from financing activities.

Point: Interest payments on a loan are classified as operating activities, but payments of loan principal are financing activities.

Noncash Investing and Financing

C3 Identify and disclose noncash investing and financing activities.

When important investing and financing activities do not affect cash receipts or payments, they are still disclosed at the bottom of the statement of cash flows or in a note to the

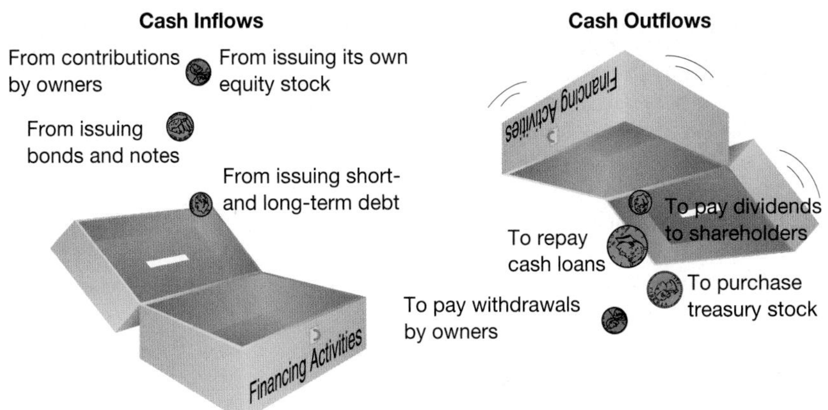

Exhibit 16.3

Cash Flows from Financing Activities

statement because of their importance and the *full-disclosure principle*. One example of such a transaction is the purchase of long-term assets using a long-term note payable. This transaction involves both investing and financing activities but does not affect any cash inflow or outflow and is not reported in any of the three sections of the statement of cash flows. This disclosure rule also extends to transactions with partial cash receipts or payments.

To illustrate, assume that Goorin purchases land for $12,000 by paying $5,000 cash and trading in used equipment with a $7,000 market value. The investing section of the statement of cash flows reports only the $5,000 cash outflow for the land purchase. The $12,000 investing transaction is only partially described in the body of the statement of cash flows, yet this information is potentially important to users because it changes the makeup of assets. Goorin could either describe the transaction in a note or include a small schedule at the bottom of its statement that lists the $12,000 land purchase along with the cash financing of $5,000 and a $7,000 trade-in of used equipment. As another example, Borg Co. acquired $900,000 of assets in exchange for $200,000 cash and a $700,000 long-term note, which is reported as follows:

Point: An income statement reports revenues, gains, expenses, and losses on an accrual basis. The statement of cash flows reports cash received and cash paid for operating, financing, and investing activities.

Point: A stock dividend transaction involving a transfer from retained earnings to common stock or a credit to contributed capital is *not* considered a noncash investing and financing activity because the company receives no consideration (asset) for shares issued.

Decision Maker

Entrepreneur You are considering purchasing a start-up business that recently reported a $110,000 annual net loss and a $225,000 annual net cash inflow. How are these results possible?

Answer—p. 656

Fair value of assets acquired	$900,000
Less cash paid	200,000
Liabilities incurred or assumed	$700,000

Exhibit 16.4 lists transactions commonly disclosed as noncash investing and financing activities.

Exhibit 16.4

Examples of Noncash Investing and Financing Activities

- Retirement of debt by issuing equity stock.
- Conversion of preferred stock to common stock.
- Lease of assets in a capital lease transaction.
- Purchase of long-term assets by issuing a note or bond.
- Exchange of noncash assets for other noncash assets.
- Purchase of noncash assets by issuing equity or debt.

Format of the Statement of Cash Flows

C4 Describe the format of the statement of cash flows.

Accounting standards require companies to include a statement of cash flows in a complete set of financial statements. This statement must report information about a company's cash receipts and cash payments during the period. Exhibit 16.5 shows the usual format. A company must report cash flows from three activities: operating, investing, and financing. The statement explains how transactions and events impact the beginning-of-period cash (and cash equivalents) balance to produce its end-of-period balance.

Exhibit 16.5

Format of the Statement of Cash Flows

COMPANY NAME Statement of Cash Flows For *period* Ended *date*	
Cash flows from operating activities	
[List of individual inflows and outflows]	
Net cash provided (used) by operating activities	$ #
Cash flows from investing activities	
[List of individual inflows and outflows]	
Net cash provided (used) by investing activities	#
Cash flows from financing activities	
[List of individual inflows and outflows]	
Net cash provided (used) by financing activities	#
Net increase (decrease) in cash	$ #
Cash (and equivalents) balance at beginning of period	#
Cash (and equivalents) balance at end of period	$ #

Note: Separate schedule or note disclosure of any "noncash investing and financing transactions" is required.

Global: International standards require a statement of cash flows separated into operating, investing, and financing activities.

Quick Check

1. Does a statement of cash flows report the cash payments to purchase cash equivalents? Does it report the cash receipts from selling cash equivalents?
2. Identify the categories of cash flows reported separately on the statement of cash flows.
3. Identify the cash activity category for each transaction: (*a*) purchase equipment for cash, (*b*) cash payment of wages, (*c*) sale of common stock for cash, (*d*) receipt of cash dividends from stock investment, (e) cash collection from customers, (*f*) bonds issuance for cash.

Answers—p. 656

Preparing the Statement of Cash Flows

P1 Prepare a statement of cash flows.

Step 1: Compute net increase or decrease in cash

Step 2: Compute net cash from operating activities

Step 3: Compute net cash from investing activities

Step 4: Compute net cash from financing activities

Step 5: Prove and report beginning and ending cash balances

Preparing a statement of cash flows involves five steps: (1) compute the net increase or decrease in cash; (2) compute and report net cash provided (used) by operating activities (using either the direct or indirect method; both are explained); (3) compute and report net cash provided (used) by investing activities; (4) compute and report net cash provided (used) by financing activities; and (5) compute net cash flow by combining net cash provided (used) by operating, investing, and financing activities and then *prove it* by adding it to the beginning cash balance to show that it equals the ending cash balance. Important noncash investing and financing activities are disclosed in either a note or a separate schedule to the statement.

Computing the net increase or net decrease in cash is a simple but crucial computation. It equals the current period's cash balance minus the prior period's cash balance. This is the *bottom-line* figure for the statement of cash flows and is a check on the accuracy of one's work. The information we need to prepare a statement of cash flows comes from various sources including comparative balance sheets at the beginning and end of the period, and an income statement for the period. There are two alternative approaches to preparing the statement: (1) analyzing the Cash account and (2) analyzing noncash accounts.

Analyzing the Cash Account A company's cash receipts and cash payments are recorded in the Cash account in its general ledger. The Cash account is therefore a natural place to look for information about cash flows from operating, investing, and financing activities. To illustrate, review the summarized Cash T-account of Genesis, Inc., in Exhibit 16.6. Individual cash transactions are summarized in this Cash account according to the major types of cash receipts and cash payments. For instance, only the total of cash receipts from all customers is listed. Individual cash transactions underlying these totals can number in the thousands. Accounting software programs are available to provide summarized cash accounts.

Preparing a statement of cash flows from Exhibit 16.6 requires determining whether an individual cash inflow or outflow is an operating, investing, or financing activity, and then

Exhibit 16.6
Summarized Cash Account

Accounting System:
File Edit Maintain Tasks Analysis Options Reports Window Help

Cash			
Balance, Dec. 31, 2004	12,000		
Receipts from customers	570,000	Payments for merchandise	319,000
Receipts from asset sales	12,000	Payments for wages and operating expenses	218,000
Receipts from stock issuance	15,000	Payments for interest	8,000
		Payments for taxes	5,000
		Payments for assets	10,000
		Payments for bond retirement	18,000
		Payments for dividends	14,000
Balance, Dec. 31, 2005	17,000		

Sales Purchases General Ledger Payroll Inventory Company Analysis

listing each by activity. This yields the statement shown in Exhibit 16.7. However, preparing the statement of cash flows from an analysis of the summarized Cash account has two limitations. First, most companies have many individual cash receipts and payments, making it difficult to review them all. Accounting software minimizes this burden, but it is still a task requiring professional judgment for many transactions. Second, the Cash account does not usually carry an adequate description of each cash transaction, making assignment of all cash transactions according to activity difficult.

Point: View the change in cash as a *target* number that you will fully explain and prove in the statement of cash flows.

Exhibit 16.7
Statement of Cash Flows—Direct Method

GENESIS
Statement of Cash Flows
For Year Ended December 31, 2005

Cash flows from operating activities		
Cash received from customers	$570,000	
Cash paid for merchandise	(319,000)	
Cash paid for wages and other operating expenses	(218,000)	
Cash paid for interest	(8,000)	
Cash paid for taxes	(5,000)	
Net cash provided by operating activities		$20,000
Cash flows from investing activities		
Cash received from sale of plant assets	12,000	
Cash paid for purchase of plant assets	(10,000)	
Net cash provided by investing activities		2,000
Cash flows from financing activities		
Cash received from issuing stock	15,000	
Cash paid to retire bonds	(18,000)	
Cash paid for dividends	(14,000)	
Net cash used in financing activities		(17,000)
Net increase in cash		$ 5,000
Cash balance at beginning of year		12,000
Cash balance at end of year		$17,000

Analyzing Noncash Accounts A second approach to preparing the statement of cash flows is analyzing noncash accounts. This approach uses the fact that when a company records cash inflows and outflows with debits and credits to the Cash account (see Exhibit 16.6), it also records credits and debits in noncash accounts (reflecting double-entry accounting). Many of these noncash accounts are balance sheet accounts, for instance, from the sale of land for cash. Others are revenue and expense accounts that are closed to equity. For instance, the sale of services for cash yields a credit to Services Revenue that is closed to Retained Earnings for a corporation. In sum, *all cash transactions eventually affect noncash balance sheet accounts.* Thus, we can determine cash inflows and outflows by analyzing changes in noncash balance sheet accounts.

Global: Some countries require a statement of funds flow instead of a statement of cash flows; *funds* are often defined as *working capital* (current assets minus current liabilities).

Exhibit 16.8 uses the accounting equation to show the relation between the Cash account and the noncash balance sheet accounts. This exhibit starts with the accounting equation at

Exhibit 16.8

Relation between Cash and Noncash Accounts

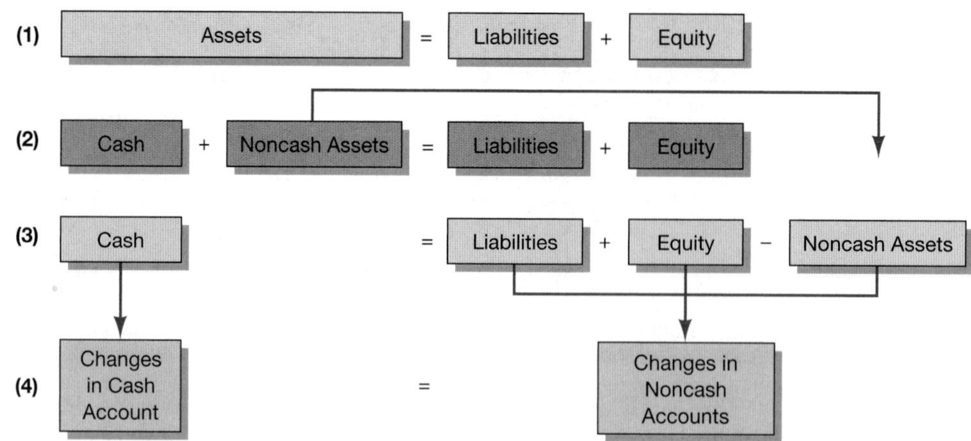

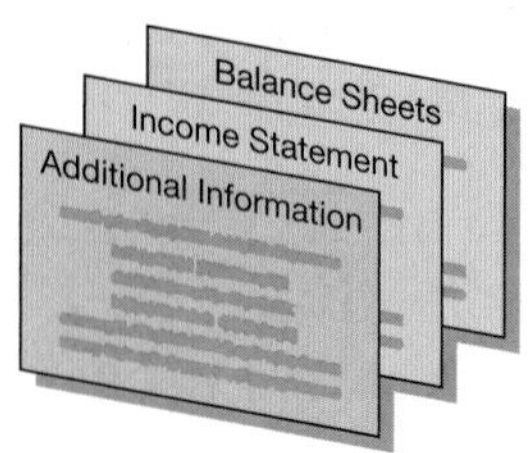

the top. It is then expanded in line (2) to separate cash from noncash asset accounts. Line (3) moves noncash asset accounts to the right-hand side of the equality where they are subtracted. This shows that cash equals the sum of the liability and equity accounts *minus* the noncash asset accounts. Line (4) points out that *changes* on one side of the accounting equation equal *changes* on the other side. It shows that we can explain changes in cash by analyzing changes in the noncash accounts consisting of liability accounts, equity accounts, and noncash assets accounts. By analyzing noncash balance sheet accounts and any related income statement accounts, we can prepare a statement of cash flows.

Information to Prepare the Statement Information to prepare the statement of cash flows usually comes from three sources: (1) comparative balance sheets, (2) current income statement, and (3) additional information. Comparative balance sheets are used to compute changes in noncash accounts from the beginning to the end of the period. The current income statement is used to help compute cash flows from operating activities. Additional information often includes details on transactions and events that help explain both the cash flows and noncash investing and financing activities.

Decision Insight

Every credit transaction on the Net leaves a trail that a hacker, a marketer, or the government can pick up. Enter e-cash—digital money that can be used anonymously. The encryption of e-cash protects your money from snoops and thieves and cannot be traced, even by the issuing bank.

Cash Flows from Operating

Indirect and Direct Methods of Reporting

Cash flows provided (used) by operating activities are reported in one of two ways: the *direct method* or the *indirect method. These two different methods apply only to the operating activities section.*

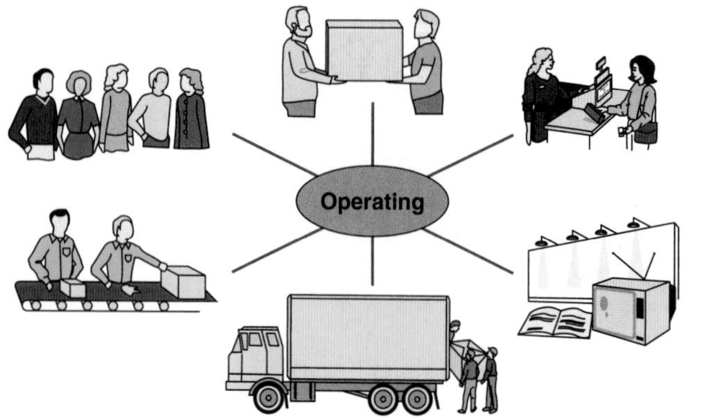

The **direct method** separately lists each major item of operating cash receipts (such as cash received from customers) and each major item of operating cash payments (such as cash paid for merchandise). The cash payments are subtracted from cash receipts to determine the net cash provided (used) by operating activities. The operating activities section of Exhibit 16.7 reflects the direct method of reporting operating cash flows.

The **indirect method** reports net income and then adjusts it for items necessary to obtain net cash provided (used) by operating activities. It does *not* report individual items of cash inflows and cash outflows from operating activities. Instead, the indirect method reports the necessary adjustments to reconcile net income to net cash provided (used) by operating activities. The operating activities section for Genesis prepared under the indirect method is shown in Exhibit 16.9.

Cash flows from operating activities		
Net income		$38,000
Adjustments to reconcile net income to net cash provided by operating activities		
Increase in accounts receivable	$(20,000)	
Increase in merchandise inventory	(14,000)	
Increase in prepaid expenses	(2,000)	
Decrease in accounts payable	(5,000)	
Decrease in interest payable	(1,000)	
Increase in income taxes payable	10,000	
Depreciation expense	24,000	
Loss on sale of plant assets	6,000	
Gain on retirement of bonds	(16,000)	
Net cash provided by operating activities		**$20,000**

Exhibit 16.9

Operating Activities Section—Indirect Method

Note that the amount of net cash provided by operating activities is *identical* under both the direct and indirect methods. This equality always exists. The difference in these methods is with the computation and presentation of this amount. The FASB recommends the direct method, but because it is not required and the indirect method is arguably easier to compute, nearly all companies report operating cash flows using the indirect method.

Point: To better understand the direct and indirect methods of reporting operating cash flows, identify similarities and differences between Exhibits 16.7 and 16.11.

To illustrate, we prepare the operating activities section of the statement of cash flows for Genesis. Exhibit 16.10 shows the December 31, 2004 and 2005, balance sheets of Genesis

Exhibit 16.10

Financial Statements

GENESIS
Balance Sheets
December 31, 2005 and 2004

	2005	2004
Assets		
Current assets		
Cash	$ 17,000	$ 12,000
Accounts receivable	60,000	40,000
Merchandise inventory	84,000	70,000
Prepaid expenses	6,000	4,000
Total current assets	167,000	126,000
Long-term assets		
Plant assets	250,000	210,000
Accumulated depreciation	(60,000)	(48,000)
Total assets	$357,000	$288,000
Liabilities		
Current liabilities		
Accounts payable	$ 35,000	$ 40,000
Interest payable	3,000	4,000
Income taxes payable	22,000	12,000
Total current liabilities	60,000	56,000
Long-term bonds payable	90,000	64,000
Total liabilities	150,000	120,000
Equity		
Common stock, $5 par	95,000	80,000
Retained earnings	112,000	88,000
Total equity	207,000	168,000
Total liabilities and equity	$357,000	$288,000

GENESIS
Income Statement
For Year Ended December 31, 2005

Sales		$590,000
Cost of goods sold	$300,000	
Wages and other operating expenses	216,000	
Interest expense	7,000	
Depreciation expense	24,000	(547,000)
		43,000
Other gains (losses)		
Gain on retirement of bonds	16,000	
Loss on sale of plant assets	(6,000)	10,000
Income before taxes		53,000
Income taxes expense		(15,000)
Net income		38,000

along with its 2005 income statement. We use this information to prepare a statement of cash flows that explains the $5,000 increase in cash for 2005 as reflected in its balance sheets. This $5,000 is computed as Cash of $17,000 at the end of 2005 minus Cash of $12,000 at the end of 2004. Genesis discloses additional information about 2005 transactions:

a. The accounts payable balances result from merchandise inventory purchases.

b. Purchased plant assets costing $70,000 by paying $10,000 cash and issuing $60,000 of bonds payable.

c. Sold plant assets with an original cost of $30,000 and accumulated depreciation of $12,000 for $12,000 cash, yielding a $6,000 loss.

d. Received cash of $15,000 from issuing 3,000 shares of common stock.

e. Paid $18,000 cash to retire bonds with a $34,000 book value, yielding a $16,000 gain.

f. Declared and paid cash dividends of $14,000.

The next section describes the indirect method. Appendix 16B describes the direct method. An instructor can choose to cover either one or both methods. Neither section depends on the other.

Topic Tackler 16-2

Application of the Indirect Method of Reporting

P2 Compute cash flows from operating activities using the indirect method.

Net income is computed using accrual accounting, which recognizes revenues when earned and expenses when incurred. Revenues and expenses do not necessarily reflect the receipt and payment of cash. The indirect method of computing and reporting net cash flows from operating activities involves adjusting the net income figure to obtain the net cash provided (used) by operating activities. This includes subtracting noncash increases (credits) from net income and adding noncash charges (debits) back to net income.

To illustrate, the indirect method begins with Genesis's net income of $38,000 and adjusts it to obtain net cash provided (used) by operating activities of $20,000. Exhibit 16.11

Exhibit 16.11

Statement of Cash Flows—Indirect Method

GENESIS Statement of Cash Flows For Year Ended December 31, 2005		
Cash flows from operating activities		
Net income		$38,000
Adjustments to reconcile net income to net cash provided by operating activities		
① Increase in accounts receivable	$(20,000)	
① Increase in merchandise inventory	(14,000)	
① Increase in prepaid expenses	(2,000)	
① Decrease in accounts payable	(5,000)	
① Decrease in interest payable	(1,000)	
① Increase in income taxes payable	10,000	
② Depreciation expense	24,000	
③ Loss on sale of plant assets	6,000	
③ Gain on retirement of bonds	(16,000)	
Net cash provided by operating activities		20,000
Cash flows from investing activities		
Cash received from sale of plant assets	12,000	
Cash paid for purchase of plant assets	(10,000)	
Net cash provided by investing activities		2,000
Cash flows from financing activities		
Cash received from issuing stock	15,000	
Cash paid to retire bonds	(18,000)	
Cash paid for dividends	(14,000)	
Net cash used in financing activities		(17,000)
Net increase in cash		$ 5,000
Cash balance at beginning of year		12,000
Cash balance at end of year		$17,000

Point: Refer to Exhibit 16.10 and identify the $5,000 change in cash. This change is what the statement of cash flows explains; it serves as a check figure.

shows the results of the indirect method of reporting operating cash flows, which adjusts net income for three types of adjustments. There are adjustments ① to reflect changes in noncash current assets and current liabilities related to operating activities, ② to income statement items involving operating activities that do not affect cash inflows or outflows, and ③ to eliminate gains and losses resulting from investing and financing activities (not part of operating activities). This section describes each of these adjustments.

Point: *Noncash credits* refer to *revenue amounts* reported on the income statement that are *not collected in cash* this period. *Noncash charges* refer to *expense amounts* reported on the income statement that are *not paid* this period.

① Adjustments for Changes in Current Assets and Current Liabilities This section describes adjustments for changes in noncash current assets and current liabilities.

Adjustments for changes in noncash current assets. Changes in noncash current assets are normally the result of operating activities. Examples are sales affecting accounts receivable and asset usage affecting prepaid rent. Decreases in noncash current assets yield the following adjustment:

Point: Operating activities are typically those that determine income, which are often reflected in changes in current assets and current liabilities.

Decreases in noncash current assets are added to net income.

To see the logic for this adjustment, consider that a decrease in a noncash current asset such as accounts receivable suggests more available cash at the end of the period compared to the beginning. This is so because a decrease in accounts receivable implies higher cash receipts than reflected in sales. We add these higher cash receipts (from decreases in noncash current assets) to net income when computing cash flow from operations.

In contrast, an increase in noncash current assets such as accounts receivable implies less cash receipts than reflected in sales. As another example, an increase in prepaid rent indicates that more cash is paid for rent than is deducted as rent expense. Increases in noncash current assets yield the following adjustment:

Increases in noncash current assets are subtracted from net income.

To illustrate, these adjustments are applied to the noncash current assets in Exhibit 16.10.

Accounts receivable. Accounts Receivable *increase* \$20,000, from a beginning balance of \$40,000 to an ending balance of \$60,000. This increase implies that Genesis collects less cash than is reported in sales. That is, some of these sales were in the form of accounts receivable and that amount increased during the period. To see this it is helpful to use *account analysis.* This usually involves setting up a T-account and reconstructing its major entries to compute cash receipts or payments. The following reconstructed Accounts Receivable T-account reveals the lower amount of cash receipts compared to sales:

Numbers in black are taken from Exhibit 16.10. The red number is the computed (plug) figure.

Accounts Receivable			
Bal., Dec. 31, 2004	40,000		
Sales	590,000	**Cash receipts =**	**570,000**
Bal., Dec. 31, 2005	60,000		

Notice that sales are \$20,000 greater than the cash receipts. This \$20,000—as reflected in the \$20,000 increase in Accounts Receivable—is subtracted from net income when computing cash provided by operating activities (see Exhibit 16.11).

Merchandise inventory. Merchandise inventory *increases* by \$14,000, from a \$70,000 beginning balance to an \$84,000 ending balance. This increase implies that Genesis had a larger amount of cash purchases than cost of goods sold. This larger amount of cash purchases is in the form of inventory, as reflected in the following account analysis:

Merchandise Inventory			
Bal., Dec. 31, 2004	70,000		
Purchases =	**314,000**	Cost of goods sold	300,000
Bal., Dec. 31, 2005	84,000		

The amount by which purchases exceed cost of goods sold—as reflected in the $14,000 increase in inventory—is subtracted from net income when computing cash provided by operating activities (see Exhibit 16.11).

Prepaid expenses. Prepaid expenses *increase* $2,000, from a $4,000 beginning balance to a $6,000 ending balance, implying that Genesis's cash payments exceed its recorded prepaid expenses. These higher cash payments increase the amount of Prepaid Expenses, as reflected in its reconstructed T-account:

Prepaid Expenses			
Bal., Dec. 31, 2004	4,000		
Cash payments =	**218,000**	Wages and other operating exp.	216,000
Bal., Dec. 31, 2005	6,000		

The amount by which cash payments exceed the recorded operating expenses—as reflected in the $2,000 increase in Prepaid Expenses—is subtracted from net income when computing cash provided by operating activities (see Exhibit 16.11).

Adjustments for changes in current liabilities. Changes in current liabilities are normally the result of operating activities. An example is a purchase that affects accounts payable. Increases in current liabilities yield the following adjustment to net income when computing operating cash flows:

Increases in current liabilities are added to net income.

To see the logic for this adjustment, consider that an increase in the Accounts Payable account suggests that cash payments are less than the related (cost of goods sold) expense. As another example, an increase in wages payable implies that cash paid for wages is less than the recorded wages expense. Since the recorded expense is greater than the cash paid, we add the increase in wages payable to net income to compute net cash flow from operations.

Conversely, when current liabilities decrease, the following adjustment is required:

Decreases in current liabilities are subtracted from net income.

To illustrate, this adjustment is applied to the current liabilities in Exhibit 16.10.

Accounts payable. Accounts Payable *decrease* $5,000, from a beginning balance of $40,000 to an ending balance of $35,000. This decrease implies that cash payments to suppliers exceed purchases by $5,000 for the period, which is reflected in the reconstructed Accounts Payable T-account:

Accounts Payable			
		Bal., Dec. 31, 2004	40,000
Cash payments =	**319,000**	Purchases	314,000
		Bal., Dec. 31, 2005	35,000

The amount by which cash payments exceed purchases—as reflected in the $5,000 decrease in Accounts Payable—is subtracted from net income when computing cash provided by operating activities (see Exhibit 16.11).

Interest payable. Interest Payable *decreases* $1,000, from a $4,000 beginning balance to a $3,000 ending balance. This decrease indicates that cash paid for interest exceeds interest expense by $1,000, which is reflected in the Interest Payable T-account:

Interest Payable			
		Bal., Dec. 31, 2004	4,000
Cash paid for interest =	**8,000**	Interest expense	7,000
		Bal., Dec. 31, 2005	3,000

The amount by which cash paid exceeds recorded expense—as reflected in the $1,000 decrease in Interest Payable—is subtracted from net income (see Exhibit 16.11).

Income taxes payable. Income Taxes Payable *increase* $10,000, from a $12,000 beginning balance to a $22,000 ending balance. This increase implies that reported income taxes exceed the cash paid for taxes, which is reflected in the Income Taxes Payable T-account:

Income Taxes Payable			
		Bal., Dec. 31, 2004	12,000
Cash paid for taxes =	**5,000**	Income taxes expense	15,000
		Bal., Dec. 31, 2005	22,000

The amount by which cash paid falls short of the reported taxes expense—as reflected in the $10,000 increase in Income Taxes Payable—is added to net income when computing cash provided by operating activities (see Exhibit 16.11).

② Adjustments for Operating Items Not Providing or Using Cash The income statement usually includes some expenses that do not reflect cash outflows in the period. Examples are depreciation, amortization, depletion, and bad debts expense. The indirect method for reporting operating cash flows requires that

Expenses with no cash outflows are added back to net income.

To see the logic of this adjustment, recall that items such as depreciation, amortization, depletion, and bad debts originate from debits to expense accounts and credits to noncash accounts. These entries have *no* cash effect, and we add them back to net income when computing net cash flows from operations. Adding them back cancels their deductions.

Similarly, when net income includes revenues that do not reflect cash inflows in the period, the indirect method for reporting operating cash flows requires that

Revenues with no cash inflows are subtracted from net income.

We apply these adjustments to the Genesis operating items that do not provide or use cash.

Depreciation. Depreciation expense is the only Genesis operating item that has no effect on cash flows in the period. We must add back the $24,000 depreciation expense to net income when computing cash provided by operating activities. (We later explain that the cash outflow to acquire a plant asset is reported as an investing activity.)

③ Adjustments for Nonoperating Items Net income often includes losses that are not part of operating activities but are part of either investing or financing activities. Examples are a loss from the sale of a plant asset and a loss from retirement of a bond payable. The indirect method for reporting operating cash flows requires that

Nonoperating losses are added back to net income.

To see the logic, consider that items such as a plant asset sale and a bond retirement are normally recorded by recognizing the cash, removing all plant asset or bond accounts, and recognizing any loss or gain. The cash received or paid is not part of operating activities but is part of either investing or financing activities. *No* operating cash flow effect occurs. However, because the nonoperating loss is a deduction in computing net income, we need to add it back to net income when computing cash flow from operations. Adding it back cancels the deduction.

Similarly, when net income includes gains not part of operating activities, the indirect method for reporting operating cash flows requires that

Nonoperating gains are subtracted from net income.

To illustrate these adjustments, we consider the nonoperating items of Genesis.

Loss on sale of plant assets. Genesis reports a $6,000 loss on sale of plant assets as part of net income. This loss is a proper deduction in computing income, but it is *not part of operating activities*. Instead, a sale of plant assets is part of investing activities. Thus, the $6,000 nonoperating loss is added back to net income (see Exhibit 16.11). Adding it back cancels the loss. We later explain how to report the cash inflow from the asset sale in investing activities.

Gain on retirement of debt. A $16,000 gain on retirement of debt is properly included in net income, but it is *not part of operating activities*. Thus, the $16,000 nonoperating gain is subtracted from net income to obtain net cash provided by operating activities (see Exhibit 16.11). Subtracting it cancels the recorded gain. We later describe how to report the cash outflow to retire debt.

Decision Insight

Cash or Income The difference between net income and operating cash flows can be large and reflect on the quality of earnings. This bar chart shows net income and operating cash flows of four companies. Operating cash flows can be either higher or lower than net income.

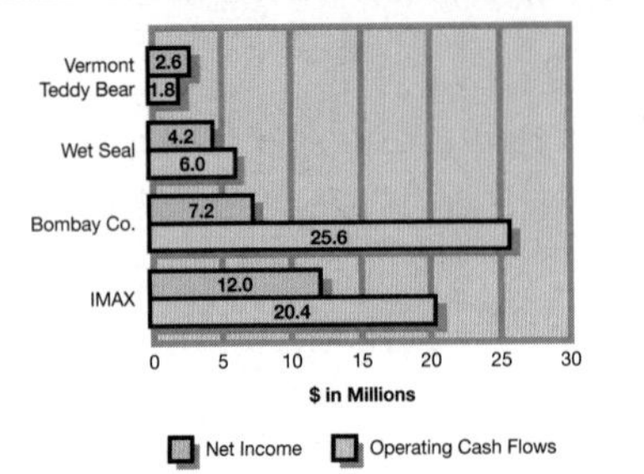

Summary of Adjustments for Indirect Method

Exhibit 16.12 summarizes the most common adjustments to net income when computing net cash provided (used) by operating activities under the indirect method.

Exhibit 16.12

Summary of Selected Adjustments for Indirect Method

Net Income	
+Decrease in noncash current asset	① Adjustments for changes in current assets and current liabilities
−Increase in noncash current asset	
+Increase in current liability*	
−Decrease in current liability*	
+Depreciation, depletion, and amortization	② Adjustments for operating items not providing or using cash
+Accrued expenses	
−Accrued revenues	
+Loss on disposal of long-term asset	③ Adjustments for nonoperating items
+Loss on retirement of debt	
−Gain on disposal of long-term asset	
−Gain on retirement of debt	
Net cash provided (used) by operating activities	

* Excludes current portion of long-term debt and any (nonsales-related) short-term notes payable—both are financing activities.

The computations in determining cash provided (used) by operating activities are different for the indirect and direct methods, but the result is identical. Both methods yield the same $20,000 figure for cash from operating activities for Genesis; see Exhibits 16.7 and 16.11.

Quick Check

4. Determine net cash provided (used) by operating activities using the following data: net income, $74,900; decrease in accounts receivable, $4,600; increase in inventory, $11,700; decrease in accounts payable, $1,000; loss on sale of equipment, $3,400; payment of cash dividends, $21,500.
5. Why are expenses such as depreciation and amortization added to net income when cash flow from operating activities is computed by the indirect method?
6. A company reports net income of $15,000 that includes a $3,000 gain on the sale of plant assets. Why is this gain subtracted from net income in computing cash flow from operating activities using the indirect method?

Answers—p. 656

Cash Flows from Investing

The third major step in preparing the statement of cash flows is to compute and report cash flows from investing activities. We normally do this by identifying changes in (1) all noncurrent asset accounts and (2) the current accounts for both notes receivable and investments in securities (excluding trading securities). We then analyze changes in these accounts to determine their effect, if any, on cash and report the cash flow effects in the investing activities section of the statement of cash flows. *Reporting of investing activities is identical under the direct method and indirect method.*

Three-Stage Process of Analysis

Information to compute cash flows from investing activities is usually taken from beginning and ending balance sheets and the income statement. We use a three-stage process to determine cash provided (used) by investing activities: (1) identify changes in investing-related accounts, (2) explain these changes using reconstruction analysis, and (3) report their cash flow effects.

Analysis of Noncurrent Assets

P3 Determine cash flows from both investing and financing activities.

Information about the Genesis transactions provided earlier reveals that the company both purchased and sold plant assets during the period. Both transactions are investing activities and are analyzed for their cash flow effects in this section.

Plant Asset Transactions The first stage in analyzing the Plant Assets account and its related Accumulated Depreciation is to identify any changes in these accounts from comparative balance sheets in Exhibit 16.10. This analysis reveals a $40,000 increase in plant assets from $210,000 to $250,000 and a $12,000 increase in accumulated depreciation from $48,000 to $60,000.

Point: Investing activities include (1) purchasing and selling long-term assets, (2) lending and collecting on notes receivable, and (3) purchasing and selling short-term investments other than cash equivalents and trading securities.

The second stage is to explain these changes. Items *b* and *c* of the additional information for Genesis (page 634) are relevant in this case. Recall that the Plant Assets account is affected by both asset purchases and sales, while its Accumulated Depreciation account is normally increased from depreciation and decreased from the removal of accumulated depreciation in asset sales. To explain changes in these accounts and to identify their cash flow effects, we prepare *reconstructed entries* from prior transactions; *they are not the actual entries by the preparer.*

Point: Financing and investing info is available in ledger accounts to help explain changes in comparative balance sheets. Post references lead to relevant entries and explanations.

To illustrate, item *b* reports that Genesis purchased plant assets of $70,000 by issuing $60,000 in bonds payable to the seller and paying $10,000 in cash. The reconstructed entry for analysis of item *b* follows:

Reconstruction	Account	Debit	Credit
	Plant Assets	70,000	
	Bonds Payable		60,000
	Cash		**10,000**

Assets	= Liabilities	+ Equity
+70,000	+60,000	
−10,000		

This entry reveals a $10,000 cash outflow for plant assets and a $60,000 noncash investing and financing transaction involving bonds exchanged for plant assets.

Next, item *c* reports that Genesis sold plant assets costing $30,000 (with $12,000 of accumulated depreciation) for $12,000 cash, resulting in a $6,000 loss. The reconstructed entry for analysis of item *c* follows:

Reconstruction	Account	Debit	Credit
	Cash	**12,000**	
	Accumulated Depreciation	12,000	
	Loss on Sale of Plant Assets	6,000	
	Plant Assets		30,000

Assets	= Liabilities	+ Equity
+12,000		−6,000
−30,000		
+12,000		

This entry reveals a $12,000 cash inflow from assets sold. The $6,000 loss is computed by comparing the asset book value to the cash received and does not reflect any cash inflow or outflow. We also reconstruct the entry for Depreciation Expense using information from the income statement:

Assets	= Liabilities +	Equity
−24,000		−24,000

Reconstruction	Depreciation Expense	24,000	
	Accumulated Depreciation		24,000

This entry shows that Depreciation Expense results in no cash flow effect. These three reconstructed entries are reflected in the following plant asset and related T-accounts.

Plant Assets			
Bal., Dec. 31, 2004	210,000		
Purchase	**70,000**	**Sale**	**30,000**
Bal., Dec. 31, 2005	250,000		

Accumulated Depreciation—Plant Assets			
		Bal., Dec. 31, 2004	48,000
Sale	**12,000**	**Depr. expense**	**24,000**
		Bal., Dec. 31, 2005	60,000

Example: If a plant asset costing $40,000 with $37,000 of accumulated depreciation is sold at a $1,000 loss, what is the cash flow? What is the cash flow if this asset is sold at a gain of $3,000? *Answers:* +$2,000; +$6,000.

This reconstruction analysis is complete in that the change in plant assets from $210,000 to $250,000 is fully explained by the $70,000 purchase and the $30,000 sale. Also, the change in accumulated depreciation from $48,000 to $60,000 is fully explained by depreciation expense of $24,000 and the removal of $12,000 in accumulated depreciation from an asset sale. (*Note:* Preparers of the statement of cash flows have the entire ledger and additional information at their disposal, but for brevity reasons only the information needed for reconstructing accounts is given.)

The third stage looks at the reconstructed entries for identification of cash flows. The two identified cash flow effects are reported in the investing section of the statement as follows (also see Exhibit 16.7 or 16.11):

Cash flows from investing activities	
Cash received from sale of plant assets	$12,000
Cash paid for purchase of plant assets	(10,000)

Also, the $60,000 portion of the purchase described in item *b* and financed by issuing bonds is a noncash investing and financing activity. It is reported in a note or in a separate schedule to the statement as follows:

Noncash investing and financing activity	
Purchased plant assets with issuance of bonds	$60,000

Analysis of Other Assets

Many other asset transactions (including those involving current notes receivable and investments in certain securities) are considered investing activities and can affect a company's cash flows. Since Genesis did not enter into other investing activities impacting assets, we do not need to extend our analysis to these other assets. If such transactions did exist, we would analyze them using the same three-stage process illustrated for plant assets.

Quick Check

7. Equipment costing $80,000 with accumulated depreciation of $30,000 is sold at a loss of $10,000. What is the cash receipt from this sale? In what section of the statement of cash flows is this transaction reported?

Answer—p. 656

Cash Flows from Financing

The fourth major step in preparing the statement of cash flows is to compute and report cash flows from financing activities. We normally do this by identifying changes in all noncurrent liability accounts (including the current portion of any notes and bonds) and the equity accounts. These accounts include long-term debt, notes payable, bonds payable, common stock, and retained earnings. Changes in these accounts are then analyzed using available information to determine their effect, if any, on cash. Results are reported in the financing activities section of the statement. *Reporting of financing activities is identical under the direct method and indirect method.*

Three-Stage Process of Analysis

We again use a three-stage process to determine cash provided (used) by financing activities: (1) identify changes in financing-related accounts, (2) explain these changes using reconstruction analysis, and (3) report their cash flow effects.

Analysis of Noncurrent Liabilities

Information about Genesis provided earlier reveals two transactions involving noncurrent liabilities. We analyzed one of those, the $60,000 issuance of bonds payable to purchase plant assets. This transaction is reported as a significant noncash investing and financing activity in a note or a separate schedule to the statement of cash flows. The other remaining transaction involving noncurrent liabilities is the cash retirement of bonds payable.

Point: Financing activities generally refer to changes in the noncurrent liability and the equity accounts. Examples are (1) receiving cash from issuing debt or repaying amounts borrowed and (2) receiving cash from or distributing cash to owners.

Bonds Payable Transactions The first stage in analysis of bonds is to review the comparative balance sheets from Exhibit 16.10. This analysis reveals an increase in bonds payable from $64,000 to $90,000.

The second stage explains this change. Item *e* of the additional information for Genesis (page 634) reports that bonds with a carrying value of $34,000 are retired for $18,000 cash, resulting in a $16,000 gain. The reconstructed entry for analysis of item *e* follows:

Reconstruction	Bonds Payable	34,000	
	Gain on retirement of debt		16,000
	Cash		**18,000**

Assets	= Liabilities	+ Equity
−18,000	−34,000	+16,000

This entry reveals an $18,000 cash outflow for retirement of bonds and a $16,000 gain from comparing the bonds payable carrying value to the cash received. This gain does not reflect any cash inflow or outflow. Also, item *b* of the additional information reports that Genesis purchased plant assets costing $70,000 by issuing $60,000 in bonds payable to the seller and paying $10,000 in cash. We reconstructed this entry when analyzing investing activities: It showed a $60,000 increase to bonds payable that is reported as a noncash investing and financing transaction. The Bonds Payable account reflects (and is fully explained by) these reconstructed entries as follows:

Bonds Payable			
		Bal., Dec. 31, 2004	64,000
Retired bonds	**34,000**	**Issued bonds**	**60,000**
		Bal., Dec. 31, 2005	90,000

The third stage is to report the cash flow effect of the bond retirement in the financing section of the statement as follows (also see Exhibit 16.7 or 16.11):

Cash flows from financing activities	
Cash paid to retire bonds	$(18,000)

Analysis of Equity

The Genesis information reveals two transactions involving equity accounts. The first is the issuance of common stock for cash. The second is the declaration and payment of cash dividends. We analyze both.

Common Stock Transactions The first stage in analyzing common stock is to review the comparative balance sheets from Exhibit 16.10, which reveals an increase in common stock from $80,000 to $95,000.

The second stage explains this change. Item *d* of the additional information (page 634) reports that 3,000 shares of common stock are issued at par for $5 per share. The reconstructed entry for analysis of item *d* follows:

Assets	= Liabilities +	Equity
+15,000		+15,000

Reconstruction	**Cash**	**15,000**	
	Common Stock		15,000

This entry reveals a $15,000 cash inflow from stock issuance and is reflected in (and explains) the Common Stock account as follows:

Common Stock			
		Bal., Dec. 31, 2004	80,000
		Issued stock	**15,000**
		Bal., Dec. 31, 2005	95,000

The third stage discloses the cash flow effect from stock issuance in the financing section of the statement as follows (also see Exhibit 16.7 or 16.11):

Cash flows from financing activities	
Cash received from issuing stock	$15,000

Retained Earnings Transactions The first stage in analyzing the Retained Earnings account is to review the comparative balance sheets from Exhibit 16.10. This reveals an increase in retained earnings from $88,000 to $112,000.

The second stage explains this change. Item *f* of the additional information (page 634) reports that cash dividends of $14,000 are paid. The reconstructed entry follows:

Assets	= Liabilities +	Equity
−14,000		−14,000

Reconstruction	Retained Earnings	14,000	
	Cash		**14,000**

This entry reveals a $14,000 cash outflow for cash dividends. Also note that the Retained Earnings account is impacted by net income of $38,000. (Net income was analyzed under the operating section of the statement of cash flows.) The reconstructed Retained Earnings account follows:

Retained Earnings			
		Bal., Dec. 31, 2004	88,000
Cash dividend	**14,000**	**Net income**	**38,000**
		Bal., Dec. 31, 2005	112,000

The third stage reports the cash flow effect from the cash dividend in the financing section of the statement as follows (also see Exhibit 16.7 or 16.11):

Cash flows from financing activities	
Cash paid for dividends	$(14,000)

Point: Financing activities not affecting cash flow include *declaration* of a cash dividend, *declaration* of a stock dividend, payment of a stock dividend, and a stock split.

Global: There are no requirements to separate domestic and international cash flows, leading some users to ask "Where in the world is cash flow?"

We now have identified and explained all of the Genesis cash inflows and cash outflows and one noncash investing and financing transaction. Specifically, our analysis has reconciled changes in all noncash balance sheet accounts.

Proving Cash Balances

The fifth and final step in preparing the statement is to report the beginning and ending cash balances and prove that the *net change in cash* is explained by operating, investing, and financing cash flows. This step is shown here for Genesis.

Net cash provided by operating activities	$20,000
Net cash provided by investing activities	2,000
Net cash used in financing activities	(17,000)
Net increase in cash	**$ 5,000**
Cash balance at beginning of 2005	12,000
Cash balance at end of 2005	$17,000

Point: The following ratio helps assess whether a company's operating cash flow is adequate to meet long-term obligations:
Cash coverage of debt = Cash flow from operations divided by noncurrent liabilities.
A low ratio suggests a higher risk of insolvency; a high ratio suggests a greater ability to meet long-term obligations.

The preceding table shows that the $5,000 net increase in cash, from $12,000 at the beginning of the period to $17,000 at the end, is reconciled by net cash flows from operating ($20,000 inflow), investing ($2,000 inflow), and financing ($17,000 outflow) activities. This is formally reported at the bottom of the statement of cash flows as shown in both Exhibits 16.7 and 16.11.

Decision Maker

Reporter Management is in labor contract negotiations and grants you an interview. It highlights a recent $600,000 net loss that involves a $930,000 extraordinary loss and a total net cash outflow of $550,000 (which includes net cash outflows of $850,000 for investing activities and $350,000 for financing activities). What is your assessment of this company?

Answer—p. 656

Cash Flow Analysis — **Decision Analysis**

Analyzing Cash Sources and Uses

A1 Analyze the statement of cash flows.

Most managers stress the importance of understanding and predicting cash flows for business decisions. Creditors evaluate a company's ability to generate cash before deciding whether to lend money. Investors also assess cash inflows and outflows before buying and selling stock. Information in the statement of cash flows helps address these and other questions such as (1) How much cash is generated from or used in operations? (2) What expenditures are made with cash from operations? (3) What is the source of cash for debt payments? (4) What is the source of cash for distributions to owners? (5) How is the increase in investing activities financed? (6) What is the source of cash for new plant assets? (7) Why is cash flow from operations different from income? (8) How is cash from financing used?

To effectively answer these questions, it is important to separately analyze investing, financing, and operating activities. To illustrate, consider data from three different companies in Exhibit 16.13. These companies operate in the same industry and have been in business for several years.

Decision Insight

Free Cash Cash-based valuation of a company is theoretically equal to earnings-based valuation, but it usually yields a different value due to practical limitations. One limitation is the measurement of cash flows that are "free" for distribution to shareholders. These *free cash flows* are defined as cash flows available to shareholders after operating asset reinvestments and debt payments. Growth and financial flexibility depend on adequate free cash flow.

Exhibit 16.13

Cash Flows of Competing Companies

($ in thousands)	BMX	ATV	Trex
Cash provided (used) by operating activities	$90,000	$40,000	$(24,000)
Cash provided (used) by investing activities			
Proceeds from sale of plant assets			26,000
Purchase of plant assets	(48,000)	(25,000)	
Cash provided (used) by financing activities			
Proceeds from issuance of debt			13,000
Repayment of debt	(27,000)		
Net increase (decrease) in cash	$15,000	$15,000	$ 15,000

Each company generates an identical $15,000 net increase in cash, but its sources and uses of cash flows are very different. BMX's operating activities provide net cash flows of $90,000, allowing it to purchase plant assets of $48,000 and repay $27,000 of its debt. ATV's operating activities provide $40,000 of cash flows, limiting its purchase of plant assets to $25,000. Trex's $15,000 net cash increase is due to selling plant assets and incurring additional debt. Its operating activities yield a net cash outflow of $24,000. Overall, analysis of these cash flows reveals that BMX is more capable of generating future cash flows than is ATV or Trex.

Cash Flow on Total Assets

A2 Compute and apply the cash flow on total assets ratio.

Cash flow information has limitations, but it can help measure a company's ability to meet its obligations, pay dividends, expand operations, and obtain financing. Users often compute and analyze a cash-based ratio similar to return on total assets except that its numerator is net cash flows from operating activities. The **cash flow on total assets** ratio is in Exhibit 16.14.

Exhibit 16.14

Cash Flow on Total Assets

$$\textbf{Cash flow on total assets} = \frac{\textbf{Cash flow from operations}}{\textbf{Average total assets}}$$

Exhibit 16.15

Nike's Cash Flow on Total Assets

Year	Cash Flow on Total Assets	Return on Total Assets
2002	17.6%	10.8%
2001	11.2	10.1
2000	12.6	10.4
1999	17.7	8.5
1998	9.6	7.4
1997	6.9	17.1

This ratio reflects actual cash flows and is not affected by accounting income recognition and measurement. It can help business decision makers estimate the amount and timing of cash flows when planning and analyzing operating activities.

To illustrate, the 2002 cash flow on total assets ratio for **Nike** is 17.6%—see Exhibit 16.15. Is a 17.6% ratio good or bad? To answer this question, we compare this ratio with the ratios of prior years (we could also compare its ratio with those of its competitors and the market). Nike's cash flow on total assets ratio for several prior years is in the second column of Exhibit 16.15. Results show that its 17.6% return is higher than all but one of the prior years' returns.

As an indicator of *earnings quality,* some analysts compare the cash flow on total assets ratio to the return on total assets ratio. Nike's return on total assets is provided in the third column of Exhibit 16.15. Nike's cash flow on total assets ratio exceeds its return on total assets in five of the six years, leading these analysts to infer that Nike's earnings quality is high for that period because more earnings are realized in the form of cash.

Decision Insight

Cash Ratios Analysts use various other cash-based ratios:

$$\textbf{(1) Cash coverage of growth} = \frac{\textbf{Operating cash flow}}{\textbf{Cash outflow for plant assets}}$$

a low ratio (less than 1) implies cash inadequacy to meet asset growth, whereas a high ratio implies cash adequacy for asset growth.

$$\textbf{(2) Operating cash flow to sales} = \frac{\textbf{Operating cash flow}}{\textbf{Net sales}}$$

when this ratio substantially and consistently differs from the operating income to net sales ratio, the risk of accounting improprieties increases.

Demonstration Problem

Umlauf's comparative balance sheets, income statement, and additional information follow.

UMLAUF COMPANY
Income Statement
For Year Ended December 31, 2005

Sales		$446,100
Cost of goods sold	$222,300	
Other operating expenses	120,300	
Depreciation expense	25,500	(368,100)
		78,000
Other gains (losses)		
Loss on sale of equipment	3,300	
Loss on retirement of bonds	825	(4,125)
Income before taxes		73,875
Income taxes expense		(13,725)
Net income		$ 60,150

UMLAUF COMPANY
Balance Sheets
December 31, 2005 and 2004

	2005	2004
Assets		
Cash	$ 43,050	$ 23,925
Accounts receivable	34,125	39,825
Merchandise inventory	156,000	146,475
Prepaid expenses	3,600	1,650
Equipment	135,825	146,700
Accum. depreciation—Equipment	(61,950)	(47,550)
Total assets	$310,650	$311,025
Liabilities and Equity		
Accounts payable	$ 28,800	$ 33,750
Income taxes payable	5,100	4,425
Dividends payable	0	4,500
Bonds payable	0	37,500
Common stock, $10 par	168,750	168,750
Retained earnings	108,000	62,100
Total liabilities and equity	$310,650	$311,025

Additional Information

a. Equipment costing $21,375 with accumulated depreciation of $11,100 is sold for cash.
b. Equipment purchases are for cash.
c. Accumulated Depreciation is affected by depreciation expense and the sale of equipment.
d. The balance of Retained Earnings is affected by dividend declarations and net income.
e. All sales are made on credit.
f. All merchandise inventory purchases are on credit.
g. Accounts Payable balances result from merchandise inventory purchases.
h. Prepaid expenses relate to "other operating expenses."

Required

1. Prepare a statement of cash flows using the indirect method for year 2005.
2.[B] Prepare a statement of cash flows using the direct method for year 2005.

Planning the Solution

- Prepare two blank statements of cash flows with sections for operating, investing, and financing activities using the (1) indirect method format and (2) direct method format.
- Compute the cash paid for equipment and the cash received from the sale of equipment using the additional information provided along with the amount for depreciation expense and the change in the balances of equipment and accumulated depreciation. Use T-accounts to help chart the effects of the sale and purchase of equipment on the balances of the Equipment account and the Accumulated Depreciation account.
- Calculate the effect of net income on the change in the Retained Earnings account balance. Assign the difference between the change in retained earnings and the amount of net income to dividends declared. Adjust the dividends declared amount for the change in the Dividends Payable balance.
- Compute cash received from customers, cash paid for merchandise, cash paid for other operating expenses, and cash paid for taxes as illustrated in the chapter.
- Enter the cash effects of reconstruction entries to the appropriate section(s) of the statement.
- Total each section of the statement, determine the total net change in cash, and add it to the beginning balance to get the ending balance of cash.

Solution to Demonstration Problem

Supporting computations for cash receipts and cash payments:

(1)	*Cost of equipment sold	$ 21,375
	Accumulated depreciation of equipment sold	(11,100)
	Book value of equipment sold	10,275
	Loss on sale of equipment	(3,300)
	Cash received from sale of equipment	$ 6,975
	Cost of equipment sold	$ 21,375
	Less decrease in the equipment account balance	(10,875)
	Cash paid for new equipment	$ 10,500
(2)	Loss on retirement of bonds	$ 825
	Carrying value of bonds retired	37,500
	Cash paid to retire bonds	$ 38,325
(3)	Net income	$ 60,150
	Less increase in retained earnings	45,900
	Dividends declared	14,250
	Plus decrease in dividends payable	4,500
	Cash paid for dividends	$ 18,750
(4)[B]	Sales	$ 446,100
	Add decrease in accounts receivable	5,700
	Cash received from customers	$451,800
(5)[B]	Cost of goods sold	$ 222,300
	Plus increase in merchandise inventory	9,525
	Purchases	231,825
	Plus decrease in accounts payable	4,950
	Cash paid for merchandise	$236,775
(6)[B]	Other operating expenses	$ 120,300
	Plus increase in prepaid expenses	1,950
	Cash paid for other operating expenses	$122,250
(7)[B]	Income taxes expense	$ 13,725
	Less increase in income taxes payable	(675)
	Cash paid for income taxes	$ 13,050

* Supporting T-account analysis for part 1:

Equipment			
Bal., Dec. 31, 2004	146,700		
Cash purchase	10,500	Sale	21,375
Bal., Dec. 31, 2005	135,825		

Accumulated Depreciation—Equipment			
		Bal., Dec. 31, 2004	47,550
Sale	11,100	Depr. expense	25,500
		Bal., Dec. 31, 2005	61,950

UMLAUF COMPANY
Statement of Cash Flows (Indirect Method)
For Year Ended December 31, 2005

Cash flows from operating activities	
Cash flows from operating activities	
Net income	$60,150
Adjustments to reconcile net income to net cash provided by operating activities	
Decrease in accounts receivable	5,700
Increase in merchandise inventory	(9,525)
Increase in prepaid expenses	(1,950)
Decrease in accounts payable	(4,950)
Increase in income taxes payable	675
Depreciation expense	25,500

[continued on next page]

[continued from previous page]

Loss on sale of plant assets	3,300	
Loss on retirement of bonds	825	
Net cash provided by operating activities		$79,725
Cash flows from investing activities		
Cash received from sale of equipment	6,975	
Cash paid for equipment	(10,500)	
Net cash used in investing activities		(3,525)
Cash flows from financing activities		
Cash paid to retire bonds payable	(38,325)	
Cash paid for dividends	(18,750)	
Net cash used in financing activities		(57,075)
Net increase in cash		$19,125
Cash balance at beginning of year		23,925
Cash balance at end of year		$43,050

UMLAUF COMPANY
Statement of Cash Flows (Direct Method)
For Year Ended December 31, 2005

Cash flows from operating activities		
Cash received from customers	$451,800	
Cash paid for merchandise	(236,775)	
Cash paid for other operating expenses	(122,250)	
Cash paid for income taxes	(13,050)	
Net cash provided by operating activities		$79,725
Cash flows from investing activities		
Cash received from sale of equipment	6,975	
Cash paid for equipment	(10,500)	
Net cash used in investing activities		(3,525)
Cash flows from financing activities		
Cash paid to retire bonds payable	(38,325)	
Cash paid for dividends	(18,750)	
Net cash used in financing activities		(57,075)
Net increase in cash		$19,125
Cash balance at beginning of year		23,925
Cash balance at end of year		$43,050

APPENDIX

Spreadsheet Preparation of the Statement of Cash Flows

16A

This appendix explains how to use a spreadsheet to prepare the statement of cash flows under the indirect method.

Preparing the Indirect Method Spreadsheet

P4 Illustrate spreadsheet use in preparing a statement of cash flows.

Analyzing noncash accounts can be challenging when a company has a large number of accounts and many operating, investing, and financing transactions. A *spreadsheet,* also called *work sheet* or *working paper,* can help us organize the information needed to prepare a statement of cash flows. A spreadsheet also makes it easier to check the accuracy of our work. To illustrate, we return to the comparative balance sheets and income statement shown in Exhibit 16.10. Information needed for the spreadsheet in preparing the statement of cash flows along with identifying letters *a* through *m* follow:

a. Net income is $38,000.

b. Accounts receivable increase by $20,000.

c. Merchandise inventory increases by $14,000.

d. Prepaid expenses increase by $2,000.

e. Accounts payable decrease by $5,000.

f. Interest payable decreases by $1,000.

g. Income taxes payable increase by $10,000.

h. Depreciation expense is $24,000.

i. Plant assets costing $30,000 with accumulated depreciation of $12,000 are sold for $12,000 cash. This yields a loss on sale of assets of $6,000.

j. Bonds with a book value of $34,000 are retired with a cash payment of $18,000, yielding a $16,000 gain on retirement.

k. Plant assets costing $70,000 are purchased with a cash payment of $10,000 and an issuance of bonds payable for $60,000.

l. Issued 3,000 shares of common stock for $15,000 cash.

m. Paid cash dividends of $14,000.

Exhibit 16A.1 shows the indirect method spreadsheet for Genesis. We enter both beginning and ending balance sheet amounts on the spreadsheet. We also enter information in the Analysis of Changes columns (keyed to the additional information items *a* through *m*) to explain changes in the accounts and determine the cash flows for operating, investing, and financing activities. Information about noncash investing and financing activities is reported near the bottom.

Entering the Analysis of Changes on the Spreadsheet

The following sequence of procedures is used to complete the spreadsheet after the beginning and ending balances of the balance sheet accounts are entered:

① Enter net income as the first item in the Statement of Cash Flows section for computing operating cash inflow (debit) and as a credit to Retained Earnings.

② In the Statement of Cash Flows section, adjustments to net income are entered as debits if they increase cash flows and as credits if they decrease cash flows. Applying this same rule, adjust net income for the change in each noncash current asset and current liability account related to operating activities. For each adjustment to net income, the offsetting debit or credit must help reconcile the beginning and ending balances of a current asset or current liability account.

③ Enter adjustments to net income for income statement items not providing or using cash in the period. For each adjustment, the offsetting debit or credit must help reconcile a noncash balance sheet account.

④ Adjust net income to eliminate any gains or losses from investing and financing activities. Because the cash from a gain must be excluded from operating activities, the gain is entered as a credit in the operating activities section. Losses are entered as debits. For each adjustment, the related debit and/or credit must help reconcile balance sheet accounts and involve reconstructed entries to show the cash flow from investing or financing activities.

⑤ After reviewing any unreconciled balance sheet accounts and related information, enter the remaining reconciling entries for investing and financing activities. Examples are purchases of plant assets, issuances of long-term debt, stock issuances, and dividend payments. Some of these may require entries in the noncash investing and financing section of the spreadsheet (reconciled).

⑥ Check accuracy by totaling the Analysis of Changes columns and by determining that the change in each balance sheet account has been explained (reconciled).

Point: Analysis of the changes on the spreadsheet are summarized as:

1. Cash flows from operating activities generally affect net income, current assets, and current liabilities.
2. Cash flows from investing activities generally affect noncurrent asset accounts.
3. Cash flows from financing activities generally affect noncurrent liability and equity accounts.

We illustrate these steps in Exhibit 16A.1 for Genesis:

Step	Entries
①	(*a*)
②	(*b*) through (*g*)
③	(*h*)
④	(*i*) through (*j*)
⑤	(*k*) through (*m*)

Exhibit 16A.1

Spreadsheet for Preparing Statement of Cash Flows—Indirect Method

	A	B	C	D	E	F	G
1	**GENESIS**						
2	**Spreadsheet for Statement of Cash Flows–Indirect Method**						
3	**For Year Ended December 31, 2005**						
5				**Analysis of Changes**			
6		**Dec. 31,**					**Dec. 31,**
7		**2004**		**Debit**		**Credit**	**2005**
8	**Balance Sheet—Debits**						
9	Cash	$ 12,000					$ 17,000
10	Accounts receivable	40,000	(b)	$ 20,000			60,000
11	Merchandise inventory	70,000	(c)	14,000			84,000
12	Prepaid expenses	4,000	(d)	2,000			6,000
13	Plant assets	210,000	(k1)	70,000	(i)	$ 30,000	250,000
14		$336,000					$417,000
16	**Balance Sheet—Credits**						
17	Accumulated depreciation	$ 48,000	(i)	12,000	(h)	24,000	$ 60,000
18	Accounts payable	40,000	(e)	5,000			35,000
19	Interest payable	4,000	(f)	1,000			3,000
20	Income taxes payable	12,000			(g)	10,000	22,000
21	Bonds payable	64,000	(j)	34,000	(k2)	60,000	90,000
22	Common stock, $5 par value	80,000			(l)	15,000	95,000
23	Retained earnings	88,000	(m)	14,000	(a)	38,000	112,000
24		$336,000					$417,000
26	**Statement of Cash Flows**						
27	Operating activities						
28	Net income		(a)	38,000			
29	Increase in accounts receivable				(b)	20,000	
30	Increase in merchandise inventory				(c)	14,000	
31	Increase in prepaid expenses				(d)	2,000	
32	Decrease in accounts payable				(e)	5,000	
33	Decrease in interest payable				(f)	1,000	
34	Increase in income taxes payable		(g)	10,000			
35	Depreciation expense		(h)	24,000			
36	Loss on sale of plant assets		(i)	6,000			
37	Gain on retirement of bonds				(j)	16,000	
38	Investing activities						
39	Receipts from sale of plant assets		(i)	12,000			
40	Payment for purchase of plant assets				(k1)	10,000	
41	Financing activities						
42	Payment to retire bonds				(j)	18,000	
43	Receipts from issuing stock		(l)	15,000			
44	Payment of cash dividends				(m)	14,000	
45							
46	**Noncash Investing and Financing Activities**						
47	Purchase of plant assets with bonds		(k2)	60,000	(k1)	60,000	
48				$337,000		$337,000	

Since adjustments *i*, *j*, and *k* are more challenging, we show them in the following debit and credit format. These entries are for purposes of our understanding; they are *not* the entries actually made in the journals. Changes in the Cash account are identified as sources or uses of cash.

		Debit	Credit
i.	Loss from sale of plant assets	6,000	
	Accumulated depreciation	12,000	
	Receipt from sale of plant assets **(source of cash)**	12,000	
	Plant assets		30,000
	To describe sale of plant assets.		

[continued on next page]

[continued from previous page]

		Debit	Credit
j.	Bonds payable	34,000	
	Payments to retire bonds **(use of cash)**		18,000
	Gain on retirement of bonds.		16,000
	To describe retirement of bonds.		
k1.	Plant assets	70,000	
	Payment to purchase plant assets **(use of cash)**		10,000
	Purchase of plant assets financed by bonds.		60,000
	To describe purchase of plant assets.		
k2.	Purchase of plant assets financed by bonds	60,000	
	Bonds payable		60,000
	To issue bonds for purchase of assets.		

APPENDIX

16B Direct Method of Reporting Operating Cash Flows

P5 Compute cash flows from operating activities using the direct method.

We compute cash flows from operating activities under the direct method by adjusting accrual-based income statement items to the cash basis. The usual approach is to adjust income statement accounts related to operating activities for changes in their related balance sheet accounts as follows:

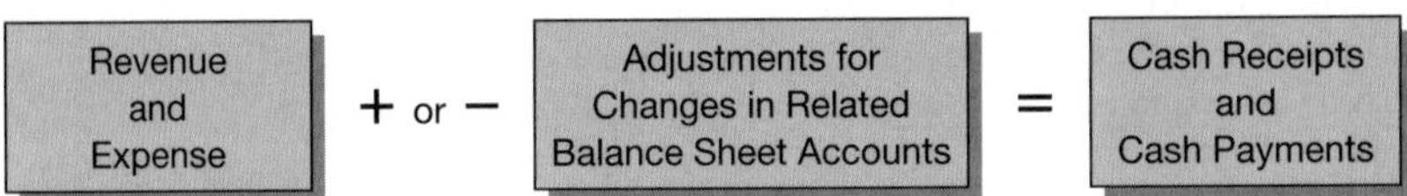

Global: Some countries such as Australia require the direct method of reporting.

The framework for reporting cash receipts and cash payments for the operating section of the cash flow statement under the direct method is as in Exhibit 16B.1. We consider cash receipts first and then cash payments.

Exhibit 16B.1

Major Classes of Operating Cash Flows

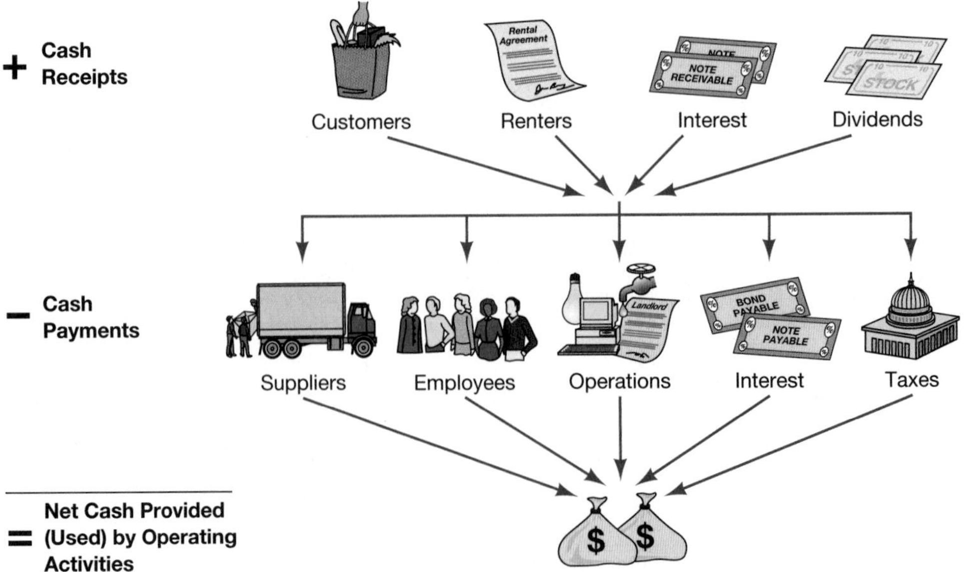

Operating Cash Receipts

A review of Exhibit 16.10 and the additional information reported by Genesis suggests only one potential cash receipt: sales to customers. This section, therefore, starts with sales to customers as reported on the income statement and then adjusts it as necessary to obtain cash received from customers to report on the statement of cash flows.

Cash Received from Customers If all sales are for cash, the amount received from customers equals the sales reported on the income statement. When some or all sales are on account, however, we must adjust the amount of sales for the change in Accounts Receivable. It is often helpful to use *account analysis* to do this. This usually involves setting up a T-account and reconstructing its major entries, with emphasis on cash receipts and payments. To illustrate, we use a T-account that includes accounts receivable balances for Genesis on December 31, 2004 and 2005. The beginning balance is $40,000 and the ending balance is $60,000. Next, the income statement shows sales of $590,000, which we enter on the debit side of this account. We now can reconstruct the Accounts Receivable account to determine the amount of cash received from customers as follows:

Point: An accounts receivable increase implies cash received from customers is less than sales (the converse is also true).

Accounts Receivable			
Bal., Dec. 31, 2004	40,000		
Sales	590,000	**Cash receipts =**	**570,000**
Bal., Dec. 31, 2005	60,000		

This T-account shows that the Accounts Receivable balance begins at $40,000 and increases to $630,000 from sales of $590,000, yet its ending balance is only $60,000. This implies that cash receipts from customers are $570,000, computed as $40,000 + $590,000 − [?] = $60,000. This computation can be rearranged to express cash received as equal to sales of $590,000 minus a $20,000 increase in accounts receivable. This computation is summarized as a general rule in Exhibit 16B.2. The statement of cash flows in Exhibit 16.7 reports the $570,000 cash received from customers as a cash inflow from operating activities.

Example: If the ending balance of accounts receivable is $20,000, what is cash received from customers? *Answer:* $610,000

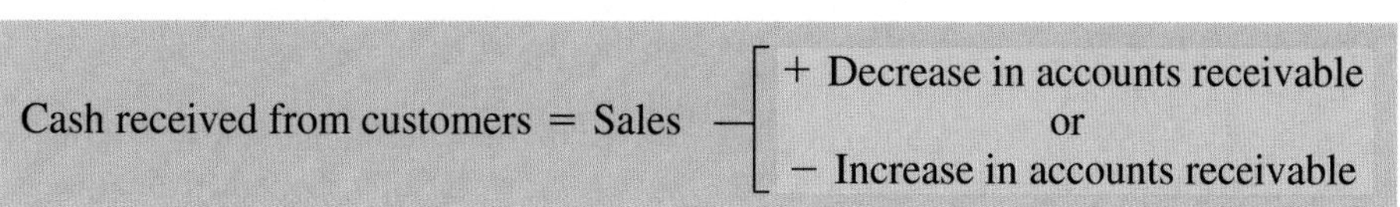

Exhibit 16B.2

Formula to Compute Cash Received from Customers—Direct Method

Other Cash Receipts While Genesis's cash receipts are limited to collections from customers, we often see other types of cash receipts, most commonly cash receipts involving rent, interest, and dividends. We compute cash received from these items by subtracting an increase in their respective receivable or adding a decrease. For instance, if rent receivable increases in the period, cash received from renters is less than rent revenue reported on the income statement. If rent receivable decreases, cash received is more than reported rent revenue. The same logic applies to interest and dividends. The formulas for these computations are summarized later in this appendix.

Point: Net income and cash flows from operations are different. Net income is measured using accrual accounting. Cash flows from operations are measured using cash basis accounting.

Operating Cash Payments

A review of Exhibit 16.10 and the additional Genesis information shows four operating expenses: cost of goods sold; wages and other operating expenses; interest expense; and taxes expense. We analyze each expense to compute its cash amounts for the statement of cash flows. (We then examine depreciation and the other losses and gains.)

Cash Paid for Merchandise We compute cash paid for merchandise by analyzing both cost of goods sold and merchandise inventory. If all merchandise purchases are for cash and the ending balance of Merchandise Inventory is unchanged from the beginning balance, the amount of cash paid for merchandise equals cost of goods sold—an uncommon situation. Instead, there normally is some change in the Merchandise Inventory balance. Also, some or all merchandise purchases are often made on credit, and this yields changes in the Accounts Payable balance. When the balances of both Merchandise Inventory and Accounts Payable change, we must adjust the cost of goods sold for changes in both accounts to compute cash paid for merchandise. This is a two-step adjustment.

First, we use the change in the account balance of Merchandise Inventory, along with the cost of goods sold amount, to compute cost of purchases for the period. An increase in merchandise inventory implies that we bought more than we sold, and we add this inventory increase to cost of goods sold to compute cost of purchases. A decrease in merchandise inventory implies that we bought less than we sold, and we subtract the inventory decrease from cost of goods sold to compute purchases. We illustrate the *first step* by reconstructing the Merchandise Inventory account of Genesis:

Merchandise Inventory			
Bal., Dec. 31, 2004	70,000		
Purchases =	**314,000**	Cost of goods sold	300,000
Bal., Dec. 31, 2005	84,000		

The beginning balance is $70,000, and the ending balance is $84,000. The income statement shows that cost of goods sold is $300,000, which we enter on the credit side of this account. With this information, we determine the amount for cost of purchases to be $314,000. This computation can be rearranged to express cost of purchases as equal to cost of goods sold of $300,000 plus the $14,000 increase in inventory.

The second step uses the change in the balance of Accounts Payable, and the amount of cost of purchases, to compute cash paid for merchandise. A decrease in accounts payable implies that we paid for more goods than we acquired this period, and we would then add the accounts payable decrease to cost of purchases to compute cash paid for merchandise. An increase in accounts payable implies that we paid for less than the amount of goods acquired, and we would subtract the accounts payable increase from purchases to compute cash paid for merchandise. The *second step* is applied to Genesis by reconstructing its Accounts Payable account:

Accounts Payable			
		Bal., Dec. 31, 2004	40,000
Cash payments =	**319,000**	Purchases	314,000
		Bal., Dec. 31, 2005	35,000

Example: If the ending balances of Inventory and Accounts Payable are $60,000 and $50,000, respectively (instead of $84,000 and $35,000), what is cash paid for merchandise? *Answer:* $280,000

Its beginning balance of $40,000 plus purchases of $314,000 minus an ending balance of $35,000 yields cash paid of $319,000 (or $40,000 + $314,000 − [?] = $35,000). Alternatively, we can express cash paid for merchandise as equal to purchases of $314,000 plus the $5,000 decrease in accounts payable. The $319,000 cash paid for merchandise is reported on the statement of cash flows in Exhibit 16.7 as a cash outflow under operating activities.

We summarize this two-step adjustment to cost of goods sold to compute cash paid for merchandise inventory in Exhibit 16B.3.

Exhibit 16B.3

Two Steps to Compute Cash Paid for Merchandise—Direct Method

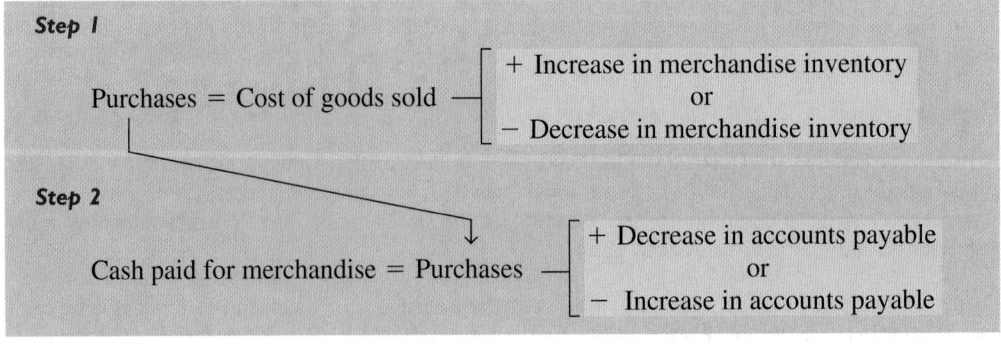

Cash Paid for Wages and Operating Expenses (excluding depreciation)

The income statement of Genesis shows wages and other operating expenses of $216,000 (see Exhibit 16.10). To compute cash paid for wages and other operating expenses, we adjust this amount for any changes in their related balance sheet accounts. We begin by looking for any prepaid expenses and accrued liabilities related to wages and other operating expenses in the balance sheets of Genesis in

Exhibit 16.10. The balance sheets show prepaid expenses but no accrued liabilities. Thus, the adjustment is limited to the change in prepaid expenses. The amount of adjustment is computed by assuming that all cash paid for wages and other operating expenses is initially debited to Prepaid Expenses. This assumption allows us to reconstruct the Prepaid Expenses account:

Prepaid Expenses			
Bal., Dec. 31, 2004	4,000		
Cash payments =	**218,000**	Wages and other operating exp.	216,000
Bal., Dec. 31, 2005	6,000		

Prepaid Expenses increase by $2,000 in the period, meaning that cash paid for wages and other operating expenses exceeds the reported expense by $2,000. Alternatively, we can express cash paid for wages and other operating expenses as equal to its reported expenses of $216,000 plus the $2,000 increase in prepaid expenses.[1]

Point: A decrease in prepaid expenses implies that reported expenses include an amount(s) that did not require a cash outflow in the period.

Exhibit 16B.4 summarizes the adjustments to wages (including salaries) and other operating expenses. The Genesis balance sheet did not report accrued liabilities, but we include them in the formula to explain the adjustment to cash when they do exist. A decrease in accrued liabilities implies that we paid cash for more goods or services than received this period, so we add the decrease in accrued liabilities to the expense amount to obtain cash paid for these goods or services. An increase in accrued liabilities implies that we paid cash for less than what was acquired, so we subtract this increase in accrued liabilities from the expense amount to get cash paid.

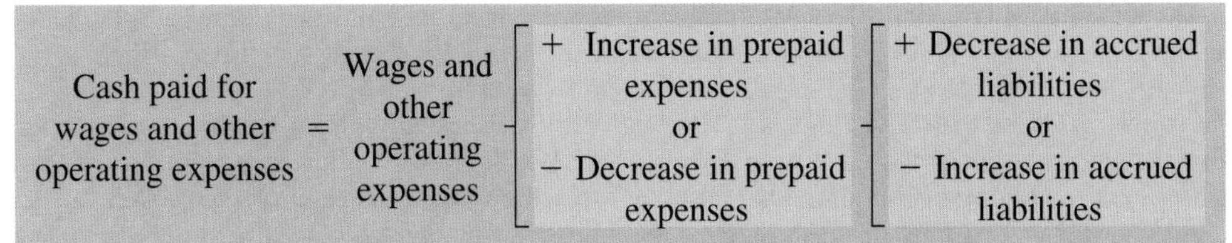

Exhibit 16B.4

Formula to Compute Cash Paid for Wages and Operating Expenses—Direct Method

Cash Paid for Interest and Income Taxes Computing operating cash flows for interest and taxes is similar to that for operating expenses. Both require adjustments to their amounts reported on the income statement for changes in their related balance sheet accounts. We begin with the Genesis income statement showing interest expense of $7,000 and income taxes expense of $15,000. To compute the cash paid, we adjust interest expense for the change in interest payable and then the income taxes expense for the change in income taxes payable. These computations involve reconstructing both liability accounts:

Interest Payable			
		Bal., Dec. 31, 2004	4,000
Cash paid for interest =	**8,000**	Interest expense	7,000
		Bal., Dec. 31, 2005	3,000

Income Taxes Payable			
		Bal., Dec. 31, 2004	12,000
Cash paid for taxes =	**5,000**	Income taxes expense	15,000
		Bal., Dec. 31, 2005	22,000

These accounts reveal cash paid for interest of $8,000 and cash paid for income taxes of $5,000. The formulas to compute these amounts are in Exhibit 16B.5. Both of these cash payments are reported as operating cash outflows on the statement of cash flows in Exhibit 16.7.

[1] The assumption that all cash payments for wages and operating expenses are initially debited to Prepaid Expenses is not necessary for our analysis to hold. If cash payments are debited directly to the expense account, the total amount of cash paid for wages and other operating expenses still equals the $216,000 expense plus the $2,000 increase in Prepaid Expenses (which arise from end-of-period adjusting entries).

Exhibit 16B.5

Formulas to Compute Cash Paid for Both Interest and Taxes—Direct Method

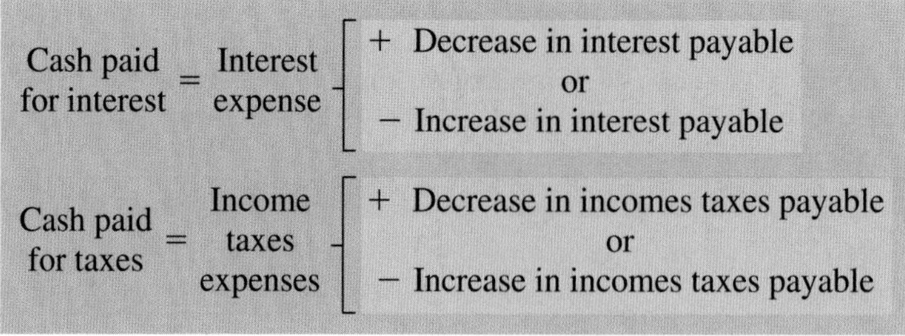

Analysis of Additional Expenses, Gains, and Losses Genesis has three additional items reported on its income statement: depreciation, loss on sale of assets, and gain on retirement of debt. We must consider each for its potential cash effects.

Depreciation Expense Depreciation expense is $24,000. It is often called a *noncash expense* because depreciation has no cash flows. Depreciation expense is an allocation of an asset's depreciable cost. The cash outflow with a plant asset is reported as part of investing activities when it is paid for. Thus, depreciation expense is *never* reported on a statement of cash flows using the direct method, nor is depletion or amortization expense.

Loss on Sale of Assets Sales of assets frequently result in gains and losses reported as part of net income, but the amount of recorded gain or loss does *not* reflect any cash flows in these transactions. Asset sales result in cash inflow equal to the cash amount received, regardless of whether the asset was sold at a gain or a loss. This cash inflow is reported under investing activities. Thus, the loss or gain on a sale of assets is *never* reported on a statement of cash flows using the direct method.

Point: The direct method is usually viewed as *user friendly* because less accounting knowledge is required to understand and use it.

Gain on Retirement of Debt Retirement of debt usually yields a gain or loss reported as part of net income, but that gain or loss does *not* reflect cash flow in this transaction. Debt retirement results in cash outflow equal to the cash paid to settle the debt, regardless of whether the debt is retired at a gain or loss. This cash outflow is reported under financing activities; the loss or gain from retirement of debt is *never* reported on a statement of cash flows using the direct method.

Summary of Adjustments for Direct Method

Exhibit 16B.6 summarizes common adjustments for net income to yield net cash provided (used) by operating activities under the direct method.

Exhibit 16B.6

Summary of Selected Adjustments for Direct Method

Item	From Income Statement	Adjustments to Obtain Cash Flow Numbers
Receipts		
From sales	Sales Revenue	+Decrease in Accounts Receivable −Increase in Accounts Receivable
From rent	Rent Revenue	+Decrease in Rent Receivable −Increase in Rent Receivable
From interest	Interest Revenue	+Decrease in Interest Receivable −Increase in Interest Receivable
From dividends	Dividend Revenue	+Decrease in Dividends Receivable −Increase in Dividends Receivable
Payments		
To suppliers	Cost of Goods Sold	+Increase in Inventory / −Decrease in Inventory; +Decrease in Accounts Payable / −Increase in Accounts Payable
For operations	Operating Expense	+Increase in Prepaids / −Decrease in Prepaids; +Decrease in Accrued Liabilities / −Increase in Accrued Liabilities
To employees	Wages (Salaries) Expense	+Decrease in Wages (Salaries) Payable −Increase in Wages (Salaries) Payable
For interest	Interest Expense	+Decrease in Interest Payable −Increase in Interest Payable
For taxes	Income Tax Expense	+Decrease in Income Tax Payable −Increase in Income Tax Payable

Direct Method Format of Operating Activities Section

Exhibit 16.7 shows the Genesis statement of cash flows using the direct method. Major items of cash inflows and cash outflows are listed separately in the operating activities section. The format requires that operating cash outflows be subtracted from operating cash inflows to get net cash provided (used) by operating activities. The FASB recommends that the operating activities section of the statement of cash flows be reported using the direct method, which is considered more useful to financial statement users. *However, the FASB requires a reconciliation of net income to net cash provided (used) by operating activities when the direct method is used* (which can be reported in the notes). This reconciliation is similar to preparation of the operating activities section of the statement of cash flows using the indirect method.

Point: Some preparers argue that it is easier to prepare a statement of cash flows using the indirect method. This likely explains its greater frequency in financial statements.

Decision Insight

B-Cash The NBA's **Boston Celtics** report operating cash flows using the direct method. The team's operating activities section from its recent statement of cash flows is shown here ($ in 000s). For this same period, its operating income is $22,953 (in 000s).

Basketball regular season receipts	
Ticket sales	$35,270
Television and radio broadcast fees	36,373
Other, advertising & playoff receipts	22,493
Costs and expenses	
Basketball season/playoff expenditures	(68,415)
General and administrative expenses	(5,124)
Selling and promotional expenses	(5,012)
Other expenses and revenues	(4,167)
Net cash flows from operations	$11,418

Quick Check

8. Net sales in a period are $590,000, beginning accounts receivable are $120,000, and ending accounts receivable are $90,000. What cash amount is collected from customers in the period?
9. The Merchandise Inventory account balance decreases in the period from a beginning balance of $32,000 to an ending balance of $28,000. Cost of goods sold for the period is $168,000. If the Accounts Payable balance increases $2,400 in the period, what is the cash amount paid for merchandise inventory?
10. Wages and other operating expenses total $112,000. Beginning-of-period prepaid expenses totaled $1,200, and its ending balance is $4,200. The end-of-period wages payable equal $5,600, whereas there were no accrued liabilities at period-end. How much cash is paid for wages and other operating expenses?

Answers—p. 656

Summary

C1 Explain the purpose and importance of cash flow information. The main purpose of the statement of cash flows is to report the major cash receipts and cash payments for a period. This includes identifying cash flows as relating to either operating, investing, or financing activities. Most business decisions involve evaluating activities that provide or use cash.

C2 Distinguish among operating, investing, and financing activities. Operating activities include transactions and events that determine net income. Investing activities include transactions and events that mainly affect long-term assets. Financing activities include transactions and events that mainly affect long-term liabilities and equity.

C3 Identify and disclose noncash investing and financing activities. Noncash investing and financing activities must be disclosed either in a note or a separate schedule to the statement of cash flows. Examples are the retirement of debt by issuing equity and the exchange of a note payable for plant assets.

C4 Describe the format of the statement of cash flows. The statement of cash flows separates cash receipts and payments into operating, investing, or financing activities.

A1 Analyze the statement of cash flows. To understand and predict cash flows, users stress identification of the sources and uses of cash flows by operating, investing, and financing activities. Emphasis is on operating cash flows since they derive from continuing operations.

A2 Compute and apply the cash flow on total assets ratio. The cash flow on total assets ratio is defined as operating cash flows divided by average total assets. Analysis of current and past values for this ratio can reflect a company's ability to yield regular and positive cash flows. It is also viewed as a measure of earnings quality.

P1 Prepare a statement of cash flows. Preparation of a statement of cash flows involves five steps: (1) Compute the net increase or decrease in cash; (2) compute net cash provided (used) by operating activities (*using either the direct or indirect method*); (3) compute net cash provided (used) by investing activities; (4) compute net cash provided (used) by financing activities; and (5) report the beginning and ending cash balance and prove that it is explained by net cash flows. Noncash investing and financing activities are also disclosed.

P2 Compute cash flows from operating activities using the indirect method. The indirect method for reporting net cash provided (used) by operating activities starts with net income and then adjusts it for three items: (1) changes in noncash current assets and current liabilities related to operating activities, (2) revenues and expenses not providing (using) cash, and (3) gains and losses from investing and financing activities.

P3 Determine cash flows from both investing and financing activities. Cash flows from both investing and financing activities are determined by identifying the cash flow effects of transactions and events affecting each balance sheet account related to these activities. All cash flows from these activities are identified when we can explain changes in these accounts from the beginning to the end of the period.

P4[A] Illustrate spreadsheet use in preparing a statement of cash flows. A spreadsheet is a useful tool in preparing a statement of cash flows. Six key steps (see appendix) are applied when using the spreadsheet to prepare the statement.

P5[B] Compute cash flows from operating activities using the direct method. The direct method for reporting net cash provided (used) by operating activities lists major operating cash inflows less cash outflows to yield net cash inflow or outflow from operations.

Guidance Answers to **Decision Maker**

Entrepreneur Several factors might explain an increase in net cash flows when a net loss is reported, including (1) early recognition of expenses relative to revenues generated (such as research and development), (2) cash advances on long-term sales contracts not yet recognized in income, (3) issuances of debt or equity for cash to finance expansion, (4) cash sale of assets, (5) delay of cash payments, and (6) cash prepayment on sales. Analysis needs to focus on the components of both the net loss and the net cash flows and their implications for future performance.

Reporter Your initial reaction based on the company's $600,000 loss with a $550,000 decrease in net cash flows is not positive. However, closer scrutiny reveals a more positive picture of this company's performance. Cash flow from operating activities is $650,000, computed as [?] – $850,000 – $350,000 = $(550,000). You also note that net income *before* the extraordinary loss is $330,000, computed as [?] – $930,000 = $(600,000).

Guidance Answers to **Quick Checks**

1. No to both. The statement of cash flows reports changes in the sum of cash plus cash equivalents. It does not report transfers between cash and cash equivalents.
2. The three categories of cash inflows and outflows are operating activities, investing activities, and financing activities.
3. **a.** Investing **c.** Financing **e.** Operating
   b. Operating **d.** Operating **f.** Financing
4. $74,900 + $4,600 – $11,700 – $1,000 + $3,400 = $70,200
5. Expenses such as depreciation and amortization do not require current cash outflows. Therefore, adding these expenses back to net income eliminates these noncash items from the net income number, converting it to a cash basis.
6. A gain on the sale of plant assets is subtracted from net income because a sale of plant assets is not an operating activity; it is an investing activity for the amount of cash received from its sale. Also, such a gain yields no cash effects.
7. $80,000 – $30,000 – $10,000 = $40,000 cash receipt. The $40,000 cash receipt is reported as an investing activity.
8. $590,000 + ($120,000 – $90,000) = $620,000
9. $168,000 – ($32,000 – $28,000) – $2,400 = $161,600
10. $112,000 + ($4,200 – $1,200) – $5,600 = $109,400

mhhe.com/larson

Key Terms

Key Terms are available at the book's Website for learning and testing in an online Flashcard Format.

Cash flow on total assets (p. 644)
Direct method (p. 632)
Financing activities (p. 628)
Indirect method (p. 632)
Investing activities (p. 628)
Operating activities (p. 627)
Statement of cash flows (p. 626)

Personal Interactive Quiz

Personal Interactive Quizzes A and B are available at the book's Website to reinforce and assess your learning.

Superscript letter A (B) denotes assignments based on Appendix 16A (16B).

Discussion Questions

1. When a statement of cash flows is prepared using the direct method, what are some of the operating cash flows?
2. What is the direct method of reporting cash flows from operating activities?
3. What is the indirect method of reporting cash flows from operating activities?
4. What are some investing activities reported on the statement of cash flows?
5. What are some financing activities reported on the statement of cash flows?
6. Where on the statement of cash flows is the payment of cash dividends reported?
7. Assume that a company purchases land for $100,000, paying $20,000 cash and borrowing the remainder with a long-term note payable. How should this transaction be reported on a statement of cash flows?
8. On June 3, a company borrows $50,000 cash by giving its bank a 160-day, interest-bearing note. On the statement of cash flows, where should this be reported?
9. If a company reports positive net income for the year, can it show a net cash outflow from operating activities? Explain.
10. Is depreciation a source of cash flow?
11. Refer to **Krispy Kreme**'s statement of cash flows in Appendix A. (*a*) Which method is used to compute its net cash provided by operating activities? (*b*) While its balance sheet shows an increase in receivables from fiscal years 2002 to 2003, why is this increase in receivables subtracted when computing net cash provided by operating activities for fiscal year 2003?
12. Refer to **Tastykake**'s statement of cash flows in Appendix A. What are its cash flows from financing activities for 2002? List items and amounts.
13. Refer to **Harley-Davidson**'s statement of cash flows in Appendix A. What investing activities result in cash outflows for the year ended January 31, 2002? List items and amounts.

Red numbers denote Discussion Questions that involve decision-making.

***Homework Manager** repeats all numerical Quick Studies on the book's Website with new numbers.*

QUICK STUDY

QS 16-1
Statement of cash flows
C1 C2 C3

The statement of cash flows is one of the four primary financial statements.

1. Describe the content and layout of a statement of cash flows, including its three sections.
2. List at least three transactions classified as investing activities in a statement of cash flows.
3. List at least three transactions classified as financing activities in a statement of cash flows.
4. List at least three transactions classified as significant noncash financing and investing activities in the statement of cash flows.

QS 16-2
Transaction classification by activity
C2

Classify the following cash flows as operating, investing, or financing activities:

1. Sold long-term investments for cash.
2. Received cash payments from customers.
3. Paid cash for wages and salaries.
4. Purchased inventories for cash.
5. Paid cash dividends.
6. Issued common stock for cash.
7. Received cash interest on a note.
8. Paid cash interest on outstanding bonds.
9. Received cash from sale of land at a loss.
10. Paid cash for property taxes on building.

QS 16-3
Computing cash from operations (indirect) P2

Use the following balance sheets and income statement to answer QS 16-3 through QS 16-8. Use the indirect method to prepare the cash provided (used) from operating activities section only of the statement of cash flows.

ORWELL, INC.
Income Statement
For Year Ended December 31, 2005

Sales		$468,000
Cost of goods sold		312,000
Gross profit		156,000
Operating expenses		
Depreciation expense	$38,600	
Other expenses	57,000	95,600
Income before taxes		60,400
Income taxes expense		24,600
Net income		$ 35,800

ORWELL, INC.
Comparative Balance Sheets
December 31, 2005

	2005	2004
Assets		
Cash	$ 95,800	$ 25,000
Accounts receivable (net)	42,000	52,000
Inventory	86,800	96,800
Prepaid expenses	6,400	5,200
Furniture	110,000	120,000
Accum. depreciation—Furniture	(18,000)	(10,000)
Total assets	$323,000	$289,000
Liabilities and Equity		
Accounts payable	$ 16,000	$ 22,000
Wages payable	10,000	6,000
Income taxes payable	2,400	3,600
Notes payable (long-term)	30,000	70,000
Common stock, $5 par value	230,000	180,000
Retained earnings	34,600	7,400
Total liabilities and equity	$323,000	$289,000

QS 16-4
Computing cash from asset sales P3

Refer to the data in QS 16-3. Furniture costing $54,000 is sold at its book value in 2005. Acquisitions of furniture total $44,000 cash, on which no depreciation is necessary because it is acquired at year-end. What is the cash inflow related to the sale of furniture?

QS 16-5
Computing financing cash outflows P3

Refer to the data in QS 16-3. (1) Assume that all common stock is issued for cash. What amount of cash dividends is paid during 2005? (2) Assume that no additional notes payable are issued in 2005. What cash amount is paid to reduce the notes payable balance in 2005?

QS 16-6[B]
Computing cash received from customers P5

Refer to the data in QS 16-3.

1. How much cash is received from sales to customers for year 2005?

2. What is the net increase or decrease in cash for year 2005?

QS 16-7[B]
Computing operating cash outflows P5

Refer to the data in QS 16-3. (1) How much cash is paid to acquire merchandise inventory during year 2005? (2) How much cash is paid for operating expenses during year 2005?

QS 16-8[B]
Computing cash from operations (direct) P5

Refer to the data in QS 16-3. Use the direct method to prepare the cash provided (used) from operating activities section only of the statement of cash flows.

QS 16-9
Analyses of sources and uses of cash A1 A2

Financial data from three competitors in the same industry follow.

1. Which of the three competitors is in the strongest position as shown by its statement of cash flows?

2. Analyze and discuss the strength of Z-Best's cash flow on total assets ratio to that of Lopez.

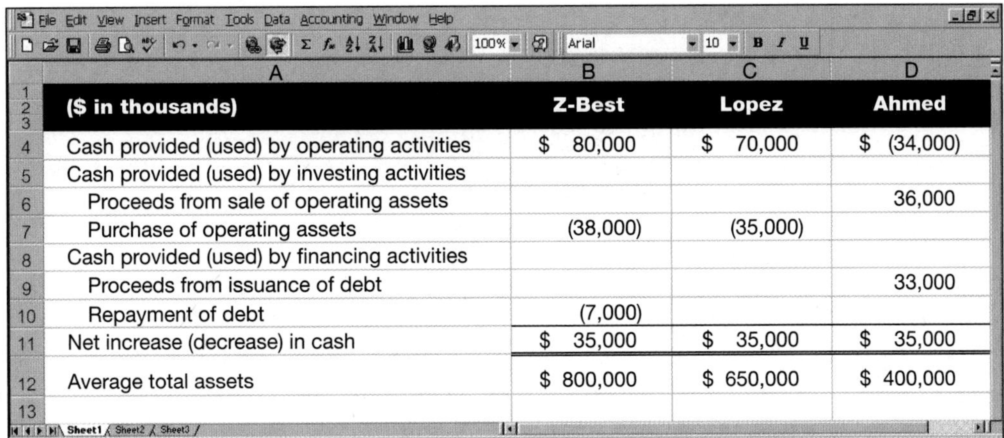

($ in thousands)	Z-Best	Lopez	Ahmed
Cash provided (used) by operating activities	$ 80,000	$ 70,000	$ (34,000)
Cash provided (used) by investing activities			
Proceeds from sale of operating assets			36,000
Purchase of operating assets	(38,000)	(35,000)	
Cash provided (used) by financing activities			
Proceeds from issuance of debt			33,000
Repayment of debt	(7,000)		
Net increase (decrease) in cash	$ 35,000	$ 35,000	$ 35,000
Average total assets	$ 800,000	$ 650,000	$ 400,000

QS 16-10A
Noncash accounts on a spreadsheet P4

When a spreadsheet for a statement of cash flows is prepared, all changes in noncash balance sheet accounts are fully explained on the spreadsheet. Explain how we use these noncash balance sheet accounts to fully account for cash flows on a spreadsheet.

***Homework Manager** repeats all numerical Exercises on the book's Website with new numbers.*

EXERCISES

Exercise 16-1
Cash flow from operations (indirect)
P2

Rasheed Company reports net income of $390,000 for the year ended December 31, 2005. It also reports $70,000 depreciation expense and a $10,000 gain on the sale of machinery. Its comparative balance sheets reveal a $30,000 increase in accounts receivable, $16,000 increase in accounts payable, $8,000 decrease in prepaid expenses, and $12,000 decrease in wages payable.

Required

Prepare only the operating activities section of the statement of cash flows for 2005 using the *indirect method.*

Exercise 16-2
Cash flow classification (indirect) C2 C3 P2

The following transactions and events occurred during the year. Assuming that this company uses the *indirect method* to report cash provided by operating activities, indicate where each item would appear on its statement of cash flows by placing an *x* in the appropriate column.

	Statement of Cash Flows			Noncash Investing and Financing Activities	Not Reported on Statement or in Notes
	Operating Activities	Investing Activities	Financing Activities		
a. Paid cash to purchase inventory.	____	____	____	____	____
b. Purchased land by issuing common stock.	____	____	____	____	____
c. Accounts receivable decreased in the year.	____	____	____	____	____
d. Sold equipment for cash, yielding a loss.	____	____	____	____	____
e. Recorded depreciation expense.	____	____	____	____	____
f. Income taxes payable increased in the year.	____	____	____	____	____
g. Declared and paid a cash dividend.	____	____	____	____	____

Exercise 16-3B
Cash flow classification (direct) C2 C3 P5

The following transactions and events occurred during the year. Assuming that this company uses the *direct method* to report cash provided by operating activities, indicate where each item would appear on the statement of cash flows by placing an *x* in the appropriate column.

	Statement of Cash Flows			Noncash Investing and Financing Activities	Not Reported on Statement or in Note
	Operating Activities	Investing Activities	Financing Activities		
a. Retired long-term bonds payable by issuing common stock. .	____	____	____	____	____
b. Recorded depreciation expense.	____	____	____	____	____
c. Paid cash dividend that was declared in a prior period. .	____	____	____	____	____
d. Sold inventory for cash. .	____	____	____	____	____
e. Borrowed cash from bank by signing a 9-month note payable.	____	____	____	____	____
f. Paid cash to purchase a patent.	____	____	____	____	____
g. Accepted six-month note receivable in exchange for plant assets.	____	____	____	____	____

Exercise 16-4[B]
Computation of cash flows (direct)
P5

For each of the following three separate cases, use the information provided about the calendar-year 2005 operations of Sahim Company to compute the required cash flow information:

Case A: Compute cash received from customers:	
Sales	$510,000
Accounts receivable, December 31, 2004	25,200
Accounts receivable, December 31, 2005	34,800
Case B: Compute cash paid for rent:	
Rent expense	$140,800
Rent payable, December 31, 2004	8,800
Rent payable, December 31, 2005	7,200
Case C: Compute cash paid for merchandise:	
Cost of goods sold	$528,000
Merchandise inventory, December 31, 2004	159,600
Accounts payable, December 31, 2004	67,800
Merchandise inventory, December 31, 2005	131,400
Accounts payable, December 31, 2005	84,000

Exercise 16-5[B]
Preparation of statement of cash flows (direct) and supporting note
C2 C3 C4 P1

Use the following information about the cash flows of Kansas Company to prepare a complete statement of cash flows (*direct method*) for the year ended December 31, 2005. Use a note disclosure for any noncash investing and financing activities.

Cash and cash equivalents balance, December 31, 2004	$ 25,000
Cash and cash equivalents balance, December 31, 2005	70,000
Cash received as interest	2,500
Cash paid for salaries	72,500
Bonds payable retired by issuing common stock (no gain or loss on retirement)	187,500
Cash paid to retire long-term notes payable	125,000
Cash received from sale of equipment	61,250
Cash received in exchange for six-month note payable	25,000
Land purchased by issuing long-term note payable	106,250
Cash paid for store equipment	23,750
Cash dividends paid	15,000
Cash paid for other expenses	40,000
Cash received from customers	485,000
Cash paid for merchandise	252,500

Exercise 16-6
Cash flows from operating activities (indirect)
P2

Use the following income statement and information about changes in noncash current assets and current liabilities to prepare only the cash flows from operating activities section of the statement of cash flows using the *indirect* method:

BECKHAM COMPANY Income Statement For Year Ended December 31, 2005	
Sales	$1,818,000
Cost of goods sold	891,000
Gross profit	927,000

[continued on next page]

[continued from previous page]

Operating expenses		
Salaries expense	$248,535	
Depreciation expense	43,200	
Rent expense	48,600	
Amortization expenses—Patents	5,400	
Utilities expense	19,125	364,860
		562,140
Gain on sale of equipment		7,200
Net income		$ 569,340

Changes in current asset and current liability accounts for the year that relate to operations follow:

Accounts receivable	$40,500 increase	Accounts payable	$13,500 decrease
Merchandise inventory	27,000 increase	Salaries payable	4,500 decrease

Exercise 16-7[B]
Cash flows from operating activities (direct) P5

Refer to the information about Beckham Company in Exercise 16-6. Use the *direct method* to prepare only the cash provided (used) by operating activities section of the statement of cash flows.

Exercise 16-8
Cash flows from operating activities (indirect)
P2

Roney Company's calendar-year 2005 income statement shows the following: Net Income, $364,000; Depreciation Expense, $45,000; Amortization Expense, $8,200; Gain on Sale of Plant Assets, $7,000. An examination of the company's current assets and current liabilities reveals the following changes (all from operating activities): Accounts Receivable decrease, $18,100; Merchandise Inventory decrease, $52,000; Prepaid Expenses increase, $3,700; Accounts Payable decrease, $9,200; Other Payables increase, $1,400. Use the *indirect method* to compute cash flow from operating activities.

Exercise 16-9
Preparation of statement of cash flows (indirect)
C2 A2 P1 P2 P3

Use the financial statements and additional information shown to (1) prepare a statement of cash flows for the year ended June 30, 2005, using the *indirect method,* and (2) compute the cash flow on total assets ratio for Gecko, Inc., for its fiscal year 2005.

GECKO INC.
Income Statement
For Year Ended June 30, 2005

Sales		$668,000
Cost of goods sold		412,000
Gross profit		256,000
Operating expenses		
Depreciation expense	$58,600	
Other expenses	67,000	
Total operating expenses		125,600
		130,400
Other gains (losses)		
Gain on sale of equipment		2,000
Income before taxes		132,400
Income taxes expense		45,640
Net income		$ 86,760

GECKO INC.
Comparative Balance Sheets
June 30, 2005

	2005	2004
Assets		
Cash	$ 85,800	$ 45,000
Accounts receivable (net)	70,000	52,000
Inventory	66,800	96,800
Prepaid expenses	5,400	5,200
Equipment	130,000	120,000
Accum. depreciation—Equip.	(28,000)	(10,000)
Total assets	$330,000	$309,000
Liabilities and Equity		
Accounts payable	$ 26,000	$ 32,000
Wages payable	7,000	16,000
Income taxes payable	2,400	3,600
Notes payable (long term)	40,000	70,000
Common stock, $5 par value	230,000	180,000
Retained earnings	24,600	7,400
Total liabilities and equity	$330,000	$309,000

Additional Information

a. A $30,000 note payable is retired at its carrying (book) value in exchange for cash.

b. The only changes affecting retained earnings are net income and cash dividends paid.

c. New equipment is acquired for $58,600 cash.

d. Received cash for the sale of equipment that had cost $48,600, yielding a $2,000 gain.

e. Prepaid Expenses and Wages Payable relate to Other Expenses on the income statement.

f. All purchases and sales of merchandise inventory are on credit.

Exercise 16-10[B]
Preparation of statement of cash flows (direct) C2 P1 P3 P5

Refer to the data in Exercise 16-9. Using the *direct method,* prepare the statement of cash flows for the year ended June 30, 2005.

Exercise 16-11[B]
Preparation of statement of cash flows (direct) from Cash T-account
C2 A1 P1 P3 P5 

The following summarized Cash T-account reflects the total debits and total credits to the Cash account of Texas Corporation for calendar year 2005. (1) Use this information to prepare a complete statement of cash flows for year 2005. The cash provided (used) by operating activities should be reported using the *direct method.* (2) Refer to the statement of cash flows prepared for part 1 to answer the following questions *a* through *d*: (*a*) Which section—operating, investing, or financing—shows the largest cash (i) inflow and (ii) outflow? (*b*) What is the largest individual item among the investing cash outflows? (*c*) Are the cash proceeds larger from issuing notes or issuing stock? (*d*) Does the company have a net cash inflow or outflow from borrowing activities?

Accounting System:
File Edit Maintain Tasks Analysis Options Reports Window Help

Cash			
Balance, Dec. 31, 2004	135,200		
Receipts from customers	6,000,000	Payments for merchandise	1,590,000
Receipts from dividends	208,400	Payments for wages	550,000
Receipts from land sale	220,000	Payments for rent	320,000
Receipts from machinery sale	710,000	Payments for interest	218,000
Receipts from issuing stock	1,540,000	Payments for taxes	450,000
Receipts from borrowing	2,600,000	Payments for machinery	2,236,000
		Payments for long-term investments	2,260,000
		Payments for note payable	386,000
		Payments for dividends	500,000
		Payments for treasury stock	218,000
Balance, Dec. 31, 2005	$?		

Sales Purchases General Ledger Payroll Inventory Company Analysis

PROBLEM SET A

Problem 16-1A
Statement of cash flows (indirect method)
C2 C3 A1 P1 P2 P3

Kazaam Company, a merchandiser, recently completed its calendar-year 2005 operations. For the year, (1) all sales are credit sales, (2) all credits to Accounts Receivable reflect cash receipts from customers, (3) all purchases of inventory are on credit, (4) all debits to Accounts Payable reflect cash payments for inventory, and (5) Other Expenses are paid in advance and are initially debited to Prepaid Expenses. Kazaam's balance sheets and income statement follow:

KAZAAM COMPANY
Comparative Balance Sheets
December 31, 2005

	2005	2004
Assets		
Cash	$ 53,875	$ 76,625
Accounts receivable	65,000	49,625
Merchandise inventory	273,750	252,500
Prepaid expenses	5,375	6,250
Equipment	159,500	110,000
Accum. depreciation—Equipment	(34,625)	(44,000)
Total assets	$522,875	$451,000
Liabilities and Equity		
Accounts payable	$ 88,125	$116,625
Short-term notes payable	10,000	6,250
Long-term notes payable	93,750	53,750
Common stock, $5 par value	168,750	156,250
Contributed capital in excess of par, common stock	32,500	0
Retained earnings	129,750	118,125
Total liabilities and equity	$522,875	$451,000

KAZAAM COMPANY
Income Statement
For Year Ended December 31, 2005

Sales		$496,250
Cost of goods sold		250,000
Gross profit		246,250
Operating expenses		
Depreciation expense	$ 18,750	
Other expenses	136,500	155,250
Other gains (losses)		
Loss on sale of equipment		5,125
Income before taxes		$ 85,875
Income taxes expense		12,125
Net income		$ 73,750

Additional Information on Year 2005 Transactions

a. The loss on the cash sale of equipment is $5,125 (details in *b*).

b. Sold equipment costing $46,875, with accumulated depreciation of $28,125, for $13,625 cash.

c. Purchased equipment costing $96,375 by paying $25,000 cash and signing a long-term note payable for the balance.

d. Borrowed $3,750 cash by signing a short-term note payable.

e. Paid $31,375 cash to reduce the long-term notes payable.

f. Issued 2,500 shares of common stock for $18 cash per share.

g. Declared and paid cash dividends of $62,125.

Required

1. Prepare a complete statement of cash flows; report its operating activities using the *indirect method*. Disclose any noncash investing and financing activities in a note.

Check Cash from operating activities, $33,375

Analysis Component

2. Analyze and discuss the statement of cash flows prepared in part 1, giving special attention to the wisdom of the cash dividend payment.

Problem 16-2A[B]
Statement of cash flows (direct method) C3 P1 P3 P5

Refer to Kazaam Company's financial statements and related information in Problem 16-1A.

Required

Prepare a complete statement of cash flows; report its operating activities according to the *direct method.* Disclose any noncash investing and financing activities in a note.

Check Cash used in financing activities, $(44,750)

Problem 16-3A[A]
Cash flows spreadsheet (indirect method)
P1 P2 P3 P4

Refer to the information reported about Kazaam Company in Problem 16-1A.

Required

Prepare a complete statement of cash flows using a spreadsheet as in Exhibit 16A.1; report its operating activities using the indirect method. Identify the debits and credits in the Analysis of Changes columns with letters that correspond to the following list of transactions and events:

a. Net income is $73,750.

b. Accounts receivable increased.

c. Merchandise inventory increased.

d. Prepaid expenses decreased.

e. Accounts payable decreased.

f. Depreciation expense is $18,750.

g. Sold equipment costing $46,875, with accumulated depreciation of $28,125, for $13,625 cash. This yielded a loss of $5,125.

h. Purchased equipment costing $96,375 by paying $25,000 cash and **(i.)** by signing a long-term note payable for the balance.

j. Borrowed $3,750 cash by signing a short-term note payable.

k. Paid $31,375 cash to reduce the long-term notes payable.

l. Issued 2,500 shares of common stock for $18 cash per share.

m. Declared and paid cash dividends of $62,125.

Check Analysis of Changes column totals, $515,375

Problem 16-4A
Statement of cash flows (indirect method) C3 P1 P2 P3

mhhe.com/larson

Galley Corp., a merchandiser, recently completed its 2005 operations. For the year, (1) all sales are credit sales, (2) all credits to Accounts Receivable reflect cash receipts from customers, (3) all purchases of inventory are on credit, (4) all debits to Accounts Payable reflect cash payments for inventory, (5) Other Expenses are all cash expenses, and (6) any change in Income Taxes Payable reflects the accrual and cash payment of taxes. Galley's balance sheets and income statement follow:

GALLEY CORPORATION Income Statement For Year Ended December 31, 2005		
Sales		$1,992,000
Cost of goods sold		1,194,000
Gross profit		798,000
Operating expenses		
Depreciation expense	$ 54,000	
Other expenses	501,000	555,000
Income before taxes		243,000
Income taxes expense		42,000
Net income		$ 201,000

GALLEY CORPORATION Comparative Balance Sheets December 31, 2005	2005	2004
Assets		
Cash	$ 174,000	$117,000
Accounts receivable	93,000	81,000
Merchandise inventory	609,000	534,000
Equipment	333,000	297,000
Accum. depreciation—Equipment	(156,000)	(102,000)
Total assets	$1,053,000	$927,000
Liabilities and Equity		
Accounts payable	$ 69,000	$ 96,000
Income taxes payable	27,000	24,000
Common stock, $2 par value	582,000	558,000
Contributed capital in excess of par value, common stock	198,000	162,000
Retained earnings	177,000	87,000
Total liabilities and equity	$1,053,000	$927,000

Additional Information on Year 2005 Transactions

a. Purchased equipment for $36,000 cash.

b. Issued 12,000 shares of common stock for $5 cash per share.

c. Declared and paid $111,000 in cash dividends.

Required

Check Cash from operating activities, $144,000

Prepare a complete statement of cash flows; report its cash inflows and cash outflows from operating activities according to the *indirect method.*

Problem 16-5A[B]
Statement of cash flows (direct method) P1 P3 P5

mhhe.com/larson

Check Cash used in financing activities, $(51,000)

Refer to Galley Corporation's financial statements and related information in Problem 16-4A.

Required

Prepare a complete statement of cash flows; report its cash flows from operating activities according to the *direct method.*

Problem 16-6A[A]
Cash flows spreadsheet (indirect method)
P1 P2 P3 P4

mhhe.com/larson

Check Analysis of Changes column totals, $579,000

Refer to the information reported about Galley Corporation in Problem 16-4A.

Required

Prepare a complete statement of cash flows using a spreadsheet as in Exhibit 16A.1; report operating activities under the indirect method. Identify the debits and credits in the Analysis of Changes columns with letters that correspond to the following list of transactions and events:

a. Net income is $201,000.

b. Accounts receivable increased.

c. Merchandise inventory increased.

d. Accounts payable decreased.

e. Income taxes payable increased.

f. Depreciation expense is $54,000.

g. Purchased equipment for $36,000 cash.

h. Issued 12,000 shares at $5 cash per share.

i. Declared and paid $111,000 of cash dividends.

PROBLEM SET B

Problem 16-1B
Statement of cash flows (indirect method)
C2 C3 A1 P1 P2 P3

Kite Corporation, a merchandiser, recently completed its calendar-year 2005 operations. For the year, (1) all sales are credit sales, (2) all credits to Accounts Receivable reflect cash receipts from customers, (3) all purchases of inventory are on credit, (4) all debits to Accounts Payable reflect cash payments for inventory, and (5) Other Expenses are paid in advance and are initially debited to Prepaid Expenses. Kite's balance sheets and income statement follow:

KITE CORPORATION
Comparative Balance Sheets
December 31, 2005

	2005	2004
Assets		
Cash	$136,500	$ 71,550
Accounts receivable	74,100	90,750
Merchandise inventory	454,500	490,200
Prepaid expenses	17,100	19,200
Equipment	278,250	216,000
Accum. depreciation—Equipment	(108,750)	(93,000)
Total assets	$851,700	$794,700
Liabilities and Equity		
Accounts payable	$117,450	$123,450
Short-term notes payable	17,250	11,250
Long-term notes payable	112,500	82,500
Common stock, $5 par	465,000	450,000
Contributed capital in excess of par, common stock	18,000	0
Retained earnings	121,500	127,500
Total liabilities and equity	$851,700	$794,700

KITE CORPORATION
Income Statement
For Year Ended December 31, 2005

Sales		$1,083,000
Cost of goods sold		585,000
Gross profit		498,000
Operating expenses		
Depreciation expense	$ 36,600	
Other expenses	392,850	
Total operating expenses		429,450
		68,550
Other gains (losses)		
Loss on sale of equipment		2,100
Income before taxes		66,450
Income taxes expense		9,450
Net income		$ 57,000

Additional Information on Year 2005 Transactions

a. The loss on the cash sale of equipment is $2,100 (details in *b*).
b. Sold equipment costing $51,000, with accumulated depreciation of $20,850, for $28,050 cash.
c. Purchased equipment costing $113,250 by paying $38,250 cash and signing a long-term note payable for the balance.
d. Borrowed $6,000 cash by signing a short-term note payable.
e. Paid $45,000 cash to reduce the long-term notes payable.
f. Issued 3,000 shares of common stock for $11 cash per share.
g. Declared and paid cash dividends of $63,000.

Required

1. Prepare a complete statement of cash flows; report its operating activities using the *indirect method.* Disclose any noncash investing and financing activities in a note.

Check Cash from operating activities, $144,150

Analysis Component

2. Analyze and discuss the statement of cash flows prepared in part 1, giving special attention to the wisdom of the cash dividend payment.

Problem 16-2B[B]
Statement of cash flows (direct method) C3 P1 P3 P5

Refer to Kite Corporation's financial statements and related information in Problem 16-1B.

Required

Prepare a complete statement of cash flows; report its operating activities according to the *direct method.* Disclose any noncash investing and financing activities in a note.

Check Cash used in financing activities, $(69,000)

Problem 16-3B^A
Cash flows spreadsheet (indirect method)
P1 P2 P3 P4

Refer to the information reported about Kite Corporation in Problem 16-1B.

Required

Prepare a complete statement of cash flows using a spreadsheet as in Exhibit 16A.1; report its operating activities using the *indirect method.* Identify the debits and credits in the Analysis of Changes columns with letters that correspond to the following list of transactions and events:

a. Net income is $57,000.
b. Accounts receivable decreased.
c. Merchandise inventory decreased.
d. Prepaid expenses decreased.
e. Accounts payable decreased.
f. Depreciation expense is $36,600.
g. Sold equipment costing $51,000, with accumulated depreciation of $20,850, for $28,050 cash. This yielded a loss of $2,100.
h. Purchased equipment costing $113,250 by paying $38,250 cash and **(i.)** by signing a long-term note payable for the balance.
j. Borrowed $6,000 cash by signing a short-term note payable.
k. Paid $45,000 cash to reduce the long-term notes payable.
l. Issued 3,000 shares of common stock for $11 cash per share.
m. Declared and paid cash dividends of $63,000.

Check Analysis of Changes column totals, $540,300

Problem 16-4B
Statement of cash flows (indirect method)
C3 P1 P2 P3

Taurasi Co., a merchandiser, recently completed its 2005 operations. For the year, (1) all sales are credit sales, (2) all credits to Accounts Receivable reflect cash receipts from customers, (3) all purchases of inventory are on credit, (4) all debits to Accounts Payable reflect cash payments for inventory, (5) Other Expenses are cash expenses, and (6) any change in Income Taxes Payable reflects the accrual and cash payment of taxes. Taurasi's balance sheets and income statement follow:

TAURASI COMPANY
Comparative Balance Sheets
December 31, 2005

	2005	2004
Assets		
Cash	$ 53,925	$ 31,800
Accounts receivable	19,425	23,250
Merchandise inventory	175,350	139,875
Equipment	105,450	76,500
Accum. depreciation—Equipment	(48,300)	(30,600)
Total assets	$305,850	$240,825
Liabilities and Equity		
Accounts payable	$ 38,475	$ 35,625
Income taxes payable	4,500	6,750
Common stock, $5 par value	165,000	150,000
Contributed capital in excess of par, common stock	42,000	15,000
Retained earnings	55,875	33,450
Total liabilities and equity	$305,850	$240,825

TAURASI COMPANY
Income Statement
For Year Ended December 31, 2005

Sales		$609,750
Cost of goods sold		279,000
Gross profit		330,750
Operating expenses		
Depreciation expense	$ 17,700	
Other expenses	179,775	197,475
Income before taxes		133,275
Income taxes expense		44,850
Net income		$ 88,425

Additional Information on Year 2005 Transactions

a. Purchased equipment for $28,950 cash.
b. Issued 3,000 shares of common stock for $14 cash per share.
c. Declared and paid $66,000 of cash dividends.

Required

Prepare a complete statement of cash flows; report its cash inflows and cash outflows from operating activities according to the *indirect method.*

Check Cash from operating activities, $75,075

Problem 16-5B[B]
Statement of cash flows (direct method) P1 P3 P5

Refer to Taurasi Company's financial statements and related information in Problem 16-4B.

Required

Prepare a complete statement of cash flows; report its cash flows from operating activities according to the *direct method.*

Check Cash used by financing activities, $(24,000)

Problem 16-6B[A]
Cash flows spreadsheet (indirect method) P1 P2 P3 P4

Refer to the information reported about Taurasi Company in Problem 16-4B.

Required

Prepare a complete statement of cash flows using a spreadsheet as in Exhibit 16A.1; report operating activities under the *indirect method.* Identify the debits and credits in the Analysis of Changes columns with letters that correspond to the following list of transactions and events:

a. Net income is $88,425.
b. Accounts receivable decreased.
c. Merchandise inventory increased.
d. Accounts payable increased.
e. Income taxes payable decreased.
f. Depreciation expense is $17,700.
g. Purchased equipment for $28,950 cash.
h. Issued 3,000 shares at $14 cash per share.
i. Declared and paid $66,000 of cash dividends.

Check Analysis of Changes column totals, $287,475

PROBLEM SET C

Problem Set C is available at the book's Website to reinforce and assess your learning.

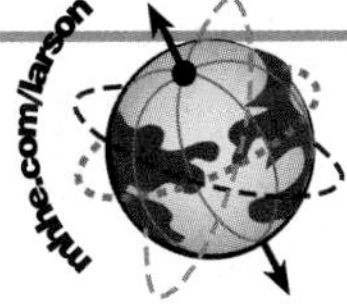

SERIAL PROBLEM

Success Systems

(This serial problem began in Chapter 1 and continues through most of the book. If previous chapter segments were not completed, the serial problem can begin at this point. It is helpful, but not necessary, for you to use the Working Papers that accompany the book.)

Kay Breeze, owner of Success Systems, decides to prepare a statement of cash flows for her business. (Although the serial problem allowed for various changes in earlier chapters and a change to the corporate form in Chapter 13, we will prepare the statement of cash flows using the proprietorship form of business for Success Systems and the following financial data.)

SUCCESS SYSTEMS
Comparative Balance Sheets
December 31, 2004 and March 31, 2005

	2005	2004
Assets		
Cash	$ 77,845	$58,160
Accounts receivable	22,720	5,668
Merchandise Inventory	704	0
Computer supplies	2,005	580
Prepaid insurance	1,110	1,665
Prepaid rent	825	825
Office equipment	8,000	8,000
Accumulated depreciation—Office equipment	(800)	(400)
Computer equipment	20,000	20,000
Accumulated depreciation—Computer equipment	(2,500)	(1,250)
Total assets	$129,909	$93,248
Liabilities		
Accounts payable	$ 0	$ 1,100
Wages payable	875	500
Unearned computer service revenue	0	1,500
Equity		
K. Breeze, Capital	129,034	90,148
Total liabilities and equity	$129,909	$93,248

SUCCESS SYSTEMS
Income Statement
For Three Months Ended March 31, 2005

Computer services revenue		$25,160
Net sales		18,693
Total revenue		43,853
Cost of goods sold	$14,052	
Depreciation expense—Office equipment	400	
Depreciation expense—Computer equipment	1,250	
Wages expense	3,250	
Insurance expense	555	
Rent expense	2,475	
Computer supplies expense	1,305	
Advertising expense	600	
Mileage expense	320	
Repairs expense—Computer	960	
Total expenses		25,167
Net income		$18,686

Required

Prepare a statement of cash flows for Success Systems using the *indirect method* for the three months ended March 31, 2005. Recall that the owner Kay Breeze contributed $25,000 to the business in the first quarter of 2005 and withdrew $4,800 for personal use.

BEYOND THE NUMBERS

REPORTING IN ACTION

C4 A1

BTN 16-1 Refer to **Krispy Kreme**'s financial statements in Appendix A to answer the following:

1. Is Krispy Kreme's statement of cash flows prepared under the direct method or the indirect method?
2. For each fiscal year 2003, 2002, and 2001, is the amount of cash provided by operating activities more or less than the cash paid for dividends?
3. What is the largest amount in reconciling the difference between net income and cash flow from operating activities in 2003? In 2002? In 2001?
4. Identify the largest cash flows for investing and for financing activities in 2003 and in 2002.

Roll On

5. Obtain Krispy Kreme's financial statements for a fiscal year ending after February 2, 2003, from either its Website (KrispyKreme.com) or the SEC's EDGAR database (www.SEC.gov). Since February 2, 2003, what are Krispy Kreme's largest cash outflows and cash inflows in the investing and in the financing sections of its statement of cash flow?

COMPARATIVE ANALYSIS

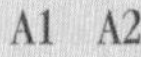

BTN 16-2 Key comparative figures ($ thousands) for **Krispy Kreme** and **Tastykake** follow:

	Krispy Kreme			Tastykake		
Key Figures	Current Year	1 Year Prior	2 Years Prior	Current Year	1 Year Prior	2 Years Prior
Operating cash flows	$ 51,036	$ 36,210	$ 32,112	$ 10,115	$ 10,905	$ 13,199
Total assets	410,487	255,376	171,493	116,560	116,136	112,192

Required

1. Compute the recent two years' cash flow on total assets ratios for both Krispy Kreme and Tastykake.
2. What does the cash flow on total assets ratio measure?
3. Which company has the higher cash flow on total assets ratio for the periods shown?
4. Does the cash flow on total assets ratio reflect on the quality of earnings? Explain.

ETHICS CHALLENGE

C1 C2 A1

BTN 16-3 Lisa Gish is preparing for a meeting with her banker. Her business is finishing its fourth year of operations. In the first year, it had negative cash flows from operations. In the second and third years, cash flows from operations was positive. However, inventory costs rose significantly in year 4, and cash flows from operations will probably be down 25%. Gish wants to secure a line of credit from her banker as a financing buffer. From experience, she knows the banker will scrutinize operating cash flows for years 1 through 4 and will want a projected number for year 5. Gish knows that a steady progression upward in operating cash flows for years 1 through 4 will help her case. She decides to use her discretion as owner and considers several business actions that will turn her operating cash flow in year 4 from a decrease to an increase over year 3.

Required

1. Identify two business actions Gish might take to improve cash flows from operations.
2. Comment on the ethics and possible consequences of Gish's decision to pursue these actions.

COMMUNICATING IN PRACTICE

C1 C4

BTN 16-4 Your friend, Jessica Willard, recently completed the second year of her business and just received annual financial statements from her accountant. Willard finds the income statement and balance sheet informative but does not understand the statement of cash flows. She says the first section is especially confusing because it contains a lot of additions and subtractions that do not make sense to her. Willard adds, "The income statement tells me the business is more profitable than last year and that's most important. If I want to know how cash changes, I can look at comparative balance sheets."

Required

Write a half-page memorandum to your friend explaining the purpose of the statement of cash flows. Speculate as to why the first section is so confusing and how it might be rectified.

TAKING IT TO THE NET

A1

mhhe.com/larson

BTN 16-5 Access the April 22, 2003, filing of the 10-K report (for fiscal year ending February 1, 2003) of **J. Crew Group, Inc.**, at www.sec.gov.

Required

1. Does J. Crew use the direct or indirect method to construct its consolidated statement of cash flows?
2. For the fiscal year ended February 1, 2003, what is the largest item recorded in reconciling the net loss to cash flow provided by operations?
3. In recent years J. Crew has recorded several net losses. Has the company been more successful in generating operating cash flows over this time period than in generating net income?
4. In the year ended February 1, 2003, what was the largest cash outflow for investing activities and for financing activities?
5. What items does J. Crew report as supplementary cash flow information?
6. Does J. Crew report any noncash financing activities?

TEAMWORK IN ACTION

C1 C4 A1 P2 P5

BTN 16-6 Team members are to coordinate and independently answer one question within each of the following three sections. Team members should then report to the team and confirm or correct teammates' answers.

1. Answer *one* of the following questions about the statement of cash flows:
   - **a.** What are this statement's reporting objectives?
   - **b.** What two methods are used to prepare it? Identify similarities and differences between them.
   - **c.** What steps are followed to prepare the statement?
   - **d.** What types of analyses are often made from this statement's information?
2. Identify and explain the adjustment from net income to obtain cash flows from operating activities using the indirect method for *one* of the following items:
   - **a.** Noncash operating revenues and expenses.
   - **b.** Nonoperating gains and losses.
   - **c.** Increases and decreases in noncash current assets.
   - **d.** Increases and decreases in current liabilities.
3. [B]Identify and explain the formula for computing cash flows from operating activities using the direct method for *one* of the following items:
   - **a.** Cash receipts from sales to customers.
   - **b.** Cash paid for merchandise inventory.
   - **c.** Cash paid for wages and operating expenses.
   - **d.** Cash paid for interest and taxes.

Note: For teams of more than four, some pairing within teams is necessary. Use as an in-class activity or as an assignment. If used in class, specify a time limit on each part. Conclude with reports to the entire class, using team rotation. Each team can prepare responses on a transparency.

BUSINESS WEEK ACTIVITY

A1

mhhe.com/larson

BTN 16-7 Read the article "Are the Golden Arches That Tarnished?" in the April 14, 2003, issue of *Business Week*. (The book's Website provides a free link.)

Required

1. The author, Robert Barker, compares **Dairy Queen** with **McDonald's**. Although the two companies vary substantially in size, in what two ways does Barker find them similar?
2. In 2002, what was McDonald's operating cash flow?
3. How does Barker compute the ratio that he calls "cash flow margin"? How does McDonald's cash flow margin compare with Dairy Queen's?
4. If free cash flow is defined as operating cash flows minus capital expenditures, what does Barker think might happen to McDonald's free cash flow in 2003?

ENTREPRENEURIAL DECISION

C2 A1

BTN 16-8 Review the chapter's opening feature involving **Atomic Toys**.

Required

1. What is the meaning of Chance Roth's remark that Atomic Toys had to increase cash outflows for manufacturing and distribution? How are such cash outflows reported in the statement of cash flows?
2. What do you believe the phrase to have *cash under control* means for a start-up business?
3. Atomic Toys's Website (AtomicToys.com) reveals that it is organized as an LLC. Given this form of business organization, identify available sources of cash financing for future expansion.

C1 A1

BTN 16-9 Jenna and Matt Wilder are completing their second year operating Mountain High, a downhill ski area and resort. Mountain High reports a net loss of $(10,000) for its second year, which includes an $85,000 extraordinary loss from fire. This past year also involved major purchases of plant assets for renovation and expansion, yielding a year-end total asset amount of $800,000. Mountain High's net cash outflow for its second year is $(5,000); a summarized version of its statement of cash flows follows:

Net cash flow provided by operating activities	$295,000
Net cash flow used by investing activities	(310,000)
Net cash flow provided by financing activities	10,000

Required

Write a one-page memorandum to the Wilders evaluating Mountain High's current performance and assessing its future. Give special emphasis to cash flow data and their interpretation.

HITTING THE ROAD

C1

BTN 16-10 Visit **The Motley Fool**'s Website (Fool.com). Click on the sidebar link titled *Fool's School*. Identify and select the link *How to Value Stocks*.

Required

1. How does the Fool's school define cash flow?
2. Per the school's instruction, why do analysts focus on earnings before interest and taxes (EBIT)?
3. Visit other links at this Website that interest you such as "A Journey through the Balance Sheet," or find out what the "Fool's Ratio" is. Write a half-page report on what you find.

BTN 16-11 Grupo Bimbo, Krispy Kreme, and Tastykake, are all competitors in the global marketplace. Access Grupo Bimbo's annual report (GrupoBimbo.com) for the year ended December 31, 2002. Review its statement of changes in financial position.

GLOBAL DECISION

C1 C2 C4

Required

1. Is Grupo Bimbo's statement of changes in financial position more similar to a statement of cash flows prepared by the direct or indirect method?

2. What title does Grupo Bimbo use in the section that reflects net income adjusted by noncash expense items and changes in noncurrent balance sheet accounts?

3. What title does Grupo Bimbo use in the section that reflects the cash flows that result from changes in the current asset and current liability accounts?

4. What "bottom-line" label is used to denote the net changes in the first major (operating) section of the statement of changes in financial position?

"*What goes on at The Motley Fool every day is similar to what goes on in a library*"—Tom Gardner (on left; David Gardner on right)

Analysis of Financial Statements

A Look Back

Chapter 16 focused on reporting and analyzing cash inflows and cash outflows. We explained how to prepare, analyze, and interpret the statement of cash flows.

A Look at This Chapter

This chapter emphasizes the analysis and interpretation of financial statement information. We learn to apply horizontal, vertical, and ratio analyses to better understand company performance and financial condition.

A Look Ahead

Chapter 18 introduces us to managerial accounting. We discuss its purposes, concepts, and roles in helping managers gather and organize information for decision making. We also explain basic management principles.

CAP

Conceptual

C1 Explain the purpose of analysis. *(p. 674)*

C2 Identify the building blocks of analysis. *(p. 675)*

C3 Describe standards for comparisons in analysis. *(p. 676)*

C4 Identify the tools of analysis. *(p. 676)*

Analytical

A1 Summarize and report results of analysis. *(p. 694)*

Procedural

P1 Explain and apply methods of horizontal analysis. *(p. 677)*

P2 Describe and apply methods of vertical analysis. *(p. 681)*

P3 Define and apply ratio analysis. *(p. 685)*

Decision Feature

Fool's Gold

ALEXANDRIA, VA—A few years ago, with less than $10,000 in start-up money, then 28-year-old David Gardner and his 26-year-old brother, Tom, launched **The Motley Fool (Fool.com).** The name derives from Elizabethan drama (Shakespeare's *As You Like It*), in which only the fool could tell the king the truth without getting his head lopped off. The Gardners view themselves as modern-day fools "dedicated to educating, amusing, and enriching individuals in the search of the truth," according to their Website. The truth to which they refer involves the financial world. Their site argues that "the financial world preys on ignorance and fear." According to Tom Gardner, "There is a great need in the general populace for financial information." Given their huge success—Website, radio shows, newspaper columns, online store, investment newsletters, and international expansion—few can argue.

Still, there is a concern that individuals fail to fully exploit the available information in financial statements. The Motley Fool's bulletin board often finds "discussions" that could be readily resolved with reference to reliable accounting data. This suggests that more "educating and enriching" of individuals is required. This chapter takes that challenge. It introduces horizontal and vertical analyses—tools that reveal crucial trends and insights from financial information. It also summarizes and expands on ratio analysis—tools that reveal insights into a company's financial condition and performance. With knowledge from this chapter, along with The Motley Fool's guidance on investing, individuals will be in a much stronger position to succeed in the financial world.

[Sources: *Motley Fool Website,* January 2004; *Entrepreneur,* July 1997; *What to Do With Your Money Now,* June 2002.]

This chapter shows how to use information in financial statements to evaluate a company's financial performance and condition. We describe the purpose of financial statement analysis, its basic building blocks, the information available, standards for comparisons, and tools of analysis. The chapter emphasizes three major analysis tools: horizontal analysis, vertical analysis, and ratio analysis. We illustrate the application of each of these tools using **Krispy Kreme**'s financial statements. We also introduce comparative analysis using **Tastykake**'s financial statements. This chapter expands and organizes the ratio analyses introduced at the end of each of the prior chapters.

Analysis of Financial Statements

Basics of Analysis	Horizontal Analysis	Vertical Analysis	Ratio Analysis
• Purpose • Building blocks • Information • Standards for comparisons • Tools	• Comparative balance sheets • Comparative income statements • Trend analysis	• Common-size balance sheet • Common-size income statement • Common-size graphics	• Liquidity and efficiency • Solvency • Profitability • Market prospects • Ratio summary

Basics of Analysis

Financial statement analysis applies analytical tools to general-purpose financial statements and related data for making business decisions. It involves transforming accounting data into more useful information. Financial statement analysis reduces our reliance on hunches, guesses, and intuition as well as our uncertainty in decision making. It does not lessen the need for expert judgment; instead, it provides us an effective and systematic basis for making business decisions. This section describes the purpose of financial statement analysis, its information sources, the use of comparisons, and some issues in computations.

Purpose of Analysis

C1 Explain the purpose of analysis.

Internal users of accounting information are those involved in strategically managing and operating the company. They include managers, officers, internal auditors, consultants, budget directors, and market researchers. The purpose of financial statement analysis for these users is to provide strategic information to improve company efficiency and effectiveness in providing products and services.

External users of accounting information are *not* directly involved in running the company. They include shareholders, lenders, directors, customers, suppliers, regulators, lawyers, brokers, and the press. External users rely on financial statement analysis to make better and more informed decisions in pursuing their own goals.

Point: Financial statement analysis tools are also used for personal financial investment decisions.

We can identify other uses of financial statement analysis. Shareholders and creditors assess company prospects to make investing and lending decisions. A board of directors analyzes financial statements in monitoring management's decisions. Employees and unions use financial statements in labor negotiations. Suppliers use financial statement information in establishing credit terms. Customers analyze financial statements in deciding whether to establish supply relationships. Public utilities set customer rates by analyzing financial statements. Auditors use financial statements in assessing the "fair presentation" of their clients' financial reports. Analyst services such as **Dun & Bradstreet**, **Moody's**, and **Standard & Poor's** use financial statements in making buy-sell recommendations and in setting credit ratings. The common goal of these users is to evaluate company performance and financial

Point: Financial statement analysis is a topic on the CPA, CMA, CIA, and CFA exams.

condition. This includes evaluating (1) past and current performance, (2) current financial position, and (3) future performance and risk.

Building Blocks of Analysis

C2 Identify the building blocks of analysis.

Financial statement analysis focuses on one or more elements of a company's financial condition or performance. Our analysis emphasizes four areas of inquiry—with varying degrees of importance. These four areas are described and illustrated in this chapter and are considered the *building blocks* of financial statement analysis:

- **Liquidity** and **efficiency**—ability to meet short-term obligations and to efficiently generate revenues.
- **Solvency**—ability to generate future revenues and meet long-term obligations.
- **Profitability**—ability to provide financial rewards sufficient to attract and retain financing.
- **Market prospects**—ability to generate positive market expectations.

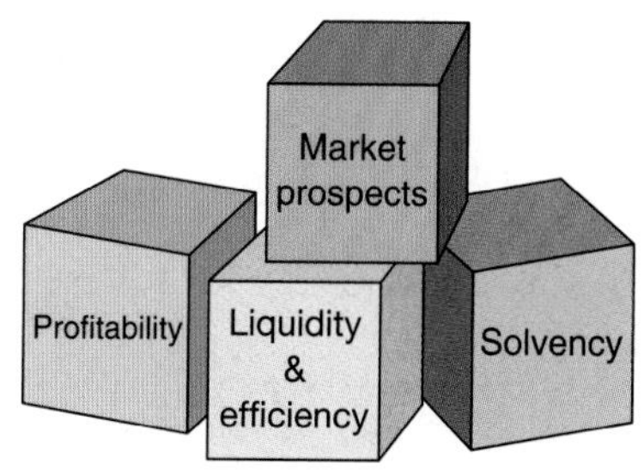

Applying the building blocks of financial statement analysis involves determining (1) the objectives of analysis and (2) the relative emphasis among the building blocks. We distinguish among these four building blocks to emphasize the different aspects of a company's financial condition or performance, yet we must remember that these areas of analysis are interrelated. For instance, a company's operating performance is affected by the availability of financing and short-term liquidity conditions. Similarly, a company's credit standing is not limited to satisfactory short-term liquidity but depends also on its profitability and efficiency in using assets. Early in our analysis, we need to determine the relative emphasis of each building block. Emphasis and analysis can later change as a result of evidence collected.

Decision Insight

Chips and Brokers The term *blue chips* refers to stock of big, profitable companies. The term comes from poker: The most valuable chips are blue. *Brokers* execute orders to buy or sell stock. The term comes from wine retailers—individuals who broach (break) wine casks.

Information for Analysis

Some users, such as managers and regulatory authorities, are able to receive special financial reports prepared to meet their analysis needs. However, most users must rely on **general-purpose financial statements** that include the (1) income statement, (2) balance sheet, (3) statement of stockholders' (owner's) equity (or statement of retained earnings), (4) statement of cash flows, and (5) notes to these statements.

Financial reporting refers to the communication of financial information useful for making investment, credit, and other business decisions. Financial reporting includes not only general-purpose financial statements but also information from SEC 10-K or other filings, press releases, shareholders' meetings, forecasts, management letters, auditors' reports, and Webcasts.

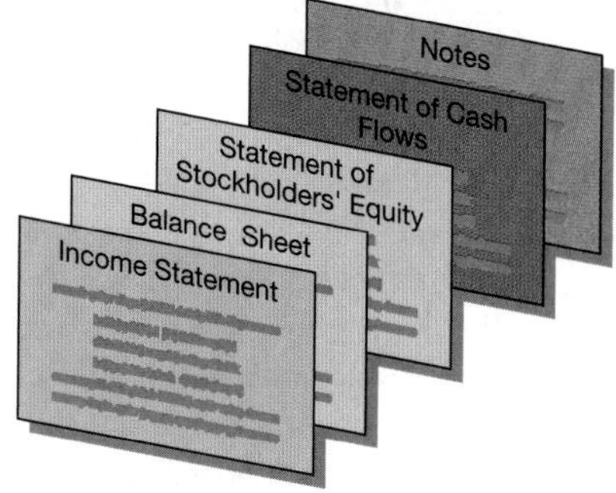

Point: Decision makers rely on financial statement analysis to help them better understand the financial position and profitability of a business. This includes estimates of the amount, timing, and uncertainty of future cash inflows and outflows.

Management's Discussion and Analysis (MD&A) is one example of useful information outside traditional financial statements. **Krispy Kreme**'s MD&A (available at KrispyKreme.com), for example, begins with critical accounting policies. It then discusses operating activities and results. The next major part examines liquidity and capital resources—roughly equivalent to investing and financing activities. The final part explains its market risks, including its exposure to currency changes, interest rates, and commodity price changes. The MD&A is an excellent starting point in understanding a company's business activities.

Decision Insight

Analysis Online Many Websites offer free access and screening of companies by key numbers such as earnings, sales, and book value. For instance, **Standard & Poor's** has information for more than 10,000 stocks (**StandardPoor.com**).

Standards for Comparisons

C3 Describe standards for comparisons in analysis.

When interpreting measures from financial statement analysis, we need to decide whether the measures indicate good, bad, or average performance. To make such judgments, we need standards (benchmarks) for comparisons that include the following:

- *Intracompany*—The company under analysis can provide standards for comparisons based on its own prior performance and relations between its financial items. **Krispy Kreme**'s current net income, for instance, can be compared with its prior years' net income and in relation to its revenues or total assets.
- *Competitor*—One or more direct competitors of the company being analyzed can provide standards for comparisons. **Coca-Cola**'s profit margin, for instance, can be compared with **PepsiCo**'s profit margin.
- *Industry*—Industry statistics can provide standards of comparisons. Such statistics are available from services such as **Dun & Bradstreet**, **Standard & Poor's**, and **Moody's**.
- *Guidelines (rules of thumb)*—General standards of comparisons can develop from experience. Examples are the 2:1 level for the current ratio or 1:1 level for the acid-test ratio. Guidelines, or rules of thumb, must be carefully applied because context is crucial.

Point: Each chapter's *Reporting in Action* problems engage students in *intracompany* analysis, whereas *Comparative Analysis* problems require competitor analysis (Krispy Kreme vs. Tastykake).

All of these comparison standards are useful when properly applied, yet measures taken from a selected competitor or group of competitors are often best. Intracompany and industry measures are also important. Guidelines or rules of thumb should be applied with care, and then only if they seem reasonable given past experience and industry norms.

Quick Check

1. Who are the intended users of general-purpose financial statements?
2. General-purpose financial statements consist of what information?
3. Which of the following is *least* useful as a basis for comparison when analyzing ratios? (*a*) Company results from a different economic setting. (*b*) Standards from past experience. (*c*) Rule-of-thumb standards. (*d*) Industry averages.
4. What is the preferred basis of comparison for ratio analysis?

Answers—p. 698

Tools of Analysis

C4 Identify the tools of analysis.

Three of the most common tools of financial statement analysis are

1. **Horizontal analysis**—Comparison of a company's financial condition and performance across time.
2. **Vertical analysis**—Comparison of a company's financial condition and performance to a base amount.
3. **Ratio analysis**—Measurement of key relations between financial statement items.

The remainder of this chapter describes these analysis tools and how to apply them.

Decision Insight

Ticker Prices *Ticker prices* refer to a band of moving data on a monitor carrying up-to-the-minute stock prices. The term comes from *ticker tape*, a 1-inch-wide strip of paper spewing stock prices from a printer that ticked as it ran. Most of today's investors have never seen actual ticker tape, but the term survives.

Horizontal Analysis

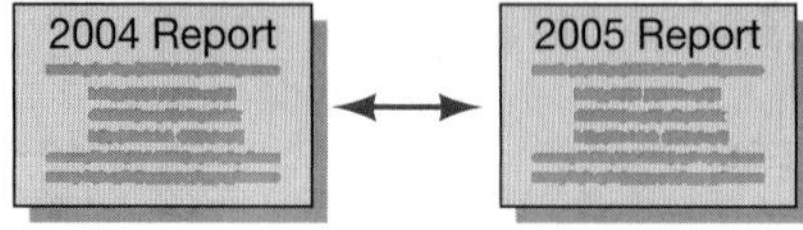

Analysis of any single financial number is of limited value. Instead, much of financial statement analysis involves identifying and describing relations between numbers, groups of numbers, and changes in those numbers. Horizontal analysis refers to examination of financial statement data *across time*. [The term *horizontal analysis*

arises from the left-to-right (or right-to-left) movement of our eyes as we review comparative financial statements across time.]

Comparative Statements

Comparing amounts for two or more successive periods often helps in analyzing financial statements. **Comparative financial statements** facilitate this comparison by showing financial amounts in side-by-side columns on a single statement, called a *comparative format.* Using figures from **Krispy Kreme**'s financial statements, this section explains how to compute dollar changes and percent changes for comparative statements.

P1 Explain and apply methods of horizontal analysis.

Topic Tackler 17-1

Computation of Dollar Changes and Percent Changes Comparing financial statements over relatively short time periods—two to three years—is often done by analyzing changes in line items. A change analysis usually includes analyzing absolute dollar amount changes and percent changes. Both analyses are relevant because dollar changes can yield large percent changes inconsistent with their importance. For instance, a 50% change from a base figure of $100 is less important than the same percent change from a base amount of $100,000 in the same statement. Reference to dollar amounts is necessary to retain a proper perspective and to assess the importance of changes. We compute the *dollar change* for a financial statement item as follows:

Example: What is a more significant change, a 70% increase on a $1,000 expense or a 30% increase on a $400,000 expense? *Answer:* The 30% increase.

Dollar change = Analysis period amount − Base period amount

Analysis period is the point or period of time for the financial statements under analysis, and *base period* is the point or period of time for the financial statements used for comparison purposes. The prior year is commonly used as a base period. We compute the *percent change* by dividing the dollar change by the base period amount and then multiplying this quantity by 100 as follows:

$$\text{Percent change (\%)} = \frac{\text{Analysis period amount} - \text{Base period amount}}{\text{Base period amount}} \times 100$$

We can always compute a dollar change, but we must be aware of a few rules in working with percent changes. To illustrate, look at four separate cases in this chart:

Case	Analysis Period	Base Period	Change Analysis: Dollar	Change Analysis: Percent
A	$ 1,500	$(4,500)	$ 6,000	—
B	(1,000)	2,000	(3,000)	—
C	8,000	—	8,000	—
D	0	10,000	(10,000)	(100%)

When a negative amount appears in the base period and a positive amount in the analysis period (or vice versa), we cannot compute a meaningful percent change; see cases A and B. Also, when no value is in the base period, no percent change is computable; see case C. Finally, when an item has a value in the base period and zero in the analysis period, the decrease is 100 percent; see case D.

Example: When there is a value in the base period and zero in the analysis period, the decrease is 100%. Why isn't the reverse situation an increase of 100%? *Answer:* A 100% increase of zero is still zero.

It is common when using horizontal analysis to compare amounts to either average or median values from prior periods (average and median values smooth out erratic or unusual fluctuations).[1] We also commonly round percents and ratios to one or two decimal places,

[1] *Median* is the middle value in a group of numbers. For instance, if five prior years' incomes are (in 000s) $15, $19, $18, $20, and $22, the median value is $19. When there are two middle numbers, we can take their average. For instance, if four prior years' sales are (in 000s) $84, $91, $96, and $93, the median is $92 (computed as the average of $91 and $93).

but practice on this matter is not uniform. Computations are as detailed as necessary, which is judged by whether rounding potentially affects users' decisions. Computations should not be excessively detailed so that important relations are lost among a mountain of decimal points and digits.

Comparative Balance Sheets Comparative balance sheets consist of balance sheet amounts from two or more balance sheet dates arranged side by side. Its usefulness is often improved by showing each item's dollar change and percent change to highlight large changes.

Analysis of comparative financial statements begins by focusing on items that show large dollar or percent changes. We then try to identify the reasons for these changes and, if possible, determine whether they are favorable or unfavorable. We also follow up on items with small changes when we expected the changes to be large.

Exhibit 17.1 shows comparative balance sheets for Krispy Kreme. A few items stand out. Nearly all asset categories substantially increase, which is probably not surprising because Krispy Kreme is a growth company. At least part of the increase in liquid assets is from more than $44,000 raised from borrowings this period; see the financing activities section

Point: Spreadsheet programs can help with horizontal, vertical, and ratio analyses, including graphical depictions of financial relations. The key is using this information effectively for business decisions.

Point: Business consultants use comparative statement analysis to provide management advice.

Exhibit 17.1

Comparative Balance Sheets

KRISPY KREME
Comparative Balance Sheets
February 2, 2003, and February 3, 2002

(in thousands)	2002	2003	Dollar Change	Percent Change
Assets				
Current assets				
Cash and cash equivalents	$ 21,904	$ 32,203	$ 10,299	47.0%
Short-term investments	15,292	22,976	7,684	50.2
Accounts receivable, net	26,894	34,373	7,479	27.8
Inventories	16,159	24,365	8,206	50.8
Prepaid expenses	2,591	3,478	887	34.2
Other current assets	18,929	23,733	4,804	25.4
Total current assets	101,769	141,128	39,359	38.7
Property and equipment, net	112,577	202,558	89,981	79.9
Long-term investments	12,700	4,344	(8,356)	(65.8)
Intangible assets	16,621	48,703	32,082	193.0
Other long-term assets	11,709	13,754	2,045	17.5
Total assets	$255,376	$410,487	$155,111	60.7
Liabilities				
Current liabilities				
Accounts payable	$ 12,095	$ 14,055	1,960	16.2
Accrued expenses	26,729	20,981	(5,748)	(21.5)
Current maturities of long-term debt	731	3,301	2,570	351.6
Other current liabilities	12,978	21,350	8,372	64.5
Total current liabilities	52,533	59,687	7,154	13.6
Long-term debt, net of current portion	3,912	49,900	45,988	1175.6
Other long-term liabilities	8,773	22,355	13,582	154.8
Total long-term liabilities	12,685	72,255	59,570	469.6
Shareholders' Equity				
Common stock	121,052	173,112	52,060	43.0
Accumulated other comprehensive income (loss)	456	(1,486)	(1,942)	—
Retained earnings	68,925	102,403	33,478	48.6
Other equity	(275)	4,516	4,791	—
Total shareholders' equity*	190,158	278,545	88,387	46.5
Total liabilities and shareholders' equity	$255,376	$410,487	155,111	60.7

* Includes any minority interest.

of the statement of cash flows. Of course, this substantial asset growth (60.7%) must be accompanied by future income to validate Krispy Kreme's growth strategy.

We likewise see substantial increases on the financing side, the most notable ones being long-term debt and stock issuances totaling about $98,000. Much of this is reflected in the $90,000 increase in property and equipment. Again, we must monitor this increase in investing and financing activities to be sure they are reflected in increased operating performance.

Comparative Income Statements Comparative income statements are prepared similarly to comparative balance sheets. Amounts for two or more periods are placed side by side, with additional columns for dollar and percent changes. Exhibit 17.2 shows Krispy Kreme's comparative income statements.

Exhibit 17.2

Comparative Income Statements

KRISPY KREME
Comparative Income Statements
For Years Ended February 2, 2003, and February 3, 2002

(in thousands, except per share data)	2002	2003	Dollar Change	Percent Change
Total revenues	$394,354	$491,549	$97,195	24.6%
Operating expenses (cost of sales)	316,946	381,489	64,543	20.4
General and administrative expenses	27,562	28,897	1,335	4.8
Depreciation and amortization expenses	7,959	12,271	4,312	54.2
Arbitration award	—	9,075	9,075	100.0
Income from operations	41,887	59,817	17,930	42.8
Interest income	2,980	1,966	(1,014)	(34.0)
Interest expense	(337)	(1,781)	(1,444)	(428.5)
Other losses	(1,749)	(4,295)	(2,546)	(145.6)
Loss on sale of property and equipment	(235)	(934)	(699)	(297.4)
Income before income taxes	42,546	54,773	12,227	28.7
Provision for income taxes	16,168	21,295	5,127	31.7
Net income	$ 26,378	$ 33,478	7,100	26.9
Basic earnings per share	$ 0.49	$ 0.61	0.12	24.5
Diluted earnings per share	$ 0.45	$ 0.56	0.11	24.4

Krispy Kreme has substantial revenue growth of 24.6% in 2003. This finding helps support management's growth strategy as revealed in the comparative balance sheets. Equally impressive is its ability to control cost of sales and general and administrative expenses, which increased only 20.4% and 4.8%, respectively. Krispy Kreme is achieving asset growth and greater returns on that growth. The substantial increase in interest expense is not surprising given the huge increase in debt financing. A net income growth of 26.9% on revenue growth of 24.6% is impressive.

Point: Percent change can also be computed by dividing the current period by the prior period and subtracting 1.0. For example, the 24.6% revenue increase of Exhibit 17.2 is computed as: ($491,549/$394,354) − 1.

Trend Analysis

Trend analysis, also called *trend percent analysis* or *index number trend analysis,* is a form of horizontal analysis that can reveal patterns in data across successive periods. It involves computing trend percents for a series of financial numbers and is a variation on the use of percent changes. The difference is that trend analysis does not subtract the base period amount in the numerator. To compute trend percents, we do the following:

1. Select a *base period* and assign each item in the base period a weight of 100%.
2. Express financial numbers as a percent of their base period number.

Specifically, a *trend percent,* also called an *index number,* is computed as follows:

Point: *Index* refers to the comparison of the analysis period to the base period. Percents determined for each period are called *index numbers.*

$$\textbf{Trend percent (\%)} = \frac{\textbf{Analysis period amount}}{\textbf{Base period amount}} \times 100$$

To illustrate trend analysis, we use the selected Krispy Kreme data in Exhibit 17.3.

Exhibit 17.3

Revenues and Expenses

(in thousands)	1999	2000	2001	2002	2003
Total revenues	$180,880	$220,243	$300,715	$394,354	$491,549
Operating expenses (cost of sales)	159,941	190,003	250,690	316,946	381,489
General and administrative expenses	10,897	14,856	20,061	27,562	28,897

These data are from Krispy Kreme's *Selected Financial Data* section in Appendix A. The base period is 1999 and the trend percent is computed in each subsequent year by dividing that year's amount by its 1999 amount. For instance, the revenue trend percent for 2003 is 271.8%, computed as $491,549/$180,880. The trend percents—using the data from Exhibit 17.3—are shown in Exhibit 17.4.

Exhibit 17.4

Trend Percents of Revenues and Expenses

(in thousands)	1999	2000	2001	2002	2003
Total revenues	100%	121.8%	166.3%	218.0%	271.8%
Operating expenses (cost of sales)	100%	118.8	156.7	198.2	238.5
General and administrative expenses	100%	136.3	184.1	252.9	265.2

Point: Trend analysis expresses a percent of base, not a percent of change.

Graphical depictions often aid analysis of trend percents. Exhibit 17.5 shows the trend percents from Exhibit 17.4 in a *line graph,* which can help us identify trends and detect changes in direction or magnitude. It reveals that the trend line for revenues consistently exceeds that for operating expenses. Moreover, the magnitude of that difference has consistently grown. This result bodes well for Krispy Kreme because its operating expenses are by far its largest cost, and the company shows an ability to control these expenses as it rapidly expands. The line graph also reveals a consistent increase in each of these accounts, which is typical of high growth companies. The trend line for general and administrative expenses is troubling because it exceeds the revenue trend line in all years except one. The good news is that the most recent year is the exception, which may show management's willingness to confront and limit such costs.

Exhibit 17.5

Trend Percent Lines for Revenues and Expenses

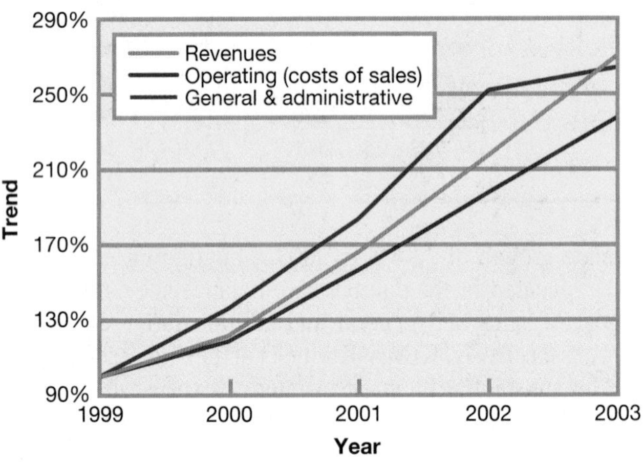

Exhibit 17.6 compares **Krispy Kreme**'s revenue trend line to that of **Tastykake** for this same period. Krispy Kreme's revenues sharply increased over this time period while those of Tastykake slightly increased. These data indicate that Krispy Kreme's products have met with considerable consumer acceptance.

Exhibit 17.6

Trend Percent Lines—Krispy Kreme vs. Tastykake

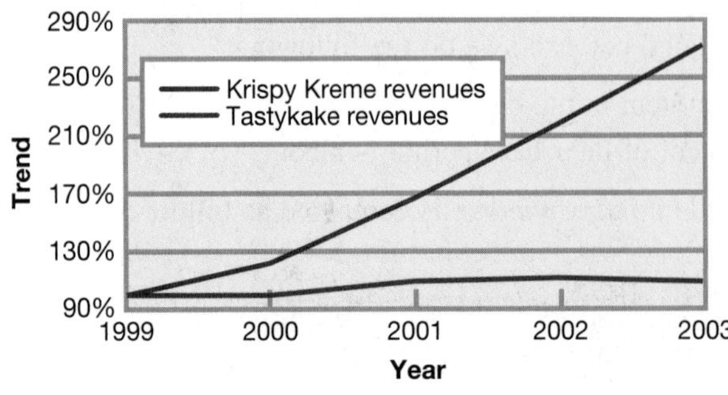

Trend analysis of financial statement items can include comparisons of relations between items on different financial statements. For instance, Exhibit 17.7 compares Krispy Kreme's revenues and total assets. The rate of increase in total assets (439.9%) is greater than the increase in revenues (271.8%). Is this result favorable or not? It suggests that Krispy Kreme was less efficient in using its assets in 2003. Management apparently is expecting future years' revenues to compensate for this asset growth.

	1999	2003	Trend Percent (1999 vs. 2003)
Total revenues	$180,880	$491,549	271.8%
Total assets	93,312	410,487	439.9

Exhibit 17.7
Revenue and Asset Data for Krispy Kreme

Overall we must remember that an important role of financial statement analysis is identifying questions and areas of interest, which often direct us to important factors bearing on a company's future. Accordingly, financial statement analysis should be seen as a continuous process of refining our understanding and expectations of company performance and financial condition.

Decision Maker

Auditor Your tests reveal a 3% increase in sales from $200,000 to $206,000 and a 4% decrease in expenses from $190,000 to $182,400. Both changes are within your "reasonableness" criterion of ±5%, and thus you don't pursue additional tests. The audit partner in charge questions your lack of follow-up and mentions the *joint relation* between sales and expenses. To what is the partner referring?

Answer—p. 697

Vertical Analysis

Vertical analysis is a tool to evaluate individual financial statement items or a group of items in terms of a specific base amount. We usually define a key aggregate figure as the base, which for an income statement is usually revenue and for a balance sheet is usually total assets. This section explains vertical analysis and applies it to **Krispy Kreme**. [The term *vertical analysis* arises from the up-down (or down-up) movement of our eyes as we review common-size financial statements. Vertical analysis is also called *common-size analysis*.]

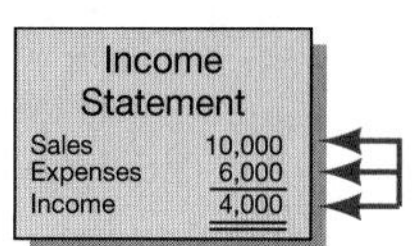

Common-Size Statements

P2 Describe and apply methods of vertical analysis.

The comparative statements in Exhibits 17.1 and 17.2 show the change in each item over time, but they do not emphasize the relative importance of each item. We use **common-size financial statements** to reveal changes in the relative importance of each financial statement item. All individual amounts in common-size statements are redefined in terms of common-size percents. A *common-size percent* is measured by dividing each individual financial statement amount under analysis by its base amount:

$$\textbf{Common-size percent (\%)} = \frac{\textbf{Analysis amount}}{\textbf{Base amount}} \times 100$$

Common-Size Balance Sheets Common-size statements express each item as a percent of a *base amount,* which for a common-size balance sheet is usually total assets. The base amount is assigned a value of 100%. (This implies that the total amount of liabilities plus equity equals 100% since this amount equals total assets.) We then compute a common-size percent for each asset, liability, and equity item using total assets as the base amount. When we present a company's successive balance sheets in this way, changes in the mixture of assets, liabilities, and equity are apparent.

Point: The *base* amount in common-size analysis is an *aggregate* amount from the same period's financial statement.

Exhibit 17.8 shows common-size comparative balance sheets for Krispy Kreme. Some relations that stand out on both a magnitude and percent basis include (1) a decrease in accounts receivable from 10.5% to 8.4%; (2) an increase in property and equipment from

Point: Common-size statements often are used to compare two or more companies in the same industry.

Exhibit 17.8

Common-Size Comparative Balance Sheets

KRISPY KREME
Common-Size Comparative Balance Sheets
February 2, 2003, and February 3, 2002

($ thousands)	2002	2003	Common-Size Percents* 2002	Common-Size Percents* 2003
Assets				
Current assets				
Cash and cash equivalents	$ 21,904	$ 32,203	8.6%	7.8%
Short-term investments	15,292	22,976	6.0	5.6
Accounts receivable, net	26,894	34,373	10.5	8.4
Inventories	16,159	24,365	6.3	5.9
Prepaid expenses	2,591	3,478	1.0	0.8
Other current assets	18,929	23,733	7.4	5.8
Total current assets	101,769	141,128	39.9	34.4
Property and equipment, net	112,577	202,558	44.1	49.3
Long-term investments	12,700	4,344	5.0	1.1
Intangible assets	16,621	48,703	6.5	11.9
Other long-term assets	11,709	13,754	4.6	3.4
Total assets	$255,376	$410,487	100.0%	100.0%
Liabilities				
Current liabilities				
Accounts payable	$ 12,095	$ 14,055	4.7%	3.4%
Accrued expenses	26,729	20,981	10.5	5.1
Current maturities of long-term debt	731	3,301	0.3	0.8
Other current liabilities	12,978	21,350	5.1	5.2
Total current liabilities	52,533	59,687	20.6	14.5
Long-term debt, net of current portion	3,912	49,900	1.5	12.2
Other long-term liabilities	8,773	22,355	3.4	5.4
Total long-term liabilities	12,685	72,255	5.0	17.6
Shareholders' Equity				
Common stock	121,052	173,112	47.4	42.2
Accumulated other comprehensive income (loss)	456	(1,486)	0.2	(0.0)
Retained earnings	68,925	102,403	27.0	24.9
Other equity	(275)	4,516	(0.1)	1.1
Total shareholders' equity**	190,158	278,545	74.5	67.9
Total liabilities and shareholders' equity	$255,376	$410,487	100.0%	100.0%

* Percents are rounded to tenths and thus may not exactly sum to totals and subtotals. ** Includes minority interest.

44.1% to 49.3%; (3) an increase in intangible assets from 6.5% to 11.9%; (4) a decrease in accrued expenses from 10.5% to 5.1%; and (5) an increase in long-term debt from 1.5% to 12.2%. These changes are characteristic of a successful growth company. The concern, if any, is whether Krispy Kreme can continue to generate sufficient revenues and income to support its asset buildup and its increased financing.

Point: Common-size statements are also useful in comparing firms that report in different currencies.

Global: International companies sometimes disclose "convenience" financial statements, which are statements translated in other languages and currencies. However, these statements rarely adjust for differences in accounting principles across countries.

Common-Size Income Statements Analysis also benefits from use of a common-size income statement. Revenues is usually the base amount, which is assigned a value of 100%. Each common-size income statement item appears as a percent of revenues. If we think of the 100% revenues amount as representing one sales dollar, the remaining items show how each revenue dollar is distributed among costs, expenses, and income.

Exhibit 17.9 shows common-size comparative income statements for each dollar of Krispy Kreme's revenues. Operating expenses (cost of sales) decreased from 80.4% to 77.6% of revenues, and so have general and administrative expenses, from 7.0% to 5.9%. This implies that management is effectively controlling costs and/or the company is reaping growth

KRISPY KREME Common-Size Comparative Income Statements For Years Ended February 2, 2003, and February 3, 2002			Common-Size Percents*	
($ thousands)	2002	2003	2002	2003
Total revenues	$394,354	$491,549	100.0%	100.0%
Operating expenses (cost of sales)	316,946	381,489	80.4	77.6
General and administrative expenses	27,562	28,897	7.0	5.9
Depreciation and amortization expenses	7,959	12,271	2.0	2.5
Arbitration award	—	9,075	—	1.8
Income from operations	41,887	59,817	10.6	12.2
Interest income	2,980	1,966	0.8	0.4
Interest expense	(337)	(1,781)	(0.1)	(0.4)
Other losses	(1,749)	(4,295)	(0.4)	(0.9)
Loss on sale of property and equipment	(235)	(934)	(0.1)	(0.2)
Income before income taxes	42,546	54,773	10.8	11.1
Provision for income taxes	16,168	21,295	4.1	4.3
Net income	$ 26,378	$ 33,478	6.7	6.8

* Percents are rounded to tenths and thus may not exactly sum totals and subtotals.

Exhibit 17.9

Common-Size Comparative Income Statements

benefits, so-called *economies of scale*. Conversely, depreciation and amortization along with interest expense have increased as a percent of revenues; again, such results are expected for a growth company. This shows that common-size percents for successive income statements can uncover potentially important changes in a company's expenses. Evidence of no changes, especially when changes are expected, is also informative.

Common-Size Graphics

Two of the most common tools of common-size analysis are trend analysis of common-size statements and graphical analysis. The trend analysis of common-size statements is similar to that of comparative statements discussed under vertical analysis. It is not illustrated here because the only difference is the substitution of common-size percents for trend percents. Instead, this section discusses graphical analysis of common-size statements.

An income statement readily lends itself to common-size graphical analysis. This is so because revenues affect nearly every item in an income statement. Exhibit 17.10 shows Krispy Kreme's 2003 common-size income statement in graphical form. This pie chart highlights the contribution of each component of revenues.

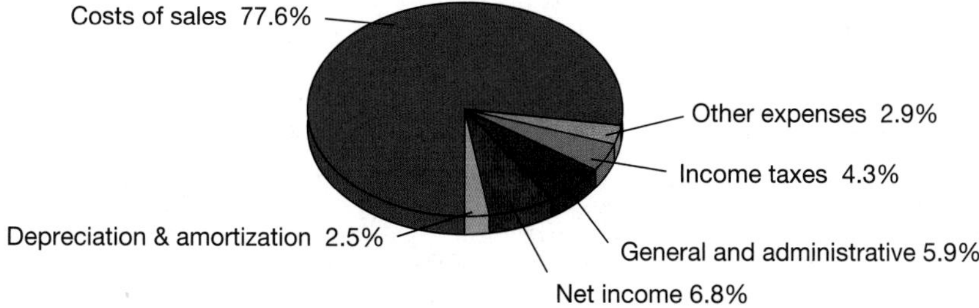

Exhibit 17.10

Common-Size Graphic of Income Statement

Exhibit 17.11 previews more complex graphical analyses available and the insights they provide. The data for this exhibit are taken from **Krispy Kreme**'s *Business Segment* footnote. Krispy Kreme has three reportable segments. The *Company Store Operations* segment refers to stores primarily operated by Krispy Kreme. *Franchise Operations* refers to royalties and fees from franchisees. The *KKM&D* segment supplies product mix, equipment, coffee, and other items to both company-owned and franchisee-owned stores.

Exhibit 17.11

Revenue and Operating Income Breakdown by Segment

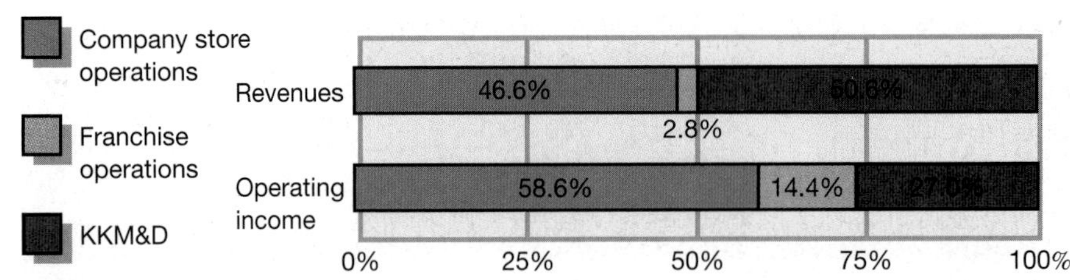

Exhibit 17.12

Common-Size Graphic of Asset Components

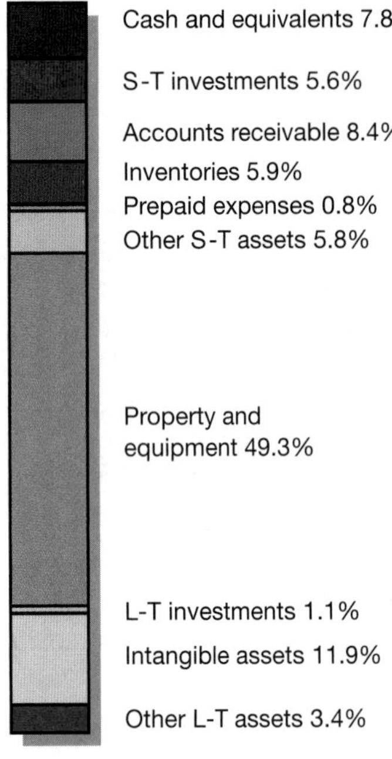

The upper bar in Exhibit 17.11 shows the percent of revenues from each segment. The two major revenue sources are Company Stores (46.6%) and KKM&D (50.6%). The lower bar shows the percent of operating income from each segment. Note that although Franchise Operations provide only 2.8% of revenues, they provide 14.4% of operating income. In contrast, KKM&D provides 50.6% of revenues but only 27.0% of operating income. This type of information can help users in determining strategic analyses and actions.

Graphical analysis is also useful in identifying (1) sources of financing including the distribution among current liabilities, noncurrent liabilities, and equity capital and (2) focuses of investing activities, including the distribution among current and noncurrent assets. As illustrative, Exhibit 17.12 shows a common-size graphical display of Krispy Kreme's assets. Common-size balance sheet analysis can be extended to examine the composition of these subgroups. For instance, in assessing liquidity of current assets, knowing what proportion of current assets consists of inventories is usually important, and not simply what proportion inventories are of total assets.

Common-size financial statements are also useful in comparing different companies. Exhibit 17.13 shows common-size graphics of both Krispy Kreme and Tastykake on financing sources. This graphic highlights the much larger percent of debt financing for Tastykake than for Krispy Kreme. Comparison of a company's common-size statements with competitors' or industry common-size statistics alerts us to differences in the structure or distribution of its financial statements but not to their dollar magnitude.

Exhibit 17.13

Common-Size Graphic of Financing Sources—Competitor Analysis

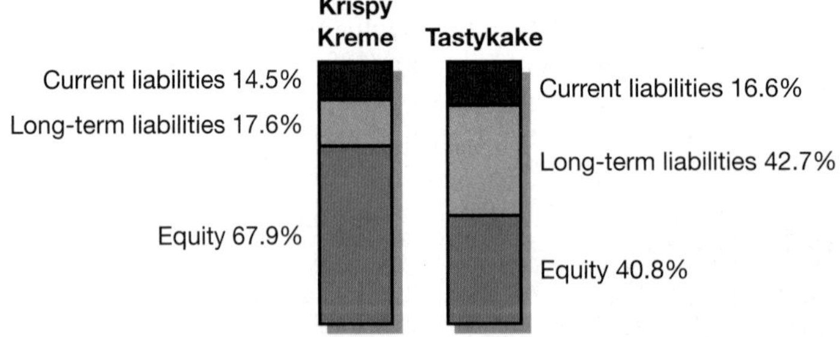

Quick Check

5. Which of the following is true for common-size comparative statements? (*a*) Each item is expressed as a percent of a base amount. (*b*) Total assets often are assigned a value of 100%. (*c*) Amounts from successive periods are placed side by side. (*d*) All are true. (*e*) None is true.
6. What is the difference between the percents shown on a comparative income statement and those shown on a common-size comparative income statement?
7. Trend percents are (*a*) shown on comparative income statements and balance sheets, (*b*) shown on common-size comparative statements, or (*c*) also called *index numbers.*

Answers—p. 698

Ratio Analysis

P3 Define and apply ratio analysis.

Ratios are among the more widely used tools of financial analysis because they provide clues to and symptoms of underlying conditions. A ratio can help us uncover conditions and trends difficult to detect by inspecting individual components making up the ratio. Ratios, like other analysis tools, are usually future oriented; that is, they are often adjusted for their probable future trend and magnitude, and their usefulness depends on skillful interpretation.

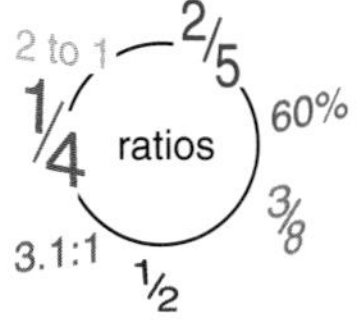

A ratio expresses a mathematical relation between two quantities. It can be expressed as a percent, rate, or proportion. For instance, a change in an account balance from $100 to $250 can be expressed as (1) 150%, (2) 2.5 times, or (3) 2.5 to 1 (or 2.5:1). Computation of a ratio is a simple arithmetic operation, but its interpretation is not. To be meaningful, a ratio must refer to an economically important relation. For example, a direct and crucial relation exists between an item's sales price and its cost. Accordingly, the ratio of cost of goods sold to sales is meaningful. In contrast, no obvious relation exists between freight costs and the balance of long-term investments.

Topic Tackler 17-2

This section describes an important set of financial ratios and its application. The selected ratios are organized into the four building blocks of financial statement analysis: (1) liquidity and efficiency, (2) solvency, (3) profitability, and (4) market prospects. All of these ratios were explained at relevant points in prior chapters. The purpose here is to organize and apply them under a summary framework. We use four common standards for comparisons: intracompany, competitor, industry, and guidelines. Our analysis of **Krispy Kreme** uses three of the four standards in varying degrees: intracompany, competitor (**Tastykake**), and guideline comparisons. Since no obvious industry comparison is available for Krispy Kreme, we do not use industry standards as we normally would. For instance, constructing industry standards using Dunkin' Donuts, Tim Hortons, Lamar's Donuts, Winchell's Donut Houses, Donut Connection, and Mister Donut would be useful, but because all are either privately held, a subsidiary, or a non-U.S. company and do not publish statements readily comparable to those of Krispy Kreme, this is not done.

Point: Some sources for industry norms are *Annual Statement Studies* by Robert Morris Associates, *Industry Norms & Key Business Ratios* by Dun & Bradstreet, *Standard & Poor's Industry Surveys*, and MarketGuide.com.

Liquidity and Efficiency

Liquidity refers to the availability of resources to meet short-term cash requirements. It is affected by the timing of cash inflows and outflows along with prospects for future performance. Analysis of liquidity is aimed at a company's funding requirements. *Efficiency* refers to how productive a company is in using its assets. Efficiency is usually measured relative to how much revenue is generated from a certain level of assets.

Both liquidity and efficiency are important and complementary. If a company fails to meet its current obligations, its continued existence is doubtful. Viewed in this light, all other measures of analysis are of secondary importance. Although accounting measurements assume the company's continued existence, our analysis must always assess the validity of this assumption using liquidity measures. Moreover, inefficient use of assets can cause liquidity problems. A lack of liquidity often precedes lower profitability and fewer opportunities. It can foretell a loss of owner control or of investment. To a company's creditors, lack of liquidity can yield delays in collecting interest and principal payments or the loss of amounts due them. A company's customers and suppliers of goods and services also are affected by short-term liquidity problems. Implications include a company's inability to execute contracts and potential damage to important customer and supplier relationships. This section describes and illustrates key ratios relevant to assessing liquidity and efficiency.

Working Capital and Current Ratio The amount of current assets less current liabilities is called **working capital,** or *net working capital.* A company needs adequate working capital to meet current debts, to carry sufficient inventories, and to take advantage of cash discounts. A company that runs low on working capital is less likely to meet current obligations or to continue operating. When evaluating a company's working capital, we must not only look at the dollar amount of current assets less current liabilities, but also at their ratio. Chapter 4 defined the *current ratio* as follows:

$$\textbf{Current ratio} = \frac{\textbf{Current assets}}{\textbf{Current liabilities}}$$

Drawing on information in Exhibit 17.1, **Krispy Kreme**'s working capital and current ratio for both 2003 and 2002 are shown in Exhibit 17.14. **Tastykake**'s current ratio of 1.87 is shown in the margin. It is lower than Krispy Kreme's current ratio (2.36), but neither company appears in danger of defaulting on loan payments. A high current ratio suggests a strong liquidity position and an ability to meet current obligations. A company can, however, have a current ratio that is too high. An excessively high current ratio means that the company has invested too much in current assets compared to its current obligations. An excessive investment in current assets is not an efficient use of funds because current assets normally generate a low return on investment (compared with long-term assets).

Exhibit 17.14

Krispy Kreme's Working Capital and Current Ratio

($ thousands)	2002	2003
Current assets	$101,769	$141,128
Current liabilities	52,533	59,687
Working capital	**$ 49,236**	**$ 81,441**
Current ratio		
$101,769/$52,533 ..	**1.94 to 1**	
$141,128/$59,687 ..		**2.36 to 1**

Tastykake
Current ratio = 1.87

Many users apply a guideline of 2:1 for the current ratio in helping evaluate a company's debt-paying ability. A company with a 2:1 or higher current ratio is generally thought to be a good credit risk in the short run. Such a guideline or any analysis of the current ratio must recognize at least three additional factors: (1) type of business, (2) composition of current assets, and (3) turnover rate of current asset components.

Type of business. A service company that grants little or no credit and carries no inventories can probably operate on a current ratio of less than 1:1 if its revenues generate enough cash to pay its current liabilities. On the other hand, a company selling high-priced clothing or furniture requires a higher ratio because of difficulties in judging customer demand and cash receipts. For instance, if demand falls, inventory may not generate as much cash as expected. Accordingly, analysis of the current ratio should include a comparison with ratios from successful companies in the same industry and from prior periods. We must also recognize that a company's accounting methods, especially choice of inventory method, affect the current ratio. For instance, when costs are rising, a company using LIFO tends to report a smaller amount of current assets than when using FIFO.

Point: When a firm uses LIFO in a period of rising costs, the standard for an adequate current ratio usually is lower than if it used FIFO.

Composition of current assets. The composition of a company's current assets is important to an evaluation of short-term liquidity. For instance, cash, cash equivalents, and short-term investments are more liquid than accounts and notes receivable. Also, short-term receivables normally are more liquid than inventory. Cash, of course, can be used to immediately pay current debts. Items such as accounts receivable and inventory, however, normally must be converted into cash before payment is made. An excessive amount of receivables and inventory weakens a company's ability to pay current liabilities. The acid-test ratio (see below) can help with this assessment.

Decision Maker

Banker A company requests a one-year, $200,000 loan for expansion. This company's current ratio is 4:1, with current assets of $160,000. Key competitors carry a current ratio of about 1.9:1. Using this information, do you approve the loan application? Does your decision change if the application is for a 10-year loan?

Answer—p. 697

Global: Ratio analysis helps overcome most currency translation problems, but it does *not* overcome differences in accounting principles.

Turnover rate of assets. Asset turnover measures a company's efficiency in using its assets. One relevant measure of asset efficiency is the revenue generated. A measure of total asset turnover is revenues divided by total assets, but evaluation of turnover for individual assets is also useful. We discuss both receivables turnover and inventory turnover below.

Acid-Test Ratio Quick assets are cash, short-term investments, and current receivables. These are the most liquid types of current assets. The *acid-test ratio,* also called *quick ratio,* was introduced in Chapter 5 and it reflects on short-term liquidity.

$$\text{Acid-test ratio} = \frac{\text{Cash + Short-term investments + Current receivables}}{\text{Current liabilities}}$$

Krispy Kreme's acid-test ratio is computed in Exhibit 17.15. Krispy Kreme's 2003 acid-test ratio (1.70) is greater than that for Tastykake (1.10) and the 1:1 common guideline for an acceptable acid-test ratio. Similar to analysis of the current ratio, we need to consider other factors. For instance, the frequency with which a company converts its current assets into cash affects its working capital requirements. This implies that analysis of short-term liquidity should also include an analysis of receivables and inventories. We next consider these analyses.

Exhibit 17.15

Acid-Test Ratio

($ thousands)	2002	2003
Cash and equivalents	$21,904	$ 32,203
Short-term investments	15,292	22,976
Current receivables	38,682	46,319
Total quick assets	$75,878	$101,498
Current liabilities	$52,533	$ 59,687
Acid-test ratio		
$75,878/$52,533	**1.44 to 1**	
$101,498/$59,687		**1.70 to 1**

Tastykake
Acid-test ratio = 1.10

Accounts Receivable Turnover We can measure how frequently a company converts its receivables into cash by computing *accounts receivable turnover*. As explained in Chapter 9, it is computed as follows:

$$\text{Accounts receivable turnover} = \frac{\text{Net sales}}{\text{Average accounts receivable}}$$

Short-term receivables from customers are often included in the denominator along with accounts receivable. Also, accounts receivable turnover is more precise if credit sales are used for the numerator, but external users generally use net sales (or net revenues) because information about credit sales is typically not reported. Krispy Kreme's 2003 accounts receivable turnover is computed as follows ($ millions):

Point: Some users prefer using gross accounts receivable (before subtracting the allowance for doubtful accounts) to avoid the influence of a manager's bad debts estimates.

$$\frac{\$491{,}549}{(\$34{,}373 + \$26{,}894)/2} = 16.0 \text{ times}$$

Tastykake
Accounts receivable turnover = 7.5

Krispy Kreme's value of 16.0 is much larger than Tastykake's 7.5. The accounts receivable turnover is high when accounts receivable are quickly collected. A high turnover is favorable because it means the company need not commit large amounts of funds to accounts receivable. However, an accounts receivable turnover can be too high; this can occur when credit terms are so restrictive that they negatively affect sales volume.

Point: Ending accounts receivable is sometimes substituted for the average balance in computing accounts receivable turnover when the difference between ending and average receivables is small.

Inventory Turnover How long a company holds inventory before selling it affects working capital requirements. One measure of this effect is the *inventory turnover,* also called *merchandise turnover* or *merchandise inventory turnover,* which is defined in Chapter 6 as:

Point: *Average collection period* is estimated by dividing 365 by the accounts receivable turnover ratio. For example, 365 divided by an accounts receivable turnover of 6.1 indicates a 60-day average collection period.

$$\text{Inventory turnover} = \frac{\text{Cost of goods sold}}{\text{Average inventory}}$$

Using operating expenses (Krispy Kreme's term for cost of goods sold) and inventories information, we compute Krispy Kreme's inventory turnover for 2003:

$$\frac{\$381{,}489}{(\$24{,}365 + \$16{,}159)/2} = 18.8 \text{ times}$$

Tastykake
Inventory turnover = 14.6

If the beginning and ending inventories for the year do not represent the usual inventory amount, an average of quarterly or monthly inventories can be used. Krispy Kreme's inventory turnover of 18.8 is slightly higher than Tastykake's 14.6. A company with a high turnover requires a smaller investment in inventory than one producing the same sales with a lower turnover. Inventory turnover can be too high, however, if the inventory a company keeps is so small that it restricts sales volume.

Days' Sales Uncollected Accounts receivable turnover provides insight into how frequently a company collects its accounts. Days' sales uncollected is one measure of this activity, which is defined in Chapter 8 as:

$$\textbf{Days' sales uncollected} = \frac{\textbf{Accounts receivable}}{\textbf{Net sales}} \times \textbf{365}$$

Any short-term notes receivable from customers are normally included in the numerator.

Krispy Kreme's 2003 days' sales uncollected follows:

Tastykake
Day's sales uncollected = 47.0

$$\frac{\$34,373}{\$491,549} \times 365 = 25.5 \text{ days}$$

Tastykake's days' sales uncollected of 47.0 days is larger than the 25.5 days for Krispy Kreme. Days' sales uncollected is more meaningful if we know the company credit terms. A rough guideline states that days' sales uncollected should not exceed $1\frac{1}{3}$ times the days in its (1) credit period, if discounts are not offered or (2) discount period, if favorable discounts are offered.

Days' Sales in Inventory Chapter 6 explained how *days' sales in inventory* is a useful measure in evaluating inventory liquidity. Days' sales in inventory is linked to inventory in a way that days' sales uncollected is linked to receivables. We compute days' sales in inventory as follows:

$$\textbf{Days' sales in inventory} = \frac{\textbf{Ending inventory}}{\textbf{Cost of goods sold}} \times \textbf{365}$$

Krispy Kreme's days' sales in inventory for 2003 follows:

Tastykake
Days' sales in inventory = 22.2

$$\frac{\$24,365}{\$381,489} \times 365 = 23.3 \text{ days}$$

If the products in Krispy Kreme's inventory are in demand by customers, this formula estimates that its inventory will be converted into receivables (or cash) in 23.3 days. If all of Krispy Kreme's sales were credit sales, the conversion of inventory to receivables in 23.3 days *plus* the conversion of receivables to cash in 25.5 days implies that inventory will be converted to cash in about 48.8 days (23.3 + 25.5).

Total Asset Turnover *Total asset turnover* reflects a company's ability to use its assets to generate sales and is an important indication of operating efficiency. We explained in Chapter 10 the computation of this ratio as follows:

$$\textbf{Total asset turnover} = \frac{\textbf{Net sales}}{\textbf{Average total assets}}$$

Krispy Kreme's total asset turnover for 2003 follows and is better than Tastykake's.

Tastykake
Total asset turnover = 1.39

$$\frac{\$491,549}{(\$410,487 + \$255,376)/2} = 1.48 \text{ times}$$

Quick Check

8. Information from Paff Co. at Dec. 31, 2005, follows: cash, $820,000; accounts receivable, $240,000; inventories, $470,000; plant assets, $910,000; accounts payable, $350,000; and income taxes payable, $180,000. Compute its (*a*) current ratio and (*b*) acid-test ratio.
9. On Dec. 31, 2004, Paff Company (question 8) had accounts receivable of $290,000 and inventories of $530,000. During 2005, net sales amounted to $2,500,000 and cost of goods sold was $750,000. Compute (*a*) accounts receivable turnover, (*b*) days' sales uncollected, (*c*) inventory turnover, and (*d*) days' sales in inventory.

Answers—p. 698

Solvency

Solvency refers to a company's long-run financial viability and its ability to cover long-term obligations. All of a company's business activities—financing, investing, and operating—affect its solvency. Analysis of solvency is long term and uses less precise but more encompassing measures than liquidity. One of the most important components of solvency analysis is the composition of a company's capital structure. *Capital structure* refers to a company's financing sources. It ranges from relatively permanent equity financing to riskier or more temporary short-term financing. Assets represent security for financiers, ranging from loans secured by specific assets to the assets available as general security to unsecured creditors. This section describes the tools of solvency analysis. Our analysis focuses on a company's ability to both meet its obligations and provide security to its creditors *over the long run*. Indicators of this ability include *debt* and *equity* ratios, the relation between *pledged assets and secured liabilities,* and the company's capacity to earn sufficient income to *pay fixed interest charges*.

Debt and Equity Ratios One element of solvency analysis is to assess the portion of a company's assets contributed by its owners and the portion contributed by creditors. This relation is reflected in the debt ratio described in Chapter 2. The *debt ratio* expresses total liabilities as a percent of total assets. The **equity ratio** provides complementary information by expressing total equity as a percent of total assets. **Krispy Kreme**'s debt and equity ratios are computed here:

Point: For analysis purposes, Minority Interest is usually added to equity.

($ thousands)	2003	Ratios	
Total liabilities	$131,942	32.1%	[Debt ratio]
Total equity	278,545	67.9	[Equity ratio]
Total liabilities and equity	$410,487	100.0%	

Tastykake
Debt ratio = 59.2%
Equity ratio = 40.8%

Krispy Kreme's financial statements reflect less debt than equity. A company is considered less risky if its capital structure (equity and long-term debt) contains more equity. One risk factor is the required payment for interest and principal when debt is outstanding. Another factor is the greater the stockholder financing, the more losses a company can absorb through equity before the assets become inadequate to satisfy creditors' claims. From the stockholders' point of view, if a company earns a return on borrowed capital that is higher than the cost of borrowing, the difference represents increased income to stockholders. The inclusion of debt is described as *financial leverage* because debt can have the effect of increasing the return to stockholders. Companies are said to be highly leveraged if a large portion of their assets is financed by debt.

Point: Bank examiners from the FDIC and other regulatory agencies use debt and equity ratios to monitor compliance with regulatory capital requirements imposed on banks and S&Ls.

Pledged Assets to Secured Liabilities We explained in Chapter 14 how to use the ratio of pledged assets to secured liabilities to evaluate the risk of nonpayment faced by secured creditors. This ratio also is relevant to unsecured creditors because of what it implies about the remaining assets available. We compute the ratio as follows:

$$\textbf{Pledged assets to secured liabilities} = \frac{\textbf{Book value of pledged assets}}{\textbf{Book value of secured liabilities}}$$

The information needed to compute this ratio is sometimes not reported in financial statements. However, persons who have the ability to obtain information directly from the company, such as bankers and lenders, nearly always examine this ratio. A generally agreed minimum value for this ratio is about 2:1 (from a secured creditor perspective), but the ratio needs careful interpretation because it is based on the *book value* of pledged assets. Book values are not necessarily intended to reflect amounts to be received from assets in event of liquidation. Also, a company's long-run earning ability is equally important. Creditors prefer that a debtor be able to pay with cash generated by operating activities rather than with cash obtained by liquidating assets.

Krispy Kreme's note 7 (*Debt*) describes several of its secured and unsecured liabilities. A complete analysis would involve assessing these details, which is left for advanced courses.

Point: The times interest earned ratio and the debt and equity ratios are of special interest to bank lending officers.

Times Interest Earned The amount of income before deductions for interest expense and income taxes is the amount available to pay interest expense. Chapter 11 explained that the following *times interest earned* ratio reflects the creditors' risk of loan repayments with interest:

$$\textbf{Times interest earned} = \frac{\textbf{Income before interest expense and income taxes}}{\textbf{Interest expense}}$$

The larger this ratio, the less risky is the company for creditors. One guideline says that creditors are reasonably safe if the company earns its fixed interest expense two or more times each year. Krispy Kreme's times interest earned ratio follows; its value suggests that its creditors have little risk of nonrepayment.

$$\frac{\$33{,}478 + \$21{,}295 + \$1{,}781}{\$1{,}781} = 31.8$$

Decision Insight

Bears and Bulls A *bear market* is a declining market. The phrase comes from bear-skin jobbers who often sold the skins before the bears were caught. The term *bear* was then used to describe investors who sold shares they did not own in anticipation of a price decline. A *bull market* is a rising market. This phrase comes from the once popular sport of bear and bull baiting. The term *bull* came to mean the opposite of *bear.*

Tastykake
Times interest earned = 2.9*
* Excludes restructuring

Profitability

We are especially interested in a company's ability to use its assets efficiently to produce profits (and positive cash flows). *Profitability* refers to a company's ability to generate an adequate return on invested capital. Return is judged by assessing earnings relative to the level and sources of financing. Profitability is also relevant to solvency. This section describes key profitability measures and their importance to financial statement analysis.

Profit Margin A company's operating efficiency and profitability can be expressed by two components. The first is *profit margin,* which Chapter 3 explained reflects a company's ability to earn net income from sales. It is measured by expressing net income as a percent of sales (*sales* and *revenues* are similar terms). **Krispy Kreme**'s profit margin follows:

Tastykake
Profit margin = 1.2%*
* Excludes restructuring

$$\textbf{Profit margin} = \frac{\textbf{Net income}}{\textbf{Net sales}} = \frac{\textbf{\$33,478}}{\textbf{\$491,549}} = 6.8\%$$

To evaluate profit margin, we must consider the industry. For instance, an appliance company might require a profit margin between 10% and 15%; a retail supermarket might require a profit margin of 1% or 2%. The second component of operating efficiency is *total asset turnover* described earlier in this section. Both profit margin and total asset turnover make up the two basic components of operating efficiency. These ratios also reflect on management because managers are ultimately responsible for operating efficiency. The next section explains how we use both measures to analyze return on total assets.

Return on Total Assets *Return on total assets* is defined as follows:

$$\textbf{Return on total assets} = \frac{\textbf{Net income}}{\textbf{Average total assets}}$$

Krispy Kreme's 2003 return on total assets is

$$\frac{\$33,478}{(\$410,487 + \$255,376)/2} = 10.1\%$$

Tastykake
Return on total assets = 1.7%*
* Excludes restructuring

Point: Many analysts add back *Interest expense* × *(1 − Tax rate)* to net income in computing return on total assets.

Krispy Kreme's 10.1% return on total assets is lower than that for many businesses but is higher than Tastykake's return of 1.7%. We need comparisons with other competitors and alternative investment opportunities, however, before drawing reliable conclusions. We also should evaluate any trend in the rate of return. The following computation shows the important relation between profit margin, total asset turnover, and return on total assets:

$$\textbf{Profit margin} \times \textbf{Total asset turnover} = \textbf{Return on total assets}$$

or

$$\frac{\textbf{Net income}}{\textbf{Net sales}} \times \frac{\textbf{Net sales}}{\textbf{Average total assets}} = \frac{\textbf{Net income}}{\textbf{Average total assets}}$$

Both profit margin and total asset turnover contribute to overall operating efficiency, as measured by return on total assets. If we apply this formula to Krispy Kreme, we get

$$6.8\% \times 1.48 = 10.1\%$$

Tastykake: 1.2% × 1.39 = 1.7%

This analysis shows that Krispy Kreme's superior return on assets to that of Tastykake is the main driver of its higher profit margin.

Return on Common Stockholders' Equity Perhaps the most important goal in operating a company is to earn net income for its owner(s). The *return on common stockholders' equity* measures a company's success in reaching this goal and is defined as follows:

$$\textbf{Return on common stockholders' equity} = \frac{\textbf{Net income} - \textbf{Preferred dividends}}{\textbf{Average common stockholders' equity}}$$

Krispy Kreme's 2003 return on common stockholders' equity is computed as follows:

$$\frac{\$33,478 - \$0.00}{(\$278,545 + \$190,158)/2} = 14.3\%$$

Tastykake
Return on common stockholders' equity = 3.9%*
* Excludes restructuring

The denominator in this computation is the book value of common equity (including any minority interest). In the numerator, the dividends on cumulative preferred stock are subtracted whether they are declared or are in arrears. If preferred stock is noncumulative, its dividends are subtracted only if declared.

Decision Insight

Wall Street *Wall Street* is synonymous with financial markets, but its name comes from the street location of the original New York Stock Exchange. The street's name derives from stockades built by early settlers to protect New York from pirate attacks.

Market Prospects

Market measures are useful for analyzing corporations with publicly traded stock. These market

measures use stock price, which reflects the market's (public's) expectations for the company. This includes expectations of both company return and risk—as the market perceives it.

Price-Earnings Ratio Computation of the *price-earnings ratio* was explained in Chapter 13 as follows:

$$\textbf{Price-earnings ratio} = \frac{\textbf{Market price per common share}}{\textbf{Earnings per share}}$$

Point: The PE ratio can be viewed as an indicator of the market's expected growth and risk for a stock. A high level of expected risk suggests a low PE ratio. A high growth rate suggests a high PE ratio.

Predicted earnings per share for the next period is often used in the denominator of this computation. Reported earnings per share for the most recent period is also commonly used. In both cases, the ratio is used as an indicator of the future growth and risk of a company's earnings as perceived by the stock's buyers and sellers.

The market price of Krispy Kreme's common stock at the start of fiscal year 2004 was $30.41. Using Krispy Kreme's $0.61 basic earnings per share, we compute its price-earnings ratio as follows (some analysts compute this ratio using the median of the low and high stock price):

Tastykake
PE (year-end) = 37.1*

* Excludes restructuring

$$\frac{\$30.41}{\$0.61} = 49.9$$

Point: Some investors avoid stocks with high PE ratios under the belief they are "overpriced." Alternatively, some investors *sell these stocks short*—hoping for price declines.

Krispy Kreme's price-earnings ratio is higher than the norm. (Tastykake's ratio is high due to abnormally low earnings.) Krispy Kreme's high ratio reflects investors' expectations of continued growth and higher than normal earnings.

Dividend Yield *Dividend yield* is used to compare the dividend-paying performance of different investment alternatives. We compute dividend yield as explained in Chapter 13 as follows:

$$\textbf{Dividend yield} = \frac{\textbf{Annual cash dividends per share}}{\textbf{Market price per share}}$$

Krispy Kreme's dividend yield, based on its fiscal year-end market price per share of $30.41 and its policy of zero cash dividends per share, is computed as follows:

Tastykake
Dividend yield = 5.2%

$$\frac{\$0.00}{\$30.41} = 0.0\%$$

Some companies do not declare and pay dividends because they wish to reinvest the cash.

Point: Corporate PE ratios and dividend yields are found in daily stock market quotations listed in *The Wall Street Journal*, *Investor's Business Daily*, or other business publications and Web services.

Summary of Ratios

Exhibit 17.16 summarizes the major financial statement analysis ratios illustrated in this chapter and throughout the book. This summary includes each ratio's title, its formula, and the purpose for which it is commonly used.

Quick Check

10. Which ratio best reflects a company's ability to meet immediate interest payments? (*a*) Debt ratio. (*b*) Equity ratio. (*c*) Times interest earned.

11. Which ratio best measures a company's success in earning net income for its owner(s)? (*a*) Profit margin. (*b*) Return on common stockholders' equity. (*c*) Price-earnings ratio. (*d*) Dividend yield.

12. If a company has net sales of $8,500,000, net income of $945,000, and total asset turnover of 1.8 times, what is its return on total assets?

Answers—p. 698

Exhibit 17.16

Financial Statement Analysis Ratios*

Ratio	Formula	Measure of
Liquidity and Efficiency		
Current ratio	$= \dfrac{\text{Current assets}}{\text{Current liabilities}}$	Short-term debt-paying ability
Acid-test ratio	$= \dfrac{\text{Cash + Short-term investments + Current receivables}}{\text{Current liabilities}}$	Immediate short-term debt-paying ability
Accounts receivable turnover	$= \dfrac{\text{Net sales}}{\text{Average accounts receivable}}$	Efficiency of collection
Inventory turnover	$= \dfrac{\text{Cost of goods sold}}{\text{Average inventory}}$	Efficiency of inventory management
Days' sales uncollected	$= \dfrac{\text{Accounts receivable}}{\text{Net sales}} \times 365$	Liquidity of receivables
Days' sales in inventory	$= \dfrac{\text{Ending inventory}}{\text{Cost of goods sold}} \times 365$	Liquidity of inventory
Total asset turnover	$= \dfrac{\text{Net sales}}{\text{Average total assets}}$	Efficiency of assets in producing sales
Solvency		
Debt ratio	$= \dfrac{\text{Total liabilities}}{\text{Total assets}}$	Creditor financing and leverage
Equity ratio	$= \dfrac{\text{Total equity}}{\text{Total assets}}$	Owner financing
Pledged assets to secured liabilities	$= \dfrac{\text{Book value of pledged assets}}{\text{Book value of secured liabilities}}$	Protection to secured creditors
Times interest earned	$= \dfrac{\text{Income before interest expense and income taxes}}{\text{Interest expense}}$	Protection in meeting interest payments
Profitability		
Profit margin ratio	$= \dfrac{\text{Net income}}{\text{Net sales}}$	Net income in each sales dollar
Gross margin ratio	$= \dfrac{\text{Net sales} - \text{Cost of goods sold}}{\text{Net sales}}$	Gross margin in each sales dollar
Return on total assets	$= \dfrac{\text{Net income}}{\text{Average total assets}}$	Overall profitability of assets
Return on common stockholders' equity	$= \dfrac{\text{Net income} - \text{Preferred dividends}}{\text{Average common stockholders' equity}}$	Profitability of owner investment
Book value per common share	$= \dfrac{\text{Shareholders' equity applicable to common shares}}{\text{Number of common shares outstanding}}$	Liquidation at reported amounts
Basic earnings per share	$= \dfrac{\text{Net income} - \text{Preferred dividends}}{\text{Weighted-average common shares outstanding}}$	Net income per common share
Market Prospects		
Price-earnings ratio	$= \dfrac{\text{Market price per common share}}{\text{Earnings per share}}$	Market value relative to earnings
Dividend yield	$= \dfrac{\text{Annual cash dividends per share}}{\text{Market price per share}}$	Cash return per common share

* Additional ratios also examined in previous chapters included credit risk ratio; plant asset useful life; plant asset age; days' cash expense coverage; cash coverage of growth; cash coverage of debt; free cash flow; cash flow on total assets; and payout ratio. Many of these are defined on the back inside cover of the book.

Decision Analysis

Analysis Reporting

A1 Summarize and report results of analysis.

Understanding the purpose of financial statement analysis is crucial to the usefulness of any analysis. This understanding leads to efficiency of effort, effectiveness in application, and relevance in focus. The purpose of most financial statement analyses is to reduce uncertainty in business decisions through a rigorous and sound evaluation. A *financial statement analysis report* helps by directly addressing the building blocks of analysis and by identifying weaknesses in inference by requiring explanation: It forces us to organize our reasoning and to verify its flow and logic. A report also serves as a communication link with readers, and the writing process reinforces our judgments and vice versa. Finally, the report helps us (re)evaluate evidence and refine conclusions on key building blocks. A good analysis report usually consists of six sections:

1. **Executive summary**—brief focus on important analysis results and conclusions.
2. **Analysis overview**—background on the company, its industry, and its economic setting.
3. **Evidential matter**—financial statements and information used in the analysis, including ratios, trends, comparisons, statistics, and all analytical measures assembled; often organized under the building blocks of analysis.
4. **Assumptions**—identification of important assumptions regarding a company's industry and economic environment, and other important assumptions for estimates.
5. **Key factors**—list of important favorable and unfavorable factors, both quantitative and qualitative, for company performance; usually organized by areas of analysis.
6. **Inferences**—forecasts, estimates, interpretations, and conclusions drawing on all sections of the report.

We must remember that the user dictates relevance, meaning that the analysis report should include a brief table of contents to help readers focus on those areas most relevant to their decisions. All irrelevant matter must be eliminated. For example, decades-old details of obscure transactions and detailed miscues of the analysis are irrelevant. Ambiguities and qualifications to avoid responsibility or hedging inferences must be eliminated. Finally, writing is important. Mistakes in grammar and errors of fact compromise the report's credibility.

Decision Insight

Short Selling *Short selling* refers to selling stock before you buy it. Here's an example: You borrow 100 shares of Nike stock, sell them in the market at $40 each, and receive money from their sale. You then wait. You hope that Nike's stock price falls to, say, $35 each and you can replace the borrowed stock for less money than you sold it for, reaping a profit of $5 each less any transaction costs.

Demonstration Problem

Use the following financial statements of Precision Co. to complete these requirements:

1. Prepare comparative income statements showing the percent increase or decrease for year 2006 in comparison to year 2005.

2. Prepare common-size comparative balance sheets for years 2006 and 2005.

3. Compute the following ratios as of December 31, 2006, or for the year ended December 31, 2006, and identify its building block category for financial statement analysis:

- **a.** Current ratio
- **b.** Acid-test ratio
- **c.** Accounts receivable turnover
- **d.** Days' sales uncollected
- **e.** Inventory turnover
- **f.** Debt ratio
- **g.** Pledged assets to secured liabilities
- **h.** Times interest earned
- **i.** Profit margin ratio
- **j.** Total asset turnover
- **k.** Return on total assets
- **l.** Return on common stockholders' equity

PRECISION COMPANY Comparative Income Statements For Years Ended December 31, 2006 and 2005	2006	2005
Sales	$2,486,000	$2,075,000
Cost of goods sold	1,523,000	1,222,000
Gross profit	963,000	853,000
Operating expenses		
Advertising expense	145,000	100,000
Sales salaries expense	240,000	280,000
Office salaries expense	165,000	200,000
Insurance expense	100,000	45,000
Supplies expense	26,000	35,000
Depreciation expense	85,000	75,000
Miscellaneous expenses	17,000	15,000
Total operating expenses	778,000	750,000
Operating income	185,000	103,000
Interest expense	44,000	46,000
Income before taxes	141,000	57,000
Income taxes	47,000	19,000
Net income	$ 94,000	$ 38,000
Earnings per share	$ 0.99	$ 0.40

PRECISION COMPANY Comparative Balance Sheets December 31, 2006 and 2005	2006	2005
Assets		
Current assets		
Cash	$ 79,000	$ 42,000
Short-term investments	65,000	96,000
Accounts receivable, net	120,000	100,000
Merchandise inventory	250,000	265,000
Total current assets	514,000	503,000
Plant assets		
Store equipment, net	400,000	350,000
Office equipment, net	45,000	50,000
Buildings, net	625,000	675,000
Land	100,000	100,000
Total plant assets	1,170,000	1,175,000
Total assets	$1,684,000	$1,678,000
Liabilities		
Current liabilities		
Accounts payable	$ 164,000	$ 190,000
Short-term notes payable	75,000	90,000
Taxes payable	26,000	12,000
Total current liabilities	265,000	292,000
Long-term liabilities		
Notes payable (secured by mortgage on buildings)	400,000	420,000
Total liabilities	665,000	712,000
Stockholders' Equity		
Common stock, $5 par value	475,000	475,000
Retained earnings	544,000	491,000
Total stockholders' equity	1,019,000	966,000
Total liabilities and equity	$1,684,000	$1,678,000

Planning the Solution

- Set up a four-column income statement; enter the 2006 and 2005 amounts in the first two columns and then enter the dollar change in the third column and the percent change from 2005 in the fourth column.
- Set up a four-column balance sheet; enter the 2006 and 2005 year-end amounts in the first two columns and then compute and enter the amount of each item as a percent of total assets.
- Compute the required ratios using the data provided. Use the average of beginning and ending amounts when appropriate (see Exhibit 17.16 for definitions).

Solution to Demonstration Problem

1.

PRECISION COMPANY Comparative Income Statements For Years Ended December 31, 2006 and 2005			Increase (Decrease) in 2006	
	2006	2005	Amount	Percent
Sales	$2,486,000	$2,075,000	**$411,000**	**19.8%**
Cost of goods sold	1,523,000	1,222,000	**301,000**	**24.6**
Gross profit	963,000	853,000	**110,000**	**12.9**
Operating expenses				
Advertising expense	145,000	100,000	**45,000**	**45.0**
Sales salaries expense	240,000	280,000	**(40,000)**	**(14.3)**
Office salaries expense	165,000	200,000	**(35,000)**	**(17.5)**

[continued on next page]

[continued from previous page]

Insurance expense	100,000	45,000	**55,000**	**122.2**
Supplies expense	26,000	35,000	**(9,000)**	**(25.7)**
Depreciation expense	85,000	75,000	**10,000**	**13.3**
Miscellaneous expenses	17,000	15,000	**2,000**	**13.3**
Total operating expenses	778,000	750,000	**28,000**	**3.7**
Operating income	185,000	103,000	**82,000**	**79.6**
Interest expense	44,000	46,000	**(2,000)**	**(4.3)**
Income before taxes	141,000	57,000	**84,000**	**147.4**
Income taxes	47,000	19,000	**28,000**	**147.4**
Net income	$ 94,000	$ 38,000	**$ 56,000**	**147.4**
Earnings per share	$ 0.99	$ 0.40	**$ 0.59**	**147.5**

2.

PRECISION COMPANY
Common-Size Comparative Balance Sheets
December 31, 2006 and 2005

	December 31		Common-Size Percents	
	2006	2005	2006*	2005*
Assets				
Current assets				
Cash	$ 79,000	$ 42,000	**4.7%**	**2.5%**
Short-term investments	65,000	96,000	**3.9**	**5.7**
Accounts receivable, net	120,000	100,000	**7.1**	**6.0**
Merchandise inventory	250,000	265,000	**14.8**	**15.8**
Total current assets	514,000	503,000	**30.5**	**30.0**
Plant Assets				
Store equipment, net	400,000	350,000	**23.8**	**20.9**
Office equipment, net	45,000	50,000	**2.7**	**3.0**
Buildings, net	625,000	675,000	**37.1**	**40.2**
Land	100,000	100,000	**5.9**	**6.0**
Total plant assets	1,170,000	1,175,000	**69.5**	**70.0**
Total assets	$1,684,000	$1,678,000	**100.0**	**100.0**
Liabilities				
Current liabilities				
Accounts payable	$ 164,000	$ 190,000	**9.7%**	**11.3%**
Short-term notes payable	75,000	90,000	**4.5**	**5.4**
Taxes payable	26,000	12,000	**1.5**	**0.7**
Total current liabilities	265,000	292,000	**15.7**	**17.4**
Long-term liabilities				
Notes payable (secured by mortgage on buildings)	400,000	420,000	**23.8**	**25.0**
Total liabilities	665,000	712,000	**39.5**	**42.4**
Stockholders' Equity				
Common stock, $5 par value	475,000	475,000	**28.2**	**28.3**
Retained earnings	544,000	491,000	**32.3**	**29.3**
Total stockholders' equity	1,019,000	966,000	**60.5**	**57.6**
Total liabilities and equity	$1,684,000	$1,678,000	**100.0**	**100.0**

* Columns do not always exactly add to 100 due to rounding.

3. Ratios for 2006:

a. Current ratio: $514,000/$265,000 = 1.9:1 (liquidity and efficiency)

b. Acid-test ratio: ($79,000 + $65,000 + $120,000)/$265,000 = 1.0:1 (liquidity and efficiency)

c. Average receivables: ($120,000 + $100,000)/2 = $110,000
Accounts receivable turnover: $2,486,000/$110,000 = 22.6 times (liquidity and efficiency)

d. Days' sales uncollected: ($120,000/$2,486,000) × 365 = 17.6 days (liquidity and efficiency)

e. Average inventory: ($250,000 + $265,000)/2 = $257,500
Inventory turnover: $1,523,000/$257,500 = 5.9 times (liquidity and efficiency)

f. Debt ratio: $665,000/$1,684,000 = 39.5% (solvency)

g. Pledged assets to secured liabilities: $625,000/$400,000 = 1.56:1 (solvency)

h. Times interest earned: $185,000/$44,000 = 4.2 times (solvency)

i. Profit margin ratio: $94,000/$2,486,000 = 3.8% (profitability)

j. Average total assets: ($1,684,000 + $1,678,000)/2 = $1,681,000
Total asset turnover: $2,486,000/$1,681,000 = 1.48 times (liquidity and efficiency)

k. Return on total assets: $94,000/$1,681,000 = 5.6% or 3.8% × 1.48 = 5.6% (profitability)

l. Average total common equity: ($1,019,000 + $966,000)/2 = $992,500
Return on common stockholders' equity: $94,000/$992,500 = 9.5% (profitability)

Summary

C1 Explain the purpose of analysis. The purpose of financial statement analysis is to help users make better business decisions. Internal users want information to improve company efficiency and effectiveness in providing products and services. External users want information to make better and more informed decisions in pursuing their goals. The common goals of all users are to evaluate a company's (1) past and current performance, (2) current financial position, and (3) future performance and risk.

C2 Identify the building blocks of analysis. Financial statement analysis focuses on four "building blocks" of analysis: (1) liquidity and efficiency—ability to meet short-term obligations and efficiently generate revenues; (2) solvency—ability to generate future revenues and meet long-term obligations; (3) profitability—ability to provide financial rewards sufficient to attract and retain financing; and (4) market prospects—ability to generate positive market expectations.

C3 Describe standards for comparisons in analysis. Standards for comparisons include (1) intracompany—prior performance and relations between financial items for the company under analysis; (2) competitor—one or more direct competitors of the company; (3) industry—industry statistics; and (4) guidelines (rules of thumb)—general standards developed from past experiences and personal judgments.

C4 Identify the tools of analysis. The three most common tools of financial statement analysis are (1) horizontal analysis—comparing a company's financial condition and performance across time; (2) vertical analysis—comparing a company's financial condition and performance to a base amount such as revenues or total assets; and (3) ratio analysis—using and quantifying key relations among financial statement items.

A1 Summarize and report results of analysis. A financial statement analysis report is often organized around the building blocks of analysis. A good report separates interpretations and conclusions of analysis from the information underlying them. An analysis report often consists of six sections: (1) executive summary, (2) analysis overview, (3) evidential matter, (4) assumptions, (5) key factors, and (6) inferences.

P1 Explain and apply methods of horizontal analysis. Horizontal analysis is a tool to evaluate changes in data across time. Two important tools of horizontal analysis are comparative statements and trend analysis. Comparative statements show amounts for two or more successive periods, often with changes disclosed in both absolute and percent terms. Trend analysis is used to reveal important changes occurring from one period to the next.

P2 Describe and apply methods of vertical analysis. Vertical analysis is a tool to evaluate each financial statement item or group of items in terms of a base amount. Two tools of vertical analysis are common-size statements and graphical analyses. Each item in common-size statements is expressed as a percent of a base amount. For the balance sheet, the base amount is usually total assets, and for the income statement, it is usually sales.

P3 Define and apply ratio analysis. Ratio analysis provides clues to and symptoms of underlying conditions. Ratios, properly interpreted, identify areas requiring further investigation. A ratio expresses a mathematical relation between two quantities such as a percent, rate, or proportion. Ratios can be organized into the building blocks of analysis: (1) liquidity and efficiency, (2) solvency, (3) profitability, and (4) market prospects.

Guidance Answers to **Decision Maker**

Auditor The *joint relation* referred to is the combined increase in sales and the decrease in expenses yielding more than a 5% increase in income. Both *individual* accounts (sales and expenses) yield percent changes within the ±5% acceptable range. However, a joint analysis suggests a different picture. For example, consider a joint analysis using the profit margin ratio. The client's profit margin is 11.46% ($206,000 − $182,400/$206,000) for the current year compared with 5.0% ($200,000 − $190,000/$200,000) for the prior year—yielding a 129% increase in profit margin! This is what concerns the partner, and it suggests expanding audit tests to verify or refute the client's figures.

Banker Your decision on the loan application is positive for at least two reasons. First, the current ratio suggests a strong ability to meet short-term obligations. Second, current assets of $160,000 and a current ratio of 4:1 imply current liabilities of $40,000 (one-fourth of current assets) and a working capital excess of $120,000. This working capital excess is 60% of the loan amount. However, if the application is for a 10-year loan, our decision is less optimistic. The current ratio and working capital suggest a good safety margin, but indications of inefficiency in operations exist. In particular, a 4:1 current ratio is more than double its key competitors' ratio. This is characteristic of inefficient asset use.

Guidance Answers to **Quick Checks**

1. General-purpose financial statements are intended for a variety of users interested in a company's financial condition and performance—users without the power to require specialized financial reports to meet their specific needs.
2. General-purpose financial statements include the income statement, balance sheet, statement of stockholders' (owner's) equity, and statement of cash flows plus the notes related to these statements.
3. *a*
4. Data from one or more direct competitors are usually preferred for comparative purposes.
5. *d*
6. Percents on comparative income statements show the increase or decrease in each item from one period to the next. On common-size comparative income statements, each item is shown as a percent of net sales for that period.
7. *c*
8. (*a*) ($820,000 + $240,000 + $470,000)/($350,000 + $180,000) = 2.9 to 1.
   (*b*) ($820,000 + $240,000)/($350,000 + $180,000) = 2:1.
9. (*a*) $2,500,000/[($290,000 + $240,000)/2] = 9.43 times.
   (*b*) ($240,000/$2,500,000) × 365 = 35 days.
   (*c*) $750,000/[($530,000 + $470,000)/2] = 1.5 times.
   (*d*) ($470,000/$750,000) × 365 = 228.7 days.
10. *c*
11. *b*
12. Profit margin × Total asset turnover = Return on total assets

$$\frac{\$945{,}000}{\$8{,}500{,}000} \times 1.8 = 20\%$$

Key Terms

Key Terms are available at the book's Website for learning and testing in an online Flashcard Format.

Common-size financial statement (p. 681)
Comparative financial statements (p. 677)
Efficiency (p. 675)
Equity ratio (p. 689)
Financial reporting (p. 675)
Financial statement analysis (p. 674)
General-purpose financial statements (p. 675)
Horizontal analysis (p. 676)
Liquidity (p. 675)
Market prospects (p. 675)
Profitability (p. 675)
Ratio analysis (p. 676)
Solvency (p. 675)
Vertical analysis (p. 676)
Working capital (p. 685)

Personal Interactive Quiz

Personal Interactive Quizzes A and B are available at the book's Website to reinforce and assess your learning.

Discussion Questions

1. What is the difference between comparative financial statements and common-size comparative statements?
2. Which items are usually assigned a 100% value on (*a*) a common-size balance sheet and (*b*) a common-size income statement?
3. Explain the difference between financial reporting and financial statements.
4. What three factors would influence your evaluation as to whether a company's current ratio is good or bad?
5. Suggest several reasons that a 2:1 current ratio may not be adequate for a particular company.
6. Why is working capital given special attention in the process of analyzing balance sheets?
7. What does the number of days' sales uncollected indicate?
8. What does a relatively high accounts receivable turnover indicate about a company's short-term liquidity?
9. Why is a company's capital structure, as measured by debt and equity ratios, important to financial statement analysts?
10. How does inventory turnover provide information about a company's short-term liquidity?
11. What ratios would you compute to evaluate management performance?

12. Why must the ratio of pledged assets to secured liabilities be interpreted with caution?

13. Why would a company's return on total assets be different from its return on common stockholders' equity?

14. Use **Krispy Kreme**'s financial statements in Appendix A to compute its return on total assets for the years ended February 2, 2003, and February 3, 2002. Total assets at January 28, 2001, were $171,493 (in thousands).

15. Refer to **Tastykake**'s financial statements in Appendix A to compute its equity ratio as of December 28, 2002, and December 29, 2001.

16. Refer to **Harley-Davidson**'s financial statements in Appendix A. Compute its profit margin for the fiscal year ended December 31, 2002.

Red numbers denote Discussion Questions that involve decision-making.

***Homework Manager** repeats all numerical Quick Studies on the book's Website with new numbers.*

QUICK STUDY

QS 17-1
Financial reporting C1

Which of the following items (1) through (9) are part of financial reporting but are *not* included as part of general-purpose financial statements? (1) stock price information and analysis, (2) statement of cash flows, (3) management discussion and analysis of financial performance, (4) income statement, (5) company news releases, (6) balance sheet, (7) financial statement notes, (8) statement of shareholders' equity, (9) prospectus.

QS 17-2
Standard of comparison C3

What are four possible standards of comparison used to analyze financial statement ratios? Which of these is generally considered to be the most useful? Which one is least likely to provide a good basis for comparison?

QS 17-3
Horizontal analysis
P1

Compute the annual dollar changes and percent changes for each of the following accounts:

	2005	2004
Short-term investments	$217,800	$165,000
Accounts receivable	42,120	48,000
Notes payable	57,000	0

QS 17-4
Common-size and trend percents
P1 P2

Use the following information for Saturn Corporation to determine (1) the 2004 and 2005 common-size percents for cost of goods sold using net sales as the base and (2) the 2004 and 2005 trend percents for net sales using 2004 as the base year.

($ thousands)	2005	2004
Net sales	$201,600	$114,800
Cost of goods sold	109,200	60,200

QS 17-5
Building blocks of analysis
C2 C4 P3

Match the ratio to the building block of financial statement analysis to which it best relates.

A. Liquidity and efficiency
B. Solvency
C. Profitability
D. Market prospects

1. _______ Gross margin ratio
2. _______ Acid-test ratio
3. _______ Equity ratio
4. _______ Return on total assets
5. _______ Dividend yield
6. _______ Book value per common share
7. _______ Days' sales in inventory
8. _______ Accounts receivable turnover
9. _______ Pledged assets to secured liabilities
10. _______ Times interest earned

QS 17-6

Identifying financial ratios
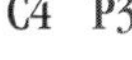
C4 P3

1. Which two ratios are key components in measuring a company's operating efficiency? Which ratio summarizes these two components?
2. Which two short-term liquidity ratios measure how frequently a company collects its accounts?
3. What measure reflects the difference between current assets and current liabilities?

QS 17-7
Ratio interpretation
P3 

For each ratio listed, identify whether the change in ratio value from 2004 to 2005 is usually regarded as favorable or unfavorable.

Ratio	2005	2004	Ratio	2005	2004
1. Profit margin	8%	6%	5. Accounts receivable turnover	5.4	6.6
2. Debt ratio	45%	40%	6. Basic earnings per share	$1.24	$1.20
3. Gross margin	33%	45%	7. Inventory turnover	3.5	3.3
4. Acid-test ratio	0.99	1.10	8. Dividend yield	1%	0.8%

***Homework Manager** repeats all numerical Exercises on the book's Website with new numbers.* 

EXERCISES

Exercise 17-1
Computation and analysis of trend percents
P1

Compute trend percents for the following financial items, using 2003 as the base year. State whether the situation as revealed by the trends appears to be favorable or unfavorable for each item.

	2007	2006	2005	2004	2003
Sales	$283,880	$271,800	$253,680	$235,560	$151,000
Cost of goods sold	129,200	123,080	116,280	107,440	68,000
Accounts receivable	19,100	18,300	17,400	16,200	10,000

Exercise 17-2
Determination of income effects from common-size and trend percents
P1 P2

Common-size and trend percents for Aziz Company's sales, cost of goods sold, and expenses follow. Determine whether net income increased, decreased, or remained unchanged in this three-year period.

	Common-Size Percents			Trend Percents		
	2006	2005	2004	2006	2005	2004
Sales	100.0%	100.0%	100.0%	104.4%	103.2%	100.0%
Cost of goods sold	62.4	60.9	58.1	102.0	108.1	100.0
Total expenses	14.3	13.8	14.1	105.9	101.0	100.0

Exercise 17-3
Common-size percent computation and interpretation

Express the following comparative income statements in common-size percents and assess whether or not this company's situation has improved in the most recent year.

GERALDO CORPORATION Comparative Income Statements For Years Ended December 31, 2005 and 2004	2005	2004
Sales	$720,000	$535,000
Cost of goods sold	475,200	280,340
Gross profit	244,800	254,660
Operating expenses	151,200	103,790
Net income	$ 93,600	$150,870

Exercise 17-4
Analysis of short-term financial condition
A1 P3 

The following information is available for Silverado Company and Titan Company, similar firms operating in the same industry. Write a half-page report comparing Silverado and Titan using the available information. Your discussion should include their ability to meet current obligations and to use current assets efficiently.

	Silverado			Titan		
	2006	2005	2004	2006	2005	2004
Current ratio	1.6	1.7	2.0	3.1	2.6	1.8
Acid-test ratio	0.9	1.0	1.1	2.7	2.4	1.5
Accounts receivable turnover	29.5	24.2	28.2	15.4	14.2	15.0
Merchandise inventory turnover	23.2	20.9	16.1	13.5	12.0	11.6
Working capital	$60,000	$48,000	$42,000	$121,000	$93,000	$68,000

Team Project: Assume that the two companies apply for a one-year loan from the team. Identify additional information the companies must provide before the team can make a loan decision.

Exercise 17-5
Analysis of efficiency and financial leverage
A1 P3

Rolf Company and Kent Company are similar firms that operate in the same industry. Kent began operations in 2005 and Rolf in 2002. In 2007, both companies pay 7% interest on their debt to creditors. The following additional information is available:

	Rolf Company			Kent Company		
	2007	2006	2005	2007	2006	2005
Total asset turnover	3.0	2.7	2.9	1.6	1.4	1.1
Return on total assets	8.9%	9.5%	8.7%	5.8%	5.5%	5.2%
Profit margin ratio	2.3%	2.4%	2.2%	2.7%	2.9%	2.8%
Sales	$400,000	$370,000	$386,000	$200,000	$160,000	$100,000

Write a half-page report comparing Rolf and Kent using the available information. Your analysis should include their ability to use assets efficiently to produce profits. Also comment on their success in employing financial leverage in 2007.

Exercise 17-6
Common-size percents
P2

Sexton Company's year-end balance sheets follow. Express the balance sheets in common-size percents. Round amounts to the nearest one-tenth of a percent. Analyze and comment on the results.

	2006	2005	2004
Cash	$ 30,800	$ 35,625	$ 36,800
Accounts receivable, net	88,500	62,500	49,200
Merchandise inventory	111,500	82,500	53,000
Prepaid expenses	9,700	9,375	4,000
Plant assets, net	277,500	255,000	229,500
Total assets	$518,000	$445,000	$372,500
Accounts payable	$128,900	$ 75,250	$ 49,250
Long-term notes payable secured by mortgages on plant assets	97,500	102,500	82,500
Common stock, $10 par value	162,500	162,500	162,500
Retained earnings	129,100	104,750	78,250
Total liabilities and equity	$518,000	$445,000	$372,500

Exercise 17-7
Liquidity analysis
P3

Refer to Sexton Company's balance sheet accounts in Exercise 17-6. Analyze its year-end short-term liquidity position at the end of 2006, 2005, and 2004 by computing (1) the current ratio and (2) the acid-test ratio. Comment on the ratio results.

Exercise 17-8
Liquidity analysis and interpretation
P3 

Refer to the Sexton Company information in Exercise 17-6. The company's income statements for the years ended December 31, 2006 and 2005, follow. Assume that all sales are on credit and then compute: (1) days' sales uncollected, (2) accounts receivable turnover, (3) inventory turnover, and (4) days' sales in inventory. Comment on the changes in the ratios from 2005 to 2006.

	2006		2005	
Sales		$672,500		$530,000
Cost of goods sold	$410,225		$344,500	
Other operating expenses	208,550		133,980	
Interest expense	11,100		12,300	
Income taxes	8,525		7,845	
Total costs and expenses		638,400		498,625
Net income		$ 34,100		$ 31,375
Earnings per share		$ 2.10		$ 1.93

Exercise 17-9
Risk and capital structure analysis
P3 

Refer to the Sexton Company information in Exercises 17-6 and 17-8. Compare the company's long-term risk and capital structure positions at the end of 2006 and 2005 by computing these ratios: (1) debt and equity ratios, (2) pledged assets to secured liabilities, and (3) times interest earned. Comment on these ratio results.

Exercise 17-10
Efficiency and profitability analysis P3 

Refer to Sexton Company's financial information in Exercises 17-6 and 17-8. Evaluate the company's efficiency and profitability by computing the following for 2006 and 2005: (1) profit margin ratio, (2) total asset turnover, and (3) return on total assets. Comment on these ratio results.

Exercise 17-11
Profitability analysis
P3  

Refer to Sexton Company's financial information in Exercises 17-6 and 17-8. Additional information about the company follows. To help evaluate the company's profitability, compute and interpret the following ratios for 2006 and 2005: (1) return on common stockholders' equity, (2) price-earnings ratio on December 31, and (3) dividend yield.

Common stock market price, December 31, 2006	$15.00
Common stock market price, December 31, 2005	14.00
Annual cash dividends per share in 2006	0.30
Annual cash dividends per share in 2005	0.15

PROBLEM SET A

Selected comparative financial statements of Bennington Company follow:

Problem 17-1A
Ratios, common-size statements, and trend percents
P1 P2 P3 

mhhe.com/larson

BENNINGTON COMPANY
Comparative Income Statements
For Years Ended December 31, 2006, 2005, and 2004

	2006	2005	2004
Sales	$444,000	$340,000	$236,000
Cost of goods sold	267,288	212,500	151,040
Gross profit	176,712	127,500	84,960
Selling expenses	62,694	46,920	31,152
Administrative expenses	40,137	29,920	19,470
Total expenses	102,831	76,840	50,622
Income before taxes	73,881	50,660	34,338
Income taxes	13,764	10,370	6,962
Net income	$ 60,117	$ 40,290	$ 27,376

BENNINGTON COMPANY Comparative Balance Sheets December 31, 2006, 2005, and 2004	2006	2005	2004
Assets			
Current assets	$ 48,480	$ 37,924	$ 50,648
Long-term investments	0	500	3,720
Plant assets, net	90,000	96,000	57,000
Total assets	$138,480	$134,424	$111,368
Liabilities and Equity			
Current liabilities	$ 20,200	$ 19,960	$ 19,480
Common stock	72,000	72,000	54,000
Other contributed capital	9,000	9,000	6,000
Retained earnings	37,280	33,464	31,888
Total liabilities and equity	$138,480	$134,424	$111,368

Required

1. Compute each year's current ratio.

2. Express the income statement data in common-size percents.

3. Express the balance sheet data in trend percents with 2004 as the base year.

Check (3) 2006, Total assets trend, 124.34%

Analysis Component

4. Comment on any significant relations revealed by the ratios and percents computed.

Problem 17-2A

Calculation and analysis of trend percents

A1 P1

Selected comparative financial statements of Sugu Company follow:

SUGU COMPANY Comparative Income Statements ($000) For Years Ended December 31, 2006–2000	2006	2005	2004	2003	2002	2001	2000
Sales	$1,594	$1,396	$1,270	$1,164	$1,086	$1,010	$828
Cost of goods sold	1,146	932	802	702	652	610	486
Gross profit	448	464	468	462	434	400	342
Operating expenses	340	266	244	180	156	154	128
Net income	$ 108	$ 198	$ 224	$ 282	$ 278	$ 246	$214

SUGU COMPANY Comparative Balance Sheets ($000) December 31, 2006–2000	2006	2005	2004	2003	2002	2001	2000
Assets							
Cash	$ 68	$ 88	$ 92	$ 94	$ 98	$ 96	$ 99
Accounts receivable, net	480	504	456	350	308	292	206
Merchandise inventory	1,738	1,264	1,104	932	836	710	515
Other current assets	46	42	24	44	38	38	19
Long-term investments	0	0	0	136	136	136	136
Plant assets, net	2,120	2,114	1,852	1,044	1,078	960	825
Total assets	$4,452	$4,012	$3,528	$2,600	$2,494	$2,232	$1,800
Liabilities and Equity							
Current liabilities	$1,120	$ 942	$ 618	$ 514	$ 446	$ 422	$ 272
Long-term liabilities	1,194	1,040	1,012	470	480	520	390
Common stock	1,000	1,000	1,000	840	840	640	640
Other contributed capital	250	250	250	180	180	160	160
Retained earnings	888	780	648	596	548	490	338
Total liabilities and equity	$4,452	$4,012	$3,528	$2,600	$2,494	$2,232	$1,800

Check (1) 2006, Total assets trend, 247.3%

Required

1. Compute trend percents for all components of both statements using 2000 as the base year.

Analysis Component

2. Analyze and comment on the financial statements and trend percents from part 1.

Problem 17-3A
Transactions, working capital, and liquidity ratios

P3

mhhe.com/larson

Check May 22: Current ratio, 2.12; Acid-test, 1.04

May 29: Current ratio, 1.82; Working capital, $320,000

Park Corporation began the month of May with $650,000 of current assets, a current ratio of 2.50:1, and an acid-test ratio of 1.10:1. During the month, it completed the following transactions (the company uses a perpetual inventory system):

May	2	Purchased $75,000 of merchandise inventory on credit.
	8	Sold merchandise inventory that cost $58,000 for $103,000 cash.
	10	Collected $19,000 cash on an account receivable.
	15	Paid $21,000 cash to settle an account payable.
	17	Wrote off a $3,000 bad debt against the Allowance for Doubtful Accounts account.
	22	Declared a $1 per share cash dividend on the 40,000 shares of outstanding common stock.
	26	Paid the dividend declared on May 22.
	27	Borrowed $75,000 cash by giving the bank a 30-day, 10% note.
	28	Borrowed $90,000 cash by signing a long-term secured note.
	29	Used the $165,000 cash proceeds from the notes to buy new machinery.

Required

Prepare a table showing Park's (1) current ratio, (2) acid-test ratio, and (3) working capital after each transaction. Round ratios to hundredths.

Problem 17-4A
Calculation of financial statement ratios

P3

mhhe.com/larson

Selected year-end financial statements of McCord Corporation follow. (*Note:* All sales are on credit; selected balance sheet amounts at December 31, 2004, were inventory, $32,400; total assets, $182,400; common stock, $90,000; and retained earnings, $31,300.)

McCORD CORPORATION
Income Statement
For Year Ended December 31, 2005

Sales	$348,600
Cost of goods sold	229,150
Gross profit	119,450
Operating expenses	52,500
Interest expense	3,100
Income before taxes	63,850
Income taxes	15,800
Net income	$ 48,050

McCORD CORPORATION
Balance Sheet
December 31, 2005

Assets		Liabilities and Equity	
Cash	$ 9,000	Accounts payable	$ 16,500
Short-term investments	7,400	Accrued wages payable	2,200
Accounts receivable, net	28,200	Income taxes payable	2,300
Notes receivable (trade)*	3,500	Long-term note payable, secured	
Merchandise inventory	31,150	by mortgage on plant assets	62,400
Prepaid expenses	1,650	Common stock, $1 par value	90,000
Plant assets, net	152,300	Retained earnings	59,800
Total assets	$233,200	Total liabilities and equity	$233,200

* These are short-term notes receivable arising from customer (trade) sales.

Required

Compute the following: (1) current ratio, (2) acid-test ratio, (3) days' sales uncollected, (4) inventory turnover, (5) days' sales in inventory, (6) ratio of pledged assets to secured liabilities, (7) times interest earned, (8) profit margin ratio, (9) total asset turnover, (10) return on total assets, and (11) return on common stockholders' equity.

Check Acid-test ratio, 2.3 to 1; Inventory turnover, 7.2

Problem 17-5A
Comparative ratio analysis
A1 P3  

Summary information from the financial statements of two companies competing in the same industry follows:

	Ryan Company	Priest Company
Data from the current year-end balance sheets		
Assets		
Cash	$ 18,500	$ 33,000
Accounts receivable, net	36,400	56,400
Current notes receivable (trade)	8,100	6,200
Merchandise inventory	83,440	131,500
Prepaid expenses	4,000	5,950
Plant assets, net	284,000	303,400
Total assets	$434,440	$536,450
Liabilities and Equity		
Current liabilities	$ 60,340	$ 92,300
Long-term notes payable	79,800	100,000
Common stock, $5 par value	175,000	205,000
Retained earnings	119,300	139,150
Total liabilities and equity	$434,440	$536,450

	Ryan Company	Priest Company
Data from the current year's income statement		
Sales	$660,000	$780,200
Cost of goods sold	485,100	532,500
Interest expense	6,900	11,000
Income tax expense	12,800	19,300
Net income	67,770	105,000
Basic earnings per share	1.94	2.56
Beginning-of-year balance sheet data		
Accounts receivable, net	$ 28,800	$ 53,200
Current notes receivable (trade)	0	0
Merchandise inventory	54,600	106,400
Total assets	388,000	372,500
Common stock, $5 par value	175,000	205,000
Retained earnings	94,300	90,600

Required

1. For both companies compute the (*a*) current ratio, (*b*) acid-test ratio, (*c*) accounts (including notes) receivable turnover, (*d*) inventory turnover, (*e*) days' sales in inventory, and (*f*) days' sales uncollected. Identify the company you consider to be the better short-term credit risk and explain why.

2. For both companies compute the (*a*) profit margin ratio, (*b*) total asset turnover, (*c*) return on total assets, and (*d*) return on common stockholders' equity. Assuming that each company paid cash dividends of $1.50 per share and each company's stock can be purchased at $25 per share, compute their (*e*) price-earnings ratios and (*f*) dividend yields. Identify which company's stock you would recommend as the better investment and explain why.

Check (1) Priest: Accounts receivable turnover, 13.5; Inventory turnover, 4.5

(2) Ryan: Profit margin, 10.3%; PE, 12.9

PROBLEM SET B

Problem 17-1B
Ratios, common-size statements, and trend percents
P1 P2 P3 

Selected comparative financial statements of Sawgrass Corporation follow:

SAWGRASS CORPORATION
Comparative Income Statements
For Years Ended December 31, 2006, 2005, and 2004

	2006	2005	2004
Sales	$199,800	$167,000	$144,800
Cost of goods sold	109,890	87,175	67,200
Gross profit	89,910	79,825	77,600
Selling expenses	23,680	20,790	19,000
Administrative expenses	17,760	15,610	16,700
Total expenses	41,440	36,400	35,700
Income before taxes	48,470	43,425	41,900
Income taxes	5,050	4,910	4,300
Net income	$ 43,420	$ 38,515	$ 37,600

SAWGRASS CORPORATION Comparative Balance Sheets December 31, 2006, 2005, and 2004	2006	2005	2004
Assets			
Current assets	$ 55,860	$ 33,660	$ 37,300
Long-term investments	0	2,700	11,600
Plant assets, net	113,810	114,660	80,000
Total assets	$169,670	$151,020	$128,900
Liabilities and Equity			
Current liabilities	$ 23,370	$ 20,180	$ 17,500
Common stock	47,500	47,500	38,000
Other contributed capital	14,850	14,850	12,300
Retained earnings	83,950	68,490	61,100
Total liabilities and equity	$169,670	$151,020	$128,900

Required

1. Compute each year's current ratio.

2. Express the income statement data in common-size percents.

3. Express the balance sheet data in trend percents with 2004 as the base year.

Check (3) 2006, Total assets trend, 131.63%

Analysis Component

4. Comment on any significant relations revealed by the ratios and percents computed.

Problem 17-2B
Calculation and analysis of trend percents
A1 P1

Selected comparative financial statements of Deuce Company follow:

DEUCE COMPANY Comparative Income Statements ($000) For Years Ended December 31, 2006–2000	2006	2005	2004	2003	2002	2001	2000
Sales	$660	$710	$730	$780	$840	$870	$960
Cost of goods sold	376	390	394	414	440	450	480
Gross profit	284	320	336	366	400	420	480
Operating expenses	184	204	212	226	240	244	250
Net income	$100	$116	$124	$140	$160	$176	$230

DEUCE COMPANY Comparative Balance Sheets ($000) December 31, 2006–2000	2006	2005	2004	2003	2002	2001	2000
Assets							
Cash	$ 34	$ 36	$ 42	$ 44	$ 50	$ 52	$ 58
Accounts receivable, net	120	126	130	134	140	144	150
Merchandise inventory	156	162	168	170	176	180	198
Other current assets	24	24	26	28	28	30	30
Long-term investments	26	20	16	100	100	100	100
Plant assets, net	410	414	420	312	320	328	354
Total assets	$770	$782	$802	$788	$814	$834	$890
Liabilities and Equity							
Current liabilities	$138	$146	$176	$180	$200	$250	$270
Long-term liabilities	82	110	132	138	184	204	250
Common stock	150	150	150	150	150	150	150
Other contributed capital	60	60	60	60	60	60	60
Retained earnings	340	316	284	260	220	170	160
Total liabilities and equity	$770	$782	$802	$788	$814	$834	$890

Required

1. Compute trend percents for all components of both statements using 2000 as the base year.

Check (1) 2006, Total assets trend, 86.5%

Analysis Component

2. Analyze and comment on the financial statements and trend percents from part 1.

Problem 17-3B
Transactions, working capital, and liquidity ratios
P3

Ready Corporation began the month of June with $280,000 of current assets, a current ratio of 2.80:1, and an acid-test ratio of 1.20:1. During the month, it completed the following transactions (the company uses a perpetual inventory system):

June 1 Sold merchandise inventory that cost $62,000 for $101,000 cash.
3 Collected $78,000 cash on an account receivable.
5 Purchased $130,000 of merchandise inventory on credit.
7 Borrowed $90,000 cash by giving the bank a 60-day, 10% note.
10 Borrowed $180,000 cash by signing a long-term secured note.
12 Purchased machinery for $280,000 cash.
15 Declared a $1 per share cash dividend on the 60,000 shares of outstanding common stock.
19 Wrote off a $7,000 bad debt against the Allowance for Doubtful Accounts account.
22 Paid $11,000 cash to settle an account payable.
30 Paid the dividend declared on June 15.

Check June 1: Current ratio, 3.19; Acid-test, 2.21

June 30: Working capital, $59,000; Current ratio, 1.19

Required

Prepare a table showing the company's (1) current ratio, (2) acid-test ratio, and (3) working capital after each transaction. Round ratios to hundredths.

Problem 17-4B
Calculation of financial statement ratios
P3

Selected year-end financial statements of Overland Corporation follow. (*Note:* All sales are on credit; selected balance sheet amounts at December 31, 2004, were inventory, $16,400; total assets, $95,900; common stock, $41,500; and retained earnings, $19,800.)

OVERLAND CORPORATION
Income Statement
For Year Ended December 31, 2005

Sales	$215,500
Cost of goods sold	136,100
Gross profit	79,400
Operating expenses	50,200
Interest expense	1,200
Income before taxes	28,000
Income taxes	2,200
Net income	$ 25,800

OVERLAND CORPORATION
Balance Sheet
December 31, 2005

Assets		**Liabilities and Equity**	
Cash	$ 5,100	Accounts payable	$ 10,500
Short-term investments	5,900	Accrued wages payable	2,300
Accounts receivable, net	11,100	Income taxes payable	1,600
Notes receivable (trade)*	2,000	Long-term note payable, secured	
Merchandise inventory	12,500	by mortgage on plant assets	25,000
Prepaid expenses	1,000	Common stock, $5 par value	41,000
Plant assets, net	72,900	Retained earnings	30,100
Total assets	$110,500	Total liabilities and equity	$110,500

* These are short-term notes receivable arising from customer (trade) sales.

Required

Compute the following: (1) current ratio, (2) acid-test ratio, (3) days' sales uncollected, (4) inventory turnover, (5) days' sales in inventory, (6) ratio of pledged assets to secured liabilities, (7) times interest earned, (8) profit margin ratio, (9) total asset turnover, (10) return on total assets, and (11) return on common stockholders' equity.

Check Acid-test ratio, 1.7 to 1; Inventory turnover, 9.4

Problem 17-5B
Comparative ratio analysis A1 P3

Summary information from the financial statements of two companies competing in the same industry follows:

	Loud Company	Clear Company
Data from the current year-end balance sheets		
Assets		
Cash	$ 22,000	$ 38,500
Accounts receivable, net	79,100	72,500
Current notes receivable (trade)	13,600	11,000
Merchandise inventory	88,800	84,000
Prepaid expenses	11,700	12,100
Plant assets, net	178,900	254,300
Total assets	$394,100	$472,400
Liabilities and Equity		
Current liabilities	$ 92,500	$ 99,000
Long-term notes payable	95,000	95,300
Common stock, $5 par value	135,000	143,000
Retained earnings	71,600	135,100
Total liabilities and equity	$394,100	$472,400

	Loud Company	Clear Company
Data from the current year's income statement		
Sales	$395,600	$669,500
Cost of goods sold	292,600	482,000
Interest expense	7,900	12,400
Income tax expense	7,700	14,300
Net income	35,850	63,700
Basic earnings per share	1.33	2.23
Beginning-of-year balance sheet data		
Accounts receivable, net	$ 74,200	$ 75,300
Current notes receivable (trade)	0	0
Merchandise inventory	107,100	82,500
Total assets	385,400	445,000
Common stock, $5 par value	135,000	143,000
Retained earnings	51,100	111,700

Required

Check (1) Loud: Accounts receivable turnover, 4.7; Inventory turnover, 3.0

(2) Clear: Profit margin, 9.5%; PE, 11.2

1. For both companies compute the (*a*) current ratio, (*b*) acid-test ratio, (*c*) accounts (including notes) receivable turnover, (*d*) inventory turnover, (*e*) days' sales in inventory, and (*f*) days' sales uncollected. Identify the company you consider to be the better short-term credit risk and explain why.

2. For both companies compute the (*a*) profit margin ratio, (*b*) total asset turnover, (*c*) return on total assets, and (*d*) return on common stockholders' equity. Assuming that each company paid cash dividends of $3.00 per share and each company's stock can be purchased at $25 per share, compute their (*e*) price-earnings ratios and (*f*) dividend yields. Identify which company's stock you would recommend as the better investment and explain why.

PROBLEM SET C

Problem Set C is available at the book's Website to reinforce and assess your learning.

SERIAL PROBLEM

Success Systems

(This serial problem began in Chapter 1 and continues through most of the book. If previous chapter segments were not completed, the serial problem can begin at this point. It is helpful, but not necessary, for you to use the Working Papers that accompany the book.)

Use the following selected data from Success Systems's income statement for the three months ended March 31, 2005, and from its March 31, 2005, balance sheet to complete the requirements below: computer services revenue, $25,160; net (goods) sales, $18,693; total revenue, $43,853; cost of goods sold, $14,052; net income, $18,686; quick assets, $100,565; current assets, $105,209; total assets, $129,909; current liabilities, $20,875; total liabilities, $20,875; and total equity, $109,034.

Required

1. Compute the gross margin ratio (both with and without services revenue) and net profit margin ratio.

2. Compute the current ratio and acid-test ratio.

3. Compute the debt ratio and equity ratio.

4. What percent of its assets are current? What percent are long term?

BEYOND THE NUMBERS

REPORTING IN ACTION

A1 P1 P2 

BTN 17-1 Refer to **Krispy Kreme**'s financial statements in Appendix A to answer the following:

1. Using 2001 as the base year, compute trend percents for 2001, 2002, and 2003 for revenues, operating expenses (cost of sales), general and administrative expenses, income taxes, and net income. (Round to the nearest whole percent.)
2. Compute common-size percents for 2003 and 2002 for the following categories of assets: (*a*) total current assets, (*b*) property and equipment, net, (*c*) intangible assets, and (*d*) accrued expenses. (Round to the nearest tenth of a percent.)
3. Comment on any significant changes across the years for the income statement trends computed in part 1 and the balance sheet percents computed in part 2.

Roll On

4. Access Krispy Kreme's financial statements for fiscal years ending after February 2, 2003, from Krispy Kreme's Website (**KrispyKreme.com**) or the SEC database (**www.sec.gov**). Update your work for parts 1, 2, and 3 using the new information accessed.

COMPARATIVE ANALYSIS

C3 P2

BTN 17-2 Key comparative figures ($ thousands) for both **Krispy Kreme** and **Tastykake** follow:

Key Figures	Krispy Kreme	Tastykake
Cash and equivalents	$ 32,203	$ 282
Accounts receivable, net	34,373	20,882
Inventories	24,365	6,777
Retained earnings	102,403	26,622
Operating expenses (Krispy Kreme)	381,489	—
Costs of sales (Tastykake)	—	111,187
Revenues (Krispy Kreme)	491,549	—
Net sales (Tastykake)	—	162,263
Total assets	410,487	116,560

Required

1. Compute common-size percents for both companies using the data provided.
2. Which company retains a higher portion of cumulative net income in the company?
3. Which company has a higher gross margin ratio on sales?
4. Which company holds a higher percent of its total assets as inventory?

ETHICS CHALLENGE

A1 

BTN 17-3 As Beacon Company controller, you are responsible for informing the board of directors about its financial activities. At the board meeting, you present the following:

	2006	2005	2004
Sales trend percent	147.0%	135.0%	100.0%
Selling expenses to sales	10.1%	14.0%	15.6%
Sales to plant assets ratio	3.8 to 1	3.6 to 1	3.3 to 1
Current ratio	2.9 to 1	2.7 to 1	2.4 to 1
Acid-test ratio	1.1 to 1	1.4 to 1	1.5 to 1
Inventory turnover	7.8 times	9.0 times	10.2 times
Accounts receivable turnover	7.0 times	7.7 times	8.5 times
Total asset turnover	2.9 times	2.9 times	3.3 times
Return on total assets	10.4%	11.0%	13.2%
Return on stockholders' equity	10.7%	11.5%	14.1%
Profit margin ratio	3.6%	3.8%	4.0%

After the meeting, the company's CEO holds a press conference with analysts in which she mentions these ratios:

	2006	2005	2004
Sales trend percent	147.0%	135.0%	100.0%
Selling expenses to sales	10.1%	14.0%	15.6%
Sales to plant assets ratio	3.8 to 1	3.6 to 1	3.3 to 1
Current ratio	2.9 to 1	2.7 to 1	2.4 to 1

Required

1. Why do you think the CEO decided to report 4 ratios instead of the 11 prepared?
2. Comment on the possible consequences of the CEO's reporting of the ratios.

COMMUNICATING IN PRACTICE

C2 A1 P3

BTN 17-4 Each team is to select a different industry, and each team member is to select a different company in that industry and acquire its financial statements. Use those statements to analyze the company, including at least one ratio from each of the four building blocks of analysis. When necessary, use the financial press to determine the market price of its stock. Communicate with teammates via a meeting, e-mail, or telephone to discuss how different companies compare to each other and to industry norms. The team is to prepare a single one-page memorandum reporting on its analysis and the conclusions reached.

TAKING IT TO THE NET

C4 P3

mhhe.com/larson

BTN 17-5 Access the March 21, 2003, filing of the 2002 10-K report of **Yahoo! Inc.** (ticker YHOO) at www.SEC.gov to complete the following requirements.

Required

Compute or locate the following profitability ratios of Yahoo! for its fiscal years ending December 31, 2002 *and* 2001. Interpret its profitability using these ratio results.

1. Profit margin ratio
2. Gross profit ratio
3. Return on total assets (*Note:* Total assets in 2000 were $2,269,576,000.)
4. Return on common stockholders' equity (*Note:* Total shareholders' equity in 2000 was $1,896,914,000.)
5. Basic earnings per share

TEAMWORK IN ACTION

C2 P1 P2 P3

BTN 17-6 A team approach to learning financial statement analysis is often useful.

Required

1. Each team should write a description of horizontal and vertical analysis that all team members agree with and understand. Illustrate each description with an example.
2. *Each* member of the team is to select *one* of the following categories of ratio analysis. Explain what the ratios in that category measure. Choose one ratio from the category selected, present its formula, and explain what it measures.
   a. Liquidity and efficiency
   b. Solvency
   c. Profitability
   d. Market prospects
3. Each team member is to present his or her notes from part 2 to teammates. Team members are to confirm or correct other teammates' presentation.

Hint: Pairing within teams may be necessary for part 2. Use as an in-class activity or as an assignment. Consider presentations to the entire class using team rotation with transparencies.

BUSINESS WEEK ACTIVITY

C1 C4

mhhe.com/larson

BTN 17-7 Read the article "Eyes Peeled for Those 'Big Red Flags'" in the September 24, 2002, issue of *Business Week*. (The book's Website provides a free link.)

Required

1. What does it mean to short sell a stock?
2. What strategies for short selling does Tom Taulli (the interviewee) advise?

3. What items does Taulli pay particular attention to on the balance sheet of a company that he might short sell?
4. If you are 100% correct in your financial analysis of a stock, are you guaranteed to make money short selling?
5. Does Taulli find the PE ratio very valuable as a factor to consider when shorting stocks?

ENTREPRENEURIAL DECISION

A1 P1 P2 P3  

BTN 17-8 Assume that David and Tom Gardner of **The Motley Fool** (Fool.com) have impressed you since you first heard of their rather improbable rise to prominence in financial circles. You learn of a staff opening at The Motley Fool and decide to apply for it. Your resume is successfully screened from the thousands received and you advance to the interview process. You learn that the interview consists of analyzing the following financial facts and answering analysis questions. (*Note:* The data are taken from a small merchandiser in outdoor recreational equipment.)

	2005	2004	2003
Sales trend percents	137.0%	125.0%	100.0%
Selling expenses to sales	9.8%	13.7%	15.3%
Sales to plant assets ratio	3.5 to 1	3.3 to 1	3.0 to 1
Current ratio	2.6 to 1	2.4 to 1	2.1 to 1
Acid-test ratio	0.8 to 1	1.1 to 1	1.2 to 1
Merchandise inventory turnover	7.5 times	8.7 times	9.9 times
Accounts receivable turnover	6.7 times	7.4 times	8.2 times
Total asset turnover	2.6 times	2.6 times	3.0 times
Return on total assets	8.8%	9.4%	11.1%
Return on equity	9.75%	11.50%	12.25%
Profit margin ratio	3.3%	3.5%	3.7%

Required

Use these data to answer each of the following questions with explanations:

1. Is it becoming easier for the company to meet its current liabilities on time and to take advantage of any available cash discounts?
2. Is the company collecting its accounts receivable more rapidly?
3. Is the company's investment in accounts receivable decreasing?
4. Is the company's investment in plant assets increasing?
5. Is the owner's investment becoming more profitable?
6. Did the dollar amount of selling expenses decrease during the three-year period?

HITTING THE ROAD

C1 P3

BTN 17-9 You are to devise an investment strategy to enable you to accumulate $1,000,000 by age 65. Start by making some assumptions about your salary. Next compute the percent of your salary that you will be able to save each year. If you will receive any lump-sum monies, include those amounts in your calculations. Historically, stocks have delivered average annual returns of 10–11%. Given this history, you should probably not assume that you will earn above 10% on the money you invest. It is not necessary to specify exactly what types of assets you will buy for your investments; just assume a rate you expect to earn. Use the future value tables in Appendix B to calculate how your savings will grow. Experiment a bit with your figures to see how much less you have to save if you start at, for example, age 25 versus age 35 or 40. (For this assignment, do not include inflation in your calculations.)

GLOBAL DECISION

A1

BTN 17-10 **Krispy Kreme**, **Tastykake**, and **Grupo Bimbo** are competitors in the global marketplace. Visit the Grupo Bimbo Website (GrupoBimbo.com) and access its most recent annual report.

Required

Review Grupo Bimbo's Website and skim through its annual report. Compare its annual report to one of its U.S. competitor's reports (Krispy Kreme or Tastykake) presented in Appendix A. Identify five ways that the Mexican company's report or its Website differs from that of its U.S. competitors.

"I wanted to have a chip company that kids from the hood could relate to"—James Lindsay

18 Managerial Accounting Concepts and Principles

A Look Back

Chapter 17 described the analysis and interpretation of financial statement information. We applied horizontal, vertical, and ratio analyses to better understand company performance and financial condition.

A Look at This Chapter

We begin our study of managerial accounting by explaining its purpose and describing its major characteristics. We also discuss cost concepts and describe how they help managers to gather and organize information they need for making decisions. The reporting of manufacturing activities is also discussed.

A Look Ahead

Chapters 19 through 25 discuss information that managers need to make informed decisions and how they obtain that information. We explain the types of decisions managers must make and how managerial accounting helps with these decisions. The first of these chapters, Chapter 19, considers how we measure costs assigned to certain types of processes.

CAP

Conceptual

C1 Explain the purpose of managerial accounting. *(p. 714)*

C2 Describe major characteristics of managerial accounting. *(p. 715)*

C3 Describe the lean business model. *(p. 717)*

C4 Describe accounting concepts useful in classifying costs. *(p. 719)*

C5 Define product and period costs and explain how they impact financial statements. *(p. 720)*

C6 Explain how the balance sheets for manufacturing and merchandising companies differ. *(p. 722)*

C7 Explain how income statements for manufacturing and merchandising companies differ. *(p. 723)*

C8 Explain manufacturing activities and the flow of manufacturing costs. *(p. 726)*

Analytical

A1 Compute unit contribution margin and describe what it reveals about a company's cost structure. *(p. 729)*

Procedural

P1 Compute cost of goods sold for a manufacturer. *(p. 724)*

P2 Prepare a manufacturing statement and explain its purpose and links to financial statements. *(p. 727)*

Decision Feature

Rap Snacks for Hip-Hop Kids

PHILADELPHIA—James "Fly" Lindsay and his three sisters were raised by their mother in North Philadelphia. "We were poor," says Lindsay, "but we were rich in the values that she set forth." One of those values was education—Lindsay was the first in his family to attend college—and another was the commitment to community. "You have everyone taking away, but you have to give back," says Lindsay. He especially saw the dollars spent on food yet noted "that dollar is not going back into our communities."

Lindsay decided to take matters into his own hands. With $40,000 collected from family and friends, he launched **Rap Snacks [RapSnacks.com],** a maker of snack foods. In the beginning, its snacks featured "M.C. Potato," a cartoon spud wearing a backward baseball cap—but nothing to distinguish them from similar snack foods. With a renewed "customer orientation" and first-hand knowledge of urban youth, Lindsay altered his packaging. He decided to sell his snacks with rappers on the wrappers to target urban youth immersed in hip-hop culture. The wrappers, importantly, were designed to instill a craving for success, commitment, and entrepreneurship, says Lindsay. The snack wrappers featured hip-hop artists such as Warren G, Lil' Romeo, and Big Tymers paired with positive messages telling buyers to "respect yourself" and "stay in school."

Rap Snacks also promoted an entrepreneurial training program for urban youth. Lindsay says that urban youth need to learn about business and how it can help a community. Basic managerial principles and concepts, product and period costs, unit contribution margin, and manufacturing statements are like another language to most urban youth. Lindsay struggles to change that and more. "You can make money," says Lindsay, "but also have a social responsibility to where you came from." Investing in urban youth is a priority, says Lindsay. Specifically, he wants to convey the knowledge of managerial principles and concepts and the belief that urban youth can be successful. Understanding manufacturing activities and cost flows is not easy, says Lindsay, but the costs of not understanding are more severe. "It feels good to make a difference," says Lindsay, "and set an example for the kids."

[Sources: *Rap Snacks Website,* January 2004; *Entrepreneur,* July 2003; *Philadelphia Inquirer,* October 2002; *Gannett News Service,* January 2003; *Source,* June 2001; *Maxim,* March 2002.]

Managerial accounting, like financial accounting, provides information to help users make better decisions. However, managerial accounting and financial accounting differ in important ways, which this chapter explains. This chapter also compares the accounting and reporting practices used by manufacturing and merchandising companies. Both types of companies earn revenues by selling products. A merchandising company sells products without changing their condition. A manufacturing company buys raw materials and turns them into finished products for sale to customers. A service company earns revenues by providing services rather than products. The skills, tools, and techniques developed for measuring a manufacturing company's activities apply to service companies as well. The chapter concludes by explaining the flow of manufacturing activities and preparing the manufacturing statement.

Managerial Accounting Concepts and Principles

Managerial Accounting Basics
- Purpose of managerial accounting
- Nature of managerial accounting
- Managerial decision making
- Focus on managerial accounting

Managerial Cost Concepts
- Types of cost classifications
- Identification of cost classifications
- Cost concepts for service companies

Reporting Manufacturing Activities
- Balance sheet
- Income statement
- Flow of activities
- Manufacturing statement

Managerial Accounting Basics

The previous chapters focused on a financial accounting system whose main purpose is to prepare general-purpose financial statements. However, this information is incomplete for internal decision makers who manage organizations. For this purpose, a managerial accounting system is required. **Managerial accounting** is an activity that provides financial and nonfinancial information to an organization's managers and other internal decision makers. This section explains the purpose of managerial accounting (also called *management accounting*) and compares it with financial accounting.

Purpose of Managerial Accounting

C1 Explain the purpose of managerial accounting.

The purpose of both managerial accounting and financial accounting is providing useful information to decision makers. They do this by collecting, managing, and reporting information in demand by their users. Both areas of accounting also share the common practice of reporting monetary information; although managerial accounting includes the reporting of nonmonetary information. They even report some of the same information. For instance, a company's financial statements contain information useful for both its managers (insiders) and other persons interested in the company (outsiders).

The remainder of this book looks carefully at managerial accounting information, how accounting professionals gather it, and how managers use it. We consider the concepts and procedures used to determine the costs of products and services as well as topics such as budgeting, break-even analysis, product costing, profit planning, and cost analysis. Information about the costs of products and services is important for many decisions that managers make. These decisions include predicting the future costs of a product or service. Predicted costs are used in product pricing, profitability analysis, and in deciding whether to make or buy a product or component. More generally, much of managerial accounting involves gathering information about costs for planning and control decisions.

Planning is the process of setting goals and making plans to achieve them. Companies formulate long-term strategic plans that usually span a 5- to 10-year horizon and then refine them with medium-term and short-term plans. Strategic plans usually set a firm's long-term direction by developing a road map for the future based on potential opportunities such as new products, new markets, and capital investments. A strategic plan's goals and objectives are often broadly defined given its long-term orientation. Medium- and short-term plans are more operational in nature. They translate the strategic plan into actions. These plans are more concrete and consist of better defined objectives and goals. A short-term plan often covers a one-year period that, when translated in monetary terms, is known as a budget (see Chapter 23).

Point: Costs are important to managers because they impact both the financial position and profitability of a business. Managerial accounting assists in analysis, planning, and control of costs.

Control is the process of monitoring planning decisions and evaluating an organization's activities and employees. It includes the measurement and evaluation of actions, processes, and outcomes. Feedback provided by the control function allows managers to revise their plans. Measurement of actions and processes also allows managers to take corrective actions to avoid undesirable outcomes. For example, managers periodically compare actual results with planned results using a process called *variance analysis* (see Chapter 24). Exhibit 18.1 portrays the important management functions of planning and control.

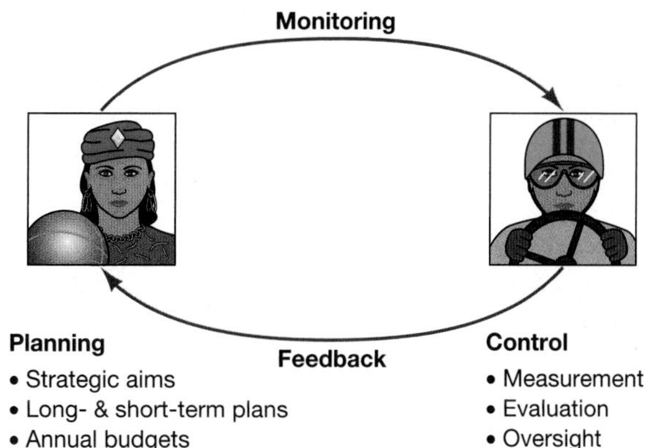

Exhibit 18.1

Planning and Control

Managers use information, including that of costs, to plan and control business activities. In later chapters, we explain how managers also use this information to direct and improve business operations.

Nature of Managerial Accounting

Managerial accounting has its own special characteristics. To understand these characteristics, we compare managerial accounting to financial accounting; they differ in at least seven important ways. These differences are summarized in Exhibit 18.2. This section discusses each of these characteristics.

C2 Describe major characteristics of managerial accounting.

	Financial Accounting	Managerial Accounting
1. Users and decision makers	Investors, creditors, and other users external to the organization	Managers, employees, and decision makers internal to the organization
2. Purpose of information	Assist external users in making investment, credit, and other decisions	Assist managers in making planning and control decisions
3. Flexibility of practice	Structured and often controlled by GAAP	Relatively flexible (no GAAP)
4. Timeliness of information	Often available only after an audit is complete	Available quickly without the need to wait for an audit
5. Time dimension	Historical information with some predictions	Many projections and estimates; historical information also presented
6. Focus of information	Emphasis on whole organization	Emphasis on an organization's projects, processes, and subdivisions
7. Nature of information	Monetary information	Mostly monetary; but also nonmonetary information

Exhibit 18.2

Major Differences between Managerial Accounting and Financial Accounting

Users and Decision Makers Companies accumulate, process, and report financial accounting and managerial accounting information for different groups of decision makers. Financial accounting information is primarily provided to external users including investors, creditors, analysts, and regulators. External users rarely have a major role in managing a company's daily activities. Managerial accounting information is primarily provided to internal users who are responsible for making and implementing decisions about a company's business activities.

Point: It is desirable to accumulate information for management reports in a database separate from financial accounting records.

Purpose of Information Investors, creditors, and other external users of financial accounting information must often decide whether to invest in or lend to a company. If they have already done so, they must decide whether to continue owning the company or carrying the loan. Internal decision makers must plan a company's future. They seek to take advantage of opportunities or to overcome obstacles. They also try to control activities and ensure their effective and efficient implementation. Managerial accounting information helps these internal users make both planning and control decisions.

Flexibility of Practice External users compare companies by using financial reports and need protection against false or misleading information. Accordingly, financial accounting relies on accepted principles that are enforced through an extensive set of rules and guidelines, or GAAP. Internal users need managerial accounting information for planning and controlling their company's activities rather than for external comparisons. They require different types of information depending on the activity. This makes standardizing managerial accounting systems across companies difficult. Instead, managerial accounting systems are flexible. The design of a company's managerial accounting system largely depends on the nature of the business and the arrangement of its internal operations. Managers can decide for themselves what information they want and how they want it reported. Even within a single company, different managers often design their own systems to meet their special needs. This flexibility allows managers to modify their systems quickly in response to changes in the environment. The important question a manager must ask is whether the information being collected and reported is useful for planning, decision-making, and control purposes.

Point: The *Institute of Management Accountants* issues statements that govern the practice of managerial accounting. Accountants who pass a qualifying exam are awarded the CMA.

Timeliness of Information Formal financial statements reporting past transactions and events are not immediately available to outside parties. Independent certified public accountants often must *audit* a company's financial statements before it provides them to external users. Thus, because audits often take several weeks to complete, financial reports to outsiders usually are not available until well after the period-end. However, managers can quickly obtain managerial accounting information. External auditors need not review it. Estimates and projections are acceptable. To get information quickly, managers often accept less precision in reports. As an example, an early internal report to management prepared right after the year-end could report net income for the year between $4.2 and $4.8 million. An audited income statement could later show net income for the year at $4.6 million. The internal report is not precise, but its information can be more useful because it is available earlier.

Internal auditing plays an important role in managerial accounting. Internal auditors evaluate the flow of information not only inside but also outside the company. Managers are responsible for preventing and detecting fraudulent activities in their companies.

Point: Financial statements are usually issued several weeks after the period-end. GAAP requires the reporting of important events that occur while the statements are being prepared. These events are called *subsequent events.*

Point: Independent auditors test the integrity of managerial accounting records when they are used in preparing financial statements.

Decision Ethics

Production Supervisor You invite three friends to a restaurant. When the dinner check arrives, David, a self-employed entrepreneur, picks it up saying, "Here, let me pay. I'll deduct it as a business expense on my tax return. It won't cost me as much." Denise, a salesperson, takes the check from David's hand and says, "I'll put this on my company's credit card. It won't cost us anything." Derek, a factory manager for a company, laughs and says, "Neither of you understands. I'll put this on my company's credit card and call it overhead on a cost-plus contract my company has with the government." (*A cost-plus contract means the company receives its costs plus a percent of those costs.*) Adds Derek, "That way, my company pays for dinner *and* makes a profit." Who should pay the bill?

Answer—p. 735

Time Dimension To protect external users from false expectations, financial reports deal primarily with results of both past activities and current conditions. While some predictions such as service lives and salvage values of plant assets are necessary, financial accounting avoids predictions whenever possible. Managerial accounting regularly includes predictions of conditions and events. As an example, one important managerial accounting report is a budget, which predicts revenues, expenses, and other items. If managerial accounting reports were restricted to the past and present, managers would be less able to plan activities and less effective in managing and evaluating current activities.

Focus of Information Companies often organize into divisions and departments, but investors rarely can buy shares in one division or department. Nor do creditors lend money to a company's single division or department. Instead, they own shares in or make loans to the entire company. Financial accounting focuses primarily on a company as a whole as depicted in Exhibit 18.3. The focus of managerial accounting is different. While top-level managers are responsible for managing the whole company, most other managers are responsible for much smaller sets of activities. These middle-level and lower-level managers need managerial accounting reports dealing with specific activities, projects, and subdivisions for which they are responsible. For instance, division sales managers are directly responsible only for the results achieved in their divisions. Accordingly, division sales managers need information about results achieved in their own divisions to improve their performance. This information includes the level of success achieved by each individual or department in each division as depicted in Exhibit 18.4.

Exhibit 18.3

Focus of External Reports

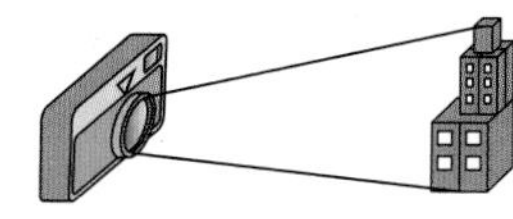

Exhibit 18.4

Focus of Internal Reports

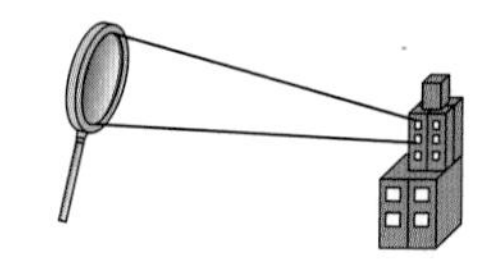

Nature of Information Both financial and managerial accounting systems report monetary information. Managerial accounting systems also report considerable nonmonetary information. Monetary information is an important part of managerial decisions, and nonmonetary information plays a crucial role, especially when monetary effects are difficult to measure. Common examples of nonmonetary information are the quality and delivery criteria of purchasing decisions.

Point: To apply these concepts, work QS 18-2.

Decision Maker

Division Manager At a recent managers' meeting, you are asked to explore the manufacturing of a component that your division has been purchasing from an outside supplier for several years. What information do you collect to evaluate these two alternative sources?

Answer—p. 735

Managerial Decision Making

The previous section emphasized differences between financial and managerial accounting, but they are not entirely separate. Similar information is useful to both external and internal users. For instance, information about costs of manufacturing products is useful to all users in making decisions. Also, both financial and managerial accounting affect peoples' actions. For example, **Harley-Davidson**'s design of a sales compensation plan affects the behavior of its salesforce. It also must estimate the dual effects of promotion and sales compensation plans on buying patterns of customers. These estimates impact the equipment purchase decisions for manufacturing and can affect the supplier selection criteria established by purchasing. Thus, financial and managerial accounting systems do more than measure; they also affect people's decisions and actions.

Focus on Managerial Accounting

C3 Describe the lean business model.

We have explained the importance of managerial accounting for internal decision making. Although the analytical tools and techniques of managerial accounting have always been useful, their relevance and importance continue to increase. This is so because of changes in the business environment. This section describes some of these changes and their impact on managerial accounting.

Lean Business Model Two important factors have encouraged companies to be more effective and efficient in running their operations. First, there is an increased emphasis on *customers* as the most important constituent of a business. Customers expect to derive a certain value for the money they spend to buy products and services. Specifically, they expect that their suppliers will offer them the right service (or product) at the right time and the right price. This implies that companies accept the notion of **customer orientation,** which means that employees understand the changing needs and wants of their customers and align their management and operating practices accordingly.

Second, our *global economy* expands competitive boundaries, thereby providing customers more choices. The global economy also produces changes in business activities. One notable case that reflects these changes in customer demand and global competition is auto manufacturing. The top three Japanese auto manufacturers (**Honda**, **Nissan**, and **Toyota**) once controlled more than 40% of the U.S. auto market. Customers perceived that Japanese auto manufacturers provided value not available from other manufacturers. Many European and North American auto manufacturers responded to this challenge and regained much of the lost market share.

Companies must be alert to these and other factors. Many companies have responded by adopting the **lean business model,** whose goal is to *eliminate waste* while "satisfying the customer" and "providing a positive return" to the company.

Point: Many industries, in addition to the automobile industry, can benefit from a JIT system.

Point: Goals of a TQM process include reduced waste, better inventory control, fewer defects, and continuous improvement. Just-in-time concepts have similar goals.

Point: The time between buying raw materials and selling the finished goods is called *throughput time.*

Lean Practices **Continuous improvement** rejects the notions of "good enough" or "acceptable" and challenges employees and managers to continuously experiment with new and improved business practices. This has led companies to adopt practices such as total quality management (TQM) and just-in-time (JIT) manufacturing. The philosophy underlying both practices is continuous improvement; the difference is in the focus.

Total quality management focuses on quality improvement and applies this standard to all aspects of business activities. In doing so, managers and employees seek to uncover waste in business activities including accounting activities such as payroll and disbursements. To encourage an emphasis on quality, the U.S. Congress established the Malcolm Baldrige National Quality Award (MBQNA). Entrants must conduct a thorough analysis and evaluation of their business using guidelines from the Baldrige committee. **Ritz Carlton Hotel Company, L.L.C** is a recent recipient of the Baldrige award in the service category. The company applies a core set of values, collectively called *The Gold Standards,* to improve customer service.

Just-in-time manufacturing is a system that acquires inventory and produces only when needed. An important aspect of JIT is that companies manufacture products only after they receive an order (a *demand-pull* system) and then deliver the customer's requirements on time. This means that processes must be aligned to eliminate any delays and inefficiencies including inferior inputs and outputs. Companies must also establish good relations and communications with their suppliers. On the downside, JIT is more susceptible to disruption than traditional systems. As one recent example, several **General Motors** plants were temporarily shut down due to a strike at an assembly division; the plants supplied components *just in time* to the assembly division.

Decision Insight

Global Lean **Toyota Motor Corporation** in Japan pioneered lean manufacturing, and it has since spread to other manufacturers throughout the world. The goals include improvements in quality, reliability, inventory turnover, productivity, exports, and—above all—sales and income.

Implications for Managerial Accounting Adopting the lean business model can be challenging because to foster its implementation, all systems and procedures that a company follows must be realigned. Managerial accounting has an important role to play by providing accurate cost and performance information. Companies must understand the nature and sources of cost and must develop systems that capture costs accurately. Developing such a system is important to measuring the "value" provided to customers. The price that customers pay for acquiring goods and services is an important determinant of value. In turn, the costs a company incurs are key determinants of price. All else being equal, the better a company is at controlling its costs, the better its performance.

Decision Insight

Balanced Scorecard The *balanced scorecard* aids continuous improvement by augmenting financial measures with information on the "drivers" (indicators) of future financial performance along four dimensions: (1) *financial*—profitability and risk, (2) *customer*—value creation and product and service differentiation, (3) *internal business processes*—businesses activities that create customer and owner satisfaction, and (4) *learning and growth*—organizational change, innovation, and growth.

Quick Check

1. Managerial accounting produces information (*a*) to meet internal users' needs, (*b*) to meet a user's specific needs, (*c*) often focusing on the future, or (*d*) all of these.
2. What is the difference between the intended users of financial and managerial accounting?
3. Do generally accepted accounting principles (GAAP) control and dictate managerial accounting?
4. What is the basic objective for a company practicing total quality management?

Answers—p. 735

Managerial Cost Concepts

Types of Cost Classifications

C4 Describe accounting concepts useful in classifying costs.

An organization incurs many different types of costs that are classified differently, depending on management needs (different costs for different purposes). Specifically, we can classify costs on the basis of their (1) behavior, (2) traceability, (3) controllability, (4) relevance, and (5) function. This section explains each concept for assigning costs to products and services.

Topic Tackler 18-1

Classification by Behavior At a basic level, a cost can be classified as fixed or variable. A **fixed cost** does not change with changes in the volume of activity (within a range of activity known as an activity's *relevant range*). For example, straight-line depreciation on equipment is a fixed cost. A **variable cost** changes in proportion to changes in the volume of activity. Sales commissions computed as a percent of sales revenue are variable costs. Additional examples of fixed and variable costs for a bike manufacturer are provided in Exhibit 18.5. When cost items are combined, total cost can be fixed, variable, or mixed. *Mixed* refers to a combination of fixed and variable costs. Equipment rental often includes a fixed cost for some minimum amount and a variable cost based on amount of usage. Classification of costs by behavior is helpful in cost-volume-profit analyses and short-term decision making. We discuss these in Chapters 22 and 25.

Exhibit 18.5
Fixed and Variable Costs

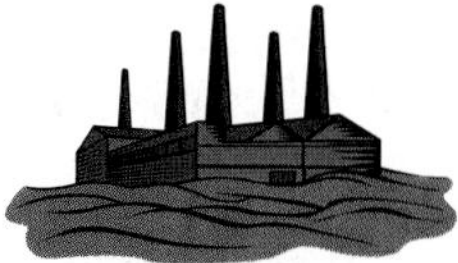

Fixed Cost: Rent for Rocky Mountain Bikes' building is $22,000, and doesn't change with the number of bikes produced.

Variable Cost: Cost of bicycle tires is variable with the number of bikes produced—this cost is $15 per pair.

Classification by Traceability A cost is often traced to a **cost object,** which is a product, process, department, or customer to which costs are assigned. When a cost is traceable to a cost object, it is classified as a direct cost. **Direct costs** are incurred for the benefit of one specific cost object. For example, if a product is a cost object, its material and labor costs are usually directly traceable. **Indirect costs** are incurred for the benefit of more than one cost object. An example of an indirect traceable cost is a maintenance plan that benefits two or more departments. Exhibit 18.6 identifies examples of both direct and indirect costs for the maintenance department in

Exhibit 18.6
Direct and Indirect Costs

Direct Costs
- Salaries of maintenance department employees
- Equipment purchased by maintenance department
- Materials purchased by maintenance department
- Maintenance department equipment depreciation

Indirect Costs
- Factory accounting
- Factory administration
- Factory rent
- Factory managers' salary
- Factory light and heat
- Factory internal audit
- Factory intranet

a manufacturing plant. Classification of costs by traceability is useful for cost allocation. This is discussed in Chapter 21.

Decision Maker

Entrepreneur You wish to trace as many of your assembly department's direct costs as possible. You can trace 90% of them in an economical manner. To trace the other 10%, you need sophisticated and costly accounting software. Do you purchase this software?

Answer—p. 735

Classification by Controllability A cost can be defined as **controllable** or **not controllable.** Whether a cost is controllable or not depends on the employee's responsibilities, as shown in Exhibit 18.7. This is referred to as *hierarchical levels* in management, or *pecking order.* For example, investments in machinery are controllable by upper-level managers but not lower-level managers. Many daily operating expenses such as overtime often are controllable by lower-level managers. Classification of costs by controllability is especially useful for assigning responsibility to and evaluating managers.

Exhibit 18.7

Controllability of Costs

Senior Manager
Controls costs of investment in land, buildings, and equipment.

Supervisor
Controls daily expenses such as supplies, maintenance, and overtime.

Classification by Relevance A cost can be classified by relevance by identifying it as either a sunk cost or an out-of-pocket cost. A **sunk cost** has already been incurred and cannot be avoided or changed. It is irrelevant to future decisions. One example is the cost of a company's office equipment previously purchased. An **out-of-pocket cost** requires a future outlay of cash and is relevant for decision making. Future purchases of equipment involve out-of-pocket costs. A discussion of relevant costs must also consider opportunity costs. An **opportunity cost** is the potential benefit lost by choosing a specific action from two or more alternatives. One example is a student giving up wages from a job to attend evening classes. Consideration of opportunity cost is important when, for example, an insurance company must decide whether to outsource its payroll function or maintain it internally. This is discussed in Chapter 25.

Point: Opportunity costs are not recorded by the accounting system.

Decision Maker

Purchase Manager You are evaluating two potential suppliers of seats for the manufacturing of motorcycles. One supplier (A) quotes a $145 price per seat and ensures 100% quality standards and on-time delivery. The second supplier (B) quotes a $115 price per seat but does not give any written assurances on quality or delivery. You decide to contract with the second supplier (B), saving $30 per seat. Does this decision have opportunity costs?

Answer—p. 735

C5 Define product and period costs and explain how they impact financial statements.

Classification by Function Another cost classification (for manufacturers) is capitalization as inventory or to expense as incurred. Costs capitalized as inventory are called **product costs,** which refer to expenditures necessary and integral to finished products. They include direct materials, direct labor, and overhead costs. Product costs pertain to activities carried out to manufacture the product. Costs expensed are called **period costs,** which refer to expenditures identified more with a time period than with finished products. They include selling and general administrative expenses. Period costs pertain to activities that are not part of the manufacturing process. A distinction between product and period costs is important because period costs are expensed in the income statement and product costs are assigned to inventory on the balance sheet. An ability to understand and identify product costs and period costs is crucial to using and interpreting a *manufacturing statement* described later in this chapter.

Exhibit 18.8 shows the different effects of product and period costs. Period costs flow directly to the current income statement as expenses. They are not reported as assets. Product costs are first assigned to inventory. Their final treatment depends on when inventory is sold or disposed of. Product costs assigned to finished goods that are sold in year 2005 are reported on the 2005 income statement as part of cost of goods sold. Product costs assigned to unsold inventory are carried forward on the balance sheet at the end of year 2005. If this inventory is sold in year 2006, product costs assigned to it are reported as part of cost of goods sold in that year's income statement.

Point: Only costs of production and purchases are classed as product costs.

Point: Product costs are either in the income statement as part of cost of goods sold or in the balance sheet as inventory. Period costs appear only on the income statement under operating expenses. See Exhibit 18.8.

The difference between period and product costs explains why the year 2005 income statement does not report operating expenses related to either factory workers' wages or

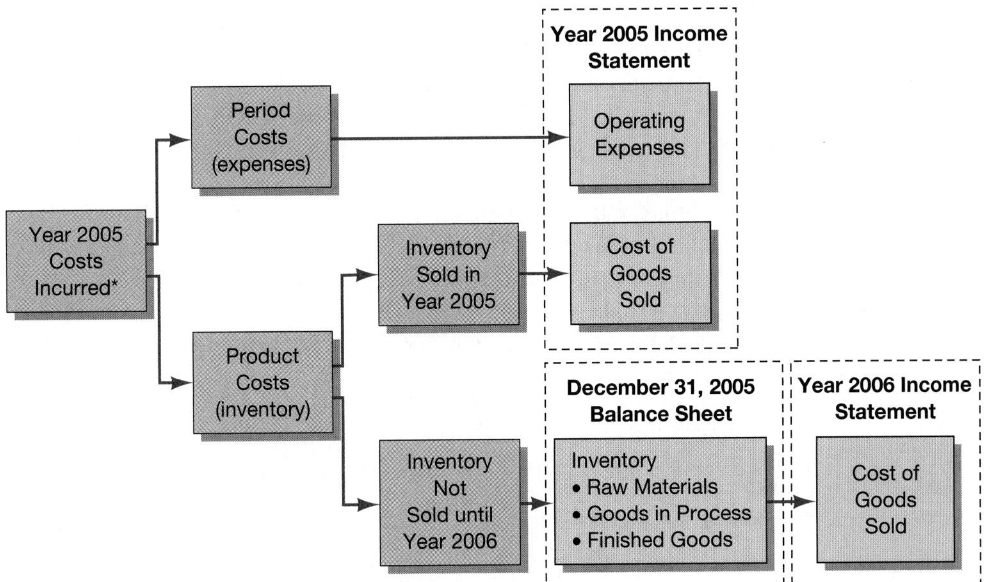

Exhibit 18.8

Period and Product Costs in Financial Statements

depreciation on factory buildings and equipment. Instead, both costs are combined with the cost of raw materials to compute the product cost of finished goods. A portion of these manufacturing costs (related to the goods sold) is reported in the year 2005 income statement as part of Cost of Goods Sold. The other portion is reported on the balance sheet at the end of that year as part of Inventory. The portion assigned to inventory could be included in any or all of raw materials, goods in process, or finished goods inventories.

Point: For a team approach to identifying period and product costs, see *Teamwork in Action* in the *Beyond the Numbers* section.

Point: To apply these concepts, work Exercise 18-6.

Identification of Cost Classification

It is important to understand that a cost can be classified using any one (or combination) of the five different means described here. To do this we must understand costs and operations. Specifically, for the five classifications, we must be able to identify the *activity* for behavior, *cost object* for traceability, *management hierarchical level* for controllability, *opportunity cost* for relevance, and *benefit period* for function. Factory rent, for instance, can be classified as a product cost; it is fixed with respect to number of units produced, it is indirect with respect to the product, and it is not controllable by a production supervisor. Potential multiple classifications are shown in Exhibit 18.9 using different cost items incurred in manufacturing mountain bikes. The finished bike is the cost object. Proper allocation of these costs and the managerial decisions based on cost data depend on a correct cost classification.

Point: All expenses of service companies are period costs because these companies do not have inventory.

Cost Item	By Behavior	By Traceability	By Function
Bicycle tires	Variable	Direct	Product
Wages of assembly worker*	Variable	Direct	Product
Advertising	Fixed	Indirect	Period
Production manager's salary	Fixed	Indirect	Product
Office depreciation	Fixed	Indirect	Period

* Although an assembly worker's wages are classified as variable costs, their actual behavior depends on how workers are paid and whether their wages are based on a union contract (such as piece rate or monthly wages).

Exhibit 18.9

Examples of Multiple Cost Classifications

Cost Concepts for Service Companies

The cost concepts described are generally applicable to service organizations. For example, consider **Delta Air Lines**. Its cost of food for passengers is a variable cost based on number

Service Costs
- Food and beverages
- Cleaning fees
- Pilot salaries
- Attendant salaries
- Fuel costs
- Travel agent fees
- Ground crew salaries

of passengers. The cost of leasing an aircraft is fixed with respect to number of passengers. We can also trace a flight crew's salary to a specific flight whereas we likely cannot trace wages for the ground crew to a specific flight. Classification by function (such as product versus period costs) is not relevant to service companies because services are not inventoried. Instead, costs incurred by a service firm are expensed in the reporting period when incurred.

Managers in service companies must understand and apply cost concepts. They seek and rely on accurate cost estimates for many decisions. For example, an airline manager must often decide between canceling or rerouting flights. The manager must also be able to estimate costs saved by canceling a flight versus rerouting. Knowledge of fixed costs is equally important. We explain more about the cost requirements for these and other managerial decisions in Chapter 25.

Quick Check

Answers—p. 736

5. Which type of cost behavior increases total costs when volume of activity increases?
6. How could traceability of costs improve managerial decisions?

Reporting Manufacturing Activities

Companies with manufacturing activities differ from both merchandising and service companies. The main difference between merchandising and manufacturing companies is that merchandisers buy goods ready for sale while manufacturers produce goods from materials and labor. **Payless** is an example of a merchandising company. It buys and sells shoes without physically changing them. **Nike** is primarily a manufacturer of shoes and apparel. It purchases materials such as leather, cloth, dye, plastic, rubber, glue, and laces and then uses employees' labor to convert these materials to products. **Delta Air Lines** is a service company that transports people and items.

Much of our focus in this book has been on the business activities of merchandising and service companies. We described their activities and how to account for them. Manufacturing activities differ from both selling merchandise and providing services. Also, the financial statements for manufacturing companies differ slightly. This section considers some of these differences and compares them to accounting for a merchandising company.

Manufacturer's Balance Sheet

C6 Explain how the balance sheets for manufacturing and merchandising companies differ.

Manufacturers carry several unique assets and usually have three inventories instead of the single inventory that merchandisers carry. Exhibit 18.10 shows three different inventories in the current asset section of the balance sheet for Rocky Mountain Bikes, a manufacturer. The three inventories are raw materials, goods in process, and finished goods.

Point: Reducing the size of inventories saves storage costs and frees money for other uses.

Raw Materials Inventory **Raw materials inventory** refers to the goods a company acquires to use in making products. It uses raw materials in two ways: directly and indirectly. Most raw materials physically become part of a product and are identified with specific units or batches of a product. Raw materials used directly in a product are called *direct materials*. Other materials used to support production processes are sometimes not as clearly identified with specific units or batches of product. These materials are called **indirect materials** because they are not clearly identified with specific product units or batches. Items used as indirect materials often appear on a balance sheet as factory supplies or are included in raw materials. Some direct materials are classified as indirect materials when their costs are low (insignificant). Examples include screws and nuts used in assembling mountain bikes and

Inventories of Rocky Mountain Bikes

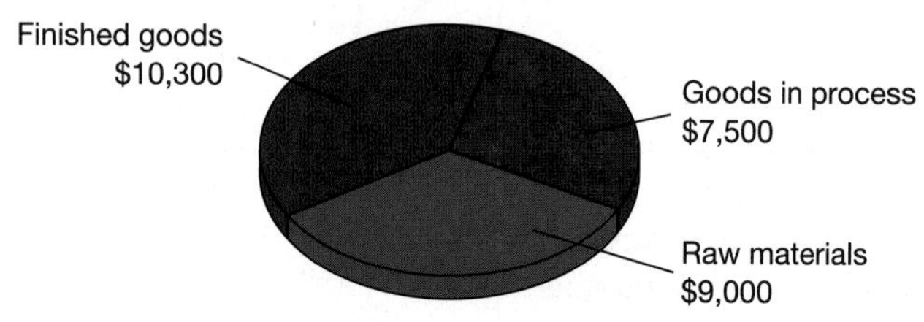

Exhibit 18.10

Balance Sheet for a Manufacturer

ROCKY MOUNTAIN BIKES
Balance Sheet
December 31, 2005

Assets		Liabilities and Equity	
Current assets		Current liabilities	
Cash	$ 11,000	Accounts payable	$ 14,000
Accounts receivable, net	30,150	Wages payable	540
Raw materials inventory	**9,000**	Interest payable	2,000
Goods in process inventory	**7,500**	Income taxes payable	32,600
Finished goods inventory	**10,300**	Total current liabilities	49,140
Factory supplies	350	Long-term liabilities	
Prepaid insurance	300	Long-term notes payable	50,000
Total current assets	68,600	Total liabilities	99,140
Plant assets			
Small tools	1,100	Stockholders' equity	
Delivery equipment, net	5,000	Common stock, $5 par	100,000
Office equipment, net	1,300	Retained earnings	49,760
Factory machinery, net	65,500	Total stockholders' equity	149,760
Factory building, net	86,700	Total liabilities and equity	$248,900
Land	9,500		
Total plant assets	169,100		
Intangible assets (patents)	11,200		
Total assets	$248,900		

staples and glue used in manufacturing shoes. Using the *materiality principle,* individually tracing the costs of each of these materials and classifying them separately as direct materials does not make much economic sense. For instance, keeping detailed records of the amount of glue used to manufacture one shoe is not cost beneficial.

Goods in Process Inventory Another inventory held by manufacturers is **goods in process inventory,** also called *work in process inventory.* It consists of products in the process of being manufactured but not yet complete. The amount of goods in process inventory depends on the type of production process. If the time required to produce a unit of product is short, the goods in process inventory is likely small, but if weeks or months are needed to produce a unit, the goods in process inventory is usually larger.

Finished Goods Inventory A third inventory owned by a manufacturer is **finished goods inventory,** which consists of completed products ready for sale. This inventory is similar to merchandise inventory owned by a merchandising company. Manufacturers also often own unique plant assets such as small tools, factory buildings, factory equipment, and patents to manufacture products. The balance sheet in Exhibit 18.10 shows that Rocky Mountain Bikes owns all of these assets. Some manufacturers invest millions or even billions of dollars in production facilities and patents. **Caterpillar**'s recent balance sheet shows a $7 billion net investment in land, buildings, machinery and equipment, much of which involves production facilities.

Manufacturer's Income Statement

C7 Explain how income statements for manufacturing and merchandising companies differ.

The main difference between the income statement of a manufacturer and that of a merchandiser involves the items making up cost of goods sold. Exhibit 18.11 compares the components of cost of goods sold for a manufacturer and a merchandiser. A merchandiser adds its cost of goods purchased to beginning merchandise inventory and then subtracts

Exhibit 18.11

Cost of Goods Sold Computation

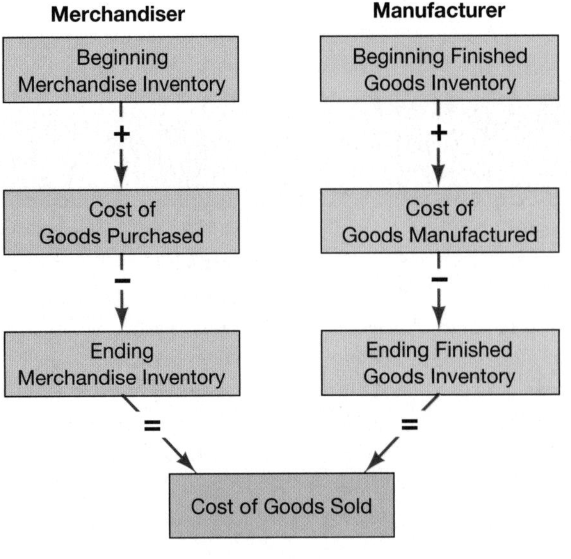

ending merchandise inventory to get cost of goods sold. A manufacturer adds its cost of goods manufactured to beginning finished goods inventory and then subtracts ending finished goods inventory to get cost of goods sold.

A merchandiser often uses the term *merchandise* inventory; a manufacturer often uses the term *finished goods* inventory. A manufacturer's inventories of raw materials and goods in process are not included in finished goods because they are not available for sale. A manufacturer also shows cost of goods *manufactured* instead of cost of goods *purchased.* This difference occurs because a manufacturer produces its goods instead of purchasing them ready for sale. We show later in this chapter how to derive cost of goods manufactured from the manufacturing statement.

P1 Compute cost of goods sold for a manufacturer.

The Cost of Goods Sold section for both a merchandiser (Tele-Mart) and a manufacturer (Rocky Mountain Bikes) is shown in Exhibit 18.12 to highlight these differences. The remaining income statement sections are similar.

Exhibit 18.12

Cost of Goods Sold for a Merchandiser and Manufacturer

Merchandising Company		Manufacturing Company	
Cost of goods sold		Cost of goods sold	
Beginning *merchandise* inventory	$ 14,200	**Beginning *finished goods* inventory**	$ 11,200
Cost of merchandise *purchased*	234,150	**Cost of goods *manufactured****	170,500
Goods available for sale	248,350	Goods available for sale	181,700
Less ending *merchandise* inventory	12,100	**Less ending *finished goods* inventory**	10,300
Cost of goods sold	$236,250	Cost of goods sold	$171,400

* Cost of goods manufactured is reported in the income statement of Exhibit 18.14.

Topic Tackler 18-2

Although the cost of goods sold computations are similar, the numbers in these computations reflect different activities. A merchandiser's cost of goods purchased is the cost of buying products to be sold. A manufacturer's cost of goods manufactured is the sum of direct materials, direct labor, and factory overhead costs incurred in producing products. The remainder of this section further explains these three manufacturing costs and describes prime and conversion costs.

Typical Manufacturing Costs in Today's Products

Direct materials 45%
Factory overhead 40%
Direct labor 15%

Direct Materials **Direct materials** are tangible components of a finished product. **Direct material costs** are the expenditures for direct materials that are separately and readily traced through the manufacturing process to finished goods. Examples of direct materials in manufacturing a mountain bike include its tires, seat, frame, pedals, brakes, cables, gears, and handlebars. The chart in the margin shows that direct materials generally make up about 45% of manufacturing costs in today's products, but this amount varies across industries and companies.

Direct Labor **Direct labor** refers to the efforts of employees who physically convert materials to finished product. **Direct labor costs** are the wages and salaries for direct labor that are separately and readily traced through the manufacturing process to finished goods. Examples of direct labor in manufacturing a mountain bike include operators directly involved in converting raw materials into finished products (welding, painting, forming) and assembly workers who attach materials such as tires, seats, pedals, and brakes to the bike frames. Costs of other workers on the assembly line who assist direct laborers are classified as **indirect labor costs. Indirect labor** refers to manufacturing workers' efforts not linked to specific units or batches of the product.

Point: Indirect labor costs are part of factory overhead.

Factory Overhead **Factory overhead** involves components or activities that support the manufacturing process but are not direct materials or direct labor. **Factory overhead costs** are the expenditures for factory overhead that cannot be separately or readily traced to finished goods. These costs include indirect materials and indirect labor, costs not directly traceable to the product. Overtime paid to direct laborers is also included in overhead because overtime is due to delays, interruptions, or constraints not necessarily identifiable to a specific product or batches of product. Factory overhead costs also include maintenance of the mountain bike factory, supervision of its employees, repairing manufacturing equipment, factory utilities (water, gas, electricity), production manager's salary, factory rent, depreciation on factory buildings and equipment, factory insurance, property taxes on factory buildings and equipment, and factory accounting and legal services. Factory overhead does *not* include selling and administrative expenses because they are not incurred in manufacturing products. These expenses are called *period costs* and are recorded as expenses on the income statement when incurred.

Point: Factory overhead is also called *manufacturing overhead.*

Prime and Conversion Costs Direct material costs and direct labor costs are also called **prime costs**—expenditures directly associated with the manufacture of finished goods. Direct labor costs and overhead costs are called **conversion costs**—expenditures incurred in the process of converting raw materials to finished goods. Direct labor costs are considered both prime costs and conversion costs. Exhibit 18.13 conveys the relation between prime and conversion costs and their components of direct material, direct labor, and factory overhead.

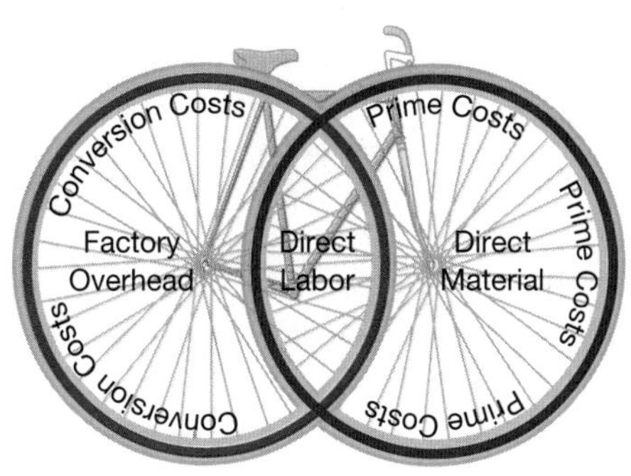

Exhibit 18.13

Prime and Conversion Costs and Their Components

Point: Prime costs = Direct materials + Direct labor. Conversion costs = Direct labor + Factory overhead.

Reporting Performance Exhibit 18.14 shows the income statement for Rocky Mountain Bikes. Its operating expenses include sales salaries, office salaries, and depreciation of delivery and office equipment. Operating expenses do not include manufacturing costs such as factory workers' wages and depreciation of production equipment and the factory buildings. These manufacturing costs are reported as part of cost of goods manufactured and included in cost of goods sold. We explained why and how this is done in the section Classification by Function.

Point: Manufacturers treat costs such as depreciation and rent as product costs if they are related to manufacturing.

Quick Check

7. What are the three types of inventory on a manufacturing company's balance sheet?
8. How does cost of goods sold differ for merchandising versus manufacturing companies?

Answers—p. 736

Exhibit 18.14

Income Statement for a Manufacturer

ROCKY MOUNTAIN BIKES Income Statement For Year Ended December 31, 2005		
Sales		$310,000
Cost of goods sold		
Finished goods inventory, Dec. 31, 2004	$ 11,200	
Cost of goods manufactured	**170,500**	
Goods available for sale	181,700	
Less finished goods inventory, Dec. 31, 2005	10,300	
Cost of goods sold		171,400
Gross profit		138,600
Operating expenses		
Selling expenses		
Sales salaries expense	18,000	
Advertising expense	5,500	
Delivery wages expense	12,000	
Shipping supplies expense	250	
Insurance expense—Delivery equipment	300	
Depreciation expense—Delivery equipment	2,100	
Total selling expenses		38,150
General and administrative expenses		
Office salaries expense	15,700	
Miscellaneous expense	200	
Bad debts expense	1,550	
Office supplies expense	100	
Depreciation expense—Office equipment	200	
Interest expense	4,000	
Total general and administrative expenses		21,750
Total operating expenses		59,900
Income before income taxes		78,700
Income taxes expense		32,600
Net income		$ 46,100
Net income per common share (20,000 shares)		$ 2.31

Flow of Manufacturing Activities

C8 Explain manufacturing activities and the flow of manufacturing costs.

To understand manufacturing and its reports, we must first understand the flow of manufacturing activities and costs. Exhibit 18.15 shows the flow of manufacturing activities for a manufacturer. This exhibit has three important sections: *materials activity, production activity,* and *sales activity.* We explain each activity in this section.

Materials Activity The far left side of Exhibit 18.15 shows the flow of raw materials. Manufacturers usually start a period with some beginning raw materials inventory carried over from the previous period. The company then acquires additional raw materials in the current period. Adding these purchases to beginning inventory gives total raw materials available for use in production. These raw materials are then either used in production in the current period or remain in inventory at the end of the period for use in future periods.

Point: Knowledge of managerial accounting provides us a means of measuring manufacturing costs and is a sound foundation for studying advanced business topics.

Production Activity The middle section of Exhibit 18.15 describes production activity. Four factors come together in production: beginning goods in process inventory, direct materials, direct labor, and overhead. Beginning goods in process inventory consists of partly assembled products from the previous period. Production activity results in products that are either finished or remain unfinished. The cost of finished products makes up the cost of goods

Point: The series of activities that add value to a company's products or services is called a **value chain.**

Exhibit 18.15

Activities and Cost Flows in Manufacturing

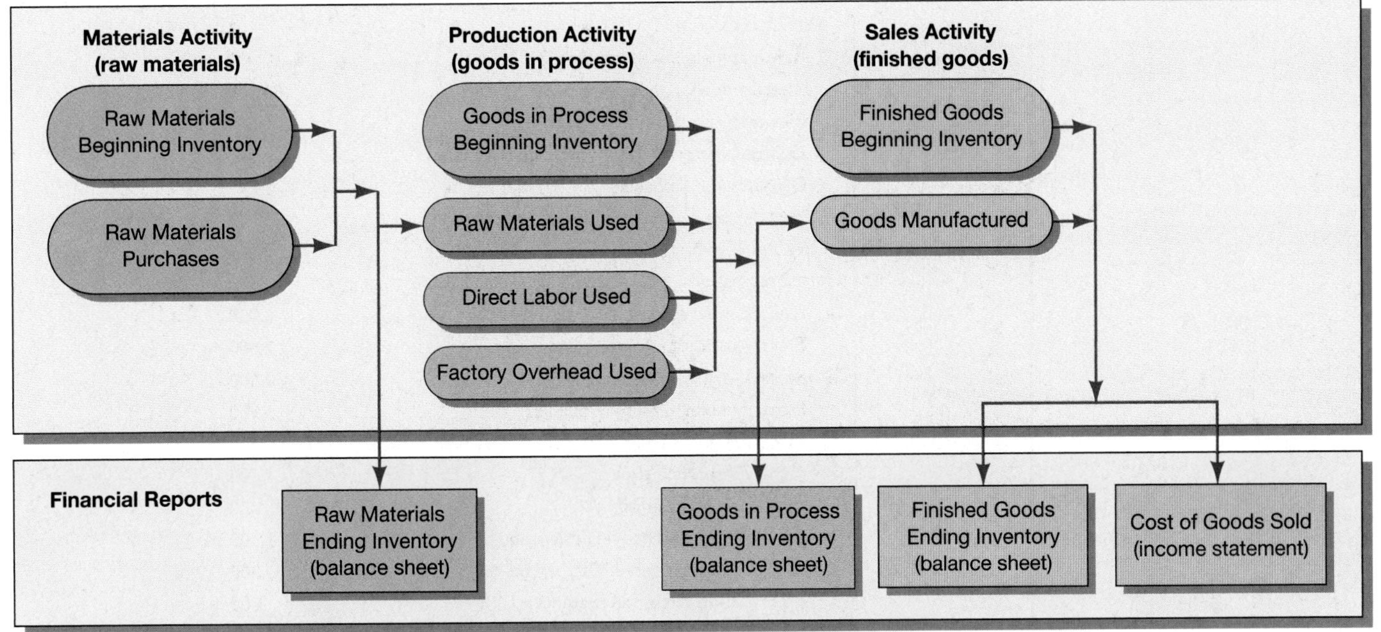

manufactured for the current period. Unfinished products are identified as ending goods in process inventory. The cost of unfinished products consists of direct materials, direct labor, and factory overhead, and is reported on the current period's balance sheet. The costs of both finished goods manufactured and goods in process are *product costs.*

Sales Activity The company's sales activity is portrayed in the far right side of Exhibit 18.15. Newly completed units are combined with beginning finished goods inventory to make up total finished goods available for sale in the current period. The cost of finished products sold is reported on the income statement as cost of goods sold. The cost of products not sold is reported on the current period's balance sheet as ending finished goods inventory.

Manufacturing Statement

A company's manufacturing activities are described in a **manufacturing statement,** also called the *schedule of manufacturing activities* or the *schedule of cost of goods manufactured.* The manufacturing statement summarizes the types and amounts of costs incurred in a company's manufacturing process. Exhibit 18.16 shows the manufacturing statement for Rocky Mountain Bikes. The statement is divided into four parts: *direct materials, direct labor, overhead,* and *computation of cost of goods manufactured.* We describe each of these parts in this section.

P2 Prepare a manufacturing statement and explain its purpose and links to financial statements.

① The manufacturing statement begins by computing direct materials used. We start by adding beginning raw materials inventory of \$8,000 to the current period's purchases of \$86,500. This yields \$94,500 of total raw materials available for use. A physical count of inventory shows \$9,000 of ending raw materials inventory. This implies a total cost of raw materials used during the period of \$85,500 (\$94,500 total raw materials available for use − \$9,000 ending inventory). (*Note:* All raw materials are direct materials for Rocky Mountain Bikes.)

② The second part of the manufacturing statement reports direct labor costs. Rocky Mountain Bikes had total direct labor costs of \$60,000 for the period. This amount includes payroll taxes and fringe benefits.

Exhibit 18.16

Manufacturing Statement

ROCKY MOUNTAIN BIKES
Manufacturing Statement
For Year Ended December 31, 2005

①	**Direct materials**		
	Raw materials inventory, Dec. 31, 2004	$ 8,000	
	Raw materials purchases	86,500	
	Raw materials available for use	94,500	
	Less raw materials inventory, Dec. 31, 2005	9,000	
	Direct materials used		$ 85,500
②	**Direct labor**		60,000
③	**Factory overhead**		
	Indirect labor	9,000	
	Factory supervision	6,000	
	Factory utilities	2,600	
	Repairs—Factory equipment	2,500	
	Property taxes—Factory building	1,900	
	Factory supplies used	600	
	Factory insurance expired	1,100	
	Small tools written off	200	
	Depreciation expense—Factory equipment	3,500	
	Depreciation expense—Factory building	1,800	
	Amortization expense—Patents	800	
	Total factory overhead		30,000
④	Total manufacturing costs		175,500
	Add goods in process inventory, Dec. 31, 2004		2,500
	Total cost of goods in process		178,000
	Less goods in process inventory, Dec. 31, 2005		7,500
	Cost of goods manufactured		$170,500

Point: Direct material and direct labor costs increase with increases in production volume and are called *variable costs*. Overhead can be both variable and fixed. When overhead costs vary with production, they are called *variable overhead*. When overhead costs don't vary with production, they are called *fixed overhead*.

③ The third part of the manufacturing statement reports overhead costs. The statement lists each important factory overhead item and its cost. Total factory overhead cost for the period is $30,000. Some companies report only *total* factory overhead on the manufacturing statement and attach a separate schedule listing individual overhead costs.

④ The final section of the manufacturing statement computes and reports the *cost of goods manufactured.* (Total manufacturing costs for the period are $175,500 [$85,500 + $60,000 + $30,000], the sum of direct materials used and direct labor and overhead costs incurred.) This amount is first added to beginning goods in process inventory. This gives the total goods in process inventory of $178,000 ($175,500 + $2,500). We then compute the current period's cost of goods manufactured of $170,500 by taking the $178,000 total goods in process and subtracting the $7,500 cost of ending goods in process inventory that consists of direct materials, direct labor, and factory overhead. The cost of goods manufactured amount is also called *net cost of goods manufactured* or *cost of goods completed.* Exhibit 18.14 shows that this item and amount are listed in the Cost of Goods Sold section of Rocky Mountain Bikes' income statement.

Point: Manufacturers sometimes report variable and fixed overhead separately in the manufacturing statement to provide more information to managers about cost behavior.

A managerial accounting system records costs and reports them in various reports that eventually determine financial statements. Exhibit 18.17 shows how overhead costs flow through the system: from an initial listing of specific costs, to a section of the manufacturing statement, to the reporting on the income statement.

Management uses information in the manufacturing statement to plan and control the company's manufacturing activities. To provide timely information for decision making, the statement is often prepared monthly, weekly, or even daily. The manufacturing statement

Exhibit 18.17

Overhead Cost Flows across Accounting Reports

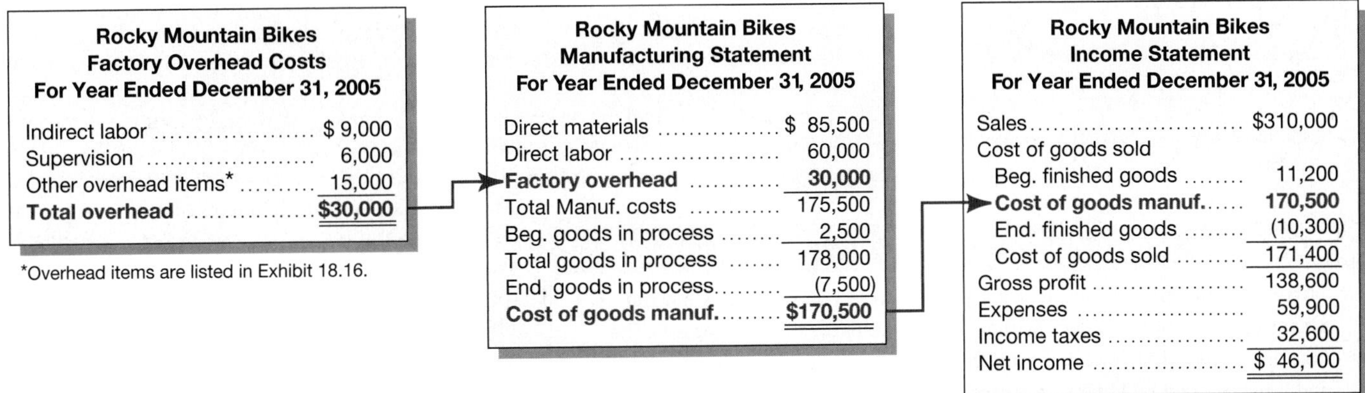

Rocky Mountain Bikes
Factory Overhead Costs
For Year Ended December 31, 2005

Indirect labor	$ 9,000
Supervision	6,000
Other overhead items*	15,000
Total overhead	**$30,000**

*Overhead items are listed in Exhibit 18.16.

Rocky Mountain Bikes
Manufacturing Statement
For Year Ended December 31, 2005

Direct materials	$ 85,500
Direct labor	60,000
Factory overhead	**30,000**
Total Manuf. costs	175,500
Beg. goods in process	2,500
Total goods in process	178,000
End. goods in process	(7,500)
Cost of goods manuf.	**$170,500**

Rocky Mountain Bikes
Income Statement
For Year Ended December 31, 2005

Sales	$310,000
Cost of goods sold	
Beg. finished goods	11,200
Cost of goods manuf.	**170,500**
End. finished goods	(10,300)
Cost of goods sold	171,400
Gross profit	138,600
Expenses	59,900
Income taxes	32,600
Net income	$ 46,100

contains information useful to external users but is not a general-purpose financial statement. Companies rarely publish the manufacturing statement because managers view this information as proprietary and potentially harmful to them if released to competitors.

Point: To apply these concepts, work Exercise 18-11.

Quick Check

9. A manufacturing statement (*a*) computes cost of goods manufactured for the period, (*b*) computes cost of goods sold for the period, or (*c*) reports operating expenses incurred for the period.

10. Are companies required to report a manufacturing statement?

11. How are both beginning and ending goods in process inventories reported on a manufacturing statement?

Answers—p. 736

Unit Contribution Margin

Decision Analysis

A1 Compute unit contribution margin and describe what it reveals about a company's cost structure.

We explained in this chapter how managers classify costs by behavior. This usually refers to costs as being fixed or variable with respect to volume of activity. In manufacturing companies, volume of activity usually refers to the number of units produced. We then classify a cost as either fixed or variable, depending on whether total cost changes as the number of units produced changes. Once we separate costs by behavior, we can then compute a product's contribution margin. **Unit contribution margin,** or *contribution margin per unit,* is the amount a product's unit selling price exceeds its total unit variable cost. This excess amount contributes to covering fixed costs and generating profits on a per unit basis. Exhibit 18.18 shows the unit contribution margin formula.

Exhibit 18.18

Unit Contribution Margin

$$\textbf{Unit contribution margin} = \textbf{Sales price per unit} - \textbf{Total variable cost per unit}$$

Users often use contribution margin in the form of a **contribution margin ratio,** which is the percent of a unit's selling price that exceeds total unit variable cost. It can be interpreted as the percent of each sales dollar that remains after deducting total unit variable cost. Exhibit 18.19 shows the formula for the contribution margin ratio.

Exhibit 18.19

Contribution Margin Ratio

$$\textbf{Contribution margin ratio} = \frac{\textbf{Unit contribution margin}}{\textbf{Sales price per unit}}$$

We use Rocky Mountain Bikes' Tracker® product to show the usefulness of these measures. The selling price of a Tracker mountain bike is $450, and the variable costs of its manufacturing and marketing are $200. The contribution margin per bike is computed as $250 ($450 − $200). This measure is useful to managers in determining the money contributed by the sale of each Tracker bike to both (1) fixed costs and (2) net income. Specifically, each sale of a Tracker bike yields a $250 contribution margin to cover fixed costs of Rocky Mountain Bikes. Once fixed costs are covered, net income is left.

We also compute the Tracker mountain bike's contribution margin ratio as 55.55% ($250/$450). This information is useful to managers working with estimates of sales in dollars. Specifically, approximately 56¢ (or 55.55%) of each sales dollar is available as contribution to fixed costs and profits. The contribution margin ratio is also useful in cost-volume-profit (CVP) analysis, a method we use to assess the volume of activity necessary to achieve different performance levels (including income, loss, and breakeven points). We explain CVP analysis in Chapter 22.

Decision Maker

Sales Manager You are evaluating orders from two customers but can accept only one of the orders because of your company's limited capacity. The first order is for 100 units of a product with a contribution margin ratio of 60% and a selling price of $1,000. The second order is for 500 units of a product with a contribution margin ratio of 20% and a selling price of $800. The incremental fixed costs are the same for both orders. Which order do you accept?

Answer—p. 735

Demonstration Problem 1: Cost Behavior

Understanding the classification and assignment of costs is important. Consider the following company, **Chip Making Systems,** that manufactures computer chips. It incurs the following costs in manufacturing chips and in operating the company:

1. Plastic board used to mount the chip, $3.50 each.
2. Assembly worker pay of $15 per hour to attach chips to plastic board.
3. Salary for factory maintenance workers who maintain factory equipment.
4. Factory supervisor pay of $55,000 per year to supervise employees.
5. Real estate taxes paid on the factory, $14,500.
6. Real estate taxes paid on the company office, $6,000.
7. Depreciation costs on machinery used by workers, $30,000.
8. Salary paid to the chief financial officer, $95,000.
9. Advertising costs of $7,800 paid to promote products.
10. Salespersons' commissions of $0.50 for each assembled chip sold.
11. CMS could rent the manufacturing plant to store medical records for six local hospitals instead of producing and assembling chips.

Classify each cost in the following table according to the categories listed across the top. A cost can be classified under more than one category. The plastic board used to mount chips, for instance, is classified as a direct material product cost and as a direct unit cost.

	Period Costs	Product Costs			Unit Cost Classification		Sunk Cost	Opportunity Cost
Cost	Selling and Administrative	Direct Material (prime cost)	Direct Labor (prime and conversion)	Factory Overhead (conversion cost)	Direct	Indirect		
1. Plastic board used to mount the chip, $3.50 each		✔			✔			

Solution to Demonstration Problem 1

	Period Costs	Product Costs			Unit Cost Classification		Sunk Cost	Opportunity Cost
Cost*	Selling and Administrative	Direct Material (prime cost)	Direct Labor (prime and conversion)	Factory Overhead (conversion cost)	Direct	Indirect		
1.		✔			✔			
2.			✔		✔			
3.				✔		✔		
4.				✔		✔		
5.				✔		✔		
6.	✔							
7.				✔		✔	✔	
8.	✔							
9.	✔							
10.	✔							
11.								✔

* Costs 1 through 11 refer to the 11 cost items described at the beginning of the problem.

Demonstration Problem 2: Reporting for Manufacturers

A manufacturing company's balance sheet and income statement differ from those for a merchandising or service company.

Required

1. Fill in the [BLANKS] on the partial balance sheets for both the manufacturing company and the merchandising company. Explain why a different presentation is required.

Manufacturing Company

CHIP MAKING SYSTEMS Partial Balance Sheet December 31, 2005	
Current assets	
Cash	$10,000
[BLANK]	8,000
[BLANK]	5,000
[BLANK]	7,000
Supplies	500
Prepaid insurance	500
Total current assets	$31,000

Merchandising Company

PAYLESS SHOE OUTLET Partial Balance Sheet December 31, 2005	
Current assets	
Cash	$ 5,000
[BLANK]	12,000
Supplies	500
Prepaid insurance	500
Total current assets	$18,000

2. Fill in the [BLANKS] on the income statements for the manufacturing company and the merchandising company. Explain why a different presentation is required.

Manufacturing Company

CHIP MAKING SYSTEMS Partial Income Statement For Year Ended December 31, 2005	
Sales	$200,000
Cost of goods sold	
Finished goods inventory, Dec. 31, 2004	10,000
[BLANK]	120,000
Goods available for sale	130,000
Finished goods inventory, Dec. 31, 2005	(7,000)
Cost of goods sold	123,000
Gross profit	$ 77,000

Merchandising Company

PAYLESS SHOE OUTLET Partial Income Statement For Year Ended December 31, 2005	
Sales	$190,000
Cost of goods sold	
Merchandise inventory, Dec. 31, 2004	8,000
[BLANK]	108,000
Net purchases	116,000
Merchandise inventory, Dec. 31, 2005	(12,000)
Cost of goods sold	104,000
Gross profit	$ 86,000

3. The manufacturer's cost of goods manufactured is the sum of (a) _______, (b) _______, and (c) _______ costs incurred in producing the product.

Solution to Demonstration Problem 2

1. Inventories for a manufacturer and for a merchandiser.

Manufacturing Company

CHIP MAKING SYSTEMS Partial Balance Sheet December 31, 2005	
Current assets	
Cash	$10,000
Raw materials inventory	8,000
Goods in process inventory	5,000
Finished goods inventory	7,000
Supplies	500
Prepaid insurance	500
Total current assets	$31,000

Merchandising Company

PAYLESS SHOE OUTLET Partial Balance Sheet December 31, 2005	
Current assets	
Cash	$ 5,000
Merchandise inventory	12,000
Supplies	500
Prepaid insurance	500
Total current assets	$18,000

Explanation: A manufacturing company must control and measure three types of inventories: raw materials, goods in process, and finished goods. In the sequence of making a product, the raw materials move into production—called *goods in process inventory*—and then to finished goods. All raw materials and goods in process inventory at the end of each accounting period are considered current assets. All unsold finished inventory is considered a current asset at the end of each accounting period. The merchandising company must control and measure only one type of inventory, purchased goods.

2. Cost of goods sold for a manufacturer and for a merchandiser.

Manufacturing Company

CHIP MAKING SYSTEMS Partial Income Statement For Year Ended December 31, 2005	
Sales	$200,000
Cost of goods sold	
Finished goods inventory, Dec. 31, 2004	10,000
Cost of goods manufactured	120,000
Goods available for sale	130,000
Finished goods inventory, Dec. 31, 2005	(7,000)
Cost of goods sold	123,000
Gross profit	$ 77,000

Merchandising Company

PAYLESS SHOE OUTLET Partial Income Statement For Year Ended December 31, 2005	
Sales	$190,000
Cost of goods sold	
Merchandise inventory, Dec. 31, 2004	8,000
Cost of purchases	108,000
Net purchases	116,000
Merchandise inventory, Dec. 31, 2005	(12,000)
Cost of goods sold	104,000
Gross profit	$ 86,000

Explanation: Manufacturing and merchandising companies use different reporting terms. In particular, the terms *finished goods* and *cost of goods manufactured* are used to reflect the production of goods, yet the concepts and techniques of reporting cost of goods sold for a manufacturing company and merchandising company are similar.

3. A manufacturer's cost of goods manufactured is the sum of (a) *direct material,* (b) *direct labor,* and (c) *factory overhead* costs incurred in producing the product.

Demonstration Problem 3: Manufacturing Statement

The following account balances and other information are from SUNN Corporation's accounting records for year-end December 31, 2005. Use this information to prepare (1) a table listing factory overhead costs, (2) a manufacturing statement (show only the total factory overhead cost), and (3) an income statement.

Advertising expense	$ 85,000	Goods in process inventory, Dec. 31, 2004	$ 8,000
Amortization expense—Patents	16,000	Goods in process inventory, Dec. 31, 2005	9,000
Bad debts expense	28,000	Income taxes	53,400
Depreciation expense—Office equipment	37,000	Indirect labor	26,000
Depreciation expense—Factory building	133,000	Interest expense	25,000
Depreciation expense—Factory equipment	78,000	Miscellaneous expense	55,000
Direct labor	250,000	Property taxes on factory equipment	14,000
Factory insurance expired	62,000	Raw materials inventory, Dec. 31, 2004	60,000
Factory supervision	74,000	Raw materials inventory, Dec. 31, 2005	78,000
Factory supplies used	21,000	Raw materials purchases	313,000
Factory utilities	115,000	Repairs expense—Factory equipment	31,000
Finished goods inventory, Dec. 31, 2004	15,000	Salaries expense	150,000
Finished goods inventory, Dec. 31, 2005	12,500	Sales	1,630,000

Planning the Solution

- Analyze the account balances and select those that are part of factory overhead costs.
- Arrange these costs in a table that lists factory overhead costs for the year.
- Analyze the remaining costs and select those related to production activity for the year; selected costs should include the materials and goods in process inventories and direct labor.
- Prepare a manufacturing statement for the year showing the calculation of the cost of materials used in production, the cost of direct labor, and the total factory overhead cost. When presenting overhead cost on this statement, report only total overhead cost from the table of overhead costs for the year. Show the costs of beginning and ending goods in process inventory to determine cost of goods manufactured.
- Organize the remaining revenue and expense items into the income statement for the year. Combine cost of goods manufactured from the manufacturing statement with the finished goods inventory amounts to compute cost of goods sold for the year.

Solution to Demonstration Problem 3

SUNN CORPORATION
Factory Overhead Costs
For Year Ended December 31, 2005

Amortization expense—Patents	$ 16,000
Depreciation expense—Factory building	133,000
Depreciation expense—Factory equipment	78,000
Factory insurance expired	62,000
Factory supervision	74,000
Factory supplies used	21,000

[continued on next page]

SUNN CORPORATION
Manufacturing Statement
For Year Ended December 31, 2005

Direct materials	
Raw materials inventory, Dec. 31, 2004	$ 60,000
Raw materials purchase	313,000
Raw materials available for use	373,000
Less raw materials inventory, Dec. 31, 2005	78,000
Direct materials used	295,000

[continued from previous page]

Factory utilities	115,000
Indirect labor	26,000
Property taxes on factory equipment	14,000
Repairs expense—Factory equipment	31,000
Total factory overhead	$570,000

Direct labor	250,000
Factory overhead	570,000
Total manufacturing costs	1,115,000
Goods in process inventory, Dec. 31, 2004	8,000
Total cost of goods in process	1,123,000
Less goods in process inventory, Dec. 31, 2005	9,000
Cost of goods manufactured	$1,114,000

SUNN CORPORATION
Income Statement
For Year Ended December 31, 2005

Sales		$1,630,000
Cost of goods sold		
Finished goods inventory, Dec. 31, 2004	$ 15,000	
Cost of goods manufactured	1,114,000	
Goods available for sale	1,129,000	
Less finished goods inventory, Dec. 31, 2005	12,500	
Cost of goods sold		1,116,500
Gross profit		513,500
Operating expenses		
Advertising expense	85,000	
Bad debts expense	28,000	
Depreciation expense—Office equipment	37,000	
Interest expense	25,000	
Miscellaneous expense	55,000	
Salaries expense	150,000	
Total operating expenses		380,000
Income before income taxes		133,500
Income taxes		53,400
Net income		$ 80,100

Summary

C1 **Explain the purpose of managerial accounting.** The purpose of managerial accounting is to provide useful information to management and other internal decision makers. It does this by collecting, managing, and reporting both monetary and nonmonetary information in a manner useful to internal users.

C2 **Describe major characteristics of managerial accounting.** Major characteristics of managerial accounting include (1) focus on internal decision makers, (2) emphasis on planning and control, (3) flexibility, (4) timeliness, (5) reliance on forecasts and estimates, (6) focus on segments and projects, and (7) reporting both monetary and nonmonetary information.

C3 **Describe the lean business model.** The main purpose of the lean business model is the elimination of waste. Concepts such as total quality management and just-in-time production often aid in effective application of the model.

C4 **Describe accounting concepts useful in classifying costs.** We can classify costs on the basis of their (1) behavior—fixed vs. variable, (2) traceability—direct vs. indirect, (3) controllability—controllable vs. uncontrollable, (4) relevance—sunk vs. out of pocket, and (5) function—product vs. period. A cost can be classified in more than one way, depending on the purpose for which the cost is being determined. These classifications help to understand cost patterns, analyze performance, and plan operations.

C5 **Define product and period costs and explain how they impact financial statements.** Costs that are capitalized because they are expected to have future value are called *product costs;* costs that are expensed are called *period costs.* This classification is important because it affects the amount of costs expensed in the income statement and the amount of costs assigned to inventory on the balance sheet. Product costs are commonly made up of direct materials, direct labor, and overhead. Period costs include selling and administrative expenses.

C6 **Explain how the balance sheets for manufacturing and merchandising companies differ.** The main difference is that manufacturers usually carry three inventories—raw materials, goods in process, and finished goods—instead of one inventory that merchandisers carry.

C7 **Explain how income statements for manufacturing and merchandising companies differ.** The main difference between income statements of manufacturers and merchandisers is the items making up cost of goods sold. A merchandiser adds beginning merchandise inventory to cost of goods purchased and then subtracts ending merchandise inventory to get cost of goods sold. A manufacturer adds beginning finished goods inventory to cost of goods manufactured and then subtracts ending finished goods inventory to get cost of goods sold.

C8 **Explain manufacturing activities and the flow of manufacturing costs.** Manufacturing activities consist of materials, production, and sales activities. The materials activity consists of the purchase and issuance of materials to production. The production activity consists of converting materials into finished goods. At this stage in the process, the materials, labor, and overhead costs have been incurred and the manufacturing statement is prepared. The sales activity consists of selling some or all of finished goods available for sale. At this stage, the cost of goods sold is determined.

A1 **Compute unit contribution margin and describe what it reveals about a company's cost structure.** Unit contribution margin is a product's sales price less its total variable costs. Contribution margin ratio is a product's unit contribution margin divided by its sales price. Unit contribution margin is the amount received from each sale that contributes to fixed costs and income. The contribution margin ratio reveals what portion of each sales dollar is available as contribution to fixed costs and income.

P1 **Compute cost of goods sold for a manufacturer.** A manufacturer adds beginning finished goods inventory to cost of goods manufactured and then subtracts ending finished goods inventory to get cost of goods sold.

P2 **Prepare a manufacturing statement and explain its purpose and links to financial statements.** The manufacturing statement reports computation of cost of goods manufactured for the period. It begins by showing the period's costs for direct materials, direct labor, and overhead and then adjusts these numbers for the beginning and ending inventories of the goods in process to yield cost of goods manufactured.

Guidance Answers to **Decision Maker** and **Decision Ethics**

Production Supervisor It appears that all three friends want to pay the bill with someone else's money. David is using money belonging to the tax authorities, Denise is taking money from her company, and Derek is defrauding the government. To prevent such practices, companies have internal audit mechanisms. Many companies also adopt ethical codes of conduct to help guide employees. We must recognize that some entertainment expenses are justifiable and even encouraged. For example, the tax law allows certain deductions for entertainment that have a business purpose. Corporate policies also sometimes allow and encourage reimbursable spending for social activities, and government contracts can include entertainment as allowable costs. Nevertheless, without further details, payment for this bill should be made from personal accounts.

Division Manager You need information pertaining to the costs of making it in-house: direct materials, direct labor, and overhead. You also need information about investments in machinery required to make the component. Regarding the possibility of continuing to buy from the outside, you need information about costs of the outside purchase: price of components, costs to place the order, and costs to receive and store components. You must also consider nonfinancial factors such as quality of components currently supplied and the quality of in-house production.

Entrepreneur Tracing all costs directly to cost objects is always desirable, but you need to be able to do so in an economically feasible manner. In this case, you are able to trace 90% of the assembly department's direct costs. It may not be economical to spend more money on a new software to trace the final 10% of costs. You need to make a cost-benefit trade-off. If the software offers benefits beyond tracing the remaining 10% of the assembly department's costs, your decision should consider this.

Purchase Manager Opportunity costs relate to the potential quality and delivery benefits given up by not choosing supplier (A). Selecting supplier (B) might involve future costs of poor-quality seats (inspection, repairs, and returns). Also, potential delivery delays could interrupt work and increase manufacturing costs. Your company could also incur sales losses if the product quality of supplier (B) is low. As purchase manager, you are responsible for these costs and must consider them in making your decision.

Sales Manager The contribution margin for the first order is $600 per unit (60% of $1,000); the contribution margin per unit for the second order is $160 (20% of $800). You are likely tempted to accept the first order based on its high contribution margin per unit, but you must compute total contribution margin based on the number of units sold for each order. Total contribution margin is $60,000 ($600 per unit × 100 units) and $80,000 ($160 per unit × 500 units) for the two orders, respectively. The second order provides the largest return in absolute dollars and is the order you would accept. Another factor to consider in your selection is the potential for a long-term relationship with these customers including repeat sales and growth.

Guidance Answers to **Quick Checks**

1. *d*
2. Financial accounting information is intended for users external to an organization such as investors, creditors, and government authorities. Managerial accounting focuses on providing information to managers, officers, and other decision makers within the organization.
3. No, GAAP do not control the practice of managerial accounting. Unlike external users, the internal users need managerial accounting information for planning and controlling business activities rather than for external comparison. Different types of information are required, depending on the activity. Therefore it is difficult to standardize managerial accounting.

4. Under TQM, all managers and employees should strive toward higher standards in their work and in the products and services they offer to customers.
5. Variable costs increase when volume of activity increases.
6. By being able to trace costs to cost objects (say, to products and departments), managers better understand the total costs associated with a cost object. This is useful when managers consider making changes to the cost object (such as when dropping the product or expanding the department).
7. Raw materials inventory, goods in process inventory, and finished goods inventory.
8. The cost of goods sold for merchandising companies includes all costs of acquiring the merchandise; the cost of goods sold for manufacturing companies includes the three costs of manufacturing: direct materials, direct labor, and overhead.
9. *a*
10. No; companies rarely report a manufacturing statement.
11. Beginning goods in process inventory is added to total manufacturing costs to yield total goods in process. Ending goods in process inventory is subtracted from total goods in process to yield cost of goods manufactured for the period.

Key Terms

Key Terms are available at the book's Website for learning and testing in an online Flashcard Format.

Continuous improvement (p. 718)
Contribution margin ratio (p. 729)
Control (p. 715)
Controllable or not controllable cost (p. 720)
Conversion costs (p. 725)
Cost object (p. 719)
Customer orientation (p. 717)
Direct costs (p. 719)
Direct labor (p. 725)
Direct labor costs (p. 725)
Direct material (p. 724)
Direct material costs (p. 724)
Factory overhead (p. 725)
Factory overhead costs (p. 725)
Finished goods inventory (p. 723)
Fixed cost (p. 719)
Goods in process inventory (p. 723)
Indirect costs (p. 719)
Indirect labor (p. 725)
Indirect labor costs (p. 725)
Indirect material (p. 722)
Just-in-time (JIT) manufacturing (p. 718)
Lean business model (p. 718)
Managerial accounting (p. 714)
Manufacturing statement (p. 727)
Opportunity cost (p. 720)
Out-of-pocket cost (p. 720)
Period costs (p. 720)
Planning (p. 714)
Prime costs (p. 725)
Product costs (p. 720)
Raw materials inventory (p. 722)
Sunk cost (p. 720)
Total quality management (TQM) (p. 718)
Unit contribution margin (p. 729)
Value chain (p. 726)
Variable cost (p. 719)

Personal Interactive Quiz

Personal Interactive Quizzes A and B are available at the book's Website to reinforce and assess your learning.

Discussion Questions

1. Discuss the managerial accountant's role in business planning, control, and decision making.
2. Distinguish between managerial and financial accounting on
   a. Users and decision makers
   b. Purpose of information
   c. Flexibility of practice
   d. Time dimension
   e. Focus of information
3. Identify the usual changes that a company must make when it adopts a customer orientation.
4. Distinguish between direct material and indirect material.
5. Distinguish between direct labor and indirect labor.
6. Distinguish between factory overhead and selling and administrative overhead.
7. What product cost is listed as both a prime cost and a conversion cost?
8. Assume that you tour Tastykake's factory where it makes its line of bakery items. List three direct costs and three indirect costs you are likely to see.

9. Should we evaluate a manager's performance on the basis of controllable or noncontrollable costs? Why?
10. Explain why knowledge of cost behavior is useful in product performance evaluation.

11. Explain why product costs are capitalized but period costs are expensed in the current accounting period.

12. Explain how business activities and inventories for a manufacturing company, a merchandising company, and a service company differ.

13. Why does managerial accounting often involve working with numerous predictions and estimates?

14. How do an income statement and a balance sheet for a manufacturing company and a merchandising company differ?

15. Refer to Appendix A and identify **Krispy Kreme**'s five inventory components (see its note 4) and reconcile this total to the amount reported on its balance sheet.

16. Besides inventories, what other assets often appear on manufacturers' balance sheets but not on merchandisers' balance sheets?

17. Why does a manufacturing company require three different inventory categories?

18. Manufacturing activities of a company are described in the ________. This statement summarizes the types and amounts of costs incurred in a company's manufacturing ________.

19. What are the three categories of manufacturing costs?

20. List several examples of factory overhead.

21. List the four components of a manufacturing statement and provide specific examples of each for **Harley-Davidson**. **Harley-Davidson**

22. Prepare a proper title for the annual "manufacturing" statement of **Harley-Davidson**. Does the date match the balance sheet or income statement? Why? **Harley-Davidson**

23. Describe the relations among the income statement, the manufacturing statement, and a detailed listing of factory overhead costs.

24. Define and describe *unit contribution margin.*

25. Define and explain the *contribution margin ratio.*

26. Describe the contribution margin ratio in layperson's terms.

27. Why is the contribution margin ratio a useful measure for **Krispy Kreme** in deciding what products to manufacture?

Red numbers denote Discussion Questions that involve decision-making.

***Homework Manager** repeats all numerical Quick Studies on the book's Website with new numbers.*

QUICK STUDY

QS 18-1
Managerial accounting defined
C1

Managerial accounting (choose one):

1. Must follow generally accepted accounting principles.
2. Provides information to aid management in planning and controlling business activities.
3. Is directed at reporting aggregate data on the company as a whole.
4. Provides information that is widely available to all interested parties.

QS 18-2
Managerial accounting versus financial accounting
C2

Identify whether each description most likely applies to managerial or financial accounting:

1. ________ Its primary focus is on the organization as a whole.
2. ________ Its principles and practices are very flexible.
3. ________ It is directed at external users in making investment, credit, and other decisions.
4. ________ Its primary users are company managers.
5. ________ Its information is often available only after an audit is complete.

QS 18-3
Lean business concepts
C3

Match each lean business concept with its best description by entering its letter in the blank:

1. ________ Customer orientation
2. ________ Total quality management
3. ________ Just-in-time manufacturing
4. ________ Continuous improvements

A. Inventory is acquired or produced only as needed.
B. Flexible product designs can be modified to accommodate customer choices.
C. Every manager and employee constantly looks for ways to improve company operations.
D. Focuses on quality throughout the production process.

QS 18-4
Fixed and variable costs
C4

Which of these statements is true regarding fixed and variable costs?

1. Fixed costs increase and variable costs decrease in total as activity volume decreases.
2. Fixed costs stay the same and variable costs increase in total as activity volume increases.
3. Both fixed and variable costs increase as activity volume increases.
4. Both fixed and variable costs stay the same in total as activity volume increases.

QS 18-5
Product and period costs
C5

Which of these statements is true regarding product and period costs?

1. Sales commission is a product cost and factory rent is a period cost.
2. Factory wages is a product cost and direct material is a period cost.
3. Factory maintenance is a product cost and sales commission is a period cost.
4. Sales commission is a product cost and depreciation on factory equipment is a product cost.

QS 18-6
Inventory reporting for manufacturers
C6

Three inventory categories are reported on a manufacturing company's balance sheet: (a) raw materials, (b) goods in process, and (c) finished goods. Identify the usual order in which these inventory items are reported on a balance sheet.

1. (a)(b)(c) 2. (b)(a)(c) 3. (b)(c)(a) 4. (c)(b)(a)

QS 18-7
Cost of goods sold P1

A company has year-end cost of goods manufactured of $5,000, beginning finished goods inventory of $700, and ending finished goods inventory of $850. Its cost of goods sold is

1. $4,250 2. $4,000 3. $4,850 4. $6,550

QS 18-8
Manufacturing flows identified
C8

Identify the usual sequence of manufacturing activities by filling in the blank (1, 2, or 3) corresponding to its order: _______ Production activities; _______ Sales activities; _______ Materials activities.

QS 18-9
Cost of goods manufactured
P2

Prepare the manufacturing statement for Triton Company using the following information.

Direct materials	$192,500
Direct labor	65,150
Factory overhead costs	26,000
Goods in process, Dec. 31, 2004	159,600
Goods in process, Dec. 31, 2005	144,750

QS 18-10
Contribution margin ratio A1

Compute and interpret the contribution margin ratio using the following data: sales, $6,000; total variable cost, $4,000.

QS 18-11
Cost of goods sold
P1

Compute cost of goods sold for year 2005 using the following information.

Finished goods inventory, Dec. 31, 2004	$321,500
Goods in process inventory, Dec. 31, 2004	74,550
Goods in process inventory, Dec. 31, 2005	81,200
Cost of goods manufactured, year 2005	972,345
Finished goods inventory, Dec. 31, 2005	297,200

***Homework Manager** repeats all numerical Exercises on the book's Website with new numbers.*

EXERCISES

Exercise 18-1
Sources of accounting information
C1

Both managerial accounting and financial accounting provide useful information to decision makers. Indicate in this chart the most likely source of information for each business decision (a decision can require major input from both sources):

Business Decision	Primary Information Source: Managerial	Primary Information Source: Financial
Estimate product cost for a new line of basketball shoes	____	____
Plan the budget for next quarter	____	____
Report financial performance to the board of directors	____	____
Measure profitability of all individual stores	____	____
Prepare financial reports according to GAAP	____	____
Determine amount of dividends to pay common stockholders	____	____
Determine location and size for a new plant	____	____
Evaluate a purchasing department's performance	____	____

Exercise 18-2
Planning and control descriptions
C1

Complete the following statements by filling in the blanks:

1. ______ is the process of setting goals and making plans to achieve them.
2. ______ ______ usually covers a period of 5 to 10 years.
3. ______ ______ usually covers a period of one year.
4. ______ is the process of monitoring planning decisions and evaluating an organization's activities and employees.

Exercise 18-3
Characteristics of financial accounting and managerial accounting
C2

In the following chart, compare financial accounting and managerial accounting by describing how each differs for the items listed. Be specific in your responses.

	Financial Accounting	Managerial Accounting
1. Users and decision makers	____	____
2. Purpose of information	____	____
3. Flexibility of practice	____	____
4. Timeliness of information	____	____
5. Time dimension	____	____
6. Focus of information	____	____
7. Nature of information	____	____

Exercise 18-4
Customer orientation in practice
C3

Customer orientation means that a company's managers and employees respond to customers' changing wants and needs. You are to stop at a restaurant, hotel, or other local business in your area and pick up a customer response card. (1) On the right hand side of a sheet of paper, write the usual competitive forces: time, quality, cost, and flexibility of service. Attach the customer response card to the left side of the sheet. Draw arrows linking questions on the customer response card to the competitive forces. (2) Identify how the response card provides information to management and employees to better meet competitive forces. Be prepared to form small groups to compare and contrast customer response cards across the types of businesses.

Exercise 18-5
Management concepts
C3

Following are three separate events affecting the managerial accounting systems for different companies. Match the management concept(s) that the company is likely to adopt for the event identified. There is some overlap in the meaning of customer orientation and total quality management and, therefore, some responses can include more than one concept.

Event	Management Concept
______ 1. The company starts measuring inventory turnover and discontinues elaborate inventory records. Its new focus is to pull inventory through the system.	a. Total quality management (TQM)
______ 2. The company starts reporting measures on customer complaints and product returns from customers.	b. Just-in-time (JIT) system
______ 3. The company starts reporting measures such as the percent of defective products and the number of units scrapped.	c. Continuous improvement (CI)
	d. Customer orientation (CO)

Exercise 18-6
Cost analysis and identification
C4 C5

Johnson & Johnson, a manufacturing company, incurs the following costs. (1) Classify each cost as either a product or a period cost. If a product cost, identify it as a prime and/or conversion cost. (2) Classify each cost as either a direct cost or an indirect cost using the product as the cost object.

Cost	Product Cost		Period Cost	Direct Cost	Indirect Cost
	Prime	Conversion			
Direct materials used	____	____	____	____	____
State and federal income taxes	____	____	____	____	____
Payroll taxes for production supervisor	____	____	____	____	____
Amortization of patents on factory machine . . .	____	____	____	____	____

[continued on next page]

[continued from previous page]

Accident insurance on factory workers	___	___	___	___	___
Wages to assembly workers	___	___	___	___	___
Factory utilities	___	___	___	___	___
Small tools used	___	___	___	___	___
Bad debts expense	___	___	___	___	___
Depreciation—Factory building	___	___	___	___	___
Advertising	___	___	___	___	___
Office supplies used	___	___	___	___	___

Exercise 18-7
Cost classifications C4

(1) Identify each of the five cost classifications discussed in the chapter. (2) List two purposes of identifying these separate cost classifications.

Exercise 18-8
Cost analysis and classification
C4

Listed here are product costs for the production of soccer balls. (1) Classify each cost (a) as either fixed or variable and (b) as either direct or indirect. (2) What pattern do you see regarding the relation between costs classified by behavior and costs classified by traceability?

	Cost by Behavior		Cost by Traceability	
Product Cost	**Variable**	**Fixed**	**Direct**	**Indirect**
Leather cover for soccer balls	___	___	___	___
Lace to hold leather together	___	___	___	___
Wages of assembly workers	___	___	___	___
Taxes on factory	___	___	___	___
Annual flat fee paid for office security	___	___	___	___
Coolants for machinery	___	___	___	___
Machinery depreciation	___	___	___	___

Exercise 18-9
Balance sheet identification and preparation
C6

Current assets for two different companies at calendar year-end 2005 are listed here. One is a manufacturer, Roller Blades Mfg., and the other, Sun Fresh Foods, is a grocery distribution company. (1) Identify which set of numbers relates to the manufacturer and which to the merchandiser. (2) Prepare the current asset section for each company from this information. Discuss why the current asset section for these two companies is different.

Account	Company 1	Company 2
Cash	$ 9,000	$ 7,000
Raw materials inventory	—	44,000
Merchandise inventory	47,000	—
Goods in process inventory	—	32,000
Finished goods inventory	—	52,000
Accounts receivable, net	64,000	77,000
Prepaid expenses	3,500	700

Exercise 18-10
Cost of goods sold computation
C7 P1

Compute cost of goods sold for each of these two companies for the year ended December 31, 2005:

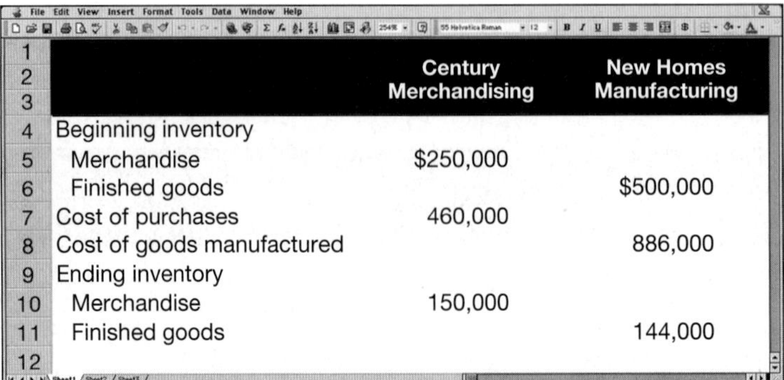

	Century Merchandising	New Homes Manufacturing
Beginning inventory		
Merchandise	$250,000	
Finished goods		$500,000
Cost of purchases	460,000	
Cost of goods manufactured		886,000
Ending inventory		
Merchandise	150,000	
Finished goods		144,000

Check Century COGS, $560,000

Exercise 18-11
Cost of goods manufactured and cost of goods sold computation
P1 P2

Using the following data, compute (1) the cost of goods manufactured and (2) the cost of goods sold for both Canyon Company and Crossings Company.

	Canyon Company	Crossings Company
Beginning finished goods inventory	$14,000	$18,450
Beginning goods in process inventory	16,500	21,950
Beginning raw materials inventory	9,250	11,000
Rental cost on factory equipment	29,000	24,750
Direct labor	21,000	37,000
Ending finished goods inventory	19,650	15,300
Ending goods in process inventory	24,000	18,000
Ending raw materials inventory	7,300	9,200
Factory utilities	11,000	14,000
Factory supplies used	10,200	5,200
General and administrative expenses	23,000	45,000
Indirect labor	3,250	9,660
Repairs—Factory equipment	6,780	3,500
Raw materials purchases	35,000	54,000
Sales salaries	52,000	48,000

Check Canyon COGS, $105,030

Exercise 18-12
Components of accounting reports
C8 P2

For each of the following account balances for a manufacturing company, place a ✔ in the appropriate column indicating that it appears on the balance sheet, the income statement, the manufacturing statement, and/or a detailed listing of factory overhead costs. Assume that the income statement shows the calculation of cost of goods sold and the manufacturing statement shows only the total amount of factory overhead. *(An account balance can appear on more than one report.)*

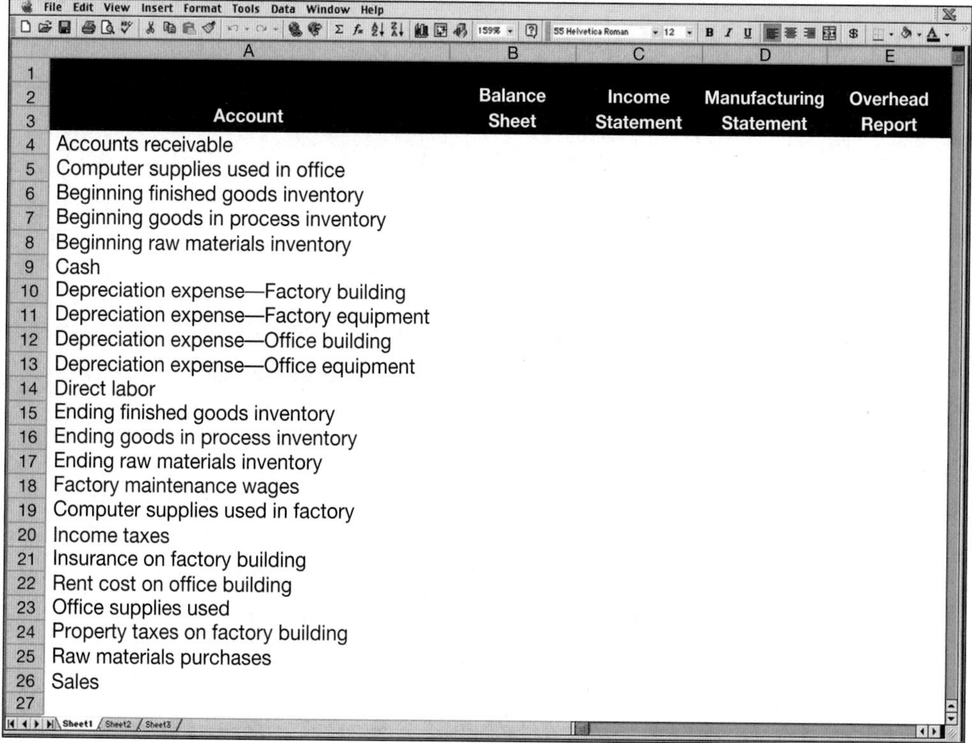

Account	Balance Sheet	Income Statement	Manufacturing Statement	Overhead Report
Accounts receivable				
Computer supplies used in office				
Beginning finished goods inventory				
Beginning goods in process inventory				
Beginning raw materials inventory				
Cash				
Depreciation expense—Factory building				
Depreciation expense—Factory equipment				
Depreciation expense—Office building				
Depreciation expense—Office equipment				
Direct labor				
Ending finished goods inventory				
Ending goods in process inventory				
Ending raw materials inventory				
Factory maintenance wages				
Computer supplies used in factory				
Income taxes				
Insurance on factory building				
Rent cost on office building				
Office supplies used				
Property taxes on factory building				
Raw materials purchases				
Sales				

Exercise 18-13
Manufacturing statement preparation P2

Given the following selected account balances of Randa Company, prepare its manufacturing statement in proper form for the year ended on December 31, 2005. Include a listing of the individual overhead account balances in this statement.

Sales	$1,252,000
Raw materials inventory, Dec. 31, 2004	39,000
Goods in process inventory, Dec. 31, 2004	55,900
Finished goods inventory, Dec. 31, 2004	64,750
Raw materials purchases	177,600
Direct labor	227,000
Factory computer supplies used	19,840
Indirect labor	49,000
Repairs—Factory equipment	7,250
Rent cost of factory building	59,000
Advertising expenses	96,000
General and administrative expenses	131,300
Raw materials inventory, Dec. 31, 2005	44,700
Goods in process inventory, Dec. 31, 2005	43,500
Finished goods inventory, Dec. 31, 2005	69,300

Check Cost of goods manufactured, $546,390

Exercise 18-14
Income statement preparation P2

Use the information in Exercise 18-13 to prepare an income statement for Randa Company (a manufacturer). Assume that its cost of goods manufactured is $546,390.

Exercise 18-15
Cost flows in manufacturing
C8 P2

The following chart shows how costs flow through a business as a product is manufactured. Some boxes in the flowchart show cost amount. Compute the cost amounts for boxes that contain question marks.

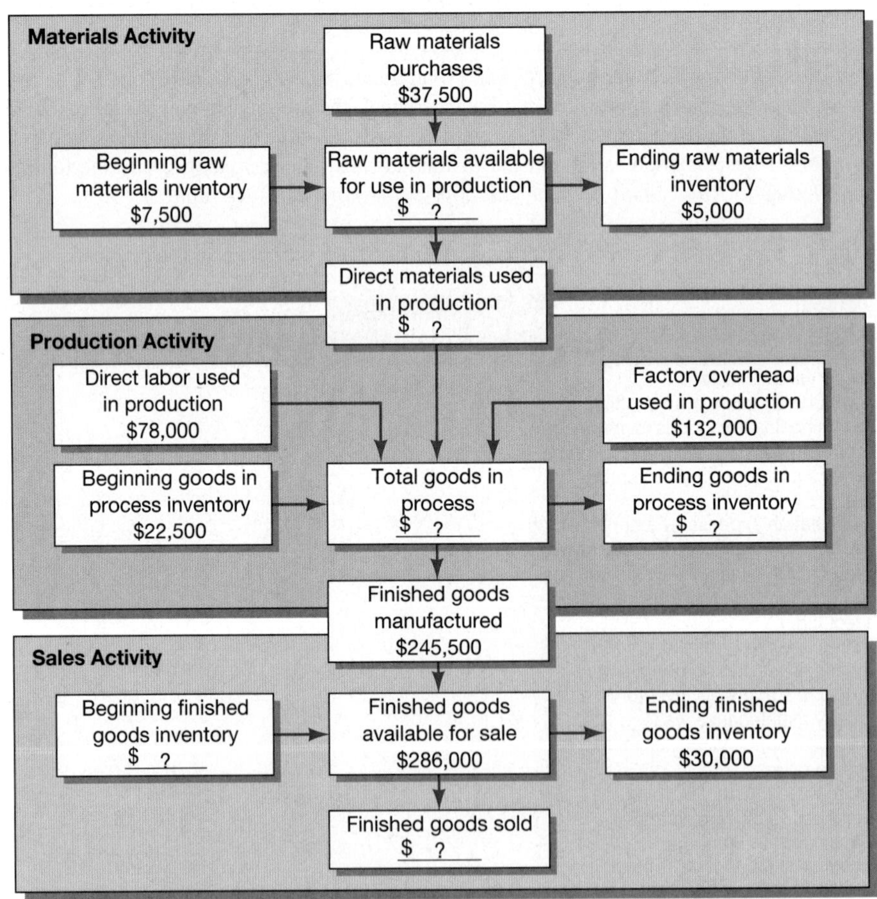

PROBLEM SET A

Problem 18-1A
Managerial accountant's role
C1 C3

This chapter discusses the purposes of managerial accounting and the current business environment. You are to look through the *automobile* section of your local newspaper; the Sunday paper is often best. Review advertisements of sport utility vehicles and note how many manufacturers offer these products and the factors on which they compete.

Required

Discuss the potential contributions and responsibilities of the managerial accounting professional in helping an automobile manufacturer succeed. (*Hint:* Think about information and estimates that a managerial accountant might provide new entrants into the sports utility market.)

Problem 18-2A
Lean business concepts
C3

A trip through a drive-up window of any leading fast-food restaurant is useful in understanding concepts such as total quality management (TQM), just-in-time (JIT), and continuous improvement (CI). Each restaurant can be viewed as a small manufacturing center. List two fast-food restaurants you are familiar with in the first column of the following table (e.g., McDonald's, Taco Bell, Burger King, and KFC). Record in the table how each company is putting each of these lean business concepts into action, both favorably and unfavorably.

Restaurant	TQM	JIT	CI
1.			
2.			

Problem 18-3A
Cost computation, classification, and analysis; contribution margin income statement
C4 A1

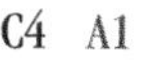

Listed here are the total costs associated with the production of 1,000 drum sets manufactured by NeatBeat. The drum sets sell for $300 each.

	Cost by Behavior		Cost by Function	
Costs	Variable	Fixed	Product	Period
Plastic for casing—$12,000	$12,000		$12,000	
Wages of assembly workers—$60,000				
Property taxes on factory—$4,500				
Accounting staff salaries—$45,000				
Drum stands (1,000 stands outsourced)—$25,000				
Rent cost of equipment for sales staff—$7,000				
Upper management salaries—$100,000				
Annual flat fee for maintenance service—$9,000				
Sales commissions—$10 per unit				
Machinery depreciation—$10,000				

Required

1. Classify each cost and its amount as (a) either fixed or variable and (b) either product or period (the first cost is completed as an example).

2. Compute the (a) contribution margin and (b) contribution margin ratio by filling in the boxes in the following report:

NeatBeat
Contribution Margin Income Statement
For Year Ended December 31, 2005

Sales ($300 × 1,000)		$[ ]		100%
Variable costs				
Plastic for casing	$[ ]			
Assembly worker wages	[ ]			
Drum stands	[ ]			
Sales commissions	[ ]	[ ]		36%
Contribution margin		$[ ]	Contribution margin ratio*	[ ]%

* Contribution margin ratio = Contribution margin/Sales.

Check Total variable cost, $107,000

Analysis Component

3. Interpret the contribution margin and the contribution margin ratio.

Problem 18-4A
Cost classification and explanation
C4 C5

Assume that you must make a presentation to the marketing staff explaining the difference between product and period costs. Your supervisor tells you the marketing staff would also like clarification regarding prime and conversion costs and an explanation of how these terms fit with product and period cost. You are told that many on the staff are unable to classify costs in their merchandising activities.

Required

Prepare a one-page memorandum to your supervisor outlining your presentation to the marketing staff.

Problem 18-5A
Opportunity cost estimation and application
C1 C4 

Refer to *Decision Maker,* **Purchase Manager,** in this chapter. Assume that you are the motorcycle manufacturer's managerial accountant. The purchasing manager asks you about preparing an estimate of the related costs for buying motorcycle seats from supplier (B). She tells you this estimate is needed because unless dollar estimates are attached to nonfinancial factors, such as lost production time, her supervisor will not give it full attention. The purchasing manager also shows you this information:

- Production output is 3,000 motorcycles per year based on 250 production days a year.
- Production time per day is 8 hours at a cost of $2,000 per hour to run the production line.
- Lost production time due to poor quality is 1%.
- Satisfied customers purchase, on average, three motorcycles during a lifetime.
- Satisfied customers recommend the product, on average, to 10 other people.
- Marketing predicts that using seat (B) will result in 10 lost customers per year from repeat business and referrals.
- Average contribution margin per motorcycle is $3,000.

Required

Estimate the costs (including opportunity costs) of buying motorcycle seats from supplier (B). This problem requires you to think creatively and make reasonable estimates and, therefore, there could be more than one correct answer. (*Hint:* Reread the answer to *Decision Maker* and compare the cost savings for buying from supplier [B] to the sum of lost customer revenue from repeat business and referrals and the cost of lost production time.)

Check Cost of lost production time, $40,000

Problem 18-6A
Ending inventory computation and evaluation
C3 C6 

Shepler's Boot Company makes specialty boots for the rodeo circuit. On December 31, 2004, the company had (a) 500 pairs of boots in finished goods inventory and (b) 1,500 heels at a cost of $5 each in raw materials inventory. During 2005, the company purchased 50,000 additional heels at $5 each and manufactured 20,000 pairs of boots.

Required

1. Determine the unit and dollar amounts of raw materials inventory in heels at December 31, 2005.

Check (1) Ending (heel) inventory, $57,500 (11,500 units)

Analysis Component

2. Write a one-half page memorandum to the production manager explaining why a just-in-time inventory system for heels should be considered. Include the amount of working capital that can be reduced at December 31, 2005, if the ending heel raw material inventory is cut in half.

Problem 18-7A
Inventory computation and reporting
C4 C7 P1

mhhe.com/larson

Shown here are the annual financial data at December 31, 2005, taken from two different companies.

	Pinnacle Retail	Slope Board Manufacturing
Beginning inventory		
Merchandise	$150,000	
Finished goods		$300,000
Cost of purchases	250,000	
Cost of goods manufactured		586,000
Ending inventory		
Merchandise	100,000	
Finished goods		200,000

Required

1. Compute the cost of goods sold section of the income statement at December 31, 2005, for each company. Include proper title and format in the solution.

2. Write a half-page memorandum to your instructor (a) identifying the inventory accounts and (b) describing where each is reported on the income statement and balance sheet for both companies.

Check (1) Slope Board's cost of goods sold, $686,000

Problem 18-8A
Manufacturing and income statements; inventory analysis P2

The following calendar year-end information is taken from the December 31, 2005, adjusted trial balance and other records of Plaza Company.

Advertising expense	$ 30,750	Direct labor	677,480
Depreciation expense—Office equipment	9,250	Income taxes expense	235,725
Depreciation expense—Selling equipment	10,600	Indirect labor	58,875
Depreciation expense—Factory equipment	35,550	Miscellaneous production costs	10,425
Factory supervision	104,600	Office salaries expense	65,000
Factory supplies used	9,350	Raw materials purchases	927,000
Factory utilities	35,000	Rent expense—Office space	24,000
Inventories		Rent expense—Selling space	28,100
Raw materials, December 31, 2004	168,850	Rent expense—Factory building	78,800
Raw materials, December 31, 2005	184,000	Maintenance expense—Factory equipment	37,400
Goods in process, December 31, 2004	17,700	Sales	4,527,000
Goods in process, December 31, 2005	21,380	Sales discounts	64,500
Finished goods, December 31, 2004	169,350	Sales salaries expense	394,560
Finished goods, December 31, 2005	138,490		

Required

1. Prepare the company's 2005 manufacturing statement.

2. Prepare the company's 2005 income statement that reports separate categories for (a) selling expenses and (b) general and administrative expenses.

Check (1) Cost of goods manufactured, $1,955,650

Analysis Component

3. Compute the (a) inventory turnover and (b) days' sales in inventory for both its raw materials inventory and its finished goods inventory (see Chapter 6). Discuss some possible reasons for differences between these ratios for the two types of inventories.

Problem 18-9A
Sales and costs estimation; contribution margin analysis
C3 A1

King grocery chain, a market leader, wants to increase sales to its existing customers by creating a customer orientation to better meet buyer needs and wants. Assume that King hires you as a consultant to analyze its operations and suggest improvements. King's goal is to increase its contribution margin by $40,000.

Required

1. To increase King's sales and contribution margin from existing customers, offer three improvements that you have observed in other stores and believe would be successful here.

2. What level of increase in sales is necessary for King to increase contribution margin by $40,000? (*Hint:* With each suggestion in part [1], identify the expected sales dollars and the contribution margin ratio to meet the $40,000 increase in contribution margin.)

PROBLEM SET B

Problem 18-1B
Managerial accountant's role
C1 C3

This chapter discusses the purposes of managerial accounting and the current business environment. You are to look through the *home electronics* section of your local newspaper; the Sunday paper is often best. Review advertisements of home electronics and note how many manufacturers offer these products and the factors on which they compete.

Required

Discuss the potential contributions and responsibilities of the managerial accounting professional in helping a home electronics manufacturer succeed. (*Hint:* Think about information and estimates that a managerial accountant might provide new entrants into the home electronics market.)

Problem 18-2B
Lean business concepts
C3 

A trip to the photography store is useful in understanding concepts such as total quality management (TQM), just-in-time (JIT), and continuous improvement (CI). List two photography stores you are familiar with in the first column of the following table. Record in the table how each store is putting each of these lean business concepts into action, both favorably and unfavorably. (*Hint:* To prepare a response to this question, you may want to watch how film is processed and prints prepared within 1 hour.)

Photography Store	TQM	JIT	CI
1.			
2.			

Problem 18-3B
Cost computation, classification, and analysis; contribution margin income statement
C4 A1 

Listed here are the total costs associated with the production of 12,000 CDs manufactured by Hip-Hop. The CDs sell for $15 each.

	Cost by Behavior		Cost by Function	
Costs	Variable	Fixed	Product	Period
Plastic for CDs—$1,000	$1,000		$1,000	
Wages of assembly workers—$20,000				
Rent cost of factory—$4,500				
Systems staff salaries—$10,000				
Labeling (12,000 outsourced)—$2,500				
Rent cost of office equipment—$700				
Upper management salaries—$100,000				
Annual fixed fee for cleaning service—$3,000				
Sales commissions—$0.50 per CD				
Machinery depreciation—$15,000				

Required

1. Classify each cost and its amount as (a) either fixed or variable and (b) either product or period.

2. Compute the (a) contribution margin and (b) contribution margin ratio by filling in the boxes in the following report:

Check Total variable cost, $29,500

HIP-HOP Contribution Margin Income Statement For Year Ended December 31, 2005			
Sales ($15 × 12,000)		$☐	100%
Variable costs			
Plastic for CDs	$☐		
Assembly worker wages	☐		
Labels outsourced	☐		
Sales commissions	☐	☐	16%
Contribution margin		$☐	Contribution margin ratio* ☐%

* Contribution margin ratio = Contribution margin/Sales.

Analysis Component

3. Interpret the contribution margin and the contribution margin ratio.

Problem 18-4B
Cost classification and explanation
C4 C5

Assume that you must make a presentation to a client explaining the difference between prime and conversion costs. The client makes and sells cookies for 50,000 customers per week. The client tells you that her sales staff also would like a clarification regarding product and period costs. She tells you that most of the staff lack training in managerial accounting.

Required

Prepare a one-page memorandum to your client outlining your planned presentation to her sales staff.

Problem 18-5B
Opportunity cost estimation and application
C1 C4

Refer to *Decision Maker,* **Purchase Manager,** in this chapter. Assume that you are the motorcycle manufacturer's managerial accountant. The purchasing manager asks you about preparing an estimate of the related costs for buying motorcycle seats from supplier (B). She tells you this estimate is needed because unless dollar estimates are attached to nonfinancial factors such as lost production time, her supervisor will not give it full attention. The purchasing manager also shows you this information:

- Production output is 2,000 motorcycles per year based on 250 production days a year.
- Production time per day is 8 hours at a cost of $500 per hour to run the production line.
- Lost production time due to poor quality is 1%.
- Satisfied customers purchase, on average, three motorcycles during a lifetime.
- Satisfied customers recommend the product, on average, to four other people.
- Marketing predicts that using seat (B) will result in eight lost customers per year from repeat business and referrals.
- Average contribution margin per motorcycle is $4,000.

Required

Estimate the costs (including opportunity costs) of buying motorcycle seats from supplier (B). This problem requires you to think creatively and make reasonable estimates and, therefore, there could be more than one correct answer. (*Hint:* Reread the answer to *Decision Maker,* and compare the cost savings for buying from supplier [B] to the sum of lost customer revenue from repeat business and referrals and the cost of lost production time.)

Check Cost of lost customer revenue, $32,000

Problem 18-6B
Ending inventory computation and evaluation
C3 C6

Icey Edges makes specialty skates for the ice skating circuit. On December 31, 2004, the company had (a) 1,500 skates in finished goods inventory and (b) 2,000 blades at a cost of $15 each in raw materials inventory. During 2005, Icey Edges purchased 45,000 additional blades at $15 each and manufactured 20,000 pairs of skates.

Required

1. Determine the unit and dollar amounts of raw materials inventory in blades at December 31, 2005.

Check (1) Ending (blade) inventory, $105,000 (7,000 units)

Analysis Component

2. Write a one-half page memorandum to the production manager explaining why a just-in-time inventory system for blades should be considered. Include the amount of working capital that can be reduced at December 31, 2005, if the ending blade raw material inventory is cut in half.

Problem 18-7B
Inventory computation and reporting
C4 C7 P1

Shown here are the annual financial data at December 31, 2005, taken from two different companies.

	Cardinal Drug Retail	Nandina Manufacturing
Beginning inventory		
Merchandise	$ 50,000	
Finished goods		$200,000
Cost of purchases	350,000	
Cost of goods manufactured		686,000
Ending inventory		
Merchandise	25,000	
Finished goods		300,000

Required

1. Compute the cost of goods sold section of the income statement at December 31, 2005, for each company. Include proper title and format in the solution.

Check (1) Cardinal Drug cost of goods sold, $375,000

2. Write a half-page memorandum to your instructor (a) identifying the inventory accounts and (b) identifying where each is reported on the income statement and balance sheet for both companies.

Problem 18-8B
Manufacturing and income statements; analysis of inventories
P2

The following calendar year-end information is taken from the December 31, 2005, adjusted trial balance and other records of Firethorn Furniture.

Advertising expense	$ 22,250	Direct labor	564,500
Depreciation expense—Office equipment	10,440	Income taxes expense	138,700
Depreciation expense—Selling equipment	12,125	Indirect labor	61,000
Depreciation expense—Factory equipment	37,400	Miscellaneous production costs	10,440
Factory supervision	123,500	Office salaries expense	72,875
Factory supplies used	8,060	Raw materials purchases	896,375
Factory utilities	39,500	Rent expense—Office space	25,625
Inventories		Rent expense—Selling space	29,000
Raw materials, December 31, 2004	42,375	Rent expense—Factory building	95,500
Raw materials, December 31, 2005	72,430	Maintenance expense—Factory equipment	32,375
Goods in process, December 31, 2004	14,500	Sales	5,002,000
Goods in process, December 31, 2005	16,100	Sales discounts	59,375
Finished goods, December 31, 2004	179,200	Sales salaries expense	297,300
Finished goods, December 31, 2005	143,750		

Required

Check (1) Cost of goods manufactured, $1,836,995

1. Prepare the company's 2005 manufacturing statement.

2. Prepare the company's 2005 income statement that reports separate categories for (a) selling expenses and (b) general and administrative expenses.

Analysis Component

3. Compute the (a) inventory turnover and (b) days' sales in inventory for both its raw materials inventory and its finished goods inventory (see Chapter 6). Discuss some possible reasons for differences between these ratios for the two types of inventories.

Problem 18-9B
Sales and costs estimation; contribution margin analysis
C3 A1 

The Hole Bagel chain, a market leader, wishes to increase sales to its existing customers by creating a customer orientation to better meet buyer needs and wants. Assume that The Hole Bagel hires you as a consultant to analyze its operations and suggest improvements. The Hole Bagel's goal is to increase its contribution margin by $10,000.

Required

1. To increase The Hole Bagel's sales and contribution margin from existing customers, offer three improvements that you have observed in other stores and believe would be successful here.

2. What level of increase in sales is necessary for The Hole Bagel to increase contribution margin by $10,000? (*Hint:* With each suggestion in part [1], identify the expected sales dollars and contribution margin ratio to meet the $10,000 increase in contribution margin.)

PROBLEM SET C

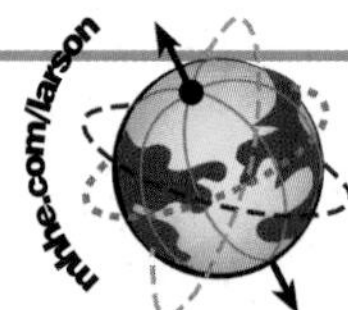

Problem Set C is available at the book's Website to reinforce and assess your learning.

SERIAL PROBLEM

Success Systems

(This serial problem began in Chapter 1 and continues through most of the book. If previous chapter segments were not completed, the serial problem can begin at this point. It is helpful, but not necessary, for you to use the Working Papers that accompany the book.)

Kay Breeze, owner of Success Systems, decides to diversify her business by manufacturing computer workstation furniture.

Required

1. Classify the following manufacturing costs of Success Systems by behavior and traceability.

	Cost by Behavior		Cost by Traceability	
Product Costs	**Variable**	**Fixed**	**Direct**	**Indirect**
Laminate coverings for desktops	___	___	___	___
Wages of desk assembler	___	___	___	___
Taxes on assembly workshop	___	___	___	___
Glue to assemble workstation component parts	___	___	___	___
Depreciation on tools	___	___	___	___
Electricity for workshop	___	___	___	___
Monthly flat fee to clean workshop	___	___	___	___

2. Prepare a manufacturing statement for Success Systems for the month ended January 31, 2006. Assume the following manufacturing costs:

Direct materials: $1,925

Factory overhead: $260

Direct labor: $652

Beginning goods in process: none (December 31, 2005)

Ending goods in process: $1,596 (January 31, 2006)

Beginning finished goods inventory: none (December 31, 2005)

Ending finished goods inventory: $144 (January 31, 2006)

3. Prepare the costs of goods sold section of a partial income statement for Success Systems for the month ended January 31, 2006.

Check COGS, $1,097

BEYOND THE NUMBERS

REPORTING IN ACTION

C1 C2

BTN 18-1 Managerial accounting is more than recording, maintaining, and reporting financial results. Managerial accountants must provide managers with both financial and nonfinancial information including estimates, projections, and forecasts. Looking into the future involves risk. **Krispy Kreme**'s managers, including its managerial accountants, must notify shareholders of this risk.

Required

1. Access and read Krispy Kreme's Management Discussion and Analysis (MD&A) section in either its annual report or its 10-K for the year ended February 3, 2002 [KrispyKreme.com]. What risks do Krispy Kreme's shareholders face as management and employees work to position the company for long-term success?

2. What are the managerial accountants' responsibilities in evaluating risk?

Roll On

3. Access **Krispy Kreme**'s annual report for a fiscal year ending after February 3, 2002, from either its Website [KrispyKreme.com] or the SEC's EDGAR database [www.sec.gov]. Answer the questions in parts (1) and (2) after reading the current MD&A section. Identify any major changes.

COMPARATIVE ANALYSIS

C3 C6

BTN 18-2 **Krispy Kreme** and **Tastykake** are both manufacturing and merchandising companies. Answer the following questions using their financial information reported in Appendix A.

Required

1. Review each company's balance sheet and then identify and record clues indicating that each performs manufacturing operations.

2. Search the notes to Krispy Kreme's financial statements for evidence that it is a manufacturer. Record your evidence.

3. Compute inventory turnover (using ending inventory in the denominator) and the days' sales in inventory for the most recent two years reported for each company. Interpret both measures.
4. What likely impact would a just-in-time inventory system have on the turnover values in part 3?

ETHICS CHALLENGE

C1 C4 C5

BTN 18-3 Assume that you are the managerial accountant at Spinex, a manufacturer of hard drives, CDs, and diskettes. Its reporting year-end is December 31. The chief financial officer is concerned about having enough cash to pay the expected income tax bill because of poor cash flow management. On November 15, the purchasing department purchased excess inventory of CD raw materials in anticipation of rapid growth of this product beginning in January. To decrease the company's tax liability, the chief financial officer tells you to record the purchase of this inventory as part of supplies and expense it in the current year; this would decrease the company's tax liability by increasing expenses.

Required

1. In which account should the purchase of CD raw materials be recorded?
2. How should you respond to this request by the chief financial officer?

COMMUNICATING IN PRACTICE

BTN 18-4 Write a one-page memorandum to a prospective college student about salary expectations for graduates in business. Compare and contrast the expected salaries for accounting (including different subfields such as public, corporate, tax, audit, and so forth), marketing, management, and finance majors. Prepare a graph showing average starting salaries (and those for experienced professionals in those fields if available). To get this information, stop by your school's career services office; libraries also have this information. The Website JobStar.org (click on *Salary Info*) also can get you started.

TAKING IT TO THE NET

C1 C2

mhhe.com/larson

BTN 18-5 Managerial accounting professionals follow a code of ethics. As a member of the Institute of Management Accountants, the managerial accountant must comply with Standards of Ethical Conduct.

Required

Identify, print, and read the *Ethical Standards* posted at www.IMAnet.org. (Search using "ethical standards.")

TEAMWORK IN ACTION

C8 P2

BTN 18-6 The following calendar-year information is taken from the December 31, 2005, adjusted trial balance and other records of Azalea Company.

Advertising expense	$ 19,125	Direct labor	650,750
Depreciation expense—Office equipment	8,750	Indirect labor	60,000
Depreciation expense—Selling equipment	10,000	Miscellaneous production costs	8,500
Depreciation expense—Factory equipment	32,500	Office salaries expense	100,875
Factory supervision	122,500	Raw materials purchases	872,500
Factory supplies used	15,750	Rent expense—Office space	21,125
Factory utilities	36,250	Rent expense—Selling space	25,750
Inventories		Rent expense—Factory building	79,750
Raw materials, December 31, 2004	177,500	Maintenance expense—Factory equipment	27,875
Raw materials, December 31, 2005	168,125	Sales	3,275,000
Goods in process, December 31, 2004	15,875	Sales discounts	57,500
Goods in process, December 31, 2005	14,000	Sales salaries expense	286,250
Finished goods, December 31, 2004	164,375		
Finished goods, December 31, 2005	129,000		

Required

1. *Each* team member is to be responsible for computing **one** of the following amounts. You are not to duplicate your teammates' work. Get any necessary amounts from teammates. Each member is to explain the computation to the team in preparation for reporting to class.
   a. Materials used.
   b. Factory overhead.
   c. Total manufacturing costs.
   d. Total cost of goods in process.
   e. Cost of goods manufactured.
2. Check your cost of goods manufactured with the instructor. If it is correct, proceed to part (3).
3. *Each* team member is to be responsible for computing **one** of the following amounts. You are not to duplicate your teammates' work. Get any necessary amounts from teammates. Each member is to explain the computation to the team in preparation for reporting to class.
   a. Net sales.
   b. Cost of goods sold.
   c. Gross profit.
   d. Total operating expenses.
   e. Net income or loss before taxes.

Point: Provide teams with transparencies and markers for presentation purposes.

BUSINESS WEEK ACTIVITY

C1 C2 C3 C8

mhhe.com/larson

BTN 18-7 Read the article "Mattel's New Toy Story" in the November 18, 2002, issue of *Business Week*. (The book's Website provides a free link.)

Required

1. Does Mattel employ just-in-time inventory management practices? (Support your answer.)
2. Identify two or three overall product strategies of Mattel.
3. Identify at least four changes that Mattel CEO Robert A. Eckert is implementing at Mattel to steady the company's performance.

ENTREPRENEURIAL DECISION

C1 C4  

BTN 18-8 James Lindsay of Rap Snacks has negotiated a deal with Universal Studios to use the image of rappers on his snack food bags. Representing the rappers, Universal pays Lindsay an advertising fee to gain exposure for the rappers. Lindsay also sponsors a summer seminar for urban youth to convey information needed to successfully own and manage entrepreneurial businesses. Assume that he has asked you to briefly speak at this year's seminar on accounting for the advertising fees that Universal pays and Rap Snacks receives. On the cost accounting side, Lindsay encourages you to emphasize the cost behavior, cost traceability, and cost function concepts when you explain how both Rap Snacks and Universal accounts for these advertising fees.

Required

Identify the main revenue and cost issues you would include in the seminar talk.

HITTING THE ROAD

C1 C5 

BTN 18-9 Visit your favorite fast-food restaurant. Observe its business operations.

Required

1. Describe all business activities from the time a customer arrives to the time that customer departs.
2. List all costs you can identify with the separate activities described in part 1.
3. Classify each cost from part 2 as fixed or variable, and explain your classification.

GLOBAL DECISION

BTN 18-10 Grupo Bimbo, Krispy Kreme, and Tastykake are competitors. Access Grupo Bimbo's annual report for the year ended December 31, 2002, at GrupoBimbo.com.

Required

1. Identify the footnote in which Grupo Bimbo provides the detail of its inventory balances.
2. Prepare a table showing dollar balances and common-size percentages (percentages of inventory item to the total inventory balance) for each inventory component for the years 2001 and 2002.
3. How do the types of manufacturing inventory accounted for by Grupo Bimbo differ from those explained in this chapter?

"*If the fear and uncertainty of risk are perceived as the enemy, then entrepreneurs ... must counter the enemy with a set of weapons called optimism and rationalization*"—Rebecca Smith

19 Job Order Cost Accounting

A Look Back

Chapter 18 introduced managerial accounting. We compared it to financial accounting and explained basic cost concepts. We also described the lean business model and the reporting of manufacturing activities, including the manufacturing statement.

A Look at This Chapter

We begin this chapter by describing a cost accounting system. We then explain the procedures used to determine costs using a job order costing system. We conclude with a discussion of over- and underapplied overhead.

A Look Ahead

Chapter 20 considers how to measure costs in process production companies. We explain process production, describe how to assign costs to processes, and compute and analyze the cost per equivalent unit.

CAP

Conceptual

C1 Explain the cost accounting system. *(p. 754)*

C2 Describe important features of job order manufacturing. *(p. 754)*

C3 Explain job cost sheets and how they are used in job order cost accounting. *(p. 756)*

Analytical

A1 Apply job order costing in pricing services. *(p. 766)*

Procedural

P1 Describe and record the flow of materials costs in job order cost accounting. *(p. 757)*

P2 Describe and record the flow of labor costs in job order cost accounting. *(p. 759)*

P3 Describe and record the flow of overhead costs in job order cost accounting. *(p. 761)*

P4 Determine adjustments for overapplied and underapplied factory overhead. *(p. 765)*

Decision Feature

Woodshop instead of Home Economics

TAMPA—Rebecca Smith's interest in construction surfaced in ninth grade, the year she elected to take woodshop instead of home economics. "I've been training for this position all of my life," says Smith. "Everything I've done has been in preparation for this." "This" is **A.D. Morgan Corporation [ADMorgan.com],** a construction company founded by Smith from her home and initially funded with a $10,000 loan from her father. "To top it off," says Smith, "I was young—29 years old—and a 'girl' going into a 'man's' business."

Smith was determined to make her business a success. "I heard so many reasons why my construction start-up would fail," says Smith. "There was only one smart thing to do—prove the naysayers wrong." She worked tirelessly to secure construction projects and wore many hats: estimator, project manager, superintendent, secretary, and accountant. She was an "army of one." Success depended not only on securing business but also on maintaining cost controls and emphasizing quality work. Smith's focus on monitoring and controlling labor, materials, and overhead costs produced consistent profits and growth. Moreover, her focus on quality helped land several lucrative jobs such as those at Brevard Community College, St. Petersburg College, Florida Atlantic University, and Poynter Institute.

Smith uses state-of-the-art job order cost accounting to track construction job costs, including the flow of materials, labor, and overhead costs. She also manages costs and prepares periodic job order cost sheets for client review. These accounting processes help A.D. Morgan avoid the pitfalls of many start-ups that fail to use cost accounting systems and experience run-away job costs. Smith also recruits top-notch personnel, which was especially crucial in the early years. "The quality of our employees was unreal," she says.

Smith still enjoys the reaction of new acquaintances when telling them she runs a construction firm. "The best part is watching their jaws drop," she says. "But I walk away knowing that it was just one more person who . . . assumed construction firms were only run by big guys with lumps of tobacco in their lips." And, by the way, who is A.D. Morgan? Turns out Smith named the company for her two golden retrievers, Addie and Morgan.

[Sources: *A.D. Morgan Website,* January 2004; *Business Week,* January 2003; *Maddux Report,* 2002; *EntreWorld.org,* January 2002.]

This chapter introduces a cost accounting system for assigning costs to the flow of goods through a production process. We then describe the details of a *job order cost accounting system*. Job order costing is frequently used by manufacturers of custom products or providers of custom services. Manufacturers that use job order costing typically base it on a perpetual inventory system, which provides a continuous record of materials, goods in process, and finished goods inventories.

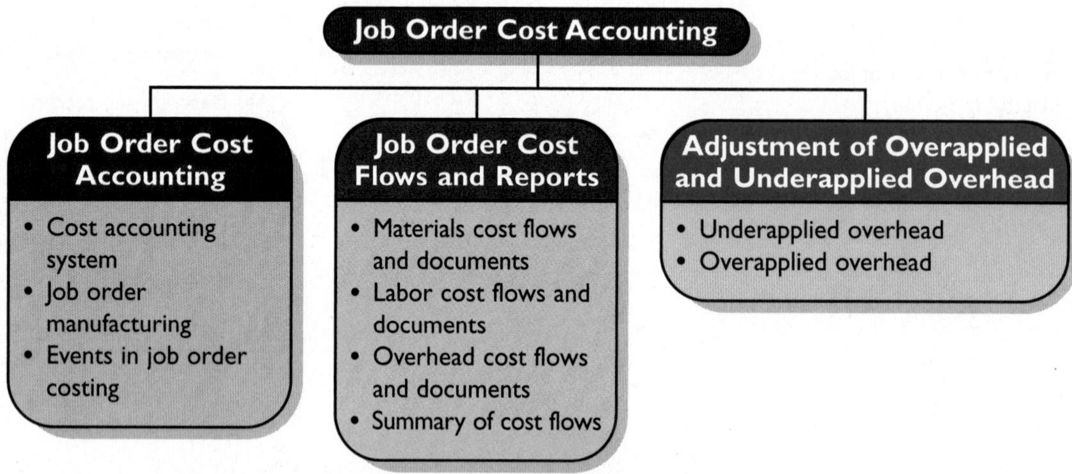

Job Order Cost Accounting

This section describes a cost accounting system and job order manufacturing and costing.

Cost Accounting System

C1 Explain the cost accounting system.

An ever-increasing number of companies use a cost accounting system to generate timely and accurate inventory information. A **cost accounting system** records manufacturing activities using a *perpetual* inventory system, which continuously updates records for costs of materials, goods in process, and finished goods inventories. A cost accounting system also provides timely information about inventories and manufacturing costs per unit of product. This is especially helpful for managers' efforts to control costs and determine selling prices. (A **general accounting system** records manufacturing activities using a *periodic* inventory system. Some companies still use a general accounting system, but its use is declining as competitive forces and customer demands have increased pressures on companies to better manage inventories.)

Point: Cost accounting systems accumulate costs and then assign them to products or services.

Point: Many professional examinations including the CPA and CMA exams require knowledge of job order and process cost accounting.

The two basic types of cost accounting systems are *job order cost accounting* and *process cost accounting*. We describe job order cost accounting in this chapter. Process cost accounting is explained in Chapter 20.

Job Order Manufacturing

C2 Describe important features of job order manufacturing.

Topic Tackler 19-1

Many companies manufacture products individually designed to meet the needs of a specific customer. Each customized product is manufactured separately and its production is called **job order manufacturing** (also called *customized production,* which is the production of products in response to special orders). Examples are special machines, a building, custom-made jewelry, and artwork. The production activities for a customized product represent a **job.** Although we use the term *job order manufacturing,* the principle of customization is equally applicable to both manufacturing *and* service companies. Most service companies meet customers' needs by performing a custom service for a specific customer. Examples of such services include an accountant auditing a client's financial statements, an interior designer remodeling an office, a wedding consultant planning and supervising a reception, and a lawyer defending a client. Whether the setting is manufacturing or services, job order operations involve meeting the needs of customers by producing or performing custom jobs.

Boeing's aerospace division is one example of a job order manufacturing system. Its primary business is twofold: (1) design, develop, and integrate space carriers and (2) provide systems engineering and integration of Department of Defense (DoD) systems. Most of its orders are customized and produced through job order manufacturing.

When a job involves producing more than one unit of a custom product, it is often called a **job lot.** Products produced as job lots could include benches for a church, imprinted T-shirts for a 10K race or company picnic, or advertising signs for a chain of stores. Although these orders involve more than one unit, the volume of production is typically low, such as 50 benches, 200 T-shirts, or 100 signs. Another feature of job order manufacturing is the diversity, often called *heterogeneity,* of the products manufactured. Namely, each customer order is likely to differ from another in some important respect. These variations can be minor or major.

Events in Job Order Costing

The initial event in a normal job order manufacturing operation is the receipt of a customer order for a custom product. This causes the manufacturer to begin work on a job. A less common case occurs when management decides to begin work on a job before it has a signed contract. This is referred to as *jobs manufactured on speculation.*

> **Decision Insight**
>
> **Custom Design** A Copernican revolution of sorts is underway. Managers once saw their companies as the center of a solar system orbited by suppliers and customers. Now the customer has become the center of the business universe. Companies such as **Dell Computer** encourage consumers to customize products. Soon consumers may be able to personalize almost any product, from cellular phones to appliances to furniture.

The first step in both cases is to predict the cost to complete the job. This cost depends on the product design prepared by either the customer or the manufacturer. The second step is to negotiate a sales price and decide whether to pursue the job. Some jobs are priced on a *cost-plus basis:* The customer pays the manufacturer for costs incurred on the job plus a negotiated amount or rate of profit. The third step is for the manufacturer to schedule production of the job to meet the customer's needs and to fit within its own production constraints. Preparation of this work schedule should consider workplace facilities including equipment, personnel, and supplies. Once this schedule is complete, the manufacturer can place orders for raw materials. Production occurs as materials and labor are applied to the job.

An overview of job order production activity is shown in Exhibit 19.1. This exhibit shows the March production activity of Road Warriors, which manufactures security-equipped cars and trucks. The company converts any vehicle by giving it a diversity of security items such as alarms, reinforced exterior, bulletproof glass, and bomb detectors. The company began by catering to high-profile celebrities, but it now caters to anyone who desires added security in a vehicle.

Job order manufacturing for Road Warriors requires materials, labor, and overhead costs. Recall that direct materials are goods used in manufacturing that are clearly identified with a particular job. Similarly, direct labor is effort devoted to a particular job. Overhead costs support production of more than one job. Common overhead items are depreciation on factory buildings and equipment, factory supplies, supervision, maintenance, cleaning, and utilities.

> **Decision Insight**
>
> **Job Order Education** Many companies invest in their employees, and the demand for executive education is strong. Annual spending on U.S. corporate training and education is nearby $20 billion. Moreover, annual revenues for providers of executive education continue to rise, with about 40% of revenues coming from custom programs designed for one or a group of companies.
>
> 

Exhibit 19.1 shows that materials, labor, and overhead are added to Jobs B15, B16, B17, B18, and B19 during March. Road Warriors completed Jobs B15, B16, and B17 in March and delivered Jobs B15 and B16 to customers. At the end of March, Jobs B18 and B19 remain

Exhibit 19.1

Job Order Manufacturing Activities

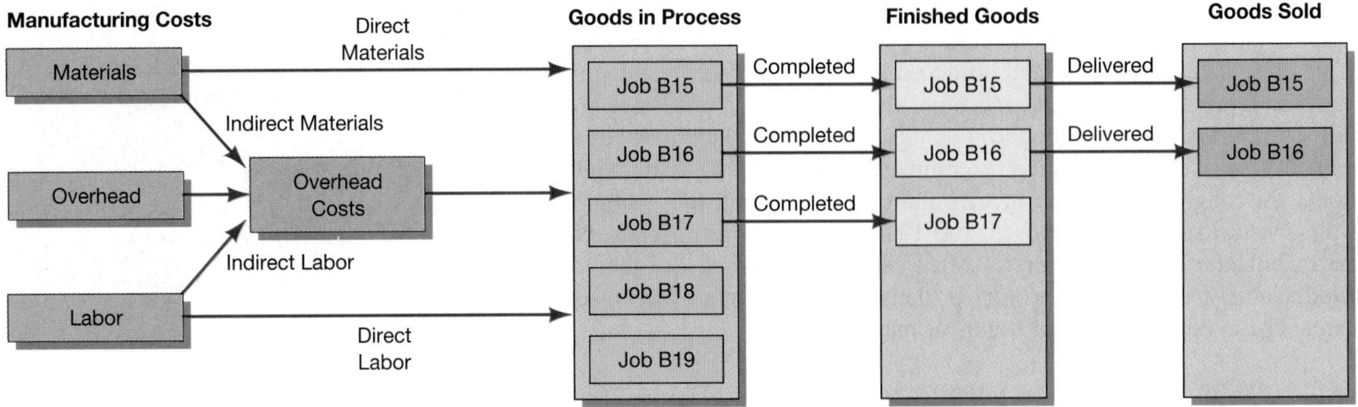

in goods in process inventory and Job B17 is in finished goods inventory. Both labor and materials costs are also separated into their direct and indirect components. Their indirect amounts are added to overhead. Total overhead cost is then allocated to the various jobs.

Decision Maker

Management Consultant One of your tasks is to control and manage costs for a consulting company. At the end of a recent month, you find that three consulting jobs were completed and two are 60% complete. Each unfinished job is estimated to cost $10,000 and to earn a revenue of $12,000. You are unsure how to recognize goods in process inventory and record costs and revenues. Do you recognize any inventory? If so, how much? Also, how much revenue is recorded for the unfinished jobs in this month?

Answer—p. 770

Job Cost Sheet

C3 Explain job cost sheets and how they are used in job order cost accounting.

General ledger accounts usually do not provide the accounting information that managers of job order cost operations need to plan and control production activities. This is so because the needed information often requires more detailed data. Such detailed data are usually stored in subsidiary records controlled by general ledger accounts. Subsidiary records store information about raw materials, overhead costs, jobs in process, finished goods, and other items. This section describes the use of these records.

Point: Factory overhead consists of costs (other than direct materials and direct labor) that ensure the production activities are carried out.

A major aim of a **job order cost accounting system** is to determine the cost of producing each job or job lot. In the case of a job lot, the system also aims to compute the cost per unit. The accounting system must include separate records for each job to accomplish this, and it must capture information about costs incurred and charge these costs to each job.

A **job cost sheet** is a separate record maintained for each job. Exhibit 19.2 shows a job cost sheet for an alarm system that Road Warriors produced for a customer. This job cost sheet identifies the customer, the job number assigned, the product, and key dates. Costs incurred on the job are immediately recorded on this sheet. When each job is complete, the supervisor enters the date of completion, records any remarks, and signs the sheet. The job cost sheet in Exhibit 19.2 classifies costs as direct materials, direct labor, or overhead. It shows that a total of $600 in direct materials is added to Job B15 on four different dates. It also shows seven entries for direct labor costs that total $1,000. Road Warriors *allocates* (also termed *applies, assigns,* or *charges*) factory overhead costs of $1,600 to this job using an allocation rate of 160% of direct labor cost (160% × $1,000)—we discuss overhead allocation later in this chapter.

While a job is being manufactured, its accumulated costs are kept in **Goods in Process Inventory.** The collection of job cost sheets for all jobs in process makes up a subsidiary ledger controlled by the Goods in Process Inventory account in the general ledger. Managers use job cost sheets to monitor costs incurred to date and to predict and control costs for each job.

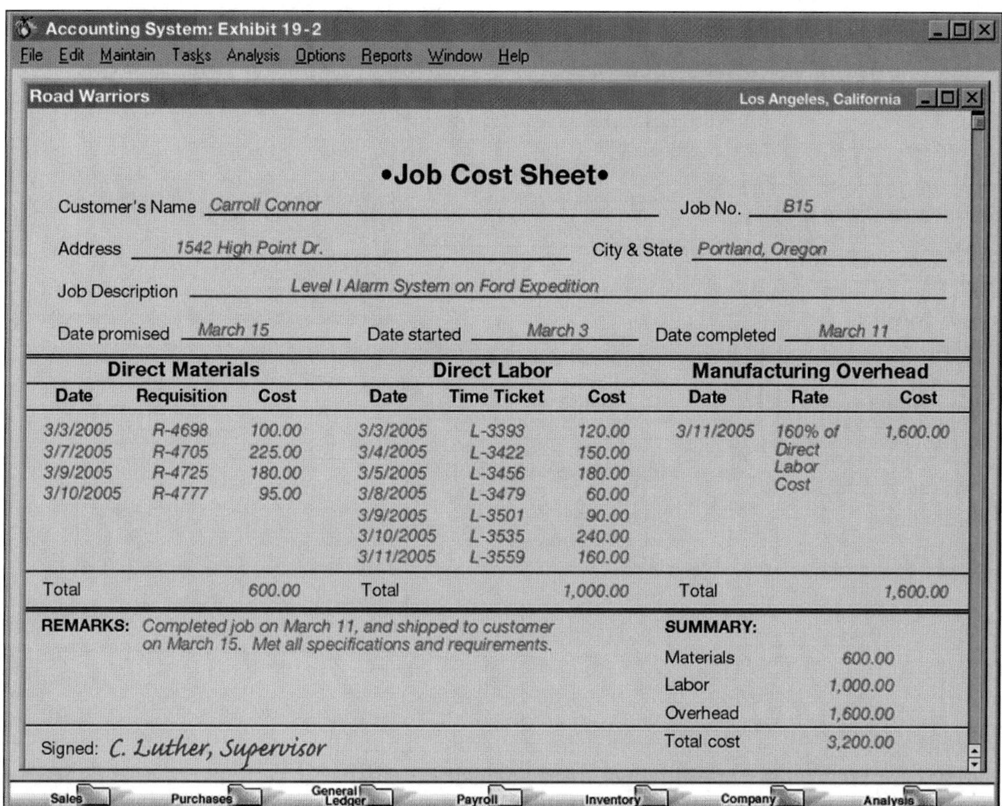

Accounting System: Exhibit 19-2

File Edit Maintain Tasks Analysis Options Reports Window Help

Road Warriors — Los Angeles, California

•Job Cost Sheet•

Customer's Name: Carroll Connor — Job No.: B15

Address: 1542 High Point Dr. — City & State: Portland, Oregon

Job Description: Level I Alarm System on Ford Expedition

Date promised: March 15 — Date started: March 3 — Date completed: March 11

Direct Materials			Direct Labor			Manufacturing Overhead		
Date	Requisition	Cost	Date	Time Ticket	Cost	Date	Rate	Cost
3/3/2005	R-4698	100.00	3/3/2005	L-3393	120.00	3/11/2005	160% of Direct Labor Cost	1,600.00
3/7/2005	R-4705	225.00	3/4/2005	L-3422	150.00			
3/9/2005	R-4725	180.00	3/5/2005	L-3456	180.00			
3/10/2005	R-4777	95.00	3/8/2005	L-3479	60.00			
			3/9/2005	L-3501	90.00			
			3/10/2005	L-3535	240.00			
			3/11/2005	L-3559	160.00			
Total		600.00	Total		1,000.00	Total		1,600.00

REMARKS: Completed job on March 11, and shipped to customer on March 15. Met all specifications and requirements.

SUMMARY:

Materials	600.00
Labor	1,000.00
Overhead	1,600.00
Total cost	3,200.00

Signed: C. Luther, Supervisor

Sales Purchases General Ledger Payroll Inventory Company Analysis

Exhibit 19.2

Job Cost Sheet

When a job is finished, its job cost sheet is completed and moved from the jobs in process file to the finished jobs file. This latter file acts as a subsidiary ledger controlled by the **Finished Goods Inventory** account. When a finished job is delivered to a customer, the job cost sheet is moved to a permanent file supporting the total cost of goods sold. This permanent file contains records from both current and prior periods.

Point: Documents are crucial in a job order system, and the job cost sheet is a cornerstone. Understanding it aids in grasping concepts of capitalizing product costs and product cost flow.

Point: To apply these concepts, work QS 19-3.

Quick Check

1. Which of these products is likely to involve job order manufacturing? (*a*) inexpensive watches, (*b*) racing bikes, or (*c*) bottled soft drinks.
2. What is the difference between a job and a job lot?
3. Which of these statements is correct? (*a*) The collection of job cost sheets for unfinished jobs makes up a subsidiary ledger controlled by the Goods in Process Inventory account, (*b*) Job cost sheets are financial statements provided to investors, or (*c*) A separate job cost sheet is maintained in the general ledger for each job in process.
4. What three costs are normally accumulated on job cost sheets?

Answers—p. 771

Job Order Cost Flows and Reports

Materials Cost Flows and Documents

P1 Describe and record the flow of materials costs in job order cost accounting.

This section focuses on the flow of materials costs and the related documents in a job order cost accounting system. We begin analysis of the flow of materials costs by examining Exhibit 19.3. When materials are first received from suppliers, the employees count and inspect them and record the items' quantity and cost on a receiving report. The receiving

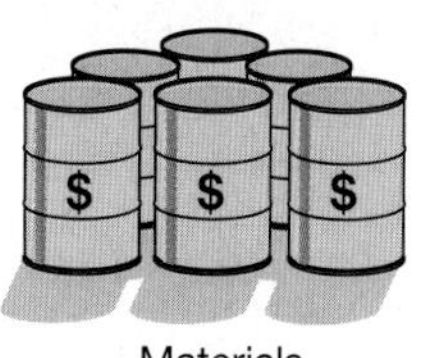

Materials

Exhibit 19.3

Materials Cost Flows through Subsidiary Records

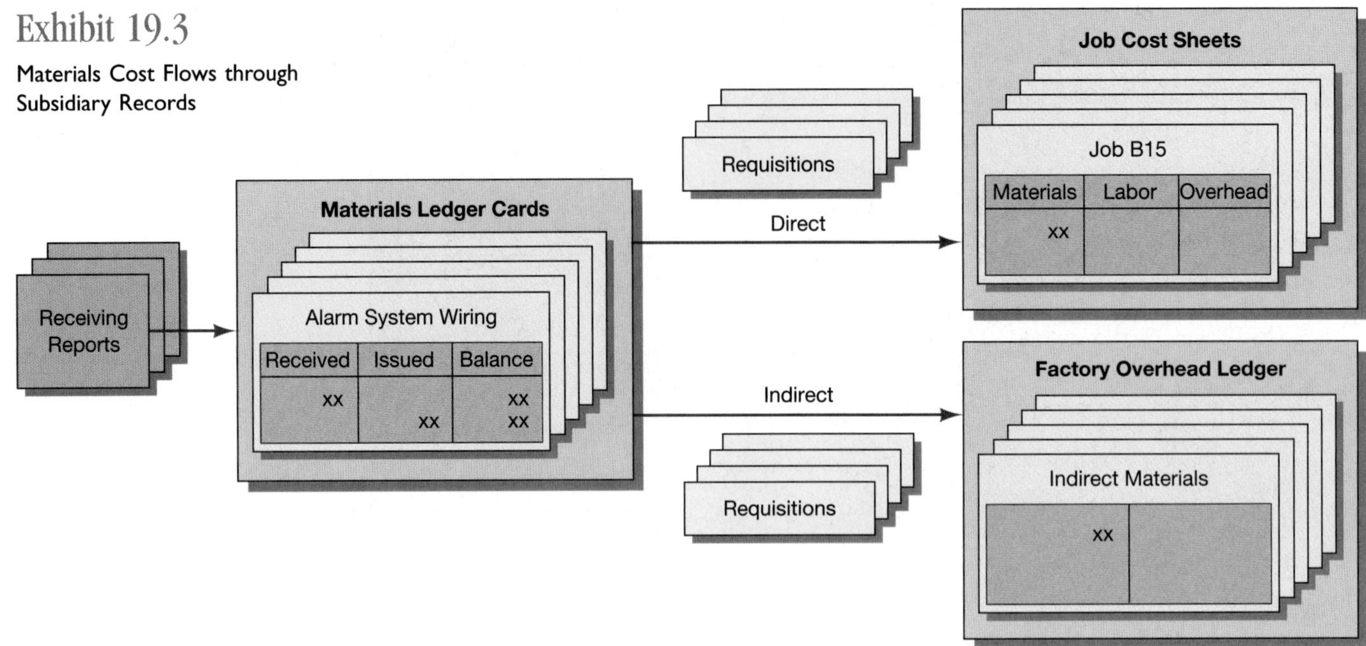

Point: Some companies certify certain suppliers based on the quality of their materials. Goods received from these suppliers are not always inspected by the purchaser to save costs.

report serves as the *source document* for recording materials received in both a materials ledger card and in the general ledger. In nearly all job order cost systems, **materials ledger cards** (or files) are perpetual records that are updated each time units are purchased and each time units are issued for use in production.

Exhibit 19.3 shows that materials can be requisitioned for use either on a specific job (direct materials) or as overhead (indirect materials). Cost of direct materials flows from the materials ledger card to the job cost sheet. The cost of indirect materials flows from the materials ledger card to the Indirect Materials account in the factory overhead ledger, which is a subsidiary ledger controlled by the Factory Overhead account in the general ledger.

Exhibit 19.4 shows a materials ledger card for material received and issued by Road Warriors. The card identifies the item as alarm system wiring and shows the item's stock number, its location in the storeroom, information about the maximum and minimum quantities that should be available, and the reorder quantity. For example, alarm system wiring is issued and recorded on March 7, 2005. The job cost sheet in Exhibit 19.2 showed that Job B15 used this wiring.

When materials are needed in production, a production manager prepares a **materials requisition** and sends it to the materials manager. The requisition shows the job number,

Exhibit 19.4

Materials Ledger Card

Road Warriors

Item *Alarm system wiring* Stock No. *M-347* Location in Storeroom *Bin 137*

Maximum quantity *5 units* Minimum quantity *1 unit* Quantity to reorder *2 units*

	Received				Issued				Balance		
Date	Receiving Report Number	Units	Unit Price	Total Price	Requisition Number	Units	Unit Price	Total Price	Units	Unit Price	Total Price
									1	225.00	225.00
3/ 4/2005	C-7117	2	225.00	450.00					3	225.00	675.00
3/ 7/2005					R-4705	1	225.00	225.00	2	225.00	450.00

the type of material, the quantity needed, and the signature of the manager authorized to make the requisition. Exhibit 19.5 shows the materials requisition for alarm system wiring for Job B15. To see how this requisition ties to the flow of costs, compare the information on the requisition with the March 7, 2005, data in Exhibits 19.2 and 19.4.

Road Warriors

MATERIALS REQUISITION NUMBER R-4705

Job No.	B15	Date	3/7/2005
Material Stock No.	M-347	Material Description	Alarm system wiring
Quantity Requested	1	Requested By	C. Luther
Quantity Provided	1	Date Provided	3/7/2005
Filled By	M. Bateman	Material Received By	C. Luther
Remarks			

Exhibit 19.5

Materials Requisition

The use of alarm system wiring on Job B15 yields the following entry (locate this cost item in the job cost sheet shown in Exhibit 19.2):

Mar. 7	Goods in Process Inventory—Job B15	225	
	Raw Materials Inventory—M-347		225
	To record use of material on Job B15.		

Assets = Liabilities + Equity
+225
−225

This entry is posted both to its general ledger accounts and to subsidiary records. Posting to subsidiary records includes a debit to a job cost sheet and a credit to a materials ledger card. (*Note:* An entry to record use of indirect materials is the same as that for direct materials *except* the debit is to Factory Overhead. In the subsidiary factory overhead ledger, this entry is posted to Indirect Materials.)

Point: Requisitions are often accumulated and recorded in one entry. The frequency of entries depends on the job, the industry, and management procedures.

Labor Cost Flows and Documents

P2 Describe and record the flow of labor costs in job order cost accounting.

Exhibit 19.6 shows the flow of labor costs from clock cards and the Factory Payroll account to subsidiary records of the job order cost accounting system. Recall that costs in subsidiary records give detailed information needed to manage and control operations.

The flow of costs in Exhibit 19.6 begins with **clock cards.** Employees commonly use these cards to record the number of hours worked, and they serve as source documents for entries to record labor costs. Clock card data on the number of hours worked is used at the end of each pay period to determine total labor cost. This amount is then debited to the Factory Payroll account, a temporary account containing the total payroll cost (both direct and indirect). Payroll cost is later allocated to both specific jobs and overhead.

Point: Indirect materials are included in overhead on the job cost sheet. Assigning overhead costs to products is described in the next section.

To assign labor costs to specific jobs and to overhead, we must know how each employee's time is used and its costs. Source documents called **time tickets** usually capture these data. Employees regularly fill out time tickets to report how much time they spent on each job. An employee who works on several jobs during a day completes a separate time ticket for each job. Tickets are also prepared for time charged to overhead as indirect labor. A supervisor signs an employee's time ticket to confirm its accuracy.

Exhibit 19.7 shows a time ticket reporting the time a Road Warrior employee spent working on Job B15. The employee's supervisor signed the ticket to confirm its accuracy. The hourly rate and total labor cost are computed after the time ticket is turned in. To see the effect of this time ticket on the job cost sheet, look at the entry dated March 8, 2005, in Exhibit 19.2.

Exhibit 19.6

Labor Cost Flows through Subsidiary Records

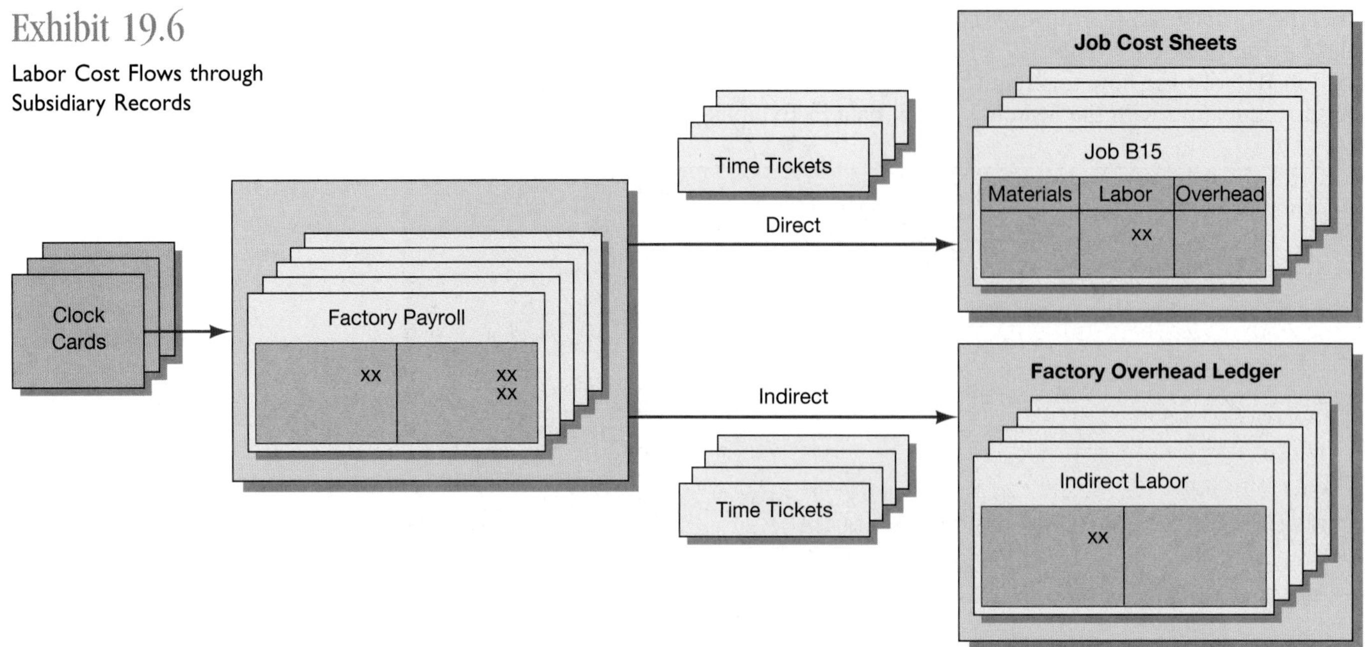

Exhibit 19.7

Time Ticket

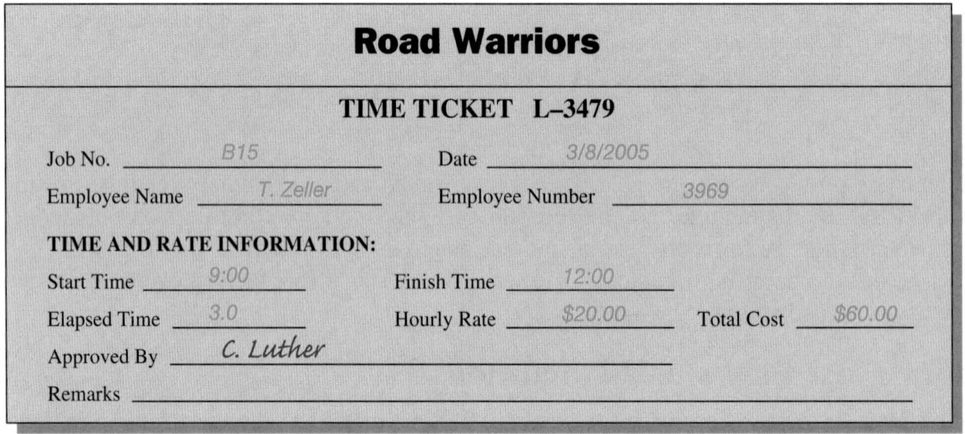

Road Warriors

TIME TICKET L–3479

Job No. B15 Date 3/8/2005

Employee Name T. Zeller Employee Number 3969

TIME AND RATE INFORMATION:

Start Time 9:00 Finish Time 12:00

Elapsed Time 3.0 Hourly Rate $20.00 Total Cost $60.00

Approved By C. Luther

Remarks

When time tickets report labor used on a specific job, this cost is recorded as direct labor. The following entry records the data from the time ticket in Exhibit 19.7:

Assets = Liabilities + Equity
+60 +60[1]

Mar. 8	Goods in Process Inventory—Job B15	60	
	Factory Payroll		60
	To record direct labor used on Job B15.		

The debit in this entry is posted both to the general ledger account and to the appropriate job cost sheet. (*Note:* An entry to record indirect labor is the same as for direct labor *except* that it debits Factory Overhead and credits Factory Payroll. In the subsidiary factory overhead ledger, the debit in this entry is posted to the Indirect Labor account.)

[1] In the accounting equation, we treat accounts such as Factory Overhead and Factory Payroll as temporary accounts, which hold various expenses until they are allocated to balance sheet or income statement accounts.

Overhead Cost Flows and Documents

P3 Describe and record the flow of overhead costs in job order cost accounting.

Factory overhead (or simply overhead) cost flows are shown in Exhibit 19.8. Factory overhead includes all manufacturing costs other than direct materials and direct labor. Two sources of overhead costs are indirect materials and indirect labor. These costs are recorded from requisitions for indirect materials and time tickets for indirect labor. Two other sources of overhead are (1) vouchers authorizing payments for items such as supplies or utilities and (2) adjusting entries for costs such as depreciation.

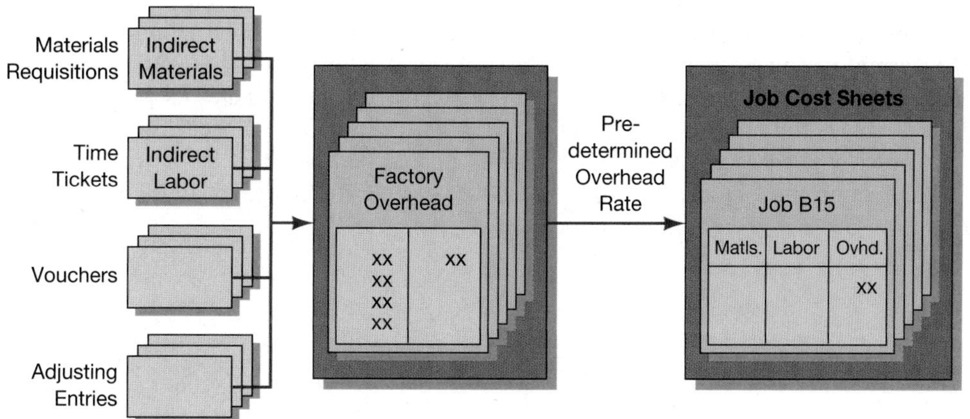

Exhibit 19.8

Overhead Cost Flows through Subsidiary Records

Factory overhead usually includes many different costs and, thus, a separate account for each is often maintained in a subsidiary factory overhead ledger. This ledger is controlled by the Factory Overhead account in the general ledger. Factory Overhead is a temporary account that accumulates costs until they are allocated to jobs.

Topic Tackler 19-2

Recall that overhead costs are recorded with debits to the Factory Overhead account and with credits to other accounts such as Cash, Accounts Payable, and Accumulated Depreciation—Equipment. In the subsidiary factory overhead ledger, the debits are posted to their respective accounts such as Depreciation Expense—Equipment, Insurance Expense—Equipment, or Amortization Expense—Patents.

Exhibit 19.8 shows that overhead costs flow from the Factory Overhead account to job cost sheets. Because overhead is made up of costs not directly associated with specific jobs or job lots, we cannot determine the dollar amount incurred on a specific job. We know, however, that overhead costs represent a necessary part of business activities. If a job cost is to include all costs needed to complete the job, some amount of overhead must be included. Given the difficulty in determining the overhead amount for a specific job, however, we allocate overhead to individual jobs in some reasonable manner.

We generally allocate overhead by linking it to another factor used in production, such as direct labor or machine hours. The factor to which overhead costs are linked is known as the *allocation base.* A manager must think carefully about how many and which allocation bases to use. This managerial decision influences the accuracy with which overhead costs are allocated to individual jobs. In Exhibit 19.2, overhead is expressed as 160% of direct labor. We then allocated overhead by multiplying 160% by the estimated amount of direct labor on the jobs.

We cannot wait until the end of a period to allocate overhead to jobs because perpetual inventory records are part of the job order costing system (demanding immediate and up-to-date costs). Instead, we must predict overhead in advance and assign it to jobs so that a job's total costs can be estimated prior to its completion. This estimated cost is useful for managers in many decisions including setting prices. Being able to estimate overhead in advance requires a **predetermined overhead rate,** or also called *predetermined overhead allocation* (or *application*) *rate.* This rate requires an estimate of total overhead cost and an allocation factor such as total direct labor cost before the start of the period.

Point: The predetermined overhead rate is computed at the start of the period and is used throughout the period to allocate overhead to jobs.

Point: Predetermined overhead rates can be estimated using mathematical equations, statistical analysis, or professional experience.

Point: To apply these concepts, work QS 19-6 and Exercise 19-3.

Exhibit 19.9 shows the usual formula for computing a predetermined overhead rate (estimates are commonly based on annual amounts). This rate is used during the period to allocate overhead to jobs. It is common for companies to use multiple allocation factors (bases) and multiple predetermined overhead rates for different types of products and services.

Exhibit 19.9

Predetermined Overhead Allocation Rate Formula

$$\textbf{Predetermined overhead rate} = \textbf{Estimated overhead costs} \div \textbf{Estimated factor costs}$$

To illustrate, Road Warriors allocates overhead by linking it to direct labor. At the start of the current period, management predicts total direct labor costs of $125,000 and total overhead costs of $200,000. Using these estimates, management computes its predetermined overhead rate as 160% of direct labor cost ($200,000 ÷ $125,000). Specifically, reviewing the job order cost sheet in Exhibit 19.2, we see that $1,000 of direct labor went into Job B15. We then use the predetermined overhead rate of 160% to allocate $1,600 of overhead to this job. The entry to record this allocation is

Example: If management predicts total direct labor costs of $100,000 and total overhead costs of $200,000, what is its predetermined overhead rate? *Answer:* 200% of direct labor cost.

Assets	=	Liabilities	+	Equity
+1,600				+1,600

Mar. 11	Goods in Process Inventory—Job B15	1,600	
	Factory Overhead		1,600
	To assign overhead to Job B15.		

Decision Ethics

Web Consultant You are working on seven client engagements. Two clients reimburse your firm for actual costs plus a 10% markup. The other five pay a fixed fee for services. Your firm's costs include overhead allocated at $47 per labor hour. The managing partner of your firm instructs you to record as many labor hours as possible to the two markup engagements by transferring labor hours from the other five. What do you do?

Answer—p. 770

Since the allocation rate for overhead is estimated at the start of a period, the total amount assigned to jobs during a period rarely equals the amount actually incurred. We explain how this difference is treated later in this chapter.

Summary of Cost Flows

We showed journal entries for charging Goods in Process Inventory (Job B15) with the cost of (1) direct materials requisitions, (2) direct labor time tickets, and (3) factory overhead. We made separate entries for each of these costs, but they are usually recorded in one entry. Specifically, materials requisitions are often collected for a day or a week and recorded with a single entry summarizing them. The same is done with labor time tickets. When summary entries are made, supporting schedules of the jobs charged and the types of materials used provide the basis for postings to subsidiary records.

Point: Study the flow of manufacturing costs through general ledger accounts and job cost sheets. Use Exhibit 19.11 as reinforcement.

To show all manufacturing cost flows for a period and their related entries, we again look at Road Warriors' activities. Exhibit 19.10 shows costs linked to all of Road Warriors' manufacturing activities for March. Road Warriors did not have any jobs in process at the beginning of March, but it did apply materials, labor, and overhead costs to five new jobs in March. Jobs B15 and B16 are completed and delivered to customers in March, Job B17 is completed but not delivered, and Jobs B18 and B19 are still in process. Exhibit 19.10 also shows purchases of raw materials for $2,750, labor costs incurred for $5,300, and overhead costs of $6,720.

Point: To apply these concepts, work Exercises 19-2 and 19-5.

Decision Maker

Entrepreneur Your division's product is facing increasing competition; competitors' prices are often lower than yours. Of the total product cost used in setting prices, 53% is factory overhead allocated using direct labor hours. You believe that product costs are distorted and wonder whether there is a better way to allocate factory overhead and to set product price. What do you suggest?

Answer—p. 771

The upper part of Exhibit 19.11 shows the flow of these costs through general ledger accounts and the end-of-month balances in key subsidiary records. Arrow lines are numbered to show the flows of costs for March. Each numbered cost flow reflects several entries made in March. The lower part of Exhibit 19.11 shows summarized job cost sheets and

Exhibit 19.10

Job Order Costs of All Manufacturing Activities

ROAD WARRIORS
Job Order Manufacturing Costs
For Month Ended March 31, 2005

Explanation	Materials	Labor	Overhead Incurred	Overhead Allocated	Goods in Process	Finished Goods	Cost of Goods Sold
Job B15	$ 600	$1,000		$1,600			$3,200
Job B16	300	800		1,280			2,380
Job B17	500	1,100		1,760		$3,360	
Job B18	150	700		1,120	$1,970		
Job B19	250	600		960	1,810		
Total job costs	1,800	4,200		$6,720	$3,780	$3,360	$5,580
Indirect materials	550		$ 550				
Indirect labor		1,100	1,100				
Other overhead			5,070				
Total costs used in production	2,350	$5,300	$6,720				
Ending materials inventory	1,400						
Materials available	3,750						
Less beginning materials inventory	(1,000)						
Materials purchased	$2,750						

Exhibit 19.11

Job Order Cost Flows and Ending Job Cost Sheets

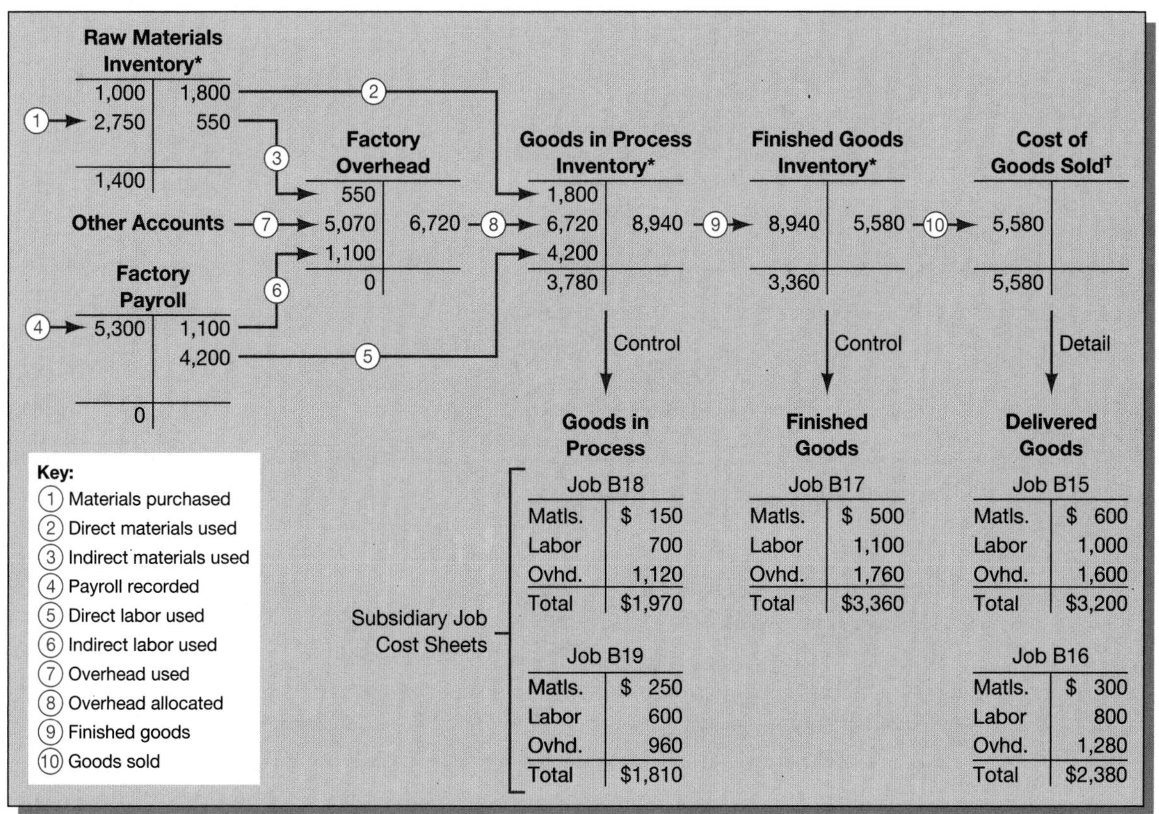

* The ending balances in the inventory accounts are carried to the balance sheet.
†The Cost of Goods Sold balance is carried to the income statement.

their status at the end of March. The sum of costs assigned to the jobs in process ($1,970 + $1,810) equals the $3,780 balance in Goods in Process Inventory shown in Exhibit 19.10. Also, costs assigned to Job B17 equal the $3,360 balance in Finished Goods Inventory. The sum of costs assigned to Jobs B15 and B16 ($3,200 + $2,380) equals the $5,580 balance in Cost of Goods Sold.

Exhibit 19.12 shows each cost flow with a single entry summarizing the actual individual entries made in March. Each entry is numbered to link with the arrow lines in Exhibit 19.11.

Exhibit 19.12

Entries for Job Order Manufacturing Costs*

①	Raw Materials Inventory	2,750	
	Accounts Payable		2,750
	Acquired materials on credit for factory use.		
②	Goods in Process Inventory	1,800	
	Raw Materials Inventory		1,800
	To assign costs of direct materials used.		
③	Factory Overhead	550	
	Raw Materials Inventory		550
	To record use of indirect materials.		
④	Factory Payroll	5,300	
	Cash (and other accounts)		5,300
	To record salaries and wages of factory workers (including various payroll liabilities).		
⑤	Goods in Process Inventory	4,200	
	Factory Payroll		4,200
	To assign costs of direct labor used.		
⑥	Factory Overhead	1,100	
	Factory Payroll		1,100
	To record indirect labor costs as overhead.		
⑦	Factory Overhead	5,070	
	Cash (and other accounts)		5,070
	To record factory overhead costs such as insurance, utilities, rent, and depreciation.		
⑧	Goods in Process Inventory	6,720	
	Factory Overhead		6,720
	To apply overhead at 160% of direct labor.		
⑨	Finished Goods Inventory	8,940	
	Goods in Process Inventory		8,940
	To record completion of Jobs B15, B16, and B17.		
⑩	Cost of Goods Sold	5,580	
	Finished Goods Inventory		5,580
	To record sale of Jobs B15 and B16.		

* Transactions are numbered to be consistent with arrow lines in Exhibit 19.11.

Point: Actual overhead is debited to Factory Overhead. Allocated overhead is credited to Factory Overhead.

Quick Check

5. In job order cost accounting, which account is debited in recording a raw materials requisition? (*a*) Raw Materials Inventory, (*b*) Raw Materials Purchases, (*c*) Goods in Process Inventory if for a job, or (*d*) Goods in Process Inventory if they are indirect materials.
6. What are four sources of information for recording costs in the Factory Overhead account?
7. Why does job order cost accounting require a predetermined overhead rate?
8. What events result in a debit to Factory Payroll? What events result in a credit?

Answers—p. 771

Adjustment of Overapplied and Underapplied Overhead

Refer to the debits in the Factory Overhead account in Exhibit 19.11 (or Exhibit 19.12). The total cost of factory overhead incurred during March is $6,720 ($550 + $5,070 + $1,100). The $6,720 exactly equals the amount assigned to goods in process inventory (see arrow line ⑧). Therefore, the overhead incurred equals the overhead applied in March. The amount of overhead incurred rarely equals the amount of overhead applied, however, because a job order cost accounting system uses a predetermined overhead rate in applying factory overhead costs to jobs. This rate is determined using estimated amounts before the period begins, and estimates rarely equal the exact amounts actually incurred. This section explains what we do when too much or too little overhead is applied to jobs.

Underapplied Overhead

P4 Determine adjustments for overapplied and underapplied factory overhead.

When less overhead is applied than is actually incurred, the remaining debit balance in the Factory Overhead account at the end of the period is called **underapplied overhead.** To illustrate, assume that Road Warriors actually incurred *other overhead costs* of $5,550 instead of the $5,070 shown in Exhibit 19.11. This yields an actual total overhead cost of $7,200 in March. Since the amount of overhead applied was only $6,720, the Factory Overhead account is left with a $480 debit balance as shown in the ledger account in Exhibit 19.13.

Exhibit 19.13

Underapplied Overhead in the Factory Overhead Ledger Account

Factory Overhead				Acct. No. 540
Date	**Explanation**	**Debit**	**Credit**	**Balance**
2005				
Mar. 31	Indirect materials cost	550		550 Dr.
31	Indirect labor cost	1,100		1,650 Dr.
31	Other overhead cost	5,550		7,200 Dr.
31	Overhead costs applied to jobs		6,720	480 Dr.

The $480 debit balance reflects manufacturing costs not assigned to jobs. This means that the balances in Goods in Process Inventory, Finished Goods Inventory, and Cost of Goods Sold do not include all manufacturing costs incurred. When the underapplied overhead amount is immaterial, it is allocated (closed) to the Cost of Goods Sold account with the following adjusting entry:[2]

Example: If we do not adjust for underapplied overhead, will net income be overstated or understated? *Answer:* Overstated.

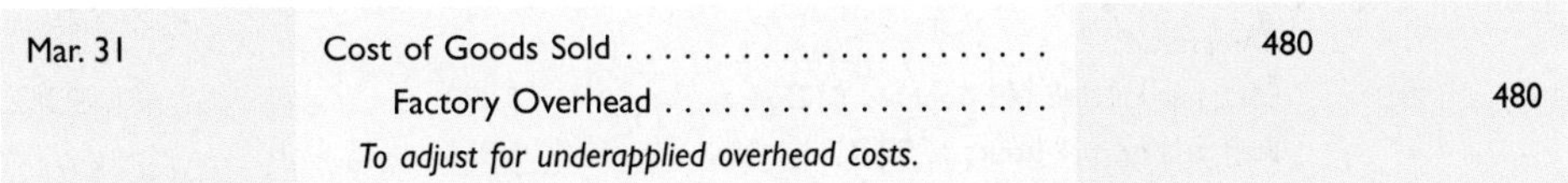

Mar. 31	Cost of Goods Sold	480	
	Factory Overhead		480
	To adjust for underapplied overhead costs.		

Assets = Liabilities + Equity
−480 +480

The $480 debit (increase) to Cost of Goods Sold reduces income by $480.

---

[2] When the underapplied (or overapplied) overhead is significant, the amount is normally allocated to the Cost of Goods Sold, Finished Goods Inventory, and Goods in Process Inventory accounts. The preferred method of allocating underapplied (or overapplied) overhead in this case is one consistent with the allocation method used in the period. For Road Warriors, underapplied overhead is allocated to jobs based on direct labor. Jobs B15 and B16, which are sold, account for 42.8% of the total direct labor cost in March. Also, 26.2% of direct labor was consumed by B17, which is in Finished Goods inventory, and the remaining 31% was consumed by Jobs B18 and B19, which are in Goods in Process inventory. These percents are multiplied by $480 to compute the amount of underapplied overhead allocated to each account (for example, 42.8% of $480, or $205, is allocated to the Cost of Goods Sold account). An adjusting entry records this allocation:

Mar. 31	Goods in Process Inventory	149	
	Finished Goods Inventory	126	
	Cost of Goods Sold.	205	
	Factory Overhead.		480
	To adjust for underapplied overhead costs.		

Overapplied Overhead

When the overhead applied in a period exceeds the overhead incurred, the resulting credit balance in the Factory Overhead account is called **overapplied overhead.** We treat overapplied overhead at the end of the period in the same way we treat underapplied overhead, except that we debit Factory Overhead and credit Cost of Good Sold for the amount.

Quick Check

9. In a job order cost accounting system, why does the Factory Overhead account usually have an overapplied or underapplied balance at period-end?

10. When the Factory Overhead account has a debit balance at period-end, does this reflect overapplied or underapplied overhead?

Answers—p. 771

Decision Analysis — Pricing for Services

A1 Apply job order costing in pricing services.

The chapter described job order costing mainly using a manufacturing setting. However, these concepts and procedures are applicable to a service setting. Consider AdWorld, an advertising agency that develops Web-based ads for small firms. Each of its customers has unique requirements, so costs for each individual job must be tracked separately.

AdWorld uses two types of labor: Web designers ($65 per hour) and computer staff ($50 per hour). It also incurs overhead costs that it assigns using two different predetermined overhead allocation rates: $125 per designer hour and $96 per staff hour. For each job, AdWorld must estimate the number of designer and staff hours needed. Then total costs pertaining to each job are determined using the procedures in the chapter. (*Note:* Most service firms have neither the category of materials cost nor inventory.)

To illustrate, a manufacturer of golf balls requested a quote from AdWorld for an advertising engagement. AdWorld estimates that the job will require 43 designer hours and 61 staff hours, with the following total estimated cost for this job:

Direct Labor		
Designers (43 hours × $65)	$ 2,795	
Staff (61 hours × $50)	3,050	
Total direct labor		$ 5,845
Overhead		
Designer related (43 hours × $125)	5,375	
Staff related (61 hours × $96)	5,856	
Total overhead		11,231
Total estimated job cost		$17,076

Decision Maker

Sales Manager As AdWorld's sales manager, assume that you estimate the costs pertaining to a proposed job to be $17,076. Your company's normal pricing policy is to apply a markup of 18% from total costs. Your assessment of the competition suggests that three other agencies are likely to bid for the same job, and that their quotes will range from $16,500 to $22,000. What price should you quote? What factors other than cost must you consider?

Answer—p. 771

AdWorld can use this cost information to help determine the price quote for the job (see *Decision Maker,* **Sales Manager**).

Another source of information that AdWorld must consider is the market, that is, how much competitors will quote for this job. Competitor information is often unavailable; therefore, AdWorld's managers must use estimates based on their assessment of the competitive environment.

Demonstration Problem—Job Order Costing

The following information reflects Peak Manufacturing Company's job order manufacturing activities for May:

Raw materials purchases	$16,000
Factory payroll cost	15,400
Overhead costs incurred	
Indirect materials	5,000
Indirect labor	3,500
Other factory overhead	9,500

The predetermined overhead rate is 150% of direct labor cost. These costs are allocated to the three jobs worked on during May as follows:

	Job 401	Job 402	Job 403
Balances on April 30			
Direct materials	$3,600		
Direct labor	1,700		
Applied overhead	2,550		
Costs during May			
Direct materials	3,550	$3,500	$1,400
Direct labor	5,100	6,000	800
Applied overhead	?	?	?
Status on May 31	**Finished (sold)**	**Finished (unsold)**	**In process**

Required

1. Determine the total cost of:
   a. The April 30 inventory of jobs in process.
   b. Materials used during May.
   c. Labor used during May.
   d. Factory overhead incurred and applied during May and the amount of any over- or underapplied overhead on May 31.
   e. Each job as of May 31, the May 31 inventories of both goods in process and finished goods, and the goods sold during May.
2. Prepare summarized journal entries for the month to record:
   a. Materials purchases (on credit), the factory payroll (paid with cash), indirect materials, indirect labor, and the other factory overhead (paid with cash).
   b. Assignment of direct materials, direct labor, and overhead costs to the Goods in Process Inventory account. (Use separate debit entries for each job.)
   c. Transfer of each completed job to the Finished Goods Inventory account.
   d. Cost of goods sold.
   e. Removal of any underapplied or overapplied overhead from the Factory Overhead account. (Assume the amount is not material.)
3. Prepare a manufacturing statement for May.

Planning the Solution

- Determine the cost of the April 30 goods in process inventory by totaling the materials, labor, and applied overhead costs for Job 401.
- Compute the cost of materials used and labor by totaling the amounts assigned to jobs and to overhead.

- Compute the total overhead incurred by totaling the amounts of the three components. Compute the amount of applied overhead by multiplying the total direct labor cost by the predetermined overhead rate. Compute the underapplied or overapplied amount as the difference between the actual cost and the applied cost.
- Determine the total cost charged to each job by adding the costs incurred in April (if any) to the cost of materials, labor, and overhead applied during May.
- Group the costs of the jobs according to their completion status.
- Record the direct materials costs assigned to the three jobs, using a separate Goods in Process Inventory account for each job; do the same for the direct labor and the applied overhead.
- Transfer costs of Jobs 401 and 402 from Goods in Process Inventory to Finished Goods.
- Record the costs of Job 401 as cost of goods sold.
- Record the transfer of underapplied overhead from the Factory Overhead account to the Cost of Goods Sold account.
- On the manufacturing statement, remember to include the beginning and ending goods in process inventories and to deduct the underapplied overhead.

Solution to Demonstration Problem

1. Total cost of

a. April 30 inventory of jobs in process (Job 401):

Direct materials	$3,600
Direct labor	1,700
Applied overhead	2,550
Total cost	$7,850

b. Materials used during May:

Direct materials	
Job 401	$ 3,550
Job 402	3,500
Job 403	1,400
Total direct materials	8,450
Indirect materials	5,000
Total materials used	$13,450

c. Labor used during May:

Direct labor	
Job 401	$ 5,100
Job 402	6,000
Job 403	800
Total direct labor	11,900
Indirect labor	3,500
Total labor used	$15,400

d. Factory overhead incurred in May:

Actual overhead	
Indirect materials	$ 5,000
Indirect labor	3,500
Other factory overhead	9,500
Total actual overhead	18,000
Overhead applied (150% × $11,900)	17,850
Underapplied overhead	$ 150

e. Total cost of each job:

	401	402	403
From April			
Direct materials	$ 3,600		
Direct labor	1,700		
Applied overhead*	2,550		
From May			
Direct materials	3,550	$ 3,500	$1,400
Direct labor	5,100	6,000	800
Applied overhead*	7,650	9,000	1,200
Total costs	$24,150	$18,500	$3,400

* Equals 150% of the direct labor cost.

Total cost of the May 31 inventory of goods in process (Job 403) = $3,400

Total cost of the May 31 inventory of finished goods (Job 402) = $18,500

Total cost of goods sold during May (Job 401) = $24,150

2. Journal entries:

a.

Account	Debit	Credit
Raw Materials Inventory	16,000	
Accounts Payable		16,000
To record materials purchases.		
Factory Payroll	15,400	
Cash		15,400
To record factory payroll.		
Factory Overhead	5,000	
Raw Materials Inventory		5,000
To record indirect materials.		
Factory Overhead	3,500	
Factory Payroll		3,500
To record indirect labor.		
Factory Overhead	9,500	
Cash		9,500
To record other factory overhead.		

b. Assignment of costs to Goods in Process Inventory:

Account	Debit	Credit
Goods in Process Inventory (Job 401)	3,550	
Goods in Process Inventory (Job 402)	3,500	
Goods in Process Inventory (Job 403)	1,400	
Raw Materials Inventory		8,450
To assign direct materials to jobs.		
Goods in Process Inventory (Job 401)	5,100	
Goods in Process Inventory (Job 402)	6,000	
Goods in Process Inventory (Job 403)	800	
Factory Payroll		11,900
To assign direct labor to jobs.		
Goods in Process Inventory (Job 401)	7,650	
Goods in Process Inventory (Job 402)	9,000	
Goods in Process Inventory (Job 403)	1,200	
Factory Overhead		17,850
To apply overhead to jobs.		

c. Transfer of completed jobs to Finished Goods Inventory:

Account	Debit	Credit
Finished Goods Inventory	42,650	
Goods in Process Inventory (Job 401)		24,150
Goods in Process Inventory (Job 402)		18,500
To record completion of jobs.		

d.

Account	Debit	Credit
Cost of Goods Sold	24,150	
Finished Goods Inventory		24,150
To record sale of Job 401.		

e.

Account	Debit	Credit
Cost of Goods Sold	150	
Factory Overhead		150
To assign underapplied overhead.		

3.

PEAK MANUFACTURING COMPANY Manufacturing Statement For Month Ended May 31		
Direct materials		$ 8,450
Direct labor		11,900
Factory overhead		
Indirect materials	$5,000	
Indirect labor	3,500	
Other factory overhead	9,500	18,000
Total manufacturing costs		38,350
Add goods in process, April 30		7,850
Total cost of goods in process		46,200
Less goods in process, May 31		3,400
Less underapplied overhead		150
Cost of goods manufactured		$42,650

Note how underapplied overhead is reported. Overapplied overhead is similarly reported, but is added.

Summary

C1 Explain the cost accounting system. A cost accounting system records manufacturing activities using a perpetual inventory system, which continuously updates records for transactions and events that affect inventory costs.

C2 Describe important features of job order manufacturing. Certain manufacturers called *job order manufacturers* produce custom-made products for customers. These customized products are manufactured in response to a customer's orders. A job order manufacturer produces products that usually are different and, typically, manufactured in low volumes. The manufacturing systems of job order companies are flexible and are not highly standardized.

C3 Explain job cost sheets and how they are used in job order cost accounting. In a job order cost accounting system, the costs of producing each job are accumulated on a separate job cost sheet. Costs of direct materials, direct labor, and overhead are accumulated separately on the job cost sheet and then added to determine the total cost of a job. Job cost sheets for jobs in process, finished jobs, and jobs sold make up subsidiary records controlled by general ledger accounts.

A1 Apply job order costing in pricing services. Job order costing can usefully be applied to a service setting. The resulting job cost estimate can then be used to help determine a price for services.

P1 Describe and record the flow of materials costs in job order cost accounting. Costs of materials flow from receiving reports to materials ledger cards and then to either job cost sheets or the Indirect Materials account in the factory overhead ledger.

P2 Describe and record the flow of labor costs in job order cost accounting. Costs of labor flow from clock cards to the Factory Payroll account and then to either job cost sheets or the Indirect Labor account in the factory overhead ledger.

P3 Describe and record the flow of overhead costs in job order cost accounting. Overhead costs are accumulated in the Factory Overhead account that controls the subsidiary factory overhead ledger. Then, using a predetermined overhead rate, overhead costs are charged to jobs.

P4 Determine adjustments for overapplied and underapplied factory overhead. At the end of each period, the Factory Overhead account usually has a residual debit (underapplied overhead); or credit (overapplied overhead) balance. If the balance is not material, it is transferred to Cost of Goods Sold, but if it is material, it is allocated to Goods in Process Inventory, Finished Goods Inventory, and Cost of Goods Sold.

Guidance Answers to **Decision Maker** and **Decision Ethics**

Management Consultant Service companies (such as this consulting firm) do not recognize goods in process inventory or finished goods inventory—an important difference between service and manufacturing companies. For the two jobs that are 60% complete, you could recognize revenues and costs at 60% of the total expected amounts. This means you could recognize revenue of \$7,200 (0.60 × \$12,000) and costs of \$6,000 (0.60 × \$10,000), yielding net income of \$1,200 from each job.

Web Consultant The partner has a monetary incentive to *manage* the numbers and assign more costs to the two cost-plus engagements. This also would reduce costs on the fixed-price engagements. To act in such a manner is unethical. As a professional and an honest person, it is your responsibility to engage in ethical behavior. You must not comply with the partner's instructions. If the partner insists you act in an unethical manner, you should report the matter to a higher authority in the organization.

Entrepreneur An inadequate cost system can distort product costs. You should review overhead costs in detail. Once you know the different cost elements in overhead, you can classify them into groups such as material related, labor related, or machine related. Other groups can also be formed (we discuss this in Chapter 21). Once you have classified overhead items into groups, you can better establish overhead allocation bases and use them to compute predetermined overhead rates. These multiple rates and bases can then be used to assign overhead costs to products. This will likely improve product pricing.

Sales Manager The price based on AdWorld's normal pricing policy is \$20,150 (\$17,076 × 1.18), which is within the price range offered by competitors. One option is to apply normal pricing policy and quote a price of \$20,150. On the other hand, assessing the competition, particularly in terms of their service quality and other benefits they might offer, would be useful. Although price is an input customers use to select suppliers, factors such as quality and timeliness (responsiveness) of suppliers are important. Accordingly, your price can reflect such factors.

Guidance Answers to **Quick Checks**

1. *b*
2. A job is a special order for a custom product. A job lot consists of a quantity of identical, special-order items.
3. *a*
4. Three costs normally accumulated on a job cost sheet are direct materials, direct labor, and factory overhead.
5. *c*
6. Four sources of factory overhead are materials requisitions, time tickets, vouchers, and adjusting entries.
7. Since a job order cost accounting system uses perpetual inventory records, overhead costs must be assigned to jobs before the end of a period. This requires the use of a predetermined overhead rate.
8. Debits are recorded when wages and salaries of factory employees are paid or accrued. Credits are recorded when direct labor costs are assigned to jobs and when indirect labor costs are transferred to the Factory Overhead account.
9. Overapplied or underapplied overhead usually exists at the end of a period because application of overhead is based on estimates of overhead and another variable such as direct labor. Estimates rarely equal actual amounts incurred.
10. A debit balance reflects underapplied factory overhead.

Key Terms

Key Terms are available at the book's Website for learning and testing in an online Flashcard Format.

Clock card (p. 759)
Cost accounting system (p. 754)
Finished Goods Inventory (p. 757)
General accounting system (p. 754)
Goods in Process Inventory (p. 756)
Job (p. 754)
Job cost sheet (p. 756)
Job lot (p. 755)
Job order cost accounting system (p. 756)
Job order manufacturing (p. 754)
Materials ledger card (p. 758)
Materials requisition (p. 758)
Overapplied overhead (p. 766)
Predetermined overhead rate (p. 761)
Time ticket (p. 759)
Underapplied overhead (p. 765)

Personal Interactive Quiz

Personal Interactive Quizzes A and B are available at the book's Website to reinforce and assess your learning.

Discussion Questions

1. Refer to Krispy Kreme's financial statements and notes in Appendix A. What are the major components and amounts of its inventory for 2003?
2. Why must a company estimate the amount of factory overhead assigned to individual jobs or job lots?
3. The chapter used a percent of labor cost to assign factory overhead to jobs. Identify another factor (or base) a company might reasonably use to assign overhead costs.
4. What information is recorded on a job cost sheet? How do management and employees use job cost sheets?
5. In a job order cost accounting system, what records serve as a subsidiary ledger for Goods in Process Inventory? For Finished Goods Inventory?
6. What journal entry is recorded when a materials manager receives a materials requisition and then issues materials (both direct and indirect) for use in the factory?

7. How does the materials requisition help safeguard a company's assets?

8. What is the difference between a clock card and a time ticket?

9. What events cause debits to be recorded in the Factory Overhead account? What events cause credits to be recorded in the Factory Overhead account?

10. What account(s) is(are) used to eliminate overapplied or underapplied overhead from the Factory Overhead account, assuming the amount is not material?

11. Assume that **Tastykake** produces a batch of 1,000 snack cakes. Does it account for this as 1,000 individual jobs or as a job lot? Explain (consider costs and benefits).

12. Why must a company prepare a predetermined overhead rate when using job order cost accounting?

13. How would a hospital apply job order costing? Explain.

14. **Harley-Davidson** manufactures 30 luxury-model motorcycles. Does it account for these motorcycles as 30 individual jobs or as a job lot? Explain.

Red numbers denote Discussion Questions that involve decision-making.

***Homework Manager** repeats all numerical Quick Studies on the book's Website with new numbers.*

QUICK STUDY

QS 19-1
Factory overhead rates P3

FasTrack Company incurred the following manufacturing costs this period: direct labor, $484,000; direct materials, $356,000; and factory overhead, $120,000. Compute overhead cost as a percent of (1) direct labor and (2) direct materials. Round percents to the nearest whole number.

QS 19-2
Jobs and job lots
C2

Determine which products are most likely to be manufactured as a job and which as a job lot:

1. A hand-crafted table.
2. A 90-foot motor yacht.
3. Wedding dresses for a chain of stores.
4. A custom-designed home.
5. Hats imprinted with company logo.
6. Little League trophies.

QS 19-3
Job cost computation
C3

The following information is from the materials requisitions and time tickets for Job 9-1005 completed by Around-The-Bay Boats. The requisitions are identified by code numbers starting with the letter Q and the time tickets start with W:

Date	Document	Amount
7/1/2005	Q-4698	$1,350
7/1/2005	W-3393	700
7/5/2005	Q-4725	1,100
7/5/2005	W-3479	550
7/10/2005	W-3559	400

At the start of the year, management estimated that overhead cost would equal 140% of direct labor cost for each job. Determine the total cost on the job cost sheet for Job 9-1005.

QS 19-4
Direct materials journal entries
P1

During the current month, a company that uses a job order cost accounting system purchases $70,000 in raw materials for cash. It then uses $22,000 of raw materials indirectly as factory supplies and uses $42,000 of raw materials as direct materials. Prepare entries to record these three transactions.

QS 19-5
Direct labor journal entries P2

During the current month, a company that uses a job order cost accounting system incurred a monthly factory payroll of $120,000, paid in cash. Of this amount, $30,000 is classified as indirect labor and the remainder as direct. Prepare entries to record these transactions.

QS 19-6
Factory overhead journal entries
P3

During the current month, a company that uses a job order cost accounting system incurred a monthly factory payroll of $120,000, paid in cash. Of this amount, $30,000 is classified as indirect labor and the remainder as direct for the production of a job lot. Factory overhead is applied at 150% of direct labor. Prepare the entry to apply factory overhead to this job lot.

QS 19-7
Entry for over- or underapplied overhead P4

Java Company allocates overhead at a rate of 140% of direct labor cost. Actual overhead cost for the current period is $745,000, and direct labor cost is $500,000. Prepare the entry to close over- or underapplied overhead to cost of goods sold.

Homework Manager repeats all numerical Exercises on the book's Website with new numbers.

EXERCISES

Exercise 19-1
Documents in job order cost accounting
C2 C3 P1 P2 P3

The left column lists the titles of documents and accounts used in job order cost accounting. The right column presents short descriptions of the purposes of the documents. Match each document in the left column to its numbered description in the right column.

A. Factory Payroll account
B. Materials ledger card
C. Time ticket
D. Voucher
E. Materials requisition
F. Factory Overhead account
G. Clock card

_____ **1.** Communicates the need for materials to complete a job.
_____ **2.** Shows only total time an employee works each day.
_____ **3.** Shows amount approved for payment of an overhead or other cost.
_____ **4.** Shows amount of time an employee works on a job.
_____ **5.** Temporarily accumulates the cost of incurred overhead until the cost is assigned to specific jobs.
_____ **6.** Temporarily accumulates incurred labor costs until they are assigned to specific jobs or to overhead.
_____ **7.** Perpetual inventory record of raw materials received, used, and available for use.

Exercise 19-2
Analysis of cost flows
C2 P1 P2 P3 

As of the end of June, the job cost sheets at Racing Wheels, Inc., show the following total costs accumulated on three custom jobs:

	Job 102	Job 103	Job 104
Direct materials	$30,000	$66,000	$54,000
Direct labor	16,000	28,400	42,000
Overhead	8,000	14,200	21,000

Job 102 was started in production in May and the following costs were assigned to it in May: direct materials, $12,000; direct labor, $3,600; and overhead, $1,800. Jobs 103 and 104 are started in June. Overhead cost is applied with a predetermined rate based on direct labor cost. Jobs 102 and 103 are finished in June, and Job 104 is expected to be finished in July. No raw materials are used indirectly in June. Using this information, answer the following questions:

1. What is the cost of the raw materials requisitioned in June for each of the three jobs?
2. How much direct labor cost is incurred during June for each of the three jobs?
3. What predetermined overhead rate is used during June?
4. How much total cost is transferred to finished goods during June?

Check (4) $162,600

Exercise 19-3
Overhead rate; costs assigned to jobs
P3

In December 2004, Kent Computer's management establishes the year 2005 predetermined overhead rate based on direct labor cost. The information used in setting this rate includes estimates that the company will incur $756,000 of overhead costs and $540,000 of direct labor cost in year 2005. During March 2005, Kent began and completed Job No. 13-56.

1. What is the predetermined overhead rate for year 2005?
2. Use the information on the following job cost sheet to determine the total cost of the job:

Check (2) $23,280

JOB COST SHEET

Customer's Name Keiser Co. **Job No.** 13-56
Job Description 5 color monitors—21 inch

	Direct Materials		Direct Labor		Overhead Costs Applied	
Date	**Requisition No.**	**Amount**	**Time-Ticket No.**	**Amount**	**Rate**	**Amount**
Mar. 8	4-129	$5,000	T-306	$ 640		
Mar. 11	4-142	7,050	T-432	1,280		
Mar. 18	4-167	3,550	T-456	1,280		
Totals						

Exercise 19-4
Analysis of costs assigned to goods in process
P3

Lopez Company uses a job order cost accounting system that charges overhead to jobs on the basis of direct material. At year-end, the Goods in Process Inventory account shows the following:

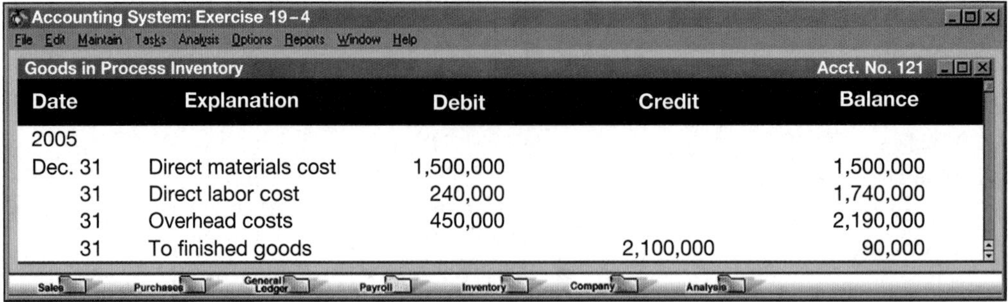

Accounting System: Exercise 19-4

Goods in Process Inventory — Acct. No. 121

Date	Explanation	Debit	Credit	Balance
2005				
Dec. 31	Direct materials cost	1,500,000		1,500,000
31	Direct labor cost	240,000		1,740,000
31	Overhead costs	450,000		2,190,000
31	To finished goods		2,100,000	90,000

1. Determine the overhead rate used (based on direct material cost).

Check (2) Direct labor cost, $51,000

2. Only one job remained in the goods in process inventory at December 31, 2005. Its direct materials cost is $30,000. How much direct labor cost and overhead cost are assigned to it?

Exercise 19-5
Cost flows in a job order cost system
C3 P3

The following information is available for Lock-Down Company, which produces special-order security products and uses a job order cost accounting system:

	April 30	May 31
Inventories		
Raw materials	$40,000	$ 50,000
Goods in process	9,600	19,500
Finished goods	60,000	33,200
Activities and information for May		
Raw materials purchases (paid with cash)		189,000
Factory payroll (paid with cash)		400,000
Factory overhead		
Indirect materials		12,000
Indirect labor		75,000
Other overhead costs		100,500
Sales (received in cash)		1,200,000
Predetermined overhead rate based on direct labor cost		65%

Compute the following amounts for the month of May:

1. Cost of direct materials used.
2. Cost of direct labor used.
3. Cost of goods manufactured.
4. Cost of goods sold.
5. Gross profit.
6. Overapplied or underapplied overhead.

Check (3) $693,350

Exercise 19-6
Journal entries for a job order cost accounting system
P1 P2 P3 P4

Use information in Exercise 19-5 to prepare journal entries for the following events in May:

1. Raw materials purchases for cash.
2. Direct materials usage.
3. Indirect materials usage.
4. Factory payroll costs in cash.
5. Direct labor usage.
6. Indirect labor usage.
7. Factory overhead other than indirect materials and indirect labor (record credit to Other Accounts).
8. Application of overhead to goods in process.
9. Transfer of finished jobs to the finished goods inventory.
10. Sale and delivery of finished goods to customers for cash.
11. Allocation (closing) of overapplied or underapplied overhead to Cost of Goods Sold.

Exercise 19-7
Factory overhead computed, applied, and adjusted
P3 P4

In December 2004, Ultravision established its predetermined overhead rate for movies produced during year 2005 by using the following cost predictions: overhead costs, $1,800,000, and direct labor costs, $450,000. At year end 2005, the company's records show that actual overhead costs for the year are $1,770,000. Actual direct labor cost had been assigned to jobs as follows:

Movies completed and released	$400,000
Movies still in production	45,000
Total actual direct labor cost	$445,000

1. Determine the predetermined overhead rate for year 2005.
2. Set up a T-account for overhead and enter the overhead costs incurred and the amounts applied to movies during the year using the predetermined overhead rate.
3. Determine whether overhead is overapplied or underapplied (and the amount) during the year.
4. Prepare the adjusting entry to allocate any over- or underapplied overhead to Cost of Goods Sold.

Check (3) $10,000 overapplied

Exercise 19-8
Factory overhead computed, applied, and adjusted
P3 P4

In December 2004, Perez Company established its predetermined overhead rate for jobs produced during year 2005 by using the following cost predictions: overhead costs, $600,000, and direct labor costs, $500,000. At year end 2005, the company's records show that actual overhead costs for the year are $680,000. Actual direct labor cost had been assigned to jobs as follows:

Jobs completed and sold	$420,000
Jobs in finished goods inventory	84,000
Jobs in goods in process inventory	56,000
Total actual direct labor cost	$560,000

1. Determine the predetermined overhead rate for year 2005.
2. Set up a T-account for Factory Overhead and enter the overhead costs incurred and the amounts applied to jobs during the year using the predetermined overhead rate.
3. Determine whether overhead is overapplied or underapplied (and the amount) during the year.
4. Prepare the adjusting entry to allocate any over- or underapplied overhead to Cost of Goods Sold.
5. Prepare the adjusting entry to allocate any over- or underapplied overhead to Cost of Goods Sold, Finished Goods Inventory, and Goods in Process Inventory.

Check (3) $8,000 underapplied

Exercise 19-9
Overhead rate calculation, allocation, and analysis
P3

Red Wing Company uses the relation between factory overhead and direct labor costs to assign factory overhead to its inventories of goods in process and finished goods. The company incurred the following costs during 2005: direct materials costs, $637,500; direct labor costs, $2,500,000; and factory overhead costs, $1,000,000.

1. Determine the company's predetermined overhead rate for year 2005.
2. Assuming that the company's $57,000 ending Goods in Process Inventory account for year 2005 had $18,000 of direct labor costs, determine the inventory's direct materials costs.
3. Assuming that the company's $337,485 ending Finished Goods Inventory account for year 2005 had $137,485 of direct materials costs, determine the inventory's direct labor costs and its overhead costs.

Check (3) $57,143 overhead costs

Exercise 19-10
Costs allocated to ending inventories
P3

Vegas Company's ending Goods in Process Inventory account consists of 4,500 units of partially completed product, and its Finished Goods Inventory account consists of 11,700 units of product. The factory manager determines that Goods in Process Inventory includes direct materials cost of $10 per unit and direct labor cost of $7 per unit. Finished goods are estimated to have $12 of direct materials cost per unit and $9 of direct labor cost per unit. The company established the predetermined overhead rate using the following predictions: estimated direct labor cost, $300,000, and estimated factory overhead, $360,000. The company allocates factory overhead to its goods in process and finished goods inventories by relating overhead to direct labor cost. During the period, the company incurred these costs: direct materials, $460,000; direct labor, $277,000; and factory overhead, $332,400.

1. Determine the predetermined overhead rate.
2. Compute the total cost of the two ending inventories.
3. Compute cost of goods sold for the year (assume no beginning inventories).

Check (3) Cost of goods sold, $583,040

Exercise 19-11
Cost-based pricing
A1 

Multiplex Corporation has requested bids from several architects to design its new corporate headquarters. Friesen Architects is one of the firms bidding on the job. Friesen estimates that the job will require the following direct labor:

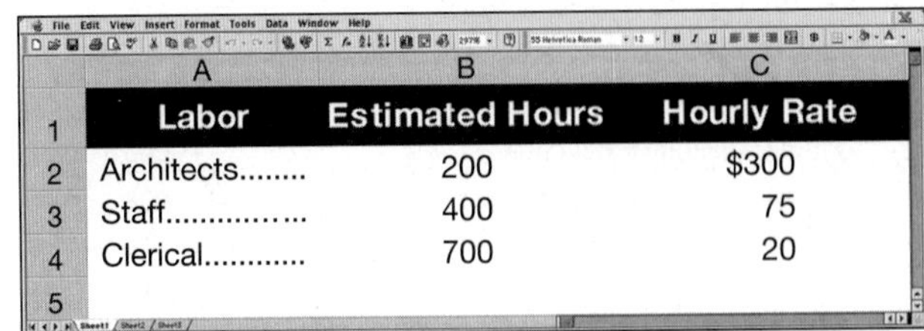

Labor	Estimated Hours	Hourly Rate
Architects........	200	$300
Staff..............	400	75
Clerical...........	700	20

Friesen applies overhead to jobs at 160% of direct labor cost. Friesen would like to earn at least $80,000 profit on the architectural job. Based on past experience and market research, it estimates that the competition will bid between $325,000 and $400,000 for the job.

Check (1) $270,400

1. What is Friesen's estimated cost of the architectural job?
2. What bid would you suggest that Friesen submit?

PROBLEM SET A

Problem 19-1A
Manufacturing costs computed and recorded; reports prepared
C3 P1 P2 P3 P4

Winfrey Co.'s March 31 inventory of raw materials is $150,000. Raw materials purchases in April are $400,000, and factory payroll cost in April is $220,000. Overhead costs incurred in April are: indirect materials, $30,000; indirect labor, $14,000; factory rent, $20,000; factory utilities, $12,000; and factory equipment depreciation, $30,000. The predetermined overhead rate is 50% of direct labor cost. Job 306 is sold for $380,000 cash in April. Costs of the three jobs worked on in April follow:

	Job 306	Job 307	Job 308
Balances on March 31			
Direct materials	$ 14,000	$ 18,000	
Direct labor	18,000	16,000	
Applied overhead	9,000	8,000	
Costs during April			
Direct materials	100,000	170,000	$ 80,000
Direct labor	30,000	56,000	120,000
Applied overhead	?	?	?
Status on April 30	Finished (sold)	Finished (unsold)	In process

Required

1. Determine the total of each manufacturing cost incurred for April (direct labor, direct materials, and applied overhead), and the total cost assigned to each job (including the balances from March 31).

2. Prepare journal entries for the month of April to record

a. Materials purchases (on credit), factory payroll (paid in cash), and actual overhead costs including indirect materials and indirect labor. (Factory rent and utilities are paid in cash.)

b. Assignment of direct materials, direct labor, and applied overhead costs to the Goods in Process Inventory.

c. Transfer of Jobs 306 and 307 to the Finished Goods Inventory.

d. Cost of goods sold for Job 306.

e. Revenue from the sale of Job 306.

Check (2f) $3,000 underapplied

f. Assignment of any underapplied or overapplied overhead to the Cost of Goods Sold account. (The amount is not material.)

(3) Cost of goods manufactured, $482,000

3. Prepare a manufacturing statement for April (use a single line presentation for direct materials and show the details of overhead cost).

4. Compute gross profit for April. Show how to present the inventories on the April 30 balance sheet.

Analysis Component

5. When the over- or underapplied overhead adjustment is made, we close Factory Overhead to Cost of Goods Sold. Discuss how this adjustment impacts business decision making regarding individual jobs or batches of jobs.

Problem 19-2A
Source documents, journal entries, overhead, and financial reports

P1 P2 P3 P4

Thai Bay's computer system generated the following trial balance on December 31, 2005. The company's manager knows something is wrong with the trial balance because it does not show any balance for Goods in Process Inventory but does show balances for the Factory Payroll and Factory Overhead accounts.

	Debit	Credit
Cash	$48,000	
Accounts receivable	42,000	
Raw materials inventory	26,000	
Goods in process inventory	0	
Finished goods inventory	9,000	
Prepaid rent	3,000	
Accounts payable		$ 10,500
Notes payable		13,500
Common stock		30,000
Retained earnings		87,000
Sales		180,000
Cost of goods sold	105,000	
Factory payroll	16,000	
Factory overhead	27,000	
Operating expenses	45,000	
Totals	$321,000	$321,000

After searching various files, the manager finds six source documents that need to be processed to bring the accounting records up to date:

Materials requisition 21-3010:	$4,600 direct materials to Job 402
Materials requisition 21-3011:	$7,600 direct materials to Job 404
Materials requisition 21-3012:	$2,100 indirect materials
Labor time ticket 6052:	$5,000 direct labor to Job 402
Labor time ticket 6053:	$8,000 direct labor to Job 404
Labor time ticket 6054:	$3,000 indirect labor

Jobs 402 and 404 are the only units in process at year-end. The predetermined overhead rate is 200% of direct labor cost.

Required

1. Use information on the six source documents to prepare journal entries to assign the following costs:
   a. Direct materials costs to Goods in Process Inventory.
   b. Direct labor costs to Goods in Process Inventory.
   c. Overhead costs to Goods in Process Inventory.
   d. Indirect materials costs to the Factory Overhead account.
   e. Indirect labor costs to the Factory Overhead account.

2. Determine the revised balance of the Factory Overhead account after making the entries in part 1. Determine whether there is any under- or overapplied overhead for the year. Prepare the adjusting entry to allocate any over- or underapplied overhead to Cost of Goods Sold, assuming the amount is not material.

Check (2) $6,100 underapplied overhead

3. Prepare a revised trial balance.

(3) T. B. totals, $321,000

4. Prepare an income statement for year 2005 and a balance sheet as of December 31, 2005.

(4) Net income, $23,900

Analysis Component

5. Assume that the $2,100 on materials requisition 21-3012 should have been direct materials charged to Job 404. Without providing specific calculations, describe the impact of this error on the income statement for 2005 and the balance sheet at December 31, 2005.

Problem 19-3A
Source documents, journal entries, and accounts in job order cost accounting

P1 P2 P3

Woodoo Watercraft's predetermined overhead rate for year 2005 is 200% of direct labor. The company's activities related to manufacturing during May 2005 follow:

a. Purchased raw materials on credit, $125,000.

b. Paid $84,000 cash for factory wages.

c. Paid $11,000 cash to a computer consultant to reprogram factory equipment.

d. Materials requisitions record use of the following materials for the month:

Job 136	$30,000
Job 137	20,000
Job 138	12,000
Job 139	14,000
Job 140	4,000
Total direct materials	80,000
Indirect materials	12,000
Total materials used	$92,000

e. Time tickets record use of the following labor for the month:

Job 136	$ 8,000
Job 137	7,000
Job 138	25,000
Job 139	26,000
Job 140	2,000
Total direct labor	68,000
Indirect labor	16,000
Total	$84,000

f. Applied overhead to Jobs 136, 138, and 139.

g. Transferred Jobs 136, 138, and 139 to Finished Goods.

h. Sold Jobs 136 and 138 on credit at a total price of $340,000.

i. Incurred the following overhead costs during the month (credit Prepaid Insurance for expired factory insurance):

Depreciation of factory building	$37,000
Depreciation of factory equipment	21,000
Expired factory insurance	7,000
Accrued property taxes payable	31,000

j. Applied overhead at month-end to the Goods in Process (Jobs 137 and 140) using the predetermined overhead rate of 200% of direct labor cost.

Required

1. Prepare a job cost sheet for each job worked on during the month. Use the following simplified form:

Job No. ________	
Materials	$
Labor	
Overhead	
Total cost	$

Check (2f) Cr. Factory Overhead, $118,000

2. Prepare journal entries to record the events and transactions *a* through *j*.

3. Set up T-accounts for each of the following general ledger accounts, each of which started the month with a zero balance: Raw Materials Inventory; Goods in Process Inventory; Finished Goods

Inventory; Factory Payroll; Factory Overhead; Cost of Goods Sold. Then post the journal entries to these T-accounts and determine the balance of each account.

4. Prepare a report showing the total cost of each job in process and prove that the sum of their costs equals the Goods in Process Inventory account balance. Prepare similar reports for Finished Goods Inventory and Cost of Goods Sold.

Check (4) Finished Goods Inventory, $92,000

Problem 19-4A
Overhead allocation and adjustment using a predetermined overhead rate

C3 P3 P4

mhhe.com/larson

In December 2004, Gomez Company's manager estimated next year's total direct labor cost assuming 50 persons working an average of 2,000 hours each at an average wage rate of $15 per hour. The manager also estimated the following manufacturing overhead costs for year 2005:

Indirect labor	$159,600
Factory supervision	120,000
Rent on factory building	70,000
Factory utilities	44,000
Factory insurance expired	34,000
Depreciation—Factory equipment	240,000
Repairs expense—Factory equipment	30,000
Factory supplies used	34,400
Miscellaneous production costs	18,000
Total estimated overhead costs	$750,000

At the end of 2005, records show the company incurred $725,000 of actual overhead costs. It completed and sold five jobs with the following direct labor costs: Job 201, $354,000; Job 202, $330,000; Job 203, $175,000; Job 204, $420,000; and Job 205, $184,000. In addition, Job 206 is in process at the end of 2005 and had been charged $10,000 for direct labor. No jobs were in process at the end of 2004. The company's predetermined overhead rate is based on direct labor cost.

Required

1. Determine the following:
   a. Predetermined overhead rate for year 2005.
   b. Total overhead cost applied to each of the six jobs during year 2005.
   c. Over- or underapplied overhead at year-end 2005.
2. Assuming that any over- or underapplied overhead is not material, prepare the adjusting entry to allocate any over- or underapplied overhead to Cost of Goods Sold at the end of year 2005.

Check (1c) $11,500 overapplied
(2) Dr. Factory Overhead $11,500

Problem 19-5A
Manufacturing transactions; subsidiary records; and source documents

P1 P2 P3 P4

If the working papers that accompany this book are not available, do not attempt to solve this problem.
Sagrillo Company manufactures variations of its product, a technopress, in response to custom orders from its customers. On May 1, the company had no inventories of goods in process or finished goods but held the following raw materials:

Material M	120 units @ $200 =	$24,000
Material R	80 units @ 160 =	12,800
Paint	44 units @ 72 =	3,168
Total cost		$39,968

On May 4, the company began working on two technopresses: Job 102 for Global Company and Job 103 for Rolf Company.

Required

Follow the instructions in this list of activities and complete the materials provided in the working papers.

a. Purchased raw materials on credit and recorded the following information from receiving reports and invoices:

Receiving Report No. 426, Material M, 150 units at $200 each.
Receiving Report No. 427, Material R, 70 units at $160 each.

Instructions: Record these purchases with a single journal entry and post it to general ledger T-accounts, using the transaction letter *a* to identify the entry. Enter the receiving report information on the materials ledger cards.

b. Requisitioned the following raw materials for production:

Requisition No. 35, for Job 102, 80 units of Material M.
Requisition No. 36, for Job 102, 60 units of Material R.
Requisition No. 37, for Job 103, 40 units of Material M.
Requisition No. 38, for Job 103, 30 units of Material R.
Requisition No. 39, for 12 units of paint.

Instructions: Enter amounts for direct materials requisitions on the materials ledger cards and the job cost sheets. Enter the indirect material amount on the materials ledger card and record a debit to the Indirect Materials account in the subsidiary factory overhead ledger. Do not record a journal entry at this time.

c. Received the following employee time tickets for work in May:

Time tickets Nos. 1 to 10 for direct labor on Job 102, $40,000.
Time tickets Nos. 11 to 30 for direct labor on Job 103, $32,000.
Time tickets Nos. 31 to 36 for equipment repairs, $12,000.

Instructions: Record direct labor from the time tickets on the job cost sheets and then debit indirect labor to the Indirect Labor account in the subsidiary factory overhead ledger. Do not record a journal entry at this time.

d. Paid cash for the following items during the month: factory payroll, $84,000, and miscellaneous overhead items, $36,000.

Instructions: Record these payments with journal entries and then post them to the general ledger accounts. Also record a debit in the Miscellaneous Overhead account in the subsidiary factory overhead ledger.

e. Finished Job 102 and transferred it to the warehouse. The company assigns overhead to each job with a predetermined overhead rate equal to 70% of direct labor cost.

Instructions: Enter the allocated overhead on the cost sheet for Job 102, fill in the cost summary section of the cost sheet, and then mark the cost sheet "Finished." Prepare a journal entry to record the job's completion and its transfer to Finished Goods and then post it to the general ledger accounts.

f. Delivered Job 102 and accepted the customer's promise to pay $290,000 within 30 days.

Instructions: Prepare journal entries to record the sale of Job 102 and the cost of goods sold. Post them to the general ledger accounts.

g. Applied overhead to Job 103 based on the job's direct labor to date.

Instructions: Enter overhead on the job cost sheet but do not make a journal entry at this time.

Check (h) Dr. Goods in Process Inventory, $38,400

h. Recorded the total direct and indirect materials costs as reported on all the requisitions for the month.

Instructions: Prepare a journal entry to record these costs and post it to general ledger accounts.

i. Recorded the total direct and indirect labor costs as reported on all time tickets for the month.

Instructions: Prepare a journal entry to record these costs and post it to general ledger accounts.

j. Recorded the total overhead costs applied to jobs.

Check Balance in Factory Overhead, $1,536 Cr., overapplied

Instructions: Prepare a journal entry to record the allocation of these overhead costs and post it to general ledger accounts.

PROBLEM SET B

Problem 19-1B

Manufacturing costs computed and recorded; reports prepared

C3 P1 P2 P3 P4 

Pak Co.'s August 31 inventory of raw materials is $16,000. Raw materials purchases in September are $60,000, and factory payroll cost in September is $68,000. Overhead costs incurred in September are: indirect materials, $6,000; indirect labor, $4,000; factory rent, $24,000; factory utilities, $22,000; and factory equipment depreciation, $25,000. The predetermined overhead rate is 130% of direct labor cost. Job 114 is sold for $100,000 cash in September. Costs for the three jobs worked on in September follow:

	Job 114	Job 115	Job 116
Balances on August 31			
Direct materials	$ 4,000	$ 6,000	
Direct labor	2,000	2,200	
Applied overhead	2,600	2,860	
Costs during September			
Direct materials	10,000	30,000	$16,000
Direct labor	16,000	28,000	20,000
Applied overhead	?	?	?
Status on September 30	Finished (sold)	Finished (unsold)	In process

Required

1. Determine the total of each manufacturing cost incurred for September (direct labor, direct materials, and applied overhead), and the total cost assigned to each job (including the balances from August 31).

2. Prepare journal entries for the month of September to record

a. Materials purchases (on credit), factory payroll (paid in cash), and actual overhead costs including indirect materials and indirect labor. (Factory rent and utilities are paid in cash.)

b. Assignment of direct materials, direct labor, and applied overhead costs to Goods in Process Inventory.

c. Transfer of Jobs 114 and 115 to the Finished Goods Inventory.

d. Cost of Job 114 in the Cost of Goods Sold account.

e. Revenue from the sale of Job 114.

f. Assignment of any underapplied or overapplied overhead to the Cost of Goods Sold account. (The amount is not material.)

Check (2f) $2,200 overapplied

3. Prepare a manufacturing statement for September (use a single line presentation for direct materials and show the details of overhead cost).

(3) Cost of goods manufactured, $160,860

4. Compute gross profit for September. Show how to present the inventories on the September 30 balance sheet.

Analysis Component

5. When the over- or underapplied overhead adjustment is made, we close Factory Overhead to Cost of Goods Sold. Discuss how this adjustment impacts business decision making regarding individual jobs or batches of jobs.

Problem 19-2B
Source documents, journal entries, overhead, and financial reports
P1 P2 P3 P4 

Metro's computer system generated the following trial balance on December 31, 2005. The company's manager knows that the trial balance is wrong because it does not show any balance for Goods in Process Inventory but does show balances for the Factory Payroll and Factory Overhead accounts.

	Debit	Credit
Cash	$ 40,000	
Accounts receivable	80,000	
Raw materials inventory	24,000	
Goods in process inventory	0	
Finished goods inventory	50,000	
Prepaid rent	4,000	
Accounts payable		$ 16,000
Notes payable		30,000
Common stock		60,000
Retained earnings		33,800
Sales		250,000
Cost of goods sold	140,000	
Factory payroll	20,000	
Factory overhead	9,800	
Operating expenses	22,000	
Totals	$389,800	$389,800

After searching various files, the manager finds six source documents that need to be processed to bring the accounting records up to date:

Materials requisition 94-231:	$ 5,000 direct materials to Job 603
Materials requisition 94-232:	$ 8,000 direct materials to Job 604
Materials requisition 94-233:	$ 1,500 indirect materials
Labor time ticket 765:	$ 6,000 direct labor to Job 603
Labor time ticket 766:	$12,000 direct labor to Job 604
Labor time ticket 777:	$ 2,000 indirect labor

Jobs 603 and 604 are the only units in process at year-end. The predetermined overhead rate is 80% of direct labor cost.

Required

1. Use information on the six source documents to prepare journal entries to assign the following costs:

a. Direct materials costs to Goods in Process Inventory.

b. Direct labor costs to Goods in Process Inventory.

c. Overhead costs to Goods in Process Inventory.

d. Indirect materials costs to the Factory Overhead account.

e. Indirect labor costs to the Factory Overhead account.

Check (2) $1,100 overapplied overhead

2. Determine the revised balance of the Factory Overhead account after making the entries in part 1. Determine whether there is under- or overapplied overhead for the year. Prepare the adjusting entry to allocate any over- or underapplied overhead to Cost of Goods Sold, assuming the amount is not material.

(3) T. B. totals, $389,800

3. Prepare a revised trial balance.

(4) Net income, $89,100

4. Prepare an income statement for year 2005 and a balance sheet as of December 31, 2005.

Analysis Component

5. Assume that the $1,500 indirect materials on materials requisition 94-233 should have been direct materials charged to Job 604. Without providing specific calculations, describe the impact of this error on the income statement for 2005 and the balance sheet at December 31, 2005.

Problem 19-3B
Source documents, journal entries, and accounts in job order cost accounting
P1 P2 P3

Troupe Company's predetermined overhead rate is 90% of direct labor. The company's activities related to manufacturing during September 2005 follow:

a. Purchased raw materials on credit, $57,000.

b. Paid $99,750 cash for factory wages.

c. Paid $11,250 cash for miscellaneous factory overhead costs.

d. Materials requisitions record use of the following materials for the month:

Job 487	$13,500
Job 488	9,000
Job 489	12,000
Job 490	10,500
Job 491	1,500
Total direct materials	46,500
Indirect materials	3,750
Total materials used	$50,250

e. Time tickets record use of the following labor for the month:

Job 487	$16,500
Job 488	19,500
Job 489	25,500
Job 490	18,000
Job 491	7,500
Total direct labor	87,000
Indirect labor	12,750
Total	$99,750

f. Allocated overhead to Jobs 487, 489, and 490.

g. Transferred Jobs 487, 489, and 490 to Finished Goods.

h. Sold Jobs 487 and 489 on credit for a total price of $225,000.

i. Incurred the following overhead costs during the month (credit Prepaid Insurance for expired factory insurance):

Depreciation of factory building	$24,750
Depreciation of factory equipment	18,750
Expired factory insurance	2,250
Accrued property taxes payable	5,250

j. Applied overhead at month-end to the Goods in Process (Jobs 488 and 491) using the predetermined overhead rate of 90% of direct labor cost.

Required

1. Prepare a job cost sheet for each job worked on during the month. Use the following simplified form:

Job No. ________	
Materials	$
Labor	
Overhead	
Total cost	$

2. Prepare journal entries to record the events and transactions *a* through *j*.

Check (2f) Cr. Factory Overhead, $54,000

3. Set up T-accounts for each of the following general ledger accounts, each of which started the month with a zero balance: Raw Materials Inventory, Goods in Process Inventory, Finished Goods Inventory, Factory Payroll, Factory Overhead, Cost of Goods Sold. Then post the journal entries to these T-accounts and determine the balance of each account.

4. Prepare a report showing the total cost of each job in process and prove that the sum of their costs equals the Goods in Process Inventory account balance. Prepare similar reports for Finished Goods Inventory and Cost of Goods Sold.

(4) Finished Goods Inventory, $44,700

Problem 19-4B
Overhead allocation and adjustment using a predetermined overhead rate
C3 P3 P4

In December 2004, Monk Company's manager estimated next year's total direct labor cost assuming 40 persons working an average of 1,500 hours each at an average wage rate of $50 per hour. The manager also estimated the following manufacturing overhead costs for year 2005.

Indirect labor	$ 540,000
Factory supervision	450,000
Rent on factory building	360,000
Factory utilities	200,000
Factory insurance expired	60,000
Depreciation—Factory equipment	300,000
Repairs expense—Factory equipment	180,000
Factory supplies used	110,000
Miscellaneous production costs	200,000
Total estimated overhead costs	$2,400,000

At the end of 2005, records show the company incurred $2,200,000 of actual overhead costs. It completed and sold five jobs with the following direct labor costs: Job 625, $300,000; Job 626, $225,000; Job 627, $975,000; Job 628, $240,000; and Job 629, $375,000. In addition, Job 630 is in process at the end of 2005 and had been charged $75,000 for direct labor. No jobs were in process at the end of 2004. The company's predetermined overhead rate is based on direct labor cost.

Required

1. Determine the following:

  a. Predetermined overhead rate for year 2005.

  b. Total overhead cost applied to each of the six jobs during year 2005.

  c. Over- or underapplied overhead at year-end 2005.

2. Assuming that any over- or underapplied overhead is not material, prepare the adjusting entry to allocate any over- or underapplied overhead to Cost of Goods Sold at the end of year 2005.

Check (1c) $448,000 underapplied

(2) Cr. Factory Overhead, $448,000

Problem 19-5B

Manufacturing transactions; subsidiary records; and source documents

P1 P2 P3 P4

If the working papers that accompany this book are not available, do not attempt to solve this problem. Sim Company manufactures variations of its product, a megatron, in response to custom orders from its customers. On June 1, the company had no inventories of goods in process or finished goods but held the following raw materials:

Material M	150 units @ $ 40 =	$ 6,000
Material R	50 units @ 160 =	8,000
Paint	20 units @ 20 =	400
Total cost		$14,400

On June 3, the company began working on two megatrons: Job 450 for Olivas Company and Job 451 for Ireland, Inc.

Required

Follow instructions in this list of activities and complete the materials provided in the working papers.

a. Purchased raw materials on credit and recorded the following information from receiving reports and invoices:

> Receiving Report No. 20, Material M, 150 units at $40 each.
> Receiving Report No. 21, Material R, 200 units at $160 each.

Instructions: Record these purchases with a single journal entry and post it to general ledger T-accounts, using the transaction letter *a* to identify the entry. Enter the receiving report information on the materials ledger cards.

b. Requisitioned the following raw materials for production:

> Requisition No. 223, for Job 450, 60 units of Material M.
> Requisition No. 224, for Job 450, 100 units of Material R.
> Requisition No. 225, for Job 451, 30 units of Material M.
> Requisition No. 226, for Job 451, 75 units of Material R.
> Requisition No. 227, for 10 units of paint.

Instructions: Enter amounts for direct materials requisitions on the materials ledger cards and the job cost sheets. Enter the indirect material amount on the materials ledger card and record a debit to the Indirect Materials account in the subsidiary factory overhead ledger. Do not record a journal entry at this time.

c. Received the following employee time tickets for work in June:

> Time tickets Nos. 1 to 10 for direct labor on Job 450, $24,000.
> Time tickets Nos. 11 to 20 for direct labor on Job 451, $20,000.
> Time tickets Nos. 21 to 24 for equipment repairs, $4,000.

Instructions: Record direct labor from the time tickets on the job cost sheets and then debit indirect labor to the Indirect Labor account in the subsidiary factory overhead ledger. Do not record a journal entry at this time.

d. Paid cash for the following items during the month: factory payroll, $48,000, and miscellaneous overhead items, $47,000.

Instructions: Record these payments with journal entries and post them to the general ledger accounts. Also record a debit in the Miscellaneous Overhead account in the subsidiary factory overhead ledger.

e. Finished Job 450 and transferred it to the warehouse. The company assigns overhead to each job with a predetermined overhead rate equal to 120% of direct labor cost.

Instructions: Enter the allocated overhead on the cost sheet for Job 450, fill in the cost summary section of the cost sheet, and then mark the cost sheet "Finished." Prepare a journal entry to record the job's completion and its transfer to Finished Goods and then post it to the general ledger accounts.

f. Delivered Job 450 and accepted the customer's promise to pay $130,000 within 30 days.

Instructions: Prepare journal entries to record the sale of Job 450 and the cost of goods sold. Post them to the general ledger accounts.

g. Applied overhead cost to Job 451 based on the job's direct labor used to date.

Instructions: Enter overhead on the job cost sheet but do not make a journal entry at this time.

h. Recorded the total direct and indirect materials costs as reported on all the requisitions for the month.

Instructions: Prepare a journal entry to record these costs and post it to general ledger accounts.

Check (h) Dr. Goods in Process Inventory, $31,600

i. Recorded the total direct and indirect labor costs as reported on all time tickets for the month.

Instructions: Prepare a journal entry to record these costs and post it to general ledger accounts.

j. Recorded the total overhead costs applied to jobs.

Instructions: Prepare a journal entry to record the allocation of these overhead costs and post it to general ledger accounts.

Check Balance in Factory Overhead, $1,600 Cr., overapplied

PROBLEM SET C

Problem Set C is available at the book's Website to reinforce and assess your learning.

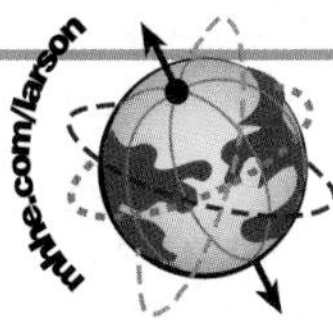

SERIAL PROBLEM

Success Systems

(This serial problem began in Chapter 1 and continues through most of the book. If previous chapter segments were not completed, the serial problem can begin at this point. It is helpful, but not necessary, for you to use the Working Papers that accompany the book.)

The computer workstation furniture manufacturing that Kay Breeze started in January 2006 is progressing well. As of the end of June, Success Systems' job cost sheets show these total costs accumulated on three furniture jobs:

	Job 6.02	Job 6.03	Job 6.04
Direct materials	$1,500	$3,300	$2,700
Direct labor	800	1,420	2,100
Overhead	400	710	1,050

Job 6.02 was started in production in May, and these costs were assigned to it in May: direct materials, $600; direct labor, $180; and overhead, $90. Jobs 6.03 and 6.04 were started in June. Overhead cost is applied with a predetermined rate based on direct labor costs. Jobs 6.02 and 6.03 are finished in June, and Job 6.04 is expected to be finished in July. No raw materials are used indirectly in June.

Required

1. What is the cost of the raw materials used in June for each of the three jobs and in total?

Check (1) Total cost, $6,900

2. How much total direct labor cost is incurred in June?

3. What predetermined overhead rate is used in June?

(3) 50%

4. How much cost is transferred to finished goods inventory in June?

BEYOND THE NUMBERS

REPORTING IN ACTION

C2 

BTN 19-1 Krispy Kreme's financial statements and notes in Appendix A provide evidence of growth potential in its domestic sales.

Required

1. Identify at least two types of costs that will predictably increase as a percent of sales with growth in domestic sales.
2. Explain why you believe the types of costs identified for part 1 will increase, and describe how you might assess Krispy Kreme's success with these costs. (*Hint:* You might consider the gross margin ratio.)

Roll On

3. Access Krispy Kreme's annual report for a fiscal year ending after February 2, 2003, from its Website [KrispyKreme.com] or the SEC's EDGAR database [www.SEC.gov]. Review and report its growth in sales along with its cost and income levels (including its gross margin ratio).

COMPARATIVE ANALYSIS

C1 

BTN 19-2 Both Krispy Kreme and Tastykake want to know the impact of a just-in-time (JIT) inventory system for their operating cash flows. Review each company's statement of cash flows in Appendix A to answer the following.

Required

1. Identify the impact on operating cash flows (increase or decrease) for changes in inventory levels (increase or decrease) for both companies for each of the three most recent years.
2. What impact would a JIT inventory system have on both Krispy Kreme's and Tastykake's level of raw materials and their operating cash flows? Link the answer to your response for part 1.
3. Would the move to a JIT system have a one-time or recurring impact on operating cash flow?

ETHICS CHALLENGE

P3 

BTN 19-3 An accounting professional requires at least two skill sets. The first is to be technically competent. Knowing how to capture, manage, and report information is a necessary skill. Second, the ability to assess manager and employee actions and biases for accounting analysis is another skill. For instance, knowing how a person is compensated helps anticipate information biases. Draw on these skills and write a one-half page memo to the financial officer on the following practice of allocating overhead.

Background: Assume that your company sells portable housing to both general contractors and the government. It sells jobs to contractors on a bid basis. A contractor asks for three bids from different manufacturers. The combination of low bid and high quality wins the job. However, jobs sold to the government are bid on a cost-plus basis. This means price is determined by adding all costs plus a profit based on cost at a specified percent, such as 10%. You observe that the amount of overhead allocated to government jobs is higher than that allocated to contract jobs. These allocations concern you and motivate your memo.

Point: Students could compare responses and discuss differences in concerns with allocating overhead.

COMMUNICATING IN PRACTICE

 C2 C3 

BTN 19-4 Assume that you are preparing for a second interview with a manufacturing company. The company is impressed with your credentials but has indicated that it has several qualified applicants. You anticipate that in this second interview, you must show what you offer over other candidates. You learn the company currently uses a periodic inventory system and is not satisfied with the timeliness of its information and its inventory management. The company manufactures custom-order holiday decorations and display items. To show your abilities, you plan to recommend that it use a cost accounting system.

Required

In preparation for the interview, prepare notes outlining the following:

1. Your cost accounting system recommendation and why it is suitable for this company.
2. A general description of the documents that the proposed cost accounting system requires.
3. How the documents in part 2 facilitate the operation of the cost accounting system.

Point: Have students present a mock interview, one assuming the role of the president of the company and the other the applicant.

BTN 19-5 Most contractors work on custom jobs that usually require a job order costing system.

TAKING IT TO THE NET

C2

Required

Access the Website AEC.Geac.com and under *Software Solutions* and then *Construction,* click on *Job Cost Accounting*. Prepare a one-page memorandum for the CEO of a construction company providing information about the job order costing software this company offers. Would you recommend that the company purchase this software?

BTN 19-6 Consider the activities undertaken by a medical clinic in your area.

TEAMWORK IN ACTION

C2

Required

1. Do you consider a job order cost accounting system appropriate for the clinic?
2. Identify as many factors as possible to lead you to conclude that it uses a job order system.

BTN 19-7 Managing materials in the production process is a challenging and crucial task for a company. Read the article "Smart Tools" in the March 24, 2003, issue of *Business Week.*

BUSINESS WEEK ACTIVITY

C1 C2

Required

1. Identify five different types of businesses that are exploring artificial intelligence applications.
2. What is DARPA? How are civilian businesses using it to improve direct materials management?

BTN 19-8 Rebecca Smith of **A.D. Morgan Corporation** already uses state-of-the-art job order cost accounting to track construction job costs on jobs in progress. Smith is considering purchasing a cost estimator *Excel* software package to help her bid competitively for new business and allow her to incorporate technology at an earlier stage of the job management process.

ENTREPRENEURIAL DECISION

C2

Required

1. Identify five features that you believe are important for the cost estimator software to possess.
2. What benefits should Smith reap from using job cost estimator software?

BTN 19-9 Job order cost accounting is frequently used by builders.

HITTING THE ROAD

C3 P2 P3 P4

Required

1. You (or your team) are to prepare a job cost sheet for a single-family home under construction. List four items of both direct materials and direct labor. Explain how you think overhead should be applied.
2. Contact a builder and compare your job cost sheet to this builder's job cost sheet. If possible, speak to that company's accountant. Write your findings in a short report.

BTN 19-10 **Grupo Bimbo, Krispy Kreme,** and **Tastykake** are competitors in the global marketplace. Access Grupo Bimbo's annual report (GrupoBimbo.com) for the year ended December 31, 2002. Review its balance sheet and its statement of changes in financial position to complete the following.

GLOBAL DECISION

C1

Required

1. Identify the impact on net resources generated by operating activities (increase or decrease) for changes in inventory levels (increase or decrease) for Grupo Bimbo for the last two years by reviewing its statement of changes in financial position.
2. Would a move to a JIT system likely impact Grupo Bimbo more significantly than it would Krispy Kreme or Tastykake? Explain.

"We don't have any superstars, just a lot of people who make the routine plays"—Shawn Buchanan

Process Cost Accounting

A Look Back

Chapter 18 introduced managerial accounting and described cost concepts and the reporting of manufacturing activities. Chapter 19 explained job order costing—an important cost accounting system for customized products and services.

A Look at This Chapter

This chapter focuses on how to measure and account for costs in process operations. We explain process production, describe how to assign costs to processes, and compute cost per equivalent unit for a process.

A Look Ahead

Chapter 21 describes managerial accounting reports useful in directing a company's operations. We explain how to allocate factory overhead costs to different products and describe the activity-based costing method of overhead allocation.

CAP

Conceptual

C1 Explain process operations and the way they differ from job order operations. *(p. 790)*

C2 Define equivalent units and explain their use in process cost accounting. *(p. 798)*

C3 Explain the four steps in accounting for production activity in a period. *(p. 799)*

C4 Define a process cost summary and describe its purposes. *(p. 803)*

Analytical

A1 Compare process cost accounting and job order cost accounting. *(p. 791)*

A2 Explain and illustrate a hybrid costing system. *(p. 809)*

Procedural

P1 Record the flow of direct materials costs in process cost accounting. *(p. 794)*

P2 Record the flow of direct labor costs in process cost accounting. *(p. 795)*

P3 Record the flow of factory overhead costs in process cost accounting. *(p. 796)*

P4 Compute equivalent units produced in a period. *(p. 798)*

P5 Prepare a process cost summary. *(p. 803)*

P6 Record the transfer of goods between departments. *(p. 803)*

P7 Record the transfer of completed goods to Finished Goods Inventory and Cost of Goods Sold. *(p. 807)*

Decision Feature

A Beef with the Entrepreneur

OMAHA—Shawn Buchanan never dreamed he would be working in the beef industry. "The funny thing is," says Buchanan, "the only thing I knew about meat or beef was that I enjoyed a good steak." That changed after he met Bill Hughes, owner of a beef-processing plant and the father of a player whom Buchanan coached in youth baseball. Before long, Buchanan was hooked by the beef business and took an unpaid management trainee job with Hughes's company. In return, Hughes mentored him in the business. Nearly one year later, with $500 in start-up capital, Buchanan launched **All American Meats [AllAmericanMeats.com],** a producer and distributor of beef products.

"As far as being an entrepreneur," says Buchanan, "it's in my blood—my dad had a machine shop." Still, a beef producer is quite a different animal than a machinist. Buchanan had to learn the beef-processing operations and the materials, labor, and overhead costs necessary to achieve high-quality meat products. His ability to monitor and control these costs was the difference between success and failure. "I learned how to operate and survive in a lean and mean situation," he says.

Buchanan's success extends to his ability to effectively prepare and interpret process cost summaries on his beef operations. Sales are important, but without cost controls, net income is quickly cut away. "When I go after something," he says, "I'm totally committed to it." This included his commitment to improving process operations and accounting for its various costs. "We hold a daily production meeting," says Buchanan. "We talk about what customers are saying about us, how we need to improve and other issues."

Buchanan encourages feedback on his process operations from his employees. "I want them to know that every idea is important." He even posts "idea boards" in the production area. "Any employee can write down an agenda item or idea on the board, and it gets discussed at the next meeting." One employee's idea, says Buchanan, "reduced the need from four to two employees on the production line." Such practices yield huge cost savings, and often kudos for the employee. "I'm a firm believer in the work ethic," says Buchanan. "You have to earn your stripes." And your steak.

[Sources: *All American Meats Website,* January 2004; *Entrepreneur,* November 2001; *PeerSpectives Report,* August 2002.]

The type of product or service a company offers determines its cost accounting system. Job order costing is used to account for custom products that meet the requirements of a particular customer. Not all products are manufactured in this way; many carry standard designs so that one unit is no different than any other unit. Such a system often produces large numbers of units on a continuous basis, all of which pass through similar manufacturing steps or processes. This chapter describes how to use a process cost accounting system to account for these types of products. It also explains how manufacturing costs are accumulated for each process and then assigned to units passing through those processes. This information helps to understand and estimate the cost of each process as well as find ways to reduce costs and improve processes.

Process Cost Accounting

Process Operations
- Comparison of job order and process operations
- Organization of process operations
- GenX Company—An Illustration

Process Cost Accounting
- Direct and indirect costs
- Accounting for materials costs
- Accounting for labor costs
- Accounting for factory overhead

Equivalent Units of Production (EUP)
- Accounting for goods in process
- Differences between EUP for materials and that for labor and overhead

Process Costing Illustration
- Physical flow of units
- EUP
- Cost per EUP
- Cost reconciliation
- Process cost summary
- Transfers between departments
- Transfers to finished goods and to cost of goods sold

Process Operations

C1 Explain process operations and the way they differ from job order operations.

Process manufacturing, also called *process operations* or *process production,* is the mass production of products in a continuous flow of steps. This means that products pass through a series of sequential processes. Petroleum refining is a common example of process operations. Crude oil passes through a series of steps before it is processed into different grades of petroleum. **Exxon Mobil**'s oil activities reflect a process operation. An important characteristic of process operations is the high level of standardization necessary if the system is to produce large volumes of products. Process operations also extend to services. Examples include mail sorting in large post offices and order processing in large mail-order firms such as **L.L. Bean**. The common feature in these service organizations is that operations are performed in a sequential manner using a series of standardized processes.

Each of these examples of products and services involves operations having a series of *processes,* or steps. Each process involves a different set of activities. A manufacturing operation that processes chemicals, for instance, might include the four steps shown in Exhibit 20.1. Understanding such processes for companies with process operations is crucial for measuring their costs.

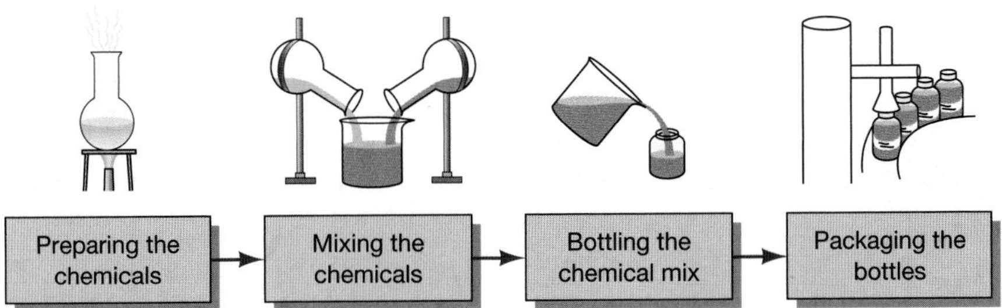

Exhibit 20.1

Process Manufacturing Operations: Chemicals

Comparing Job Order and Process Operations

A1 Compare process cost accounting and job order cost accounting.

Job order and process operations can be considered as two ends of a continuum. Important features of both systems are shown in Exhibit 20.2. We often describe job order and process operations with manufacturing examples, but they both apply to service companies. In a job order costing system, the measurement focus is on the individual job or batch. In a process costing system, the measurement focus is on the process itself and the standardized units produced.

Exhibit 20.2

Comparing Job Order and Process Operations

Job Order Systems	Process Systems
• Custom orders	• Repetitive operations
• Heterogeneous products	• Homogeneous products
• Low production volume	• High production volume
• High product flexibility	• Low product flexibility
• Low to medium standardization	• High standardization

Organization of Process Operations

In a process manufacturing operation, each process is identified as a separate *production department, workstation,* or *work center.* With the exception of the first process or department, each receives the output from the prior department as a partially processed product. Depending on the nature of the process, a company applies direct labor, overhead, and, perhaps, additional direct materials to move the product toward completion. Only the final process or department in the series produces finished goods ready for sale to customers.

Exhibit 20.3 shows an operation that manufactures components of a final product in three parallel processes (each shown in sequential layout) and combines them at different production stages. In the context of parallel and sequential processes, many operations involve numerous components and related production processes.

GenX Company—An Illustration

The GenX Company illustrates process operations. It produces Profen®, an over-the-counter pain reliever for athletes. GenX sells Profen to wholesale distributors who in turn sell it to retailers. Profen is produced in two steps. Step 1 uses a grinding process to pulverize blocks of its active ingredient, Profelene. Step 2 mixes the resulting powder with flavorings and preservatives, molds it into Profen tablets, and

Decision Insight

Accounting for Health Many service companies use process departments to perform specific tasks for consumers. Hospitals, for instance, have radiology and physical therapy facilities with special equipment and trained employees. When patients need services, they are processed through departments to receive prescribed care. Service companies need process cost accounting information as much as manufacturers to estimate costs of providing services, to plan future operations, to control costs, and to determine charges to customers.

Exhibit 20.3

Manufacturing Operations with Parallel and Sequential Processes

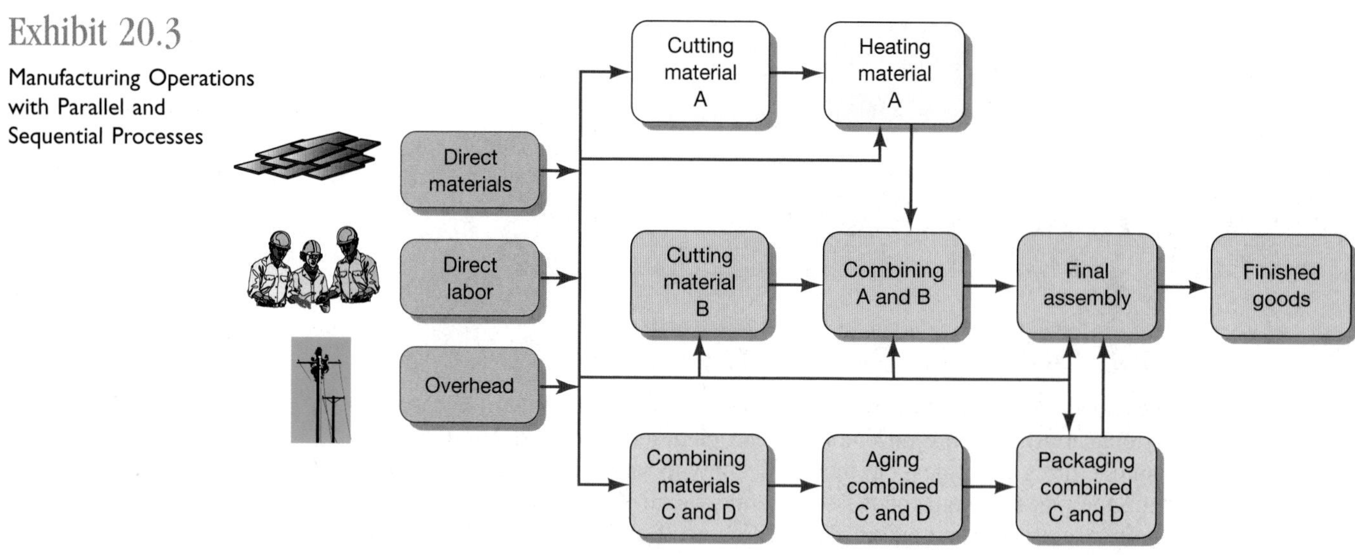

packages the tablets. Exhibit 20.4 shows a summary floor plan of the GenX factory, which has five areas:

1. *Storeroom*—materials are received and then distributed when requisitioned.
2. *Production support offices*—used by administrative and maintenance employees who support manufacturing operations.
3. *Locker rooms*—workers change from street clothes into sanitized uniforms before working in the factory.
4. *Production floor*—areas divided between the grinding and mixing departments.
5. *Warehouse*—finished products are stored before being shipped to wholesalers.

Point: Robots, computers, and online information are common in today's factory.

Exhibit 20.4

Floor Plan of GenX's Factory

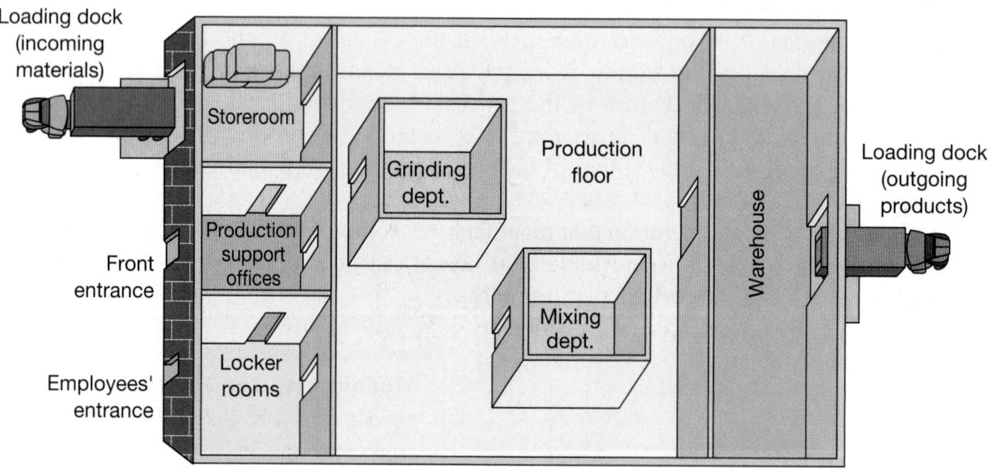

The first step in process manufacturing is to decide to produce a product. Management determines the types and quantities of materials and labor needed and then schedules the work for departments. Based on these plans, production begins. The flowchart in Exhibit 20.5 shows the production steps for GenX. The table in part B of the exhibit summarizes GenX's April costs of its manufacturing processes. This includes costs at the beginning of April and costs incurred in April and the application of those costs to the grinding and mixing departments. The following sections explain how GenX uses a process cost accounting system to compute these costs. Many of the explanations refer to this exhibit and its numbered cost flows.

A. Process Manufacturing Operations

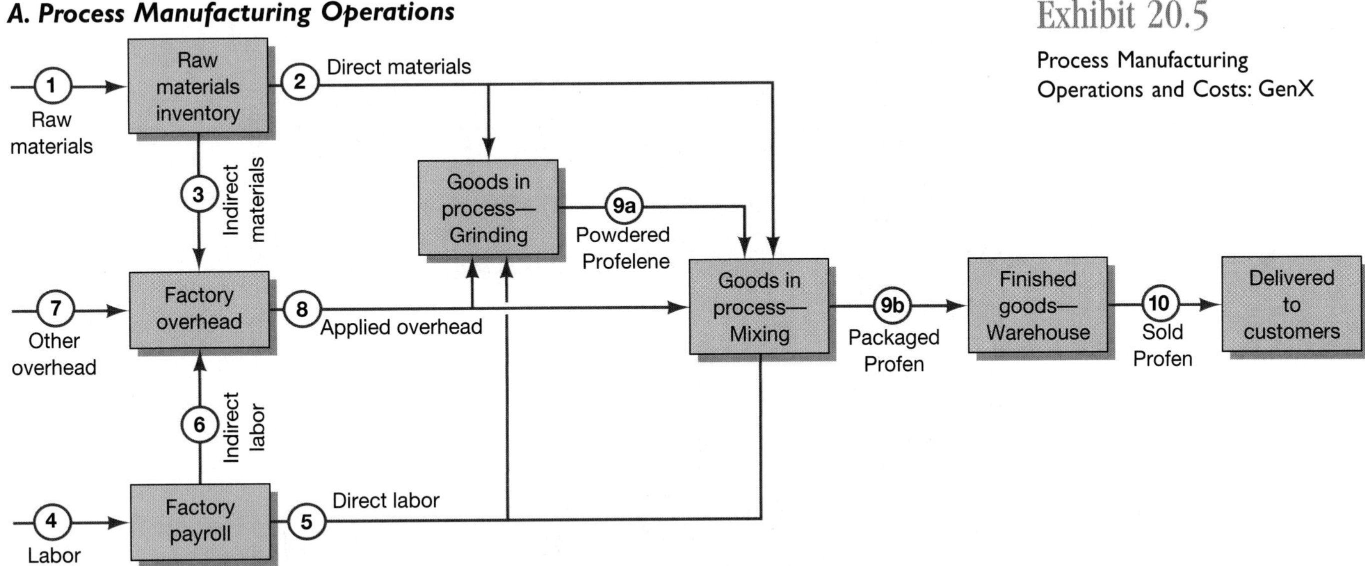

Exhibit 20.5

Process Manufacturing Operations and Costs: GenX

B. Manufacturing Costs of Goods Transferred and Sold in April

	Grinding Department	Mixing Department	Finished Goods
Beginning inventory	$ 4,250	$ 3,520	$ 6,440
Direct materials	9,900	2,040	
Direct labor	5,700	5,100	
Overhead applied*	4,275	1,020	
Total costs—Grinding	24,125		
Less ending inventory—Grinding	2,725		
Transferred to Mixing	$21,400 →	21,400	
Total costs—Mixing		33,080	
Less ending inventory—Mixing		3,610	
Transferred to finished goods		$29,470 →	29,470
Less ending inventory—Finished goods			5,251
Cost of goods sold			$30,659

* Overhead is applied to the two production departments using predetermined overhead rates based on direct labor dollars. Actual overhead incurred: Indirect materials, $1,195; indirect labor, $3,220; other overhead purchases and costs, $880.

Process Cost Accounting

Process and job order manufacturing operations are similar in that both combine materials, labor, and overhead in the process of producing products. They differ in how they are organized and managed. The measurement focus in a job order costing system is on the individual job or batch, whereas in a process costing system, it is on the individual process. Regardless of the measurement focus, we are ultimately interested in determining the cost per unit of product (or service) resulting from either system.

Specifically, the **job order cost accounting system** assigns direct materials, direct labor, and overhead to jobs. The total job cost is then divided by the number of units to compute a cost per unit for that job. The **process cost accounting system** assigns direct materials, direct labor, and overhead to specific processes. The total costs associated with each process are then divided by the number of units passing through that process to determine the cost per equivalent unit (defined later in the chapter) for that process. The cost per equivalent unit for each process is summed for all processes to determine the total cost per unit of a product. The differences in the way these two systems apply materials, labor, and overhead costs are highlighted in Exhibit 20.6.

Point: The cost object in a job order system is the specific job; the cost object in a process costing system is the process.

Exhibit 20.6

Comparing Job Order and Process Cost Accounting Systems

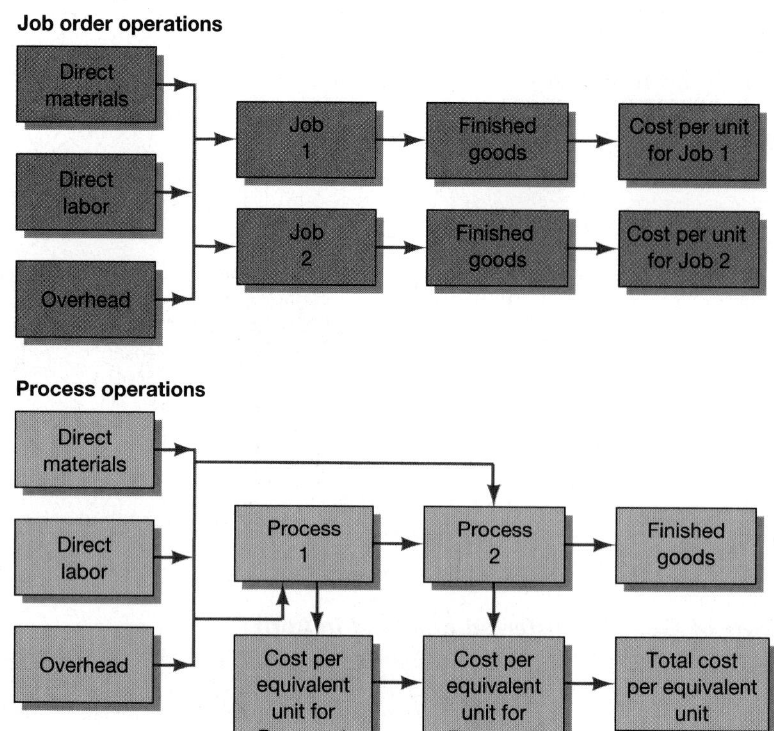

Direct and Indirect Costs

Point: If a cost can be directly linked to the cost object, it is direct; if it cannot, it is indirect.

Like job order operations, process cost accounting systems use the concepts of direct and indirect costs. Materials and labor that are clearly linked with specific processes are assigned to those processes as direct costs. Materials and labor not clearly linked with a specific process are indirect costs and are assigned to overhead. Some costs classified as overhead in a job order system may be classified as direct costs in process cost accounting. For example, depreciation of a machine used entirely by one process is a direct cost of that process. The next three subsections explain the accounting for materials, labor, and overhead in a process cost accounting system.

Decision Insight

JIT Boon to Process Operations Companies that adopt JIT manufacturing often organize their production system as a series of sequential processes. One survey found 60% of companies that converted to JIT used process operations; this compares to only 20% before converting to JIT.

Accounting for Materials Costs

P1 Record the flow of direct materials costs in process cost accounting.

In Exhibit 20.5, arrow line ① reflects the arrival of materials at GenX's factory. These materials include Profelene, flavorings, preservatives, and packaging. They also include supplies for the production support office. GenX uses a perpetual inventory system and makes all purchases on credit. The summary entry for receipts of raw materials in April follows (dates in journal entries numbered ① through ⑩ are omitted because they are summary entries, often reflecting two or more transactions or events):

Assets = Liabilities + Equity
+14,135 +14,135

①	Raw Materials Inventory	14,135	
	Accounts Payable.		14,135
	Acquired materials on credit for factory use.		

Arrow line ② in Exhibit 20.5 reflects the flow of direct materials to the grinding and mixing departments, where they are used to produce Profen. Most direct materials are physically combined into the finished product; the remaining direct materials include those used and clearly linked with a specific process. The manager of a process usually obtains materials by submitting a *materials requisition* to the materials storeroom manager. In some situations, materials move continuously from raw materials inventory through the manufacturing process. **Pepsi Bottling**, for instance, uses a process in which inventory moves continuously through the system. In these cases, a **materials consumption report** summarizes the materials used by a department during a reporting period and replaces materials requisitions. The entry to record the use of direct materials by GenX's two production departments in April follows:

②	Goods in Process Inventory—Grinding	9,900	
	Goods in Process Inventory—Mixing	2,040	
	Raw Materials Inventory		11,940
	To assign costs of direct materials used in the grinding and mixing departments.		

Assets = Liabilities + Equity
+9,900
+2,040
−11,940

This entry transfers costs from one asset account to two other asset accounts. Use of two Goods in Process Inventory accounts allows the costs incurred by each process to be separately accumulated.

In Exhibit 20.5, the arrow line ③ reflects the flow of indirect materials from the storeroom to factory overhead. These materials are not clearly linked with either the grinding or the mixing departments but are used to support overall production activity. The following entry records the cost of indirect materials used by GenX in April:

Example: What types of materials might the flow of arrow line ③ in Exhibit 20.5 reflect? *Answer:* Goggles, gloves, protective clothing, recordkeeping supplies, and cleaning supplies.

③	Factory Overhead	1,195	
	Raw Materials Inventory		1,195
	To record indirect materials used in April.		

Assets = Liabilities + Equity
−1,195 −1,195

After the entries for both direct and indirect materials are posted, the Raw Materials Inventory account appears as shown in Exhibit 20.7. The April 30 balance sheet reports the $5,000 Raw Materials Inventory account as a current asset.

Raw Materials Inventory					Acct. No. 132
Date		**Explanation**	**Debit**	**Credit**	**Balance**
2005					
Mar.	31	Balance			4,000
Apr.	30	Materials purchases	14,135		18,135
	30	Direct materials usage		11,940	6,195
	30	Indirect materials usage		1,195	5,000

Exhibit 20.7
Raw Materials Inventory

Accounting for Labor Costs

P2 Record the flow of direct labor costs in process cost accounting.

Exhibit 20.5 shows GenX factory payroll costs as reflected in arrow line ④. Total labor costs of $14,020 are paid in cash and are recorded in the Factory Payroll account:

④	Factory Payroll	14,020	
	Cash		14,020
	To record factory wages for April.		

Assets = Liabilities + Equity
−14,020 −14,020

Time reports from the two production departments and the production support office triggered this entry. (For simplicity, we do not separately identify withholdings and additional payroll taxes for employees.) In a process operation, the direct labor of a production department (such as mixing) includes all labor used exclusively by that department. This is the case even if the labor is not applied to the product itself. If a production department in a process operation, for instance, has a full-time manager and a full-time maintenance worker, their salaries are direct labor costs of a process, not factory overhead.

Arrow line ⑤ in Exhibit 20.5 shows GenX's use of direct labor in the grinding and mixing departments. The following entry transfers April's direct labor costs from the Factory Payroll account to the two Goods in Process Inventory accounts:

Assets	=	Liabilities	+	Equity
+5,700				+10,800
+5,100				

		Debit	Credit
⑤	Goods in Process Inventory—Grinding	5,700	
	Goods in Process Inventory—Mixing	5,100	
	Factory Payroll		10,800
	To assign costs of direct labor used in the grinding and mixing departments.		

Point: A department's indirect labor cost might include an allocated portion of the salary of a manager who supervises two departments. Allocation of costs between departments is discussed in Chapter 21.

Arrow line ⑥ in Exhibit 20.5 reflects GenX's indirect labor costs. These employees provide clerical, maintenance, and other services that help both the grinding *and* mixing departments produce Profen efficiently. For example, they order materials, deliver them to the factory floor, repair equipment, operate and program computers used in production, keep payroll and other production records, clean up, and move the finished goods to the warehouse. The following entry charges these indirect labor costs to factory overhead:

Assets	=	Liabilities	+	Equity
				−3,220
				+3,220

		Debit	Credit
⑥	Factory Overhead	3,220	
	Factory Payroll		3,220
	To record indirect labor as overhead.		

After these entries for both direct and indirect labor are posted, the Factory Payroll account appears as shown in Exhibit 20.8. The Factory Payroll account is now closed and ready to receive entries for May.

Exhibit 20.8

Factory Payroll

Factory Payroll					Acct. No. 530
Date		Explanation	Debit	Credit	Balance
2005					
Mar.	31	Balance			0
Apr.	30	Total payroll for April	14,020		14,020
	30	Direct labor costs		10,800	3,220
	30	Indirect labor costs		3,220	0

Accounting for Factory Overhead

P3 Record the flow of factory overhead costs in process cost accounting.

Overhead costs other than indirect materials and indirect labor are reflected by arrow line ⑦ in Exhibit 20.5. These overhead items include the costs of insuring manufacturing assets, renting the factory building, using factory utilities, and depreciating equipment not directly related to a specific process. The following entry records overhead costs for April:

Assets	=	Liabilities	+	Equity
−80		+200		−880
−250				
−350				

		Debit	Credit
⑦	Factory Overhead	880	
	Prepaid Insurance		80
	Utilities Payable		200
	Cash		250
	Accumulated Depreciation—Factory Equipment		350
	To record overhead items incurred in April.		

After this entry is posted, the Factory Overhead account balance is $5,295, comprising indirect materials of $1,195, indirect labor of $3,220, and $880 of other overhead.

Arrow line ⑧ in Exhibit 20.5 reflects the application of factory overhead to the two production departments. Factory overhead is applied to processes by relating overhead cost to another variable such as direct labor hours or machine hours used. In many situations, a single allocation basis such as direct labor hours (or a single rate for the entire plant) fails to provide useful allocations. As a result, management may use different rates for different production departments. Based on an analysis of each department's operations, GenX applies its April overhead on the basis of direct labor cost but with different predetermined rates, as shown in Exhibit 20.9.

Point: The time it takes to process (cycle) products through a process can also be used to allocate costs.

Exhibit 20.9

Applying Factory Overhead

Production Department	Direct Labor Cost	Predetermined Rate*	Overhead Applied
Grinding	$5,700	75%	$4,275
Mixing	5,100	20	1,020
Total			$5,295

* Predetermined overhead rates: Grinding department, 75% of direct labor cost; and Mixing department, 20% of direct labor cost.

Example: If grinding uses a 70% rate (instead of 75%), what balance remains in the factory overhead account after overhead is applied to both departments? *Answer:*

Overhead costs	$5,295
Overhead applied	5,010
Underapplied overhead	$ 285

GenX records its applied overhead with the following entry:

		Debit	Credit
⑧	Goods in Process Inventory—Grinding	4,275	
	Goods in Process Inventory—Mixing	1,020	
	Factory Overhead		5,295
	Allocated overhead costs to grinding department at 75% of direct labor cost and to mixing department at 20% of direct labor cost.		

Assets	=	Liabilities	+	Equity
+4,275				+5,295
+1,020				

After posting this entry, the Factory Overhead account appears as shown in Exhibit 20.10. For GenX, the amount of overhead applied equals the actual overhead incurred during April. In most cases, using a predetermined overhead rate leaves an overapplied or underapplied balance in the Factory Overhead account. At the end of the period, this overapplied or underapplied balance should be either closed to the Cost of Goods Sold account or allocated among the Cost of Goods Sold, the Goods in Process Inventory, and the Finished Goods Inventory. Procedures for this allocation are the same as that described in Chapter 19 for job order cost accounting systems.

Decision Ethics

Budget Officer You are working to identify the direct and indirect costs of a new processing department that has several machines. This department's manager instructs you to classify a majority of the costs as indirect to take advantage of the direct labor–based overhead allocation method so it will be charged a lower amount of overhead (because of its small direct labor cost). This would penalize other departments charged with higher allocations. It also will cause the performance ratings of managers in these other departments to suffer. What action do you take?

Answer—p. 814

Exhibit 20.10

Factory Overhead

Factory Overhead					Acct. No. 540
Date		Explanation	Debit	Credit	Balance
2005					
Mar.	31	Balance			0
Apr.	30	Indirect materials usage	1,195		1,195
	30	Indirect labor costs	3,220		4,415
	30	Other overhead costs	880		5,295
	30	Applied to production departments		5,295	0

Example: If applied overhead results in a $5,400 credit to the factory overhead account, does it yield an over- or underapplied overhead amount? *Answer:* $105 overapplied overhead

Quick Check

1. A process manufacturing operation (*a*) is another name for a job order operation, (*b*) does not use the concepts of direct materials or direct labor, or (*c*) typically produces large quantities of homogenous products.
2. Under what conditions is a process cost accounting system more suitable for measuring manufacturing costs than a job order cost accounting system?
3. When direct materials are assigned and used in both Department X and Department Y, the entry to record their use includes (*a*) a credit to Goods in Process Inventory—Department X, (*b*) a debit to Goods in Process Inventory—Department Y, or (*c*) a credit to Goods in Process Inventory—Department Y.
4. What are the three cost categories incurred by both job order and process operations?
5. How many Goods in Process Inventory accounts are needed in a process cost system?

Answers—p. 814

Equivalent Units of Production

C2 Define equivalent units and explain their use in process cost accounting.

We explained how materials, labor, and overhead costs for a period are accumulated in separate Goods in Process Inventory accounts for each process, but we have not explained the arrow lines labeled ⑨a, ⑨b, and ⑩ in Exhibit 20.5. These lines reflect the transfer of products from the grinding department to the mixing department, from the mixing department to finished goods inventory, and from finished goods inventory to cost of goods sold. To determine the costs recorded for these flows, we must first determine the cost per unit of product and then apply this result to the number of units transferred.

Topic Tackler 20-1

Accounting for Goods in Process

If a process has *no beginning and no ending goods in process inventory,* the unit cost of goods transferred out of a process is defined as follows:

$$\frac{\textbf{Total cost assigned to the process (direct materials, direct labor, and overhead)}}{\textbf{Total number of units started and finished in the period}}$$

If a process has a beginning or ending inventory of partially processed units (or both), however, the total cost assigned to the process must be allocated to all completed and incomplete units worked on during the period. Therefore, the denominator must measure the entire production activity of the process for the period, called **equivalent units of production** (or **EUP**), a term that refers to the number of units that would be completed if all effort during a period had been applied to only those units started in that period. This measure is then used to compute the cost per equivalent unit and to assign costs to finished goods and goods in process inventory.

To illustrate, assume that GenX adds (or introduces) 100 units into the grinding process during a period. Suppose at the end of that period, the production supervisor determines that those 100 units are 60% processed. Therefore, equivalent units of production for that period total 60 units (100 units × 60%). This means that if we had introduced 60 units into the process, we would have completely processed these 60 units.

Differences between Equivalent Units for Materials and that for Labor and Overhead

P4 Compute the equivalent units produced in a period.

In many processes, the equivalent units of production for materials are not the same with respect to labor and overhead. To illustrate, consider the 5-step process operation shown in Exhibit 20.11.

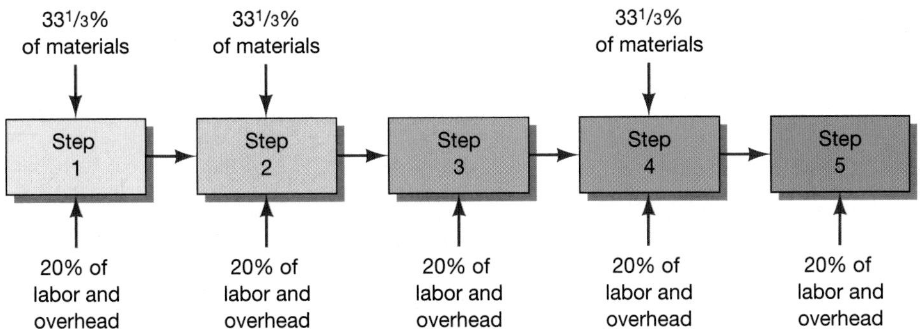

Exhibit 20.11

Process Manufacturing: An Example

This exhibit shows that one-third of the direct material cost is added at each of three steps: 1, 2, and 4. One-fifth of the direct labor cost is added at each of the five steps. One-fifth of the overhead also is added at each step because overhead is applied as a percent of direct labor for this company.

When units finish step 1, they are one-third complete with respect to materials but only one-fifth complete with respect to labor and overhead. When they finish step 2, they are two-thirds complete with respect to materials but only two-fifths complete with respect to labor and overhead. When they finish step 3, they remain two-thirds complete with respect to materials but are now three-fifths complete with respect to labor and overhead. When they finish step 4, they are 100% complete with respect to materials (all materials have been added) but only four-fifths complete with respect to labor and overhead.

Decision Insight

Process Services Customer-interaction software is a hot item in customer-service processes. Whether in insurance, delivery, or technology services, companies are finding that this software can turn their customer-service process into an asset. How does it work? For starters, it cuts time spent on service calls because a customer describes a problem only once. It also yields a database of customer questions and complaints that gives insights into needed improvements. It also recognizes incoming phone numbers and accesses previous dealings.

As an example, if 300 units of product are started and processed through step 1 of Exhibit 20.11, they are said to be one-third complete *with respect to materials*. Expressed in terms of equivalent finished units, the processing of these 300 units is equal to finishing 100 units with respect to materials (300 units × 33⅓%). However, only one-fifth of direct labor and overhead has been applied to the 300 units at the end of step 1. This means that the equivalent units of production *with respect to labor and overhead* total 60 units (300 units × 20%).

Process Costing Illustration

This section applies the process costing concepts and procedures to GenX.

Accounting for First (Grinding) Department

C3 Explain the four steps in accounting for production activity in a period.

Exhibit 20.12 shows selected information from the first (grinding) department for the month of April. In computing equivalent units, assume that each of GenX's production departments processes units on a first-in, first-out basis.[1] Accounting for a department's activity for a period includes four steps involving analysis of (1) physical flow, (2) equivalent units, (3) cost per equivalent unit, and (4) cost reconciliation. The next sections describe each step.

[1] Assume a FIFO flow for all computations and assignments in this chapter unless explicitly stated differently. Weighted average and LIFO also can be used, but they are less useful for measuring how effectively costs are controlled during a period. When using a just-in-time inventory system, the different inventory methods yield similar results because inventories are immaterial.

Exhibit 20.12

Production Data—First (Grinding) Department

Beginning inventory (March 31)	
Units of product	30,000
Percentage of completion—Direct materials	100%
Percentage of completion—Direct labor	33⅓%
Direct materials costs	$ 2,780
Direct labor costs	$ 700
Factory overhead costs	$ 770
Activities during the current period	
Units started this period (April)	90,000
Units transferred to mixing (during April)	100,000
Direct materials costs	$ 9,900
Direct labor costs	$ 5,700
Factory overhead costs	$ 4,275
Ending inventory (April 30)	
Units of product	20,000
Percentage of completion—Direct materials	100%
Percentage of completion—Direct labor	25%

Physical Flow of Units—First Department *Physical flow* is a reconciliation of (1) the physical units started in a period with (2) the physical units completed in that period. A physical flow reconciliation for GenX is shown in Exhibit 20.13 for April.

Exhibit 20.13

Physical Flow Reconciliation—First (Grinding) Department

Units to Account For		Units Accounted For	
Beginning inventory	30,000 units	Units transferred from grinding to mixing	100,000 units
Units started (in April)	90,000 units	Ending inventory	20,000 units
Total number of units	**120,000 units**	Total number of units	**120,000 units**

reconciled

The 100,000 units transferred from grinding to mixing during April include the 30,000 units from the beginning goods in process inventory (or simply beginning inventory) because of the FIFO assumption. The remaining 70,000 units transferred out are from units started in April. Of the total 90,000 units started in April, 70,000 of these are completed, and 20,000 remain unfinished at period-end.

Equivalent Units of Production—First Department The second step is to compute *equivalent units of production* in the grinding department for direct materials, direct labor, and factory overhead for April. Overhead is applied using direct labor as the allocation base. This means that the equivalent units are the same for both labor and overhead for GenX.

Equivalent units—Direct materials Direct materials (the Profelene blocks) are added at the *beginning* of the process. A unit of product is 100% complete with respect to materials as soon as it is started. This means that beginning goods in process inventory for April received all its materials in March and is not assigned any additional materials. The 70,000 units started and completed in April and the 20,000 units in ending goods in process inventory on April 30 received all of their materials in April. The grinding department's equivalent units of production for materials are computed in Exhibit 20.14.

Equivalent units—Direct labor and factory overhead. Direct labor and factory overhead, both conversion costs, are assigned uniformly throughout the GenX process. Recall that beginning inventory of 30,000 units is partially completed in March. In April, additional labor and overhead are assigned to these units to complete them. Based on percent of

Point: To apply these concepts, work QS 20-3.

EUP for Materials	Units of Product		Percent Added This Period		Equivalent Units
Beginning goods in process	30,000	×	0%	=	0
Goods started and completed	70,000	×	100	=	70,000
Ending goods in process	20,000	×	100	=	20,000
Total units	120,000				90,000

Exhibit 20.14

Equivalent Units of Production for Direct Materials—First (Grinding) Department

completion (see Exhibit 20.12), 33⅓% of labor and overhead was assigned in March. The remaining 66⅔% is assigned in April. The 70,000 units started and completed in April are assigned 100% of labor and overhead. The 20,000 partly completed units in ending inventory are assigned only 25% of labor at the end of April. Exhibit 20.15 shows these computations.

EUP for Labor and Overhead	Units of Product		Percent Added This Period		Equivalent Units
Beginning goods in process	30,000	×	66⅔%	=	20,000
Goods started and completed	70,000	×	100	=	70,000
Ending goods in process	20,000	×	25	=	5,000
Total units	120,000				95,000

Exhibit 20.15

Equivalent Units of Production for Direct Labor and Overhead—First (Grinding) Department

Example: If ending goods in process are 20% complete, what are total equivalent units for labor and overhead for April? *Answer:* 94,000 units

A summary of April's equivalent units of production for the grinding department is shown in Exhibit 20.16.[2]

EUP Summary	Equivalent Units of Production		
	Direct Materials	Direct Labor*	Factory Overhead*
Beginning goods in process	0	20,000	20,000
Goods started and completed in current period	70,000	70,000	70,000
Ending goods in process	20,000	5,000	5,000
Equivalent units of production for period	90,000	95,000	95,000

* The columns for direct labor and factory overhead are sometimes combined and termed *conversion costs;* when this is done, these columns in all other reports should be similarly combined.

Exhibit 20.16

Equivalent Units of Production Summary—First (Grinding) Department*

Cost per Equivalent Unit—First Department The third step is to compute the *cost per equivalent unit* for direct materials, direct labor, and factory overhead as shown in Exhibit 20.17. Specifically, the $9,900 direct materials costs for April (from Exhibit 20.5) are assigned to the 90,000 equivalent units for materials, yielding a cost per equivalent unit of $0.11. The $5,700 direct labor costs and the $4,275 factory overhead costs for April (from Exhibit 20.5) are assigned to 95,000 equivalent units for direct labor and factory overhead,

Activities during April	Direct Materials	Direct Labor	Factory Overhead
Costs assigned to grinding in current period	$ 9,900	$ 5,700	$ 4,275
Equivalent units of production in current period	90,000	95,000	95,000
Cost per equivalent unit for period	$ 0.11	$ 0.06	$ 0.045

Exhibit 20.17

Cost per Equivalent Unit—First (Grinding) Department

[2] Under the *weighted-average method,* the 100,000 units transferred out during April are *not* separated into their two components of 30,000 from beginning inventory and 70,000 started and completed during the month. Thus, the equivalent units for direct materials equal 120,000 [(100,000 × 100%) + (20,000 × 100%)], and for direct labor and overhead would equal 105,000 [(100,000 × 100%) + (20,000 × 25%)].

Topic Tackler 20-2

yielding costs per equivalent unit of $0.06 and $0.045, respectively. Total cost per equivalent unit for the grinding department amounts to $0.215 ($0.11 + $0.06 + $0.045).[3]

Cost Reconciliation—First Department The fourth and final step in this process is to reconcile the *costs to account for* with the *costs accounted for* in the period. We do this by identifying the costs to (1) process beginning inventory, (2) start and complete units transferred from grinding to mixing, and (3) process ending inventory. Exhibit 20.18 shows this cost reconciliation.

Exhibit 20.18

Cost Reconciliation for April—First (Grinding) Department

Costs to Account For		
From beginning inventory		$ 4,250
Assigned in period (direct materials, direct labor, and overhead)		19,875
Total costs		**$24,125**
Costs Accounted For		
Beginning inventory completed in period (April)		
Costs from prior period	$4,250	
Costs assigned in current period		
Direct materials (0 units × $0.11)	0	
Direct labor (20,000 units × $0.06)	1,200	
Factory overhead (20,000 units × $0.045)	900	
Costs to process beginning inventory in period (April)		$ 6,350
Cost of units started and completed in period (April) (70,000 × $0.215)		15,050
Ending inventory for period (April)		
Direct materials (20,000 units × $0.11)	2,200	
Direct labor (5,000 units × $0.06)	300	
Factory overhead (5,000 units × $0.045)	225	
Costs of ending inventory for period (April)		2,725
Total costs		**$24,125**

The total *costs to account for* must equal the total *costs accounted for* in a cost reconciliation (minor differences can exist due to rounding). Also, the cost of each unit transferred out of the department must include the cost of completing beginning inventory in the current period ($6,350) and the cost of units started and completed in the current period ($15,050)—yielding $21,400 for 100,000 units actually transferred out, or $0.214 per unit. This leaves ending inventory at $2,725, which is carried over to the next period.[4]

[3] The cost per equivalent units computation is slightly different under the *weighted-average method* because costs of beginning inventory are added to the costs incurred in the current period. This means the cost of direct materials is $12,680 ($9,900 + $2,780), and the cost per equivalent unit for direct materials is $0.106 ($12,680/120,000 equivalent units). Similarly, the costs of direct labor and factory overhead are $6,400 ($5,700 + $700) and $5,045 ($4,275 + $770), respectively. Then the costs per equivalent unit for direct labor and factory overhead are $0.061 ($6,400/105,000 equivalent units) and $0.048 ($5,045/105,000 equivalent units), respectively. The total cost per equivalent unit is $0.215, which is the same as in the FIFO method. Note that the cost per equivalent unit for direct materials under the weighted-average method is lower than under FIFO; the reverse is the case for direct labor and factory overhead. This implies that costs incurred for direct materials in the prior period were lower than those incurred in the current period but were higher for direct labor and factory overhead. When end-of-period inventories are large and costs fluctuate, FIFO is the superior method for controlling and monitoring costs because it focuses on the activities and costs for the current period.

[4] Using the *weighted-average method,* the *costs to account for* are $24,125—the same as with FIFO—but the *costs accounted for* are computed differently (note a $40 difference from rounding):

Costs of units transferred during period (April) (100,000 units × $0.215)		$21,500
Ending inventory for period (April)		
Direct materials (20,000 units × $0.106)	$2,120	
Direct labor (5,000 units × $0.061)	305	
Factory overhead (5,000 units × $0.048)	240	
Costs of ending inventory for period (April)		2,665
Total costs		$24,165

Exhibit 20.17 showed that total cost per equivalent unit for April is $0.215, but the cost per unit for the units transferred out is $0.214. The difference of $0.001 exists because the total cost per equivalent unit is different for March; recall that $4,250 of the $21,400 is carried forward from March. As we explained earlier, the FIFO method uses only the current period's costs and activities to compute the cost per equivalent unit for that period.

C4 Define a process cost summary and describe its purposes.

Process Cost Summary—First Department An important managerial accounting report for a process cost accounting system is the **process cost summary** prepared separately for each process or production department. Three purposes of the summary are to (1) help department managers control and monitor their departments, (2) help factory managers evaluate department managers' performances, and (3) provide cost information for financial statements. A process cost summary achieves these purposes by describing the costs charged to each department, reporting the equivalent units of production achieved by each department, and determining the costs assigned to each department's output. For our purposes, it is prepared using a combination of Exhibits 20.13, 20.16, 20.17, and 20.18.

The process cost summary for GenX is shown in Exhibit 20.19. The summary is divided into three sections. Section ① lists the total costs charged to the department, including direct materials, direct labor, and overhead costs incurred, as well as the cost of the beginning goods in process inventory. Section ② describes the equivalent units of production for the department. Equivalent units for materials, labor, and overhead are often in separate columns. GenX reports equivalent units for labor and overhead in one column because it applies overhead using labor as the allocation base. It also reports direct materials, direct labor, and overhead costs per equivalent unit. Section ③ allocates total costs among units worked on in the period. Costs of completing beginning inventory units are computed and added to the cost carried forward from March to get total processing cost of $6,350 for beginning inventory units. Also, costs of processing 70,000 units from start to finish are computed and added to get their total $15,050 processing cost. The $21,400 ($6,350 + $15,050) is the total cost of goods transferred out of the department. The final part of section 3 computes the $2,725 cost of partially processed ending inventory units. The assigned costs are then added to show that the total $24,125 cost charged to the department in section ① is now assigned to the units in section ③.

Decision Maker

Cost Manager As cost manager for an electronics manufacturer, you apply a process costing system using FIFO. Your company plans to adopt a just-in-time system and eliminate inventories. What is the impact of the use of FIFO (versus the weighted-average method) given these plans?

Answer—p. 814

P5 Prepare a process cost summary.

Point: To apply these concepts, work Exercise 20-9.

Quick Check

6. Equivalent units are (*a*) a measure of a production department's productivity in using direct materials, direct labor, or overhead; (*b*) units of a product produced by a foreign competitor that are similar to units produced by a domestic company; or (*c*) generic units of a product similar to brand name units of a product.
7. Interpret the meaning of a department's equivalent units with respect to direct labor.
8. A department began the period with 8,000 units that were one-fourth complete. It also started and completed 50,000 units and ended with 6,000 units that were one-third complete. How many equivalent units did it produce during the period?
9. A process cost summary for a department has three sections. What information is presented in each of them?

Answers—p. 814

P6 Record the transfer of goods between departments.

Transfers between Departments Arrow line ⑨a in Exhibit 20.5 reflects the transfer of units (powdered Profelene) from the grinding department to the mixing department. This transfer's $21,400 cost, as computed in Section 3 of the process cost summary of Exhibit 20.19, is recorded with the following entry:

Assets = Liabilities + Equity
+21,400
−21,400

		Debit	Credit
(9a)	Goods in Process Inventory—Mixing	21,400	
	Goods in Process Inventory—Grinding		21,400
	To record transfer of partially completed goods from the grinding department to the mixing department.		

Exhibit 20.19

Process Cost Summary—First (Grinding) Department

GENX COMPANY
Process Cost Summary (Grinding Department)
For Month Ended April 30, 2005

(1)

Costs Charged to Department	
Direct materials requisitioned	$ 9,900
Direct labor charged	5,700
Overhead allocated (at predetermined rate)	4,275
Total processing costs for the period	19,875
Goods in process at the beginning of the period	4,250
Total costs to be accounted for	**$24,125**

(2)

		Equivalent Units	
Equivalent Unit Processing Costs	**Units of Product**	**Direct Materials**	**Labor and Overhead**
Units processed			
Beginning goods in process	30,000	0	20,000
Units started and completed	70,000	70,000	70,000
Ending goods in process	20,000	20,000	5,000
Total	120,000	90,000	95,000
Total direct materials cost for the period			$9,900
Direct materials cost per equivalent unit ($9,900/90,000 units)			$0.110
Total direct labor cost for the period			$5,700
Direct labor cost per equivalent unit ($5,700/95,000 units)			$0.060
Total overhead cost for the period			$4,275
Overhead cost per equivalent unit ($4,275/95,000 units)			$0.045

(3)

Assignment of Costs to Output of Department	**Equivalent Units**	**Cost per Unit**	**Total Cost**
Goods in process, March 31, 2005, and completed in the period			
Costs from prior period			$ 4,250
Direct materials added	0	$0.110	0
Direct labor added	20,000	0.060	1,200
Overhead applied	20,000	0.045	900
Total costs to process			6,350
Goods started and completed in the period			
Direct materials added	70,000	$0.110	7,700
Direct labor added	70,000	0.060	4,200
Overhead applied	70,000	0.045	3,150
Total costs to process			15,050
Total costs transferred to next department (unit cost = $21,400/100,000 units = $0.214)			21,400
Goods in process, April 30, 2005			
Direct materials added	20,000	$0.110	2,200
Direct labor added	5,000	0.060	300
Overhead applied	5,000	0.045	225
Total costs to process			2,725
Total costs accounted for ($21,400 + $2,725)			**$24,125**

After this entry is posted, the Goods in Process Inventory—Grinding account appears as shown in Exhibit 20.20. The $2,725 ending balance in this account equals the cost assigned to partially completed units as shown in section 3 of the process cost summary.

Exhibit 20.20

Goods in Process Inventory—Grinding

Goods in Process Inventory—Grinding					Acct. No. 133
Date		Explanation	Debit	Credit	Balance
2005					
Mar.	31	Balance			4,250
Apr.	30	Direct materials usage	9,900		14,150
	30	Direct labor costs	5,700		19,850
	30	Applied overhead	4,275		24,125
	30	Transfer to mixing department		21,400	2,725

Accounting for Second (Mixing) Department

The mixing department begins work on Profelene when it is received from the grinding department. Most of its costs are in the form of labor for specialists mixing the compounds and laborers packaging the product. Direct labor and overhead are added at the same rate as direct materials for this department.

Equivalent Units of Production—Second Department The mixing department requires only one computation of equivalent units of production because direct materials, direct labor, and overhead are used at the same rate. Exhibit 20.21 provides the data needed to compute equivalent units of production for the mixing department for April.

Exhibit 20.21

Production Data—Second (Mixing) Department

Beginning inventory (March 31)	
Units of product	16,000
Percentage of completion—Direct materials, direct labor, and overhead	25%
Activities during the current period	
Units received from grinding (in April)	100,000
Units transferred to finished goods (in April)	101,000
Ending inventory (April 30)	
Units of product	15,000
Percentage of completion—Direct materials, direct labor, and overhead	33⅓%

A total of 101,000 units is transferred from the mixing department to finished goods in the period. Based on a FIFO assumption, this implies that 16,000 of these units are from beginning goods in process inventory and another 85,000 are received and completed in the current period. Since 100,000 units are received from the grinding department this period and only 85,000 of these units are completed, this explains the 15,000 units in the ending goods in process inventory.

Exhibit 20.22 computes the mixing department's equivalent units of production for direct materials, direct labor, and overhead for the month of April. (Recall that because materials, labor, and overhead are added at the same rate in this department, only one report is needed.)

Exhibit 20.22

Equivalent Units of Production for Materials, Labor, and Overhead—Second (Mixing) Department

EUP for Materials, Labor, and Overhead	Units of Product		Percent Added This Period		Equivalent Units
Beginning goods in process	16,000	×	75%	=	12,000
Goods started and completed	85,000	×	100	=	85,000
Ending goods in process	15,000	×	33⅓	=	5,000
Total units	116,000				102,000

Exhibit 20.23

Process Cost Summary—Second (Mixing) Department

GENX COMPANY
Process Cost Summary (Mixing Department)
For Month Ended April 30, 2005

①

Costs Charged to Department	
Direct materials requisitioned	$ 2,040
Direct labor charged	5,100
Overhead allocated (at predetermined rate)	1,020
Total processing costs for the period	8,160
Goods in process at the beginning of the period	3,520
Costs transferred in from grinding department (100,000 units at $0.214 each)	21,400
Total costs to be accounted for	**$33,080**

②

Equivalent Unit Processing Costs	**Units of Product**	**Equivalent Units of Production**
Units processed		
Beginning goods in process	16,000	12,000
Units received and completed	85,000	85,000
Ending goods in process	15,000	5,000
Total	116,000	102,000
Total direct materials cost for the period		$2,040
Direct materials cost per equivalent unit ($2,040/102,000 units)		$0.020
Total direct labor cost for the period		$5,100
Direct labor cost per equivalent unit ($5,100/102,000 units)		$0.050
Total overhead cost for the period		$1,020
Overhead cost per equivalent unit ($1,020/102,000 units)		$0.010

③

Assignment of Costs to Output of Department	**Equivalent Units**	**Cost per Unit**	**Total Cost**
Goods in process, March 31, 2005, and completed in the period			
Costs from prior period			$ 3,520
Direct materials added	12,000	$0.020	240
Direct labor added	12,000	0.050	600
Overhead applied	12,000	0.010	120
Total costs to process			4,480
Goods received and completed in the period			
Costs transferred in (85,000 × $0.214)			18,190
Direct materials added	85,000	$0.020	1,700
Direct labor added	85,000	0.050	4,250
Overhead applied	85,000	0.010	850
Total costs to process			24,990
Total costs transferred to finished goods (unit cost = $29,470/101,000 units = $0.2918)			29,470
Goods in process, April 30, 2005			
Costs transferred in (15,000 × $0.214)			3,210
Direct materials added	5,000	$0.020	100
Direct labor added	5,000	0.050	250
Overhead applied	5,000	0.010	50
Total costs to process			3,610
Total costs accounted for ($29,470 + $3,610)			**$33,080**

Process Cost Summary—Second Department Exhibit 20.23 shows the mixing department's process cost summary. The costs charged to the department in section ① include $21,400 transferred in from the grinding department. Section ② shows the equivalent units of production for the direct materials, direct labor, and overhead for the mixing department. Section ② also computes the costs per equivalent unit. Section ③ shows how costs charged to the department are assigned to its output. The $29,470 cost of the 101,000 units transferred to finished goods is computed as the combined cost of the 16,000 beginning units in process and the 85,000 units received and completed in the period. Also, the $21,400 cost transferred in from Grinding (see ①) during April relates to the 100,000 units that the mixing department received in April. Section ③ shows that $18,190 of this $21,400 is assigned to the 85,000 units received and completed in April (85,000 × $0.214), while the remaining $3,210 is assigned to the 15,000 units remaining in ending inventory (15,000 × $0.214).

Quick Check

10. What effect does the transfer of a partially completed product from one production department to another have on the company's total assets?
11. A ski manufacturer's total processing costs for its waxing department in December are $262,500. To complete beginning goods in process, this department added 20,000 equivalent units of materials, labor, and overhead, and it started and completed 70,000 units during the month. It had 15,000 equivalent units remaining in process at month-end. Costs transferred in from the sanding department for December total $300,000, of which 25% relates to units the waxing department had not finished by month-end. What does the waxing department's process cost summary show as the total costs to process goods received and completed?

Answers—p. 814

Transfers to Finished Goods Inventory and Cost of Goods Sold

P7 Record the transfer of completed goods to Finished Goods Inventory and Cost of Goods Sold.

Arrow line ⑨b in Exhibit 20.5 reflects the transfer of completed products from the mixing department to finished goods inventory. The process cost summary for the mixing department shows that the 101,000 units of finished Profen are assigned a cost of $29,470. The entry to record this transfer is:

⑨b	Finished Goods Inventory	29,470	
	Goods in Process Inventory—Mixing		29,470
	To record transfer of completed units.		

Assets = Liabilities + Equity
+29,470
−29,470

After this entry is posted, the Goods in Process Inventory—Mixing account appears as shown in Exhibit 20.24. The ending balance of this account equals the cost assigned to the partially completed units in section ③ of Exhibit 20.23.

Exhibit 20.24

Goods in Process Inventory—Mixing

Goods in Process Inventory—Mixing					Acct. No. 134
Date		Explanation	Debit	Credit	Balance
2005					
Mar.	31	Balance			3,520
Apr.	30	Direct materials usage	2,040		5,560
	30	Direct labor costs	5,100		10,660
	30	Applied overhead	1,020		11,680
	30	Transfer in from grinding department	21,400		33,080
	30	Transfer to warehouse		29,470	3,610

Arrow line ⑩ in Exhibit 20.5 reflects the sale of finished goods. GenX sold 106,000 units of Profen in April. The beginning inventory of finished goods consists of 23,000 units with a cost of $6,440. All 23,000 units are sold in April. The remaining 83,000 units sold are from the 101,000 units completed in April. Ending finished goods inventory equals the 18,000 units remaining. Section ③ of Exhibit 20.23 shows that total cost per unit of finished goods in April is $0.2918 ($29,470/101,000 units). Using this information, we can compute cost of goods sold for April as shown in Exhibit 20.25.

Exhibit 20.25
Cost of Goods Sold

23,000 units from beginning inventory*	$ 6,440
83,000 units processed in period (83,000 × $0.2918)	24,219
Total cost of goods sold	$30,659

* Computations assume a FIFO inventory system.

The summary entry to record cost of goods sold for April is:

Assets	= Liabilities +	Equity
−30,659		−30,659

		Debit	Credit
⑩	Cost of Goods Sold	30,659	
	Finished Goods Inventory		30,659
	To record cost of goods sold for April.		

The Finished Goods Inventory account now appears as shown in Exhibit 20.26.

Exhibit 20.26
Finished Goods Inventory

Finished Goods Inventory					Acct. No. 135
Date		Explanation	Debit	Credit	Balance
2005					
Mar.	31	Balance			6,440
Apr.	30	Transfer in from mixing department	29,470		35,910
	30	Cost of goods sold		30,659	5,251

Summary of Cost Flows Exhibit 20.27 shows GenX's manufacturing cost flows for April. Each of these cost flows and the entries to record them have been explained. The flow of costs through the accounts reflects the flow of manufacturing activities and products.

Effect of Lean Business Model on Process Operations

Adopting lean business practices often yields changes in process operations. Management concerns with throughput and just-in-time manufacturing, for instance, cause boundary lines between departments to become less distinct. In some cases, higher quality and better efficiency are obtained by entirely reorganizing production processes. For example, instead of producing different types of computers in a series of departments, a separate work center for each computer can be established in one department. When such a rearrangement occurs, the process cost accounting system is changed to account for each work center's costs.

To illustrate, when a company adopts a just-in-time inventory system, its inventories can be minimal. For example, if raw materials are

Decision Insight

Lean Machine Attention to customer orientation has led to improved processes for companies. A manufacturer of control devices improved quality and reduced production time by forming teams to study processes and suggest improvements. Another company set up project groups to evaluate its manufacturing processes. Still another company uses statistical process control to identify problems and implement corrective actions.

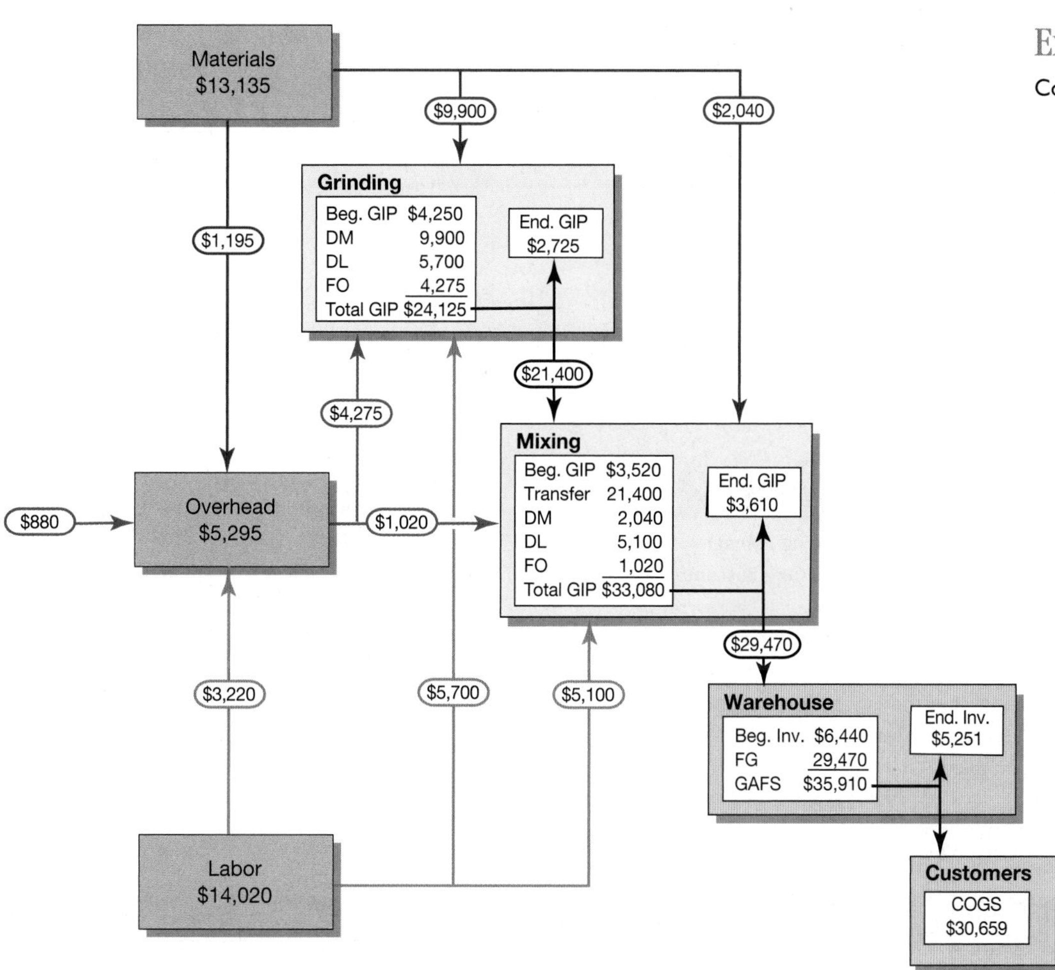

Exhibit 20.27*

Cost Flows through GenX

*Abbreviations: GIP (goods in process); DM (direct materials); DL (direct labor); FO (factory overhead); FG (finished goods); GAFS (goods available for sale); COGS (cost of goods sold).

not ordered or received until needed, a Raw Materials Inventory account may be unnecessary. Instead, materials cost is immediately debited to the Goods in Process Inventory account. Similarly, a Finished Goods Inventory account may not be needed. Instead, cost of finished goods may be immediately debited to the Cost of Goods Sold account.

Decision Insight

Best of Both Customer orientation demands both flexibility and standardization. Flexibility allows companies to supply products or services to a customer's specifications as in a job order setting, and standardization helps achieve efficiencies and lower costs as in a process operation. Companies that successfully combine flexibility and standardization can better satisfy customers.

Hybrid Costing System

Decision Analysis

A2 Explain and illustrate a hybrid costing system.

This chapter explained the process costing system and contrasted it with the job order costing system. Many organizations use a *hybrid system* that contains features of both process and job order operations. A recent survey of manufacturers revealed that a majority use hybrid systems.

To illustrate, consider a car manufacturer's assembly line. On one hand, the line resembles a process operation in that the assembly steps for each car are nearly identical. On the other hand, the specifications of most cars have several important differences. At the **Ford** Mustang plant in Michigan, each car assembled on a given day can be different from the previous car and the next car. This means that the costs of materials (subassemblies or components) for each car can differ. Accordingly, while the conversion costs (direct labor and overhead) can be accounted for using a process costing system, the component costs (direct materials) are accounted for using a job order system (separately for each car or type of car).

A hybrid system of processes requires a *hybrid costing system* to properly cost products or services. In the Ford assembly plant case, the assembly costs per car are readily determined using process costing. The costs of additional components can then be added to the assembly costs to determine each car's total cost (as in job order costing). To illustrate, consider the following information for the assembly process at Ford for a recent day:

Assembly process costs	
Direct materials	$10,600,000
Direct labor	$5,800,000
Factory overhead	$6,200,000
Number of cars assembled	1,000
Costs of three different types of steering wheels	$240, $330, $480
Costs of three different types of seats	$620, $840, $1,360

The assembly process costs $22,600 per car. Depending on the type of steering wheel and seats the customer requests, the cost of a car can range from $23,460 to $24,440 (a $980 difference).

Today companies are increasingly trying to standardize processes while attempting to meet individual customer needs. To the extent that differences among individual customers' requests are large, understanding the costs to satisfy those requests is important. Thus, monitoring and controlling both process and job order costs are important.

Decision Ethics

Entrepreneur You operate a process manufacturing company making similar products for three different customers. One customer demands 100% quality inspection of the products at your location before shipping them. The added costs of the quality inspection are spread across all customers, not just the one using the service. If you charge the added costs to that customer, the company could lose the customer and experience a loss. Moreover, your other two customers have agreed to pay 110% of full costs. What actions (if any) do you take?

Answer—p. 814

Demonstration Problem

Pennsylvania Company produces a product that passes through a molding process and then through an assembly process. Information related to its manufacturing activities for July follows:

Raw Materials	
Beginning inventory	$100,000
Raw materials purchased on credit	300,000
Direct materials—Molding	(190,000)
Direct materials—Assembly	(88,600)
Indirect materials used	(51,400)
Ending inventory	$ 70,000
Factory Payroll	
Direct labor—Molding	$ 42,000
Direct labor—Assembly	55,375
Indirect labor used	50,625
Total payroll cost (paid in cash)	$148,000
Factory Overhead	
Indirect materials used	$ 51,400
Indirect labor used	50,625
Other overhead costs	71,725
Total factory overhead incurred	$173,750
Factory Overhead Applied	
Molding (150% of direct labor)	$ 63,000
Assembly (200% of direct labor)	110,750
Total factory overhead applied	$173,750

Molding Department	
Beginning goods in process inventory (units)	5,000
Percentage completed—Materials	100%
Percentage completed—Labor and overhead	60%
Units started and completed	17,000
Ending goods in process inventory (units)	8,000
Percentage completed—Materials	100%
Percentage completed—Labor and overhead	25%
Costs	
Beginning goods in process inventory	$ 53,000
Direct materials added	190,000
Direct labor added	42,000
Overhead applied (150% of direct labor)	63,000
Total costs	$348,000
Assembly Department	
Beginning goods in process inventory	$154,800
Ending goods in process inventory	108,325
Finished Goods Inventory	
Beginning inventory	$ 96,400
Cost transferred in from assembly	578,400
Cost of goods sold	(506,100)
Ending Inventory	$168,700

Required

1. Compute the equivalent units of production for the molding department for July and determine the costs per equivalent unit for direct materials, direct labor, and factory overhead.
2. Compute the cost of the units transferred from molding to assembly in July and the cost of the ending goods in process inventory for the molding department.
3. Prepare summary journal entries to record the transactions and events of July for (a) raw materials purchases, (b) direct materials usage, (c) indirect materials usage, (d) factory payroll costs, (e) direct labor usage, (f) indirect labor usage, (g) other overhead costs (credit Other Accounts), (h) application of overhead to the two departments, (i) transfer of partially completed goods from molding to assembly, (j) transfer of finished goods out of assembly, and (k) the cost of goods sold.

Planning the Solution

- Compute the molding department's equivalent units of production and cost per unit with respect to direct materials.
- Compute the molding department's equivalent units of production with respect to direct labor and overhead and determine the cost per unit for each.
- Compute the total cost of the goods transferred to the assembly department by using the equivalent units and unit costs to determine (a) the cost of the beginning in-process inventory, (b) the materials, labor, and overhead costs added to the beginning in-process inventory, and (c) the materials, labor, and overhead costs added to the units started and completed in the month.
- Use the information to record the summary journal entries for July.

Solution to Demonstration Problem

1. **Equivalent units of production—direct materials**

EUP for Materials	Units of Product		Percent Added This Period		Equivalent Units
Beginning goods in process	5,000	×	0%	=	0
Goods started and completed	17,000	×	100	=	17,000
Ending goods in process	8,000	×	100	=	8,000
Total units	30,000				**25,000**

The direct materials used in molding total $190,000. Therefore,
Materials cost per equivalent unit = $190,000/25,000 units = $7.60 per unit

Equivalent units of production—direct labor and overhead

EUP for Labor and Overhead	Units of Product		Percent Added This Period		Equivalent Units
Beginning goods in process	5,000	×	40%	=	2,000
Goods started and completed	17,000	×	100	=	17,000
Ending goods in process	8,000	×	25	=	2,000
Total units	30,000				**21,000**

The direct labor used in molding totals $42,000. Therefore,
Labor cost per equivalent unit = $42,000/21,000 units = $2 per unit

The overhead applied in molding totals 150% of direct labor cost. Therefore,
Overhead cost per equivalent unit = $63,000/21,000 units = $3 per unit

2. Cost of units transferred from molding to assembly in July

	Equivalent Units	Cost per Unit	Total Cost
Beginning goods in process			
Costs from prior month			$ 53,000
Direct materials added	0	$7.60	0
Direct labor added	2,000	2.00	4,000
Overhead applied	2,000	3.00	6,000
Total cost to process			$ 63,000
Goods started and completed			
Direct materials added	17,000	$7.60	$ 129,200
Direct labor added	17,000	2.00	34,000
Overhead applied	17,000	3.00	51,000
Total cost to process			214,200
Cost of transferred units			**$277,200**

Cost of the July ending goods in process inventory for the molding department

	Equivalent Units	Cost per Unit	Total Cost
Direct materials added	8,000	$7.60	$ 60,800
Direct labor added	2,000	2.00	4,000
Overhead applied	2,000	3.00	6,000
Cost of ending goods in process inventory			**$70,800**

3. Summary journal entries for the transactions and events in July:

		Debit	Credit
a.	Raw Materials Inventory	300,000	
	Accounts Payable		300,000
	To record raw materials purchases.		
b.	Goods in Process Inventory—Molding	190,000	
	Goods in Process Inventory—Assembly	88,600	
	Raw Materials Inventory		278,600
	To record direct materials usage.		
c.	Factory Overhead	51,400	
	Raw Materials Inventory		51,400
	To record indirect materials usage.		
d.	Factory Payroll	148,000	
	Cash		148,000
	To record factory payroll costs.		
e.	Goods in Process Inventory—Molding	42,000	
	Goods in Process Inventory—Assembly	55,375	
	Factory Payroll		97,375
	To record direct labor usage.		
f.	Factory Overhead	50,625	
	Factory Payroll		50,625
	To record indirect labor usage.		
g.	Factory Overhead	71,725	
	Other Accounts		71,725
	To record other overhead costs.		

[continued on next page]

[continued from previous page]

		Debit	Credit
h.	Goods in Process Inventory—Molding	63,000	
	Goods in Process Inventory—Assembly.	110,750	
	Factory Overhead		173,750
	To record application of overhead.		
i.	Goods in Process Inventory—Assembly.	277,200	
	Goods in Process Inventory—Molding		277,200
	To record transfer of partially completed goods from molding to assembly.		
j.	Finished Goods Inventory	578,400	
	Goods in Process Inventory—Assembly		578,400
	To record transfer of finished goods out of assembly.		
k.	Cost of Goods Sold	506,100	
	Finished Goods Inventory.		506,100
	To record cost of goods sold.		

Summary

C1 **Explain process operations and the way they differ from job order operations.** Process operations produce large quantities of similar products or services by passing them through a series of processes, or steps, in production. Like job order operations, they combine direct materials, direct labor, and overhead in the operations. Unlike job order operations that assign the responsibility for each job to a manager, process operations assign the responsibility for each *process* to a manager.

C2 **Define equivalent units and explain their use in process cost accounting.** Equivalent units of production measure the activity of a process as the number of units that would be completed in a period if all effort had been applied to units that were started and finished. This measure of production activity is used to compute the cost per equivalent unit and to assign costs to finished goods and goods in process inventory.

C3 **Explain the four steps in accounting for production activity in a period.** The four steps involved in accounting for production activity in a period are (1) recording the physical flow of units, (2) computing the equivalent units of production, (3) computing the cost per equivalent unit of production, and (4) reconciling costs. The last step involves assigning costs to finished goods and goods in process inventory for the period.

C4 **Define a process cost summary and describe its purposes.** A process cost summary reports on the activities of a production process or department for a period. It describes the costs charged to the department, the equivalent units of production for the department, and the costs assigned to the output. The report aims to (1) help managers control their departments, (2) help factory managers evaluate department managers' performances, and (3) provide cost information for financial statements.

A1 **Compare process cost accounting and job order cost accounting.** Process and job order manufacturing operations are similar in that both combine materials, labor, and factory overhead to produce products or services. They differ in the way they are organized and managed. In job order operations, the job order cost accounting system assigns materials, labor, and overhead to specific jobs. In process operations, the process cost accounting system assigns materials, labor, and overhead to specific processes. The total costs associated with each process are then divided by the number of units passing through that process to get cost per equivalent unit. The costs per equivalent unit for all processes are added to determine the total cost per unit of a product or service.

A2 **Explain and illustrate a hybrid costing system.** A hybrid costing system contains features of both job order and process costing systems. Generally, certain direct materials are accounted for by individual products as in job order costing, but direct labor and overhead costs are accounted for similar to process costing.

P1 **Record the flow of direct materials costs in process cost accounting.** Materials purchased are debited to a Raw Materials Inventory account. As direct materials are issued to processes, they are separately accumulated in a Goods in Process Inventory account for that process.

P2 **Record the flow of direct labor costs in process cost accounting.** Direct labor costs are initially debited to the Factory Payroll account. The total amount in it is then assigned to the goods in process inventory account pertaining to each process.

P3 **Record the flow of factory overhead costs in process cost accounting.** The different factory overhead items are first accumulated in the Factory Overhead account and are then allocated, using a predetermined overhead rate, to the different processes. The allocated amount is debited to the goods in process inventory account pertaining to each process.

P4 **Compute equivalent units produced in a period.** To compute equivalent units, determine the number of units that would have been finished if all materials (or labor or overhead) had been used to produce units that were started and completed during the period. The costs incurred by a process are divided by its equivalent units to yield cost per unit.

P5 Prepare a process cost summary. A process cost summary includes the physical flow of units, equivalent units of production, costs per equivalent unit, and a cost reconciliation. It reports the units and costs to account for during the period and how they were accounted for during the period. In terms of units, the summary includes the beginning goods in process inventory and the units started during the month. These units are accounted for in terms of the goods completed and transferred out, and the ending goods in process inventory. With respect to costs, the summary includes materials, labor, and overhead costs assigned to the process during the period. It shows how these costs are assigned to goods completed and transferred out, and to ending goods in process inventory.

P6 Record the transfer of goods between departments. As units of product are transferred from one process to the next, the accumulated cost of those units is transferred from one goods in process account to the next. Once the goods are completed in the preceding process, they are transferred out to the next process in the sequence. Costs associated with goods completed in the preceding process are then debited to the goods in process inventory of the next process.

P7 Record the transfer of completed goods to Finished Goods Inventory and Cost of Goods Sold. As units complete the final process and are eventually sold, their accumulated cost is transferred to Finished Goods Inventory and finally to Cost of Goods Sold.

Guidance Answers to **Decision Maker** and **Decision Ethics**

Budget Officer By instructing you to classify a majority of costs as indirect, the manager is passing some of his department's costs to a common overhead pool that other departments will partially absorb. Since overhead costs are allocated on the basis of direct labor for this company and the new department has a relatively low direct labor cost, the new department will be assigned less overhead. Such action suggests unethical behavior by this manager. You must object to such reclassification. If this manager refuses to comply, you must inform someone in a more senior position.

Cost Manager Differences between the FIFO and weighted-average methods are greatest when large work in process inventories exist and when costs fluctuate. The method used if inventories are eliminated does not matter; both produce identical costs.

Entrepreneur By spreading the added quality-related costs across three customers, the entrepreneur is probably trying to remain competitive with respect to the customer that demands the 100% quality inspection. Moreover, the entrepreneur is partly covering the added costs by recovering 2/3 of them from the other two customers who are paying 110% of total costs. This act likely breaches the trust placed by the two customers in this entrepreneur's application of its costing system. The costing system should be changed, and the entrepreneur should consider renegotiating the pricing and/or quality-test agreement with this one customer (at the risk of losing this currently loss-producing customer).

Guidance Answers to **Quick Checks**

1. *c*
2. When a company produces large quantities of similar products/services, a process cost system is often more suitable.
3. *b*
4. The costs are direct materials, direct labor, and overhead.
5. A goods in process inventory account is needed for *each* production department.
6. *a*
7. Equivalent units with respect to direct labor are the number of units that would have been produced if all labor had been used on units that were started and finished during the period.
8.

	Units of Product		Percent Added		Equivalent Units
Beginning Inventory	8,000	×	75%	=	6,000
Units started and finished	50,000	×	100	=	50,000
Ending inventory	6,000	×	33⅓	=	2,000
Equivalent units					58,000

9. The first section shows the costs charged to the department. The second section describes the equivalent units produced by the department. The third section shows the assignment of total costs to units worked on during the period.
10. The transfer decreases one Goods in Process Inventory account and increases another. This has no effect on total assets.
11. Equivalent unit processing cost:

$$\$262{,}500/(20{,}000 + 70{,}000 + 15{,}000) \text{ units} = \$2.50.$$

Costs to process goods received and completed follow:

Costs transferred in	$225,000
Total costs added (70,000 × $2.50)	175,000
Total costs to process	$400,000

Key Terms

Key Terms are available at the book's Website for learning and testing in an online Flashcard Format.

Equivalent units of production (EUP) (p. 798)
Job order cost accounting system (p. 793)
Materials consumption report (p. 795)
Process cost accounting system (p. 793)
Process cost summary (p. 803)
Process manufacturing (p. 790)

Personal Interactive Quiz

Personal Interactive Quizzes A and B are available at the book's Website to reinforce and assess your learning.

Assume FIFO inventory method is used for all assignments unless stated differently.

Discussion Questions

1. Can services be delivered by means of process operations? Support your answer with an example.
2. What is the main factor for a company in choosing between the job order costing and process costing accounting systems? Give two likely applications of each system.
3. Identify the control document for materials flow when a materials requisition slip is not used.
4. The focus in a job order costing system is the job or batch. Identify the main focus in process costing.
5. Are the journal entries that match cost flows to product flows in process costing primarily the same or much different than those in job order costing? Explain.
6. Explain in simple terms the notion of equivalent units of production (EUP). Why is it necessary to use EUP in process costing?
7. What are the two main inventory methods used in process costing? What are the differences between these methods?
8. Why is it possible for direct labor in process operations to include the labor of employees who do not work directly on products or services?
9. Assume that a company produces a single product by processing it first through a mixing department and next through a cutting department. Direct labor costs flow through what accounts in this company's process cost system?
10. After all labor costs for a period are allocated, what balance should remain in the Factory Payroll account?
11. Is it possible to have under- or overapplied overhead costs in a process cost accounting system? Explain.
12. Explain why equivalent units of production for both direct labor and overhead can be the same as, and why they can be different from, equivalent units for direct materials.
13. List the four steps in accounting for production activity in a reporting period (for process operations).
14. What purposes does a process cost summary serve?
15. Assume that **Krispy Kreme** takes a special order to produce donuts for all employees of Andrews Air Force Base. Chart Krispy Kreme's production process, assuming it has three production departments: (1) mixing and shaping, (2) baking, and (3) glazing. Begin the flowchart with delivery of raw materials and finish with shipment of the goods (see Exhibit 20.5 for guidance).
16. **Harley-Davidson** produces motorcycles with a multiple process production line. Starting with assembling the motor cycles from inventory parts, list some of the motorcycle manufacturing processes.

Red numbers denote Discussion Questions that involve decision-making.

Homework Manager *repeats all numerical Quick Studies on the book's Website with new numbers.*

QUICK STUDY

QS 20-1
Matching of product to cost accounting system
C1

For each of the following products and services, indicate whether it is most likely produced in a process operation or in a job order operation:

1. Door hinges
2. Cut flower arrangements
3. House paints
4. Concrete swimming pools
5. Custom tailored suits
6. Grand pianos
7. Wall clocks
8. Sport shirts
9. Bolts and nuts
10. Folding chairs

QS 20-2
Identifying and recording cost flows
P1 P2 P3 P7

Jeans Co. manufactures a product requiring two processes, cutting and sewing. During August, partially completed units with a cost of $287,200 are transferred from cutting to sewing. The sewing department requisitions $58,200 of direct materials and incurs direct labor of $96,000. Overhead is applied to the sewing department at 100% of direct labor. Finally, units with a cost of $102,400 are completed and transferred from sewing to finished goods. Prepare journal entries dated August 31 to record these August activities of the sewing department: (1) goods transferred from cutting to sewing, (2) direct materials used, (3) direct labor used, (4) overhead applied, and (5) goods transferred from sewing to finished goods.

QS 20-3
Computing equivalent units of production—FIFO
C2 P4

This information refers to units processed in Sunflower Printing's binding department in March:

	Units of Product	Percent of Labor Added
Beginning goods in process	150,000	25%
Goods started and completed	340,000	100
Ending goods in process	120,000	40

Compute the total equivalent units of production with respect to labor for March using the FIFO inventory method.

QS 20-4
Computing equivalent units—weighted average C2 P4

Refer to QS 20-3 and compute the total equivalent units of production with respect to labor for March using the weighted average inventory method.

QS 20-5
Computing EUP cost C4 P5

The cost of beginning inventory plus the costs added during the period should equal the cost of units ____________________ plus the cost of ____________________.

QS 20-6
Hybrid costing system A2

Explain a hybrid costing system. Identify a product or service operation that might well fit a hybrid costing system.

***Homework Manager** repeats all numerical Exercises on the book's Website with new numbers.*

EXERCISES

Exercise 20-1
Terminology in process cost accounting
C1 A1 P1 P2 P3

Match each of the following items A through H with the best numbered description of its purpose.

A. Materials consumption report
B. Process cost summary
C. Equivalent units of production
D. Goods in Process Inventory—Dept. A
E. Raw Materials Inventory account
F. Materials requisition
G. Finished Goods Inventory account
H. Factory Overhead account

_______ **1.** Notifies the materials manager to send materials to a production department.
_______ **2.** Holds costs of indirect materials, indirect labor, and similar costs until assigned to production.
_______ **3.** Holds costs of direct materials, direct labor, and applied overhead until products are transferred from Department A to another department.
_______ **4.** Describes the direct materials used in a production department.
_______ **5.** Standardizes partially completed units into equivalent completed units.
_______ **6.** Holds costs of finished products until sold to customers.
_______ **7.** Describes the activity and output of a production department for a period.
_______ **8.** Holds costs of materials until they are used in production or as factory overhead.

Exercise 20-2
Journal entries in process cost accounting
P1 P2 P3

Wooden Toy Company manufactures products with two processes: sanding and painting. Prepare journal entries to record its following production activities for January.

1. Purchased $40,000 of raw materials on credit.
2. Used $19,000 of direct materials in the sanding department and $5,000 in the painting department.
3. Used $20,500 of indirect materials.
4. Incurred total labor cost of $75,000, which is paid in cash.
5. Used $30,000 of direct labor in the sanding department and $24,000 in the painting department.

6. Used $21,000 of indirect labor.
7. Incurred overhead costs of $24,000 (paid in cash).
8. Applied overhead at 125% of direct labor in the sanding department and at 75% of direct labor in the painting department.
9. Transferred partially completed products with a cost of $79,900 from the sanding department to the painting department.
10. Transferred completed products with a cost of $145,000 from the painting department to the finished goods inventory.
11. Sold $300,000 of products on credit. Their accumulated cost is $150,000.

Check (8) Cr. Factory Overhead, $55,500

Exercise 20-3
Interpretation of journal entries in process cost accounting

P1 P2 P3 P6 P7

The following journal entries are recorded in Kiera Co.'s process cost accounting system. Kiera produces clothing items by passing them through a cutting department and an assembly department. Overhead is applied to production departments based on direct labor cost for the period. Prepare a brief explanation (including any overhead rates applied) for each journal entry *a* through *k*.

a.	Raw Materials Inventory	26,000	
	Accounts Payable		26,000
b.	Goods in Process Inventory—Cutting	12,000	
	Goods in Process Inventory—Assembly	9,000	
	Raw Materials Inventory		21,000
c.	Goods in Process Inventory—Cutting	8,000	
	Goods in Process Inventory—Assembly	5,000	
	Factory Payroll		13,000
d.	Factory Payroll	16,000	
	Cash		16,000
e.	Factory Overhead	5,000	
	Cash		5,000
f.	Factory Overhead	5,000	
	Raw Materials Inventory		5,000
g.	Factory Overhead	3,000	
	Factory Payroll		3,000
h.	Goods in Process Inventory—Cutting	6,000	
	Goods in Process Inventory—Assembly	7,000	
	Factory Overhead		13,000
i.	Goods in Process Inventory—Assembly	30,000	
	Goods in Process Inventory—Cutting		30,000
j.	Finished Goods Inventory	44,000	
	Goods in Process Inventory—Assembly		44,000
k.	Accounts Receivable	125,000	
	Sales		125,000
	Cost of Goods Sold	50,000	
	Finished Goods Inventory		50,000

Exercise 20-4
Recording cost flows in a process cost system

P1 P2 P3 P6 P7

Lowes Lumber produces shredded bark using a two-step process. The system begins by processing bark chips through the shredding department and then through the bagging department. The following information describes production operations for October.

	A	B	C
1–2		Shredding Department	Bagging Department
3	Direct materials used	$ 40,000	$ 460,000
4	Direct labor used	$ 45,000	$ 75,000
5	Predetermined overhead rate (based on direct labor)	120%	200%
6	Goods transferred from shredding to bagging	$(145,000)	
7	Goods transferred from bagging to finished goods		$(403,000)
8			

The company's revenue for the month totaled $900,000 from credit sales, and its cost of goods sold for the month is $300,000. Prepare summary journal entries dated October 31 to record its October production activities for (1) direct material usage, (2) direct labor usage, (3) overhead allocation, (4) goods transfer from shredding to bagging, (5) goods transfer from bagging to finished goods, and (6) sales.

Check (3) Cr. Factory Overhead, $204,000

Exercise 20-5
Computing equivalent units of production—FIFO
C2 P4

During April, the production department of a process manufacturing system completed a number of units of a product and transferred them to finished goods. Of these transferred units, 50,000 were in process in the department at the beginning of April and 220,000 were started and completed in April. April's beginning inventory units were 60% complete with respect to materials and 40% complete with respect to labor. At the end of April, 66,000 additional units were in process in the department and were 80% complete with respect to materials and 30% complete with respect to labor. Compute (1) the number of units transferred to finished goods and (2) the number of equivalent units with respect to both materials used and labor used in the department for April using the FIFO method.

Check (2) EUP for materials, 292,800 units

Exercise 20-6
Computing equivalent units of production—weighted average
C2 P4

Refer to the information in Exercise 20-5 to compute the number of equivalent units with respect to both materials used and labor used in the department for April using the weighted average method.

Exercise 20-7
Costs assigned to output and inventories—FIFO
C3 P4 P5 

The production department described in Exercise 20-5 had $700,000 of direct materials and $500,000 of direct labor cost charged to it during April. Also, its beginning inventory included $90,000 of direct materials cost and $40,000 of direct labor. (1) Compute the direct materials cost and the direct labor cost per equivalent unit for the department—see Exhibit 20.17 for guidance. (2) Assign costs to the department's output; specifically, its beginning inventory, its goods started and completed, and its ending goods in process inventory for April using the FIFO method—see section ③ of Exhibit 20.19 for guidance.

Check (2) Costs accounted for, $1,200,000

Exercise 20-8
Costs assigned to output—weighted average C3 P4 P5

Refer to the information in Exercise 20-7 and complete its parts (1) and (2) using the weighted average method.

Exercise 20-9
Equivalent units computed
C2 P4 P5 

The production department in a process manufacturing system completed 250,000 units of product and transferred them to finished goods during a recent period. Of these units, 75,000 were in process at the beginning of the period. The other 175,000 units were started and completed during the period. At period-end, 50,000 units were in process. Compute the department's equivalent units of production with respect to direct materials under each of three separate assumptions: (1) All direct materials are added to products when processing begins. (2) Direct materials are added to products evenly throughout the process. Beginning goods in process inventory was 50% complete, and ending goods in process inventory was 70% complete. (3) One-half of direct materials is added to products when the process begins and the other half is added when the process is 75% complete as to direct labor. Beginning goods in process inventory is 40% complete as to direct labor and ending goods in process inventory is 60% complete as to direct labor.

Check (3) EUP for materials, 237,500 units

Exercise 20-10
Flowchart of costs for a process operation P1 P2 P3 P6 P7

The flowchart on the opposite page shows the August production activity of the punching and bending departments of Utility Box Company. Use the amounts shown on the flowchart to compute the missing numbers identified by question marks.

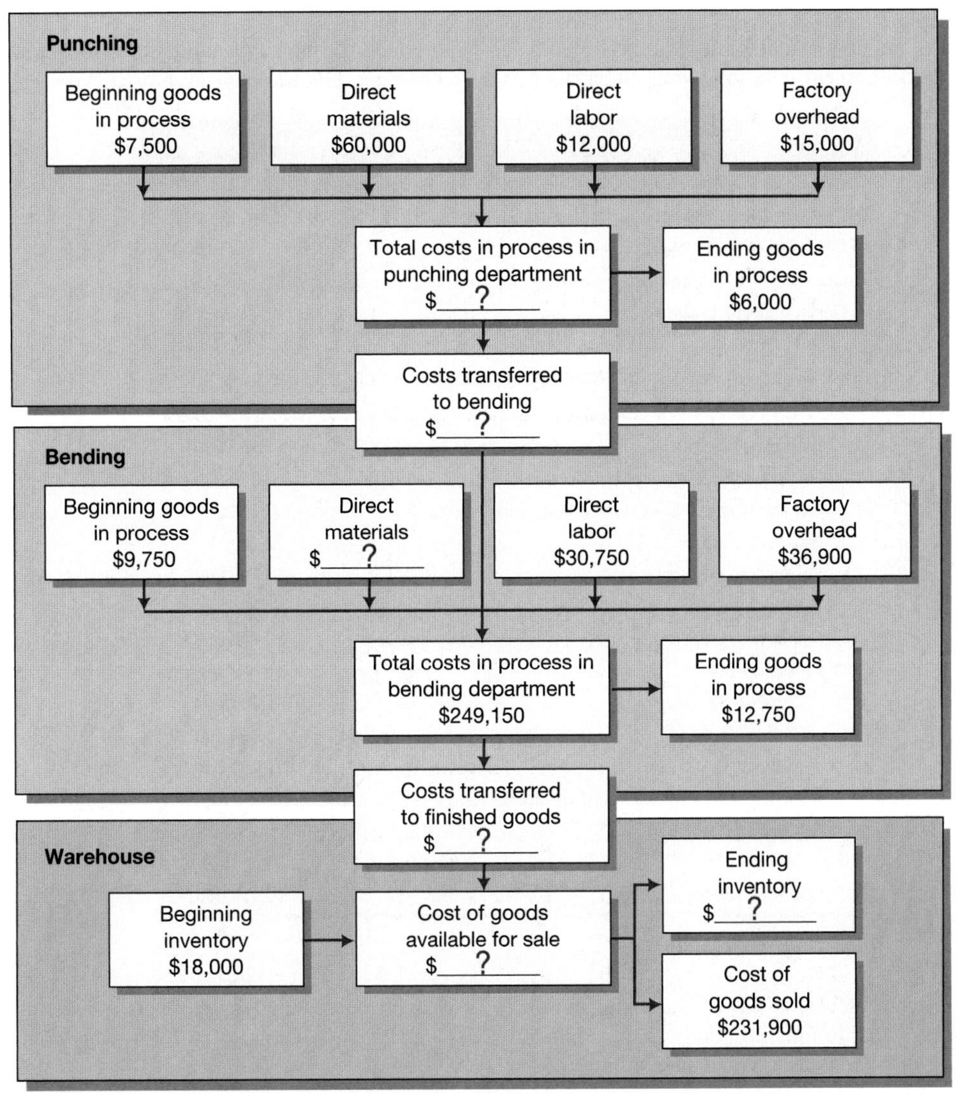

Exercise 20-11
Completing a process cost summary
P5  

The following partially completed process cost summary describes the July activities of Soriano Company's slicing department. Its output is sent to the canning department, which sends the finished goods to the warehouse for shipping.

Costs Charged to the Department	
Direct materials requisitioned	$224,000
Direct labor charged	39,000
Overhead allocated (at 200% of direct labor)	78,000
Total processing costs for the month	341,000
Goods in process at the beginning of the month	24,000
Total costs to be accounted for	$365,000

		Equivalent Units	
Equivalent Unit Processing Costs	**Units of Product**	**Direct Materials**	**Labor and Overhead**
Units processed			
Beginning goods in process	1,600	0	1,200
Units started and completed	20,000	20,000	20,000
Ending goods in process	2,400	2,400	1,800
Total	24,000	22,400	23,000

Prepare the process cost summary for the slicing department by completing both (1) the *Equivalent Unit Processing Costs* section and (2) the *Assignment of Costs to Output of Department* sections.

PROBLEM SET A

Problem 20-1A

Production cost flow and measurement; journal entries prepared

P1 P2 P3 P6 P7

Sullivan Company manufactures blankets by passing the products through a weaving department and a sewing department. The following information is available regarding its May inventories:

	Beginning Inventory	Ending Inventory
Raw materials inventory	$ 120,000	$ 185,000
Goods in process inventory—Weaving	300,000	330,000
Goods in process inventory—Sewing	570,000	700,000
Finished goods inventory	1,266,000	1,206,000

The following additional information describes the company's manufacturing activities for May:

Raw materials purchases (on credit)	$ 500,000
Factory payroll cost (paid in cash)	3,060,000
Other overhead cost (Other Accounts credited)	156,000
Materials used	
Direct—Weaving	$ 240,000
Direct—Sewing	75,000
Indirect	120,000
Labor used	
Direct—Weaving	$1,200,000
Direct—Sewing	360,000
Indirect	1,500,000
Overhead rates as a percent of direct labor	
Weaving	80%
Sewing	150%
Sales (on credit)	$4,000,000

Check (1c) Cost of goods sold $3,275,000

Required

1. Compute the cost of (a) products transferred from weaving to sewing, (b) products transferred from sewing to finished goods, and (c) goods sold. (*Hint:* Prepare a table of cost flows and computations like that in part B of Exhibit 20.5.)
2. Prepare summary journal entries dated May 31 to record the following production activities during May: (a) raw materials purchases, (b) direct materials usage, (c) indirect materials usage, (d) payroll costs, (e) direct labor costs, (f) indirect labor costs, (g) other overhead costs, (h) overhead applied, (i) goods transferred from weaving to sewing, (j) goods transferred from sewing to finished goods, and (k) sale of finished goods.

Problem 20-2A

Cost per equivalent unit; costs assigned to products

P4 P5

mhhe.com/larson

Liberty Company's product passes through several departments, the last of which is the carving department where direct labor is added evenly throughout the process. Also, one-fourth of direct materials is added at the beginning of the carving process and the remaining three-fourths is added when the process is 50% complete with respect to direct labor. During November, the carving department transferred 575,000 units of product to finished goods. Of these units, 100,000 were 40% complete with respect to labor at the beginning of the period; also, 475,000 were started and completed during the period. At the end of November, the goods in process inventory consists of 300,000 units that are 25% complete with respect to labor. The carving department's direct labor cost for November is $1,220,000, and its direct materials cost is $1,875,000.

Required

1. Determine the carving department's equivalent units of production with respect to (a) direct labor and (b) direct materials.
2. Compute both the direct labor cost and the direct materials cost per equivalent unit (see Exhibit 20.17 for guidance).
3. Compute both direct labor cost and direct materials cost assigned to the (a) beginning goods in process inventory, (b) units started and completed, and (c) ending goods in process inventory (see section ③ of Exhibit 20.19 for guidance).

Check (2) Direct labor cost per equivalent unit, $2

(3c) $375,000

Analysis Component

4. Liberty sells and ships all units to customers as soon as they are completed. Assume that an error is made in determining the percentage of completion for units in ending inventory. Instead of being 25% complete with respect to labor, they are actually 60% complete. Write a one-page memo to the plant manager describing how this error affects its November financial statements.

Problem 20-3A
Journalizing in process cost accounting; equivalent units and costs P1 P2 P3 P4 P6 P7

Newman Company produces large quantities of a product that pass through two processes, spinning and cutting. The following information is available on its manufacturing activities for March:

Raw materials		**Factory overhead incurred**	
Beginning inventory	$ 32,000	Indirect materials used	$ 40,560
Raw materials purchased (on credit)	221,120	Indirect labor used	36,320
Direct materials—Spinning	(160,000)	Other overhead costs	91,640
Direct materials—Cutting	(37,120)	Total factory overhead incurred	$168,520
Indirect materials used	(40,560)	**Factory overhead applied**	
Ending inventory	$ 15,440	Spinning (125% of direct labor)	$ 85,000
Factory payroll		Cutting (150% of direct labor)	83,520
Direct labor—Spinning	$ 68,000	Total factory overhead applied	$168,520
Direct labor—Cutting	55,680		
Indirect labor used	36,320		
Total payroll cost (paid in cash)	$160,000		

Information about the inventory in the *spinning department* follows:

Units		**Costs**	
Beginning goods in process inventory	4,000	Beginning goods in process inventory	$ 41,000
Started and completed	12,000	Direct materials added	160,000
Ending goods in process inventory	8,000	Direct labor added	68,000
Beginning goods in process inventory		Overhead applied (125% of direct labor)	85,000
Materials—Percent complete	100%	Total costs	354,000
Labor and overhead—Percent complete	25%	Costs transferred from spinning to cutting department	(272,000)
Ending goods in process inventory		Ending goods in process inventory	$ 82,000
Materials—Percent complete	100%		
Labor and overhead—Percent complete	25%		

Information about the goods in process inventories for the *cutting department* follows: beginning goods in process inventory, $174,000; and ending goods in process inventory, $177,120. Also, information regarding finished goods follows:

Beginning finished goods inventory	$148,400
Cost transferred in from cutting	445,200
Cost of goods sold	(530,000)
Ending finished goods inventory	$ 63,600

During March, 10,000 units of finished goods are sold for $120 cash each.

Required

1. Prepare journal entries dated March 31 to record the following March activities: (a) raw materials purchases, (b) direct materials usage, (c) indirect materials usage, (d) payroll costs, (e) direct labor costs, (f) indirect labor costs, (g) other overhead costs—credit Other Accounts, (h) overhead applied, (i) goods transferred from spinning to cutting, (j) goods transferred from cutting to finished goods, (k) sale of finished goods.

2. Compute the spinning department's equivalent units of production and its cost per equivalent unit for direct materials, direct labor, and overhead for March.

Check (2) Cost per equivalent unit: materials, $8; labor, $4; overhead, $5

3. Compute the cost of the ending goods in process inventory for the spinning department.

(3) $82,000

Analysis Component

4. Newman provides incentives to its department managers by paying monthly bonuses based on their success in controlling costs per equivalent unit of production. Assume that the spinning department underestimates the percentage of completion for units in ending inventory with the result that its equivalent units of production in ending inventory for March are understated. What impact does this error have on the March bonuses paid to the managers of the spinning department and the cutting department? What impact, if any, does this error have on April bonuses?

Problem 20-4A
Process cost summary; equivalent units
P4 P5 P7

mhhe.com/larson

RSTN Co. produces its product through a single processing department. Direct materials, direct labor, and overhead are added to the product evenly throughout the process. The company uses monthly reporting periods for its process cost accounting system. The Goods in Process Inventory account appears as follows after entries for direct materials, direct labor, and overhead costs for October:

Goods in Process Inventory					Acct. No. 133
Date		Explanation	Debit	Credit	Balance
Oct.	1	Balance			40,800
	31	Direct materials	100,200		141,000
	31	Direct labor	400,500		541,500
	31	Applied overhead	123,000		664,500

During October, the company finished and transferred 150,000 units of its product to finished goods. Of these units, 30,000 were in process at the beginning of the month and 120,000 were started and completed during the month. The beginning goods in process inventory was 30% complete. At the end of the month, the goods in process inventory consisted of 20,000 units that were 80% complete.

Required

Check (1) 157,000 units
(2) Total cost transferred to finished goods, $600,570

1. Compute the number of equivalent units of production for October.
2. Prepare the department's process cost summary for October.
3. Prepare the journal entry dated October 31 to transfer the cost of the completed units to finished goods inventory.

Problem 20-5A
Process cost summary; equivalent units; cost estimates
P4 P5 P7 

Vista Co. manufactures a single product in one department. All direct materials are added at the beginning of the manufacturing process. Direct labor and overhead are added evenly throughout the process. Vista uses monthly reporting periods for its process cost accounting system. During May, the company completed and transferred 22,200 units of product to finished goods inventory. The beginning goods in process inventory consisted of 3,000 units that were 100% complete with respect to direct materials and 40% complete with respect to direct labor and overhead. The other 19,200 completed units were started during the month. Also, another 2,400 units (100% complete with respect to direct materials and 80% complete with respect to direct labor and overhead) are in process at month-end. After entries to record direct materials, direct labor, and overhead for May, the company's Goods in Process Inventory account appears as follows:

Goods in Process Inventory					Acct. No. 133
Date		Explanation	Debit	Credit	Balance
May	1	Balance			181,320
	31	Direct materials	496,800		678,120
	31	Direct labor	1,185,600		1,863,720
	31	Applied overhead	948,480		2,812,200

Required

Check (1) EUP for labor and overhead, 22,920 units
(2) Cost transferred to finished goods, $2,578,230

1. Compute the equivalent units of production in May for direct materials and for direct labor and overhead.
2. Prepare the department's process cost summary for May.
3. Prepare the journal entry dated May 31 to transfer the cost of completed units to finished goods inventory.

Analysis Components

4. The cost accounting process depends on numerous estimates.

a. Identify two major estimates that determine the cost per equivalent unit.

b. In what direction might you anticipate a bias from management for each estimate in part 4a (assume that management compensation is based on maintaining low inventory amounts)? Explain your answer.

PROBLEM SET B

Problem 20-1B
Production cost flow and measurement; journal entries prepared

P1 P2 P3 P6 P7

Dream Toys Company manufactures dolls by passing the products through a molding department and an assembly department. The following information is available regarding its June inventories:

	Beginning Inventory	Ending Inventory
Raw materials inventory	$36,000	$45,000
Goods in process inventory—Molding	12,000	21,000
Goods in process inventory—Assembly	66,000	54,000
Finished goods inventory	78,000	99,000

The following additional information describes the company's manufacturing activities for June:

Raw materials purchases (on credit)	$100,000
Factory payroll cost (paid in cash)	200,000
Other overhead cost (Other Accounts credited)	50,000
Materials used	
Direct—molding	$ 6,000
Direct—assembly	54,000
Indirect	21,000
Labor used	
Direct—molding	$100,000
Direct—assembly	75,000
Indirect	25,000
Overhead rates as a percent of direct labor	
Molding	80%
Assembly	75%
Sales (on credit)	$500,000

Required

1. Compute the cost of (a) products transferred from molding to assembly, (b) products transferred from assembly to finished goods, and (c) goods sold. (*Hint:* Prepare a table of cost flows and computations like that in part B of Exhibit 20.5.)

Check (1c) Cost of goods sold, $353,250

2. Prepare journal entries dated June 30 to record the following production activities during June: (a) raw materials purchases, (b) direct materials usage, (c) indirect materials usage, (d) payroll costs, (e) direct labor costs, (f) indirect labor costs, (g) other overhead costs, (h) overhead applied, (i) goods transferred from molding to assembly, (j) goods transferred from assembly to finished goods, and (k) sale of finished goods.

Problem 20-2B
Cost per equivalent unit; costs assigned to products

P4 P5

Packard Company's product passes through several departments, the last of which is the bagging department where direct materials are added evenly throughout the process. Also, one-half of the direct labor is added at the beginning of the bagging process and the other half is added when the process is 50% complete with respect to materials. During September, the bagging department transferred 40,000 units of product to finished goods. Of these units, 9,000 were 60% complete with respect to materials at the beginning of the period; also, 31,000 were started and completed during the period. At the end of September, the goods in process inventory consists of 4,000 units that are 25% complete with respect to materials. The bagging department's direct materials cost for September is $356,000, and its direct labor cost is $990,000.

Required

Check (2) Direct labor cost per equivalent unit, $30

(3c) $70,000

1. Determine the bagging department's equivalent units of production with respect to (a) direct labor and (b) direct materials.
2. Compute both the direct labor cost and the direct materials cost per equivalent unit (see Exhibit 20.17 for guidance).
3. Compute both direct labor cost and direct materials cost assigned to the (a) beginning goods in process inventory, (b) units started and completed, and (c) ending goods in process inventory (see section ③ of Exhibit 20.19 for guidance).

Analysis Component

4. Packard sells and ships all units to customers as soon as they are completed. Assume that an error is made in determining the percentage of completion for units in ending inventory. Instead of being 25% complete with respect to materials, they are actually 75% complete. Write a one-page memo to the plant manager describing how this error affects its September financial statements.

Problem 20-3B
Journalizing in process cost accounting; equivalent units and costs

P1 P2 P3 P4 P6 P7

Sox Company produces large quantities of a product that pass through two processes, tooling and machining. The following information is available on its manufacturing activities for May:

Raw materials		**Factory overhead incurred**	
Beginning inventory	$ 84,000	Indirect materials used	$101,600
Raw materials purchased (on credit)	500,000	Indirect labor used	46,360
Direct materials—Tooling	(248,200)	Other overhead costs	50,520
Direct materials—Machining	(178,200)	Total factory overhead incurred	$198,480
Indirect materials used	(101,600)	**Factory overhead applied**	
Ending inventory	$ 56,000	Tooling (40% of direct labor)	$127,200
Factory payroll		Machining (200% of direct labor)	71,280
Direct labor—Tooling	$ 318,000	Total factory overhead applied	$198,480
Direct labor—Machining	35,640		
Indirect labor used	46,360		
Total payroll cost (paid in cash)	$ 400,000		

Information about the inventory in the *tooling department* follows:

Units		**Costs**	
Beginning goods in process inventory	40,000	Beginning goods in process inventory	$ 99,200
Started and completed	120,000	Direct materials added	248,200
Ending goods in process inventory	20,000	Direct labor added	318,000
Beginning goods in process inventory		Overhead applied (40% of direct labor)	127,200
Materials—percent complete	80%	Total costs	792,600
Labor and overhead—Percent complete	40%	Costs transferred from tooling to machining department	(720,000)
Ending goods in process inventory		Ending goods in process inventory	$ 72,600
Materials—Percent complete	90%		
Labor and overhead—Percent complete	75%		

Information about the goods in process inventories for the *machining department* follows: beginning goods in process inventory, $249,000; and ending goods in process inventory, $229,320. Also, information regarding finished goods follows:

Beginning finished goods inventory	$ 36,600
Cost transferred in from machining	1,024,800
Cost of goods sold	(1,000,400)
Ending finished goods inventory	$ 61,000

During May, 80,000 units of finished goods are sold for $20 cash each.

Required

1. Prepare journal entries dated May 31 to record the following May activities: (a) raw materials purchases, (b) direct materials usage, (c) indirect materials usage, (d) payroll costs, (e) direct labor costs, (f) indirect labor costs, (g) other overhead costs—credit Other Accounts, (h) overhead applied, (i) goods transferred from tooling to machining, (j) goods transferred from machining to finished goods, (k) sale of finished goods.

2. Compute the tooling department's equivalent units of production and its cost per equivalent unit for direct materials, direct labor, and overhead for May, assuming that all product costs are added evenly throughout the process.

3. Compute the cost of the ending goods in process inventory for the tooling department.

Check (2) Cost per equivalent unit: materials, $1.70; labor, $2; overhead, $0.80

(3) $72,600

Analysis Component

4. Sox provides incentives to its department managers by paying monthly bonuses based on their success in controlling costs per equivalent unit of production. Assume that the tooling department overestimates the percentage of completion for units in ending inventory with the result that its equivalent units of production in ending inventory for May are overstated. What impact does this error have on bonuses paid to the managers of the tooling department and the machining department? What impact, if any, does this error have on these managers' June bonuses?

Problem 20-4B
Process cost summary; equivalent units
P4 P5 P7

Oxford Company produces its product through a single processing department. Direct materials, direct labor, and overhead are added to the product evenly throughout the process. The company uses monthly reporting periods for its process cost accounting system. The Goods in Process Inventory account appears as follows after entries for direct materials, direct labor, and overhead costs for November:

Goods in Process Inventory					Acct. No. 133
Date		Explanation	Debit	Credit	Balance
Nov.	1	Balance			70,000
	30	Direct materials	115,000		185,000
	30	Direct labor	425,000		610,000
	30	Applied overhead	600,000		1,210,000

During November, the company finished and transferred 100,000 units of its product to finished goods. Of these units, 7,500 were in process at the beginning of the month, and 92,500 were started and completed during the month. The beginning goods in process inventory was 80% complete. At the end of the month, the goods in process inventory consisted of 12,000 units that were 25% completed.

Required

1. Compute the number of equivalent units of production for November.

2. Prepare the department's process cost summary for November.

3. Prepare the journal entry dated November 30 to transfer the cost of the completed units to finished goods inventory.

Check (1) 97,000 units

(2) Cost of goods transferred to finished goods, $1,175,440

Problem 20-5B
Process cost summary; equivalent units; cost estimates
P4 P5 P7 

Roadrunner Co. manufactures a single product in one department. Direct labor and overhead are added evenly throughout the process. Direct materials are added as needed. The company uses monthly reporting periods for its process cost accounting system. During January, Roadrunner completed and transferred 110,000 units of product to finished goods inventory. The beginning goods in process inventory consisted of 10,000 units (75% complete with respect to direct materials and 60% complete with respect to direct labor and overhead). The other 100,000 completed units were started during the month. Also, another 20,000 units (50% complete with respect to direct materials and 30% complete with respect to direct labor and overhead) are in process at month-end. After entries for direct materials, direct labor, and overhead for January, the company's Goods in Process Inventory account appears as follows:

Goods in Process Inventory					Acct. No. 133
Date		Explanation	Debit	Credit	Balance
Jan.	1	Balance			20,550
	31	Direct materials	56,250		76,800
	31	Direct labor	88,000		164,800
	31	Applied overhead	220,000		384,800

Required

Check (1) EUP for labor and overhead, 110,000 units
(2) Cost of goods transferred to finished goods, $363,000

1. Compute the equivalent units of production for direct materials and for direct labor and overhead.
2. Prepare the department's process cost summary for January.
3. Prepare the journal entry dated January 31 to transfer the cost of completed units to finished goods inventory.

Analysis Components

4. The cost accounting process depends on several estimates.
- **a.** Identify two major estimates that affect the cost per equivalent unit.
- **b.** In what direction might you anticipate a bias from management for each estimate in part 4a (assume that management compensation is based on maintaining low inventory amounts)? Explain your answer.

PROBLEM SET C

Problem Set C is available at the book's Website to further reinforce and assess your learning.

COMPREHENSIVE PROBLEM

Corked Bat Company
(Review of Chapters 2, 5, 18, 20)

Corked Bat Company manufactures baseball bats. The bats go through two processes: one cuts the wood into bats and drills a hole for the cork (department 1), and the other fills the hole with cork and stamps the company's logo on the bat (department 2). All of department 1's output is transferred to department 2. In addition to the goods in process inventories in departments 1 and 2, Corked Bat maintains inventories of raw materials and finished goods. It uses raw materials as direct materials in both departments and as indirect materials. Its factory payroll costs include direct labor for each department and indirect labor. All materials are added at the beginning of the process in each department, and direct labor and factory overhead are applied uniformly throughout each department's process.

Required

You are to maintain records and produce measures of inventories to reflect the July events of this company. All computations of unit costs are rounded to the nearest penny and all other dollar amounts to the nearest whole dollar. Set up the following general ledger accounts and enter their June 30 balances: Raw Materials Inventory, $25,000; Goods in Process Inventory—Department 1, $65,000; Goods in Process Inventory—Department 2, $25,000; Finished Goods Inventory, $110,000; Sales, $0; Cost of Goods Sold, $0; Factory Payroll, $0; and Factory Overhead, $0.

1. Prepare journal entries to record the following July transactions and events:
- **a.** Purchased raw materials for $125,000 cash (the company uses a perpetual inventory system).
- **b.** Used raw materials as follows: department 1, $30,000; department 2, $22,440; and indirect materials, $10,000.
- **c.** Incurred factory payroll cost of $227,250 paid in cash (ignore taxes).
- **d.** Assigned factory payroll costs as follows: department 1, $135,000; department 2, $67,250; and indirect labor, $25,000.
- **e.** Incurred additional factory overhead costs of $80,000 paid in cash.
- **f.** Allocated factory overhead to departments 1 and 2 at 50% of direct labor costs.

Check (1f) Cr. Factory Overhead, $101,125

2. Information about the July inventories for the two departments follows:

	Department 1	Department 2
Units		
Beginning inventory	500 units	1,000 units
Started and finished	2,000 units	1,800 units
Ending inventory	1,000 units	1,600 units
Beginning inventory		
Materials—Percent complete	100%	100%
Labor and overhead—Percent complete	20%	75%
Ending inventory		
Materials—Percent complete	100%	100%
Labor and overhead—Percent complete	30%	40%

Use this information with that from part 1 to compute the following:

a. Department 1's equivalent units of production and its per unit costs for labor, materials, and overhead.

b. Department 2's equivalent units of production and its per unit costs for labor, materials, and overhead.

Check (2b) EUP for overhead, 2,690 units

3. Using results from part 2 and the available information, make computations and prepare journal entries to record the following:

a. Total costs transferred from department 1 to department 2 for July (label entry *g*).

b. Total costs transferred from department 2 to finished goods for July (label entry *h*).

c. Sale of finished goods costing $265,700 for $625,000 in cash (label entry *i*).

(3a) $265,000
(3b) $378,755

4. Post entries from parts 1 and 3 to the ledger accounts set up at the beginning of the problem.

5. Compute the amount of gross profit from the sales in July. (*Note:* Add any underapplied overhead to, or deduct any overapplied overhead from, cost of goods sold. Ignore the corresponding journal entry.)

BEYOND THE NUMBERS

REPORTING IN ACTION

C2

BTN 20-1 A company must consider the costs and benefits of reporting externally the precise estimates of the percentage complete for goods in process inventory. It must also consider whether reasonable estimates are acceptable. Review **Krispy Kreme**'s inventory (Note 4 in Appendix A) and assume that its work in process inventory value for 2003 is overstated by 10% and for 2002 is understated by 15% due to estimation errors.

Required

1. Compute the dollar amount that work in process inventory is (a) overstated for 2003 and (b) understated for 2002. Separately consider each error and compute the impact on net income for only the year of the error (assume a 40% tax rate).

2. Compute the amount (in percent) that Krispy Kreme's net income increased or decreased for 2003 and for 2002 due to the estimation errors. (*Hint:* Work a simple example to see how an error in inventory impacts income.)

3. Are amounts in part 2 material? Explain in reference to costs and benefits of decision makers.

Roll On

4. Access Krispy Kreme's annual report for fiscal years ending after February 2, 2003, from its Website [KrispyKreme.com] or the SEC's EDGAR database [www.sec.gov]. Identify its current period work in process inventory value and assume a 10% understatement and a 40% tax rate. Recompute answers for parts 1 through 3 using this current information.

COMPARATIVE ANALYSIS

C1

BTN 20-2 Leading process manufacturers such as **Krispy Kreme** and **Tastykake** usually work to maintain a high-quality and low-cost operation. One ratio routinely computed for this assessment is the cost of goods sold divided by total expenses. A decline in this ratio can mean that the company is spending too much on selling and administrative activities and not enough on production. An increase in this ratio beyond a reasonable level can mean that the company is spending too much on production or not enough on selling activities. (Assume for this analysis that total expenses equal cost of goods sold plus selling, general, and administrative expenses.)

Required

1. For both Krispy Kreme and Tastykake, refer to Appendix A and compute the ratio of cost of goods sold to total expenses for their two most recent fiscal years.
2. Comment on the similarities or differences in the ratio results across both years and companies.

ETHICS CHALLENGE

C1 C3

BTN 20-3 Many accounting and accounting-related professionals are skilled in financial analysis, but most are not skilled in manufacturing. This is especially the case for process manufacturing environments (for example, a bottling plant or chemical factory). To provide professional accounting and financial services, one must understand the industry, product, and processes. We have an ethical responsibility to develop this understanding before offering services to clients in these areas.

Required

Write a one-page action plan, in memorandum format, on how you would obtain an understanding of key business processes of a company that hires you to provide financial services. The memorandum should specify an industry, product, and one selected process and should draw on at least one reference, such as a professional journal or industry magazine.

COMMUNICATING IN PRACTICE

A1 C1 P1 P2

BTN 20-4 You hire a new assistant production manager whose prior experience is with a company that produced goods to order. Your company engages in continuous production of homogeneous products that go through various manufacturing processes. Your new assistant e-mails you questioning some cost classifications on an internal report, specifically why the costs of some materials that do not actually become part of the finished product, including some labor costs not directly associated with producing the product, are classified as direct costs. Respond to this concern via memorandum.

TAKING IT TO THE NET

C1 C3

mhhe.com/larson

BTN 20-5 Teamwork is essential for business success and for the effective application of accounting software. Software products must work together to be useful in providing information in support of decision making. Check the Website for **QPR Management Software [QPR.com]** and complete the following requirements.

Required

1. Give examples of common business processes.
2. Click on ***Products*** and then on ***QPR Management Software.*** Explain how such software is helpful to business.

TEAMWORK IN ACTION

C1 P1 P2 P3 P6 P7

BTN 20-6 The purpose of this team activity is to ensure that each team member understands process operations and the related accounting entries. Find the activities and flows identified in Exhibit 20.5 with numbers ①–⑩. Pick a member of the team to start by describing activity number ① in this exhibit, then verbalizing the related journal entry, and describing how the amounts in the entry are computed. The other members of the team are to agree or disagree; discussion is to continue until all members express understanding. Rotate to the next numbered activity and next team member until all activities and entries have been discussed. If at any point a team member is uncertain about an answer, the team member may pass and get back in the rotation when he or she can contribute to the team's discussion.

BUSINESS WEEK ACTIVITY

C1 C3

mhhe.com/larson

BTN 20-7 Read the article "A Mass Market of One" in the December 2, 2002, issue of ***Business Week***. (The book's Website provides a free link to the article.)

Required

1. Provide examples of goods that have formerly been mass-produced but are now being offered on a customized basis.
2. What are some of the challenges that manufacturers have encountered in customizing goods?
3. Why did customization of goods emerge in the late 1990s but not earlier?

ENTREPRENEURIAL DECISION

C4  

BTN 20-8 Shawn Buchanan of **All American Meats** welcomes ideas for improvements from employees via the "idea boards" posted in the production area of his plant. Recently, an employee suggested that cost savings might be achieved if Buchanan outsourced selected parts of the plant's processes such as payroll.

Required

How should Buchanan evaluate which processes to retain and which to outsource?

HITTING THE ROAD

C3 

BTN 20-9 In process costing, the process is analyzed first and then a unit measure is computed in the form of equivalent units for direct materials, direct labor, overhead, and all three combined. The same analysis applies to both manufacturing and service processes.

Required

Visit your local **U.S. Mail** center. Look into the backroom and you will see several ongoing processes. Select one process, such as sorting, and list the costs associated with this process. Your list should include materials, labor, and overhead; be specific. Classify each cost as fixed or variable. At the bottom of your list, outline how overhead should be assigned to your identified process. The following format (with an example) is suggested:

Point: The class can compare and discuss the different processes studied and the answers provided.

Cost Description	Direct Material	Direct Labor	Overhead	Variable Cost	Fixed Cost
Manual sorting		X		X	
⋮					
Overhead allocation suggestions:					

GLOBAL DECISION

C1 

BTN 20-10 **Grupo Bimbo**, **Krispy Kreme**, and **Tastykake** are competitors in the global marketplace. Selected data for each of these companies follow.

	Grupo Bimbo*		Krispy Kreme†		Tastykake†	
	Current Year	Prior Year	Current Year	Prior Year	Current Year	Prior Year
Cost of goods sold ...	19,155,865	15,707,809	$381,489	$316,946	$111,187	$103,297
General, selling, and administrative expenses	19,220,603	15,816,046	28,897	27,562	44,983	43,236
Total expenses	38,376,468	31,523,855	410,386	344,508	156,170	146,533

* thousands of pesos
† thousands of dollars

Required

1. Review the discussion of the importance of the cost of goods sold divided by total expenses ratio in BTN 20-2. Compute the cost of goods sold to total expenses ratio for all three companies for the two years of data provided.
2. Comment on the similarities or differences in the ratio results across years and companies.

"*People are drawn to Jake usually with a grin or a big laugh. … Jake rules!*"—Bert Jacobs (on left; John Jacobs on right)

Cost Allocation and Performance Measurement

A Look Back

Chapter 20 focused on how to measure and account for costs in process operations. It explained process production, described how to assign costs to processes, and computed cost per equivalent unit for a process.

A Look at This Chapter

This chapter describes cost allocation and activity-based costing. It identifies managerial reports useful in directing a company's activities. It also describes responsibility accounting, measuring departmental performance, and allocating common costs across departments.

A Look Ahead

Chapter 22 looks at cost behavior and explains how its identification is useful to managers in performing cost-volume-profit analyses. It also describes break-even analysis and how to apply cost-volume-profit analysis for managerial decisions.

CAP

Conceptual

C1 Explain departmentalization and the role of departmental accounting. *(p. 838)*

C2 Distinguish between direct and indirect expenses. *(p. 839)*

C3 Identify bases for allocating indirect expenses to departments. *(p. 840)*

C4 Explain controllable costs and responsibility accounting. *(p. 845)*

C5 Describe allocation of joint costs across products. *(p. 848)*

Analytical

A1 Analyze investment centers using return on total assets. *(p. 849)*

Procedural

P1 Assign overhead costs using two-stage cost allocation. *(p. 832)*

P2 Assign overhead costs using activity-based costing. *(p. 834)*

P3 Prepare departmental income statements. *(p. 841)*

P4 Prepare departmental contribution reports. *(p. 844)*

Decision Feature

Life Is Good . . . and So Is Business

BOSTON—Bert and John Jacobs launched their T-shirt company, **Life Is Good® [LifeIsGood.com]**, with as Bert says, "nothing in our bank account and $78 in cash." The brothers spent early days visiting college campuses and street fairs peddling T-shirts. Although they lived and slept out of their van and made only enough to eat and pay for gas, they stayed the course. Then, as they like to say, "We created Jake, and he showed us the way!"

Jake is the smiling stick figure that now adorns their products. The brothers initially drew him on their apartment wall and then transferred the figure to a batch of T-shirts that sold out in less than an hour at a Cambridge street fair. "It scared the hell out of us," says Bert. "We looked at each other and said, 'Oh my God, what do we have here?'" What they had was a Hollywood story in the making. Within a few years, their Jake-adorned T-shirts, sweatshirts, and headwear produced annual sales exceeding $10 million.

Bert and John have also successfully merged their fun and quirky style with business. The Life Is Good factory comes with loud music, popcorn machines, free-roaming dogs, and giant murals on bright-colored walls. "We have a great team, so we encourage autonomy," says John, "and people know how to mix laughs into their day." The brothers have also successfully merged cost controls and departmental and individual responsibility into their factory. They identify and monitor costs—including direct, indirect, joint, and controllable costs—and allocate them to departments and products. The brothers know which products are selling and their contribution margins. Says John, "Consistent performance is what has enhanced and strengthened" our products.

Yet these cost management realities have not curtailed their fun-loving approach. This past year featured a factory talent show, bowling tournament, and watermelon seed-spitting contest. Our factory is "kind of like your favorite neighbor's basement," says John. "It just has a good vibe." The tight-knit factory crew works across departments and centers for the common good of both the workers and bottom-line income. "We want to make products we're proud of," says Bert, "and kind of enjoy the ride the whole time." And that ride is through the roof.

[Sources: *Life Is Good Website,* January 2004; *New Hampshire Business Review,* February 2003; *Boston Magazine,* 2003; *Improper Bostonian,* 2003.]

This chapter describes how to allocate costs shared by more than one product across those different products and how to allocate indirect costs of shared items such as utilities, advertising, and rent. The chapter also describes activity-based costing and how it traces the costs of individual activities. This knowledge helps managers better understand how to assign costs and assess company performance. The chapter also introduces additional managerial accounting reports useful in managing a company's activities and explains how and why management divides companies into departments.

Cost Allocation and Performance Measurement

Overhead Cost Allocation Methods
- Two-stage cost allocation
- Activity-based cost allocation
- Comparison of allocation methods

Departmental Accounting
- Motivation for departmentalization
- Departmental evaluation
- Departmental reporting and analysis

Departmental Expense Allocation
- Direct and indirect expenses
- Allocation of indirect expenses
- Departmental income statements
- Departmental contribution to overhead

Responsibility Accounting
- Controllable versus direct costs
- Responsibility accounting system
- Joint costs and their allocation

Overhead Cost Allocation Methods

P1 Assign overhead costs using two-stage cost allocation.

We previously explained how to assign overhead costs to jobs (and processes) by using a predetermined overhead rate per unit of an allocation base such as direct labor cost. When a single overhead rate is used on a companywide basis, all overhead is lumped together, and a predetermined overhead rate per unit of an allocation base is computed and used to assign overhead to jobs (and processes). The use of a single predetermined overhead rate suggests that this allocation process is simple. In reality, it can be complicated. This chapter explains the traditional two-stage cost allocation procedure and then introduces the activity-based cost allocation procedure.

Point: Use of a single overhead allocation rate is known as using a *plantwide rate*.

Two-Stage Cost Allocation

An organization incurs overhead costs in many activities. These activities can be identified with various departments, which can be broadly classified as either *operating* or *service* departments. *Operating departments* perform an organization's main functions. For example, an accounting firm's main functions usually include auditing, tax, and advisory services. Similarly, the production and selling departments of a manufacturing firm perform its main functions and serve as operating departments. *Service departments* provide support to an organization's operating departments. Examples of service departments are payroll, human resource management, accounting, and executive management. Service departments do not engage in activities that generate revenues, yet their support is crucial for the operating departments' success. In this section, we apply a two-stage cost allocation procedure to assign (1) service department costs to operating departments and (2) operating department costs, including those assigned from service departments, to the organization's output.

Illustration of Two-Stage Cost Allocation Exhibit 21.1 shows the two-stage cost allocation procedure. This exhibit uses data from **AutoGrand,** a custom automobile manufacturer. AutoGrand has five manufacturing-related departments: janitorial, maintenance, factory accounting, machining, and assembly. Expenses incurred by each of these departments are considered product costs. There are three service departments—janitorial,

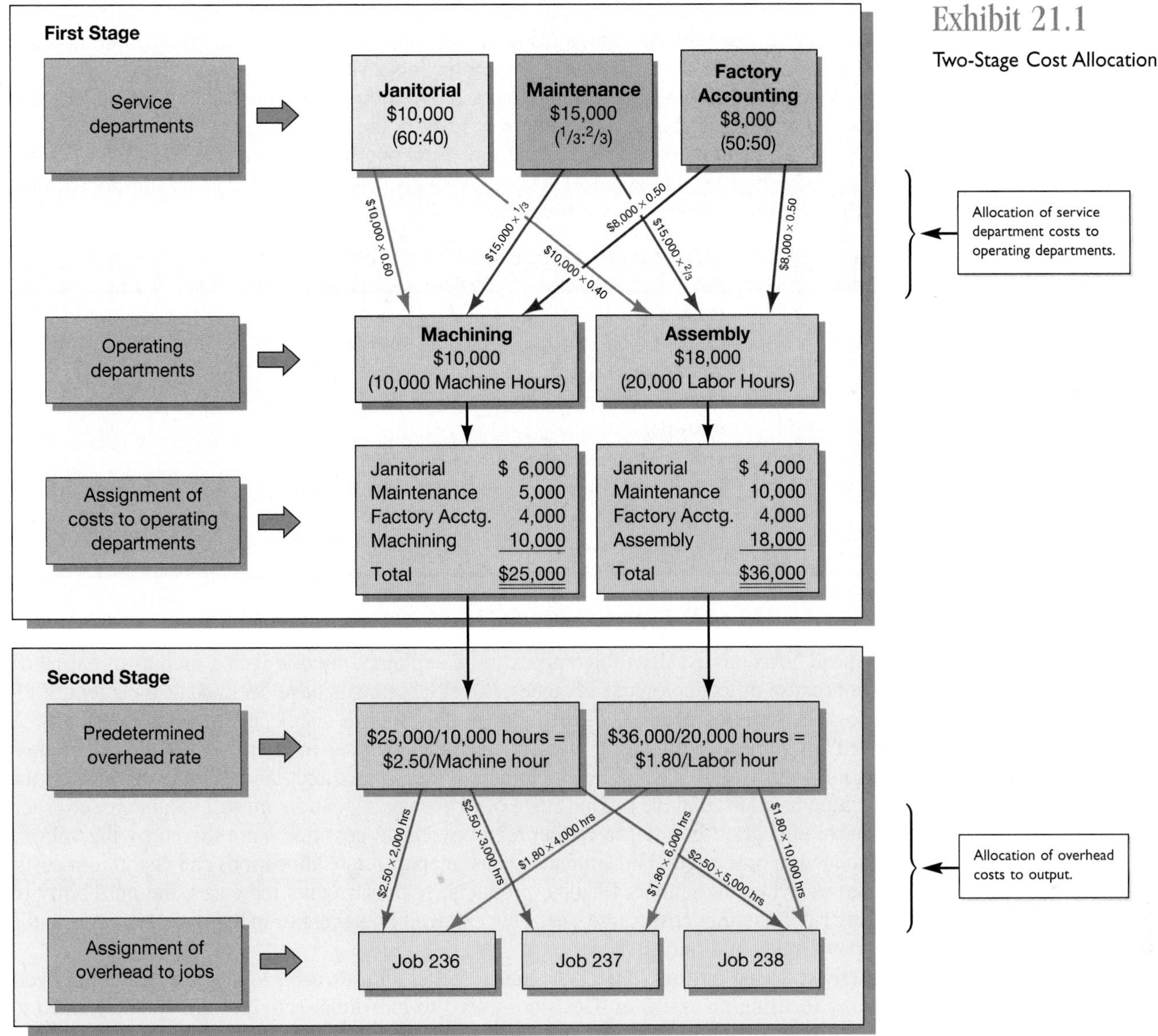

Exhibit 21.1

Two-Stage Cost Allocation

maintenance, and factory accounting; each incurs expenses of $10,000, $15,000 and $8,000, respectively. As shown in Exhibit 21.1, the first stage of the two-stage procedure involves allocating the costs of the three service departments to the two operating departments (machining and assembly). The two operating departments use the resources of these service departments.

To illustrate the first stage of cost allocation, we use the janitorial department. Its costs are allocated to machining and assembly in the ratio 60 : 40. This means that 60%, or $6,000, of janitorial costs are assigned to the machining department and 40%, or $4,000, to the assembly department. The expenses incurred by the maintenance and factory accounting departments are similarly assigned to machining and assembly. We then add the expenses directly incurred by each operating department to these assigned costs to determine the total expenses for each operating department. This yields total costs of $25,000 for machining and $36,000 for assembly.

Point: Use of a separate overhead allocation rate for each department is known as using *departmental rates.*

In the second stage, predetermined overhead rates are computed for each operating department. The allocation base is machine hours for machining and labor hours for assembly. The predetermined overhead rate is $2.50 per machine hour for the machining department and $1.80 per labor hour for the assembly department. These predetermined overhead rates are then used to assign overhead to output.

To illustrate this second stage, assume that three jobs were started and finished in a recent month. These jobs consumed resources as follows: Job 236—2,000 machine hours in machining and 4,000 labor hours in assembly; Job 237—3,000 machine hours and 6,000 labor hours; Job 238—5,000 machine hours and 10,000 labor hours. The overhead assigned to these three jobs is shown with the arrow lines in the bottom row of Exhibit 21.1.

Exhibit 21.2 summarizes these allocations. Total overhead allocated to Jobs 236, 237, and 238, is $12,200, $18,300, and $30,500, respectively. These allocated costs sum to $61,000, which is the total amount of overhead started with.

Exhibit 21.2

Assignment of Overhead Costs to Output

	Job 236	Job 237	Job 238
Machining			
$2.50 × 2,000 hours	$ 5,000		
$2.50 × 3,000 hours		$ 7,500	
$2.50 × 5,000 hours			$12,500
Assembly			
$1.80 × 4,000 hours	7,200		
$1.80 × 6,000 hours		10,800	
$1.80 × 10,000 hours			18,000
Total overhead assigned	$12,200	$18,300	$30,500

Activity-Based Cost Allocation

P2 Assign overhead costs using activity-based costing.

Overhead costs are usually too complex to be explained by one factor such as direct labor. Also, because of technological advances, direct labor costs have declined as a percent of total cost. In some companies, direct labor cost is such a small part of total cost that it is treated as overhead. Computing multiple overhead rates, as in the two-stage cost allocation, is an improvement over a single allocation rate based on direct labor. However, because the allocation bases used in the second stage of two-stage allocation are still volume based (such as machine hours), they fail to reflect many overhead cost items not driven by the volume of production or services. Unfortunately, such inappropriate allocations can distort unit costs. Moreover, when the number of jobs, products, or departments increases, the possibility of improperly assigning costs increases. This can lead managers to make poor decisions and a company's eventual failure.

Topic Tackler 21-1

Point: A recent survey found that most respondents believe that activity-based costing is worth the investment because of improved management decisions.

Activity-based costing (ABC) attempts to better allocate costs to the proper users of overhead by focusing on *activities.* Costs are traced to individual activities and then allocated to cost objects. Exhibit 21.3 shows the (two-stage) activity-based cost allocation method. The first stage identifies the activities involved in processing Jobs 236, 237, and 238 and then forms activity cost *pools* by combining these activities into sets. The second stage involves computing predetermined overhead cost rates for each cost pool and then assigning costs to jobs.

We begin our explanation at the top of Exhibit 21.3. The first stage identifies individual activities, which are then pooled in a logical manner into homogenous groups, or *cost pools.* A homogenous cost pool consists of activities that belong to the same process and/or are caused by the same cost driver. A **cost driver** is a factor that causes the cost of an activity to go up or down. For example, preparing an invoice, checking it, and dispatching it are activities of the "invoicing" process and can therefore be grouped in a single cost pool. Moreover, the number of invoices processed likely drives the costs of these activities.

An **activity cost pool** is a temporary account accumulating the costs a company incurs to support an identified set of activities. Costs accumulated in an activity cost pool include the variable and fixed costs of the activities in the pool. Variable costs pertain to resources acquired as needed (such as materials); fixed costs pertain

Decision Insight

Misled by Overhead **Futura Computer** outsourced 2 million units of a "money-losing" product to a Korean firm for manufacturing. Its own manufacturing facility was retooled to produce extra units of a "more profitable" product. Profits did not materialize, and losses grew to more than $20 million! What went wrong? It seems the better product was a loser and the losing product was a winner. Poor overhead allocations misled Futura's management.

Exhibit 21.3

Activity-Based Cost Allocation

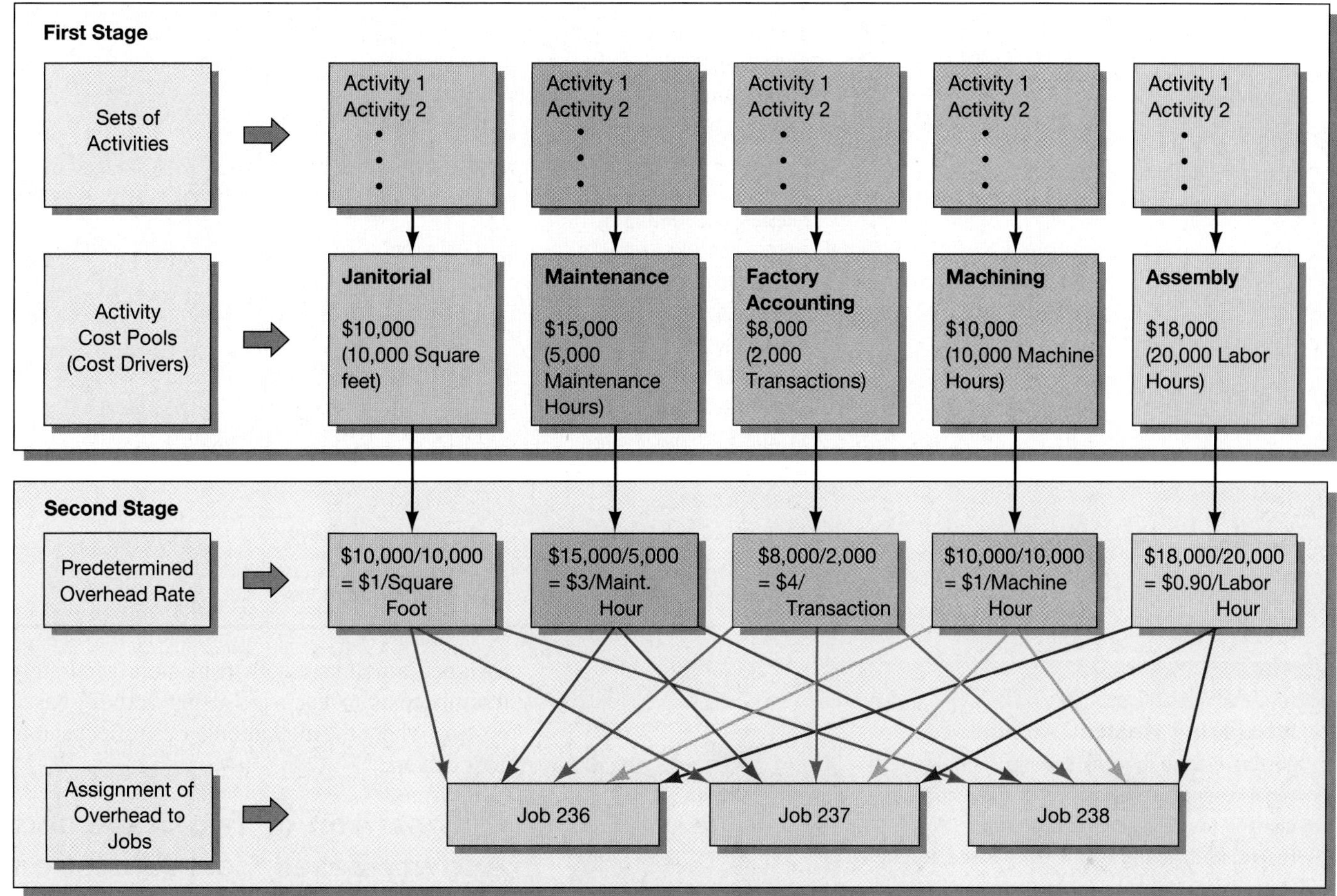

to resources acquired in advance (such as equipment). An activity cost pool account is handled like a factory overhead account.

In the second stage, after all activity costs are accumulated in an activity cost pool account, overhead rates are computed. Then, costs are allocated to cost objects (users) based on cost drivers (allocation bases).

Point: A cost driver is different from an allocation base. An allocation base is used as a basis for assigning overhead but need not have a cause-effect relation with the costs assigned. However, a cost driver has a cause-effect relation with the cost assigned.

Illustration of Activity-Based Costing To illustrate, let's return to AutoGrand's three jobs. Assume that resources used to complete Jobs 236, 237, and 238 are shown in Exhibit 21.4.

Exhibit 21.4

Activity Resource Use

Resources Used	Job 236	Job 237	Job 238
Square feet of space	5,000	3,000	2,000
Maintenance hours	2,500	1,500	1,000
Number of transactions	500	700	800
Machine hours	2,000	3,000	5,000
Direct labor hours	4,000	6,000	10,000

The $61,000 of total costs are assigned to these three jobs using activity-based costing as shown in Exhibit 21.5 (rates are taken from the second stage of Exhibit 21.3). Comparing Exhibits 21.2 and 21.5, we see that the costs assigned to the three jobs vary markedly depending on whether two-stage cost allocation or activity-based costing is used. Costs assigned to Job 236 go from $12,200 using two-stage cost allocation to $20,100 under activity-based costing. Costs assigned to Job 238 decline from $30,500 to $22,200. These differences in

Exhibit 21.5

Activity-Based Assignment of Overhead to Output

	Job 236	Job 237	Job 238
Janitorial			
$1.00 × 5,000 sq. ft.	$ 5,000		
$1.00 × 3,000 sq. ft.		$ 3,000	
$1.00 × 2,000 sq. ft.			$ 2,000
Maintenance			
$3.00 × 2,500 maint. hrs.	7,500		
$3.00 × 1,500 maint. hrs.		4,500	
$3.00 × 1,000 maint. hrs.			3,000
Factory Accounting			
$4.00 × 500 transactions	2,000		
$4.00 × 700 transactions		2,800	
$4.00 × 800 transactions			3,200
Machining			
$1.00 × 2,000 machine hrs.	2,000		
$1.00 × 3,000 machine hrs.		3,000	
$1.00 × 5,000 machine hrs.			5,000
Assembly			
$0.90 × 4,000 labor hrs.	3,600		
$0.90 × 6,000 labor hrs.		5,400	
$0.90 × 10,000 labor hrs.			9,000
Total overhead assigned	$20,100	$18,700	$22,200

assigned amounts result from more accurately tracing costs to each job using activity-based costing where the allocation bases reflect actual cost drivers.

Decision Insight

Measuring Health Activity-based costing is used in many settings. Its only requirements are existence of costs and demand for reliable cost information. A recent study found that activity-based costing improves health care costing accuracy, enabling improved profitability analysis and decision making. However, identifying cost drivers in a health care setting is challenging.

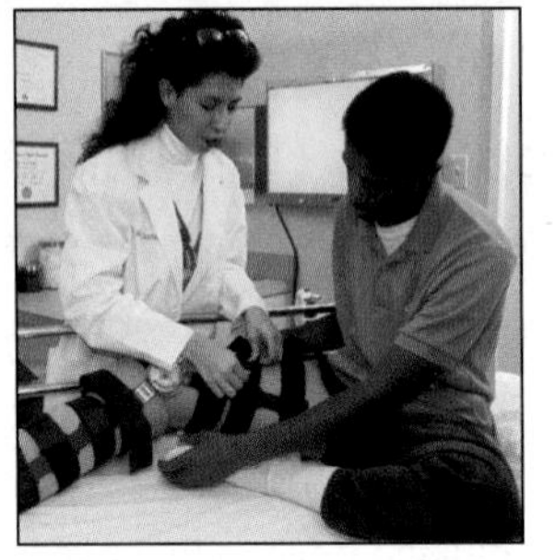

Comparison of Two-Stage and Activity-Based Cost Allocation

Traditional cost systems capture overhead costs by individual department (or function) and accumulate these costs in one or more overhead accounts. Companies then assign these overhead costs using a single allocation base such as direct labor or multiple allocation bases. Unfortunately, traditional cost systems have tended to use allocation bases that are often not closely related to the way these costs are actually incurred.

In contrast, activity-based cost systems capture costs by individual activity. These activities and their costs are then accumulated into activity cost pools. A company selects a cost driver (allocation base) for each activity pool. It uses this cost driver to assign the accumulated activity costs to cost objects (such as jobs or products) benefiting from the activity.

An activity-based costing system commonly consists of more allocation bases as compared to a traditional cost system. For example, a Chicago-based manufacturer currently uses nearly 20 different activity cost drivers to assign overhead costs to its products. Also, **Perkin-Elmer**, a maker of analytical instruments, uses an activity-based cost system. The company's controller reports that at first they tried to analyze too many cost drivers. Eventually, they set up cross-functional teams able to identify the important cost drivers for each pool. Exhibit 21.6 lists examples of overhead cost pools and their usual cost drivers.

Decision Maker

Director of Operations Two department managers at your ad agency complain to you that overhead costs assigned to them are too high. Overhead is currently assigned on the basis of labor hours for artwork designers. These managers argue that overhead depends not only on the designers' hours but on many activities unrelated to these hours. What is your response?

Answer—p. 853

Activity Cost Pool	Cost Driver
Materials purchasing	Number of purchase orders
Materials handling	Number of materials requisitions
Personnel processing	Number of employees hired or laid off
Equipment depreciation	Number of products produced or hours of use
Quality inspection	Number of units inspected
Indirect labor in setting up equipment	Number of setups required
Engineering costs for product modifications	Number of modifications (engineering change orders)

Exhibit 21.6

Cost Pools and Cost Drivers in Activity-Based Costing

Activity-based costing is especially effective when the same department or departments produce many different types of products. For instance, more complex products often require more help from service departments such as engineering, maintenance, and materials handling. If the same amount of direct labor is applied to the complex and simple products, a traditional overhead allocation system assigns the same overhead cost to both. With activity-based costing, however, the complex products are assigned a larger portion of overhead. The difference in overhead assigned can affect product pricing, make-or-buy, and other managerial decisions. Activity-based costing allows production managers to focus on managing activities that drive overhead cost instead of reducing allocated overhead by reducing direct labor cost.

Activity-based costing causes managers to pay closer attention to all activities. If overhead costs are accumulated in one account, attention is less likely to be directed at controlling any individual item. Activity-based costing requires managers to look at each item and encourages them to manage each cost to increase the benefit from each dollar spent. It also encourages managers to cooperate because it shows how their efforts are interrelated. This results in *activity-based management.*

Decision Ethics

Accounting Officer You work for a company that produces expensive garments, whose production involves many complex and specialized activities. The company's general manager recently learned about activity-based costing (ABC) and requests your opinion. However, your supervisor does not want to disturb the existing cost system and instructs you to prepare a report stating that "implementation of ABC is a complicated process involving too many steps and not worth the effort." You believe ABC will actually help the company to identify sources of costs and control them. What action do you take?

Answer—p. 853

Point: To apply these concepts, work QS 21-3.

Quick Check

1. What is a cost driver?
2. When activity-based costing is used rather than traditional allocation methods, (*a*) managers must identify cost drivers for various items of overhead cost, (*b*) individual cost items in service departments are allocated directly to products or services, (*c*) managers can direct their attention to the activities that drive overhead cost, or (*d*) all of the above.

Answers—p. 853

Departmental Accounting

Companies are divided into *departments,* also called *subunits,* when they are too large to be managed effectively as a single unit. Managerial accounting for departments has two main goals. The first is to set up a **departmental accounting system** to provide information for managers to use to evaluate the profitability or cost effectiveness of each department's activities. The second goal is to set up a **responsibility accounting system** to control costs and expenses and evaluate managers' performances by assigning costs and expenses to the managers responsible for controlling them. Departmental and responsibility accounting systems are related and share much information. We discuss departmental accounting in this and the next section. Then we describe responsibility accounting.

Motivation for Departmentalization

C1 Explain departmentalization and the role of departmental accounting.

Many companies are so large and complex that they are broken into separate divisions for efficiency and/or effectiveness purposes. Divisions then are usually organized into separate departments. When a company is departmentalized, each department is often placed under the direction of a manager. As a company grows, management often divides departments into new departments so that responsibilities for a department's activities do not overwhelm the manager's ability to oversee and control them. A company also creates departments to take advantage of the skills of individual managers. Departments are broadly classified as either operating or service departments.

Departmental Evaluation

Point: To improve profitability, **Sears, Roebuck & Co.** eliminated several departments, including its catalog division.

When a company is divided into departments, managers need to know how each department is performing. The accounting system must supply information about resources used and outputs achieved by each department. This requires a system to measure and accumulate revenue and expense information for each department whenever possible.

Topic Tackler 21-2

Departmental information is rarely distributed publicly because of its potential usefulness to competitors. Information about departments is prepared for internal managers to help control operations, appraise performance, allocate resources, and plan strategy. If a department is highly profitable, management may decide to expand its operations, or if a department is performing poorly, information about revenues or expenses can suggest useful changes.

More companies are emphasizing customer satisfaction as a main responsibility of many departments. This has led to changes in the measures reported. Increasingly, financial measurements are being supplemented with quality and customer satisfaction indexes. **Motorola**, for instance, uses two key measures: the number of defective parts per million parts produced and the percent of orders delivered on time to customers. (Note that some departments have only "internal customers.")

Financial information used to evaluate a department depends on whether it is evaluated as a profit center or a cost center. A **profit center** incurs costs and generates revenues; selling departments are often evaluated as profit centers. A **cost center** incurs costs without directly generating revenues. The manufacturing departments of a manufacturer and its service departments such as accounting, advertising, and purchasing, are all cost centers. Evaluating managers' performance depends on whether they are responsible for profit centers or cost centers. Profit center managers are judged on their abilities to generate revenues in excess of the department's costs. They are assumed to influence both revenue generation and cost incurrence. Cost center managers are judged on their abilities to control costs by keeping them within a satisfactory range under an assumption that only they influence costs.

Point: Selling departments are often treated as *revenue centers;* their managers are responsible for maximizing sales revenues.

Decision Insight

Nonfinancial Measures Survey data show that a majority of companies now report nonfinancial performance measures to management. The nonfinancial measures commonly used are cycle time, defect rate, on-time deliveries, inventory turnover, customer satisfaction, and safety. When nonfinancial measures are used with financial measures, the performance measurement system resembles a ***balanced scorecard.*** Also, many of these companies are implementing activity-based management as part of their performance measurement system.

Departmental Reporting and Analysis

Companies use various measures (financial and nonfinancial) and reporting formats to evaluate their departments. The type and form of information depend on management's focus and philosophy. **Hewlett-Packard**'s statement of corporate objectives, for instance, indicates that its goal is to satisfy customer needs. Its challenge is to set up managerial accounting systems to provide relevant feedback for evaluating performance in terms of its stated objectives. Also, the means used to obtain information about departments depend on how extensively a company uses computer and information technology.

When accounts are not maintained separately in the general ledger by department, a company can create departmental information by using a *departmental spreadsheet analysis*. For example, after recording sales in its usual manner, a company can compute daily total sales by department and enter these totals on a sales spreadsheet. At period-end, column totals of the spreadsheet show sales by department. The combined total of all columns equals the balance of the Sales account. A merchandiser that uses a spreadsheet analysis of department sales often uses separate spreadsheets to accumulate sales, sales returns, purchases, and purchases returns by department. If each department keeps a count of its inventory, it can also compute its gross profit (assuming it's a profit center).

Point: Some retailers use a point-of-sales system capturing sales data and creating documents to release inventory from the warehouse and order additional merchandise. **Wal-Mart**'s sales system not only collects data for internal use but also is used by **Procter & Gamble** to plan its production and product delivery schedule to **Wal-Mart.**

Point: **Link Wood Products,** a manufacturer of lawn and garden products, records each sale by department on a spreadsheet. Daily totals are accumulated in another spreadsheet to obtain monthly totals by department.

Quick Check

3. What is the difference between a departmental accounting system and a responsibility accounting system?
4. Service departments (*a*) manufacture products, (*b*) make sales directly to customers, (*c*) produce revenues, (*d*) assist operating departments.
5. Explain the difference between a cost center and a profit center. Cite an example of each.

Answers—p. 853

Departmental Expense Allocation

When a company computes departmental profits, it confronts some accounting challenges that involve allocating its expenses across its operating departments.

Direct and Indirect Expenses

C2 Distinguish between direct and indirect expenses.

Direct expenses are costs readily traced to a department because they are incurred for that department's sole benefit. They require no allocation across departments. For example, the salary of an employee who works in only one department is a direct expense of that one department.

Indirect expenses are costs that are incurred for the joint benefit of more than one department and cannot be readily traced to only one department. For example, if two or more departments share a single building, all enjoy the benefits of the expenses for rent, heat, and light. Indirect expenses are allocated across departments benefiting from them when we need information about departmental profits. Ideally, we allocate indirect expenses by using a cause-effect relation. When we cannot identify cause-effect relations, we allocate each indirect expense on a basis approximating the relative benefit each department receives. Measuring the benefit for each department from an indirect expense can be difficult or sometimes impossible.

Point: Utility expense has elements of both direct and indirect expenses.

Illustration of Indirect Expense Allocation To illustrate how to allocate an indirect expense, we consider a retail store that purchases janitorial services from an outside company. Management allocates this cost across the store's three departments according to the floor space each occupies. Costs of janitorial services for a recent month are $300. Exhibit 21.7 shows the square feet of floor space each department occupies. The store computes the percent of total square feet alloted to each department and uses it to allocate the $300 cost.

Exhibit 21.7

Indirect Expense Allocation

Department	Square Feet	Percent of Total	Allocated Cost
Jewelry	2,400	60%	$180
Watch repair	600	15	45
China and silver	1,000	25	75
Totals	4,000	100%	$300

Specifically, because the jewelry department occupies 60% of the floor space, 60% of the total $300 cost is assigned to it. The same procedure is applied to the other departments. When the allocation process is complete, these and other allocated costs are deducted from the gross profit for each department to determine net income for each. One consideration in allocating costs is to motivate managers and employees to behave as desired. As a result, a cost incurred in one department might be best allocated to other departments when one of the other departments caused the cost.

Allocation of Indirect Expenses

C3 Identify bases for allocating indirect expenses to departments.

Point: Expense allocations cannot always avoid some arbitrariness.

This section describes how to identify the bases used to allocate indirect expenses across departments. No standard rule identifies the best basis because expense allocation involves several factors, and the relative importance of these factors varies across departments and organizations. Judgment is required, and people do not always agree. In our discussion, note the parallels between activity-based costing and the departmental expense allocation procedures described here.

Wages and Salaries Employee wages and salaries can be either direct or indirect expenses. If their time is spent entirely in one department, their wages are direct expenses of that department. However, if employees work for the benefit of more than one department, their wages are indirect expenses and must be allocated across the departments benefited. An employee's contribution to a department usually depends on the number of hours worked in contributing to that department. Thus, a reasonable basis for allocating employee wages and salaries is the *relative amount of time spent in each department.* In the case of a supervisor who manages more than one department, recording the time spent in each department may not always be practical. Instead, a company can allocate the supervisor's salary to departments on the basis of the number of employees in each department—a reasonable basis if a supervisor's main task is managing people. Another basis of allocation is on sales across departments, also a reasonable basis if a supervisor's job reflects on departmental sales.

Point: Some companies ask supervisors to estimate time spent supervising specific departments for purposes of expense allocation.

Rent and Related Expenses Rent expense for a building is reasonably allocated to a department on the basis of floor space it occupies. Location can often make some floor space more valuable than other space. Thus, the allocation method can charge departments that occupy more valuable space a higher expense per square foot. Ground floor retail space, for instance, is often more valuable than basement or upper-floor space because all customers pass departments near the entrance but fewer go beyond the first floor. When no precise measures of floor space values exist, basing allocations on data such as customer traffic and real estate assessments are helpful. When a company owns its building, its expenses for depreciation, taxes, insurance, and other related building expenses are allocated like rent expense.

Advertising Expenses Effective advertising of a department's products increases its sales and customer traffic. Moreover, advertising products for some departments usually helps other departments' sales because customers also often buy unadvertised products. Thus, many stores treat advertising as an indirect expense allocated on the basis of each department's proportion of total sales. For example, a department with 10% of a store's total sales is assigned 10% of advertising expense. Another method is to analyze each advertisement to compute the Web/newspaper space or TV/radio time devoted to the products of a department and charge that department for the proportional costs of advertisements. Management must consider whether this more detailed and costly method is justified.

Point: To apply these concepts, work QS 21-2.

Equipment and Machinery Depreciation Depreciation on equipment and machinery used only in one department is a direct expense of that department. Depreciation on equipment and machinery used by more than one department is an indirect expense to be allocated across departments. Accounting for each department's depreciation expense requires a company to keep records showing which departments use specific assets. The number of hours that a department uses equipment and machinery is a reasonable basis for allocating depreciation.

Point: Employee morale suffers when allocations are perceived as unfair. Thus, it is important to carefully design and explain the allocation of service department costs.

Utilities Expenses Utilities expenses such as heating and lighting are usually allocated on the basis of floor space occupied by departments. This practice assumes their use is uniform across departments. When this is not so, a more involved allocation can be necessary, although there is often a trade-off between the usefulness of more precise allocations and the effort to compute them.

Point: Manufacturers often allocate electricity cost to departments on the basis of the horsepower of equipment located in each department.

Service Department Expenses To generate revenues, operating departments require support services provided by departments such as personnel, payroll, advertising, and purchasing. Such service departments are typically evaluated as cost centers because they do not produce revenues. (Evaluating them as profit centers requires the use of a system that "charges" user departments a price that then serves as the "revenue" generated by service departments.) A departmental accounting system can accumulate and report costs incurred directly by each service department for this purpose. The system then allocates a service department's expenses to operating departments benefiting from them. This is often done, for example, using traditional two-stage cost allocation (see Exhibit 21.1). Exhibit 21.8 shows some commonly used bases for allocating service department expenses to operating departments.

Point: When a service department "charges" its user departments within a company, a *transfer pricing system* must be set up to determine the "revenue" from its services provided.

Exhibit 21.8

Bases for Allocating Service Department Expenses

Service Department	Common Allocation Bases
Office expenses	Number of employees or sales in each department
Personnel expenses	Number of employees in each department
Payroll expenses	Number of employees in each department
Advertising expenses	Sales or amount of advertising charged directly to each department
Purchasing costs	Dollar amounts of purchases or number of purchase orders processed
Cleaning expenses	Square feet of floor space occupied
Maintenance expenses	Square feet of floor space occupied

Departmental Income Statements

P3 Prepare departmental income statements.

An income statement can be prepared for each operating department once expenses have been assigned to it. Its expenses include both direct expenses and its share of indirect expenses. For this purpose, compiling all expenses incurred in service departments before assigning them to operating departments is useful. We illustrate the steps to prepare departmental income statements using **A-1 Hardware** and its five departments. Two of them (office and purchasing) are service departments and the other three (hardware, housewares, and appliances) are operating (selling) departments. Allocating costs to operating departments and preparing departmental income statements involves four steps.

Step 1 Step 1 accumulates direct expenses for each service and operating department as shown in Exhibit 21.9. Direct expenses include salaries, wages, and other expenses that each department incurs but does not share with any other department. This information is accumulated in departmental expense accounts.

Exhibit 21.9

Step 1: Direct Expense Accumulation

Direct Expenses → General office

Direct Expenses → Purchasing

Direct Expenses → Hardware

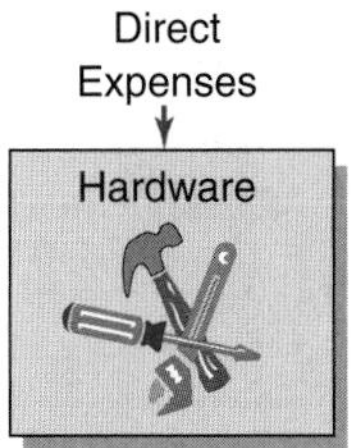

Direct Expenses → Housewares

Direct Expenses → Appliances

Step 2 Step 2 allocates indirect expenses across all departments using the allocation base identified for each expense as shown in Exhibit 21.10. Indirect expenses can include items such as depreciation, rent, advertising, and any other expenses that cannot be directly assigned to a department. Indirect expenses are recorded in expense accounts, and costs are allocated using a *departmental expense allocation spreadsheet* described in step 3.

Point: We sometimes allocate service department costs across other service departments before allocating them to operating departments. This "step-wise" process is in advanced courses.

Exhibit 21.10

Step 2: Indirect Expense Allocation

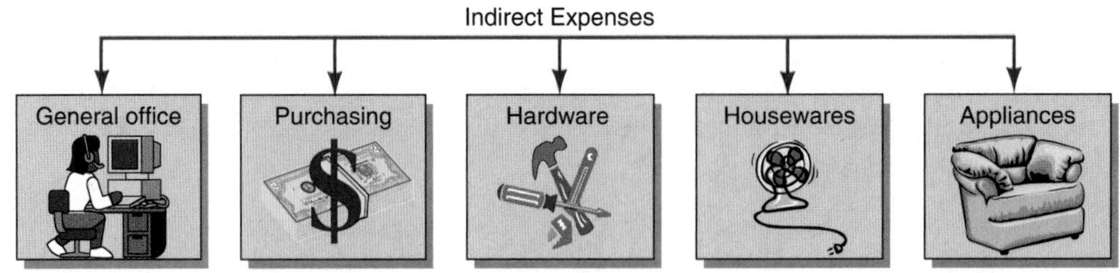

Step 3 Step 3 allocates expenses of the service departments (office and purchasing) to the operating departments. Exhibit 21.11 reflects the allocation of service department expenses using the allocation base(s).

Exhibit 21.11

Step 3: Service Department Expense Allocation to Operating Departments

General Office Department Expense Allocation

General office | Purchasing | Hardware | Housewares | Appliances

Purchasing Department Expense Allocation

Point: To apply these concepts, work Exercise 21-1.

Exhibit 21.12

Departmental Expense Allocation Spreadsheet

Computations for both steps 2 and 3 are commonly made using a departmental expense allocation spreadsheet as shown in Exhibit 21.12.[1] The first two sections of this spreadsheet list direct expenses and indirect expenses by department. The third section lists the service

A-1 HARDWARE
Departmental Expense Allocations
For Year Ended December 31, 2005

	Allocation Base	Expense Account Balance	General Office Dept.	Purchasing Dept.	Hardware Dept.	Housewares Dept.	Appliances Dept.
			Allocation of Expenses to Departments				
Direct expenses							
Salaries expense	Payroll records	$51,900	$13,300	$8,200	$15,600	$ 7,000	$ 7,800
Depreciation—Equipment	Depreciation records	1,500	500	300	400	100	200
Supplies expense	Requisitions	900	200	100	300	200	100
Indirect expenses							
Rent expense	Amount and value of space	12,000	600	600	4,860	3,240	2,700
Utilities expense	Floor space	2,400	300	300	810	540	450
Advertising expense	Sales	1,000			500	300	200
Insurance expense	Value of insured assets	2,500	400	200	900	600	400
Total department expenses		72,200	15,300	9,700	23,370	11,980	11,850
Service department expenses							
General office department	Sales		15,300		7,650	4,590	3,060
Purchasing department	Purchase orders			9,700	3,880	2,630	3,190
Total expenses allocated to operating departments		$72,200	$ 0	$ 0	$34,900	$19,200	$18,100

[1] In some cases we allocate a service department's expenses to other service departments when they use its services. For example, expenses of a payroll office benefit all service and operating departments and can be assigned to all departments. Nearly all examples and assignment materials in this book allocate service expenses only to operating departments for simplicity.

department expenses and their allocations to operating departments. The allocation bases are identified in the second column, and total expense amounts are reported in the third column.

The departmental expense allocation spreadsheet is useful in implementing the first three steps. To illustrate, first (step 1) the three direct expenses of salaries, depreciation, and supplies are accumulated in each of the five departments.

Second (step 2), the four indirect expenses of rent, utilities, advertising, and insurance are allocated to all departments using the allocation bases identified. For example, consider rent allocation. Exhibit 21.13 lists the five departments' square footage of space occupied. The two service departments (office and purchasing) occupy 25% of the total space (3,000 sq. feet/12,000 sq. feet). However, they are located near the back of the building, which is of lower value than space near the front that is occupied by operating departments. Management estimates that space near the back accounts for $1,200 of the total rent expense of $12,000. Exhibit 21.14 shows how we allocate the $1,200 rent expense between these two service departments in proportion to their square footage. We then allocate the remaining $10,800 of rent expense to the three operating departments as shown in Exhibit 21.15. We continue step 2 by allocating the $2,400 of utilities expense to all departments based on the square footage occupied as shown in Exhibit 21.16. The rows in Exhibit 21.12 for rent and utilities expenses show the amounts from Exhibits 21.14, 21.15, and 21.16. The allocations of the two other indirect expenses of advertising and insurance are similarly computed. Note that because advertising expense is allocated on the basis of sales and because service departments do not have sales, it is allocated only to the three operating departments.

Exhibit 21.13

Departments' Square Footages

General office	1,500 sq. ft.
Purchasing	1,500 sq. ft.
Hardware	4,050 sq. ft.
Housewares	2,700 sq. ft.
Appliances	2,250 sq. ft.
Total	12,000 sq. ft.

Exhibit 21.14

Allocating Indirect (Rent) Expense to Service Departments

Department	Square Feet	Percent of Total	Allocated Cost
General office	1,500	50.0%	$ 600
Purchasing	1,500	50.0	600
Totals	3,000	100.0%	$1,200

Exhibit 21.15

Allocating Indirect (Rent) Expense to Operating Departments

Department	Square Feet	Percent of Total	Allocated Cost
Hardware	4,050	45.0%	$ 4,860
Housewares	2,700	30.0	3,240
Appliances	2,250	25.0	2,700
Totals	9,000	100.0%	$10,800

Exhibit 21.16

Allocating Indirect (Utilities) Expense to All Departments

Department	Square Feet	Percent of Total	Allocated Cost
General office	1,500	12.50%	$ 300
Purchasing	1,500	12.50	300
Hardware	4,050	33.75	810
Housewares	2,700	22.50	540
Appliances	2,250	18.75	450
Totals	12,000	100.00%	$2,400

Example: If the $15,300 general office expenses in Exhibit 21.12 are allocated equally across departments, what is net income for the hardware department and for the combined company? *Answer:* Hardware income, $13,350; combined income, $19,000.

Third (step 3), total expenses of the two service departments are allocated to the three operating departments using the allocation bases shown in the final three rows of Exhibit 21.12.

Step 4 When the departmental expense spreadsheet is complete, the amounts in the operating department columns are used to prepare departmental income statements as shown in Exhibit 21.17. This exhibit uses the spreadsheet for its operating expenses; information on sales and cost of goods sold comes from departmental records.

Exhibit 21.17

Departmental Income Statements

A-1 HARDWARE
Departmental Income Statements
For Year Ended December 31, 2005

	Hardware Department	Housewares Department	Appliances Department	Combined
Sales	$119,500	$71,700	$47,800	$239,000
Cost of goods sold	73,800	43,800	30,200	147,800
Gross profit	45,700	27,900	17,600	91,200
Operating expenses				
Salaries expense	15,600	7,000	7,800	30,400
Depreciation expense—Equipment	400	100	200	700
Supplies expense	300	200	100	600
Rent expense	4,860	3,240	2,700	10,800
Utilities expense	810	540	450	1,800
Advertising expense	500	300	200	1,000
Insurance expense	900	600	400	1,900
Share of general office expenses	7,650	4,590	3,060	15,300
Share of purchasing expenses	3,880	2,630	3,190	9,700
Total operating expenses	34,900	19,200	18,100	72,200
Net income (loss)	**$ 10,800**	**$ 8,700**	**$ (500)**	**$ 19,000**

Departmental Contribution to Overhead

P4 Prepare departmental contribution reports.

Data from departmental income statements are not always best for evaluating each department's performance, especially when indirect expenses are a large portion of total expenses and when weaknesses in assumptions and decisions in allocating indirect expenses can markedly affect net income. In these and other cases, we might better evaluate department performance using the **departmental contribution to overhead,** which is a report of the amount of sales less *direct* expenses.[2]

Point: Net income is the same in Exhibits 21.17 and 21.18. The method of reporting indirect expenses in Exhibit 21.18 does not change total net income but does identify each department's contribution to overhead and net income.

The upper half of Exhibit 21.18 shows a departmental contribution to overhead as part of an expanded income statement. This format is common when reporting departmental contributions to overhead. Using the information in Exhibits 21.17 and 21.18, we can evaluate the profitability of the three operating departments. For instance, let's compare the performance of the appliances department as described in these two exhibits. Exhibit 21.17 shows a $500 net loss resulting from this department's operations, but Exhibit 21.18 shows a $9,500 positive contribution to overhead, which is 19.9% of sales. The contribution of the appliances department is not as large as that of the other selling departments, but a $9,500 contribution to overhead is better than a $500 loss. This tells us that the appliances department is not a money loser. On the contrary, it is contributing $9,500 toward defraying total indirect expenses of $40,500.

[2] A department's contribution is said to be "to overhead" because of the practice of considering all indirect expenses as overhead. Thus, the excess of a department's sales over direct expenses is a contribution toward at least a portion of its total overhead.

Exhibit 21.18

Departmental Contribution to Overhead

A-1 HARDWARE
Income Statement Showing Departmental Contribution to Overhead
For Year Ended December 31, 2005

	Hardware Department	Housewares Department	Appliances Department	Combined
Sales	$119,500	$ 71,700	$47,800	$239,000
Cost of goods sold	73,800	43,800	30,200	147,800
Gross profit	45,700	27,900	17,600	91,200
Direct expenses				
Salaries expense	15,600	7,000	7,800	30,400
Depreciation expense—Equipment	400	100	200	700
Supplies expense	300	200	100	600
Total direct expenses	16,300	7,300	8,100	31,700
Departmental contributions to overhead	**$ 29,400**	**$20,600**	**$ 9,500**	**$ 59,500**
Indirect expenses				
Rent expense				10,800
Utilities expense				1,800
Advertising expense				1,000
Insurance expense				1,900
General office department expense				15,300
Purchasing department expense				9,700
Total indirect expenses				40,500
Net income				$ 19,000
Contribution as percent of sales	24.6%	28.7%	19.9%	24.9%

Quick Check

6. If a company has two operating (selling) departments (shoes and hats) and two service departments (payroll and advertising), which of the following statements is correct? (*a*) Wages incurred in the payroll department are direct expenses of the shoe department, (*b*) Wages incurred in the payroll department are indirect expenses of the operating departments, or (*c*) Advertising department expenses are allocated to the other three departments.
7. Which of the following bases can be used to allocate supervisors' salaries across operating departments? (*a*) Hours spent in each department, (*b*) number of employees in each department, (*c*) sales achieved in each department, or (*d*) any of the above, depending on which information is most relevant and accessible.
8. What three steps are used to allocate expenses to operating departments?
9. An income statement showing departmental contribution to overhead, (*a*) subtracts indirect expenses from each department's revenues, (*b*) subtracts only direct expenses from each department's revenues, or (*c*) shows net income for each department.

Answers—p. 853

Responsibility Accounting

C4 Explain controllable costs and responsibility accounting.

Departmental accounting reports often provide data used to evaluate a department's performance, but are they useful in assessing how well a department *manager* performs? Neither departmental income nor its contribution to overhead may be useful because many expenses can be outside a manager's control. Instead, we often evaluate a manager's performance using responsibility accounting reports that describe a department's activities in terms of **controllable costs.**[3] A cost is controllable if a manager has the power to determine or at

[3] The terms *cost* and *expense* are often used interchangeably in managerial accounting, but they are not necessarily the same. *Cost* often refers to the monetary outlay to acquire some resource that can have present and future benefit. *Expense* usually refers to an expired cost. That is, as the benefit of a resource expires, a portion of its cost is written off as an expense.

least significantly affect the amount incurred. **Uncontrollable costs** are not within the manager's control or influence.

Controllable versus Direct Costs

Controllable costs are not always the same as direct costs. Direct costs are readily traced to a department, but the department manager might or might not control their amounts. For example, department managers often have little or no control over depreciation expense because they cannot affect the amount of equipment assigned to their departments. Also, department managers rarely control their own salaries. However, they can control or influence items such as the cost of supplies used in their department. When evaluating managers' performances, we should use data reflecting their departments' outputs along with their controllable costs and expenses.

Distinguishing between controllable and uncontrollable costs depends on the particular manager and time period under analysis. For example, the cost of property insurance is usually not controllable at the department manager's level but by the executive responsible for obtaining the company's insurance coverage. Likewise, this executive might not control costs resulting from insurance policies already in force. However, when a policy expires, this executive can renegotiate a replacement policy and then controls these costs. Therefore, all costs are controllable at some management level if the time period is sufficiently long. We must use good judgment in identifying controllable costs.

Point: To apply these concepts, work Exercise 21-8.

Responsibility Accounting System

A *responsibility accounting system* uses the concept of controllable costs to assign managers the responsibility for costs and expenses under their control. Prior to each reporting period, a company prepares plans that identify costs and expenses under each manager's control. These plans are called **responsibility accounting budgets.** To ensure the cooperation of managers and the reasonableness of budgets, managers should be involved in preparing their budgets.

Exhibit 21.19

Organizational Responsibility Chart

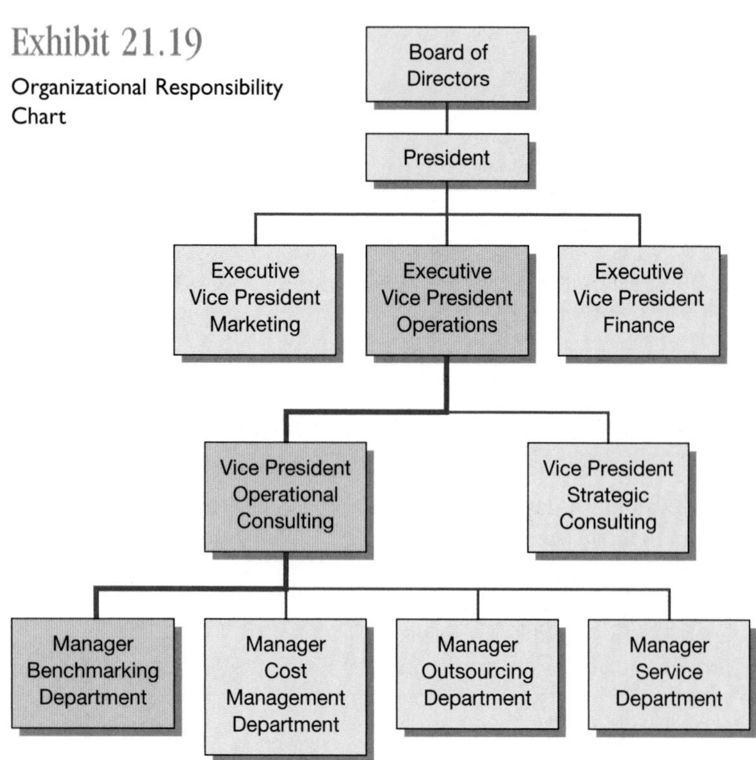

A responsibility accounting system also involves performance reports. A **responsibility accounting performance report** accumulates and reports costs and expenses that a manager is responsible for and their budgeted amounts. Management's analysis of differences between budgeted amounts and actual costs and expenses often results in corrective or strategic managerial actions. Upper-level management uses performance reports to evaluate the effectiveness of lower-level managers in controlling costs and expenses and keeping them within budgeted amounts.

A responsibility accounting system recognizes that control over costs and expenses belongs to several levels of management. We illustrate this by considering the organization chart in Exhibit 21.19. The lines in this chart connecting the managerial positions reflect channels of authority. For example, the four department managers of this consulting firm (benchmarking, cost management, outsourcing, and service) are responsible for controllable costs and expenses incurred in their departments, but these same costs are subject to the overall control of the vice president (VP) for operational consulting. Similarly, this VP's costs are subject to the control of the executive vice president (EVP) for operations, the president, and, ultimately, the board of directors.

At lower levels, managers have limited responsibility and relatively little control over costs and expenses. Performance reports for low-level management typically cover few controllable costs. Responsibility and control broaden for higher-level managers; therefore, their reports span a wider range of costs. However, reports to higher-level managers seldom contain the details reported to their subordinates but are summarized for two reasons: (1) lower-level managers are often responsible for these detailed costs and (2) detailed reports can obscure broader, more important issues facing a company.

Exhibit 21.20 shows summarized performance reports for the three management levels identified in Exhibit 21.19. Exhibit 21.20 shows that costs under the control of the benchmarking department manager are totaled and included among controllable costs of the VP for operational consulting. Also, costs under the control of the VP are totaled and included among controllable costs of the EVP for operations. In this way, a responsibility accounting system provides relevant information for each management level.

Point: Responsibility accounting does not place blame. Instead, responsibility accounting is used to identify opportunities for improving performance.

Exhibit 21.20

Responsibility Accounting Performance Reports

Executive Vice President, Operations	**For July**		
Controllable Costs	**Budgeted Amount**	**Actual Amount**	**Over (Under) Budget**
Salaries, VPs	$ 80,000	$ 80,000	$ 0
Quality control costs	21,000	22,400	1,400
Office costs	29,500	28,800	(700)
Operational consulting	**276,700**	**279,500**	**2,800**
Strategic consulting	390,000	380,600	(9,400)
Totals	$ 797,200	$ 791,300	$(5,900)

Vice President, Operational Consulting	**For July**		
Controllable Costs	**Budgeted Amount**	**Actual Amount**	**Over (Under) Budget**
Salaries, department managers	$ 75,000	$ 78,000	$ 3,000
Depreciation	10,600	10,600	0
Insurance	6,800	6,300	(500)
Benchmarking department	**79,600**	**79,900**	**300**
Cost management department	61,500	60,200	(1,300)
Outsourcing department	24,300	24,700	400
Service department	18,900	19,800	900
Totals	**$276,700**	**$279,500**	**$2,800**

Manager, Benchmarking Department	**For July**		
Controllable Costs	**Budgeted Amount**	**Actual Amount**	**Over (Under) Budget**
Salaries	$ 51,600	$ 52,500	$ 900
Supplies	8,000	7,800	(200)
Other controllable costs	20,000	19,600	(400)
Totals	**$ 79,600**	**$ 79,900**	**$ 300**

Technological advances increase our ability to produce vast amounts of information that often exceeds our ability to use it. Good managers select relevant data for planning and controlling the areas under their responsibility. A good responsibility accounting system makes every effort to provide relevant information to the right person (the one who controls the cost) at the right time (before a cost is out of control).

Point: A responsibility accounting system usually divides a company into subunits called *responsibility centers*. The manager of each center is evaluated on how well the center performs, as reported in responsibility accounting reports.

Quick Check

10. Are the reports of departmental net income and the departmental contribution to overhead useful in assessing a department manager's performance? Explain.
11. Performance reports to evaluate managers should (*a*) include data about controllable expenses, (*b*) compare actual results with budgeted levels, or (*c*) both (*a*) and (*b*).

Answers—p. 854

Joint Costs and Their Allocation

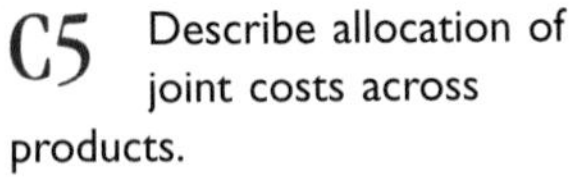

C5 Describe allocation of joint costs across products.

Most manufacturing processes involve **joint costs,** which refer to costs incurred to produce or purchase two or more products at the same time. A joint cost is like an indirect expense in the sense that more than one cost object share it. For example, a sawmill company incurs a joint cost when it buys logs that it cuts into lumber as shown in Exhibit 21.21. The joint cost includes the logs (raw material) and its cutting (conversion) into boards classified as Clear (FAS), Select, No. 1 Common, No. 2 Common, No. 3 Common, and other types of lumber and by-products.

Exhibit 21.21

Joint Products from Logs

Joint Cost: Cutting of Logs | Split-off Point | Joint Products: Clear, Select, No. 1 Common, No. 2 Common, No. 3 Common

When a joint cost is incurred, a question arises as to whether to allocate it to different products resulting from it. The answer is that when management wishes to estimate the costs of individual products, joint costs are included and must be allocated to these joint products. However, when management needs information to help decide whether to sell a product at a certain point in the production process or to process it further, the joint costs are ignored.

Financial statements prepared according to GAAP must assign joint costs to products. To do this, management must decide how to allocate joint costs across products benefiting from these costs. If some products are sold and others remain in inventory, allocating joint costs involves assigning costs to both cost of goods sold and ending inventory.

The two usual methods to allocate joint costs are the (1) *physical basis* and (2) the *value basis.* The physical basis typically involves allocating joint cost using physical characteristics such as the ratio of pounds, cubic feet, or gallons of each joint product to the total pounds, cubic feet, or gallons of all joint products flowing from the cost. This method is not preferred because the resulting cost allocations do not reflect the relative market values the joint cost generates. The preferred approach is the value basis, which allocates joint cost in proportion to the sales value of the output produced by the process at the "split-off point"; see Exhibit 21.21.

Physical Basis Allocation of Joint Cost To illustrate the physical basis of allocating a joint cost, we consider a sawmill that bought logs for $30,000. When cut, these logs produce 100,000 board feet of lumber in the grades and amounts shown in Exhibit 21.22. The logs produce 20,000 board feet of No. 3 Common lumber, which is 20% of the total. With physical allocation, the No. 3 Common lumber is assigned 20% of the $30,000 cost of the logs, or $6,000 ($30,000 × 20%). Because this low-grade lumber sells for $4,000, this allocation gives a $2,000 loss from its production and sale. The physical basis for allocating joint costs does not reflect the extra value flowing into some products or the inferior value flowing into others. That is, the portion of a log that produces Clear and Select grade lumber is worth more than the portion used to produce the three grades of common lumber, but the physical basis fails to reflect this.

Grade of Lumber	Board Feet Produced	Percent of Total	Allocated Cost	Sales Value	Gross Profit
Clear and Select	10,000	10.0%	$ 3,000	$12,000	$ 9,000
No. 1 Common	30,000	30.0	9,000	18,000	9,000
No. 2 Common	40,000	40.0	12,000	16,000	4,000
No. 3 Common	20,000	20.0	6,000	4,000	(2,000)
Totals	100,000	100.0%	$30,000	$50,000	$20,000

Exhibit 21.22

Allocating Joint Costs on a Physical Basis

Value Basis Allocation of Joint Cost Exhibit 21.23 illustrates the value basis method of allocation. It determines the percents of the total costs allocated to each grade by the ratio of each grade's sales value to the total sales value of $50,000 (sales value is the unit selling price multiplied by the number of units produced). The Clear and Select lumber grades receive 24% of the total cost ($12,000/$50,000) instead of the 10% portion using a physical basis. The No. 3 Common lumber receives only 8% of the total cost, or $2,400, which is much less than the $6,000 assigned to it using the physical basis.

Grade of Lumber	Sales Value	Percent of Total	Allocated Cost	Gross Profit
Clear and Select	$12,000	24.0%	$ 7,200	$ 4,800
No. 1 Common	18,000	36.0	10,800	7,200
No. 2 Common	16,000	32.0	9,600	6,400
No. 3 Common	4,000	8.0	2,400	1,600
Totals	$50,000	100.0%	$30,000	$20,000

Exhibit 21.23

Allocating Joint Costs on a Value Basis

Example: Refer to Exhibit 21.23. If the sales value of Clear and Select lumber is changed to $10,000, what is the revised ratio of the market value of No. 1 Common to the total?
Answer: $18,000/$48,000 = 37.5%

An outcome of value basis allocation is that *each* grade produces exactly the same 40% gross profit at the split-off point. This 40% rate equals the gross profit rate from selling all the lumber made from the $30,000 logs for a combined price of $50,000.

Quick Check

12. A company produces three products, B1, B2, and B3. The joint cost incurred for the current month for these products is $180,000. The following data relate to this month's production:

Product	Units Produced	Unit Sales Value
B1	96,000	$3.00
B2	64,000	6.00
B3	32,000	9.00

The amount of joint cost allocated to product B3 using the value basis allocation is (*a*) $30,000, (*b*) $54,000, or (*c*) $90,000.

Answer—p. 854

Investment Center Return on Total Assets

Decision Analysis

A1 Analyze investment centers using return on total assets.

We discussed the classification of departments and divisions as profit centers or cost centers. Another way is to classify (and evaluate) a department as an **investment center.** An investment center manager is responsible for effectively using the center's assets to generate income for the center.

A measure often used to evaluate the performance of an investment center manager is the **investment center return on total assets,** also called *return on investment*. This measure is computed as a center's net income divided by the center's average total assets. To illustrate, if a center with an average investment of $1 million yields a net income of $210,000, its return on total assets is 21%.

Top management can use a center's return on total assets to assess how well its manager has utilized the center's assets to generate returns for the company. Top management can also compare performance

Topic Tackler 21-3

Decision Maker

Center Manager Your center's usual return on total assets is 19%. You are considering two new investing opportunities for your center. The first requires a $250,000 average investment and is expected to yield annual net income of $50,000. The second requires a $1 million average investment with an expected annual net income of $175,000. Do you pursue either opportunity?

Answer—p. 853

across departments and/or divisions using this measure. Many companies establish a center's target return on total assets and reward managers based on whether they meet targets. In addition, center managers often use the center's return on total assets to decide whether to invest additional resources in the center.

Demonstration Problem

We must prepare departmental income statements for Hacker's Haven, a computer store that has five departments. Three are operating departments (hardware, software, and repairs) and two are service departments (general office and purchasing).

	General Office	Purchasing	Hardware	Software	Repairs
Sales	—	—	$960,000	$600,000	$840,000
Cost of goods sold	—	—	500,000	300,000	200,000
Direct expenses					
Payroll	$60,000	$45,000	80,000	25,000	325,000
Depreciation	6,000	7,200	33,000	4,200	9,600
Supplies	15,000	10,000	10,000	2,000	25,000

The departments incur several indirect expenses. To prepare departmental income statements, the indirect expenses must be allocated across the five departments. Then the expenses of the two service departments must be allocated to the three operating departments. Total cost amounts and the allocation bases for each indirect expense are as follows:

Indirect Expense	Total Cost	Allocation Basis
Rent	$150,000	Square footage occupied
Utilities	50,000	Square footage occupied
Advertising	125,000	Dollars of sales
Insurance	30,000	Value of assets insured
Service departments		
General office	?	Number of employees
Purchasing	?	Dollars of cost of goods sold

The following additional information is needed for indirect expense allocations:

Department	Square Feet	Sales	Insured Assets	Employees	Cost of Goods Sold
General office	500		$ 60,000		
Purchasing	500		72,000		
Hardware	4,000	$ 960,000	330,000	5	$ 500,000
Software	3,000	600,000	42,000	5	300,000
Repairs	2,000	840,000	96,000	10	200,000
Totals	10,000	$2,400,000	$600,000	20	$1,000,000

Required

1. Prepare a departmental expense allocation spreadsheet for Hacker's Haven.

2. Prepare a departmental income statement reporting net income for each operating department and for all operating departments combined.

Planning the Solution

- Set up and complete four tables to allocate the indirect expenses—one each for rent, utilities, advertising, and insurance.
- Allocate the departments' indirect expenses using a spreadsheet like the one in Exhibit 21.12. Enter the given amounts of the direct expenses for each department. Then enter the allocated amounts of the indirect expenses that you computed.
- Complete two tables for allocating the general office and purchasing department costs to the three operating departments. Enter these amounts on the spreadsheet and determine the total expenses allocated to the three operating departments.
- Prepare departmental income statements like the one in Exhibit 21.17. Show sales, cost of goods sold, gross profit, individual expenses, and net income for each of the three operating departments and for the combined company.

Solution to Demonstration Problem

Allocations of the four indirect expenses across the five departments:

Rent	Square Feet	Percent of Total	Allocated Cost
General office	500	5.0%	$ 7,500
Purchasing	500	5.0	7,500
Hardware	4,000	40.0	60,000
Software	3,000	30.0	45,000
Repairs	2,000	20.0	30,000
Totals	10,000	100.0%	$150,000

Utilities	Square Feet	Percent of Total	Allocated Cost
General office	500	5.0%	$ 2,500
Purchasing	500	5.0	2,500
Hardware	4,000	40.0	20,000
Software	3,000	30.0	15,000
Repairs	2,000	20.0	10,000
Totals	10,000	100.0%	$50,000

Advertising	Sales Dollars	Percent of Total	Allocated Cost
Hardware	$ 960,000	40.0%	$ 50,000
Software	600,000	25.0	31,250
Repairs	840,000	35.0	43,750
Totals	$2,400,000	100.0%	$125,000

Insurance	Assets Insured	Percent of Total	Allocated Cost
General office	$ 60,000	10.0%	$ 3,000
Purchasing	72,000	12.0	3,600
Hardware	330,000	55.0	16,500
Software	42,000	7.0	2,100
Repairs	96,000	16.0	4,800
Totals	$600,000	100.0%	$30,000

1. Allocations of service department expenses to the three operating departments:

General Office Allocations to	Employees	Percent of Total	Allocated Cost
Hardware	5	25.0%	$23,500
Software	5	25.0	23,500
Repairs	10	50.0	47,000
Totals	20	100.0%	$94,000

Purchasing Allocations to	Cost of Goods Sold	Percent of Total	Allocated Cost
Hardware	$ 500,000	50.0%	$37,900
Software	300,000	30.0	22,740
Repairs	200,000	20.0	15,160
Totals	$1,000,000	100.0%	$75,800

HACKER'S HAVEN
Departmental Expense Allocations
For Year Ended December 31, 2005

	Allocation Base	Expense Account Balance	General Office Dept.	Purchasing Dept.	Hardware Dept.	Software Dept.	Repairs Dept.
Direct Expenses							
Payroll		$ 535,000	$ 60,000	$ 45,000	$ 80,000	$ 25,000	$ 325,000
Depreciation		60,000	6,000	7,200	33,000	4,200	9,600
Supplies		62,000	15,000	10,000	10,000	2,000	25,000
Indirect Expenses							
Rent	Square ft.	150,000	7,500	7,500	60,000	45,000	30,000
Utilities	Square ft.	50,000	2,500	2,500	20,000	15,000	10,000
Advertising	Sales	125,000	—	—	50,000	31,250	43,750
Insurance	Assets	30,000	3,000	3,600	16,500	2,100	4,800
Total expenses		**1,012,000**	**94,000**	**75,800**	269,500	124,550	448,150
Service Department Expenses							
General office	Employees		**94,000**		23,500	23,500	47,000
Purchasing	Goods sold			**75,800**	37,900	22,740	15,160
Total expenses allocated to operating departments		**$1,012,000**	**$ 0**	**$ 0**	**$330,900**	**$170,790**	**$510,310**

2. Departmental income statements for Hacker's Haven:

HACKER'S HAVEN
Departmental Income Statements
For Year Ended December 31, 2005

	Hardware	Software	Repairs	Combined
Sales	$ 960,000	$ 600,000	$ 840,000	$2,400,000
Cost of goods sold	500,000	300,000	200,000	1,000,000
Gross profit	460,000	300,000	640,000	1,400,000
Expenses				
Payroll	80,000	25,000	325,000	430,000
Depreciation	33,000	4,200	9,600	46,800
Supplies	10,000	2,000	25,000	37,000
Rent	60,000	45,000	30,000	135,000
Utilities	20,000	15,000	10,000	45,000
Advertising	50,000	31,250	43,750	125,000
Insurance	16,500	2,100	4,800	23,400
Share of general office	23,500	23,500	47,000	94,000
Share of purchasing	37,900	22,740	15,160	75,800
Total expenses	330,900	170,790	510,310	1,012,000
Net income	**$129,100**	**$129,210**	**$129,690**	**$ 388,000**

Summary

C1 Explain departmentalization and the role of departmental accounting. Companies are divided into departments when they are too large to be effectively managed as a single unit. Operating departments carry out an organization's main functions. Service departments support the activities of operating departments. Departmental accounting systems provide information for evaluating departmental performance.

C2 Distinguish between direct and indirect expenses. Direct expenses are traced to a specific department and are incurred for the sole benefit of that department. Indirect expenses benefit more than one department. Indirect expenses are allocated to departments when computing departmental net income.

C3 Identify bases for allocating indirect expenses to departments. Ideally, we allocate indirect expenses by using a cause-effect relation for the allocation base. When a cause-effect relation is not identifiable, each indirect expense is allocated on a basis reflecting the relative benefit received by each department.

C4 **Explain controllable costs and responsibility accounting.** A controllable cost is one that is influenced by a specific management level. The total expenses of operating a department often include some items a department manager does not control. Responsibility accounting systems provide information for evaluating the performance of department managers. A responsibility accounting system's performance reports for evaluating department managers should include only the expenses (and revenues) that each manager controls.

C5 **Describe allocation of joint costs across products.** A joint cost refers to costs incurred to produce or purchase two or more products at the same time. When income statements are prepared, joint costs are usually allocated to the resulting joint products using either a physical or value basis.

A1 **Analyze investment centers using return on total assets.** A measure often used to evaluate an investment center manager is the *investment center return on total assets,* also called *return on investment*. This measure is computed as the center's net income divided by the center's average total assets.

P1 **Assign overhead costs using two-stage cost allocation.** In the traditional two-stage cost allocation procedure, service department costs are first assigned to operating departments. Then, in the second stage, a predetermined overhead allocation rate is computed for each operating department and is used to assign overhead to output.

P2 **Assign overhead costs using activity-based costing.** In activity-based costing, the costs of related activities are collected and then pooled in some logical manner into activity cost pools. After all activity costs have been accumulated in an activity cost pool account, users of the activity, termed *cost objects,* are assigned a portion of the total activity cost using a cost driver (allocation base).

P3 **Prepare departmental income statements.** Each profit center (department) is assigned its expenses to yield its own income statement. These costs include its direct expenses and its share of indirect expenses. The departmental income statement lists its revenues and costs of goods sold to determine gross profit. Its operating expenses (direct expenses and its indirect expenses allocated to the department) are deducted from gross profit to yield departmental net income.

P4 **Prepare departmental contribution reports.** The departmental contribution report is similar to the departmental income statement in terms of computing the gross profit for each department. Then the direct operating expenses for each department are deducted from gross profit to determine the contribution generated by each department. Indirect operating expenses are deducted *in total* from the company's combined contribution.

Guidance Answers to **Decision Maker** and **Decision Ethics**

Director of Operations You should collect details on overhead items and review them to see whether direct labor does indeed drive these costs. If it does not, overhead might be improperly assigned to departments. The situation also provides an opportunity to consider other overhead allocation bases, including the use of activity-based costing.

Accounting Officer You should not author a report that you disagree with. You are responsible for ascertaining all the facts of ABC (implementation procedures, advantages and disadvantages, and costs). You should then approach your supervisor with these facts and suggest that you would like to modify the report to request, for example, a pilot implementation. The pilot test will allow you to further assess the suitability of ABC. Your suggestion might be rejected, at which time you may wish to speak with a more senior-level manager.

Center Manager We must first realize that the two investment opportunities are not comparable on the basis of absolute dollars of income or on assets. For instance, the second investment provides a higher income in absolute dollars but requires a higher investment. Accordingly, we need to compute return on total assets for each alternative: (1) $50,000 ÷ $250,000 = 20%, and (2) $175,000 ÷ $1 million = 17.5%. Alternative 1 has the higher return and is preferred over alternative 2. Do you pursue one, both, or neither? Because alternative 1's return is higher than the center's usual return of 19%, it should be pursued, assuming its risks are acceptable. Also, since alternative 1 requires a small investment, top management is likely to be more agreeable to pursuing it. Alternative 2's return is lower than the usual 19% and is not likely to be acceptable.

Guidance Answers to **Quick Checks**

1. Cost drivers are the factors that have a cause-effect relation with costs (or activities that pertain to costs).
2. *d*
3. A departmental accounting system provides information used to evaluate the performance of *departments.* A responsibility accounting system provides information used to evaluate the performance of *department managers.*
4. *d*
5. A cost center, such as a service department, incurs costs without directly generating revenues. A profit center, such as a product division, incurs costs but also generates revenues.
6. *b*
7. *d*
8. (1) Assign the direct expenses to each department. (2) Allocate indirect expenses to all departments. (3) Allocate the service department expenses to the operating departments.

9. *b*

10. No, because many expenses that enter into these calculations are beyond the manager's control, and managers should not be evaluated using costs they do not control.

11. *c*

12. *b*; $180,000 × ([32,000 × $9]/[96,000 × $3 + 64,000 × $6 + 32,000 × $9]) = $54,000.

Key Terms

Key Terms are available at the book's Website for learning and testing in an online Flashcard Format.

Activity-based costing (ABC) (p. 834)
Activity cost pool (p. 834)
Controllable costs (p. 845)
Cost center (p. 838)
Cost driver (p. 834)
Departmental accounting system (p. 837)
Departmental contribution to overhead (p. 844)
Direct expenses (p. 839)
Indirect expenses (p. 839)
Investment center (p. 849)
Investment center return on total assets (p. 849)
Joint cost (p. 848)
Profit center (p. 838)
Responsibility accounting budget (p. 846)
Responsibility accounting performance report (p. 846)
Responsibility accounting system (p. 838)
Uncontrollable costs (p. 846)

Personal Interactive Quiz

Personal Interactive Quizzes A and B are available at the book's Website to reinforce and assess your learning.

Discussion Questions

1. Why are many companies divided into departments?

2. Complete the following for a traditional two-stage allocation system: In the first stage, service department costs are assigned to _____ departments. In the second stage, a predetermined overhead rate is computed for each operating department and used to assign overhead to _____.

3. What is the difference between operating departments and service departments?

4. What is activity-based costing? What is its goal?

5. Identify at least four common cost pools for activity-based costing in most organizations.

6. In activity-based costing, costs in a cost pool are allocated to _____ using predetermined overhead rates.

7. What company circumstances especially encourage use of activity-based costing?

8. What are two main goals in managerial accounting for reporting on and analyzing departments?

9. Is it possible to evaluate a cost center's profitability? Explain.

10. What is the difference between direct and indirect expenses?

11. Suggest a reasonable basis for allocating each of the following indirect expenses to departments: (a) salary of a supervisor who manages several departments, (b) rent, (c) heat, (d) electricity for lighting, (e) janitorial services, (f) advertising, (g) expired insurance on equipment, and (h) property taxes on equipment.

12. How is a department's contribution to overhead measured?

13. What are controllable costs?

14. Controllable and uncontrollable costs must be identified with a particular _____ and a definite _____ period.

15. Why should managers be closely involved in preparing their responsibility accounting budgets?

16. In responsibility accounting, who receives timely cost reports and specific cost information? Explain.

17. What is a joint cost? How are joint costs usually allocated among the products produced from them?

18. Give two examples of products with joint costs.

19. **Krispy Kreme** receives orders for donuts from different types of stores, such as grocery stores and convenience stores. Why is it useful to (a) collect information for each particular store category and (b) treat each category as a profit center?

Krispy Kreme DOUGHNUTS

20. **Harley-Davidson** delivers its products to locations around the world. List three controllable and three uncontrollable costs for its delivery department.

Harley-Davidson

Red numbers denote Discussion Questions that involve decision-making.

Homework Manager repeats all numerical Quick Studies on the book's Website with new numbers.

QUICK STUDY

QS 21-1
Allocation and measurement terms
C1 C2 C3 C4 A1

In each blank next to the following terms, place the identifying letter of its best description.

1. ______ Cost center
2. ______ Investment center
3. ______ Departmental accounting system
4. ______ Operating department
5. ______ Profit center
6. ______ Responsibility accounting system
7. ______ Service department

A. Incurs costs without directly yielding revenues.
B. Provides information used to evaluate the performance of a department manager.
C. Holds manager responsible for revenues, costs, and investments.
D. Engages directly in manufacturing or in making sales directly to customers.
E. Does not directly manufacture products but contributes to profitability of the entire company.
F. Incurs costs and also generates revenues.
G. Provides information used to evaluate the performance of a department.

QS 21-2
Basis for cost allocation
C3

For each of the following types of indirect expenses and service department expenses, identify one allocation basis that could be used to distribute it to the departments indicated.

1. Computer service expenses of production scheduling for operating departments.
2. Electric utility expenses of all departments.
3. Maintenance department expenses of the operating departments.
4. General office department expenses of the operating departments.

QS 21-3
Activity-based costing and overhead cost allocation
P2

The following is taken from Rankin Co.'s internal records of its factory with two operating departments. The cost driver for indirect labor and supplies is direct labor costs, and the cost driver for the remaining overhead items is number of hours of machine use. Compute the total amount of overhead cost allocated to Operating Department 1 using activity-based costing.

	Direct Labor	Hours of Machine Use
Operating department 1	$10,400	2,200
Operating department 2	9,600	3,000
Totals	$20,000	5,200
Factory overhead costs		
Rent and utilities		$ 7,100
Indirect labor		3,700
General office expense		2,700
Depreciation—Equipment		4,500
Supplies		300
Total factory overhead		$18,300

Check Dept. 1 allocation, $8,130

QS 21-4
Joint cost allocation
C5

A company purchases a 12,000 square foot commercial building for $322,000 and spends an additional $50,000 to divide the space into two separate rental units and prepare it for rent. Unit A, which has the desirable location on the corner and contains 4,000 square feet, will be rented for $1.00 per square foot. Unit B contains 8,000 square feet and will be rented for $0.75 per square foot. How much of the joint cost should be assigned to Unit B using the value basis of allocation?

QS 21-5
Departmental contribution to overhead P4

Use the information in the following table to compute each department's contribution to overhead (both in dollars and as a percent). Which department contributes the highest dollar amount to total overhead? Which contributes the highest percent (as a percent of sales)?

	Dept. A	Dept. B	Dept. C
Sales	$53,000	$170,000	$84,000
Cost of goods sold	34,185	103,700	49,560
Gross profit	18,815	66,300	34,440
Total direct expenses	6,360	37,060	8,736
Contribution to overhead	$ ____	$ ____	$ ____
Contribution percent	____%	____%	____%

QS 21-6
Investment center analysis
A1

Compute return on assets for each of these Reebok shoe divisions (each is an investment center). Comment on the relative performance of each investment center.

Investment Center	Net Income	Average Assets	Return on Assets
Basketball	$4,000,000	$20,000,000	____
Soccer	1,500,000	15,000,000	____
Cross-trainer	750,000	10,000,000	____

Homework Manager *repeats all numerical Exercises on the book's Website with new numbers.*

EXERCISES

Exercise 21-1
Departmental expense allocations
P1 C3

Won Han Co. has four departments: materials, personnel, manufacturing, and packaging. In a recent month, the four departments incurred three shared indirect expenses. The amounts of these indirect expenses and the bases used to allocate them follow:

Indirect Expense	Cost	Allocation Base
Supervision	$ 75,000	Number of employees
Utilities	60,000	Square feet occupied
Insurance	16,500	Value of assets in use
Total	$151,500	

Departmental data for the company's recent reporting period follow:

Department	Employees	Square Feet	Asset Values
Materials	18	27,000	$ 6,000
Personnel	6	4,500	1,200
Manufacturing	66	45,000	37,800
Packaging	30	13,500	15,000
Total	120	90,000	$60,000

Check (2) $30,900 assigned to materials

(1) Use this information to allocate each of the three indirect expenses across the four departments.
(2) Prepare a summary table that reports the indirect expenses assigned to each of the four departments.

Exercise 21-2
Activity-based costing of overhead
P2

Pane Company manufactures two types of glass shelving, rounded edge and squared edge, on the same production line. For the current period, the company reports the following data:

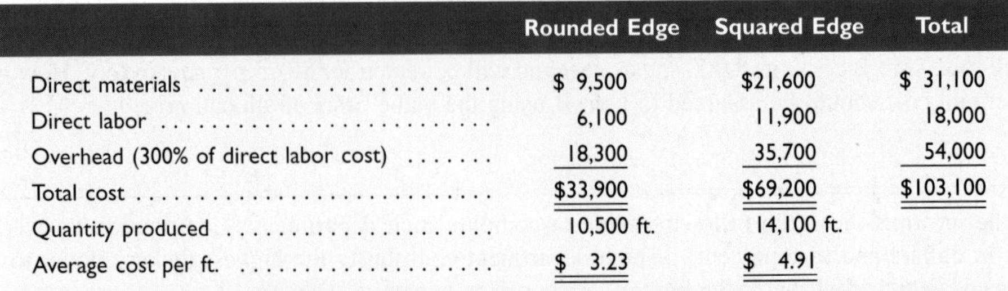

	Rounded Edge	Squared Edge	Total
Direct materials	$ 9,500	$21,600	$ 31,100
Direct labor	6,100	11,900	18,000
Overhead (300% of direct labor cost)	18,300	35,700	54,000
Total cost	$33,900	$69,200	$103,100
Quantity produced	10,500 ft.	14,100 ft.	
Average cost per ft.	$ 3.23	$ 4.91	

Pane's controller wishes to apply activity-based costing (ABC) to the $54,000 of overhead costs incurred by the two product lines to see whether cost per foot would change significantly from that recorded above. She has collected the following information:

Overhead Cost Category (Activity Cost Pool)	Cost
Supervision	$ 2,160
Depreciation of machinery	28,840
Assembly line preparation	23,000
Total overhead	$54,000

She has also collected the following information about the cost drivers for each category (cost pool) and the amount of each driver used by the two product lines:

Overhead Cost Category (Activity Cost Pool)	Driver	Usage		
		Rounded Edge	Squared Edge	Total
Supervision	Direct labor cost($)	$6,100	$11,900	$18,000
Depreciation of machinery	Machine hours	300 hours	700 hours	1,000 hours
Assembly line preparation	Setups (number)	31 times	94 times	125 times

Use this information to (1) assign these three overhead cost pools to each of the two products using ABC, (2) determine average cost per foot for each of the two products using ABC, and (3) compare the average cost per foot under ABC with the average cost per foot under the current method for each product. For part 3, explain why a difference between the two cost allocation methods exists.

Check (2) Rounded edge, $2.92; Squared edge, $5.14

Exercise 21-3
Rent expense allocated to departments
P1 C3

Auto Market pays $128,000 rent each year for its two-story building. The space in this building is occupied by five departments as specified here:

Paint department	1,390 square feet of first-floor space
Engine department	3,410 square feet of first-floor space
Window department	2,040 square feet of second-floor space
Electrical department	960 square feet of second-floor space
Accessory department	1,800 square feet of second-floor space

The company allocates 65% of total rent expense to the first floor and 35% to the second floor and then allocates rent expense for each floor to the departments occupying that floor on the basis of space occupied. Determine the rent expense to be allocated to each department. (Round percents to the nearest one-tenth and dollar amounts to the nearest whole dollar.)

Check Paint dept., $24,128

Exercise 21-4
Departmental expense allocation spreadsheet
C3 P1

Overroad Cycle Shop has two service departments (advertising and administration) and two operating departments (cycles and clothing). During 2005, the departments had the following direct expenses and occupied the following amount of floor space:

Department	Direct Expenses	Square Feet
Advertising	$ 16,000	1,088
Administrative	18,500	1,152
Cycles	101,600	6,336
Clothing	11,900	4,224

The advertising department developed and distributed 100 advertisements during the year. Of these, 76 promoted cycles and 24 promoted clothing. The store sold $300,000 of merchandise during the year. Of this amount, $225,000 is from the cycles department, and $75,000 is from the clothing department. The utilities expense of $64,000 is an indirect expense to all departments. Prepare a departmental expense allocation spreadsheet for Overroad Cycle Shop. The spreadsheet should assign

(1) direct expenses to each of the four departments, (2) the $64,000 of utilities expense to the four departments on the basis of floor space occupied, (3) the advertising department's expenses to the two operating departments on the basis of the number of ads placed that promoted a department's products, and (4) the administrative department's expenses to the two operating departments based on the amount of sales. Provide supporting computations for the expense allocations.

Check Total expenses allocated to Cycles, $167,769

Exercise 21-5
Service department expenses allocated to operating departments P3

The following is a partially completed lower section of a departmental expense allocation spreadsheet for Bookworm Bookstore. It reports the total amounts of direct and indirect expenses allocated to its five departments.

	A	B	C	D	E	F	G	H
1				Allocation of Expenses to Departments				
2-4		Allocation Base	Expense Account Balance	Advertising Dept.	Purchasing Dept.	Books Dept.	Magazines Dept.	Newspapers Dept.
5	Total department expenses		$654,000	$22,000	$30,000	$425,000	$86,000	$91,000
6	**Service department expenses**							
7	Advertising department	Sales		?		?	?	?
8	Purchasing department	Purch. orders			?	?	?	?
9	Total expenses allocated to							
10	operating departments		?	$ 0	$ 0	?	?	?
11								

Complete the spreadsheet by allocating the expenses of the two service departments (advertising and purchasing) to the three operating departments. Advertising and purchasing department expenses are allocated to operating departments on the basis of dollar sales and purchase orders, respectively. Information about the allocation bases for the three operating departments follows:

Check Total expenses allocated to Books Dept., $450,040

Department	Sales	Purchase Orders
Books	$448,000	424
Magazines	144,000	312
Newspapers	208,000	264
Total	$800,000	1,000

Exercise 21-6
Indirect payroll expense allocated to departments
C3

Monica Gellar works in both the jewelry department and the hosiery department of a retail store. Gellar assists customers in both departments and arranges and stocks merchandise in both departments. The store allocates Gellar's $30,000 annual wages between the two departments based on a sample of the time worked in the two departments. The sample is obtained from a diary of hours worked that Gellar kept in a randomly chosen two-week period. The diary showed the following hours and activities spent in the two departments. Allocate Gellar's annual wages between the two departments.

Selling in jewelry department	64 hours
Arranging and stocking merchandise in jewelry department	6 hours
Selling in hosiery department	14 hours
Arranging and stocking merchandise in hosiery department	12 hours
Idle time spent waiting for a customer to enter one of the selling departments	4 hours

Check Assign $8,130 to hosiery

Exercise 21-7
Joint product costs assigned
C5

First Mate's Seafood Company purchases lobsters and processes them into tails and flakes. It sells the lobster tails for $21 per pound and the flakes for $14 per pound. On average, 100 pounds of lobster are processed into 52 pounds of tails and 22 pounds of flakes, with 26 pounds of waste. Assume that First Mate's purchased 4,800 pounds of lobster for $4.50 per pound and processed the lobsters with an additional labor cost of $3,600. No materials or labor costs are assigned to the waste. If 2,192 pounds of tails and 648 pounds of flakes are sold, what is (1) the allocated cost of the sold items and (2) the allocated cost of the ending inventory? First Mate's allocates joint costs on a value basis. (Round the dollar cost per pound to the nearest thousandth.)

Check (2) Inventory cost, $4,536

Exercise 21-8
Managerial performance evaluation
C4 

Beth Daniel manages an auto dealership's service department. The recent month's income statement for her department follows. (1) Analyze the items on the income statement and identify those that definitely should be included on a performance report used to evaluate Daniel's performance. List them and explain why you chose them. (2) List and explain the items that should definitely be excluded. (3) List the items that are not definitely included or excluded and explain why they fall into that category.

Revenues		
Sales of parts	$144,000	
Sales of services	210,000	$354,000
Costs and expenses		
Cost of parts sold	60,000	
Building depreciation	18,600	
Income taxes allocated to department	17,400	
Interest on long-term debt	15,000	
Manager's salary	24,000	
Payroll taxes	16,200	
Supplies	31,800	
Utilities	8,800	
Wages (hourly)	32,000	
Total costs and expenses		223,800
Departmental net income		$130,200

Exercise 21-9
Joint real estate costs assigned
C5

Windsboro Properties is developing a subdivision that includes 400 home lots. The 300 lots in the Canyon section are below a ridge and do not have views of the neighboring canyons and hills; the 100 lots in the Hilltop section offer unobstructed views. The expected selling price for each Canyon lot is $50,000 and for each Hilltop lot is $90,000. The developer acquired the land for $2,500,000 and spent another $2,500,000 on street and utilities improvements. Assign the joint land and improvement costs to the lots using the value basis of allocation and determine the average cost per lot.

Check Total Hilltop cost, $1,875,000

Exercise 21-10
Investment center analysis
A1 

You must prepare a return on investment analysis for the regional manager of Out-and-In Burgers. This growing chain is trying to decide which outlet of two alternatives to open. The first location (A) requires a $500,000 investment and is expected to yield annual net income of $80,000. The second location (B) requires a $200,000 investment and is expected to yield annual net income of $38,000. Compute the return on investment for each Out-and-In Burgers alternative and then make your recommendation in a one-half page memorandum to the regional manager. (The chain currently generates an 18% return on total assets.)

PROBLEM SET A

Problem 21-1A
Allocation of building occupancy costs to departments
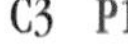  

mhhe.com/larson

City Bank has several departments that occupy both floors of a two-story building. The departmental accounting system has a single account, Building Occupancy Cost, in its ledger. The types and amounts of occupancy costs recorded in this account for the current period follow:

Depreciation—Building	$18,000
Interest—Building mortgage	27,000
Taxes—Building and land	8,000
Gas (heating) expense	2,500
Lighting expense	3,000
Maintenance expense	5,500
Total occupancy cost	$64,000

The building has 4,000 square feet on each floor. In prior periods, the accounting manager merely divided the $64,000 occupancy cost by 8,000 square feet to find an average cost of $8 per square foot and then charged each department a building occupancy cost equal to this rate times the number of square feet that it occupied.

Laura Diaz manages a first-floor department that occupies 1,000 square feet, and Lauren Wright manages a second-floor department that occupies 1,800 square feet of floor space. In discussing the departmental reports, they question whether using the same rate per square foot for all departments makes sense because the first-floor space is more valuable. The two managers also check a recent real estate study of average local rental costs for similar space that shows first-floor space worth $30 per square foot and second-floor space worth $20 per square foot (excluding costs for heating, lighting, and maintenance).

Required

1. Allocate all occupancy costs to the Diaz and Wright departments using the current allocation method.

Check (2) Total occupancy cost to Diaz, $9,330

2. Allocate the depreciation, interest, and taxes occupancy costs to the Diaz and Wright departments in proportion to the relative market values of the floor space. Allocate the heating, lighting, and maintenance costs to the Diaz and Wright departments in proportion to the square feet occupied (ignoring floor space market values).

Analysis Component

3. Which allocation method would you prefer if you were a manager of a second-floor department? Explain.

Problem 21-2A
Activity-based costing

P2 

We Care is an outpatient surgical clinic that was profitable for many years, but Medicare has cut its reimbursements by as much as 50%. As a result, the clinic wants to better understand its costs. It decides to prepare an activity-based cost analysis, including an estimate of the average cost of both general surgery and orthopedic surgery. The clinic's three cost centers and their cost drivers follow:

Cost Center	Cost	Cost Driver	Driver Quantity
Professional salaries	$1,500,000	Professional hours	10,000
Patient services and supplies	25,000	Number of patients	500
Building cost	150,000	Square feet	1,500

The two main surgical units and their related data follow:

Service	Hours	Square Feet*	Patients
General surgery	2,500	500	400
Orthopedic surgery	7,500	1,000	100

* Orthopedic surgery requires more space for patients, supplies, and equipment.

Required

1. Compute the cost per cost driver for each of the three cost centers.

Check (2) Average cost of general (orthopedic) surgery, $1,113 ($12,300) per patient

2. Use the results from part 1 to allocate costs from each of the three cost centers to both the general surgery and the orthopedic surgery units. Compute total cost and average cost per patient for both the general surgery and the orthopedic surgery units.

Analysis Component

3. Without providing computations, would the average cost of general surgery be higher or lower if all center costs were allocated based on the number of patients? Explain.

Problem 21-3A
Departmental income statements; forecasts

P3 

mhhe.com/larson

Time-To-See Co. began operations in January 2005 with two operating (selling) departments and one service (office) department. Its departmental income statements follow:

TIME-TO-SEE Co. Departmental Income Statements For Year Ended December 31, 2005	Clock	Mirror	Combined
Sales	$122,500	$52,500	$175,000
Cost of goods sold	60,000	32,000	92,000
Gross profit	62,500	20,500	83,000
Direct expenses			
Sales salaries	20,000	7,000	27,000
Advertising	1,200	500	1,700
Store supplies used	900	400	1,300
Depreciation—Equipment	1,500	300	1,800
Total direct expenses	23,600	8,200	31,800
Allocated expenses			
Rent expense	7,020	3,780	10,800
Utilities expense	2,600	1,400	4,000
Share of office department expenses	10,500	4,500	15,000
Total allocated expenses	20,120	9,680	29,800
Total expenses	43,720	17,880	61,600
Net income	$ 18,780	$ 2,620	$ 21,400

Time-To-See plans to open a third department in January 2006 that will sell paintings. Management predicts that the new department will generate $35,000 in sales with a 55% gross profit margin and will require the following direct expenses: sales salaries, $8,000; advertising, $800; store supplies, $500; and equipment depreciation, $200. It will fit the new department into the current rented space by taking some square footage from the other two departments. When opened the new painting department will fill one-fifth of the space presently used by the clock department and one-sixth used by the mirror department. Management does not predict any increase in utilities costs, which are allocated to the departments in proportion to occupied space (or rent expense). The company allocates office department expenses to the operating departments in proportion to their sales. It expects the painting department to increase total office department expenses by $7,000. Since the painting department will bring new customers into the store, management expects sales in both the clock and mirror departments to increase by 7%. No changes for those departments' gross profit percents or their direct expenses are expected except for store supplies used, which will increase in proportion to sales.

Required

Prepare departmental income statements that show the company's predicted results of operations for calendar year 2006 for the three operating (selling) departments and their combined totals. (Round percents to the nearest one-tenth and dollar amounts to the nearest whole dollar.)

Check 2006 forecasted combined net income (sales), $29,869 ($222,250)

Problem 21-4A
Responsibility accounting performance reports; controllable and budgeted costs

C4 P4

Becky Hofer, the plant manager of Travel Far's Indiana plant, is responsible for all of that plant's costs other than her own salary. The plant has two operating departments and one service department. The camper and trailer operating departments manufacture different products and have their own managers. The office department, which Hofer also manages, provides services equally to the two operating departments. A budget is prepared for each operating department and the office department. The company's responsibility accounting system must assemble information to present budgeted and actual costs in performance reports for each operating department manager and the plant manager. Each performance report includes only those costs that a particular operating department manager can control: raw materials, wages, supplies used, and equipment depreciation. The plant manager is responsible for the department managers' salaries, utilities, building rent, office salaries other than her own, and other office costs plus all costs controlled by the two operating department managers. The annual departmental budgets and actual costs for the two operating departments follow:

	Budget			Actual		
	Campers	Trailers	Combined	Campers	Trailers	Combined
Raw materials	$160,000	$250,000	$ 410,000	$159,400	$246,500	$ 405,900
Employee wages	99,000	191,000	290,000	102,300	193,700	296,000
Dept. manager salary	40,000	44,000	84,000	41,000	47,000	88,000
Supplies used	34,000	83,000	117,000	31,900	84,600	116,500
Depreciation—Equip.	58,000	110,000	168,000	58,000	110,000	168,000
Utilities	2,800	4,200	7,000	2,700	3,800	6,500
Building rent	5,000	8,000	13,000	4,800	7,200	12,000
Office department costs	56,000	56,000	112,000	54,450	54,450	108,900
Totals	$454,800	$746,200	$1,201,000	$454,550	$747,250	$1,201,800

The office department's annual budget and its actual costs follow:

	Budget	Actual
Plant manager salary	$ 60,000	$ 62,000
Other office salaries	30,000	27,700
Other office costs	22,000	19,200
Totals	$112,000	$108,900

Required

1. Prepare responsibility accounting performance reports like those in Exhibit 21.20 that list costs controlled by the following:

Check (a) $600 total over budget

a. Manager of the camper department.

b. Manager of the trailer department.

(c) Indiana plant controllable costs, $1,200 total under budget

c. Manager of the Indiana plant.

In each report, include the budgeted and actual costs and show the amount that each actual cost is over or under the budgeted amount.

Analysis Component

2. Did the plant manager or the operating department managers better manage costs? Explain.

Problem 21-5A
Allocation of joint costs

C5 

Bloom Orchards produced a good crop of peaches this year. After preparing the following income statement, Bloom believes it should have given its No. 3 peaches to charity and saved its efforts.

BLOOM ORCHARDS
Income Statement
For Year Ended December 31, 2005

	No. 1	No. 2	No. 3	Combined
Sales (by grade)				
No. 1: 300,000 lbs. @ $1.50/lb	$450,000			
No. 2: 300,000 lbs. @ $1.00/lb		$300,000		
No. 3: 750,000 lbs. @ $0.20/lb			$ 150,000	
Total sales				$900,000
Costs				
Tree pruning and care @ $0.20/lb	60,000	60,000	150,000	270,000
Picking, sorting, and grading @ $0.12/lb	36,000	36,000	90,000	162,000
Delivery costs @ $0.03/lb	9,000	9,000	22,500	40,500
Total costs	105,000	105,000	262,500	472,500
Net income (loss)	$345,000	$195,000	$(112,500)	$427,500

In preparing this statement, Bloom allocated joint costs among the grades on a physical basis as an equal amount per pound. Bloom's delivery cost records show that $30,000 of the $40,500 relates to crating the No. 1 and No. 2 peaches and hauling them to the buyer. The remaining $10,500 of delivery costs is for crating the No. 3 peaches and hauling them to the cannery.

Required

1. Prepare reports showing cost allocations on a sales value basis to the three grades of peaches. Separate the delivery costs into the amounts directly identifiable with each grade. Then allocate any shared delivery costs on the basis of the relative sales value of each grade. (Round percents to the nearest one-tenth and dollar amounts to the nearest whole dollar.)

2. Using your answers to part 1, prepare an income statement using the joint costs allocated on a sales value basis.

Check (1) $89,910 tree pruning and care costs allocated to No. 2

(2) Net income from No. 1 & No. 2 peaches, $216,000 & $144,144

Analysis Component

3. Do you think delivery costs fit the definition of a joint cost? Explain.

PROBLEM SET B

Problem 21-1B
Allocation of building occupancy costs to departments
C3 P1 

Dixon's has several departments that occupy all floors of a two-story building that includes a basement floor. Dixon rented this building under a long-term lease negotiated when rental rates were low. The departmental accounting system has a single account, Building Occupancy Cost, in its ledger. The types and amounts of occupancy costs recorded in this account for the current period follow:

Building rent	$300,000
Lighting expense	24,000
Cleaning expense	16,000
Total occupancy cost	$340,000

The building has 7,500 square feet on each of the upper two floors but only 5,000 square feet in the basement. In prior periods, the accounting manager merely divided the $340,000 occupancy cost by 20,000 square feet to find an average cost of $17 per square foot and then charged each department a building occupancy cost equal to this rate times the number of square feet that it occupies.

Alex Ferrero manages a department that occupies 2,000 square feet of basement floor space. In discussing the departmental reports with other managers, he questions whether using the same rate per square foot for all departments makes sense because different floor space has different values. Ferrero checked a recent real estate report of average local rental costs for similar space that shows first-floor space worth $40 per square foot, second-floor space worth $20 per square foot, and basement space worth $10 per square foot (excluding costs for lighting and cleaning).

Required

1. Allocate all occupancy costs to Ferrero's department using the current allocation method.

2. Allocate the building rent cost to Ferrero's department in proportion to the relative market value of the floor space. Allocate to Ferrero's department the lighting and heating costs in proportion to the square feet occupied (ignoring floor space market values).

Check (2) Total costs allocated to Ferrero, $16,000

Analysis Component

3. Which allocation method would you prefer if you were a manager of a basement department?

Problem 21-2B
Activity-based costing
P2 

Prairie Landscaping has enjoyed profits for many years, but new competition has cut service revenue by as much as 30%. As a result, the company wants to better understand its costs. It decides to prepare an activity-based cost analysis, including an estimate of the average cost of both general landscaping services and custom design landscaping services. The company's three cost centers and their cost drivers follow:

Cost Center	Cost	Cost Driver	Driver Quantity
Professional salaries	$500,000	Professional hours	10,000
Customer supplies	125,000	Number of customers	500
Building cost	150,000	Square feet	1,500

The two main landscaping units and their related data follow:

Service	Hours	Square Feet*	Customers
General landscaping	2,500	500	400
Custom design landscaping	7,500	1,000	100

* Custom design landscaping requires more space for equipment, supplies, and planning.

Required

1. Compute the cost per cost driver for each of the three cost centers.

Check (2) Average cost of general (custom) landscaping, $687.50 ($5,000) per customer

2. Use the results from part 1 to allocate costs from each of the three cost centers to both the general landscaping and the custom design landscaping units. Compute total cost and average cost per customer for both the general landscaping and the custom design landscaping units.

Analysis Component

3. Without providing computations, would the average cost of general landscaping be higher or lower if all center costs were allocated based on the number of customers? Explain.

Problem 21-3B

Departmental income statements; forecasts

P3

Hollywood Entertainment began operations in January 2005 with two operating (selling) departments and one service (office) department. Its departmental income statements follow:

HOLLYWOOD ENTERTAINMENT
Departmental Income Statements
For Year Ended December 31, 2005

	Movies	Video Games	Combined
Sales	$540,000	$180,000	$720,000
Cost of goods sold	378,000	138,600	516,600
Gross profit	162,000	41,400	203,400
Direct expenses			
Sales salaries	35,000	14,000	49,000
Advertising	10,500	5,500	16,000
Store supplies used	3,300	700	4,000
Depreciation—Equipment	4,200	2,800	7,000
Total direct expenses	53,000	23,000	76,000
Allocated expenses			
Rent expense	29,520	6,480	36,000
Utilities expense	4,100	900	5,000
Share of office department expenses	39,000	14,000	53,000
Total allocated expenses	72,620	21,380	94,000
Total expenses	125,620	44,380	170,000
Net income (loss)	$ 36,380	$ (2,980)	$ 33,400

Hollywood plans to open a third department in January 2006 that will sell compact discs. Management predicts that the new department will generate $250,000 in sales with a 35% gross profit margin and will require the following direct expenses: sales salaries, $18,000; advertising, $10,000; store supplies, $1,500; and equipment depreciation, $1,000. The company will fit the new department into the current rented space by taking some square footage from the other two departments. When opened, the new compact disc department will fill one-fourth of the space presently used by the movie department and one-third of the space used by the video game department. Management does not predict any increase in utilities costs, which are allocated to the departments in proportion to occupied space (or rent expense). The company allocates office department expenses to the operating departments in proportion to their sales. It expects the compact disc department to increase total office department expenses by $8,000. Since the compact disc department will bring new customers into the store, management expects sales in both the movie and video game departments to increase by 10%.

No changes for those departments' gross profit percents or for their direct expenses are expected, except for store supplies used, which will increase in proportion to sales.

Required

Prepare departmental income statements that show the company's predicted results of operations for calendar year 2006 for the three operating (selling) departments and their combined totals. (Round percents to the nearest one-tenth and dollar amounts to the nearest whole dollar.)

Check 2006 forecasted movies net income (sales), $64,885 ($594,000)

Problem 21-4B
Responsibility accounting performance reports; controllable and budgeted costs
C4 P4

Ann Braun, the plant manager of SOS Co.'s Chicago plant, is responsible for all of that plant's costs other than her own salary. The plant has two operating departments and one service department. The refrigerator and dishwasher operating departments manufacture different products and have their own managers. The office department, which Braun also manages, provides services equally to the two operating departments. A monthly budget is prepared for each operating department and the office department. The company's responsibility accounting system must assemble information to present budgeted and actual costs in performance reports for each operating department manager and the plant manager. Each performance report includes only those costs that a particular operating department manager can control: raw materials, wages, supplies used, and equipment depreciation. The plant manager is responsible for the department managers' salaries, utilities, building rent, office salaries other than her own, and other office costs plus all costs controlled by the two operating department managers. The April departmental budgets and actual costs for the two operating departments follow:

	Budget			Actual		
	Refrigerators	Dishwashers	Combined	Refrigerators	Dishwashers	Combined
Raw materials	$400,000	$200,000	$ 600,000	$375,000	$200,000	$ 575,000
Employee wages	172,000	80,000	252,000	174,700	76,800	251,500
Dept. manager salary	55,000	49,000	104,000	55,000	46,500	101,500
Supplies used	15,000	9,000	24,000	14,000	10,000	24,000
Depreciation—Equip.	53,000	37,000	90,000	53,000	37,000	90,000
Utilities	30,000	18,000	48,000	34,500	20,700	55,200
Building rent	63,000	17,000	80,000	61,000	15,000	76,000
Office department costs	70,500	70,500	141,000	75,000	75,000	150,000
Totals	$858,500	$480,500	$1,339,000	$842,200	$481,000	$1,323,200

The office department's budget and its actual costs for April follow:

	Budget	Actual
Plant manager salary	$ 80,000	$ 85,000
Other office salaries	40,000	35,200
Other office costs	21,000	29,800
Totals	$141,000	$150,000

Required

1. Prepare responsibility accounting performance reports like those in Exhibit 21.20 that list costs controlled by the following:

a. Manager of the refrigerator department.

b. Manager of the dishwasher department.

c. Manager of the Chicago plant.

In each report, include the budgeted and actual costs for the month and show the amount by which each actual cost is over or under the budgeted amount.

Check (a) $23,300 total under budget

(c) Chicago plant controllable costs, $20,800 total under budget

Analysis Component

2. Did the plant manager or the operating department managers better manage costs? Explain.

Problem 21-5B
Allocation of joint costs
C5 

Sarah and Stew Salsa own and operate a tomato grove. After preparing the following income statement, Sarah believes they should have offered the No. 3 tomatoes to the public for free and saved themselves time and money.

SARAH AND STEW SALSA Income Statement For Year Ended December 31, 2005	No. 1	No. 2	No. 3	Combined
Sales (by grade)				
No. 1: 400,000 lbs. @ $1.50/lb	$600,000			
No. 2: 300,000 lbs. @ $1.00/lb		$300,000		
No. 3: 100,000 lbs. @ $0.30/lb			$ 30,000	
Total sales				$930,000
Costs				
Land preparation, seeding, and cultivating @ $0.50/lb	200,000	150,000	50,000	400,000
Harvesting, sorting, and grading @ $0.02/lb	8,000	6,000	2,000	16,000
Delivery costs @ $0.01/lb	4,000	3,000	1,000	8,000
Total costs	212,000	159,000	53,000	424,000
Net income (loss)	$388,000	$141,000	$(23,000)	$506,000

In preparing this statement, Sarah and Stew allocated joint costs among the grades on a physical basis as an equal amount per pound. Also, their delivery cost records show that $7,000 of the $8,000 relates to crating the No. 1 and No. 2 tomatoes and hauling them to the buyer. The remaining $1,000 of delivery costs is for crating the No. 3 tomatoes and hauling them to the cannery.

Required

Check (1) $512 harvesting, sorting and grading costs allocated to No. 3

(2) Net income from No. 1 & No. 2 tomatoes, $327,011 & $163,301

1. Prepare reports showing cost allocations on a sales value basis to the three grades of tomatoes. Separate the delivery costs into the amounts directly identifiable with each grade. Then allocate any shared delivery costs on the basis of the relative sales value of each grade. (Round percents to the nearest one-tenth and dollar amounts to the nearest whole dollar.)
2. Using your answers to part 1, prepare an income statement using the joint costs allocated on a sales value basis.

Analysis Component

3. Do you think delivery costs fit the definition of a joint cost? Explain.

PROBLEM SET C

Problem Set C is available at the book's Website to further reinforce and assess your learning.

BEYOND THE NUMBERS

REPORTING IN ACTION

C4 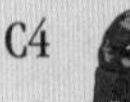

BTN 21-1 A careful review of **Krispy Kreme**'s financial statements in Appendix A offers clues to its growth in revenues. In particular, you should read its note 14.

Required

1. Compute the growth (in percent) for Krispy Kreme's revenues using 2001 as the base for 2002 and 2002 as the base for 2003. Do this for each of the three business segments listed in its note and for total revenue.
2. Which business segment in part 1 is growing the fastest for Krispy Kreme?
3. How can Krispy Kreme's managers use this information?

Roll On

4. Access Krispy Kreme's annual report for a fiscal year ending after February 2, 2003, from its Website [KrispyKreme.com] or the SEC's EDGAR database [www.SEC.gov]. Compute its growth in revenues by business segment and for total revenue for the most recent reporting period(s). Compare results to those from part 1. What growth patterns, if any, do you observe?

COMPARATIVE ANALYSIS

P3 

BTN 21-2 Krispy Kreme and Tastykake compete in several markets. The most common competitive markets for these two companies are likely grocery stores and convenience stores.

Required

1. Design a three-tier responsibility accounting organizational chart assuming that you have available internal information for both companies. Use Exhibit 21.19 as an example. The goal of this assignment is to design a reporting framework for the companies; numbers are not required. Limit your reporting framework to sales activity only.
2. Explain why it is important to have similar performance reports when comparing performance within a company (and across different companies). Be specific in your response.

ETHICS CHALLENGE

P3 

BTN 21-3 Senior Security Co. offers a range of security services for senior citizens. Each type of service is considered within a separate department. Gary Pinkel, the overall manager, is compensated partly on the basis of departmental performance by staying within the quarterly cost budget. He often revises operations to make sure departments stay within budget. Says Pinkel, "I will not go over budget even if it means slightly compromising the level and quality of service. These are minor compromises that don't significantly affect my clients, at least in the short term."

Required

1. Is there an ethical concern in this situation? If so, which parties are affected? Explain.
2. Can Gary Pinkel take action to eliminate or reduce any ethical concerns? Explain.
3. What is Senior Security's ethical responsibility in offering professional services?

COMMUNICATING IN PRACTICE

C4 C5 P3 

BTN 21-4 Home Station is a national home improvement chain with more than 100 stores throughout the country. The manager of each store receives a salary plus a bonus equal to a percent of the store's net income for the reporting period. The following net income calculation is on the Denver store manager's performance report for the recent monthly period:

Sales	$5,000,000
Cost of goods sold	1,600,000
Wages expense	1,000,000
Utilities expense	400,000
Home office expense	150,000
Net income	$1,850,000
Manager's bonus (0.5%)	$ 9,250

In previous periods, the bonus had also been 0.5%, but the performance report had not included any charges for the home office expense, which is now assigned to each store as a percent of its sales.

Required

Assume that you are the national office manager. Write a one-half page memorandum to your store managers explaining why home office expense is in the new performance report.

TAKING IT TO THE NET

A1

mhhe.com/larson

BTN 21-5 This chapter described and used spreadsheets to prepare various managerial reports (see Exhibit 21-12). You can download from Websites various tutorials showing how spreadsheets are used in managerial accounting and other business applications.

Required

1. Check out the Website Lacher.com. Scroll down and open its table of contents. Select "Business Solutions Tutorials" and identify and list three tutorials for review.
2. Describe in a one-half page memorandum to your instructor how the applications described in each tutorial are helpful in business and managerial decision making.

TEAMWORK IN ACTION

C1 C2 

BTN 21-6 Activity-based costing (ABC) is increasingly popular as a useful managerial tool to (1) measure the cost of resources consumed and (2) assign cost to products and services. This managerial tool has been available to accounting and business decision makers for more than 25 years.

Required

Break into teams and identify at least three likely reasons that activity-based costing has gained popularity in recent years. Be prepared to present your answers in a class discussion. (*Hint:* What changes have occurred in products and services over the past 25 years?)

BUSINESS WEEK ACTIVITY

C4

mhhe.com/larson

BTN 21-7 Read the article "The Measure of Your Management" in the April 23, 2003, issue of *Business Week*. (The book's Website provides free access to the article.)

Required

1. At **TriNet**, what activity indicators are closely monitored?
2. How does TriNet use its *set measuring system* to monitor executive performance?
3. What benefits does TriNet feel its set measuring system provides to the company as a whole?

ENTREPRENEURIAL DECISION

C1 C2 C3  

BTN 21-8 Bert and John Jacobs of **Life Is Good** have come a long way from their start-up's initial cash balance of $78. As the business grew, the Jacobs began to understand how effective organizational structure can improve managerial control. Assume that Life Is Good recently created three departments (cutting, sewing, and screening) to produce the T-shirts. The Jacobs are not sure how to determine the costs associated with each department's activity, particularly because several costs are common across the entire business.

Required

1. As a consultant to the Jacobs, how would you suggest they address the cost allocation issue?
2. What type of costing system would you implement to monitor each department's performance? Explain.

HITTING THE ROAD

P3 

BTN 21-9 Visit a local movie theater and check out both its concession area and its showing areas. The manager of a theater must confront questions such as:

- How much return do we earn on concessions?
- What types of movies generate the greatest sales?
- What types of movies generate the greatest net income?

Required

Assume that you are the new accounting manager for a 16-screen movie theater. You are to set up a responsibility accounting reporting framework for the theater.

1. Recommend how to segment the different departments of a movie theater for responsibility reporting.
2. Propose an expense allocation system for heat, rent, insurance, and maintenance costs of the theater.

BTN 21-10 Key segment data of **Grupo Bimbo** (GrupoBimbo.com) follows.

GLOBAL DECISION

	Net Sales		Operating Income	
Segment	2002	2001	2002	2001
Mexico	27,964	26,297	3,207	3,612
United States	10,810	6,238	30	(53)
Latin America	2,599	2,433	(240)	(115)
Totals	41,373	34,968	2,997	3,444

In millions of pesos in accordance with generally accepted accounting standards in Mexico.

Required

1. Compute the growth (in percent) for Grupo Bimbo's total net sales from year 2001 to 2002.
2. Compute the growth (in percent) for each segment's net sales from 2001 to 2002.
3. Which segment's net sales grew the fastest?
4. Which segment was most profitable?
5. How can Grupo Bimbo's managers use this information?

"*I began to dream up sweet/spice concoctions, and that was the start of it all!*"—Katrina Markoff

22 Cost-Volume-Profit Analysis

A Look Back

Chapter 21 focused on cost allocation, activity-based costing, and performance measurement. We identified several managerial reports useful in measuring and analyzing the activities of a company, its departments, and its managers.

A Look at This Chapter

This chapter shows how information on both costs and sales behavior is useful to managers in performing cost-volume-profit analysis. This analysis is an important part of successful management and sound business decisions.

A Look Ahead

Chapter 23 introduces and describes the budgeting process and its importance to management. It also explains the master budget and its usefulness to the planning of future company activities.

CAP

Conceptual

C1 Describe different types of cost behavior in relation to production and sales volume. *(p. 872)*

C2 Identify assumptions in cost-volume-profit analysis and explain their impact. *(p. 880)*

C3 Describe several applications of cost-volume-profit analysis. *(p. 881)*

Analytical

A1 Compare the scatter diagram, high-low, and regression methods of estimating costs. *(p. 877)*

A2 Analyze changes in sales using the degree of operating leverage. *(p. 885)*

Procedural

P1 Determine cost estimates using three different methods. *(p. 875)*

P2 Compute the break-even point for a single product company. *(p. 878)*

P3 Graph costs and sales for a single product company. *(p. 879)*

P4 Compute break-even point for a multiproduct company. *(p. 884)*

Decision Feature

Sweet and Spice and . . . Culinary Adventures

CHICAGO—"My heritage is Macedonian," says Katrina Markoff, "and my love of cooking has been with me from childhood. I began to think why not combine international spices and chocolate?" It is no surprise that Markoff created a chocolate confectionary company, **Vosges Haut Chocolat [VosgesChocolate.com]**, with an "East-meets-West" feel. "I noticed a lack of creativity in chocolate," says Markoff. "They were all gold boxes with chocolate that tasted lousy and raspberry and strawberry filling."

Markoff's chocolates are far from the norm. With ingredients such as wasabi, balsamic vinegar, jasmine flower, curry, and anise, you won't confuse her chocolate with that of Hershey. "When I tell people stories about the ingredients," says Markoff, "they tend to slow down and pay attention to what they're putting in their mouths."

Markoff is also a businessperson. Her use of exotic spices, seasonings, and chocolates is combined with a keen business sense. "I couldn't help it," says Markoff; "my mother is an entrepreneur." That business sense mixed with her culinary skills gives her unique insights on how materials and labor costs relate to sales volume and profits. She not only achieves the break-even level but also markedly exceeds it, with this year's sales projected to exceed $2 million. Markoff also tracks the individual products in her multiproduct offerings. "Best sellers include Naga, Black Pearl, and Absinthe," she notes. Such results foretell even further growth. "I'd like to just keep expanding," Markoff says.

Cost management is crucial to Markoff's past and future success. She personally inspects and purchases each spice, flower, and chocolate used. "Right now, I'm trying out a Jamaican-style truffle, flavored with rum and allspice." Once new products meet her culinary standards, they are appropriately priced to reflect expected costs and sales volume. "Vosges is very expensive and is not something that can be everywhere," says Markoff.

"We want people to experience chocolate through the use of their senses—all six!" exclaims Markoff. One of her newer products is the Aztec collection that combines chocolate with spices of the vanilla bean, ancho chili pepper, Ceylon cinnamon, and cashews. Adds Markoff, both chocolate and spices have a long history as aphrodisiacs. Now we're cooking!

[Sources: *Vosges Haut Chocolat Website,* January 2004; *Entrepreneur,* November 2002; *Chicago Business,* November 2002; *Victoria,* February 2003; *Recipes Today Website,* 2003.]

This chapter describes different types of costs and shows how changes in a company's operating volume affect these costs. The chapter also analyzes a company's costs and sales to understand how different operating strategies affect profit or loss. Managers use this type of analysis to forecast what will happen if changes are made to costs, sales volume, selling prices, or product mix. They then use these forecasts to select the best business strategy for the company.

Cost-Volume-Profit Analysis

Identifying Cost Behavior	Measuring Cost Behavior	Using Break-Even Analysis	Applying Cost-Volume-Profit Analysis
• Fixed costs • Variable costs • Mixed costs • Step-wise costs • Curvilinear costs	• Scatter diagrams • High-low method • Least-squares regression • Comparison of cost estimation methods	• Computing break-even point • Preparing a cost-volume-profit chart • Making assumptions in cost-volume-profit analysis	• Computing income from sales and costs • Computing sales for a target income • Computing margin of safety • Using sensitivity analysis • Computing multiproduct break-even point

Identifying Cost Behavior

Planning a company's future activities and events is a crucial phase in successful management. One of the first steps in planning is to predict the volume of activity, the costs to be incurred, sales to be made, and profit to be received. An important tool to help managers carry out this step is **cost-volume-profit (CVP) analysis,** which helps them predict how changes in costs and sales levels affect income. In its basic form, CVP analysis involves computing the sales level at which a company neither earns an income nor incurs a loss, called the *break-even point.* For this reason, this basic form of cost-volume-profit analysis is often called *break-even analysis.* Managers use variations of CVP analysis to answer questions such as these:

- What sales volume is needed to earn a target income?
- What is the change in income if selling prices decline and sales volume increases?
- How much does income increase if we install a new machine to reduce labor costs?
- What is the income effect if we change the sales mix of our products or services?

Point: *Profit* is another term for *income.*

Decision Insight

No Free Lunch Hardly a week goes by without a company announcing some scheme to give away a free product with the purchase of another. Examples are a free printer with a digital camera purchase or a free monitor with a computer purchase. Can these companies break-even, let alone earn profits? We are reminded of the *no-free-lunch* adage, meaning that these companies must expect profits from the companion or add-on purchase to make up for the free product.

Consequently, cost-volume-profit analysis is useful in a wide range of business decisions.

Conventional cost-volume-profit analysis requires management to classify all costs as either *fixed* or *variable* with respect to production or sales volume. The remainder of this section discusses the concepts of fixed and variable cost behavior as they relate to CVP analysis.

Topic Tackler 22-1

Fixed Costs

C1 Describe different types of cost behavior in relation to production and sales volume.

A *fixed cost* remains unchanged in amount when the volume of activity varies from period to period within a relevant range. For example, $5,000 in monthly rent paid for a factory building remains the same whether the factory operates with a single eight-hour shift or around the clock with three shifts. This means that rent cost is the same each month at any level of output from zero to the plant's full productive capacity. Notice that while *total* fixed cost does not change as the level of production changes the fixed cost *per unit* of output decreases as volume increases. For instance, if 20 units are produced when monthly rent is $5,000, the average rent cost per unit is $250 (computed as $5,000/20 units). When production increases to 100 units per month, the average cost per unit decreases to $50 (computed as $5,000/100 units). The average cost decreases to $10 per unit if production increases to 500 units per month. Common examples of fixed costs include depreciation, property taxes, office salaries, and many service department costs.

Point: Fixed costs do not change when volume changes, but the per unit cost declines as volume increases.

Decision Insight

Cost Driven Fixed costs were a driving force behind the **Daimler-Benz** and **Chrysler** merger. The auto business has huge fixed costs, mainly in plant and equipment. This means that with higher sales volume, fixed costs can be spread over more units. This yields lower fixed costs (and price) per auto.

When production volume and costs are graphed, units of product are usually plotted on the *horizontal axis* and dollars of cost are plotted on the *vertical axis.* Fixed costs then are represented as a horizontal line because they remain constant at all levels of production. To illustrate, the graph in Exhibit 22.1 shows that fixed costs remain at $32,000 at all production levels up to the company's monthly capacity of 2,000 units of output. The *relevant range* for fixed costs in Exhibit 22.1 is 0 to 2,000 units. If the relevant range changes (that is, production capacity extends beyond this range), the amount of fixed costs will likely change.

Example: If the fixed cost line in Exhibit 22.1 is shifted upward, does the total cost line shift up, down, or remain in the same place? *Answer:* It shifts up by the same amount.

Exhibit 22.1

Relations of Fixed and Variable Costs to Volume

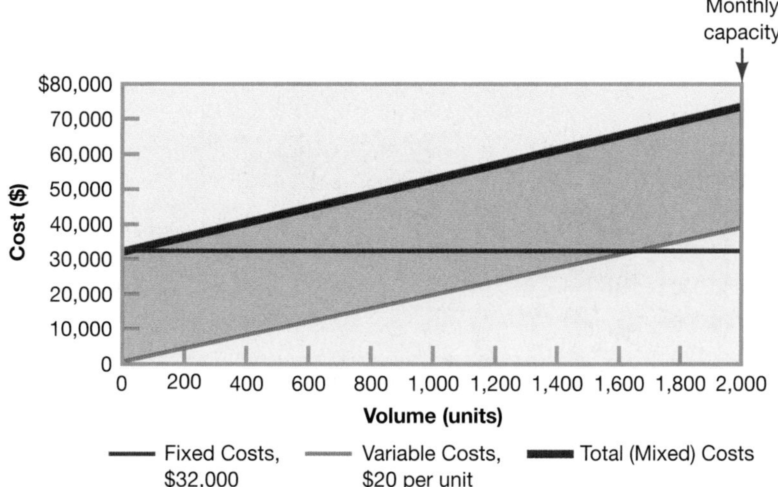

Variable Costs

A *variable cost* changes in proportion to changes in volume of activity. The direct material cost of a product is one example of a variable cost. If one unit of product requires material costing $20, total material costs are $200 when 10 units of product are manufactured, $400 for 20 units, $600 for 30 units, and so on. Notice that variable cost *per unit* remains constant but the *total* amount of variable cost changes with the level of production. In addition to direct material, common variable costs include direct labor (if employees are paid per unit), sales commissions, shipping costs, and some overhead costs.

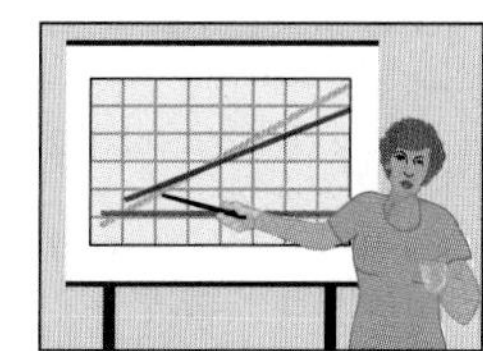

When variable costs are plotted on a graph of cost and volume, they appear as a straight line starting at the zero cost level. This straight line is upward (positive) sloping. The line rises as volume of activity increases. A variable cost line using a $20 per unit cost is graphed in Exhibit 22.1.

Point: Fixed costs are constant in total but vary (decline) per unit as more units are produced. Variable costs vary in total but are fixed per unit.

Mixed Costs

A **mixed cost** includes both fixed and variable cost components. For example, compensation for sales representatives often includes a fixed monthly salary and a variable commission based on sales. The total cost line in Exhibit 22.1 is a mixed cost. Like a fixed cost, it is greater than zero when volume is zero, but unlike a fixed cost, it increases steadily in proportion to increases in volume. The mixed cost line in Exhibit 22.1 starts on the vertical axis at the $32,000 fixed cost point. Thus, at the zero volume level, total cost equals the fixed costs. As the activity level increases, the mixed cost line increases at an amount equal to the variable cost per unit. This line is highest when volume of activity is at 2,000 units (the end point of the relevant range). In CVP analysis, mixed costs are often separated into fixed and variable components. The fixed component is added to other fixed costs, and the variable component is added to other variable costs.

Example: If the level of fixed costs in Exhibit 22.1 changes, does the slope of the total cost line change? *Answer:* No, the slope doesn't change. The total cost line is simply shifted upward or downward.

Step-Wise Costs

A **step-wise cost** reflects a step pattern in costs. Salaries of production supervisors often behave in a step-wise manner in that their salaries are fixed within a *relevant range* of the current production volume. However, if production volume expands significantly (for example, with the addition of another shift), additional supervisors must be hired. This means that the total cost for supervisory salaries goes up by a lump-sum amount. Similarly, if volume takes another significant step up, supervisory salaries will increase by another lump sum. This behavior reflects a step-wise cost, also known as *stair-step costs,* which is graphed in Exhibit 22.2. See how it is flat within ranges (steps). Then, when volume significantly changes, it shifts to another level for that range (step).

Exhibit 22.2

Step-Wise and Curvilinear Costs

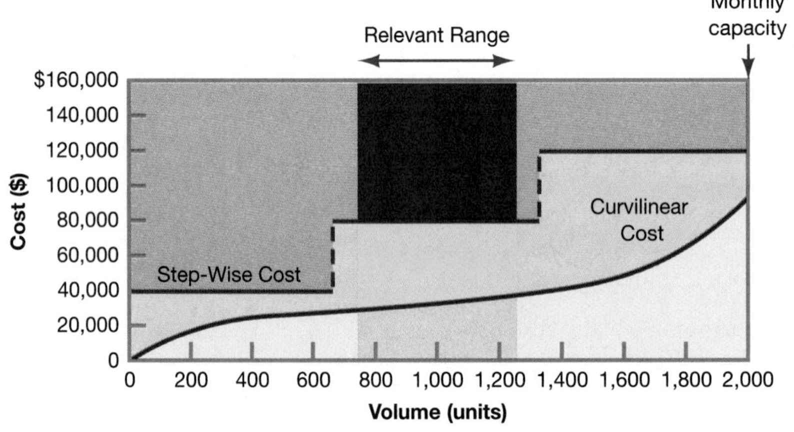

In a conventional CVP analysis, a step-wise cost is usually treated as either a fixed cost or a variable cost. This treatment involves manager judgment and depends on the width of the range and the expected volume. To illustrate, suppose after the production of every 25 snowboards, an operator lubricates the finishing machine. The cost of this lubricant reflects a step-wise pattern. Also, suppose that after the production of every 1,000 units, the snowboard cutting tool is replaced. Again, this is a step-wise cost. Note that the range of 25 snowboards is much narrower than the range of 1,000 snowboards. Some managers might treat the lubricant cost as a variable cost and the cutting tool cost as a fixed cost.

Point: Computer spreadsheets are important and effective tools for CVP analysis and for analyzing alternative "what-if" strategies.

Curvilinear Costs

A variable cost, as explained, is a *linear* cost; that is, it increases at a constant rate as volume of activity increases. A **curvilinear cost,** also called *nonlinear cost,* increases at a nonconstant rate as volume increases. When graphed, curvilinear costs appear as a curved line. Exhibit 22.2 shows a curvilinear cost beginning at zero when production is zero and then increasing at different rates.

An example of a curvilinear cost is total direct labor cost when workers are paid by the hour. At low to medium levels of production, adding more employees allows each of them to specialize by doing certain tasks repeatedly instead of doing several different tasks. This

Point: To apply these concepts, work QS 22-1 and QS 22-2.

often yields additional units of output at lower costs. A point is eventually reached at which adding more employees creates inefficiencies. For instance, a large crew demands more time and effort in communicating and coordinating their efforts. While adding employees in this case increases output, the labor cost per unit increases, and the total labor cost goes up at a steeper slope. This pattern is seen in Exhibit 22.2 where the curvilinear cost curve starts at zero, rises, flattens out, and then increases at a faster rate as output nears the maximum.

Point: Cost-volume-profit analysis helped Rod Canion, Jim Harris, and Bill Murto raise start-up capital of $20 million to launch **Compaq Computer.** They showed that break-even volumes were attainable within the first year.

Quick Check

1. Which of the following statements is typically true? (*a*) Variable cost per unit increases as volume increases, (*b*) fixed cost per unit decreases as volume increases, or (*c*) a curvilinear cost includes both fixed and variable elements.
2. Describe the behavior of a fixed cost.
3. If cost per unit of activity remains constant (fixed), why is it called a variable cost?

Answers—p. 888

Measuring Cost Behavior

P1 Determine cost estimates using three different methods.

Identifying and measuring cost behavior requires careful analysis and judgment. An important part of this process is to identify costs that can be classified as either fixed or variable, which often requires analysis of past cost behavior. Three methods are commonly used to analyze past costs: scatter diagrams, high-low method, and least-squares regression. Each method is discussed in this section using the sales and cost data shown in Exhibit 22.3, which is taken from a start-up company, which uses sales volume (in dollars) as the activity base in estimating cost behavior.

Scatter Diagrams

Scatter diagrams display past cost data in graphical form. In preparing a scatter diagram, sales volume ($) is plotted on the horizontal axis and cost is plotted on the vertical axis. Each individual point on a scatter diagram reflects the cost and sales levels for a prior period. In Exhibit 22.4, the prior 12 months' cost and sales figures are graphed. Each point reflects total costs incurred and sales volume for one of those months. For instance, the point labeled March had sales of $25,000 and costs of $25,000.

Exhibit 22.3

Data for Estimating Cost Behavior

Month	Sales Volume ($)	Total Cost ($)
January	$17,500	$20,500
February	27,500	21,500
March	25,000	25,000
April	35,000	21,500
May	47,500	25,500
June	22,500	18,500
July	30,000	23,500
August	52,500	28,500
September ..	37,500	26,000
October	57,500	26,000
November ..	62,500	31,000
December ...	67,500	29,000

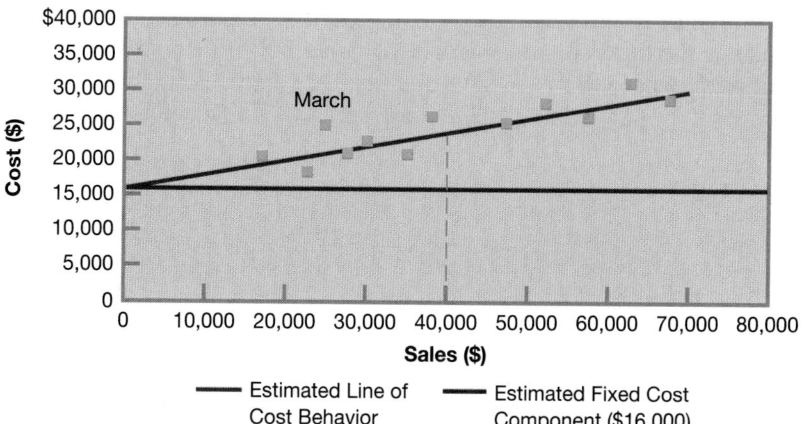

Exhibit 22.4

Scatter Diagram

The **estimated line of cost behavior** is drawn on a scatter diagram to reflect the relation between cost and sales volume. This line best visually "fits" the points in a scatter diagram. Fitting this line demands judgment. The line drawn in Exhibit 22.4 intersects the vertical axis at approximately $16,000, which reflects fixed cost. To compute variable cost per unit, or the slope, we perform three steps. First, we select any two points on the horizontal axis (sales), say $0 and $40,000. Second, we draw a vertical line from each of these points to intersect the estimated line of cost behavior. The point on the vertical axis (cost) corresponding to the $40,000 sales point that intersects the estimated line is roughly $24,000. Similarly, the cost corresponding to zero sales is $16,000 (the fixed cost point). Third, we compute the slope of the line, or variable cost, as the change in cost divided by the change in sales. Exhibit 22.5 shows this computation.

Point: To apply these concepts, work QS 22-3.

Exhibit 22.5

Variable Cost per Unit (Scatter Diagram)

$$\frac{\text{Change in cost}}{\text{Change in sales}} = \frac{\$24{,}000 - \$16{,}000}{\$40{,}000 - \$0} = \frac{\$8{,}000}{\$40{,}000} = \$0.20 \text{ per sales dollar}$$

Variable cost is $0.20 per sales dollar. Thus, the cost equation that management will use to estimate costs for different sales levels is **$16,000 plus $0.20 per sales dollar**.

Example: In Exhibits 22.4 and 22.5, if sales are projected at $30,000, what is predicted cost? *Answer:* Approximately $22,000.

High-Low Method

The **high-low method** is a way to estimate the cost equation by graphically connecting the two cost amounts at the highest and lowest sales volumes. In our case, the lowest sales volume is $17,500, and the highest is $67,500. The costs corresponding to these sales volumes are $20,500 and $29,000, respectively (see data in Exhibit 22.3). The estimated line of cost behavior for the high-low method is then drawn by connecting these two points on the scatter diagram corresponding to the lowest and highest sales volumes as follows:

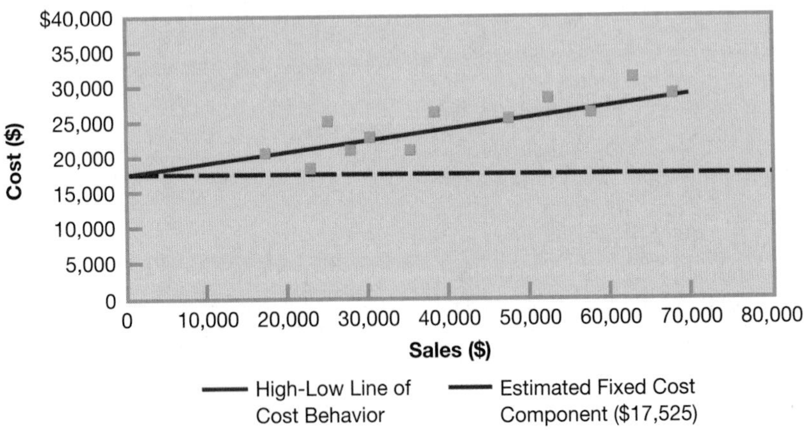

If we extend this line to the vertical axis, it intersects the vertical axis at a cost of about $17,525, which is the fixed cost. The variable cost per unit is determined as the change in cost divided by the change in sales and uses the data from the high and low sales volumes. This results in a slope, or variable cost per sales dollar, of $0.17 as computed in Exhibit 22.6.

Point: Note that the high-low method identifies the high and low points of the volume (activity) base, and the costs linked with those extremes—which may not be the highest and lowest costs.

Exhibit 22.6

Variable Cost per Unit (High-Low Method)

$$\frac{\text{Change in cost}}{\text{Change in sales}} = \frac{\$29{,}000 - \$20{,}500}{\$67{,}500 - \$17{,}500} = \frac{\$8{,}500}{\$50{,}000} = \$0.17 \text{ per sales dollar}$$

Thus, the cost equation used to estimate costs at different sales levels is **$17,525 plus $0.17 per sales dollar**. This cost equation differs slightly from that determined from the scatter diagram method. Note that a deficiency of the high-low method is that it ignores all sales points except the highest and lowest. The result is less precision because the high-low method uses the most extreme points rather than the more usual conditions likely to recur.

Least-Squares Regression

Least-squares regression is a statistical method for identifying cost behavior. For our purposes, we use the cost equation estimated from this method but leave the computational details for more advanced courses. Such computations for least-squares regression are readily done using most spreadsheet programs and calculators.

The regression cost equation for the data presented in Exhibit 22.3 is **$16,947 plus $0.19 per sales dollar**; that is, fixed cost is estimated as $16,947 and variable cost at $0.19 per sales dollar. Both costs are reflected in the following graph:

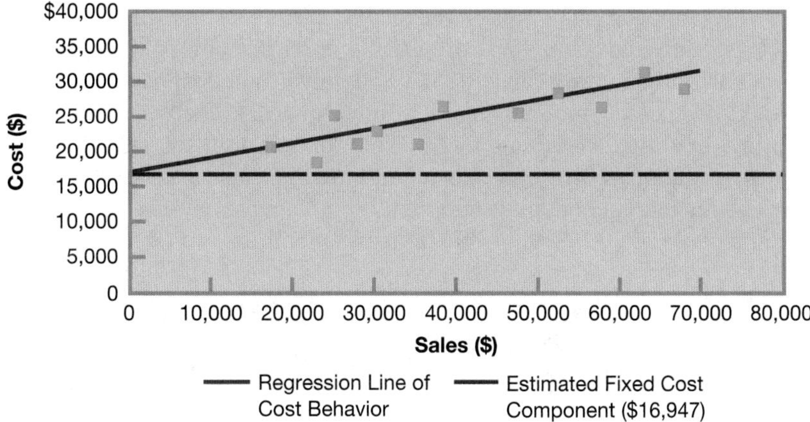

Comparison of Cost Estimation Methods

A1 Compare the scatter diagram, high-low, and regression methods of estimating costs.

The three cost estimation methods result in slightly different estimates of fixed and variable costs as summarized in Exhibit 22.7. Estimates from the scatter diagram are based on a visual fit of the cost line and are subject to interpretation. Estimates from the high-low method use only two sets of values corresponding to the lowest and highest sales volumes. Estimates from least-squares regression use a statistical technique and all available data points.

Exhibit 22.7
Comparison of Cost Estimation Methods

Estimation Method	Fixed Cost	Variable Cost
Scatter diagram	$16,000	$0.20 per sales dollar
High-low method	17,525	0.17 per sales dollar
Least-squares regression	16,947	0.19 per sales dollar

We must remember that all three methods use *past data*. Thus, cost estimates resulting from these methods are only as good as the data used for estimation. Managers must establish that the data are reliable in deriving cost estimates for future costs.

Quick Check

4. Which of the following methods is likely to yield the most precise estimated line of cost behavior? (*a*) high-low, (*b*) least-squares regression, or (*c*) scatter diagram.
5. What is the primary weakness of the high-low method?
6. Using conventional CVP analysis, a mixed cost should be (*a*) disregarded, (*b*) treated as a fixed cost, or (*c*) separated into fixed and variable components.

Answers—p. 888

Using Break-Even Analysis

P2 Compute break-even point for a single product company.

Break-even analysis is a special case of cost-volume-profit analysis. This section describes break-even analysis by computing the break-even point and preparing a CVP (or break-even) chart.

Computing Break-Even Point

Topic Tackler 22-2

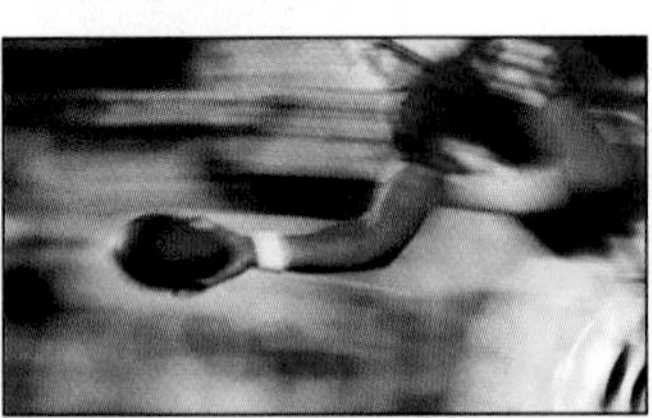

The **break-even point** is the sales level at which a company neither earns a profit nor incurs a loss. The concept of breakeven is applicable to nearly all organizations, activities, and events. One of the most important items of information when launching a project is whether it will break even, that is, whether sales will at least cover total costs. The break-even point can be expressed in either units or dollars of sales.

To illustrate the computation of break-even analysis, let's look at **Rydell,** which sells footballs for $100 per unit and incurs $70 of variable costs per unit sold. Its fixed costs are $24,000 per month with monthly capacity of 1,800 units (footballs). Rydell breaks even for the month when it sells 800 footballs (sales volume of $80,000). We compute this break-even point using the formula in Exhibit 22.8. This formula uses the **contribution margin per unit,** which is the difference between selling price per unit and variable cost per unit. Rydell's contribution margin per unit is $30 ($100 − $70). From this we can compute break-even sales volume as $24,000/$30, or 800 units per month.

Exhibit 22.8

Formula for Computing Break-Even Sales (in units)[1]

$$\textbf{Break-even point in units} = \frac{\textbf{Fixed costs}}{\textbf{Contribution margin per unit}}$$

Point: The break-even point is where total expenses equal total sales and the profit is zero.

At a price of $100 per unit, monthly sales of 800 units yields sales dollars of $80,000 (called *break-even sales dollars*). This $80,000 break-even sales can be computed directly using the formula in Exhibit 22.9. The **contribution margin ratio** is the proportion of a unit's selling price that exceeds its unit variable cost, which is defined as contribution margin per unit divided by unit selling price.

Exhibit 22.9

Formula for Computing Break-Even Sales (in dollars)[2]

$$\textbf{Break-even point in dollars} = \frac{\textbf{Fixed costs}}{\textbf{Contribution margin ratio}}$$

Point: While a company may operate at a level in excess of its break-even point, management may decide to stop operating because it is not earning a reasonable return on investment.

Rydell's contribution margin ratio is 30%, computed as $30/$100. Break-even sales dollars are then computed as $24,000/0.30, or $80,000 of monthly sales. To verify that Rydell's break-even point equals $80,000 (or 800 units), we prepare a simplified income statement in Exhibit 22.10. It shows that the $80,000 revenue from sales of 800 units exactly equals the sum of variable and fixed costs.

---

[1] To obtain this formula, we define S = Sales in units; R = Revenue per unit; F = Fixed costs per period; V = Variable cost per unit; $S \times R$ = Dollar sales; $S \times V$ = Total variable cost; and contribution margin per unit = $R - V$. At breakeven, net income is zero, so therefore,

$$\begin{aligned} \text{Sales} &= \text{Fixed costs} + \text{Variable costs} \\ (S \times R) &= F + (S \times V) \\ (S \times R) - (S \times V) &= F \\ S \times (R - V) &= F \\ S &= F/(R - V) \\ S &= F/\text{Contribution margin per unit} \end{aligned}$$

[2] To obtain this formula, recall that: Contribution margin ratio = $(R - V)/R$. Then, at breakeven,

$$\begin{aligned} S &= F/(R - V) \text{ [from footnote 1]} \\ S \times R &= (F \times R)/(R - V) \\ S \times R &= F \times [R/(R - V)] \\ S \times R &= F/[(R - V)/R] \\ S \times R &= F/\text{Contribution margin ratio} \end{aligned}$$

The statement in Exhibit 22.10 is called a *contribution margin income statement.* It differs in format from a conventional income statement in two ways. First, it separately classifies costs and expenses as variable or fixed. Second, it reports contribution margin (Sales − Variable costs). The contribution margin income statement format is used in this chapter's assignment materials because of its usefulness in CVP analysis.

Point: A *contribution margin income statement* groups variable and fixed expenses separately and reports the contribution margin.

RYDELL COMPANY
Contribution Margin Income Statement (at Breakeven)
For Month Ended January 31, 2005

Sales (800 units @ $100 each)	$80,000
Variable costs (800 units @ $70 each)	56,000
Contribution margin	24,000
Fixed costs	24,000
Net income	$ 0

Exhibit 22.10

Contribution Margin Income Statement for Break-Even Sales

Preparing a Cost-Volume-Profit Chart

P3 Graph costs and sales for a single product company.

Exhibit 22.11 is a graph of Rydell's cost-volume-profit relations. This graph is called a **cost-volume-profit (CVP) chart,** or a *break-even chart* or a *break-even graph.* The horizontal axis is the number of units sold and the vertical axis is dollars of sales and costs. The lines in the chart depict both sales and costs at different output levels.

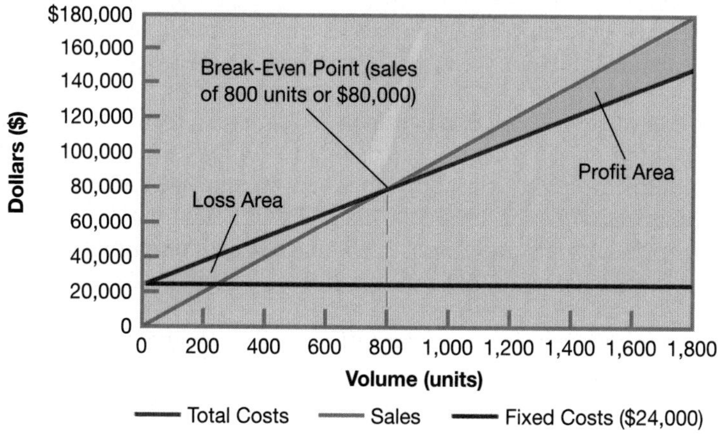

Exhibit 22.11

Cost-Volume-Profit Chart

We follow three steps to prepare a CVP chart, which can also be drawn with computer programs that convert numeric data to graphs:

1. Plot fixed costs on the vertical axis ($24,000 for Rydell). Draw a horizontal line at this level to show that fixed costs remain unchanged regardless of sales volume (drawing this fixed cost line is not essential to the chart).
2. Draw the total (variable plus fixed) costs line for a relevant range of sales levels. This line starts at the fixed costs level on the vertical axis because total costs equal fixed costs at zero sales. The slope of the total cost line equals the variable cost per unit ($70). To draw the line, compute the total costs for any sales level, and connect this point with the vertical axis intercept ($24,000). Do not draw this line beyond the productive capacity for the planning period (1,800 units for Rydell).
3. Draw the sales line. Start at the origin (zero units and zero dollars of sales) and make the slope of this line equal to the selling price per unit ($100). To sketch the line, compute dollar sales for any sales level and connect this point with the origin. Do not extend this line beyond the productive capacity. Total sales will be at the highest level at maximum capacity.

Point: A contribution margin income statement is also referred to as a ***variable costing income statement.*** This differs from the traditional ***absorption costing*** approach where product costs are assigned to units sold and to units in ending inventory. Recall that variable costing expenses all product costs. Thus, income for the two approaches differs depending on the level of finished goods inventory; the lower is inventory, the more similar the two approaches.

The total costs line and the sales line intersect at 800 units in Exhibit 22.11, which is the break-even point, the point where total dollar sales of $80,000 equals the sum of both fixed and variable costs ($80,000).

Example: In Exhibit 22.11, the sales line intersects the total cost line at 800 units. At what point would the two lines intersect if selling price is increased by 20% to $120 per unit? *Answer:* $24,000/($120 − $70) = 480 units

Decision Maker

Operations Manager As a start-up manufacturer, one of your tasks is to identify the behavior of manufacturing costs to develop a production cost budget. You know three methods can be used to identify cost behavior from past data, but past data are not available because this is a start-up. What do you do?

Answer—p. 888

On either side of the break-even point, the vertical distance between the sales line and the total costs line at any specific volume measures the profit or loss expected at that point. At volume levels to the left of the break-even point, this vertical distance is the amount of the expected loss because the total costs line is above the total sales line. At volume levels to the right of the break-even point, the vertical distance represents the expected profit because the total sales line is above the total costs line.

Making Assumptions in Cost-Volume-Profit Analysis

C2 Identify assumptions in cost-volume-profit analysis and explain their impact.

Cost-volume-profit analysis assumes that relations can normally be expressed as simple lines similar to those in Exhibits 22.1 and 22.11. Such assumptions allow users to answer several important questions, but the usefulness of the answers depends on the validity of three assumptions: (1) constant selling price per unit, (2) constant variable costs per unit, and (3) constant total fixed costs. These assumptions are not always realistic, but they do not necessarily limit the usefulness of CVP analysis as a way to better understand costs and sales. This section discusses these assumptions and other issues for CVP analysis.

Point: CVP analysis can be very useful for business decision making even when its assumptions are not strictly met.

Working with Assumptions The behavior of individual costs and sales often is not perfectly consistent with CVP assumptions. If the expected costs and sales behavior differ from the assumptions, the results of CVP analysis can be limited. Still, we can perform useful analyses in spite of limitations with these assumptions for several reasons.

Summing costs can offset individual deviations. Deviations from assumptions with individual costs are often minor when these costs are summed. That is, individual variable cost items may not be perfectly variable, but when we sum these variable costs, their individual deviations can offset each other. This means the assumption of variable cost behavior can be proper for total variable costs. Similarly, an assumption that total fixed costs are constant can be proper even when individual fixed cost items are not exactly constant.

CVP is applied to a relevant range of operations. Sales, variable costs, and fixed costs often are reasonably reflected in straight lines on a graph when the assumptions are applied over a relevant range. The **relevant range of operations** is the normal operating range for a business. Except for unusually difficult or prosperous times, management typically plans for operations within a range of volume neither close to zero nor at maximum capacity. The relevant range excludes extremely high and low operating levels that are unlikely to occur. The validity of assuming that a specific cost is fixed or variable is more acceptable when operations are within the relevant range. As shown in Exhibit 22.2, a curvilinear cost can be treated as variable and linear if the relevant range covers volumes where it has a nearly constant slope. Management must plan according to the normal relevant range of activity. If the normal range of activity changes, some costs might need reclassification.

Point: To apply these concepts, work QS 22-7.

CVP analysis yields estimates. CVP analysis yields approximate answers to questions about costs, volumes, and profits. These answers do not have to be precise because the analysis makes rough estimates about the future. As long as managers understand that CVP analysis gives estimates, it can be a useful tool for starting the planning process. Other qualitative factors also must be considered.

Working with Output Measures CVP analysis usually describes the level of activity in terms of *sales volume,* which can be expressed in terms of either units sold or dollar sales. However, other measures of output exist. For instance, a manufacturer can use the number of units produced as a measure of output. Also, to simplify analysis, we sometimes assume that production level is the same as the sales level. That is, inventory levels are ignored. This often is justified by arguing that CVP analysis provides only approximations.

Example: If selling price declines, what happens to the break-even point? *Answer:* It increases.

Quick Check

7. Fixed cost divided by the contribution margin ratio yields the (*a*) break-even point in dollars, (*b*) contribution margin per unit, or (*c*) break-even point in units.
8. A company sells a product for $90 per unit with variable costs of $54 per unit. What is the contribution margin ratio?
9. Refer to Quick Check (8). If fixed costs for the period are $90,000, what is the break-even point in dollars?
10. What three basic assumptions are used in CVP analysis?

Answers—p. 888

Applying Cost-Volume-Profit Analysis

Managers consider a variety of strategies in planning business operations. Cost-volume-profit analysis is useful in helping managers evaluate the likely effects of these strategies, which is the focus of this section.

Computing Income from Sales and Costs

C3 Describe several applications of cost-volume-profit analysis.

An important question managers often need an answer to is "What is the predicted income from a predicted level of sales?" To answer this, we look at four variables in CVP analysis. These variables and their relations to income (pretax) are shown in Exhibit 22.12. We use these relations to compute expected income from predicted sales and cost levels.

Exhibit 22.12
Income Relations in CVP Analysis

Income (pretax) = Sales − Variable costs − Fixed costs

To illustrate, let's assume that Rydell's management expects to sell 1,500 units this month. What is the amount of income if this sales level is achieved? At this level, sales are $150,000 (1,500 units × $100). Also, Rydell's fixed costs are $24,000 per month, its variable costs per unit are $70, and its total variable costs for 1,500 units are $105,000 (1,500 units × $70). Following Exhibit 22.12, we compute Rydell's expected income in Exhibit 22.13.

Exhibit 22.13
Computing Expected Income from Expected Sales

Income (pretax) = [1,500 units × $100] − [1,500 units × $70] − $24,000
= $21,000

The $21,000 income does not include the effects of income taxes. To find the amount of *after-tax* income from selling 1,500 units, management must apply the proper tax rate to the $21,000. If the tax rate is 25%, income tax is $5,250 and net income is $15,750. Management then assesses whether this net income is an adequate return on assets invested. Management should also consider whether sales and income can be increased by raising or lowering prices. CVP analysis is a good tool for addressing these kinds of "what-if" questions.

Computing Sales for a Target Income

Many companies' annual plans are based on certain income targets (sometimes called *budgets*). Rydell's income target for this year is to increase income by 10% over the prior year. When prior year income is known, Rydell easily computes its target income. CVP analysis helps to determine the sales level needed to achieve the target income. Computing this sales level is important because planning for the year is then based on this level. We use the formula shown in Exhibit 22.14 to compute sales for a target *after-tax* income.

Exhibit 22.14

Computing Sales (dollars) for a Target After-Tax Income[3]

$$\text{Dollar sales at target after-tax income} = \frac{\text{Fixed costs} + \text{Target after-tax income} + \text{Income taxes}}{\text{Contribution margin ratio}} \text{ or } = \frac{\text{Fixed costs} + \text{Target pretax income}}{\text{Contribution margin ratio}}$$

Example: If variable costs decline, what happens to the break-even point? *Answer:* It decreases.

To illustrate, Rydell has monthly fixed costs of \$24,000 and a 30% contribution margin ratio. Assume that it sets a target monthly after-tax income of \$9,000 when the tax rate is 25%. This means the pretax income is targeted at \$12,000 [\$9,000/(1 − 0.25)] with a tax expense of \$3,000. Using the formula in Exhibit 22.14, we find that \$120,000 of sales is needed to produce a \$9,000 after-tax income as shown in Exhibit 22.15.

Exhibit 22.15

Rydell's Dollar Sales for a Target Income

$$\text{Dollar sales at target after-tax income} = \frac{\$24{,}000 + \$9{,}000 + \$3{,}000}{30\%} = \$120{,}000$$

We can alternatively compute *unit sales* instead of dollar sales. To do this, we substitute *contribution margin per unit* for the contribution margin ratio in the denominator. This gives the number of units to sell to reach the target after-tax income. Exhibit 22.16 illustrates this for Rydell. The two computations in Exhibits 22.15 and 22.16 are equivalent because sales of 1,200 units at \$100 per unit equals \$120,000 of sales.

Exhibit 22.16

Computing Sales (units) for a Target After-Tax Income

$$\text{Unit sales at target after-tax income} = \frac{\text{Fixed costs} + \text{Target after-tax income} + \text{Income taxes}}{\text{Contribution margin per unit}} \text{ or } = \frac{\text{Fixed costs} + \text{Target pretax income}}{\text{Contribution margin per unit}}$$

$$= \frac{\$24{,}000 + \$9{,}000 + \$3{,}000}{\$30} = 1{,}200 \text{ units}$$

Point: If a company is not subject to taxes, then substitute *pretax income* for *after-tax income* and delete *income taxes* in both Exhibits 22.14 and 22.16.

Computing the Margin of Safety

All companies wish to sell more than the break-even number of units. The excess of expected sales over the break-even sales level is called a company's **margin of safety,** the amount that sales can drop before the company incurs a loss. It can be expressed in units, dollars, or even as a percent of the predicted level of sales. To illustrate, if Rydell's expected sales are \$100,000, the margin of safety is \$20,000, above break-even sales of \$80,000. As a percent, the margin of safety is 20% of expected sales as shown in Exhibit 22.17.

Decision Ethics

Supervisor You are part of a team debating a new product. Different sales projections have a range of income levels. One member suggests picking numbers yielding favorable income because any estimate is "as good as any other." Another member points to a scatter diagram of 20 months' production on a comparable product and suggests dropping unfavorable data points for cost estimation. Your task is to conduct a cost-volume-profit analysis to reflect these suggestions. What do you do?

Answer—p. 888

[3] To obtain this formula, we define S = Sales in units; R = Revenue per unit; F = Fixed costs per period; V = Variable cost per unit; N = Target net income; T = Income taxes; $S \times R$ = Dollar sales; $S \times V$ = Total variable cost; and the Contribution margin ratio = $(R - V)/R$. The after-tax target net income is then defined as:

$$(S \times R) - F - (S \times V) - T = N$$
$$(S \times R) - (S \times V) = F + N + T$$
$$S \times (R - V) = F + N + T$$
$$S = (F + N + T)/(R - V)$$
$$S \times R = [(F + N + T) \times R]/(R - V)$$
$$S \times R = (F + N + T) \times [R/(R - V)]$$
$$S \times R = (F + N + T)/[(R - V)/R]$$
$$S \times R = (F + N + T)/\text{Contribution margin ratio}$$

$$\text{Margin of safety (in percent)} = \frac{\text{Expected sales} - \text{Break-even sales}}{\text{Expected sales}} = \frac{\$100{,}000 - \$80{,}000}{\$100{,}000} = 20\%$$

Exhibit 22.17

Computing Margin of Safety (in percent)

Management must assess whether the margin of safety is adequate in light of factors such as sales variability, competition, consumer tastes, and economic conditions.

Using Sensitivity Analysis

Knowing the effects of changing some estimates used in CVP analysis is often useful because they are *estimates,* not actual values. For instance, we might want to know what happens if we reduce a product's selling price to increase sales. Or we might want to know what happens to income if we automate a currently manual process. We can use CVP analysis to predict income if we can describe how these changes affect a company's fixed costs, variable costs, selling price, and volume.

To illustrate, assume that Rydell Company is looking into buying a new machine that would increase monthly fixed costs from $24,000 to $30,000 but decrease variable costs from $70 per unit to $60 per unit. The machine is used to produce output whose selling price will remain unchanged at $100. This results in increases in both the unit contribution margin and the contribution margin ratio. The revised contribution margin per unit is $40 ($100 − $60), and the revised contribution margin ratio is 40% of selling price ($40/$100). Using CVP analysis, Rydell's revised break-even point in dollars would be $75,000 as computed in Exhibit 22.18.

Decision Insight

Eco-CVP Ford Escape, Toyota Prius, and Honda Insight are hybrids powered by a small gas engine and an electric motor. Many promise to save owners $500 a year in fuel costs relative to comparables and they generate less carbon dioxide and other greenhouse gases. Are these models economically feasible? Analysts estimate that **Ford** can break even with its Escape when a $3,000 premium is paid over comparable gas-based models.

Example: If fixed costs decline, what happens to the break-even point? *Answer:* It decreases.

$$\text{Revised break-even point in dollars} = \frac{\text{Revised fixed costs}}{\text{Revised contribution margin ratio}} = \frac{\$30{,}000}{40\%} = \$75{,}000$$

Exhibit 22.18

Revising Breakeven When Changes Occur

The revised fixed costs and the revised contribution margin ratio can also be used to address other issues including computation of (1) expected income for a given sales level and (2) the sales level needed to earn a target income. Another use of sensitivity analysis is to generate different sets of revenue and cost estimates that are *optimistic, pessimistic,* and *most likely.* Different CVP analyses based on these estimates provide different scenarios that management can analyze and use in planning business strategy.

Point: Price competition led paging companies to give business to resellers—companies that lease services at a discount and then resell to subscribers. **Paging Network** charged some resellers under $1 per month, less than a third of what is needed to break even. Its CEO now admits the low-price strategy was flawed.

Quick Check

11. A firm has fixed costs of $50,000 and a 25% contribution margin ratio. What dollar sales are necessary to achieve an after-tax net income of $120,000 if the tax rate is 20%? (*a*) $800,000, (*b*) $680,000, or (*c*) $600,000.
12. If the contribution margin ratio decreases from 50% to 25%, what can be said about unit sales needed to achieve the same target income level?
13. What is a company's margin of safety?

Answers—p. 888

Computing Multiproduct Break-Even Point

P4 Compute break-even point for a multiproduct company.

To this point, we have looked only at cases where the company sells a single product or service. This was to keep the basic CVP analysis simple. However, many companies sell multiple products or services, and we can modify the CVP analysis for use in these cases. An important assumption in a multiproduct setting is that the sales mix of different products is known and remains constant during the planning period. **Sales mix** is the ratio (proportion) of the sales volumes for the various products. For instance, if a company normally sells 10,000 footballs, 5,000 softballs, and 4,000 basketballs per month, its sales mix can be expressed as 10:5:4 for footballs, softballs, and basketballs.

To apply multiproduct CVP analysis, we need to estimate the break-even point by using a **composite unit,** which consists of a specific number of units of each product in proportion to their expected sales mix. Multiproduct CVP analysis treats this composite unit as a single product. To illustrate, let's look at **Hair-Today,** a styling salon that offers three cuts: basic, ultra, and budget in the ratio of 4 basic units to 2 ultra units to 1 budget unit (expressed as 4:2:1). Management wants to estimate its break-even point for next year. Unit selling prices for these three cuts are basic, $10; ultra, $16; and budget, $8. Using the 4:2:1 sales mix, the selling price of a composite unit of the three products is computed as follows:

4 units of basic @ $10 per unit	$40
2 units of ultra @ $16 per unit	32
1 unit of budget @ $8 per unit	8
Selling price of a composite unit	$80

Point: Selling prices and variable costs are usually expressed in per unit amounts. Fixed costs are usually expressed in total amounts.

Hair-Today's fixed costs are $96,000 per year, and its variable costs of the three products are basic, $6.50; ultra, $9.00; and budget, $4.00. Variable costs for a composite unit of these products follow:

4 units of basic @ $6.50 per unit	$26
2 units of ultra @ $9.00 per unit	18
1 unit of budget @ $4.00 per unit	4
Variable costs of a composite unit	$48

Point: To apply these concepts, work QS 22-9.

Hair-Today's $32 contribution margin for a composite unit is computed by subtracting the variable costs of a composite unit ($48) from its selling price ($80). We then use the contribution margin to determine Hair-Today's break-even point in composite units in Exhibit 22.19.

Exhibit 22.19
Break-Even Point in Composite Units

$$\textbf{Break-even point in composite units} = \frac{\textbf{Fixed costs}}{\textbf{Contribution margin per composite unit}}$$

$$= \frac{\$96{,}000}{\$32} = 3{,}000 \text{ composite units}$$

Point: The break-even point in dollars for Exhibit 22.19 is: $96,000/($32/$80) = $240,000.

This computation implies that Hair-Today breaks even when it sells 3,000 composite units. To determine how many units of each product it must sell to break even, we multiply the number of units of each product in the composite by 3,000:

Basic:	4 × 3,000	12,000 units
Ultra:	2 × 3,000	6,000 units
Budget:	1 × 3,000	3,000 units

Exhibit 22.20 verifies these results by showing Hair-Today's sales and costs at this break-even point using a contribution margin income statement.

Exhibit 22.20

Multiproduct Break-Even Income Statement

HAIR-TODAY Forecasted Contribution Margin Income Statement (at Breakeven)	Basic	Ultra	Budget	Combined
Sales				
Basic (12,000 @ $10)	$120,000			
Ultra (6,000 @ $16)		$96,000		
Budget (3,000 @ $8)			$24,000	
Total sales				$240,000
Variable costs				
Basic (12,000 @ $6.50)	78,000			
Ultra (6,000 @ $9)		54,000		
Budget (3,000 @ $4)			12,000	
Total variable costs				144,000
Contribution margin	$ 42,000	$42,000	$12,000	96,000
Fixed costs				96,000
Net income				$ 0

A CVP analysis using composite units can be used to answer a variety of planning questions. Once a product mix is set, all answers are based on the assumption that the mix remains constant at all relevant sales levels as other factors in the analysis do. We also can vary the sales mix to see what happens under alternative strategies.

Decision Maker

Entrepreneur A CVP analysis indicates that your start-up, which markets electronic products, will break even with the current sales mix and price levels. You have a target income in mind. What analysis might you perform to assess likelihood for achieving this income?

Answer—p. 888

Quick Check

14. The sales mix of a company's two products, X and Y, is 2:1. Unit variable costs for both products are $2, and unit sales price is $5 for X and $4 for Y. What is the contribution margin per composite unit? (*a*) $5, (*b*) $10, or (*c*) $8.

15. What additional assumption about sales mix must be made in doing a conventional CVP analysis for a company that produces and sells more than one product?

Answers—p. 888

Degree of Operating Leverage

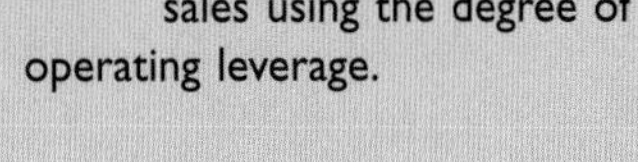

A2 Analyze changes in sales using the degree of operating leverage.

CVP analysis is especially useful when management begins the planning process and wishes to predict outcomes of alternative strategies. These strategies can involve changes in selling prices, fixed costs, variable costs, sales volume, and product mix. Managers are interested in seeing the effects of changes in some or all of these factors.

One goal of all managers is to get maximum benefits from their fixed costs. Managers would like to use 100% of their output capacity so that fixed costs are spread over the largest number of units. This would decrease fixed cost per unit and increase income. The extent, or relative size, of fixed costs in the total cost structure is known as **operating leverage.** Companies having a higher proportion of fixed costs in their total cost structure are said to have higher operating leverage. An example of this is a company that chooses to automate its processes instead of using direct labor, increasing its fixed costs and lowering its variable costs. A useful managerial measure to help assess the effect of changes in the level of sales on income is the **degree of operating leverage (DOL)** defined as:

DOL = Total contribution margin (in dollars)/Pretax income

To illustrate, let's return to Rydell Company. At a sales level of 1,200 units, Rydell's total contribution margin is \$36,000 (1,200 units × \$30 contribution margin per unit). Its pretax income, after subtracting fixed costs of \$24,000, is \$12,000 (\$36,000 − \$24,000). Rydell's degree of operating leverage at this sales level is 3.0, computed as contribution margin divided by pretax income (\$36,000/\$12,000). We then use DOL to measure the effect of changes in the level of sales on pretax income. For instance, suppose Rydell expects sales to increase by 10%. If this increase is within the relevant range of operations, we can expect this 10% increase in sales to result in a 30% increase in pretax income computed as DOL multiplied by the increase in sales (3.0 × 10%). Similar analyses can be done for expected decreases in sales.

Demonstration Problem

Sport Caps Co. manufactures and sells caps for different sporting events. The fixed costs of operating the company are \$150,000 per month, and the variable costs for caps are \$5 per unit. The caps are sold for \$8 per unit. The fixed costs provide a production capacity of up to 100,000 caps per month.

Required

1. Use the formulas in the chapter to compute the following:
   - **a.** Contribution margin per cap.
   - **b.** Break-even point in terms of the number of caps produced and sold.
   - **c.** Amount of net income at 30,000 caps sold per month (ignore taxes).
   - **d.** Amount of net income at 85,000 caps sold per month (ignore taxes).
   - **e.** Number of caps to be produced and sold to provide \$45,000 of after-tax income, assuming an income tax rate of 25%.

2. Draw a CVP chart for the company, showing cap output on the horizontal axis. Identify (*a*) the break-even point and (*b*) the amount of pretax income when the level of cap production is 70,000. (Omit the fixed cost line.)

3. Use the formulas in the chapter to compute the
   - **a.** Contribution margin ratio.
   - **b.** Break-even point in terms of sales dollars.
   - **c.** Amount of net income at \$250,000 of sales per month (ignore taxes).
   - **d.** Amount of net income at \$600,000 of sales per month (ignore taxes).
   - **e.** Dollars of sales needed to provide \$45,000 of after-tax income, assuming an income tax rate of 25%.

Planning the Solution

- Identify the formulas in the chapter for the required items expressed in units and solve them using the data given in the problem.
- Draw a CVP chart that reflects the facts in the problem. The horizontal axis should plot the volume in units up to 100,000, and the vertical axis should plot the total dollars up to \$800,000. Plot the total cost line as upward sloping, starting at the fixed cost level (\$150,000) on the vertical axis and increasing until it reaches \$650,000 at the maximum volume of 100,000 units. Verify that the break-even point (where the two lines cross) equals the amount you computed in part 1.
- Identify the formulas in the chapter for the required items expressed in dollars and solve them using the data given in the problem.

Solution to Demonstration Problem

1. a. Contribution margin per cap = Selling price per unit − Variable cost per unit
= \$8 − \$5 = \$3

b. Break-even point in caps $= \dfrac{\text{Fixed costs}}{\text{Contribution margin per cap}} = \dfrac{\$150{,}000}{\$3} = \underline{\underline{50{,}000 \text{ caps}}}$

c. Net income at 30,000 caps sold = (Units × Contribution margin per unit) − Fixed costs
= (30,000 × \$3) − \$150,000 = \$(60,000) loss

d. Net income at 85,000 caps sold = (Units × Contribution margin per unit) − Fixed costs
= (85,000 × $3) − $150,000 = $105,000 profit

e. Pretax income = $45,000/(1 − 0.25) = $60,000
Income taxes = $60,000 × 25% = $15,000

Units needed for $45,000 income = $\frac{\text{Fixed costs + Target income + Income taxes}}{\text{Contribution margin per cap}}$

$= \frac{\$150{,}000 + \$45{,}000 + \$15{,}000}{\$3} = \underline{\underline{70{,}000 \text{ caps}}}$

2. CVP chart:

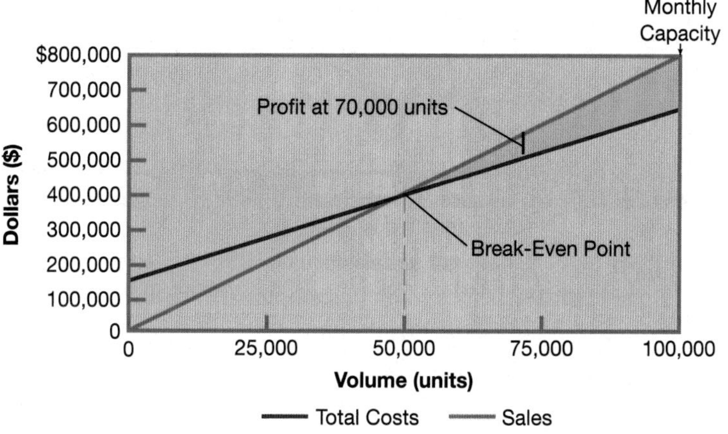

3. a. Contribution margin ratio $= \frac{\text{Contribution margin per unit}}{\text{Selling price per unit}} = \frac{\$3}{\$8} = \underline{\underline{0.375}}$, or $\underline{\underline{37.5\%}}$

b. Break-even point in dollars $= \frac{\text{Fixed costs}}{\text{Contribution margin ratio}} = \frac{\$150{,}000}{37.5\%} = \underline{\underline{\$400{,}000}}$

c. Net income at sales of $250,000 = (Sales × Contribution margin ratio) − Fixed costs
= ($250,000 × 37.5%) − $150,000 = $(56,250) loss

d. Net income at sales of $600,000 = (Sales × Contribution margin ratio) − Fixed costs
= ($600,000 × 37.5%) − $150,000 = $75,000 income

e. Dollars of sales to yield $45,000 income $= \frac{\text{Fixed costs + Target income + Income taxes}}{\text{Contribution margin ratio}}$

$= \frac{\$150{,}000 + \$45{,}000 + \$15{,}000}{37.5\%} = \underline{\underline{\$560{,}000}}$

Summary

C1 **Describe different types of cost behavior in relation to production and sales volume.** Cost behavior is described in terms of how its amount changes in relation to volume of activity changes within a relevant range. Fixed costs remain constant to changes in volume. Total variable costs change in direct proportion to volume changes. Mixed costs display the effects of both fixed and variable components. Step-wise costs remain constant over a small volume range, then change by a lump sum and remain constant over another volume range, and so on. Curvilinear costs change in a nonlinear relation to volume changes.

C2 **Identify assumptions in cost-volume-profit analysis and explain their impact.** Conventional cost-volume-profit analysis is based on assumptions that the product's selling price remains constant and that variable and fixed costs behave in a manner consistent with their variable and fixed classifications.

C3 **Describe several applications of cost-volume-profit analysis.** Cost-volume-profit analysis can be used to predict what can happen under alternative strategies concerning sales volume, selling prices, variable costs, or fixed costs. Applications include "what-if" analysis, computing sales for a target income, and break-even analysis.

A1 **Compare the scatter diagram, high-low, and regression methods of estimating costs.** Cost estimates from a scatter diagram are based on a visual fit of the cost line. Estimates from the high-low method are based only on costs corresponding to the lowest and highest sales. The least-squares regression method is a statistical technique and uses all data points.

A2 **Analyze changes in sales using the degree of operating leverage.** The extent, or relative size, of fixed costs in a company's total cost structure is known as *operating leverage.*

One tool useful in assessing the effect of changes in sales on income is the degree of operating leverage, or DOL. DOL is the ratio of the contribution margin divided by pretax income. This ratio can be used to determine the expected percent change in income given a percent change in sales.

P1 Determine cost estimates using three different methods. Three different methods used to estimate costs are the scatter diagram, the high-low method, and least-squares regression. All three methods use past data to estimate costs.

P2 Compute break-even point for a single product company. A company's break-even point for a period is the sales volume at which total revenues equal total costs. To compute a break-even point in terms of sales units, we divide total fixed costs by the contribution margin per unit. To compute a break-even point in terms of sales dollars, divide total fixed costs by the contribution margin ratio.

P3 Graph costs and sales for a single product company. The costs and sales for a company can be graphically illustrated using a CVP chart. In this chart, the horizontal axis represents the number of units sold and the vertical axis represents dollars of sales or costs. Straight lines are used to depict both costs and sales on the CVP chart.

P4 Compute break-even point for a multiproduct company. CVP analysis can be applied to a multiproduct company by expressing sales volume in terms of composite units. A composite unit consists of a specific number of units of each product in proportion to their expected sales mix. Multiproduct CVP analysis treats this composite unit as a single product.

Guidance Answers to **Decision Maker** and **Decision Ethics**

Operations Manager Without the availability of past data, none of the three methods described in the chapter can be used to measure cost behavior. Instead, the manager must investigate whether data from similar manufacturers can be accessed. This is likely difficult due to the sensitive nature of such data. In the absence of data, the manager should develop a list of the different production inputs and identify input-output relations. This provides guidance to the manager in measuring cost behavior. After several months, actual cost data will be available for analysis.

Supervisor Your dilemma is whether to go along with the suggestions to "manage" the numbers to make the project look like it will achieve sufficient profits. You should not succumb to these suggestions. Many people will likely be affected negatively if you manage the predicted numbers and the project eventually is unprofitable. Moreover, if it does fail, an investigation would likely reveal that data in the proposal were "fixed" to make it look good. Probably the only benefit from managing the numbers is the short-term payoff of pleasing those who proposed the product. One way to deal with this dilemma is to prepare several analyses showing results under different assumptions and then let senior management make the decision.

Entrepreneur You must first compute the level of sales required to achieve the desired net income. Then you must conduct sensitivity analysis by varying the price, sales mix, and cost estimates. Results from the sensitivity analysis provide information you can use to assess the possibility of reaching the target sales level. For instance, you might have to pursue aggressive marketing strategies to push the high-margin products, or you might have to cut prices to increase sales and profits, or another strategy might emerge.

Guidance Answers to **Quick Checks**

1. *b*
2. A fixed cost remains unchanged in total amount regardless of output levels. However, fixed *cost per unit* declines with increased output.
3. Such a cost is considered variable because the *total* cost changes in proportion to volume changes.
4. *b*
5. The high-low method ignores all costs and sales (activity-base) volume data points except the costs corresponding to the highest and lowest (most extreme) sales (activity-base) volume.
6. *c*
7. *a*
8. (\$90 − \$54)/\$90 = 40%
9. \$90,000/40% = \$225,000
10. Three basic CVP assumptions are that (1) selling price per unit is constant, (2) variable costs per unit are constant, and (3) total fixed costs are constant.
11. a; Two steps are required for explanation:
    (1) Pretax income = \$120,000/(1 − 0.20) = \$150,000
    (2) $\frac{\$50{,}000 + \$120{,}000 + (\$150{,}000 \times 20\%)}{25\%} = \$800{,}000$
12. If the contribution margin ratio decreases from 50% to 25%, unit sales would have to double.
13. A company's margin of safety is the excess of the predicted sales level over its break-even sales level.
14. *c*; Selling price of a composite unit:

2 units of X @ \$5 per unit	\$10
1 unit of Y @ \$4 per unit	4
Selling price of a composite unit	\$14

Variable costs of a composite unit:

2 units of X @ \$2 per unit	\$4
1 unit of Y @ \$2 per unit	2
Variable costs of a composite unit	\$6

Therefore, contribution margin per composite unit is \$8.

15. It must be assumed that the sales mix remains unchanged at all sales levels in the relevant range.

Key Terms

Key Terms are available at the book's Website for learning and testing in an online Flashcard Format.

Break-even point (p. 878)
Composite unit (p. 884)
Contribution margin per unit (p. 878)
Contribution margin ratio (p. 878)
Cost-volume-profit (CVP) analysis (p. 872)
Cost-volume-profit (CVP) chart (p. 879)
Curvilinear cost (p. 874)
Degree of operating leverage (DOL) (p. 885)
Estimated line of cost behavior (p. 876)
High-low method (p. 876)
Least-squares regression (p. 877)
Margin of safety (p. 882)
Mixed cost (p. 873)
Operating leverage (p. 885)
Relevant range of operations (p. 880)
Sales mix (p. 884)
Scatter diagram (p. 875)
Step-wise cost (p. 874)

Personal Interactive Quiz

Personal Interactive Quizzes A and B are available at the book's Website to reinforce and assess your learning.

Discussion Questions

1. How is cost-volume-profit analysis useful?
2. What is a variable cost? Identify two variable costs.
3. When output volume increases, do variable costs per unit increase, decrease, or stay the same within the relevant range of activity? Explain.
4. When output volume increases, do fixed costs per unit increase, decrease, or stay the same within the relevant range of activity? Explain.
5. How do step-wise costs and curvilinear costs differ?
6. In performing CVP analysis for a manufacturing company, what simplifying assumption is usually made about the volume of production and the volume of sales?
7. What two arguments tend to justify classifying all costs as either fixed or variable even though individual costs might not behave perfectly consistently with these classifications?
8. How does assuming that operating activity occurs within a relevant range affect cost-volume-profit analysis?
9. List three methods to measure cost behavior.
10. How is a scatter diagram used to identify and measure the behavior of a company's costs?
11. In cost-volume-profit analysis, what is the estimated profit at the break-even point?
12. Assume that a straight line on a CVP chart intersects the vertical axis at the level of fixed costs and has a positive slope that rises with each additional unit of volume by the amount of the variable costs per unit. What does this line represent?
13. Why are fixed costs depicted as a horizontal line on a CVP chart?
14. Each of two similar companies has sales of $20,000 and total costs of $15,000 for a month. Company A's total costs include $10,000 of variable costs and $5,000 of fixed costs. If Company B's total costs include $4,000 of variable costs and $11,000 of fixed costs, which company will enjoy more profit if sales double?
15. _______ of _______ reflects expected sales in excess of the level of break-even sales.
16. **Krispy Kreme** produced donuts for sale during the Olympic games. Identify some of the variable and fixed product costs associated with that production. [*Hint:* Limit costs to product costs.]

17. Should **Tastykake** use single product or multi-product break-even analysis? Explain.

TASTYKAKE

18. **Harley-Davidson** is thinking of expanding sales of its most popular motorcycle model by 65%. Do you expect its variable and fixed costs for this model to stay within the relevant range? Explain.

Harley-Davidson

Red numbers denote Discussion Questions that involve decision-making.

***Homework Manager** repeats all numerical Quick Studies on the book's Website with new numbers.*

QUICK STUDY

QS 22-1
Cost behavior identification
C1

Determine whether each of the following is best described as a fixed, variable, or mixed cost with respect to product units:

1. Factory supervisor's salary.
2. Taxes on factory building.
3. Rubber used to manufacture athletic shoes.
4. Maintenance of factory machinery.
5. Packaging expense.
6. Wages of an assembly-line worker paid on the basis of acceptable units produced.

QS 22-2
Cost behavior identification
C1 

Listed here are four series of separate costs measured at various volume levels. Examine each series and identify whether it is best described as a fixed, variable, step-wise, or curvilinear cost. (It may help to graph the cost series.)

Volume (Units)	Series 1	Series 2	Series 3	Series 4
0	$ 0	$900	$ 400	$200
100	400	900	400	210
200	800	900	400	240
300	1,200	900	800	290
400	1,600	900	800	380
500	2,000	900	1,200	500
600	2,400	900	1,200	640

QS 22-3
Cost behavior estimation
C1 P1

This scatter diagram reflects past maintenance hours and their corresponding maintenance costs.

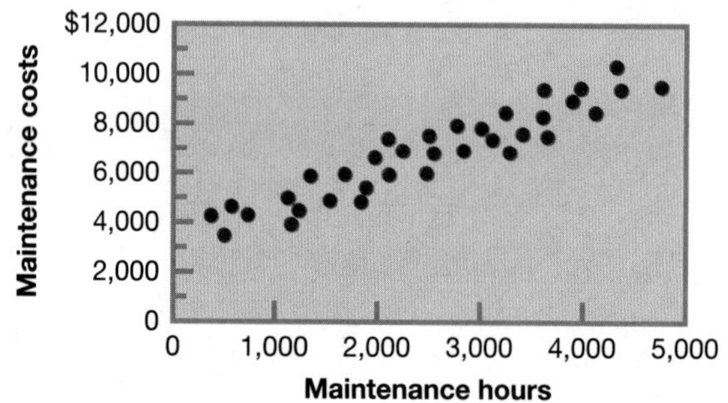

1. Draw an estimated line of cost behavior.
2. Estimate the fixed and variable components of maintenance costs.

QS 22-4
Contribution margin per unit and break-even units P2

MCU Phone Company sells its cordless phone for $100 per unit. Fixed costs total $180,000, and variable costs are $40 per unit. Determine (1) contribution margin per unit and (2) break-even point in units.

QS 22-5
Contribution margin ratio and break-even dollars P2

Refer to QS 22-4. Determine (1) contribution margin ratio and (2) break-even point in dollars.

QS 22-6
CVP analysis and target income
C3 P2

Refer to QS 22-4. Assume that MCU Phone Co. is subject to a 30% income tax rate. Compute the units of product that must be sold to earn after-tax income of $140,000.

QS 22-7
CVP assumptions
C2

Which one of the following is an assumption that underlies cost-volume-profit analysis?

1. Selling price per unit must change in proportion to the number of units sold.
2. All costs have approximately the same relevant range.
3. For costs classified as variable, the costs per unit of output must change constantly.
4. For costs classified as fixed, the costs per unit of output must remain constant.

QS 22-8
Operating leverage analysis A2

A high proportion of Company A's total costs are variable with respect to units sold; a high proportion of Company B's total costs are fixed with respect to units sold. Which company is likely to have a higher degree of operating leverage (DOL)? Explain.

QS 22-9
Multiproduct break-even
P4

Hot Pager Company manufactures and sells two products, green beepers and gold beepers, in the ratio of 5:3. Fixed costs are $85,000, and the contribution margin per composite unit is $170. What number of both green and gold beepers is sold at the break-even point?

Homework Manager repeats all numerical Exercises on the book's Website with new numbers.

EXERCISES

Exercise 22-1
Measurement of cost behavior using a scatter diagram
P1

A company reports the following information about its sales and its cost of sales. Each unit of its product sells for $500. Use these data to prepare a scatter diagram. Draw an estimated line of cost behavior and determine whether the cost appears to be variable, fixed, or mixed.

Period	Sales	Cost of Sales
1	$15,000	$10,100
2	11,500	7,500
3	10,500	7,000
4	7,500	5,500
5	9,000	6,000
6	12,500	9,500

Exercise 22-2
Cost behavior in graphs
C1 

Following are five graphs representing various cost behaviors. (1) Identify whether the cost behavior in each graph is mixed, step-wise, fixed, variable, or curvilinear. (2) Identify the graph (by number) that best illustrates each cost behavior: (a) Factory policy requires one supervisor for every 30 factory workers; (b) real estate taxes on factory; (c) electricity charge that includes the standard monthly charge plus a charge for each kilowatt hour; (d) commissions to salespersons; and (e) costs of hourly paid workers that provide substantial gains in efficiency when a few workers are added but gradually smaller gains in efficiency when more workers are added.

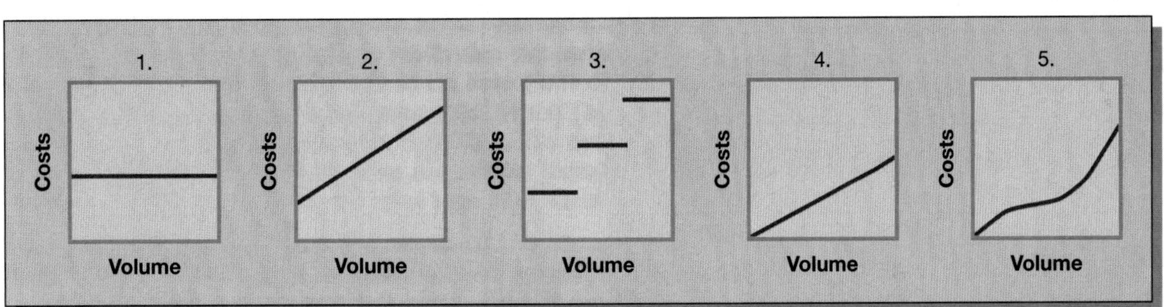

Exercise 22-3
Cost behavior defined
C1

The left column lists several categories of costs. The right column presents short definitions of those costs. In the blank space beside each of the numbers in the right column, write the letter of the cost best described by the definition.

A. Total cost
B. Mixed cost
C. Variable cost
D. Curvilinear cost
E. Step-wise cost
F. Fixed cost

______ **1.** This cost remains constant over all volume levels within the productive capacity for the planning period.

______ **2.** This cost increases in direct proportion to increases in volume; its amount is constant for each unit produced.

______ **3.** This cost is the combined amount of all the other costs.

______ **4.** This cost remains constant over a limited range of volume; when it reaches the end of its limited range, it changes by a lump sum and remains at that level until it exceeds another limited range.

______ **5.** This cost has a component that remains the same over all volume levels and another component that increases in direct proportion to increases in volume.

______ **6.** This cost increases when volume increases, but the increase is not constant for each unit produced.

Exercise 22-4
Cost behavior identification

C1  

Following are five series of costs *A* through *E* measured at various volume levels. Examine each series and identify which is fixed, variable, mixed, step-wise, or curvilinear.

	Volume (Units)	Series A	Series B	Series C	Series D	Series E
1	0	$ 0	$2,500	$ 0	$2,000	$4,000
2	200	3,600	3,100	6,000	2,000	4,000
3	400	7,200	3,700	6,600	4,000	4,000
4	600	10,800	4,300	7,200	4,000	4,000
5	800	14,400	4,900	8,200	6,000	4,000
6	1,000	18,000	5,500	9,600	6,000	4,000
7	1,200	21,600	6,100	13,500	8,000	4,000

Exercise 22-5
Scatter diagram and measurement of cost behavior

P1 

Use the following information about sales and costs to prepare a scatter diagram. Draw a cost line that reflects the behavior displayed by this cost. Determine whether the cost is variable, step-wise, fixed, mixed, or curvilinear.

Period	Sales	Costs	Period	Sales	Costs
1	$760	$590	9	$580	$390
2	800	560	10	320	240
3	200	230	11	240	230
4	400	400	12	720	550
5	480	390	13	280	260
6	620	550	14	440	410
7	680	590	15	380	260
8	540	430			

Exercise 22-6
Predicting sales and variable costs using contribution margin

C3

Orlando Company management predicts that it will incur fixed costs of $250,000 and earn pretax income of $350,000 in the next period. Its expected contribution margin ratio is 60%. Use this information to compute the amounts of (1) total dollar sales and (2) total variable costs.

Exercise 22-7
Contribution margin, break-even, and CVP chart P2 P3

Apollo Company manufactures a single product that sells for $168 per unit and whose total variable costs are $126 per unit. The company's annual fixed costs are $630,000. (1) Use this information to compute the company's (a) contribution margin, (b) contribution margin ratio, (c) break-even point in units, and (d) break-even point in dollars of sales. (2) Draw a CVP chart for the company.

Exercise 22-8
Income reporting and break-even analysis C3

Refer to Exercise 22-7. (1) Prepare a contribution margin income statement for Apollo Company showing sales, variable costs, and fixed costs at the break-even point. (2) If Apollo's fixed costs increase by $135,000, what amount of sales (in dollars) is needed to break even?

Exercise 22-9
Computing sales to achieve target income

C3

Apollo Company management (in Exercise 22-7) targets an annual after-tax income of $840,000. The company is subject to a 20% income tax rate. Assume that fixed costs remain at $630,000. Compute the (1) unit sales to earn the target after-tax net income and (2) dollar sales to earn the target after-tax net income.

Exercise 22-10
Forecasted income statement

C3

Apollo Company sales manager (in Exercise 22-7) predicts that annual sales of the company's product will soon reach 40,000 units and its price will increase to $200 per unit. According to the production manager, the variable costs are expected to increase to $140 per unit but fixed costs will remain at $630,000. The income tax rate is 20%. What amounts of pretax and after-tax income can the company expect to earn from these predicted changes? (*Hint:* Prepare a forecasted contribution margin income statement as in Exhibit 22.20.)

Check Forecast income, $1,416,000

Exercise 22-11
Predicting unit and dollar sales
C3

Greenspan Company management predicts $500,000 of variable costs, $800,000 of fixed costs, and a pretax income of $100,000 in the next period. Management also predicts that the contribution margin per unit will be $60. Use this information to compute the (1) total expected dollar sales for next period and (2) number of units expected to be sold next period.

Exercise 22-12
Computation of variable and fixed costs; CVP chart P3

Cinquante Company expects to sell 100,000 units of its product next year, which would generate total sales of $12 million. Management predicts that pretax net income for next year will be $3,000,000 and that the contribution margin per unit will be $40. (1) Use this information to compute next year's total expected (a) variable costs and (b) fixed costs. (2) Prepare a CVP chart from this information.

Exercise 22-13
Operating leverage computed and applied
A2 

Company A is a manufacturer with current sales of $1,000,000 and a 65% contribution margin. Its fixed costs equal $500,000. Company B is a consulting firm with current service revenues of $1,000,000 and a 25% contribution margin. Its fixed costs equal $100,000. Compute the degree of operating leverage (DOL) for each company. Identify which company benefits more from a 20% increase in sales and explain why.

Exercise 22-14
CVP analysis using composite units P4

Home Builders sells windows and doors in the ratio of 8:2 (windows:doors). The selling price of each window is $100 and of each door is $250. The variable cost of a window is $62.50 and of a door is $175. Fixed costs are $450,000. Use this information to determine the (1) selling price per composite unit, (2) variable costs per composite unit, (3) break-even point in composite units, and (4) number of units of each product that will be sold at the break-even point.

Check (3) 1,000 units

PROBLEM SET A

Problem 22-1A
CVP analysis and charting
P2 P3 
mhhe.com/larson

Edge Equipment Co. manufactures and markets a number of rope products. Management is considering the future of Product XT, a special rope for hang gliding, that has not been as profitable as planned. Since Product XT is manufactured and marketed independently of the other products, its total costs can be precisely measured. Next year's plans call for a $150 selling price per 100 yards of XT rope. Its fixed costs for the year are expected to be $200,000, up to a maximum capacity of 550,000 yards. Forecasted variable costs are $100 per 100 yards of XT rope.

Required

1. Estimate Product XT's break-even point in terms of (a) sales units and (b) sales dollars.
2. Prepare a CVP chart for Product XT like that in Exhibit 22.11. Use 550,000 yards as the maximum number of sales units on the horizontal axis of the graph, and $900,000 as the maximum dollar amount on the vertical axis.
3. Prepare a contribution margin income statement showing sales, variable costs, and fixed costs for Product XT at the break-even point.

Check (1) Break-even sales, 4,000 units or $600,000

Problem 22-2A
Scatter diagram and cost behavior estimation
P1

Lazra Co.'s monthly sales and cost data for its operating activities of the past year follow. Management wants to use these data to predict future fixed and variable costs.

Period	Sales	Total Cost
1	$160,000	$ 80,000
2	80,000	50,000
3	140,000	110,000
4	100,000	50,000
5	150,000	115,000
6	100,000	60,000
7	170,000	110,000
8	140,000	80,000
9	10,000	40,000
10	80,000	70,000
11	50,000	50,000
12	55,000	40,000

Required

1. Prepare a scatter diagram for these data with sales volume (in $) plotted on the horizontal axis and total cost plotted on the vertical axis.

2. Estimate the line of cost behavior by a visual inspection and draw it on the scatter diagram. (Assume a linear relation, which means that you should draw a straight cost line on the graph.)

Check (3) Variable costs, $0.50 per sales dollar; Fixed costs, $22,000

3. Using the estimated line of cost behavior from part 2 and the assumption that the future will be like the past, predict the monthly fixed costs. Also predict variable costs *per sales dollar*.

4. Use the estimated line of cost behavior and results from part 3 to predict future total costs when sales volume is (a) $100,000 and (b) $150,000.

Problem 22-3A
Break-even analysis; income targeting and forecasting
C3 P2

Jetson Co. sold 20,000 units of its only product and incurred a $50,000 loss (ignoring taxes) for the current year as shown below. During a planning session for year 2006's activities, the production manager notes that variable costs can be reduced 50% by installing a machine that automates several operations. To obtain these savings, the company must increase its annual fixed costs by $150,000. The maximum output capacity of the company is 40,000 units per year.

JETSON COMPANY
Contribution Margin Income Statement
For Year Ended December 31, 2005

Sales	$750,000
Variable costs	600,000
Contribution margin	150,000
Fixed costs	200,000
Net loss	$ (50,000)

Required

1. Compute the break-even point in dollar sales for year 2005.

2. Compute the predicted break-even point in dollar sales for year 2006 assuming the machine is installed and there is no change in unit sales price.

Check (3) Net income, $100,000

3. Prepare a forecasted contribution margin income statement for 2006 that shows the expected results with the machine installed. Assume that the unit sales price and the number of units sold will not change and no income taxes.

(4) Required sales, $916,667 or 24,445 units

4. Compute the sales level required in both dollars and units to earn $140,000 of after-tax income in 2006 with the machine installed and no change in unit sales price. Assume that the income tax rate is 30%. (*Hint:* Use procedures in Exhibits 22.14 and 22.16.)

(5) Net income, $140,000 (rounded)

5. Prepare a forecasted contribution margin income statement that shows the results at the sales level computed in part 4. Assume an income tax rate of 30%.

Problem 22-4A
Break-even analysis, different cost structures, and income calculations
C3  

Letter Co. produces and sells two products, T and O. It manufactures these products in separate factories and markets them through different channels. They have no shared costs. This year, Letter sold 50,000 units of each product. Sales and costs for each product follow.

	Product T	Product O
Sales	$800,000	$800,000
Variable costs	560,000	100,000
Contribution margin	240,000	700,000
Fixed costs	100,000	560,000
Income before taxes	140,000	140,000
Income taxes (32% rate)	44,800	44,800
Net income	$ 95,200	$ 95,200

Required

1. Compute the break-even point in dollar sales for each product.
2. Assume that the company expects sales of each product to decline to 33,000 units next year with no change in unit sales price. Prepare forecasted financial results for next year following the format of the contribution margin income statement as shown above with columns for each of the two products (assume a 32% tax rate). Also, assume that any loss before taxes yields a 32% tax savings.
3. Assume that the company expects sales of each product to increase to 64,000 units next year with no change in unit sales price. Prepare forecasted financial results for next year following the format of the contribution margin income statement as shown above with columns for each of the two products (assume a 32% tax rate).

Check (2) After-tax income: T, $39,712; O, $(66,640)

(3) After-tax income: T, $140,896; O, $228,480

Analysis Component

4. If sales greatly decrease, which product would experience a greater loss? Explain.
5. Describe some factors that might have created the different cost structures for these two products.

Problem 22-5A
Analysis of price, cost, and volume changes for contribution margin and net income

C3 P2

mhhe.com/larson

This year Cairo Company sold 35,000 units of its only product for $16 per unit. Manufacturing and selling the product required $120,000 of fixed manufacturing costs and $180,000 of fixed selling and administrative costs. Its per unit variable costs were as follows:

Material	$4.00
Direct labor (paid on the basis of completed units)	3.00
Variable overhead costs	0.40
Variable selling and administrative costs	0.20

Next year the company will use new material that is easier to work. The new material will reduce material costs by 60% and direct labor costs by 40% and will not affect product quality or marketability. Management is considering an increase in the unit sales price to reduce the number of units sold because the factory's output is nearing its annual output capacity of 40,000 units. Two plans are being considered. Under plan 1, the company will keep the price at the current level and sell the same volume as last year. This plan will increase income because of the reduced costs from using the new material. Under plan 2, the company will increase price by 25%. This plan will decrease unit sales volume by 10%. Under both plans 1 and 2, the total fixed costs and the variable costs per unit for overhead and for selling and administrative costs will remain the same.

Required

1. Compute the break-even point in dollar sales for both (a) plan 1 and (b) plan 2.
2. Prepare a forecasted contribution margin income statement with two columns showing the expected results of plan 1 and plan 2. The statements should report sales, total variable costs, contribution margin, total fixed costs, income before taxes, income taxes (30% rate), and net income.

Check (1) Breakeven: Plan 1, $400,000; Plan 2, $375,000

(2) Net income: Plan 1, $84,000; Plan 2, $142,800

Problem 22-6A
Break-even analysis with composite units

P4 C3

National Co. manufactures and sells three products: red, white, and blue. Their unit sales prices are red, $55; white, $85; and blue, $110. The per unit variable costs to manufacture and sell these products are red, $40; white, $60; and blue, $80. Their sales mix is reflected in a ratio of 5:4:2 (red:white:blue). Annual fixed costs shared by all three products are $150,000. One type of raw material has been used to manufacture all three products. The company has developed a new material of equal quality for less cost. The new material would reduce variable costs per unit as follows: red, by $10; white, by $20; and blue, by $10. However, the new material requires new equipment, which will increase annual fixed costs by $20,000. (Round answers to whole composite unit.)

Required

1. If it continues to use the old material, determine the company's break-even point in both sales units and sales dollars of each individual product.
2. If it uses the new material, determine the company's new break-even point in both sales units and sales dollars of each individual product.

Check (1) Old plan breakeven, 639 composite units

(2) New plan breakeven, 442 composite units

Analysis Component

3. What insight does this analysis offer management for long-term planning?

PROBLEM SET B

Problem 22-1B
CVP analysis and charting

P2 P3

Jammin Co. manufactures and markets a number of products. Management is considering the future of one product, electronic keyboards, that has not been as profitable as planned. Since this product is manufactured and marketed independently of the other products, its total costs can be precisely measured. Next year's plans call for a $225 selling price per unit. The fixed costs for the year are expected to be $30,000, up to a maximum capacity of 700 units. Forecasted variable costs are $150 per unit.

Required

Check (1) Break-even sales, 400 units or $90,000

1. Estimate the keyboards' break-even point in terms of (a) sales units and (b) sales dollars.
2. Prepare a CVP chart for keyboards like that in Exhibit 22.11. Use 700 keyboards as the maximum number of sales units on the horizontal axis of the graph, and $180,000 as the maximum dollar amount on the vertical axis.
3. Prepare a contribution margin income statement showing sales, variable costs, and fixed costs for keyboards at the break-even point.

Problem 22-2B
Scatter diagram and cost behavior estimation

P1

Koto Co.'s monthly sales and costs data for its operating activities of the past year follow. Management wants to use these data to predict future fixed and variable costs.

Period	Sales	Total Costs
1	$390	$194
2	250	174
3	210	146
4	310	178
5	190	162
6	430	220
7	290	186
8	370	210
9	270	170
10	170	130
11	350	190
12	230	158

Required

1. Prepare a scatter diagram for these data with sales volume (in $) plotted on the horizontal axis and total costs plotted on the vertical axis.
2. Estimate the line of cost behavior by a visual inspection and draw it on the scatter diagram. (Assume a linear relation, which means that you should draw a straight cost line on the graph.)

Check (3) Variable costs, $0.30 per sales dollar; Fixed costs, $90

3. Use the estimated line of cost behavior from part 2 and the assumption that the future will be like the past, to predict the monthly fixed costs. Also predict variable costs *per sales dollar*.
4. Use the estimated line of cost behavior and results from part 3 to predict future total costs when sales volume is (a) $150 and (b) $250.

Problem 22-3B
Break-even analysis; income targeting and forecasting

C3 P2

Caruso Co. sold 40,000 units of its only product and incurred a $100,000 loss (ignoring taxes) for the current year as shown below.

CARUSO COMPANY Contribution Margin Income Statement For Year Ended December 31, 2005	
Sales	$1,500,000
Variable costs	1,200,000
Contribution margin	300,000
Fixed costs	400,000
Net loss	$ (100,000)

During a planning session for year 2006's activities, the production manager notes that variable costs can be reduced 50% by installing a machine that automates several operations. To obtain these savings, the company must increase its annual fixed costs by $300,000. The maximum output capacity of the company is 80,000 units per year.

Required

1. Compute the break-even point in dollar sales for year 2005.
2. Compute the predicted break-even point in dollar sales for year 2006 assuming the machine is installed and no change in unit sales price. (Round the change in variable costs to a whole number.)
3. Prepare a forecasted contribution margin income statement for 2006 that shows the expected results with the machine installed. Assume that the unit sales price and the number of units sold will not change and no income taxes.
4. Compute the sales level required in both dollars and units to earn $280,000 of after-tax income in 2006 with the machine installed and no change in unit sales price. Assume that the income tax rate is 30%. (*Hint:* Use procedures in Exhibits 22.14 and 22.16.)
5. Prepare a forecasted contribution margin income statement that shows the results at the sales level computed in part 4. Assume an income tax rate of 30%.

Check (3) Net income, $200,000

(4) Required sales, $1,833,333 or 48,889 units

(5) Net income, $280,000

Problem 22-4B
Break-even analysis, different cost structures, and income calculations
C3

Dominico Co. produces and sells two products, BB and TT. It manufactures these products in separate factories and markets them through different channels. They have no shared costs. This year, Dominico Co. sold 120,000 units of each product. Sales and costs for each product follow.

	Product BB	Product TT
Sales	$3,000,000	$3,000,000
Variable costs	1,800,000	600,000
Contribution margin	1,200,000	2,400,000
Fixed costs	600,000	1,800,000
Income before taxes	600,000	600,000
Income taxes (35% rate)	210,000	210,000
Net income	$ 390,000	$ 390,000

Required

1. Compute the break-even point in dollar sales for each product.
2. Assume that the company expects sales of each product to decline to 104,000 units next year with no change in unit sales price. Prepare forecasted financial results for next year following the format of the contribution margin income statement as shown above with columns for each of the two products (assume a 35% tax rate).
3. Assume that the company expects sales of each product to increase to 190,000 units next year with no change in unit sales price. Prepare forecasted financial results for next year following the format of the contribution margin income statement as shown above with columns for each of the two products (assume a 35% tax rate).

Check (2) After-tax income: BB, $286,000; TT, $182,000

(3) After-tax income: BB, $845,000; TT, $1,300,000

Analysis Component

4. If sales greatly increase, which product would experience a greater increase in profit? Explain.
5. Describe some factors that might have created the different cost structures for these two products.

Problem 22-5B
Analysis of price, cost, and volume changes for contribution margin and net income
C3 P2

This year Jostens Company earned a disappointing 4.2% after-tax return on sales from marketing 100,000 units of its only product. The company buys its product in bulk and repackages it for resale at the price of $25 per unit. Jostens incurred the following costs this year:

Total variable unit costs	$1,000,000
Total variable packaging costs	$ 100,000
Fixed costs	$1,250,000
Income tax rate	30%

The marketing manager claims that next year's results will be the same as this year's unless some changes are made. The manager predicts the company can increase the number of units sold by 80% if it reduces the selling price by 20% and upgrades the packaging. This change would increase variable packaging costs by 25%. Increased sales would allow the company to take advantage of a 20% quantity purchase discount on the cost of the bulk product. Neither the packaging change nor the volume discount would affect fixed costs, which provide an annual output capacity of 200,000 units.

Required

Check (1) Breakeven for new strategy, $2,325,581

(2) Net income: Existing strategy, $105,000; New strategy, $479,500

1. Compute the break-even point in dollar sales under the (a) existing business strategy and (b) new strategy that alters both unit sales price and variable costs.
2. Prepare a forecasted contribution margin income statement with two columns showing the expected results of (a) the existing strategy and (b) changing to the new strategy. The statements should report sales, total variable costs (unit and packaging), contribution margin, fixed costs, income before taxes, income taxes, and net income. Also determine the after-tax return on sales for these two strategies.

Problem 22-6B
Break-even analysis with composite units
P4 C3 

Texon Co. manufactures and sells three products: product 1, product 2, and product 3. Their unit sales prices are product 1, $40; product 2, $30; and product 3, $14. The per unit variable costs to manufacture and sell these products are product 1, $30; product 2, $20; and product 3, $8. Their sales mix is reflected in a ratio of 6:3:5. Annual fixed costs shared by all three products are $200,000. One type of raw material has been used to manufacture products 1 and 2. The company has developed a new material of equal quality for less cost. The new material would reduce variable costs per unit as follows: product 1 by $10, and product 2, by $5. However, the new material requires new equipment, which will increase annual fixed costs by $50,000.

Required

Check (1) Old plan breakeven, 1,667 composite units

(2) New plan breakeven, 1,282 composite units

1. If it continues to use the old material, determine the company's break-even point in both sales units and sales dollars of each individual product.
2. If it uses the new material, determine the company's new break-even point in both sales units and sales dollars of each individual product.

Analysis Component

3. What insight does this analysis offer management for long-term planning?

PROBLEM SET C

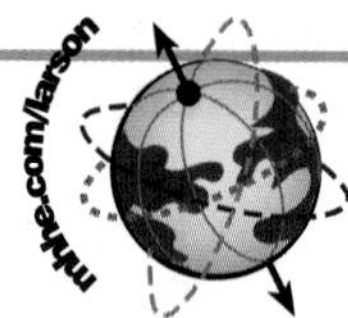

Problem Set C is available at the book's Website to further reinforce and assess your learning.

SERIAL PROBLEM

Success Systems

(This serial problem began in Chapter 1 and continues through most of the book. If previous chapter segments were not completed, the serial problem can begin at this point. It is helpful, but not necessary, for you to use the Working Papers that accompany the book.)

Success Systems sells upscale modular desk units and office chairs in the ratio of 2:1 (desk unit: chair). The selling price is $2,500 per desk unit and $1,000 per chair. The variable cost is $1,500 per desk unit and $500 per chair. Fixed costs are $60,000.

Required

1. Compute the selling price per composite unit.
2. Compute the variable costs per composite unit.
3. Compute the break-even point in composite units.
4. Compute the number of units of each product that would be sold at the break-even point.

Check (3) 24 units

BEYOND THE NUMBERS

REPORTING IN ACTION

C1 

BTN 22-1 Krispy Kreme has expanded its product line from the original hot glazed yeast-raised donut to 19 varieties of donuts. Assume that you are to head Krispy Kreme's new product, special blended "America's Cup of Coffee," to be sold through its chain of stores. You have permission to use all existing resources, such as its purchasing department, legal department, and buildings and equipment, to get the coffee to market.

Required

1. What costs, variable or fixed, are your most immediate concern? Explain.
2. Identify the coffee's direct costs and where they are primarily reflected in the financial reports.
3. Assume that the contribution margin per package of coffee is 60% and you anticipate coffee sales of $5 million this year. Explain why gross margin on the income statement will not fully reflect your success. (*Hint:* Consider the difference between gross margin and contribution margin.)

COMPARATIVE ANALYSIS

P2 C3 A2 

BTN 22-2 Both Krispy Kreme and Tastykake make baked goods, but one company is usually more profitable than the other with its products. We know that each company makes decisions about purchasing plant assets and that the fixed costs along with the variable costs of manufacturing and selling determine the break-even point and profitability of these companies.

Required

1. Using the following data, compute the total cost per each dozen (or unit) of baked goods for Krispy Kreme and Tastykake. (Assume that sales volume equals production volume.)

	Krispy Kreme	Tastykake
Estimated sales units and price	10,000 units @ $6/unit	10,000 units @ $6/unit
Direct material per unit	$1.00/unit	$1.00/unit
Direct labor per unit	$3.00/unit	$3.40/unit
Factory rent per month	$ 3,000	$ 1,000
Factory equipment (depreciation)	$ 5,000	$ 6,000

2. Compare Krispy Kreme and Tastykake using the results from your analysis of part 1 to explain why one company is more profitable than the other.
3. If sales decline to very low levels, which company will yield the higher net income (computations are unnecessary)?

ETHICS CHALLENGE

C1 

BTN 22-3 Labor costs of an auto repair mechanic are seldom based on actual hours worked. Instead, the amount paid a mechanic is based on an industry average of time estimated to complete a repair job. The repair shop bills the customer for the industry average amount of time at the repair center's billable cost per hour. This means a customer can pay, for example, $120 for two hours of work on a car when the actual time worked was only one hour. Many experienced mechanics can complete repair jobs well under the industry average. The average data are compiled by engineering studies and surveys conducted in the auto repair business. Assume that you are asked to complete such a survey for a repair center. The survey calls for objective input, and many questions require detailed cost data and analysis. The mechanics and owners know you have the survey and encourage you to complete it in a way that increases the average billable cost per hour for repair work.

Required

Write a one-page memorandum to the mechanics and owners that describes the direct labor analysis you will undertake in completing this survey.

COMMUNICATING IN PRACTICE

C2

BTN 22-4 Several important assumptions underlie CVP analysis. Assumptions often help simplify and focus our analysis of sales and costs. A common application of CVP analysis is as a tool to forecast sales, costs, and income.

Required

Assume that you are actively searching for a job. Prepare a one-half page report identifying (1) three assumptions relating to your expected revenue (salary) and (2) three assumptions relating to your expected costs for the first year of your new job. Be prepared to discuss your assumptions in class.

TAKING IT TO THE NET

C1 C3

mhhe.com/larson

BTN 22-5 Access and review the entrepreneurial information at **Business Owner's Toolkit** [Toolkit.cch.com]. Access and review its *Initial Cash Requirements Worksheet* for a business start-up [Toolkit.cch.com/tools/CashNe_m.asp] or similar worksheets related to controls of cash and costs.

Required

Write a one-half page report that describes the information and resources available at the Business Owner's Toolkit to help the owner of a start-up business to control and monitor its costs.

TEAMWORK IN ACTION

C2 

BTN 22-6 A local movie theater owner explains to you that ticket sales on weekends and evenings are strong, but attendance during the weekdays, Monday through Thursday, is poor. The owner proposes to offer a contract to the local grade school to show educational materials at the theater for a set charge per student during school hours. The owner asks your help to prepare a CVP analysis listing the cost and sales projections for the proposal. The owner must propose to the school's administration a charge per child. At a minimum, the charge per child needs to be sufficient for the theater to break even.

Required

Your team is to prepare two separate lists of questions that enable you to complete a reliable CVP analysis of this situation. One list is to be answered by the school's administration, the other by the owner of the movie theater.

BUSINESS WEEK ACTIVITY

C3

BTN 22-7 Read the article "Cooking Up a Global Empire" in the May 19, 2003, issue of ***Business Week***. (The book's Website provides free access to the article.)

Required

1. What does the term *haute cuisine* mean?
2. What percent of haute cuisine restaurants fail?
3. Why is it so difficult for haute cuisine restaurants to break even or earn a profit?
4. What formula has **Chef Ducasse** found to make haute cuisine profitable?

ENTREPRENEURIAL DECISION

C1  

BTN 22-8 Katrina Markoff of **Vosges Haut Chocolat** has always packaged her chocolates with only one exotic flavor per box. She now is considering offering a new variety box to allow her customers to sample each flavor. Markoff is concerned that offering the variety box in addition to the individually packaged flavors could change costs.

Required

1. What information do you recommend that Markoff collect to help address her concern?
2. What managerial accounting tools might be especially useful to her in this situation?

HITTING THE ROAD

P4 

BTN 22-9 Multiproduct break-even analysis is often viewed differently when actually applied in practice. You are to visit a local fast-food restaurant and count the number of items on the menu. To apply multiproduct break-even analysis to the restaurant, similar menu items must often be fit into groups. A reasonable approach is to classify menu items into approximately five groups, for example, drink group. We then estimate average selling price and average variable cost to compute average contribution margin. (*Hint:* The contribution margin ratio on drinks is about 90%.)

Required

1. Prepare a one-year multiproduct break-even analysis for the restaurant you visit. Begin by establishing groups. Next, estimate each group's volume and contribution margin. These estimates are necessary to compute each group's contribution margin. Assume that annual fixed costs in total are $500,000 per year. (*Hint:* You must develop your own estimates on volume and contribution margin for each group to obtain the break-even point and sales.)
2. Prepare a one-page report on the results of your analysis. Comment on the volume of sales necessary to break even at a fast-food restaurant.

GLOBAL DECISION

C3 

BTN 22-10 Access and review **Grupo Bimbo**'s Website (GrupoBimbo.com) to answer the following questions:

1. Do you believe that Grupo Bimbo managers use single product CVP analysis or multiproduct break-even point analysis? Explain.
2. Identify at least seven products as part of Grupo Bimbo's sales mix.
3. On January 21, 2003, Grupo Bimbo added variety to its existing sales mix by entering into an exclusive distributor agreement with what world-famous company?

"The way you grow a large company is by growing it a little bit each year, the next thing you know, it's a huge amount"—John Chuang (far left)

Master Budgets and Planning

A Look Back

Chapter 22 looked at cost behavior and described its relevance for managers in performing cost-volume-profit analysis. That chapter also explained and illustrated the application of cost-volume-profit analysis.

A Look at This Chapter

This chapter explains the importance of budgeting and describes the master budget and its preparation. It also discusses the value of the master budget to the planning of future business activities.

A Look Ahead

Chapter 24 focuses on flexible budgets, standard costs, and variance reporting. It explains the usefulness of these procedures and reports for business decisions.

CAP

Conceptual

C1 Describe the importance and benefits of budgeting. *(p. 904)*

C2 Explain the process of budget administration. *(p. 906)*

C3 Describe a master budget and the process of preparing it. *(p. 908)*

Analytical

A1 Analyze expense planning using activity-based budgeting. *(p. 917)*

Procedural

P1 Prepare each component of a master budget and link each to the budgeting process. *(p. 910)*

P2 Link both operating and capital expenditures budgets to budgeted financial statements. *(p. 914)*

Decision Feature

Big Budgets and Bigger Plans

BOSTON—John Chuang, Mia Wenjen, and Steve Kapner started with a PC in their college dorm room. "We formed a business doing typesetting work," says Chuang. "We soon became known . . . as people who knew how to do desktop publishing." The phone rang off the hook. In spite of what Wenjen says was a college term of "serious grade point average tankage and serious parent freakage," the three pushed forward. Their start-up survived and is now called **Aquent [Aquent.com],** which helps its clients with staffing, consulting, outsourcing, and technology.

The three friends always had big plans and even bigger dreams. "We had a sign on our dorm room that read 'Worldwide Headquarters,'" says Chuang. With those plans and dreams came budgets. However, in the early stages, Wenjen admits that their budgeting process and planning were not ideal. We would hire someone, says Wenjen, and then say "you're going to be getting a budget . . . one big number of money to spend. Spend it how you see fit, but be smart about it." She would then add, "Spend on things that grow the business."

The friends now more seriously attend to master budgets and the budgeting process. They say budgets help formalize business expectations and objectives. Budgets also help direct employees and put everyone on the same page. "Every manager, for example, has the ability to make monetary decisions without going through various levels of approvals," says Chuang. To make such a system successful requires trust, an understanding of the process, and knowledge of how decisions impact the budgeted financial statements.

The three friends continue to expand their business. Master budgets and planning are an important part of their expansion decisions. "With each new unit we create," says Chuang, "we examine the marketplace first to see if the market has a need for our service and can sustain it." This includes analysis of plans and budgets of both costs and revenues. This approach, says Chuang, has been successful; the company "performs very well." Still, the three want more. "We have a long way to go," adds Chuang. "We're just getting started!"

[Sources: *Aquent Website,* January 2004; *Asian Business News,* Summer 2002; *Staffing Today Website,* February 2002; *Asian American Supersite—Goldsea 100,* 2003.]

After management applies cost-volume-profit analysis or other techniques in devising a strategy for future periods, it then seeks to turn this strategy into action plans. These action plans include financial details that are compiled in a master budget. The budgeting process serves several purposes, including motivating employees and effectively communicating with them. The budget process also helps coordinate a company's activities toward common goals and is useful in evaluating actual results and management performance. In this chapter, we explain how to prepare a master budget and use it as a formal plan of a company's future activities. The ability to prepare this type of formal plan is of enormous help in starting and operating a company. Such planning gives managers a glimpse into the future, and it can help translate ideas into actions.

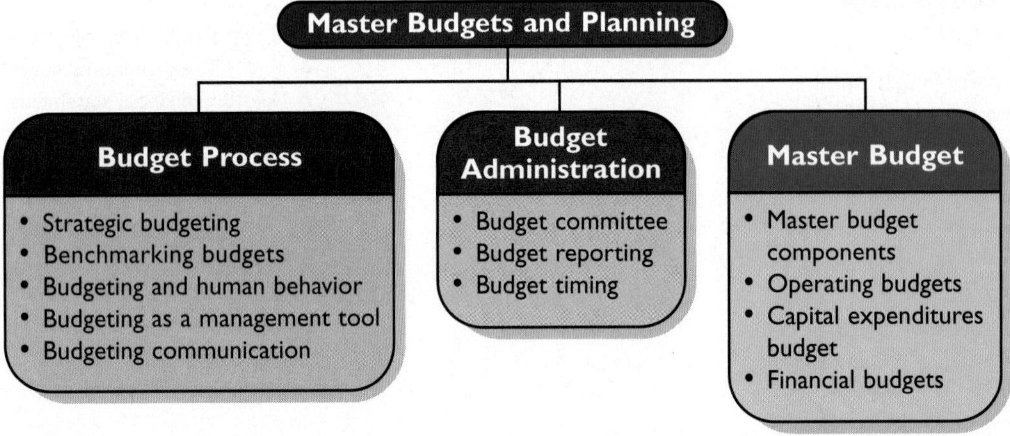

Budget Process

Strategic Budgeting

Most companies prepare long-term strategic plans spanning 5 to 10 years. They then fine-tune them in preparing medium-term and short-term plans. Strategic plans usually set a company's long-term direction. They provide a road map for the future about potential opportunities such as new products, markets, and investments. The strategic plan can be inexact, given its long-term focus. Medium- and short-term plans are more operational and translate strategic plans into actions. These action plans are fairly concrete and consist of defined objectives and goals.

C1 Describe the importance and benefits of budgeting.

Short-term plans are usually called *budgets* and typically cover a one-year period. A **budget** is a formal statement of a company's future plans. It is usually expressed in monetary terms because the economic or financial aspects of the business are the primary factors driving management's decisions. All managers should be involved in **budgeting,** the process of planning future business actions and expressing them as formal plans. Managers who plan carefully and formalize plans in a budgeting process increase the likelihood of both personal and company success. (Although most firms prepare annual budgets, it is not unusual for organizations to prepare three-year and five-year budgets that are revised at least annually.)

The relevant focus of a budgetary analysis is the future. Management must focus on future transactions and events and the opportunities available. A focus on the future is important because the pressures of daily operating problems often divert management's attention and take precedence over planning. A good budgeting system counteracts this tendency by formalizing the planning process and demanding relevant input. Budgeting makes planning an explicit management responsibility.

Benchmarking Budgets

The control function requires management to evaluate (benchmark) business operations against some norm. Evaluation involves comparing actual results against one of two usual alternatives: (1) past performance or (2) expected performance.

An evaluation assists management in identifying problems and taking corrective actions if necessary. Evaluation using expected, or budgeted, performance is potentially superior to using past performance to decide whether actual results trigger a need for corrective actions. This is so because past performance is often an inferior standard for evaluation because it fails to consider several changes that can affect current and future activities. Changes in economic conditions, shifts in competitive advantages within the industry, new product developments, increased or decreased advertising, and other factors reduce the usefulness of comparisons with past results. In hi-tech industries, for instance, increasing competition, technological advances, and other innovations often reduce the usefulness of performance comparisons across years.

Budgeted performance is computed after careful analysis and research that attempts to anticipate and adjust for changes in important company, industry, and economic factors. Therefore, budgets usually provide management an effective control and monitoring system.

Point: Managers can evaluate performance by preparing reports that compare actual results to budgeted plans.

Budgeting and Human Behavior

Budgeting provides standards for evaluating performance and can affect the attitudes of employees evaluated by them. It can be used to create a positive effect on employees' attitudes, but it can also create negative effects if not properly applied. Budgeted levels of performance, for instance, must be realistic to avoid discouraging employees. Personnel who will be evaluated should be consulted and involved in preparing the budget to increase their commitment to meeting it. Performance evaluations must allow the affected employees to explain the reasons for apparent performance deficiencies.

The budgeting process has three important guidelines: (1) Employees affected by a budget should be consulted when it is prepared (*participatory budgeting*), (2) goals reflected in a budget should be attainable, and (3) evaluations should be made carefully with opportunities to explain any failures. Budgeting can be a positive motivating force when these guidelines are followed. Budgeted performance levels can provide goals for employees to attain or even exceed as they carry out their responsibilities. This is especially important in organizations that consider the annual budget a "sacred" document.

Point: The practice of involving employees in the budgeting process is known as *participatory budgeting.*

Decision Insight

Budgets Exposed When companies go public and trade their securities on an organized exchange, management usually develops specific future plans and budgets. For this purpose, companies often develop detailed six- to twelve-month budgets and less-detailed budgets spanning 2 to 5 years.

Budgeting as a Management Tool

An important management objective in large companies is to ensure that activities of all departments contribute to meeting the company's overall goals. This requires coordination. Budgeting provides a way to achieve this coordination.

We describe later in this chapter that a company's budget, or operating plan, is based on its objectives. This operating plan starts with the sales budget, which drives all other budgets including production, materials, labor, and overhead. The budgeting process coordinates the activities of these various departments to meet the company's overall goals.

Budgeting Communication

Managers of small companies can adequately explain business plans directly to employees through conversations and other informal communications. However, conversations can create uncertainty and confusion if not supported by clear documentation of the plans. A written budget is preferred and can inform employees in all types of organizations about management's plans. The budget can also communicate management's specific action plans for the employees in the budget period.

Decision Ethics

Budget Staffer You learn that your company's earnings for the current period will be far below the budgeted amount reported in the press. You also know that one of your superiors, who is also aware of the earnings shortfall, has accepted a management position with a competitor. This superior is selling her shares of the company. Does this situation present ethical concerns for you?

Answer—p. 925

Budget Administration

Budget Committee

C2 Explain the process of budget administration.

The task of preparing a budget should not be the sole responsibility of any one department. Similarly, the budget should not be simply handed down as top management's final word. Instead, budget figures and budget estimates developed through a *bottom-up* process usually are more useful. This includes, for instance, involving the sales department in preparing sales estimates. Likewise, the production department should have initial responsibility for preparing its own expense budget. Without active employee involvement in preparing budget figures, there is a risk these employees will feel that the numbers fail to reflect their special problems and needs.

Most budgets should be developed by a bottom-up process, but the budgeting system requires central guidance. This guidance is supplied by a budget committee of department heads and other executives responsible for seeing that budgeted amounts are realistic and coordinated. If a department submits initial budget figures not reflecting efficient performance, the budget committee should return them with explanatory comments on how to improve them. Then the originating department must either adjust its proposals or explain why they are acceptable. Communication between the originating department and the budget committee should continue as needed to ensure that both parties accept the budget as reasonable, attainable, and desirable.

Point: In a large company, developing a budget through a bottom-up process can involve hundreds of employees and take several weeks to finalize.

The concept of continuous improvement applies to budgeting as well as production. **BP** streamlined its monthly budget report from a one-inch-thick stack of monthly control reports to a tidy, two-page flash report on monthly earnings and key production statistics. The key to this efficiency gain was the integration of new budgeting and cost allocation processes with its strategic planning process. BP's controller explained the new role of the finance department with respect to the budgetary control process as follows: "there's less of an attitude that finance's job is to control. People really have come to see that our job is to help attain business objectives."

Budget Reporting

The budget period usually coincides with the accounting period. Most companies prepare at least an annual budget, which reflects the objectives for the next year. To provide specific guidance, the annual budget usually is separated into quarterly or monthly budgets. These short-term budgets allow management to periodically evaluate performance and take needed corrective action.

Managers can compare actual results to budgeted amounts in a report such as that shown in Exhibit 23.1. This report shows actual amounts, budgeted amounts, and their differences. A difference is called a *variance*. Management examines variances to identify areas for improvement and corrective action.

Budget Timing

The time period required for the annual budgeting process can vary considerably. For example, budgeting for 2006 can begin as early as January 2005 or as late as December 2005. Large, complex organizations usually require a longer time to prepare their budgets than do smaller organizations. This is so because considerable effort is required to coordinate the different units (departments) within large organizations.

Many companies apply **continuous budgeting** by preparing **rolling budgets.** As each monthly or quarterly budget period goes by, these companies revise their entire set of budgets for the months or quarters remaining and add new monthly or quarterly budgets to replace the ones that have lapsed. At any point in time, monthly or quarterly budgets are

ECCENTRIC MUSIC Income Statement with Variations from Budget For Month Ended April 30, 2005	Actual	Budget	Variance
Net sales	$60,500	$57,150	$+3,350
Cost of goods sold	41,350	39,100	+2,250
Gross profit	19,150	18,050	+1,100
Operating expenses			
Selling expenses			
Sales salaries	6,250	6,000	+250
Advertising	900	800	+100
Store supplies	550	500	+50
Depreciation—Store equipment	1,600	1,600	
Total selling expenses	9,300	8,900	+400
General and administrative expenses			
Office salaries	2,000	2,000	
Office supplies used	165	150	+15
Rent	1,100	1,100	
Insurance	200	200	
Depreciation—Office equipment	100	100	
Total general and administrative expenses	3,565	3,550	+15
Total operating expenses	12,865	12,450	+415
Net income	$ 6,285	$ 5,600	$ +685

Exhibit 23.1

Comparing Actual Performance with Budgeted Performance

Example: Assume that you must explain variances to top management. Which variances in Exhibit 23.1 would you research and why? *Answer:* Sales and cost of goods sold—due to their large variances.

available for the next 12 months or four quarters. Exhibit 23.2 shows rolling budgets prepared at the end of five consecutive periods. The first set (at top) is prepared in December 2004 and covers the four calendar quarters of 2005. In March 2005, the company prepares another rolling budget for the next four quarters through March 2006. This same process is repeated every three months. As a result, management is continuously planning ahead.

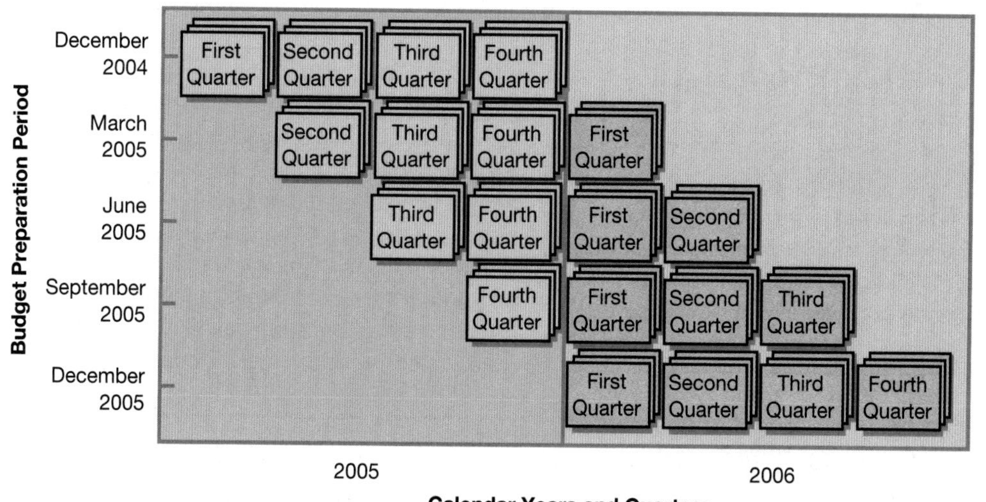

Exhibit 23.2

Rolling Budgets

Exhibit 23.2 reflects an annual budget composed of four quarters prepared four times per year using the most recent information available. For example, the budget for the fourth quarter of 2005 is prepared in December 2004 and revised in March, June, and September of 2005. When continuous budgeting is not used, the fourth-quarter budget is nine months old and perhaps out of date when applied.

Decision Insight

Budget Calendar Many companies use long-range operating budgets. For large companies, three groups usually determine or influence the budgets: creditors, directors, and management. All three are interested in the companies' future cash flows and earnings. The annual budget process often begins six months or more before the budget is due to the board of directors. A typical budget calendar, shown here, provides insight into the budget process during this period.

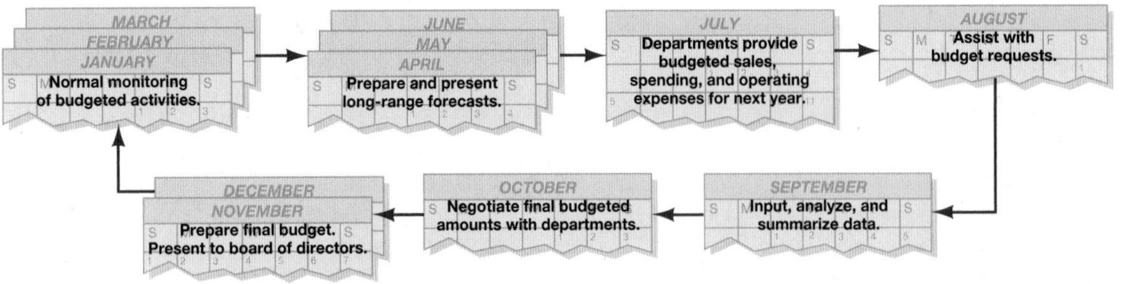

Quick Check

1. What are the major benefits of budgeting?
2. What is the main responsibility of the budget committee?
3. What is the usual time period covered by a budget?
4. What are rolling budgets?

Answers—p. 925

Master Budget

C3 Describe a master budget and the process of preparing it.

A **master budget** is a formal, comprehensive plan for a company's future. It contains several individual budgets that are linked with each other to form a coordinated plan.

Master Budget Components

The master budget typically includes individual budgets for sales, purchases, production, various expenses, capital expenditures, and cash. Managers often express the expected financial results of these planned activities with both a budgeted income statement for the budget period and a budgeted balance sheet for the end of the budget period. The usual number and types of budgets included in a master budget depend on the company's size and complexity. A master budget should include, at a minimum, the budgets listed in Exhibit 23.3. In addition to these individual budgets, managers often include supporting calculations and additional tables with the master budget.

Decision Insight

Budgeting Targets Budgeting is a crucial part of any acquisitions or takeover analyses. Analysis begins by projecting annual sales volume and prices. It then estimates cost of sales, expenses, and income for the next several years. By computing the present value of this projected income stream, buyers determine an offer price.

Exhibit 23.3

Basic Components of a Master Budget

- **Operating budgets**
  - *Sales budget*
  - For merchandisers add: *Merchandise purchases budget* (units to be purchased)
  - For manufacturers add: *Production budget* (units to be produced)
    Manufacturing budget (manufacturing costs)
  - *Selling expense budget*
  - *General and administrative expense budget*
- **Capital expenditures budget** (expenditures for plant assets)
- **Financial budgets**
  - *Cash budget* (cash receipts and disbursements)
  - *Budgeted income statement*
  - *Budgeted balance sheet*

Some budgets require the input of other budgets. For example, the merchandise purchases budget cannot be prepared until the sales budget has been prepared because the number of units to be purchased depends on how many units are expected to be sold. As a result, we often must sequentially prepare budgets within the master budget.

Topic Tackler 23-1

A typical sequence for a quarterly budget consists of the five steps in Exhibit 23.4. Any stage in this budgeting process might reveal undesirable outcomes, so changes often must be made to prior budgets by repeating the previous steps. For instance, an early version of the cash budget could show an insufficient amount of cash unless cash outlays are reduced. This could yield a reduction in planned equipment purchases. A preliminary budgeted balance sheet could also reveal too much debt from an ambitious capital expenditures budget. Findings such as these often result in revised plans and budgets.

Exhibit 23.4

Master Budget Sequence

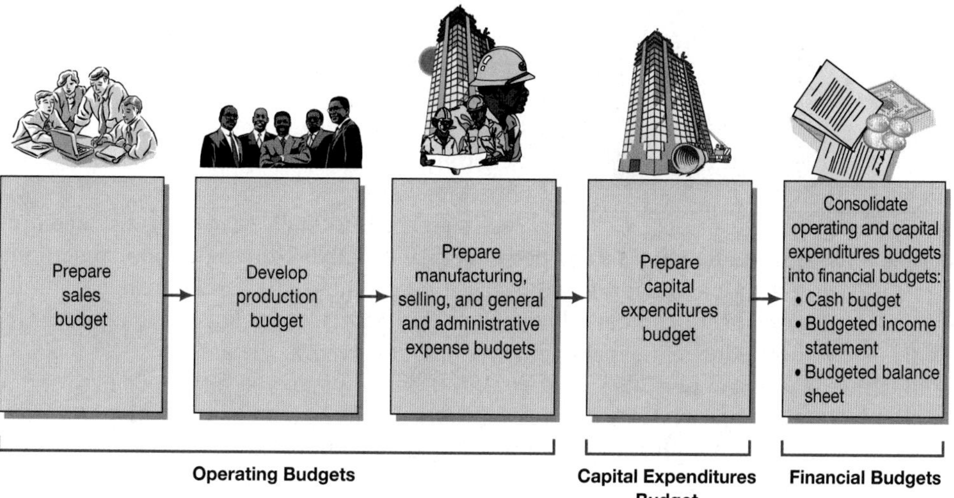

The remainder of this section explains how Hockey Den (HD), a retailer of youth hockey sticks, prepares its master budget. Its master budget includes operating, capital expenditures, and cash budgets for each month in each quarter. It also includes a budgeted income statement for each quarter and a budgeted balance sheet as of the last day of each quarter. We show how HD prepares budgets for October, November, and December 2005. Exhibit 23.5 presents HD's balance sheet at the start of this budgeting period, which we often refer to as we prepare the component budgets.

Exhibit 23.5

Balance Sheet Prior to the Budgeting Periods

HOCKEY DEN
Balance Sheet
September 30, 2005

Assets		
Cash		$ 20,000
Accounts receivable		42,000
Inventory (900 units @ $60)		54,000
Equipment*	$200,000	
Less accumulated depreciation	36,000	164,000
Total assets		$280,000
Liabilities and Equity		
Liabilities		
Accounts payable	$ 58,200	
Income taxes payable (due 10/31/2005)	20,000	
Note payable to bank	10,000	$ 88,200
Stockholders' equity		
Common stock	150,000	
Retained earnings	41,800	191,800
Total liabilities and equity		$280,000

* Equipment is depreciated on a straight-line basis over 10 years (salvage value is $20,000).

P1 Prepare each component of a master budget and link each to the budgeting process.

Operating Budgets

This section explains HD's preparation of operating budgets. Its operating budgets consist of the sales budget, merchandise purchases budget, selling expense budget, and general and administrative expense budget. HD does not prepare production and manufacturing budgets because it is a merchandiser. (The preparation of production budgets and manufacturing budgets is described in Appendix 23A.)

Decision Insight

No Biz Like Snow Biz Ski resorts' costs of making snow are in the tens of millions of dollars for equipment alone. Snowmaking involves spraying droplets of water into the air, causing them to freeze and come down as snow. Making snow can cost more than $2,000 an hour. Snowmaking accounts for 40 to 50 percent of the operating budgets for many ski resorts.

Sales Budget The first step in preparing the master budget is planning the **sales budget,** which shows the planned sales units and the expected dollars from these sales. The sales budget is the starting point in the budgeting process because plans for most departments are linked to sales.

The sales budget should emerge from a careful analysis of forecasted economic and market conditions, business capacity, proposed selling expenses (such as advertising), and predictions of unit sales. A company's sales personnel are usually asked to develop predictions of sales for each territory and department because people normally feel a greater commitment to goals they help set. Another advantage to this participatory budgeting approach is that it draws on knowledge and experience of people involved in the activity.

Example: Assume a company's sales force receives a bonus when sales exceed the budgeted amount. How would this arrangement affect the bottom-up process of sales forecasts? *Answer:* Sales reps may understate their budgeted sales.

To illustrate, in September 2005, HD sold 700 hockey sticks at $100 per unit. After considering sales predictions and market conditions, HD prepares its sales budget for the next quarter (three months) plus one extra month (see Exhibit 23.6). The sales budget includes January 2006 because the purchasing department relies on estimated January sales to decide on December 2005 inventory purchases. The sales budget in Exhibit 23.6 includes forecasts of both unit sales and unit prices. Some sales budgets are expressed only in total sales dollars, but most are more detailed. Management finds it useful to know budgeted units and unit prices for many different products, regions, departments, and sales representatives.

Exhibit 23.6

Sales Budget for Planned Unit and Dollar Sales

HOCKEY DEN
Monthly Sales Budget
October 2005–January 2006

	Budgeted Unit Sales	Budgeted Unit Price	Budgeted Total Sales
September 2005 (actual)	700	$100	$ 70,000
October 2005	1,000	$100	$100,000
November 2005	800	100	80,000
December 2005	1,400	100	140,000
Total for the quarter	3,200	100	$320,000
January 2006	900	100	$ 90,000

Merchandise Purchases Budget Companies use various methods to help managers make inventory purchasing decisions. These methods recognize that the number of units added to inventory depends on budgeted sales volume. Whether a company manufactures or purchases the product it sells, budgeted future sales volume is the primary factor in most inventory management decisions. A company must also consider its inventory system and other factors that we discuss next.

Decision Maker

Entrepreneur You run a start-up that manufactures designer clothes. Business is seasonal, and fashions and designs quickly change. How do you prepare reliable annual sales budgets?

Answer—p. 925

Just-in-time inventory systems. Managers of *just-in-time* (JIT) inventory systems use sales budgets for short periods (often as few as one or two days) to order just enough merchandise or materials to satisfy the immediate sales demand. This keeps the amount of inventory to a minimum (or zero in an ideal situation). A JIT system minimizes the costs of maintaining inventory, but it is practical only if customers are content to order in advance or if managers can accurately determine short-term sales demand. Suppliers also must be able and willing to ship small quantities regularly and promptly.

Point: Accurate estimates of future sales are crucial in a JIT system.

Topic Tackler 23-2

Safety stock inventory systems. Market conditions and manufacturing processes for some products do not allow use of a just-in-time system. Companies in these cases maintain sufficient inventory to reduce the risk and cost of running short. This practice requires enough purchases to satisfy the budgeted sales amounts and to maintain a **safety stock,** a quantity of inventory that provides protection against lost sales caused by unfulfilled demands from customers or delays in shipments from suppliers.

Merchandise purchases budget preparation. A merchandiser usually expresses a **merchandise purchases budget** in both units and dollars. Exhibit 23.7 shows the general layout for this budget in equation form. If this formula is expressed in units and only one product is involved, we can compute the number of dollars of inventory to be purchased for the budget by multiplying the units to be purchased by the cost per unit.

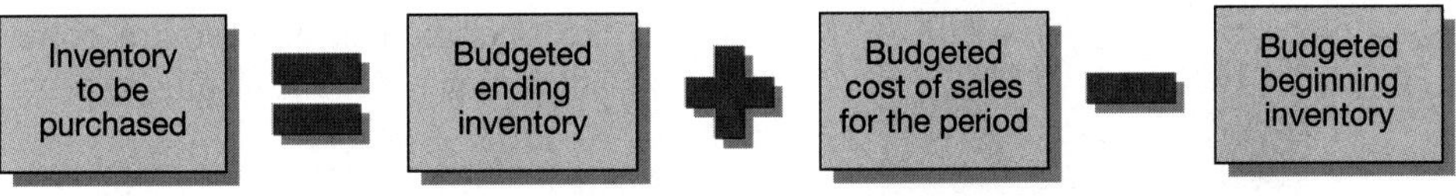

Exhibit 23.7

Formula for a Merchandise Purchases Budget

To illustrate, after assessing the cost of keeping inventory along with the risk and cost of inventory shortages, HD decided that the number of units in its inventory at each month-end should equal 90% of next month's predicted sales. For example, inventory at the end of October should equal 90% of budgeted November sales, and the November ending inventory should equal 90% of budgeted December sales, and so on. Also, HD's suppliers expect the September 2005 per unit cost of $60 to remain unchanged through January 2006. This information along with knowledge of 900 units in inventory at September 30 (see Exhibit 23.5) allows the company to prepare the merchandise purchases budget shown in Exhibit 23.8.

Example: Assume Hockey Den adopts a JIT system in purchasing merchandise. How will its sales budget differ from its merchandise purchases budget? *Answer:* The two budgets will be similar because future inventory should be near zero.

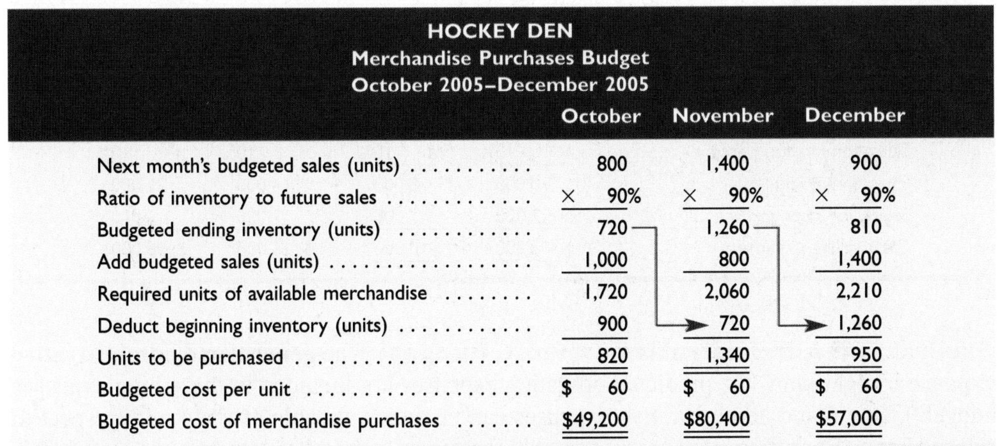

HOCKEY DEN
Merchandise Purchases Budget
October 2005–December 2005

	October	November	December
Next month's budgeted sales (units)	800	1,400	900
Ratio of inventory to future sales	× 90%	× 90%	× 90%
Budgeted ending inventory (units)	720	1,260	810
Add budgeted sales (units)	1,000	800	1,400
Required units of available merchandise	1,720	2,060	2,210
Deduct beginning inventory (units)	900	720	1,260
Units to be purchased	820	1,340	950
Budgeted cost per unit	$ 60	$ 60	$ 60
Budgeted cost of merchandise purchases	$49,200	$80,400	$57,000

Exhibit 23.8

Merchandise Purchases Budget

The first three lines of HD's merchandise purchases budget determine the required ending inventories (in units). Budgeted unit sales are then added to the desired ending inventory to give the required units of available merchandise. We then subtract beginning inventory to determine the budgeted number of units to be purchased. The last line is the budgeted cost of the purchases, computed by multiplying the number of units to be purchased by the predicted cost per unit.

Example: If ending inventory in Exhibit 23.8 is required to equal 80% of next month's predicted sales, how many units must be purchased each month? *Answer:* Budgeted ending inventory: Oct. = 640 units; Nov. = 1,120 units; Dec. = 720 units. Required purchases: Oct. = 740 units; Nov. = 1,280 units; Dec. = 1,000 units.

We already indicated that some budgeting systems describe only the total dollars of budgeted sales. Likewise, a system can express a merchandise purchases budget only in terms of the total cost of merchandise to be purchased, omitting the number of units to be purchased. This method assumes a constant relation between sales and cost of goods sold. HD, for instance, might assume the expected cost of goods sold to be 60% of sales, computed from the budgeted unit cost of $60 and the budgeted sales price of $100. However, it still must consider the effects of changes in beginning and ending inventories in determining the amounts to be purchased.

Point: To apply these concepts, work Exercise 23-1.

Selling Expense Budget The **selling expense budget** is a plan listing the types and amounts of selling expenses expected during the budget period. Its initial responsibility usually rests with the vice president of marketing or an equivalent sales manager. The selling expense budget is normally created to provide sufficient selling expenses to meet sales goals reflected in the sales budget. Predicted selling expenses are based on both the sales budget and the experience of previous periods. After some or all of the master budget is prepared, management might decide that projected sales volume is inadequate. If so, subsequent adjustments in the sales budget can require corresponding adjustments in the selling expense budget.

To illustrate, HD's selling expense budget is in Exhibit 23.9. The firm's selling expenses consist of commissions paid to sales personnel and a $2,000 monthly salary paid to the sales manager. Sales commissions equal 10% of total sales and are paid in the month sales occur. Sales commissions are variable with respect to sales volume, but the sales manager's salary is fixed. No advertising expenses are budgeted for this particular quarter.

Decision Insight

Goals and Budgets **France Telecom** failed to properly budget and coordinate its efforts for World Cup ticket sales. According to the company, it assigned 60 of its operators to take orders for the few thousand tickets available to U.K. citizens. In the first 60 minutes after the phone lines opened, **British Telecom** logged an amazing four million call attempts. The odds of a U.K. soccer fan getting through to the ticket hotline were around one in two million.

Exhibit 23.9

Selling Expense Budget

HOCKEY DEN
Selling Expense Budget
October 2005–December 2005

	October	November	December	Total
Budgeted sales	$100,000	$80,000	$140,000	$320,000
Sales commission percent	× 10%	× 10%	× 10%	× 10%
Sales commissions	10,000	8,000	14,000	32,000
Salary for sales manager	2,000	2,000	2,000	6,000
Total selling expenses	$ 12,000	$10,000	$ 16,000	$ 38,000

Example: If sales commissions in Exhibit 23.9 are increased, which budgets are affected? *Answer:* Selling expenses budget, cash budget, and budgeted income statement.

General and Administrative Expense Budget The **general and administrative expense budget** plans the predicted operating expenses not included in the selling expenses budget. General and administrative expenses can be either variable or fixed with respect to sales volume. The office manager responsible for general administration often is responsible for preparing the initial general and administrative expense budget.

Interest expense and income tax expense are often classified as general and administrative expenses in published income statements, but normally cannot be planned at this stage of the budgeting process. The prediction of interest expense follows the preparation of the cash budget and the decisions regarding debt. The predicted income tax expense depends on the budgeted amount of pretax income. Both interest and income taxes are usually beyond the control of the office manager. As a result, they are not used in comparison to the budget to evaluate that person's performance.

Exhibit 23.10 shows HD's general and administrative expense budget. It includes salaries of $54,000 per year, or $4,500 per month (paid each month when they are earned). Using information in Exhibit 23.5, the depreciation on equipment is computed as $18,000 per year [($200,000 − $20,000)/10 years], or $1,500 per month ($18,000/12 months).

Exhibit 23.10

General and Administrative Expense Budget

HOCKEY DEN General and Administrative Expense Budget October 2005–December 2005	October	November	December	Total
Administrative salaries	$4,500	$4,500	$4,500	$13,500
Depreciation of equipment	1,500	1,500	1,500	4,500
Total general and administrative expenses	$6,000	$6,000	$6,000	$18,000

Example: In Exhibit 23.10, how would a rental agreement of $5,000 per month plus 1% of sales affect the general and administrative expense budget? (Budgeted sales are in Exhibit 23.6.)
Answer: Rent expense: Oct. = $6,000; Nov. = $5,800; Dec. = $6,400; Total = 18,200; *Revised total general and administrative expenses:* Oct. = $12,000; Nov. = $11,800; Dec. = $12,400; Total = $36,200.

Quick Check

5. What is a master budget?
6. A master budget (*a*) always includes a manufacturing budget specifying the units to be produced, (*b*) is prepared with a process starting with the operating budgets and continues with the capital expenditures budget, and then financial budgets, or (*c*) is prepared with a process ending with the sales budget.
7. What are the three primary categories of budgets in the master budget?
8. In preparing monthly budgets for the third quarter, a company budgeted sales of 120 units for July and 140 units for August. Management wants each month's ending inventory to be 60% of next month's sales. The June 30 inventory consists of 50 units. How many units of product for July acquisition should the merchandise purchases budget specify for the third quarter? (*a*) 84, (*b*) 120, (*c*) 154, or (*d*) 204.
9. How do the operating budgets for merchandisers and manufacturers differ?
10. How does a just-in-time inventory system differ from a safety stock system?

Answers—p. 925

Capital Expenditures Budget

The **capital expenditures budget** lists dollar amounts to be both received from plant asset disposals and spent to purchase additional plant assets to carry out the budgeted business activities. It is usually prepared after the operating budgets. Since a company's plant assets determine its productive capacity, this budget is usually affected by long-range plans for the business. Yet the process of preparing a sales or purchases budget can reveal that the company requires more (or less) capacity, which implies more (or less) plant assets.

Capital budgeting is the process of evaluating and planning for capital (plant asset) expenditures. This is an important management task because these expenditures often involve long-run commitments of large amounts, affect predicted cash flows, and impact future debt and equity financing. This means that the capital expenditures budget is often linked with management's evaluation of the company's ability to take on more debt. We describe capital budgeting in Chapter 25.

Hockey Den does not anticipate disposal of any plant assets through December 2005, but it does plan to acquire additional equipment for $25,000 cash near the end of December 2005. This is the only budgeted capital expenditure from October 2005 through January 2006. Thus, no separate budget is shown. The cash budget in Exhibit 23.11 reflects this $25,000 planned expenditure.

Exhibit 23.11
Cash Budget

HOCKEY DEN Cash Budget October 2005–December 2005	October	November	December
Beginning cash balance	$ 20,000	$ 20,000	$ 22,272
Cash receipts from customers (Exhibit 23.12)	82,000	92,000	104,000
Total cash available	102,000	112,000	126,272
Cash disbursements			
Payments for merchandise (Exhibit 23.13)	58,200	49,200	80,400
Sales commissions (Exhibit 23.9)	10,000	8,000	14,000
Salaries			
Sales (Exhibit 23.9)	2,000	2,000	2,000
Administrative (Exhibit 23.10)	4,500	4,500	4,500
Income taxes payable (Exhibit 23.5)	20,000		
Dividends ($150,000 × 2%)		3,000	
Interest on bank loan			
October ($10,000 × 1%)	100		
November ($22,800 × 1%)		228	
Purchase of equipment			25,000
Total cash disbursements	94,800	66,928	125,900
Preliminary cash balance	$ 7,200	$ 45,072	$ 372
Additional loan from bank	12,800		19,628
Repayment of loan to bank		22,800	
Ending cash balance	$ 20,000	$ 22,272	$ 20,000
Loan balance, end of month	$ 22,800	$ 0	$ 19,628

Financial Budgets

P2 Link both operating and capital expenditures budgets to budgeted financial statements.

After preparing its operating and capital expenditures budgets, a company uses information from these budgets to prepare at least three financial budgets: the cash budget, budgeted income statement, and budgeted balance sheet.

Cash Budget After developing budgets for sales, merchandise purchases, expenses, and capital expenditures, the next step is to prepare the **cash budget,** which shows expected cash inflows and outflows during the budget period. It is especially important to maintain a cash balance necessary to meet ongoing obligations. By preparing a cash budget, management can prearrange loans to cover anticipated cash shortages before they are needed. A cash budget also helps management avoid a cash balance that is too large. Too much cash is undesirable because it earns a relatively low (if any) return.

When preparing a cash budget, we add expected cash receipts to the beginning cash balance and deduct expected cash disbursements. If the expected ending cash balance is inadequate, additional cash requirements appear in the budget as planned increases from short-term loans. If the expected ending cash balance exceeds the desired balance, the excess is used to repay loans or to acquire short-term investments. Information for preparing the cash budget is mainly taken from the operating and capital expenditures budgets.

To illustrate, Exhibit 23.11 presents HD's cash budget. The beginning cash balance for October is taken from the September 30, 2005, balance sheet in Exhibit 23.5. The remainder of this section describes the computations in the cash budget.

We begin with reference to HD's budgeted sales (Exhibit 23.6). Analysis of past sales indicates that 40% of the firm's sales are for cash. The remaining 60% are credit sales; these customers are expected to pay in full in the month following the sales. We now can compute the budgeted cash receipts from customers as shown in Exhibit 23.12. October's budgeted cash receipts consist of $40,000 from expected cash sales ($100,000 × 40%) plus the anticipated collection of $42,000 of accounts receivable from the end of

	September	October	November	December
Sales	$70,000	$100,000	$80,000	$140,000
Less ending accounts receivable (60%)	42,000	60,000	48,000	84,000
Cash receipts from				
Cash sales (40% of sales)		40,000	32,000	56,000
Collections of prior month's receivables		42,000	60,000	48,000
Total cash receipts		$ 82,000	$92,000	$104,000

Exhibit 23.12

Computing Budgeted Cash Receipts

September. Each month's cash receipts from customers are transferred to the second line of Exhibit 23.11.

Next, we note that HD's merchandise purchases are entirely on account. It makes full payments during the month following the purchases. Therefore, cash disbursements for purchases can be computed from the September 30, 2005, balance sheet (Exhibit 23.5) and the merchandise purchases budget (Exhibit 23.8). This computation is shown in Exhibit 23.13.

October payments (September 30 balance)	$58,200
November payments (October purchases)	49,200
December payments (November purchases)	80,400

Exhibit 23.13

Computing Cash Disbursements for Purchases

The monthly budgeted cash disbursements for sales commissions and salaries are taken from the selling expense budget (Exhibit 23.9) and the general and administrative expense budget (Exhibit 23.10). The cash budget is unaffected by depreciation as reported in the general and administrative expenses budget.

Income taxes are due and payable in October as shown in the September 30, 2005, balance sheet (Exhibit 23.5). The cash budget in Exhibit 23.11 shows this $20,000 expected payment in October. Predicted income tax expense for the quarter ending December 31 is 40% of net income and is due in January 2006. It is therefore not reported in the October–December 2005 cash budget but in the budgeted income statement as income tax expense and on the budgeted balance sheet as income tax liability.

Hockey Den also pays a cash dividend equal to 2% of the par value of common stock in the second month of each quarter. The cash budget in Exhibit 23.11 shows a November payment of $3,000 for this purpose (2% of $150,000; see Exhibit 23.5).

Hockey Den has an agreement with its bank that promises additional loans at each month-end, if necessary, to keep a minimum cash balance of $20,000. If the cash balance exceeds $20,000 at a month-end, HD uses the excess to repay loans. Interest is paid at each month-end at the rate of 1% of the beginning balance of these loans. For October, this payment is 1% of the $10,000 amount reported in the balance sheet of Exhibit 23.5. For November, HD expects to pay interest of $228, computed as 1% of the $22,800 expected loan balance at October 31. No interest is budgeted for December because the company expects to repay the loans in full at the end of November. Exhibit 23.11 shows that the October 31 cash balance declines to $7,200 (before any loan-related activity). This amount is less than the $20,000 minimum. Hockey Den will bring this balance up to the minimum by borrowing $12,800 with a short-term note. At the end of November, the budget shows an expected cash balance of $45,072 before any loan activity. This means that HD expects to repay $22,800 of debt. The equipment purchase budgeted for December reduces the expected cash

Example: If the minimum ending cash balance in Exhibit 23.11 is changed to $25,000 for each month, what is the projected loan balance at Dec. 31, 2005? *Answer:*

Loan balance, Oct. 31	$27,800
November interest	278
November payment	25,022
Loan balance, Nov. 30	2,778
December interest	28
Additional loan in Dec.	21,928
Loan balance, Dec. 31	24,706

Example: Give one reason for maintaining a minimum cash balance when the budget shows extra cash is not needed. *Answer:* For unexpected events.

Point: To apply these concepts, work Exercises 23-2 and 23-3.

Decision Insight

Netting Cash The **Hockey Company**—whose brands include CCM, JOFA, and KOHO—reported net cash outflows for investing activities of $1.9 million this past year. The entire amount was for capital expenditures.

Decision Insight

Plan Ahead Most companies allocate dollars based on budgets submitted by department managers. These managers verify the numbers and monitor the budget. Managers must remember, however, that a budget is judged by its success in helping achieve the company's mission. One analogy is that a hiker must know the route to properly plan a hike and monitor hiking progress.

balance to $372, far below the $20,000 minimum. The company expects to borrow $19,628 in that month to reach the minimum desired ending balance.

Budgeted Income Statement One of the final steps in preparing the master budget is to summarize the income effects. The **budgeted income statement** is a managerial accounting report showing predicted amounts of sales and expenses for the budget period. Information needed for preparing a budgeted income statement is primarily taken from already prepared budgets. The volume of information summarized in the budgeted income statement is so large for some companies that they often use spreadsheets to accumulate the budgeted transactions and classify them by their effects on income. We condense HD's budgeted income statement and show it in Exhibit 23.14. All information in this exhibit is taken from earlier budgets. Also, we now can predict the amount of income tax expense for the quarter, computed as 40% of the budgeted pretax income. This amount is included in the cash budget and/or the budgeted balance sheet as necessary.

Exhibit 23.14

Budgeted Income Statement

HOCKEY DEN
Budgeted Income Statement
For Three Months Ended December 31, 2005

Sales (Exhibit 23.6, 3,200 units @ $100)		$320,000
Cost of goods sold (3,200 units @ $60)		192,000
Gross profit		128,000
Operating expenses		
Sales commissions (Exhibit 23.9)	$32,000	
Sales salaries (Exhibit 23.9)	6,000	
Administrative salaries (Exhibit 23.10)	13,500	
Depreciation on equipment (Exhibit 23.10)	4,500	
Interest expense (Exhibit 23.11)	328	56,328
Income before income taxes		71,672
Income tax expense ($71,672 × 40%)		28,669
Net income		$ 43,003

Point: Lending institutions often require potential borrowers to provide cash budgets, budgeted income statements, and budgeted balance sheets, as well as data on past performance.

Point: To apply these concepts, work Exercise 23-4.

Budgeted Balance Sheet The final step in preparing the master budget is summarizing the company's financial position. The **budgeted balance sheet** shows predicted amounts for the company's assets, liabilities, and equity as of the end of the budget period. HD's budgeted balance sheet in Exhibit 23.15 is prepared using information from the other budgets. The sources of amounts are reported in the notes to the budgeted balance sheet.[1]

[1] An eight-column spreadsheet, or work sheet, can be used to prepare a budgeted balance sheet (and income statement). The first two columns show the ending balance sheet amounts from the period prior to the budget period. The budgeted transactions and adjustments are entered in the third and fourth columns in the same manner as adjustments are entered on an ordinary work sheet. After all budgeted transactions and adjustments have been entered, the amounts in the first two columns are combined with the budget amounts in the third and fourth columns and sorted to the proper Income Statement (fifth and sixth columns) and Balance Sheet columns (seventh and eighth columns). Amounts in these columns are used to prepare the budgeted income statement and balance sheet.

Exhibit 23.15

Budgeted Balance Sheet

HOCKEY DEN Budgeted Balance Sheet December 31, 2005		
Assets		
Cash[a]		$ 20,000
Accounts receivable[b]		84,000
Inventory (810 unit @ $60)[c]		48,600
Equipment[d]	$225,000	
Less accumulated depreciation[e]	40,500	184,500
Total assets		$337,100
Liabilities and Equity		
Liabilities		
Accounts payable[f]	$ 57,000	
Income taxes payable[g]	28,669	
Bank loan payable[h]	19,628	$105,297
Stockholders' equity		
Common stock[i]	150,000	
Retained earnings[j]	81,803	231,803
Total liabilities and equity		$337,100

[a] Ending balance for December from the cash budget in Exhibit 23.11.
[b] 60% of $140,000 sales budgeted for December from the sales budget in Exhibit 23.6.
[c] 810 units in budgeted December ending inventory at the budgeted cost of $60 per unit (from the purchases budget in Exhibit 23.8).
[d] September 30 balance of $200,000 from the beginning balance sheet in Exhibit 23.5 plus $25,000 cost of new equipment from the cash budget in Exhibit 23.11.
[e] September 30 balance of $36,000 from the beginning balance sheet in Exhibit 23.5 plus $4,500 expense from the general and administrative expense budget in Exhibit 23.10.
[f] Budgeted cost of purchases for December from the purchases budget in Exhibit 23.8.
[g] Income tax expense from the budgeted income statement for the fourth quarter in Exhibit 23.14.
[h] Budgeted December 31 balance from the cash budget in Exhibit 23.11.
[i] Unchanged from the beginning balance sheet in Exhibit 23.5.
[j] September 30 balance of $41,800 from the beginning balance sheet in Exhibit 23.5 plus budgeted net income of $43,003 from the budgeted income statement in Exhibit 23.14 minus budgeted cash dividends of $3,000 from the cash budget in Exhibit 23.11.

Quick Check

11. In preparing a budgeted balance sheet, (*a*) plant assets are determined by analyzing the capital expenditures budget and the balance sheet from the beginning of the budget period, (*b*) liabilities are determined by analyzing the general and administrative expense budget, or (*c*) retained earnings are determined from information contained in the cash budget and the balance sheet from the beginning of the budget period.
12. What sequence is followed in preparing the budgets that constitute the master budget?

Answers—p. 925

Activity-Based Budgeting

Decision Analysis

A1 Analyze expense planning using activity-based budgeting.

Activity-based budgeting (ABB) is a budget system based on expected activities. Knowledge of expected activities and their levels for the budget period enables management to plan for resources required to perform the activities. To illustrate, we consider the budget of a company's accounting department. Traditional budgeting systems list items such as salaries, supplies, equipment, and utilities. Such an itemized budget informs management of the use of the funds budgeted (for example, salaries), but management cannot assess the basis for increases or decreases in budgeted amounts as compared to prior periods. Accordingly, management often makes across-the-board cuts or increases. In contrast, ABB requires management to list activities performed by, say, the accounting department such as auditing, tax reporting, financial reporting, and cost accounting. Exhibit 23.16 contrasts a

Exhibit 23.16

Activity-Based Budgeting versus Traditional Budgeting (for an accounting department)

Activity-Based Budget		Traditional Budget	
Auditing	$ 58,000	Salaries	$152,000
Tax reporting	71,000	Supplies	22,000
Financial reporting	63,000	Depreciation	36,000
Cost accounting	32,000	Utilities	14,000
Total	$224,000	Total	$224,000

traditional budget with an activity-based budget for a company's accounting department. An understanding of the resources required to perform the activities, the costs associated with these resources, and the way resource use changes with changes in activity levels allows management to better assess how expenses will change to accommodate changes in activity levels. Moreover, by knowing the relation between activities and costs, management can attempt to reduce costs by eliminating nonvalue-added activities.

Decision Maker

Environmental Manager You hold the new position of environmental control manager for a chemical company. You are asked to develop a budget for your job and identify job responsibilities. How do you proceed?

Answer—p. 925

Demonstration Problem

Wild Wood Co's management asks you to prepare its master budget using the following information. The budget is to cover the months of April, May, and June 2005.

WILD WOOD COMPANY
Balance Sheet
March 31, 2005

Assets			Liabilities and Equity	
Cash		$ 50,000	Accounts payable	$156,000
Accounts receivable		175,000	Short-term notes payable	12,000
Inventory		126,000	Total current liabilities	168,000
Total current assets		351,000	Long-term note payable	200,000
Equipment	$480,000		Total liabilities	368,000
Accumulated depreciation	(90,000)	390,000	Common stock	235,000
			Retained earnings	138,000
			Total stockholders' equity	373,000
Total assets		$741,000	Total liabilities and equity	$741,000

Additional Information

a. Sales for March total 10,000 units. Each month's sales are expected to exceed the prior month's results by 5%. The product's selling price is $25 per unit.

b. Company policy calls for a given month's ending inventory to equal 80% of the next month's expected unit sales. The March 31 inventory is 8,400 units, which complies with the policy. The purchase price is $15 per unit.

c. Sales representatives' commissions are 12.5% of sales and are paid in the month of the sales. The sales manager's monthly salary will be $3,500 in April and $4,000 per month thereafter.

d. Monthly general and administrative expenses include $8,000 administrative salaries, $5,000 depreciation, and 0.9% monthly interest on the long-term note payable.

e. The company expects 30% of sales to be for cash and the remaining 70% on credit. Receivables are collected in full in the month following the sale (none is collected in the month of the sale).

f. All merchandise purchases are on credit, and no payables arise from any other transactions. One month's purchases are fully paid in the next month.

g. The minimum ending cash balance for all months is $50,000. If necessary, the company borrows enough cash using a short-term note to reach the minimum. Short-term notes require an interest payment of 1% at each month-end (before any repayment). If the ending cash balance exceeds the minimum, the excess will be applied to repaying the short-term notes payable balance.

h. Dividends of $100,000 are to be declared and paid in May.

i. No cash payments for income taxes are to be made during the second calendar quarter. Income taxes will be assessed at 35% in the quarter.

j. Equipment purchases of $55,000 are scheduled for June.

Required

Prepare the following budgets and other financial information as required:

1. Sales budget, including budgeted sales for July.
2. Purchases budget, the budgeted cost of goods sold for each month and quarter, and the cost of the June 30 budgeted inventory.
3. Selling expense budget.
4. General and administrative expense budget.
5. Expected cash receipts from customers and the expected June 30 balance of accounts receivable.
6. Expected cash payments for purchases and the expected June 30 balance of accounts payable.
7. Cash budget.
8. Budgeted income statement.
9. Budgeted statement of retained earnings.
10. Budgeted balance sheet.

Planning the Solution

- The sales budget shows expected sales for each month in the quarter. Start by multiplying March sales by 105% and then do the same for the remaining months. July's sales are needed for the purchases budget. To complete the budget, multiply the expected unit sales by the selling price of $25 per unit.
- Use these results and the 80% inventory policy to budget the size of ending inventory for April, May, and June. Add the budgeted sales to these numbers and subtract the actual or expected beginning inventory for each month. The result is the number of units to be purchased each month. Multiply these numbers by the per unit cost of $15. Find the budgeted cost of goods sold by multiplying the unit sales in each month by the $15 cost per unit. Compute the cost of the June 30 ending inventory by multiplying the expected units available at that date by the $15 cost per unit.
- The selling expense budget has only two items. Find the amount of the sales representatives' commissions by multiplying the expected dollar sales in each month by the 12.5% commission rate. Then include the sales manager's salary of $3,500 in April and $4,000 in May and June.
- The general and administrative expense budget should show three items. Administrative salaries are fixed at $8,000 per month, and depreciation is $5,000 per month. Budget the monthly interest expense on the long-term note by multiplying its $200,000 balance by the 0.9% monthly interest rate.
- Determine the amounts of cash sales in each month by multiplying the budgeted sales by 30%. Add to this amount the credit sales of the prior month (computed as 70% of prior month's sales). April's cash receipts from collecting receivables equals the March 31 balance of $175,000. The expected June 30 accounts receivable balance equals 70% of June's total budgeted sales.
- Determine expected cash payments on accounts payable for each month by making them equal to the merchandise purchases in the prior month. The payments for April equal the March 31 balance of accounts payable shown on the beginning balance sheet. The June 30 balance of accounts payable equals merchandise purchases for June.
- Prepare the cash budget by combining the given information and the amounts of cash receipts and cash payments on account that you computed. Complete the cash budget for each month by either borrowing enough to raise the preliminary balance to the minimum or paying off short-term debt as much as the balance allows without falling below the minimum. Show the ending balance of the short-term note in the budget.
- Prepare the budgeted income statement by combining the budgeted items for all three months. Determine the income before income taxes and multiply it by the 35% rate to find the quarter's income tax expense.
- The budgeted statement of retained earnings should show the March 31 balance plus the quarter's net income minus the quarter's dividends.

- The budgeted balance sheet includes updated balances for all items that appear in the beginning balance sheet and an additional liability for unpaid income taxes. Amounts for all asset, liability, and equity accounts can be found either in the budgets, other calculations, or by adding amounts found there to the beginning balances.

Solution to Demonstration Problem

1. Sales budget

	April	May	June	July
Prior month's sales	10,000	10,500	11,025	11,576
Plus 5% growth	500	525	551	579
Projected unit	10,500	11,025	11,576	12,155

	April	May	June	Quarter
Projected unit sales	10,500	11,025	11,576	
Selling price per unit	× $25	× $25	× $25	
Projected sales	$262,500	$275,625	$289,400	$827,525

2. Purchases budget

	April	May	June	Quarter
Next month's unit sales (part 1)	11,025	11,576	12,155	
Ending inventory percent	× 80%	× 80%	× 80%	
Desired ending inventory	8,820	9,261	9,724	
This month's unit sales (part 1)	10,500	11,025	11,576	
Units to be available	19,320	20,286	21,300	
Less beginning inventory	8,400	8,820	9,261	
Units to be purchased	10,920	11,466	12,039	
Budgeted cost per unit	× $15	× $15	× $15	
Projected purchases	$163,800	$171,990	$180,585	$516,375

Budgeted cost of goods sold

	April	May	June	Quarter
This month's unit sales (part 1)	10,500	11,025	11,576	
Budgeted cost per unit	× $15	× $15	× $15	
Projected cost of goods sold	$157,500	$165,375	$173,640	$496,515

Budgeted inventory for June 30

Units (part 2)	9,724
Cost per unit	× $15
Total	$145,860

3. Selling expense budget

	April	May	June	Quarter
Budgeted sales (part 1)	$262,500	$275,625	$289,400	$827,525
Commission percent	× 12.5%	× 12.5%	× 12.5%	× 12.5%
Sales commissions	32,813	34,453	36,175	103,441
Manager's salary	3,500	4,000	4,000	11,500
Projected selling expenses	$ 36,313	$ 38,453	$ 40,175	$114,941

4. General and administrative expense budget

	April	May	June	Quarter
Administrative salaries	$ 8,000	$ 8,000	$ 8,000	$24,000
Depreciation	5,000	5,000	5,000	15,000
Interest on long-term note payable (0.9% × $200,000)	1,800	1,800	1,800	5,400
Projected expenses	$14,800	$14,800	$14,800	$44,400

5. Expected cash receipts from customers

	April	May	June	Quarter
Budgeted sales (part 1)	$262,500	$275,625	$289,400	
Ending accounts receivable (70%)	$183,750	$192,938	$202,580	
Cash receipts				
Cash sales (30%)	$ 78,750	$ 82,687	$ 86,820	$248,257
Collections of prior month's receivables	175,000	183,750	192,938	551,688
Total cash to be collected	$253,750	$266,437	$279,758	$799,945

6. Expected cash payments to suppliers

	April	May	June	Quarter
Cash payments (equal to prior month's purchases)	$156,000	$163,800	$171,990	$491,790
Expected June 30 balance of accounts payable (June purchases)			$180,585	

7. Cash budget

	April	May	June
Beginning cash balance	$ 50,000	$ 89,517	$ 50,000
Cash receipts (part 5)	253,750	266,437	279,758
Total cash available	303,750	355,954	329,758
Cash payments			
Payments for merchandise (part 6)	156,000	163,800	171,990
Sales commissions (part 3)	32,813	34,453	36,175
Salaries			
Sales (part 3)	3,500	4,000	4,000
Administrative (part 4)	8,000	8,000	8,000
Interest on long-term note (part 4)	1,800	1,800	1,800
Dividends		100,000	
Equipment purchase			55,000
Interest on short-term notes			
April ($12,000 × 1.0%)	120		
June ($6,099 × 1.0%)			61
Total cash payments	202,233	312,053	277,026
Preliminary balance	101,517	43,901	52,732
Additional loan		6,099	
Loan repayment	(12,000)		(2,732)
Ending cash balance	$ 89,517	$ 50,000	$ 50,000
Ending short-term notes	$ 0	$ 6,099	$ 3,367

8.

WILD WOOD COMPANY Budgeted Income Statement For Quarter Ended June 30, 2005		
Sales (part 1)		$ 827,525
Cost of goods sold (part 2)		496,515
Gross profit		331,010
Operating expenses		
Sales commissions (part 3)	$103,441	
Sales salaries (part 3)	11,500	
Administrative salaries (part 4)	24,000	
Depreciation (part 4)	15,000	
Interest on long-term note (part 4)	5,400	
Interest on short-term notes (part 7)	181	
Total operating expenses		159,522
Income before income taxes		171,488
Income taxes (35%)		60,021
Net income		$ 111,467

9.

WILD WOOD COMPANY Budgeted Statement of Retained Earnings For Quarter Ended June 30, 2005	
Beginning retained earnings (given)	$138,000
Net income (part 8)	111,467
	249,467
Less cash dividends (given)	100,000
Ending retained earnings	$149,467

10.

WILD WOOD COMPANY Budgeted Balance Sheet June 30, 2005		
Assets		
Cash (part 7)		$ 50,000
Accounts receivable (part 5)		202,580
Inventory (part 2)		145,860
Total current assets		398,440
Equipment (given plus purchase)	$535,000	
Less accumulated depreciation (given plus expense)	105,000	430,000
Total assets		$828,440
Liabilities and Equity		
Accounts payable (part 6)		$180,585
Short-term notes payable (part 7)		3,367
Income taxes payable (part 8)		60,021
Total current liabilities		243,973
Long-term note payable (given)		200,000
Total liabilities		443,973
Common stock (given)		235,000
Retained earnings (part 9)		149,467
Total stockholders' equity		384,467
Total liabilities and equity		$828,440

APPENDIX

Production and Manufacturing Budgets

23A

P3 Prepare production and manufacturing budgets.

Unlike a merchandising company, a manufacturer must prepare a **production budget** instead of a merchandise purchases budget. A production budget, which shows the number of units to be produced each month, is similar to merchandise purchases budgets except that the number of units to be purchased each month (as shown in Exhibit 23.8) is replaced by the number of units to be manufactured each month. A production budget does not show costs; it is *always expressed in units of product.* Exhibit 23A.1 shows the production budget for **Toronto Sticks Company** (**TSC**), a manufacturer of hockey sticks. TSC is an exclusive supplier of hockey sticks to Hockey Den, meaning that TSC uses HD's budgeted sales figures (Exhibit 23.6) to determine its production and manufacturing budgets.

Exhibit 23A.1

Production Budget

TSC
Production Budget
October 2005–December 2005

	October	November	December
Next month's budgeted sales (units)	800	1,400	900
Ratio of inventory to future sales	× 90%	× 90%	× 90%
Budgeted ending inventory (units)	720	1,260	810
Add budgeted sales for the month (units)	1,000	800	1,400
Required units of available production	1,720	2,060	2,210
Deduct beginning inventory (units)	(900)	(720)	(1,260)
Units to be produced	820	1,340	950

A **manufacturing budget** shows the budgeted costs for direct materials, direct labor, and overhead. It is based on the budgeted production volume from the production budget. The manufacturing budget for most companies consists of three individual budgets: direct materials budget, direct labor budget, and overhead budget. Exhibits 23A.2–23A.4 show these three manufacturing budgets for TSC. These budgets yield the total expected cost of goods to be manufactured in the budget period.

The *direct materials budget* is driven by the budgeted materials needed to satisfy each month's production requirement. To this we must add the desired ending inventory requirements. The desired ending inventory of direct materials as shown in Exhibit 23A.2 is 50% of next month's budgeted materials requirements of wood. For instance, in October 2005, an ending inventory of 335 units of material is desired (50% of November's 670 units). The desired ending inventory for December 2005

Exhibit 23A.2

Direct Materials Budget

TSC
Direct Materials Budget
October 2005–December 2005

	October	November	December
Budget production (units)	820	1,340	950
Materials requirements per unit	× 0.5	× 0.5	× 0.5
Materials needed for production (units)	410	670	475
Add budgeted ending inventory (units)	335	237.5	225
Total materials requirements (units)	745	907.5	700
Deduct beginning inventory (units)	(205)	(335)	(237.5)
Materials to be purchased (units)	540	572.5	462.5
Material price per unit	$ 20	$ 20	$ 20
Total cost of direct materials purchases	$10,800	$11,450	$9,250

is 225 units, computed from the direct material requirement of 450 units for a production level of 900 units in January 2006. The total materials requirements are computed by adding the desired ending inventory figures to that month's budgeted production material requirements. For October 2005, the total materials requirement is 745 units (335 + 410). From the total materials requirement, we then subtract the units of materials available in beginning inventory. For October 2005, the materials available from September 2005 are computed as 50% of October's materials requirements to satisfy production, or 205 units (50% of 410). Therefore, direct materials purchases in October 2005 are budgeted at 540 units (745 − 205). See Exhibit 23A.2.

TSC's *direct labor budget* is shown in Exhibit 23A.3. About 15 minutes of labor time is required to produce one unit. Labor is paid at the rate of $12 per hour. Budgeted labor hours are computed by multiplying the budgeted production level for each month by one-quarter (0.25) of an hour. Direct labor cost is then computed by multiplying budgeted labor hours by the labor rate of $12 per hour.

Exhibit 23A.3

Direct Labor Budget

TSC
Direct Labor Budget
October 2005–December 2005

	October	November	December
Budgeted production (units)	820	1,340	950
Labor requirements per unit (hours)	× 0.25	× 0.25	× 0.25
Total labor hours needed	205	335	237.5
Labor rate (per hour)	$ 12	$ 12	$ 12
Labor dollars	$2,460	$4,020	$2,850

TSC's *factory overhead budget* is shown in Exhibit 23A.4. The variable portion of overhead is assigned at the rate of $2.50 per unit of production. The fixed portion stays constant at $1,500 per month. The budget in Exhibit 23A.4 is in condensed form; most overhead budgets are more detailed, listing each overhead cost item.

Exhibit 23A.4

Factory Overhead Budget

TSC
Factory Overhead Budget
October 2005–December 2005

	October	November	December
Budgeted production (units)	820	1,340	950
Variable factory overhead rate	× $2.50	× $2.50	× $2.50
Budgeted variable overhead	2,050	3,350	2,375
Budgeted fixed overhead	1,500	1,500	1,500
Budgeted total overhead	$3,550	$4,850	$3,875

Summary

C1 Describe the importance and benefits of budgeting. Planning is a management responsibility of critical importance to business success. Budgeting is the process management uses to formalize its plans. Budgeting promotes management analysis and focuses its attention on the future. Budgeting also provides a basis for evaluating performance, serves as a source of motivation, is a means of coordinating activities, and communicates management's plans and instructions to employees.

C2 Explain the process of budget administration. Budgeting is a detailed activity that requires administration. At least three aspects are important: budget committee, budget reporting, and budget timing. A budget committee oversees the budget preparation. The budget period pertains to the time period for which the budget is prepared such as a year or month.

C3 Describe a master budget and the process of preparing it. A master budget is a formal overall plan for a company. It consists of plans for business operations and capital expenditures, plus the financial results of those activities. The budgeting process begins with a sales budget. Based on expected sales volume, companies can budget purchases, selling expenses, and administrative expenses. Next, the capital expenditures budget is prepared, followed by the cash budget and budgeted financial statements. Manufacturers also must budget production quantities, materials purchases, labor costs, and overhead.

A1 Analyze expense planning using activity-based budgeting. Activity-based budgeting requires management to identify activities performed by departments, plan necessary activity levels, identify resources required to perform these activities, and budget the resources.

P1 Prepare each component of a master budget and link each to the budgeting process. The term *master budget* refers to a collection of individual component budgets. Each component budget is designed to guide persons responsible for activities covered by that component. A master budget must reflect the components of a company and their interaction in pursuit of company goals.

P2 Link both operating and capital expenditures budgets to budgeted financial statements. The operating budgets, capital expenditures budget, and cash budget contain much of the information to prepare a budgeted income statement for the budget period and a budgeted balance sheet at the end of the budget period. Budgeted financial statements show the expected financial consequences of the planned activities described in the budgets.

P3[A] Prepare production and manufacturing budgets. A manufacturer must prepare a *production budget* instead of a purchases budget. A *manufacturing budget* shows the budgeted production costs for direct materials, direct labor, and overhead.

Guidance Answers to **Decision Maker** and **Decision Ethics**

Budget Staffer Your superior's actions appear unethical because she is using private information for personal gain. As a budget staffer, you are low in the company's hierarchical structure and probably unable to confront this superior directly. You should inform an individual with a position of authority within the organization about your concerns.

Entrepreneur You must deal with two issues. First, because fashions and designs frequently change, you cannot heavily rely on previous budgets. As a result, you must carefully analyze the market to understand what designs are in vogue. This will help you plan the product mix and estimate demand. The second issue is the budgeting period. An annual sales budget may be unreliable because tastes can quickly change. Your best bet might be to prepare monthly and quarterly sales budgets that you continuously monitor and revise.

Environmental Manager You are unlikely to have data on this new position to use in preparing your budget. In this situation, you can use activity-based budgeting. This requires developing a list of activities to conduct, the resources required to perform these activities, and the expenses associated with these resources. You should challenge yourself to be absolutely certain that the listed activities are necessary and that the listed resources are required.

Guidance Answers to **Quick Checks**

1. Major benefits include promoting a focus on the future; providing a basis for evaluating performance; providing a source of motivation; coordinating the departments of a business; and communicating plans and instructions.
2. The budget committee's responsibility is to provide guidance to ensure that budget figures are realistic and coordinated.
3. Budget periods usually coincide with accounting periods and therefore cover a month, quarter, or a year. Budgets can also be prepared for longer time periods, such as five years.
4. Rolling budgets are budgets that are periodically revised in the ongoing process of continuous budgeting.
5. A master budget is a comprehensive or overall plan for the company that is generally expressed in monetary terms.
6. *b*
7. The master budget includes operating budgets, the capital expenditures budget, and financial budgets.
8. *c*; Computed as $(60\% \times 140) + 120 - 50 = 154$.
9. Merchandisers prepare merchandise purchases budgets; manufacturers prepare production and manufacturing budgets.
10. A just-in-time system keeps the level of inventory to a minimum and orders merchandise or materials to meet immediate sales demand. A safety stock system maintains an inventory that is large enough to meet sales demands plus an amount to satisfy unexpected sales demands and an amount to cover delayed shipments from suppliers.
11. *a*
12. (a) Operating budgets (such as sales, selling expense, and administrative budgets), (b) capital expenditures budget, (c) financial budgets: cash budget, budgeted income statement, and budgeted balance sheet.

mhhe.com/larson

Key Terms

Key Terms are available at the book's Website for learning and testing in an online Flashcard Format.

Activity-based budgeting (ABB) (p. 917)
Budget (p. 904)
Budgeted balance sheet (p. 916)
Budgeted income statement (p. 916)
Budgeting (p. 904)
Capital expenditures budget (p. 913)
Cash budget (p. 914)
Continuous budgeting (p. 906)
General and administrative expense budget (p. 912)
Manufacturing budget (p. 923)
Master budget (p. 908)
Merchandise purchases budget (p. 911)
Production budget (p. 923)
Rolling budgets (p. 906)
Safety stock (p. 911)
Sales budget (p. 910)
Selling expense budget (p. 912)

Personal Interactive Quiz

Personal Interactive Quizzes A and B are available at the book's Website to reinforce and assess your learning.

Superscript letter A denotes assignments based on Appendix 23A.

Discussion Questions

1. Identify at least three roles that budgeting plays in helping managers control and monitor a business.
2. What two common benchmarks can be used to evaluate actual performance? Which of the two is generally more useful?
3. What is the benefit of continuous budgeting?
4. Identify three usual time horizons for short-term planning and budgets.
5. Why should each department participate in preparing its own budget?
6. How does budgeting help management coordinate and plan business activities?
7. Why is the sales budget so important to the budgeting process?
8. What is a selling expense budget? What is a capital expenditures budget?
9. Budgeting promotes good decision making by requiring managers to conduct ______ and by focusing their attention on the ______.
10. What is a cash budget? Why must operating budgets and the capital expenditures budget be prepared before the cash budget?
11. [A]What is the difference between a production budget and a manufacturing budget?
12. Would a franchise owner of a **Krispy Kreme** store participate more in budgeting than a manager for a corporate owned Krispy Kreme retail store? Explain.

13. Does the manager of a local **Tastykake** retail outlet participate in long-term budgeting? Explain.

14. Assume that **Harley-Davidson**'s V-Rod division is charged with preparing a master budget. Identify the participants—for example, the sales manager for the sales budget—and describe the information each person provides in preparing the master budget.

Harley-Davidson

Red numbers denote Discussion Questions that involve decision-making.

***Homework Manager** repeats all numerical Quick Studies on the book's Website with new numbers.*

QUICK STUDY

QS 23-1
Budgeting process C2

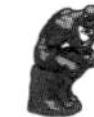

Good management includes good budgeting. (1) Explain why the bottom-up approach to budgeting is considered a more successful management technique than a top-down approach. (2) Provide an example of implementation of the bottom-up approach to budgeting.

QS 23-2
Purchases budget P1

Rockgate Company's July sales budget calls for sales of $400,000. The store expects to begin July with $40,000 of inventory and to end the month with $50,000 of inventory. Gross margin is typically 30% of sales. Determine the budgeted cost of merchandise purchases for July.

QS 23-3
Components of a master budget C3

Which one of the following sets of items are all necessary components of the master budget?

1. Sales budget, operating budgets, and historical financial budgets.
2. Operating budgets, historical income statement, and budgeted balance sheet.
3. Operating budgets, financial budgets, and capital expenditures budget.
4. Prior sales reports, capital expenditures budget, and financial budgets.

QS 23-4
Budget motivation C1

The motivation of employees is one goal of budgeting. Identify three guidelines that organizations should follow if budgeting is to serve effectively as a source of motivation for employees.

QS 23-5
Computing budgeted accounts receivable P2

Treehouse Company anticipates total sales for June and July of $420,000 and $398,000, respectively. Cash sales are normally 60% of total sales. Of the credit sales, 10% are collected in the same month as the sale, 70% are collected during the first month after the sale, and the remaining 20% are collected in the second month. Determine the amount of accounts receivable reported on Treehouse's budgeted balance sheet as of July 31.

Use the following information to prepare a cash budget for the month ended on March 31 for Sosa Company. The budget should show expected cash receipts and cash disbursements for the month of March and the balance expected on March 31.

a. Beginning cash balance on March 1, $82,000.
b. Cash receipts from sales, $300,000.
c. Budgeted cash disbursements for purchases, $120,000.
d. Budgeted cash disbursements for salaries, $80,000.
e. Other budgeted cash expenses, $55,000.
f. Cash repayment of bank loan, $30,000.

QS 23-6
Cash budget
P1 P2

Activity-based budgeting is a budget system based on *expected activities.* (1) Describe activity-based budgeting, and explain its preparation of budgets. (2) How does activity-based budgeting differ from traditional budgeting?

QS 23-7
Activity-based budgeting
A1

Goldenlook Company manufactures watches and has a JIT policy that ending inventory must equal 20% of the next month's sales. Goldenlook estimates that October's actual ending inventory will consist of 95,000 watches. November and December sales are estimated to be 350,000 and 400,000 watches, respectively. Calculate the number of watches to be produced that would appear on Goldenlook's production budget for the month of November.

QS 23-8A
Production budget
P3

Homework Manager repeats all numerical Exercises on the book's Website with new numbers.

EXERCISES

Formworks Company prepares monthly budgets. The current budget plans for a September ending inventory of 15,000 units. Company policy is to end each month with merchandise inventory equal to a specified percent of budgeted sales for the following month. Budgeted sales and merchandise purchases for the three most recent months follow. (1) Prepare the merchandise purchases budget for the months of July, August, and September. (2) Compute the ratio of ending inventory to the next month's sales for each budget prepared in part 1. (3) How many units are budgeted for sale in October?

Exercise 23-1
Preparation of merchandise purchases budgets (for three periods)
C3 P1

	Sales (Units)	Purchases (Units)
July	120,000	138,000
August	210,000	204,000
September	180,000	159,000

Check July budgeted purchases, $138,000

Kasik Co. budgeted the following cash receipts and cash disbursements for the first three months of next year.

Exercise 23-2
Preparation of cash budgets (for three periods)
C3 P2

	Cash Receipts	Cash Disbursements
January	$500,000	$450,000
February	300,000	250,000
March	400,000	500,000

Check January ending cash balance, $30,000

According to a credit agreement with the company's bank, Kasik promises to have a minimum cash balance of $30,000 at each month-end. In return, the bank has agreed that the company can borrow up to $150,000 at an annual interest rate of 12%, paid on the last day of each month. The interest is computed based on the beginning balance of the loan for the month. The company has a cash balance of $30,000 and a loan balance of $60,000 at January 1. Prepare monthly cash budgets for each of the first three months of next year.

Exercise 23-3
Preparation of a cash budget
C3 P2

Use the following information to prepare the July cash budget for Sanchez Co. It should show expected cash receipts and cash disbursements for the month and the cash balance expected on July 31.

a. Beginning cash balance on July 1: $50,000.
b. Cash receipts from sales: 30% is collected in the month of sale, 50% in the next month, and 20% in the second month after sale (uncollectible accounts are negligible and can be ignored). Sales amounts are: May (actual), $1,720,000; June (actual), $1,200,000; and July (budgeted), $1,400,000.
c. Payments on merchandise purchases: 60% in the month of purchase and 40% in the month following purchase. Purchases amounts are: June (actual), $430,000; and July (budgeted), $600,000.
d. Budgeted cash disbursements for salaries in July: $211,000.
e. Budgeted depreciation expense for July: $12,000.
f. Other cash expenses budgeted for July: $150,000.
g. Accrued income taxes due in July: $80,000.
h. Bank loan interest due in July: $6,600.

Check Ending cash balance, $434,400

Exercise 23-4
Preparing a budgeted income statement and balance sheet
C3 P2

Use the information in Exercise 23-3 and the following additional information to prepare a budgeted income statement for the month of July and a budgeted balance sheet for July 31:

a. Cost of goods sold is 44% of sales.
b. Inventory at the end of June is $80,000 and at the end of July is $64,000.
c. Salaries payable on June 30 are $50,000 and are expected to be $40,000 on July 31.
d. The equipment account balance is $1,600,000 on July 31. On June 30, the accumulated depreciation on equipment is $280,000.
e. The $6,600 cash payment of interest represents the 1% monthly expense on a bank loan of $660,000.
f. Income taxes payable on July 31 are $124,320, and the income tax rate applicable to the company is 30%.
g. The only other balance sheet accounts are: Common Stock, with a balance of $600,000 on June 30; and Retained Earnings, with a balance of $1,072,000 on June 30.

Check Net income, $290,080; Total assets, $3,026,400

Exercise 23-5
Computing budgeted cash payments for purchases
C3 P2

Powerdyne Company's cost of goods sold is consistently 60% of sales. The company plans to carry ending merchandise inventory for each month equal to 40% of the next month's budgeted cost of goods sold. All merchandise is purchased on credit, and 50% of the purchases made during a month is paid for in that month. Another 35% is paid for during the first month after purchase, and the remaining 15% is paid for during the second month after purchase. Expected sales are: August (actual), $150,000; September (actual), $350,000; October (estimated), $200,000; November (estimated), $300,000. Use this information to determine October's expected cash payments for purchases. (*Hint:* Use the layout of Exhibit 23.8, but revised for the facts given here.)

Check Budgeted purchases: August, $138,000; October, $144,000

Exercise 23-6
Computing budgeted purchases and costs of goods sold
C3 P1 P2

Sand Dollar Company purchases all merchandise on credit. It recently budgeted the following month-end accounts payable balances and merchandise inventory balances. Cash payments on accounts payable during each month are expected to be: May, $1,300,000; June, $1,450,000; July, $1,350,000; and August, $1,400,000. Use the available information to compute the budgeted amounts of (1) merchandise purchases for June, July, and August, and (2) cost of goods sold for June, July, and August.

	Accounts Payable	Merchandise Inventory
May 31	$120,000	$250,000
June 30	170,000	400,000
July 31	200,000	300,000
August 31	160,000	330,000

Check June purchases, $1,500,000; June cost of goods sold, $1,350,000

Exercise 23-7
Computing budgeted accounts payable and purchases P1 P2

Sound Check, a merchandising company specializing in home computer speakers, budgets its monthly cost of goods sold to equal 70% of sales. Its inventory policy calls for ending inventory in each month to equal 25% of the next month's budgeted cost of goods sold. All purchases are on credit, and 20% of the purchases in a month is paid for in the same month. Another 50% is paid for during the first month after purchase, and the remaining 30% is paid for in the second month after purchase. The following sales budgets are set: July, $300,000; August, $240,000; September, $270,000; October, $240,000; and November, $210,000. Compute the following: (1) budgeted merchandise purchases for July, August, September, and October; (2) budgeted payments on accounts payable for September and October; and (3) budgeted ending balances of accounts payable for September and October.

Check July purchases, $199,500; Sept. payments on accts. pay., $183,225

Exercise 23-8[A]
Preparing production budgets (for two periods) P3

Nascar Company manufactures an innovative automobile transmission for electric cars. Management predicts that ending inventory for the first quarter will be 37,500 units. The following unit sales of the transmissions are expected during the rest of the year: second quarter, 225,000 units; third quarter, 262,500 units; and fourth quarter, 237,500 units. Company policy calls for the ending inventory of a quarter to equal 20% of the next quarter's budgeted sales. Prepare a production budget for both the second and third quarters that shows the number of transmissions to manufacture.

Check Second quarter production, 240,000

PROBLEM SET A

Problem 23-1A
Preparation and analysis of merchandise purchases budgets

C3 P1

eXcel

mhhe.com/larson

Pinsetter's Supply is a merchandiser of three different products. The company's February 28 inventories are footwear, 15,500 units; sports equipment, 70,000 units; and apparel, 40,000 units. Management believes that excessive inventories have accumulated for all three products. As a result, a new policy dictates that ending inventory in any month should equal 40% of the expected unit sales for the following month. Expected sales in units for March, April, May, and June follow:

	Budgeted Sales in Units			
	March	April	May	June
Footwear	10,000	20,000	30,000	33,000
Sports equipment	66,000	85,000	90,000	80,000
Apparel	36,000	30,000	30,000	18,000

Required

1. Prepare a merchandise purchases budget (in units) for each product for each of the months of March, April, and May.

Check (1) March budgeted purchases: Footwear, 2,500; Sports equip., 30,000; Apparel, 8,000

Analysis Component

2. The purchases budgets in part 1 should reflect fewer purchases of all three products in March compared to those in April and May. What factor caused fewer purchases to be planned? Suggest business conditions that would cause this factor to both occur and impact the company in this way.

Problem 23-2A
Preparation of cash budgets (for three periods)

C3 P2

eXcel

mhhe.com/larson

During the last week of August, Apache Arts Company's owner approaches the bank for an $80,000 loan to be made on September 2 and repaid on November 30 with annual interest of 12%, for an interest cost of $2,400. The owner plans to increase the store's inventory by $60,000 during September and needs the loan to pay for inventory acquisitions. The bank's loan officer needs more information about Apache Arts' ability to repay the loan and asks the owner to forecast the store's November 30 cash position. On September 1, Apache Arts is expected to have a $3,000 cash balance, $135,000 of accounts receivable, and $100,000 of accounts payable. Its budgeted sales, merchandise purchases, and various cash disbursements for the next three months follow:

	Budgeted Figures*	September	October	November
2	Sales	$220,000	$300,000	$380,000
3	Merchandise purchases	210,000	180,000	220,000
4	Cash disbursements			
5	Payroll	16,000	17,000	18,000
6	Rent	6,000	6,000	6,000
7	Other cash expenses	64,000	8,000	7,000
8	Repayment of bank loan			80,000
9	Interest on the bank loan			2,400
10				

* Operations began in August; August sales were $180,000 and purchases were $100,000.

The budgeted September merchandise purchases include the inventory increase. All sales are on account. Company experience is that 25% of credit sales is collected in the month of the sale, 45% in the month following the sale, 20% in the second month, 9% in the third, and the remainder is uncollectible. Applying these percents to the August credit sales, for example, shows that $81,000 of the $180,000 will be collected in September, $36,000 in October, and $16,200 in November. All merchandise is purchased on credit; 80% of the balance is paid in the month following a purchase, and the remaining 20% is paid in the second month. For example, of the $100,000 August purchases, $80,000 will be paid in September and $20,000 in October.

Required

Check Budgeted cash balance: September, $53,000; October, $44,000; November, $34,800

Prepare a cash budget for September, October, and November for Apache Arts Company. Show supporting calculations as needed.

Problem 23-3A
Preparation and analysis of cash budgets with supporting inventory and purchases budgets

C3 P2  

Abacus Company sells its product for $125 per unit. Its actual and projected sales follow:

	Units	Dollars
April (actual)	8,000	$1,000,000
May (actual)	4,000	500,000
June (budgeted)	12,000	1,500,000
July (budgeted)	6,000	750,000
August (budgeted)	7,600	950,000

All sales are on credit. Recent experience shows that 20% of credit sales is collected in the month of the sale, 30% in the month after the sale, 48% in the second month after the sale, and 2% proves to be uncollectible. The product's purchase price is $100 per unit. All purchases are payable within 12 days. Thus, 60% of purchases made in a month is paid in that month and the other 40% is paid in the next month. Abacus has a policy to maintain an ending monthly inventory of 25% of the next month's unit sales plus a safety stock of 100 units. The April 30 and May 31 actual inventory levels are consistent with this policy. Selling and administrative expenses for the year are $1,200,000 and are paid evenly throughout the year in cash. The company's minimum cash balance at month-end is $60,000. This minimum is maintained, if necessary, by borrowing cash from the bank. If the balance exceeds $60,000, the company repays as much of the loan as it can without going below the minimum. This type of loan carries an annual 9% interest rate. On May 31, the loan balance is $32,000, and the company's cash balance is $60,000.

Required

Check (1) Cash collections: June, $930,000; July, $840,000

1. Prepare a table that shows the computation of cash collections of its credit sales (accounts receivable) in each of the months of June and July.
2. Prepare a table that shows the computation of budgeted ending inventories (in units) for April, May, June, and July.

(3) Budgeted purchases: May, $600,000; June, $1,050,000

3. Prepare the merchandise purchases budget for May, June, and July. Report calculations in units and then show the dollar amount of purchases for each month.
4. Prepare a table showing the computation of cash payments on product purchases for June and July.

(5) Budgeted ending loan balance: June, $72,240; July, $136,782

5. Prepare a cash budget for June and July, including any loan activity and interest expense. Compute the loan balance at the end of each month.

Analysis Component

6. Refer to your answer to part 5. Abacus's cash budget indicates the company will need to borrow more than $40,000 in June and more than $60,000 in July. Suggest some reasons that knowing this information in May would be helpful to management.

Problem 23-4A
Preparation and analysis of budgeted income statements

Lilliput, a one-product mail-order firm, buys its product for $60 per unit and sells it for $130 per unit. The sales staff receives a 10% commission on the sale of each unit. Its December income statement follows:

LILLIPUT COMPANY Income Statement For Month Ended December 31, 2005	
Sales	$1,300,000
Cost of goods sold	600,000
Gross profit	700,000
Expenses	
Sales commissions (10%)	130,000
Advertising	200,000
Store rent	24,000
Administrative salaries	40,000
Depreciation	50,000
Other expenses	12,000
Total expenses	456,000
Net income	$ 244,000

Management expects December's results to be repeated in January, February, and March of 2006 without any changes in strategy. Management, however, has an alternative plan. It believes that unit sales will increase at a rate of 10% *each* month for the next three months (beginning with January) if the item's selling price is reduced to $115 per unit and advertising expenses are increased by 25% and remain at that level for all three months. The cost of its product will remain at $60 per unit, the sales staff will continue to earn a 10% commission, and the remaining expenses will stay the same.

Required

1. Prepare budgeted income statements for each of the months of January, February, and March that show the expected results from implementing the proposed changes. Use a three-column format, with one column for each month.

Check (1) Budgeted net income: January, $102,500; February, $150,350; March, $202,985

Analysis Component

2. Use the budgeted income statements from part 1 to recommend whether management should implement the proposed changes. Explain.

Problem 23-5A
Preparation of a complete master budget
C2 C3 P1 P2

Near the end of 2005, the management of Simid Sports Co., a merchandising company, prepared the following estimated balance sheet for December 31, 2005:

SIMID SPORTS COMPANY Estimated Balance Sheet December 31, 2005		
Assets		
Cash		$ 18,000
Accounts receivable		262,500
Inventory		75,000
Total current assets		355,500
Equipment	$270,000	
Less accumulated depreciation	33,750	236,250
Total assets		$591,750
Liabilities and Equity		
Accounts payable	$180,000	
Bank loan payable	7,500	
Taxes payable (due 3/15/2006)	45,000	
Total liabilities		$232,500
Common stock	236,250	
Retained earnings	123,000	
Total stockholders' equity		359,250
Total liabilities and equity		$591,750

To prepare a master budget for January, February, and March of 2006, management gathers the following information:

a. Simid Sports' single product is purchased for $30 per unit and resold for $55 per unit. The expected inventory level of 2,500 units on December 31, 2005, is more than management's desired level for 2006, which is 20% of the next month's expected sales (in units). Expected sales are: January, 3,500 units; February, 4,500 units; March, 5,500 units; and April, 5,000 units.

b. Cash sales and credit sales represent 25% and 75%, respectively, of total sales. Of the credit sales, 60% is collected in the first month after the month of sale and 40% in the second month after the month of sale. For the December 31, 2005, accounts receivable balance, $62,500 is collected in January and the remaining $200,000 is collected in February.

c. Merchandise purchases are paid for as follows: 20% in the first month after the month of purchase and 80% in the second month after the month of purchase. For the December 31, 2005, accounts payable balance, $40,000 is paid in January and the remaining $140,000 is paid in February.

d. Sales commissions equal to 20% of sales are paid each month. Sales salaries (excluding commissions) are $30,000 per year.

e. General and administrative salaries are $72,000 per year. Maintenance expense equals $1,000 per month and is paid in cash.

f. Equipment reported in the December 31, 2005, balance sheet was purchased in January 2005. It is being depreciated over eight years under the straight-line method with no salvage value. The following amounts for new equipment purchases are planned in the coming quarter: January, $18,000; February, $48,000; and March, $14,400. This equipment will be depreciated under the straight-line method over eight years with no salvage value. A full month's depreciation is taken for the month in which equipment is purchased.

g. The company plans to acquire land at the end of March at a cost of $75,000, which will be paid with cash on the last day of the month.

h. Simid Sports has a working arrangement with its bank to obtain additional loans as needed. The interest rate is 12% per year, and interest is paid at each month-end based on the beginning balance. Partial or full payments on these loans can be made on the last day of the month. The company has agreed to maintain a minimum ending cash balance of $12,500 in each month.

i. The income tax rate for the company is 40%. Income taxes on the first quarter's income will not be paid until April 15.

Required

Prepare a master budget for each of the first three months of 2006; include the following component budgets (show supporting calculations as needed, and round amounts to the nearest dollar):

1. Monthly sales budgets (showing both budgeted unit sales and dollar sales).

2. Monthly merchandise purchases budgets.

3. Monthly selling expense budgets.

4. Monthly general and administrative expense budgets.

5. Monthly capital expenditures budgets.

6. Monthly cash budgets.

7. Budgeted income statement for the entire first quarter (not for each month).

8. Budgeted balance sheet as of March 31, 2006.

Check (2) Budgeted purchases: January, $57,000; February, $141,000
(3) Budgeted selling expenses: January, $41,000; February, $52,000
(6) Ending cash bal.: January, $15,050; February, $105,150
(8) Budgeted total assets at March 31, $784,325

Problem 23-6A[A]
Preparing production and direct materials budgets
C3 P3

Diamond Slope Company produces snow skis. Each ski requires 2 pounds of carbon fiber. The company's management predicts that 7,000 skis and 10,000 pounds of carbon fiber will be in inventory on June 30 of the current year and that 120,000 skis will be sold during the next (third) quarter. Management wants to end the third quarter with 4,000 skis and 5,000 pounds of carbon fiber in inventory. Carbon fiber can be purchased for $12 per pound.

Required

1. Prepare the third-quarter production budget for skis.

2. Prepare the third-quarter direct materials (carbon fiber) budget; include the dollar cost of purchases.

Check (1) Units manuf., 117,000;
(2) Cost of carbon fiber purchases, $2,748,000

PROBLEM SET B

Problem 23-1B
Preparation and analysis of merchandise purchases budgets

C3 P1 

H2O Sports Corp. is a merchandiser of three different products. The company's March 31 inventories are water skis, 40,000 units; tow ropes, 90,000 units; and life jackets, 250,000 units. Management believes that excessive inventories have accumulated for all three products. As a result, a new policy dictates that ending inventory in any month should equal 10% of the expected unit sales for the following month. Expected sales in units for April, May, June, and July follow:

	Budgeted Sales in Units			
	April	May	June	July
Water skis	70,000	90,000	130,000	140,000
Tow ropes	100,000	90,000	110,000	100,000
Life jackets	300,000	260,000	310,000	260,000

Required

1. Prepare a merchandise purchases budget (in units) for each product for each of the months of April, May, and June.

Check (1) April budgeted purchases: Water skis, 39,000; Tow ropes, 19,000; Life jackets, 76,000

Analysis Component

2. The purchases budgets in part 1 should reflect fewer purchases of all three products in April compared to those in May and June. What factor caused fewer purchases to be planned? Suggest business conditions that would cause this factor to both occur and affect the company as it has.

Problem 23-2B
Preparation of cash budgets (for three periods)

C3 P2

During the last week of March, Siro Stereo's owner approaches the bank for a $125,000 loan to be made on April 1 and repaid on June 30 with annual interest of 10%, for an interest cost of $3,125. The owner plans to increase the store's inventory by $100,000 in April and needs the loan to pay for inventory acquisitions. The bank's loan officer needs more information about Siro Stereo's ability to repay the loan and asks the owner to forecast the store's June 30 cash position. On April 1, Siro Stereo is expected to have a $12,000 cash balance, $121,500 of accounts receivable, and $90,000 of accounts payable. Its budgeted sales, merchandise purchases, and various cash disbursements for the next three months follow:

	Budgeted Figures*	April	May	June
2	Sales	$350,000	$500,000	$550,000
3	Merchandise purchases	250,000	200,000	190,000
4	Cash disbursements			
5	Payroll	22,500	30,000	37,500
6	Rent	12,000	12,000	12,000
7	Other cash expenses	9,000	13,500	16,500
8	Repayment of bank loan			125,000
9	Interest on the bank loan			3,125
10				

* Operations began in March; March sales were $135,000 and purchases were $90,000.

The budgeted April merchandise purchases include the inventory increase. All sales are on account. Company experience is that 10% of credit sales is collected in the month of the sale, 60% in the month following the sale, 25% in the second month, 3% in the third, and the remainder is uncollectible. Applying these percents to the March credit sales, for example, shows that $81,000 of the $135,000 will be collected in April, $33,750 in May, and $4,050 in June. All merchandise is purchased on credit; 80% of the balance is paid in the month following a purchase and the remaining 20% is paid in the second month. For example, of the $90,000 March purchases, $72,000 will be paid in April and $18,000 in May.

Required

Prepare a cash budget for April, May, and June for Siro Stereo. Show supporting calculations as needed.

Check Budgeted cash balance: April, $137,500; May, $157,750; June, $200,175

Problem 23-3B
Preparation and analysis of cash budgets with supporting inventory and purchases budgets

 P2 

LaRocca Company sells its product for $20 per unit. Its actual and projected sales follow:

	Units	Dollars
January (actual)	18,000	$360,000
February (actual)	27,000	540,000
March (budgeted)	15,000	300,000
April (budgeted)	27,000	540,000
May (budgeted)	33,000	660,000

All sales are on credit. Recent experience shows that 40% of credit sales is collected in the month of the sale, 30% in the month after the sale, 25% in the second month after the sale, and 5% proves to be uncollectible. The product's purchase price is $12 per unit. All purchases are payable within 21 days. Thus, 30% of purchases made in a month is paid in that month and the other 70% is paid in the next month. LaRocca has a policy to maintain an ending monthly inventory of 30% of the next month's unit sales plus a safety stock of 300 units. The January 31 and February 28 actual inventory levels are consistent with this policy. Selling and administrative expenses for the year are $1,440,000 and are paid evenly throughout the year in cash. The company's minimum cash balance for month-end is $45,000. This minimum is maintained, if necessary, by borrowing cash from the bank. If the balance exceeds $45,000, the company repays as much of the loan as it can without going below the minimum. This type of loan carries an annual 12% interest rate. At February 28, the loan balance is $12,000, and the company's cash balance is $45,000.

Required

Check (1) Cash collections: March, $372,000; April, $441,000

1. Prepare a table that shows the computation of cash collections of its credit sales (accounts receivable) in each of the months of March and April.

2. Prepare a table showing the computations of budgeted ending inventories (units) for January, February, March, and April.

(3) Budgeted purchases: February, $280,800; March, $223,200

3. Prepare the merchandise purchases budget for February, March, and April. Report calculations in units and then show the dollar amount of purchases for each month.

4. Prepare a table showing the computation of cash payments on product purchases for March and April.

(5) Ending cash balance: March, $45,000, April, $82,204

5. Prepare a cash budget for March and April, including any loan activity and interest expense. Compute the loan balance at the end of each month.

Analysis Component

6. Refer to your answer to part 5. LaRocca's cash budget indicates the company must borrow additional funds at the end of March. Suggest some reasons that knowing this information in February would be helpful to management.

Problem 23-4B
Preparation and analysis of budgeted income statements

C3 P2 

Computa-Cations buys its product for $20 and sells it for $50 per unit. The sales staff receives a 10% commission on the sale of each unit. Its June income statement follows:

COMPUTA-CATIONS COMPANY Income Statement For Month Ended June 30, 2005	
Sales	$1,000,000
Cost of goods sold	400,000
Gross profit	600,000
Expenses	
Sales commissions (10%)	100,000
Advertising	100,000
Store rent	10,000
Administrative salaries	20,000
Depreciation	12,000
Other expenses	24,000
Total expenses	266,000
Net income	$ 334,000

Management expects June's results to be repeated in July, August, and September without any changes in strategy. Management, however, has another plan. It believes that unit sales will increase at a rate of 10% *each* month for the next three months (beginning with July) if the item's selling price is reduced to $45 per unit and advertising expenses are increased by 20% and remain at that level for all three months. The cost of its product will remain at $20 per unit, the sales staff will continue to earn a 10% commission, and the remaining expenses will stay the same.

Required

1. Prepare budgeted income statements for each of the months of July, August, and September that show the expected results from implementing the proposed changes. Use a three-column format, with one column for each month.

Check Budgeted net income: July, $265,000; August, $310,100; September, $359,710

Analysis Component

2. Use the budgeted income statements from part 1 to recommend whether management should implement the proposed plan. Explain.

Problem 23-5B
Preparation of a complete master budget
C2 C3 P1 P2

Near the end of 2005, the management of Oasis Corp., a merchandising company, prepared the following estimated balance sheet for December 31, 2005:

OASIS CORPORATION
Estimated Balance Sheet
December 31, 2005

Assets		
Cash		$ 160,000
Accounts receivable		400,000
Inventory		180,000
Total current assets		740,000
Equipment	$1,200,000	
Less accumulated depreciation	120,000	1,080,000
Total assets		$1,820,000
Liabilities and Equity		
Accounts payable	$ 300,000	
Bank loan payable	20,000	
Taxes payable (due 3/15/2006)	200,000	
Total liabilities		$ 520,000
Common stock	1,500,000	
Retained earnings (deficit)	(200,000)	
Total stockholders' equity		1,300,000
Total liabilities and equity		$1,820,000

To prepare a master budget for January, February, and March of 2006, management gathers the following information:

a. Oasis Corp.'s single product is purchased for $10 per unit and resold for $24 per unit. The expected inventory level of 18,000 units on December 31, 2005, is more than management's desired level for 2006, which is 40% of the next month's expected sales (in units). Expected sales are: January, 30,000 units; February, 24,000 units; March, 40,000 units; and April, 50,000 units.

b. Cash sales and credit sales represent 40% and 60%, respectively, of total sales. Of the credit sales, 70% is collected in the first month after the month of sale and 30% in the second month after the month of sale. For the $400,000 accounts receivable balance at December 31, 2005, $280,000 is collected in January 2006 and the remaining $120,000 is collected in February 2006.

c. Merchandise purchases are paid for as follows: 80% in the first month after the month of purchase and 20% in the second month after the month of purchase. For the $300,000 accounts payable balance at December 31, 2005, $240,000 is paid in January 2006 and the remaining $60,000 is paid in February 2006.

d. Sales commissions equal to 10% of sales are paid each month. Sales salaries (excluding commissions) are $288,000 per year.

e. General and administrative salaries are $336,000 per year. Maintenance expense equals $6,000 per month and is paid in cash.

f. Equipment reported in the December 31, 2005, balance sheet was purchased in January 2005. It is being depreciated over 10 years under the straight-line method with no salvage value. The following amounts for new equipment purchases are planned in the coming quarter: January, $240,000; February, $120,000; and March, $96,000. This equipment will be depreciated using the straight-line method over 10 years with no salvage value. A full month's depreciation is taken for the month in which equipment is purchased.

g. The company plans to acquire land at the end of March at a cost of $232,000, which will be paid with cash on the last day of the month.

h. Oasis Corp. has a working arrangement with its bank to obtain additional loans as needed. The interest rate is 12% per year, and interest is paid at each month-end based on the beginning balance. Partial or full payments on these loans can be made on the last day of the month. Oasis has agreed to maintain a minimum ending cash balance of $160,000 in each month.

i. The income tax rate for the company is 30%. Income taxes on the first quarter's income will not be paid until April 15.

Required

Prepare a master budget for each of the first three months of 2006; include the following component budgets (show supporting calculations as needed, and round amounts to the nearest dollar):

1. Monthly sales budgets (showing both budgeted unit sales and dollar sales).
2. Monthly merchandise purchases budgets.
3. Monthly selling expense budgets.
4. Monthly general and administrative expense budgets.
5. Monthly capital expenditures budgets.
6. Monthly cash budgets.
7. Budgeted income statement for the entire first quarter (not for each month).
8. Budgeted balance sheet as of March 31, 2006.

Check (2) Budgeted purchases: January, $216,000; February, $304,000; (3) Budgeted selling expenses: January, $96,000; February, $81,600

(6) Ending cash bal.: January, $160,000; February, $281,578 (8) Budgeted total assets at March 31, $2,768,880

Problem 23-6B^A
Preparing production and direct materials budgets
C3 P3

RBI Company produces baseball bats. Each bat requires 4 pounds of aluminum alloy. Management predicts that 10,000 bats and 28,000 pounds of aluminum alloy will be in inventory on March 31 of the current year and that 100,000 bats will be sold during this year's second quarter. Management wants to end the second quarter with 3,000 finished bats and 2,000 pounds of aluminum alloy in inventory. Aluminum alloy can be purchased for $3 per pound.

Required

1. Prepare the second-quarter production budget for bats.
2. Prepare the second-quarter direct materials (aluminum alloy) budget; include the dollar cost of purchases.

Check (1) Units manuf., 93,000; (2) Cost of aluminum purchases, $1,038,000

PROBLEM SET C

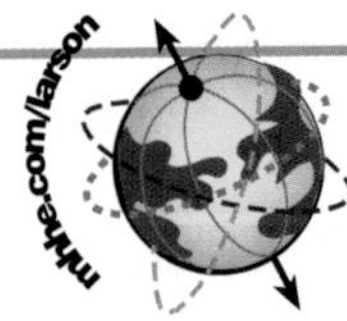

Problem Set C is available at the book's Website to further reinforce and assess your learning.

SERIAL PROBLEM

Success Systems

(This serial problem began in Chapter 1 and continues through most of the book. If previous chapter segments were not completed, the serial problem can begin at this point. It is helpful, but not necessary, for you to use the Working Papers that accompany the book.)

Kay Breeze expects second quarter 2006 sales of her new line of computer furniture to be the same as the first quarter's sales (reported below) without any changes in strategy. Monthly sales averaged 20 desk units (sales price of $2,500) and 10 chairs (sales price of $1,000).

SUCCESS SYSTEMS Segment Income Statement* For the Quarter Ended March 31, 2006	
Sales†	$180,000
Cost of goods sold‡	105,000
Gross profit	75,000
Expenses	
Sales commissions (10%)	18,000
Advertising expenses	12,000
Other fixed expenses	15,000
Total expenses	45,000
Net income	$ 30,000

* Reflects revenue and expense activity only related to the computer furniture segment.

† Revenue: (60 desks × $2,500) + (30 chairs × $1,000) = $150,000 + $30,000 = $180,000

‡ Cost of goods sold: (60 desks × $1,500) + (30 chairs × $500) = $90,000 + $15,000 = $105,000

Breeze believes that sales will increase each month for the next three months (April, 22 desks, 11 chairs; May, 24 desks, 12 chairs; June, 26 desks, 13 chairs) *if* selling prices are reduced to $2,250 for desks and $750 for chairs and advertising expenses are increased by 25% and remain at that level for all three months. The products' cost will remain at $1,500 for desks and $500 for chairs. The sales staff will continue to earn a 10% commission, and the fixed costs per month will remain at $5,000.

Required

1. Prepare budgeted income statements for each of the months of April, May, and June that show the expected results from implementing the proposed changes. Use a three-column format, with one column for each month.
2. Use the budgeted income statements from part 1 to recommend whether Breeze should implement the proposed changes. Explain.

Check (1) Budgeted income: April, $3,475; May, $4,700

BEYOND THE NUMBERS

REPORTING IN ACTION

P2 C2 C3

BTN 23-1 Financial statements often serve as a starting point in formulating the budget. You are assigned to review **Krispy Kreme**'s financial statements to determine its cash paid for dividends in the current year and the budgeted cash needed to pay its next year's dividend.

Required

1. Which financial statement(s) reports the amount of (a) cash dividends paid and (b) annual cash dividends declared? Explain where on the statement(s) this information is reported.
2. Indicate the amount of cash dividends (a) paid in the year ended February 2, 2003, and (b) to be paid (budgeted for) next year under the assumption that annual cash dividends equal 25% of the prior year's net income.

Roll On

3. Access Krispy Kreme's financial statements for a fiscal year ending after February 2, 2003, from either its Website [KrispyKreme.com] or the SEC's EDGAR database [www.SEC.gov]. Compare your answer for part 2 with actual cash dividends paid for the year ended February 2, 2003. Compute the error, if any, in your estimate. Speculate as to why dividends were higher or lower than budgeted.

COMPARATIVE ANALYSIS

P2 

BTN 23-2 One source of cash savings for a company is improved management of inventory. To illustrate, assume that **Krispy Kreme** and **Tastykake** both have $250,000 per month in sales in the Virginia area, and both forecast this level of sales per month for the next 24 months. Also assume that both Krispy Kreme and Tastykake have a 20% contribution margin and equal fixed costs, and that cost per dozen of baked goods is the only variable cost. Assume that the main difference between Krispy Kreme and Tastykake is the distribution system. Krispy Kreme bakes onsite without preservatives and requires ending inventory of only 10% of next month's sales of nonperishable items (for example, coffee) in inventory at each month-end. However, Tastykake's retail outlets are mostly offsite from the factory. Tastykake is building an improved distribution system and requires 40% of next month's sales in inventory at each month-end.

Required

1. Compute the amount by which Tastykake can reduce its inventory level if it can match Krispy Kreme's system of maintaining an inventory equal to 10% of next month's sales. (*Hint:* Focus on the facts given and only on the Virginia area.)
2. Explain how the analysis in part 1 that shows ending inventory levels for both the 40% and 10% required inventory policies can help justify a just-in-time inventory system. You can assume a 15% interest cost for resources that are tied up in ending inventory.

ETHICS CHALLENGE

C1 C2 

BTN 23-3 Both the budget process and budgets themselves can impact management actions, both positively and negatively. For instance, a common practice among not-for-profit organizations and government agencies is for management to spend any amounts remaining in a budget at the end of the budget period, a practice often called "use it or lose it." The view is that if a department manager does not spend the budgeted amount, top management will reduce next year's budget by the amount not spent. To avoid losing budget dollars, department managers often spend all budgeted amounts regardless of the value added to products or services. All of us pay for the costs associated with this budget system.

Required

Write a one-half page report to a local not-for-profit organization or government agency offering a solution to the "use it or lose it" budgeting problem.

COMMUNICATING IN PRACTICE

P1

BTN 23-4 The sales budget is usually the first and most crucial of the component budgets in a master budget because all other budgets usually rely on it for planning purposes.

Required

Assume that your company's sales staff provides information on expected sales and selling prices for items making up the sales budget. Prepare a one-page memorandum to your supervisor outlining concerns with the sales staff's input in the sales budget when its compensation is at least partly tied to these budgets. More generally, explain the importance of assessing any potential bias in information provided to the budget process.

TAKING IT TO THE NET

C2 P1 P2 

mhhe.com/larson

BTN 23-5 Access an e-budgets Website at **HelmsmanGroup.com** (by **FRx Corporation**). Review the information at this site; click on the link *CFO Tour* and examine the information provided.

Required

1. Assume the role of a senior manager in a large, multidivision company. What are the benefits of using e-budgets?
2. As a senior manager, what concerns do you have with the concept and application of e-budgets?

TEAMWORK IN ACTION

A1 

BTN 23-6 Your team is to prepare a budget report outlining the costs of attending college (full-time) for the next two semesters (30 hours) or three quarters (45 hours). This budget's focus is solely on attending college; do not include personal items in the team's budget. Your budget must include tuition, books, supplies, club fees, food, housing, and all costs associated with travel to and from college. This budgeting exercise is similar to the initial phase in activity-based budgeting. Include a list of any assumptions you use in completing the budget. Be prepared to present your budget in class.

BUSINESS WEEK ACTIVITY

C2 A1 

BTN 23-7 Read the article "A Wrong Turn for Pro Cycling" in the June 23, 2003, issue of *Business Week*. (This book's Website provides free access to this article.)

Required

1. Which corporate budget is the subject of this article?
2. Would Krispy Kreme or Tastykake be potential good fits for pro cycle sponsoring given the types of companies that have sponsored teams in the past? Explain.
3. Is sponsoring a pro cycling team ever a good investment? Explain.

ENTREPRENEURIAL DECISION

C1  

BTN 23-8 Chuang, Wenjen, and Kapner are continually in an expansion mode with their entrepreneurial business, Aquent. Their vision for expansion will require outside financing. Assume that the three Aquent owners call on a financial institution for backing and have been asked by the bankers for a detailed business plan.

Required

1. What should Aquent's business plan include?
2. How can budgeting help the three owners effectively develop and operate their business?

HITTING THE ROAD

C3 P1 

BTN 23-9 To help understand the factors impacting a sales budget, you are to visit three businesses with the same ownership or franchise membership. Record the selling prices of two identical products at each location, such as regular and premium gas sold at Texaco stations. You are likely to find a difference in prices for at least one of the three locations you visit.

Required

1. Identify at least three external factors that must be considered when setting the sales budget. (*Note:* There is a difference between internal and external factors that impact the sales budget.)
2. What factors might explain any differences identified in the prices of the businesses you visited?

GLOBAL DECISION

BTN 23-10 Access Grupo Bimbo's income statement (GrupoBimbo.com) for the year ended December 31, 2002.

Required

1. Is Grupo Bimbo's selling expense budget likely to be an important budget in its master budgeting process? Explain.
2. Identify three types of expenses that would be reported as distribution and selling expenses on Grupo Bimbo's income statement.
3. Who likely has the initial responsibility for Grupo Bimbo's selling expense budget? Explain.

"All my friends told me it was ridiculous"—Scott Jordan

24 Flexible Budgets and Standard Costs

A Look Back

Chapter 23 explained the importance of budgeting. It also described the master budget and its component budgets as well as their usefulness for planning and monitoring company activities.

A Look at This Chapter

This chapter describes flexible budgets, variance analysis, and standard costs. It explains how each is used for purposes of better controlling and monitoring business activities.

A Look Ahead

Chapter 25 focuses on capital budgeting decisions. It explains and illustrates several procedures used in evaluating short-term managerial decisions.

CAP

Conceptual

C1 Define *standard costs* and explain their computation and uses. *(p. 947)*

C2 Describe variances and what they reveal about performance. *(p. 949)*

C3 Explain how standard cost information is useful for management by exception. *(p. 958)*

Analytical

A1 Compare fixed and flexible budgets. *(p. 944)*

A2 Analyze changes in sales from expected amounts. *(p. 960)*

Procedural

P1 Prepare a flexible budget and interpret a flexible budget performance report. *(p. 945)*

P2 Compute materials and labor variances. *(p. 950)*

P3 Compute overhead variances. *(p. 954)*

P4 Prepare journal entries for standard costs and account for price and quantity variances. *(p. 958)*

Decision Feature

Vested Interest in Geek Chic

CHICAGO—Success for clothing and accessory companies usually depends on the current fad. Scott Jordan has taken a different tack, however. Jordan, a former corporate lawyer, created **Technology Enabled Clothing, LLC [TechnologyEnabledClothing.com]** and **SCOTTeVEST, LLC**, which focus on functionality. "I couldn't carry all of my electronic gadgets," says Jordan. "So the idea of technology-enabled clothing came to me." This led to another problem, he says: "The difficult part was finding a way to use the gadgets while on the go."

Jordan then assembled an expert design team to fit conduits throughout a garment that did not look "geeky." The result was *SCOTTeVEST,* a stylish, lightweight jacket with zip off sleeves, which comes in different versions, colors, and styles. Says Jordan, "I view our product as the convergence of apparel, luggage, and technology." On the first day the Website went live, he says, "I got 50,000 hits and more than 100 orders. I didn't even have a manufacturer lined up!"

The realities of business quickly became apparent. Jordan admits that he didn't have "any real management experience—so that was the tough part, having to learn about business and management from scratch." He persisted and quickly learned the importance of cost analysis and variances, flexible and fixed budgets, and performance reports. He also learned to keep tabs on sales variances because production pricing is one key to his successful performance. Complicating Jordan's analysis was the garment industry. "We had trouble to get a retailer to stock our goods," he admits. "They're so risk averse."

The company has outperformed Jordan's most optimistic budget goals. Disneyland even helped by including his vest in its "Tomorrow Land" exhibit. "We continue to create new and improved versions," says Jordan. With budgeted sales projections of $5 million for his two-year-old company, he has seemingly grasped business principles.

"I'm told the president got one [*eVEST*] with the presidential seal on it," exclaims Jordan. Now, that's one big *seal of approval!*

[Sources: *Technology Enabled Clothing Website,* January 2004; *Entrepreneur,* February 2003; *The Wall Street Journal,* January 2003; *Business Week,* September 2002; *Computer User,* January 2003.]

Budgeting helps organize and formalize management's planning activities. This chapter extends the study of budgeting to look more closely at the use of budgets to evaluate performance. Evaluations are important for controlling and monitoring business activities. This chapter also describes and illustrates the use of standard costs and variance analyses. These managerial tools are useful for both evaluating and controlling organizations and for the planning of future activities.

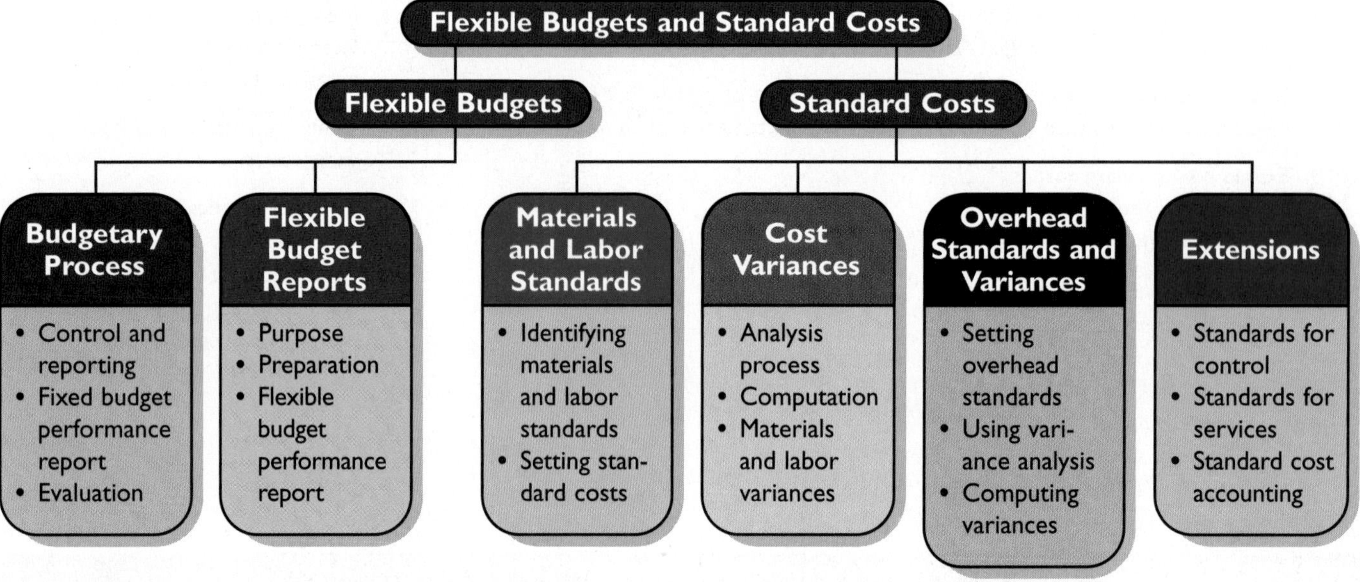

Section 1—Flexible Budgets

This section introduces fixed budgets and fixed budget performance reports. It then introduces flexible budgets and flexible budget performance reports and illustrates their advantages.

Budgetary Process

A master budget reflects management's planned objectives for a future period. The preparation of a master budget is based on a predicted level of activity such as sales volume for the budget period. This section discusses the effects on the usefulness of budget reports when the actual level of activity differs from the predicted level.

Budgetary Control and Reporting

Budgetary control refers to management's use of budgets to monitor and control a company's operations. This includes using budgets to see that planned objectives are met. **Budget reports** contain relevant information that compares actual results to planned activities. This comparison is motivated by a need to both monitor performance and control activities. Budget reports are sometimes viewed as progress reports, or *report cards,* on management's performance in achieving planned objectives. These reports can be prepared at any time and for any period. Three common periods for a budget report are a month, quarter, and year.

Point: Budget reports are often used as a base to determine bonuses of managers.

The budgetary control process involves at least four steps: (1) develop the budget from planned objectives, (2) compare actual results to budgeted amounts and analyze any differences, (3) take corrective and strategic actions, and (4) establish new planned objectives and prepare a new budget. Exhibit 24.1 shows this continual process of budgetary control. Budget

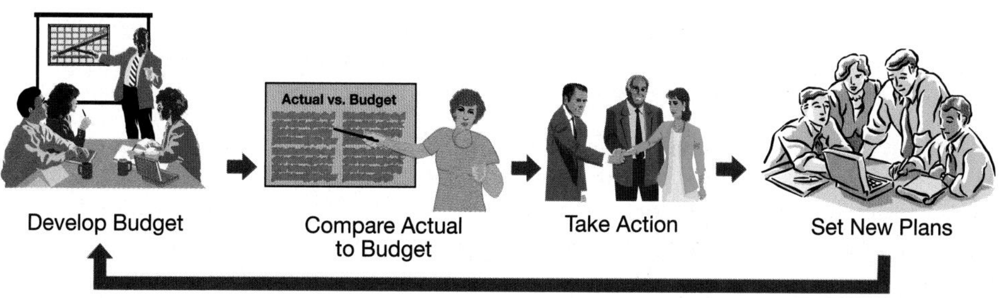

Exhibit 24.1

Process of Budgetary Control

reports and related documents are effective tools for managers to obtain the greatest benefits from this budgetary process.

Fixed Budget Performance Report

In a fixed budgetary control system, the master budget is based on a single prediction for sales volume or other activity level. The budgeted amount for each cost essentially assumes that a specific (or *fixed*) amount of sales will occur. A **fixed budget,** also called *static budget,* is based on a single predicted amount of sales or other measure of activity.

One benefit of a budget is its usefulness in comparing actual results with planned activities. Information useful for analysis is often presented for comparison in a performance report. As shown in Exhibit 24.2, a **fixed budget performance report** for Optel compares actual results for January 2005 with the results expected under its fixed budget that predicted 10,000 (composite) units of sales. Optel manufactures inexpensive eyeglasses, frames, contact lens, and related supplies. For this report, its production volume equals sales volume (its inventory level did not change).

Exhibit 24.2

Fixed Budget Performance Report

OPTEL
Fixed Budget Performance Report
For Month Ended January 31, 2005

	Fixed Budget	Actual Results	Variances*
Sales (in units)	10,000	12,000	
Sales (in dollars)	$100,000	$125,000	**$25,000 F**
Cost of goods sold			
Direct materials	10,000	13,000	**3,000 U**
Direct labor	15,000	20,000	**5,000 U**
Overhead			
Factory supplies	2,000	2,100	**100 U**
Utilities	3,000	4,000	**1,000 U**
Depreciation—Machinery	8,000	8,000	**0**
Supervisory salaries	11,000	11,000	**0**
Selling expenses			
Sales commissions	9,000	10,800	**1,800 U**
Shipping expenses	4,000	4,300	**300 U**
General and administrative expenses			
Office supplies	5,000	5,200	**200 U**
Insurance expenses	1,000	1,200	**200 U**
Depreciation—Office equipment	7,000	7,000	**0**
Administrative salaries	13,000	13,000	**0**
Total expenses	88,000	99,600	**11,600 U**
Income from operations	$ 12,000	$ 25,400	**$13,400 F**

* F = Favorable variance; and U = Unfavorable variance.

This type of performance report designates differences between budgeted and actual results as variances. We see the letters *F* and *U* located beside the numbers in the third number column of this report. Their meanings are as follows:

F = **Favorable variance** When compared to budget, the actual cost or revenue contributes to a *higher* income. That is, actual revenue is higher than budgeted revenue, or actual cost is lower than budgeted cost.

U = **Unfavorable variance** When compared to budget, the actual cost or revenue contributes to a *lower* income; actual revenue is lower than budgeted revenue, or actual cost is higher than budgeted cost.

Example: How is it that the favorable sales variance in Exhibit 24.2 is linked with so many unfavorable cost and expense variances? *Answer:* Costs have increased with the increase in sales.

This convention is common in practice and is used throughout this chapter.

Budget Reports for Evaluation

A primary use of budget reports is as a tool for management to monitor and control operations. Evaluation by Optel management is likely to focus on a variety of questions that might include these:

- Why is actual income from operations $13,400 higher than budgeted?
- Are amounts paid for each expense item too high?
- Is manufacturing using too much direct material?
- Is manufacturing using too much direct labor?

The performance report in Exhibit 24.2 provides little help in answering these questions because actual sales volume is 2,000 units higher than budgeted. A manager does not know if this higher level of sales activity is the cause of variations in total dollar sales and expenses or if other factors have influenced these amounts. This inability of fixed budget reports to adjust for changes in activity levels is a major limitation of a fixed budget performance report. That is, it fails to show whether actual costs are out of line due to a change in actual sales volume or some other factor.

Decision Insight

Natural Budget Budget reporting and evaluation are used at the **Environmental Protection Agency (EPA).** It regularly prepares performance plans and budget requests that describe performance goals, measure outcomes, and analyze variances.

Flexible Budget Reports

Purpose of Flexible Budgets

A1 Compare fixed and flexible budgets.

Topic Tackler 24-1

To help address limitations with the fixed budget performance report, particularly from the effects of changes in sales volume, management can use a flexible budget. A **flexible budget,** also called a *variable budget,* is a report based on predicted amounts of revenues and expenses corresponding to the actual level of output. Unlike fixed budgets, a flexible budget is prepared after a period's activities are complete. A flexible budget can be viewed as a fixed budget prepared at the activity level corresponding to the actual level of activity.

A flexible budget's primary purpose is to help managers evaluate past performance. It is especially useful for such an evaluation because it reflects budgeted revenues and costs based on the actual level of activity. Thus, comparisons of actual results with budgeted performance are more likely to identify the causes of any differences. This can help managers focus attention on real problem areas and implement corrective actions. This is in contrast to a fixed budget, whose primary purpose is to assist managers in planning future activities and whose numbers are based on a single predicted amount of budgeted sales or production.

Preparation of Flexible Budgets

A flexible budget is designed to reveal the effects of volume of activity on revenues and costs. To prepare a flexible budget, management relies on the distinctions between fixed and variable costs. Recall that the cost per unit of activity remains constant for variable costs so that the total amount of a variable cost changes in direct proportion to a change in activity level. The total amount of fixed cost remains unchanged regardless of changes in the level of activity within a relevant (normal) operating range. (Assume that costs can be reasonably classified as variable or fixed within a relevant range.)

P1 Prepare a flexible budget and interpret a flexible budget performance report.

When we create the numbers constituting a flexible budget, we express each variable cost as either a constant amount per unit of sales or as a percent of a sales dollar. In the case of a fixed cost, we express its budgeted amount as the total amount expected to occur at any sales volume within the relevant range.

Exhibit 24.3 shows a set of flexible budgets for Optel in January 2005. Seven of its expenses are classified as variable costs. Its remaining five expenses are fixed costs. These classifications result from management's investigation of each expense. Variable and fixed expense categories are *not* the same for every company, and we must avoid drawing conclusions from specific cases. For example, depending on the nature of a company's operations, office supplies expense can be either fixed or variable with respect to sales.

Point: Usefulness of a flexible budget depends on valid classification of variable and fixed costs. Some costs are mixed and must be analyzed to determine their variable and fixed portions.

Point: To apply these concepts, work Exercise 24-2.

Exhibit 24.3

Flexible Budgets

OPTEL
Flexible Budgets
For Month Ended January 31, 2005

	Flexible Budget				
	Variable Amount per Unit	Total Fixed Cost	Flexible Budget for Unit Sales of 10,000	Flexible Budget for Unit Sales of 12,000	Flexible Budget for Unit Sales of 14,000
Sales	$10.00		$100,000	$120,000	$140,000
Variable costs					
Direct materials	1.00		10,000	12,000	14,000
Direct labor	1.50		15,000	18,000	21,000
Factory supplies	0.20		2,000	2,400	2,800
Utilities	0.30		3,000	3,600	4,200
Sales commissions	0.90		9,000	10,800	12,600
Shipping expenses	0.40		4,000	4,800	5,600
Office supplies	0.50		5,000	6,000	7,000
Total variable costs	4.80		48,000	57,600	67,200
Contribution margin	$ 5.20		$ 52,000	$ 62,400	$ 72,800
Fixed costs					
Depreciation—Machinery		$ 8,000	8,000	8,000	8,000
Supervisory salaries		11,000	11,000	11,000	11,000
Insurance expense		1,000	1,000	1,000	1,000
Depreciation—Office equipment		7,000	7,000	7,000	7,000
Administrative salaries		13,000	13,000	13,000	13,000
Total fixed costs		$40,000	40,000	40,000	40,000
Income from operations			$ 12,000	$ 22,400	$ 32,800

The layout for the flexible budgets in Exhibit 24.3 begins with sales followed by variable costs and then fixed costs. Both the expected individual and total variable costs are reported and then subtracted from sales. The difference between sales and variable costs equals contribution margin. The expected amounts of fixed costs are listed next, followed by the expected income from operations before taxes.

Example: Using Exhibit 24.3, what is the budgeted income from operations for unit sales of (a) 11,000 and (b) 13,000? *Answers:* $17,200 for unit sales of 11,000. $27,600 for unit sales of 13,000.

The first and second number columns of Exhibit 24.3 show the flexible budget amounts for variable costs per unit and each fixed cost for any volume of sales in the relevant range. The third, fourth, and fifth columns show the flexible budget amounts computed for three different sales volumes. For instance, the third column's flexible budget is based on 10,000 units. These numbers are the same as those in the fixed budget of Exhibit 24.2 because the expected volumes are the same for these two budgets.

Point: Flexible budgeting allows a budget to be prepared at the *actual* output level. Performance reports are then prepared comparing the flexible budget to actual revenues and costs.

Point: A flexible budget yields an "apples to apples" comparison because budgeted activity levels are the same as the actual.

Recall that Optel's actual sales volume for January is 12,000 units. This sales volume is 2,000 units more than the 10,000 units originally predicted in the master budget. When differences between actual and predicted volume arise, the usefulness of a flexible budget is apparent. For instance, compare the flexible budget for 10,000 units in the third column (which is the same as the fixed budget in Exhibit 24.2) with the flexible budget for 12,000 units in the fourth column. The higher levels for both sales and variable costs reflect nothing more than the increase in sales activity. Any budget analysis comparing actual with planned results that ignores this information is less useful to management.

To illustrate, when we evaluate Optel's performance, we need to prepare a flexible budget showing actual and budgeted values at 12,000 units. As part of a complete profitability analysis, managers could compare the actual income of $25,400 (from Exhibit 24.2) with the $22,400 income expected at the actual sales volume of 12,000 units (from Exhibit 24.3). This results in a total income variance of $3,000 to be explained and interpreted. This variance is markedly different from the $13,400 variance identified in Exhibit 24.2 using a fixed budget. After receiving the flexible budget based on January's actual volume, management must determine what caused this $3,000 difference. The next section describes a flexible budget performance report that provides guidance in this analysis.

Flexible Budget Performance Report

A **flexible budget performance report** lists differences between actual performance and budgeted performance based on actual sales volume or other activity level. This report helps direct management's attention to those costs or revenues that differ substantially from budgeted amounts. Exhibit 24.4 shows Optel's flexible budget performance report for January. We prepare this report after the actual volume is known to be 12,000 units. This report shows a $5,000 favorable variance in total dollar sales. Because actual and budgeted volumes are both 12,000 units, the $5,000 sales variance must have resulted from a higher than expected selling price. Further analysis of the facts surrounding this $5,000 sales variance reveals a favorable sales variance per unit of nearly $0.42 as shown here:

Point: To apply these concepts, work QS 24-1.

Actual average price per unit (rounded to cents)	$125,000/12,000 = $10.42
Budgeted price per unit	$120,000/12,000 = 10.00
Favorable sales variance per unit	$5,000/12,000 = $ 0.42

Decision Maker

Entrepreneur The heads of both strategic consulting and tax consulting divisions of your financial services firm complain to you about the unfavorable variances on their performance reports. "We worked on more consulting assignments than planned. It's not surprising our costs are higher than expected. To top it off, this report characterizes our work as *poor!*" How do you respond?

Answer—p. 966

The other variances in Exhibit 24.4 also direct management's attention to areas where corrective actions can help control Optel's operations. Each expense variance is analyzed as the sales variance was. We can think of each expense as the joint result of using a given number of units and paying a specific price per unit.

More generally, each variance in Exhibit 24.4 is due in part to a difference between *actual price* per unit of input and *budgeted price* per unit of input. This is a **price variance.** Each variance also can be due in part to a difference between *actual quantity* of input used and *budgeted quantity* of input. This is a **quantity variance.** We explain more about this breakdown, known as **variance analysis,** later in the standard costs section.

Exhibit 24.4

Flexible Budget Performance Report

OPTEL Flexible Budget Performance Report For Month Ended January 31, 2005	Flexible Budget	Actual Results	Variances*
Sales (12,000 units)	$120,000	$125,000	$5,000 F
Variable costs			
Direct materials	12,000	13,000	1,000 U
Direct labor	18,000	20,000	2,000 U
Factory supplies	2,400	2,100	300 F
Utilities	3,600	4,000	400 U
Sales commissions	10,800	10,800	0
Shipping expenses	4,800	4,300	500 F
Office supplies	6,000	5,200	800 F
Total variable costs	57,600	59,400	1,800 U
Contribution margin	62,400	65,600	3,200 F
Fixed costs			
Depreciation—Machinery	8,000	8,000	0
Supervisory salaries	11,000	11,000	0
Insurance expense	1,000	1,200	200 U
Depreciation—Office equipment	7,000	7,000	0
Administrative salaries	13,000	13,000	0
Total fixed costs	40,000	40,200	200 U
Income from operations	$ 22,400	$ 25,400	$3,000 F

* F = Favorable variance; and U = Unfavorable variance.

Quick Check

1. A flexible budget (*a*) shows fixed costs as constant amounts of cost per unit of activity, (*b*) shows variable costs as constant amounts of cost per unit of activity, or (*c*) is prepared based on one expected amount of budgeted sales or production.
2. What is the initial step in preparing a flexible budget?
3. What is the main difference between a fixed and a flexible budget?
4. What is contribution margin?

Answers—p. 966

Section 2—Standard Costs

C1 Define *standard costs* and explain their computation and uses.

Standard costs are preset costs for delivering a product or service under normal conditions. These costs are established by personnel, engineering, and accounting studies using past experiences and data. Management uses these costs to assess the reasonableness of actual costs incurred for producing the product or service. When actual costs vary from standard costs, management follows up to identify potential problems and take corrective actions.

Standard costs are often used in preparing budgets because they are the anticipated costs incurred under normal conditions. Terms such as *standard materials cost, standard labor cost,* and *standard overhead cost* are often used to refer to amounts budgeted for direct materials, direct labor, and overhead.

Point: Since standard costs are often budgeted costs, they can be used to prepare both fixed budgets and flexible budgets.

Materials and Labor Standards

This section explains how to set materials and labor standards and how to prepare a standard cost card.

Identifying Standard Costs

Managerial accountants, engineers, personnel administrators, and other managers combine their efforts to set standard costs. To identify standards for direct labor costs, we can conduct time and motion studies for each labor operation in the process of providing a product or service. From these studies, management can learn the best way to perform the operation and then sets the standard labor time required for the operation under normal conditions. Similarly, standards for materials are set by studying the quantity, grade, and cost of each material used. Standards for overhead costs are explained later in the chapter.

Point: Business practice often uses the word *budget* when speaking of total values and *standard* when discussing per unit values.

Decision Insight

Cruis'n Standards The **Corvette** convertible consists of hundreds of parts for which engineers establish standards. Various types of labor are also involved in its production, including machining, assembly, painting, and welding, and standards are established for each. Actual results are periodically compared with standards to assess production performance.

Regardless of the care used in setting standard costs and in revising them as conditions change, actual costs frequently differ from standard costs, often as a result of one or more factors. For instance, the actual quantity of material used can differ from the standard, or the price paid per unit of material can differ from the standard. Quantity and price differences from standard amounts can also occur for labor. That is, the actual labor time and actual labor rate can vary from what was expected. The same analysis applies to overhead costs.

Setting Standard Costs

Example: What factors might be considered when deciding whether to revise standard costs? *Answer:* Changes in the processes and/or resources needed to carry out the processes.

Point: Companies promoting continuous improvement strive to achieve ideal standards by eliminating inefficiencies and waste.

To illustrate the setting of a standard cost, we consider a professional league baseball bat manufactured by ProBat. Its engineers have determined that manufacturing one bat requires 0.90 kgs. of high-grade wood. They also expect some loss of material as part of the process because of inefficiencies and waste. This results in adding an *allowance* of 0.10 kgs., making the standard requirement 1.0 kg. of wood for each bat.

The 0.90 kgs. portion is called an *ideal standard;* it is the quantity of material required if the process is 100% efficient without any loss or waste. Reality suggests that some loss of material usually occurs with any process. The standard of 1.0 kg. is known as the *practical standard,* the quantity of material required under normal application of the process.

High-grade wood can be purchased at a standard price of $25 per kg. The purchasing department sets this price as the expected price for the budget period. To determine this price, the purchasing department considers factors such as the quality of materials, future economic conditions, supply factors (shortages and excesses), and any available discounts. The engineers also decide that two hours of labor time (after including allowances) are required to manufacture a bat. The wage rate is $20 per hour (better than average skilled labor is required). ProBat assigns all overhead at the rate of $10 per labor hour. The standard costs of direct materials, direct labor, and overhead for one bat are as shown in Exhibit 24.5 in what is called a *standard cost card.* These cost amounts are then used to prepare manufacturing budgets for a budgeted level of production.

Exhibit 24.5

Standard Cost Card

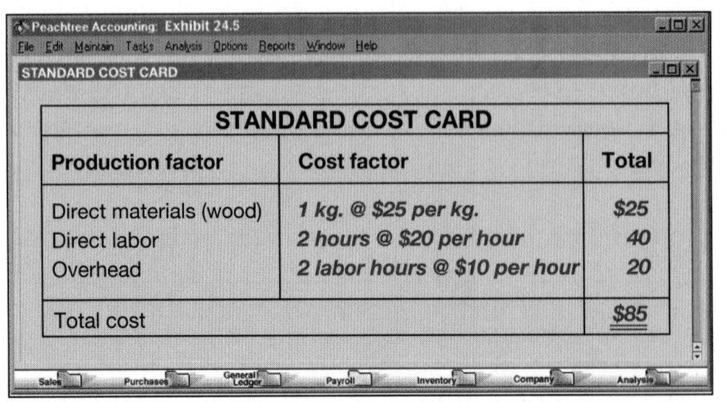

STANDARD COST CARD

Production factor	Cost factor	Total
Direct materials (wood)	*1 kg. @ $25 per kg.*	$25
Direct labor	*2 hours @ $20 per hour*	40
Overhead	*2 labor hours @ $10 per hour*	20
Total cost		$85

Cost Variances

C2 Describe variances and what they reveal about performance.

A **cost variance,** also simply called a *variance,* is the difference between actual and standard costs. A cost variance can be favorable or unfavorable. A variance from standard cost is considered favorable if actual cost is less than standard cost. It is considered unfavorable if actual cost is more than standard cost.[1] This section discusses variance analysis.

Cost Variance Analysis

Variances are usually identified in performance reports. When a variance occurs, management wants to determine the factors causing it. This often involves analysis, evaluation, and explanation. The results of these efforts should enable management to assign responsibility for the variance and then to take actions to correct the situation.

To illustrate, Optel's standard materials cost for producing 12,000 units of its product is \$12,000. Its actual materials cost for January proved to be \$13,000. The \$1,000 unfavorable variance raises questions that call for answers that, in turn, can lead to changes to correct the situation and eliminate this variance in the next period. A performance report often identifies the existence of a problem, but we must follow up with further investigation to see what can be done to improve future performance.

Exhibit 24.6 shows the flow of events in the effective management of variance analysis. It shows four steps: (1) preparing a standard cost performance report, (2) computing and analyzing variances, (3) identifying questions and their explanations, and (4) taking corrective and strategic actions. These variance analysis steps are interrelated and are frequently applied in good organizations.

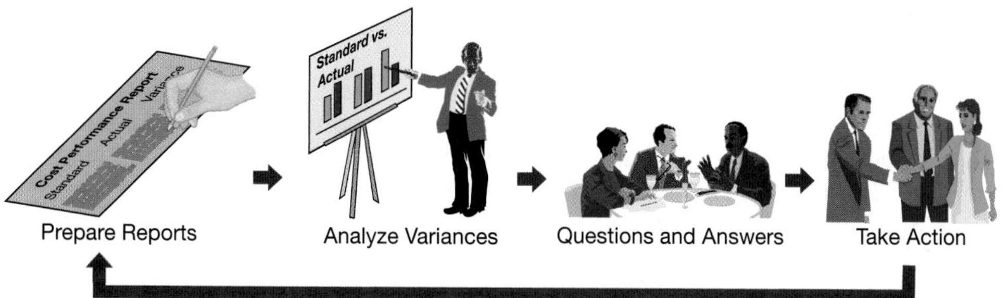

Exhibit 24.6

Variance Analysis

Cost Variance Computation

Management needs information about the factors causing a cost variance, but first it must properly compute the variance. In its most simple form, a cost variance (CV) is computed as the difference between actual cost (AC) and standard cost (SC) as shown in Exhibit 24.7.

Cost Variance (CV) = **Actual Cost** (AC) − **Standard Cost** (SC)

where:

Actual Cost (AC) = **Actual Quantity** (AQ) × **Actual Price** (AP)

Standard Cost (SC) = **Standard Quantity** (SQ) × **Standard Price** (SP)

Exhibit 24.7

Cost Variance Formulas

A cost variance is further defined by its components. Actual quantity (AQ) is the input (material or labor) used to manufacture the quantity of output. Standard quantity (SQ) is the expected input for the quantity of output. Actual price (AP) is the amount paid to acquire the input (material or labor), and standard price (SP) is the expected price.

[1] Short-term favorable variances can sometimes lead to long-term unfavorable variances. For instance, if management spends less than the budgeted amount on maintenance or insurance, the performance report would show a favorable variance. Cutting these expenses can lead to major losses in the long run if machinery wears out prematurely or insurance coverage proves inadequate.

Point: Price and quantity variances for direct labor are nearly always referred to as *rate* and *efficiency variances*, respectively.

Two main factors cause a cost variance: (1) the difference between actual price and standard price results in a *price* (or rate) *variance* and (2) the difference between actual quantity and standard quantity results in a *quantity* (or usage or efficiency) *variance*. To assess the impacts of these two factors on a cost variance, we use the formula in Exhibit 24.8.

Exhibit 24.8

Price Variance and Quantity Variance Formulas

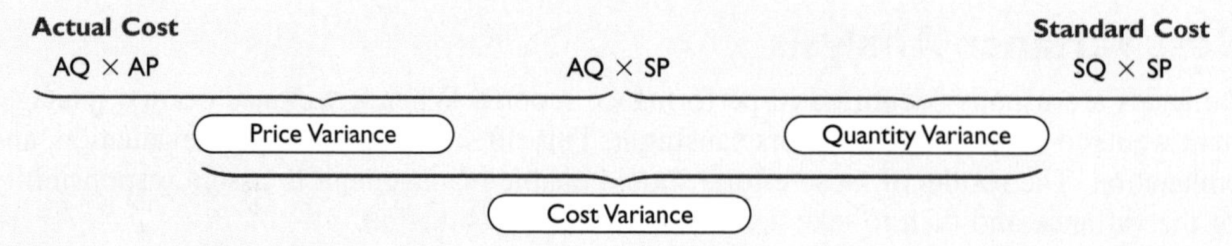

These formulas identify the sources of the cost variance. Managers sometimes find it useful to apply an alternative (but equivalent) computation for the price and quantity variances as shown in Exhibit 24.9.

Exhibit 24.9

Alternative Price Variance and Quantity Variance Formulas

Price Variance (PV) = [**Actual Price** (AP) − **Standard Price** (SP)] × **Actual Quantity** (AQ)

Quantity Variance (QV) = [**Actual Quantity** (AQ) − **Standard Quantity** (SQ)] × **Standard Price** (SP)

The results from applying the formulas in Exhibits 24.8 and 24.9 are identical.

Materials and Labor Variances

P2 Compute materials and labor variances.

We illustrate the computation of the materials and labor cost variances using data from **G-Max,** a company that makes specialty golf equipment and accessories for individual customers. This company has set the following standard quantities and prices for materials and labor per unit for one of its hand-crafted golf clubheads:

Direct materials (1 lb. per unit at $1 per lb.)	$1.00
Direct labor (1 hr. per unit at $8 per hr.)	8.00
Total standard direct cost per unit	$9.00

Materials Cost Variances During May 2005, G-Max budgeted to produce 4,000 clubheads (units). It actually produced only 3,500 units. It used 3,600 pounds of direct materials (titanium) costing $1.05 per pound, meaning its total materials cost was $3,780. This information allows us to compute both actual and standard direct materials costs for G-Max's 3,500 units and its direct materials cost variance:

Topic Tackler 24-2

Actual cost	3,600 lbs. @ $1.05 per lb.	= $3,780
Standard cost	3,500 lbs. @ $1.00 per lb.	= 3,500
Direct materials cost variance (unfavorable)		= $ 280

The materials price and quantity variances for these G-Max clubheads are computed and shown in Exhibit 24.10.

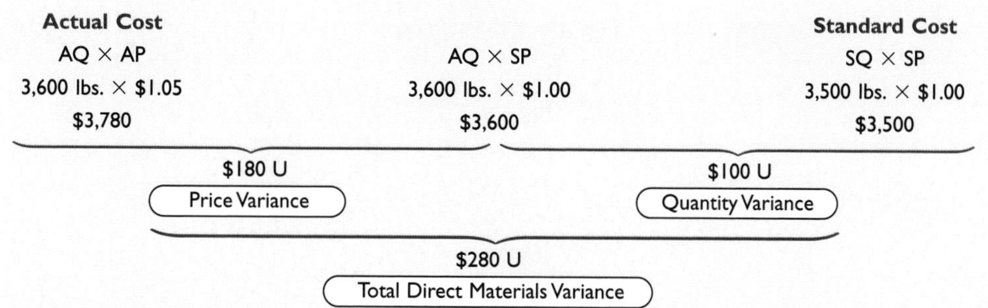

Exhibit 24.10

Materials Price and Quantity Variances

Example: Identify at least two factors that might have caused the $100 unfavorable quantity variance and the $180 unfavorable price variance in Exhibit 24.10. *Answer:* Poor quality materials or untrained workers for the former; poor price negotiation or higher quality materials for the latter.

The $180 unfavorable price variance results from paying 5 cents more than the standard price, computed as 3,600 lbs. × $0.05. The $100 unfavorable quantity variance is due to using 100 lbs. more materials than the standard quantity, computed as 100 lbs. × $1. The total direct materials variance is $280 and is unfavorable. This information allows management to ask the responsible individuals for explanations and corrective actions.

The purchasing department is usually responsible for the price paid for materials. Responsibility for explaining the price variance in this case rests with the purchasing manager if a price higher than standard caused the variance. The production department is usually responsible for the amount of material used and in this case is responsible for explaining why the process used more than the standard amount of materials.

Example: Give an example of a manufacturing situation in which a favorable price variance for material might be the cause of an unfavorable quantity variance. *Answer:* Buying cheap materials.

Variance analysis presents challenges. For instance, the production department could have used more than the standard amount of material because its quality did not meet specifications and led to excessive waste. In this case, the purchasing manager is responsible for explaining why inferior materials were acquired. However, the production manager is responsible for explaining what happened if analysis shows that waste was due to inefficiencies, not poor quality material.

In evaluating price variances, managers must recognize that a favorable price variance can indicate a problem with poor product quality. **Redhook Ale**, a micro brewery in the Pacific Northwest, can probably save 10% to 15% in material prices by buying six-row barley malt instead of the better two-row from Washington's Yakima valley. Attention to quality, however, has helped Redhook Ale become the only craft brewer to be "kosher" certified. Redhook's purchasing activities are judged on both the quality of the materials and the purchase price variance. This stand on quality has helped Redhook report increases in both sales and gross margin.

Labor Cost Variances Labor cost for a specific product or service depends on the number of hours worked (quantity) and the wage rate paid to employees (price). When actual amounts for a task differ from standard, the labor cost variance can be divided into a rate (price) variance and an efficiency (quantity) variance.

To illustrate, G-Max's direct labor standard for 3,500 units of its hand-crafted clubheads is one hour per unit, or 3,500 hours at $8 per hour. Since only 3,400 hours at $8.30 per hour were actually used to complete the units, the actual and standard labor costs are

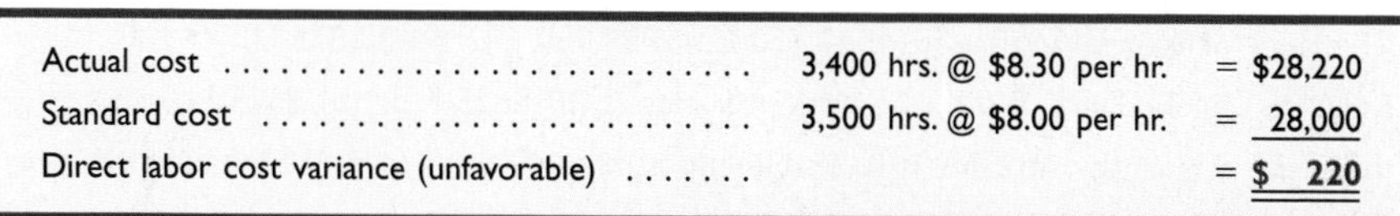

Actual cost	3,400 hrs. @ $8.30 per hr.	= $28,220
Standard cost	3,500 hrs. @ $8.00 per hr.	= 28,000
Direct labor cost variance (unfavorable)		= $ 220

This analysis shows that actual cost is merely $220 over the standard and suggests no immediate concern. Computing both the labor rate and efficiency variances reveals a different picture, however, as shown in Exhibit 24.11.

Exhibit 24.11

Labor Rate and Efficiency Variances*

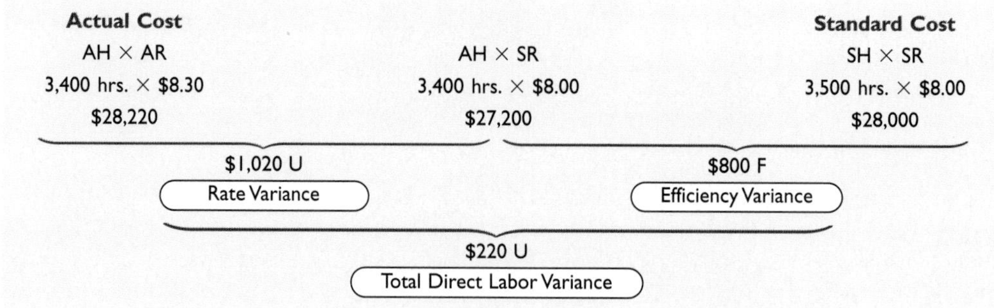

* AH is actual direct labor hours: AR is actual wage rate; SH is standard direct labor hours allowed for actual output; SR is standard wage rate.

Example: Compute the rate variance and the efficiency variance for Exhibit 24.11 if 3,700 actual hours are used at an actual price of $7.50 per hour. *Answer:* $1,850 favorable labor rate variance and $1,600 unfavorable labor efficiency variance.

Point: To apply these concepts, work Exercise 24-5.

The analysis in Exhibit 24.11 shows that an $800 favorable efficiency variance results from using 100 fewer direct labor hours than standard for the units produced, but this favorable variance is more than offset by a wage rate that is $0.30 higher than standard. The personnel administrator or possibly the production manager needs to explain why the wage rate is higher than expected. The production manager should also explain how the labor hours were reduced. If this experience can be repeated and transferred to other departments, more savings are possible.

One possible explanation of these labor rate and efficiency variances is the use of workers with different skill levels. If this is the reason, senior management must discuss the implications with the production manager who has the responsibility to assign workers to tasks with the appropriate skill level. In this case, an investigation might show that higher skilled workers were used to produce 3,500 units of hand-crafted clubheads. As a result, fewer labor hours might be required for the work, but the wage rate paid these workers is higher than standard because of their greater skills. The effect of this strategy is a higher than standard total cost, which would require actions to remedy the situation or adjust the standard.

Decision Maker

Human Resource Manager You receive the manufacturing variance report for June and discover a large unfavorable labor efficiency (quantity) variance. What factors do you investigate to identify its possible causes?

Answer—p. 966

Quick Check

5. A standard cost (*a*) changes in direct proportion to changes in the level of activity, (*b*) is an amount incurred at the actual level of production for the period, or (*c*) is an amount incurred under normal conditions to provide a product or service.
6. What is a cost variance?
7. The following information is available for York Company:

Actual direct labor hours per unit	2.5 hours
Standard direct labor hours per unit	2.0 hours
Actual production (units)	2,500 units
Budgeted production (units)	3,000 units
Actual rate per hour	$3.10
Standard rate per hour	$3.00

The labor efficiency variance is (*a*) $3,750 U, (*b*) $3,750 F, or (*c*) $3,875 U.

8. Refer to Quick Check 7; the labor rate variance is (*a*) $625 F or (*b*) $625 U.
9. If a material quantity variance is favorable and a material price variance is unfavorable, can the total material cost variance be favorable?

Answers—p. 966

Overhead Standards and Variances

When standard costs are used, a predetermined overhead rate is used to assign standard overhead costs to products or services produced. This predetermined rate is often based on some overhead allocation base (such as standard labor cost, standard labor hours, or standard machine hours).

Setting Overhead Standards

Standard overhead costs are the amounts expected to occur at a certain activity level. Unlike direct materials and direct labor, overhead includes fixed costs and variable costs. This results in the average overhead cost per unit changing as the predicted volume changes. Since standard costs are also budgeted costs, they must be established before the reporting period begins. Standard overhead costs are therefore average per unit costs based on the predicted activity level.

To establish the standard overhead cost rate, management uses the same cost structure it used to construct a flexible budget at the end of a period. This cost structure identifies the different overhead cost components and classifies them as variable or fixed. To get the standard overhead rate, management selects a level of activity (volume) and predicts total overhead cost. It then divides this total by the allocation base to get the standard rate. Standard direct labor hours expected to be used to produce the predicted volume is a common allocation base and is used in this section.

Point: Managers consider the types of overhead costs when choosing the basis for assigning overhead costs to products.

To illustrate, Exhibit 24.12 shows the overhead cost structure used to develop G-Max's flexible overhead budgets for May 2005. The predetermined standard overhead rate for May is set before the month begins. The first two number columns list the per unit amounts of variable costs and the monthly amounts of fixed costs. The four rightmost columns show the costs expected to occur at four different levels of activity. The predetermined overhead rate per labor hour is smaller as volume of activity increases because fixed costs remain constant.

G-Max managers predicted an 80% activity level for May, or a production volume of 4,000 clubheads. At this volume, they budget $8,000 as the May total overhead. This choice implies a $2 per unit (labor hour) average overhead cost ($8,000/4,000 units). Since G-Max has a standard of one direct labor hour per unit, the predetermined standard overhead rate for May is $2 per standard direct labor hour. The variable overhead rate remains constant at $1 per direct labor hour regardless of the budgeted production level. The fixed overhead rate changes according to the budgeted production volume. For instance, for the predicted level of 4,000 units of production, the fixed rate is $1 per hour ($4,000 fixed costs/4,000 units). For a production level of 5,000 units, however, the fixed rate is $0.80 per hour.

Point: Variable costs per unit remain constant, but fixed costs per unit decline with increases in volume. This means the average total overhead cost per unit declines with increases in volume.

When choosing the predicted activity level, management considers many factors. The level can be set as high as 100% of capacity, but this is rare. Factors causing the activity level to be less than full capacity include difficulties in scheduling work, equipment under repair or maintenance, and insufficient product demand. Good long-run management practices often call for some plant capacity in excess of current operating needs to allow for special opportunities and demand changes.

Decision Insight

Measuring Up In the spirit of continuous improvement, competitors compare their processes and performance standards against benchmarks established by industry leaders. Those that use **benchmarking** include Precision Lube, Jiffy Lube, All Tune and Lube, and Speedee Oil Change and Tune-Up.

Exhibit 24.12

Flexible Overhead Budgets

G-MAX Flexible Overhead Budgets For Month Ended May 31, 2005	Flexible Budget					
	Variable Amount per Unit	Total Fixed Cost	Flexible Budget at 70% Capacity	Flexible Budget at 80% Capacity	Flexible Budget at 90% Capacity	Flexible Budget at 100% Capacity
Production (in units)	1 unit		3,500	**4,000**	4,500	5,000
Factory overhead						
Variable costs						
Indirect labor	$0.40/unit		$1,400	**$1,600**	$1,800	$2,000
Indirect materials	0.30/unit		1,050	**1,200**	1,350	1,500
Power and lights	0.20/unit		700	**800**	900	1,000
Maintenance	0.10/unit		350	**400**	450	500
Total variable overhead costs	$1.00/unit		3,500	**4,000**	4,500	5,000
Fixed costs (per month)						
Building rent		$1,000	1,000	**1,000**	1,000	1,000
Depreciation—Machinery		1,200	1,200	**1,200**	1,200	1,200
Supervisory salaries		1,800	1,800	**1,800**	1,800	1,800
Total fixed overhead costs		$4,000	4,000	**4,000**	4,000	4,000
Total factory overhead			$7,500	**$8,000**	$8,500	$9,000
Standard direct labor hours	1 hr./unit		3,500 hrs.	**4,000 hrs.**	4,500 hrs.	5,000 hrs.
Predetermined overhead rate per standard direct labor hour			$ 2.14	**$ 2.00**	$ 1.89	$ 1.80

P3 Compute overhead variances.

Using Overhead Cost Variance Analysis

When standard costs are used, the cost accounting system applies overhead to the good units produced using the predetermined standard overhead rate. At period-end, the difference between the total overhead cost applied to products and the total overhead cost actually incurred is called an **overhead cost variance,** which is defined in Exhibit 24.13.

Exhibit 24.13

Overhead Cost Variance

Overhead cost variance (OCV) = Actual overhead incurred (AOI) − Standard overhead applied (SOA)

To help identify factors causing the overhead cost variance, managers analyze this variance separately for variable and fixed overhead. The results provide information useful for taking strategic actions to improve company performance. Similar to analysis of direct materials and direct labor variances, both the variable and fixed overhead variances can be separated into useful components as shown in Exhibit 24.14.

A **spending variance** occurs when management pays an amount different than the standard price to acquire an item. For instance, the actual wage rate paid to indirect labor might be higher than the standard rate. Similarly, actual supervisory salaries might be different than expected. Spending variances such as these cause management to investigate the reasons that the amount paid differs from the standard. Both variable and fixed overhead costs can yield their own spending variances. Analyzing variable overhead includes computing an **efficiency variance,** which occurs when standard direct labor hours (the allocation base) expected for actual production differ from the actual direct labor hours used.

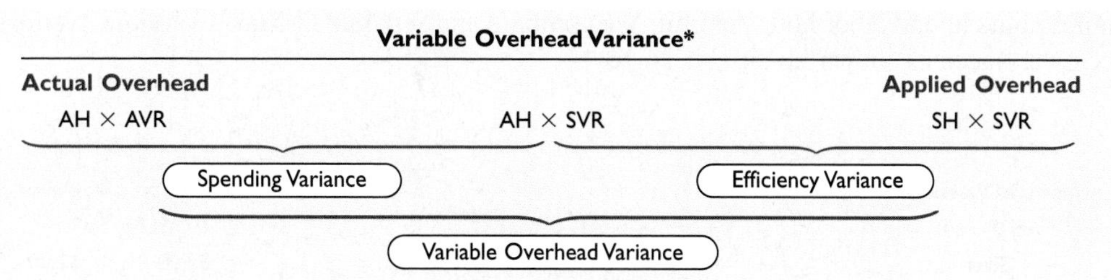

* AH = actual direct labor hours; AVR = actual variable overhead rate; SH = standard direct labor hours; SVR = standard variable overhead rate.

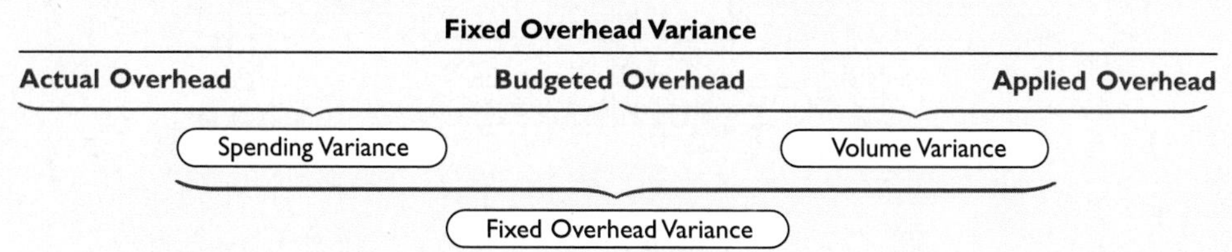

Exhibit 24.14

Variable and Fixed Overhead Variances

This efficiency variance reflects on the cost-effectiveness in using the overhead allocation base (such as direct labor).

A **volume variance** occurs when a difference occurs between the actual volume of production and the standard volume of production. The budgeted fixed overhead amount is the same regardless of the volume of production (within the relevant range). This budgeted amount is computed based on standard direct labor hours that the budgeted production volume allows. The applied overhead is based, however, on the standard direct labor hours allowed for the actual volume of production. A difference between budgeted and actual production volumes results in a difference in the standard direct labor hours allowed for these two production levels. This situation yields a volume variance different from zero.

We can combine the variable overhead spending variance, the fixed overhead spending variance, and the variable overhead efficiency variance to get **controllable variance;** see Exhibit 24.15. The controllable variance is so named because it refers to activities usually under management control.

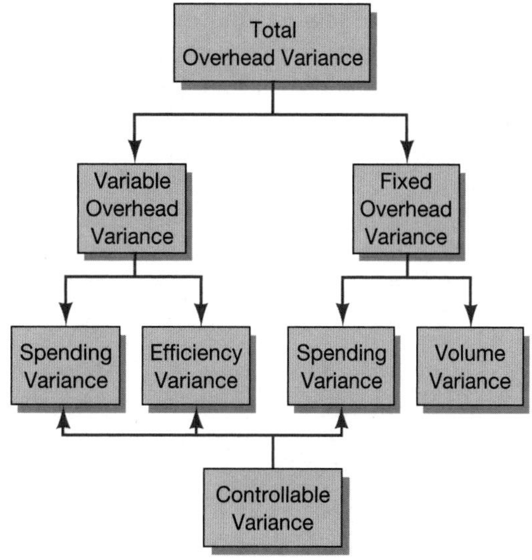

Exhibit 24.15

Framework for Understanding Total Overhead Variance

Computing Overhead Cost Variances

To illustrate how to compute overhead cost variances, return to the G-Max data. We know that it actually produced 3,500 units when 4,000 units were budgeted. Additional G-Max data show that actual overhead cost incurred is $7,650 (variable portion of $3,650; fixed portion of $4,000). Using this information, we can compute overhead variances for both variable and fixed overhead.

Variable Overhead Cost Variances Recall that G-Max applies overhead based on direct labor hours as the allocation base. We know that it used 3,400 direct labor hours to produce 3,500 units. This compares favorably to the standard requirement of 3,500 direct labor hours at one labor hour per unit. We compute and separate G-Max's variable overhead cost variances as shown in Exhibit 24.16.

Exhibit 24.16

Computing Variable Overhead Cost Variances

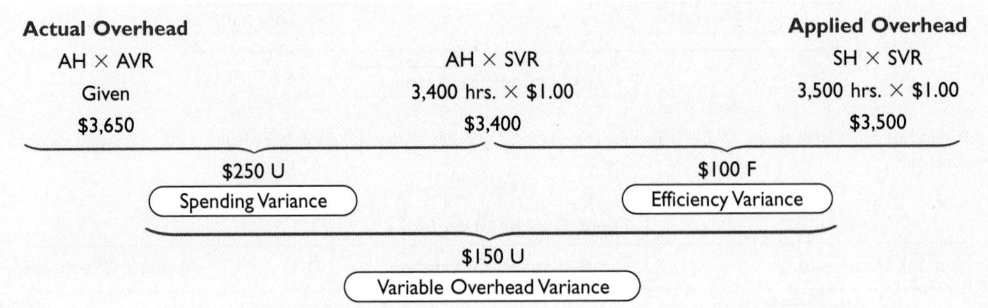

The $3,650 actual variable overhead from G-Max's cost records is used to compute the actual variable overhead rate of $1.07 per direct labor hour ($3,650/3,400 direct labor hours). This reveals that, on average, G-Max incurred $0.07 more per direct labor hour in variable overhead than the standard rate. The middle column of Exhibit 24.16 is computed by multiplying the 3,400 actual direct labor hours by the $1 standard rate per direct labor hour. The applied overhead is computed by multiplying the 3,500 standard hours allowed for actual production by the $1 standard rate per direct labor hour.

Fixed Overhead Cost Variances G-Max reports that it incurred $4,000 in actual fixed overhead ; this amount equals the budgeted fixed overhead for May (see Exhibit 24.12). G-Max's budgeted fixed overhead application rate is $1 per hour ($4,000/4,000 direct labor hours), but the actual production level is only 3,500 units. Using this information, we can compute the fixed overhead cost variances shown in Exhibit 24.17. The applied fixed overhead is computed by multiplying 3,500 standard hours allowed for the actual production by the $1 fixed overhead allocation rate. Exhibit 24.17 reveals that the fixed overhead spending variance is zero and the volume variance is $500. The volume variance occurs because 500 fewer units are produced than budgeted; namely, 80% of the manufacturing capacity is budgeted but only 70% is used.

Exhibit 24.17

Computing Fixed Overhead Cost Variances

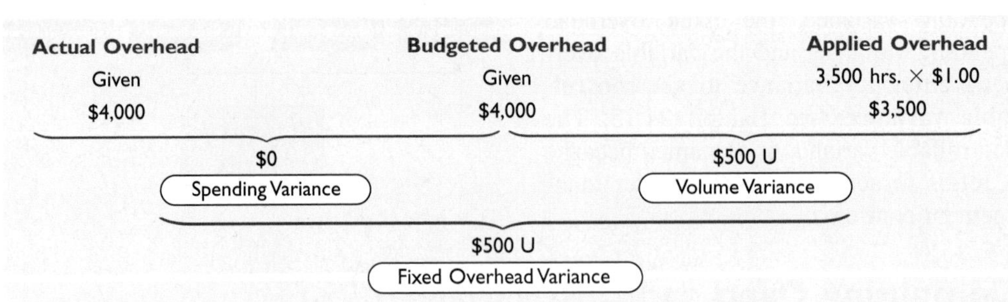

We show this volume variance graphically in Exhibit 24.18. The upward-sloping line reflects the amount of fixed overhead costs applied to the units produced in May using the predetermined fixed overhead rate. The uppermost horizontal line reflects the $4,000 of total fixed costs budgeted for May. These two lines cross at the planned operating volume of 4,000 units. When unit volume is 3,500 units, the overhead-costs-applied line falls $500 below the budgeted fixed overhead line. This shortfall is the volume variance.

An unfavorable volume variance implies that the company did not reach its predicted operating level. Management needs to know why the actual level of performance differs

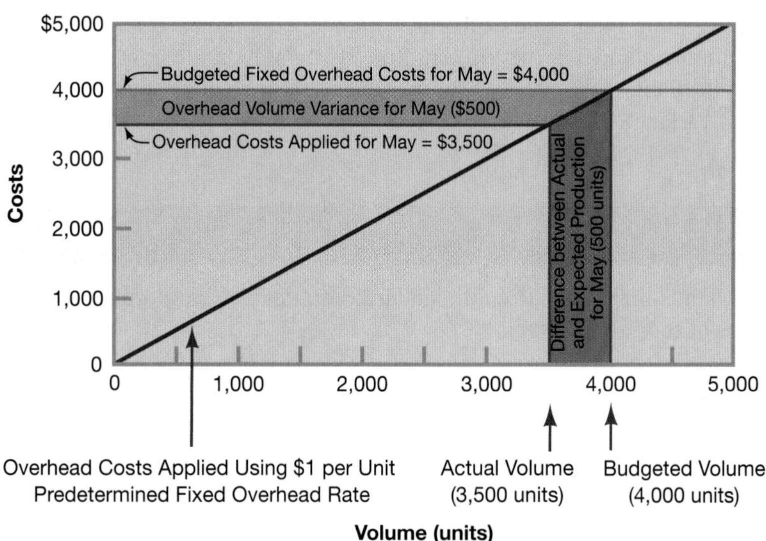

Exhibit 24.18

Fixed Overhead Volume Variance

from the expected level. The main purpose of the volume variance is to identify what portion of the total variance is caused by failing to meet the expected volume level. This information permits management to focus on the controllable variance.

A complete overhead variance report provides managers information about specific overhead costs and how they differ from budgeted amounts. Exhibit 24.19 shows G-Max's overhead variance report for May. It reveals that (1) fixed costs and maintenance cost were incurred as expected, (2) costs for indirect labor and power and lights were higher than expected, and (3) indirect materials cost was less than expected.

Using information from Exhibits 24.16 and 24.17, we can compute the total controllable overhead variance as $150 unfavorable ($250 U + $100 F + $0). This amount is also readily

Exhibit 24.19

Overhead Variance Report

G-MAX
Overhead Variance Report
For Month Ended May 31, 2005

Volume Variance			
Expected production level	80% of capacity		
Production level achieved	70% of capacity		
Volume variance	**$500 (unfavorable)**		

Controllable Variance	**Flexible Budget**	**Actual Results**	**Variances***
Variable overhead costs			
Indirect labor	$1,400	$1,525	$125 U
Indirect materials	1,050	1,025	25 F
Power and lights	700	750	50 U
Maintenance	350	350	0
Total variable overhead costs	3,500	3,650	150 U†
Fixed overhead costs			
Building rent	1,000	1,000	0
Depreciation—Machinery	1,200	1,200	0
Supervisory salaries	1,800	1,800	0
Total fixed overhead costs	4,000	4,000	0‡
Total overhead costs	$7,500	$7,650	**$150 U**

* F = Favorable variance; and U = Unfavorable variance.

† Total variable overhead (spending and efficiency) variance.

‡ Fixed overhead spending variance.

available from Exhibit 24.19. The overhead variance report shows the total volume variance as $500 unfavorable (shown at the top) and the $150 unfavorable controllable variance. The sum of the controllable variance and the volume variance equals the total (fixed and variable) overhead variance of $650 unfavorable.

Extensions of Standard Costs

This section extends the application of standard costs for control purposes, for service companies, and for accounting systems.

Standard Costs for Control

C3 Explain how standard cost information is useful for management by exception.

To control business activities, top management must be able to affect the actions of lower-level managers responsible for the company's revenues and costs. After preparing a budget and establishing standard costs, management should take actions to gain control when actual costs differ from standard or budgeted amounts.

Reports such as the ones illustrated in this chapter call management's attention to variances from business plans and other standards. When managers use these reports to focus on problem areas, the budgeting process contributes to the control function. In using budgeted performance reports, practice of management by exception is often useful. **Management by exception** means that managers focus attention on the most significant variances and give less attention to areas where performance is reasonably close to the standard. This practice leads management to concentrate on the exceptional or irregular situations. Management by exception is especially useful when directed at controllable items.

Decision Ethics

Internal Auditor You discover a manager who always spends exactly what is budgeted for supplies, and about 30% of her budget is spent just before the period-end. She admits to spending what is budgeted, whether or not supplies are needed. She offers three reasons for her actions. First, she doesn't want her budget cut. Second, "management by exception" calls attention to budget deviations. Third, she believes the money is budgeted to be spent. What action do you take?

Answer—p. 966

Standard Costs for Services

Many managers use standard costs and variance analysis to investigate manufacturing costs. Many managers also recognize that standard costs and variances can help them control *non* manufacturing costs. Companies providing services instead of products can benefit from the use of standard costs. Application of standard costs and variances can be readily adapted to nonmanufacturing situations. To illustrate, many service providers use standard costs to help control expenses. First, they use standard costs as a basis for budgeting all services. Second, they use periodic performance reports to compare actual results to standards. Third, they use these reports to identify significant variances within specific areas of responsibility. Fourth, they implement the appropriate control procedures.

Decision Insight

Health Budget Medical professionals continue to struggle with business realities. Quality medical service is paramount, but efficiency in providing that service also is important. The use of budgeting and standard costing is touted as an effective means to control and monitor medical costs, especially overhead.

Standard Cost Accounting System

P4 Prepare journal entries for standard costs and account for price and quantity variances.

We have shown how companies use standard costs in management reports. Most standard cost systems also record these costs and variances in accounts. This practice simplifies recordkeeping and helps in preparing reports. Although we do not need knowledge of standard cost accounting practices to understand standard costs and their use, we must know how to interpret the accounts in which standard costs and variances are recorded. The entries in this section briefly illustrate the important aspects of this process for G-Max's standard costs and variances for May.

The first of these entries records standard materials cost incurred in May in the Goods in Process Inventory account. This part of the entry is similar to the usual accounting entry, but the amount of the debit equals the standard cost ($3,500) instead of the actual cost ($3,780). This entry credits Raw Materials Inventory for actual cost. The difference between standard and actual costs is recorded with debits to two separate materials variance accounts (recall Exhibit 24.10). Both the materials price and quantity variances are recorded as debits because they reflect additional costs higher than the standard cost (if actual costs were less than the standard, they are recorded as credits). This treatment (debit) reflects their unfavorable effect because they represent higher costs and lower income.

May 31	Goods in Process Inventory	3,500	
	Direct Materials Price Variance*	**180**	
	Direct Materials Quantity Variance	**100**	
	Raw Materials Inventory		3,780
	To charge production for standard quantity of materials used (3,500 lbs.) at the standard price ($1 per lb.), and to record material price and material quantity variances.		

Assets	= Liabilities +	Equity
+3,500		−100
−3,780		−180

* Many companies record the materials price variance when materials are purchased. For simplicity, we record both the materials price and quantity variances when materials are issued to production.

The second entry debits Goods in Process Inventory for the standard labor cost of the goods manufactured during May ($28,000). Actual labor cost ($28,220) is recorded with a credit to the Factory Payroll account. The difference between standard and actual labor costs is explained by two variances (see Exhibit 24.11). The direct labor rate variance is unfavorable and is debited to that account. The direct labor efficiency variance is favorable and is credited. The direct labor efficiency variance is favorable because it represents a lower cost and a higher net income.

May 31	Goods in Process Inventory	28,000	
	Direct Labor Rate Variance	**1,020**	
	Direct Labor Efficiency Variance		**800**
	Factory Payroll		28,220
	To charge production with 3,500 standard hours of direct labor at the standard $8 per hour rate, and to record the labor rate and efficiency variances.		

Assets	= Liabilities +	Equity
+28,000		+28,220
		− 1,020
		+ 800

The entry to assign standard predetermined overhead to the cost of goods manufactured must debit the $7,000 predetermined amount to the Goods in Process Inventory account. The $7,650 actual overhead costs are debited to the Factory Overhead account. Thus, when Factory Overhead is applied to Goods in Process Inventory, the amount applied is debited to the Goods in Process Inventory account and credited to the Factory Overhead account. To account for the difference between actual and standard costs, the entry includes a $250 debit to the Variable Overhead Spending Variance, a $100 credit to the Variable Overhead Efficiency Variance, and a $500 debit to the Volume Variance (recall Exhibits 24.16 and 24.17). An alternative (simpler) approach, shown here, is to record the difference with a $150 debit to the Controllable Variance account and a $500 debit to the Volume Variance account (recall from Exhibit 24.15 that controllable variance is the sum of both variable overhead variances and the fixed overhead spending variance).

Assets = Liabilities + Equity
+7,000 +7,650
− 150
− 500

May 31	Goods in Process Inventory.	7,000	
	Controllable Variance	**150**	
	Volume Variance	**500**	
	Factory Overhead		7,650
	To apply overhead at the standard rate of $2 per standard direct labor hour (3,500 hours), and to record overhead variances.		

Point: To apply these concepts, work Exercises 24-8 and 24-9.

The balances of these six different variance accounts accumulate until the end of the accounting period. As a result, the unfavorable variances of some months offset the favorable variances of others.

These variance account balances, which reflect results of the period's various transactions and events, are closed at period-end. If the variances are *material,* they are added to or subtracted from the balances of the Goods in Process Inventory, the Finished Goods Inventory, and the Cost of Goods Sold accounts. If the amounts are *immaterial,* they are added to or subtracted from the balance of the Cost of Goods Sold account. This process is similar to that shown in Chapter 19 for eliminating an underapplied or overapplied balance in the Factory Overhead account. (*Note:* These variance balances, which represent differences between actual and standard costs, must be added to or subtracted from the materials, labor, and overhead costs recorded. In this way, the recorded costs equal the actual costs incurred in the period; a company must use actual costs in external financial statements prepared in accordance with generally accepted accounting principles.)

Quick Check

10. Under what conditions is an overhead volume variance considered favorable?

11. To use management by exception with standard costs, a company (*a*) must record standard costs in its accounting, (*b*) should compute variances from flexible budget amounts to allow management to focus its attention on significant differences between actual and budgeted results, or (*c*) should analyze only variances for direct materials and direct labor.

12. A company uses a standard cost accounting system. Prepare the journal entry to record these direct materials variances:

Direct materials cost actually incurred	$73,200
Direct materials quantity variance (favorable)	3,800
Direct materials price variance (unfavorable)	1,300

13. If standard costs are recorded in the manufacturing accounts, how are recorded variances treated at the end of an accounting period?

Answers—p. 966

Decision Analysis — Sales Variances

A2 Analyze changes in sales from expected amounts.

This chapter explained the computation and analysis of cost variances. A similar variance analysis can be applied to sales. To illustrate, consider the following sales data from G-Max for two of its golf products, fluorescent Excel balls and Big Bert® drivers.

	Budgeted	Actual
Sales of Excel golf balls (units)	1,000	1,100
Sales price per Excel golf ball	$ 10	$ 10.50
Sales of Big Bert® drivers (units)	150	140
Sales price per Big Bert® driver	$ 200	$ 190

Using this information, we compute both the *sales price variance* and the *sales volume variance* as shown in Exhibit 24.20. The total sales price variance is $850 unfavorable, and the total sales volume variance is $1,000 unfavorable. Neither variance implies anything positive about these two products. Further analysis of these total sales variances reveals that both the sales price and sales volume variances for Excel golf balls are favorable, meaning that both the unfavorable total sales price variance and the unfavorable total sales volume variance are due to the Big Bert driver.

Exhibit 24.20

Computing Sales Variances

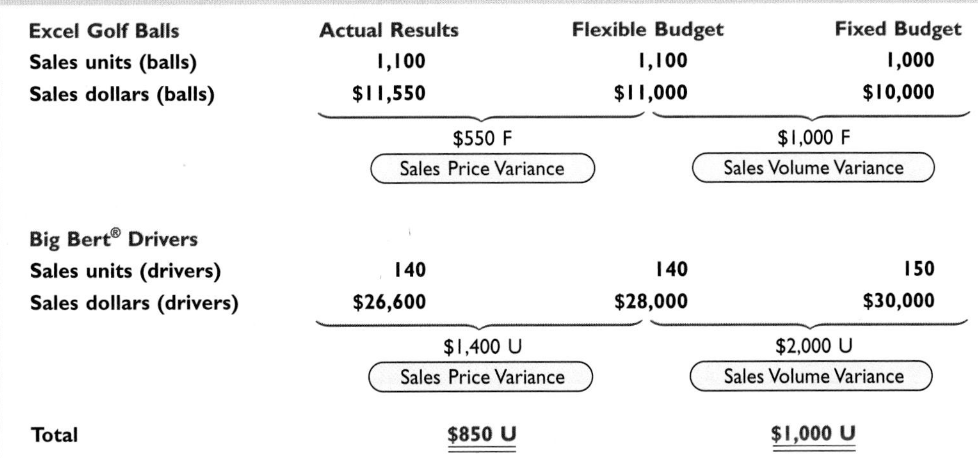

Excel Golf Balls	Actual Results	Flexible Budget	Fixed Budget
Sales units (balls)	1,100	1,100	1,000
Sales dollars (balls)	$11,550	$11,000	$10,000
	$550 F Sales Price Variance		$1,000 F Sales Volume Variance
Big Bert® Drivers			
Sales units (drivers)	140	140	150
Sales dollars (drivers)	$26,600	$28,000	$30,000
	$1,400 U Sales Price Variance		$2,000 U Sales Volume Variance
Total	$850 U		$1,000 U

Managers use sales variances for planning and control purposes. The sales variance information is used to plan future actions to avoid unfavorable variances. G-Max sold 90 total combined units (both balls and drivers) more than planned, but these 90 units were not sold in the proportion budgeted. G-Max sold fewer than the budgeted quantity of the higher priced driver, which contributed to the unfavorable total sales variances. Managers use such detail to question what caused the company to sell more golf balls and fewer drivers. Managers also use this information to evaluate and even reward their salespeople. Extra compensation is paid to salespeople who contribute to a higher profit margin. Finally, with multiple products, the sales volume variance can be separated into a *sales mix variance* and a *sales quantity variance*. The sales mix variance is the difference between the actual and budgeted sales mix of the products. The sales quantity variance is the difference between the total actual and total budgeted quantity of units sold.

Decision Maker

Sales Manager The current performance report reveals a large favorable sales volume variance but an unfavorable sales price variance. You did not expect to see a large increase in sales volume. What steps do you take to analyze this situation?

Answer—p. 966

Demonstration Problem

Pacific Company provides the following information about its budgeted and actual results for June 2005. Although the expected June volume was 25,000 units produced and sold, the company actually produced and sold 27,000 units as detailed here:

	Budget (25,000 units)	Actual (27,000 units)
Selling price	$5.00 per unit	$5.23 per unit
Variable costs (per unit)		
Direct materials	1.24 per unit	1.12 per unit
Direct labor	1.50 per unit	1.40 per unit
Factory supplies*	0.25 per unit	0.37 per unit
Utilities*	0.50 per unit	0.60 per unit
Selling costs	0.40 per unit	0.34 per unit

[continued on next page]

[continued from previous page]

Fixed costs (per month)		
Depreciation—Machinery*	$3,750	$3,710
Depreciation—Building*	2,500	2,500
General liability insurance	1,200	1,250
Property taxes on office equipment	500	485
Other administrative expense	750	900

* Indicates factory overhead item; $0.75 per unit or $3 per direct labor hour for variable overhead, and $0.25 per unit or $1 per direct labor hour for fixed overhead.

Standard costs based on expected output of 25,000 units

	Per Unit of Output	Quantity to Be Used	Total Cost
Direct materials, 4 oz. @ $0.31/oz.	$1.24/unit	100,000 oz.	$31,000
Direct labor, 0.25 hrs. @ $6.00/hr.	1.50/unit	6,250 hrs.	37,500
Overhead	1.00/unit		25,000

Actual costs incurred to produce 27,000 units

	Per Unit of Output	Quantity Used	Total Cost
Direct materials, 4 oz. @ $0.28/oz.	$1.12/unit	108,000 oz.	$30,240
Direct labor, 0.20 hrs. @ $7.00/hr.	1.40/unit	5,400 hrs.	37,800
Overhead	1.20/unit		32,400

Standard costs based on expected output of 27,000 units

	Per Unit of Output	Quantity to Be Used	Total Cost
Direct materials, 4 oz. @ $0.31/oz.	$1.24/unit	108,000 oz.	$33,480
Direct labor, 0.25 hrs. @ $6.00/hr.	1.50/unit	6,750 hrs.	40,500
Overhead			26,500

Required

1. Prepare June flexible budgets showing expected sales, costs, and net income assuming 20,000, 25,000, and 30,000 units of output produced and sold.
2. Prepare a flexible budget performance report that compares actual results with the amounts budgeted if the actual volume had been expected.
3. Apply variance analysis for direct materials, for direct labor, and for overhead.

Planning the Solution

- Prepare a table showing the expected results at the three specified levels of output. Compute the variable costs by multiplying the per unit variable costs by the expected volumes. Include fixed costs at the given amounts. Combine the amounts in the table to show total variable costs, contribution margin, total fixed costs, and income from operations.
- Prepare a table showing the actual results and the amounts that should be incurred at 27,000 units. Show any differences in the third column and label them with an *F* for favorable if they increase income or a *U* for unfavorable if they decrease income.
- Using the chapter's format, compute these total variances and the individual variances requested:
  - Total materials variance (including the direct materials quantity variance and the direct materials price variance).

- Total direct labor variance (including the direct labor efficiency variance and rate variance).
- Total overhead variance (including both variable and fixed overhead variances and their component variances).

Solution to Demonstration Problem

1.

PACIFIC COMPANY
Flexible Budgets
For Month Ended June 30, 2005

	Flexible Budget				
	Variable Amount per Unit	Total Fixed Cost	Flexible Budget for Unit Sales of 20,000	Flexible Budget for Unit Sales of 25,000	Flexible Budget for Unit Sales of 30,000
Sales	$5.00		$100,000	$125,000	$150,000
Variable costs					
Direct materials	1.24		24,800	31,000	37,200
Direct labor	1.50		30,000	37,500	45,000
Factory supplies	0.25		5,000	6,250	7,500
Utilities	0.50		10,000	12,500	15,000
Selling costs	0.40		8,000	10,000	12,000
Total variable costs	3.89		77,800	97,250	116,700
Contribution margin	$1.11		22,200	27,750	33,300
Fixed costs					
Depreciation—Machinery		$3,750	3,750	3,750	3,750
Depreciation—Building		2,500	2,500	2,500	2,500
General liability insurance		1,200	1,200	1,200	1,200
Property taxes on office equipment		500	500	500	500
Other administrative expense		750	750	750	750
Total fixed costs		$8,700	8,700	8,700	8,700
Income from operations			$ 13,500	$ 19,050	$ 24,600

2.

PACIFIC COMPANY
Flexible Budget Performance Report
For Month Ended June 30, 2005

	Flexible Budget	Actual Results	Variance*
Sales (27,000 units)	$135,000	$141,210	**$6,210 F**
Variable costs			
Direct materials	33,480	30,240	**3,240 F**
Direct labor	40,500	37,800	**2,700 F**
Factory supplies	6,750	9,990	**3,240 U**
Utilities	13,500	16,200	**2,700 U**
Selling costs	10,800	9,180	**1,620 F**
Total variable costs	105,030	103,410	**1,620 F**
Contribution margin	29,970	37,800	**7,830 F**
Fixed costs			
Depreciation—Machinery	3,750	3,710	**40 F**
Depreciation—Building	2,500	2,500	**0**
General liability insurance	1,200	1,250	**50 U**
Property taxes on office equipment	500	485	**15 F**
Other administrative expense	750	900	**150 U**
Total fixed costs	8,700	8,845	**145 U**
Income from operations	$ 21,270	$ 28,955	**$7,685 F**

* F = Favorable variance; and U = Unfavorable variance.

3. Variance analysis of materials, labor, and overhead costs.

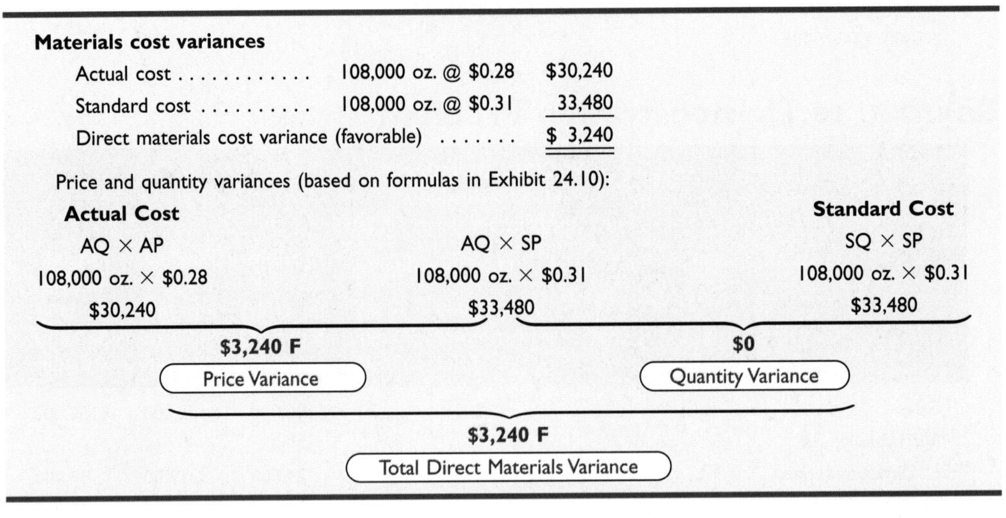

Materials cost variances

Actual cost	108,000 oz. @ $0.28	$30,240
Standard cost	108,000 oz. @ $0.31	33,480
Direct materials cost variance (favorable)		$ 3,240

Price and quantity variances (based on formulas in Exhibit 24.10):

Actual Cost		Standard Cost
AQ × AP	AQ × SP	SQ × SP
108,000 oz. × $0.28	108,000 oz. × $0.31	108,000 oz. × $0.31
$30,240	$33,480	$33,480

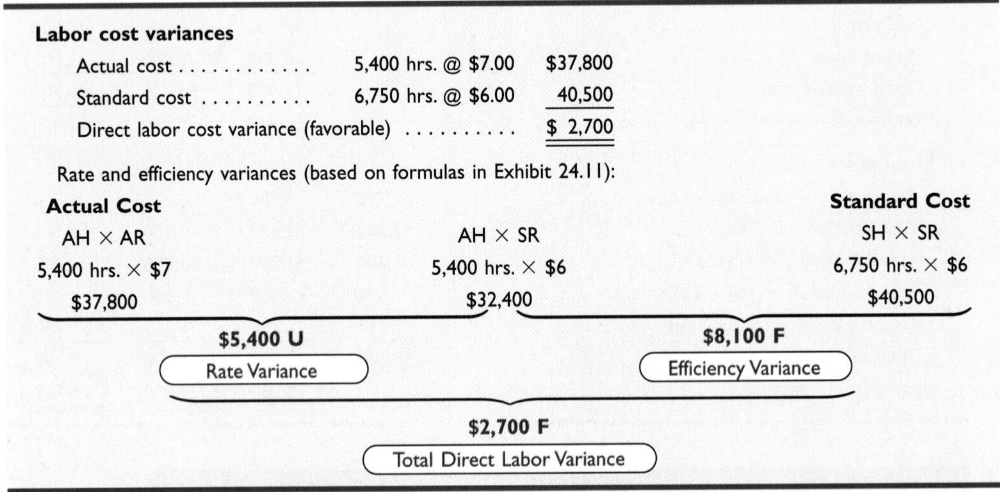

Labor cost variances

Actual cost	5,400 hrs. @ $7.00	$37,800
Standard cost	6,750 hrs. @ $6.00	40,500
Direct labor cost variance (favorable)		$ 2,700

Rate and efficiency variances (based on formulas in Exhibit 24.11):

Actual Cost		Standard Cost
AH × AR	AH × SR	SH × SR
5,400 hrs. × $7	5,400 hrs. × $6	6,750 hrs. × $6
$37,800	$32,400	$40,500

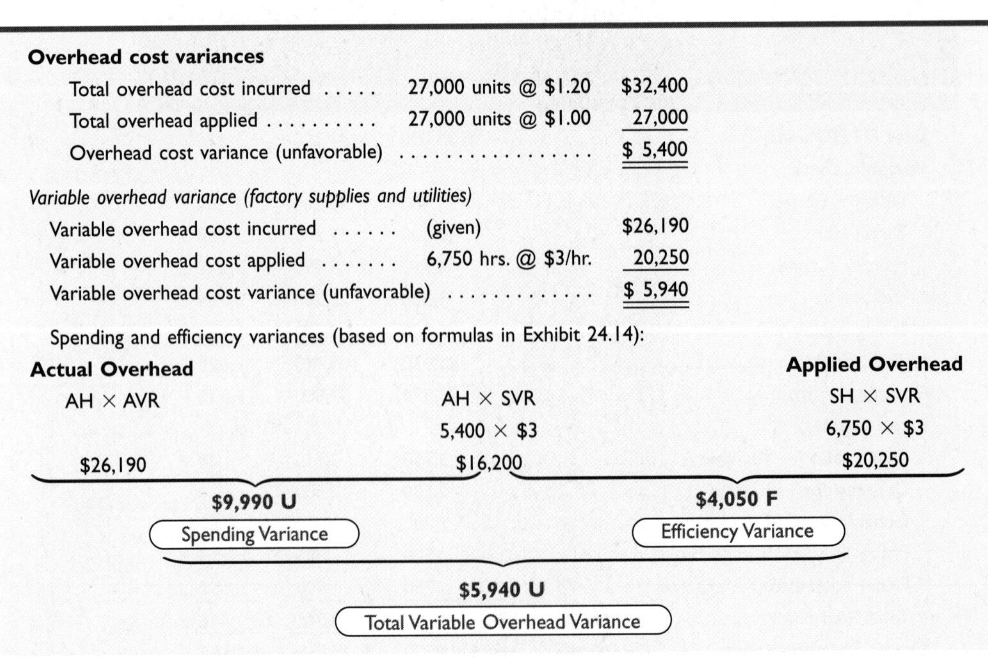

Overhead cost variances

Total overhead cost incurred	27,000 units @ $1.20	$32,400
Total overhead applied	27,000 units @ $1.00	27,000
Overhead cost variance (unfavorable)		$ 5,400

Variable overhead variance (factory supplies and utilities)

Variable overhead cost incurred	(given)	$26,190
Variable overhead cost applied	6,750 hrs. @ $3/hr.	20,250
Variable overhead cost variance (unfavorable)		$ 5,940

Spending and efficiency variances (based on formulas in Exhibit 24.14):

Actual Overhead		Applied Overhead
AH × AVR	AH × SVR	SH × SVR
	5,400 × $3	6,750 × $3
$26,190	$16,200	$20,250

[continued on next page]

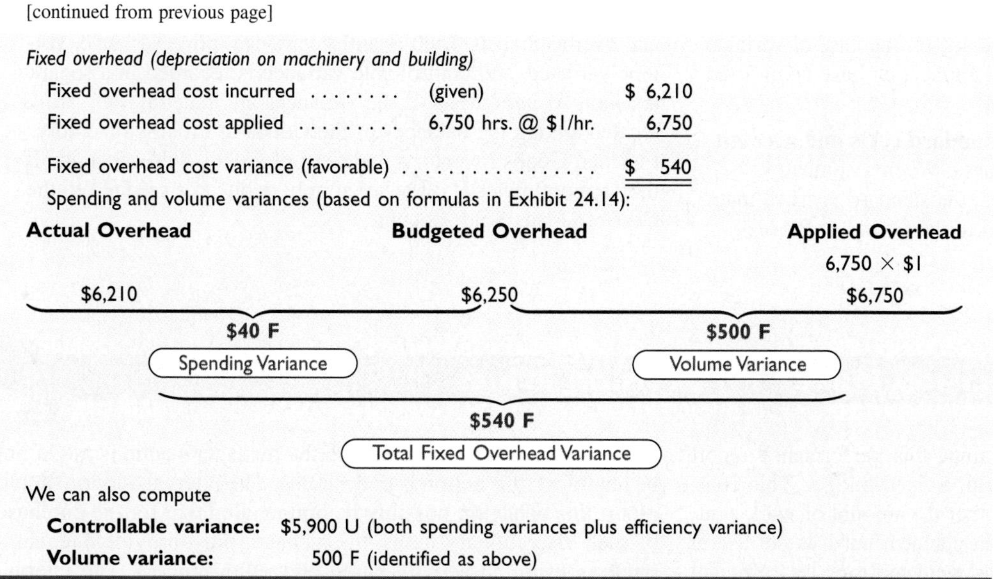

[continued from previous page]

Fixed overhead (depreciation on machinery and building)

Fixed overhead cost incurred	(given)	$ 6,210
Fixed overhead cost applied	6,750 hrs. @ $1/hr.	6,750
Fixed overhead cost variance (favorable)		$ 540

Spending and volume variances (based on formulas in Exhibit 24.14):

We can also compute

Controllable variance: $5,900 U (both spending variances plus efficiency variance)

Volume variance: 500 F (identified as above)

Summary

C1 Define standard costs and explain their computation and uses. Standard costs are the normal costs that should be incurred to produce a product or perform a service. They should be based on a careful examination of the processes used to produce a product or perform a service as well as the quantities and prices that should be incurred in carrying out those processes. On a performance report, standard costs (which are flexible budget amounts) are compared to actual costs, and the differences are presented as variances.

C2 Describe variances and what they reveal about performance. Management can use variances to monitor and control activities. Total cost variances can be broken into price and quantity variances to direct management's attention to those responsible for quantities used and prices paid.

C3 Explain how standard cost information is useful for management by exception. Standard cost accounting provides management information about costs that differ from budgeted (expected) amounts. Performance reports disclose the costs or areas of operations that have significant variances from budgeted amounts. This allows managers to focus attention on the exceptions and less attention on areas proceeding normally.

A1 Compare fixed and flexible budgets. A fixed budget shows the revenues and costs expected to occur at a specified volume level. If actual volume is at some other level, the amounts in the fixed budget do not provide a reasonable basis for evaluating actual performance. A flexible budget expresses variable costs in per unit terms so that it can be used to develop budgeted amounts for any volume level within the relevant range. Thus, managers compute budgeted amounts for evaluation after a period for the volume that actually occurred.

A2 Analyze changes in sales from expected amounts. Actual sales can differ from budgeted sales, and managers can investigate this difference by computing both the sales price and sales volume variances. The *sales price variance* refers to that portion of total variance resulting from a difference between actual and budgeted selling prices. The *sales volume variance* refers to that portion of total variance resulting from a difference between actual and budgeted sales quantities.

P1 Prepare a flexible budget and interpret a flexible budget performance report. To prepare a flexible budget, we express each variable cost as a constant amount per unit of sales (or as a percent of sales dollar). In contrast, the budgeted amount of each fixed cost is expressed as a total amount expected to occur at any sales volume within the relevant range. The flexible budget is then determined using these computations and amounts for fixed and variable costs at the expected sales volume.

P2 Compute materials and labor variances. Materials and labor variances are due to differences between the actual costs incurred and the budgeted costs. The price (or rate) variance is computed by comparing the actual cost with the flexible budget amount that should have been incurred to acquire the actual quantity of resources. The quantity (or efficiency) variance is computed by comparing the flexible budget amount that should have been incurred to acquire the actual quantity of resources with the flexible budget amount that should have been incurred to acquire the standard quantity of resources.

P3 Compute overhead variances. Overhead variances are due to differences between the actual overhead costs incurred and the overhead applied to production. An overhead spending variance arises when the actual amount incurred differs from the budgeted amount of overhead. An overhead efficiency (or volume) variance arises when the flexible overhead budget amount differs from the overhead applied to production. It is important to realize that overhead is assigned using an overhead allocation base, meaning that an efficiency variance (in the case of variable overhead) is a result of the overhead application base being used more or less efficiently than planned.

P4 **Prepare journal entries for standard costs and account for price and quantity variances.** When a company records standard costs in its accounts, the standard costs of materials, labor, and overhead are debited to the Goods in Process Inventory account. Based on an analysis of the material, labor, and overhead costs, each quantity variance, price variance, volume variance, and controllable variance is recorded in a separate account. At period-end, if the variances are material, they are allocated among the balances of the Goods in Process Inventory, Finished Goods Inventory, and Cost of Goods Sold accounts. If they are not material, they are simply debited or credited to the Cost of Goods Sold account.

Guidance Answers to **Decision Maker** and **Decision Ethics**

Entrepreneur From the complaints, this performance report appears to compare actual results with a fixed budget. This comparison is useful in determining whether the amount of work actually performed was more or less than planned, but it is not useful in determining whether the divisions were more or less efficient than planned. If the two consulting divisions worked on more assignments than expected, some costs will certainly increase. Therefore, you should prepare a flexible budget using the actual number of consulting assignments and then compare actual performance to the flexible budget.

Human Resource Manager As HR manager, you should investigate the causes for any labor-related variances although you may not be responsible for them. An unfavorable labor efficiency variance occurs because more labor hours than standard were used during the period. There are at least three possible reasons for this: (1) materials quality could be poor, resulting in more labor consumption due to rework, (2) unplanned interruptions (strike, breakdowns, accidents) could have occurred during the period, and (3) the production manager could have used a different labor mix to expedite orders. This new labor mix could have consisted of a larger proportion of untrained labor, which resulted in more labor hours.

Internal Auditor Although the manager's actions might not be unethical, this action is undesirable. The internal auditor should report this behavior, possibly recommending that for the purchase of such discretionary items, the manager must provide budgetary requests using an activity-based budgeting process. The internal auditor would then be given full authority to verify this budget request.

Sales Manager The unfavorable sales price variance suggests that actual prices were lower than budgeted prices. As the sales manager, you want to know the reasons for a lower than expected price. Perhaps your salespeople lowered the price of certain products by offering quantity discounts. You then might want to know what prompted them to offer the quantity discounts (perhaps competitors were offering discounts). You want to break the sales volume variance into both the sales mix and sales quantity variances. You could find that although the sales quantity variance is favorable, the sales mix variance is not. Then you need to investigate why actual sales mix differs from budgeted sales mix.

Guidance Answers to **Quick Checks**

1. *b*
2. The first step is classifying each cost as variable or fixed.
3. A fixed budget is prepared using an expected volume of sales or production. A flexible budget is prepared using the actual volume of activity.
4. Contribution margin equals sales less variable costs.
5. *c*
6. It is the difference between actual cost and standard cost.
7. *a*; Total actual hours: 2,500 × 2.5 = 6,250
   Total standard hours: 2,500 × 2.0 = 5,000
   Efficiency variance = (6,250 − 5,000) × $3.00
   = $3,750 U
8. *b*; Rate variance = ($3.10 − $3.00) × 6,250 = $625 U
9. Yes, this will occur when the materials quantity variance is more than the materials price variance.
10. The overhead volume variance is favorable when the actual operating level is higher than the expected level.
11. *b*
12.

Goods in Process Inventory	75,700	
Direct Materials Price Variance	1,300	
Direct Materials Quantity Variance		3,800
Raw Materials Inventory		73,200

13. If the variances are material, they should be prorated among the Goods in Process Inventory, Finished Goods Inventory, and Cost of Goods Sold accounts. If they are not material, they can be closed to Cost of Goods Sold.

Key Terms

Key Terms are available at the book's Website for learning and testing in an online Flashcard Format.

Budgetary control (p. 942)
Budget report (p. 942)
Controllable variance (p. 955)
Cost variance (p. 949)
Efficiency variance (p. 954)
Favorable variance (p. 944)
Fixed budget (p. 943)
Fixed budget performance report (p. 943)
Flexible budget (p. 944)
Flexible budget performance report (p. 946)
Management by exception (p. 958)
Overhead cost variance (p. 954)
Price variance (p. 946)
Quantity variance (p. 946)
Spending variance (p. 954)
Standard costs (p. 947)
Unfavorable variance (p. 944)
Variance analysis (p. 946)
Volume variance (p. 955)

Personal Interactive Quiz

Personal Interactive Quizzes A and B are available at the book's Website to reinforce and assess your learning.

Discussion Questions

1. What limits the usefulness to managers of fixed budget performance reports?
2. Identify the main purpose of a flexible budget for managers.
3. Prepare a flexible budget performance report title (in proper form) for Spalding Company for the calendar year 2005. Why is a proper title important for this or any report?
4. What type of analysis does a flexible budget performance report help management perform?
5. In what sense can a variable cost be considered constant?
6. What department is usually responsible for a direct labor rate variance? What department is usually responsible for a direct labor efficiency variance? Explain.
7. What is a price variance? What is a quantity variance?
8. What is the purpose of using standard costs?
9. In an analysis of fixed overhead cost variances, what is the volume variance?
10. What is the predetermined standard overhead rate? How is it computed?
11. In general, variance analysis is said to provide information about ________ and ________ variances.
12. In an analysis of overhead cost variances, what is the controllable variance and what causes it?
13. What is the relation among standard costs, flexible budgets, variance analysis, and management by exception?
14. **Krispy Kreme** has a standard cost for a special type of donut. List several factors that might cause the actual cost incurred to vary from the standard cost.
15. Assume that **Tastykake**'s overhead costs consist only of variable costs and its actual sales volume is 10% higher than its budgeted sales volume. What type of volume variance would it experience?
16. Assume that **Harley-Davidson** is budgeted to operate at 80% of capacity but actually operates at 75% of capacity. What effect will the 5% deviation have on the controllable variance? The volume variance?

Red numbers denote Discussion Questions that involve decision-making.

***Homework Manager** repeats all numerical Quick Studies on the book's Website with new numbers.*

QUICK STUDY

QS 24-1
Flexible budget performance report
P1

Santana Company reports the following selected financial results for May. For the level of production achieved in May, the budgeted amounts would be: sales, $650,000; variable costs, $375,000; and fixed costs, $150,000. Prepare a flexible budget performance report for May.

Sales (150,000 units)	$637,500
Variable costs	356,250
Fixed costs	150,000

QS 24-2
Labor cost variances
C2 P2

Reflection Company's output for the current period results in a $40,000 unfavorable direct labor rate variance and a $20,000 unfavorable direct labor efficiency variance. Production for the current period was assigned an $800,000 standard direct labor cost. What is the actual total direct labor cost for the current period?

QS 24-3
Materials cost variances
C2 P2

Jacomo Company's output for the current period was assigned a $300,000 standard direct materials cost. The direct materials variances included a $24,000 favorable price variance and a $4,000 favorable quantity variance. What is the actual total direct materials cost for the current period?

QS 24-4
Materials cost variances
C2 P2

For the current period, Kawaga Company's manufacturing operations yield a $4,000 favorable price variance on its direct materials usage. The actual price per pound of material is $77; the standard price is $77.50. How many pounds of material are used in the current period?

QS 24-5
Management by exception
C3

Managers use *management by exception* for control purposes. (1) Describe the concept of management by exception. (2) Explain how standard costs help managers apply this concept to monitor and control costs.

QS 24-6
Overhead cost variances
P3

Hewitt Company's output for the current period yields a $30,000 favorable overhead volume variance and a $50,400 unfavorable overhead controllable variance. Standard overhead charged to production for the period is $225,000. What is the actual total overhead cost incurred for the period?

QS 24-7
Preparing overhead entries P4

Refer to the information in QS 24-6. Hewitt records standard costs in its accounts. Prepare the journal entry to charge overhead costs to the Goods in Process Inventory account and to record any variances.

QS 24-8
Computing sales price and volume variances
A2

VanWay, Inc., specializes in selling used SUVs. During the first six months of 2005, the dealership sold 100 SUVs at an average price of $10,000 each. The budget for the first six months of 2005 was to sell 90 SUVs at an average price of $10,500 each. Compute the dealership's sales price variance and sales volume variance for the first six months of 2005.

Homework Manager *repeats all numerical Exercises on the book's Website with new numbers.*

EXERCISES

Exercise 24-1
Preparation of flexible budgets
P1

Mesa Company's fixed budget for the first quarter of calendar year 2005 reveals the following. Prepare flexible budgets following the format of Exhibit 24.3 that show variable costs per unit, fixed costs, and three different flexible budgets for sales volumes of 7,500, 10,000, and 12,500 units.

Sales (10,000 units)		$3,000,000
Cost of goods sold		
Direct materials	$320,000	
Direct labor	680,000	
Production supplies	264,000	
Plant manager salary	60,000	1,324,000
Gross profit		1,676,000
Selling expenses		
Sales commissions	120,000	
Packaging	210,000	
Advertising	100,000	430,000
Administrative expenses		
Administrative salaries	80,000	
Depreciation—Office equip.	30,000	
Insurance	18,000	
Office rent	24,000	152,000
Income from operations		$1,094,000

Check Income (at 7,500 units), $742,500

Exercise 24-2
Classification of costs as fixed or variable
P1 

KMAR Company manufactures and sells mountain bikes. It normally operates eight hours a day, five days a week. Using this information, classify each of the following costs as fixed or variable. If additional information would affect your decision, describe the information.

a. Incoming shipping expenses
b. Office supplies
c. Depreciation on tools
d. Taxes on property
e. Pension cost
f. Gas used for heating
g. Bike frames
h. Direct labor
i. Screws for assembly
j. Repair expense for tools
k. Management salaries

Exercise 24-3
Preparation of a flexible budget performance report
A1

Daytec Company's fixed budget performance report for June follows. The $440,000 budgeted expenses include $300,000 variable expenses and $140,000 fixed expenses. Actual expenses include $130,000 fixed expenses. Prepare a flexible budget performance report that shows any variances between budgeted results and actual results. List fixed and variable expenses separately.

	Fixed Budget	Actual Results	Variances
Sales (in units)	6,000	4,800	
Sales (in dollars)	$480,000	$422,400	$57,600 U
Total expenses	440,000	394,000	46,000 F
Income from operations	$ 40,000	$ 28,400	$11,600 U

Check Income variance, $24,400 F

Exercise 24-4
Preparation of a flexible budget performance report
A1

Cimarron Company's fixed budget performance report for July follows. The $630,000 budgeted expenses include $588,000 variable expenses and $42,000 fixed expenses. Actual expenses include $54,000 fixed expenses. Prepare a flexible budget performance report showing any variances between budgeted and actual results. List fixed and variable expenses separately.

	Fixed Budget	Actual Results	Variances
Sales (in units)	8,400	10,800	
Sales (in dollars)	$840,000	$1,080,000	$240,000 F
Total expenses	630,000	756,000	126,000 U
Income from operations	$210,000	$ 324,000	$114,000 F

Check Income variance, $42,000 F

Exercise 24-5
Computation and interpretation of labor variances
C2 P2 

After evaluating Zero Company's manufacturing process, management decides to establish standards of 1.5 hours of direct labor per unit of product and $11 per hour for the labor rate. During October, the company uses 3,780 hours of direct labor at a $45,360 total cost to produce 2,700 units of product. In November, the company uses 4,480 hours of direct labor at a $47,040 total cost to produce 2,800 units of product. (1) Compute the rate variance, the efficiency variance, and the total direct labor cost variance for each of these two months. (2) Interpret the October direct labor variances.

Exercise 24-6
Computation and interpretation of overhead variances
C2 P3 

Sonic Company set the following standard costs for one unit of its product for 2005:

Direct material (20 lbs. @ $2.50 per lb.)	$ 50.00
Direct labor (15 hrs. @ $8.00 per hr.)	120.00
Factory variable overhead (15 hrs. @ $2.50 per hr.)	37.50
Factory fixed overhead (15 hrs. @ $0.50 per hr.)	7.50
Standard cost	$215.00

The $3.00 ($2.50 + $0.50) total overhead rate per direct labor hour is based on an expected operating level equal to 75% of the factory's capacity of 50,000 units per month. The following monthly flexible budget information is also available:

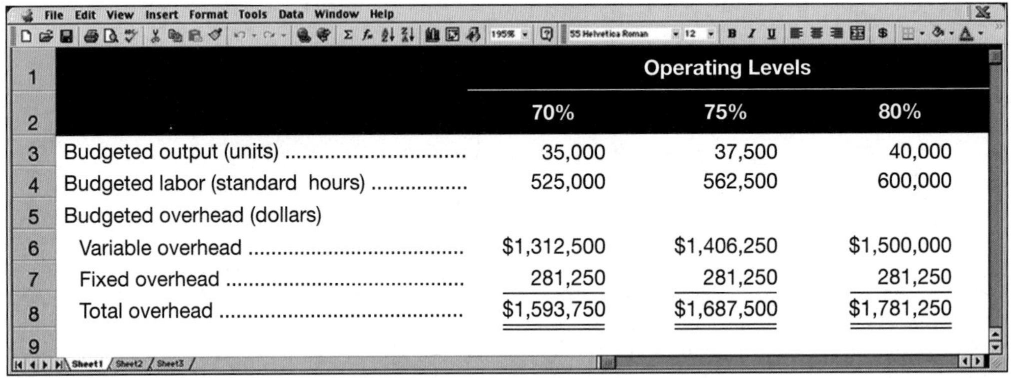

	Operating Levels		
	70%	75%	80%
Budgeted output (units)	35,000	37,500	40,000
Budgeted labor (standard hours)	525,000	562,500	600,000
Budgeted overhead (dollars)			
Variable overhead	$1,312,500	$1,406,250	$1,500,000
Fixed overhead	281,250	281,250	281,250
Total overhead	$1,593,750	$1,687,500	$1,781,250

During the current month, the company operated at 70% of capacity, employees worked 500,000 hours, and the following actual overhead costs are incurred:

Variable overhead costs	$1,267,500
Fixed overhead costs	285,000
Total overhead costs	$1,552,500

Check (2) Variable overhead: Spending, $17,500 U; Efficiency, $62,500 F

(1) Show how the company computed its predetermined overhead application rate per hour for total overhead, variable overhead, and fixed overhead. (2) Compute and interpret the variable overhead spending and efficiency variances. (3) Compute and interpret the fixed overhead spending and volume variances.

Exercise 24-7
Computation and interpretation of materials variances

C2 P2 

BTS Company made 6,000 bookshelves using 88,000 board feet of wood costing $607,200. The company's direct materials standards for one bookshelf are 16 board feet of wood at $7 per board foot. (1) Compute the direct materials variances incurred in manufacturing these bookshelves. (2) Interpret the direct materials variances.

Exercise 24-8
Materials variances recorded and closed

C3 P4 

Refer to Exercise 24-7. BTS Company records standard costs in its accounts and its material variances in separate accounts when it assigns materials costs to the Goods in Process Inventory account. (1) Show the journal entry that both charges the direct materials costs to the Goods in Process Inventory account and records the materials variances in their proper accounts. (2) Assume that BTS's material variances are the only variances accumulated in the accounting period and that they are immaterial. Prepare the adjusting journal entry to close the variance accounts at period-end. (3) Identify the variance that should be investigated according to the management by exception concept. Explain.

Exercise 24-9
Computation of volume and controllable overhead variances

P3

Earth Company expects to operate at 80% of its productive capacity of 25,000 units per month. At this planned level, the company expects to use 40,000 standard hours of direct labor. Overhead is allocated to products using a predetermined standard rate based on direct labor hours. At the 80% capacity level, the total budgeted cost includes $40,000 fixed overhead cost and $280,000 variable overhead cost. In the current month, the company incurred $340,000 actual overhead and 39,000 actual labor hours while producing 19,500 units. Compute the (1) total overhead variance, (2) overhead volume variance, and (3) overhead controllable variance.

Check (3) $27,000 U

Exercise 24-10
Computing and interpreting sales variances A2

Comp Wiz sells computers. During May 2005, it sold 500 computers at a $900 average price each. The May 2005 budget included sales of 550 computers at an average price of $850 each. (1) Compute the sales price variance and the sales volume variance for May 2005. (2) Interpret the findings.

PROBLEM SET A

Problem 24-1A
Computation of materials, labor, and overhead variances
C2 P2 P3

eXcel
mhhe.com/larson

Tuna Company set the following standard unit costs for its single product:

Direct materials (25 lbs. @ $4 per lb.)	$100.00
Direct labor (6 hrs. @ $8 per hr.)	48.00
Factory overhead—Variable (6 hrs. @ $5 per hr.)	30.00
Factory overhead—Fixed (6 hrs. @ $7 per hr.)	42.00
Total standard cost	$220.00

The predetermined overhead rate is based on a planned operating volume of 80% of the productive capacity of 60,000 units per quarter. The following flexible budget information is available:

	Operating Levels		
	70%	80%	90%
Production in units	42,000	48,000	54,000
Standard direct labor hours	252,000	288,000	324,000
Budgeted overhead			
Fixed factory overhead	$2,016,000	$2,016,000	$2,016,000
Variable factory overhead	$1,260,000	$1,440,000	$1,620,000

During the current quarter, the company operated at 70% of capacity and produced 42,000 units of product; actual direct labor totaled 250,000 hours. Units produced are assigned the following standard costs:

Direct materials (1,050,000 lbs. @ $4 per lb.)	$4,200,000
Direct labor (252,000 hrs. @ $8 per hr.)	2,016,000
Factory overhead (252,000 hrs. @ $12 per hr.)	3,024,000
Total standard cost	$9,240,000

Actual costs incurred during the current quarter follow:

Direct materials (1,000,000 lbs. @ $4.25)	$4,250,000
Direct labor (250,000 hrs. @ $7.75)	1,937,500
Fixed factory overhead costs	1,960,000
Variable factory overhead costs	1,200,000
Total actual costs	$9,347,500

Required

1. Compute the direct materials cost variance, including its price and quantity variances.
2. Compute the direct labor variance including its rate and efficiency variances.
3. Compute these variances: (a) variable overhead spending and efficiency, (b) fixed overhead spending and volume, and (c) total overhead controllable.

Check (1) Materials variances: Price, $250,000 U; Quantity, $200,000 F. (2) Labor variances: Rate, $62,500 F; Efficiency, $16,000 F

Problem 24-2A
Preparation and analysis of a flexible budget
P1 A1

Pebco Company's 2005 master budget included the following fixed budget performance report. It is based on an expected production and sales volume of 20,000 units.

PEBCO COMPANY Fixed Budget Performance Report For Year Ended December 31, 2005		
Sales		$3,000,000
Cost of goods sold		
Direct materials	$1,200,000	
Direct labor	260,000	
Machinery repairs (variable cost)	57,000	
Depreciation—Plant equipment	250,000	
Utilities ($50,000 is variable)	200,000	
Plant management salaries	140,000	2,107,000
Gross profit		893,000

[continued on next page]

[continued from previous page]

Selling expenses		
Packaging	80,000	
Shipping	116,000	
Sales salary (fixed annual amount)	160,000	356,000
General and administrative expenses		
Advertising expense	81,000	
Salaries	241,000	
Entertainment expense	90,000	412,000
Income from operations		$ 125,000

Required

1. Classify all items listed in the fixed budget as variable or fixed. Also determine their amounts per unit or their amounts for the year, as appropriate.
2. Prepare flexible budgets (see Exhibit 24.3) for the company at sales volumes of 18,000 and 24,000 units.
3. The company's business conditions are improving. One possible result is a sales volume of approximately 28,000 units. The company president is confident that this volume is within the relevant range of existing capacity. How much would operating income increase over the 2005 budgeted amount of $125,000 if this level is reached without increasing capacity?
4. An unfavorable change in business is remotely possible; in this case, production and sales volume for 2005 could fall to 14,000 units. How much income (or loss) from operations would occur if sales volume falls to this level?

Check (2) Budgeted income at 24,000 units, $372,400

(4) Potential operating loss, $(246,100)

Problem 24-3A
Preparation and analysis of a flexible budget performance report

P1 A2

mhhe.com/larson

Refer to information in Problem 24-2A. Pebco Company's actual income statement for 2005 follows:

PEBCO COMPANY
Statement of Income from Operations
For Year Ended December 31, 2005

Sales (24,000 units)		$3,648,000
Cost of goods sold		
Direct materials	$1,400,000	
Direct labor	360,000	
Machinery repairs (variable cost)	60,000	
Depreciation—Plant equipment	250,000	
Utilities (fixed cost is $154,000)	218,000	
Plant management salaries	155,000	2,443,000
Gross profit		1,205,000
Selling expenses		
Packaging	90,000	
Shipping	124,000	
Sales salary (annual)	162,000	376,000
General and administrative expenses		
Advertising expense	104,000	
Salaries	232,000	
Entertainment expense	100,000	436,000
Income from operations		$ 393,000

Required

1. Prepare a flexible budget performance report for 2005.

Check (1) Variances: Fixed costs, $45,000 U; Income, $20,600 F

Analysis Component

2. Analyze and interpret both the (a) sales variance and (b) direct materials variance.

Problem 24-4A
Flexible budget preparation; computation of materials, labor, and overhead variances; and overhead variance report
P1 P2 P3 C2

Kwikeze Company set the following standard costs for one unit of its product:

Direct materials (4.5 lbs. @ $6 per lb.)	$27.00
Direct labor (1.5 hrs. @ $12 per hr.)	18.00
Overhead (1.5 hrs. @ $16 per hr.)	24.00
Total standard cost	$69.00

The predetermined overhead rate ($16 per direct labor hour) is based on expected volume of 75% of the factory's capacity of 20,000 units per month. Following are the company's budgeted overhead costs per month at the 75% level:

Overhead Budget (75% capacity)		
Variable overhead costs		
Indirect materials	$22,500	
Indirect labor	90,000	
Power	22,500	
Repairs and maintenance	45,000	
Total variable overhead costs		$180,000
Fixed overhead costs		
Depreciation—Building	24,000	
Depreciation—Machinery	72,000	
Taxes and insurance	18,000	
Supervision	66,000	
Total fixed overhead costs		180,000
Total overhead costs		$360,000

The company incurred the following actual costs when it operated at 75% of capacity in October:

Direct materials (69,000 lbs. @ $6.10 per lb.)		$ 420,900
Direct labor (22,800 hrs. @ $12.30 per hr.)		280,440
Overhead costs		
Indirect materials	$21,600	
Indirect labor	82,260	
Power	23,100	
Repairs and maintenance	46,800	
Depreciation—Building	24,000	
Depreciation—Machinery	75,000	
Taxes and insurance	16,500	
Supervision	66,000	355,260
Total costs		$1,056,600

Required

1. Examine the monthly overhead budget to (a) determine the costs per unit for each variable overhead item and its total per unit costs, and (b) identify the total fixed costs per month.
2. Prepare flexible overhead budgets (as in Exhibit 24.12) for October showing the amounts of each variable and fixed cost at the 65%, 75%, and 85% capacity levels.
3. Compute the direct materials cost variance, including its price and quantity variances.
4. Compute the direct labor cost variance, including its rate and efficiency variances.
5. Compute the (a) variable overhead spending and efficiency variances, (b) fixed overhead spending and volume variances, and (c) total overhead controllable variance.
6. Prepare a detailed overhead variance report (as in Exhibit 24.19) that shows the variances for individual items of overhead.

Check (2) Budgeted total overhead at 13,000 units, $336,000.

(3) Materials variances: Price, $6,900 U; Quantity, $9,000 U.

(4) Labor variances: Rate, $6,840 U; Efficiency, $3,600 U

Problem 24-5A
Materials, labor, and overhead variances; and overhead variance report
C2 P2 P3

Kudos Company has set the following standard costs per unit for the product it manufactures:

Direct materials (10 lbs. @ $3 per lb.)	$30.00
Direct labor (4 hrs. @ $6 per hr.)	24.00
Overhead (4 hrs. @ $2.50 per hr.)	10.00
Total standard cost	$64.00

The predetermined overhead rate is based on a planned operating volume of 80% of the productive capacity of 10,000 units per month. The following flexible budget information is available:

	Operating Levels		
	70%	80%	90%
Production in units	7,000	8,000	9,000
Standard direct labor hours	28,000	32,000	36,000
Budgeted overhead			
Variable overhead costs			
Indirect materials	$ 8,750	$ 10,000	$11,250
Indirect labor	14,000	16,000	18,000
Power	3,500	4,000	4,500
Maintenance	1,750	2,000	2,250
Total variable costs	28,000	32,000	36,000
Fixed overhead costs			
Rent of factory building	12,000	12,000	12,000
Depreciation—Machinery	20,000	20,000	20,000
Supervisory salaries	16,000	16,000	16,000
Total fixed costs	48,000	48,000	48,000
Total overhead costs	$76,000	$ 80,000	$84,000

During May, the company operated at 90% of capacity and produced 9,000 units, incurring the following actual costs:

Direct materials (92,000 lbs. @ $2.95 per lb.)		$271,400
Direct labor (37,600 hrs. @ $6.05 per hr.)		227,480
Overhead costs		
Indirect materials	$10,000	
Indirect labor	16,000	
Power	4,500	
Maintenance	3,000	
Rent of factory building	12,000	
Depreciation—Machinery	19,200	
Supervisory salaries	17,000	81,700
Total costs		$580,580

Required

Check (1) Materials variances: Price, $4,600 F; Quantity, $6,000 U. (2) Labor variances: Rate, $1,880 U; Efficiency, $9,600 U.

1. Compute the direct materials variance, including its price and quantity variances.
2. Compute the direct labor variance, including its rate and efficiency variances.
3. Compute these variances: (a) variable overhead spending and efficiency, (b) fixed overhead spending and volume, and (c) total overhead controllable.
4. Prepare a detailed overhead variance report (as in Exhibit 24.19) that shows the variances for individual items of overhead.

Problem 24-6A
Materials, labor, and overhead variances recorded and analyzed
C3 P4 

Loretto Company's standard cost accounting system recorded this information from its December operations.

Standard direct materials cost	$130,000
Direct materials quantity variance (unfavorable)	5,000
Direct materials price variance (favorable)	1,500
Actual direct labor cost	65,000

[continued on next page]

[continued from previous page]

Direct labor efficiency variance (favorable)	7,000
Direct labor rate variance (unfavorable)	500
Actual overhead cost	250,000
Volume variance (unfavorable)	12,000
Controllable variance (unfavorable)	8,000

Required

1. Prepare December 30 journal entries to record the company's costs and variances for the month.

Check (1) Dr. Goods in Process Inventory (for overhead), $230,000

Analysis Component

2. Identify the areas that would attract the attention of a manager who uses management by exception. Explain what action(s) the manager should consider.

PROBLEM SET B

Problem 24-1B

Computation of materials, labor, and overhead variances

C2 P2 P3

Sabates Company set the following standard unit costs for its single product:

Direct materials (5 lbs. @ $10 per lb.)	$ 50.00
Direct labor (3 hrs. @ $15 per hr.)	45.00
Factory overhead—Variable (3 hrs. @ $5 per hr.)	15.00
Factory overhead—Fixed (3 hrs. @ $3 per hr.)	9.00
Total standard cost	$119.00

The predetermined overhead rate is based on a planned operating volume of 90% of the productive capacity of 100,000 units per quarter. The following flexible budget information is available:

	Operating Levels		
	80%	90%	100%
Production in units	32,000	36,000	40,000
Standard direct labor hours	96,000	108,000	120,000
Budgeted overhead			
Fixed factory overhead	$324,000	$324,000	$324,000
Variable factory overhead	480,000	540,000	600,000

During the current quarter, the company operated at 80% of capacity and produced 32,000 units of product; direct labor hours worked were 100,000. Units produced are assigned the following standard costs:

Direct materials (160,000 lbs. @ $10 per lb.)	$1,600,000
Direct labor (96,000 hrs. @ $15 per hr.)	1,440,000
Factory overhead (96,000 hrs. @ $8.00 per hr.)	768,000
Total standard cost	$3,808,000

Actual costs incurred during the current quarter follow:

Direct materials (155,000 lbs. @ $10.20)	$1,581,000
Direct labor (100,000 hrs. @ $14.00)	1,400,000
Fixed factory overhead costs	370,000
Variable factory overhead costs	480,000
Total actual costs	$3,831,000

Required

1. Compute the direct materials cost variance, including its price and quantity variances.

2. Compute the direct labor variance, including its rate and efficiency variances.

3. Compute these variances: (a) variable overhead spending and efficiency, (b) fixed overhead spending and volume, and (c) total overhead controllable.

Check (1) Materials variances: Price, $31,000 U; Quantity, $50,000 F. (2) Labor variances: Rate, $100,000 F; Efficiency, $60,000 U

Problem 24-2B
Preparation and analysis of a flexible budget
P1 A1

Razorback Company's 2005 master budget included the following fixed budget performance report. It is based on an expected production and sales volume of 10,000 units.

RAZORBACK COMPANY Fixed Budget Performance Report For Year Ended December 31, 2005		
Sales		$250,000
Cost of goods sold		
Direct materials	$100,000	
Direct labor	20,000	
Machinery repairs (variable cost)	3,000	
Depreciation—Machinery	11,920	
Utilities (80% is variable cost)	8,000	
Plant manager salaries	6,000	148,920
Gross profit		101,080
Selling expenses		
Packaging	9,000	
Shipping	30,000	
Sales salary (fixed annual amount)	18,000	57,000
General and administrative expenses		
Advertising	4,000	
Salaries	9,360	
Entertainment expense	10,000	23,360
Income from operations		$ 20,720

Required

1. Classify all items listed in the fixed budget as variable or fixed. Also determine their amounts per unit or their amounts for the year, as appropriate.
2. Prepare flexible budgets (see Exhibit 24.3) for the company at sales volumes of 8,000 and 12,000 units.
3. The company's business conditions are improving. One possible result is a sales volume of approximately 14,400 units. The company president is confident that this volume is within the relevant range of existing capacity. How much would operating income increase over the 2005 budgeted amount of $20,720 if this level is reached without increasing capacity?
4. An unfavorable change in business is remotely possible; in this case, production and sales volume for 2005 could fall to 5,000 units. How much income (or loss) from operations would occur if sales volume falls to this level?

Check (2) Budgeted income at 12,000 units, $37,040

(4) Potential operating loss, $(20,080)

Problem 24-3B
Preparation and analysis of a flexible budget performance report
P1 A2

Refer to information in Problem 24-2B. Razorback Company's actual income statement for 2005 follows:

RAZORBACK COMPANY Statement of Income from Operations For Year Ended December 31, 2005		
Sales (12,000 units)		$288,000
Cost of goods sold		
Direct materials	$95,000	
Direct labor	16,000	
Machinery repairs (variable cost)	3,300	
Depreciation—Machinery	11,920	
Utilities (variable cost, $7,160)	8,520	
Plant manager salaries	6,720	141,460
Gross profit		146,540
Selling expenses		
Packaging	10,800	
Shipping	37,200	
Sales salary (annual)	19,200	67,200
General and administrative expenses		
Advertising expense	4,200	
Salaries	9,360	
Entertainment expense	10,000	23,560
Income from operations		$ 55,780

Required

1. Prepare a flexible budget performance report for 2005.

Check (1) Variances: Fixed costs, $1,880 U; Income, $18,740 F

Analysis Component

2. Analyze and interpret both the (a) sales variance and (b) direct materials variance.

Problem 24-4B

Flexible budget preparation; computation of materials, labor, and overhead variances; and overhead variance report

P1 P2 P3 C2

Sunburst Company set the following standard costs for one unit of its product:

Direct materials (48 kgs. @ $4 per kg.)	$192.00
Direct labor (12 hrs. @ $9 per hr.)	108.00
Overhead (12 hrs. @ $4.50 per hr.)	54.00
Total standard cost	$354.00

The predetermined overhead rate ($4.50 per direct labor hour) is based on an expected volume of 50% of the factory's capacity of 10,000 units per month. Following are the company's budgeted overhead costs per month at the 50% level:

Overhead Budget (50% capacity)		
Variable overhead costs		
Indirect materials	$40,000	
Indirect labor	80,000	
Power	20,000	
Repairs and maintenance	30,000	
Total variable overhead costs		$170,000
Fixed overhead costs		
Depreciation—Building	20,000	
Depreciation—Machinery	30,000	
Taxes and insurance	10,000	
Supervision	40,000	
Total fixed overhead costs		100,000
Total overhead costs		$270,000

The company incurred the following actual costs when it operated at 40% of capacity in December:

Direct materials (196,000 kgs. @ $4.00)		$ 784,000
Direct labor (46,000 hrs. @ $9.15)		420,900
Overhead costs		
Indirect materials	$30,000	
Indirect labor	66,000	
Power	15,600	
Repairs and maintenance	21,000	
Depreciation—Building	20,000	
Depreciation—Machinery	30,000	
Taxes and insurance	9,600	
Supervision	39,600	231,800
Total costs		$1,436,700

Required

1. Examine the monthly overhead budget to (a) determine the costs per unit for each variable overhead item and its total per unit costs, and (b) identify the total fixed costs per month.

2. Prepare flexible overhead budgets (as in Exhibit 24.12) for December showing the amounts of each variable and fixed cost at the 40%, 50%, and 60% capacity levels.

Check (2) Budgeted total overhead at 6,000 units, $304,000;

3. Compute the direct materials cost variance, including its price and quantity variances.

(3) Materials variances: Price, $0; Quantity, $16,000 U

4. Compute the direct labor cost variance, including its rate and efficiency variances.

(4) Labor variances: Rate, $6,900 U; Efficiency, $18,000 F

5. Compute the (a) variable overhead spending and efficiency variances, (b) fixed overhead spending and volume variances, and (c) total overhead controllable variance.

6. Prepare a detailed overhead variance report (as in Exhibit 24.19) that shows the variances for individual items of overhead.

Problem 24-5B
Materials, labor, and overhead variances; and overhead variance report
C2 P2 P3

Carlsbad Company has set the following standard costs per unit for the product it manufactures:

Direct materials (40 oz. @ $0.75 per oz.)	$ 30.00
Direct labor (2 hr. @ $20 per hr.)	40.00
Overhead (2 hr. @ $53.50 per hr.)	107.00
Total standard cost	$177.00

The predetermined overhead rate is based on a planned operating volume of 60% of the productive capacity of 3,000 units per month. The following flexible budget information is available:

	Operating Levels		
	50%	60%	70%
Production in units	1,500	1,800	2,100
Standard direct labor hours	3,000	3,600	4,200
Budgeted overhead			
Variable overhead costs			
Indirect materials	$ 18,000	$21,600	$25,200
Indirect labor	10,500	12,600	14,700
Power	7,500	9,000	10,500
Maintenance	4,500	5,400	6,300
Total variable costs	40,500	48,600	56,700
Fixed overhead costs			
Rent of factory building	48,000	48,000	48,000
Depreciation—Machinery	44,000	44,000	44,000
Taxes and insurance	20,000	20,000	20,000
Supervisory salaries	32,000	32,000	32,000
Total fixed costs	144,000	144,000	144,000
Total overhead costs	$184,500	$192,600	$200,700

During March, the company operated at 70% of capacity and produced 2,100 units, incurring the following actual costs:

Direct materials (88,000 ozs. @ $0.70 per oz.)		$ 61,600
Direct labor (4,000 hrs. @ $19.50 per hr.)		78,000
Overhead costs		
Indirect materials	$23,600	
Indirect labor	14,800	
Power	10,000	
Maintenance	3,200	
Rent of factory building	48,000	
Depreciation—Machinery	44,000	
Taxes and insurance	24,000	
Supervisory salaries	31,600	199,200
Total costs		$338,800

Check (1) Materials variances: Price, $4,400 F; Quantity, $3,000 U.
(2) Labor variances: Rate, $2,000 F; Efficiency, $4,000 F

Required

1. Compute the direct materials cost variance, including its price and quantity variances.
2. Compute the direct labor variance, including its rate and efficiency variances.

3. Compute these variances: (a) variable overhead spending and efficiency, (b) fixed overhead spending and volume, and (c) total overhead controllable.
4. Prepare a detailed overhead variance report (as in Exhibit 24.19) that shows the variances for individual items of overhead.

Problem 24-6B
Materials, labor, and overhead variances recorded and analyzed

C3 P4

Kincaid Company's standard cost accounting system recorded this information from its June operations:

Standard direct materials cost	$220,500
Direct materials quantity variance (favorable)	20,250
Direct materials price variance (favorable)	14,500
Actual direct labor cost	335,000
Direct labor efficiency variance (favorable)	26,700
Direct labor rate variance (unfavorable)	3,500
Actual overhead cost	359,000
Volume variance (unfavorable)	1,650
Controllable variance (unfavorable)	32,500

Required

1. Prepare journal entries dated June 30 to record the company's costs and variances for the month.

Check (1) Dr. Goods in Process Inventory (for overhead), $324,850

Analysis Component

2. Identify the areas that would attract the attention of a manager who uses management by exception. Describe what action(s) the manager should consider.

PROBLEM SET C

Problem Set C is available at the book's Website to further reinforce and assess your learning.

SERIAL PROBLEM
Success Systems

(This serial problem began in Chapter 1 and continues through most of the book. If previous chapter segments were not completed, the serial problem can begin at this point. It is helpful, but not necessary, for you to use the Working Papers that accompany the book.)

Success Systems' second quarter 2006 fixed budget performance report for its computer furniture operations follows. The $174,900 budgeted expenses include $159,900 variable expenses and $15,000 fixed expenses. The actual expenses include $18,000 fixed expenses. Prepare a flexible budget performance report that shows any variances between budgeted results and actual results. List fixed and variable expenses separately.

	Fixed Budget	Actual Results	Variances
Desk sales (in units)	72	90	
Chair sales (in units)	36	45	
Desk sales (in dollars)	$162,000	$207,000	$45,000 F
Chair sales (in dollars)	$ 27,000	$ 33,750	$ 6,750 F
Total expenses	$174,900	$162,300	$12,600 F
Income from operations	$ 14,100	$ 78,450	$64,350 F

Check Variances: Fixed expenses, $3,000 U

BEYOND THE NUMBERS

REPORTING IN ACTION

C1 

BTN 24-1 Analysis of flexible budgets and standard costs emphasizes the importance of a similar unit of measure for meaningful comparisons and evaluations. When **Krispy Kreme** compiles its financial reports in compliance with GAAP, it applies the same unit of measurement, U.S. dollars, for most measures of business operations. One issue for Krispy Kreme is how best to adjust account values for its subsidiaries that compile financial reports in currencies other than the U.S. dollar.

Required

1. Read Krispy Kreme's Note 2 in Appendix A and identify the financial statement where it reports foreign currency translation.
2. Record the annual amount of its foreign currency translation adjustment and its ending balance for the three fiscal years 2001–2003.

Roll On

3. Access Krispy Kreme's financial statements for a fiscal year ending after February 2, 2003, from either its Website [KrispyKreme.com] or the SEC's EDGAR database [www.sec.gov]. (a) Identify its foreign currency translation adjustment. (b) Does this adjustment increase or decrease net income? Explain.

COMPARATIVE ANALYSIS

A2 

BTN 24-2 The usefulness of budgets, variances, and related analyses often depends on the accuracy of management's estimates of future sales activity.

Required

1. Identify and record the prior three years' sales (in dollars) for both **Krispy Kreme** and **Tastykake** using their financial statements in Appendix A.
2. Using the data in part 1, predict both companies' sales activity for the next two to three years. (If possible, compare your predictions to actual sales figures for these years.)

ETHICS CHALLENGE

C1 

BTN 24-3 Setting materials, labor, and overhead standards is challenging. If standards are set too low, companies might purchase inferior products and employees might not work to their full potential. If standards are set too high, companies could be unable to offer a quality product at a profitable rate and employees could be overworked. The ethical challenge is to set a high but reasonable standard. Assume that as a manager, you are asked to set the standard materials price and quantity for the new 1,000 CKB Mega-Max chip, a technically advanced product. To properly set the price and quantity standards, you assemble a team of specialists to provide input.

Required

Identify four types of specialists that you would assemble to provide information to help set the materials price and quantity standards. Briefly explain why you chose each individual.

COMMUNICATING IN PRACTICE

P4 C2 

BTN 24-4 The reason we use the words *favorable* and *unfavorable* when evaluating variances is made clear when we look at the closing of accounts. To see this, consider that (1) all variance accounts are closed at the end of each period (temporary accounts), (2) a favorable variance is always a credit balance, and (3) an unfavorable variance is always a debit balance. Write a one-half page memorandum to your instructor with three parts that answer the three following requirements. (Assume that variance accounts are closed to Cost of Goods Sold.)

Required

1. Does Cost of Goods Sold increase or decrease when closing a favorable variance? Does gross margin increase or decrease when a favorable variance is closed to Cost of Goods Sold? Explain.
2. Does Cost of Goods Sold increase or decrease when closing an unfavorable variance? Does gross margin increase or decrease when an unfavorable variance is closed to Cost of Goods Sold? Explain.
3. Explain the meaning of a favorable variance and an unfavorable variance.

TAKING IT TO THE NET

C1

mhhe.com/larson

BTN 24-5 Access **Hoover's Online** Website (Hoovers.com) or other Websites such as BestPracticeDatabase.com and SMThacker.Co.UK to search for and read information about *benchmarking* to complete the requirements.

Required

1. Write a one-paragraph explanation (in layperson's terms) of benchmarking.
2. How does standard costing relate to benchmarking?

TEAMWORK IN ACTION

C2 

BTN 24-6 Many service industries link labor rate and time (quantity) standards with their processes. One example is the standard time to board an aircraft. The reason time plays such an important role in the service industry is that it is viewed as a competitive advantage: best service in the shortest amount of time. Although the labor rate component is difficult to observe, the time component of a service delivery standard is often readily apparent, for example, "Lunch will be served in less than five minutes, or it is free."

Required

Break into teams and select two service industries for your analysis. Identify and describe all the time elements each industry uses to create a competitive advantage.

BUSINESS WEEK ACTIVITY

C2

mhhe.com/larson

BTN 24-7 Read the article "Doing a Job on Labor" in the October 30, 2002, issue of ***Business Week***. (The book's Website provides free access to the article.)

Required

1. Identify two ways that Internet use has impacted labor markets.
2. How might Internet hiring impact labor markets in Europe and other international locations?
3. Does the Internet impact union/member communications? Explain.

ENTREPRENEURIAL DECISION

C1 C2  

BTN 24-8 Entrepreneur Scott Jordan of **Technology Enabled Clothing** has implemented a costing system with standard costs for direct materials, direct labor, and overhead costs. Two comments frequently are mentioned in relation to standard costing and variance analysis: "Variances are not explanations" and "Management's goal is not to minimize variances."

Required

Write Scott Jordan a short memo interpreting these two comments.

HITTING THE ROAD

C1 

BTN 24-9 Training employees to use standard amounts of materials in production is common. Typically, large companies invest in this training but small organizations do not. One can observe these different practices in a trip to two different pizza businesses. Visit both a local pizza business and a national pizza chain business and then complete the following.

Required

1. Observe and record the number of raw material items used to make a typical cheese pizza. Also observe how the person making the pizza applies each item when preparing the pizza.
2. Record any differences in how items are applied between the two businesses.
3. Estimate which business is more profitable from your observations. Explain.

GLOBAL DECISION

BTN 24-10 Access the annual report of **Grupo Bimbo** (at GrupoBimbo.com) for the year ended December 31, 2002. The usefulness of its budgets, variances, and related analyses depends on the accuracy of management's estimates of future sales activity.

Required

1. Identify and record the prior two years' sales (in pesos) for Grupo Bimbo from its income statement.
2. Using the data in part 1, predict sales activity for Grupo Bimbo for the next two years. Explain your prediction process.

"We're taking advantage of the revolution in consumer electronics and communications, and that has not been done in the medical field"—Corinna Lathan

25 Capital Budgeting and Managerial Decisions

A Look Back

Chapter 24 discussed flexible budgets, variance analysis, and standard costs. It explained how management uses each to control and monitor business activities.

A Look at This Chapter

This chapter focuses on evaluating capital budgeting decisions. It also explains several tools and procedures used in making and evaluating short-term managerial decisions.

CAP

Conceptual

C1 Explain the importance of capital budgeting. *(p. 984)*

C2 Describe the selection of a hurdle rate for an investment. *(p. 992)*

C3 Describe the importance of relevant costs for short-term decisions. *(p. 995)*

Analytical

A1 Evaluate short-term managerial decisions using relevant costs. *(p. 995)*

A2 Analyze a capital investment project using break-even time. *(p. 1002)*

Procedural

P1 Compute payback period and describe its use. *(p. 985)*

P2 Compute accounting rate of return and explain its use. *(p. 987)*

P3 Compute net present value and describe its use. *(p. 989)*

P4 Compute internal rate of return and explain its use. *(p. 991)*

Decision Feature

Therapist, Technician, Teacher . . . and Entrepreneur

COLLEGE PARK, MD—"No one knows how to categorize **AnthroTronix**," says Corinna Lathan, its founder. "That's kind of the story of my life: 'What are you?'" Lathan is an entrepreneur. Her company **[AnthroTronix.com]** develops practical applications from research in virtual reality, robotics, and telecommunications. Her personal focus is on interactive, rehabilitative technologies for children with disabilities. "I was appalled at the lack of technology available for kids with disabilities," says Lathan. "I saw a huge opportunity in rehabilitation."

Lathan's pet project, CosmoBot, is a twenty first century version of a short C-3PO. Wearing an ordinary-looking glove or cap embedded with sensors, a child can direct the robot to perform various movements and activities. "This is absolutely revolutionary in the world of rehab," says Lathan. The robot can be programmed to respond to voice commands, to record a child's movements, and to download new software from the Internet. Plans are to sell an enhanced CosmoBot model to clinics and therapists for $2,500 and a home model to individuals for $500. "I'm interested in problem solving . . . using technology," says Lathan. "How can you enable . . . a person with a disability to complete an activity of daily living?" That's her goal.

To achieve this goal, Lathan must overcome business realities such as making capital budgeting and managerial decisions. She has several projects in the works and a diverse client base, including companies in the rehabilitation and entertainment fields as well as private and government defense agencies. She also confronts financing requirements and the realities of hurdle rates, payback periods, rates of returns, net present values, and break-even time. "Because there's nothing out there like this, it's a real battle with venture capitalists," says Lathan. The key for her is to identify the successful projects from those that are not.

In spite of these tough capital budgeting and managerial decisions, Lathan loves what she's doing. "I love working with new technologies and new applications. I'm designing robotic technology to motivate children to increase their progress with physical and educational therapy programs." Many would say the payback on Lathan's investment is priceless.

[Sources: *AnthroTronix Website,* January 2004; *Inc. Magazine,* September 2002; *Daily Record,* June and September 2002; *Washington City Paper,* October 2001; *Technology Review,* June 2002.]

Making business decisions involves choosing between alternative courses of action. Many factors affect business decisions, yet analysis typically focuses on finding the alternative that offers the highest return on investment or the greatest reduction in costs. Some decisions are based on little more than an intuitive understanding of the situation because available information is too limited to allow a more systematic analysis. In other cases, intangible factors such as convenience, prestige, and environmental considerations are more important than strictly quantitative factors. In all situations, managers can reach a sounder decision if they identify the consequences of alternative choices in financial terms. This chapter explains several methods of analysis that can help managers make business decisions.

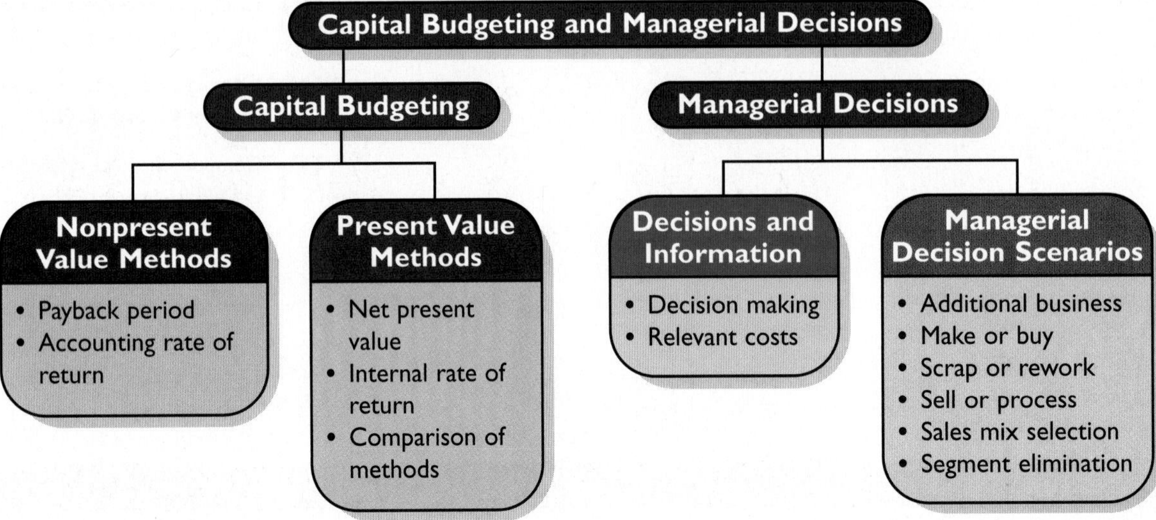

Section 1—Capital Budgeting

C1 Explain the importance of capital budgeting.

The capital expenditures budget is management's plan for acquiring and selling plant assets. **Capital budgeting** is the process of analyzing alternative long-term investments and deciding which assets to acquire or sell. These decisions can involve developing a new product or process, buying a new machine or a new building, or acquiring an entire company. An objective for these decisions is to earn a satisfactory return on investment.

Capital budgeting decisions require careful analysis because they are usually the most difficult and risky decisions that managers make. These decisions are difficult because they require predicting events that will not occur until well into the future. Many of these predictions are tentative and potentially unreliable. Specifically, a capital budgeting decision is risky because (1) the outcome is uncertain, (2) large amounts of money are usually involved, (3) the investment involves a long-term commitment, and (4) the decision could be difficult or impossible to reverse, no matter how poor it turns out to be. Risk is especially high for investments in technology due to innovations and uncertainty.

Managers use several methods to evaluate capital budgeting decisions. Nearly all of these methods involve predicting cash inflows and cash outflows of proposed investments, assessing the risk of and returns on those flows, and then choosing the investments to make. Management often restates future cash flows in terms of their present value. This approach applies the time value of money: A dollar today is worth more than a dollar tomorrow. Similarly, a dollar tomorrow is worth less than a dollar today. The process of restating future cash flows in terms of their present value is called *discounting*. The time value of money is important when evaluating capital investments, but managers sometimes apply evaluation methods that ignore present value. This section describes four methods for comparing alternative investments.

Point: The nature of capital spending has changed with the business environment. Budgets for information technology have increased from about 25% of corporate capital spending 20 years ago to an estimated 35% today.

Methods Not Using Time Value of Money

All investments, whether they involve the purchase of a machine or another long-term asset, are expected to produce net cash flows. *Net cash flow* is cash inflows minus cash outflows. Sometimes managers perform simple analyses of the financial feasibility of an investment's net cash flow without using the time value of money. This section explains two of the most common methods in this category: (1) payback period and (2) accounting rate of return.

Payback Period

P1 Compute payback period and describe its use.

An investment's **payback period (PBP)** is the expected time period to recover the initial investment amount. Managers prefer investing in assets with shorter payback periods to reduce the risk of an unprofitable investment over the long run. Acquiring assets with short payback periods reduces a company's risk from potentially inaccurate long-term predictions of future cash flows.

Computing Payback Period with Even Cash Flows To illustrate use of the payback period for an investment with even cash flows,[1] we look at data from FasTrac, a manufacturer of exercise equipment and supplies. It is considering several different capital investments, one of which is to purchase a machine to use in manufacturing a new product. This machine costs $16,000 and is expected to have an eight-year life with no salvage value. Management predicts this machine will produce 1,000 units of product each year and that the new product will be sold for $30 per unit. Exhibit 25.1 shows the expected annual net cash flows for this asset over its life as well as the expected annual revenues and expenses (including depreciation and income taxes) from investing in the machine.

Decision Insight

Telecom Decisions Profits of telecoms are dropping as too much capital investment chases too little revenue. Telecoms' success depends on keeping up with technology. Communications gear is evolving at a rate that is dizzying, even when compared to the computer industry. Consequently, managers of telecoms often demand short payback periods and large expected net cash flows to compensate for the investment risk.

Exhibit 25.1
Cash Flow Analysis

FASTRAC
Cash Flow Analysis—New Machinery
January 15, 2005

	Expected Accrual Figures	Expected Net Cash Flows
Annual sales of new product	$30,000	$30,000
Deduct annual expenses		
Cost of materials, labor, and overhead (except depr.)	15,500	15,500
Depreciation—Machinery	2,000	
Additional selling and administrative expenses	9,500	9,500
Annual pretax accrual income	3,000	
Income taxes (30%)	900	900
Annual net income	$ 2,100	
Annual net cash flow		**$ 4,100**

The amount of net cash flow from the machinery is computed by subtracting expected cash outflows from expected cash inflows. The cash flows column of Exhibit 25.1 excludes all noncash revenues and expenses. Depreciation is FasTrac's, only noncash item. Alternatively,

Point: Annual net cash flow in Exhibit 25.1 equals net income plus depreciation (a noncash expense).

[1] *Even cash flows* refers to cash flows that are the same each and every year. *Uneven cash flows* refers to cash flows that are not all equal in amount.

managers can adjust the projected net income for revenue and expense items that do not affect cash flows. For FasTrac, this means taking the $2,100 net income and adding back the $2,000 depreciation.

The formula for computing the payback period of an investment that yields even net cash flows is in Exhibit 25.2.

Exhibit 25.2

Payback Period Formula with Even Cash Flows

$$\textbf{Payback period} = \frac{\textbf{Cost of investment}}{\textbf{Annual net cash flow}}$$

The payback period reflects the amount of time for the investment to generate enough net cash flow to return (or pay back) the cash initially invested to purchase it. FasTrac's payback period for this machine is just under four years:

Example: If an alternative machine (with different technology) yields a payback period of 3.5 years, which one do you choose? *Answer:* The alternative (3.5 is less than 3.9).

$$\text{Payback period} = \frac{\$16{,}000}{\$4{,}100} = 3.9 \text{ years}$$

The initial investment is fully recovered in 3.9 years, or just before reaching the halfway point of this machine's useful life of eight years.

Point: To apply these concepts, work Exercise 25-1.

Computing Payback Period with Uneven Cash Flows Computing the payback period in the prior section assumed even net cash flows. What happens if the net cash flows are uneven? In this case, the payback period is computed using the *cumulative total of net cash flows.* The word *cumulative* refers to the addition of each period's net cash flows as we progress through time. To illustrate, consider data for another investment that FasTrac is considering. This machine is predicted to generate uneven net cash flows over the next eight years. The relevant data and payback period computation are shown in Exhibit 25.3.

Exhibit 25.3

Payback Period Calculation with Uneven Cash Flows

Period*	Expected Net Cash Flows	Cumulative Net Cash Flows
Year 0	$(16,000)	$(16,000)
Year 1	3,000	(13,000)
Year 2	4,000	(9,000)
Year 3	4,000	(5,000)
Year 4	4,000	(1,000)
Year 5	5,000	4,000
Year 6	3,000	7,000
Year 7	2,000	9,000
Year 8	2,000	11,000
		Payback period = 4.2 years

* All cash inflows and outflows occur uniformly during the year.

Example: Find the payback period in Exhibit 25.3 if net cash flows for the first 4 years are:
Year 1 = $6,000; Year 2 = $5,000;
Year 3 = $4,000; Year 4 = $3,000.
Answer: 3.33 years

Year 0 refers to the period of initial investment in which the $16,000 cash outflow occurs at the end of year 0 to acquire the machinery. By the end of year 1, the cumulative net cash flow is reduced to $(13,000), computed as the $(16,000) initial cash outflow plus year 1's $3,000 cash inflow. This process continues throughout the asset's life. The cumulative net cash flow amount changes from negative to positive in year 5. Specifically, at the end of year 4, the cumulative net cash flow is $(1,000). As soon as FasTrac receives net cash inflow of $1,000 during the fifth year, it has fully recovered the investment. If we assume that cash flows are received uniformly *within* each year, receipt of the $1,000 occurs about one-fifth of the way through the year. This is computed as $1,000 divided by year 5's total net cash flow of $5,000, or 0.20. This yields a payback period of 4.2 years, computed as 4 years plus 0.20 of year 5.

Point: To apply these concepts, work Exercise 25-2.

Using the Payback Period Companies desire a short payback period to increase return and reduce risk. The more quickly a company receives cash, the sooner it is available for other uses and the less time it is at risk of loss. A shorter payback period also improves the company's ability to respond to unanticipated changes and lowers its risk of having to keep an unprofitable investment.

Payback period should never be the only consideration in evaluating investments. This is so because it ignores at least two important factors. First, it fails to reflect differences in the timing of net cash flows within the payback period. In Exhibit 25.3, FasTrac's net cash flows in the first five years were $3,000, $4,000, $4,000, $4,000, and $5,000. If another investment had predicted cash flows of $9,000, $3,000, $2,000, $1,800, and $1,000 in these five years, its payback period would also be 4.2 years, but this second alternative could be more desirable because it provides cash more quickly. The second important factor is that the payback period ignores *all* cash flows after the point where its costs are fully recovered. For example, one investment might pay back its cost in 3 years but stop producing cash after 4 years. A second investment might require 5 years to pay back its cost yet continue to produce net cash flows for another 15 years. A focus on only the payback period would mistakenly lead management to choose the first investment over the second.

Point: To apply these concepts, work QS 25-1.

Quick Check

1. Capital budgeting is (*a*) concerned with analyzing alternative sources of capital, including debt and equity, (*b*) an important activity for companies when considering what assets to acquire or sell, or (*c*) best done by intuitive assessments of the value of assets and their usefulness.
2. Why are capital budgeting decisions often difficult?
3. A company is considering purchasing equipment costing $75,000. Future annual net cash flows from this equipment are $30,000, $25,000, $15,000, $10,000, and $5,000. The payback period is (*a*) 4 years, (*b*) 3.5 years, or (*c*) 3 years.
4. If depreciation is an expense, why is it added back to an investment's net income to compute the net cash flow from that investment?
5. If two investments have the same payback period, are they equally desirable? Explain.

Answers—p. 1006

Accounting Rate of Return

P2 Compute accounting rate of return and explain its use.

The **accounting rate of return,** also called *return on average investment,* is computed by dividing a project's after-tax net income by the average amount invested in it. To illustrate, we return to FasTrac's $16,000 machinery investment described in Exhibit 25.1. We first compute (1) the after-tax net income and (2) the average amount invested. The $2,100 after-tax net income is already available from Exhibit 25.1. To compute the average amount invested, we assume that net cash flows are received evenly throughout each year. Thus, the average investment for each year is computed as the average of its beginning and ending book values. If FasTrac's $16,000 machine is depreciated $2,000 each year, the average amount invested in the machine for each year is computed as shown in Exhibit 25.4. The average for any year is the average of the beginning and ending book values.

Exhibit 25.4

Computing Average Amount Invested

	Beginning Book Value	Annual Depreciation	Ending Book Value	Average Book Value
Year 1	$16,000	$2,000	$14,000	$15,000
Year 2	14,000	2,000	12,000	13,000
Year 3	12,000	2,000	10,000	11,000
Year 4	10,000	2,000	8,000	9,000
Year 5	8,000	2,000	6,000	7,000
Year 6	6,000	2,000	4,000	5,000
Year 7	4,000	2,000	2,000	3,000
Year 8	2,000	2,000	0	1,000
Years 1—8				$ 8,000

Next we need the average book value for the asset's entire life. This amount is computed by taking the average of the individual yearly averages. This average equals $8,000, computed as $64,000 (the sum of the individual years' averages) divided by eight years (see last column of Exhibit 25.4).

Point: General formula for *annual average investment* is the sum of individual years' average book values divided by the number of years of the planned investment.

If a company uses straight-line depreciation, we can find the average amount invested by using the formula in Exhibit 25.5. Because FasTrac uses straight-line depreciation, its average amount invested for the eight years equals the sum of the book value at the beginning of the asset's investment period and the book value at the end of its investment period, divided by 2, as shown in Exhibit 25.5.

Exhibit 25.5

Computing Average Amount Invested under Straight-Line Depreciation

$$\textbf{Annual average investment} = \frac{\textbf{Beginning book value + Ending book value}}{\textbf{2}}$$

(straight-line case only)

$$= \frac{\$16{,}000 + \$0}{2} = \$8{,}000$$

Note that if an investment carries a salvage value, the average amount invested when using straight-line depreciation is computed as (Beginning book value + Salvage value)/2.

Once we determine the after-tax net income and the average amount invested, the accounting rate of return on the investment can be computed as Annual after-tax net income/Average amount invested, as shown in Exhibit 25.6.

Exhibit 25.6

Accounting Rate of Return Formula

$$\textbf{Accounting rate of return} = \frac{\textbf{Annual after-tax net income}}{\textbf{Annual average investment}}$$

This yields an accounting rate of return of 26.25% ($2,100/$8,000). FasTrac management must decide whether a 26.25% accounting rate of return is satisfactory. To make this decision, we must factor in the investment's risk. For instance, we cannot say an investment with a 26.25% return is preferred over one with a lower return unless we recognize any differences in risk. Thus, an investment's return is satisfactory or unsatisfactory only when it is related to returns from other investments with similar lives and risk.

When accounting rate of return is used to choose among capital investments, the one with the least risk, the shortest payback period, and the highest return for the longest time period is often identified as the best. However, use of accounting rate of return to evaluate investment opportunities is limited because it bases the amount invested on book values (not predicted market values) in future periods. Accounting rate of return is also limited when an asset's net incomes are expected to vary from year to year. This requires computing the rate using *average* annual net incomes, yet this accounting rate of return fails to distinguish between two investments with the same average annual net income but different amounts of income in early years versus later years or different levels of income variability.

Point: To apply these concepts, work QS 25-4 and Exercise 25-4.

Quick Check

6. The following data relate to a company's decision on whether to purchase a machine:

Cost	$180,000
Salvage value	15,000
Annual after-tax net income	40,000

The machine's accounting rate of return, assuming even receipt of its net cash flows during the year and use of straight-line depreciation, is (*a*) 22%, (*b*) 41%, or (*c*) 21%.

7. Is a 15% accounting rate of return for a machine a good rate?

Answers—p. 1006

Methods Using Time Value of Money

This section describes two methods that help managers with capital budgeting decisions and that use the time value of money: (1) net present value and (2) internal rate of return. *(To apply these methods, you need a basic understanding of the concept of present value. An*

expanded explanation of present value concepts is in Appendix B near the end of the book. You can use the present value tables at the end of Appendix B to solve many of this chapter's assignments that use the time value of money.)

P3 Compute net present value and describe its use.

Net Present Value

Net present value analysis applies the time value of money to future cash inflows and cash outflows so management can evaluate a project's benefits and costs at one point in time. Specifically, **net present value (NPV)** is computed by discounting the future net cash flows from the investment at the project's required rate of return and then subtracting the initial amount invested.

To illustrate, let's return to FasTrac's proposed machinery purchase described in Exhibit 25.1. Does this machine provide a satisfactory return while recovering the amount invested? Recall that the machine requires a $16,000 investment and is expected to provide $4,100 annual net cash inflows for the next eight years. If we assume that net cash flows from this machine are received at each year-end and that FasTrac requires a 12% annual return, net present value can be computed as in Exhibit 25.7.

Topic Tackler 25-1

Point: The assumption of end-of-year cash flows simplifies computations and is common in practice.

Exhibit 25.7

Net Present Value Calculation with Equal Cash Flows

	Net Cash Flows*	Present Value of 1 at 12%†	Present Value of Net Cash Flows
Year 1	$ 4,100	0.8929	$ 3,661
Year 2	4,100	0.7972	3,269
Year 3	4,100	0.7118	2,918
Year 4	4,100	0.6355	2,606
Year 5	4,100	0.5674	2,326
Year 6	4,100	0.5066	2,077
Year 7	4,100	0.4523	1,854
Year 8	4,100	0.4039	1,656
Totals	$32,800		$20,367
Amount invested			(16,000)
Net present value			$ 4,367

* Cash flows occur at the end of each year.

† Present value of 1 factors are taken from Table B.1 in Appendix B.

The first number column of Exhibit 25.7 shows the annual net cash flows. Present value of 1 factors, also called *discount factors,* are shown in the second column. Taken from Table B.1 in Appendix B, they assume that net cash flows are received at each year-end. *(To simplify present value computations and for assignment material at the end of this chapter, we assume that net cash flows are received at each year-end.)* Annual net cash flows from the first column of Exhibit 25.7 are multiplied by the discount factors in the second column to give present values shown in the third column. The last three lines of this exhibit show the final NPV computations. The asset's $16,000 initial cost is deducted from the $20,367 total present value of all future net cash flows to give this asset's NPV of $4,367. The machine is thus expected to (1) recover its cost, (2) provide a 12% compounded return, and (3) generate $4,367 above cost. We summarize this analysis by saying the present value of this machine's future net cash flows to FasTrac exceeds the $16,000 investment by $4,367.

Point: The amount invested includes all costs that must be incurred to get the asset in its proper location and ready for use.

Example: What is the net present value in Exhibit 25.7 if a 10% return is applied? *Answer:* $5,873

Net Present Value Decision Rule The decision rule in applying NPV is as follows: When an asset's expected cash flows are discounted at the required rate and yield a *positive* net present value, the asset should be acquired. This decision rule is reflected in the graphic at the right. When comparing several investment opportunities of about the same cost and same risk, we prefer the one with the highest positive net present value.

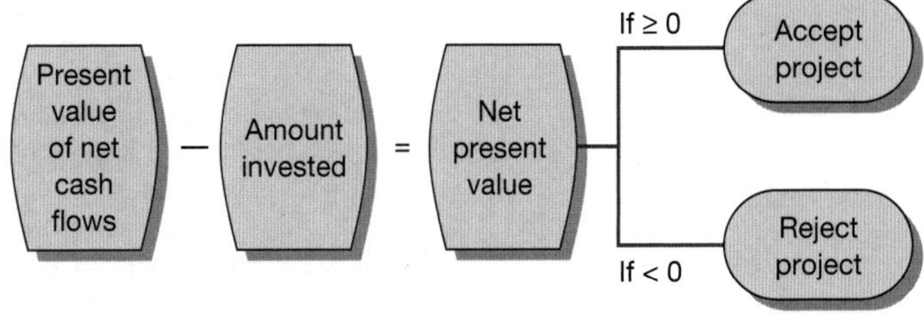

Example: Why does the net present value of an investment increase when a lower discount rate is used? *Answer:* Time value of money.

Simplifying Computations The computations in Exhibit 25.7 use separate present value of 1 factors for each of the eight years. Each year's net cash flow is multiplied by its present value of 1 factor to determine its present value. The individual present values for each of the eight net cash flows are added to give the asset's total present value. This computation can be simplified in two ways if annual net cash flows are equal in amount. One way is to add the eight annual present value of 1 factors for a total of 4.9676 and multiply this amount by the annual $4,100 net cash flow to get the $20,367 total present value of net cash flows.[2] A second simplification is to use a calculator with compound interest functions or a spreadsheet program. Whatever procedure you use, it is important to understand the concepts behind these computations.

Decision Ethics

Systems Manager Top management recently adopted a new policy requiring all proposals for purchases in excess of $5,000 to be submitted with cash flow predictions to the financial analysis group for capital budget analysis and approval. As systems manager, you want to upgrade your department's computers at a $25,000 cost. You are considering submitting several orders all under $5,000 to avoid the proposal process. You believe the computers will increase profits and wish to avoid a delay. What do you do?

Answer—p. 1006

Point: To apply these concepts, work Exercise 25-7.

Uneven Cash Flows Net present value analysis can also be applied when net cash flows are uneven (unequal). To illustrate, assume that FasTrac can choose only one capital investment from among projects A, B, and C. Each project requires the same $12,000 initial investment. Future net cash flows for each project are shown in the first three number columns of Exhibit 25.8.

Exhibit 25.8

Net Present Value Calculation with Uneven Cash Flows

	Net Cash Flows			Present Value of 1 at 10%	Present Value of Net Cash Flows		
	A	B	C		A	B	C
Year 1	$ 5,000	$ 8,000	$ 1,000	0.9091	$ 4,546	$ 7,273	$ 909
Year 2	5,000	5,000	5,000	0.8264	4,132	4,132	4,132
Year 3	5,000	2,000	9,000	0.7513	3,757	1,503	6,762
Totals	$15,000	$15,000	$15,000		12,435	12,908	11,803
Amount invested					(12,000)	(12,000)	(12,000)
Net present value					**$ 435**	**$ 908**	**$ (197)**

Example: If 12% is the required return in Exhibit 25.8, which project is preferred? *Answer:* Project B. Net present values are: A = $10; B = $553; C = $(715).

The three projects in Exhibit 25.8 have the same expected total net cash flows of $15,000. Project A is expected to produce equal amounts of $5,000 each year. Project B is expected to produce a larger amount in the first year. Project C is expected to produce a larger amount in the third year. The fourth column of Exhibit 25.8 shows the present value of 1 factors from Table B.1 assuming 10% required return.

Example: Will the rankings of Projects A, B, and C change with the use of different discount rates, assuming the same rate is used for all projects? *Answer:* No; only the NPV amounts will change.

Computations in the right-most columns show that Project A has a $435 positive NPV. Project B has the largest NPV of $908 because it brings in cash more quickly. Project C has a $(197) *negative* NPV because its larger cash inflows are delayed. If FasTrac requires a 10% return, it should reject Project C because its NPV implies a return *under* 10%. If only one project can be accepted, project B appears best because it yields the highest NPV.

Point: Projects with higher cash flows in earlier years generally yield higher net present values.

Salvage Value and Accelerated Depreciation FasTrac predicted the $16,000 machine to have zero salvage value at the end of its useful life (recall Exhibit 25.1). In many

[2] We can simplify this computation even further using Table B.3, which gives the present value of 1 to be received periodically for a number of periods. To determine the present value of these eight annual receipts discounted at 12%, go down the 12% column of Table B.3 to the factor on the eighth line. This cumulative discount factor, also known as an *annuity* factor, is 4.9676. We then compute the $20,367 present value for these eight annual $4,100 receipts, computed as 4.9676 × $4,100.

cases, assets are expected to have salvage values. If so, this amount is an additional net cash inflow received at the end of the final year of the asset's life. All other computations remain the same.

Depreciation computations also affect net present value analysis. FasTrac computes depreciation using the straight-line method. Accelerated depreciation is also commonly used, especially for income tax reports. Accelerated depreciation produces larger depreciation deductions in the early years of an asset's life and smaller deductions in later years. This pattern results in smaller income tax payments in early years and larger payments in later years. Accelerated depreciation does not change the basics of a present value analysis, but it can change the result. Using accelerated depreciation for tax reporting affects the NPV of an asset's cash flows because it produces larger net cash inflows in the early years of the asset's life and smaller ones in later years. Being able to use accelerated depreciation for tax reporting always makes an investment more desirable because early cash flows are more valuable than later ones.

Example: When is it appropriate to use different discount rates for different projects? *Answer:* When risk levels are different.

Use of Net Present Value In deciding whether to proceed with a capital investment project, we approve the proposal if the NPV is positive but reject it if the NPV is negative. When considering several projects of similar investment amounts and risk levels, we can compare the different projects' NPVs and rank them on the basis of their NPVs. However, if the amount invested differs substantially across projects, the NPV is of limited value for comparison purposes. To illustrate, suppose that Project X requires a $1 million investment and provides a $100,000 NPV. Project Y requires an investment of only $100,000 and returns a $75,000 NPV. Ranking on the basis of NPV puts Project X ahead of Y, yet X's NPV is only 10% of the initial investment whereas Y's NPV is 75% of its investment. We must also remember that when reviewing projects with different risks, we computed the NPV of individual projects using different discount rates. The higher the risk, the higher the discount rate.

Internal Rate of Return

P4 Compute internal rate of return and explain its use.

Another means to evaluate capital investments is to use the **internal rate of return,** which equals the rate that yields an NPV of zero for an investment. This means that if we compute the total present value of a project's net cash flows using the IRR as the discount rate and then subtract the initial investment from this total present value, we get a zero NPV.

To illustrate, we use the data for FasTrac's Project A from Exhibit 25.8 to compute its IRR. Exhibit 25.9 shows the two-step process in computing IRR.

Exhibit 25.9

Computing Internal Rate of Return (with even cash flows)

Step 1: Compute the present value factor for the investment project.

$$\textbf{Present value factor} = \frac{\textbf{Amount invested}}{\textbf{Net cash flows}} = \frac{\$12{,}000}{\$5{,}000} = 2.4000$$

Step 2: Identify the discount rate (IRR) yielding the present value factor

Search Table B.3 for a present value factor of 2.4000 in the three-year row (equaling the 3-year project duration). The 12% discount rate yields a present value factor of 2.4018. This implies that the IRR is approximately 12%.*

* Since the present value factor of 2.4000 is not exactly equal to the 12% factor of 2.4018, we can more precisely estimate the IRR as follows:

Discount rate	Present Value Factor from Table B.3
12%	2.4018
15%	2.2832
	0.1186 = difference

$$\text{Then, IRR} = 12\% + \left[(15\% - 12\%) \times \frac{2.4018 - 2.4000}{0.1186}\right] = \underline{\underline{12.05\%}}$$

When cash flows are equal, as with Project A, we compute the present value factor (as shown in Exhibit 25.9) by dividing the initial investment by its annual net cash flows. We then use an annuity table to determine the discount rate equal to this present value factor. For FasTrac's Project A, we look across the three-period row of Table B.3 and find that the discount rate corresponding to the present value factor of 2.4000 roughly equals the 2.4018 value for the 12% rate. This row is reproduced here:

Present Value of an Annuity of 1 for Three Periods

	Rate				
Periods	1%	5%	10%	12%	15%
3	2.9410	2.7232	2.4869	2.4018	2.2832

The 12% rate is the Project's IRR. A more precise IRR estimate can be computed following the procedure shown in the note to Exhibit 25.9. Spreadsheet software and calculators can also compute this IRR.

Uneven Cash Flows If net cash flows are uneven, we must use trial and error to compute the IRR. We do this by selecting any reasonable discount rate and computing the NPV. If the amount is positive (negative), we recompute the NPV using a higher (lower) discount rate. We continue these steps until we reach a point where two consecutive computations result in NPVs having different signs (positive and negative). Because the NPV is zero using IRR, we know that the IRR lies between these two discount rates. We can then estimate its value. Spreadsheet programs and calculators can do these computations for us.

Decision Insight

Fun-IRR Many theme parks use both financial and nonfinancial criteria to evaluate their investments in new rides and activities. The use of IRR is a major part of this evaluation. This requires good estimates of future cash inflows and outflows. It also requires risk assessments of the uncertainty of the future cash flows.

C2 Describe the selection of a hurdle rate for an investment.

Use of Internal Rate of Return When we use the IRR to evaluate a project, we compare it to a predetermined **hurdle rate,** which is a minimum acceptable rate of return and is applied as follows:

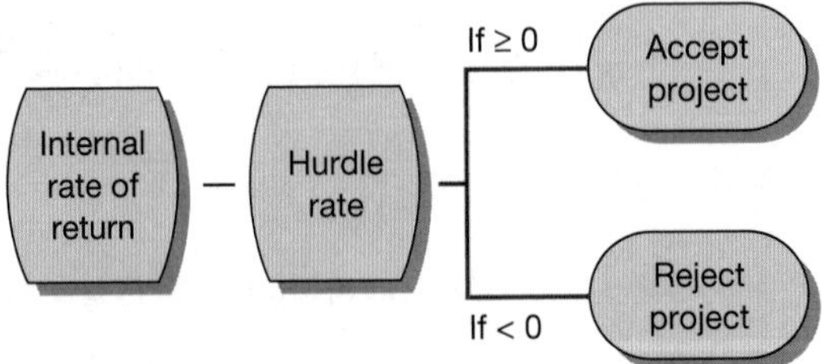

Example: How can management evaluate the risk of an investment? *Answer:* It must assess the uncertainty of future cash flows.

Top management selects the hurdle rate to use in evaluating capital investments. Financial formulas aid in this selection, but the choice of a minimum rate is subjective and left to management. For projects financed from borrowed funds, the hurdle rate must exceed the interest rate paid on these funds. The return on an investment must cover its interest and provide an additional profit to reward the company for its risk. For instance, if money is borrowed at 10%, an average risk investment often requires an after-tax return of 15% (or 5% above the borrowing rate). Remember that lower-risk investments require a lower rate of return compared with higher-risk investments.

Point: To apply these concepts, work Exercise 25-7.

If the project is internally financed, the hurdle rate is often based on actual returns from comparable projects. If the IRR is higher than the hurdle rate, the project is accepted. Multiple projects are often ranked by the extent to which their IRR exceeds the hurdle rate. The hurdle rate for individual projects is often different, depending on the risk involved. IRR is not subject to the limitations of NPV when comparing projects with different amounts invested because the IRR is expressed as a percent rather than as an absolute dollar value in NPV.

Decision Maker

Entrepreneur For a new product being developed, you use a 12% discount rate to compute its NPV. Your banker, with whom you share your analysis, expresses concern that your discount rate is too low. How do you respond?

Answer—p. 1006

Comparison of Capital Budgeting Methods

We explained four methods that managers use to evaluate capital investment projects. How do these methods compare with each other? Exhibit 25.10 addresses that question. Note that neither the payback period nor the accounting rate of return considers the time value of money. On the other hand, both the net present value and the internal rate of return do.

Exhibit 25.10

Comparing Capital Budgeting Methods

	Payback Period	Accounting Rate of Return	Net Present Value	Internal Rate of Return
Measurement basis	■ Cash flows	■ Accrual income	■ Cash flows ■ Profitability	■ Cash flows ■ Profitability
Measurement unit	■ Years	■ Percent	■ Dollars	■ Percent
Strengths	■ Easy to understand ■ Allows comparison of projects	■ Easy to understand ■ Allows comparison of projects	■ Reflects time value of money ■ Reflects varying risks over project's life	■ Reflects time value of money ■ Allows comparisons of dissimilar projects
Limitations	■ Ignores time value of money ■ Ignores cash flows after payback period	■ Ignores time value of money ■ Ignores annual rates over life of project	■ Difficult to compare dissimilar projects	■ Ignores varying risks over life of project

The payback period is probably the simplest method. It gives managers an estimate of how soon they will recover their initial investment. Managers sometimes use this method when they have limited cash to invest and a number of projects to choose from. The accounting rate of return yields a percent measure computed using accrual income instead of cash flows. The accounting rate of return is an average rate for the entire investment period. Net present value considers all estimated net cash flows for the project's expected life. It can be applied to even and uneven cash flows and can reflect changes in the level of risk over a project's life. Since it yields a dollar measure, comparing projects of unequal sizes is more difficult. The internal rate of return considers all cash flows from a project. It is readily computed when the cash flows are even but requires some trial and error estimation when cash flows are uneven. Because the IRR is a percent measure, it is readily used to compare projects with different investment amounts. However, IRR does not reflect changes in risk over a project's life.

Decision Insight

And the Winner Is . . . 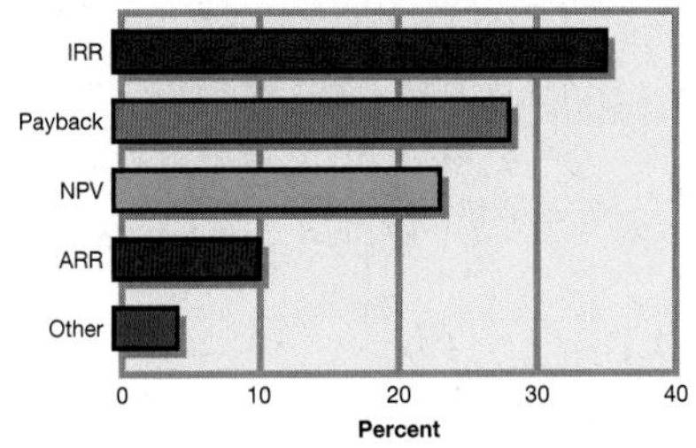
How do we choose among the methods for evaluating capital investments? Management surveys consistently show the internal rate of return (IRR) as the most popular method followed by the payback period and net present value (NPV). Few companies use the accounting rate of return (ARR), but nearly all use more than one method.

Quick Check

8. A company can invest in only one of two projects, A or B. Each project requires a $20,000 investment and is expected to generate end-of-period, annual cash flows as follows:

	Year 1	Year 2	Year 3	Total
Project A	$12,000	$8,500	$4,000	$24,500
Project B	4,500	8,500	13,000	26,000

Assuming a discount rate of 10%, which project has the higher net present value?

9. Two investment alternatives are expected to generate annual cash flows with the same net present value (assuming the same discount rate applied to each). Using this information, can you conclude that the two alternatives are equally desirable?

10. When two investment alternatives have the same total expected cash flows but differ in the timing of those flows, which method of evaluating those investments is superior, (*a*) accounting rate of return or (*b*) net present value?

Answers—p. 1006

Section 2—Managerial Decisions

This section focuses on the use of accounting information to make several important managerial decisions. It emphasizes the use of quantitative measures to help managers make business decisions. Most of these involve short-term decisions. Methods for long-term managerial decisions are described in the first section of this chapter and in several other chapters of this book.

Decisions and Information

This section explains how managers make decisions and the information relevant to these decisions.

Decision Making

Managerial decision making involves five steps: (1) define the decision task, (2) identify alternative courses of action, (3) collect relevant information and evaluate each alternative, (4) select the preferred course of action, and (5) analyze and assess decisions made. These five steps are illustrated in Exhibit 25.11.

Exhibit 25.11

Managerial Decision Making

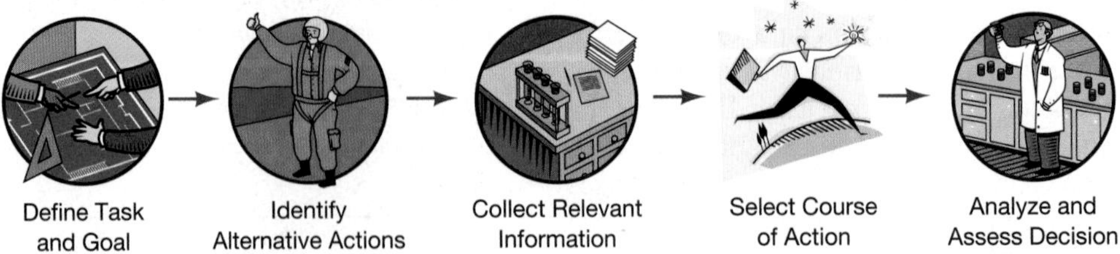

Both managerial and financial accounting information play an important role in most management decisions. The accounting system is expected to provide primarily *financial* information such as performance reports and budget analyses for decision making. *Nonfinancial* information is also relevant, however; it includes information on environmental effects, political sensitivities, and social responsibility.

Relevant Costs

C3 Describe the importance of relevant costs for short-term decisions.

Most financial measures of revenues and costs from cost accounting systems are based on historical costs. Although historical costs are important and useful for many tasks such as product pricing and the control and monitoring of business activities, we sometimes find that an analysis of *relevant costs,* or *avoidable costs,* is especially useful for certain managerial decisions. Three types of costs are pertinent to our discussion of relevant costs: sunk costs, out-of-pocket costs, and opportunity costs.

A *sunk cost* arises from a past decision and cannot be avoided or changed; it is irrelevant to future decisions. An example is the cost of computer equipment previously purchased by a company. Most of a company's allocated costs, including fixed overhead items such as depreciation and administrative expenses, are sunk costs.

Example: Depreciation and amortization are allocations of the original cost of plant and intangible assets. Are they out-of-pocket costs? *Answer:* No; they are sunk costs.

An *out-of-pocket cost* requires a future outlay of cash and is relevant for current and future decision making. These costs are usually the direct result of management's decisions. For instance, future purchases of computer equipment involve out-of-pocket costs.

An *opportunity cost* is the potential benefit lost by taking a specific action when two or more alternative choices are available. An example is a student giving up wages from a job to attend summer school. Companies continually must choose from alternative courses of action. For instance, a company making standardized products might be approached by a customer to supply a special (nonstandard) product. A decision to accept or reject the special order must consider not only the profit to be made from the special order but also the profit given up by devoting time and resources to this order instead of pursuing an alternative project. The profit given up is an opportunity cost. Consideration of opportunity costs is important. The implications extend to internal resource allocation decisions. For instance, a computer manufacturer must decide between internally manufacturing a chip versus buying it externally. In another case, management of a multidivisional company must decide whether to continue operating or close a particular division.

Point: Opportunity costs are not entered in accounting records. This does not reduce their relevance for managerial decisions.

Besides relevant costs, management must also consider the relevant benefits associated with a decision. **Relevant benefits** refer to the additional or *incremental* revenue generated by selecting a particular course of action over another. For instance, a student must decide the relevant benefits of taking one course over another. In sum, both relevant costs and relevant benefits are crucial to managerial decision making.

Managerial Decision Scenarios

Managers experience many different scenarios that require analyzing alternative actions and making a decision. We describe several different types of decision scenarios in this section. We set these tasks in the context of FasTrac, the exercise supplies and equipment manufacturer introduced earlier. *We treat each of these decision tasks as separate from each other.*

Additional Business

A1 Evaluate short-term managerial decisions using relevant costs.

FasTrac is operating at its normal level of 80% of full capacity. At this level, it produces and sells approximately 100,000 units of product annually. Its per unit and annual total costs are shown in Exhibit 25.12.

Exhibit 25.12
Selected Operating Income Data

	Per Unit	Annual Total
Sales (100,000 units)	$10.00	$1,000,000
Direct materials	(3.50)	(350,000)
Direct labor	(2.20)	(220,000)
Overhead	(1.10)	(110,000)
Selling expenses	(1.40)	(140,000)
Administrative expenses	(0.80)	(80,000)
Total costs and expenses	(9.00)	(900,000)
Operating income	$ 1.00	$ 100,000

A current buyer of FasTrac's products wants to purchase additional units of its product and export them to another country. This buyer offers to buy 10,000 units of the product at $8.50 per unit, or $1.50 less than the current price. The offer price is low, but FasTrac is considering the proposal because this sale would be several times larger than any single previous sale. Also, the units will be exported, so this new business will not affect current sales.

To determine whether to accept or reject this order, management needs to know whether accepting the offer will increase net income. The analysis in Exhibit 25.13 shows that if management relies on per unit historical costs, it would reject the sale because it yields a loss. However, historical costs are *not* relevant to this decision. Instead, the relevant costs are the additional costs called **incremental costs.** These costs, also called *differential costs,* are the additional costs incurred if a company pursues a certain course of action. FasTrac's incremental costs are those related to the added volume that this new order would bring.

Exhibit 25.13

Analysis of Additional Business Using Historical Costs

	Per Unit	Total
Sales (10,000 additional units)	$ 8.50	$ 85,000
Direct materials	(3.50)	(35,000)
Direct labor	(2.20)	(22,000)
Overhead	(1.10)	(11,000)
Selling expenses	(1.40)	(14,000)
Administrative expenses	(0.80)	(8,000)
Total costs and expenses	(9.00)	(90,000)
Operating loss	$(0.50)	**$ (5,000)**

To make its decision, FasTrac must analyze the costs of this new business in a different manner. The following information regarding the order is available:

- Manufacturing 10,000 additional units requires direct materials of $3.50 per unit and direct labor of $2.20 per unit (same as for all other units).
- Manufacturing 10,000 additional units adds $5,000 of incremental overhead costs for power, packaging, and indirect labor (all variable costs).
- Incremental commissions and selling expenses from this sale of 10,000 additional units would be $2,000 (all variable costs).
- Incremental administrative expenses of $1,000 for clerical efforts are needed (all fixed costs) with the sale of 10,000 additional units.

We use this information, as shown in Exhibit 25.14, to assess how accepting this new business will affect FasTrac's income.

Exhibit 25.14

Analysis of Additional Business Using Relevant Costs

	Current Business	Additional Business	Combined
Sales	$1,000,000	**$ 85,000**	$1,085,000
Direct materials	(350,000)	**(35,000)**	(385,000)
Direct labor	(220,000)	**(22,000)**	(242,000)
Overhead	(110,000)	**(5,000)**	(115,000)
Selling expenses	(140,000)	**(2,000)**	(142,000)
Administrative expense	(80,000)	**(1,000)**	(81,000)
Total costs and expenses	(900,000)	**(65,000)**	(965,000)
Operating income	$ 100,000	**$ 20,000**	$ 120,000

Example: Exhibit 25.14 uses quantitative information. Suggest some qualitative factors to be considered when deciding whether to accept this project. *Answer:* (1) Impact on relationships with other customers and (2) Improved relationship with customer buying additional units.

The analysis of relevant costs in Exhibit 25.14 suggests that the additional business be accepted. It would provide $85,000 of added revenue while incurring only $65,000 of added costs. This would yield $20,000 of additional pretax income, or a pretax profit margin of 23.5%. More generally, FasTrac would increase its income with any price that exceeded $6.50 per unit ($65,000 incremental cost/10,000 additional units).

An analysis of the incremental costs pertaining to the additional volume is always relevant for this type of decision. We must proceed cautiously, however, when the additional volume approaches or exceeds the factory's existing available capacity. If the additional volume requires the company to expand its capacity by obtaining more equipment, more space, or more personnel, the incremental costs could quickly exceed the incremental revenue. Another cautionary note is the effect on existing sales. All new units of the extra business will be sold outside FasTrac's normal domestic sales channels. If accepting additional business would cause existing sales to decline, this information must be included in our analysis. The contribution margin lost from a decline in sales is an opportunity cost. If future cash flows over several time periods are affected, their net present value also must be computed and used in this analysis.

Point: To apply these concepts, work Exercise 25-8.

The key point is that management must not blindly use historical costs, especially allocated overhead costs. Instead, the accounting system needs to provide information about the incremental costs to be incurred if the additional business is accepted.

Decision Maker

Partner You are a partner in a small accounting firm that specializes in keeping the books and preparing taxes for clients such as doctors and lawyers. A local restaurant is interested in obtaining these services from your firm. Identify factors that are relevant in deciding whether to accept the engagement.

Answer—p. 1006

Make or Buy

The managerial decision to make or buy a component for one of its current products is commonplace and depends on incremental costs. To illustrate, FasTrac has excess productive capacity it can use to manufacture Part 417, a component of the main product it sells. The part is currently purchased and delivered to the plant at a cost of $1.20 per unit. FasTrac estimates that making Part 417 would cost $0.45 for direct materials, $0.50 for direct labor, and an undetermined amount for overhead. The task is to determine how much overhead to add to these costs so we can decide whether to make or buy Part 417. If FasTrac's normal predetermined overhead application rate is 100% of direct labor cost, we might be tempted to conclude that overhead cost is $0.50 per unit, computed as 100% of the $0.50 direct labor cost. We would then mistakenly conclude that total cost is $1.45 ($0.45 of materials + $0.50 of labor + $0.50 of overhead). A wrong decision in this case would be to conclude that the company is better off buying the part at $1.20 each than making it for $1.45 each.

Topic Tackler 25-2

Instead, as we explained earlier, only incremental overhead costs are relevant in this situation. Thus, we must compute an *incremental overhead rate.* Incremental overhead costs might include, for example, additional power for operating machines, extra supplies, added cleanup costs, materials handling, and quality control. We can prepare a per unit analysis in this case as shown in Exhibit 25.15.

We can see that if incremental overhead costs are less than $0.25 per unit, the total cost of making the component is less than the purchase price of $1.20 and FasTrac should make the part. FasTrac's decision rule in this case is that any amount of overhead less than $0.25 per unit yields a total cost for Part 417 that is less than the $1.20 purchase price. FasTrac must consider several factors in the make or buy decision, including product quality, timeliness of delivery (especially in a just-in-time setting), reactions of customers and suppliers, and other intangibles such as employee morale and workload. It must also consider whether making the part requires incremental fixed costs to expand plant capacity. When these added factors are considered, small cost differences may not matter.

Exhibit 25.15

Make or Buy Analysis

	Make	Buy
Direct materials	$0.45	—
Direct labor	0.50	—
Overhead costs	**[?]**	**—**
Purchase price	—	$ 1.20
Total incremental costs	**$0.95 + [?]**	**$1.20**

Point: To apply these concepts, work QS 25-6.

Decision Insight

Make or Buy Services Companies also apply make or buy decisions to services. Many now outsource their payroll activities to a payroll service provider. Many argue the prices paid for such service are close to what it costs them to do it but without the headaches.

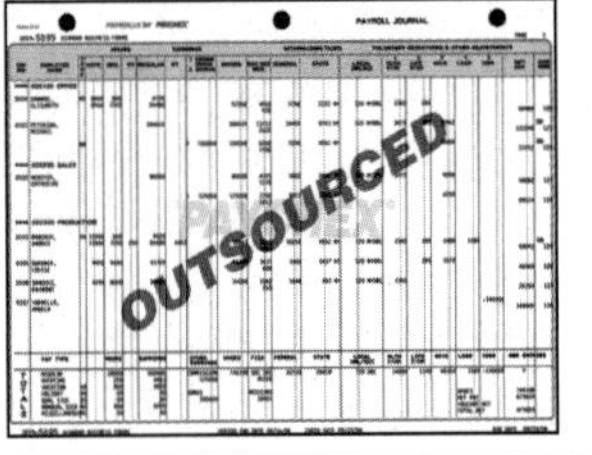

Scrap or Rework

Managers often must make a decision on whether to scrap or rework products in process. Remember that costs already incurred in manufacturing the units of a product that do not meet quality standards are sunk costs that have been incurred and cannot be changed. Sunk costs are irrelevant in any decision on whether to sell the substandard units as scrap or to rework them to meet quality standards.

To illustrate, assume that FasTrac has 10,000 defective units of a product that have already cost $1 per unit to manufacture. These units can be sold as is (as scrap) for $0.40 each, or they can be reworked for $0.80 per unit and then sold for their full price of $1.50 each. Should FasTrac sell the units as scrap or rework them?

To make this decision, management must recognize that the already incurred manufacturing costs of $1 per unit are sunk (unavoidable). These costs are *entirely irrelevant* to the decision. In addition, we must be certain that all costs of reworking defects, including interfering with normal operations, are accounted for in our analysis. For instance, reworking the defects means that FasTrac is unable to manufacture 10,000 *new* units with an incremental cost of $1 per unit and a selling price of $1.50 per unit, meaning it incurs an opportunity cost equal to the lost $5,000 net return from making and selling 10,000 new units. This opportunity cost is the difference between the $15,000 revenue (10,000 units × $1.50) from selling these new units and their $10,000 manufacturing costs (10,000 units × $1). Our analysis is reflected in Exhibit 25.16.

Exhibit 25.16

Scrap or Rework Analysis

	Scrap	Rework
Sale of scrapped/reworked units	$ 4,000	$ 15,000
Less costs to rework defects		(8,000)
Less opportunity cost of not making new units		**(5,000)**
Incremental net income	**$4,000**	**$ 2,000**

The analysis yields a $2,000 difference in favor of scrapping the defects, yielding a total incremental net income of $4,000. If we had failed to include the opportunity costs of $5,000, the rework option would have shown an income of $7,000 instead of $2,000, mistakenly making the reworking appear more favorable than scrapping.

Quick Check

11. A company receives a special order for 200 units that requires stamping the buyer's name on each unit, yielding an additional fixed cost of $400 to its normal costs. Without the order, the company is operating at 75% of capacity and produces 7,500 units of product at the following costs:

Direct materials	$37,500
Direct labor	60,000
Overhead (30% variable)	20,000
Selling expenses (60% variable)	25,000

The special order will not affect normal unit sales and will not increase fixed overhead and selling expenses. Variable selling expenses on the special order are reduced to one-half the normal amount. The price per unit necessary to earn $1,000 on this order is (*a*) $14.80, (*b*) $15.80, (*c*) $19.80, (*d*) $20.80, or (*e*) $21.80.

12. What are the incremental costs of accepting additional business?

Answers—p. 1006

Sell or Process

The managerial decision to sell partially completed products as is or to process them further for sale depends significantly on relevant costs. To illustrate, suppose that FasTrac has 40,000 units of partially finished Product Q. It has already spent $0.75 per unit to manufacture these 40,000 units at a $30,000 total cost. FasTrac can sell the 40,000 units to another manufacturer as raw material for $50,000. Alternatively, it can process them further and produce finished products X, Y, and Z at an incremental cost of $2 per unit. The added processing yields the products and revenues shown in Exhibit 25.17. FasTrac must decide whether the added revenues from selling finished products X, Y, and Z exceed the costs of finishing them.

Exhibit 25.17
Revenues from Processing Further

Product	Price	Units	Revenues
Product X	$4.00	10,000	$ 40,000
Product Y	6.00	22,000	132,000
Product Z	8.00	6,000	48,000
Spoilage	—	2,000	0
Totals		40,000	$220,000

Point: To apply these concepts, work Exercise 25-10.

Exhibit 25.18 shows the two-step analysis for this decision. First, FasTrac computes its incremental revenue from further processing Q into products X, Y, and Z. This amount is the difference between the $220,000 revenue from the further processed products and the $50,000 FasTrac will give up by not selling Q as is (a $50,000 opportunity cost). Second, FasTrac computes its incremental costs from further processing Q into X, Y, and Z. This amount is $80,000 (40,000 units × $2 incremental cost). The analysis shows that FasTrac can earn incremental net income of $90,000 from a decision to further process Q. (Notice that the earlier incurred $30,000 manufacturing cost for the 40,000 units of Product Q does not appear in Exhibit 25.18 because it is a sunk cost and as such is irrelevant to the decision.)

Exhibit 25.18
Sell or Process Analysis

Revenue if processed	$220,000
Revenue if sold as is	(50,000)
Incremental revenue	170,000
Cost if processed	(80,000)
Incremental net income	**$ 90,000**

Example: Does the decision change if incremental costs in Exhibit 25.18 increase to $4 per unit and the opportunity cost increases to $95,000? *Answer:* Yes. There is now an incremental net loss of $35,000.

Quick Check

13. A company has already incurred a $1,000 cost in partially producing its four products. Their selling prices when partially and fully processed follow with additional costs necessary to finish these partially processed units:

Product	Unfinished Selling Price	Finished Selling Price	Further Processing Costs
Alpha	$300	$600	$150
Beta	450	900	300
Gamma	275	425	125
Delta	150	210	75

Which product(s) should *not* be processed further, (*a*) Alpha, (*b*) Beta, (*c*) Gamma, or (*d*) Delta?

14. Under what conditions is a sunk cost relevant to decision making?

Answers—p. 1006

Sales Mix Selection

When a company sells a mix of products, some are likely to be more profitable than others. Management is often wise to concentrate sales efforts on more profitable products. If production facilities or other factors are limited, an increase in the production and sale of one product usually requires reducing the production and sale of others. In this case, management must identify the most profitable combination, or *sales mix* of products. To identify the best sales mix, management must know the contribution

Decision Insight

The **Estee Lauder Companies** must continuously monitor and manage the sales mix of its enormous product list. Selling its products in more than 130 countries and territories further complicates this decision process. The contribution margin of each product is crucial to its product mix strategy.

margin of each product, the facilities required to produce each product, any constraints on these facilities, and its markets.

To illustrate, assume that FasTrac makes and sells two products, A and B. The same machines are used to produce both products. A and B have the following selling prices and variable costs per unit:

	Product A	Product B
Selling price per unit	$5.00	$7.50
Variable costs per unit	3.50	5.50
Contribution margin per unit	$1.50	$2.00

The variable costs are included in the analysis because they are the incremental costs of producing these products within the existing capacity of 100,000 machine hours per month. We consider three separate cases.

Case 1: Assume that (1) each product requires 1 machine hour per unit for production and (2) the markets for these products are unlimited. Under these conditions, FasTrac should produce as much of Product B as it can because of its larger contribution margin of $2 per unit. At full capacity, FasTrac would produce $200,000 of total contribution margin per month, computed as $2 per unit times 100,000 machine hours.

Case 2: Assume that (1) Product A requires 1 machine hour per unit, (2) Product B requires 2 machine hours per unit, and (3) the markets for these products are unlimited. Under these conditions, FasTrac should produce as much of Product A as it can because it has a contribution margin of $1.50 per machine hour compared with only $1 per machine hour for Product B. Exhibit 25.19 shows the relevant analysis.

Exhibit 25.19

Sales Mix Analysis

	Product A	Product B
Selling price per unit	$ 5.00	$ 7.50
Variable costs per unit	3.50	5.50
Contribution margin per unit	$ 1.50	$ 2.00
Machine hours per unit	1.0	2.0
Contribution margin per machine hour	**$1.50**	**$1.00**

Example: For Case 2, if Product B's variable costs per unit increase to $6, Product A's variable costs per unit decrease to $3, and the same machine hours per unit are used, which product should FasTrac produce? *Answer:* Product A. Its contribution margin of $2 per machine hour is higher than B's $.75 per machine hour.

Point: To apply these concepts, work QS 25-5.

At its full capacity of 100,000 machine hours, FasTrac would produce 100,000 units of Product A, yielding $150,000 of total contribution margin per month. In contrast, if it uses all 100,000 hours to produce Product B, only 50,000 units would be produced yielding a contribution margin of $100,000. These results suggest that when a company faces excess demand and limited capacity, only the most profitable product per input should be manufactured.

Case 3: The need for a mix of different products arises when market demand is not sufficient to allow a company to sell all that it produces. For instance, assume that (1) Product A requires 1 machine hour per unit, (2) Product B requires 2 machine hours per unit, and (3) the market for Product A is limited to 80,000 units. Under these conditions, FasTrac should produce no more than 80,000 units of Product A. This would leave another 20,000 machine hours of capacity for making Product B. FasTrac should use this spare capacity to produce 10,000 units of Product B. This sales mix would maximize FasTrac's total contribution margin per month at an amount of $140,000.

Segment Elimination

Point: A method called *linear programming* is useful for finding the optimal sales mix for several products subject to many market and production constraints. This method is described in advanced courses.

When a segment such as a department or division is performing poorly, management must consider eliminating it. Segment information on either net income (loss) or its contribution to overhead is not sufficient for this decision. Instead, we must look at the segment's avoidable expenses and unavoidable expenses. **Avoidable expenses,** also called *escapable expenses,* are amounts the company would not incur if it eliminated the segment. **Unavoidable**

expenses, also called *inescapable expenses,* are amounts that would continue even if the segment is eliminated.

To illustrate, FasTrac considers eliminating its treadmill division because its $48,300 total expenses are higher than its $47,800 sales. Classification of this division's operating expenses into avoidable or unavoidable expenses is shown in Exhibit 25.20.

	Total	Avoidable Expenses	Unavoidable Expenses
Cost of goods sold	$ 30,000	$ 30,000	—
Direct expenses			
Salaries expense	7,900	7,900	—
Depreciation expense—Equipment	200	—	$ 200
Indirect expenses			
Rent and utilities expense	3,150	—	3,150
Advertising expense	400	400	—
Insurance expense	400	300	100
Service department costs			
Share of office department expenses	3,060	2,200	860
Share of purchasing expenses	3,190	1,000	2,190
Total	**$48,300**	**$41,800**	**$6,500**

Exhibit 25.20

Classification of Segment Operating Expenses for Analysis

FasTrac's analysis shows that it can avoid $41,800 expenses if it eliminates the treadmill division. Because this division's sales are $47,800, eliminating it will cause FasTrac to lose $6,000 of income. *Our decision rule is that a segment is a candidate for elimination if its revenues are less than its avoidable expenses.* Avoidable expenses can be viewed as the costs to generate this segment's revenues.

When considering elimination of a segment, we must assess its impact on other segments. A segment could be unprofitable on its own, but it might still contribute to other segments' revenues and profits. It is possible then to continue a segment even when its revenues are less than its avoidable expenses. Similarly, a profitable segment might be discontinued if its space, assets, or staff can be more profitably used by expanding existing segments or by creating new ones. Our decision to keep or eliminate a segment requires a more complex analysis than simply looking at a segment's performance report. Such reports provide useful information, but they do not provide all the information necessary for this decision.

Example: How can insurance be classified as either avoidable or unavoidable? *Answer:* Depends on whether the assets insured can be removed and the premiums canceled.

Example: Give an example of a segment that a company might profitably use to attract customers even though it might incur a loss. *Answer:* Warranty and post-sales services.

Point: To apply these concepts, work Exercise 25-11.

Qualitative Decision Factors

Managers must consider qualitative factors in making managerial decisions. Consider a decision on whether to buy a component from an outside supplier or continue to make it. Several qualitative decision factors must be considered. For example, the quality, delivery, and reputation of the proposed supplier are important. The effects from deciding not to make the component can include potential layoffs and impaired worker morale. Consider another situation in which a company is considering a one-time sale to a new customer at a special low price. Qualitative factors to consider in this situation include the effects of a low price on the company's image and the threat that regular customers might demand a similar price. The company must also consider whether this customer is really a one-time customer. If not, can it continue to offer this low price in the long run? Clearly, management cannot rely solely on financial data to make such decisions.

Quick Check

15. What is the difference between avoidable and unavoidable expenses?

16. A segment is a candidate for elimination if (*a*) its revenues are less than its avoidable expenses, (*b*) it has a net loss, (*c*) its unavoidable expenses are higher than its revenues.

Answers—p. 1006

Decision Analysis — Break-Even Time

A2 Analyze a capital investment project using break-even time.

The first section of this chapter explained several methods to evaluate capital investments. Break-even time of an investment project is a variation of the payback period method that overcomes the limitation of not using the time value of money. **Break-even time (BET)** is a time-based measure used to evaluate a capital investment's acceptability. Its computation yields a measure of expected time, reflecting the time period until the *present value* of the net cash flows from an investment equals the initial cost of the investment. In basic terms, break-even time is computed by restating future cash flows in terms of present values and then determining the payback period using these present values.

To illustrate, we return to the FasTrac case described in Exhibit 25.1 involving a $16,000 investment in machinery. The annual net cash flows from this investment are projected at $4,100 for eight years. Exhibit 25.21 shows the computation of break-even time for this investment decision.

Exhibit 25.21

Break-Even Time Analysis*

Year	Cash Flows	Present Value of 1 at 10%	Present Value of Cash Flows	Cumulative Present Value of Cash Flows
0	$(16,000)	1.0000	$(16,000)	$(16,000)
1	4,100	0.9091	3,727	(12,273)
2	4,100	0.8264	3,388	(8,885)
3	4,100	0.7513	3,080	(5,805)
4	4,100	0.6830	2,800	(3,005)
5	4,100	0.6209	2,546	**(459)**
6	4,100	0.5645	2,314	**1,855**
7	4,100	0.5132	2,104	3,959
8	4,100	0.4665	1,913	5,872

* The time of analysis is the start of year 1 (same as end of year 0). All cash flows occur at the end of each year.

The right-most column of this exhibit shows that break-even time is between 5 and 6 years, or about 5.2 years. This is the time the project takes to break even after considering the time value of money (recall that the payback period computed without considering the time value of money was 3.9 years). We interpret this as cash flows earned after 5.2 years contribute to a positive net present value that, in this case, eventually amounts to $5,872.

Break-even time is a useful measure for managers because it identifies the point in time when they can expect the cash flows to begin to yield net positive returns. Managers expect a positive net present value from an investment if break-even time is less than the investment's estimated life. The method allows managers to compare and rank alternative investments, giving the project with the shortest break-even time the highest rank.

Decision Maker

Investment Manager As the investment manager, management asks you to evaluate three alternative investments. Investment recovery time is crucial because cash is scarce. The time value of money is also important. Which capital budgeting method(s) do you choose to evaluate the investments?

Answers—p. 1006

Demonstration Problem

Determine the appropriate action in each of the following managerial decision situations.

1. Packer Company is operating at 80% of its manufacturing capacity of 100,000 product units per year. A chain store has offered to buy an additional 10,000 units at $22 each and sell them to customers so as not to compete with Packer Co. The following data are available:

Costs at 80% Capacity	Per Unit	Total
Direct materials	$ 8.00	$ 640,000
Direct labor	7.00	560,000
Overhead (fixed and variable)	12.50	1,000,000
Totals	$27.50	$2,200,000

In producing 10,000 additional units, fixed overhead costs would remain at their current level but incremental variable overhead costs of $3 per unit would be incurred. Should the company accept or reject this order?

2. Green Company uses Part JR3 in manufacturing its products. It has always purchased this part from a supplier for $40 each. It recently upgraded its own manufacturing capabilities and has enough excess capacity (including trained workers) to begin manufacturing Part JR3 instead of buying it. The company prepares the following cost projections of making the part, assuming that overhead is allocated to the part at the normal predetermined rate of 200% of direct labor cost.

Direct materials	$11
Direct labor	15
Overhead (fixed and variable) (200% of direct labor)	30
Total	$56

The required volume of output to produce the part will not require any incremental fixed overhead. Incremental variable overhead cost will be $17 per unit. Should the company make or buy this part?

3. Gold Company's manufacturing process causes a relatively large number of defective parts to be produced. The defective parts can be (a) sold for scrap, (b) melted to recover the recycled metal for reuse, or (c) reworked to be good units. Reworking defective parts reduces the output of other good units because no excess capacity exists. Each unit reworked means that one new unit cannot be produced. The following information reflects 500 defective parts currently available:

Proceeds of selling as scrap	$2,500
Additional cost of melting down defective parts	400
Cost of purchases avoided by using recycled metal from defects	4,800
Cost to rework 500 defective parts	
Direct materials	0
Direct labor	1,500
Incremental overhead	1,750
Cost to produce 500 new parts	
Direct materials	6,000
Direct labor	5,000
Incremental overhead	3,200
Selling price per good unit	40

Should the company melt the parts, sell them as scrap, or rework them?

4. White Company can invest in one of two projects, TD1 or TD2. Each project requires an initial investment of $100,000 and produces the year-end cash inflows shown in the following table. Use net present values to determine which project, if any, should be chosen. Assume that the company requires a 10% return from its investments.

	Net Cash Flows	
	TD1	TD2
Year 1	$ 20,000	$ 40,000
Year 2	30,000	40,000
Year 3	70,000	40,000
Totals	$120,000	$120,000

Planning the Solution

- Determine whether Packer Company should accept the additional business by finding the incremental costs of materials, labor, and overhead that will be incurred if the order is accepted. Omit fixed costs that the order will not increase. If the incremental revenue exceeds the incremental cost, accept the order.
- Determine whether Green Company should make or buy the component by finding the incremental cost of making each unit. If the incremental cost exceeds the purchase price, the component should be purchased. If the incremental cost is less than the purchase price, make the component.

- Determine whether Gold Company should sell the defective parts, melt them down and recycle the metal, or rework them. To compare the three choices, examine all costs incurred and benefits received from the alternatives in working with the 500 defective units versus the production of 500 new units. For the scrapping alternative, include the costs of producing 500 new units and subtract the $2,500 proceeds from selling the old ones. For the melting alternative, include the costs of melting the defective units, add the net cost of new materials in excess over those obtained from recycling, and add the direct labor and overhead costs. For the reworking alternative, add the costs of direct labor and incremental overhead. Select the alternative that has the lowest cost. The cost assigned to the 500 defective units is sunk and not relevant in choosing among the three alternatives.
- Compute White Company's net present value of each investment using a 10% discount rate.

Solution to Demonstration Problem

1. This decision involves accepting additional business. Since current unit costs are $27.50, it appears initially as if the offer to sell for $22 should be rejected, but the $27.50 cost includes fixed costs. When the analysis includes only *incremental* costs, the per unit cost is as shown in the following table. The offer should be accepted because it will produce $4 of additional profit per unit (computed as $22 price less $18 incremental cost), which yields a total profit of $40,000 for the 10,000 additional units.

Direct materials	$ 8.00
Direct labor	7.00
Variable overhead (given)	3.00
Total incremental cost	$18.00

2. For this make or buy decision, the analysis must not include the $13 nonincremental overhead per unit ($30 − $17). When only the $17 incremental overhead is included, the relevant unit cost of manufacturing the part is shown in the following table. It would be better to continue buying the part for $40 instead of making it for $43.

Direct materials	$11.00
Direct labor	15.00
Variable overhead	17.00
Total incremental cost	$43.00

3. The goal of this scrap or rework decision is to identify the alternative that produces the greatest net benefit to the company. To compare the alternatives, we determine the net cost of obtaining 500 marketable units as follows:

Incremental Cost to Produce 500 Marketable Units	Sell as Is	Melt and Recycle	Rework Units
Direct materials			
New materials	$ 6,000	$6,000	
Recycled metal materials		(4,800)	
Net materials cost		1,200	
Melting costs		400	
Total direct materials cost	6,000	1,600	
Direct labor	5,000	5,000	$1,500
Incremental overhead	3,200	3,200	1,750
Cost to produce 500 marketable units	14,200	9,800	3,250
Less proceeds of selling defects as scrap	(2,500)		
Opportunity costs*			5,800
Net cost	$11,700	$9,800	$9,050

* The $5,800 opportunity cost is the lost contribution margin from not being able to produce and sell 500 units because of reworking, computed as ($40 − $28.40) × 500 units.

The incremental cost of 500 marketable parts is smallest if the defects are reworked.

4. **TD1:**

	Net Cash Flows	Present Value of 1 at 10%	Present Value of Net Cash Flows
Year 1	$ 20,000	0.9091	$ 18,182
Year 2	30,000	0.8264	24,792
Year 3	70,000	0.7513	52,591
Totals	$120,000		95,565
Amount invested			(100,000)
Net present value			**$ (4,435)**

TD2:

	Net Cash Flows	Present Value of 1 at 10%	Present Value of Net Cash Flows
Year 1	$ 40,000	0.9091	$ 36,364
Year 2	40,000	0.8264	33,056
Year 3	40,000	0.7513	30,052
Totals	$120,000		99,472
Amount invested			(100,000)
Net present value			**$ (528)**

White Co. should not invest in either project. Both are expected to yield a negative net present value, and it should invest only in positive net present value projects.

Summary

C1 Explain the importance of capital budgeting. Capital budgeting is the process of analyzing alternative investments and deciding which assets to acquire or sell. It involves predicting the cash flows to be received from the alternatives, evaluating their merits, and then choosing which ones to pursue.

C2 Describe the selection of a hurdle rate for an investment. Top management should select the hurdle (discount) rate to use in evaluating capital investments. The required hurdle rate should be at least higher than the interest rate on money borrowed because the return on an investment must cover the interest and provide an additional profit to reward the company for risk.

C3 Describe the importance of relevant costs for short-term decisions. A company must rely on relevant costs pertaining to alternative courses of action rather than historical costs. Out-of-pocket expenses and opportunity costs are relevant because these are avoidable; sunk costs are irrelevant because they result from past decisions and are therefore unavoidable. Managers must also consider the relevant benefits associated with alternative decisions.

A1 Evaluate short-term managerial decisions using relevant costs. Relevant costs are useful in making decisions such as to accept additional business, make or buy, and sell as is or process further. For example, the relevant factors in deciding whether to produce and sell additional units of product are incremental costs and incremental revenues from the additional volume.

A2 Analyze a capital investment project using break-even time. Break-even time (BET) is a method for evaluating capital investments by restating future cash flows in terms of their present values (discounting the cash flows) and then calculating the payback period using these present values of cash flows.

P1 Compute payback period and describe its use. One way to compare potential investments is to compute and compare their payback periods. The payback period is an estimate of the expected time before the cumulative net cash inflow from the investment equals its initial cost. A payback period analysis fails to reflect risk of the cash flows, differences in the timing of cash flows within the payback period, and cash flows that occur after the payback period.

P2 Compute accounting rate of return and explain its use. A project's accounting rate of return is computed by dividing the expected annual after-tax net income by the average amount of investment in the project. When the net cash flows are received evenly throughout each period and straight-line depreciation is used, the average investment is computed as the average of the investment's initial book value and its salvage value.

P3 Compute net present value and describe its use. An investment's net present value is determined by predicting the future cash flows it is expected to generate, discounting them at a rate that represents an acceptable return, and then by subtracting the investment's initial cost from the sum of the present values. This technique can deal with any pattern of expected cash flows and applies a superior concept of return on investment.

P4 Compute internal rate of return and explain its use. The internal rate of return (IRR) is the discount rate that results in a zero net present value. When the cash flows are equal, we can compute the present value factor corresponding to the IRR by dividing the initial investment by the annual cash flows. We then use the annuity tables to determine the discount rate corresponding to this present value factor.

Guidance Answers to **Decision Maker** and **Decision Ethics**

Systems Manager Your dilemma is whether to abide by rules designed to prevent abuse or to bend them to acquire an investment that you believe will benefit the firm. You should not pursue the latter action because breaking up the order into small components is dishonest and there are consequences of being caught at a later stage. Develop a proposal for the entire package and then do all you can to expedite its processing, particularly by pointing out its benefits. When faced with controls that are not working, there is rarely a reason to overcome its shortcomings by dishonesty. A direct assault on those limitations is more sensible and ethical.

Entrepreneur The banker is probably concerned because new products are risky and should therefore be evaluated using a higher rate of return. You should conduct a thorough technical analysis and obtain detailed market data and information about any similar products available in the market. These factors might provide sufficient information to support the use of a lower return. You must convince yourself that the risk level is consistent with the discount rate used. You should also be confident that your company has the capacity and the resources to handle the new product.

Partner You should identify the differences between existing clients and this potential client. A key difference is that the restaurant business has additional inventory components (groceries, vegetables, meats, etc.) and is likely to have a higher proportion of depreciable assets. These differences imply that the partner must spend more hours auditing the records and understanding the business, regulations, and standards that pertain to the restaurant business. Such differences suggest that the partner must use a different "formula" for quoting a price to this potential client vis-à-vis current clients.

Investment Manager You should probably focus on either the payback period or break-even time because both the time value of money and recovery time are important. Break-even time method is superior because it accounts for the time value of money, which is an important consideration in this decision.

Guidance Answers to **Quick Checks**

1. *b*

2. A capital budgeting decision is difficult because (1) the outcome is uncertain, (2) large amounts of money are usually involved, (3) a long-term commitment is required, and (4) the decision could be difficult or impossible to reverse.

3. *b*

4. Depreciation expense is subtracted from revenues in computing net income but does not use cash and should be added back to net income to compute net cash flows.

5. Not necessarily. One investment can continue to generate cash flows beyond the payback period for a longer time period than the other. The timing of their cash flows within the payback period also can differ.

6. *b*; Annual average investment = ($180,000 + $15,000)/2 = $97,500
Accounting rate of return = $40,000/$97,500 = 41%

7. For this determination, we need to compare it to the returns expected from alternative investments with similar risk.

8. Project A has the higher net present value as shown:

		Project A		Project B	
Year	Present Value of 1 at 10%	Net Cash Flows	Present Value of Net Cash Flows	Net Cash Flows	Present Value of Net Cash Flows
1	0.9091	$12,000	$10,909	$ 4,500	$ 4,091
2	0.8264	8,500	7,024	8,500	7,024
3	0.7513	4,000	3,005	13,000	9,767
Totals		$24,500	$20,938	$26,000	$20,882
Amount invested			(20,000)		(20,000)
Net present value			$ 938		$ 882

9. No, the information is too limited to draw that conclusion. For example, one investment could be riskier than the other, or one could require a substantially larger initial investment.

10. *b*

11. *e*; Variable costs per unit for this order of 200 units follow:

Direct materials ($37,500/7,500)	$ 5.00
Direct labor ($60,000/7,500)	8.00
Variable overhead [(0.30 × $20,000)/7,500]	0.80
Variable selling expenses [(0.60 × $25,000 × 0.5)/7,500]	1.00
Total variable costs per unit	$14.80

Cost to produce special order: (200 × $14.80) + $400 = $3,360.

Price per unit to earn $1,000: ($3,360 + $1,000)/200 = 21.80.

12. They are the additional (new) costs of accepting new business.

13. *d*;

	Incremental benefits		Incremental costs
Alpha	$300 ($600 − $300)	>	$150 (given)
Beta	$450 ($900 − $450)	>	$300 (given)
Gamma	$150 ($425 − $275)	>	$125 (given)
Delta	$ 60 ($210 − $150)	<	$ 75 (given)

14. A sunk cost is *never* relevant because it results from a past decision and is already incurred.

15. Avoidable expenses are ones a company will not incur by eliminating a segment; unavoidable expenses will continue even after a segment is eliminated.

16. *a*

Key Terms

Key Terms are available at the book's Website for learning and testing in an online Flashcard Format.

Accounting rate of return (p. 987)
Avoidable expense (p. 1000)
Break-even time (BET) (p. 1002)
Capital budgeting (p. 984)
Hurdle rate (p. 992)
Incremental cost (p. 996)
Internal rate of return (IRR) (p. 991)
Net present value (NPV) (p. 989)
Payback period (PBP) (p. 985)
Relevant benefits (p. 995)
Unavoidable expense (p. 1000)

Personal Interactive Quiz

Personal Interactive Quizzes A and B are available at the book's Website to reinforce and assess your learning.

Discussion Questions

1. What is capital budgeting?
2. Identify four reasons that capital budgeting decisions by managers are risky.
3. Capital budgeting decisions require careful analysis because they are generally the ________ ________ and ________ decisions that management faces.
4. Identify two disadvantages of using the payback period for comparing investments.
5. Why is an investment more attractive to management if it has a shorter payback period?
6. What is the average amount invested in a machine during its predicted five-year life if it costs $200,000 and has a $20,000 salvage value? Assume that net income is received evenly throughout each year and straight-line depreciation is used.
7. If the present value of the expected net cash flows from a machine, discounted at 10%, exceeds the amount to be invested, what can you say about the investment's expected rate of return? What can you say about the expected rate of return if the present value of the net cash flows, discounted at 10%, is less than the investment amount?
8. Why is the present value of $100 that you expect to receive one year from today worth less than $100 received today? What is the present value of $100 that you expect to receive one year from today, discounted at 12%?
9. Why should managers set the required rate of return higher than the rate at which money can be borrowed when making a typical capital budgeting decision?
10. Why does the use of the accelerated depreciation method (instead of straight line) for income tax reporting increase an investment's value?
11. What is an out-of-pocket cost? What is an opportunity cost? Are opportunity costs recorded in the accounting records?
12. Why are sunk costs irrelevant in deciding whether to sell a product in its present condition or to make it into a new product through additional processing?
13. Identify the incremental costs incurred by Krispy Kreme for shipping one additional dozen donuts to a convenience store along with the store's normal order of 6 dozen donuts.
14. Tastykake is considering purchasing five new ovens for its factory. Identify three methods management can use to evaluate whether to purchase the new ovens.
15. Assume that Harley-Davidson manufactures and sells 500,000 units of a memorabilia product at $30 per unit in domestic markets. It costs $20 per unit to manufacture ($13 variable cost per unit, $7 fixed cost per unit). Can you describe a situation under which the company is willing to sell an additional 25,000 units of the product in an international market at $15 per unit?

Red numbers denote Discussion Questions that involve decision-making.

***Homework Manager** repeats all numerical Quick Studies on the book's Website with new numbers.*

QUICK STUDY

QS 25-1
Analyzing payback periods P1

Ortega Company is considering two alternative investments. The payback period is 4.5 years for Investment A and 5 years for Investment B. (1) If management relies on the payback period, which investment is preferred? (2) Why might Ortega's analysis of these two alternatives lead to the selection of B over A?

QS 25-2
Payback period P1

Rivera Company is considering an investment that requires immediate payment of $18,000 and provides expected cash inflows of $6,000 annually for four years. What is the investment's payback period?

QS 25-3
Computation of net present value P3

If VHS Company invests $100,000 today, it can expect to receive $20,000 at the end of each year for the next seven years plus an extra $12,000 at the end of the seventh year. What is the net present value of this investment assuming a required 10% return on investments?

QS 25-4
Computation of accounting rate of return P2

Cardinal Company is considering an investment expected to generate an average net income after taxes of $1,300 for three years. The investment costs $30,000 and has an estimated $4,000 salvage value. Compute the accounting rate of return for this investment.

QS 25-5
Selection of sales mix
C3 A1

Memory Lane Company can sell all units of computer memory X and Y that it can produce, but it has limited production capacity. It can produce two units of X per hour *or* three units of Y per hour, and it has 8,000 production hours available. Contribution margin is $10 for Product X and $8 for Product Y. What is the most profitable sales mix for Memory Lane Company?

QS 25-6
Analysis of incremental costs
C3 A1

Mo-Kan Company incurs a $6 per unit cost for Product A, which it currently manufactures and sells for $9 per unit. Instead of manufacturing and selling this product, Mo-Kan can purchase Product B for $5 per unit and sell it for $8 per unit. If it does so, unit sales would remain unchanged and $5 of the $6 per unit costs assigned to Product A would be eliminated. Should Mo-Kan continue to manufacture Product A or purchase Product B for resale?

QS 25-7
Computation of break-even time
A2

Soles, a shoe manufacturer, is evaluating the costs and benefits of new equipment that would custom fit each pair of athletic shoes. The customer would have his or her foot scanned by digital computer equipment; this information would be used to cut the raw materials to provide the customer a perfect fit. The new equipment costs $100,000 and is expected to generate an additional $35,000 in cash flows for five years. A bank will make a $100,000 loan to Soles at a 10% interest rate for this equipment's purchase. Use the following table to determine the break-even time for this equipment.

Year	Cash Flows*	Present Value of 1 at 10%	Present Value of Cash Flows	Cumulative Present Value of Cash Flows
0	$(100,000)	1.0000		
1	35,000	0.9091		
2	35,000	0.8264		
3	35,000	0.7513		
4	35,000	0.6830		
5	35,000	0.6209		

* All cash flows occur at year-end.

***Homework Manager** repeats all numerical Exercises on the book's Website with new numbers.*

EXERCISES

Exercise 25-1
Payback period computation; even cash flows
P1

Compute the payback period for each of these two separate investments:

a. A new operating system for an existing machine is expected to cost $260,000 and have a useful life of five years. The system yields an incremental after-tax income of $75,000 each year after deducting its straight-line depreciation. The predicted salvage value of the system is $10,000.

b. A machine costs $190,000, has a $10,000 salvage value, is expected to last nine years, and will generate an after-tax income of $30,000 per year after straight-line depreciation.

Exercise 25-2
Payback period computation; uneven cash flows
P1

Wenro Company is considering the purchase of an asset for $90,000. It is expected to produce the following net cash flows. The cash flows occur evenly throughout each year. Compute the payback period for this investment.

	Year 1	Year 2	Year 3	Year 4	Year 5	Total
Net cash flows	$30,000	$20,000	$30,000	$60,000	$19,000	$159,000

Check 3.167 years

Exercise 25-3
Payback period computation; declining-balance depreciation
P1

A machine can be purchased for $300,000 and used for 5 years, yielding the following net incomes. In projecting net incomes, double-declining balance depreciation is applied, using a 5-year life and a $50,000 salvage value. Compute the machine's payback period. Ignore taxes.

	Year 1	Year 2	Year 3	Year 4	Year 5
Net incomes	$20,000	$50,000	$100,000	$75,000	$200,000

Check 2.265 years

Exercise 25-4
Accounting rate of return P2

A machine costs $500,000 and is expected to yield an after-tax net income of $15,000 each year. Management predicts this machine has a 10-year service life and a $100,000 salvage value. Compute this machine's accounting rate of return.

Exercise 25-5
Payback period and accounting rate of return on investment
P1 P2

K2B Co. is considering the purchase of equipment that would allow the company to add a new product to its line. The equipment is expected to cost $240,000 with a 12-year life and no salvage value. It will be depreciated on a straight-line basis. The company expects to sell 96,000 units of the equipment's product each year. The expected annual income related to this equipment follows. Compute the (1) payback period and (2) accounting rate of return for this equipment.

Sales	$150,000
Costs	
Materials, labor, and overhead (except depreciation)	80,000
Depreciation on new equipment	20,000
Selling and administrative expenses	15,000
Total costs and expenses	115,000
Pretax income	35,000
Income taxes (30%)	10,500
Net income	$ 24,500

Check (1) 5.39 years (2) 20.42%

Exercise 25-6
Computing net present value P3

After evaluating the risk of the investment described in Exercise 25-5, K2B Co. concludes that it must earn at least an 8% return on this investment. Compute the net present value of this investment.

Exercise 25-7
Computation and interpretation of net present value and internal rate of return
P3 P4 

Kase Company can invest in each of three cheese-making projects: C1, C2, and C3. Each project requires an initial investment of $190,000 and would yield the following annual cash flows:

	C1	C2	C3
Year 1	$ 10,000	$ 80,000	$150,000
Year 2	90,000	80,000	50,000
Year 3	140,000	80,000	40,000
Totals	$240,000	$240,000	$240,000

(1) Assuming that the company requires a 12% return from its investments, use net present value to determine which projects, if any, should be acquired. (2) Using the answer from part 1, explain whether the internal rate of return is higher or lower than 12% for project C2? (3) Compute the internal rate of return for project C2.

Check (3) IRR = 13%

Exercise 25-8
Decision to accept additional business or not
C3 A1

Feist Co. expects to sell 200,000 units of its product in the next period with the following results:

Sales (200,000 units)	$3,000,000
Costs and expenses	
Direct materials	400,000
Direct labor	800,000
Overhead	200,000
Selling expenses	300,000
Administrative expenses	514,000
Total costs and expenses	2,214,000
Net income	$ 786,000

The company has an opportunity to sell 20,000 additional units at $12 per unit. The additional sales would not affect its current expected sales. Direct materials and labor costs would be the same for the additional units as they are for the regular units. However, the additional volume would create the following incremental costs: (1) total overhead would increase by 15% and (2) administrative expenses would increase by $86,000. Prepare an analysis to determine whether the company should accept or reject the offer to sell additional units at the reduced price of $12 per unit.

Check Income increase, $4,000

Exercise 25-9
Make or buy decision
C3 A1

Santos Company currently manufactures one of its crucial parts at a cost of $3.40 per unit. This cost is based on a normal production rate of 50,000 units per year. Variable costs are $1.50 per unit, fixed costs related to making this part are $50,000 per year, and allocated fixed costs are $45,000 per year. Allocated fixed costs are unavoidable whether the company makes or buys the part. Santos is considering buying the part from a supplier for a quoted price of $2.70 per unit guaranteed for a three-year period. Should the company continue to manufacture the part, or should it buy the part from the outside supplier? Support your answer with analyses.

Check $10,000 increased costs to buy

Exercise 25-10
Sell or process decision
C3 A1

Cantrell Company has already manufactured 20,000 units of Product A at a cost of $20 per unit. The 20,000 units can be sold at this stage for $500,000. Alternatively, it can be further processed at a $300,000 total additional cost and be converted into 4,000 units of Product B and 8,000 units of Product C. Per unit selling price for Product B is $75 and for Product C is $50. Prepare an analysis that shows whether the 20,000 units of Product A should be processed further or not.

Exercise 25-11
Analysis of income effects from eliminating departments
C3 A1

Suresh Co. expects its five departments to yield the following income for next year:

		Dept. M	Dept. N	Dept. O	Dept. P	Dept. T
2	Sales	$31,500	$17,500	$28,000	$21,000	$14,000
3	Expenses					
4	Avoidable	4,900	18,200	11,200	7,000	18,900
5	Unavoidable	25,900	6,300	2,100	14,700	4,900
6	Total expenses	30,800	24,500	13,300	21,700	23,800
7	Net income (loss)	$ 700	$ (7,000)	$14,700	$ (700)	$ (9,800)

Recompute and prepare the departmental income statements (including a combined total column) for the company under each of the following separate scenarios: Management (1) does not eliminate any department, (2) eliminates departments with expected net losses, and (3) eliminates departments with sales dollars that are less than avoidable expenses. Explain your answers to parts 2 and 3.

Check Total income (loss): (2) $(10,500), (3) $3,500

Exercise 25-12
Sales mix determination and analysis
C3 A1

Bethel Company owns a machine that can produce two specialized products. Production time for Product TLX is two units per hour and for Product MTV is five units per hour. The machine's capacity is 2,200 hours per year. Both products are sold to a single customer who has agreed to buy all of the company's output up to a maximum of 3,750 units of Product TLX and 2,000 units of Product

MTV. Selling prices and variable costs per unit to produce the products follow. Determine (1) the company's most profitable sales mix and (2) the contribution margin that results from that sales mix.

	Product TLX	Product MTV
Selling price per unit	$12.50	$7.50
Variable costs per unit	3.75	4.50

Check (2) $37,688

Exercise 25-13
Comparison of payback and BET
P1 A2 

This chapter explained two methods to evaluate investments using recovery time, the payback period and break-even time (BET). Refer to QS 25-7 and (1) compute the recovery time for both the payback period and break-even time, (2) discuss the advantage(s) of break-even time over the payback period, and (3) list two conditions under which payback period and break-even time are similar.

PROBLEM SET A

Problem 25-1A
Computation of payback period, accounting rate of return, and net present value
P1 P2 P3

mhhe.com/larson

Elite Company is planning to add a new product to its line. To manufacture this product, the company needs to buy a new machine at a $300,000 cost with an expected four-year life and a $20,000 salvage value. All sales are for cash, and all costs are out of pocket except for depreciation on the new machine. Additional information includes the following:

Expected annual sales of new product	$1,150,000
Expected annual costs of new product	
Direct materials	300,000
Direct labor	420,000
Overhead excluding straight-line depreciation on new machine	210,000
Selling and administrative expenses	100,000
Income taxes	30%

Required

1. Compute straight-line depreciation for each year of this new machine's life.
2. Determine expected net income and net cash flow for each year of this machine's life.
3. Compute this machine's payback period, assuming that cash flows occur evenly throughout each year.
4. Compute this machine's accounting rate of return, assuming that income is earned evenly throughout each year.
5. Compute the net present value for this machine using a discount rate of 7% and assuming that cash flows occur at each year-end. (*Hint:* Salvage value is a cash inflow at the end of the asset's life.)

Check (4) 21.88%

(5) $70,915

Problem 25-2A
Analysis and computation of payback period, accounting rate of return, and net present value
P1 P2 P3 

Pleasant Company has an opportunity to invest in one of two new projects. Project Y requires a $700,000 investment for new machinery with a four-year life and no salvage value. Project Z requires a $700,000 investment for new machinery with a three-year life and no salvage value. The two projects yield the following predicted annual results. The company uses straight-line depreciation, and cash flows occur evenly throughout each year.

	Project Y	Project Z
Sales	$700,000	$560,000
Expenses		
Direct materials	98,000	70,000
Direct labor	140,000	84,000
Overhead including depreciation	252,000	252,000
Selling and administrative expenses	50,000	50,000
Total expenses	540,000	456,000
Pretax income	160,000	104,000
Income taxes (30%)	48,000	31,200
Net income	$112,000	$ 72,800

Required

Check For Project Y: (2) 2.44 years, (3) 32%, (4) $250,573

1. Compute each project's annual expected net cash flows.
2. Determine each project's payback period.
3. Compute each project's accounting rate of return.
4. Determine each project's net present value using 8% as the discount rate. For part 4 only, assume that cash flows occur at each year-end.

Analysis Component

5. Identify the project you would recommend to management and explain your choice.

Problem 25-3A
Computation of cash flows and net present values with alternative depreciation methods

P3 

Angiletta Corporation is considering a new project requiring a $30,000 investment in test equipment with no salvage value. The project would produce $12,000 of pretax income before depreciation at the end of each of the next six years. The company's income tax rate is 40%. In compiling its tax return and computing its income tax payments, the company can choose between the two alternative depreciation schedules shown in the table.

	Straight-Line Depreciation	MACRS Depreciation*
Year 1	$ 3,000	$ 6,000
Year 2	6,000	9,600
Year 3	6,000	5,760
Year 4	6,000	3,456
Year 5	6,000	3,456
Year 6	3,000	1,728
Totals	$30,000	$30,000

* The modified accelerated cost recovery system (MACRS) for depreciation is discussed in Chapter 10.

Required

1. Prepare a five-column table that reports amounts (assuming use of straight-line depreciation) for each of the following for each of the six years: (a) pretax income before depreciation, (b) straight-line depreciation expense, (c) taxable income, (d) income taxes, and (e) net cash flow. Net cash flow equals the amount of income before depreciation minus the income taxes.
2. Prepare a five-column table that reports amounts (assuming use of MACRS depreciation) for each of the following for each of the six years: (a) pretax income before depreciation, (b) MACRS depreciation expense, (c) taxable income, (d) income taxes, and (e) net cash flow. Net cash flow equals the income amount before depreciation minus the income taxes.

Check Net present value: (3) $10,041, (4) $10,635

3. Compute the net present value of the investment if straight-line depreciation is used. Use 10% as the discount rate.
4. Compute the net present value of the investment if MACRS depreciation is used. Use 10% as the discount rate.

Analysis Component

5. Explain why the MACRS depreciation method increases this project's net present value.

Problem 25-4A
Analysis of income effects of additional business

C3 A1

mhhe.com/larson

Cayman Products manufactures and sells to wholesalers approximately 300,000 packages per year of underwater markers at $4 per package. Annual costs for the production and sale of this quantity are shown in the table.

Direct materials	$384,000
Direct labor	96,000
Overhead	288,000
Selling expenses	120,000
Administrative expenses	80,000
Total costs and expenses	$968,000

A new wholesaler has offered to buy 50,000 packages for $3.44 each. These markers would be marketed under the wholesaler's name and would not affect Cayman Products' sales through its normal channels. A study of the costs of this additional business reveals the following:

- Direct materials costs are 100% variable.
- Per unit direct labor costs for the additional units would be 50% higher than normal because their production would require overtime pay at one-and-one-half times the usual labor rate.
- 25% of the normal annual overhead costs are fixed at any production level from 250,000 to 400,000 units. The remaining 75% of the annual overhead cost is variable with volume.
- Accepting the new business would involve no additional selling expenses.
- Accepting the new business would increase administrative expenses by a $4,000 fixed amount.

Required

Prepare a three-column comparative income statement that shows the following:

1. Annual operating income without the special order (column 1).

2. Annual operating income received from the new business only (column 2).

3. Combined annual operating income from normal business and the new business (column 3).

Check Operating income: (1) $232,000, (2) $44,000

Problem 25-5A
Analysis of sales mix strategies

C3 A1

Ortiz Company is able to produce two products, G and B, with the same machine in its factory. The following information is known:

	Product G	Product B
Selling price per unit	$120	$160
Variable costs per unit	40	90
Contribution margin per unit	$ 80	$ 70
Machine hours to produce 1 unit	0.8 hours	2.0 hours
Maximum unit sales per month	400 units	350 units

Ortiz presently operates the machine for a single eight-hour shift for 22 working days each month. Management is thinking about operating the machine for two shifts, which will increase its productivity by another eight hours per day for 22 days per month. This change would require $6,500 additional fixed costs per month.

Required

1. Determine the contribution margin per machine hour that each product generates.

2. How many units of Product G and Product B should the company produce if it continues to operate with only one shift? How much total contribution margin does this mix produce each month?

3. If the company adds another shift, how many units of Product G and Product B should it produce? How much total contribution margin would this mix produce each month? Should the company add the new shift? Explain.

4. Suppose that the company determines that it can increase Product G's maximum sales to 440 units per month by spending $2,000 per month in marketing efforts. Should the company pursue this strategy and the double shift? Explain.

Check Units of Product G: (2) 220, (3) 400, (4) 440

Problem 25-6A
Analysis of possible elimination of a department

C3 A1

Home Decor Company's management is trying to decide whether to eliminate Department 200, which has produced losses or low profits for several years. The company's 2005 departmental income statement shows the following:

HOME DECOR COMPANY
Departmental Income Statements
For Year Ended December 31, 2005

	Dept. 100	Dept. 200	Combined
Sales	$872,000	$580,000	$1,452,000
Cost of goods sold	524,000	414,000	938,000
Gross profit	348,000	166,000	514,000
Operating expenses			
Direct expenses			
Advertising	34,000	24,000	58,000
Store supplies used	8,000	7,600	15,600
Depreciation—Store equipment	10,000	6,600	16,600
Total direct expenses	52,000	38,200	90,200

[continued on next page]

[continued from previous page]

Allocated expenses			
Sales salaries	130,000	78,000	208,000
Rent expense	18,880	9,440	28,320
Bad debts expense	19,800	16,200	36,000
Office salary	37,440	24,960	62,400
Insurance expense	4,000	2,200	6,200
Miscellaneous office expenses	4,800	3,200	8,000
Total allocated expenses	214,920	134,000	348,920
Total expenses	266,920	172,200	439,120
Net income (loss)	$ 81,080	$ (6,200)	$ 74,880

In analyzing whether to eliminate Department 200, management considers the following:

a. The company has one office worker who earns $1,200 per week, or $62,400 per year, and four salesclerks who each earn $1,000 per week, or $52,000 per year.

b. The full salaries of two salesclerks are charged to Department 100. The full salary of one sales clerk is charged to Department 200. The salary of the fourth clerk, who works half-time in both departments, is divided evenly between the two departments.

c. Eliminating Department 200 would avoid the sales salaries and the office salary currently allocated to it. However, management prefers another plan. Two salesclerks have indicated that they will be quitting soon. Management believes that their work can be done by the other two clerks if the one office worker works in sales half-time. Eliminating Department 200 will allow this shift of duties. If this change is implemented, half the office worker's salary would be reported as sales salaries and half would be reported as office salary.

d. The store building is rented under a long-term lease that cannot be changed. Therefore, Department 100 will use the space and equipment currently used by Department 200.

e. Closing Department 200 will eliminate its expenses for advertising, bad debts, and store supplies; 70% of the insurance expense allocated to it to cover its merchandise inventory; and 25% of the miscellaneous office expenses presently allocated to it.

Required

Check (1) Total expenses: (a) $1,377,120, (b) $568,140

1. Prepare a three-column report that lists items and amounts for (a) the company's total expenses (including cost of goods sold)—in column 1, (b) the expenses that would be eliminated by closing Department 200—in column 2, and (c) the expenses that will continue—in column 3.

(2) Forecasted net income without Department 200, $63,020

2. Prepare a forecasted annual income statement for the company reflecting the elimination of Department 200 assuming that it will not affect Department 100's sales and gross profit. The statement should reflect the reassignment of the office worker to one-half time as a salesclerk.

Analysis Component

3. Reconcile the company's combined net income with the forecasted net income assuming that Department 200 is eliminated (list both items and amounts). Analyze the reconciliation and explain why you think the department should or should not be eliminated.

PROBLEM SET B

Problem 25-1B

Computation of payback period, accounting rate of return, and net present value

P1 P2 P3

Concorde Company is planning to add a new product to its line. To manufacture this product, the company needs to buy a new machine at a $100,000 cost with an expected five-year life and a $25,000 salvage value. All sales are for cash and all costs are out of pocket, except for depreciation on the new machine. Additional information includes the following:

Expected annual sales of new product	$350,000
Expected annual costs of new product	
Direct materials	150,000
Direct labor	50,000
Overhead excluding straight-line depreciation on new machine	100,000
Selling and administrative expenses	23,000
Income taxes	20%

Required

1. Compute straight-line depreciation for each year of this new machine's life.

2. Determine expected net income and net cash flow for each year of this machine's life.

3. Compute this machine's payback period, assuming that cash flows occur evenly throughout each year.

4. Compute this machine's accounting rate of return, assuming that income is earned evenly throughout each year.

5. Compute the net present value for this machine using a discount rate of 12% and assuming that cash flows occur at each year-end. (*Hint:* Salvage value is a cash inflow at the end of the asset's life.)

Check (4) 15.36%

(5) $2,862

Problem 25-2B
Analysis and computation of payback period, accounting rate of return, and net present value

P1 P2 P3 

Micelli Company has an opportunity to invest in one of two projects. Project A requires a $480,000 investment for new machinery with a three-year life and no salvage value. Project B also requires a $480,000 investment for new machinery with a four-year life and no salvage value. The two projects yield the following predicted annual results. The company uses straight-line depreciation, and cash flows occur evenly throughout each year.

	Project A	Project B
Sales	$750,000	$800,000
Expenses		
Direct materials	125,000	250,000
Direct labor	130,000	80,000
Overhead including depreciation	330,000	276,000
Selling and administrative expenses	120,000	120,000
Total expenses	705,000	726,000
Pretax income	45,000	74,000
Income taxes (30%)	13,500	22,200
Net income	$ 31,500	$ 51,800

Required

1. Compute each project's annual expected net cash flows.

2. Determine each project's payback period.

3. Compute each project's accounting rate of return.

4. Determine each project's net present value using 10% as the discount rate. For part 4 only, assume that cash flows occur at each year-end.

Check For Project A: (2) 2.5 years, (3) 13.1%, (4) $(3,759)

Analysis Component

5. Identify the project you would recommend to management and explain your choice.

Problem 25-3B
Computation of cash flows and net present values with alternative depreciation methods

P3 

Cologne Corporation is considering a new project requiring a $25,000 investment in an asset having no salvage value. The project would produce $15,000 of pretax income before depreciation at the end of each of the next six years. The company's income tax rate is 30%. In compiling its tax return and computing its income tax payments, the company can choose between two alternative depreciation schedules as shown in the table.

	Straight-Line Depreciation	MACRS Depreciation*
Year 1	$ 2,500	$ 5,000
Year 2	5,000	8,000
Year 3	5,000	4,800
Year 4	5,000	2,880
Year 5	5,000	2,880
Year 6	2,500	1,440
Totals	$25,000	$25,000

* The modified accelerated cost recovery system (MACRS) for depreciation is discussed in Chapter 10.

Required

1. Prepare a five-column table that reports amounts (assuming use of straight-line depreciation) for each of the following items for each of the six years: (a) pretax income before depreciation, (b) straight-line depreciation expense, (c) taxable income, (d) income taxes, and (e) net cash flow. Net cash flow equals the amount of income before depreciation minus the income taxes.

2. Prepare a five-column table that reports amounts (assuming use of MACRS depreciation) for each of the following items for each of the six years: (a) income before depreciation, (b) MACRS depreciation expense, (c) taxable income, (d) income taxes, and (e) net cash flow. Net cash flow equals the amount of income before depreciation minus the income taxes.

Check Net present value: (3) $19,437, (4) $19,914

3. Compute the net present value of the investment if straight-line depreciation is used. Use 15% as the discount rate.

4. Compute the net present value of the investment if MACRS depreciation is used. Use 15% as the discount rate.

Analysis Component

5. Explain why the MACRS depreciation method increases the net present value of this project.

Problem 25-4B
Analysis of income effects of additional business

C3 A1

Windtrax Company manufactures and sells to local wholesalers approximately 200,000 units per month at a sales price of $1 per unit. Monthly costs for the production and sale of this quantity follow.

Direct materials	$ 30,000
Direct labor	12,000
Overhead	50,000
Selling expenses	7,500
Administrative expenses	31,500
Total costs and expenses	$131,000

A new out-of-state distributor has offered to buy 20,000 units next month for $0.80 each. These units would be marketed in other states and would not affect Windtrax's sales through its normal channels. A study of the costs of this new business reveals the following:

- Direct materials costs are 100% variable.
- Per unit direct labor costs for the additional units would be 100% higher than normal because their production would require double overtime pay to meet the distributor's deadline.
- Eighty percent of the normal annual overhead costs are fixed at any production level from 120,000 to 300,000 units. The remaining 20% is variable with volume.
- Accepting the new business would involve no additional selling expenses.
- Accepting the new business would increase administrative expenses by a $750 fixed amount.

Required

Prepare a three-column comparative income statement that shows the following:

Check Operating income: (1) $69,000, (2) $8,850

1. Monthly operating income without the special order (column 1).

2. Monthly operating income received from the new business only (column 2).

3. Combined monthly operating income from normal business and the new business (column 3).

Problem 25-5B
Analysis of sales mix strategies

C3 A1 

Digits Company is able to produce two products, 22 and 44, with the same machine in its factory. The following information is known:

	Product 22	Product 44
Selling price per unit	$175	$200
Variable costs per unit	100	150
Contribution margin per unit	$ 75	$ 50
Machine hours to produce 1 unit	0.8 hours	0.5 hours
Maximum unit sales per month	525 units	450 units

Digits presently operates the machine for a single eight-hour shift for 23 working days each month. Management is thinking about operating the machine for two shifts, which will increase its productivity by another eight hours per day for 23 days per month. This change would require $5,000 additional fixed costs per month.

Required

1. Determine the contribution margin per machine hour that each product generates.
2. How many units of Product 22 and Product 44 should the company produce if it continues to operate with only one shift? How much total contribution margin does this mix produce each month?
3. If the company adds another shift, how many units of Product 22 and Product 44 should it produce? How much total contribution margin would this mix produce each month? Should the company add the new shift? Explain.
4. Suppose that the company determines that it can increase Product 44's maximum sales to 500 units per month by spending $500 per month in marketing efforts. Should the company pursue this strategy and the double shift? Explain.

Check Units of Product 44: (2) 368, (3) 450, (4) 500

Problem 25-6B
Analysis of possible elimination of a department

C3 A1

Turftime Company's management is trying to decide whether to eliminate Department Z, which has produced low profits or losses for several years. The company's 2005 departmental income statement shows the following:

TURFTIME COMPANY
Departmental Income Statements
For Year Ended December 31, 2005

	Dept. A	Dept. Z	Combined
Sales	$350,000	$87,500	$437,500
Cost of goods sold	230,650	62,550	293,200
Gross profit	119,350	24,950	144,300
Operating expenses			
Direct expenses			
Advertising	13,500	1,500	15,000
Store supplies used	2,800	700	3,500
Depreciation—Store equipment	7,000	3,500	10,500
Total direct expenses	23,300	5,700	29,000
Allocated expenses			
Sales salaries	35,100	11,700	46,800
Rent expense	11,040	2,760	13,800
Bad debts expense	10,500	2,000	12,500
Office salary	10,400	2,600	13,000
Insurance expense	2,100	700	2,800
Miscellaneous office expenses	850	1,250	2,100
Total allocated expenses	69,990	21,010	91,000
Total expenses	93,290	26,710	120,000
Net income (loss)	$ 26,060	$(1,760)	$ 24,300

In analyzing whether to eliminate Department Z, management considers the following items:

a. The company has one office worker who earns $250 per week or $13,000 per year and four salesclerks who each earn $225 per week or $11,700 per year.

b. The full salaries of three salesclerks are charged to Department A. The full salary of one salesclerk is charged to Department Z.

c. Eliminating Department Z would avoid the sales salaries and the office salary currently allocated to it. However, management prefers another plan. Two salesclerks have indicated that they will be quitting soon. Management believes that their work can be done by the two remaining clerks if the one office worker works in sales half time. Eliminating Department Z will allow this shift of duties. If this change is implemented, half the office worker's salary would be reported as sales salaries and half would be reported as office salary.

d. The store building is rented under a long-term lease that cannot be changed. Therefore, Department A will use the space and equipment currently used by Department Z.

e. Closing Department Z will eliminate its expenses for advertising, bad debts, and store supplies; 65% of the insurance expense allocated to it to cover its merchandise inventory; and 30% of the miscellaneous office expenses presently allocated to it.

Required

Check (1) Total expenses: (a) $413,200, (b) $90,980

1. Prepare a three-column report that lists items and amounts for (a) the company's total expenses (including cost of goods sold)—in column 1, (b) the expenses that would be eliminated by closing Department Z—in column 2, and (c) the expenses that will continue—in column 3.

(2) Forecasted net income without Department Z, $27,780

2. Prepare a forecasted annual income statement for the company reflecting the elimination of Department Z assuming that it will not affect Department A's sales and gross profit. The statement should reflect the reassignment of the office worker to one-half time as a salesclerk.

Analysis Component

3. Reconcile the company's combined net income with the forecasted net income assuming that Department Z is eliminated (list both items and amounts). Analyze the reconciliation and explain why you think the department should or should not be eliminated.

PROBLEM SET C

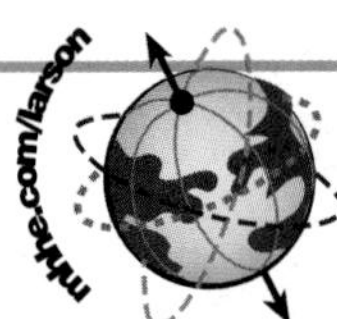

Problem Set C is available at the book's Website to further reinforce and assess your learning.

SERIAL PROBLEM

Success Systems

Kay Breeze is considering the purchase of equipment for Success Systems that would allow the company to add a new product to its computer furniture line. The equipment is expected to cost $120,000 and to have a six-year life and no salvage value. It will be depreciated on a straight-line basis. Success Systems expects to sell 50 units of the equipment's product each year. The expected annual income related to this equipment follows:

Sales	$150,000
Costs	
Materials, labor, and overhead (except depreciation)	80,000
Depreciation on new equipment	20,000
Selling and administrative expenses	15,000
Total costs and expenses	115,000
Pretax income	35,000
Income taxes (30%)	10,500
Net income	$ 24,500

Required

Compute the (1) payback period and (2) accounting rate of return for this equipment.

BEYOND THE NUMBERS

REPORTING IN ACTION

C1 A1 P3

BTN 25-1 Advertising is an important component of product mix decisions because it helps drive product sales. In 2003 Krispy Kreme's stores in the Kansas City area ran a unique promotion associated with the performance of the Kansas City Royals major league baseball team. If the Royals scored 12 hits (not runs) in a home game, each person with a ticket stub for that game could redeem it for a free dozen Krispy Kreme donuts at a local Krispy Kreme store.

Required

1. Can you compute Krispy Kreme's incremental product cost for this advertisement? Explain.
2. Assume that the average attendance for home games at Royals stadium is 20,000 fans. How many dozen donuts must Krispy Kreme give away every time the Royals score 12 hits if 5% of fans redeem ticket stubs? Explain.
3. What would Krispy Kreme's total promotional cost be if the Royals score 12 hits in 15 home games? Assume the same attendance and redemption rates as in part 2, and that the cost to produce one dozen donuts is $2 per dozen. Explain.
4. What does Krispy Kreme potentially gain by this unique promotion? What behavior does management hope results from people redeeming ticket stubs for free donuts?

Roll On

5. Do research on the Internet to determine whether Krispy Kreme extended this promotion to the 2004 (or later) baseball season. Offer possible reasons that such a popular promotion would be discontinued or continued.

COMPARATIVE ANALYSIS

C3 

BTN 25-2 Krispy Kreme and Tastykake sell several different products; most are profitable but some are not. Teams of employees in each company make advertising, investment, and product mix decisions. A certain portion of advertising for both companies is on a local basis to a target audience.

Required

1. Find one major advertisement of a product or group of products for each company in your local newspaper. Contact the newspaper and ask the approximate cost of this ad space (for example, cost of one page or one-half page of advertising).
2. Estimate how many products this advertisement must sell to justify its cost. Begin by taking the product's sales price advertised for each company and assume a 20% contribution margin.
3. Prepare a one-half page memorandum explaining the importance of effective advertising when making a product mix decision. Be prepared to present your ideas in class.

ETHICS CHALLENGE

P3

BTN 25-3 A consultant commented that "too often the numbers look good but feel bad." This comment stems from estimation error common to capital budgeting proposals that relate to future cash flows. Three reasons for this error often exist. First, reliably predicting cash flows several years into the future is very difficult. Second, the present value of cash flows many years into the future (say, beyond 10 years) is often very small. Third, it is difficult for personal biases and expectations not to unduly influence present value computations.

Required

1. Compute the present value of $100 to be received in 10 years assuming a 12% discount rate.
2. Why is understanding the three reasons mentioned for estimation errors important when evaluating investment projects? Link this response to your answer for part 1.

COMMUNICATING IN PRACTICE

P1 P2 P3 P4

BTN 25-4 Payback period, accounting rate of return, net present value, and internal rate of return are common methods to evaluate capital investment opportunities. Assume that your manager asks you to identify the type of measurement basis and unit that each method offers and to list the advantages and disadvantages of each. Present your response in memorandum format of less than one page.

TAKING IT TO THE NET

mhhe.com/larson

BTN 25-5 Capital budgeting is an important issue for every organization, particularly as it relates to an organization's future. The United States set up a commission to study capital budgeting at the federal government level. Access the report of *The President's Commission to Study Capital Budgeting* from the following Website: **http://Clinton2.nara.gov/pcscb**.

Required

1. Does the commission's concept of *capital* for federal government differ from that used by the private sector?
2. Are the investment analysis techniques explained in the chapter relevant to the government?

TEAMWORK IN ACTION

P1 P3 

BTN 25-6 Break into teams and identify four reasons that an international airline such as **Southwest**, **Northwest**, or **American** would invest in a project when its direct analysis using both payback period and net present value indicate it to be a poor investment. (*Hint:* Think about qualitative factors.) Provide an example of an investment project supporting your answer.

BUSINESS WEEK ACTIVITY

mhhe.com/larson

BTN 25-7 Read the article "An MBA: Is It Still Worth It?" in the October 21, 2002, issue of ***Business Week***. (The book's Website provides free access to the article.)

Required

1. Describe how deciding to obtain graduate education is similar to a capital budgeting decision.
2. Explain the calculation used by Professor Jens Stephan in the article to determine the payback on an investment in an MBA degree.
3. How long will it take for an average 2002 MBA graduate to break even on the investment in graduate business education?
4. Do European or U.S. MBA graduates have a shorter payback period on their investment in education?
5. What is the annual return on investment over a 10-year period for an average MBA graduate?

ENTREPRENEURIAL DECISION

mhhe.com/larson

BTN 25-8 In the chapter's opening feature, Corinna Lathan of **AnthroTronix** says she hopes to produce and sell two models of CosmoBot. The selling price of the enhanced model available to clinics and therapists is $2,500. The selling price of the home model to individuals is $500. Assume that AnthroTronix can sell all units of both CosmoBot models that it can produce but that it has limited production capacity. Specifically, it estimates that it can produce two units of the enhanced model per hour or, alternatively, four units of the home model per hour. The company has 2,080 production hours available. Contribution margin is $500 for the enhanced model and $400 for the home model.

Required

What is the most profitable sales mix for AnthroTronix? Explain.

HITTING THE ROAD

C1 P3 

BTN 25-9 Visit or call a local auto dealership and inquire about leasing a car. Ask about the down payment and the required monthly payments. You will likely find the salesperson does not discuss the cost to purchase this car but focuses on the affordability of the monthly payments. This chapter gives you the tools to compute the cost of this car using the lease payment schedule in present dollars and to estimate the profit from leasing for an auto dealership.

Required

1. Compare the cost of leasing the car to buying it in present dollars using the information from the dealership you contact. (Assume you will make a final payment at the end of the lease and then own the car.)
2. Is it more costly to lease or buy the car? Support your answer with computations.

GLOBAL DECISION

C1 

BTN 25-10 Access **Grupo Bimbo**'s 2002 annual report from its Website GrupoBimbo.com. Read the message from its Chief Executive Officer Daniel M. Servitje near the beginning of the report.

Required

1. What tool did Grupo Bimbo provide to its entire sales force to improve productivity?
2. Did Grupo Bimbo close any of its plants in 2002 to improve operating efficiency?
3. Identify two new products that Grupo Bimbo added to its product mix in 2002.
4. In what markets did Grupo Bimbo increase its sales volume in 2002?
5. What does it identify as its most outstanding promotional and advertising activity in 2002?

Financial Statement Information

This appendix includes financial information for (1) **Krispy Kreme**, (2) **Tastykake**, and (3) **Harley-Davidson**. This information is taken from their annual reports. An **annual report** is a summary of a company's financial results for the year along with its current financial condition and future plans. This report is directed to external users of financial information, but it also affects the actions and decisions of internal users.

A company uses an annual report to showcase itself and its products. Many annual reports include attractive photos, diagrams, and illustrations related to the company. The primary objective of annual reports, however, is the *financial section,* which communicates much information about a company, with most data drawn from the accounting information system. The layout of an annual report's financial section is fairly established and typically includes the following:

- Letter to Shareholders
- Financial History and Highlights
- Management Discussion and Analysis
- Management's Report
- Report of Independent Accountants (Auditor's Report)
- Financial Statements
- Notes to Financial Statements
- List of Directors and Officers

This appendix provides the financial statements for Krispy Kreme (plus selected notes), Tastykake, and Harley-Davidson. The appendix is organized as follows:

- **Krispy Kreme A-2** through **A-17**
- **Tastykake A-18** through **A-24**
- **Harley-Davidson A-25** through **A-30**

Many assignments at the end of each chapter refer to information in this appendix. We encourage readers to spend time with these assignments; they are especially useful in showing the relevance and diversity of financial accounting and reporting.

> *Special note:* The SEC maintains the EDGAR (**E**lectronic **D**ata **G**athering, **A**nalysis, and **R**etrieval) database at **www.sec.gov.** The **Form 10-K** is the annual report form for most companies. It provides electronically accessible information. The **Form 10-KSB** is the annual report form filed by "small businesses." It requires slightly less information than the Form 10-K. One of these forms must be filed within 90 days after the company's fiscal year-end. (Forms 10-K405, 10-KT, 10-KT405, and 10-KSB405 are slight variations of the usual form due to certain regulations or rules.)

KRISPY KREME
2003 ANNUAL REPORT

SELECTED FINANCIAL DATA

The following table shows selected financial data for Krispy Kreme. The selected historical statement of operations data for each of the years ended, and the selected historical balance sheet data as of January 31, 1999, January 30, 2000, January 28, 2001, February 3, 2002 and February 2, 2003 have been derived from our audited consolidated financial statements. Please note that our fiscal year ended February 3, 2002 contained 53 weeks.

Systemwide sales include the sales by both our company and franchised stores and exclude the sales by our KKM&D business segment and the royalties and fees received from our franchised stores. Our consolidated financial statements appearing elsewhere in this annual report exclude franchised store sales and include royalties and fees received from our franchisees. The consolidated financial statements also include the results of Freedom Rings, LLC, the area developer in Philadelphia, and Golden Gate Doughnuts, LLC, the area developer in Northern California, in which Krispy Kreme has a majority ownership interest, as well as the results of Glazed Investments, LLC, the area developer in Colorado, Minnesota and Wisconsin, for periods subsequent to August 22, 2002, the date the Company acquired a controlling interest in this area developer.

You should read the following selected financial data in conjunction with "Management's Discussion and Analysis of Financial Condition and Results of Operations," the consolidated financial statements and accompanying notes and the other financial data included elsewhere herein. All references to per share amounts and any other reference to shares in "Selected Financial Data," unless otherwise noted, have been adjusted to reflect a two-for-one stock split paid on March 19, 2001 to shareholders of record as of March 5, 2001 and a two-for-one stock split paid on June 14, 2001 to shareholders of record as of May 29, 2001. Unless otherwise specified, references in this annual report to "Krispy Kreme," the "Company," "we," "us" or "our" refer to Krispy Kreme Doughnuts, Inc. and its subsidiaries.

IN THOUSANDS, EXCEPT PER SHARE DATA AND STORE NUMBERS

YEAR ENDED	Jan. 31, 1999	Jan. 30, 2000	Jan. 28, 2001	Feb. 3, 2002	Feb. 2, 2003
Statement of Operations Data:					
Total revenues	$180,880	$220,243	$300,715	$394,354	$491,549
Operating expenses	159,941	190,003	250,690	316,946	381,489
General and administrative expenses	10,897	14,856	20,061	27,562	28,897
Depreciation and amortization expenses	4,278	4,546	6,457	7,959	12,271
Arbitration award	—	—	—	—	9,075
Provision for restructuring	9,466	—	—	—	—
Income (loss) from operations	(3,702)	10,838	23,507	41,887	59,817
Interest expense (income), net, and other	1,577	1,232	(1,698)	(2,408)	749
Equity loss in joint ventures	—	—	706	602	2,008
Minority interest	—	—	716	1,147	2,287
Income (loss) before income taxes	(5,279)	9,606	23,783	42,546	54,773
Provision (benefit) for income taxes	(2,112)	3,650	9,058	16,168	21,295
Net income (loss)	$ (3,167)	$ 5,956	$ 14,725	$ 26,378	$ 33,478
Net income (loss) per share:					
Basic	$ (.09)	$ .16	$ .30	$ .49	$ .61
Diluted	(.09)	.15	.27	.45	.56
Shares used in calculation of net income (loss) per share:					
Basic	32,996	37,360	49,184	53,703	55,093
Diluted	32,996	39,280	53,656	58,443	59,492
Cash dividends declared per common share	$ .04	$ —	$ —	$ —	$ —
Operating Data (Unaudited):					
Systemwide sales	$240,316	$318,854	$448,129	$621,665	$778,573
Number of stores at end of period:					
Company	61	58	63	75	99
Franchised	70	86	111	143	177
Systemwide	131	144	174	218	276
Average weekly sales per store:					
Company	$ 47	$ 54	$ 69	$ 72	$ 76
Franchised	28	38	43	53	58
Balance Sheet Data (at end of period):					
Working capital	$ 8,387	$ 11,452	$ 29,443	$ 49,236	$ 81,441
Total assets	93,312	104,958	171,493	255,376	410,487
Long-term debt, including current maturities	21,020	22,902	—	4,643	60,489
Total shareholders' equity	42,247	47,755	125,679	187,667	273,352

KRISPY KREME DOUGHNUTS, INC.
REPORT OF INDEPENDENT ACCOUNTANTS

To the Board of Directors and Shareholders of Krispy Kreme Doughnuts, Inc.

In our opinion, the accompanying consolidated balance sheets and the related consolidated statements of operations, of shareholders' equity and of cash flows present fairly, in all material respects, the financial position of Krispy Kreme Doughnuts, Inc. and its subsidiaries (the Company) at February 3, 2002 and February 2, 2003, and the results of their operations and their cash flows for each of the three years in the period ended February 2, 2003, in conformity with accounting principles generally accepted in the United States of America. These financial statements are the responsibility of the Company's management; our responsibility is to express an opinion on these financial statements based on our audits. We conducted our audits of these statements in accordance with auditing standards generally accepted in the United States of America, which require that we plan and perform the audit to obtain reasonable assurance about whether the financial statements are free of material misstatement. An audit includes examining, on a test basis, evidence supporting the amounts and disclosures in the financial statements, assessing the accounting principles used and significant estimates made by management, and evaluating the overall financial statement presentation. We believe that our audits provide a reasonable basis for the opinion expressed above.

As discussed in Note 2 to the consolidated financial statements, effective February 4, 2002, the Company changed its method of accounting for goodwill and other intangible assets to conform to Statement of Financial Accounting Standards No. 142, "Goodwill and Other Intangible Assets."

Greensboro, North Carolina
March 13, 2003

KRISPY KREME DOUGHNUTS, INC.
CONSOLIDATED STATEMENTS OF OPERATIONS

In Thousands, Except Per Share Amounts

YEAR ENDED	Jan. 28, 2001	Feb. 3, 2002	Feb. 2, 2003
Total revenues	$300,715	$394,354	$491,549
Operating expenses*	250,690	316,946	381,489
General and administrative expenses	20,061	27,562	28,897
Depreciation and amortization expenses	6,457	7,959	12,271
Arbitration award (Note 18)	—	—	9,075
Income from operations	23,507	41,887	59,817
Interest income	2,325	2,980	1,966
Interest expense	(607)	(337)	(1,781)
Equity loss in joint ventures	(706)	(602)	(2,008)
Minority interest	(716)	(1,147)	(2,287)
Loss on sale of property and equipment	(20)	(235)	(934)
Income before income taxes	23,783	42,546	54,773
Provision for income taxes	9,058	16,168	21,295
Net income	$ 14,725	$ 26,378	$ 33,478
Basic earnings per share	$ 0.30	$ 0.49	$ 0.61
Diluted earnings per share	$ 0.27	$ 0.45	$ 0.56

* Operating expenses consist entirely of cost of goods sold.

The accompanying notes are an integral part of these consolidated financial statements.

KRISPY KREME DOUGHNUTS, INC.
CONSOLIDATED BALANCE SHEETS

	IN THOUSANDS	
	Feb. 3, 2002	**Feb. 2, 2003**
ASSETS		
Current Assets:		
Cash and cash equivalents	$ 21,904	$ 32,203
Short-term investments	15,292	22,976
Accounts receivable, less allowance for doubtful accounts of $1,182 (2002) and $1,453 (2003)	26,894	34,373
Accounts receivable, affiliates	9,017	11,062
Other receivables	2,771	884
Inventories	16,159	24,365
Prepaid expenses	2,591	3,478
Income taxes refundable	2,534	1,963
Deferred income taxes	4,607	9,824
Total current assets	101,769	141,128
Property and equipment, net	112,577	202,558
Long-term investments	12,700	4,344
Investments in unconsolidated joint ventures	3,400	6,871
Intangible assets	16,621	48,703
Other assets	8,309	6,883
Total assets	$255,376	$410,487
LIABILITIES AND SHAREHOLDERS' EQUITY		
Current Liabilities:		
Accounts payable	$ 12,095	$ 14,055
Book overdraft	9,107	11,375
Accrued expenses	26,729	20,981
Arbitration award	—	9,075
Revolving line of credit	3,871	—
Current maturities of long-term debt	731	3,301
Short-term debt — related party	—	900
Total current liabilities	52,533	59,687
Deferred income taxes	3,930	9,849
Long-term debt, net of current portion	3,912	49,900
Revolving lines of credit	—	7,288
Other long-term obligations	4,843	5,218
Total long-term liabilities	12,685	72,255
Commitments and contingencies		
Minority interest	2,491	5,193
Shareholders' Equity:		
Preferred stock, no par value, 10,000 shares authorized; none issued and outstanding	—	—
Common stock, no par value, shares authorized — 100,000 (2002) and 300,000 (2003); issued and outstanding — 54,271 (2002) and 56,295 (2003)	121,052	173,112
Unearned compensation	(186)	(119)
Notes receivable, employees	(2,580)	(558)
Nonqualified employee benefit plan assets	(138)	(339)
Nonqualified employee benefit plan liability	138	339
Accumulated other comprehensive income (loss)	456	(1,486)
Retained earnings	68,925	102,403
Total shareholders' equity	187,667	273,352
Total liabilities and shareholders' equity	$255,376	$410,487

The accompanying notes are an integral part of these consolidated financial statements.

KRISPY KREME DOUGHNUTS, INC.
CONSOLIDATED STATEMENTS OF SHAREHOLDERS' EQUITY

	KRISPY KREME DOUGHNUT CORPORATION			KRISPY KREME DOUGHNUTS, INC.			
	Common Shares	Common Stock	Additional Paid-In Capital	Preferred Shares	Preferred Stock	Common Shares	Common Stock
Balance at January 30, 2000	467	$ 4,670	$ 10,805	—	$ —	—	$ —
Comprehensive income:							
Net income for the year ended January 28, 2001							
Unrealized holding gain, net							
Total comprehensive income							
Proceeds from public offering						13,800	65,637
Conversion of Krispy Kreme Doughnut Corporation shares to Krispy Kreme Doughnuts, Inc. shares	(467)	(4,670)	(10,805)			37,360	15,475
Cash dividend to shareholders							
Issuance of shares to employee stock ownership plan						580	3,039
Contribution to the nonqualified employee benefit plan							
Liability under the nonqualified employee benefit plan							
Issuance of restricted common shares						12	210
Exercise of stock options, including tax benefit of $595						80	699
Amortization of restricted common shares							
Collection of notes receivable							
Balance at January 28, 2001	—	$ —	$ —	—	$ —	51,832	$ 85,060
Comprehensive income:							
Net income for the year ended February 3, 2002							
Unrealized holding loss, net							
Foreign currency translation adjustment, net							
Total comprehensive income							
Proceeds from public offering						1,086	17,202
Exercise of stock options, including tax benefit of $9,772						1,183	13,678
Issuance of shares in conjunction with acquisition of franchise market						115	4,183
Adjustment of nonqualified employee benefit plan investments							
Issuance of restricted common shares						1	50
Amortization of restricted common shares							
Issuance of stock for notes receivable						54	879
Collection of notes receivable							
Balance at February 3, 2002	—	$ —	$ —	—	$ —	54,271	$121,052
Comprehensive income:							
Net income for the year ended February 2, 2003							
Unrealized holding loss, net of tax benefit of $241							
Foreign currency translation adjustment, net of tax expense of $7							
Unrealized loss from cash flow hedge, net of tax benefit of $982							
Total comprehensive income							
Exercise of stock options, including tax benefit of $13,795						1,187	20,935
Issuance of shares in conjunction with acquisition of franchise markets						837	30,975
Adjustment of nonqualified employee benefit plan investments							
Amortization of restricted common shares							
Issuance of stock options in exchange for services							150
Collection of notes receivable							
Balance at February 2, 2003	—	$ —	$ —	—	$ —	56,295	$173,112

The accompanying notes are an integral part of these consolidated financial statements.

In Thousands

Unearned Compensation	Notes Receivable, Employees	Nonqualified Employee Benefit Plan Assets	Nonqualified Employee Benefit Plan Liability	Accumulated Other Comprehensive Income (Loss)	Retained Earnings	Total
$ —	$(2,547)	$ —	$ —	$ —	$ 34,827	$ 47,755
					14,725	14,725
				609		609
						15,334
						65,637
						—
					(7,005)	(7,005)
						3,039
		(126)				(126)
			126			126
(210)						—
						699
22						22
	198					198
$(188)	$(2,349)	$(126)	$126	$ 609	$ 42,547	$125,679
					26,378	26,378
				(111)		(111)
				(42)		(42)
						26,225
						17,202
						13,678
						4,183
		(12)	12			—
(50)						—
52						52
	(879)					—
	648					648
$(186)	$(2,580)	$(138)	$138	$ 456	$ 68,925	$187,667
					33,478	33,478
				(385)		(385)
				11		11
				(1,568)		(1,568)
						31,536
						20,935
						30,975
		(201)	201			—
67						67
						150
	2,022					2,022
$(119)	$ (558)	$(339)	$339	$ (1,486)	$102,403	$273,352

KRISPY KREME DOUGHNUTS, INC.
CONSOLIDATED STATEMENTS OF CASH FLOWS

IN THOUSANDS

YEAR ENDED	Jan. 28, 2001	Feb. 3, 2002	Feb. 2, 2003
Cash Flow From Operating Activities:			
Net income	$ 14,725	$ 26,378	$ 33,478
Items not requiring cash:			
Depreciation and amortization	6,457	7,959	12,271
Deferred income taxes	1,668	2,553	1,632
Loss on disposal of property and equipment, net	20	235	934
Compensation expense related to restricted stock awards	22	52	67
Tax benefit from exercise of nonqualified stock options	595	9,772	13,795
Provision for store closings and impairment	318	—	—
Minority interest	716	1,147	2,287
Equity loss in joint ventures	706	602	2,008
Change in assets and liabilities:			
Receivables	(3,434)	(13,317)	(7,390)
Inventories	(2,052)	(3,977)	(7,866)
Prepaid expenses	1,239	(682)	(331)
Income taxes, net	902	(2,575)	571
Accounts payable	2,279	3,884	(33)
Accrued expenses	7,966	4,096	(9,296)
Arbitration award	—	—	9,075
Other long-term obligations	(15)	83	(166)
Net cash provided by operating activities	32,112	36,210	51,036
Cash Flow From Investing Activities:			
Purchase of property and equipment	(25,655)	(37,310)	(83,196)
Proceeds from disposal of property and equipment	1,419	3,196	701
Proceeds from disposal of assets held for sale	—	—	1,435
Acquisition of franchise markets, net of cash acquired	—	(20,571)	(4,965)
Investments in unconsolidated joint ventures	(4,465)	(1,218)	(7,869)
Purchases of investments	(41,375)	(10,128)	(32,739)
Proceeds from investments	6,004	18,005	33,097
Increase in other assets	(3,216)	(4,237)	(1,038)
Net cash used for investing activities	(67,288)	(52,263)	(94,574)
Cash Flow From Financing Activities:			
Borrowings of long-term debt	—	4,643	44,234
Repayment of long-term debt	(3,600)	—	(2,170)
Net (repayments) borrowings from revolving line of credit	(15,775)	345	(121)
Repayment of short-term debt — related party	—	—	(500)
Debt issue costs	—	—	(194)
Proceeds from exercise of stock options	104	3,906	7,140
Proceeds from stock offering	65,637	17,202	—
Book overdraft	(941)	3,960	2,268
Collection of notes receivable	198	648	3,612
Minority interest	401	227	(432)
Cash dividends paid	(7,005)	—	—
Net cash provided by financing activities	39,019	30,931	53,837
Net increase in cash and cash equivalents	3,843	14,878	10,299
Cash and cash equivalents at beginning of year	3,183	7,026	21,904
Cash and cash equivalents at end of year	$ 7,026	$ 21,904	$ 32,203
Supplemental schedule of non-cash investing and financing activities:			
Issuance of stock in conjunction with acquisition of franchise markets	$ —	$ 4,183	$ 8,727
Issuance of stock in conjunction with acquisition of additional interest in area developer franchisee	—	—	22,248
Unrealized gain (loss) on investments	609	(111)	(385)
Issuance of stock options in exchange for services	—	—	150
Issuance of stock to Krispy Kreme Profit-Sharing Stock Ownership Plan	3,039	—	—
Issuance of restricted common shares	210	50	—
Issuance of stock in exchange for employee notes receivable	—	879	—

The accompanying notes are an integral part of these consolidated financial statements.

KRISPY KREME DOUGHNUTS, INC.
SELECTED NOTES TO CONSOLIDATED FINANCIAL STATEMENTS

1. ORGANIZATION AND PURPOSE

Krispy Kreme Doughnuts, Inc. was incorporated in North Carolina on December 2, 1999 as a wholly-owned subsidiary of Krispy Kreme Doughnut Corporation ("KKDC"). Pursuant to a plan of merger approved by shareholders on November 10, 1999, the shareholders of KKDC became shareholders of Krispy Kreme Doughnuts, Inc. on April 4, 2000. Each shareholder received 80 shares of Krispy Kreme Doughnuts, Inc. common stock and $15 in cash for each share of KKDC common stock they held. As a result of the merger, KKDC became a wholly-owned subsidiary of Krispy Kreme Doughnuts, Inc. Krispy Kreme Doughnuts, Inc. closed a public offering of its common stock on April 10, 2000.

All consolidated financial statements prior to the merger are those of KKDC and all consolidated financial statements after the merger are those of Krispy Kreme Doughnuts, Inc.

2. NATURE OF BUSINESS AND SIGNIFICANT ACCOUNTING POLICIES

Nature of Business. Krispy Kreme Doughnuts, Inc. and its subsidiaries (the "Company") are engaged principally in the sale of doughnuts and related items through Company-owned stores. The Company also derives revenue from franchise and development fees and the collection of royalties from franchisees. Additionally, the Company sells doughnut-making equipment, mix, coffee and other ingredients and supplies used in operating a doughnut store to Company-owned and franchised stores.

The significant accounting policies followed by the Company in preparing the accompanying consolidated financial statements are as follows:

Basis of Consolidation. The consolidated financial statements include the accounts of the Company and its wholly-owned subsidiaries. All significant intercompany accounts and transactions are eliminated in consolidation. Generally, investments greater than 50 percent in affiliates for which the Company maintains control are also consolidated and the portion not owned by the Company is shown as a minority interest. As of February 2, 2003, the Company consolidated the accounts of three joint ventures which the Company controlled: Freedom Rings, LLC ("Freedom Rings"), the joint venture with the rights to develop stores in the Philadelphia market; Glazed Investments, LLC ("Glazed Investments"), the joint venture with the rights to develop stores in Colorado, Minnesota and Wisconsin; and Golden Gate Doughnuts, LLC ("Golden Gate"), the joint venture with the rights to develop stores in Northern California. Generally, investments in 20- to 50-percent owned affiliates for which the Company has the ability to exercise significant influence over operating and financial policies are accounted for by the equity method of accounting, whereby the investment is carried at the cost of acquisition, plus the Company's equity in undistributed earnings or losses since acquisition, less any distributions received by the Company. Accordingly, the Company's share of the net earnings of these companies is included in consolidated net income. Investments in less than 20-percent owned affiliates are accounted for by the cost method of accounting.

Fiscal Year. The Company's fiscal year is based on a fifty-two/fifty-three week year. The fiscal year ends on the Sunday closest to the last day in January. The years ended January 28, 2001, February 3, 2002 and February 2, 2003 contained 52, 53 and 52 weeks, respectively.

Cash and Cash Equivalents. The Company considers cash on hand, deposits in banks, and all highly liquid debt instruments with a maturity of three months or less at date of acquisition to be cash and cash equivalents.

Inventories. Inventories are recorded at the lower of average cost (first-in, first-out) or market.

Investments. Investments consist of United States Treasury notes, mortgage-backed government securities, corporate debt securities, municipal securities and certificates of deposit and are included in short-term and long-term investments in the accompanying consolidated balance sheets. Certificates of deposit are carried at cost which approximates fair value. All other marketable securities are stated at market value as determined by the most recently traded price of each security at the balance sheet date.

Management determines the appropriate classification of its investments in marketable securities at the time of the purchase and reevaluates such determination at each balance sheet date. At February 2, 2003, all marketable securities are classified as available-for-sale. Available-for-sale securities are carried at fair value with the unrealized gains and losses reported as a separate component of shareholders' equity in accumulated other comprehensive income (loss). The cost of investments sold is determined on the specific identification or the first-in, first-out method.

Property and Equipment. Property and equipment are stated at cost less accumulated depreciation. Major renewals and betterments are charged to the property accounts while replacements, maintenance and repairs which do not improve or extend the lives of the respective assets are expensed currently. Interest is capitalized on major capital expenditures during the period of construction.

Depreciation of property and equipment is provided on the straight-line method over the estimated useful lives: Buildings — 15 to 35 years; Machinery and equipment — 3 to 15 years; Leasehold improvements — lesser of useful lives of assets or lease term.

Intangible Assets. In July 2001, the Financial Accounting Standards Board ("FASB") issued Statement of Financial Accounting Standards ("SFAS") No. 141, "Business Combinations," and SFAS No. 142, "Goodwill and Other Intangible Assets." These pronouncements provide guidance on accounting for the acquisition of businesses and other intangible assets, including goodwill, which arise from such activities. SFAS No. 141 affirms that only the purchase method of accounting may be applied to a business combination and provides guidance on the allocation of purchase price to the assets acquired. SFAS No. 141 applies to all business combinations initiated after June 30, 2001. Under SFAS No. 142, goodwill and intangible assets that have indefinite useful lives are no longer amortized but are reviewed at least annually for impairment. SFAS No. 142 is effective for the Company's fiscal 2003, although goodwill and intangible assets acquired after June 30, 2001 were subject immediately to the non-amortization provisions of SFAS No. 142. The Company has evaluated its intangible assets, which at February 2, 2003 consist of goodwill recorded in connection with a business acquisition ($201,000) and the value assigned to reacquired franchise rights in connection with the acquisition of rights to certain markets from franchisees ($48,502,000), and determined that all such assets have indefinite lives and, as a result, are not subject to amortization provisions. For the fiscal year ended February 3, 2002, the Company recorded an expense of $100,000 to amortize intangible assets related to an acquisition completed prior to June 30, 2001. The Company completed impairment analyses of its intangible assets in fiscal 2003 and found no instances of impairment.

Use of Estimates in Preparation of Financial Statements. The preparation of financial statements in conformity with generally accepted accounting principles requires management to make estimates and assumptions that affect the reported amounts of assets and liabilities and disclosure of contingent assets and liabilities at the date of the financial statements and the reported amounts of revenues and expenses during the reporting period. Actual results could differ from those estimates.

Revenue Recognition. A summary of the revenue recognition policies for each segment of the Company (see Note 14) is as follows:

- Company Store Operations revenue is derived from the sale of doughnuts and related items to on-premises and off-premises customers. Revenue is recognized at the time of sale for on-premises sales. For off-premises sales, revenue is recognized at the time of delivery.

- Franchise Operations revenue is derived from: (1) development and franchise fees from the opening of new stores; and (2) royalties charged to franchisees based on sales. Development and franchise fees are charged for certain new stores and are deferred until the store is opened and the Company has performed substantially all of the initial services it is required to provide. The royalties recognized in each period are based on the sales in that period.

- KKM&D revenue is derived from the sale of doughnut-making equipment, mix, coffee and other supplies needed to operate a doughnut store to Company-owned and franchised stores. Revenue is recognized at the time the title and the risk of loss pass to the customer, generally upon delivery of the goods. Revenue from Company-owned stores and consolidated joint venture stores is eliminated in consolidation.

Income Taxes. The Company uses the asset and liability method to account for income taxes, which requires the recognition of deferred tax assets and liabilities for the expected future tax consequences of temporary differences between tax bases and financial reporting bases for assets and liabilities.

Fair Value Of Financial Instruments. Cash, accounts receivable, accounts payable, accrued liabilities and debt are reflected in the financial statements at carrying amounts which approximate fair value.

Advertising Costs. All costs associated with advertising and promoting products are expensed in the period incurred.

Store Opening Costs. All costs, both direct and indirect, incurred to open either Company or franchise stores are expensed in the period incurred. Direct costs to open stores amounted to $464,000, $551,000 and $845,000 in fiscal 2001, 2002 and 2003, respectively.

Asset Impairment. When a store is identified as underperforming or when a decision is made to close a store, the Company makes an assessment of the potential impairment of the related assets. The assessment is based upon a comparison of the carrying amount of the assets, primarily property and equipment, to the estimated undiscounted cash flows expected to be generated from those assets. To estimate cash flows, management projects the net cash flows anticipated from continuing operation of the store until its closing as well as cash flows anticipated from disposal of the related assets, if any. If the carrying amount of the assets exceeds the sum of the undiscounted cash flows, the Company records an impairment charge measured as the excess of the carrying value over the fair value of the assets. The resulting net book value of the assets less estimated net realizable value at disposition, is depreciated over the remaining term that the store will continue in operation.

Comprehensive Income. SFAS No. 130, "Reporting Comprehensive Income," requires that certain items such as foreign currency translation adjustments, unrealized gains and losses on certain investments in debt and equity securities and minimum pension liability adjustments be presented as separate components of shareholders' equity. SFAS No. 130 defines these as items of other comprehensive income which must be reported in a financial statement displayed with the same prominence as other financial statements. Accumulated other comprehensive income (loss), as reflected in the consolidated statements of shareholders' equity, was comprised of net unrealized holding gains on marketable securities of $498,000 at February 3, 2002 and $113,000 at February 2, 2003 and foreign currency translation adjustment, net, of $42,000 at February 3, 2002 and $31,000 at February 2, 2003. At February 2, 2003, accumulated other comprehensive income (loss) also included the unrealized loss from a cash flow hedge, net of related tax benefits, of $1,568,000. Total comprehensive income for fiscal 2001, 2002 and 2003 was $15,334,000, $26,225,000 and $31,536,000, respectively.

Foreign Currency Translation. For all non-U.S. joint ventures, the functional currency is the local currency. Assets and liabilities of those operations are translated into U.S. dollars using exchange rates at the balance sheet date. Revenue and expenses are translated using the average exchange rates for the reporting period. Translation adjustments are deferred in accumulated other comprehensive income (loss), a separate component of shareholders' equity.

3. INVESTMENTS

The following table provides certain information about investments at February 3, 2002 and February 2, 2003.

IN THOUSANDS

	Amortized Cost	Gross Unrealized Holding Gains	Gross Unrealized Holding Losses	Fair Value
February 3, 2002				
U.S. government notes	$ 9,049	$ —	$ (17)	$ 9,032
Federal government agencies	10,959	442	(166)	11,235
Corporate debt securities	6,475	317	(88)	6,704
Other bonds	1,043	—	(22)	1,021
Total	$27,526	$759	$(293)	$27,992
February 2, 2003				
U.S. government notes	$16,657	$152	$ (97)	$16,712
Federal government agencies	7,485	289	(197)	7,577
Corporate debt securities	1,000	76	(45)	1,031
Certificate of deposit	2,000	—	—	2,000
Total	$27,142	$517	$(339)	$27,320

Maturities of investments were as follows at February 2, 2003:

IN THOUSANDS

	Amortized Cost	Fair Value
Due within one year	$22,844	$22,976
Due after one year through five years	4,298	4,344
Total	$27,142	$27,320

4. INVENTORIES

The components of inventories are as follows:

IN THOUSANDS

	Distribution Center	Equipment Department	Mix Department	Company Stores	Total
February 3, 2002					
Raw materials	$ —	$3,060	$ 788	$1,826	$ 5,674
Work in progress	—	28	—	—	28
Finished goods	1,318	2,867	95	—	4,280
Purchased merchandise	5,503	—	—	613	6,116
Manufacturing supplies	—	—	61	—	61
Totals	$ 6,821	$5,955	$ 944	$2,439	$16,159
February 2, 2003					
Raw materials	$ —	$3,828	$1,069	$1,922	$ 6,819
Work in progress	—	234	—	—	234
Finished goods	2,222	3,616	172	—	6,010
Purchased merchandise	10,191	—	—	966	11,157
Manufacturing supplies	—	—	145	—	145
Totals	$12,413	$7,678	$1,386	$2,888	$24,365

5. PROPERTY AND EQUIPMENT

Property and equipment consists of the following:

IN THOUSANDS

	Feb. 3, 2002	Feb. 2, 2003
Land	$ 14,823	$ 24,741
Buildings	39,566	88,641
Machinery and equipment	86,683	118,332
Leasehold improvements	13,463	19,522
Construction in progress	1,949	1,534
	156,484	252,770
Less: accumulated depreciation	43,907	50,212
Property and equipment, net	$112,577	$202,558

Depreciation expense was $6,141,000, $7,398,000 and $11,570,000 for fiscal 2001, fiscal 2002 and fiscal 2003, respectively.

6. ACCRUED EXPENSES

Accrued expenses consist of the following:

IN THOUSANDS

	Feb. 3, 2002	Feb. 2, 2003
Insurance	$ 4,891	$ 6,150
Salaries, wages and incentive compensation	11,686	6,034
Deferred revenue	2,082	1,485
Taxes, other than income	1,632	1,865
Other	6,438	5,447
Total	$ 26,729	$ 20,981

7. DEBT

The Company's debt, including debt of consolidated joint ventures, consists of the following:

	IN THOUSANDS	
	Feb. 3, 2002	**Feb. 2, 2003**
Krispy Kreme Doughnut Corporation:		
$40 million revolving line of credit	$ —	$ —
Golden Gate:		
$6.75 million revolving line of credit	3,871	4,750
Freedom Rings:		
$5 million revolving line of credit	—	2,538
Revolving lines of credit	$ 3,871	$ 7,288
Glazed Investments:		
Short-term debt — related party	$ —	$ 900
Krispy Kreme Doughnut Corporation:		
$33 million term loan	$ —	$ 31,763
Golden Gate:		
$4.5 million term loan	4,418	3,926
$3 million term loan	—	2,976
Glazed Investments:		
Real Estate and Equipment loans	—	14,400
Subordinated notes	—	136
Freedom Rings:		
Other debt	225	—
	4,643	53,201
Current maturities of long-term debt	(731)	(3,301)
Long-term debt, net of current portion	$ 3,912	$ 49,900

$40 Million Revolving Line of Credit

On December 29, 1999, the Company entered into an unsecured loan agreement ("Agreement") with a bank to increase borrowing availability and extend the maturity of its revolving line of credit. The Agreement provides a $40 million revolving line of credit and expires on June 30, 2004.

Under the terms of the Agreement, interest on the revolving line of credit is charged, at the Company's option, at either the lender's prime rate less 110 basis points or at the one-month LIBOR plus 100 basis points. There was no interest, fee or other charge for the unadvanced portion of the line of credit until July 1, 2002 at which time the Company began paying a fee of 0.10% on the unadvanced portion. No amounts were outstanding on the revolving line of credit at February 3, 2002 or February 2, 2003. The amount available under the revolving line of credit is reduced by letters of credit, amounts outstanding under certain loans made by the bank to franchisees which are guaranteed by the Company and certain amounts available or outstanding in connection with credit cards issued by the lender on behalf of the Company and was $31,695,000 at February 2, 2003. Outstanding letters of credit, primarily for insurance purposes, totaled $6,626,000, amounts outstanding under the loans guaranteed by the Company totaled $152,000 and amounts available in connection with credit cards issued by the lender totaled $1,527,000 at February 2, 2003.

The Agreement contains provisions that, among other requirements, restrict capital expenditures, require the maintenance of certain financial ratios, place various restrictions on the sale of properties, restrict the Company's ability to enter into collateral repurchase agreements and guarantees, restrict the payment of dividends and require compliance with other customary financial and nonfinancial covenants. At February 2, 2003, the Company was in compliance with each of these covenants.

8. LEASE COMMITMENTS

The Company conducts some of its operations from leased facilities and, additionally, leases certain equipment under operating leases. Generally, these leases have initial terms of 5 to 18 years and contain provisions for renewal options of 5 to 10 years.

At February 2, 2003, future minimum annual rental commitments, gross, under noncancelable operating leases, including lease commitments of consolidated joint ventures, are as follows:

IN THOUSANDS

FISCAL YEAR ENDING IN	Amount
2004	$10,969
2005	9,187
2006	6,707
2007	5,018
2008	5,433
Thereafter	32,397
	$69,711

Rental expense, net of rental income, totaled $8,540,000 in fiscal 2001, $10,576,000 in fiscal 2002 and $13,169,000 in fiscal 2003.

9. INCOME TAXES

The components of the provision for federal and state income taxes are summarized as follows:

IN THOUSANDS

YEAR ENDED	Jan. 28, 2001	Feb. 3, 2002	Feb. 2, 2003
Currently payable	$7,390	$13,615	$19,663
Deferred	1,668	2,553	1,632
	$9,058	$16,168	$21,295

A reconciliation of the statutory federal income tax rate with the company's effective rate is as follows:

IN THOUSANDS

YEAR ENDED	Jan. 28, 2001	Feb. 3, 2002	Feb. 2, 2003
Federal taxes at statutory rate	$8,321	$14,891	$19,170
State taxes, net of federal benefit	673	1,158	1,405
Other	64	119	720
	$9,058	$16,168	$21,295

Income tax payments, net of refunds, were $5,894,000 in fiscal 2001, $6,616,000 in fiscal 2002 and $5,298,000 in fiscal 2003. The income tax payments in fiscal 2002 and fiscal 2003 were lower than the current provision due to the income tax benefit of stock option exercises of $9,772,000 and $13,795,000 during fiscal 2002 and fiscal 2003, respectively.

The net current and non-current components of deferred income taxes recognized in the balance sheet are as follows:

IN THOUSANDS

	Feb. 3, 2002	Feb. 2, 2003
Net current assets	$ 4,607	$ 9,824
Net non-current liabilities	(3,930)	(9,849)
	$ 677	$ (25)

The tax effects of the significant temporary differences which comprise the deferred tax assets and liabilities are as follows:

IN THOUSANDS

	Feb. 3, 2002	Feb. 2, 2003
ASSETS		
Compensation deferred (unpaid)	$ 676	$ 663
Insurance	1,859	2,368
Other long-term obligations	659	395
Accrued restructuring expenses	1,183	501
Deferred revenue	791	1,165
Accounts receivable	449	556
Inventory	436	278
Charitable contributions carryforward	—	714
Gain/loss on hedging transactions	—	982
Accrued litigation	—	3,494
Accrued payroll	—	1,018
State tax credit carryforwards	—	179
State NOL carryforwards	2,524	2,463
Other	676	687
Gross deferred tax assets	9,253	15,463
LIABILITIES		
Property and equipment	5,589	11,628
Goodwill	198	1,037
Prepaid expenses	265	360
Gross deferred tax liabilities	6,052	13,025
Valuation allowance — State NOL carryforwards	(2,524)	(2,463)
Net asset/(liability)	$ 677	$ (25)

At February 2, 2003, the Company has recorded a valuation allowance against the state NOL carryforwards of $2,463,000. If these carryforwards are realized in the future, $2,232,000 of the tax benefit would be recorded as an addition to common stock as this portion of the carryforwards were a result of the tax benefits of stock option exercises in fiscal 2002 and 2003.

The Company records deferred tax assets reflecting the benefit of future deductible amounts. Realization of these assets is dependent on generating sufficient future taxable income and the ability to carryback losses to previous years in which there was taxable income. Although realization is not assured, management believes it is more likely than not that all of the deferred tax assets, for which a valuation allowance has not been established, will be realized. The amount of the deferred tax assets considered realizable, however, could be reduced in the near term if estimates of future taxable income are reduced.

10. EARNINGS PER SHARE

The computation of basic earnings per share is based on the weighted average number of common shares outstanding during the period. The computation of diluted earnings per share reflects the potential dilution that would occur if stock options were exercised and the dilution from the issuance of restricted shares. The treasury stock method is used to calculate dilutive shares. This reduces the gross number of dilutive shares by the number of shares purchasable from the proceeds of the options assumed to be exercised, the proceeds of the tax benefits recognized by the Company in conjunction with nonqualified stock plans and from the amounts of unearned compensation associated with the restricted shares.

The following table sets forth the computation of basic and diluted earnings per share:

IN THOUSANDS, EXCEPT SHARE AMOUNTS

YEAR ENDED	Jan. 28, 2001	Feb. 3, 2002	Feb. 2, 2003
Numerator:			
Net income	$ 14,725	$ 26,378	$ 33,478
Denominator:			
Basic earnings per share — weighted average shares	49,183,916	53,702,916	55,092,542
Effect of dilutive securities:			
Stock options	4,471,576	4,734,371	4,395,864
Restricted stock	—	5,698	3,967
Diluted earnings per share — adjusted weighted average shares	53,655,492	58,442,985	59,492,373

14. BUSINESS SEGMENT INFORMATION

The Company has three reportable business segments. The Company Store Operations segment is comprised of the operating activities of the stores owned by the Company and those in consolidated joint ventures. These stores sell doughnuts and complementary products through both on-premises and off-premises sales. The majority of the ingredients and materials used by Company Store Operations is purchased from the KKM&D business segment.

The Franchise Operations segment represents the results of the Company's franchise program. Under the terms of the franchise agreements, the licensed operators pay royalties and fees to the Company in return for the use of the Krispy Kreme name. Expenses for this business segment include costs incurred to recruit new franchisees and to open, monitor and aid in the performance of these stores and direct general and administrative expenses.

The KKM&D segment supplies mix, equipment, coffee and other items to both Company and franchisee-owned stores. All intercompany transactions between the KKM&D business segment and Company stores and consolidated joint venture stores are eliminated in consolidation.

Segment information for total assets and capital expenditures is not presented as such information is not used in measuring segment performance or allocating resources among segments.

Segment operating income is income before general corporate expenses and income taxes.

Information about the Company's operations by business segment is as follows:

IN THOUSANDS

YEAR ENDED	Jan. 28, 2001	Feb. 3, 2002	Feb. 2, 2003
Revenues:			
Company Store Operations	$ 213,677	$ 266,209	$ 319,592
Franchise Operations	9,445	14,008	19,304
KKM&D	201,406	269,396	347,642
Intercompany sales eliminations	(123,813)	(155,259)	(194,989)
Total revenues	$ 300,715	$ 394,354	$ 491,549
Operating income:			
Company Store Operations	$ 27,370	$ 42,932	$ 58,214
Franchise Operations	5,730	9,040	14,319
KKM&D	11,712	18,999	26,843
Unallocated general and administrative expenses	(21,305)	(29,084)	(30,484)
Arbitration award	—	—	(9,075)
Total operating income	$ 23,507	$ 41,887	$ 59,817
Depreciation and Amortization Expenses:			
Company Store Operations	$ 4,838	$ 5,859	$ 8,854
Franchise Operations	72	72	108
KKM&D	303	507	1,723
Corporate administration	1,244	1,521	1,586
Total depreciation and amortization expenses	$ 6,457	$ 7,959	$ 12,271

16. COMMITMENTS AND CONTINGENCIES

In order to assist certain associate and franchise operators in obtaining third-party financing, the Company from time-to-time enters into collateral repurchase agreements involving both Company stock and doughnut-making equipment. The Company's contingent liability related to these agreements was approximately $70,000 at February 3, 2002. The Company was not contingently liable under any such agreements at February 2, 2003. Additionally, primarily for the purpose of providing financing guarantees in a percentage equivalent to the Company's ownership percentage in various joint venture investments, the Company has guaranteed certain leases and loans from third-party financial institutions on behalf of franchise operators. The Company's contingent liability related to these guarantees was approximately $3,805,000 at February 3, 2002 and $7,652,000 at February 2, 2003. Of the total guaranteed amount of $7,652,000 at February 2, 2003, $6,450,000 are for franchisees in which we have an ownership interest and $1,202,000 are for franchisees in which we have no ownership interest. The expirations of these guarantees for the five fiscal years ending after February 2, 2003 are $2,903,000, $498,000, $517,000, $357,000 and $355,000, respectively.

Because the Company enters into long-term contracts with its suppliers, in the event that any of these relationships terminate unexpectedly, even where it has multiple suppliers for the same ingredient, the Company's ability to obtain adequate quantities of the same high quality ingredient at the same competitive price could be negatively impacted.

COMPANY PROFILE

Krispy Kreme is a leading branded specialty retailer of premium quality doughnuts which are made throughout the day in our stores. We opened our first store in 1937, and there were 276 Krispy Kreme stores, consisting of 99 company-owned and 177 franchised stores, as of February 2, 2003. Our principal business is the high volume production and sale of over 20 varieties of premium quality doughnuts, including our signature Hot Original Glazed. We have established Krispy Kreme as a leading consumer brand with a loyal customer base through our longstanding commitment to quality and consistency. Our place in American society was recognized in 1997 with the induction of Krispy Kreme artifacts into the Smithsonian Institution's National Museum of American History. We differentiate ourselves by combining quality ingredients, vertical integration and a unique retail experience featuring our stores' fully displayed production process, or doughnut-making theater.

Krispy Kreme has been a publicly held company since April 5, 2000. Our stock is listed on the New York Stock Exchange with shares trading under the ticker symbol KKD.

BOARD OF DIRECTORS

Scott A. Livengood
Krispy Kreme Doughnuts, Inc.
Chairman of the Board,
President and Chief Executive Officer

Erskine Bowles
Senior Advisor
Carousel Capital

Mary Davis Holt
Senior Executive Vice President
of Time Life Inc.

William T. Lynch Jr.
Liam Holdings LLC, President
and Chief Executive Officer
Retired Chief Executive Officer of
Leo Burnett Company

John N. (Jack) McAleer
Krispy Kreme Doughnuts, Inc.
Vice Chairman of the Board
and Executive Vice President
of Concept Development

James H. Morgan
Chairman of Morgan, Semones and Associates
and former Chairman and Chief Executive
Officer of Wachovia Securities, Inc.

Dr. Su Hua Newton
Co-owner Newton Vineyard

Robert L. Strickland
Chairman Emeritus of
Lowe's Companies, Inc.

Togo D. West Jr.
Of Counsel, Covington and Burling

OFFICERS

Scott A. Livengood
Chairman of the Board,
President and Chief Executive Officer

John W. Tate
Chief Operating Officer

Randy S. Casstevens
Chief Financial Officer and Treasurer

R. Frank Murphy
Executive Vice President,
General Counsel and Secretary

John N. (Jack) McAleer
Vice Chairman of the Board
and Executive Vice President
of Concept Development

Stephen E. Gorman
Executive Vice President
of Operations Support

Steve A. Martin
Executive Vice President,
Dean of the Learning Institute

Philip R.S. Waugh Jr.
Executive Vice President
of Worldwide Development

Tasty Baking Company 2002 Annual Report

FIVE YEAR SELECTED FINANCIAL DATA

All amounts presented are in thousands except for per share amounts.

	2002(a)	2001(b)	2000	1999(c)	1998
Operating Results					
Gross sales	$ $255,504	$ 255,336	$ 249,691	$ 226,350	$ 228,453
Net sales **(d)**	162,263	166,245	162,877	148,830	149,054
Net income (loss)	(4,341)	6,320	8,144	4,703	5,729
Per Share Amounts					
Net income:					
Basic	$ (.54)	$ .79	$ 1.04	$ .60	$ .73
Diluted	(.54)	.78	1.04	.60	.72
Cash dividends	.48	.48	.48	.48	.48
Shareholders' equity	5.86	6.84	6.40	5.81	5.67
Financial Position					
Working capital	$ 16,788	$ 18,284	$ 15,474	$ 14,406	$ 15,830
Total assets	116,560	116,137	112,192	111,753	101,744
Long-term obligations	12,486	14,603	16,843	21,060	13,761
Shareholders' equity	47,525	55,065	50,174	45,422	44,357
Shares of common stock Outstanding	8,104	8,052	7,845	7,823	7,822
Statistical Information					
Capital expenditures	$ 5,359	$ 7,314	$ 8,116	$ 14,038	$ 11,328
Depreciation	6,807	7,204	7,759	7,016	6,650
Average common shares Outstanding:					
Basic	8,075	7,998	7,837	7,824	7,808
Diluted	8,159	8,140	7,861	7,865	7,953

(a) During the second quarter of 2002, the company incurred a $1,405 restructure charge related to its decision to close six thrift stores and to eliminate certain manufacturing and administrative positions.

During the fourth quarter of 2002, the company incurred a $4,936 restructure charge related to the closing of the remaining twelve thrift stores and the specific arrangements made with senior executives who departed the company in the fourth quarter of 2002.

Also, during the fourth quarter of 2002, the company recorded additional pension expense in the amount of $4,656 in connection with the company's method of immediately recognizing gains and losses that fall outside the pension corridor.

(b) During the fourth quarter of 2001, the company incurred a $1,728 restructure charge related to its decision to close its Dutch Mill Baking Company production facility and two company thrift stores.

(c) During 1999 the company incurred a route restructure charge of $950. Also included is an after-tax charge of $205 that is the cumulative effect of an accounting change that required the write-off of start-up costs. Long-term obligations reflect the renewal of a capital lease with the trustees of the company pension plan.

(d) For comparative purposes net sales for 2001, 2000, 1999 and 1998 have been reclassified to reflect changes in accounting for thrift stores and cooperative advertising. The change was an increase of $1,637 for 2001 and a decrease of $1,406, $1,832 and $1,675, for 2000, 1999 and 1998 respectively.

CONSOLIDATED FINANCIAL STATEMENTS
Tasty Baking Company and Subsidiaries

Consolidated Statements of Operations and Retained Earnings

	52 Weeks Ended Dec. 28, 2002	52 Weeks Ended Dec. 29, 2001(a)	53 Weeks Ended Dec. 30, 2000(a)
Operations			
Gross sales	$ 255,503,818	$ 255,335,587	$ 249,690,639
Less discounts and allowances	(93,240,612)	(89,090,607)	(86,813,226)
Net sales	162,263,206	166,244,980	162,877,413
Costs and expenses:			
Cost of sales	111,187,357	103,297,040	105,036,081
Depreciation	6,807,369	7,203,688	7,759,345
Selling, general and administrative	44,982,205	43,236,117	35,959,008
Restructure charges	6,340,810	1,727,844	–
Interest expense	1,066,250	1,102,777	1,540,242
Provision for doubtful accounts	958,365	772,372	1,250,385
Other income, net	(1,165,548)	(1,189,606)	(1,420,557)
	170,176,808	156,150,232	150,124,504
Income (loss) before provision for income taxes	(7,913,602)	10,094,748	12,752,909
Provision for (benefit from) income taxes:			
Federal	(11,432)	3,284,796	2,562,171
State	(315,262)	(89,526)	(269,625)
Deferred	(3,246,179)	579,276	2,316,823
	(3,572,873)	3,774,546	4,609,369
Net income (loss)	(4,340,729)	6,320,202	8,143,540
Retained Earnings			
Balance, beginning of year	34,838,636	32,351,894	27,968,811
Cash dividends paid on common shares ($.48 per share in 2002, 2001 and 2000)	(3,875,855)	(3,833,460)	(3,760,457)
Balance, end of year	$ 26,622,052	$ 34,838,636	$ 32,351,894
Per share of common stock:			
Net income:			
Basic	$ (.54)	$ .79	$ 1.04
Diluted	$ (.54)	$ .78	$ 1.04

(a) 2001 and 2000 have been reclassified for comparative purposes to reflect the changes in accounting for thrift stores and cooperative advertising.

See accompanying notes to consolidated financial statements.

Consolidated Statements of Cash Flows

	52 Weeks Ended Dec. 28, 2002	52 Weeks Ended Dec. 29, 2001	53 Weeks Ended Dec. 30, 2000
Cash flows from (used for) operating activities			
Net income (loss)	$ (4,340,729)	$ 6,320,202	$ 8,143,540
Adjustments to reconcile net income to net cash provided by operating activities:			
Depreciation	6,807,369	7,203,688	7,759,345
Restructure charges, net of cash expenditures	5,133,794	850,879	–
Conditional stock grant	–	804,759	319,016
Provision for doubtful accounts	958,365	772,372	1,250,385
Pension expense	5,456,000	(216,770)	(2,318,000)
Deferred taxes	(3,246,179)	579,276	2,316,823
Other	(547,841)	(420,277)	(154,683)
Changes in assets and liabilities:			
Decrease (increase) in receivables	393,451	(2,233,932)	(2,339,505)
Decrease (increase) in inventories	1,634,632	(2,481,235)	(1,424,770)
Increase in prepayments and other	(1,839,688)	(197,658)	(948,500)
Increase (decrease) in accrued payroll, accrued income taxes, accounts payable and other current liabilities	(294,575)	(76,690)	594,924
Net cash from operating activities	10,114,599	10,904,614	13,198,575
Cash flows from (used for) investing activities			
Proceeds from owner/operator loan repayments	3,987,420	3,494,763	4,065,144
Purchase of property, plant and equipment	(5,359,051)	(7,313,982)	(8,116,213)
Loans to owner/operators	(3,881,472)	(4,043,379)	(3,038,759)
Other	(46,359)	46,131	40,402
Net cash used for investing activities	(5,299,462)	(7,816,467)	(7,049,426)
Cash flows from (used for) financing activities			
Dividends paid	(3,875,855)	(3,833,460)	(3,760,457)
Payment of long-term debt	(2,117,092)	(3,216,821)	(10,196,240)
Net increase in short-term debt	600,000	1,700,000	1,450,000
Additional long-term debt	–	1,000,000	6,000,000
Net proceeds from sale of common stock	492,275	1,318,112	(36,704)
Net cash used for financing activities	(4,900,672)	(3,032,169)	(6,543,401)
Net increase (decrease) in cash	(85,535)	55,978	(394,252)
Cash, beginning of year	367,220	311,242	705,494
Cash, end of year	$ 281,685	$ 367,220	$ 311,242
Supplemental cash flow information			
Cash paid during the year for:			
Interest	$ 1,084,322	$ 1,231,521	$ 1,750,990
Income taxes	$ 1,011,650	$ 3,065,069	$ 4,819,057

See accompanying notes to consolidated financial statements.

Consolidated Balance Sheets

	Dec. 28, 2002	Dec. 29, 2001
Assets		
Current Assets:		
Cash	$ 281,685	$ 367,220
Receivables, less allowance of $3,606,117 and $3,751,854, respectively	20,881,597	22,233,413
Inventories	6,777,152	8,411,784
Deferred income taxes	5,213,847	3,055,410
Prepayments and other	2,941,033	1,101,345
Total current assets	36,095,314	35,169,172
Property, plant and equipment:		
Land	1,097,987	1,097,987
Buildings and improvements	37,831,789	37,103,226
Machinery and equipment	148,990,425	146,023,373
	187,920,021	184,224,586
Less accumulated depreciation and amortization	129,528,979	124,522,610
	58,391,222	59,701,976
Other assets:		
Long-term receivables from owner/operators	10,095,101	10,201,049
Deferred income taxes	8,229,612	7,381,934
Spare parts inventory	3,698,780	3,632,687
Miscellaneous	50,001	50,001
	22,073,494	21,265,671
	$ 116,560,030	$ 116,136,819

See accompanying notes to consolidated financial statements.

	Dec. 28, 2002	Dec. 29, 2001
Liabilities		
Current Liabilities:		
Current obligations under capital leases	$ 175,715	$ 239,593
Notes payable, banks	4,500,000	3,900,000
Accounts payable	6,074,193	5,306,976
Accrued payroll and employee benefits	5,158,820	6,208,889
Reserve for restructures	2,417,178	850,879
Other	981,459	378,982
Total current liabilities	19,307,365	16,885,319
Long-term debt	9,000,000	11,000,000
Long-term obligations under capital leases, less current portion	3,486,218	3,603,310
Reserve for restructures-less current portion	3,567,495	–
Accrued pensions and other liabilities	15,923,020	11,506,969
Postretirement benefits other than pensions	17,750,696	18,076,719
Total liabilities	69,034,794	61,072,317
Shareholders' Equity		
Common stock, par value $.50 per share, and entitled to one vote per share: Authorized 15,000,000 shares, issued 9,116,483 shares	4,558,243	4,558,243
Capital in excess of par value of stock	29,432,917	29,388,567
Retained earnings	26,622,052	34,838,636
	60,613,212	68,785,446
Less:		
Treasury stock, at cost: 1,012,798 shares and 1,064,539 shares, respectively	12,538,632	13,167,082
Management Stock Purchase Plan receivables and deferrals	549,344	553,862
	47,525,236	55,064,502
	$ 116,560,030	$ 116,136,819

See accompanying notes to consolidated financial statements.

Consolidated Statements of Changes in Capital Accounts

	Dec. 28, 2002		Dec. 29, 2001		Dec. 30, 2000	
	Shares	**Amount**	**Shares**	**Amount**	**Shares**	**Amount**
Common Stock:						
Balance, beginning of year	9,116,483	$ 4,558,243	9,116,483	$ 4,558,243	9,116,483	$ 4,558,243
Balance, end of year	9,116,483	$ 4,558,243	9,116,483	$ 4,558,243	9,116,483	$ 4,558,243
Capital in Excess of Par Value of Stock:						
Balance, beginning of year		$ 29,388,567		$ 29,742,434		$ 29,778,768
Issuances:						
Management Stock Purchase Plan		16,975		53,766		(4,211)
Stock Option Plan		(24,777)		(599,642)		–
Conditional Stock Grant		–		(11,535)		(35,573)
Tax benefits related to Management Stock Purchase Plan and Stock Option Plan		52,152		203,544		3,450
Balance, end of year		$ 29,432,917		$ 29,388,567		$ 29,742,434
Treasury Stock:						
Balance, beginning of year	1,064,539	$ 13,167,082	1,271,171	$ 16,106,361	1,293,135	$ 16,408,808
Management Stock Purchase Plan:						
Reissued	(11,900)	(159,117)	(20,345)	(270,021)	(1,400)	(20,048)
Reacquired	7,634	128,490	5,775	64,790	2,365	35,488
Net shares reissued in connection with:						
Stock Option Plan	(47,475)	(597,823)	(155,820)	(2,141,247)	–	–
Conditional Stock Grant	–	–	(36,242)	(592,801)	(22,929)	(317,887)
Balance, end of year	1,012,798	$ 12,538,632	1,064,539	$ 13,167,082	1,271,171	$ 16,106,361
Management Stock Purchase Plan Receivables and Deferrals:						
Balance, beginning of year		$ 553,862		$ 372,532		$ 475,470
Common stock issued		176,092		323,787		15,837
Common stock repurchased		(98,861)		(60,083)		(29,904)
Note payments and amortization of deferred compensation		(81,749)		(82,374)		(88,871)
Balance, end of year		$ 549,344		$ 553,862		$ 372,532

See accompanying notes to consolidated financial statements.

Harley-Davidson

CONSOLIDATED STATEMENTS *of* INCOME

(In thousands, except per share amounts) Years ended December 31,	**2002**	2001	2000
Net revenue	**$4,090,970**	$3,406,786	$2,943,346
Cost of goods sold	**2,673,129**	2,253,815	1,979,572
Gross profit	**1,417,841**	1,152,971	963,774
Financial services income	**211,500**	181,545	140,135
Financial services expense	**107,273**	120,272	102,957
Operating income from financial services	**104,227**	61,273	37,178
Selling, administrative and engineering expense	**(639,366)**	(551,743)	(485,980)
Income from operations	**882,702**	662,501	514,972
Gain on sale of credit card business	**—**	—	18,915
Interest income, net	**16,541**	17,478	17,583
Other, net	**(13,416)**	(6,524)	(2,914)
Income before provision for income taxes	**885,827**	673,455	548,556
Provision for income taxes	**305,610**	235,709	200,843
Net income	**$ 580,217**	$ 437,746	$ 347,713
Basic earnings per common share	**$1.92**	$1.45	$1.15
Diluted earnings per common share	**$1.90**	$1.43	$1.13
Cash dividends per common share	**$ .14**	$ .12	$ .10

The accompanying notes are an integral part of the consolidated financial statements.

REPORT *of* ERNST & YOUNG LLP, INDEPENDENT AUDITORS

We have audited the accompanying consolidated balance sheets of Harley-Davidson, Inc. as of December 31, 2002 and 2001, and the related consolidated statements of income, shareholders' equity and cash flows for each of the three years in the period ended December 31, 2002. These financial statements are the responsibility of the Company's management. Our responsibility is to express an opinion on these financial statements based on our audits.

We conducted our audits in accordance with auditing standards generally accepted in the United States. Those standards require that we plan and perform the audit to obtain reasonable assurance about whether the financial statements are free of material misstatement. An audit includes examining, on a test basis, evidence supporting the amounts and disclosures in the financial statements. An audit also includes assessing the accounting principles used and significant estimates made by management, as well as evaluating the overall financial statement presentation. We believe that our audits provide a reasonable basis for our opinion.

In our opinion, the consolidated financial statements referred to above present fairly, in all material respects, the consolidated financial position of Harley-Davidson, Inc. at December 31, 2002 and 2001, and the consolidated results of its operations and its cash flows for each of the three years in the period ended December 31, 2002, in conformity with accounting principles generally accepted in the United States.

As discussed in Note 1 to the consolidated financial statements, on January 1, 2002, the Company changed its method of accounting for goodwill.

Ernst & Young LLP

Milwaukee, Wisconsin
January 16, 2003

CONSOLIDATED BALANCE SHEETS

(In thousands, except share amounts) December 31,	2002	2001
ASSETS		
Current assets:		
Cash and cash equivalents	**$ 280,928**	$ 439,438
Marketable securities	**514,800**	196,011
Accounts receivable, net	**108,694**	118,843
Current portion of finance receivables, net	**855,771**	656,421
Inventories	**218,156**	181,115
Deferred income taxes	**41,430**	38,993
Prepaid expenses & other current assets	**46,807**	34,443
Total current assets	**2,066,586**	1,665,264
Finance receivables, net	**589,809**	379,335
Property, plant, and equipment, net	**1,032,596**	891,820
Goodwill, net	**49,930**	49,711
Other assets	**122,296**	132,365
	$3,861,217	$3,118,495
LIABILITIES *and* SHAREHOLDERS' EQUITY		
Current liabilities:		
Accounts payable	**$ 226,977**	$ 194,683
Accrued expenses and other liabilities	**380,496**	304,376
Current portion of finance debt	**382,579**	217,051
Total current liabilities	**990,052**	716,110
Finance debt	**380,000**	380,000
Other long-term liabilities	**123,353**	158,374
Postretirement health care benefits	**105,419**	89,912
Deferred income taxes	**29,478**	17,816
Commitments and contingencies (Note 7)		
Shareholders' equity:		
Series A Junior participating preferred stock, none issued	**—**	—
Common stock, 325,298,404 and 324,340,432 shares issued in 2002 and 2001, respectively	**3,254**	3,242
Additional paid-in capital	**386,284**	359,165
Retained earnings	**2,372,095**	1,833,335
Accumulated other comprehensive loss	**(46,266)**	(13,728)
	2,715,367	2,182,014
Less:		
Treasury stock (22,636,295 and 21,550,923 shares in 2002 and 2001, respectively), at cost	**(482,360)**	(425,546)
Unearned compensation	**(92)**	(185)
Total shareholders' equity	**2,232,915**	1,756,283
	$3,861,217	$3,118,495

The accompanying notes are an integral part of the consolidated financial statements.

CONSOLIDATED STATEMENTS *of* SHAREHOLDERS' EQUITY

(In thousands, except share amounts)

	Common Stock	
	Issued Shares	Balance
BALANCE DECEMBER 31, 1999	**318,586,144**	**$3,184**
Comprehensive income:		
Net income	—	—
Other comprehensive income (loss):		
Foreign currency translation adjustment	—	—
Change in net unrealized gains on investment in retained securitization interests, net of taxes of $(3,759)	—	—
Minimum pension liability adjustment, net of tax benefit of $120	—	—
Comprehensive income		
Dividends	—	—
Repurchase of common stock	—	—
Amortization of unearned compensation	—	—
Exercise of stock options	2,599,423	26
Tax benefit of stock options	—	—
BALANCE DECEMBER 31, 2000	**321,185,567**	**$3,210**
Comprehensive income:		
Net income	—	—
Other comprehensive income (loss):		
Foreign currency translation adjustment	—	—
Change in net unrealized gains on investment in retained securitization interests, net of taxes of $(6,117)	—	—
Change in net unrealized gains on derivative financial instruments, net of taxes of $(407)	—	—
Minimum pension liability adjustment, net of tax benefit of $11,515	—	—
Comprehensive income		
Dividends	—	—
Repurchase of common stock	—	—
Amortization of unearned compensation	—	—
Exercise of stock options	3,154,865	32
Tax benefit of stock options	—	—
BALANCE DECEMBER 31, 2001	**324,340,432**	**$3,242**
Comprehensive income:		
Net income	—	—
Other comprehensive income (loss):		
Foreign currency translation adjustment	—	—
Change in net unrealized gains on investment in retained securitization interests, net of taxes of $(6,113)	—	—
Change in net unrealized losses on derivative financial instruments, net of tax benefit of $5,929	—	—
Change in net unrealized gains on marketable securities, net of taxes of $(377)	—	—
Minimum pension liability adjustment, net of tax benefit of $29,896	—	—
Comprehensive income		
Dividends	—	—
Repurchase of common stock	—	—
Amortization of unearned compensation	—	—
Exercise of stock options	957,972	12
Tax benefit of stock options	—	—
BALANCE DECEMBER 31, 2002	**325,298,404**	**$3,254**

The accompanying notes are an integral part of the consolidated financial statements.

CONSOLIDATED STATEMENTS *of* SHAREHOLDERS' EQUITY

Additional Paid-In Capital	Retained Earnings	Other Comprehensive Income (Loss)	Treasury Balance	Unearned Compensation	Total
$234,948	**$ 1,113,376**	**$ (2,067)**	**$ (187,992)**	**$(369)**	**$ 1,161,080**
—	347,713	—	—	—	347,713
—	—	(4,383)	—	—	(4,383)
—	—	6,981	—	—	6,981
—	—	(223)	—	—	(223)
					350,088
—	(30,072)	—	—	—	(30,072)
—	—	—	(126,002)	—	(126,002)
—	—	—	—	93	93
14,566	—	—	—	—	14,592
35,876	—	—	—	—	35,876
$285,390	**$ 1,431,017**	**$ 308**	**$ (313,994)**	**$(276)**	**$1,405,655**
—	437,746	—	—	—	437,746
—	—	(6,143)	—	—	(6,143)
—	—	11,115	—	—	11,115
—	—	668	—	—	668
—	—	(19,676)	—	—	(19,676)
					423,710
—	(35,428)	—	—	—	(35,428)
—	—	—	(111,552)	—	(111,552)
—	—	—	—	91	91
28,807	—	—	—	—	28,839
44,968	—	—	—	—	44,968
$ 359,165	**$ 1,833,335**	**$ (13,728)**	**$(425,546)**	**$ (185)**	**$1,756,283**
—	580,217	—	—	—	580,217
—	—	14,545	—	—	14,545
—	—	11,108	—	—	11,108
—	—	(9,824)	—	—	(9,824)
—	—	618	—	—	618
—	—	(48,985)	—	—	(48,985)
					547,679
—	(41,457)	—	—	—	(41,457)
—	—	—	(56,814)	—	(56,814)
—	—	—	—	93	93
12,667	—	—	—	—	12,679
14,452	—	—	—	—	14,452
$386,284	**$2,372,095**	**$(46,266)**	**$(482,360)**	**$ (92)**	**$2,232,915**

CONSOLIDATED STATEMENTS *of* CASH FLOWS

(In thousands) Years ended December 31,	**2002**	2001	2000
Cash flows from operating activities:			
Net income	**$ 580,217**	$ 437,746	$ 347,713
Adjustments to reconcile net income to net cash provided by operating activities:			
Depreciation and amortization	**175,778**	153,061	133,348
Gain on sale of credit card business	**—**	—	(18,915)
Tax benefit from the exercise of stock options	**14,452**	44,968	35,876
Provision for finance credit losses	**6,167**	22,178	9,919
Deferred income taxes	**38,560**	(3,539)	1,363
Long-term employee benefits	**57,124**	40,882	17,433
Contributions to pension plans	**(153,636)**	(19,294)	(12,802)
Other	**7,057**	3,045	1,800
Net changes in current assets and current liabilities	**53,827**	77,761	49,609
Total adjustments	**199,329**	319,062	217,631
Net cash provided by operating activities	**779,546**	756,808	565,344
Cash flows from investing activities:			
Capital expenditures	**(323,866)**	(290,381)	(203,611)
Finance receivables acquired or originated	**(5,611,217)**	(4,387,371)	(3,556,195)
Finance receivables collected	**3,933,125**	3,123,941	2,727,746
Finance receivables sold	**1,279,324**	987,676	723,928
Net proceeds from sale of credit card business	**—**	—	170,146
Purchase of marketable securities	**(1,508,285)**	(247,989)	—
Sales and redemptions of marketable securities	**1,190,114**	51,978	—
Purchase of Italian distributor	**—**	(1,873)	(18,777)
Other, net	**22,813**	(7,488)	(14,124)
Net cash used in investing activities	**(1,017,992)**	(771,507)	(170,887)
Cash flows from financing activities:			
Net increase (decrease) in finance debt	**165,528**	152,542	(16,654)
Dividends paid	**(41,457)**	(35,428)	(30,072)
Purchase of common stock for treasury	**(56,814)**	(111,552)	(126,002)
Issuance of common stock under employee stock option plans	**12,679**	28,839	14,592
Net cash provided by (used in) financing activities	**79,936**	34,401	(158,136)
Net (decrease) increase in cash and cash equivalents	**(158,510)**	19,702	236,321
Cash and cash equivalents:			
At beginning of year	**439,438**	419,736	183,415
At end of year	**$ 280,928**	$ 439,438	$ 419,736

The accompanying notes are an integral part of the consolidated financial statements.

Present and Future Values in Accounting

Learning Objectives

CAP

Conceptual

C1 Describe the earning of interest and the concepts of present and future values. *(p. B-2)*

Procedural

P1 Apply present value concepts to a single amount by using interest tables. *(p. B-3)*

P2 Apply future value concepts to a single amount by using interest tables. *(p. B-5)*

P3 Apply present value concepts to an annuity by using interest tables. *(p. B-6)*

P4 Apply future value concepts to an annuity by using interest tables. *(p. B-7)*

The concepts of present and future values are important to modern business activity. The purpose of this appendix is to explain, illustrate, and compute present and future values. This appendix applies these concepts with reference to both business and everyday activities.

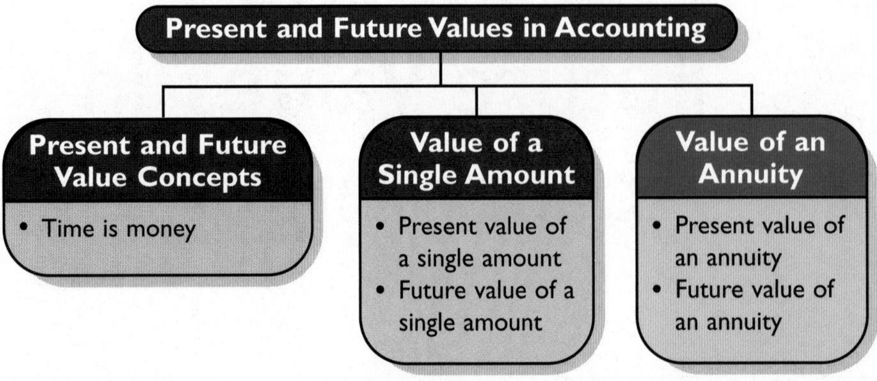

Present and Future Value Concepts

C1 Describe the earning of interest and the concepts of present and future values.

The old saying "Time is money" reflects the notion that as time passes, the values of our assets and liabilities change. This change is due to *interest,* which is a borrower's payment to the owner of an asset for its use. The most common example of interest is a savings account asset. As we keep a balance of cash in the account, it earns interest that the financial institution pays us. An example of a liability is a car loan. As we carry the balance of the loan, we accumulate interest costs on it. We must ultimately repay this loan with interest.

Present and future value computations enable us to measure or estimate the interest component of holding assets or liabilities over time. The present value computation is important when we want to know the value of future-day assets *today.* The future value computation is important when we want to know the value of present-day assets *at a future date.* The first section focuses on the present value of a single amount. The second section focuses on the future value of a single amount. Then both the present and future values of a series of amounts (called an *annuity*) are defined and explained.

Present Value of a Single Amount

We graphically express the present value, called p, of a single future amount, called f, that is received or paid at a future date in Exhibit B.1.

Exhibit B.1

Present Value of a Single Amount Diagram

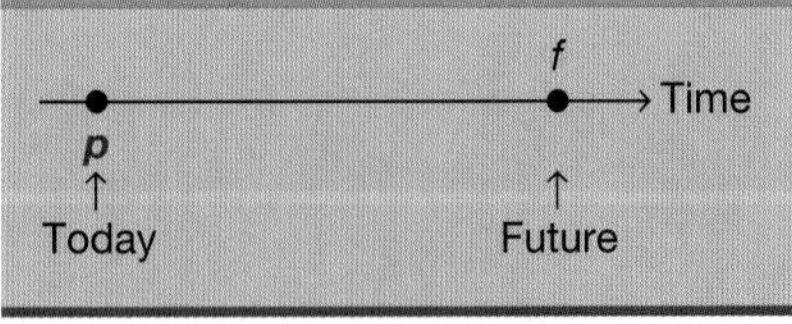

The formula to compute the present value of a single amount is shown in Exhibit B.2, where p = present value; f = future value; i = rate of interest per period; and n = number of periods. (Interest is also called the *discount,* and an interest rate is also called the *discount rate.*)

Exhibit B.2

Present Value of a Single Amount Formula

$$p = \frac{f}{(1 + i)^n}$$

To illustrate present value concepts, assume that we need \$220 one period from today. We want to know how much we must invest now, for one period, at an interest rate of 10% to provide for this \$220. For this illustration, the p, or present value, is the unknown amount—the specifics are shown graphically as follows:

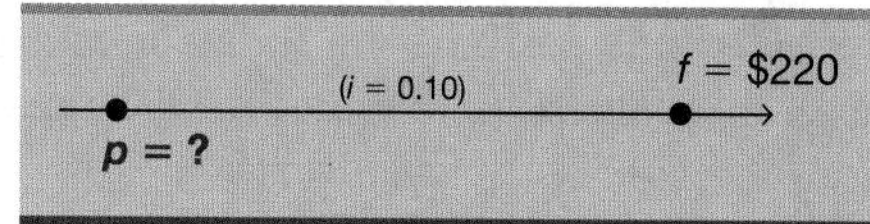

Conceptually, we know p must be less than \$220. This is obvious from the answer to this question: Would we rather have \$220 today or \$220 at some future date? If we had \$220 today, we could invest it and see it grow to something more than \$220 in the future. Therefore, we would prefer the \$220 today. This means that if we were promised \$220 in the future, we would take less than \$220 today. But how much less? To answer that question, we compute an estimate of the present value of the \$220 to be received one period from now using the formula in Exhibit B.2 as follows:

$$p = \frac{f}{(1+i)^n} = \frac{\$220}{(1+0.10)^1} = \$200$$

We interpret this result to say that given an interest rate of 10%, we are indifferent between \$200 today or \$220 at the end of one period.

We can also use this formula to compute the present value for *any number of periods.* To illustrate, consider a payment of \$242 at the end of two periods at 10% interest. The present value of this \$242 to be received two periods from now is computed as follows:

$$p = \frac{f}{(1+i)^n} = \frac{\$242}{(1+0.10)^2} = \$200$$

Together, these results tell us we are indifferent between \$200 today, or \$220 one period from today, or \$242 two periods from today given a 10% interest rate per period.

I will pay your allowance at the end of the month. Do you want to wait or receive its present value today?

The number of periods (n) in the present value formula does not have to be expressed in years. Any period of time such as a day, a month, a quarter, or a year can be used. Whatever period is used, the interest rate (i) must be compounded for the same period. This means that if a situation expresses n in months and i equals 12% per year, then i is transformed into interest earned per month (or 1%). In this case, interest is said to be *compounded monthly.*

A present value table helps us with present value computations. It gives us present values (factors) for a variety of both interest rates (i) and periods (n). Each present value in a present value table assumes that the future value (f) equals 1. When the future value (f) is different from 1, we simply multiply the present value (p) from the table by that future value to give us the estimate. The formula used to construct a table of present values for a single future amount of 1 is shown in Exhibit B.3.

$$p = \frac{1}{(1+i)^n}$$

Exhibit B.3

Present Value of 1 Formula

This formula is identical to that in Exhibit B.2 except that f equals 1. Table B.1 at the end of this appendix is such a present value table. It is often called a **present value of 1 table.** A present value table involves three factors: p, i, and n. Knowing two of these three factors allows us to compute the third. (A fourth is f, but as already explained, we need only multiply the 1 used in the formula by f.) To illustrate the use of a present value table, consider three cases.

P1 Apply present value concepts to a single amount by using interest tables.

Case 1 (solve for p when knowing i and n). To show how we use a present value table, let's look again at how we estimate the present value of \$220 (the f value) at the end of one period ($n = 1$) where the interest rate (i) is 10%. To solve this case, we go to the present value table (Table B.1) and look in the row for 1 period and in the column for 10% interest. Here we find a present value (p) of 0.9091 based on a future value of 1. This means, for instance, that \$1 to be received one period from today at 10% interest is worth \$0.9091 today. Since the future value in this case is not \$1 but \$220, we multiply the 0.9091 by \$220 to get an answer of \$200.

Case 2 (solve for n when knowing p and i). To illustrate, assume a \$100,000 future value (f) that is worth \$13,000 today (p) using an interest rate of 12% (i) but where n is unknown. In particular, we want to know how many periods (n) there are between the present value and the future value. To put this in context, it would fit a situation in which we want to retire with \$100,000 but currently have only \$13,000 that is earning a 12% return. How long will it be before we can retire? To answer this, we go to Table B.1 and look in the 12% interest column. Here we find a column of present values (p) based on a future value of 1. To use the present value table for this solution, we must divide \$13,000 (p) by \$100,000 (f), which equals 0.1300. This is necessary because *a present value table defines* f *equal to 1, and* p *as a fraction of 1*. We look for a value nearest to 0.1300 (p), which we find in the row for 18 periods (n). This means that the present value of \$100,000 at the end of 18 periods at 12% interest is \$13,000 or, alternatively stated, we must work 18 more years.

Decision Insight

Keep That Job Lottery winners often never work again. Kenny Dukes, a recent Georgia lottery winner, doesn't have that option. He is serving parole for burglary charges, and Georgia requires its parolees to be employed (or in school). Dukes had to choose between \$31 million in 30 annual payments or \$16 million in one lump sum (\$10.6 million after-tax); he chose the latter.

Case 3 (solve for i when knowing p and n). In this case, we have, say, a \$120,000 future value (f) worth \$60,000 today (p) when there are nine periods (n) between the present and future values, but the interest rate is unknown. As an example, suppose we want to retire with \$120,000, but we have only \$60,000 and hope to retire in nine years. What interest rate must we earn to retire with \$120,000 in nine years? To answer this, we go to the present value table (Table B.1) and look in the row for nine periods. To use the present value table, we must divide \$60,000 (p) by \$120,000 (f), which equals 0.5000. Recall that this step is necessary because a present value table defines f equal to 1 and p as a fraction of 1. We look for a value in the row for nine periods that is nearest to 0.5000 (p), which we find in the column for 8% interest (i). This means that the present value of \$120,000 at the end of nine periods at 8% interest is \$60,000 or, in our example, we must earn 8% annual interest to retire in nine years.

Quick Check

1. A company is considering an investment expected to yield \$70,000 after six years. If this company demands an 8% return, how much is it willing to pay for this investment?

Answer—p. B-8

Future Value of a Single Amount

We must modify the formula for the present value of a single amount to obtain the formula for the future value of a single amount. In particular, we multiply both sides of the equation in Exhibit B.2 by $(1 + i)^n$ to get the result shown in Exhibit B.4.

Exhibit B.4

Future Value of a Single Amount Formula

$$f = p \times (1 + i)^n$$

The future value (f) is defined in terms of p, i, and n. We can use this formula to determine that \$200 (p) invested for 1 (n) period at an interest rate of 10% (i) yields a future value of \$220 as follows:

$$f = p \times (1 + i)^n$$
$$= \$200 \times (1 + 0.10)^1$$
$$= \$220$$

This formula can also be used to compute the future value of an amount for *any number of periods* into the future. To illustrate, assume that \$200 is invested for three periods at 10%. The future value of this \$200 is \$266.20, computed as follows:

$$f = p \times (1 + i)^n$$
$$= \$200 \times (1 + 0.10)^3$$
$$= \$266.20$$

P2 Apply future value concepts to a single amount by using interest tables.

A future value table makes it easier for us to compute future values (f) for many different combinations of interest rates (i) and time periods (n). Each future value in a future value table assumes the present value (p) is 1. As with a present value table, if the future amount is something other than 1, we simply multiply our answer by that amount. The formula used to construct a table of future values (factors) for a single amount of 1 is in Exhibit B.5.

Exhibit B.5

Future Value of 1 Formula

$$f = (1 + i)^n$$

Table B.2 at the end of this appendix shows a table of future values for a current amount of 1. This type of table is called a **future value of 1 table.**

There are some important relations between Tables B.1 and B.2. In Table B.2, for the row where $n = 0$, the future value is 1 for each interest rate. This is so because no interest is earned when time does not pass. Also notice that Tables B.1 and B.2 report the same information but in a different manner. In particular, one table is simply the *inverse* of the other. To illustrate this inverse relation, let's say we invest \$100 annually for a period of five years at 12% per year. How much do we expect to have after five years? We can answer this question using Table B.2 by finding the future value (f) of 1, for five periods from now, compounded at 12%. From that table we find $f = 1.7623$. If we start with \$100, the amount it accumulates to after five years is \$176.23 (\$100 × 1.7623). We can alternatively use Table B.1. Here we find that the present value (p) of 1, discounted five periods at 12%, is 0.5674. Recall the inverse relation between present value and future value. This means that $p = 1/f$ (or equivalently, $f = 1/p$). We can compute the future value of \$100 invested for five periods at 12% as follows: $f = \$100 \times (1/0.5674) = \$176.24$.

A future value table involves three factors: f, i, and n. Knowing two of these three factors allows us to compute the third. To illustrate, consider these three possible cases.

Case 1 (solve for f when knowing i and n). Our preceding example fits this case. We found that \$100 invested for five periods at 12% interest accumulates to \$176.24.

Case 2 (solve for n when knowing f and i). In this case, we have, say, \$2,000 (p) and we want to know how many periods (n) it will take to accumulate to \$3,000 (f) at 7% (i) interest. To answer this, we go to the future value table (Table B.2) and look in the 7% interest column. Here we find a column of future values (f) based on a present value of 1. To use a future value table, we must divide \$3,000 (f) by \$2,000 (p), which equals 1.500. This is necessary because *a future value table defines* p *equal to 1, and* f *as a multiple of 1.* We look for a value nearest to 1.50 (f), which we find in the row for six periods (n). This means that \$2,000 invested for six periods at 7% interest accumulates to \$3,000.

Case 3 (solve for i when knowing f and n). In this case, we have, say, \$2,001 (p) and in nine years (n), we want to have \$4,000 (f). What rate of interest must we earn to accomplish this? To answer that, we go to Table B.2 and search in the row for nine periods. To use a future value table, we must divide \$4,000 (f) by \$2,001 (p), which equals 1.9990. Recall that this is necessary because a future value table defines p equal to 1 and f as a multiple of 1. We look for a value nearest to 1.9990 (f), which we find in the column for 8% interest (i). This means that \$2,001 invested for nine periods at 8% interest accumulates to \$4,000.

Quick Check

2. Assume that you win a $150,000 cash sweepstakes. You decide to deposit this cash in an account earning 8% annual interest, and you plan to quit your job when the account equals $555,000. How many years will it be before you can quit working?

Answer—p. B-8

Present Value of an Annuity

An *annuity* is a series of equal payments occurring at equal intervals. One example is a series of three annual payments of $100 each. An *ordinary annuity* is defined as equal end-of-period payments at equal intervals. An ordinary annuity of $100 for 3 periods and its present value (p) are illustrated in Exhibit B.6.

Exhibit B.6

Present Value of an Ordinary Annuity Diagram

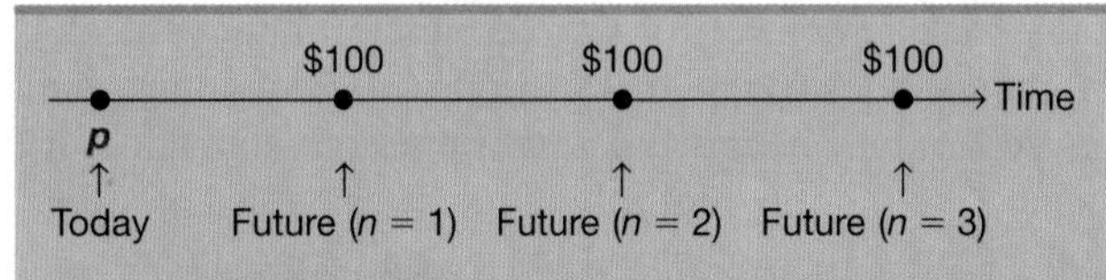

P3 Apply present value concepts to an annuity by using interest tables.

One way to compute the present value of an ordinary annuity is to find the present value of each payment using our present value formula from Exhibit B.3. We then add each of the three present values. To illustrate, let's look at three $100 payments at the end of each of the next three periods with an interest rate of 15%. Our present value computations are

$$p = \frac{\$100}{(1 + 0.15)^1} + \frac{\$100}{(1 + 0.15)^2} + \frac{\$100}{(1 + 0.15)^3} = \$228.32$$

This computation is identical to computing the present value of each payment (from Table B.1) and taking their sum or, alternatively, adding the values from Table B.1 for each of the three payments and multiplying their sum by the $100 annuity payment.

A more direct way is to use a present value of annuity table. Table B.3 at the end of this appendix is one such table. This table is called a **present value of an annuity of 1 table.** If we look at Table B.3 where $n = 3$ and $i = 15\%$, we see the present value is 2.2832. This means that the present value of an annuity of 1 for three periods, with a 15% interest rate, equals 2.2832.

Decision Insight

Aw-Shucks "I don't have good luck—I'm blessed," proclaimed Andrew "Jack" Whittaker, 55, a sewage treatment contractor, after winning the largest-ever, undivided jackpot in a U.S. lottery. Whittaker had to choose between $315 million in 30 annual installments or $170 million in one lump sum ($112 million after-tax). Says Whittaker, "My biggest problem is to keep my daughter and granddaughter from spending all their money in one week."

A present value of an annuity formula is used to construct Table B.3. It can also be constructed by adding the amounts in a present value of 1 table. To illustrate, we use Table B.1 and B.3 to confirm this relation for the prior example:

From Table B.1		From Table B.3	
$i = 15\%, n = 1$	0.8696		
$i = 15\%, n = 2$	0.7561		
$i = 15\%, n = 3$	0.6575		
Total	2.2832	$i = 15\%, n = 3$	2.2832

We can also use business calculators or spreadsheet programs to find the present value of an annuity.

Quick Check

3. A company is considering an investment paying $10,000 every six months for three years. The first payment would be received in six months. If this company requires an 8% annual return, what is the maximum amount it is willing to pay for this investment?

Answer—p. B-8

Future Value of an Annuity

The future value of an *ordinary annuity* is the accumulated value of each annuity payment with interest as of the date of the final payment. To illustrate, let's consider the earlier annuity of three annual payments of $100. Exhibit B.7 shows the point in time for the future value (f). The first payment is made two periods prior to the point when future value is determined, and the final payment occurs on the future value date.

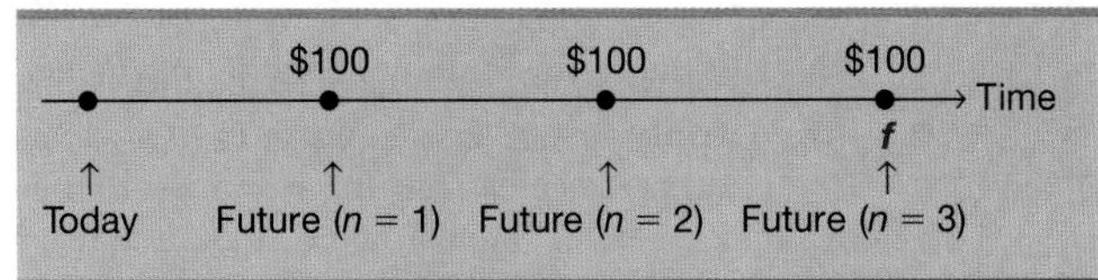

Exhibit B.7

Future Value of an Ordinary Annuity Diagram

One way to compute the future value of an annuity is to use the formula to find the future value of *each* payment and add them. If we assume an interest rate of 15%, our calculation is

$$f = \$100 \times (1 + 0.15)^2 + \$100 \times (1 + 0.15)^1 + \$100 \times (1 + 0.15)^0 = \$347.25$$

This is identical to using Table B.2 and summing the future values of each payment, or by adding the future values of the three payments of 1 and multiplying the sum by $100.

P4 Apply future value concepts to an annuity by using interest tables.

A more direct way is to use a table showing future values of annuities. Such a table is called a **future value of an annuity of 1 table**. Table B.4 at the end of this appendix is one such table. Note that in Table B.4 when $n = 1$, the future values equal 1 ($f = 1$) for all rates of interest. This is so because such an annuity consists of only one payment and the future value is determined on the date of that payment—no time passes between the payment and its future value. The future value of an annuity formula is used to construct Table B.4. We can also construct it by adding the amounts from a future value of 1 table. To illustrate, we use Tables B.2 and B.4 to confirm this relation for the prior example:

From Table B.2		From Table B.4	
i = 15%, n = 0	1.0000		
i = 15%, n = 1	1.1500		
i = 15%, n = 2	1.3225		
Total	3.4725	i = 15%, n = 3	3.4725

Note that the future value in Table B.2 is 1.0000 when $n = 0$, but the future value in Table B.4 is 1.0000 when $n = 1$. Is this a contradiction? No. When $n = 0$ in Table B.2, the future value is determined on the date when a single payment occurs. This means that no interest is earned because no time has passed, and the future value equals the payment. Table B.4 describes annuities with equal payments occurring at the end of each period. When $n = 1$, the annuity has one payment, and its future value equals 1 on the date of its final and only payment. Again, no time passes from the payment and its future value date.

Quick Check

4. A company invests $45,000 per year for five years at 12% annual interest. Compute the value of this annuity investment at the end of five years.

Answer—p. B-8

Summary

C1 Describe the earning of interest and the concepts of present and future values. Interest is payment by a borrower to the owner of an asset for its use. Present and future value computations are a way for us to estimate the interest component of holding assets or liabilities over a period of time.

P1 Apply present value concepts to a single amount by using interest tables. The present value of a single amount received at a future date is the amount that can be invested now at the specified interest rate to yield that future value.

P2 Apply future value concepts to a single amount by using interest tables. The future value of a single amount invested at a specified rate of interest is the amount that would accumulate by the future date.

P3 Apply present value concepts to an annuity by using interest tables. The present value of an annuity is the amount that can be invested now at the specified interest rate to yield that series of equal periodic payments.

P4 Apply future value concepts to an annuity by using interest tables. The future value of an annuity invested at a specific rate of interest is the amount that would accumulate by the date of the final payment.

Guidance Answers to Quick Checks

1. $70,000 × 0.6302 = $44,114 (use Table B.1, $i = 8\%$, $n = 6$).
2. $555,000/$150,000 = 3.7000; Table B.2 shows this value is not achieved until after 17 years at 8% interest.
3. $10,000 × 5.2421 = $52,421 (use Table B.3, $i = 4\%$, $n = 6$).
4. $45,000 × 6.3528 = $285,876 (use Table B.4, $i = 12\%$, $n = 5$).

Homework Manager *repeats all numerical Quick Studies on the book's Website with new numbers.* HM

QUICK STUDY

QS B-1
Identifying interest rates in tables
C1

Assume that you must make future value estimates using the *future value of 1 table* (Table B.2). Which interest rate column do you use when working with the following rates?

1. 8% compounded quarterly
2. 12% compounded annually
3. 6% compounded semiannually
4. 12% compounded monthly

QS B-2
Interest rate on an investment P1

Ken Francis is offered the possibility of investing $2,745 today and in return to receive $10,000 after 15 years. What is the annual rate of interest for this investment? (Use Table B.1.)

QS B-3
Number of periods of an investment P1

Megan Brink is offered the possibility of investing $6,651 today at 6% interest per year in a desire to accumulate $10,000. How many years must Brink wait to accumulate $10,000? (Use Table B.1.)

QS B-4
Present value of an amount P1

Flaherty is considering an investment that, if paid for immediately, is expected to return $140,000 five years from now. If Flaherty demands a 9% return, how much is she willing to pay for this investment?

CII, Inc., invests $630,000 in a project expected to earn a 12% annual rate of return. The earnings will be reinvested in the project each year until the entire investment is liquidated 10 years later. What will the cash proceeds be when the project is liquidated?

QS B-5
Future value of an amount P2

Beene Distributing is considering a project that will return $150,000 annually at the end of each year for six years. If Beene demands an annual return of 7% and pays for the project immediately, how much is it willing to pay for the project?

QS B-6
Present value of an annuity P3

Claire Fitch is planning to begin an individual retirement program in which she will invest $1,500 at the end of each year. Fitch plans to retire after making 30 annual investments in the program earning a return of 10%. What is the value of the program on the date of the last payment?

QS B-7
Future value of an annuity P4

Homework Manager *repeats all numerical Exercises on the book's Website with new numbers.*

EXERCISES

Bill Thompson expects to invest $10,000 at 12% and, at the end of a certain period, receive $96,463. How many years will it be before Thompson receives the payment? (Use Table B.2.)

Exercise B-1
Number of periods of an investment P2

Ed Summers expects to invest $10,000 for 25 years, after which he wants to receive $108,347. What rate of interest must Summers earn? (Use Table B.2.)

Exercise B-2
Interest rate on an investment P2

Jones expects an immediate investment of $57,466 to return $10,000 annually for eight years, with the first payment to be received one year from now. What rate of interest must Jones earn? (Use Table B.3.)

Exercise B-3
Interest rate on an investment P3

Keith Riggins expects an investment of $82,014 to return $10,000 annually for several years. If Riggins earns a return of 10%, how many annual payments will he receive? (Use Table B.3.)

Exercise B-4
Number of periods of an investment P3

Algoe expects to invest $1,000 annually for 40 years to yield an accumulated value of $154,762 on the date of the last investment. For this to occur, what rate of interest must Algoe earn? (Use Table B.4.)

Exercise B-5
Interest rate on an investment P4

Kate Beckwith expects to invest $10,000 annually that will earn 8%. How many annual investments must Beckwith make to accumulate $303,243 on the date of the last investment? (Use Table B.4.)

Exercise B-6
Number of periods of an investment P4

Sam Weber finances a new automobile by paying $6,500 cash and agreeing to make 40 monthly payments of $500 each, the first payment to be made one month after the purchase. The loan bears interest at an annual rate of 12%. What is the cost of the automobile?

Exercise B-7
Present value of an annuity P3

Spiller Corp. plans to issue 10%, 15-year, $500,000 par value bonds payable that pay interest semiannually on June 30 and December 31. The bonds are dated December 31, 2005, and are issued on that date. If the market rate of interest for the bonds is 8% on the date of issue, what will be the total cash proceeds from the bond issue?

Exercise B-8
Present value of bonds P1 P3

McAdams Company expects to earn 10% per year on an investment that will pay $606,773 six years from now. Use Table B.1 to compute the present value of this investment.

Exercise B-9
Present value of an amount P1

Exercise B-10
Present value of an amount and of an annuity P1 P3

Compute the amount that can be borrowed under each of the following circumstances:

1. A promise to repay $90,000 seven years from now at an interest rate of 6%.

2. An agreement made on February 1, 2005, to make three separate payments of $20,000 on February 1 of 2006, 2007, and 2008. The annual interest rate is 10%.

Exercise B-11
Present value of an amount P1

On January 1, 2005, a company agrees to pay $20,000 in three years. If the annual interest rate is 10%, determine how much cash the company can borrow with this agreement.

Exercise B-12
Present value of an amount P1

Find the amount of money that can be borrowed today with each of the following separate debt agreements *a* through *f*:

Case	Single Future Payment	Number of Periods	Interest Rate
a.	$40,000	3	4%
b.	75,000	7	8
c.	52,000	9	10
d.	18,000	2	4
e.	63,000	8	6
f.	89,000	5	2

Exercise B-13
Present values of annuities
P3

C&H Ski Club recently borrowed money and agrees to pay it back with a series of six annual payments of $5,000 each. C&H subsequently borrows more money and agrees to pay it back with a series of four annual payments of $7,500 each. The annual interest rate for both loans is 6%.

1. Use Table B.1 to find the present value of these two separate annuities. (Round amounts to the nearest dollar.)

2. Use Table B.3 to find the present value of these two separate annuities.

Exercise B-14
Present value with semiannual compounding
C1 P3

Otto Co. borrows money on April 30, 2005, by promising to make four payments of $13,000 each on November 1, 2005; May 1, 2006; November 1, 2006; and May 1, 2007.

1. How much money is Otto able to borrow if the interest rate is 8%, compounded semiannually?

2. How much money is Otto able to borrow if the interest rate is 12%, compounded semiannually?

3. How much money is Otto able to borrow if the interest rate is 16%, compounded semiannually?

Exercise B-15
Future value of an amount P2

Mark Welsch deposits $7,200 in an account that earns interest at an annual rate of 8%, compounded quarterly. The $7,200 plus earned interest must remain in the account 10 years before it can be withdrawn. How much money will be in the account at the end of 10 years?

Exercise B-16
Future value of an annuity P4

Kelly Malone plans to have $50 withheld from her monthly paycheck and deposited in a savings account that earns 12% annually, compounded monthly. If Malone continues with her plan for two and one-half years, how much will be accumulated in the account on the date of the last deposit?

Exercise B-17
Future value of an amount plus an annuity P2 P4

Starr Company decides to establish a fund that it will use 10 years from now to replace an aging production facility. The company will make a $100,000 initial contribution to the fund and plans to make quarterly contributions of $50,000 beginning in three months. The fund earns 12%, compounded quarterly. What will be the value of the fund 10 years from now?

Exercise B-18
Future value of an amount P2

Catten, Inc., invests $163,170 today earning 7% per year for nine years. Use Table B.2 to compute the future value of the investment nine years from now.

Exercise B-19
Using present and future value tables

C1 P1 P2 P3 P4

For each of the following situations, identify (1) the case as either (*a*) a present or a future value and (*b*) a single amount or an annuity, (2) the table you would use in your computations (but do not solve the problem), and (3) the interest rate and time periods you would use.

a. You need to accumulate $10,000 for a trip you wish to take in four years. You are able to earn 8% compounded semiannually on your savings. You plan to make only one deposit and let the money accumulate for four years. How would you determine the amount of the one-time deposit?

b. Assume the same facts as in part (*a*) except that you will make semiannual deposits to your savings account.

c. You want to retire after working 40 years with savings in excess of $1,000,000. You expect to save $4,000 a year for 40 years and earn an annual rate of interest of 8%. Will you be able to retire with more than $1,000,000 in 40 years? Explain.

d. A sweepstakes agency names you a grand prize winner. You can take $225,000 immediately or elect to receive annual installments of $30,000 for 20 years. You can earn 10% annually on any investments you make. Which prize do you choose to receive?

Table B.1

Present Value of 1

$$p = 1/(1 + i)^n$$

	Rate											
Periods	**1%**	**2%**	**3%**	**4%**	**5%**	**6%**	**7%**	**8%**	**9%**	**10%**	**12%**	**15%**
1	0.9901	0.9804	0.9709	0.9615	0.9524	0.9434	0.9346	0.9259	0.9174	0.9091	0.8929	0.8696
2	0.9803	0.9612	0.9426	0.9246	0.9070	0.8900	0.8734	0.8573	0.8417	0.8264	0.7972	0.7561
3	0.9706	0.9423	0.9151	0.8890	0.8638	0.8396	0.8163	0.7938	0.7722	0.7513	0.7118	0.6575
4	0.9610	0.9238	0.8885	0.8548	0.8227	0.7921	0.7629	0.7350	0.7084	0.6830	0.6355	0.5718
5	0.9515	0.9057	0.8626	0.8219	0.7835	0.7473	0.7130	0.6806	0.6499	0.6209	0.5674	0.4972
6	0.9420	0.8880	0.8375	0.7903	0.7462	0.7050	0.6663	0.6302	0.5963	0.5645	0.5066	0.4323
7	0.9327	0.8706	0.8131	0.7599	0.7107	0.6651	0.6227	0.5835	0.5470	0.5132	0.4523	0.3759
8	0.9235	0.8535	0.7894	0.7307	0.6768	0.6274	0.5820	0.5403	0.5019	0.4665	0.4039	0.3269
9	0.9143	0.8368	0.7664	0.7026	0.6446	0.5919	0.5439	0.5002	0.4604	0.4241	0.3606	0.2843
10	0.9053	0.8203	0.7441	0.6756	0.6139	0.5584	0.5083	0.4632	0.4224	0.3855	0.3220	0.2472
11	0.8963	0.8043	0.7224	0.6496	0.5847	0.5268	0.4751	0.4289	0.3875	0.3505	0.2875	0.2149
12	0.8874	0.7885	0.7014	0.6246	0.5568	0.4970	0.4440	0.3971	0.3555	0.3186	0.2567	0.1869
13	0.8787	0.7730	0.6810	0.6006	0.5303	0.4688	0.4150	0.3677	0.3262	0.2897	0.2292	0.1625
14	0.8700	0.7579	0.6611	0.5775	0.5051	0.4423	0.3878	0.3405	0.2992	0.2633	0.2046	0.1413
15	0.8613	0.7430	0.6419	0.5553	0.4810	0.4173	0.3624	0.3152	0.2745	0.2394	0.1827	0.1229
16	0.8528	0.7284	0.6232	0.5339	0.4581	0.3936	0.3387	0.2919	0.2519	0.2176	0.1631	0.1069
17	0.8444	0.7142	0.6050	0.5134	0.4363	0.3714	0.3166	0.2703	0.2311	0.1978	0.1456	0.0929
18	0.8360	0.7002	0.5874	0.4936	0.4155	0.3503	0.2959	0.2502	0.2120	0.1799	0.1300	0.0808
19	0.8277	0.6864	0.5703	0.4746	0.3957	0.3305	0.2765	0.2317	0.1945	0.1635	0.1161	0.0703
20	0.8195	0.6730	0.5537	0.4564	0.3769	0.3118	0.2584	0.2145	0.1784	0.1486	0.1037	0.0611
25	0.7798	0.6095	0.4776	0.3751	0.2953	0.2330	0.1842	0.1460	0.1160	0.0923	0.0588	0.0304
30	0.7419	0.5521	0.4120	0.3083	0.2314	0.1741	0.1314	0.0994	0.0754	0.0573	0.0334	0.0151
35	0.7059	0.5000	0.3554	0.2534	0.1813	0.1301	0.0937	0.0676	0.0490	0.0356	0.0189	0.0075
40	0.6717	0.4529	0.3066	0.2083	0.1420	0.0972	0.0668	0.0460	0.0318	0.0221	0.0107	0.0037

Table B.2

Future Value of 1

$$f = (1 + i)^n$$

	Rate											
Periods	**1%**	**2%**	**3%**	**4%**	**5%**	**6%**	**7%**	**8%**	**9%**	**10%**	**12%**	**15%**
0	1.0000	1.0000	1.0000	1.0000	1.0000	1.0000	1.0000	1.0000	1.0000	1.0000	1.0000	1.0000
1	1.0100	1.0200	1.0300	1.0400	1.0500	1.0600	1.0700	1.0800	1.0900	1.1000	1.1200	1.1500
2	1.0201	1.0404	1.0609	1.0816	1.1025	1.1236	1.1449	1.1664	1.1881	1.2100	1.2544	1.3225
3	1.0303	1.0612	1.0927	1.1249	1.1576	1.1910	1.2250	1.2597	1.2950	1.3310	1.4049	1.5209
4	1.0406	1.0824	1.1255	1.1699	1.2155	1.2625	1.3108	1.3605	1.4116	1.4641	1.5735	1.7490
5	1.0510	1.1041	1.1593	1.2167	1.2763	1.3382	1.4026	1.4693	1.5386	1.6105	1.7623	2.0114
6	1.0615	1.1262	1.1941	1.2653	1.3401	1.4185	1.5007	1.5869	1.6771	1.7716	1.9738	2.3131
7	1.0721	1.1487	1.2299	1.3159	1.4071	1.5036	1.6058	1.7138	1.8280	1.9487	2.2107	2.6600
8	1.0829	1.1717	1.2668	1.3686	1.4775	1.5938	1.7182	1.8509	1.9926	2.1436	2.4760	3.0590
9	1.0937	1.1951	1.3048	1.4233	1.5513	1.6895	1.8385	1.9990	2.1719	2.3579	2.7731	3.5179
10	1.1046	1.2190	1.3439	1.4802	1.6289	1.7908	1.9672	2.1589	2.3674	2.5937	3.1058	4.0456
11	1.1157	1.2434	1.3842	1.5395	1.7103	1.8983	2.1049	2.3316	2.5804	2.8531	3.4785	4.6524
12	1.1268	1.2682	1.4258	1.6010	1.7959	2.0122	2.2522	2.5182	2.8127	3.1384	3.8960	5.3503
13	1.1381	1.2936	1.4685	1.6651	1.8856	2.1329	2.4098	2.7196	3.0658	3.4523	4.3635	6.1528
14	1.1495	1.3195	1.5126	1.7317	1.9799	2.2609	2.5785	2.9372	3.3417	3.7975	4.8871	7.0757
15	1.1610	1.3459	1.5580	1.8009	2.0789	2.3966	2.7590	3.1722	3.6425	4.1772	5.4736	8.1371
16	1.1726	1.3728	1.6047	1.8730	2.1829	2.5404	2.9522	3.4259	3.9703	4.5950	6.1304	9.3576
17	1.1843	1.4002	1.6528	1.9479	2.2920	2.6928	3.1588	3.7000	4.3276	5.0545	6.8660	10.7613
18	1.1961	1.4282	1.7024	2.0258	2.4066	2.8543	3.3799	3.9960	4.7171	5.5599	7.6900	12.3755
19	1.2081	1.4568	1.7535	2.1068	2.5270	3.0256	3.6165	4.3157	5.1417	6.1159	8.6128	14.2318
20	1.2202	1.4859	1.8061	2.1911	2.6533	3.2071	3.8697	4.6610	5.6044	6.7275	9.6463	16.3665
25	1.2824	1.6406	2.0938	2.6658	3.3864	4.2919	5.4274	6.8485	8.6231	10.8347	17.0001	32.9190
30	1.3478	1.8114	2.4273	3.2434	4.3219	5.7435	7.6123	10.0627	13.2677	17.4494	29.9599	66.2118
35	1.4166	1.9999	2.8139	3.9461	5.5160	7.6861	10.6766	14.7853	20.4140	28.1024	52.7996	133.176
40	1.4889	2.2080	3.2620	4.8010	7.0400	10.2857	14.9745	21.7245	31.4094	45.2593	93.0510	267.864

$$p = \left[1 - \frac{1}{(1 + i)^n}\right] / i$$

Table B.3

Present Value of an Annuity of 1

Periods	1%	2%	3%	4%	5%	6%	7%	8%	9%	10%	12%	15%
1	0.9901	0.9804	0.9709	0.9615	0.9524	0.9434	0.9346	0.9259	0.9174	0.9091	0.8929	0.8696
2	1.9704	1.9416	1.9135	1.8861	1.8594	1.8334	1.8080	1.7833	1.7591	1.7355	1.6901	1.6257
3	2.9410	2.8839	2.8286	2.7751	2.7232	2.6730	2.6243	2.5771	2.5313	2.4869	2.4018	2.2832
4	3.9020	3.8077	3.7171	3.6299	3.5460	3.4651	3.3872	3.3121	3.2397	3.1699	3.0373	2.8550
5	4.8534	4.7135	4.5797	4.4518	4.3295	4.2124	4.1002	3.9927	3.8897	3.7908	3.6048	3.3522
6	5.7955	5.6014	5.4172	5.2421	5.0757	4.9173	4.7665	4.6229	4.4859	4.3553	4.1114	3.7845
7	6.7282	6.4720	6.2303	6.0021	5.7864	5.5824	5.3893	5.2064	5.0330	4.8684	4.5638	4.1604
8	7.6517	7.3255	7.0197	6.7327	6.4632	6.2098	5.9713	5.7466	5.5348	5.3349	4.9676	4.4873
9	8.5660	8.1622	7.7861	7.4353	7.1078	6.8017	6.5152	6.2469	5.9952	5.7590	5.3282	4.7716
10	9.4713	8.9826	8.5302	8.1109	7.7217	7.3601	7.0236	6.7101	6.4177	6.1446	5.6502	5.0188
11	10.3676	9.7868	9.2526	8.7605	8.3064	7.8869	7.4987	7.1390	6.8052	6.4951	5.9377	5.2337
12	11.2551	10.5753	9.9540	9.3851	8.8633	8.3838	7.9427	7.5361	7.1607	6.8137	6.1944	5.4206
13	12.1337	11.3484	10.6350	9.9856	9.3936	8.8527	8.3577	7.9038	7.4869	7.1034	6.4235	5.5831
14	13.0037	12.1062	11.2961	10.5631	9.8986	9.2950	8.7455	8.2442	7.7862	7.3667	6.6282	5.7245
15	13.8651	12.8493	11.9379	11.1184	10.3797	9.7122	9.1079	8.5595	8.0607	7.6061	6.8109	5.8474
16	14.7179	13.5777	12.5611	11.6523	10.8378	10.1059	9.4466	8.8514	8.3126	7.8237	6.9740	5.9542
17	15.5623	14.2919	13.1661	12.1657	11.2741	10.4773	9.7632	9.1216	8.5436	8.0216	7.1196	6.0472
18	16.3983	14.9920	13.7535	12.6593	11.6896	10.8276	10.0591	9.3719	8.7556	8.2014	7.2497	6.1280
19	17.2260	15.6785	14.3238	13.1339	12.0853	11.1581	10.3356	9.6036	8.9501	8.3649	7.3658	6.1982
20	18.0456	16.3514	14.8775	13.5903	12.4622	11.4699	10.5940	9.8181	9.1285	8.5136	7.4694	6.2593
25	22.0232	19.5235	17.4131	15.6221	14.0939	12.7834	11.6536	10.6748	9.8226	9.0770	7.8431	6.4641
30	25.8077	22.3965	19.6004	17.2920	15.3725	13.7648	12.4090	11.2578	10.2737	9.4269	8.0552	6.5660
35	29.4086	24.9986	21.4872	18.6646	16.3742	14.4982	12.9477	11.6546	10.5668	9.6442	8.1755	6.6166
40	32.8347	27.3555	23.1148	19.7928	17.1591	15.0463	13.3317	11.9246	10.7574	9.7791	8.2438	6.6418

$$f = [(1 + i)^n - 1] / i$$

Table B.4

Future Value of an Annuity of 1

Periods	1%	2%	3%	4%	5%	6%	7%	8%	9%	10%	12%	15%
1	1.0000	1.0000	1.0000	1.0000	1.0000	1.0000	1.0000	1.0000	1.0000	1.0000	1.0000	1.0000
2	2.0100	2.0200	2.0300	2.0400	2.0500	2.0600	2.0700	2.0800	2.0900	2.1000	2.1200	2.1500
3	3.0301	3.0604	3.0909	3.1216	3.1525	3.1836	3.2149	3.2464	3.2781	3.3100	3.3744	3.4725
4	4.0604	4.1216	4.1836	4.2465	4.3101	4.3746	4.4399	4.5061	4.5731	4.6410	4.7793	4.9934
5	5.1010	5.2040	5.3091	5.4163	5.5256	5.6371	5.7507	5.8666	5.9847	6.1051	6.3528	6.7424
6	6.1520	6.3081	6.4684	6.6330	6.8019	6.9753	7.1533	7.3359	7.5233	7.7156	8.1152	8.7537
7	7.2135	7.4343	7.6625	7.8983	8.1420	8.3938	8.6540	8.9228	9.2004	9.4872	10.0890	11.0668
8	8.2857	8.5830	8.8923	9.2142	9.5491	9.8975	10.2598	10.6366	11.0285	11.4359	12.2997	13.7268
9	9.3685	9.7546	10.1591	10.5828	11.0266	11.4913	11.9780	12.4876	13.0210	13.5795	14.7757	16.7858
10	10.4622	10.9497	11.4639	12.0061	12.5779	13.1808	13.8164	14.4866	15.1929	15.9374	17.5487	20.3037
11	11.5668	12.1687	12.8078	13.4864	14.2068	14.9716	15.7836	16.6455	17.5603	18.5312	20.6546	24.3493
12	12.6825	13.4121	14.1920	15.0258	15.9171	16.8699	17.8885	18.9771	20.1407	21.3843	24.1331	29.0017
13	13.8093	14.6803	15.6178	16.6268	17.7130	18.8821	20.1406	21.4953	22.9534	24.5227	28.0291	34.3519
14	14.9474	15.9739	17.0863	18.2919	19.5986	21.0151	22.5505	24.2149	26.0192	27.9750	32.3926	40.5047
15	16.0969	17.2934	18.5989	20.0236	21.5786	23.2760	25.1290	27.1521	29.3609	31.7725	37.2797	47.5804
16	17.2579	18.6393	20.1569	21.8245	23.6575	25.6725	27.8881	30.3243	33.0034	35.9497	42.7533	55.7175
17	18.4304	20.0121	21.7616	23.6975	25.8404	28.2129	30.8402	33.7502	36.9737	40.5447	48.8837	65.0751
18	19.6147	21.4123	23.4144	25.6454	28.1324	30.9057	33.9990	37.4502	41.3013	45.5992	55.7497	75.8364
19	20.8109	22.8406	25.1169	27.6712	30.5390	33.7600	37.3790	41.4463	46.0185	51.1591	63.4397	88.2118
20	22.0190	24.2974	26.8704	29.7781	33.0660	36.7856	40.9955	45.7620	51.1601	57.2750	72.0524	102.444
25	28.2432	32.0303	36.4593	41.6459	47.7271	54.8645	63.2490	73.1059	84.7009	98.3471	133.334	212.793
30	34.7849	40.5681	47.5754	56.0849	66.4388	79.0582	94.4608	113.283	136.308	164.494	241.333	434.745
35	41.6603	49.9945	60.4621	73.6522	90.3203	111.435	138.237	172.317	215.711	271.024	431.663	881.170
40	48.8864	60.4020	75.4013	95.0255	120.800	154.762	199.635	259.057	337.882	442.593	767.091	1,779.09

Glossary

Absorption costing Costing method that assigns both variable and fixed costs to products. *(p. 879)*

Accelerated depreciation method Method that produces larger depreciation charges in the early years of an asset's life and smaller charges in its later years. *(p. 388)*

Account Record within an accounting system in which increases and decreases are entered and stored in a specific asset, liability, equity, revenue, or expense. *(p. 49)*

Account balance Difference between total debits and total credits (including the beginning balance) for an account. *(p. 53)*

Account form balance sheet Balance sheet that lists assets on the left side and liabilities and equity on the right. *(p. 18)*

Account payable Liability created by buying goods or services on credit; backed by the buyer's general credit standing. *(p. 50)*

Accounting Information and measurement system that identifies, records, and communicates relevant information about a company's business activities. *(p. 4)*

Accounting cycle Recurring steps performed each accounting period, starting with analyzing transactions and continuing through the post-closing trial balance (or reversing entries). *(p. 143)*

Accounting equation Equality involving a company's assets, liabilities, and equity; Assets = Liabilities + Equity; also called *balance sheet equation*. *(p. 12)*

Accounting information system People, records, and methods that collect and process data from transactions and events, organize them in useful forms, and communicate results to decision makers. *(p. 262)*

Accounting period Length of time covered by financial statements; also called *reporting period*. *(p. 94)*

Accounting rate of return Rate used to evaluate the acceptability of an investment; equals the after-tax periodic income from a project divided by the average investment in the asset; also called *rate of return on average investment*. *(p. 987)*

Accounts payable ledger Subsidiary ledger listing individual creditor (supplier) accounts. *(p. 267)*

Accounts receivable Amounts due from customers for credit sales; backed by the customer's general credit standing. *(p. 350)*

Accounts receivable ledger Subsidiary ledger listing individual customer accounts. *(p. 267)*

Accounts receivable turnover Measure of both the quality and liquidity of accounts receivable; indicates how often receivables are received and collected during the period; computed by dividing net sales by average accounts receivable. *(p. 364)*

Accrual basis accounting Accounting system that recognizes revenues when earned and expenses when incurred; the basis for GAAP. *(p. 95)*

Accrued expenses Costs incurred in a period that are both unpaid and unrecorded; adjusting entries for recording accrued expenses involve increasing expenses and increasing liabilities. *(p. 101)*

Accrued revenues Revenues earned in a period that are both unrecorded and not yet received in cash (or other assets); adjusting entries for recording accrued revenues involve increasing assets and increasing revenues. *(p. 103)*

Accumulated depreciation Cumulative sum of all depreciation expense recorded for an asset. *(p. 99)*

Acid-test ratio Ratio used to assess a company's ability to settle its current debts with its most liquid assets; defined as quick assets (cash, short-term investments, and current receivables) divided by current liabilities. *(p. 193)*

Activity-based budgeting (ABB) Budget system based on expected activities. *(p. 917)*

Activity-based costing (ABC) Cost allocation method that focuses on activities performed; traces costs to activities and then assigns them to cost objects. *(p. 834)*

Activity cost pool Temporary account that accumulates costs a company incurs to support an activity. *(p. 834)*

Adjusted trial balance List of accounts and balances prepared after period-end adjustments are recorded and posted. *(p. 105)*

Adjusting entry Journal entry at the end of an accounting period to bring an asset or liability account to its proper amount and update the related expense or revenue account. *(p. 97)*

Aging of accounts receivable Process of classifying accounts receivable by how long they are past due for purposes of estimating uncollectible accounts. *(p. 358)*

Allowance for Doubtful Accounts Contra asset account with a balance approximating uncollectible accounts receivable; also called *Allowance for Uncollectible Accounts*. *(p. 355)*

Allowance method Procedure that (a) estimates and matches bad debts expense with its sales for the period and/or (b) reports accounts receivable at estimated realizable value. *(p. 354)*

Amortization Process of allocating the cost of an intangible asset to expense over its estimated useful life. *(p. 398)*

Annual financial statements Financial statements covering a one-year period; often based on a calendar year, but any consecutive 12-month (or 52-week) period is acceptable. *(p. 95)*

Annual report Summary of a company's financial results for the year with its current financial condition and future planes; directed to external users of financial information. *(p. A-1)*

Annuity Series of equal payments at equal intervals. *(p. 570)*

Appropriated retained earnings Retained earnings separately reported to inform stockholders of funding needs. *(p. 517)*

Assets Resources a business owns or controls that are expected to provide current and future benefits to the business. *(p. 12)*

Audit Analysis and report of an organization's accounting system, its records, and its reports using various tests. *(p. 9)*

Authorized stock Total amount of stock that a corporation's charter authorizes it to issue. *(p. 499)*

Available-for-sale (AFS) securities Investments in debt and equity securities that are not classified as trading securities or held-to-maturity securities. *(p. 596)*

Average cost See *weighted average. (p. 228)*

Avoidable expense Expense (or cost) that is relevant for decision making; expense that is not incurred if a department, product, or service is eliminated. *(p. 1000)*

Bad debts Accounts of customers who do not pay what they have promised to pay; an expense of selling on credit; also called *uncollectible accounts. (p. 353)*

Balance column account Account with debit and credit columns for recording entries and another column for showing the balance of the account after each entry. *(p. 56)*

Balance sheet Financial statement that lists types and dollar amounts of assets, liabilities, and equity at a specific date. *(p. 17)*

Balance sheet equation (See *accounting equation.*) *(p. 12)*

Bank reconciliation Report that explains the difference between the book (company) balance of cash and the cash balance reported on the bank statement. *(p. 322)*

Bank statement Bank report on the depositor's beginning and ending cash balances, and a listing of its changes, for a period. *(p. 320)*

Basic earnings per share Net income less any preferred dividends and then divided by weighted-average common shares outstanding. *(p. 514)*

Batch processing Accumulating source documents for a period of time and then processing them all at once such as once a day, week, or month. *(p. 277)*

Bearer bonds Bonds made payable to whoever holds them (the *bearer*); also called *unregistered bonds. (p. 550)*

Benchmarking Practice of comparing and analyzing company financial performance or position with other companies or standards. *(p. 676)*

Betterments Expenditures to make a plant asset more efficient or productive; also called *improvements. (p. 393)*

Bond Written promise to pay the bond's par (or face) value and interest at a stated contract rate; often issued in denominations of $1,000. *(p. 548)*

Bond certificate Document containing bond specifics such as issuer's name, bond par value, contract interest rate, and maturity date. *(p. 551)*

Bond indenture Contract between the bond issuer and the bondholders; identifies the parties' rights and obligations. *(p. 551)*

Bookkeeping (See *recordkeeping.*) *(p. 5)*

Book value Asset's acquisition costs less its accumulated depreciation (or depletion, or amortization); also sometimes used synonymously as the *carrying value* of an account. *(p. 387)*

Book value per common share Recorded amount of equity applicable to common shares divided by the number of common shares outstanding. *(p. 518)*

Book value per preferred share Equity applicable to preferred shares (equals its call price [or par value if it is not callable] plus any cumulative dividends in arrears) divided by the number of preferred shares outstanding. *(p. 518)*

Break-even point Output level at which sales equals fixed plus variable costs; where income equals zero. *(p. 878)*

Break-even time (BET) Time-based measurement used to evaluate the acceptability of an investment; equals the time expected to pass before the present value of the net cash flows from an investment equals its initial cost. *(p. 1002)*

Budget Formal statement of future plans, usually expressed in monetary terms. *(p. 904)*

Budget report Report comparing actual results to planned objectives; sometimes used as a progress report. *(p. 942)*

Budgetary control Management use of budgets to monitor and control company operations. *(p. 942)*

Budgeted balance sheet Accounting report that presents predicted amounts of the company's assets, liabilities, and equity balances as of the end of the budget period. *(p. 916)*

Budgeted income statement Accounting report that presents predicted amounts of the company's revenues and expenses for the budget period. *(p. 916)*

Budgeting Process of planning future business actions and expressing them as formal plans. *(p. 904)*

Business An organization of one or more individuals selling products and/or services for profit. *(p. 10)*

Business entity principle Principle that requires a business to be accounted for separately from its owner(s) and from any other entity. *(p. 10)*

Business segment Part of a company that can be separately identified by the products or services that it provides or by the geographic markets that it serves; also called *segment. (p. 512)*

C corporation Corporation that does not qualify for nor elect to be treated as a proprietorship or partnership for income tax purposes and therefore is subject to income taxes; also called *C corp. (p. 470)*

Call price Amount that must be paid to call and retire a callable preferred stock or a callable bond. *(p. 505)*

Callable bonds Bonds that give the issuer the option to retire them at a stated amount prior to maturity. *(p. 550)*

Callable preferred stock Preferred stock that the issuing corporation, at its option, may retire by paying the call price plus any dividends in arrears. *(p. 505)*

Canceled checks Checks that the bank has paid and deducted from the depositor's account. *(p. 321)*

Capital budgeting Process of analyzing alternative investments and deciding which assets to acquire or sell. *(p. 984)*

Capital expenditures Additional costs of plant assets that provide material benefits extending beyond the current period; also called *balance sheet expenditures. (p. 392)*

Capital expenditures budget Plan that lists dollar amounts to be both received from disposal of plant assets and spent to purchase plant assets. *(p. 913)*

Capital leases Long-term leases in which the lessor transfers substantially all risk and rewards of ownership to the lessee. *(p. 573)*

Capital stock General term referring to a corporation's stock used in obtaining capital (owner financing). *(p. 499)*

Capitalize Record the cost as part of a permanent account and allocate it over later periods. *(p. 392)*

Carrying value of bonds Net amount at which bonds are reported on the balance sheet; equals the par value of the bonds less any unamortized discount or plus any unamortized premium; also called *carrying amount* or *book value. (p. 553)*

Cash Includes currency, coins, and amounts on deposit in bank checking or savings accounts. *(p. 312)*

Cash basis accounting Accounting system that recognizes revenues when cash is received and records expenses when cash is paid. *(p. 95)*

Cash budget Plan that shows expected cash inflows and outflows during the budget period, including receipts from loans needed to maintain a minimum cash balance and repayments of such loans. *(p. 914)*

Cash disbursements journal Special journal normally used to record all payments of cash; also called *cash payments journal. (p. 274)*

Cash discount Reduction in the price of merchandise granted by a seller to a buyer when payment is made within the discount period. *(p. 181)*

Cash equivalents Short-term, investment assets that are readily convertible to a known cash amount or sufficiently close to their maturity date (usually within 90 days) so that market value is not sensitive to interest rate changes. *(p. 312)*

Cash flow on total assets Ratio of operating cash flows to average total assets; not sensitive to income recognition and measurement; partly reflects earnings quality. *(p. 644)*

Cash Over and Short Income statement account used to record cash overages and cash shortages arising from errors in cash receipts or payments. *(p. 313)*

Cash receipts journal Special journal normally used to record all receipts of cash. *(p. 271)*

Change in an accounting estimate Change in an accounting estimate that results from new information, subsequent developments, or improved judgment that impacts current and future periods. *(p. 391 & 517)*

Chart of accounts List of accounts used by a company; includes an identification number for each account. *(p. 52)*

Check Document signed by a depositor instructing the bank to pay a specified amount to a designated recipient. *(p. 319)*

Check register Another name for a cash disbursements journal when the journal has a column for check numbers. *(p. 275 & 330)*

Classified balance sheet Balance sheet that presents assets and liabilities in relevant subgroups, including current and noncurrent classifications. *(p. 146)*

Clock card Source document used to record the number of hours an employee works and to determine the total labor cost for each pay period. *(p. 759)*

Closing entries Entries recorded at the end of each accounting period to transfer end-of-period balances in revenue, gain, expense, loss, and withdrawal (dividend for a corporation) accounts to the capital account (to retained earnings for a corporation). *(p. 141)*

Closing process Necessary end-of-period steps to prepare the accounts for recording the transactions of the next period. *(p. 140)*

Columnar journal Journal with more than one column. *(p. 268)*

Common stock Corporation's basic ownership share; also generically called *capital stock. (p. 11 & 498)*

Common-size financial statement Statement that expresses each amount as a percent of a base amount. In the balance sheet, total assets is usually the base and is expressed as 100%. In the income statement, net sales is usually the base. *(p. 681)*

Comparative financial statement Statement with data for two or more successive periods placed in side-by-side columns, often with changes shown in dollar amounts and percents. *(p. 677)*

Compatibility principle Information system principle that requires an accounting system to conform with a company's activities, personnel, and structure. *(p. 263)*

Complex capital structure Capital structure that includes outstanding rights or options to purchase common stock, or securities that are convertible into common stock. *(p. 516)*

Composite unit Generic unit consisting of a specific number of units of each product; unit comprised in proportion to the expected sales mix of its products. *(p. 884)*

Compound journal entry Journal entry that affects at least three accounts. *(p. 59)*

Comprehensive income Net change in equity for a period, excluding owner investments and distributions. *(p. 600)*

Computer hardware Physical equipment in a computerized accounting information system. *(p. 277)*

Computer network Linkage giving different users and different computers access to common databases and programs. *(p. 277)*

Computer software Programs that direct operations of computer hardware. *(p. 276)*

Conservatism principle Principle that prescribes the less optimistic estimate when two estimates are about equally likely. *(p. 232)*

Consignee Receiver of goods owned by another who holds them for purposes of selling them for the owner. *(p. 222)*

Consignor Owner of goods who ships them to another party who will sell them for the owner. *(p. 222)*

Consistency principle Principle that prescribes use of the same accounting method(s) over time so that financial statements are comparable across periods. *(p. 230)*

Consolidated financial statements Financial statements that show all (combined) activities under the parent's control, including those of any subsidiaries. *(p. 599)*

Contingent liability Obligation to make a future payment if, and only if, an uncertain future event occurs. *(p. 436)*

Continuous budgeting Practice of preparing budgets for a selected number of future periods and revising those budgets as each period is completed. *(p. 906)*

Continuous improvement Concept requiring every manager and employee continually to look to improve operations. *(p. 718)*

Contra account Account linked with another account and having an opposite normal balance; reported as a subtraction from the other account's balance. *(p. 99)*

Contract rate Interest rate specified in a bond indenture (or note); multiplied by the par value to determine the interest paid each period; also called *coupon rate, stated rate,* or *nominal rate. (p. 552)*

Contributed capital Total amount of cash and other assets received from stockholders in exchange for stock; also called *paid-in capital. (p. 500)*

Contributed capital in excess of par value Difference between the par value of stock and its issue price when issued at a price above par. *(p. 500)*

Contribution margin Sales revenue less total variable costs. *(p. 729)*

Contribution margin income statement Income statement that separates variable and fixed costs; highlights the contribution margin, which is sales less variable expenses. *(p. 878)*

Contribution margin per unit Amount that the sale of one unit contributes toward recovering fixed costs and earning profit; defined as sales price per unit minus variable expense per unit. *(p. 878)*

Contribution margin ratio Product's contribution margin divided by its sale price. *(p. 729 & 878)*

Control Process of monitoring planning decisions and evaluating the organization's activities and employees. *(p. 715)*

Control principle Information system principle that requires an accounting system to aid managers in controlling and monitoring business activities. *(p. 262)*

Controllable costs Costs that a manager has the power to control or at least strongly influence. *(p. 720 & 845)*

Controllable variance Combination of both overhead spending variances (variable and fixed) and the variable overhead efficiency variance. *(p. 955)*

Controlling account General ledger account, the balance of which (after posting) equals the sum of the balances in its related subsidiary ledger. *(p. 267)*

Conversion costs Expenditures incurred in converting raw materials to finished goods; includes direct labor costs and overhead costs. *(p. 725)*

Convertible bonds Bonds that bondholders can exchange for a set number of the issuer's shares. *(p. 550)*

Convertible preferred stock Preferred stock with an option to exchange it for common stock at a specified rate. *(p. 505)*

Copyright Right giving the owner the exclusive privilege to publish and sell musical, literary, or artistic work during the creator's life plus 70 years. *(p. 399)*

Corporation Business that is a separate legal entity under state or federal laws with owners called *shareholders* or *stockholders. (p. 11 & 496)*

Cost All normal and reasonable expenditures necessary to get an asset in place and ready for its intended use. *(p. 383)*

Cost accounting system Accounting system for manufacturing activities based on the perpetual inventory system. *(p. 754)*

Cost-benefit principle Information system principle that requires the benefits from an activity in an accounting system to outweigh the costs of that activity. *(p. 263)*

Cost center Department that incurs costs but generates no revenues; common example is the accounting or legal department. *(p. 838)*

Cost driver Variable that causes an activity's cost to go up or down; a causal factor. *(p. 834)*

Cost object Product, process, department, or customer to which costs are assigned. *(p. 719)*

Cost of goods available for sale Consists of beginning inventory plus net purchases of a period. *(p. 179)*

Cost of goods sold Cost of inventory sold to customers during a period; also called *cost of sales. (p. 179)*

Cost principle Accounting principle that prescribes financial statement information to be based on actual costs incurred in business transactions. *(p. 9)*

Cost variance Difference between the actual incurred cost and the standard cost. *(p. 949)*

Cost-volume-profit (CVP) analysis Planning method that includes predicting the volume of activity, the costs incurred, sales earned, and profits received. *(p. 872)*

Coupon bonds Bonds with interest coupons attached to their certificates; bondholders detach coupons when they mature and present them to a bank or broker for collection. *(p. 550)*

Credit Recorded on the right side; an entry that decreases asset and expense accounts, and increases liability, revenue, and most equity accounts; abbreviated Cr. *(p. 53)*

Credit memorandum Notification that the sender has credited the recipient's account in the sender's records. *(p. 187)*

Credit period Time period that can pass before a customer's payment is due. *(p. 181)*

Credit terms Description of the amounts and timing of payments that a buyer (debtor) agrees to make in the future. *(p. 181)*

Creditors Individuals or organizations entitled to receive payments. *(p. 50)*

Cumulative preferred stock Preferred stock on which undeclared dividends accumulate until paid; common stockholders cannot receive dividends until cumulative dividends are paid. *(p. 503)*

Current assets Cash and other assets expected to be sold, collected, or used within one year or the company's operating cycle, whichever is longer. *(p. 146)*

Current liabilities Obligations due to be paid or settled within one year or the company's operating cycle, whichever is longer. *(p. 148 & 425)*

Current portion of long-term debt Portion of long-term debt due within one year or the operating cycle, whichever is longer; reported under current liabilities. *(p. 433)*

Current ratio Ratio used to evaluate a company's ability to pay its short-term obligations, calculated by dividing current assets by current liabilities. *(p. 148)*

Curvilinear cost Cost that changes with volume but not at a constant rate. *(p. 874)*

Customer orientation Company position that its managers and employees be in tune with the changing wants and needs of consumers. *(p. 717)*

CVP chart Graphic representation of cost-volume-profit relations. *(p. 879)*

Date of declaration Date the directors vote to pay a dividend. *(p. 506)*

Date of payment Date the corporation makes the dividend payment. *(p. 506)*

Date of record Date directors specify for identifying stockholders to receive dividends. *(p. 506)*

Days' sales in inventory Estimate of number of days needed to convert inventory into receivables or cash; equals ending inventory divided by cost of goods sold and then multiplied by 365; also called *days' stock on hand. (p. 234)*

Days' sales uncollected Measure of the liquidity of receivables computed by dividing the current balance of receivables by the annual credit (or net) sales and then multiplying by 365; also called *days' sales in receivables. (p. 325)*

Debit Recorded on the left side; an entry that increases asset and expense accounts, and decreases liability, revenue, and most equity accounts; abbreviated Dr. *(p. 53)*

Debit memorandum Notification that the sender has debited the recipient's account in the sender's records. *(p. 182)*

Debt ratio Ratio of total liabilities to total assets; used to reflect risk associated with a company's debts. *(p. 67)*

Debtors Individuals or organizations that owe money. *(p. 49)*

Declining-balance method Method that determines depreciation charge for the period by multiplying a depreciation rate (often twice the straight-line rate) by the asset's beginning-period book value. *(p. 388)*

Deferred income tax liability Corporation income taxes that are deferred until future years because of temporary differences between GAAP and tax rules. *(p. 447)*

Degree of operating leverage (DOL) Ratio of contribution margin divided by pretax income; used to assess the effect on income of changes in sales. *(p. 885)*

Departmental accounting system Accounting system that provides information useful in evaluating the profitability or cost effectiveness of a department. *(p. 837)*

Departmental contribution to overhead Amount by which a department's revenues exceed its direct expenses. *(p. 844)*

Depletion Process of allocating the cost of natural resources to periods when they are consumed and sold. *(p. 397)*

Deposit ticket Lists items such as currency, coins, and checks deposited and their corresponding dollar amounts. *(p. 319)*

Deposits in transit Deposits recorded by the company but not yet recorded by its bank. *(p. 322)*

Depreciable cost Cost of a plant asset less its salvage value. *(p. 386)*

Depreciation Expense created by allocating the cost of plant and equipment to periods in which they are used; represents the expense of using the asset. *(p. 385)*

Diluted earnings per share Earnings per share calculation that requires dilutive securities be added to the denominator of the basic EPS calculation. *(p. 516)*

Dilutive securities Securities having the potential to increase common shares outstanding; examples are options, rights, convertible bonds, and convertible preferred stock. *(p. 516)*

Direct costs Costs incurred for the benefit of one specific cost object. *(p. 719)*

Direct expenses Expenses traced to a specific department (object) that are incurred for the sole benefit of that department. *(p. 839)*

Direct labor Efforts of employees who physically convert materials to finished product. *(p. 725)*

Direct labor costs Wages and salaries for direct labor that are separately and readily traced through the production process to finished goods. *(p. 725)*

Direct material Raw material that physically becomes part of the product and is clearly identified with specific products or batches of product. *(p. 724)*

Direct material costs Expenditures for direct material that are separately and readily traced through the production process to finished goods. *(p. 724)*

Direct method Presentation of net cash from operating activities for the statement of cash flows that lists major operating cash receipts less major operating cash payments. *(p. 632)*

Direct write-off method Method that records the loss from an uncollectible account receivable at the time it is determined to be uncollectible; no attempt is made to estimate bad debts. *(p. 354)*

Discount on bonds payable Difference between a bond's par value and its lower issue price or carrying value; occurs when the contract rate is less than the market rate. *(p. 552)*

Discount on note payable Difference between the face value of a note payable and the (lesser) amount borrowed; reflects the added interest to be paid on the note over its life.

Discount on stock Difference between the par value of stock and its issue price when issued at a price below par value. *(p. 501)*

Discount period Time period in which a cash discount is available and the buyer can make a reduced payment. *(p. 181)*

Discount rate Expected rate of return on investments; also called *cost of capital, hurdle rate,* or *required rate of return. (p. B-2)*

Discounts lost Expenses resulting from not taking advantage of cash discounts on purchases. *(p. 331)*

Dividend in arrears Unpaid dividend on cumulative preferred stock; must be paid before any regular dividends on preferred stock and before any dividends on common stock. *(p. 504)*

Dividend yield Ratio of the annual amount of cash dividends distributed to common shareholders relative to the common stock's market value (price). *(p. 519)*

Dividends Corporation's distributions of assets to its owners. *(p. 506)*

Double-declining-balance (DDB) depreciation Depreciation equals beginning book value multiplied by 2 times the straight-line rate. *(p. 388)*

Double-entry accounting Accounting system in which each transaction affects at least two accounts and has at least one debit and one credit. *(p. 53)*

Double taxation Corporate income is taxed and then its later distribution through dividends is normally taxed again for shareholders. *(p. 11)*

Earnings (See *net income.*) *(p. 13)*

Earnings per share (EPS) Amount of income earned by each share of a company's outstanding common stock; also called *net income per share. (p. 514)*

Effective interest method Allocates interest expense over the bond life to yield a constant rate of interest; interest expense for a period is found by multiplying the balance of the liability at the beginning of the period by the bond market rate at issuance; also called *interest method. (p. 571)*

Efficiency Company's productivity in using its assets; usually measured relative to how much revenue a certain level of assets generates. *(p. 675)*

Efficiency variance Difference between the actual quantity of an input and the standard quantity of that input. *(p. 954)*

Electronic funds transfer (EFT) Use of electronic communication to transfer cash from one party to another. *(p. 320)*

Employee benefits Additional compensation paid to or on behalf of employees, such as premiums for medical, dental, life, and disability insurance, and contributions to pension plans. *(p. 433)*

Employee earnings report Record of an employee's net pay, gross pay, deductions, and year-to-date payroll information. *(p. 444)*

Enterprise resource planning (ERP) software Programs that manage a company's vital operations, which range from order taking to production to accounting. *(p. 277)*

Entity Organization that, for accounting purposes, is separate from other organizations and individuals. *(p. 10)*

EOM Abbreviation for *end of month;* used to describe credit terms for credit transactions. *(p. 181)*

Equity Owner's claim on the assets of a business; equals the residual interest in an entity's assets after deducting liabilities; also called *net assets. (p. 12)*

Equity method Accounting method used for long-term investments when the investor has "significant influence" over the investee. *(p. 598)*

Equity ratio Portion of total assets provided by equity, computed as total equity divided by total assets. *(p. 689)*

Equity securities with controlling influence Long-term investment when the investor is able to exert controlling influence over the investee; investors owning 50% or more of voting stock are presumed to exert controlling influence. *(p. 599)*

Equity securities with significant influence Long-term investment when the investor is able to exert significant influence over the investee; investors owning 20 percent or more (but less than 50 percent) of voting stock are presumed to exert significant influence. *(p. 597)*

Equivalent units of production (EUP) Number of units that would be completed if all effort during a period had been applied to units that were started and finished. *(p. 798)*

Estimated liability Obligation of an uncertain amount that can be reasonably estimated. *(p. 433)*

Estimated line of cost behavior Line drawn on a graph to visually fit the relation between cost and sales. *(p. 876)*

Ethics Codes of conduct by which actions are judged as right or wrong, fair or unfair, honest or dishonest. *(p. 8)*

Events Happenings that both affect an organization's financial position and can be reliably measured. *(p. 13)*

Expanded accounting equation Assets = Liabilities + Equity; Equity equals [Owner capital − Owner withdrawals + Revenues − Expenses] for a noncorporation; Equity equals [Contributed capital + Retained earnings + Revenues − Expenses] for a corporation where dividends are subtracted from retained earnings. *(p. 13)*

Expenses Outflows or using up of assets as part of operations of a business to generate sales. *(p. 13)*

External transactions Exchanges of economic value between one entity and another entity. *(p. 13)*

External users Persons using accounting information who are not directly involved in running the organization. *(p. 5)*

Extraordinary gains or losses Gains or losses reported separately from continuing operations because they are both unusual and infrequent. *(p. 512)*

Extraordinary repairs Major repairs that extend the useful life of a plant asset beyond prior expectations; treated as a capital expenditure. *(p. 393)*

Factory overhead Factory activities supporting the production process that are not direct material or direct labor; also called *overhead* and *manufacturing overhead. (p. 725)*

Factory overhead costs Expenditures for factory overhead that cannot be separately or readily traced to finished goods; also called *overhead costs. (p. 725)*

Favorable variance Difference in actual revenues or expenses from the budgeted amount that contributes to a higher income. *(p. 944)*

Federal depository bank Bank authorized to accept deposits of amounts payable to the federal government. *(p. 442)*

Federal Insurance Contributions Act (FICA) Taxes Taxes assessed on both employers and employees; for Social Security and Medicare programs. *(p. 430)*

Federal Unemployment Taxes (FUTA) Payroll taxes on employers assessed by the federal government to support its unemployment insurance program. *(p. 432)*

Financial accounting Area of accounting mainly aimed at serving external users. *(p. 5)*

Financial Accounting Standards Board (FASB) Independent group of full-time members responsible for setting accounting rules. *(p. 9)*

Financial leverage Earning a higher return on equity by paying dividends on preferred stock or interest on debt at a rate lower than the return earned with the assets from issuing preferred stock or debt; also called *trading on the equity. (p. 505)*

Financial reporting Process of communicating information relevant to investors, creditors, and others in making investment, credit, and business decisions. *(p. 675)*

Financial statement analysis Application of analytical tools to general-purpose financial statements and related data for making business decisions. *(p. 674)*

Financial statements Includes the balance sheet, income statement, statement of owner's (or stockholder's) equity, and statement of cash flows. *(p. 17)*

Financing activities Transactions with owners and creditors that include obtaining cash from issuing long-term debt, repaying amounts borrowed, and obtaining cash from or distributing cash to owners. *(p. 628)*

Finished goods inventory Account that controls the finished goods files, which acts as a subsidiary ledger (of the Inventory account) in which the costs of finished goods that are ready for sale are recorded. *(p. 723 & 757)*

First-in, first-out (FIFO) Method to assign cost to inventory that assumes items are sold in the order acquired; earliest items purchased are the first sold. *(p. 227)*

Fiscal year Consecutive 12-month (or 52-week) period chosen as the organization's annual accounting period. *(p. 95)*

Fixed budget Planning budget based on a single predicted amount of volume; unsuitable for evaluations if the actual volume differs from predicted volume. *(p. 943)*

Fixed budget performance report Report that compares actual revenues and costs with fixed budgeted amounts and identifies the differences as favorable or unfavorable variances. *(p. 943)*

Fixed cost Cost that does not change with changes in the volume of activity. *(p. 719)*

Flexibility principle Information system principle that requires an accounting system be able to adapt to changes in the company, its operations, and needs of decision makers. *(p. 263)*

Flexible budget Budget prepared (using actual volume) once a period is complete that helps managers evaluate past performance; uses fixed and variable costs in determining total costs. *(p. 944)*

Flexible budget performance report Report that compares actual revenues and costs with their variable budgeted amounts based on actual sales volume (or other level of activity) and identifies the differences as variances. *(p. 946)*

FOB Abbreviation for *free on board;* the point when ownership of goods passes to the buyer; *FOB shipping point* (or *factory*) means the buyer pays shipping costs and accepts ownership of goods when the seller transfers goods to carrier; *FOB destination* means the seller pays shipping costs and buyer accepts ownership of goods at the buyer's place of business. *(p. 183)*

Foreign exchange rate Price of one currency stated in terms of another currency. *(p. 605)*

Form 940 IRS form used to report an employer's federal unemployment taxes (FUTA) on an annual filing basis. *(p. 442)*

Form 941 IRS form filed to report FICA taxes owed and remitted. *(p. 440)*

Form 10-K (or 10-KSB) Annual report form filed with SEC by businesses (small businesses) with publicly-traded securities. *(p. A-1)*

Form W-2 Annual report by an employer to each employee showing the employee's wages subject to FICA and federal income taxes along with amounts withheld. *(p. 442)*

Form W-4 Withholding allowance certificate, filed with the employer, identifying the number of withholding allowances claimed. *(p. 444)*

Franchises Privileges granted by a company or government to sell a product or service under specified conditions. *(p. 400)*

Full-disclosure principle Principle that prescribes financial statements (including notes) to report all relevant information about an entity's operations and financial condition. *(p. 362)*

GAPP (See *generally accepted accounting principles.*) *(p. 9)*

General accounting system Accounting system for manufacturing activities based on the *periodic* inventory system. *(p. 754)*

General and administrative expenses Expenses that support the operating activities of a business. *(p. 191)*

General and administrative expense budget Plan that shows predicted operating expenses not included in the selling expenses budget. *(p. 912)*

General journal All-purpose journal for recording the debits and credits of transactions and events. *(p. 55 & 266)*

General ledger (See *ledger.*) *(p. 49)*

General partner Partner who assumes unlimited liability for the debts of the partnership; responsible for partnership management. *(p. 469)*

General partnership Partnership in which all partners have mutual agency and unlimited liability for partnership debts. *(p. 469)*

Generally accepted accounting principles (GAAP) Rules that specify acceptable accounting practices. *(p. 9)*

Generally accepted auditing standards (GAAS) Rules that specify acceptable auditing practices. *(p. 5 & 9)*

General-purpose financial statements Statements published periodically for use by a variety of interested parties; includes the income statement, balance sheet, statement of owner's equity (or statement of retained earnings for a corporation), statement of cash flows, and notes to these statements. *(p. 675)*

Going-concern principle Principle that requires financial statements to reflect the assumption that the business will continue operating. *(p. 10)*

Goods in process inventory Account in which costs are accumulated for products that are in the process of being produced but are not yet complete; also called *work in process inventory. (p. 723 & 756)*

Goodwill Amount by which a company's (or a segment's) value exceeds the value of its individual assets less its liabilities. *(p. 400)*

Gross margin (See *gross profit.*) *(p. 179)*

Gross margin ratio Gross margin (net sales minus cost of goods sold) divided by net sales; also called *gross profit ratio. (p. 193)*

Gross method Method of recording purchases at the full invoice price without deducting any cash discounts. *(p. 331)*

Gross pay Total compensation earned by an employee. *(p. 429)*

Gross profit Net sales minus cost of goods sold; also called *gross margin. (p. 179)*

Gross profit method Procedure to estimate inventory when the past gross profit rate is used to estimate cost of goods sold, which is then subtracted from the cost of goods available for sale. *(p. 244)*

Held-to-maturity (HTM) securities Debt securities that a company has the intent and ability to hold until they mature. *(p. 596)*

High-low method Procedure that yields an estimated line of cost behavior by graphically connecting costs associated with the highest and lowest sales volume. *(p. 876)*

Horizontal analysis Comparison of a company's financial condition and performance across time. *(p. 676)*

Hurdle rate Minimum acceptable rate of return (set by management) for an investment. *(p. 992)*

Impairment Diminishment of an asset value. *(p. 399)*

Imprest system Method to account for petty cash; maintains a constant balance in the fund, which equals cash plus petty cash receipts. *(p. 316)*

Inadequacy Condition in which the capacity of plant assets is too small to meet the company's production demands. *(p. 385)*

Income (See *net income.*) *(p. 13)*

Income statement Financial statement that subtracts expenses from revenues to yield a net income or loss over a specified period of time; also includes any gains or losses. *(p. 17)*

Income Summary Temporary account used only in the closing process to which the balances of revenue and expense accounts (including any gains or losses) are transferred; its balance is transferred to the capital account (or retained earnings for a corporation). *(p. 141)*

Incremental cost Additional cost incurred only if a company pursues a specific course of action. *(p. 996)*

Indefinite useful life Asset life that is not limited by legal, regulatory, contractural, competitive, economic, or other factors. *(p. 398)*

Indirect costs Costs incurred for the benefit of more than one cost object. *(p. 719)*

Indirect expenses Expenses incurred for the joint benefit of more than one department (or cost object). *(p. 839)*

Indirect labor Efforts of production employees who do not work specifically on converting direct materials into finished products and who are not clearly identified with specific units or batches of product. *(p. 725)*

Indirect material Material used to support the production process but not clearly identified with products or batches of product. *(p. 722)*

Indirect method Presentation that reports net income and then adjusts it by adding and subtracting items to yield net cash from operating activities on the statement of cash flows. *(p. 632)*

Information processor Component of an accounting system that interprets, transforms, and summarizes information for use in analysis and reporting. *(p. 264)*

Information storage Component of an accounting system that keeps data in a form accessible to information processors. *(p. 264)*

Infrequent gain or loss Gain or loss not expected to recur given the operating environment of the business. *(p. 512)*

Input device Means of capturing information from source documents that enables its transfer to information processors. *(p. 264)*

Installment note Liability requiring a series of periodic payments to the lender. *(p. 561)*

Intangible assets Long-term assets (resources) used to produce or sell products or services; usually lack physical form and have uncertain benefits. *(p. 148 & 398)*

Interest Charge for using money (or other assets) loaned from one entity to another. *(p. 360)*

Interim financial statements Financial statements covering periods of less than one year; usually based on one-, three-, or six-month periods. *(p. 95 & 243)*

Internal control system All policies and procedures used to protect assets, ensure reliable accounting, promote efficient operations, and urge adherence to company policies. *(p. 262 & 308)*

Internal rate of return (IRR) Rate used to evaluate the acceptability of an investment; equals the rate that yields a net present value of zero for an investment. *(p. 991)*

Internal transactions Activities within an organization that can affect the accounting equation. *(p. 13)*

Internal users Persons using accounting information who are directly involved in managing the organization. *(p. 6)*

International Accounting Standards Board (IASB) Group that identifies preferred accounting practices and encourages global acceptance; issues International Financial Reporting Standards (IFRS). *(p. 9)*

Inventory Goods a company owns and expects to sell in its normal operations. *(p. 179)*

Inventory turnover Number of times a company's average inventory is sold during a period; computed by dividing cost of goods sold by average inventory; also called *merchandise turnover*. *(p. 233)*

Investing activities Transactions that involve purchasing and selling of long-term assets, includes making and collecting notes receivable and investments in other than cash equivalents. *(p. 628)*

Investment center Center of which a manager is responsible for revenues, costs, and asset investments. *(p. 849)*

Investment center return on total assets Center net income divided by average total assets for the center. *(p. 849)*

Invoice Itemized record of goods prepared by the vendor that lists the customer's name, items sold, sales prices, and terms of sale. *(p. 328)*

Invoice approval Document containing a checklist of steps necessary for approving the recording and payment of an invoice; also called *check authorization*. *(p. 329)*

Job Production of a customized product or service. *(p. 754)*

Job cost sheet Separate record maintained for each job. *(p. 756)*

Job lot Production of more than one unit of a customized product or service. *(p. 755)*

Job order cost accounting system Cost accounting system to determine the cost of producing each job or job lot. *(p. 756 & 793)*

Job order manufacturing Production of special-order products; also called *customized production*. *(p. 754)*

Joint cost Cost incurred to produce or purchase two or more products at the same time. *(p. 848)*

Journal Record in which transactions are entered before they are posted to ledger accounts; also called *book of original entry*. *(p. 55)*

Journalizing Process of recording transactions in a journal. *(p. 55)*

Just-in-time (JIT) manufacturing Process of acquiring or producing inventory only when needed. *(p. 718)*

Known liabilities Obligations of a company with little uncertainty; set by agreements, contracts, or laws; also called *definitely determinable liabilities*. *(p. 426)*

Land improvements Assets that increase the benefits of land, have a limited useful life, and are depreciated. *(p. 384)*

Large stock dividend Stock dividend that is more than 25% of the previously outstanding shares. *(p. 507)*

Last-in, first-out (LIFO) Method to assign cost to inventory that assumes costs for the most recent items purchased are sold first and charged to cost of goods sold. *(p. 227)*

Lean business model Practice of eliminating waste while meeting customer needs and yielding positive company returns. *(p. 718)*

Lease Contract specifying the rental of property. *(p. 400 & 573)*

Leasehold Rights the lessor grants to the lessee under the terms of a lease. *(p. 400)*

Leasehold improvements Alterations or improvements to leased property such as partitions and storefronts. *(p. 400)*

Least-squares regression Statistical method for deriving an estimated line of cost behavior that is more precise than the high-low method and the scatter diagram. *(p. 877)*

Ledger Record containing all accounts (with amounts) for a business; also called *general ledger*. *(p. 49)*

Lessee Party to a lease who secures the right to possess and use the property from another party (the lessor). *(p. 400)*

Lessor Party to a lease who grants another party (the lessee) the right to possess and use its property. *(p. 400)*

Liabilities Creditors' claims on an organization's assets; involves a probable future payment of assets, products, or services that a company is obligated to make due to past transactions or events. *(p. 12)*

Licenses (See *franchises*.) *(p. 400)*

Limited liability Owner can lose no more than the amount invested. *(p. 11)*

Limited liability company Organization form that combines select features of a corporation and a limited partnership; provides limited liability to its members (owners), is free of business tax, and allows members to actively participate in management. *(p. 470)*

Limited liability partnership Partnership in which a partner is not personally liable for malpractice or negligence unless that partner is responsible for providing the service that resulted in the claim. *(p. 469)*

Limited partners Partners who have no personal liability for partnership debts beyond the amounts they invested in the partnership. *(p. 469)*

Limited partnership Partnership that has two classes of partners, limited partners and general partners. *(p. 469)*

Liquid assets Resources such as cash that are easily converted into other assets or used to pay for goods, services, or liabilities. *(p. 312)*

Liquidating cash dividend Distribution of assets that returns part of the original investment to stockholders; deducted from contributed capital accounts. *(p. 507)*

Liquidation Process of going out of business; involves selling assets, paying liabilities, and distributing remainder to owners. *(p. 477 & 1001)*

Liquidity Availability of resources to meet short-term cash requirements. *(p. 312 & 675)*

List price Catalog (full) price of an item before any trade discount is deducted. *(p. 180)*

Long-term investments Long-term assets not used in operating activities such as notes receivable and investments in stocks and bonds. *(p. 147 & 592)*

Long-term liabilities Obligations not due to be paid within one year or the operating cycle, whichever is longer. *(p. 148 & 425)*

Lower of cost or market (LCM) Required method to report inventory at market replacement cost when that market cost is lower than recorded cost. *(p. 231)*

Maker of the note Entity who signs a note and promises to pay it at maturity. *(p. 360)*

Management by exception Management process to focus on significant variances and give less attention to areas where performance is close to the standard. *(p. 958)*

Managerial accounting Area of accounting mainly aimed at serving the decision-making needs of internal users; also called *management accounting*. *(p. 6 & 714)*

Manufacturer Company that uses labor and operating assets to convert raw materials to finished goods. *(p. 13)*

Manufacturing budget Plan that shows the predicted costs for direct materials, direct labor, and overhead to be incurred in manufacturing units in the production budget. *(p. 923)*

Manufacturing statement Report that summarizes the types and amounts of costs incurred in a company's production process for a period; also called *cost of goods manufacturing statement*. *(p. 727)*

Margin of safety Excess of expected sales over the level of break-even sales. *(p. 882)*

Market prospects Expectations (both good and bad) about a company's future performance as assessed by users and other interested parties. *(p. 675)*

Market rate Interest rate that borrowers are willing to pay and lenders are willing to accept for a specific lending agreement given the borrowers' risk level. *(p. 552)*

Market value per share Price at which stock is bought or sold. *(p. 499)*

Master budget Comprehensive business plan that includes specific plans for expected sales, product units to be produced, merchandise (or materials) to be purchased, expenses to be incurred, plant assets to be purchased, and amounts of cash to be borrowed or loans to be repaid, as well as a budgeted income statement and balance sheet. *(p. 908)*

Matching principle Prescribes expenses to be reported in the same period as the revenues that were earned as a result of the expenses. *(p. 96 & 354)*

Materiality Prescribes that accounting for items that significantly impact financial statement and any inferences from them adhere strictly to GAAP. *(p. 354)*

Materials consumption report Document that summarizes the materials a department uses during a reporting period; replaces materials requisitions. *(p. 795)*

Materials ledger card Perpetual record updated each time units are purchased or issued for production use. *(p. 758)*

Materials requisition Source document production managers use to request materials for production; used to assign materials costs to specific jobs or overhead. *(p. 758)*

Maturity date of a note Date when a note's principal and interest are due. *(p. 360)*

Merchandise (See *merchandise inventory*.) *(p. 178)*

Merchandise inventory Goods that a company owns and expects to sell to customers; also called *merchandise* or *inventory*. *(p. 179)*

Merchandise purchases budget Plan that shows the units or costs of merchandise to be purchased by a merchandising company during the budget period. *(p. 911)*

Merchandiser Entity that earns net income by buying and selling merchandise. *(p. 178)*

Merit rating Rating assigned to an employer by a state based on the employer's record of employment. *(p. 432)*

Minimum legal capital Amount of assets defined by law that stockholders must (potentially) invest in a corporation; usually defined as par value of the stock; intended to protect creditors. *(p. 499)*

Mixed cost Cost that behaves like a combination of fixed and variable costs. *(p. 873)*

Modified Accelerated Cost Recovery System (MACRS) Depreciation system required by federal income tax law. *(p. 390)*

Monetary unit principle Principle that assumes transactions and events can be expressed in money units. *(p. 10)*

Mortgage Legal loan agreement that protects a lender by giving the lender the right to be paid from the cash proceeds from the sale of a borrower's assets identified in the mortgage. *(p. 564)*

Multinational Company that operates in several countries. *(p. 605)*

Multiple-step income statement Income statement format that shows subtotals between sales and net income, categorizes expenses, and often reports the details of net sales and expenses. *(p. 190)*

Mutual agency Legal relationship among partners whereby each partner is an agent of the partnership and is able to bind the partnership to contracts within the scope of the partnership's business. *(p. 469)*

Natural business year Twelve-month period that ends when a company's sales activities are at their lowest point. *(p. 95)*

Natural resources Assets physically consumed when used; examples are timber, mineral deposits, and oil and gas fields; also called *wasting assets*. *(p. 397)*

Net assets (See *equity*.) *(p. 12)*

Net income Amount earned after subtracting all expenses necessary for and matched with sales for a period; also called *income, profit,* or *earnings*. *(p. 13)*

Net loss Excess of expenses over revenues for a period. *(p. 13)*

Net method Method of recording purchases at the full invoice price less any cash discounts. *(p. 331)*

Net pay Gross pay less all deductions; also called *take-home pay*. *(p. 430)*

Net present value (NPV) Dollar estimate of an asset's value that is used to evaluate the acceptability of an investment; computed by discounting future cash flows from the investment at a satisfactory rate and then subtracting the initial cost of the investment. *(p. 989)*

Net realizable value Expected selling price (value) of an item minus the cost of making the sale. *(p. 223)*

Noncontrollable costs Costs that a manager does not have the power to control or strongly influence. *(p. 720)*

Noncumulative preferred stock Preferred stock on which the right to receive dividends is lost for any period when dividends are not declared. *(p. 504)*

Noninterest-bearing note Note with no stated (contract) rate of interest; interest is implicitly included in the note's face value.

Nonparticipating preferred stock Preferred stock on which dividends are limited to a maximum amount each year. *(p. 504)*

No-par value stock Stock class that has not been assigned a par (or stated) value by the corporate charter. *(p. 500)*

Nonsufficient funds (NSF) check Maker's bank account has insufficient money to pay the check; also called *hot check*. *(p. 322)*

Note (See promissory note.) *(p. 359)*

Note payable Liability expressed by a written promise to pay a definite sum of money on demand or on a specific future date(s). *(p. 360)*

Note receivable Asset consisting of a written promise to receive a definite sum of money on demand or on a specific future date(s). *(p. 49)*

Objectivity principle Principle that prescribes independent, unbiased evidence to support financial statement information. *(p. 9)*

Obsolescence Condition in which, because of new inventions and improvements, a plant asset can no longer be used to produce goods or services with a competitive advantage. *(p. 385)*

Off-balance-sheet financing Acquisition of assets by agreeing to liabilities not reported on the balance sheet. *(p. 574)*

Online processing Approach to inputting data from source documents as soon as the information is available. *(p. 277)*

Operating activities Activities that involve the production or purchase of merchandise and the sale of goods or services to customers, including expenditures related to administering the business. *(p. 627)*

Operating cycle Normal time between paying cash for merchandise or employee services and receiving cash from customers. *(p. 146)*

Operating leases Short-term (or cancelable) leases in which the lessor retains risks and rewards of ownership. *(p. 573)*

Operating leverage Extent, or relative size, of fixed costs in the total cost structure. *(p. 885)*

Opportunity cost Potential benefit lost by choosing a specific action from two or more alternatives. *(p. 720)*

Ordinary repairs Repairs to keep a plant asset in normal, good operating condition; treated as a revenue expenditure and immediately expensed. *(p. 393)*

Organization expenses (costs) Costs such as legal fees and promoter fees to bring an entity into existence. *(p. 502)*

Out-of-pocket cost Cost incurred or avoided as a result of management's decisions. *(p. 720)*

Output devices Means by which information is taken out of the accounting system and made available for use. *(p. 265)*

Outsourcing Manager decision to buy a product or service from another entity; part of a *make-or-buy* decision; also called *make or buy*. *(p. 997)*

Outstanding checks Checks written and recorded by the depositor but not yet paid by the bank at the bank statement date. *(p. 322)*

Outstanding stock Corporation's stock held by its shareholders. *(p. 509)*

Overapplied overhead Amount by which the overhead applied to production in a period using the predetermined overhead rate exceeds the actual overhead incurred in a period. *(p. 766)*

Overhead cost variance Difference between the total overhead cost applied to products and the total overhead cost actually incurred. *(p. 954)*

Owner, capital Account showing the owner's claim on company assets; equals owner investments plus net income (or less net losses) minus owner withdrawals since the company's inception; also referred to as *equity*. *(p. 51)*

Owner investment Assets put into the business by the owner. *(p. 13)*

Owner's equity (See *equity*.) *(p. 12)*

Owner withdrawals (See *withdrawals*.) *(p. 13)*

Paid-in capital (See *contributed capital*.) *(p. 500)*

Par value Value assigned a share of stock by the corporate charter when the stock is authorized. *(p. 499)*

Par value of a bond Amount the bond issuer agrees to pay at maturity and the amount on which cash interest payments are based; also called *face amount* or *face value* of a bond. *(p. 548)*

Par value stock Class of stock assigned a par value by the corporate charter. *(p. 499)*

Parent Company that owns a controlling interest in a corporation (requires more than 50% of voting stock). *(p. 599)*

Participating preferred stock Preferred stock that shares with common stockholders any dividends paid in excess of the percent stated on preferred stock. *(p. 504)*

Partner return on equity Partner net income divided by average partner equity for the period. *(p. 480)*

Partnership Unincorporated association of two or more persons to pursue a business for profit as co-owners. *(p. 10 & 468)*

Partnership contract Agreement among partners that sets terms under which the affairs of the partnership are conducted; also called *articles of partnership*. *(p. 468)*

Partnership liquidation Dissolution of a partnership by (1) selling noncash assets and allocating any gain or loss according to partners' income-and-loss ratio, (2) paying liabilities, and (3) distributing any remaining cash according to partners' capital balances. *(p. 478)*

Patent Exclusive right granted to its owner to produce and sell an item or to use a process for 17 years. *(p. 399)*

Payback period (PBP) Time-based measurement used to evaluate the acceptability of an investment; equals the time expected to pass before an investment's net cash flows equal its initial cost. *(p. 985)*

Payee of the note Entity to whom a note is made payable. *(p. 360)*

Payroll bank account Bank account used solely for paying employees; each pay period an amount equal to the total employees' net pay is deposited in it and the payroll checks are drawn on it. *(p. 446)*

Payroll deductions Amounts withheld from an employee's gross pay; also called *withholdings*. *(p. 430)*

Payroll register Record for a pay period that shows the pay period dates, regular and overtime hours worked, gross pay, net pay, and deductions. *(p. 442)*

Pension plan Contractual agreement between an employer and its employees for the employer to provide benefits to employees after they retire; expensed when incurred. *(p. 575)*

Period costs Expenditures identified more with a time period than with finished products costs; includes selling and general administrative expenses. *(p. 720)*

Periodic inventory system Method that records the cost of inventory purchased but does not continuously track the quantity available or sold to customers; records are updated at the end of each period to reflect the physical count and costs of goods available. *(p. 180)*

Permanent accounts Accounts that reflect activities related to one or more future periods; balance sheet accounts whose balances are not closed; also called *real accounts*. *(p. 141)*

Perpetual inventory system Method that maintains continuous records of the cost of inventory available and the cost of goods sold. *(p. 179)*

Petty cash Small amount of cash in a fund to pay minor expenses; accounted for using an imprest system. *(p. 316)*

Planning Process of setting goals and preparing to achieve them. *(p. 714)*

Plant assets Tangible long-lived assets used to produce or sell products and services; also called *property, plant and equipment (PP&E)* or *fixed assets*. *(p. 99 & 382)*

Pledged assets to secured liabilities Ratio of the book value of a company's pledged assets to the book value of its secured liabilities. *(p. 565)*

Post-closing trial balance List of permanent accounts and their balances from the ledger after all closing entries are journalized and posted. *(p. 143)*

Posting Process of transferring journal entry information to the ledger; computerized systems automate this process. *(p. 55)*

Posting reference (PR) column A column in journals in which individual ledger account numbers are entered when entries are posted to those ledger accounts. *(p. 56)*

Predetermined overhead rate Rate established prior to the beginning of a period that relates estimated overhead to another variable, such as estimated direct labor, and is used to assign overhead cost to production. *(p. 761)*

Preemptive right Stockholders' right to maintain their proportionate interest in a corporation with any additional shares issued. *(p. 498)*

Preferred stock Stock with a priority status over common stockholders in one or more ways, such as paying dividends or distributing assets. *(p. 503)*

Premium on bonds Difference between a bond's par value and its higher carrying value; occurs when the contract rate is higher than the market rate; also called *bond premium*. *(p. 555)*

Premium on stock (See *contributed capital in excess of par value*.) *(p. 500)*

Prepaid expenses Items paid for in advance of receiving their benefits; classified as assets. *(p. 97)*

Price-earnings (PE) ratio Ratio of a company's current market value per share to its earnings per share; also called *price-to-earnings*. *(p. 519)*

Price variance Difference between actual and budgeted revenue or cost caused by the difference between the actual price per unit and the budgeted price per unit. *(p. 946)*

Prime costs Expenditures directly identified with the production of finished goods; include direct materials costs and direct labor costs. *(p. 725)*

Principal of a note Amount that the signer of a note agrees to pay back when it matures, not including interest. *(p. 360)*

Principles of internal control Principles prescribing management to establish responsibility, maintain records, insure assets, separate recordkeeping from custody of assets, divide responsibility for related transactions, apply technological controls, and perform reviews. *(p. 309)*

Prior period adjustment Correction of an error in a prior year that is reported in the statement of retained earnings (or statement of stockholders' equity) net of any income tax effects. *(p. 517)*

Pro forma financial statements Statements that show the effects of proposed transactions and events as if they had occurred. *(p. 140)*

Process cost accounting system System of assigning direct materials, direct labor, and overhead to specific processes; total costs associated with each process are then divided by the number of units passing through that process to determine the cost per equivalent unit. *(p. 793)*

Process cost summary Report of costs charged to a department, its equivalent units of production achieved, and the costs assigned to its output. *(p. 803)*

Process manufacturing Processing of products in a continuous (sequential) flow of steps; also called *process operations* or *process production. (p. 790)*

Product costs Costs that are capitalized as inventory because they produce benefits expected to have future value; include direct materials, direct labor, and overhead. *(p. 720)*

Production budget Plan that shows the units to be produced each period. *(p. 923)*

Profit (See *net income.*) *(p. 13)*

Profit center Business unit that incurs costs and generates revenues. *(p. 838)*

Profit margin Ratio of a company's net income to its net sales; the percent of income in each dollar of revenue; also called *net profit margin. (p. 108)*

Profitability Company's ability to generate an adequate return on invested capital. *(p. 675)*

Promissory note (or **note**) Written promise to pay a specified amount either on demand or at a definite future date; is a *note receivable* for the lender but a *note payable* for the lendee. *(p. 359)*

Proprietorship (See *sole proprietorship.*) *(p. 10)*

Proxy Legal document giving a stockholder's agent the power to exercise the stockholder's voting rights. *(p. 498)*

Purchase discount Term used by a purchaser to describe a cash discount granted to the purchaser for paying within the discount period. *(p. 181)*

Purchase order Document used by the purchasing department to place an order with a seller (vendor). *(p. 328)*

Purchase requisition Document listing merchandise needed by a department and requesting it be purchased. *(p. 328)*

Purchases journal Journal normally used to record all purchases on credit. *(p. 273)*

Quantity variance Difference between actual and budgeted revenue or cost caused by the difference between the actual number of units and the budgeted number of units. *(p. 946)*

Ratio analysis Determination of key relations between financial statement items as reflected in numerical measures. *(p. 676)*

Raw materials inventory Goods a company acquires to use in making products. *(p. 722)*

Realizable value Expected proceeds from converting an asset into cash. *(p. 355)*

Receiving report Form used to report that ordered goods are received and to describe their quantity and condition. *(p. 329)*

Recordkeeping Part of accounting that involves recording transactions and events, either manually or electronically; also called *bookkeeping. (p. 5)*

Registered bonds Bonds owned by investors whose names and addresses are recorded by the issuer; interest payments are made to the registered owners. *(p. 550)*

Relevance principle Information system principle prescribing that its reports be useful, understandable, timely, and pertinent for decision making. *(p. 262)*

Relevant benefits Additional or incremental revenue generated by selecting a particular course of action over another. *(p. 995)*

Relevant range of operations Company's normal operating range; excludes extremely high and low volumes not likely to occur. *(p. 880)*

Report form balance sheet Balance sheet that lists accounts vertically in the order of assets, liabilities, and equity. *(p. 18)*

Responsibility accounting budget Report of expected costs and expenses under a manager's control. *(p. 846)*

Responsibility accounting performance report Responsibility report that compares actual costs and expenses for a department with budgeted amounts. *(p. 846)*

Responsibility accounting system System that provides information that management can use to evaluate the performance of a department's manager. *(p. 838)*

Restricted retained earnings Retained earnings that are not available for dividends because of legal or contractual limitations. *(p. 517)*

Retail inventory method Method to estimate ending inventory based on the ratio of the amount of goods for sale at cost to the amount of goods for sale at retail. *(p. 243)*

Retailer Intermediary that buys products from manufacturers or wholesalers and sells them to consumers. *(p. 178)*

Retained earnings Cumulative income less cumulative losses and dividends. *(p. 500)*

Retained earnings deficit Debit (abnormal) balance in Retained Earnings; occurs when cumulative losses and dividends exceed cumulative income; also called *accumulated deficit. (p. 507)*

Return Monies received from an investment; often in percent form. *(p. 23)*

Return on assets (See *return on total assets*) *(p. 20)*

Return on total assets Ratio reflecting operating efficiency; defined as net income divided by average total assets for the period; also called *return on assets* or *return on investment. (p. 600)*

Return on equity Ratio of net income to average equity for the period. *(p. 549)*

Revenue expenditures Expenditures reported on the current income statement as an expense because they do not provide benefits in future periods. *(p. 392)*

Revenue recognition principle The principle prescribing that revenue is recognized when earned. *(p. 10)*

Revenues Gross increase in equity from a company's business activities that earn income; also called *sales. (p. 13)*

Reverse stock split Occurs when a corporation calls in its stock and replaces each share with less than one new share; increases both market value per share and any par or stated value per share. *(p. 509)*

Reversing entries Optional entries recorded at the beginning of a period that prepare the accounts for the usual journal entries as if adjusting entries had not occurred in the prior period. *(p. 152)*

Risk Uncertainty about an expected return. *(p. 24)*

Rolling budget New set of budgets a firm adds for the next period (with revisions) to replace the ones that have lapsed. *(p. 906)*

S corporation Corporation that meets special tax qualifications so as to be treated like a partnership for income tax purposes. *(p. 470)*

Safety stock Quantity of inventory or materials over the minimum needed to satisfy budgeted demand. *(p. 911)*

Sales (See *revenues.*) *(p. 13)*

Sales budget Plan showing the units of goods to be sold or services to be provided; the starting point in the budgeting process for most departments. *(p. 910)*

Sales discount Term used by a seller to describe a cash discount granted to buyers who pay within the discount period. *(p. 181)*

Sales journal Journal normally used to record sales of goods on credit. *(p. 267)*

Sales mix Ratio of sales volumes for the various products sold by a company. *(p. 884)*

Salvage value Estimate of amount to be recovered at the end of an asset's useful life; also called *residual value* or *scrap value*. *(p. 385)*

Sarbanes-Oxley Act Created the *Public Company Accounting Oversight Board,* regulates analyst conflicts, imposes corporate governance requirements, enhances accounting and control disclosures, impacts insider transactions and executive loans, establishes new types of criminal conduct, and expands penalties for violations of federal securities laws.

Scatter diagram Graph used to display data about past cost behavior and sales as points on a diagram. *(p. 875)*

Schedule of accounts payable List of the balances of all accounts in the accounts payable ledger and their total. *(p. 274)*

Schedule of accounts receivable List of the balances for all accounts in the accounts receivable ledger and their total. *(p. 269)*

Secured bonds Bonds that have specific assets of the issuer pledged as collateral. *(p. 549)*

Securities and Exchange Commission (SEC) Federal agency Congress has charged to set reporting rules for organizations that sell ownership shares to the public. *(p. 9)*

Segment return on assets Segment operating income divided by segment average (identifiable) assets for the period. *(p. 278)*

Selling expense budget Plan that lists the types and amounts of selling expenses expected in the budget period. *(p. 912)*

Selling expenses Expenses of promoting sales, such as displaying and advertising merchandise, making sales, and delivering goods to customers. *(p. 191)*

Serial bonds Bonds consisting of separate amounts that mature at different dates. *(p. 550)*

Service company Organization that provides services instead of tangible products. *(p. 178)*

Shareholders Owners of a corporation; also called *stockholders*. *(p. 11)*

Shares Equity of a corporation divided into ownership units; also called *stock*. *(p. 11)*

Short-term investments Debt and equity securities that management expects to convert to cash within the next 3 to 12 months (or the operating cycle if longer); also called *temporary investments* or *marketable securities*. *(p. 592)*

Short-term note payable Current obligation in the form of a written promissory note. *(p. 427)*

Shrinkage Inventory losses that occur as a result of theft or deterioration. *(p. 188)*

Signature card Includes the signatures of each person authorized to sign checks on the bank account. *(p. 319)*

Simple capital structure Capital structure that consists of only common stock and nonconvertible preferred stock; consists of no dilutive securities. *(p. 516)*

Single-step income statement Income statement format that includes cost of goods sold as an expense and shows only one subtotal for total expenses. *(p. 192)*

Sinking fund bonds Bonds that require the issuer to make deposits to a separate account; bondholders are repaid at maturity from that account. *(p. 550)*

Small stock dividend Stock dividend that is 25% or less of a corporation's previously outstanding shares. *(p. 507)*

Social responsibility Being accountable for the impact that one's actions might have on society. *(p. 8)*

Sole proprietorship Business owned by one person that is not organized as a corporation; also called *proprietorship*. *(p. 10)*

Solvency Company's long-run financial viability and its ability to cover long-term obligations. *(p. 675)*

Source documents Source of information for accounting entries that can be in either paper or electronic form; also called *business papers*. *(p. 49)*

Special journal Any journal used for recording and posting transactions of a similar type. *(p. 266)*

Specific identification Method to assign cost to inventory when the purchase cost of each item in inventory is identified and used to compute cost of inventory. *(p. 225)*

Spending variance Difference between the actual price of an item and its standard price. *(p. 954)*

Spreadsheet Computer program that organizes data by means of formulas and format; also called *electronic work sheet*. *(p. 136)*

Standard costs Costs that should be incurred under normal conditions to produce a product or component or to perform a service. *(p. 947)*

State Unemployment Taxes (SUTA) State payroll taxes on employers to support its unemployment programs. *(p. 432)*

Stated value stock No-par stock assigned a stated value per share; this amount is recorded in the stock account when the stock is issued. *(p. 500)*

Statement of cash flows A financial statement that lists cash inflows (receipts) and cash outflows (payments) during a period; arranged by operating, investing, and financing. *(p. 17 & 626)*

Statement of owner's equity Report of changes in equity over a period; adjusted for increases (owner investment and net income) and for decreases (withdrawals and net loss). *(p. 17)*

Statement of partners' equity Financial statement that shows total capital balances at the beginning of the period, any additional investment by partners, the income or loss of the period, the partners' withdrawals, and the partners' ending capital balances; also called *statement of partners' capital*. *(p. 473)*

Statement of retained earnings Report of changes in retained earnings over a period; adjusted for increases (net income), for decreases (dividends and net loss), and for any prior period adjustment. *(p. 517)*

Statement of stockholders' equity Financial statement that lists the beginning and ending balances of each major equity account and describes all changes in those accounts. *(p. 517)*

Statements of Financial Accounting Standards (SFAS) FASB publications that establish U.S. GAAP. *(p. 9)*

Step-wise cost Cost that remains fixed over limited ranges of volumes but changes by a lump sum when volume changes occur outside these limited ranges. *(p. 874).*

Stock (See *shares.*) *(p. 11)*

Stock dividend Corporation's distribution of its own stock to its stockholders without the receipt of any payment. *(p. 507)*

Stock options Rights to purchase common stock at a fixed price over a specified period of time. *(p. 516)*

Stock split Occurs when a corporation calls in its stock and replaces each share with more than one new share; decreases both the market value per share and any par or stated value per share. *(p. 509)*

Stock subscription Investor's contractual commitment to purchase unissued shares at future dates and prices. *(p. 502)*

Stockholders' equity A corporation's equity; also called *shareholders' equity* or *corporate capital.* *(p. 500)*

Stockholders (See *shareholders.*) *(p. 11)*

Straight-line depreciation Method that allocates an equal portion of the depreciable cost of plant asset (cost minus salvage) to each accounting period in its useful life. *(p. 99 & 386)*

Straight-line bond amortization Method allocating an equal amount of bond interest expense to each period of the bond life. *(p. 553)*

Subsidiary Entity controlled by another entity (parent) in which the parent owns more than 50% of the subsidiary's voting stock. *(p. 599)*

Subsidiary ledger List of individual sub-accounts and amounts with a common characteristic; linked to a controlling account in the general ledger. *(p. 266)*

Sunk cost Cost already incurred and cannot be avoided or changed. *(p. 720)*

Supplementary records Information outside the usual accounting records; also called *supplemental records.* *(p. 184)*

Supply chain Linkages of services or goods extending from suppliers, to the company itself, and on to customers. *(p. 718)*

T-account Tool used to show the effects of transactions and events on individual accounts. *(p. 53)*

Temporary accounts Accounts used to record revenues, expenses, and withdrawals (dividends for a corporation); they are closed at the end of each period; also called *nominal accounts.* *(p. 141)*

Term bonds Bonds scheduled for payment (maturity) at a single specified date. *(p. 550)*

Time period principle Assumption that an organization's activities can be divided into specific time periods such as months, quarters, or years. *(p. 94)*

Time ticket Source document used to report the time an employee spent working on a job or on overhead activities and then to determine the amount of direct labor to charge to the job or the amount of indirect labor to charge to overhead. *(p. 759)*

Times interest earned Ratio of income before interest expense (and any income taxes) divided by interest expense; reflects risk of covering interest commitments when income varies. *(p. 437)*

Total asset turnover Measure of a company's ability to use its assets to generate sales; computed by dividing net sales by average total assets. *(p. 401)*

Total quality management (TQM) Concept calling for all managers and employees at all stages of operations to strive toward higher standards and reduce number of defects. *(p. 718)*

Trade discount Reduction from a list or catalog price that can vary for wholesalers, retailers, and consumers. *(p. 180)*

Trademark or **Trade (Brand) name** Symbol, name, phrase, or jingle identified with a company, product, or service. *(p. 400)*

Trading on the equity (See *financial leverage.*) *(p. 505)*

Trading securities Investments in debt and equity securities that the company intends to actively trade for profit. *(p. 595)*

Transaction Exchange of economic consideration affecting an entity's financial position that can be reliably measured. *(p. 13)*

Treasury stock Corporation's own stock that it reacquired and still holds. *(p. 510)*

Trial balance List of accounts and their balances at a point in time; total debit balances equal total credit balances. *(p. 63)*

Unadjusted trial balance List of accounts and balances prepared before accounting adjustments are recorded and posted. *(p. 105)*

Unavoidable expense Expense (or cost) that is not relevant for business decisions; an expense that would continue even if a department, product, or service is eliminated. *(p. 1000)*

Unclassified balance sheet Balance sheet that broadly groups assets, liabilities, and equity accounts. *(p. 146)*

Uncontrollable costs Costs that a manager does not have the power to determine or strongly influence. *(p. 846)*

Underapplied overhead Amount by which overhead incurred in a period exceeds the overhead applied to that period's production using the predetermined overhead rate. *(p. 765)*

Unearned revenue Liability created when customers pay in advance for products or services; earned when the products or services are later delivered. *(p. 51 & 100)*

Unfavorable variance Difference in revenues or costs, when the actual amount is compared to the budgeted amount, that contributes to a lower income. *(p. 944)*

Unit contribution margin Amount a product's unit selling price exceeds its total unit variable cost. *(p. 729)*

Units-of-production depreciation Method that charges a varying amount to depreciation expense for each period of an asset's useful life depending on its usage. *(p. 387)*

Unlimited liability Legal relationship among general partners that makes each of them responsible for partnership debts if the other partners are unable to pay their shares. *(p. 469)*

Unrealized gain (loss) Gain (loss) not yet realized by an actual transaction or event such as a sale. *(p. 595)*

Unsecured bonds Bonds backed only by the issuer's credit standing; almost always riskier than secured bonds; also called *debentures.* *(p. 549)*

Unusual gain or loss Gain or loss that is abnormal or unrelated to the company's ordinary activities and environment. *(p. 512)*

Useful life Length of time an asset will be productively used in the operations of a business; also called *service life*. *(p. 385)*

Value chain Sequential activities that add value to an entity's products or services; includes design, production, marketing, distribution, and service. *(p. 726)*

Variable cost Cost that changes in proportion to changes in the activity output volume. *(p. 719)*

Variance analysis Process of examining differences between actual and budgeted revenues or costs and describing them in terms of price and quantity differences. *(p. 946)*

Vendee Buyer of goods or services. *(p. 328)*

Vendor Seller of goods or services. *(p. 328)*

Vertical analysis Evaluation of each financial statement item or group of items in terms of a specific base amount. *(p. 676)*

Volume variance Difference between two dollar amounts of fixed overhead cost; one amount is the total budgeted overhead cost, and the other is the overhead cost allocated to products using the predetermined fixed overhead rate. *(p. 955)*

Voucher Internal file used to store documents and information to control cash disbursements and to ensure that a transaction is properly authorized and recorded. *(p. 315)*

Voucher system Procedures and approvals designed to control cash disbursements and acceptance of obligations. *(p. 315)*

Wage bracket withholding table Table of the amounts of income tax withheld from employees' wages. *(p. 444)*

Warranty Agreement that obligates the seller to correct or replace a product or service when it fails to perform properly within a specified period. *(p. 434)*

Weighted average Method to assign inventory cost to sales; the cost of available-for-sale units is divided by the number of units available to determine per unit cost prior to each sale that is then multiplied by the units sold to yield the cost of that sale. *(p. 228)*

Wholesaler Intermediary that buys products from manufacturers or other wholesalers and sells them to retailers or other wholesalers. *(p. 178)*

Withdrawals Payment of cash or other assets from a proprietorship or partnership to its owner or owners. *(p. 13)*

Work sheet Spreadsheet used to draft an unadjusted trial balance, adjusting entries, adjusted trial balance, and financial statements. *(p. 136)*

Working capital Current assets minus current liabilities at a point in time. *(p. 685)*

Working papers Analyses and other informal reports prepared by accountants and managers when organizing information for formal reports and financial statements. *(p. 136)*

Credits

Page 2 © Neal Stafford/The Chocolate Farm, LLC
Page 6 © Reuters/New Media CORBIS
Page 10 top AP/Wide World Photos
Page 10 bottom AP/Wide World Photos
Page 11 AP/Wide World Photos

Page 46 Courtesy of York Entertainment, Inc.
Page 51 AP/Wide World Photos
Page 64 © David Young-Wolff/PhotoEdit

Page 92 left and right Courtesy of Mellies
Page 95 AP/Wide World Photos
Page 96 © Getty Images
Page 108 © ASHBY DON/CORBIS SYGMA

Page 134 Courtesy of Premier Snowskates
Page 143 © Firefly Productions/CORBIS
Page 146 © Peter Barrett/CORBIS

Page 176 Courtesy of Damani Dada
Page 180 © Flip Chalfant/Getty Images/The Image Bank
Page 183 © David Woods/CORBIS
Page 186 top © David Young-Wolff/PhotoEdit
Page 186 bottom © Robert Ginn/Index Stock Imagery, Inc.
Page 192 © Martin Harvey; Gallo Images/CORBIS

Page 220 Courtesy of FunKo, Inc.
Page 223 © Kwame Zikomo/SuperStock
Page 229 AP/Wide World Photos
Page 230 AP/Wide World Photos

Page 260 left and right Zach Cordner/Courtesy of Rap-Up
Page 264 top AP/Wide World Photos
Page 264 bottom AP/Wide World Photos
Page 265 © Benjamin Shearn/Getty Images/Taxi
Page 267 © Duomo/CORBIS
Page 272 PhotoDisc Blue/Getty Images
Page 276 (c) Ralph Mercer/Getty Images/Stone
Page 277 © 1997–1998 Federal Express Corporation. All Rights Reserved.

Page 306 left Courtesy of Dylan's Candy Bar
Page 306 right Courtesy of Dylan's Candy Bar
Page 310 © Lawrence Manning/CORBIS
Page 311 PhotoDisc Green/Getty Images
Page 313 © Bob Rowan/CORBIS
Page 314 © Darrell Gulin/CORBIS

Page 348 left Courtesy of Manzi Metals Inc.
Page 348 right © James L. Amos/CORBIS
Page 352 © Topham/The Image Works
Page 353 © David McNew/Getty Images
Page 358 © Thierry Dosogne/Getty Images/The Image Bank
Page 364 © Royalty Free/Corbis

Page 380 left © Cable Risdon Photography/Courtesy of Queston Construction
Page 380 right © photolibrary.com pty. ltd../Index Stock Photography
Page 383 AP/Wide World Photos
Page 384 © Michael J. Doolittle/The Image Works
Page 386 © Neil Rabinowitz/Corbis
Page 391 AP/Wide World Photos
Page 393 © DOUG KNUTSON/Time Life Pictures/Getty Images
Page 397 © Jan Stromme/PhotoEdit
Page 399 AP/Wide World Photos

Page 422 © Doby Photography
Page 427 AP/Wide World Photos
Page 429 © Michael Keller/Corbis
Page 433 AP/Wide World Photos
Page 436 © David Muench/Getty Images/Stone

Page 466 Courtesy of KOCH Entertainment
Page 469 AP/Wide World Photos
Page 471 © James L. Amos/Corbis
Page 474 © Rick Doyle/Corbis
Page 477 © Chuck Keeler, Jr./Corbis

Page 494 © Shmuel Thaler/Santa Cruz Sentinel
Page 497 © Chuck Savage/Corbis
Page 498 Courtesy of Green Bay Packers, Inc.
Page 499 © Rob Crandall/The Image Works
Page 516 THE KOBAL COLLECTION/ORION/SEAGOAT

Page 546 left Dennis Kleiman/Courtesy of Noodles & Company
Page 546 right Joseph Hancock Studio/Courtesy of Noodles & Company
Page 550 © Paul Conklin/PhotoEdit
Page 551 Courtesy of Dow Chemicals.

Page 590 left and center Courtesy of TradeStation Group
Page 590 right © Rick Gayle/CORBIS
Page 594 Courtesy of Scripophily.com
Page 595 © Alan Schein Photography/Corbis
Page 599 © Neil Selkirk/Getty Images/Stone

Page 624 Courtesy of Atomic Toys, LLC
Page 627 © Joseph Sohm/CORBIS
Page 632 © Royalty-Free/CORBIS
Page 643 © Charles O'Rear/CORBIS
Page 655 AP/Wide World Photos

Page 672 © Peter Serling, 2003 ALL RIGHTS RESERVED
Page 675 © Charles O'Rear/CORBIS
Page 676 AP/Wide World Photos
Page 688 © Arnold Gold/New Haven Register/The Image Works
Page 691 Mary Evans Picture Library

Page 712 © James Wasserman
Page 718 © Rick Rusing/Getty Images/Stone
Page 722 © Syracuse Newspapers/The Image Works
Page 723 © David Stoecklein/CORBIS

Page 752 left Tom Berndt
Page 752 right © Jeremy Walker/Getty Images/Stone
Page 755 top Courtesy of NASA
Page 755 bottom PhotoDisc/Getty Images
Page 756 © Mark Peterson/CORBIS
Page 759 © Michael Newman/PhotoEdit
Page 761 © Steve Dunwell/Getty Images/The Image Bank
Page 788 © Geoff Johnson
Page 790 © Steve Lesch/Getty Images/The Image Bank
Page 791 © Bruce Ayers/Getty Images/Stone
Page 795 © Karim Shamsi-Basha/The Image Works
Page 799 © Chris Haigh/Getty Images/Stone
Page 808 © Bisson Bernard/CORBIS SYGMA

Page 830 Courtesy of Life is Good® Inc.
Page 832 © David Madison/Getty Images/The Image Bank
Page 834 © David Young-Wolff/PhotoEdit
Page 836 © Bob Daemmrich/The Image Works
Page 838 © Reuters NewMedia Inc./CORBIS
Page 841 © Spencer Grant/PhotoEdit
Page 844 © Susan Van Etten/PhotoEdit
Page 848 © Bob Rowan; Progressive Image/CORBIS

Page 870 left © egon douglas photography 2003/Courtesy of Vosges Haut-Chocolat
Page 870 right Courtesy of Vosges Haut-Chocolat
Page 873 © Reuters NewMedia Inc./CORBIS
Page 878 © David Madison/Getty Images/The Image Bank
Page 883 AP/Wide World Photos
Page 884 © Alan Abramowitz/Getty Images/Stone

Page 902 all Courtesy of Aquent.com
Page 906 © RO-MA Stock/Index Stock
Page 910 © Jeff Greenberg/PhotoEdit
Page 912 AP/Wide World Photos
Page 915 © David Madison/Getty Images/Stone
Page 916 © Royalty-Free/CORBIS

Page 940 left and right Courtesy of SCOTTeVEST, LLC
Page 944 © Dorothy Littel Greco/The Image Works
Page 948 © John Kelly/Getty Images/The Image Bank
Page 950 © Chuck Carlton/Index Stock
Page 953 © Chuck Carlton/Index Stock
Page 951 © Paul A. Souders/CORBIS
Page 953 © Helen King/CORBIS
Page 958 © Tony Freeman/PhotoEdit

Page 982 Courtesy of AnthroTronix
Page 985 © Karsten de Risso/plus 49/The Image Works
Page 992 © Syracuse Newspapers/The Image Works
Page 999 © Susan Van Etten/PhotoEdit

Index

Note: Page numbers followed by *n* indicate material found in footnotes; page numbers in **boldface** indicate defined terms; underlined items are URLs.

Chart of Accounts

Following is a typical chart of accounts. Each company has its own unique accounts and numbering system.

Assets

Current Assets

101 Cash
102 Petty cash
103 Cash equivalents
104 Short-term investments
105 Market adjustment, _______ securities (S-T)
106 Accounts receivable
107 Allowance for doubtful accounts
108 Legal fees receivable
109 Interest receivable
110 Rent receivable
111 Notes receivable
119 Merchandise inventory
120 _________ inventory
121 _________ inventory
124 Office supplies
125 Store supplies
126 _______ supplies
128 Prepaid insurance
129 Prepaid interest
131 Prepaid rent
132 Raw materials inventory
133 Goods in process inventory, _______
134 Goods in process inventory, _______
135 Finished goods inventory

Long-Term Investments

141 Long-term investments
142 Market adjustment, _______ securities (L-T)
144 Investment in _______
145 Bond sinking fund

Plant Assets

151 Automobiles
152 Accumulated depreciation—Automobiles
153 Trucks
154 Accumulated depreciation—Trucks
155 Boats
156 Accumulated depreciation—Boats
157 Professional library
158 Accumulated depreciation—Professional library
159 Law library
160 Accumulated depreciation—Law library
161 Furniture
162 Accumulated depreciation—Furniture
163 Office equipment
164 Accumulated depreciation—Office equipment
165 Store equipment
166 Accumulated depreciation—Store equipment
167 _______ equipment
168 Accumulated depreciation—_______ equipment
169 Machinery
170 Accumulated depreciation—Machinery
173 Building _______
174 Accumulated depreciation—Building _______
175 Building _______
176 Accumulated depreciation—Building _______
179 Land improvements _______
180 Accumulated depreciation—Land improvements _______
181 Land improvements _______
182 Accumulated depreciation—Land improvements _______
183 Land

Natural Resources

185 Mineral deposit
186 Accumulated depletion—Mineral deposit

Intangible Assets

191 Patents
192 Leasehold
193 Franchise
194 Copyrights
195 Leasehold improvements
196 Licenses
197 Accumulated amortization—_______

Liabilities

Current Liabilities

201 Accounts payable
202 Insurance payable
203 Interest payable
204 Legal fees payable
207 Office salaries payable
208 Rent payable
209 Salaries payable
210 Wages payable
211 Accrued payroll payable
214 Estimated warranty liability
215 Income taxes payable
216 Common dividend payable
217 Preferred dividend payable
218 State unemployment taxes payable
219 Employee federal income taxes payable
221 Employee medical insurance payable
222 Employee retirement program payable
223 Employee union dues payable
224 Federal unemployment taxes payable
225 FICA taxes payable
226 Estimated vacation pay liability

Unearned Revenues

230 Unearned consulting fees
231 Unearned legal fees
232 Unearned property management fees
233 Unearned _______ fees
234 Unearned _______ fees
235 Unearned janitorial revenue
236 Unearned _______ revenue
238 Unearned rent

Notes Payable

240 Short-term notes payable
241 Discount on short-term notes payable
245 Notes payable
251 Long-term notes payable
252 Discount on long-term notes payable

Long-Term Liabilities

253 Long-term lease liability
255 Bonds payable
256 Discount on bonds payable
257 Premium on bonds payable
258 Deferred income tax liability

Equity

Owner's Equity

301 ____________, Capital
302 ____________, Withdrawals
303 ____________, Capital
304 ____________, Withdrawals
305 ____________, Capital
306 ____________, Withdrawals

Contributed Capital

307 Common stock, $ _______ par value
308 Common stock, no-par value
309 Common stock, $ _______ stated value
310 Common stock dividend distributable
311 Contributed capital in excess of par value, Common stock
312 Contributed capital in excess of stated value, No-par common stock
313 Contributed capital from retirement of common stock
314 Contributed capital, Treasury stock
315 Preferred stock
316 Contributed capital in excess of par value, Preferred stock

Retained Earnings

318 Retained earnings
319 Cash dividends (or Dividends)
320 Stock dividends

Other Equity Accounts

321 Treasury stock, Common
322 Unrealized gain—Equity
323 Unrealized loss—Equity

Revenues

401 ____________ fees earned
402 ____________ fees earned
403 ____________ services revenue
404 ____________ services revenue
405 Commissions earned
406 Rent revenue (or Rent earned)
407 Dividends revenue (or Dividend earned)
408 Earnings from investment in ______
409 Interest revenue (or Interest earned)
410 Sinking fund earnings
413 Sales
414 Sales returns and allowances
415 Sales discounts

Cost of Sales

Cost of Goods Sold

502 Cost of goods sold
505 Purchases
506 Purchases returns and allowances
507 Purchases discounts
508 Transportation-in

Manufacturing

520 Raw materials purchases
521 Freight-in on raw materials
530 Factory payroll
531 Direct labor
540 Factory overhead
541 Indirect materials
542 Indirect labor
543 Factory insurance expired
544 Factory supervision
545 Factory supplies used
546 Factory utilities
547 Miscellaneous production costs
548 Property taxes on factory building
549 Property taxes on factory equipment
550 Rent on factory building
551 Repairs, factory equipment
552 Small tools written off
560 Depreciation of factory equipment
561 Depreciation of factory building

Standard Cost Variance

580 Direct material quantity variance
581 Direct material price variance
582 Direct labor quantity variance
583 Direct labor price variance
584 Factory overhead volume variance
585 Factory overhead controllable variance

Expenses

Amortization, Depletion, and Depreciation

601 Amortization expense—______
602 Amortization expense—______
603 Depletion expense—______
604 Depreciation expense—Boats
605 Depreciation expense—Automobiles
606 Depreciation expense—Building ______
607 Depreciation expense—Building ______
608 Depreciation expense—Land improvements ______
609 Depreciation expense—Land improvements ______
610 Depreciation expense—Law library
611 Depreciation expense—Trucks
612 Depreciation expense—______ equipment
613 Depreciation expense—______ equipment
614 Depreciation expense—______
615 Depreciation expense—______

Employee-Related Expenses

620 Office salaries expense
621 Sales salaries expense
622 Salaries expense
623 ______ wages expense
624 Employees' benefits expense
625 Payroll taxes expense

Financial Expenses

630 Cash over and short
631 Discounts lost
632 Factoring fee expense
633 Interest expense

Insurance Expenses

635 Insurance expense—Delivery equipment
636 Insurance expense—Office equipment
637 Insurance expense—______

Rental Expenses

640 Rent expense
641 Rent expense—Office space
642 Rent expense—Selling space
643 Press rental expense
644 Truck rental expense
645 ______ rental expense

Supplies Expenses

650 Office supplies expense
651 Store supplies expense
652 ______ supplies expense
653 ______ supplies expense

Miscellaneous Expenses

655 Advertising expense
656 Bad debts expense
657 Blueprinting expense
658 Boat expense
659 Collection expense
661 Concessions expense
662 Credit card expense
663 Delivery expense
664 Dumping expense
667 Equipment expense
668 Food and drinks expense
671 Gas and oil expense
672 General and administrative expense
673 Janitorial expense
674 Legal fees expense
676 Mileage expense
677 Miscellaneous expenses
678 Mower and tools expense
679 Operating expense
680 Organization expense
681 Permits expense
682 Postage expense
683 Property taxes expense
684 Repairs expense—______
685 Repairs expense—______
687 Selling expense
688 Telephone expense
689 Travel and entertainment expense
690 Utilities expense
691 Warranty expense
695 Income taxes expense

Gains and Losses

701 Gain on retirement of bonds
702 Gain on sale of machinery
703 Gain on sale of investments
704 Gain on sale of trucks
705 Gain on ______
706 Foreign exchange gain or loss
801 Loss on disposal of machinery
802 Loss on exchange of equipment
803 Loss on exchange of ______
804 Loss on sale of notes
805 Loss on retirement of bonds
806 Loss on sale of investments
807 Loss on sale of machinery
808 Loss on ______
809 Unrealized gain—Income
810 Unrealized loss—Income

Clearing Accounts

901 Income summary
902 Manufacturing summary

A Rose by Any Other Name

The same financial statement sometimes receives different titles. Below are some of the more common aliases.†

Balance Sheet	Statement of Financial Position Statement of Financial Condition
Income Statement	Statement of Income Operating Statement Statement of Operations Statement of Operating Activity Earnings Statement Statement of Earnings Profit and Loss (P&L) Statement
Statement of Cash Flows	Statement of Cash Flow Cash Flows Statement Statement of Changes in Cash Position Statement of Changes in Financial Position
Statement of Owner's Equity	Statement of Changes in Owner's Equity Statement of Changes in Owner's Capital Statement of Shareholders' Equity* Statement of Changes in Shareholders' Equity* Statement of Changes in Capital Accounts*

† The term "**Consolidated**" often precedes or follows these statement titles to reflect the combination of different entities, such as a parent company and its subsidiaries.
* Corporation only.

We thank Dr. Louella Moore from Arkansas State University for suggesting this listing.

FUNDAMENTALS

① Accounting Equation

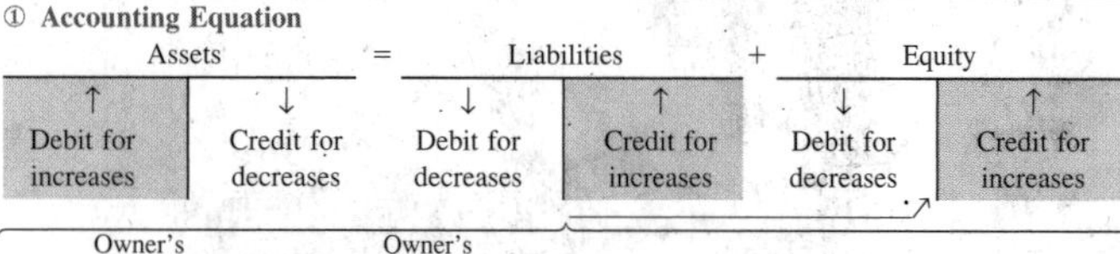

Owner's Capital*		−	Owner's Withdrawals*		+	Revenues		−	Expenses	
↓ Dr. for decreases	↑ Cr. for increases		↑ Dr. for increases	↓ Cr. for decreases		↓ Dr. for decreases	↑ Cr. for increases		↑ Dr. for increases	↓ Cr. for decreases

Indicates normal balance.

*Comparable corporate accounts are Contributed Capital and Dividends.

② Accounting Cycle

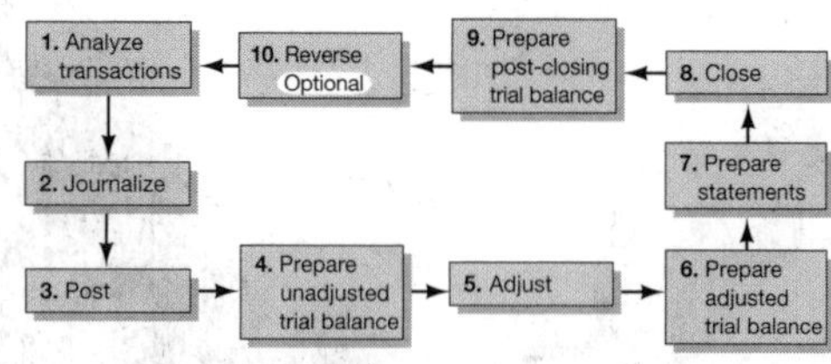

③ Adjustments and Entries

Type	Adjusting Entry	
Prepaid Expenses	Dr. Expense	Cr. Asset*
Unearned Revenues	Dr. Liability	Cr. Revenue
Accrued Expenses	Dr. Expense	Cr. Liability
Accrued Revenues	Dr. Asset	Cr. Revenue

*For depreciation, credit Accumulated Depreciation (contra asset).

④ 4-Step Closing Process

<1>Transfer revenue and gain account balances to Income Summary.
<2>Transfer expense and loss account balances to Income Summary.
<3>Transfer Income Summary balance to Owner's Capital.
<4>Transfer Withdrawals balance to Owner's Capital.

⑤ Accounting Concepts

Characteristics	Assumptions	Principles	Constraints
Relevance	Business entity	Historical cost	Cost-benefit
Reliability	Going concern	Revenue recognition	Materiality
Comparability	Monetary unit	Matching	Industry practice
Consistency	Periodicity	Full disclosure	Conservatism

⑥ Ownership of Inventory

	Ownership transfers when goods passed to	Transportation costs paid by
FOB Shipping Point	Carrier	Buyer
FOB Destination	Buyer	Seller

⑦ Inventory Costing Methods

Specific Identification
First-In, First-Out (FIFO)
Last-In, First-Out (LIFO)
Weighted-Average

⑧ Depreciation and Depletion

Straight-Line: $\frac{\text{Cost} - \text{Salvage value}}{\text{Useful life in periods}} \times \text{Periods expired}$

Units-of-Production: $\frac{\text{Cost} - \text{Salvage value}}{\text{Useful life in units}} \times \text{Units produced}$

Declining-Balance: Rate* × Beginning-of-period book value

*Rate is often double the straight-line rate, or 2 × (1/useful life)

Depletion: $\frac{\text{Cost} - \text{Salvage value}}{\text{Total capacity in units}} \times \text{Units extracted}$

⑨ Interest Computation

Interest = Principal (face) × Rate × Time

⑩ Accounting for Investment Securities

Trading (debt and equity) securities	Market value (with market adjustment to income)
Held-to-maturity (debt) securities	
Short-term	Cost (without any discount or premium amortization)
Long-term	Cost (with any discount or premium amortization)
Available-for-sale (debt and equity) securities ...	Market value (with market adjustment to equity)
Equity securities with significant influence	Equity method

ANALYSES

① Liquidity and Efficiency

Current ratio $= \frac{\text{Current assets}}{\text{Current liabilities}}$ p. 148

Working capital = Current assets − Current liabilities p. 685

Acid-test ratio $= \frac{\text{Cash} + \text{Short-term investments} + \text{Current receivables}}{\text{Current liabilities}}$ p. 193

Accounts receivable turnover $= \frac{\text{Net sales}}{\text{Average accounts receivable}}$ p. 364

Credit risk ratio $= \frac{\text{Allowance for doubtful accounts}}{\text{Accounts receivable}}$ p. 364

Inventory turnover $= \frac{\text{Cost of goods sold}}{\text{Average inventory}}$ p. 233

Days' sales uncollected $= \frac{\text{Accounts receivable}}{\text{Net sales}} \times 365^*$ p. 325

Days' sales in inventory $= \frac{\text{Ending inventory}}{\text{Cost of goods sold}} \times 365^*$ p. 234

Total asset turnover $= \frac{\text{Net sales}}{\text{Average total assets}}$ p. 401

Plant asset useful life $= \frac{\text{Plant asset cost}}{\text{Depreciation expense}}$ p. 401

Plant asset age $= \frac{\text{Accumulated depreciation}}{\text{Depreciation expense}}$ p. 401

Days' cash expense coverage $= \frac{\text{Cash and cash equivalents}}{\text{Average daily cash expenses}}$ p. 313

*360 days is also commonly used.

② Solvency

Debt ratio $= \frac{\text{Total liabilities}}{\text{Total assets}}$ Equity ratio $= \frac{\text{Total equity}}{\text{Total assets}}$ p. 67 & p. 689

Pledged assets to secured liabilities $= \frac{\text{Book value of pledged assets}}{\text{Book value of secured liabilities}}$ p. 565

Times interest earned $= \frac{\text{Income before interest expense and income taxes}}{\text{Interest expense}}$ p. 437

Cash coverage of growth $= \frac{\text{Operating cash flow}}{\text{Cash outflow for plant assets}}$ p. 644

Cash coverage of debt $= \frac{\text{Cash flow from operations}}{\text{Total noncurrent liabilities}}$ p. 643

③ Profitability

Profit margin ratio $= \frac{\text{Net income}}{\text{Net sales}}$ p. 108

Gross margin ratio $= \frac{\text{Net sales} - \text{Cost of goods sold}}{\text{Net sales}}$ p. 193

Return on total assets $= \frac{\text{Net income}}{\text{Average total assets}}$ p. 20

= Profit margin ratio × Total asset turnover p. 600

Return on common stockholders' equity $= \frac{\text{Net income} - \text{Preferred dividends}}{\text{Average common stockholders' equity}}$ p. 691

Book value per common share $= \frac{\text{Stockholders' equity applicable to common shares}}{\text{Number of common shares outstanding}}$ p. 518

Basic earnings per share $= \frac{\text{Net income} - \text{Preferred dividends}}{\text{Weighted-average common shares outstanding}}$ p. 514

Cash flow on total assets $= \frac{\text{Cash flow from operations}}{\text{Average total assets}}$ p. 644

Payout ratio $= \frac{\text{Cash dividends declared on common stock}}{\text{Net income}}$ p. 519

④ Market

Price-earnings ratio $= \frac{\text{Market price per common share}}{\text{Earnings per share}}$ p. 520

Dividend yield $= \frac{\text{Annual cash dividends per share}}{\text{Market price per share}}$ p. 519

⑤ Costing Ratios

Contribution margin ratio = (Net sales − Variable costs)/Net sales p. 878
Predetermined overhead rate = Estimated overhead costs/Estimated "factor" costs p. 762
Costs per unit = Material, labor, and overhead costs per unit p. 798

⑥ Planning and Control

Break-even point in units = Fixed costs/Contribution margin per unit p. 878
Cost variance = Actual cost − Budgeted cost p. 949
Sales (revenue) variance = Actual sales − Budgeted sales p. 961
Payback period = Time expected to recover initial investment p. 986
Net present value = Present value of cash flows − Initial investment p. 989